The Handbook For
No-Load
FUND
INVESTORS

Eighteenth Annual Edition

By Sheldon Jacobs and the editors of
*The No-Load Fund Investor—the complete
no-load mutual fund advisory service.*

Editor-in-chief/**Sheldon Jacobs**

Statistical editor/**Lawrence Solomon**

Directory editor/**Layne Aurand**

Eighteenth Edition. Printed in the United States of America

The No-Load Fund Investor, Inc. is not associated with the management or sale of any mutual fund, nor with any mutual fund association. The *Investor*'s sole objective is to present unbiased information about funds. The data contained herein have been obtained from the mutual funds themselves and from other sources believed reliable. Although carefully verified, data and compilations are not guaranteed. Readers desiring information about a particular fund should examine the fund's prospectus. Performance results do not take into account any tax consequences and are not, in or of themselves, predictive of future performance. *The Handbook For No-Load Fund Investors* is designed to provide accurate and authoritative information in regard to the subject matter covered. It is sold with the understanding that neither the author nor the publisher renders legal or accounting advice. If legal advice or other expert assistance is required, the services of a competent professional person should be sought.

If you have any suggestions for future editions of this *Handbook,* or have spotted any mistakes, we would be glad to hear from you. Important corrections will be made in our monthly *No-Load Fund Investor* newsletter.

ISBN 0-9664627-1-8

Library of Congress Catalog Card No. 85—645285

Acknowledgments

Numerous people and organizations gave their assistance and support in the preparation of this Handbook. In particular we would like to thank the Investment Company Institute, the mutual funds' industry association, Lipper Analytical Services and all the no-load mutual funds which provided us with prospectuses, annual reports and directory information.

Additional copies of the *Handbook* can be obtained from *The No-Load Fund Investor* at $45 each.
The *Handbook* with twelve monthly *No-Load Fund Investor* newsletter supplements is $155. Monthly *Investor*
supplements are $135 per year; a sample issue of the *Investor* newsletter
can be obtained free by writing *The No-Load Fund Investor.*

    The No-Load Fund Investor also publishes *Sheldon Jacobs' Guide to Successful No-Load Fund Investing* at $25.

    For updated information on *The No-Load Fund Investor* newsletter, including current model portfolios, visit our
site on the World Wide Web at the following address: http://www.sheldonjacobs.com

THE NO-LOAD FUND INVESTOR, INC., Post Office Box 318,
Irvington-on-Hudson, NY 10533, Telephone: 914-693-7420
800-252-2042

The Handbook For No–Load Fund Investors
1998 EDITION

Contents

Preface: Covering the wide world of no-load mutual funds

SECTION I. 1997 In Review

SECTION II. No-load Fund Performance Tables

SECTION III. Directory of No-load Funds

SECTION IV. Appendixes

Covering the wide world of no-load mutual funds

Just exactly, what is a no-load? Very simple, it's a type of mutual fund sold without a sales commission (which in the jargon of the industry is called a "load"). Selling funds without a sales charge is possible when no salespeople are involved in the purchase. By going directly to no-load fund companies, you can save substantial sums of money while still enjoying outstanding returns. That's because, on average, no-load funds perform as well as the more expensive load funds.

Years ago, the difference between loads and no-loads was clear cut. That's no longer the case. Seeing the increasing popularity of no-loads, load fund companies have blurred the line. There are now load funds without front-end loads. Instead, they have back-end loads and ongoing sales charges (called 12b-1 fees.) More recently load fund companies have developed "level-load" funds. They don't have either front- or back-end loads. They still have high continuing fees. Load funds, by whatever name, are more costly, and thus inferior, to no-loads.

This book, *The Handbook For No-Load Fund Investors*, is designed to provide meaningful coverage of virtually all no-load stock and bond funds available to the public, as well as coverage of the important money market funds. In various chapters you will find detailed performance data and rankings, going back ten years, as well as a complete directory that gives you all the purchase information you need. This edition of the *Handbook* reports on 2,428 funds ranging from speculative aggressive growth funds to conservative money-market funds—and includes international funds, domestic funds, bond funds, and stocks funds.

The *Handbook* also has separate sections that cover load funds that are available no-load through certain discount stock brokers, and low-load funds that are marketed directly to the public, meaning that you buy without the help of a broker or financial adviser. Fidelity Magellan is an example of a low-load marketed directly to the public. We exclude low-load funds that are distributed through brokers, salesmen or financial advisers. We provide data on these direct marketed low-loads because we perform a vital information function in the absence of a salesmen. We do not recommend these funds.

While virtually all money market funds are no-load, the *Handbook* focuses on money funds that are part of no-load groups or allow you to switch into or out of no-load stock funds. We also include most of the large independent and stockbroker affiliated funds. We've generally excluded those money funds that are part of load fund families.

The *Handbook*, which has been published annually since 1981, complements two other publications published by *The No-Load Fund Investor*. In addition, there is *Sheldon Jacobs' Guide to Successful No-Load Fund Investing* (the "*Guide*"), which provides in-depth strategic information on how to select the best performing funds that suit your own needs. Finally, there is our monthly newsletter, *The No-Load Fund Investor*, which updates the performance data in this book and issues continuing recommendations. The *Investor* newsletter, which has been published since 1979, covers 794 of the most popular funds each month.

How to use the Handbook

With its wealth of statistical and directory data, the *Handbook* can satisfy all your no-load mutual fund investing needs with concise to-the-point information.

How do I look up a fund to see how it has done?

Chapter 4 has all funds in alphabetical order. The left hand pages allow you to see how consistent a fund's performance has been over the last ten years. The right hand pages report on the fund's size, prices, dividends, risk and portfolio composition.

If you want to see a fund's performance over a three- or five-year period, you have two choices. We provide it on an annualized basis, which is an easy number to grasp, and also in terms of how much an investment would have grown over those years.

One of the most important criteria in determining the right fund for you is the fund's objective. It's listed in Chapter 4. In addition, the Directory provides a short extract of the objective as stated in each fund's prospectus. Here are capsule explanations of the meaning of each objective category. For a more definitive discussion of this important topic see the *Guide*.

Aggressive growth funds aim at maximum capital appreciation, and may take great risks to achieve this goal. They frequently invest in small company and less seasoned stocks. They may have high turnover of port-

folio securities, leverage, or hold large amounts of cash. They are for investors willing to take a substantial amount of risk.

Growth funds are less risky and less volatile than aggressive growth funds. They typically invest in the growth stocks of larger companies and are suitable for a wide range of growth-oriented investors.

Growth-income funds combine a growth of earnings orientation with level or rising dividends. They offer more stable performance than either the aggressive growth or growth categories. Growth-income funds frequently hold a small portion of their portfolios in fixed-income securities.

Income funds seek stocks paying generous dividends, but may also hold fixed-income securities. It is the policy of the *Handbook* to use the Income category as a catch-all for a number of different types of mutual funds that have the common attributes of relatively low volatility and reasonable dividend income. These include the equity income funds, income funds (which may have up to 40% of their portfolios in fixed-income securities), balanced funds, domestic asset allocation funds and convertible securities funds.

Sector funds are non-diversified funds investing in specific industries. We include in this category the Fidelity, Invesco, and Vanguard sector portfolios as well as stand-alone funds investing in real estate, utilities and other industries.

Precious metals funds invest primarily in gold bullion or gold mining shares. While, technically, they could be included with the sector funds, we give them their own category because of their large numbers and the fact they frequently perform differently than other industry funds.

Global funds invest in both foreign and U.S. equity securities.

International funds invest in securities whose primary trading markets are outside the U.S. International funds can invest in any foreign country, regionally, or in specific countries.

Fixed-income funds hold taxable long-term fixed-income investments. International bond funds are included in this category.

Tax-free bond funds own municipal securities. Both fixed-income and tax-free bond funds have variable prices.

Money market funds hold short-term money market instruments. They have a fixed price, almost always $1. We sub-divide this category into general, government and muni money market funds. Money market funds with variable prices are put in the fixed-income category.

How do I compare a fund to other funds?

The best way to select top-performing funds is to go by our unique quintile ranking system. The *Handbook* uses superscript numbers (exponents) above each performance figure to show the fund's rank *within its objective category*. For example, an aggressive growth fund with a "1" above its performance figure is in the top 20% of all aggressive growth funds for the indicated period. A "2" indicates the fund was in the second 20% (or top 40%) of all funds that have the same investment objective. A "3" indicates the third or middle quintile. These are average funds. Funds ranked "4" or "5" are below average. Funds that have quintiles in the top two ranks are best.

In addition, Chapters 5 and 6 show fund performance in rank order for direct comparison.

How do I identify "pure" no-loads?

Pure no-load funds are identified in the Directory by a diamond after the fund's name. They have no front-end, back-end or 12b-1 fees. Funds without a diamond may still be called no-loads under current federal regulations if there 12b-1 fees are .25% or less.

How do I contact a fund?

The Directory section has the phone numbers, both toll-free and local, and the funds' mail and internet addresses.

Where do I get purchase information?

The Directory tells you minimum investments, if the fund is available in your state, whether it will accept wire orders.

How do I sell a fund?

Directory section provides some information, but see the prospectus.

Who manages the fund?

The Directory section lists each fund's manager or co-managers. Chapter 14 has an alphabetical listing of portfolio managers so you can see how many funds they manage, or simply match the manager to the fund.

Sheldon Jacobs, Editor
Irvington-on-Hudson, NY

Section I

1997
In
Review

CHAPTER 1

The trend is your friend

Mea culpa. Sort of.

Last year in this space, looking back on two memorable years in the investment markets—one great, one good—I was cautious about the outlook for 1997. I wrote: "Perhaps we'll have a gloomier headline to write when we chronicle 1997 this time next year." (This chapter's headlines for the past two years: How Sweet It Was!—1995; Stocks Keep Rolling—1996.)

Well, time flies, and it *is* "this time next year." I should have kept in mind that old Wall Street maxim: the trend is your friend. Meaning that a body in motion tends to stay in motion. And stay in motion the markets certainly did in 1997.

	Avg equity fund fund	Avg diversified equity fund
1995	25.4	29.3
1996	18.0	18.6
1997	17.9	22.9

Happily, I'm spared for another year having to write a gloomy headline for this annual Year in Review chapter. 1997 provided yet another hospitable environment for investors. To show you how

the financial markets have confounded the experts, consider Federal Reserve Chairman Alan Greenspan's to-ing and frow-ing. In late 1996, His Majesty grumped about "irrational exuberance" in the stock markets. In February 1997, he complained that "history is strewn with visions of 'new eras' that in the end have proven to be a mirage." But by the middle of last year, Greenspan had become more cheerful, talking about how we are in the midst of a once in a lifetime convergence of positive circumstances: low inflation despite low unemployment, declining interest rates and a Goldilocks economy (not too cold, not too hot . . .) that moves indomitably ahead. Of course, Greenspan's optimism came at a time when the chairman was marrying television reporter Andrea Mitchell, which could account for his improved mood.

Nor have investors, especially those of a more skeptical bent, known quite what to make of the doughtily resilient stock market. I recall speaking with a man early last year, as the Dow Jones Industrial Average was plowing through 7000 for the first time. He was absolutely not, he scoffed, about to take money out of his bank account and invest it in stocks with the Dow at 7000! I didn't say anything,

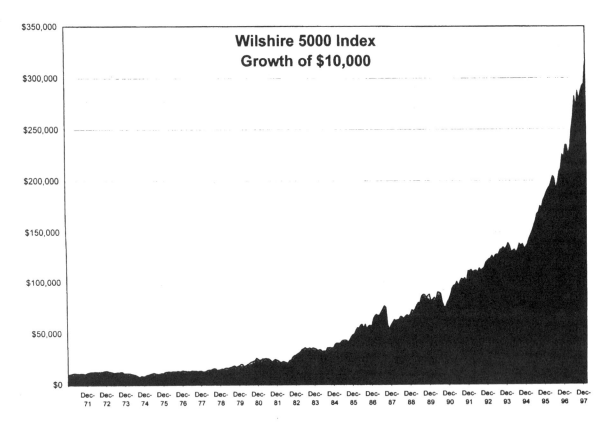

Prepared by Wilshire Associates Inc. 1998

2

but I was thinking about a comment supposedly made by our generation's legendary investor, Warren Buffet. He was asked, so the story goes, "Mr. Buffet, when's the best time to invest?", and supposedly he replied, "When the market's open." Meaning, don't try to time the market. (PS, the Dow finished the year at 7908, and as I write this in early 1998, it's above 8500.)

Boomers Buy Funds

There are, of course, plausible explanations. The economic climate that Chairman Greenspan praised is fertile for financial assets. And an aging population is likely to be thriftier than gangs of twenty- and thirty-somethings, frantically investing in pampers and power tools.

The growth of mutual fund investing among individual investors has also played a large role. Focused on their future, erstwhile Baby Boomers are starting to crank up their savings rate. Not only are investors turning to mutual funds as the investment of choice in general, but also more specifically the proliferation of corporate retirement plans has provided a ready-made investment arena.

That trend is favorable to the stock market because it ensures a steady supply of new money streaming continuously into stocks. Moreover, money that is invested for retirement is not likely to be withdrawn prematurely because of the stiff penalties on participants who take their chips home before 59 1/2.

Mutual funds, of course, are the obvious beneficiaries of all these trends. Some statistics to ponder: mutual funds in 1996 and 1997 had back-to-back years of $200 billion inflows. Last year for the first time, the fund industry broke the $4 trillion mark. The industry is four times as large as it was at the beginning of the decade. And during that time, the average stock fund has had a total return of 350%, more than 16% per year.

So the good news for stocks will be endless, right? And every year at this time I'll be straining to think up still another congratulatory headline, right? Maybe, but I think this year I'll be more discreet, and simply say, as I did in the January issue of my newsletter, *The No-Load Fund Investor*: I'm not bearish, but considering that stocks have scored enormous gains three years in a row—an unprecedented occurrence—common sense dictates that you take a prudent approach in 1998.

For one thing, this year is likely to see more of the volatility that gave investors fits in 1997. Early in the year, interest rates spiked, depressing both bond and stock values. By mid-April, the 30-year Treasury bond was yielding just above 7.15%. But then rates began sliding, and the long bond ended the year at 5.92%, although it popped back over 6% early in 1998.

In the fall, a calamity in Asia threatened to gore the long bull market. With Korea's economy next to bankrupt, Japan's financial system still in disarray and Indonesia, Malaysia, Singapore and Thailand all experiencing serious economic problems, the average Pacific fund was down 24.7% in the fourth quarter, 32.1% for the full year.

Asia's problems gave the U.S. stock market a serious case of the jitters in the fall. On Oct. 27th, the Dow plunged 554 points, or 7.18%, its worst drop in almost exactly 10 years. The New York Stock Exchange's trading curb program, devised after that 1987 meltdown, was activated for the first time, although I think it made matters worse, not better.

For investors, one strategy that seemed to work well all year was an investment approach that has come into vogue the past few years. It's called "buy on the dips." The very next day after the big plunge, the Dow regained 335 of the points it had lost as bargain hunters gleefully dived into stocks. Buying when stocks drop is perhaps an inevitable strategy to cope with one of the longest bull markets in history. The stock market has been rising—with only a few breaks—since August 1982. The Dow Jones Industrial Average has risen a record-setting seven straight years. Only the 20-year bull market that began in the late 1940s was longer than the current spree.

That isn't to say that favor has smiled on all types of investments alike, of course. Decidedly, 1997 favored the Dow-like stocks of large companies. For example, the S&P 500 index was up 31%; but the blue chips' smaller cousins that make up the NASDAQ Composite rose 21.6%.

U.S. stocks generally had an excellent time of it. Only one growth fund in 14 declined last year (although only one in 20 beat the S&P 500). In the world at large, though, it was a different story. The EAFE (Europe, Australia, and Far East) Index managed only to break even, up 0.2%. And for some very specific market sectors, 1997 was a disastrous year. Gold once again was dross; the average no-load precious metals fund lost 46.1% of its value in 1997.

Specific segments of the U.S. stock market varied wildly. The average diversified no-load stock fund was up 22.9% last year. But with interest rates in decline for most of the year, and a major consolidation underway in the banking industry, financial services stocks were big winners. The average no-load financial services fund soared 46.3%.

On the other hand, technology stocks brought up the rear. Hailed as the growth area of the economy, technology stocks stumbled badly, particularly in the fourth quarter, after the Asian crisis hit. The average no-load technology fund advanced 16.7 for the year after losing 13.9% in the final three months.

Flush with success, the mutual fund industry last year continued several trends that have been gathering steam. Of course, as always, the big got bigger, while the small were being gobbled up. It was a year

of unprecedented consolidation. Yet, while large banks and insurance companies were swallowing small no-load families, at the other end of the spectrum Fidelity and Vanguard, the super novas of the mutual fund universe, grew still larger.

Vanguard especially was a winner again. Both because of its squeeky clean image, and because it is riding the crest of a trend (indexing), the firm closed a bit more ground on Fidelity. There is still a large difference between $650 billion Fidelity and $350 billion Vanguard. But in another sense, a lot of the difference is between a fund family that's having a good time and one that constantly seems to be putting out fires. For example, three Fidelity funds — **Contrafund** and two precious metals funds — were among the biggest buyers of Bre-X stock. That Canadian "gold mining" company turned out to be a hoax.

Spooky Funds

For mutual fund investors eager to leave the well-trod path and try something entirely else, the industry became increasingly obliging—to an almost bizarre extent. New specialty funds ranged from the sublime to the macabre. Tiny **Meyers Pride Value Fund,** for instance, invests only in companies that appear tolerant of gays and lesbians. **Timothy Plan,** which takes its name from the letters to Timothy in the New Testament, will not invest in alcohol, tobacco or gambling stocks, or those linked to abortion, pornography or gay rights. **Pauze Tombstone Fund** invests in 10 stocks that it calls "death equities;" that's funeral homes, casket makers, and the like.

While those funds may seem frivolous or even downright spooky, a concept that is gaining popularity is the "select" or "focus" fund. The notion is that a fund manager might not have an unlimited number of great investment ideas. So, diversifying too broadly dilutes the impact of excellent ideas.

And the Winner Is . . .

The trouble with an undiversified approach is that the fund's performance can be very uneven. Take the number one performing no-load fund for 1997, **American Heritage.** This is the classic soar or crash fund. While it was up 75% last year, here is the fund's performance for the prior three years: 1994—(-35.33%); 1995—(-30.59%); 1996—(-5.09%). In other words, a four-year investor would still be well under water, and 1998 did not begin encouragingly, either. In January, **American Heritage** was off 13.27%.

Manager Heiko H. Thieme takes a cheerful approach, noting that his 1997 success was attributable to exactly the same factors that caused his earlier calamity, intense concentration. In Thieme's case, that meant putting up to 69% of his investors' money into a British biotech firm, Senetek PLC. And, a

dozen stocks can comprise 90% of his portfolio, among them the illiquid stocks of tiny corporations as well as private placements.

Of Heroes and Goats

In previous editions of this book, I've commented on the rotational nature of the stock market. Revisiting some of the specialized no-loads that had heroic performances in years past is instructive. For instance:

	1995	1996	1997
Fidel. Sel. Air Tr.	59.5%	1.2%	31.1%
Invesco Str. Health	58.9%	11.4%	18.4%
Price Sci & Tech	55.5%	14.2%	1.7%

Only a few of this year's Top Twenty are solid portfolio foundation investments, rather than roller-coaster riders. Among that handful the best perhaps are **SAFECO Growth** and **Gabelli Growth.** Not that they haven't had off years; but these two have had double-digit positive years fairly consistently. If they are similar in that respect, however, the two funds are a study in contrasts in other ways.

Both are run by well-regarded managers. Tom Maguire, who in early 1998 received Mutual Funds magazine's Fund of the Year award for his stewardship, has been managing the comparatively modest **SAFECO Growth** (it grew from $200 million to $400 last year) for the past eight years. Maguire portrays himself as a stock picker, rather than an adherent of any particular investment discipline. He looks for small companies in out-of-favor industries, and he's had a consistent record of finding bargains.

Howard Ward, the proprietor of **Gabelli Growth,** contrasts with Maguire in several respects. Rather than investing in small companies, he concentrates on large and giant corporations. Rather than being oriented to value, as Maguire is, Ward focuses on strong earnings growth. He tries to buy stocks when they are on sale. As a result, his fund usually is less risky than the stock market as a whole.

What About Bonds?

In a year in which interest rates declined steadily from April on, you might have thought that bond funds would be among the top performers. And, indeed, some of the long-term American Century/Benham Target funds turned in excellent total returns. These funds buy zero-coupon bonds of a particular maturity. They are not for unwitting investors, however, since zeros have far more volatility than coupon-bearing bonds. And in a turbulent interest-rate environment, these funds are to diversified bond funds as the specialized stock funds are to diversified stock funds.

The **Target: 2025** was the best-performing bond fund last year, with a 30.1% return, followed closely

by **Target: 2020,** up 28.6% and **Target 2015,** up 22.9%. Those were terrific total returns, but not enough to overtake the best stock funds. If you take a three-year view, however, you see an eerie similarity to the specialty stock funds.

	1995	**1996**	**1997**
Target: 2025	30.1%		
Target: 2020	61.3%	-8.7%	28.6%
Target: 2015	52.6%	-6.4%	22.9%

(Note: Target 2025 was inaugurated in mid-1996)

Zeros being the high rollers of the bond world, those fantastic numbers (for bonds) aren't really reflective of fixed-income investments in general. The typical no-load taxable bond fund last year was up 9.2%, a somewhat better than average year for bonds historically, but not exactly a barn-burner, especially compared with stocks. The average no-load muni bond fund was up 8.4% in 1997.

And the Loser Is . . .

International. While diversified no-load U.S. growth-stock funds were climbing 25.0%, the typical international stock fund gained only 4.8% in 1997. And that's because of good performances in Europe. The emerging markets international funds *lost* 3.6%. Japan only funds declined 22.6% while Pacific Basin funds that hold both Japan and the Southeast Asia emerging markets suffered a double-whammy.

Obviously, a receding tide doesn't necessarily strand all boats. While the **Fidelity Emerging Markets** and **Matthews Pacific Tiger** funds were each losing 40.9% last year, **Fidelity Latin America** was up 32.9% and **Vanguard Index Europe** was ahead 24.2%. The Latin American funds, especially, enjoyed a good year. As always, a few highly focused funds — like the **Lexington Troika Russia Fund** — bobbed to the top.

As a no-load investor, can you draw any lessons from 1997 that will help your 1998 portfolio? Not especially. Unless the lesson is: protect yourself. In my newsletter, my public appearances and in fact all of my work, I constantly preach the virtues of diversification. Maybe that is the lesson of 1997. You cannot possibly know whether a particular year will favor a focused bank-stock fund, a fund that invests exclusively in Russian stocks or a manager who puts most of his chips on one tiny biotech stock.

I began this chapter with a Wall Street maxim, so it's fitting to end with one: Bulls win, bears win, pigs get slaughtered. If it proved anything, 1997 probably was still another object lesson in the art of building a broad portfolio of no-load funds. Hire a handful of superb managers with long records of investment success. Supplement them with a couple of more specialized funds. Keep the risk level at your sleep-at-night threshold. And then hope that we have a few more years like 1997! Oh, and don't take a lot of the credit for great performance. After all, you were just riding the trend.

THE WINNERS

Top ranked no- or low-load each year

Year	Fund	Objective	% Gain	What happened
1997	American Heritage	aggressive growth	75.0	Heiko Thieme made the comeback of the year with 69% of his assets in one British biotech stock, Senetek.
1996	Interactive Inv. Tech Value	sector	60.9	Two Silicon Valley medical and technology scientists put their expertise to work in the market.
1995	Fidelity Select Electronics	sector	69.4	Technology led the way in the great 1995 bull market.
1994	DFA Japan Small Co.	international	29.5	In a generally down year, Japanese small stocks recover some of their bear market losses.
1993	United Services Gold Shares	precious metals	123.9	U.S. Gold wins for the fourth time.
1992	Fidelity Home Finance	sector	57.8	S&L stocks recover from the scandals of the 80s.
1991	CGM Capital Development	aggressive growth	99.1	Ken Heebner, one of the all-time pro's, turned in the best performance for a diversified fund since 1975. Unfortunately, the fund is closed.
1990	Fidelity Select Biotechnology	sector	44.3	Fidelity's youngest manager, 26 year old Michael Gordon, rode the crest of 1990s only equity group to show gains
1989	United Services Gold Shares	precious metals	64.7	Investing in risky South African shares pays off; U. S. Gold won for the third time.
1988	Kaufmann	aggressive growth	58.6	A small-cap fund, heavy in medical stocks, benefitted from takeover situations.
1987	DFA Japan Small Co.	international	87.6	Dimensional Fund Advisors' institutional fund, that required purchases be made in yen, achieved the biggest gain of the decade.
1986	Nomura Pacific Basin	international	74.5	For the second straight year, internationals benefit from a declining dollar and strong overseas markets.
1985	Fidelity Overseas	international	78.7	A bull market in foreign stocks and a declining dollar propelled this new fund, managed by a 29 year old Yale economics graduate, to the top.
1984	Vanguard Qual Div Port I	income	25.2	A fund designed to provide tax-sheltered income won; its gain was the smallest for a #1 fund since 1974.
1983	Fidelity Select Technology	aggressive growth	52.4	Rode the crest of the 1982-83 bull market in technology stocks.
1982	United Services Gold Shares	precious metals	64.1	In a year when stocks finished strong, U. S. Gold won out for the second time.
1981	Lindner Fund	growth	34.0	Money funds were the big winners in a down market, but a portfolio half in cash and a sizeable position in utilities brought Lindner honors.
1980	Hartwell Leverage	aggressive growth	93.9	A great year for equities; the most aggressive funds really shined.
1979	United Services Gold Shares	precious metals	172.9	Gold wins during an inflationary year.
1978	G. T. Pacific	international	50.9	A roller coaster year for U. S. stocks, the Far East was the place to invest.
1977	Value Line Leverage Growth	aggressive growth	51.1	Blue chips were battered, but secondaries and special situations had a great year.
1976	Sequoia	aggressive growth	70.8	Aggressive growth funds dominated in the second year of a powerful bull market. Sequoia achieved its best annual gain ever.
1975	44 Wall Street	aggressive growth	184.1	Leverage made for top performance in the year that began the great bull run.
1974	Sherman, Dean	aggressive growth	24.8	While money funds were the place to be, a non-diversified fund with 12 stocks gained an easy win by zooming to a 79% gain in the first quarter before succumbing to the bear.
1973	Wade Fund	growth	17.6	In a terrible year, Maury Wade got lucky by adding some gold stocks to his portfolio.
1972	Twentieth Century Growth	aggressive growth	42.4	The steady winner from Kansas City began its streak.
1971	Nicholas Strong Fund	aggressive growth	85.5	Both Nicholas and Strong have done very well managing their own funds since the split-up.

CHAPTER 2

Highlights from *The No-Load Fund Investor*

■ Our monthly publication, *The No-Load Fund Investor* newsletter publishes articles of lasting interest. In this chapter, we reprise those articles published since the 1997 Edition of the *Handbook* that we believe are particularly noteworthy.

Portfolio commission costs

(February 1997 *Investor*)

Those of you who actually study the numbers in your funds' annual reports may have noticed a new line at the bottom of the per share table (also called the Financial Highlights table). Starting with fiscal years beginning Sept. 1, 1995, the SEC now requires funds to disclose their average per share commissions for security trades on which commissions are charged. Based on the new data received so far, we have observed an interesting pattern. Domestic funds are paying $0.04 to $0.15 a share to trade stocks, while the per share commission costs for international funds are considerably lower—less than two cents a share. (There are exceptions in both categories.)

Since investment transaction costs are known to be higher overseas, how is this possible? The explanation: Foreign stocks often trade at very low prices in dollar terms. For example, **Founders Passport** owns ten million shares of a Philippine stock with a per share price of 23 cents (when translated from the local currency). Outside the U.S. and Canada, commissions are figured as a percentage of trade value, not on a per share basis. Therefore, if you paid 1% brokerage commission to buy a stock selling for 23 cents per share, your cost would be about a quarter of a cent a share. By focusing on per share cost, the SEC requirements make funds with low-priced shares look like a bargain!

In retrospect, the SEC should have mandated that commission costs be expressed as a percent of the stocks's trade value, not as cents per share. I would hope the SEC will notice and change their reporting standard in the interest of providing meaningful disclosure to investors.

While the funds' commission costs are very low—particularly in contrast to what most individuals pay—that's not the whole story by any means. The real cost of trading is the spread between the bid and ask prices, which can be many times the commission cost. The ask price is what you pay to buy

shares "at the market." The bid price is what you get for selling them "at the market." So, the spread is what you lose if you buy and immediately sell back the same shares.

Bid-ask spreads are not reported anywhere, but the Dimensional Fund Advisors group (DFA) has done an extensive analysis of their impact. DFA says spreads vary considerably based on market cap size. Among the largest and most actively traded blue chip stocks, the bid/ask spread is nominal; among micro cap stocks, however, it is frighteningly large. As shown in the table below, the DFA study ranked stocks by the decile size of their market caps. For the first decile (the 10% of stocks with the largest market caps), the spread was 0.5%. For the last decile of very small stocks, it was 6.2%—twelve times as large. The table also includes the average daily trading volume (per stock) by decile. The daily trading volume of an average decile-one stock is $47 million, roughly 400 times that of an average decile-ten stock.

Per share commissions in cents
Selected funds

Fund name	cents per share	Fund name	cents per share
Invesco Technology	15.6	Lindner Dividend	5.1
Price Dividend Gr	12.7	Strong Common Stock	4.4
Dreyfus Gro & Inc	10.7	Montgomery Equity Inc	4.2
Bonnel Growth	7.2	Fidelity Emerging Growth	4.1
Lexington Gr & Inc	7.0	Fidelity Magellan	3.8
Strong Growth	6.7	Vanguard Wellington	2.7
Founders Balanced	6.3	Founders WrldWide Gro	2.3
Vanguard Equity Inc	6.0	Lexington Int'l	2.0
Vanguard Conv Securities	6.0	Vanguard Int'l Growth	1.9
Baron Gr & Inc	6.0	Founders Intl Equity	1.7
Founders Discovery	5.7	Founders Passport	1.7
Janus Twenty	5.7	Rowe Price Int'l Stk	0.2
Yacktman	5.5	Montgomery Emerg Mkts	0.1
Price Science & Tech	5.3	Invesco Latin Amer	0.01

Daily trading volume

Size Decile	Average Price	Percent Spread	per issue Shares	Dollars
1	$53.92	0.53%	904,445	$47,294,212
2	42.70	0.60	506,539	19,300,213
3	38.19	0.71	336,778	10,772,236
4	33.12	0.98	211,360	5,354,680
5	27.32	1.25	164,897	3,697,177
6	25.79	1.26	117,658	2,645,244
7	22.87	1.61	88,745	1,636,101
8	19.16	2.21	60,099	846,424
9	14.84	2.99	37,894	415,914
10	8.35	6.19	17,462	119,259

DFA is an institutional fund group that manages money passively, through index funds. That's why

they research the costs of active management. If you buy a small cap index fund, it will have a lower turnover than a typical actively-managed small cap fund, and this means lower trading costs. For example, the **Vanguard Small Cap Index Fund** has annual turnover of 28%. In contrast, the average small cap fund has an 84% turnover, with some funds turning over their portfolios in excess of 200% a year. In small stocks, that's expensive.

These data may explain why small cap index funds do well versus the actively managed competition over the long term. Conventional wisdom holds that good small cap active managers have an easier time picking winners than their large cap counterparts because the small cap universe is not as well researched, hence less efficient. But even if this holds true, trading costs may offset any advantage relating to market efficiency. It also follows that small cap funds are not desirable holds in a bear market, because their managers may incur sizable losses if they have to sell stocks to meet redemptions. Most small cap funds should be sold in anticipation of a bear market.

Inflation-adjusted Treasury notes

(March 1997 *Investor*)

On January 29th, the U. S. Treasury, for the first time, auctioned off the ultimate worry-free investment—inflation-adjusted 10-year notes. The notes were sold at an average yield of 3.449% and a coupon of 3 3/8% fixed for the life of the note. As soon as the Treasury broke the ice, four government agencies and three corporations also brought out inflation-adjusted bonds. The FHLB and the Federal Farm Credit Bank issued 5-year notes, The FHLB and the TVA issued 10-year notes and the SLMA issued a 3-year note. Toyota Motor Credit and Salomon, Inc. issued 5-year notes; JP Morgan, a 15-year note.

The Treasury inflation-adjusted notes differ from regular Treasury securities in one important aspect. Twice a year, the face value of the bonds is adjusted for inflation. For example, if the Consumer Price Index rises 3% annually, the note's $1,000 original face value will rise to $1,030, a 3% increase over the year. The following year, the bond will pay 3.375% interest on the larger principal amount, or $34.76. Thus, investors are protected from inflation eroding the bonds' purchasing power. But even if we have deflation, investors will get back no less than the $1,000 face value at maturity. If Congress changes the computation of the CPI (a real possibility), the Treasury will base the adjustment on an appropriate alternate index. In periods of high inflation these

bonds should deliver a higher total return than regular bonds. In periods of falling inflation, deflation, or even a constant inflation rate, the reverse will be true, but you will have bought insurance against higher inflation.

Bear in mind that all you are getting is inflation protection. There is no protection from market forces. For example, if foreigners stop buying our Treasury bonds, values on the indexed Treasuries could fall along with other bonds.

In designing these notes, the U.S. Treasury unfortunately slipped in two ways. 1) You don't get the inflation adjustment in cash. It's added to the face value, which you won't get until sale or maturity, and 2) As in zero coupon bond funds, you will pay taxes on the annual adjustment as if you had actually received it in cash. This makes holding the bonds in regular accounts somewhat less attractive than in tax-sheltered accounts.

Given their lower yields, these notes will not generate much current income for many years. So why buy them? Three reasons: They provide the ultimate in safety. Unlike regular bonds or bank savings accounts, you are guaranteed the return of your principal in real terms. 2) They may be less volatile than regular bonds, because inflation fears create much of the volatility in today's bond market. 3) They offer great diversification, providing either low positive correlation or negative correlation with regular bonds.

By the way, this concept is not untried. The United Kingdom has issued inflation-adjusted bonds for ten years and they now account for 10% of all government borrowing. (Canada and Australia have also issued inflation-adjusted bonds for some time.) A study of these inflation-linked bonds found that in the last five years, a period of declining inflation, the indexed bonds had a correlation coefficient of .56 with regular bonds (Gilts) and of .46 with stocks. (A coefficient of 1.0 is perfect; zero is random, and below zero is negative.) If inflation were increasing, we would expect negative correlations, since the value of the adjusted bonds would rise while that of regular bonds and stocks would fall.

Notes or funds

You can buy individual inflation-adjusted notes with a $1,000 minimum face value, through either Treasury direct or brokers including discount brokers at Fidelity, Rowe Price or Vanguard. Interest is paid twice a year. Small amounts of individual notes may be relatively illiquid because if you need to sell them before maturity, you may not get a good price. notes bought through Treasury Direct are "book entry" and may not be held in an IRA. On the plus side, by buying individual notes you will avoid mutual fund fees and receive the adjusted face value at maturity. Bond funds, as usual, have no maturity.

At this point bond funds have the advantage of greater liquidity, monthly distributions which can be reinvested, and the ease of dealing through a fund group. In the future as more notes are issued, the ability to manage maturities (the Treasury plans quarterly borrowings) will be an another advantage.

First fund out is the **American Century—Benham Inflation-Adjusted Treasury Fund.** Its monthly distributions will represent both interest and an inflation adjustment. Thus, fund investors taking cash distributions will avoid the possible mismatch between distributions and imputed taxes. (If you reinvest, the tax mismatch is academic since, as with all reinvestments, the taxes come 100% out of your pocket.) Benham estimates a .50% expense ratio. Minimum investment is $2,500, IRA minimum $1,000. Dave Schroeder, the fund's manager, notes the ten year inflation-adjusted Treasury note should be about as a volatile as a regular five-year note. For now, he is stuck with the 10-year maturities, but eventually he is aiming for average maturities of less than ten years, giving the fund the volatility of a typical short-intermediate term fund. Also, he will eventually include government agency bonds, but not corporates.

The **PIMCO Real Return Bond Fund,** which also invests in foreign inflation-hedged bonds, can be purchased through Jack White, NTF, for a $25,000 minimum.

We queried three other large groups with heavy fixed-income involvement to determine their plans. Basically, Vanguard is studying the merits of these new bonds, but hasn't filed a registration. Fidelity and Rowe Price are waiting to see how much investor demand develops.

Who should buy them

At this time, inflation-adjusted notes or funds seem best suited for conservative investors who are overweighted with traditional fixed-income investments without inflation protection. These investors can benefit from additional diversification of bond or bond fund holdings, particularly in tax-sheltered plans. However, these notes should be avoided by investors who need high current income to live on. (The Benham fund, with its monthly distributions of the adjustment, may prove attractive to income-seekers.) The notes may also be appropriate for wealthy older investors who can live comfortably off the smaller interest.

Book reviews

(April 1997 *Investor*)

Here are two books that are worthy of your consideration:

John Bogle and the Vanguard Experiment. This isn't an investment how-to book, but rather a biography of John Bogle and a corporate history of Vanguard. Written by Robert Slater, it's a paean to Bogle's quest to market mutual funds at the lowest possible cost. One interesting fact the book unearths is the reason why the **Wellesley Income Fund** has an asset allocation of two-thirds bonds vs. one-third stocks, a rare allocation that has never made much sense to me. The answer, not surprisingly, is that it was the result of a compromise. Back in 1970, Bogle wanted to launch a bond fund, which would have been a first for Wellington. But in 1970 bond funds didn't have much public acceptance. (There were only ten in existence). Since balanced and income funds were popular, the board of directors insisted on some balance. The book is published by Irwin.

Against the Gods, The Remarkable Story of Risk, by Peter Bernstein (one of my heroes), is a treasure. It tells the history of risk management beginning with the ancient Greeks. While they were great mathematical innovators, particularly in geometry, the Greeks didn't understand the principles of uncertainty. (They thought risk was an area controlled by the gods.) Therefore, great strides forward were not made until the 16th century with the work of Pascal and de Fermat in probability theory. Their breakthroughs laid the mathematical and conceptual foundation for such diverse modern industries as investing (including modern portfolio theory and derivatives), gambling, insurance, bridge design, drug-testing, and hundreds of other facets of modern life. None of these modern developments would have occurred if we still called on the oracles or the gods for forecasts. Don't be put off by the subject matter; it's a lively book that includes tales ranging from Omar Khayyam (a skilled mathematician) to Florence Nightingale, Lord Keynes and the Defense Department's notorious Pentagon papers leaker, Daniel Ellsberg. Bernstein is a gifted story-teller and also the former editor of the Journal of Portfolio Management. The book is published by John Wiley.

Large cap vs. small cap

(April 1997 *Investor*)

Small cap stocks continue to disappoint investors. Ever since small cap began lagging large cap three years ago, many investment professionals began predicting small cap's time would soon come. But it hasn't happened yet. The Russell 2000, a prominent small cap index, has lagged badly. Since its 1996 high on May 22nd, the index has declined 6.0%. In contrast, the S&P 500—heavily large cap weighted—gained 11.6% in this same period. In the first quarter of this year, the S&P 500 has gained 2.2%. Meanwhile, the Russell 2000 has lost 5.5%. At some

point, it would seem reasonable that small cap stocks will become more attractive than large cap, then go on to outperform them. But based on history, it's almost impossible to say when.

Students of the market know that since 1926, the earliest year for which we have rigorous, detailed measurement of stocks prices and distributions, small cap has outperformed large cap. $1 invested in the S&P 500 in 1926 grew to $1,371 by the end of 1996; $1 invested in the CRSP 9-10 grew to $2,783. (The CRSP 9-10, an outstanding long-term measure of small cap prices, includes the bottom 20% of NYSE, AMEX and OTC stocks, as measured by market cap.) Annualized, small caps have averaged 11.8% per year vs. 10.7% for large caps, a 10% advantage.

Does that mean small cap is always a good buy? Hardly. The long-term averages mask a multitude of variations. In fact, in the last thirteen years, it's been a completely different story. Since 1984, large cap stocks have surged well ahead of small caps. From 1926 through 1983, small cap stocks averaged 12.3% a year. Since then, they've averaged 9.5% a year—23% less. In contrast, large cap stocks averaged 9.6% a year from 1926 to 1983 and 16.0% since then—67% better. So the small cap stocks' long-term advantage has turned into a 40.6% disadvantage.

	Avg. ann. return		
	CRSP 9-10	S&P 500	% adv.
1926-1996	11.8	10.7	+10.2%
1926-1983	12.3	9.6	+28.1%
1984-1996	9.5	16.0	-40.6%

Some of the small caps' outstanding long-term advantage is due to terrific performances years ago. In three separate years (each in a different decade), small caps more than doubled in value. In contrast, the best annual performance for the S&P 500 was +54%.

Best years			
CRSP 9-10		S&P 500	
Year	return	Year	return
1933	161.4%	1933	54.0%
1943	100.9%	1954	52.6%
1967	100.7%	1935	47.7%

A look at standard deviations confirms that small cap investing is more volatile than large cap. Since 1926, the annualized standard deviation for small cap stocks has been 38.8% versus only 20.3% for the S&P. This means the "normal" variation among small caps falls between plus or minus 38.8% of the long-term average. That's a huge range of returns—between 50.6% and -27.0%. In contrast, large cap varies between 31.0% and -9.6%. Confirming this, small caps have had many more losing years than the S&P during this 71-year period—26 versus 20.

Of course, the overall large cap advantage since 1984 doesn't mean that large cap outperformed small

cap every year. In four years out of 13 since 1984, small caps excelled—the most recent being 1993. In the following table, the winner is in bold-face. The "point diff" column shows the advantage of large cap over small cap.

	Average annual return		
	S&P 500	CRSP 9-10	point diff
1984	**6.3**	-11.6	17.9
1985	**32.2**	26.2	6.0
1986	**18.5**	3.5	15.0
1987	**5.2**	-14.2	19.4
1988	16.8	**19.9**	-3.1
1989	**31.5**	8.2	23.3
1990	**-3.2**	-28.0	24.8
1991	30.5	**51.6**	-21.1
1992	7.7	**26.0**	-18.3
1993	10.0	**19.9**	-9.9
1994	**1.3**	-2.3	3.6
1995	**37.4**	33.3	4.1
1996	**23.0**	18.4	4.6
Average	16.0	9.5	6.5

Small caps underperform in bear markets

One could argue that after three consecutive years of underperformance, the small caps' time has come. But I think it's unlikely. With the market still high, and the Fed just having raised rates, many professionals are nervous. Some feel they have to keep fully invested or they will lag their peers, but they want to be able to sell readily if they perceive a top. They want liquidity! Large cap stocks are simply far more liquid than small cap stocks. Secondly, the pros know that small cap will almost certainly underperform in a bear market. Here's the record for the last four downturns.

	Total return %	
	CRSP 9-10	S&P 500
October 1987	-28.5	-21.5
Third quarter 1990	-24.5	-13.8
1994	-2.3	1.3
June-July 1996	-14.0	-4.1

Then there's the matter of valuations. The Price/Earnings ratio for the Russell 2000 at end of March was 22, while the P/E for the S&P 500 was 19.6. Now, the faster growing small caps traditionally have higher P/E ratios; but still, on an absolute basis, they're more pricey than large caps. Finally, IPO's, at times a significant source of profits for small cap funds, are drying up. According to *Barron's*, 135 initial public offerings were brought to market this past quarter, versus 170 issues floated in the first quarter of 1996. The $5.9 billion in first-quarter 1997 IPO dollar volume represented a 30% decline from last year's $8.3 billion.

Growth vs. value

There are two kinds of small cap funds: those buying growth and those buying value. It's the growth funds that have been hard hit this year; value has been okay.

	Total return %	
	March 97	**1Q 97**
Small cap growth	-8.2	-13.4
Small cap value	-2.7	-0.8

With these huge declines, it would not be surprising, perhaps even likely, that the small cap growth funds will recover some of these losses in the weeks ahead. Nevertheless, given the possibility of a bear market sometime in the next twelve months, I think small cap growth funds will continue to underperform growth funds without market cap restrictions, even those with similar risk levels (as denoted by betas).

Allocating your assets

(May 1997 *Investor*)

Everybody's getting into the asset allocation game. Several fund groups now offer a variety of pre-packaged asset allocation programs, and many leading personal finance magazines offer asset allocation models. Frequently these programs or models are based on an underlying premise that the amount of risk you can take declines with age. For example, a 30-year old investor might be advised to place 70% of a portfolio in equities, while a 50-year old may be guided to a 50% equity weighting.

Unfortunately, such age-based allocation models are far too simplistic. Funds fall back upon simplistic formulae because they can't possibly know the personal needs of each shareholder. So, they reduce the allocation design process to three or four convenient baskets—take your pick. Investment publications simplify the concept for much the same reason, and also because they have space limitations. The *Investor* does not believe in a simplistic age-based asset allocation formula. However, we also are limited by space and lack of knowledge regarding each readers' objectives. Our solution is to offer three model portfolios, each designed for a different risk tolerance: *Wealth Builder, Pre-Retirement*, and *Retirement*.

Therefore, although we hope you find our model portfolios and their allocations useful, we think there is more to this concept than any "cookie cutter" solution can offer you. After all, your needs are unique. That's why we believe that you should give time and thought to the design of your personal asset allocation portfolio.

But how? What investment characteristics should you take into account?

Your time horizon. How much time do you expect to have before you need to begin using the money for either income (e.g., retirement) or a lump-sum payment (e.g., a house)? This is more important than your age, because financial objectives vary for people of the same age. A twenty-year-old could be saving for a retirement decades from now, or to buy a house in just a few years. The investment guidelines for reaching these objectives differ because the cost of a bad investment varies with the time horizon. In the first case, the investor can afford to take a substantial risk because even if the investment is made at the worst time, a mistake can be overcome by holding on. The second investor, who needs his money in a few years, should invest more conservatively because it's difficult to overcome bad timing in such a brief time frame.

Don't assume that you must be conservative because you are older, or aggressive because you are younger. It's truly your time horizon that counts the most. For purposes of establishing your investment time horizon, focus on when you expect to need access to all your income or assets, assuming all goes well. Bear in mind that a person retiring at age 65 doesn't need all his retirement funds at once. Assuming a 20-year life expectancy, the average retirement dollar is needed ten years later, or at age 75.

In asset allocation, a commonly accepted way to adjust investment risk is through the mix of assets placed in bonds and stocks. Stocks are considered more volatile in price than bonds, and stock dividends do not match bond interest as a steady component of return. Hence, stocks carry more risk than bonds. Over the last 40 years, the greatest three-month loss for stocks (the S&P 500) was -25.2%; the greatest loss over a six-month period was 30.8%. In contrast, the greatest losses for five-year government bonds were -5.7% and -3.3% respectively; for 20-year Treasuries, -14.5% and -18.8% respectively.

Your wealth. Another premise of asset allocation is that risk can increase with wealth. For example, if you are retired and living on investment income and the return on your assets is just sufficient to make ends meet, then you can't afford much risk. On the other hand, if your assets are great enough that a major loss won't affect your lifestyle, then you can afford greater risks.

A simple yet effective way of determining how much risk you can afford, based on your accumulated assets, is to multiply your equity assets by 8%. Consider this a middle-of-the-road estimate of what assets might earn, after inflation, over a long period of time. For example, if you have $1 million in equity-based assets, that should provide a total return of $80,000 a year. Add, say, $20,000 in social security or a pension, and you might generate an annual retirement income of $100,000. Now, suppose you

lose one-fourth of it. The $1 million shrinks to $750,000, and your 8% return declines to $60,000 per year, or a total of $80,000 with the pension. For many people that would still be sufficient.

On the other hand, if you have $400,000 of financial assets all invested in equities, your total return would be $32,000 plus $20,000 or $52,000. In this case, a 25% loss slices away $100,000. Your return is now $24,000 plus $20,000 for a total of $44,000. That might not be enough to maintain your standard of living.

For money invested in bonds, a comparable test is to multiply assets by 4%, which represents a rough estimate of what fixed income assets can return after inflation. It would be unusual for short-intermediate-term bonds to decline more than 6%. This loss would reduce a $1 million portfolio to $940,000 and, assuming a 4% after-inflation return, the income from $40,000 to $37,600 or, adding in the $20,000 social security, from $60,000 to $57,600. In most cases this reduction would be tolerable.

Your propensity for risk. No matter how great your need for income, you shouldn't take risks you can't tolerate. This principle might be called "investing up to your sleeping point." Last September, I received a letter from a middle-aged subscriber asking that I cancel his subscription. The letter said he had first invested in stock mutual funds in May 1996, just before the 10% correction. Then "after losing thousands of dollars," he sold out two months later. Unfortunately, if he had just stayed with his investments a few weeks longer, he could have recouped his loss and gone on to greater profits.

It was obvious to me that this subscriber had invested beyond his sleeping point. He remarked that he was comfortable in fixed-income investments but could not handle the volatility of equities.

Your investing goals. Do you want to live off your capital or build an estate which can be distributed to charities or heirs? If your goal is to die broke (and you'd be surprised how many people have that goal), then you should probably take fewer investing risks because you will be making large withdrawals. A table of financial life expectancy in the *Guide* (on page 321) tells how many years your money will last at various withdrawal rates. If you match the withdrawal rate to your life expectancy (and live just that long), you will enjoy your money for all it's worth, and leave nothing behind.

However, if you want to leave money to heirs or charity, then you have a longer time frame and perhaps more flexibility in assuming risk. For example, a few years ago a doctor went to a financial advisor I know and asked that the $500,000 in his pension plan be invested as aggressively as possible. The advisor demurred since it was pension money that is normally invested conservatively. The doctor explained that he didn't need the money; he had other sources of wealth to support his retirement

lifestyle. "If I can make a killing with the money, I can endow a wing in my hospital and be remembered a long time. And if I lose, let someone else be remembered," explained the doctor.

How much money do you want to amass? Like the doctor above, if you're goals are lofty, you'll want a heavier allocation to risky equities (aggressive growth, small-cap and international funds or stocks), the best bet for the highest returns over the long run.

Amount of diversification needed. This goes hand-in-hand with the amount of risk you want to take. Less diversification among asset classes will enhance the possibility of greater returns. Less diversification within an asset class (i.e., owning one fund or stock instead of many) gives you a greater chance to outperform the equity averages. In general, the more investments you own, the more your portfolio tends to "return to an average" return.

Relative valuations in the market. While the primary reason for selecting various asset classes is to implement your personal strategy, asset classes should on occasion be adjusted to maximize returns under varying market conditions. From time to time, *The Wall Street Journal* publishes the asset allocation weightings recommended by the major brokerage firms and investment banks. These allocations vary based on the firms' perception of the relative value of stocks versus bonds. For example, on April 30 the *Journal* published allocations from 14 investment firms. At one extreme Prudential had 70% allocated to stocks, 30% to cash. At the other end, Merrill Lynch had 40% in stocks, 55% in bonds, and 5% in cash. The overall average: 56% stocks, 30% bonds, 5% cash.

Investment Experience. In asset allocation, there is something to be said for having been through the ups and downs of investment markets. The first time an investor experiences a sudden dip in net worth, it is a little like that first plunge on a roller coaster. In general, it's better to gain this experience with a small portion of assets in equities instead of a huge portion.

The Investor has three model portfolios, *Wealth Builder, Pre-Retirement,* and *Retirement. Wealth Builder* has been 100% in equities since 1990 while *Pre-Retirement* and *Retirement* have had 20% and 35% fixed-income allocations since May 1994. All three portfolios have been re-allocated from time to time based on our view of market conditions, and will certainly be reallocated again in the future.

What is a smart way to use these model portfolios while heeding my advice to design your own allocation? While generally speaking, the *Pre-Retirement* portfolio is for investors within ten years of retirement, and the *Retirement* portfolio is for investors who expect to live on their capital for many years, the real difference between the portfolios is in their risk levels. Currently, the *Wealth Builder* portfolio has an average beta of 0.75 and the *Pre-Retirement* portfolio 0.50. The stock market average beta (S&P

500) is 1.00. Therefore, the *Wealth Builder* has about three-quarters of the market's volatility, while *Pre-Retirement* has about half.

Suppose you decide to seek a risk level somewhere between these two models. Then look at the betas for the individual funds listed in each portfolio and seek to "mix and match." For example, you might basically follow the *Wealth Builder* portfolio. However, if you replaced the highest beta fund in that portfolio (Neuberger Berman Partners, 1.08) with a lower beta growth fund recommended in the *Pre-Retirement* portfolio (Third Avenue Value, .73), you would have your own tailor-made portfolio at a risk level between our two models. All funds in any of our three Master Portfolios currently meet our quality criteria, and each portfolio is diversified across several asset classes. So feel free to add, subtract, or replace individual funds to create your own allocation; focus on fund betas in doing so. The higher the beta, the higher the volatility and risk.

Finally, monitor your allocation periodically. Soon you will know the risk level that feels comfortable to you and helps you progress towards your goals.

Importance of fund supermarkets

(June 1997 *Investor*)

Mutual fund supermarkets, such as Charles Schwab Mutual Fund Marketplace, now control a huge amount of assets and are changing the character of fund marketing. For example, we have obtained data for the **Montgomery** funds from their just-issued proxy statement, in connection with their forthcoming sale to Commerzbank AG. The following table shows the percent of each Montgomery stock and bond funds' shares held in Schwab omnibus accounts.

% of Montgomery funds' assets held by Schwab

Emerging Markets	45%	Asset Allocation	34%
Equity Income	44%	Short Duration Gov. Bond	30%
Global Communications	42%	CA Tax Free Inter Bond	29%
International Small Cap	40%	Select 50	26%
Global Opportunities	39%	Emerging Asia	22%
Micro Cap	36%	International Growth	17%
Growth	36%	Small Cap	15%
Small Cap Opportunities	36%	Global Asset Allocation	5%

The relevance of these data are that assets held at Schwab are far more likely to be liquidated in the event of a bear market than assets held directly at the fund. Heavy redemptions, particularly among small-cap funds, are likely to impair performance. Again,

the Montgomery funds are cited because of the availability of data. They are not being singled out; many other fund groups have similar percentages.

What investing is all about

(July 1997 *Investor*)

First of all, it's not about any of the following topics.

How To Get Rich Quick...Six Aggressive Fund Strategies...If You Dare
World's Best Fund?
The 6 Best Investments For '97
Superstar Funds
Double Your Money in 5 Years
Best Mutual Funds to Buy Now
The 7 Best New Mutual Funds
25 Best Funds to Buy Today
The Greatest Funds of All Time
How to Find POWER FUNDS

The excerpts above are from headlines found on the covers of our best-known personal finance magazines. They were all written simply to sell magazines, particularly on the newsstands. And these headlines work, too, or else the magazines wouldn't stick with this format.

The reason these "grabber" headlines work is that most investors still focus on the "recommendation." I get this all the time—when I'm interviewed for print or broadcast media and by individuals. "Sheldon, what's your favorite fund? Which small-cap fund will be top-rated next year?" etc. I think this tradition goes back to the old days when most investors held stock portfolios bought on the advice of brokers. Push a stock; make a commission. That's how brokers paid the rent. Perhaps it's also human nature to converse along these lines—"What's the best movie you've seen lately?...The best book you've read?

After much academic research (which resulted in several Nobel prizes) we know today that successful investing requires more than a steady stream of stocks-du-jour. We know that it's important to diversify, and we know how to diversify. We know how to establish appropriate portfolio risk levels.

Today, the task of investment professionals should be to get investors to realize that their primary goal is to build a *properly diversified portfolio* with the *appropriate risk level*. That is far more important than picking the best individual securities—or funds. Various studies have shown that the asset allocation you choose will determine 90% or more of your total returns. So it's very important not to lose sight of the big picture.

Each of the *Investor's* model portfolios is designed to be a complete investment program. The

Wealth Builder, Pre-Retirement and Retirement portfolios are differentiated by risk levels.

A number of new subscribers have joined us this month. So let's address a common question from new subscribers: "Should I sell my other securities to own one of the model portfolios? There's no pat answer. To make that determination, I would first segregate securities that are performing well from those that are not. Then I would calculate the risk level of your current holdings where possible, using betas. If you hold no-load funds not included in Best Buys, you can find recent betas in the statistical pages of our May or forthcoming August issue or in the *Handbook*. (For bond funds, betas are in the *Handbook* only.) If you own load funds, you can make an estimate or check another source.

You should weight your individual fund betas by your portfolio percent distributions, but if that's too much work, just take a straight average. Then, if after computing the average beta of your portfolio, you find it is seriously out of whack from the *Investor* portfolio you think is best suited for you, more substantial changes should be made.

If the assets are in a tax-sheltered account, you have the freedom to make all the necessary changes without any tax consequences. When in doubt, make the changes. Don't cling to a status quo portfolio for emotional reasons.

If the assets are in a taxable account and there are significant unrealized capital gains involved, I would sell only the extreme underperformers. I would not sell funds recommended in our model portfolios or bold-faced in the tables. You may also need to sell off funds to establish the proper risk level. For example, if you own nothing but aggressive-growth funds, lower your risk level.

If the reduction in the capital gains tax becomes law, I would be quick to sell. In the past, reductions in the capital gains tax have depressed stock prices in the short run as investors rushed to unlock capital gains on favorable terms.

The *Investor* replicates its Master portfolio with single family portfolios for Schwab, Fidelity, Rowe Price and Vanguard. If you prefer, you can concentrate your holdings at another mutual fund group by simply utilizing our risk levels and asset allocations. Your first choice should be funds that are bold-faced in the tables. However, if you still haven't achieved the proper risk level and allocations, then fill in with non-recommended funds from that group.

Should you dollar-cost average a lump sum? Dollar-cost averaging is a strategy in which you make regular purchases, usually of the same amount, over a period of time—usually measured in months or even years. It works very well when saving out of earned income. Investing in a 401(k) is a good example of dollar-cost averaging. But dollar-cost averaging a lump sum often doesn't work out nearly as well. When the market is in a long-term uptrend, it is more profitable to invest a lump sum immediately than to spread it out over an extended period of time.

However, with the market at today's lofty levels, it makes sense to do some dollar-cost averaging. What we currently recommend is that 50% of the money be deployed immediately in relatively conservative funds—the equity income or growth-income funds in any of the three *Investor* lifestyle portfolios. Then, invest the remaining sums over no more than a six-month period or, even better, during market dips.

Of course, investor preference also plays a role in the decision whether to dollar-cost average. Last year a subscriber joined our BJ Group, which manages money on a discretionary basis. We began investing his money using the above strategy. Two weeks later he called, asking me when the remaining 50% would be invested. I explained the strategy and he responded saying, "I'm 82 years old. I'm too old to dollar-cost average! Dump it in!"

Risk-adjusted performance

(August 1997 *Investor*)

I was recently interviewed on KFNN, the fine business radio station in Phoenix AZ. In the course of the discussion, I noted that the *Investor's* model portfolios are currently rated #1 in "Hulbert" for the last eight years *on a risk-adjusted basis*. The station promptly received a call from a listener asking, "What is risk-adjusted performance?" This reminded me that as professionals we must constantly be on guard against slipping into trade jargon (unless talking to the trade). And it also prompted the following answer to a very good question.

It is an investment truism that risk and reward go hand-in-hand. That means riskier investments usually offer greater growth potential than more conservative investments. (Sometimes conservative investments actually outperform riskier ones, but that's another article.) A highly leveraged investment in options and futures obviously has greater potential than, say, investing in an AAA-rated bond. The reason is that investors expect greater compensation for taking greater risks and price securities accordingly. If the stock market didn't return more than a totally safe Treasury note, it would be foolish to choose the market (with all its risk) over the note.

However, before we can explain risk-adjusted performance, we need to explain how risk is measured. For stock funds, the *Investor* prefers betas, which measure historic price volatility in relation to the S&P 500, even though a good case can be made for using standard deviation (which is discussed in the next paragraph). The reason I prefer betas is that they are more understandable than standard devia-

tions. The market has a beta of one. A fund—or a portfolio—with a beta of 1.10 is 10% riskier than the market. A fund with a beta of .75 is one-fourth less risky than the market. The disadvantage: in some cases a low beta simply means there is a low correlation with the U.S. stock market, not that the fund carries little risk. For example, **U.S. Global Shares,** a gold fund with a heavy concentration of South African investments, has a beta of .31. However, as the worst performing fund over the last three years, it's obviously quite risky. Another disadvantage of using beta is that sometimes a fund will change its policies or strategies, lessening the predictive value of the data.

In contrast, standard deviation measures volatility within the investment itself, independent of an index. A fund whose NAVs range from $7 to $14 over a period of time will have a greater standard deviation than a fund whose NAVs vary from $9 to $11 over the same period. The disadvantage of standard deviations, in my opinion, is that they are harder for investors to grasp. Standard deviation, while it has a precise statistical meaning, doesn't mean much to laymen unless compared to a benchmark. For example, it's hard to tell in non-technical terms just how risky a fund is with a standard deviation of, say, 5.22.

Since bonds have a low relationship to the S&P 500, beta is not very meaningful for them. Therefore, we use standard deviations as a measure of risk for bond funds in this issue and the other quarterly issues that carry betas. As a general rule, bond funds with longer maturities will have greater standard deviations. Standard deviations for stock funds are published annually in the *Handbook.*

Morningstar, the mutual fund rating service, offers yet another way of measuring risk. Unlike both beta and standard deviation, which take into account both upside and downside risk, *Morningstar* assigns its risk percentile rankings (and stars) based on downside risk only. Downside risk is assumed by *Morningstar* to be any month in which a fund's return is below the Treasury bill return. As a practical matter, most investors *love* upside volatility; it's only downside volatility that we *hate.* So, *Morningstar's* exclusion of upside volatility in computing their star ratings makes a lot of sense.

Note also, the securities industry uses volatility as a proxy for risk because it can be computed precisely. But it's really a very imperfect measure of risk. There are many, many risks that volatility doesn't measure. For example, the likelihood of a company going bankrupt. It's quite possible that a stock's price will be relatively flat (i.e. have low volatility) until an announcement is made, and then fall off a cliff. Similarly volatility can fail to capture chronic underperformance. A fund that *consistently* gains 10% a year isn't any more volatile than a fund that *consistently* gains 5% a year.

In a long-term bull market, a decision to take greater risks for higher returns will frequently prove profitable. Yet, only a minority of investors can or should seek maximum risk. Most of us must moderate our risk profile because we can't take a chance of losing substantial portions of our nest eggs. That's why the *Investor* has three lifestyle portfolios, two of which include fixed-income investments.

I think it's unlikely that the *Retirement* portfolio, and probably even the *Pre-Retirement* portfolio, will ever totally avoid fixed-income investments. It's just not prudent. So, as long as these portfolios include bonds, it's unlikely the *Investor* will ever outperform our competitors on the basis of performance only. Most top-rated newsletter portfolios have all-equity, or even riskier, model portfolios. However, when our performance is risk-adjusted (i.e., our lower risk level is taken into account), we shine!

The *Hulbert Financial Digest* computes risk-adjusted performance using the Sharpe ratio, the same calculation which we publish for mutual funds in this issue and quarterly. Data used in Sharpe ratio calculations for this issue are based on the three years ending June, 1997.

The Sharpe ratio is a measure of reward per unit of risk. Reward is considered to be the fund's performance minus a constant (U.S. Treasury bill yield) that reflects a risk-free rate of return. Risk is considered to be the fund's standard deviation—i.e., variability of returns. Divide reward by risk and you have the Sharpe ratio. In order to simplify Sharpe ratings, we have assigned letter grades — from A to F. Funds graded "A" have posted the best gains with the least risk within their objective category. For convenience, these grades are shown next to the betas, but are a totally separate measure. Additional explanations of these risk-measuring devices are contained in the *Guide.*

Insights into '97 tax act

(September 1997 *Investor*)

On August 5, President Clinton signed into law the Taxpayer Relief Act of 1997, one of the most complex tax acts of modern times. Here's a review of the new tax rules affecting mutual fund investors:

Lower capital gains rates

The biggest change in the new tax bill is the reduction—and complication—of capital gains taxes. There will now be three different maximum rates on capital gains, (with a fourth one to come in the year 2001):

1) For assets sold after 7/28/97, the new capital gains rate on assets held at least 18 months is 20% if

your ordinary income bracket is 28% or higher. If you're in the 15% bracket, the new capital gains rate is 10%.

2) Assets sold between May 7 and July 28, 1997 qualify for the new rates if they were held for more than 12 months.

3) For assets sold after 7/28/97, and held between 12 and 18 months, the old rates apply: 28% for investors in the 28% bracket or higher; 15% for investors in the 15% bracket.

4) Short-term capital gains—held less than 12 months—along with mutual fund dividends and interest are still taxed at ordinary income rates.

5) Assets purchased in 2001 or later, and held for five years, will be subjected to a maximum rate of 18% (8% in the 15% bracket). Assets purchased earlier can qualify by "marking to market" and paying the tax based on market value on Jan. 1, 2001. However, the five-year holding period after 1/1/01 will still apply for assets marked-to-market.

There hasn't been much of an incentive in recent years to hold long term, because the 28% maximum capital gains rate was about the same as the 28% or 31% ordinary income rate that most investors paid. As a result, many fund managers paid little attention to their holding periods. Of course, if your funds are held in a tax-deferred account, the holding period is irrelevant. But if they're not sheltered, under the new law the extent to which a fund manager takes his profits short-term will have a great impact on your after-tax return. It's now far more important to pick funds whose managers are predisposed to holding stocks long-term in order to obtain more favorable tax treatment.

Pay attention to turnover

The funds that are likeliest to hold stocks 18 months or more are those funds with low portfolio turnover. The turnover statistic is readily available; it's published in the funds' prospectuses and annual reports. We show it in the *Handbook* and, this issue only, in the *Investor.*

The turnover rate can be used to approximate the holding period. A fund with a turnover ratio of 100% is holding its positions, on average, for one year. A fund with a 67% turnover ratio is holding stocks 18 months on average.

Recognize, though, that turnover is only a rough measure. Whether funds sell low-cost basis or high-cost basis stocks also makes a big difference. Some funds use FIFO accounting, others LIFO. And, keep in mind, even a low turnover fund can turn into a high turnover fund if a lot of investors redeem. Hopefully, turnover rates will decline as managers adjust to the new law. (Technically, the turnover rate is calculated by computing the value of securities sold or purchased over a given time divided by the fund's average net assets.)

In this issue we've averaged the turnover ratios for the latest three years' data available. For newer funds, it's either the latest year or an average of the latest two years. (You can find annual data in the *Handbook.*) We've shown an average because significant year-to-year differences do occur. Half of all equity funds in this issue have annual turnovers under 75%.

Index funds almost always have low turnover, as do a new breed of funds designed specifically to be tax-efficient. Following is a partial list of low turnover funds that we are currently recommending. With the exception of the **Schwab 1000 Fund**, we've excluded index funds, which would otherwise dominate the list, to make more room for actively managed funds. **Schwab 1000** is highlighted because, unlike most index funds, it does not rebalance. In total, this issue recommends 118 equity funds with average turnovers under 75%.

Recommended low turnover funds excluding index and multifunds

	Avg Ann % Turnover		Avg Ann % Turnover
Schwab 1000	2	Vangd Spec-Energy	16
Longleaf Partners Realty	4	USAA Gro & Inc	16
Vangd Tax Mngd: Balanced	5	Invesco Total Ret	17
Dreyfus Apprec	6	Tweedy Brwn Glob Val	18
Vangd Tax Mngd: Gro & Inc	7	Price Int'l Stk	18
Vangd Primecap	8	Babson Enterprise II	18
Salomon Opportunity	9	Price Balanced	18
Vangd Spec-Gold	9	Papp L Roy Stock	19
Vangd Tax Mngd:Cap App	10	Price European	18
Tweedy Brwn Amer Val	10	Dodge & Cox Balanced	19
Dodge & Cox Stock	10	Htchks & Wly Int'l	20
Babson Value	10	Babson Growth	20
Third Ave Value	11	Gabelli Asset	20
Vangd Spec-Health	15	Vanguard Equity Inc	23

In addition to **Vanguard's Tax-Managed Funds,** another fund that makes a special effort to limit the tax bite is the two-month old **T. Rowe Price Tax-Efficient Balanced Fund**. Another fund of interest is **Selected American Shares** with a 26% turnover. Run by the Davis', it has a lot of their own money in it.

Even under the new tax laws, don't automatically exclude high-turnover funds from your portfolio. Many have superior performance that will more than compensate for the tax disadvantage. Some do a lot of trading, but are careful to take losses to offset their gains. This issue recommends 68 funds with turnovers over 100%. If you maintain both taxable and tax-sheltered accounts, the easy solution is to own high-turnover funds in tax-sheltered accounts and low-turnover funds in regular accounts. Also, for mutual fund traders the lower rates are largely academic. If you sell a fund within 18 months of buying it, you'll pay regular tax rates on all profits, except any long-term gains distributed by the fund (usually in December).

Other investing considerations

The new tax rates narrow the appeal of tax-deferred accounts over taxable accounts. That's because the long-term capital gains portion of your total return in a taxable account will now be taxed at rates from 10% to 20%, while distributions from tax-deferred accounts will be taxed at ordinary income rates as high as 39.6%. For most investors, this means emphasizing equities in taxable accounts and holding taxable fixed-income investments in tax-deferred accounts. (Muni bonds or muni bond funds, already tax-free, should never be placed in tax-sheltered accounts!) Typically, a far higher portion of an equity investment's total return comes from capital gains than is the case with bonds.

When calculating the 18-month holding period for long-term capital gains, don't forget to look at each reinvestment. For example, shares purchased last December via reinvestment plans won't turn long term until next June.

I've never been a fan of the short-trading strategies sometimes encouraged by brokers or Internet trading programs. With the new rate differentials, day trades, scalping a few points on a stock, taking a flyer on a hot tip, etc. are strictly for gamblers. Their chances of making real after-tax money are in line with Las Vegas odds. The only place such strategies make any sense for individual investors is in self-directed IRAs.

The Roth IRA, which becomes effective in 1998, is a new type of non-deductible IRA available to couples with incomes less than $160,000 and individuals with incomes under $110,000. If you hold more than five years, tax-free withdrawals (without penalty) are permitted to buy a first home, pay for higher education and, after age 59 1/2, fund retirement. The Roth has some advantages over other types of IRAs, and in many instances is superior to muni-bond funds, particularly if equities continue to outperform munis. Unfortunately, the Roth has the usual $2,000/$4,000 annual limits. Investors will be permitted to roll over traditional IRAs to Roth IRAs by paying all tax (as if on a withdrawal, but without 10% penalty). For these rollovers made in 1998, the tax may be paid in installments over four years. With a Roth IRA, you can continue to make contributions after age 70 1/2, with no minimum distribution requirements, but for older investors this advantage may be offset by having to pay the tax now.

If you want help deciding whether the Roth IRA is right for you, check the internet. The Strong funds have launched a Roth IRA Analyzer on the company's web site at www.strong-funds.com. You simply enter your own financial and demographic information and the Analyzer determines whether you are eligible for the Roth, the education IRA or the deductible IRA and which produces the best returns. You can also call a Strong fund IRA specialist at 800-588-4472.

Consider slanting your asset allocation towrds growth and total return funds and away from income-oriented funds.

Lower capital gains rates benefit real estate investment trusts because a portion of REIT dividends is typically classified as a nontaxable return of capital. That lowers the cost basis and essentially converts current income into capital gains when the REITs are sold. At **Cohen & Steers Realty Fund,** 15% to 35% of the fund's income distributions are return of capital. This is noted at year-end when the fund sends out its 1099s.

To our great relief, the act does *not* incorporate President Clinton's earlier proposal to require an average cost basis to calculate gains or losses when selling securities. If you are making a partial sale of a fund, it usually pays to identify and sell those specific shares with the highest cost basis.

Variable annuities less attractive

The prime attraction of variable annuities is their ability to shelter income and capital gains distributions. With a lower long-term capital gains rate, that advantage isn't as important. That's particularly true for investors in the higher brackets since regular income tax rates apply on variable annuity withdrawals of earnings. In other words, capital gains that would be taxed at 20% outside a tax-shelter will be taxed as high as 39.6% when distributed from an annuity. Due to the costs of higher internal fees, variable annuity holders have always had lengthy holding periods before their tax-deferral advantages offset their higher expense ratios. Vanguard estimates that under the old tax law, a person in the 28% tax bracket needed six years to break even. Under the new law, 19 years is needed to break even, assuming that internal fees on variable annuities stay the same. If you're in the 39.6% bracket, your break-even period went from 20 years to 31 years. Bear in mind, Vanguard's variable annuities are among the lowest cost in the business. For higher-cost sponsors, the holding periods will be even longer.

Consider variable annuities only if: You are young, have already funded your IRA and 401(k) to the limit, and think you'll retire 20-30 years from now in a lower tax bracket. Of course, salespeople will probably recommend otherwise. On the other hand, if you already own an annuity, you shouldn't rush to sell it. You'll need to work out the numbers—redemption penalties, 10% federal tax penalty (if you are under 59 1/2), your tax rate, amount of gains, etc.—to see if you'll benefit.

Short-short rule eliminated

One relatively obscure tax law change passed in the 1997 Budget Act is the elimination of the short-short rule. This rule deprived funds of their pass-

through tax status if more than 30% of their gross income came from short-term investments held less than 90 days. As a practical matter, this inhibited funds from utilizing short-term strategies since they couldn't always foresee the size of their long-term profits and thus keep the ratio under 30%. With the short-short rule repealed, mutual funds are now free to do more short-term trading, hedging, short-selling, and writing of covered call options.

The industry opposed the short-short rule for years, arguing that it was archaic and unfairly limited flexibility. I agreed with the industry position, but it wouldn't surprise me if some funds will now overuse their new-found flexibility.

Manager turnover

(October 1997 *Investor*)

Fidelity Investments frequently has been criticized for its management turnover, which is indeed high. We've just completed a special study and found that the median fund manager at Fidelity has been running his or her current fund for only 17 months.

We've separated sector funds from other equity funds, because Fidelity seems to use them as a training ground before giving a manager responsibility for a diversified fund. We found that only 18% of all Fidelity fund managers were in place before 1995 and, in the case of sector funds, only 6%. Here's the breakdown:

Tenure of Fidelity portfolio managers*
Percent distribution As of September 1997

Year began	Sector	Other equity	Fixed-income	All
1992 & earlier	3%	13%	9%	8%
1993-94	3%	20%	7%	10%
1995-96	38%	45%	51%	45%
1997	56%	22%	33%	37%
Total	100%	100%	100%	100%
Median start	Jan '97	Mar '96	Jan '96	May '96
Median tenure	9 mos	19 mos	21 mos	17 mos
# managers/funds	36	60	43	139

Source: Fidelity Mutual Fund Guide. Money funds excluded.

Bear in mind that we are measuring manager tenure with the current fund. Many Fidelity managers managed other Fidelity funds before assuming the helm of their present funds.

A number of Fidelity funds had mediocre performances in 1995 and 1996, and the recent high turnover of managers is partly Fidelity's response to fixing that problem. Also, Fidelity made switches as part its plan to get managers to hew to their funds' stated objectives. Nevertheless, we previously conducted this study in early 1995, when neither poor performance nor

objectives slippage was a big concern, and we found similar results. Another independent study found high turnover in 1992 and 1993, two years in which Fidelity funds turned in outstanding performances.

The *Fidelity Monitor* newsletter, has done a study that seems to show that Fidelity has not been hurt by management turnover. The *Monitor* found that Fidelity funds with only one manager over the five-year period ending 12/31/96 performed only fractionally better than funds with several managers. In fact, given the small amount of performance difference and the limited number of funds in the sample, it appears that manager turnover at Fidelity has had far less impact on performance than critics charge.

Performance vs. Manager turnover at Fidelity
Annual return for the five years ending 12/31/96

# Managers	# Funds	Avg. return over 5 yrs
One	5	17.2%
Two	17	16.1%
Three	18	17.1%
Four	12	16.7%
Five	5	16.7%

Source: Fidelity Monitor, Feb. 1997. The study encompassed Fidelity's domestic funds (growth, growth & income and Selects except Electronics) that were at least five years old. Select Electronics was excluded from the study because it had an unusually high return for the period. (It had five managers.)

One explanation for these results is that Fidelity managers are supported by a group of 231 analysts and researchers who have a vested interest in the quality of their recommendations. Fund managers often do research as a team, such as questioning company managers during face-to-face meetings. Findings are well documented and shared internally so every manager at Fidelity can benefit. This is also true at several other large complexes. It's a good reason to prefer these large fund complexes, other things being equal.

Objective classifications

Recently, a subscriber asked us why we classify **Neuberger-Berman Guardian Fund** a growth fund, since other publications classify it as a growth-income fund and the fund's prospectus says it is a growth-income fund. Our response to that subscriber explains our thinking about how we evaluate funds for purposes of assigning categories.

We replied that most fund groups like to position funds in the most conservative category possible, because that makes it easier for them to excel vis-a-vis their peers. Our job is to give subscribers more objectivity; in many cases, more than the funds do.

We use the categories in the *Investor* and *Handbook* primarily to establish risk levels which allow for "apples-to-apples" comparisons amongst similar funds.

Guardian has a beta of 1.05. That makes it riskier than the average diversified equity fund (.81) and even the average aggressive-growth fund (.94). With a higher beta than 87% of all equity funds, Guardian does not fit in with the more conservative growth-income funds, in our book.

Secondly, **Guardian** has a yield of 0.6%, less than the yield of the average growth fund (0.7%), and far below the 1.6% yield of the average growth-income fund. (The Vanguard S&P 500, often considered a quintessential growth-income fund, now yields 1.6%.) If this is a growth-income fund, where's the income?

Investors typically comparison shop within the growth-income category when they are seeking a fund that will provide less volatility and more income than the stock market average. We don't believe **Guardian** fits these criteria. That, in a nutshell, is our rationale for including this fund in the growth category, and for laying an objective eye on all fund classifications.

The *Investor's* objective classifications are designed to group funds by risk levels. Typically, aggressive growth funds are riskier than growth funds, etc. From time to time we have been asked to group funds by style (growth versus value) or by capitalization size. Small-cap funds are noted by an "SC" next to the name, but we've resisted labeling for growth or value because so many funds pursue a blend of styles, and styles do change from time to time. *Morningstar* publications, an excellent source for this information, categorizes 41% of the domestic stock funds it follows as having portfolios that hold a blend of both growth and value stocks. It's their largest category. (31% of funds are in the growth category, 28% in the value category.) Information on styles is certainly helpful, but I'd rather concentrate on risk.

Selected or focus funds

(December 1997 *Investor*)

"Selected" or "focus" funds are the new vogue terms for concentrated mutual funds with a limited number of stocks in their portfolios. The concept: Individual money managers have a limited number of great investment ideas. When managers are too widely diversified, the impact of their best selections will be diluted. A concentrated portfolio therefore allows managers to get the greatest mileage out of their best ideas; it's a way to stand out from the pack. It's also a resurrection of an old idea—with "fewer eggs in the basket," the manager can watch each one more closely.

The concept seems to be gaining popularity. We now have **Montgomery Select 50, PBHG Select**

Equity, Oakmark Select, Masters Select Equity, and **Vanguard Selected Value**, as well as the **Neuberger-Berman, CGM**, and **Yacktman Focus** funds. (Such older funds as **American Century Select, Selected American** and **Special Shares,** and **Fidelity Stock Selector** are not particularly concentrated, despite their names. The 36 **Fidelity Select** sector funds are concentrated, but by industry.)

As a test-tube illustration of how good the concept can be when things are working, look at the performance of the **Masters Select Equity Fund** run by Litman/Gregory. This 11-month old fund is sub-advised by six veteran portfolio managers, each contributing up to 15 stocks to the portfolio. Each manager serving as a sub-advisor independently runs one or more successful funds. The Masters fund has gained 27.8% year-to-date, a better performance than four of the six sub-advisors' own funds.

Sub-advisor	Fund	YTD return	Wgt
Shelby Davis	NY Venture	30.8%	20.1%
Jean-Marie Eveillard	SoGen Overseas	3.7	19.8
	SoGen Int'l	8.6	
Mason Hawkins	Longleaf Partners	27.3	19.8
Spiros Segalas	Harbor Cap. Appr.	30.3	20.5
Foster Friess	Brandywine	20.1	9.9
	Brandywine Blue	26.8	
Richard Weiss	Strong Common Stk	21.6	9.9

We're not really sure what defines a selected or focus fund. Like many terms in this business, the definitions are something less than precise. However, after checking several sources, we find a working definition might be: "Either 1) a fund holding 25 or fewer stocks; or 2) a fund in which the top ten holdings account for 50% or more of the fund's total assets." In the case of funds with multiple managers, such as **Montgomery Select 50** or **Masters Select Equity Fund**, it would be stocks per manager.

I asked Ken Heebner, manager of the CGM funds, how his new **CGM Focus Fund** differs from his other three funds, all of which have concentrated portfolios. His answer was that all four funds are essentially run the same. So, in some cases the difference is marketing. Nevertheless, there are significant investment differences between concentrated and widely diversified funds. Heavily concentrated funds will have more price volatility than widely diversified funds. Good stock selections will goose performance more; poor selections will hurt more.

The range of performance among focus funds can be particularly wide. Of the funds we carry, year-to-date performances have been as high as 61.5% for **American Heritage** and as low as -10.1% for **Vanguard Horizons Capital Opportunities.** So regardless of the theory (or the marketing hype), concentrating a portfolio doesn't necessarily guarantee better performance. While wide diversification dilutes your winners, it also limits your downside risk.

That said, I should quickly add that many of these focus funds have turned in outstanding performances this year. The focus funds in the accompanying table averaged 25.5%. Twenty-two of the 34 funds bettered the average diversified fund, which gained 21.0%.

I tried to see if there was a pattern to the exceptional performances. One factor: 24 of the 34 focus funds included in the accompanying table bought large-cap stocks. Given the great performances of some of these stocks, this may have made the stock selection process easier. Even then, only four of these concentrated funds have over a billion dollars in assets. And of the four, **Yacktman**, in terms of its concentration, is a borderline focused fund. Long-closed **Sequoia**, a fund with a Warren Buffet-like focus on a few value stocks, is a special case. Focus funds oriented toward mid-cap and small-cap stocks performed more in line with their group averages.

Two-thirds of the concentrated funds had below-average turnover ratios. Since portfolio managers who concentrate their portfolios all believe they are superior stock pickers, this isn't surprising. However, it's not clear that having a low turnover helped performance much.

During bear markets, expect a wide disparity of performance among these funds. In the big bear of October 1987, **Sequoia** declined 12.2% and **Clipper** declined 7.3% versus a 21.0% decline for the average diversified fund. On the other hand, **Fairmont** declined 29.2%. A focus fund's objective and style have more to do with its bear market performance than its concentration.

I think the bottom line here is you will likely find greater consistency of performance in diversified funds than in concentrated funds. However, if the manager is a great stock picker, there is the potential to do better in a concentrated fund. The corollary, of course, is if the manager isn't a great stock picker, or runs hot and cold (as some of these managers always do), you'll wind up with inferior or spotty performances. Witness: **American Heritage**, the top-ranked fund this year, was dead last only two years ago. Ken Heebner is considered a very good manager, but his new **CGM Focus Fund** is not off to a fast start.

I think 1998 may be a good year for select and focus funds. In the early years of this great bull market, virtually all stocks were undervalued, and it didn't require great brains to pick stocks that were going up. But with the market no longer undervalued, I think there will be a greater disparity between great stock pickers and run-of-the-mill managers. While I think this will hold true whether funds are diversified or concentrated, the funds that should benefit the most from truly expert stock picking will be concentrated funds.

Some of the concentrated funds I like for the long-term are: **Robertson Stephens Partners, Vontobel U.S. Value, L. Roy Papp America Abroad, Masters Select Equity, Montgomery Select 50** (a global fund), and **CGM Realty**. Three other funds that have potential, but are too new to recommend, are: **CGM Focus, Yacktman Focus** and **Marsico Focus**.

Concentrated funds							
Fund	Obj	Total holdings	% Assets in top 10 holdings	Net assets $M	Assets/ holding $M	Average turnover %	1997 11 mo return
American Heritage SC	agg gr	50	75.0%	$ 23.1	$ 0.5	565%	62.5%
Cappiello-Rushmore Gro	growth	22	45.3	31.6	1.4	88	24.8
CGM Focus	agg gr	24	58.0	37.0	1.5	—	—
Clipper	growth	19	74.9	751.1	39.5	33	28.9
Fairmont	agg gr	37	53.1	34.8	0.9	253	20.0
Fidelity Fifty	agg gr	59	40.3	180.1	3.1	217	20.5
Gintel	growth	41	74.6	174.9	4.3	61	29.9
Janus Olympus	agg gr	33	59.0	615.8	18.7	303	25.2
Janus Twenty	agg gr	24	57.2	5,969.7	248.7	151	28.6
Lexington Corporate Leaders	gr-inc	26	60.6	532.0	20.5	—	20.7
Longleaf Partners Sm Cap SC‡	growth	33	39.5	883.5	26.8	27	26.9
Masters' Select Equity	agg gr	75	28.6	272.5	3.6	62	27.8
Montgomery Select 50	global	55	34.8	251.3	4.6	106	29.7
Nicholas Equity Income	income	25	44.5	25.6	1.0	34	15.3
Oakmark	growth	46	55.6	6,614.9	143.8	24	28.2
Oakmark Select#	growth	16	71.4	384.6	24.0	—	44.3
Papp L Roy America-Abroad	growth	29	43.3	279.8	9.6	26	29.9
Papp L Roy Stock	growth	27	53.6	80.1	3.0	19	32.6
PBHG Large Cap 20	growth	20	56.6	110.2	5.5	44	27.0
Philadelphia	gr-inc	24	68.1	110.1	4.6	37	29.5
Reynolds Blue Chip Growth	gr-inc	110	50.1	62.3	0.6	38	31.3
Robertson Stephens Partners SC	agg gr	44	78.8	216.7	4.9	86	19.7
Rydex Nova	agg gr	13	152.1	767.6	59.0	0	39.3
Rydex OTC	agg gr	79	73.5	449.6	5.7	1997	29.4
Salomon Opportunity	growth	88	57.3	201.6	2.3	9	30.0
Sequoia‡	growth	15	91.5	3,327.4	221.8	23	35.3
Van Wagoner Mid-Cap	growth	43	50.3	115.6	2.7	173	-6.2
Vanguard Horizon Cap Opp	agg gr	23	55.9	81.0	3.5	128	-10.1
Vanguard Selected Value	growth	27	43.8	193.4	7.2	25	17.0
Vontobel U.S. Value	gr-inc	19	73.8	103.0	5.4	101	29.0
Wasatch Growth	growth	35	59.8	135.4	3.9	104	25.7
Wasatch Mid-Cap	agg gr	48	51.4	77.3	1.6	84	7.0
Yacktman	gr-inc	43	47.7	1,160.3	27.0	54	16.6
Yacktman Focused	growth	15	72.9	41.1	2.7	*65	—
Average focused fund							25.5
Average diversified fund							21.0

* estimated   # Not carried in the Investor

Section II

No-Load Fund Performance Tables

CHAPTER 3

Explanation of tables

Alphabetical tables of no-load funds

The statistical tables that follow show all no-loads in existence since the beginning of 1997. Other funds, started in late 1997 and early 1998, are listed in the Handbook's Directory Sections.

Explanation of symbols: A † sign to the right of a fund name indicates the fund has a low load or sales charge applicable to some purchases. A ‡ sign next to the fund name indicates the fund is in some way limiting sales—it may be closed to new shareholders, or restricting share ownership to certain classes such as corporations, institutions, or only to clients of a brokerage house. See the Directory Section for specifics. An asterisk beside a fund (in Chapter 7) indicates there is switching between a fund group and an unaffiliated money fund. In Chapter 4, right-hand pages, percent distribution of portfolio columns: Parenthesis around a cash percentage figure indicates the fund is leveraged.

Performance computations: The *Handbook* shows performance on a total return basis. This is the percent gain or loss for a fund, including distributions, over the stated period. For example: for the AARP Balanced Stock & Bond Fund we show a total return in 1997 of 21.9, meaning that, including distributions, AARP Balanced Fund gained 21.9% from Jan. 1 through Dec. 31, 1997. It is important to note that the *Handbook's* figures rate the funds' performance—not the investors' experience. The calculations do not take into account front-end low loads or redemption fees, nor taxes you might have to pay on distributions.

Three, five and ten year performance figures are compounded. This means you cannot average the individual years arithmetically to get the compounded results.

Quintile ranking system: The *Handbook* uses superscript numbers (exponents) above each performance figure to show the fund's rank *within its objective category*. For example, an aggressive growth fund with a "1" above its performance figure is in the top 20% of all aggressive growth funds for the indicated period. A "2" indicates the fund was in the second 20% (or top 40%) of all funds that have the same investment objective. A "3" indicates the third or middle quintile. These are average funds. Funds ranked "4" or "5" are below average. If you don't know a fund's objective, check the right-hand pages of Chapter 4, which lists all stock and bond funds in alphabetical order.

Yield and Distributions: Are based on the income distributions for the latest twelve months divided by ending NAV. An adjustment is made for capital gains distributions by adding them back into the ending NAV. For investment analysis, long and short-term capital gains distributions are totaled in the capital gains column.

In the case of the American Century Benham Zero Coupon Bond Funds, we show a yield-to-maturity even though no actual interest is paid. It's the yield you would receive if you held the fund until it was liquidated at maturity.

Portfolio distribution: Shows the percent of each fund's year-end total assets invested in stocks, bonds, preferreds, and cash. Stocks include both common stocks and convertibles. The bond category includes fixed-income as well as preferred securities. Cash means cash and cash equivalents, including CDs, repurchase agreements, money markets, and any bonds with maturities of less than one year. This information can be used in conjunction with the investing principles described in the *Guide*, and with the cash position data published in *The No-Load Fund Investor* newsletter.

NAVs and total assets are shown for two years. If a fund's assets have grown at a faster rate than its per share NAV, the fund has had net sales. If the asset growth was less than the per share growth, the fund is in net redemptions. See the *Guide* for investment implications.

Betas are computed using least squares correlation and regression analysis. Monthly percentage returns (adjusted for reinvestment of all distributions) are computed for both the funds and the S&P 500, a large company market index reflecting fund portfolios for the latest 36 months. Second, these returns are expressed in "risk premium" form by subtracting from each the return on risk-free Treasury bills, thus reducing the observations to data reflective of the rewards attained for bearing risk. Betas, the funds' objectives, year-to-year variations in prices and the yield are all factors to consider in determining the amount of risk you wish to take.

As a benchmark, following are the average betas by objective for funds in this edition of the *Handbook*.

Betas ranked by objective
3 yrs ending 1997

Aggressive growth	.84
Growth	.80
Growth-income	.78
Sector	.75
Small company	.73
International equity	.72
Global equity	.65
Income	.57
Precious metals	.40
Fixed-income	.16
Tax-free	.15
Avg diversified stock	.77
Avg stock	.75

Beta has two companions: the *coefficient of determination* and the *alpha*. The coefficient of determination, notated as "R^2," measures the percentage of variability due to the market. Index funds have R^2's approaching 100. All their variability is due to the market. Gold funds have low R^2's. Their variability is only slightly related to the overall stock market. The other measure, alpha, which measures non-market-related variability, is considered by some to be an indicator of management ability.

The *Handbook* shows the beta and R^2, but not the alpha. Instead, we include the *Sharpe* ratio, which measures the reward per unit of risk, with risk being defined as variability. It is the fund's performance, minus a risk free constant, divided by the fund's standard deviation. The Sharpe ratio, developed by Nobel prize winning economist William F. Sharpe, attempts to reduce all portfolio results to the same risk level in order to assess management's ability. That is, a management which produces a mediocre return while taking a large risk with your capital is inferior to one which can produce that same return with much lower risk. In order to simplify the resulting ratings they are shown with letter grades—from A to F. Funds with an "A" have posted the best gains with the least risk within their objective category.

Chapter 4 also includes a fourth measure of risk, *standard deviation*, which measures a security's periodic variations from its own average performance. This differs from beta which measures the variation in relation to a separate index. The standard deviations are particularly useful for evaluating the risk of bond funds, because regressing their performance to a stock market index has limited value. We show betas for bond funds basically for consistency's sake. The greater the standard deviation, the greater the volatility and therefore the greater the risk. As a benchmark, the annualized standard deviation for the latest three year period is 3.80 for the average fixed-income fund and 3.51 for the average tax-free fund.

The *Handbook's* alphabetical listing enables you to easily locate your fund and determine its performance, objective, risk, price, size and yield. Expense and turnover ratios can be found in the Directory section.

Additional stock and bond funds available no-load through discount brokers

Chapter 10 lists funds available through discount brokerage firms that are normally not available to individual investors. They include the following:

• Institutional funds that either have minimum initial investments of $100,000 or more, or are not available to individual investors, that can be purchased through discount brokerage firms at lower ($25,000 or less) initial minimums.

• Load funds that are available through discount brokerage firms at NAV.

With some minor exceptions, we do not follow institutional or load funds that are available at discount brokers only through financial advisors.

Ranking tables

To pinpoint a fund's performance with other funds of the same objective, consult the ranking tables which immediately follow the alphabetical tables. In Chapter 5, separate tables rank all no-loads by percent change within objective category for 1997, and for the three and five year periods ending in 1997. International funds are divided into four categories, but there is only one set of quintile rankings for all. Next the *Handbook's* Chapter 6 shows the top 50 no-loads for the one, three, five, and ten-year periods. These tables enable you to spot the best performers without regard to their objective category.

Funds by fund group

The *Handbook* has a special statistical chapter designed to help you select the family best suited to your needs. The performance data in Chapter 7 are arrayed by fund group. No-load and low-load funds are listed from the most speculative to the most conservative. Each fund is shown with its objective; assets; one-, three-, and five-year returns; and also quintile rankings. We then give you space in adjacent columns to post the quintile ranks of funds that interest you. You can conveniently average the rankings and compare fund groups. For example, let's say you anticipate investing in an aggressive growth fund, an income fund and a municipal bond fund during the course of a full market cycle. In addition, you plan to use the group's money market fund for "parking lot" purposes. You decide that in the Strong group you are interested in Strong Growth, Schafer Value, Equity Income and Money Market. In the 1997 performance column, you post Growth's quintile ranking of "3," Schafer Value's "2" and Equity Income's ranking of "1." Average the three numbers (3, 2, 1) to get a 2.0. Repeat this process for the other periods where data is available. Then do the same for other fund groups. The lower the average number, obviously, the better the family is for you. If you plan to use a group's money fund as a significant part of your investment strategy in a meaningful way for yield, then it too should be averaged in. In this case Money Market has a quintile ranking of "1."

As you evaluate these funds' quintile rankings, bear in mind that there are a limited number of no-load gold funds. In this case the actual performances are more relevant than their quintile rankings. Similarly, not all internationals are the same. The top emerging markets fund might be only average among all international funds.

Money Market Funds

Annual yields are given in compounded, not simple, interest. They show the total return an investor

would receive for shares held a full calendar year. Annual compounded yields are higher than an average of weekly or monthly yields.

The *Handbook* provides data for money market funds that are part of groups having no-load mutual funds, for money market funds that have switching arrangements with no-load mutual funds, and for some of the major independent- and stockbroker-affiliated money market funds. Yields are shown for funds that have been in existence for a full year. The Directory Section provides further information on these money market funds and other money market funds first offered during 1997.

Funds covered

The No-Load Fund Investor, Inc. uses a two-tiered structure in covering mutual funds. The annual *Handbook* covers virtually all no-load stock and bond funds available to the individual investor, and many money market funds.

The No-Load Fund Investor newsletter covers 794 funds in each monthly issue. Funds are selected for the newsletter on the basis of investor interest (sometimes evidenced by size), performance, availability, uniqueness, newsworthiness and how they cooperate with us in providing data on a timely basis.

Using the Investor newsletter tables

The monthly *No-Load Fund Investor* updates provide important timely information not in the *Handbook*. In addition, the data differ from the *Handbook* in some minor respects. Since the number of funds differs, quintile ranks, top fund ranks and fund averages can vary between the two publications. The top 20s are for funds reported in the *Investor* only. Other no-loads might have made the top rankings lists had they met our criteria for inclusion in the newsletter.

Performances, quintile ranks and yields are computed the same way in the *Investor* as in the *Handbook*. Because funds report total net assets slowly, the total net assets shown in the updates lag a month. Note also, that there are three separate sets of quintile rankings for the fixed-income and tax-free bond funds: Short maturity funds, intermediate maturity, and long maturity each have their own rankings. If they were lumped together, most short maturity funds would be in the bottom quintile during times of falling interest rates, and most long maturity funds would be at the bottom during times of rising interest

rates. Speculative high-yield and zero coupon bond funds are ranked in the long-term section no matter what their maturities.

Cash % is the percentage of an equity fund's portfolio in cash or cash equivalents. Parentheses indicate fund is leveraged. Data is generally for the last day of the month but may be up to five days earlier. In the case of bond funds, the *average maturity* in years is shown. This is a more meaningful measure which includes the impact of cash.

Betas for equity funds and *standard deviations* for bond funds are included in the newsletter in its February, May, July and November issues. They are computed on a one month lag. Also in the newsletter is the *Sharpe* ratio, which measures the reward per unit of risk. For convenience they are shown next to the betas in the newsletter, but the two have nothing to do with one another. They are completely separate measures.

Explanation of symbols and data

Following is the explanation of symbols and data as shown in small type at the bottom of page 3 of the *Investor* newsletter:

Funds in bold face are recommended in appropriate market climate. ℗ telephone switch funds. † fund has a low load; as a matter of principle these funds are not bold faced. †† Fidelity low-load waiving fee for certain retirement accounts. ‡ Fund is not selling shares or has restricted its sale to certain investors. * after restricted sale or low-load fund indicates a hold or recommended on a no-load basis. (r) redemption fee. SC Small company funds. X Stock fund with an expense ratio 2%+, bond fund, 1.5%+ C indicates a change in recommendation from previous month. NAV is the fund's price. f previous day's price. Total return is % change with distributions reinvested for measured period. Periods over 1 yr are shown compounded annually. Superscript numbers next to performance figures indicate each fund's quintile rank within objective. "1" top 20% of all aggr grth funds rated, "2" next 20%, to "5" the bottom 20%, same for other objective categories except fixed which is ranked within S, I, L. Yield is latest 12 months dividends divided by current NAV. Cash % is the % of a fund's portfolio in cash or cash equivalents, generally at month-end. Parentheses indicate fund is leveraged. Betas and std. deviations are computed for the 3 yrs ending previous quarter. See the *Guide,* Chapter 21, and the *Handbook,* Chapter 3, for further explanation, addresses and phone numbers.

Performance Summary

Fund averages by objective and indices

No-Load Fund averages	Total # of Funds	Total return percent 1988	1989	1990	1991	1992	1993	1994	1995	1996	1997	Annualized 3 years	5 years	Yield %
All Stock Funds	1321	14.8	24.1	-6.7	32.0	8.0	18.7	-1.5	25.6	18.0	17.9	20.1	15.1	1.1
All Diversified Stock*	950	16.1	23.8	-5.8	35.1	10.0	13.5	-1.0	29.6	18.6	22.9	23.4	16.0	1.1
Aggressive Growth	264	15.3	27.4	-8.8	49.3	10.2	15.8	-1.9	32.1	18.5	18.8	22.1	15.1	0.3
Growth	319	16.8	23.7	-5.7	33.3	11.0	12.9	-0.5	29.2	19.8	25.0	24.3	16.7	0.6
Growth-Income	219	16.6	22.3	-5.2	28.8	9.1	12.7	-0.2	30.2	20.2	26.1	25.6	17.2	1.5
Income	148	14.5	19.4	-1.8	25.0	9.1	12.5	-2.2	25.9	14.0	20.4	20.1	13.7	2.9
Asset Allocation	85	10.1	15.3	-1.5	23.4	9.8	14.2	-2.4	26.3	13.9	18.7	20.5	14.4	2.7
Balanced	76	13.9	19.4	-0.1	25.8	7.8	11.4	-0.8	25.6	14.8	20.1	20.2	13.7	2.6
Convertible	8	15.9	15.8	-4.7	34.9	15.8	14.9	-4.3	20.1	13.6	15.0	16.0	12.3	3.2
Financial	16	17.8	26.5	-14.4	59.5	32.9	19.0	-4.0	37.8	28.8	46.3	36.6	25.0	0.4
Health/Biotech	8	14.6	47.4	25.5	79.7	-11.2	2.4	6.7	46.3	15.3	23.8	26.5	17.0	0.2
Global Equity	51	7.9	18.9	-5.0	15.1	2.1	25.0	-4.3	15.8	16.6	12.0	13.8	11.4	1.4
International Equity-General	106	16.6	22.5	-11.2	11.7	-4.8	36.8	-1.4	10.4	14.0	4.8	9.5	12.4	1.1
International Equity-Europe	23	8.2	28.3	-2.0	8.4	-5.6	24.1	4.0	19.3	24.1	17.0	20.8	18.4	0.8
International Equity-Emg Mkts	47	10.5	28.1	-14.4	16.4	7.0	65.9	-14.6	-6.5	14.7	-3.6	0.7	5.9	0.7
Natural Resources	12	7.3	33.2	-8.6	3.5	-6.1	11.3	-5.2	22.6	29.4	6.8	19.5	13.3	0.6
Precious Metals	16	-19.0	24.5	-22.2	-4.5	-15.2	87.9	-13.0	5.3	9.1	-46.1	-15.2	0.0	1.0
Real Estate	19	13.7	13.3	-10.8	43.2	13.7	9.5	-3.4	16.2	34.3	22.0	23.3	13.4	3.3
Small Company	187	21.5	22.6	-10.0	48.3	13.9	15.7	-0.5	31.6	20.1	21.1	23.2	16.2	0.2
Technology	25	6.9	23.5	3.8	50.1	20.5	27.9	6.5	38.7	22.5	16.7	24.1	22.1	0.2
Utility	13	15.6	33.6	-5.4	17.6	10.3	14.7	-8.3	31.1	10.4	26.7	22.2	13.3	2.5
Fixed Income-Total	375	8.0	11.4	6.5	16.1	7.2	10.1	-3.2	16.1	4.8	8.2	9.5	6.9	5.9
Fixed Income-Corp Short	47	6.9	10.1	7.4	11.8	6.2	6.0	-0.2	10.2	4.8	6.3	7.1	5.3	5.7
Fixed Income-Corp Inter	64	7.9	11.3	6.5	16.2	7.1	10.0	-3.3	17.0	3.7	8.7	9.7	7.0	5.9
Fixed Income-Corp Long	72	8.0	12.2	6.3	16.4	7.4	11.6	-4.4	19.4	3.3	9.6	10.7	7.8	5.9
Fixed Income-High Yld	26	13.7	0.8	-6.7	30.0	15.3	17.7	-2.0	16.1	13.6	13.1	13.6	10.8	7.9
Fixed Income-Gov Short	45	6.5	10.7	7.9	12.5	5.6	6.7	-0.8	11.1	4.3	5.5	6.9	5.2	5.6
Fixed Income-Gov Inter	43	7.4	13.0	9.0	14.9	6.6	8.3	-3.5	16.1	3.4	8.5	9.3	6.4	6.1
Fixed Income-Gov Long	28	7.3	13.5	8.2	15.4	6.7	10.5	-5.7	20.7	1.9	9.7	10.6	7.0	5.6
Fixed Inc-World,(Glob & Int'l)	34	1.2	4.0	16.5	13.9	4.4	14.2	-5.8	16.6	10.4	2.0	9.9	5.5	5.5
Tax-Free-Total	231	10.0	9.1	6.3	11.3	8.3	11.4	-5.1	15.0	3.7	8.0	8.8	6.4	4.6
Tax-Free-Short	30	11.5	9.6	6.4	8.4	5.9	6.2	0.0	7.7	3.8	5.1	5.5	4.6	4.1
Tax-Free-Intermediate	65	7.0	10.1	6.7	10.4	7.6	10.0	-3.8	13.3	3.9	7.1	8.0	6.0	4.3
Tax-Free-Long	139	9.1	9.5	6.2	11.8	8.8	12.5	-6.6	17.2	3.6	9.0	9.8	6.8	4.8
Tax-Free-High Yld	13	9.3	8.8	5.4	11.4	8.3	11.6	-6.7	18.0	4.5	11.4	11.0	7.3	5.0
Tax-Free-NY	20	6.5	6.9	5.0	12.0	8.8	11.8	-6.7	15.7	3.0	7.9	8.7	5.9	4.5
Tax-Free-CA	29	7.0	9.1	6.5	10.6	8.0	12.6	-5.9	15.7	3.7	8.3	9.5	6.8	4.6
Tax-Free-MA	6	0.0	0.0	5.4	9.2	6.8	9.2	-5.0	14.7	3.8	8.1	8.8	6.4	4.7
Money Market-General	103	7.2	8.9	7.9	5.8	3.4	2.7	3.8	5.5	5.0	5.1	5.2	4.4	5.1
Money Market-Government	75	6.8	8.5	7.6	5.6	3.3	2.6	3.6	5.4	4.8	5.0	5.0	4.3	5.0
Money Market-Tax-Free	123	4.7	5.9	5.5	4.2	2.6	2.0	2.4	3.4	3.3	3.1	3.3	2.8	3.1

Stock Market Indices

														Close
S&P 500 w/reinvestment	—	16.6	32.2	-3.1	30.4	7.6	10.1	1.3	37.5	23.0	33.4	31.2	18.1	970.43
Dow Jones Industrials**	—	11.8	27.0	-4.3	20.3	4.2	13.7	2.1	33.5	26.0	22.6	27.3	19.1	7,908.25
S&P 500**	—	12.4	27.3	-6.6	26.3	4.5	7.1	-1.5	34.1	20.3	31.0	28.3	17.4	970.43
NYSE Composite	—	13.0	24.8	-7.5	27.1	4.7	7.9	-3.1	31.3	19.1	30.3	26.8	16.3	511.19
AMEX Index**	—	17.5	23.5	-18.5	28.2	1.1	19.5	-9.1	26.4	6.4	17.4	16.4	11.4	684.61
Value Line Composite**	—	15.4	11.2	-24.3	27.2	7.0	10.7	-6.0	19.3	13.4	21.1	17.9	11.2	454.35
NASDAQ Composite**	—	15.4	19.3	-17.8	56.8	15.5	14.7	-3.2	39.9	22.7	21.6	27.8	18.3	1,570.35
Russell 2000**	—	22.5	14.2	-21.3	43.4	16.5	17.3	-3.2	26.2	14.8	20.5	20.4	14.6	437.02
Wilshire 5000**	—	13.3	24.9	-9.3	30.3	6.2	8.6	-2.5	33.4	18.8	29.2	27.0	16.7	9,298.19
MSCI EAFE**	—	26.7	9.2	-24.7	10.1	-13.9	30.4	6.4	9.4	4.4	0.2	4.6	9.7	1,188.17
MSCI Gold Mines (Developed)**	—	-33.5	49.6	-25.9	-8.1	-27.5	130.4	-11.2	5.9	-2.8	-39.8	-14.7	4.9	443.15

Consumer Price Index

Consumer Price Index	—	4.1	4.7	6.1	3.1	2.9	2.8	2.7	3.0	3.3	1.8	2.7	2.7	—

*Average of aggressive growth, growth, growth-income, and income funds.
**Without dividends reinvested

25

CHAPTER 4

Stock and bond funds — comprehensive summary

Arranged in alphabetical order

No-Load Fund	Total return percent with quintile ranks by objective										Annualized 3 yrs.	Annualized 5 yrs.	What $10,000 grew to after 3 yrs.	5 yrs.
	1988	1989	1990	1991	1992	1993	1994	1995	1996	1997				
AARP Bal Stk & Bd	—	—	—	—	—	—	—	23.9[4]	13.2[3]	21.9[2]	19.6[3]	—	17,093	—
AARP Bond Fd Inc	—	—	—	—	—	—	—	—	—	—	—	—	—	—
AARP Capital Growth	27.3[1]	33.5[2]	-15.8[4]	40.5[4]	4.7[4]	16.0[3]	-10.0[5]	30.5[3]	20.6[3]	35.1[1]	28.6[1]	17.3[2]	21,256	22,191
AARP Divsfd Gro	—	—	—	—	—	—	—	—	—	—	—	—	—	—
AARP Divsfd Inc w/Gro	—	—	—	—	—	—	—	—	—	—	—	—	—	—
AARP Global Growth	—	—	—	—	—	—	—	—	—	14.6[2]	—	—	—	—
AARP GNMA & Trsy	7.1[2]	11.7[1]	9.7[1]	14.4[2]	6.6[2]	6.0[3]	-1.9[4]	12.8[1]	4.4[3]	8.0[1]	8.3[1]	5.8[2]	12,718	13,225
AARP Gro & Inc	10.9[4]	26.7[2]	-2.0[2]	26.5[4]	9.2[3]	15.7[2]	3.1[1]	31.8[3]	21.6[3]	31.0[2]	28.1[2]	20.2[1]	21,000	25,050
AARP Hi Qual ST Bond	8.1[3]	12.3[3]	7.6[2]	15.4[4]	6.2[5]	11.0[4]	-4.5[3]	17.3[4]	2.8[4]	7.9[4]	9.2[4]	6.6[4]	13,013	13,794
AARP Insur TF Gen	12.2[2]	10.8[1]	6.3[4]	12.3[2]	8.5[4]	12.7[3]	-6.2[3]	16.1[4]	3.7[3]	8.9[3]	9.5[4]	6.8[4]	13,114	13,863
AARP Int'l Gro & Inc	—	—	—	—	—	—	—	—	—	—	—	—	—	—
AARP Sm Co Stk SC	—	—	—	—	—	—	—	—	—	—	—	—	—	—
AARP US Stk Idx	—	—	—	—	—	—	—	—	—	—	—	—	—	—
Academy Value	—	—	—	—	—	—	—	4.5[5]	14.6[5]	19.5[4]	12.7[5]	—	14,309	—
Accessor Growth	—	—	—	—	—	14.2[3]	4.0[1]	34.3[2]	20.4[3]	33.2[1]	29.2[2]	20.7[1]	21,546	25,588
Accessor Int'l Eqty	—	—	—	—	—	—	—	7.6[3]	13.8[3]	11.0[2]	10.8[2]	—	13,588	—
Accessor Inter Fix Inc	—	—	—	—	—	9.5[3]	-5.2[5]	18.3[2]	2.6[4]	8.6[3]	9.6[3]	6.5[4]	13,173	13,673
Accessor Mort Sec	—	—	—	—	—	7.3[4]	-1.7[1]	16.0[3]	5.0[2]	9.5[1]	10.1[2]	7.1[2]	13,338	14,071
Accessor S-I Fix Inc	—	—	—	—	—	5.6[5]	-1.4[1]	11.4[5]	3.6[3]	6.3[5]	7.1[5]	5.0[5]	12,277	12,784
Accessor Sm\Mid Cap	—	—	—	—	—	14.4[3]	-4.1[4]	32.0[3]	24.7[2]	36.2[1]	30.9[1]	19.7[1]	22,412	24,595
Accessor Val & Inc	—	—	—	—	—	14.7[2]	-1.9[4]	33.2[2]	23.9[2]	33.0[1]	30.0[2]	19.8[2]	21,955	24,694
Acorn Int'l	—	—	—	—	—	—	-3.8[4]	8.9[3]	21.7[2]	0.2[3]	9.9[2]	13.8[2]	13,279	19,046
Acorn SC	24.8[1]	24.8[3]	-17.5[5]	47.3[1]	24.2[1]	32.3[1]	-7.4[5]	20.8[5]	21.2[3]	25.0[3]	22.3[4]	17.5[3]	18,297	22,415
Acorn USA SC	—	—	—	—	—	—	—	—	—	32.3[1]	—	—	—	—
Advance Cap Balanced	17.6[2]	18.6[4]	-1.1[3]	18.3[5]	3.1[5]	5.0[5]	-2.7[4]	31.5[1]	14.5[3]	20.5[3]	22.0[2]	13.1[3]	18,144	18,530
Advance Cap Bond	5.1[5]	12.7[3]	8.4[2]	14.4[4]	7.0[4]	11.5[3]	-4.7[3]	20.1[2]	2.9[4]	9.4[3]	10.6[3]	7.5[3]	13,519	14,369
Advance Cap Eqty Gro	—	—	—	—	—	—	-4.0[4]	38.0[1]	17.5[4]	17.7[5]	24.0[3]	—	19,078	—
Advance Cap Ret Inc	—	—	—	—	—	13.9[2]	-5.3[4]	23.0[1]	4.5[3]	12.2[2]	13.0[2]	9.2[2]	14,426	15,558
AFBA Five Star Balanced	—	—	—	—	—	—	—	—	—	—	—	—	—	—
AFBA Five Star Equity	—	—	—	—	—	—	—	—	—	—	—	—	—	—
AFBA Five Star Hi Yld	—	—	—	—	—	—	—	—	—	—	—	—	—	—
AFBA Five Star US Global	—	—	—	—	—	—	—	—	—	—	—	—	—	—
AIT Vision: US Equity	—	—	—	—	—	—	—	—	27.2[1]	29.1[2]	—	—	—	—
Alliance World Inc	—	—	—	5.7[5]	1.7[5]	4.0[5]	-4.2[3]	0.9[5]	7.3[2]	3.6[5]	3.9[5]	2.3[5]	11,217	11,175
Amana Growth	—	—	—	—	—	—	—	35.0[2]	5.4[5]	15.7[5]	18.1[1]	—	16,469	—
Amana Income	14.7[3]	18.4[4]	-3.4[4]	24.0[3]	1.6[5]	11.6[4]	-6.5[5]	27.5[2]	12.4[3]	24.5[2]	21.3[2]	13.2[3]	17,841	18,625
Amer AAdv Mileage Bal	—	—	—	—	—	—	—	28.3[2]	13.5[3]	19.5[3]	20.3[3]	—	17,401	—
Amer AAdv Mileage Gro & Inc	—	—	—	—	—	—	—	33.9[2]	20.7[3]	26.1[3]	26.7[3]	—	20,361	—
Amer AAdv Mileage Int'l	—	—	—	—	—	—	—	17.1[1]	19.0[2]	8.8[2]	14.9[1]	—	15,167	—
Amer AAdv Mileage Ltd Inc	—	—	—	—	—	—	—	9.4[4]	3.3[5]	6.5[3]	6.4[5]	—	12,034	—
Amer AAdv Mileage S&P 500 Idx	—	—	—	—	—	—	—	—	—	33.1[1]	—	—	—	—
Amer Cent Balanced	—	25.7[2]	1.8[1]	46.8[1]	-6.1[5]	7.2[5]	-0.1[3]	21.4[5]	13.3[5]	16.9[5]	17.2[5]	11.5[5]	16,082	17,222
Amer Cent Equity Growth	—	—	—	—	4.1[5]	11.4[3]	-0.2[3]	34.6[2]	27.3[1]	36.1[1]	32.6[1]	21.0[1]	23,313	25,919
Amer Cent Equity Inc	—	—	—	—	—	—	—	29.6[3]	24.3[1]	28.3[3]	27.4[3]	—	20,660	—
Amer Cent Glob Gold	—	30.4[2]	-19.7[2]	-11.2[5]	-8.7[3]	81.2[4]	-16.7[4]	9.3[3]	-2.8[5]	-41.5[3]	-14.7[1]	-1.3[4]	6,216	9,383
Amer Cent Glob Nat Res	—	—	—	—	—	—	—	14.4[3]	15.5[3]	2.5[5]	10.6[5]	—	13,541	—
Amer Cent Inc & Gro	—	—	—	38.7[1]	7.9[3]	11.1[3]	-0.5[3]	36.9[1]	23.9[2]	34.3[1]	31.6[1]	20.3[1]	22,780	25,182
Amer Cent New Opp SC	—	—	—	—	—	—	—	—	—	3.1[5]	—	—	—	—
Amer Cent Real Est	—	—	—	—	—	—	—	—	40.8[1]	25.2[3]	—	—	—	—
Amer Cent Strat Asst: Agg	—	—	—	—	—	—	—	—	—	16.2[4]	—	—	—	—
Amer Cent Strat Asst: Cons	—	—	—	—	—	—	—	—	—	12.8[5]	—	—	—	—
Amer Cent Strat Asst: Mod	—	—	—	—	—	—	—	—	—	15.2[5]	—	—	—	—
Amer Cent Util	—	—	—	—	—	—	-10.0[5]	35.7[1]	4.5[5]	35.7[1]	24.4[1]	—	19,249	—
Amer Cent Value	—	—	—	—	—	—	4.0[1]	32.8[2]	24.8[1]	26.0[3]	27.8[2]	—	20,884	—
Amer Cent-20th Cent Emg Mkts	—	—	—	—	—	—	—	—	—	—	—	—	—	—
Amer Cent-20th Cent Giftrust	11.1[4]	50.2[1]	-17.0[5]	84.6[1]	18.0[1]	31.4[1]	13.5[1]	38.3[2]	5.8[5]	-1.2[5]	13.1[5]	16.6[3]	14,456	21,560
Amer Cent-20th Cent Growth	2.7[5]	43.1[1]	-3.8[2]	69.0[1]	-4.3[5]	3.8[5]	-1.5[3]	20.3[5]	15.0[4]	29.3[2]	21.4[4]	12.8[4]	17,885	18,286
Amer Cent-20th Cent Heritage	16.4[3]	35.1[1]	-9.2[4]	35.9[2]	10.1[3]	20.4[1]	-6.3[5]	26.7[4]	15.3[3]	19.3[4]	20.3[4]	14.5[4]	17,431	19,665
Amer Cent-20th Cent Int'l Disc	—	—	—	—	—	—	—	9.9[3]	31.2[1]	17.5[1]	19.2[1]	—	16,939	—
Amer Cent-20th Cent Int'l Gr	—	—	—	—	4.8[1]	42.6[2]	-4.8[4]	11.9[2]	14.4[3]	19.7[1]	15.3[1]	15.8[1]	15,325	20,804

See Chapter 3 for explanation of symbols

Total Net Assets $Million		NAV per share		1997 per share distributions		Yield %	Risk Analysis				% Distribution of Portfolio 12/31/97			Objective	No-Load Fund
December 31 1996	1997	December 31 1996	1997	Income	Capital gains	12/31/97	beta	R²	Std. Dev.	Sharpe Ratio	Stocks	Bonds	Cash		
446.5	667.6	18.32	20.56	0.71	0.99	3.3	0.55	0.88	6.47	B	63	33	4	income	AARP Bal Stk & Bd
—	81.0	—	15.30	0.94	0.02	—	—	—	—	—	0	73	27	fix-inc	AARP Bond Fd Inc
877.2	1,217.9	42.07	52.11	0.31	4.31	0.5	1.09	0.91	12.73	A	96	0	4	agg gr	AARP Capital Growth
—	72.0	—	17.09	0.32	0.10	—	—	—	—	—	62	36	2	growth	AARP Divsfd Gro
—	53.3	—	15.94	0.64	0.05	—	—	—	—	—	25	61	14	income	AARP Divsfd Inc w/Gro
92.3	144.6	16.30	17.99	0.15	0.53	0.9	—	—	—	—	79	16	5	global	AARP Global Gro
4,826.1	4,539.4	15.04	15.22	0.98	0.00	6.5	0.12	0.28	2.43	B	0	97	3	fix-inc	AARP GNMA & Trsy
4,606.5	6,671.3	45.38	53.04	1.16	5.07	2.0	0.79	0.88	9.44	A	100	0	0	gr-inc	AARP Gro & Inc
502.0	450.0	15.99	16.27	0.94	0.00	5.8	0.16	0.24	3.73	C	0	85	15	fix-inc	AARP Hi Qual ST Bond
1,742.3	1,698.4	17.98	18.61	0.88	0.05	4.7	0.19	0.24	4.25	D	0	99	1	tax-free	AARP Insur TF Gen
—	23.8	—	16.46	0.11	0.15	—	—	—	—	—	96	0	4	int'l	AARP Int'l Gro & Inc
—	62.3	—	19.93	0.04	0.08	—	—	—	—	—	98	0	2	agg gr	AARP Sm Co Stk SC
—	44.4	—	18.29	0.26	0.13	—	—	—	—	—	96	0	4	gr-inc	AARP US Stk Idx
4.8	6.8	11.97	12.98	0.00	1.30	0.0	0.37	0.14	11.07	F	87	0	13	growth	Academy Value
60.7	87.9	19.51	21.57	0.11	3.76	0.5	1.05	0.95	11.97	B	100	0	0	growth	Accessor Growth
76.4	151.4	13.83	14.83	0.00	0.47	0.0	0.68	0.37	12.24	B	95	0	5	int'l	Accessor Int'l Eqty
52.3	55.1	11.91	12.19	0.71	0.00	5.8	0.20	0.25	4.36	D	96	0	4	fix-inc	Accessor Inter Fix Inc
73.8	109.7	12.24	12.60	0.72	0.05	5.7	0.16	0.28	3.27	A	0	99	1	fix-inc	Accessor Mort Sec
36.8	40.9	12.16	12.27	0.64	0.00	5.2	0.09	0.22	2.18	F	0	99	1	fix-inc	Accessor S-I Fix Inc
65.7	124.8	18.82	21.82	0.02	3.46	0.1	0.81	0.51	12.71	A	100	0	0	agg gr	Accessor Sm\Mid Cap
36.5	81.1	17.75	20.88	0.24	2.27	1.1	0.94	0.92	10.92	B	100	0	0	gr-inc	Accessor Val & Inc
1,771.7	1,628.3	19.61	18.39	0.38	0.90	2.0	0.48	0.31	9.40	B	88	0	12	int'l	Acorn Int'l
2,853.7	3,687.1	15.04	16.99	0.16	1.61	0.9	0.63	0.43	10.64	D	91	0	9	growth	Acorn SC
52.7	184.4	11.65	15.12	0.00	0.29	0.0	—	—	—	—	93	0	7	growth	Acorn USA SC
75.2	99.4	13.68	15.69	0.44	0.31	2.8	0.66	0.92	7.66	B	61	38	1	income	Advance Cap Balanced
4.4	4.2	10.37	10.52	0.69	0.09	6.6	0.22	0.27	4.72	C	0	100	0	fix-inc	Advance Cap Bond
38.8	54.3	14.72	17.25	0.00	0.07	0.0	0.98	0.51	15.35	D	99	0	1	growth	Advance Cap Eqty Gro
170.8	200.5	10.20	10.65	0.74	0.00	7.0	0.26	0.31	5.20	B	0	99	1	fix-inc	Advance Cap Ret Inc
—	1.0	—	10.76	0.15	0.04	—	—	—	—	—	39	38	24	income	AFBA Five Star Balanced
—	2.7	—	10.87	0.04	0.06	—	—	—	—	—	97	0	3	growth	AFBA Five Star Equity
—	0.9	—	10.26	0.21	0.00	—	—	—	—	—	8	35	57	fix-inc	AFBA Five Star Hi Yld
—	2.3	—	10.45	0.05	0.00	—	—	—	—	—	87	0	13	global	AFBA Five Star US Global
0.7	4.9	11.22	13.26	0.06	1.11	0.4	—	—	—	—	—	—	—	growth	AIT Vision: US Equity
44.2	20.9	1.66	1.62	0.10	0.00	6.2	0.00	0.00	2.87	F	0	100	0	fix-inc	Alliance World Inc
5.5	7.7	6.43	7.44	0.00	0.00	0.0	0.83	0.46	13.62	F	80	0	20	growth	Amana Growth
14.7	18.6	14.94	17.79	0.32	0.47	1.8	0.62	0.73	8.00	C	0	90	10	income	Amana Income
2.6	3.7	15.90	17.24	0.54	1.16	3.1	0.56	0.86	6.75	B	57	36	7	income	Amer AAdv Mileage Balanced
6.7	9.9	19.68	23.12	0.37	1.27	1.6	0.77	0.86	9.23	B	97	0	3	gr-inc	Amer AAdv Mileage Gro & Inc
3.7	4.8	15.97	16.69	0.26	0.42	1.6	0.53	0.37	9.52	A	92	0	8	int'l	Amer AAdv Mileage Int'l
1.0	1.3	9.63	9.62	0.61	0.00	6.4	0.08	0.21	1.89	F	0	90	10	fix-inc	Amer AAdv Mileage Ltd Inc
0.1	7.6	10.00	13.16	0.14	0.00	1.1	—	—	—	—	99	0	1	dgr-inc	Amer AAdv Mileage S&P 500 Idx
878.4	936.7	17.26	18.14	0.39	1.60	2.0	0.71	0.76	8.95	F	56	39	5	gr-inc	Amer Cent Balanced
274.3	770.7	15.96	19.04	0.24	2.31	1.1	0.95	0.91	11.12	A	99	0	1	growth	Amer Cent Equity Growth
187.2	296.8	6.34	6.66	0.26	1.16	3.3	0.53	0.66	7.22	A	79	19	2	gr-inc	Amer Cent Equity Inc
433.5	249.0	11.33	6.34	0.09	0.20	1.4	0.59	0.04	31.17	A	98	0	2	prec met	Amer Cent Glob Gol
66.1	46.7	11.91	11.48	0.23	0.50	1.9	0.48	0.26	10.45	F	98	0	2	global	Amer Cent Glob Nat Res
715.2	1,786.2	20.16	24.30	0.39	2.29	1.4	0.94	0.96	10.68	A	99	0	1	gr-inc	Amer Cent Inc & Gro
1.5	233.1	5.09	5.25	0.00	0.00	0.0	—	—	—	—	95	0	5	agg gr	Amer Cent New Opp SC
10.2	105.1	13.80	16.26	0.39	0.52	2.4	—	—	—	—	97	0	3	sector	Amer Cent Real Est
53.4	112.6	5.45	6.03	0.09	0.21	1.4	—	—	—	—	73	26	1	agg gr	Amer Cent Strat Asst: Agg
37.7	157.5	5.17	5.30	0.17	0.26	3.3	—	—	—	—	40	59	1	gr-inc	Amer Cent Strat Asst: Cons
66.8	206.6	5.35	5.82	0.13	0.20	2.3	—	—	—	—	58	40	2	growth	Amer Cent Strat Asst: Mod
144.6	206.5	11.51	14.24	0.42	0.85	2.8	0.58	0.34	11.22	D	99	0	1	income	Amer Cent Util
1,548.2	2,418.6	6.59	6.95	0.12	1.20	1.4	0.65	0.62	9.16	A	98	0	2	gr-inc	Amer Cent Value
—	15.4	—	4.18	0.00	0.00	—	—	—	—	—	83	7	10	int'l	Amer Cent-20th Cent Emg Mkts
874.4	986.0	24.39	23.30	0.00	0.75	0.0	1.26	0.26	27.39	F	89	0	11	agg gr	Amer Cent-20th Cent Giftrust
4,667.2	5,165.8	21.88	24.01	0.00	4.17	0.0	1.21	0.74	15.74	D	96	1	3	agg gr	Amer Cent-20th Cent Growth
1,125.5	1,277.4	12.07	11.50	0.07	2.70	0.5	0.93	0.53	14.27	F	94	3	3	growth	Amer Cent-20th Cent Heritage
390.0	622.1	7.36	8.15	0.02	0.47	0.2	0.47	0.22	11.02	A	94	3	3	int'l	Amer Cent-20th Cent Int'l Disc
1,364.8	1,784.3	7.96	8.19	0.03	1.28	0.3	0.73	0.42	12.25	A	93	2	5	int'l	Amer Cent-20th Cent Int'l Gr

Arranged in alphabetical order

No-Load Fund	1988	1989	1990	1991	1992	1993	1994	1995	1996	1997	Annualized 3 yrs.	Annualized 5 yrs.	What $10,000 grew to after 3 yrs.	grew to after 5 yrs.
Amer Cent-20th Cent Select...	5.6 [5]	39.5 [1]	-0.4 [2]	31.6 [3]	-4.4 [5]	14.7 [2]	-8.0 [5]	22.7 [5]	19.2 [3]	32.2 [1]	24.6 [3]	15.3 [4]	19,332	20,400
Amer Cent-20th Cent Ultra...........	13.3 [3]	36.9 [1]	9.4 [1]	86.5 [1]	1.3 [5]	21.8 [2]	-3.6 [4]	37.7 [2]	13.8 [4]	23.1 [3]	24.5 [2]	17.8 [2]	19,294	22,655
Amer Cent-20th Cent Vista...	2.4 [5]	52.2 [1]	-15.7 [4]	73.7 [1]	-2.1 [5]	5.4 [5]	4.7 [1]	46.1 [1]	7.6 [5]	-8.7 [5]	12.8 [5]	9.6 [5]	14,356	15,842
Amer Cent-Benham AZ Inter.........	—	—	—	—	—	—	—	13.2 [4]	3.7 [3]	6.9 [4]	7.9 [4]	—	12,553	—
Amer Cent-Benham Bd.............	8.3 [2]	14.0 [2]	6.0 [5]	17.5 [1]	5.5 [4]	10.1 [2]	-4.6 [5]	20.3 [1]	2.5 [4]	8.6 [3]	10.2 [2]	7.1 [2]	13,396	14,070
Amer Cent-Benham CA Hi Yld......	12.4 [2]	9.7 [3]	5.6 [5]	10.9 [4]	9.2 [2]	13.2 [2]	-5.3 [2]	18.3 [2]	5.9 [1]	10.4 [1]	11.4 [1]	8.2 [1]	13,833	14,829
Amer Cent-Benham CA Insured...	10.2 [4]	10.3 [2]	6.8 [2]	11.3 [4]	9.2 [2]	13.5 [1]	-6.6 [3]	19.0 [1]	3.7 [3]	9.3 [2]	10.5 [2]	7.4 [1]	13,482	14,292
Amer Cent-Benham CA Inter... ...	6.4 [4]	7.9 [4]	7.0 [2]	10.4 [3]	7.1 [4]	10.7 [2]	-3.7 [3]	13.5 [3]	4.2 [1]	7.4 [2]	8.3 [2]	6.2 [2]	12,699	13,538
Amer Cent-Benham CA Long.......	10.4 [4]	9.8 [3]	6.6 [3]	11.8 [3]	8.2 [4]	13.7 [1]	-6.5 [3]	19.8 [1]	3.6 [3]	9.6 [2]	10.8 [1]	7.7 [1]	13,609	14,467
Amer Cent-Benham CA Ltd Term.....	—	—	—	—	—	—	-0.6 [4]	8.3 [2]	3.9 [2]	5.3 [3]	5.8 [2]	4.5 [3]	11,846	12,470
Amer Cent-Benham FL Inter...	—	—	—	—	—	—	—	13.6 [3]	3.7 [4]	8.2 [1]	8.4 [2]	—	12,745	—
Amer Cent-Benham GNMA	8.5 [2]	13.9 [2]	10.2 [1]	15.6 [2]	7.7 [2]	6.6 [5]	-1.7 [2]	15.9 [3]	5.2 [1]	8.7 [3]	9.8 [3]	6.8 [3]	13,252	13,887
Amer Cent-Benham Hi Yld............	—	—	—	—	—	—	—	—	—	—	—	—	—	—
Amer Cent-Benham Inflat Adj Trsy......	—	—	—	—	—	—	—	—	—	—	—	—	—	—
Amer Cent-Benham Int'l Bd.........	—	—	—	—	—	—	1.5 [1]	24.4 [1]	6.4 [1]	-5.9 [5]	7.6 [5]	7.2 [2]	12,458	14,137
Amer Cent-Benham Inter Bd........	5.3 [5]	12.0 [4]	9.2 [2]	13.7 [5]	6.7 [3]	7.9 [4]	-2.3 [2]	13.7 [5]	4.1 [3]	8.4 [3]	8.7 [4]	6.2 [4]	12,826	13,516
Amer Cent-Benham Inter TF.........	6.6 [3]	8.3 [3]	6.8 [2]	11.7 [1]	7.2 [3]	10.2 [3]	-3.5 [2]	12.7 [4]	3.8 [3]	7.4 [3]	7.9 [4]	6.0 [3]	12,560	13,357
Amer Cent-Benham Inter-Trm Treas.....	5.2 [5]	11.9 [4]	9.2 [2]	13.7 [5]	6.6 [3]	7.9 [4]	-2.3 [2]	13.7 [5]	4.1 [3]	8.3 [3]	8.6 [4]	6.2 [4]	12,818	13,512
Amer Cent-Benham Long TF.........	11.2 [3]	9.6 [3]	6.7 [3]	12.9 [1]	9.2 [2]	14.3 [1]	-6.1 [3]	17.7 [3]	2.3 [5]	9.5 [2]	9.7 [3]	7.2 [2]	13,185	14,151
Amer Cent-Benham LT Trsy...........	—	—	—	—	—	—	-9.1 [5]	29.3 [1]	-1.4 [5]	14.7 [1]	13.5 [2]	9.3 [2]	14,618	15,626
Amer Cent-Benham Ltd Term TF......	—	—	—	—	—	—	2.5 [1]	6.7 [4]	3.7 [3]	5.5 [2]	5.3 [4]	—	11,677	—
Amer Cent-Benham Ltd Trm Bd......	—	—	—	—	—	—	—	10.9 [3]	4.4 [3]	6.3 [3]	7.2 [3]	—	12,315	—
Amer Cent-Benham ST Gov.........	5.6 [4]	10.0 [3]	7.5 [4]	11.6 [4]	4.4 [5]	4.2 [4]	-0.5 [3]	10.5 [3]	4.1 [4]	6.0 [4]	6.8 [4]	4.8 [4]	12,191	12,639
Amer Cent-Benham ST Trsy...........	—	—	—	—	—	—	0.3 [2]	9.9 [4]	4.1 [4]	6.0 [4]	6.6 [4]	5.1 [4]	12,130	12,812
Amer Cent-Benham Target 2000......	11.5 [2]	19.8 [1]	6.3 [3]	20.7 [2]	8.5 [2]	15.5 [2]	-6.9 [4]	20.7 [2]	8.9 [1]	7.0 [5]	12.1 [2]	8.6 [2]	14,071	15,130
Amer Cent-Benham Target 2005......	14.5 [1]	23.9 [1]	3.6 [4]	21.5 [2]	9.6 [2]	21.6 [1]	-8.9 [5]	32.6 [1]	5.8 [2]	11.6 [2]	16.1 [1]	11.6 [1]	15,661	17,349
Amer Cent-Benham Target 2010......	15.7 [1]	28.0 [1]	0.3 [4]	21.1 [2]	9.8 [1]	26.3 [1]	-11.6 [5]	42.1 [1]	5.8 [2]	16.7 [1]	20.6 [1]	14.4 [1]	17,552	19,597
Amer Cent-Benham Target 2015...	11.1 [2]	33.5 [1]	-3.4 [5]	22.5 [1]	7.8 [3]	30.5 [1]	-14.1 [5]	52.7 [1]	0.9 [5]	22.9 [1]	23.7 [1]	16.2 [1]	18,939	21,230
Amer Cent-Benham Target 2020...	—	—	-4.5 [5]	17.4 [3]	8.3 [2]	35.6 [1]	-17.7 [5]	61.3 [1]	-2.5 [5]	28.6 [1]	26.5 [1]	17.7 [1]	20,228	22,574
Amer Cent-Benham Target 2025...	—	—	—	—	—	—	—	—	—	30.1 [1]	—	—	—	—
Amer Trust Allegiance................	—	—	—	—	—	—	—	—	—	—	—	—	—	—
America's Utility..............	—	—	—	—	—	13.3 [3]	-13.1 [5]	32.3 [1]	5.5 [5]	23.4 [2]	19.8 [3]	11.1 [5]	17,210	16,938
American Heritage Gro...............	—	—	—	—	—	—	—	24.2 [4]	-3.0 [5]	-2.9 [5]	5.4 [5]	—	11,693	—
American Heritage................	1.9 [5]	-2.8 [5]	-30.8 [5]	96.6 [1]	18.9 [1]	41.4 [1]	-35.3 [5]	-30.6 [5]	-5.1 [5]	75.0 [1]	4.8 [5]	1.1 [5]	11,526	10,544
Ameristock................	—	—	—	—	—	—	—	—	27.7 [1]	32.9 [1]	—	—	—	—
AMEX-Strategist Balanced............	—	—	—	—	—	—	—	—	—	20.7 [3]	—	—	—	—
AMEX-Strategist Emg Mkts...........	—	—	—	—	—	—	—	—	—	5.4 [3]	—	—	—	—
AMEX-Strategist Eqty Inc............	—	—	—	—	—	—	—	—	—	23.6 [2]	—	—	—	—
AMEX-Strategist Equity....	—	—	—	—	—	—	—	—	—	19.6 [5]	—	—	—	—
AMEX-Strategist Gov Inc....	—	—	—	—	—	—	—	—	—	8.6 [3]	—	—	—	—
AMEX-Strategist Growth Trend......	—	—	—	—	—	—	—	—	—	24.7 [3]	—	—	—	—
AMEX-Strategist Growth..........	—	—	—	—	—	—	—	—	—	20.6 [4]	—	—	—	—
AMEX-Strategist Hi Yld............	—	—	—	—	—	—	—	—	—	14.0 [1]	—	—	—	—
AMEX-Strategist Qual Inc............	—	—	—	—	—	—	—	—	—	8.6 [4]	—	—	—	—
AMEX-Strategist Spec Gr..............	—	—	—	—	—	—	—	—	—	26.3 [2]	—	—	—	—
AMEX-Strategist TF HY..........	—	—	—	—	—	—	—	—	—	14.1 [1]	—	—	—	—
AMEX-Strategist Total Ret............	—	—	—	—	—	—	—	—	—	10.3 [5]	—	—	—	—
AMEX-Strategist World Gro...........	—	—	—	—	—	—	—	—	—	7.0 [4]	—	—	—	—
AMEX-Strategist World Inc............	—	—	—	—	—	—	—	—	—	5.8 [5]	—	—	—	—
Amtrust Value SC......	—	—	—	—	—	—	1.9 [2]	7.5 [5]	-2.9 [5]	-20.1 [5]	-5.9 [5]	—	8,343	—
Analysts Inv Fix Inc..............	—	—	—	—	—	—	-6.4 [5]	18.2 [2]	6.2 [1]	9.1 [2]	11.1 [1]	—	13,694	—
Analysts Inv Stk................	—	—	—	—	—	—	-3.2 [4]	19.8 [5]	14.6 [5]	19.4 [4]	17.9 [5]	—	16,382	—
Analytic Defnsve Eqty................	15.6 [3]	17.7 [4]	1.5 [1]	13.3 [5]	6.2 [4]	6.7 [5]	2.5 [2]	20.8 [5]	16.2 [4]	19.1 [5]	18.7 [5]	12.8 [5]	16,720	18,286
Analytic Enhncd Eqty................	—	—	—	—	—	—	-0.4 [3]	35.4 [2]	23.0 [2]	29.9 [2]	29.3 [1]	—	21,612	—
Analytic Master Fix Inc...............	—	—	—	—	—	—	-3.1 [3]	16.4 [3]	5.6 [1]	10.1 [1]	10.6 [1]	—	13,531	—
Analytic ST Gov................	—	—	—	—	—	—	0.0 [3]	10.5 [3]	5.4 [1]	5.5 [5]	7.1 [3]	—	12,280	—
AON Asst Alloc	—	—	—	—	—	—	—	33.8 [1]	10.5 [4]	31.5 [1]	24.8 [1]	—	19,426	—
AON Gov Sec................	—	—	—	—	—	—	—	—	—	10.0 [1]	—	—	—	—
AON Int'l Eqty................	—	—	—	—	—	—	—	—	—	6.5 [2]	—	—	—	—
AON REIT Idx................	—	—	—	—	—	—	—	—	—	18.8 [4]	—	—	—	—

See Chapter 3 for explanation of symbols

Stock and bond funds — comprehensive summary *continued*
Arranged in alphabetical order

Total Net Assets $Million		NAV per share		1997 per share distributions			Risk Analysis				% Distribution of Portfolio				
December 31		December 31			Capital	Yield %			Std.	Sharpe	12/31/97				
1996	1997	1996	1997	Income	gains	12/31/97	beta	R²	Dev.	Ratio	Stocks	Bonds	Cash	Objective	No-Load Fund
4,060.5	5,006.2	38.53	42.59	0.20	7.93	0.4	1.00	0.85	12.14	D	98	0	2	growth	Amer Cent-20th Cent Select
18,418.6	22,420.3	28.09	27.30	0.01	7.07	0.0	1.34	0.67	18.26	C	97	1	2	agg gr	Amer Cent-20th Cent Ultra
2,236.1	1,650.9	14.51	12.42	0.00	0.80	0.0	1.09	0.26	23.70	F	98	0	2	agg gr	Amer Cent-20th Cent Vista
27.3	37.2	10.49	10.69	0.45	0.05	4.2	0.14	0.28	2.89	C	0	99	1	tax-free	Amer Cent-Benham AZ Inter
136.6	127.9	9.51	9.69	0.59	0.03	6.0	0.22	0.28	4.68	C	0	98	2	fix-inc	Amer Cent-Benham Bd
158.6	219.2	9.48	9.79	0.54	0.12	5.4	0.17	0.23	3.92	A	0	96	4	tax-free	Amer Cent-Benham CA Hi Yld
192.2	197.6	10.24	10.48	0.53	0.16	4.9	0.21	0.22	5.03	D	0	99	1	tax-free	Amer Cent-Benham CA Insured
439.1	437.0	11.16	11.29	0.53	0.15	4.6	0.14	0.26	3.02	B	0	98	2	tax-free	Amer Cent-Benham CA Inter
296.9	311.8	11.32	11.58	0.61	0.20	5.1	0.20	0.21	4.78	B	0	99	1	tax-free	Amer Cent-Benham CA Long
108.1	130.2	10.25	10.36	0.43	0.00	4.1	0.07	0.29	1.43	B	0	101	-1	tax-free	Amer Cent-Benham CA Ltd Ter
14.8	22.7	10.32	10.53	0.45	0.16	4.2	0.13	0.23	2.90	A	0	102	-2	tax-free	Amer Cent-Benham FL Inter
1,130.8	1,233.4	10.49	10.68	0.70	0.00	6.5	0.14	0.27	3.03	A	0	99	1	fix-inc	Amer Cent-Benham GNMA
—	0.1	—	9.98	0.18	0.00	—	—	—	—	—	0	100	0	fix-inc	Amer Cent-Benham Hi Yld
—	4.2	—	9.67	0.43	0.00	—	—	—	—	—	0	100	0	fix-inc	Amer Cent-Benham Inflat Adj Trsy
252.4	166.0	11.79	10.92	0.04	0.14	0.3	-0.12	0.03	7.99	F	0	97	3	fix-inc	Amer Cent-Benham Int'l Bd
337.0	361.2	10.31	10.55	0.59	0.00	5.6	0.16	0.29	3.39	D	0	104	-4	fix-inc	Amer Cent-Benham Inter Bd
63.6	132.6	10.37	10.54	0.49	0.09	4.5	0.13	0.28	2.79	C	0	98	2	tax-free	Amer Cent-Benham Inter TF
337.0	361.2	10.31	10.55	0.59	0.00	5.6	0.16	0.29	3.39	D	0	99	1	fix-inc	Amer Cent-Benham Inter-Trm Treas
55.6	110.3	10.63	10.83	0.54	0.24	4.9	0.20	0.25	4.49	D	0	105	-5	tax-free	Amer Cent-Benham Long TF
121.1	129.4	9.78	10.56	0.60	0.00	5.6	0.35	0.21	8.54	D	0	99	1	fix-inc	Amer Cent-Benham LT Trsy
49.3	35.2	10.08	10.15	0.41	0.07	4.0	0.07	0.38	1.21	D	0	103	-3	tax-free	Amer Cent-Benham Ltd Term TF
8.4	25.2	9.91	9.96	0.55	0.00	5.5	0.07	0.25	1.62	B	0	102	-2	fix-inc	Amer Cent-Benham Ltd Trm Bd
344.9	509.5	9.45	9.48	0.53	0.00	5.5	0.06	0.18	1.57	C	0	100	0	fix-inc	Amer Cent-Benham ST Gov
36.4	40.0	9.75	9.80	0.53	0.00	5.3	0.06	0.21	1.60	F	0	100	0	fix-inc	Amer Cent-Benham ST Trsy
267.3	243.3	82.01	87.79	0.00	0.00	5.2	0.17	0.17	4.53	B	0	101	-1	fix-inc	Amer Cent-Benham Target 2000
242.3	301.2	60.35	67.37	0.00	0.00	5.4	0.36	0.22	8.60	B	0	100	0	fix-inc	Amer Cent-Benham Target 2005
109.3	157.9	45.20	52.77	0.00	0.00	5.5	0.48	0.20	11.95	B	0	100	0	fix-inc	Amer Cent-Benham Target 2010
117.7	134.0	34.60	42.53	0.00	0.00	5.6	0.63	0.19	15.85	B	0	100	0	fix-inc	Amer Cent-Benham Target 2015
869.7	599.4	24.04	30.92	0.00	0.00	5.7	0.74	0.19	18.92	B	0	100	0	fix-inc	Amer Cent-Benham Target 2020
45.6	193.1	19.63	25.54	0.00	0.00	5.5	—	—	—	—	0	100	0	fix-inc	Amer Cent-Benham Target 2025
—	5.3	—	12.48	0.00	0.00	—	—	—	—	—	96	0	4	growth	Amer Trust Allegiance
143.2	152.1	25.07	29.04	0.94	0.79	3.2	0.47	0.31	9.41	F	89	6	5	income	America's Utility
3.1	1.3	0.15	0.14	0.01	0.00	4.0	1.03	0.35	19.33	F	10	0	90	growth	American Heritage Gro
12.3	20.6	0.56	0.98	0.00	0.00	0.0	0.41	0.03	28.38	F	100	0	0	agg gr	American Heritage
4.8	7.3	21.18	26.81	0.41	0.83	1.5	—	—	—	—	95	0	5	growth	Ameristock
0.6	0.9	14.41	15.54	0.63	1.12	4.1	—	—	—	—	53	36	11	income	AMEX-Strategist Balanced
0.5	0.7	5.11	4.49	0.01	0.86	0.2	—	—	—	—	83	0	17	int'l	AMEX-Strategist Emg Mkts
0.6	0.8	23.92	28.16	0.38	0.97	1.4	—	—	—	—	79	14	7	income	AMEX-Strategist Eqty Inc
0.6	0.8	9.69	10.33	0.36	0.82	3.4	—	—	—	—	89	13	-2	gr-inc	AMEX-Strategist Equity
0.5	0.6	4.93	4.96	0.32	0.05	6.5	—	—	—	—	120	0	-20	fix-inc	AMEX-Strategist Gov Inc
27.1	21.2	21.39	26.44	0.21	0.00	0.8	—	—	—	—	92	0	8	growth	AMEX-Strategist Growth Trend
27.5	21.9	27.72	33.44	0.00	0.00	0.0	—	—	—	—	98	0	2	growth	AMEX-Strategist Growth
0.6	1.1	4.40	4.57	0.42	0.00	9.2	—	—	—	—	1	97	2	fix-inc	AMEX-Strategist Hi Yld
0.5	0.6	9.24	9.33	0.62	0.06	6.7	—	—	—	—	0	97	3	fix-inc	AMEX-Strategist Qual Inc
0.9	1.5	5.43	5.57	0.02	1.24	0.3	—	—	—	—	97	0	3	agg gr	AMEX-Strategist Spec Gr
0.6	0.7	12.78	13.06	0.24	1.24	1.8	—	—	—	—	0	98	2	tax-free	AMEX-Strategist TF HY
0.6	0.7	4.53	4.68	0.30	1.24	6.5	—	—	—	—	62	24	14	gr-inc	AMEX-Strategist Total Ret
0.5	0.6	7.29	7.76	0.04	0.00	0.5	—	—	—	—	102	0	-2	global	AMEX-Strategist World Gro
0.6	0.6	6.36	6.13	0.26	0.29	4.3	—	—	—	—	0	101	-1	fix-inc	AMEX-Strategist World Inc
0.7	0.6	9.61	7.68	0.00	0.00	0.0	0.51	0.07	21.30	F	—	—	—	growth	Amtrust Value SC
3.5	4.5	14.06	14.51	0.80	0.00	5.5	0.22	0.33	4.26	B	15	71	14	fix-inc	Analysts Inv Fix Inc
4.5	7.2	20.12	23.58	0.27	0.15	1.1	0.68	0.79	8.50	D	87	0	13	growth	Analysts Inv Stk
52.5	46.3	14.38	13.02	0.13	3.97	0.8	0.58	0.92	6.72	D	99	0	1	gr-inc	Analytic Defnsve Eqty
3.5	7.3	12.09	13.72	0.14	1.81	1.0	0.91	0.88	10.85	B	96	0	4	growth	Analytic Enhncd Eqty
28.9	5.7	10.27	8.84	0.59	1.84	5.5	0.22	0.47	3.53	A	0	66	34	fix-inc	Analytic Master Fix Inc
1.0	3.0	9.83	9.81	0.54	0.00	5.5	0.06	0.20	1.56	B	0	100	0	fix-inc	Analytic ST Gov
133.6	166.7	13.16	16.42	0.29	0.55	1.8	0.74	0.74	9.60	C	75	16	9	income	AON Asst Alloc
71.2	106.8	10.17	10.55	0.60	0.00	5.7	—	—	—	—	0	98	2	fix-inc	AON Gov Sec
36.2	50.4	10.65	10.79	0.42	0.12	3.9	—	—	—	—	93	0	7	int'l	AON Int'l Eqty
49.5	102.1	12.03	13.74	0.45	0.09	3.3	—	—	—	—	100	0	0	sector	AON REIT Idx

Stock and bond funds — comprehensive summary *continued*
Arranged in alphabetical order

No-Load Fund	1988	1989	1990	1991	1992	1993	1994	1995	1996	1997	Annualized 3 yrs.	5 yrs.	What $10,000 grew to after 3 yrs.	5 yrs.
AON S & P 500	—	—	—	—	—	—	—	—	—	32.8[1]	—	—	—	—
API Cap Inc	—	—	—	—	4.4[5]	9.9[4]	-0.8[4]	27.2[4]	17.7[4]	25.2[4]	23.3[4]	15.4[4]	18,757	20,444
API T-1 Trsy	—	—	—	—	—	—	—	5.7[5]	3.7[5]	2.8[5]	4.1[5]	—	11,266	—
Aquinas Balanced	—	—	—	—	—	—	—	23.1[4]	15.3[2]	19.9[3]	19.4[3]	—	17,024	—
Aquinas Eqty Gro	—	—	—	—	—	—	—	30.3[3]	22.9[2]	29.0[2]	27.4[2]	—	20,652	—
Aquinas Eqty Inc	—	—	—	—	—	—	—	35.6[2]	20.4[3]	27.9[3]	27.8[2]	—	20,881	—
Aquinas Fix Inc	—	—	—	—	—	—	—	16.3[4]	2.8[4]	8.5[4]	9.1[5]	—	12,975	—
Ariel Apprec	—	—	—	33.2[3]	13.2[2]	7.9[4]	-8.4[5]	24.1[4]	23.7[2]	37.9[1]	28.4[2]	15.9[4]	21,176	20,930
Ariel Growth SC	40.0[1]	25.1[3]	-16.1[5]	32.9[5]	11.9[3]	8.8[4]	-4.2[4]	18.5[5]	23.5[2]	36.4[1]	25.9[2]	15.8[3]	19,973	20,803
Ariel Premier Bond	—	—	—	—	—	—	—	—	—	—	—	—	—	—
Armstrong Assoc	15.7[4]	14.3[5]	-6.7[4]	18.7[5]	6.8[4]	15.1[2]	5.4[1]	19.1[5]	9.5[5]	14.2[5]	14.2[5]	12.5[5]	14,880	18,047
Artisan International	—	—	—	—	—	—	—	—	—	3.5[3]	—	—	—	—
Artisan Mid Cap	—	—	—	—	—	—	—	—	—	—	—	—	—	—
Artisan Small Cap SC‡	—	—	—	—	—	—	—	—	11.9[5]	22.7[4]				
Artisan Small Cap Val SC	—	—	—	—	—	—	—	—	—	—	—	—	—	—
ASM Idx 30	—	—	—	—	5.7[4]	13.3[2]	1.1[2]	29.0[3]	24.8[1]	24.5[4]	26.1[3]	18.1[3]	20,043	22,959
Asset Mgmt ARM	—	—	—	—	4.4[4]	4.7[4]	2.0[1]	9.1[4]	5.9[1]	6.5[2]	7.2[3]	5.6[2]	12,312	13,144
Asset Mgmt Inter Mrtg	11.0[1]	12.1[3]	6.1[4]	16.2[2]	7.8[1]	6.9[5]	-1.6[1]	13.9[5]	2.9[4]	8.4[3]	8.3[4]	6.0[4]	12,697	13,349
Asset Mgmt ST US Gov	6.3[3]	10.8[3]	9.4[1]	11.8[4]	6.5[2]	5.8[3]	0.4[2]	11.3[2]	3.6[5]	6.3[3]	7.0[5]	5.4[3]	12,257	13,016
Asset Mgmt US Mrtg Sec	8.6[2]	14.4[1]	10.0[2]	14.8[3]	6.5[4]	6.8[5]	-2.4[2]	16.2[3]	2.8[4]	9.7[1]	9.4[3]	6.4[4]	13,100	13,662
Austin Global Eqty	—	—	—	—	—	—	2.1[2]	22.6[1]	5.8[5]	23.9[1]	17.1[3]	—	16,075	—
Avondale Total Ret	—	14.5[4]	0.7[2]	26.9[2]	-1.5[5]	7.2[5]	2.3[1]	28.6[2]	4.7[5]	20.1[3]	17.4[5]	12.1[5]	16,158	17,713
Babson Bond-Port L	5.8[5]	13.1[3]	7.8[2]	15.0[4]	8.0[3]	11.1[3]	-3.3[2]	15.9[4]	3.2[3]	9.3[3]	9.3[4]	7.0[4]	13,072	14,044
Babson Bond-Port S	—	10.8[4]	8.1[4]	14.5[4]	7.0[2]	8.4[3]	-2.1[2]	13.6[5]	4.4[2]	8.2[3]	8.7[4]	6.4[4]	12,833	13,619
Babson Enterprise II SC	—	—	—	—	17.2[2]	19.8[2]	-7.4[5]	19.9[5]	27.6[1]	33.3[1]	26.8[2]	17.7[2]	20,388	22,618
Babson Enterprise‡ SC	32.5[1]	22.5[4]	-15.9[5]	43.0[4]	24.6[1]	16.3[3]	2.5[2]	16.5[4]	21.3[2]	32.4[1]	23.2[3]	17.4[2]	18,696	22,287
Babson Growth	15.9[3]	22.1[3]	-9.4[4]	26.1[4]	9.1[3]	10.3[4]	-0.6[3]	31.4[3]	21.8[2]	28.0[2]	27.0[2]	17.6[3]	20,484	22,458
Babson Shadow Stk SC	22.5[2]	11.2[5]	-19.3[5]	40.0[2]	17.4[1]	15.3[2]	-4.3[5]	23.6[4]	21.4[2]	27.6[3]	24.2[3]	16.1[4]	19,144	21,123
Babson Stew Ivry Int'l	3.4[5]	27.0[2]	-9.4[2]	15.1[2]	-1.7[2]	33.5[3]	1.3[2]	12.6[2]	13.4[3]	1.7[3]	9.1[3]	11.9[3]	12,992	17,569
Babson TF Long	11.6[3]	8.8[4]	6.2[4]	12.2[3]	8.4[4]	12.3[4]	-7.4[4]	16.2[4]	3.5[4]	8.7[4]	9.4[4]	6.3[4]	13,077	13,599
Babson TF Short	5.3[4]	7.0[3]	6.6[2]	9.5[2]	5.2[4]	6.7[2]	-1.7[5]	9.3[1]	3.4[5]	5.1[3]	5.9[2]	4.5[4]	11,878	12,459
Babson Value	19.0[2]	18.2[4]	-11.4[5]	28.9[3]	15.4[1]	22.9[1]	2.5[1]	31.7[3]	22.7[2]	26.5[3]	26.9[3]	20.8[1]	20,444	25,754
Baron Asset SC	34.4[1]	25.0[2]	-18.5[5]	34.0[3]	13.9[2]	23.5[1]	7.4[1]	35.2[2]	22.0[2]	33.9[1]	30.2[1]	24.0[1]	22,085	29,293
Baron Gro & Inc	—	—	—	—	—	—	—	52.5[1]	27.7[1]	31.1[2]	36.7[1]	—	25,534	—
Baron Sm Cap SC	—	—	—	—	—	—	—	—	—	—	—	—	—	—
Barr Rosnbrg Int'l Sm Cap†	—	—	—	—	—	—	—	—	—	-13.4[4]	—	—	—	—
Barr Rosnbrg Japan†	—	—	—	—	—	—	—	—	—	-34.9[5]	—	—	—	—
Barr Rosnbrg US Sm Cap† ‡SC	—	—	—	—	—	—	—	—	—	30.4[1]	—	—	—	—
BBK Diversa	6.6[4]	12.7[4]	-9.5[4]	16.0[3]	4.4[2]	21.6[4]	-9.4[4]	20.1[2]	11.1[4]	13.2[2]	14.7[4]	10.7[3]	15,108	16,644
BBK Int'l Bond	—	—	—	14.0[5]	7.0[4]	14.8[2]	-19.2[5]	20.6[2]	8.5[2]	2.6[5]	10.3[3]	4.5[5]	13,421	12,448
BBK Int'l Equity	11.8[4]	14.0[5]	-19.2[5]	1.8[5]	-11.4[4]	37.8[3]	-12.6[5]	12.5[2]	9.6[4]	10.0[2]	10.7[4]	10.3[3]	13,552	16,332
BEA Advs:Emg Mkts	—	—	—	—	—	—	—	—	—	-3.6[4]	—	—	—	—
BEA Advs:Glob Telecomm	—	—	—	—	—	—	—	—	—	32.3[1]	—	—	—	—
BEA Advs:Hi Yld	—	—	—	—	—	—	—	—	—	14.5[1]	—	—	—	—
BEA Advs:Int'l Eqty	—	—	—	—	—	—	—	—	—	14.9[1]	—	—	—	—
Bender Growth	—	—	—	—	—	—	—	—	—	20.8[4]	—	—	—	—
Berger 100	1.7[5]	48.3[1]	-5.6[3]	88.8[1]	8.5[3]	21.2[2]	-6.7[5]	21.3[5]	13.7[4]	13.6[4]	16.1[5]	12.1[5]	15,664	17,713
Berger Balanced	—	—	—	—	—	—	—	—	—	—	—	—	—	—
Berger Gro & Inc	5.3[5]	20.3[3]	-8.0[4]	61.0[1]	4.8[5]	23.3[1]	-9.1[5]	23.9[5]	15.6[5]	22.7[4]	20.7[5]	14.5[5]	17,572	19,694
Berger New Generation	—	—	—	—	—	—	—	—	—	24.2[3]	—	—	—	—
Berger Sm Cap Val SC	20.1[2]	26.4[3]	-22.0[5]	24.9[5]	19.7[1]	16.3[3]	6.7[1]	26.1[4]	25.6[1]	36.4[1]	29.3[1]	21.8[1]	21,596	26,799
Berger Sm Co Gro SC	—	—	—	—	—	—	13.7[1]	33.8[3]	16.8[4]	16.2[4]	22.0[4]	—	18,154	—
Berger/BIAM Int'l	—	—	—	—	—	—	—	—	—	2.9[3]	—	—	—	—
Bernstein CA Muni	—	—	—	9.5[5]	6.8[5]	8.3[5]	-3.2[2]	13.8[3]	3.7[3]	6.3[5]	7.9[4]	5.6[4]	12,547	13,156
Bernstein CA Short Dur Muni	—	—	—	—	—	—	—	6.3[5]	3.6[4]	3.6[5]	4.5[5]	—	11,409	—
Bernstein Dvsfd Muni	—	—	6.8[3]	10.2[3]	6.5[5]	8.3[5]	-2.5[1]	13.0[4]	3.6[4]	6.7[4]	7.7[4]	5.7[4]	12,488	13,187
Bernstein Emg Mkts	—	—	—	—	—	—	—	—	7.1[5]	-23.8[5]	—	—	—	—
Bernstein Gov Sht Dur	—	—	8.9[2]	11.3[4]	5.5[4]	4.6[4]	0.4[2]	10.2[3]	4.1[4]	5.7[5]	6.6[4]	4.9[4]	12,119	12,727
Bernstein Int'l Value	—	—	—	—	34.6[3]	3.8[2]	8.1[3]	17.5[2]	9.3[2]	11.5[2]	14.2[2]	13,874	19,384	
Bernstein Inter Dur	—	—	7.3[4]	17.1[2]	7.7[2]	10.2[2]	-3.2[3]	17.8[2]	3.6[3]	7.6[4]	9.5[3]	7.0[2]	13,131	14,007

See Chapter 3 for explanation of symbols

Total Net Assets $Million		NAV per share		1997 per share distributions		Yield %	Risk Analysis				% Distribution of Portfolio			Objective	No-Load Fund
December 31		December 31			Capital				Std.	Sharpe	12/31/97				
1996	1997	1996	1997	Income	gains	12/31/97	beta	R²	Dev.	Ratio	Stocks	Bonds	Cash		
95.7	123.7	11.33	14.34	0.22	0.48	1.5	—	—	—	—	95	0	5	gr-inc	AON S & P 500
5.7	9.9	18.29	21.07	0.65	1.08	3.1	0.73	0.84	8.91	D	95	0	5	gr-inc	API Cap Inc
6.5	2.2	4.68	4.64	0.17	0.00	3.7	0.01	0.02	0.65	F	0	99	1	fix-inc	API T-1 Trsy
29.6	29.2	11.53	11.58	0.26	1.91	2.3	0.52	0.76	6.61	C	58	35	7	income	Aquinas Balanced
22.6	36.0	13.45	15.12	0.00	2.21	0.0	0.88	0.67	12.05	C	95	0	5	growth	Aquinas Eqty Gro
54.2	73.6	13.26	14.89	0.23	1.77	1.6	0.74	0.83	9.09	A	92	1	7	gr-inc	Aquinas Eqty Inc
37.2	40.7	9.90	10.17	0.55	0.00	5.4	0.18	0.26	3.83	D	0	84	16	fix-inc	Aquinas Fix Inc
146.3	204.4	26.07	32.82	0.07	3.07	0.2	0.58	0.44	9.73	A	97	0	3	growth	Ariel Apprec
120.0	174.2	31.96	39.88	0.13	3.57	0.3	0.53	0.38	9.60	A	92	0	8	agg gr	Ariel Growth SC
—	0.6	—	10.33	0.52	0.07	—	—	—	—	—	0	80	20	fix-inc	Ariel Premier Bond
12.6	13.6	10.12	10.66	0.05	0.83	0.4	0.75	0.82	9.19	F	87	0	13	growth	Armstrong Assoc
191.6	322.5	13.32	12.46	0.20	1.13	1.5	—	—	—	—	96	0	4	int'l	Artisan International
—	9.7	—	12.01	0.00	0.79	—	—	—	—	—	96	0	4	growth	Artisan Mid Cap
296.1	292.4	13.64	14.15	0.00	2.58	0.0	—	—	—	—	97	0	3	growth	Artisan Small Cap SC‡
—	—	—	10.31	0.00	0.00	—	—	—	—	—	95	0	5	growth	Artisan Small Cap Val SC
21.1	40.2	14.91	17.50	0.27	0.78	1.5	1.02	0.88	12.07	D	98	0	2	gr-inc	ASM Idx 30
749.9	762.0	9.95	9.98	0.60	0.00	6.0	0.03	0.16	0.71	A	0	91	9	fix-inc	Asset Mgmt ARM
87.5	79.1	9.48	9.59	0.66	0.00	6.9	0.13	0.23	2.92	D	0	91	9	fix-inc	Asset Mgmt Inter Mrtg
175.6	105.8	10.52	10.53	0.63	0.00	6.0	0.08	0.19	1.91	D	0	72	28	fix-inc	Asset Mgmt ST US Gov
55.2	52.0	10.45	10.66	0.76	0.00	7.2	0.16	0.25	3.54	C	0	100	0	fix-inc	Asset Mgmt US Mrtg Sec
10.8	13.7	12.96	14.55	0.00	0.00	0.0	0.99	0.75	15.33	D	92	0	8	global	Austin Global Eqty
10.2	10.9	26.81	31.58	0.11	0.49	0.4	0.80	0.75	10.19	F	86	10	4	income	Avondale Total Ret
137.0	132.4	1.53	1.57	0.10	0.00	6.2	0.17	0.24	3.84	C	0	97	3	fix-inc	Babson Bond-Port L
35.0	39.0	9.67	9.82	0.62	0.00	6.3	0.12	0.26	2.69	B	0	95	5	fix-inc	Babson Bond-Port S
49.7	87.7	20.37	24.99	0.05	2.05	0.2	0.56	0.32	11.05	A	96	0	4	agg gr	Babson Enterprise II SC
191.6	217.6	16.31	19.03	0.06	2.42	0.3	0.37	0.16	10.28	B	98	0	2	agg gr	Babson Enterprise‡ SC
311.1	395.8	15.43	18.08	0.09	1.50	0.5	0.97	0.94	11.25	B	93	0	7	growth	Babson Growth
39.6	49.7	11.70	12.70	0.13	2.00	0.9	0.43	0.26	9.52	B	97	0	3	growth	Babson Shadow Stk SC
89.7	98.0	18.41	17.69	0.08	0.96	0.4	0.54	0.29	10.87	B	97	0	3	int'l	Babson Stew Ivry Int'l
27.0	27.4	8.91	9.23	0.42	0.02	4.5	0.18	0.25	3.91	D	0	100	0	tax-free	Babson TF Long
24.3	22.5	10.75	10.82	0.44	0.03	4.0	0.09	0.28	1.90	B	0	91	9	tax-free	Babson TF Short
781.9	1,421.1	37.74	45.71	0.49	1.47	1.0	0.81	0.80	10.08	C	95	0	5	gr-inc	Babson Value
1,326.0	3,793.0	36.23	48.51	0.00	0.00	0.0	0.85	0.40	14.85	C	97	2	1	growth	Baron Asset SC
244.0	415.1	19.04	24.88	0.02	0.06	0.1	0.80	0.43	13.69	A	97	3	0	gr-inc	Baron Gro & Inc
—	267.0	—	10.31	0.00	0.00	—	—	—	—	—	96	0	4	agg gr	Baron Sm Cap SC
0.1	0.5	10.22	8.62	0.04	0.20	0.4	—	—	—	—	101	0	-1	int'l	Barr Rosnbrg Int'l Sm Cap†
0.1	1.0	7.05	4.59	0.00	0.00	0.0	—	—	—	—	100	0	0	int'l	Barr Rosnbrg Japan†
0.2	17.9	7.19	8.86	0.00	0.52	0.0	—	—	—	—	97	0	3	agg gr	Barr Rosnbrg US Sm Cap† ‡SC
37.2	36.8	12.43	12.66	0.34	1.05	2.5	0.57	0.89	6.71	C	66	27	7	global	BBK Diversa
49.5	50.7	8.15	7.49	0.87	0.00	11.6	0.06	0.02	4.33	C	0	91	9	fix-inc	BBK Int'l Bond
119.4	132.1	5.94	6.26	0.13	0.14	2.1	0.65	0.43	10.79	B	97	0	3	int'l	BBK Int'l Equity
0.1	0.1	18.87	17.01	0.12	1.04	0.7	—	—	—	—	99	0	1	int'l	BEA Advs:Emg Mkts
0.3	0.8	16.24	18.77	0.00	1.04	0.0	—	—	—	—	89	0	11	sector	BEA Advs:Glob Telecomm
0.1	1.0	16.16	17.11	1.32	0.00	7.7	—	—	—	—	0	97	3	fix-inc	BEA Advs:Hi Yld
0.1	1.3	20.35	20.44	0.00	2.93	0.0	—	—	—	—	100	0	0	int'l	BEA Advs:Int'l Eqty
0.1	5.1	—	11.97	0.00	—	0.0	—	—	—	—	95	0	5	growth	Bender Growth
2,003.0	1,718.6	17.83	13.45	0.00	6.95	0.0	0.95	0.63	13.17	D	91	0	9	agg gr	Berger 100
—	17.1	—	11.81	0.06	1.90	—	—	—	—	—	41	43	16	income	Berger Balanced
321.0	340.5	13.30	13.45	0.08	2.82	0.5	0.66	0.60	9.56	F	93	7	0	gr-inc	Berger Gro & Inc
105.5	130.9	10.94	13.59	0.00	0.00	0.0	—	—	—	—	94	0	6	growth	Berger New Generation
36.0	74.2	16.48	19.94	0.17	2.37	0.7	0.53	0.33	10.36	A	89	0	11	agg gr	Berger Sm Cap Val SC
782.0	784.3	4.24	4.43	0.00	0.48	0.0	0.86	0.22	20.44	D	95	0	5	agg gr	Berger Sm Co Gro SC
13.2	17.1	10.59	10.45	0.32	0.12	3.0	—	—	—	—	93	0	7	int'l	Berger/BIAM In
310.7	429.5	13.71	13.97	0.57	0.01	4.1	0.13	0.24	2.88	C	0	100	0	tax-free	Bernstein CA Muni
76.5	82.9	12.55	12.55	0.43	0.01	3.4	0.03	0.17	0.77	F	0	102	-2	tax-free	Bernstein CA Short Dur Muni
890.1	1,161.0	13.55	13.83	0.60	0.01	4.3	0.12	0.25	2.67	C	0	100	0	tax-free	Bernstein Dvsfd Muni
311.7	339.0	21.83	15.93	0.10	0.61	0.7	—	—	—	—	97	3	0	int'l	Bernstein Emg Mkts
134.0	144.6	12.51	12.53	0.65	0.00	5.2	0.05	0.15	1.37	D	0	98	2	fix-inc	Bernstein Gov Sht Dur
3,495.2	4,697.8	17.85	17.72	1.07	0.71	6.0	0.52	0.34	9.78	B	93	4	3	int'l	Bernstein Int'l Value
1,594.1	2,136.6	13.24	13.22	0.73	0.27	5.4	0.15	0.19	3.70	C	0	123	-23	fix-inc	Bernstein Inter Dur

Stock and bond funds — comprehensive summary *continued*

Arranged in alphabetical order

No-Load Fund	Total return percent with quintile ranks by objective										Annualized		What $10,000 grew to after	
	1988	1989	1990	1991	1992	1993	1994	1995	1996	1997	3 yrs.	5 yrs.	3 yrs.	5 yrs.
Bernstein NY Muni	—	—	6.6[4]	10.4[3]	6.9[4]	8.4[5]	-2.5[1]	13.0[4]	3.5[4]	6.5[4]	7.6[5]	5.7[4]	12,458	13,167
Bernstein NY Short Dur Muni	—	—	—	—	—	—	—	6.1[5]	3.5[4]	3.8[5]	4.5[5]	—	11,397	—
Bernstein Short Dur Plus	—	9.9[4]	8.3[3]	12.4[3]	6.4[2]	5.3[4]	0.5[2]	10.1[4]	4.8[2]	5.5[5]	6.8[4]	5.2[3]	12,172	12,882
Bernstein Sht Dur Divsfd Muni	—	—	—	—	—	—	—	6.4[5]	3.6[4]	4.0[5]	4.6[5]	—	11,456	—
Berwyn Income	11.3[4]	11.9[5]	-0.2[2]	23.0[4]	21.6[1]	16.9[1]	-1.1[2]	21.1[5]	14.0[3]	13.3[5]	16.1[5]	12.6[4]	15,644	18,087
Berwyn‡	21.6[2]	16.5[4]	-23.8[5]	43.6[1]	20.6[1]	23.0[1]	3.9[1]	19.2[5]	14.3[5]	26.1[3]	19.8[5]	17.0[3]	17,174	21,948
Bjurman Micro Cap Gro SC	—	—	—	—	—	—	—	—	—	—	—	—	—	—
Blanchard Flex Inc‡	—	—	—	—	—	—	-5.6[5]	15.4[4]	5.8[1]	9.4[2]	10.1[2]	7.4[2]	13,352	14,319
Blanchard Flex TF‡	—	—	—	—	—	—	-5.6[2]	22.1[1]	4.2[2]	8.8[3]	11.5[1]	—	13,845	—
Blanchard Glob Gro‡	7.4[4]	15.7[4]	-6.4[3]	10.7[4]	0.8[4]	24.5[3]	-7.5[4]	12.7[4]	13.3[4]	6.5[5]	10.8[5]	9.4[4]	13,595	15,656
Blanchard Gro & Inc‡	—	—	—	—	—	—	—	24.6[4]	18.7[4]	28.9[3]	24.0[4]	—	19,058	—
Blanchard Prec Met‡	—	8.0[5]	-22.9[4]	-2.3[2]	-18.5[4]	100.4[1]	-15.0[3]	4.4[3]	24.2[1]	-47.1[4]	-11.8[1]	3.2[2]	6,865	11,693
Blanchard ST Flex‡	—	—	—	—	—	—	1.0[2]	9.1[4]	6.7[1]	7.2[1]	7.7[2]	—	12,482	—
BNY Hamilton Eqty Inc	—	—	—	—	—	11.9[4]	-2.6[4]	25.8[3]	19.6[1]	25.9[1]	23.7[1]	15.6[2]	18,929	20,644
BNY Hamilton Int'l Eqty	—	—	—	—	—	—	—	—	—	—	—	—	—	—
BNY Hamilton Inter Gov	—	—	—	—	—	8.0[4]	-5.2[5]	15.4[1]	3.1[4]	7.5[4]	8.6[4]	5.6[5]	12,801	13,115
BNY Hamilton Inter Inv Grd	—	—	—	—	—	—	—	—	—	—	—	—	—	—
BNY Hamilton Inter TE	—	—	—	—	—	—	—	—	—	—	—	—	—	—
BNY Hamilton Inter NY TE	—	—	—	—	—	8.0[5]	-3.8[3]	12.1[5]	3.5[4]	6.2[5]	7.2[5]	5.1[5]	12,316	12,791
BNY Hamilton Lg Cap Gro	—	—	—	—	—	—	—	—	—	—	—	—	—	—
BNY Hamilton Sm Cap Gro SC	—	—	—	—	—	—	—	—	—	—	—	—	—	—
Boston Prtnrs Fix Inc	—	—	—	—	—	—	—	—	—	—	—	—	—	—
Boston Prtnrs Large Cap	—	—	—	—	—	—	—	—	—	31.1[2]	—	—	—	—
Boston Prtnrs Mid Cap Val	—	—	—	—	—	—	—	—	—	—	—	—	—	—
Boston-1784 Asst Alloc	—	—	—	—	—	—	-0.7[4]	29.6[3]	10.5[5]	20.7[4]	20.0[5]	—	17,281	—
Boston-1784 CT TE Inc	—	—	—	—	—	—	—	14.6[5]	3.6[3]	8.5[4]	8.8[4]	—	12,893	—
Boston-1784 FL TE	—	—	—	—	—	—	—	—	—	—	—	—	—	—
Boston 1784 Growth	—	—	—	—	—	—	—	—	—	13.9[5]	—	—	—	—
Boston-1784 Gro & Inc	—	—	—	—	—	—	-0.2[3]	30.6[3]	23.6[2]	19.7[5]	24.5[4]	—	19,315	—
Boston-1784 Income	—	—	—	—	—	—	—	17.9[3]	2.6[4]	7.8[4]	9.3[4]	—	13,048	—
Boston-1784 Int'l Eqty	—	—	—	—	—	—	—	13.3[2]	13.7[3]	-0.9[4]	8.5[3]	—	12,757	—
Boston-1784 MA TE Inc	—	—	—	—	—	—	-5.5[2]	13.7[5]	3.3[4]	8.9[3]	8.6[5]	—	12,792	—
Boston-1784 RI TE Inc	—	—	—	—	—	—	—	14.2[5]	4.7[1]	8.3[4]	9.0[4]	—	12,940	—
Boston-1784 ST Income	—	—	—	—	—	—	—	11.3[2]	4.3[3]	6.3[3]	7.3[2]	—	12,337	—
Boston-1784 TE Med Term	—	—	—	—	—	—	-3.0[2]	14.3[2]	4.2[2]	9.1[1]	9.1[1]	—	12,994	—
Boston-1784 US Gov Med	—	—	—	—	—	—	-3.7[4]	15.8[4]	2.0[5]	8.1[4]	8.5[4]	—	12,763	—
Bramwell Growth	—	—	—	—	—	—	—	32.5[3]	12.8[4]	33.7[1]	25.9[2]	—	19,978	—
Brandywine Blue	—	—	—	—	13.1[2]	27.2[1]	2.3[2]	32.3[2]	23.2[2]	19.3[4]	24.8[3]	20.4[1]	19,446	25,308
Brandywine	17.7[3]	33.0[2]	0.6[1]	49.2[3]	15.7[2]	22.6[1]	0.0[2]	35.7[3]	24.9[2]	12.0[4]	23.8[3]	18.4[2]	18,987	23,278
Brazos/JMIC Real Est	—	—	—	—	—	—	—	—	—	28.6[2]	—	—	—	—
Brazos/JMIC Sm Cap Gro SC	—	—	—	—	—	—	—	—	—	54.5[1]	—	—	—	—
Bridges Investment	7.0[5]	22.4[3]	1.9[1]	20.8[5]	5.9[4]	6.2[5]	0.4[3]	30.7[3]	17.9[4]	21.1[4]	23.1[4]	14.8[4]	18,666	19,896
Bridgeway Agg Gro	—	—	—	—	—	—	—	27.2[4]	32.2[1]	18.3[3]	25.7[2]	—	19,882	—
Bridgeway Soc Resp	—	—	—	—	—	—	—	30.3[3]	16.2[4]	22.9[4]	23.0[4]	—	18,605	—
Bridgeway Ult Lg 35 Idx	—	—	—	—	—	—	—	—	—	—	—	—	—	—
Bridgeway Ult Sm Co SC	—	—	—	—	—	—	—	39.8[2]	29.7[1]	38.0[1]	35.8[1]	—	25,037	—
Bridgeway Ult Sm Idx SC	—	—	—	—	—	—	—	—	—	—	—	—	—	—
Brown Cap Balanced	—	—	—	—	—	8.2[5]	-3.2[4]	29.8[2]	13.8[3]	21.0[3]	21.4[2]	13.4[3]	17,878	18,735
Brown Cap Equity	—	—	—	—	—	7.4[4]	-1.9[4]	32.0[1]	19.4[3]	22.7[4]	24.6[3]	15.3[4]	19,336	20,375
Brown Cap Sm Co SC	—	—	—	—	—	5.8[5]	4.8[1]	33.9[1]	17.1[3]	15.8[4]	22.0[4]	15.0[3]	18,152	20,134
Bruce	12.9[3]	15.7[5]	-1.1[2]	1.4[5]	10.6[3]	19.4[2]	-16.1[5]	64.8[1]	-2.3[5]	30.2[1]	28.0[1]	16.0[3]	20,963	21,011
BSR Equity	—	—	—	—	2.5[5]	10.3[3]	-0.5[3]	27.2[4]	19.3[4]	27.3[3]	24.5[4]	16.2[4]	19,313	21,179
BSR S-I Fix Inc	—	—	—	—	6.5[2]	8.4[1]	-2.3[5]	15.5[1]	4.1[4]	7.6[1]	9.0[1]	6.5[1]	12,943	13,702
BT Advs:EAFE Eqty Indx	—	—	—	—	—	—	—	—	—	1.9[3]	—	—	—	—
BT Advs:Sm Cap Idx SC	—	—	—	—	—	—	—	—	—	25.1[2]	—	—	—	—
BT Advs:US Bond Idx	—	—	—	—	—	—	—	—	—	—	—	—	—	—
BT Invest:Cap App	—	—	—	—	—	—	3.2[2]	37.4[1]	8.7[5]	14.5[5]	19.6[5]	—	17,095	—
BT Invest:Glob Hi Yld	—	—	—	—	—	—	-3.1[2]	18.6[3]	21.4[1]	10.1[2]	16.6[1]	—	15,848	—
BT Invest:Int'l Eqty	—	—	—	—	—	37.4[3]	4.1[2]	16.1[1]	21.3[2]	17.4[1]	18.2[1]	18.8[1]	16,531	23,642
BT Invest:Inter TF	—	—	—	—	—	9.9[3]	-3.8[3]	13.7[3]	3.3[5]	7.5[2]	8.1[3]	6.0[3]	12,627	13,352

See Chapter 3 for explanation of symbols

Total Net Assets $Million		NAV per share		1997 per share distributions		Yield %	Risk Analysis				% Distribution of Portfolio 12/31/97				
December 31 1996	1997	December 31 1996	1997	Income	Capital gains	12/31/97	beta	R^2	Std. Dev.	Sharpe Ratio	Stocks	Bonds	Cash	Objective	No-Load Fund
570.1	693.6	13.46	13.71	0.60	0.01	4.4	0.11	0.23	2.70	D	0	100	0	tax-free	Bernstein NY Muni
60.9	81.5	12.49	12.45	0.47	0.01	3.8	0.03	0.22	0.75	F	0	96	4	tax-free	Bernstein NY Short Dur Muni
550.3	597.2	12.50	12.42	0.67	0.08	5.3	0.04	0.13	1.31	C	0	98	2	fix-inc	Bernstein Short Dur Plus
121.3	153.2	12.54	12.53	0.45	0.03	3.6	0.03	0.22	0.76	F	0	100	0	tax-free	Bernstein Sht Dur Divsfd Muni
137.2	180.8	12.31	12.51	0.77	0.64	5.8	0.25	0.36	4.67	B	32	68	0	income	Berwyn Income
94.1	100.4	19.69	22.01	0.00	2.74	0.0	0.52	0.24	11.95	F	99	0	1	gr-inc	Berwyn‡
—	3.5	—	17.91	0.00	0.00	—	—	—	—	—	96	0	4	agg gr	Bjurman Micro Cap Gro SC
176.8	151.3	4.90	5.04	0.30	0.00	6.0	0.15	0.28	3.14	A	0	97	3	fix-inc	Blanchard Flex Inc‡
22.5	23.9	5.41	5.64	0.23	0.00	4.2	0.23	0.21	5.58	B	0	96	4	tax-free	Blanchard Flex TF‡
65.8	56.3	9.52	8.58	0.22	1.31	2.2	0.61	0.59	8.67	D	56	38	6	global	Blanchard Glob Gro‡
15.4	17.9	9.52	10.73	0.03	1.45	0.3	0.87	0.90	10.21	D	89	2	9	gr-inc	Blanchard Gro & Inc‡
80.1	39.6	6.46	3.42	0.00	0.00	0.0	0.32	0.01	35.18	A	99	1	0	prec met	Blanchard Prec Met‡
151.4	125.0	3.01	3.05	0.17	0.00	5.6	0.08	0.42	1.33	A	0	80	20	fix-inc	Blanchard ST Flex‡
203.4	34.2	14.12	15.53	0.26	1.92	1.7	0.73	0.89	8.58	B	78	18	4	income	BNY Hamilton Eqty In
—	2.6	—	10.66	0.00	0.00	—	—	—	—	—	98	0	2	int'l	BNY Hamilton Int'l Eqty
64.2	10.5	9.70	9.87	0.54	0.00	5.5	0.13	0.21	3.24	D	0	99	1	fix-inc	BNY Hamilton Inter Gov
—	347.0	—	10.45	0.47	0.00	—	—	—	—	—	0	98	2	fix-inc	BNY Hamilton Inter Inv Grd
—	268.0	—	10.27	0.34	0.04	—	—	—	—	—	0	98	2	tax-free	BNY Hamilton Inter TE
36.7	10.4	10.29	10.52	0.39	0.00	3.7	0.12	0.26	2.65	F	0	93	7	tax-free	BNY Hamilton Inter NY TE
—	6.5	—	10.92	0.01	1.88	—	—	—	—	—	99	0	1	growth	BNY Hamilton Lg Cap Gro
—	1.2	—	11.94	0.00	0.85	—	—	—	—	—	97	0	3	agg gr	BNY Hamilton Sm Cap Gro SC
—	—	—	—	—	—	—	—	—	—	—	—	—	—	fix-inc	Boston Prtnrs Fix Inc
0.3	34.5	10.00	12.40	0.08	0.61	0.7	—	—	—	—	95	0	5	gr-inc	Boston Prtnrs Large Cap
—	17.3	—	11.44	0.00	0.00	—	—	—	—	—	97	0	3	growth	Boston Prtnrs Mid Cap Val
21.4	42.5	12.58	14.25	0.36	0.53	2.5	0.61	0.87	7.25	D	52	39	9	gr-inc	Boston-1784 Asst Alloc
93.7	119.9	10.39	10.73	0.50	0.02	4.7	0.14	0.24	3.19	C	0	94	6	tax-free	Boston-1784 CT TE Inc
—	49.8	—	10.27	0.24	0.02	—	—	—	—	—	93	2	5	tax-free	Boston-1784 FL TE
244.0	294.7	11.69	12.53	0.00	0.80	0.0	—	—	—	—	96	0	4	agg gr	Boston 1784 Growth
375.2	504.2	16.30	19.04	0.11	0.35	0.6	0.83	0.70	11.02	D	87	7	6	gr-inc	Boston-1784 Gro & Inc
321.6	376.8	10.11	10.25	0.63	0.00	6.1	0.21	0.27	4.52	F	0	89	11	fix-inc	Boston-1784 Income
433.5	438.5	12.36	11.96	0.14	0.14	1.2	0.66	0.37	11.84	C	97	0	3	int'l	Boston-1784 Int'l Eqty
130.4	184.3	9.99	10.39	0.47	0.00	4.5	0.15	0.27	3.21	D	0	98	2	tax-free	Boston-1784 MA TE Inc
47.4	66.9	10.31	10.61	0.49	0.04	4.6	0.14	0.26	3.08	B	0	91	9	tax-free	Boston-1784 RI TE Inc
145.2	193.7	10.04	10.08	0.57	0.00	5.7	0.09	0.27	1.95	C	0	87	13	fix-inc	Boston-1784 ST Income
231.6	287.1	10.18	10.49	0.49	0.10	4.6	0.16	0.29	3.30	A	0	94	6	tax-free	Boston-1784 TE Med Term
196.8	240.5	9.45	9.61	0.58	0.00	6.0	0.16	0.26	3.52	F	0	88	12	fix-inc	Boston-1784 US Gov Med
128.7	149.4	15.02	18.93	0.00	1.17	0.0	1.12	0.77	14.20	B	90	0	10	agg gr	Bramwell Growth
383.0	589.8	26.47	26.58	0.00	5.09	0.0	0.94	0.43	16.10	D	47	0	53	growth	Brandywine Blue
6,547.0	8,414.5	33.69	30.89	0.00	7.02	0.0	0.99	0.42	16.98	C	46	0	54	agg gr	Brandywine
0.1	59.7	10.00	11.40	0.31	1.07	2.5	—	—	—	—	97	0	3	sector	Brazos/JMIC Real Est
0.1	92.4	10.00	14.07	0.00	1.27	0.0	—	—	—	—	91	0	9	agg gr	Brazos/JMIC Sm Cap Gro SC
29.2	36.6	24.56	29.02	0.39	0.31	1.3	0.76	0.96	8.61	D	85	13	2	gr-inc	Bridges Investment
2.3	5.5	16.72	18.11	0.00	1.63	0.0	0.88	0.30	17.89	C	90	0	10	agg gr	Bridgeway Agg Gro
0.4	0.9	14.15	17.39	0.00	0.00	0.0	0.89	0.58	12.89	D	74	0	26	growth	Bridgeway Soc Resp
—	0.1	—	5.00	—	—	—	—	—	—	—	100	0	0	gr-inc	Bridgeway Ult Lg 35 Idx
13.7	41.0	17.15	21.83	0.00	1.79	0.0	0.90	0.26	19.75	B	100	0	0	agg gr	Bridgeway Ult Sm Co SC
—	1.3	—	4.98	—	—	—	—	—	—	—	100	0	0	agg gr	Bridgeway Ult Sm Idx SC
4.1	5.4	14.29	15.73	0.17	—	1.1	0.72	0.72	11.29	F	83	10	7	income	Brown Cap Balanced
2.9	6.9	17.06	19.98	0.00	—	0.0	0.86	0.69	14.16	D	90	0	10	growth	Brown Cap Equity
5.3	9.7	16.00	18.29	0.00	—	0.0	0.64	0.27	16.53	D	79	0	21	agg gr	Brown Cap Sm Co SC
2.6	3.2	138.05	175.51	4.28	0.00	2.4	0.77	0.28	16.51	B	35	64	1	agg gr	Bruce
27.7	36.5	15.67	17.86	0.05	1.94	0.3	0.92	0.85	11.10	D	97	1	2	gr-inc	BSR Equity
33.0	37.3	10.58	10.74	0.62	0.00	5.8	0.13	0.25	2.91	B	0	94	6	fix-inc	BSR S-I Fix Inc
0.7	3.2	10.14	9.63	0.08	0.61	0.8	—	—	—	—	99	0	1	int'l	BT Advs:EAFE Eqty Indx
0.1	1.3	11.04	11.69	0.09	1.95	0.8	—	—	—	—	96	0	4	agg gr	BT Advs:Sm Cap Idx SC
—	0.2	—	10.25	0.31	0.04	—	—	—	—	—	0	98	2	fix-inc	BT Advs:US Bond Idx
58.1	39.9	13.95	12.26	0.00	3.61	0.0	0.98	0.34	18.80	F	99	0	1	growth	BT Invest:Cap App
21.6	26.7	11.08	10.72	0.70	0.72	6.5	0.46	0.28	9.69	B	18	82	0	fix-inc	BT Invest:Glob Hi Yld
210.3	573.8	17.61	20.06	0.01	0.59	0.1	0.74	0.52	11.40	A	87	0	13	int'l	BT Invest:Int'l Eqty
21.3	19.7	10.46	10.78	0.44	0.00	4.1	0.17	0.29	3.46	F	0	100	0	tax-free	BT Invest:Inter TF

Stock and bond funds — comprehensive summary *continued*

Arranged in alphabetical order

No-Load Fund	Total return percent with quintile ranks by objective										Annualized		What $10,000 grew to after	
	1988	1989	1990	1991	1992	1993	1994	1995	1996	1997	3 yrs.	5 yrs.	3 yrs.	5 yrs.
BT Invest:Lat Am Eqty	—	—	—	—	—	—	-11.0[5]	-24.3[5]	32.8[1]	30.8[1]	9.6[3]	—	13,155	—
BT Invest:Lifecycle Long Range	—	—	—	—	—	—	-2.9[4]	23.0[5]	15.8[4]	23.0[4]	20.6[4]	—	17,526	—
BT Invest:Lifecycle Mid Range	—	—	—	—	—	—	-3.4[5]	18.5[5]	11.7[5]	18.5[5]	16.2[5]	—	15,695	—
BT Invest:Lifecycle Sht Range	—	—	—	—	—	—	-2.8[4]	14.4[5]	7.8[5]	13.7[5]	12.0[5]	—	14,029	—
BT Invest:Pac Basin	—	—	—	—	—	—	-16.9[5]	7.3[3]	13.0[3]	-45.9[5]	-13.1[5]	—	6,553	—
BT Invest:Sm Cap SC	—	—	—	—	—	—	19.3[1]	58.6[1]	6.9[5]	13.2[4]	24.3[3]	—	19,182	—
BT Pyramid:Eqty 500 Idx	—	—	—	—	—	9.5[4]	1.1[2]	37.2[1]	22.8[2]	33.0[1]	30.9[1]	19.9[1]	22,408	24,825
BT Pyramid:Eqty App	—	—	—	—	—	—	3.5[1]	37.6[2]	9.6[5]	15.4[4]	20.3[4]	—	17,406	—
BT Pyramid:Instit Asst Mgt	—	—	—	—	—	—	-3.2[4]	23.5[5]	16.2[4]	23.5[4]	21.0[4]	—	17,733	—
BT Pyramid:Ltd Trm US Gov	—	—	—	—	—	6.2[3]	-0.1[3]	9.8[4]	4.4[3]	6.0[4]	6.72[4]	5.22[3]	12,153	—
Buffalo Balanced	—	—	—	—	—	—	—	20.3[5]	19.3[1]	15.1[5]	18.2[4]	—	16,516	—
Buffalo Equity	—	—	—	—	—	—	—	—	29.3[1]	24.2[3]	—	—	—	—
Buffalo High Yield	—	—	—	—	—	—	—	—	16.7[1]	15.8[1]	—	—	—	—
Buffalo USA Global	—	—	—	—	—	—	—	—	36.8[1]	19.0[2]	—	—	—	—
Bull & Bear Gold	-13.5[1]	19.3[4]	-22.1[3]	-1.1[2]	-17.2[3]	87.6[3]	-13.8[3]	-5.4[5]	4.3[3]	-55.7[5]	-24.1[2]	-6.7[5]	4,369	7,064
Bull & Bear Spec Eqty	22.7[2]	42.3[1]	-36.4[5]	40.5[4]	28.4[1]	16.4[3]	-16.5[5]	40.5[2]	1.1[5]	5.2[5]	14.3[5]	7.8[5]	14,948	14,528
Bull & Bear US & Overs	8.0[3]	11.0[5]	-8.6[4]	22.6[1]	-2.6[4]	26.7[3]	-13.1[5]	25.1[1]	5.3[5]	6.7[4]	12.0[4]	9.1[4]	14,056	15,473
Bullfinch Unrestrcd	—	—	—	—	—	—	—	—	—	—	—	—	—	—
C&O Market Opport	—	—	—	—	15.3[2]	14.9[3]	-1.0[3]	16.5[5]	27.3[1]	29.4[2]	24.3[3]	16.9[3]	19,187	21,832
C\FUNDS:Adams Equity	—	—	—	—	—	—	—	—	26.3[1]	18.5[5]	—	—	—	—
C\FUNDS:C\FUND	11.4[4]	17.8[4]	-1.5[2]	22.7[4]	10.3[2]	10.9[3]	-1.1[4]	26.2[4]	16.2[4]	21.0[4]	21.0[5]	14.2[5]	17,726	19,444
C\FUNDS:Gov	—	—	—	—	—	6.8[5]	-0.5[1]	12.1[5]	4.1[3]	7.3[5]	7.8[5]	5.9[5]	12,509	13,299
C\FUNDS:Growth Stk	—	—	—	—	—	2.7[5]	-8.9[5]	22.8[5]	20.3[3]	25.5[3]	22.9[4]	11.7[5]	18,539	17,356
C\FUNDS:Tax-Free	—	—	—	—	—	4.1[5]	-2.2[1]	10.3[5]	3.5[4]	—	—	—	—	—
CA Inv Tr-CA Insur Inter	—	—	—	—	—	10.5[3]	-5.0[5]	14.4[2]	3.9[3]	6.4[5]	8.1[3]	5.8[4]	12,642	13,275
CA Inv Tr-CA TF	10.7[4]	9.9[2]	6.7[3]	12.1[3]	8.8[3]	14.8[1]	-8.6[5]	20.6[1]	3.1[4]	9.3[2]	10.8[1]	7.3[2]	13,584	14,247
CA Inv Tr-Eqty Inc	—	—	—	—	—	—	—	—	—	29.3[1]	—	—	—	—
CA Inv Tr-S&P 500	—	—	—	—	—	9.8[4]	1.0[2]	37.2[1]	22.6[2]	33.0[1]	30.8[1]	19.9[1]	22,378	24,815
CA Inv Tr-S&P MidCap	—	—	—	—	—	12.9[3]	-3.9[4]	30.6[3]	18.9[3]	31.9[2]	27.0[2]	17.3[3]	20,474	22,199
CA Inv Tr-Sm Cap Idx SC	—	—	—	—	—	—	—	—	—	24.1[2]	—	—	—	—
CA Inv Tr-US Gov	7.3[4]	13.5[2]	8.6[1]	17.5[3]	8.4[2]	15.8[2]	-7.0[4]	23.4[1]	-0.5[5]	9.3[3]	10.3[3]	7.7[3]	13,421	14,454
Capp-Rush Emg Growth SC	—	—	—	—	—	—	-6.9[5]	36.0[2]	2.0[5]	4.7[5]	13.3[5]	10.6[5]	14,526	16,567
Capp-Rush Gold	—	—	—	—	—	—	—	4.1[3]	-6.3[5]	-45.2[4]	-18.9[2]	—	5,341	—
Capp-Rush Growth	—	—	—	—	—	—	4.6[1]	37.1[1]	7.2[5]	22.2[4]	21.5[4]	16.5[3]	17,955	21,486
Capp-Rush Util	—	—	—	—	—	6.1[5]	-13.4[5]	29.8[2]	4.4[5]	25.3[2]	19.3[4]	9.3[5]	16,972	15,608
Capstone Gov Inc	12.0[1]	7.3[5]	-1.2[5]	6.6[5]	3.6[5]	3.3[5]	1.2[2]	5.7[5]	3.9[4]	4.4[5]	4.7[5]	3.7[5]	11,471	11,988
Capstone Growth	12.4[4]	30.9[2]	-3.3[3]	34.8[3]	0.8[5]	6.1[4]	-7.8[5]	29.2[3]	17.2[4]	28.7[2]	24.9[3]	13.8[5]	19,498	19,081
Capstone New Zealand	—	—	—	—	2.8[1]	14.0[5]	-8.4[4]	11.8[2]	26.4[1]	-23.1[5]	2.8[4]	2.6[5]	10,864	11,350
Capstone Nikko Japan	—	—	-37.0[5]	-0.3[5]	-28.9[5]	25.3[5]	24.3[1]	-3.2[5]	-16.1[5]	-24.6[5]	-15.1[5]	-0.9[5]	6,127	9,540
Carl Domino Eqty Inc	—	—	—	—	—	—	—	—	24.4[1]	35.4[1]	—	—	—	—
Century Shares	15.7[3]	41.6[2]	-7.8[3]	31.5[4]	27.0[1]	-0.4[5]	-3.9[4]	35.2[2]	17.2[3]	50.1[1]	33.5[1]	17.9[3]	23,789	22,770
CGM American TF	—	—	—	—	—	—	-8.2[4]	18.0[2]	2.9[5]	9.0[3]	9.8[3]	—	13,234	—
CGM Capital Dev‡	-0.3[5]	17.9[5]	1.5[1]	99.1[1]	17.5[2]	28.7[1]	-22.9[5]	41.1[2]	28.1[1]	23.9[2]	30.8[1]	17.3[2]	22,393	22,209
CGM Fixed Inc	—	—	—	—	—	—	-8.0[5]	27.3[1]	15.4[1]	3.7[5]	15.0[1]	10.7[1]	15,228	16,657
CGM Focus	—	—	—	—	—	—	—	—	—	—	—	—	—	—
CGM Mutual	3.2[5]	21.7[3]	1.1[1]	40.9[1]	6.1[4]	21.8[1]	-9.7[5]	24.3[5]	23.7[2]	8.2[5]	18.5[5]	12.8[5]	16,633	18,294
CGM Realty	—	—	—	—	—	—	—	19.8[4]	44.1[1]	26.7[3]	29.8[2]	—	21,876	—
Chicago Tr Balanced	—	—	—	—	—	—	—	—	16.6[2]	20.9[3]	—	—	—	—
Chicago Tr Bond	—	—	—	—	—	—	-2.8[3]	17.5[2]	3.8[3]	9.0[2]	10.0[2]	—	13,298	—
Chicago Tr Gro & Inc	—	—	—	—	—	—	0.5[3]	35.6[2]	25.4[1]	26.7[3]	29.2[2]	—	21,545	—
Chicago Tr Muni	—	—	—	—	—	—	-2.2[1]	11.1[5]	3.1[5]	5.5[5]	6.5[5]	—	12,078	—
Chicago Tr Talon	—	—	—	—	—	—	—	27.4[4]	26.2[1]	26.5[3]	26.7[2]	—	20,316	—
CitiSelect 200	—	—	—	—	—	—	—	—	—	8.3[5]	—	—	—	—
CitiSelect 300	—	—	—	—	—	—	—	—	—	9.9[5]	—	—	—	—
CitiSelect 400	—	—	—	—	—	—	—	—	—	10.3[5]	—	—	—	—
CitiSelect 500	—	—	—	—	—	—	—	—	—	12.0[5]	—	—	—	—
Citizens Tr Emg Gr SC	—	—	—	—	—	—	—	40.7[2]	13.9[4]	17.7[4]	23.6[3]	—	18,866	—
Citizens Tr Global	—	—	—	—	—	—	—	13.7[4]	13.2[4]	19.9[2]	15.6[4]	—	15,433	—
Citizens Tr Idx	—	—	—	—	—	—	—	—	23.1[2]	35.0[1]	—	—	—	—
Citizens Tr Income	—	—	—	—	—	10.0[2]	-3.1[3]	17.5[2]	4.9[2]	10.5[1]	10.8[1]	7.7[1]	13,606	14,500

See Chapter 3 for explanation of symbols

Arranged in alphabetical order

Total Net Assets $Million		NAV per share		1997 per share distributions		Yield % 12/31/97	Risk Analysis				% Distribution of Portfolio 12/31/97			Objective	No-Load Fund
December 31 1996	1997	December 31 1996	1997	Income	Capital gains		beta	R^2	Std. Dev.	Sharpe Ratio	Stocks	Bonds	Cash		
20.6	32.5	10.98	14.33	0.03	0.00	0.2	0.85	0.13	25.32	C	95	0	5	int'l	BT Invest:Lat Am Eqty
72.4	114.6	11.86	13.36	0.23	0.95	1.7	0.72	0.96	8.17	C	47	12	41	growth	BT Invest:Lifecycle Long Range
60.1	84.8	10.80	11.55	0.35	0.84	3.0	0.55	0.92	6.33	F	30	20	50	gr-inc	BT Invest:Lifecycle Mid Range
32.3	41.0	10.35	10.31	0.52	0.86	5.0	0.37	0.83	4.54	F	14	31	55	income	BT Invest:Lifecycle Sht Range
31.7	11.2	11.82	5.40	0.00	0.99	0.0	1.20	0.26	24.16	F	84	0	16	int'l	BT Invest:Pac Basin
188.1	229.0	18.17	18.15	0.00	2.30	0.0	1.19	0.26	25.64	D	95	0	5	agg gr	BT Invest:Sm Cap SC
447.4	646.1	99.06	124.95	1.78	4.73	1.4	1.00	1.00	11.14	B	99	0	1	gr-inc	BT Pyramid:Eqty 500 Idx
152.8	163.7	13.88	15.00	0.00	0.97	0.0	0.97	0.34	18.47	D	95	0	5	agg gr	BT Pyramid:Eqty App
250.7	384.7	11.96	13.29	0.27	1.15	2.0	0.72	0.96	8.21	C	47	12	41	growth	BT Pyramid:Instit Asst Mgt
12,897.0	48.0	9.85	9.89	0.53	0.00	5.4	0.06	0.20	1.48	D	0	93	7	fix-inc	BT Pyramid:Ltd Trm US Gov
42.7	50.9	10.86	10.89	0.65	0.91	5.5	0.37	0.53	5.67	B	53	40	7	income	Buffalo Balanced
17.3	33.6	14.19	15.65	0.09	1.82	0.6	—	—	—	—	100	0	0	growth	Buffalo Equity
16.8	35.9	11.80	12.57	0.80	0.24	6.3	—	—	—	—	2	98	0	fix-inc	Buffalo High Yield
19.5	48.4	14.09	15.66	0.06	1.02	0.4	—	—	—	—	100	0	0	global	Buffalo USA Global
23.0	9.4	10.33	4.16	0.00	0.41	0.0	0.31	0.01	31.87	B	98	0	2	prec met	Bull & Bear Gold
49.8	44.3	22.96	23.38	0.00	0.75	0.0	1.25	0.39	21.83	F	106	0	-6	agg gr	Bull & Bear Spec Eqty
10.0	8.5	7.91	7.42	0.00	0.87	0.0	1.04	0.47	16.61	F	99	0	1	global	Bull & Bear US & Overs
—	0.6	—	10.65	—	—	—	—	—	—	—	—	—	—	growth	Bullfinch Unrestrcd
43.5	141.1	14.65	17.85	0.20	0.88	1.1	-0.07	0.01	7.49	A	95	0	5	agg gr	C&O Market Opport
0.2	1.3	11.82	13.90	0.10	0.00	0.7	—	—	—	—	—	—	—	gr-inc	C\FUNDS:Adams Equity
5.4	7.1	17.71	20.61	0.25	0.55	1.2	—	—	—	—	—	—	—	gr-inc	C\FUNDS:C\FUND
4.7	4.5	9.87	10.01	0.55	0.00	5.5	0.13	0.30	2.61	D	—	—	—	fix-inc	C\FUNDS:Gov
2.2	2.5	12.38	13.65	0.14	1.73	1.0	—	—	—	—	—	—	—	growth	C\FUNDS:Growth Stk
3.8	3.3	9.81	—	0.46	—	—	—	—	—	—	—	—	—	tax-free	C\FUNDS:Tax-Free
26.3	22.3	10.62	10.78	0.55	0.05	4.2	0.16	0.28	3.28	D	0	99	1	tax-free	CA Inv Tr-CA Insur Inter
209.3	221.1	12.64	13.00	0.59	0.19	4.5	0.24	0.26	5.22	C	0	95	5	tax-free	CA Inv Tr-CA TF
2.9	9.8	10.69	13.00	0.35	0.41	2.7	—	—	—	—	71	0	29	income	CA Inv Tr-Eqty Inc
52.6	79.6	16.46	21.13	0.33	0.38	1.5	0.99	1.00	11.05	B	94	0	6	gr-inc	CA Inv Tr-S&P 500
37.2	49.6	15.11	18.22	0.23	1.40	1.2	0.84	0.64	11.68	C	90	0	10	growth	CA Inv Tr-S&P MidCap
2.5	9.2	10.27	12.15	0.17	0.39	1.4	—	—	—	—	80	0	20	agg gr	CA Inv Tr-Sm Cap Idx SC
30.1	34.3	10.50	10.74	0.62	0.07	5.8	0.24	0.18	6.29	F	0	99	1	fix-inc	CA Inv Tr-US Gov
29.3	18.2	13.36	13.99	0.00	0.00	0.0	1.16	0.30	23.35	F	98	0	2	agg gr	Capp-Rush Emg Growth SC
4.4	2.6	8.58	4.70	0.00	0.00	0.0	0.51	0.03	30.94	B	82	0	18	prec met	Capp-Rush Gold
24.2	24.9	17.05	20.83	0.00	0.00	0.0	1.08	0.52	16.64	F	96	0	4	growth	Capp-Rush Growth
11.3	14.0	10.44	12.50	0.49	0.00	3.9	0.43	0.22	10.31	F	67	0	33	income	Capp-Rush Util
20.0	8.6	23.95	24.28	0.73	0.00	3.0	0.02	0.11	0.54	F	92	0	8	fix-inc	Capstone Gov Inc
60.6	70.1	13.74	13.87	0.13	3.65	0.9	0.90	0.98	10.10	B	82	0	18	growth	Capstone Growth
10.0	6.0	13.17	9.92	0.20	0.00	2.0	0.24	0.03	14.22	D	95	2	3	int'l	Capstone New Zealand
2.6	1.8	6.15	4.64	0.00	0.00	0.0	0.58	0.12	18.39	F	92	0	8	int'l	Capstone Nikko Japan
1.5	4.7	12.59	15.93	0.13	0.94	0.8	—	—	—	—	100	0	0	income	Carl Domino Eqty Inc
270.8	413.7	31.30	44.66	0.38	1.90	0.8	0.86	0.59	12.66	A	96	0	4	sector	Century Shares
12.4	14.4	9.46	9.70	0.58	0.00	6.0	0.17	0.22	3.93	B	0	96	4	tax-free	CGM American TF
631.3	722.6	29.08	26.96	0.00	9.08	0.0	0.97	0.41	16.97	B	101	0	-1	agg gr	CGM Capital Dev‡
40.6	43.9	11.60	11.24	0.78	0.00	7.0	0.25	0.19	6.42	B	10	88	2	fix-inc	CGM Fixed Inc
—	95.0	—	9.38	0.00	0.00	—	—	—	—	—	99	0	1	agg gr	CGM Focus
1,217.7	1,192.2	31.42	25.52	0.70	7.78	2.1	0.76	0.56	11.39	F	75	26	-1	gr-inc	CGM Mutual
161.7	489.6	14.50	15.60	0.73	1.98	4.2	0.25	0.06	11.69	B	98	0	2	sector	CGM Realty
162.5	191.0	9.70	10.73	0.29	0.68	2.5	—	—	—	—	55	36	9	income	Chicago Tr Balanced
84.3	131.8	9.86	10.11	0.61	0.00	6.0	0.17	0.27	3.68	B	0	91	9	fix-inc	Chicago Tr Bond
215.2	289.9	16.49	19.42	0.06	1.37	0.3	0.92	0.89	10.91	C	95	0	5	gr-inc	Chicago Tr Gro & Inc
11.2	12.5	10.09	10.23	0.40	0.00	3.9	0.10	0.23	2.40	F	0	93	7	tax-free	Chicago Tr Muni
18.9	30.2	14.05	14.83	0.10	2.83	0.7	0.92	0.45	15.20	D	70	21	9	growth	Chicago Tr Talon
93.2	184.9	10.50	10.95	0.22	0.19	2.0	—	—	—	—	32	38	30	income	CitiSelect 200
174.6	349.6	10.66	11.30	0.14	0.27	1.2	—	—	—	—	44	36	20	income	CitiSelect 300
220.4	469.6	10.82	11.57	0.08	0.27	0.7	—	—	—	—	60	22	18	gr-inc	CitiSelect 400
70.9	201.5	10.69	11.73	0.08	0.15	0.7	—	—	—	—	77	10	13	growth	CitiSelect 500
52.9	71.8	13.39	14.70	0.00	1.00	0.0	0.92	0.41	15.92	C	92	0	8	agg gr	Citizens Tr Emg Gr SC
20.2	35.0	12.30	14.19	0.00	0.56	0.0	0.80	0.64	11.04	D	93	0	7	global	Citizens Tr Global
161.9	257.0	15.01	19.30	0.00	0.95	0.0	—	—	—	—	99	0	1	growth	Citizens Tr Idx
34.5	45.8	10.53	10.93	0.66	0.01	6.0	0.19	0.37	3.50	A	0	100	0	fix-inc	Citizens Tr Income

No-Load Fund	1988	1989	1990	1991	1992	1993	1994	1995	1996	1997	Annualized 3 yrs.	5 yrs.	What $10,000 grew to after 3 yrs.	5 yrs.
Clipper	19.7[2]	22.1[3]	-7.6[4]	32.7[3]	15.9[2]	11.3[3]	-2.5[4]	45.2[1]	19.4[3]	30.4[2]	31.3[1]	19.7[2]	22,611	24,537
Cohen & Steers Realty	—	—	—	—	20.1[2]	18.8[3]	8.3[2]	11.1[5]	38.5[1]	21.1[3]	23.0[4]	19.1[2]	18,631	23,971
Cohen & Steers Spec Eqty	—	—	—	—	—	—	—	—	—	—	—	—	—	—
Columbia Balanced	—	—	—	—	8.9[3]	13.6[3]	0.1[2]	25.1[3]	11.8[4]	18.8[3]	18.4[4]	13.6[3]	16,609	18,887
Columbia Common Stk	—	—	—	—	10.5[2]	16.4[2]	2.1[2]	30.8[3]	20.7[3]	25.4[3]	25.6[3]	18.7[3]	19,794	23,524
Columbia Fix Inc	7.7[3]	14.3[1]	8.3[3]	16.8[2]	8.0[1]	10.5[2]	-3.4[4]	18.9[2]	3.4[3]	9.6[1]	10.4[1]	7.5[2]	13,469	14,377
Columbia Growth	10.8[4]	29.1[3]	-3.3[2]	34.3[4]	11.8[3]	13.0[4]	-0.6[2]	33.0[3]	20.8[2]	26.3[2]	26.6[2]	17.9[2]	20,295	22,795
Columbia High Yld	—	—	—	—	—	—	-0.9[1]	19.1[3]	9.4[1]	12.7[2]	13.7[2]	—	14,688	—
Columbia Int'l Stk	—	—	—	—	—	—	-2.5[3]	5.1[4]	16.6[2]	11.5[2]	11.0[2]	12.2[3]	13,660	17,768
Columbia Muni Bd	10.2[4]	8.9[4]	6.9[2]	11.7[3]	6.5[5]	10.7[5]	-4.7[1]	14.1[5]	3.8[3]	8.4[4]	8.7[5]	6.2[5]	12,833	13,539
Columbia Real Est Eqty	—	—	—	—	—	—	—	19.8[4]	38.3[1]	24.7[3]	27.4[2]	—	20,668	—
Columbia Small Cap SC	—	—	—	—	—	—	—	—	—	34.1[1]	—	—	—	—
Columbia Special	42.5[1]	31.9[2]	-12.4[4]	50.5[3]	13.6[2]	21.6[2]	2.3[2]	29.5[3]	13.1[4]	12.6[4]	18.2[4]	15.5[3]	16,498	20,524
Columbia US Gov	5.3[5]	9.6[4]	9.3[1]	12.8[3]	5.8[3]	5.9[3]	0.0[3]	10.2[4]	3.9[4]	5.6[5]	6.5[5]	5.1[4]	12,095	12,808
Concorde Income	—	—	—	—	—	—	—	—	—	6.8[5]	—	—	—	—
Concorde Value	13.9[4]	4.6[5]	-16.7[5]	27.5[3]	14.7[1]	10.5[3]	-4.0[5]	24.0[5]	18.0[4]	29.1[3]	23.6[4]	14.9[4]	18,899	20,049
Copley	19.9[2]	17.8[4]	-1.5[2]	17.1[5]	17.7[1]	10.2[3]	-7.7[5]	26.1[4]	4.8[5]	25.1[4]	18.2[5]	10.9[5]	16,528	16,811
Corbin Sm Cap Val SC	—	—	—	—	—	—	—	—	—	—	—	—	—	—
Cornercap Growth	7.0[4]	8.2[5]	-16.1[5]	34.6[4]	-3.8[5]	5.3[5]	8.1[1]	9.7[5]	28.9[1]	32.9[1]	23.4[3]	16.4[3]	18,806	21,402
Crabbe Hsn Asst Alloc	—	7.5[5]	-0.8[3]	21.2[4]	12.2[2]	18.2[1]	-0.8[2]	20.2[5]	6.7[5]	19.2[3]	15.2[5]	12.4[4]	15,286	17,924
Crabbe Hsn Equity	—	—	-1.5[2]	35.1[2]	16.4[1]	26.0[1]	1.6[2]	26.4[4]	11.7[5]	25.7[3]	21.1[4]	17.8[3]	17,752	22,725
Crabbe Hsn Income	—	—	5.9[3]	15.4[4]	6.3[4]	6.3[5]	-3.3[2]	17.0[4]	2.0[4]	11.6[2]	10.0[4]	6.5[5]	13,312	13,685
Crabbe Hsn OR Muni	7.6[3]	7.5[4]	6.4[4]	9.8[4]	7.3[3]	8.9[4]	-2.7[2]	12.1[5]	3.0[5]	7.0[3]	7.3[5]	5.5[5]	12,358	13,094
Crabbe Hsn Real Est	—	—	—	—	—	—	—	9.5[5]	36.0[2]	18.8[4]	20.9[4]	—	17,685	—
Crabbe Hsn Small Cap SC	—	—	—	—	—	—	—	—	—	26.1[2]	—	—	—	—
Crabbe Hsn Special SC	19.9[2]	16.9[5]	3.8[1]	17.1[5]	33.4[1]	34.5[1]	11.7[1]	10.8[5]	5.9[5]	11.2[4]	9.3[5]	14.4[4]	13,049	19,605
Crabbe Hsn US Gov Bd	—	—	7.4[4]	13.2[2]	5.5[4]	5.9[3]	-2.1[4]	12.0[2]	2.9[5]	7.1[1]	7.2[3]	5.0[4]	12,331	12,782
CRM Small Cap Value SC	—	—	—	—	—	—	—	—	39.0[1]	21.7[4]	—	—	—	—
Croft Leom Income	—	—	—	—	—	—	—	—	7.1[5]	13.0[5]	—	—	—	—
Croft Leom Value	—	—	—	—	—	—	—	—	19.9[3]	32.5[1]	—	—	—	—
Crowley Dvsfd Mngmt	—	—	—	—	—	—	—	—	12.3[5]	13.0[5]	—	—	—	—
Crowley Gro & Inc	—	—	-0.8[2]	15.9[5]	3.6[5]	3.2[5]	3.9[1]	13.4[5]	4.4[5]	9.0[5]	8.9[5]	6.7[5]	12,902	13,834
Crowley Income	—	—	9.0[1]	11.4[5]	7.2[3]	9.6[4]	-1.8[1]	10.6[5]	3.0[3]	—	—	—	—	—
Cruelty Free Val	—	—	—	—	—	—	—	—	—	—	—	—	—	—
Cutler Approved List	—	—	—	—	—	5.0[5]	0.8[2]	33.2[2]	16.9[4]	33.3[1]	27.5[2]	17.0[3]	20,746	21,957
Cutler Eqty Income	—	—	—	—	—	5.1[5]	-2.9[4]	34.4[1]	18.3[1]	33.4[1]	28.5[1]	16.7[1]	21,202	21,637
Daruma MidCap Value	—	—	—	—	—	—	—	—	—	35.9[1]	—	—	—	—
Dean Witter ST Bond	—	—	—	—	—	—	—	11.9[2]	4.5[2]	6.4[3]	7.6[2]	—	12,444	—
Dean Witter ST US Treas	—	—	—	—	5.4[4]	5.0[4]	-1.2[4]	9.8[4]	3.9[5]	6.1[4]	6.6[5]	4.6[5]	12,099	12,544
Delafield Fund	—	—	—	—	—	—	5.6[1]	27.4[4]	26.4[1]	19.7[4]	24.4[3]	—	19,264	—
Dodge & Cox Balanced	11.5[4]	23.0[2]	0.9[2]	20.7[5]	10.6[2]	16.0[2]	2.0[1]	28.0[2]	14.8[3]	21.2[3]	21.2[2]	16.1[2]	17,807	21,070
Dodge & Cox Income	—	14.1[2]	7.4[2]	17.9[3]	7.8[3]	11.3[3]	-2.9[2]	20.2[2]	3.6[3]	10.0[2]	11.1[3]	8.2[3]	13,699	14,804
Dodge & Cox Stock	13.8[4]	26.9[2]	-5.1[3]	21.5[4]	10.8[2]	·18.3[2]	5.2[1]	33.4[2]	22.3[2]	28.4[3]	28.0[2]	21.1[1]	20,947	26,069
Domini Social Eqty	—	—	—	—	12.1[3]	6.5[4]	-0.4[3]	35.2[2]	21.8[2]	36.0[1]	30.8[1]	18.9[2]	22,399	23,760
Drey-Basic GNMA	10.6[2]	8.4[4]	8.5[2]	13.3[5]	7.0[3]	8.8[4]	-1.0[1]	16.4[4]	4.8[2]	9.5[3]	10.2[3]	7.6[3]	13,390	14,416
Drey-Basic Inter Muni	—	—	—	—	—	—	—	13.8[3]	4.9[1]	8.8[1]	9.1[1]	—	12,978	—
Drey-Basic Muni	—	—	—	—	—	—	—	19.3[1]	4.6[1]	10.9[1]	11.4[1]	—	13,836	—
Drey-General CA	—	—	7.7[1]	10.9[4]	8.6[3]	13.7[1]	-7.0[3]	18.0[2]	4.3[2]	8.8[3]	10.2[2]	7.2[2]	13,393	14,161
Drey-General Muni	12.6[2]	11.5[1]	7.6[1]	14.7[1]	9.8[1]	13.3[2]	-7.3[4]	17.3[3]	3.1[5]	8.1[5]	9.3[4]	6.5[4]	13,068	13,725
Drey-General NY	6.0[5]	6.6[5]	6.7[3]	14.1[1]	10.1[1]	14.2[1]	-7.2[4]	16.5[4]	3.1[5]	9.6[2]	9.6[3]	6.9[3]	13,161	13,948
Dreyfus 100% US Inter	5.8[5]	12.9[3]	8.6[3]	15.2[3]	7.2[2]	11.1[2]	-4.0[4]	15.8[4]	3.1[4]	7.6[4]	8.7[4]	6.5[3]	12,850	13,705
Dreyfus 100% US Long	8.2[3]	16.2[1]	7.0[3]	18.3[1]	7.5[3]	16.6[1]	-9.2[5]	24.9[1]	0.9[5]	11.7[2]	12.1[2]	8.3[2]	14,077	14,903
Dreyfus 100% US Short	7.9[1]	12.8[1]	6.2[5]	12.9[3]	7.0[1]	7.0[2]	-0.3[1]	11.4[2]	4.1[4]	6.1[4]	7.2[3]	5.6[2]	12,306	13,128
Dreyfus A Bonds Plus	9.0[3]	14.2[2]	4.8[4]	18.8[2]	8.2[2]	15.0[2]	-6.2[4]	20.3[2]	3.1[3]	9.5[3]	10.7[3]	7.9[3]	13,583	14,652
Dreyfus Agg Gr SC	—	—	—	—	—	—	—	—	20.6[3]	-15.8[5]	—	—	—	—
Dreyfus Agg Val SC	—	—	—	—	—	—	—	—	38.9[1]	21.6[3]	—	—	—	—
Dreyfus Apprec	16.6[3]	27.2[3]	-1.8[2]	38.4[4]	4.6[4]	0.7[5]	3.6[1]	37.9[2]	25.7[1]	27.8[2]	30.4[1]	18.2[2]	22,160	23,119
Dreyfus Asst Alloc	—	—	—	—	—	—	1.7[1]	23.5[4]	14.9[3]	28.9[1]	22.3[2]	—	18,295	—
Dreyfus Balanced	—	—	—	—	—	—	4.0[1]	25.0[3]	11.6[4]	17.4[4]	17.9[4]	13.5[3]	16,381	18,876
Dreyfus Bond Mkt Idx	—	—	—	—	—	—	—	18.1[2]	1.9[5]	9.2[2]	9.5[3]	—	13,145	—

See Chapter 3 for explanation of symbols

Stock and bond funds — comprehensive summary *continued*
Arranged in alphabetical order

Total Net Assets $Million		NAV per share		1997 per share distributions		Yield % 12/31/97	Risk Analysis				% Distribution of Portfolio 12/31/97			Objective	No-Load Fund
December 31 1996	1997	December 31 1996	1997	Income	Capital gains		beta	R²	Std. Dev.	Sharpe Ratio	Stocks	Bonds	Cash		
542.8	824.1	67.57	76.86	1.36	9.83	1.6	0.76	0.79	9.54	A	59	11	30	growth	Clipper
2,025.1	3,433.0	45.09	50.18	1.88	2.30	3.6	0.16	0.03	11.51	C	98	0	2	sector	Cohen & Steers Realty
—	135.9	—	32.25	0.27	2.71	—	—	—	—	—	92	0	8	sector	Cohen & Steers Spec Eqty
672.6	792.4	20.32	21.42	0.83	1.83	3.6	0.52	0.90	6.17	C	52	47	1	income	Columbia Balanced
536.8	783.9	19.26	22.02	0.27	1.84	1.1	0.73	0.82	9.03	C	93	0	7	gr-inc	Columbia Common Stk
356.4	381.3	13.08	13.41	0.85	0.03	6.3	0.19	0.26	4.10	B	1	93	6	fix-inc	Columbia Fix Inc
1,064.1	1,324.9	30.74	34.34	0.17	4.32	0.4	0.94	0.79	11.75	A	98	0	2	agg gr	Columbia Growth
28.8	39.3	9.94	10.04	0.79	0.30	7.9	0.20	0.43	3.29	A	0	100	0	fix-inc	Columbia High Yld
125.5	146.3	13.86	13.70	0.00	1.75	0.0	0.64	0.34	12.08	B	89	0	11	int'l	Columbia Int'l Stk
375.7	404.5	12.15	12.47	0.60	0.07	4.8	0.14	0.24	3.20	D	0	97	3	tax-free	Columbia Muni Bd
68.1	151.6	16.16	18.80	0.79	0.51	4.1	0.28	0.08	11.14	B	93	0	7	sector	Columbia Real Est Eqty
21.1	96.4	12.99	16.65	0.00	0.77	0.0	—	—	—	—	97	0	3	agg gr	Columbia Small Cap SC
1,585.3	1,249.7	19.85	20.26	0.00	2.10	0.0	0.84	0.40	14.68	D	98	0	2	agg gr	Columbia Special
40.8	37.8	8.24	8.28	0.41	0.00	5.0	0.07	0.21	1.77	F	0	100	0	fix-inc	Columbia US Gov
2.6	4.2	10.08	10.28	0.47	0.00	4.6	—	—	—	—	20	76	4	income	Concorde Income
13.4	17.3	14.90	17.63	0.05	1.53	0.3	0.78	0.79	9.83	D	89	0	11	gr-inc	Concorde Value
74.7	82.8	26.05	32.58	0.00	0.00	0.0	0.42	0.31	8.48	F	96	1	3	gr-inc	Copley
—	1.7	—	10.25	0.01	0.63	—	—	—	—	—	100	0	0	agg gr	Corbin Sm Cap Val SC
12.2	15.6	11.71	13.37	0.03	2.09	0.2	0.54	0.34	10.30	B	96	0	4	agg gr	Cornercap Growth
118.1	93.3	13.01	13.33	0.32	1.80	2.1	0.54	0.62	7.70	F	56	39	5	income	Crabbe Hsn Asst Alloc
410.1	377.6	18.85	18.76	0.05	4.74	0.2	0.79	0.51	12.47	D	98	0	2	growth	Crabbe Hsn Equity
3.7	3.5	10.17	10.42	0.88	0.00	8.5	0.22	0.29	4.59	D	0	101	-1	fix-inc	Crabbe Hsn Income
25.8	26.4	12.56	12.85	0.54	0.03	4.2	0.14	0.28	3.01	F	0	100	0	tax-free	Crabbe Hsn OR Muni
31.7	32.2	12.57	12.77	0.34	1.69	2.7	0.18	0.04	9.91	C	94	0	6	sector	Crabbe Hsn Real Est
25.0	39.1	11.76	13.51	0.00	1.24	0.0	—	—	—	—	88	0	12	agg gr	Crabbe Hsn Small Cap SC
435.6	352.7	14.33	13.98	0.16	1.69	1.0	0.17	0.03	10.15	F	79	0	21	agg gr	Crabbe Hsn Special SC
7.9	4.4	10.64	10.77	0.60	0.00	5.6	0.10	0.22	2.34	D	0	95	5	fix-inc	Crabbe Hsn US Gov Bd
57.8	163.5	14.02	16.18	0.00	0.86	0.0	—	—	—	—	98	0	2	growth	CRM Small Cap Value SC
7.2	9.7	10.56	10.90	0.85	0.11	7.8	—	—	—	—	4	94	2	income	Croft Leom Income
1.8	3.9	12.69	15.02	0.00	1.78	0.0	—	—	—	—	89	0	11	growth	Croft Leom Value
1.6	2.2	11.50	12.59	0.08	0.32	0.6	—	—	—	—	—	—	—	gr-inc	Crowley Dvsfd Mngmt
6.6	6.5	10.50	10.48	0.64	0.30	6.1	—	—	—	—	—	—	—	growth	Crowley Gro & Inc
9.3	9.3	10.21	—	—	—	—	—	—	—	—	—	—	—	fix-inc	Crowley Income
—	1.2	—	27.49	0.00	0.30	—	—	—	—	—	86	0	14	gr-inc	Cruelty Free Value
31.2	35.6	15.29	18.66	0.15	1.50	0.8	0.91	0.95	10.41	C	98	0	2	gr-inc	Cutler Approved List
49.7	65.8	13.19	15.82	0.19	1.51	1.2	0.87	0.81	10.82	B	88	0	12	income	Cutler Eqty Income
1.0	1.9	10.76	13.02	0.00	1.55	0.0	—	—	—	—	93	0	7	growth	Daruma MidCap Value
43.3	80.6	9.53	9.49	0.63	0.00	6.6	0.06	0.19	1.61	A	0	66	34	fix-inc	Dean Witter ST Bond
299.4	280.5	9.91	9.96	0.53	0.00	5.3	0.08	0.24	1.81	F	0	81	19	fix-inc	Dean Witter ST US Tr
61.3	146.3	13.49	14.88	0.19	1.03	1.3	0.29	0.23	6.84	A	67	1	32	growth	Delafield Fund
3,629.8	5,076.6	59.82	66.78	2.22	3.27	3.2	0.60	0.83	7.35	B	58	37	5	income	Dodge & Cox Balanced
532.8	705.5	11.68	12.08	0.73	0.00	6.0	0.22	0.27	4.68	B	0	93	7	fix-inc	Dodge & Cox Income
2,252.1	4,087.0	79.81	94.57	1.49	6.09	1.5	0.82	0.80	10.25	C	89	0	11	gr-inc	Dodge & Cox Stock
115.0	282.3	19.35	26.22	0.06	0.03	0.2	1.05	0.97	11.84	B	99	0	1	growth	Domini Social Eqty
57.4	75.6	15.14	15.32	0.97	0.22	6.4	0.17	0.30	3.52	B	0	122	-22	fix-inc	Drey-Basic GNMA
54.1	72.9	13.05	13.36	0.64	0.16	4.8	0.15	0.27	3.11	A	0	100	0	tax-free	Drey-Basic Inter Muni
75.2	138.9	13.28	13.78	0.71	0.19	5.1	0.19	0.20	4.62	A	0	102	-2	tax-free	Drey-Basic Muni
302.2	292.7	13.29	13.66	0.69	0.07	5.0	0.17	0.17	4.65	C	0	100	0	tax-free	Drey-General CA
811.2	700.4	14.59	14.94	0.77	0.02	5.2	0.16	0.19	4.12	D	0	103	-3	tax-free	Drey-General Muni
312.7	307.2	19.66	20.33	0.98	0.18	4.8	0.20	0.21	4.75	D	0	101	-1	tax-free	Drey-General NY
191.6	187.7	12.69	12.70	0.91	0.00	7.2	0.17	0.25	3.79	D	0	98	2	fix-inc	Dreyfus 100% US Inter
136.0	133.8	14.61	15.30	0.93	0.00	6.1	0.29	0.22	7.09	D	0	99	1	fix-inc	Dreyfus 100% US Long
187.6	194.6	14.82	14.77	0.93	0.00	6.3	0.09	0.25	1.94	C	0	99	1	fix-inc	Dreyfus 100% US Short
605.4	633.3	14.41	14.68	0.89	0.17	6.0	0.21	0.27	4.62	C	0	105	-5	fix-inc	Dreyfus A Bonds Plus
92.2	94.0	19.70	16.58	0.00	0.00	0.0	—	—	—	—	98	0	2	agg gr	Dreyfus Agg Gr SC
33.6	157.0	20.71	23.50	0.02	1.70	0.1	—	—	—	—	99	0	1	agg gr	Dreyfus Agg Val SC
876.7	1,978.8	25.58	32.38	0.26	0.06	0.8	0.97	0.94	11.09	A	100	0	0	agg gr	Dreyfus Apprec
59.7	82.3	13.98	14.16	0.24	3.59	1.4	0.68	0.69	9.16	D	76	21	3	income	Dreyfus Asst Alloc
292.2	372.0	16.04	16.27	0.45	2.09	2.4	0.57	0.79	7.19	D	60	42	-2	income	Dreyfus Balanced
0.1	0.5	9.75	9.99	0.57	0.05	5.7	0.20	0.25	4.39	D	0	97	3	fix-inc	Dreyfus Bond Mkt Idx

Stock and bond funds — comprehensive summary *continued*

Arranged in alphabetical order

No-Load Fund	\[Total return percent with quintile ranks by objective\] 1988	1989	1990	1991	1992	1993	1994	1995	1996	1997	Annualized 3 yrs.	5 yrs.	What $10,000 grew to after 3 yrs.	5 yrs.
Dreyfus CA Inter...	—	—	—	—	—	—	-5.5⁵	13.4³	3.7³	7.6²	8.2³	6.5¹	12,656	13,682
Dreyfus CA TE	9.7⁵	8.6⁴	6.7³	10.3⁵	6.7⁵	11.9⁴	-7.1⁴	14.1⁵	3.4⁴	8.3⁴	8.5⁵	5.8⁵	12,773	13,278
Dreyfus Premier Core Value‡	19.5³	25.0²	-13.4⁵	22.9⁵	4.0⁵	16.5²	0.3³	35.6¹	21.4²	25.2³	27.3²	19.2²	20,610	24,083
Dreyfus CT Inter	—	—	—	—	—	—	-4.7⁴	14.3²	3.7⁴	7.6²	8.4²	6.5¹	12,750	13,706
DreyfusPremier Lrg Co Stk‡	—	—	—	—	—	—	—	35.4²	22.3²	34.6¹	30.6¹	—	22,279	—
Dreyfus Discpl Inter Bd	—	—	—	—	—	—	—	—	2.4⁵	9.0²	—	—	—	—
Dreyfus Premier MidCap Stk‡	—	—	—	—	—	—	—	37.7¹	26.4¹	35.6¹	33.2¹	—	23,608	—
Dreyfus Discpl Stock	10.7⁵	34.3¹	0.2²	33.6²	7.6³	11.8³	-1.0⁴	36.9¹	24.9¹	31.9²	31.2¹	20.1¹	22,560	24,970
Dreyfus Emg Ldrs SC	—	—	—	—	—	—	—	—	37.4¹	33.9¹	—	—	—	—
Dreyfus Emg Mkts	—	—	—	—	—	—	—	—	—	-1.5⁴	—	—	—	—
Dreyfus Eqty Div	—	—	—	—	—	—	—	—	19.6¹	25.5²	—	—	—	—
Dreyfus FL Inter	—	—	—	—	—	—	-4.9⁴	14.0²	3.4⁵	6.3⁵	7.8⁴	6.1²	12,536	13,447
Dreyfus Fund	8.7⁵	23.6³	-3.3³	28.0³	5.5⁴	6.4⁵	-4.3⁵	23.8⁵	15.8⁴	10.7⁵	16.7⁵	10.1⁵	15,876	16,166
Dreyfus Global Bd	—	—	—	—	—	—	—	18.5³	8.0²	6.8⁵	11.0³	—	13,674	—
Dreyfus Global Gro	15.8²	21.0³	5.8¹	17.5²	-2.7⁵	22.0³	-7.5⁴	12.1⁴	12.0⁴	12.3³	12.1⁴	9.7⁴	14,094	15,905
Dreyfus GNMA	6.4⁴	11.6³	9.7¹	14.5⁴	6.3⁴	7.2⁵	-2.8²	15.1⁵	5.0²	8.8⁴	9.6⁴	6.5⁵	13,149	13,701
Dreyfus Gro & Inc	—	—	—	—	20.1¹	18.6¹	-5.2⁵	25.0⁴	14.4⁵	16.0⁵	18.4⁵	13.3⁵	16,581	18,642
Dreyfus Growth Opp	17.9³	14.8⁵	-6.6⁴	51.5¹	-4.2⁵	1.8⁵	-6.3⁵	28.3⁴	22.3²	15.1⁵	21.8⁴	11.5⁵	18,074	17,240
Dreyfus Hi Yld Secs	—	—	—	—	—	—	—	—	—	16.7¹	—	—	—	—
Dreyfus Insur Muni	10.2⁴	8.7⁴	7.1²	11.4⁴	7.7⁵	12.6³	-8.6⁵	15.6⁴	2.3⁵	8.4⁴	8.6⁵	5.7⁵	12,818	13,192
Dreyfus Int'l Eqty Alloc	—	—	—	—	—	—	—	10.9²	7.1⁵	0.6³	6.1³	—	11,938	—
Dreyfus Int'l Gro	—	—	—	—	—	—	-5.4⁴	0.7⁴	8.5⁴	-1.5⁴	2.5⁴	—	10,764	—
Dreyfus Int'l Stk Idx	—	—	—	—	—	—	—	—	—	—	—	—	—	—
Dreyfus Int'l Val	—	—	—	—	—	—	—	—	10.4⁴	9.0²	—	—	—	—
Dreyfus Inter Inc	—	—	—	—	—	—	—	—	—	14.6¹	—	—	—	—
Dreyfus Inter Muni	8.0²	8.7²	6.8²	11.1¹	8.7¹	11.6¹	-4.6⁴	14.2²	3.8³	7.6²	8.5²	6.3²	12,757	13,581
Dreyfus Lg Co Gr	—	—	—	—	—	—	-0.8³	24.8⁴	22.3²	11.7⁵	19.4⁵	—	17,037	—
Dreyfus Lg Co Val	—	—	—	—	—	—	-1.0⁴	43.1¹	31.4¹	16.0⁵	29.7²	—	21,805	—
Dreyfus LifeTime Gr & Inc	—	—	—	—	—	—	—	—	16.5⁴	20.4⁴	—	—	—	—
Dreyfus LifeTime Growth	—	—	—	—	—	—	—	—	21.3²	27.0³	—	—	—	—
Dreyfus LifeTime Income	—	—	—	—	—	—	—	—	6.8⁵	11.9⁵	—	—	—	—
Dreyfus MA Inter	—	—	—	—	—	—	-6.4⁵	14.6¹	3.5⁴	7.5²	8.4²	6.1³	12,753	13,440
Dreyfus MA TE	10.5⁴	7.7⁵	6.1⁴	12.7²	7.5⁵	12.4⁴	-6.0³	15.5⁴	4.0²	9.1³	9.4⁴	6.7⁴	13,100	13,840
Dreyfus MidCap Idx	—	—	—	—	12.0³	13.5³	-4.0⁴	30.3³	18.5³	31.6²	26.6²	17.2³	20,313	22,133
Dreyfus MidCap Val	—	—	—	—	—	—	—	—	37.3¹	28.0²	—	—	—	—
Dreyfus Muni Bond	11.5³	9.4³	6.4³	12.0³	8.4⁴	12.7³	-7.0⁴	15.7⁴	3.8³	7.9⁵	9.0⁴	6.3⁵	12,964	13,587
Dreyfus New Leaders SC	23.3¹	31.3²	-11.9⁴	45.4³	9.4³	17.1³	-0.1²	29.8³	17.3³	19.5³	22.1⁴	16.3³	18,200	21,291
Dreyfus NJ Inter	—	—	—	—	—	—	-5.2⁵	14.1²	3.3⁵	6.9³	8.0³	6.1²	12,605	13,443
Dreyfus NJ Muni	12.6²	9.1⁴	7.9¹	12.0³	8.8³	13.0²	-6.0³	15.3⁴	3.4⁴	8.8³	9.1⁴	6.6⁴	12,975	13,782
Dreyfus NY Insur	11.3³	8.8⁴	5.9⁴	13.1¹	8.5³	11.1⁵	-6.6³	15.4⁴	2.1⁵	7.4⁵	8.2⁵	5.6⁵	12,655	13,131
Dreyfus NY Inter	9.6¹	9.3¹	6.1⁵	11.1²	9.4¹	11.5¹	-5.1⁵	14.0²	4.2²	8.2¹	8.7¹	6.4²	12,857	13,605
Dreyfus NY TE	10.1⁴	8.9⁴	5.5⁵	12.4²	8.9³	12.6⁴	-7.0⁴	16.2⁴	2.5⁵	9.1²	9.1⁴	6.4⁴	12,997	13,610
Dreyfus PA Inter Muni	—	—	—	—	—	—	-1.5¹	15.2¹	4.2²	8.3¹	9.2¹	—	13,003	—
Dreyfus Real Estate Mrtg	—	—	—	—	—	—	—	—	—	—	—	—	—	—
Dreyfus S&P 500 Idx	—	—	—	29.9²	7.7³	9.5⁴	0.7²	36.7¹	22.3²	32.6¹	30.4¹	19.6²	22,170	24,446
Dreyfus S-I Gov	5.6⁵	11.3²	10.0¹	13.5²	7.0¹	7.3²	-0.8⁴	12.6¹	4.0⁴	6.1⁴	7.5²	5.8²	12,429	13,230
Dreyfus S-I Muni	5.8²	6.5⁵	6.7¹	8.3³	6.7¹	6.7²	-0.3⁴	7.1⁴	4.2¹	5.2³	5.5⁴	4.5³	11,736	12,485
Dreyfus Sm Cap Stk Idx	—	—	—	—	—	—	—	—	—	—	—	—	—	—
Dreyfus Sm Co Val SC	—	—	—	—	—	—	-1.5⁴	36.1¹	34.2¹	26.0³	32.0¹	—	22,999	—
Dreyfus ST Hi Yld	—	—	—	—	—	—	—	—	—	12.6¹	—	—	—	—
Dreyfus ST Income	—	—	—	—	—	—	0.1¹	11.2⁵	6.2¹	8.2³	8.5⁴	6.9³	12,781	13,971
Dreyfus Strat Income	11.1²	13.9²	5.5⁴	19.1²	9.0²	15.1²	-6.3⁴	20.8²	6.6²	11.2²	12.7²	9.1²	14,321	15,440
Dreyfus Tech Growth	—	—	—	—	—	—	—	—	—	—	—	—	—	—
Dreyfus Third Cent	23.2²	17.3⁵	3.5¹	38.1²	1.9⁵	5.2⁵	-7.5⁵	35.8¹	24.3²	29.4²	29.7¹	16.3³	21,838	21,251
Dupree Inter Gov	—	—	—	—	—	11.9¹	-5.9⁵	17.6²	3.2⁴	9.4²	9.9³	6.9³	13,268	13,967
Dupree KY Sht-Med	5.1⁵	7.3⁵	6.8³	7.3⁵	6.8⁵	5.7⁵	1.0¹	6.1⁵	4.0²	5.2⁵	5.1⁵	4.4⁵	11,606	12,390
Dupree KY TF Inc	10.3⁴	10.7¹	7.4¹	10.7⁴	9.0³	12.7³	-2.9¹	13.4⁵	3.7³	8.0⁵	8.3⁵	6.8³	12,704	13,902
Dupree NC TF Inc	—	—	—	—	—	—	—	—	5.4¹	9.8¹	—	—	—	—
Dupree NC TF Sht-Med	—	—	—	—	—	—	—	—	4.6¹	5.0⁵	—	—	—	—
Dupree TN TF Inc	—	—	—	—	—	—	-1.2¹	18.3²	5.2¹	8.9³	10.7¹	—	13,551	—

See Chapter 3 for explanation of symbols

Total Net Assets $Million		NAV per share		1997 per share distributions		Yield % 12/31/97	Risk Analysis				% Distribution of Portfolio 12/31/97			Objective	No-Load Fund
December 31 1996	1997	December 31 1996	1997	Income	Capital gains		beta	R²	Std. Dev.	Sharpe Ratio	Stocks	Bonds	Cash		
219.8	200.9	13.44	13.84	0.60	0.00	4.3	0.15	0.26	3.25	D	0	105	-5	tax-free	Dreyfus CA Inter
1,400.7	1,338.5	14.43	14.87	0.71	0.00	4.8	0.16	0.19	4.13	F	0	99	1	tax-free	Dreyfus CA TE
488.9	585.7	30.40	30.11	0.24	7.25	0.7	0.87	0.84	10.64	B	97	0	3	growth	Dreyfus Premier Core Value‡
129.5	129.8	13.51	13.91	0.60	0.00	4.3	0.15	0.25	3.37	C	0	99	1	tax-free	Dreyfus CT Inter
4.6	9.0	14.63	18.39	0.16	1.09	0.9	0.96	0.98	10.73	A	98	0	2	gr-inc	Dreyfus Premier Lrg Co Stk‡
0.1	0.4	12.24	12.56	0.74	0.00	5.9	—	—	—	—	0	99	1	fix-inc	Dreyfus Discpl Inter Bd
3.5	9.5	13.19	15.30	0.01	2.47	0.1	0.90	0.66	12.35	A	98	0	2	growth	Dreyfus Premier MidCap‡
874.9	1,645.6	26.40	31.12	0.23	3.37	0.7	1.02	0.98	11.46	B	98	0	2	gr-inc	Dreyfus Discpl Stock
61.4	129.0	20.39	24.57	0.00	2.67	0.0	—	—	—	—	98	0	2	agg gr	Dreyfus Emg Ldrs SC
16.0	63.3	12.42	11.76	0.02	0.44	0.2	—	—	—	—	97	0	3	int'l	Dreyfus Emg Mkts
3.1	4.5	14.37	16.42	0.29	1.29	1.7	—	—	—	F	99	0	1	income	Dreyfus Eqty Div
385.9	341.7	13.45	13.64	0.60	0.04	4.4	0.14	0.22	3.40	F	0	98	2	tax-free	Dreyfus FL Inter
2,711.7	2,614.8	10.82	9.93	0.08	1.92	0.7	0.94	0.73	12.10	F	100	0	0	gr-inc	Dreyfus Fund
10.7	12.4	12.70	12.51	0.90	0.12	7.2	0.22	0.27	4.65	B	0	97	3	fix-inc	Dreyfus Global Bd
96.2	89.8	34.62	34.53	0.11	4.17	0.3	0.83	0.64	11.40	D	93	0	7	global	Dreyfus Global Gro
1,310.2	1,199.1	14.53	14.87	0.90	0.00	6.1	0.15	0.31	3.07	B	0	122	-22	fix-inc	Dreyfus GNMA.
2,008.7	1,944.0	18.16	17.60	0.31	3.09	1.5	0.74	0.73	9.57	F	88	13	-1	gr-inc	Dreyfus Gro & Inc
464.4	499.9	9.71	9.60	0.07	1.44	0.6	0.90	0.74	11.72	D	94	2	4	growth	Dreyfus Growth Opp
39.9	139.3	13.98	14.54	1.63	0.02	11.2	—	—	—	—	1	97	2	fix-inc	Dreyfus Hi Yld Secs
204.4	195.3	17.62	18.19	0.86	0.00	4.7	0.18	0.20	4.52	F	0	99	1	tax-free	Dreyfus Insur Muni
1.5	1.4	10.68	9.59	0.07	1.06	0.8	0.65	0.38	11.61	C	79	0	21	int'l	Dreyfus Int'l Eqty Alloc
91.6	77.1	14.85	12.76	0.01	1.90	0.1	0.74	0.39	12.84	D	98	0	2	int'l	Dreyfus Int'l Gro
—	9.6	—	11.21	0.10	0.00	—	—	—	—	—	82	0	18	int'l	Dreyfus Int'l Stk Idx
41.0	114.7	13.82	14.60	0.08	0.40	0.5	—	—	—	—	92	0	8	int'l	Dreyfus Int'l Val
15.2	22.1	12.58	13.10	0.89	0.34	6.8	—	—	—	—	1	103	-4	fix-inc	Dreyfus Inter Inc.
1,430.3	1,372.7	13.91	14.12	0.70	0.12	4.9	0.14	0.24	3.27	B	0	99	1	tax-free	Dreyfus Inter Muni
9.4	11.8	17.06	17.25	0.00	1.83	0.0	1.02	0.52	15.68	F	100	0	0	growth	Dreyfus Lg Co Gr
51.6	165.5	18.46	20.31	0.05	1.06	0.3	0.83	0.70	11.09	C	97	0	3	gr-inc	Dreyfus Lg Co Val
0.2	0.9	16.04	16.35	0.61	2.34	3.3	—	—	—	—	26	59	15	gr-inc	Dreyfus LifeTime Gr & Inc
15.4	6.3	16.28	15.60	0.46	4.58	2.3	—	—	—	—	45	31	24	growth	Dreyfus LifeTime Growth
9.0	10.3	12.77	12.87	0.66	0.71	5.2	—	—	—	—	0	64	36	income	Dreyfus LifeTime Income
64.1	64.0	13.26	13.64	0.59	0.00	4.3	0.15	0.24	3.33	C	0	102	-2	tax-free	Dreyfus MA Inter
156.6	154.5	16.39	16.98	0.85	0.00	5.0	0.17	0.21	4.06	D	0	99	1	tax-free	Dreyfus MA TE
184.1	257.3	21.23	25.64	0.23	1.99	0.8	0.84	0.64	11.78	C	94	0	6	growth	Dreyfus MidCap Idx
8.4	124.0	16.83	20.52	0.00	1.05	0.0	—	—	—	—	100	0	0	growth	Dreyfus MidCap Val
3,603.7	3,505.8	12.48	12.71	0.66	0.07	5.2	0.16	0.22	3.74	D	0	101	-1	tax-free	Dreyfus Muni Bond
795.5	866.1	40.74	44.35	0.00	4.24	0.0	0.65	0.33	12.59	C	100	0	0	agg gr	Dreyfus New Leaders SC
224.4	214.0	13.53	13.85	0.60	0.00	4.3	0.14	0.23	3.19	D	0	99	1	tax-free	Dreyfus NJ Inter
595.8	591.2	13.01	13.35	0.68	0.09	5.1	0.18	0.27	3.83	D	0	98	2	tax-free	Dreyfus NJ Muni
142.5	135.1	11.19	11.37	0.50	0.12	4.3	0.19	0.20	4.61	F	0	101	-1	tax-free	Dreyfus NY Insur
364.7	363.2	18.08	18.62	0.83	0.09	4.4	0.15	0.25	3.49	B	0	100	0	tax-free	Dreyfus NY Inter
1,761.3	1,704.5	14.99	15.43	0.75	0.14	4.8	0.20	0.23	4.58	F	0	99	1	tax-free	Dreyfus NY TE
50.1	65.8	13.11	13.57	0.60	0.01	4.4	0.14	0.23	3.24	A	0	98	2	tax-free	Dreyfus PA Inter Muni
—	10.9	—	12.79	0.22	0.15	—	—	—	—	—	28	100	-28	sector	Dreyfus Real Estate Mrtg
653.3	1,430.9	22.22	28.70	0.30	0.46	1.0	1.00	1.00	11.13	B	97	0	3	gr-inc	Dreyfus S&P 500 Idx
561.1	477.5	10.87	10.84	0.67	0.00	6.2	0.09	0.22	2.21	C	0	109	-9	fix-inc	Dreyfus S-I Gov
314.4	290.0	12.97	13.08	0.54	0.00	4.2	0.05	0.35	0.97	C	0	99	1	tax-free	Dreyfus S-I Muni
—	18.8	—	13.88	0.02	0.16	—	—	—	—	—	97	0	3	agg gr	Dreyfus Sm Cap Stk Idx
23.8	402.3	17.04	21.07	0.01	0.39	0.1	0.51	0.26	11.21	A	97	0	3	growth	Dreyfus Sm Co Val SC
30.7	156.0	12.69	12.84	1.26	0.12	9.8	—	—	—	—	0	-3	103	fix-inc	Dreyfus ST Hi Yld
214.4	294.6	11.95	12.04	0.86	0.00	7.1	0.08	0.30	1.67	A	0	104	-4	fix-inc	Dreyfus ST Income
293.5	277.0	14.42	14.96	1.01	0.00	6.8	0.21	0.32	4.03	A	1	102	-3	fix-inc	Dreyfus Strat Income
—	4.7	—	10.51	0.00	0.00	—	—	—	—	—	85	0	15	sector	Dreyfus Tech Growth
562.4	804.1	8.82	10.51	0.02	0.90	0.2	1.11	0.88	13.22	C	89	0	11	growth	Dreyfus Third Cent
8.0	8.8	9.92	10.13	0.69	0.00	6.8	0.16	0.20	4.12	C	0	100	0	fix-inc	Dupree Inter Gov
57.0	54.2	5.24	5.29	0.22	0.00	4.1	0.06	0.16	1.52	F	0	91	9	tax-free	Dupree KY Sht-Med
312.3	346.2	7.49	7.68	0.40	0.00	5.2	0.10	0.11	3.37	F	0	100	0	tax-free	Dupree KY TF Inc
2.4	6.1	10.28	10.73	0.53	0.00	5.0	—	—	—	—	0	100	0	tax-free	Dupree NC TF Inc
1.4	1.5	10.11	10.21	0.40	0.00	3.9	—	—	—	—	0	94	6	tax-free	Dupree NC TF Sht-Med
10.1	17.3	10.50	10.87	0.54	0.00	5.0	0.13	0.14	3.67	A	0	99	1	tax-free	Dupree TN TF Inc

Stock and bond funds — comprehensive summary *continued*

Arranged in alphabetical order

No-Load Fund	1988	1989	1990	1991	1992	1993	1994	1995	1996	1997	Annualized 3 yrs.	5 yrs.	What $10,000 grew to after 3 yrs.	5 yrs.
Dupree TN TF Sht-Med	—	—	—	—	—	—	—	7.1[5]	3.9[3]	5.4[5]	5.5[5]	—	11,733	—
Eastcliff Growth	—	—	—	—	—	—	—	—	16.9[4]	22.4[4]	—	—	—	—
Eastcliff Reg Sm Cap Val	—	—	—	—	—	—	—	—	—	21.1[3]	—	—	—	—
Eastcliff Total Ret	20.8[1]	13.2[5]	-4.4[4]	30.1[1]	10.4[2]	11.1[4]	-2.0[3]	23.2[4]	20.5[1]	30.0[1]	24.5[1]	16.0[2]	19,300	21,002
Eclipse Balanced	—	—	1.5[2]	20.9[5]	12.0[2]	17.1[1]	-0.1[2]	23.1[4]	12.9[4]	23.4[2]	19.7[3]	14.9[2]	17,148	20,061
Eclipse Equity SC	12.7[4]	16.4[5]	-13.6[4]	31.2[5]	19.4[1]	17.0[3]	-4.7[4]	19.6[5]	29.9[1]	33.3[1]	27.5[2]	18.2[2]	20,710	23,091
Eclipse Gro & Inc	—	—	—	—	—	—	—	26.8[4]	22.4[2]	32.5[1]	27.2[3]	—	20,561	—
Eclipse Ultra Short	—	—	—	—	—	—	—	7.8[5]	5.5[1]	6.2[3]	6.5[5]	—	12,082	—
Eighteen - 1838 Fix Inc	—	—	—	—	—	—	—	—	—	—	—	—	—	—
Eighteen - 1838 Int'l Eqty	—	—	—	—	—	—	—	—	8.0[4]	10.0[2]	—	—	—	—
Eighteen - 1838 Sm Cap SC	—	—	—	—	—	—	—	—	—	29.9[1]	—	—	—	—
Elite Gr & Inc	16.2[3]	29.0[2]	-3.8[3]	25.6[4]	10.3[2]	11.9[3]	-1.8[4]	37.5[1]	21.2[3]	28.2[3]	28.8[2]	18.6[3]	21,360	23,463
Elite Bond	6.0[5]	11.7[4]	8.2[3]	9.5[5]	6.9[2]	9.2[3]	-2.9[3]	15.7[4]	3.1[4]	9.8[1]	9.4[3]	6.8[3]	13,099	13,890
Emerald Balanced	—	—	—	—	—	—	—	27.7[2]	11.3[4]	16.4[4]	18.3[4]	—	16,546	—
Emerald Eqty Val	—	—	—	—	—	—	—	—	23.8[2]	29.4[2]	—	—	—	—
Emerald Eqty	—	—	—	—	4.2[5]	4.3[5]	-6.6[5]	35.3[2]	19.5[3]	25.4[3]	26.6[2]	14.6[4]	20,277	19,753
Emerald FL TE	—	—	—	—	10.4[1]	14.1[1]	-6.9[3]	16.1[4]	2.7[5]	9.1[3]	9.2[4]	6.7[4]	13,010	13,823
Emerald Int'l Eqty	—	—	—	—	—	—	—	—	15.3[3]	20.4[1]	—	—	—	—
Emerald Mndg Bd	—	—	—	—	—	—	—	19.5[2]	3.0[4]	8.2[4]	10.0[4]	—	13,317	—
Emerald Small Cap SC	—	—	—	—	—	—	—	33.9[3]	10.1[5]	12.6[4]	18.4[4]	—	16,596	—
Emerald ST Inc	—	—	—	—	—	—	—	10.9[3]	4.2[3]	5.7[5]	6.9[4]	—	12,211	—
Emerald US Gov Sec	—	—	—	—	6.8[3]	9.1[3]	-3.3[3]	14.2[5]	3.5[3]	7.4[4]	8.3[5]	6.0[4]	12,695	13,396
Empire Builder TF Bond	9.9[5]	7.3[5]	6.0[4]	11.3[4]	8.0[5]	12.2[4]	-4.5[1]	14.6[5]	3.2[4]	7.9[5]	8.5[5]	6.5[4]	12,766	13,680
Excelsior Blended Eqty	18.8[3]	27.7[2]	-12.3[5]	34.5[3]	16.6[1]	16.3[2]	0.2[3]	28.9[3]	19.9[3]	29.8[2]	26.1[3]	18.5[2]	20,059	23,376
Excelsior CA TE	—	—	—	—	—	—	—	—	—	5.7[5]	—	—	—	—
Excelsior Enrgy & Nat Resc	—	—	—	—	—	14.7[4]	-2.7[3]	20.1[4]	38.4[1]	18.5[4]	25.4[3]	17.1[3]	19,701	21,987
Excelsior Inc & Gro	24.0[1]	21.2[3]	-18.2[5]	26.4[4]	20.4[1]	19.4[1]	-4.3[5]	30.0[3]	18.8[4]	22.1[4]	23.6[4]	16.6[4]	18,861	21,549
Excelsior Instit Balanced	—	—	—	—	—	—	—	23.3[4]	13.8[3]	18.3[4]	18.4[4]	—	16,594	—
Excelsior Instit Eqty	—	—	—	—	—	—	—	—	19.8[3]	31.7[2]	—	—	—	—
Excelsior Instit Income	—	—	—	—	—	—	—	—	2.5[4]	9.3[3]	—	—	—	—
Excelsior Instit Tot Ret Bd	—	—	—	—	—	—	—	—	2.7[4]	9.2[3]	—	—	—	—
Excelsior Inter Mgd Inc	—	—	—	—	—	8.4[3]	-3.7[4]	19.2[1]	1.9[5]	8.5[3]	9.6[3]	6.6[3]	13,177	13,758
Excelsior Inter TE	7.0[3]	8.7[2]	6.4[4]	10.2[3]	8.5[2]	10.8[2]	-4.2[3]	15.1[1]	4.3[1]	7.3[3]	8.8[1]	6.5[2]	12,887	13,684
Excelsior International	13.2[3]	23.0[3]	-9.4[2]	5.9[5]	-9.4[4]	36.5[3]	-2.0[3]	7.3[3]	7.3[3]	9.3[2]	8.0[3]	11.0[3]	12,578	16,828
Excelsior Lat Amer	—	—	—	—	—	39.7[2]	-10.6[5]	-10.6[5]	24.9[1]	25.2[1]	11.8[2]	11.8[3]	13,979	17,461
Excelsior LT TE	12.8[1]	11.8[1]	6.9[2]	12.7[2]	10.0[1]	15.6[1]	-5.8[2]	23.4[1]	3.7[3]	9.4[2]	11.9[1]	8.8[1]	14,002	15,257
Excelsior Mgd Inc	9.1[3]	15.8[2]	8.6[2]	16.7[3]	5.8[5]	12.6[3]	-5.5[4]	22.4[2]	0.6[5]	9.8[3]	10.5[3]	7.5[3]	13,508	14,376
Excelsior NY Inter TE	—	—	—	9.5[5]	6.6[5]	9.3[4]	-4.2[3]	13.6[3]	4.3[1]	6.7[4]	8.1[3]	5.8[4]	12,639	13,232
Excelsior Pac Asia	—	—	—	—	—	66.3[1]	-14.7[5]	8.5[3]	7.2[5]	-32.2[5]	-7.6[5]	2.3[5]	7,893	11,201
Excelsior Pan Europe	—	—	—	—	—	17.3[1]	0.0[1]	14.9[5]	21.6[1]	24.4[1]	20.2[1]	15.3[1]	17,382	20,389
Excelsior Sm Cap SC	—	—	—	—	—	27.9[1]	5.3[1]	22.8[4]	-2.3[5]	14.2[4]	11.1[5]	13.0[4]	13,698	18,448
Excelsior ST Gov	—	—	—	—	—	4.3[4]	1.2[1]	10.2[3]	4.0[4]	5.9[4]	6.7[4]	5.1[4]	12,131	12,801
Excelsior ST TE	—	—	—	—	—	5.5[4]	-0.3[3]	7.4[4]	3.7[3]	4.6[4]	5.2[4]	4.1[4]	11,639	12,243
Excelsior Val & Restruc	—	—	—	—	—	40.0[1]	2.6[2]	38.8[1]	25.0[1]	33.6[1]	32.4[1]	27.2[1]	23,182	33,284
Fairmont	3.1[5]	6.8[5]	-22.1[5]	40.6[4]	14.0[2]	15.6[3]	7.3[1]	27.9[4]	9.5[5]	15.3[4]	17.3[5]	14.9[4]	16,144	20,025
Fairport Gov Sec	—	—	—	—	—	—	-6.5[5]	17.9[2]	2.3[5]	7.5[4]	9.1[3]	—	12,969	—
Fairport Gr & Inc	—	—	—	—	—	—	1.7[2]	28.9[3]	17.7[4]	30.3[2]	25.5[3]	—	19,772	—
Fairport Midwest Gr	—	—	—	—	—	—	7.2[1]	23.3[5]	20.6[3]	27.7[3]	23.8[4]	—	18,983	—
FAM Equity Income	—	—	—	—	—	—	—	—	—	26.9[1]	—	—	—	—
FAM Value SC	35.5[1]	20.3[4]	-5.4[3]	47.6[1]	25.0[1]	0.2[5]	6.8[1]	19.7[5]	11.2[5]	39.1[1]	22.8[4]	14.6[4]	18,510	19,808
Fasciano SC	—	22.4[3]	-1.2[2]	32.6[3]	7.7[3]	8.1[4]	3.7[1]	31.1[3]	26.5[1]	21.5[4]	26.3[2]	17.7[3]	20,152	22,590
FBP Contrn Balanced	—	—	-7.8[5]	27.3[2]	14.4[1]	10.0[4]	1.9[1]	25.7[3]	16.6[2]	20.7[3]	20.9[2]	14.7[2]	17,682	19,806
FBP Contrn Eqty	—	—	—	—	—	—	4.6[1]	30.4[3]	22.8[2]	25.4[3]	26.2[3]	—	20,079	—
FBR Fin'l Svcs‡	—	—	—	—	—	—	—	—	—	47.7[1]	—	—	—	—
FBR Sm Cap Finl Svcs‡	—	—	—	—	—	—	—	—	—	58.1[1]	—	—	—	—
FBR Sm Cap Gr/Val‡	—	—	—	—	—	—	—	—	—	44.3[1]	—	—	—	—
Federated ARMS	7.3[1]	15.9[1]	6.6[5]	15.7[1]	3.7[5]	4.3[4]	0.3[2]	8.8[5]	6.5[1]	6.3[3]	7.2[3]	5.2[3]	12,323	12,888
Federated Bond Idx	—	—	—	—	—	—	—	—	—	9.0[4]	—	—	—	—
Federated GNMA	8.2[2]	15.1[1]	10.3[1]	15.3[3]	6.5[3]	6.5[5]	-2.5[2]	16.1[3]	5.0[2]	8.8[3]	9.9[3]	6.6[3]	13,261	13,773
Federated Hi Yld	16.2[1]	-1.1[5]	-12.7[5]	52.5[1]	15.0[1]	17.4[1]	-2.4[2]	18.4[3]	13.5[1]	13.3[2]	15.0[1]	11.8[1]	15,217	17,430

See Chapter 3 for explanation of symbols

Arranged in alphabetical order

Total Net Assets $Million		NAV per share		1997 per share distributions		Yield % 12/31/97	Risk Analysis				% Distribution of Portfolio 12/31/97			Objective	No-Load Fund
December 31 1996	1997	December 31 1996	1997	Income	Capital gains		beta	R²	Std. Dev.	Sharpe Ratio	Stocks	Bonds	Cash		
2.6	3.8	10.33	10.46	0.41	0.00	4.0	0.05	0.17	1.21	F	0	6	94	tax-free	Dupree TN TF Sht-Med
45.5	49.8	12.69	14.88	0.00	0.63	0.0	—	—	—	—	100	0	0	growth	Eastcliff Growth
17.6	53.8	10.89	13.09	0.01	0.09	0.0	—	—	—	—	90	0	10	agg gr	Eastcliff Reg Sm Cap Val
18.6	23.0	14.36	17.86	0.25	0.53	1.4	0.81	0.78	10.29	C	76	20	4	income	Eastcliff Total Ret
83.7	88.7	21.00	22.15	0.66	2.99	2.6	0.52	0.82	6.45	B	57	42	1	income	Eclipse Balanced
170.7	192.9	13.47	14.19	0.00	3.66	0.0	0.60	0.36	11.20	A	98	0	2	agg gr	Eclipse Equity SC
9.7	110.0	13.49	17.76	0.03	0.07	0.2	0.71	0.74	9.23	B	99	0	1	gr-inc	Eclipse Gro & Inc
4.5	5.4	10.03	10.00	0.64	0.00	6.4	0.02	0.08	0.86	A	0	97	3	fix-inc	Eclipse Ultra Short
—	45.0	—	10.15	0.13	0.02	—	—	—	—	—	0	100	0	fix-inc	Eighteen - 1838 Fix Inc
46.1	52.7	10.93	11.33	0.00	0.67	0.0	—	—	—	—	97	0	3	int'l	Eighteen - 1838 Int'l Eqty
7.8	31.5	10.25	12.33	0.00	0.95	0.0	—	—	—	—	99	0	1	agg gr	Eighteen - 1838 Sm Cap SC
48.8	68.9	19.32	22.30	0.27	2.14	1.2	0.83	0.77	10.52	—	61	29	10	gr-inc	Elite Gr & Inc
13.5	16.9	9.85	10.18	0.60	0.00	5.9	0.19	0.30	3.80	—	0	98	2	fix-inc	Elite Bond
5.6	8.4	12.21	12.10	0.26	1.78	2.1	0.71	0.82	8.72	F	63	37	1	income	Emerald Balanced
0.1	4.8	12.07	15.10	0.15	0.34	1.0	—	—	—	—	96	0	4	gr-inc	Emerald Eqty Val
32.0	47.3	14.27	14.41	0.00	3.42	0.0	1.11	0.82	13.72	D	99	0	1	growth	Emerald Eqty
84.6	84.5	10.94	11.39	0.52	0.00	4.5	0.19	0.21	4.71	F	0	98	2	tax-free	Emerald FL TE
0.1	4.7	11.38	13.34	0.06	0.29	0.5	—	—	—	—	96	0	3	int'l	Emerald Int'l Eqty
1.7	2.7	10.16	10.32	0.57	0.08	5.5	0.20	0.26	4.25	C	0	99	1	fix-inc	Emerald Mndg Bd
8.8	15.3	11.69	12.86	0.00	0.29	0.0	0.85	0.23	19.64	F	92	0	8	agg gr	Emerald Small Cap SC
1.1	4.2	9.99	10.02	0.52	0.00	5.2	0.08	0.23	1.84	D	0	99	1	fix-inc	Emerald ST Inc
22.5	21.5	10.18	10.32	0.58	0.00	5.7	0.14	0.26	3.04	D	0	98	2	fix-inc	Emerald US Gov
60.3	58.4	17.75	18.24	0.80	0.07	4.4	0.17	0.26	3.77	F	0	97	3	tax-free	Empire Builder TF Bond
307.9	542.2	26.30	31.66	0.15	2.29	0.5	0.97	0.84	11.71	C	90	0	10	growth	Excelsior Blended Eqty
7.6	30.5	7.03	7.15	0.27	0.00	3.8	—	—	—	—	0	93	7	tax-free	Excelsior CA TE
33.8	44.5	11.43	12.32	0.09	1.14	0.7	0.41	0.11	13.63	C	92	0	8	sector	Excelsior Enrgy & Nat Resc
134.9	143.6	15.46	16.64	0.30	1.85	1.8	0.66	0.67	9.05	D	71	26	3	gr-inc	Excelsior Inc & Gro
95.2	79.5	8.26	8.53	0.27	0.92	3.2	0.49	0.73	6.39	C	59	36	5	income	Excelsior Instit Balanced
135.9	118.9	9.67	11.05	0.05	1.62	0.5	—	—	—	—	98	0	2	growth	Excelsior Instit Eqty
51.9	54.7	7.05	7.21	0.44	0.02	6.2	—	—	—	—	0	97	3	fix-inc	Excelsior Instit Income
145.1	152.5	7.34	7.49	0.44	0.06	5.9	—	—	—	—	0	86	14	fix-inc	Excelsior Instit Tot Ret Bd
76.3	91.4	7.04	7.21	0.41	0.00	5.6	0.19	0.24	4.36	D	0	98	2	fix-inc	Excelsior Inter Mgd Inc
248.9	253.5	9.22	9.46	0.41	0.01	4.3	0.14	0.24	3.23	A	0	95	5	tax-free	Excelsior Inter TE
110.5	177.7	11.07	11.61	0.05	0.43	0.5	0.70	0.42	11.89	C	96	0	4	int'l	Excelsior International
55.6	95.9	8.58	10.55	0.02	0.16	0.2	1.03	0.22	23.53	C	94	0	6	int'l	Excelsior Lat Amer
111.2	134.0	9.70	10.03	0.44	0.12	4.3	0.22	0.20	5.48	A	0	76	24	tax-free	Excelsior LT TE
187.4	197.6	8.83	9.15	0.50	0.01	5.5	0.25	0.25	5.53	D	0	98	2	fix-inc	Excelsior Mgd Inc
100.3	121.9	8.55	8.75	0.36	0.00	4.1	0.15	0.26	3.29	D	0	95	5	tax-free	Excelsior NY Inter TE
88.0	41.6	9.60	6.45	0.06	0.00	1.0	0.92	0.36	16.10	F	97	0	3	int'l	Excelsior Pac Asia
84.7	168.7	10.18	11.84	0.00	0.81	0.0	0.47	0.31	9.47	A	91	0	9	int'l	Excelsior Pan Europe
68.9	65.7	9.78	11.17	0.00	0.00	0.0	1.05	0.34	19.83	F	89	0	11	agg gr	Excelsior Sm Cap SC
29.6	32.3	6.97	7.00	0.37	0.00	5.3	0.06	0.20	1.49	D	0	95	5	fix-inc	Excelsior ST Gov
38.6	38.5	7.06	7.11	0.27	0.00	3.7	0.06	0.25	1.32	D	0	98	2	tax-free	Excelsior ST TE
113.1	230.0	15.87	20.82	0.09	0.27	0.5	0.88	0.66	12.14	A	93	0	7	growth	Excelsior Val & Restruc
30.7	31.9	26.45	27.68	0.00	2.81	0.0	0.83	0.30	16.83	D	97	0	3	agg gr	Fairmont
5.2	4.3	9.71	9.93	0.49	0.00	4.9	0.17	0.23	4.02	D	0	98	2	fix-inc	Fairport Gov Sec
22.9	29.5	14.13	16.54	0.03	1.84	0.2	0.75	0.76	9.60	C	108	0	-8	gr-inc	Fairport Gr & Inc
57.5	76.8	15.42	18.59	0.00	1.10	0.0	0.77	0.51	12.00	D	104	0	-4	growth	Fairport Midwest Gr
2.5	4.4	10.99	13.20	0.26	0.44	2.0	—	—	—	—	76	0	24	income	FAM Equity Inc
254.0	333.2	26.53	35.76	0.08	1.06	0.2	0.57	0.36	10.66	C	89	0	11	growth	FAM Value SC
33.9	55.8	26.20	30.31	0.00	1.49	0.0	0.53	0.28	11.08	C	95	0	5	growth	Fasciano SC
41.4	50.6	15.83	17.87	0.41	0.76	2.3	0.64	0.90	7.51	C	66	22	12	income	FBP Contrn Balanced
14.5	28.3	15.93	19.33	0.20	0.42	1.0	0.77	0.85	9.39	B	85	0	15	growth	FBP Contrn Eqty
0.1	33.6	12.00	17.49	0.04	0.19	0.2	—	—	—	—	98	0	2	sector	FBR Fin'l Svcs‡
0.1	72.1	12.00	18.78	0.03	0.15	0.2	—	—	—	—	92	0	8	sector	FBR Sm Cap Finl Svcs‡
0.1	9.6	12.00	16.82	0.00	0.49	0.0	—	—	—	—	93	0	7	agg gr	FBR Sm Cap Gr/Val‡
597.8	466.0	9.73	9.74	0.59	0.00	6.0	0.03	0.12	0.93	A	0	99	1	fix-inc	Federated ARMS
15.1	27.2	7.10	7.25	0.46	0.00	6.4	—	—	—	—	0	95	5	fix-inc	Federated Bond
1,204.1	1,116.0	11.12	11.33	0.74	0.00	6.5	0.15	0.29	3.17	B	0	98	2	fix-inc	Federated GNMA
887.4	1,121.2	9.29	9.64	0.83	0.00	8.6	0.20	0.34	3.72	A	1	96	3	fix-inc	Federated Hi Yld

Stock and bond funds — comprehensive summary *continued*

Arranged in alphabetical order

No-Load Fund	1988	1989	1990	1991	1992	1993	1994	1995	1996	1997	Annualized 3 yrs.	Annualized 5 yrs.	$10,000 grew to 3 yrs.	$10,000 grew to 5 yrs.
Federated Income	7.7[3]	12.5[3]	10.4[1]	13.9[4]	5.7[4]	5.9[5]	-1.6[1]	15.4[4]	4.7[2]	8.9[3]	9.6[3]	6.5[3]	13,163	13,713
Federated Inter Inc	—	—	—	—	—	—	-2.4[2]	20.1[1]	3.3[3]	8.6[3]	10.5[1]	—	13,484	—
Federated Inter Muni	5.1[5]	9.0[2]	6.5[4]	10.8[2]	7.1[3]	9.7[4]	-3.8[3]	11.5[5]	4.0[2]	6.9[4]	7.4[5]	5.5[5]	12,391	13,081
Federated Max Cap	—	—	—	30.0[2]	7.2[3]	9.5[4]	1.2[2]	36.6[1]	22.8[2]	32.7[1]	30.6[1]	19.8[2]	22,255	24,670
Federated Mgd Agg Gro	—	—	—	—	—	—	—	22.3[5]	12.4[4]	14.9[4]	16.4[5]	—	15,782	—
Federated Mgd Gro & Inc	—	—	—	—	—	—	—	19.8[5]	6.3[5]	13.0[5]	12.9[5]	—	14,393	—
Federated Mgd Growth	—	—	—	—	—	—	—	22.3[5]	10.5[5]	14.3[5]	15.6[5]	—	15,440	—
Federated Mgd Inc	—	—	—	—	—	—	—	15.7[5]	5.6[5]	10.5[5]	10.5[5]	—	13,493	—
Federated Mid Cap	—	—	—	—	—	11.2[3]	-4.3[5]	29.0[3]	18.3[4]	31.1[2]	26.0[3]	16.3[3]	19,997	21,282
Federated Mini Cap SC	—	—	—	—	—	15.3[3]	-2.8[3]	26.3[4]	15.3[4]	20.4[3]	20.6[4]	14.5[4]	17,535	19,640
Federated PA Inter	—	—	—	—	—	—	-6.2[5]	14.6[1]	4.1[2]	7.5[2]	8.7[2]	—	12,883	—
Federated ST Income	8.6[1]	9.4[4]	1.9[5]	13.9[2]	6.1[3]	5.5[4]	-0.5[3]	10.9[3]	5.4[1]	6.4[3]	7.5[2]	5.5[2]	12,434	13,045
Federated ST Muni	5.6[3]	6.5[4]	6.3[4]	7.3[5]	5.1[5]	4.1[5]	0.1[3]	8.1[3]	4.0[2]	4.5[4]	5.5[3]	4.1[5]	11,745	12,237
Federated Stock	12.7[4]	13.1[5]	-5.0[3]	29.0[3]	11.9[2]	12.5[3]	-0.5[3]	35.6[2]	21.2[3]	34.4[1]	30.2[1]	19.9[2]	22,090	24,736
Federated US Gov 1-3	—	—	—	—	—	4.3[4]	0.4[2]	9.3[4]	4.4[3]	5.7[5]	6.5[5]	4.8[5]	12,064	12,631
Federated US Gov 2-5	—	—	—	—	—	6.8[3]	-2.2[4]	13.3[1]	3.3[3]	6.9[2]	7.8[2]	5.5[2]	12,510	13,076
Federated US Gov 5-10	—	—	—	—	—	—	—	—	1.5[5]	9.3[2]	—	—	—	—
Federated US Gov Bd	6.0[5]	13.7[2]	8.7[1]	13.6[5]	8.2[2]	13.3[3]	-6.2[4]	25.8[1]	-0.3[5]	11.7[2]	11.9[2]	8.3[3]	14,015	14,894
Fidelity Asst Mgr Gro	—	—	—	—	19.1[1]	26.3[1]	-7.4[5]	20.0[5]	17.6[4]	26.4[3]	21.3[4]	15.8[4]	17,839	20,863
Fidelity Asst Mgr Inc	—	—	—	—	—	—	-1.4[3]	16.7[5]	7.8[5]	12.4[5]	12.2[5]	10.0[5]	14,138	16,087
Fidelity Asst Mgr	—	15.3[4]	5.4[1]	23.6[3]	12.7[4]	23.3[1]	-6.6[5]	18.2[5]	12.7[4]	22.3[2]	17.7[4]	13.4[3]	16,288	18,758
Fidelity Balanced	15.8[3]	19.7[3]	-0.5[3]	26.8[2]	7.9[4]	19.3[1]	-5.3[4]	14.9[5]	9.3[5]	23.4[2]	15.7[5]	11.9[5]	15,502	17,514
Fidelity Blue Chip Gro††	5.9[5]	36.2[1]	3.5[1]	54.8[1]	6.2[4]	24.5[1]	9.8[1]	28.4[3]	15.4[4]	27.0[3]	23.5[4]	20.8[1]	18,819	25,725
Fidelity Canada††	19.5[1]	27.0[1]	-5.5[1]	17.7[1]	-2.9[2]	25.5[5]	-12.0[5]	19.4[1]	16.0[2]	6.1[2]	13.7[4]	10.2[3]	14,697	16,231
Fidelity Cap & Inc	12.6[1]	-3.2[5]	-3.8[5]	29.8[1]	28.0[1]	24.9[1]	-4.6[3]	16.1[4]	11.4[1]	14.7[1]	14.1[1]	12.1[1]	14,835	17,677
Fidelity Cap Apprec	37.6[1]	26.9[2]	-15.7[5]	10.0[5]	16.4[2]	33.4[1]	2.5[2]	18.8[5]	15.1[4]	26.5[3]	20.0[4]	18.8[2]	17,300	23,655
Fidelity Contrafund†††‡	21.0[2]	43.2[1]	3.9[1]	54.9[2]	15.9[2]	21.4[2]	-1.1[3]	36.3[2]	21.9[2]	23.0[3]	26.9[2]	19.7[1]	20,431	24,530
Fidelity Convert	15.9[2]	26.3[1]	-2.9[4]	38.7[1]	22.0[1]	17.8[1]	-1.8[3]	19.4[5]	15.0[2]	14.4[5]	16.3[5]	12.7[4]	15,711	18,174
Fidelity Discpl Eqty	—	36.3[1]	-0.8[2]	36.0[2]	13.2[2]	13.9[3]	3.0[2]	29.0[3]	15.1[4]	33.3[1]	25.6[3]	18.4[2]	19,795	23,223
Fidelity Divnd Growth	—	—	—	—	—	—	4.3[1]	37.5[1]	30.1[1]	27.9[3]	31.8[1]	—	22,876	—
Fidelity Dvsfd Int'l	—	—	—	—	—	—	1.1[2]	18.0[1]	20.0[2]	13.7[1]	17.2[1]	17.4[1]	16,104	22,256
Fidelity Emg Gro††	—	—	—	67.1[1]	8.4[3]	19.9[2]	-0.2[5]	35.9[2]	15.8[4]	19.4[3]	23.4[3]	17.6[2]	18,798	22,493
Fidelity Emg Mkts††	—	—	—	6.8[4]	5.9[1]	81.8[1]	-17.9[5]	-3.2[5]	10.0[4]	-40.9[5]	-14.3[5]	-1.2[5]	6,298	9,400
Fidelity Eqty Inc II	—	—	—	46.6[1]	19.1[1]	18.9[1]	3.2[1]	26.4[4]	18.7[4]	27.2[3]	24.0[4]	18.5[3]	19,081	23,413
Fidelity Eqty Inc	22.5[1]	18.7[4]	-14.0[5]	29.4[3]	14.7[1]	21.3[1]	0.2[3]	31.8[3]	21.0[3]	30.0[2]	27.5[2]	20.3[1]	20,728	25,193
Fidelity Europe Cap App††	—	—	—	—	—	—	6.9[1]	14.7[2]	25.9[1]	24.9[1]	21.7[1]	—	18,041	—
Fidelity Europe††	5.8[5]	32.3[1]	-4.6[1]	4.2[5]	-2.5[2]	27.2[4]	6.3[1]	18.8[1]	25.6[1]	22.9[1]	22.4[1]	19.9[1]	18,335	24,791
Fidelity Export & Multi††SC	—	—	—	—	—	—	—	32.2[3]	38.6[1]	23.7[3]	31.4[1]	—	22,664	—
Fidelity Fifty	—	—	—	—	—	—	4.0[1]	32.1[3]	14.4[4]	23.0[3]	22.9[3]	—	18,585	—
Fidelity France	—	—	—	—	—	—	—	—	25.4[1]	14.5[1]	—	—	—	—
Fidelity Freedom 2000	—	—	—	—	—	—	—	—	—	15.3[4]	—	—	—	—
Fidelity Freedom 2010	—	—	—	—	—	—	—	—	—	19.4[3]	—	—	—	—
Fidelity Freedom 2020	—	—	—	—	—	—	—	—	—	21.2[4]	—	—	—	—
Fidelity Freedom 2030	—	—	—	—	—	—	—	—	—	21.4[4]	—	—	—	—
Fidelity Freedom Inc	—	—	—	—	—	—	—	—	—	10.7[5]	—	—	—	—
Fidelity Fund	17.8[3]	28.8[2]	-5.1[3]	24.1[4]	8.5[3]	18.4[2]	2.6[1]	32.8[2]	19.8[3]	32.1[2]	28.1[2]	20.6[1]	21,010	25,523
Fidelity Germany	—	—	—	—	—	—	—	—	18.5[2]	20.3[1]	—	—	—	—
Fidelity Glob Bal	—	—	—	—	—	—	-11.5[5]	11.5[4]	7.7[5]	12.4[3]	10.5[5]	—	13,503	—
Fidelity Int'l Bond	3.7[5]	7.9[5]	12.3[1]	12.8[5]	7.3[2]	21.9[1]	-16.3[5]	6.7[5]	3.5[3]	-1.3[5]	2.9[5]	2.1[5]	10,898	11,120
Fidelity GNMA	7.2[3]	13.8[2]	10.5[1]	13.6[5]	6.7[3]	6.1[5]	-2.0[2]	16.6[3]	4.9[2]	8.7[3]	10.0[2]	6.7[3]	13,296	13,825
Fidelity Gov Sec	6.4[5]	12.6[3]	9.5[1]	16.0[4]	8.0[2]	12.3[3]	-5.2[4]	18.1[3]	2.1[4]	8.9[4]	9.5[4]	6.9[4]	13,135	13,984
Fidelity Gro & Inc‡	23.0[1]	29.6[2]	-6.8[4]	41.8[1]	11.5[2]	19.5[1]	2.3[2]	35.4[2]	20.0[3]	30.2[2]	28.4[2]	20.9[1]	21,151	25,857
Fidelity Growth Co	16.1[3]	41.6[1]	3.6[1]	48.3[1]	7.9[4]	16.2[3]	-2.2[3]	39.6[2]	16.8[4]	18.9[3]	24.7[2]	17.1[2]	19,384	22,029
Fidelity HK & China	—	—	—	—	—	—	—	—	41.0[1]	-22.1[5]	—	—	—	—
Fidelity Int'l Gr & Inc	11.6[4]	19.1[4]	-3.2[1]	8.0[4]	-3.3[2]	35.1[3]	-2.9[3]	12.2[2]	12.7[3]	7.1[2]	10.6[2]	12.2[2]	13,547	17,771
Fidelity Int'l Value	—	—	—	—	—	—	—	13.9[2]	9.6[4]	7.8[2]	10.4[2]	—	13,462	—
Fidelity Inter Bond	7.2[4]	11.8[4]	7.5[4]	14.5[4]	6.1[4]	12.0[1]	-2.0[2]	12.8[5]	3.6[3]	7.6[4]	7.9[5]	6.7[3]	12,571	13,798
Fidelity Inv Grd Bd	7.9[3]	13.0[3]	6.1[3]	18.9[2]	8.3[2]	16.2[1]	-5.4[4]	15.5[5]	3.0[4]	8.9[4]	9.0[5]	7.3[4]	12,956	14,242
Fidelity Japan Sm Cap††	—	—	—	—	—	—	—	—	-24.6[5]	-30.4[5]	—	—	—	—
Fidelity Japan††	—	—	—	—	—	—	16.5[1]	-2.1[5]	-11.2[5]	-10.7[4]	-8.1[5]	1.7[5]	7,765	10,900

See Chapter 3 for explanation of symbols

Stock and bond funds — comprehensive summary *continued*
Arranged in alphabetical order

Total Net Assets $Million		NAV per share		1997 per share distributions		Yield %	Risk Analysis				% Distribution of Portfolio				
December 31 1996	1997	December 31 1996	1997	Income	Capital gains	12/31/97	beta	R²	Std. Dev.	Sharpe Ratio	12/31/97 Stocks	Bonds	Cash	Objective	No-Load Fund
841.1	759.2	10.15	10.35	0.68	0.00	6.5	0.14	0.26	3.02	B	0	99	1	fix-inc	Federated Income
123.7	152.6	9.96	10.15	0.64	0.00	6.3	0.20	0.26	4.36	B	0	98	2	fix-inc	Federated Inter Inc
221.6	213.2	10.56	10.73	0.53	0.00	5.0	0.13	0.28	2.59	D	0	100	0	tax-free	Federated Inter Muni
953.1	1,233.9	15.97	20.23	0.30	0.62	1.5	1.00	1.00	11.09	B	96	0	4	gr-inc	Federated Max Cap
51.3	76.9	12.09	12.89	0.28	0.69	2.2	0.58	0.70	7.71	C	73	18	9	agg gr	Federated Mgd Agg Gro
157.8	163.5	11.07	11.38	0.46	0.62	4.0	0.32	0.69	4.33	F	36	57	7	gr-inc	Federated Mgd Gro & Inc
136.2	160.7	11.79	12.19	0.35	0.88	2.9	0.47	0.77	5.98	D	54	40	6	growth	Federated Mgd Growth
67.0	71.6	10.40	10.73	0.59	0.13	5.5	0.18	0.47	2.83	D	16	78	6	income	Federated Mgd Inc
61.8	77.2	13.88	16.56	0.17	1.38	1.1	0.83	0.64	11.59	C	92	0	8	growth	Federated Mid Cap
157.9	140.7	14.04	15.24	0.13	1.46	0.9	0.71	0.36	13.20	C	96	0	4	agg gr	Federated Mini Cap SC
16.0	19.5	10.22	10.47	0.49	0.00	4.7	0.13	0.22	3.16	B	0	99	1	fix-inc	Federated PA Inter
228.7	199.1	8.73	8.74	0.53	0.00	6.1	0.06	0.21	1.46	A	0	95	5	fix-inc	Federated ST Income
206.8	177.9	10.30	10.31	0.44	0.00	4.3	0.05	0.21	1.25	C	0	99	1	tax-free	Federated ST Muni
839.8	1,216.4	31.85	35.09	0.36	7.22	0.9	0.84	0.89	9.96	A	98	0	2	gr-inc	Federated Stock
28.4	29.8	10.35	10.40	0.53	0.00	5.1	0.05	0.17	1.33	D	0	98	2	fix-inc	Federated US Gov 1-3
28.4	35.1	10.49	10.63	0.56	0.00	5.3	0.12	0.24	2.76	D	0	98	2	fix-inc	Federated US Gov 2-5
1.4	2.3	9.85	10.16	0.56	0.02	5.5	—	—	—	—	0	94	6	fix-inc	Federated US Gov 5-10
77.1	74.2	10.25	10.50	0.58	0.31	5.5	0.30	0.22	7.05	D	0	96	4	fix-inc	Federated US Gov Bd
3,377.8	4,662.9	16.35	18.48	0.40	1.75	2.0	0.75	0.82	9.22	D	77	18	5	gr-inc	Fidelity Asst Mgr Gro
588.4	687.3	11.61	12.18	0.55	0.29	4.4	0.31	0.77	3.90	D	22	48	30	income	Fidelity Asst Mgr Inc
10,971.9	12,099.0	16.47	18.35	0.61	1.11	3.1	0.59	0.86	7.08	D	58	32	10	income	Fidelity Asst Mgr
3,919.2	4,283.9	14.08	15.27	0.56	1.46	3.3	0.61	0.82	7.47	F	57	38	5	income	Fidelity Balanced
9,569.7	13,428.4	32.69	39.46	0.26	1.75	0.6	0.98	0.81	12.18	D	96	0	4	growth	Fidelity Blue Chip Gro††
129.6	87.9	17.62	16.53	0.05	2.08	0.3	0.84	0.43	14.08	B	93	0	7	int'l	Fidelity Canada††
2,162.8	2,096.1	9.36	10.01	0.68	0.00	6.8	0.23	0.25	5.05	A	29	60	11	fix-inc	Fidelity Cap & Inc
1,642.0	2,109.6	17.64	19.38	0.08	2.85	0.4	0.87	0.65	12.02	D	96	0	4	growth	Fidelity Cap Apprec
23,797.9	30,808.5	42.15	46.63	0.35	4.56	0.7	0.79	0.63	11.11	A	86	5	9	agg gr	Fidelity Contrafund†††‡
1,119.6	1,002.6	17.56	17.51	0.70	1.77	3.6	0.64	0.64	8.86	F	95	0	5	income	Fidelity Convert
2,099.0	2,557.4	22.04	25.86	0.25	3.30	0.9	0.96	0.83	11.83	C	98	0	2	growth	Fidelity Discpl Eqty
2,345.2	4,480.4	20.09	23.27	0.15	2.19	0.6	0.90	0.78	11.31	A	95	0	5	growth	Fidelity Divnd Growth
754.1	1,536.4	14.71	16.13	0.19	0.41	1.1	0.61	0.42	10.45	A	92	0	7	int'l	Fidelity Dvsfd Int'l
1,854.0	1,981.5	25.19	23.75	0.00	6.00	0.0	1.14	0.48	18.33	D	97	0	3	agg gr	Fidelity Emg Gro††
1,161.3	446.5	16.62	9.60	0.23	0.00	2.4	1.29	0.32	23.72	F	96	0	4	int'l	Fidelity Emg Mkts††
15,238.4	16,977.5	23.75	27.01	0.43	2.63	1.5	0.85	0.88	10.08	D	94	0	6	gr-inc	Fidelity Eqty Inc II
14,258.9	21,177.7	42.83	52.41	0.96	2.04	1.8	0.81	0.91	9.51	B	96	0	4	gr-inc	Fidelity Eqty Inc
189.4	371.6	13.59	14.68	0.16	2.09	1.0	0.64	0.42	10.92	A	98	0	2	int'l	Fidelity Europe Cap App††
773.2	951.5	26.61	29.94	0.39	2.35	1.2	0.45	0.30	9.17	A	94	0	6	int'l	Fidelity Europe††
397.5	465.3	16.75	17.02	0.00	3.79	0.0	1.05	0.36	19.84	B	92	0	8	agg gr	Fidelity Export & Multi††SC
147.4	175.0	14.04	15.21	0.05	2.00	0.3	1.09	0.83	13.19	C	98	0	2	agg gr	Fidelity Fifty
5.4	5.6	12.02	12.55	0.04	1.15	0.3	—	—	—	—	95	0	5	int'l	Fidelity France
1.6	81.4	10.15	11.24	0.33	0.10	2.9	—	—	—	—	43	44	13	income	Fidelity Freedom 2000
0.5	123.2	10.19	11.69	0.37	0.08	3.1	—	—	—	—	67	32	1	income	Fidelity Freedom 2010
0.6	84.0	10.24	11.93	0.34	0.11	2.8	—	—	—	—	82	18	0	gr-inc	Fidelity Freedom 2020
0.5	57.0	10.24	11.99	0.31	0.12	2.6	—	—	—	—	85	15	0	growth	Fidelity Freedom 2030
0.7	29.6	10.08	10.62	0.46	0.05	4.3	—	—	—	—	20	40	40	income	Fidelity Freedom Inc
4,450.8	6,529.6	24.70	29.81	0.32	2.35	1.0	0.92	0.91	10.70	C	95	0	5	gr-inc	Fidelity Fund
8.5	13.1	11.64	12.74	0.00	1.25	0.0	—	—	—	—	96	0	4	int'l	Fidelity Germany
77.1	68.9	13.36	14.63	0.40	0.00	2.7	0.53	0.53	8.03	D	57	28	15	global	Fidelity Glob Bal
121.7	78.2	9.72	9.09	0.50	0.00	5.5	0.03	0.00	4.80	F	0	100	0	fix-inc	Fidelity Int'l Bond
793.1	862.5	10.70	10.89	0.71	0.00	6.5	0.14	0.27	3.11	A	0	97	3	fix-inc	Fidelity GNMA
972.5	1,164.9	9.69	9.91	0.61	0.00	6.2	0.18	0.24	4.24	D	0	97	3	fix-inc	Fidelity Gov Sec
23,896.5	36,656.8	30.73	38.10	0.43	1.36	1.1	0.88	0.96	9.95	B	92	1	7	gr-inc	Fidelity Gro & Inc‡
9,272.6	10,509.4	40.46	43.32	0.22	4.35	0.5	1.04	0.76	13.33	B	95	0	5	agg gr	Fidelity Growth Co
197.2	180.1	14.21	11.02	0.06	0.00	0.5	—	—	—	—	96	0	4	int'l	Fidelity HK & China
1,080.5	1,030.3	19.55	19.70	0.37	0.88	1.8	0.53	0.37	9.61	B	75	17	8	int'l	Fidelity Int'l Gr & Inc
267.2	390.7	11.55	12.11	0.06	0.28	0.5	0.63	0.37	11.31	B	93	0	7	int'l	Fidelity Int'l Value
3,079.7	3,193.4	10.08	10.17	0.65	0.00	6.4	0.13	0.26	2.75	D	0	98	2	fix-inc	Fidelity Inter Bond
1,455.4	1,649.6	7.12	7.28	0.45	0.00	6.2	0.17	0.27	3.77	D	0	95	5	fix-inc	Fidelity Inv Grd Bd
78.4	76.4	7.94	5.52	0.01	0.00	0.2	—	—	—	—	92	0	8	int'l	Fidelity Japan Sm Cap††
255.3	215.8	11.42	10.02	0.18	0.00	1.8	0.73	0.20	17.78	F	93	0	7	int'l	Fidelity Japan††

Arranged in alphabetical order

No-Load Fund	Total return percent with quintile ranks by objective										Annualized		What $10,000 grew to after	
	1988	1989	1990	1991	1992	1993	1994	1995	1996	1997	3 yrs.	5 yrs.	3 yrs.	5 yrs.
Fidelity Large Cap	—	—	—	—	—	—	—	—	21.5^{2}	24.7^{3}	—	—	—	—
Fidelity Latin Amer††	—	—	—	—	—	—	-23.2^{5}	-16.5^{5}	30.7^{1}	32.9^{1}	13.2^{2}	—	14,501	—
Fidelity Low Pr Stk†† SC‡	—	—	-0.1^{2}	46.3^{1}	29.0^{1}	20.2^{1}	4.8^{1}	24.9^{4}	26.9^{1}	26.7^{3}	26.2^{3}	20.4^{1}	20,080	25,295
Fidelity Ltd Muni Inc	8.2^{2}	7.8^{4}	7.0^{1}	11.2^{1}	8.2^{2}	12.2^{1}	-4.8^{4}	14.8^{1}	4.3^{1}	8.3^{1}	9.1^{1}	6.7^{1}	12,972	13,856
Fidelity Magellan†‡	22.8^{2}	34.6^{2}	-4.5^{2}	41.0^{4}	7.0^{4}	24.7^{1}	-1.8^{3}	36.8^{2}	11.7^{5}	26.5^{2}	24.6^{2}	18.8^{2}	19,337	23,679
Fidelity Mid-Cap Stk	—	—	—	—	—	—	—	33.9^{2}	18.1^{4}	27.1^{3}	26.2^{3}	—	20,095	—
Fidelity Mortg Sec(Init Class)‡	6.7^{4}	13.7^{2}	10.3^{1}	13.6^{5}	5.5^{5}	6.7^{5}	1.9^{1}	17.0^{3}	5.4^{1}	9.1^{2}	10.4^{1}	7.9^{1}	13,463	14,646
Fidelity Muni Bd(Init Class)‡	12.3^{2}	9.6^{3}	6.9^{2}	11.9^{3}	8.9^{3}	13.2^{2}	-8.5^{5}	18.2^{2}	4.1^{2}	9.2^{2}	10.3^{2}	6.8^{3}	13,433	13,912
Fidelity New Millnm††‡	—	—	—	—	—	—	0.8^{2}	52.1^{1}	23.1^{2}	24.6^{2}	32.6^{1}	24.0^{1}	23,336	29,333
Fidelity New Mkts Inc	—	—	—	—	—	—	-16.6^{5}	8.0^{5}	41.4^{1}	17.2^{1}	21.4^{1}	—	17,900	—
Fidelity Nordic	—	—	—	—	—	—	—	—	41.7^{1}	12.1^{2}	—	—	—	—
Fidelity NY Insur Muni Inc‡	11.3^{3}	9.1^{4}	6.2^{4}	12.5^{2}	8.6^{3}	12.8^{3}	-8.0^{4}	18.5^{2}	3.8^{3}	8.8^{3}	10.2^{2}	6.8^{3}	13,379	13,892
Fidelity NY Muni Inc	11.9^{3}	9.3^{3}	5.1^{5}	13.4^{1}	9.0^{3}	12.9^{3}	-8.0^{4}	19.6^{1}	3.8^{3}	9.7^{2}	10.9^{1}	7.2^{3}	13,621	14,148
Fidelity OTC††	22.9^{2}	30.4^{3}	-4.8^{2}	49.2^{3}	14.9^{2}	8.3^{5}	-2.7^{3}	38.2^{2}	23.7^{2}	9.9^{4}	23.4^{3}	14.6^{4}	18,790	19,800
Fidelity Overseas	8.3^{5}	16.9^{4}	-6.6^{1}	8.6^{4}	-11.5^{5}	40.1^{2}	1.3^{2}	9.1^{3}	13.1^{3}	10.9^{2}	11.0^{2}	14.2^{2}	13,688	19,426
Fidelity Pacific Bas††	10.4^{5}	11.4^{5}	-27.2^{5}	12.5^{2}	-7.6^{4}	63.9^{1}	-2.8^{3}	-6.1^{5}	-2.5^{5}	-15.1^{4}	-8.2^{5}	4.3^{4}	7,749	12,345
Fidelity Puritan	18.9^{2}	19.6^{3}	-6.4^{4}	24.5^{3}	15.4^{1}	21.4^{1}	1.8^{1}	21.5^{5}	15.2^{2}	22.4^{2}	19.6^{3}	16.2^{1}	17,127	21,167
Fidelity Real Est	10.4^{4}	13.8^{4}	-8.7^{3}	39.2^{3}	19.5^{2}	12.5^{4}	2.0^{2}	10.9^{5}	36.2^{2}	21.3^{3}	22.4^{4}	16.0^{4}	18,323	21,025
Fidelity Retrmnt Gro	15.5^{4}	30.4^{2}	-10.2^{4}	45.6^{1}	10.6^{3}	22.1^{1}	0.1^{3}	24.3^{4}	8.3^{5}	18.5^{4}	16.9^{5}	14.3^{4}	15,955	19,500
Fidelity S-I Gov	—	—	—	—	4.7^{4}	5.3^{4}	-1.4^{4}	11.9^{2}	4.1^{4}	6.6^{2}	7.5^{2}	5.2^{3}	12,418	12,893
Fidelity SE Asia††	—	—	—	—	—	—	-21.8^{5}	12.2^{2}	10.2^{4}	-38.9^{5}	-8.9^{5}	—	7,560	—
Fidelity Sel Air Trans†	29.1^{1}	26.3^{3}	-18.2^{5}	37.1^{3}	6.6^{4}	30.9^{2}	-21.7^{5}	59.5^{1}	1.2^{5}	31.1^{2}	28.4^{2}	16.8^{4}	21,167	21,695
Fidelity Sel Amer Gold†	-12.5^{1}	22.0^{3}	-17.2^{1}	-6.1^{3}	-3.1^{1}	78.7^{4}	-15.5^{4}	11.2^{2}	19.9^{2}	-39.4^{2}	-6.9^{1}	4.1^{1}	8,081	12,202
Fidelity Sel Auto†	20.1^{2}	4.1^{5}	-6.7^{3}	37.3^{3}	41.6^{1}	35.4^{1}	-12.8^{5}	13.4^{5}	16.1^{3}	16.7^{4}	15.4^{5}	12.7^{5}	15,370	18,147
Fidelity Sel Biotech†	4.1^{5}	43.9^{1}	44.3^{1}	99.0^{1}	-10.3^{5}	0.7^{5}	-18.2^{5}	49.1^{1}	5.6^{5}	15.4^{4}	22.0^{4}	8.4^{5}	18,167	14,965
Fidelity Sel Broker†	18.5^{2}	14.1^{4}	-16.2^{4}	82.3^{1}	5.1^{4}	49.3^{1}	-17.3^{5}	23.6^{4}	39.6^{1}	62.3^{1}	41.0^{1}	28.2^{1}	28,003	34,576
Fidelity Sel Chemical†	21.0^{2}	17.3^{4}	-4.1^{2}	38.7^{3}	8.9^{4}	12.8^{4}	14.8^{1}	21.4^{2}	21.5^{3}	16.5^{4}	19.8^{4}	17.3^{3}	17,185	22,254
Fidelity Sel Computer†	-5.0^{5}	6.8^{5}	18.4^{1}	30.7^{4}	22.0^{2}	28.9^{2}	20.5^{1}	51.8^{1}	31.5^{2}	-1.1^{5}	25.5^{2}	25.1^{1}	19,751	30,678
Fidelity Sel Consmr Ind†	—	—	—	38.5^{3}	8.6^{4}	24.7^{2}	-7.1^{4}	28.3^{3}	13.1^{4}	38.0^{1}	26.0^{2}	18.3^{3}	20,025	23,198
Fidelity Sel Const/Hous†	29.2^{1}	16.6^{4}	-9.6^{3}	41.3^{3}	18.7^{2}	33.6^{1}	-15.9^{5}	28.8^{3}	13.2^{4}	29.6^{2}	23.6^{3}	16.2^{4}	18,893	21,228
Fidelity Sel Cycl Indust†	—	—	—	—	—	—	—	—	—	—	—	—	—	—
Fidelity Sel Defense†	4.3^{5}	8.8^{5}	-4.6^{3}	26.9^{5}	0.0^{5}	28.9^{2}	1.8^{3}	47.4^{1}	24.9^{3}	23.5^{3}	31.5^{1}	24.4^{1}	22,741	29,841
Fidelity Sel Devel Comm†	—	—	—	61.4^{2}	17.2^{3}	31.8^{1}	15.1^{1}	17.4^{5}	14.5^{4}	5.6^{5}	12.4^{5}	16.6^{4}	14,189	21,525
Fidelity Sel Electronics†	-8.5^{5}	15.7^{4}	5.8^{2}	35.5^{4}	27.4^{1}	32.1^{1}	17.2^{1}	69.0^{1}	41.7^{1}	14.2^{5}	39.8^{1}	33.5^{1}	27,339	42,326
Fidelity Sel Energy Serv†	-0.4^{5}	59.4^{1}	1.9^{2}	-23.5^{5}	3.4^{1}	21.0^{3}	0.6^{3}	40.9^{2}	49.0^{1}	51.9^{1}	47.2^{1}	31.2^{1}	31,896	38,826
Fidelity Sel Energy†	15.9^{3}	42.8^{1}	-4.5^{3}	0.0^{5}	-2.4^{5}	19.2^{3}	0.4^{3}	21.4^{4}	32.5^{2}	10.5^{5}	21.1^{4}	16.3^{4}	17,771	21,268
Fidelity Sel Envir Serv†	—	—	-2.5^{2}	7.7^{5}	-1.4^{5}	-0.6^{5}	-9.6^{4}	26.1^{3}	15.6^{4}	17.9^{4}	19.8^{4}	9.1^{5}	17,182	15,439
Fidelity Sel Financial†	12.0^{4}	19.3^{4}	-24.3^{5}	61.6^{2}	42.8^{1}	17.6^{3}	-3.6^{4}	47.3^{1}	32.1^{2}	41.9^{1}	40.3^{1}	25.6^{1}	27,615	31,306
Fidelity Sel Food/Agr†	26.8^{1}	38.9^{2}	9.3^{1}	34.1^{4}	6.0^{4}	8.8^{4}	6.1^{2}	36.6^{2}	13.3^{4}	30.3^{2}	26.3^{2}	18.4^{3}	20,159	23,271
Fidelity Sel Health†	8.8^{4}	42.5^{2}	24.3^{1}	83.7^{1}	-17.4^{5}	2.4^{5}	21.5^{1}	45.9^{2}	15.4^{4}	31.1^{2}	30.2^{2}	22.4^{2}	22,078	27,469
Fidelity Sel Home Finc†	18.5^{2}	9.3^{5}	-15.1^{4}	64.6^{2}	57.9^{1}	27.3^{2}	2.7^{2}	53.5^{1}	36.8^{1}	45.8^{1}	45.2^{1}	32.0^{1}	30,620	40,032
Fidelity Sel Indust Equip†	4.9^{5}	18.0^{4}	-15.5^{4}	26.8^{5}	11.3^{3}	43.3^{1}	3.1^{2}	27.8^{3}	26.7^{2}	18.8^{4}	24.4^{3}	23.2^{1}	19,232	28,414
Fidelity Sel Indust Mat†	10.8^{4}	4.4^{5}	-17.2^{5}	35.8^{3}	12.4^{3}	21.4^{3}	8.2^{3}	15.4^{5}	14.0^{4}	1.9^{5}	10.3^{5}	12.0^{5}	13,411	17,616
Fidelity Sel Insurance†	17.4^{3}	37.8^{2}	-9.8^{4}	36.7^{3}	22.5^{2}	8.2^{5}	-0.3^{3}	34.8^{2}	23.7^{3}	42.5^{1}	33.5^{1}	20.7^{2}	23,769	25,641
Fidelity Sel Leisure†	26.0^{2}	31.2^{3}	-22.3^{5}	32.9^{4}	16.2^{3}	39.6^{1}	-6.8^{4}	27.0^{3}	13.4^{4}	41.3^{1}	26.7^{2}	21.5^{2}	20,352	26,479
Fidelity Sel Medical Del†	15.8^{3}	58.0^{1}	16.3^{1}	77.8^{1}	-13.2^{5}	5.5^{4}	19.8^{1}	32.2^{3}	11.0^{5}	20.5^{3}	20.9^{4}	17.5^{3}	17,685	22,352
Fidelity Sel Multimedia†	26.8^{2}	32.5^{3}	-26.2^{5}	37.8^{3}	21.5^{2}	38.0^{1}	4.0^{2}	33.7^{3}	1.1^{5}	30.9^{2}	21.0^{4}	20.5^{2}	17,699	25,401
Fidelity Sel Nat Gas†	—	—	—	—	—	—	-6.8^{4}	30.4^{3}	34.9^{2}	-8.0^{5}	17.4^{5}	—	16,179	—
Fidelity Sel Nat Rescs†	—	—	—	—	—	—	—	—	—	—	—	—	—	—
Fidelity Sel Pap/Forest†	6.8^{5}	4.1^{5}	-15.1^{4}	34.8^{4}	12.1^{3}	18.6^{3}	14.1^{1}	21.9^{4}	7.0^{5}	9.4^{5}	12.6^{5}	14.1^{5}	14,272	19,313
Fidelity Sel Prec Met†	-23.9^{1}	32.2^{1}	-21.3^{1}	1.5^{1}	-21.9^{5}	111.6^{1}	-1.1^{1}	-3.3^{1}	5.4^{3}	-44.9^{3}	-17.5^{2}	3.3^{2}	5,617	11,754
Fidelity Sel Reg Banks†	25.7^{2}	26.6^{3}	-20.7^{5}	65.8^{1}	48.5^{1}	11.2^{4}	0.2^{3}	46.8^{1}	35.8^{2}	45.5^{1}	42.6^{1}	26.4^{1}	29,009	32,322
Fidelity Sel Retail†	38.7^{1}	29.5^{3}	-5.0^{3}	68.1^{1}	22.1^{2}	13.0^{4}	-5.0^{4}	12.0^{5}	20.9^{3}	41.7^{1}	24.3^{3}	15.6^{4}	19,192	20,603
Fidelity Sel Software†	9.0^{4}	12.0^{5}	0.9^{2}	45.8^{3}	35.5^{1}	32.7^{1}	0.4^{3}	46.3^{2}	21.6^{3}	14.9^{4}	26.9^{2}	22.2^{2}	20,447	27,242
Fidelity Sel Technology†	-2.7^{5}	17.0^{4}	10.5^{1}	59.0^{2}	8.7^{4}	28.7^{2}	11.1^{1}	43.8^{2}	15.6^{4}	10.4^{5}	22.4^{4}	21.3^{2}	18,347	26,234
Fidelity Sel Telecomm†	27.8^{1}	50.9^{1}	-16.4^{4}	30.9^{4}	15.3^{3}	29.7^{2}	4.3^{2}	29.7^{3}	5.3^{5}	25.8^{3}	19.8^{5}	18.4^{3}	17,179	23,240
Fidelity Sel Transport†	38.5^{1}	28.5^{3}	-21.6^{5}	54.1^{2}	23.8^{1}	29.3^{2}	3.9^{2}	15.2^{5}	9.5^{5}	32.1^{1}	18.6^{5}	17.5^{3}	16,662	22,384
Fidelity Sel Util Gro†	16.5^{3}	39.0^{2}	0.6^{2}	21.0^{5}	10.6^{3}	12.5^{4}	-7.4^{4}	34.4^{3}	11.3^{5}	30.3^{2}	24.9^{3}	15.2^{4}	19,496	20,310
Fidelity Small Cap Selector†† SC	—	—	—	—	—	—	-3.3^{4}	26.6^{4}	13.6^{4}	27.2^{2}	22.3^{3}	—	18,298	—
Fidelity Spart Agg Muni‡	13.4^{1}	9.5^{3}	7.5^{1}	11.8^{3}	9.2^{2}	13.6^{1}	-5.8^{2}	14.9^{5}	3.6^{3}	10.3^{1}	9.5^{4}	7.0^{3}	13,129	14,049

See Chapter 3 for explanation of symbols

Total Net Assets $Million		NAV per share		1997 per share distributions		Yield % 12/31/97	Risk Analysis				% Distribution of Portfolio 12/31/97			Objective	No-Load Fund
December 31 1996	1997	December 31 1996	1997	Income	Capital gains		beta	R^2	Std. Dev.	Sharpe Ratio	Stocks	Bonds	Cash		
111.7	139.3	12.51	14.41	0.06	1.07	0.4	—	—	—	—	94	0	6	growth	Fidelity Large Cap
535.1	860.6	13.11	17.22	0.20	0.00	1.2	1.12	0.22	25.55	C	94	0	6	int'l	Fidelity Latin Amer††
5,664.3	10,691.1	21.35	25.13	0.28	1.58	1.0	0.48	0.38	8.80	A	79	0	21	growth	Fidelity Low Pr Stk†† SC‡
901.0	911.8	9.69	9.94	0.49	0.05	4.9	0.14	0.26	3.12	A	0	98	2	tax-free	Fidelity Ltd Muni Inc
53,988.7	63,766.2	80.65	95.27	1.25	5.21	1.3	0.92	0.73	12.11	B	94	0	6	agg gr	Fidelity Magellan††
1,695.1	1,763.1	14.64	16.69	0.01	1.77	0.1	0.85	0.60	12.27	C	95	0	5	growth	Fidelity Mid-Cap Stk
521.3	483.6	10.85	11.01	0.68	0.03	6.2	0.14	0.25	3.04	A	0	100	0	fix-inc	Fidelity Mortg Sec(Init Class)‡
944.3	932.8	8.19	8.52	0.40	0.00	4.7	0.18	0.24	4.16	A	0	98	2	tax-free	Fidelity Muni Bd(Init Class)‡
1,252.9	1,564.2	20.25	22.19	0.00	2.89	0.0	1.03	0.44	17.37	B	95	0	5	agg gr	Fidelity New Millnm††‡
305.8	371.3	12.96	12.96	1.32	0.87	9.5	0.64	0.19	15.71	C	0	90	10	fix-inc	Fidelity New Mkts Inc
43.5	64.8	13.80	14.22	0.06	1.18	0.5	—	—	—	—	97	0	3	int'l	Fidelity Nordic
318.1	302.7	11.71	12.07	0.55	0.08	4.6	0.19	0.23	4.38	C	0	99	1	tax-free	Fidelity NY Insur Muni Inc‡
411.4	444.6	12.33	12.85	0.62	0.02	4.9	0.20	0.23	4.61	B	0	98	2	tax-free	Fidelity NY Muni Inc
3,387.2	3,858.1	32.71	33.45	0.00	2.52	0.0	1.07	0.58	15.70	A	95	0	5	agg gr	Fidelity OTC††
3,247.1	3,704.9	30.84	32.54	0.34	1.34	1.0	0.66	0.45	10.79	B	92	0	8	int'l	Fidelity Overseas
446.9	213.6	14.70	12.23	0.25	0.00	2.0	0.85	0.32	16.21	F	95	0	5	int'l	Fidelity Pacific Bas††
18,501.7	22,821.8	17.24	19.38	0.68	0.96	3.3	0.65	0.47	7.88	D	61	32	7	income	Fidelity Puritan
1,721.6	2,480.2	18.03	20.45	0.79	0.56	3.8	0.25	0.07	10.63	B	95	0	5	sector	Fidelity Real Est
4,045.9	3,932.2	17.29	16.85	0.13	3.41	0.6	0.99	0.83	12.03	F	99	0	1	growth	Fidelity Retrmnt Gro
121.5	126.2	9.37	9.40	0.57	0.00	6.1	0.09	0.19	2.25	C	0	95	5	fix-inc	Fidelity S-I Gov
762.0	263.4	15.03	9.14	0.05	0.00	0.5	1.39	0.37	23.65	F	92	0	8	int'l	Fidelity SE Asi
150.5	61.1	19.41	23.95	0.00	1.43	0.0	0.87	0.21	21.04	D	92	0	8	sector	Fidelity Sel Air Trans†
354.7	211.6	26.04	14.93	0.00	1.29	0.0	0.51	0.03	30.97	A	96	0	4	prec met	Fidelity Sel Amer Gold†
67.7	59.6	24.55	25.30	0.08	3.09	0.3	0.59	0.37	10.60	F	94	0	6	sector	Fidelity Sel Auto†
635.0	551.0	32.51	32.54	0.00	4.71	0.0	0.72	0.23	16.54	D	97	0	3	sector	Fidelity Sel Biotech†
111.4	647.6	23.17	36.86	0.09	0.61	0.2	1.31	0.70	17.60	A	90	0	10	sector	Fidelity Sel Broker†
109.8	68.3	41.53	43.70	0.01	4.53	0.0	0.65	0.47	10.46	C	91	0	9	sector	Fidelity Sel Chemical†
664.0	569.4	48.68	34.48	0.00	13.39	0.0	1.59	0.38	28.77	F	90	0	10	sector	Fidelity Sel Computer†
16.5	40.4	19.62	25.51	0.00	1.52	0.0	0.85	0.53	12.80	B	90	0	10	sector	Fidelity Sel Consmr Ind†
84.0	18.1	21.09	22.78	0.02	3.87	0.1	0.72	0.52	11.27	B	93	0	7	sector	Fidelity Sel Const/Hous†
—	3.7	—	11.00	0.00	0.46	—	—	—	—	—	90	0	10	sector	Fidelity Sel Cycl Indust†
39.1	50.0	29.12	32.74	0.00	3.04	0.0	0.68	0.30	13.87	B	94	0	6	sector	Fidelity Sel Defense†
275.3	203.7	21.26	18.00	0.00	4.35	0.0	1.36	0.43	22.68	F	93	0	8	sector	Fidelity Sel Devel Comm†
1,565.2	2,302.0	36.48	30.81	0.00	10.20	0.0	1.54	0.37	28.71	C	91	0	9	sector	Fidelity Sel Electronics†
562.8	1,133.4	21.73	30.45	0.00	1.85	0.0	0.42	0.04	21.34	A	97	0	3	sector	Fidelity Sel Energy Serv†
239.7	158.2	23.21	21.15	0.09	4.09	0.4	0.53	0.17	14.31	D	94	0	6	sector	Fidelity Sel Energy†
28.1	26.6	13.99	16.49	0.00	0.00	0.0	0.87	0.40	15.03	F	94	0	6	sector	Fidelity Sel Envir Serv†
337.5	548.7	76.59	95.98	0.64	10.51	0.6	1.09	0.79	13.81	A	85	0	15	sector	Fidelity Sel Financial†
252.8	309.1	41.41	47.87	0.37	4.95	0.7	0.67	0.60	9.71	B	96	0	4	sector	Fidelity Sel Food/Agr†
1,242.3	1,631.5	95.40	101.87	0.25	20.73	0.2	0.89	0.70	11.86	A	91	0	9	sector	Fidelity Sel Health†
794.3	1,664.0	40.79	52.09	0.29	5.84	0.5	0.88	0.50	13.88	A	95	0	5	sector	Fidelity Sel Home Finc†
86.2	47.7	24.93	23.87	0.02	5.26	0.1	0.83	0.45	13.89	C	90	0	10	sector	Fidelity Sel Indust Equip†
84.5	22.4	27.04	23.33	0.03	4.00	0.1	0.70	0.28	14.67	F	94	0	6	sector	Fidelity Sel Indust Mat†
35.0	111.7	30.67	39.49	0.00	3.54	0.0	0.92	0.74	11.95	A	87	0	13	sector	Fidelity Sel Insurance†
107.0	229.1	46.06	57.55	0.00	6.46	0.0	0.79	0.48	12.71	B	89	0	11	sector	Fidelity Sel Leisure†
182.9	141.8	26.42	26.05	0.00	5.23	0.0	0.95	0.42	16.29	D	91	0	9	sector	Fidelity Sel Medical Del†
72.6	70.6	25.37	31.44	0.00	1.52	0.0	0.90	0.49	14.18	D	88	0	12	sector	Fidelity Sel Multimedia†
153.1	69.3	14.84	13.27	0.00	0.33	0.0	0.38	0.06	17.29	F	96	0	4	sector	Fidelity Sel Nat Gas†
—	8.6	—	10.38	0.00	0.26	—	—	—	—	—	94	0	6	sector	Fidelity Sel Nat Rescs†
20.6	17.1	21.36	21.18	0.04	2.07	0.2	0.76	0.31	15.15	F	89	0	11	sector	Fidelity Sel Pap/Forest††
258.8	142.1	17.91	9.87	0.00	0.00	0.0	0.37	0.02	30.79	B	98	0	2	prec met	Fidelity Sel Prec Met†
510.6	1,351.8	29.29	41.05	0.28	1.23	0.7	0.99	0.74	12.89	A	87	0	13	sector	Fidelity Sel Reg Banks†
157.2	191.2	32.24	45.06	0.00	0.51	0.0	0.77	0.29	15.76	D	101	0	-1	sector	Fidelity Sel Retail†
401.5	426.2	39.62	38.58	0.00	6.61	0.0	1.13	0.44	19.08	D	93	0	7	sector	Fidelity Sel Software†
491.3	526.5	55.68	45.28	0.00	15.69	0.0	1.46	0.45	24.04	F	92	0	8	sector	Fidelity Sel Technology†
437.0	441.0	41.16	45.13	0.00	6.44	0.0	0.95	0.50	15.18	F	97	0	3	sector	Fidelity Sel Telecomm†
13.0	54.6	22.28	26.59	0.00	2.80	0.0	0.65	0.35	12.37	D	96	0	4	sector	Fidelity Sel Transport†
255.7	358.9	43.90	48.88	0.58	7.30	1.0	0.67	0.53	10.16	B	88	0	12	sector	Fidelity Sel Util Gro†
538.0	824.8	13.56	15.93	0.13	1.14	0.8	0.69	0.25	15.37	C	97	0	3	agg gr	Fidelity Small Cap Selector†† SC
848.9	954.6	11.36	11.86	0.63	0.00	5.3	0.16	0.23	3.79	C	0	97	3	tax-free	Fidelity Spart Agg Muni‡

Stock and bond funds — comprehensive summary *continued*

Arranged in alphabetical order

| No-Load Fund | Total return percent with quintile ranks by objective | | | | | | | | | | Annualized | | What $10,000 grew to after | |
	1988	1989	1990	1991	1992	1993	1994	1995	1996	1997	3 yrs.	5 yrs.	3 yrs.	5 yrs.
Fidelity Spart AZ Muni	—	—	—	—	—	—	—	18.5[2]	3.5[4]	8.0[5]	9.8[3]	—	13,242	—
Fidelity Spart CA Muni Inc	11.8[3]	9.7[3]	7.0[2]	10.2[5]	8.7[3]	13.4[2]	-8.9[5]	19.2[1]	4.8[1]	9.8[1]	11.1[1]	7.2[2]	13,717	14,171
Fidelity Spart CT Muni	10.1[4]	10.4[2]	6.7[3]	10.6[5]	8.2[4]	13.0[2]	-7.0[3]	17.1[3]	4.2[2]	9.1[2]	10.0[3]	7.0[3]	13,316	13,994
Fidelity Spart Extd Market Idx†	—	—	—	—	—	—	—	—	—	—	—	—	—	—
Fidelity Spart FL Muni	—	—	—	—	—	—	-6.7[3]	18.6[2]	4.0[2]	8.7[4]	10.3[2]	7.5[1]	13,414	14,380
Fidelity Spart GNMA	—	—	—	13.8[5]	6.5[4]	6.3[5]	-1.5[1]	16.7[3]	5.0[2]	8.9[2]	10.1[2]	6.9[2]	13,350	13,978
Fidelity Spart Gov Inc	—	—	9.2[1]	15.1[4]	7.1[3]	7.3[5]	-3.6[3]	18.2[3]	2.6[4]	9.2[3]	9.8[4]	6.5[4]	13,245	13,701
Fidelity Spart Hi Inc	—	—	—	34.3[1]	21.5[1]	21.9[1]	3.2[1]	16.9[4]	14.2[1]	15.9[1]	15.7[1]	14.2[1]	15,470	19,461
Fidelity Spart Insur Muni Inc‡	11.2[3]	9.4[3]	7.1[1]	11.6[4]	7.9[5]	13.8[1]	-7.7[4]	18.7[2]	3.7[3]	9.5[2]	10.5[2]	7.2[2]	13,483	14,162
Fidelity Spart Int'l Idx†	—	—	—	—	—	—	—	—	—	—	—	—	—	—
Fidelity Spart Inter Muni	—	—	—	—	—	—	-5.0[5]	14.4[2]	4.6[1]	8.0[1]	8.9[1]	—	12,921	—
Fidelity Spart Inv Grd	—	—	—	—	—	—	-5.2[4]	18.6[3]	3.1[3]	9.3[3]	10.1[3]	8.0[3]	13,363	14,669
Fidelity Spart Ltd Mat Gov	—	10.4[3]	9.1[2]	11.9[4]	5.8[3]	6.4[3]	-0.9[4]	13.9[1]	4.1[4]	7.3[1]	8.3[1]	6.0[1]	12,718	13,410
Fidelity Spart MA Muni Inc	10.7[4]	9.2[4]	7.4[1]	11.3[4]	9.3[2]	12.9[3]	-6.1[3]	18.1[2]	3.6[3]	9.3[2]	10.2[3]	7.2[2]	13,375	14,180
Fidelity Spart Market Idx	—	—	—	30.3[2]	7.3[3]	9.6[4]	1.0[2]	37.0[1]	22.6[2]	33.0[1]	30.7[1]	19.9[2]	22,327	24,738
Fidelity Spart MD Muni Inc	—	—	—	—	—	—	-7.5[4]	17.8[2]	3.9[3]	8.8[3]	10.0[3]	—	13,318	—
Fidelity Spart MI Muni Inc	13.0[1]	10.2[2]	5.1[5]	12.0[3]	9.5[1]	13.8[1]	-7.5[4]	15.4[4]	3.4[4]	9.1[3]	9.2[4]	6.5[4]	13,018	13,707
Fidelity Spart MN Muni Inc	12.6[2]	9.2[4]	7.2[1]	8.5[5]	7.6[5]	12.4[4]	-6.0[3]	16.0[4]	3.8[3]	8.8[3]	9.4[4]	6.7[4]	13,106	13,848
Fidelity Spart Muni Inc	12.2[2]	11.4[1]	8.5[1]	10.2[5]	8.4[4]	12.6[4]	-7.4[4]	16.2[4]	4.9[1]	9.2[2]	10.0[3]	6.8[4]	13,314	13,882
Fidelity Spart NJ Muni Inc	—	10.3[2]	7.1[2]	12.3[2]	8.7[3]	13.1[2]	-5.7[2]	15.4[4]	4.1[2]	8.3[4]	9.2[4]	6.8[4]	13,016	13,882
Fidelity Spart NY Inter Muni Inc‡	—	—	—	—	—	—	-4.3[3]	14.4[1]	3.9[3]	8.1[1]	8.7[1]	—	12,858	—
Fidelity Spart NY Muni Inc‡	—	—	—	14.4[1]	9.5[1]	13.4[2]	-8.3[4]	19.1[1]	4.3[2]	10.0[1]	11.0[1]	7.3[2]	13,667	14,208
Fidelity Spart OH Muni Inc	12.9[1]	10.0[2]	7.5[1]	11.4[4]	8.7[3]	12.6[4]	-5.5[2]	16.4[4]	4.2[2]	8.7[4]	9.7[3]	7.0[3]	13,188	14,033
Fidelity Spart PA Muni Inc	14.2[1]	9.8[3]	7.2[1]	12.5[2]	9.1[2]	13.2[2]	-5.0[1]	17.4[3]	4.0[2]	8.3[4]	9.8[3]	7.3[2]	13,228	14,225
Fidelity Spart S-I Gov	—	—	—	—	—	—	-0.5[3]	12.3[2]	4.3[3]	6.6[2]	7.7[2]	5.6[2]	12,487	13,133
Fidelity Spart S-I Muni	4.9[5]	6.3[5]	6.4[3]	8.9[2]	6.2[2]	7.1[1]	-0.1[3]	8.5[2]	3.9[3]	5.5[2]	5.9[2]	4.9[1]	11,888	12,719
Fidelity Spart ST Bd	—	—	—	—	—	—	-4.6[5]	9.9[4]	5.0[2]	6.5[2]	7.1[3]	5.0[4]	12,295	12,785
Fidelity ST Bond	5.7[4]	10.5[3]	6.1[5]	14.0[2]	7.4[1]	9.1[1]	-4.1[5]	9.8[4]	4.8[2]	6.2[4]	6.9[3]	5.0[4]	12,221	12,787
Fidelity Stk Selector	—	—	—	45.9[1]	15.4[2]	14.0[3]	0.8[2]	36.5[1]	17.1[4]	28.9[2]	27.2[2]	18.8[2]	20,603	23,675
Fidelity Target Timeline 1999	—	—	—	—	—	—	—	—	—	6.7[5]	—	—	—	—
Fidelity Target Timeline 2001	—	—	—	—	—	—	—	—	—	8.2[4]	—	—	—	—
Fidelity Target Timeline 2003	—	—	—	—	—	—	—	—	—	10.1[2]	—	—	—	—
Fidelity TechnoQuant Gro	—	—	—	—	—	—	—	—	—	17.9[3]	—	—	—	—
Fidelity Trend	24.3[1]	31.7[2]	-12.7[4]	36.3[4]	16.8[2]	19.1[1]	-6.7[5]	22.1[5]	17.0[4]	8.5[5]	15.7[5]	11.5[5]	15,504	17,228
Fidelity UK	—	—	—	—	—	—	—	—	—	—	28.6[1]	16.8[1]	—	—
Fidelity Utilities	14.8[3]	25.9[1]	1.8[2]	21.2[4]	10.9[2]	15.6[2]	-5.3[5]	30.6[2]	11.4[4]	31.6[1]	24.2[1]	16.0[2]	19,146	20,959
Fidelity Value	29.0[1]	22.9[3]	-12.8[5]	26.2[4]	21.2[1]	22.9[1]	7.6[1]	27.1[4]	16.9[4]	21.1[4]	21.6[4]	18.9[2]	17,991	23,791
Fidelity Worldwide	—	—	—	7.9[5]	6.2[1]	36.5[1]	3.0[1]	7.2[5]	18.7[2]	12.1[3]	12.6[4]	14.9[2]	14,259	20,048
Fiduciary Cap Growth SC	18.8[3]	17.9[4]	-11.7[4]	36.3[2]	14.4[2]	14.7[2]	0.4[3]	26.5[4]	17.1[4]	29.2[2]	24.2[3]	17.1[3]	19,139	22,041
First Eagle America	22.7[2]	26.7[3]	-17.6[5]	20.9[5]	24.3[1]	23.9[1]	-2.6[3]	36.4[2]	29.3[1]	29.5[2]	31.7[1]	22.5[1]	22,839	27,552
First Eagle Int'l	—	—	—	—	—	—	—	11.6[2]	15.9[3]	9.3[2]	12.2[2]	—	14,139	—
First Hawaii Muni Bd	—	8.9[4]	5.3[5]	10.6[5]	8.8[3]	10.6[5]	-5.8[2]	14.4[5]	4.2[2]	7.1[5]	8.5[5]	5.9[5]	12,770	13,295
First Omaha Balanced	—	—	—	—	—	—	—	—	—	15.0[5]	—	—	—	—
First Omaha Eqty	—	—	—	—	—	10.9[3]	7.4[1]	26.9[4]	15.8[4]	19.3[5]	20.6[5]	15.9[4]	17,536	20,882
First Omaha Fix Inc	—	—	—	—	—	11.1[3]	-4.7[3]	20.4[2]	0.9[5]	9.5[2]	10.0[4]	7.1[4]	13,300	14,074
First Omaha S-I Fix	—	—	—	—	—	6.4[3]	-1.3[4]	12.7[1]	3.4[5]	6.7[2]	7.5[2]	5.5[2]	12,438	13,055
First Omaha Small Cap Val	—	—	—	—	—	—	—	—	—	21.8[4]	—	—	—	—
FL Hough ST	—	—	—	—	—	—	1.2[1]	7.3[4]	4.0[2]	4.9[4]	5.4[4]	—	11,710	—
FL Street Bond	—	—	—	—	—	—	—	—	—	—	—	—	—	—
FL Street Growth	—	—	—	—	—	—	—	—	—	—	—	—	—	—
Flex-Fund Highlands Gro	-5.8[5]	10.2[5]	4.3[1]	21.5[5]	6.4[4]	7.2[4]	-0.7[3]	24.6[4]	9.1[5]	29.3[2]	20.7[4]	13.3[5]	17,574	18,708
Flex-Fund Muirfield	—	14.0[5]	2.3[1]	29.8[2]	6.9[4]	8.1[4]	2.7[1]	25.8[4]	6.0[5]	18.6[5]	16.5[5]	11.9[5]	15,814	17,556
Flex-Fund Tot Ret Util	—	—	—	—	—	—	—	—	13.3[3]	28.7[1]	—	—	—	—
Flex-Fund US Gov Bond	2.8[5]	8.7[5]	8.3[3]	15.3[3]	3.3[5]	8.3[4]	-1.0[1]	18.3[2]	0.2[5]	7.8[4]	8.5[4]	6.5[4]	12,773	13,691
Flex-Partners Int'l Eqty†	—	—	—	—	—	—	—	—	—	—	—	—	—	—
FMC Select Fund	—	—	—	—	—	—	—	—	20.2[3]	34.1[1]	—	—	—	—
FMI Focus	—	—	—	—	—	—	—	—	—	69.7[1]	—	—	—	—
Focus Trust	—	—	—	—	—	—	—	—	17.1[4]	29.1[2]	—	—	—	—
Fontaine Cap App	—	—	6.1[1]	11.8[5]	-3.9[5]	14.1[4]	2.3[2]	15.5[5]	15.0[4]	-27.3[5]	-1.2[5]	2.4[5]	9,654	11,272

See Chapter 3 for explanation of symbols

Stock and bond funds — comprehensive summary *continued*
Arranged in alphabetical order

Total Net Assets $Million		NAV per share		1997 per share distributions		Yield %	Risk Analysis				% Distribution of Portfolio 12/31/97			Objective	No-Load Fund
December 31 1996	1997	December 31 1996	1997	Income	Capital gains	12/31/97	beta	R^2	Std. Dev.	Sharpe Ratio	Stocks	Bonds	Cash		
21.7	20.5	10.61	10.91	0.48	0.04	4.4	0.18	0.23	4.09	C	0	91	9	tax-free	Fidelity Spart AZ Muni
481.9	1,209.7	11.77	12.30	0.59	0.00	4.8	0.20	0.25	4.47	A	0	100	0	tax-free	Fidelity Spart CA Muni Inc
330.1	344.1	11.13	11.45	0.56	0.11	4.8	0.18	0.26	3.97	B	0	97	3	tax-free	Fidelity Spart CT Muni
—	21.6	—	25.19	0.07	0.00	—	—	—	—	—	97	0	3	growth	Fidelity Spart Extd Market Idx†
392.7	419.0	11.12	11.48	0.54	0.05	4.7	0.19	0.25	4.27	B	0	95	5	tax-free	Fidelity Spart FL Muni
442.5	593.7	9.99	10.17	0.68	0.00	6.7	0.14	0.26	3.15	A	0	97	3	fix-inc	Fidelity Spart GNMA
276.9	279.8	10.20	10.46	0.64	0.00	6.2	0.17	0.22	4.05	C	0	100	0	fix-inc	Fidelity Spart Gov Inc
1,717.3	2,446.9	12.54	13.03	1.11	0.31	8.4	0.24	0.41	4.18	A	0	95	5	fix-inc	Fidelity Spart Hi Inc
330.4	331.4	11.89	12.41	0.58	0.00	4.7	0.20	0.23	4.57	B	0	99	1	tax-free	Fidelity Spart Insur Muni Inc‡
—	21.3	—	24.87	0.06	0.00	—	—	—	—	—	99	0	1	int'l	Fidelity Spart Int'l Idx†
211.3	196.8	10.23	10.54	0.49	0.00	4.6	0.15	0.29	3.02	A	0	99	1	tax-free	Fidelity Spart Inter Muni
359.9	658.3	10.11	10.37	0.65	0.00	6.2	0.18	0.25	4.02	C	0	93	7	fix-inc	Fidelity Spart Inv Grd
712.9	758.1	9.74	9.78	0.64	0.00	6.6	0.12	0.24	2.64	B	0	97	3	fix-inc	Fidelity Spart Ltd Mat Gov
1,138.1	1,210.2	11.46	11.90	0.60	0.00	5.0	0.17	0.21	4.23	B	0	97	3	tax-free	Fidelity Spart MA Muni Inc
1,597.5	3,869.7	53.42	68.50	0.97	1.38	1.4	1.00	1.00	11.11	B	100	0	0	gr-inc	Fidelity Spart Market Idx
45.4	39.4	10.03	10.43	0.46	0.00	4.4	0.19	0.26	4.03	B	0	100	0	tax-free	Fidelity Spart MD Muni Inc
452.7	456.2	11.30	11.64	0.57	0.09	4.9	0.17	0.22	4.17	D	0	98	2	tax-free	Fidelity Spart MI Muni Inc
293.7	295.8	10.94	11.33	0.55	0.00	4.9	0.16	0.25	3.67	B	0	97	3	tax-free	Fidelity Spart MN Muni In
1,796.2	2,347.1	12.27	12.68	0.61	0.08	4.8	0.17	0.23	4.07	B	0	98	2	tax-free	Fidelity Spart Muni In
350.9	363.7	11.16	11.44	0.56	0.07	4.9	0.16	0.26	3.42	B	0	98	2	tax-free	Fidelity Spart NJ Muni Inc
55.6	53.9	9.85	10.18	0.45	0.00	4.4	0.15	0.28	3.13	A	0	94	6	tax-free	Fidelity Spart NY Inter Muni Inc‡
313.7	314.0	10.62	11.11	0.54	0.00	4.8	0.19	0.23	4.47	A	0	97	3	tax-free	Fidelity Spart NY Muni Inc‡
381.1	387.8	11.43	11.72	0.55	0.12	4.7	0.18	0.26	3.89	C	0	96	4	tax-free	Fidelity Spart OH Muni Inc
270.5	263.6	10.49	10.81	0.50	0.03	4.6	0.17	0.25	3.85	B	0	97	3	tax-free	Fidelity Spart PA Muni Inc
71.8	75.5	9.38	9.40	0.58	0.00	6.2	0.08	0.20	2.06	B	0	98	2	fix-inc	Fidelity Spart S-I Gov
737.2	699.5	10.00	10.11	0.42	0.00	4.2	0.07	0.31	1.44	A	0	99	1	tax-free	Fidelity Spart S-I Muni
319.8	284.1	9.05	9.04	0.58	0.00	6.5	0.06	0.22	1.38	B	0	98	2	fix-inc	Fidelity Spart ST Bd
—	20.0	—	25.72	0.08	0.00	—	—	—	—	—	97	0	3	growth	Fidelity Spart Total Mkt Idx†
995.6	875.3	8.72	8.70	0.54	0.00	6.3	0.06	0.25	1.41	C	0	98	2	fix-inc	Fidelity ST Bond
1,601.9	1,895.5	23.85	27.13	0.33	3.32	1.1	0.95	0.70	12.66	C	97	0	3	growth	Fidelity Stk Selector
9.3	12.6	9.60	9.52	0.70	0.00	7.4	—	—	—	—	0	98	2	fix-inc	Fidelity Target Timeline 1999
8.0	11.3	9.55	9.62	0.68	0.00	7.1	—	—	—	—	0	97	3	fix-inc	Fidelity Target Timeline 2001
10.7	15.7	9.47	9.75	0.64	0.00	6.6	—	—	—	—	0	98	2	fix-inc	Fidelity Target Timeline 2003
35.5	82.9	10.33	11.56	0.00	0.61	0.0	—	—	—	—	98	0	2	agg gr	Fidelity TechnoQuant Gro
1,333.9	1,428.0	56.81	54.10	0.05	7.19	0.1	1.00	0.51	15.52	F	99	0	1	agg gr	Fidelity Trend
3.8	6.1	12.56	13.68	0.18	0.80	1.3	—	—	—	—	95	0	5	int'l	Fidelity UK
1,267.9	1,708.7	16.91	19.46	0.44	2.20	2.0	0.60	0.54	9.13	B	84	0	16	income	Fidelity Utilities
7,080.1	7,913.8	51.54	54.04	0.48	7.95	0.8	0.73	0.65	9.99	D	94	0	6	growth	Fidelity Value
925.5	1,145.3	15.39	15.95	0.11	1.16	0.6	0.67	0.50	10.45	D	83	0	17	global	Fidelity Worldwide
43.6	52.0	20.73	22.66	0.01	3.86	0.0	0.65	0.49	10.32	C	94	0	6	growth	Fiduciary Cap Growth SC
171.4	268.9	18.30	19.33	0.00	4.10	0.0	0.82	0.72	10.75	A	97	1	2	agg gr	First Eagle America
32.1	37.4	15.04	15.45	0.00	0.97	0.0	0.52	0.31	10.17	B	77	1	22	int'l	First Eagle Int'l
55.4	108.9	10.97	11.18	0.55	0.00	4.9	0.12	0.22	2.86	C	0	95	5	tax-free	First Hawaii Muni Bd
3.7	21.1	10.45	11.55	0.36	0.07	3.2	—	—	—	—	52	39	9	income	First Omaha Balanced
256.2	287.3	13.51	14.72	0.28	1.05	1.9	0.63	0.79	7.89	D	86	0	14	gr-inc	First Omaha Eqty
80.9	80.0	10.11	10.44	0.59	0.00	5.7	0.23	0.24	5.16	D	0	94	6	fix-inc	First Omaha Fix Inc
21.1	19.5	9.87	9.96	0.55	0.00	5.6	0.12	0.26	2.67	D	0	83	17	fix-inc	First Omaha S-I Fix
3.8	12.8	10.65	12.30	0.18	0.46	1.4	—	—	—	—	87	0	13	growth	First Omaha Small Cap Val
20.6	26.5	10.01	10.07	0.42	0.00	4.2	0.05	0.26	1.03	D	0	87	13	tax-free	FL Hough ST
—	8.6	—	9.96	0.26	0.00	—	—	—	—	—	0	91	9	fix-inc	FL Street Bond
—	2.1	—	10.05	0.02	0.03	—	—	—	—	—	79	12	9	growth	FL Street Gro
24.3	29.0	16.41	18.55	0.06	2.59	0.3	0.88	0.92	10.24	D	98	0	2	growth	Flex-Fund Highlands Gro
106.4	111.2	5.47	5.47	0.11	0.91	1.7	0.90	0.75	11.42	F	38	0	62	gr-inc	Flex-Fund Muirfield
4.9	7.6	14.98	17.72	0.24	1.25	1.3	—	—	—	—	97	0	3	income	Flex-Fund Tot Ret Util
17.7	16.8	20.64	21.19	1.00	0.00	4.7	0.17	0.14	4.94	F	0	91	9	fix-inc	Flex-Fund US Gov Bond
—	12.2	—	12.18	0.00	0.00	—	—	—	—	—	92	0	8	int'l	Flex-Partners Int'l Eqty†
52.2	83.4	13.57	16.99	0.15	0.99	0.9	—	—	—	—	82	13	5	agg gr	FMC Select Fund
0.1	8.9	10.23	14.77	0.00	2.38	0.0	—	—	—	—	113	0	-13	growth	FMI Focus
7.3	8.1	13.01	16.32	0.00	0.47	0.0	—	—	—	—	95	0	5	growth	Focus Trust
6.4	4.0	9.37	6.71	0.10	0.00	1.5	0.52	0.08	19.84	F	55	36	9	agg gr	Fontaine Cap App

Arranged in alphabetical order

No-Load Fund	1988	1989	1990	1991	1992	1993	1994	1995	1996	1997	Annualized 3 yrs.	Annualized 5 yrs.	What $10,000 grew to after 3 yrs.	What $10,000 grew to after 5 yrs.
Fontaine Glob Gro	—	—	—	—	—	13.4 [5]	-0.4 [2]	14.0 [3]	37.1 [1]	-44.9 [5]	-4.9 [5]	-0.5 [5]	8,613	9,731
Fontaine Glob Inc	—	—	—	—	—	20.5 [1]	1.5 [1]	12.6 [1]	15.2 [1]	-27.3 [5]	-1.9 [5]	2.9 [5]	9,436	11,543
Founders Balanced	11.1 [4]	25.3 [1]	-5.0 [4]	22.6 [4]	5.2 [5]	21.8 [1]	-1.9 [3]	29.3 [2]	24.9 [1]	16.9 [4]	23.6 [1]	17.7 [1]	18,874	22,552
Founders Blue Chip	10.1 [5]	35.6 [1]	0.4 [2]	28.3 [3]	-0.5 [5]	14.5 [2]	0.5 [3]	29.1 [3]	24.4 [1]	19.0 [5]	24.1 [4]	17.1 [3]	19,116	21,997
Founders Discovery SC	—	—	13.2 [1]	62.5 [2]	15.2 [2]	10.8 [4]	-7.7 [5]	31.3 [3]	21.2 [2]	11.9 [4]	21.2 [4]	12.7 [4]	17,814	18,219
Founders Frontier SC	29.2 [1]	44.3 [1]	-7.5 [3]	49.3 [3]	8.9 [3]	16.5 [3]	-2.8 [3]	37.0 [2]	14.3 [4]	6.2 [5]	18.5 [4]	13.5 [4]	16,633	18,834
Founders Gov Sec	—	13.3 [2]	4.4 [5]	14.7 [4]	5.3 [5]	9.3 [3]	-7.5 [5]	11.1 [5]	2.3 [5]	7.9 [4]	7.0 [5]	4.4 [5]	12,262	12,397
Founders Growth	4.8 [5]	41.7 [1]	-10.6 [4]	47.4 [3]	4.3 [4]	25.5 [1]	-3.3 [4]	45.6 [1]	16.6 [4]	26.5 [2]	29.0 [1]	21.1 [1]	21,479	26,067
Founders Int'l Equity	—	—	—	—	—	—	—	—	18.6 [2]	16.1 [1]	—	—	—	—
Founders Passport	—	—	—	—	—	—	-10.4 [5]	24.4 [1]	20.0 [2]	1.7 [3]	14.9 [1]	—	15,177	—
Founders Special	13.2 [3]	39.2 [1]	-10.4 [4]	63.7 [1]	8.3 [3]	16.0 [3]	-4.9 [4]	25.7 [4]	15.3 [4]	16.4 [4]	19.1 [4]	13.2 [4]	16,875	18,615
Founders Worldwide Gr	—	—	6.7 [1]	34.8 [1]	1.5 [3]	29.9 [2]	-2.2 [3]	20.6 [1]	14.0 [3]	10.5 [3]	15.0 [4]	14.1 [2]	15,196	19,305
Fountainhead Spec Val	—	—	—	—	—	—	—	—	—	36.7 [1]	—	—	—	—
Fremont Bond	—	—	—	—	—	—	-4.0 [4]	21.3 [1]	5.2 [1]	9.7 [1]	11.9 [1]	—	13,994	—
Fremont CA Inter	—	—	—	10.7 [2]	7.3 [3]	10.0 [3]	-4.9 [5]	14.9 [1]	4.1 [2]	7.3 [3]	8.6 [2]	6.1 [3]	12,822	13,411
Fremont Emg Mkts	—	—	—	—	—	—	—	—	—	10.4 [2]	—	—	—	—
Fremont Global	—	15.9 [3]	-1.8 [2]	19.3 [1]	4.7 [2]	19.6 [4]	-4.2 [3]	19.3 [2]	14.0 [3]	9.9 [4]	14.3 [4]	11.4 [3]	14,950	17,129
Fremont Growth	—	—	—	—	—	6.4 [4]	0.4 [3]	33.6 [2]	25.1 [3]	29.0 [2]	29.2 [2]	18.2 [2]	21,553	23,029
Fremont Int'l Gro	—	—	—	—	—	—	—	7.2 [4]	13.0 [3]	-8.4 [4]	3.5 [4]	—	11,100	—
Fremont Int'l Sm Cap	—	—	—	—	—	—	—	2.8 [4]	12.2 [3]	-26.5 [5]	-5.4 [5]	—	8,469	—
Fremont Real Estate	—	—	—	—	—	—	—	—	—	—	—	—	—	—
Fremont Select	—	—	—	—	—	—	—	—	—	—	—	—	—	—
Fremont US Micro Cap SC	—	—	—	—	—	—	—	54.0 [1]	48.7 [1]	7.0 [5]	34.8 [1]	—	24,500	—
Fremont US Sm Cap SC	—	—	—	—	—	—	—	—	—	—	—	—	—	—
FTI Global Bond	—	—	—	—	—	—	—	—	4.9 [2]	-0.2 [5]	—	—	—	—
FTI Int'l Bond	—	—	—	—	—	—	—	—	3.6 [3]	-6.1 [5]	—	—	—	—
FTI Int'l Eqty	—	—	—	—	—	—	—	—	12.8 [3]	13.3 [1]	—	—	—	—
FTI Small Cap Eqty SC	—	—	—	—	—	—	—	—	23.4 [2]	17.8 [3]	—	—	—	—
Fundamental CA Muni	12.1 [2]	8.0 [5]	4.4 [5]	8.8 [5]	7.2 [5]	16.8 [1]	-19.9 [5]	32.0 [1]	-8.0 [5]	11.3 [1]	10.6 [2]	4.8 [5]	13,520	12,649
Fundamental HY Muni	3.2 [5]	5.9 [5]	-5.9 [5]	10.2 [5]	6.3 [5]	5.1 [5]	-12.9 [5]	25.7 [1]	4.1 [2]	15.7 [1]	14.8 [1]	6.7 [4]	15,129	13,845
Fundamental NY Muni	11.2 [3]	9.6 [3]	-0.9 [5]	15.8 [1]	11.9 [1]	12.6 [4]	-20.5 [5]	15.9 [4]	-7.7 [5]	1.5 [5]	2.8 [5]	-0.6 [5]	10,851	9,716
Fundamental US Gov Strat	—	—	—	—	—	8.2 [5]	-25.6 [5]	15.4 [5]	5.0 [2]	5.5 [5]	8.5 [5]	0.6 [5]	12,785	10,293
FundMngr Agg Gro†	11.8 [4]	20.9 [4]	-6.7 [3]	43.9 [3]	0.6 [5]	14.4 [4]	-1.2 [3]	24.8 [4]	16.6 [4]	16.7 [4]	19.3 [4]	13.9 [4]	16,964	19,178
FundMngr Bond†	9.1 [1]	7.7 [5]	4.2 [5]	14.7 [4]	7.3 [2]	10.6 [2]	-3.9 [4]	16.3 [3]	2.7 [4]	7.8 [4]	8.8 [4]	6.5 [4]	12,881	13,686
FundMngr Gro & Inc†	19.5 [2]	18.4 [4]	-7.7 [4]	22.6 [4]	9.9 [2]	12.7 [3]	-0.1 [3]	32.6 [2]	15.6 [5]	25.3 [4]	24.3 [4]	16.7 [4]	19,194	21,603
FundMngr Growth†	14.4 [4]	17.7 [4]	-5.5 [3]	22.6 [5]	14.4 [2]	12.5 [3]	-0.5 [3]	28.2 [4]	19.3 [3]	27.5 [3]	24.9 [3]	16.9 [3]	19,492	21,828
FundMngr Mgd Tot Ret†	—	14.2 [5]	0.6 [2]	18.8 [5]	6.3 [4]	9.0 [4]	-1.2 [4]	19.3 [5]	8.3 [5]	13.5 [5]	13.6 [5]	9.6 [5]	14,653	15,788
Gabelli ABC	—	—	—	—	—	—	4.5 [1]	11.1 [5]	7.9 [5]	12.8 [5]	10.6 [5]	—	13,513	—
Gabelli Asset	31.1 [1]	26.2 [2]	-5.0 [3]	18.1 [5]	14.9 [2]	21.8 [1]	-0.1 [3]	24.9 [4]	13.4 [5]	38.1 [1]	25.1 [3]	18.9 [2]	19,555	23,795
Gabelli Eqty Inc	—	—	—	—	—	17.9 [1]	1.1 [2]	28.3 [2]	17.9 [2]	27.9 [1]	24.6 [1]	18.2 [1]	19,341	23,046
Gabelli Glbl Conv Sec	—	—	—	—	—	—	—	12.6 [4]	5.5 [5]	2.8 [5]	6.9 [5]	—	12,212	—
Gabelli Glbl Telecomm	—	—	—	—	—	—	-3.7 [3]	16.2 [3]	9.0 [5]	31.9 [1]	18.6 [3]	—	16,695	—
Gabelli Gold	—	—	—	—	—	—	—	3.1 [4]	8.0 [3]	-51.9 [4]	-18.8 [2]	—	5,358	—
Gabelli Growth	39.2 [1]	40.1 [1]	-2.0 [2]	34.3 [3]	4.5 [5]	11.3 [3]	-3.4 [4]	32.7 [2]	19.4 [3]	42.6 [1]	31.2 [1]	19.4 [2]	22,598	24,297
Gabelli Glbl Couch Potato	—	—	—	—	—	—	—	17.9 [1]	12.5 [3]	41.7 [1]	23.4 [1]	—	18,794	—
Gabelli Int'l Growth	—	—	—	—	—	—	—	—	22.1 [2]	7.3 [2]	—	—	—	—
Gabelli Sm Cap Gro SC	—	—	—	—	20.3 [1]	22.8 [1]	-2.9 [4]	25.2 [4]	12.0 [4]	36.5 [1]	24.1 [3]	17.9 [2]	19,128	22,806
Galaxy II Lg Co Idx	—	—	—	29.1 [3]	7.1 [4]	9.6 [4]	1.0 [2]	37.1 [1]	22.5 [2]	32.8 [1]	30.7 [1]	19.8 [2]	22,311	24,690
Galaxy II Sm Co Idx SC	—	—	—	45.5 [3]	12.2 [2]	11.3 [4]	-3.7 [4]	33.1 [3]	19.7 [3]	23.6 [3]	25.3 [2]	16.1 [3]	19,683	21,109
Galaxy II US Trsy Idx	—	—	—	—	6.8 [1]	10.2 [4]	-3.7 [3]	18.1 [3]	2.2 [4]	9.3 [3]	9.7 [4]	7.0 [4]	13,185	13,997
Galaxy II Util Idx	—	—	—	—	—	—	-8.6 [5]	37.1 [1]	3.5 [5]	28.5 [1]	22.2 [2]	—	18,227	—
Gateway Cincinnati	—	—	—	—	—	—	—	35.3 [2]	20.0 [3]	29.0 [2]	27.9 [2]	—	20,938	—
Gateway Idx Plus	19.8 [2]	19.4 [3]	10.3 [1]	17.8 [5]	5.1 [4]	7.4 [5]	5.6 [1]	11.0 [5]	10.5 [5]	12.3 [5]	11.3 [5]	9.3 [5]	13,780	15,628
Gateway MidCap Idx	—	—	—	—	—	5.2 [5]	-5.1 [5]	25.7 [4]	15.3 [4]	25.0 [3]	21.9 [4]	12.6 [5]	18,123	18,086
Gateway Sm Cap Idx SC	—	—	—	—	—	—	-6.0 [5]	21.8 [5]	17.0 [3]	20.6 [3]	19.8 [4]	—	17,199	—
General Securities	14.0 [3]	20.5 [4]	-0.2 [5]	35.8 [4]	6.1 [4]	6.2 [5]	5.4 [1]	27.9 [4]	20.4 [3]	13.4 [4]	20.4 [4]	14.3 [4]	17,459	19,540
Gintel	32.7 [1]	20.6 [4]	-6.7 [4]	15.6 [5]	24.7 [1]	2.0 [5]	-16.5 [5]	31.0 [3]	31.0 [1]	31.5 [2]	31.2 [1]	14.0 [4]	22,560	19,214
Globalt Growth	—	—	—	—	—	—	—	—	20.0 [3]	27.8 [3]	—	—	—	—
GMO: Pelican	—	—	-8.8 [4]	24.9 [4]	12.7 [2]	20.1 [1]	3.1 [2]	29.8 [3]	20.7 [3]	26.5 [3]	25.6 [3]	19.7 [2]	19,825	24,544
Gov Street AL TF	—	—	—	—	—	—	-3.2 [1]	12.4 [5]	3.8 [3]	6.3 [5]	7.4 [5]	—	12,404	—

See Chapter 3 for explanation of symbols

Total Net Assets $Million		NAV per share		1997 per share distributions		Yield %	Risk Analysis				% Distribution of Portfolio				
December 31		December 31			Capital				Std.	Sharpe	12/31/97				
1996	1997	1996	1997	Income	gains	12/31/97	beta	R^2	Dev.	Ratio	Stocks	Bonds	Cash	Objective	No-Load Fund
4.8	2.0	12.50	6.89	0.00	0.00	0.0	0.45	0.04	23.19	F	74	13	13	global	Fontaine Glob Gro
2.8	1.1	10.89	7.47	0.48	0.00	6.4	0.24	0.04	12.52	F	57	38	5	fix-inc	Fontaine Glob Inc
394.0	937.2	10.61	11.35	0.30	0.73	2.5	0.52	0.77	6.52	A	58	41	1	income	Founders Balanced
535.9	543.3	7.23	6.92	0.13	1.56	1.6	0.68	0.73	8.86	C	72	28	0	gr-inc	Founders Blue Chip
250.7	247.3	24.22	23.45	0.00	3.53	0.0	1.06	0.32	20.92	D	89	0	11	agg gr	Founders Discovery SC
108.2	222.7	32.34	27.99	0.00	6.10	0.0	0.73	0.30	14.71	D	90	10	0	agg gr	Founders Frontier SC
15.0	12.7	9.04	9.28	0.45	0.00	4.9	0.17	0.29	3.56	F	0	98	2	fix-inc	Founders Gov Sec
1,032.1	1,758.3	15.87	17.28	0.07	2.68	0.4	1.03	0.72	13.56	A	87	0	13	agg gr	Founders Growth
10.1	15.6	11.86	12.05	0.00	1.69	0.0	—	—	—	—	85	0	15	int'l	Founders Int'l Equity.
179.0	123.3	13.91	13.64	0.03	0.48	0.2	0.40	0.20	9.80	A	94	0	6	int'l	Founders Passport
364.0	320.3	7.66	7.72	0.00	1.16	0.0	0.89	0.50	13.93	D	84	0	16	agg gr	Founders Special
342.0	308.9	21.79	21.11	0.04	2.88	0.1	0.59	0.43	9.97	D	91	0	9	global	Founders Worldwide Gr
0.1	3.3	10.00	13.52	0.00	0.14	0.0	—	—	—	—	—	—	—	growth	Fountainhead Spec Val
72.7	109.4	9.95	10.13	0.63	0.11	6.2	0.21	0.25	4.66	B	0	79	21	fix-inc	Fremont Bond
59.3	64.8	10.84	11.09	0.51	0.00	4.6	0.13	0.20	3.31	B	0	93	7	tax-free	Fremont CA Inter
4.1	13.8	9.77	9.46	0.00	0.32	0.0	—	—	—	—	71	0	29	int'l	Fremont Emg Mkts
597.0	661.6	13.77	14.04	0.48	0.61	3.2	0.63	0.77	7.87	C	66	28	6	global	Fremont Global
96.4	155.5	12.76	15.43	0.15	0.82	1.0	0.91	0.89	10.76	B	95	0	5	growth	Fremont Growth
38.2	36.3	11.10	10.06	0.00	0.11	0.0	0.82	0.43	13.46	D	71	0	29	int'l	Fremont Int'l Gro
9.7	6.5	9.93	6.85	0.37	0.11	5.4	0.52	0.18	13.34	F	100	0	0	int'l	Fremont Int'l Sm Cap
—	1.0	—	10.00	—	—	—	—	—	—	—	—	—	—	sector	Fremont Real Estate
—	5.0	—	10.00	—	—	—	—	—	—	—	—	—	—	agg gr	Fremont Select
142.9	166.9	21.50	20.28	0.00	2.76	0.0	0.80	0.24	18.27	A	82	0	18	agg gr	Fremont US Micro Cap SC
—	5.6	—	9.53	0.00	0.00	—	—	—	—	—	88	0	12	agg gr	Fremont US Sm Cap SC
1.2	1.4	9.92	9.61	0.29	0.00	3.0	—	—	—	—	0	97	3	fix-inc	FTI Global Bond
5.1	7.3	9.97	9.22	0.14	0.00	1.6	—	—	—	—	0	90	10	fix-inc	FTI Int'l Bond
12.4	43.5	11.10	12.46	0.12	0.00	1.0	—	—	—	—	95	0	5	int'l	FTI Int'l Eqty
20.4	42.3	12.34	14.17	0.00	0.35	0.0	—	—	—	—	97	0	3	agg gr	FTI Small Cap Eqty SC
16.3	8.9	7.79	8.27	0.38	0.00	4.6	0.37	0.17	10.01	F	0	100	0	tax-free	Fundamental CA Muni
1.9	1.8	6.86	7.53	0.37	0.00	4.9	0.24	0.18	6.27	A	0	100	0	tax-free	Fundamental HY Muni
197.1	77.1	0.87	0.86	0.02	0.00	2.6	0.17	0.11	5.77	F	0	100	0	tax-free	Fundamental NY Muni
13.2	10.0	1.43	1.41	0.09	0.00	6.7	0.18	0.12	5.62	F	0	100	0	fix-inc	Fundamental US Gov Strat
39.3	38.0	17.30	17.84	0.06	1.92	0.4	0.83	0.60	11.90	C	86	2	12	agg gr	FundMngr Agg Gro†
69.4	50.6	10.15	10.37	0.54	0.00	5.2	0.19	0.29	3.84	D	4	90	6	fix-inc	FundMngr Bond†
31.1	40.9	17.95	19.03	0.40	2.33	2.1	0.84	0.92	9.72	D	88	5	7	gr-inc	FundMngr Gro & Inc†
27.2	39.6	16.24	17.97	0.29	1.83	1.6	0.83	0.94	9.50	B	90	1	9	growth	FundMngr Growth†
12.4	10.7	11.85	12.12	0.31	0.85	2.6	0.45	0.88	5.36	F	40	46	14	gr-inc	FundMngr Mgd Tot Ret†
28.2	35.2	9.84	10.23	0.08	0.77	0.8	0.07	0.10	2.33	B	56	3	41	growth	Gabelli ABC
1,080.6	1,334.2	26.42	31.85	0.07	4.54	0.2	0.74	0.75	9.56	B	92	0	8	growth	Gabelli Asset
60.3	76.3	14.16	16.12	0.25	1.67	1.5	0.60	0.79	7.60	A	89	6	5	income	Gabelli Eqty Inc
13.7	9.4	10.18	9.39	0.12	0.93	1.3	0.49	0.47	7.91	F	31	68	1	global	Gabelli Glbl Conv Sec
108.6	117.9	11.28	13.32	0.00	1.55	0.0	0.76	0.57	11.12	C	91	1	8	global	Gabelli Glbl Telecomm
17.1	8.1	12.32	5.87	0.06	0.00	1.0	0.12	0.00	30.71	B	94	0	6	prec met	Gabelli Gold
609.4	951.5	24.14	28.63	0.00	5.79	0.0	1.05	0.88	12.57	B	97	0	3	growth	Gabelli Growth
31.8	40.6	11.75	14.28	0.00	2.37	0.0	0.76	0.45	12.55	A	93	3	4	global	Gabelli Glbl Couch Potato
12.8	18.1	13.42	14.40	0.00	0.00	0.0	—	—	—	—	98	2	0	int'l	Gabelli Int'l Growth
216.7	293.0	18.53	21.58	0.00	3.66	0.0	0.54	0.33	10.44	A	91	0	9	agg gr	Gabelli Sm Cap Gro SC
352.5	547.1	22.52	28.07	0.42	1.36	1.5	1.00	1.00	11.08	B	87	0	13	gr-inc	Galaxy II Lg Co Idx
326.3	379.2	23.38	18.73	0.33	9.49	1.2	0.71	0.51	11.16	A	84	0	16	agg gr	Galaxy II Sm Co Idx SC
114.3	115.5	10.23	10.51	0.63	0.00	6.0	0.18	0.23	4.25	D	0	97	3	fix-inc	Galaxy II US Trsy Idx
50.6	55.2	11.88	13.64	0.51	0.91	3.7	0.56	0.34	10.64	D	100	0	0	income	Galaxy II Util Idx
9.0	17.5	15.40	18.98	0.07	0.81	0.4	0.61	0.59	8.88	A	99	0	1	growth	Gateway Cincinnati
194.0	254.9	18.48	18.85	0.18	1.73	0.9	0.28	0.69	3.78	F	97	-5	8	gr-inc	Gateway Idx Plus
6.3	8.0	12.78	15.13	0.00	0.85	0.0	0.71	0.61	10.17	D	97	0	3	growth	Gateway MidCap Idx
10.9	15.8	12.06	13.48	0.00	1.07	0.0	0.64	0.39	11.34	C	98	0	2	agg gr	Gateway Sm Cap Idx SC
42.4	49.7	16.22	16.59	0.16	1.61	1.0	0.73	0.64	10.23	B	79	0	21	agg gr	General Securities
147.9	178.6	18.10	21.78	0.16	1.82	0.7	0.49	0.25	10.89	A	92	0	8	growth	Gintel
4.1	8.8	12.60	14.70	0.01	1.39	0.1	—	—	—	—	96	0	4	growth	Globalt Growth
201.5	225.5	15.82	16.92	0.40	2.58	2.1	0.75	0.85	9.11	B	82	12	6	growth	GMO: Pelican
16.7	19.4	10.32	10.52	0.44	0.00	4.2	—	—	—	—	0	100	0	tax-free	Gov Street AL TF

Arranged in alphabetical order

No-Load Fund	Total return percent with quintile ranks by objective										Annualized		What $10,000 grew to after	
	1988	1989	1990	1991	1992	1993	1994	1995	1996	1997	3 yrs.	5 yrs.	3 yrs.	5 yrs.
Govt Street Bond	—	—	—	—	6.4[4]	8.8[3]	-2.7[3]	15.5[4]	3.7[3]	7.8[4]	8.9[4]	6.5[4]	12,906	13,668
Govt Street Equity	—	—	—	—	6.0[4]	3.2[5]	-2.8[4]	27.4[4]	21.5[2]	27.8[3]	25.6[3]	14.7[4]	19,789	19,845
Gradison Estab Value	15.1[4]	16.1[4]	-8.1[4]	22.2[4]	10.2[2]	22.6[1]	0.3[3]	26.4[4]	18.9[4]	22.6[4]	22.6[4]	17.8[3]	18,430	22,663
Gradison Gro & Inc	—	—	—	—	—	—	—	—	18.8[4]	30.1[2]	—	—	—	—
Gradison International	—	—	—	—	—	—	—	—	5.9[5]	5.1[3]	—	—	—	—
Gradison Oppty Value SC	23.6[1]	23.1[4]	-13.1[4]	35.9[4]	14.3[2]	11.1[4]	-2.2[3]	26.7[4]	19.5[3]	31.1[1]	25.7[2]	16.6[3]	19,857	21,576
Green Cent Balanced	—	—	—	—	—	-0.7[5]	-4.1[4]	18.3[5]	25.0[1]	19.0[3]	20.7[3]	10.9[5]	17,595	16,762
Green Cent Equity	—	—	—	—	—	—	—	—	21.3[3]	35.7[1]	—	—	—	—
Greenspring	16.0[3]	10.6[5]	-6.5[3]	19.3[5]	16.5[1]	14.6[2]	2.9[1]	18.7[5]	22.6[2]	23.9[4]	21.7[4]	16.3[4]	18,029	21,260
Guinness Flt Asia Blue Chip	—	—	—	—	—	—	—	—	—	-37.7[5]	—	—	—	—
Guinness Flt Asia Small Cap	—	—	—	—	—	—	—	—	—	-30.8[5]	—	—	—	—
Guinness Flt China & HK	—	—	—	—	—	—	—	20.5[1]	34.4[1]	-20.3[5]	8.9[3]	—	12,901	—
Guinness Flt Glob Gov	—	—	—	—	—	—	—	14.5[5]	6.2[2]	2.9[5]	7.8[5]	—	12,510	
Guinness Flt Mainland China	—	—	—	—	—	—	—	—	—	—	—	—	—	—
Harbor Bond	7.2[4]	13.7[2]	7.9[4]	19.6[1]	9.1[1]	12.4[1]	-3.8[4]	19.2[2]	4.9[2]	9.4[2]	11.0[1]	8.1[1]	13,680	14,792
Harbor Cap App	15.4[3]	24.2[3]	-1.8[2]	54.8[2]	10.0[3]	12.1[4]	3.4[2]	37.8[2]	19.9[3]	31.4[1]	29.5[1]	20.3[1]	21,718	25,173
Harbor Growth	14.3[3]	23.0[4]	-6.7[3]	50.5[3]	-6.3[5]	18.4[2]	-11.4[5]	38.2[2]	11.0[5]	20.9[3]	22.9[3]	14.2[4]	18,542	19,451
Harbor Int'l Gro	—	—	—	—	—	—	-7.7[4]	24.3[1]	32.0[1]	3.6[3]	19.3[1]	—	16,990	—
Harbor Int'l II	—	—	—	—	—	—	—	—	—	9.7[2]	—	—	—	—
Harbor Int'l‡	37.7[1]	36.9[1]	-9.8[3]	21.5[1]	-0.2[2]	45.4[1]	5.4[1]	16.1[1]	20.1[2]	15.5[1]	17.2[1]	19.8[1]	16,100	24,673
Harbor Short Dur	—	—	—	—	—	—	2.7[1]	7.4[5]	6.3[1]	6.3[3]	6.7[4]	5.4[3]	12,134	13,010
Harbor Value	19.8[2]	29.8[1]	-5.7[3]	21.3[4]	7.4[3]	8.4[4]	0.7[2]	35.4[2]	20.0[3]	31.2[2]	28.7[2]	18.4[3]	21,318	23,271
Haven Fund	16.3[3]	20.9[4]	-2.4[2]	31.0[4]	13.1[2]	12.7[3]	-0.6[3]	26.8[4]	27.4[1]	19.1[4]	24.4[3]	16.6[3]	19,243	21,553
Heartland Hi Yld Muni	—	—	—	—	—	—	—	—	—	—	—	—	—	—
Heartland Large Cap Val	—	—	—	—	—	—	—	—	—	22.9[4]	—	—	—	—
Heartland Mid Cap Val	—	—	—	—	—	—	—	—	—	22.8[4]	—	—	—	—
Heartland Sht Dur Hi Yld Muni	—	—	—	—	—	—	—	—	—	7.4[1]	—	—	—	—
Heartland Small Cap Contra‡SC	—	—	—	—	—	—	—	—	18.9[3]	13.7[4]	—	—	—	—
Heartland US Gov	6.5[3]	11.3[2]	9.9[1]	17.0[1]	10.1[1]	17.8[1]	-9.6[5]	19.0[1]	2.0[5]	9.7[1]	10.0[1]	7.2[1]	13,314	14,173
Heartland Val Plus	—	—	—	—	—	—	-4.9[5]	24.4[5]	33.8[1]	30.6[2]	29.5[2]	—	21,731	—
Heartland Value‡SC	27.0[1]	6.6[5]	-17.1[5]	49.4[1]	42.5[1]	18.8[2]	1.7[2]	29.8[3]	21.0[3]	23.2[4]	24.6[3]	18.5[2]	19,347	23,375
Heartland WI TF	—	—	—	—	—	10.8[5]	-6.5[3]	17.8[3]	3.8[3]	8.1[5]	9.7[3]	6.5[4]	13,211	13,689
Henlopen Fund	—	—	—	—	—	29.9[1]	-2.7[4]	38.0[1]	21.4[2]	22.6[4]	27.1[2]	21.0[1]	20,540	25,945
Hennessey Balanced	—	—	—	—	—	—	—	—	—	13.0[5]	—	—	—	—
HGK Fix Inc	—	—	—	—	—	—	—	17.9[3]	2.4[4]	9.4[3]	9.7[4]	—	13,205	—
Highland Growth	—	—	—	—	—	—	—	—	—	—	—	—	—	—
Holland Balanced	—	—	—	—	—	—	—	—	16.5[2]	12.1[5]	—	—	—	—
Homestead ST Bond	—	—	—	—	6.3[2]	6.6[3]	0.1[3]	10.8[3]	5.2[2]	6.6[2]	7.5[2]	5.8[1]	12,424	13,259
Homestead ST Gov	—	—	—	—	—	—	—	—	4.5[3]	5.7[5]	—	—	—	—
Homestead Value	—	—	—	17.2[5]	11.7[2]	18.1[1]	2.5[1]	33.8[2]	17.9[4]	26.7[3]	26.0[3]	19.5[2]	19,991	24,349
Htchks & Wly Balanced	14.6[3]	17.9[4]	-0.4[3]	20.5[5]	9.4[3]	12.5[3]	0.8[2]	24.8[3]	11.7[4]	16.8[4]	17.6[4]	13.0[4]	16,276	18,457
Htchks & Wly Eq Inc	21.1[2]	23.7[3]	-18.1[5]	34.6[2]	14.0[1]	15.8[2]	-3.5[5]	34.4[2]	17.4[4]	31.2[2]	27.3[4]	18.3[3]	20,695	23,126
Htchks & Wly Glob Eqty	—	—	—	—	—	—	—	—	—	—	—	—	—	—
Htchks & Wly Int'l	—	—	—	20.3[1]	-2.7[2]	45.8[1]	-2.9[3]	19.9[1]	18.3[2]	5.3[3]	14.3[1]	16.2[1]	14,938	21,149
Htchks & Wly Low Dur	—	—	—	—	—	—	5.2[1]	12.7[1]	6.2[1]	7.6[1]	8.8[1]	—	12,878	—
Htchks & Wly Midcap	—	—	—	—	—	—	—	—	—	39.5[1]	—	—	—	—
Htchks & Wly Sm Cap SC	8.9[4]	20.5[4]	-9.0[4]	48.3[1]	13.5[2]	12.5[3]	1.1[2]	18.5[5]	14.3[5]	39.5[1]	23.6[4]	16.5[3]	18,895	21,490
Htchks & Wly ST Invest	—	—	—	—	—	—	4.4[1]	7.8[5]	6.2[1]	6.5[2]	6.8[4]	—	12,196	—
Htchks & Wly Tot Ret	—	—	—	—	—	—	—	21.3[1]	4.4[2]	10.8[1]	12.0[1]	—	14,030	—
IAA Trust Asst Alloc	7.4[5]	13.5[4]	7.9[1]	13.0[5]	6.1[4]	9.0[4]	-1.0[2]	25.3[3]	13.0[4]	17.9[4]	18.6[4]	12.5[4]	16,698	18,022
IAA Trust Growth	13.7[4]	26.2[2]	-4.1[3]	27.9[5]	2.1[5]	6.3[4]	0.3[3]	31.1[3]	22.0[2]	19.7[4]	24.2[3]	15.3[4]	19,143	20,415
IAA Trust LT Bd	—	—	—	—	—	—	—	—	—	—	—	—	—	—
IAA Trust ST Gov	—	—	—	—	—	—	—	—	—	—	—	—	—	—
IAA Trust TE Bd	10.1[4]	8.1[5]	6.7[3]	10.1[5]	8.2[4]	8.8[5]	-6.1[3]	15.9[4]	3.0[5]	9.0[3]	9.1[4]	5.8[5]	13,001	13,287
IAI Balanced	—	—	—	—	—	—	—	-1.4[3]	18.6[5]	25.7[1]	19.6[3]	12.1[4]	17,110	17,714
IAI Bond	6.4[5]	15.9[1]	7.1[3]	17.3[3]	6.8[4]	12.3[3]	-4.9[3]	16.2[4]	4.1[3]	10.8[2]	10.3[3]	7.4[3]	13,407	14,319
IAI Cap Apprec SC	—	—	—	—	—	—	—	—	—	17.8[3]	—	—	—	—
IAI Develop Countries	—	—	—	—	—	—	—	—	8.5[4]	-14.1[4]	—	—	—	—
IAI Emg Growth SC	—	—	—	—	22.4[1]	14.8[3]	0.2[2]	49.6[1]	6.9[5]	-2.9[5]	15.8[5]	12.3[5]	15,535	17,869
IAI Gov Bond	—	—	—	—	5.7[3]	8.5[1]	-2.3[5]	11.5[2]	2.9[5]	6.4[3]	6.9[4]	5.3[3]	12,206	12,939

See Chapter 3 for explanation of symbols

Total Net Assets $Million		NAV per share		1997 per share distributions		Yield % 12/31/97	Risk Analysis				% Distribution of Portfolio 12/31/97			Objective	No-Load Fund
December 31 1996	1997	December 31 1996	1997	Income	Capital gains		beta	R²	Std. Dev.	Sharpe Ratio	Stocks	Bonds	Cash		
29.3	34.4	20.82	21.06	1.34	0.00	6.3	0.13	0.21	3.09	C	0	91	9	fix-inc	Govt Street Bond
48.3	66.2	32.16	39.63	0.32	1.08	0.8	0.88	0.93	10.21	B	95	0	5	growth	Govt Street Equity
416.0	522.3	28.19	31.37	0.49	2.57	1.5	0.72	0.79	8.99	D	73	0	27	gr-inc	Gradison Estab Value
20.9	47.6	20.79	26.48	0.35	0.17	1.3	—	—	—	—	96	0	4	gr-inc	Gradison Gro & Inc
22.3	27.9	16.04	16.68	0.00	0.17	0.0	—	—	—	—	82	0	18	int'l	Gradison International
116.0	157.2	23.07	26.10	0.27	3.56	0.9	0.62	0.49	9.80	A	74	0	26	agg gr	Gradison Oppty Value SC
8.8	13.2	12.65	13.52	0.12	1.35	0.9	0.48	0.19	12.45	F	71	26	3	income	Green Cent Balanced
1.5	7.6	12.85	17.42	0.01	0.01	0.0	—	—	—	—	100	0	0	growth	Green Cent Equity
91.5	180.9	17.24	20.04	0.68	0.60	3.3	0.35	0.41	6.15	A	61	33	6	gr-inc	Greenspring
3.7	6.9	12.98	8.08	0.01	0.00	0.1	—	—	—	—	88	0	12	int'l	Guinness Flt Asia Blue Chip
50.8	109.4	14.10	9.73	0.05	0.00	0.5	—	—	—	—	94	0	6	int'l	Guinness Flt Asia Small Cap
308.2	242.8	17.71	12.91	0.20	1.09	1.4	1.61	0.41	25.93	C	96	0	4	int'l	Guinness Flt China & HK
6.5	10.0	12.72	12.37	0.58	0.11	4.7	0.09	0.06	4.22	F	0	83	17	fix-inc	Guinness Flt Glob Gov
—	16.3	—	11.79	0.02	0.00	—	—	—	—	—	36	0	64	int'l	Guinness Flt Mainland China
288.2	384.6	11.24	11.37	0.66	0.23	5.7	0.22	0.33	4.21	B	0	107	-7	fix-inc	Harbor Bond
1,681.7	2,906.3	26.33	29.47	0.07	4.85	0.2	1.22	0.74	15.90	B	95	0	5	agg gr	Harbor Cap App
111.8	109.8	12.17	12.27	0.00	2.28	0.0	0.80	0.38	14.27	C	86	0	14	agg gr	Harbor Growth
645.6	943.8	16.24	16.09	0.12	0.59	0.7	0.71	0.32	13.85	A	98	0	2	int'l	Harbor Int'l Gro
15.2	130.2	11.03	11.45	0.09	0.54	0.8	—	—	—	—	100	0	0	int'l	Harbor Int'l II
4,318.6	5,276.6	32.20	35.86	0.40	0.90	1.1	0.71	0.43	11.94	A	96	1	3	int'l	Harbor Int'l‡
177.3	165.5	8.62	8.60	0.55	0.00	6.4	0.03	0.08	1.17	B	0	103	-3	fix-inc	Harbor Short Dur
116.8	174.8	14.79	15.20	0.33	3.74	1.7	0.72	0.86	8.74	A	96	0	4	gr-inc	Harbor Value
69.3	74.8	13.53	14.46	0.09	1.52	0.6	0.68	0.63	9.52	B	92	0	8	growth	Haven Fund
0.1	30.6	—	10.45	0.65	0.03	—	—	—	—	—	0	101	-1	tax-free	Heartland Hi Yld Muni
2.4	7.7	10.50	12.30	0.10	0.48	0.9	—	—	—	—	98	0	2	growth	Heartland Large Cap Val
6.9	36.6	10.66	12.78	0.05	0.26	0.4	—	—	—	—	96	0	4	growth	Heartland Mid Cap Val
0.1	116.3	—	10.15	0.57	0.00	5.7	—	—	—	—	0	97	3	tax-free	Heartland Sht Dur Hi Yld Mun
263.0	276.6	13.40	12.64	0.05	2.52	0.3	—	—	—	—	92	4	4	agg gr	Heartland Small Cap Contra‡SC
51.5	48.6	9.54	9.85	0.58	0.00	5.9	0.21	0.20	5.15	C	0	93	7	fix-inc	Heartland US Gov
66.6	336.3	13.73	16.13	0.47	1.26	2.7	0.24	0.11	8.39	A	68	26	6	gr-inc	Heartland Val Plus
1,626.8	2,126.7	31.65	33.87	0.17	4.87	0.4	0.48	0.26	10.45	C	85	5	10	growth	Heartland Value‡SC
124.1	131.3	10.16	10.44	0.52	0.00	5.0	0.13	0.14	4.00	C	0	101	-1	tax-free	Heartland WI TF
31.2	33.2	14.89	14.80	0.00	3.31	0.0	0.88	0.27	18.63	D	96	0	4	growth	Henlopen Fund
11.3	21.5	10.85	11.83	0.26	0.16	2.2	—	—	—	—	51	49	0	income	Hennessey Balanced
13.1	13.3	10.28	10.56	0.61	0.04	5.7	0.21	0.29	4.38	D	0	84	16	fix-inc	HGK Fix Inc
—	0.5	—	10.18	0.00	0.00	—	—	—	—	—	100	0	0	growth	Highland Growth
9.3	26.7	11.98	13.17	0.26	0.00	2.0	—	—	—	—	56	35	9	income	Holland Balanced
81.1	108.6	5.15	5.18	0.29	0.00	5.7	0.06	0.18	1.53	A	0	98	2	fix-inc	Homestead ST Bond
7.7	16.1	5.05	5.07	0.26	0.00	5.1	—	—	—	—	0	99	1	fix-inc	Homestead ST Gov
232.4	367.0	20.99	25.50	0.36	0.71	1.4	0.74	0.75	9.44	C	92	0	8	gr-inc	Homestead Value
70.5	104.1	18.33	19.29	0.93	1.11	4.6	0.41	0.77	5.24	B	40	57	3	income	Htcks & Wly Balanced
203.8	196.9	18.75	20.75	0.48	3.25	2.0	0.87	0.81	10.77	C	100	0	0	gr-inc	Htcks & Wly Eq Inc
0.1	5.3	—	10.25	0.35	0.18	—	—	—	—	—	98	0	2	global	Htcks & Wly Glob Eqty
521.8	1,041.9	22.19	22.67	0.71	0.00	3.1	0.51	0.36	9.41	A	92	0	8	int'l	Htcks & Wly Int'l
170.3	194.1	10.18	10.19	0.68	0.06	6.7	0.06	0.21	1.48	A	0	89	11	fix-inc	Htcks & Wly Low Dur
0.1	5.2	—	12.77	0.13	0.32	—	—	—	—	—	100	0	0	agg gr	Htcks & Wly Midcap
17.6	60.0	19.65	24.92	0.05	2.37	0.2	0.60	0.23	14.04	D	96	0	4	growth	Htcks & Wly Sm Cap SC
17.3	22.2	10.15	10.14	0.62	0.00	6.1	0.02	0.13	0.51	A	0	90	10	fix-inc	Htcks & Wly ST Invest
27.8	18.3	12.97	13.31	1.00	0.00	7.5	0.16	0.21	3.90	A	0	96	4	fix-inc	Htcks & Wly Tot Ret
11.1	15.3	13.29	14.62	0.35	0.67	2.4	0.58	0.90	6.73	C	54	41	5	income	IAA Trust Asst Alloc
92.9	145.8	19.33	21.34	0.14	1.68	0.7	0.84	0.86	10.05	C	87	0	13	growth	IAA Trust Growth
0.1	36.5	—	10.35	0.48	0.01	—	—	—	—	—	0	90	10	fix-inc	IAA Trust LT Bd
0.1	26.4	—	10.09	0.47	0.00	—	—	—	—	—	0	92	8	fix-inc	IAA Trust ST Gov
—	17.9	—	8.95	0.37	0.00	4.1	—	—	4.61	F	0	96	4	tax-free	IAA Trust TE Bd
32.2	31.9	10.64	11.97	0.37	1.01	2.9	0.57	0.48	9.31	F	72	28	0	income	IAI Balanced
82.5	68.7	9.16	9.56	0.56	0.00	5.9	0.24	0.41	4.10	B	0	100	0	fix-inc	IAI Bond
53.7	57.5	15.09	15.52	0.00	2.14	0.0	—	—	—	—	101	0	-1	agg gr	IAI Cap Apprec SC
10.5	8.6	9.81	7.58	0.15	0.68	2.0	—	—	—	—	96	0	4	int'l	IAI Develop Countries
617.6	324.7	19.96	16.61	0.00	2.63	0.0	1.17	0.29	23.90	F	100	0	0	agg gr	IAI Emg Growth SC
28.8	18.0	9.78	9.74	0.65	0.00	6.6	0.15	0.34	2.87	F	0	99	1	fix-inc	IAI Gov Bond

Stock and bond funds — comprehensive summary *continued*

Arranged in alphabetical order

| No-Load Fund | Total return percent with quintile ranks by objective | | | | | | | | | | Annualized | | What $10,000 grew to after | |
	1988	1989	1990	1991	1992	1993	1994	1995	1996	1997	3 yrs.	5 yrs.	3 yrs.	5 yrs.
IAI Gro & Inc	8.5[5]	29.8[1]	-6.7[4]	26.7[3]	4.0[5]	10.0[4]	-4.8[5]	27.1[4]	20.2[3]	23.9[4]	23.7[4]	14.7[4]	18,932	19,825
IAI Growth	—	—	—	—	—	—	0.7[2]	23.2[5]	15.3[4]	19.2[4]	19.2[5]	—	16,927	—
IAI International	18.0[2]	18.4[4]	-13.1[3]	16.6[2]	-6.3[4]	39.5[2]	0.5[2]	9.1[3]	8.4[4]	-4.2[4]	4.2[4]	9.7[4]	11,327	15,881
IAI Latin Amer	—	—	—	—	—	—	—	—	—	18.7[1]	—	—	—	—
IAI MidCap	—	—	—	—	—	—	5.7[1]	26.1[4]	16.6[4]	8.9[5]	17.0[5]	15.7[4]	16,005	20,774
IAI Regional	18.6[3]	31.3[1]	-0.3[2]	35.4[2]	3.5[5]	8.6[4]	0.7[2]	32.6[2]	15.7[4]	18.9[4]	22.2[4]	14.8[4]	18,235	19,942
IAI Reserve	6.8[2]	8.8[5]	8.4[3]	8.0[5]	3.3[5]	3.1[5]	2.7[1]	6.9[5]	4.4[3]	4.6[5]	5.3[5]	4.3[5]	11,676	12,362
IAI Value	24.3[2]	22.6[3]	-11.5[4]	19.8[5]	11.9[3]	22.1[1]	-9.1[5]	24.4[4]	21.9[2]	19.6[4]	21.9[4]	15.0[4]	18,133	20,125
IBJ Blend Tot Ret	—	—	—	—	—	—	—	—	11.4[4]	17.8[4]	—	—	—	—
IBJ Core Eqty	—	—	—	—	—	—	—	—	20.6[3]	29.9[2]	—	—	—	—
IBJ Core Fix Inc	—	—	—	—	—	—	—	—	2.2[4]	8.9[4]	—	—	—	—
ICAP Discret Equity	—	—	—	—	—	—	—	35.2[2]	25.6[1]	28.6[3]	29.7[2]	—	21,831	—
ICAP Equity	—	—	—	—	—	—	—	38.9[1]	26.3[1]	29.1[3]	31.3[1]	—	22,629	—
IMS Cap Val	—	—	—	—	—	—	—	—	—	6.7[5]	—	—	—	—
Independence One Eqty Plus	—	—	—	—	—	—	—	—	24.5[1]	28.7[3]	—	—	—	—
Independence One Fix Inc	—	—	—	—	—	—	—	—	3.5[3]	7.5[4]	—	—	—	—
Independence One MI Muni	—	—	—	—	—	—	—	—	4.5[1]	7.7[5]	—	—	—	—
Independence One US Gov Sec	—	—	—	—	—	—	-3.0[3]	18.1[2]	2.3[5]	9.1[2]	9.6[3]	—	13,180	—
Information Tech 100	—	—	—	—	—	—	—	—	—	-38.5[5]	—	—	—	—
Invesco Asia Growth	—	—	—	—	—	—	—	—	—	—	—	—	—	—
Invesco Balanced	—	—	—	—	—	—	9.4[1]	36.5[1]	14.7[3]	19.5[3]	23.2[2]	—	18,714	—
Invesco Dynamics	9.1[4]	22.7[4]	-6.4[3]	67.0[1]	13.2[2]	19.1[2]	-1.9[3]	37.6[2]	15.7[4]	24.1[2]	25.5[2]	18.2[2]	19,755	23,081
Invesco Europe Sm Co	—	—	—	—	—	—	—	—	31.0[1]	-3.1[4]	—	—	—	—
Invesco Europe	10.6[4]	24.2[2]	0.7[1]	8.0[4]	-7.6[4]	24.6[5]	-3.0[4]	19.2[1]	29.7[1]	15.1[1]	21.2[1]	16.6[1]	17,802	21,516
Invesco Growth	5.9[5]	31.2[1]	-1.2[2]	42.1[2]	2.9[5]	17.9[2]	-8.8[5]	29.5[3]	21.0[3]	27.2[3]	25.9[3]	16.5[3]	19,936	21,436
Invesco High Yld	13.4[1]	3.7[5]	-4.6[5]	23.5[1]	14.6[1]	15.8[2]	-5.0[3]	17.9[3]	14.1[1]	17.1[1]	16.3[1]	11.6[1]	15,746	17,323
Invesco Indust Inc	15.3[3]	31.9[1]	0.9[1]	46.3[1]	1.0[5]	16.7[2]	-3.9[5]	27.3[4]	16.7[4]	26.4[3]	23.4[4]	16.1[4]	18,782	21,064
Invesco Int'l Gro	16.6[3]	16.1[4]	-14.6[4]	7.2[4]	-12.5[5]	27.9[4]	0.6[2]	8.3[3]	12.0[3]	-1.9[4]	6.0[3]	8.9[4]	11,895	15,305
Invesco Inter Gov	5.4[5]	10.5[3]	9.1[2]	14.2[2]	6.0[3]	8.4[1]	-1.7[4]	16.8[1]	1.4[5]	6.2[4]	7.9[1]	6.0[1]	12,575	13,400
Invesco Latin Amer	—	—	—	—	—	—	—	—	25.9[1]	19.3[1]	—	—	—	—
Invesco Multi-Asst	—	—	—	—	—	—	-2.0[3]	23.9[4]	18.1[1]	19.1[3]	20.3[3]	—	17,426	—
Invesco Pacific Bas	23.2[1]	20.2[3]	-24.4[5]	13.2[2]	-13.6[5]	42.6[2]	4.7[1]	4.0[4]	-1.2[5]	-36.9[5]	-13.4[5]	-0.6[5]	6,488	9,687
Invesco Realty	—	—	—	—	—	—	—	—	—	21.1[3]	—	—	—	—
Invesco S&P 500 Idx II	—	—	—	—	—	—	—	—	—	—	—	—	—	—
Invesco Select Inc	10.4[2]	8.2[4]	4.9[4]	18.7[3]	10.4[1]	11.4[3]	-1.2[1]	20.2[2]	4.9[2]	11.7[2]	12.1[2]	9.2[2]	14,085	15,503
Invesco Sm Co Gro SC	—	—	—	—	25.7[1]	23.4[1]	-3.7[4]	30.0[3]	11.6[5]	18.3[3]	19.7[4]	15.3[3]	17,164	20,397
Invesco Small Co Val SC	—	—	—	—	—	—	-1.0[3]	27.1[4]	12.5[4]	25.0[2]	21.4[4]	—	17,877	—
Invesco ST Bond	—	—	—	—	—	—	-0.6[3]	9.8[4]	4.7[2]	6.7[2]	7.1[3]	—	12,268	—
Invesco Strat Enrgy	15.0[3]	43.5[1]	-16.5[5]	-3.5[5]	-13.2[5]	16.7[3]	-7.3[4]	19.8[4]	38.8[1]	19.1[3]	25.6[2]	16.5[4]	19,802	21,421
Invesco Strat Envrn	—	—	—	—	-18.7[5]	-4.7[5]	-11.4[5]	41.1[2]	18.8[3]	16.6[4]	25.0[3]	10.5[5]	19,537	16,497
Invesco Strat Fncl	17.1[4]	36.9[2]	-7.2[3]	74.0[1]	26.8[1]	19.7[3]	-5.9[4]	39.8[2]	30.3[2]	44.8[1]	38.2[1]	24.3[1]	26,374	29,707
Invesco Strat Gold	-20.0[4]	21.3[3]	-23.0[4]	-7.2[5]	-8.2[2]	72.6[5]	-27.9[5]	12.7[2]	40.6[1]	-55.5[4]	-11.0[1]	-2.6[5]	7,047	8,770
Invesco Strat Hlth	16.0[3]	59.5[1]	25.8[1]	91.8[1]	-13.7[5]	-8.4[5]	0.9[3]	58.9[1]	11.4[5]	18.4[4]	28.0[2]	14.1[5]	20,964	19,376
Invesco Strat Leis	28.5[1]	38.3[2]	-11.0[4]	52.7[2]	23.4[1]	35.7[1]	-5.0[4]	15.8[5]	9.1[5]	26.5[3]	16.9[5]	15.5[4]	15,977	20,597
Invesco Strat Tech	14.2[4]	21.4[3]	8.6[1]	76.9[1]	18.8[2]	15.0[4]	5.3[2]	45.8[2]	21.8[3]	8.8[5]	24.6[3]	18.5[3]	19,329	23,407
Invesco Strat Util	14.2[4]	31.5[3]	-10.0[4]	28.1[4]	10.7[3]	21.2[3]	-9.9[5]	25.3[4]	12.8[5]	24.4[3]	20.7[4]	13.9[5]	17,579	19,197
Invesco TF Inter	—	—	—	—	—	—	-4.4[4]	13.0[4]	2.9[5]	6.4[5]	7.3[5]	—	12,363	—
Invesco TF Long	15.1[1]	11.7[1]	7.1[1]	12.7[2]	8.8[3]	12.6[4]	-5.5[2]	15.6[4]	2.4[5]	8.7[4]	8.8[5]	6.5[4]	12,864	13,688
Invesco Total Ret	11.5[4]	19.1[3]	-0.3[3]	24.9[3]	9.8[2]	12.4[3]	2.5[1]	28.6[2]	13.1[3]	25.0[2]	22.1[2]	15.9[2]	18,186	20,952
Invesco US Gov Sec	6.3[5]	12.4[3]	7.3[3]	15.5[4]	5.8[5]	10.2[4]	-7.2[5]	22.1[2]	0.5[5]	12.2[2]	11.3[3]	7.1[4]	13,774	14,086
Invesco Value Eqty	16.9[3]	21.3[3]	-5.8[3]	35.8[2]	5.0[5]	10.4[3]	4.0[1]	30.6[3]	18.5[4]	28.0[3]	25.6[3]	17.9[3]	19,809	22,744
Invesco Wrld Cap Gds	—	—	—	—	—	—	—	7.8[5]	15.0[4]	27.8[2]	16.6[5]	—	15,852	—
Invesco Wrld Comm	—	—	—	—	—	—	—	27.4[1]	16.8[3]	30.3[1]	24.7[2]	—	19,387	—
Investek Fix Inc	—	—	—	—	7.9[1]	10.6[2]	-3.8[3]	16.8[3]	4.1[3]	9.2[2]	9.9[3]	7.2[2]	13,273	14,157
IPS Millenium	—	—	—	—	—	—	—	24.8[4]	24.5[1]	21.4[4]	23.6[4]	—	18,867	—
Jamestown Int'l Eqty	—	—	—	—	—	—	—	—	—	12.4[1]	—	—	—	—
Jamestown VA Tax-Free	—	—	—	—	—	—	-3.7[1]	12.2[5]	4.0[2]	7.0[5]	7.7[5]	—	12,485	—
Janus Balanced	—	—	—	—	—	—	0.0[2]	27.3[3]	15.3[2]	21.8[3]	21.4[2]	14.6[2]	17,876	19,770
Janus Enterprise	—	—	—	—	—	—	8.9[1]	27.3[4]	11.6[5]	10.8[5]	16.3[5]	14.7[4]	15,744	19,820
Janus Equity Inc	—	—	—	—	—	—	—	—	—	31.1[2]	—	—	—	—

See Chapter 3 for explanation of symbols

Total Net Assets $Million December 31		NAV per share December 31		1997 per share distributions		Yield % 12/31/97	Risk Analysis				% Distribution of Portfolio 12/31/97			Objective	No-Load Fund
1996	1997	1996	1997	Income	Capital gains		beta	R²	Std. Dev.	Sharpe Ratio	Stocks	Bonds	Cash		
93.7	88.7	15.01	17.66	0.07	0.83	0.4	0.85	0.80	10.52	D	99	0	1	gr-inc	IAI Gro & Inc
15.1	13.2	10.19	10.72	0.00	1.34	0.0	0.97	0.78	12.17	F	98	0	2	growth	IAI Growth
119.5	73.1	12.35	10.13	0.32	1.39	2.8	0.57	0.32	10.96	D	98	0	2	int'l	IAI International
1.0	2.6	10.39	10.22	0.03	1.94	0.3	—	—	—		94	0	6	int'l	IAI Latin Amer
140.3	95.4	17.62	14.97	0.00	4.01	0.0	0.78	0.42	13.22	F	99	0	1	growth	IAI MidCap
565.2	501.7	23.19	24.44	0.00	3.00	0.0	0.78	0.52	11.95	D	100	0	0	growth	IAI Regional
60.1	32.3	9.86	9.79	0.52	0.00	5.3	0.03	0.15	0.94	F	0	98	2	fix-inc	IAI Reserve
36.7	27.2	12.57	12.21	0.11	2.59	0.8	0.47	0.24	10.73	D	99	0	1	growth	IAI Value
63.3	63.1	12.09	11.73	0.33	1.91	2.8	—	—	—		52	45	3	income	IBJ Blend Tot Ret
88.8	109.5	13.56	15.34	0.22	1.96	1.4	—	—	—		97	0	3	growth	IBJ Core Eqty
26.5	31.8	10.09	10.31	0.57	0.08	5.5	—	—	—		0	96	4	fix-inc	IBJ Core Fix Inc
110.3	157.1	29.55	30.34	0.49	7.00	1.3	0.88	0.86	10.63	B	90	3	8	gr-inc	ICAP Discret Equity
149.1	371.4	31.16	35.12	0.34	4.60	1.0	0.93	0.85	11.25	B	95	3	2	gr-inc	ICAP Equity
5.2	10.0	11.14	11.03	0.03	0.81	0.3	—	—	—		100	0	0	gr-inc	IMS Cap Val
161.4	186.7	12.89	15.69	0.21	0.65	1.3	—	—	—		98	0	2	gr-inc	Independence One Eqty Plus
70.3	77.7	9.91	10.04	0.59	0.00	5.8	—	—	—		0	99	1	fix-inc	Independence One Fix Inc
24.9	26.0	10.11	10.45	0.42	0.00	4.0	—	—	—		0	96	4	fix-inc	Independence One MI Muni
72.4	72.3	10.12	10.42	0.58	0.00	5.6	0.18	0.23	4.30	D	0	97	3	fix-inc	Independence One US Gov Sec
—	1.4	—	26.66	0.00	0.00	—	—	—	—		90	0	10	sector	Information Tech 100
36.8	12.8	10.22	4.95	0.00	1.32	0.0	—	—	—		87	0	13	int'l	Invesco Asia Growth
134.2	167.7	13.82	14.48	0.35	1.63	2.2	0.48	0.63	6.84	A	61	35	4	income	Invesco Balanced
856.2	1,120.5	12.89	13.96	0.00	1.95	0.0	0.94	0.56	14.03	B	95	0	5	agg gr	Invesco Dynamics
129.0	51.4	16.03	12.04	0.00	3.45	0.0	—	—	—		94	0	6	int'l	Invesco Europe Sm Co
326.0	331.3	15.86	14.82	0.10	3.28	0.5	0.47	0.24	10.53	A	95	0	5	int'l	Invesco Europe
651.3	53.5	5.19	4.96	0.43	0.17	0.1	1.08	0.89	12.71	C	99	0	1	growth	Invesco Growth
437.9	753.3	7.10	7.23	0.01	1.60	8.3	0.27	0.40	4.70	A	2	92	6	fix-inc	Invesco High Yld
4,281.8	588.3	13.46	14.91	0.63	0.40	2.2	0.74	0.95	8.46	C	77	18	5	gr-inc	Invesco Indust Inc
91.2	4,858.8	16.63	13.46	0.37	1.67	1.9	0.73	0.41	12.27	C	75	0	25	int'l	Invesco Int'l Gro
46.9	50.3	12.46	12.55	0.30	2.49	5.2	0.11	0.13	3.32	F	91	0	9	fix-inc	Invesco Inter Gov
28.7	47.9	13.26	13.79	0.66	0.00	0.8	—	—	—		98	0	2	int'l	Invesco Latin Amer
16.9	80.3	12.11	12.57	0.12	1.78	1.8	0.57	0.81	7.00	B	72	20	8	income	Invesco Multi-Asst
153.8	16.6	13.60	8.27	0.25	1.54	1.4	1.02	0.32	18.88	F	89	0	11	int'l	Invesco Pacific Bas
0.1	47.6	10.00	10.77	0.43	0.87	4.0	—	—	—		83	0	17	sector	Invesco Realty
—	1.0	—	10.33	0.00	0.00	—	—	—	—		98	0	2	gr-inc	Invesco S&P 500 Idx II
269.7	53.1	6.55	6.67	0.12	0.20	6.6	0.22	0.34	4.24	B	0	98	2	fix-inc	Invesco Select Inc
267.9	331.8	12.52	11.21	0.45	0.17	0.0	0.91	0.26	19.88	D	89	0	11	agg gr	Invesco Sm Co Gro SC
85.0	313.6	12.42	11.69	0.00	3.42	0.5	0.63	0.43	10.65	B	88	0	12	agg gr	Invesco Small Co Val SC
10.7	15.5	9.50	9.57	0.55	0.00	5.8	0.08	0.29	1.57	C	0	84	16	fix-inc	Invesco ST Bond
233.0	67.3	14.46	14.01	0.08	3.63	0.4	0.39	0.06	17.59	D	101	0	-1	sector	Invesco Strat Enrgy
26.9	212.1	9.95	8.39	0.06	3.03	0.1	0.69	0.27	14.34	C	91	0	9	sector	Invesco Strat Envrn
622.2	20.5	22.22	28.11	0.01	3.07	0.8	0.95	0.67	12.90	A	90	0	10	sector	Invesco Strat Fncl
229.6	1,307.2	5.56	2.44	0.25	3.70	1.3	0.37	0.01	35.08	A	88	5	7	prec met	Invesco Strat Gold
936.2	127.6	49.36	49.17	0.03	0.00	0.3	0.92	0.46	14.96	B	81	0	19	sector	Invesco Strat Hlth
237.5	945.8	22.58	25.43	0.18	8.80	0.1	0.60	0.42	10.25	D	92	1	7	sector	Invesco Strat Leis
838.5	222.7	30.99	26.89	0.02	2.98	0.4	0.95	0.40	16.68	D	98	0	2	sector	Invesco Strat Tech
157.4	1,021.3	11.38	13.47	0.13	6.45	2.4	0.52	0.45	8.56	B	91	0	9	sector	Invesco Strat Util
5.6	4.7	9.88	10.09	0.40	0.00	4.0	0.14	0.29	2.87	F	0	95	5	tax-free	Invesco TF Inter
236.8	212.5	15.19	15.67	0.33	0.29	4.0	0.20	0.22	4.62	F	0	88	12	tax-free	Invesco TF Long
1,227.4	218.7	24.30	29.09	0.63	0.17	2.5	0.59	0.92	6.91	A	66	28	6	income	Invesco Total Ret
57.4	2,160.7	7.42	7.70	0.74	0.48	5.5	0.29	0.26	6.30	D	0	91	9	fix-inc	Invesco US Gov Sec
251.8	379.1	23.74	27.88	0.24	2.19	0.8	0.85	0.93	9.79	C	94	0	6	gr-inc	Invesco Value Eqty
4.5	16.9	9.59	11.00	0.01	1.21	0.1	0.78	0.41	13.58	F	93	0	7	sector	Invesco Wrld Cap Gds
54.1	83.6	12.63	15.34	0.05	1.04	0.3	0.81	0.60	11.76	B	91	0	9	global	Invesco Wrld Comm
0.1	0.7	10.10	10.35	0.65	0.00	6.3	—	—	—		0	92	8	fix-inc	Investek Fix Inc
5.9	11.8	18.28	22.20	0.00	0.00	0.0	1.11	0.69	14.87	F	95	0	5	gr-inc	IPS Millenium
28.3	35.5	9.73	10.87	0.07	0.00	0.6	—	—	—		100	0	0	int'l	Jamestown Int'l Eqty
—	16.4	—	10.19	0.45	0.00	4.4	—	—	2.92	F	0	97	3	fix-inc	Jamestown VA Tax-Free
219.7	369.4	14.14	15.33	0.36	1.49	2.1	0.45	0.71	6.02	A	52	40	8	income	Janus Balanced
721.7	573.1	29.34	30.48	0.00	1.96	0.0	0.67	0.23	15.62	F	98	0	2	growth	Janus Enterprise
29.3	88.6	11.08	13.54	0.07	0.88	0.5	—	—	—		82	11	7	gr-inc	Janus Equity Inc

Arranged in alphabetical order

| No-Load Fund | Total return percent with quintile ranks by objective | | | | | | | | | | Annualized | | What $10,000 grew to after | |
	1988	1989	1990	1991	1992	1993	1994	1995	1996	1997	3 yrs.	5 yrs.	3 yrs.	5 yrs.
Janus Federal TE	—	—	—	—	—	—	-7.8⁴	15.8⁴	4.7¹	9.0³	9.7³	—	13,213	—
Janus Flex Inc	10.7¹	4.1⁵	-4.6⁵	26.0¹	12.0¹	15.7¹	-2.9³	21.1¹	6.9¹	11.4¹	13.0¹	10.1¹	14,423	16,204
Janus Fund	16.6³	46.3¹	-0.7²	42.8²	6.9⁴	10.9³	-1.1³	29.4³	19.6³	22.7⁴	23.8⁴	15.8⁴	18,988	20,826
Janus Gro & Inc	—	—	—	—	5.4⁴	6.7⁴	-4.9⁵	36.4¹	26.0¹	34.7¹	32.3¹	18.6²	23,143	23,484
Janus High Yld	—	—	—	—	—	—	—	—	24.0¹	15.4¹	—	—	—	—
Janus Mercury	—	—	—	—	—	—	15.9¹	33.0³	17.7³	11.9⁴	20.5⁴	—	17,513	—
Janus Olympus	—	—	—	—	—	—	—	—	21.7²	26.7³	—	—	—	—
Janus Overseas	—	—	—	—	—	—	—	22.1¹	28.8¹	18.2¹	23.0¹	—	18,592	—
Janus Spec Situations	—	—	—	—	—	—	—	—	—	46.0¹	—	—	—	—
Janus ST Bond	—	—	—	—	—	—	0.4²	7.9⁵	6.2¹	6.6²	6.9³	5.4²	12,218	13,028
Janus Twenty	19.1²	50.8¹	0.6¹	69.2¹	2.0⁴	3.4⁵	-6.7⁵	36.2²	27.9¹	29.7²	31.2¹	16.9³	22,593	21,796
Janus Venture‡SC	19.6²	38.7¹	-0.4²	47.8¹	7.4⁴	9.1⁴	5.5¹	26.5⁴	8.0⁵	13.1⁵	15.6⁵	12.2⁵	15,449	17,782
Janus Worldwide	—	—	—	—	9.0¹	28.4²	3.6¹	21.9¹	26.4¹	20.5¹	22.9²	19.8¹	18,563	24,693
Japan (Scudder)	19.5²	11.6⁵	-16.4⁵	3.1⁵	-16.7⁵	23.6⁵	10.0¹	-9.1⁵	-10.9⁵	-14.5⁴	-11.5⁵	-1.2⁵	6,928	9,419
Japan Alpha‡	—	—	—	—	—	—	—	—	-17.0⁵	-42.1⁵	—	—	—	—
Jensen Portfolio	—	—	—	—	—	-7.3⁵	-1.8⁴	27.6⁴	21.1³	23.0⁴	23.9⁴	11.6⁵	18,999	17,305
Jhaveri Value	—	—	—	—	—	—	—	—	15.7⁴	17.2⁵	—	—	—	—
JP Morgan Bond	—	10.3⁴	10.1¹	13.4⁵	6.5⁴	9.9⁴	-3.0²	18.2³	3.1³	9.1³	10.0⁴	7.2⁴	13,299	14,172
JP Morgan Diversified	—	—	—	—	—	—	0.6²	26.5³	13.4³	18.5⁴	19.3⁴	—	16,993	—
JP Morgan Emg Mkts Debt	—	—	—	—	—	—	—	—	—	—	—	—	—	—
JP Morgan Emg Mkts Eqty	—	—	—	—	—	—	-7.6⁴	-10.0⁵	8.5⁴	-7.6⁴	-3.4⁴	—	9,016	—
JP Morgan Euro Eqty	—	—	—	—	—	—	—	—	—	22.1¹	—	—	—	—
JP Morgan Int'l Eqty	—	—	—	10.6³	-10.8⁴	24.4⁵	5.7¹	7.6³	8.4⁴	1.2³	5.7⁴	9.2⁴	11,801	15,508
JP Morgan Int'l Oppty	—	—	—	—	—	—	—	—	—	—	—	—	—	—
JP Morgan Japan Eqty	—	—	—	—	—	—	—	—	—	-30.8⁵	—	—	—	—
JP Morgan NY Tot Ret	—	—	—	—	—	—	—	13.0⁵	4.0³	7.4⁵	8.1⁵	—	12,621	—
JP Morgan Shrs CA Bond	—	—	—	—	—	—	—	—	—	—	—	—	—	—
JP Morgan Shrs Tax Aware Disc Eqty	—	—	—	—	—	—	—	—	—	—	—	—	—	—
JP Morgan Shrs Tax Aware Eqty	—	—	—	—	—	—	—	—	—	30.3²	—	—	—	—
JP Morgan ST Bond	—	—	—	—	—	—	0.1²	10.6³	4.9²	6.1⁴	7.2³	—	12,316	—
JP Morgan TE Bond	7.4⁵	8.3⁵	6.8²	10.9⁴	7.5⁵	9.6⁵	-2.7¹	13.4⁵	3.5⁴	7.4⁵	8.0⁵	6.1⁵	12,612	13,446
JP Morgan US Eqty	14.1⁴	31.4¹	1.4¹	34.1²	8.8³	11.0³	-0.6⁴	32.5³	21.1³	28.4³	27.2³	17.8³	20,595	22,725
JP Morgan US Sm Co Opp SC	—	—	—	—	—	—	—	—	—	—	—	—	—	—
JP Morgan US Sm Co SC	13.7³	29.0³	-24.2⁵	59.6²	19.0¹	8.6⁴	-5.9⁵	31.9³	20.8³	22.8³	25.0²	14.8⁴	19,545	19,972
Jurika & Voyles Balanced	—	—	—	—	—	17.1¹	-2.2³	25.4³	15.5²	16.7⁴	19.1⁴	14.1²	16,898	19,351
Jurika & Voyles MiniCap SC	—	—	—	—	—	—	—	52.2¹	32.2¹	23.9²	35.6¹	—	24,916	—
Kalmar Gr\Val Sm Cap SC	—	—	—	—	—	—	—	—	—	—	—	—	—	—
Kaminski Poland	—	—	—	—	—	—	—	—	—	—	—	—	—	—
Kaufmann SC	58.6¹	46.8¹	-6.1³	79.5¹	11.3³	18.2²	9.0¹	36.9²	20.9²	12.6⁴	23.0³	19.1¹	18,630	24,002
Kayne Anderson Int'l Ris Div	—	—	—	—	—	—	—	—	—	17.4¹	—	—	—	—
Kayne Anderson Inter TF	—	—	—	—	—	—	—	—	—	4.2⁵	—	—	—	—
Kayne Anderson Inter Tot Ret	—	—	—	—	—	—	—	—	—	7.2⁵	—	—	—	—
Kayne Anderson Ris Div	—	—	—	—	—	—	—	—	19.1⁴	31.0²	—	—	—	—
Kayne Anderson Sm-Mid Cap Ris Div	—	—	—	—	—	—	—	—	—	19.5³	—	—	—	—
Kent Gro & Inc	—	—	—	—	—	14.4²	0.5³	34.6²	19.1⁴	23.9⁴	25.7³	18.0³	19,866	22,843
Kent Idx Eqty	—	—	—	—	—	9.6⁴	0.8³	35.8²	21.9³	32.2²	29.8²	19.3²	21,891	24,168
Kent Income	—	—	—	—	—	—	—	—	1.2⁵	10.0³	—	—	—	—
Kent Int'l Gro	—	—	—	—	—	29.7⁴	5.5¹	12.9²	5.6⁵	2.3⁵	6.8³	10.8³	12,183	16,669
Kent Inter Bd	—	—	—	—	—	8.2⁴	-3.0³	15.8⁴	2.8⁴	7.6⁴	8.6⁴	6.1⁴	12,802	13,433
Kent Inter TF	—	—	—	—	—	8.3⁵	-3.0²	12.8⁴	3.2⁵	6.8⁴	7.5⁵	5.5⁵	12,426	13,048
Kent Ltd Trm TF	—	—	—	—	—	—	—	8.4²	3.5⁴	4.6⁴	5.5³	—	11,739	—
Kent MI Muni	—	—	—	—	—	—	0.2²	8.0³	3.4⁵	5.4²	5.6³	—	11,765	—
Kent Sm Co Gro SC	—	—	—	—	—	17.3²	-0.1²	23.5⁴	19.2³	27.7²	23.4³	17.1²	18,791	22,029
Kent ST Bd	—	—	—	—	—	3.0⁵	1.0²	10.3³	4.1⁴	6.3³	6.8⁴	4.9⁴	12,197	12,694
Kent TF Inc	—	—	—	—	—	—	—	—	3.5⁴	8.3⁴	—	—	—	—
Kenwood Gro & Inc	—	—	—	—	—	—	—	—	—	30.2²	—	—	—	—
Key Choice:Growth‡	—	—	—	—	—	—	—	—	—	16.9⁵	—	—	—	—
Key Choice:Inc & Gro‡	—	—	—	—	—	—	—	—	—	12.7⁵	—	—	—	—
Key Choice:Mod Gro‡	—	—	—	—	—	—	—	—	—	14.8⁵	—	—	—	—
Key SBSF Capital Gro‡	—	—	—	—	—	—	-4.5⁵	33.7²	3.5⁵	9.1⁵	14.7⁵	—	15,096	—

See Chapter 3 for explanation of symbols

Total Net Assets $Million		NAV per share		1997 per share distributions		Yield % 12/31/97	Risk Analysis				% Distribution of Portfolio 12/31/97			Objective	No-Load Fund
December 31 1996	1997	December 31 1996	1997	Income	Capital gains		beta	R²	Std. Dev.	Sharpe Ratio	Stocks	Bonds	Cash		
47.9	62.8	6.98	7.24	0.35	0.00	4.8	0.19	0.23	4.36	D	0	92	8	tax-free	Janus Federal TE
625.0	766.4	9.69	9.87	0.68	0.21	6.7	0.22	0.33	4.36	A	0	95	5	fix-inc	Janus Flex Inc
15,890.3	19,200.2	24.45	24.90	0.23	4.75	0.8	0.82	0.83	10.02	C	96	0	4	growth	Janus Fund
1,100.5	2,004.6	19.05	23.15	0.07	2.38	0.3	1.05	0.79	13.34	B	89	1	10	growth	Janus Gro & Inc
238.2	367.4	11.23	11.39	0.95	0.56	7.9	—	—	—	—	0	87	13	fix-inc	Janus High Yld
2,061.3	1,911.5	16.52	16.50	0.04	1.90	0.2	1.00	0.60	14.34	D	93	1	6	agg gr	Janus Mercury
412.9	629.2	14.48	17.58	0.04	0.71	0.2	—	—	—	—	95	1	4	growth	Janus Olympus
955.4	3,240.9	15.22	17.39	0.10	0.50	0.5	0.59	0.38	10.55	A	89	1	10	int'l	Janus Overseas
0.5	389.4	10.00	13.93	0.00	0.66	0.0	—	—	—	—	99	0	1	agg gr	Janus Spec Situations
44.4	69.1	2.88	2.89	0.18	0.00	6.1	0.08	0.28	1.68	D	0	84	16	fix-inc	Janus ST Bond
4,070.7	6,003.6	27.47	30.99	0.01	4.55	0.0	1.15	0.84	14.10	A	84	0	16	agg gr	Janus Twenty
1,705.5	1,234.3	53.06	50.26	0.07	9.29	0.1	0.64	0.22	15.00	F	87	0	13	growth	Janus Venture‡SC
5,046.3	10,567.8	33.69	37.78	0.19	2.61	0.5	0.69	0.49	10.85	B	97	1	2	global	Janus Worldwide
383.7	270.8	8.33	6.77	0.37	0.00	5.4	0.50	0.08	19.68	F	94	2	4	int'l	Japan (Scudder)
3.9	2.6	7.60	4.40	0.00	0.00	0.0	—	—	—	—	0	0	100	int'l	Japan Alpha‡
12.6	17.8	13.49	16.14	0.08	0.37	0.5	0.87	0.79	10.92	D	96	0	4	gr-inc	Jensen Portfolio
11.1	14.0	12.58	12.27	0.00	2.45	0.0	—	—	—	—	75	0	25	growth	Jhaveri Value
148.0	176.6	10.21	10.45	0.66	0.00	6.3	0.19	0.26	4.04	C	0	98	2	fix-inc	JP Morgan Bond
60.4	100.3	12.44	13.69	0.35	0.66	2.6	0.61	0.95	6.98	C	57	39	4	income	JP Morgan Diversified
—	12.0	—	9.76	0.59	0.17	—	—	—	—	—	0	91	9	fix-inc	JP Morgan Emg Mkts Debt
54.7	58.1	10.32	9.45	0.08	0.00	0.8	0.88	0.28	17.56	D	84	1	15	int'l	JP Morgan Emg Mkts Eqty
2.1	4.8	11.61	13.35	0.07	0.74	0.5	—	—	—	—	97	0	3	int'l	JP Morgan Euro Eqty
203.2	113.6	10.93	10.15	0.40	0.47	4.0	0.54	0.29	10.98	D	92	0	8	int'l	JP Morgan Int'l Eqty
—	72.7	—	10.08	0.07	0.00	—	—	—	—	—	88	0	12	int'l	JP Morgan Int'l Oppty
0.6	0.6	7.83	5.42	0.00	0.00	0.0	—	—	—	—	81	4	15	int'l	JP Morgan Japan Eqty
55.0	75.7	10.44	10.67	0.46	0.06	4.3	0.16	0.30	3.29	F	0	96	4	tax-free	JP Morgan NY Tot Ret
—	4.3	—	10.50	0.04	0.00	—	—	—	—	—	0	90	10	tax-free	JP Morgan Shrs CA Bond
0.1	30.0	—	12.73	0.00	0.00	—	—	—	—	—	100	0	0	growth	JP Morgan Shrs Tax Aware Disc Eqty
5.4	32.9	10.10	13.10	0.06	0.00	0.5	—	—	—	—	99	0	1	growth	JP Morgan Shrs Tax Aware Eqty
12.5	19.3	9.84	9.84	0.59	0.00	6.0	0.07	0.23	1.58	B	0	95	5	fix-inc	JP Morgan ST Bond
366.0	390.3	11.76	12.06	0.55	0.00	4.5	0.15	0.29	3.11	F	0	97	3	tax-free	JP Morgan TE Bond
332.1	398.5	21.60	22.54	0.20	4.84	0.8	0.94	0.89	11.06	D	97	1	2	gr-inc	JP Morgan US Eqty
—	112.2	—	11.84	0.00	0.00	—	—	—	—	—	91	0	9	agg gr	JP Morgan US Sm Co Opp SC
224.9	264.2	24.98	26.42	0.14	3.91	0.5	0.68	0.38	12.18	B	95	0	5	agg gr	JP Morgan US Sm Co SC
54.0	68.3	14.43	14.81	0.33	1.67	2.2	0.62	0.68	8.36	D	51	35	14	income	Jurika & Voyles Balanced
119.0	122.4	19.50	19.16	0.00	4.96	0.0	0.70	0.23	16.39	A	93	0	7	agg gr	Jurika & Voyles MiniCap SC
—	226.8	—	13.70	0.00	0.92	—	—	—	—	—	88	0	12	agg gr	Kalmar Gr\Val Sm Cap SC
—	0.8	—	9.06	0.00	0.00	—	—	—	—	—	84	0	16	int'l	Kaminski Poland
5,300.0	6,105.0	5.84	6.37	0.00	0.21	0.0	0.85	0.37	15.78	C	89	0	11	agg gr	Kaufmann SC
1.1	7.0	10.91	12.61	0.05	0.14	0.4	—	—	—	—	94	0	6	int'l	Kayne Anderson Int'l Ris Div
5.1	6.0	10.64	10.74	0.35	0.00	3.3	—	—	—	—	0	100	0	fix-inc	Kayne Anderson Inter TF
5.0	6.3	10.59	10.75	0.58	0.00	5.4	—	—	—	—	0	97	3	fix-inc	Kayne Anderson Inter Tot
26.1	35.3	14.32	17.28	0.11	1.36	0.7	—	—	—	—	97	0	3	gr-inc	Kayne Anderson Ris Div
0.8	6.5	11.06	13.12	0.05	0.05	0.4	—	—	—	—	98	0	2	agg gr	Kayne Anderson Sm-Mid Cap Ris Div
15.1	35.3	13.81	15.44	0.20	1.39	1.3	0.78	0.86	9.31	C	98	0	2	gr-inc	Kent Gro & Inc
9.9	27.9	14.72	19.15	0.21	0.07	1.1	0.99	1.00	11.02	B	97	0	3	gr-inc	Kent Idx Eqty
2.7	5.6	10.16	10.29	0.62	0.14	6.1	—	—	—	—	0	97	3	fix-inc	Kent Income
8.8	9.8	14.69	14.79	0.14	0.08	1.0	0.57	0.31	11.18	C	99	0	1	int'l	Kent Int'l Gro
7.3	7.0	9.78	9.93	0.57	0.00	5.7	0.16	0.25	3.59	D	0	95	5	fix-inc	Kent Inter Bd
3.4	3.5	10.42	10.68	0.43	0.00	4.0	0.15	0.29	3.03	F	0	98	2	tax-free	Kent Inter TF
0.1	0.5	10.20	10.23	0.38	0.04	3.7	0.07	0.28	1.54	D	0	97	3	tax-free	Kent Ltd Trm TF
2.4	4.4	10.07	10.20	0.40	0.00	3.9	0.09	0.31	1.75	C	0	98	2	tax-free	Kent MI Muni
14.4	22.8	15.61	18.33	0.03	1.05	0.2	0.63	0.36	11.68	B	99	0	1	agg gr	Kent Sm Co Gro SC
1.7	7.4	9.74	9.74	0.59	0.00	6.1	0.08	0.24	1.80	D	0	93	7	fix-inc	Kent ST Bd
0.9	1.7	10.29	10.67	0.42	0.03	4.0	—	—	—	—	0	98	2	tax-free	Kent TF Inc
0.5	2.4	10.67	12.97	0.09	0.83	0.7	—	—	—	—	95	0	5	gr-inc	Kenwood Gro & Inc
0.1	7.1	10.00	11.37	0.14	—	1.2	—	—	—	—	70	26	4	growth	Key Choice:Growth‡
0.2	3.2	10.00	10.85	0.37	—	3.5	—	—	—	—	36	59	5	income	Key Choice:Inc & Gro‡
1.7	7.2	10.00	11.14	0.25	—	2.2	—	—	—	—	49	46	5	gr-inc	Key Choice:Mod Gro‡
37.5	33.6	10.03	9.54	0.00	1.45	0.0	0.96	0.26	20.78	F	98	0	2	growth	Key SBSF Capital Gro‡

Stock and bond funds — comprehensive summary *continued*

Arranged in alphabetical order

No-Load Fund	1988	1989	1990	1991	1992	1993	1994	1995	1996	1997	Annualized 3 yrs.	Annualized 5 yrs.	Grew to after 3 yrs.	Grew to after 5 yrs.
Key SBSF Convert‡	—	18.9[3]	-5.1[4]	27.7[2]	11.3[2]	20.1[1]	-6.5[5]	24.3[3]	19.2[1]	16.3[4]	19.9[3]	14.1[2]	17,238	19,357
Key SBSF Fund‡	17.2[3]	34.0[1]	-2.7[2]	19.3[5]	6.7[4]	20.4[1]	-5.6[5]	32.6[2]	20.5[3]	12.3[5]	21.5[4]	15.3[4]	17,948	20,399
Key Stock Idx‡	—	—	—	—	—	—	—	—	—	32.4[1]	—	—	—	—
Kiewit Eqty Fund	—	—	—	—	—	—	—	—	16.6[4]	26.1[3]	—	—	—	—
Kiewit Inter Bond	—	—	—	—	—	—	—	14.2[5]	3.4[3]	8.1[4]	8.5[4]	—	12,763	—
Kiewit Sht Term Gov	—	—	—	—	—	—	—	9.7[4]	4.5[3]	6.3[3]	6.8[4]	—	12,182	—
Kiewit Tax Exempt	—	—	—	—	—	—	—	10.5[5]	3.1[4]	6.2[5]	6.5[5]	—	12,094	—
Kobren Insight:Cons Alloc	—	—	—	—	—	—	—	—	—	20.7[3]	—	—	—	—
Kobren Insight:Growth	—	—	—	—	—	—	—	—	—	15.0[5]	—	—	—	—
Kobren Insight:Mod Gro	—	—	—	—	—	—	—	—	—	23.3[4]	—	—	—	—
KPM Equity	—	—	—	—	—	—	—	32.6[2]	29.0[1]	20.1[4]	27.1[2]	—	20,538	—
KPM Fixed Inc	—	—	—	—	—	—	—	16.6[4]	3.2[3]	8.4[4]	9.3[4]	—	13,047	—
Lake Forest Core Eqty	—	—	—	—	—	—	—	—	21.1[3]	29.2[2]	—	—	—	—
Lancaster Cap Builder	—	—	—	—	—	—	—	—	19.1[3]	19.4[4]	—	—	—	—
Lancaster Convert	—	—	—	—	—	16.4[2]	-8.0[5]	26.3[3]	14.8[3]	22.4[2]	21.1[2]	13.7[2]	17,742	19,000
Lancaster Gov Qual	—	—	—	—	—	8.2[5]	-3.4[2]	13.6[5]	2.3[4]	7.0[5]	7.5[5]	5.4[5]	12,434	12,996
Lancaster Crest Sm Cap SC	—	—	—	—	—	12.3[4]	2.5[2]	21.1[5]	24.2[4]	8.5[5]	17.8[4]	13.5[4]	16,342	18,806
Lazard Bantam Val SC(O shrs)	—	—	—	—	—	—	—	—	—	33.9[1]	—	—	—	—
Lazard Bond(O shrs)	—	—	—	—	5.8[5]	8.6[4]	-4.5[3]	16.2[4]	4.4[3]	8.4[4]	9.6[4]	6.4[5]	13,151	13,643
Lazard Emg Mkt(O shrs)	—	—	—	—	—	—	—	-5.9[5]	23.6[2]	-9.8[4]	1.6[4]	—	10,491	—
Lazard Equity(O shrs)	20.5[2]	23.7[3]	-4.8[3]	27.5[4]	5.3[4]	18.6[2]	4.3[1]	37.7[1]	19.9[3]	25.1[3]	27.4[2]	20.6[1]	20,657	25,543
Lazard Global Eqty(O shrs)	—	—	—	—	—	—	—	—	—	15.3[2]	—	—	—	—
Lazard Int'l Eqty(O shrs)	—	—	—	—	-6.6[4]	31.1[4]	0.3[3]	13.1[2]	15.6[3]	11.8[2]	13.5[2]	14.0[2]	14,632	19,232
Lazard Int'l Fix Inc(O shrs)	—	—	—	—	2.1[5]	15.7[2]	4.2[1]	19.4[2]	5.5[2]	-5.7[5]	5.9[5]	7.4[3]	11,878	14,317
Lazard Int'l Sm Cap(O shrs)	—	—	—	—	—	—	-4.4[4]	1.8[4]	15.7[3]	0.3[3]	5.7[3]	—	11,803	—
Lazard Mid Cap(O shrs)	—	—	—	—	—	—	—	—	—	—	—	—	—	—
Lazard Small Cap SC(O shrs)	—	—	—	—	24.8[1]	30.2[1]	2.0[2]	21.5[5]	23.9[2]	28.1[2]	24.5[2]	20.7[1]	19,288	25,617
Lazard Strat Yld(O shrs)	—	—	—	—	6.3[4]	15.4[2]	-2.4[1]	13.6[5]	13.8[1]	5.2[5]	10.8[3]	8.9[2]	13,595	15,313
Legg Mason Amer Lead	—	—	—	—	—	—	-4.2[4]	22.9[5]	28.4[1]	23.8[4]	25.0[3]	—	19,529	—
Legg Mason Balanced	—	—	—	—	—	—	—	—	—	18.7[4]	—	—	—	—
Legg Mason Emg Mkts	—	—	—	—	—	—	—	—	—	-6.2[4]	—	—	—	—
Legg Mason Glob Gov	—	—	—	—	—	—	-1.4[1]	20.8[1]	8.2[1]	-1.7[5]	8.7[4]	—	12,852	—
Legg Mason Gov Inter	6.5[4]	12.8[3]	9.0[3]	14.4[4]	6.1[4]	6.8[5]	-1.9[2]	13.9[5]	4.5[2]	7.0[5]	8.4[4]	5.9[5]	12,727	13,334
Legg Mason High Yld	—	—	—	—	—	—	—	18.0[3]	14.9[1]	15.9[1]	16.3[1]	—	15,712	—
Legg Mason Int'l Eqty	—	—	—	—	—	—	—	—	16.5[2]	1.8[3]	—	—	—	—
Legg Mason Invest Grd	7.7[4]	13.0[3]	5.8[3]	16.0[4]	6.8[4]	11.2[3]	-4.8[3]	20.1[2]	4.3[3]	10.3[2]	11.4[2]	7.9[3]	13,824	14,632
Legg Mason Spec Invest SC	19.7[2]	32.1[2]	0.5[1]	39.4[4]	15.4[2]	24.1[1]	-13.1[5]	22.5[4]	28.7[1]	22.1[3]	24.4[3]	15.7[3]	19,246	20,766
Legg Mason Total Ret	21.8[2]	16.4[5]	-16.8[5]	40.5[2]	14.3[2]	14.1[3]	-7.1[5]	30.4[3]	31.1[1]	37.5[1]	33.0[1]	20.0[1]	23,507	24,908
Legg Mason Value	25.8[1]	20.2[4]	-17.0[5]	34.7[3]	11.4[3]	11.3[3]	1.4[2]	40.8[1]	38.4[1]	37.1[1]	38.7[1]	24.7[1]	26,705	30,124
Leonetti Balanced	—	—	—	—	—	—	—	—	6.8[5]	20.9[3]	—	—	—	—
Lepercq-Istel	7.1[5]	21.8[3]	-6.7[4]	17.3[5]	5.5[4]	13.5[3]	-5.0[5]	27.1[4]	26.3[1]	8.9[5]	20.5[4]	13.5[5]	17,489	18,857
Leuthold Asst Alloc	—	—	—	—	—	—	—	—	9.3[5]	17.3[5]	—	—	—	—
Lexington Convert	—	7.2[5]	-3.4[4]	45.1[1]	12.8[1]	6.5[5]	1.3[1]	18.6[5]	4.9[5]	13.2[5]	12.1[5]	8.7[5]	14,080	15,194
Lexington Corp Ldrs	20.1[2]	30.3[1]	-3.9[3]	23.7[4]	9.6[2]	17.6[2]	-1.0[4]	39.2[1]	22.4[2]	23.1[4]	28.0[2]	19.5[2]	20,973	24,417
Lexington Crsby Sm Cap Asia	—	—	—	—	—	—	—	—	25.7[1]	-42.3[5]	—	—	—	—
Lexington Global	16.3[1]	25.1[1]	-16.7[5]	15.5[3]	-3.5[5]	31.9[1]	1.8[2]	10.7[5]	16.4[3]	6.9[4]	11.3[5]	13.1[3]	13,773	18,494
Lexington GNMA	6.9[4]	15.6[1]	9.3[2]	15.7[2]	4.5[5]	8.1[4]	-2.1[2]	15.9[4]	5.6[1]	10.2[1]	10.5[1]	7.4[2]	13,488	14,274
Lexington Goldfund	-15.0[2]	23.6[2]	-20.6[3]	-6.1[4]	-20.5[5]	87.0[3]	-7.3[2]	-1.9[4]	7.8[3]	-43.0[5]	-15.5[2]	0.9[3]	6,030	10,452
Lexington Gro & Inc	9.5[5]	27.6[2]	-10.3[5]	24.9[4]	12.4[2]	13.2[3]	-3.1[5]	22.6[5]	26.5[1]	30.3[2]	26.4[3]	17.3[3]	20,210	22,169
Lexington Int'l	—	—	—	—	—	—	—	5.8[4]	13.6[3]	1.6[3]	6.9[3]	—	12,211	—
Lexington Ramrz Glob Inc	—	—	—	—	—	—	—	20.1[2]	13.3[1]	5.0[5]	12.6[2]	—	14,291	—
Lexington Sm Cap Value SC	—	—	—	—	—	—	—	—	17.6[4]	10.5[5]	—	—	—	—
Lexington Trka Dlg Russia	—	—	—	—	—	—	—	—	—	67.5[1]	—	—	—	—
Lexington World Emg	10.5[4]	28.1[1]	-14.4[4]	24.2[1]	3.8[5]	63.4[1]	-13.8[5]	-5.9[5]	7.4[5]	-11.4[4]	-3.6[5]	4.8[4]	8,954	12,612
Lighthouse Growth	—	—	—	—	—	—	—	—	25.8[1]	9.0[5]	—	—	—	—
Lindner Bulwark	—	—	—	—	—	—	—	-11.2[5]	28.8[1]	-22.3[5]	-3.8[5]	—	8,890	—
Lindner Dividend	24.2[1]	11.9[5]	-6.5[4]	27.4[2]	21.1[1]	14.9[2]	-3.3[4]	21.5[5]	11.5[4]	13.9[5]	15.6[5]	11.4[5]	15,433	17,148
Lindner Growth	20.4[2]	21.2[4]	-11.3[4]	23.4[4]	12.8[2]	19.8[1]	-0.7[3]	19.9[5]	21.0[3]	8.7[5]	16.4[5]	13.4[5]	15,765	18,754
Lindner International	—	—	—	—	—	—	—	—	18.7[2]	2.6[3]	—	—	—	—
Lindner Utility	—	—	—	—	—	—	-1.0[2]	23.9[4]	23.2[1]	19.8[3]	22.3[2]	—	18,281	—

See Chapter 3 for explanation of symbols

| Total Net Assets $Million | | NAV per share | | 1997 per share distributions | | Yield % | Risk Analysis | | | | % Distribution of Portfolio | | | | |
December 31 1996	1997	December 31 1996	1997	Income	Capital gains	12/31/97	beta	R^2	Std. Dev.	Sharpe Ratio	12/31/97 Stocks	Bonds	Cash	Objective	No-Load Fund
63.6	113.7	12.90	13.29	0.59	1.07	4.1	0.40	0.57	5.96	A	82	11	7	income	Key SBSF Convert‡
109.1	84.7	16.54	14.54	0.01	3.90	0.0	0.72	0.63	10.10	D	96	0	4	growth	Key SBSF Fund‡
16.7	39.8	10.80	13.34	0.39	0.51	3.0	—	—	—	—	91	0	9	gr-inc	Key Stock Idx‡
75.5	98.2	17.85	15.88	0.11	6.36	0.7	—	—	—	—	99	0	1	growth	Kiewit Eqty Fund
117.4	247.5	10.20	10.35	0.62	0.03	6.0	0.17	0.27	3.57	F	0	100	0	fix-inc	Kiewit Inter Bond
140.7	255.5	10.05	10.08	0.57	0.01	5.7	0.06	0.22	1.48	C	0	99	1	fix-inc	Kiewit Sht Term Gov
136.8	157.3	10.20	10.25	0.43	0.13	4.2	0.07	0.13	2.11	F	0	96	4	tax-free	Kiewit Tax Exempt
0.2	17.5	9.98	11.39	0.61	0.03	5.3	—	—	—	—	77	21	2	income	Kobren Insight:Cons Alloc
0.3	62.6	10.24	11.51	0.27	0.00	2.3	—	—	—	—	99	0	1	growth	Kobren Insight:Growth
0.2	43.4	10.06	11.94	0.46	0.00	3.8	—	—	—	—	83	15	2	gr-inc	Kobren Insight:Mod Gro
33.7	51.7	15.83	16.88	0.08	2.03	0.5	0.65	0.66	8.99	A	89	0	11	growth	KPM Equity
7.9	10.0	10.44	10.70	0.59	0.00	5.6	0.16	0.23	3.80	C	0	99	1	fix-inc	KPM Fixed Inc
2.1	6.6	19.14	24.42	0.29	0.00	1.2	—	—	—	—	98	2	0	growth	Lake Forest Core Eqty
9.3	9.3	12.13	12.47	0.01	1.99	0.1	—	—	—	—	93	0	7	growth	Lancaster Cap Builder
1.8	3.4	12.59	14.13	0.30	0.97	2.1	—	—	—	—	69	23	8	income	Lancaster Convert
2.5	1.2	10.22	10.30	0.60	0.00	5.8	—	—	—	—	0	94	6	fix-inc	Lancaster Gov Qual
9.1	7.5	15.62	13.37	0.00	3.28	0.0	0.91	0.24	20.87	F	94	0	6	agg gr	Lancaster Crest Sm Cap SC
—	8.4	—	14.26	0.00	2.07	0.0	—	—	—	—	95	0	5	agg gr	Lazard Bantam Val SC(O shrs)
—	7.3	—	10.02	0.58	0.07	5.8	0.14	0.24	3.27	B	0	89	11	fix-inc	Lazard Bond(O shrs)
—	7.8	—	9.20	0.09	0.66	0.9	0.93	0.27	18.83	D	71	0	29	int'l	Lazard Emg Mkt(O shrs)
—	22.9	—	19.99	0.19	3.54	0.9	0.90	0.88	10.60	B	97	0	3	growth	Lazard Equity(O shrs)
—	2.3	—	11.91	0.16	1.14	1.2	—	—	—	—	96	0	4	global	Lazard Global Eqty(O shrs)
—	10.9	—	13.95	0.32	0.84	2.3	0.50	0.26	10.89	A	90	0	10	int'l	Lazard Int'l Eqty(O shrs)
—	2.8	—	9.65	0.52	0.00	5.4	0.01	0.00	7.95	F	1	88	11	fix-inc	Lazard Int'l Fix Inc(O shrs)
—	1.9	—	11.69	0.06	0.12	0.5	0.41	0.23	9.40	C	92	0	8	int'l	Lazard Int'l Sm Cap(O shrs)
—	1.8	—	10.30	0.00	0.00	—	—	—	—	—	96	0	4	agg gr	Lazard Mid Cap(O sh)
—	46.2	—	20.02	0.05	2.95	0.3	0.70	0.43	11.80	B	94	0	6	agg gr	Lazard Small Cap SC(O shrs)
—	15.3	—	9.66	0.80	0.06	8.3	0.13	0.29	2.74	A	1	69	30	fix-inc	Lazard Strat Yld(O shrs)
90.9	172.0	14.40	15.90	0.00	1.85	0.0	0.97	0.88	11.63	C	93	0	7	growth	Legg Mason Amer Lead
14.9	34.5	10.34	11.93	0.21	0.10	1.7	—	—	—	—	59	38	3	income	Legg Mason Balan
21.1	65.3	10.51	9.85	0.01	0.00	0.1	—	—	—	—	86	9	5	int'l	Legg Mason Emg Mkts
161.2	136.7	10.41	9.60	0.52	0.11	5.5	0.16	0.11	5.43	F	0	89	11	fix-inc	Legg Mason Glob Gov
294.6	300.3	10.31	10.40	0.58	0.00	5.6	0.13	0.26	2.78	C	0	98	2	fix-inc	Legg Mason Gov Inter
232.9	380.4	15.37	16.29	1.33	0.08	8.2	0.10	0.17	2.78	A	16	75	9	fix-inc	Legg Mason High Yld
167.5	228.6	12.09	11.78	0.08	0.44	0.7	—	—	—	—	96	1	3	int'l	Legg Mason Int'l Eqty
91.7	121.7	10.22	10.59	0.62	0.00	5.9	0.21	0.29	4.37	B	0	93	7	fix-inc	Legg Mason Invest Grd
964.4	1,366.8	27.83	32.27	0.00	1.50	0.0	0.82	0.41	14.10	C	94	0	6	agg gr	Legg Mason Spec Invest SC
344.7	598.6	19.01	23.31	0.38	2.03	1.6	0.70	0.64	9.80	A	89	5	6	growth	Legg Mason Total Ret
1,978.0	3,683.1	32.99	42.74	0.03	2.32	0.1	1.08	0.80	13.58	A	91	1	8	growth	Legg Mason Value
10.3	12.5	11.19	12.41	0.03	1.06	0.2	—	—	—	—	68	18	14	income	Leonetti Balanced
24.2	28.4	19.03	19.21	0.00	1.44	0.0	0.66	0.24	14.90	F	80	0	20	growth	Lepercq-Istel
31.8	32.8	10.37	11.35	0.39	0.36	3.4	—	—	—	—	28	60	12	growth	Leuthold Asst Alloc
11.2	10.3	13.66	15.08	0.11	0.26	0.7	0.44	0.33	8.34	F	88	0	12	income	Lexington Convert
391.7	526.7	16.05	14.88	0.26	4.45	12.7	0.86	0.89	10.11	C	90	0	10	gr-inc	Lexington Corp Ldrs
25.2	14.0	12.24	7.06	0.00	0.00	0.1	—	—	—	—	97	0	3	int'l	Lexington Crsby Sm Cap Asia
37.2	35.1	11.28	10.59	0.09	1.36	0.7	0.64	0.47	10.27	F	90	0	10	global	Lexington Global
133.7	151.6	8.12	8.40	0.52	0.00	6.2	0.15	0.32	3.07	A	0	94	6	fix-inc	Lexington GNMA
109.2	53.9	5.97	3.24	0.01	0.21	0.3	0.29	0.01	26.58	B	96	0	4	prec met	Lexington Goldfund
200.2	228.1	18.56	20.27	0.33	3.47	1.4	0.80	0.83	9.84	C	97	0	3	gr-inc	Lexington Gro & Inc
18.9	19.9	10.86	10.10	0.13	0.80	1.2	0.58	0.32	11.20	C	85	0	15	int'l	Lexington Int'l
29.0	23.6	11.22	10.58	0.89	0.27	8.4	0.12	0.09	4.35	A	0	96	4	fix-inc	Lexington Ramrz Glob Inc.
8.1	9.6	11.73	11.39	0.13	1.41	1.1	—	—	—	—	98	0	2	growth	Lexington Sm Cap Value SC
13.8	137.6	11.24	17.50	0.01	1.29	0.1	—	—	—	—	74	4	22	int'l	Lexington Trka Dlg Russia
256.5	138.0	11.49	10.18	0.00	0.00	0.0	0.92	0.32	17.50	F	83	0	17	int'l	Lexington World Emg
17.6	33.8	14.86	15.59	0.00	0.61	0.0	—	—	—	—	170	0	-35	growth	Lighthouse Contrarian
75.3	42.1	7.97	5.81	0.39	0.00	6.6	-0.12	0.01	18.54	F	38	4	58	agg gr	Lindner Bulwark
2,281.5	1,800.0	27.50	26.99	1.68	2.49	5.7	0.35	0.43	5.84	D	75	23	2	income	Lindner Dividend
1,495.1	1,300.0	24.60	22.85	0.34	3.48	1.3	0.47	0.23	10.80	F	87	2	11	growth	Lindner Growth
2.0	3.5	9.70	9.72	0.00	0.22	0.0	—	—	—	—	99	0	1	int'l	Lindner International
35.1	47.0	14.64	16.15	0.37	0.93	2.1	0.53	0.20	13.16	F	89	6	5	income	Lindner Utility

Arranged in alphabetical order

No-Load Fund	1988	1989	1990	1991	1992	1993	1994	1995	1996	1997	Annualized 3 yrs.	Annualized 5 yrs.	What $10,000 grew to after 3 yrs.	5 yrs.
Lindner/Ryback Small Cap SC	—	—	—	—	—	—	—	8.9[5]	41.2[1]	31.7[2]	26.5[2]	—	20,246	—
Lipper Hi Inc Bd	—	—	—	—	—	—	—	—	—	11.0[2]	—	—	—	—
Lipper Prime Europe Eqty	—	—	—	—	—	—	—	—	—	18.6[1]	—	—	—	—
Lipper US Eqty	—	—	—	—	—	—	—	—	—	18.6[5]	—	—	—	—
LKCM Eqty	—	—	—	—	—	—	—	—	17.0[4]	23.6[4]	—	—	—	—
LKCM Sm Cap SC	—	—	—	—	—	—	—	31.8[3]	25.7[1]	23.1[3]	26.8[2]	—	20,387	—
Longleaf Partners Realty	—	—	—	—	—	—	—	—	—	29.7[2]	—	—	—	—
Longleaf Partners Sm Cap‡SC	—	—	-30.0[5]	26.2[4]	6.8[4]	19.8[2]	3.7[1]	18.6[5]	30.6[1]	29.0[2]	26.0[3]	19.9[1]	19,987	24,830
Longleaf Partners‡	35.3[1]	23.3[3]	-16.4[5]	39.2[2]	20.5[1]	22.2[1]	9.0[1]	27.5[4]	21.0[3]	28.2[2]	25.5[3]	21.4[1]	19,786	26,354
Mairs & Power Gro	10.2[4]	28.1[2]	3.7[1]	42.1[2]	7.8[3]	12.9[3]	5.6[1]	49.3[1]	26.1[2]	28.7[2]	34.4[1]	23.7[1]	24,282	28,947
Mairs & Power Inc	—	—	—	—	—	—	—	—	—	29.4[1]	—	—	—	—
Managers Bond	8.1[3]	13.1[3]	7.6[2]	19.1[2]	7.9[3]	11.9[3]	-7.3[5]	30.9[1]	5.0[2]	10.4[2]	14.9[1]	9.5[2]	15,174	15,745
Managers Cap App	19.2[2]	21.1[4]	-1.9[2]	33.2[5]	10.7[3]	16.7[3]	-1.5[3]	33.4[3]	13.7[4]	12.7[4]	19.6[4]	14.5[4]	17,097	19,644
Managers Glob Bd	—	—	—	—	—	—	—	19.1[3]	4.4[3]	0.2[5]	7.6[5]	—	12,451	—
Managers Inc Eqty	26.1[1]	22.3[2]	-13.1[5]	29.7[1]	10.0[2]	12.5[3]	1.0[2]	34.4[1]	17.1[2]	27.2[1]	26.0[1]	17.8[1]	20,007	22,719
Managers Int'l Eqty	9.9[5]	15.2[5]	-9.8[3]	18.1[1]	4.3[1]	38.2[3]	2.0[2]	16.3[1]	12.7[3]	10.8[2]	13.3[2]	15.4[1]	14,528	20,484
Managers Inter Mortg	7.4[3]	14.7[1]	10.1[2]	18.2[1]	10.5[1]	11.7[2]	-25.1[5]	17.3[2]	3.3[4]	8.2[3]	9.5[3]	1.9[5]	13,115	10,972
Managers Sht & Int Bd	5.8[4]	10.6[3]	6.5[5]	12.8[3]	11.6[1]	8.5[1]	-8.4[5]	15.5[1]	4.3[3]	5.9[4]	8.4[1]	4.8[4]	12,750	12,668
Managers Spec Eqty SC	26.0[1]	33.9[2]	-15.8[4]	49.8[3]	16.1[2]	17.4[2]	-2.0[3]	33.9[3]	24.8[2]	24.5[2]	27.6[1]	19.1[1]	20,794	23,917
Managers ST Gov	6.0[4]	8.7[5]	7.1[4]	10.8[5]	3.9[5]	3.7[5]	-6.1[5]	9.7[4]	3.9[5]	5.5[5]	6.3[5]	3.2[5]	12,022	11,707
Markman Agg Alloc	—	—	—	—	—	—	—	11.6[5]	19.0[3]	—	—	—	—	—
Markman Conserv Alloc	—	—	—	—	—	—	—	13.0[5]	14.3[5]	—	—	—	—	—
Markman Moderate Alloc	—	—	—	—	—	—	—	10.7[5]	19.4[1]	—	—	—	—	—
Marshall Eqty Inc	—	—	—	—	—	—	-1.6[4]	34.2[2]	21.3[2]	27.5[3]	27.5[2]	—	20,742	—
Marshall Gov Inc	—	—	—	—	—	6.0[5]	-2.7[2]	16.9[4]	3.0[3]	8.4[4]	9.3[4]	6.1[5]	13,063	13,466
Marshall Int'l Stk	—	—	—	—	—	—	—	11.6[2]	19.7[2]	10.9[2]	14.0[1]	—	14,796	—
Marshall Inter Bd	—	—	—	—	—	6.9[4]	-3.1[3]	15.4[4]	2.4[4]	7.2[5]	8.2[5]	5.6[5]	12,669	13,126
Marshall Inter TF	—	—	—	—	—	—	—	11.5[5]	3.8[3]	6.8[4]	7.3[5]	—	12,365	—
Marshall Lg Cap Gr & Inc	—	—	—	—	—	3.4[5]	-5.8[5]	33.2[2]	14.7[5]	26.2[3]	24.5[4]	13.4[5]	19,280	18,773
Marshall Mid-Cap Gro	—	—	—	—	—	—	-5.6[5]	33.7[2]	20.6[3]	22.7[4]	25.6[3]	—	19,796	—
Marshall Mid-Cap Val	—	—	—	—	—	—	2.1[2]	25.4[4]	13.9[5]	23.4[4]	20.8[5]	—	17,622	—
Marshall Sm Cap Gro SC	—	—	—	—	—	—	—	—	—	23.2[3]	—	—	—	—
Marshall ST Inc	—	—	—	—	—	3.7[5]	1.8[1]	8.9[5]	5.0[2]	6.4[3]	6.8[4]	5.1[3]	12,167	12,847
Masters Sel Equity	—	—	—	—	—	—	—	—	—	29.1[2]	—	—	—	—
Masters Sel International	—	—	—	—	—	—	—	—	—	—	—	—	—	—
Mathers	13.7[4]	10.4[5]	10.4[1]	9.4[5]	3.1[5]	2.1[5]	-5.9[5]	7.0[5]	-0.1[5]	3.0[5]	3.3[5]	1.1[5]	11,012	10,579
Matrix Emg Growth SC	—	—	—	—	—	—	—	—	10.5[5]	16.6[4]	—	—	—	—
Matrix Growth	-2.0[5]	36.3[1]	-4.5[3]	34.2[3]	4.9[4]	9.3[4]	-4.8[5]	23.5[5]	17.9[4]	34.6[1]	25.2[3]	15.3[4]	19,602	20,396
Matrix\LMH Value	18.0[2]	12.1[5]	-18.6[5]	18.8[5]	8.3[3]	7.2[5]	2.6[1]	26.2[4]	15.6[5]	17.9[5]	19.8[5]	13.6[5]	17,190	18,911
Matterhorn Growth	32.3[1]	23.5[4]	-8.6[3]	25.7[5]	18.2[1]	25.8[1]	-11.3[5]	25.3[4]	10.5[5]	13.7[4]	16.3[5]	11.9[5]	15,735	17,564
Matthew 25	—	—	—	—	—	—	—	—	—	39.7[1]	—	—	—	—
Matthews Asian Cnvrt	—	—	—	—	—	—	—	8.2[3]	13.9[3]	-23.2[5]	-1.8[4]	—	9,463	—
Matthews Korea	—	—	—	—	—	—	—	—	-31.8[5]	-64.8[5]	—	—	—	—
Matthews Pac Tiger	—	—	—	—	—	—	—	3.1[4]	24.2[1]	-40.9[5]	-8.9[5]	—	7,570	—
Maxus Equity	—	—	-10.8[5]	36.5[1]	13.5[2]	24.5[1]	0.6[2]	22.4[5]	19.1[4]	28.4[3]	23.3[4]	18.6[3]	18,727	23,461
Maxus Income	7.7[4]	11.5[4]	-0.2[4]	19.2[2]	7.8[3]	8.7[4]	-4.4[3]	16.0[4]	9.2[1]	11.8[2]	12.3[2]	8.1[3]	14,161	14,726
Maxus Laureate	—	—	—	—	—	—	-3.2[4]	14.1[5]	21.0[2]	6.0[5]	13.6[5]	—	14,643	—
McM Balanced	—	—	—	—	—	—	—	28.7[2]	16.3[2]	23.7[2]	22.8[2]	—	18,504	—
McM Eqty Invest	—	—	—	—	—	—	—	35.9[1]	26.8[1]	33.8[1]	32.1[1]	—	23,070	—
McM Fixed Inc	—	—	—	—	—	—	—	19.3[2]	3.0[4]	9.5[3]	10.4[3]	—	13,459	—
McM Inter Fix	—	—	—	—	—	—	—	15.0[4]	4.1[2]	7.9[4]	8.9[4]	—	12,916	—
Merger‡	18.3[3]	9.6[5]	1.1[1]	16.8[5]	5.3[4]	17.7[2]	7.1[1]	14.2[5]	10.0[5]	11.7[5]	11.9[5]	12.1[5]	14,026	17,680
Meridian Value	—	—	—	—	—	—	—	23.8[5]	32.3[1]	21.4[4]	25.7[3]	—	19,876	—
Meridian	18.1[3]	19.6[4]	4.6[1]	56.9[1]	15.6[2]	13.1[3]	0.6[3]	21.8[5]	11.2[5]	19.2[4]	17.3[5]	12.9[5]	16,146	18,371
Merriman Asst Alloc	—	—	0.8[2]	12.3[4]	2.8[3]	18.5[4]	-2.9[3]	10.5[5]	10.5[4]	5.8[5]	8.9[5]	8.3[5]	12,923	14,869
Merriman Cap App	—	—	3.1[1]	21.9[5]	4.2[5]	3.6[5]	-0.6[3]	14.8[5]	10.3[5]	9.9[5]	11.6[5]	7.5[5]	13,915	14,329
Merriman Flex Bd	—	8.5[5]	6.1[5]	13.3[5]	4.5[5]	14.4[1]	-2.9[3]	14.6[4]	7.6[1]	5.7[5]	9.2[3]	7.7[1]	13,032	14,477
Merriman Gro & Inc	—	9.8[5]	3.8[1]	19.2[5]	-1.3[5]	2.8[5]	-0.2[3]	17.7[5]	15.0[5]	13.1[5]	15.3[5]	9.4[5]	15,309	15,706
Merriman Levgd Gro	—	—	—	—	—	—	-0.1[2]	17.1[5]	12.0[4]	12.2[4]	13.8[5]	8.8[5]	14,718	15,248
Metro West Low Dur	—	—	—	—	—	—	—	—	—	—	—	—	—	—

See Chapter 3 for explanation of symbols

Total Net Assets $Million		NAV per share		1997 per share distributions		Yield %	Risk Analysis				% Distribution of Portfolio			Objective	No-Load Fund
December 31		December 31		Income	Capital gains	12/31/97	beta	R²	Std. Dev.	Sharpe Ratio	Stocks	12/31/97 Bonds	Cash		
1996	1997	1996	1997												
14.5	44.3	6.72	8.50	0.04	0.30	0.5	0.36	0.09	13.29	C	88	0	12	growth	Lindner/Ryback Small Cap SC
0.8	4.7	10.18	10.11	0.86	0.26	8.5	—	—	—	—	0	85	15	fix-inc	Lipper Hi Inc Bd
0.6	1.1	11.25	11.73	0.00	1.51	0.0	—	—	—	—	98	0	2	int'l	Lipper Prime Europe Eqty
0.6	0.9	11.37	12.02	0.12	1.30	1.0	—	—	—	—	79	0	21	gr-inc	Lipper US Eqty
34.6	50.5	11.70	13.18	0.24	0.46	1.8	—	—	—	—	96	0	4	growth	LKCM Eqty
199.1	255.3	16.20	16.89	0.06	1.33	0.4	0.54	0.28	11.40	A	90	0	10	agg gr	LKCM Sm Cap SC
156.0	737.3	13.97	17.35	0.13	0.64	0.7	—	—	—	—	90	3	7	sector	Longleaf Partners Realty
252.1	915.3	17.86	22.18	0.18	0.69	0.8	0.27	0.18	7.05	A	89	0	11	growth	Longleaf Partners Sm Cap‡SC
2,300.1	2,605.1	22.85	25.98	0.21	3.11	0.7	0.75	0.68	10.24	B	97	0	3	growth	Longleaf Partners‡
150.2	412.6	69.48	86.67	0.98	1.69	1.1	0.83	0.76	10.63	A	100	0	0	growth	Mairs & Power Gro
510.7	568.4	11.17	12.91	0.14	1.09	1.1	—	—	—	—	67	29	4	income	Mairs & Power Inc
31.8	41.4	22.83	23.73	1.40	0.00	5.9	0.36	0.32	7.12	B	2	94	4	fix-inc	Managers Bond
101.0	73.4	26.33	24.25	0.00	5.12	0.0	0.93	0.67	12.62	C	95	0	5	agg gr	Managers Cap App
16.8	17.4	21.40	20.93	0.17	0.34	0.8	0.13	0.04	6.99	F	0	93	7	fix-inc	Managers Glob Bd
52.8	64.8	30.49	31.07	0.57	6.16	1.8	0.74	0.87	8.81	A	97	0	3	income	Managers Inc Eqty
270.4	379.4	43.69	45.58	0.62	2.15	1.4	0.55	0.33	10.57	A	91	0	9	int'l	Managers Int'l Eqty
25.2	21.6	15.17	15.52	0.86	0.00	5.5	0.15	0.23	3.49	B	0	103	-3	fix-inc	Managers Inter Mortg
22.4	15.2	19.46	19.52	1.05	0.00	5.4	0.10	0.22	2.35	A	0	97	3	fix-inc	Managers Sht & Int Bd
270.6	719.9	50.95	61.17	0.07	2.07	0.1	0.69	0.30	13.89	B	91	0	9	agg gr	Managers Spec Eqty SC
6.1	5.0	17.40	17.37	0.97	0.00	5.6	0.06	0.20	1.57	F	0	99	1	fix-inc	Managers ST Gov
84.0	84.4	12.26	12.74	0.20	1.65	1.4	—	—	—	—	77	12	11	agg gr	Markman Agg Alloc
43.0	36.7	11.49	11.82	0.45	0.86	3.6	—	—	—	—	55	32	13	gr-inc	Markman Conserv Alloc
84.0	86.4	11.49	11.90	0.47	1.35	3.6	—	—	—	—	67	21	12	growth	Markman Moderate Alloc
231.4	526.3	13.55	15.62	0.31	1.27	2.0	0.71	0.87	8.44	A	89	0	11	gr-inc	Marshall Eqty Inc
157.2	219.0	9.45	9.59	0.63	0.00	6.6	0.16	0.25	3.61	C	0	100	0	fix-inc	Marshall Gov Inc
169.9	225.3	11.80	12.58	0.21	0.29	1.7	0.59	0.40	10.32	A	90	0	10	int'l	Marshall Int'l Stk
431.6	554.2	9.44	9.51	0.59	0.00	6.2	0.13	0.19	3.21	F	0	100	0	fix-inc	Marshall Inter Bd
74.7	95.7	10.00	10.23	0.43	0.00	4.2	0.14	0.32	2.69	F	0	98	2	tax-free	Marshall Inter TF
236.1	288.5	11.81	13.63	0.08	1.18	0.6	1.00	0.95	11.40	D	97	0	3	gr-inc	Marshall Lg Cap Gr & Inc
161.0	216.1	13.10	14.21	0.00	1.81	0.0	1.05	0.49	16.67	D	96	0	4	growth	Marshall Mid-Cap Gro
175.1	184.5	11.09	11.57	0.10	1.95	0.9	0.68	0.60	9.76	F	92	0	8	gr-inc	Marshall Mid-Cap Val
33.6	70.0	10.76	12.75	0.00	0.49	0.0	—	—	—	—	96	0	4	agg gr	Marshall Sm Cap Gro SC
104.0	150.4	9.65	9.63	0.62	0.00	6.4	0.05	0.26	1.19	B	0	96	4	fix-inc	Marshall ST Inc
0.1	296.1	10.00	11.84	0.03	1.06	0.2	—	—	—	—	90	0	10	agg gr	Masters Sel Equity
—	10.0	—	9.88	0.00	0.00	—	—	—	—	—	—	—	—	int'l	Masters Sel International
171.6	138.4	13.27	13.06	0.61	0.00	4.7	0.11	0.04	5.52	F	20	64	16	growth	Mathers
5.6	7.0	14.24	16.33	0.00	0.26	0.0	—	—	—	—	91	0	9	agg gr	Matrix Emg Growth SC
10.5	12.5	15.09	18.64	0.00	1.63	0.0	0.93	0.80	11.68	C	98	0	2	growth	Matrix Growth
—	9.1	26.33	30.86	0.17	0.00	0.6	0.54	0.47	8.75	F	91	0	9	gr-inc	Matrix\LMH Value
8.6	8.9	6.17	6.74	0.00	0.27	0.0	0.70	0.52	10.78	D	84	0	16	agg gr	Matterhorn Growth
1.4	10.6	6.11	8.50	0.01	0.02	0.2	—	—	—	—	99	0	1	growth	Matthew 25
3.9	4.7	11.12	8.01	0.06	0.48	0.8	0.60	0.23	13.62	F	10	81	9	int'l	Matthews Asian Cnvrt
2.8	25.7	5.90	2.08	0.00	0.00	0.0	—	—	—	—	84	0	16	int'l	Matthews Korea
32.9	37.3	12.12	7.15	0.01	0.02	0.1	1.30	0.37	22.36	F	95	0	5	int'l	Matthews Pac Tiger
38.8	55.6	16.00	18.23	0.17	2.10	0.9	0.65	0.64	9.10	D	77	5	18	gr-inc	Maxus Equity
35.7	38.6	10.78	11.31	0.70	0.00	6.2	0.16	0.31	3.23	A	2	87	11	fix-inc	Maxus Income
3.2	3.4	10.82	10.38	0.55	0.46	5.3	0.65	0.57	9.48	D	73	24	3	agg gr	Maxus Laureate
23.6	64.6	13.79	16.57	0.45	0.00	2.7	0.67	0.93	7.80	B	59	39	2	income	McM Balanced
39.5	91.2	16.70	22.05	0.23	0.04	1.1	0.97	0.96	11.18	A	99	0	1	growth	McM Eqty Invest
9.0	13.8	10.45	10.76	0.67	0.02	6.2	—	—	—	—	0	100	0	fix-inc	McM Fixed Inc
89.1	110.5	10.25	10.44	0.60	0.00	5.7	0.13	0.22	3.16	C	0	98	2	fix-inc	McM Inter Fix
473.8	435.5	14.11	14.15	0.03	1.58	0.2	0.05	0.05	2.41	A	113	0	-13	growth	Merger‡
5.4	8.7	14.85	15.86	1.23	0.99	7.5	0.58	0.24	13.27	F	95	0	5	gr-inc	Meridian Value
377.6	330.2	30.08	30.73	0.32	4.81	0.9	0.54	0.37	9.91	F	88	0	12	growth	Meridian
15.8	14.6	10.61	9.41	0.37	1.45	3.4	0.54	0.61	7.63	F	64	0	36	global	Merriman Asst Alloc
14.3	13.6	10.12	8.72	0.19	2.21	1.7	0.71	0.59	10.15	F	64	0	36	growth	Merriman Cap App
8.6	9.0	10.50	10.21	0.65	0.23	6.2	0.15	0.30	3.08	B	0	96	4	fix-inc	Merriman Flex Bd
7.9	8.9	11.00	9.20	0.27	2.97	2.2	0.63	0.77	7.90	F	56	0	44	gr-inc	Merriman Gro & Inc
14.5	16.2	11.87	10.25	0.29	2.78	2.2	0.98	0.61	13.91	F	84	0	16	agg gr	Merriman Levgd Gro
—	78.0	—	10.17	0.49	0.01	—	—	—	—	—	0	71	29	fix-inc	Metro West Low Dur

Stock and bond funds — comprehensive summary *continued*
Arranged in alphabetical order

No-Load Fund	Total return percent with quintile ranks by objective										Annualized		What $10,000 grew to after	
	1988	1989	1990	1991	1992	1993	1994	1995	1996	1997	3 yrs.	5 yrs.	3 yrs.	5 yrs.
Metro West Tot Ret Bd...	—	—	—	—	—	—	—	—	—	—	—	—	—	—
Meyers Sheppard Pride...	—	—	—	—	—	—	—	—	—	21.8 [4]	—	—	—	—
Midas Gold...	-19.0 [4]	21.9 [3]	-17.0 [1]	-0.2 [1]	-7.2 [1]	98.8 [2]	-17.3 [5]	37.1 [1]	21.2 [2]	-59.0 [5]	-12.0 [1]	2.3 [3]	6,808	11,193
Monetta Balanced...	—	—	—	—	—	—	—	—	25.9 [1]	21.2 [3]	—	—	—	—
Monetta Fund...	23.0 [2]	15.2 [5]	11.4 [1]	55.9 [1]	5.5 [4]	0.5 [5]	-6.2 [5]	28.0 [4]	1.6 [5]	26.2 [3]	18.0 [5]	9.1 [5]	16,409	15,469
Monetta Inter Bd...	—	—	—	—	—	—	-1.0 [1]	14.8 [4]	6.5 [1]	8.9 [3]	10.0 [2]	—	13,315	—
Monetta Large Cap Eqty...	—	—	—	—	—	—	—	—	—	26.6 [3]	—	—	—	—
Monetta MidCap...	—	—	—	—	—	—	2.2 [2]	24.5 [4]	24.2 [2]	29.1 [2]	25.9 [3]	—	19,968	—
Monetta Sm Cap Eqty SC...	—	—	—	—	—	—	—	—	—	—	—	—	—	—
Montag & Cldwl Balanced...	—	—	—	—	—	—	—	29.4 [2]	20.4 [1]	23.5 [2]	24.4 [1]	—	19,232	—
Montag & Cldwl Growth...	—	—	—	—	—	—	—	38.7 [1]	32.7 [1]	31.9 [2]	34.4 [1]	—	24,267	—
Montgmry CA TF Inter...	—	—	—	—	—	—	0.1 [1]	11.4 [5]	4.5 [1]	7.5 [2]	7.8 [4]	—	12,516	—
Montgmry Emg Asia...	—	—	—	—	—	—	—	—	—	-28.3 [5]	—	—	—	—
Montgmry Emg Mkts...	—	—	—	—	—	—	-7.7 [4]	-9.1 [5]	12.3 [3]	-3.2 [4]	-0.4 [5]	7.7 [4]	9,883	14,477
Montgmry Eqty Inc...	—	—	—	—	—	—	—	35.2 [2]	18.3 [4]	26.1 [3]	26.3 [3]	—	20,169	—
Montgmry Glob Asst Alloc...	—	—	—	—	—	—	—	—	—	11.2 [3]	—	—	—	—
Montgmry Glob Comm...	—	—	—	—	—	—	-13.4 [5]	16.9 [3]	8.0 [5]	15.8 [2]	13.5 [4]	—	14,624	—
Montgmry Glob Oppty...	—	—	—	—	—	—	-8.6 [4]	17.3 [3]	20.2 [2]	11.0 [3]	16.1 [3]	—	15,657	—
Montgmry Growth...	—	—	—	—	—	—	20.9 [1]	23.6 [4]	20.2 [3]	24.1 [3]	22.6 [4]	—	18,444	—
Montgmry Int'l Growth...	—	—	—	—	—	—	—	—	21.0 [2]	10.2 [2]	—	—	—	—
Montgmry Int'l Sm Cap...	—	—	—	—	—	—	-13.3 [5]	11.7 [2]	15.0 [3]	-0.8 [4]	8.4 [3]	—	12,745	—
Montgmry Latin Amer...	—	—	—	—	—	—	—	—	—	—	—	—	—	—
Montgmry Micro Cap‡ SC...	—	—	—	—	—	—	—	28.7 [4]	19.1 [3]	27.1 [2]	24.9 [2]	—	19,475	—
Montgmry Select 50...	—	—	—	—	—	—	—	—	20.5 [2]	29.3 [1]	—	—	—	—
Montgmry Sht Dur Gov...	—	—	—	—	—	8.1 [1]	1.1 [2]	11.5 [2]	5.1 [2]	7.0 [2]	7.8 [1]	6.5 [1]	12,539	13,709
Montgmry Sm Cap Opp SC...	—	—	—	—	—	—	—	—	37.3 [1]	16.5 [4]	—	—	—	—
Montgmry Sm Cap‡ SC...	—	—	—	98.7 [1]	9.6 [3]	24.3 [1]	-10.0 [5]	35.1 [3]	18.7 [3]	23.9 [2]	25.7 [2]	17.3 [2]	19,863	22,221
Montgmry Total Ret Bd...	—	—	—	—	—	—	—	—	—	—	—	—	—	—
Montgmry US Asst Alloc...	—	—	—	—	—	—	—	32.6 [1]	12.9 [4]	18.9 [3]	21.2 [2]	—	17,795	—
Mosaic Balanced...	7.8 [5]	12.1 [5]	-7.3 [5]	25.1 [3]	8.4 [3]	4.2 [5]	1.1 [1]	21.5 [4]	16.5 [2]	25.5 [2]	21.1 [2]	13.4 [3]	17,757	18,715
Mosaic Bond...	—	—	—	14.0 [4]	4.1 [5]	6.0 [5]	-2.0 [2]	14.1 [5]	2.6 [4]	6.0 [5]	7.4 [5]	5.2 [5]	12,399	12,878
Mosaic Gov...	7.2 [4]	11.1 [4]	7.1 [4]	13.9 [5]	5.4 [5]	9.7 [3]	-3.6 [4]	14.3 [4]	0.4 [5]	7.7 [4]	7.3 [5]	5.5 [5]	12,354	13,059
Mosaic Hi Yld...	10.3 [2]	2.8 [5]	-7.5 [5]	25.6 [1]	12.0 [1]	15.0 [2]	-2.6 [2]	14.4 [5]	6.8 [2]	9.9 [3]	10.3 [3]	8.5 [2]	13,433	15,041
Mosaic Investors...	12.8 [4]	16.0 [4]	-14.2 [5]	32.1 [2]	11.0 [2]	2.9 [5]	3.9 [1]	24.6 [4]	22.8 [2]	34.8 [1]	27.3 [3]	17.1 [3]	20,628	22,061
Mosaic Mid-Cap Gro...	24.7 [1]	25.2 [3]	-15.9 [5]	25.7 [5]	6.7 [4]	14.9 [3]	-4.0 [4]	22.2 [5]	6.1 [5]	17.1 [4]	14.9 [5]	10.9 [5]	15,172	16,736
Mosaic TF AZ...	—	—	6.7 [3]	9.8 [5]	8.4 [4]	11.9 [4]	-8.6 [5]	14.9 [5]	3.2 [4]	7.9 [5]	8.6 [5]	5.5 [5]	12,792	13,077
Mosaic TF MD...	—	—	—	—	—	—	-8.9 [5]	15.3 [4]	2.1 [5]	8.0 [5]	8.4 [5]	—	12,720	—
Mosaic TF MO...	—	—	5.9 [4]	9.7 [5]	8.0 [5]	11.1 [5]	-8.5 [5]	16.2 [4]	2.7 [5]	8.1 [5]	8.9 [4]	5.6 [5]	12,908	13,120
Mosaic TF Nat...	8.5 [5]	7.3 [5]	5.4 [5]	10.3 [5]	8.2 [4]	11.9 [4]	-8.8 [5]	15.3 [4]	2.9 [5]	8.2 [4]	8.7 [5]	5.6 [5]	12,850	13,102
Mosaic TF VA...	8.3 [5]	7.3 [5]	5.9 [4]	9.9 [5]	7.5 [5]	12.5 [4]	-8.3 [4]	16.1 [4]	3.2 [4]	8.4 [4]	9.1 [4]	6.0 [5]	12,984	13,394
Mosaic Foresight...	—	—	—	—	—	—	-24.1 [5]	-4.7 [5]	9.3 [5]	2.5 [5]	2.2 [5]	—	10,671	—
MSB...	9.8 [5]	28.1 [2]	-7.4 [4]	17.0 [5]	10.7 [2]	20.6 [1]	-1.7 [4]	25.0 [4]	21.2 [3]	28.9 [3]	25.0 [3]	18.3 [3]	19,515	23,145
Muhlenkamp...	—	12.9 [5]	-14.9 [5]	45.4 [1]	15.8 [1]	18.1 [2]	-7.3 [5]	33.3 [2]	29.9 [1]	33.3 [1]	32.1 [1]	20.4 [1]	23,066	25,259
Munder NetNet...	—	—	—	—	—	—	—	—	—	30.1 [2]	—	—	—	—
Mutual Beacon Z‡...	28.9 [1]	17.4 [4]	-8.1 [4]	17.6 [5]	22.9 [1]	22.9 [1]	5.6 [1]	25.9 [4]	21.2 [3]	22.9 [4]	23.3 [4]	19.5 [2]	18,753	24,339
Mutual Discovery Z‡...	—	—	—	—	—	—	3.6 [1]	28.6 [1]	24.9 [1]	22.8 [1]	25.4 [2]	—	19,730	—
Mutual European Z‡...	—	—	—	—	—	—	—	—	—	23.2 [1]	—	—	—	—
Mutual Finl Servs Z‡...	—	—	—	—	—	—	—	—	—	—	—	—	—	—
Mutual Qualified Z‡...	30.4 [1]	14.4 [5]	-10.1 [4]	21.1 [5]	22.7 [1]	22.7 [1]	5.7 [1]	26.6 [4]	21.2 [3]	24.8 [4]	24.2 [4]	20.0 [1]	19,153	24,840
Mutual Shares Z‡...	30.7 [1]	14.9 [5]	-9.8 [4]	21.0 [5]	21.3 [1]	21.0 [1]	4.5 [1]	29.1 [4]	20.8 [3]	26.3 [3]	25.4 [3]	20.0 [1]	19,700	24,909
Nations Balanced Assts...	—	—	—	—	—	9.7 [4]	-3.3 [4]	26.1 [4]	14.4 [3]	21.4 [2]	20.5 [3]	13.2 [3]	17,498	18,556
Nations Cap Gro...	—	—	—	—	—	7.5 [4]	-1.6 [4]	28.6 [3]	18.3 [4]	30.4 [2]	25.6 [3]	16.0 [4]	19,824	20,986
Nations Disc Eqty...	—	—	—	—	—	—	-6.4 [5]	27.3 [4]	21.9 [2]	29.6 [2]	26.2 [3]	—	20,109	—
Nations Divsfd Inc...	—	—	—	—	—	15.7 [2]	-2.8 [2]	20.6 [2]	2.2 [4]	8.3 [4]	10.1 [3]	8.5 [2]	13,352	15,015
Nations Emg Gro SC...	—	—	—	—	—	11.7 [4]	0.4 [2]	29.7 [3]	18.3 [3]	20.5 [3]	22.7 [3]	15.7 [3]	18,489	20,726
Nations Emg Mkts...	—	—	—	—	—	—	—	—	8.5 [4]	-3.2 [4]	—	—	—	—
Nations Eqty Idx...	—	—	—	—	—	—	—	—	22.3 [3]	32.0 [2]	—	—	—	—
Nations Eqty Inc...	—	—	—	9.8 [2]	12.5 [3]	-1.3 [3]	27.4 [2]	19.6 [1]	25.7 [1]	24.2 [1]	16.3 [1]	19,151	21,260	
Nations FL Int Muni...	—	—	—	—	—	11.2 [2]	-4.3 [3]	14.1 [2]	3.5 [4]	7.0 [3]	8.1 [3]	6.1 [3]	12,637	13,440
Nations FL Muni...	—	—	—	—	—	—	-8.2 [4]	19.7 [1]	3.0 [5]	8.7 [4]	10.2 [2]	—	13,395	—

See Chapter 3 for explanation of symbols

Arranged in alphabetical order

Total Net Assets $Million		NAV per share		1997 per share distributions		Yield %	Risk Analysis				% Distribution of Portfolio			Objective	No-Load Fund
December 31 1996	1997	December 31 1996	1997	Income	Capital gains	12/31/97	beta	R^2	Std. Dev.	Sharpe Ratio	Stocks	12/31/97 Bonds	Cash	Objective	No-Load Fund
—	16.7	—	10.51	0.54	0.11	—	—	—	—	—	0	80	20	fix-inc	Metro West Tot Ret Bd
0.9	2.1	10.81	11.59	0.00	1.54	0.0	—	—	—	—	—	—	—	gr-inc	Meyers Sheppard Pride
200.7	100.8	5.15	2.11	0.00	0.00	0.0	0.42	0.01	36.19	A	88	0	12	prec met	Midas Gold
2.3	12.1	12.64	14.08	0.21	1.00	1.5	—	—	—	—	62	33	5	income	Monetta Balanced
212.0	163.4	15.84	17.27	0.00	2.75	0.0	0.82	0.29	17.07	F	96	0	4	growth	Monetta Fund
2.8	3.9	10.21	10.45	0.59	0.05	5.7	0.15	0.27	3.16	A	0	97	3	fix-inc	Monetta Inter Bd
2.3	4.3	12.27	13.36	0.00	2.15	0.0	—	—	—	—	92	0	8	gr-inc	Monetta Large Cap Eqty
17.0	21.9	14.81	14.98	0.00	4.09	0.0	0.64	0.39	11.43	C	93	0	7	growth	Monetta MidCap
—	2.5	—	13.90	0.00	0.83	—	—	—	—	—	97	0	3	agg gr	Monetta Sm Cap Eqty SC
33.0	89.7	13.46	15.96	0.25	0.38	1.5	0.75	0.82	9.25	C	61	38	1	income	Montag & Cldwl Balanced
196.1	548.6	17.80	23.25	0.00	0.21	0.0	1.07	0.78	13.62	A	96	0	4	growth	Montag & Cldwl Growth
18.0	28.0	12.47	12.86	0.52	0.00	4.1	0.14	0.37	2.53	B	0	100	0	tax-free	Montgmry CA TF Inter
19.0	33.9	14.50	9.30	0.17	0.95	1.7	—	—	—	—	90	0	10	int'l	Montgmry Emg Asia
912.5	988.6	13.87	12.93	0.15	0.33	1.2	1.00	0.34	17.99	D	97	0	3	int'l	Montgmry Emg Mkts
29.9	42.2	16.04	17.78	0.46	1.92	2.3	0.68	0.77	8.68	B	96	0	4	gr-inc	Montgmry Eqty Inc
0.1	1.6	12.00	12.21	0.47	0.61	3.9	—	—	—	—	100	0	0	global	Montgmry Glob Asst Alloc
165.4	136.0	16.74	15.57	0.00	3.75	0.0	0.95	0.56	14.03	D	87	0	13	global	Montgmry Glob Comm
29.2	22.7	16.73	14.63	0.00	3.85	0.0	0.85	0.54	12.69	D	102	0	-2	global	Montgmry Glob Oppty
994.9	1,364.4	20.15	21.89	0.15	2.92	0.6	0.79	0.60	11.38	D	80	0	20	growth	Montgmry Growth
25.4	31.8	14.40	14.76	0.02	1.07	0.2	—	—	—	—	98	0	2	int'l	Montgmry Int'l Growth
40.5	45.0	15.13	12.68	0.13	2.19	0.8	0.43	0.20	10.50	C	84	0	16	int'l	Montgmry Int'l Sm Cap
—	7.7	—	11.00	0.07	0.15	—	—	—	—	—	101	0	-1	int'l	Montgmry Latin Amer
298.7	368.1	16.91	20.31	0.00	1.14	0.0	0.65	0.23	15.07	C	89	0	11	agg gr	Montgmry Micro Cap‡ SC
89.1	230.7	16.03	18.83	0.00	1.85	0.0	—	—	—	—	100	0	0	global	Montgmry Select 50
39.0	53.4	10.00	10.10	0.58	0.00	5.7	0.08	0.24	1.72	A	0	100	0	fix-inc	Montgmry Sht Dur Gov
200.2	243.9	16.47	18.74	0.00	0.42	0.0	—	—	—	—	96	0	4	agg gr	Montgmry Sm Cap Opp SC
220.9	207.6	18.40	19.64	0.00	2.97	0.0	0.82	0.31	16.59	C	96	0	4	agg gr	Montgmry Sm Cap‡ SC
—	75.5	—	12.29	0.36	0.12	—	—	—	—	—	0	100	0	fix-inc	Montgmry Total Ret Bd
141.8	136.2	18.09	18.01	1.63	1.83	8.2	0.55	0.63	7.80	C	49	51	0	income	Montgmry US Asst Alloc
11.0	16.0	18.09	19.48	0.79	1.70	4.0	0.64	0.83	7.88	C	65	30	5	income	Mosaic Balanced
4.1	1.1	20.63	20.75	1.07	0.00	5.2	0.15	0.26	3.29	F	0	90	10	fix-inc	Mosaic Bond
6.2	5.5	9.68	9.89	0.51	0.00	5.2	0.21	0.27	4.35	F	0	98	2	fix-inc	Mosaic Gov
6.3	6.5	7.10	7.21	0.57	0.00	7.9	0.18	0.43	3.04	A	0	98	2	fix-inc	Mosaic Hi Yld
13.2	22.9	19.16	22.37	0.49	2.82	2.0	0.87	0.81	10.85	C	94	0	6	gr-inc	Mosaic Investors
12.7	10.6	10.64	9.25	0.00	2.72	0.0	0.81	0.46	13.23	F	86	0	14	agg gr	Mosaic Mid-Cap Gro
9.0	8.4	10.25	10.58	0.46	0.00	4.3	0.16	0.23	3.57	F	0	97	3	tax-free	Mosaic TF AZ
2.1	2.1	9.78	10.13	0.42	0.00	4.1	0.16	0.22	3.85	F	0	98	2	tax-free	Mosaic TF MD
11.4	11.4	10.31	10.67	0.46	0.00	4.3	0.17	0.22	4.00	F	0	98	2	tax-free	Mosaic TF MO
29.3	26.9	10.39	10.80	0.43	0.00	3.9	0.18	0.25	3.89	F	0	97	3	tax-free	Mosaic TF Nat
33.1	32.2	11.31	11.72	0.51	0.00	4.4	0.18	0.24	4.04	D	0	97	3	tax-free	Mosaic TF VA
2.4	1.9	10.21	10.46	0.00	0.00	0.0	0.94	0.33	17.51	F	0	0	100	global	Mosaic Foresight
37.4	49.3	14.60	17.73	0.07	0.97	0.4	0.78	0.82	9.56	C	95	0	5	gr-inc	MSB
41.6	125.1	27.52	36.55	0.13	0.00	0.4	0.80	0.75	10.32	A	87	9	4	gr-inc	Muhlenkamp
1.3	4.7	12.64	14.21	0.00	2.20	0.0	—	—	—	—	96	0	4	sector	Munder NetNet
4,950.8	5,684.6	38.95	14.12	0.54	1.26	3.5	0.54	0.65	7.45	B	78	3	18	gr-inc	Mutual Beacon Z‡
2,974.4	3,878.0	17.18	18.89	0.81	1.36	4.0	0.47	0.57	6.98	B	78	4	18	global	Mutual Discovery Z‡
450.2	546.5	11.39	12.60	0.81	0.52	6.4	—	—	—	—	77	3	20	int'l	Mutual European Z‡
—	134.6	—	12.28	0.03	0.09	—	—	—	—	—	82	1	17	sector	Mutual Finl Servs Z‡
4,999.1	5,239.7	32.47	18.18	0.64	1.40	3.3	0.53	0.64	7.40	A	77	3	20	gr-inc	Mutual Qualified Z‡
9,107.5	7,918.5	92.85	21.29	0.54	1.58	2.4	0.54	0.60	7.76	A	74	3	23	gr-inc	Mutual Shares Z‡
9.2	14.4	11.06	10.59	0.26	2.34	2.5	0.55	0.84	6.73	B	58	37	5	income	Nations Balanced Assts
22.3	38.3	11.85	11.41	0.00	0.00	3.68	1.07	0.90	12.53	C	63	34	3	growth	Nations Cap Gro
7.0	19.2	18.47	19.32	0.03	4.23	0.1	0.93	0.76	11.99	C	99	0	1	growth	Nations Disc Eqty
12.2	11.5	10.36	10.56	0.63	0.00	6.0	0.20	0.22	4.68	C	0	99	1	fix-inc	Nations Divsfd Inc
12.3	17.0	13.77	14.71	0.00	1.79	0.0	0.90	0.42	15.39	C	96	0	4	agg gr	Nations Emg Gro SC
0.7	1.6	10.47	10.07	0.08	0.00	0.8	—	—	—	—	99	0	1	int'l	Nations Emg Mkts
1.5	3.3	15.54	19.66	0.22	0.59	1.1	—	—	—	—	100	0	0	gr-inc	Nations Eqty Idx
45.6	63.5	12.11	12.57	0.24	2.16	1.9	0.70	0.87	8.40	A	83	3	14	income	Nations Eqty Inc
3.4	7.6	10.55	10.79	0.48	0.00	4.4	0.14	0.23	3.14	C	0	101	-1	tax-free	Nations FL Int Muni
2.1	2.0	9.64	10.00	0.46	0.00	4.6	0.18	0.19	4.70	C	0	97	3	tax-free	Nations FL Muni

Stock and bond funds — comprehensive summary *continued*

Arranged in alphabetical order

| No-Load Fund | Total return percent with quintile ranks by objective |||||||||| Annualized || What $10,000 grew to after ||
	1988	1989	1990	1991	1992	1993	1994	1995	1996	1997	3 yrs.	5 yrs.	3 yrs.	5 yrs.
Nations GA Int Muni	—	—	—	—	—	10.9[2]	-4.8[4]	14.1[2]	3.5[4]	7.0[3]	8.1[3]	5.9[4]	12,623	13,326
Nations GA Muni	—	—	—	—	—	—	-8.6[5]	19.4[1]	3.2[4]	8.6[4]	10.2[2]	—	13,380	—
Nations GI Gov	—	—	—	—	—	—	—	—	6.7[1]	-1.3[5]	—	—	—	—
Nations Int Muni	—	—	—	—	—	—	-4.8[4]	14.6[1]	3.8[3]	7.1[3]	8.4[2]	—	12,744	—
Nations Int'l Eqty	—	—	—	—	—	26.9[5]	2.2[2]	8.2[3]	8.1[4]	1.0[3]	5.8[3]	8.9[4]	11,825	15,337
Nations Int'l Gro	21.0[1]	23.0[3]	-14.8[4]	11.8[3]	-3.4[3]	28.5[4]	-0.3[3]	13.7[2]	10.9[4]	1.9[3]	8.7[3]	10.5[3]	12,847	16,460
Nations LifeGoal Bal Gro	—	—	—	—	—	—	—	—	—	11.2[5]	—	—	—	—
Nations LifeGoal Gro	—	—	—	—	—	—	—	—	—	14.6[5]	—	—	—	—
Nations LifeGoal Inc & Gro	—	—	—	—	—	—	—	—	—	8.5[5]	—	—	—	—
Nations MD Int Muni	—	—	—	10.2[4]	7.1[4]	10.0[3]	-4.7[4]	13.6[3]	3.4[5]	6.5[5]	7.8[4]	5.6[5]	12,513	13,118
Nations MD Muni	—	—	—	—	—	—	-9.3[5]	19.0[1]	3.0[5]	9.0[3]	10.2[3]	—	13,366	—
Nations Mngd Idx	—	—	—	—	—	—	—	—	—	33.2[1]	—	—	—	—
Nations Mngd Sm Cap Val Idx SC	—	—	—	—	—	—	—	—	—	—	—	—	—	—
Nations Mngd Small Cap Idx SC	—	—	—	—	—	—	—	—	—	27.6[3]	—	—	—	—
Nations Mngd Val Idx	—	—	—	—	—	—	—	—	—	—	—	—	—	—
Nations Muni Inc	—	—	—	—	8.2[4]	13.4[2]	-7.6[4]	19.3[1]	4.5[1]	9.3[2]	10.9[1]	7.4[2]	13,626	14,268
Nations NC Int Muni	—	—	—	—	—	10.3[3]	-4.3[3]	13.9[3]	3.6[4]	7.0[3]	8.1[3]	5.9[3]	12,634	13,338
Nations NC Muni	—	—	—	—	—	—	-9.2[5]	20.1[1]	2.5[5]	8.8[3]	10.3[2]	—	13,404	—
Nations Pacific Gro	—	—	—	—	—	—	—	—	10.3[4]	-33.0[5]	—	—	—	—
Nations S-I Gov	—	—	—	—	5.7[4]	7.8[4]	-2.6[3]	12.2[5]	3.0[4]	7.0[5]	7.3[5]	5.4[5]	12,367	12,991
Nations SC Int Muni	—	—	—	—	—	9.9[4]	-3.1[2]	13.4[3]	3.8[3]	6.6[4]	7.9[4]	6.0[3]	12,550	13,356
Nations SC Muni	—	—	—	—	—	—	-6.3[5]	19.4[1]	3.3[5]	8.4[1]	10.2[1]	—	13,369	—
Nations ST Inc	—	—	—	—	—	7.4[2]	-0.5[3]	11.1[3]	4.7[2]	5.8[4]	7.2[3]	5.6[2]	12,304	13,143
Nations ST Muni	—	—	—	—	—	—	0.3[2]	8.1[3]	3.9[2]	4.6[4]	5.5[3]	—	11,742	—
Nations Strat Inc	—	—	—	—	—	10.6[4]	-3.5[3]	17.1[4]	1.9[4]	8.3[3]	8.9[5]	6.4[4]	12,914	13,783
Nations TN Int Muni	—	—	—	—	—	—	-4.7[4]	13.9[2]	3.7[3]	6.7[4]	8.0[3]	—	12,609	—
Nations TN Muni	—	—	—	—	—	—	-6.7[3]	19.2[1]	3.6[4]	9.0[3]	10.4[2]	—	13,461	—
Nations TX Int Muni	—	—	—	—	—	—	-3.5[2]	12.7[4]	3.4[5]	6.9[3]	7.6[4]	—	12,463	—
Nations TX Muni	—	—	—	—	—	—	-8.4[5]	19.6[1]	3.6[4]	8.8[3]	10.5[2]	—	13,481	—
Nations US Gov Sec	—	—	—	—	—	—	—	—	1.8[5]	8.0[4]	—	—	—	—
Nations VA Int Muni	—	—	7.2[1]	9.7[4]	6.9[5]	9.9[3]	-4.5[4]	13.2[4]	3.6[4]	6.6[4]	7.7[4]	5.6[5]	12,503	13,129
Nations VA Muni	—	—	—	—	—	—	-9.5[5]	19.6[1]	3.5[4]	9.2[2]	10.6[2]	—	13,517	—
Nations Value	—	—	3.5[1]	25.9[4]	7.1[3]	16.1[2]	-3.1[4]	35.8[2]	20.9[3]	26.3[3]	27.5[2]	18.4[3]	20,723	23,310
Navellier Perf: Agg Gro SC	—	—	—	—	—	—	—	—	22.6[2]	9.8[4]	—	—	—	—
Navellier Perf: Agg Sm Cap SC	—	—	—	—	—	—	—	—	—	—	—	—	—	—
Navellier Perf: Lg Cap Gro	—	—	—	—	—	—	—	—	—	—	—	—	—	—
Navellier Perf: Lg Cap Val	—	—	—	—	—	—	—	—	—	—	—	—	—	—
Navellier Perf: Mid Cap	—	—	—	—	—	—	—	—	—	26.2[2]	—	—	—	—
Navellier Perf: Sm Cap Val SC	—	—	—	—	—	—	—	—	—	—	—	—	—	—
Navellier Ser: Sm Cap Eq SC	—	—	—	—	—	—	—	43.9[1]	15.5[4]	11.2[4]	22.7[3]	—	18,486	—
Nbrgr-Ber Focus	16.5[3]	29.8[2]	-5.9[3]	24.7[4]	21.1[1]	16.3[2]	0.9[2]	36.2[1]	16.2[4]	24.1[3]	25.2[3]	18.2[2]	19,648	23,056
Nbrgr-Ber Genesis SC‡	—	17.2[5]	-16.2[5]	41.5[2]	15.6[2]	13.9[3]	-1.8[4]	27.3[4]	29.9[1]	34.9[1]	30.7[1]	20.1[1]	22,305	24,948
Nbrgr-Ber Guardian	28.0[1]	21.5[3]	-4.7[3]	34.3[3]	19.0[1]	14.4[3]	0.6[3]	32.1[2]	17.9[4]	17.9[5]	22.5[4]	16.1[4]	18,362	21,132
Nbrgr-Ber Int'l Eqty	—	—	—	—	—	—	—	7.9[3]	23.7[1]	11.2[2]	14.1[1]	—	14,843	—
Nbrgr-Ber Ltd Mat	6.7[3]	11.1[2]	8.7[2]	11.8[4]	5.2[4]	6.8[3]	-0.3[3]	10.6[3]	4.5[3]	6.9[2]	7.3[3]	5.6[2]	12,350	13,150
Nbrgr-Ber Manhtn	18.3[2]	29.1[3]	-8.0[3]	30.9[5]	17.8[1]	10.0[4]	-3.6[4]	31.0[3]	9.8[5]	29.2[2]	22.9[3]	14.5[4]	18,584	19,707
Nbrgr-Ber Muni	6.8[3]	8.3[3]	6.9[2]	9.1[5]	6.9[4]	9.5[4]	-4.0[3]	12.7[5]	3.6[4]	7.4[3]	7.8[4]	5.7[4]	12,536	13,178
Nbrgr-Ber Partners	15.5[4]	22.8[3]	-5.1[3]	22.4[5]	17.5[1]	16.5[2]	-1.9[4]	35.2[2]	26.5[1]	29.2[2]	30.3[1]	20.4[1]	22,097	25,254
Nbrgr-Ber Social Resp	—	—	—	—	—	—	—	38.9[1]	18.5[3]	24.4[3]	27.0[2]	—	20,483	—
Nbrgr-Ber Ultra Sht‡	6.8[2]	9.4[4]	8.4[3]	7.4[5]	3.7[5]	3.2[5]	2.2[1]	6.9[5]	4.8[2]	6.2[4]	6.0[5]	4.6[5]	11,898	12,549
Needham Growth	—	—	—	—	—	—	—	—	51.6[1]	15.7[5]	—	—	—	—
New Providence Cap Gro	—	—	—	—	—	—	—	—	—	—	—	—	—	—
NewCap Contrarian	—	—	—	—	—	—	—	—	—	-13.1[5]	—	—	—	—
ni Growth and Value	—	—	—	—	—	—	—	—	—	33.1[1]	—	—	—	—
ni Growth SC‡	—	—	—	—	—	—	—	—	—	15.6[5]	—	—	—	—
ni Larger Cap Val	—	—	—	—	—	—	—	—	—	—	—	—	—	—
ni Micro-Cap‡SC	—	—	—	—	—	—	—	—	—	30.9[1]	—	—	—	—
Nicholas Eqty Inc	—	—	—	—	—	—	4.1[1]	17.2[5]	15.9[2]	19.3[3]	17.5[5]	—	16,208	—
Nicholas Fund	18.0[3]	24.5[3]	-4.8[3]	41.9[2]	12.6[3]	5.9[4]	-2.8[4]	35.4[2]	19.8[3]	37.0[1]	30.5[1]	18.0[3]	22,223	22,875
Nicholas II SC	17.3[3]	17.7[4]	-6.1[4]	39.6[2]	9.4[3]	6.4[4]	1.0[2]	28.6[3]	19.4[3]	37.0[1]	28.1[2]	17.7[3]	21,037	22,607

See Chapter 3 for explanation of symbols

Total Net Assets $Million December 31		NAV per share December 31		1997 per share distributions		Yield %	Risk Analysis				% Distribution of Portfolio 12/31/97			Objective	No-Load Fund
1996	1997	1996	1997	Income	Capital gains	12/31/97	beta	R²	Std. Dev.	Sharpe Ratio	Stocks	Bonds	Cash		
8.9	9.8	10.74	10.95	0.47	0.05	4.3	0.14	0.23	3.11	C	0	96	4	tax-free	Nations GA Int Muni
0.2	0.5	9.65	10.00	0.45	0.00	4.5	0.17	0.17	4.66	D	0	97	3	tax-free	Nations GA Muni
15.7	14.8	10.27	9.74	0.36	0.03	3.7	—	—	—	—	0	96	4	fix-inc	Nations GI Gov
1.6	4.9	10.13	10.34	0.45	0.04	4.4	0.13	0.23	3.04	B	0	99	1	tax-free	Nations Int Muni
11.7	13.4	13.20	12.99	0.18	0.16	1.4	0.63	0.38	11.05	C	95	1	5	int'l	Nations Int'l Eqty
26.9	23.9	17.02	17.01	0.00	0.00	0.0	0.64	0.36	11.70	C	98	0	2	int'l	Nations Int'l Gro
0.1	0.4	10.14	10.15	0.58	—	5.7	—	—	—	—	—	—	—	income	Nations LifeGoal Bal Gro
0.1	1.5	10.30	11.20	0.38	—	3.4	—	—	—	—	—	—	—	growth	Nations LifeGoal Gro
0.1	0.1	9.97	10.27	0.47	—	4.5	—	—	—	—	—	—	—	gr-inc	Nations LifeGoal Inc & Gro
15.6	15.9	10.86	11.06	0.48	0.00	4.4	0.13	0.25	2.98	D	0	97	3	tax-free	Nations MD Int Muni
1.4	1.8	9.55	9.95	0.44	0.00	4.4	0.17	0.18	4.54	C	0	95	5	tax-free	Nations MD Mun
1.2	17.0	11.61	15.13	0.17	0.15	0.9	—	—	—	—	100	0	0	gr-inc	Nations Mngd Idx
—	1.1	—	10.40	0.00	0.00	—	—	—	—	—	97	0	3	growth	Nations Mngd Sm Cap Val Idx SC
0.1	11.3	10.30	12.77	0.04	0.31	0.3	—	—	—	—	98	0	2	growth	Nations Mngd Small Cap Idx SC
—	1.5	—	10.25	0.00	0.00	—	—	—	—	—	99	0	1	gr-inc	Nations Mngd Val Idx
15.9	16.3	11.07	11.47	0.55	0.05	4.8	0.17	0.21	4.24	A	0	98	2	tax-free	Nations Muni Inc
8.4	7.3	10.48	10.73	0.47	0.00	4.3	0.13	0.25	3.01	C	0	97	3	tax-free	Nations NC Int Muni
0.6	0.7	9.63	10.01	0.45	0.00	4.5	0.19	0.20	4.59	C	0	96	4	tax-free	Nations NC Muni
3.3	0.7	10.66	7.01	0.17	0.00	2.4	—	—	—	—	87	0	13	int'l	Nations Pacific Gro
45.3	50.1	4.06	4.12	0.22	0.00	5.3	0.12	0.25	2.62	F	0	84	16	fix-inc	Nations S-I
11.3	12.6	10.63	10.82	0.49	0.01	4.5	0.13	0.24	2.88	C	0	99	1	tax-free	Nations SC Int Muni
0.8	1.6	9.94	10.28	0.47	0.00	4.5	0.17	0.19	4.23	A	0	95	5	tax-free	Nations SC Muni
6.0	11.9	9.76	9.77	0.54	0.00	5.6	0.06	0.21	1.52	B	0	94	6	tax-free	Nations ST Inc
5.8	25.2	10.01	10.05	0.41	0.00	4.1	0.05	0.23	1.16	C	0	98	2	tax-free	Nations ST Muni
6.9	26.2	9.84	10.06	0.57	0.00	5.6	0.18	0.24	4.05	F	0	96	4	fix-inc	Nations Strat Inc
6.9	7.3	10.20	10.42	0.45	0.00	4.3	0.13	0.24	2.86	B	0	98	2	tax-free	Nations TN Int Muni
1.0	1.4	9.85	10.26	0.46	0.00	4.5	0.19	0.21	4.57	B	0	93	7	tax-free	Nations TN Muni
0.9	2.2	10.30	10.53	0.46	0.00	4.4	0.13	0.25	2.82	D	0	98	2	tax-free	Nations TX Int Muni
0.4	0.4	9.66	10.03	0.46	0.00	4.6	0.18	0.21	4.46	B	0	99	1	tax-free	Nations TX Muni
1.1	1.8	10.29	10.42	0.53	0.13	5.1	—	—	—	—	0	99	1	fix-inc	Nations US Gov Sec
55.5	52.7	10.76	10.96	0.49	0.00	4.5	0.13	0.25	2.95	D	0	97	3	tax-free	Nations VA Int Muni
0.6	1.2	9.55	9.95	0.46	0.00	4.6	0.19	0.21	4.55	B	0	98	2	tax-free	Nations VA Muni
67.9	127.9	17.51	17.82	0.16	3.94	0.8	0.87	0.90	10.24	C	99	0	1	gr-inc	Nations Value
95.2	101.7	12.25	13.29	0.00	0.16	0.0	—	—	—	—	93	0	7	agg gr	Navellier Perf: Agg Gro SC
—	10.2	—	20.40	0.00	0.36	—	—	—	—	—	94	0	6	agg gr	Navellier Perf: Agg Sm Cap SC
—	0.1	—	10.25	0.00	0.00	—	—	—	—	—	84	0	16	growth	Navellier Perf: Lg Cap Gro
—	0.1	—	10.11	0.00	0.00	—	—	—	—	—	90	0	10	gr-inc	Navellier Perf: Lg Cap Val
1.0	8.4	10.27	12.43	0.00	0.53	0.0	—	—	—	—	94	0	6	agg gr	Navellier Perf: Mid Cap
—	0.1	—	10.12	0.00	0.00	—	—	—	—	—	86	0	14	growth	Navellier Perf: Sm Cap Val SC
195.4	214.9	17.79	16.00	0.00	3.54	0.0	0.96	0.18	31.74	F	94	0	6	agg gr	Navellier Ser: Sm Cap Eq SC
1,179.0	1,368.9	30.82	33.08	0.06	4.93	0.2	1.16	0.75	14.98	D	100	0	0	growth	Nbrgr-Ber Focus
299.0	1,246.4	12.03	16.03	0.00	0.19	0.0	0.54	0.26	11.80	B	101	0	-1	growth	Nbrgr-Ber Genesis SC‡
5,473.0	5,987.3	25.63	25.90	0.17	4.00	0.6	1.01	0.71	13.39	D	97	0	3	growth	Nbrgr-Ber Guardian
73.4	111.7	13.14	14.47	0.00	0.14	0.0	0.74	0.46	12.01	B	100	0	0	int'l	Nbrgr-Ber Int'l Eqty
239.6	252.4	9.98	10.01	0.63	0.00	6.3	0.09	0.31	1.83	C	0	94	6	fix-inc	Nbrgr-Ber Ltd Mat
531.7	571.3	11.68	11.01	0.00	3.84	0.0	1.05	0.57	15.32	C	100	0	0	agg gr	Nbrgr-Ber Manhtn
38.5	31.8	10.83	11.14	0.47	0.00	4.2	0.14	0.26	3.00	D	0	97	3	tax-free	Nbrgr-Ber Muni
2,218.3	3,230.3	25.19	26.30	0.19	5.84	0.6	0.87	0.76	11.16	A	98	0	2	growth	Nbrgr-Ber Partners
42.6	71.4	15.02	18.24	0.03	0.40	0.2	0.91	0.79	11.39	B	95	0	5	growth	Nbrgr-Ber Social Resp
82.4	48.1	9.47	9.51	0.53	0.00	5.6	—	—	1.00	F	0	94	6	fix-inc	Nbrgr-Ber Ultra Sht‡
14.4	21.8	14.49	14.42	0.04	2.34	0.3	—	—	—	—	94	3	3	growth	Needham Growth
—	11.9	—	11.11	0.00	0.00	0.0	—	—	—	—	—	—	—	growth	New Providence Cap
1.8	1.4	9.01	7.62	0.00	0.21	0.0	—	—	—	—	95	0	5	agg gr	NewCap Contrarian
14.2	89.5	13.31	15.08	0.05	2.61	0.3	—	—	—	—	93	0	7	growth	ni Growth and Value
54.0	116.2	13.24	12.91	0.00	2.49	0.0	—	—	—	—	92	0	8	growth	ni Growth SC‡
—	5.6	—	12.07	0.00	0.00	—	—	—	—	—	87	0	13	gr-inc	ni Larger Cap Val
27.1	131.9	14.01	15.68	0.00	2.65	0.0	—	—	—	—	91	0	9	agg gr	ni Micro-Cap‡SC
21.0	27.2	12.27	13.40	0.56	0.60	4.1	0.50	0.54	7.58	F	69	22	9	income	Nicholas Eqty Inc
3,984.0	5,257.1	65.94	83.80	0.34	5.82	0.4	0.87	0.87	10.33	A	96	1	3	growth	Nicholas Fund
784.0	1,025.0	30.99	36.94	0.07	5.24	0.2	0.69	0.44	11.46	B	98	1	1	growth	Nicholas II SC

Stock and bond funds — comprehensive summary *continued*
Arranged in alphabetical order

| No-Load Fund | Total return percent with quintile ranks by objective | | | | | | | | | | Annualized | | What $10,000 grew to after | |
	1988	1989	1990	1991	1992	1993	1994	1995	1996	1997	3 yrs.	5 yrs.	3 yrs.	5 yrs.
Nicholas Income	11.5[2]	3.9[5]	-1.0[4]	23.0[1]	10.3[1]	13.0[3]	-0.2[1]	16.2[4]	12.4[1]	13.1[2]	13.9[2]	10.8[1]	14,775	16,662
Nicholas Ltd Edit SC	27.3[1]	17.3[5]	-1.7[2]	43.2[1]	16.8[1]	9.0[4]	-3.0[4]	30.2[3]	21.8[2]	33.0[1]	28.3[2]	17.4[3]	21,095	22,304
Nomura Pacific Bas	15.2[3]	22.7[3]	-15.3[4]	11.7[3]	-12.3[5]	39.2[2]	4.7[1]	3.6[4]	3.0[5]	-28.7[5]	-8.7[5]	2.1[5]	7,614	11,096
North Carolina TF	—	—	—	—	—	—	-4.0[1]	15.8[4]	3.8[3]	8.0[5]	9.1[4]	—	12,985	—
Northeast Inv Growth	12.8[4]	32.9[1]	1.4[1]	37.0[2]	-0.7[5]	2.4[5]	0.0[3]	36.5[1]	24.6[1]	37.3[1]	32.7[1]	19.0[2]	23,347	23,908
Northeast Inv Trust	14.1[1]	0.0[5]	-9.2[5]	26.4[1]	17.5[1]	23.6[1]	2.2[1]	17.3[4]	20.2[1]	13.9[2]	17.1[1]	15.2[1]	16,054	20,280
Northern CA TE	—	—	—	—	—	—	—	—	—	—	—	—	—	—
Northern Fix Inc	—	—	—	—	—	—	—	18.8[3]	2.6[4]	9.5[3]	10.1[3]	—	13,348	—
Northern FL Inter TE	—	—	—	—	—	—	—	—	—	7.7[1]	—	—	—	—
Northern Growth Eqty	—	—	—	—	—	—	—	26.1[4]	17.9[4]	30.2[2]	24.6[3]	—	19,349	—
Northern Inc Eqty	—	—	—	—	—	—	—	19.0[5]	20.0[3]	20.8[4]	19.9[5]	—	17,251	—
Northern Int'l Fix Inc	—	—	—	—	—	—	—	19.8[2]	5.4[2]	-2.5[5]	7.2[5]	—	12,311	—
Northern Int'l Gro Eq	—	—	—	—	—	—	—	2.0[4]	5.0[5]	6.3[2]	4.4[4]	—	11,394	—
Northern Int'l Sel Eq	—	—	—	—	—	—	—	-0.8[4]	2.9[5]	9.1[2]	3.7[4]	—	11,135	—
Northern Inter TE	—	—	—	—	—	—	—	12.0[5]	3.3[5]	5.8[5]	7.0[5]	—	12,246	—
Northern Select Eqty	—	—	—	—	—	—	—	29.0[3]	21.5[2]	31.9[2]	27.4[2]	—	20,674	—
Northern Sm Cap SC	—	—	—	—	—	—	—	22.5[4]	19.0[3]	29.8[2]	23.7[3]	—	18,920	—
Northern Stock Idx	—	—	—	—	—	—	—	—	—	32.7[1]	—	—	—	—
Northern TE Bond	—	—	—	—	—	—	—	17.5[3]	2.8[5]	8.7[4]	9.5[4]	—	13,121	—
Northern Technology	—	—	—	—	—	—	—	—	—	16.8[4]	—	—	—	—
Northern US Gov	—	—	—	—	—	—	—	12.6[1]	3.1[5]	7.2[1]	7.6[2]	—	12,452	—
O'Shaughnessy Agg Gr	—	—	—	—	—	—	—	—	—	22.3[3]	—	—	—	—
O'Shaughnessy Cornrstn Gro	—	—	—	—	—	—	—	—	—	31.3[2]	—	—	—	—
O'Shaughnessy Cornrstn Val	—	—	—	—	—	—	—	—	—	15.3[5]	—	—	—	—
O'Shaughnessy Dogs Of Mkt	—	—	—	—	—	—	—	—	—	25.8[1]	—	—	—	—
Oak Hall Equity	—	—	—	—	—	42.1[1]	-11.6[5]	9.9[5]	17.2[4]	14.5[5]	13.8[5]	13.1[5]	14,743	18,519
Oak Value	—	—	—	—	—	—	-1.4[4]	28.3[3]	29.0[1]	37.7[1]	31.8[1]	—	22,883	—
Oakmark Eqty & Inc	—	—	—	—	—	—	—	—	15.3[2]	26.6[1]	—	—	—	—
Oakmark Int'l Small Cap	—	—	—	—	—	—	—	—	25.0[1]	-19.9[5]	—	—	—	—
Oakmark Int'l	—	—	—	—	—	—	-9.1[4]	8.3[3]	28.0[1]	3.4[3]	12.7[2]	14.9[2]	14,329	20,006
Oakmark Select	—	—	—	—	—	—	—	—	—	55.0[1]	—	—	—	—
Oakmark Small Cap SC‡	—	—	—	—	—	—	—	—	39.8[1]	40.5[1]	—	—	—	—
Oakmark	—	—	—	—	48.9[1]	30.5[1]	3.3[1]	34.4[2]	16.2[4]	32.6[1]	27.5[2]	22.8[1]	20,704	27,911
Oberweis Emg Growth SC	5.7[5]	25.0[3]	0.4[1]	87.1[1]	13.7[2]	9.7[4]	-3.5[4]	42.6[2]	23.2[2]	-8.6[5]	17.1[5]	11.2[5]	16,066	17,007
Oberweis MicroCap SC	—	—	—	—	—	—	—	—	22.8[2]	10.7[4]	—	—	—	—
Oberweis Midcap	—	—	—	—	—	—	—	—	—	5.5[5]	—	—	—	—
OVB Cap App	—	—	—	—	—	—	-5.5[5]	33.3[2]	16.2[4]	27.0[3]	25.3[3]	—	19,675	—
OVB Emg Gro SC	—	—	—	—	—	—	-18.4[5]	47.5[1]	3.2[5]	0.5[5]	15.2[5]	—	15,300	—
OVB Eqty Inc	—	—	—	—	—	—	—	—	—	23.0[2]	—	—	—	—
OVB Gov	—	—	—	—	—	—	-5.1[3]	19.4[2]	2.3[4]	9.3[3]	10.1[3]	—	13,347	—
OVB WV TE	—	—	—	—	—	—	-5.0[2]	16.0[4]	3.7[3]	8.9[3]	9.4[4]	—	13,101	—
Papp Amer Pac Rim	—	—	—	—	—	—	—	—	—	—	—	—	—	—
Papp L Roy Amer Abroad	—	—	—	—	7.4[4]	-0.6[5]	7.8[1]	37.1[1]	27.7[1]	29.9[2]	31.5[1]	19.5[2]	22,746	24,373
Papp L Roy Stock	—	—	2.6[1]	33.9[3]	13.5[2]	1.7[5]	-1.4[4]	32.9[2]	21.8[2]	33.1[1]	29.2[2]	16.7[3]	21,548	21,608
Parnassus Balanced	—	—	—	—	—	15.9[2]	-5.4[5]	31.1[1]	7.1[5]	20.2[3]	19.1[4]	13.1[4]	16,872	18,502
Parnassus CA TE	—	—	—	—	—	13.0[2]	-6.4[3]	18.6[2]	4.8[1]	9.3[2]	10.8[1]	7.5[1]	13,587	14,378
Parnassus Fix Inc	—	—	—	—	—	10.6[4]	-6.8[4]	21.6[2]	4.1[3]	10.6[2]	11.9[2]	7.6[3]	13,996	14,431
Pathfinder SC	12.7[4]	-2.6[5]	-37.6[5]	63.8[2]	1.0[5]	3.1[5]	-8.9[5]	39.0[1]	5.6[5]	24.9[2]	22.4[3]	11.5[5]	18,319	17,198
Pax World	11.5[4]	24.9[2]	10.5[1]	20.8[5]	0.6[5]	-1.1[5]	2.6[1]	29.2[1]	10.4[4]	25.1[2]	21.3[2]	12.6[4]	17,839	18,102
Payden & Rygel Euro Gro & Inc	—	—	—	—	—	—	—	—	—	—	—	—	—	—
Payden & Rygel Glob Bal	—	—	—	—	—	—	—	—	—	12.5[3]	—	—	—	—
Payden & Rygel Glob Fl	—	—	—	—	—	13.2[1]	-3.0[3]	18.0[2]	5.8[1]	9.1[2]	10.8[1]	8.4[1]	13,609	14,935
Payden & Rygel Glob ST Bd	—	—	—	—	—	—	—	—	—	6.6[5]	—	—	—	—
Payden & Rygel Gro & Inc	—	—	—	—	—	—	—	—	—	26.9[3]	—	—	—	—
Payden & Rygel Int'l Bd.‡	—	—	—	—	—	—	—	—	4.3[2]	-3.2[5]	—	—	—	—
Payden & Rygel Int'l Eqty	—	—	—	—	—	—	—	—	—	5.5[3]	—	—	—	—
Payden & Rygel Inter Bd	—	—	—	—	—	—	-3.3[4]	15.4[4]	2.1[5]	7.5[4]	8.2[5]	—	12,668	—
Payden & Rygel Inv Qual Bd	—	—	—	—	—	—	-4.7[5]	19.7[1]	1.7[5]	9.0[2]	9.9[2]	—	13,276	—
Payden & Rygel Ltd Mat	—	—	—	—	—	—	—	7.1[5]	5.2[2]	5.5[5]	5.9[5]	—	11,883	—
Payden & Rygel Mkt Ret	—	—	—	—	—	—	—	—	17.4[4]	30.7[2]	—	—	—	—

See Chapter 3 for explanation of symbols

Stock and bond funds — comprehensive summary *continued*
Arranged in alphabetical order

Total Net Assets $Million		NAV per share		1997 per share distributions		Yield %	Risk Analysis				% Distribution of Portfolio 12/31/97			Objective	No-Load Fund
December 31 1996	1997	December 31 1996	1997	Income	Capital gains	12/31/97	beta	R^2	Std. Dev.	Sharpe Ratio	Stocks	Bonds	Cash		
186.0	254.2	3.53	3.69	0.29	0.00	7.9	0.16	0.36	3.05	A	10	88	2	fix-inc	Nicholas Income
233.0	328.0	20.74	25.07	0.00	2.49	0.0	0.57	0.25	12.75	C	89	4	7	growth	Nicholas Ltd Edit SC
28.6	13.7	14.70	10.42	0.04	0.03	0.4	0.96	0.37	16.69	F	90	0	10	int'l	Nomura Pacific Bas.
6.8	10.5	10.57	10.93	0.47	0.00	4.3	0.19	0.22	4.42	F	0	91	9	tax-free	North Carolina TF
60.3	108.6	36.45	15.84	0.09	0.80	0.5	1.07	0.92	12.49	A	100	0	0	growth	Northeast Inv Growth
1,354.8	2,161.0	11.12	11.65	0.96	0.00	8.2	0.17	0.24	3.80	A	14	81	5	fix-inc	Northeast Inv Trust
—	29.2	—	10.77	0.30	0.00	—	—	—	—	—	0	98	2	tax-free	Northern CA TE
114.5	163.7	10.10	10.41	0.59	0.03	5.7	0.20	0.24	4.49	C	0	96	4	fix-inc	Northern Fix Inc
15.3	24.3	10.14	10.49	0.40	0.01	3.8	—	—	—	—	0	97	3	tax-free	Northern FL Inter TE
289.1	422.0	14.11	16.54	0.05	1.67	0.3	1.03	0.90	12.10	C	97	0	3	growth	Northern Growth Eqty
71.1	103.7	11.77	12.69	0.44	1.03	3.2	0.53	0.75	6.79	C	20	76	4	gr-inc	Northern Inc Eqty
16.9	14.6	10.83	9.84	0.62	0.09	6.3	0.01	0.00	6.87	F	0	94	6	fix-inc	Northern Int'l Fix Inc
179.4	163.9	10.07	10.24	0.16	0.29	1.6	0.53	0.29	10.85	D	92	0	8	int'l	Northern Int'l Gro Eq
109.8	105.0	10.22	10.89	0.26	0.00	2.4	0.60	0.25	13.05	D	94	0	6	int'l	Northern Int'l Sel Eq
254.3	290.6	10.19	10.37	0.40	0.00	3.8	0.12	0.25	2.59	F	0	98	2	tax-free	Northern Inter TE
54.7	104.4	14.65	16.98	0.02	2.20	0.1	1.08	0.87	12.95	C	99	0	1	growth	Northern Select Eqty
193.4	336.5	12.33	15.26	0.04	0.68	0.3	0.64	0.36	11.78	B	98	0	2	agg gr	Northern Sm Cap SC
14.4	66.9	10.50	13.24	0.14	0.52	1.0	—	—	—	—	95	0	5	gr-inc	Northern Stock Idx
132.1	154.1	10.43	10.75	0.48	0.08	4.4	0.20	0.24	4.64	D	0	99	1	tax-free	Northern TE Bond
34.3	80.9	13.11	14.35	0.00	0.90	0.0	—	—	—	—	98	0	2	sector	Northern Technology
171.7	214.5	10.03	10.19	0.53	0.01	5.2	0.11	0.23	2.59	D	0	85	15	fix-inc	Northern US Gov
0.5	6.7	10.41	12.53	0.00	0.20	0.0	—	—	—	—	98	0	2	agg gr	O'Shaughnessy Agg Gr
1.1	54.4	10.07	11.43	0.00	1.78	0.0	—	—	—	—	101	0	-1	growth	O'Shaughnessy Cornrstn Gro
0.8	15.9	10.01	11.37	0.17	0.00	1.5	—	—	—	—	95	0	5	gr-inc	O'Shaughnessy Cornrstn Val
0.6	9.7	10.02	11.93	0.09	0.59	0.7	—	—	—	—	95	0	5	income	O'Shaughnessy Dogs Of Mkt
9.2	6.1	14.66	16.78	0.00	0.00	0.0	0.62	0.21	17.26	F	93	0	7	growth	Oak Hall Equity
32.0	139.9	17.49	23.19	0.00	0.81	0.0	0.65	0.58	9.50	A	88	0	12	growth	Oak Value
14.8	40.6	11.55	13.76	0.23	0.59	1.6	—	—	—	—	59	33	8	income	Oakmark Eqty & Inc
46.8	50.2	11.59	8.09	0.06	1.34	0.6	—	—	—	—	98	0	2	int'l	Oakmark Int'l Small Cap
1,232.8	1,237.5	15.68	12.83	0.58	2.86	3.7	0.55	0.23	12.59	B	95	0	5	int'l	Oakmark Int'l
50.3	981.6	11.42	17.52	0.00	0.17	0.0	—	—	—	—	92	0	8	agg gr	Oakmark Select
316.5	1,492.0	14.44	19.42	0.00	0.84	0.0	—	—	—	—	94	0	6	growth	Oakmark Small Cap‡ SC
4,195.0	7,301.4	32.35	40.41	0.40	1.98	0.9	0.79	0.84	9.55	A	90	0	10	growth	Oakmark
185.6	140.1	32.86	25.71	0.00	4.64	0.0	1.29	0.27	27.66	F	97	1	2	agg gr	Oberweis Emg Growth SC
31.0	36.9	12.28	13.59	0.00	0.00	0.0	—	—	—	—	102	1	-3	agg gr	Oberweis MicroCap SC
7.3	6.3	10.28	10.51	0.00	0.35	0.0	—	—	—	—	98	0	2	agg gr	Oberweis Midcap
110.1	112.2	14.04	13.91	0.00	3.87	0.0	1.17	0.75	15.07	D	100	0	0	growth	OVB Cap App
56.6	32.6	12.45	10.66	0.00	4.64	0.0	0.95	0.19	23.74	F	99	0	1	agg gr	OVB Emg Gro SC
38.5	48.6	10.93	12.76	0.26	0.39	2.0	—	—	—	—	90	6	4	income	OVB Eqty Inc
59.9	49.9	9.80	10.10	0.57	0.01	5.6	0.22	0.26	4.71	D	0	98	2	fix-inc	OVB Gov
94.8	84.8	9.97	10.28	0.50	0.05	4.9	0.18	0.26	3.80	C	0	100	0	tax-free	OVB WV TE
—	13.7	—	12.10	0.00	0.01	—	—	—	—	—	100	0	0	int'l	Papp Amer Pac Rim
29.6	288.2	20.11	25.98	0.02	0.13	0.1	1.01	0.81	12.58	B	99	0	1	growth	Papp L Roy Amer Abroad
53.3	79.8	22.70	29.78	0.00	0.43	0.0	1.04	0.83	12.77	C	99	0	1	growth	Papp L Roy Stock
33.4	38.9	18.56	20.68	0.76	0.74	3.7	0.39	0.50	6.21	B	66	23	11	income	Parnassus Balanced
5.8	6.5	16.02	16.72	0.75	0.00	4.5	0.16	0.16	4.48	A	0	98	2	tax-free	Parnassus CA TE
8.4	9.7	15.43	16.04	0.89	0.07	5.6	0.26	0.26	5.67	C	0	68	32	fix-inc	Parnassus Fix Inc
2.8	3.0	7.41	8.81	0.00	0.43	0.0	0.66	0.14	19.74	D	100	0	0	agg gr	Pathfinder SC
518.5	628.8	16.56	18.52	0.50	1.65	2.5	0.47	0.63	6.50	A	53	24	23	income	Pax World
—	13.2	—	10.51	0.00	0.00	—	—	—	—	—	100	0	0	int'l	Payden & Rygel Euro Gro & Inc
6.7	8.9	10.02	10.45	0.19	0.61	1.8	—	—	—	—	45	52	3	global	Payden & Rygel Glob Bal
658.6	493.6	10.30	10.24	0.95	0.00	9.3	0.18	0.32	3.58	A	0	100	0	fix-inc	Payden & Rygel Glob Fl
37.6	293.2	10.14	10.14	0.65	0.00	6.4	—	—	—	—	0	100	0	fix-inc	Payden & Rygel Glob ST Bd
12.9	188.7	10.61	13.26	0.19	0.00	1.4	—	—	—	—	100	0	0	gr-inc	Payden & Rygel Gro & Inc
18.7	0.1	10.40	9.67	0.36	0.05	3.7	—	—	—	—	0	100	0	fix-inc	Payden & Rygel Int'l Bd‡
7.0	16.6	10.10	10.65	0.00	0.00	0.0	—	—	—	—	93	0	7	int'l	Payden & Rygel Int'l Eqty
29.1	110.0	9.57	9.67	0.54	0.05	5.6	0.14	0.24	3.12	D	0	100	0	fix-inc	Payden & Rygel Inter Bd
36.9	119.2	9.76	9.97	0.59	0.05	5.9	0.19	0.21	4.65	D	0	99	1	fix-inc	Payden & Rygel Inv Qual Bd
53.0	138.4	10.05	10.05	0.54	0.00	5.4	0.02	0.10	0.54	D	0	14	86	fix-inc	Payden & Rygel Ltd Mat
6.1	24.0	10.82	12.42	0.60	0.97	4.8	—	—	—	—	5	51	44	gr-inc	Payden & Rygel Mkt Ret

Stock and bond funds — comprehensive summary *continued*

Arranged in alphabetical order

| No-Load Fund | Total return percent with quintile ranks by objective | | | | | | | | | | Annualized | | What $10,000 grew to after | |
	1988	1989	1990	1991	1992	1993	1994	1995	1996	1997	3 yrs.	5 yrs.	3 yrs.	5 yrs.
Payden & Rygel Sht Dur TE	—	—	—	—	—	—	—	6.9 [4]	2.9 [5]	4.5 [4]	4.8 [5]	—	11,500	—
Payden & Rygel ST Bd	—	—	—	—	—	—	0.4 [2]	11.4 [2]	3.7 [5]	5.8 [4]	6.9 [3]	—	12,225	—
Payden & Rygel TE Bd	—	—	—	—	—	—	—	—	3.0 [5]	6.6 [5]	—	—	—	—
Payden & Rygel Tot Ret	—	—	—	—	—	—	-7.9 [5]	15.9 [4]	2.4 [5]	7.7 [4]	8.5 [4]	—	12,772	—
Payden & Rygel US Trsy	—	—	—	—	—	—	—	—	—	8.8 [1]	—	—	—	—
PBHG Core Growth	—	—	—	—	—	—	—	—	32.8 [1]	-9.7 [5]	—	—	—	—
PBHG Emg Growth SC	—	—	—	—	—	—	23.8 [1]	48.4 [1]	17.1 [3]	-3.7 [5]	18.7 [4]	—	16,739	—
PBHG Growth	6.9 [4]	29.4 [3]	-9.7 [3]	52.5 [2]	28.5 [1]	46.6 [1]	4.8 [1]	50.3 [1]	9.8 [5]	-3.3 [5]	16.8 [5]	19.6 [1]	15,950	24,505
PBHG International	—	—	—	—	—	—	—	2.1 [4]	12.7 [3]	3.5 [5]	6.0 [3]	—	11,910	—
PBHG Large Cap 20	—	—	—	—	—	—	—	—	—	33.0 [1]	—	—	—	—
PBHG Large Cap Gro	—	—	—	—	—	—	—	—	23.4 [2]	22.4 [4]	—	—	—	—
PBHG Large Cap Val	—	—	—	—	—	—	—	—	—	25.6 [3]	—	—	—	—
PBHG Limited‡ SC	—	—	—	—	—	—	—	—	—	16.1 [4]	—	—	—	—
PBHG Mid Cap Val	—	—	—	—	—	—	—	—	—	—	—	—	—	—
PBHG Select Eqty	—	—	—	—	—	—	—	—	28.0 [1]	6.8 [5]	—	—	—	—
PBHG Sm Cap Val SC	—	—	—	—	—	—	—	—	—	—	—	—	—	—
PBHG Strat Small Co SC	—	—	—	—	—	—	—	—	—	25.7 [2]	—	—	—	—
PBHG Tech & Comm	—	—	—	—	—	—	—	—	54.4 [1]	3.3 [5]	—	—	—	—
PC&J Performance	12.6 [4]	33.4 [2]	-5.9 [3]	30.5 [5]	8.1 [4]	14.2 [4]	0.8 [2]	22.8 [4]	19.8 [3]	35.6 [1]	25.9 [2]	18.1 [2]	19,938	22,952
PC&J Preservation	5.1 [5]	11.3 [4]	9.3 [1]	12.5 [5]	6.3 [4]	8.5 [5]	-2.4 [2]	15.2 [5]	2.8 [4]	7.4 [5]	8.3 [5]	6.1 [5]	12,710	13,454
Peregrine Asia Pac Growth‡	—	—	—	—	—	—	—	—	16.0 [2]	-33.1 [5]	—	—	—	—
Permanent Agg Growth	—	—	—	30.4 [5]	19.9 [1]	21.9 [2]	1.0 [2]	32.6 [3]	14.5 [4]	32.7 [1]	26.3 [2]	19.9 [1]	20,149	24,821
Permanent Portfolio†	1.3 [5]	6.4 [5]	-3.9 [2]	8.1 [5]	2.5 [3]	15.5 [5]	-2.9 [3]	15.5 [3]	1.7 [5]	5.6 [5]	7.5 [5]	6.8 [5]	12,407	13,915
Permanent Treasy†	6.4 [3]	8.1 [5]	7.3 [4]	5.3 [5]	2.9 [5]	2.3 [5]	3.3 [1]	4.9 [5]	4.3 [3]	4.1 [5]	4.4 [5]	3.8 [5]	11,386	12,033
Permanent Vers Bd†	—	—	—	—	5.7 [4]	3.8 [5]	2.6 [1]	7.6 [5]	4.8 [2]	5.1 [5]	5.8 [5]	4.8 [5]	11,856	12,626
Perritt Micro Cap Opp SC	—	2.0 [5]	-16.8 [5]	38.7 [4]	6.5 [4]	5.3 [5]	-5.1 [4]	27.9 [4]	18.0 [3]	22.1 [3]	22.6 [3]	13.0 [4]	18,431	18,418
Philadelphia	15.2 [3]	32.7 [1]	-11.4 [5]	5.7 [5]	19.7 [1]	17.6 [2]	-8.6 [5]	27.4 [4]	12.7 [5]	35.8 [1]	24.9 [3]	15.9 [4]	19,494	20,953
PIC Growth	—	—	—	—	—	0.8 [5]	-2.6 [4]	23.5 [4]	20.7 [3]	28.0 [2]	24.0 [3]	13.4 [5]	19,078	18,740
PIC Sm Co Gro SC	—	—	—	—	—	—	—	—	—	-1.4 [5]	—	—	—	—
PIC:Pinnacle Balanced	—	—	—	—	—	2.7 [5]	-3.1 [4]	22.3 [4]	15.6 [2]	22.3 [2]	20.0 [3]	11.5 [5]	17,288	17,198
PIC:Pinnacle Growth	—	—	—	—	—	—	—	—	—	—	—	—	—	—
PIC:Pinnacle Sm Co Gro SC	—	—	—	—	—	—	—	—	—	—	—	—	—	—
Pin Oak Agg Stk SC	—	—	—	—	—	1.8 [5]	0.0 [2]	37.2 [2]	10.8 [5]	1.3 [5]	15.5 [5]	9.4 [5]	15,399	15,669
Pinnacle Fund	6.8 [5]	31.0 [1]	-3.1 [3]	39.9 [2]	-0.7 [5]	3.3 [5]	-1.1 [4]	35.4 [2]	22.4 [2]	35.4 [1]	31.0 [1]	18.1 [3]	22,454	22,939
Preferred Asst Alloc	—	—	—	—	—	10.6 [3]	-2.6 [4]	32.8 [2]	15.1 [5]	21.0 [4]	22.8 [4]	14.8 [4]	18,496	19,931
Preferred Fix Inc	—	—	—	—	—	10.3 [4]	-2.4 [2]	17.7 [4]	3.0 [4]	8.5 [4]	9.5 [4]	7.2 [4]	13,141	14,149
Preferred Growth	—	—	—	—	—	16.1 [2]	-1.1 [4]	28.4 [3]	18.7 [3]	31.9 [2]	26.2 [3]	18.2 [2]	20,103	23,071
Preferred Int'l	—	—	—	—	—	41.5 [2]	3.3 [2]	9.9 [3]	17.2 [2]	6.8 [2]	11.2 [2]	15.0 [2]	13,761	20,114
Preferred Small Cap SC	—	—	—	—	—	—	—	—	20.5 [3]	31.9 [1]	—	—	—	—
Preferred ST Gov	—	—	—	—	—	5.6 [3]	-0.7 [4]	9.1 [4]	4.7 [2]	6.2 [4]	6.6 [4]	4.9 [4]	12,127	12,714
Preferred Value	—	—	—	—	—	8.8 [4]	0.5 [3]	37.8 [1]	25.3 [1]	28.0 [3]	30.2 [1]	19.3 [2]	22,093	24,152
Price Balanced	9.0 [5]	20.6 [2]	4.7 [1]	22.0 [4]	8.8 [3]	13.3 [3]	-2.1 [3]	24.9 [3]	14.6 [3]	19.0 [3]	19.4 [3]	13.6 [3]	17,029	18,889
Price Blue Chip	—	—	—	—	—	—	0.8 [2]	37.9 [1]	27.8 [1]	27.5 [3]	31.0 [1]	—	22,478	—
Price CA TF	9.5 [5]	8.5 [4]	5.8 [4]	12.1 [3]	8.9 [3]	12.5 [4]	-5.7 [2]	17.4 [3]	4.5 [1]	9.1 [3]	10.2 [2]	7.3 [2]	13,382	14,197
Price Cap App	21.2 [2]	21.4 [4]	-1.2 [2]	21.6 [5]	9.4 [3]	15.7 [2]	3.8 [1]	22.6 [5]	16.8 [4]	16.2 [5]	18.5 [5]	14.8 [4]	16,634	19,977
Price Cap Oppty	—	—	—	—	—	—	—	46.5 [1]	16.8 [4]	15.9 [4]	25.6 [2]	—	19,826	—
Price Corp Inc	—	—	—	—	—	—	—	—	4.7 [2]	12.6 [2]	—	—	—	—
Price Div Gro	—	—	—	—	—	—	2.2 [2]	31.7 [3]	25.4 [1]	30.8 [2]	29.3 [2]	21.4 [1]	21,597	26,354
Price Divsfd Sm Cap Gro SC	—	—	—	—	—	—	—	—	—	—	—	—	—	—
Price Emg Mkt Bond	—	—	—	—	—	—	—	25.1 [1]	36.8 [1]	16.8 [1]	26.0 [1]	—	19,994	—
Price Emg Mkts Stk	—	—	—	—	—	—	—	—	11.8 [4]	1.2 [3]	—	—	—	—
Price Eqty 500 Idx	—	—	—	29.2 [3]	7.2 [3]	9.4 [4]	1.0 [2]	37.2 [1]	22.7 [2]	32.9 [1]	30.8 [1]	19.8 [2]	22,371	24,718
Price Eqty Inc	27.6 [1]	13.7 [4]	-6.8 [5]	25.3 [3]	14.1 [1]	14.8 [2]	4.5 [1]	33.4 [1]	20.4 [1]	28.8 [1]	27.4 [1]	19.9 [1]	20,692	24,824
Price Europe	—	—	—	7.3 [4]	-5.6 [3]	27.2 [5]	4.1 [2]	21.9 [1]	25.9 [1]	17.0 [1]	21.5 [1]	18.9 [1]	17,958	23,779
Price Finl Serv	—	—	—	—	—	—	—	—	—	41.4 [1]	—	—	—	—
Price FL Ins Inter	—	—	—	—	—	—	-2.8 [2]	13.2 [4]	3.7 [4]	6.7 [4]	7.8 [4]	—	12,531	—
Price GA TF	—	—	—	—	—	—	-5.9 [3]	17.8 [3]	3.9 [3]	9.7 [2]	10.3 [2]	—	13,425	—
Price Glob Gov	—	—	—	11.3 [5]	3.7 [5]	10.7 [2]	-3.1 [3]	18.1 [2]	6.6 [1]	1.6 [5]	8.6 [4]	6.5 [3]	12,792	13,722
Price Glob Stk	—	—	—	—	—	—	—	—	20.0 [2]	13.2 [2]	—	—	—	—
Price GNMA	6.0 [5]	14.0 [2]	10.0 [2]	15.0 [3]	6.5 [3]	6.2 [5]	-1.6 [1]	17.8 [2]	3.1 [4]	9.5 [1]	10.0 [2]	6.8 [3]	13,297	13,895

See Chapter 3 for explanation of symbols

Arranged in alphabetical order

Total Net Assets $Million December 31 1996	1997	NAV per share December 31 1996	1997	1997 per share distributions Income	Capital gains	Yield % 12/31/97	beta	R²	Std. Dev.	Sharpe Ratio	Stocks	Bonds	Cash	Objective	No-Load Fund
31.6	33.5	10.03	10.09	0.38	0.01	3.8	0.05	0.23	1.15	F	0	75	25	tax-free	Payden & Rygel Sht Dur TE
107.1	82.0	9.94	9.92	0.58	0.00	5.9	0.07	0.18	1.72	D	0	66	34	fix-inc	Payden & Rygel ST Bd
25.7	24.4	10.50	10.60	0.57	0.00	5.4	—	—	—		0	100	0	tax-free	Payden & Rygel TE B
48.1	64.0	9.53	9.81	0.61	0.08	4.4	0.15	0.20	3.82	F	0	90	10	fix-inc	Payden & Rygel Tot Ret
4.0	77.1	9.94	10.11	0.60	0.08	6.0	—	—	—		0	81	19	fix-inc	Payden & Rygel US Trsy
455.7	192.3	13.28	11.99	0.00	0.00	0.0	—	—	—		97	0	3	agg gr	PBHG Core Growth
1,518.2	1,516.2	24.23	23.34	0.00	0.00	0.0	1.02	0.21	24.89	F	94	0	6	agg gr	PBHG Emg Growth SC
5,931.2	5,463.5	26.27	25.39	0.00	0.00	0.0	1.03	0.29	20.97	F	95	0	5	agg gr	PBHG Growth
19.6	17.1	11.21	10.56	0.00	1.02	0.0	0.70	0.40	12.00	C	95	0	5	int'l	PBHG International
48.5	116.5	9.83	13.07	0.00	0.00	0.0	—	—	—		92	0	8	growth	PBHG Large Cap 20
154.6	141.3	15.99	19.36	0.00	0.20	0.0	—	—	—		95	0	5	growth	PBHG Large Cap Gro
0.1	70.5	10.00	11.59	0.06	0.90	0.5	—	—	—		96	0	4	gr-inc	PBHG Large Cap Val
199.8	172.1	11.04	12.40	0.00	0.40	0.0	—	—	—		89	0	11	agg gr	PBHG Limited‡ SC
—	40.4	—	13.44	0.00	0.69	—	—	—	—		94	0	6	agg gr	PBHG Mid Cap Val
580.1	348.6	19.59	20.93	0.00	0.00	0.0	—	—	—		96	0	4	agg gr	PBHG Select Eqty
—	80.6	—	13.78	0.00	0.74	—	—	—	—		93	0	7	agg gr	PBHG Sm Cap Val SC
0.1	117.2	10.00	11.67	0.00	0.87	0.0	—	—	—		97	0	3	agg gr	PBHG Strat Small Co SC
562.6	551.0	17.56	17.28	0.00	0.85	0.0	—	—	—		94	0	6	sector	PBHG Tech & Comm
28.6	37.5	21.11	27.01	0.00	1.61	0.0	—	—	—	F	93	0	7	agg gr	PC&J Performance
16.2	16.1	10.97	11.14	0.64	0.00	5.7	0.15	0.24	3.34	F	0	94	6	fix-inc	PC&J Preservation
22.7	14.1	11.31	7.33	0.03	0.21	0.4	—	—	—		—	—	—	int'l	Peregrine Asia Pac Growth‡
16.0	20.2	45.27	56.97	0.18	2.89	0.3	1.13	0.68	15.19	B	96	0	4	agg gr	Permanent Agg Growth
74.4	70.7	18.53	18.87	0.34	0.36	1.8	0.34	0.46	5.60	F	45	46	9	global	Permanent Portfolio†
106.2	93.3	67.33	67.33	2.74	0.00	4.1	0.00	0.01	0.16	F	0	0	100	fix-inc	Permanent Treasy†
18.9	23.9	57.05	58.28	1.70	0.00	2.9	0.03	0.25	0.69	F	0	100	0	fix-inc	Permanent Vers Bd†
8.4	14.1	13.47	14.32	0.00	2.26	0.0	0.63	0.16	18.09	D	100	0	0	agg gr	Perritt Micro Cap Opp SC
95.8	116.9	7.82	9.67	0.09	0.82	0.9	0.84	0.79	10.49	D	93	6	1	gr-inc	Philadelphia
113.5	119.3	14.60	15.21	0.00	3.37	0.0	1.19	0.77	15.06	D	96	0	4	growth	PIC Growth
9.7	30.1	9.53	9.40	0.00	0.00	0.0	—	—	—		99	0	1	agg gr	PIC Sm Co Gro SC
13.1	36.1	13.04	14.75	0.17	1.01	1.1	0.94	0.80	11.73	F	72	22	6	income	PIC:Pinnacle Balanced
—	2.3	—	11.72	0.00	0.00	—	—	—	—		96	0	4	growth	PIC:Pinnacle Growth
—	3.3	—	9.88	0.00	0.00	—	—	—	—		98	0	2	agg gr	PIC:Pinnacle Sm Co Gro SC
26.9	30.5	18.50	18.74	0.00	0.00	0.0	1.62	0.44	27.17	F	98	0	2	agg gr	Pin Oak Agg Stk SC
16.5	22.3	23.96	27.71	0.11	4.50	0.4	0.98	0.91	11.44	A	94	0	6	growth	Pinnacle Fund
107.8	138.9	13.37	14.28	0.43	1.38	3.0	0.63	0.85	7.60	C	46	33	21	gr-inc	Preferred Asst Alloc
131.1	148.0	10.24	10.32	0.64	0.11	6.2	0.18	0.27	3.94	C	0	95	5	fix-inc	Preferred Fix Inc
381.9	448.1	17.23	18.23	0.00	4.38	0.0	1.16	0.68	15.78	D	97	0	3	growth	Preferred Growth
209.5	241.3	14.10	14.10	0.23	0.72	1.6	0.51	0.29	10.53	B	91	0	9	int'l	Preferred Int'l
68.9	121.6	12.45	14.45	0.08	1.83	0.5	—	—	—		99	0	1	agg gr	Preferred Small Cap SC
53.7	56.7	9.80	9.83	0.56	0.00	5.7	0.06	0.25	1.44	D	0	87	13	fix-inc	Preferred ST Gov
307.2	342.3	18.02	22.85	0.22	0.00	1.0	0.84	0.88	9.95	A	96	0	4	gr-inc	Preferred Value
876.0	1,219.2	14.48	16.54	0.53	0.12	3.2	0.58	0.93	6.70	C	61	40	-1	income	Price Balanced
539.7	2,344.6	19.06	24.17	0.12	0.02	0.5	0.85	0.91	9.91	A	90	0	10	growth	Price Blue Chip
156.3	184.0	10.48	10.86	0.54	0.00	5.0	0.18	0.91	4.41	C	0	95	5	tax-free	Price CA TF
959.9	1,059.9	14.47	14.71	0.50	1.58	3.1	0.37	0.68	5.08	A	53	36	11	growth	Price Cap App
125.1	109.1	15.75	16.62	0.00	1.59	0.0	0.68	0.31	13.63	B	91	0	9	agg gr	Price Cap Oppty
15.7	32.7	9.95	10.39	0.75	0.00	7.3	—	—	—		0	95	5	fix-inc	Price Corp Inc
209.5	747.0	16.37	20.13	0.44	0.75	2.1	0.63	0.85	7.67	A	84	5	11	gr-inc	Price Div Gro
—	72.1	—	10.70	0.00	0.01	—	—	—	—		98	0	2	growth	Price Divsfd Sm Cap Gro SC
40.0	113.4	12.97	13.71	1.15	0.24	8.2	0.60	0.25	13.08	A	0	93	7	fix-inc	Price Emg Mkt Bond
73.3	123.7	11.69	11.68	0.00	0.15	0.0	—	—	—		83	15	2	int'l	Price Emg Mkts Stk
807.7	1,908.3	20.34	26.38	0.34	0.25	1.3	1.00	1.00	11.11	B	98	0	2	gr-inc	Price Eqty 500 Idx
7,818.1	12,771.2	22.54	26.07	0.66	2.14	2.4	0.63	0.88	7.50	A	89	3	8	income	Price Eqty Inc
765.1	1,020.8	17.62	19.36	0.25	1.01	1.2	0.47	0.31	9.40	A	97	0	3	int'l	Price Europe
30.0	177.3	11.31	15.56	0.10	0.33	0.6	—	—	—		89	0	11	sector	Price Finl Serv
89.7	83.1	10.51	10.74	0.46	0.00	4.3	0.13	0.23	3.06	D	0	86	14	tax-free	Price FL Ins Inter
37.5	46.0	10.43	10.90	0.51	0.00	4.7	0.19	0.23	4.29	B	0	99	1	tax-free	Price GA TF
55.9	44.1	10.35	9.90	0.53	0.07	5.4	0.11	0.07	4.72	F	0	96	4	fix-inc	Price Glob Gov
17.2	33.6	11.76	12.72	0.06	0.53	0.5	—	—	—		95	2	3	global	Price Glob Stk
927.6	1,063.3	9.37	9.58	0.65	0.00	6.7	0.18	0.27	3.86	B	0	107	-7	fix-inc	Price GNMA

Stock and bond funds — comprehensive summary *continued*

Arranged in alphabetical order

No-Load Fund	Total return percent with quintile ranks by objective										Annualized		What $10,000 grew to after	
	1988	1989	1990	1991	1992	1993	1994	1995	1996	1997	3 yrs.	5 yrs.	3 yrs.	5 yrs.
Price Gro & Inc	25.1[1]	19.3[4]	-11.1[5]	31.5[2]	15.3[1]	13.0[3]	-0.1[3]	30.9[3]	25.6[1]	23.5[4]	26.6[3]	18.1[3]	20,311	22,928
Price Gro Stk	6.1[5]	25.4[2]	-4.3[3]	33.8[3]	6.0[4]	15.6[2]	0.9[2]	31.0[3]	21.7[2]	26.6[3]	26.4[2]	18.7[2]	20,176	23,534
Price Health Sciences	—	—	—	—	—	—	—	—	26.8[2]	19.4[3]	—	—	—	—
Price High Yld	17.9[1]	-1.5[5]	-11.0[5]	30.9[1]	14.7[1]	21.7[1]	-8.0[5]	15.8[4]	11.6[1]	14.5[1]	13.9[1]	10.6[1]	14,793	16,562
Price Int'l Bond	-1.3[5]	-3.2[5]	16.0[1]	17.7[1]	2.9[5]	19.4[1]	-1.8[2]	20.3[1]	7.1[1]	-3.2[5]	7.7[5]	7.9[1]	12,475	14,627
Price Int'l Disc	—	41.4[1]	-11.1[3]	10.7[3]	-8.3[4]	49.8[1]	-7.6[4]	-4.4[5]	13.9[1]	-5.7[4]	0.9[4]	7.3[4]	10,272	14,218
Price Int'l Stk	17.9[3]	23.7[2]	-8.9[2]	15.9[2]	-3.5[3]	40.1[2]	-0.8[3]	11.4[2]	16.0[3]	2.7[3]	9.9[3]	13.0[2]	13,271	18,444
Price Japan	—	—	—	—	-13.4[5]	20.6[5]	15.1[1]	-3.1[5]	-11.0[5]	-22.1[5]	-12.4[5]	-1.4[5]	6,720	9,327
Price Latin Amer	—	—	—	—	—	—	-15.9[5]	-18.7[5]	23.4[2]	31.8[1]	9.8[3]	—	13,227	—
Price MD ST TF	—	—	—	—	—	—	0.6[2]	7.6[3]	3.4[5]	4.2[5]	5.0[5]	—	11,591	—
Price MD TF	8.9[5]	9.6[3]	6.2[4]	11.2[4]	8.5[4]	12.7[3]	-5.0[1]	16.5[3]	3.8[3]	8.6[4]	9.5[4]	7.1[3]	13,139	14,067
Price Media & Telecomm	—	—	—	—	—	—	-0.9[3]	43.3[2]	1.8[5]	28.1[2]	23.1[3]	—	18,674	—
Price Mid Cap Gro	—	—	—	—	—	—	0.3[3]	41.0[1]	24.8[1]	18.3[5]	27.7[2]	21.4[1]	20,822	26,357
Price Mid Cap Val	—	—	—	—	—	—	—	—	—	27.1[3]	—	—	—	—
Price New Amer	18.5[2]	38.4[1]	-12.2[4]	62.0[2]	9.9[3]	17.4[2]	-7.4[5]	44.3[1]	20.0[3]	21.1[3]	28.0[1]	17.9[2]	20,969	22,796
Price New Asia	—	—	—	18.1[1]	11.2[1]	78.8[1]	-19.2[5]	3.8[4]	13.5[3]	-37.1[5]	-9.5[5]	1.5[5]	7,405	10,698
Price New Era	10.3[4]	24.3[3]	-8.8[4]	14.7[5]	2.1[5]	15.3[2]	5.2[1]	20.8[5]	24.2[2]	10.9[5]	18.5[5]	15.1[4]	16,644	20,189
Price New Horizon‡ SC	14.0[3]	26.2[3]	-9.5[3]	52.2[2]	10.6[3]	22.0[2]	0.3[2]	55.4[1]	17.0[3]	9.8[4]	25.9[2]	19.6[1]	19,959	24,423
Price New Inc	7.6[3]	12.1[3]	8.8[3]	15.5[2]	5.0[5]	9.6[3]	-2.2[2]	18.4[2]	2.4[5]	9.3[2]	9.8[3]	7.3[2]	13,255	14,207
Price NJ TF	—	—	—	—	9.6[1]	14.0[1]	-6.1[3]	17.0[3]	3.2[4]	9.1[2]	9.6[3]	7.1[3]	13,175	14,103
Price NY TF	10.5[4]	8.0[5]	5.3[5]	12.4[2]	10.4[1]	13.3[2]	-5.9[3]	17.3[3]	3.7[3]	9.5[2]	10.0[3]	7.3[2]	13,323	14,205
Price Pers Str-Bal	—	—	—	—	—	—	—	28.2[4]	14.2[5]	17.8[5]	19.9[5]	—	17,246	—
Price Pers Str-Gro	—	—	—	—	—	—	—	31.4[3]	17.7[4]	20.5[4]	23.1[4]	—	18,643	—
Price Pers Str-Inc	—	—	—	—	—	—	—	24.7[3]	11.8[4]	15.0[5]	17.0[5]	—	16,036	—
Price Real Est	—	—	—	—	—	—	—	—	—	—	—	—	—	—
Price Sci/Tech	13.3[4]	40.7[2]	-1.3[2]	60.2[2]	18.8[2]	24.2[2]	15.8[1]	55.5[1]	14.2[4]	1.7[5]	21.8[4]	21.0[2]	18,062	25,977
Price Sm Cap Stk	27.2[1]	19.1[4]	-20.5[5]	38.6[2]	13.9[2]	18.4[2]	0.1[3]	33.8[2]	21.1[3]	28.8[2]	27.8[2]	19.9[1]	20,871	24,736
Price Sm Cap Value‡ SC	—	18.1[4]	-11.3[4]	34.2[3]	20.9[1]	23.3[1]	-1.4[4]	29.3[1]	24.6[2]	27.9[3]	27.3[2]	20.2[1]	20,605	25,051
Price Spect-Gro	—	—	—	23.6[4]	7.2[4]	21.0[1]	1.4[2]	30.0[3]	20.5[3]	17.4[5]	22.5[4]	17.7[3]	18,387	22,559
Price Spect-Inc	—	—	—	19.6[1]	7.8[1]	12.4[1]	-1.9[2]	19.4[1]	7.6[1]	12.2[1]	13.0[1]	9.7[1]	14,413	15,892
Price Spect-Int'l	—	—	—	—	—	—	—	—	—	2.4[3]	—	—	—	—
Price ST Bond	5.5[5]	9.9[4]	8.6[3]	11.2[4]	5.0[4]	6.6[3]	-2.9[5]	9.7[4]	3.9[4]	6.3[3]	6.6[4]	4.6[5]	12,115	12,540
Price ST Gov	—	—	—	—	4.0[5]	2.8[5]	-0.6[3]	11.1[3]	4.3[3]	6.7[2]	7.3[2]	4.8[5]	12,359	12,628
Price Summit GNMA	—	—	—	—	—	—	-2.3[2]	17.8[2]	3.4[3]	9.8[1]	10.2[2]	—	13,370	—
Price Summit Ltd Trm	—	—	—	—	—	—	-3.1[5]	10.2[4]	3.9[4]	7.2[1]	7.1[3]	—	12,269	—
Price Summit Muni Inc	—	—	—	—	—	—	-4.7[1]	17.9[2]	5.0[1]	11.6[1]	11.4[1]	—	13,821	—
Price Summit Muni Inter	—	—	—	—	—	—	-1.7[1]	13.7[3]	4.7[1]	8.4[1]	8.9[1]	—	12,907	—
Price Tax-Efficnt Bal	—	—	—	—	—	—	—	—	—	—	—	—	—	—
Price TF Hi Yld	11.2[3]	10.5[2]	7.1[2]	11.7[3]	9.6[1]	13.0[3]	-4.4[1]	16.6[3]	5.0[1]	10.2[1]	10.5[2]	7.8[1]	13,488	14,571
Price TF Inc	7.9[5]	9.2[4]	5.9[4]	12.2[3]	9.4[2]	12.8[3]	-5.5[2]	17.7[3]	3.3[4]	9.3[2]	10.0[3]	7.2[2]	13,292	14,169
Price TF Ins Inter	—	—	—	—	—	—	-2.6[1]	13.0[4]	4.2[2]	7.2[3]	8.1[3]	6.7[1]	12,628	13,861
Price TF S-I	4.9[5]	6.9[3]	6.1[5]	7.9[4]	6.0[3]	6.3[3]	0.3[2]	8.1[3]	4.0[2]	5.3[2]	5.8[3]	4.8[2]	11,839	12,622
Price Trsy Inter	—	—	9.0[2]	14.8[1]	6.3[2]	8.0[2]	-2.2[5]	15.9[1]	2.4[5]	8.2[1]	8.7[1]	6.3[1]	12,838	13,560
Price Trsy Long	—	—	6.7[3]	16.3[4]	5.8[5]	12.9[3]	-5.7[4]	28.6[1]	-2.4[5]	14.7[1]	12.9[2]	8.9[2]	14,400	15,331
Price VA ST	—	—	—	—	—	—	—	7.6[3]	3.5[4]	4.3[5]	5.1[4]	—	11,613	—
Price VA TF	—	—	—	—	9.2[2]	12.5[4]	-5.1[2]	16.8[3]	4.1[2]	9.0[3]	9.8[3]	7.2[3]	13,253	14,149
Price Value	—	—	—	—	—	—	—	39.8[1]	28.5[1]	29.2[2]	32.4[1]	—	23,218	—
Primary Income	—	—	3.7[1]	21.5[4]	2.3[5]	15.3[2]	-2.6[4]	20.5[5]	20.0[1]	25.5[1]	22.0[2]	15.3[2]	18,153	20,401
Primary Trend	18.4[2]	8.9[5]	-1.7[2]	19.5[5]	0.2[5]	11.4[3]	-0.1[5]	16.2[5]	30.0[1]	18.2[5]	21.3[4]	14.7[4]	17,850	19,865
Primary US Gov	—	—	8.2[3]	14.5[4]	3.6[5]	8.3[3]	-3.2[5]	14.0[5]	3.8[3]	6.1[5]	7.9[5]	5.7[5]	12,555	13,172
Profit Value	—	—	—	—	—	—	—	—	—	23.6[4]	—	—	—	—
ProFunds Bear	—	—	—	—	—	—	—	—	—	—	—	—	—	—
ProFunds Bull	—	—	—	—	—	—	—	—	—	—	—	—	—	—
ProFunds Ultra Bear	—	—	—	—	—	—	—	—	—	—	—	—	—	—
ProFunds Ultra Bull	—	—	—	—	—	—	—	—	—	—	—	—	—	—
ProFunds Ultra OTC	—	—	—	—	—	—	—	—	—	—	—	—	—	—
Prudent Bear	—	—	—	—	—	—	—	—	-13.7[5]	-4.3[5]	—	—	—	—
Prudential Gov Sec S-I	6.1[3]	11.0[2]	7.8[4]	13.2[2]	6.2[3]	7.4[2]	-2.5[5]	12.9[1]	4.0[4]	7.1[1]	7.9[1]	5.6[2]	12,573	13,159
Purisima Total Ret	—	—	—	—	—	—	—	—	—	22.4[2]	—	—	—	—
Quaker Agg Gro	—	—	—	—	—	—	—	—	—	20.3[3]	—	—	—	—

See Chapter 3 for explanation of symbols

Arranged in alphabetical order

Total Net Assets $Million		NAV per share		1997 per share distributions		Yield %	Risk Analysis				% Distribution of Portfolio 12/31/97				
December 31 1996	1997	December 31 1996	1997	Income	Capital gains	12/31/97	beta	R^2	Std. Dev.	Sharpe Ratio	Stocks	Bonds	Cash	Objective	No-Load Fund
2,480.1	3,446.7	22.63	26.36	0.56	0.97	2.1	0.68	0.88	8.12	A	87	4	9	gr-inc	Price Gro & Inc
3,430.8	3,988.4	26.18	28.99	0.20	3.87	0.6	0.83	0.88	9.88	B	93	0	7	growth	Price Gro Stk
194.0	271.4	12.27	13.66	0.00	0.97	0.0	—	—	—	—	90	6	4	sector	Price Health Sciences
1,325.2	1,571.7	8.34	8.74	0.76	0.00	8.7	0.19	0.36	3.63	A	8	88	4	fix-inc	Price High Yld
969.5	825.8	10.46	9.58	0.53	0.02	5.5	0.04	0.00	7.29	F	0	96	4	fix-inc	Price Int'l Bond
322.4	228.2	16.22	15.05	0.00	0.25	0.0	0.39	0.17	10.27	D	92	3	5	int'l	Price Int'l Disc
9,340.8	9,720.6	13.80	13.42	0.20	0.55	1.4	0.69	0.40	11.83	B	95	4	1	int'l	Price Int'l Stk
147.0	152.2	8.83	6.88	0.00	0.00	0.0	0.65	0.15	18.39	F	95	0	5	int'l	Price Japan
211.0	432.7	8.26	10.77	0.12	0.00	1.1	1.16	0.24	25.44	C	63	35	2	int'l	Price Latin Amer
94.6	106.4	5.11	5.12	0.20	0.00	3.9	0.05	0.21	1.14	F	0	96	4	tax-free	Price MD ST TF
807.8	889.7	10.35	10.66	0.56	0.00	5.2	0.16	0.25	3.65	B	0	99	1	tax-free	Price MD TF
—	133.9	15.22	17.40	0.03	2.02	0.2	0.80	0.31	16.07	D	93	1	6	sector	Price Media & Telecomm
1,021.0	1,838.7	24.43	28.60	0.00	0.30	0.0	0.69	0.40	12.16	C	92	0	8	growth	Price Mid Cap Gro
49.2	218.0	11.56	14.47	0.08	0.14	0.6	—	—	—	—	90	0	10	growth	Price Mid Cap Val
1,440.2	1,757.9	38.37	44.19	0.00	2.20	0.0	0.83	0.52	12.82	A	94	0	6	agg gr	Price New Amer
2,181.7	782.0	9.26	5.74	0.08	0.00	1.4	1.42	0.40	23.08	F	94	0	6	int'l	Price New Asia
1,467.7	1,492.7	26.06	25.95	0.37	2.54	1.3	0.58	0.35	11.02	F	95	1	4	growth	Price New Era
4,363.5	5,103.7	21.77	23.30	0.00	0.58	0.0	0.88	0.36	16.31	C	94	0	6	agg gr	Price New Horizon‡ SC
1,688.3	1,945.0	8.89	9.07	0.58	0.04	6.3	0.20	0.27	4.30	D	0	92	8	fix-inc	Price New Inc
79.2	93.0	11.08	11.49	0.57	0.00	5.0	0.17	0.22	4.00	C	0	100	0	tax-free	Price NJ TF
141.7	165.4	10.81	11.24	0.57	0.00	5.1	0.18	0.23	4.29	C	0	100	0	tax-free	Price NY TF
179.7	281.5	13.29	14.82	0.44	0.35	2.9	0.57	0.88	6.71	C	58	42	0	gr-inc	Price Pers Str-Bal
41.8	98.3	14.08	16.52	0.26	0.19	1.6	0.68	0.91	7.96	B	75	25	0	growth	Price Pers Str-Gro
33.3	66.2	11.56	12.45	0.53	0.28	4.2	0.42	0.81	5.24	B	40	49	11	income	Price Pers Str-Inc
—	6.9	—	10.69	0.09	0.00	—	—	—	—	—	90	0	10	sector	Price Real Est
3,291.8	3,538.5	29.71	27.26	0.00	2.87	0.0	1.17	0.38	21.16	F	93	0	7	sector	Price Sci/Tech
415.6	816.4	18.07	22.20	0.04	1.01	0.2	0.50	0.24	11.41	B	89	1	10	growth	Price Sm Cap Stk
1,409.8	2,088.2	19.56	23.40	0.20	1.39	0.8	0.39	0.25	8.78	A	87	3	10	growth	Price Sm Cap Value‡ SC
2,104.1	2,605.3	15.13	15.93	0.20	1.60	1.1	0.73	0.74	9.45	C	93	1	6	growth	Price Spect-Gro
1,356.0	2,022.2	11.20	11.66	0.71	0.15	6.0	0.24	0.56	3.52	A	15	79	6	fix-inc	Price Spect-Inc
0.1	51.1	10.00	9.74	0.15	0.35	1.5	—	—	—	—	85	12	3	int'l	Price Spect-Int'l
446.9	345.0	4.67	4.68	0.28	0.00	5.9	0.07	0.25	1.59	F	0	93	7	fix-inc	Price ST Bond
95.8	102.1	4.64	4.66	0.28	0.00	6.0	0.09	0.23	2.04	C	0	92	8	fix-inc	Price ST Gov
25.1	32.2	9.61	9.85	0.66	0.00	6.7	0.17	0.24	3.87	B	0	105	-5	fix-inc	Price Summit GNMA
26.9	30.5	4.58	4.61	0.29	0.00	6.2	0.10	0.33	1.98	D	0	94	6	fix-inc	Price Summit Ltd Trm
16.1	32.1	10.04	10.63	0.54	0.00	5.1	0.17	0.21	4.04	A	0	94	6	tax-free	Price Summit Muni Inc
30.7	49.0	10.26	10.58	0.48	0.04	4.5	0.13	0.27	2.86	A	0	91	9	tax-free	Price Summit Muni Inter
—	13.9	—	10.77	0.02	0.00	—	—	—	—	—	48	47	5	income	Price Tax-Efficnt Bal
1,033.2	1,171.8	12.12	12.62	0.69	0.00	5.5	0.15	0.23	3.49	A	0	96	4	tax-free	Price TF Hi Yld
1,344.8	1,372.0	9.59	9.94	0.52	0.00	5.2	0.18	0.21	4.29	C	0	98	2	tax-free	Price TF Inc
97.0	104.6	10.79	11.04	0.48	0.03	4.4	0.14	0.27	3.01	C	0	98	2	tax-free	Price TF Ins Inter
439.3	439.9	5.34	5.36	0.23	0.03	4.2	0.07	0.30	1.48	B	0	99	1	tax-free	Price TF S-I
193.6	199.5	5.18	5.28	0.31	0.00	5.8	0.15	0.23	3.51	C	0	98	2	fix-inc	Price Trsy Inter
73.1	206.8	10.43	11.27	0.63	0.00	5.6	0.36	0.22	8.63	D	0	98	2	fix-inc	Price Trsy Long
14.9	19.2	5.13	5.14	0.20	0.01	3.8	0.04	0.13	1.16	D	0	96	4	tax-free	Price VA ST
189.9	220.5	11.06	11.45	0.58	0.00	5.0	0.17	0.23	3.93	B	0	101	-1	tax-free	Price VA TF
197.9	546.4	15.76	18.24	0.21	1.83	1.1	0.61	0.56	9.12	A	91	0	9	gr-inc	Price Value
5.0	4.9	13.28	13.93	0.40	0.42	2.9	0.46	0.51	7.19	A	72	17	11	income	Primary Income
23.6	24.4	13.66	13.47	0.30	2.27	1.9	0.67	0.48	10.71	F	81	4	15	gr-inc	Primary Trend
0.8	0.8	9.94	9.93	0.60	0.00	6.1	0.11	0.17	3.02	F	0	84	16	fix-inc	Primary US Gov
0.4	1.9	10.24	12.51	0.09	0.05	0.7	—	—	—	—	99	0	1	gr-inc	Profit Value
—	3.0	—	10.00	0.00	0.00	—	—	—	—	—	100	0	0	agg gr	ProFunds Bear
—	0.1	—	9.89	0.00	0.00	—	—	—	—	—	100	0	0	agg gr	ProFunds Bull
—	0.2	—	10.36	0.00	0.00	—	—	—	—	—	100	0	0	agg gr	ProFunds Ultra Bear
—	6.0	—	10.29	0.00	0.00	—	—	—	—	—	100	0	0	agg gr	ProFunds Ultra Bull
—	0.3	—	8.36	0.00	0.00	—	—	—	—	—	100	0	0	agg gr	ProFunds Ultra OTC
10.3	62.1	8.48	7.88	0.23	0.00	3.0	—	—	—	—	87	0	13	agg gr	Prudent Bear
180.9	149.0	9.62	9.76	0.52	0.00	5.4	0.11	0.22	2.47	C	0	102	-2	fix-inc	Prudential Gov Sec S-I
0.2	8.3	10.10	12.36	0.00	0.00	0.0	—	—	—	—	97	0	3	income	Purisima Total Ret
0.3	1.3	10.33	10.48	0.03	1.91	0.2	—	—	—	—	84	0	16	agg gr	Quaker Agg Gro

Stock and bond funds — comprehensive summary *continued*

Arranged in alphabetical order

No-Load Fund	Total return percent with quintile ranks by objective										Annualized		What $10,000 grew to after	
	1988	1989	1990	1991	1992	1993	1994	1995	1996	1997	3 yrs.	5 yrs.	3 yrs.	5 yrs.
Quaker Core Eqty	—	—	—	—	—	—	—	—	—	29.6 [2]	—	—	—	—
Quaker Enhnd Stk Market	—	—	—	—	—	—	—	—	—	30.2 [2]	—	—	—	—
Quaker Fixed Inc	—	—	—	—	—	—	—	—	—	8.1 [4]	—	—	—	—
Quaker Sector Alloc	—	—	—	—	—	—	—	—	—	18.5 [4]	—	—	—	—
Quaker Sm Cap Val	—	—	—	—	—	—	—	—	—	41.5 [1]	—	—	—	—
Quant Frgn Frntr	—	—	—	—	—	—	—	-2.3 [5]	8.8 [4]	-9.2 [4]	-1.2 [4]	—	9,648	—
Quant Gro & Inc	17.0 [3]	37.2 [1]	-1.1 [2]	28.0 [3]	6.3 [4]	11.9 [3]	-0.7 [4]	29.4 [3]	18.8 [4]	36.7 [1]	28.1 [2]	18.5 [3]	21,019	23,360
Quant Int'l Eqty	29.0 [1]	17.2 [4]	-28.2 [5]	10.1 [3]	-13.8 [5]	32.5 [4]	9.1 [1]	3.4 [4]	5.3 [5]	-1.6 [4]	2.3 [4]	9.1 [4]	10,715	15,482
Quant Numeric II	—	—	—	—	—	—	—	—	27.5 [1]	28.6 [2]	—	—	—	—
Quant Numeric SC	—	—	—	—	—	—	4.3 [1]	35.0 [3]	23.3 [2]	7.2 [5]	21.3 [4]	19.1 [1]	17,844	23,990
Rainbow Fund	18.1 [3]	9.4 [5]	-9.7 [3]	38.0 [4]	-2.7 [5]	-4.7 [5]	-4.7 [4]	20.8 [5]	24.1 [2]	5.0 [5]	16.3 [5]	7.4 [5]	15,733	14,292
Rainier Balanced	—	—	—	—	—	—	—	33.2 [1]	14.0 [3]	23.9 [2]	23.5 [2]	—	18,822	—
Rainier Core Eqty	—	—	—	—	—	—	—	47.2 [1]	23.3 [2]	33.9 [1]	34.4 [1]	—	24,286	—
Rainier Inter Fix Inc	—	—	—	—	—	—	—	13.4 [5]	2.9 [4]	7.3 [4]	7.8 [5]	—	12,521	—
Rainier Sm/Mid Cap	—	—	—	—	—	—	—	47.5 [1]	22.6 [2]	32.2 [1]	33.7 [1]	—	23,901	—
RCM Global Health Care	—	—	—	—	—	—	—	—	—	30.0 [2]	—	—	—	—
RCM Global Small Cap	—	—	—	—	—	—	—	—	—	25.5 [1]	—	—	—	—
RCM Global Tech	—	—	—	—	—	—	—	—	26.4 [3]	27.1 [2]	—	—	—	—
RCM Large Cap Growth	—	—	—	—	—	—	—	—	—	31.9 [2]	—	—	—	—
Reich & Tang Eqty	23.0 [2]	18.0 [4]	-5.8 [3]	23.1 [4]	16.4 [2]	13.8 [3]	1.7 [2]	28.2 [4]	16.9 [4]	13.8 [5]	19.5 [5]	14.6 [4]	17,044	19,730
Reserve Blue Chip Gro	—	—	—	—	—	—	—	35.9 [1]	8.6 [5]	25.5 [3]	22.8 [4]	—	18,529	—
Reserve Conv Secs	—	—	—	—	—	—	—	—	—	17.5 [4]	—	—	—	—
Reserve Infmd Invstr	—	—	—	—	—	—	—	30.4 [3]	1.3 [5]	19.0 [4]	16.3 [5]	—	15,714	—
Reserve Int'l Eqty	—	—	—	—	—	—	—	—	15.9 [3]	-8.7 [4]	—	—	—	—
Reserve Lrg Cap Val	—	—	—	—	—	—	—	—	—	32.7 [1]	—	—	—	—
Reserve Mid Cap Gro	—	—	—	—	—	—	—	—	14.8 [5]	7.9 [5]	—	—	—	—
Reserve Sm Cap Gr SC	—	—	—	—	—	—	—	67.5 [1]	2.8 [5]	-0.5 [5]	19.6 [4]	—	17,115	—
Reynolds Blue Chip Gr	—	20.7 [3]	0.1 [2]	35.9 [1]	0.1 [5]	-5.2 [5]	-0.6 [4]	32.9 [2]	28.1 [1]	31.5 [2]	30.8 [1]	16.1 [4]	22,401	21,109
Reynolds Opportunity	—	—	—	—	—	0.1 [5]	1.7 [2]	36.3 [1]	14.1 [5]	14.6 [5]	21.2 [4]	12.7 [5]	17,820	18,139
Reynolds US Gov	—	—	—	—	—	9.3 [1]	-5.6 [5]	12.2 [2]	3.5 [5]	5.4 [5]	7.0 [3]	4.8 [5]	12,247	12,638
Ridgeway Helms Millenium	—	—	—	—	—	—	—	—	—	—	—	—	—	—
Rightime	-1.3 [5]	11.8 [5]	0.7 [1]	31.3 [3]	3.4 [5]	7.9 [4]	0.8 [2]	26.9 [4]	8.6 [5]	-3.3 [5]	10.0 [5]	7.7 [5]	13,323	14,490
RNC Equity	—	—	—	—	—	—	—	—	—	27.7 [3]	—	—	—	—
Robrtsn Stph Contrn	—	—	—	—	—	—	-5.5 [4]	30.9 [3]	21.7 [2]	-29.5 [5]	3.9 [5]	—	11,230	—
Robrtsn Stph Devlp Cnt	—	—	—	—	—	—	-14.5 [5]	—	21.1 [2]	-15.2 [4]	-4.2 [5]	—	8,793	—
Robrtsn Stph Divrsfd Gro	—	—	—	—	—	—	—	—	—	29.6 [2]	—	—	—	—
Robrtsn Stph Emg Gro SC	14.1 [3]	44.5 [1]	9.6 [1]	58.5 [2]	-2.4 [5]	7.2 [5]	8.0 [1]	20.3 [5]	21.5 [2]	18.5 [3]	20.1 [4]	14.9 [3]	17,327	20,060
Robrtsn Stph Glob Low Pr	—	—	—	—	—	—	—	—	29.4 [1]	-13.5 [5]	—	—	—	—
Robrtsn Stph Glob Nat Res	—	—	—	—	—	—	—	—	41.2 [1]	-17.1 [5]	—	—	—	—
Robrtsn Stph Glob Val	—	—	—	—	—	—	—	—	—	—	—	—	—	—
Robrtsn Stph Gro & Inc	—	—	—	—	—	—	—	—	24.2 [2]	22.3 [4]	—	—	—	—
Robrtsn Stph Info Age	—	—	—	—	—	—	—	—	26.7 [3]	6.1 [5]	—	—	—	—
Robrtsn Stph MicroCap Gro SC	—	—	—	—	—	—	—	—	—	30.5 [1]	—	—	—	—
Robrtsn Stph Partners SC	—	—	—	—	—	—	—	—	43.3 [1]	18.1 [3]	—	—	—	—
Robrtsn Stph Val Gro	—	—	—	—	—	—	23.1 [1]	42.7 [2]	14.1 [4]	13.9 [4]	22.8 [3]	22.0 [1]	18,538	27,065
Rockhaven Fund	—	—	—	—	—	—	—	—	—	—	—	—	—	—
Rockhaven Premier Divd	—	—	—	—	—	—	—	—	—	—	—	—	—	—
Rockwood	26.8 [1]	19.1 [4]	-31.7 [5]	6.4 [5]	28.0 [1]	14.3 [3]	1.6 [2]	32.8 [2]	18.7 [3]	3.5 [5]	17.7 [5]	13.6 [5]	16,321	18,949
Royce Finl Servs	—	—	—	—	—	—	—	21.4 [2]	14.6 [4]	19.4 [3]	18.4 [5]	—	16,592	—
Royce GiftShares	—	—	—	—	—	—	—	—	25.6 [2]	26.0 [2]	—	—	—	—
Royce Low Priced Stk SC	—	—	—	—	—	—	3.0 [2]	22.5 [2]	22.8 [2]	19.5 [4]	21.6 [4]	—	17,973	—
Royce Micro-Cap SC	—	—	—	—	29.4 [1]	23.7 [1]	3.6 [1]	19.1 [5]	15.5 [4]	24.7 [2]	19.7 [4]	17.1 [2]	17,153	21,982
Royce Penn Mutual SC	24.6 [1]	16.7 [5]	-11.5 [4]	31.8 [3]	16.2 [2]	11.3 [3]	-0.7 [3]	18.7 [5]	12.8 [5]	24.9 [3]	18.7 [5]	13.1 [5]	16,730	18,490
Royce PMF II SC	—	—	—	—	—	—	—	—	—	20.8 [4]	—	—	—	—
Royce Premier SC	—	—	—	—	15.8 [2]	19.0 [2]	3.3 [1]	17.8 [5]	18.1 [4]	18.4 [5]	18.1 [5]	15.2 [4]	16,474	20,250
Royce REvest Gro & Inc	—	—	—	—	—	—	—	16.2 [5]	22.3 [3]	23.5 [4]	20.6 [5]	—	17,551	—
Royce Total Ret	—	—	—	—	—	—	5.1 [1]	26.9 [4]	25.5 [1]	23.7 [4]	25.3 [3]	—	19,691	—
RSI Tr-Act Mgd Bd	6.5 [4]	11.2 [4]	7.6 [2]	17.3 [3]	6.7 [4]	11.2 [3]	-4.2 [3]	17.7 [3]	3.2 [3]	9.7 [3]	10.0 [4]	7.2 [4]	13,318	14,186
RSI Tr-Core Eqty	16.3 [3]	33.5 [1]	-3.2 [2]	21.5 [4]	6.3 [4]	10.3 [3]	1.3 [2]	40.2 [1]	21.5 [3]	25.3 [3]	28.8 [2]	19.0 [2]	21,348	23,866
RSI Tr-Emg Gro SC	20.5 [2]	12.6 [5]	-9.9 [3]	53.5 [2]	15.8 [2]	21.0 [2]	3.5 [1]	42.8 [1]	27.1 [1]	8.3 [5]	25.3 [2]	19.7 [1]	19,651	24,615

See Chapter 3 for explanation of symbols

Stock and bond funds — comprehensive summary *continued*
Arranged in alphabetical order

Total Net Assets $Million December 31 1996	1997	NAV per share December 31 1996	1997	1997 per share distributions Income	Capital gains	Yield % 12/31/97	Risk Analysis beta	R^2	Std. Dev.	Sharpe Ratio	% Distribution of Portfolio 12/31/97 Stocks	Bonds	Cash	Objective	No-Load Fund
0.1	0.8	9.78	12.66	0.16	0.00	0.1	—	—	—	—	99	0	1	agg gr	Quaker Core Eqty
0.3	1.3	10.13	12.14	0.08	0.94	0.7	—	—	—	—	99	0	1	gr-inc	Quaker Enhnd Stk Market
0.3	1.0	9.92	10.25	0.45	0.00	4.4	—	—	—	—	0	88	12	fix-inc	Quaker Fixed Inc
0.1	0.8	9.83	10.11	0.05	1.45	0.5	—	—	—	—	96	0	4	growth	Quaker Sector Alloc
0.7	1.9	9.95	12.42	0.01	1.52	0.1	—	—	—	—	98	0	2	growth	Quaker Sm Cap Val
8.7	9.0	8.45	7.67	0.00	0.00	0.0	0.87	0.31	16.73	D	99	0	1	int'l	Quant Frgn Frntr
43.3	55.8	14.94	18.46	0.04	1.93	0.2	0.98	0.87	11.86	D	100	0	0	gr-inc	Quant Gro & Inc
27.2	28.0	11.02	10.42	0.17	0.26	1.6	0.65	0.37	11.75	D	87	0	13	int'l	Quant Int'l Eqty
8.1	12.5	13.72	14.36	0.00	3.37	0.0	—	—	—	—	88	0	12	agg gr	Quant Numeric II SC
69.0	64.5	17.30	15.93	0.16	2.45	0.9	0.97	0.31	19.69	D	98	0	2	agg gr	Quant Numeric SC
1.4	1.4	6.25	4.38	0.00	2.12	0.0	0.67	0.52	10.22	D	60	15	25	agg gr	Rainbow Fund
38.3	60.2	14.75	15.42	0.36	2.44	2.0	0.61	0.90	7.20	A	60	33	7	income	Rainier Balanced
220.1	497.8	18.73	21.79	0.07	3.16	0.3	0.91	0.88	10.92	A	98	0	2	growth	Rainier Core Eqty
16.5	21.5	12.27	12.45	0.69	0.00	5.5	0.12	0.24	2.70	F	0	89	11	fix-inc	Rainier Inter Fix Inc
124.6	353.1	18.78	22.45	0.00	2.31	0.0	0.80	0.65	11.11	A	97	0	3	agg gr	Rainier Sm/Mid Cap
4.0	4.6	10.00	11.65	0.00	1.32	0.0	—	—	—	—	100	0	0	sector	RCM Global Health Care
4.0	4.5	10.00	11.09	0.00	1.42	0.0	—	—	—	—	101	0	-1	global	RCM Global Small Cap
5.1	6.9	12.60	13.69	0.00	2.21	0.0	—	—	—	—	76	0	24	sector	RCM Global Tech
4.0	5.0	10.00	12.52	0.01	0.64	0.1	—	—	—	—	98	0	2	growth	RCM Large Cap Growth
91.1	88.7	18.10	17.25	0.09	3.23	0.5	0.58	0.46	9.43	D	94	0	6	growth	Reich & Tang Eqty
5.1	6.5	14.24	14.57	0.00	3.19	0.0	0.91	0.56	13.46	D	97	0	3	growth	Reserve Blue Chip Gro
14.1	21.8	10.30	10.79	0.52	0.71	4.9	—	—	—	—	99	1	1	income	Reserve Conv Secs
5.4	6.2	10.94	10.06	0.00	2.91	0.0	1.22	0.29	25.39	F	97	0	3	growth	Reserve Infmd Invstr
9.5	10.5	12.18	11.12	0.00	0.00	0.0	—	—	—	—	96	0	4	int'l	Reserve Int'l Eqty
2.3	5.9	12.49	16.26	0.00	0.31	0.0	—	—	—	—	93	0	7	gr-inc	Reserve Lrg Cap Val
2.0	4.6	12.82	12.33	0.00	1.46	0.0	—	—	—	—	97	0	3	growth	Reserve Mid Cap Gro
6.3	6.1	16.80	16.71	0.00	0.00	0.0	1.09	0.29	22.34	F	99	0	1	agg gr	Reserve Sm Cap Gr SC
34.6	60.5	24.27	31.50	0.01	0.38	0.0	1.17	0.80	14.71	D	100	0	0	gr-inc	Reynolds Blue Chip Gr
18.1	20.9	15.91	18.23	0.00	0.00	0.0	1.37	0.62	19.44	F	98	0	2	growth	Reynolds Opportunity
2.7	2.7	9.79	9.77	0.53	0.00	5.5	0.06	0.10	1.99	D	0	60	40	fix-inc	Reynolds US Gov
—	6.5	—	8.94	0.00	0.00	—	—	—	—	—	71	0	29	agg gr	Ridgeway Helms Millenium
162.2	120.6	31.67	30.57	0.05	0.00	0.2	0.49	0.36	8.98	F	100	0	0	growth	Rightime
0.9	4.3	12.14	15.48	0.02	0.00	0.1	—	—	—	—	—	—	—	growth	RNC Equity
1,063.4	402.9	16.57	11.61	0.05	0.03	0.4	0.06	0.00	16.84	F	97	1	2	agg gr	Robrtsn Stph Contrn
50.4	30.0	9.68	8.02	0.20	0.00	2.5	0.60	0.13	17.93	F	74	0	26	int'l	Robrtsn Stph Devlp Cnt
59.6	79.6	12.41	14.04	0.00	1.93	0.0	—	—	—	—	99	0	1	growth	Robrtsn Stph Divrsfd Gro
210.4	248.9	20.07	18.71	0.00	5.02	0.0	1.05	0.28	21.98	F	87	0	13	agg gr	Robrtsn Stph Emg Gro SC
31.4	14.3	13.52	11.17	0.00	0.56	0.0	—	—	—	—	99	0	1	global	Robrtsn Stph Glob Low Pr
120.5	79.3	14.29	11.67	0.18	0.00	1.5	—	—	—	—	94	1	5	sector	Robrtsn Stph Glob Nat Res
—	21.0	—	11.15	0.22	0.60	—	—	—	—	—	71	0	29	global	Robrtsn Stph Glob Val
309.8	298.4	13.62	13.51	0.04	3.04	0.2	—	—	—	—	81	16	3	growth	Robrtsn Stph Gro & Inc
106.3	118.6	11.51	11.80	0.43	0.01	3.7	—	—	—	—	98	0	2	sector	Robrtsn Stph Info Age
9.5	104.7	11.00	14.35	0.00	0.00	0.0	—	—	—	—	77	0	23	agg gr	Robrtsn Stph MicroCap Gro SC
127.3	196.3	14.60	16.49	0.12	0.64	0.7	—	—	—	—	85	0	15	agg gr	Robrtsn Stph Partners SC
643.2	756.8	24.15	23.18	0.00	4.43	0.0	1.35	0.49	21.48	D	98	0	2	agg gr	Robrtsn Stph Val Gro
—	0.7	—	10.27	0.03	0.00	—	—	—	—	—	67	32	1	growth	Rockhaven Fund
—	0.8	—	10.07	0.04	0.00	—	—	—	—	—	51	48	1	gr-inc	Rockhaven Premier Divd
1.3	1.4	20.43	19.36	0.00	1.80	0.0	0.80	0.15	22.51	F	100	0	0	growth	Rockwood
2.0	2.4	6.03	6.21	0.01	0.97	0.2	0.44	0.31	8.71	C	78	2	20	sector	Royce Finl Servs
1.0	3.5	5.83	6.91	0.00	0.43	0.0	—	—	—	—	76	0	24	agg gr	Royce GiftShares
15.9	18.1	6.30	6.82	0.00	0.71	0.0	0.38	0.11	13.08	D	90	0	10	growth	Royce Low Priced Stk SC
141.4	199.5	8.14	9.40	0.00	0.75	0.0	0.48	0.25	10.73	C	89	0	11	agg gr	Royce Micro-Cap SC
456.1	507.7	7.11	7.82	0.06	1.00	0.7	0.43	0.30	8.71	D	94	0	6	growth	Royce Penn Mutual SC
17.8	22.2	5.26	5.92	0.08	0.36	1.3	—	—	—	—	94	0	6	growth	Royce PMF II SC
316.8	533.5	7.81	8.70	0.09	0.46	1.0	0.38	0.29	7.96	D	93	0	7	growth	Royce Premier SC
42.1	34.3	12.21	13.00	0.19	1.87	1.3	0.36	0.23	8.48	D	89	9	2	gr-inc	Royce REvest Gro & Inc
6.2	120.6	6.29	7.52	0.11	0.15	1.5	0.18	0.12	5.85	A	73	5	22	gr-inc	Royce Total Ret
156.0	145.4	31.76	34.84	0.00	0.00	0.0	0.22	0.27	4.69	D	0	99	1	fix-inc	RSI Tr-Act Mgd Bd
223.9	196.5	60.39	75.68	0.00	0.00	0.0	1.07	0.93	12.37	D	99	0	1	gr-inc	RSI Tr-Core Eqty
91.4	75.4	67.60	73.18	0.00	0.00	0.0	0.79	0.18	20.70	D	96	0	4	agg gr	RSI Tr-Emg Gro SC

Arranged in alphabetical order

No-Load Fund	1988	1989	1990	1991	1992	1993	1994	1995	1996	1997	Annualized 3 yrs.	Annualized 5 yrs.	What $10,000 grew to after 3 yrs.	5 yrs.
RSI Tr-Int'l Eqty	12.4[3]	13.6[5]	-13.9[4]	9.4[4]	-5.4[3]	30.4[4]	0.8[2]	12.5[2]	10.9[4]	0.9[3]	8.0[3]	10.6[3]	12,581	16,527
RSI Tr-Inter Bd	7.2[3]	11.0[4]	9.5[2]	14.7[3]	6.0[4]	7.6[4]	-2.5[2]	14.0[5]	4.0[3]	7.1[5]	8.3[5]	5.9[5]	12,696	13,317
RSI Tr-ST Invest	7.1[2]	9.1[5]	8.1[3]	5.7[5]	3.1[5]	2.4[5]	3.4[1]	5.4[5]	4.7[2]	4.9[5]	5.0[5]	4.2[5]	11,579	12,259
RSI Tr-Value Eqty	24.4[1]	14.4[5]	-9.0[4]	24.3[4]	8.4[3]	8.1[4]	-1.1[4]	34.0[2]	25.9[1]	31.7[2]	30.5[1]	18.9[2]	22,212	23,736
Rushmore Amer Gas Idx	—	—	-10.5[4]	3.3[5]	11.4[3]	16.6[4]	-9.8[5]	30.5[3]	20.8[3]	24.2[3]	25.1[3]	15.5[4]	19,578	20,590
Rushmore MD TF	9.7[5]	6.7[5]	2.9[5]	10.2[5]	8.0[5]	11.9[4]	-5.2[2]	14.2[5]	3.2[4]	7.9[5]	8.3[5]	6.2[5]	12,711	13,484
Rushmore US Gov	7.9[3]	18.9[1]	4.4[4]	16.6[3]	6.1[5]	15.4[3]	-9.9[5]	32.0[1]	-2.9[5]	13.1[2]	13.2[2]	8.5[2]	14,491	15,068
Rushmore VA TF	7.6[5]	8.0[5]	4.4[5]	10.8[4]	8.0[4]	11.8[5]	-5.0[2]	14.9[5]	2.9[5]	8.5[4]	8.6[5]	6.4[4]	12,822	13,619
Rydex Gov Bd	—	—	—	—	—	—	—	37.4[1]	-7.0[5]	16.4[1]	14.1[1]	—	14,864	—
Rydex High Yld	—	—	—	—	—	—	—	—	—	—	—	—	—	—
Rydex Juno	—	—	—	—	—	—	—	—	8.0[2]	-5.6[5]	—	—	—	—
Rydex Nova	—	—	—	—	—	—	-4.8[4]	50.4[1]	25.5[2]	42.3[1]	39.0[1]	—	26,866	—
Rydex OTC	—	—	—	—	—	—	—	41.5[2]	43.5[1]	21.9[3]	35.3[1]	—	24,750	—
Rydex Prec Met	—	—	—	—	—	—	-25.4[5]	11.5[2]	-2.6[4]	-37.6[1]	-12.2[1]	—	6,776	—
Rydex Ursa	—	—	—	—	—	—	—	-20.1[5]	-12.4[5]	-21.0[5]	-17.9[5]	—	5,530	—
SAFECO Balanced	—	—	—	—	—	—	—	—	—	16.6[4]	—	—	—	—
SAFECO CA TF	12.8[1]	9.4[3]	7.0[2]	12.6[2]	8.0[4]	13.2[2]	-9.2[5]	26.1[1]	2.5[5]	11.6[1]	13.0[1]	8.2[1]	14,418	14,820
SAFECO Equity	25.3[1]	35.8[1]	-8.6[4]	27.9[3]	9.3[3]	30.9[1]	9.9[1]	25.3[4]	25.0[1]	24.2[4]	24.8[3]	22.9[1]	19,454	27,986
SAFECO GNMA	7.8[2]	12.9[3]	8.7[3]	14.8[3]	6.7[3]	7.1[4]	-4.3[4]	15.5[4]	4.0[3]	9.0[2]	9.4[3]	6.1[4]	13,090	13,416
SAFECO Growth SC	22.1[2]	19.2[5]	-15.0[4]	62.6[2]	-3.1[5]	22.2[2]	-1.6[3]	26.1[4]	22.9[2]	50.0[1]	32.5[1]	22.8[1]	23,241	27,946
SAFECO Hi Yld Bd	—	2.0[5]	-3.6[5]	24.3[1]	13.9[1]	16.9[1]	-2.3[1]	15.6[5]	10.4[1]	12.8[2]	12.9[2]	10.5[1]	14,395	16,441
SAFECO Income	19.0[1]	19.2[3]	-10.8[5]	23.3[4]	11.5[2]	12.6[3]	-1.1[3]	30.4[2]	24.0[1]	26.4[1]	26.9[1]	17.9[1]	20,443	22,766
SAFECO Insur Muni	—	—	—	—	—	—	-10.4[5]	24.4[1]	2.6[5]	10.7[1]	12.2[1]	—	14,120	—
SAFECO Int'l Stk	—	—	—	—	—	—	—	—	—	4.6[3]	—	—	—	—
SAFECO Inter Muni	—	—	—	—	—	—	-5.6[5]	15.2[1]	3.8[3]	7.5[2]	8.7[1]	—	12,850	—
SAFECO Inter Trsy	—	10.3[4]	7.2[4]	13.5[5]	6.6[3]	10.8[2]	-3.6[4]	16.7[3]	0.4[5]	8.3[3]	8.3[5]	6.3[4]	12,688	13,552
SAFECO Managed Bond	—	—	—	—	—	—	—	17.4[2]	0.0[5]	8.2[3]	8.3[5]	—	12,702	—
SAFECO Muni Bd	13.9[1]	10.1[2]	6.7[3]	13.8[1]	8.7[3]	12.7[3]	-8.2[4]	21.5[1]	3.2[4]	10.7[1]	11.5[1]	7.5[1]	13,878	14,358
SAFECO Northwest Gr	—	—	—	—	14.1[2]	1.0[5]	-1.6[4]	20.2[5]	15.0[5]	31.1[2]	21.9[4]	12.5[5]	18,125	18,013
SAFECO Sm Cap Stk SC	—	—	—	—	—	—	—	—	—	23.4[3]	—	—	—	—
SAFECO US Value	—	—	—	—	—	—	—	—	—	—	—	—	—	—
SAFECO WA Muni	—	—	—	—	—	—	-8.7[5]	19.9[1]	3.0[5]	9.0[3]	10.4[2]	—	13,458	—
Salomon Opportunity	23.3[2]	21.0[4]	-16.0[5]	30.6[4]	13.9[2]	12.8[3]	0.8[2]	35.1[2]	19.6[3]	33.0[1]	29.0[2]	19.6[2]	21,489	24,433
Sand Hill Port Mgr	—	—	—	—	—	—	—	11.6[5]	19.6[3]	17.8[5]	16.3[5]	—	15,721	—
Schroder Cap:Emg Mkts	—	—	—	—	—	—	—	—	7.9[4]	-5.2[4]	—	—	—	—
Schroder Cap:Int'l Sm Cap	—	—	—	—	—	—	—	—	—	-14.1[4]	—	—	—	—
Schroder Cap:Int'l	19.5[2]	22.1[3]	-11.5[3]	4.6[5]	-4.0[3]	45.7[1]	-0.3[3]	11.6[2]	9.9[4]	3.2[3]	8.2[3]	12.9[2]	12,655	18,383
Schroder Cap:Micro Cap SC	—	—	—	—	—	—	—	—	—	—	—	—	—	—
Schroder Cap:US Eqty	12.2[4]	24.1[4]	-4.0[2]	38.3[4]	15.2[2]	12.5[4]	-5.2[4]	28.0[4]	21.5[2]	23.3[3]	24.3[3]	15.4[3]	19,182	20,454
Schroder Cap:US Sm Co SC	—	—	—	—	—	—	4.5[1]	49.1[1]	22.3[2]	26.9[2]	32.2[1]	—	23,127	—
Schroder Ser:Inv Grd Inc	—	—	—	—	—	—	—	18.3[3]	2.0[4]	7.7[4]	9.2[4]	—	13,004	—
Schroder Ser:Lg Cap Eqty	—	—	—	—	—	—	—	28.3[4]	19.9[3]	26.3[3]	24.8[3]	—	19,426	—
Schroder Ser:Sm Cap Val SC	—	—	—	—	—	—	—	23.4[4]	23.9[2]	32.1[1]	26.4[2]	—	20,202	—
Schroder Ser:ST Invest	—	—	—	—	—	—	—	5.2[5]	4.5[2]	4.9[5]	4.9[5]	—	11,537	—
Schwab 1000(Inv)	—	—	—	—	8.5[3]	9.6[4]	-0.1[3]	36.6[1]	21.6[3]	31.9[2]	29.9[2]	19.1[2]	21,905	23,984
Schwab Analytics	—	—	—	—	—	—	—	—	—	31.8[1]	—	—	—	—
Schwab Asst Dir: Balanced	—	—	—	—	—	—	—	—	11.2[4]	17.8[4]	—	—	—	—
Schwab Asst Dir: Cons Gr	—	—	—	—	—	—	—	—	8.1[5]	14.7[5]	—	—	—	—
Schwab Asst Dir: Hi Gro	—	—	—	—	—	—	—	—	14.5[5]	21.0[4]	—	—	—	—
Schwab CA Long	—	—	—	—	—	—	-8.9[5]	19.9[1]	4.3[2]	10.2[1]	11.3[1]	7.2[2]	13,776	14,169
Schwab CA S-I	—	—	—	—	—	—	-2.1[5]	10.5[1]	3.9[3]	5.3[2]	6.5[1]	—	12,088	—
Schwab Int'l Idx(Inv)	—	—	—	—	—	—	3.8[2]	14.2[2]	9.1[4]	7.3[2]	10.2[2]	—	13,366	—
Schwab LT TF	—	—	—	—	—	—	-7.0[4]	18.1[2]	4.2[2]	9.9[1]	10.6[2]	7.4[1]	13,522	14,286
Schwab OneSource Bal Alloc	—	—	—	—	—	—	—	—	—	16.5[4]	—	—	—	—
Schwab OneSource Gro Alloc	—	—	—	—	—	—	—	—	—	18.4[5]	—	—	—	—
Schwab OneSource Int'l	—	—	—	—	—	—	—	—	—	6.8[2]	—	—	—	—
Schwab OneSource Sm Co SC	—	—	—	—	—	—	—	—	—	—	—	—	—	—
Schwab S & P 500(Inv)	—	—	—	—	—	—	—	—	—	32.5[1]	—	—	—	—
Schwab S-I TF	—	—	—	—	—	—	-1.1[4]	9.3[1]	3.5[4]	5.3[3]	6.0[1]	—	11,907	—
Schwab Sm Cap Idx(Inv) SC	—	—	—	—	—	—	-3.1[4]	27.7[4]	15.5[4]	25.7[2]	22.8[3]	—	18,536	—

See Chapter 3 for explanation of symbols

Total Net Assets $Million		NAV per share		1997 per share distributions		Yield %	Risk Analysis				% Distribution of Portfolio			Objective	No-Load Fund
December 31		December 31			Capital				Std.	Sharpe	12/31/97				
1996	1997	1996	1997	Income	gains	12/31/97	beta	R²	Dev.	Ratio	Stocks	Bonds	Cash		
42.1	29.8	45.84	46.26	0.00	0.00	0.0	0.68	0.41	11.63	C	97	0	3	int'l	RSI Tr-Int'l Eqty
77.0	63.8	30.00	32.12	0.00	0.00	0.0	0.12	0.24	2.75	C	0	100	0	fix-inc	RSI Tr-Inter Bd
26.5	24.8	20.48	21.49	0.00	0.00	0.0	0.00	0.07	0.15	F	0	100	0	fix-inc	RSI Tr-ST Invest
56.4	57.8	43.85	57.75	0.00	0.00	0.0	0.86	0.92	10.05	A	94	5	1	gr-inc	RSI Tr-Value Eqty
228.0	245.7	15.22	18.25	0.46	0.12	2.5	0.43	0.31	8.60	A	94	0	6	sector	Rushmore Amer Gas Idx
46.6	46.3	10.79	11.10	0.51	0.00	4.6	0.14	0.23	3.33	F	0	100	0	tax-free	Rushmore MD TF
17.7	16.5	9.90	10.60	0.54	0.00	5.1	0.38	0.21	9.22	F	0	99	1	fix-inc	Rushmore US Gov
32.1	32.3	11.09	11.46	0.53	0.02	4.6	0.17	0.25	3.73	F	0	100	0	tax-free	Rushmore VA TF
4.2	57.8	9.19	10.03	0.51	0.08	5.0	0.55	0.24	12.38	F	0	90	10	fix-inc	Rydex Gov Bd
0.1	18.4	—	9.88	0.73	0.00	—	—	—	—	—	3	97	1	fix-inc	Rydex High Yld
17.8	12.9	9.19	8.60	0.08	0.00	0.9	—	—	—	—	0	0	100	fix-inc	Rydex Juno
360.5	776.9	17.55	24.93	0.00	0.05	0.0	1.50	0.99	16.75	A	150	0	-50	agg gr	Rydex Nova
174.5	206.1	18.43	22.36	0.10	0.01	0.4	1.32	0.52	20.79	B	100	0	0	agg gr	Rydex OTC
28.6	24.9	8.56	5.34	0.00	0.00	0.0	0.83	0.08	32.20	A	100	0	0	prec met	Rydex Prec Met
298.7	278.9	7.04	5.54	0.02	0.00	0.4	-0.96	0.98	10.66	F	100	0	0	agg gr	Rydex Ursa
8.4	13.7	10.70	11.61	0.30	0.54	2.6	—	—	—	—	59	39	2	income	SAFECO Balanced
72.1	86.0	12.22	12.93	0.60	0.05	4.7	0.29	0.19	7.39	C	0	100	0	tax-free	SAFECO CA TF
821.6	1,490.2	16.60	19.54	0.23	0.84	1.1	0.86	0.89	10.16	D	99	0	1	gr-inc	SAFECO Equity
39.5	38.1	9.36	9.57	0.60	0.00	6.3	0.16	0.31	3.24	B	0	98	2	fix-inc	SAFECO GNMA
192.9	638.6	16.97	22.45	0.00	3.00	0.0	0.75	0.29	15.64	A	98	0	2	agg gr	SAFECO Growth SC
50.4	71.1	8.82	9.13	0.77	0.00	8.4	0.18	0.37	3.21	A	0	99	1	fix-inc	SAFECO Hi Yld Bd
281.7	402.0	21.13	23.89	0.65	2.11	2.5	0.69	0.83	8.42	A	98	2	0	income	SAFECO Income
13.2	16.5	10.74	11.36	0.50	0.00	4.4	0.27	0.18	7.05	D	0	100	0	tax-free	SAFECO Insur Muni
11.4	14.8	11.29	11.50	0.29	0.02	2.5	—	—	—	—	99	0	1	int'l	SAFECO Int'l Stk
14.2	13.8	10.61	10.92	0.47	0.00	4.3	0.15	0.22	3.43	B	0	100	0	tax-free	SAFECO Inter Muni
15.6	15.7	10.11	10.34	0.58	0.00	5.6	0.17	0.22	4.13	F	0	100	0	fix-inc	SAFECO Inter Trsy
2.0	4.8	8.32	8.60	0.42	0.00	4.9	—	—	4.43	F	0	97	3	fix-inc	SAFECO Managed Bond
480.8	496.1	13.98	14.52	0.75	0.16	5.1	0.24	0.21	5.85	C	0	100	0	tax-free	SAFECO Muni Bd
44.0	64.6	14.07	17.31	0.00	1.14	0.0	0.79	0.57	11.60	D	100	0	0	growth	SAFECO Northwest Gr
13.6	22.7	11.81	14.23	0.00	0.34	0.0	—	—	—	—	86	2	12	agg gr	SAFECO Sm Cap Stk SC
—	9.2	—	11.19	0.03	0.05	—	—	—	—	—	100	0	0	gr-inc	SAFECO US Value
7.1	7.3	10.53	10.95	0.50	0.00	4.5	0.21	0.19	5.20	D	0	100	0	tax-free	SAFECO WA Muni
158.8	203.1	41.53	53.44	0.39	1.40	0.7	0.86	0.82	10.66	B	87	0	13	growth	Salomon Opportunity
6.5	9.8	12.80	14.57	0.08	1.40	0.5	0.64	0.74	9.50	F	72	24	4	growth	Sand Hill Port Mgr
175.4	177.1	11.57	10.93	0.04	0.00	0.3	—	—	—	—	83	8	9	int'l	Schroder Cap:Emg Mkt
6.9	5.9	9.91	8.00	0.01	0.50	0.2	—	—	—	—	91	6	3	int'l	Schroder Cap:Int'l Sm Ca
188.2	174.0	17.57	16.28	0.29	1.55	1.6	0.63	0.35	11.64	C	89	2	9	int'l	Schroder Cap:Int'
—	2.1	—	10.57	0.00	0.19	—	—	—	—	—	83	0	17	agg gr	Schroder Cap:Micro Cap SC
17.1	13.5	8.36	7.52	0.00	2.75	0.0	1.01	0.90	11.91	B	100	0	0	agg gr	Schroder Cap:US Eqty
13.6	42.2	12.05	13.99	0.00	1.26	0.0	0.69	0.34	13.21	A	86	0	14	agg gr	Schroder Cap:US Sm Co SC
22.2	27.0	9.56	9.79	0.49	0.00	5.0	—	—	4.72	F	0	85	15	fix-inc	Schroder Ser:Inv Grd Inc
46.1	48.0	12.16	12.62	0.07	2.64	0.6	0.98	0.91	11.46	D	93	0	7	gr-inc	Schroder Ser:Lg Cap Eqty.
62.1	94.6	13.23	14.73	0.00	2.69	0.0	0.72	0.31	14.23	B	95	0	5	agg gr	Schroder Ser:Sm Cap Val SC
30.4	27.3	9.86	9.86	0.47	0.00	4.8	0.00	0.01	0.28	F	0	23	77	fix-inc	Schroder Ser:ST Invest
1,908.7	2,823.1	20.34	26.56	0.26	0.00	1.0	0.97	0.99	10.86	B	99	0	1	gr-inc	Schwab 1000(Inv)
104.0	160.0	11.17	13.21	0.12	1.33	0.9	—	—	—	—	97	0	3	agg gr	Schwab Analytics
97.6	162.1	11.15	12.58	0.23	0.31	1.8	—	—	—	—	56	30	14	income	Schwab Asst Dir: Balanced
23.4	46.7	10.66	11.63	0.33	0.24	2.9	—	—	—	—	38	48	13	gr-inc	Schwab Asst Dir: Cons Gr
112.9	184.0	11.56	13.20	0.15	0.62	1.2	—	—	—	—	75	16	10	growth	Schwab Asst Dir: Hi Gro
108.4	132.9	10.90	11.40	0.58	0.00	5.0	0.21	0.23	4.98	B	0	100	0	tax-free	Schwab CA Long
48.9	61.2	10.12	10.21	0.44	0.00	4.2	0.08	0.24	1.82	A	0	98	2	tax-free	Schwab CA S-I
259.6	325.0	12.54	13.30	0.15	0.00	1.2	0.66	0.38	11.74	B	98	0	2	int'l	Schwab Int'l Idx(Inv)
43.4	51.5	10.41	10.87	0.54	0.00	4.9	0.21	0.24	4.72	B	0	99	1	tax-free	Schwab LT TF
40.8	68.1	9.93	11.01	0.34	0.21	3.1	—	—	—	—	60	35	5	income	Schwab OneSource Bal Alloc
84.2	132.2	9.94	11.16	0.29	0.31	2.6	—	—	—	—	80	15	5	growth	Schwab OneSource Gro Alloc
67.6	76.5	10.14	10.19	0.33	0.30	3.2	—	—	—	—	98	0	2	int'l	Schwab OneSource Int'l
—	206.0	—	9.61	0.27	0.00	—	—	—	—	—	99	0	1	agg gr	Schwab OneSource Sm Co SC
292.3	1,032.4	11.37	14.93	0.13	0.00	0.9	—	—	—	—	97	0	3	gr-inc	Schwab S & P 500(Inv)
51.9	53.8	10.13	10.23	0.42	0.00	4.1	0.07	0.25	1.68	B	0	100	0	tax-free	Schwab S-I TF
232.8	427.5	14.27	17.87	0.06	0.00	0.4	0.79	0.40	13.93	C	99	0	1	agg gr	Schwab Sm Cap Idx(Inv) SC

Arranged in alphabetical order

| No-Load Fund | Total return percent with quintile ranks by objective | | | | | | | | | | Annualized | | What $10,000 grew to after | |
	1988	1989	1990	1991	1992	1993	1994	1995	1996	1997	3 yrs.	5 yrs.	3 yrs.	5 yrs.
Schwab ST Bd Mkt Idx..........	—	—	—	—	6.1³	7.8²	-2.8⁵	10.9³	4.0⁴	7.1¹	7.3²	5.3³	12,350	12,940
Schwab Tot Bd Mkt Idx..........	—	—	—	—	—	—	-5.8⁴	22.5²	1.1⁵	10.0³	10.8³	—	13,613	—
Schwartz Value SC..........	—	—	—	—	—	—	-6.8⁵	16.9⁵	18.3⁴	28.0²	21.0⁴	—	17,700	—
SCM Portfolio..........	—	—	4.6¹	9.8⁵	2.1⁵	6.2⁵	-0.8⁴	14.1⁵	11.5⁵	16.3⁵	14.0⁵	9.3⁵	14,803	15,601
Scout Balanced..........	—	—	—	—	—	—	—	—	6.1⁵	10.1⁵	—	—	—	—
Scout Bond..........	5.9⁵	11.3⁴	8.0²	13.2⁵	6.6⁴	8.3⁵	-3.1²	14.0⁵	3.5³	7.3⁵	8.2⁵	5.9⁵	12,663	13,291
Scout Regional SC..........	—	—	—	—	11.0³	6.0⁵	0.7²	20.0⁵	12.6⁴	23.0³	18.4⁴	12.1⁵	16,609	17,723
Scout Stock..........	13.9⁴	19.1⁴	-2.4²	24.8⁴	7.1⁴	10.7⁴	2.8²	19.7⁵	10.7⁵	21.0⁴	17.0⁵	12.8⁵	16,030	18,227
Scout Worldwide..........	—	—	—	—	—	—	3.8¹	14.7³	18.4⁵	18.4²	17.1³	—	16,061	—
Scudder 21st Cent Gro SC..........	—	—	—	—	—	—	—	—	—	9.7⁴	—	—	—	—
Scudder Balanced..........	—	—	—	—	—	—	-2.4⁴	26.5⁴	11.5⁵	22.7⁴	20.1⁵	—	17,313	—
Scudder CA TF..........	12.1²	10.3²	6.4³	12.7²	9.4²	13.8¹	-7.3⁴	18.9²	3.6³	10.2¹	10.7¹	7.4¹	13,574	14,319
Scudder Classic Gro‡..........	—	—	—	—	—	—	—	—	—	34.9¹	—	—	—	—
Scudder Development SC..........	11.1⁴	23.2⁴	1.5¹	71.9¹	-2.0⁵	9.0⁴	-5.3⁴	50.7¹	10.0⁵	6.9⁵	21.0⁴	12.8⁴	17,726	18,297
Scudder Emg Mkts Gro..........	—	—	—	—	—	—	—	—	—	3.6³	—	—	—	—
Scudder Emg Mkts Inc..........	—	—	—	—	—	—	-8.1⁵	19.5²	34.6¹	13.1²	22.1¹	—	18,188	—
Scudder Finl Srvcs..........	—	—	—	—	—	—	—	—	—	—	—	—	—	—
Scudder Glob Bond..........	—	—	—	—	5.5⁵	6.7⁵	-1.1¹	7.7⁵	3.1³	0.4⁵	3.7⁵	3.3⁵	11,144	11,760
Scudder Glob Disc‡..........	—	—	—	—	-0.1⁴	38.2¹	-7.7⁴	17.8²	21.5¹	9.9⁴	16.3³	14.9¹	15,723	20,056
Scudder Global..........	19.2¹	37.4¹	-6.4³	17.3²	4.5²	31.2²	-4.2³	20.5²	13.6⁴	17.2²	17.1³	15.1¹	16,047	20,169
Scudder GNMA..........	6.8⁴	12.8³	10.1²	15.0³	7.0²	6.0⁵	-3.1³	16.6³	4.2²	8.4³	9.6³	6.2⁴	13,166	13,523
Scudder Gold..........	—	10.7⁵	-16.7¹	-6.9⁴	-9.1³	59.5⁵	-7.4²	13.2¹	32.1¹	-40.9²	-4.0¹	5.5¹	8,845	13,064
Scudder Gro & Inc..........	11.9⁴	26.5²	-2.3²	28.2³	9.6²	15.6²	2.6¹	31.2³	22.3²	30.3²	27.8²	19.9²	20,886	24,773
Scudder Grt Europe..........	—	—	—	—	—	—	—	23.6¹	30.9¹	24.0¹	26.1¹	—	20,062	—
Scudder Hi Yld Bd..........	—	—	—	—	—	—	—	—	—	14.8¹	—	—	—	—
Scudder Hi Yld TF..........	13.5¹	10.3²	6.0⁴	13.4¹	10.8¹	13.9¹	-8.4⁵	18.8²	4.4¹	12.0¹	11.6¹	7.7¹	13,894	14,496
Scudder Income..........	8.9³	12.7³	8.3²	17.3³	6.7⁴	12.7³	-4.5³	18.5³	3.4³	8.7⁴	10.0³	7.5³	13,321	14,337
Scudder Int'l Bond..........	—	7.2⁵	21.1¹	21.4¹	7.6²	15.9¹	-8.6⁵	8.5⁵	3.5³	-4.2⁵	2.5⁵	2.7⁵	10,763	11,402
Scudder Int'l Gro & Inc..........	—	—	—	—	—	—	—	—	—	—	—	—	—	—
Scudder Int'l Stk..........	18.8²	27.0²	-8.9²	11.8³	-2.6²	36.5³	-3.0⁴	12.2²	14.6³	8.0²	11.6²	12.9²	13,884	18,383
Scudder Large Cap Gro..........	—	—	—	—	6.7⁴	0.0⁵	-1.3³	32.5³	18.2³	32.8¹	27.6¹	15.5³	20,798	20,528
Scudder Large Cap Val..........	29.7¹	33.8¹	-17.0⁵	43.0¹	7.1⁴	20.1¹	-9.9⁵	31.6³	19.5³	32.5¹	27.7²	17.7³	20,841	22,552
Scudder Latin Amer..........	—	—	—	—	—	—	-9.4⁴	-9.8⁵	28.3¹	31.3¹	15.0¹	19.1¹	15,191	23,989
Scudder Ltd TF..........	—	—	—	—	—	—	—	9.3¹	4.0²	5.9¹	6.4¹	—	12,036	—
Scudder MA Ltd TF..........	—	—	—	—	—	—	—	9.5¹	3.4⁵	5.7²	6.2¹	—	11,961	—
Scudder MA TF..........	12.4²	9.8³	6.3⁴	12.3²	10.8¹	14.3¹	-6.2³	17.9²	4.1²	8.5⁴	10.0³	7.4²	13,317	14,278
Scudder Medium TF..........	4.9⁵	6.0⁵	6.3⁵	12.1¹	8.9¹	10.7²	-3.5²	14.3²	4.0²	7.7²	8.6²	6.5²	12,797	13,671
Scudder Micro-Cap SC..........	—	—	—	—	—	—	—	—	—	35.2¹	—	—	—	—
Scudder Mngd Muni..........	12.3²	11.2¹	6.8³	12.2²	9.1²	13.3²	-6.0³	16.8³	4.1²	9.3²	9.9³	7.2³	13,286	14,150
Scudder NY TF..........	10.9³	10.1²	4.3⁵	14.4¹	10.2¹	12.9³	-7.2⁴	17.9²	3.3⁴	9.9¹	10.2³	7.0³	13,381	14,019
Scudder OH TF..........	12.8¹	9.6³	6.6³	11.9³	8.8³	12.3⁴	-5.5²	17.2³	4.2²	8.7⁴	9.9³	7.1³	13,274	14,087
Scudder PA TF..........	13.5¹	10.1²	5.8⁴	12.5²	9.1²	13.2²	-5.9³	17.4³	3.5⁴	8.9³	9.8³	7.1³	13,238	14,101
Scudder Pacific Opp..........	—	—	—	—	—	—	-17.1⁵	1.3⁴	6.5⁵	-37.8⁵	-12.4⁵	-2.3⁵	6,716	8,913
Scudder Pathway Balanced..........	—	—	—	—	—	—	—	—	—	13.4⁵	—	—	—	—
Scudder Pathway Cons..........	—	—	—	—	—	—	—	—	—	14.4⁵	—	—	—	—
Scudder Pathway Growth..........	—	—	—	—	—	—	—	—	—	14.9⁵	—	—	—	—
Scudder Pathway Int'l..........	—	—	—	—	—	—	—	—	—	7.0²	—	—	—	—
Scudder S&P 500 Idx..........	—	—	—	—	—	—	—	—	—	—	—	—	—	—
Scudder Small Co Val SC..........	—	—	—	—	—	—	—	—	23.8²	37.0¹	—	—	—	—
Scudder ST Bond..........	6.3³	13.3¹	9.9¹	14.4¹	5.6⁴	8.2¹	-2.9⁵	10.7³	3.9⁴	6.1⁴	6.9⁴	5.1³	12,209	12,827
Scudder US Zero 2000..........	11.7¹	20.4¹	4.6⁴	20.0²	8.1²	16.0²	-7.9⁵	19.1³	0.7⁵	6.5⁵	8.5³	6.4⁵	12,776	13,649
Scudder Value‡..........	—	—	—	—	—	—	1.6²	30.2³	23.0²	35.3¹	29.4¹	19.7¹	21,672	24,573
Sefton CA Tax-Free..........	—	—	—	—	—	—	—	—	4.6¹	8.5⁴	—	—	—	—
Sefton Sm Co Val SC..........	—	—	—	—	—	—	—	—	—	—	—	—	—	—
Sefton US Gov..........	—	—	—	—	—	—	—	—	1.7⁵	8.4³	—	—	—	—
Sefton Value Eqty..........	—	—	—	—	—	—	—	—	30.7¹	25.3³	—	—	—	—
Selected Amer Shares..........	22.0²	20.1³	-3.9³	46.3¹	5.8⁴	5.5⁵	-3.3⁵	38.1¹	30.7¹	37.3¹	35.3¹	20.4¹	24,774	25,274
Selected Spec Shares..........	19.6²	28.9²	-6.9⁴	25.5⁴	8.4³	10.8⁴	-2.5⁴	32.3²	11.9⁵	26.9³	23.4⁴	15.2⁴	18,787	20,296
Selected US Gov Inc..........	3.0⁵	9.3⁴	8.5²	13.6⁵	5.0⁵	8.4⁵	-2.5²	15.6⁴	2.8⁴	7.2⁵	8.4⁵	6.2⁵	12,748	13,483
Seneca Bond..........	—	—	—	—	—	—	—	—	—	12.8¹	—	—	—	—

See Chapter 3 for explanation of symbols

Total Net Assets $Million		NAV per share		1997 per share distributions		Yield %	Risk Analysis				% Distribution of Portfolio				
December 31		December 31			Capital				Std.	Sharpe	12/31/97				
1996	1997	1996	1997	Income	gains	12/31/97	beta	R^2	Dev.	Ratio	Stocks	Bonds	Cash	Objective	No-Load Fund
131.5	138.1	9.75	9.82	0.60	0.00	6.1	0.09	0.30	1.92	C	0	98	2	fix-inc	Schwab ST Bd Mkt Idx
21.6	94.2	9.71	10.01	0.62	0.00	6.2	0.26	0.24	5.80	D	0	95	5	fix-inc	Schwab Tot Bd Mkt Idx
55.1	70.0	21.19	23.99	0.05	3.08	0.2	0.50	0.33	9.76	D	89	0	11	growth	Schwartz Value SC
1.0	1.1	11.69	13.05	0.26	0.28	2.0	0.45	0.85	5.44	F	50	10	40	gr-inc	SCM Portfolio
7.4	9.1	10.33	10.62	0.40	0.33	3.8	—	—	—	—	33	49	18	income	Scout Balanced
79.8	79.5	11.02	11.17	0.62	0.00	5.6	0.12	0.24	2.79	D	0	98	2	fix-inc	Scout Bond
47.6	49.9	10.43	11.89	0.21	0.46	1.8	0.34	0.23	7.97	B	89	0	11	agg gr	Scout Regional SC
178.9	198.5	16.97	19.01	0.40	1.04	2.1	0.60	0.73	7.75	D	81	0	19	growth	Scout Stock
41.0	57.0	13.94	16.02	0.24	0.22	1.5	0.57	0.53	8.78	C	82	0	18	global	Scout Worldwide
9.6	29.1	11.81	12.96	0.00	0.00	0.0	—	—	—	—	95	0	5	agg gr	Scudder 21st Cent Gro SC
112.7	158.0	14.60	16.85	0.37	0.68	2.1	0.77	0.93	8.85	F	58	33	9	gr-inc	Scudder Balanced
296.6	310.1	10.57	11.08	0.52	0.02	4.7	0.20	0.23	4.79	B	0	96	4	tax-free	Scudder CA TF
16.7	72.0	13.39	17.73	0.03	0.29	0.2	—	—	—	—	92	0	8	growth	Scudder Classic Gro‡
971.5	862.2	39.79	38.55	0.00	3.88	0.0	1.06	0.33	20.26	D	99	0	1	agg gr	Scudder Development SC
99.0	205.7	13.80	14.23	0.06	0.00	0.4	—	—	—	—	90	0	10	int'l	Scudder Emg Mkts Gro
323.5	345.6	12.28	11.26	1.06	1.50	8.3	0.54	0.22	12.53	B	0	80	20	fix-inc	Scudder Emg Mkts Inc
—	27.0	—	12.94	0.00	0.00	—	—	—	—	—	96	0	4	sector	Scudder Finl Srvcs
201.6	124.9	10.20	9.61	0.61	0.00	6.4	0.06	0.04	3.65	F	0	100	0	fix-inc	Scudder Glob Bond
362.5	339.5	19.95	19.84	0.64	1.41	3.0	0.51	0.26	11.13	C	92	0	8	global	Scudder Glob Disc‡
1,409.3	1,570.5	28.80	28.28	0.88	4.58	2.7	0.67	0.56	9.86	C	81	15	4	global	Scudder Global
402.9	389.9	14.59	14.82	0.95	0.00	6.4	0.15	0.24	3.37	B	0	100	0	fix-inc	Scudder GNMA
184.3	124.7	12.68	7.36	0.14	0.00	1.9	0.22	0.01	27.16	A	78	0	22	prec met	Scudder Gold
4,201.0	6,832.8	23.23	27.33	0.58	2.20	2.0	0.78	0.89	9.25	A	93	4	3	gr-inc	Scudder Gro & Inc
150.7	228.5	18.08	20.58	0.54	1.30	2.5	0.45	0.32	8.93	A	87	0	13	int'l	Scudder Grt Europe
52.8	155.7	12.53	13.00	1.16	0.12	8.9	—	—	—	—	5	91	4	fix-inc	Scudder Hi Yld Bd
292.9	324.8	12.04	12.78	0.67	0.00	5.2	0.17	0.19	4.29	A	0	95	5	tax-free	Scudder Hi Yld TF
580.4	695.6	13.15	13.47	0.79	0.01	5.9	0.19	0.29	3.91	B	0	82	18	fix-inc	Scudder Income
359.5	176.7	11.20	10.16	0.57	0.00	5.6	0.02	0.00	4.97	F	0	99	1	fix-inc	Scudder Int'l Bond
—	46.9	—	11.71	0.02	0.00	—	—	—	—	—	97	0	3	int'l	Scudder Int'l Gro & Inc
2,644.9	2,617.0	47.56	45.75	0.25	5.35	0.5	0.69	0.44	11.45	B	94	0	6	int'l	Scudder Int'l Stk
217.9	307.4	20.04	25.12	0.00	1.46	0.0	1.15	0.92	13.30	B	97	0	3	agg gr	Scudder Large Cap Gro
1,774.1	2,230.2	22.11	27.17	0.24	1.86	0.8	0.87	0.89	10.31	B	99	0	1	growth	Scudder Large Cap Val
636.9	962.4	21.40	26.67	0.25	1.14	0.9	1.11	0.26	23.57	B	97	0	3	int'l	Scudder Latin Amer
122.7	116.4	11.99	12.15	0.52	0.01	4.3	0.08	0.26	1.73	A	0	83	17	tax-free	Scudder Ltd TF
66.4	83.9	12.02	12.16	0.53	0.00	4.4	0.08	0.22	1.85	A	0	88	12	tax-free	Scudder MA Ltd TF
330.8	356.0	13.90	14.35	0.70	0.00	4.9	0.17	0.22	4.05	B	0	97	3	tax-free	Scudder MA TF
649.8	651.6	11.15	11.41	0.52	0.05	4.5	0.14	0.26	3.06	B	0	95	5	tax-free	Scudder Medium TF
35.4	134.7	12.99	17.49	0.00	0.07	0.0	—	—	—	—	98	0	2	agg gr	Scudder Micro-Cap SC
736.1	719.2	8.84	9.13	0.46	0.05	5.0	0.19	0.25	4.16	C	0	97	3	tax-free	Scudder Mngd Muni
188.1	189.1	10.81	11.32	0.51	0.02	4.5	0.21	0.23	4.83	D	0	99	1	tax-free	Scudder NY TF
85.9	89.5	13.15	13.55	0.68	0.03	5.0	0.17	0.23	4.08	B	0	98	2	tax-free	Scudder OH TF
75.9	75.5	13.46	13.89	0.71	0.03	5.1	0.17	0.22	4.05	C	0	92	8	tax-free	Scudder PA TF
344.3	127.4	16.82	10.17	0.30	0.00	2.9	1.12	0.38	18.68	F	89	0	11	int'l	Scudder Pacific Opp
0.7	207.3	11.92	12.91	0.37	0.21	2.9	—	—	—	—	55	43	2	income	Scudder Pathway Balance
0.7	17.9	11.86	12.77	0.76	0.02	5.9	—	—	—	—	32	59	9	income	Scudder Pathway Con
0.7	50.0	11.92	13.23	0.21	0.26	1.6	—	—	—	—	74	23	3	growth	Scudder Pathway Growt
0.4	9.7	11.90	12.22	0.16	0.35	1.3	—	—	—	—	86	11	3	int'l	Scudder Pathway Int'
—	26.5	—	12.94	0.06	0.00	—	—	—	—	—	99	0	1	gr-inc	Scudder S&P 500 Idx
56.4	211.5	15.44	20.83	0.02	0.30	0.1	—	—	—	—	95	0	5	growth	Scudder Small Co Val SC
1,466.1	1,165.5	11.05	11.04	0.67	0.00	6.1	0.06	0.14	1.87	D	0	97	3	fix-inc	Scudder ST Bond
25.5	352.5	11.77	11.88	0.24	1.65	5.3	0.17	0.18	4.49	F	0	99	1	fix-inc	Scudder US Zero 2000
102.4	20.4	17.81	22.18	0.63	0.00	1.0	0.81	0.83	9.98	A	82	0	18	growth	Scudder Value‡
43.2	40.3	12.46	12.84	0.57	0.07	4.5	—	—	—	—	0	100	0	tax-free	Sefton CA Tax-Free
—	29.7	—	12.74	0.07	0.00	—	—	—	—	—	—	—	—	agg gr	Sefton Sm Co Val SC
25.2	35.3	12.31	12.62	0.69	0.00	5.5	—	—	—	—	94	0	6	fix-inc	Sefton US Gov
51.5	85.3	16.05	17.45	0.16	2.42	0.9	—	—	—	—	89	0	11	growth	Sefton Value Eqty
1,378.1	2,218.1	21.53	27.18	0.21	2.03	0.7	0.99	0.89	11.82	A	97	0	3	gr-inc	Selected Amer Shares
62.4	74.9	10.89	13.03	0.00	0.62	0.0	0.99	0.51	15.58	F	90	0	10	growth	Selected Spec Shares
6.9	6.0	8.90	9.01	0.52	0.00	5.8	0.15	0.18	3.81	F	0	96	4	fix-inc	Selected US Gov Inc
0.1	8.9	10.23	10.62	0.62	0.00	5.8	—	—	—	—	0	99	1	fix-inc	Seneca Bond

Stock and bond funds — comprehensive summary *continued*

Arranged in alphabetical order

| No-Load Fund | Total return percent with quintile ranks by objective | | | | | | | | | | Annualized | | What $10,000 grew to after | |
	1988	1989	1990	1991	1992	1993	1994	1995	1996	1997	3 yrs.	5 yrs.	3 yrs.	5 yrs.
Seneca Growth	—	—	—	—	—	—	—	—	—	27.9[3]	—	—	—	—
Seneca Mid-Cap Edge	—	—	—	—	—	—	—	—	—	16.2[4]	—	—	—	—
Seneca Real Estate	—	—	—	—	—	—	—	—	—	16.6[4]	—	—	—	—
Sentry	16.9[3]	24.2[3]	5.2[1]	29.3[4]	7.5[4]	6.0[4]	-1.1[4]	27.8[4]	22.8[2]	29.7[2]	26.7[2]	16.4[3]	20,349	21,320
Sequoia‡	11.0[4]	27.9[2]	-3.8[3]	40.0[2]	9.4[3]	10.8[4]	3.3[1]	41.4[1]	21.7[2]	43.2[1]	35.1[1]	23.0[1]	24,643	28,205
Sextant Bond Inc	—	—	—	—	—	—	-6.4[4]	16.7[4]	-0.6[5]	12.1[2]	9.2[4]	—	13,006	—
Sextant Growth	5.3[5]	5.6[5]	6.3[1]	23.6[4]	-1.3[5]	10.0[4]	-11.4[5]	29.3[3]	8.5[5]	26.6[3]	21.1[4]	11.6[5]	17,761	17,315
Sextant Idaho TE	—	9.0[4]	5.7[5]	8.8[5]	6.9[5]	8.4[5]	-3.3[1]	13.6[5]	3.5[4]	7.1[5]	8.0[5]	5.7[5]	12,594	13,201
Sextant International	—	—	—	—	—	—	—	—	16.9[2]	15.9[1]	—	—	—	—
Sextant ST Bond	—	—	—	—	—	—	—	—	3.8[5]	6.5[2]	—	—	—	—
Shelby Fund SC	—	—	—	—	—	—	—	35.2[2]	14.0[5]	6.2[5]	17.9[5]	—	16,368	—
Sit Balanced	—	—	—	—	—	—	-0.3[2]	25.4[3]	15.8[2]	21.7[3]	20.9[2]	—	17,681	—
Sit Bond	—	—	—	—	—	—	-1.3[1]	16.9[3]	4.3[2]	9.4[2]	10.1[2]	—	13,328	—
Sit Develop Mkts Gro	—	—	—	—	—	—	—	-4.3[5]	17.3[2]	-5.2[4]	2.1[4]	—	10,641	—
Sit Int'l Growth	—	—	—	—	2.7[1]	48.4[1]	-3.0[3]	9.4[3]	10.3[4]	4.8[3]	8.1[3]	12.7[2]	12,644	18,201
Sit Large Cap Gro	5.3[5]	32.0[1]	-2.4[2]	29.4[4]	4.9[4]	3.1[5]	2.8[2]	31.7[2]	23.1[2]	31.7[2]	28.8[2]	17.7[3]	21,351	22,629
Sit Mid Cap Gro	9.8[4]	35.2[2]	-2.0[2]	65.5[1]	-2.1[5]	8.5[4]	-0.5[2]	33.6[3]	21.9[2]	17.7[3]	24.2[3]	15.7[3]	19,168	20,693
Sit MN TF Inc	—	—	—	—	—	—	0.6[1]	11.9[5]	5.9[1]	8.2[4]	8.6[5]	—	12,815	—
Sit Regional Gro	—	—	—	—	—	—	—	—	—	—	—	—	—	—
Sit Sci & Tech Gro	—	—	—	—	—	—	—	—	—	—	—	—	—	—
Sit Sm Cap Gro SC	—	—	—	—	—	—	—	52.2[1]	15.0[4]	7.6[5]	23.5[3]	—	18,829	—
Sit TF Income	—	8.4[5]	7.1[2]	9.4[5]	7.5[5]	10.4[5]	-0.6[1]	12.9[5]	5.7[1]	9.8[1]	9.4[4]	7.5[1]	13,106	14,382
Sit US Gov	7.9[4]	11.0[4]	10.9[1]	11.1[5]	5.4[5]	7.4[5]	1.8[1]	11.5[5]	5.0[2]	8.2[4]	8.2[5]	6.7[4]	12,667	13,849
Skyline Sm Cap Contra SC	—	—	—	—	—	—	—	—	—	—	—	—	—	—
Skyline Spcl Eqty II	—	—	—	—	—	—	-1.5[3]	20.9[5]	26.6[1]	26.2[2]	24.5[2]	—	19,317	—
Skyline Special Eqty SC‡	29.7[1]	24.0[4]	-9.3[3]	47.4[3]	42.3[1]	22.8[1]	-1.1[3]	13.8[5]	30.4[1]	35.4[1]	26.2[2]	19.5[1]	20,098	24,408
Smith Brdn Eqty Plus	—	—	—	—	—	13.2[3]	1.8[2]	36.8[1]	24.4[1]	32.3[2]	31.0[1]	21.0[1]	22,503	25,936
Smith Brdn Finl Srvcs	—	—	—	—	—	—	—	—	—	—	—	—	—	—
Smith Brdn Inter Dur US Gov	—	—	—	—	—	11.2[2]	-1.7[1]	16.4[3]	5.1[2]	9.0[2]	10.1[2]	7.8[1]	13,333	14,568
Smith Brdn Sh Dur US Gov	—	—	—	—	—	4.3[4]	4.1[1]	6.1[5]	6.3[1]	6.3[3]	6.2[5]	5.4[3]	11,993	13,027
Sound Shore	21.1[2]	22.5[3]	-10.6[4]	32.2[3]	21.2[1]	12.0[3]	0.3[3]	29.9[3]	33.3[1]	36.4[1]	33.2[1]	21.5[1]	23,618	26,531
Spectra	6.7[4]	31.4[2]	0.4[1]	48.9[3]	4.7[4]	20.8[2]	-1.9[3]	47.7[1]	19.5[3]	24.7[2]	30.1[1]	21.1[1]	22,004	26,080
SSgA Active Int'l	—	—	—	—	—	—	—	—	3.9[5]	-10.1[4]	—	—	—	—
SSgA Bond Mkt	—	—	—	—	—	—	—	—	—	8.9[4]	—	—	—	—
SSgA Emg Mkts	—	—	—	—	—	—	—	-7.9[5]	14.9[3]	-8.8[4]	-1.2[4]	—	9,649	—
SSgA Gro & Inc	—	—	—	—	—	—	-0.3[3]	28.6[3]	21.4[3]	37.7[1]	29.1[2]	—	21,498	—
SSgA Inter Fix	—	—	—	—	—	—	-4.5[5]	16.7[3]	3.7[3]	7.4[4]	9.1[3]	—	12,997	—
SSgA LifeSol Bal	—	—	—	—	—	—	—	—	—	—	—	—	—	—
SSgA LifeSol Gro	—	—	—	—	—	—	—	—	—	—	—	—	—	—
SSgA LifeSol Inc & Gro	—	—	—	—	—	—	—	—	—	—	—	—	—	—
SSgA Matrix Eqty	—	—	—	—	—	16.3[2]	-0.4[3]	28.2[4]	23.7[2]	34.2[1]	28.6[2]	19.8[1]	21,279	24,649
SSgA S&P 500	—	—	—	—	—	9.6[4]	1.3[2]	37.0[1]	22.7[2]	33.1[1]	30.8[1]	20.0[1]	22,369	24,838
SSgA Sm Cap SC	—	—	—	—	—	13.0[4]	-1.0[3]	41.8[2]	28.8[1]	23.6[3]	31.2[1]	20.4[1]	22,577	25,259
SSgA Yld Plus	—	—	—	—	—	3.4[5]	4.1[1]	6.6[5]	5.5[1]	5.5[5]	5.9[5]	5.0[4]	11,867	12,779
Stagecoach Eqty Idx	15.2[4]	29.8[1]	-4.0[3]	28.7[3]	6.6[4]	8.9[4]	0.4[3]	36.0[2]	21.7[3]	31.9[2]	29.7[2]	19.0[2]	21,821	23,863
State Farm Balanced‡	11.5[4]	25.8[1]	10.1[1]	39.4[1]	5.4[4]	3.3[5]	5.0[1]	25.1[3]	13.2[3]	22.2[2]	20.1[3]	13.4[3]	17,305	18,775
State Farm Growth‡	11.8[4]	32.1[1]	4.4[1]	42.0[2]	2.1[5]	0.5[5]	6.0[1]	30.7[3]	17.4[4]	31.2[2]	26.3[2]	16.5[3]	20,132	21,464
State Farm Interm‡	6.0[5]	12.1[3]	9.4[2]	12.3[5]	6.4[4]	6.9[4]	-0.8[1]	12.5[5]	4.2[2]	7.1[5]	7.9[5]	5.9[5]	12,547	13,308
State Farm Muni Bd‡	9.7[5]	10.3[2]	7.2[1]	11.1[4]	7.8[5]	9.9[5]	-2.5[1]	13.4[5]	4.2[2]	7.3[5]	8.2[5]	6.3[5]	12,675	13,570
Steadman Amer Indust	-11.1[5]	5.8[5]	-31.4[5]	1.3[5]	-6.5[5]	9.1[4]	-37.2[5]	-18.4[5]	1.3[5]	-12.4[5]	-10.2[5]	-13.1[5]	7,245	4,965
Steadman Associated	1.5[5]	34.1[1]	-25.0[5]	24.6[3]	5.6[4]	10.7[4]	-20.5[5]	-1.5[5]	15.4[2]	-1.3[5]	3.9[5]	-0.3[5]	11,212	9,867
Steadman Investment	-6.6[5]	8.2[5]	-15.2[5]	33.0[3]	-7.4[5]	2.9[5]	-33.8[5]	9.6[5]	-14.6[5]	1.1[5]	-1.8[5]	-8.4[5]	9,468	6,449
Steadman Tech & Gro	-25.9[5]	29.9[3]	-43.8[5]	27.9[5]	-5.3[5]	-7.8[5]	-37.1[5]	-28.2[5]	-30.4[5]	-28.2[5]	-28.9[5]	-26.9[5]	3,590	2,082
Stein Roe Balanced	7.9[5]	20.3[3]	-1.7[3]	29.6[1]	7.9[3]	12.3[4]	-4.1[4]	22.6[4]	16.3[2]	17.5[4]	18.8[4]	12.5[4]	16,749	18,038
Stein Roe Cap Opp	-3.9[5]	36.8[1]	-29.1[5]	62.8[2]	2.4[4]	27.5[1]	0.0[2]	50.8[1]	20.4[3]	6.2[5]	24.4[3]	19.7[1]	19,274	24,574
Stein Roe Emg Mkts	—	—	—	—	—	—	—	—	—	—	—	—	—	—
Stein Roe Gro & Inc	9.0[5]	31.0[1]	-1.7[2]	32.4[2]	10.0[2]	12.9[3]	-0.1[3]	30.2[3]	21.8[3]	25.7[3]	25.9[3]	17.6[3]	19,935	22,484
Stein Roe Growth Opp	—	—	—	—	—	—	—	—	—	—	—	—	—	—
Stein Roe Growth Stk‡	0.7[5]	35.5[2]	0.9[1]	46.0[3]	8.2[3]	2.8[5]	-3.8[4]	35.6[3]	20.9[2]	31.6[1]	29.2[1]	16.4[3]	21,577	21,339
Stein Roe Hi Yld Bd	—	—	—	—	—	—	—	—	—	15.9[1]	—	—	—	—

See Chapter 3 for explanation of symbols

Stock and bond funds — comprehensive summary *continued*
Arranged in alphabetical order

Total Net Assets $Million		NAV per share		1997 per share distributions		Yield %	Risk Analysis				% Distribution of Portfolio			Objective	No-Load Fund
December 31		December 31			Capital				Std.	Sharpe	12/31/97				
1996	1997	1996	1997	Income	gains	12/31/97	beta	R²	Dev.	Ratio	Stocks	Bonds	Cash		
1.1	5.9	12.92	15.26	0.00	1.23	0.0	—	—	—	—	94	0	6	growth	Seneca Growth
2.8	2.5	13.86	14.10	0.00	1.85	0.0	—	—	—	—	95	0	5	agg gr	Seneca Mid-Cap Edge
0.7	3.0	12.54	13.80	0.19	0.60	1.4	—	—	—	—	99	0	1	sector	Seneca Real Estate
105.2	120.6	18.84	20.39	0.09	3.80	0.5	0.62	0.50	9.98	B	96	0	4	growth	Sentry
2,568.3	3,672.6	88.44	125.63	0.11	0.88	0.1	0.89	0.58	13.08	A	96	0	4	growth	Sequoia‡
1.2	1.2	4.62	4.88	0.27	0.00	5.6	0.34	0.32	6.67	F	0	95	5	fix-inc	Sextant Bond Inc
1.6	2.2	8.01	9.41	0.00	0.00	0.1	0.99	0.52	15.33	F	98	0	2	growth	Sextant Growth
5.1	5.4	5.23	5.33	—	0.00	—	—	—	—	—	0	100	0	tax-free	Sextant Idaho TE
0.7	0.9	5.91	6.79	0.06	0.00	0.8	—	—	—	—	91	0	9	int'l	Sextant International
2.1	2.7	4.97	5.01	0.27	0.00	5.4	—	—	—	—	0	97	3	fix-inc	Sextant ST Bond
109.6	101.3	12.95	12.12	0.00	1.72	0.0	1.09	0.26	24.04	F	98	0	2	growth	Shelby Fund SC
4.3	5.7	13.33	14.60	0.33	1.23	2.3	0.70	0.88	8.25	D	58	38	4	income	Sit Balanced
5.5	8.5	9.82	10.06	0.63	0.02	6.3	0.21	0.31	4.15	C	0	97	3	fix-inc	Sit Bond
10.8	12.8	10.93	10.35	0.01	0.00	0.1	1.00	0.35	17.81	D	87	0	13	int'l	Sit Develop Mkts Gro
87.4	90.5	16.45	16.53	0.19	0.51	1.1	0.76	0.41	12.88	C	93	0	7	int'l	Sit Int'l Growth
57.7	81.5	33.68	40.04	0.07	4.17	0.2	1.03	0.82	12.71	C	96	0	4	growth	Sit Large Cap Gro
398.7	382.3	14.27	14.69	0.00	2.02	0.0	1.02	0.50	16.17	C	93	0	7	agg gr	Sit Mid Cap Gro
82.7	128.2	10.24	10.50	0.55	0.00	5.3	0.08	0.16	2.21	A	0	92	8	tax-free	Sit MN TF Inc
—	0.1	—	10.00	—	—	—	—	—	—	—	—	—	—	growth	Sit Regional Gro
—	0.1	—	10.00	—	—	—	—	—	—	—	—	—	—	sector	Sit Sci & Tech Gro
58.0	60.1	18.43	19.13	0.00	0.68	0.0	0.93	0.27	20.20	D	88	0	12	agg gr	Sit Sm Cap Gro SC
305.5	445.2	10.05	10.39	0.55	0.07	5.3	0.11	0.27	2.39	A	0	97	3	tax-free	Sit TF Income
64.9	92.9	10.45	10.64	0.64	0.00	6.0	0.10	0.29	2.07	B	0	99	1	fix-inc	Sit US Gov
—	4.7	—	10.00	0.00	0.00	—	—	—	—	—	89	0	11	agg gr	Skyline Sm Cap Contra SC
105.5	165.5	11.94	12.75	0.00	2.29	0.0	0.67	0.38	12.15	A	94	0	6	agg gr	Skyline Spcl Eqty II
218.7	466.5	18.16	21.66	0.00	2.89	0.0	0.43	0.16	12.10	A	95	0	5	agg gr	Skyline Special Eqty SC‡
8.9	86.5	12.25	14.86	0.62	0.40	4.1	0.97	0.99	10.87	A	0	80	20	gr-inc	Smith Brdn Eqty Plus
—	0.1	—	10.00	—	—	—	—	—	—	—	100	0	0	sector	Smith Brdn Finl Srvcs
37.4	32.3	9.86	9.97	0.56	0.00	5.6	0.13	0.23	3.08	A	0	100	0	fix-inc	Smith Brdn Inter Dur US Gov
188.7	89.5	9.81	9.90	0.51	0.00	5.2	0.01	0.01	0.77	B	0	102	-2	fix-inc	Smith Brdn Sh Dur US Gov
131.5	1,303.5	21.71	28.57	0.12	0.89	0.4	0.81	0.74	10.58	A	74	0	26	growth	Sound Shore
17.1	96.6	13.86	17.14	0.00	0.14	0.0	1.12	0.49	18.22	B	91	0	9	agg gr	Spectra
67.1	142.1	10.84	9.17	0.15	0.49	1.5	—	—	—	—	91	0	9	int'l	SSgA Active Int'l
41.0	108.6	9.77	10.03	0.55	0.03	5.5	—	—	—	—	0	82	18	fix-inc	SSgA Bond Mkt
148.1	254.9	10.98	9.69	0.15	0.26	1.5	0.89	0.30	17.37	D	100	0	0	int'l	SSgA Emg Mkts
71.4	80.5	14.54	18.07	0.08	1.81	0.5	0.97	0.91	11.38	C	96	0	4	gr-inc	SSgA Gro & Inc
46.0	60.6	9.60	9.75	0.54	0.00	5.6	0.14	0.22	3.25	C	0	98	2	fix-inc	SSgA Inter Fix
—	52.6	—	13.21	0.56	0.52	—	—	—	—	—	60	40	0	income	SSgA LifeSol Bal
—	46.2	—	13.62	0.71	0.69	—	—	—	—	—	79	21	0	growth	SSgA LifeSol Gro
—	16.0	—	12.57	0.41	0.32	—	—	—	—	—	39	61	0	gr-inc	SSgA LifeSol Inc & Gro
314.9	470.1	14.73	16.47	0.21	3.00	1.1	1.01	0.92	11.83	B	100	0	0	growth	SSgA Matrix Eqty
860.7	1,452.7	15.57	19.66	0.29	0.71	1.5	1.00	1.00	11.12	B	100	0	0	gr-inc	SSgA S&P 500
76.3	281.5	18.30	21.02	0.04	1.59	0.2	0.72	0.35	13.55	A	97	0	3	agg gr	SSgA Sm Cap SC
1,001.9	704.2	10.00	9.99	0.55	0.00	5.5	0.00	0.04	0.22	A	0	81	19	fix-inc	SSgA Yld Plus
396.4	515.8	48.55	61.95	0.45	1.59	0.7	0.99	1.00	11.05	C	99	0	1	gr-inc	Stagecoach Eqty Idx
585.7	764.4	39.36	45.86	1.44	0.69	3.1	0.61	0.88	7.18	C	66	27	7	income	State Farm Balanced‡
1,237.3	1,826.1	31.36	39.32	0.61	1.13	1.6	0.82	0.87	9.78	B	93	0	7	growth	State Farm Growth‡
107.8	110.9	9.89	9.87	0.69	0.00	7.0	0.10	0.23	2.25	C	0	100	0	fix-inc	State Farm Interm‡
317.7	338.6	8.38	8.50	0.47	0.00	5.6	0.13	0.25	2.83	D	0	98	2	tax-free	State Farm Muni Bd‡
1.1	0.8	0.81	0.71	0.00	0.00	0.0	1.30	0.34	24.58	F	100	0	0	agg gr	Steadman Amer Indust
4.6	3.5	0.75	0.74	0.00	0.00	0.0	1.52	0.50	23.94	F	98	0	2	income	Steadman Associated
1.8	1.6	0.88	0.89	0.00	0.00	0.0	1.22	0.52	18.91	F	4	0	96	growth	Steadman Investment
0.4	0.3	0.78	0.56	0.00	0.00	0.0	1.16	0.28	23.35	F	76	0	24	agg gr	Steadman Tech & Gro
257.3	278.6	29.18	31.31	0.88	2.00	2.6	0.60	0.87	7.12	D	56	39	5	income	Stein Roe Balanced
1,423.9	1,012.6	28.11	29.84	0.00	0.00	0.0	1.14	0.37	20.46	D	93	0	7	agg gr	Stein Roe Cap Opp
—	20.7	—	5.72	0.17	0.93	—	—	—	—	—	92	0	8	int'l	Stein Roe Emg Mkts
241.0	340.0	18.73	22.28	0.28	0.97	1.2	0.80	0.94	9.23	C	84	1	15	gr-inc	Stein Roe Gro & Inc
—	50.3	—	10.96	0.00	0.00	—	—	—	—	—	92	0	8	growth	Stein Roe Growth Opp
443.3	623.4	27.90	34.50	0.00	2.15	0.0	1.09	0.88	12.84	A	96	0	4	agg gr	Stein Roe Growth Stk‡
6.8	31.1	10.16	10.72	0.81	0.15	7.6	—	—	—	—	0	98	2	fix-inc	Stein Roe Hi Yld Bd

Stock and bond funds — comprehensive summary *continued*

Arranged in alphabetical order

No-Load Fund	1988	1989	1990	1991	1992	1993	1994	1995	1996	1997	Annualized 3 yrs.	5 yrs.	What $10,000 grew to after 3 yrs.	5 yrs.
Stein Roe Hi Yld Muni...	13.7 [1]	11.4 [1]	7.7 [1]	9.8 [5]	5.4 [5]	10.6 [5]	-4.2 [1]	17.7 [3]	4.5 [1]	9.5 [2]	10.4 [2]	7.4 [2]	13,471	14,274
Stein Roe Income...	11.5 [1]	7.0 [5]	6.1 [5]	17.2 [1]	9.0 [1]	13.4 [1]	-4.1 [4]	19.7 [1]	4.9 [2]	9.6 [1]	11.2 [1]	8.4 [1]	13,760	14,964
Stein Roe Int'l...	—	—	—	—	—	—	—	3.9 [4]	8.3 [4]	-3.5 [4]	2.8 [4]	—	10,855	—
Stein Roe Inter Bd...	7.2 [4]	12.6 [3]	7.1 [4]	15.1 [3]	7.7 [2]	9.2 [3]	-2.8 [3]	16.8 [3]	4.6 [2]	9.3 [2]	10.1 [2]	7.2 [2]	13,353	14,173
Stein Roe Inter Muni...	6.1 [4]	8.1 [3]	7.5 [1]	10.7 [3]	7.6 [2]	11.1 [2]	-3.5 [2]	13.0 [4]	4.2 [2]	7.5 [2]	8.2 [3]	6.3 [2]	12,658	13,570
Stein Roe Mgd Muni...	10.9 [4]	10.6 [1]	7.0 [2]	11.9 [3]	8.3 [4]	11.2 [5]	-5.5 [2]	16.6 [3]	3.8 [3]	9.3 [2]	9.8 [3]	6.8 [3]	13,230	13,902
Stein Roe Spec Venture SC...	—	—	—	—	—	—	—	27.2 [4]	28.7 [1]	9.7 [4]	21.5 [4]	—	17,942	—
Stein Roe Special...	20.2 [2]	37.8 [1]	-5.8 [3]	34.0 [3]	14.0 [2]	20.4 [1]	-3.3 [4]	18.7 [5]	18.8 [3]	25.9 [3]	21.1 [4]	15.6 [4]	17,760	20,677
Stein Roe Young Invest...	—	—	—	—	—	—	—	39.8 [1]	35.1 [1]	26.3 [3]	33.6 [1]	—	23,851	—
Stonebridge Growth...	12.6 [4]	24.5 [2]	2.6 [1]	32.6 [2]	-0.6 [5]	1.4 [5]	-0.3 [1]	21.3 [5]	18.5 [4]	23.7 [4]	21.2 [4]	12.5 [5]	17,786	17,982
Stratton Growth...	22.6 [1]	23.8 [3]	-6.7 [4]	22.2 [4]	6.7 [4]	6.4 [5]	7.2 [1]	37.7 [1]	14.2 [5]	36.1 [1]	28.9 [2]	19.5 [2]	21,396	24,404
Stratton Month Div REIT Sh...	9.8 [4]	18.8 [4]	-3.8 [2]	35.1 [4]	10.3 [3]	6.6 [5]	-12.1 [5]	23.4 [4]	8.6 [5]	17.3 [4]	16.3 [5]	8.1 [5]	15,725	14,735
Stratton Sm Cap Yld SC...	—	—	—	—	—	—	-2.7 [4]	27.3 [4]	15.0 [5]	42.6 [1]	27.8 [2]	—	20,880	—
Strong 500 Idx...	—	—	—	—	—	—	—	—	—	—	—	—	—	—
Strong Advantage...	—	9.4 [4]	6.6 [4]	10.6 [5]	8.6 [1]	8.1 [2]	3.6 [1]	7.5 [5]	6.7 [1]	6.5 [2]	6.9 [4]	6.5 [1]	12,216	13,681
Strong Amer Util...	—	—	—	—	—	—	-2.6 [4]	37.0 [1]	8.4 [5]	27.6 [1]	23.7 [1]	—	18,945	—
Strong Asia Pacific...	—	—	—	—	—	—	-5.3 [4]	5.9 [4]	2.1 [5]	-31.0 [5]	-9.3 [5]	—	7,461	—
Strong Asst Alloc...	9.2 [5]	11.2 [5]	2.8 [2]	19.6 [5]	3.2 [5]	14.5 [3]	-1.5 [3]	22.0 [4]	10.5 [4]	16.7 [4]	16.3 [5]	12.1 [4]	15,729	17,740
Strong Blue Chip 100...	—	—	—	—	—	—	—	—	—	—	—	—	—	—
Strong Common Stk‡...	—	—	1.0 [1]	56.9 [1]	20.8 [1]	25.2 [1]	-0.5 [3]	32.4 [2]	20.5 [3]	24.0 [4]	25.5 [3]	19.8 [1]	19,785	24,647
Strong Corp Bond...	12.5 [1]	0.4 [5]	-6.2 [5]	14.8 [4]	9.6 [2]	17.1 [1]	-1.3 [1]	25.4 [1]	5.5 [2]	11.9 [2]	14.0 [1]	11.3 [1]	14,802	17,107
Strong Discovery SC...	24.4 [1]	24.0 [4]	-2.7 [2]	67.6 [1]	1.9 [4]	22.2 [2]	-5.7 [4]	34.8 [3]	1.5 [5]	10.8 [4]	14.9 [5]	11.8 [5]	15,166	17,477
Strong Eqty Inc...	—	—	—	—	—	—	—	—	28.1 [1]	31.3 [1]	—	—	—	—
Strong Gov Sec...	10.5 [1]	9.9 [4]	8.1 [4]	16.6 [2]	9.4 [1]	13.0 [1]	-3.4 [4]	19.9 [1]	2.8 [4]	9.1 [2]	10.4 [2]	8.0 [1]	13,441	14,672
Strong Gr & Inc...	—	—	—	—	—	—	—	—	31.9 [1]	30.4 [2]	—	—	—	—
Strong Growth 20...	—	—	—	—	—	—	—	—	—	—	—	—	—	—
Strong Growth...	—	—	—	—	—	—	17.3 [1]	41.0 [2]	19.5 [3]	19.1 [3]	26.1 [2]	—	20,060	—
Strong Hi Yld Bd...	—	—	—	—	—	—	—	—	26.8 [1]	16.0 [1]	—	—	—	—
Strong Hi Yld Muni...	—	—	—	—	—	—	-1.0 [1]	14.6 [5]	5.1 [1]	13.9 [1]	11.1 [1]	—	13,718	—
Strong Int'l Bond...	—	—	—	—	—	—	—	19.1 [3]	8.0 [2]	-4.8 [5]	7.0 [5]	—	12,237	—
Strong Int'l Stk...	—	—	—	—	—	—	-1.6 [3]	7.8 [3]	8.2 [4]	-14.2 [4]	0.0 [4]	7.8 [4]	10,005	14,551
Strong Limited Rescs...	—	—	—	—	—	—	—	—	—	—	—	—	—	—
Strong MidCap...	—	—	—	—	—	—	—	—	—	13.9 [5]	—	—	—	—
Strong Muni Advantage...	—	—	—	—	—	—	—	—	4.9 [1]	5.1 [3]	—	—	—	—
Strong Muni Bond...	7.6 [5]	7.1 [5]	4.6 [5]	13.3 [1]	12.4 [1]	12.0 [4]	-4.6 [1]	11.4 [5]	2.4 [5]	12.1 [1]	8.5 [5]	6.4 [4]	12,789	13,665
Strong Opportunity...	16.5 [3]	18.5 [4]	-11.3 [4]	31.7 [3]	17.4 [1]	21.2 [1]	3.2 [2]	27.3 [4]	18.1 [4]	23.4 [4]	22.9 [4]	18.3 [2]	18,559	23,213
Strong Schafer Value...	18.0 [3]	30.1 [2]	-13.5 [5]	46.4 [1]	18.7 [1]	24.0 [1]	-4.3 [4]	34.1 [2]	23.2 [2]	29.3 [2]	28.8 [2]	20.4 [1]	21,360	25,348
Strong Small Cap SC...	—	—	—	—	—	—	—	—	22.7 [2]	-4.5 [5]	—	—	—	—
Strong ST Bond...	10.1 [1]	8.2 [5]	5.3 [5]	14.6 [1]	6.8 [1]	9.6 [1]	-1.6 [4]	12.0 [2]	6.8 [1]	7.2 [1]	8.6 [1]	6.7 [1]	12,818	13,823
Strong ST Global...	—	—	—	—	—	—	—	10.5 [3]	10.0 [1]	6.1 [4]	8.8 [1]	—	12,892	—
Strong ST Hi Yld Muni...	—	—	—	—	—	—	—	—	—	—	—	—	—	—
Strong ST Hi Yld...	—	—	—	—	—	—	—	—	—	—	—	—	—	—
Strong ST Muni...	—	—	—	—	—	—	-1.6 [5]	5.4 [5]	4.9 [1]	6.9 [1]	5.7 [3]	4.4 [5]	11,823	12,425
Strong Total Ret...	15.6 [3]	2.6 [5]	-7.1 [4]	33.6 [2]	0.5 [5]	22.5 [1]	-1.4 [4]	27.0 [4]	14.1 [5]	24.2 [4]	21.6 [4]	16.8 [4]	17,995	21,735
Strong Value...	—	—	—	—	—	—	—	—	16.8 [4]	25.9 [3]	—	—	—	—
SwissKey Glob Bd...	—	—	—	—	—	—	—	—	8.7 [2]	1.2 [5]	—	—	—	—
SwissKey Glob Eqty...	—	—	—	—	—	—	—	—	16.3 [3]	9.9 [4]	—	—	—	—
SwissKey Global...	—	—	—	—	—	—	—	—	13.5 [4]	10.2 [4]	—	—	—	—
SwissKey Non-US Eqty...	—	—	—	—	—	—	—	—	11.8 [3]	5.0 [3]	—	—	—	—
SwissKey US Balanced...	—	—	—	—	—	—	—	—	10.9 [4]	12.6 [5]	—	—	—	—
SwissKey US Bd...	—	—	—	—	—	—	—	—	3.1 [3]	9.1 [4]	—	—	—	—
SwissKey US Eqty...	—	—	—	—	—	—	—	—	24.9 [1]	24.2 [3]	—	—	—	—
Technology Value...	—	—	—	—	—	—	—	61.2 [1]	60.9 [1]	6.5 [5]	40.3 [1]	—	27,612	—
Third Ave Small Cap SC...	—	—	—	—	—	—	—	—	—	—	—	—	—	—
Third Ave Value...	—	—	—	34.4 [3]	21.3 [1]	23.7 [1]	-1.5 [4]	31.7 [2]	21.9 [2]	23.9 [4]	25.8 [3]	19.4 [2]	19,886	24,230
Thomas White Wld Fd...	—	—	—	—	—	—	—	19.0 [2]	16.5 [3]	11.7 [3]	15.7 [3]	—	15,490	—
Thompson Plumb Balanced...	13.7 [4]	20.0 [3]	3.1 [1]	27.0 [3]	2.3 [5]	4.5 [5]	1.5 [2]	20.0 [5]	23.1 [2]	22.5 [4]	21.9 [4]	13.9 [4]	18,104	19,189
Thompson Plumb Bond...	—	—	—	—	—	8.2 [5]	-2.7 [2]	14.5 [5]	1.8 [5]	7.4 [5]	7.8 [5]	5.7 [5]	12,521	13,183
Thompson Plumb Growth...	—	—	—	—	1.6 [5]	0.4 [3]	30.5 [3]	33.1 [1]	32.4 [1]	32.0 [1]	18.6 [2]	22,980	23,446	
TIP:Clover Cap Eqty Val...	—	—	—	—	7.3 [3]	12.5 [3]	16.0 [1]	21.4 [5]	22.9 [2]	17.5 [5]	20.6 [5]	18.0 [3]	17,532	22,893

See Chapter 3 for explanation of symbols

Total Net Assets $Million		NAV per share		1997 per share distributions		Yield %	Risk Analysis				% Distribution of Portfolio			Objective	No-Load Fund
December 31 1996	1997	December 31 1996	1997	Income	Capital gains	12/31/97	beta	R²	Std. Dev.	Sharpe Ratio	12/31/97 Stocks	Bonds	Cash		
294.9	137.6	11.61	12.00	0.11	0.58	5.7	0.14	0.20	3.59	A	0	100	0	tax-free	Stein Roe Hi Yld Muni
337.7	1,267.6	9.83	10.04	0.00	3.32	7.0	0.23	0.40	4.13	B	0	99	1	fix-inc	Stein Roe Income
140.0	532.2	10.76	9.68	0.00	0.32	1.0	0.58	0.28	11.92	D	94	0	6	int'l	Stein Roe Int'l
312.4	323.1	8.72	8.92	0.68	0.00	6.5	0.19	0.35	3.64	B	0	96	4	fix-inc	Stein Roe Inter Bd
240.0	425.3	11.36	11.61	0.70	0.00	4.7	0.15	0.29	3.05	C	0	99	1	tax-free	Stein Roe Inter Muni
612.9	393.7	9.07	9.41	0.58	0.00	5.1	0.18	0.25	4.11	C	0	100	0	tax-free	Stein Roe Mgd Muni
158.0	222.8	14.70	14.29	0.00	1.77	0.0	0.60	0.27	12.88	C	94	0	6	agg gr	Stein Roe Spec Venture SC
1,149.5	200.0	26.01	29.36	0.55	0.03	0.0	0.75	0.55	11.26	D	90	0	10	growth	Stein Roe Special
271.3	591.7	18.71	23.29	0.48	0.00	0.0	0.93	0.65	12.85	A	97	0	3	growth	Stein Roe Young Invest
38.7	42.7	14.50	14.99	0.22	2.69	1.2	0.78	0.82	9.59	F	97	0	3	gr-inc	Stonebridge Growth
44.8	60.0	27.00	33.39	0.54	2.52	1.5	0.76	0.78	9.65	A	90	0	10	gr-inc	Stratton Growth
103.8	102.0	27.43	30.25	1.76	0.00	5.8	0.26	0.15	7.54	C	94	2	4	sector	Stratton Month Div REIT Sh
21.7	39.4	33.58	22.47	0.41	2.25	1.7	0.50	0.33	9.82	A	94	0	6	growth	Stratton Sm Cap Yld SC
—	19.7	—	12.16	0.09	0.01	—					95	0	5	gr-inc	Strong 500 Idx
1,417.1	2,041.0	10.07	10.08	0.63	0.00	6.2	0.01	0.08	0.49	A	0	96	4	fix-inc	Strong Advantage
134.8	187.4	12.54	14.82	0.36	0.76	2.3	0.53	0.40	9.31	C	93	0	7	income	Strong Amer Util
70.4	24.7	9.54	6.52	0.07	0.00	1.1	0.75	0.29	14.91	F	73	5	22	int'l	Strong Asia Pacific
271.4	278.8	19.40	19.83	0.67	2.06	3.1	0.56	0.73	7.34	F	69	27	4	income	Strong Asst Alloc
—	12.7	—	10.84	0.03	0.00	—					99	0	1	gr-inc	Strong Blue Chip 100
1,243.7	1,564.8	20.24	21.02	0.04	3.86	0.2	0.71	0.52	10.90	C	93	0	7	growth	Strong Common Stk‡
305.3	560.5	10.73	11.20	0.76	0.00	6.8	0.24	0.31	4.90	A	3	89	8	fix-inc	Strong Corp Bond
513.8	383.0	17.45	17.00	0.00	2.29	0.0	0.98	0.47	15.97	F	88	0	12	agg gr	Strong Discovery SC
38.2	145.8	12.64	15.76	0.13	0.69	0.8	—	—	—	—	92	2	6	income	Strong Eqty Inc
659.9	907.4	10.48	10.75	0.65	0.00	6.0	0.18	0.25	4.08	B	3	91	6	fix-inc	Strong Gov Sec
48.5	246.2	13.11	16.31	0.07	0.69	0.4	—	—	—	—	98	0	2	gr-inc	Strong Gr & Inc
—	59.7	—	11.31	0.08	0.00	—	—	—	—	—	90	0	10	agg gr	Strong Growth 20
1,308.2	1,597.1	18.50	18.31	0.00	3.52	0.0	1.13	0.54	17.06	C	93	0	7	agg gr	Strong Growth
282.5	568.9	11.45	11.84	1.04	0.32	8.6	—	—	—		6	85	9	fix-inc	Strong Hi Yld Bd
244.8	323.1	9.74	10.43	0.60	0.02	5.8	0.16	0.25	3.47	A	0	100	0	tax-free	Strong Hi Yld Muni
35.3	25.3	11.77	10.43	0.51	0.26	4.9	0.01	0.00	8.11	F	3	67	30	fix-inc	Strong Int'l Bond
296.3	147.3	13.23	10.76	0.37	0.26	3.3	0.64	0.30	12.69	D	95	0	5	int'l	Strong Int'l Stk
—	5.4	—	9.30	0.00	0.00	—	—	—	—	—	95	0	5	sector	Strong Limited Rescs
0.1	15.7	10.00	11.38	0.00	0.00	0.0	—	—	—	—	96	0	4	growth	Strong MidCap
501.4	986.5	5.01	5.03	0.23	0.00	4.6	—	—	—	—	0	100	0	tax-free	Strong Muni Advantage
233.8	240.8	9.24	9.82	0.51	0.00	5.1	0.18	0.27	3.78	F	0	95	5	tax-free	Strong Muni Bond
1,769.6	1,924.9	35.26	37.41	0.10	5.75	0.2	0.70	0.57	10.25	C	90	0	10	growth	Strong Opportunity
514.2	1,511.2	51.02	63.90	0.35	1.68	0.5	0.80	0.77	10.21	A	98	0	2	growth	Strong Schafer Value
157.1	181.9	12.08	11.45	0.10	0.00	0.9	—	—	—	—	94	0	6	agg gr	Strong Small Cap SC
1,181.0	1,320.7	9.79	9.78	0.69	0.00	7.0	0.06	0.18	1.65	A	7	89	4	fix-inc	Strong ST Bond
77.6	106.8	10.71	10.43	0.89	0.08	8.0	0.09	0.26	1.92	A	1	84	15	fix-inc	Strong ST Global
—	11.6	—	10.05	0.03	0.00	—	—	—	—	—	0	95	5	fix-inc	Strong ST Hi Yld Muni
—	56.5	—	10.35	0.31	0.05	—	—	—	—	—	0	92	8	fix-inc	Strong ST Hi Yld
145.4	182.1	9.74	9.92	0.48	0.00	4.8	0.06	0.20	1.46	C	0	88	12	tax-free	Strong ST Muni
759.1	848.7	27.23	26.46	0.20	6.99	0.6	0.99	0.85	11.98	F	93	2	5	gr-inc	Strong Total Ret
55.5	93.5	11.55	13.77	0.10	0.63	0.7	—	—	—	—	95	0	5	growth	Strong Value
3.5	4.5	9.56	9.32	0.18	0.17	1.9	—	—	—	—	0	90	10	fix-inc	SwissKey Glob Bd
42.4	63.6	11.38	11.34	0.09	1.04	0.8	—	—	—	—	80	0	20	global	SwissKey Glob Eqty
17.3	28.4	12.03	12.08	0.46	0.70	3.6	—	—	—	—	49	40	11	global	SwissKey Global
1.9	8.1	11.02	10.72	0.10	0.74	1.0	—	—	—	—	93	1	6	int'l	SwissKey Non-US Eqty
1.5	1.7	11.75	11.84	0.43	0.94	3.4	—	—	—	—	37	54	9	income	SwissKey US Balanced
0.5	1.9	10.06	10.33	0.48	0.14	4.7	—	—	—	—	0	87	13	fix-inc	SwissKey US Bd
10.7	44.1	15.11	17.53	0.08	1.13	0.5	—	—	—	—	97	0	3	growth	SwissKey US Eqty
35.1	194.3	26.66	26.06	0.00	2.24	0.0	1.15	0.22	28.50	C	98	0	2	sector	Technology Valu
—	106.1	—	11.64	0.06	0.00	—	—	—	—	—	81	0	19	agg gr	Third Ave Small Cap SC
644.0	1,676.0	25.86	31.46	0.41	0.16	1.3	0.60	0.52	9.28	B	56	8	36	growth	Third Ave Value
42.2	49.0	12.09	12.76	0.19	0.54	1.4	0.65	0.65	8.89	C	91	0	9	global	Thomas White Wld Fd
21.5	36.8	14.84	16.29	0.12	1.71	0.7	0.80	0.81	9.92	F	68	17	14	gr-inc	Thompson Plumb Balanced
22.5	32.2	10.25	10.46	0.53	0.00	5.1	0.19	0.28	4.07	F	0	97	3	fix-inc	Thompson Plumb Bond
24.2	47.3	30.17	36.44	0.00	3.36	0.0	1.00	0.85	12.24	B	98	0	2	growth	Thompson Plumb Growth
93.1	122.2	16.88	17.60	0.17	2.02	0.9	0.45	0.28	9.44	F	94	3	3	gr-inc	TIP:Clover Cap Eqty Val

No-Load Fund	Total return percent with quintile ranks by objective										Annualized 3 yrs.	Annualized 5 yrs.	What $10,000 grew to after 3 yrs.	5 yrs.
	1988	1989	1990	1991	1992	1993	1994	1995	1996	1997				
TIP:Clover Cap Fix Inc...	—	—	—	—	7.4[3]	11.5[3]	-2.8[2]	18.0[3]	4.4[3]	9.6[3]	10.5[3]	7.9[3]	13,495	14,617
TIP:Clover Cap Sm Cap Val SC...	—	—	—	—	—	—	—	—	—	15.5[5]	—	—	—	—
TIP:Clover Max Cap Val...	—	—	—	—	—	—	—	—	—	—	—	—	—	—
TIP:Penn Cap Sel Finl Srvcs...	—	—	—	—	—	—	—	—	—	—	—	—	—	—
TIP:Penn Cap Strat Hi Yld...	—	—	—	—	—	—	—	—	—	—	—	—	—	—
TIP:Penn Cap Value Plus...	—	—	—	—	—	—	—	—	—	—	—	—	—	—
TIP:Target Sel Eqty...	—	—	—	—	—	—	—	—	—	—	—	—	—	—
TIP:Turner Growth Eqty...	—	—	—	—	—	15.4[2]	-6.7[5]	30.3[3]	19.2[3]	31.4[2]	26.9[2]	17.1[3]	20,415	21,969
TIP:Turner Mid Cap...	—	—	—	—	—	—	—	—	—	40.6[1]	—	—	—	—
TIP:Turner Small Cap SC‡...	—	—	—	—	—	—	—	68.2[1]	28.9[1]	14.8[4]	35.5[1]	—	24,879	—
TIP:Turner Ultra Large Cap...	—	—	—	—	—	—	—	—	—	—	—	—	—	—
Titan Finl Svcs...	—	—	—	—	—	—	—	—	—	55.6[1]	—	—	—	—
Torray...	—	—	—	20.0[5]	21.1[1]	6.3[4]	2.5[2]	50.4[1]	29.1[1]	37.1[1]	38.6[1]	23.7[1]	26,626	29,011
Trainer-Wrthm First Mutual...	9.1[4]	35.1[2]	-4.5[2]	26.2[5]	2.2[4]	15.2[3]	-15.1[5]	45.9[1]	21.4[2]	23.1[3]	29.7[1]	16.3[3]	21,801	21,316
Trainer-Wrthm Tot Ret Bd...	—	—	—	—	—	—	—	—	—	7.6[4]	—	—	—	—
Transamerica Premr Agg Gr...	—	—	—	—	—	—	—	—	—	—	—	—	—	—
Transamerica Premr Balanced...	—	—	—	—	—	—	—	—	15.3[2]	35.4[1]	—	—	—	—
Transamerica Premr Bond...	—	—	—	—	—	—	—	—	1.2[5]	10.0[3]	—	—	—	—
Transamerica Premr Eqty...	—	—	—	—	—	—	—	—	29.1[1]	47.5[1]	—	—	—	—
Transamerica Premr Idx...	—	—	—	—	—	—	—	—	22.3[2]	33.1[1]	—	—	—	—
Transamerica Premr Sm Cap SC...	—	—	—	—	—	—	—	—	—	—	—	—	—	—
Trent Equity...	—	—	—	—	—	5.4[5]	-10.6[5]	14.3[5]	20.4[3]	25.2[2]	19.9[4]	10.2[5]	17,225	16,236
Tweedy Brown Amer Val...	—	—	—	—	—	—	-0.6[4]	36.2[2]	22.4[2]	38.9[1]	32.3[1]	—	23,149	—
Tweedy Brwn Glob Val...	—	—	—	—	—	—	4.4[1]	10.7[5]	20.2[2]	22.9[1]	17.8[3]	—	16,351	—
U.S. Global Leaders...	—	—	—	—	—	—	—	—	23.0[1]	40.7[1]	—	—	—	—
UAM BHM&S Tot Ret Bd...	—	—	—	—	—	—	—	—	3.5[3]	8.8[4]	—	—	—	—
UAM C & B Balanced...	—	—	7.8[1]	25.8[2]	5.5[4]	6.4[5]	-0.9[2]	24.3[4]	13.0[3]	19.7[3]	18.9[4]	12.1[4]	16,810	17,719
UAM C & B Eqty...	—	—	—	31.1[2]	4.4[5]	4.2[5]	1.4[2]	31.9[2]	20.2[3]	28.0[3]	26.6[3]	16.5[4]	20,295	21,435
UAM C&B Eqty Taxable Invst...	—	—	—	—	—	—	—	—	—	—	—	—	—	—
UAM Chi Asst Mgmt Int Bd...	—	—	—	—	—	—	—	—	3.2[4]	7.2[5]	—	—	—	—
UAM Chi Asst Mgmt Val Contra...	—	—	—	—	—	—	—	26.5[4]	13.8[5]	18.9[4]	19.6[5]	—	17,116	—
UAM DSI Balanced...	—	—	—	—	—	—	—	—	—	—	—	—	—	—
UAM DSI Discpnd Val...	—	—	-10.2[4]	24.1[4]	10.1[3]	16.8[2]	-1.6[4]	32.3[2]	22.2[2]	23.4[4]	25.9[3]	18.1[2]	19,953	22,944
UAM DSI Ltd Mat...	—	—	8.1[4]	14.9[1]	7.4[1]	3.7[5]	-1.2[4]	11.0[3]	5.0[2]	6.7[2]	7.5[2]	5.0[4]	12,435	12,745
UAM FMA Small Co SC...	—	—	—	—	5.5[4]	28.3[1]	-2.9[4]	24.0[4]	26.2[1]	40.4[1]	30.0[1]	22.3[1]	21,966	27,358
UAM FPA Crescent...	—	—	—	—	—	—	4.3[1]	26.0[4]	22.9[2]	22.0[4]	23.6[4]	—	18,887	—
UAM Hanson Eqty...	—	—	—	—	—	—	—	—	—	—	—	—	—	—
UAM ICM Equity...	—	—	—	—	—	—	0.6[2]	30.7[3]	29.2[1]	29.6[2]	29.8[2]	—	21,889	—
UAM IRC Enhncd Idx...	—	—	—	—	—	—	—	—	—	27.2[3]	—	—	—	—
UAM Jacobs Int'l Octgn...	—	—	—	—	—	—	—	—	—	—	—	—	—	—
UAM Mckee Domestic Eqty...	—	—	—	—	—	—	—	—	22.5[2]	20.9[4]	—	—	—	—
UAM McKee Int'l...	—	—	—	—	—	—	—	8.9[3]	10.5[4]	11.3[2]	10.2[2]	—	13,392	—
UAM McKee Sm Cap SC...	—	—	—	—	—	—	—	—	—	—	—	—	—	—
UAM Mckee US Gov...	—	—	—	—	—	—	—	—	1.1[5]	8.5[3]	—	—	—	—
UAM MJI Int'l...	—	—	—	—	—	—	—	9.6[3]	7.8[5]	6.0[2]	7.8[3]	—	12,529	—
UAM NWQ Balanced...	—	—	—	—	—	—	—	25.0[3]	11.6[4]	20.9[3]	19.0[4]	—	16,846	—
UAM NWQ Value Eqty...	—	—	—	—	—	—	—	29.2[3]	21.9[3]	30.8[2]	27.2[3]	—	20,590	—
UAM RHJ Sm Cap SC...	—	—	—	—	—	—	—	52.4[1]	17.2[3]	20.7[3]	29.2[1]	—	21,560	—
UAM RHJ Small\MidCap SC...	—	—	—	—	—	—	—	—	—	25.7[2]	—	—	—	—
UAM SAMI Pref Stck Inc...	—	—	—	—	—	6.0[5]	-1.7[1]	6.2[5]	10.1[1]	8.3[4]	8.2[5]	5.7[5]	12,655	13,192
UAM Sirach Bond...	—	—	—	—	—	—	—	—	—	—	—	—	—	—
UAM Sirach Eqty...	—	—	—	—	—	—	—	—	—	30.0[2]	—	—	—	—
UAM Sirach Growth...	—	—	—	—	—	—	-7.5[5]	29.4[3]	23.2[2]	32.1[2]	28.2[2]	—	21,056	—
UAM Sirach Spec Eqty...	—	—	5.3[1]	53.6[1]	10.0[2]	18.9[1]	-6.8[5]	36.2[1]	12.1[5]	11.3[5]	19.3[5]	13.5[5]	16,988	18,834
UAM Sirach Strat Balanced...	—	—	—	—	—	—	-6.9[5]	26.0[3]	13.2[3]	21.9[2]	20.2[3]	—	17,379	—
UAM Strlng Part Balanced...	—	—	—	—	8.7[3]	10.0[4]	-1.9[3]	20.7[5]	18.3[1]	18.3[4]	19.1[4]	12.7[4]	16,890	18,211
UAM Strlng Part Eqty...	—	—	—	—	11.8[3]	11.0[3]	-2.4[4]	27.6[4]	30.1[1]	24.9[3]	27.6[2]	17.6[3]	20,767	22,497
UAM Strlng Sm Cap Val SC...	—	—	—	—	—	—	—	—	—	38.8[1]	—	—	—	—
UAM TJ Core Eqty...	—	—	—	—	—	—	—	—	18.2[4]	30.7[2]	—	—	—	—
UAM TS&W Eqty...	—	—	—	—	—	12.8[3]	-0.6[3]	26.3[4]	21.3[3]	26.0[3]	24.5[4]	16.7[4]	19,310	21,653

See Chapter 3 for explanation of symbols

Stock and bond funds — comprehensive summary *continued*
Arranged in alphabetical order

Total Net Assets $Million		NAV per share		1997 per share distributions		Yield %	Risk Analysis				% Distribution of Portfolio 12/31/97				
December 31 1996	1997	December 31 1996	1997	Income	Capital gains	12/31/97	beta	R²	Std. Dev.	Sharpe Ratio	Stocks	Bonds	Cash	Objective	No-Load Fund
20.8	27.8	9.75	10.04	0.59	0.02	5.9	0.18	0.29	3.77	B	0	99	1	fix-inc	TIP:Clover Cap Fix Inc
5.8	15.3	12.11	12.80	0.00	1.17	0.0	—	—	—	—	97	0	3	growth	TIP:Clover Cap Sm Cap Val SC
—	0.7	—	10.08	0.00	0.00	0.0	—	—	—	—	92	0	7	gr-inc	TIP:Clover Max Cap Val
—	0.4	—	12.47	0.01	0.20	—	—	—	—	—	—	—	—	sector	TIP:Penn Cap Sel Finl Srvcs
—	0.1	—	10.00	0.00	0.00	—	—	—	—	—	—	—	—	fix-inc	TIP:Penn Cap Strat Hi Yld
—	—	—	—	—	—	—	—	—	—	—	—	—	—	gr-inc	TIP:Penn Cap Value Plus
—	0.1	—	10.00	0.00	0.00	—	—	—	—	—	97	0	3	agg gr	TIP:Target Sel Eqty
90.5	89.6	12.76	11.71	0.00	4.82	0.0	1.08	0.74	13.96	D	99	0	1	growth	TIP:Turner Growth Eqty
1.7	13.0	10.22	13.84	0.00	0.50	0.0	—	—	—	—	94	0	6	agg gr	TIP:Turner Mid Cap
74.1	153.5	21.86	24.62	0.00	0.44	0.0	1.05	0.30	21.58	B	98	0	2	agg gr	TIP:Turner Small Cap SC‡
0.1	0.9	—	11.81	0.01	1.02	—	—	—	—	—	99	0	1	gr-inc	TIP:Turner Ultra Large Cap
5.5	22.4	11.85	17.55	0.00	0.86	0.0	—	—	—	—	99	0	1	sector	Titan Finl Svcs
116.4	608.6	25.22	33.85	0.13	0.58	0.4	0.83	0.76	10.67	A	98	0	2	growth	Torray
30.9	36.1	11.30	11.20	0.00	2.53	0.0	0.80	0.43	13.48	A	98	0	2	agg gr	Trainer-Wrthm First Mutual
5.0	10.0	—	—	—	—	—	—	—	—	—	0	100	0	fix-inc	Trainer-Wrthm Tot Ret Bd
—	12.8	—	12.18	0.00	0.00	—	—	—	—	—	94	0	6	agg gr	Transamerica Premr Agg Gr
16.0	26.7	11.57	15.54	0.11	0.00	0.7	—	—	—	—	67	31	2	income	Transamerica Premr Balanced
12.5	14.2	9.86	10.19	0.62	0.00	6.1	—	—	—	—	0	98	2	fix-inc	Transamerica Premr Bond
30.5	110.2	12.65	18.53	0.00	0.13	0.0	—	—	—	—	90	0	10	growth	Transamerica Premr Eqty
10.2	23.9	11.96	15.49	0.32	0.07	2.1	—	—	—	—	98	0	2	gr-inc	Transamerica Premr Idx
—	11.1	—	12.49	0.00	0.00	—	—	—	—	—	89	0	11	agg gr	Transamerica Premr Sm Cap SC
3.2	3.6	10.44	13.07	0.00	0.00	0.0	0.92	0.61	12.93	C	100	0	0	agg gr	Trent Equity
277.6	721.3	15.64	21.11	0.17	0.43	0.8	0.75	0.76	9.63	A	89	0	11	gr-inc	Tweedy Brown Amer Val
1,211.3	1,985.3	14.45	16.39	0.87	0.49	5.2	0.51	0.49	7.95	C	92	0	8	global	Tweedy Brwn Glob Val
10.4	44.2	12.98	18.26	0.00	0.00	0.0	—	—	—	—	100	0	0	global	U.S. Global Leaders
12.9	19.9	10.01	10.26	0.57	0.04	5.5	—	—	—	—	94	0	6	fix-inc	UAM BHM&S Tot Ret Bd
22.3	24.0	12.08	12.44	0.42	1.57	3.0	0.57	0.87	6.74	C	60	38	2	income	UAM C & B Balanced
132.0	152.4	13.61	13.28	0.22	3.88	1.3	0.85	0.87	10.11	C	97	0	3	gr-inc	UAM C & B Eqty
—	2.1	—	11.85	0.04	0.00	—	—	—	—	—	65	0	35	growth	UAM C&B Eqty Taxable Invst
—	10.8	—	10.46	0.59	0.00	5.6	—	—	—	—	0	94	6	fix-inc	UAM Chi Asst Mgmt Int B
—	19.1	—	14.38	0.14	1.78	1.0	0.75	0.70	11.82	F	98	0	2	growth	UAM Chi Asst Mgmt Val Contra
—	30.4	—	10.09	0.01	0.00	—	—	—	—	—	33	31	36	income	UAM DSI Balanced
66.7	78.2	11.84	12.21	0.16	2.19	1.3	0.76	0.78	9.66	B	95	0	5	growth	UAM DSI Discpnd Val
30.7	32.7	9.32	9.37	0.56	0.00	6.0	0.07	0.21	1.67	B	0	90	10	fix-inc	UAM DSI Ltd Mat
26.5	56.0	12.66	15.89	0.05	1.77	0.3	0.42	0.24	9.57	A	89	0	11	agg gr	UAM FMA Small Co SC
37.3	173.1	13.02	15.20	0.39	0.26	2.6	0.30	0.33	5.91	A	45	26	29	gr-inc	UAM FPA Crescent
—	19.9	—	9.98	0.00	0.00	—	—	—	—	—	95	3	2	growth	UAM Hanson Eqty
12.6	47.9	14.60	18.26	0.26	0.38	1.4	0.85	0.83	10.50	B	100	0	0	gr-inc	UAM ICM Equity
5.3	2.5	11.49	3.10	0.00	11.44	0.0	—	—	—	—	95	0	5	gr-inc	UAM IRC Enhncd Idx
—	84.9	—	10.40	0.09	0.15	—	—	—	—	—	86	0	14	int'l	UAM Jacobs Int'l Octgn
75.6	102.3	14.05	15.60	0.07	1.29	0.5	—	—	—	—	81	0	19	growth	UAM Mckee Domestic Eqty
90.4	114.3	11.01	10.97	0.09	1.17	0.8	0.80	0.46	12.89	B	94	0	6	int'l	UAM McKee Int'l
—	57.0	—	9.96	0.01	0.00	—	—	—	—	—	96	0	4	agg gr	UAM McKee Sm Cap SC
55.4	26.0	10.72	10.49	0.56	0.07	5.3	—	—	—	—	0	74	26	fix-inc	UAM Mckee US Gov
25.1	29.9	10.53	10.70	0.04	0.41	0.4	0.72	0.46	11.57	C	94	0	6	int'l	UAM MJI Int'l
8.5	14.1	12.67	14.51	0.31	0.46	2.1	0.57	0.77	7.22	D	56	25	19	income	UAM NWQ Balanced
3.5	4.9	14.42	18.03	0.09	0.72	0.5	0.83	0.77	10.59	C	92	0	8	gr-inc	UAM NWQ Value Eqty
36.4	48.0	15.03	15.79	0.00	2.29	0.0	0.52	0.10	18.26	C	95	0	5	agg gr	UAM RHJ Sm Cap SC
2.3	13.4	10.33	12.80	0.01	0.16	0.1	—	—	—	—	98	0	2	agg gr	UAM RHJ Small\MidCap
32.9	25.1	9.31	9.50	0.56	0.00	5.9	-0.01	0.01	1.59	A	96	0	4	fix-inc	UAM SAMI Pref Stck Inc
—	39.0	—	10.10	0.09	0.00	—	—	—	—	—	0	94	6	fix-inc	UAM Sirach Bond
7.2	33.0	11.27	14.24	0.02	0.38	0.1	—	—	—	—	97	0	3	growth	UAM Sirach Eqty
121.0	138.9	12.36	12.99	0.11	3.13	0.7	0.85	0.85	10.26	B	88	0	12	growth	UAM Sirach Growth
422.4	314.1	13.38	11.82	0.00	2.86	0.0	1.11	0.33	21.43	F	93	0	7	gr-inc	UAM Sirach Spec Eqty
79.7	88.4	10.79	10.99	0.30	1.75	2.8	0.57	0.86	6.85	B	53	41	6	income	UAM Sirach Strat Balanced
60.0	78.9	12.32	12.62	0.28	1.62	2.3	0.53	0.81	6.58	C	62	35	3	income	UAM Strlng Part Balanced
37.6	52.3	15.69	16.91	0.13	2.52	0.8	0.74	0.78	9.43	A	98	0	2	growth	UAM Strlng Part Eqty
1.1	27.6	10.00	13.40	0.01	0.44	0.1	—	—	—	—	93	0	7	growth	UAM Strlng Sm Cap Val SC
2.3	9.9	12.06	15.42	0.05	0.29	0.3	—	—	—	—	96	0	4	growth	UAM TJ Core Eqty
85.2	100.2	14.08	14.57	0.28	2.83	1.6	0.80	0.88	9.52	D	91	0	9	gr-inc	UAM TS&W Eqty

Stock and bond funds — comprehensive summary *continued*

Arranged in alphabetical order

No-Load Fund	1988	1989	1990	1991	1992	1993	1994	1995	1996	1997	Annualized 3 yrs.	Annualized 5 yrs.	Grew to after 3 yrs.	Grew to after 5 yrs.
UAM TS&W Fix Inc	—	—	—	—	—	9.6[4]	-4.2[3]	17.1[4]	2.3[4]	9.2[3]	9.4[4]	6.6[4]	13,088	13,749
UAM TS&W Int'l Eqty	—	—	—	—	—	32.7[4]	-0.8[3]	7.2[4]	10.7[4]	2.5[3]	6.7[3]	9.9[4]	12,155	16,005
UBS Bond	—	—	—	—	—	—	—	—	—	7.2[5]	—	—	—	—
UBS Int'l Eqty	—	—	—	—	—	—	—	—	—	-3.7[4]	—	—	—	—
UBS US Eqty	—	—	—	—	—	—	—	—	—	29.6[2]	—	—	—	—
Unified First Lexgtn Bal	—	—	—	—	—	—	—	—	—	—	—	—	—	—
Unified Laidlaw	—	—	—	—	—	—	—	—	—	32.8[1]	—	—	—	—
Unified Starwood Strat	—	—	—	—	—	—	—	—	—	23.1[4]	—	—	—	—
US Glb:Adrian Day Glob Oppty	—	—	—	—	—	—	—	—	—	—	—	—	—	—
US Glb:All-Amer Eqty	-3.1[5]	16.8[4]	-11.3[5]	26.6[4]	5.6[4]	10.0[4]	-5.3[5]	30.9[3]	22.3[2]	30.3[2]	27.8[2]	16.8[4]	20,860	21,730
US Glb:Bonnel Growth	—	—	—	—	—	—	—	45.2[1]	27.9[1]	10.3[4]	27.0[2]	—	20,487	—
US Glb:China Region Oppty	—	—	—	—	—	—	—	-14.1[5]	27.8[1]	-22.5[5]	-5.2[5]	—	8,513	—
US Glb:Glob Resrcs	-12.2[5]	22.1[4]	-10.7[5]	-1.6[5]	-2.7[5]	18.5[5]	-9.7[5]	9.0[5]	34.1[1]	-2.8[5]	12.4[4]	8.7[4]	14,214	15,210
US Glb:Gold Shares	-35.7[5]	64.7[1]	-34.2[5]	-15.6[5]	-50.8[5]	123.9[1]	-2.7[1]	-26.8[5]	-25.5[5]	-57.4[5]	-38.5[2]	-12.7[5]	2,326	5,066
US Glb:Income	16.9[2]	37.9[1]	-8.7[5]	14.3[5]	8.1[3]	17.7[1]	-10.3[5]	22.3[4]	10.4[5]	23.1[2]	18.4[4]	11.9[5]	16,618	17,545
US Glb:MegaTrends	—	—	—	—	6.2[4]	2.9[5]	-3.1[4]	24.2[5]	15.4[5]	15.6[5]	18.3[5]	10.6[5]	16,568	16,518
US Glb:Near Term TF	—	—	—	9.7[1]	6.6[1]	9.8[1]	-0.1[3]	6.5[5]	4.3[1]	6.6[1]	5.8[2]	5.4[1]	11,845	12,997
US Glb:Real Estate	20.8[2]	7.4[5]	-19.8[5]	55.3[2]	4.7[4]	0.2[5]	-11.6[5]	18.9[5]	31.6[2]	19.3[3]	23.1[3]	10.6[5]	18,664	16,532
US Glb:Regent East Europe	—	—	—	—	—	—	—	—	—	—	—	—	—	—
US Glb:Tax Free	12.0[1]	8.2[3]	5.5[5]	9.9[4]	7.2[3]	11.8[1]	-5.2[5]	14.6[1]	3.4[5]	9.1[1]	8.9[1]	6.5[1]	12,927	13,700
US Glb:World Gold	-18.8[3]	16.5[5]	-27.9[5]	-3.4[3]	-4.7[1]	89.8[3]	-16.9[4]	15.9[1]	19.5[2]	-41.1[2]	-6.6[1]	5.2[1]	8,160	12,871
USAA Agg Growth SC	14.3[3]	16.6[5]	-11.9[4]	71.7[1]	-8.5[5]	8.1[5]	-0.8[2]	50.4[1]	16.5[4]	7.6[5]	23.5[3]	15.1[3]	18,846	20,210
USAA Balanced Strat	—	—	—	—	—	—	—	—	13.5[5]	19.1[5]	—	—	—	—
USAA CA Bond	—	—	8.2[1]	10.9[1]	8.3[4]	12.7[3]	-9.3[5]	21.9[1]	5.4[1]	10.3[1]	12.3[1]	7.7[1]	14,176	14,490
USAA Cornerstone Strat	8.4[2]	21.9[2]	-9.2[4]	16.2[3]	6.4[1]	23.7[3]	-1.0[2]	18.4[2]	17.9[2]	15.6[2]	17.3[2]	14.6[2]	16,136	19,760
USAA Emg Mkts	—	—	—	—	—	—	—	3.7[4]	16.6[2]	-3.5[4]	5.3[4]	—	11,667	—
USAA First Start Gro	—	—	—	—	—	—	—	—	—	—	—	—	—	—
USAA FL TF	—	—	—	—	—	—	-10.0[5]	18.9[2]	4.4[2]	11.2[1]	11.3[1]	—	13,796	—
USAA GNMA	—	—	—	—	6.1[4]	7.1[4]	0.0[1]	16.8[3]	2.9[4]	9.5[1]	9.6[3]	7.1[2]	13,162	14,096
USAA Gold	-17.1[3]	18.1[4]	-26.6[5]	-4.4[3]	-7.9[2]	58.3[5]	-9.4[2]	4.0[3]	0.0[4]	-38.2[1]	-13.7[1]	-1.6[4]	6,429	9,220
USAA Gro & Inc	—	—	—	—	—	—	1.3[2]	31.6[3]	23.0[2]	26.0[3]	26.8[3]	—	20,400	—
USAA Growth & Tax Strat	—	—	1.4[2]	14.5[5]	5.1[5]	13.7[3]	-2.6[4]	22.7[4]	11.1[4]	16.1[4]	16.6[5]	11.9[5]	15,833	17,534
USAA Growth Strat	—	—	—	—	—	—	—	—	22.1[2]	9.1[5]	—	—	—	—
USAA Growth	6.6[5]	27.3[2]	-0.1[1]	27.8[4]	10.0[3]	7.4[4]	3.3[2]	32.1[1]	17.8[4]	3.7[5]	17.3[5]	12.4[5]	16,136	17,902
USAA Income Stk	19.4[1]	27.1[1]	-1.4[3]	27.3[2]	7.8[4]	11.6[4]	-0.7[2]	28.6[2]	17.9[1]	26.9[1]	24.4[1]	16.4[1]	19,244	21,326
USAA Income Strat	—	—	—	—	—	—	—	—	3.0[5]	15.2[5]	—	—	—	—
USAA Income	10.0[1]	16.1[1]	7.7[4]	19.4[1]	8.4[1]	9.9[2]	-5.2[5]	24.5[1]	1.3[5]	11.0[1]	11.9[1]	7.8[1]	14,003	14,589
USAA International	—	17.4[4]	-9.3[2]	13.4[2]	-0.2[2]	39.8[2]	2.7[2]	8.3[3]	19.1[2]	9.0[2]	12.0[2]	15.1[1]	14,057	20,183
USAA NY Bond	—	—	—	13.8[1]	9.0[2]	13.5[1]	-9.0[5]	18.1[2]	3.7[3]	10.6[1]	10.7[2]	7.0[3]	13,550	13,995
USAA S & P Idx	—	—	—	—	—	—	—	—	—	33.0[1]	—	—	—	—
USAA Science & Tech	—	—	—	—	—	—	—	—	—	—	—	—	—	—
USAA ST Bond	—	—	—	—	—	—	0.0[3]	11.2[2]	6.3[1]	7.2[1]	8.2[1]	—	12,667	—
USAA TE Inter	8.7[2]	9.2[1]	6.7[3]	11.1[2]	8.5[1]	11.5[1]	-4.0[3]	15.1[1]	4.5[1]	9.4[1]	9.6[1]	7.1[1]	13,158	14,084
USAA TE Long	12.5[2]	10.6[1]	6.6[3]	12.4[2]	8.6[3]	12.5[4]	-7.9[4]	18.6[2]	4.5[1]	10.4[1]	11.0[1]	7.2[2]	13,681	14,175
USAA TE Short	6.1[1]	7.4[1]	5.9[5]	7.7[4]	6.0[4]	5.5[4]	0.8[1]	8.1[2]	4.4[1]	5.9[1]	6.1[1]	4.9[2]	11,946	12,704
USAA Texas TF	—	—	—	—	—	—	—	22.2[1]	5.3[1]	11.7[1]	12.9[1]	—	14,370	—
USAA VA Bond	—	—	—	11.7[3]	8.5[4]	12.7[3]	-6.3[3]	17.1[3]	5.1[1]	9.5[2]	10.5[2]	7.3[2]	13,476	14,231
USAA World Growth	—	—	—	—	—	—	0.6[2]	12.8[4]	19.1[2]	12.9[3]	14.9[4]	13.6[2]	15,162	18,914
Valley Forge	7.3[5]	13.0[5]	-5.4[3]	7.9[5]	9.3[3]	17.1[2]	5.9[1]	10.6[5]	6.2[5]	6.0[5]	7.6[5]	9.1[5]	12,454	15,444
Value Line Agg Inc	6.3[5]	2.4[5]	-3.7[5]	26.6[1]	12.2[1]	19.0[1]	-4.1[3]	20.1[2]	19.8[1]	14.1[1]	18.0[1]	13.4[1]	16,416	18,734
Value Line Asst Alloc	—	—	—	—	—	—	3.4[1]	36.1[1]	26.6[1]	20.9[3]	27.7[1]	—	20,838	—
Value Line Convert	16.0[2]	10.7[5]	-3.7[4]	28.7[1]	13.8[1]	14.8[2]	-5.3[5]	22.7[4]	20.2[1]	17.0[4]	19.9[3]	13.4[3]	17,258	18,762
Value Line Fund	9.7[4]	31.4[1]	-0.8[2]	48.9[1]	4.7[4]	6.8[4]	-4.5[5]	32.1[2]	22.5[2]	21.6[4]	25.3[3]	15.0[4]	19,678	20,071
Value Line Income	12.2[3]	22.5[2]	2.0[2]	28.5[1]	1.8[5]	8.3[4]	-4.4[4]	26.2[3]	17.4[2]	18.5[4]	20.7[3]	12.7[4]	17,564	18,184
Value Line Levergd Gro	6.4[5]	32.3[2]	-1.6[2]	46.4[3]	-2.5[5]	16.2[3]	-3.7[4]	37.1[2]	22.3[2]	23.8[2]	27.6[2]	18.4[2]	20,766	23,238
Value Line Multi-Nat'l Co	—	—	—	—	—	—	—	—	32.5[1]	19.0[3]	—	—	—	—
Value Line NY TE	10.8[4]	8.2[5]	4.1[5]	14.3[1]	9.5[1]	13.9[1]	-7.7[4]	17.3[3]	2.4[5]	9.3[2]	9.5[4]	6.7[4]	13,134	13,808
Value Line Sm Cap SC	—	—	—	—	—	—	-0.6[2]	24.0[4]	10.4[5]	11.5[4]	15.2[5]	—	15,268	—
Value Line Spec Sit	3.2[5]	21.9[4]	-4.4[2]	36.6[4]	-3.5[5]	13.0[4]	1.0[2]	29.0[4]	7.2[5]	32.2[1]	22.3[3]	15.8[3]	18,280	20,863
Value Line TE Hi Yld	11.0[3]	8.4[4]	6.6[3]	12.2[3]	7.8[5]	11.5[5]	-6.9[3]	16.7[3]	3.6[4]	8.8[3]	9.6[3]	6.4[4]	13,153	13,654

See Chapter 3 for explanation of symbols

Stock and bond funds — comprehensive summary *continued*
Arranged in alphabetical order

Total Net Assets $Million December 31 1996	1997	NAV per share December 31 1996	1997	1997 per share distributions Income	Capital gains	Yield % 12/31/97	beta	R^2	Std. Dev.	Sharpe Ratio	% Distribution of Portfolio 12/31/97 Stocks	Bonds	Cash	Objective	No-Load Fund
61.1	67.9	10.27	10.59	0.59	0.00	5.6	0.19	0.26	4.15	D	95	0	5	fix-inc	UAM TS&W Fix Inc
109.2	110.2	14.66	14.59	0.08	0.34	0.5	0.66	0.39	11.52	C	85	7	8	int'l	UAM TS&W Int'l Eqty
7.5	13.5	100.13	101.50	5.53	0.11	5.5	—	—	—	—	0	97	3	fix-inc	UBS Bond
26.6	23.2	102.84	95.37	1.23	2.34	1.3	—	—	—	—	86	1	13	int'l	UBS Int'l Eqty
9.5	26.5	106.70	129.17	2.27	6.75	1.7	—	—	—	—	97	0	3	gr-inc	UBS US Eqty
—	6.3	—	10.78	0.28	0.01	—	—	—	—	—	85	0	15	income	Unified First Lexgtn Bal
0.1	2.8	1.73	1.95	0.00	0.35	0.0	—	—	—	—	99	0	1	gr-inc	Unified Laidlaw
0.1	1.2	7.78	9.44	0.00	0.13	0.0	—	—	—	—	93	0	7	growth	Unified Starwood Strat
—	3.2	—	8.16	0.00	0.00	—	—	—	—	—	60	0	40	global	US Glb:Adrian Day Glob Op
16.7	27.4	26.08	33.13	0.40	0.42	1.2	0.90	0.97	10.22	C	86	0	14	gr-inc	US Glb:All-Amer Eqty
98.8	103.6	17.68	16.04	0.00	3.56	0.0	1.06	0.34	20.12	C	99	0	1	agg gr	US Glb:Bonnel Growth
30.0	25.6	7.54	5.80	0.05	0.00	0.8	0.62	0.09	21.36	D	98	0	2	int'l	US Glb:China Region Oppty
25.9	25.0	7.08	5.98	0.00	0.91	0.0	0.41	0.07	17.11	F	99	0	1	global	US Glb:Glob Resrcs
153.3	66.1	1.40	0.57	0.04	0.00	6.3	0.38	0.01	33.69	B	65	0	35	prec met	US Glb:Gold Shares
8.3	9.3	13.34	14.00	0.24	2.15	1.5	0.59	0.66	8.06	D	88	4	8	income	US Glb:Income
24.8	21.1	12.01	11.86	0.01	2.01	0.1	0.77	0.74	9.88	F	91	0	9	gr-inc	US Glb:MegaTrends
6.2	7.7	10.47	10.68	0.47	0.00	4.4	0.09	0.41	1.58	C	98	0	2	tax-free	US Glb:Near Term TF
19.2	16.3	13.67	15.54	0.48	0.27	3.0	0.29	0.10	10.71	B	89	0	11	sector	US Glb:Real Estate
—	9.3	—	11.18	0.01	0.05	—	—	—	—	—	75	0	25	int'l	US Glb:Regent East Europe
19.2	19.7	11.78	12.24	0.58	0.00	4.8	0.15	0.27	3.21	A	94	0	6	tax-free	US Glb:Tax Free
225.5	131.3	19.16	11.15	0.14	0.00	1.2	0.39	0.02	28.10	A	93	0	7	prec met	US Glb:World Gold
716.0	732.4	29.81	29.73	0.00	2.34	0.0	1.03	0.26	22.66	D	84	0	16	agg gr	USAA Agg Growth SC
25.9	47.4	11.26	12.74	0.34	0.29	2.7	—	—	—	—	55	43	2	gr-inc	USAA Balanced Strat
439.0	511.0	10.71	11.18	0.60	0.00	5.4	0.18	0.18	4.77	A	0	100	0	tax-free	USAA CA Bond
1,171.3	1,413.9	26.59	28.06	0.72	1.90	2.4	0.51	0.58	7.38	C	77	21	2	global	USAA Cornerstone Strat
55.5	305.9	10.29	9.79	0.00	0.18	0.0	0.92	0.31	17.99	D	95	0	5	int'l	USAA Emg Mkts
—	22.6	—	9.98	0.00	0.00	—	—	—	—	—	99	0	1	growth	USAA First Start Gro
95.1	137.4	9.45	9.96	0.51	0.00	5.2	0.18	0.19	4.57	A	0	94	6	tax-free	USAA FL TF
307.0	347.0	9.99	10.23	0.68	0.00	6.6	0.16	0.22	3.68	C	0	130	-30	fix-inc	USAA GNMA
129.7	84.5	8.93	5.52	0.00	0.00	0.0	0.44	0.03	28.49	A	93	0	7	prec met	USAA Gold
513.2	936.4	15.26	18.31	0.23	0.66	1.2	0.78	0.87	9.30	B	94	3	3	gr-inc	USAA Gro & Inc
172.6	211.6	14.31	15.51	0.52	0.54	3.2	0.43	0.84	5.26	C	48	48	4	income	USAA Growth & Tax Strat
142.5	228.7	12.38	13.15	0.12	0.23	0.9	—	—	—	—	81	18	1	growth	USAA Growth Strat
1,316.6	1,356.9	18.84	17.40	0.09	2.23	0.5	0.91	0.46	15.01	F	96	0	4	growth	USAA Growth
1,922.2	2,397.5	16.95	19.55	0.78	1.02	3.8	0.58	0.69	7.78	A	83	15	2	income	USAA Income Stk
13.3	24.1	10.60	11.64	0.49	0.04	4.2	—	—	—	—	24	75	1	income	USAA Income Strat
1,738.0	1,722.1	12.31	12.78	0.83	0.00	6.5	0.25	0.24	5.71	C	7	92	1	fix-inc	USAA Income
513.1	575.3	19.15	19.22	0.12	1.57	0.6	0.64	0.37	11.50	B	94	1	5	int'l	USAA International
56.1	66.0	11.09	11.60	0.63	0.00	5.5	0.17	0.20	4.15	A	0	98	2	tax-free	USAA NY Bond
178.1	628.6	11.57	15.16	0.21	0.00	1.4	—	—	—	—	99	0	1	gr-inc	USAA S & P Idx
—	62.4	—	9.07	0.00	0.00	—	—	—	—	—	96	0	4	sector	USAA Science & Tech
111.6	144.9	9.92	10.00	0.61	0.00	6.1	0.09	0.22	2.04	A	0	81	19	fix-inc	USAA ST Bond
1,711.2	1,936.0	12.92	13.38	0.72	0.00	5.4	0.14	0.26	3.14	A	0	98	2	tax-free	USAA TE Inter
1,872.7	2,002.0	13.42	13.99	0.78	0.00	5.6	0.17	0.21	4.17	A	0	100	0	tax-free	USAA TE Long
785.9	937.0	10.62	10.74	0.49	0.00	4.5	0.05	0.27	1.14	A	0	81	19	tax-free	USAA TE Short
10.2	17.4	10.58	11.10	0.58	0.10	5.2	0.20	0.19	5.07	A	0	103	-3	tax-free	USAA Texas TF
284.9	331.0	11.11	11.51	0.62	0.00	5.4	0.18	0.25	3.99	A	0	99	1	tax-free	USAA VA Bond
266.8	321.5	15.30	16.19	0.08	1.02	0.4	0.71	0.51	10.88	D	94	1	5	global	USAA World Growth
11.4	10.8	9.36	8.96	0.31	0.63	3.4	0.23	0.33	4.41	F	30	7	63	growth	Valley Forge
74.2	134.3	8.16	8.53	0.73	0.00	8.5	0.17	0.28	3.65	A	1	89	10	fix-inc	Value Line Agg Inc
69.2	101.7	13.73	14.47	0.26	1.83	1.6	0.39	0.40	6.99	A	59	26	15	income	Value Line Asst Alloc
67.6	85.6	13.10	13.86	0.68	0.75	4.6	0.43	0.51	6.65	B	5	80	15	income	Value Line Convert
348.9	382.4	19.29	19.29	0.14	3.79	0.6	0.82	0.65	11.29	C	88	0	12	growth	Value Line Fund
147.2	160.4	7.37	7.98	0.15	0.57	1.8	0.72	0.73	9.43	D	70	28	2	income	Value Line Income
371.1	432.6	31.51	35.58	0.00	3.24	0.0	1.14	0.70	15.25	B	91	0	9	agg gr	Value Line Levergd Gro
16.3	26.3	12.90	14.54	0.00	0.79	0.0	—	—	—	—	86	0	14	agg gr	Value Line Multi-Nat'l Co
33.0	33.9	10.03	10.48	0.46	0.00	4.4	0.19	0.20	4.70	F	0	94	6	tax-free	Value Line NY TE
18.1	21.8	13.54	12.50	0.00	2.49	0.0	0.80	0.33	15.44	F	97	0	3	agg gr	Value Line Sm Cap SC
89.6	116.6	13.34	14.48	0.01	2.99	0.0	0.72	0.34	13.86	C	93	0	7	agg gr	Value Line Spec Sit
201.9	187.5	10.77	11.05	0.54	0.10	4.9	0.16	0.21	3.92	C	0	95	5	tax-free	Value Line TE Hi Yld

Arranged in alphabetical order

No-Load Fund	Total return percent with quintile ranks by objective										Annualized		What $10,000 grew to after	
	1988	1989	1990	1991	1992	1993	1994	1995	1996	1997	3 yrs.	5 yrs.	3 yrs.	5 yrs.
Value Line US Gov...	7.9[4]	12.0[3]	10.3[1]	16.4[3]	6.3[4]	9.8[4]	-10.7[5]	14.4[5]	3.9[3]	9.2[3]	9.1[5]	4.9[5]	12,984	12,731
Van Wagoner Emg Gr...	—	—	—	—	—	—	—	—	26.9[1]	-20.0[5]	—	—	—	—
Van Wagoner Micro-Cap SC...	—	—	—	—	—	—	—	—	24.5[2]	-19.8[5]	—	—	—	—
Van Wagoner Mid-Cap...	—	—	—	—	—	—	—	—	23.9[2]	-13.9[5]	—	—	—	—
Van Wagoner Post Venture...	—	—	—	—	—	—	—	—	—	-12.2[5]	—	—	—	—
Vangd Asst Alloc...	—	23.7[2]	0.9[2]	25.6[2]	7.5[4]	13.5[3]	-2.3[3]	35.5[1]	15.7[2]	27.3[1]	25.9[1]	17.2[1]	19,956	22,129
Vangd Bond Idx Inter...	—	—	—	—	—	—	—	21.1[1]	2.6[4]	9.4[1]	10.8[1]	—	13,594	—
Vangd Bond Idx Long...	—	—	—	—	—	—	—	29.7[1]	-0.3[5]	14.3[1]	13.9[1]	—	14,780	—
Vangd Bond Idx Short...	—	—	—	—	—	—	—	12.9[1]	4.5[3]	7.0[1]	8.1[1]	—	12,628	—
Vangd Bond Idx Total...	7.4[3]	13.6[2]	8.6[3]	15.3[3]	7.2[2]	9.7[3]	-2.7[3]	18.2[2]	3.6[3]	9.4[1]	10.3[2]	7.4[2]	13,402	14,305
Vangd CA Insur Inter...	—	—	—	—	—	—	—	13.1[4]	5.4[1]	7.7[2] ·	8.7[2]	—	12,839	—
Vangd CA Insur LT...	12.1[3]	10.5[1]	7.0[2]	11.1[4]	9.4[2]	12.8[3]	-5.7[2]	18.6[2]	5.0[1]	8.9[3]	10.7[1]	7.6[1]	13,564	14,428
Vangd Convert...	15.7[3]	15.8[4]	-8.2[5]	34.3[1]	19.0[1]	13.5[3]	-5.7[5]	16.7[5]	15.4[2]	16.3[4]	16.1[5]	10.9[5]	15,669	16,770
Vangd Equity Inc...	—	26.5[1]	-11.9[5]	25.4[2]	9.2[3]	14.7[2]	-1.6[3]	37.3[1]	17.4[2]	31.2[1]	28.4[1]	19.0[1]	21,144	23,864
Vangd Explorer SC...	25.8[1]	9.4[5]	-10.8[4]	55.9[2]	13.0[2]	15.4[3]	0.5[2]	26.6[4]	14.0[4]	14.6[4]	18.2[4]	13.9[4]	16,533	19,174
Vangd FL Insur...	—	—	—	—	—	—	-4.7[1]	17.7[3]	4.2[2]	8.9[3]	10.1[3]	7.6[1]	13,360	14,439
Vangd GNMA...	8.8[1]	14.8[1]	10.3[1]	16.8[2]	6.9[3]	6.0[5]	-1.0[1]	17.0[3]	5.2[2]	9.5[1]	10.4[1]	7.2[2]	13,474	14,139
Vangd Gro & Inc...	16.8[3]	32.0[1]	-2.4[2]	29.8[2]	7.0[4]	13.8[2]	-0.6[4]	35.9[2]	23.1[2]	35.6[1]	31.4[1]	20.7[1]	22,677	25,652
Vangd Hi Yld Corp...	13.6[1]	1.9[5]	-5.8[5]	29.0[1]	14.3[1]	18.2[1]	-1.7[1]	19.2[3]	9.5[1]	11.9[2]	13.5[2]	11.2[1]	14,607	16,971
Vangd Hrzn:Agg Gro...	—	—	—	—	—	—	—	—	25.1[2]	25.5[2]	—	—	—	—
Vangd Hrzn:Cap Opp...	—	—	—	—	—	—	—	—	13.4[4]	-8.0[5]	—	—	—	—
Vangd Hrzn:Glob Asst...	—	—	—	—	—	—	—	—	10.0[4]	9.3[4]	—	—	—	—
Vangd Hrzn:Glob Eqty...	—	—	—	—	—	—	—	—	15.6[3]	6.7[4]	—	—	—	—
Vangd Idx 500...	16.2[3]	31.4[1]	-3.3[3]	30.2[2]	7.5[3]	9.9[4]	1.2[2]	37.4[1]	22.9[2]	33.2[1]	31.0[1]	20.1[1]	22,494	25,017
Vangd Idx Balanced...	—	—	—	—	—	—	-1.6[3]	28.6[2]	13.9[3]	22.2[2]	21.4[2]	14.1[2]	17,904	19,379
Vangd Idx Emg Mkt†	—	—	—	—	—	—	—	0.5[4]	15.9[3]	-16.8[5]	-1.0[4]	—	9,694	—
Vangd Idx Europe†	—	—	—	12.4[2]	-3.3[2]	29.1[4]	1.9[2]	22.3[1]	21.3[2]	24.2[1]	22.6[1]	19.4[1]	18,431	24,246
Vangd Idx Extend Mkt†	19.7[2]	24.0[3]	-14.0[5]	41.8[2]	12.5[3]	14.5[3]	-1.8[4]	33.8[2]	17.6[4]	26.7[3]	25.9[3]	17.5[3]	19,934	22,414
Vangd Idx Growth...	—	—	—	—	—	—	2.9[1]	38.1[1]	23.8[2]	36.3[1]	32.6[1]	19.5[2]	23,296	24,331
Vangd Idx Pacific†	—	—	—	10.6[3]	-18.2[5]	35.5[3]	12.9[1]	2.8[4]	-7.8[5]	-25.7[5]	-11.0[5]	1.5[5]	7,043	10,775
Vangd Idx Sm Capt† SC...	24.6[1]	10.5[5]	-18.1[5]	45.3[1]	18.2[1]	18.7[2]	-0.5[3]	28.7[3]	18.1[4]	24.5[3]	23.7[4]	17.5[3]	18,930	22,357
Vangd Idx Total Mkt...	—	—	—	—	—	—	-0.2[3]	35.8[1]	21.0[3]	31.0[2]	29.1[2]	18.9[2]	21,523	23,757
Vangd Idx Value...	—	—	—	—	—	—	-0.6[4]	37.0[1]	21.8[3]	29.8[2]	29.4[2]	20.5[1]	21,652	25,439
Vangd Int'l Growth...	11.6[4]	24.8[2]	-12.0[3]	4.7[5]	-5.8[3]	44.7[2]	0.8[2]	14.9[1]	14.6[3]	4.1[3]	11.1[2]	14.9[2]	13,706	19,991
Vangd Int'l Value...	18.8[2]	26.0[2]	-12.3[3]	10.0[4]	-8.7[4]	30.5[4]	5.3[1]	9.6[3]	10.2[4]	-4.6[4]	4.8[4]	9.6[4]	11,522	15,834
Vangd Inter Corp...	—	—	—	—	—	—	-4.2[4]	21.4[1]	2.8[4]	8.9[2]	10.8[1]	—	13,595	—
Vangd Inter Trsy...	—	—	—	—	7.8[1]	12.5[1]	-4.3[4]	20.4[1]	1.9[5]	9.0[2]	10.2[2]	7.6[2]	13,368	14,392
Vangd LifeStrat:Cons Gro...	—	—	—	—	—	—	—	24.3[4]	10.4[5]	16.8[4]	17.0[5]	—	16,025	—
Vangd LifeStrat:Growth...	—	—	—	—	—	—	—	29.2[3]	15.4[4]	22.1[4]	22.1[4]	—	18,211	—
Vangd LifeStrat:Income...	—	—	—	—	—	—	—	23.0[4]	7.6[5]	14.2[5]	14.8[5]	—	15,117	—
Vangd LifeStrat:Mod Gr...	—	—	—	—	—	—	—	27.9[4]	12.7[5]	19.7[4]	19.9[5]	—	17,255	—
Vangd LT Corp...	9.7[2]	15.2[2]	6.2[3]	20.9[2]	9.8[2]	14.5[2]	-5.3[4]	26.4[1]	1.2[5]	13.8[2]	13.3[2]	9.6[2]	14,555	15,782
Vangd LT Trsy...	9.2[2]	17.9[1]	5.8[3]	17.5[3]	7.5[3]	16.8[1]	-7.0[4]	30.1[1]	-1.3[5]	13.9[1]	13.5[2]	9.7[2]	14,626	15,888
Vangd Morgan...	22.3[2]	22.7[4]	-1.5[2]	29.3[5]	9.5[3]	7.3[5]	-1.7[3]	36.0[2]	23.3[2]	30.8[1]	29.9[1]	18.3[2]	21,929	23,130
Vangd Muni Hi Yld...	13.8[1]	11.1[1]	5.9[4]	14.7[1]	9.9[1]	12.7[3]	-5.1[2]	18.1[2]	4.5[1]	9.2[2]	10.5[2]	7.6[1]	13,481	14,419
Vangd Muni Insur LT...	12.8[1]	10.6[1]	7.0[2]	13.1[1]	9.2[2]	13.1[2]	-5.6[2]	18.6[2]	4.0[2]	8.6[4]	10.2[2]	7.4[1]	13,401	14,308
Vangd Muni Inter...	10.0[1]	10.0[1]	7.2[1]	12.1[1]	8.9[1]	11.6[1]	-2.1[1]	13.6[3]	4.2[2]	7.1[3]	8.2[2]	6.7[1]	12,676	13,849
Vangd Muni Long...	12.2[2]	11.5[1]	6.8[2]	13.5[1]	9.3[2]	13.5[2]	-5.8[2]	18.7[2]	4.4[1]	9.3[2]	10.6[2]	7.7[1]	13,543	14,480
Vangd Muni Ltd Trm...	6.4[1]	8.2[1]	7.0[1]	9.5[1]	6.4[2]	6.3[3]	0.1[3]	8.6[2]	4.1[1]	5.1[3]	5.9[2]	4.8[2]	11,882	12,643
Vangd Muni Short...	5.6[3]	7.1[2]	6.6[3]	7.2[5]	4.7[5]	3.9[5]	1.7[1]	5.9[5]	3.7[3]	4.1[5]	4.5[5]	3.8[5]	11,429	12,077
Vangd NJ Insur LT...	—	10.4[2]	7.7[1]	11.3[4]	9.4[2]	13.4[2]	-5.2[2]	17.3[3]	3.2[4]	8.6[4]	9.4[4]	7.2[3]	13,143	14,129
Vangd NY Insur LT...	12.0[3]	10.4[2]	6.2[4]	12.9[1]	9.8[1]	13.1[2]	-5.6[2]	17.7[3]	4.1[2]	8.7[4]	10.0[3]	7.3[2]	13,324	14,225
Vangd OH Insur LT...	—	—	—	12.0[3]	9.4[2]	12.8[3]	-5.1[2]	16.9[3]	4.2[2]	8.5[4]	9.7[3]	7.2[3]	13,214	14,145
Vangd PA Insur LT...	12.3[2]	10.6[1]	6.9[2]	12.2[2]	10.2[1]	12.8[3]	-4.5[1]	16.4[4]	4.3[2]	8.3[4]	9.5[4]	7.2[2]	13,142	14,157
Vangd Prefrd Stk...	8.0[3]	18.7[1]	6.4[3]	20.9[2]	8.4[2]	13.0[3]	-7.9[5]	25.9[1]	8.4[2]	13.0[2]	15.5[1]	9.9[2]	15,424	16,052
Vangd Primecap...	14.7[4]	21.6[3]	-2.8[2]	33.1[3]	9.0[3]	18.0[2]	11.4[1]	35.5[2]	18.3[4]	36.8[1]	29.9[1]	23.6[1]	21,929	28,827
Vangd Selected Val...	—	—	—	—	—	—	—	—	—	17.4[5]	—	—	—	—
Vangd Spec-Energy...	21.4[2]	43.5[1]	-1.4[2]	0.3[5]	6.2[4]	26.4[2]	-1.6[3]	25.3[4]	34.0[2]	14.8[5]	24.5[3]	19.1[2]	19,280	23,980
Vangd Spec-Gold...	-14.2[2]	30.4[1]	-19.9[2]	4.4[1]	-19.4[4]	93.4[2]	-5.4[1]	-4.5[5]	-0.7[4]	-39.0[1]	-16.7[2]	1.1[3]	5,786	10,587
Vangd Spec-Health...	28.4[1]	33.0[2]	16.8[1]	46.3[1]	-1.6[5]	11.8[4]	9.5[1]	45.2[2]	21.4[3]	28.5[2]	31.3[2]	22.6[2]	22,656	27,736

See Chapter 3 for explanation of symbols

Stock and bond funds — comprehensive summary *continued*
Arranged in alphabetical order

Total Net Assets $Million December 31 1996	1997	NAV per share December 31 1996	1997	1997 per share distributions Income	Capital gains	Yield % 12/31/97	beta	R²	Std. Dev.	Sharpe Ratio	Stocks	Bonds	Cash	Objective	No-Load Fund
203.7	188.7	10.93	11.18	0.73	0.00	6.5	0.18	0.32	3.63	C	0	98	2	fix-inc	Value Line US Gov
638.2	313.2	12.69	10.15	0.00	0.00	0.0	—	—	—	—	102	0	-2	agg gr	Van Wagoner Emg Gr
140.7	71.9	12.45	9.99	0.00	0.00	0.0	—	—	—	—	90	0	10	agg gr	Van Wagoner Micro-Cap SC
137.7	73.8	12.39	10.67	0.00	0.00	0.0	—	—	—	—	92	0	8	growth	Van Wagoner Mid-Cap
0.5	20.5	10.00	8.78	0.00	0.00	0.0	—	—	—	—	92	0	8	agg gr	Van Wagoner Post Venture
2,596.9	4,099.0	17.94	21.05	0.74	1.01	3.4	0.73	0.89	8.60	A	40	29	31	income	Vangd Asst Alloc
460.4	684.3	9.96	10.20	0.66	0.00	6.5	0.22	0.24	4.96	C	0	96	4	fix-inc	Vangd Bond Idx Inter
44.1	87.3	10.08	10.78	0.68	0.00	6.3	0.36	0.24	8.22	C	0	98	2	fix-inc	Vangd Bond Idx Long
328.3	438.3	9.92	10.00	0.60	0.00	6.0	0.09	0.23	2.16	B	0	98	2	fix-inc	Vangd Bond Idx Short
2,961.6	5,010.0	9.84	10.09	0.64	0.00	6.4	0.18	0.25	3.99	B	0	98	2	fix-inc	Vangd Bond Idx Total
353.2	622.9	10.49	10.77	0.50	0.00	4.7	0.13	0.24	2.90	A	0	95	5	tax-free	Vangd CA Insur Inter
1,060.9	1,198.3	11.22	11.53	0.59	0.07	5.1	0.20	0.20	5.04	C	0	91	9	tax-free	Vangd CA Insur LT
166.1	186.7	11.63	11.82	0.54	1.12	4.2	0.49	0.42	8.47	F	0	98	2	income	Vangd Convert
1,424.9	2,099.7	18.32	22.39	0.67	0.89	2.9	0.69	0.84	8.40	A	92	2	7	income	Vangd Equity Inc
2,263.7	2,541.0	53.83	55.30	0.25	5.85	0.4	0.69	0.31	13.62	D	89	1	10	agg gr	Vangd Explorer SC
549.8	614.0	10.96	11.35	0.56	0.00	4.9	0.19	0.20	4.68	D	0	90	10	tax-free	Vangd FL Insur
7,441.2	8,689.8	10.22	10.43	0.72	0.00	6.9	0.15	0.27	3.35	A	0	99	1	fix-inc	Vangd GNMA
1,285.4	2,141.8	22.23	26.19	0.42	3.18	1.5	1.04	0.96	11.91	C	96	0	4	gr-inc	Vangd Gro & Inc
3,582.6	4,543.9	7.87	8.08	0.69	0.00	8.5	0.18	0.35	3.37	A	0	97	3	fix-inc	Vangd Hi Yld Corp
153.2	474.1	12.57	14.60	0.14	1.08	0.9	—	—	—	—	99	0	1	agg gr	Vangd Hrzn:Agg Gro
117.4	63.4	11.13	10.20	0.05	0.00	0.4	—	—	—	—	91	0	9	agg gr	Vangd Hrzn:Cap Opp
77.1	80.1	10.59	10.28	0.71	0.54	6.9	—	—	—	—	6	56	39	global	Vangd Hrzn:Glob Asst
106.6	126.4	11.84	11.98	0.23	0.44	1.9	—	—	—	—	96	0	4	global	Vangd Hrzn:Glob Eqty
30,331.8	49,357.6	69.16	90.07	1.32	0.59	1.5	1.00	1.00	11.13	B	99	0	1	gr-inc	Vangd Idx 500
826.2	1,260.4	13.92	16.29	0.53	0.15	3.2	0.63	0.95	7.21	B	57	40	3	income	Vangd Idx Balanced
637.1	660.9	12.28	9.99	0.23	0.00	2.3	1.17	0.41	19.31	D	96	0	4	int'l	Vangd Idx Emg Mkt†
1,594.7	2,432.4	16.57	20.13	0.37	0.08	1.8	0.52	0.34	10.03	A	98	0	2	int'l	Vangd Idx Europe†
2,098.8	2,722.8	26.19	30.75	0.36	1.91	1.1	0.78	0.51	12.08	C	97	0	3	growth	Vangd Idx Extend Mkt†
786.9	2,365.3	16.91	22.53	0.23	0.25	1.0	1.08	0.96	12.25	B	99	0	1	gr-inc	Vangd Idx Growth
977.5	827.2	10.51	7.72	0.09	0.00	1.2	0.77	0.22	17.92	F	100	0	0	int'l	Vangd Idx Pacific†
1,713.4	2,652.4	20.23	23.75	0.27	1.12	1.1	0.72	0.37	13.27	D	97	0	3	growth	Vangd Idx Sm Cap† SC
3,530.9	5,092.0	17.77	22.64	0.32	0.27	1.4	0.94	0.94	10.76	B	95	0	5	growth	Vangd Idx Total Mkt
1,015.7	1,795.5	17.02	20.85	0.37	0.75	1.7	0.92	0.94	10.56	B	99	0	1	gr-inc	Vangd Idx Value
5,568.7	6,809.0	16.46	16.39	0.21	0.52	1.2	0.74	0.41	12.55	B	92	0	8	int'l	Vangd Int'l Growth
916.6	776.8	27.54	22.64	0.69	2.96	2.8	0.48	0.23	10.87	D	98	1	1	int'l	Vangd Int'l Value
621.5	860.1	9.75	9.94	0.64	0.01	6.4	0.22	0.25	4.84	C	0	97	3	fix-inc	Vangd Inter Corp
1,274.2	1,498.5	10.42	10.67	0.65	0.00	6.1	0.20	0.22	4.89	D	0	98	2	fix-inc	Vangd Inter Trsy
462.5	802.9	12.14	13.40	0.56	0.19	4.1	0.47	0.90	5.56	C	50	50	0	income	Vangd LifeStrat:Cons Gro
628.7	1,183.7	13.68	16.04	0.38	0.29	2.3	0.77	0.96	8.72	C	90	10	0	growth	Vangd LifeStrat:Growth
151.5	243.9	11.55	12.43	0.63	0.10	5.0	0.34	0.66	4.68	D	30	69	1	income	Vangd LifeStrat:Income
825.7	1,358.2	12.97	14.81	0.49	0.22	3.3	0.63	0.95	7.24	D	70	30	0	gr-inc	Vangd LifeStrat:Mod Gr
3,460.7	3,599.2	8.79	9.26	0.61	0.08	6.6	0.34	0.28	7.15	C	0	96	4	fix-inc	Vangd LT Corp
918.5	1,030.2	9.96	10.64	0.64	0.00	6.1	0.35	0.21	8.38	D	0	92	8	fix-inc	Vangd LT Trsy
2,053.8	2,795.3	15.63	17.54	0.16	2.53	0.8	0.93	0.74	12.15	A	91	0	9	agg gr	Vangd Morgan
2,041.8	2,266.4	10.63	10.93	0.60	0.05	5.5	0.17	0.20	4.26	A	0	95	5	tax-free	Vangd Muni Hi Yld
1,964.7	2,051.7	12.34	12.62	0.67	0.08	5.3	0.19	0.21	4.78	D	0	97	3	tax-free	Vangd Muni Insur LT
6,139.1	6,793.1	13.23	13.42	0.67	0.05	5.0	0.13	0.24	2.92	B	0	92	8	tax-free	Vangd Muni Inter
1,147.4	1,260.1	10.95	11.29	0.59	0.06	5.2	0.19	0.22	4.42	A	0	94	6	tax-free	Vangd Muni Long
1,792.4	1,978.5	10.71	10.77	0.47	0.00	4.4	0.06	0.25	1.44	B	0	92	8	tax-free	Vangd Muni Ltd Trm
1,455.8	1,489.3	15.58	15.58	0.62	0.01	4.0	0.02	0.18	0.63	F	0	50	50	tax-free	Vangd Muni Short
843.7	936.9	11.51	11.85	0.61	0.01	5.1	0.18	0.21	4.27	D	0	93	7	tax-free	Vangd NJ Insur LT
950.2	1,129.5	10.84	11.17	0.57	0.02	5.1	0.19	0.22	4.51	C	0	95	5	tax-free	Vangd NY Insur LT
216.1	252.1	11.52	11.87	0.60	0.02	5.0	0.18	0.21	4.28	D	0	95	5	tax-free	Vangd OH Insur LT
1,640.5	1,741.0	11.11	11.40	0.60	0.00	5.2	0.16	0.21	3.96	C	0	98	2	tax-free	Vangd PA Insur LT
297.5	329.5	9.66	10.23	0.65	0.00	6.4	0.21	0.22	4.96	A	0	99	1	fix-inc	Vangd Prefrd Stk
4,203.9	8,186.2	30.08	39.57	0.20	1.30	0.5	0.99	0.62	14.19	C	87	0	13	growth	Vangd Primecap
101.0	191.0	10.91	12.28	0.05	0.46	0.4	—	—	—	—	98	0	2	gr-inc	Vangd Selected Val
847.9	1,181.4	22.54	24.14	0.32	1.33	1.3	0.52	0.15	14.72	C	95	1	4	sector	Vangd Spec-Energy
496.5	293.0	11.63	6.97	0.13	0.00	1.9	0.38	0.02	26.62	B	90	1	9	prec met	Vangd Spec-Gold
2,661.7	4,466.2	58.35	71.88	0.78	2.14	1.1	0.69	0.63	9.71	A	90	0	10	sector	Vangd Spec-Health

Arranged in alphabetical order

Total return percent with quintile ranks by objective / Annualized / What $10,000 grew to after

No-Load Fund	1988	1989	1990	1991	1992	1993	1994	1995	1996	1997	Ann. 3 yrs.	Ann. 5 yrs.	$10,000 after 3 yrs.	$10,000 after 5 yrs.
Vangd Spec-REIT Idx	—	—	—	—	—	—	—	—	—	18.6[4]	—	—	—	—
Vangd Spec-Util	—	—	—	—	—	—	-8.6[5]	34.0[1]	5.3[5]	25.1[2]	20.8[3]	13.2[3]	17,648	18,566
Vangd ST Corp	6.9[2]	11.4[1]	9.2[2]	13.1[3]	7.3[1]	7.0[2]	-0.1[3]	12.7[1]	4.8[2]	6.9[2]	8.1[1]	6.2[1]	12,631	13,502
Vangd ST Federal	5.7[4]	11.3[2]	9.3[1]	12.3[4]	6.2[3]	7.0[2]	-0.9[4]	12.3[2]	4.8[2]	6.5[3]	7.8[1]	5.8[1]	12,530	13,286
Vangd ST Trsy	—	—	—	—	6.7[2]	6.4[3]	-0.6[3]	12.1[2]	4.4[3]	6.4[3]	7.6[2]	5.7[2]	12,451	13,169
Vangd Star:Star	19.0[2]	18.8[4]	-3.7[3]	24.5[4]	10.5[2]	11.0[3]	-0.3[3]	28.7[3]	16.2[4]	20.5[4]	21.7[4]	14.8[4]	18,028	19,951
Vangd Tax Mgd:Balanced	—	—	—	—	—	—	—	24.5[3]	12.2[4]	16.6[4]	17.6[4]	—	16,281	—
Vangd Tax Mgd:Cap App	—	—	—	—	—	—	—	34.4[2]	20.9[3]	27.3[3]	27.4[2]	—	20,680	—
Vangd Tax Mgd:Gro & Inc	—	—	—	—	—	—	—	37.5[1]	23.0[2]	33.3[1]	31.1[1]	—	22,548	—
Vangd Tot Int'l Port†	—	—	—	—	—	—	—	—	—	-0.8[4]	—	—	—	—
Vangd Trust US	24.6[1]	17.2[4]	-8.3[4]	26.6[3]	6.5[4]	17.2[2]	-3.9[5]	33.2[2]	21.3[3]	29.5[2]	27.9[2]	18.7[2]	20,917	23,559
Vangd US Growth	8.8[4]	37.7[1]	4.6[1]	46.8[1]	2.8[5]	-1.4[5]	3.9[1]	38.4[1]	26.0[1]	25.9[3]	30.0[1]	17.6[3]	21,954	22,491
Vangd Wellesley Inc	13.6[3]	20.9[2]	3.8[1]	21.5[4]	8.7[3]	14.6[2]	-4.4[4]	28.9[2]	9.4[5]	20.3[3]	19.2[4]	13.2[3]	16,952	18,572
Vangd Wellington	16.1[2]	21.6[2]	-2.8[3]	23.7[3]	7.9[4]	13.5[3]	-0.5[2]	32.9[1]	16.2[2]	23.2[2]	23.9[1]	16.5[1]	19,032	21,493
Vangd Windsor II	24.7[1]	27.8[2]	-10.0[4]	28.7[3]	12.0[2]	13.6[2]	-1.2[4]	38.8[1]	24.2[2]	32.3[2]	31.6[1]	20.7[1]	22,814	25,606
Vangd Windsor‡	28.7[1]	15.0[5]	-15.5[5]	28.6[3]	16.5[1]	19.4[1]	-0.1[3]	30.1[3]	26.4[1]	22.0[4]	26.1[3]	19.1[2]	20,060	23,927
Vangd-Adml Inter	—	—	—	—	—	—	-4.2[4]	20.5[1]	2.1[5]	9.0[2]	10.3[2]	7.4[2]	13,413	14,301
Vangd-Adml Long	—	—	—	—	—	—	-6.8[4]	30.0[1]	-1.1[5]	14.0[1]	13.6[2]	9.9[2]	14,654	16,034
Vangd-Adml Short	—	—	—	—	—	—	-0.3[3]	12.3[2]	4.5[3]	6.5[2]	7.7[2]	5.8[1]	12,497	13,269
Vintage Agg Gro	—	—	—	—	—	—	—	—	19.3[3]	26.2[2]	—	—	—	—
Vintage Balanced	—	—	—	—	—	—	—	—	13.5[3]	22.8[2]	—	—	—	—
Vintage Bond	—	—	—	—	—	—	—	—	2.4[4]	9.2[3]	—	—	—	—
Vintage Eqty	—	—	—	—	—	5.5[5]	2.0[2]	35.7[1]	21.3[2]	30.1[2]	28.9[2]	18.2[2]	21,420	23,043
Vintage Fix Inc	—	—	—	—	—	9.0[3]	-3.1[3]	14.5[4]	2.8[4]	7.1[5]	8.1[5]	5.9[5]	12,615	13,322
Vintage Fix Tot Ret	—	—	—	—	—	—	—	—	1.8[5]	6.7[5]	—	—	—	—
Vintage Inter TF	—	—	—	—	—	—	-5.4[5]	15.1[1]	3.1[5]	6.6[4]	8.1[3]	—	12,643	—
Vista Amer Value	—	—	—	—	—	—	—	—	15.7[4]	21.8[4]	—	—	—	—
Volumetric	19.9[2]	15.9[5]	-5.0[3]	35.1[2]	10.6[3]	2.2[5]	-2.1[4]	17.1[5]	15.5[4]	18.3[5]	17.0[5]	9.9[5]	16,006	16,017
Vontobel East Europe Debt	—	—	—	—	—	—	—	—	—	—	—	—	—	—
Vontobel East Europe	—	—	—	—	—	—	—	—	—	8.7[2]	—	—	—	—
Vontobel Emg Mkts Eqty	—	—	—	—	—	—	—	—	—	—	—	—	—	—
Vontobel Int'l Bd	—	—	—	—	—	—	—	17.6[4]	7.5[2]	-6.0[5]	5.9[5]	—	11,880	—
Vontobel Int'l Eqty	—	—	—	—	-2.4[2]	40.8[2]	-5.3[4]	10.9[2]	17.0[2]	9.2[2]	12.3[2]	13.6[2]	14,167	18,890
Vontobel US Value	—	—	—	38.2[1]	16.0[1]	6.0[5]	0.0[3]	40.4[1]	21.3[3]	34.3[1]	31.8[1]	19.4[2]	22,873	24,245
Wade	-10.2[5]	26.2[2]	-3.8[3]	15.7[5]	7.6[4]	9.3[4]	-1.3[4]	20.8[5]	13.0[5]	20.3[4]	18.0[5]	12.1[5]	16,413	17,701
Warbg Pincus Balanced	—	19.6[3]	3.1[1]	25.1[3]	7.5[4]	10.7[4]	1.3[1]	31.6[1]	12.9[4]	16.4[4]	20.0[3]	14.2[2]	17,287	19,386
Warbg Pincus Cap App	21.4[2]	26.8[2]	-5.5[3]	26.3[4]	7.6[3]	15.9[2]	-2.9[4]	38.1[1]	23.2[2]	31.4[2]	30.8[1]	20.3[1]	22,370	25,175
Warbg Pincus Emg Gro SC	—	21.8[4]	-9.9[3]	56.1[2]	12.1[3]	18.1[2]	-1.4[3]	46.2[1]	9.9[5]	21.3[3]	24.9[2]	17.8[2]	19,484	22,689
Warbg Pincus Emg Mkts	—	—	—	—	—	—	—	17.2[1]	9.9[4]	-20.0[5]	1.0[4]	—	10,306	—
Warbg Pincus Fix Inc	8.6[2]	9.3[5]	2.9[5]	16.8[2]	6.7[3]	11.2[2]	-0.7[1]	15.1[4]	6.2[1]	8.8[3]	10.0[2]	8.0[1]	13,300	14,686
Warbg Pincus Glob Fix Inc	—	—	—	14.7[4]	2.1[5]	19.6[1]	-5.5[5]	16.0[3]	10.0[1]	2.2[5]	9.3[3]	8.1[1]	13,040	14,738
Warbg Pincus Glob Post Vent	—	—	—	—	—	—	—	—	—	8.7[4]	—	—	—	—
Warbg Pincus Gro & Inc	—	20.7[3]	4.0[1]	13.0[5]	8.5[3]	37.0[1]	7.6[1]	20.4[5]	-1.2[5]	30.2[2]	15.7[5]	18.0[3]	15,494	22,839
Warbg Pincus Health Sci	—	—	—	—	—	—	—	—	—	27.4[2]	—	—	—	—
Warbg Pincus Int'l Eqty	—	—	-4.6[1]	20.6[1]	-4.3[3]	51.3[1]	0.2[3]	10.4[3]	10.6[4]	-4.4[4]	5.3[4]	12.1[3]	11,670	17,692
Warbg Pincus Inter Gov	—	11.5[1]	8.9[2]	15.0[1]	6.7[2]	7.9[2]	-1.8[4]	15.8[1]	2.3[5]	7.6[1]	8.4[1]	6.2[1]	12,741	13,500
Warbg Pincus Japan Growth	—	—	—	—	—	—	—	—	—	—	—	—	—	—
Warbg Pincus Japan OTC	—	—	—	—	—	—	—	-1.1[4]	-13.1[5]	-25.5[5]	-13.8[5]	—	6,399	—
Warbg Pincus Maj For Mkts	—	—	—	—	—	—	—	—	—	—	—	—	—	—
Warbg Pincus NY Inter Muni	6.4[4]	6.9[5]	5.9[5]	9.5[5]	7.5[2]	9.9[4]	-0.6[1]	9.5[5]	4.3[1]	5.9[5]	6.5[5]	5.7[4]	12,092	13,210
Warbg Pincus Post Vent	—	—	—	—	—	—	—	—	17.3[3]	9.7[5]	—	—	—	—
Warbg Pincus Small Co Gro SC	—	—	—	—	—	—	—	—	—	22.3[3]	—	—	—	—
Warbg Pincus Small Co Val SC	—	—	—	—	—	—	—	—	56.2[1]	19.2[3]	—	—	—	—
Warbg Pincus Strat Val	—	—	—	—	—	—	—	—	—	24.2[2]	—	—	—	—
Wasatch Agg Eqty‡ SC	-1.4[5]	32.0[2]	7.7[1]	50.6[2]	-0.6[5]	22.6[1]	5.5[1]	28.1[4]	5.2[5]	19.2[3]	17.1[5]	15.8[3]	16,067	20,782
Wasatch Growth	3.2[5]	24.8[3]	10.3[1]	48.9[1]	-1.4[5]	11.1[3]	2.7[2]	40.4[1]	16.5[4]	27.5[3]	27.8[2]	18.9[2]	20,861	23,803
Wasatch Hosington US Treas	8.5[3]	14.7[2]	10.4[1]	13.6[5]	4.7[5]	4.0[5]	1.6[1]	11.5[5]	7.8[2]	15.7[1]	11.6[2]	8.0[3]	13,914	14,699
Wasatch Micro Cap SC	—	—	—	—	—	—	—	—	13.7[4]	35.3[1]	—	—	—	—
Wasatch Micro Cap Val SC	—	—	—	—	—	—	—	—	—	—	—	—	—	—
Wasatch MidCap	—	—	—	—	—	—	8.1[1]	58.8[1]	3.6[5]	-0.5[5]	17.9[4]	11.5[5]	16,368	17,269

See Chapter 3 for explanation of symbols

Total Net Assets $Million		NAV per share		1997 per share distributions		Yield %	Risk Analysis				% Distribution of Portfolio			Objective	No-Load Fund
December 31		December 31			Capital				Std.	Sharpe	12/31/97				
1996	1997	1996	1997	Income	gains	12/31/97	beta	R²	Dev.	Ratio	Stocks	Bonds	Cash		
469.1	1,277.7	12.62	14.16	0.72	0.05	5.1	—	—	—	—	98	0	2	sector	Vangd Spec-REIT Idx
658.6	684.6	12.74	14.98	0.60	0.26	3.9	0.44	0.34	8.48	D	83	15	2	income	Vangd Spec-Util
4,608.7	4,595.5	10.75	10.81	0.66	0.00	6.1	0.09	0.25	1.98	A	0	98	2	fix-inc	Vangd ST Corp
1,337.9	1,413.6	10.11	10.13	0.61	0.00	6.1	0.08	0.22	1.88	B	0	99	1	fix-inc	Vangd ST Federal
960.0	993.8	10.17	10.21	0.59	0.00	5.8	0.08	0.20	1.93	B	0	98	2	fix-inc ·	Vangd ST Trsy
5,863.4	7,355.4	15.86	17.38	0.59	1.20	3.2	0.59	0.91	6.84	B	63	25	12	gr-inc	Vangd Star:Star
63.1	119.8	12.92	14.67	0.37	0.00	2.5	0.55	0.87	6.60	D	49	51	0	income	Vangd Tax Mgd:Balanced
517.4	892.5	15.95	20.18	0.12	0.00	0.6	1.04	0.87	12.45	C	100	0	0	growth	Vangd Tax Mgd:Cap App
234.5	579.3	15.89	20.88	0.28	0.00	1.3	1.00	0.99	11.16	B	100	0	0	gr-inc	Vangd Tax Mgd:Gro & Inc
280.4	903.1	10.14	9.87	0.17	0.02	1.7	—	—	—	—	100	0	0	int'l	Vangd Tot Int'l Port†
157.7	174.0	37.08	36.82	0.43	9.91	1.0	0.97	0.93	11.21	C	100	0	0	gr-inc	Vangd Trust US
5,532.0	8,054.6	23.74	28.70	0.27	0.89	0.9	0.99	0.89	11.65	B	95	0	5	growth	Vangd US Growth
7,012.7	7,645.9	20.51	21.86	1.20	1.45	5.2	0.46	0.58	6.74	C	36	62	1	income	Vangd Wellesley Inc
16,189.8	21,811.8	26.15	29.45	1.12	1.57	3.6	0.69	0.86	8.23	A	61	38	2	income	Vangd Wellington
15,700.0	24,376.5	23.83	28.62	0.66	2.19	2.1	0.83	0.92	9.67	A	93	0	7	gr-inc	Vangd Windsor II
16,738.1	20,914.6	16.59	16.98	0.32	2.88	1.6	0.76	0.64	10.66	D	97	2	1	gr-inc	Vangd Windsor‡
655.3	866.4	10.22	10.46	0.65	0.00	6.2	0.20	0.22	4.88	D	0	98	2	fix-inc	Vangd-Adml Inter
189.7	311.2	10.26	10.96	0.67	0.00	6.1	0.35	0.21	8.36	C	0	92	8	fix-inc	Vangd-Adml Long
531.0	743.6	10.05	10.09	0.59	0.00	5.9	0.07	0.19	1.95	B	0	98	2	fix-inc	Vangd-Adml Short
41.0	86.4	12.24	15.20	0.00	0.24	0.0	—	—	—	—	95	0	5	agg gr	Vintage Agg Gro
18.0	47.0	11.77	14.09	0.18	0.17	1.3	—	—	—	—	63	28	9	income	Vintage Balanced
3.9	2.9	9.93	10.12	0.64	0.05	6.3	—	—	—	—	0	98	2	fix-inc	Vintage Bond
252.2	389.5	16.15	18.84	0.02	2.15	0.1	1.06	0.94	12.15	B	99	0	1	growth	Vintage Eqty
90.2	102.7	9.87	10.04	0.51	0.00	5.1	0.15	0.25	3.33	F	0	94	6	fix-inc	Vintage Fix Inc
41.6	42.1	9.84	9.98	0.50	0.00	5.0	—	—	—	—	0	88	12	fix-inc	Vintage Fix Tot Ret
44.9	47.3	10.37	10.64	0.39	0.01	3.7	0.15	0.22	3.47	D	0	93	7	tax-free	Vintage Inter TF
10.2	12.0	13.46	14.41	0.21	1.75	1.3	—	—	—	—	90	0	10	gr-inc	Vista Amer Value
14.3	17.8	18.38	20.30	0.03	1.18	0.1	0.76	0.82	9.34	F	86	0	14	growth	Volumetric
—	14.0	—	9.70	0.24	0.00	—	—	—	—	—	0	81	19	fix-inc	Vontobel East Europe Debt
61.3	139.9	14.89	15.25	0.00	0.92	0.0	—	—	—	—	99	0	1	int'l	Vontobel East Europe
—	3.6	—	9.42	0.00	0.00	—	—	—	—	—	80	3	17	int'l	Vontobel Emg Mkts Eqty
26.9	10.8	10.93	9.89	0.00	0.38	0.0	-0.10	0.03	5.76	F	0	93	7	fix-inc	Vontobel Int'l Bd
151.7	160.9	18.22	18.15	0.00	1.78	0.0	0.66	0.41	11.28	B	92	0	8	int'l	Vontobel Int'l Eqty
69.6	201.3	13.78	16.51	0.10	1.88	0.5	0.57	0.70	7.62	A	58	0	42	gr-inc	Vontobel US Value
0.6	0.7	34.81	38.88	0.05	2.91	0.1	0.81	0.60	11.56	F	74	0	26	growth	Wade
33.3	38.2	12.63	13.10	0.26	1.29	1.8	0.60	0.56	8.94	D	62	32	6	income	Warbg Pincus Balanced
464.9	623.4	16.94	18.27	0.08	3.81	0.4	0.87	0.83	10.75	A	100	0	0	growth	Warbg Pincus Cap App
1,151.0	1,578.0	33.22	37.77	0.00	2.39	0.0	0.80	0.32	15.71	C	88	1	12	agg gr	Warbg Pincus Emg Gro SC
212.4	116.5	12.59	9.58	0.00	0.47	0.0	1.08	0.37	18.57	D	91	0	9	int'l	Warbg Pincus Emg Mkts
158.1	312.1	10.15	10.32	0.61	0.09	5.9	0.15	0.30	3.12	A	0	100	0	fix-inc	Warbg Pincus Fix Inc
142.5	174.5	11.01	10.37	0.89	0.00	8.5	0.13	0.16	3.59	C	0	92	8	fix-inc	Warbg Pincus Glob Fix Inc
4.0	3.1	10.06	10.53	0.28	0.11	2.7	—	—	—	—	94	0	6	global	Warbg Pincus Glob Post Vent
460.7	616.4	15.15	16.48	0.20	2.95	1.0	0.91	0.58	13.13	F	93	1	6	gr-inc	Warbg Pincus Gro & Inc
0.1	20.3	10.00	11.99	0.04	0.68	0.3	—	—	—	—	92	0	8	sector	Warbg Pincus Health Sci
2,953.0	1,956.2	20.84	17.01	0.29	2.57	1.5	0.75	0.33	14.05	D	94	0	6	int'l	Warbg Pincus Int'l Eqty
46.9	49.3	9.91	10.06	0.58	0.00	5.7	0.13	0.19	3.28	C	0	99	1	fix-inc	Warbg Pincus Inter Gov
17.5	26.6	9.21	9.35	0.00	0.00	0.0	—	—	—	—	81	0	19	int'l	Warbg Pincus Japan Growth
94.6	37.6	7.85	5.72	0.12	0.00	2.2	0.36	0.04	18.46	F	73	4	23	int'l	Warbg Pincus Japan OTC
—	8.9	—	9.95	0.21	0.24	—	—	—	—	—	87	0	13	int"l	Warbg Pincus Maj For Mkts
115.1	91.7	10.26	10.40	0.45	0.00	4.3	0.08	0.21	1.91	F	0	100	0	tax-free	Warbg Pincus NY Inter Muni
165.2	104.5	16.24	17.81	0.00	0.00	0.0	—	—	—	—	93	1	6	agg gr	Warbg Pincus Post Vent
0.1	11.5	10.00	12.16	0.06	0.00	0.5	—	—	—	—	94	0	6	agg gr	Warbg Pincus Small Co Gro SC
120.9	200.6	15.44	16.40	0.00	1.93	0.0	—	—	—	—	94	1	5	agg gr	Warbg Pincus Small Co Val SC
0.1	12.7	10.00	11.66	0.14	0.58	1.2	—	—	—	—	88	0	12	agg gr	Warbg Pincus Strat Val
219.2	172.2	23.86	24.60	0.00	3.69	0.0	0.69	0.25	15.32	D	98	0	2	agg gr	Wasatch Agg Eqty‡ SC
89.9	146.7	17.19	20.22	0.03	1.62	0.1	0.43	0.17	11.64	B	96	0	4	growth	Wasatch Growth
9.2	14.0	10.49	11.58	0.56	0.00	4.9	0.36	0.34	6.90	D	0	94	6	fix-inc	Wasatch Hosington US Treas
82.0	120.6	3.03	3.76	0.00	0.33	0.0	—	—	—	—	98	0	2	agg gr	Wasatch Micro Cap SC
—	2.3	—	2.01	0.00	0.00	—	—	—	—	—	74	0	26	agg gr	Wasatch Micro Cap Val SC
100.5	61.1	18.94	16.71	0.00	2.00	0.0	1.02	0.30	20.74	F	100	1	-1	agg gr	Wasatch MidCap

Stock and bond funds — comprehensive summary *continued*

Arranged in alphabetical order

No-Load Fund	\$10,000 Total return percent with quintile ranks by objective — 1988	1989	1990	1991	1992	1993	1994	1995	1996	1997	Annualized 3 yrs	Annualized 5 yrs	grew to after 3 yrs	grew to after 5 yrs
Wayne Hummer Growth	7.0[5]	24.0[3]	5.0[1]	27.8[4]	10.4[3]	3.1[5]	-0.9[3]	24.8[4]	11.9[5]	30.2[2]	22.1[4]	13.2[5]	18,184	18,579
Wayne Hummer Income	—	—	—	—	—	10.6[4]	-2.5[2]	15.5[5]	3.5[3]	9.0[4]	9.2[4]	7.0[4]	13,028	14,055
Weitz Ser Fix Inc	—	9.1[4]	9.1[1]	11.2[5]	5.5[5]	8.0[5]	-2.4[2]	15.8[4]	4.4[3]	8.6[4]	9.5[4]	6.7[4]	13,128	13,844
Weitz Ser Hickory	—	—	—	—	—	—	-17.2[5]	40.5[1]	35.4[1]	39.2[1]	38.3[1]	—	26,466	—
Weitz Ser Partners Value	—	—	—	—	—	—	—	38.7[1]	19.0[3]	40.6[1]	32.4[1]	—	23,214	—
Weitz Value	16.4[3]	22.1[3]	-5.2[3]	27.6[3]	13.6[2]	20.0[1]	-9.8[5]	38.4[1]	18.7[4]	38.9[1]	31.7[1]	19.8[2]	22,816	24,694
West University Fd	—	—	—	—	—	—	—	—	—	9.7[5]	—	—	—	—
Westcore Blue Chip	—	20.6[4]	-0.3[2]	34.5[3]	2.0[5]	12.4[3]	0.4[3]	36.4[1]	21.2[3]	30.9[2]	29.4[1]	19.6[2]	21,654	24,432
Westcore CO TE	—	—	—	—	8.1[4]	9.9[5]	-3.2[1]	13.0[5]	4.3[2]	7.4[5]	8.2[5]	6.1[5]	12,655	13,457
Westcore Gro & Inc	—	26.4[2]	-2.8[2]	31.2[2]	5.0[5]	11.3[3]	-8.4[5]	22.5[5]	23.3[2]	27.3[3]	24.3[4]	14.4[5]	19,203	19,585
Westcore Inter Bond	—	11.2[4]	1.6[5]	20.2[1]	7.1[2]	9.9[3]	-3.4[4]	15.0[4]	3.8[3]	8.3[3]	8.9[4]	6.5[3]	12,922	13,717
Westcore LT Bond	—	15.7[2]	5.1[4]	19.4[2]	8.9[2]	15.9[2]	-7.1[4]	26.7[1]	0.7[5]	14.0[1]	13.3[2]	9.4[2]	14,543	15,655
Westcore MIDCO Gro	7.5[4]	29.2[2]	4.4[1]	67.0[1]	6.5[4]	17.5[2]	-1.0[3]	27.4[4]	17.0[4]	14.9[5]	19.6[4]	14.8[4]	17,126	19,916
Westcore Sm Cap Oppty SC	—	—	—	—	—	—	-2.0[3]	29.5[3]	25.6[1]	27.8[2]	27.6[2]	—	20,788	—
Weston: New Cent Cap	—	—	-4.8[3]	36.5[1]	0.6[5]	13.8[2]	0.1[3]	28.1[4]	14.5[5]	26.1[3]	22.8[4]	16.1[4]	18,496	21,066
Weston: New Cent Inc	—	—	-0.7[3]	22.9[4]	2.8[5]	15.5[2]	-2.4[3]	22.9[4]	12.2[4]	18.6[4]	17.8[4]	13.0[4]	16,346	18,428
Westwood Balanced	—	—	—	—	5.9[4]	16.8[2]	0.1[2]	31.2[1]	18.1[1]	22.5[2]	23.8[1]	17.3[1]	18,969	22,169
Westwood Equity	12.7[4]	28.4[2]	-6.2[3]	21.2[4]	6.0[4]	17.2[2]	2.3[2]	36.9[1]	26.8[1]	29.6[2]	31.0[1]	21.9[1]	22,480	26,940
Westwood Inter Bd	—	—	—	—	6.1[4]	10.5[2]	-5.6[5]	16.2[3]	3.7[3]	10.7[1]	10.1[2]	6.8[3]	13,342	13,920
Westwood Realty	—	—	—	—	—	—	—	—	—	—	—	—	—	—
Westwood Sm Cap Eqty SC	—	—	—	—	—	—	—	—	—	—	—	—	—	—
White Oak Gro	—	—	—	—	—	-0.3[5]	6.3[1]	52.7[1]	32.3[1]	24.3[3]	35.9[1]	21.6[1]	25,115	26,624
Wilshire Target Lg Gro	—	—	—	—	—	—	2.3[2]	36.6[1]	25.7[1]	32.2[1]	31.4[1]	18.2[2]	22,704	23,063
Wilshire Target Lg Val	—	—	—	—	—	—	-5.2[5]	39.9[1]	18.1[4]	30.2[2]	29.1[2]	18.3[2]	21,507	23,101
Wilshire Target Sm Gro SC	—	—	—	—	—	—	-1.4[3]	28.2[4]	14.0[4]	11.7[4]	17.7[5]	13.2[4]	16,321	18,619
Wilshire Target Sm Val SC	—	—	—	—	—	—	-4.5[5]	25.2[4]	13.5[5]	31.2[2]	23.2[4]	14.7[4]	18,710	19,869
Wm Blair Growth	7.1[5]	30.4[2]	-2.0[2]	44.4[1]	7.6[3]	15.5[2]	6.5[1]	29.1[3]	18.0[4]	20.1[4]	22.3[4]	17.6[3]	18,292	22,501
Wm Blair Income	—	—	—	16.4[2]	7.2[2]	7.8[4]	-0.7[1]	14.4[4]	3.1[4]	8.0[4]	8.4[4]	6.4[4]	12,740	13,638
Wm Blair Int'l Gro	—	—	—	—	—	33.4[3]	0.0[3]	7.2[4]	10.2[4]	8.4[2]	8.6[3]	11.3[3]	12,806	17,082
Wm Blair Val Disc SC	—	—	—	—	—	—	—	—	—	33.5[1]	—	—	—	—
Women's Equity	—	—	—	—	—	—	-0.1[3]	17.0[5]	14.5[5]	28.6[2]	19.9[4]	—	17,219	—
WPG Core Bd	7.9[2]	13.9[2]	8.9[3]	13.9[4]	7.9[1]	8.9[3]	-9.0[5]	12.8[5]	4.4[2]	7.4[4]	8.2[5]	4.6[5]	12,650	12,536
WPG Growth & Inc	9.4[5]	27.6[2]	-10.4[5]	40.7[1]	13.8[2]	9.5[4]	-5.5[5]	32.7[2]	24.1[4]	36.3[1]	31.0[1]	18.4[3]	22,494	23,277
WPG Growth SC	11.7[4]	24.9[3]	-12.8[4]	56.8[2]	6.3[4]	14.9[3]	-14.0[5]	39.7[2]	18.0[3]	9.7[5]	21.8[4]	12.3[5]	18,080	17,855
WPG Inter Muni	—	—	—	—	—	—	-2.3[1]	12.1[5]	4.2[2]	7.9[1]	8.0[3]	—	12,594	—
WPG International	—	—	-14.8[4]	0.9[5]	-5.5[3]	37.2[3]	-6.3[4]	10.9[2]	4.6[5]	2.9[3]	6.1[3]	9.0[4]	11,943	15,355
WPG Quant Eqty	—	—	—	—	—	—	0.3[3]	33.4[2]	18.5[3]	25.5[3]	25.6[3]	—	19,834	—
WPG Tudor SC	15.1[3]	25.1[3]	-5.2[3]	45.8[3]	5.1[4]	13.4[4]	-9.8[5]	41.2[2]	18.8[3]	11.1[4]	23.1[3]	13.8[4]	18,639	19,065
Wright Curr Inc	8.7[2]	14.2[1]	9.7[2]	15.4[3]	6.7[3]	6.6[5]	-3.3[4]	17.4[2]	4.3[2]	8.6[3]	10.0[2]	6.5[3]	13,301	13,708
Wright Equifund Belg\Lux	—	—	—	—	—	—	—	20.3[1]	20.9[2]	11.4[2]	17.5[1]	—	16,203	—
Wright Equifund Britain	—	—	—	—	—	—	—	—	26.8[1]	13.3[1]	—	—	—	—
Wright Equifund Germany	—	—	—	—	—	—	—	—	15.0[3]	9.9[2]	—	—	—	—
Wright Equifund Hong Kong	—	—	—	33.1[1]	16.3[1]	84.2[1]	-37.0[5]	1.6[4]	28.0[1]	-27.2[5]	-1.8[4]	1.9[5]	9,468	10,979
Wright Equifund Italian	—	—	—	—	—	—	—	—	—	19.3[1]	—	—	—	—
Wright Equifund Japan	—	—	—	—	—	—	—	-9.1[5]	-9.1[5]	-14.2[4]	-10.8[5]	—	7,091	—
Wright Equifund Mexico	—	—	—	—	—	—	—	-33.4[5]	27.5[1]	42.4[1]	6.6[3]	—	12,095	—
Wright Equifund Netherland	—	—	—	10.2[3]	-9.2[4]	19.5[5]	11.7[1]	18.8[1]	36.3[1]	15.4[1]	23.2[1]	20.1[1]	18,692	24,949
Wright Equifund Nordic	—	—	—	—	—	—	—	19.8[1]	32.1[1]	5.2[3]	18.5[1]	—	16,650	—
Wright Equifund Swiss	—	—	—	—	—	—	—	18.4[1]	0.5[5]	22.7[1]	13.4[2]	—	14,584	—
Wright Int'l Blue Ch	—	—	-6.9[2]	17.2[2]	-3.9[3]	28.2[4]	-1.6[3]	13.6[2]	20.7[2]	1.5[3]	11.7[2]	11.9[3]	13,927	17,565
Wright Jr Blue Ch SC	15.2[3]	15.6[5]	-10.6[4]	37.0[4]	3.4[4]	7.9[5]	-2.8[3]	20.5[5]	17.5[3]	28.9[2]	22.2[3]	13.9[4]	18,261	19,167
Wright Major Blue Chip	16.7[3]	23.0[3]	-2.9[2]	38.9[1]	8.0[3]	1.0[5]	-0.7[4]	29.0[3]	17.6[4]	33.9[1]	26.3[3]	15.3[4]	20,311	20,365
Wright Sel Blue Chip	21.3[2]	24.7[2]	-3.3[3]	36.0[1]	4.7[5]	2.1[5]	-3.5[5]	30.3[3]	18.6[4]	32.7[1]	27.1[3]	15.1[4]	20,508	20,194
Wright Total Ret Bd	7.0[4]	13.3[2]	5.3[4]	15.4[2]	7.1[3]	11.0[4]	-6.6[4]	22.0[2]	0.9[5]	9.2[3]	10.4[3]	6.9[4]	13,440	13,942
Wright US Treas Near Term	5.4[5]	11.2[2]	8.2[3]	13.1[3]	6.3[2]	8.0[2]	-3.1[5]	11.9[2]	3.9[4]	5.9[4]	7.2[3]	5.2[3]	12,320	12,885
Wright US Treas	7.3[4]	16.3[1]	6.3[3]	17.6[3]	7.1[3]	15.9[2]	-8.7[5]	28.2[1]	-1.3[5]	9.1[3]	11.3[3]	7.9[3]	13,803	14,613
WWW Internet Fund	—	—	—	—	—	—	—	—	—	0.4[5]	—	—	—	—
Yachtman Focused	—	—	—	—	—	—	—	—	—	—	—	—	—	—
Yacktman	—	—	—	—	—	—	8.8[1]	30.4[3]	26.0[1]	18.3[5]	24.8[3]	14.6[5]	19,434	19,749
ZSA Asst Alloc	—	—	—	—	—	16.7[2]	-12.8[5]	22.5[5]	13.8[5]	12.3[5]	16.1[5]	9.8[5]	15,657	15,933

See Chapter 3 for explanation of symbols

Total Net Assets $Million		NAV per share		1997 per share distributions		Yield % 12/31/97	Risk Analysis				% Distribution of Portfolio			Objective	No-Load Fund
December 31 1996	1997	December 31 1996	1997	Income	Capital gains		beta	R^2	Std. Dev.	Sharpe Ratio	12/31/97 Stocks	Bonds	Cash		
104.6	128.5	27.50	32.80	0.20	2.49	0.6	0.75	0.68	10.18	C	95	0	5	growth	Wayne Hummer Growth
22.9	22.4	14.98	15.37	0.92	0.00	6.0	0.19	0.33	3.67	C	0	98	2	fix-inc	Wayne Hummer Income
17.3	28.1	10.79	11.07	0.63	0.00	5.7	0.16	0.26	3.49	C	0	97	3	fix-inc	Weitz Ser Fix Inc
10.2	21.6	18.80	23.70	0.07	1.90	0.3	0.61	0.26	13.44	A	88	0	12	growth	Weitz Ser Hickory
94.8	133.7	11.52	15.45	0.00	0.53	0.0	0.63	0.48	10.15	A	80	6	14	growth	Weitz Ser Partners Value
260.7	366.0	20.59	25.15	0.31	2.61	1.2	0.60	0.46	9.86	A	77	10	13	gr-inc	Weitz Value
2.0	3.5	10.21	10.35	0.85	0.00	8.2	—	—	—	—	65	0	35	income	West University Fd
56.6	62.2	15.96	16.70	0.12	3.99	0.7	0.90	0.91	10.57	A	95	0	5	growth	Westcore Blue Chip
18.7	26.7	10.81	11.08	0.50	0.00	4.6	0.14	0.25	3.05	D	0	100	0	tax-free	Westcore CO TE
20.3	17.1	11.81	13.10	0.09	1.77	0.7	0.80	0.70	10.54	D	81	3	16	gr-inc	Westcore Gro & Inc
67.9	51.4	10.27	10.47	0.62	0.00	5.9	0.14	0.27	3.03	C	0	86	14	fix-inc	Westcore Inter Bond
22.1	17.2	9.79	10.22	0.60	0.27	5.9	0.31	0.24	7.06	C	0	97	3	fix-inc	Westcore LT Bond
569.8	602.5	20.06	19.66	0.00	3.24	0.0	0.99	0.49	15.78	F	94	0	6	growth	Westcore MIDCO Gro
36.7	46.0	22.53	24.70	0.03	3.97	0.1	0.57	0.33	11.18	A	95	0	5	agg gr	Westcore Sm Cap Oppty SC
64.1	81.0	13.99	13.59	0.36	3.14	2.3	0.87	0.79	10.93	F	100	0	0	gr-inc	Weston: New Cent Cap
41.8	49.1	12.61	12.40	0.79	1.55	5.9	—	—	—	—	60	39	1	income	Weston: New Cent Inc
30.8	80.6	9.68	11.00	0.25	0.56	2.3	0.55	0.85	6.59	A	61	39	0	income	Westwood Balanced
38.1	150.5	7.41	9.15	0.06	0.37	0.7	0.76	0.82	9.32	A	91	2	7	gr-inc	Westwood Equity
5.4	6.2	10.09	10.44	0.69	0.00	6.6	0.21	0.31	4.09	C	0	100	0	fix-inc	Westwood Inter Bd
—	1.8	—	10.06	0.12	0.24	—	—	—	—	—	100	0	0	sector	Westwood Realty
—	9.2	—	13.01	0.09	0.74	—	—	—	—	—	100	0	0	agg gr	Westwood Sm Cap Eqty SC
40.4	391.9	23.55	29.18	0.02	0.06	0.1	1.33	0.66	18.37	C	95	0	5	growth	White Oak Gro
18.9	74.6	19.27	24.90	0.06	0.52	0.2	1.13	0.94	12.92	B	100	0	1	growth	Wilshire Target Lg Gro
14.9	14.3	17.25	20.86	0.38	1.21	1.7	0.80	0.81	10.00	B	100	0	1	gr-inc	Wilshire Target Lg Val
15.9	14.3	14.61	15.64	0.00	0.67	0.0	0.80	0.32	15.74	D	100	0	1	agg gr	Wilshire Target Sm Gro SC
15.8	21.1	14.30	16.42	0.37	1.97	2.0	0.55	0.57	8.12	B	100	0	1	growth	Wilshire Target Sm Val SC
501.8	591.4	13.48	15.35	0.00	0.80	0.0	0.98	0.66	13.38	D	94	0	6	growth	Wm Blair Growth
150.1	160.1	10.27	10.41	0.66	0.00	6.3	0.11	0.22	2.65	C	0	100	0	fix-inc	Wm Blair Income
105.2	128.8	13.95	13.14	0.07	1.86	0.5	0.61	0.37	10.91	C	99	0	1	int'l	Wm Blair Int'l Gro
2.2	30.4	10.00	12.97	0.02	0.34	0.2	—	—	—	—	100	0	0	agg gr	Wm Blair Val Disc SC
4.3	5.8	12.39	15.78	0.00	0.15	0.0	0.99	0.80	12.33	F	99	0	1	growth	Women's Equity
127.5	107.7	9.19	9.34	0.51	0.00	5.5	0.13	0.28	2.76	D	0	100	0	fix-inc	WPG Core Bd
82.9	117.1	29.32	35.11	0.26	4.51	0.7	0.95	0.88	11.24	B	97	0	3	gr-inc	WPG Growth & Inc
62.9	61.0	118.47	113.74	0.00	16.00	0.0	0.86	0.28	18.16	D	80	0	20	agg gr	WPG Growth SC
15.2	23.5	10.14	10.45	0.47	0.00	4.5	0.12	0.27	2.64	B	0	107	-7	tax-free	WPG Inter Muni
13.2	8.6	10.29	10.15	0.01	0.43	0.1	0.62	0.36	11.37	C	111	0	-11	int'l	WPG International
102.3	96.0	5.89	5.84	0.08	1.47	1.1	0.90	0.92	10.41	B	95	0	5	growth	WPG Quant Eqty
182.3	170.7	23.28	21.90	0.00	3.90	0.0	0.94	0.31	18.78	D	87	0	13	agg gr	WPG Tudor SC
65.6	75.6	10.43	10.63	0.66	0.00	6.2	0.16	0.24	3.61	B	0	98	2	fix-inc	Wright Curr Inc
19.2	1.5	13.39	9.54	0.00	5.33	0.0	0.48	0.25	10.59	A	93	0	7	int'l	Wright Equifund Belg\Lux
3.8	0.7	9.09	8.98	0.00	1.31	0.0	—	—	—	—	100	0	-1	int'l	Wright Equifund Britain
23.1	1.4	10.63	11.68	0.00	0.00	0.0	—	—	—	—	97	0	3	int'l	Wright Equifund Germany
34.5	6.6	16.47	11.99	0.00	0.00	0.0	1.55	0.39	24.72	D	90	0	10	int'l	Wright Equifund Hong Kong
0.1	0.6	10.67	11.04	0.00	1.67	0.0	—	—	—	—	95	0	5	int'l	Wright Equifund Italian
17.1	3.9	7.98	6.85	0.00	0.00	0.0	0.54	0.13	16.37	F	95	0	5	int'l	Wright Equifund Japan
22.1	28.5	5.38	7.66	0.00	0.00	0.0	1.14	0.12	35.23	C	95	0	5	int'l	Wright Equifund Mexico
7.5	13.0	8.97	9.80	0.00	0.55	0.0	0.49	0.22	11.57	A	99	0	1	int'l	Wright Equifund Netherland
7.0	2.7	14.78	12.68	0.00	2.83	0.0	0.46	0.16	12.94	A	102	0	-2	int'l	Wright Equifund Nordic
6.1	1.3	10.85	11.99	0.00	1.27	0.0	0.44	0.16	12.35	B	116	0	-16	int'l	Wright Equifund Swiss
268.9	212.7	16.69	16.02	0.16	0.74	1.0	0.49	0.30	9.87	B	98	0	2	int'l	Wright Int'l Blue Ch
14.1	33.5	8.86	10.48	0.03	0.88	0.3	0.62	0.44	10.32	B	98	0	2	agg gr	Wright Jr Blue Ch SC
25.8	27.7	12.45	12.02	0.09	3.96	0.6	0.87	0.87	10.34	C	95	0	5	gr-inc	Wright Major Blue Chip
205.8	259.5	17.73	19.20	0.15	3.69	0.7	0.68	0.75	8.78	A	97	0	3	gr-inc	Wright Sel Blue Ch
91.1	79.7	12.50	12.93	0.69	0.00	5.3	0.24	0.22	5.62	F	0	99	1	fix-inc	Wright Total Ret Bd
132.2	102.3	10.24	10.24	0.59	0.00	5.8	0.07	0.16	1.91	C	0	98	2	fix-inc	Wright US Treas Near Term
54.4	74.2	13.58	13.95	0.70	0.11	5.0	0.24	0.15	6.85	F	0	97	3	fix-inc	Wright US Treas
—	2.6	11.09	9.57	0.00	1.53	0.0	—	—	—	—	90	0	10	sector	WWW Internet Fund
—	58.4	—	11.21	0.07	0.26	—	—	—	—	—	82	0	18	growth	Yachtman Focused
755.6	1,082.1	13.34	14.05	0.22	1.50	1.4	0.52	0.53	8.00	B	93	0	7	gr-inc	Yacktman
9.4	6.2	13.61	14.28	0.28	0.70	2.0	0.51	0.82	6.22	F	73	26	1	gr-inc	ZSA Asst Alloc

CHAPTER 5

Stock and bond funds — ranked within objective

By 1997 performance

No-Load Fund	Total return percent with quintile ranks by objective		
	1997	Annualized 3 years	5 years
AGGRESSIVE GROWTH FUNDS			
American Heritage	**75.0**[1]	4.8[5]	1.1[5]
Oakmark Select	**55.0**[1]	—	—
Brazos/JMIC Sm Cap Gro SC	**54.5**[1]	—	—
SAFECO Growth SC	**50.0**[1]	32.5[1]	22.8[1]
Janus Spec Situations	**46.0**[1]	—	—
FBR Sm Cap Gr/Val‡	**44.3**[1]	—	—
Rydex Nova	**42.3**[1]	39.0[1]	—
TIP:Turner Mid Cap	**40.6**[1]	—	—
UAM FMA Small Co SC	**40.4**[1]	30.0[1]	22.3[1]
Bridgeway Ult Sm Co SC	**38.0**[1]	35.8[1]	—
Gabelli Sm Cap Gro SC	**36.5**[1]	24.1[3]	17.9[2]
Ariel Growth SC	**36.4**[1]	25.9[2]	15.8[3]
Berger Sm Cap Val SC	**36.4**[1]	29.3[1]	21.8[1]
Accessor Sm\Mid Cap SC	**36.2**[1]	30.9[1]	19.7[1]
PC&J Performance	**35.6**[1]	25.9[2]	18.1[2]
Skyline Special Eqty SC‡	**35.4**[1]	26.2[2]	19.5[1]
Wasatch Micro Cap SC	**35.3**[1]	—	—
Scudder Micro-Cap SC	**35.2**[1]	—	—
AARP Capital Growth	**35.1**[1]	28.6[1]	17.3[2]
Columbia Small Cap SC	**34.1**[1]	—	—
FMC Select Fund	**34.1**[1]	—	—
Lazard Bantam Val SC(O shrs)	**33.9**[1]	—	—
Dreyfus Emg Ldrs SC	**33.9**[1]	—	—
Bramwell Growth	**33.7**[1]	25.9[2]	—
Wm Blair Val Disc SC	**33.5**[1]	—	—
Eclipse Equity SC	**33.3**[1]	27.5[2]	18.2[2]
Babson Enterprise II SC	**33.3**[1]	26.8[2]	17.7[2]
Cornercap Growth	**32.9**[1]	23.4[3]	16.4[3]
Scudder Large Cap Gro	**32.8**[1]	27.6[1]	15.5[3]
Permanent Agg Growth	**32.7**[1]	26.3[2]	19.9[1]
Babson Enterprise‡ SC	**32.4**[1]	23.2[3]	17.4[2]
Rainier Sm/Mid Cap	**32.2**[1]	33.7[1]	—
Value Line Spec Sit	**32.2**[1]	22.3[3]	15.8[3]
Schroder Ser:Sm Cap Val SC	**32.1**[1]	26.4[2]	—
Preferred Small Cap SC	**31.9**[1]	—	—
Schwab Analytics	**31.8**[1]	—	—
Stein Roe Growth Stk‡	**31.6**[1]	29.2[1]	16.4[3]
Harbor Cap App	**31.4**[1]	29.5[1]	20.3[1]
Gradison Oppty Value SC	**31.1**[1]	25.7[2]	16.6[3]
ni Micro-Cap‡SC	**30.9**[1]	—	—
Vangd Morgan	**30.8**[1]	29.9[1]	18.3[2]
Robrtsn Stph MicroCap Gro SC	**30.5**[1]	—	—
Barr Rosnbrg US Sm Cap††SC	**30.4**[1]	—	—
Bruce	**30.2**[1]	28.0[1]	16.0[3]
Eighteen - 1838 Sm Cap SC	**29.9**[1]	—	—
Northern Sm Cap SC	**29.8**[2]	23.7[3]	—
Janus Twenty	**29.7**[2]	31.2[1]	16.9[3]
Quaker Core Eqty	**29.6**[2]	—	—
First Eagle America	**29.5**[2]	31.7[1]	22.5[1]
C&O Market Opport	**29.4**[2]	24.3[3]	16.9[3]
Amer Cent-20th Cent Growth	**29.3**[2]	21.4[4]	12.8[4]
Nbrgr-Ber Manhtn	**29.2**[2]	22.9[3]	14.5[4]
Masters Sel Equity	**29.1**[2]	—	—
Wright Jr Blue Ch SC	**28.9**[2]	22.2[3]	13.9[4]
Quant Numeric II	**28.6**[2]	—	—
Lazard Small Cap SC(O shrs)	**28.1**[2]	24.5[2]	20.7[1]
Dreyfus Apprec	**27.8**[2]	30.4[1]	18.2[2]
Westcore Sm Cap Oppty SC	**27.8**[2]	27.6[2]	—
Kent Sm Co Gro SC	**27.7**[2]	23.4[3]	17.1[2]
Fidelity Small Cap Selector†† SC	**27.2**[2]	22.3[3]	—
Montgmry Micro Cap‡ SC	**27.1**[2]	24.9[2]	—
Schroder Cap:US Sm Co SC	**26.9**[2]	32.2[1]	—
Fidelity Magellan†‡	**26.5**[2]	24.6[2]	18.8[2]
Founders Growth	**26.5**[2]	29.0[1]	21.1[1]
Columbia Growth	**26.3**[2]	26.6[2]	17.9[2]
AMEX-Strategist Spec Gr	**26.3**[2]	—	—
Skyline Spcl Eqty II	**26.2**[2]	24.5[2]	—
Navellier Perf: Mid Cap	**26.2**[2]	—	—
Vintage Agg Gro	**26.2**[2]	—	—
Crabbe Hsn Small Cap SC	**26.1**[2]	—	—
Royce GiftShares	**26.0**[2]	—	—
Schwab Sm Cap Idx(Inv) SC	**25.7**[2]	22.8[3]	—
PBHG Strat Small Co SC	**25.7**[2]	—	—
UAM RHJ Small\MidCap SC	**25.7**[2]	—	—
Vangd Hrzn:Agg Gro	**25.5**[2]	—	—
Trent Equity	**25.2**[2]	19.9[4]	10.2[5]
BT Advs:Sm Cap Idx SC	**25.1**[2]	—	—
Invesco Small Co Val SC	**25.0**[2]	21.4[4]	—
Pathfinder SC	**24.9**[2]	22.4[3]	11.5[5]
Royce Micro-Cap SC	**24.7**[2]	19.7[4]	17.1[2]
Spectra	**24.7**[2]	30.1[1]	21.1[1]
Fidelity New Millnm†‡	**24.6**[2]	32.6[1]	24.0[1]
Managers Spec Eqty SC	**24.5**[2]	27.6[1]	19.1[1]
Warbg Pincus Strat Val	**24.2**[2]	—	—
Invesco Dynamics	**24.1**[2]	25.5[2]	18.2[2]
CA Inv Tr-Sm Cap Idx SC	**24.1**[2]	—	—
CGM Capital Dev‡	**23.9**[2]	30.8[1]	17.3[2]
Montgmry Sm Cap‡ SC	**23.9**[2]	25.7[2]	17.3[2]
Jurika & Voyles MiniCap SC	**23.9**[2]	35.6[1]	—
Value Line Levergd Gro	**23.8**[2]	27.6[2]	18.4[2]
Fidelity Export & Multi††SC	**23.7**[2]	31.4[1]	—
SSgA Sm Cap SC	**23.6**[3]	31.2[1]	20.4[1]
Galaxy II Sm Co Idx SC	**23.6**[3]	25.3[2]	16.1[3]
SAFECO Sm Cap Stk SC	**23.4**[3]	—	—
Schroder Cap:US Eqty	**23.3**[3]	24.3[3]	15.4[3]
Marshall Sm Cap Gro SC	**23.2**[3]	—	—
Amer Cent-20th Cent Ultra	**23.1**[3]	24.5[2]	17.8[2]
Trainer-Wrthm First Mutual	**23.1**[3]	29.7[1]	16.3[3]
LKCM Sm Cap SC	**23.1**[3]	26.8[2]	—
Scout Regional SC	**23.0**[3]	18.4[4]	12.1[5]
Fidelity Fifty	**23.0**[3]	22.9[3]	—
Fidelity Contrafund††‡	**23.0**[3]	26.9[2]	19.7[1]
JP Morgan US Sm Co SC	**22.8**[3]	25.0[2]	14.8[4]
O'Shaughnessy Agg Gr	**22.3**[3]	—	—
Warbg Pincus Small Co Gro SC	**22.3**[3]	—	—
Perritt Micro Cap Opp SC	**22.1**[3]	22.6[3]	13.0[4]
Legg Mason Spec Invest SC	**22.1**[3]	24.4[3]	15.7[3]
Rydex OTC	**21.9**[3]	35.3[1]	—
Dreyfus Agg Val SC	**21.6**[3]	—	—
Warbg Pincus Emg Gro SC	**21.3**[3]	24.9[2]	17.8[2]
Price New Amer	**21.1**[3]	28.0[1]	17.9[2]
Eastcliff Reg Sm Cap Val	**21.1**[3]	—	—
Harbor Growth	**20.9**[3]	22.9[3]	14.2[4]
UAM RHJ Sm Cap SC	**20.7**[3]	29.2[1]	—
Gateway Sm Cap Idx SC	**20.6**[3]	19.8[4]	—
Nations Emg Gro SC	**20.5**[3]	22.7[3]	15.7[3]
Federated Mini Cap SC	**20.4**[3]	20.6[4]	14.5[4]
Quaker Agg Gro	**20.3**[3]	—	—
Dreyfus New Leaders SC	**19.5**[3]	22.1[4]	16.3[3]

No-Load Fund	Total return percent with quintile ranks by objective			No-Load Fund	Total return percent with quintile ranks by objective		
	1997	Annualized 3 years	5 years		1997	Annualized 3 years	5 years
Kayne Anderson Sm-Mid Cap Ris Div....	19.5³	—	—	WPG Growth SC	9.7⁵	21.8⁴	12.3⁵
Fidelity Emg Gro††	19.4³	23.4³	17.6²	Stein Roe Spec Venture SC	9.7⁴	21.5⁴	—
Wasatch Agg Eqty‡ SC	19.2³	17.1⁵	15.8³	Warbg Pincus Post Vent	9.7⁵	—	—
Warbg Pincus Small Co Val SC	19.2³	—	—	Fidelity Trend	8.5⁵	15.7⁵	11.5⁵
Strong Growth	19.1³	26.1²	—	Lancaster Crest Sm Cap SC	8.5⁵	17.8⁴	13.5⁴
Markman Agg Alloc	19.0³	—	—	RSI Tr-Emg Gro SC	8.3⁵	25.3²	19.7¹
Value Line Multi-Nat'l Co	19.0³	—	—	Sit Sm Cap Gro SC	7.6⁵	23.5³	—
Fidelity Growth Co	18.9³	24.7²	17.1²	USAA Agg Growth SC	7.6⁵	23.5³	15.1³
Robrtsn Stph Emg Gro SC	18.5³	20.1⁴	14.9³	Quant Numeric SC	7.2⁵	21.3⁴	19.1¹
Invesco Sm Co Gro SC	18.3³	19.7⁴	15.3³	Fremont US Micro Cap SC	7.0⁵	34.8¹	—
Bridgeway Agg Gro	18.3³	25.7²	—	Scudder Development SC	6.9⁵	21.0⁴	12.8⁴
Robrtsn Stph Partners SC	18.1³	—	—	PBHG Select Eqty	6.8⁵	—	—
Fidelity TechnoQuant Gro	17.9³	—	—	Founders Frontier SC	6.2⁵	18.5⁴	13.5⁴
FTI Small Cap Eqty SC	17.8³	—	—	Stein Roe Cap Opp	6.2⁵	24.4³	19.7¹
IAI Cap Apprec SC	17.8³	—	—	Maxus Laureate	6.0⁵	13.6⁵	—
Sit Mid Cap Gro	17.7³	24.2³	15.7³	Oberweis Midcap	5.5⁵	—	—
Citizens Tr Emg Gr SC	17.7⁴	23.6³	—	Bull & Bear Spec Eqty	5.2⁵	14.3⁵	7.8⁵
Mosaic Mid-Cap Gro	17.1⁴	14.9⁵	10.9⁵	Rainbow Fund	5.0⁵	16.3⁵	7.4⁵
FundMngr Agg Gro†	16.7⁴	19.3⁴	13.9⁴	Capp-Rush Emg Growth SC	4.7⁵	13.3⁵	10.6⁵
Matrix Emg Growth SC	16.6⁴	—	—	Amer Cent New Opp SC	3.1⁵	—	—
Montgmry Sm Cap Opp SC	16.5⁴	—	—	Pin Oak Agg Stk SC	1.3⁵	15.5⁵	9.4⁵
Founders Special	16.4⁴	19.1⁴	13.2⁴	OVB Emg Gro SC	0.5⁵	15.2⁵	—
Amer Cent Strat Asst: Agg	16.2⁴	—	—	Wasatch MidCap	-0.5⁵	17.9⁴	11.5⁵
Seneca Mid-Cap Edge	16.2⁴	—	—	Reserve Sm Cap Gr SC	-0.5⁵	19.6⁴	—
Berger Sm Co Gro SC	16.2⁴	22.0⁴	—	Amer Cent-20th Cent Giftrust	-1.2⁵	13.1⁵	16.6³
PBHG Limited‡ SC	16.1⁴	—	—	PIC Sm Co Gro SC	-1.4⁵	—	—
Price Cap Oppty	15.9⁴	25.6²	—	IAI Emg Growth SC	-2.9⁵	15.8⁵	12.3⁵
Brown Cap Sm Co SC	15.8⁴	22.0⁴	15.0³	PBHG Growth	-3.3⁵	16.8⁵	19.6¹
BT Pyramid:Eqty App	15.4⁴	20.3⁴	—	PBHG Emg Growth SC	-3.7⁵	18.7⁴	—
Fairmont	15.3⁴	17.3⁵	14.9⁴	Prudent Bear	-4.3⁵	—	—
Federated Mgd Agg Gro	14.9⁴	16.4⁵	—	Strong Small Cap SC	-4.5⁵	—	—
TIP:Turner Small Cap SC‡	14.8⁴	35.5¹	—	Vangd Hrzn:Cap Opp	-8.0⁵	—	—
Vangd Explorer SC	14.6⁴	18.2⁴	13.9⁴	Oberweis Emg Growth SC	-8.6⁵	17.1⁵	11.2⁵
Excelsior Sm Cap SC	14.2⁴	11.1⁵	13.0⁴	Amer Cent-20th Cent Vista	-8.7⁵	12.8⁵	9.6⁵
Robrtsn Stph Val Gro	13.9⁴	22.8³	22.0¹	PBHG Core Growth	-9.7⁵	—	—
Heartland Small Cap Contra‡SC	13.7⁴	—	—	Van Wagoner Post Venture	-12.2⁵	—	—
Matterhorn Growth	13.7⁴	16.3⁵	11.9⁵	Steadman Amer Indust	-12.4⁵	-10.2⁵	-13.1⁵
Berger 100	13.6⁴	16.1⁵	12.1⁵	NewCap Contrarian	-13.1⁵	—	—
General Securities	13.4⁴	20.4⁴	14.3⁴	Dreyfus Agg Gr SC	-15.8⁵	—	—
BT Invest:Sm Cap SC	13.2⁴	24.3³	—	Van Wagoner Micro-Cap SC	-19.8⁵	—	—
Managers Cap App	12.7⁴	19.6⁴	14.5⁴	Van Wagoner Emg Gr	-20.0⁵	—	—
Columbia Special	12.6⁴	18.2⁴	15.5³	Rydex Ursa	-21.0⁵	-17.9⁵	—
Emerald Small Cap SC	12.6⁴	18.4⁴	—	Lindner Bulwark	-22.3⁵	-3.8⁵	—
Kaufmann SC	12.6⁴	23.0³	19.1¹	Fontaine Cap App	-27.3⁵	-1.2⁵	2.4⁵
Merriman Levgd Gro	12.2⁴	13.8⁵	8.8⁵	Steadman Tech & Gro	-28.2⁵	-28.9⁵	-26.9⁵
Brandywine	12.0⁴	23.8³	18.4²	Robrtsn Stph Contrn	-29.5⁵	3.9⁵	—
Founders Discovery SC	11.9⁴	21.2⁴	12.7⁴	**GROWTH FUNDS**			
Janus Mercury	11.9⁴	20.5⁴	—	FMI Focus	69.7¹	—	—
Wilshire Target Sm Gro SC	11.7⁴	17.7⁵	13.2⁴	Transamerica Premr Eqty	47.5¹	—	—
Value Line Sm Cap SC	11.5⁴	15.2⁵	—	Sequoia‡	43.2¹	35.1¹	23.0¹
Navellier Ser: Sm Cap Eq SC	11.2⁴	22.7³	—	Stratton Sm Cap Yld SC	42.6¹	27.8²	—
Crabbe Hsn Special SC	11.2⁴	9.3⁵	14.4⁴	Gabelli Growth	42.6¹	31.2¹	19.4²
WPG Tudor SC	11.1⁴	23.1³	13.8⁴	Quaker Sm Cap Val	41.5¹	—	—
Strong Discovery SC	10.8⁴	14.9⁵	11.8⁵	Weitz Ser Partners Value	40.6¹	32.4¹	—
Oberweis MicroCap SC	10.7⁴	—	—	Oakmark Small Cap ‡SC	40.5¹	—	—
US Glb:Bonnel Growth	10.3⁴	27.0²	—	Matthew 25	39.7¹	—	—
Fidelity OTC††	9.9⁴	23.4³	14.6⁴	Htchks & Wly Sm Cap SC	39.5¹	23.6⁴	16.5³
Price New Horizon‡ SC	9.8⁴	25.9²	19.6¹	Weitz Ser Hickory	39.2¹	38.3¹	—
Navellier Perf: Agg Gro SC	9.8⁴	—	—	FAM Value SC	39.1¹	22.8⁴	14.6⁴
Scudder 21st Cent GroSC	9.7⁴	—	—	UAM Strlng Sm Cap Val SC	38.8¹	—	—

| No-Load Fund | Total return percent with quintile ranks by objective | | | No-Load Fund | Total return percent with quintile ranks by objective | | |
	1997	Annualized 3 years	5 years		1997	Annualized 3 years	5 years
Gabelli Asset...	38.1[1]	25.1[3]	18.9[2]	State Farm Growth‡...	31.2[2]	26.3[2]	16.5[3]
Ariel Apprec...	37.9[1]	28.4[2]	15.9[4]	SAFECO Northwest Gr...	31.1[2]	21.9[4]	12.5[5]
Oak Value...	37.7[1]	31.8[1]	—	Federated Mid Cap...	31.1[2]	26.0[3]	16.3[3]
Legg Mason Total Ret...	37.5[1]	33.0[1]	20.0[1]	Vangd Idx Total Mkt...	31.0[2]	29.1[2]	18.9[2]
Northeast Inv Growth...	37.3[1]	32.7[1]	19.0[2]	Westcore Blue Chip...	30.9[2]	29.4[1]	19.6[2]
Torray...	37.1[1]	38.6[1]	23.7[1]	UAM TJ Core Eqty...	30.7[2]		
Legg Mason Value...	37.1[1]	38.7[1]	24.7[1]	Clipper...	30.4[2]	31.3[1]	19.7[2]
Scudder Small Cap Val SC...	37.0[1]	—	—	Nations Cap Gro...	30.4[2]	25.6[3]	16.0[4]
Nicholas II SC...	37.0[1]	28.1[2]	17.7[3]	JP Morgan Shrs Tax Aware Eqty...	30.3[2]	—	—
Nicholas Fund...	37.0[1]	30.5[1]	18.0[3]	Wayne Hummer Growth...	30.2[2]	22.1[4]	13.2[5]
Vangd Primecap...	36.8[1]	29.9[1]	23.6[1]	Northern Growth Eqty...	30.2[2]	24.6[3]	
Fountainhead Spec Val...	36.7[1]	—	—	Vintage Eqty...	30.1[2]	28.9[2]	18.2[2]
Sound Shore...	36.4[1]	33.2[1]	21.5[1]	UAM Sirach Eqty...	30.0[2]	—	—
Amer Cent Equity Growth...	36.1[1]	32.6[1]	21.0[1]	IBJ Core Eqty...	29.9[2]	—	—
Domini Social Eqty...	36.0[1]	30.8[1]	18.9[2]	Papp L Roy Amer Abroad...	29.9[2]	31.5[1]	19.5[2]
Daruma MidCap Value...	35.9[1]	—	—	Analytic Enhncd Eqty...	29.9[2]	29.3[1]	—
Green Cent Equity...	35.7[1]	—	—	Excelsior Blended Eqty...	29.8[2]	26.1[3]	18.5[2]
Dreyfus Premier MidCap‡...	35.6[1]	33.2[1]	—	Sentry...	29.7[2]	26.7[2]	16.4[3]
Pinnacle Fund...	35.4[1]	31.0[1]	18.1[3]	Nations Disc Eqty...	29.6[2]	26.2[3]	—
Scudder Value...	35.3[1]	29.4[1]	19.7[1]	Robrtsn Stph Divrsfd Gro...	29.6[2]	—	—
Citizens Tr Idx...	35.0[1]	—	—	Dreyfus Third Cent...	29.4[2]	29.7[1]	16.3[3]
Nbrgr-Ber Genesis ‡SC...	34.9[1]	30.7[1]	20.1[1]	Strong Schafer Value...	29.3[2]	28.8[2]	20.4[1]
Scudder Classic Gro‡...	34.9[1]	—	—	Flex-Fund Highlands Gro...	29.3[2]	20.7[4]	13.3[5]
Janus Gro & Inc...	34.7[1]	32.3[1]	18.6[2]	Lake Forest Core Eqty...	29.2[2]	—	—
Matrix Growth...	34.6[1]	25.2[3]	15.3[4]	Fiduciary Cap Growth SC...	29.2[2]	24.2[3]	17.1[3]
SSgA Matrix Eqty...	34.2[1]	28.6[2]	19.8[1]	Nbrgr-Ber Partners...	29.2[2]	30.3[1]	20.4[1]
Baron Asset SC...	33.9[1]	30.2[1]	24.0[1]	Monetta MidCap...	29.1[2]	25.9[3]	—
Rainier Core Eqty...	33.9[1]	34.4[1]	—	Focus Trust...	29.1[2]	—	—
McM Eqty Invest...	33.8[1]	32.1[1]	—	AIT Vision: US Equity...	29.1[2]	—	—
Excelsior Val & Restruc...	33.6[1]	32.4[1]	27.2[1]	Longleaf Partners Sm Cap‡SC...	29.0[2]	26.0[3]	19.9[1]
Fidelity Discpl Eqty...	33.3[1]	25.6[3]	18.4[2]	Gateway Cincinnati...	29.0[2]	27.9[2]	—
Accessor Growth...	33.2[1]	29.2[2]	20.7[1]	Aquinas Eqty Gro...	29.0[2]	27.4[2]	—
Papp L Roy Stock...	33.1[1]	29.2[2]	16.7[3]	Fremont Growth...	29.0[2]	29.2[2]	18.2[2]
ni Growth and Value...	33.1[1]	—	—	Fidelity Stk Selector...	28.9[2]	27.2[2]	18.8[2]
Nicholas Ltd Edit SC...	33.0[1]	28.3[2]	17.4[3]	Price Sm Cap Stk...	28.8[2]	27.8[2]	19.9[1]
Salomon Opportunity...	33.0[1]	29.0[2]	19.6[2]	Capstone Growth...	28.7[2]	24.9[3]	13.8[5]
PBHG Large Cap 20...	33.0[1]	—	—	Mairs & Power Gro...	28.7[2]	34.4[1]	23.7[1]
Ameristock...	32.9[1]	—	—	Women's Equity...	28.6[2]	19.9[4]	—
Oakmark...	32.6[1]	27.5[2]	22.8[1]	Longleaf Partners‡...	28.2[2]	25.5[3]	21.4[1]
Scudder Large Cap Val...	32.5[1]	27.7[2]	17.7[3]	Schwartz Value SC...	28.0[2]	21.0[4]	—
Croft Leom Value...	32.5[1]	—	—	Dreyfus MidCap Val...	28.0[2]	—	—
Thompson Plumb Growth...	32.4[1]	32.0[1]	18.6[2]	Babson Growth...	28.0[2]	27.0[2]	17.6[3]
Acorn USA SC...	32.3[1]	—	—	PIC Growth...	28.0[2]	24.0[3]	13.4[5]
Wilshire Target Lg Gro...	32.2[1]	31.4[1]	18.2[2]	Price Sm Cap Value‡ SC...	27.9[3]	27.3[2]	20.2[1]
Amer Cent-20th Cent Select...	32.2[1]	24.6[3]	15.3[4]	Fidelity Divnd Growth...	27.9[3]	31.8[1]	—
UAM Sirach Growth...	32.1[2]	28.2[2]	—	Seneca Growth...	27.9[3]		
Preferred Growth...	31.9[2]	26.2[3]	18.2[2]	Govt Street Equity...	27.8[3]	25.6[3]	14.7[4]
CA Inv Tr-S&P MidCap...	31.9[2]	27.0[2]	17.3[3]	Globalt Growth...	27.8[3]	—	—
RCM Large Cap Growth...	31.9[2]	—	—	Fairport Midwest Gr...	27.7[3]	23.8[4]	—
Northern Select Eqty...	31.9[2]	27.4[2]	—	RNC Equity...	27.7[3]	—	—
Montag & Cldwl Growth...	31.9[2]	34.4[1]	—	Babson Shadow Stk SC...	27.6[3]	24.2[3]	16.1[4]
Excelsior Instit Eqty...	31.7[2]	—	—	Nations Mngd Small Cap Idx SC...	27.6[3]	—	—
Sit Large Cap Gro...	31.7[2]	28.8[2]	17.7[3]	Price Blue Chip...	27.5[3]	31.0[1]	—
Lindner/Ryback Small Cap SC...	31.7[2]	26.5[2]	—	Wasatch Growth...	27.5[3]	27.8[2]	18.9[2]
Dreyfus MidCap Idx...	31.6[2]	26.6[2]	17.2[3]	FundMngr Growth†...	27.5[3]	24.9[3]	16.9[3]
Gintel...	31.5[2]	31.2[1]	14.0[4]	Vangd Tax Mgd:Cap App...	27.3[3]	27.4[2]	—
Warbg Pincus Cap App...	31.4[2]	30.8[1]	20.3[1]	Invesco Growth...	27.2[3]	25.9[3]	16.5[3]
TIP:Turner Growth Eqty...	31.4[2]	26.9[2]	17.1[3]	Price Mid Cap Val...	27.1[3]	—	—
O'Shaughnessy Cornrstn Gro...	31.3[2]	—	—	Fidelity Mid-Cap Stk...	27.1[3]	26.2[3]	—
Wilshire Target Sm Val SC...	31.2[2]	23.2[4]	14.7[4]	OVB Cap App...	27.0[3]	25.3[3]	—

Stock and bond funds – ranked within objective *continued*

By 1997 performance

No-Load Fund	Total return percent with quintile ranks by objective			No-Load Fund	Total return percent with quintile ranks by objective		
	1997	Annualized 3 years	5 years		1997	Annualized 3 years	5 years
Fidelity Blue Chip Gro††	27.0[3]	23.5[4]	20.8[1]	PBHG Large Cap Gro	22.4[4]	—	—
Dreyfus LifeTime Growth	27.0[3]	—	—	Robrtsn Stph Gro & Inc	22.3[4]	—	—
Selected Spec Shares	26.9[3]	23.4[4]	15.2[4]	Capp-Rush Growth	22.2[4]	21.5[4]	16.5[3]
Janus Olympus	26.7[3]	—	—	Vangd LifeStrat:Growth	22.1[4]	22.1[4]	—
Fidelity Low Pr Stk†† ‡SC	26.7[3]	26.2[3]	20.4[1]	First Omaha Small Cap Val	21.8[4]	—	—
Vangd Idx Extend Mkt†	26.7[3]	25.9[3]	17.5[3]	CRM Small Cap Value SC	21.7[4]	—	—
Price Gro Stk	26.6[3]	26.4[2]	18.7[2]	Value Line Fund	21.6[4]	25.3[3]	15.0[4]
Sextant Growth	26.6[3]	21.1[4]	11.6[5]	Fasciano SC	21.5[4]	26.3[2]	17.7[3]
GMO: Pelican	26.5[3]	25.6[3]	19.7[2]	Fidelity Freedom 2030	21.4[4]	—	—
Fidelity Cap Apprec	26.5[3]	20.0[4]	18.8[2]	Fidelity Value	21.1[4]	21.6[4]	18.9[2]
Chicago Tr Talon	26.5[3]	26.7[2]	—	Scout Stock	21.0[4]	17.0[5]	12.8[5]
Stein Roe Young Invest	26.3[3]	33.6[1]	—	Schwab Asst Dir: Hi Gro	21.0[4]	—	—
Monetta Fund	26.2[3]	18.0[5]	9.1[5]	UAM Mckee Domestic Eqty	20.9[4]	—	—
Kiewit Eqty Fund	26.1[3]	—	—	Royce PMF II SC	20.8[4]	—	—
Dreyfus Sm Co Val SC	26.0[3]	32.0[1]	—	Bender Growth	20.8[4]	—	—
Stein Roe Special	25.9[3]	21.1[4]	15.6[4]	AMEX-Strategist Growth	20.6[4]	—	—
Strong Value	25.9[3]	—	—	Price Pers Str-Gro	20.5[4]	23.1[4]	—
Vangd US Growth	25.9[3]	30.0[1]	17.6[3]	Wade	20.3[4]	18.0[5]	12.1[5]
Crabbe Hsn Equity	25.7[3]	21.1[4]	17.8[3]	KPM Equity	20.1[4]	27.1[2]	—
C\FUNDS:Growth Stk	25.5[3]	22.9[4]	11.7[5]	Wm Blair Growth	20.1[4]	22.3[4]	17.6[3]
Reserve Blue Chip Gro	25.5[3]	22.8[4]	—	IAA Trust Growth	19.7[4]	24.2[3]	15.3[4]
WPG Quant Eqty	25.5[3]	25.6[3]	—	Delafield Fund	19.7[4]	24.4[3]	—
Emerald Eqty	25.4[3]	26.6[2]	14.6[4]	IAI Value	19.6[4]	21.9[4]	15.0[4]
FBP Contrn Eqty	25.4[3]	26.2[3]	—	Academy Value	19.5[4]	12.7[5]	—
Sefton Value Eqty	25.3[3]	—	—	Royce Low Priced Stk SC	19.5[4]	21.6[4]	—
Dreyfus Premier Core Value‡	25.2[3]	27.3[2]	19.2[2]	Markman Moderate Alloc	19.4[4]	—	—
Lazard Equity(O shrs)	25.1[3]	27.4[2]	20.6[1]	Lancaster Cap Builder	19.4[4]	—	—
Gateway MidCap Idx	25.0[3]	21.9[4]	12.6[5]	Analysts Inv Stk	19.4[4]	17.9[5]	—
Acorn SC	25.0[3]	22.3[4]	17.5[3]	Amer Cent-20th Cent Heritage	19.3[4]	20.3[4]	14.5[4]
Royce Penn Mutual SC	24.9[3]	18.7[5]	13.1[5]	Brandywine Blue	19.3[4]	24.8[3]	20.4[1]
UAM Strlng Part Eqty	24.9[3]	27.6[2]	17.6[3]	Meridian	19.2[4]	17.3[5]	12.9[5]
Fidelity Large Cap	24.7[3]	—	—	IAI Growth	19.2[4]	19.2[5]	—
AMEX-Strategist Growth Trend	24.7[3]	—	—	IMG Core Stock Fd	19.1[4]	—	—
Vangd Idx Sm Cap† SC	24.5[3]	23.7[4]	17.5[3]	Haven Fund	19.1[4]	24.4[3]	16.6[3]
Nbrgr-Ber Social Resp	24.4[3]	27.0[2]	—	Reserve Infmd Invstr	19.0[4]	16.3[5]	—
White Oak Gro	24.3[3]	35.9[1]	21.6[1]	UAM Chi Asst Mgmt Val Contra	18.9[4]	19.6[5]	—
SwissKey US Eqty	24.2[3]	—	—	IAI Regional	18.9[4]	22.2[4]	14.8[4]
Berger New Generation	24.2[3]	—	—	Quaker Sector Alloc	18.5[4]	—	—
Buffalo Equity	24.2[3]	—	—	Fidelity Retrmnt Gro	18.5[4]	16.9[5]	14.3[4]
Montgmry Growth	24.1[3]	22.6[4]	—	Royce Premier SC	18.4[5]	18.1[5]	15.2[4]
Nbrgr-Ber Focus	24.1[3]	25.2[3]	18.2[2]	Schwab OneSource Gro Alloc	18.4[5]	—	—
Strong Common Stk‡	24.0[4]	25.5[3]	19.8[1]	Price Mid Cap Gro	18.3[5]	27.7[2]	21.4[1]
Third Ave Value	23.9[4]	25.8[3]	19.4[2]	Volumetric	18.3[5]	17.0[5]	9.9[5]
Legg Mason Amer Lead	23.8[4]	25.0[3]	—	Nbrgr-Ber Guardian	17.9[5]	22.5[4]	16.1[4]
LKCM Eqty	23.6[4]	—	—	Sand Hill Port Mgr	17.8[5]	16.3[5]	—
BT Pyramid:Instit Asst Mgt	23.5[4]	21.0[4]	—	Advance Cap Eqty Gro	17.7[5]	24.0[3]	—
Strong Opportunity	23.4[4]	22.9[4]	18.3[2]	Price Spect-Gro	17.4[5]	22.5[4]	17.7[3]
UAM DSI Discpnd Val	23.4[4]	25.9[3]	18.1[2]	Leuthold Asst Alloc	17.3[5]	—	—
Heartland Value‡SC	23.2[4]	24.6[3]	18.5[2]	Jhaveri Value	17.2[5]	—	—
Unified Starwood Strat	23.1[4]	—	—	Key Choice:Growth‡	16.9[5]	—	—
BT Invest:Lifecycle Long Range	23.0[4]	20.6[4]	—	Price Cap App	16.2[5]	18.5[5]	14.8[4]
Bridgeway Soc Resp	22.9[4]	23.0[4]	—	Amana Growth	15.7[5]	18.1[5]	—
Heartland Large Cap Val	22.9[4]	—	—	Needham Growth	15.7[5]	—	—
Heartland Mid Cap Val	22.8[4]	—	—	ni Growth SC‡	15.6[5]	—	—
Marshall Mid-Cap Gro	22.7[4]	25.6[3]	—	TIP:Clover Cap Sm Cap Val SC	15.5[5]	—	—
Janus Fund	22.7[4]	23.8[4]	15.8[4]	Amer Cent Strat Asst: Mod	15.2[5]	—	—
Artisan Small Cap SC‡	22.7[4]	—	—	Dreyfus Growth Opp	15.1[5]	21.8[4]	11.5[5]
Brown Cap Equity	22.7[4]	24.6[3]	15.3[4]	Kobren Insight:Growth	15.0[5]	—	—
Henlopen Fund	22.6[4]	27.1[2]	21.0[1]	Scudder Pathway Growth	14.9[5]	—	—
Eastcliff Growth	22.4[4]	—	—	Westcore MIDCO Gro	14.9[5]	19.6[4]	14.8[4]

No-Load Fund	Total return percent with quintile ranks by objective			No-Load Fund	Total return percent with quintile ranks by objective		
		Annualized				Annualized	
	1997	3 years	5 years		1997	3 years	5 years
Reynolds Opportunity	14.6[5]	21.2[4]	12.7[5]	SSgA S&P 500	33.1[1]	30.8[1]	20.0[1]
Nations LifeGoal Gro	14.6[5]	—	—	Amer AAdv Mileage S&P 500 Idx	33.1[1]	—	—
Oak Hall Equity	14.5[5]	13.8[5]	13.1[5]	USAA S & P Idx	33.0[1]	—	—
BT Invest:Cap App	14.5[5]	19.6[5]	—	BT Pyramid:Eqty 500 Idx	33.0[1]	30.9[1]	19.9[1]
Federated Mgd Growth	14.3[5]	15.6[5]	—	Fidelity Spart Market Idx	33.0[1]	30.7[1]	19.9[2]
Armstrong Assoc	14.2[5]	14.2[5]	12.5[5]	CA Inv Tr-S&P 500	33.0[1]	30.8[1]	19.9[1]
Strong MidCap	13.9[5]	—	—	Accessor Val & Inc	33.0[1]	30.0[2]	19.8[2]
Reich & Tang Eqty	13.8[5]	19.5[5]	14.6[5]	Price Eqty 500 Idx	32.9[1]	30.8[1]	19.8[2]
Janus Venture‡SC	13.1[5]	15.6[5]	12.2[5]	AON S & P 500	32.8[1]	—	—
Pragma Provident	13.0[5]	—	—	Galaxy II Lg Co Idx	32.8[1]	30.7[1]	19.8[2]
Gabelli ABC	12.8[5]	10.6[5]	—	Unified Laidlaw	32.8[1]	—	—
Key SBSF Fund‡	12.3[5]	21.5[4]	15.3[4]	Reserve Lrg Cap Val	32.7[1]	—	—
CitiSelect 500	12.0[5]	—	—	Wright Sel Blue Ch	32.7[1]	27.1[3]	15.1[4]
Dreyfus Lg Co Gr	11.7[5]	19.4[5]	—	Federated Max Cap	32.7[1]	30.6[1]	19.8[2]
Merger‡	11.7[5]	11.9[5]	12.1[5]	Northern Stock Idx	32.7[1]	—	—
Price New Era	10.9[5]	18.5[5]	15.1[4]	Dreyfus S&P 500 Idx	32.6[1]	30.4[1]	19.6[2]
Janus Enterprise	10.8[5]	16.3[5]	14.7[4]	Schwab S & P 500(Inv)	32.5[1]	—	—
Lexington Sm Cap Value SC	10.5[5]	—	—	Eclipse Gro & Inc	32.5[1]	27.2[3]	—
Merriman Cap App	9.9[5]	11.6[5]	7.5[5]	Key Stock Idx‡	32.4[1]	—	—
Key SBSF Capital Gro‡	9.1[5]	14.7[5]	—	Vangd Windsor II	32.3[2]	31.6[1]	20.7[1]
USAA Growth Strat	9.1[5]	—	—	Smith Brdn Eqty Plus	32.3[2]	31.0[1]	21.0[1]
Lighthouse Growth	9.0[5]	—	—	Kent Idx Eqty	32.2[2]	29.8[2]	19.3[2]
Crowley Gro & Inc	9.0[5]	8.9[5]	6.7[5]	Fidelity Fund	32.1[2]	28.1[2]	20.6[1]
Lepercq-Istel	8.9[5]	20.5[4]	13.5[5]	Nations Eqty Idx	32.0[2]	—	—
IAI MidCap	8.9[5]	17.0[5]	15.7[4]	Dreyfus Discpl Stock	31.9[2]	31.2[1]	20.1[1]
Lindner Growth	8.7[5]	16.4[5]	13.4[5]	Stagecoach Eqty Idx Stk	31.9[2]	29.7[2]	19.0[2]
Reserve Mid Cap Gro	7.9[5]	—	—	Schwab 1000(Inv)	31.9[2]	29.9[2]	19.1[2]
Shelby Fund SC	6.2[5]	17.9[5]	—	RSI Tr-Value Eqty	31.7[2]	30.5[1]	18.9[2]
Valley Forge	6.0[5]	7.6[5]	9.1[5]	Reynolds Blue Chip Gr	31.5[2]	30.8[1]	16.1[4]
USAA Growth	3.7[5]	17.3[5]	12.4[5]	Harbor Value	31.2[2]	28.7[2]	18.4[3]
Rockwood	3.5[5]	17.7[5]	13.6[5]	Htchks & Wly Eq Inc	31.2[2]	27.4[3]	18.3[3]
Mathers	3.0[5]	3.3[5]	1.1[5]	Boston Prtnrs Large Cap	31.1[2]	—	—
Steadman Investment	1.1[5]	-1.8[5]	-8.4[5]	Janus Equity Inc	31.1[2]	—	—
American Heritage Gro	-2.9[5]	5.4[5]	—	Baron Gro & Inc	31.1[2]	36.7[1]	—
Rightime	-3.3[5]	10.0[5]	7.7[5]	AARP Gro & Inc	31.0[2]	28.1[2]	20.2[1]
Van Wagoner Mid-Cap	-13.9[5]	—	—	Kayne Anderson Ris Div	31.0[2]	—	—
Amtrust Value SC	-20.1[5]	-5.9[5]	—	Price Div Gro	30.8[2]	29.3[2]	21.4[1]
GROWTH-INCOME FUNDS				UAM NWQ Value Eqty	30.8[2]	27.2[3]	—
Weitz Value	38.9[1]	31.7[1]	19.8[2]	Payden & Rygel Mkt Ret	30.7[2]	—	—
Tweedy Brown Amer Val	38.9[1]	32.3[1]	—	Heartland Val Plus	30.6[2]	29.5[2]	—
SSgA Gro & Inc	37.7[1]	29.1[2]	—	Strong Gr & Inc	30.4[2]	—	—
Selected Amer Shares	37.3[1]	35.3[1]	20.4[1]	Lexington Gro & Inc	30.3[2]	26.4[3]	17.3[3]
Quant Gro & Inc	36.7[1]	28.1[2]	18.5[3]	Fairport Gr & Inc	30.3[2]	25.5[3]	—
WPG Growth & Inc	36.3[1]	31.0[1]	18.4[3]	US Glb:All-Amer Eqty	30.3[2]	27.8[2]	16.8[4]
Vangd Idx Growth	36.3[1]	32.6[1]	19.5[2]	Scudder Gro & Inc	30.3[2]	27.8[2]	19.9[2]
Stratton Growth	36.1[1]	28.9[2]	19.5[2]	Warbg Pincus Gro & Inc	30.2[2]	15.7[5]	18.0[3]
Philadelphia	35.8[1]	24.9[3]	15.9[4]	Kenwood Gro & Inc	30.2[2]	—	—
Vangd Gro & Inc	35.6[1]	31.4[1]	20.7[1]	Quaker Enhnd Stk Market	30.2[2]	—	—
Mosaic Investors	34.8[1]	27.3[3]	17.1[3]	Fidelity Gro & Inc‡	30.2[2]	28.4[2]	20.9[1]
Dreyfus Premier Lrg Co‡	34.6[1]	30.6[1]	—	Wilshire Target Lg Val	30.2[2]	29.1[2]	18.2[3]
Federated Stock	34.4[1]	30.2[1]	19.9[2]	Gradison Gro & Inc	30.1[2]	—	—
Vontobel US Value	34.3[1]	31.8[1]	19.4[2]	Fidelity Eqty Inc	30.0[2]	27.5[2]	20.3[1]
Amer Cent Inc & Gro	34.3[1]	31.6[1]	20.3[1]	Vangd Idx Value	29.8[2]	29.4[2]	20.5[1]
Wright Major Blue Chip	33.9[1]	26.6[3]	15.3[4]	UAM ICM Equity	29.6[2]	29.8[2]	—
Vangd Tax Mgd:Gro & Inc	33.3[1]	31.1[1]	—	Westwood Equity	29.6[2]	31.0[1]	21.9[1]
Muhlenkamp	33.3[1]	32.1[1]	20.4[1]	UBS US Eqty	29.6[2]	—	—
Cutler Approved List	33.3[1]	27.5[2]	17.0[3]	Vangd Trust US	29.5[2]	27.9[2]	18.7[2]
Vangd Idx 500	33.2[1]	31.0[1]	20.1[1]	Emerald Eqty Val	29.4[2]	—	—
Nations Mngd Idx	33.2[1]	—	—	Price Value	29.2[2]	32.4[1]	—
Transamerica Premr Idx	33.1[1]	—	—	Concorde Value	29.1[3]	23.6[4]	14.9[4]

No-Load Fund	Total return percent with quintile ranks by objective			No-Load Fund	Total return percent with quintile ranks by objective		
	1997	Annualized 3 years	5 years		1997	Annualized 3 years	5 years
ICAP Equity...	29.1[3]	31.3[1]	—	Mutual Beacon Z‡...	22.9[4]	23.3[4]	19.5[2]
MSB...	28.9[3]	25.0[3]	18.3[3]	Scudder Balanced...	22.7[4]	20.1[5]	—
Blanchard Gro & Inc‡...	28.9[3]	24.0[4]	—	Berger Gro & Inc...	22.7[4]	20.7[5]	14.5[5]
Independence One Eqty Plus...	28.7[3]	—	—	Gradison Estab Value...	22.6[4]	22.6[4]	17.8[3]
ICAP Discret Equity...	28.6[3]	29.7[2]	—	Thompson Plumb Balanced...	22.5[4]	21.9[4]	13.9[5]
JP Morgan US Eqty...	28.4[3]	27.2[3]	17.8[3]	Excelsior Inc & Gro...	22.1[4]	23.6[4]	16.6[4]
Maxus Equity...	28.4[3]	23.3[4]	18.6[3]	Vangd Windsor‡...	22.0[4]	26.1[3]	19.1[2]
Dodge & Cox Stock...	28.4[3]	28.0[2]	21.1[1]	UAM FPA Crescent...	22.0[4]	23.6[4]	—
Amer Cent Equity Inc...	28.3[3]	27.4[3]	—	Meyers Sheppard Pride...	21.8[4]	—	—
Elite Gro & Inc...	28.2[3]	28.8[2]	18.6[3]	Vista Amer Value...	21.8[4]	—	—
Preferred Value...	28.0[3]	30.2[1]	19.3[2]	IPS Millenium...	21.4[4]	23.6[4]	—
Invesco Value Eqty...	28.0[3]	25.6[3]	17.9[3]	Meridian Value...	21.4[4]	25.7[3]	—
UAM C & B Eqty...	28.0[3]	26.6[3]	16.5[4]	Fidelity Freedom 2020...	21.2[4]	—	—
Aquinas Eqty Inc...	27.9[3]	27.8[2]	—	Bridges Investment...	21.1[4]	23.1[4]	14.8[4]
Marshall Eqty Inc...	27.5[3]	27.5[2]	—	Preferred Asst Allocc...	21.0[4]	22.8[4]	14.8[4]
BSR Equity...	27.3[3]	24.5[4]	16.2[4]	C\FUNDS:C\FUND...	21.0[4]	21.0[5]	14.2[5]
Westcore Gro & Inc...	27.3[3]	24.3[4]	14.4[5]	Northern Inc Eqty...	20.8[4]	19.9[5]	—
Fidelity Eqty Inc II...	27.2[3]	24.0[4]	18.5[3]	Boston-1784 Asst Alloc...	20.7[4]	20.0[5]	—
UAM IRC Enhcd Idx...	27.2[3]	—	—	Vangd Star:Star...	20.5[4]	21.7[4]	14.8[4]
Payden & Rygel Gro & Inc...	26.9[3]	—	—	Dreyfus LifeTime Gr & Inc...	20.4[4]	—	—
Chicago Tr Gro & Inc...	26.7[3]	29.2[2]	—	Vangd LifeStrat:Mod Gr...	19.7[4]	19.9[5]	—
Homestead Value...	26.7[3]	26.0[3]	19.5[2]	Boston-1784 Gro & Inc...	19.7[5]	24.5[4]	—
Monetta Large Cap Eqty...	26.6[3]	—	—	AMEX-Strategist Equity...	19.6[5]	—	—
Babson Value...	26.5[3]	26.9[3]	20.8[1]	First Omaha Eqty...	19.3[5]	20.6[5]	15.9[4]
Invesco Indust Inc...	26.4[3]	23.4[4]	16.1[4]	Analytic Defnsve Eqty...	19.1[5]	18.7[5]	12.8[5]
Fidelity Asst Mgr Gro...	26.4[3]	21.3[4]	15.8[4]	USAA Balanced Strat...	19.1[5]	—	—
Mutual Shares Z‡...	26.3[3]	25.4[3]	20.0[1]	Founders Blue Chip...	19.0[5]	24.1[4]	17.1[3]
Nations Value...	26.3[3]	27.5[2]	18.4[3]	Lipper US Eqty...	18.6[5]	—	—
Schroder Ser:Lg Cap Eqty...	26.3[3]	24.8[3]	—	Flex-Fund Muirfield...	18.6[5]	16.5[5]	11.9[5]
Marshall Lg Cap Gr & Inc...	26.2[3]	24.5[4]	13.4[5]	BT Invest:Lifecycle Mid Range...	18.5[5]	16.2[5]	—
Montgmry Eqty Inc...	26.1[3]	26.3[3]	—	C\FUNDS:Adams Equity...	18.5[5]	—	—
Amer AAdv Mileage Gro & Inc...	26.1[3]	26.7[3]	—	Yacktman...	18.3[5]	24.8[3]	14.6[5]
Weston: New Cent Cap...	26.1[3]	22.8[4]	16.1[4]	Primary Trend...	18.2[5]	21.3[4]	14.7[4]
Berwyn‡...	26.1[3]	19.8[5]	17.0[3]	Matrix\LMH Value...	17.9[5]	19.8[5]	13.6[5]
USAA Gro & Inc...	26.0[3]	26.8[3]	—	Price Pers Str-Bal...	17.8[5]	19.9[5]	—
Amer Cent Value...	26.0[3]	27.8[2]	—	TIP:Clover Cap Eqty Val...	17.5[5]	20.6[5]	18.0[3]
UAM TS&W Eqty...	26.0[3]	24.5[4]	16.7[4]	Vangd Selected Val...	17.4[5]	—	—
Stein Roe Gro & Inc...	25.7[3]	25.9[3]	17.6[3]	Amer Cent Balanced...	16.9[5]	17.2[5]	11.5[5]
PBHG Large Cap Val...	25.6[3]	—	—	SCM Portfolio...	16.3[5]	14.0[5]	9.3[5]
Columbia Common Stk...	25.4[3]	25.6[3]	18.7[3]	Dreyfus Lg Co Val...	16.0[5]	29.7[2]	—
RSI Tr-Core Eqty...	25.3[3]	28.8[2]	19.0[2]	Dreyfus Gro & Inc...	16.0[5]	18.4[5]	13.3[5]
FundMngr Gro & Inc†...	25.3[4]	24.3[4]	16.7[4]	US Glb:MegaTrends...	15.6[5]	18.3[5]	10.6[5]
API Cap Inc...	25.2[4]	23.3[4]	15.4[4]	O'Shaughnessy Cornrstn Val...	15.3[5]	—	—
Copley...	25.1[4]	18.2[5]	10.9[5]	Key Choice:Mod Gro‡...	14.8[5]	—	—
Mutual Qualified Z‡...	24.8[4]	24.2[4]	20.0[1]	Schwab Asst Dir: Cons Gr...	14.7[5]	—	—
ASM Idx 30...	24.5[4]	26.1[3]	18.1[3]	Markman Conserv Alloc...	14.3[5]	—	—
SAFECO Equity...	24.2[4]	24.8[3]	22.9[1]	FundMngr Mgd Tot Ret†...	13.5[5]	13.6[5]	9.6[5]
Strong Total Ret...	24.2[4]	21.6[4]	16.8[4]	Merriman Gro & Inc...	13.1[5]	15.3[5]	9.4[5]
IAI Gro & Inc...	23.9[4]	23.7[4]	14.7[4]	Federated Gro & Inc...	13.0[5]	12.9[5]	—
Kent Gro & Inc...	23.9[4]	25.7[3]	18.0[3]	Crowley Dvsfd Mngmt...	13.0[5]	—	—
Greenspring...	23.9[4]	21.7[4]	16.3[4]	Amer Cent Strat Asst: Cons...	12.8[5]	—	—
Stonebridge Growth...	23.7[4]	21.2[4]	12.5[5]	Gateway Idx Plus...	12.3[5]	11.3[5]	9.3[5]
Royce Total Ret...	23.7[4]	25.3[3]	—	ZSA Asst Alloc...	12.3[5]	16.1[5]	9.8[5]
Profit Value...	23.6[4]	—	—	UAM Sirach Spec Eqty...	11.3[5]	19.3[5]	13.5[5]
Price Gro & Inc...	23.5[4]	26.6[3]	18.1[3]	Dreyfus Fund...	10.7[5]	16.7[5]	10.1[5]
Royce REvest Gro & Inc...	23.5[4]	20.6[5]	—	AMEX-Strategist Total Ret...	10.3[5]	—	—
Marshall Mid-Cap Val...	23.4[4]	20.8[5]	—	CitiSelect 400...	10.3[5]	—	—
Kobren Insight:Mod Gro...	23.3[4]	—	—	Nations LifeGoal Inc & Gro...	8.5[5]	—	—
Lexington Corp Ldrs...	23.1[4]	28.0[2]	19.5[2]	CGM Mutual...	8.2[5]	18.5[5]	12.8[5]
Jensen Portfolio...	23.0[4]	23.9[4]	11.6[5]	IMS Cap Val...	6.7[5]	—	—

No-Load Fund	Total return percent with quintile ranks by objective			No-Load Fund	Total return percent with quintile ranks by objective		
	1997	Annualized 3 years	5 years		1997	Annualized 3 years	5 years
INCOME FUNDS				Monetta Balanced	**21.2**[3]	—	—
Amer Cent Util	**35.7**[1]	24.4[1]	—	Dodge & Cox Balanced	**21.2**[3]	21.2[2]	16.1[2]
Transamerica Premr Balanced	**35.4**[1]	—	—	Brown Cap Balanced	**21.0**[3]	21.4[2]	13.4[3]
Carl Domino Eqty Inc	**35.4**[1]	—	—	Value Line Asst Alloc	**20.9**[3]	27.7[1]	—
Cutler Eqty Income	**33.4**[1]	28.5[1]	16.7[1]	Leonetti Balanced	**20.9**[3]	—	—
Fidelity Utilities	**31.6**[1]	24.2[1]	16.0[2]	UAM NWQ Balanced	**20.9**[3]	19.0[4]	—
AON Asst Alloc	**31.5**[1]	24.8[1]	—	FBP Contrn Balanced	**20.7**[3]	20.9[2]	14.7[2]
Strong Eqty Inc	**31.3**[1]	—	—	AMEX-Strategist Balanced	**20.7**[3]	—	—
Vangd Equity Inc	**31.2**[1]	28.4[1]	19.0[1]	Kobren Insight:Cons Alloc	**20.7**[3]	—	—
Eastcliff Total Ret	**30.0**[1]	24.5[1]	16.0[2]	Advance Cap Balanced	**20.5**[3]	22.0[2]	13.1[3]
Mairs & Power Inc	**29.4**[1]	—	—	Vangd Wellesley Inc	**20.2**[3]	19.2[4]	13.2[3]
CA Inv Tr-Eqty Inc	**29.3**[1]	—	—	Parnassus Balanced	**20.2**[3]	19.1[4]	13.1[4]
Dreyfus Asst Alloc	**28.9**[1]	22.3[2]	—	Avondale Total Ret	**20.1**[3]	17.4[5]	12.1[5]
Price Eqty Inc	**28.8**[1]	27.4[1]	19.9[1]	Aquinas Balanced	**19.9**[3]	19.4[3]	—
Flex-Fund Tot Ret Util	**28.7**[1]	—	—	Lindner Utility	**19.8**[3]	22.3[2]	—
Galaxy II Util Idx	**28.5**[1]	22.2[2]	—	UAM C & B Balanced	**19.7**[3]	18.9[4]	.12.1[4]
Gabelli Eqty Inc	**27.9**[1]	24.6[1]	18.2[1]	Invesco Balanced	**19.5**[3]	23.2[2]	—
Strong Amer Util	**27.6**[1]	23.7[1]	—	Amer AAdv Mileage Bal	**19.5**[3]	20.3[3]	—
Vangd Asst Alloc	**27.3**[1]	25.9[1]	17.2[1]	Fidelity Freedom 2010	**19.4**[3]	—	—
Managers Inc Eqty	**27.2**[1]	26.0[1]	17.8[1]	Nicholas Eqty Inc	**19.3**[3]	17.5[5]	—
USAA Income Stk	**26.9**[1]	24.4[1]	16.4[1]	Crabbe Hsn Asst Alloc	**19.2**[3]	15.2[5]	12.4[4]
FAM Equity Income	**26.9**[1]	—	—	Invesco Multi-Asst	**19.1**[3]	20.3[3]	—
Oakmark Eqty & Inc	**26.6**[1]	—	—	Green Cent Balanced	**19.0**[3]	20.7[3]	10.9[5]
SAFECO Income	**26.4**[1]	26.9[1]	17.9[1]	Price Balanced	**19.0**[3]	19.4[3]	13.6[3]
BNY Hamilton Eqty Inc	**25.9**[1]	23.7[1]	15.6[2]	Montgmry US Asst Alloc	**18.9**[3]	21.2[2]	—
O'Shaughnessy Dogs Of Mkt	**25.8**[1]	—	—	Columbia Balanced	**18.8**[3]	18.4[4]	13.6[3]
Nations Eqty Inc	**25.7**[1]	24.2[1]	16.3[1]	Legg Mason Balanced	**18.7**[4]	—	—
IAI Balanced	**25.7**[1]	19.6[3]	12.1[4]	Weston: New Cent Inc	**18.6**[4]	17.8[4]	13.0[4]
Primary Income	**25.5**[1]	22.0[2]	15.3[2]	Value Line Income	**18.5**[4]	20.7[3]	12.7[4]
Dreyfus Eqty Div	**25.5**[2]	—	—	JP Morgan Diversified	**18.5**[4]	19.3[4]	—
Mosaic Balanced	**25.5**[2]	21.1[2]	13.4[3]	UAM Strng Part Balanced	**18.3**[4]	19.1[4]	12.7[4]
Capp-Rush Util	**25.3**[2]	19.3[4]	9.3[5]	Excelsior Instit Balanced	**18.3**[4]	18.4[4]	—
Vangd Spec-Util	**25.1**[2]	20.8[3]	13.2[3]	IAA Trust Asst Alloc	**17.9**[4]	18.6[4]	12.5[4]
Pax World	**25.1**[2]	21.3[2]	12.6[4]	IBJ Blend Tot Ret	**17.8**[4]	—	—
Invesco Total Ret	**25.0**[2]	22.1[2]	15.9[2]	Schwab Asst Dir: Balanced	**17.8**[4]	—	—
Amana Income	**24.5**[2]	21.3[2]	13.2[3]	Reserve Conv Secs	**17.5**[4]	—	—
Rainier Balanced	**23.9**[2]	23.5[2]	—	Stein Roe Balanced	**17.5**[4]	18.8[4]	12.5[4]
McM Balanced	**23.7**[2]	22.8[2]	—	Dreyfus Balanced	**17.4**[4]	17.9[4]	13.5[3]
AMEX-Strategist Eqty Inc	**23.6**[2]	—	—	Value Line Convert	**17.0**[4]	19.9[3]	13.4[3]
Montag & Cldwl Balanced	**23.5**[2]	24.4[1]	—	Founders Balanced	**16.9**[4]	23.6[1]	17.7[1]
Fidelity Balanced	**23.4**[2]	15.7[5]	11.9[5]	Vangd LifeStrat:Cons Gro	**16.8**[4]	17.0[5]	—
Eclipse Balanced	**23.4**[2]	19.7[3]	14.9[2]	Htchks & Wly Balanced	**16.8**[4]	17.6[4]	13.0[4]
America's Utility	**23.4**[2]	19.8[3]	11.1[5]	Jurika & Voyles Balanced	**16.7**[4]	19.1[4]	14.1[2]
Vangd Wellington	**23.2**[2]	23.9[1]	16.5[1]	Strong Asst Alloc	**16.7**[4]	16.3[5]	12.1[4]
US Glb:Income	**23.1**[2]	18.4[4]	11.9[5]	SAFECO Balanced	**16.6**[4]	—	—
OVB Eqty Inc	**23.0**[2]	—	—	Vangd Tax Mgd:Balanced	**16.6**[4]	17.6[4]	—
Vintage Balanced	**22.8**[2]	—	—	Schwab OneSource Bal Alloc	**16.5**[4]	—	—
Westwood Balanced	**22.5**[2]	23.8[1]	17.3[1]	Emerald Balanced	**16.4**[4]	18.3[4]	—
Lancaster Convert	**22.4**[2]	21.1[2]	13.7[2]	Warbg Pincus Balanced	**16.4**[4]	20.0[3]	14.2[2]
Purisima Total Ret	**22.4**[2]	—	—	Vangd Convert	**16.3**[4]	16.1[5]	10.9[5]
Fidelity Puritan	**22.4**[2]	19.6[3]	16.2[1]	Key SBSF Convert‡	**16.3**[4]	19.9[3]	14.1[2]
PIC:Pinnacle Balanced	**22.3**[2]	20.0[3]	11.5[5]	USAA Growth & Tax Strat	**16.1**[4]	16.6[5]	11.9[5]
Fidelity Asst Mgr	**22.3**[2]	17.7[4]	13.4[3]	Fidelity Freedom 2000	**15.3**[4]	—	—
Vangd Idx Balanced	**22.2**[2]	21.4[2]	14.1[2]	USAA Income Strat	**15.2**[5]	—	—
State Farm Balanced‡	**22.2**[2]	20.1[3]	13.4[3]	Buffalo Balanced	**15.1**[5]	18.2[4]	—
UAM Sirach Strat Balanced	**21.9**[2]	20.2[3]	—	Price Pers Str-Inc	**15.0**[5]	17.0[5]	—
AARP Bal Stk & Bd	**21.9**[2]	19.6[3]	—	First Omaha Balanced	**15.0**[5]	—	—
Janus Balanced	**21.8**[3]	21.4[2]	14.6[2]	Fidelity Convert	**14.4**[5]	16.3[5]	12.7[4]
Sit Balanced	**21.7**[3]	20.9[2]	—	Scudder Pathway Cons	**14.4**[5]	—	—
Nations Balanced Assts	**21.4**[3]	20.5[3]	13.2[3]	Vangd LifeStrat:Income	**14.2**[5]	14.8[5]	—

By 1997 performance

No-Load Fund	Total return percent with quintile ranks by objective		
	1997	Annualized 3 years	5 years
Lindner Dividend	13.9[5]	15.6[5]	11.4[5]
BT Invest:Lifecycle Sht Range	13.7[5]	12.0[5]	—
Scudder Pathway Balanced	13.4[5]	—	—
Berwyn Income	13.3[5]	16.1[5]	12.6[4]
Lexington Convert	13.2[5]	12.1[5]	8.7[5]
Croft Leom Income	13.0[5]	—	—
Hennessey Balanced	13.0[5]	—	—
Key Choice:Inc & Gro‡	12.7[5]	—	—
SwissKey US Balanced	12.6[5]	—	—
Fidelity Asst Mgr Inc	12.4[5]	12.2[5]	10.0[5]
Holland Balanced	12.1[5]	—	—
Dreyfus LifeTime Income	11.9[5]	—	—
Nations LifeGoal Bal Gro	11.2[5]	—	—
Fidelity Freedom Inc	10.7[5]	—	—
Federated Mgd Inc	10.5[5]	10.5[5]	—
Scout Balanced	10.1[5]	—	—
CitiSelect 300	9.9[5]	—	—
West University Fd	9.7[5]	—	—
CitiSelect 200	8.3[5]	—	—
Concorde Income	6.8[5]	—	—
Steadman Associated	-1.3[5]	3.9[5]	-0.3[5]
SECTOR & INDUSTRY FUNDS			
Fidelity Sel Broker†	62.3[1]	41.0[1]	28.2[1]
FBR Sm Cap Finl Svcs‡	58.1[1]	—	—
Titan Finl Svcs	55.6[1]	—	—
Fidelity Sel Energy Serv†	51.9[1]	47.2[1]	31.2[1]
Century Shares	50.1[1]	33.5[1]	17.9[3]
FBR Fin'l Svcs‡	47.7[1]	—	—
Fidelity Sel Home Finc†	45.8[1]	45.2[1]	32.0[1]
Fidelity Sel Reg Banks†	45.5[1]	42.6[1]	26.4[1]
Invesco Strat Fncl	44.8[1]	38.2[1]	24.3[1]
Fidelity Sel Insurance†	42.5[1]	33.5[1]	20.7[2]
Fidelity Sel Financial†	41.9[1]	40.3[1]	25.6[1]
Fidelity Sel Retail†	41.7[1]	24.3[3]	15.6[4]
Price Finl Serv	41.4[1]	—	—
Fidelity Sel Leisure†	41.3[1]	26.7[2]	21.5[2]
Fidelity Sel Consmr Ind†	38.0[1]	26.0[2]	18.3[3]
Fidelity Sel Transport†	32.1[1]	18.6[5]	17.5[3]
Fidelity Sel Air Trans†	31.1[2]	28.4[2]	16.8[4]
Fidelity Sel Health†	31.1[2]	30.2[2]	22.4[2]
Fidelity Sel Multimedia†	30.9[2]	21.0[4]	20.5[2]
Fidelity Sel Util Gro†	30.3[2]	24.9[3]	15.2[4]
Fidelity Sel Food/Agr†	30.3[2]	26.3[2]	18.4[3]
Munder NetNet	30.1[2]	—	—
RCM Global Health Care	30.0[2]	—	—
Longleaf Partners Realty	29.7[2]	—	—
Fidelity Sel Const/Hous†	29.6[2]	23.6[3]	16.2[4]
Brazos/JMIC Real Est	28.6[2]	—	—
Vangd Spec-Health	28.5[2]	31.3[2]	22.6[2]
Price Media & Telecomm	28.1[2]	23.1[3]	—
Invesco Wrld Cap Gds	27.8[2]	16.6[5]	—
Warbg Pincus Health Sci	27.4[2]	—	—
RCM Global Tech	27.1[2]	—	—
CGM Realty	26.7[3]	29.8[2]	—
Invesco Strat Leis	26.5[3]	16.9[5]	15.5[4]
Fidelity Sel Telecomm†	25.8[3]	19.8[5]	18.4[3]
Amer Cent Real Est	25.2[3]	—	—
Columbia Real Est Eqty	24.7[3]	27.4[2]	—
Invesco Strat Util	24.4[3]	20.7[4]	13.9[5]
Rushmore Amer Gas Idx	24.2[3]	25.1[3]	15.4[4]

No-Load Fund	Total return percent with quintile ranks by objective		
	1997	Annualized 3 years	5 years
Fidelity Sel Defense†	23.5[3]	31.5[1]	24.4[1]
Fidelity Real Est	21.3[3]	22.4[4]	16.0[4]
Cohen & Steers Realty	21.1[3]	23.0[4]	19.1[2]
Invesco Realty	21.1[3]	—	—
Fidelity Sel Medical Del†	20.5[3]	20.9[4]	17.5[3]
Price Health Sciences	19.4[3]	—	—
Royce Finl Servs	19.4[3]	18.4[5]	—
US Glb:Real Estate	19.3[3]	23.1[3]	10.6[5]
Invesco Strat Enrgy	19.1[3]	25.6[2]	16.5[4]
Fidelity Sel Indust Equip†	18.8[4]	24.4[3]	23.2[1]
Crabbe Hsn Real Est	18.8[4]	20.9[4]	—
AON REIT Idx	18.8[4]	—	—
Vangd Spec-REIT Idx	18.6[4]	—	—
Excelsior Enrgy & Nat Resc	18.5[4]	25.4[3]	17.1[3]
Invesco Strat Hlth	18.4[4]	28.0[2]	14.1[5]
Fidelity Sel Envir Serv†	17.9[4]	19.8[4]	9.1[5]
Stratton Month Div REIT Sh	17.3[4]	16.3[5]	8.1[5]
Northern Technology	16.8[4]	—	—
Fidelity Sel Auto†	16.7[4]	15.4[5]	12.7[5]
Seneca Real Estate	16.6[4]	—	—
Invesco Strat Envrn	16.6[4]	25.0[3]	10.5[5]
Fidelity Sel Chemical†	16.5[4]	19.8[4]	17.3[3]
Fidelity Sel Biotech†	15.4[4]	22.0[4]	8.4[5]
Fidelity Sel Software†	14.9[4]	26.9[2]	22.2[2]
Vangd Spec-Energy	14.8[5]	24.5[3]	19.1[2]
Fidelity Sel Electronics†	14.2[5]	39.8[1]	33.5[1]
Fidelity Sel Energy†	10.5[5]	21.1[4]	16.3[4]
Fidelity Sel Technology†	10.4[5]	22.4[4]	21.3[2]
Fidelity Sel Pap/Forest†	9.4[5]	12.6[5]	14.1[5]
Invesco Strat Tech	8.8[5]	24.6[3]	18.5[3]
Technology Value	6.5[5]	40.3[1]	—
Robrtsn Stph Info Age	6.1[5]	—	—
Fidelity Sel Devel Comm†	5.6[5]	12.4[5]	16.6[4]
PBHG Tech & Comm	3.3[5]	—	—
Fidelity Sel Indust Mat†	1.9[5]	10.3[5]	12.0[5]
Price Sci/Tech	1.7[5]	21.8[4]	21.0[2]
WWW Internet Fund	0.4[5]	—	—
Fidelity Sel Computer†	-1.1[5]	25.5[2]	25.1[1]
Fidelity Sel Nat Gas†	-8.0[5]	17.4[5]	—
Robrtsn Stph Glob Nat Res	-17.1[5]	—	—
PRECIOUS METALS FUNDS			
Rydex Prec Met	-37.6[1]	-12.2[1]	—
USAA Gold	-38.2[1]	-13.7[1]	-1.6[4]
Vangd Spec-Gold	-39.0[1]	-16.7[2]	1.1[3]
Fidelity Sel Amer Gold†	-39.4[2]	-6.9[1]	4.1[1]
Scudder Gold	-40.9[2]	-4.0[1]	5.5[1]
US Glb:World Gold	-41.1[2]	-6.6[1]	5.2[1]
Amer Cent Glob Gold	-41.5[3]	-14.7[1]	-1.3[4]
Lexington Goldfund	-43.0[3]	-15.5[2]	0.9[3]
Fidelity Sel Prec Met†	-44.9[3]	-17.5[2]	3.3[2]
Capp-Rush Gold	-45.2[4]	-18.9[2]	—
Blanchard Prec Met.‡	-47.1[4]	-11.8[1]	3.2[2]
Gabelli Gold	-51.9[4]	-18.8[2]	—
Invesco Strat Gold	-55.5[4]	-11.0[1]	-2.6[5]
Bull & Bear Gold	-55.7[5]	-24.1[2]	-6.7[5]
US Glb:Gold Shares	-57.4[5]	-38.5[2]	-12.7[5]
Midas Gold	-59.0[5]	-12.0[1]	2.3[3]
GLOBAL EQUITY FUNDS			
Gabelli Glbl Couch Potato	41.7[1]	23.4[1]	—
U.S. Global Leaders	40.7[1]	—	—

Stock and bond funds – ranked within objective *continued*

By 1997 performance

No-Load Fund	Total return percent with quintile ranks by objective			No-Load Fund	Total return percent with quintile ranks by objective		
		Annualized				Annualized	
	1997	3 years	5 years		1997	3 years	5 years
Gabelli Glbl Telecomm..........................	31.9[1]	18.6[3]	—	Lazard Int'l Eqty(O shrs).....................	11.8[2]	13.5[2]	14.0[2]
Invesco Wrld Comm..............................	30.3[1]	24.7[2]	—	Columbia Int'l Stk..............................	11.5[2]	11.0[2]	12.2[3]
Montgmry Select 50.............................	29.3[1]	—	—	UAM McKee Int'l................................	11.3[2]	10.2[2]	—
RCM Global Small Cap........................	25.5[1]	—	—	Nbrgr-Ber Int'l Eqty...........................	11.2[2]	14.1[1]	—
Austin Global Eqty..............................	23.9[1]	17.1[3]	—	Accessor Int'l Eqty............................	11.0[2]	10.8[2]	—
Tweedy Brwn Glob Val.........................	22.9[1]	17.8[3]	—	Fidelity Overseas..............................	10.9[2]	11.0[2]	14.2[2]
Mutual Discovery Z‡...........................	22.8[1]	25.4[2]	—	Marshall Int'l Stk..............................	10.9[2]	14.0[1]	—
Janus Worldwide................................	20.5[1]	22.9[2]	19.8[1]	Managers Int'l Eqty...........................	10.8[2]	13.3[2]	15.4[1]
Citizens Tr Global..............................	19.9[2]	15.6[4]	—	Montgmry Int'l Growth........................	10.2[2]	—	—
Buffalo USA Global............................	19.0[2]	—	—	Eighteen - 1838 Int'l Eqty...................	10.0[2]	—	—
Scout Worldwide................................	18.4[2]	17.1[3]	—	BBK Int'l Equity...............................	10.0[2]	10.7[2]	10.3[3]
Scudder Global..................................	17.2[2]	17.1[3]	15.1[1]	Harbor Int'l II..................................	9.7[2]	—	—
Montgmry Glob Comm..........................	15.8[2]	13.5[4]	—	Bernstein Int'l Value..........................	9.3[2]	11.5[2]	14.2[2]
USAA Cornerstone Strat......................	15.6[2]	17.3[3]	14.6[2]	Excelsior International........................	9.3[2]	8.0[3]	11.0[3]
Lazard Global Eqty(O shrs)...................	15.3[2]	—	—	First Eagle Int'l................................	9.3[2]	12.2[2]	—
AARP Global Growth...........................	14.6[2]	—	—	Vontobel Int'l Eqty............................	9.2[2]	12.3[2]	13.6[2]
Price Glob Stk...................................	13.2[2]	—	—	Northern Int'l Sel Eq.........................	9.1[2]	3.7[4]	—
BBK Diversa......................................	13.2[2]	14.7[4]	10.7[3]	Dreyfus Int'l Val...............................	9.0[2]	—	—
USAA World Growth...........................	12.9[3]	14.9[4]	13.6[2]	USAA International............................	9.0[2]	12.0[2]	15.1[1]
Payden & Rygel Glob Bal....................	12.5[3]	—	—	Amer AAdv Mileage Int'l.....................	8.8[2]	14.9[1]	—
Fidelity Glob Bal...............................	12.4[3]	10.5[5]	—	Wm Blair Int'l Gro.............................	8.4[2]	8.6[3]	11.3[3]
Dreyfus Global Gro............................	12.3[3]	12.1[4]	9.7[4]	Scudder Int'l Stk..............................	8.0[2]	11.6[2]	12.9[2]
Fidelity Worldwide.............................	12.1[3]	12.6[4]	14.9[2]	Fidelity Int'l Value............................	7.8[2]	10.4[2]	—
Thomas White Wld Fd........................	11.7[3]	15.7[3]	—	Gabelli Int'l Growth...........................	7.3[2]	—	—
Montgmry Glob Asst Alloc...................	11.2[3]	—	—	Schwab Int'l Idx(Inv).........................	7.3[2]	10.2[2]	—
Montgmry Glob Oppty.........................	11.0[3]	16.1[3]	—	Fidelity Int'l Gr & Inc........................	7.1[2]	10.6[2]	12.2[2]
Founders Worldwide Gr.......................	10.5[3]	15.0[4]	14.1[2]	Scudder Pathway Int'l........................	7.0[2]	—	—
SwissKey Global...............................	10.2[4]	—	—	Schwab OneSource Int'l......................	6.8[2]	—	—
Fremont Global..................................	9.9[4]	14.3[4]	11.4[3]	Preferred Int'l..................................	6.8[2]	11.2[2]	15.0[2]
SwissKey Glob Eqty...........................	9.9[4]	—	—	AON Int'l Eqty..................................	6.5[2]	—	—
Scudder Glob Disc.‡..........................	9.9[4]	16.3[3]	14.9[1]	Northern Int'l Gro Eq.........................	6.3[2]	4.4[4]	—
Vangd Hrzn:Glob Asst........................	9.3[4]	—	—	Fidelity Canada††..............................	6.1[2]	13.7[2]	10.2[3]
Warbg Pincus Glob Post Vent..............	8.7[4]	—	—	UAM MJI Int'l...................................	6.0[2]	7.8[3]	—
AMEX-Strategist World Gro.................	7.0[4]	—	—	Payden & Rygel Int'l Eqty...................	5.5[3]	—	—
Lexington Global...............................	6.9[4]	11.3[5]	13.1[3]	Htchks & Wly Int'l............................	5.3[3]	14.3[1]	16.2[1]
Vangd Hrzn:Glob Eqty........................	6.7[4]	—	—	Gradison International........................	5.1[3]	—	—
Bull & Bear US & Overs......................	6.7[4]	12.0[4]	9.1[4]	SwissKey Non-US Eqty.......................	5.0[3]	—	—
Blanchard Glob Gro‡.........................	6.5[5]	10.8[5]	9.4[4]	Sit Int'l Growth................................	4.8[3]	8.1[3]	12.7[2]
Merriman Asst Alloc..........................	5.8[5]	8.9[5]	8.3[5]	SAFECO Int'l Stk..............................	4.6[3]	—	—
Permanent Portfolio†.........................	5.6[5]	7.5[5]	6.8[5]	Vangd Int'l Growth............................	4.1[3]	11.1[2]	14.9[2]
Gabelli Glbl Conv Sec.......................	2.8[5]	6.9[5]	—	Harbor Int'l Gro...............................	3.6[3]	19.3[1]	—
Amer Cent Glob Nat Res.....................	2.5[5]	10.6[5]	—	PBHG International............................	3.5[3]	6.0[3]	—
Mosaic Foresight...............................	2.5[5]	2.2[5]	—	Artisan International..........................	3.5[3]	—	—
US Glb:Glob Resrcs...........................	-2.8[5]	12.4[3]	8.7[4]	Oakmark Int'l...................................	3.4[3]	12.7[2]	14.9[2]
Robrtsn Stph Glob Low Pr...................	-13.5[5]	—	—	Schroder Cap:Int'l............................	3.2[3]	8.2[3]	12.9[2]
Fontaine Glob Gro..............................	-44.9[5]	-4.9[5]	-0.5[5]	Berger/BIAM Int'l..............................	2.9[3]	—	—
INT'L EQUITY FUNDS - GENERAL				WPG International.............................	2.9[3]	6.1[3]	9.0[4]
Emerald Int'l Eqty.............................	20.4[1]	—	—	Price Int'l Stk..................................	2.7[3]	9.9[3]	13.0[2]
Amer Cent-20th Cent Int'l Gr...............	19.7[1]	15.3[1]	15.8[1]	Lindner International..........................	2.6[3]	—	—
Janus Overseas................................	18.2[1]	23.0[1]	—	UAM TS&W Int'l Eqty.........................	2.5[3]	6.7[3]	9.9[4]
Amer Cent-20th Cent Int'l Disc.............	17.5[1]	19.2[1]	—	Price Spect-Int'l...............................	2.4[3]	—	—
Kayne Anderson Int'l Ris Div...............	17.4[1]	—	—	Kent Int'l Gro...................................	2.3[3]	6.8[3]	10.8[3]
BT Invest:Int'l Eqty...........................	17.4[1]	18.2[1]	18.8[1]	BT Advs:EAFE Eqty Indx.....................	1.9[3]	—	—
Founders Int'l Equity.........................	16.1[1]	—	—	Nations Int'l Gro..............................	1.9[3]	8.7[3]	10.5[3]
Sextant International..........................	15.9[1]	—	—	Legg Mason Int'l Eqty........................	1.8[3]	—	—
Harbor Int'l‡....................................	15.5[1]	17.2[1]	19.8[1]	Babson Stew Ivry Int'l........................	1.7[3]	9.1[3]	11.9[3]
BEA Advs:Int'l Eqty...........................	14.9[1]	—	—	Founders Passport............................	1.7[3]	14.9[1]	—
Fidelity Dvsfd Int'l............................	13.7[1]	17.2[1]	17.4[1]	Lexington Int'l.................................	1.6[3]	6.9[3]	—
FTI Int'l Eqty...................................	13.3[1]	—	—	Wright Int'l Blue Ch..........................	1.5[3]	11.7[2]	11.9[3]
Jamestown Int'l Eqty.........................	12.4[1]	—	—	JP Morgan Int'l Eqty..........................	1.2[3]	5.7[4]	9.2[4]

Stock and bond funds – ranked within objective *continued*

By 1997 performance

No-Load Fund	Total return percent with quintile ranks by objective 1997	Annualized 3 years	Annualized 5 years
Nations Int'l Eqty	**1.0**^{3}	5.8^{3}	8.9^{4}
RSI Tr-Int'l Eqty	**0.9**^{3}	8.0^{3}	10.6^{3}
Dreyfus Int'l Eqty Alloc	**0.6**^{3}	6.1^{3}	—
Lazard Int'l Sm Cap(O shrs)	**0.3**^{3}	5.7^{3}	—
Acorn Int'l	**0.2**^{3}	9.9^{2}	13.8^{2}
Montgmry Int'l Sm Cap	**-0.8**^{4}	8.4^{3}	—
Vangd Tot Int'l Port†	**-0.8**^{4}	—	—
Boston-1784 Int'l Eqty	**-0.9**^{4}	8.5^{3}	—
Dreyfus Int'l Growth	**-1.5**^{4}	2.5^{4}	—
Quant Int'l Eqty	**-1.6**^{4}	2.3^{4}	9.1^{4}
Invesco Int'l Gro	**-1.9**^{4}	6.0^{3}	8.9^{4}
Stein Roe Int'l	**-3.5**^{4}	2.8^{4}	—
UBS Int'l Eqty	**-3.7**^{4}	—	—
IAI International	**-4.2**^{4}	4.2^{4}	9.7^{4}
Warbg Pincus Int'l	**-4.4**^{4}	5.3^{4}	12.1^{3}
Vangd Int'l Value	**-4.6**^{4}	4.8^{4}	9.6^{4}
Price Int'l Disc	**-5.7**^{4}	0.9^{4}	7.3^{4}
Fremont Int'l Gro	**-8.4**^{4}	3.5^{4}	—
Reserve Int'l Eqty	**-8.7**^{4}	—	—
SSgA Active Int'l	**-10.1**^{4}	—	—
Barr Rosnbrg Int'l Sm Cap†	**-13.4**^{4}	—	—
Schroder Cap:Int'l Sm Cap	**-14.1**^{4}	—	—
Strong Int'l Stk	**-14.2**^{4}	0.0^{4}	7.8^{4}
Fremont Int'l Sm Cap	**-26.5**^{5}	-5.4^{5}	—
INT'L EQUITY FUNDS - EUROPE			
Fidelity Europe Cap App††	**24.9**^{1}	21.7^{1}	—
Excelsior Pan Europe	**24.4**^{1}	20.2^{1}	15.3^{1}
Vangd Idx Europe†	**24.2**^{1}	22.6^{1}	19.4^{1}
Scudder Grt Europe	**24.0**^{1}	26.1^{1}	—
Mutual European Z‡	**23.2**^{1}	—	—
Fidelity Europe††	**22.9**^{1}	22.4^{1}	19.9^{1}
Wright Equifund Swiss	**22.7**^{1}	13.4^{2}	—
JP Morgan Euro Eqty	**22.1**^{1}	—	—
Fidelity Germany	**20.3**^{1}	—	—
Lipper Prime Europe Eqty	**18.6**^{1}	—	—
Price Europe	**17.0**^{1}	21.5^{1}	18.9^{1}
Fidelity UK	**16.8**^{1}	—	—
Wright Equifund Netherland	**15.4**^{1}	23.2^{1}	20.1^{1}
Invesco Europe	**15.1**^{1}	21.2^{1}	16.6^{1}
Fidelity France	**14.5**^{1}	—	—
Wright Equifund Britain	**13.3**^{1}	—	—
Fidelity Nordic	**12.1**^{2}	—	—
Wright Equifund Belg\Lux	**11.4**^{2}	17.5^{1}	—
Wright Equifund Germany	**9.9**^{2}	—	—
Wright Equifund Nordic	**5.2**^{3}	18.5^{1}	—
Invesco Europe Sm Co	**-3.1**^{4}	—	—
INT'L EQUITY FUNDS - EMG MKTS			
Lexington Trka Dlg Russia	**67.5**^{1}	—	—
Wright Equifund Mexico	**42.4**^{1}	6.6^{3}	—
Fidelity Latin Amer††	**32.9**^{1}	13.2^{2}	—
Price Latin Amer	**31.8**^{1}	9.8^{3}	—
Scudder Latin Amer	**31.3**^{1}	15.0^{1}	19.1^{1}
BT Invest:Lat Am Eqty	**30.8**^{1}	9.6^{3}	—
Excelsior Lat Amer	**25.2**^{1}	11.8^{2}	11.8^{3}
Invesco Latin Amer	**19.3**^{1}	—	—
IAI Latin Amer	**18.7**^{1}	—	—
Fremont Emg Mkts	**10.4**^{2}	—	—
Vontobel East Europe	**8.7**^{2}	—	—
AMEX-Strategist Emg Mkts	**5.4**^{3}	—	—
Scudder Emg Mkts Gro	**3.6**^{3}	—	—

No-Load Fund	Total return percent with quintile ranks by objective 1997	Annualized 3 years	Annualized 5 years
Price Emg Mkts Stk	**1.2**^{3}	—	—
Dreyfus Emg Mkts	**-1.5**^{4}	—	—
Montgmry Emg Mkts	**-3.2**^{4}	-0.4^{4}	7.7^{4}
Nations Emg Mkts	**-3.2**^{4}	—	—
USAA Emg Mkts	**-3.5**^{4}	5.3^{4}	—
BEA Advs:Emg Mkts	**-3.6**^{4}	—	—
Sit Develop Mkts Gro	**-5.2**^{4}	2.1^{4}	—
Schroder Cap:Emg Mkts	**-5.2**^{4}	—	—
Legg Mason Emg Mkts	**-6.2**^{4}	—	—
JP Morgan Emg Mkts Eqty	**-7.6**^{4}	-3.4^{4}	—
SSgA Emg Mkts	**-8.8**^{4}	-1.2^{4}	—
Quant Frgn Frntr	**-9.2**^{4}	-1.2^{4}	—
Lazard Emg Mkt(O shrs)	**-9.8**^{4}	1.6^{4}	—
Lexington World Emg	**-11.4**^{4}	-3.6^{5}	4.8^{4}
IAI Develop Countries	**-14.1**^{4}	—	—
Robrtsn Stph Devlp Cnt	**-15.2**^{4}	-4.2^{5}	—
Vangd Idx Emg Mkt†	**-16.8**^{5}	-1.0^{4}	—
Oakmark Int'l Small Cap	**-19.9**^{5}	—	—
Warbg Pincus Emg Mkts	**-20.0**^{5}	1.0^{4}	—
Capstone New Zealand	**-23.1**^{5}	2.8^{4}	2.6^{5}
Bernstein Emg Mkts	**-23.8**^{5}	—	—
Montgmry Emg Asia	**-28.3**^{5}	—	—
Price New Asia	**-37.1**^{5}	-9.5^{5}	1.4^{5}
Invesco Asia Growth	**-38.5**^{5}	—	—
Fidelity SE Asia††	**-38.9**^{5}	-8.9^{5}	—
Fidelity Emg Mkts††	**-40.9**^{5}	-14.3^{5}	-1.2^{5}
INT'L EQUITY FUNDS - PACIFIC			
Warbg Pincus Japan Growth	**1.5**^{3}	—	—
Fidelity Japan††	**-10.7**^{4}	-8.1^{5}	1.7^{5}
Wright Equifund Japan	**-14.2**^{4}	-10.8^{5}	—
Japan (Scudder)	**-14.5**^{4}	-11.5^{5}	-1.2^{5}
Fidelity Pacific Bas††	**-15.1**^{4}	-8.2^{5}	4.3^{4}
Guinness Flt China & HK	**-20.3**^{5}	8.9^{3}	—
Fidelity HK & China	**-22.1**^{5}	—	—
Price Japan	**-22.1**^{5}	-12.4^{5}	-1.4^{5}
US Glb:China Region Oppty	**-22.5**^{5}	-5.2^{5}	—
Matthews Asian Cnvrt	**-23.2**^{5}	-1.8^{4}	—
Capstone Nikko Japan	**-24.6**^{5}	-15.1^{5}	-0.9^{5}
Warbg Pincus Japan OTC	**-25.5**^{5}	-13.8^{5}	—
Vangd Idx Pacific†	**-25.7**^{5}	-11.0^{5}	1.5^{5}
Wright Equifund Hong Kong	**-27.2**^{5}	-1.8^{4}	1.9^{5}
Nomura Pacific Bas	**-28.7**^{5}	-8.7^{5}	2.1^{5}
Fidelity Japan Sm Cap	**-30.4**^{5}	—	—
Guinness Flt Asia Small Cap	**-30.8**^{5}	—	—
JP Morgan Japan Eqty	**-30.8**^{5}	—	—
Strong Asia Pacific	**-31.0**^{5}	-9.3^{5}	—
Excelsior Pac Asia	**-32.2**^{5}	-7.6^{5}	2.3^{5}
Nations Pacific Gro	**-33.0**^{5}	—	—
Peregrine Asia Pac Growth‡	**-33.1**^{5}	—	—
Barr Rosnbrg Japan†	**-34.9**^{5}	—	—
Invesco Pacific Bas	**-36.9**^{5}	-13.4^{5}	-0.6^{5}
Guinness Flt Asia Blue Chip	**-37.7**^{5}	—	—
Scudder Pacific Opp	**-37.8**^{5}	-12.4^{5}	-2.3^{5}
Matthews Pac Tiger	**-40.9**^{5}	-8.9^{5}	—
Japan Alpha‡	**-42.1**^{5}	—	—
Lexington Crsby Sm Cap Asia	**-42.3**^{5}	—	—
BT Invest:Pac Basin	**-45.9**^{5}	-13.1^{5}	—
Matthews Korea	**-64.8**^{5}	—	—
FIXED-INCOME - LONG TERM			
Amer Cent-Benham Target 2025	**30.1**^{1}	—	—

Stock and bond funds – ranked within objective continued

By 1997 performance

No-Load Fund	Total return percent with quintile ranks by objective			No-Load Fund	Total return percent with quintile ranks by objective		
	1997	Annualized 3 years	5 years		1997	Annualized 3 years	5 years
Amer Cent-Benham Target 2020	**28.6**[1]	26.5[1]	17.7[1]	Mosaic Hi Yld	**9.9**[3]	10.3[3]	8.5[2]
Amer Cent-Benham Target 2015	**22.9**[1]	23.7[1]	16.2[1]	Excelsior Mgd Inc	**9.8**[3]	10.5[3]	7.5[3]
Fidelity New Mkts Inc	**17.2**[1]	21.4[1]	—	RSI Tr-Act Mgd Bd	**9.7**[3]	10.0[4]	7.2[4]
Invesco High Yld	**17.1**[1]	16.3[1]	11.6[1]	TIP:Clover Cap Fix Inc	**9.6**[3]	10.5[3]	7.9[3]
Price Emg Mkt Bond	**16.8**[1]	26.0[1]	—	Drey-Basic GNMA	**9.5**[3]	10.2[3]	7.6[3]
Amer Cent-Benham Target 2010	**16.7**[1]	20.6[1]	14.4[1]	McM Fixed Inc	**9.5**[3]	10.4[3]	—
Dreyfus Hi Yld Secs	**16.7**[1]	—	—	Dreyfus A Bonds Plus	**9.5**[3]	10.7[3]	7.9[3]
Rydex Gov Bd	**16.4**[1]	14.1[1]	—	Northern Fix Inc	**9.5**[3]	10.1[3]	—
Strong Hi Yld Bd	**16.0**[1]	—	—	First Omaha Fix Inc	**9.5**[3]	10.0[4]	7.1[4]
Fidelity Spart Hi Inc	**15.9**[1]	15.7[1]	14.2[1]	Advance Cap Bond	**9.4**[3]	10.6[3]	7.5[3]
Legg Mason High Yld	**15.9**[1]	16.3[1]	—	HGK Fix Inc	**9.4**[3]	9.7[4]	—
Stein Roe Hi Yld Bd	**15.9**[1]	—	—	CA Inv Tr-US Gov	**9.3**[3]	10.3[3]	7.7[3]
Buffalo High Yield	**15.8**[1]	—	—	Babson Bond-Port L	**9.3**[3]	9.3[4]	7.0[4]
Wasatch Hosington US Treas	**15.7**[1]	11.6[2]	8.0[3]	Fidelity Spart Inv Grd	**9.3**[3]	10.1[3]	8.0[3]
Janus High Yld	**15.4**[1]	—	—	Excelsior Instit Income	**9.3**[3]	—	—
Scudder Hi Yld Bd	**14.8**[1]	—	—	Galaxy II US Trsy Idx	**9.3**[3]	9.7[4]	7.0[4]
Price Trsy Long	**14.7**[1]	12.9[2]	8.9[2]	OVB Gov	**9.3**[3]	10.1[3]	—
Fidelity Cap & Inc	**14.7**[1]	14.1[1]	12.1[1]	Wright Total Ret Bd	**9.2**[3]	10.4[3]	6.9[4]
Amer Cent-Benham LT Trsy	**14.7**[1]	13.5[2]	9.3[2]	Value Line US Gov	**9.2**[3]	9.1[5]	4.9[5]
BEA Advs:Hi Yld	**14.5**[1]	—	—	Excelsior Instit Tot Ret Bd	**9.2**[3]	—	—
Price High Yld	**14.5**[1]	13.9[1]	10.6[1]	Fidelity Spart Gov Inc	**9.2**[3]	9.8[4]	6.5[4]
Vangd Bond Idx Long	**14.3**[1]	13.9[1]	—	UAM TS&W Fix Inc	**9.2**[3]	9.4[4]	6.6[4]
Value Line Agg Inc	**14.1**[1]	18.0[1]	13.4[1]	Vintage Bond	**9.2**[3]	—	—
AMEX-Strategist Hi Yld	**14.0**[1]	—	—	JP Morgan Bond	**9.1**[3]	10.0[4]	7.2[4]
Vangd-Adml Long	**14.0**[1]	13.6[2]	9.9[2]	Wright US Treas	**9.1**[3]	11.3[3]	7.9[3]
Westcore LT Bond	**14.0**[1]	13.3[2]	9.4[2]	SwissKey US Bd	**9.1**[4]	—	—
Vangd LT Trsy	**13.9**[1]	13.5[2]	9.7[2]	Federated Bond Idx	**9.0**[4]	—	—
Northeast Inv Trust	**13.9**[2]	17.1[1]	15.2[1]	Wayne Hummer Income	**9.0**[4]	9.2[4]	7.0[4]
Vangd LT Corp	**13.8**[2]	13.3[2]	9.6[2]	Fidelity Gov Sec	**8.9**[4]	9.5[4]	6.9[4]
Federated Hi Yld	**13.3**[2]	15.0[1]	11.8[1]	SSgA Bond Mkt	**8.9**[4]	—	—
Nicholas Income	**13.1**[2]	13.9[2]	10.8[1]	IBJ Core Fix Inc	**8.9**[4]	—	—
Scudder Emg Mkts Inc	**13.1**[2]	22.1[1]	—	Fidelity Inv Grd Bd	**8.9**[4]	9.0[5]	7.3[4]
Rushmore US Gov	**13.1**[2]	13.2[2]	8.5[2]	UAM BHM&S Tot Ret Bd	**8.8**[4]	—	—
Vangd Prefrd Stk	**13.0**[2]	15.5[1]	9.9[2]	Dreyfus GNMA	**8.8**[4]	9.6[4]	6.5[5]
SAFECO Hi Yld Bd	**12.8**[2]	12.9[2]	10.5[1]	Vontobel East Europe Debt	**8.7**[4]	—	—
Columbia High Yld	**12.7**[2]	13.7[2]	—	Scudder Income	**8.7**[4]	10.0[3]	7.5[3]
Price Corp Inc	**12.6**[2]	—	—	Weitz Ser Fix Inc	**8.6**[4]	9.5[4]	6.7[4]
Invesco US Gov Sec	**12.2**[2]	11.3[3]	7.1[4]	AMEX-Strategist Qual Inc	**8.6**[4]	—	—
Advance Cap Ret Inc	**12.2**[2]	13.0[2]	9.2[2]	Aquinas Fix Inc	**8.5**[4]	9.1[5]	—
Sextant Bond Inc	**12.1**[2]	9.2[4]	—	Preferred Fix Inc	**8.5**[4]	9.5[4]	7.2[4]
Vangd Hi Yld Corp	**11.9**[2]	13.5[2]	11.2[1]	Lazard Bond(O shrs)	**8.4**[4]	9.6[4]	6.4[5]
Strong Corp Bond	**11.9**[2]	14.0[1]	11.3[1]	Marshall Gov Inc	**8.4**[4]	9.3[4]	6.1[5]
Maxus Income	**11.8**[2]	12.3[2]	8.1[3]	KPM Fixed Inc	**8.4**[4]	9.3[4]	—
Federated US Gov Bd	**11.7**[2]	11.9[2]	8.3[3]	Nations Divsfd Inc	**8.3**[4]	10.1[3]	8.5[2]
Invesco Select Inc	**11.7**[2]	12.1[2]	9.2[2]	UAM SAMI Pref Stck Inc	**8.3**[4]	8.2[5]	5.7[5]
Dreyfus 100% US Long	**11.7**[2]	12.1[2]	8.3[2]	Nations Strat Inc	**8.3**[4]	8.9[5]	6.6[4]
Amer Cent-Benham Target 2005	**11.6**[2]	16.1[1]	11.6[1]	Fidelity Target Timeline 2001	**8.2**[4]	—	—
Crabbe Hsn Income	**11.6**[2]	10.0[4]	6.5[5]	Emerald Mndg Bd	**8.2**[4]	10.0[4]	—
Dreyfus Strat Income	**11.2**[2]	12.7[2]	9.1[2]	Sit US Gov	**8.2**[4]	8.2[5]	6.7[4]
Lipper Hi Inc Bd	**11.0**[2]	—	—	Quaker Fixed Inc	**8.1**[4]	—	—
IAI Bond	**10.8**[2]	10.3[3]	7.4[3]	Nations US Gov Sec	**8.0**[4]	—	—
Parnassus Fix Inc	**10.6**[2]	11.9[2]	7.6[3]	AARP Hi Qual ST Bond	**7.9**[4]	9.2[4]	6.6[4]
Managers Bond	**10.4**[2]	14.9[1]	9.5[2]	Boston-1784 Income	**7.8**[4]	9.3[4]	—
Legg Mason Invest Grd	**10.3**[2]	11.4[2]	7.9[3]	Schroder Ser:Inv Grd Inc	**7.7**[4]	9.2[4]	—
Fidelity Target Timeline 2003	**10.1**[2]	—	—	Trainer-Wrthm Tot Ret Bd	**7.6**[4]	—	—
BT Invest:Glob Hi Yld	**10.1**[2]	16.6[1]	—	Thompson Plumb Bond	**7.4**[5]	7.8[5]	5.7[5]
Dodge & Cox Income	**10.0**[2]	11.1[3]	8.2[3]	PC&J Preservation	**7.4**[5]	8.3[5]	6.1[5]
Schwab Tot Bd Mkt Idx	**10.0**[3]	10.8[3]	—	C\FUNDS:Gov	**7.3**[5]	7.8[5]	5.9[5]
Transamerica Premr Bond	**10.0**[3]	—	—	Scout Bond	**7.3**[5]	8.2[5]	5.9[5]
Kent Income	**10.0**[3]	—	—	Selected US Gov Inc	**7.2**[5]	8.4[5]	6.2[5]

By 1997 performance

No-Load Fund	1997	Annualized 3 years	Annualized 5 years
Amer Cent-Benham Target 2000	7.0[5]	12.1[2]	8.6[2]
Lancaster Gov Qual	7.0[5]	7.5[5]	5.4[5]
Dreyfus Global Bd	6.8[5]	11.0[3]	—
Fidelity Target Timeline 1999	6.7[5]	—	—
Payden & Rygel Glob ST Bd	6.6[5]	—	—
Scudder US Zero 2000	6.5[5]	8.5[5]	6.4[5]
AMEX-Strategist World Inc	5.8[5]	—	—
Payden & Rygel Ltd Mat	5.5[5]	5.9[5]	—
Fundamental US Gov Strat	5.5[5]	8.5[5]	0.6[5]
Lazard Strat Yld(O shrs)	5.2[5]	10.8[3]	8.9[2]
Lexington Ramrz Glob Inc	5.0[5]	12.6[2]	—
CGM Fixed Inc	3.7[5]	15.0[1]	10.7[1]
Alliance World Inc	3.6[5]	3.9[5]	2.3[5]
Guinness Flt Glob Gov	2.9[5]	7.8[5]	—
BBK Int'l Bond	2.6[5]	10.3[3]	4.5[5]
SwissKey Glob Bd	1.2[5]	—	—
Scudder Glob Bond	0.4[5]	3.7[5]	3.3[5]
Managers Glob Bd	0.2[5]	7.6[5]	—
Northern Int'l Fix Inc	-2.5[5]	7.2[5]	—
Strong Int'l Bond	-4.8[5]	7.0[5]	—
Rydex Juno	-5.6[5]	—	—
Lazard Int'l Fix Inc(O shrs)	-5.7[5]	5.9[5]	7.4[3]
Vontobel Int'l Bd	-6.0[5]	5.9[5]	—
FTI Int'l Bond	-6.1[5]	—	—

FIXED-INCOME - INTERMEDIATE TERM

No-Load Fund	1997	Annualized 3 years	Annualized 5 years
Dreyfus Inter Inc	14.6[1]	—	—
Seneca Bond	12.8[1]	—	—
Price Spect-Inc	12.2[1]	13.0[1]	9.7[1]
Janus Flex Inc	11.4[1]	13.0[1]	10.1[1]
USAA Income	11.0[1]	11.9[1]	7.8[1]
Htchks & Wly Tot Ret	10.8[1]	12.0[1]	—
Westwood Inter Bd	10.7[1]	10.1[2]	6.8[3]
Citizens Tr Income	10.5[1]	10.8[1]	7.7[1]
Lexington GNMA	10.2[1]	10.5[1]	7.4[2]
Analytic Master Fix Inc	10.1[1]	10.6[1]	—
AON Gov Sec	10.0[1]	—	—
Price Summit GNMA	9.8[1]	10.2[2]	—
Elite Bond	9.8[1]	9.4[3]	6.8[3]
Asset Mgmt US Mrtg Sec	9.7[1]	9.4[3]	6.4[4]
Fremont Bond	9.7[1]	11.9[1]	—
Stein Roe Income	9.6[1]	11.2[1]	8.4[1]
Columbia Fix Inc	9.6[1]	10.4[1]	7.5[2]
Accessor Mort Sec	9.5[1]	10.1[2]	7.1[2]
USAA GNMA	9.5[1]	9.6[3]	7.1[2]
Price GNMA	9.5[1]	10.0[2]	6.8[3]
Vangd GNMA	9.5[1]	10.4[1]	7.2[2]
Vangd Bond Idx Total	9.4[1]	10.3[2]	7.4[2]
Vangd Bond Idx Inter	9.4[1]	10.8[1]	—
Harbor Bond	9.4[2]	11.0[1]	8.1[1]
Sit Bond	9.4[2]	10.1[2]	—
Dupree Inter Gov	9.4[2]	9.9[3]	6.9[3]
Blanchard Flex Inc.‡	9.4[2]	10.1[2]	7.4[2]
Price New Inc	9.3[2]	9.8[3]	7.3[2]
Stein Roe Inter Bd	9.3[2]	10.1[2]	7.2[2]
Federated US Gov 5-10	9.3[2]	—	—
Dreyfus Bond Mkt Idx	9.2[2]	9.5[3]	—
Analysts Inv Fix Inc	9.1[2]	11.1[1]	—
Fidelity Mortg Sec(Init Class)‡	9.1[2]	10.4[1]	7.9[1]
Payden & Rygel Glob Fl	9.1[2]	10.8[1]	8.4[1]
Independence One US Gov Sec	9.1[2]	9.6[3]	—
Strong Gov Sec	9.1[2]	10.4[2]	8.0[1]
Vangd-Adml Inter	9.0[2]	10.3[2]	7.4[2]
Smith Brdn Inter Dur US Gov	9.0[2]	10.1[2]	7.8[1]
Payden & Rygel Inv Qual Bd	9.0[2]	9.9[2]	—
Chicago Tr Bond	9.0[2]	10.0[2]	—
SAFECO GNMA	9.0[2]	9.4[3]	6.1[4]
Dreyfus Discpl Inter Bd	9.0[2]	—	—
Vangd Inter Trsy	9.0[2]	10.2[2]	7.6[2]
Fidelity Spart GNMA	8.9[2]	10.1[2]	6.9[2]
Vangd Inter Corp	8.9[2]	10.8[1]	—
Federated Income	8.9[2]	9.6[3]	6.5[3]
Monetta Inter Bd	8.9[2]	10.0[2]	—
Federated GNMA	8.8[3]	9.9[3]	6.6[3]
Warbg Pincus Fix Inc	8.8[3]	10.0[2]	8.0[1]
Fidelity GNMA	8.7[3]	10.0[2]	6.7[3]
Amer Cent-Benham GNMA	8.7[3]	9.8[3]	6.8[3]
Federated Inter Inc	8.6[3]	10.5[1]	—
Amer Cent-Benham Bd	8.6[3]	10.2[2]	7.1[2]
Accessor Inter Fix Inc	8.6[3]	9.6[3]	6.5[4]
AMEX-Strategist Gov Inc	8.6[3]	—	—
Wright Curr Inc	8.6[3]	10.0[2]	6.5[3]
UAM Mckee US Gov	8.5[3]	—	—
Excelsior Inter Mgd Inc	8.5[3]	9.6[3]	6.6[3]
Sefton US Gov	8.4[3]	—	—
Asset Mgmt Inter Mrtg	8.4[3]	8.3[4]	6.0[4]
Amer Cent-Benham Inter Bd	8.4[3]	8.7[4]	6.2[4]
Scudder GNMA	8.4[3]	9.6[3]	6.2[4]
Amer Cent-Benham Inter-Trm Treas	8.3[3]	8.6[4]	6.2[4]
SAFECO Inter Trsy	8.3[3]	8.3[5]	6.3[4]
Westcore Inter Bond	8.3[3]	8.9[4]	6.5[3]
Managers Inter Mortg	8.2[3]	9.5[3]	1.9[5]
Dreyfus ST Income	8.2[3]	8.5[4]	6.9[3]
Babson Bond-Port S	8.2[3]	8.7[4]	6.4[4]
Kiewit Inter Bond	8.1[4]	8.5[4]	—
Boston-1784 US Gov Med	8.1[4]	8.5[4]	—
Wm Blair Income	8.0[4]	8.4[4]	6.4[4]
McM Inter Fix	7.9[4]	8.9[4]	—
Founders Gov Sec	7.9[4]	7.0[5]	4.4[5]
Govt Street Bond	7.8[4]	8.9[4]	6.5[4]
FundMngr Bond	7.8[4]	8.8[4]	6.5[4]
Flex-Fund US Gov Bond	7.8[4]	8.5[4]	6.5[4]
Mosaic Gov	7.7[4]	7.3[5]	5.5[5]
Payden & Rygel Tot Ret	7.7[4]	8.5[4]	—
Dreyfus 100% US Inter	7.6[4]	8.7[4]	6.5[3]
Kent Inter Bd	7.6[4]	8.6[4]	6.1[4]
Bernstein Inter Dur	7.6[4]	9.5[3]	7.0[2]
Fidelity Inter Bond	7.6[4]	7.9[5]	6.7[3]
BNY Hamilton Inter Gov	7.5[4]	8.6[4]	5.6[5]
Fairport Gov Sec	7.5[4]	9.1[3]	—
Payden & Rygel Inter Bd	7.5[4]	8.2[5]	—
Independence One Fix Inc	7.5[4]	—	—
SSgA Inter Fix	7.4[4]	9.1[3]	—
WPG Core Bd	7.4[4]	8.2[5]	4.6[5]
Emerald US Gov Sec	7.4[4]	8.3[5]	6.0[4]
Rainier Inter Fix Inc	7.3[4]	7.8[5]	—
UBS Bond	7.2[5]	—	—
UAM Chi Asst Mgmt Int Bd	7.2[5]	—	—
Kayne Anderson Inter Tot Ret	7.2[5]	—	—
Marshall Inter Bd	7.2[5]	8.2[5]	5.6[5]
Vintage Fix Inc	7.1[5]	8.1[5]	5.9[5]

Stock and bond funds – ranked within objective *continued*

By 1997 performance

No-Load Fund	Total return percent with quintile ranks by objective		
	1997	Annualized 3 years	5 years
RSI Tr-Inter Bd	7.1[5]	8.3[5]	5.9[5]
State Farm Interm‡	7.1[5]	7.9[5]	5.9[5]
Nations S-I Gov	7.0[5]	7.3[5]	5.4[5]
Legg Mason Gov Inter	7.0[5]	8.4[4]	5.9[5]
Vintage Fix Tot Ret	6.7[5]	—	—
Primary US Gov	6.1[5]	7.9[5]	5.7[5]
Mosaic Bond	6.0[5]	7.4[5]	5.2[5]
Merriman Flex Bd	5.7[5]	9.2[3]	7.7[1]
Warbg Pincus Glob Fix Inc	2.2[5]	9.3[3]	8.1[1]
Price Glob Gov	1.6[5]	8.6[4]	6.5[3]
FTI Global Bond	-0.2[5]	—	—
Fidelity Int'l Bond	-1.3[5]	2.9[5]	2.1[5]
Nations Gl Gov	-1.3[5]	—	—
Legg Mason Glob Gov	-1.7[5]	8.7[4]	—
Payden & Rygel Int'l Bd	-3.2[5]	—	—
Price Int'l Bond	-3.2[5]	7.7[5]	7.9[1]
Scudder Int'l Bond	-4.2[5]	2.5[5]	2.7[5]
Amer Cent-Benham Int'l Bd	-5.9[5]	7.6[5]	7.2[2]
FIXED-INCOME · SHORT TERM			
Dreyfus ST Hi Yld	12.6[1]	—	—
Heartland US Gov	9.7[1]	10.0[1]	7.2[1]
Payden & Rygel US Trsy	8.8[1]	—	—
Price Trsy Inter	8.2[1]	8.7[1]	6.3[1]
AARP GNMA & Trsy	8.0[1]	8.3[1]	5.8[2]
BSR S-I Fix Inc	7.6[1]	9.0[1]	6.5[1]
Htchks & Wly Low Dur	7.6[1]	8.8[1]	—
Warbg Pincus Inter Gov	7.6[1]	8.4[1]	6.2[1]
Fidelity Spart Ltd Mat Gov	7.3[1]	8.3[1]	6.0[1]
Blanchard ST Flex‡	7.2[1]	7.7[2]	—
Northern US Gov	7.2[1]	7.6[2]	—
USAA ST Bond	7.2[1]	8.2[1]	—
Strong ST Bond	7.2[1]	8.6[1]	6.7[1]
Price Summit Ltd Trm	7.2[1]	7.1[3]	—
Prudential Gov Sec S-I	7.1[1]	7.9[1]	5.6[2]
Schwab ST Bd Mkt Idx	7.1[1]	7.3[2]	5.3[3]
Crabbe Hsn US Gov Bd	7.1[1]	7.2[3]	5.0[4]
Vangd Bond Idx Short	7.0[1]	8.1[1]	—
Montgmry Sht Dur Gov	7.0[2]	7.8[1]	6.5[1]
Vangd ST Corp	6.9[2]	8.1[1]	6.2[1]
Federated US Gov 2-5	6.9[2]	7.8[2]	5.5[2]
Nbrgr-Ber Ltd Mat	6.9[2]	7.3[2]	5.6[2]
Invesco ST Bond	6.7[2]	7.1[3]	—
UAM DSI Ltd Mat	6.7[2]	7.5[2]	5.0[4]
First Omaha S-I Fix	6.7[2]	7.5[2]	5.5[2]
Price ST Gov	6.7[2]	7.3[2]	4.8[5]
Janus ST Bond	6.6[2]	6.9[3]	5.4[2]
Fidelity Spart S-I Gov	6.6[2]	7.7[2]	5.6[2]
Fidelity S-I Gov	6.6[2]	7.5[2]	5.2[3]
Homestead ST Bond	6.6[2]	7.5[2]	5.8[1]
Fidelity Spart ST Bd	6.5[2]	7.1[3]	5.0[4]
Asset Mgmt ARM	6.5[2]	7.2[3]	5.6[2]
Strong Advantage	6.5[2]	6.9[4]	6.5[1]
Htchks & Wly ST Invest	6.5[2]	6.8[4]	—
Vangd-Adml Short	6.5[2]	7.7[2]	5.8[1]
Amer AAdv Mileage Ltd Inc	6.5[3]	6.4[5]	—
Sextant Bond	6.5[2]	—	—
Vangd ST Federal	6.5[3]	7.8[1]	5.8[1]
Federated ST Income	6.4[3]	7.5[2]	5.5[2]
Dean Witter ST Bond	6.4[3]	7.6[2]	—
Marshall ST Inc	6.4[3]	6.8[4]	5.1[3]

No-Load Fund	Total return percent with quintile ranks by objective		
	1997	Annualized 3 years	5 years
Vangd ST Trsy	6.4[3]	7.6[2]	5.7[2]
IAI Gov Bond	6.4[3]	6.9[4]	5.3[3]
Federated ARMS	6.3[3]	7.2[3]	5.2[3]
Smith Brdn Sh Dur US Gov	6.3[3]	6.2[5]	5.4[3]
Amer Cent-Benham Ltd Trm Bd	6.3[3]	7.2[3]	—
Boston-1784 ST Income	6.3[3]	7.3[2]	—
Price ST Bond	6.3[3]	6.6[4]	4.6[5]
Kiewit Sht Term Gov	6.3[3]	6.8[4]	—
Harbor Short Dur	6.3[3]	6.7[4]	5.4[3]
Kent ST Bd	6.3[3]	6.8[4]	4.9[4]
Asset Mgmt ST US Gov	6.3[3]	7.0[3]	5.4[3]
Eclipse Ultra Short	6.2[3]	6.5[5]	—
Fidelity ST Bond	6.2[4]	6.9[3]	5.0[4]
Nbrgr-Ber Ultra Sht‡	6.2[4]	6.0[5]	4.6[5]
Preferred ST Gov	6.2[4]	6.6[4]	4.9[4]
Invesco Inter Gov	6.2[4]	7.9[1]	6.0[1]
Scudder ST Bond	6.1[4]	6.9[4]	5.1[3]
Dreyfus S-I Gov	6.1[4]	7.5[2]	5.8[2]
JP Morgan ST Bond	6.1[4]	7.2[3]	—
Dreyfus 100% US Short	6.1[4]	7.2[3]	5.6[2]
Strong ST Global	6.1[4]	8.8[1]	—
Dean Witter ST US Treas	6.1[4]	6.6[5]	4.6[5]
Amer Cent-Benham ST Trsy	6.0[4]	6.6[4]	5.1[4]
BT Pyramid:Ltd Trm US Gov	6.0[4]	6.7[4]	5.2[3]
Amer Cent-Benham ST Gov	6.0[4]	6.8[4]	4.8[4]
Wright US Treas Near Term	5.9[4]	7.2[3]	5.2[3]
Managers Sht & Int Bd	5.9[4]	8.4[1]	4.8[4]
Excelsior ST Gov	5.9[4]	6.7[4]	5.1[4]
Payden & Rygel ST Bd	5.8[4]	6.9[3]	—
Nations ST Inc	5.8[4]	7.2[3]	5.6[2]
Federated US Gov 1-3	5.7[5]	6.5[5]	4.8[5]
Homestead ST Gov	5.7[5]	—	—
Emerald ST Inc	5.7[5]	6.9[4]	—
Bernstein Gov Sht Dur	5.7[5]	6.6[4]	4.9[4]
Columbia US Gov	5.6[5]	6.5[5]	5.1[4]
Managers ST Gov	5.5[5]	6.3[5]	3.2[5]
SSgA Yld Plus	5.5[5]	5.9[5]	5.0[4]
Bernstein Short Dur Plus	5.5[5]	6.8[4]	5.2[3]
Analytic ST Gov	5.5[5]	7.1[3]	—
Reynolds US Gov	5.4[5]	7.0[3]	4.8[5]
Permanent Vers Bd†	5.1[5]	5.8[5]	4.8[5]
RSI Tr-ST Invest	4.9[5]	5.0[5]	4.2[5]
Schroder Ser:ST Invest	4.9[5]	4.9[5]	—
IAI Reserve	4.6[5]	5.3[5]	4.3[5]
Capstone Gov Inc	4.4[5]	4.7[5]	3.7[5]
Permanent Treasy†	4.1[5]	4.4[5]	3.8[5]
API T-1 Trsy	2.8[5]	4.1[5]	—
Fontaine Glob Inc	-27.3[5]	-1.9[5]	2.9[5]
TAX-FREE · LONG TERM			
Fundamental HY Muni	15.7[1]	14.8[1]	6.7[4]
AMEX-Strategist TF HY	14.1[1]	—	—
Strong Hi Yld Muni	13.9[1]	11.1[1]	—
Strong Muni Bond	12.1[1]	8.5[5]	6.4[4]
Scudder Hi Yld TF	12.0[1]	11.6[1]	7.7[1]
USAA Texas TF	11.7[1]	12.9[1]	—
Price Summit Muni Inc	11.6[1]	11.4[1]	—
SAFECO CA TF	11.6[1]	13.0[1]	8.2[1]
Fundamental CA Muni	11.3[1]	10.6[2]	4.8[5]
USAA FL TF	11.2[1]	11.3[1]	—
Drey-Basic Muni	10.9[1]	11.4[1]	—

Stock and bond funds – ranked within objective *continued*

By 1997 performance

No-Load Fund	Total return percent with quintile ranks by objective			No-Load Fund	Total return percent with quintile ranks by objective		
	1997	Annualized 3 years	5 years		1997	Annualized 3 years	5 years
SAFECO Insur Muni	10.7[1]	12.2[1]	—	Boston-1784 MA TE Inc	8.9[3]	8.6[5]	—
SAFECO Muni Bd	10.7[1]	11.5[1]	7.5[1]	Fidelity Spart MN Muni Inc	8.8[3]	9.4[4]	6.7[4]
USAA NY Bond	10.6[1]	10.7[2]	7.0[3]	Fidelity Spart MD Muni Inc	8.8[3]	10.0[3]	—
Amer Cent-Benham CA Hi Yld	10.4[1]	11.4[1]	8.2[1]	Nations NC Muni	8.8[3]	10.3[2]	—
USAA TE Long	10.4[1]	11.0[1]	7.2[2]	Dreyfus NJ Muni	8.8[3]	9.1[4]	6.6[4]
USAA CA Bond	10.3[1]	12.3[1]	7.7[1]	Blanchard Flex TF‡	8.8[3]	11.5[1]	—
Fidelity Spart Agg Muni‡	10.3[1]	9.5[4]	7.0[3]	Fidelity NY Insur Muni Inc‡	8.8[3]	10.2[2]	6.8[3]
Scudder CA TF	10.2[1]	10.7[1]	7.4[1]	Nations TX Muni	8.8[3]	10.5[2]	—
Price TF Hi Yld	10.2[1]	10.5[2]	7.8[1]	Drey-General CA	8.8[3]	10.2[2]	7.2[2]
Schwab CA Long	10.2[1]	11.3[1]	7.2[2]	Value Line TE Hi Yld	8.8[3]	9.6[3]	6.4[4]
Fidelity Spart NY Muni Inc‡	10.0[1]	11.0[1]	7.3[2]	Fidelity Spart FL Muni	8.7[4]	10.3[2]	7.5[1]
Schwab LT TF	9.9[1]	10.6[1]	7.4[1]	Vangd NY Insur LT	8.7[4]	10.0[3]	7.3[2]
Scudder NY TF	9.9[1]	10.2[1]	7.0[3]	Fidelity Spart OH Muni Inc	8.7[4]	9.7[3]	7.0[3]
Sit TF Income	9.8[1]	9.4[4]	7.5[1]	Babson TF Long	8.7[4]	9.4[4]	6.3[4]
Dupree NC TF Inc	9.8[1]	—	—	Nations FL Muni	8.7[4]	10.2[2]	—
Fidelity Spart CA Muni Inc	9.8[1]	11.1[1]	7.2[2]	Scudder OH TF	8.7[4]	9.9[3]	7.1[3]
Fidelity NY Muni Inc	9.7[2]	10.9[1]	7.2[3]	Invesco TF Long	8.7[4]	8.8[5]	6.5[4]
Price GA TF	9.7[2]	10.3[2]	—	Northern TE Bond	8.7[4]	9.5[4]	—
Amer Cent-Benham CA Long	9.6[2]	10.8[1]	7.7[1]	Price MD TF	8.6[4]	9.5[4]	7.1[3]
Drey-General NY	9.6[2]	9.6[3]	6.9[3]	Vangd Muni Insur LT	8.6[4]	10.2[2]	7.4[1]
Fidelity Spart Insur Muni Inc	9.5[2]	10.5[2]	7.2[2]	Vangd NJ Insur LT	8.6[4]	9.5[4]	7.2[3]
Price NY TF	9.5[2]	10.0[3]	7.3[2]	Nations GA Muni	8.6[4]	10.2[2]	—
Stein Roe Hi Yld Muni	9.5[2]	10.4[2]	7.4[2]	Boston-1784 CT TE Inc	8.5[4]	8.8[4]	—
Amer Cent-Benham Long TF	9.5[2]	9.7[3]	7.2[2]	Scudder MA TF	8.5[4]	10.0[3]	7.4[2]
USAA VA Bond	9.5[2]	10.5[2]	7.3[2]	Vangd OH Insur LT	8.5[4]	9.7[3]	7.2[3]
Excelsior LT TE	9.4[2]	11.9[1]	8.8[1]	Rushmore VA TF	8.5[4]	8.6[5]	6.4[4]
Value Line NY TE	9.3[2]	9.5[4]	6.7[4]	Sefton CA Tax-Free	8.5[4]	—	—
Nations Muni Inc	9.3[2]	10.9[1]	7.4[2]	Dreyfus Insur Muni	8.4[4]	8.6[5]	5.7[5]
Parnassus CA TE	9.3[2]	10.8[1]	7.5[1]	Mosaic TF VA	8.4[4]	9.1[4]	6.0[5]
Price TF Inc	9.3[2]	10.0[3]	7.2[2]	Columbia Muni Bd	8.4[4]	8.7[5]	6.2[5]
Fidelity Spart MA Muni Inc	9.3[2]	10.2[3]	7.2[2]	Fidelity Spart NJ Muni Inc	8.3[4]	9.2[4]	6.8[4]
Stein Roe Mgd Muni	9.3[2]	9.8[3]	6.8[3]	Fidelity Spart PA Muni Inc	8.3[4]	9.8[3]	7.3[2]
CA Inv Tr-CA TF	9.3[2]	10.8[1]	7.3[2]	Kent TF Inc	8.3[4]	—	—
Vangd Muni Long	9.3[2]	10.6[2]	7.7[1]	Boston-1784 RI TE Inc	8.3[4]	9.0[4]	—
Scudder Mngd Muni	9.3[2]	9.9[3]	7.2[3]	Dreyfus CA TE	8.3[4]	8.5[5]	5.8[5]
Amer Cent-Benham CA Insured	9.3[2]	10.5[2]	7.4[1]	Vangd PA Insur LT	8.3[4]	9.5[4]	7.2[2]
Nations VA Muni	9.2[2]	10.6[2]	—	Mosaic TF Nat	8.2[4]	8.7[5]	5.6[5]
Vangd Muni Hi Yld	9.2[2]	10.5[2]	7.6[1]	Sit MN TF Inc	8.2[4]	8.6[5]	—
Fidelity Spart Muni Inc	9.2[2]	10.0[3]	6.8[4]	Mosaic TF MO	8.1[5]	8.9[4]	5.6[5]
Fidelity Muni Bd(Init Class)‡	9.2[2]	10.3[2]	6.8[3]	Heartland WI TF	8.1[5]	9.7[3]	6.5[4]
Fidelity Spart CT Muni	9.1[2]	10.0[3]	7.0[3]	Drey-General Muni	8.1[5]	9.3[4]	6.5[4]
Dreyfus NY TE	9.1[2]	9.1[4]	6.4[4]	North Carolina TF	8.0[5]	9.1[4]	—
Price NJ TF	9.1[2]	9.6[3]	7.1[3]	Dupree KY TF Inc	8.0[5]	8.3[5]	6.8[3]
Fidelity Spart MI Muni Inc	9.1[3]	9.2[4]	6.5[4]	Mosaic TF MD	8.0[5]	8.4[5]	—
Emerald FL TE	9.1[3]	9.2[4]	6.7[4]	Fidelity Spart AZ Muni	8.0[5]	9.8[3]	—
Price CA TF	9.1[3]	10.2[2]	7.3[2]	Dreyfus Muni Bond	7.9[5]	9.0[4]	6.3[5]
Dreyfus MA TE	9.1[3]	9.4[4]	6.7[4]	Empire Builder TF Bond	7.9[5]	8.5[5]	6.5[4]
Nations TN Muni	9.0[3]	10.4[2]	—	Mosaic TF AZ	7.9[5]	8.6[5]	5.5[5]
Price VA TF	9.0[3]	9.8[3]	7.2[3]	Rushmore MD TF	7.9[5]	8.3[5]	6.2[5]
Nations MD Muni	9.0[3]	10.2[3]	—	Independence One MI Muni	7.7[5]	—	—
IAA Trust TE Bd	9.0[3]	9.1[4]	5.8[5]	JP Morgan TE Bond	7.4[5]	8.0[5]	6.1[5]
Janus Federal TE	9.0[3]	9.7[3]	—	JP Morgan NY Tot Ret	7.4[5]	8.1[5]	—
CGM American TF	9.0[3]	9.8[3]	—	Dreyfus NY Insur	7.4[5]	8.2[5]	5.6[5]
SAFECO WA Muni	9.0[3]	10.4[2]	—	Westcore CO TE	7.4[5]	8.2[5]	6.1[5]
Scudder PA TF	8.9[3]	9.8[3]	7.1[3]	State Farm Muni Bd‡	7.3[5]	8.2[5]	6.3[5]
Vangd FL Insur	8.9[3]	10.1[3]	7.6[1]	First Hawaii Muni Bd	7.1[5]	8.5[5]	5.9[5]
OVB WV TE	8.9[3]	9.4[4]	—	Sextant Idaho TE	7.1[5]	8.0[5]	5.7[5]
AARP Insur TF Gen	8.9[3]	9.5[4]	6.8[4]	Jamestown VA Tax-Free	7.0[5]	7.7[5]	—
Vangd CA Insur LT	8.9[3]	10.7[1]	7.6[1]	Payden & Rygel TE Bd	6.6[5]	—	—
Dupree TN TF Inc	8.9[3]	10.7[1]	—	Accessor S-I Fix Inc	6.3[5]	7.1[5]	5.0[5]

Stock and bond funds – ranked within objective *continued*

By 1997 performance

No-Load Fund	Total return percent with quintile ranks by objective		
	1997	Annualized 3 years	5 years
Gov Street AL TF....	6.3[5]	7.4[5]	—
Kiewit Tax Exempt....	6.2[5]	6.5[5]	—
Excelsior CA TE....	5.7[5]	—	—
Fundamental NY Muni....	1.5[5]	2.8[5]	-0.6[5]
TAX-FREE - INTERMEDIATE TERM			
USAA TE Inter....	9.4[1]	9.6[1]	7.1[1]
Boston-1784 TE Med Term....	9.1[1]	9.1[1]	—
US Glb:Tax Free....	9.1[1]	8.9[1]	6.5[1]
Drey-Basic Inter Muni....	8.8[1]	9.1[1]	—
Price Summit Muni Inter....	8.4[1]	8.9[1]	—
Fidelity Ltd Muni Inc....	8.3[1]	9.1[1]	6.7[1]
Dreyfus PA Inter Muni....	8.3[1]	9.2[1]	—
Dreyfus NY Inter....	8.2[1]	8.7[1]	6.4[2]
Amer Cent-Benham FL Inter....	8.2[1]	8.4[2]	—
Fidelity Spart NY Inter Muni Inc‡....	8.1[1]	8.7[1]	—
Fidelity Spart Inter Muni....	8.0[1]	8.9[1]	—
WPG Inter Muni....	7.9[1]	8.0[3]	—
Northern FL Inter TE....	7.7[1]	—	—
Vangd CA Insur Inter....	7.7[2]	8.7[2]	—
Scudder Medium TF....	7.7[2]	8.6[2]	6.5[2]
Dreyfus CA Inter....	7.6[2]	8.2[3]	6.5[1]
Dreyfus Inter Muni....	7.6[2]	8.5[2]	6.3[2]
Dreyfus CT Inter....	7.6[2]	8.4[2]	6.5[1]
Dreyfus MA Inter....	7.5[2]	8.4[2]	6.1[3]
Federated PA Inter....	7.5[2]	8.7[2]	—
Montgmry CA TF Inter....	7.5[2]	7.8[4]	—
SAFECO Inter Muni....	7.5[2]	8.7[1]	—
Stein Roe Inter Muni....	7.5[2]	8.2[2]	6.3[2]
BT Invest:Inter TF....	7.5[2]	8.1[3]	6.0[3]
Amer Cent-Benham CA Inter....	7.4[2]	8.3[2]	6.2[2]
Nbrgr-Ber Muni....	7.4[3]	7.8[4]	5.7[4]
Amer Cent-Benham Inter TF....	7.4[3]	7.9[4]	6.0[3]
Excelsior Inter TE....	7.3[3]	8.8[1]	6.5[2]
Fremont CA Inter....	7.3[3]	8.6[2]	6.1[3]
Price TF Ins Inter....	7.2[3]	8.1[3]	6.7[1]
Nations Int Muni....	7.1[3]	8.4[2]	—
Vangd Muni Inter....	7.1[3]	8.2[2]	6.7[1]
Crabbe Hsn OR Muni....	7.0[3]	7.3[5]	5.5[5]
Nations NC Int Muni....	7.0[3]	8.1[3]	5.9[3]
Nations FL Int Muni....	7.0[3]	8.1[3]	6.1[3]
Nations GA Int Muni....	7.0[3]	8.1[3]	5.9[4]
Dreyfus NJ Inter....	6.9[3]	8.0[3]	6.1[2]
Nations TX Int Muni....	6.9[3]	7.6[4]	—
Amer Cent-Benham AZ Inter....	6.9[4]	7.9[4]	—
Federated Inter Muni....	6.9[4]	7.4[5]	5.5[5]
Kent Inter TF....	6.8[4]	7.5[5]	5.5[5]
Marshall Inter TF....	6.8[4]	7.3[5]	—
Price FL Ins Inter....	6.7[4]	7.8[4]	—
Nations TN Int Muni....	6.7[4]	8.0[3]	—
Bernstein Dvsfd Muni....	6.7[4]	7.7[4]	5.7[4]
Excelsior NY Inter TE....	6.7[4]	8.1[3]	5.8[4]

No-Load Fund	Total return percent with quintile ranks by objective		
	1997	Annualized 3 years	5 years
Nations VA Int Muni....	6.6[4]	7.7[4]	5.6[5]
Nations SC Int Muni....	6.6[4]	7.9[4]	6.0[3]
Vintage Inter TF....	6.6[4]	8.1[3]	—
Bernstein NY Muni....	6.5[4]	7.6[5]	5.7[4]
Nations MD Int Muni....	6.5[5]	7.8[4]	5.6[5]
CA Inv Tr-CA Insur Inter....	6.4[5]	8.1[3]	5.8[4]
Invesco TF Inter....	6.4[5]	7.3[5]	—
Dreyfus FL Inter....	6.3[5]	7.8[4]	6.1[2]
Bernstein CA Muni....	6.3[5]	7.9[4]	5.6[4]
BNY Hamilton Inter NY TE....	6.2[5]	7.2[5]	5.1[5]
Warbg Pincus NY Inter....	5.9[5]	6.5[5]	5.7[4]
Northern Inter TE....	5.8[5]	7.0[5]	—
Chicago Tr Muni....	5.5[5]	6.5[5]	—
Dupree TN TF Sht-Med....	5.4[5]	5.5[5]	—
Dupree KY Sht-Med....	5.2[5]	5.1[5]	4.4[5]
Dupree NC TF Sht-Med....	5.0[5]	—	—
Kayne Anderson Inter TF....	4.2[5]	—	—
TAX-FREE - SHORT TERM			
Nations SC Muni....	8.4[1]	10.2[1]	—
Heartland Sht Dur Hi Yld Muni....	7.4[1]	—	—
Strong ST Muni....	6.9[1]	5.7[3]	4.4[4]
US Glb:Near Term TF....	6.6[1]	5.8[2]	5.4[1]
Scudder Ltd TF....	5.9[1]	6.4[1]	—
USAA TE Short....	5.9[1]	6.1[1]	4.9[2]
Scudder MA Ltd TF....	5.7[2]	6.2[1]	—
Amer Cent-Benham Ltd Term TF....	5.5[2]	5.3[4]	—
Fidelity Spart S-I Muni....	5.5[2]	5.9[2]	4.9[1]
Kent MI Muni....	5.4[2]	5.6[3]	—
Price TF S-I....	5.3[2]	5.8[3]	4.8[2]
Schwab CA S-I....	5.3[2]	6.5[1]	—
Amer Cent-Benham CA Ltd Term....	5.3[3]	5.8[2]	4.5[3]
Schwab S-I TF....	5.3[3]	6.0[1]	—
Dreyfus S-I Muni....	5.2[3]	5.5[4]	4.5[3]
Strong Muni Advantage....	5.1[3]	—	—
Vangd Muni Ltd Trm....	5.1[3]	5.9[2]	4.8[2]
Babson TF Short....	5.1[3]	5.9[2]	4.5[4]
FL Hough ST....	4.9[4]	5.4[4]	—
Kent Ltd Trm TF....	4.6[4]	5.5[3]	—
Excelsior ST TE....	4.6[4]	5.2[4]	4.1[4]
Nations ST Muni....	4.6[4]	5.5[3]	—
Payden & Rygel Sht Dur TE....	4.5[4]	4.8[5]	—
Federated ST Muni....	4.5[4]	5.5[3]	4.1[5]
Price VA ST....	4.3[5]	5.1[4]	—
Price MD ST TF....	4.2[5]	5.0[5]	—
Vangd Muni Short....	4.1[5]	4.6[5]	3.8[5]
Bernstein Sht Dur Divsfd Muni....	4.0[5]	4.6[5]	—
Bernstein NY Short Dur Muni....	3.8[5]	4.5[5]	—
Bernstein CA Short Dur Muni....	3.6[5]	4.5[5]	—

Stock and bond funds – ranked within objective *continued*

By 1995-1997 performance

| No-Load Fund | Total return percent with quintile ranks by objective | | | No-Load Fund | Total return percent with quintile ranks by objective | | |
	1997	Annualized 3 years	5 years		1997	Annualized 3 years	5 years
AGGRESSIVE GROWTH FUNDS				Skyline Spcl Eqty II	26.2[2]	**24.5[2]**	—
Rydex Nova	42.3[1]	**39.0[1]**	—	Amer Cent-20th Cent Ultra	23.1[3]	**24.5[2]**	17.8[2]
Bridgeway Ult Sm Co SC	38.0[1]	**35.8[1]**	—	Lazard Small Cap SC(O shrs)	28.1[2]	**24.5[2]**	20.7[1]
Jurika & Voyles MiniCap SC	23.9[2]	**35.6[1]**	—	Stein Roe Cap Opp	6.2[5]	**24.4[3]**	19.7[1]
TIP:Turner Small Cap SC‡	14.8[4]	**35.5[1]**	—	Legg Mason Spec Invest SC	22.1[3]	**24.4[3]**	15.7[3]
Rydex OTC	21.9[3]	**35.3[1]**	—	C&O Market Opport	29.4[2]	**24.3[3]**	16.9[3]
Fremont US Micro Cap SC	7.0[5]	**34.8[1]**	—	Schroder Cap:US Eqty	23.3[3]	**24.3[3]**	15.4[3]
Rainier Sm/Mid Cap	32.2[1]	**33.7[1]**	—	BT Invest:Sm Cap SC	13.2[4]	**24.3[3]**	—
Fidelity New Millnm††‡	24.6[2]	**32.6[1]**	24.0[1]	Sit Mid Cap Gro	17.7[3]	**24.2[3]**	15.7[3]
SAFECO Growth SC	50.0[1]	**32.5[1]**	22.8[1]	Gabelli Sm Cap Gro SC	36.5[1]	**24.1[3]**	17.9[2]
Schroder Cap:US Sm Co SC	26.9[2]	**32.2[1]**	—	Brandywine	12.0[4]	**23.8[3]**	18.4[2]
First Eagle America	29.5[2]	**31.7[1]**	22.5[1]	Northern Sm Cap SC	29.8[2]	**23.7[3]**	—
Fidelity Export & Multi††SC	23.7[3]	**31.4[1]**	—	Citizens Tr Emg Gr SC	17.7[4]	**23.6[3]**	—
Janus Twenty	29.7[2]	**31.2[1]**	16.9[1]	USAA Agg Growth SC	7.6[5]	**23.5[3]**	15.1[3]
SSgA Sm Cap SC	23.6[3]	**31.2[1]**	20.4[1]	Sit Sm Cap Gro SC	7.6[5]	**23.5[3]**	—
Accessor Sm\Mid Cap	36.2[1]	**30.9[1]**	19.7[1]	Cornercap Growth	32.9[1]	**23.4[3]**	16.4[3]
CGM Capital Dev‡	23.9[2]	**30.8[1]**	17.3[2]	Fidelity Emg Gro††	19.4[3]	**23.4[3]**	17.6[2]
Dreyfus Apprec	27.8[2]	**30.4[1]**	18.2[2]	Kent Sm Co Gro SC	27.7[2]	**23.4[3]**	17.1[2]
Spectra	24.7[2]	**30.1[1]**	21.1[1]	Fidelity OTC††	9.9[4]	**23.4[3]**	14.6[4]
UAM FMA Small Co SC	40.4[1]	**30.0[1]**	22.3[1]	Babson Enterprise‡ SC	32.4[1]	**23.2[3]**	17.4[2]
Vangd Morgan	30.8[1]	**29.9[1]**	18.3[2]	WPG Tudor SC	11.1[4]	**23.1[3]**	13.8[4]
Trainer-Wrthm First Mutual	23.1[3]	**29.7[1]**	16.3[3]	Kaufmann SC	12.6[4]	**23.0[3]**	19.1[1]
Harbor Cap App	31.4[1]	**29.5[1]**	20.3[1]	Fidelity Fifty	23.0[3]	**22.9[3]**	—
Berger Sm Cap Val SC	36.4[1]	**29.3[1]**	21.8[1]	Nbrgr-Ber Manhtn	29.2[2]	**22.9[3]**	14.5[4]
Stein Roe Growth Stk‡	31.6[1]	**29.2[1]**	16.4[3]	Harbor Growth	20.9[3]	**22.9[3]**	14.2[4]
UAM RHJ Sm Cap SC	20.7[3]	**29.2[1]**	—	Robrtsn Stph Val Gro	13.9[4]	**22.8[3]**	22.0[1]
Founders Growth	26.5[2]	**29.0[1]**	21.1[1]	Schwab Sm Cap Idx(Inv) SC	25.7[2]	**22.8[3]**	—
AARP Capital Growth	35.1[1]	**28.6[1]**	17.3[2]	Nations Emg Gro SC	20.5[3]	**22.7[3]**	15.7[3]
Price New Amer	21.1[3]	**28.0[1]**	17.9[2]	Navellier Ser: Sm Cap Eq SC	11.2[4]	**22.7[3]**	—
Bruce	30.2[1]	**28.0[1]**	16.0[3]	Perritt Micro Cap Opp SC	22.1[3]	**22.6[3]**	13.0[4]
Scudder Large Cap Gro	32.8[1]	**27.6[1]**	15.5[3]	Pathfinder SC	24.9[2]	**22.4[3]**	11.5[5]
Managers Spec Eqty SC	24.5[2]	**27.6[1]**	19.1[1]	Fidelity Small Cap Selector†† SC	27.2[2]	**22.3[3]**	—
Westcore Sm Cap Oppty SC	27.8[2]	**27.6[2]**	—	Value Line Spec Sit	32.2[1]	**22.3[3]**	15.8[3]
Value Line Levergd Gro	23.8[2]	**27.6[2]**	18.4[2]	Wright Jr Blue Ch SC	28.9[2]	**22.2[3]**	13.9[4]
Eclipse Equity SC	33.3[1]	**27.5[2]**	18.2[2]	Dreyfus New Leaders SC	19.5[3]	**22.1[4]**	16.3[3]
US Glb:Bonnel Growth	10.3[4]	**27.0[2]**	—	Berger Sm Co Gro SC	16.2[4]	**22.0[4]**	—
Fidelity Contrafund††‡	23.0[3]	**26.9[2]**	19.7[1]	Brown Cap Sm Co SC	15.8[4]	**22.0[4]**	15.0[3]
Babson Enterprise II SC	33.3[1]	**26.8[2]**	17.7[2]	WPG Growth SC	9.7[5]	**21.8[4]**	12.3[5]
LKCM Sm Cap SC	23.1[3]	**26.8[2]**	—	Stein Roe Spec Venture SC	9.7[4]	**21.5[4]**	—
Columbia Growth	26.3[2]	**26.6[2]**	17.9[2]	Amer Cent-20th Cent Growth	29.3[2]	**21.4[4]**	12.8[4]
Schroder Ser:Sm Cap Val SC	32.1[1]	**26.4[2]**	—	Invesco Small Co Val SC	25.0[2]	**21.4[4]**	—
Permanent Agg Growth	32.7[1]	**26.3[2]**	19.9[1]	Quant Numeric SC	7.2[5]	**21.3[4]**	19.1[1]
Skyline Special Eqty SC‡	35.4[1]	**26.2[2]**	19.5[1]	Founders Discovery SC	11.9[4]	**21.2[4]**	12.7[4]
Strong Growth	19.1[3]	**26.1[2]**	—	Scudder Development SC	6.9[5]	**21.0[4]**	12.8[4]
Bramwell Growth	33.7[1]	**25.9[2]**	—	Federated Mini Cap SC	20.4[3]	**20.6[4]**	14.5[4]
Ariel Growth SC	36.4[1]	**25.9[2]**	15.8[3]	Janus Mercury	11.9[4]	**20.5[4]**	—
Price New Horizon‡ SC	9.8[4]	**25.9[2]**	19.6[1]	General Securities	13.4[4]	**20.4[4]**	14.3[4]
PC&J Performance	35.6[1]	**25.9[2]**	18.1[2]	BT Pyramid:Eqty App	15.4[4]	**20.3[4]**	—
Bridgeway Agg Gro	18.3[3]	**25.7[2]**	—	Robrtsn Stph Emg Gro SC	18.5[3]	**20.1[4]**	14.9[3]
Montgmry Sm Cap‡ SC	23.9[2]	**25.7[2]**	17.3[2]	Trent Equity	25.2[2]	**19.9[4]**	10.2[5]
Gradison Oppty Value SC	31.1[1]	**25.7[2]**	16.6[3]	Gateway Sm Cap Idx SC	20.6[3]	**19.8[4]**	—
Price Cap Oppty	15.9[4]	**25.6[2]**	—	Invesco Sm Co Gro SC	18.3[3]	**19.7[4]**	15.3[3]
Invesco Dynamics	24.1[2]	**25.5[2]**	18.2[2]	Royce Micro-Cap SC	24.7[2]	**19.7[4]**	17.1[2]
Galaxy II Sm Co Idx SC	23.6[3]	**25.3[2]**	16.1[3]	Reserve Sm Cap Gr SC	-0.5[5]	**19.6[4]**	—
RSI Tr-Emg Gro SC	8.3[5]	**25.3[2]**	19.7[1]	Managers Cap App	12.7[4]	**19.6[4]**	14.5[4]
JP Morgan US Sm Co SC	22.8[3]	**25.0[2]**	14.8[4]	FundMngr Agg Gro†	16.7[4]	**19.3[4]**	13.9[4]
Warbg Pincus Emg Gro SC	21.3[3]	**24.9[2]**	17.8[2]	Founders Special	16.4[4]	**19.1[4]**	13.2[4]
Montgmry Micro Cap‡ SC	27.1[2]	**24.9[2]**	—	PBHG Emg Growth SC	-3.7[5]	**18.7[4]**	—
Fidelity Growth Co	18.9[3]	**24.7[2]**	17.1[2]	Founders Frontier SC	6.2[5]	**18.5[4]**	13.5[4]
Fidelity Magellan††‡	26.5[2]	**24.6[2]**	18.8[2]	Scout Regional SC	23.0[3]	**18.4[4]**	12.1[5]

Stock and bond funds – ranked within objective *continued*

By 1995-1997 performance

No-Load Fund	Total return percent with quintile ranks by objective			No-Load Fund	Total return percent with quintile ranks by objective		
	1997	Annualized 3 years	5 years		1997	Annualized 3 years	5 years
Emerald Small Cap SC...	12.6[4]	**18.4[4]**	—	Wilshire Target Lg Gro...	32.2[1]	**31.4[1]**	18.2[2]
Vangd Explorer SC...	14.6[4]	**18.2[4]**	13.9[4]	Clipper...	30.4[2]	**31.3[1]**	19.7[2]
Columbia Special...	12.6[4]	**18.2[4]**	15.5[3]	Gabelli Growth...	42.6[1]	**31.2[1]**	19.4[2]
Wasatch MidCap...	-0.5[5]	**17.9[4]**	11.5[5]	Gintel...	31.5[2]	**31.2[1]**	14.0[4]
Lancaster Crest Sm Cap SC...	8.5[5]	**17.8[4]**	13.5[4]	Price Blue Chip...	27.5[3]	**31.0[1]**	—
Wilshire Target Sm Gro SC...	11.7[4]	**17.7[5]**	13.2[4]	Pinnacle Fund...	35.4[1]	**31.0[1]**	18.1[3]
Fairmont...	15.3[4]	**17.3[5]**	14.9[4]	Domini Social Eqty...	36.0[1]	**30.8[1]**	18.9[2]
Wasatch Agg Eqty‡ SC...	19.2[3]	**17.1[5]**	15.8[3]	Warbg Pincus Cap App...	31.4[2]	**30.8[1]**	20.3[1]
Oberweis Emg Growth SC...	-8.6[5]	**17.1[5]**	11.2[5]	Nbrgr-Ber Genesis SC...	34.9[1]	**30.7[1]**	20.1[1]
PBHG Growth...	-3.3[5]	**16.8[5]**	19.6[1]	Nicholas Fund...	37.0[1]	**30.5[1]**	18.0[3]
Federated Mgd Agg Gro...	14.9[4]	**16.4[5]**	—	Nbrgr-Ber Partners...	29.2[2]	**30.3[1]**	20.4[1]
Matterhorn Growth...	13.7[4]	**16.3[5]**	11.9[5]	Baron Asset SC...	33.9[1]	**30.2[1]**	24.0[1]
Rainbow Fund...	5.0[5]	**16.3[5]**	7.4[5]	Vangd US Growth...	25.9[3]	**30.0[1]**	17.6[3]
Berger 100...	13.6[4]	**16.1[5]**	12.1[5]	Vangd Primecap...	36.8[1]	**29.9[1]**	23.6[1]
IAI Emg Growth SC...	-2.9[5]	**15.8[5]**	12.3[5]	Dreyfus Third Cent...	29.4[2]	**29.7[1]**	16.3[3]
Fidelity Trend...	8.5[5]	**15.7[5]**	11.5[5]	Scudder Value‡...	35.3[1]	**29.4[1]**	19.7[1]
Pin Oak Agg Stk SC...	1.3[5]	**15.5[5]**	9.4[5]	Westcore Blue Chip...	30.9[2]	**29.4[1]**	19.6[2]
Arbor OVB Emg Gro SC...	0.5[5]	**15.2[5]**	—	Analytic Enhncd Eqty...	29.9[2]	**29.3[1]**	—
Value Line Sm Cap SC...	11.5[4]	**15.2[5]**	—	Fremont Growth...	29.0[2]	**29.2[2]**	18.2[2]
Mosaic Mid-Cap Gro...	17.1[4]	**14.9[5]**	10.9[5]	Papp L Roy Stock...	33.1[1]	**29.2[2]**	16.7[3]
Strong Discovery SC...	10.8[4]	**14.9[5]**	11.8[5]	Accessor Growth...	33.2[1]	**29.2[2]**	20.7[1]
Bull & Bear Spec Eqty...	5.2[5]	**14.3[5]**	7.8[5]	Vangd Idx Total Mkt...	31.0[2]	**29.1[2]**	18.9[2]
Merriman Levgd Gro...	12.2[4]	**13.8[5]**	8.8[5]	Salomon Opportunity...	33.0[1]	**29.0[2]**	19.6[2]
Maxus Laureate...	6.0[5]	**13.6[5]**	—	Vintage Eqty...	30.1[2]	**28.9[2]**	18.2[2]
Capp-Rush Emg Growth SC...	4.7[5]	**13.3[5]**	10.6[5]	Strong Schafer Value...	29.3[2]	**28.8[2]**	20.4[1]
Amer Cent-20th Cent Giftrust...	-1.2[5]	**13.1[5]**	16.6[3]	Sit Large Cap Gro...	31.7[2]	**28.8[2]**	17.7[3]
Amer Cent-20th Cent Vista...	-8.7[5]	**12.8[5]**	9.6[5]	SSgA Matrix Eqty...	34.2[1]	**28.6[2]**	19.8[1]
Excelsior Sm Cap SC...	14.2[4]	**11.1[5]**	13.0[4]	Ariel Apprec...	37.9[1]	**28.4[2]**	15.9[4]
Crabbe Hsn Special SC...	11.2[4]	**9.3[5]**	14.4[4]	Nicholas Ltd Edit SC...	33.0[1]	**28.3[2]**	17.4[3]
American Heritage...	75.0[1]	**4.8[5]**	1.1[5]	UAM Sirach Growth...	32.1[2]	**28.2[2]**	—
Robrtsn Stph Contrn...	-29.5[5]	**3.9[5]**	—	Nicholas II SC...	37.0[1]	**28.1[2]**	17.7[3]
Fontaine Cap App...	-27.3[5]	**-1.2[5]**	2.4[5]	Gateway Cincinnati...	29.0[2]	**27.9[2]**	—
Lindner Bulwark...	-22.3[5]	**-3.8[5]**	—	Stratton Sm Cap Yld SC...	42.6[1]	**27.8[2]**	—
Steadman Amer Indust...	-12.4[5]	**-10.2[5]**	-13.1[5]	Price Sm Cap Stk...	28.8[2]	**27.8[2]**	19.9[1]
Rydex Ursa...	-21.0[5]	**-17.9[5]**	—	Wasatch Growth...	27.5[3]	**27.8[2]**	18.9[2]
Steadman Tech & Gro...	-28.2[5]	**-28.9[5]**	-26.9[5]	Scudder Large Cap Val...	32.5[1]	**27.7[2]**	17.7[3]
GROWTH FUNDS				Price Mid Cap Gro...	18.3[5]	**27.7[2]**	21.4[1]
Legg Mason Value...	37.1[1]	**38.7[1]**	24.7[1]	UAM Strlng Part Eqty...	24.9[3]	**27.6[2]**	17.6[3]
Torray...	37.1[1]	**38.6[1]**	23.7[1]	Oakmark...	32.6[1]	**27.5[2]**	22.8[1]
Weitz Ser Hickory...	39.2[1]	**38.3[1]**	—	Vangd Tax Mgd:Cap App...	27.3[3]	**27.4[2]**	—
White Oak Gro...	24.3[3]	**35.9[1]**	21.6[1]	Northern Select Eqty...	31.9[2]	**27.4[2]**	—
Sequoia‡...	43.2[1]	**35.1[1]**	23.0[1]	Lazard Equity(O shrs)...	25.1[3]	**27.4[2]**	20.6[1]
Rainier Core Eqty...	33.9[1]	**34.4[1]**	—	Aquinas Eqty Gro...	29.0[2]	**27.4[2]**	—
Mairs & Power Gro...	28.7[2]	**34.4[1]**	23.7[1]	Dreyfus Premier Core Value‡...	25.2[3]	**27.3[2]**	19.2[2]
Montag & Cldwl Growth...	31.9[2]	**34.4[1]**	—	Price Sm Cap Value‡ SC...	27.9[3]	**27.3[2]**	20.2[1]
Stein Roe Young Invest...	26.3[3]	**33.6[1]**	—	Fidelity Stk Selector...	28.9[2]	**27.2[2]**	18.8[2]
Sound Shore...	36.4[1]	**33.2[1]**	21.5[1]	Henlopen Fund...	22.6[4]	**27.1[2]**	21.0[1]
Dreyfus Premier MidCap Stk‡...	35.6[1]	**33.2[1]**	—	KPM Equity...	20.1[4]	**27.1[2]**	—
Legg Mason Total Ret...	37.5[1]	**33.0[1]**	20.0[1]	Babson Growth...	28.0[2]	**27.0[2]**	17.6[3]
Northeast Inv Growth...	37.3[1]	**32.7[1]**	19.0[2]	Nbrgr-Ber Social Resp...	24.3[3]	**27.0[2]**	—
Amer Cent Equity Growth...	36.1[1]	**32.6[1]**	21.0[1]	CA Inv Tr-S&P MidCap...	31.9[2]	**27.0[2]**	17.3[3]
Weitz Ser Partners Value...	40.6[1]	**32.4[1]**	—	TIP:Turner Growth Eqty...	31.4[2]	**26.9[2]**	17.1[3]
Excelsior Val & Restruc...	33.6[1]	**32.4[1]**	27.2[1]	Sentry...	29.7[2]	**26.7[2]**	16.4[3]
Janus Gro & Inc...	34.7[1]	**32.3[1]**	18.6[2]	Chicago Tr Talon...	26.5[3]	**26.7[2]**	—
McM Eqty Invest...	33.8[1]	**32.1[1]**	—	Dreyfus MidCap Idx...	31.6[2]	**26.6[2]**	17.2[3]
Dreyfus Sm Co Val SC...	26.0[3]	**32.0[1]**	—	Emerald Eqty...	25.4[3]	**26.6[2]**	14.6[4]
Thompson Plumb Growth...	32.4[1]	**32.0[1]**	18.6[2]	Lindner/Ryback Small Cap SC...	31.7[2]	**26.5[2]**	—
Oak Value...	37.7[1]	**31.8[1]**	—	Price Gro Stk...	26.6[3]	**26.4[2]**	18.7[2]
Fidelity Divnd Growth...	27.9[3]	**31.8[1]**	—	Fasciano SC...	21.5[4]	**26.3[2]**	17.7[3]
Papp L Roy Amer Abroad...	29.9[2]	**31.5[1]**	19.5[2]	State Farm Growth‡...	31.2[2]	**26.3[2]**	16.5[3]

No-Load Fund	Total return percent with quintile ranks by objective			No-Load Fund	Total return percent with quintile ranks by objective		
	1997	Annualized 3 years	5 years		1997	Annualized 3 years	5 years
Nations Disc Eqty	29.6[2]	**26.2[3]**	—	Vangd LifeStrat:Growth	22.1[4]	**22.1[4]**	—
Preferred Growth	31.9[2]	**26.2[3]**	18.2[2]	Wayne Hummer Growth	30.2[2]	**22.1[4]**	13.2[5]
Fidelity Mid-Cap Stk	27.1[3]	**26.2[3]**	—	IAI Value	19.6[4]	**21.9[4]**	15.0[4]
FBP Contrn Eqty	25.4[3]	**26.2[3]**	—	SAFECO Northwest Gr	31.1[2]	**21.9[4]**	12.5[5]
Fidelity Low Pr Stk†††SC	26.7[3]	**26.2[3]**	20.4[1]	Gateway MidCap Idx	25.0[3]	**21.9[4]**	12.6[5]
Excelsior Blended Eqty	29.8[2]	**26.1[3]**	18.5[2]	Dreyfus Growth Opp	15.1[5]	**21.8[4]**	11.5[5]
Federated Mid Cap	31.1[2]	**26.0[3]**	16.3[3]	Fidelity Value	21.1[4]	**21.6[4]**	18.9[2]
Longleaf Partners Sm Cap‡SC	29.0[2]	**26.0[3]**	19.9[1]	Royce Low Priced Stk SC	19.5[4]	**21.6[4]**	—
Monetta MidCap	29.1[2]	**25.9[3]**	—	Capp-Rush Growth	22.2[4]	**21.5[4]**	16.5[3]
UAM DSI Discpnd Val	23.4[4]	**25.9[3]**	18.1[2]	Key SBSF Fund‡	12.3[5]	**21.5[4]**	15.3[4]
Invesco Growth	27.2[3]	**25.9[3]**	16.5[3]	Reynolds Opportunity	14.6[5]	**21.2[4]**	12.7[5]
Vangd Idx Extend Mkt†	26.7[3]	**25.9[3]**	17.5[3]	Stein Roe Special	25.9[3]	**21.1[4]**	15.6[4]
Third Ave Value	23.9[4]	**25.8[3]**	19.4[2]	Sextant Growth	26.6[3]	**21.1[4]**	11.6[5]
WPG Quant Eqty	25.5[3]	**25.6[3]**	—	Crabbe Hsn Equity	25.7[3]	**21.1[4]**	17.8[3]
Nations Cap Gro	30.4[2]	**25.6[3]**	16.0[4]	BT Pyramid:Instit Asst Mgt	23.5[4]	**21.0[4]**	—
GMO: Pelican	26.5[3]	**25.6[3]**	19.7[2]	Schwartz Value SC	28.0[2]	**21.0[4]**	—
Fidelity Discpl Eqty	33.3[1]	**25.6[3]**	18.4[2]	Flex-Fund Highlands Gro	29.3[2]	**20.7[4]**	13.3[5]
Marshall Mid-Cap Gro	22.7[4]	**25.6[3]**	—	BT Invest:Lifecycle Long Range	23.0[4]	**20.6[4]**	—
Govt Street Equity	27.8[3]	**25.6[3]**	14.7[4]	Lepercq-Istel	8.9[5]	**20.5[4]**	13.5[5]
Longleaf Partners‡	28.2[2]	**25.5[3]**	21.4[1]	Amer Cent-20th Cent Heritage	19.3[4]	**20.3[4]**	14.5[4]
Strong Common Stk‡	24.0[4]	**25.5[3]**	19.8[1]	Fidelity Cap Apprec	26.5[3]	**20.0[4]**	18.8[2]
Value Line Fund	21.6[4]	**25.3[3]**	15.0[4]	Women's Equity	28.6[2]	**19.9[4]**	—
Arbor OVB Cap App	27.0[3]	**25.3[3]**	—	Westcore MIDCO Gro	14.9[5]	**19.6[4]**	14.8[4]
Nbrgr-Ber Focus	24.1[3]	**25.2[3]**	18.2[2]	UAM Chi Asst Mgmt Val Contra	18.9[4]	**19.6[5]**	—
Matrix Growth	34.6[1]	**25.2[3]**	15.3[4]	BT Invest:Cap App	14.5[5]	**19.6[5]**	—
Gabelli Asset	38.1[1]	**25.1[3]**	18.9[2]	Reich & Tang Eqty	13.8[5]	**19.5[5]**	14.6[4]
Legg Mason Amer Lead	23.8[4]	**25.0[3]**	—	Dreyfus Lg Co Gr	11.7[5]	**19.4[5]**	—
Capstone Growth	28.7[2]	**24.9[3]**	13.8[5]	IAI Growth	19.2[4]	**19.2[5]**	—
FundMngr Growth†	27.5[3]	**24.9[3]**	16.9[3]	Royce Penn Mutual SC	24.9[3]	**18.7[5]**	13.1[5]
Brandywine Blue	19.3[4]	**24.8[3]**	20.4[1]	Price New Era	10.9[5]	**18.5[5]**	15.1[4]
Northern Growth Eqty	30.2[2]	**24.6[3]**	—	Price Cap App	16.2[5]	**18.5[5]**	14.8[4]
Heartland Value‡SC	23.2[4]	**24.6[3]**	18.5[2]	Royce Premier SC	18.4[5]	**18.1[5]**	15.2[4]
Brown Cap Equity	22.7[4]	**24.6[3]**	15.3[4]	Amana Growth	15.7[5]	**18.1[5]**	—
Amer Cent-20th Cent Select	32.2[1]	**24.6[3]**	15.3[4]	Wade	20.3[4]	**18.0[5]**	12.1[5]
Delafield Fund	19.7[4]	**24.4[3]**	—	Monetta Fund	26.2[3]	**18.0[5]**	9.1[5]
Haven Fund	19.1[4]	**24.4[3]**	16.6[3]	Analysts Inv Stk	19.4[4]	**17.9[5]**	—
IAA Trust Growth	19.7[4]	**24.2[3]**	15.3[4]	Shelby Fund SC	6.2[5]	**17.9[5]**	—
Babson Shadow Stk SC	27.6[3]	**24.2[3]**	16.1[4]	Rockwood	3.5[5]	**17.7[5]**	13.6[5]
Fiduciary Cap Growth SC	29.2[2]	**24.2[3]**	17.1[3]	Meridian	19.2[4]	**17.3[5]**	12.9[5]
PIC Growth	28.0[2]	**24.0[3]**	13.4[5]	USAA Growth	3.7[5]	**17.3[5]**	12.4[5]
Advance Cap Eqty Gro	17.7[5]	**24.0[3]**	—	Scout Stock	21.0[4]	**17.0[5]**	12.8[5]
Janus Fund	22.7[4]	**23.8[4]**	15.8[4]	Volumetric	18.3[5]	**17.0[5]**	9.9[5]
Fairport Midwest Gr	27.7[3]	**23.8[4]**	—	IAI MidCap	8.9[5]	**17.0[5]**	15.7[4]
Vangd Idx Sm Cap† SC	24.5[3]	**23.7[4]**	17.5[3]	Fidelity Retrmnt Gro	18.5[4]	**16.9[5]**	14.3[4]
Htchks & Wly Sm Cap SC	39.5[1]	**23.6[4]**	16.5[3]	Lindner Growth	8.7[5]	**16.4[5]**	13.4[5]
Fidelity Blue Chip Gro††	27.0[3]	**23.5[4]**	20.8[1]	Janus Enterprise	10.8[5]	**16.3[5]**	14.7[4]
Selected Spec Shares	26.9[3]	**23.4[4]**	15.2[4]	Sand Hill Port Mgr	17.8[5]	**16.3[5]**	—
Wilshire Target Sm Val SC	31.2[2]	**23.2[4]**	14.7[4]	Reserve Infmd Invstr	19.0[4]	**16.3[5]**	—
Price Pers Str-Gro	20.5[4]	**23.1[4]**	—	Janus Venture‡SC	13.1[5]	**15.6[5]**	12.2[5]
Bridgeway Soc Resp	22.9[4]	**23.0[4]**	—	Federated Mgd Growth	14.3[5]	**15.6[5]**	—
Strong Opportunity	23.4[4]	**22.9[4]**	18.3[2]	Key SBSF Capital Gro‡	9.1[5]	**14.7[5]**	—
C\FUNDS:Growth Stk	25.5[3]	**22.9[4]**	11.7[5]	Armstrong Assoc	14.2[5]	**14.2[5]**	12.5[5]
Reserve Blue Chip Gro	25.5[3]	**22.8[4]**	—	Oak Hall Equity	14.5[5]	**13.8[5]**	13.1[5]
FAM Value SC	39.1[1]	**22.8[4]**	14.6[4]	Academy Value	19.5[4]	**12.7[5]**	—
Montgmry Growth	24.1[3]	**22.6[4]**	—	Merger‡	11.7[5]	**11.9[5]**	12.1[5]
Price Spect-Gro	17.4[5]	**22.5[4]**	17.7[3]	Merriman Cap App	9.9[5]	**11.6[5]**	7.5[5]
Nbrgr-Ber Guardian	17.9[5]	**22.5[4]**	16.1[4]	Gabelli ABC	12.8[5]	**10.6[5]**	—
Acorn SC	25.0[3]	**22.3[4]**	17.5[3]	Rightime	-3.3[5]	**10.0[5]**	7.7[5]
Wm Blair Growth	20.1[4]	**22.3[4]**	17.6[3]	Crowley Gro & Inc	9.0[5]	**8.9[5]**	6.7[5]
IAI Regional	18.9[4]	**22.2[4]**	14.8[4]	Valley Forge	6.0[5]	**7.6[5]**	9.1[5]

Stock and bond funds – ranked within objective *continued*

By 1995-1997 performance

No-Load Fund	Total return percent with quintile ranks by objective			No-Load Fund	Total return percent with quintile ranks by objective		
	1997	Annualized 3 years	5 years		1997	Annualized 3 years	5 years
American Heritage Gro...	-2.9[5]	**5.4**[5]	—	Scudder Gro & Inc...	30.3[2]	**27.8**[2]	19.9[2]
Mathers...	3.0[5]	**3.3**[5]	1.1[5]	Amer Cent Value...	26.0[3]	**27.8**[2]	—
Steadman Investment...	1.1[5]	**-1.8**[5]	-8.4[5]	Aquinas Eqty Inc...	27.9[3]	**27.8**[2]	—
Amtrust Value SC...	-20.1[5]	**-5.9**[5]	—	US Glb:All-Amer Eqty...	30.3[2]	**27.8**[2]	16.8[4]
GROWTH-INCOME FUNDS				Cutler Approved List...	33.3[1]	**27.5**[2]	17.0[3]
Baron Gro & Inc...	31.1[2]	**36.7**[1]	—	Marshall Eqty Inc...	27.5[3]	**27.5**[2]	—
Selected Amer Shares...	37.3[1]	**35.3**[1]	20.4[1]	Fidelity Eqty Inc...	30.0[2]	**27.5**[2]	20.3[1]
Vangd Idx Growth...	36.3[1]	**32.6**[1]	19.5[2]	Nations Value...	26.3[3]	**27.5**[2]	18.4[3]
Price Value...	29.2[2]	**32.4**[1]	—	Htchks & Wly Eq Inc...	31.2[2]	**27.4**[3]	18.3[3]
Tweedy Brown Amer Val...	38.9[1]	**32.3**[1]	—	Amer Cent Equity Inc...	28.3[3]	**27.4**[3]	—
Muhlenkamp...	33.3[1]	**32.1**[1]	20.4[1]	Mosaic Investors...	34.8[1]	**27.3**[3]	17.1[3]
Vontobel US Value...	34.3[1]	**31.8**[1]	19.4[2]	JP Morgan US Eqty...	28.4[3]	**27.2**[3]	17.8[3]
Weitz Value...	38.9[1]	**31.7**[1]	19.8[2]	UAM NWQ Value Eqty...	30.8[2]	**27.2**[3]	—
Vangd Windsor II...	32.3[2]	**31.6**[1]	20.7[1]	Eclipse Gro & Inc...	32.5[1]	**27.2**[3]	—
Amer Cent Inc & Gro...	34.3[1]	**31.6**[1]	20.3[1]	Wright Sel Blue Ch...	32.7[1]	**27.1**[3]	15.1[4]
Vangd Gro & Inc...	35.6[1]	**31.4**[1]	20.7[1]	Babson Value...	26.5[3]	**26.9**[3]	20.8[1]
ICAP Equity...	29.1[3]	**31.3**[1]	—	USAA Gro & Inc...	26.0[3]	**26.8**[3]	—
Dreyfus Discpl Stock...	31.9[2]	**31.2**[1]	20.1[1]	Amer AAdv Mileage Gro & Inc...	26.1[3]	**26.7**[3]	—
Vangd Tax Mgd:Gro & Inc...	33.3[1]	**31.1**[1]	—	Price Gro & Inc...	23.5[4]	**26.6**[3]	18.1[3]
Smith Brdn Eqty Plus...	32.3[2]	**31.0**[1]	21.0[1]	Wright Major Blue Chip...	33.9[1]	**26.6**[3]	15.3[4]
WPG Growth & Inc...	36.3[1]	**31.0**[1]	18.4[3]	UAM C & B Eqty...	28.0[3]	**26.6**[3]	16.5[4]
Vangd Idx 500...	33.2[1]	**31.0**[1]	20.1[1]	Lexington Gro & Inc...	30.3[2]	**26.4**[3]	17.3[3]
Westwood Equity...	29.6[2]	**31.0**[1]	21.9[1]	Montgmry Eqty Inc...	26.1[3]	**26.3**[3]	—
BT Pyramid:Eqty 500 Idx...	33.0[1]	**30.9**[1]	19.9[1]	Vangd Windsor‡...	22.0[4]	**26.1**[3]	19.1[2]
Reynolds Blue Chip Gr...	31.5[2]	**30.8**[1]	16.1[4]	ASM Idx 30...	24.5[4]	**26.1**[3]	18.1[3]
CA Inv Tr-S&P 500...	33.0[1]	**30.8**[1]	19.9[1]	Homestead Value...	26.7[3]	**26.0**[3]	19.5[2]
Price Eqty 500 Idx...	32.9[1]	**30.8**[1]	19.8[2]	Stein Roe Gro & Inc...	25.7[3]	**25.9**[3]	17.6[3]
SSgA S&P 500...	33.1[1]	**30.8**[1]	20.0[1]	Meridian Value...	21.4[4]	**25.7**[3]	—
Fidelity Spart Market Idx...	33.0[1]	**30.7**[1]	19.9[2]	Kent Gro & Inc...	23.9[4]	**25.7**[3]	18.0[3]
Galaxy II Lg Co Idx...	32.8[1]	**30.7**[1]	19.8[2]	Invesco Value Eqty...	28.0[3]	**25.6**[3]	17.9[3]
Dreyfus Premier Lrg Co‡...	34.6[1]	**30.6**[1]	—	Columbia Common Stk...	25.4[3]	**25.6**[3]	18.7[3]
Federated Max Cap...	32.7[1]	**30.6**[1]	19.8[2]	Fairport Gr & Inc...	30.3[2]	**25.5**[3]	—
RSI Tr-Value Eqty...	31.7[2]	**30.5**[1]	18.9[2]	Mutual Shares Z‡...	26.3[3]	**25.4**[3]	20.0[1]
Dreyfus S&P 500 Idx...	32.6[1]	**30.4**[1]	19.6[2]	Royce Total Ret...	23.7[4]	**25.3**[3]	—
Federated Stock...	34.4[1]	**30.2**[1]	19.9[2]	MSB...	28.9[3]	**25.0**[3]	18.3[3]
Preferred Value...	28.0[3]	**30.2**[1]	19.3[2]	Philadelphia...	35.8[1]	**24.9**[3]	15.9[4]
Accessor Val & Inc...	33.0[1]	**30.0**[2]	19.8[2]	SAFECO Equity...	24.2[4]	**24.8**[3]	22.9[1]
Schwab 1000(Inv)...	31.9[2]	**29.9**[2]	19.1[2]	Yacktman...	18.3[5]	**24.8**[3]	14.6[5]
Kent Idx Eqty...	32.2[2]	**29.8**[2]	19.3[2]	Schroder Ser:Lg Cap Eqty...	26.3[3]	**24.8**[3]	—
UAM ICM Equity...	29.6[2]	**29.8**[2]	—	Boston-1784 Gro & Inc...	19.7[5]	**24.5**[4]	—
ICAP Discret Equity...	28.6[3]	**29.7**[2]	—	BSR Equity...	27.3[3]	**24.5**[4]	16.2[4]
Stagecoach Eqty Idx...	31.9[2]	**29.7**[2]	19.0[2]	UAM TS&W Eqty...	26.0[3]	**24.5**[4]	16.7[4]
Dreyfus Lg Co Val...	16.0[5]	**29.7**[2]	—	Marshall Lg Cap Gr & Inc...	26.2[3]	**24.5**[4]	13.4[5]
Heartland Val Plus...	30.6[2]	**29.5**[2]	—	Westcore Gro & Inc...	27.3[3]	**24.3**[4]	14.4[5]
Vangd Idx Value...	29.8[2]	**29.4**[2]	20.5[1]	FundMngr Gro & Inc†...	25.3[4]	**24.3**[4]	16.7[4]
Price Div Gro...	30.8[2]	**29.3**[2]	21.4[1]	Mutual Qualified Z‡...	24.8[4]	**24.2**[4]	20.0[1]
Chicago Tr Gro & Inc...	26.7[3]	**29.2**[2]	—	Founders Blue Chip...	19.0[5]	**24.1**[4]	17.1[3]
Wilshire Target Lg Val...	30.2[2]	**29.1**[2]	18.2[3]	Fidelity Eqty Inc II...	27.2[3]	**24.0**[4]	18.5[3]
SSgA Gro & Inc...	37.7[1]	**29.1**[2]	—	Blanchard Gro & Inc†...	28.9[3]	**24.0**[4]	—
Stratton Growth...	36.1[1]	**28.9**[2]	19.5[2]	Jensen Portfolio...	23.0[4]	**23.9**[4]	11.6[5]
RSI Tr-Core Eqty...	25.3[3]	**28.8**[2]	19.0[2]	IAI Gro & Inc...	23.9[4]	**23.7**[4]	14.7[4]
Elite Gr & Inc...	28.2[3]	**28.8**[2]	18.6[3]	Concorde Value...	29.1[3]	**23.6**[4]	14.9[4]
Harbor Value...	31.2[2]	**28.7**[2]	18.4[3]	UAM FPA Crescent...	22.0[4]	**23.6**[4]	—
Fidelity Gro & Inc‡...	30.2[2]	**28.4**[2]	20.9[1]	IPS Millenium...	21.4[4]	**23.6**[4]	—
Quant Gro & Inc...	36.7[1]	**28.1**[2]	18.5[3]	Excelsior Inc & Gro...	22.1[4]	**23.6**[4]	16.6[4]
Fidelity Fund...	32.1[2]	**28.1**[2]	20.6[1]	Invesco Indust Inc...	26.4[3]	**23.4**[4]	16.1[4]
AARP Gro & Inc...	31.0[2]	**28.1**[2]	20.2[1]	API Cap Inc...	25.2[4]	**23.3**[4]	15.4[4]
Lexington Corp Ldrs...	23.1[4]	**28.0**[2]	19.5[2]	Mutual Beacon Z‡...	22.9[4]	**23.3**[4]	19.5[2]
Dodge & Cox Stock...	28.4[3]	**28.0**[2]	21.1[1]	Maxus Equity...	28.4[3]	**23.3**[4]	18.6[3]
Vangd Trust US...	29.5[2]	**27.9**[2]	18.7[2]	Bridges Investment...	21.1[4]	**23.1**[4]	14.8[4]

108

Stock and bond funds – ranked within objective continued

By 1995-1997 performance

No-Load Fund	Total return percent with quintile ranks by objective		
	1997	Annualized 3 years	5 years
Weston: New Cent Cap...	26.1[3]	**22.8[4]**	16.1[4]
Preferred Asst Allocc...	21.0[4]	**22.8[4]**	14.8[4]
Gradison Estab Value...	22.6[4]	**22.6[4]**	17.8[3]
Thompson Plumb Balanced...	22.5[4]	**21.9[4]**	13.9[5]
Greenspring...	23.9[4]	**21.7[4]**	16.3[4]
Vangd Star:Star...	20.5[4]	**21.7[4]**	14.8[4]
Strong Total Ret...	24.2[4]	**21.6[4]**	16.8[4]
Primary Trend...	18.2[5]	**21.3[4]**	14.7[4]
Fidelity Asst Mgr Gro...	26.4[3]	**21.3[4]**	15.8[4]
Stonebridge Growth...	23.7[4]	**21.2[4]**	12.5[5]
C\FUNDS:C\FUND...	21.0[4]	**21.0[5]**	14.2[5]
Marshall Mid-Cap Val...	23.4[4]	**20.8[5]**	—
Berger Gro & Inc...	22.7[4]	**20.7[5]**	14.5[5]
Royce REvest Gro & Inc...	23.5[4]	**20.6[5]**	—
First Omaha Eqty...	19.3[5]	**20.6[5]**	15.9[4]
TIP:Clover Cap Eqty Val...	17.5[5]	**20.6[5]**	18.0[3]
Scudder Balanced...	22.7[4]	**20.1[5]**	—
Boston-1784 Asst Alloc...	20.7[4]	**20.0[5]**	—
Vangd LifeStrat:Mod Gr...	19.7[4]	**19.9[5]**	—
Northern Inc Eqty...	20.8[4]	**19.9[5]**	—
Price Pers Str-Bal...	17.8[5]	**19.9[5]**	—
Matrix\LMH Value...	17.9[5]	**19.8[5]**	13.6[5]
Berwyn‡...	26.1[3]	**19.8[5]**	17.0[3]
UAM Sirach Spec Eqty...	11.3[5]	**19.3[5]**	13.5[5]
Analytic Defnsve Eqty...	19.1[5]	**18.7[5]**	12.8[5]
CGM Mutual...	8.2[5]	**18.5[5]**	12.8[5]
Dreyfus Gro & Inc...	16.0[5]	**18.4[5]**	13.3[5]
US Glb:MegaTrends...	15.6[5]	**18.3[5]**	10.6[5]
Copley...	25.1[4]	**18.2[5]**	10.9[5]
Amer Cent Balanced...	16.9[5]	**17.2[5]**	11.5[5]
Dreyfus Fund...	10.7[5]	**16.7[5]**	10.1[5]
Flex-Fund Muirfield...	18.6[5]	**16.5[5]**	11.9[5]
BT Invest:Lifecycle Mid Range...	18.5[5]	**16.2[5]**	—
ZSA Asst Alloc...	12.3[5]	**16.1[5]**	9.8[5]
Warbg Pincus Gro & Inc...	30.2[2]	**15.7[5]**	18.0[3]
Merriman Gro & Inc...	13.1[5]	**15.3[5]**	9.4[5]
SCM Portfolio...	16.3[5]	**14.0[5]**	9.3[5]
FundMngr Mgd Tot Ret.†...	13.5[5]	**13.6[5]**	9.6[5]
Federated Mgd Gro & Inc...	13.0[5]	**12.9[5]**	—
Gateway Idx Plus...	12.3[5]	**11.3[5]**	9.3[5]
INCOME FUNDS			
Cutler Eqty Income...	33.4[1]	**28.5[1]**	16.7[1]
Vangd Equity Inc...	31.2[1]	**28.4[1]**	19.0[1]
Value Line Asst Alloc...	20.9[3]	**27.7[1]**	—
Price Eqty Inc...	28.8[1]	**27.4[1]**	19.9[1]
SAFECO Income...	26.4[1]	**26.9[1]**	17.9[1]
Managers Inc Eqty...	27.2[1]	**26.0[1]**	17.8[1]
Vangd Asst Alloc...	27.3[1]	**25.9[1]**	17.2[1]
AON Asst Alloc...	31.5[1]	**24.8[1]**	—
Gabelli Eqty Inc...	27.9[1]	**24.6[1]**	18.2[1]
Eastcliff Total Ret...	30.0[1]	**24.5[1]**	16.0[2]
Amer Cent Util Inc...	35.7[1]	**24.4[1]**	—
USAA Income Stk...	26.9[1]	**24.4[1]**	16.4[1]
Montag & Cldwl Balanced...	23.5[2]	**24.4[1]**	—
Nations Eqty Inc...	25.7[1]	**24.2[1]**	16.3[1]
Fidelity Utilities...	31.6[1]	**24.2[1]**	16.0[2]
Vangd Wellington...	23.2[2]	**23.9[1]**	16.5[1]
Westwood Balanced...	22.5[2]	**23.8[1]**	17.3[1]
Strong Amer Util...	27.6[1]	**23.7[1]**	—
BNY Hamilton Eqty Inc...	25.9[1]	**23.7[1]**	15.6[2]

No-Load Fund	Total return percent with quintile ranks by objective		
	1997	Annualized 3 years	5 years
Founders Balanced...	16.9[4]	**23.6[1]**	17.7[1]
Rainier Balanced...	23.9[2]	**23.5[2]**	—
Invesco Balanced...	19.5[3]	**23.2[2]**	—
McM Balanced...	23.7[2]	**22.8[2]**	—
Dreyfus Asst Alloc...	28.9[1]	**22.3[2]**	—
Lindner Utility...	19.8[3]	**22.3[2]**	—
Galaxy II Util Idx...	28.5[1]	**22.2[2]**	—
Invesco Total Ret...	25.0[2]	**22.1[2]**	15.9[2]
Primary Income...	25.5[1]	**22.0[2]**	15.3[2]
Advance Cap Balanced...	20.5[3]	**22.0[2]**	13.1[3]
Vangd Idx Balanced...	22.2[2]	**21.4[2]**	14.1[2]
Brown Cap Balanced...	21.0[3]	**21.4[2]**	13.4[3]
Janus Balanced...	21.8[3]	**21.4[2]**	14.6[2]
Amana Income...	24.5[2]	**21.3[2]**	13.2[3]
Pax World...	25.1[2]	**21.3[2]**	12.6[4]
Dodge & Cox Balanced...	21.2[3]	**21.2[2]**	16.1[2]
Montgmry US Asst Alloc...	18.9[3]	**21.2[2]**	—
Mosaic Balanced...	25.5[2]	**21.1[2]**	13.4[3]
Lancaster Convert...	22.4[2]	**21.1[2]**	13.7[2]
Sit Balanced...	21.7[3]	**20.9[2]**	—
FBP Contrn Balanced...	20.7[3]	**20.9[2]**	14.7[2]
Vangd Spec-Util...	25.1[2]	**20.8[3]**	13.2[3]
Green Cent Balanced...	19.0[3]	**20.7[3]**	10.9[5]
Value Line Income...	18.5[4]	**20.7[3]**	12.7[4]
Nations Balanced Assts...	21.4[3]	**20.5[3]**	13.2[3]
Invesco Multi-Asst...	19.1[3]	**20.3[3]**	—
Amer AAdv Mileage Bal...	19.5[3]	**20.3[3]**	—
UAM Sirach Strat Balanced...	21.9[2]	**20.2[3]**	—
State Farm Balanced‡...	22.2[2]	**20.1[3]**	13.4[3]
PIC:Pinnacle Balanced...	22.3[2]	**20.0[3]**	11.5[5]
Warbg Pincus Balanced...	16.4[4]	**20.0[3]**	14.2[2]
Value Line Convert...	17.0[4]	**19.9[3]**	13.4[3]
Key SBSF Convert‡...	16.3[4]	**19.9[3]**	14.1[2]
America's Utility...	23.4[2]	**19.8[3]**	11.1[5]
Eclipse Balanced...	23.4[2]	**19.7[3]**	14.9[2]
Fidelity Puritan...	22.4[2]	**19.6[3]**	16.2[1]
IAI Balanced...	25.7[1]	**19.6[3]**	12.1[4]
AARP Bal Stk & Bd...	21.9[2]	**19.6[3]**	—
Price Balanced...	19.0[3]	**19.4[3]**	13.6[3]
Aquinas Balanced...	19.9[3]	**19.4[3]**	—
JP Morgan Diversified...	18.5[4]	**19.3[4]**	—
Capp-Rush Util...	25.3[2]	**19.3[4]**	9.3[5]
Vangd Wellesley Inc...	20.2[3]	**19.2[4]**	13.2[3]
Jurika & Voyles Balanced...	16.7[4]	**19.1[4]**	14.1[2]
UAM Strlng Part Balanced...	18.3[4]	**19.1[4]**	12.7[4]
Parnassus Balanced...	20.2[3]	**19.1[4]**	13.1[4]
UAM NWQ Balanced...	20.9[3]	**19.0[4]**	—
UAM C & B Balanced...	19.7[3]	**18.9[4]**	12.1[4]
Stein Roe Balanced...	17.5[4]	**18.8[4]**	12.5[4]
IAA Trust Asst Alloc...	17.9[4]	**18.6[4]**	12.5[4]
US Glb:Income...	23.1[2]	**18.4[4]**	11.9[5]
Columbia Balanced...	18.8[3]	**18.4[4]**	13.6[3]
Excelsior Instit Balanced...	18.3[4]	**18.4[4]**	—
Emerald Balanced...	16.4[4]	**18.3[4]**	—
Buffalo Balanced...	15.1[5]	**18.2[4]**	—
Dreyfus Balanced...	17.4[4]	**17.9[4]**	13.5[3]
Weston: New Cent Inc...	18.6[4]	**17.8[4]**	13.0[4]
Fidelity Asst Mgr...	22.3[2]	**17.7[4]**	13.4[3]
Vangd Tax Mgd:Balanced...	16.6[4]	**17.6[4]**	—
Htchks & Wly Balanced...	16.8[4]	**17.6[4]**	13.0[4]

By 1995-1997 performance

No-Load Fund	Total return percent with quintile ranks by objective		
	1997	Annualized 3 years	5 years
Nicholas Eqty Inc...	19.3[3]	**17.5[5]**	—
Avondale Total Ret...	20.1[3]	**17.4[5]**	12.1[5]
Price Pers Str-Inc...	15.0[5]	**17.0[5]**	—
Vangd LifeStrat:Cons Gro...	16.8[4]	**17.0[5]**	—
USAA Growth & Tax Strat...	16.1[4]	**16.6[5]**	11.9[5]
Strong Asst Alloc...	16.7[4]	**16.3[5]**	12.1[4]
Fidelity Convert...	14.4[5]	**16.3[5]**	12.7[4]
Vangd Convert...	16.3[4]	**16.1[5]**	10.9[5]
Berwyn Income...	13.3[5]	**16.1[5]**	12.6[4]
Fidelity Balanced...	23.4[2]	**15.7[5]**	11.9[5]
Lindner Dividend...	13.9[5]	**15.6[5]**	11.4[5]
Crabbe Hsn Asst Alloc...	19.2[3]	**15.2[5]**	12.4[4]
Vangd LifeStrat:Income...	14.2[5]	**14.8[5]**	—
Fidelity Asst Mgr Inc...	12.4[5]	**12.2[5]**	10.0[5]
Lexington Convert...	13.2[5]	**12.1[5]**	8.7[5]
BT Invest:Lifecycle Sht Range...	13.7[5]	**12.0[5]**	—
Federated Mgd Inc...	10.5[5]	**10.5[5]**	—
Steadman Associated...	-1.3[5]	**3.9[5]**	-0.3[5]
SECTOR & INDUSTRY FUNDS			
Fidelity Sel Energy Serv†	51.9[1]	**47.2[1]**	31.2[1]
Fidelity Sel Home Finc†...	45.8[1]	**45.2[1]**	32.0[1]
Fidelity Sel Reg Banks†...	45.5[1]	**42.6[1]**	26.4[1]
Fidelity Sel Broker†...	62.3[1]	**41.0[1]**	28.2[1]
Fidelity Sel Financial†...	41.9[1]	**40.3[1]**	25.6[1]
Technology Value...	6.5[5]	**40.3[1]**	—
Fidelity Sel Electronics†...	14.2[5]	**39.8[1]**	33.5[1]
Invesco Strat Fncl...	44.8[1]	**38.2[1]**	24.3[1]
Century Shares...	50.1[1]	**33.5[1]**	17.9[3]
Fidelity Sel Insurance†...	42.5[1]	**33.5[1]**	20.7[2]
Fidelity Sel Defense†...	23.5[3]	**31.5[1]**	24.4[1]
Vangd Spec-Health...	28.5[2]	**31.3[1]**	22.6[2]
Fidelity Sel Health†...	31.1[2]	**30.2[1]**	22.4[2]
CGM Realty...	26.7[3]	**29.8[1]**	—
Fidelity Sel Air Trans†...	31.1[2]	**28.4[1]**	16.8[4]
Invesco Strat Hlth...	18.4[4]	**28.0[1]**	14.1[5]
Columbia Real Est Eqty...	24.7[3]	**27.4[2]**	—
Fidelity Sel Software†...	14.9[4]	**26.9[2]**	22.2[2]
Fidelity Sel Leisure†...	41.3[1]	**26.7[2]**	21.5[2]
Fidelity Sel Food/Agr†...	30.3[2]	**26.3[2]**	18.4[3]
Fidelity Sel Consmr Ind†...	38.0[1]	**26.0[2]**	18.3[3]
Invesco Strat Enrgy...	19.1[3]	**25.6[2]**	16.5[4]
Fidelity Sel Computer†...	-1.1[5]	**25.5[2]**	25.1[1]
Excelsior Enrgy & Nat Resc...	18.5[4]	**25.4[3]**	17.1[3]
Rushmore Amer Gas Idx...	24.2[3]	**25.1[3]**	15.5[4]
Invesco Strat Envrn...	16.6[4]	**25.0[3]**	10.5[5]
Fidelity Sel Util Gro†...	30.3[2]	**24.9[3]**	15.2[4]
Invesco Strat Tech...	8.8[5]	**24.6[3]**	18.5[3]
Vangd Spec-Energy...	14.8[5]	**24.5[3]**	19.1[2]
Fidelity Sel Indust Equip†...	18.8[4]	**24.4[3]**	23.2[1]
Fidelity Sel Retail†...	41.7[1]	**24.3[3]**	15.6[4]
Fidelity Sel Const/Hous†...	29.6[2]	**23.6[3]**	16.2[4]
Price Media & Telecomm...	28.1[2]	**23.1[3]**	—
US Glb:Real Estate...	19.3[3]	**23.1[3]**	10.6[5]
Cohen & Steers Realty...	21.1[3]	**23.0[4]**	19.1[2]
Fidelity Sel Technology†...	10.4[5]	**22.4[4]**	21.3[2]
Fidelity Real Est...	21.3[3]	**22.4[4]**	16.0[4]
Fidelity Sel Biotech†...	15.4[4]	**22.0[4]**	8.4[5]
Price Sci/Tech...	1.7[5]	**21.8[4]**	21.0[2]
Fidelity Sel Energy†...	10.5[5]	**21.4[4]**	16.3[4]
Fidelity Sel Multimedia†...	30.9[2]	**21.0[4]**	20.5[2]

No-Load Fund	Total return percent with quintile ranks by objective		
	1997	Annualized 3 years	5 years
Fidelity Sel Medical Del†...	20.5[3]	**20.9[4]**	17.5[3]
Crabbe Hsn Real Est...	18.8[4]	**20.9[4]**	—
Invesco Strat Util...	24.4[3]	**20.7[4]**	13.9[5]
Fidelity Sel Chemical†...	16.5[4]	**19.8[4]**	17.3[3]
Fidelity Sel Envir Serv†...	17.9[4]	**19.8[4]**	9.1[5]
Fidelity Sel Telecomm†...	25.8[3]	**19.8[5]**	18.4[3]
Fidelity Sel Transport†...	32.1[1]	**18.6[5]**	17.5[3]
Royce Finl Servs...	19.4[3]	**18.4[5]**	—
Fidelity Sel Nat Gas†...	-8.0[5]	**17.4[5]**	—
Invesco Strat Leis...	26.5[3]	**16.9[5]**	15.5[4]
Invesco Wrld Cap Gds...	27.8[2]	**16.6[5]**	—
Stratton Month Div REIT Sh...	17.3[4]	**16.3[5]**	8.1[5]
Fidelity Sel Auto†...	16.7[4]	**15.4[5]**	12.7[5]
Fidelity Sel Pap/Forest†...	9.4[5]	**12.6[5]**	14.1[5]
Fidelity Sel Devel Comm†...	5.6[5]	**12.4[5]**	16.6[4]
Fidelity Sel Indust Mat†...	1.9[5]	**10.3[5]**	12.0[5]
PRECIOUS METALS FUNDS			
Scudder Gold...	-40.9[2]	**-4.0[1]**	5.5[1]
US Glb:World Gold...	-41.1[2]	**-6.6[1]**	5.2[1]
Fidelity Sel Amer Gold†...	-39.4[2]	**-6.9[1]**	4.1[1]
Invesco Strat Gold...	-55.5[4]	**-11.0[1]**	-2.6[5]
Blanchard Prec Met.‡...	-47.1[4]	**-11.8[1]**	3.2[2]
Midas Gold...	-59.0[5]	**-12.0[1]**	2.3[3]
Rydex Prec Met...	-37.6[1]	**-12.2[1]**	—
USAA Gold...	-38.2[1]	**-13.7[1]**	-1.6[4]
Amer Cent Glob Gold...	-41.5[3]	**-14.7[1]**	-1.3[4]
Lexington Goldfund...	-43.0[3]	**-15.5[2]**	0.9[3]
Vangd Spec-Gold...	-39.0[1]	**-16.7[2]**	1.1[3]
Fidelity Sel Prec Met†...	-44.9[3]	**-17.5[2]**	3.3[2]
Gabelli Gold...	-51.9[4]	**-18.8[2]**	—
Capp-Rush Gold...	-45.2[4]	**-18.9[2]**	—
Bull & Bear Gold...	-55.7[5]	**-24.1[1]**	-6.7[5]
US Glb:Gold Shares...	-57.4[5]	**-38.5[2]**	-12.7[5]
GLOBAL EQUITY FUNDS			
Mutual Discovery Z‡...	22.8[1]	**25.4[2]**	—
Invesco Wrld Comm...	30.3[1]	**24.7[2]**	—
Gabelli Glbl Couch Potato...	41.7[1]	**23.4[1]**	—
Janus Worldwide...	20.5[1]	**22.9[2]**	19.8[1]
Gabelli Glbl Telecomm...	31.9[1]	**18.6[3]**	—
Tweedy Brwn Glob Val...	22.9[1]	**17.8[3]**	—
USAA Cornerstone Strat...	15.6[2]	**17.3[3]**	14.6[2]
Austin Global Eqty...	23.9[1]	**17.1[3]**	—
Scout Worldwide...	18.4[2]	**17.1[3]**	—
Scudder Global...	17.2[2]	**17.1[3]**	15.1[1]
Scudder Glob Disc‡...	9.9[4]	**16.3[3]**	14.9[1]
Montgmry Glob Oppty...	11.0[3]	**16.1[3]**	—
Thomas White Wld Fd...	11.7[3]	**15.7[3]**	—
Citizens Tr Global...	19.9[2]	**15.6[4]**	—
Founders Worldwide Gr...	10.5[3]	**15.0[4]**	14.1[2]
USAA World Growth...	12.9[3]	**14.9[4]**	13.6[2]
BBK Diversa...	13.2[2]	**14.7[4]**	10.7[3]
Fremont Global...	9.9[4]	**14.3[4]**	11.4[3]
Montgmry Glob Comm...	15.8[2]	**13.5[4]**	—
Fidelity Worldwide...	12.1[3]	**12.6[4]**	14.9[2]
US Glb:Glob Resrcs...	-2.8[5]	**12.4[4]**	8.7[4]
Dreyfus Global Gro...	12.3[3]	**12.1[4]**	9.7[4]
Bull & Bear US & Overs...	6.7[4]	**12.0[4]**	9.1[4]
Lexington Global...	6.9[4]	**11.3[5]**	13.1[3]
Blanchard Glob Gro‡...	6.5[5]	**10.8[5]**	9.4[4]
Amer Cent Glob Nat Res...	2.5[5]	**10.6[5]**	—

By 1995-1997 performance

No-Load Fund	1997	Annualized 3 years	Annualized 5 years
Fidelity Glob Bal	12.4[3]	10.5[5]	—
Merriman Asst Alloc	5.8[5]	8.9[5]	8.3[5]
Permanent Portfolio†	5.6[5]	7.5[5]	6.8[5]
Gabelli Glbl Conv Sec	2.8[5]	6.9[5]	—
Mosaic Foresight	2.5[5]	2.2[5]	—
Fontaine Glob Gro	-44.9[5]	-4.9[5]	-0.5[5]
INT'L EQUITY FUNDS - GENERAL			
Janus Overseas	18.2[1]	23.0[1]	—
Harbor Int'l Gro	3.6[3]	19.3[1]	—
Amer Cent-20th Cent Int'l Disc	17.5[1]	19.2[1]	—
BT Invest:Int'l Eqty	17.4[1]	18.2[1]	18.8[1]
Fidelity Dvsfd Int'l	13.7[1]	17.2[1]	17.4[1]
Harbor Int'l‡	15.5[1]	17.2[1]	19.8[1]
Amer Cent-20th Cent Int'l Gr	19.7[1]	15.3[1]	15.8[1]
Founders Passport	1.7[3]	14.9[1]	—
Amer AAdv Mileage Int'l	8.8[2]	14.9[1]	—
Htchks & Wly Int'l	5.3[3]	14.3[1]	16.2[1]
Nbrgr-Ber Int'l Eqty	11.2[2]	14.1[1]	—
Marshall Int'l Stk	10.9[2]	14.0[1]	—
Fidelity Canada††	6.1[2]	13.7[2]	10.2[3]
Lazard Int'l Eqty(O shrs)	11.8[2]	13.5[2]	14.0[2]
Managers Int'l Eqty	10.8[2]	13.3[2]	15.4[1]
Oakmark Int'l	3.4[3]	12.7[2]	14.9[2]
Vontobel Int'l Eqty	9.2[2]	12.3[2]	13.6[2]
First Eagle Int'l	9.3[2]	12.2[2]	—
USAA International	9.0[2]	12.0[2]	15.1[1]
Wright Int'l Blue Ch	1.5[3]	11.7[2]	11.9[3]
Scudder Int'l Stk	8.0[2]	11.6[2]	12.9[2]
Bernstein Int'l Value	9.3[2]	11.5[2]	14.2[2]
Preferred Int'l	6.8[2]	11.2[2]	15.0[2]
Vangd Int'l Growth	4.1[3]	11.1[2]	14.9[2]
Fidelity Overseas	10.9[2]	11.0[2]	14.2[2]
Columbia Int'l Stk	11.5[2]	11.0[2]	12.2[3]
Accessor Int'l Eqty	11.0[2]	10.8[2]	—
BBK Int'l Equity	10.0[2]	10.7[2]	10.3[3]
Fidelity Int'l Gr & Inc	7.1[2]	10.6[2]	12.2[2]
Fidelity Int'l Value	7.8[2]	10.4[2]	—
UAM McKee Int'l	11.3[2]	10.2[2]	—
Schwab Int'l Idx(Inv)	7.3[2]	10.2[2]	—
Acorn Int'l	0.2[3]	9.9[2]	13.8[2]
Price Int'l Stk	2.7[3]	9.9[3]	13.0[2]
Babson Stew Ivry Int'l	1.7[3]	9.1[3]	11.9[3]
Nations Int'l Gro	1.9[3]	8.7[3]	10.5[3]
Wm Blair Int'l Gro	8.4[2]	8.6[3]	11.3[3]
Boston-1784 Int'l Eqty	-0.9[4]	8.5[3]	—
Montgmry Int'l Sm Cap	-0.8[4]	8.4[3]	—
Schroder Cap:Int'l	3.2[3]	8.2[3]	12.9[2]
Sit Int'l Growth	4.8[3]	8.1[3]	12.7[2]
Excelsior International	9.3[2]	8.0[3]	11.0[3]
RSI Tr-Int'l Eqty	0.9[3]	8.0[3]	10.6[3]
UAM MJI Int'l	6.0[2]	7.8[3]	—
Lexington Int'l	1.6[3]	6.9[3]	—
Kent Int'l Gro	2.3[3]	6.8[3]	10.8[3]
UAM TS&W Int'l Eqty	2.5[3]	6.7[3]	9.9[4]
WPG International	2.9[3]	6.1[3]	9.0[4]
Dreyfus Int'l Eqty Alloc	0.6[3]	6.1[3]	—
PBHG International	3.5[3]	6.0[3]	—
Invesco Int'l Gro	-1.9[4]	6.0[3]	8.9[4]
Nations Int'l Eqty	1.0[3]	5.8[3]	8.9[4]
Lazard Int'l Sm Cap(O shrs)	0.3[3]	5.7[3]	—

No-Load Fund	1997	Annualized 3 years	Annualized 5 years
JP Morgan Int'l Eqty	1.2[3]	5.7[4]	9.2[4]
Warbg Pincus Int'l	-4.4[4]	5.3[4]	12.1[3]
Vangd Int'l Value	-4.6[4]	4.8[4]	9.6[4]
Northern Int'l Gro Eq	6.3[2]	4.4[4]	—
IAI International	-4.2[4]	4.2[4]	9.7[4]
Northern Int'l Sel Eq	9.1[2]	3.7[4]	—
Fremont Int'l Gro	-8.4[4]	3.5[4]	—
Stein Roe Int'l	-3.5[4]	2.8[4]	—
Dreyfus Int'l Growth	-1.5[4]	2.5[4]	—
Quant Int'l Eqty	-1.6[4]	2.3[4]	9.1[4]
Price Int'l Disc	-5.7[4]	0.9[4]	7.3[4]
Strong Int'l Stk	-14.2[4]	0.0[4]	7.8[4]
Fremont Int'l Sm Cap	-26.5[5]	-5.4[5]	—
INT'L EQUITY FUNDS - EUROPE			
Scudder Grt Europe	24.0[1]	26.1[1]	
Wright Equifund Netherland	15.4[1]	23.2[1]	20.1[1]
Vangd Idx Europe†	24.2[1]	22.6[1]	19.4[1]
Fidelity Europe††	22.9[1]	22.4[1]	19.9[1]
Fidelity Europe Cap App††	24.9[1]	21.7[1]	—
Price Europe	17.0[1]	21.5[1]	18.9[1]
Invesco Europe	15.1[1]	21.2[1]	16.6[1]
Excelsior Pan Europe	24.4[1]	20.2[1]	15.3[1]
Wright Equifund Nordic	5.2[3]	18.5[1]	—
Wright Equifund Belg\Lux	11.4[2]	17.5[1]	—
Wright Equifund Swiss	22.7[1]	13.4[2]	—
INT'L EQUITY FUNDS - EMG MKTS			
Scudder Latin Amer	31.3[1]	15.0[1]	19.1[1]
Fidelity Latin Amer††	32.9[1]	13.2[2]	—
Excelsior Lat Amer	25.2[1]	11.8[2]	11.8[3]
Price Latin Amer	31.8[1]	9.8[3]	—
BT Invest:Lat Am Eqty	30.8[1]	9.6[3]	—
Wright Equifund Mexico	42.4[1]	6.6[3]	—
USAA Emg Mkts	-3.5[4]	5.3[4]	—
Capstone New Zealand	-23.1[5]	2.8[4]	2.6[5]
Sit Develop Mkts Gro	-5.2[4]	2.1[4]	—
Lazard Emg Mkt(O shrs)	-9.8[4]	1.6[4]	—
Warbg Pincus Emg Mkts	-20.0[5]	1.0[4]	—
Montgmry Emg Mkts	-3.2[4]	-0.4[4]	7.7[4]
Vangd Idx Emg Mkt†	-16.8[5]	-1.0[4]	—
SSgA Emg Mkts	-8.8[4]	-1.2[4]	—
Quant Frgn Frntr	-9.2[4]	-1.2[4]	—
JP Morgan Emg Mkts Eqty	-7.6[4]	-3.4[4]	—
Lexington World Emg	-11.4[4]	-3.6[5]	4.8[4]
Robrtsn Stph Devlp Cnt	-15.2[4]	-4.2[5]	—
Fidelity SE Asia††	-38.9[5]	-8.9[5]	—
Price New Asia	-37.1[5]	-9.5[5]	1.4[5]
Fidelity Emg Mkts††	-40.9[5]	-14.3[5]	-1.2[5]
INT'L EQUITY FUNDS - PACIFIC			
Guinness Flt China & HK	-20.3[5]	8.9[3]	—
Wright Equifund Hong Kong	-27.2[5]	-1.8[4]	1.9[5]
Matthews Asian Cnvrt	-23.2[5]	-1.8[4]	—
US Glb:China Region Oppty	-22.5[5]	-5.2[5]	—
Excelsior Pac Asia	-32.2[5]	-7.6[5]	2.3[5]
Fidelity Japan††	-10.7[4]	-8.1[5]	1.7[5]
Fidelity Pacific Bas††	-15.1[4]	-8.2[5]	4.3[4]
Nomura Pacific Bas	-28.7[5]	-8.7[5]	2.1[5]
Matthews Pac Tiger	-40.9[5]	-8.9[5]	—
Strong Asia Pacific	-31.0[5]	-9.3[5]	—
Wright Equifund Japan	-14.2[4]	-10.8[5]	—
Vangd Idx Pacific†	-25.7[5]	-11.0[5]	1.5[5]

Stock and bond funds – ranked within objective continued
By 1995-1997 performance

No-Load Fund	1997	Annualized 3 years	5 years	No-Load Fund	1997	Annualized 3 years	5 years
Japan (Scudder)........................	-14.5[4]	**-11.5[5]**	-1.2[5]	Excelsior Mgd Inc...............	9.8[3]	**10.5[3]**	7.5[3]
Price Japan.............................	-22.1[5]	**-12.4[5]**	-1.4[5]	TIP:Clover Cap Fix Inc........	9.6[3]	**10.5[3]**	7.9[3]
Scudder Pacific Opp...............	-37.8[5]	**-12.4[5]**	-2.3[5]	McM Fixed Inc.....................	9.5[3]	**10.4[3]**	—
BT Invest:Pac Basin...............	-45.9[5]	**-13.1[5]**	—	Wright Total Ret Bd..............	9.2[3]	**10.4[3]**	6.9[4]
Invesco Pacific Bas...............	-36.9[5]	**-13.4[5]**	-0.6[5]	Mosaic Hi Yld......................	9.9[3]	**10.3[3]**	8.5[2]
Warbg Pincus Japan OTC......	-25.5[5]	**-13.8[5]**	—	CA Inv Tr-US Gov..................	9.3[3]	**10.3[3]**	7.7[3]
Capstone Nikko Japan............	-24.6[5]	**-15.1[5]**	-0.9[5]	BBK Int'l Bond.....................	2.6[5]	**10.3[3]**	4.5[5]
FIXED-INCOME - LONG TERM				IAI Bond...............................	10.8[2]	**10.3[3]**	7.4[3]
Amer Cent-Benham Target 2020.........	28.6[1]	**26.5[1]**	17.7[1]	Drey-Basic GNMA.................	9.5[3]	**10.2[3]**	7.6[3]
Price Emg Mkt Bond...............	16.8[1]	**26.0[1]**	—	Dreyfus Basic GNMA............	9.5[3]	**10.2[3]**	7.6[3]
Amer Cent-Benham Target 2015.........	22.9[1]	**23.7[1]**	16.2[1]	Fidelity Spart Inv Grd..........	9.3[3]	**10.1[3]**	8.0[3]
Scudder Emg Mkts Inc...........	13.1[2]	**22.1[1]**	—	Nations Divsfd Inc...............	8.3[4]	**10.1[3]**	8.5[2]
Fidelity New Mkts Inc............	17.2[1]	**21.4[1]**	—	Northern Fix Inc...................	9.5[3]	**10.1[3]**	—
Amer Cent-Benham Target 2010.........	16.7[1]	**20.6[1]**	14.4[1]	Arbor OVB Gov.....................	9.3[3]	**10.1[3]**	—
Value Line Agg Inc................	14.1[1]	**18.0[1]**	13.4[1]	Scudder Income..................	8.7[4]	**10.0[3]**	7.5[3]
Northeast Inv Trust...............	13.9[2]	**17.1[1]**	15.2[1]	RSI Tr-Act Mgd Bd...............	9.7[3]	**10.0[4]**	7.2[4]
BT Invest:Glob Hi Yld............	10.1[2]	**16.6[1]**	—	Emerald Mndg Bd................	8.2[4]	**10.0[4]**	—
Invesco High Yld...................	17.1[1]	**16.3[1]**	11.6[1]	Crabbe Hsn Income.............	11.6[2]	**10.0[4]**	6.5[5]
Legg Mason High Yld............	15.9[1]	**16.3[1]**	—	First Omaha Fix Inc.............	9.5[3]	**10.0[4]**	7.1[4]
Amer Cent-Benham Target 2005.........	11.6[2]	**16.1[1]**	11.6[1]	JP Morgan Bond...................	9.1[3]	**10.0[4]**	7.2[4]
Fidelity Spart Hi Inc.............	15.9[1]	**15.7[1]**	14.2[1]	Fidelity Spart Gov Inc..........	9.2[3]	**9.8[4]**	6.5[4]
Vangd Prefrd Stk..................	13.0[2]	**15.5[1]**	9.9[2]	HGK Fix Inc..........................	9.4[3]	**9.7[4]**	—
CGM Fixed Inc.....................	3.7[5]	**15.0[1]**	10.7[1]	Galaxy II US Trsy Idx...........	9.3[3]	**9.7[4]**	7.0[4]
Federated Hi Yld..................	13.3[2]	**15.0[1]**	11.8[1]	Lazard Bond(O shrs)............	8.4[4]	**9.6[4]**	6.4[5]
Managers Bond....................	10.4[2]	**14.9[1]**	9.5[2]	Dreyfus GNMA.....................	8.8[4]	**9.6[4]**	6.5[5]
Rydex Gov Bd......................	16.4[1]	**14.1[1]**	—	Preferred Fix Inc.................	8.5[4]	**9.5[4]**	7.2[4]
Fidelity Cap & Inc................	14.7[1]	**14.1[1]**	12.1[1]	Fidelity Gov Sec..................	8.9[4]	**9.5[4]**	6.9[4]
Strong Corp Bond................	11.9[2]	**14.0[1]**	11.3[1]	Weitz Ser Fix Inc.................	8.6[4]	**9.5[4]**	6.7[4]
Price High Yld.....................	14.5[1]	**13.9[1]**	10.6[1]	UAM TS&W Fix Inc..............	9.2[3]	**9.4[4]**	6.6[4]
Vangd Bond Idx Long...........	14.3[1]	**13.9[1]**	—	Babson Bond-Port L............	9.3[3]	**9.3[4]**	7.0[4]
Nicholas Income..................	13.1[2]	**13.9[2]**	10.8[1]	Marshall Gov Inc.................	8.4[4]	**9.3[4]**	6.1[5]
Columbia High Yld...............	12.7[2]	**13.7[2]**	—	Boston-1784 Income...........	7.8[4]	**9.3[4]**	—
Vangd-Adml Long................	14.0[1]	**13.6[2]**	9.9[2]	KPM Fixed Inc.....................	8.4[4]	**9.3[4]**	—
Vangd LT Trsy.....................	13.9[1]	**13.5[2]**	9.7[2]	Wayne Hummer Income.......	9.0[4]	**9.2[4]**	7.0[4]
Amer Cent-Benham LT Trsy...	14.7[1]	**13.5[2]**	9.3[2]	AARP Hi Qual ST Bond.........	7.9[4]	**9.2[4]**	6.6[4]
Vangd Hi Yld Corp...............	11.9[2]	**13.5[2]**	11.2[1]	Sextant Bond Inc.................	12.1[2]	**9.2[4]**	—
Vangd LT Corp....................	13.8[2]	**13.3[2]**	9.6[2]	Schroder Ser:Inv Grd Inc......	7.7[4]	**9.2[4]**	—
Westcore LT Bond...............	14.0[1]	**13.3[2]**	9.4[2]	Value Line US Gov...............	9.2[3]	**9.1[5]**	4.9[5]
Rushmore US Gov................	13.1[2]	**13.2[2]**	8.5[2]	Aquinas Fix Inc...................	8.5[4]	**9.1[5]**	—
Advance Cap Ret Inc............	12.2[2]	**13.0[2]**	9.2[2]	Fidelity Inv Grd Bd..............	8.9[4]	**9.0[5]**	7.3[4]
Price Trsy Long...................	14.7[1]	**12.9[2]**	8.9[2]	Nations Strat Inc.................	8.3[4]	**8.9[5]**	6.6[4]
SAFECO Hi Yld Bd...............	12.8[2]	**12.9[2]**	10.5[1]	Fundamental US Gov Strat...	5.5[5]	**8.5[5]**	0.6[5]
Dreyfus Strat Income...........	11.2[2]	**12.7[2]**	9.1[2]	Scudder US Zero 2000.........	6.5[5]	**8.5[5]**	6.4[5]
Lexington Ramrz Glob Inc.....	5.0[5]	**12.6[2]**	—	Selected US Gov Inc............	7.2[5]	**8.4[5]**	6.2[5]
Maxus Income......................	11.8[2]	**12.3[2]**	8.1[3]	PC&J Preservation...............	7.4[5]	**8.3[5]**	6.1[5]
Invesco Select Inc...............	11.7[2]	**12.1[2]**	9.2[2]	Sit US Gov..........................	8.2[4]	**8.2[5]**	6.7[4]
Dreyfus 100% US Long.........	11.7[2]	**12.1[2]**	8.3[2]	Scout Bond........................	7.3[5]	**8.2[5]**	5.9[5]
Amer Cent-Benham Target 2000....	7.0[5]	**12.1[2]**	8.6[2]	UAM SAMI Pref Stck Inc.......	8.3[4]	**8.2[5]**	5.7[5]
Federated US Gov Bd...........	11.7[2]	**11.9[2]**	8.3[3]	Thompson Plumb Bond........	7.4[5]	**7.8[5]**	5.7[5]
Parnassus Fix Inc................	10.6[2]	**11.9[2]**	7.6[3]	C\FUNDS:Gov......................	7.3[5]	**7.8[5]**	5.9[5]
Wasatch Hosington US Treas...	15.7[1]	**11.6[2]**	8.0[3]	Guinness Flt Glob Gov.........	2.9[5]	**7.8[5]**	—
Legg Mason Invest Grd.........	10.3[2]	**11.4[2]**	7.9[3]	Managers Glob Bd...............	0.2[5]	**7.6[5]**	—
Wright US Treas...................	9.1[3]	**11.3[3]**	7.9[3]	Lancaster Gov Qual.............	7.0[5]	**7.5[5]**	5.4[5]
Invesco US Gov Sec.............	12.2[2]	**11.3[3]**	7.1[4]	Northern Int'l Fix Inc...........	-2.5[5]	**7.2[5]**	—
Dodge & Cox Income............	10.0[2]	**11.1[3]**	8.2[3]	Strong Int'l Bond.................	-4.8[5]	**7.0[5]**	—
Dreyfus Global Bd...............	6.8[5]	**11.0[3]**	—	Payden & Rygel Ltd Mat......	5.5[5]	**5.9[5]**	—
Schwab Tot Bd Mkt Idx.........	10.0[3]	**10.8[3]**	—	Vontobel Int'l Bd.................	-6.0[5]	**5.9[5]**	—
Lazard Strat Yld(O shrs).......	5.2[5]	**10.8[3]**	8.9[2]	Lazard Int'l Fix Inc(O shrs)....	-5.7[5]	**5.9[5]**	7.4[3]
Dreyfus A Bonds Plus...........	9.5[3]	**10.7[3]**	7.9[3]	Alliance World Inc...............	3.6[5]	**3.9[5]**	2.3[5]
Advance Cap Bond...............	9.4[3]	**10.6[3]**	7.5[3]	Scudder Glob Bond..............	0.4[5]	**3.7[5]**	3.3[5]

No-Load Fund	Total return percent with quintile ranks by objective			No-Load Fund	Total return percent with quintile ranks by objective		
	1997	Annualized 3 years	5 years		1997	Annualized 3 years	5 years
FIXED-INCOME - INTERMEDIATE TERM				McM Inter Fix	7.9[4]	**8.9[4]**	—
Janus Flex Inc	11.4[1]	**13.0[1]**	10.1[1]	Govt Street Bond	7.8[4]	**8.9[4]**	6.5[4]
Price Spect-Inc	12.2[1]	**13.0[1]**	9.7[1]	FundMngr Bond†	7.8[4]	**8.8[4]**	6.5[4]
Htchks & Wly Tot Ret	10.8[1]	**12.0[1]**	—	Legg Mason Glob Gov	-1.7[5]	**8.7[4]**	—
USAA Income	11.0[1]	**11.9[1]**	7.8[1]	Dreyfus 100% US Inter	7.6[4]	**8.7[4]**	6.5[3]
Fremont Bond	9.7[1]	**11.9[1]**	—	Babson Bond-Port S	8.2[3]	**8.7[4]**	6.4[4]
Stein Roe Income	9.6[1]	**11.2[1]**	8.4[1]	Amer Cent-Benham Inter Bd	8.4[3]	**8.7[4]**	6.2[4]
Analysts Inv Fix Inc	9.1[2]	**11.1[1]**	—	Amer Cent-Benham Inter-Trm Treas	8.3[3]	**8.6[4]**	6.2[4]
Harbor Bond	9.4[2]	**11.0[1]**	8.1[1]	BNY Hamilton Inter Gov	7.5[4]	**8.6[4]**	5.6[5]
Payden & Rygel Glob Fl	9.1[2]	**10.8[1]**	8.4[1]	Kent Inter Bd	7.6[4]	**8.6[4]**	6.1[4]
Citizens Tr Income	10.5[1]	**10.8[1]**	7.7[1]	Price Glob Gov	1.6[5]	**8.6[4]**	6.5[3]
Vangd Inter Corp	8.9[2]	**10.8[1]**	—	Dreyfus ST Income	8.2[3]	**8.5[4]**	6.9[3]
Vangd Bond Idx Inter	9.4[1]	**10.8[1]**	—	Flex-Fund US Gov Bond	7.8[4]	**8.5[4]**	6.5[4]
Analytic Master Fix Inc	10.1[1]	**10.6[1]**	—	Payden & Rygel Tot Ret	7.7[4]	**8.5[4]**	—
Lexington GNMA	10.2[1]	**10.5[1]**	7.4[2]	Boston-1784 US Gov Med	8.1[4]	**8.5[4]**	—
Federated Inter Inc	8.6[3]	**10.5[1]**	—	Kiewit Inter Bond	8.1[4]	**8.5[4]**	—
Vangd GNMA	9.5[1]	**10.4[1]**	7.2[2]	Wm Blair Income	8.0[4]	**8.4[4]**	6.4[4]
Columbia Fix Inc	9.6[1]	**10.4[1]**	7.5[2]	Legg Mason Gov Inter	7.0[5]	**8.4[4]**	5.9[5]
Fidelity Mortg Sec(Init Class)‡	9.1[2]	**10.4[1]**	7.9[1]	RSI Tr-Inter Bd	7.1[5]	**8.3[5]**	5.9[5]
Strong Gov Sec	9.1[2]	**10.4[2]**	8.0[1]	Asset Mgmt Inter Mrtg	8.4[3]	**8.3[4]**	6.0[4]
Vangd-Adml Inter	9.0[2]	**10.3[2]**	7.4[2]	Emerald US Gov Sec	7.4[4]	**8.3[5]**	6.0[4]
Vangd Bond Idx Total	9.4[1]	**10.3[2]**	7.4[2]	SAFECO Inter Trsy	8.3[3]	**8.3[5]**	6.3[4]
Amer Cent-Benham Bd	8.6[3]	**10.2[2]**	7.1[2]	Marshall Inter Bd	7.2[5]	**8.2[5]**	5.6[5]
Price Summit GNMA	9.8[1]	**10.2[2]**	—	Payden & Rygel Inter Bd	7.5[4]	**8.2[5]**	—
Vangd Inter Trsy	9.0[2]	**10.2[2]**	7.6[2]	WPG Core Bd	7.4[4]	**8.2[5]**	4.6[5]
Stein Roe Inter Bd	9.3[2]	**10.1[2]**	7.2[2]	Vintage Fix Inc	7.1[5]	**8.1[5]**	5.9[5]
Blanchard Flex Inc‡	9.4[2]	**10.1[2]**	7.4[2]	Fidelity Inter Bond‡	7.6[4]	**7.9[5]**	6.7[3]
Fidelity Spart GNMA	8.9[2]	**10.1[2]**	6.9[2]	Primary US Gov	6.1[5]	**7.9[5]**	5.7[5]
Westwood Inter Bd	10.7[1]	**10.1[2]**	6.8[3]	State Farm Interm‡	7.1[5]	**7.9[5]**	5.9[5]
Accessor Mort Sec	9.5[1]	**10.1[2]**	7.1[2]	Rainier Inter Fix Inc	7.3[4]	**7.8[5]**	—
Smith Brdn Inter Dur US Gov	9.0[2]	**10.1[2]**	7.8[1]	Price Int'l Bond	-3.2[5]	**7.7[5]**	7.9[1]
Sit Bond	9.4[2]	**10.1[2]**	—	Amer Cent-Benham Int'l Bd	-5.9[5]	**7.6[5]**	7.2[1]
Monetta Inter Bd	8.9[3]	**10.0[2]**	—	Mosaic Bond	6.0[5]	**7.4[5]**	5.2[5]
Wright Curr Inc	8.6[3]	**10.0[2]**	6.5[3]	Nations S-I Gov	7.0[5]	**7.3[5]**	5.4[5]
Warbg Pincus Fix Inc	8.8[3]	**10.0[2]**	8.0[1]	Mosaic Gov	7.7[4]	**7.3[5]**	5.5[5]
Chicago Tr Bond	9.0[2]	**10.0[2]**	—	Founders Gov Sec	7.9[4]	**7.0[5]**	4.4[5]
Price GNMA	9.5[1]	**10.0[2]**	6.8[3]	Fidelity Int'l Bond	-1.3[5]	**2.9[5]**	2.1[5]
Fidelity GNMA	8.7[3]	**10.0[2]**	6.7[3]	Scudder Int'l Bond	-4.2[5]	**2.5[5]**	2.7[5]
Payden & Rygel Inv Qual Bd	9.0[2]	**9.9[2]**	—	**FIXED-INCOME - SHORT TERM**			
Dupree Inter Gov	9.4[2]	**9.9[3]**	6.9[3]	Heartland US Gov	9.7[1]	**10.0[1]**	7.2[1]
Federated GNMA	8.8[3]	**9.9[3]**	6.6[3]	BSR S-I Fix Inc	7.6[1]	**9.0[1]**	6.5[1]
Price New Inc	9.3[2]	**9.8[3]**	7.3[2]	Strong ST Global	6.1[4]	**8.8[1]**	—
Amer Cent-Benham GNMA	8.7[3]	**9.8[3]**	6.8[3]	Htchks & Wly Low Dur	7.6[1]	**8.8[1]**	—
Independence One US Gov Sec	9.1[2]	**9.6[3]**	—	Price Trsy Inter	8.2[1]	**8.7[1]**	6.3[1]
Excelsior Inter Mgd Inc	8.5[3]	**9.6[3]**	6.6[3]	Strong ST Bond	7.2[1]	**8.6[1]**	6.7[1]
Accessor Inter Fix Inc	8.6[3]	**9.6[3]**	6.5[4]	Managers Sht & Int Bd	5.9[4]	**8.4[1]**	4.8[4]
Scudder GNMA	8.4[3]	**9.6[3]**	6.2[4]	Warbg Pincus Inter Gov	7.6[1]	**8.4[1]**	6.2[1]
Federated Income	8.9[3]	**9.6[3]**	6.5[3]	AARP GNMA & Trsy	8.0[1]	**8.3[1]**	5.8[2]
USAA GNMA	9.5[1]	**9.6[3]**	7.1[2]	Fidelity Spart Ltd Mat Gov	7.3[1]	**8.3[1]**	6.0[1]
Dreyfus Bond Mkt Idx	9.2[2]	**9.5[3]**	—	USAA ST Bond	7.2[1]	**8.2[1]**	—
Bernstein Inter Dur	7.6[4]	**9.5[3]**	7.0[2]	Vangd ST Corp	6.9[2]	**8.1[1]**	6.2[1]
Managers Inter Mortg	8.2[3]	**9.5[3]**	1.9[5]	Vangd Bond Idx Short	7.0[1]	**8.1[1]**	—
Asset Mgmt US Mrtg Sec	9.7[1]	**9.4[3]**	6.4[4]	Invesco Inter Gov	6.2[4]	**7.9[1]**	6.0[1]
SAFECO GNMA	9.0[2]	**9.4[3]**	6.1[4]	Prudential Gov Sec S-I	7.1[1]	**7.9[1]**	5.6[2]
Elite Bond	9.8[1]	**9.4[3]**	6.8[3]	Montgmry Sht Dur Gov	7.0[2]	**7.8[1]**	6.5[1]
Warbg Pincus Glob Fix Inc	2.2[5]	**9.3[3]**	8.1[1]	Vangd ST Federal	6.5[3]	**7.8[1]**	5.8[1]
Merriman Flex Bd	5.7[5]	**9.2[3]**	7.7[1]	Federated US Gov 2-5	6.9[2]	**7.8[2]**	5.5[2]
SSgA Inter Fix	7.4[4]	**9.1[3]**	—	Vangd-Adml Short	6.5[2]	**7.7[2]**	5.8[1]
Fairport Gov Sec	7.5[4]	**9.1[3]**	—	Fidelity Spart S-I Gov	6.6[2]	**7.7[2]**	5.6[2]
Westcore Inter Bond	8.3[3]	**8.9[4]**	6.5[3]	Blanchard ST Flex.†	7.2[1]	**7.7[2]**	—

By 1995-1997 performance

No-Load Fund	1997	Annualized 3 years	5 years	No-Load Fund	1997	Annualized 3 years	5 years
Vangd ST Trsy...	6.4³	7.6²	5.7²	Capstone Gov Inc...	4.4⁵	4.7⁵	3.7⁵
Northern US Gov...	7.2¹	7.6²	—	Permanent Treasy†	4.1⁵	4.4⁵	3.8⁵
Dean Witter ST Bond	6.4³	7.6²	—	API T-1 Trsy...	2.8⁵	4.1⁵	—
First Omaha S-I Fix...	6.7²	7.5²	5.5²	Fontaine Glob Inc...	-27.3⁵	-1.9⁵	2.9⁵
UAM DSI Ltd Mat...	6.7²	7.5²	5.0⁴	**TAX-FREE - LONG TERM**			
Federated ST Income...	6.4³	7.5²	5.5²	Fundamental HY Muni...	15.7¹	14.8¹	6.7⁴
Dreyfus S-I Gov...	6.1⁴	7.5²	5.8²	SAFECO CA TF...	11.6¹	13.0¹	8.2¹
Homestead ST Bond...	6.6²	7.5²	5.8¹	USAA Texas TF...	11.7¹	12.9¹	—
Fidelity S-I Gov...	6.6²	7.5²	5.2³	USAA CA Bond...	10.3¹	12.3¹	7.7¹
Price ST Gov...	6.7²	7.3²	4.8⁵	SAFECO Insur Muni...	10.7¹	12.2¹	—
Schwab ST Bd Mkt Idx...	7.1¹	7.3²	5.3³	Excelsior LT TE...	9.4²	11.9¹	8.8¹
Nbrgr-Ber Ltd Mat...	6.9²	7.3²	5.6²	Scudder Hi Yld TF...	12.0¹	11.6¹	7.7¹
Boston-1784 ST Income...	6.3³	7.3²	—	SAFECO Muni Bd...	10.7¹	11.5¹	7.5¹
Crabbe Hsn US Gov Bd...	7.1¹	7.2³	5.0⁴	Blanchard Flex TF...	8.8³	11.5¹	—
Federated ARMS...	6.3³	7.2³	5.2³	Drey-Basic Muni...	10.9¹	11.4¹	—
Wright US Treas Near Term...	5.9⁴	7.2³	5.2³	Amer Cent-Benham CA Hi Yld...	10.4¹	11.4¹	8.2¹
Amer Cent-Benham Ltd Trm Bd...	6.3³	7.2³	—	Price Summit Muni Inc...	11.6¹	11.4¹	—
JP Morgan ST Bond...	6.1⁴	7.2³	—	USAA FL TF...	11.2¹	11.3¹	—
Asset Mgmt ARM...	6.5²	7.2³	5.6²	Schwab CA Long...	10.2¹	11.3¹	7.2²
Dreyfus 100% US Short...	6.1⁴	7.2³	5.6²	Strong Hi Yld Muni...	13.9¹	11.1¹	—
Nations ST Inc...	5.8⁴	7.2³	5.6²	Fidelity Spart CA Muni Inc...	9.8¹	11.1¹	7.2²
Fidelity Spart ST Bd...	6.5²	7.1³	5.0⁴	USAA TE Long...	10.4¹	11.0¹	7.2²
Analytic ST Gov...	5.5⁵	7.1³	—	Fidelity Spart NY Muni Inc‡...	10.0¹	11.0¹	7.3²
Price Summit Ltd Trm...	7.2¹	7.1³	—	Nations Muni Inc...	9.3²	10.9¹	7.4²
Invesco ST Bond...	6.7²	7.1³	—	Fidelity NY Muni Inc...	9.7²	10.9¹	7.2³
Asset Mgmt ST US Gov...	6.3³	7.0³	5.4³	Amer Cent-Benham CA Long...	9.6²	10.8¹	7.7¹
Reynolds US Gov...	5.4⁵	7.0³	4.8⁵	Parnassus CA TE...	9.3²	10.8¹	7.5¹
Payden & Rygel ST Bd...	5.8⁴	6.9³	—	CA Inv Tr-CA TF...	9.3²	10.8¹	7.3²
Fidelity ST Bond...	6.2⁴	6.9³	5.0⁴	Scudder CA TF...	10.2¹	10.7¹	7.4¹
Janus ST Bond...	6.6²	6.9³	5.4²	Vangd CA Insur LT...	8.9³	10.7¹	7.6¹
Strong Advantage...	6.5²	6.9⁴	6.5¹	Dupree TN TF Inc...	8.9³	10.7¹	—
Emerald ST Inc...	5.7⁵	6.9⁴	—	USAA NY Bond...	10.6¹	10.7²	7.0³
Scudder ST Bond...	6.1⁴	6.9⁴	5.1³	Vangd Muni Long...	9.3²	10.6²	7.7¹
IAI Gov Bond...	6.4³	6.9⁴	5.3³	Schwab LT TF...	9.9¹	10.6²	7.4¹
Kent ST Bd...	6.3³	6.8⁴	4.9⁴	Fundamental CA Muni...	11.3¹	10.6²	4.8⁵
Htchks & Wly ST Invest...	6.5²	6.8⁴	—	Nations VA Muni...	9.2²	10.6²	—
Amer Cent-Benham ST Gov...	6.0⁴	6.8⁴	4.8⁴	Price TF Hi Yld...	10.2¹	10.5²	7.8¹
Kiewit Sht Term Gov...	6.3³	6.8⁴	—	Fidelity Spart Insur Muni Inc.‡...	9.5²	10.5²	7.2²
Bernstein Short Dur Plus...	5.5⁵	6.8⁴	5.2³	Amer Cent-Benham CA Insured...	9.3²	10.5²	7.4¹
Marshall ST Inc...	6.4³	6.8⁴	5.1³	Vangd Muni Hi Yld...	9.2²	10.5²	7.6¹
BT Pyramid:Ltd Trm US Gov...	6.0⁴	6.7⁴	5.2³	Nations TX Muni...	8.8³	10.5²	—
Harbor Short Dur...	6.3³	6.7⁴	5.4³	USAA VA Bond...	9.5²	10.5²	7.3²
Excelsior ST Gov...	5.9⁴	6.7⁴	5.1⁴	Stein Roe Hi Yld Muni...	9.5²	10.4²	7.4²
Amer Cent-Benham ST Trsy...	6.0⁴	6.6⁴	5.1⁴	Nations TN Muni...	9.0³	10.4²	—
Preferred ST Gov...	6.2⁴	6.6⁴	4.9⁴	SAFECO WA Muni...	9.0³	10.4²	—
Bernstein Gov Sht Dur...	5.7⁵	6.6⁴	4.9⁴	Fidelity Muni Bd(Init Class)...	9.2²	10.3²	6.8³
Price ST Bond...	6.3³	6.6⁴	4.6⁵	Price GA TF...	9.7²	10.3²	—
Dean Witter ST US Treas...	6.1⁴	6.6⁵	4.6⁵	Fidelity Spart FL Muni...	8.7⁴	10.3²	7.5¹
Columbia US Gov...	5.6⁵	6.5⁵	5.1⁴	Nations NC Muni...	8.8³	10.3²	—
Eclipse Ultra Short...	6.2³	6.5⁵	—	Vangd Muni Insur LT...	8.6⁴	10.2²	7.4¹
Federated US Gov 1-3...	5.7⁵	6.5⁵	4.8⁵	Nations FL Muni...	8.7⁴	10.2²	—
Amer AAdv Mileage Ltd Inc...	6.5²	6.4⁵	—	Drey-General CA...	8.8³	10.2²	7.2²
Managers ST Gov...	5.5⁵	6.3⁵	3.2⁵	Price CA TF...	9.1³	10.2²	7.3²
Smith Brdn Sh Dur US Gov...	6.3³	6.2⁵	5.4³	Scudder NY TF...	9.9¹	10.2²	7.0³
Nbrgr-Ber Ultra Sht‡...	6.2⁴	6.0⁵	4.6⁵	Fidelity NY Insur Muni Inc...	8.8³	10.2²	6.8³
SSgA Yld Plus...	5.5⁵	5.9⁵	5.0⁴	Nations GA Muni...	8.6⁴	10.2²	—
Permanent Vers Bd†...	5.1⁵	5.8⁵	4.8⁵	Fidelity Spart MA Muni Inc...	9.3²	10.2³	7.2²
IAI Reserve...	4.6⁵	5.3⁵	4.3⁵	Nations MD Muni...	9.0³	10.2³	—
RSI Tr-ST Invest...	4.9⁵	5.0⁵	4.2⁵	Vangd FL Insur...	8.9³	10.1³	7.6¹
Schroder Ser:ST Invest...	4.9⁵	4.9⁵	—	Vangd NY Insur LT...	8.7⁴	10.0³	7.3²

No-Load Fund	Total return percent with quintile ranks by objective			No-Load Fund	Total return percent with quintile ranks by objective		
	1997	Annualized 3 years	5 years		1997	Annualized 3 years	5 years
Price NY TF	9.5^2	$\mathbf{10.0^3}$	7.3^2	Rushmore MD TF	7.9^5	$\mathbf{8.3^5}$	6.2^5
Scudder MA TF	8.5^4	$\mathbf{10.0^3}$	7.4^2	Dupree KY TF Inc	8.0^5	$\mathbf{8.3^5}$	6.8^3
Fidelity Spart MD Muni Inc	8.8^3	$\mathbf{10.0^3}$	—	State Farm Muni Bd‡	7.3^5	$\mathbf{8.2^5}$	6.3^5
Fidelity Spart CT Muni	9.1^2	$\mathbf{10.0^3}$	7.0^3	Westcore CO TE	7.4^5	$\mathbf{8.2^5}$	6.1^5
Fidelity Spart Muni Inc	9.2^2	$\mathbf{10.0^3}$	6.8^4	Dreyfus NY Insur	7.4^5	$\mathbf{8.2^5}$	5.6^5
Price TF Inc	9.3^2	$\mathbf{10.0^3}$	7.2^2	JP Morgan NY Tot Ret	7.4^5	$\mathbf{8.1^5}$	—
Scudder Mngd Muni	9.3^2	$\mathbf{9.9^3}$	7.2^3	JP Morgan TE Bond	7.4^5	$\mathbf{8.0^5}$	6.1^5
Scudder OH TF	8.7^4	$\mathbf{9.9^3}$	7.1^3	Sextant Idaho TE	7.1^5	$\mathbf{8.0^5}$	5.7^5
Price VA TF	9.0^3	$\mathbf{9.8^3}$	7.2^3	Jamestown VA Tax-Free	7.0^5	$\mathbf{7.7^5}$	—
Fidelity Spart AZ Muni	8.0^5	$\mathbf{9.8^3}$	—	Gov Street AL TF	6.3^5	$\mathbf{7.4^5}$	—
Scudder PA TF	8.9^3	$\mathbf{9.8^3}$	7.1^3	Accessor S-I Fix Inc	6.3^5	$\mathbf{7.1^5}$	5.0^5
CGM American TF	9.0^3	$\mathbf{9.8^3}$	—	Kiewit Tax Exempt	6.2^5	$\mathbf{6.5^5}$	—
Stein Roe Mgd Muni	9.3^2	$\mathbf{9.8^3}$	6.8^3	Fundamental NY Muni	1.5^5	$\mathbf{2.8^5}$	-0.6^5
Fidelity Spart PA Muni Inc	8.3^4	$\mathbf{9.8^3}$	7.3^2	**TAX-FREE - INTERMEDIATE TERM**			
Vangd OH Insur LT	8.5^4	$\mathbf{9.7^3}$	7.2^3	USAA TE Inter	9.4^1	$\mathbf{9.6^1}$	7.1^1
Janus Federal TE	9.0^3	$\mathbf{9.7^3}$	—	Dreyfus PA Inter Muni	8.3^1	$\mathbf{9.2^1}$	—
Heartland WI TF	8.1^5	$\mathbf{9.7^3}$	6.5^4	Boston-1784 TE Med Term	9.1^1	$\mathbf{9.1^1}$	—
Fidelity Spart OH Muni Inc	8.7^4	$\mathbf{9.7^3}$	7.0^3	Drey-Basic Inter Muni	8.8^1	$\mathbf{9.1^1}$	—
Amer Cent-Benham Long TF	9.5^2	$\mathbf{9.7^3}$	7.2^2	Fidelity Ltd Muni Inc	8.3^1	$\mathbf{9.1^1}$	6.7^1
Price NJ TF	9.1^2	$\mathbf{9.6^3}$	7.1^3	US Glb:Tax Free	9.1^1	$\mathbf{8.9^1}$	6.5^1
Drey-General NY	9.6^2	$\mathbf{9.6^3}$	6.9^3	Fidelity Spart Inter Muni	8.0^1	$\mathbf{8.9^1}$	—
Value Line TE Hi Yld	8.8^3	$\mathbf{9.6^3}$	6.4^4	Price Summit Muni Inter	8.4^1	$\mathbf{8.9^1}$	—
Vangd NJ Insur LT	8.6^4	$\mathbf{9.5^4}$	7.2^3	Excelsior Inter TE	7.3^3	$\mathbf{8.8^1}$	6.5^2
Vangd PA Insur LT	8.3^4	$\mathbf{9.5^4}$	7.2^3	Fidelity Spart NY Inter Muni Inc‡	8.1^1	$\mathbf{8.7^1}$	—
Price MD TF	8.6^4	$\mathbf{9.5^4}$	7.1^3	Dreyfus NY Inter	8.2^1	$\mathbf{8.7^1}$	6.4^2
Value Line NY TE	9.3^2	$\mathbf{9.5^4}$	6.7^4	SAFECO Inter Muni	7.5^2	$\mathbf{8.7^1}$	—
Fidelity Spart Agg Muni.‡	10.3^1	$\mathbf{9.5^4}$	7.0^3	Vangd CA Insur Inter	7.7^2	$\mathbf{8.7^2}$	—
Northern TE Bond	8.7^4	$\mathbf{9.5^4}$	—	Federated PA Inter	7.5^2	$\mathbf{8.7^2}$	—
AARP Insur TF Gen	8.9^3	$\mathbf{9.5^4}$	6.8^4	Fremont CA Inter	7.3^3	$\mathbf{8.6^2}$	6.1^3
Fidelity Spart MN Muni Inc	8.8^3	$\mathbf{9.4^4}$	6.7^4	Scudder Medium TF	7.7^2	$\mathbf{8.6^2}$	6.5^2
Sit TF Income	9.8^1	$\mathbf{9.4^4}$	7.5^1	Dreyfus Inter Muni	7.6^2	$\mathbf{8.5^2}$	6.3^2
Arbor OVB WV TE	8.9^3	$\mathbf{9.4^4}$	—	Dreyfus MA Inter	7.5^2	$\mathbf{8.4^2}$	6.1^3
Dreyfus MA TE	9.1^3	$\mathbf{9.4^4}$	6.7^4	Dreyfus CT Inter	7.6^2	$\mathbf{8.4^2}$	6.5^2
Babson TF Long	8.7^4	$\mathbf{9.4^4}$	6.3^4	Amer Cent-Benham FL Inter	8.2^1	$\mathbf{8.4^2}$	—
Drey-General Muni	8.1^5	$\mathbf{9.3^4}$	6.5^4	Nations Int Muni	7.1^3	$\mathbf{8.4^2}$	—
Fidelity Spart MI Muni Inc	9.1^3	$\mathbf{9.2^4}$	6.5^4	Amer Cent-Benham CA Inter	7.4^2	$\mathbf{8.3^2}$	6.2^2
Fidelity Spart NJ Muni Inc	8.3^4	$\mathbf{9.2^4}$	6.8^4	Vangd Muni Inter	7.1^3	$\mathbf{8.2^2}$	6.7^1
Emerald FL TE	9.1^3	$\mathbf{9.2^4}$	6.7^4	Stein Roe Inter Muni	7.5^2	$\mathbf{8.2^2}$	6.3^2
IAA Trust TE Bd	9.0^3	$\mathbf{9.1^4}$	5.8^5	Dreyfus CA Inter	7.6^2	$\mathbf{8.2^3}$	6.5^1
Dreyfus NY TE	9.1^2	$\mathbf{9.1^4}$	6.4^4	CA Inv Tr-CA Insur Inter	6.4^5	$\mathbf{8.1^3}$	5.8^4
North Carolina TF	8.0^5	$\mathbf{9.1^4}$	—	Vintage Inter TF	6.6^4	$\mathbf{8.1^3}$	—
Mosaic TF VA	8.4^4	$\mathbf{9.1^4}$	6.0^5	Excelsior NY Inter TE	6.7^4	$\mathbf{8.1^3}$	5.8^4
Dreyfus NJ Muni	8.8^3	$\mathbf{9.1^4}$	6.6^4	Nations FL Int Muni	7.0^3	$\mathbf{8.1^3}$	6.1^3
Dreyfus Muni Bond	7.9^5	$\mathbf{9.0^4}$	6.3^5	Nations NC Int Muni	7.0^3	$\mathbf{8.1^3}$	5.9^3
Boston-1784 RI TE Inc	8.3^4	$\mathbf{9.0^4}$	—	Price TF Ins Inter	7.2^3	$\mathbf{8.1^3}$	6.7^1
Mosaic TF MO	8.1^5	$\mathbf{8.9^4}$	5.6^5	BT Invest:Inter TF	7.5^2	$\mathbf{8.1^3}$	6.0^3
Boston-1784 CT TE Inc	8.5^4	$\mathbf{8.8^4}$	—	Nations GA Int Muni	7.0^3	$\mathbf{8.1^3}$	5.9^4
Invesco TF Long	8.7^4	$\mathbf{8.8^5}$	6.5^4	Nations TN Int Muni	6.7^4	$\mathbf{8.0^3}$	—
Mosaic TF Nat	8.2^4	$\mathbf{8.7^5}$	5.6^5	Dreyfus NJ Inter	6.9^3	$\mathbf{8.0^3}$	6.1^2
Columbia Muni Bd	8.4^4	$\mathbf{8.7^5}$	6.2^5	WPG Inter Muni	7.9^1	$\mathbf{8.0^3}$	—
Rushmore VA TF	8.5^4	$\mathbf{8.6^5}$	6.4^4	Amer Cent-Benham Inter TF	7.4^3	$\mathbf{7.9^4}$	6.0^3
Dreyfus Insur Muni	8.4^4	$\mathbf{8.6^5}$	5.7^5	Nations SC Int Muni	6.6^4	$\mathbf{7.9^4}$	6.0^3
Sit MN TF Inc	8.2^4	$\mathbf{8.6^5}$	—	Amer Cent-Benham AZ Inter	6.9^4	$\mathbf{7.9^4}$	—
Mosaic TF AZ	7.9^5	$\mathbf{8.6^5}$	5.5^5	Bernstein CA Muni	6.3^5	$\mathbf{7.9^4}$	5.6^4
Boston-1784 MA TE Inc	8.9^3	$\mathbf{8.6^5}$	—	Nbrgr-Ber Muni	7.4^3	$\mathbf{7.8^4}$	5.7^4
Strong Muni Bond	12.1^1	$\mathbf{8.5^5}$	6.4^4	Dreyfus FL Inter	6.3^5	$\mathbf{7.8^4}$	6.1^2
Dreyfus CA TE	8.3^4	$\mathbf{8.5^5}$	5.8^5	Price FL Ins Inter	6.7^4	$\mathbf{7.8^4}$	—
First Hawaii Muni Bd	7.1^5	$\mathbf{8.5^5}$	5.9^5	Montgmry CA TF Inter	7.5^2	$\mathbf{7.8^4}$	—
Empire Builder TF Bond	7.9^5	$\mathbf{8.5^5}$	6.5^4	Nations MD Int Muni	6.5^5	$\mathbf{7.8^4}$	5.6^5
Mosaic TF MD	8.0^5	$\mathbf{8.4^5}$	—	Nations VA Int Muni	6.6^4	$\mathbf{7.7^4}$	5.6^5

Stock and bond funds – ranked within objective *continued*

By 1995-1997 performance

No-Load Fund	Total return percent with quintile ranks by objective			No-Load Fund	Total return percent with quintile ranks by objective		
	1997	Annualized 3 years	5 years		1997	Annualized 3 years	5 years
Bernstein Dvsfd Muni	6.7[4]	**7.7[4]**	5.7[4]	Vangd Muni Ltd Trm	5.1[3]	**5.9[2]**	4.8[2]
Nations TX Int Muni	6.9[3]	**7.6[4]**	—	Babson TF Short	5.1[3]	**5.9[2]**	4.5[4]
Bernstein NY Muni	6.5[4]	**7.6[5]**	5.7[4]	Amer Cent-Benham CA Ltd Term	5.3[3]	**5.8[2]**	4.5[3]
Kent Inter TF	6.8[4]	**7.5[5]**	5.5[5]	US Glb:Near Term TF	6.6[1]	**5.8[2]**	5.4[1]
Federated Inter Muni	6.9[4]	**7.4[5]**	5.5[5]	Price TF S-I	5.3[2]	**5.8[3]**	4.8[2]
Invesco TF Inter	6.4[5]	**7.3[5]**	—	Strong ST Muni	6.9[1]	**5.7[3]**	4.4[4]
Marshall Inter TF	6.8[4]	**7.3[5]**	—	Kent MI Muni	5.4[2]	**5.6[3]**	—
Crabbe Hsn OR Muni	7.0[3]	**7.3[5]**	5.5[5]	Federated ST Muni	4.5[4]	**5.5[3]**	4.1[5]
BNY Hamilton Inter NY TE	6.2[5]	**7.2[5]**	5.1[5]	Nations ST Muni	4.6[4]	**5.5[3]**	—
Northern Inter TE	5.8[5]	**7.0[5]**	—	Kent Ltd Trm TF	4.6[4]	**5.5[3]**	—
Warbg Pincus NY Inter	5.9[5]	**6.5[5]**	5.7[4]	Dreyfus S-I Muni	5.2[3]	**5.5[4]**	4.5[3]
Chicago Tr Muni	5.5[5]	**6.5[5]**	—	FL Hough ST	4.9[4]	**5.4[4]**	—
Dupree TN TF Sht-Med	5.4[5]	**5.5[5]**	—	Amer Cent-Benham Ltd Term TF	5.5[2]	**5.3[4]**	—
Dupree KY Sht-Med	5.2[5]	**5.1[5]**	4.4[5]	Excelsior ST TE	4.6[4]	**5.2[4]**	4.1[4]
TAX-FREE · SHORT TERM				Price VA ST	4.3[5]	**5.1[4]**	—
Nations SC Muni	8.4[1]	**10.2[1]**	—	Price MD ST TF	4.2[5]	**5.0[5]**	—
Schwab CA S-I	5.3[2]	**6.5[1]**	—	Payden & Rygel Sht Dur TE	4.5[4]	**4.8[5]**	—
Scudder Ltd TF	5.9[1]	**6.4[1]**	—	Bernstein Sht Dur Divsfd Muni	4.0[5]	**4.6[5]**	—
Scudder MA Ltd TF	5.7[2]	**6.2[1]**	—	Vangd Muni Short	4.1[5]	**4.6[5]**	3.8[5]
USAA TE Short	5.9[1]	**6.1[1]**	4.9[2]	Bernstein CA Short Dur Muni	3.6[5]	**4.5[5]**	—
Schwab S-I TF	5.3[3]	**6.0[1]**	—	Bernstein NY Short Dur Muni	3.8[5]	**4.5[5]**	—
Fidelity Spart S-I Muni	5.5[2]	**5.9[2]**	4.9[1]				

By 1993-1997 performance

AGGRESSIVE GROWTH FUNDS

No-Load Fund	Total return percent with quintile ranks by objective		
	1997	Annualized 3 years	Annualized 5 years
Fidelity New Millnm†‡	24.6[2]	32.6[1]	**34.0[1]**
SAFECO Growth SC	50.0[1]	32.5[1]	**32.8[1]**
First Eagle America	29.5[2]	31.7[1]	**32.5[1]**
UAM FMA Small Co SC	40.4[1]	30.0[1]	**22.3[1]**
Robrtsn Stph Val Gro	13.9[4]	22.8[3]	**22.0[1]**
Berger Sm Cap Val SC	36.4[1]	29.3[1]	**21.8[1]**
Spectra	24.7[2]	30.1[1]	**21.1[1]**
Founders Growth	26.5[2]	29.0[1]	**21.1[1]**
Lazard Small Cap SC(O shrs)	28.1[2]	24.5[2]	**20.7[1]**
SSgA Sm Cap SC	23.6[3]	31.2[1]	**20.4[1]**
Harbor Cap App	31.4[1]	29.5[1]	**20.3[1]**
Permanent Agg Growth	32.7[1]	26.3[2]	**19.9[1]**
RSI Tr-Emg Gro SC	8.3[5]	25.3[2]	**19.7[1]**
Accessor Sm\Mid Cap	36.2[1]	30.9[1]	**19.7[1]**
Stein Roe Cap Opp	6.2[5]	24.4[3]	**19.7[1]**
Fidelity Contrafund†††	23.0[3]	26.9[2]	**19.7[1]**
PBHG Growth	-3.3[5]	16.8[5]	**19.6[1]**
Price New Horizon‡ SC	9.8[4]	25.9[2]	**19.6[1]**
Skyline Special Eqty SC‡	35.4[1]	26.2[2]	**19.5[1]**
Kaufmann SC	12.6[4]	23.0[3]	**19.1[1]**
Quant Numeric SC	7.2[5]	21.3[4]	**19.1[1]**
Managers Spec Eqty SC	24.5[2]	27.6[1]	**19.1[1]**
Fidelity Magellan†‡	26.5[2]	24.6[2]	**18.8[2]**
Brandywine	12.0[4]	23.8[3]	**18.4[2]**
Value Line Levergd Gro	23.8[2]	27.6[2]	**18.4[2]**
Vangd Morgan	30.8[1]	29.9[1]	**18.3[2]**
Dreyfus Apprec	27.8[2]	30.4[1]	**18.2[2]**
Eclipse Equity SC	33.3[1]	27.5[2]	**18.2[2]**
Invesco Dynamics	24.1[2]	25.5[2]	**18.2[2]**
PC&J Performance	35.6[1]	25.9[2]	**18.1[2]**
Gabelli Sm Cap Gro SC	36.5[1]	24.1[3]	**17.9[2]**
Price New Amer	21.1[3]	28.0[1]	**17.9[2]**
Columbia Growth	26.3[2]	26.6[2]	**17.9[2]**
Warbg Pincus Emg Gro SC	21.3[3]	24.9[2]	**17.8[2]**
Amer Cent-20th Cent Ultra	23.1[3]	24.5[2]	**17.8[2]**
Babson Enterprise II SC	33.3[1]	26.8[2]	**17.7[2]**
Fidelity Emg Gro††	19.4[3]	23.4[3]	**17.6[2]**
Babson Enterprise‡ SC	32.4[1]	23.2[3]	**17.4[2]**
Montgmry Sm Cap‡ SC	23.9[2]	25.7[2]	**17.3[2]**
CGM Capital Dev‡	23.9[2]	30.8[1]	**17.3[2]**
AARP Capital Growth	35.1[1]	28.6[1]	**17.3[2]**
Fidelity Growth Co	18.9[3]	24.7[2]	**17.1[2]**
Kent Sm Co Gro SC	27.7[2]	23.4[3]	**17.1[2]**
Royce Micro-Cap SC	24.7[2]	19.7[4]	**17.1[2]**
C&O Market Opport	29.4[2]	24.3[3]	**16.9[3]**
Janus Twenty	29.7[2]	31.2[1]	**16.9[3]**
Gradison Oppty Value SC	31.1[1]	25.7[2]	**16.6[3]**
Amer Cent-20th Cent Giftrust	-1.2[5]	13.1[5]	**16.6[3]**
Cornercap Growth	32.9[1]	23.4[3]	**16.4[3]**
Stein Roe Growth Stk‡	31.6[1]	29.2[1]	**16.4[3]**
Trainer-Wrthm First Mutual	23.1[3]	29.7[1]	**16.3[3]**
Dreyfus New Leaders SC	19.5[3]	22.1[4]	**16.3[3]**
Galaxy II Sm Co Idx SC	23.6[3]	25.3[2]	**16.1[3]**
Bruce	30.2[1]	28.0[1]	**16.0[3]**
Value Line Spec Sit	32.2[1]	22.3[3]	**15.8[3]**
Ariel Growth SC	36.4[1]	25.9[2]	**15.8[3]**
Wasatch Agg Eqty‡ SC	19.2[3]	17.1[5]	**15.8[3]**
Legg Mason Spec Invest SC	22.1[3]	24.4[3]	**15.7[3]**
Nations Emg Gro SC	20.5[3]	22.7[3]	**15.7[3]**
Sit Mid Cap Gro	17.7[3]	24.2[3]	**15.7[3]**
Scudder Large Cap Gro	32.8[1]	27.6[1]	**15.5[3]**
Columbia Special	12.6[4]	18.2[4]	**15.5[3]**
Schroder Cap:US Eqty	23.3[3]	24.3[3]	**15.4[3]**
Invesco Sm Co Gro SC	18.3[3]	19.7[4]	**15.3[3]**
USAA Agg Growth SC	7.6[5]	23.5[3]	**15.1[3]**
Brown Cap Sm Co SC	15.8[4]	22.0[4]	**15.0[3]**
Robrtsn Stph Emg Gro SC	18.5[3]	20.1[4]	**14.9[3]**
Fairmont	15.3[4]	17.3[5]	**14.9[4]**
JP Morgan US Sm Co SC	22.8[3]	25.0[2]	**14.8[3]**
Fidelity OTC††	9.9[4]	23.4[3]	**14.6[4]**
Nbrgr-Ber Manhtn	29.2[2]	22.9[3]	**14.5[4]**
Managers Cap App	12.7[4]	19.6[4]	**14.5[4]**
Federated Mini Cap SC	20.4[3]	20.6[4]	**14.5[4]**
Crabbe Hsn Special SC	11.2[4]	9.3[5]	**14.4[4]**
General Securities	13.4[4]	20.4[4]	**14.3[4]**
Harbor Growth	20.9[3]	22.9[3]	**14.2[4]**
FundMngr Agg Gro‡	16.7[4]	19.3[4]	**13.9[4]**
Vangd Explorer SC	14.6[4]	18.2[4]	**13.9[4]**
Wright Jr Blue Ch SC	28.9[2]	22.2[3]	**13.9[4]**
WPG Tudor SC	11.1[4]	23.1[3]	**13.8[4]**
Founders Frontier SC	6.2[5]	18.5[4]	**13.5[4]**
Lancaster Crest Sm Cap SC	8.5[5]	17.8[4]	**13.5[4]**
Wilshire Target Sm Gro SC	11.7[4]	17.7[5]	**13.2[4]**
Founders Special	16.4[4]	19.1[4]	**13.2[4]**
Excelsior Sm Cap SC	14.2[4]	11.1[5]	**13.0[4]**
Perritt Micro Cap Opp SC	22.1[3]	22.6[3]	**13.0[4]**
Scudder Development SC	6.9[5]	21.0[4]	**12.8[4]**
Amer Cent-20th Cent Growth	29.3[2]	21.4[4]	**12.8[4]**
Founders Discovery	11.9[4]	21.2[4]	**12.7[4]**
IAI Emg Growth SC	-2.9[5]	15.8[5]	**12.3[5]**
WPG Growth SC	9.7[5]	21.8[4]	**12.3[5]**
Scout Regional SC	23.0[3]	18.4[4]	**12.1[5]**
Berger 100	13.6[4]	16.1[5]	**12.1[5]**
Matterhorn Growth	13.7[4]	16.3[5]	**11.9[5]**
Strong Discovery SC	10.8[4]	14.9[5]	**11.8[5]**
Wasatch MidCap	-0.5[5]	17.9[4]	**11.5[5]**
Fidelity Trend	8.5[5]	15.7[5]	**11.5[5]**
Pathfinder SC	24.9[2]	22.4[3]	**11.5[5]**
Oberweis Emg Growth SC	-8.6[5]	17.1[5]	**11.2[5]**
Mosaic Mid-Cap Gro	17.1[4]	14.9[5]	**10.9[5]**
Capp-Rush Emg Growth SC	4.7[5]	13.3[5]	**10.6[5]**
Trent Equity	25.2[2]	19.9[4]	**10.2[5]**
Amer Cent-20th Cent Vista	-8.7[5]	12.8[5]	**9.6[5]**
Pin Oak Agg Stk SC	1.3[5]	15.5[5]	**9.4[5]**
Merriman Levgd Gro	12.2[4]	13.8[5]	**8.8[5]**
Bull & Bear Spec Eqty	5.2[5]	14.3[5]	**7.8[5]**
Rainbow Fund	5.0[5]	16.3[5]	**7.4[5]**
Fontaine Cap App	-27.3[5]	-1.2[5]	**2.4[5]**
American Heritage	75.0[1]	4.8[5]	**1.1[5]**
Steadman Amer Indust	-12.4[5]	-10.2[5]	**-13.1[5]**
Steadman Tech & Gro	-28.2[5]	-28.9[5]	**-26.9[5]**

GROWTH FUNDS

No-Load Fund	1997	Annualized 3 years	Annualized 5 years
Excelsior Val & Restruc	33.6[1]	32.4[1]	**27.2[1]**
Legg Mason Value	37.1[1]	38.7[1]	**24.7[1]**
Baron Asset SC	33.9[1]	30.2[1]	**24.0[1]**
Torray	37.1[1]	38.6[1]	**23.7[1]**
Mairs & Power Gro	28.7[2]	34.4[1]	**23.7[1]**
Vangd Primecap	36.8[1]	29.9[1]	**23.6[1]**
Sequoia‡	43.2[1]	35.1[1]	**23.0[1]**

Stock and bond funds – ranked within objective *continued*

No-Load Fund	Total return percent with quintile ranks by objective			No-Load Fund	Total return percent with quintile ranks by objective		
	1997	Annualized 3 years	5 years		1997	Annualized 3 years	5 years
Oakmark	32.6[1]	27.5[2]	**22.8[1]**	UAM Strlng Part Eqty	24.9[3]	27.6[2]	**17.6[3]**
White Oak Gro	24.3[3]	35.9[1]	**21.6[1]**	Wm Blair Growth	20.1[4]	22.3[4]	**17.6[3]**
Sound Shore	36.4[1]	33.2[1]	**21.5[1]**	Vangd US Growth	25.9[3]	30.0[1]	**17.6[3]**
Price Mid Cap Gro	18.3[5]	27.7[2]	**21.4[1]**	Babson Growth	28.0[2]	27.0[2]	**17.6[3]**
Longleaf Partners‡	28.2[2]	25.5[3]	**21.4[1]**	Acorn SC	25.0[3]	22.3[4]	**17.5[3]**
Henlopen Fund	22.6[4]	27.1[2]	**21.0[1]**	Vangd Idx Extend Mkt†	26.7[3]	25.9[3]	**17.5[3]**
Amer Cent Equity Growth	36.1[1]	32.6[1]	**21.0[1]**	Vangd Idx Sm Cap† SC	24.5[3]	23.7[4]	**17.5[3]**
Fidelity Blue Chip Gro††	27.0[3]	23.5[4]	**20.8[1]**	Nicholas Ltd Edit SC	33.0[1]	28.3[2]	**17.4[3]**
Accessor Growth	33.2[1]	29.2[2]	**20.7[1]**	CA Inv Tr-S&P MidCap	31.9[2]	27.0[2]	**17.3[3]**
Lazard Equity(O shrs)	25.1[3]	27.4[2]	**20.6[1]**	Dreyfus MidCap Idx	31.6[2]	26.6[2]	**17.2[3]**
Strong Schafer Value	29.3[2]	28.8[2]	**20.4[1]**	Fiduciary Cap Growth SC	29.2[2]	24.2[3]	**17.1[3]**
Brandywine Blue	19.3[4]	24.8[3]	**20.4[1]**	TIP:Turner Growth Eqty	31.4[2]	26.9[2]	**17.1[3]**
Fidelity Low Pr Stk††‡ SC	26.7[3]	26.2[3]	**20.4[1]**	FundMngr Growth†	27.5[3]	24.9[3]	**16.9[3]**
Nbrgr-Ber Partners	29.2[2]	30.3[1]	**20.4[1]**	Papp L Roy Stock	33.1[1]	29.2[2]	**16.7[3]**
Warbg Pincus Cap App	31.4[2]	30.8[1]	**20.3[1]**	Haven Fund	19.1[4]	24.4[3]	**16.6[3]**
Price Sm Cap Value‡ SC	27.9[3]	27.3[2]	**20.2[1]**	Htchks & Wly Sm Cap SC	39.5[1]	23.6[4]	**16.5[3]**
Nbrgr-Ber Genesis ‡ SC	34.9[1]	30.7[1]	**20.1[1]**	Capp-Rush Growth	22.2[4]	21.5[4]	**16.5[3]**
Legg Mason Total Ret	37.5[1]	33.0[1]	**20.0[1]**	State Farm Growth‡	31.2[2]	26.3[2]	**16.5[3]**
Longleaf Partners Sm Cap‡SC	29.0[2]	26.0[3]	**19.9[1]**	Invesco Growth	27.2[3]	25.9[3]	**16.5[3]**
Price Sm Cap Stk	28.8[2]	27.8[2]	**19.9[1]**	Sentry	29.7[2]	26.7[2]	**16.4[3]**
Strong Common Stk‡	24.0[4]	25.5[3]	**19.8[1]**	Federated Mid Cap	31.1[2]	26.0[3]	**16.3[3]**
SSgA Matrix Eqty	34.2[1]	28.6[2]	**19.8[1]**	Dreyfus Third Cent	29.4[2]	29.7[1]	**16.3[3]**
Scudder Value	35.3[1]	29.4[1]	**19.7[1]**	Nbrgr-Ber Guardian	17.9[5]	22.5[4]	**16.1[4]**
GMO: Pelican	26.5[3]	25.6[3]	**19.7[2]**	Babson Shadow Stk SC	27.6[3]	24.2[3]	**16.1[4]**
Clipper	30.4[2]	31.3[1]	**19.7[2]**	Nations Cap Gro	30.4[2]	25.6[3]	**16.0[4]**
Salomon Opportunity	33.0[1]	29.0[2]	**19.6[2]**	Ariel Apprec	37.9[1]	28.4[2]	**15.9[4]**
Westcore Blue Chip	30.9[2]	29.4[1]	**19.6[2]**	Janus Fund	22.7[4]	23.8[4]	**15.8[4]**
Papp L Roy Amer Abroad	29.9[2]	31.5[1]	**19.5[2]**	IAI MidCap	8.9[5]	17.0[5]	**15.7[4]**
Gabelli Growth	42.6[1]	31.2[1]	**19.4[2]**	Stein Roe Special	25.9[3]	21.1[4]	**15.6[4]**
Third Ave Value	23.9[4]	25.8[3]	**19.4[2]**	IAA Trust Growth	19.7[4]	24.2[3]	**15.3[4]**
Dreyfus Premier Core Value‡	25.2[3]	27.3[2]	**19.2[2]**	Amer Cent-20th Cent Select	32.2[1]	24.6[3]	**15.3[4]**
Northeast Inv Growth	37.3[1]	32.7[1]	**19.0[2]**	Key SBSF Fund‡	12.3[5]	21.5[4]	**15.3[4]**
Wasatch Growth	27.5[3]	27.8[2]	**18.9[2]**	Matrix Growth	34.6[1]	25.2[3]	**15.3[4]**
Gabelli Asset	38.1[1]	25.1[3]	**18.9[2]**	Brown Cap Equity	22.7[4]	24.6[3]	**15.3[4]**
Fidelity Value	21.1[4]	21.6[4]	**18.9[2]**	Selected Spec Shares	26.9[3]	23.4[4]	**15.2[4]**
Domini Social Eqty	36.0[1]	30.8[1]	**18.9[2]**	Royce Premier SC	18.4[5]	18.1[5]	**15.2[4]**
Vangd Idx Total Mkt	31.0[2]	29.1[2]	**18.9[2]**	Price New Era	10.9[5]	18.5[5]	**15.1[4]**
Fidelity Stk Selector	28.9[2]	27.2[2]	**18.8[2]**	IAI Value	19.6[4]	21.9[4]	**15.0[4]**
Fidelity Cap Apprec	26.5[3]	20.0[4]	**18.8[2]**	Value Line Fund	21.6[4]	25.3[3]	**15.0[4]**
Price Gro Stk	26.6[3]	26.4[2]	**18.7[2]**	Price Cap App	16.2[5]	18.5[5]	**14.8[4]**
Janus Gro & Inc	34.7[1]	32.3[1]	**18.6[2]**	IAI Regional	18.9[4]	22.2[4]	**14.8[4]**
Thompson Plumb Growth	32.4[1]	32.0[1]	**18.6[2]**	Westcore MIDCO Gro	14.9[5]	19.6[4]	**14.8[4]**
Excelsior Blended Eqty	29.8[2]	26.1[3]	**18.5[2]**	Wilshire Target Sm Val SC	31.2[2]	23.2[4]	**14.7[4]**
Heartland Value‡SC	23.2[4]	24.6[3]	**18.5[2]**	Govt Street Equity	27.8[3]	25.6[3]	**14.7[4]**
Fidelity Discpl Eqty	33.3[1]	25.6[3]	**18.4[2]**	Janus Enterprise	10.8[5]	16.3[5]	**14.7[4]**
Strong Opportunity	23.4[4]	22.9[4]	**18.3[2]**	FAM Value SC	39.1[1]	22.8[4]	**14.6[4]**
Preferred Growth	31.9[2]	26.2[3]	**18.2[2]**	Emerald Eqty	25.4[3]	26.6[2]	**14.6[4]**
Wilshire Target Lg Gro	32.2[1]	31.4[1]	**18.2[2]**	Reich & Tang Eqty	13.8[5]	19.5[5]	**14.6[4]**
Nbrgr-Ber Focus	24.1[3]	25.2[3]	**18.2[2]**	Amer Cent-20th Cent Heritage	19.3[4]	20.3[4]	**14.5[4]**
Vintage Eqty	30.1[2]	28.9[2]	**18.2[2]**	Fidelity Retrmnt Gro	18.5[4]	16.9[5]	**14.3[4]**
Fremont Growth	29.0[2]	29.2[2]	**18.2[2]**	Gintel	31.5[2]	31.2[1]	**14.0[4]**
UAM DSI Discpnd Val	23.4[4]	25.9[3]	**18.1[2]**	Capstone Growth	28.7[2]	24.9[3]	**13.8[5]**
Pinnacle Fund	35.4[1]	31.0[1]	**18.1[3]**	Rockwood	3.5[5]	17.7[5]	**13.6[5]**
Nicholas Fund	37.0[1]	30.5[1]	**18.0[3]**	Lepercq-Istel	8.9[5]	20.5[4]	**13.5[5]**
Crabbe Hsn Equity	25.7[3]	21.1[4]	**17.8[3]**	Lindner Growth	8.7[5]	16.4[5]	**13.4[5]**
Sit Large Cap Gro	31.7[2]	28.8[2]	**17.7[3]**	PIC Growth	28.0[2]	24.0[3]	**13.4[5]**
Nicholas II SC	37.0[1]	28.1[2]	**17.7[3]**	Flex-Fund Highlands Gro	29.3[2]	20.7[4]	**13.3[5]**
Fasciano SC	21.5[4]	26.3[2]	**17.7[3]**	Wayne Hummer Growth	30.2[2]	22.1[4]	**13.2[5]**
Price Spect-Gro	17.4[5]	22.5[4]	**17.7[3]**	Oak Hall Equity	14.5[5]	13.8[5]	**13.1[5]**
Scudder Large Cap Val	32.5[1]	27.7[2]	**17.7[3]**	Royce Penn Mutual SC	24.9[3]	18.7[5]	**13.1[5]**

Stock and bond funds – ranked within objective continued

By 1993-1997 performance

No-Load Fund	1997	3 years	5 years	No-Load Fund	1997	3 years	5 years
Meridian	19.2^4	17.3^5	**12.9^5**	Kent Idx Eqty	32.2^2	29.8^2	**19.3^2**
Scout Stock	21.0^4	17.0^5	**12.8^5**	Preferred Value	28.0^3	30.2^1	**19.3^2**
Reynolds Opportunity	14.6^5	21.2^4	**12.7^5**	Schwab 1000(Inv)	31.9^2	29.9^2	**19.1^2**
Gateway MidCap Idx	25.0^3	21.9^4	**12.6^5**	Vangd Windsor‡	22.0^4	26.1^3	**19.1^2**
Armstrong Assoc	14.2^5	14.2^5	**12.5^5**	RSI Tr-Core Eqty	25.3^3	28.8^2	**19.0^2**
SAFECO Northwest Gr	31.1^2	21.9^4	**12.5^5**	Stagecoach Eqty IdxStk	31.9^2	29.7^2	**19.0^2**
USAA Growth	3.7^5	17.3^5	**12.4^5**	RSI Tr-Value Eqty	31.7^2	30.5^1	**18.9^2**
Janus Venture‡SC	13.1^5	15.6^5	**12.2^5**	Vangd Trust US	29.5^2	27.9^2	**18.7^2**
Wade	20.3^4	18.0^5	**12.1^5**	Columbia Common Stk	25.4^3	25.6^3	**18.7^3**
Merger‡	11.7^5	11.9^5	**12.1^5**	Maxus Equity	28.4^3	23.3^4	**18.6^3**
C\FUNDS:Growth Stk	25.5^3	22.9^4	**11.7^5**	Elite Gr & Inc	28.2^3	28.8^2	**18.6^3**
Sextant Growth	26.6^3	21.1^4	**11.6^5**	Fidelity Eqty Inc II	27.2^3	24.0^4	**18.5^3**
Dreyfus Growth Opp	15.1^5	21.8^4	**11.5^5**	Quant Gro & Inc	36.7^1	28.1^2	**18.5^3**
Volumetric	18.3^5	17.0^5	**9.9^5**	Nations Value	26.3^3	27.5^2	**18.4^3**
Monetta Fund	26.2^3	18.0^5	**9.1^5**	WPG Growth & Inc	36.3^1	31.0^1	**18.4^3**
Valley Forge	6.0^5	7.6^5	**9.1^5**	Harbor Value	31.2^2	28.7^2	**18.4^3**
Rightime	-3.3^5	10.0^5	**7.7^5**	MSB	28.9^3	25.0^3	**18.3^3**
Merriman Cap App	9.9^5	11.6^5	**7.5^5**	Htchks & Wly Eq Inc	31.2^2	27.4^3	**18.3^3**
Crowley Gro & Inc	9.0^5	8.9^5	**6.7^5**	Wilshire Target Lg Val	30.2^2	29.1^2	**18.2^3**
Mathers	3.0^5	3.3^5	**1.1^5**	ASM Idx 30	24.5^4	26.1^3	**18.1^3**
Steadman Investment	1.1^5	-1.8^5	**-8.4^5**	Price Gro & Inc	23.5^4	26.6^3	**18.1^3**
GROWTH-INCOME FUNDS				TIP:Clover Cap Eqty Val	17.5^5	20.6^5	**18.0^3**
SAFECO Equity	24.2^4	24.8^3	**22.9^1**	Warbg Pincus Gro & Inc	30.2^2	15.7^5	**18.0^3**
Westwood Equity	29.6^2	31.0^1	**21.9^1**	Kent Gro & Inc	23.9^4	25.7^3	**18.0^3**
Price Div Gro	30.8^2	29.3^2	**21.4^1**	Invesco Value Eqty	28.0^3	25.6^3	**17.9^3**
Dodge & Cox Stock	28.4^3	28.0^2	**21.1^1**	JP Morgan US Eqty	28.4^3	27.2^3	**17.8^3**
Smith Brdn Eqty Plus	32.3^2	31.0^1	**21.0^1**	Gradison Estab Value	22.6^4	22.6^4	**17.8^3**
Fidelity Gro & Inc‡	30.2^2	28.4^2	**20.9^1**	Stein Roe Gro & Inc	25.7^3	25.9^3	**17.6^3**
Babson Value	26.5^3	26.9^3	**20.8^1**	Lexington Gro & Inc	30.3^2	26.4^3	**17.3^3**
Vangd Gro & Inc	35.6^1	31.4^1	**20.7^1**	Mosaic Investors	34.8^1	27.3^3	**17.1^3**
Vangd Windsor II	32.3^2	31.6^1	**20.7^1**	Founders Blue Chip	19.0^5	24.1^4	**17.1^3**
Fidelity Fund	32.1^2	28.1^2	**20.6^1**	Cutler Approved List	33.3^1	27.5^2	**17.0^3**
Vangd Idx Value	29.8^2	29.4^2	**20.5^1**	Berwyn‡	26.1^3	19.8^5	**17.0^3**
Selected Amer Shares	37.3^1	35.3^1	**20.4^1**	Strong Total Ret	24.2^4	21.6^4	**16.8^4**
Muhlenkamp	33.3^1	32.1^1	**20.4^1**	US Glb:All-Amer Eqty	30.3^2	27.8^2	**16.8^4**
Fidelity Eqty Inc	30.0^2	27.5^2	**20.3^1**	UAM TS&W Eqty	26.0^3	24.5^4	**16.7^4**
Amer Cent Inc & Gro	34.3^1	31.6^1	**20.3^1**	FundMngr Gro & Inc†	25.3^4	24.3^4	**16.7^4**
AARP Gro & Inc	31.0^2	28.1^2	**20.2^1**	Excelsior Inc & Gro	22.1^4	23.6^4	**16.6^4**
Vangd Idx 500	33.2^1	31.0^1	**20.1^1**	UAM C & B Eqty	28.0^3	26.6^3	**16.5^4**
Dreyfus Discpl Stock	31.9^2	31.2^1	**20.1^1**	Greenspring	23.9^4	21.7^4	**16.3^4**
Mutual Shares Z‡	26.3^3	25.4^3	**20.0^1**	BSR Equity	27.3^3	24.5^4	**16.2^4**
SSgA S&P 500	33.1^1	30.8^1	**20.0^1**	Reynolds Blue Chip Gr	31.5^2	30.8^1	**16.1^4**
Mutual Qualified Z‡	24.8^4	24.2^4	**20.0^1**	Weston: New Cent Cap	26.1^3	22.8^4	**16.1^4**
BT Pyramid:Eqty 500 Idx	33.0^1	30.9^1	**19.9^1**	Invesco Indust Inc	26.4^3	23.4^4	**16.1^4**
CA Inv Tr-S&P 500	33.0^1	30.8^1	**19.9^1**	Philadelphia	35.8^1	24.9^3	**15.9^4**
Scudder Gro & Inc	30.3^2	27.8^2	**19.9^2**	First Omaha Eqty	19.3^5	20.6^5	**15.9^4**
Federated Stock	34.4^1	30.2^1	**19.9^2**	Fidelity Asst Mgr Gro	26.4^3	21.3^4	**15.8^4**
Fidelity Spart Market Idx	33.0^1	30.7^1	**19.9^2**	API Cap Inc	25.2^4	23.3^4	**15.4^4**
Price Eqty 500 Idx	32.9^1	30.8^1	**19.8^2**	Wright Major Blue Chip	33.9^1	26.6^3	**15.3^4**
Accessor Val & Inc	33.0^1	30.0^2	**19.8^2**	Wright Sel Blue Ch	32.7^1	27.1^3	**15.1^4**
Weitz Value	38.9^1	31.7^1	**19.8^2**	Concorde Value	29.1^3	23.6^4	**14.9^4**
Galaxy II Lg Co Idx	32.8^1	30.7^1	**19.8^2**	Vangd Star:Star	20.5^4	21.7^4	**14.8^4**
Federated Max Cap	32.7^1	30.6^1	**19.8^2**	Preferred Asst Alloc	21.0^4	22.8^4	**14.8^4**
Dreyfus S&P 500 Idx	32.6^1	30.4^1	**19.6^2**	Bridges Investment	21.1^4	23.1^4	**14.8^4**
Lexington Corp Ldrs	23.1^4	28.0^2	**19.5^2**	Primary Trend	18.2^5	21.3^4	**14.7^4**
Stratton Growth	36.1^1	28.9^1	**19.5^2**	IAI Gro & Inc	23.9^4	23.7^4	**14.7^4**
Homestead Value	26.7^3	26.0^3	**19.5^2**	Yacktman	18.3^5	24.8^3	**14.6^5**
Mutual Beacon Z‡	22.9^4	23.3^4	**19.5^2**	Berger Gro & Inc	22.7^4	20.7^5	**14.5^5**
Vangd Idx Growth	36.3^1	32.6^1	**19.5^2**	Westcore Gro & Inc	27.3^3	24.3^4	**14.4^5**
Vontobel US Value	34.3^1	31.8^1	**19.4^2**	C\FUNDS:C\FUND	21.0^4	21.0^5	**14.2^5**

Stock and bond funds – ranked within objective *continued*

By 1993-1997 performance

No-Load Fund	Total return percent with quintile ranks by objective			No-Load Fund	Total return percent with quintile ranks by objective		
	1997	Annualized 3 years	5 years		1997	Annualized 3 years	5 years
Thompson Plumb Balanced	22.5[4]	21.9[4]	**13.9[5]**	Parnassus Balanced	20.2[3]	19.1[4]	**13.1[4]**
Matrix\LMH Value	17.9[5]	19.8[5]	**13.6[5]**	Htchks & Wly Balanced	16.8[4]	17.6[4]	**13.0[4]**
UAM Sirach Spec Eqty	11.3[5]	19.3[5]	**13.5[5]**	Weston: New Cent Inc	18.6[4]	17.8[4]	**13.0[4]**
Marshall Lg Cap Gr & Inc	26.2[3]	24.5[4]	**13.4[5]**	UAM StrIng Part Balanced	18.3[4]	19.1[4]	**12.7[4]**
Dreyfus Gro & Inc	16.0[5]	18.4[5]	**13.3[5]**	Value Line Income	18.5[4]	20.7[3]	**12.7[4]**
CGM Mutual	8.2[5]	18.5[5]	**12.8[5]**	Fidelity Convert	14.4[5]	16.3[5]	**12.7[4]**
Analytic Defnsve Eqty	19.1[5]	18.7[5]	**12.8[5]**	Pax World	25.1[2]	21.3[2]	**12.6[4]**
Stonebridge Growth	23.7[4]	21.2[4]	**12.5[5]**	Berwyn Income	13.3[5]	16.1[5]	**12.6[4]**
Flex-Fund Muirfield	18.6[5]	16.5[5]	**11.9[5]**	Stein Roe Balanced	17.5[4]	18.8[4]	**12.5[4]**
Jensen Portfolio	23.0[4]	23.9[4]	**11.6[5]**	IAA Trust Asst Alloc	17.9[4]	18.6[4]	**12.5[4]**
Amer Cent Balanced	16.9[5]	17.2[5]	**11.5[5]**	Crabbe Hsn Asst Alloc	19.2[3]	15.2[5]	**12.4[4]**
Copley	25.1[4]	18.2[5]	**10.9[5]**	Strong Asst Alloc	16.7[4]	16.3[5]	**12.1[4]**
US Glb:MegaTrends	15.6[5]	18.3[5]	**10.6[5]**	UAM C & B Balanced	19.7[3]	18.9[4]	**12.1[4]**
Dreyfus Fund	10.7[5]	16.7[5]	**10.1[5]**	IAI Balanced	25.7[1]	19.6[3]	**12.1[4]**
ZSA Asst Alloc	12.3[5]	16.1[5]	**9.8[5]**	Avondale Total Ret	20.1[3]	17.4[5]	**12.1[5]**
FundMngr Mgd Tot Ret†	13.5[5]	13.6[5]	**9.6[5]**	US Glb:Income	23.1[2]	18.4[4]	**11.9[5]**
Merriman Gro & Inc	13.1[5]	15.3[5]	**9.4[5]**	USAA Growth & Tax Strat	16.1[4]	16.6[5]	**11.9[5]**
Gateway Idx Plus	12.3[5]	11.3[5]	**9.3[5]**	Fidelity Balanced	23.4[2]	15.7[5]	**11.9[5]**
SCM Portfolio	16.3[5]	14.0[5]	**9.3[5]**	PIC:Pinnacle Balanced	22.3[2]	20.0[3]	**11.5[5]**
INCOME FUNDS				Lindner Dividend	13.9[5]	15.6[5]	**11.4[5]**
Price Eqty Inc	28.8[1]	27.4[1]	**19.9[1]**	America's Utility	23.4[2]	19.8[3]	**11.1[5]**
Vangd Equity Inc	31.2[1]	28.4[1]	**19.0[1]**	Vangd Convert	16.3[4]	16.1[5]	**10.9[5]**
Gabelli Eqty Inc	27.9[1]	24.6[1]	**18.2[1]**	Green Cent Balanced	19.0[3]	20.7[3]	**10.9[5]**
SAFECO Income	26.4[1]	26.9[1]	**17.9[1]**	Fidelity Asst Mgr Inc	12.4[5]	12.2[5]	**10.0[5]**
Managers Inc Eqty	27.2[1]	26.0[1]	**17.8[1]**	Capp-Rush Util	25.3[2]	19.3[4]	**9.3[5]**
Founders Balanced	16.9[4]	23.6[1]	**17.7[1]**	Lexington Convert	13.2[5]	12.1[5]	**8.7[5]**
Westwood Balanced	22.5[2]	23.8[1]	**17.3[1]**	Steadman Associated	-1.3[5]	3.9[5]	**-0.3[5]**
Vangd Asst Alloc	27.3[1]	25.9[1]	**17.2[1]**	**SECTOR & INDUSTRY FUNDS**			
Cutler Eqty Income	33.4[1]	28.5[1]	**16.7[1]**	Fidelity Sel Electronics†	14.2[5]	39.8[1]	**33.5[1]**
Vangd Wellington	23.2[2]	23.9[1]	**16.5[1]**	Fidelity Sel Home Finc†	45.8[1]	45.2[1]	**32.0[1]**
USAA Income Stk	26.9[1]	24.4[1]	**16.4[1]**	Fidelity Sel Energy Serv†	51.9[1]	47.2[1]	**31.2[1]**
Nations Eqty Inc	25.7[1]	24.2[1]	**16.3[1]**	Fidelity Sel Broker†	62.3[1]	41.0[1]	**28.2[1]**
Fidelity Puritan	22.4[2]	19.6[3]	**16.2[1]**	Fidelity Sel Reg Banks†	45.5[1]	42.6[1]	**26.4[1]**
Dodge & Cox Balanced	21.2[3]	21.2[2]	**16.1[2]**	Fidelity Sel Financial†	41.9[1]	40.3[1]	**25.6[1]**
Eastcliff Total Ret	30.0[1]	24.5[1]	**16.0[2]**	Fidelity Sel Computer†	-1.1[5]	25.5[2]	**25.1[1]**
Fidelity Utilities	31.6[1]	24.2[1]	**16.0[2]**	Fidelity Sel Defense†	23.5[3]	31.5[1]	**24.4[1]**
Invesco Total Ret	25.0[2]	22.1[2]	**15.9[2]**	Invesco Strat Fncl	44.8[1]	38.2[1]	**24.3[1]**
BNY Hamilton Eqty Inc	25.9[1]	23.7[1]	**15.6[2]**	Fidelity Sel Indust Equip†	18.8[4]	24.4[3]	**23.2[1]**
Primary Income	25.5[1]	22.0[2]	**15.3[2]**	Vangd Spec-Health	28.5[2]	31.3[2]	**22.6[2]**
Eclipse Balanced	23.4[2]	19.7[3]	**14.9[2]**	Fidelity Sel Health†	31.1[2]	30.2[2]	**22.4[2]**
FBP Contrn Balanced	20.7[3]	20.9[2]	**14.7[2]**	Fidelity Sel Software†	14.9[4]	26.9[2]	**22.2[2]**
Janus Balanced	21.8[3]	21.4[2]	**14.6[2]**	Fidelity Sel Leisure†	41.3[1]	26.7[2]	**21.5[2]**
Warbg Pincus Balanced	16.4[4]	20.0[3]	**14.2[2]**	Fidelity Sel Technology†	10.4[5]	22.4[4]	**21.3[2]**
Vangd Idx Balanced	22.2[2]	21.4[2]	**14.1[2]**	Price Sci/Tech	1.7[5]	21.8[4]	**21.0[2]**
Key SBSF Convert‡	16.3[4]	19.9[3]	**14.1[2]**	Fidelity Sel Insurance†	42.5[1]	33.5[1]	**20.7[2]**
Jurika & Voyles Balanced	16.7[4]	19.1[3]	**14.1[2]**	Fidelity Sel Multimedia†	30.9[2]	21.0[4]	**20.5[2]**
Lancaster Convert	22.4[2]	21.1[2]	**13.7[2]**	Vangd Spec-Energy	14.8[5]	24.5[3]	**19.1[2]**
Price Balanced	19.0[3]	19.4[3]	**13.6[3]**	Cohen & Steers Realty	21.1[3]	23.0[4]	**19.1[2]**
Columbia Balanced	18.8[3]	18.4[4]	**13.6[3]**	Invesco Strat Tech	8.8[5]	24.6[3]	**18.5[3]**
Dreyfus Balanced	17.4[4]	17.9[4]	**13.5[3]**	Fidelity Sel Food/Agr†	30.3[2]	26.3[2]	**18.4[3]**
State Farm Balanced‡	22.2[2]	20.1[3]	**13.4[3]**	Fidelity Sel Telecomm†	25.8[3]	19.8[5]	**18.4[3]**
Value Line Convert	17.0[4]	19.9[3]	**13.4[3]**	Fidelity Sel Consmr Ind†	38.0[1]	26.0[2]	**18.3[3]**
Fidelity Asst Mgr	22.3[2]	17.7[4]	**13.4[3]**	Century Shares	50.1[1]	33.5[1]	**17.9[3]**
Brown Cap Balanced	21.0[3]	21.4[2]	**13.4[3]**	Fidelity Sel Transport†	32.1[1]	18.6[5]	**17.5[3]**
Mosaic Balanced	25.5[2]	21.1[2]	**13.4[3]**	Fidelity Sel Medical Del†	20.5[3]	20.9[4]	**17.5[3]**
Amana Income	24.5[2]	21.3[2]	**13.2[3]**	Fidelity Sel Chemical†	16.5[4]	19.8[4]	**17.3[3]**
Vangd Wellesley Inc	20.2[3]	19.2[4]	**13.2[3]**	Excelsior Enrgy & Nat Resc	18.5[4]	25.4[3]	**17.1[3]**
Vangd Spec-Util	25.1[2]	20.8[3]	**13.2[3]**	Fidelity Sel Air Trans†	31.1[2]	28.4[2]	**16.8[4]**
Nations Balanced Assts	21.4[3]	20.5[3]	**13.2[3]**	Fidelity Sel Devel Comm†	5.6[5]	12.4[5]	**16.6[4]**
Advance Cap Balanced	20.5[3]	22.0[2]	**13.1[3]**	Invesco Strat Enrgy	19.1[3]	25.6[2]	**16.5[4]**

No-Load Fund	Total return percent with quintile ranks by objective			No-Load Fund	Total return percent with quintile ranks by objective		
	1997	Annualized 3 years	5 years		1997	Annualized 3 years	5 years
Fidelity Sel Energy†...	10.5[5]	21.1[4]	**16.3[4]**	Fidelity Overseas...	10.9[2]	11.0[2]	**14.2[2]**
Fidelity Sel Const/Hous†...	29.6[2]	23.6[3]	**16.2[4]**	Bernstein Int'l Value...	9.3[2]	11.5[2]	**14.2[2]**
Fidelity Real Est...	21.3[3]	22.4[4]	**16.0[4]**	Lazard Int'l Eqty(O shrs)...	11.8[2]	13.5[2]	**14.0[2]**
Fidelity Sel Retail†...	41.7[1]	24.3[3]	**15.6[4]**	Acorn Int'l...	0.2[3]	9.9[2]	**13.8[2]**
Invesco Strat Leis...	26.5[3]	16.9[5]	**15.5[4]**	Vontobel Int'l Eqty...	9.2[2]	12.3[2]	**13.6[2]**
Rushmore Amer Gas Idx...	24.2[3]	25.1[3]	**15.5[4]**	Price Int'l Stk...	2.7[3]	9.9[3]	**13.0[2]**
Fidelity Sel Util Gro†...	30.3[2]	24.9[3]	**15.2[4]**	Scudder Int'l Stk...	8.0[2]	11.6[2]	**12.9[2]**
Invesco Strat Hlth...	18.4[4]	28.0[2]	**14.1[5]**	Schroder Cap:Int'l...	3.2[3]	8.2[3]	**12.9[2]**
Fidelity Sel Pap/Forest†...	9.4[5]	12.6[5]	**14.1[5]**	Sit Int'l Growth...	4.8[3]	8.1[3]	**12.7[2]**
Invesco Strat Util...	24.4[3]	20.7[4]	**13.9[5]**	Fidelity Int'l Gr & Inc...	7.1[2]	10.6[2]	**12.2[2]**
Fidelity Sel Auto†...	16.7[4]	15.4[5]	**12.7[5]**	Columbia Int'l Stk...	11.5[2]	11.0[2]	**12.2[3]**
Fidelity Sel Indust Mat†...	1.9[5]	10.3[5]	**12.0[5]**	Warbg Pincus Int'l...	-4.4[4]	5.3[4]	**12.1[3]**
US Glb:Real Estate...	19.3[3]	23.1[3]	**10.6[5]**	Babson Stew Ivry Int'l...	1.7[3]	9.1[3]	**11.9[3]**
Invesco Strat Envrn...	16.6[4]	25.0[3]	**10.5[5]**	Wright Int'l Blue Ch...	1.5[3]	11.7[2]	**11.9[3]**
Fidelity Sel Envir Serv†...	17.9[4]	19.8[4]	**9.1[5]**	Wm Blair Int'l Gro...	8.4[2]	8.6[3]	**11.3[3]**
Fidelity Sel Biotech†...	15.4[4]	22.0[4]	**8.4[5]**	Excelsior International...	9.3[2]	8.0[3]	**11.0[3]**
Stratton Month Div REIT Sh...	17.3[4]	16.3[5]	**8.1[5]**	Kent Int'l Gro...	2.3[3]	6.8[3]	**10.8[3]**
PRECIOUS METALS FUNDS				RSI Tr-Int'l Eqty...	0.9[3]	8.0[3]	**10.6[3]**
Scudder Gold...	-40.9[2]	-4.0[1]	**5.5[1]**	Nations Int'l Gro...	1.9[3]	8.7[3]	**10.5[3]**
US Glb:World Gold...	-41.1[2]	-6.6[1]	**5.2[1]**	BBK Int'l Equity...	10.0[2]	10.7[2]	**10.3[3]**
Fidelity Sel Amer Gold†...	-39.4[2]	-6.9[1]	**4.1[1]**	Fidelity Canada††	6.1[2]	13.7[2]	**10.2[3]**
Fidelity Sel Prec Met†...	-44.9[3]	-17.5[2]	**3.3[2]**	UAM TS&W Int'l Eqty...	2.5[3]	6.7[3]	**9.9[4]**
Blanchard Prec Met‡...	-47.1[4]	-11.8[1]	**3.2[2]**	IAI International...	-4.2[4]	4.2[4]	**9.7[4]**
Midas Gold...	-59.0[5]	-12.0[1]	**2.3[3]**	Vangd Int'l Value...	-4.6[4]	4.8[4]	**9.6[4]**
Vangd Spec-Gold...	-39.0[1]	-16.7[2]	**1.1[3]**	JP Morgan Int'l Eqty...	1.2[3]	5.7[4]	**9.2[4]**
Lexington Goldfund...	-43.0[3]	-15.5[2]	**0.9[3]**	Quant Int'l Eqty...	-1.6[4]	2.3[4]	**9.1[4]**
Amer Cent Glob Gold...	-41.5[3]	-14.7[1]	**-1.3[4]**	WPG International...	2.9[3]	6.1[3]	**9.0[4]**
USAA Gold...	-38.2[1]	-13.7[1]	**-1.6[4]**	Nations Int'l Eqty...	1.0[3]	5.8[3]	**8.9[4]**
Invesco Strat Gold...	-55.5[4]	-11.0[1]	**-2.6[5]**	Invesco Int'l Gro...	-1.9[4]	6.0[3]	**8.9[4]**
Bull & Bear Gold...	-55.7[5]	-24.1[2]	**-6.7[5]**	Strong Int'l Stk...	-14.2[4]	0.0[4]	**7.8[4]**
US Glb:Gold Shares...	-57.4[5]	-38.5[2]	**-12.7[5]**	Price Int'l Disc...	-5.7[4]	0.9[4]	**7.3[4]**
GLOBAL EQUITY FUNDS				**INT'L EQUITY FUNDS - EUROPE**			
Janus Worldwide...	20.5[1]	22.9[2]	**19.8[1]**	Wright Equifund Netherland...	15.4[1]	23.2[1]	**20.1[1]**
Scudder Global...	17.2[2]	17.1[3]	**15.1[1]**	Fidelity Europe††	22.9[1]	22.4[1]	**19.9[1]**
Scudder Glob Disc‡...	9.9[4]	16.3[3]	**14.9[1]**	Vangd Idx Europe†...	24.2[1]	22.6[1]	**19.4[1]**
Fidelity Worldwide...	12.1[3]	12.6[4]	**14.9[2]**	Price Europe...	17.0[1]	21.5[1]	**18.9[1]**
USAA Cornerstone Strat...	15.6[2]	17.3[3]	**14.6[2]**	Invesco Europe...	15.1[1]	21.2[1]	**16.6[1]**
Founders Worldwide Gr...	10.5[3]	15.0[4]	**14.1[2]**	Excelsior Pan Europe...	24.4[1]	20.2[1]	**15.3[1]**
USAA World Growth...	12.9[3]	14.9[4]	**13.6[2]**	**INT'L EQUITY FUNDS - EMG MKTS**			
Lexington Global...	6.9[4]	11.3[5]	**13.1[3]**	Scudder Latin Amer...	31.3[1]	15.0[1]	**19.1[1]**
Fremont Global...	9.9[4]	14.3[4]	**11.4[3]**	Excelsior Lat Amer...	25.2[1]	11.8[2]	**11.8[3]**
BBK Diversa...	13.2[2]	14.7[4]	**10.7[3]**	Montgmry Emg Mkts...	-3.2[4]	-0.4[4]	**7.7[4]**
Dreyfus Global Gro...	12.3[3]	12.1[4]	**9.7[4]**	Lexington World Emg...	-11.4[4]	-3.6[5]	**4.8[4]**
Blanchard Glob Gro‡...	6.5[5]	10.8[5]	**9.4[4]**	Capstone New Zealand...	-23.1[5]	2.8[4]	**2.6[5]**
Bull & Bear US & Overs...	6.7[4]	12.0[4]	**9.1[4]**	Price New Asia...	-37.1[5]	-9.5[5]	**1.4[5]**
US Glb:Glob Resrcs...	-2.8[5]	12.4[4]	**8.7[4]**	Fidelity Emg Mkts††	-40.9[5]	-14.3[5]	**-1.2[5]**
Merriman Asst Alloc...	5.8[5]	8.9[5]	**8.3[5]**	**INT'L EQUITY FUNDS - PACIFIC**			
Permanent Portfolio†...	5.6[5]	7.5[5]	**6.8[5]**	Fidelity Pacific Bas††	-15.1[4]	-8.2[5]	**4.3[4]**
Fontaine Glob Gro...	-44.9[5]	-4.9[5]	**-0.5[5]**	Excelsior Pac Asia...	-32.2[5]	-7.6[5]	**2.3[5]**
INT'L EQUITY FUNDS - GENERAL				Nomura Pacific Bas...	-28.7[5]	-8.7[5]	**2.1[5]**
Harbor Int'l‡...	15.5[1]	17.2[1]	**19.8[1]**	Wright Equifund Hong Kong...	-27.2[5]	-1.8[4]	**1.9[5]**
BT Invest:Int'l Eqty...	17.4[1]	18.2[1]	**18.8[1]**	Fidelity Japan††	-10.7[4]	-8.1[5]	**1.7[5]**
Fidelity Dvsfd Int'l...	13.7[1]	17.2[1]	**17.4[1]**	Vangd Idx Pacific†...	-25.7[5]	-11.0[5]	**1.5[5]**
Htchks & Wly Int'l...	5.3[3]	14.3[1]	**16.2[1]**	Invesco Pacific Bas...	-36.9[5]	-13.4[5]	**-0.6[5]**
Amer Cent-20th Cent Int'l Gr...	19.7[1]	15.3[1]	**15.8[1]**	Capstone Nikko Japan...	-24.6[5]	-15.1[5]	**-0.9[5]**
Managers Int'l Eqty...	10.8[2]	13.3[2]	**15.4[1]**	Japan (Scudder)...	-14.5[4]	-11.5[5]	**-1.2[5]**
USAA International...	9.0[2]	12.0[2]	**15.1[1]**	Price Japan...	-22.1[5]	-12.4[5]	**-1.4[5]**
Preferred Int'l...	6.8[2]	11.2[2]	**15.0[2]**	Scudder Pacific Opp...	-37.8[5]	-12.4[5]	**-2.3[5]**
Oakmark Int'l...	3.4[3]	12.7[2]	**14.9[2]**	**FIXED-INCOME - LONG TERM**			
Vangd Int'l Growth...	4.1[3]	11.1[2]	**14.9[2]**	Amer Cent-Benham Target 2020...	28.6[1]	26.5[1]	**17.7[1]**

By 1993-1997 performance

No-Load Fund	Total return percent with quintile ranks by objective			No-Load Fund	Total return percent with quintile ranks by objective		
	1997	Annualized 3 years	5 years		1997	Annualized 3 years	5 years
Amer Cent-Benham Target 2015	22.9¹	23.7¹	**16.2¹**	Fidelity Gov Sec	8.9⁴	9.5⁴	**6.9⁴**
Northeast Inv Trust	13.9²	17.1¹	**15.2¹**	Wright Total Ret Bd	9.2³	10.4³	**6.9⁴**
Amer Cent-Benham Target 2010	16.7¹	20.6¹	**14.4¹**	Sit US Gov	8.2⁴	8.2⁵	**6.7⁴**
Fidelity Spart Hi Inc	15.9¹	15.7¹	**14.2¹**	Weitz Ser Fix Inc	8.6⁴	9.5⁴	**6.7⁴**
Value Line Agg Inc	14.1¹	18.0¹	**13.4¹**	AARP Hi Qual ST Bond	7.9⁴	9.2⁴	**6.6⁴**
Fidelity Cap & Inc	14.7¹	14.1¹	**12.1¹**	Nations Strat Inc	8.3⁴	8.9⁵	**6.6⁴**
Federated Hi Yld	13.3²	15.0¹	**11.8¹**	UAM TS&W Fix Inc	9.2³	9.4⁴	**6.6⁴**
Amer Cent-Benham Target 2005	11.6²	16.1¹	**11.6¹**	Fidelity Spart Gov Inc	9.2³	9.8⁴	**6.5⁴**
Invesco High Yld	17.1¹	16.3¹	**11.6¹**	Dreyfus GNMA	8.8⁴	9.6⁴	**6.5⁵**
Strong Corp Bond	11.9²	14.0¹	**11.3¹**	Crabbe Hsn Income	11.6²	10.0⁴	**6.5⁵**
Vangd Hi Yld Corp	11.9²	13.5²	**11.2¹**	Scudder US Zero 2000	6.5⁵	8.5⁵	**6.4⁵**
Nicholas Income	13.1²	13.9²	**10.8¹**	Lazard Bond(O shrs)	8.4⁴	9.6⁴	**6.4⁵**
CGM Fixed Inc	3.7⁵	15.0¹	**10.7¹**	Selected US Gov Inc	7.2⁵	8.4⁵	**6.2⁵**
Price High Yld	14.5¹	13.9¹	**10.6¹**	Marshall Gov Inc	8.4⁴	9.3⁴	**6.1⁵**
SAFECO Hi Yld Bd	12.8²	12.9²	**10.5¹**	PC&J Preservation	7.4⁵	8.3⁵	**6.1⁵**
Vangd Prefrd Stk	13.0²	15.5¹	**9.9²**	C\FUNDS:Gov	7.3⁵	7.8⁵	**5.9⁵**
Vangd-Adml Long	14.0¹	13.6²	**9.9²**	Scout Bond	7.3⁵	8.2⁵	**5.9⁵**
Vangd LT Trsy	13.9¹	13.5²	**9.7²**	UAM SAMI Pref Stck Inc	8.3⁴	8.2⁵	**5.7⁵**
Vangd LT Corp	13.8²	13.3²	**9.6²**	Thompson Plumb Bond	7.4⁵	7.8⁵	**5.7⁵**
Managers Bond	10.4²	14.9¹	**9.5²**	Lancaster Gov Qual	7.0⁵	7.5⁵	**5.4⁵**
Westcore LT Bond	14.0¹	13.3²	**9.4²**	Value Line US Gov	9.2³	9.1⁵	**4.9⁵**
Amer Cent-Benham LT Trsy	14.7¹	13.5²	**9.3²**	BBK Int'l Bond	2.6⁵	10.3³	**4.5⁵**
Advance Cap Ret Inc	12.2²	13.0²	**9.2²**	Scudder Glob Bond	0.4⁵	3.7⁵	**3.3⁵**
Invesco Select Inc	11.7²	12.1²	**9.2²**	Alliance World Inc	3.6⁵	3.9⁵	**2.3⁵**
Dreyfus Strat Income	11.2²	12.7²	**9.1²**	Fundamental US Gov Strat	5.5⁵	8.5⁵	**0.6⁵**
Price Trsy Long	14.7¹	12.9²	**8.9²**	**FIXED-INCOME - INTERMEDIATE TERM**			
Lazard Strat Yld(O shrs)	5.2⁵	10.8³	**8.9²**	Janus Flex Inc	11.4¹	13.0¹	**10.1¹**
Amer Cent-Benham Target 2000	7.0⁵	12.1²	**8.6²**	Price Spect-Inc	12.2¹	13.0¹	**9.7¹**
Rushmore US Gov	13.1²	13.2²	**8.5²**	Stein Roe Income	9.6¹	11.2¹	**8.4¹**
Mosaic Hi Yld	9.9³	10.3³	**8.5²**	Payden & Rygel Glob Fl	9.1²	10.8¹	**8.4¹**
Nations Divsfd Inc	8.3⁴	10.1³	**8.5²**	Harbor Bond	9.4²	11.0¹	**8.1¹**
Dreyfus 100% US Long	11.7²	12.1²	**8.3²**	Warbg Pincus Glob Fix Inc	2.2⁵	9.3³	**8.1¹**
Federated US Gov Bd	11.7²	11.9²	**8.3³**	Warbg Pincus Fix Inc	8.8³	10.0²	**8.0¹**
Dodge & Cox Income	10.0²	11.1³	**8.2³**	Strong Gov Sec	9.1²	10.4²	**8.0¹**
Maxus Income	11.8²	12.3²	**8.1³**	Fidelity Mortg Sec(Init Class)‡	9.1²	10.4¹	**7.9¹**
Wasatch Hosington US Treas	15.7¹	11.6²	**8.0³**	Price Int'l Bond	-3.2⁵	7.7⁵	**7.9¹**
Fidelity Spart Inv Grd	9.3³	10.1³	**8.0³**	USAA Income	11.0¹	11.9¹	**7.8¹**
Dreyfus A Bonds Plus	9.5³	10.7³	**7.9³**	Smith Brdn Inter Dur US Gov	9.0²	10.1²	**7.8¹**
Legg Mason Invest Grd	10.3²	11.4²	**7.9³**	Citizens Tr Income	10.5¹	10.8¹	**7.7¹**
TIP:Clover Cap Fix Inc	9.6³	10.5³	**7.9³**	Merriman Flex Bd	5.7⁵	9.2³	**7.7¹**
Wright US Treas	9.1³	11.3³	**7.9³**	Vangd Inter Trsy	9.0²	10.2²	**7.6²**
CA Inv Tr-US Gov	9.3³	10.3³	**7.7³**	Columbia Fix Inc	9.6¹	10.4¹	**7.5²**
Parnassus Fix Inc	10.6²	11.9²	**7.6³**	Blanchard Flex Inc‡	9.4²	10.1²	**7.4²**
Dreyfus Basic GNMA	9.5³	10.2³	**7.6³**	Vangd Bond Idx Total	9.4¹	10.3²	**7.4²**
Drey-Basic GNMA	9.5³	10.2³	**7.6³**	Vangd-Adml Inter	9.0²	10.3²	**7.4²**
Excelsior Mgd Inc	9.8³	10.5³	**7.5³**	Lexington GNMA	10.2¹	10.5¹	**7.4²**
Advance Cap Bond	9.4³	10.6³	**7.5³**	Price New Inc	9.3²	9.8³	**7.3²**
Scudder Income	8.7⁴	10.0³	**7.5³**	Stein Roe Inter Bd	9.3²	10.1²	**7.2²**
IAI Bond	10.8²	10.3³	**7.4³**	Vangd GNMA	9.5¹	10.4¹	**7.2²**
Lazard Int'l Fix Inc(O shrs)	-5.7⁵	5.9⁵	**7.4³**	Amer Cent-Benham Int'l Bd	-5.9⁵	7.6⁵	**7.2²**
Fidelity Inv Grd Bd	8.9⁴	9.0⁵	**7.3⁴**	USAA GNMA	9.5¹	9.6³	**7.1²**
RSI Tr-Act Mgd Bd	9.7³	10.0⁴	**7.2⁴**	Accessor Mort Sec	9.5¹	10.1²	**7.1²**
JP Morgan Bond	9.1³	10.0⁴	**7.2⁴**	Amer Cent-Benham Bd	8.6³	10.2²	**7.1²**
Preferred Fix Inc	8.5⁴	9.5⁴	**7.2⁴**	Bernstein Inter Dur	7.6⁴	9.5³	**7.0²**
Invesco US Gov Sec	12.2²	11.3³	**7.1⁴**	Fidelity Spart GNMA	8.9²	10.1²	**6.9²**
First Omaha Fix Inc	9.5³	10.0⁴	**7.1⁴**	Dreyfus ST Income	8.2³	8.5⁴	**6.9³**
Wayne Hummer Income	9.0⁴	9.2⁴	**7.0⁴**	Dupree Inter Gov	9.4²	9.9³	**6.9³**
Babson Bond-Port L	9.3³	9.3⁴	**7.0⁴**	Westwood Inter Bd	10.7¹	10.1²	**6.8³**
Galaxy II US Trsy Idx	9.3³	9.7⁴	**7.0⁴**	Price GNMA	9.5¹	10.0²	**6.8³**

By 1993-1997 performance

| No-Load Fund | Total return percent with quintile ranks by objective | | | No-Load Fund | Total return percent with quintile ranks by objective | | |
	1997	Annualized 3 years	5 years		1997	Annualized 3 years	5 years
Amer Cent-Benham GNMA	8.7[3]	9.8[3]	**6.8[3]**	Asset Mgmt ARM	6.5[2]	7.2[3]	**5.6[2]**
Elite Bond	9.8[1]	9.4[3]	**6.8[3]**	Nations ST Inc	5.8[4]	7.2[3]	**5.6[2]**
Fidelity GNMA	8.7[3]	10.0[2]	**6.7[3]**	Fidelity Spart S-I Gov	6.6[2]	7.7[2]	**5.6[2]**
Fidelity Inter Bond	7.6[4]	7.9[5]	**6.7[3]**	Dreyfus 100% US Short	6.1[4]	7.2[3]	**5.6[2]**
Federated GNMA	8.8[3]	9.9[3]	**6.6[3]**	Federated US Gov 2-5	6.9[2]	7.8[2]	**5.5[2]**
Excelsior Inter Mgd Inc	8.5[3]	9.6[3]	**6.6[3]**	First Omaha S-I Fix	6.7[2]	7.5[2]	**5.5[2]**
Price Glob Gov	1.6[5]	8.6[4]	**6.5[3]**	Federated ST Income	6.4[3]	7.5[2]	**5.5[2]**
Westcore Inter Bond	8.3[3]	8.9[4]	**6.5[3]**	Janus ST Bond	6.6[2]	6.9[3]	**5.4[2]**
Federated Income	8.9[3]	9.6[3]	**6.5[3]**	Smith Brdn Sh Dur US Gov	6.3[3]	6.2[5]	**5.4[3]**
Wright Curr Inc	8.6[3]	10.0[2]	**6.5[3]**	Asset Mgmt ST US Gov	6.3[3]	7.0[3]	**5.4[3]**
Dreyfus 100% US Inter	7.6[4]	8.7[4]	**6.5[3]**	Harbor Short Dur	6.3[3]	6.7[4]	**5.4[3]**
Flex-Fund US Gov Bond	7.8[4]	8.5[4]	**6.5[4]**	Schwab ST Bd Mkt Idx	7.1[1]	7.3[2]	**5.3[3]**
FundMngr Bond†	7.8[4]	8.8[4]	**6.5[4]**	IAI Gov Bond	6.4[3]	6.9[4]	**5.3[3]**
Accessor Inter Fix Inc	8.6[3]	9.6[3]	**6.5[4]**	BT Pyramid:Ltd Trm US Gov	6.0[4]	6.7[4]	**5.2[3]**
Govt Street Bond	7.8[4]	8.9[4]	**6.5[4]**	Fidelity S-I Gov	6.6[2]	7.5[2]	**5.2[3]**
Asset Mgmt US Mrtg Sec	9.7[1]	9.4[3]	**6.4[4]**	Federated ARMS	6.3[3]	7.2[3]	**5.2[3]**
Wm Blair Income	8.0[4]	8.4[4]	**6.4[4]**	Wright US Treas Near Term	5.9[4]	7.2[3]	**5.2[3]**
Babson Bond-Port S	8.2[3]	8.7[4]	**6.4[4]**	Bernstein Short Dur Plus	5.5[5]	6.8[4]	**5.2[3]**
SAFECO Inter Trsy	8.3[3]	8.3[5]	**6.3[4]**	Marshall ST Inc	6.4[3]	6.8[4]	**5.1[3]**
Scudder GNMA	8.4[3]	9.6[3]	**6.2[4]**	Scudder ST Bond	6.1[4]	6.9[4]	**5.1[3]**
Amer Cent-Benham Inter Bd	8.4[3]	8.7[4]	**6.2[4]**	Amer Cent-Benham ST Trsy	6.0[4]	6.6[4]	**5.1[4]**
Amer Cent-Benham Inter-Trm Treas	8.3[3]	8.6[4]	**6.2[4]**	Columbia US Gov	5.6[5]	6.5[5]	**5.1[4]**
Kent Inter Bd	7.6[4]	8.6[4]	**6.1[4]**	Excelsior ST Gov	5.9[4]	6.7[4]	**5.1[4]**
SAFECO GNMA	9.0[2]	9.4[3]	**6.1[4]**	Fidelity ST Bond	6.2[4]	6.9[3]	**5.0[4]**
Emerald US Gov Sec	7.4[4]	8.3[5]	**6.0[4]**	Fidelity Spart ST Bd	6.5[2]	7.1[3]	**5.0[4]**
Asset Mgmt Inter Mrtg	8.4[3]	8.4[4]	**6.0[4]**	Crabbe Hsn US Gov Bd	7.1[1]	7.2[3]	**5.0[4]**
Legg Mason Gov Inter	7.0[5]	8.4[4]	**5.9[5]**	SSgA Yld Plus	5.5[5]	5.9[5]	**5.0[4]**
Vintage Fix Inc	7.1[5]	8.1[5]	**5.9[5]**	UAM DSI Ltd Mat	6.7[2]	7.5[2]	**5.0[4]**
RSI Tr-Inter Bd	7.1[5]	8.3[5]	**5.9[5]**	Bernstein Gov Sht Dur	5.7[5]	6.4[5]	**4.9[4]**
State Farm Interm‡	7.1[5]	7.9[5]	**5.9[5]**	Preferred ST Gov	6.2[4]	6.4[5]	**4.9[4]**
Primary US Gov	6.1[5]	7.9[5]	**5.7[5]**	Kent ST Bd	6.3[3]	6.8[4]	**4.9[4]**
Marshall Inter Bd	7.2[5]	8.2[5]	**5.6[5]**	Managers Sht & Int Bd	5.9[4]	8.4[1]	**4.8[4]**
BNY Hamilton Inter Gov	7.5[4]	8.6[4]	**5.6[5]**	Amer Cent-Benham ST Gov	6.0[4]	6.8[4]	**4.8[4]**
Mosaic Gov	7.7[4]	7.3[5]	**5.5[5]**	Reynolds US Gov	5.4[5]	7.0[3]	**4.8[5]**
Nations S-I Gov	7.0[5]	7.3[5]	**5.4[5]**	Federated US Gov 1-3	5.7[5]	6.5[5]	**4.8[5]**
Mosaic Bond	6.0[5]	7.4[5]	**5.2[5]**	Price ST Gov	6.7[2]	7.3[2]	**4.8[5]**
WPG Core Bd	7.4[4]	8.2[5]	**4.6[5]**	Permanent Vers Bd†	5.1[5]	5.8[5]	**4.8[5]**
Founders Gov Sec	7.9[4]	7.0[5]	**4.4[5]**	Nbrgr-Ber Ultra Sht‡	6.2[4]	6.0[5]	**4.6[5]**
Scudder Int'l Bond	-4.2[5]	2.5[5]	**2.7[5]**	Dean Witter ST US Treas	6.1[4]	6.6[5]	**4.6[5]**
Fidelity Int'l Bond	-1.3[5]	2.9[5]	**2.1[5]**	Price ST Bond	6.3[3]	6.6[4]	**4.6[5]**
Managers Inter Mortg	8.2[3]	9.5[3]	**1.9[5]**	IAI Reserve	4.6[5]	5.3[5]	**4.3[5]**
FIXED-INCOME - SHORT TERM				RSI Tr-ST Invest	4.9[5]	5.0[5]	**4.2[5]**
Heartland US Gov	9.7[1]	10.0[1]	**7.2[1]**	Permanent Treasy†	4.1[5]	4.4[5]	**3.8[5]**
Strong ST Bond	7.2[1]	8.6[1]	**6.7[1]**	Capstone Gov Inc	4.4[5]	4.7[5]	**3.7[5]**
Montgmry Sht Dur Gov	7.0[2]	7.8[1]	**6.5[1]**	Managers ST Gov	5.5[5]	6.3[5]	**3.2[5]**
BSR S-I Fix Inc	7.6[1]	9.0[1]	**6.5[1]**	Fontaine Glob Inc	-27.3[5]	-1.9[5]	**2.9[5]**
Strong Advantage	6.5[2]	6.9[4]	**6.5[1]**	**TAX-FREE - LONG TERM**			
Price Trsy Inter	8.2[1]	8.7[1]	**6.3[1]**	Excelsior LT TE	9.4[2]	11.9[1]	**8.8[1]**
Vangd ST Corp	6.9[2]	8.1[1]	**6.2[1]**	Amer Cent-Benham CA Hi Yld	10.4[1]	11.4[1]	**8.2[1]**
Warbg Pincus Inter Gov	7.6[1]	8.4[1]	**6.2[1]**	SAFECO CA TF	11.6[1]	13.0[1]	**8.2[1]**
Fidelity Spart Ltd Mat Gov	7.3[1]	8.3[1]	**6.0[1]**	Price TF Hi Yld	10.2[1]	10.5[2]	**7.8[1]**
Invesco Inter Gov	6.2[4]	7.9[1]	**6.0[1]**	Scudder Hi Yld TF	12.0[1]	11.6[1]	**7.7[1]**
Vangd ST Federal	6.5[3]	7.8[1]	**5.8[1]**	USAA CA Bond	10.3[1]	12.3[1]	**7.7[1]**
Vangd-Adml Short	6.5[2]	7.7[2]	**5.8[1]**	Vangd Muni Long	9.3[2]	10.6[2]	**7.7[1]**
Homestead ST Bond	6.6[2]	7.5[2]	**5.8[1]**	Amer Cent-Benham CA Long	9.6[2]	10.8[1]	**7.7[1]**
Dreyfus S-I Gov	6.1[4]	7.5[2]	**5.8[2]**	Vangd FL Insur	8.9[3]	10.1[3]	**7.6[1]**
AARP GNMA & Trsy	8.0[1]	8.3[1]	**5.8[2]**	Vangd CA Insur LT	8.9[3]	10.7[1]	**7.6[1]**
Vangd ST Trsy	6.4[3]	7.6[2]	**5.7[2]**	Vangd Muni Hi Yld	9.2[2]	10.5[2]	**7.6[1]**
Prudential Gov Sec S-I	7.1[1]	7.9[1]	**5.6[2]**	Sit TF Income	9.8[1]	9.4[4]	**7.5[1]**
Nbrgr-Ber Ltd Mat	6.9[2]	7.3[2]	**5.6[2]**	Fidelity Spart FL Muni	8.7[4]	10.3[2]	**7.5[1]**

By 1993-1997 performance

No-Load Fund	Total return percent with quintile ranks by objective		
	1997	**Annualized 3 years**	**Annualized 5 years**
Parnassus CA TE	9.3[2]	10.8[1]	**7.5[1]**
SAFECO Muni Bd	10.7[1]	11.5[1]	**7.5[1]**
Scudder CA TF	10.2[1]	10.7[1]	**7.4[1]**
Vangd Muni Insur LT	8.6[4]	10.2[2]	**7.4[1]**
Amer Cent-Benham CA Insured	9.3[2]	10.5[2]	**7.4[1]**
Schwab LT TF	9.9[1]	10.6[2]	**7.4[1]**
Scudder MA TF	8.5[4]	10.0[3]	**7.4[2]**
Stein Roe Hi Yld Muni	9.5[2]	10.4[2]	**7.4[2]**
Nations Muni Inc	9.3[2]	10.9[1]	**7.4[2]**
CA Inv Tr-CA TF	9.3[2]	10.8[1]	**7.3[2]**
USAA VA Bond	9.5[2]	10.5[2]	**7.3[2]**
Vangd NY Insur LT	8.7[4]	10.0[3]	**7.3[2]**
Fidelity Spart PA Muni Inc	8.3[4]	9.8[3]	**7.3[2]**
Fidelity Spart NY Muni Inc‡	10.0[1]	11.0[1]	**7.3[2]**
Price NY TF	9.5[2]	10.0[3]	**7.3[2]**
Price CA TF	9.1[3]	10.2[2]	**7.3[2]**
Fidelity Spart MA Muni Inc	9.3[2]	10.2[3]	**7.2[2]**
USAA TE Long	10.4[1]	11.0[1]	**7.2[2]**
Fidelity Spart CA Muni Inc	9.8[1]	11.1[1]	**7.2[2]**
Price TF Inc	9.3[2]	10.0[3]	**7.2[2]**
Schwab CA Long	10.2[1]	11.3[1]	**7.2[2]**
Fidelity Spart Insur Muni Inc	9.5[2]	10.5[2]	**7.2[2]**
Drey-General CA	8.8[3]	10.2[2]	**7.2[2]**
Vangd PA Insur LT	8.3[4]	9.5[4]	**7.2[2]**
Amer Cent-Benham Long TF	9.5[2]	9.7[3]	**7.2[2]**
Scudder Mngd Muni	9.3[2]	9.9[3]	**7.2[3]**
Price VA TF	9.0[3]	9.8[3]	**7.2[3]**
Fidelity NY Muni Inc	9.7[2]	10.9[1]	**7.2[3]**
Vangd OH Insur LT	8.5[4]	9.7[3]	**7.2[3]**
Vangd NJ Insur LT	8.6[4]	9.5[4]	**7.2[3]**
Price NJ TF	9.1[2]	9.6[3]	**7.1[3]**
Scudder PA TF	8.9[3]	9.8[3]	**7.1[3]**
Scudder OH TF	8.7[4]	9.9[3]	**7.1[3]**
Price MD TF	8.6[4]	9.5[4]	**7.1[3]**
Fidelity Spart Agg Muni‡	10.3[1]	9.5[4]	**7.0[3]**
Fidelity Spart OH Muni Inc	8.7[4]	9.7[3]	**7.0[3]**
Scudder NY TF	9.9[1]	10.2[2]	**7.0[3]**
USAA NY Bond	10.6[1]	10.7[2]	**7.0[3]**
Fidelity Spart CT Muni	9.1[2]	10.0[3]	**7.0[3]**
Drey-General NY	9.6[2]	9.6[3]	**6.9[3]**
Fidelity Muni Bd(Init Class)	9.2[2]	10.3[2]	**6.8[3]**
Stein Roe Mgd Muni	9.3[2]	9.8[3]	**6.8[3]**
Dupree KY TF Inc	8.0[5]	8.3[5]	**6.8[3]**
Fidelity NY Insur Muni Inc	8.8[3]	10.2[2]	**6.8[3]**
Fidelity Spart NJ Muni Inc	8.3[4]	9.2[4]	**6.8[4]**
Fidelity Spart Muni Inc	9.2[2]	10.0[3]	**6.8[4]**
AARP Insur TF Gen	8.9[3]	9.5[4]	**6.8[4]**
Fidelity Spart MN Muni Inc	8.8[3]	9.4[4]	**6.7[4]**
Fundamental HY Muni	15.7[1]	14.8[1]	**6.7[4]**
Dreyfus MA TE	9.1[3]	9.4[4]	**6.7[4]**
Emerald FL TE	9.1[3]	9.2[4]	**6.7[4]**
Value Line NY TE	9.3[2]	9.5[4]	**6.7[4]**
Dreyfus NJ Muni	8.8[3]	9.1[4]	**6.6[4]**
Drey-General Muni	8.1[5]	9.3[4]	**6.5[4]**
Fidelity Spart MI Muni Inc	9.1[3]	9.2[4]	**6.5[4]**
Heartland WI TF	8.1[5]	9.7[3]	**6.5[4]**
Invesco TF Long	8.7[4]	8.8[5]	**6.5[4]**
Empire Builder TF Bond	7.9[5]	8.5[5]	**6.5[4]**
Strong Muni Bond	12.1[1]	8.5[5]	**6.4[4]**
Value Line TE Hi Yld	8.8[3]	9.6[3]	**6.4[4]**
Rushmore VA TF	8.5[4]	8.6[5]	**6.4[4]**
Dreyfus NY TE	9.1[2]	9.1[4]	**6.4[4]**
Babson TF Long	8.7[4]	9.4[4]	**6.3[4]**
Dreyfus Muni Bond	7.9[5]	9.0[4]	**6.3[5]**
State Farm Muni Bd‡	7.3[5]	8.2[5]	**6.3[5]**
Columbia Muni Bd	8.4[4]	8.7[5]	**6.2[5]**
Rushmore MD TF	7.9[5]	8.3[5]	**6.2[5]**
Westcore CO TE	7.4[5]	8.2[5]	**6.1[5]**
JP Morgan TE Bond	7.4[5]	8.0[5]	**6.1[5]**
Mosaic TF VA	8.4[4]	9.1[4]	**6.0[5]**
First Hawaii Muni Bd	7.1[5]	8.5[5]	**5.9[5]**
IAA Trust TE Bd	9.0[3]	9.1[4]	**5.8[5]**
Dreyfus CA TE	8.3[4]	8.5[5]	**5.8[5]**
Sextant Idaho TE	7.1[5]	8.0[5]	**5.7[5]**
Dreyfus Insur Muni‡	8.4[4]	8.6[5]	**5.7[5]**
Dreyfus NY Insur	7.4[5]	8.2[5]	**5.6[5]**
Mosaic TF MO	8.1[5]	8.9[4]	**5.6[5]**
Mosaic TF Nat	8.2[4]	8.7[5]	**5.6[5]**
Mosaic TF AZ	7.9[5]	8.6[5]	**5.5[5]**
Accessor S-I Fix Inc	6.3[5]	7.1[5]	**5.0[5]**
Fundamental CA Muni	11.3[1]	10.6[2]	**4.8[5]**
Fundamental NY Muni	1.5[5]	2.8[5]	**-0.6[5]**

TAX-FREE - INTERMEDIATE TERM

No-Load Fund	1997	Annualized 3 years	Annualized 5 years
USAA TE Inter	9.4[1]	9.6[1]	**7.1[1]**
Price TF Ins Inter	7.2[3]	8.1[3]	**6.7[1]**
Fidelity Ltd Muni Inc	8.3[1]	9.1[1]	**6.7[1]**
Vangd Muni Inter	7.1[3]	8.2[2]	**6.7[1]**
Dreyfus CT Inter	7.6[2]	8.4[2]	**6.5[1]**
US Glb:Tax Free	9.1[1]	8.9[1]	**6.5[1]**
Dreyfus CA Inter	7.6[2]	8.2[3]	**6.5[1]**
Excelsior Inter TE	7.3[3]	8.8[1]	**6.5[2]**
Scudder Medium TF	7.7[2]	8.6[2]	**6.5[2]**
Dreyfus NY Inter	8.2[1]	8.7[1]	**6.4[2]**
Dreyfus Inter Muni	7.6[2]	8.5[2]	**6.3[2]**
Stein Roe Inter Muni	7.5[2]	8.2[2]	**6.3[2]**
Amer Cent-Benham CA Inter	7.4[2]	8.3[2]	**6.2[2]**
Dreyfus FL Inter	6.3[5]	7.8[4]	**6.1[2]**
Dreyfus NJ Inter	6.9[3]	8.0[3]	**6.1[2]**
Dreyfus MA Inter	7.5[2]	8.4[2]	**6.1[3]**
Nations FL Int Muni	7.0[3]	8.1[3]	**6.1[3]**
Fremont CA Inter	7.3[3]	8.6[2]	**6.1[3]**
Nations SC Int Muni	6.6[4]	7.9[4]	**6.0[3]**
Amer Cent-Benham Inter TF	7.4[3]	7.9[4]	**6.0[3]**
BT Invest:Inter TF	7.5[2]	8.1[3]	**6.0[3]**
Nations NC Int Muni	7.0[3]	8.1[3]	**5.9[3]**
Nations GA Int Muni	7.0[3]	8.1[3]	**5.9[4]**
CA Inv Tr-CA Insur Inter	6.4[5]	8.1[3]	**5.8[4]**
Excelsior NY Inter TE	6.7[4]	8.1[3]	**5.8[4]**
Warbg Pincus NY Inter	5.9[5]	6.5[5]	**5.7[4]**
Bernstein Dvsfd Muni	6.7[4]	7.7[4]	**5.7[4]**
Nbrgr-Ber Muni	7.4[3]	7.8[4]	**5.7[4]**
Bernstein NY Muni	6.5[4]	7.6[5]	**5.7[4]**
Bernstein CA Muni	6.3[5]	7.9[4]	**5.6[4]**
Nations VA Int Muni	6.6[4]	7.7[4]	**5.6[5]**
Nations MD Int Muni	6.5[5]	7.8[4]	**5.6[5]**
Crabbe Hsn OR Muni	7.0[3]	7.3[5]	**5.5[5]**
Federated Inter Muni	6.9[4]	7.4[5]	**5.5[5]**
Kent Inter TF	6.8[4]	7.5[5]	**5.5[5]**
BNY Hamilton Inter NY TE	6.2[5]	7.2[5]	**5.1[5]**
Dupree KY Sht-Med	5.2[5]	5.1[5]	**4.4[5]**

Stock and bond funds – ranked within objective *continued*

By 1993-1997 performance

No-Load Fund	Total return percent with quintile ranks by objective			No-Load Fund	Total return percent with quintile ranks by objective		
	1997	Annualized 3 years	5 years		1997	Annualized 3 years	5 years
TAX-FREE · SHORT TERM							
US Glb:Near Term TF............................	6.6[1]	5.8[2]	**5.4[1]**	Amer Cent-Benham CA Ltd Term...........	5.3[3]	5.8[2]	**4.5[3]**
Fidelity Spart S-I Muni........................	5.5[2]	5.9[2]	**4.9[1]**	Babson TF Short.................................	5.1[3]	5.9[2]	**4.5[4]**
USAA TE Short..................................	5.9[1]	6.1[1]	**4.9[2]**	Strong ST Muni...................................	6.9[1]	5.7[3]	**4.4[4]**
Vangd Muni Ltd Trm..........................	5.1[3]	5.9[2]	**4.8[2]**	Excelsior ST TE..................................	4.6[4]	5.2[4]	**4.1[4]**
Price TF S-I......................................	5.3[2]	5.8[3]	**4.8[2]**	Federated ST Muni..............................	4.5[4]	5.5[3]	**4.1[5]**
Dreyfus S-I Muni...............................	5.2[3]	5.5[4]	**4.5[3]**	Vangd Muni Short...............................	4.1[5]	4.6[5]	**3.8[5]**

CHAPTER 6

Stock and bond funds — top 50

Ranked by 1997 performance   *Ranked by 1995-1997 performance*

	No-Load Fund	Objective	1997	3 yrs.		No-Load Fund	Objective	1997	3 yrs.
			Total return percent (Annualized)					**Total return percent** (Annualized)	
1	American Heritage	agg gr	**75.0**	4.8	1	Fidelity Sel Energy Serv†	sector	51.9	**47.2**
2	FMI Focus	growth	**69.7**	—	2	Fidelity Sel Home Finc†	sector	45.8	**45.2**
3	Lexington Trka Dlg Russia	int'l	**67.5**	—	3	Fidelity Sel Reg Banks†	sector	45.5	**42.6**
4	Fidelity Sel Broker†	sector	**62.3**	41.0	4	Fidelity Sel Broker†	sector	62.3	**41.0**
5	FBR Sm Cap Finl Svcs‡	sector	**58.1**	—	5	Fidelity Sel Financial†	sector	41.9	**40.3**
6	Titan Finl Svcs	sector	**55.6**	—	6	Technology Value	sector	6.5	**40.3**
7	Oakmark Select	agg gr	**55.0**	—	7	Fidelity Sel Electronics†	sector	14.2	**39.8**
8	Brazos/JMIC Sm Cap Gro SC	agg gr	**54.5**	—	8	Rydex Nova	agg gr	42.3	**39.0**
9	Fidelity Sel Energy Serv†	sector	**51.9**	47.2	9	Legg Mason Value	growth	37.1	**38.7**
10	Century Shares	sector	**50.1**	33.5	10	Torray	growth	37.1	**38.6**
11	SAFECO Growth SC	agg gr	**50.0**	32.5	11	Weitz Ser Hickory	growth	39.2	**38.3**
12	FBR Fin'l Svcs‡	sector	**47.7**	—	12	Invesco Strat Fncl	sector	44.8	**38.2**
13	Transamerica Premr Eqty	growth	**47.5**	—	13	Baron Gro & Inc	gr-inc	31.1	**36.7**
14	Janus Spec Situations	agg gr	**46.0**	—	14	White Oak Gro	growth	24.3	**35.9**
15	Fidelity Sel Home Finc†	sector	**45.8**	45.2	15	Bridgeway Ult Sm Co SC	agg gr	38.0	**35.8**
16	Fidelity Sel Reg Banks†	sector	**45.5**	42.6	16	Jurika & Voyles MiniCap SC	agg gr	23.9	**35.6**
17	Invesco Strat Fncl	sector	**44.8**	38.2	17	TIP:Turner Small Cap SC‡	agg gr	14.8	**35.5**
18	FBR Sm Cap Gr/Val‡	agg gr	**44.3**	—	18	Selected Amer Shares	gr-inc	37.3	**35.3**
19	Sequoia‡	growth	**43.2**	35.1	19	Rydex OTC	agg gr	21.9	**35.3**
20	Stratton Sm Cap Yld SC	growth	**42.6**	27.8	20	Sequoia‡	growth	43.2	**35.1**
21	Gabelli Growth	growth	**42.6**	31.2	21	Fremont US Micro Cap SC	agg gr	7.0	**34.8**
22	Fidelity Sel Insurance†	sector	**42.5**	33.5	22	Rainier Core Eqty	growth	33.9	**34.4**
23	Wright Equifund Mexico	int'l	**42.4**	6.6	23	Mairs & Power Gro	growth	28.7	**34.4**
24	Rydex Nova	agg gr	**42.3**	39.0	24	Montag & Cldwl Growth	growth	31.9	**34.4**
25	Fidelity Sel Financial†	sector	**41.9**	40.3	25	Rainier Sm/Mid Cap	agg gr	32.2	**33.7**
26	Fidelity Sel Retail†	sector	**41.7**	24.3	26	Stein Roe Young Invest	growth	26.3	**33.6**
27	Gabelli Glbl Couch Potato	int'l	**41.7**	23.4	27	Century Shares	sector	50.1	**33.5**
28	Quaker Sm Cap Val SC	growth	**41.5**	—	28	Fidelity Sel Insurance†	sector	42.5	**33.5**
29	Price Finl Serv	sector	**41.4**	—	29	Sound Shore	growth	36.4	**33.2**
30	Fidelity Sel Leisure†	sector	**41.3**	26.7	30	Dreyfus Premier MidCap‡	growth	35.6	**33.2**
31	U.S. Global Leaders	global	**40.7**	—	31	Legg Mason Total Ret	growth	37.5	**33.0**
32	Weitz Ser Partners Value	growth	**40.6**	32.4	32	Northeast Inv Growth	growth	37.3	**32.7**
33	TIP:Turner Mid Cap	agg gr	**40.6**	—	33	Fidelity New Millnm†‡	agg gr	24.6	**32.6**
34	Oakmark Small Cap‡ SC	growth	**40.5**	—	34	Amer Cent Equity Growth	growth	36.1	**32.6**
35	UAM FMA Small Co SC	agg gr	**40.4**	30.0	35	Vangd Idx Growth	gr-inc	36.3	**32.6**
36	Matthew 25	growth	**39.7**	—	36	SAFECO Growth SC	agg gr	50.0	**32.5**
37	Htchks & Wly Sm Cap SC	growth	**39.5**	23.6	37	Price Value	gr-inc	29.2	**32.4**
38	Weitz Ser Hickory	growth	**39.2**	38.3	38	Weitz Ser Partners Value	growth	40.6	**32.4**
39	FAM Value SC	growth	**39.1**	22.8	39	Excelsior Val & Restruc	growth	33.6	**32.4**
40	Weitz Value	gr-inc	**38.9**	31.7	40	Tweedy Brown Amer Val	gr-inc	38.9	**32.3**
41	Tweedy Brown Amer Val	gr-inc	**38.9**	32.3	41	Janus Gro & Inc	growth	34.7	**32.3**
42	UAM Strlng Sm Cap Val SC	growth	**38.8**	—	42	Schroder Cap:US Sm Co SC	agg gr	26.9	**32.2**
43	Gabelli Asset	growth	**38.1**	25.1	43	Muhlenkamp	gr-inc	33.3	**32.1**
44	Fidelity Sel Consmr Ind†	sector	**38.0**	26.0	44	McM Eqty Invest	growth	33.8	**32.1**
45	Bridgeway Ult Sm Co SC	agg gr	**38.0**	35.8	45	Dreyfus Sm Co Val SC	growth	26.0	**32.0**
46	Ariel Apprec	growth	**37.9**	28.4	46	Thompson Plumb Growth	growth	32.4	**32.0**
47	Oak Value	growth	**37.7**	31.8	47	Oak Value	growth	37.7	**31.8**
48	SSgA Gro & Inc	gr-inc	**37.7**	29.1	48	Fidelity Divnd Growth	growth	27.9	**31.8**
49	Legg Mason Total Ret	growth	**37.5**	33.0	49	Vontobel US Value	gr-inc	34.3	**31.8**
50	Northeast Inv Growth	growth	**37.3**	32.7	50	First Eagle America	agg gr	29.5	**31.7**

Ranked by 1993-1997 performance

No-Load Fund	Objective	Total return percent 1997	Annualized 5 yrs.
1 Fidelity Sel Electronics†	sector	14.2	**33.5**
2 Fidelity Sel Home Finc†	sector	45.8	**32.0**
3 Fidelity Sel Energy Serv†	sector	51.9	**31.2**
4 Fidelity Sel Broker†	sector	62.3	**28.2**
5 Excelsior Val & Restruc	growth	33.6	**27.2**
6 Fidelity Sel Reg Banks†	sector	45.5	**26.4**
7 Fidelity Sel Financial†	sector	41.9	**25.6**
8 Fidelity Sel Computer†	sector	-1.1	**25.1**
9 Legg Mason Value	growth	37.1	**24.7**
10 Fidelity Sel Defense†	sector	23.5	**24.4**
11 Invesco Strat Fncl	sector	44.8	**24.3**
12 Fidelity New Millnm†‡	agg gr	24.6	**24.0**
13 Baron Asset SC	growth	33.9	**24.0**
14 Torray	growth	37.1	**23.7**
15 Mairs & Power Gro	growth	28.7	**23.7**
16 Vangd Primecap	growth	36.8	**23.6**
17 Fidelity Sel Indust Equip†	sector	18.8	**23.2**
18 Sequoia‡	growth	43.2	**23.0**
19 SAFECO Equity	gr-inc	24.2	**22.9**
20 SAFECO Growth SC	agg gr	50.0	**22.8**
21 Oakmark	growth	32.6	**22.8**
22 Vangd Spec-Health	sector	28.5	**22.6**
23 First Eagle America	agg gr	29.5	**22.5**
24 Fidelity Sel Health†	sector	31.1	**22.4**
25 UAM FMA Small Co SC	agg gr	40.4	**22.3**
26 Fidelity Sel Software†	sector	14.9	**22.2**
27 Robrtsn Stph Val Gro	agg gr	13.9	**22.0**
28 Westwood Equity	gr-inc	29.6	**21.9**
29 Berger Sm Cap Val SC	agg gr	36.4	**21.8**
30 White Oak Gro	growth	24.3	**21.6**
31 Sound Shore	growth	36.4	**21.5**
32 Fidelity Sel Leisure†	sector	41.3	**21.5**
33 Price Mid Cap Gro	growth	18.3	**21.4**
34 Price Div Gro	gr-inc	30.8	**21.4**
35 Longleaf Partners‡	growth	28.2	**21.4**
36 Fidelity Sel Technology†	sector	10.4	**21.3**
37 Spectra	agg gr	24.7	**21.1**
38 Dodge & Cox Stock	gr-inc	28.4	**21.1**
39 Founders Growth	agg gr	26.5	**21.1**
40 Price Sci/Tech	sector	1.7	**21.0**
41 Henlopen Fund	growth	22.6	**21.0**
42 Smith Brdn Eqty Plus	gr-inc	32.3	**21.0**
43 Amer Cent Equity Growth	growth	36.1	**21.0**
44 Fidelity Gro & Inc‡	gr-inc	30.2	**20.9**
45 Babson Value	gr-inc	26.5	**20.8**
46 Fidelity Blue Chip Gro††	growth	27.0	**20.8**
47 Vangd Gro & Inc	gr-inc	35.6	**20.7**
48 Fidelity Sel Insurance†	sector	42.5	**20.7**
49 Lazard Small Cap SC(O shrs)	agg gr	28.1	**20.7**
50 Vangd Windsor II	gr-inc	32.3	**20.7**

Ranked by 1988-1997 performance

No-Load Fund	Objective	Total return percent 1997	Annualized 10 yrs.
1 Fidelity Sel Home Finc†	sector	45.8	**27.6**
2 Kaufmann SC	agg gr	12.6	**26.5**
3 Fidelity Sel Reg Banks†	sector	45.5	**25.9**
4 Invesco Strat Fncl	sector	44.8	**25.6**
5 Fidelity Sel Electronics†	sector	14.2	**23.4**
6 Fidelity Sel Health†	sector	31.1	**23.2**
7 Vangd Spec-Health	sector	28.5	**23.1**
8 Fidelity Contrafund††	agg gr	23.0	**23.0**
9 Price Sci/Tech	sector	1.7	**22.8**
10 Fidelity Sel Broker†	sector	62.3	**22.3**
11 Skyline Special Eqty SC‡	agg gr	35.4	**22.3**
12 Invesco Strat Hlth	sector	18.4	**22.3**
13 Invesco Strat Tech	sector	8.8	**22.2**
14 Fidelity Sel Medical Del†	sector	20.5	**22.1**
15 Fidelity Sel Financial†	sector	41.9	**22.0**
16 Amer Cent-20th Cent Ultra	agg gr	23.1	**21.9**
17 Fidelity Sel Retail†	sector	41.7	**21.9**
18 Janus Twenty	agg gr	29.7	**21.1**
19 Fidelity Sel Software†	sector	14.9	**20.8**
20 Gabelli Growth	growth	42.6	**20.6**
21 Amer Cent-20th Cent Giftrust	agg gr	-1.2	**20.6**
22 Mairs & Power Gro	growth	28.7	**20.6**
23 Fidelity Sel Food/Agr†	sector	30.3	**20.3**
24 Brandywine	agg gr	12.0	**20.3**
25 Fidelity Blue Chip Gro††	growth	27.0	**20.2**
26 Fidelity Sel Insurance†	sector	42.5	**20.1**
27 CGM Capital Dev‡	agg gr	23.9	**20.0**
28 Longleaf Partners‡	growth	28.2	**19.9**
29 Invesco Strat Leis	sector	26.5	**19.9**
30 Baron Asset SC	growth	33.9	**19.9**
31 SAFECO Equity	gr-inc	24.2	**19.8**
32 Fidelity Gro & Inc‡	gr-inc	30.2	**19.8**
33 Harbor Cap App	agg gr	31.4	**19.7**
34 Fidelity Growth Co	agg gr	18.9	**19.6**
35 PBHG Growth	agg gr	-3.3	**19.6**
36 Fidelity Sel Transport†	sector	32.1	**19.5**
37 Managers Spec Eqty SC	agg gr	24.5	**19.5**
38 Sequoia‡	growth	43.2	**19.4**
39 Fidelity Sel Computer†	sector	-1.1	**19.4**
40 Strong Schafer Value	growth	29.3	**19.3**
41 Price New Amer	agg gr	21.1	**19.3**
42 Columbia Special	agg gr	12.6	**19.2**
43 Fidelity Sel Biotech†	sector	15.4	**19.2**
44 Century Shares	sector	50.1	**19.1**
45 Spectra	agg gr	24.7	**19.1**
46 Fidelity Sel Technology†	sector	10.4	**19.0**
47 Legg Mason Value	growth	37.1	**19.0**
48 Vangd Primecap	growth	36.8	**18.9**
49 Fidelity Sel Telecomm†	sector	25.8	**18.9**
50 Fidelity Magellan††‡	agg gr	26.5	**18.9**

CHAPTER 7

No-load fund groups

Families with 3 or more funds including one stock or bond fund
Arranged in alphabetical order by group and risk within group

Fund group/fund	Objective	Total Net Assets $ Millions 12/31/97	Annualized Total Return % with quintile ranks by obj			Post quintile ranks for your funds here		
			1997	3 years 1995-1997	5 years 1993-1997	1997	3 years ending 1997	5 years ending 1997
American Assoc of Retired Persons (Scudder)								
AARP Capital Growth	agg gr	1,217.9	35.1[1]	28.6[1]	17.3[2]	_____	_____	_____
AARP Sm Co Stk SC	agg gr	62.3	—	—	—	_____	_____	_____
AARP Divsfd Gro	growth	72.0	—	—	—	_____	_____	_____
AARP Int'l Gr & Inc	int'l	23.8	—	—	—	_____	_____	_____
AARP Global Growth	global	144.6	14.6[2]	—	—	_____	_____	_____
AARP Gro & Inc	gr-inc	6,671.3	31.0[2]	28.1[2]	20.2[1]	_____	_____	_____
AARP US Stk Idx	gr-inc	44.4	—	—	—	_____	_____	_____
AARP Bal Stk & Bd	income	667.6	21.9[2]	19.6[3]	—	_____	_____	_____
AARP Divsfd Inc w/Gro	income	53.3	—	—	—	_____	_____	_____
AARP Bond Fd for Inc	fix-inc	81.0	—	—	—	_____	_____	_____
AARP Hi Qual ST Bond	fix-inc	450.0	7.9[4]	9.2[4]	6.6[4]	_____	_____	_____
AARP GNMA & Trsy	fix-inc	4,539.4	8.0[1]	8.3[1]	5.8[2]	_____	_____	_____
AARP Insur TF Gen	tax-free	1,698.4	8.9[3]	9.5[4]	6.8[4]	_____	_____	_____
AARP Hi Qual MM	money mkt gen	467.4	4.8[5]	4.8[5]	4.0[5]	_____	_____	_____
AARP Hi Qual TF MM	money mkt TF	100.7	2.9[5]	3.0[5]	2.5[5]	_____	_____	_____
Your average		16,294.1				_____	_____	_____
Accessor Funds								
Accessor Sm/Mid Cap	agg gr	124.8	36.2[1]	30.9[1]	19.7[1]	_____	_____	_____
Accessor Int'l Eqty	int'l	151.4	11.0[2]	10.8[2]	—	_____	_____	_____
Accessor Growth	growth	87.9	33.2[1]	29.2[2]	20.7[1]	_____	_____	_____
Accessor Val & Inc	gr-inc	81.1	33.0[1]	30.0[2]	19.8[2]	_____	_____	_____
Accessor Inter Fix Inc	fix-inc	55.1	8.6[3]	9.6[3]	6.5[4]	_____	_____	_____
Accessor Mort Sec	fix-inc	109.7	9.5[1]	10.1[2]	7.1[2]	_____	_____	_____
Accessor S-I Fix Inc	fix-inc	40.9	6.3[5]	7.1[5]	5.0[5]	_____	_____	_____
Accessor US Gov MM	money mkt gov	50.9	5.1[2]	—	—	_____	_____	_____
Your average		701.8				_____	_____	_____
Acorn Funds								
Acorn SC	growth	3,687.1	25.0[3]	22.3[4]	17.5[3]	_____	_____	_____
Acorn USA SC	growth	184.4	32.3[1]	—	—	_____	_____	_____
Acorn Int'l	int'l	1,628.3	0.2[3]	9.9[2]	13.8[2]	_____	_____	_____
Short Tm Inc-MM(R&T)*	money mkt gen	853.4	4.8[5]	4.8[5]	4.1[5]	_____	_____	_____
Your average		5,499.8				_____	_____	_____
Advance Capital								
Advance Cap Eqty Gro	growth	54.3	17.7[5]	24.0[3]	—	_____	_____	_____
Advance Cap Balanced	income	99.4	20.5[3]	22.0[2]	13.1[3]	_____	_____	_____
Advance Cap Bond	fix-inc	4.2	9.4[3]	10.6[3]	7.5[3]	_____	_____	_____
Advance Cap Ret Inc	fix-inc	200.5	12.2[2]	13.0[2]	9.2[2]	_____	_____	_____
Your average		358.4				_____	_____	_____
American AAdvantage Funds								
Amer AAdv Mileage Gro & Inc	gr-inc	9.9	26.1[3]	26.7[3]	—	_____	_____	_____
Amer AAdv Mileage S&P 500 Idx	gr-inc	7.6	33.1[1]	—	—	_____	_____	_____
Amer AAdv Mileage Int'l	int'l	4.8	8.8[2]	14.9[1]	—	_____	_____	_____

See Chapter 3 for explanation of symbols

No-load fund groups *continued*

Families with 3 or more funds including one stock or bond fund
arranged in alphabetical order by group and risk within group

Fund group/fund	Objective	Total Net Assets $ Millions 12/31/97	Annualized Total Return % with quintile ranks by obj			Post quintile ranks for your funds here		
			1997	3 years 1995-1997	5 years 1993-1997	1997	3 years ending 1997	5 years ending 1997
Amer AAdv Mileage Bal..	income	3.7	19.5³	20.3³	—			
Amer AAdv Mileage Ltd Inc...	fix-inc	1.3	6.5³	6.4⁵	—			
Amer AAdv Mileage MM.	money mkt gen	100.1	5.2³	5.3²	4.6²			
Amer AAdv Muni Miles...	money mkt TF	26.3	3.2²	3.4²	—			
Amer AAdv US Gov't MM...	money mkt gov	31.4	5.0²	5.2²	—			
Your average		185.1						
American Century Mutual Funds								
Amer Cent Glob Gold..	prec met	249.0	-41.5³	-14.7¹	-1.3⁴			
Amer Cent-20th Cent Emg Mkts...	int'l	15.4	—	—	—			
Amer Cent-20th Cent Int'l Disc...	int'l	622.1	17.5¹	19.2¹	—			
Amer Cent-20th Cent Int'l Gr...	int'l	1,784.3	19.7¹	15.3¹	15.8¹			
Amer Cent New Opp SC...	agg gr	233.1	3.1⁵	—	—			
Amer Cent Strat Asst: Agg...	agg gr	112.6	16.2⁴	—	—			
Amer Cent-20th Cent Giftrust...	agg gr	986.0	-1.2⁵	13.1⁵	16.6³			
Amer Cent-20th Cent Growth...	agg gr	5,165.8	29.3²	21.4⁴	12.8⁴			
Amer Cent-20th Cent Ultra...	agg gr	22,420.3	23.1³	24.5²	17.8²			
Amer Cent-20th Cent Vista...	agg gr	1650.9	-8.7⁵	12.8⁵	9.6⁵			
Amer Cent Equity Growth...	growth	770.7	36.1¹	32.6¹	21.0¹			
Amer Cent Strat Asst: Mod...	growth	206.6	15.2⁵	—	—			
Amer Cent-20th Cent Heritage...	growth	1,277.4	19.3⁴	20.3⁴	14.5⁴			
Amer Cent-20th Cent Select...	growth	5,006.2	32.2¹	24.6³	15.3⁴			
Amer Cent Glob Nat Res...	global	46.7	2.5⁵	10.6⁵	—			
Amer Cent Balanced...	gr-inc	936.7	16.9⁵	17.2⁵	11.5⁵			
Amer Cent Equity Inc...	gr-inc	296.8	28.3³	27.4³	—			
Amer Cent Inc & Gro...	gr-inc	1,786.2	34.3¹	31.6¹	20.3¹			
Amer Cent Strat Asst: Cons...	gr-inc	157.5	12.8⁵	—	—			
Amer Cent Value...	gr-inc	2,418.6	26.0³	27.8²	—			
Amer Cent Util...	income	206.5	35.7¹	24.4¹	—			
Amer Cent Real Est...	sector	105.1	25.2³	—	—			
Amer Cent-Benham Hi Yld...	fix-inc	0.1	—	—	—			
Amer Cent-Benham Target 2000...	fix-inc	243.3	7.0⁵	12.1²	8.6²			
Amer Cent-Benham Target 2005...	fix-inc	301.2	11.6²	16.1¹	11.6¹			
Amer Cent-Benham Target 2010...	fix-inc	157.9	16.7¹	20.6¹	14.4¹			
Amer Cent-Benham Target 2015...	fix-inc	134.0	22.9¹	23.7¹	16.2¹			
Amer Cent-Benham Target 2020...	fix-inc	599.4	28.6¹	26.5¹	17.7¹			
Amer Cent-Benham Target 2025...	fix-inc	193.1	30.1¹	—	—			
Amer Cent-Benham LT Trsy...	fix-inc	129.4	14.7¹	13.5²	9.3²			
Amer Cent-Benham Int'l Bd...	fix-inc	166.0	-5.9⁵	7.6⁵	7.2²			
Amer Cent-Benham Bd...	fix-inc	127.9	8.6³	10.2²	7.1²			
Amer Cent-Benham Inter Bd...	fix-inc	361.2	8.4³	8.7⁴	6.2⁴			
Amer Cent-Benham GNMA...	fix-inc	1,233.4	8.7³	9.8³	6.8³			
Amer Cent-Benham Inflat Adj Trsy...	fix-inc	4.2	—	—	—			
Amer Cent-Benham Inter-Trm Treas...	fix-inc	361.2	8.3³	8.6⁴	6.2⁴			
Amer Cent-Benham Ltd Trm Bd...	fix-inc	25.2	6.3³	7.2³	—			
Amer Cent-Benham ST Gov...	fix-inc	509.5	6.0⁴	6.8⁴	4.8⁴			
Amer Cent-Benham ST Trsy...	fix-inc	40.0	6.0⁴	6.6⁴	5.1⁴			

129

No-load fund groups *continued*

Families with 3 or more funds including one stock or bond fund
Arranged in alphabetical order by group and risk within group

| Fund group/fund | Objective | Total Net Assets $ Millions 12/31/97 | Annualized Total Return % with quintile ranks by obj | | | Post quintile ranks for your funds here | | |
			1997	3 years 1995-1997	5 years 1993-1997	1997	3 years ending 1997	5 years ending 1997
Amer Cent-Benham CA Hi Yld...	tax-free	219.2	10.4[1]	11.4[1]	8.2[1]	_____	_____	_____
Amer Cent-Benham CA Insured...	tax-free	197.6	9.3[2]	10.5[2]	7.4[1]	_____	_____	_____
Amer Cent-Benham CA Long...	tax-free	311.8	9.6[2]	10.8[1]	7.7[1]	_____	_____	_____
Amer Cent-Benham Long TF...	tax-free	110.3	9.5[2]	9.7[3]	7.2[2]	_____	_____	_____
Amer Cent-Benham AZ Inter...	tax-free	37.2	6.9[4]	7.9[4]	—	_____	_____	_____
Amer Cent-Benham CA Inter...	tax-free	437.0	7.4[2]	8.3[2]	6.2[2]	_____	_____	_____
Amer Cent-Benham FL Inter...	tax-free	22.7	8.2[1]	8.4[2]	—	_____	_____	_____
Amer Cent-Benham Inter TF...	tax-free	132.6	7.4[3]	7.9[4]	6.0[3]	_____	_____	_____
Amer Cent-Benham CA Ltd Term...	tax-free	130.2	5.3[3]	5.8[2]	4.5[3]	_____	_____	_____
Amer Cent-Benham Ltd Term TF...	tax-free	35.2	5.5[2]	5.3[4]	—	_____	_____	_____
Amer Cent-Benham Cash Res...	money mkt gen	1,146.3	5.1[3]	5.2[3]	4.3[4]	_____	_____	_____
Amer Cent-Benham Prime MM...	money mkt gen	1,344.2	5.3[2]	5.3[2]	—	_____	_____	_____
Amer Cent-Benham CA Muni MM...	money mkt TF	172.8	3.2[2]	3.4[2]	3.0[2]	_____	_____	_____
Amer Cent-Benham CA TF MM...	money mkt TF	410.5	3.2[2]	3.4[2]	2.9[2]	_____	_____	_____
Amer Cent-Benham FL Muni MM...	money mkt TF	211.3	3.4[1]	3.8[1]	—	_____	_____	_____
Amer Cent-Benham TF MM...	money mkt TF	232.7	3.4[1]	3.4[2]	2.9[2]	_____	_____	_____
Amer Cent-Benham Cap Presv I...	money mkt gov	3,106.7	4.9[3]	5.0[3]	4.3[3]	_____	_____	_____
Amer Cent-Benham Gov Agcy MM...	money mkt gov	483.7	5.1[2]	5.1[2]	4.4[2]	_____	_____	_____
Your average		59,783.5	0			_____	_____	_____
American Express Strategist Funds								
AMEX-Strategist Emg Mkts...	int'l	0.7	5.4[3]	—	—	_____	_____	_____
AMEX-Strategist Spec Gr...	agg gr	1.5	26.3[2]	—	—	_____	_____	_____
AMEX-Strategist Growth Trend...	growth	21.2	24.7[3]	—	—	_____	_____	_____
AMEX-Strategist Growth...	growth	21.9	20.6[4]	—	—	_____	_____	_____
AMEX-Strategist World Gro...	global	0.6	7.0[4]	—	—	_____	_____	_____
AMEX-Strategist Equity...	gr-inc	0.8	19.6[5]	—	—	_____	_____	_____
AMEX-Strategist Total Ret...	gr-inc	0.7	10.3[5]	—	—	_____	_____	_____
AMEX-Strategist Balanced...	income	0.9	20.7[3]	—	—	_____	_____	_____
AMEX-Strategist Eqty Inc...	income	0.8	23.6[2]	—	—	_____	_____	_____
AMEX-Strategist World Inc...	fix-inc	0.6	5.8[5]	—	—	_____	_____	_____
AMEX-Strategist Hi Yld...	fix-inc	1.1	14.0[1]	—	—	_____	_____	_____
AMEX-Strategist Qual Inc...	fix-inc	0.6	8.6[4]	—	—	_____	_____	_____
AMEX-Strategist Gov Inc...	fix-inc	0.6	8.6[3]	—	—	_____	_____	_____
AMEX-Strategist TF HY...	tax-free	0.7	14.1[1]	—	—	_____	_____	_____
AMEX-Strategist MM...	money mkt gen	64.2	5.5[1]	—	—	_____	_____	_____
Your average		116.9				_____	_____	_____
Analytic Investment Management								
Analytic Enhncd Eqty...	growth	7.3	29.9[2]	29.3[1]	—	_____	_____	_____
Analytic Defnsve Eqty...	gr-inc	46.3	19.1[5]	18.7[5]	12.8[5]	_____	_____	_____
Analytic Master Fix Inc...	fix-inc	5.7	10.1[1]	10.6[1]	—	_____	_____	_____
Analytic ST Gov...	fix-inc	3.0	5.5[5]	7.1[3]	—	_____	_____	_____
Your average		62.3				_____	_____	_____

Families with 3 or more funds including one stock or bond fund
Arranged in alphabetical order by group and risk within group

Fund group/fund	Objective	Total Net Assets $ Millions 12/31/97	1997	3 years 1995-1997	5 years 1993-1997	1997	3 years ending 1997	5 years ending 1997
AON Mutual Funds								
AON Int'l Eqty...	int'l	50.4	6.5[2]	—	—			
AON S & P 500...	gr-inc	123.7	32.8[1]	—	—			
AON Asst Alloc...	income	166.7	31.5[1]	24.8[1]	—			
AON REIT Idx...	sector	102.1	18.8[4]	—	—			
AON Gov Sec...	fix-inc	106.8	10.0[1]	—	—			
AON MM...	money mkt gen	583.9	5.5[1]	—	—			
Your average...		1,133.6						
Aquinas Funds								
Aquinas Eqty Gro...	growth	36.0	29.0[2]	27.4[2]	—			
Aquinas Eqty Inc...	gr-inc	73.6	27.9[3]	27.8[2]	—			
Aquinas Balanced...	income	29.2	19.9[3]	19.4[3]	—			
Aquinas Fix Inc...	fix-inc	40.7	8.5[4]	9.1[5]	—			
Your average...		179.5						
Ariel Funds								
Ariel Growth SC...	agg gr	174.2	36.4[1]	25.9[2]	15.8[3]			
Ariel Apprec...	growth	204.4	37.9[1]	28.4[2]	15.9[4]			
Ariel Premier Bond...	fix-inc	0.6	—	—	—			
Your average...		379.2						
Artisan Funds								
Artisan International...	int'l	322.5	3.5[3]	—	—			
Artisan Mid Cap...	growth	9.7	—	—	—			
Artisan Small Cap SC‡...	growth	292.4	22.7[4]	—	—			
Artisan Small Cap Val SC...	growth	—	—	—	—			
Your average...		624.6						
Asset Management Financial								
Asset Mgmt Inter Mrtg...	fix-inc	79.1	8.4[3]	8.3[4]	6.0[4]			
Asset Mgmt US Mrtg Sec...	fix-inc	52.0	9.7[1]	9.4[3]	6.4[4]			
Asset Mgmt ARM...	fix-inc	762.0	6.5[2]	7.2[3]	5.6[2]			
Asset Mgmt ST US Gov...	fix-inc	105.8	6.3[3]	7.0[3]	5.4[3]			
Asset Mgmt Money Mkt...	money mkt gen	74.8	5.3[2]	—	—			
Your average...		1,073.7						
Jones & Babson Funds								
Babson Bond-Port L...	fix-inc	132.4	9.3[3]	9.3[4]	7.0[4]			
Babson Bond-Port S...	fix-inc	39.0	8.2[3]	8.7[4]	6.4[4]			
Babson Enterprise II SC...	agg gr	87.7	33.3[1]	26.8[2]	17.7[2]			
Babson Enterprise‡ SC...	agg gr	217.6	32.4[1]	23.2[3]	17.4[2]			
Babson Fed MM...	money mkt gov	13.8	4.7[5]	4.8[5]	4.0[5]			
Babson Growth...	growth	395.8	28.0[2]	27.0[2]	17.6[3]			
Babson Prime MM...	money mkt gen	36.5	4.7[5]	4.9[5]	4.1[5]			
Babson Shadow Stk SC...	growth	49.7	27.6[3]	24.2[3]	16.1[4]			
Babson Stew Ivry Int'l...	int'l	98.0	1.7[3]	9.1[3]	11.9[3]			

Post quintile ranks for your funds here

No-load fund groups *continued*

Families with 3 or more funds including one stock or bond fund
Arranged in alphabetical order by group and risk within group

Fund group/fund	Objective	Total Net Assets $ Millions 12/31/97	Annualized Total Return % with quintile ranks by obj			Post quintile ranks for your funds here		
			1997	3 years 1995-1997	5 years 1993-1997	1997	3 years ending 1997	5 years ending 1997
Babson TF Long	tax-free	27.4	8.7[4]	9.4[4]	6.3[4]			
Babson TF MM	money mkt TF	11.2	3.1[3]	3.3[3]	2.8[3]			
Babson TF Short	tax-free	22.5	5.1[3]	5.9[2]	4.5[4]			
Babson Value	gr-inc	1,421.1	26.5[3]	26.9[3]	20.8[1]			
Your average		2,552.7						
Bailard, Biehl & Kaiser Funds								
BBK Int'l Equity	int'l	132.1	10.0[2]	10.7[2]	10.3[3]			
BBK Diversa	global	36.8	13.2[2]	14.7[4]	10.7[3]			
BBK Int'l Bond	fix-inc	50.7	2.6[5]	10.3[3]	4.5[5]			
Your average		219.6						
Baron Funds								
Baron Sm Cap SC	agg gr	267.0	—	—	—			
Baron Asset SC	growth	3,793.0	33.9[1]	30.2[1]	24.0[1]			
Baron Gro & Inc	gr-inc	415.1	31.1[2]	36.7[1]	—			
Your average		4,475.1						
Barr Rosenberg Series Trust								
Barr Rosnbrg Japan†	int'l	1.0	-34.9[5]	—	—			
Barr Rosnbrg Int'l Sm Cap†	int'l	0.5	-13.4[4]	—	—			
Barr Rosnbrg US Sm Cap†‡SC	agg gr	17.9	30.4[1]	—	—			
Your average		19.4						
BEA Associates								
BEA Advs:Glob Telecomm	sector	0.8	32.3[1]	—	—			
BEA Advs:Emg Mkts	int'l	0.1	-3.6[4]	—	—			
BEA Advs:Int'l Eqty	int'l	1.3	14.9[1]	—	—			
BEA Advs:Hi Yld	fix-inc	1.0	14.5[1]	—	—			
Your average		3.2						
Berger Funds								
Berger 100	agg gr	1,718.6	13.6[4]	16.1[5]	12.1[5]			
Berger Sm Cap Val SC	agg gr	74.2	36.4[1]	29.3[1]	21.8[1]			
Berger Sm Co Gro SC	agg gr	784.3	16.2[4]	22.0[4]	—			
Berger/BIAM Int'l	int'l	17.1	2.9[3]	—	—			
Berger New Generation	growth	130.9	24.2[3]	—	—			
Berger Gro & Inc	gr-inc	340.5	22.7[4]	20.7[5]	14.5[5]			
Berger Balanced	income	17.1	—	—	—			
Kemper-Cash Acct Tr MM*	money mkt gen	1,574.1	4.8[5]	4.9[5]	4.1[5]			
Kemper-Cash Acct Tr TF MM*	money mkt TF	349.4	2.9[5]	3.1[4]	2.7[4]			
Kemper-Cash Acct Tr Gov MM*	money mkt gov	707.5	4.8[4]	4.9[4]	4.1[4]			
Your average		5,713.7						

Families with 3 or more funds including one stock or bond fund
Arranged in alphabetical order by group and risk within group

| Fund group/fund | Objective | Total Net Assets $ Millions 12/31/97 | Annualized Total Return % with quintile ranks by obj | | | Post quintile ranks for your funds here | | |
			1997	3 years 1995-1997	5 years 1993-1997	1997	3 years ending 1997	5 years ending 1997
Sanford Bernstein & Co								
Bernstein Emg Mkts	int'l	339.0	-23.8[5]	—	—			
Bernstein Int'l Value	int'l	4,697.8	9.3[2]	11.5[2]	14.2[2]			
Bernstein Inter Dur	fix-inc	2,136.6	7.6[4]	9.5[3]	7.0[2]			
Bernstein Short Dur Plus	fix-inc	597.2	5.5[5]	6.8[4]	5.2[3]			
Bernstein Gov Sht Dur	fix-inc	144.6	5.7[5]	6.6[4]	4.9[4]			
Bernstein CA Muni	tax-free	429.5	6.3[5]	7.9[4]	5.6[4]			
Bernstein NY Muni	tax-free	693.6	6.5[4]	7.6[5]	5.7[4]			
Bernstein Dvsfd Muni	tax-free	1,161.0	6.7[4]	7.7[4]	5.7[4]			
Bernstein Short Dur Muni CA	tax-free	82.9	3.6[5]	4.5[5]	—			
Bernstein Short Dur Muni NY	tax-free	81.5	3.8[5]	4.5[5]	—			
Bernstein Sht Dur Divsfd Muni	tax-free	153.2	4.0[5]	4.6[5]	—			
Your average		10,516.9						
BNY Hamilton Funds								
BNY Hamilton Sm Cap Gro SC	agg gr	1.2	—	—	—			
BNY Hamilton Int'l Eqty	int'l	2.6	—	—	—			
BNY Hamilton Lg Cap Gro	growth	6.5	—	—	—			
BNY Hamilton Eqty Inc	income	34.2	25.9[1]	23.7[1]	15.6[2]			
BNY Hamilton Inter Inv Grd	fix-inc	346.7	—	—	—			
BNY Hamilton Inter Gov	fix-inc	10.5	7.5[4]	8.6[4]	5.6[5]			
BNY Hamilton Inter NY TE	tax-free	10.4	6.2[5]	7.2[5]	5.1[5]			
BNY Hamilton Inter TE	tax-free	267.7	—	—	—			
BNY Hamilton MF Classic		23.8	5.1[3]	—	—			
Your average		703.6						
Boston 1784 Funds								
Boston-1784 Int'l Eqty	int'l	438.5	-0.9[4]	8.5[3]	—			
Boston-1784 Growth	growth	294.7	13.9[5]	—	—			
Boston-1784 Asst Alloc	gr-inc	42.5	20.7[4]	20.0[5]	—			
Boston-1784 Gro & Inc	gr-inc	504.2	19.7[5]	24.5[4]	—			
Boston-1784 Income	fix-inc	376.8	7.8[4]	9.3[4]	—			
Boston-1784 US Gov Med	fix-inc	240.5	8.1[4]	8.5[4]	—			
Boston-1784 ST Income	fix-inc	193.7	6.3[3]	7.3[2]	—			
Boston-1784 CT TE Inc	tax-free	119.9	8.5[4]	8.8[4]	—			
Boston-1784 MA TE Inc	tax-free	184.3	8.9[3]	8.6[5]	—			
Boston-1784 RI TE Inc	tax-free	66.9	8.3[4]	9.0[4]	—			
Boston-1784 FL TE	tax-free	49.8	—	—	—			
Boston-1784 TE Med Term	tax-free	287.1	9.1[1]	9.1[1]	—			
Boston-1784 TF MM	money mkt TF	909.4	3.3[1]	4.1[1]	—			
Boston-1784 Trsy MM	money mkt gov	364.4	5.0[3]	5.2[1]	4.5[1]			
Your average		4,072.7						

No-load fund groups *continued*

Families with 3 or more funds including one stock or bond fund
Arranged in alphabetical order by group and risk within group

Fund group/fund	Objective	Total Net Assets $ Millions 12/31/97	Annualized Total Return % with quintile ranks by obj 1997	3 years 1995-1997	5 years 1993-1997	Post quintile ranks for your funds here 1997	3 years ending 1997	5 years ending 1997
Bridgeway Funds								
Bridgeway Agg Gro	agg gr	5.5	18.3[3]	25.7[2]	—	___	___	___
Bridgeway Ult Sm Co SC	agg gr	41.0	38.0[1]	35.8[1]	—	___	___	___
Bridgeway Ult Sm Idx SC	agg gr	1.3	—	—	—	___	___	___
Bridgeway Soc Resp	growth	0.9	22.9[4]	23.0[4]	—	___	___	___
Bridgeway Ult Lg 35 Idx	gr-inc	0.1	—	—	—	___	___	___
Your average		48.8				___	___	___
Brown Capital Funds								
Brown Cap Balanced	income	5.4	21.0[3]	21.4[2]	13.4[3]	___	___	___
Brown Cap Equity	growth	6.9	22.7[4]	24.6[3]	15.3[4]	___	___	___
Brown Cap Sm Co SC	agg gr	9.7	15.8[4]	22.0[4]	15.0[3]	___	___	___
Your average		22.0				___	___	___
Banker's Trust Mutual Funds								
BT Invest:Pac Basin	int'l	11.2	-45.9[5]	-13.1[5]	—	___	___	___
BT Invest:Lat Am Eqty	int'l	32.5	30.8[1]	9.6[3]	—	___	___	___
BT Advs:EAFE Eqty Indx	int'l	3.2	1.9[3]	—	—	___	___	___
BT Invest:Int'l Eqty	int'l	573.8	17.4[1]	18.2[1]	18.8[1]	___	___	___
BT Advs:Sm Cap Idx SC	agg gr	1.3	25.1[2]	—	—	___	___	___
BT Invest:Sm Cap SC	agg gr	229.0	13.2[4]	24.3[3]	—	___	___	___
BT Pyramid:Eqty App	agg gr	163.7	15.4[4]	20.3[4]	—	___	___	___
BT Invest:Cap App	growth	39.9	14.5[5]	19.6[5]	—	___	___	___
BT Invest:Lifecycle Long Range	growth	114.6	23.0[4]	20.6[4]	—	___	___	___
BT Pyramid:Instit Asst Mgt	growth	384.7	23.5[4]	21.0[4]	—	___	___	___
BT Invest:Lifecycle Mid Range	gr-inc	84.8	18.5[5]	16.2[5]	—	___	___	___
BT Pyramid:Eqty 500 Idx	gr-inc	646.1	33.0[1]	30.9[1]	19.9[1]	___	___	___
BT Invest:Lifecycle Sht Range	income	41.0	13.7[5]	12.0[5]	—	___	___	___
BT Invest:Glob Hi Yld	fix-inc	26.7	10.1[2]	16.6[1]	—	___	___	___
BT Advs:US Bond Idx	fix-inc	0.2	—	—	—	___	___	___
BT Pyramid:Ltd Trm US Gov	fix-inc	48.0	6.0[4]	6.7[4]	5.2[3]	___	___	___
BT Invest:Inter TF	tax-free	19.7	7.5[2]	8.1[3]	6.0[3]	___	___	___
BT Invest Cash Mgt	money mkt gen	138.2	5.0[4]	—	—	___	___	___
BT Pyramid MM	money mkt gen	423.3	5.4[1]	—	—	___	___	___
BT Invest NY TF MM	money mkt TF	85.3	2.9[5]	—	—	___	___	___
BT Invest TF MM	money mkt TF	150.4	2.9[5]	—	—	___	___	___
BT Invest Treas MM	money mkt gov	267.4	4.9[4]	—	—	___	___	___
Your average		3,485.0				___	___	___
Buffalo Funds								
Buffalo Equity	growth	33.6	24.2[3]	—	—	___	___	___
Buffalo USA Global	global	48.4	19.0[2]	—	—	___	___	___
Buffalo Balanced	income	50.9	15.1[5]	18.2[4]	—	___	___	___
Buffalo High Yield	fix-inc	35.9	15.8[1]	—	—	___	___	___
Your average		168.8				___	___	___

Families with 3 or more funds including one stock or bond fund
Arranged in alphabetical order by group and risk within group

Fund group/fund	Objective	Total Net Assets $ Millions 12/31/97	1997	3 years 1995-1997	5 years 1993-1997	Post quintile ranks for your funds here 1997	3 years ending 1997	5 years ending 1997
Bull & Bear Mutual Funds								
Bull & Bear Gold	prec met	9.4	-55.7[5]	-24.1[2]	-6.7[5]	___	___	___
Bull & Bear Spec Eqty	agg gr	44.3	5.2[5]	14.3[5]	7.8[5]	___	___	___
Bull & Bear US & Overs	global	8.5	6.7[4]	12.0[4]	9.1[4]	___	___	___
Bull & Bear Dollar	money mkt gov	61.4	4.9[4]	4.9[5]	4.1[5]	___	___	___
Your average		123.6				___	___	___
C/FUNDS								
C/FUNDS:Growth Stk	growth	2.5	25.5[3]	22.9[4]	11.7[5]	___	___	___
C/FUNDS:Adams Equity	gr-inc	1.3	18.5[5]	—	—	___	___	___
C/FUNDS:C/FUND	gr-inc	7.1	21.0[4]	21.0[5]	14.2[5]	___	___	___
C/FUNDS:Gov	fix-inc	4.5	7.3[5]	7.8[5]	5.9[5]	___	___	___
C/FUNDS:Tax-Free	tax-free	3.3	—	—	—	___	___	___
Your average		18.7				___	___	___
California Investment Trust								
CA Inv Tr-S&P Sm Cap Idx SC	agg gr	9.2	24.1[2]	—	—	___	___	___
CA Inv Tr-S&P MidCap	growth	49.6	31.9[2]	27.0[2]	17.3[3]	___	___	___
CA Inv Tr-S&P 500	gr-inc	79.6	33.0[1]	30.8[1]	19.9[1]	___	___	___
CA Inv Tr-Eqty Inc	income	9.8	29.3[1]	—	—	___	___	___
CA Inv Tr-US Gov	fix-inc	34.3	9.3[3]	10.3[3]	7.7[3]	___	___	___
CA Inv Tr-CA TF Inc	tax-free	221.1	9.3[2]	10.8[1]	7.3[2]	___	___	___
CA Inv Tr-CA Insur Inter	tax-free	22.3	6.4[5]	8.1[3]	5.8[4]	___	___	___
CA Inv Tr-CA TF MM	money mkt TF	110.4	3.1[3]	3.3[3]	2.9[3]	___	___	___
CA Inv Tr-US Trsy MM	money mkt gov	33.8	4.9[4]	—	—	___	___	___
Your average		570.1				___	___	___
Capiello-Rushmore Funds								
Capp-Rush Gold	prec met	2.6	-45.2[4]	-18.9[2]	—	___	___	___
Capp-Rush Emg Growth SC	agg gr	18.2	4.7[5]	13.3[5]	10.6[5]	___	___	___
Capp-Rush Growth	growth	24.9	22.2[4]	21.5[4]	16.5[3]	___	___	___
Rushmore Amer Gas Idx	sector	245.7	24.2[3]	25.1[3]	15.5[4]	___	___	___
Capp-Rush Util	income	14.0	25.3[2]	19.3[4]	9.3[5]	___	___	___
Rushmore US Gov	fix-inc	16.5	13.1[2]	13.2[2]	8.5[2]	___	___	___
Rushmore MD TF	tax-free	46.3	7.9[5]	8.3[5]	6.2[5]	___	___	___
Rushmore VA TF	tax-free	32.3	8.5[4]	8.6[5]	6.4[4]	___	___	___
Rushmore Fd TF Inv MM	money mkt TF	19.1	2.9[5]	—	—	___	___	___
Rushmore Fd Gov Inv MM	money mkt gov	567.6	4.5[5]	—	—	___	___	___
Your average		987.2				___	___	___
Capstone Funds								
Capstone New Zealand	int'l	6.0	-23.1[5]	2.8[4]	2.6[5]	___	___	___
Capstone Nikko Japan	int'l	1.8	-24.6[5]	-15.1[5]	-0.9[5]	___	___	___
Capstone Growth	growth	70.1	28.7[2]	24.9[3]	13.8[5]	___	___	___
Capstone Gov Inc	fix-inc	8.6	4.4[5]	4.7[5]	3.7[5]	___	___	___
Your average		86.5				___	___	___

Families with 3 or more funds including one stock or bond fund
Arranged in alphabetical order by group and risk within group

Fund group/fund	Objective	Total Net Assets $ Millions 12/31/97	Annualized Total Return % with quintile ranks by obj			Post quintile ranks for your funds here		
			1997	3 years 1995-1997	5 years 1993-1997	1997	3 years ending 1997	5 years ending 1997
Capital Growth Management(CGM)								
CGM Capital Dev‡	agg gr	722.6	23.9[2]	30.8[1]	17.3[2]	____	____	____
CGM Focus	agg gr	95.0	—	—	—	____	____	____
CGM Mutual	gr-inc	1,192.2	8.2[5]	18.5[5]	12.8[5]	____	____	____
CGM Realty	sector	489.6	26.7[3]	29.8[2]	—	____	____	____
CGM Fixed Inc	fix-inc	43.9	3.7[5]	15.0[1]	10.7[1]	____	____	____
CGM American TF	tax-free	14.4	9.0[3]	9.8[3]	—	____	____	____
Your average		2,557.7				____	____	____
Chicago Trust Funds								
Chicago Tr Talon	growth	30.2	26.5[3]	26.7[2]	—	____	____	____
Montag & Cldwl Growth	growth	548.6	31.9[2]	34.4[1]	—	____	____	____
Chicago Tr Gro & Inc	gr-inc	289.9	26.7[3]	29.2[2]	—	____	____	____
Montag & Cldwl Balanced	income	89.7	23.5[2]	24.4[1]	—	____	____	____
Chicago Tr Balanced	income	191.1	20.9[3]	—	—	____	____	____
Chicago Tr Bond	fix-inc	131.8	9.0[2]	10.0[2]	—	____	____	____
Chicago Tr Muni	tax-free	12.5	5.5[5]	6.5[5]	—	____	____	____
Chicago Tr MM	money mkt gen	246.0	5.2[2]	5.3[2]	—	____	____	____
Your average		1,539.8				____	____	____
CitiSelect Funds								
CitiSelect 500	growth	201.5	12.0[5]	—	—	____	____	____
CitiSelect 400	gr-inc	469.6	10.3[5]	—	—	____	____	____
CitiSelect 200	income	184.9	8.3[5]	—	—	____	____	____
CitiSelect 300	income	349.6	9.9[5]	—	—	____	____	____
Your average		1,205.6				____	____	____
Citizens Trust								
Citizens Tr Emg Gr SC	agg gr	71.8	17.7[4]	23.6[3]	—	____	____	____
Citizens Tr Idx	growth	257.0	35.0[1]	—	—	____	____	____
Citizens Tr Global	global	35.0	19.9[2]	15.6[4]	—	____	____	____
Citizens Tr Income	fix-inc	45.8	10.5[1]	10.8[1]	7.7[1]	____	____	____
Working Asst MM(Citizen's)	money mkt gen	102.9	4.4[5]	4.6[5]	3.8[5]	____	____	____
Your average		512.5				____	____	____
Columbia Funds								
Columbia Growth	agg gr	1,324.9	26.3[2]	26.6[2]	17.9[2]	____	____	____
Columbia Small Cap SC	agg gr	96.4	34.1[1]	—	—	____	____	____
Columbia Special	agg gr	1,249.7	12.6[4]	18.2[4]	15.5[3]	____	____	____
Columbia Int'l Stk	int'l	146.3	11.5[2]	11.0[2]	12.2[3]	____	____	____
Columbia Common Stk	gr-inc	783.9	25.4[3]	25.6[3]	18.7[3]	____	____	____
Columbia Balanced	income	792.4	18.8[3]	18.4[4]	13.6[3]	____	____	____
Columbia Real Est Eqty	sector	151.6	24.7[3]	27.4[2]	—	____	____	____
Columbia High Yld	fix-inc	39.3	12.7[2]	13.7[2]	—	____	____	____
Columbia Fix Inc	fix-inc	381.3	9.6[1]	10.4[1]	7.5[2]	____	____	____
Columbia US Gov	fix-inc	37.8	5.6[5]	6.5[5]	5.1[4]	____	____	____
Columbia Muni Bd	tax-free	404.5	8.4[4]	8.7[5]	6.2[5]	____	____	____
Columbia Daily Inc	money mkt gen	1,169.0	5.1[3]	5.2[3]	4.3[4]	____	____	____
Your average		6,577.1				____	____	____

No-load fund groups *continued*

Families with 3 or more funds including one stock or bond fund
Arranged in alphabetical order by group and risk within group

Fund group/fund	Objective	Total Net Assets $ Millions 12/31/97	1997	3 years 1995-1997	5 years 1993-1997	1997	3 years ending 1997	5 years ending 1997
Crabbe Huson Funds								
Crabbe Hsn Small Cap SC	agg gr	39.1	26.1[2]	—	—			
Crabbe Hsn Special SC	agg gr	352.7	11.2[4]	9.3[5]	14.4[4]			
Crabbe Hsn Equity	growth	377.6	25.7[3]	21.1[4]	17.8[3]			
Crabbe Hsn Asst Alloc	income	93.3	19.2[3]	15.2[5]	12.4[4]			
Crabbe Hsn Real Est	sector	32.2	18.8[4]	20.9[4]	—			
Crabbe Hsn Income	fix-inc	3.5	11.6[2]	10.0[4]	6.5[5]			
Crabbe Hsn US Gov Inc	fix-inc	4.4	7.1[1]	7.2[3]	5.0[4]			
Crabbe Hsn OR TF	tax-free	26.4	7.0[3]	7.3[5]	5.5[5]			
Crabbe Hsn Gov MM	money mkt gov	30.8	4.9[4]	—	—			
Your average		960.0						
Dodge & Cox								
Dodge & Cox Balanced	income	5,076.6	21.2[3]	21.2[2]	16.1[2]			
Dodge & Cox Income	fix-inc	705.5	10.0[2]	11.1[3]	8.2[3]			
Dodge & Cox Stock	gr-inc	4,087.0	28.4[3]	28.0[2]	21.1[1]			
Your average		9,869.1						
Dreyfus Mutual Funds								
Dreyfus Tech Growth	sector	4.7	—	—	—			
Dreyfus Emg Mkts	int'l	63.3	-1.5[4]	—	—			
Dreyfus Int'l Eqty Alloc	int'l	1.4	0.6[3]	6.1[3]	—			
Dreyfus Int'l Gro	int'l	77.1	-1.5[4]	2.5[4]	—			
Dreyfus Int'l Stk Idx	int'l	9.6	—	—	—			
Dreyfus Int'l Val	int'l	114.7	9.0[2]	—	—			
Dreyfus Agg Gr SC	agg gr	94.0	-15.8[5]	—	—			
Dreyfus Agg Val SC	agg gr	157.0	21.6[3]	—	—			
Dreyfus Apprec	agg gr	1,978.8	27.8[2]	30.4[1]	18.2[2]			
Dreyfus Emg Ldrs SC	agg gr	129.0	33.9[1]	—	—			
Dreyfus New Leaders SC	agg gr	866.1	19.5[3]	22.1[4]	16.3[3]			
Dreyfus Sm Cap Stk Idx	agg gr	18.8	—	—	—			
Dreyfus Premier Core Value‡	growth	585.7	25.2[3]	27.3[2]	19.2[2]			
Dreyfus Premier MidCap Stk‡	growth	9.5	35.6[1]	33.2[1]	—			
Dreyfus Growth Opp	growth	499.9	15.1[5]	21.8[4]	11.5[5]			
Dreyfus Lg Co Gr	growth	11.8	11.7[5]	19.4[5]	—			
Dreyfus LifeTime Growth	growth	6.3	27.0[3]	—	—			
Dreyfus MidCap Idx	growth	257.3	31.6[2]	26.6[2]	17.2[3]			
Dreyfus MidCap Val	growth	124.0	28.0[2]	—	—			
Dreyfus Sm Co Val SC	growth	402.3	26.0[3]	32.0[1]	—			
Dreyfus Third Cent	growth	804.1	29.4[2]	29.7[1]	16.3[3]			
Dreyfus Global Gro	global	89.8	12.3[3]	12.1[4]	9.7[4]			
Dreyfus Premier Lg Co Stk‡	gr-inc	9.0	34.6[1]	30.6[1]	—			
Dreyfus Discpl Stock	gr-inc	1,645.6	31.9[2]	31.2[1]	20.1[1]			
Dreyfus Fund	gr-inc	2,614.8	10.7[5]	16.7[5]	10.1[5]			
Dreyfus Gro & Inc	gr-inc	1,944.0	16.0[5]	18.4[5]	13.3[5]			
Dreyfus Lg Co Val	gr-inc	165.5	16.0[5]	29.7[2]	—			
Dreyfus LifeTime Gr & Inc	gr-inc	0.9	20.4[4]	—	—			

137

Families with 3 or more funds including one stock or bond fund
Arranged in alphabetical order by group and risk within group

| Fund group/fund | Objective | Total Net Assets $ Millions 12/31/97 | Annualized Total Return % with quintile ranks by obj | | | Post quintile ranks for your funds here | | |
			1997	3 years 1995-1997	5 years 1993-1997	1997	3 years ending 1997	5 years ending 1997
Dreyfus S&P 500 Idx	gr-inc	1,430.9	32.6[1]	30.4[1]	19.6[2]			
Dreyfus Asst Alloc	income	82.3	28.9[1]	22.3[2]	—			
Dreyfus Balanced	income	372.0	17.4[4]	17.9[4]	13.5[3]			
Dreyfus Eqty Div	income	4.5	25.5[2]	—	—			
Dreyfus LifeTime Income	income	10.3	11.9[5]	—	—			
Dreyfus Real Estate Mrtg	sector	10.9	—	—	—			
Dreyfus Global Bd	fix-inc	12.4	6.8[5]	11.0[3]	—			
Dreyfus Hi Yld Secs	fix-inc	139.3	16.7[1]	—	—			
Dreyfus A Bonds Plus	fix-inc	633.3	9.5[3]	10.7[3]	7.9[3]			
Dreyfus Strat Income	fix-inc	277.0	11.2[2]	12.7[2]	9.1[2]			
Dreyfus 100% US Long	fix-inc	133.8	11.7[2]	12.1[2]	8.3[2]			
Dreyfus Basic GNMA	fix-inc	75.6	9.5[3]	10.2[3]	7.6[3]			
Dreyfus GNMA	fix-inc	1,199.1	8.8[4]	9.6[4]	6.5[5]			
Dreyfus Bond Mkt Idx	fix-inc	0.5	9.2[2]	9.5[3]	—			
Dreyfus Discpl Inter Bd	fix-inc	0.4	9.0[2]	—	—			
Dreyfus Inter Inc	fix-inc	22.1	14.6[1]	—	—			
Dreyfus ST Income	fix-inc	294.6	8.2[3]	8.5[4]	6.9[3]			
Dreyfus 100% US Inter	fix-inc	187.7	7.6[4]	8.7[4]	6.5[3]			
Dreyfus ST Hi Yld	fix-inc	156.0	12.6[1]	—	—			
Dreyfus 100% US Short	fix-inc	194.6	6.1[4]	7.2[3]	5.6[2]			
Dreyfus S-I Gov	fix-inc	477.5	6.1[4]	7.5[2]	5.8[2]			
Drey-General CA Muni	tax-free	292.7	8.8[3]	10.2[2]	7.2[2]			
Drey-General NY Muni	tax-free	307.2	9.6[2]	9.6[3]	6.9[3]			
Dreyfus CA TE	tax-free	1,338.5	8.3[4]	8.5[5]	5.8[5]			
Dreyfus MA TE	tax-free	154.5	9.1[3]	9.4[4]	6.7[4]			
Dreyfus NJ Muni	tax-free	591.2	8.8[3]	9.1[4]	6.6[4]			
Dreyfus NY Insur TE	tax-free	135.1	7.4[5]	8.2[5]	5.6[5]			
Dreyfus NY TE	tax-free	1,704.5	9.1[2]	9.1[4]	6.4[4]			
Drey-Basic Muni	tax-free	138.9	10.9[1]	11.4[1]	—			
Drey-General Muni	tax-free	700.4	8.1[5]	9.3[4]	6.5[4]			
Dreyfus Insur Muni	tax-free	195.3	8.4[4]	8.6[5]	5.7[5]			
Dreyfus Muni Bond	tax-free	3,505.8	7.9[5]	9.0[4]	6.3[5]			
Dreyfus CA Inter	tax-free	200.9	7.6[2]	8.2[3]	6.5[1]			
Dreyfus CT Inter	tax-free	129.8	7.6[2]	8.4[2]	6.5[1]			
Dreyfus FL Inter	tax-free	341.7	6.3[5]	7.8[4]	6.1[2]			
Dreyfus MA Inter	tax-free	64.0	7.5[2]	8.4[2]	6.1[3]			
Dreyfus NJ Inter	tax-free	214.0	6.9[3]	8.0[3]	6.1[2]			
Dreyfus NY Inter TE	tax-free	363.2	8.2[1]	8.7[1]	6.4[2]			
Dreyfus PA Inter Muni	tax-free	65.8	8.3[1]	9.2[1]	—			
Drey-Basic Inter Muni	tax-free	72.9	8.8[1]	9.1[1]	—			
Dreyfus Inter Muni	tax-free	1,372.7	7.6[2]	8.5[2]	6.3[2]			
Dreyfus S-I Muni	tax-free	290.0	5.2[3]	5.5[4]	4.5[3]			
Drey-Basic MM	money mkt gen	1,679.0	5.4[1]	5.6[1]	4.9[1]			
Drey-General MM	money mkt gen	885.6	5.0[4]	5.1[4]	4.3[4]			
Dreyfus Liq Asst	money mkt gen	4,567.5	5.0[4]	5.1[4]	4.3[4]			
Dreyfus MM Instr MM Ser	money mkt gen	118.3	4.8[5]	5.0[5]	4.2[5]			
Dreyfus Wrld Dollar MM	money mkt gen	1,634.5	5.1[4]	5.2[4]	4.3[4]			

amilies with 3 or more funds including one stock or bond fund
rranged in alphabetical order by group and risk within group

| Fund group/fund | Objective | Total Net Assets $ Millions 12/31/97 | Annualized Total Return % with quintile ranks by obj | | | Post quintile ranks for your funds here | | |
			1997	3 years 1995-1997	5 years 1993-1997	1997	3 years ending 1997	5 years ending 1997
Drey-Basic CA Muni MM...	money mkt TF	86.3	3.2³	—	—	___	___	___
Drey-Basic MA Muni MM...	money mkt TF	165.8	3.2²	—	—	___	___	___
Drey-Basic Muni MM...	money mkt TF	623.5	3.4¹	3.6¹	3.3¹	___	___	___
Drey-Basic NJ Muni MM...	money mkt TF	134.5	3.2³	—	—	___	___	___
Drey-Basic NY Muni MM...	money mkt TF	317.4	3.2²	—	—	___	___	___
Drey-General CA Muni MM...	money mkt TF	356.4	3.0⁴	3.2⁴	2.9³	___	___	___
Drey-General Muni MM...	money mkt TF	262.2	3.2³	3.3³	2.9³	___	___	___
Drey-General NY Muni MM...	money mkt TF	431.8	3.0⁴	3.2⁴	2.8³	___	___	___
Dreyfus CA TE MM...	money mkt TF	206.5	2.9⁵	3.1⁵	2.7⁴	___	___	___
Dreyfus CT Muni MM...	money mkt TF	189.5	3.0⁴	3.2⁴	2.9³	___	___	___
Dreyfus FL Muni MM...	money mkt TF	367.9	3.1³	3.3²	—	___	___	___
Dreyfus MA Muni MM...	money mkt TF	178.7	3.0⁴	3.2⁴	2.9³	___	___	___
Dreyfus Muni MM...	money mkt TF	971.1	3.1³	3.3³	2.9³	___	___	___
Dreyfus NJ Muni MM...	money mkt TF	533.5	3.0⁴	3.1⁴	2.8³	___	___	___
Dreyfus NY TE MM...	money mkt TF	299.0	3.0⁴	3.2⁴	2.6⁵	___	___	___
Dreyfus PA Muni MM...	money mkt TF	128.1	3.1⁴	3.3³	3.0¹	___	___	___
Drey-Basic US Gov MM...	money mkt gov	1,222.4	5.3¹	5.5¹	4.8¹	___	___	___
Drey-General Gov MM...	money mkt gov	524.0	4.9⁴	5.0³	4.3³	___	___	___
Dreyfus 100% US MM...	money mkt gov	1,194.2	4.7⁵	4.9⁵	4.1⁴	___	___	___
Dreyfus MM Instr Gov...	money mkt gov	377.9	4.7⁵	4.9⁵	4.1⁵	___	___	___
Your average		48,034.2				___	___	___
Dupree Funds								
Dupree Inter Gov...	fix-inc	8.8	9.4²	9.9³	6.9³	___	___	___
Dupree KY TF Inc...	tax-free	346.2	8.0⁵	8.3⁵	6.8³	___	___	___
Dupree NC TF Inc...	tax-free	6.1	9.8¹	—	—	___	___	___
Dupree TN TF Inc...	tax-free	17.3	8.9³	10.7¹	—	___	___	___
Dupree KY TF Sht-Med...	tax-free	54.2	5.2⁵	5.1⁵	4.4⁵	___	___	___
Dupree NC TF Sht-Med...	tax-free	1.5	5.0⁵	—	—	___	___	___
Dupree TN TF Sht-Med...	tax-free	3.8	5.4⁵	5.5⁵	—	___	___	___
Your average		437.9				___	___	___
Eastcliff Funds								
Eastcliff Reg Sm Cap Val...	agg gr	53.8	21.1³	—	—	___	___	___
Eastcliff Growth...	growth	49.8	22.4⁴	—	—	___	___	___
Eastcliff Total Ret...	income	23.0	30.0¹	24.5¹	16.0²	___	___	___
Your average		126.6				___	___	___
Eclipse Funds								
Eclipse Equity SC...	agg gr	192.9	33.3¹	27.5²	18.2²	___	___	___
Eclipse Gro & Inc...	gr-inc	110.0	32.5¹	27.2³	—	___	___	___
Eclipse Balanced...	income	88.7	23.4²	19.7³	14.9²	___	___	___
Eclipse Ultra Short...	fix-inc	5.4	6.2³	6.5⁵	—	___	___	___
Your average		397.0				___	___	___

No-load fund groups *continued*

Families with 3 or more funds including one stock or bond fund
Arranged in alphabetical order by group and risk within group

Fund group/fund	Objective	Total Net Assets $ Millions 12/31/97	Annualized Total Return % with quintile ranks by obj 1997	3 years 1995-1997	5 years 1993-1997	Post quintile ranks for your funds here 1997	3 years ending 1997	5 years ending 1997
Emerald Funds								
Emerald Small Cap SC	agg gr	15.3	12.6[4]	18.4[4]	—	_____	_____	_____
Emerald Int'l Eqty	int'l	4.7	20.4[1]	—	—	_____	_____	_____
Emerald Eqty	growth	47.3	25.4[3]	26.6[2]	14.6[4]	_____	_____	_____
Emerald Eqty Val	gr-inc	4.8	29.4[2]	—	—	_____	_____	_____
Emerald Balanced	income	8.4	16.4[4]	18.3[4]	—	_____	_____	_____
Emerald Mndg Bd	fix-inc	2.7	8.2[4]	10.0[4]	—	_____	_____	_____
Emerald US Gov Sec	fix-inc	21.5	7.4[4]	8.3[5]	6.0[4]	_____	_____	_____
Emerald ST Inc	fix-inc	4.2	5.7[5]	6.9[4]	—	_____	_____	_____
Emerald FL TE	tax-free	84.5	9.1[3]	9.2[4]	6.7[4]	_____	_____	_____
Emerald Prime MM	money mkt gen	351.5	4.9[5]	—	—	_____	_____	_____
Emerald TE MM	money mkt TF	26.8	2.9[5]	—	—	_____	_____	_____
Emerald Treas MM	money mkt gov	367.2	4.6[5]	—	—	_____	_____	_____
Your average		938.9				_____	_____	_____
Excelsior Funds								
Excelsior Enrgy & Nat Resc	sector	44.5	18.5[4]	25.4[3]	17.1[3]	_____	_____	_____
Excelsior Pac Asia	int'l	41.6	-32.2[5]	-7.6[5]	2.3[5]	_____	_____	_____
Excelsior Lat Amer	int'l	95.9	25.2[1]	11.8[2]	11.8[3]	_____	_____	_____
Excelsior Pan Europe	int'l	168.7	24.4[1]	20.2[1]	15.3[1]	_____	_____	_____
Excelsior International	int'l	177.7	9.3[2]	8.0[3]	11.0[3]	_____	_____	_____
Excelsior Sm Cap SC	agg gr	65.7	14.2[4]	11.1[5]	13.0[4]	_____	_____	_____
Excelsior Blended Eqty	growth	542.2	29.8[2]	26.1[3]	18.5[2]	_____	_____	_____
Excelsior Val & Restruc	growth	230.0	33.6[1]	32.4[1]	27.2[1]	_____	_____	_____
Excelsior Inc & Gro	gr-inc	143.6	22.1[4]	23.6[4]	16.6[4]	_____	_____	_____
Excelsior Mgd Inc	fix-inc	197.6	9.8[3]	10.5[3]	7.5[3]	_____	_____	_____
Excelsior Inter Mgd Inc	fix-inc	91.4	8.5[3]	9.6[3]	6.6[3]	_____	_____	_____
Excelsior ST Gov	fix-inc	32.3	5.9[4]	6.7[4]	5.1[4]	_____	_____	_____
Excelsior CA TE Inc	tax-free	30.5	5.7[5]	—	—	_____	_____	_____
Excelsior LT TE	tax-free	134.0	9.4[2]	11.9[1]	8.8[1]	_____	_____	_____
Excelsior NY Inter TE	tax-free	121.9	6.7[4]	8.1[3]	5.8[4]	_____	_____	_____
Excelsior Inter TE	tax-free	253.5	7.3[3]	8.8[1]	6.5[2]	_____	_____	_____
Excelsior ST TE	tax-free	38.5	4.6[4]	5.2[4]	4.1[4]	_____	_____	_____
Excelsior MM	money mkt gen	493.3	5.2[2]	5.3[2]	4.5[2]	_____	_____	_____
Excelsior TE MM	money mkt TF	1,119.2	3.3[2]	—	—	_____	_____	_____
Excelsior Govt MM	money mkt gov	559.8	5.1[2]	5.2[2]	4.4[2]	_____	_____	_____
Excelsior Treas MM	money mkt gov	437.1	4.9[3]	—	—	_____	_____	_____
Your average		5,019.0				_____	_____	_____
Fairport Funds								
Fairport Midwest Gr	growth	76.8	27.7[3]	23.8[4]	—	_____	_____	_____
Fairport Gr & Inc	gr-inc	29.5	30.3[2]	25.5[3]	—	_____	_____	_____
Fairport Gov Sec	fix-inc	4.3	7.5[4]	9.1[3]	—	_____	_____	_____
Kemper-Cash Acct Tr MM*	money mkt gen	1,574.1	4.8[5]	4.9[5]	4.1[5]	_____	_____	_____
Kemper-Cash Acct Tr TF MM*	money mkt TF	349.4	2.9[5]	3.1[4]	2.7[4]	_____	_____	_____
Kemper-Cash Acct Tr Gov MM*	money mkt gov	707.5	4.8[4]	4.9[4]	4.1[4]	_____	_____	_____
Your average		110.6				_____	_____	_____

Families with 3 or more funds including one stock or bond fund
Arranged in alphabetical order by group and risk within group

Fund group/fund	Objective	Total Net Assets $ Millions 12/31/97	Annualized Total Return % with quintile ranks by obj 1997	3 years 1995-1997	5 years 1993-1997	Post quintile ranks for your funds here 1997	3 years ending 1997	5 years ending 1997
FBR Funds								
FBR Fin'l Svcs‡	sector	33.6	47.7[1]	—	—			
FBR Sm Cap Finl Svcs‡	sector	72.1	58.1[1]	—	—			
FBR Sm Cap Gr/Val‡	agg gr	9.6	44.3[1]	—	—			
FBR Mny Mkt(RBB)*	money mkt gen	1,363.3	4.8[5]	—	—			
Your average		115.3						
Federated Funds								
Federated Mgd Agg Gro	agg gr	76.9	14.9[4]	16.4[5]	—			
Federated Mini Cap SC	agg gr	140.7	20.4[3]	20.6[4]	14.5[4]			
Federated Mgd Growth	growth	160.7	14.3[5]	15.6[5]	—			
Federated Mid Cap	growth	77.2	31.1[2]	26.0[3]	16.3[3]			
Federated Max Cap	gr-inc	1,233.9	32.7[1]	30.6[1]	19.8[2]			
Federated Mgd Gro & Inc	gr-inc	163.5	13.0[5]	12.9[5]	—			
Federated Stock	gr-inc	1,216.4	34.4[1]	30.2[1]	19.9[2]			
Federated Mgd Inc	income	71.6	10.5[5]	10.5[5]	—			
Federated Hi Yld	fix-inc	1,121.2	13.3[2]	15.0[1]	11.8[1]			
Federated Bond Idx	fix-inc	27.2	9.0[4]	—	—			
Federated US Gov Bd	fix-inc	74.2	11.7[2]	11.9[2]	8.3[3]			
Federated Inter Inc	fix-inc	152.6	8.6[3]	10.5[1]	—			
Federated GNMA	fix-inc	1,116.0	8.8[3]	9.9[3]	6.6[3]			
Federated Income	fix-inc	759.2	8.9[3]	9.6[3]	6.5[3]			
Federated US Gov 5-10	fix-inc	2.3	9.3[2]	—	—			
Federated ST Income	fix-inc	199.1	6.4[3]	7.5[2]	5.5[2]			
Federated ARMS	fix-inc	466.0	6.3[3]	7.2[3]	5.2[3]			
Federated US Gov 1-3	fix-inc	29.8	5.7[5]	6.5[5]	4.8[5]			
Federated US Gov 2-5	fix-inc	35.1	6.9[2]	7.8[2]	5.5[2]			
Federated PA Inter	fix-inc	19.5	7.5[2]	8.7[2]	—			
Federated Inter Muni	tax-free	213.2	6.9[4]	7.4[5]	5.5[5]			
Federated ST Muni	tax-free	177.9	4.5[4]	5.5[3]	4.1[5]			
Municipal Cash Res(Federated)MM	money mkt TF	548.5	3.3[1]	—	—			
Govt Cash Series(Federated)MM	money mkt gov	734.4	5.2[1]	—	—			
Your average		7,534.2						
Fidelity Investments								
Fidelity Sel Air Trans†	sector	61.1	31.1[2]	28.4[2]	16.8[4]			
Fidelity Sel Auto†	sector	59.6	16.7[4]	15.4[5]	12.7[5]			
Fidelity Sel Biotech†	sector	551.0	15.4[4]	22.0[4]	8.4[5]			
Fidelity Sel Broker†	sector	647.6	62.3[1]	41.0[1]	28.2[1]			
Fidelity Sel Chemical†	sector	68.3	16.5[4]	19.8[4]	17.3[3]			
Fidelity Sel Computer†	sector	569.4	-1.1[5]	25.5[2]	25.1[1]			
Fidelity Sel Consmr Ind†	sector	40.4	38.0[1]	26.0[2]	18.3[3]			
Fidelity Sel Const/Hous†	sector	18.1	29.6[2]	23.6[3]	16.2[4]			
Fidelity Sel Cycl Indust†	sector	3.7	—	—	—			
Fidelity Sel Defense†	sector	50.0	23.5[3]	31.5[1]	24.4[1]			
Fidelity Sel Devel Comm†	sector	203.7	5.6[5]	12.4[5]	16.6[4]			
Fidelity Sel Electronics†	sector	2,302.0	14.2[5]	39.8[1]	33.5[1]			

No-load fund groups *continued*

Families with 3 or more funds including one stock or bond fund
Arranged in alphabetical order by group and risk within group

Fund group/fund	Objective	Total Net Assets $ Millions 12/31/97	Annualized Total Return % with quintile ranks by obj			Post quintile ranks for your funds here		
			1997	3 years 1995-1997	5 years 1993-1997	1997	3 years ending 1997	5 years ending 1997
Fidelity Sel Energy Serv†	sector	1,133.4	51.9[1]	47.2[1]	31.2[1]	_____	_____	_____
Fidelity Sel Energy†	sector	158.2	10.5[5]	21.1[4]	16.3[4]	_____	_____	_____
Fidelity Sel Envir Serv†	sector	26.6	17.9[4]	19.8[4]	9.1[5]	_____	_____	_____
Fidelity Sel Financial†	sector	548.7	41.9[1]	40.3[1]	25.6[1]	_____	_____	_____
Fidelity Sel Food/Agr†	sector	309.1	30.3[2]	26.3[2]	18.4[3]	_____	_____	_____
Fidelity Sel Health†	sector	1,631.5	31.1[2]	30.2[2]	22.4[2]	_____	_____	_____
Fidelity Sel Home Finc†	sector	1,664.0	45.8[1]	45.2[1]	32.0[1]	_____	_____	_____
Fidelity Sel Indust Equip†	sector	47.7	18.8[4]	24.4[3]	23.2[1]	_____	_____	_____
Fidelity Sel Indust Mat†	sector	22.4	1.9[5]	10.3[5]	12.0[5]	_____	_____	_____
Fidelity Sel Insurance†	sector	111.7	42.5[1]	33.5[1]	20.7[2]	_____	_____	_____
Fidelity Sel Leisure†	sector	229.1	41.3[1]	26.7[2]	21.5[2]	_____	_____	_____
Fidelity Sel Medical Del†	sector	141.8	20.5[3]	20.9[4]	17.5[3]	_____	_____	_____
Fidelity Sel Multimedia†	sector	70.6	30.9[2]	21.0[4]	20.5[2]	_____	_____	_____
Fidelity Sel Nat Gas†	sector	69.3	-8.0[5]	17.4[5]	—	_____	_____	_____
Fidelity Sel Nat Rescs†	sector	8.6	—	—	—	_____	_____	_____
Fidelity Sel Pap/Forest†	sector	17.1	9.4[5]	12.6[5]	14.1[5]	_____	_____	_____
Fidelity Sel Reg Banks†	sector	1,351.8	45.5[1]	42.6[1]	26.4[1]	_____	_____	_____
Fidelity Sel Retail†	sector	191.2	41.7[1]	24.3[3]	15.6[4]	_____	_____	_____
Fidelity Sel Software†	sector	426.2	14.9[4]	26.9[2]	22.2[2]	_____	_____	_____
Fidelity Sel Technology†	sector	526.5	10.4[5]	22.4[4]	21.3[2]	_____	_____	_____
Fidelity Sel Telecomm†	sector	441.0	25.8[3]	19.8[5]	18.4[3]	_____	_____	_____
Fidelity Sel Transport†	sector	54.6	32.1[1]	18.6[5]	17.5[3]	_____	_____	_____
Fidelity Sel Amer Gold†	prec met	211.6	-39.4[2]	-6.9[1]	4.1[1]	_____	_____	_____
Fidelity Sel Prec Met†	prec met	142.1	-44.9[3]	-17.5[2]	3.3[2]	_____	_____	_____
Fidelity HK & China	int'l	180.1	-22.1[3]	—[2]	—[2]	_____	_____	_____
Fidelity Japan Sm Cap††	int'l	76.4	-30.4[5]	—	—	_____	_____	_____
Fidelity Japan††	int'l	215.8	-10.7[4]	-8.1[5]	1.7[5]	_____	_____	_____
Fidelity Pacific Bas††	int'l	213.6	-15.1[4]	-8.2[5]	4.3[4]	_____	_____	_____
Fidelity Emg Mkts††	int'l	446.5	-40.9[5]	-14.3[5]	-1.2[5]	_____	_____	_____
Fidelity Latin Amer††	int'l	860.6	32.9[1]	13.2[2]	—	_____	_____	_____
Fidelity SE Asia††	int'l	263.4	-38.9[5]	-8.9[5]	—	_____	_____	_____
Fidelity Europe Cap App††	int'l	371.6	24.9[1]	21.7[1]	—	_____	_____	_____
Fidelity Europe††	int'l	951.5	22.9[1]	22.4[1]	19.9[1]	_____	_____	_____
Fidelity France	int'l	5.6	14.5[1]	—	—	_____	_____	_____
Fidelity Germany	int'l	13.1	20.3[1]	—	—	_____	_____	_____
Fidelity Nordic	int'l	64.8	12.1[2]	—	—	_____	_____	_____
Fidelity UK	int'l	6.1	16.8[1]	—	—	_____	_____	_____
Fidelity Canada††	int'l	87.9	6.1[2]	13.7[2]	10.2[3]	_____	_____	_____
Fidelity Dvsfd Int'l	int'l	1,536.4	13.7[1]	17.2[1]	17.4[1]	_____	_____	_____
Fidelity Int'l Gr & Inc	int'l	1,030.3	7.1[2]	10.6[2]	12.2[2]	_____	_____	_____
Fidelity Int'l Value	int'l	390.7	7.8[2]	10.4[2]	—	_____	_____	_____
Fidelity Overseas	int'l	3,704.9	10.9[2]	11.0[2]	14.2[2]	_____	_____	_____
Fidelity Spart Int'l Idx†	int'l	21.3	—	—	—	_____	_____	_____
Fidelity Contrafund††‡	agg gr	30,808.5	23.0[3]	26.9[2]	19.7[1]	_____	_____	_____
Fidelity Emg Gro††	agg gr	1,981.5	19.4[3]	23.4[3]	17.6[2]	_____	_____	_____
Fidelity Export & Multi††SC	agg gr	465.3	23.7[3]	31.4[1]	—	_____	_____	_____
Fidelity Fifty	agg gr	175.0	23.0[3]	22.9[3]	—	_____	_____	_____

142

families with 3 or more funds including one stock or bond fund
arranged in alphabetical order by group and risk within group

| Fund group/fund | Objective | Total Net Assets $ Millions 12/31/97 | Annualized Total Return % with quintile ranks by obj | | | Post quintile ranks for your funds here | | |
			1997	3 years 1995-1997	5 years 1993-1997	1997	3 years ending 1997	5 years ending 1997
Fidelity Growth Co...	agg gr	10,509.4	18.9[2]	24.7[2]	17.1[1]			
Fidelity Magellan†‡	agg gr	63,766.2	26.5[2]	24.6[2]	18.8[2]			
Fidelity New Millnm†‡	agg gr	1,564.2	24.6[2]	32.6[1]	24.0[1]			
Fidelity OTC††	agg gr	3,858.1	9.9[4]	23.4[3]	14.6[4]			
Fidelity Small Cap Selector†† SC	agg gr	824.8	27.2[2]	22.3[3]	—			
Fidelity TechnoQuant Gro	agg gr	82.9	17.9[3]	—	—			
Fidelity Trend	agg gr	1,428.0	8.5[5]	15.7[5]	11.5[5]			
Fidelity Blue Chip Gro††	growth	13,428.4	27.0[3]	23.5[4]	20.8[1]			
Fidelity Cap Apprec	growth	2,109.6	26.5[3]	20.0[4]	18.8[2]			
Fidelity Discpl Eqty	growth	2,557.4	33.3[1]	25.6[3]	18.4[2]			
Fidelity Divnd Growth	growth	4,480.4	27.9[3]	31.8[1]	—			
Fidelity Freedom 2030	growth	57.0	21.4[4]	—	—			
Fidelity Large Cap	growth	139.3	24.7[3]	—	—			
Fidelity Low Pr Stk†††‡ SC	growth	10,691.1	26.7[3]	26.2[3]	20.4[1]			
Fidelity Mid-Cap Stk	growth	1,763.1	27.1[3]	26.2[3]	—			
Fidelity Retrmnt Gro	growth	3,932.2	18.5[4]	16.9[5]	14.3[4]			
Fidelity Spart Extd Market Idx†	growth	21.6	—	—	—			
Fidelity Spart Total Market Idx†	growth	20.0	—	—	—			
Fidelity Stk Selector	growth	1,895.5	28.9[2]	27.2[2]	18.8[2]			
Fidelity Value	growth	7,913.8	21.1[4]	21.6[4]	18.9[2]			
Fidelity Glob Bal	global	68.9	12.4[3]	10.5[5]	—			
Fidelity Worldwide	global	1,145.3	12.1[3]	12.6[4]	14.9[2]			
Fidelity Asst Mgr Gro	gr-inc	4,662.9	26.4[3]	21.3[4]	15.8[4]			
Fidelity Eqty Inc II	gr-inc	16,977.5	27.2[3]	24.0[4]	18.5[3]			
Fidelity Eqty Inc	gr-inc	21,177.7	30.0[2]	27.5[2]	20.3[1]			
Fidelity Freedom 2020	gr-inc	84.0	21.2[4]	—	—			
Fidelity Fund	gr-inc	6,529.6	32.1[2]	28.1[2]	20.6[1]			
Fidelity Gro & Inc‡	gr-inc	36,656.8	30.2[4]	28.4[4]	20.9[4]			
Fidelity Spart Market Idx	gr-inc	3,869.7	33.0[1]	30.7[1]	19.9[2]			
Fidelity Asst Mgr Inc	income	687.3	12.4[5]	12.2[5]	10.0[5]			
Fidelity Asst Mgr	income	12,099.0	22.3[2]	17.7[4]	13.4[3]			
Fidelity Balanced	income	4,283.9	23.4[2]	15.7[5]	11.9[5]			
Fidelity Convert	income	1,002.6	14.4[5]	16.3[5]	12.7[4]			
Fidelity Freedom 2000	income	81.4	15.3[4]	—	—			
Fidelity Freedom 2010	income	123.2	19.4[3]	—	—			
Fidelity Freedom Inc	income	29.6	10.7[5]	—	—			
Fidelity Puritan	income	22,821.8	22.4[2]	19.6[3]	16.2[1]			
Fidelity Sel Util Gro†	sector	358.9	30.3[2]	24.9[3]	15.2[4]			
Fidelity Utilities	income	1,708.7	31.6[1]	24.2[1]	16.0[2]			
Fidelity Real Est	sector	2,480.2	21.3[3]	22.4[4]	16.0[4]			
Fidelity New Mkts Inc	fix-inc	371.3	17.2[1]	21.4[1]	—			
Fidelity Cap & Inc	fix-inc	2,096.1	14.7[1]	14.1[1]	12.1[1]			
Fidelity Spart Hi Inc	fix-inc	2,446.9	15.9[1]	15.7[1]	14.2[1]			
Fidelity Target Timeline 1999	fix-inc	12.6	6.7[5]	—	—			
Fidelity Target Timeline 2001	fix-inc	11.3	8.2[4]	—	—			
Fidelity Target Timeline 2003	fix-inc	15.7	10.1[2]	—	—			
Fidelity Inv Grd Bd	fix-inc	1,649.6	8.9[4]	9.0[5]	7.3[4]			

No-load fund groups   *continued*

Families with 3 or more funds including one stock or bond fund
Arranged in alphabetical order by group and risk within group

| | | | Annualized Total Return % with quintile ranks by obj | | | Post quintile ranks for your funds here | | |
| | | Total Net Assets $ Millions 12/31/97 | 1997 | 3 years 1995-1997 | 5 years 1993-1997 | 1997 | 3 years ending 1997 | 5 years ending 1997 |
Fund group/fund	Objective							
Fidelity Spart Inv Grd	fix-inc	658.3	9.3[3]	10.1[3]	8.0[3]			
Fidelity Gov Sec	fix-inc	1,164.9	8.9[3]	9.5[2]	6.9[3]			
Fidelity Spart Gov Inc	fix-inc	279.8	9.2[3]	9.8[4]	6.5[4]			
Fidelity Int'l Bond	fix-inc	78.2	-1.3[5]	2.9[5]	2.1[5]			
Fidelity Inter Bond	fix-inc	3,193.4	7.6[4]	7.9[5]	6.7[3]			
Fidelity GNMA	fix-inc	862.5	8.7[5]	10.0[5]	6.7[5]			
Fidelity Mortg Sec(Init Class)‡	fix-inc	483.6	9.1[2]	10.4[1]	7.9[1]			
Fidelity Spart GNMA	fix-inc	593.7	8.9[2]	10.1[2]	6.9[2]			
Fidelity Spart ST Bd	fix-inc	284.1	6.5[2]	7.1[3]	5.0[4]			
Fidelity ST Bond	fix-inc	875.3	6.2[4]	6.9[3]	5.0[4]			
Fidelity S-I Gov	fix-inc	126.2	6.6[2]	7.5[2]	5.2[3]			
Fidelity Spart Ltd Mat Gov	fix-inc	758.1	7.3[1]	8.3[1]	6.0[1]			
Fidelity Spart S-I Gov	fix-inc	75.5	6.6[2]	7.7[2]	5.6[2]			
Fidelity NY Insur Muni Inc	tax-free	302.7	8.8[3]	10.2[2]	6.8[3]			
Fidelity NY Muni Inc	tax-free	444.6	9.7[2]	10.9[1]	7.2[3]			
Fidelity Spart AZ Muni	tax-free	20.5	8.0[5]	9.8[3]	—			
Fidelity Spart CA Muni Inc	tax-free	1,209.7	9.8[1]	11.1[1]	7.2[2]			
Fidelity Spart CT Muni	tax-free	344.1	9.1[2]	10.0[3]	7.0[3]			
Fidelity Spart FL Muni	tax-free	419.0	8.7[4]	10.3[2]	7.5[1]			
Fidelity Spart MA Muni Inc	tax-free	1,210.2	9.3[2]	10.2[3]	7.2[2]			
Fidelity Spart MD Muni Inc	tax-free	39.4	8.8[3]	10.0[3]	—			
Fidelity Spart MI Muni Inc	tax-free	456.2	9.1[3]	9.2[4]	6.5[4]			
Fidelity Spart MN Muni Inc	tax-free	295.8	8.8[3]	9.4[4]	6.7[4]			
Fidelity Spart NJ Muni Inc	tax-free	363.7	8.3[4]	9.2[4]	6.8[4]			
Fidelity Spart NY Muni Inc‡	tax-free	314.0	10.0[1]	11.0[1]	7.3[2]			
Fidelity Spart OH Muni Inc	tax-free	387.8	8.7[4]	9.7[3]	7.0[3]			
Fidelity Spart PA Muni Inc	tax-free	263.6	8.3[4]	9.8[3]	7.3[2]			
Fidelity Spart Agg Muni	tax-free	954.6	10.3[1]	9.5[4]	7.0[3]			
Fidelity Spart Muni Inc	tax-free	2,347.1	9.2[2]	10.0[3]	6.8[4]			
Fidelity Muni Bd(Init Class)‡	tax-free	932.8	9.2[2]	10.3[2]	6.8[3]			
Fidelity Spart Insur Muni Inc	tax-free	331.4	9.5[2]	10.5[2]	7.2[2]			
Fidelity Spart NY Inter Muni Inc‡	tax-free	53.9	8.1[1]	8.7[1]	—			
Fidelity Ltd Muni Inc	tax-free	911.8	8.3[1]	9.1[1]	6.7[1]			
Fidelity Spart Inter Muni	tax-free	196.8	8.0[1]	8.9[1]	—			
Fidelity Spart S-I Muni	tax-free	699.5	5.5[2]	5.9[2]	4.9[1]			
Fidelity Cash Res MM	money mkt gen	23,337.9	5.3[2]	5.4[2]	4.6[1]			
Fidelity Daily Inc MM	money mkt gen	2,491.9	5.3[2]	5.4[2]	4.5[2]			
Fidelity Select MM	money mkt gen	775.7	5.2[3]	5.2[3]	4.4[3]			
Fidelity Spart MM	money mkt gen	8,605.1	5.4[1]	5.5[1]	4.7[1]			
Fidelity CA Muni MM	money mkt TF	910.0	3.1[4]	3.2[3]	2.8[3]			
Fidelity CT Muni MM	money mkt TF	407.1	3.1[4]	3.2[4]	2.8[4]			
Fidelity MA Muni MM	money mkt TF	1,156.8	3.1[3]	3.2[4]	2.7[5]			
Fidelity MI Muni MM	money mkt TF	285.8	3.2[2]	3.3[3]	2.9[3]			
Fidelity Muni MM	money mkt TF	4,307.0	3.3[1]	3.4[2]	3.0[1]			
Fidelity NJ Muni MM	money mkt TF	506.3	3.0[4]	3.2[4]	2.8[4]			
Fidelity NY Muni MM	money mkt TF	998.7	3.1[3]	3.3[3]	2.8[3]			
Fidelity OH Muni MM	money mkt TF	361.6	3.3[2]	3.4[2]	3.0[2]			

*milies with 3 or more funds including one stock or bond fund
ranged in alphabetical order by group and risk within group*

| Fund group/fund | Objective | Total Net Assets $ Millions 12/31/97 | Annualized Total Return % with quintile ranks by obj | | | Post quintile ranks for your funds here | | |
			1997	3 years 1995-1997	5 years 1993-1997	1997	3 years ending 1997	5 years ending 1997
Fidelity Spart AZ MM	money mkt TF	84.5	3.5[1]	3.7[1]	—	___	___	___
Fidelity Spart CA Muni MM	money mkt TF	1,367.6	3.3[2]	3.5[1]	3.2[1]	___	___	___
Fidelity Spart CT Muni MM	money mkt TF	160.4	3.1[3]	3.3[3]	2.9[2]	___	___	___
Fidelity Spart FL Muni MM	money mkt TF	990.9	3.3[2]	3.5[1]	3.1[1]	___	___	___
Fidelity Spart MA MM	money mkt TF	729.3	3.2[3]	3.3[3]	2.8[3]	___	___	___
Fidelity Spart Muni MM	money mkt TF	2,124.3	3.5[1]	3.6[1]	3.2[1]	___	___	___
Fidelity Spart NJ Muni MM	money mkt TF	508.5	3.2[2]	3.5[1]	3.0[2]	___	___	___
Fidelity Spart NY Muni MM	money mkt TF	752.7	3.3[2]	3.4[2]	2.9[2]	___	___	___
Fidelity Spart PA Muni MM	money mkt TF	228.9	3.4[1]	3.5[1]	3.1[1]	___	___	___
Fidelity Spart US Gov MM	money mkt gov	778.2	5.3[1]	5.4[1]	4.6[1]	___	___	___
Fidelity Spart US Trsy MM	money mkt gov	2,059.9	5.0[2]	5.1[2]	4.4[2]	___	___	___
Fidelity US Gov Res	money mkt gov	1219.5	5.3[1]	5.3[1]	4.5[1]	___	___	___
Your average		409,557.7				___	___	___
First Omaha Funds								
First Omaha Small Cap Val	growth	12.8	21.8[4]	—	—	___	___	___
First Omaha Eqty	gr-inc	287.3	19.3[5]	20.6[5]	15.9[4]	___	___	___
First Omaha Balanced	income	21.1	15.0[5]	—	—	___	___	___
First Omaha Fix Inc	fix-inc	80.0	9.5[3]	10.0[4]	7.1[4]	___	___	___
First Omaha S-I Fix	fix-inc	19.5	6.7[2]	7.5[2]	5.5[2]	___	___	___
First Omaha US Gov Oblg MM	money mkt gov	93.9	4.9[3]	5.0[3]	4.2[3]	___	___	___
Your average		514.6				___	___	___
Flex-Funds								
Flex-Partners Int'l Eqty†	int'l	12.2	—	—	—	___	___	___
Flex-Fund Highlands Gro	growth	29.0	29.3[2]	20.7[4]	13.3[5]	___	___	___
Flex-Fund Muirfield	gr-inc	111.2	18.6[5]	16.5[5]	11.9[5]	___	___	___
Flex-Fund Tot Ret Util	income	7.6	28.7[1]	—	—	___	___	___
Flex-Fund US Gov Bond	fix-inc	16.8	7.8[4]	8.5[4]	6.5[4]	___	___	___
Flex-Fund MM	money mkt gen	168.6	5.4[1]	5.5[1]	4.7[1]	___	___	___
Your average		345.4				___	___	___
Fontaine Funds								
Fontaine Cap App	agg gr	4.0	-27.3[5]	-1.2[5]	2.4[5]	___	___	___
Fontaine Glob Gro	global	2.0	-44.9[5]	-4.9[5]	-0.5[5]	___	___	___
Fontaine Glob Inc	fix-inc	1.1	-27.3[5]	-1.9[5]	2.9[5]	___	___	___
Your average		7.1				___	___	___
Founders Funds								
Founders Discovery SC	agg gr	247.3	11.9[4]	21.2[4]	12.7[4]	___	___	___
Founders Frontier SC	agg gr	222.7	6.2[5]	18.5[4]	13.5[4]	___	___	___
Founders Growth	agg gr	1,758.3	26.5[2]	29.0[1]	21.1[1]	___	___	___
Founders Special	agg gr	320.3	16.4[4]	19.1[4]	13.2[4]	___	___	___
Founders Int'l Equity	int'l	15.6	16.1[1]	—	—	___	___	___
Founders Passport	int'l	123.3	1.7[3]	14.9[1]	—	___	___	___

No-load fund groups *continued*

Families with 3 or more funds including one stock or bond fund
Arranged in alphabetical order by group and risk within group

| Fund group/fund | Objective | Total Net Assets $ Millions 12/31/97 | Annualized Total Return % with quintile ranks by obj | | | Post quintile ranks for your funds here | | |
			1997	3 years 1995-1997	5 years 1993-1997	1997	3 years ending 1997	5 years ending 1997
Founders Worldwide Gr	global	308.9	10.5³	15.0⁴	14.1²	___	___	___
Founders Blue Chip	gr-inc	543.3	19.0⁵	24.1⁴	17.1³	___	___	___
Founders Balanced	income	937.2	16.9⁴	23.6¹	17.7¹	___	___	___
Founders Gov Sec	fix-inc	12.7	7.9⁴	7.0⁵	4.4⁵	___	___	___
Founders Money Mkt	money mkt gen	105.5	4.8⁵	4.9⁵	4.1⁵	___	___	___
Your average		4,595.1				___	___	___
Fremont Funds								
Fremont Emg Mkts	int'l	13.8	10.4²	—	—	___	___	___
Fremont Int'l Gro	int'l	36.3	-8.4⁴	3.5⁴	—	___	___	___
Fremont Int'l Sm Cap	int'l	6.5	-26.5⁵	-5.4⁵	—	___	___	___
Fremont Select	agg gr	5.0	—	—	—	___	___	___
Fremont US Micro Cap SC	agg gr	166.9	7.0⁵	34.8¹	—	___	___	___
Fremont US Sm Cap SC	agg gr	5.6	—	—	—	___	___	___
Fremont Growth	growth	155.5	29.0²	29.2²	18.2²	___	___	___
Fremont Global	global	661.6	9.9⁴	14.3⁴	11.4³	___	___	___
Fremont Real Estate	sector	1.0	—	—	—	___	___	___
Fremont Bond	fix-inc	109.4	9.7¹	11.9¹	—	___	___	___
Fremont CA Inter TF	tax-free	64.8	7.3³	8.6²	6.1³	___	___	___
Fremont Money Mkt	money mkt gen	484.2	5.4¹	5.5¹	4.6¹	___	___	___
Your average		1,710.5				___	___	___
FTI Funds								
FTI Small Cap Eqty SC	agg gr	42.3	17.8³	—	—	___	___	___
FTI Int'l Eqty	int'l	43.5	13.3¹	—	—	___	___	___
FTI Int'l Bond	fix-inc	7.3	-6.1⁵	—	—	___	___	___
FTI Global Bond	fix-inc	1.4	-0.2⁵	—	—	___	___	___
Your average		94.5				___	___	___
Fundamental Funds								
Fundamental US Gov Strat	fix-inc	10.0	5.5⁵	8.5⁵	0.6⁵	___	___	___
Fundamental CA Muni	tax-free	8.9	11.3¹	10.6²	4.8⁵	___	___	___
Fundamental NY Muni	tax-free	77.1	1.5⁵	2.8⁵	-0.6⁵	___	___	___
Fundamental HY Muni	tax-free	1.8	15.7¹	14.8¹	6.7⁴	___	___	___
Fundamental TF MM	money mkt TF	76.8	2.2⁵	2.5⁵	2.1⁵	___	___	___
Your average		174.6				___	___	___
FundManager Funds								
FundManager Agg Gro†	agg gr	38.0	16.7⁴	19.3⁴	13.9⁴	___	___	___
FundManager Growth†	growth	39.6	27.5³	24.9³	16.9³	___	___	___
FundManager Gro & Inc†	gr-inc	40.9	25.3⁴	24.3⁴	16.7⁴	___	___	___
FundManager Mgd Tot Ret†	gr-inc	10.7	13.5⁵	13.6⁵	9.6⁵	___	___	___
FundManager Bond†	fix-inc	50.6	7.8⁴	8.8⁴	6.5⁴	___	___	___
Your average		179.8				___	___	___

o-load fund groups *continued*

milies with 3 or more funds including one stock or bond fund
ranged in alphabetical order by group and risk within group

Fund group/fund	Objective	Total Net Assets $ Millions 12/31/97	Annualized Total Return % with quintile ranks by obj			Post quintile ranks for your funds here		
			1997	3 years 1995-1997	5 years 1993-1997	1997	3 years ending 1997	5 years ending 1997
Gabelli Funds								
Gabelli Gold	prec met	8.1	-51.9[4]	-18.8[2]	—	____	____	____
Gabelli Glbl Interact Couch Potato	global	40.6	41.7[1]	23.4[1]	—	____	____	____
Gabelli Int'l Growth	int'l	18.1	7.3[2]	—	—	____	____	____
Gabelli Sm Cap Gro SC	agg gr	293.0	36.5[1]	24.1[3]	17.9[2]	____	____	____
Westwood Sm Cap Eqty SC	agg gr	9.2	—	—	—	____	____	____
Gabelli ABC	growth	35.2	12.8[5]	10.6[5]	—	____	____	____
Gabelli Asset	growth	1,334.2	38.1[1]	25.1[3]	18.9[2]	____	____	____
Gabelli Growth	growth	951.5	42.6[1]	31.2[1]	19.4[2]	____	____	____
Gabelli Glbl Conv Sec	global	9.4	2.8[5]	6.9[5]	—	____	____	____
Gabelli Glbl Telecomm	global	117.9	31.9[1]	18.6[3]	—	____	____	____
Westwood Equity	gr-inc	150.5	29.6[2]	31.0[1]	21.9[1]	____	____	____
Gabelli Eqty Inc	income	76.3	27.9[1]	24.6[1]	18.2[1]	____	____	____
Westwood Balanced	income	80.6	22.5[2]	23.8[1]	17.3[1]	____	____	____
Westwood Realty	sector	1.8	—	—	—	____	____	____
Westwood Inter Bd	fix-inc	6.2	10.7[1]	10.1[2]	6.8[3]	____	____	____
Gabelli Treas MM	money mkt gov	283.2	5.3[1]	5.2[2]	4.5[2]	____	____	____
Your average		3,415.8				____	____	____
Galaxy Funds								
Galaxy II Sm Co Idx SC	agg gr	379.2	23.6[3]	25.3[2]	16.1[3]	____	____	____
Galaxy II Lg Co Idx	gr-inc	547.1	32.8[1]	30.7[1]	19.8[2]	____	____	____
Galaxy II Util Idx	income	55.2	28.5[1]	22.2[2]	—	____	____	____
Galaxy II US Trsy Idx	fix-inc	115.5	9.3[3]	9.7[4]	7.0[4]	____	____	____
Galaxy Money Mkt	money mkt gen	1,937.2	5.0[4]	5.0[4]	4.3[4]	____	____	____
Your average		3,034.2				____	____	____
Gateway Funds								
Gateway Sm Cap Idx SC	agg gr	15.8	20.6[3]	19.8[4]	—	____	____	____
Gateway Cincinnati	growth	17.5	29.0[2]	27.9[2]	—	____	____	____
Gateway MidCap Idx	growth	8.0	25.0[3]	21.9[4]	12.6[5]	____	____	____
Gateway Idx Plus	gr-inc	254.9	12.3[5]	11.3[5]	9.3[5]	____	____	____
Your average		296.2				____	____	____
Government Street Funds								
Govt Street Equity	growth	66.2	27.8[3]	25.6[3]	14.7[4]	____	____	____
Govt Street Bond	fix-inc	34.4	7.8[4]	8.9[4]	6.5[4]	____	____	____
Gov Street AL TF	tax-free	19.4	6.3[5]	7.4[5]	—	____	____	____
Your average		120.0				____	____	____
Gradison Mutual Funds								
Gradison Oppty Value SC	agg gr	157.2	31.1[1]	25.7[2]	16.6[3]	____	____	____
Gradison International	int'l	27.9	5.1[3]	—	—	____	____	____
Gradison Estab Value	gr-inc	522.3	22.6[4]	22.6[4]	17.8[3]	____	____	____
Gradison Gro & Inc	gr-inc	47.6	30.1[2]	—	—	____	____	____
Gradison US Gov MM	money mkt gov	1,650.6	4.9[3]	5.0[4]	4.2[4]	____	____	____
Your average		2,405.6				____	____	____

No-load fund groups *continued*

Families with 3 or more funds including one stock or bond fund
Arranged in alphabetical order by group and risk within group

| Fund group/fund | Objective | Total Net Assets $ Millions 12/31/97 | Annualized Total Return % with quintile ranks by obj | | | Post quintile ranks for your funds here | | |
			1997	3 years 1995-1997	5 years 1993-1997	1997	3 years ending 1997	5 years ending 1997
Guinness Flight Funds								
Guinness Flt Asia Blue Chip	int'l	6.9	-37.7[5]	—	—			
Guinness Flt Asia Small Cap	int'l	109.4	-30.8[5]	—	—			
Guinness Flt China & HK	int'l	242.8	-20.3[5]	8.9[3]	—			
Guinness Flt Mainland China	int'l	16.3	—	—	—			
Guinness Flt Glob Gov	fix-inc	10.0	2.9[5]	7.8[5]	—			
Your average		385.4						
Harbor Funds								
Harbor Cap App	agg gr	2,906.3	31.4[1]	29.5[1]	20.3[1]			
Harbor Growth	agg gr	109.8	20.9[3]	22.9[3]	14.2[4]			
Harbor Int'l Gro	int'l	943.8	3.6[3]	19.3[1]	—			
Harbor Int'l II	int'l	130.2	9.7[2]	—	—			
Harbor Int'l‡	int'l	5,276.6	15.5[1]	17.2[1]	19.8[1]			
Harbor Value	gr-inc	174.8	31.2[2]	28.7[2]	18.4[3]			
Harbor Bond	fix-inc	384.6	9.4[2]	11.0[1]	8.1[1]			
Harbor Short Dur	fix-inc	165.5	6.3[3]	6.7[4]	5.4[3]			
Harbor Money Mkt	money mkt gen	85.2	5.2[3]	5.3[3]	4.5[2]			
Your average		10,176.8						
Heartland Funds								
Heartland Small Cap Contra‡SC	agg gr	276.6	13.7[4]	—	—			
Heartland Large Cap Val	growth	7.7	22.9[4]	—	—			
Heartland Mid Cap Val	growth	36.6	22.8[4]	—	—			
Heartland Value‡SC	growth	2,126.7	23.2[4]	24.6[3]	18.5[2]			
Heartland Val Plus	gr-inc	336.3	30.6[2]	29.5[2]	—			
Heartland US Gov	fix-inc	48.6	9.7[1]	10.0[1]	7.2[1]			
Heartland WI TF	tax-free	131.3	8.1[5]	9.7[3]	6.5[4]			
Heartland Hi Yld Muni	tax-free	30.6	—	—	—			
Heartland Sht Dur Hi Yld Muni	tax-free	116.3	7.4[1]	—	—			
Firstar Money Mkt*	money mkt gen	254.0	5.1[3]	5.2[3]	4.4[3]			
Your average		3,110.7						
Homestead Funds								
Homestead Value	gr-inc	367.0	26.7[3]	26.0[3]	19.5[2]			
Homestead ST Bond	fix-inc	108.6	6.6[2]	7.5[2]	5.8[1]			
Homestead ST Gov	fix-inc	16.1	5.7[5]	—	—			
Homestead Daily Inc MM	money mkt gen	53.0	5.0[4]	—	—			
Your average		544.7						
Hotchkis & Wiley Funds								
Htchks & Wly Midcap	agg gr	5.2	—	—	—			
Htchks & Wly Int'l	int'l	1,041.9	5.3[3]	14.3[1]	16.2[1]			
Htchks & Wly Sm Cap SC	growth	60.0	39.5[1]	23.6[4]	16.5[3]			
Htchks & Wly Glob Eqty	global	5.3	—	—	—			

milies with 3 or more funds including one stock or bond fund
ranged in alphabetical order by group and risk within group

| Fund group/fund | Objective | Total Net Assets $ Millions 12/31/97 | Annualized Total Return % with quintile ranks by obj | | | Post quintile ranks for your funds here | | |
			1997	3 years 1995-1997	5 years 1993-1997	1997	3 years ending 1997	5 years ending 1997
Htchks & Wly Eq Inc	gr-inc	196.9	31.2[2]	27.4[3]	18.3[3]	___	___	___
Htchks & Wly Balanced	income	104.1	16.8[4]	17.6[4]	13.0[4]	___	___	___
Htchks & Wly Tot Ret	fix-inc	18.3	10.8[1]	12.0[1]	—	___	___	___
Htchks & Wly Low Dur	fix-inc	194.1	7.6[1]	8.8[1]	—	___	___	___
Htchks & Wly ST Invest	fix-inc	22.2	6.5[2]	6.8[4]	—	___	___	___
Your average		1,648.0				___	___	___
AA Funds								
IAA Trust Growth	growth	145.8	19.7[4]	24.2[3]	15.3[4]	___	___	___
IAA Trust Asst Alloc	income	15.3	17.9[4]	18.6[4]	12.5[4]	___	___	___
IAA Trust LT Bd	fix-inc	36.5	—	—	—	___	___	___
IAA Trust ST Gov	fix-inc	26.4	—	—	—	___	___	___
IAA Trust TE Bd	tax-free	17.9	9.0[3]	9.1[4]	5.8[5]	___	___	___
IAA Trust MM	money mkt gen	59.0	4.8[5]	—	—	___	___	___
Your average		300.9				___	___	___
AI Funds								
IAI Develop Countries	int'l	8.6	-14.1[4]	—	—	___	___	___
IAI Latin Amer	int'l	2.6	18.7[1]	—	—	___	___	___
IAI International	int'l	73.1	-4.2[4]	4.2[4]	9.7[4]	___	___	___
IAI Cap Apprec SC	agg gr	57.5	17.8[3]	—	—	___	___	___
IAI Emg Growth SC	agg gr	324.7	-2.9[5]	15.8[5]	12.3[5]	___	___	___
IAI Growth	growth	13.2	19.2[4]	19.2[5]	—	___	___	___
IAI MidCap	growth	95.4	8.9[5]	17.0[5]	15.7[4]	___	___	___
IAI Regional	growth	501.7	18.9[4]	22.2[4]	14.8[4]	___	___	___
IAI Value	growth	27.2	19.6[4]	21.9[4]	15.0[4]	___	___	___
IAI Gro & Inc	gr-inc	88.7	23.9[4]	23.7[4]	14.7[4]	___	___	___
IAI Balanced	income	31.9	25.7[1]	19.6[3]	12.1[4]	___	___	___
IAI Bond	fix-inc	68.7	10.8[2]	10.3[3]	7.4[3]	___	___	___
IAI Reserve	fix-inc	32.3	4.6[5]	5.3[5]	4.3[5]	___	___	___
IAI Gov Bond	fix-inc	18.0	6.4[3]	6.9[4]	5.3[3]	___	___	___
IAI Money Mkt	money mkt gen	23.4	5.1[4]	5.1[4]	4.4[3]	___	___	___
Your average		1,367.0				___	___	___
ndependence One Funds								
Independence One Eqty Plus	gr-inc	186.7	28.7[3]	—	—	___	___	___
Independence One Fix Inc	fix-inc	77.7	7.5[4]	—	—	___	___	___
Independence One US Gov Sec	fix-inc	72.3	9.1[2]	9.6[3]	—	___	___	___
Independence One MI Muni	fix-inc	26.0	7.7[5]	—	—	___	___	___
Independence One Prime MM	money mkt gen	374.5	5.1[3]	—	—	___	___	___
Independence One MI Muni MM	money mkt TF	91.9	3.2[2]	—	—	___	___	___
Indepence One US Treas MM	money mkt gov	259.6	5.0[3]	—	—	___	___	___
Your average		1,088.7				___	___	___

No-load fund groups *continued*

Families with 3 or more funds including one stock or bond fund
Arranged in alphabetical order by group and risk within group

Fund group/fund	Objective	Total Net Assets $ Millions 12/31/97	Annualized Total Return % with quintile ranks by obj — 1997	3 years 1995-1997	5 years 1993-1997	Post quintile ranks for your funds here — 1997	3 years ending 1997	5 years ending 1997
Invesco Funds Group								
Invesco Strat Enrgy	sector	67.3	19.1[3]	25.6[2]	16.5[4]	_____	_____	_____
Invesco Strat Envrn	sector	212.1	16.6[4]	25.0[3]	10.5[5]	_____	_____	_____
Invesco Strat Fncl	sector	20.5	44.8[1]	38.2[1]	24.3[1]	_____	_____	_____
Invesco Strat Hlth	sector	127.6	18.4[4]	28.0[2]	14.1[5]	_____	_____	_____
Invesco Strat Leis	sector	945.8	26.5[3]	16.9[5]	15.5[4]	_____	_____	_____
Invesco Strat Tech	sector	222.7	8.8[5]	24.6[3]	18.5[3]	_____	_____	_____
Invesco Wrld Cap Gds	sector	16.9	27.8[2]	16.6[5]	—	_____	_____	_____
Invesco Strat Gold	prec met	1,307.2	-55.5[4]	-11.0[1]	-2.6[5]	_____	_____	_____
Invesco Pacific Bas	int'l	16.6	-36.9[5]	-13.4[5]	-0.6[5]	_____	_____	_____
Invesco Asia Growth	int'l	12.8	-38.5[5]	—	—	_____	_____	_____
Invesco Latin Amer	int'l	47.9	19.3[1]	—	—	_____	_____	_____
Invesco Europe Sm Co	int'l	51.4	-3.1[4]	—	—	_____	_____	_____
Invesco Europe	int'l	331.3	15.1[1]	21.2[1]	16.6[1]	_____	_____	_____
Invesco Int'l Gro	int'l	4,858.8	-1.9[4]	6.0[3]	8.9[4]	_____	_____	_____
Invesco Dynamics	agg gr	1,120.5	24.1[2]	25.5[2]	18.2[2]	_____	_____	_____
Invesco Sm Co Gro SC	agg gr	331.8	18.3[3]	19.7[4]	15.3[3]	_____	_____	_____
Invesco Small Co Val SC	agg gr	313.6	25.0[2]	21.4[4]	—	_____	_____	_____
Invesco Growth	growth	53.5	27.2[3]	25.9[3]	16.5[3]	_____	_____	_____
Invesco Wrld Comm	global	83.6	30.3[1]	24.7[2]	—	_____	_____	_____
Invesco Indust Inc	gr-inc	588.3	26.4[3]	23.4[4]	16.1[4]	_____	_____	_____
Invesco S&P 500 Idx II	gr-inc	1.0	—	—	—	_____	_____	_____
Invesco Value Eqty	gr-inc	379.1	28.0[3]	25.6[3]	17.9[3]	_____	_____	_____
Invesco Balanced	income	167.7	19.5[3]	23.2[2]	—	_____	_____	_____
Invesco Multi-Asst	income	80.3	19.1[3]	20.3[3]	—	_____	_____	_____
Invesco Total Ret	income	218.7	25.0[2]	22.1[2]	15.9[2]	_____	_____	_____
Invesco Strat Util	sector	1,021.3	24.4[3]	20.7[4]	13.9[5]	_____	_____	_____
Invesco Realty	sector	47.6	21.1[3]	—	—	_____	_____	_____
Invesco High Yld	fix-inc	753.3	17.1[1]	16.3[1]	11.6[1]	_____	_____	_____
Invesco Select Inc	fix-inc	53.1	11.7[2]	12.1[2]	9.2[2]	_____	_____	_____
Invesco US Gov Sec	fix-inc	2,160.7	12.2[2]	11.3[3]	7.1[4]	_____	_____	_____
Invesco ST Bond	fix-inc	15.5	6.7[2]	7.1[3]	—	_____	_____	_____
Invesco Inter Gov	fix-inc	50.3	6.2[4]	7.9[1]	6.0[1]	_____	_____	_____
Invesco TF Long	tax-free	212.5	8.7[4]	8.8[5]	6.5[4]	_____	_____	_____
Invesco TF Inter	tax-free	4.7	6.4[5]	7.3[5]	—	_____	_____	_____
Invesco Cash Res	money mkt gen	599.0	4.8[5]	4.9[5]	4.2[5]	_____	_____	_____
Invesco TF MM	money mkt TF	47.8	3.0[4]	3.2[4]	2.7[4]	_____	_____	_____
Invesco Gov MM	money mkt gov	64.7	4.7[5]	4.8[5]	4.0[5]	_____	_____	_____
Your average		16,607.5				_____	_____	_____
Janus Funds								
Janus Mercury	agg gr	1,911.5	11.9[4]	20.5[4]	—	_____	_____	_____
Janus Spec Situations	agg gr	389.4	46.0[1]	—	—	_____	_____	_____
Janus Twenty	agg gr	6,003.6	29.7[2]	31.2[1]	16.9[3]	_____	_____	_____
Janus Overseas	int'l	3,240.9	18.2[1]	23.0[1]	—	_____	_____	_____
Janus Enterprise	growth	573.1	10.8[5]	16.3[5]	14.7[4]	_____	_____	_____
Janus Fund	growth	19,200.2	22.7[4]	23.8[4]	15.8[4]	_____	_____	_____

150

milies with 3 or more funds including one stock or bond fund
ranged in alphabetical order by group and risk within group

Fund group/fund	Objective	Total Net Assets $ Millions 12/31/97	Annualized Total Return % with quintile ranks by obj 1997	3 years 1995-1997	5 years 1993-1997	Post quintile ranks for your funds here 1997	3 years ending 1997	5 years ending 1997
Janus Gro & Inc	growth	2004.6	34.7[1]	32.3[1]	18.6[2]			
Janus Olympus	growth	629.2	26.7[3]	—	—			
Janus Venture‡SC	growth	1,234.3	13.1[5]	15.6[5]	12.2[5]			
Janus Worldwide	global	10,567.8	20.5[1]	22.9[2]	19.8[1]			
Janus Equity Inc	gr-inc	88.6	31.1[2]	—	—			
Janus Balanced	income	369.4	21.8[3]	21.4[2]	14.6[2]			
Janus High Yld	fix-inc	367.4	15.4[1]	—	—			
Janus Flex Inc	fix-inc	766.4	11.4[1]	13.0[1]	10.1[1]			
Janus ST Bond	fix-inc	69.1	6.6[2]	6.9[3]	5.4[2]			
Janus Federal TE	tax-free	62.8	9.0[3]	9.7[3]	—			
Janus MM	money mkt gen	947.7	5.3[2]	—	—			
Janus TE MM	money mkt TF	80.7	3.2[2]	—	—			
Janus Gov MM	money mkt gov	129.7	5.1[2]	—	—			
Your average		48,636.4						
P Morgan Funds								
JP Morgan Japan Eqty	int'l	0.8	-30.8[5]	—	—			
JP Morgan Emg Mkts Eqty	int'l	58.1	-7.6[4]	-3.4[4]	—			
JP Morgan Euro Eqty	int'l	4.8	22.1[1]	—	—			
JP Morgan Int'l Eqty	int'l	113.6	1.2[3]	5.7[4]	9.2[4]			
JP Morgan Int'l Oppty	int'l	72.7	—	—	—			
JP Morgan US Sm Co SC	agg gr	264.2	22.8[3]	25.0[2]	14.8[4]			
JP Morgan US Sm Co Opp SC	agg gr	112.2	—	—	—			
JP Morgan Shrs Tax Aware Disc Eqty	growth	30.0	—	—	—			
JP Morgan Shrs Tax Aware US Eqty	growth	32.9	30.3[2]	—	—			
JP Morgan US Eqty	gr-inc	398.5	28.4[3]	27.2[3]	17.8[3]			
JP Morgan Diversified	income	100.3	18.5[4]	19.3[4]	—			
JP Morgan Emg Mkts Debt	fix-inc	12.0	—	—	—			
JP Morgan Bond	fix-inc	176.6	9.1[3]	10.0[4]	7.2[4]			
JP Morgan ST Bond	fix-inc	19.3	6.1[4]	7.2[3]	—			
JP Morgan NY Tot Ret	tax-free	75.7	7.4[5]	8.1[5]	—			
JP Morgan TE Bond	tax-free	390.3	7.4[5]	8.0[5]	6.1[5]			
JP Morgan Shrs CA Bond	tax-free	4.3	—	—	—			
JP Morgan Prime MM	money mkt gen	2,076.8	5.4[1]	—	—			
JP Morgan TE MM	money mkt TF	1,034.5	3.3[2]	—	—			
JP Morgan Fed MM	money mkt gov	375.7	5.2[1]	—	—			
Your average		5,353.3						
Kayne Anderson Funds								
Kayne Anderson Int'l Ris Div	int'l	7.0	17.4[1]	—	—			
Kayne Anderson Sm-Mid Cap Ris Div	agg gr	6.5	19.5[3]	—	—			
Kayne Anderson Ris Div	gr-inc	35.3	31.0[2]	—	—			
Kayne Anderson Inter Tot Ret	fix-inc	6.3	7.2[5]	—	—			
Kayne Anderson Inter TF	fix-inc	6.0	4.2[5]	—	—			
Your average		61.1						

No-load fund groups *continued*

Families with 3 or more funds including one stock or bond fund
Arranged in alphabetical order by group and risk within group

| Fund group/fund | Objective | Total Net Assets $ Millions 12/31/97 | Annualized Total Return % with quintile ranks by obj | | | Post quintile ranks for your funds here | | |
			1997	3 years 1995-1997	5 years 1993-1997	1997	3 years ending 1997	5 years ending 1997
Kent Funds								
Kent Sm Co Gro SC...............	agg gr	22.8	27.7[2]	23.4[3]	17.1[2]	_____	_____	_____
Kent Int'l Gro..................	int'l	9.8	2.3[3]	6.8[3]	10.8[3]	_____	_____	_____
Kent Gro & Inc.................	gr-inc	35.3	23.9[4]	25.7[3]	18.0[3]	_____	_____	_____
Kent Idx Eqty..................	gr-inc	27.9	32.2[2]	29.8[2]	19.3[2]	_____	_____	_____
Kent Income...................	fix-inc	5.6	10.0[3]	—	—	_____	_____	_____
Kent Inter Bd..................	fix-inc	7.0	7.6[4]	8.6[4]	6.1[4]	_____	_____	_____
Kent ST Bd....................	fix-inc	7.4	6.3[3]	6.8[4]	4.9[4]	_____	_____	_____
Kent TF Inc...................	tax-free	1.7	8.3[4]	—	—	_____	_____	_____
Kent Inter TF.................	tax-free	3.5	6.8[4]	7.5[5]	5.5[5]	_____	_____	_____
Kent MI Muni Bond.............	tax-free	4.4	5.4[2]	5.6[3]	—	_____	_____	_____
Kent Ltd Trm TF...............	tax-free	0.5	4.6[4]	5.5[3]	—	_____	_____	_____
Kent MM......................	money mkt gen	563.0	5.2[2]	—	—	_____	_____	_____
Kent MI Muni MM..............	money mkt TF	211.7	3.3[2]	—	—	_____	_____	_____
Kent Gov MM..................	money mkt gov	98.0	5.1[2]	—	—	_____	_____	_____
Your average................		998.6				_____	_____	_____
Kiewit Funds								
Kiewit Eqty Fund..............	growth	98.2	26.1[3]	—	—	_____	_____	_____
Kiewit Inter Bond.............	fix-inc	247.5	8.1[4]	8.5[4]	—	_____	_____	_____
Kiewit Sht Term Gov...........	fix-inc	255.5	6.3[3]	6.8[4]	—	_____	_____	_____
Kiewit Tax Exempt.............	tax-free	157.3	6.2[5]	6.5[5]	—	_____	_____	_____
Kiewit MMP...................	money mkt gen	518.0	5.5[1]	—	—	_____	_____	_____
Your average................		1,276.5				_____	_____	_____
Kobren Insight Funds								
Kobren Insight:Growth.........	growth	62.6	15.0[5]	—	—	_____	_____	_____
Kobren Insight:Mod Gro........	gr-inc	43.4	23.3[4]	—	—	_____	_____	_____
Kobren Insight:Cons Alloc.....	income	17.5	20.7[3]	—	—	_____	_____	_____
Your average................		123.5				_____	_____	_____
Lancaster Funds								
Lancaster Crestone Sm Cap SC..	agg gr	7.5	8.5[5]	17.8[4]	13.5[4]	_____	_____	_____
Lancaster Cap Builder.........	growth	9.3	19.4[4]	—	—	_____	_____	_____
Lancaster Convert.............	income	3.4	22.4[2]	21.1[2]	13.7[2]	_____	_____	_____
Lancaster Gov Qual Bond.......	fix-inc	1.2	7.0[5]	7.5[5]	5.4[5]	_____	_____	_____
Lancaster MM.................	money mkt gen	47.9	5.1[3]	5.1[4]	4.3[4]	_____	_____	_____
Your average................		69.3				_____	_____	_____
The Lazard Portfolios								
Lazard Emg Mkt(O shrs)........	int'l	7.8	-9.8[4]	1.6[4]	—	_____	_____	_____
Lazard Int'l Eqty(O shrs).....	int'l	10.9	11.8[2]	13.5[2]	14.0[2]	_____	_____	_____
Lazard Int'l Sm Cap(O shrs)...	int'l	1.9	0.3[3]	5.7[3]	—	_____	_____	_____
Lazard Bantam Val SC(O shrs)..	agg gr	8.4	33.9[1]	—	—	_____	_____	_____
Lazard Mid Cap(O shrs)........	agg gr	1.8	—	—	—	_____	_____	_____
Lazard Small Cap SC(O shrs)...	agg gr	46.2	28.1[2]	24.5[2]	20.7[1]	_____	_____	_____
Lazard Equity(O shrs).........	growth	22.9	25.1[3]	27.4[2]	20.6[1]	_____	_____	_____

amilies with 3 or more funds including one stock or bond fund
rranged in alphabetical order by group and risk within group

Fund group/fund	Objective	Total Net Assets $ Millions 12/31/97	Annualized Total Return % with quintile ranks by obj			Post quintile ranks for your funds here		
			1997	3 years 1995-1997	5 years 1993-1997	1997	3 years ending 1997	5 years ending 1997
Lazard Global Eqty(O shrs)	global	2.3	15.3^{2}	—	—			
Lazard Int'l Fix Inc(O shrs)	fix-inc	2.8	-5.7^{5}	5.9^{5}	7.4^{3}			
Lazard Strat Yld(O shrs)	fix-inc	15.3	5.2^{5}	10.8^{3}	8.9^{2}			
Lazard Bond(O shrs)	fix-inc	7.3	8.4^{4}	9.6^{4}	6.4^{5}			
Your average		127.6						
egg Mason Funds								
Legg Mason Emg Mkts	int'l	65.3	-6.2^{4}	—	—			
Legg Mason Int'l Eqty	int'l	228.6	1.8^{3}	—	—			
Legg Mason Spec Invest SC	agg gr	1,366.8	22.1^{3}	24.4^{3}	15.7^{3}			
Legg Mason Amer Lead	growth	172.0	23.8^{4}	25.0^{3}	—			
Legg Mason Total Ret	growth	598.6	37.5^{1}	33.0^{1}	20.0^{1}			
Legg Mason Value	growth	3,683.1	37.1^{1}	38.7^{1}	24.7^{1}			
Legg Mason Balanced	income	34.5	18.7^{4}	—	—			
Legg Mason High Yld	fix-inc	380.4	15.9^{1}	16.3^{1}	—			
Legg Mason Invest Grd	fix-inc	121.7	10.3^{2}	11.4^{2}	7.9^{3}			
Legg Mason Glob Gov	fix-inc	136.7	-1.7^{5}	8.7^{4}	—			
Legg Mason Gov Inter	fix-inc	300.3	7.0^{5}	8.4^{4}	5.9^{5}			
Legg Msn Cash Res	money mkt gen	1,207.1	4.9^{5}	5.0^{5}	4.3^{4}			
Legg Msn TE MM	money mkt TF	307.4	3.0^{5}	3.0^{5}	2.6^{5}			
Legg Msn Gov MM	money mkt gov	324.7	4.9^{4}	5.0^{3}	4.3^{3}			
Your average		8,927.2						
Lexington Funds								
Lexington Goldfund	prec met	53.9	-43.0^{3}	-15.5^{2}	0.9^{3}			
Lexington Crsby Sm Cap Asia	int'l	14.0	-42.3^{5}	—	—			
Lexington Trka Dlg Russia	int'l	137.6	67.5^{1}	—	—			
Lexington World Emg	int'l	138.0	-11.4^{4}	-3.6^{5}	4.8^{4}			
Lexington Int'l	int'l	19.9	1.6^{3}	6.9^{3}	—			
Lexington Sm Cap Value SC	growth	9.6	10.5^{5}	—	—			
Lexington Global	global	35.1	6.9^{4}	11.3^{5}	13.1^{3}			
Lexington Corp Ldrs	gr-inc	526.7	23.1^{4}	28.0^{2}	19.5^{2}			
Lexington Gro & Inc	gr-inc	228.1	30.3^{2}	26.4^{3}	17.3^{3}			
Lexington Convert	income	10.3	13.2^{5}	12.1^{5}	8.7^{5}			
Lexington Ramrz Glob Inc	fix-inc	23.6	5.0^{5}	12.6^{2}	—			
Lexington GNMA	fix-inc	151.6	10.2^{1}	10.5^{1}	7.4^{2}			
Lexington MM	money mkt gen	94.3	4.7^{5}	4.8^{5}	4.0^{5}			
Your average		1,442.7						
Lindner/Ryback Management								
Lindner Bulwark	agg gr	42.1	-22.3^{5}	-3.8^{5}	—			
Lindner International	int'l	3.5	2.6^{3}	—	—			
Lindner Growth	growth	1,300.0	8.7^{5}	16.4^{5}	13.4^{5}			
Lindner/Ryback Small Cap SC	growth	44.3	31.7^{2}	26.5^{2}	—			
Lindner Dividend	income	1,800.0	13.9^{5}	15.6^{5}	11.4^{5}			
Lindner Utility	income	47.0	19.8^{3}	22.3^{2}	—			
Lindner Govt MM	money mkt gov	36.8	5.3^{2}	—	—			
Your average		3,273.7						

No-load fund groups *continued*

Families with 3 or more funds including one stock or bond fund
Arranged in alphabetical order by group and risk within group

| Fund group/fund | Objective | Total Net Assets $ Millions 12/31/97 | Annualized Total Return % with quintile ranks by obj | | | Post quintile ranks for your funds here | | |
			1997	3 years 1995-1997	5 years 1993-1997	1997	3 years ending 1997	5 years ending 1997
Longleaf Partners Funds								
Longleaf Partners Sm Cap‡SC	growth	915.3	29.0²	26.0³	19.9¹			
Longleaf Partners‡	growth	2,605.1	28.2²	25.5³	21.4¹			
Longleaf Partners Realty	sector	737.3	29.7²	—	—			
Your average		4,257.7						
Managers Funds								
Managers Cap App	agg gr	73.4	12.7⁴	19.6⁴	14.5⁴			
Managers Spec Eqty SC	agg gr	719.9	24.5²	27.6¹	19.1¹			
Managers Int'l Eqty	int'l	379.4	10.8²	13.3²	15.4¹			
Managers Inc Eqty	income	64.8	27.2¹	26.0¹	17.8¹			
Managers Glob Bd	fix-inc	17.4	0.2⁵	7.6⁵	—			
Managers Bond	fix-inc	41.4	10.4²	14.9¹	9.5²			
Managers Inter Mortg	fix-inc	21.6	8.2³	9.5³	1.9⁵			
Managers Sht & Int Bd	fix-inc	15.2	5.9⁴	8.4¹	4.8⁴			
Managers ST Gov	fix-inc	5.0	5.5⁵	6.3⁵	3.2⁵			
Managers Money Mkt	money mkt gen	30.7	5.4¹	5.5¹	4.6¹			
Your average		1,368.8						
Markman Funds								
Markman Agg Alloc	agg gr	84.4	19.0³	—	—			
Markman Moderate Alloc	growth	86.4	19.4⁴	—	—			
Markman Conserv Alloc	gr-inc	36.7	14.3⁵	—	—			
Your average		207.5						
Marshall Funds								
Marshall Sm Cap Gro SC	agg gr	70.0	23.2³	—	—			
Marshall Int'l Stk	int'l	225.3	10.9²	14.0¹	—			
Marshall Mid-Cap Gro	growth	216.1	22.7⁴	25.6³	—			
Marshall Eqty Inc	gr-inc	526.3	27.5³	27.5²	—			
Marshall Lg Cap Gr & Inc	gr-inc	288.5	26.2³	24.5⁴	13.4⁵			
Marshall Mid-Cap Val	gr-inc	184.5	23.4⁴	20.8⁵	—			
Marshall Gov Inc	fix-inc	219.0	8.4⁴	9.3⁴	6.1⁵			
Marshall Inter Bd	fix-inc	554.2	7.2⁵	8.2⁵	5.6⁵			
Marshall ST Inc	fix-inc	150.4	6.4³	6.8⁴	5.1³			
Marshall Inter TF	tax-free	95.7	6.8⁴	7.3⁵	—			
Marshall MM Invest A	money mkt gen	1,365.5	5.4¹	5.5¹	4.6²			
Marshall MM Trust B	money mkt gen	100.7	5.1³	5.2³	4.5²			
Your average		3,996.2						
Matthews International Funds								
Matthews Asian Cnvrt	int'l	4.7	-23.2⁵	-1.8⁴	—			
Matthews Korea	int'l	25.7	-64.8⁵	—	—			
Matthews Pac Tiger	int'l	37.3	-40.9⁵	-8.9⁵	—			
Your average		67.7						

No-load fund groups *continued*

Families with 3 or more funds including one stock or bond fund
Arranged in alphabetical order by group and risk within group

Fund group/fund	Objective	Total Net Assets $ Millions 12/31/97	1997	3 years 1995-1997	5 years 1993-1997	Post quintile ranks for your funds here 1997	3 years ending 1997	5 years ending 1997
Maxus Funds								
Maxus Laureate	agg gr	3.4	6.0[5]	13.6[5]	—	___	___	___
Maxus Equity	gr-inc	55.6	28.4[3]	23.3[4]	18.6[3]	___	___	___
Maxus Income	fix-inc	38.6	11.8[2]	12.3[2]	8.1[3]	___	___	___
Your average		97.6				___	___	___
McM Funds								
McM Eqty Invest	growth	91.2	33.8[1]	32.1[1]	—	___	___	___
McM Balanced	income	64.6	23.7[2]	22.8[2]	—	___	___	___
McM Fixed Inc	fix-inc	13.8	9.5[3]	10.4[3]	—	___	___	___
McM Inter Fix	fix-inc	110.5	7.9[4]	8.9[4]	—	___	___	___
McM Princ Pres	money mkt gen	32.1	5.4[1]	—	—	___	___	___
Your average		312.2				___	___	___
Merriman Funds								
Merriman Levgd Gro	agg gr	16.2	12.2[4]	13.8[5]	8.8[5]	___	___	___
Merriman Cap App	growth	13.6	9.9[5]	11.6[5]	7.5[5]	___	___	___
Merriman Asst Alloc	global	14.6	5.8[5]	8.9[5]	8.3[5]	___	___	___
Merriman Gro & Inc	gr-inc	8.9	13.1[5]	15.3[5]	9.4[5]	___	___	___
Merriman Flex Bd	fix-inc	9.0	5.7[5]	9.2[3]	7.7[1]	___	___	___
Firstar Money Mkt*	money mkt gen	254.0	5.1[3]	5.2[3]	4.4[3]	___	___	___
Firstar TE MM*	money mkt TF	123.5	3.1[3]	3.4[2]	2.9[2]	___	___	___
Firstar Gov MM*	money mkt gov	193.1	5.0[3]	5.1[3]	4.3[2]	___	___	___
Firstar US Treas MM*	money mkt gov	66.7	4.8[4]	4.9[4]	4.2[4]	___	___	___
Your average		62.3				___	___	___
Monetta Funds								
Monetta Sm Cap Eqty SC	agg gr	2.5	—	—	—	___	___	___
Monetta Fund	growth	163.4	26.2[3]	18.0[5]	9.1[5]	___	___	___
Monetta MidCap	growth	21.9	29.1[2]	25.9[3]	—	___	___	___
Monetta Large Cap Eqty	gr-inc	4.3	26.6[3]	—	—	___	___	___
Monetta Balanced	income	12.1	21.2[3]	—	—	___	___	___
Monetta Inter Bd	fix-inc	3.9	8.9[3]	10.0[2]	—	___	___	___
Monetta Gov MM	money mkt gov	4.5	5.1[2]	—	—	___	___	___
Your average		212.6				___	___	___
Montgomery Funds								
Montgmry Emg Asia	int'l	33.9	-28.3[5]	—	—	___	___	___
Montgmry Emg Mkts	int'l	988.6	-3.2[4]	-0.4[4]	7.7[4]	___	___	___
Montgmry Latin Amer	int'l	7.7	—	—	—	___	___	___
Montgmry Int'l Growth	int'l	31.8	10.2[2]	—	—	___	___	___
Montgmry Int'l Sm Cap	int'l	45.0	-0.8[4]	8.4[3]	—	___	___	___
Montgmry Micro Cap‡ SC	agg gr	368.1	27.1[2]	24.9[2]	—	___	___	___
Montgmry Sm Cap Opp SC	agg gr	243.9	16.5[4]	—	—	___	___	___
Montgmry Sm Cap‡ SC	agg gr	207.6	23.9[2]	25.7[2]	17.3[2]	___	___	___
Montgmry Growth	growth	1,364.4	24.1[3]	22.6[4]	—	___	___	___
Montgmry Glob Asst Alloc	global	1.6	11.2[3]	—	—	___	___	___

Families with 3 or more funds including one stock or bond fund
Arranged in alphabetical order by group and risk within group

Fund group/fund	Objective	Total Net Assets $ Millions 12/31/97	1997	3 years 1995-1997	5 years 1993-1997	Post quintile ranks for your funds here 1997	3 years ending 1997	5 years ending 1997
Montgmry Glob Comm...	global	136.0	15.8[2]	13.5[4]	—	___	___	___
Montgmry Glob Oppty...	global	22.7	11.0[3]	16.1[3]	—	___	___	___
Montgmry Select 50...	global	230.7	29.3[1]	—	—	___	___	___
Montgmry Eqty Inc...	gr-inc	42.2	26.1[3]	26.3[3]	—	___	___	___
Montgmry US Asst Alloc...	income	136.2	18.9[3]	21.2[2]	—	___	___	___
Montgmry Total Ret Bd...	fix-inc	75.5	—	—	—	___	___	___
Montgmry Sht Dur Gov...	fix-inc	53.4	7.0[2]	7.8[1]	6.5[1]	___	___	___
Montgmry CA TF Inter...	tax-free	28.0	7.5[2]	7.8[4]	—	___	___	___
Montgmry CA TF MM...	money mkt TF	178.1	3.0[4]	3.2[3]	—	___	___	___
Montgmry Fed TF MM...	money mkt TF	113.2	3.2[3]	—	—	___	___	___
Montgmry Gov Res MM...	money mkt gov	666.0	5.2[2]	5.3[1]	4.5[1]	___	___	___
Your average		4,974.6				___	___	___
Mosaic Funds								
Mosaic Foresight...	int'l	1.9	2.5[5]	2.2[5]	—	___	___	___
Mosaic Mid-Cap Gro...	agg gr	10.6	17.1[4]	14.9[5]	10.9[5]	___	___	___
Mosaic Investors...	gr-inc	22.9	34.8[1]	27.3[3]	17.1[3]	___	___	___
Mosaic Balanced...	income	16.0	25.5[2]	21.1[2]	13.4[3]	___	___	___
Mosaic Hi Yld...	fix-inc	6.5	9.9[3]	10.3[3]	8.5[2]	___	___	___
Mosaic Bond...	fix-inc	1.1	6.0[5]	7.4[5]	5.2[5]	___	___	___
Mosaic Gov...	fix-inc	5.5	7.7[4]	7.3[5]	5.5[5]	___	___	___
Mosaic TF AZ...	tax-free	8.4	7.9[5]	8.6[5]	5.5[5]	___	___	___
Mosaic TF MD...	tax-free	2.1	8.0[5]	8.4[5]	—	___	___	___
Mosaic TF MO...	tax-free	11.4	8.1[5]	8.9[4]	5.6[5]	___	___	___
Mosaic TF VA...	tax-free	32.2	8.4[4]	9.1[4]	6.0[5]	___	___	___
Mosaic TF Nat...	tax-free	26.9	8.2[4]	8.7[5]	5.6[5]	___	___	___
Mosaic TF MM...	money mkt TF	6.4	2.6[5]	2.8[5]	2.3[5]	___	___	___
Mosaic Gov Tr MM ...	money mkt gov	48.8	4.3[5]	4.5[5]	3.8[5]	___	___	___
Your average		200.7				___	___	___
Mutual Series Funds(Franklin)								
Mutual Finl Svcs Z‡...	sector	134.6	—	—	—	___	___	___
Mutual European Z‡...	int'l	546.5	23.2[1]	—	—	___	___	___
Mutual Discovery Z‡...	global	3,878.0	22.8[1]	25.4[2]	—	___	___	___
Mutual Beacon Z‡...	gr-inc	5,684.6	22.9[4]	23.3[4]	19.5[2]	___	___	___
Mutual Qualified Z‡...	gr-inc	5,239.7	24.8[4]	24.2[4]	20.0[1]	___	___	___
Mutual Shares Z‡...	gr-inc	7,918.5	26.3[3]	25.4[3]	20.0[1]	___	___	___
Franklin Money Fund*...	money mkt gen	1,614.9	5.0[4]	—	—	___	___	___
Your average		23,401.9				___	___	___
Nations Funds								
Nations Pacific Gro...	int'l	0.7	-33.0[5]	—	—	___	___	___
Nations Emg Mkts...	int'l	1.6	-3.2[4]	—	—	___	___	___
Nations Int'l Eqty...	int'l	13.4	1.0[3]	5.8[3]	8.9[4]	___	___	___
Nations Int'l Gro...	int'l	23.9	1.9[3]	8.7[3]	10.5[3]	___	___	___
Nations Emg Gro SC...	agg gr	17.0	20.5[3]	22.7[3]	15.7[3]	___	___	___
Nations Cap Gro...	growth	38.3	30.4[2]	25.6[3]	16.0[4]	___	___	___

Families with 3 or more funds including one stock or bond fund
arranged in alphabetical order by group and risk within group

Fund group/fund	Objective	Total Net Assets $ Millions 12/31/97	1997	3 years 1995-1997	5 years 1993-1997	Post quintile ranks for your funds here 1997	3 years ending 1997	5 years ending 1997
Nations Disc Eqty	growth	19.2	29.6[2]	26.2[3]	—			
Nations LifeGoal Gro	growth	1.5	14.6[5]	—	—			
Nations Mngd Sm Cap Val Idx SC	growth	1.1	—	—	—			
Nations Mngd Small Cap Idx SC	growth	11.3	27.6[3]	—	—			
Nations Eqty Idx	gr-inc	3.3	32.0[2]	—	—			
Nations LifeGoal Inc & Gro	gr-inc	0.1	8.5[5]	—	—			
Nations Mngd Idx	gr-inc	17.0	33.2[1]	—	—			
Nations Mngd Val Idx	gr-inc	1.5	—	—	—			
Nations Value	gr-inc	127.9	26.3[3]	27.5[2]	18.4[3]			
Nations Balanced Assts	income	14.4	21.4[3]	20.5[3]	13.2[3]			
Nations Eqty Inc	income	63.5	25.7[1]	24.2[1]	16.3[1]			
Nations LifeGoal Bal Gro	income	0.4	11.2[5]	—	—			
Nations Divsfd Inc	fix-inc	11.5	8.3[4]	10.1[3]	8.5[2]			
Nations Strat Inc	fix-inc	26.2	8.3[4]	8.9[5]	6.6[4]			
Nations US Gov Sec	fix-inc	1.8	8.0[4]	—	—			
Nations Gl Gov	fix-inc	14.8	-1.3[5]	—	—			
Nations S-I Gov	fix-inc	50.1	7.0[5]	7.3[5]	5.4[5]			
Nations ST Inc	tax-free	11.9	5.8[4]	7.2[3]	5.6[2]			
Nations FL Muni	tax-free	2.0	8.7[4]	10.2[2]	—			
Nations GA Muni	tax-free	0.5	8.6[4]	10.2[2]	—			
Nations MD Muni	tax-free	1.8	9.0[3]	10.2[3]	—			
Nations NC Muni	tax-free	0.7	8.8[3]	10.3[2]	—			
Nations SC Muni	tax-free	1.6	8.4[1]	10.2[1]	—			
Nations TN Muni	tax-free	1.4	9.0[3]	10.4[2]	—			
Nations TX Muni	tax-free	0.4	8.8[3]	10.5[2]	—			
Nations VA Muni	tax-free	1.2	9.2[2]	10.6[2]	—			
Nations Muni Inc	tax-free	16.3	9.3[2]	10.9[1]	7.4[2]			
Nations FL Int Muni	tax-free	7.6	7.0[3]	8.1[3]	6.1[3]			
Nations GA Int Muni	tax-free	9.8	7.0[3]	8.1[3]	5.9[4]			
Nations MD Int Muni	tax-free	15.9	6.5[5]	7.8[4]	5.6[5]			
Nations NC Int Muni	tax-free	7.3	7.0[3]	8.1[3]	5.9[3]			
Nations SC Int Muni	tax-free	12.6	6.4[4]	7.9[4]	6.0[3]			
Nations TN Int Muni	tax-free	7.3	6.7[4]	8.0[3]	—			
Nations TX Int Muni	tax-free	2.2	6.9[3]	7.6[4]	—			
Nations VA Int Muni	tax-free	52.7	6.4[4]	7.7[4]	5.6[5]			
Nations Int Muni	tax-free	4.9	7.1[3]	8.4[2]	—			
Nations ST Muni	tax-free	25.2	4.6[4]	5.5[3]	—			
Nations Prime MM	money mkt gen	1,396.0	5.2[3]	—	—			
Nations TE MM	money mkt TF	154.9	3.2[2]	—	—			
Nations Gov MM	money mkt gov	45.5	5.0[3]	—	—			
Nations Treas MM	money mkt gov	1,299.6	5.0[2]	—	—			
Your average		3,539.8						
Navellier Funds								
Navellier Perf: Agg Gro SC	agg gr	101.7	9.8[4]	—	—			
Navellier Perf: Agg Sm Cap SC	agg gr	10.2	—	—	—			
Navellier Perf: Mid Cap	agg gr	8.4	26.2[2]	—	—			

Families with 3 or more funds including one stock or bond fund
Arranged in alphabetical order by group and risk within group

| Fund group/fund | Objective | Total Net Assets $ Millions 12/31/97 | Annualized Total Return % with quintile ranks by obj | | | Post quintile ranks for your funds here | | |
			1997	3 years 1995-1997	5 years 1993-1997	1997	3 years ending 1997	5 years ending 1997
Navellier Series: Sm Cap Eq SC	agg gr	214.9	11.2[4]	22.7[3]	—	___	___	___
Navellier Perf: Lg Cap Gr	growth	0.1	—	—	—	___	___	___
Navellier Perf: Sm Cap Val SC	growth	0.1	—	—	—	___	___	___
Navellier Perf: Lg Cap Val	gr-inc	0.1	—	—	—	___	___	___
Your average		335.5				___	___	___
Neuberger & Berman Funds								
Nbrgr-Ber Manhtn	agg gr	571.3	29.2[2]	22.9[3]	14.5[4]	___	___	___
Nbrgr-Ber Int'l Eqty	int'l	111.7	11.2[2]	14.1[1]	—	___	___	___
Nbrgr-Ber Focus	growth	1,368.9	24.1[3]	25.2[3]	18.2[2]	___	___	___
Nbrgr-Ber Guardian	growth	5,987.3	17.9[5]	22.5[4]	16.1[4]	___	___	___
Nbrgr-Ber Genesis SC‡	growth	1,246.4	34.9[1]	30.7[1]	20.1[1]	___	___	___
Nbrgr-Ber Partners	growth	3,230.3	29.2[2]	30.3[1]	20.4[1]	___	___	___
Nbrgr-Ber Social Resp	growth	71.4	24.4[3]	27.0[2]	—	___	___	___
Nbrgr-Ber Ltd Mat	fix-inc	252.4	6.9[2]	7.3[2]	5.6[2]	___	___	___
Nbrgr-Ber Ultra Sht‡	fix-inc	48.1	6.2[4]	6.0[5]	4.6[5]	___	___	___
Nbrgr-Ber Muni	tax-free	31.8	7.4[3]	7.8[4]	5.7[4]	___	___	___
Nbrgr-Ber Cash Res	money mkt gen	660.0	5.1[3]	5.2[3]	4.4[3]	___	___	___
Nbrgr-Ber Muni MM	money mkt TF	166.0	3.0[4]	3.1[4]	2.7[4]	___	___	___
Nbrgr-Ber Gov MM	money mkt gov	396.0	4.8[5]	4.9[4]	4.1[4]	___	___	___
Your average		14,141.6				___	___	___
ni Numeric Funds								
ni Numeric Micro-Cap‡SC	agg gr	131.9	30.9[1]	—	—	___	___	___
ni Numeric Gr and Val	growth	89.5	33.1[1]	—	—	___	___	___
ni Numeric Growth SC‡	growth	116.2	15.6[5]	—	—	___	___	___
ni Numeric Larger Cap Val	gr-inc	5.6	—	—	—	___	___	___
Your average		343.2				___	___	___
Nicholas Funds								
Nicholas Fund	growth	5,257.1	37.0[1]	30.5[1]	18.0[3]	___	___	___
Nicholas II SC	growth	1,025.0	37.0[1]	28.1[2]	17.7[3]	___	___	___
Nicholas Ltd Edit SC	growth	328.0	33.0[1]	28.3[2]	17.4[3]	___	___	___
Nicholas Eqty Inc	income	27.2	19.3[3]	17.5[5]	—	___	___	___
Nicholas Income	fix-inc	254.2	13.1[2]	13.9[2]	10.8[1]	___	___	___
Nicholas Money Mkt	money mkt gen	117.8	5.3[2]	5.3[2]	4.5[2]	___	___	___
Your average		7,009.3				___	___	___
Northern Funds								
Northern Technology	sector	80.9	16.8[4]	—	—	___	___	___
Northern Int'l Gro Eq	int'l	163.9	6.3[2]	4.4[4]	—	___	___	___
Northern Int'l Sel Eq	int'l	105.0	9.1[2]	3.7[4]	—	___	___	___
Northern Sm Cap SC	agg gr	336.5	29.8[2]	23.7[3]	—	___	___	___
Northern Growth Eqty	growth	422.0	30.2[2]	24.6[3]	—	___	___	___
Northern Select Eqty	growth	104.4	31.9[2]	27.4[2]	—	___	___	___
Northern Inc Eqty	gr-inc	103.7	20.8[4]	19.9[5]	—	___	___	___
Northern Stock Idx	gr-inc	66.9	32.7[1]	—	—	___	___	___

No-load fund groups _continued_

Families with 3 or more funds including one stock or bond fund
Arranged in alphabetical order by group and risk within group

Fund group/fund	Objective	Total Net Assets $ Millions 12/31/97	Annualized Total Return % with quintile ranks by obj			Post quintile ranks for your funds here		
			1997	3 years 1995-1997	5 years 1993-1997	1997	3 years ending 1997	5 years ending 1997
Northern Int'l Fix Inc	fix-inc	14.6	-2.5[5]	7.2[5]	—			
Northern Fix Inc	fix-inc	163.7	9.5[3]	10.1[3]	—			
Northern US Gov	fix-inc	214.5	7.2[1]	7.6[2]	—			
Northern CA TE	tax-free	29.2	—	—	—			
Northern TE Bond	tax-free	154.1	8.7[4]	9.5[4]	—			
Northern FL Inter TE	tax-free	24.3	7.7[1]	—	—			
Northern Inter TE	tax-free	290.6	5.8[5]	7.0[5]	—			
Northern Money Mkt	money mkt gen	2,579.7	5.1[3]	—	—			
Northern CA Muni MM	money mkt TF	227.8	3.4[1]	—	—			
Northern Muni MM	money mkt TF	1,227.2	3.3[2]	3.4[2]	—			
Northern US Gov MM	money mkt gov	311.3	5.0[2]	—	—			
Northern US Gov Sel MM	money mkt gov	211.0	5.4[1]	—	—			
Your average		6,831.3						
Oakmark Funds								
Oakmark Select	agg gr	981.6	55.0[1]	—	—			
Oakmark Int'l Small Cap	int'l	50.2	-19.9[5]	—	—			
Oakmark Int'l	int'l	1,237.5	3.4[3]	12.7[2]	14.9[2]			
Oakmark Small Cap‡ SC	growth	1,492.0	40.5[1]	—	—			
Oakmark	growth	7,301.4	32.6[1]	27.5[2]	22.8[1]			
Oakmark Eqty & Inc	income	40.6	26.6[1]	—	—			
Oakmark Units Gov MM	money mkt gen	70.0	5.3[2]	—	—			
Oakmark Units TE Div MM	money mkt TF	4.6	3.4[1]	—	—			
Your average		11,177.9						
Oberweis Funds								
Oberweis Emg Growth SC	agg gr	140.1	-8.6[5]	17.1[5]	11.2[5]			
Oberweis MicroCap SC	agg gr	36.9	10.7[4]	—	—			
Oberweis MidCap	agg gr	6.3	5.5[5]	—	—			
Your average		183.3						
O'Shaughnessy Funds								
O'Shaughnessy Agg Gr	agg gr	6.7	22.3[3]	—	—			
O'Shaughnessy Cornrstn Gro	growth	54.4	31.3[2]	—	—			
O'Shaughnessy Cornrstn Val	gr-inc	15.9	15.3[5]	—	—			
O'Shaughnessy Dogs Of Mkt	income	9.7	25.8[1]	—	—			
Your average		86.7						
OVB Funds								
OVB Emg Gro SC	agg gr	32.6	0.5[5]	15.2[5]	—			
OVB Cap App	growth	112.2	27.0[3]	25.3[3]	—			
OVB Eqty Inc	income	48.6	23.0[2]	—	—			
OVB Gov	fix-inc	49.9	9.3[3]	10.1[3]	—			
OVB WV TE	tax-free	84.8	8.9[3]	9.4[4]	—			
OVB Prime Obl	money mkt gen	6.3	5.0[4]	5.1[4]	—			
Your average		334.4						

No-load fund groups *continued*

Families with 3 or more funds including one stock or bond fund
Arranged in alphabetical order by group and risk within group

Fund group/fund	Objective	Total Net Assets $ Millions 12/31/97	1997	3 years 1995-1997	5 years 1993-1997	1997	3 years ending 1997	5 years ending 1997
				Annualized Total Return % with quintile ranks by obj			Post quintile ranks for your funds here	
L Roy Papp Funds								
Papp Amer Pac Rim...	int'l	13.7	—	—	—	____	____	____
Papp L Roy Amer Abroad...	growth	288.2	29.9²	31.5¹	19.5²	____	____	____
Papp L Roy Stock...	growth	79.8	33.1¹	29.2²	16.7³	____	____	____
Your average...		381.7				____	____	____
Parnassus Income Fund Portfolios								
Parnassus Balanced...	income	38.9	20.2³	19.1⁴	13.1⁴	____	____	____
Parnassus Fix Inc...	fix-inc	9.7	10.6²	11.9²	7.6³	____	____	____
Parnassus CA TE...	tax-free	6.5	9.3²	10.8¹	7.5¹	____	____	____
Your average...		55.1				____	____	____
Payden & Rygel Funds								
Payden & Rygel Euro Gro & Inc...	int'l	13.2	—	—	—	____	____	____
Payden & Rygel Int'l Eqty...	int'l	16.6	5.5³	—	—	____	____	____
Payden & Rygel Glob Bal...	global	8.9	12.5³	—	—	____	____	____
Payden & Rygel Gro & Inc...	gr-inc	188.7	26.9³	—	—	____	____	____
Payden & Rygel Mkt Ret...	gr-inc	24.0	30.7²	—	—	____	____	____
Payden & Rygel Int'l Bd‡...	fix-inc	0.1	-3.2⁵	—	—	____	____	____
Payden & Rygel Glob FI...	fix-inc	493.6	9.1²	10.8¹	8.4¹	____	____	____
Payden & Rygel Inter Bd...	fix-inc	110.0	7.5⁴	8.2⁵	—	____	____	____
Payden & Rygel Inv Qual Bd...	fix-inc	119.2	9.0²	9.9²	—	____	____	____
Payden & Rygel Tot Ret...	fix-inc	64.0	7.7⁴	8.5⁴	—	____	____	____
Payden & Rygel Glob ST Bd...	fix-inc	293.2	6.6⁵	—	—	____	____	____
Payden & Rygel Ltd Mat...	fix-inc	138.4	5.5⁵	5.9⁵	—	____	____	____
Payden & Rygel ST Bd...	fix-inc	82.0	5.8⁴	6.9³	—	____	____	____
Payden & Rygel US Govt...	int'l	77.1	8.8¹	—	—	____	____	____
Payden & Rygel TE Bd...	tax-free	24.4	6.6⁵	—	—	____	____	____
Payden & Rygel Sht Dur TE...	tax-free	33.5	4.5⁴	4.8⁵	—	____	____	____
Your average...		1,686.9				____	____	____
Permanent Portfolio Funds								
Permanent Agg Growth†...	agg gr	20.2	32.7¹	26.3²	19.9¹	____	____	____
Permanent Portfolio†...	global	70.7	5.6⁵	7.5⁵	6.8⁵	____	____	____
Permanent Vers Bd†...	fix-inc	23.9	5.1⁵	5.8⁵	4.8⁵	____	____	____
Permanent Treasy†...	fix-inc	93.3	4.1⁵	4.4⁵	3.8⁵	____	____	____
Your average...		208.1				____	____	____
Pilgrim, Baxter Mutual Funds (PBHG)								
PBHG Tech & Comm...	sector	551.0	3.3⁵	—	—	____	____	____
PBHG International...	int'l	17.1	3.5³	6.0³	—	____	____	____
PBHG Core Growth...	agg gr	192.3	-9.7⁵	—	—	____	____	____
PBHG Emg Growth SC...	agg gr	1,516.2	-3.7⁵	18.7⁴	—	____	____	____
PBHG Growth...	agg gr	5,463.5	-3.3⁵	16.8⁵	19.6¹	____	____	____
PBHG Limited‡ SC...	agg gr	172.1	16.1⁴	—	—	____	____	____
PBHG Mid Cap Val...	agg gr	40.4	—	—	—	____	____	____
PBHG Select Eqty...	agg gr	348.6	6.8⁵					

Families with 3 or more funds including one stock or bond fund
Arranged in alphabetical order by group and risk within group

| Fund group/fund | Objective | Total Net Assets $ Millions 12/31/97 | Annualized Total Return % with quintile ranks by obj | | | Post quintile ranks for your funds here | | |
			1997	3 years 1995-1997	5 years 1993-1997	1997	3 years ending 1997	5 years ending 1997
PBHG Sm Cap Val SC	agg gr	80.6	—	—	—			
PBHG Strat Small Co SC	agg gr	117.2	25.7[2]	—	—			
PBHG Large Cap 20	growth	116.5	33.0[1]	—	—			
PBHG Large Cap Gro	growth	141.3	22.4[4]	—	—			
PBHG Large Cap Val	gr-inc	70.5	25.6[3]	—	—			
PBHG Cash Res	money mkt gen	155.3	5.1[4]	—	—			
Your average		8,982.6						
PIC Funds								
PIC Sm Co Gro SC	agg gr	30.1	-1.4[5]	—	—			
PIC:Pinnacle Sm Co Gro SC	agg gr	3.3	—	—	—			
PIC Growth	growth	119.3	28.0[2]	24.0[3]	13.4[5]			
PIC:Pinnacle Growth	growth	2.3	—	—	—			
PIC:Pinnacle Balanced	income	36.1	22.3[2]	20.0[3]	11.5[5]			
Your average		191.1						
Preferred Funds								
Preferred Small Cap SC	agg gr	121.6	31.9[1]	—	—			
Preferred Int'l	int'l	241.3	6.8[2]	11.2[2]	15.0[2]			
Preferred Growth	growth	448.1	31.9[2]	26.2[3]	18.2[2]			
Preferred Asst Alloc	gr-inc	138.9	21.0[4]	22.8[4]	14.8[4]			
Preferred Value	gr-inc	342.3	28.0[3]	30.2[1]	19.3[2]			
Preferred Fix Inc	fix-inc	148.0	8.5[4]	9.5[4]	7.2[4]			
Preferred ST Gov	fix-inc	56.7	6.2[4]	6.6[4]	4.9[4]			
Preferred Money Mkt	money mkt gen	87.0	5.2[3]	5.4[2]	4.5[2]			
Your average		1,583.9						
T. Rowe Price Funds								
Price Finl Serv	sector	177.3	41.4[1]	—	—			
Price Health Sciences	sector	271.4	19.4[3]	—	—			
Price Media & Telecomm	sector	133.9	28.1[2]	23.1[3]	—			
Price Sci/Tech	sector	3,538.5	1.7[5]	21.8[4]	21.0[2]			
Price Japan	int'l	152.2	-22.1[5]	-12.4[5]	-1.4[5]			
Price Emg Mkts Stk	int'l	123.7	1.2[3]	—	—			
Price Latin Amer	int'l	432.7	31.8[1]	9.8[3]	—			
Price New Asia	int'l	782.0	-37.1[5]	-9.5[5]	1.4[5]			
Price Europe Stk	int'l	1,020.8	17.0[1]	21.5[1]	18.9[1]			
Price Int'l Disc	int'l	228.2	-5.7[4]	0.9[4]	7.3[4]			
Price Int'l Stk	int'l	9,720.6	2.7[3]	9.9[3]	13.0[2]			
Price Spect-Int'l	int'l	51.1	2.4[3]	—	—			
Price Cap Oppty	agg gr	109.1	15.9[4]	25.6[2]	—			
Price New Amer	agg gr	1,757.9	21.1[3]	28.0[1]	17.9[2]			
Price New Horizon‡ SC	agg gr	5,103.7	9.8[4]	25.9[2]	19.6[1]			
Price Blue Chip	growth	2,344.6	27.5[3]	31.0[1]	—			
Price Cap App	growth	1,059.9	16.2[5]	18.5[5]	14.8[4]			
Price Divsfd Sm Cap Gro SC	growth	72.1	—	—	—			
Price Gro Stk	growth	3,988.4	26.6[3]	26.4[2]	18.7[2]			

Families with 3 or more funds including one stock or bond fund
Arranged in alphabetical order by group and risk within group

| Fund group/fund | Objective | Total Net Assets $ Millions 12/31/97 | Annualized Total Return % with quintile ranks by obj | | | Post quintile ranks for your funds here | | |
			1997	3 years 1995-1997	5 years 1993-1997	1997	3 years ending 1997	5 years ending 1997
Price Mid Cap Gro...	growth	1,838.7	18.3[5]	27.7[2]	21.4[1]	___	___	___
Price Mid Cap Val...	growth	218.0	27.1[3]	—	—	___	___	___
Price New Era...	growth	1,492.7	10.9[5]	18.5[5]	15.1[4]	___	___	___
Price Pers Str-Gro...	growth	98.3	20.5[4]	23.1[4]	—	___	___	___
Price Sm Cap Stk...	growth	816.4	28.8[2]	27.8[2]	19.9[1]	___	___	___
Price Sm Cap Value‡ SC...	growth	2,088.2	27.9[3]	27.3[2]	20.2[1]	___	___	___
Price Spect-Gro...	growth	2,605.3	17.4[5]	22.5[4]	17.7[3]	___	___	___
Price Glob Stk...	global	33.6	13.2[2]	—	—	___	___	___
Price Div Gro...	gr-inc	747.0	30.8[2]	29.3[2]	21.4[1]	___	___	___
Price Eqty Idx 500...	gr-inc	1,908.3	32.9[1]	30.8[1]	19.8[2]	___	___	___
Price Gro & Inc...	gr-inc	3,446.7	23.5[4]	26.6[3]	18.1[3]	___	___	___
Price Pers Str-Bal...	gr-inc	281.5	17.8[5]	19.9[5]	—	___	___	___
Price Value...	gr-inc	546.4	29.2[2]	32.4[1]	—	___	___	___
Price Balanced...	income	1,219.2	19.0[3]	19.4[3]	13.6[3]	___	___	___
Price Eqty Inc...	income	12,771.2	28.8[1]	27.4[1]	19.9[1]	___	___	___
Price Pers Str-Inc...	income	66.2	15.0[5]	17.0[5]	—	___	___	___
Price Tax-Effient Bal...	income	13.9	—	—	—	___	___	___
Price Real Est...	sector	6.9	—	—	—	___	___	___
Price Emg Mkt Bond...	fix-inc	113.4	16.8[1]	26.0[1]	—	___	___	___
Price High Yld...	fix-inc	1,571.7	14.5[1]	13.9[1]	10.6[1]	___	___	___
Price Corp Inc...	fix-inc	32.7	12.6[2]	—	—	___	___	___
Price Trsy Long...	fix-inc	206.8	14.7[1]	12.9[2]	8.9[2]	___	___	___
Price Int'l Bond...	fix-inc	825.8	-3.2[5]	7.7[5]	7.9[1]	___	___	___
Price Glob Gov Bd...	fix-inc	44.1	1.6[5]	8.6[4]	6.5[3]	___	___	___
Price New Inc...	fix-inc	1,945.0	9.3[2]	9.8[3]	7.3[2]	___	___	___
Price Spect-Inc...	fix-inc	2,022.2	12.2[1]	13.0[1]	9.7[1]	___	___	___
Price GNMA...	fix-inc	1,063.3	9.5[1]	10.0[2]	6.8[3]	___	___	___
Price Summit GNMA...	fix-inc	32.2	9.8[1]	10.2[2]	—	___	___	___
Price ST Bond...	fix-inc	345.0	6.3[3]	6.6[4]	4.6[5]	___	___	___
Price Summit Ltd Trm...	fix-inc	30.5	7.2[1]	7.1[3]	—	___	___	___
Price ST U.S. Gov...	fix-inc	102.1	6.7[2]	7.3[2]	4.8[5]	___	___	___
Price Trsy Inter...	fix-inc	199.5	8.2[1]	8.7[1]	6.3[1]	___	___	___
Price CA TF Bond...	tax-free	184.0	9.1[3]	10.2[2]	7.3[2]	___	___	___
Price GA TF Bond...	tax-free	46.0	9.7[2]	10.3[2]	—	___	___	___
Price MD TF Bond...	tax-free	889.7	8.6[4]	9.5[4]	7.1[3]	___	___	___
Price NJ TF Bond...	tax-free	93.0	9.1[2]	9.6[3]	7.1[3]	___	___	___
Price NY TF Bond...	tax-free	165.4	9.5[2]	10.0[3]	7.3[2]	___	___	___
Price VA TF Bond...	tax-free	220.5	9.0[3]	9.8[3]	7.2[3]	___	___	___
Price TF Hi Yld...	tax-free	1,171.8	10.2[1]	10.5[2]	7.8[1]	___	___	___
Price Summit Muni Inc...	tax-free	32.1	11.6[1]	11.4[1]	—	___	___	___
Price TF Inc...	tax-free	1,372.0	9.3[2]	10.0[3]	7.2[2]	___	___	___
Price FL Ins Inter...	tax-free	83.1	6.7[4]	7.8[4]	—	___	___	___
Price Summit Muni Inter...	tax-free	49.0	8.4[1]	8.9[1]	—	___	___	___
Price TF Ins Inter...	tax-free	104.6	7.2[3]	8.1[3]	6.7[1]	___	___	___
Price MD ST TF...	tax-free	106.4	4.2[5]	5.0[5]	—	___	___	___
Price VA ST TF Bond...	tax-free	19.2	4.3[5]	5.1[4]	—	___	___	___
Price TF S-I...	tax-free	439.9	5.3[2]	5.8[3]	4.8[2]	___	___	___

Families with 3 or more funds including one stock or bond fund
Arranged in alphabetical order by group and risk within group

| Fund group/fund | Objective | Total Net Assets $ Millions 12/31/97 | Annualized Total Return % with quintile ranks by obj | | | Post quintile ranks for your funds here | | |
			1997	3 years 1995-1997	5 years 1993-1997	1997	3 years ending 1997	5 years ending 1997
Price Prime Res...	money mkt gen	4,535.5	5.2[3]	5.2[3]	4.4[3]			
Price Summit Cash Res...	money mkt gen	1,272.6	5.4[1]	5.4[1]	4.6[2]			
Price CA TF MM...	money mkt TF	84.9	3.0[4]	3.2[4]	2.8[4]			
Price NY TF MM...	money mkt TF	91.1	3.1[3]	3.2[3]	2.8[4]			
Price Summit Muni MM...	money mkt TF	139.9	3.4[1]	3.5[1]	—			
Price TE MM...	money mkt TF	713.8	3.2[2]	3.4[2]	2.9[2]			
Price Trsy MM...	money mkt gov	827.5	4.9[3]	5.0[3]	4.2[4]			
Your average...		82,442.9						
Primary Funds								
Primary Trend...	gr-inc	24.4	18.2[5]	21.3[4]	14.7[4]			
Primary Income...	income	4.9	25.5[1]	22.0[2]	15.3[2]			
Primary US Gov...	fix-inc	0.8	6.1[5]	7.9[5]	5.7[5]			
Your average...		30.1						
Quaker Funds								
Quaker Aggr Gro...	agg gr	1.3	20.3[3]	—	—			
Quaker Core Eqty...	agg gr	0.8	29.6[2]	—	—			
Quaker Sector Alloc‡...	growth	0.8	18.5[4]	—	—			
Quaker Sm Cap Val SC...	growth	1.9	41.5[1]	—	—			
Quaker Enhncd Stk Market...	gr-inc	1.3	30.2[2]	—	—			
Quaker Fixed Inc...	fix-inc	1.0	8.1[4]	—	—			
Your average...		7.1						
Quantitative Funds								
Quant Foreign Frontier...	int'l	9.0	-9.2[4]	-1.2[4]	—			
Quant Int'l Eqty...	int'l	28.0	-1.6[4]	2.3[4]	9.1[4]			
Quant Numeric II SC...	agg gr	12.5	28.6[2]	—	—			
Quant Numeric SC...	agg gr	64.5	7.2[5]	21.3[4]	19.1[1]			
Quant Gro & Inc...	gr-inc	55.8	36.7[1]	28.1[2]	18.5[3]			
Your average...		169.8						
Rainier Portfolios								
Rainier Sm/Mid Cap...	agg gr	353.1	32.2[1]	33.7[1]	—			
Rainier Core Eqty...	growth	497.8	33.9[1]	34.4[1]	—			
Rainier Balanced...	income	60.2	23.9[2]	23.5[2]	—			
Rainier Inter Fix Inc...	fix-inc	21.5	7.3[4]	7.8[5]	—			
Firstar Money Mkt*...	money mkt gen	254.0	5.1[3]	5.2[3]	4.4[3]			
Firstar Gov MM*...	money mkt gov	193.1	5.0[3]	5.1[3]	4.3[2]			
Your average...		932.6						
RCM Global Investment Funds								
RCM Global Health Care...	sector	4.6	30.0[2]	—	—			
RCM Global Tech...	sector	6.9	27.1[2]	—	—			
RCM Large Cap Growth...	growth	5.0	31.9[2]	—	—			
RCM Global Small Cap...	global	4.5	25.5[1]	—	—			
Your average...		21.0						

No-load fund groups *continued*

Families with 3 or more funds including one stock or bond fund
Arranged in alphabetical order by group and risk within group

| Fund group/fund | Objective | Total Net Assets $ Millions 12/31/97 | Annualized Total Return % with quintile ranks by obj | | | Post quintile ranks for your funds here | | |
			1997	3 years 1995-1997	5 years 1993-1997	1997	3 years ending 1997	5 years ending 1997
Reserve Funds								
Reserve Sm Cap Gr SC...............	agg gr	6.1	-0.5[5]	19.6[4]	—	___	___	___
Reserve Int'l Eqty....................	int'l	10.5	-8.7[4]	—	—	___	___	___
Reserve Blue Chip Gro...............	growth	6.5	25.5[3]	22.8[4]	—	___	___	___
Reserve Informd Invstr...............	growth	6.2	19.0[4]	16.3[5]	—	___	___	___
Reserve Mid Cap Gro.................	growth	4.6	7.9[5]	—	—	___	___	___
Reserve Lrg Cap Val.................	gr-inc	5.9	32.7[1]	—	—	___	___	___
Reserve Conv Secs....................	income	21.8	17.5[4]	—	—	___	___	___
Reserve Primary MM..................	money mkt gen	2,333.0	4.8[5]	4.8[5]	4.2[5]	___	___	___
Reserve CA TE MM....................	money mkt TF	32.8	2.8[5]	2.8[5]	—	___	___	___
Reserve CT TE MM....................	money mkt TF	40.7	2.6[5]	2.7[5]	2.4[5]	___	___	___
Reserve TE Interstate MM...........	money mkt TF	299.6	2.7[5]	2.9[5]	2.5[5]	___	___	___
Reserve MA TE MM...................	money mkt TF	9.9	2.8[5]	3.0[5]	2.5[5]	___	___	___
Reserve NJ TE MM....................	money mkt TF	38.2	2.7[5]	—	—	___	___	___
Reserve NY TE MM....................	money mkt TF	165.5	2.6[5]	2.8[5]	2.4[5]	___	___	___
Reserve PA TE MM....................	money mkt TF	11.4	2.6[5]	—	—	___	___	___
Reserve FL TE MM....................	money mkt TF	20.2	2.3[5]	—	—	___	___	___
Reserve Treas MM....................	money mkt gov	324.4	4.5[5]	4.6[5]	3.9[5]	___	___	___
Reserve US Gov MM..................	money mkt gov	623.2	4.7[5]	—	—	___	___	___
Your average........................		3,960.5				___	___	___
Reynolds Funds								
Reynolds Opportunity................	growth	20.9	14.6[5]	21.2[4]	12.7[5]	___	___	___
Reynolds Blue Chip Gr..............	gr-inc	60.5	31.5[2]	30.8[1]	16.1[4]	___	___	___
Reynolds US Gov.....................	fix-inc	2.7	5.4[5]	7.0[3]	4.8[5]	___	___	___
Reynolds Money Mkt.................	money mkt gen	3.3	4.9[4]			___	___	___
Your average........................		87.4				___	___	___
Robertson Stephens Funds								
Robrtsn Stph Glob Nat Res.........	sector	79.3	-17.1[5]	—	—	___	___	___
Robrtsn Stph Info Age..............	sector	118.6	6.1[5]	—	—	___	___	___
Robrtsn Stph Devlp Countries.....	int'l	30.0	-15.2[4]	-4.2[5]	—	___	___	___
Robrtsn Stph Contrn................	agg gr	402.9	-29.5[5]	3.9[5]	—	___	___	___
Robrtsn Stph Emg Gro SC..........	agg gr	248.9	18.5[3]	20.1[4]	14.9[3]	___	___	___
Robrtsn Stph MicroCap Gro SC.....	agg gr	104.7	30.5[1]	—	—	___	___	___
Robrtsn Stph Partners SC..........	agg gr	196.3	18.1[3]	—	—	___	___	___
Robrtsn Stph Val Gro...............	agg gr	756.8	13.9[4]	22.8[3]	22.0[1]	___	___	___
Robrtsn Stph Divrsfd Gro..........	growth	79.6	29.6[2]	—	—	___	___	___
Robrtsn Stph Gro & Inc............	growth	298.4	22.3[4]	—	—	___	___	___
Robrtsn Stph Glob Low Pr.........	global	14.3	-13.5[5]	—	—	___	___	___
Robrtsn Stph Glob Val.............	global	21.0	—	—	—	___	___	___
Your average........................		2,350.8				___	___	___
Royce Funds								
Royce Finl Svcs.....................	sector	2.4	19.4[3]	18.4[5]	—	___	___	___
Royce GiftShares....................	agg gr	3.5	26.0[2]	—	—	___	___	___
Royce Micro-Cap SC.................	agg gr	199.5	24.7[2]	19.7[4]	17.1[2]	___	___	___
Royce Low Priced Stk SC...........	growth	18.1	19.5[4]	21.6[4]	—	___	___	___

164

No-load fund groups *continued*

Families with 3 or more funds including one stock or bond fund
Arranged in alphabetical order by group and risk within group

Fund group/fund	Objective	Total Net Assets $ Millions 12/31/97	Annualized Total Return % with quintile ranks by obj			Post quintile ranks for your funds here		
			1997	3 years 1995-1997	5 years 1993-1997	1997	3 years ending 1997	5 years ending 1997
Royce Penn Mutual SC	growth	507.7	24.9[3]	18.7[5]	13.1[5]			
Royce PMF II SC	growth	22.2	20.8[4]	—	—			
Royce Premier SC	growth	533.5	18.4[5]	18.1[5]	15.2[4]			
Royce REvest Gro & Inc	gr-inc	34.3	23.5[4]	20.6[5]	—			
Royce Total Ret	gr-inc	120.6	23.7[4]	25.3[3]	—			
Your average		1,441.8						
RSI Retirement Trust Funds								
RSI Tr-Emg Gro SC	agg gr	75.4	8.3[5]	25.3[2]	19.7[1]			
RSI Tr-Int'l Eqty	int'l	29.8	0.9[3]	8.0[3]	10.6[3]			
RSI Tr-Core Eqty	gr-inc	196.5	25.3[3]	28.8[2]	19.0[2]			
RSI Tr-Value Eqty	gr-inc	57.8	31.7[2]	30.5[1]	18.9[2]			
RSI Tr-Act Mgd Bd	fix-inc	145.4	9.7[3]	10.0[4]	7.2[4]			
RSI Tr-Inter Bd	fix-inc	63.8	7.1[5]	8.3[5]	5.9[5]			
RSI Tr-ST Invest	fix-inc	24.8	4.9[5]	5.0[5]	4.2[5]			
Rydex Series Funds								
Rydex Prec Met	prec met	24.9	-37.6[1]	-12.2[1]	—			
Rydex Nova	agg gr	776.9	42.3[1]	39.0[1]	—			
Rydex OTC	agg gr	206.1	21.9[3]	35.3[1]	—			
Rydex Ursa	agg gr	278.9	-21.0[5]	-17.9[5]	—			
Rydex High Yld	fix-inc	18.4	—	—	—			
Rydex US Gov Bd	fix-inc	57.8	16.4[1]	14.1[1]	—			
Rydex Juno	fix-inc	12.9	-5.6[5]	—	—			
Rydex US Gov MM	money mkt gov	282.9	4.9[4]	—	—			
Your average		1,658.8						
SAFECO Funds								
SAFECO Growth SC	agg gr	638.6	50.0[1]	32.5[1]	22.8[1]			
SAFECO Sm Cap Stk SC	agg gr	22.7	23.4[3]	—	—			
SAFECO Int'l Stk	int'l	14.8	4.6[3]	—	—			
SAFECO Northwest Gr	growth	64.6	31.1[2]	21.9[4]	12.5[5]			
SAFECO Equity	gr-inc	1,490.2	24.2[4]	24.8[3]	22.9[1]			
SAFECO US Value	gr-inc	9.2	—	—	—			
SAFECO Balanced	income	13.7	16.6[4]	—	—			
SAFECO Income	income	402.0	26.4[1]	26.9[1]	17.9[1]			
SAFECO Hi Yld Bd	fix-inc	71.1	12.8[2]	12.9[2]	10.5[1]			
SAFECO Managed Bd	fix-inc	4.8	8.3[3]	8.3[3]	—			
SAFECO GNMA	fix-inc	38.1	9.0[2]	9.4[3]	6.1[4]			
SAFECO Inter Trsy	fix-inc	15.7	8.3[3]	8.3[5]	6.3[4]			
SAFECO CA TF Inc	tax-free	86.0	11.6[1]	13.0[1]	8.2[1]			
SAFECO WA Muni	tax-free	7.3	9.0[3]	10.4[2]	—			
SAFECO Insur Muni Bd	tax-free	16.5	10.7[1]	12.2[1]	—			
SAFECO Muni Bd	tax-free	496.1	10.7[1]	11.5[1]	7.5[1]			
SAFECO Inter Muni Bd	tax-free	13.8	7.5[2]	8.7[1]	—			
SAFECO Money Mkt	money mkt gen	179.0	4.9[5]	5.0[5]	4.2[5]			
SAFECO TF MM	money mkt TF	75.7	3.2[3]	3.3[2]	2.9[2]			
Your average		3,659.9						

No-load fund groups *continued*

Families with 3 or more funds including one stock or bond fund
Arranged in alphabetical order by group and risk within group

| Fund group/fund | Objective | Total Net Assets $ Millions 12/31/97 | Annualized Total Return % with quintile ranks by obj | | | Post quintile ranks for your funds here | | |
			1997	3 years 1995-1997	5 years 1993-1997	1997	3 years ending 1997	5 years ending 1997
Schroder Capital Funds								
Schroder Cap:Emg Mkts..........	int'l	177.1	-5.2[4]	—	—	___	___	___
Schroder Cap:Int'l Sm Cap..........	int'l	5.9	-14.1[4]	—	—	___	___	___
Schroder Cap:Int'l..........	int'l	174.0	3.2[3]	8.2[3]	12.9[2]	___	___	___
Schroder Cap:Micro Cap SC..........	agg gr	2.1	—	—	—	___	___	___
Schroder Cap:US Eqty..........	agg gr	13.5	23.3[3]	24.3[3]	15.4[3]	___	___	___
Schroder Cap:US Sm Co SC..........	agg gr	42.2	26.9[2]	32.2[1]	—	___	___	___
Your average		414.8				___	___	___
Schroder Series Funds								
Schroder Ser:Sm Cap Val SC..........	agg gr	94.6	32.1[1]	26.4[2]	—	___	___	___
Schroder Ser:Lg Cap Eqty..........	gr-inc	48.0	26.3[3]	24.8[3]	—	___	___	___
Schroder Ser:Inv Grd Inc..........	fix-inc	27.0	7.7[4]	9.2[4]	—	___	___	___
Schroder Ser:ST Invest..........	fix-inc	27.3	4.9[5]	4.9[5]	—	___	___	___
Your average		196.9				___	___	___
Schwab Funds								
Schwab Analytics..........	agg gr	160.0	31.8[1]	—	—	___	___	___
Schwab OneSource Sm Co SC..........	agg gr	206.0	—	—	—	___	___	___
Schwab Sm Cap Idx(Inv) SC..........	agg gr	427.5	25.7[2]	22.8[3]	—	___	___	___
Schwab Int'l Idx(Inv)..........	int'l	325.0	7.3[2]	10.2[2]	—	___	___	___
Schwab OneSource Int'l..........	int'l	76.5	6.8[2]	—	—	___	___	___
Schwab Asst Dir: Hi Gro..........	growth	184.0	21.0[4]	—	—	___	___	___
Schwab OneSource Gro Alloc..........	growth	132.2	18.4[5]	—	—	___	___	___
Schwab 1000(Inv)..........	gr-inc	2,823.1	31.9[2]	29.9[2]	19.1[2]	___	___	___
Schwab Asst Dir: Cons Gr..........	gr-inc	46.7	14.7[5]	—	—	___	___	___
Schwab S & P 500(Inv)..........	gr-inc	1,032.4	32.5[1]	—	—	___	___	___
Schwab Asst Dir: Balanced..........	income	162.1	17.8[4]	—	—	___	___	___
Schwab OneSource Bal Alloc..........	income	68.1	16.5[4]	—	—	___	___	___
Schwab Tot Bd Mkt Idx..........	fix-inc	94.2	10.0[3]	10.8[3]	—	___	___	___
Schwab ST Bd Mkt Idx..........	fix-inc	138.1	7.1[1]	7.3[2]	5.3[3]	___	___	___
Schwab CA Long TF..........	tax-free	132.9	10.2[1]	11.3[1]	7.2[2]	___	___	___
Schwab LT TF Bd..........	tax-free	51.5	9.9[1]	10.6[2]	7.4[1]	___	___	___
Schwab CA S-I TF Bd..........	tax-free	61.2	5.3[2]	6.5[1]	—	___	___	___
Schwab S-I TF..........	tax-free	53.8	5.3[3]	6.0[1]	—	___	___	___
Schwab Inst Adv MM..........	money mkt gen	275.3	5.3[2]	5.4[2]	—	___	___	___
Schwab Money Mkt..........	money mkt gen	21,421.4	5.0[4]	5.1[4]	4.3[4]	___	___	___
Schwab Retirement MM..........	money mkt gen	154.9	5.1[4]	5.1[4]	—	___	___	___
Schwab Value Adv MM..........	money mkt gen	13,662.2	5.4[1]	5.5[1]	4.7[1]	___	___	___
Schwab CA Muni MM Sweep Shrs..........	money mkt TF	2,154.5	3.0[5]	—	—	___	___	___
Schwab CA Muni MM Val Adv..........	money mkt TF	936.8	3.2[3]	3.1[5]	2.7[4]	___	___	___
Schwab Muni MM Sweep Shrs..........	money mkt TF	4,423.6	3.1[3]	—	—	___	___	___
Schwab Muni MM Val Adv..........	money mkt TF	1,085.2	3.3[2]	3.3[3]	2.8[3]	___	___	___
Schwab NY Muni MM Sweep..........	money mkt TF	357.2	3.0[4]	—	—	___	___	___
Schwab NY Muni MM Val Adv..........	money mkt TF	125.6	3.2[2]	—	—	___	___	___
Schwab Gov MM..........	money mkt gov	1,981.9	5.0[3]	5.0[3]	4.3[3]	___	___	___
Schwab US Trsy MM..........	money mkt gov	1,765.4	4.9[4]	5.0[3]	4.2[3]	___	___	___
Your average		54,519.3				:-	:-	:-

Families with 3 or more funds including one stock or bond fund
Arranged in alphabetical order by group and risk within group

Fund group/fund	Objective	Total Net Assets $ Millions 12/31/97	Annualized Total Return % with quintile ranks by obj			Post quintile ranks for your funds here		
			1997	3 years 1995-1997	5 years 1993-1997	1997	3 years ending 1997	5 years ending 1997
Scout Funds								
Scout Regional SC	agg gr	49.9	23.0[3]	18.4[4]	12.1[5]	___	___	___
Scout Stock	growth	198.5	21.0[4]	17.0[5]	12.8[5]	___	___	___
Scout Worldwide	global	57.0	18.4[2]	17.1[3]	—	___	___	___
Scout Balanced	income	9.1	10.1[5]	—	—	___	___	___
Scout Bond	fix-inc	79.5	7.3[5]	8.2[5]	5.9[5]	___	___	___
Scout Prime MM	money mkt gen	555.7	5.2[3]	5.3[2]	4.5[2]	___	___	___
Scout TF MM	money mkt TF	150.8	3.1[3]	3.2[4]	2.8[3]	___	___	___
Scout Fed MMF	money mkt gov	312.8	5.1[2]	5.2[2]	4.4[2]	___	___	___
Your average		1,413.3				___	___	___
Scudder Funds								
Scudder Finl Svcs	sector	27.0	—	—	—	___	___	___
Scudder Gold	prec met	124.7	-40.9[2]	-4.0[1]	5.5[1]	___	___	___
Scudder Emg Mkts Gro	int'l	205.7	3.6[3]	—	—	___	___	___
Scudder Latin Amer	int'l	962.4	31.3[1]	15.0[1]	19.1[1]	___	___	___
Scudder Pacific Opps	int'l	127.4	-37.8[5]	-12.4[5]	-2.3[5]	___	___	___
Scudder Grtr Europe	int'l	228.5	24.0[1]	26.1[1]	—	___	___	___
Scudder Int'l Gro & Inc	int'l	46.9	—	—	—	___	___	___
Scudder Int'l Stk	int'l	2,617.0	8.0[2]	11.6[2]	12.9[2]	___	___	___
Scudder Pathway Int'l	int'l	9.7	7.0[2]	—	—	___	___	___
Scudder Development SC	agg gr	862.2	6.9[5]	21.0[4]	12.8[4]	___	___	___
Scudder Large Cap Gro	agg gr	307.4	32.8[1]	27.6[1]	15.5[3]	___	___	___
Scudder Micro-Cap SC	agg gr	134.7	35.2[1]	—	—	___	___	___
Scudder 21st Cent Gro	agg gr	29.1	9.7[4]	—	—	___	___	___
Scudder Classic Gro‡	growth	72.0	34.9[1]	—	—	___	___	___
Scudder Large Cap Val	growth	2,230.2	32.5[1]	27.7[2]	17.7[3]	___	___	___
Scudder Pathway Growth	growth	50.0	14.9[5]	—	—	___	___	___
Scudder Small Co Val SC	growth	211.5	37.0[1]	—	—	___	___	___
Scudder Value‡	growth	20.4	35.3[1]	29.4[1]	19.7[1]	___	___	___
Scudder Glob Disc‡	global	339.5	9.9[4]	16.3[3]	14.9[1]	___	___	___
Scudder Global	global	1,570.5	17.2[2]	17.1[3]	15.1[1]	___	___	___
Scudder Balanced	gr-inc	158.0	22.7[4]	20.1[5]	—	___	___	___
Scudder Gro & Inc	gr-inc	6,832.8	30.3[2]	27.8[2]	19.9[2]	___	___	___
Scudder S&P 500 Idx	gr-inc	26.5	—	—	—	___	___	___
Scudder Pathway Balanced	income	207.3	13.4[5]	—	—	___	___	___
Scudder Pathway Cons	income	17.9	14.4[5]	—	—	___	___	___
Scudder Emg Mkts Inc	fix-inc	345.6	13.1[2]	22.1[1]	—	___	___	___
Scudder Glob Bond	fix-inc	124.9	0.4[5]	3.7[5]	3.3[5]	___	___	___
Scudder Hi Yld Bd	fix-inc	155.7	14.8[1]	—	—	___	___	___
Scudder US Zero 2000	fix-inc	352.5	6.5[5]	8.5[5]	6.4[5]	___	___	___
Scudder Income	fix-inc	695.6	8.7[4]	10.0[3]	7.5[3]	___	___	___
Scudder Int'l Bond	fix-inc	176.7	-4.2[5]	2.5[5]	2.7[5]	___	___	___
Scudder GNMA	fix-inc	389.9	8.4[3]	9.6[3]	6.2[4]	___	___	___
Scudder ST Bond	fix-inc	1,165.5	6.1[4]	6.9[4]	5.1[3]	___	___	___
Scudder CA TF Bd	tax-free	310.1	10.2[1]	10.7[1]	7.4[1]	___	___	___
Scudder MA TF Bd	tax-free	356.0	8.5[4]	10.0[3]	7.4[2]	___	___	___

No-load fund groups *continued*

Families with 3 or more funds including one stock or bond fund
Arranged in alphabetical order by group and risk within group

| Fund group/fund | Objective | Total Net Assets $ Millions 12/31/97 | Annualized Total Return % with quintile ranks by obj | | | Post quintile ranks for your funds here | | |
			1997	3 years 1995-1997	5 years 1993-1997	1997	3 years ending 1997	5 years ending 1997
Scudder NY TF Bd	tax-free	189.1	9.9[1]	10.2[2]	7.0[3]	_____	_____	_____
Scudder OH TF Bd	tax-free	89.5	8.7[4]	9.9[3]	7.1[3]	_____	_____	_____
Scudder PA TF Bd	tax-free	75.5	8.9[3]	9.8[3]	7.1[3]	_____	_____	_____
Scudder Hi Yld TF	tax-free	324.8	12.0[1]	11.6[1]	7.7[1]	_____	_____	_____
Scudder Mngd Muni	tax-free	719.2	9.3[2]	9.9[3]	7.2[3]	_____	_____	_____
Scudder Medium TF	tax-free	651.6	7.7[2]	8.6[2]	6.5[2]	_____	_____	_____
Scudder MA Ltd TF	tax-free	83.9	5.7[2]	6.2[1]	—	_____	_____	_____
Scudder Ltd TF	tax-free	116.4	5.9[1]	6.4[1]	—	_____	_____	_____
Scudder Cash Inv Tr	money mkt gen	1,231.7	4.9[5]	4.9[5]	4.2[4]	_____	_____	_____
Scudder Premium MM	money mkt gen	334.8	—	—	—	_____	_____	_____
Scudder CA TF MM	money mkt TF	80.9	3.0[4]	3.2[4]	2.8[4]	_____	_____	_____
Scudder NY TF MM	money mkt TF	86.7	3.1[4]	3.2[4]	2.7[5]	_____	_____	_____
Scudder TF MM	money mkt TF	280.2	3.1[3]	3.2[3]	2.8[4]	_____	_____	_____
Scudder Trsy MM	money mkt gov	412.4	4.7[5]	4.8[5]	4.1[5]	_____	_____	_____
Your average		26,168.5				_____	_____	_____
Sefton Funds								
Sefton Sm Co Val SC	agg gr	29.7	—	—	—	_____	_____	_____
Sefton Equity Value	growth	85.3	25.3[3]	—	—	_____	_____	_____
Sefton US Gov	fix-inc	35.3	8.4[3]	—	—	_____	_____	_____
Sefton CA Tax-Free	tax-free	40.3	8.5[4]	—	—	_____	_____	_____
Your average		190.6				_____	_____	_____
The Selected Funds								
Selected Spec Shares	growth	74.9	26.9[3]	23.4[4]	15.2[4]	_____	_____	_____
Selected Amer Shares	gr-inc	2,218.1	37.3[1]	35.3[1]	20.4[1]	_____	_____	_____
Selected US Gov Inc	fix-inc	6.0	7.2[5]	8.4[5]	6.2[5]	_____	_____	_____
Selected Daily Gov MM	money mkt gov	117.6	4.9[3]	5.0[4]	4.1[4]	_____	_____	_____
Your average		2,416.6				_____	_____	_____
Seneca Funds								
Seneca Mid-Cap Edge	agg gr	2.5	16.2[4]	—	—	_____	_____	_____
Seneca Growth	growth	5.9	27.9[3]	—	—	_____	_____	_____
Seneca Real Estate	sector	3.0	16.6[4]	—	—	_____	_____	_____
Seneca Bond	fix-inc	8.9	12.8[1]	—	—	_____	_____	_____
Your average		20.3				_____	_____	_____
Sextant Funds								
Sextant International	int'l	0.9	15.9[1]	—	—	_____	_____	_____
Sextant Growth	growth	2.2	26.6[3]	21.1[4]	11.6[5]	_____	_____	_____
Sextant Bond Inc	fix-inc	1.2	12.1[2]	9.2[4]	—	_____	_____	_____
Sextant ST Bond	fix-inc	2.7	6.5[2]	—	—	_____	_____	_____
Sextant Idaho TE	tax-free	5.4	7.1[5]	8.0[5]	5.7[5]	_____	_____	_____
Your average		12.4				:-	:-	:-

o-load fund groups *continued*

families with 3 or more funds including one stock or bond fund
arranged in alphabetical order by group and risk within group

Fund group/fund	Objective	Total Net Assets $ Millions 12/31/97	Annualized Total Return % with quintile ranks by obj			Post quintile ranks for your funds here		
			1997	3 years 1995-1997	5 years 1993-1997	1997	3 years ending 1997	5 years ending 1997
Sit Funds								
Sit Sci & Tech Gro...	sector	0.1	—	—	—	____	____	____
Sit Develop Mkts Gro...	int'l	12.8	-5.2[4]	2.1[4]	—	____	____	____
Sit Int'l Growth...	int'l	90.5	4.8[3]	8.1[3]	12.7[2]	____	____	____
Sit Mid Cap Gro...	agg gr	382.3	17.7[3]	24.2[3]	15.7[3]	____	____	____
Sit Sm Cap Gro SC...	agg gr	60.1	7.6[5]	23.5[3]	—	____	____	____
Sit Large Cap Gro...	growth	81.5	31.7[2]	28.8[2]	17.7[3]	____	____	____
Sit Regional Gro...	growth	0.1	—	—	—	____	____	____
Sit Balanced...	income	5.7	21.7[3]	20.9[2]	—	____	____	____
Sit US Gov...	fix-inc	92.9	8.2[4]	8.2[5]	6.7[4]	____	____	____
Sit Bond...	fix-inc	8.5	9.4[2]	10.1[2]	—	____	____	____
Sit MN TF Inc...	tax-free	128.2	8.2[4]	8.6[5]	—	____	____	____
Sit TF Income...	tax-free	445.2	9.8[1]	9.4[4]	7.5[1]	____	____	____
Sit Money Mkt...	money mkt gen	30.7	5.2[2]	—	—	____	____	____
Your average		1,338.6				____	____	____
Skyline Funds								
Skyline Sm Cap Contra SC...	agg gr	4.7	—	—	—	____	____	____
Skyline Spcl Eqty II...	agg gr	165.5	26.2[2]	24.5[2]	—	____	____	____
Skyline Special Eqty SC‡...	agg gr	466.5	35.4[1]	26.2[2]	19.5[1]	____	____	____
Firstar Money Mkt*...	money mkt gen	254.0	5.1[3]	5.2[3]	4.4[3]	____	____	____
Firstar Gov MM*...	money mkt gov	193.1	5.0[3]	5.1[3]	4.3[2]	____	____	____
Your average		890.7				____	____	____
Smith Breeden Funds								
Smith Brdn Finl Srvcs...	sector	0.1	—	—	—	____	____	____
Smith Brdn Eqty Plus...	gr-inc	86.5	32.3[2]	31.0[1]	21.0[1]	____	____	____
Smith Brdn Inter Dur US Gov...	fix-inc	32.3	9.0[2]	10.1[2]	7.8[1]	____	____	____
Smith Brdn Sh Dur US Gov...	fix-inc	89.5	6.3[3]	6.2[5]	5.4[3]	____	____	____
Your average		208.4				____	____	____
SSgA Funds								
SSgA Emg Mkts...	int'l	254.9	-8.8[4]	-1.2[4]	—	____	____	____
SSgA Active Int'l...	int'l	142.1	-10.1[4]	—	—	____	____	____
SSgA Sm Cap SC...	agg gr	281.5	23.6[3]	31.2[1]	20.4[1]	____	____	____
SSgA LifeSol Gro...	growth	46.2	—	—	—	____	____	____
SSgA Matrix Eqty...	growth	470.1	34.2[1]	28.6[2]	19.8[1]	____	____	____
SSgA Gro & Inc...	gr-inc	80.5	37.7[1]	29.1[2]	—	____	____	____
SSgA LifeSol Inc & Gro...	gr-inc	16.0	—	—	—	____	____	____
SSgA S&P 500 Index...	gr-inc	1,452.7	33.1[1]	30.8[1]	20.0[1]	____	____	____
SSgA LifeSol Bal...	income	52.6	—	—	—	____	____	____
SSgA Bond Mkt...	fix-inc	108.6	8.9[4]	—	—	____	____	____
SSgA Inter Fix...	fix-inc	60.6	7.4[4]	9.1[3]	—	____	____	____
SSgA Yld Plus...	fix-inc	704.2	5.5[5]	5.9[5]	5.0[4]	____	____	____
SSgA MM...	money mkt gen	4,757.9	5.4[1]	5.5[1]	—	____	____	____
SSgA TF MM...	money mkt TF	219.4	3.1[4]	3.2[3]	—	____	____	____
SSgA Gov MM...	money mkt gov	707.0	5.3[1]	5.4[1]	—	____	____	____
Your average		9,354.3				____	____	____

Families with 3 or more funds including one stock or bond fund
Arranged in alphabetical order by group and risk within group

| Fund group/fund | Objective | Total Net Assets $ Millions 12/31/97 | Annualized Total Return % with quintile ranks by obj | | | Post quintile ranks for your funds here | | |
			1997	3 years 1995-1997	5 years 1993-1997	1997	3 years ending 1997	5 years ending 1997
State Farm Funds								
State Farm Balanced‡	income	764.4	22.2[2]	20.1[3]	13.4[3]	___	___	___
State Farm Growth‡	growth	1,826.1	31.2[2]	26.3[2]	16.5[3]	___	___	___
State Farm Interm‡	fix-inc	110.9	7.1[5]	7.9[5]	5.9[5]	___	___	___
State Farm Muni Bd‡	tax-free	338.6	7.3[5]	8.2[5]	6.3[5]	___	___	___
Your average		3,040.0				___	___	___
Steadman Funds								
Steadman Amer Indust	agg gr	0.8	-12.4[5]	-10.2[5]	-13.1[5]	___	___	___
Steadman Tech & Gro	agg gr	0.3	-28.2[5]	-28.9[5]	-26.9[5]	___	___	___
Steadman Investment	growth	1.6	1.1[5]	-1.8[5]	-8.4[5]	___	___	___
Steadman Associated	income	3.5	-1.3[5]	3.9[5]	-0.3[5]	___	___	___
Your average		6.2				___	___	___
Stein Roe Funds								
Stein Roe Emg Mkts	int'l	20.7	—	—	—	___	___	___
Stein Roe Int'l	int'l	532.2	-3.5[4]	2.8[4]	—	___	___	___
Stein Roe Cap Opp	agg gr	1,012.6	6.2[5]	24.4[3]	19.7[1]	___	___	___
Stein Roe Growth Stk‡	agg gr	623.4	31.6[1]	29.2[1]	16.4[3]	___	___	___
Stein Roe Spec Venture SC	agg gr	222.8	9.7[4]	21.5[4]	—	___	___	___
Stein Roe Growth Opp	growth	50.3	—	—	—	___	___	___
Stein Roe Special	growth	200.0	25.9[3]	21.1[4]	15.6[4]	___	___	___
Stein Roe Young Invest	growth	591.7	26.3[3]	33.6[1]	—	___	___	___
Stein Roe Gro & Inc	gr-inc	340.0	25.7[3]	25.9[3]	17.6[3]	___	___	___
Stein Roe Balanced	income	278.6	17.5[4]	18.8[4]	12.5[4]	___	___	___
Stein Roe Hi Yld Bd	fix-inc	31.1	15.9[1]	—	—	___	___	___
Stein Roe Income	fix-inc	1,267.6	9.6[1]	11.2[1]	8.4[1]	___	___	___
Stein Roe Inter Bd	fix-inc	323.1	9.3[2]	10.1[2]	7.2[2]	___	___	___
Stein Roe Hi Yld Muni	tax-free	137.6	9.5[2]	10.4[2]	7.4[2]	___	___	___
Stein Roe Mgd Muni	tax-free	393.7	9.3[2]	9.8[3]	6.8[3]	___	___	___
Stein Roe Inter Muni	tax-free	425.3	7.5[2]	8.2[2]	6.3[2]	___	___	___
Stein Roe Cash Res	money mkt gen	507.5	5.0[4]	5.2[3]	4.4[3]	___	___	___
Stein Roe Muni MM	money mkt TF	129.7	3.1[3]	3.3[3]	2.8[3]	___	___	___
Your average		7,087.9				___	___	___
Stratton Funds								
Stratton Sm Cap Yld SC	growth	39.4	42.6[1]	27.8[2]	—	___	___	___
Stratton Growth	gr-inc	60.0	36.1[1]	28.9[2]	19.5[2]	___	___	___
Stratton Month Div REIT Sh	sector	102.0	17.3[4]	16.3[5]	8.1[5]	___	___	___
Your average		201.4				___	___	___
Strong Funds								
Strong Limited Rescs	sector	5.4	—	—	—	___	___	___
Strong Asia Pacific	int'l	24.7	-31.0[5]	-9.3[5]	—	___	___	___
Strong Int'l Stk	int'l	147.3	-14.2[4]	0.0[4]	7.8[4]	___	___	___
Strong Discovery SC	agg gr	383.0	10.8[4]	14.9[5]	11.8[5]	___	___	___
Strong Growth 20	agg gr	59.7	—	—	—	___	___	___

milies with 3 or more funds including one stock or bond fund
ranged in alphabetical order by group and risk within group

| | | | Annualized Total Return % with quintile ranks by obj | | | Post quintile ranks for your funds here | | |
| | | Total Net Assets $ Millions 12/31/97 | 1997 | 3 years 1995-1997 | 5 years 1993-1997 | 1997 | 3 years ending 1997 | 5 years ending 1997 |
Fund group/fund	Objective							
Strong Growth	agg gr	1,597.1	19.1[3]	26.1[2]	—	___	___	___
Strong Small Cap SC	agg gr	181.9	-4.5[5]	—	—	___	___	___
Strong Common Stk‡	growth	1,564.8	24.0[4]	25.5[3]	19.8[1]	___	___	___
Strong MidCap	growth	15.7	13.9[5]	—	—	___	___	___
Strong Opportunity	growth	1,924.9	23.4[4]	22.9[4]	18.3[2]	___	___	___
Strong Schafer Value	growth	1,511.2	29.3[2]	28.8[2]	20.4[1]	___	___	___
Strong Value	growth	93.5	25.9[3]	—	—	___	___	___
Strong 500 Idx	gr-inc	19.7	—	—	—	___	___	___
Strong Blue Chip 100	gr-inc	12.7	—	—	—	___	___	___
Strong Gr & Inc	gr-inc	246.2	30.4[2]	—	—	___	___	___
Strong Total Ret	gr-inc	848.7	24.2[4]	21.6[4]	16.8[4]	___	___	___
Strong Asst Alloc	income	278.8	16.7[4]	16.3[5]	12.1[4]	___	___	___
Strong Eqty Inc	income	145.8	31.3[1]	—	—	___	___	___
Strong Amer Util	income	187.4	27.6[1]	23.7[1]	—	___	___	___
Strong Int'l Bond	fix-inc	25.3	-4.8[5]	7.0[5]	—	___	___	___
Strong Hi Yld Bd	fix-inc	568.9	16.0[1]	—	—	___	___	___
Strong Corp Bond	fix-inc	560.5	11.9[2]	14.0[1]	11.3[1]	___	___	___
Strong Gov Sec	fix-inc	907.4	9.1[2]	10.4[2]	8.0[1]	___	___	___
Strong ST Global Bd	fix-inc	106.8	6.1[4]	8.8[1]	—	___	___	___
Strong ST Hi Yld Bd	fix-inc	56.5	—	—	—	___	___	___
Strong Advantage	fix-inc	2,041.0	6.5[2]	6.9[4]	6.5[1]	___	___	___
Strong ST Bond	fix-inc	1,320.7	7.2[1]	8.6[1]	6.7[1]	___	___	___
Strong Hi Yld Muni	tax-free	323.1	13.9[1]	11.1[1]	—	___	___	___
Strong Muni Bond	tax-free	240.8	12.1[1]	8.5[5]	6.4[4]	___	___	___
Strong Muni Advantage	tax-free	986.5	5.1[3]	—	—	___	___	___
Strong ST Hi Yld Muni	fix-inc	11.6	—	—	—	___	___	___
Strong ST Muni	tax-free	182.1	6.9[1]	5.7[3]	4.4[4]	___	___	___
Strong Heritage MM	money mkt gen	1,480.5	5.6[1]	—	—	___	___	___
Strong Money Mkt	money mkt gen	1,818.9	5.3[2]	5.6[1]	4.7[1]	___	___	___
Strong Muni MM	money mkt TF	1,807.1	3.6[1]	3.9[1]	3.4[1]	___	___	___
Your average		21,686.2				___	___	___
SwissKey Funds								
SwissKey Non-US Eqty	int'l	8.1	5.0[3]	—	—	___	___	___
SwissKey US Eqty	growth	44.1	24.2[3]	—	—	___	___	___
SwissKey Glob Eqty	global	63.6	9.9[4]	—	—	___	___	___
SwissKey Global	global	28.4	10.2[4]	—	—	___	___	___
SwissKey US Balanced	income	1.7	12.6[5]	—	—	___	___	___
SwissKey Glob Bd	fix-inc	4.5	1.2[5]	—	—	___	___	___
SwissKey US Bd	fix-inc	1.9	9.1[4]	—	—	___	___	___
Your average		152.3				___	___	___
Thompson Plumb Funds								
Thompson Plumb Growth	growth	47.3	32.4[1]	32.0[1]	18.6[2]	___	___	___
Thompson Plumb Balanced	gr-inc	36.8	22.5[4]	21.9[4]	13.9[5]	___	___	___
Thompson Plumb Bond	fix-inc	32.2	7.4[5]	7.8[5]	5.7[5]	___	___	___
Your average		116.3				___	___	___

No-load fund groups *continued*

Families with 3 or more funds including one stock or bond fund
Arranged in alphabetical order by group and risk within group

| Fund group/fund | Objective | Total Net Assets $ Millions 12/31/97 | Annualized Total Return % with quintile ranks by obj | | | Post quintile ranks for your funds here | | |
			1997	3 years 1995-1997	5 years 1993-1997	1997	3 years ending 1997	5 years ending 1997
TIP Mutual Funds								
TIP:Penn Cap Sel Finl Srvcs...	sector	0.4	—	—	—			
TIP:Target Sel Eqty...	agg gr	0.1	—	—	—			
TIP:Turner Mid Cap...	agg gr	13.0	40.6[1]	—	—			
TIP:Turner Small Cap SC‡	agg gr	153.5	14.8[4]	35.5[1]	—			
TIP:Clover Cap Sm Cap Val SC	growth	15.3	15.5[5]	—	—			
TIP:Turner Growth Eqty...	growth	89.6	31.4[2]	26.9[2]	17.1[3]			
TIP:Clover Cap Eqty Val...	gr-inc	122.2	17.5[5]	20.6[5]	18.0[3]			
TIP:Clover Max Cap Val...	gr-inc	0.7	—	—	—			
TIP:Turner Ultra Large Cap...	gr-inc	0.9	—	—	—			
TIP:Penn Cap Strat Hi Yld...	fix-inc	0.1	—	—	—			
TIP:Clover Cap Fix Inc...	fix-inc	27.8	9.6[3]	10.5[3]	7.9[3]			
Your average		423.6						
Transamerica Premier Funds								
Transamerica Premr Agg Gr...	agg gr	12.8	—	—	—			
Transamerica Premr Sm Cap SC...	agg gr	11.1	—	—	—			
Transamerica Premr Eqty...	growth	110.2	47.5[1]	—	—			
Transamerica Premr Idx...	gr-inc	23.9	33.1[1]	—	—			
Transamerica Premr Balanced...	income	26.7	35.4[1]	—	—			
Transamerica Premr Bond...	fix-inc	14.2	10.0[3]	—	—			
Transamerica Premr Cash Res...	money mkt gen	51.2	5.5[1]	—	—			
Your average		250.1						
UAM Funds								
UAM FMA Small Co SC...	agg gr	56.0	40.4[1]	30.0[1]	22.3[1]			
UAM McKee Sm Cap SC...	agg gr	57.0	—	—	—			
UAM RHJ Sm Cap SC...	agg gr	48.0	20.7[3]	29.2[1]	—			
UAM RHJ Small to MidCap SC...	agg gr	13.4	25.7[2]	—	—			
UAM Jacobs Int'l Octgn...	int'l	84.9	—	—	—			
UAM McKee Int'l...	int'l	114.3	11.3[2]	10.2[2]	—			
UAM MJI Int'l...	int'l	29.9	6.0[2]	7.8[3]	—			
UAM TS&W Int'l Eqty...	int'l	110.2	2.5[3]	6.7[3]	9.9[4]			
UAM C&B Eqty Taxable Invst...	growth	2.1	—	—	—			
UAM Chi Asst Mgmt Val Contra...	growth	19.1	18.9[4]	19.6[5]	—			
UAM DSI Discpnd Val...	growth	78.2	23.4[4]	25.9[3]	18.1[2]			
UAM Hanson Eqty...	growth	19.9	—	—	—			
UAM McKee Domestic Eqty...	growth	108.0	20.9[4]	—	—			
UAM Sirach Eqty...	growth	33.0	30.0[2]	—	—			
UAM Sirach Growth...	growth	138.9	32.1[2]	28.2[2]	—			
UAM Strlng Part Eqty...	growth	52.3	24.9[3]	27.6[2]	17.6[3]			
UAM Strlng Sm Cap Val SC...	growth	27.6	38.8[1]	—	—			
UAM TJ Core Eqty...	growth	9.9	30.7[2]	—	—			
UAM C & B Eqty...	gr-inc	152.4	28.0[3]	26.6[3]	16.5[4]			
UAM FPA Crescent...	gr-inc	173.1	22.0[4]	23.6[4]	—			
UAM ICM Equity...	gr-inc	47.9	29.6[2]	29.8[2]	—			
UAM IRC Enhncd Idx...	gr-inc	2.5	27.2[3]	—	—			
UAM NWQ Value Eqty...	gr-inc	4.9	30.8[2]	27.2[3]	—			

milies with 3 or more funds including one stock or bond fund
rranged in alphabetical order by group and risk within group

| | | Total Net Assets $ Millions 12/31/97 | Annualized Total Return % with quintile ranks by obj | | | Post quintile ranks for your funds here | | |
			1997	3 years 1995-1997	5 years 1993-1997	1997	3 years ending 1997	5 years ending 1997
Fund group/fund	Objective							
UAM Sirach Spec Eqty	gr-inc	314.1	11.3[5]	19.3[5]	13.5[5]	____	____	____
UAM TS&W Eqty	gr-inc	100.2	26.0[3]	24.5[4]	16.7[4]	____	____	____
UAM C & B Balanced	income	24.0	19.7[3]	18.9[4]	12.1[4]	____	____	____
UAM DSI Balanced	income	30.4	—	—	—	____	____	____
UAM NWQ Balanced	income	14.1	20.9[3]	19.0[4]	—	____	____	____
UAM Sirach Strat Balanced	income	88.4	21.9[2]	20.2[3]	—	____	____	____
UAM Strlng Part Balanced	income	78.9	18.3[4]	19.1[4]	12.7[4]	____	____	____
UAM SAMI Pref Stck Inc	fix-inc	25.1	8.3[4]	8.2[5]	5.7[5]	____	____	____
UAM BHM&S Tot Ret Bd	fix-inc	19.9	8.8[4]	—	—	____	____	____
UAM Sirach Bond	fix-inc	39.0	—	—	—	____	____	____
UAM TS&W Fix Inc	fix-inc	67.9	9.2[3]	9.4[4]	6.6[4]	____	____	____
UAM Chi Asst Mgmt Int Bd	fix-inc	10.8	7.2[5]	—	—	____	____	____
UAM Mckee US Gov	fix-inc	26.0	8.5[3]	—	—	____	____	____
UAM DSI Ltd Mat	fix-inc	32.7	6.7[2]	7.5[2]	5.0[4]	____	____	____
UAM DSI MM	money mkt gen	149.0	5.3[2]	—	—	____	____	____
Your average		2,479.6				____	____	____
JBS Funds								
UBS Int'l Eqty	int'l	23.2	-3.7[4]	—	—	____	____	____
UBS US Eqty	gr-inc	26.5	29.6[2]	—	—	____	____	____
UBS Bond	fix-inc	13.5	7.2[5]	—	—	____	____	____
Your average		63.2				____	____	____
Unified Funds								
Unified Starwood Strat	growth	1.2	23.1[4]	—	—	____	____	____
Unified Laidlaw	gr-inc	2.8	32.8[1]	—	—	____	____	____
Unified First Lexgtn Bal	income	6.3	—	—	—	____	____	____
Unified Taxable MM	money mkt gen	50.0	4.5[5]	—	—	____	____	____
Your average		60.3				____	____	____
US Global Investors Funds								
US Glb:Gold Shares	prec met	66.1	-57.4[5]	-38.5[2]	-12.7[5]	____	____	____
US Glb:World Gold	prec met	131.3	-41.1[2]	-6.6[1]	5.2[1]	____	____	____
US Glb:China Region Oppty	int'l	25.6	-22.5[5]	-5.2[5]	—	____	____	____
US Glb:Regents East Europe	int'l	9.3	—	—	—	____	____	____
US Glb:Bonnel Growth	agg gr	103.6	10.3[4]	27.0[2]	—	____	____	____
US Glb:Adrian Day Glob Oppty	global	3.2	—	—	—	____	____	____
US Glb:Glob Resrcs	global	25.0	-2.8[5]	12.4[4]	8.7[4]	____	____	____
US Glb:All-Amer Eqty	gr-inc	27.4	30.3[2]	27.8[2]	16.8[4]	____	____	____
US Glb:MegaTrends	gr-inc	21.1	15.6[5]	18.3[5]	10.6[5]	____	____	____
US Glb:Income	income	9.3	23.1[2]	18.4[4]	11.9[5]	____	____	____
US Glb:Real Estate	sector	16.3	19.3[3]	23.1[3]	10.6[5]	____	____	____
US Glb:Tax Free	tax-free	19.7	9.1[1]	8.9[1]	6.5[1]	____	____	____
US Glb:Near Term TF	tax-free	7.7	6.6[1]	5.8[2]	5.4[1]	____	____	____
US Glb:US Gov Sec Svgs MM	money mkt gov	732.9	5.3[1]	5.4[1]	4.7[1]	____	____	____
US Glb:US Trsy Sec Csh MM	money mkt gov	182.4	4.5[5]	4.3[5]	3.7[5]	____	____	____
Your average		1,380.9				____	____	____

No-load fund groups *continued*

Families with 3 or more funds including one stock or bond fund
Arranged in alphabetical order by group and risk within group

Fund group/fund	Objective	Total Net Assets $ Millions 12/31/97	Annualized Total Return % with quintile ranks by obj			Post quintile ranks for your funds here		
			1997	3 years 1995-1997	5 years 1993-1997	1997	3 years ending 1997	5 years ending 1997
USAA Investment Management								
USAA Science & Tech	sector	62.4	—	—	—			
USAA Gold	prec met	84.5	-38.2[1]	-13.7[1]	-1.6[4]			
USAA Emg Mkts	int'l	305.9	-3.5[4]	5.3[4]	—			
USAA International	int'l	575.3	9.0[2]	12.0[2]	15.1[1]			
USAA Agg Growth SC	agg gr	732.4	7.6[5]	23.5[3]	15.1[3]			
USAA First Start Gro	growth	22.6	—	—	—			
USAA Growth Strat	growth	228.7	9.1[5]	—	—			
USAA Growth	growth	1,356.9	3.7[5]	17.3[5]	12.4[5]			
USAA Cornerstone Strat	global	1,413.9	15.6[2]	17.3[3]	14.6[2]			
USAA World Growth	global	321.5	12.9[3]	14.9[4]	13.6[2]			
USAA Balanced Strat	gr-inc	47.4	19.1[5]	—	—			
USAA Gro & Inc	gr-inc	936.4	26.0[3]	26.8[3]	—			
USAA S&P 500 Idx	gr-inc	628.6	33.0[1]	—	—			
USAA Growth & Tax Strat	income	211.6	16.1[4]	16.6[5]	11.9[5]			
USAA Income Stk	income	2,397.5	26.9[1]	24.4[1]	16.4[1]			
USAA Income Strat	income	24.1	15.2[5]	—	—			
USAA Income	fix-inc	1,722.1	11.0[1]	11.9[1]	7.8[1]			
USAA GNMA	fix-inc	347.0	9.5[1]	9.6[3]	7.1[2]			
USAA ST Bond	fix-inc	144.9	7.2[1]	8.2[1]	—			
USAA CA Bond	tax-free	511.0	10.3[1]	12.3[1]	7.7[1]			
USAA FL TF Inc	tax-free	137.4	11.2[1]	11.3[1]	—			
USAA NY Bond	tax-free	66.0	10.6[1]	10.7[2]	7.0[3]			
USAA Texas TF Inc	tax-free	17.4	11.7[1]	12.9[1]	—			
USAA VA Bond	tax-free	331.0	9.5[2]	10.5[2]	7.3[2]			
USAA TE Long	tax-free	2,002.0	10.4[1]	11.0[1]	7.2[2]			
USAA TE Inter	tax-free	1,936.0	9.4[1]	9.6[1]	7.1[1]			
USAA TE Short	tax-free	937.0	5.9[1]	6.1[1]	4.9[2]			
USAA Money Mkt	money mkt gen	2,215.1	5.4[1]	5.5[1]	4.7[1]			
USAA CA MM	money mkt TF	389.2	3.4[1]	3.4[2]	3.0[1]			
USAA FL MM	money mkt TF	170.8	3.3[1]	3.4[2]	—			
USAA NY MM	money mkt TF	51.0	3.3[2]	3.4[2]	2.9[2]			
USAA TE MM	money mkt TF	1,502.1	3.5[1]	3.5[1]	3.1[1]			
USAA TX TF MM	money mkt TF	5.4	3.4[1]	—	—			
USAA VA MM	money mkt TF	117.3	3.3[2]	3.3[2]	3.0[2]			
USAA Trsy MM	money mkt gov	95.6	5.2[1]	5.3[1]	4.5[1]			
Your average		22,048.0						
Value Line Funds								
Value Line Levergd Gro	agg gr	432.6	23.8[2]	27.6[2]	18.4[2]			
Value Line US Multi-Nat'l Co	agg gr	26.3	19.0[3]	—	—			
Value Line Sm Cap Gro SC	agg gr	21.8	11.5[4]	15.2[5]	—			
Value Line Spec Sit	agg gr	116.6	32.2[1]	22.3[3]	15.8[3]			
Value Line Fund	growth	382.4	21.6[4]	25.3[3]	15.0[4]			
Value Line Asst Alloc	income	101.7	20.9[3]	27.7[1]	—			
Value Line Convert	income	85.6	17.0[4]	19.9[3]	13.4[3]			
Value Line Income	income	160.4	18.5[4]	20.7[3]	12.7[4]			

milies with 3 or more funds including one stock or bond fund
ranged in alphabetical order by group and risk within group

| | | Total Net Assets $ Millions 12/31/97 | Annualized Total Return % with quintile ranks by obj | | | Post quintile ranks for your funds here | | |
			1997	3 years 1995-1997	5 years 1993-1997	1997	3 years ending 1997	5 years ending 1997
Fund group/fund	Objective							
Value Line Agg Inc	fix-inc	134.3	14.1¹	18.0¹	13.4¹	_____	_____	_____
Value Line US Gov	fix-inc	188.7	9.2³	9.1⁵	4.9⁵	_____	_____	_____
Value Line NY TE	tax-free	33.9	9.3²	9.5⁴	6.7⁴	_____	_____	_____
Value Line TE Hi Yld	tax-free	187.5	8.8³	9.6³	6.4⁴	_____	_____	_____
Value Line Cash	money mkt gen	303.1	5.1³	5.4¹	4.6¹	_____	_____	_____
Value Line TE MM	money mkt TF	17.7	2.5⁵	2.7⁵	2.3⁵	_____	_____	_____
Your average		2,192.6				_____	_____	_____
an Wagoner Funds								
Van Wagoner Emg Gr	agg gr	313.2	-20.0⁵	—	—	_____	_____	_____
Van Wagoner Micro-Cap SC	agg gr	71.9	-19.8⁵	—	—	_____	_____	_____
Van Wagoner Post Venture	agg gr	20.5	-12.2⁵	—	—	_____	_____	_____
Van Wagoner Mid-Cap	growth	73.8	-13.9⁵	—	—	_____	_____	_____
Northern US Gov MM*	money mkt gov	311.3	5.0²	—	—	_____	_____	_____
Your average		479.4				_____	_____	_____
anguard Funds Group								
Vangd Spec-Energy	sector	1,181.4	14.8⁵	24.5³	19.1²	_____	_____	_____
Vangd Spec-Health	sector	4,466.2	28.5²	31.3²	22.6²	_____	_____	_____
Vangd Spec-Gold	prec met	293.0	-39.0¹	-16.7²	1.1³	_____	_____	_____
Vangd Idx Pacific†	int'l	827.2	-25.7⁵	-11.0⁵	1.5⁵	_____	_____	_____
Vangd Idx Emg Mkt†	int'l	660.9	-16.8⁵	-1.0⁴	—	_____	_____	_____
Vangd Idx Europe†	int'l	2,432.4	24.2¹	22.6¹	19.4¹	_____	_____	_____
Vangd Int'l Growth	int'l	6,809.0	4.1³	11.1²	14.9²	_____	_____	_____
Vangd Int'l Value	int'l	776.8	-4.6⁴	4.8⁴	9.6⁴	_____	_____	_____
Vangd Tot Int'l Port†	int'l	903.1	-0.8⁴	—	—	_____	_____	_____
Vangd Explorer SC	agg gr	2,541.0	14.6⁴	18.2⁴	13.9⁴	_____	_____	_____
Vangd Hrzn:Agg Gro	agg gr	474.1	25.5²	—	—	_____	_____	_____
Vangd Hrzn:Cap Opp	agg gr	63.4	-8.0⁵	—	—	_____	_____	_____
Vangd Morgan	agg gr	2,795.3	30.8¹	29.9¹	18.3²	_____	_____	_____
Vangd Idx Extend Mkt†	growth	2,722.8	26.7³	25.9³	17.5³	_____	_____	_____
Vangd Idx Sm Cap† SC	growth	2,652.4	24.5³	23.7⁴	17.5³	_____	_____	_____
Vangd Idx Total Mkt	growth	5,092.0	31.0²	29.1²	18.9²	_____	_____	_____
Vangd LifeStrat:Growth	growth	1,183.7	22.1⁴	22.1⁴	—	_____	_____	_____
Vangd Primecap	growth	8,186.2	36.8¹	29.9¹	23.6¹	_____	_____	_____
Vangd Tax Mgd:Cap App	growth	892.5	27.3³	27.4²	—	_____	_____	_____
Vangd US Growth	growth	8,054.6	25.9³	30.0¹	17.6³	_____	_____	_____
Vangd Hrzn:Glob Asst	global	80.1	9.3⁴	—	—	_____	_____	_____
Vangd Hrzn:Glob Eqty	global	126.4	6.7⁴	—	—	_____	_____	_____
Vangd Gro & Inc	gr-inc	2,141.8	35.6¹	31.4¹	20.7¹	_____	_____	_____
Vangd Idx 500	gr-inc	49,357.6	33.2¹	31.0¹	20.1¹	_____	_____	_____
Vangd Idx Growth	gr-inc	2,365.3	36.3¹	32.6¹	19.5²	_____	_____	_____
Vangd Idx Value	gr-inc	1,795.5	29.8²	29.4²	20.5¹	_____	_____	_____
Vangd LifeStrat:Mod Gr	gr-inc	1,358.2	19.7⁴	19.9⁵	—	_____	_____	_____
Vangd Selected Val	gr-inc	191.0	17.4⁵	—	—	_____	_____	_____
Vangd Star:Star	gr-inc	7,355.4	20.5⁴	21.7⁴	14.8⁴	_____	_____	_____
Vangd Tax Mgd:Gro & Inc	gr-inc	579.3	33.3¹	31.1¹		_____	_____	_____

No-load fund groups   *continued*

Families with 3 or more funds including one stock or bond fund
Arranged in alphabetical order by group and risk within group

Fund group/fund	Objective	Total Net Assets $ Millions 12/31/97	1997	3 years 1995-1997	5 years 1993-1997	1997	3 years ending 1997	5 years ending 1997
Vangd Trust US...	gr-inc	174.0	29.5²	27.9²	18.7²			
Vangd Windsor II...	gr-inc	24,376.5	32.3²	31.6¹	20.7¹			
Vangd Windsor‡...	gr-inc	20,914.6	22.0⁴	26.1³	19.1²			
Vangd Asst Alloc...	income	4,099.0	27.3¹	25.9¹	17.2¹			
Vangd Convert...	income	186.7	16.3⁴	16.1⁵	10.9⁶			
Vangd Equity Inc...	income	2,099.7	31.2¹	28.4¹	19.0¹			
Vangd Idx Balanced...	income	1,260.4	22.2²	21.4²	14.1²			
Vangd LifeStrat:Cons Gro...	income	802.9	16.8⁴	17.0⁵	—			
Vangd LifeStrat:Income...	income	243.9	14.2⁵	14.8⁵	—			
Vangd Tax Mgd:Balanced...	income	119.8	16.6⁴	17.6⁴	—			
Vangd Wellesley Inc...	income	7,645.9	20.2³	19.2⁴	13.2³			
Vangd Wellington...	income	21,811.8	23.2²	23.9¹	16.5¹			
Vangd Spec-Util...	income	684.6	25.1²	20.8³	13.2³			
Vangd Spec-REIT Idx...	sector	1,277.7	18.6⁴	—	—			
Vangd Hi Yld Corp...	fix-inc	4,543.9	11.9²	13.5²	11.2¹			
Vangd Prefrd Stk...	fix-inc	329.5	13.0²	15.5¹	9.9²			
Vangd Bond Idx Long...	fix-inc	87.3	14.3¹	13.9¹	—			
Vangd LT Corp...	fix-inc	3,599.2	13.8²	13.3²	9.6²			
Vangd-Adml Long...	fix-inc	311.2	14.0¹	13.6²	9.9²			
Vangd LT Trsy...	fix-inc	1,030.2	13.9¹	13.5²	9.7²			
Vangd Bond Idx Inter...	fix-inc	684.3	9.4¹	10.8¹	—			
Vangd Bond Idx Total...	fix-inc	5,010.0	9.4¹	10.3²	7.4²			
Vangd Inter Corp...	fix-inc	860.1	8.9²	10.8¹	—			
Vangd-Adml Inter...	fix-inc	866.4	9.0²	10.3²	7.4²			
Vangd GNMA...	fix-inc	8,689.8	9.5¹	10.4¹	7.2²			
Vangd Inter Trsy...	fix-inc	1,498.5	9.0²	10.2²	7.6²			
Vangd Bond Idx Short...	fix-inc	438.3	7.0¹	8.1¹	—			
Vangd ST Corp...	fix-inc	4,595.5	6.9²	8.1¹	6.2¹			
Vangd-Adml Short...	fix-inc	743.6	6.5²	7.7²	5.8¹			
Vangd ST Federal...	fix-inc	1,413.6	6.5³	7.8¹	5.8¹			
Vangd ST Trsy...	fix-inc	993.8	6.4³	7.6²	5.7²			
Vangd CA Insur LT...	tax-free	1,198.3	8.9³	10.7¹	7.6¹			
Vangd FL Insur...	tax-free	614.0	8.9³	10.1³	7.6¹			
Vangd NJ Insur LT...	tax-free	936.9	8.6⁴	9.5⁴	7.2³			
Vangd NY Insur LT...	tax-free	1,129.5	8.7⁴	10.0³	7.3²			
Vangd OH Insur LT...	tax-free	252.1	8.5⁴	9.7³	7.2³			
Vangd PA Insur LT...	tax-free	1,741.0	8.3⁴	9.5⁴	7.2²			
Vangd Muni Hi Yld...	tax-free	2,266.4	9.2²	10.5²	7.6¹			
Vangd Muni Insur LT...	tax-free	2,051.7	8.6⁴	10.2²	7.4¹			
Vangd Muni Long...	tax-free	1,260.1	9.3²	10.6²	7.7¹			
Vangd CA Insur Inter...	tax-free	622.9	7.7²	8.7²	—			
Vangd Muni Inter...	tax-free	6,793.1	7.1³	8.2²	6.7¹			
Vangd Muni Ltd Trm...	tax-free	1,978.5	5.1³	5.9²	4.8²			
Vangd Muni Short...	tax-free	1,489.3	4.1⁵	4.6⁵	3.8⁵			
Vangd MM Resvs Prime...	money mkt gen	26,474.0	5.4¹	5.5¹	4.7¹			
Vangd CA MM...	money mkt TF	1,821.9	3.4¹	3.6¹	3.2¹			
Vangd Muni MM...	money mkt TF	5,296.9	3.5¹	3.7¹	3.2¹			

Table header note:
- **Annualized Total Return %** with quintile ranks by obj
- **Post quintile ranks for your funds here**

milies with 3 or more funds including one stock or bond fund
ranged in alphabetical order by group and risk within group

| Fund group/fund | Objective | Total Net Assets $ Millions 12/31/97 | Annualized Total Return % with quintile ranks by obj | | | Post quintile ranks for your funds here | | |
			1997	3 years 1995-1997	5 years 1993-1997	1997	3 years ending 1997	5 years ending 1997
Vangd NJ TF MM	money mkt TF	1,038.5	3.3[1]	3.5[1]	3.1[1]	___	___	___
Vangd NY TF MM	money mkt TF	185.6	—	—	—	___	___	___
Vangd OH TF MM	money mkt TF	291.8	3.5[1]	3.7[1]	3.2[1]	___	___	___
Vangd PA TF MM	money mkt TF	1,642.9	3.5[1]	3.7[1]	3.2[1]	___	___	___
Vangd MM Resvs Federal	money mkt gov	3,480.9	5.4[1]	5.5[1]	4.7[1]	___	___	___
Vangd MM US Trsy	money mkt gov	3,805.0	5.1[2]	5.2[2]	4.5[2]	___	___	___
Vangd-Adml Trsy MM	money mkt gov	3,742.6	5.3[1]	5.4[1]	4.6[1]	___	___	___
Your average		309,865.2				___	___	___
intage Funds								
Vintage Agg Gro	agg gr	86.4	26.2[2]	—	—	___	___	___
Vintage Eqty	growth	389.5	30.1[2]	28.9[2]	18.2[2]	___	___	___
Vintage Balanced	income	47.0	22.8[2]	—	—	___	___	___
Vintage Income	fix-inc	102.7	7.1[5]	8.1[5]	5.9[5]	___	___	___
Vintage Fix Tot Ret	fix-inc	42.1	6.7[5]	—	—	___	___	___
Vintage Bond	fix-inc	2.9	9.2[3]	—	—	___	___	___
Vintage Muni Bd	tax-free	47.3	6.6[4]	8.1[3]	—	___	___	___
Vintage Assets MM	money mkt gov	73.3	4.8[5]	5.0[4]	—	___	___	___
Your average		791.2				___	___	___
ontobel Funds								
Vontobel East Europe	int'l	139.9	8.7[2]	—	—	___	___	___
Vontobel Emg Mkts Eqty	int'l	3.6	—	—	—	___	___	___
Vontobel Int'l Eqty	int'l	160.9	9.2[2]	12.3[2]	13.6[2]	___	___	___
Sand Hill Port Mgr	growth	9.8	17.8[5]	16.3[5]	—	___	___	___
Vontobel US Value	gr-inc	201.3	34.3[1]	31.8[1]	19.4[2]	___	___	___
Vontobel East Europe Debt	fix-inc	14.0	—	—	—	___	___	___
Vontobel Int'l Bd	fix-inc	10.8	-6.0[5]	5.9[5]	—	___	___	___
Kemper-Cash Acct Tr MM*	money mkt gen	1,574.1	4.8[5]	4.9[5]	4.1[5]	___	___	___
Kemper-Cash Acct Tr TF MM*	money mkt TF	349.4	2.9[5]	3.1[4]	2.7[4]	___	___	___
Kemper-Cash Acct Tr Gov MM*	money mkt gov	707.5	4.8[4]	4.9[4]	4.1[4]	___	___	___
Your average		540.3				___	___	___
Varburg Pincus Funds								
Warbg Pincus Health Sci	sector	20.3	27.4[2]	—	—	___	___	___
Warbg Pincus Japan Growth	int'l	26.6	1.5[3]	—	—	___	___	___
Warbg Pincus Japan OTC	int'l	37.6	-25.5[5]	-13.8[5]	—	___	___	___
Warbg Pincus Emg Mkts	int'l	116.5	-20.0[5]	1.0[4]	—	___	___	___
Warbg Pincus Int'l Eqty	int'l	1,956.2	-4.4[4]	5.3[4]	12.1[3]	___	___	___
Warbg Pincus Major Forgn Mkts	int'l	8.9	—	—	—	___	___	___
Warbg Pincus Emg Gro SC	agg gr	1,578.0	21.3[3]	24.9[2]	17.8[2]	___	___	___
Warbg Pincus Post Vent	agg gr	104.5	9.7[5]	—	—	___	___	___
Warbg Pincus Small Co Gro SC	agg gr	11.5	22.3[3]	—	—	___	___	___
Warbg Pincus Small Co Val SC	agg gr	200.6	19.2[3]	—	—	___	___	___
Warbg Pincus Strat Val	agg gr	12.7	24.2[2]	—	—	___	___	___

No-load fund groups   *continued*

Families with 3 or more funds including one stock or bond fund
Arranged in alphabetical order by group and risk within group

| Fund group/fund | Objective | Total Net Assets $ Millions 12/31/97 | Annualized Total Return % with quintile ranks by obj | | | Post quintile ranks for your funds here | | |
			1997	3 years 1995-1997	5 years 1993-1997	1997	3 years ending 1997	5 years ending 1997
Warbg Pincus Cap App	growth	623.4	31.4[2]	30.8[1]	20.3[1]			
Warbg Pincus Glob Post Vent	global	3.1	8.7[4]	—	—			
Warbg Pincus Gro & Inc	gr-inc	616.4	30.2[2]	15.7[5]	18.0[3]			
Warbg Pincus Balanced	income	38.2	16.4[4]	20.0[3]	14.2[2]			
Warbg Pincus Glob Fix Inc	fix-inc	174.5	2.2[5]	9.3[3]	8.1[1]			
Warbg Pincus Fix Inc	fix-inc	312.1	8.8[3]	10.0[2]	8.0[1]			
Warbg Pincus Inter Gov	fix-inc	49.3	7.6[1]	8.4[1]	6.2[1]			
Warbg Pincus NY Inter Muni	tax-free	91.7	5.9[5]	6.5[5]	5.7[4]			
Warbg Pincus Cash Res	money mkt gen	472.7	5.2[3]	5.3[2]	4.5[2]			
Warbg Pincus NY TE MM	money mkt TF	151.2	3.1[3]	3.1[5]	2.7[5]			
Your average		6,606.0						
Wasatch Funds								
Wasatch Agg Eqty‡ SC	agg gr	172.2	19.2[3]	17.1[5]	15.8[3]			
Wasatch Micro Cap‡ SC	agg gr	120.6	35.3[1]	—	—			
Wasatch Micro Cap Val SC	agg gr	2.3	—	—	—			
Wasatch MidCap	agg gr	61.1	-0.5[5]	17.9[4]	11.5[5]			
Wasatch Growth	growth	146.7	27.5[3]	27.8[2]	18.9[2]			
Wasatch Hosington US Treas	fix-inc	14.0	15.7[1]	11.6[2]	8.0[3]			
Northern US Gov MM*	money mkt gov	311.3	5.0[2]	—	—			
Your average		516.9						
Wayne Hummer Funds								
Wayne Hummer Growth	growth	128.5	30.2[2]	22.1[4]	13.2[5]			
Wayne Hummer Income	fix-inc	22.4	9.0[4]	9.2[4]	7.0[4]			
Wayne Hummer MM	money mkt gen	261.4	5.0[4]	5.1[4]	4.2[4]			
Your average		412.3						
Weitz Series Funds								
Weitz Hickory	growth	21.6	39.2[1]	38.3[1]	—			
Weitz Partners Value	growth	133.7	40.6[1]	32.4[1]	—			
Weitz Value	gr-inc	366.0	38.9[1]	31.7[1]	19.8[2]			
Weitz Fix Inc	fix-inc	28.1	8.6[4]	9.5[4]	6.7[4]			
Weitz Gov Port MM	money mkt gov	8.6	5.0[3]	—	—			
Your average		558.0						
Westcore Funds								
Westcore Sm Cap Oppty SC	agg gr	46.0	27.8[2]	27.6[2]	—			
Westcore Blue Chip	growth	62.2	30.9[2]	29.4[1]	19.6[2]			
Westcore MIDCO Gro	growth	602.5	14.9[5]	19.6[4]	14.8[4]			
Westcore Gro & Inc	gr-inc	17.1	27.3[3]	24.3[4]	14.4[5]			
Westcore LT Bond	fix-inc	17.2	14.0[1]	13.2[2]	9.4[2]			
Westcore Inter Bond	fix-inc	51.4	8.3[3]	8.9[4]	6.5[3]			
Westcore CO TE	tax-free	26.7	7.4[5]	8.2[5]	6.1[5]			
Your average		823.1						

milies with 3 or more funds including one stock or bond fund
ranged in alphabetical order by group and risk within group

| | | | Annualized Total Return % with quintile ranks by obj | | | Post quintile ranks for your funds here | | |
| | | Total Net Assets $ Millions 12/31/97 | 1997 | 3 years 1995-1997 | 5 years 1993-1997 | 1997 | 3 years ending 1997 | 5 years ending 1997 |
Fund group/fund	Objective							
liam Blair Mutual Funds								
Wm Blair Val Disc SC	agg gr	30.4	33.5[1]	—	—			
Wm Blair Int'l Gro	int'l	128.8	8.4[2]	8.6[3]	11.3[3]			
Wm Blair Growth	growth	591.4	20.1[4]	22.3[4]	17.6[3]			
Wm Blair Income	fix-inc	160.1	8.0[4]	8.4[4]	6.4[4]			
Wm Blair Ready Res	money mkt gen	919.4	5.0[4]	5.1[4]	4.3[4]			
Your average		1,830.1						
ilshire Target Funds								
Wilshire Target Sm Gro SC	agg gr	14.3	11.7[4]	17.7[5]	13.2[4]			
Wilshire Target Lg Gro	growth	74.6	32.2[1]	31.4[1]	18.2[2]			
Wilshire Target Sm Val SC	growth	21.1	31.2[2]	23.2[4]	14.7[4]			
Wilshire Target Lg Val	gr-inc	14.3	30.2[2]	29.1[2]	18.2[3]			
Your average		124.3						
eiss, Peck, & Greer (WPG) Funds								
WPG Growth SC	agg gr	61.0	9.7[5]	21.8[4]	12.3[5]			
WPG Tudor SC	agg gr	170.7	11.1[4]	23.1[3]	13.8[4]			
WPG International	int'l	8.6	2.9[3]	6.1[3]	9.0[4]			
WPG Quant Eqty	growth	96.0	25.5[3]	25.6[3]	—			
WPG Gro & Inc	gr-inc	117.1	36.3[1]	31.0[1]	18.4[3]			
WPG Core Bd	fix-inc	107.7	7.4[4]	8.2[5]	4.6[5]			
WPG Inter Muni	tax-free	23.5	7.9[1]	8.0[3]	—			
WPG TF MM	money mkt TF	129.7	3.2[2]	3.4[2]	3.0[1]			
WPG Gov MM	money mkt gov	183.5	4.8[5]	4.9[5]	4.2[4]			
Your average		897.8						
he Wright Managed Funds								
Wright Equifund Hong Kong	int'l	6.6	-27.2[5]	-1.8[4]	1.9[5]			
Wright Equifund Japan	int'l	3.9	-14.2[4]	-10.8[5]	—			
Wright Equifund Mexico	int'l	28.5	42.4[1]	6.6[3]	—			
Wright Equifund Belg/Lux	int'l	1.5	11.4[2]	17.5[1]	—			
Wright Equifund Britain	int'l	0.7	13.3[1]	—	—			
Wright Equifund Germany	int'l	1.4	9.9[2]	—	—			
Wright Equifund Netherland	int'l	13.0	15.4[1]	23.2[1]	20.1[1]			
Wright Equifund Nordic	int'l	2.7	5.2[3]	18.5[1]	—			
Wright Equifund Swiss	int'l	1.3	22.7[1]	13.4[2]	—			
Wright Equifund Italian	int'l	0.6	19.1[1]	—	—			
Wright Int'l Blue Ch	int'l	212.7	1.5[3]	11.7[2]	11.9[3]			
Wright Jr Blue Ch SC	agg gr	33.5	28.9[2]	22.2[3]	13.9[4]			
Wright Major Blue Chip	gr-inc	27.7	33.9[1]	26.6[3]	15.3[4]			
Wright Sel Blue Ch	gr-inc	259.5	32.7[1]	27.1[3]	15.1[4]			
Wright Total Ret Bd	fix-inc	79.7	9.2[3]	10.4[3]	6.9[4]			
Wright US Treas	fix-inc	74.2	9.1[3]	11.3[3]	7.9[3]			
Wright Curr Inc	fix-inc	75.6	8.6[3]	10.0[2]	6.5[3]			
Wright US Treas Near Term	fix-inc	102.3	5.9[4]	7.2[3]	5.2[3]			
Wright Trsy MM	money mkt gov	86.8	4.8[4]	5.0[3]	4.2[3]			
Your average		1,012.2						

CHAPTER 8

No-load fund charts

■ It's often said a picture is worth a thousand words. And that's certainly true when it comes to getting a quick, easy fix on mutual fund performance. Charts show you a fund's volatility, resistance to downturns, and growth potential, all at a glance. A buy or sell point is often indicated when a fund's graph crosses its moving average.

The first two charts provide your key to making the greatest use of these valuable tools. These charts (for Neuberger & Berman Partners and Price Equity Income Funds) show the location of data for net assets, distributions, weekly highs, lows and closings, 13 and 39 week moving averages. All other charts in this chapter are in alphabetical order. Charts for precious metals and international funds are grouped separately at the end.

All charts in this chapter were provided by *Mutual Fund Trends,* a publication of Growth Fund Research, a long-established publisher of mutual fund data. *Mutual Fund Trends* shows all the funds included in this chapter, updated weekly. Trends regularly costs $139 per year for 12 monthly issues. A single copy of this fine publication is available to *Handbook* readers for $5 from Growth Fund Research. Their address is on the Price Equity Income Fund chart.

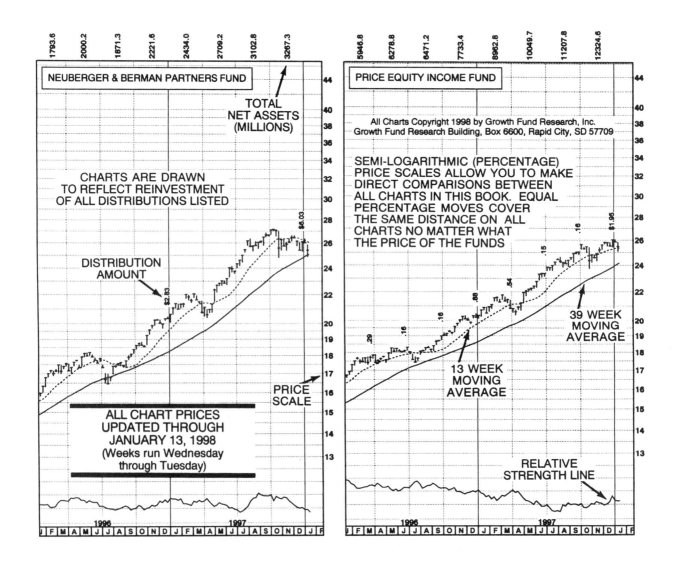

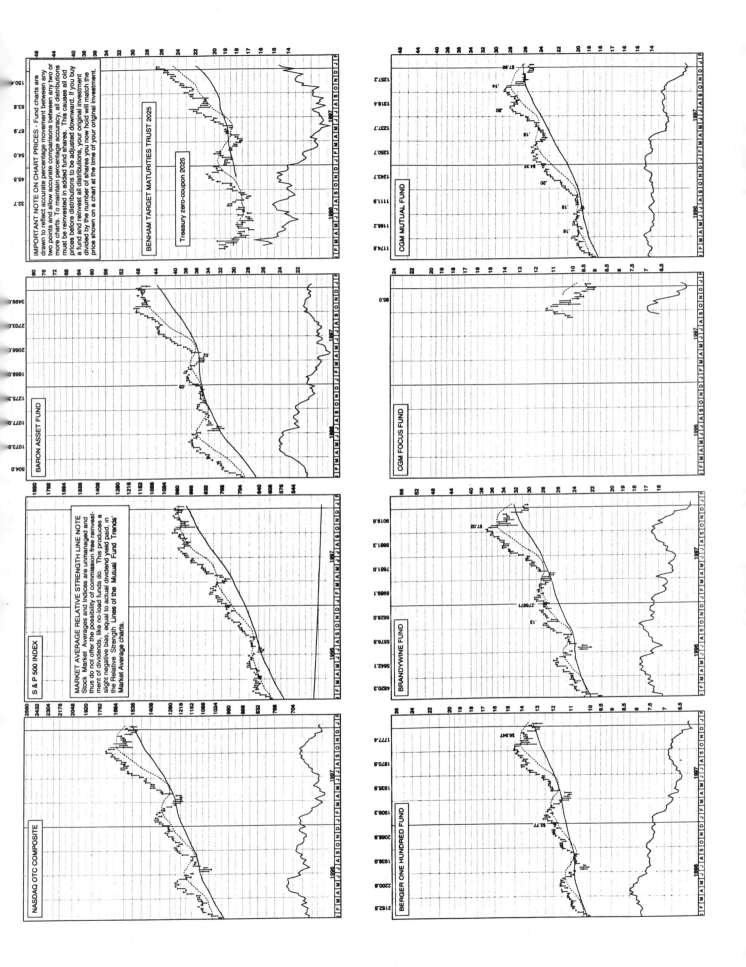

IMPORTANT NOTE ON CHART PRICES - Fund charts are drawn to reflect accurate percentage movement between any two points and allow accurate comparisons between any two or more charts. To maintain percentage accuracy, all distributions must be reinvested in added fund shares. This causes all old prices before distributions to be adjusted downward. If you buy a fund and reinvest all distributions, your original investment divided by the number of shares you now hold will match the price shown on a chart at the time of your original investment.

BENHAM TARGET MATURITIES TRUST 2025

Treasury zero-coupon 2025

BARON ASSET FUND

CGM MUTUAL FUND

CGM FOCUS FUND

S & P 500 INDEX

MARKET AVERAGE RELATIVE STRENGTH LINE NOTE
Stock Market Averages and Indices are unmanaged and thus do not offer the possibility of commission free reinvestment of dividends, like no-load funds do. This produces a slight negative bias, equal to actual dividend yield paid, in the Relative Strength Lines of the Mutual Fund Trends' Market Average charts.

BRANDYWINE FUND

NASDAQ OTC COMPOSITE

BERGER ONE HUNDRED FUND

181

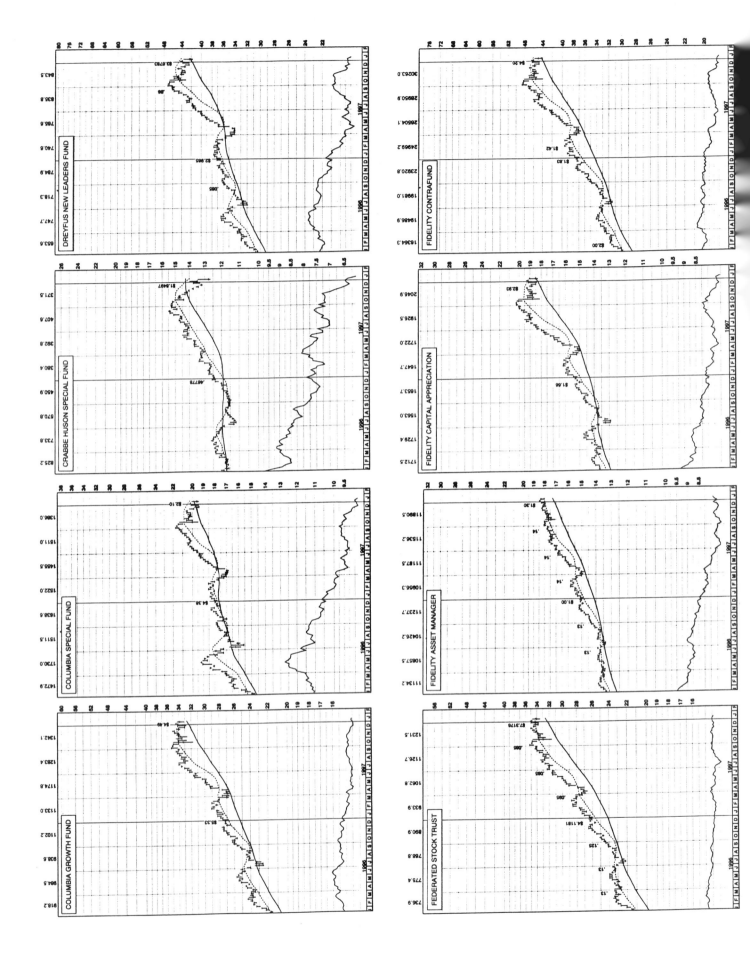

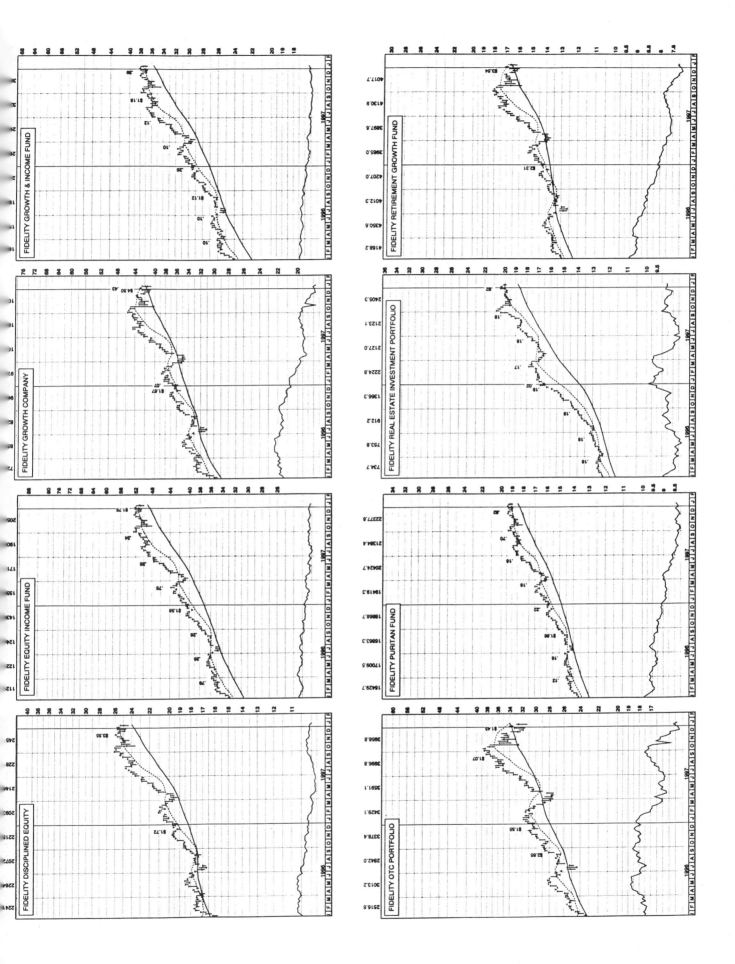

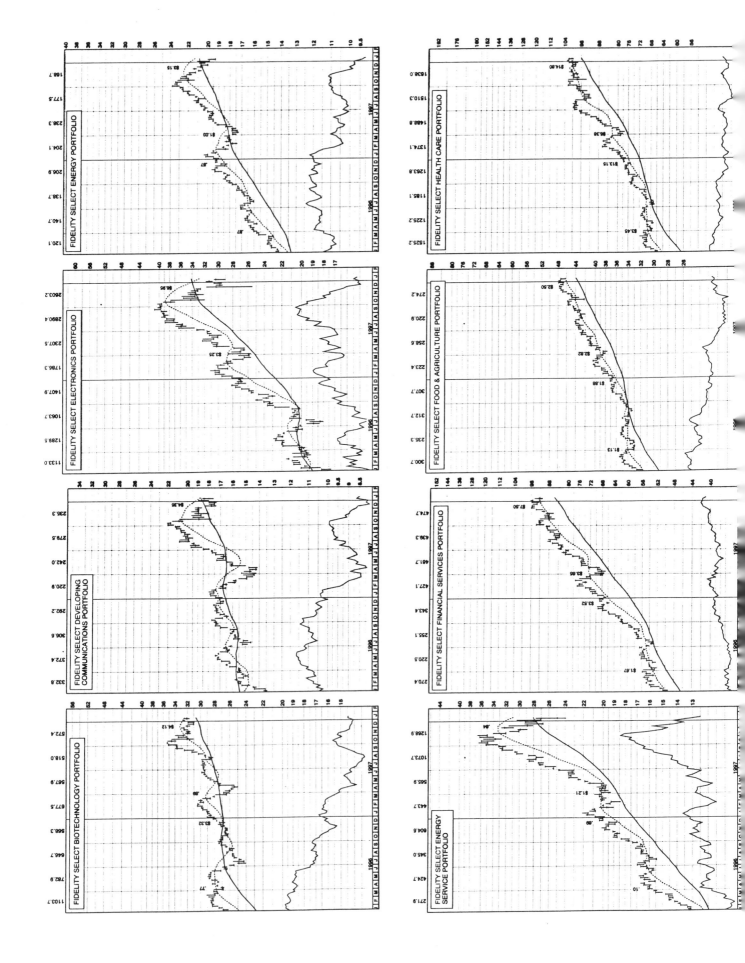

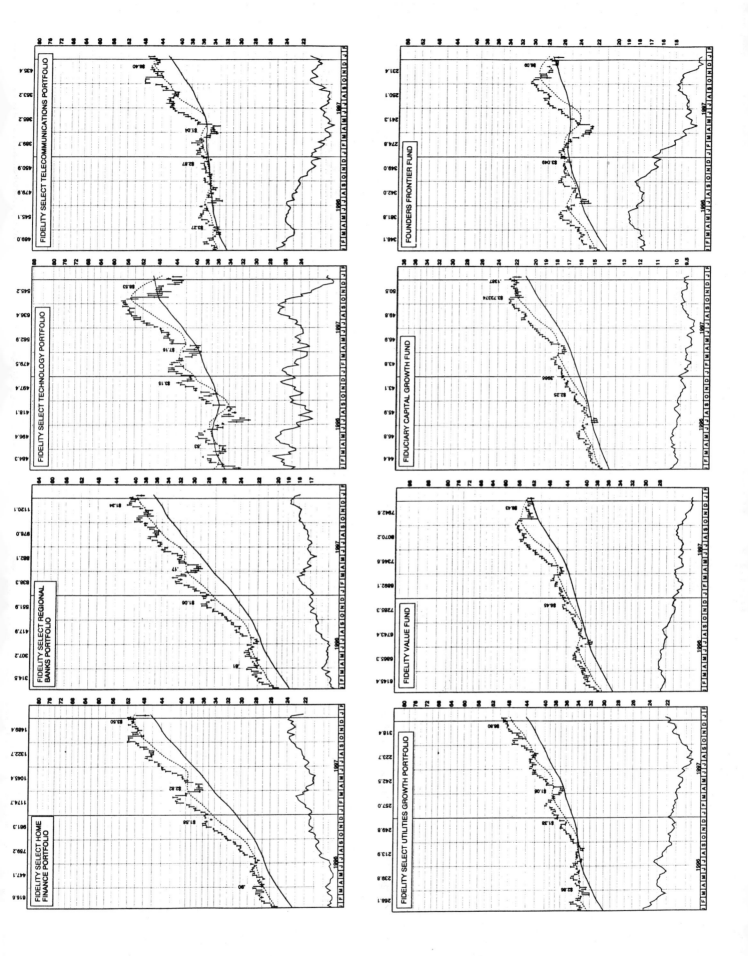

185

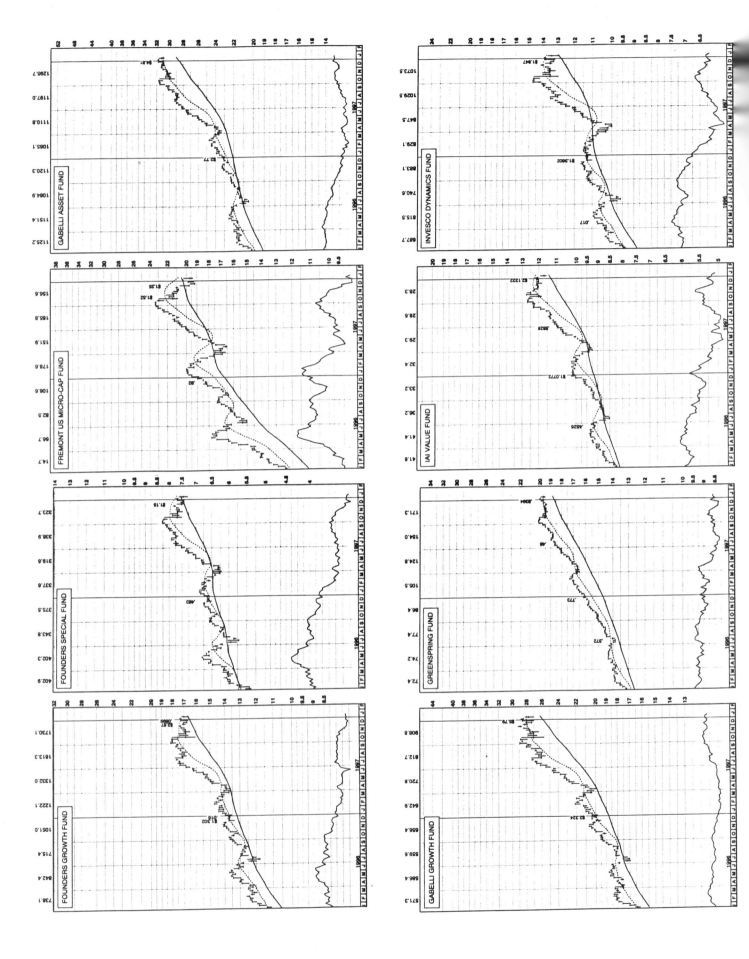

186

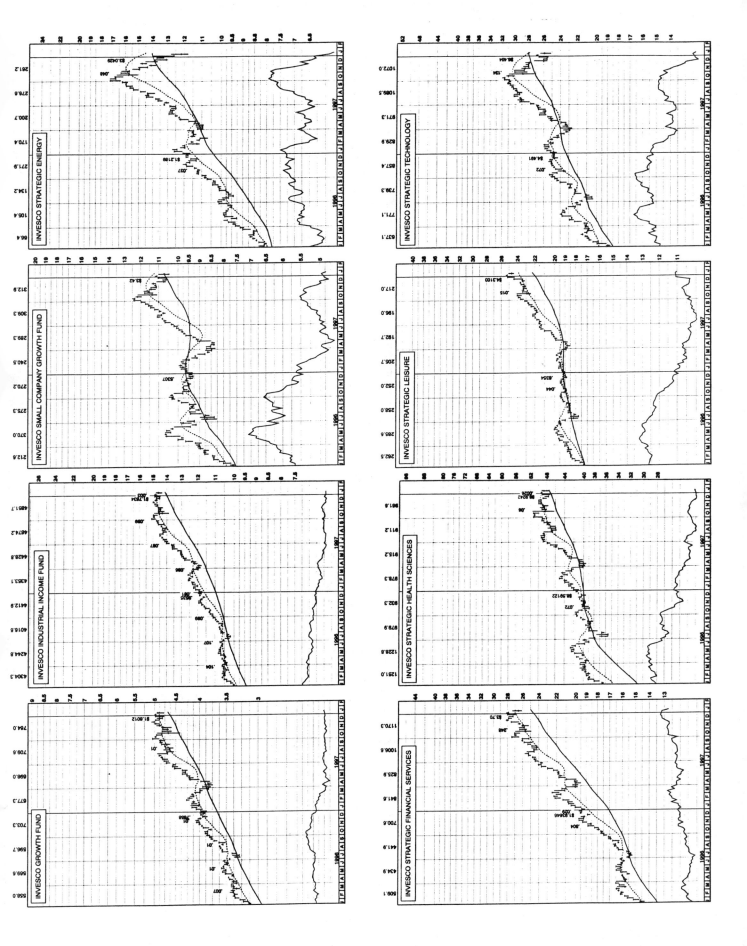

187

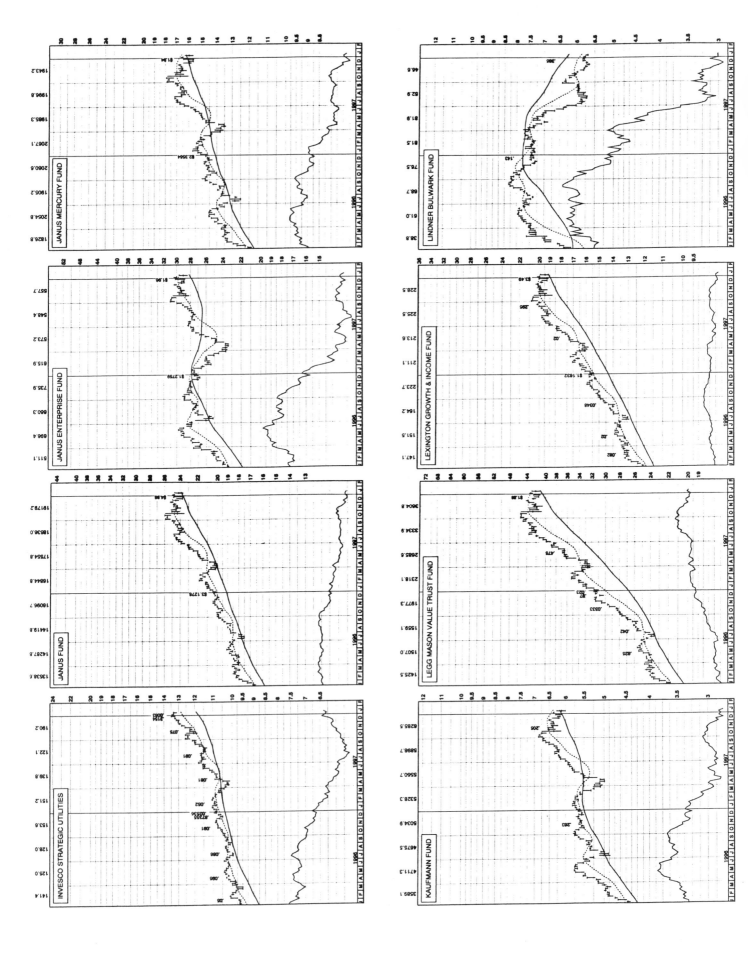

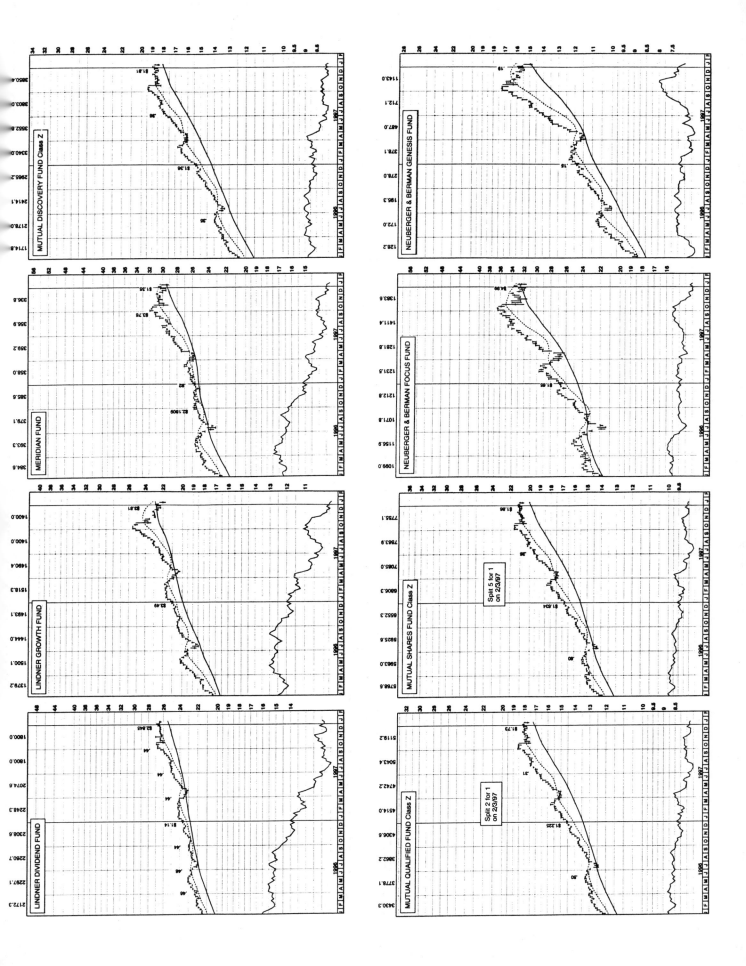

189

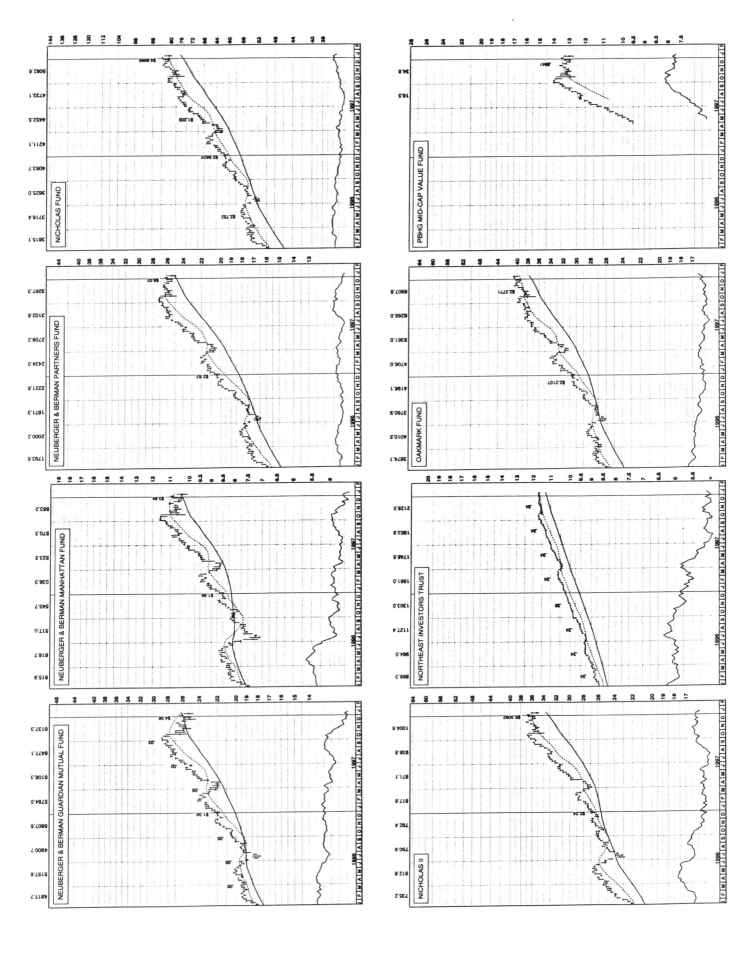

190

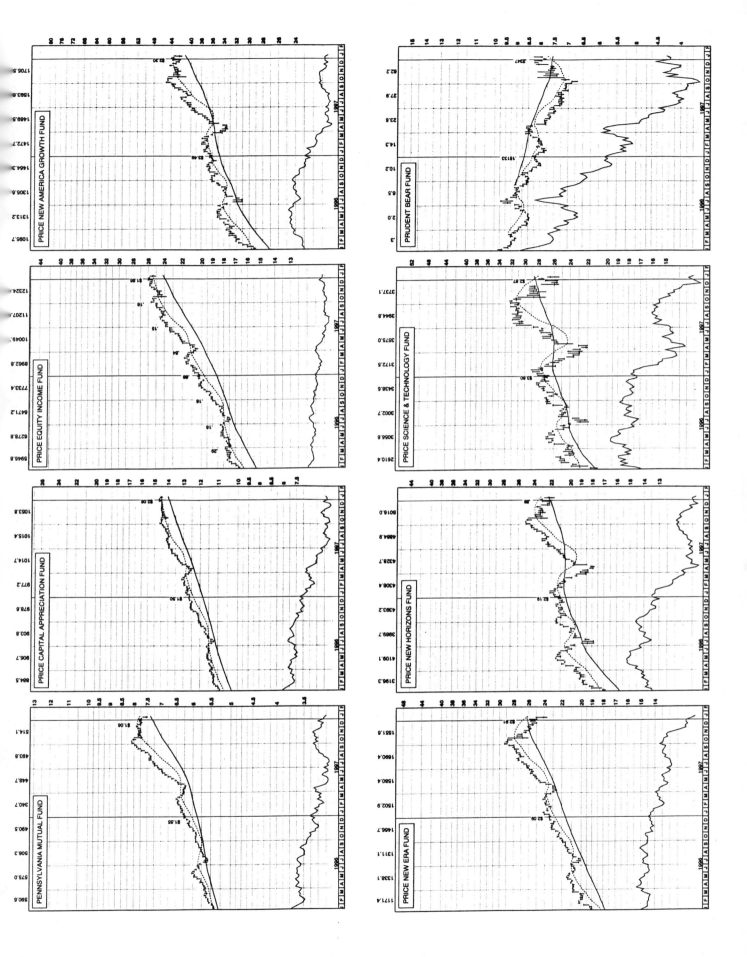

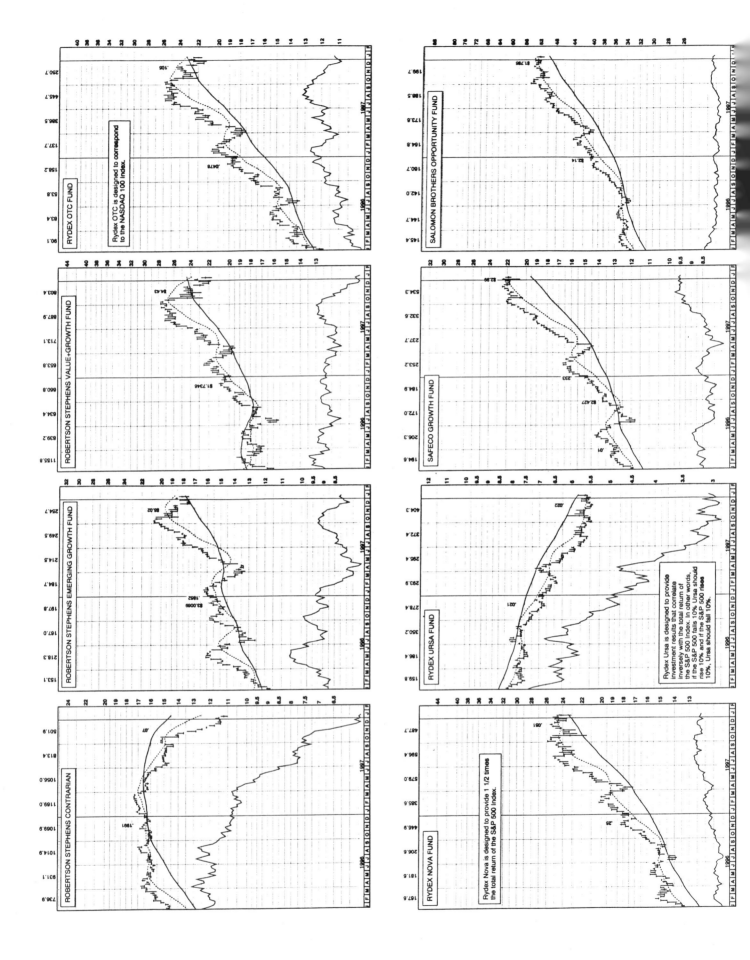

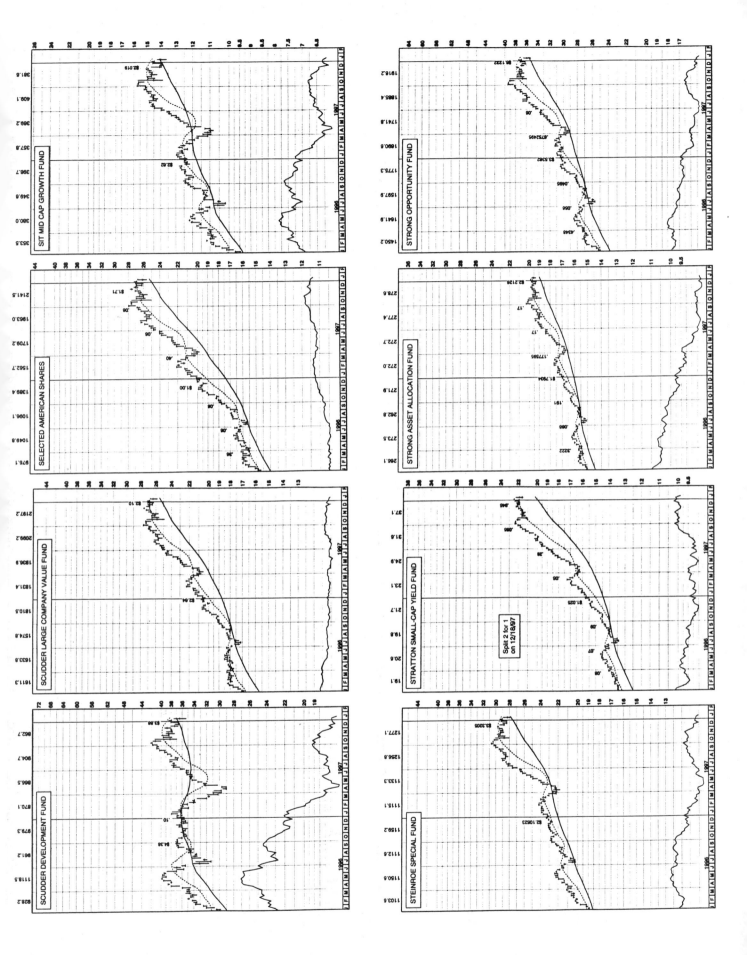

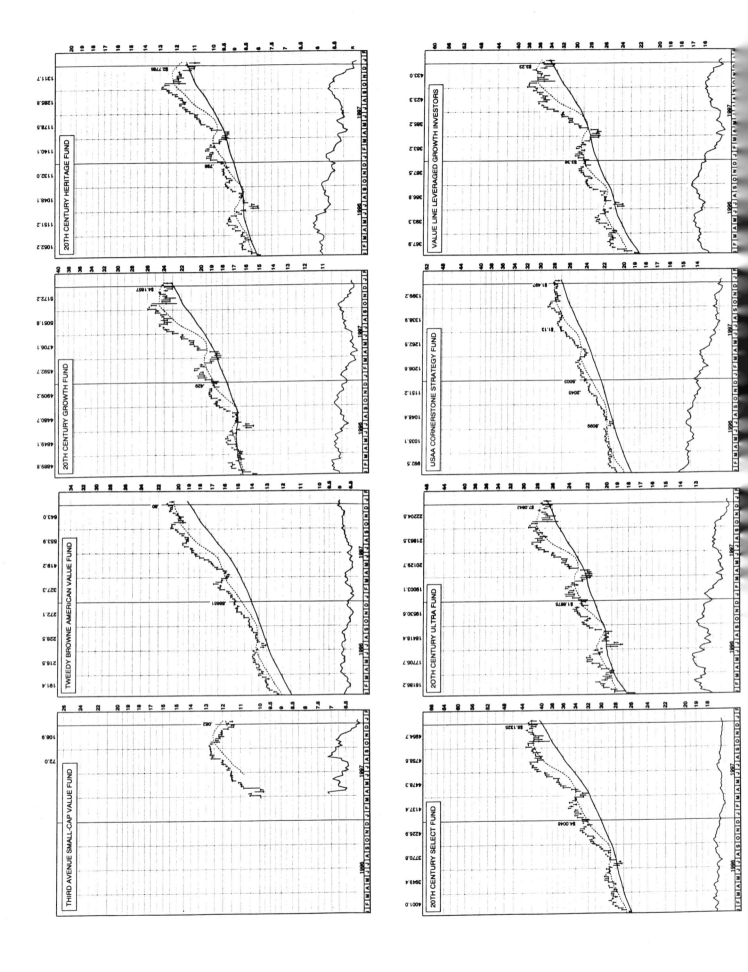

194

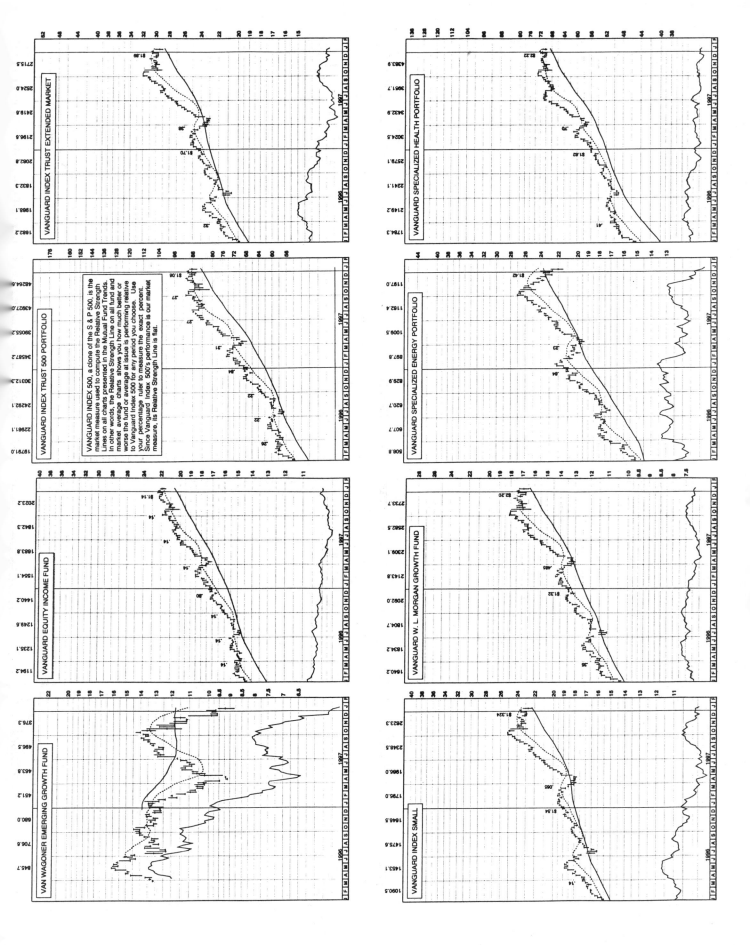

VANGUARD INDEX TRUST EXTENDED MARKET

VANGUARD SPECIALIZED HEALTH PORTFOLIO

VANGUARD INDEX TRUST 500 PORTFOLIO

VANGUARD INDEX 500, a clone of the S & P 500, is the market measure used to compute the Relative Strength Lines on all charts presented in the Mutual Fund Trends. In other words, the Relative Strength Line on all fund and market average charts shows you how much better or worse the fund or average at issue is performing relative to Vanguard Index 500 for any period you choose. Use your percentage ruler to measure the exact percent. Since Vanguard Index 500's performance is our market measure, its Relative Strength Line is flat.

VANGUARD SPECIALIZED ENERGY PORTFOLIO

VANGUARD EQUITY INCOME FUND

VANGUARD W. L. MORGAN GROWTH FUND

VAN WAGONER EMERGING GROWTH FUND

VANGUARD INDEX SMALL

195

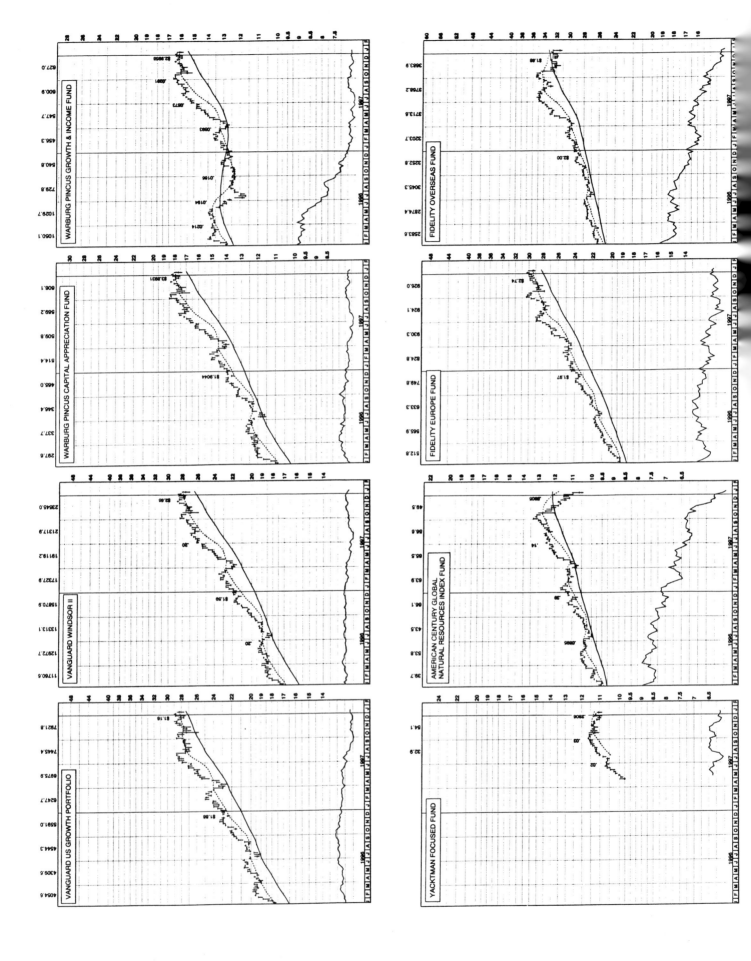

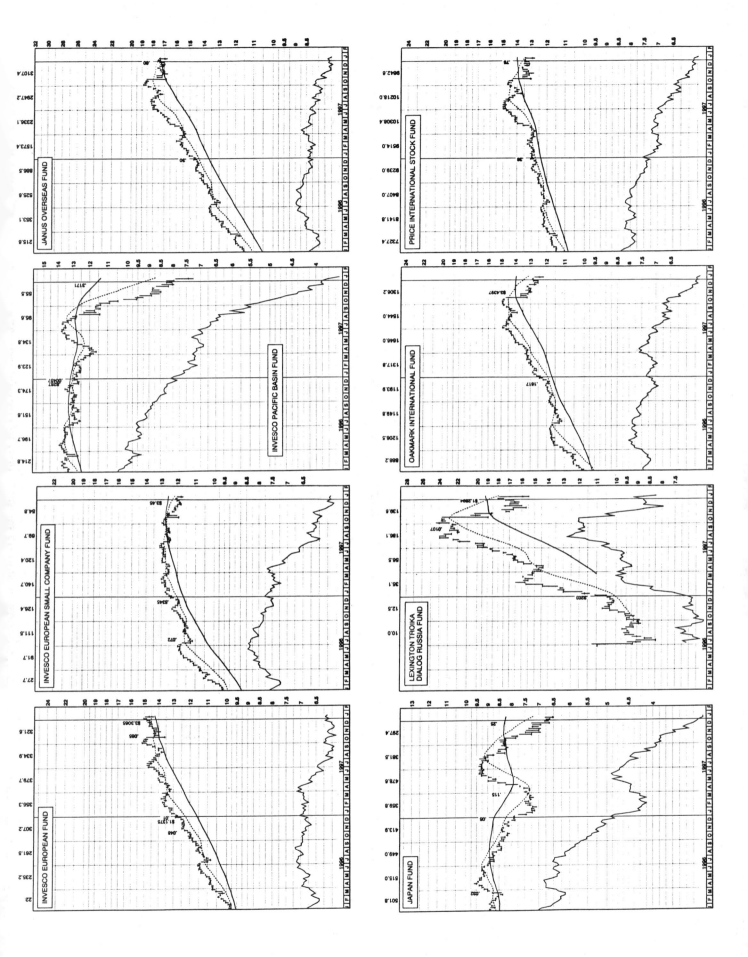

197

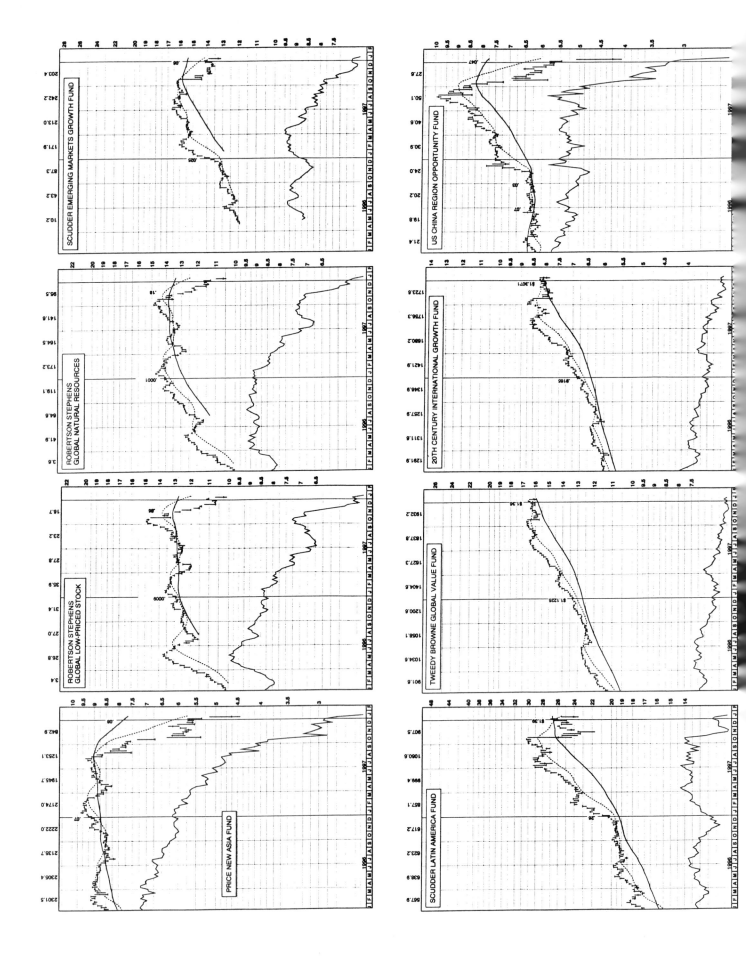

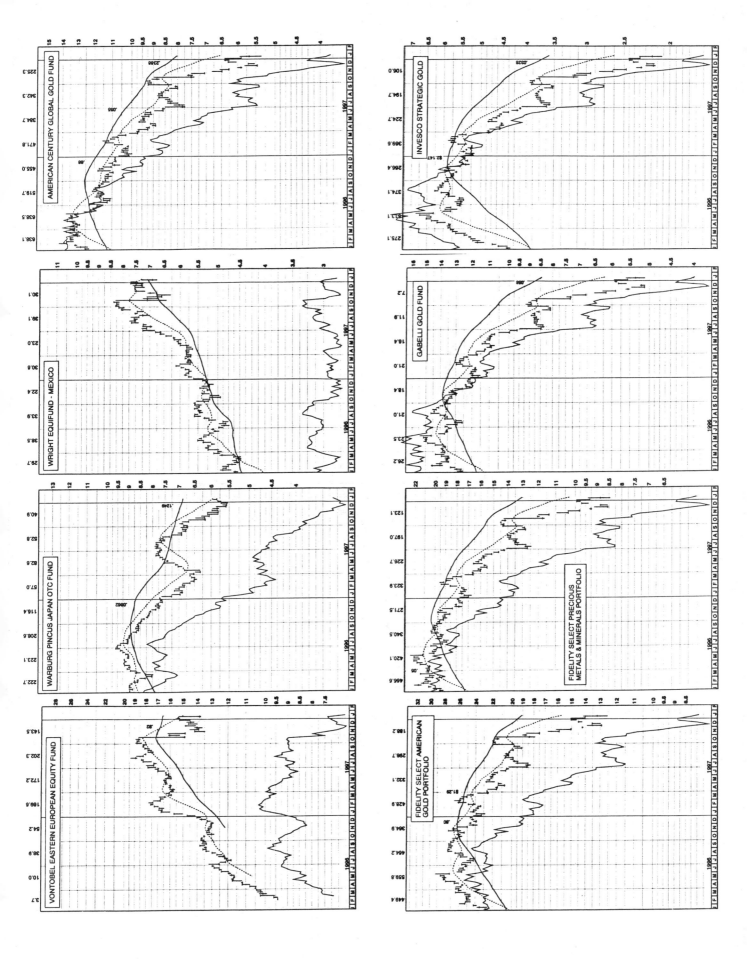

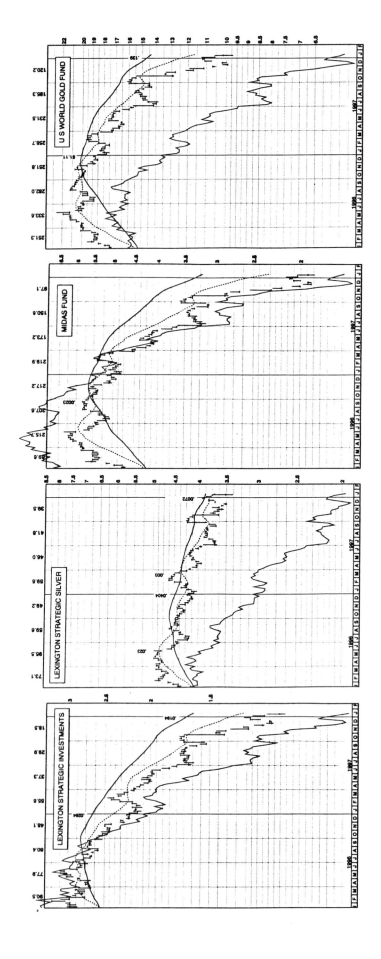

Money market funds

arranged in alphabetical order within objective

No-Load Fund	Compound yield percent with quintile ranks by objective										Annualized	
	1988	1989	1990	1991	1992	1993	1994	1995	1996	1997	3 years	5 years
GENERAL MONEY MARKET FUNDS												
AARP Hi Qual MM	6.6^5	8.4^5	7.4^5	5.9^2	2.9^5	2.1^5	3.5^5	5.1^5	4.7^5	4.8^5	4.8^5	4.0^5
Amer AAdv Mileage MM	—	—	—	—	3.8^1	3.0^1	3.9^2	5.7^2	5.1^2	5.2^3	5.3^2	4.6^2
Amer Cent-Benham Cash Res	6.9^5	8.7^5	7.6^5	5.9^3	3.0^5	2.3^5	3.7^4	5.4^4	5.0^4	5.1^3	5.2^3	4.3^4
Amer Cent-Benham Prime MM	—	—	—	—	—	—	4.5^1	5.7^1	5.0^3	5.3^2	5.3^2	—
AMEX-Strategist MM	—	—	—	—	—	—	—	—	5.7^1	5.5^1	—	—
AON MM	—	—	—	—	—	—	—	—	—	5.5^1	—	—
Asset Mgmt Money Mkt	—	—	—	—	3.3^4	2.8^2	3.9^2	—	5.1^3	5.3^2	—	—
Babson Prime MM	6.9^5	8.7^5	7.6^5	5.4^5	3.1^5	2.3^5	3.4^5	5.2^5	4.7^5	4.7^5	4.9^5	4.1^5
BT Invest Cash Mgt	—	—	—	—	—	—	—	—	—	5.0^4	—	—
BT Pyramid MM	—	—	—	—	—	—	—	—	—	5.4^1	—	—
Cash Resource MM	—	—	—	—	—	—	—	—	—	4.9^5	—	—
Chicago Tr MM	—	—	—	—	—	—	3.9^2	5.6^2	5.1^3	5.2^2	5.3^2	—
CMA Money Mkt‡	7.2^3	9.0^2	8.0^2	6.0^1	3.5^2	2.9^2	3.8^2	5.6^2	5.0^3	5.2^3	5.3^3	4.5^2
Columbia Daily Inc	7.1^4	8.9^3	7.8^3	5.7^4	3.3^4	2.5^5	3.7^4	5.5^3	5.0^3	5.1^3	5.2^3	4.3^4
Dean Witter Liq Asst	7.3^2	9.1^1	7.9^3	5.7^4	3.4^3	2.7^3	3.8^3	5.6^2	5.1^2	5.2^2	5.3^2	4.5^3
Drey-Basic MM	—	—	—	—	—	3.4^1	4.3^1	6.1^1	5.2^2	5.4^1	5.6^1	4.9^1
Drey-General MM	7.0^5	8.8^4	7.7^4	5.8^3	3.4^3	2.6^4	3.5^5	5.4^4	4.8^4	5.0^4	5.1^4	4.3^4
Dreyfus Liq Asst	7.1^3	9.1^1	7.9^3	5.9^3	3.5^2	2.6^4	3.5^4	5.5^4	5.0^4	5.0^4	5.1^4	4.3^4
Dreyfus MM Instr MM Ser	—	—	—	6.0^2	3.5^2	2.6^4	3.4^5	5.5^4	4.7^5	4.8^5	5.0^5	4.2^5
Dreyfus Wrld Dollar MM	—	—	8.7^1	6.4^1	3.8^1	2.7^3	3.5^5	5.5^3	5.0^4	5.1^4	5.2^4	4.3^4
Emerald Prime MM	—	—	—	—	—	—	—	—	4.8^5	4.9^5	—	—
Excelsior MM	7.4^1	8.7^5	8.1^1	6.0^2	3.6^1	2.8^2	3.9^2	5.6^2	5.1^2	5.2^2	5.3^2	4.5^2
FBR Mny Mkt(RBB)	—	—	—	—	—	—	—	—	—	4.8^5	—	—
Fidelity Cash Res MM	7.3^2	8.9^3	7.8^4	6.0^2	3.8^1	2.9^1	4.0^2	5.7^2	5.1^2	5.3^2	5.4^2	4.6^1
Fidelity Daily Inc MM	7.3^2	8.9^4	7.9^3	5.8^3	3.6^1	2.8^2	3.9^2	5.7^2	5.1^2	5.3^2	5.4^2	4.5^2
Fidelity Select MM	7.1^4	9.0^2	7.8^4	5.8^3	3.5^2	2.7^3	3.7^3	5.7^2	4.7^5	5.2^3	5.2^3	4.4^3
Fidelity Spart MM	—	—	8.4^1	6.2^1	4.0^1	3.1^1	4.1^1	5.8^1	5.3^1	5.4^1	5.5^1	4.7^1
Firstar Money Mkt	—	9.0^2	8.1^1	5.7^4	3.4^3	2.7^3	3.8^3	5.6^3	5.0^3	5.1^3	5.2^3	4.4^3
Flex-Fund MM	7.6^1	9.4^1	8.2^1	6.1^1	3.7^1	3.0^1	4.1^1	5.9^1	5.4^1	5.4^1	5.5^1	4.7^1
Forum Dly Asst Cash	—	—	—	—	—	—	—	—	—	5.3^2	—	—
Founders Money Mkt	6.9^5	8.6^5	7.5^5	5.3^5	2.9^5	2.3^5	3.5^5	5.2^5	4.7^5	4.8^5	4.9^5	4.1^5
Franklin Money Fund	—	—	—	—	—	—	—	—	4.9^4	5.0^4	—	—
Fremont Money Mkt	—	8.9^3	8.0^2	6.0^1	3.4^3	2.6^4	4.0^2	5.9^1	5.3^1	5.4^1	5.5^1	4.6^1
Galaxy Money Mkt	7.4^1	8.9^3	8.0^2	5.9^2	3.5^2	2.7^3	3.7^4	5.3^4	4.8^4	5.0^4	5.0^4	4.3^4
Harbor Money Mkt	7.1^4	9.3^1	8.0^2	5.8^3	3.2^4	2.8^2	3.9^2	5.7^2	4.9^4	5.2^3	5.3^3	4.5^2
Homestead Daily Inc MM	—	—	—	—	—	—	—	—	—	5.0^4	—	—
IAA Trust MM	—	—	—	—	—	—	—	—	—	4.8^5	—	—
IAI Money Mkt	—	—	—	—	—	2.9^2	3.7^3	5.3^5	5.0^3	5.1^4	5.1^4	4.4^3
Independence One Prime MM	—	—	—	—	—	—	—	—	5.1^3	5.1^3	—	—
Invesco Cash Res	7.1^4	8.9^4	7.8^4	5.6^5	3.1^5	2.4^5	3.7^4	5.3^5	4.7^5	4.8^5	4.9^5	4.2^5
Janus MM	—	—	—	—	—	—	—	—	5.2^2	5.3^2	—	—
JP Morgan Prime MM	—	—	—	—	—	—	—	—	—	5.4^1	—	—
Kemper-Cash Acct Tr MM‡	—	—	—	5.4^5	3.0^5	2.4^5	3.5^5	5.1^5	4.6^5	4.8^5	4.9^5	4.1^5
Kemper-Cash Equiv Fd MM‡	—	—	—	—	—	—	—	—	—	4.9^5	—	—
Kent MM	—	—	—	—	—	—	—	—	—	5.2^2	—	—
Key Money Mkt‡	—	8.9^4	7.9^3	5.8^3	3.3^4	2.6^4	3.6^4	5.3^5	5.0^3	5.0^4	5.1^4	4.3^4
Kiewit MMP	—	—	—	—	—	—	—	—	—	5.5^1	—	—
Lancaster MM	—	—	—	—	—	2.8^3	3.4^5	5.2^5	4.9^4	5.1^3	5.1^4	4.3^4
Legg Msn Cash Res	7.0^4	8.4^5	7.7^4	5.8^3	3.5^3	2.8^2	3.7^4	5.3^4	4.8^5	4.9^5	5.0^5	4.3^4
Lexington MM	7.0^4	8.6^5	7.6^5	5.5^5	3.0^5	2.3^5	3.4^5	5.1^5	4.6^5	4.7^5	4.8^5	4.0^5
Lindner MM	—	—	—	—	—	—	—	—	5.2^2	5.3^2	—	—
Managers Money Mkt	7.3^2	8.7^5	7.7^5	5.4^5	3.1^5	2.9^2	3.6^4	5.9^1	5.4^1	5.4^1	5.5^1	4.6^1
Marshall MM Invest A	—	—	—	—	—	2.7^3	3.8^3	5.8^1	5.3^1	5.4^1	5.5^1	4.6^2
Marshall MM Trust B	—	—	—	—	—	3.0^1	4.1^1	5.5^3	5.0^3	5.1^3	5.2^3	4.5^2
McM Princ Pres	—	—	—	—	—	—	—	—	5.3^1	5.4^1	—	—
Merrill Lynch Rdy Asst	7.2^3	9.0^2	8.0^2	6.0^1	3.5^3	2.8^2	3.7^3	5.5^3	5.1^3	5.2^3	5.3^3	4.5^3
Merrill Lynch Ret Res	—	—	—	6.1^1	3.5^2	2.9^2	3.9^2	5.7^2	5.2^2	5.3^2	5.4^2	4.6^2
Nations Prime MM	—	—	—	—	—	—	—	—	5.0^3	5.2^3	—	—
Nbrgr-Ber Cash Res	—	9.0^2	7.8^4	5.7^4	3.4^4	2.7^3	3.7^3	5.5^3	5.0^4	5.1^3	5.2^3	4.3^4

Money market funds *continued*
Arranged in alphabetical order within objective

No-Load Fund	Compound yield percent with quintile ranks by objective										Annualized	
	1988	1989	1990	1991	1992	1993	1994	1995	1996	1997	3 years	5 years
New England Cash Mgt MM	7.2[3]	8.9[3]	7.9[3]	5.9[2]	3.5[3]	2.5[4]	3.5[5]	5.3[4]	4.8[4]	4.9[5]	5.0[5]	4.2[5]
Nicholas Money Mkt	—	9.0[3]	8.1[1]	5.8[4]	3.3[4]	2.7[3]	3.9[2]	5.7[2]	5.1[2]	5.3[2]	5.3[2]	4.5[2]
Northern Money Mkt	—	—	—	—	—	—	—	—	5.2[2]	5.1[3]	—	—
Oakmark Units Gov MM	—	—	—	—	—	—	—	—	5.3[1]	5.3[2]	—	—
OVB Prime Obl	—	—	—	—	—	—	—	5.4[1]	4.9[4]	5.0[4]	5.1[4]	—
Pacific Hzn Prime MM	—	—	—	—	—	—	3.7[3]	5.6[3]	5.2[2]	5.2[2]	5.3[2]	—
Paine Webber Cashfund	7.3[2]	9.1[2]	8.0[2]	5.9[3]	3.5[2]	2.8[2]	3.8[3]	5.5[3]	5.0[3]	5.2[3]	5.2[3]	4.4[3]
PBHG Cash Res	—	—	—	—	—	—	—	—	5.0[3]	5.1[4]	—	—
Preferred Money Mkt	—	—	—	—	—	2.6[4]	3.9[2]	5.8[1]	5.2[2]	5.2[3]	5.4[2]	4.5[2]
Price Prime Res	7.2[3]	8.9[3]	7.7[4]	5.7[4]	3.4[4]	2.6[4]	3.7[3]	5.5[3]	5.0[3]	5.2[3]	5.2[3]	4.4[3]
Price Summit Cash Res	—	—	—	—	—	2.5[5]	4.0[1]	5.7[1]	5.3[1]	5.4[1]	5.4[1]	4.6[2]
Prime Cash Oblig MM (Federated)	—	—	—	—	—	—	—	—	4.8[5]	5.3[2]	—	—
ProFunds MM	—	—	—	—	—	—	—	—	—	—	—	—
Prudential Moneymart	7.2[3]	9.0[2]	7.9[3]	6.0[2]	3.6[2]	2.7[3]	3.8[3]	5.5[3]	4.8[4]	5.1[4]	5.1[4]	4.4[3]
Reserve Primary MM	7.2[2]	8.8[4]	7.6[5]	5.4[5]	3.1[5]	2.4[5]	4.0[1]	5.1[5]	4.6[5]	4.8[5]	4.8[5]	4.2[5]
Reynolds Money Mkt	—	—	—	—	3.2[4]	2.8[2]	—	—	4.8[5]	4.9[4]	—	—
RNC MM	—	—	—	—	—	—	—	—	—	5.1[3]	—	—
SAFECO Money Mkt	7.0[5]	9.1[2]	8.0[2]	5.7[4]	3.3[4]	2.5[5]	3.5[4]	5.3[5]	4.8[4]	4.9[5]	5.0[5]	4.2[5]
Schwab Inst Adv MM	—	—	—	—	—	—	—	5.7[2]	5.2[2]	5.3[2]	5.4[2]	—
Schwab Money Mkt	—	—	—	5.7[4]	3.5[3]	2.7[3]	3.7[4]	5.4[4]	4.9[4]	5.0[4]	5.1[4]	4.3[4]
Schwab Retirement MM	—	—	—	—	—	—	—	5.4[4]	4.9[4]	5.1[4]	5.1[4]	—
Schwab Value Adv MM	—	—	—	—	—	3.0[1]	4.1[1]	5.8[1]	5.3[1]	5.4[1]	5.5[1]	4.7[1]
Scout Prime MM	7.3[2]	9.1[2]	8.0[2]	5.8[3]	3.5[3]	2.8[3]	3.8[3]	5.6[3]	5.2[2]	5.2[3]	5.3[2]	4.5[2]
Scudder Cash Inv Tr	7.2[3]	8.9[4]	7.8[4]	6.0[2]	3.5[2]	2.6[4]	3.7[4]	5.3[5]	4.7[5]	4.9[5]	4.9[5]	4.2[4]
Scudder Premium MM	—	—	—	—	—	—	—	—	—	—	—	—
Short Tm Inc-MM(R&T)	7.0[4]	8.8[4]	7.7[4]	5.7[4]	3.4[3]	2.6[4]	3.5[5]	5.1[5]	4.6[5]	4.8[5]	4.8[5]	4.1[5]
Sit Money Mkt	—	—	—	—	—	—	—	—	5.0[3]	5.2[2]	—	—
Smith Barney Cash Port MM	7.2[3]	9.0[3]	7.9[3]	5.7[4]	3.3[4]	2.6[4]	3.7[3]	5.5[3]	5.0[3]	5.0[4]	5.2[3]	4.4[3]
SSgA MM	—	—	—	—	—	—	4.0[1]	5.8[1]	5.3[1]	5.4[1]	5.5[1]	—
Stagecoach Money Mkt	—	—	—	—	—	3.0[1]	3.8[2]	5.6[2]	4.8[4]	5.0[4]	5.2[4]	4.5[3]
Stein Roe Cash Res	7.1[4]	8.9[4]	7.8[4]	5.7[4]	3.4[3]	2.6[4]	3.7[4]	5.4[4]	5.1[2]	5.0[4]	5.2[3]	4.4[3]
Strong Heritage MM	—	—	—	—	—	—	—	—	5.8[1]	5.6[1]	—	—
Strong Money Mkt	7.5[1]	9.2[1]	8.1[1]	6.1[1]	3.7[1]	2.9[1]	4.0[1]	6.3[1]	5.3[1]	5.3[2]	5.6[1]	4.7[1]
Transamerica Prem Cash Res	—	—	—	—	—	—	—	—	5.5[1]	5.5[1]	—	—
UAM DSI MM	—	—	—	—	—	—	—	—	—	5.3[2]	—	—
USAA Money Mkt	7.3[2]	8.9[3]	8.0[2]	6.1[1]	3.8[1]	3.0[1]	4.1[1]	5.8[1]	5.2[2]	5.4[1]	5.5[1]	4.7[1]
Value Line Cash	7.4[1]	9.1[1]	7.9[3]	5.9[2]	3.7[1]	3.1[1]	3.7[4]	5.4[4]	5.8[1]	5.1[3]	5.4[1]	4.6[1]
Vangd MM Resvs Prime	7.6[1]	9.4[1]	8.3[1]	6.1[1]	3.7[1]	3.0[1]	4.1[1]	5.8[1]	5.3[1]	5.4[1]	5.5[1]	4.7[1]
Vintage Taxable MM	—	—	—	—	—	—	—	—	4.2[5]	4.5[5]	—	—
Warbg Pincus Cash Res	7.4[1]	9.2[1]	8.0[2]	5.9[2]	3.6[2]	2.8[2]	3.9[2]	5.6[3]	5.2[2]	5.2[3]	5.3[2]	4.5[2]
Wayne Hummer MM	7.0[5]	8.7[5]	7.7[5]	5.4[5]	3.1[5]	2.5[5]	3.5[4]	5.3[4]	4.8[4]	5.0[4]	5.1[4]	4.2[4]
Wm Blair Ready Res	—	—	—	5.6[5]	3.3[4]	2.6[4]	3.5[5]	5.5[4]	4.9[4]	5.0[4]	5.1[4]	4.3[4]
Working Asst MM(Citizen's)	6.7[5]	8.4[5]	7.5[5]	5.5[5]	3.0[5]	2.2[5]	3.2[5]	5.0[5]	4.3[5]	4.4[5]	4.6[5]	3.8[5]
Zurich Money Mkt	7.5[1]	9.2[1]	8.2[1]	6.0[1]	3.5[2]	2.9[1]	4.0[1]	5.7[2]	5.3[1]	5.4[1]	5.4[1]	4.6[1]
GOVERNMENT MONEY MARKET FUNDS												
Accessor US Gov MM	—	—	—	—	—	—	—	—	—	5.1[2]	—	—
Amer AAdv US Gov't MM	—	—	—	—	—	—	3.8[2]	5.4[3]	5.2[1]	5.0[2]	5.2[2]	—
Amer Cent-Benham Cap Presv I	6.5[4]	8.4[4]	7.7[3]	5.6[3]	3.3[3]	2.7[3]	3.6[3]	5.4[3]	4.8[3]	4.9[3]	5.0[3]	4.3[3]
Amer Cent-Benham Gov Agcy MM	—	—	8.4[1]	6.0[1]	3.4[3]	2.7[2]	3.8[2]	5.5[2]	4.8[3]	5.1[2]	5.1[2]	4.4[2]
Babson Fed MM	6.8[3]	8.5[4]	7.4[4]	5.3[5]	3.1[4]	2.3[5]	3.3[5]	5.1[5]	4.5[5]	4.7[5]	4.8[5]	4.0[5]
Boston-1784 Trsy MM	—	—	—	—	—	3.0[1]	4.0[1]	5.7[1]	5.0[2]	5.0[3]	5.2[1]	4.5[1]
BT Invest Treas MM	—	—	—	—	—	—	—	—	—	4.9[4]	—	—
Bull & Bear Dollar	7.1[2]	8.5[3]	7.4[5]	5.4[4]	3.2[4]	2.4[5]	3.4[5]	5.0[5]	4.8[4]	4.9[4]	4.9[5]	4.1[5]
CA Inv Tr-US Trsy MM	—	—	7.8[2]	5.6[3]	3.2[4]	2.6[3]	3.5[4]	—	4.8[3]	4.9[4]	—	—
Cash Resource US MM	—	—	—	—	—	—	—	—	—	4.8[4]	—	—
Crabbe Hsn Gov MM	—	8.9[1]	7.5[4]	5.3[5]	3.1[4]	2.6[3]	3.6[3]	—	4.8[3]	4.9[4]	—	—
Drey-Basic US Gov MM	—	—	—	—	—	3.3[1]	4.2[1]	6.1[1]	5.2[1]	5.3[1]	5.5[1]	4.8[1]
Drey-General Gov MM	6.8[3]	8.6[3]	7.5[3]	5.7[3]	3.5[2]	2.7[2]	3.7[3]	5.4[3]	4.7[4]	4.9[4]	5.0[3]	4.3[3]
Dreyfus 100% US MM	6.9[3]	8.2[5]	7.9[1]	6.2[1]	3.6[1]	2.6[3]	3.4[5]	5.2[4]	4.7[5]	4.7[5]	4.9[5]	4.1[4]
Dreyfus MM Instr Gov	6.8[3]	8.7[2]	7.6[3]	5.7[3]	3.5[2]	2.5[4]	3.3[5]	5.2[5]	4.7[5]	4.7[5]	4.9[5]	4.1[5]

No-Load Fund	Compound yield percent with quintile ranks by objective										Annualized	
	1988	1989	1990	1991	1992	1993	1994	1995	1996	1997	3 years	5 years
Emerald Treas MM	—	—	—	—	—	—	—	—	4.6^5	4.6^5	—	—
Excelsior Govt MM	7.2^1	8.6^3	8.0^1	5.8^2	3.6^1	2.8^2	3.8^1	5.5^2	5.0^2	5.1^2	5.2^2	4.4^2
Excelsior Treas MM	—	—	—	—	—	—	—	—	—	4.9^3	—	—
Fidelity Spart US Gov MM	—	—	—	6.1^1	3.8^1	2.8^1	3.9^1	5.7^1	5.2^1	5.3^1	5.4^1	4.6^1
Fidelity Spart US Trsy MM	—	8.3^5	7.9^1	6.1^1	3.7^1	2.7^2	3.7^2	5.4^2	4.9^2	5.0^2	5.1^2	4.4^2
Fidelity US Gov Res	7.0^2	8.7^2	7.7^3	5.7^3	3.4^3	2.6^3	3.9^1	5.6^1	5.1^2	5.3^1	5.3^1	4.5^1
First Omaha Gov MM	—	—	—	—	—	2.6^3	3.6^3	5.4^3	4.8^4	4.9^3	5.0^3	4.2^3
Firstar Gov MM	—	8.7^2	7.7^2	5.4^4	3.3^3	2.6^3	3.7^2	5.4^2	4.8^3	5.0^3	5.1^3	4.3^2
Firstar US Treas MM	—	—	—	—	3.2^4	2.6^4	3.5^4	5.2^4	4.7^4	4.8^4	4.9^4	4.2^4
Forum Dly Asst Trsy	—	—	—	—	—	2.8^1	3.8^2	5.4^3	4.7^5	4.9^4	5.0^4	4.3^3
Gabelli Treas MM	—	—	—	—	—	2.8^2	3.8^1	5.5^2	4.9^3	5.3^1	5.2^2	4.5^2
Gov't Cash Series(Federated) MM	—	—	—	—	—	—	—	—	—	5.2^1	—	—
Gradison US Gov MM	6.3^5	8.4^4	7.3^5	5.3^5	3.1^4	2.5^4	3.5^5	5.3^4	4.7^4	4.9^3	5.0^4	4.2^4
Indepence One US Treas	—	—	—	—	—	—	—	—	5.1^2	5.0^3	—	—
Invesco Gov MM	—	—	—	4.0^5	3.0^5	2.4^5	3.6^3	5.2^4	4.4^5	4.7^5	4.8^5	4.0^5
Janus Gov MM	—	—	—	—	—	—	—	—	5.2^1	5.1^2	—	—
JP Morgan Fed MM	—	—	—	—	—	—	—	—	—	5.2^1	—	—
Kemper-Cash Acct Tr Gov MM‡	—	—	—	5.3^5	3.0^5	2.4^5	3.5^4	5.2^4	4.8^4	4.8^4	4.9^4	4.1^4
Kemper-Cash Equiv Fd Gov MM‡	—	—	—	—	—	—	—	—	—	4.9^4	—	—
Kent Gov MM	—	—	—	—	—	—	—	—	—	5.1^2	—	—
Lake Forest MM	—	—	—	—	—	—	—	—	5.5^1	5.4^1	—	—
Legg Msn Gov MM	—	—	7.6^3	5.9^1	3.5^2	2.8^1	3.7^3	5.3^3	4.8^3	4.9^4	5.0^3	4.3^3
Monetta Gov MM	—	—	—	—	—	—	4.0^1	—	5.3^1	5.1^2	—	—
Montgmry Gov Res MM	—	—	—	—	—	2.7^2	3.8^2	5.6^1	5.2^1	5.2^2	5.3^1	4.5^1
Mosaic Gov Tr MM	6.9^2	8.6^3	7.3^5	5.1^5	2.8^5	2.1^5	3.1^5	4.8^5	4.6^5	4.3^5	4.5^5	3.8^5
Nations Gov MM	—	—	—	—	—	—	—	—	4.9^3	5.0^3	—	—
Nations Treas MM	—	—	—	—	—	—	—	—	5.1^2	5.0^2	—	—
Nbrgr-Ber Gov MM	6.2^5	7.9^5	7.3^5	5.5^3	3.3^3	2.5^4	3.4^5	5.2^5	4.7^4	4.8^5	4.9^4	4.1^4
New England Cash Mgt Gov MM	6.7^4	8.5^3	7.5^4	5.7^2	3.4^2	2.5^4	3.4^5	5.2^5	4.6^5	4.9^4	4.9^4	4.1^5
Northern US Gov MM	—	—	—	—	—	—	—	—	5.0^2	5.0^2	—	—
Northern US Gov Sel MM	—	—	—	—	—	—	—	—	5.1^1	5.4^1	—	—
Price Trsy MM	6.5^4	8.3^4	7.4^4	5.4^4	3.2^4	2.5^4	3.5^4	5.3^4	4.8^4	4.9^3	5.0^3	4.2^4
Prudential Gov MM	7.1^2	8.8^1	7.8^2	5.7^2	3.4^2	2.6^3	3.5^4	5.3^3	4.8^4	4.9^3	5.0^3	4.2^3
Reserve Treas MM	7.2^1	8.7^2	7.5^3	5.2^5	3.1^5	2.3^5	3.4^5	5.1^5	4.3^5	4.5^5	4.6^5	3.9^5
Reserve US Gov MM	—	—	—	—	—	—	—	—	—	4.7^5	—	—
Riverfront Gov MM	—	—	—	—	—	—	—	5.5^2	5.1^2	5.0^2	5.2^2	—
Rushmore Fd Gov Inv MM	6.7^4	8.5^3	7.4^5	5.4^4	3.0^5	2.4^5	3.6^3	—	4.3^5	4.5^5	—	—
Rydex US Gov MM	—	—	—	—	—	—	3.6^3	—	4.3^5	4.9^4	—	—
Schwab Gov MM	—	—	—	5.3^4	3.4^2	2.7^2	3.6^3	5.3^3	4.9^3	5.0^3	5.0^3	4.3^3
Schwab Trsy MM	—	—	—	—	—	2.5^4	3.5^4	5.3^4	4.9^2	4.9^4	5.0^3	4.2^3
Scout Fed MMF	7.2^1	8.9^1	7.8^2	5.7^2	3.4^2	2.7^2	3.8^2	5.5^2	5.0^2	5.1^2	5.2^2	4.4^2
Scudder Trsy MM	6.3^5	8.3^5	7.8^2	5.7^2	3.4^3	2.6^4	3.5^4	5.2^4	4.4^5	4.7^5	4.8^5	4.1^5
Selected Daily Gov MM	7.0^2	8.7^2	7.4^5	5.4^4	3.0^5	2.3^5	3.5^4	5.3^4	4.8^4	4.9^3	5.0^4	4.1^4
Short Tm Inc-Gov(R&T)	6.4^5	8.2^5	7.5^4	5.5^3	3.3^3	2.5^4	3.4^5	5.2^5	4.8^3	4.8^5	4.9^4	4.1^4
SSgA Gov MM	—	—	—	—	—	—	3.9^1	5.6^1	5.2^1	5.3^1	5.4^1	—
Treas Cash Oblig (Federated)	—	—	—	—	—	—	—	—	4.9^3	5.4^1	—	—
US Glb:US Gov Sec Svgs MM	—	—	—	6.3^1	4.4^1	3.4^1	4.0^1	5.6^1	5.2^1	5.3^1	5.4^1	4.7^1
US Glb:US Trsy Sec Csh MM	6.8^4	8.3^4	7.5^4	5.8^2	3.1^4	2.3^5	3.2^5	5.0^5	3.5^5	4.5^5	4.3^5	3.7^5
USAA Trsy MM	—	—	—	—	3.5^1	2.8^1	3.8^2	5.6^1	5.1^2	5.2^1	5.3^1	4.5^1
Vangd MM Resvs Federal	7.3^1	9.2^1	8.1^1	6.0^1	3.7^1	3.0^1	4.0^1	5.8^1	5.3^1	5.4^1	5.5^1	4.7^1
Vangd MM US Trsy	—	—	7.9^1	5.7^2	3.5^2	2.9^1	3.8^2	5.5^2	5.0^2	5.1^2	5.2^2	4.5^2
Vangd-Adml Trsy MM	—	—	—	—	—	3.0^1	4.0^1	5.7^1	5.2^1	5.3^1	5.4^1	4.6^1
Vintage Gov Obl MM	—	—	—	—	—	—	3.7^2	5.4^2	4.7^4	4.8^5	5.0^4	—
Vista Cash Mgt:100% US Trsy MM	—	—	—	—	—	—	—	—	—	4.9^3	—	—
Vista Cash Mgt:Trsy Plus MM	—	—	—	—	—	—	—	—	—	5.0^3	—	—
Vista Cash Mgt:US Gov MM	—	—	—	—	3.1^5	2.4^5	3.6^3	5.3^3	5.1^1	5.1^2	5.2^2	4.3^2
Weitz Gov Port MM	—	—	—	—	3.6^1	2.6^3	3.5^4	—	4.8^3	5.0^3	—	—
WPG Gov MM	—	8.8^1	7.7^2	5.4^4	2.9^5	2.8^2	3.6^3	5.2^5	4.7^4	4.8^5	4.9^5	4.2^4
Wright Trsy MM	—	—	—	—	3.3^3	2.6^3	3.5^4	5.3^3	4.9^3	4.8^4	5.0^3	4.2^3
Zurich Gov MM	—	—	—	—	—	—	—	—	—	5.3^1	—	—

Money market funds *continued*

Arranged in alphabetical order within objective

No-Load Fund	Compound yield percent with quintile ranks by objective										Annualized	
	1988	1989	1990	1991	1992	1993	1994	1995	1996	1997	3 years	5 years
TAX-FREE MONEY MARKET FUNDS												
AARP Hi Qual TF MM	—	—	—	—	2.1^5	1.6^5	2.0^5	3.1^5	3.1^5	2.9^5	3.0^5	2.5^5
Amer AAdv Muni Miles	—	—	—	—	—	—	2.4^3	3.5^2	3.6^1	3.2^2	3.4^2	—
Amer Cent-Benham CA Muni MM	—	—	—	—	3.0^1	2.1^2	2.5^2	3.5^2	3.6^1	3.2^2	3.4^2	3.0^2
Amer Cent-Benham CA TF MM	4.6^4	5.7^4	5.2^4	3.8^5	2.5^4	2.0^2	2.4^3	3.4^3	3.6^1	3.2^2	3.4^2	2.9^2
Amer Cent-Benham FL TF MM	—	—	—	—	—	—	—	4.1^1	4.0^1	3.4^1	3.8^1	—
Amer Cent-Benham Nat TF MM	4.8^2	6.1^2	5.6^2	4.2^3	2.5^4	1.9^4	2.3^4	3.4^3	3.4^2	3.4^1	3.4^2	2.9^2
Babson TF MM	5.0^1	6.0^2	5.5^3	4.2^3	2.7^3	2.0^3	2.4^3	3.4^3	3.4^2	3.1^3	3.3^3	2.8^3
Boston-1784 TF MM	—	—	—	—	—	—	2.7^1	3.8^1	5.3^1	3.3^1	4.1^1	—
BT Invest NY TF MM	—	—	—	—	—	—	—	—	—	2.9^5	—	—
BT Invest TF MM	—	—	—	—	—	—	—	—	—	2.9^5	—	—
CA Daily TF Inc (R&T)	4.7^3	5.8^4	5.2^4	3.8^5	2.3^5	2.2	2.4^3	3.3^4	3.2^4	2.8^5	3.1^5	2.8^4
CA Inv Tr-CA MM	5.0^1	6.1^2	5.6^2	4.1^3	2.7^3	2.2	2.5^2	3.4^3	3.3^3	3.1^3	3.3^3	2.9^3
Cash Resource TE MM	—	—	—	—	—	—	—	—	—	3.0^4	—	—
CT Daily TF (R&T)	4.5^5	5.6^4	5.1^5	3.7^5	2.2^5	1.7^5	2.2^5	3.0^5	2.8^5	2.7^5	2.9^5	2.5^5
Daily TF Inc(R&T)	5.0^1	6.1^2	5.5^3	4.4^2	2.7^2	2.2^2	2.6^2	3.5^2	3.4^2	3.1^3	3.3^3	2.9^2
Drey-Basic CA Muni MM	—	—	—	—	—	—	—	—	3.4^2	3.2^3	—	—
Drey-Basic MA Muni MM	—	—	—	—	—	—	—	—	3.5^2	3.2^2	—	—
Drey-Basic Muni MM	—	—	—	—	—	2.6^1	2.9^1	3.9^1	3.6^1	3.4^1	3.6^1	3.3^1
Drey-Basic NJ Muni MM	—	—	—	—	—	—	—	—	3.5^2	3.2^3	—	—
Drey-Basic NY Muni MM	—	—	—	—	—	—	—	—	3.4^2	3.2^2	—	—
Drey-General CA MM	4.8^3	5.8^4	5.9^1	4.7^1	2.9^1	2.3^1	2.6^2	3.2^4	3.3^3	3.0^4	3.2^4	2.9^3
Drey-General Muni MM	4.8^3	5.9^3	5.5^3	4.2^3	2.6^3	2.1^3	2.4^3	3.4^3	3.4^2	3.2^3	3.3^3	2.9^3
Drey-General NY MM	4.4^5	5.4^5	5.8^2	4.3^2	2.6^3	2.0^3	2.5^3	3.3^4	3.2^4	3.0^4	3.2^4	2.8^3
Dreyfus CA TE MM	4.7^3	5.8^4	5.2^4	4.0^4	2.6^3	2.0^3	2.3^4	3.2^5	3.2^4	2.9^5	3.1^5	2.7^4
Dreyfus CT Muni MM	—	—	—	4.4^2	2.9^2	2.2^2	2.6^2	3.4^3	3.3^4	3.0^4	3.2^4	2.9^3
Dreyfus FL Muni MM	—	—	—	—	—	—	—	3.6^2	3.3^3	3.1^3	3.3^2	—
Dreyfus MA Muni MM	—	—	—	—	2.9^1	2.1^2	2.6^1	3.4^3	3.2^4	3.0^4	3.2^4	2.9^3
Dreyfus Muni MM	4.8^3	6.0^2	5.6^2	4.1^3	2.5^4	2.0^2	2.4^3	3.4^3	3.4^3	3.1^3	3.3^3	2.9^3
Dreyfus NJ Muni MM	—	6.4^1	5.9^1	4.4^2	2.8^2	2.1^2	2.5^2	3.3^4	3.2^4	3.0^4	3.1^4	2.8^3
Dreyfus NY TE MM	4.5^4	5.5^5	5.2^4	3.8^5	2.3^5	1.6^5	2.1^5	3.2^4	3.3^3	3.0^4	3.2^4	2.6^5
Dreyfus PA Muni MM	—	—	—	4.7^1	3.0^1	2.4^1	2.8^1	3.5^2	3.3^3	3.1^4	3.3^3	3.0^1
Emerald TE MM	—	—	—	—	—	—	—	—	3.0^5	2.9^5	—	—
Excelsior ST TE MM	—	—	—	—	—	—	—	—	—	3.3^2	—	—
Fidelity CA Muni MM	4.8^2	5.8^3	5.2^4	4.0^4	2.6^3	2.0^3	2.4^3	3.3^4	3.4^2	3.1^4	3.2^3	2.8^3
Fidelity CT Muni MM	—	—	5.7^2	4.4^2	2.6^3	1.9^4	2.3^4	3.3^4	3.3^3	3.1^4	3.2^4	2.8^4
Fidelity MA Muni MM	4.6^4	5.9^3	5.3^4	4.0^4	2.2^5	1.7^5	2.2^5	3.2^5	3.2^4	3.1^3	3.2^4	2.7^5
Fidelity MI Muni MM	—	—	—	4.5^1	2.7^3	2.0^3	2.4^3	3.4^3	3.4^2	3.2^2	3.3^3	2.9^3
Fidelity Muni MM	4.9^2	6.0^2	5.6^2	4.4^2	2.9^2	2.2^2	2.5^2	3.5^2	3.5^2	3.3^1	3.4^2	3.0^1
Fidelity NJ Muni MM	—	6.4^1	5.7^2	4.1^3	2.7^3	1.9^4	2.3^4	3.3^4	3.3^3	3.0^4	3.2^4	2.8^4
Fidelity NY Muni MM	4.5^4	5.5^5	5.1^5	3.9^4	2.5^4	1.9^4	2.3^4	3.3^3	3.4^3	3.1^3	3.3^3	2.8^3
Fidelity OH Muni MM	—	—	5.9^1	4.5^1	2.8^2	2.1^2	2.5^2	3.5^2	3.5^2	3.3^2	3.4^2	3.0^2
Fidelity Spart AZ MM	—	—	—	—	—	—	—	3.9^1	3.7^1	3.5^1	3.7^1	—
Fidelity Spart CA Muni MM	—	—	5.9^1	4.6^1	3.0^1	2.4^1	2.8^1	3.7^1	3.7^1	3.3^2	3.5^1	3.2^1
Fidelity Spart CT Muni MM	—	—	—	—	3.0^1	2.2^2	2.4^3	3.4^3	3.4^2	3.1^3	3.3^3	2.9^2
Fidelity Spart FL Muni MM	—	—	—	—	—	2.3^1	2.6^2	3.6^2	3.5^2	3.3^2	3.5^1	3.1^1
Fidelity Spart MA MM	—	—	—	—	2.7^2	2.0^3	2.3^4	3.3^3	3.3^3	3.2^3	3.3^3	2.8^3
Fidelity Spart Muni MM	—	—	—	—	3.3^1	2.5^1	2.8^1	3.7^1	3.7^1	3.5^1	3.6^1	3.2^1
Fidelity Spart NJ Muni MM	—	—	—	4.6^1	3.0^1	1.9^4	2.7^1	3.7^1	3.5^2	3.2^2	3.5^1	3.0^2
Fidelity Spart NY Muni MM	—	—	—	4.3^2	2.7^2	2.0^3	2.5^3	3.5^2	3.4^2	3.3^2	3.4^2	2.9^2
Fidelity Spart PA Muni MM	5.1^1	6.3^1	6.1^1	4.6^1	2.9^2	2.2^2	2.6^1	3.6^2	3.6^1	3.4^1	3.5^1	3.1^1
Firstar TE MM	—	6.0^2	5.5^3	4.2^3	2.6^3	2.1^2	2.5^2	3.5^2	3.5^2	3.1^3	3.4^2	2.9^2
FL Daily Muni (R&T)	—	—	—	—	—	—	—	—	3.2^4	3.1^4	—	—
FL Hough TF MM	—	—	—	—	—	—	3.1^1	3.9^1	3.7^1	3.5^1	3.7^1	—
Fundamental TF MM	4.5^5	5.5^5	5.1^5	4.8^1	2.8^2	1.4^5	1.7^5	2.6^5	2.7^5	2.2^5	2.5^5	2.1^5
Independence One MI Muni MM	—	—	—	—	—	—	—	—	—	3.2^3	—	—
Invesco TF MM	4.7^3	5.7^4	5.3^4	3.7^5	2.4^4	1.9^4	2.2^5	3.3^4	3.2^4	3.0^4	3.2^4	2.7^4
Janus TE MM	—	—	—	—	—	—	—	—	3.6^1	3.2^2	—	—
JP Morgan TE MM	—	—	—	—	—	—	—	—	—	3.3^2	—	—
Kemper-Cash Acct Tr TF MM‡	—	—	—	3.9^4	2.4^4	1.8^4	2.3^4	3.3^4	3.2^4	2.9^5	3.1^4	2.7^4

No-Load Fund	Compound yield percent with quintile ranks by objective										Annualized	
	1988	1989	1990	1991	1992	1993	1994	1995	1996	1997	3 years	5 years
emper-Cash Equiv Fd TE MM‡	—	—	—	—	—	—	—	—	—	3.1^3	—	—
ent MI Muni MM	—	—	—	—	—	—	—	—	—	3.3^2	—	—
egg Msn TE MM	4.6^4	5.9^3	5.3^4	3.9^4	2.3^5	1.8^5	2.3^4	3.2^5	2.9^5	3.0^5	3.0^5	2.6^5
* Daily TF (R&T)	4.7^3	6.3^1	5.9^1	4.1^3	2.4^4	1.9^4	2.3^4	3.3^4	3.2^4	3.0^4	3.2^4	2.7^4
ontgmry CA TF MM	—	—	—	—	—	—	—	3.4^3	3.3^3	3.0^4	3.2^3	—
ontgmry Fed TF MM	—	—	—	—	—	—	—	—	4.0^1	3.2^3	—	—
osaic TF MM	4.4^5	5.8^4	5.3^4	3.5^5	2.2^5	1.4^5	1.8^5	2.9^5	2.9^5	2.6^5	2.8^5	2.3^5
unicipal Cash Resrvs(Federated)	—	—	—	—	—	—	—	—	3.2^4	3.3^1	—	—
ations TE MM	—	—	—	—	—	—	—	—	3.6^1	3.2^2	—	—
orgr-Ber Muni MM	5.0^1	6.1^2	5.5^3	4.1^3	2.4^5	1.8^5	2.3^4	3.3^4	3.0^5	3.0^4	3.1^4	2.7^4
C Daily Muni (R&T)	—	—	—	—	2.5^4	1.8^5	2.2^5	3.2^5	3.1^5	2.9^5	3.1^5	2.6^5
ew England TE MM	4.8^2	5.8^3	5.5^3	4.2^3	2.6^3	2.0^3	2.5^2	3.5^2	3.6^2	3.3^2	3.4^2	3.0^2
J Daily Muni (R&T)	—	—	—	4.4^2	2.7^2	1.9^4	2.2^5	3.1^5	3.0^5	2.7^5	2.9^5	2.6^5
orthern CA Muni MM	—	—	—	—	—	—	—	—	3.7^1	3.4^1	—	—
orthern Muni MM	—	—	—	—	—	—	—	3.5^2	3.6^2	3.3^2	3.4^2	—
Y Daily TF Inc(R&T)	4.5^5	5.6^5	5.1^5	4.2^2	2.6^3	1.9^4	2.3^4	3.2^5	3.2^4	2.9^5	3.1^5	2.7^4
akmark Units TE Div MM	—	—	—	—	—	—	—	—	3.6^1	3.4^1	—	—
A Daily Muni (R&T)	—	—	—	—	—	2.3^1	2.6^2	3.5^2	3.4^3	3.1^4	3.3^3	2.9^2
acific Hzn CA TE MM	—	—	—	—	—	—	—	—	—	3.1^4	—	—
rice CA TF MM	4.6^4	5.5^5	4.9^5	3.7^5	2.5^4	1.9^3	2.4^3	3.3^4	3.3^3	3.0^4	3.2^4	2.8^4
rice NY TF MM	4.3^5	5.3^5	4.9^5	3.8^5	2.4^5	1.8^4	2.3^4	3.3^4	3.3^3	3.1^3	3.2^3	2.8^4
rice Summit Muni MM	—	—	—	—	—	—	2.6^2	3.6^2	3.6^1	3.4^1	3.5^1	—
rice TE MM	4.9^2	6.0^2	5.4^4	3.9^4	2.5^4	2.0^3	2.5^2	3.4^3	3.4^2	3.2^2	3.4^2	2.9^2
rudential TF MM	4.8^2	5.8^4	5.4^3	4.2^3	2.6^3	1.9^4	2.3^4	3.2^5	3.3^3	3.0^4	3.2^4	2.7^4
eserve TE CA MM	—	—	—	—	—	—	—	3.3^4	2.2^5	2.8^5	2.8^5	—
eserve TE CT MM	4.5^5	5.6^4	5.1^5	3.6^5	2.2^5	1.6^5	2.0^5	2.8^5	2.7^5	2.6^5	2.7^5	2.4^5
eserve TE Interstate	4.9^2	5.9^3	5.4^4	4.1^3	2.6^3	1.7^5	2.0^5	3.0^5	3.0^5	2.7^5	2.9^5	2.5^5
eserve TE MA MM	—	—	—	4.1^3	2.4^4	1.8^4	2.0^5	2.9^5	3.1^4	2.8^5	3.0^5	2.5^5
eserve TE NJ MM	—	—	—	—	—	—	—	—	2.3^5	2.7^5	—	—
eserve TE NY MM	4.4^5	5.4^5	5.0^5	3.7^5	2.2^5	1.5^5	2.0^5	2.9^5	2.8^5	2.6^5	2.8^5	2.4^5
eserve TE PA MM	—	—	—	—	—	—	—	—	—	2.6^5	—	—
ushmore Fd TF Inv MM	4.6^4	5.8^4	5.6^2	4.0^4	2.3^5	1.7^5	2.3^4	—	2.6^5	2.9^5	—	—
AFECO TF MM	4.8^3	6.1^2	5.6^2	4.3^2	2.7^2	2.0^3	2.5^3	3.5^2	3.3^3	3.2^3	3.3^2	2.9^2
chwab CA Muni Sweep Shrs	—	—	—	—	—	—	—	—	2.8^5	3.0^5	—	—
chwab CA Muni Val Adv	—	—	—	3.8^5	2.4^5	1.9^4	2.2^5	3.2^5	3.0^5	3.2^3	3.1^5	2.7^4
chwab Muni Sweep Shrs	—	—	—	—	—	—	—	—	2.9^5	3.1^3	—	—
chwab Muni Val Adv MM	—	—	—	4.0^4	2.5^4	1.9^3	2.3^4	3.3^4	3.1^4	3.3^2	3.3^3	2.8^3
chwab NY Muni Sweep MM	—	—	—	—	—	—	—	—	2.7^5	3.0^4	—	—
chwab NY Muni Val Adv MM	—	—	—	—	—	—	—	—	3.0^5	3.2^2	—	—
cout TF MM	4.8^2	5.9^3	5.4^3	4.0^4	2.6^3	2.0^3	2.4^3	3.3^4	3.2^4	3.1^3	3.2^4	2.8^3
cudder CA TF MM	4.7^3	5.6^5	5.0^5	3.9^4	2.5^3	2.0^3	2.4^3	3.4^3	3.2^4	3.0^4	3.2^4	2.8^4
cudder NY TF MM	4.4^5	5.4^5	5.0^5	3.7^5	2.5^4	1.8^5	2.2^5	3.2^5	3.2^4	3.1^4	3.2^4	2.7^5
cudder TF MM	4.7^3	5.8^3	5.4^3	3.8^5	2.5^4	1.9^4	2.3^4	3.3^4	3.3^3	3.1^3	3.2^3	2.8^4
SgA TF MM	—	—	—	—	—	—	—	3.4^3	3.3^4	3.1^4	3.2^3	—
tagecoach Nat'l TF MM	—	—	—	—	—	—	—	—	—	3.0^4	—	—
tein Roe Muni MM	4.8^2	5.9^3	5.4^3	3.9^4	2.4^5	1.9^4	2.3^4	3.4^3	3.4^2	3.1^3	3.3^3	2.8^3
trong Muni MM	5.2^1	6.1^2	6.1^1	5.2^1	3.4^1	2.5^1	2.9^1	4.1^1	3.9^1	3.6^1	3.9^1	3.4^1
SAA CA MM	—	—	5.6^2	4.4^2	2.9^1	2.3^1	2.6^2	3.7^1	3.3^3	3.4^1	3.4^2	3.0^1
SAA FL MM	—	—	—	—	—	—	2.5^2	3.6^2	3.2^4	3.3^1	3.4^2	—
SAA NY MM	—	—	—	4.2^3	2.8^2	2.0^3	2.4^3	3.6^1	3.2^4	3.3^2	3.4^2	2.9^2
SAA TE MM	5.2^1	6.3^1	6.1^1	4.8^1	3.1^1	2.4^1	2.6^1	3.7^1	3.3^3	3.5^1	3.5^1	3.1^1
SAA TX TF MM	—	—	—	—	—	—	—	—	3.3^3	3.4^1	—	—
SAA VA MM	—	—	—	4.5^1	2.9^1	2.2^2	2.6^2	3.5^2	3.2^4	3.3^2	3.3^2	3.0^2
alue Line TE MM	4.6^4	5.9^3	5.4^3	4.1^4	2.5^4	1.6^5	2.0^5	2.9^5	2.8^5	2.5^5	2.7^5	2.3^5
angd CA MM	5.1^1	6.2^1	5.6^3	4.3^2	2.9^2	2.4^1	2.7^1	3.7^1	3.8^1	3.4^1	3.6^1	3.2^1
angd Muni MM	5.2^1	6.3^1	5.8^1	4.6^1	3.0^1	2.4^1	2.8^1	3.8^1	3.8^1	3.5^1	3.7^1	3.2^1
angd NJ TF MM	—	6.3^1	5.8^1	4.4^2	2.9^1	2.3^1	2.6^1	3.6^1	3.6^2	3.3^1	3.5^1	3.1^1
angd NY TF MM	—	—	—	—	—	—	—	—	—	—	—	—
angd OH TF MM	—	—	—	—	2.9^2	2.3^1	2.7^1	3.8^1	3.8^1	3.5^1	3.7^1	3.2^1
angd PA TF MM	—	6.4^1	5.9^1	4.4^1	2.8^2	2.4^1	2.7^1	3.7^1	3.8^1	3.5^1	3.7^1	3.2^1

Money market funds *continued*

Arranged in alphabetical order within objective

| No-Load Fund | Compound yield percent with quintile ranks by objective | | | | | | | | | | Annualized | |
	1988	1989	1990	1991	1992	1993	1994	1995	1996	1997	3 years	5 years
Vista Cash Mgt:TF MM............................	—	—	—	—	—	—	—	—	—	3.2[3]	—	—
Warbg Pincus NY MM.............................	4.5[4]	5.6[4]	5.2[5]	3.6[5]	2.4[5]	1.8[5]	2.2[5]	3.3[3]	2.9[5]	3.1[3]	3.1[5]	2.7[5]
WPG TF MM...	—	6.3[1]	5.7[2]	4.6[1]	3.0[1]	2.3[1]	2.6[1]	3.6[1]	3.4[3]	3.2[2]	3.4[2]	3.0[1]
Zurich TF MM...	—	—	—	—	—	—	—	—	—	3.5[1]	—	—

Additional funds available no-load through discount brokers

Arranged in alphabetical order

No-Load Fund	Objective	Total return percent 1988	1989	1990	1991	1992	1993	1994	1995	1996	1997	Annualized 3 yrs.	5 yrs.
BlackRock Core Bd	fix-inc	—	—	—	—	—	9.8	-2.3	18.3	3.6	9.0	10.1	7.5
BlackRock Low Dur Bd	fix-inc	—	—	—	—	—	5.7	1.4	10.6	5.1	6.1	7.2	5.7
Brinson Global Bd	fix-inc	—	—	—	—	—	—	-3.5	20.3	9.3	1.6	10.2	—
Brinson Global Eqty	global	—	—	—	—	—	—	—	21.9	17.3	10.7	16.6	—
Brinson Global	global	—	—	—	—	—	11.2	-1.9	24.1	14.1	11.0	16.3	11.4
Brinson Non US Eqty	int'l	—	—	—	—	—	—	0.9	15.6	12.8	5.7	11.3	—
Brinson US Balanced	income	—	—	—	—	—	—	—	25.5	11.3	13.2	16.5	—
Brinson US Bond	fix-inc	—	—	—	—	—	—	—	—	3.5	9.6	—	—
Brinson US Eqty	growth	—	—	—	—	—	—	—	40.6	25.7	24.8	30.1	—
DFA 1 Yr Fix‡	fix-inc	7.4	9.6	9.1	8.7	5.2	4.4	2.5	8.0	5.8	6.1	6.6	5.3
DFA 2 Yr Glbl Fix Inc‡	fix-inc	—	—	—	—	—	—	—	—	—	5.9	—	—
DFA 5 Yr Gov‡	fix-inc	6.3	9.5	10.9	14.6	7.3	8.3	-3.2	9.6	6.6	6.4	7.5	5.4
DFA Cont Sm Co‡	int'l	—	44.7	-4.1	-4.2	-19.8	25.3	11.0	0.0	14.3	11.7	8.5	12.2
DFA Emg Mkts‡	int'l	—	—	—	—	—	—	—	2.2	11.4	-18.9	-2.6	—
DFA Enhancd US Lg Cap‡	gr-inc	—	—	—	—	—	—	—	—	—	32.7	—	—
DFA Glob Fix Inc‡	fix-inc	—	—	—	12.8	6.5	11.6	-4.3	16.0	10.8	8.3	11.7	8.2
DFA Int'l High BTM‡	int'l	—	—	—	—	—	—	8.8	11.5	7.9	-3.2	5.2	—
DFA Int'l Sm Cap Val‡	int'l	—	—	—	—	—	—	—	1.2	1.0	-22.7	-5.2	—
DFA Int'l Sm Cap‡	int'l	—	—	—	—	—	—	—	1.1	1.0	-22.7	-7.6	—
DFA Int'l Value‡	int'l	—	—	—	—	—	—	—	11.5	7.8	-3.1	5.2	—
DFA Inter Gov‡	fix-inc	—	—	—	16.9	7.6	11.6	-4.8	19.1	2.4	9.2	10.0	7.2
DFA Japan Sm Co‡	int'l	32.2	38.5	-33.4	7.1	-26.1	14.2	29.5	-3.6	-22.8	-54.9	-30.5	-13.1
DFA Lrg Cap Int'l‡	int'l	—	—	—	—	-13.1	25.8	5.3	13.1	6.4	5.5	8.3	11.0
DFA Pac Rim Sm Co‡	int'l	—	—	—	—	—	—	-12.1	-2.9	14.4	-42.1	-13.7	—
DFA Real Estate‡	sector	—	—	—	—	—	—	-8.4	12.1	33.8	19.3	21.4	—
DFA UK Sm Co‡	int'l	6.6	-6.3	-6.7	14.8	-14.0	30.6	4.7	10.7	29.8	3.5	14.2	15.3
DFA US 6-10 Sm Co‡	agg gr	—	—	—	—	—	13.7	-1.4	30.2	17.7	24.2	23.9	16.4
DFA US 9-10 Sm Co‡	agg gr	22.9	10.2	-21.6	44.4	23.5	21.0	3.1	34.5	17.7	22.8	24.8	19.4
DFA US Lrg Cap Val‡	gr-inc	—	—	—	—	—	—	-4.6	38.4	20.2	28.1	28.7	—
DFA US Lrg Co‡	growth	—	—	—	30.1	7.4	9.6	1.3	37.1	22.6	33.1	30.8	20.0
DFA US Sm Cap Val‡	growth	—	—	—	—	—	—	1.2	29.3	22.3	30.8	27.4	—
Fifty - 59 Wall European Eqty	int'l	—	—	—	9.3	7.5	27.1	-3.9	16.5	19.3	15.3	17.0	14.4
Fifty - 59 Wall Inflat Idx Sec	fix-inc	—	—	—	—	—	7.0	-2.4	12.8	3.4	2.3	6.1	4.5
Fifty - 59 Wall Pac Basin	int'l	—	—	—	13.6	6.2	74.9	-21.5	3.5	-0.7	-20.1	-6.4	2.4
Fifty - 59 Wall S-I TF	tax-free	—	—	—	—	—	6.0	0.3	7.2	3.7	4.0	5.0	4.2
Fifty - 59 Wall Sm Co SC	agg gr	—	—	—	—	10.6	12.2	-10.5	22.0	19.1	19.9	20.3	11.8
Fifty - 59 Wall US Eqty	growth	—	—	—	—	—	10.3	0.7	38.4	15.6	30.3	27.8	18.3
Harding-Loevner Glob Eqty	global	—	—	—	—	—	—	—	—	—	9.3	—	—
Harding-Loevner Int'l Eqty	int'l	—	—	—	—	—	—	—	12.0	15.4	-4.2	7.4	—
Harding-Loevner Multi Asst Glob	global	—	—	—	—	—	—	—	—	—	11.9	—	—
Lexington Strat Invest	prec met	-43.0	61.2	-42.4	-18.9	-60.7	269.8	11.3	-14.7	-11.1	-45.7	-25.6	11.1
Lexington Strat Silver	prec met	-15.9	16.1	-32.1	-14.5	-11.5	76.5	-8.4	12.4	2.4	-8.1	1.9	11.3
Loomis Syls Bond	fix-inc	—	—	—	—	14.3	22.2	-4.1	32.0	10.3	12.7	17.9	14.0
Loomis Syls Core Val	growth	—	—	—	—	14.1	11.9	-0.9	35.2	21.2	29.2	28.4	18.6
Loomis Syls Glob Bd	fix-inc	—	—	—	—	0.8	14.6	-8.7	23.9	15.0	2.3	13.4	8.8
Loomis Syls Growth	growth	—	—	—	—	3.8	9.2	-3.7	30.9	19.9	24.1	24.9	15.4
Loomis Syls Hi Yld	fix-inc	—	—	—	—	—	—	—	—	—	11.5	—	—
Loomis Syls Int'l Eq	int'l	—	—	—	—	-5.1	38.5	-1.8	8.7	18.3	-1.0	8.4	11.6
Loomis Syls Inter Mat	fix-inc	—	—	—	—	—	—	—	—	—	6.4	—	—
Loomis Syls Inv Gr Bd	fix-inc	—	—	—	—	—	—	—	30.3	11.0	10.6	16.9	—
Loomis Syls Mid Cap Gro	agg gr	—	—	—	—	—	—	—	—	—	22.2	—	—
Loomis Syls Mid Cap Val	growth	—	—	—	—	—	—	—	—	—	26.3	—	—
Loomis Syls Muni Bd	tax-free	—	—	—	—	9.4	11.5	-5.4	16.5	3.3	9.8	9.8	6.9
Loomis Syls Sm Cap Gro SC	agg gr	—	—	—	—	—	—	—	—	—	19.4	—	—
Loomis Syls Sm Cap Val SC	agg gr	—	—	—	—	13.1	24.7	-8.3	32.2	30.4	26.0	29.5	19.9
Loomis Syls ST Bd	fix-inc	—	—	—	—	—	6.9	1.8	10.6	4.7	7.1	7.5	6.2
Loomis Syls Strat Val	growth	—	—	—	—	—	—	—	—	—	19.7	—	—
Loomis Syls US Gov	fix-inc	—	—	—	—	8.8	15.7	-6.3	23.0	1.3	12.7	12.0	8.8
Loomis Syls Worldwide	global	—	—	—	—	—	—	—	—	—	3.5	—	—

Arranged in alphabetical order

No-Load Fund	Objective	Total return percent										Annualized	
		1988	1989	1990	1991	1992	1993	1994	1995	1996	1997	3 yrs.	5 yrs.
Mainstay Inst EAFE Idx.............	int'l	—	—	—	10.1	-12.2	29.0	6.8	9.0	6.5	0.4	5.2	9.9
Mainstay Inst Val Eqty...............	gr-inc	0.0	0.0	0.0	36.6	20.7	14.9	1.2	29.4	22.4	22.6	24.8	17.7
MAS Balanced......................	income	—	—	—	—	—	10.4	-1.9	27.3	15.4	19.6	20.7	13.7
MAS Equity	growth	13.1	28.3	-0.1	40.0	7.8	6.7	0.5	33.1	20.5	25.8	26.4	16.7
MAS Fix Inc II.....................	fix-inc	—	—	—	19.3	7.0	12.6	-5.2	18.7	5.5	9.3	11.0	7.9
MAS Fix Inc........................	fix-inc	8.8	11.2	7.2	21.5	8.5	13.9	-5.5	19.0	7.4	9.6	11.9	8.6
MAS Glob Fix Inc.................	fix-inc	—	—	—	—	—	—	-1.6	20.0	6.0	0.0	8.4	—
MAS High Yld.......................	fix-inc	—	—	-10.9	44.2	18.5	24.6	-7.1	23.9	15.3	16.0	18.3	13.9
MAS Int'l Eqty......................	int'l	—	26.1	-15.4	21.2	-3.5	42.7	-10.1	6.2	10.4	13.0	9.8	11.2
MAS Int'l Fix Inc..................	fix-inc	—	—	—	—	—	—	—	19.6	6.2	-4.0	6.9	—
MAS Ltd Dur Fix Inc..................	fix-inc	—	—	—	—	—	6.0	-0.1	10.4	5.3	6.3	7.3	5.5
MAS MidCap Gro...................	agg gr	—	—	—	59.2	3.0	18.3	-5.4	36.3	18.8	33.1	29.2	19.3
MAS MidCap Val.....................	growth	—	—	—	—	—	—	—	32.7	40.8	39.6	37.6	—
MAS Mortg Bckd Sec............	fix-inc	—	—	—	—	—	—	8.2	-3.4	17.4	5.8	9.3	10.7	7.3
MAS Multi-Asset...................	income	—	—	—	—	—	—	—	24.6	15.9	17.5	19.3	—
MAS Muni...........................	tax-free	—	—	—	—	—	14.4	-6.3	20.0	5.6	8.7	11.3	8.1
MAS PA Muni.......................	tax-free	—	—	—	—	—	14.9	-6.9	21.1	5.2	8.4	11.4	8.1
MAS Sm Cap Val+	growth	21.3	17.6	-16.6	63.8	22.7	21.2	2.2	21.0	35.2	30.6	28.8	21.5
MAS Value...........................	gr-inc	22.2	20.7	-6.2	37.7	14.7	14.3	3.5	38.8	27.6	23.4	29.8	20.9
Morgan Grenfell Emg Mkts Debt...	fix-inc	—	—	—	—	—	—	—	18.6	33.5	12.5	21.2	—
Morgan Grenfell Emg Mkts Eq...	int'l	—	—	—	—	—	—	—	-10.0	10.6	-12.1	-4.3	—
Morgan Grenfell Europe Sm Co.....	int'l	—	—	—	—	—	—	—	18.9	12.8	-5.3	8.3	—
Morgan Grenfell Fix Inc...........	fix-inc	—	—	—	—	—	13.6	-1.9	18.1	4.5	9.3	10.5	8.5
Morgan Grenfell Glob Fix Inc.....	fix-inc	—	—	—	—	—	—	-2.4	17.8	5.2	1.0	7.8	—
Morgan Grenfell Int'l Eq...........	int'l	—	—	—	—	—	—	—	—	10.3	0.5	—	—
Morgan Grenfell Int'l Fix Inc.......	fix-inc	—	—	—	—	—	—	—	17.2	5.5	-3.3	6.2	—
Morgan Grenfell Int'l Sm Co...	int'l	—	—	—	—	—	—	-3.2	2.8	1.9	-14.3	-3.6	—
Morgan Grenfell Muni..............	tax-free	—	—	—	—	11.7	12.4	-1.0	13.3	5.8	8.2	9.1	7.6
Morgan Grenfell Sm Co............	agg gr	—	—	—	—	—	—	—	—	22.2	15.1	—	—
Morgan Grenfell ST Fix Inc.........	fix-inc	—	—	—	—	—	—	—	—	5.5	6.8	—	—
Morgan Grenfell ST Muni...........	tax-free	—	—	—	—	—	—	—	—	5.6	6.9	—	—
PIMCO Balanced......................	income	—	—	—	—	—	6.4	-1.0	27.0	13.1	21.9	20.5	13.0
PIMCO Cap App......................	agg gr	—	—	—	—	7.5	17.7	-4.3	37.1	26.8	34.2	32.7	21.3
PIMCO Core Eqty....................	growth	—	—	—	—	—	—	—	—	17.7	24.9	—	—
PIMCO Emg Mkts....................	int'l	—	—	—	—	—	—	-7.8	-12.5	4.8	-2.0	-3.5	—
PIMCO Eqty Inc.....................	income	—	—	—	—	14.8	8.5	-1.6	33.5	21.5	31.4	28.7	17.9
PIMCO Foreign Bd..................	fix-inc	—	—	—	—	—	16.4	-7.3	21.2	18.9	10.5	16.8	11.4
PIMCO Global Bd....................	fix-inc	—	—	—	—	—	—	-1.6	23.0	10.3	-0.9	10.4	—
PIMCO Hi Yield......................	fix-inc	—	—	—	—	—	—	—	—	11.4	12.9	—	—
PIMCO Innovation....................	sector	—	—	—	—	—	—	—	45.3	23.6	9.0	25.1	—
PIMCO Int'l Devlpd...................	int'l	—	—	—	—	—	—	7.1	17.1	5.8	1.9	8.1	—
PIMCO Int'l Gro......................	int'l	—	—	—	—	-5.0	34.4	-7.5	6.5	6.6	2.6	5.2	7.7
PIMCO Low Dur II...................	fix-inc	—	—	—	—	6.2	6.6	0.3	11.8	5.2	7.6	8.2	6.2
PIMCO Low Dur Mortg............	fix-inc	—	—	—	—	—	—	—	—	—	—	—	—
PIMCO Low Dur......................	fix-inc	8.2	11.6	9.0	13.5	7.7	7.8	0.6	11.9	6.1	8.2	8.7	6.9
PIMCO LT US Gov...................	fix-inc	—	—	—	—	12.0	18.6	-7.4	31.6	0.7	15.0	15.1	10.9
PIMCO Micro Cap Gro	agg gr	—	—	—	—	—	—	1.0	36.3	23.8	36.7	32.1	—
PIMCO MidCap Eqty................	growth	—	—	—	—	—	—	—	31.7	17.3	16.2	21.6	—
PIMCO MidCap Gro.................	agg gr	—	—	—	—	9.7	15.8	-2.4	37.3	23.4	34.2	31.5	20.8
PIMCO Real Return Bd.............	fix-inc	—	—	—	—	—	—	—	—	—	—	—	—
PIMCO Short Term...................	fix-inc	7.6	9.4	8.5	6.7	3.6	4.6	2.9	9.2	7.0	6.5	7.6	6.0
PIMCO Sm Cap Val.................	growth	—	—	—	—	18.6	13.8	-3.7	25.5	27.7	35.0	29.3	18.9
PIMCO Small Cap Gro..............	agg gr	—	—	—	—	16.7	24.5	0.5	21.8	16.8	26.7	21.7	17.7
PIMCO Stocks Plus..................	gr-inc	—	—	—	—	—	—	2.9	40.5	23.1	32.9	32.0	—
PIMCO Strat Balanced..............	income	—	—	—	—	—	—	—	—	—	24.2	—	—
PIMCO Total Return II..............	fix-inc	—	—	—	—	9.4	10.9	-2.2	19.0	3.9	10.0	10.8	8.1
PIMCO Total Return III.............	fix-inc	—	—	—	—	9.1	12.7	-3.4	19.2	4.6	10.2	11.2	8.4
PIMCO Total Return Mortg.........	fix-inc	—	—	—	—	—	—	—	—	—	—	—	—
PIMCO Total Return...	fix-inc	9.4	14.3	8.1	19.6	9.8	12.5	-3.6	19.8	4.7	10.2	11.4	8.4

Additional funds available no-load through discount brokers *continued*
Arranged in alphabetical order

No-Load Fund	Objective	Total return percent										Annualized	
		1988	1989	1990	1991	1992	1993	1994	1995	1996	1997	3 yrs.	5 yrs.
PIMCO Value...............	gr-inc	—	—	—	—	13.2	16.4	-4.1	38.9	20.3	26.2	28.3	18.7
Rea-Graham Blncd..........	income	11.0	7.9	-5.7	14.7	4.2	0.2	-5.3	15.6	6.8	9.3	10.5	5.1
Rembrandt Asian Tiger......	int'l	—	—	—	—	—	—	—	11.6	14.6	-36.0	-6.5	—
Rembrandt Balanced.........	income	—	—	—	—	—	—	-2.1	21.9	13.2	22.1	19.0	—
Rembrandt Fix Inc...........	fix-inc	—	—	—	—	—	—	-3.8	17.8	3.4	9.2	10.0	—
Rembrandt Glob Fl...........	fix-inc	—	—	—	—	—	—	-1.5	21.0	2.8	-5.9	5.4	—
Rembrandt Growth Eqty......	growth	—	—	—	—	—	—	-2.1	31.6	21.7	24.0	25.7	—
Rembrandt Int'l Eq...........	int'l	—	—	—	—	—	—	3.3	14.0	10.1	4.6	9.5	—
Rembrandt Inter Gov........	fix-inc	—	—	—	—	—	—	-2.8	13.9	3.5	7.9	8.4	—
Rembrandt Small Cap........	agg gr	—	—	—	—	—	—	-6.3	32.1	19.4	15.9	22.3	—
Rembrandt Tax Exempt......	tax-free	—	—	—	—	—	—	-4.9	15.7	3.0	9.4	9.2	—
Rembrandt Value............	gr-inc	—	—	—	—	—	—	0.0	32.0	20.4	30.6	27.6	—
SEI Bond Idx................	fix-inc	7.0	13.9	8.3	13.5	7.1	9.3	-3.2	17.9	2.9	9.4	9.9	7.0
SEI Bond....................	fix-inc	12.6	17.5	5.5	17.4	7.6	15.4	-6.3	20.8	1.9	13.0	11.7	8.5
SEI Core Fix Inc............	fix-inc	7.1	11.6	7.2	15.2	6.0	8.8	-4.9	20.0	3.7	9.5	10.9	7.1
SEI Corp Daily Inc..........	fix-inc	—	—	—	—	—	—	2.9	8.6	5.2	5.7	6.5	—
SEI Daily Govt..............	fix-inc	—	—	—	—	—	—	—	—	5.4	5.5	—	—
SEI Emg Mkts...............	int'l	—	—	—	—	—	—	—	—	8.7	-9.1	—	—
SEI Eqty Inc	income	—	25.2	-9.0	30.6	10.0	13.2	-0.2	36.1	16.6	28.0	26.6	18.1
SEI GNMA..................	fix-inc	8.0	14.1	10.4	15.8	7.3	6.6	-3.4	16.9	4.5	9.2	10.1	6.6
SEI Idx S&P 500............	gr-inc	—	—	—	—	—	—	—	—	—	32.8	—	—
SEI Instit Balanced..........	income	—	—	—	15.3	13.3	7.9	-6.6	24.3	13.5	21.0	19.5	11.5
SEI Instit Cap Apprec.......	agg gr	—	35.5	0.0	35.1	7.7	9.2	-7.5	30.8	20.9	31.7	27.7	16.0
SEI Int'l Eqty..............	int'l	—	—	-12.6	10.2	-2.9	22.8	0.0	11.3	9.0	-1.9	6.0	7.9
SEI Int'l Fl.................	fix-inc	—	—	—	—	—	—	3.6	22.1	4.7	-3.6	7.2	—
SEI Inter Gov..............	fix-inc	5.5	11.5	9.4	13.7	6.4	7.1	-2.8	15.7	3.0	8.2	8.9	6.1
SEI Inter Muni.............	tax-free	—	—	6.9	8.7	7.3	8.8	-3.1	12.7	3.9	7.8	8.1	5.9
SEI Lrg Cap Gro...........	growth	—	—	—	—	—	—	—	35.5	22.7	34.8	30.9	—
SEI Lrg Cap Val...........	gr-inc	22.5	19.3	-5.3	26.8	7.3	2.5	-3.8	37.8	20.5	36.7	31.4	17.5
SEI MidCap Gro...........	agg gr	—	—	—	—	—	—	-10.8	23.0	26.7	31.9	27.1	—
SEI PA Muni	tax-free	—	—	6.1	10.4	7.1	8.5	-2.0	11.2	4.3	8.0	7.8	5.9
SEI Sm Cap Gro...........	agg gr	—	—	—	—	—	13.3	1.7	39.9	19.1	8.4	21.8	15.8
SEI Sm Cap Val...........	growth	—	—	—	—	—	—	—	18.2	22.1	35.1	24.9	—
SEI ST Gov................	fix-inc	5.8	9.9	9.1	11.2	5.3	4.8	0.3	10.8	4.6	6.9	7.4	5.4
Solon Gov 1 Yr............	fix-inc	—	—	—	—	—	—	—	7.6	6.4	6.2	6.8	—
Solon Gov 3 Yr............	fix-inc	—	—	—	—	—	—	—	11.2	5.3	6.9	7.7	—
Touchstone Balanced.......	income	—	—	—	—	—	—	—	23.2	16.9	19.6	19.9	—
Touchstone Bond..........	fix-inc	—	—	—	—	—	—	—	17.0	2.9	7.3	8.9	—
Touchstone Emg Gro.......	agg gr	—	—	—	—	—	—	—	22.6	10.1	32.2	21.3	—
Touchstone Gro & Inc......	gr-inc	—	—	—	—	—	—	—	35.1	17.0	20.7	24.0	—
Touchstone Inc Oppty......	fix-inc	—	—	—	—	—	—	—	23.2	26.7	9.5	19.6	—
Touchstone Int'l Eqty.......	int'l	—	—	—	—	—	—	—	5.3	11.6	15.6	10.7	—
Touchstone Standby Inc....	fix-inc	—	—	—	—	—	—	—	5.4	4.8	5.2	5.1	—
UAM Acdn Emg Mkts.......	int'l	—	—	—	—	—	—	-2.7	-10.3	12.1	-15.9	-5.5	—
UAM Acdn Int'l Eqty........	int'l	—	—	—	—	—	—	6.8	6.1	11.1	-6.9	3.2	—
UAM ICM Fix Inc...........	fix-inc	—	—	—	—	—	9.0	-3.6	18.1	3.0	8.8	9.8	6.8
Western Asst Core.........	fix-inc	—	—	—	18.0	7.9	13.9	-4.3	21.0	3.7	10.2	11.4	8.5
Western Asst Inter Dur.....	fix-inc	—	—	—	—	—	—	—	15.5	4.7	8.4	9.4	—

Section III

Directory of No-Load Funds

Explanation of directory data

Fund name: An ◆ after the fund name indicates the fund is a pure no-load. This is defined as a fund without any front- or back-end sales charges or 12b-1 fees. Funds with front- or back-end fees payable to the *fund* and not the adviser; or funds with redemption fees of 2% or less or fees in force for no more than 90 days, are considered pure no-loads. An ◆ after the initial group listing indicates all the group's funds are pure no-load.

Master listings: Any fund family with three or more funds begins with a master listing showing all information common to each fund.

Addresses: The *Handbook* usually shows the fund's address. In some cases the address of the custodial bank or the transfer agent is shown if investments must be made there.

Phone numbers: TDD phone numbers are "Telecommunications Device for the Deaf." Funds without 800 numbers may accept collect calls. Additional specialized numbers are noted as such.

Internet addresses: Most large fund company information can now be found by pointing your net browser to the address listed here.

Americans are a mobile people, and mutual funds are no exception. Consequently, addresses and phone numbers can change without warning. If the phone listed in our Directory section is out of date, call the regular area code or the toll-free information operator (800-555-1212) for the new number.

Hours of service: Full service means all services including transactions are handled by a person. After hours service, either live, on tape, or computerized, is generally available at all other times. This information is only given for large fund groups.

Fund adviser: The management company overseeing the operations of the fund.

Administrator: Listed separately if a fund or its transfer agent does not handle its own back office functions.

Portfolio manager: The date after the manager's name indicates the year he or she began managing the fund. Portfolio managers are listed alphabetically in a separate table in Chapter 14. Use this table to find out which fund(s) a manager runs.

Transfer agent: The firm that maintains shareholder transaction records.

Investment objective and policies: Growth or income is an example of an objective. A policy explains how the objective is achieved. E.g., the fund buys gold stocks to achieve a growth objective. If a fund leverages or sells short, it is noted in this section.

Year organized: In most cases, the year shown is when a fund was first offered to the public.

Ticker symbol: The five letter code used to identify any listed fund through computerized tracking or trading systems.

Special sales restrictions: Any unusual information or requirements explaining restricted or closed access to a given fund.

Minimum investments: The amount required for regular accounts is listed first. If there are no special listings for IRAs, Keoghs, or automatic investment plans, regular minimums apply.

Group fund code: Codes required to use many computerized or telephone access systems provided by the major fund companies.

Wire orders accepted: *Yes* means you get end-of-day NAV. In some cases, pre-notification by phone may be required.

Deadline for same day wire purchase: Shown in Eastern Standard Time.

Discount broker availability: Fund trading through several brokers is shown: Charles Schwab & Co. (Schwab), Jack White & Co. (White), Fidelity FundsNetwork Brokerage (Fidelity) and Muriel Siebert (Siebert). NTF funds traded without brokerage fees have asterisks. See Chapter 13 for more details.

Telephone redemptions: This means the fund will sell your shares at that day's price with the proceeds wired or mailed to

you, or occasionally to your bank. This is different from telephone switch, which may be available even if the fund does not redeem directly by phone.

Redemption fee: If redemption fees are payable to the fund, they have no effect on the fund's "pure no-load" status.

Telephone switching: Any family or non-affiliated funds and money markets to which you may move your holdings simply by calling.

Dividends paid: The *Handbook* shows the specific months by date of record (not pay date), or the frequency. Capital gains are paid only if realized.

Portfolio turnover: The turnover rate for the last three fiscal years is shown, with the most recent year shown first. The period covered generally ends on the same date as is shown for the expense ratio.

Shareholder services: Generally lists retirement, withdrawal options, and systematic investment and withdrawal plans. A number of funds that do not have Keogh or IRA plans will accept tax-sheltered accounts from investors with their own plans. Since tax-free mutual funds are inappropriate for tax-sheltered accounts, their availability, or unavailability, is not noted.

Management fee: Percentage of the fund's average daily net assets. M equals millions, B equals billions. Where there are several breakpoints at different asset levels, only the first and last are shown.

12b-1 distribution fee: Percentage of the fund's average daily net assets, paid annually unless otherwise indicated. Where the listing states, "Maximum of %", the fund pays only the amounts actually expended for the allowed purposes. Expenditures can be, and often are, considerably less than the maximum. See Chapter 2 of the *Guide* for a detailed discussion of 12b-1 plans. We note whether the fund or the advisor is paying the fee.

Expense ratio: Ratio of expenses to average net assets. When fiscal period is less than one year, annualized data are shown. The **Turnover ratio** is shown for the same fiscal period as the expense ratio.

No information listed: If specific purchase or redemption services are not listed, that generally means they are unavailable. Missing data for group funds may often be found in the first generic listing for the group.

Qualified for sale in: States where the fund is registered to sell its shares. The *Handbook* uses official two-letter postal abbreviations for the states. These are:

Alabama	AL	Montana	MT
Alaska	AK	Nebraska	NE
Arizona	AZ	Nevada	NV
Arkansas	AR	New Hampshire	NH
California	CA	New Jersey	NJ
Colorado	CO	New Mexico	NM
Connecticut	CT	New York	NY
Delaware	DE	North Carolina	NC
Dist. of Col.	DC	North Dakota	ND
Florida	FL	Ohio	OH
Georgia	GA	Oklahoma	OK
Hawaii	HI	Oregon	OR
Idaho	ID	Pennsylvania	PA
Illinois	IL	Puerto Rico	PR
Indiana	IN	Rhode Island	RI
Iowa	IA	South Carolina	SC
Kansas	KS	South Dakota	SD
Kentucky	KY	Tennessee	TN
Louisiana	LA	Texas	TX
Maine	ME	Utah	UT
Maryland	MD	Vermont	VT
Massachusetts	MA	Virginia	VA
Michigan	MI	Washington	WA
Minnesota	MN	West Virginia	WV
Mississippi	MS	Wisconsin	WI
Missouri	MO	Wyoming	WY

Chapter 11

Directory of no-load mutual funds

AARP FUNDS ◆
(Data common to all AARP funds are shown below. See subsequent listings for data specific to individual funds.)

P.O. Box 2540
Boston, MA 02208-2540
800-253-2277, 617-792-4000
prices/yields 800-631-4636
TDD 800-634-9454, fax 800-821-6234
Internet: http://www.aarp.scudder.com

Shareholder service hours: Full service: M-F 8 A.M.-8 P.M.; Sat 10 A.M.-2 P.M. EST; After hours service: prices, yields, balances, exchanges, last transaction
Adviser: Scudder, Kemper Investments, Inc.
Transfer agent: Scudder Service Corp.
Special sales restrictions: Designed for members of the American Association of Retired Persons, but open to all investors
Minimum purchase: Initial: $2,000 (exceptions noted), Subsequent: None; IRA/Keogh: Initial: $250; Automatic investment plan: Initial: $500, Subsequent: $100
Wire orders accepted: Yes
Deadline for same day wire purchase: 4 P.M.
Qualified for sale in: All states
Telephone redemptions: Yes
Wire redemptions: Yes, $50,000 maximum, $5 fee
Letter redemptions: Signature guarantee required over $100,000
Telephone switching: With other AARP Funds
Number of switches permitted: 4 round trips per year
Shareholder services: IRA, SEP-IRA, Keogh, electronic funds transfer, directed dividends, systematic withdrawal plan min. bal. req. $10,000
IRA/Keogh fees: None

AARP BALANCED STOCK AND BOND FUND ◆
(See first AARP listing for data common to all funds)

Portfolio managers: Robert T. Hoffman (1994), Stephen A. Wohler (1998), Lori J. Ensinger (1998)
Investment objective and policies: Long-term growth of capital and income, consistent with a degree of stability greater than that of other balanced funds. Invests a maximum of 70% of assets in common stocks and at least 30% in investment grade fixed-income securities and cash equivalents. Allocation of assets will vary depending on perceived economic and market conditions. May invest in foreign securities without limit, and use foreign currency exchange contracts, futures and options for hedging purposes.
Year organized: 1994
Ticker symbol: ABSBX
Group fund code: 099
Minimum purchase: Initial: $500
Discount broker availability: White
Dividends paid: Income - March, June, September, December; Capital gains - December
Portfolio turnover (3 yrs): 27%, 35%, 64%
Management fee: 0.19% + group fee of 0.35% first $2B to 0.24% over $14B
Expense ratio: 0.91% (year ending 9/30/97)

AARP BOND FUND FOR INCOME ◆
(See first AARP listing for data common to all funds)

Portfolio managers: Stephen A. Wohler (1998), Kelly D. Babson (1997), Robert S. Cessine (1998)
Investment objective and policies: High level of current income consistent with share price stability. Invests at least 65% of assets in corporate and government debt securities rated in the top four categories by the agencies. May also invest as much as 35% of assets in the next two lower grades, although no more

than 10% of assets may be rated as low as B. May invest up to 20% of assets in foreign debt securities denominated in other currencies besides the dollar, and use options and futures for hedging purposes.
Year organized: 1997
Ticker symbol: AABIX
Group fund code: 017
Discount broker availability: White
Dividends paid: Income - declared daily, paid monthly; Capital gains - annually
Portfolio turnover (1 yr): 14%
Management fee: 0.28% + group fee of 0.35% first $2B to 0.24% over $14B
Expense ratio: 0.00% (eight months ending 9/30/97) (1.53% without waiver)

AARP CAPITAL GROWTH FUND ◆
(See first AARP listing for data common to all funds)

Portfolio managers: William F. Gadsden (1989), Bruce F. Beaty (1994)
Investment objective and policies: Long-term capital growth consistent with stability of share value. Invests in a broadly diversified portfolio of common stocks and securities convertible into common stocks of companies of all sizes. Securities may be deemed to be "undervalued" and may have above-average stock market risk. May invest in foreign securities without limit and use currency exchange contracts, futures and options for hedging purposes.
Year organized: 1984
Ticker symbol: ACGFX
Group fund code: 098
Discount broker availability: White
Dividends paid: Income - December; Capital gains - December
Portfolio turnover (3 yrs): 39%, 65%, 98%
Management fee: 0.32% + group fee of 0.35% first $2B to 0.24% over $14B
Expense ratio: 0.92% (year ending 9/30/97)

AARP DIVERSIFIED GROWTH PORTFOLIO ◆
(See first AARP listing for data common to all funds)

Portfolio managers: Philip S. Fortuna (1997), Salvatore J. Bruno (1997), Shahram Tajbakhsh (1997), Karla D. Grant (1997)
Investment objective and policies: Long-term capital growth. A "fund of funds," the portfolio invests in a select mix of other AARP mutual funds, consisting of 60% to 80% stock mutual funds, and secondarily, 20% to 40% bond and 0% to 20% in cash or money market funds. Reallocation may occur in light of changing market conditions or if imbalances occur to move the percentages outside the stated ranges.
Year organized: 1997
Ticker symbol: AADGX
Group fund code: 086
Discount broker availability: White
Dividends paid: Income - December; Capital gains - December
Portfolio turnover (1 yr): 8%
Management fee: None (pro rata portion of underlying fund fees)
Expense ratio: None (pro rata portion of underlying fund fees)

AARP DIVERSIFIED INCOME WITH GROWTH PORTFOLIO ◆
(See first AARP listing for data common to all funds)

Portfolio managers: Philip S. Fortuna (1997), Salvatore J. Bruno (1997), Shahram Tajbakhsh (1997), Karla D. Grant (1997)
Investment objective and policies: Current income and modest long-term capital appreciation. A "fund of funds," the portfolio invests in a select mix of other

AARP mutual funds consisting of 60% to 80% bond funds, and secondarily, of 20% to 40% stock and 0% to 20% in cash or money market funds. Reallocation may occur in light of changing market conditions or if imbalances occur to move the percentages outside the stated ranges.
Year organized: 1997 (name changed from Diversified Income 2/1/98)
Ticker symbol: ARDIX
Group fund code: 072
Discount broker availability: White
Dividends paid: Income - March, June, September, December; Capital gains - December
Portfolio turnover (1 yr): (6%)
Management fee: None (pro rata portion of underlying fund fees)
Expense ratio: None (pro rata portion of underlying fund fees)

AARP GLOBAL GROWTH FUND ◆
(See first AARP listing for data common to all funds)

Portfolio managers: William E. Holzer (1996), Nicholas Bratt (1996), Diego Espinosa (1997)
Investment objective and policies: Long-term capital growth consistent with stability of share value. Invests in a diversified portfolio of equity securities from 100 or more well established, financially sound companies. Will invest in at least three countries including the U.S., but intends to be invested in companies located throughout twenty or more countries. May be 100% invested in non-U.S. issues. May invest in government or supranational agency investment grade debt securities without limit when perceived to offer greater capital appreciation than equity securities. May use derivative instruments for hedging purposes.
Year organized: 1996
Ticker symbol: ARGGX
Group fund code: 091
Discount broker availability: White
Dividends paid: Income - December; Capital gains - December
Portfolio turnover (2 yrs): 31%, 13%
Management fee: 0.55% + group fee of 0.35% first $2B to 0.24% over $14B
Expense ratio: 1.75% (year ending 9/30/97)

AARP GNMA AND U.S. TREASURY FUND ◆
(See first AARP listing for data common to all funds)

Lead portfolio manager: Richard L. Vandenberg (1998)
Investment objective and policies: High level of current income consistent with a more stable share price than that of a long-term bond. Invests primarily in GNMA securities and U.S. Treasury obligations. Average duration and maturity of the portfolio will vary according to perceived market conditions. May use futures contracts and covered call options on up to 25% of assets in an effort to enhance returns.
Year organized: 1984
Ticker symbol: AGNMX
Group fund code: 093
Minimum purchase: Initial: $500
Discount broker availability: White
Dividends paid: Income - declared daily, paid monthly; Capital gains - December
Portfolio turnover (3 yrs): 87%, 83%, 70%
Management fee: 0.12% + group fee of 0.35% first $2B to 0.24% over $14B
Expense ratio: 0.65% (year ending 9/30/97)

AARP GROWTH AND INCOME FUND ◆
(See first AARP listing for data common to all funds)

Portfolio managers: Robert T. Hoffman (1991), Kathleen T. Millard (1991), Benjamin W. Thorndike (1986), Lori J. Ensinger (1996)

Investment objective and policies: Long-term capital growth, current income and growth of income. Invests primarily in a diversified portfolio of common stocks and securities convertible into common stocks with above average dividend yields that are perceived to offer greater long-term growth potential. May also invest in preferred stocks and foreign securities without limit. May use currency exchange contracts, covered call options and options on stock indices for hedging purposes. Fund seeks to keep value of its shares more stable than other growth and income mutual funds.
Year organized: 1984
Ticker symbol: AGIFX
Group fund code: 097
Minimum purchase: Initial: $500
Discount broker availability: White
Dividends paid: Income - March, June, September, December; Capital gains - December
Portfolio turnover (3 yrs): 33%, 25%, 31%
Management fee: 0.19% + group fee of 0.35% first $2B to 0.24% over $14B
Expense ratio: 0.71% (year ending 9/30/97)

AARP HIGH QUALITY MONEY FUND ◆
(See first AARP listing for data common to all funds)

Lead portfolio manager: Frank J. Rachwalski, Jr. (1998)
Investment objective and policies: Current income and liquidity consistent with maintaining stability and safety of capital. Invests in money market obligations which are issued, guaranteed or insured by the U.S. Government, its agencies or instrumentalities; or supranational organizations such as the World Bank; or domestic banks and their foreign branches. May also use repurchase agreements and corporate obligations.
Year organized: 1985 (name changed from AARP Money Fund in March 1991)
Ticker symbol: ARPXX
Group fund code: 092
Check redemptions: $100 minimum
Dividends paid: Income - declared daily, paid monthly
Management fee: 0.10% + group fee of 0.35% first $2B to 0.24% over $14B
Expense ratio: 0.91% (year ending 9/30/97)

AARP HIGH QUALITY SHORT TERM BOND FUND ◆
(See first AARP listing for data common to all funds)

Portfolio managers: Stephen A. Wohler (1998), Robert S. Cessine (1998)
Investment objective and policies: High level of income while keeping price more stable than that of a long-term bond. Invests primarily in U.S. Government, corporate, and other notes and bonds in the three highest rating categories, with at least 65% of assets in the top two categories. There is no limit as to the stated remaining duration required for any individual security as long as the average effective duration of the portfolio does not exceed three years. May invest in up to 20% of assets in foreign debt securities denominated in other currencies than the dollar. May use futures contracts and covered call options on up to 25% of assets for hedging purposes.
Year organized: 1984 (formerly AARP General Bond Fund; name and objective changed from High Quality Bond 2/1/98. Duration secured at less than three years.)
Ticker symbol: AGBFX
Group fund code: 094
Discount broker availability: White
Dividends paid: Income - declared daily, paid monthly; Capital gains - December
Portfolio turnover (3 yrs): 83%, 170%, 201%
Management fee: 0.19% + group fee of 0.35% first $2B to 0.24% over $14B
Expense ratio: 0.93% (year ending 9/30/97)

AARP HIGH QUALITY TAX FREE MONEY FUND ◆
(See first AARP listing for data common to all funds)

Lead portfolio manager: Frank J. Rachwalski, Jr. (1998)
Investment objective and policies: Current income

exempt from federal income tax, and liquidity consistent with stability and safety of principal. Invests at least 80% of assets in high quality municipal money market securities. Up to 20% may be in taxable securities.
Year organized: 1984 (formerly AARP Insured Short-Term TF Bond Fund. Name and objectives changed on 9/30/91.)
Ticker symbol: AHTXX
Group fund code: 095
Check redemptions: $100 minimum
Dividends paid: Income - declared daily, paid monthly
Management fee: 0.10% + group fee of 0.35% first $2B to 0.24% over $14B
Expense ratio: 0.85% (year ending 9/30/97)

AARP INSURED TAX FREE GENERAL BOND FUND ◆
(See first AARP listing for data common to all funds)

Portfolio managers: Philip G. Condon (1989), M. Ashton Patton (1998)
Investment objective and policies: High income exempt from federal income taxes, with share price stability exceeding that of a long-term municipal bond. Invests in a mix of short-, intermediate- and long-term municipal securities that are insured against default by private insurers. May use futures contracts and covered call options on up to 25% of assets.
Year organized: 1984
Ticker symbol: AITGX
Group fund code: 096
Discount broker availability: White
Dividends paid: Income - declared daily, paid monthly; Capital gains - December
Portfolio turnover (3 yrs): 8%, 19%, 17%
Management fee: 0.19% + group fee of 0.35% first $2B to 0.24% over $14B
Expense ratio: 0.66% (year ending 9/30/97)

AARP INTERNATIONAL GROWTH AND INCOME FUND ◆
(See first AARP listing for data common to all funds)

Portfolio managers: Sheridan Reilly (1997), Irene T. Cheng (1997), Marc Joseph (1997), Deborah A. Chaplin (1997)
Investment objective and policies: Long-term capital growth with relatively stable share price. Invests in a diversified portfolio of established, dividend paying foreign equity securities, focusing only on the 21 countries identified as 'developed' markets. Will diversify at least 65% of assets in at least three different countries. May invest up to 20% of assets in investment grade foreign debt obligations, including supranational agencies and ECU denominated issues.
Year organized: 1997 (name changed from International Stock 2/1/98)
Ticker symbol: AAISX
Group fund code: 070
Discount broker availability: White
Dividends paid: Income - December; Capital gains - December
Management fee: 0.60% + group fee of 0.35% first $2B to 0.24% over $14B
Expense ratio: 1.75% (eight months ending 9/30/97) (4.28% without waiver)

AARP SMALL COMPANY STOCK FUND ◆
(See first AARP listing for data common to all funds)

Portfolio managers: James M. Eysenbach (1997), Philip S. Fortuna (1997)
Investment objective and policies: Long-term capital growth with relatively stable share price. Invests in a broadly diversified portfolio of common stocks of domestic companies with market capitalizations below $1B who demonstrate a higher than average dividend yield and are perceived to be undervalued. Will probably hold at least 100 different companies. May invest up to 20% of assets in U.S. treasury, agency and instrumentality obligations, and use options and futures for hedging purposes.
Year organized: 1997
Ticker symbol: ASCSX
Group fund code: 039
Discount broker availability: White

Dividends paid: Income - December; Capital gains - December
Portfolio turnover (1 yr): 5%
Management fee: 0.55% + group fee of 0.35% first $2B to 0.24% over $14B
Expense ratio: 1.75% (eight months ending 9/30/97) (2.79% without waiver)

AARP U.S. STOCK INDEX FUND ◆
(See first AARP listing for data common to all funds)

Sub-adviser: Bankers Trust Co.
Portfolio managers: Philip S. Fortuna (1997), James M. Eysenbach (1997)
Investment objective and policies: Long-term capital growth and income with a relatively stable share price. Invests at least 95% of assets in common stocks and futures and options on those companies found in the S&P 500 which have the highest dividend paying yield. Will hold between 400 and 470 of the companies. May invest up to 20% of assets in futures contracts and options to invest uncommitted cash balances, to maintain liquidity, and to minimize trading costs. Will not take steps to minimize losses in market declines.
Year organized: 1997
Ticker symbol: AUSSX
Group fund code: 040
Discount broker availability: White
Dividends paid: Income - March, June, September, December; Capital gains - annually
Portfolio turnover (1 yr): 15%
Management fee: 0.00% + group fee of 0.35% first $2B to 0.24% over $14B
Expense ratio: 0.50% (eight months ending 9/30/97) (2.38% without waiver)

ACADEMY VALUE FUND ◆
500 North Valley Mills Drive, Suite 208
Waco, TX 60606
800-385-7003, 817-751-0555

Adviser: Academy Capital Management
Administrator: Southampton Investment Management Co.
Portfolio manager: Joel Adam (1994)
Transfer agent: American Data Services, Inc.
Investment objective and policies: Capital growth. Invests primarily in a diversified portfolio of common stocks perceived to be undervalued. Will normally remain 70% invested in common stocks, but may use convertibles and debt obligations. May use short sales, options and futures.
Year organized: 1994
Ticker symbol: ACVFX
Minimum purchase: Initial: $1,000, Subsequent: $100; IRA: Initial: $500
Wire orders accepted: Yes
Deadline for same day wire purchase: 4 P.M.
Qualified for sale in: AR, CA, CO, CT, DC, FL, GA, HI, IL, IN, MN, NE, NY, OK, PA, TX, VA, WY
Telephone redemptions: Yes, $1,000 minimum
Wire redemptions: Yes, $1,000 minimum
Letter redemptions: Signature guarantee required
Dividends paid: Income - August, December; Capital gains - July, December
Portfolio turnover (1 yr): 21%
Shareholder services: IRA, automatic investment plan, electronic funds transfer, systematic withdrawal plan min. bal. req. $10,000
Management fee: 1.00%
Administration fee: 0.25%
12b-1 distribution fee: 0.25% (paid by fund)
Expense ratio: 2.00% (year ending 8/31/97) (includes waiver)
IRA fees: None

ACCESSOR PORTFOLIOS ◆
(Data common to all Accessor portfolios are shown below. See subsequent listings for data specific to individual portfolios.)

1420 Fifth Avenue, Suite 3130
Seattle, WA 98101
800-759-3504, 206-224-7420
fax 206-224-4274

Adviser: Bennington Capital Management, L.P.
Transfer agent: Bennington Capital Management, L.P.
Special sales restrictions: Generally sold through

financial intermediaries such as banks or registered financial advisers, but individuals may invest directly or through discount brokerage firms.
Minimum purchase: Initial: $1,000, Subsequent: $1,000; IRA: Subsequent: $100; Automatic investment plan: Subsequent: $500 (all minimums are aggregate amounts required through all portfolios)
Wire orders accepted: Yes
Deadline for same day wire purchase: 4 P.M.
Qualified for sale in: All states
Telephone redemptions: Only for account holders with over $1M in assets; faxes redemptions for any amount are, however, acceptable
Wire redemptions: Yes, same terms as telephone
Redemption fee: $10 per check
Telephone switching: With other Accessor funds, subject to same minimums as other telephone services
Number of switches permitted: Unlimited
Shareholder services: IRA, directed dividends, electronic funds transfer, systematic withdrawal plan
IRA fees: Annual $25 for balances of less than $10,000

ACCESSOR GROWTH PORTFOLIO ◆
(See first Accessor listing for data common to all portfolios)

Sub-adviser: Geewax, Terker & Co.
Portfolio managers: John J. Geewax (1997), Christopher P. Ouimet (1997)
Investment objective and policies: Capital growth. Invests at least 80% of assets in equity securities perceived to have above-average growth characteristics. Securities are selected from S&P 500 issuers with the goal of total return exceeding the S&P/BARRA Growth Index. May invest up to 20% of assets in foreign issues. May use options and futures for hedging purposes.
Year organized: 1992
Ticker symbol: AGROX
Discount broker availability: Fidelity, Schwab, Siebert, White
Dividends paid: Income - March, June, September, December; Capital gains - December
Portfolio turnover (3 yrs): 82%, 100%, 58%
Management fee: 0.45%
12b-1 distribution fee: 0.45% (not currently imposed, paid by adviser)
Expense ratio: 1.13% (year ending 12/31/96)

ACCESSOR INTERMEDIATE FIXED-INCOME PORTFOLIO ◆
(See first Accessor listing for data common to all portfolios)

Sub-adviser: Smith Barney Capital Management
Portfolio managers: Joshua H. Lane (1992), Patrick Sheehan (1995), Robert Kopprasch (1995)
Investment objective and policies: Current income. Invests in bonds, debentures and other fixed-income securities. Portfolio maintains a weighted average maturity of three to ten years. May use U.S. dollar-denominated securities of foreign issuers.
Year organized: 1992
Ticker symbol: AIFIX
Discount broker availability: Fidelity, Schwab, Siebert, White
Dividends paid: Income - monthly; Capital gains - December
Portfolio turnover (3 yrs): 95%, 188%, 255%
Management fee: 0.36%
12b-1 distribution fee: 0.36% (not currently imposed, paid by adviser)
Expense ratio: 0.88% (year ending 12/31/96)

ACCESSOR INTERNATIONAL EQUITY PORTFOLIO ◆
(See first Accessor listing for data common to all portfolios)

Sub-adviser: Nicholas-Applegate Capital Management
Portfolio manager: Team managed
Investment objective and policies: Capital growth. Invests in equity securities of companies domiciled in countries other than the U.S. and traded on foreign stock exchanges - primarily in Western Europe and the

Pacific Rim. May, however, invest in emerging markets without limit. Up to 20% of assets may be in fixed-income securities. May use options, futures and forward foreign currency exchange contracts for hedging purposes.
Year organized: 1994
Ticker symbol: ACIEX
Discount broker availability: Fidelity, Schwab, Siebert, White
Dividends paid: Income - December; Capital gains - December
Portfolio turnover (2 yrs): 158%, 85%
Management fee: 0.55%
12b-1 distribution fee: 0.55% (not currently imposed, paid by adviser)
Expense ratio: 1.52% (year ending 12/31/96)

ACCESSOR MORTGAGE SECURITIES PORTFOLIO ◆
(See first Accessor listing for data common to all portfolios)

Sub-adviser: BlackRock Financial Management, Inc. (a wholly owned indirect subsidiary of PNC Bank, N.A.)
Portfolio manager: Team managed
Investment objective and policies: High current income consistent with capital preservation. Invests in mortgage-related securities, primarily issued or guaranteed by the U.S. Government, its agencies or instrumentalities.
Year organized: 1992
Ticker symbol: AMSFX
Discount broker availability: Fidelity, Schwab, Siebert, White
Dividends paid: Income - monthly; Capital gains - December
Portfolio turnover (3 yrs): 356%, 423%, 604%
Management fee: 0.36%
12b-1 distribution fee: 0.36% (not currently imposed, paid by adviser)
Expense ratio: 0.95% (year ending 12/31/96)

ACCESSOR SHORT-INTERMEDIATE FIXED-INCOME PORTFOLIO ◆
(See first Accessor listing for data common to all portfolios)

Sub-adviser: Bankers Trust Co.
Portfolio manager: Louis M. Hudson (1992)
Investment objective and policies: Current income consistent with capital preservation. Invests in bonds, debentures and other fixed-income securities. Portfolio maintains a weighted average maturity of two to five years. May use U.S. dollar-denominated securities of foreign issuers.
Year organized: 1992
Ticker symbol: ASIFX
Discount broker availability: Fidelity, Schwab, Siebert, White
Dividends paid: Income - monthly; Capital gains - December
Portfolio turnover (3 yrs): 31%, 42%, 37%
Management fee: 0.36%
12b-1 distribution fee: 0.36% (not currently imposed, paid by adviser)
Expense ratio: 0.93% (year ending 12/31/96)

ACCESSOR SMALL TO MID CAP PORTFOLIO ◆
(See first Accessor listing for data common to all portfolios)

Sub-adviser: Symphony Asset Management, Inc.
Portfolio manager: Praveen K. Gottipalli (1995)
Investment objective and policies: Capital growth. Invests primarily in equity securities of companies with market capitalizations under $5B, with the goal of total return exceeding the Wilshire 4500 Index. Up to 20% of assets may be in securities of small cap foreign issuers. May use options and futures for hedging purposes.
Year organized: 1992 (sub-adviser, objective and name changed from Small Cap Portfolio, 9/15/95)
Ticker symbol: ASMCX
Discount broker availability: Fidelity, Schwab, Siebert, White

Dividends paid: Income - March, June, September, December; Capital gains - December
Portfolio turnover (3 yrs): 113%, 84%, 30%
Management fee: 0.60%
12b-1 distribution fee: 0.60% (not currently imposed, paid by adviser)
Expense ratio: 1.17% (year ending 12/31/96)

ACCESSOR U.S. GOVERNMENT MONEY PORTFOLIO ◆
(See first Accessor listing for data common to all portfolios)

Portfolio manager: Ravindra A. Deo (1992)
Investment objective and policies: Maximum current income consistent with the preservation of principal and liquidity. Invests in short-term money market instruments issued or guaranteed by the U.S. Government, its agencies or instrumentalities.
Year organized: 1992
Dividends paid: Income - declared daily, paid monthly
Management fee: 0.25%
12b-1 distribution fee: 0.25% (not currently imposed, paid by adviser)
Expense ratio: 0.59% (year ending 12/31/96)

ACCESSOR VALUE AND INCOME PORTFOLIO ◆
(See first Accessor listing for data common to all portfolios)

Sub-adviser: Martingale Asset Management, L.P.
Portfolio managers: William E. Jacques (1992), Douglas E. Stark (1996)
Investment objective and policies: Current income and capital growth. Invests in income producing equity securities selected from S&P 500 issuers, with the goal of total return exceeding the S&P/BARRA Value Index over a five year market cycle. Up to 20% of assets may be in income producing securities of foreign issuers. May use options and futures for hedging purposes.
Year organized: 1992
Ticker symbol: AVAIX
Discount broker availability: Fidelity, Schwab, Siebert, White
Dividends paid: Income - March, June, September, December; Capital gains - December
Portfolio turnover (3 yrs): 94%, 101%, 54%
Management fee: 0.45%
12b-1 distribution fee: 0.45% (not currently imposed, paid by adviser)
Expense ratio: 1.21% (year ending 12/31/96)

ACORN FUNDS ◆
(Data common to all Acorn funds are shown below. See subsequent listings for data specific to individual funds.)

227 West Monroe Street, Suite 3000
Chicago, IL 60606
800-922-6769, 312-634-9200
prices/yields 800-962-1585
fax 312-634-0016, TDD 800-306-4567
Internet: http://www.wanger.com
e-mail: acorn@wanger.com

Shareholder service hours: Full service: M-F 8 A.M.-4:30 P.M. CST; After hours service: prices, account balances, news and views, prospectuses
Adviser: Wanger Asset Management, L.P.
Transfer agent: State Street Bank & Trust Co.
Minimum purchase: Initial: $1,000, Subsequent: $100
Wire orders accepted: Yes
Deadline for same day wire purchase: 4 P.M.
Qualified for sale in: All states
Telephone redemptions: Yes, $100 minimum
Wire redemptions: Yes, $1,000 minimum
Letter redemptions: Signature guarantee required over $50,000
Telephone switching: With other Acorn funds and certain Reich & Tang money market and income funds; $1,000 minimum to new account or to money market, $100 minimum otherwise
Number of switches permitted: 4 round trips/year

Shareholder services: IRA, SEP-IRA, corporate retirement plans, automatic investment plan, electronic funds transfer, systematic withdrawal plan min. bal. req. $25,000
IRA fees: Annual $10, Initial $5, Closing $10

ACORN FUND ◆
(See first Acorn listing for data common to all funds)

Portfolio managers: Ralph L. Wanger, Jr. (1970), Terence M. Hogan (1995), Charles P. McQuaid (1995)
Investment objective and policies: Capital growth. Seeks areas of economy that will benefit from favorable trends for a number of years. Emphasizes common stocks of smaller companies worldwide with market capitalizations under $800M. Up to 33% of assets may be in foreign securities.
Year organized: 1970 (split 5 for 1 on 12/15/93)
Ticker symbol: ACRNX
Group fund code: 90
Discount broker availability: Fidelity, Schwab, Siebert, White
Dividends paid: Income - July, December; Capital gains - December
Portfolio turnover (3 yrs): 32%, 33%, 29%
Management fee: 0.75% first $700M to 0.65% over $2B
Expense ratio: 0.56% (year ending 12/31/97)

ACORN INTERNATIONAL ◆
(See first Acorn listing for data common to all funds)

Portfolio managers: Ralph L. Wanger, Jr. (1992), Leah Joy Zell (1995)
Investment objective and policies: Long-term capital growth. Invests at least 75% of assets in equity securities of small and medium size non-U.S. companies in mature and emerging markets. May invest in ADRs, EDRs or other securities representing shares of foreign issuers. May invest up to 20% of assets in debt securities, including junk bonds, and use futures and options for hedging purposes.
Year organized: 1992
Ticker symbol: ACINX
Group fund code: 100
Discount broker availability: Fidelity, Schwab, Siebert, White
Dividends paid: Income - July, December; Capital gains - December
Portfolio turnover (3 yrs): 39%, 34%, 26%
Management fee: 1.20% first $100M to 0.75% over $500M
Expense ratio: 1.19% (year ending 12/31/97)

ACORN USA ◆
(See first Acorn listing for data common to all funds)

Portfolio manager: Robert A. Mohn (1996)
Investment objective and policies: Long-term capital growth. Invests primarily in small and mid-sized U.S. companies of less than $1B market capitalizations that the advisers believe will benefit from favorable long-term social, economic or political trends. May, however, hold debt securities without any limit, of any rating, although it is not expected that any more than 20% of assets will be in debt, or more than 5% will be in junk bonds. May hold up to 10% of assets in foreign securities, 10% in other investment companies, 15% in illiquid securities, and lend up to 33% of its portfolio securities. May use options and futures and currency exchange contracts for hedging purposes.
Year organized: 1996
Ticker symbol: AUSAX
Group fund code: 820
Discount broker availability: Fidelity, Schwab, Siebert, White
Dividends paid: Income - December; Capital gains - December
Portfolio turnover (2 yrs): 33%, 20%
Management fee: 0.95% first $200M to 0.90% over $200M
Expense ratio: 1.35% (year ending 12/31/97)

ADVANCE CAPITAL I FUNDS
(Fund family will not provide data. Data common to all Advance Capital I funds are shown below. See subsequent listings for data specific to individual funds.)

One Towne Square, Suite 444
Southfield, MI 48076
800-345-4783, 248-350-8543
fax 248-350-0115

Adviser: Advance Capital Management, Inc.
Transfer agent: Advance Capital Group, Inc.
Minimum purchase: Initial: $10,000 (aggregate total for all funds, $1,000 for individual fund), Subsequent: None; IRA: Initial: $2,000
Wire orders accepted: Yes
Deadline for same day wire purchase: 4 P.M.
Qualified for sale in: FL, IL, IN, MI, MO, NJ, OH, PA, TX
Telephone redemptions: Yes, $25,000 maximum
Letter redemptions: Signature guarantee required over $25,000
Telephone switching: With other Advance Capital I funds
Number of switches permitted: Unlimited
Shareholder services: IRA
IRA fees: Closing $50

ADVANCE CAPITAL BALANCED FUND
(See first Advance Capital I listing for data common to all funds)

Sub-adviser: T. Rowe Price Assocs., Inc.
Portfolio managers: John C. Shoemaker (1987), Robert J. Cappelli (1991), Richard T. Whitney (1993)
Investment objective and policies: Capital growth, current income and capital preservation. Normally invests 60% (but at least 25%) of assets in common stocks of companies expected to outperform the S&P 500 over a three to five year horizon, and remaining 40% (range 25% to 75%) in investment grade debt securities. Allocation of assets adjusted to changes in market and economic conditions. Fund may hedge.
Year organized: 1987
Ticker symbol: ADBAX
Dividends paid: Income - declared daily, paid monthly; Capital gains - December
Management fee: 0.70%
12b-1 distribution fee: 0.25%

ADVANCE CAPITAL I BOND FUND ◆
(See first Advance Capital I listing for data common to all funds)

Portfolio managers: John C. Shoemaker (1987), Robert J. Cappelli (1991)
Investment objective and policies: High current income consistent with relative stability of principal and liquidity. Invests at least 65% of assets in investment grade corporate debt securities and U.S. Government bonds. Remainder may be in preferred stocks, U.S. Government agency securities, U.S. Government obligations and money market instruments. Fund maintains a weighted average maturity of three to ten years.
Year organized: 1987
Dividends paid: Income - declared daily, paid monthly; Capital gains - December
Management fee: 0.40%
12b-1 distribution fee: 0.25% (not currently imposed)

ADVANCE CAPITAL I EQUITY GROWTH FUND
(See first Advance Capital I listing for data common to all funds)

Sub-adviser: T. Rowe Price Assocs., Inc.
Portfolio manager: Richard T. Whitney (1993)
Investment objective and policies: Long-term capital growth. Invests primarily in common stocks of small (capitalizations under $1.5B), rapidly growing companies. May also invest in convertible securities,

preferred stocks and restricted securities. Fund may hedge.
Year organized: 1987 (name changed from Equity Universe fund in 1994)
Ticker symbol: ADEGX
Dividends paid: Income - December; Capital gains - December
Management fee: 0.70%
12b-1 distribution fee: 0.25%

ADVANCE CAPITAL I LONG-TERM INCOME FUND ◆
(Fund liquidated 8/15/97)

ADVANCE CAPITAL I RETIREMENT INCOME FUND
(See first Advance Capital I listing for data common to all funds)

Portfolio managers: John C. Shoemaker (1992), Robert J. Cappelli (1992)
Investment objective and policies: High current income without undue risk to principal. Invests at least 50% of assets in investment grade corporate debt securities and U.S. Government bonds. Remainder may be in preferred stocks, U.S. Government agency securities, U.S. Government obligations and money market instruments. Up to 33% of assets may be in junk bonds. Fund maintains a weighted average maturity of 5 to 22 years.
Year organized: 1992
Ticker symbol: ADRIX
Dividends paid: Income - declared daily, paid monthly; Capital gains - December
Management fee: 0.50%
12b-1 distribution fee: 0.25%

ADVISORS' INNER CIRCLE FUND - PIN OAK AGGRESSIVE STOCK FUND ◆
(See Pin Oak Aggressive Stock Fund)

ADVISORS' INNER CIRCLE FUND - WHITE OAK GROWTH STOCK FUND ◆
(See White Oak Growth Stock Fund)

AFBA FIVE STAR FUNDS ◆
(Data common to all AFBA Five Star funds are shown below. See subsequent listings for data specific to individual funds.)

909 North Washington Street
Alexandria, VA 22314
800-243-9865, 800-776-2264
shareholder services 888-578-2733

Adviser: AFBA Investment Management Co. (a wholly-owned subsidiary of Armed Forces Benefit Services, Inc., which is, in turn, owned by the Armed Forces Benefit Association.)
Sub-adviser: Kornitzer Capital Management, Inc.
Transfer agent and administrator: Jones & Babson, Inc.
Minimum purchase: Initial: $500, Subsequent: $100; IRA: Initial: $250; Automatic investment plan: Initial: $100, Subsequent: $50
Wire orders accepted: Yes, $500 subsequent minimum
Deadline for same day wire purchase: 4 P.M.
Qualified for sale in: All states
Letter redemptions: Signature guarantee required over $10,000
Telephone switching: With other AFBA Five Star funds and the D.L. Babson Money Market Fund
Number of switches permitted: Unlimited, 15 day hold
Shareholder services: IRA, SEP-IRA, electronic funds transfer (purchase only), systematic withdrawal plan min. bal. req. $10,000
Administration fee: 0.33%
IRA fees: Annual $10, Closing $10

AFBA FIVE STAR BALANCED FUND ◆
(See first AFBA Five Star listing for data common to all funds)

Portfolio manager: Team managed
Investment objective and policies: Long-term capital growth and high current income. Invests in a diversified array of common and preferred stocks, convertible bonds and convertible preferred stocks, and corporate and government bonds. The majority of stocks purchased will be of companies with market capitalizations exceeding $1B. May invest up to 75% of assets, and will always invest at least 25%, in debt issues, with up to 20% of assets in junk bonds. Will always invest at least 25% of assets in equity securities. May use covered call options for hedging purposes.
Year organized: 1997
Dividends paid: Income - March, June, September, December; Capital gains - December
Management fee: 1.00%

AFBA FIVE STAR EQUITY FUND ◆
(See first AFBA Five Star listing for data common to all funds)

Portfolio manager: Team managed
Investment objective and policies: Long-term capital appreciation; dividend income secondary. Invests at least 65% of assets in a broadly diversified portfolio of common stocks of companies with market capitalizations exceeding $1B. May invest in foreign issues through ADRs only. May use covered call options for hedging purposes.
Year organized: 1997
Dividends paid: Income - June, December; Capital gains - June, December
Management fee: 1.00%

AFBA FIVE STAR HIGH YIELD FUND ◆
(See first AFBA Five Star listing for data common to all funds)

Portfolio manager: Team managed
Investment objective and policies: High current income; capital growth secondary. Invests at least 65% of assets in high yielding debt securities, but may invest up to 10% of assets in preferred stock as well. May invest in junk bonds without limit. The portfolio average maturity generally will not exceed ten years. May use covered call options for hedging purposes.
Year organized: 1997
Dividends paid: Income - March, June, September, December; Capital gains - June, December
Management fee: 1.00%

AFBA FIVE STAR USA GLOBAL FUND ◆
(See first AFBA Five Star listing for data common to all funds)

Portfolio manager: Team managed
Investment objective and policies: Capital growth. Invest at least 65% of assets in common stocks of companies based in the U.S. that receive greater than 40% of their revenues or pre-tax income from international operations. At least three different countries must be represented. May use covered call options for hedging purposes.
Year organized: 1997
Dividends paid: Income - June, December; Capital gains - June, December
Management fee: 1.00%

AIT VISION: U.S. EQUITY PORTFOLIO ◆
311 Park Place Blvd., Suite 250
Clearwater, FL 34619
800-507-9922, 888-248-8324
813-799-3671
fax 813-799-1232

Adviser: Advanced Investment Technology, Inc.
Portfolio managers: Douglas W. Case (1995), Dean S. Barr (1995), Susan L. Reigel (1995)

Transfer agent: AmeriPrime Financial Services, Inc.
Investment objective and policies: Long-term capital growth. Invests in a diversified portfolio of equity securities perceived to be undervalued. Management focuses on companies whose earnings trends appear to be superior to others over time.
Year organized: 1995
Minimum purchase: Initial: $5,000, Subsequent: $5,000; IRA: Initial: $2,000, Subsequent: $2,000
Wire orders accepted: Yes
Discount broker availability: Fidelity, Siebert, White
Qualified for sale in: All states
Wire redemptions: Yes
Letter redemptions: Signature guarantee required
Dividends paid: Income - annually; Capital gains - annually
Portfolio turnover (2 yrs): 0%, 239%
Shareholder services: IRA
Management fee: 0.70%
Expense ratio: 0.70% (year ending 10/31/97) (0.74% without waiver)
IRA fees: Annual $15

ALLIANCE WORLD INCOME TRUST
1345 Ave. of the Americas
New York, NY 10105
800-247-4154, 800-221-5672,
800-227-4618, 212-969-1000
yields 800-251-0539
TDD 800-367-1684
Internet: http://www.alliancecapital.com

Adviser: Alliance Capital Management, L.P. (a wholly-owned subsidiary of The Equitable Life Assurance Society of the United States)
Portfolio manager: Douglas J. Peebles (1990)
Transfer agent: Alliance Fund Services, Inc.
Investment objective and policies: High current income consistent with prudent investment risk. Invests in high quality debt securities denominated in the U.S. dollar and selected foreign currencies, with remaining maturities of one year or less. At least 35% of assets are denominated in U.S. dollars and 35% in currencies of countries participating in the European Monetary System. May use futures and options. Fund seeks higher yields than money market funds with less fluctuation than longer-term bond funds.
Year organized: 1990
Ticker symbol: AWITX
Minimum purchase: Initial: $10,000, Subsequent: $50
Wire orders accepted: Yes
Deadline for same day wire purchase: 3 P.M.
Discount broker availability: Fidelity, Schwab, Siebert, White
Qualified for sale in: All states
Wire redemptions: Yes, $1,000 minimum
Letter redemptions: Signature guarantee required over $25,000
Telephone switching: With Class A shares of other Alliance funds (which carry loads)
Number of switches permitted: Unlimited
Dividends paid: Income - declared daily, paid monthly
Shareholder services: IRA, SEP-IRA, Keogh, 403(b), corporate retirement plans, automatic investment plan, directed dividends, electronic funds transfer, systematic withdrawal plan
Management fee: 0.65%
12b-1 distribution fee: Maximum of 0.90%
Expense ratio: 2.25% (year ending 10/31/97) (includes waiver)
IRA/Keogh fees: Annual $10, Initial $5

AMANA GROWTH FUND ◆
1300 N. State Street
Bellingham, WA 98225-4730
800-728-8762, 360-734-9900
prices/yields 888-732-6262
fax 360-734-0755
Internet: http://www.saturna.com
e-mail: amana@saturna.com

Adviser: Saturna Capital Corp.
Portfolio manager: Nicholas F. Kaiser (1994)
Transfer agent: Saturna Capital Corp.

Investment objective and policies: Long-term capital growth. In accordance with Islamic principles, the fund will not make any investments which pay interest. Fund invests primarily in common stocks believed to have potential for above average increases in earnings and share price. May purchase preferred stocks and write covered options.
Year organized: 1994 (a portfolio of Amana Mutual Funds Trust)
Ticker symbol: AMAGX
Group fund code: 11
Special sales restrictions: Fund is designed to meet the special needs of Muslims by investing in accordance with Islamic principles, but is open to all investors.
Minimum purchase: Initial: $100, Subsequent: $25
Wire orders accepted: No
Discount broker availability: Fidelity, Siebert
Qualified for sale in: All states except AL, AK, AR, DE, ME, MT, NE, NV, NH, RI, SD, UT, VT, WY
Telephone redemptions: Yes
Wire redemptions: Yes, $5,000 minimum, $25 fee
Letter redemptions: Signature guarantee not required
Check redemptions: $500 minimum
Telephone switching: With Amana Income Fund and Sextant funds, $25 minimum
Number of switches permitted: Unlimited
Dividends paid: Income - May, December; Capital gains - May, December
Portfolio turnover (3 yrs): 25%, 22%, 38%
Shareholder services: IRA, Keogh, 401(k), corporate retirement plans, automatic investment plan, electronic funds transfer
Management fee: 0.95%
Expense ratio: 1.62% (year ending 5/31/97)
IRA/Keogh fees: None

AMANA INCOME FUND ◆
1300 N. State Street
Bellingham, WA 98225-4730
800-728-8762, 360-734-9900
prices/yields 888-732-6262
fax 360-734-0755
Internet: http://www.saturna.com
e-mail: amana@saturna.com

Adviser: Saturna Capital Corp.
Portfolio manager: Nicholas F. Kaiser (1986)
Transfer agent: Saturna Capital Corp.
Investment objective and policies: High current income and capital preservation. In accordance with Islamic principles, the fund will not make any investments which pay interest. Fund invests primarily in income-producing securities such as common stock. May purchase preferred stocks and write covered options.
Year organized: 1984 (a portfolio of Amana Mutual Funds Trust)
Ticker symbol: AMANX
Group fund code: 10
Special sales restrictions: Fund is designed to meet the special needs of Muslims by investing in accordance with Islamic principles, but is open to all investors.
Minimum purchase: Initial: $100, Subsequent: $25; IRA: Initial: $25
Wire orders accepted: No
Discount broker availability: Fidelity, Siebert
Qualified for sale in: All states except AK, AR, DE, ME, MT, NE, NV, NH, RI, SD, UT, VT, WY
Telephone redemptions: Yes
Wire redemptions: Yes, $5,000 minimum, $25 fee
Letter redemptions: Signature guarantee not required
Check redemptions: $500 minimum
Telephone switching: With Amana Growth Fund and Sextant funds, $25 minimum
Number of switches permitted: Unlimited
Dividends paid: Income - May, December; Capital gains - May, December
Portfolio turnover (3 yrs): 14%, 24%, 29%
Shareholder services: IRA, Keogh, 401(k), corporate retirement plans, automatic investment plan, electronic funds transfer
Management fee: 0.95%
Expense ratio: 1.55% (year ending 5/31/97)
IRA/Keogh fees: None

AMCORE VINTAGE MUTUAL FUNDS ◆
(Merged with the IMG Funds effective 2/16/98 and became The Vintage Funds.)

AMERICAN AADVANTAGE FUNDS
(Data common to all American Aadvantage funds are shown below. See subsequent listings for data specific to individual funds.)

4333 Amon Carter Blvd.
MD5645
Fort Worth, TX 76155
800-388-3344, 800-231-4252
fax 312-655-4489
Internet: http://www.amrcorp.com/amr/amr_invest

Fund manager: AMR Investment Services, Inc. (a wholly-owned subsidiary of AMR Corp.)
Adviser: AMR Investment Services, Inc.
Transfer agent: Goldman, Sachs & Co.
Objectives and policies: All funds invest their assets in underlying portfolios of the same objective. Expense ratios and administrative fees given here represent the 'fund;' portfolio turnover, management fees and largest holdings represent the underlying 'portfolio.'
Sales restrictions: Funds have three classes of shares - Mileage, PlanAhead, and Institutional; the first two are available to individuals directly from the company. Mileage Class shares are only for taxable accounts. PlanAhead Class shares are primarily for tax-deferred accounts (but are available for taxable accounts) and are also offered through discount brokerage firms. Some Institutional class shares are available at lower minimums through discount brokers. Each shareholder of Mileage Class gains mileage in the American Airlines Aadvantage Travel Awards Program at the rate of one mile for every $10 invested on an annualized basis. There are no mileage credits for PlanAhead shares. Mileage shares have 12b-1 fees; PlanAhead and Institutional shares do not.
Minimum purchase: Initial: $10,000, Subsequent: $250; Automatic investment plan: Initial: $50 (not available to Mileage Class), Subsequent: $50 (PlanAhead Class), $100 (Mileage Class)
Wire orders accepted: Yes, $1,000 subsequent minimum
Deadline for same day wire purchase: 4 P.M. (except money market funds)
Qualified for sale in: All states except LA
Telephone redemptions: Yes
Wire redemptions: Yes, 1,000 minimum, $12 fee
Letter redemptions: Signature guarantee required over $25,000
Telephone switching: With other American Aadvantage Mileage Class and PlanAhead Class funds, $250 minimum
Number of switches permitted: Unlimited, 15 day hold
Deadline for same day switch: 4 P.M. (3 P.M. for money market funds)
Shareholder services: IRA, SEP-IRA, Keogh, (for PlanAhead Class shares only), automatic investment plan, electronic funds transfer (purchase only), systematic withdrawal plan
12b-1 distribution fee: Maximum of 0.25% (Mileage Class shares only)
Shareholder services fee: 0.25% (PlanAhead Class shares only)
IRA/Keogh fees: Annual $12 total for all funds, Closing $12 (PlanAhead Class shares only)

AMERICAN AADVANTAGE
BALANCED FUND
(See first American Aadvantage listing for data common to all funds)

Sub-advisers: Barrow, Hanley, Mewhinney & Strauss, Inc.; Brandywine Asset Management, Inc.; GSB Investment Management, Inc.; Hotchkis and Wiley; Independence Investment Assocs., Inc.
Portfolio managers: William F. Quinn (1987), Nancy A. Eckl (1995)
Investment objective and policies: Total return: income and capital appreciation. Normally invests 50% to 65% of assets in equity securities and 35% to 50% in investment grade fixed-income securities, with allocation adjusted to reflect perceived changes in market and economic conditions. Will have a minimum of 30% each of debt or equity securities, and a maximum of 70% of either type. May invest in convertible securities and ADRs of foreign issuers. Up to 15% of assets may be in illiquid securities. Fund may hedge.
Year organized: 1987 (Mileage: 1995, PlanAhead: 1994)
Ticker symbol: AABPX (PlanAhead)
Discount broker availability: *Fidelity, *Schwab, *Siebert, *White
Dividends paid: Income - December; Capital gains - December
Portfolio turnover (3 yrs): 105%, 76%, 73%
Management fee: from 0.60% of the first $10M (highest)
Administration fee: 0.25%
Expense ratio: PlanAhead Class: 0.97% (year ending 10/31/96), Mileage Class: 0.99% (year ending 10/31/97) (1.83% without waiver)

AMERICAN AADVANTAGE GROWTH
AND INCOME FUND
(See first American Aadvantage listing for data common to all funds)

Sub-advisers: Barrow, Hanley, Mewhinney & Strauss, Inc.; Brandywine Asset Management, Inc.; GSB Investment Management, Inc.; Hotchkis and Wiley; Independence Investment Assocs., Inc.
Portfolio managers: William F. Quinn (1987), Nancy A. Eckl (1995)
Investment objective and policies: Long-term capital appreciation and current income. Invests at least 80% of assets in a diversified portfolio of equity securities. Foreign issues amy be represented by ADRs. Securities selection emphasizes perceived undervaluations and above average growth expectations. May invest in other investment companies and up to 15% of assets may be in illiquid securities.
Year organized: 1987 (Mileage: 1995, PlanAhead: 1994. Name changed from Equity Fund in 1994)
Ticker symbol: AAGPX (PlanAhead)
Discount broker availability: *Fidelity, *Schwab, *Siebert, *White
Dividends paid: Income - December; Capital gains - December
Portfolio turnover (3 yrs): 35%, 40%, 26%
Management fee: from 0.60% of the first $10M (highest)
Administration fee: 0.25%
Expense ratio: PlanAhead Class: 0.94% (year ending 10/31/96) (0.96% without waiver), Mileage Class: 0.99% (year ending 10/31/97) (1.31% without waiver)

AMERICAN AADVANTAGE
INTERNATIONAL EQUITY FUND
(See first American Aadvantage listing for data common to all funds)

Sub-advisers: Hotchkis and Wiley; Morgan Stanley Asset Management, Inc.; Templeton Investment Counsel, Inc.
Portfolio managers: William F. Quinn (1991), Nancy A. Eckl (1995)
Investment objective and policies: Long-term capital appreciation. Invests at least 65% of assets in common stocks and convertible securities of foreign issuers in at least three countries other than the U.S. Security selection is based on the country's economic outlook, market valuation and potential changes in currency exchange rates. The balance of the fund is invested in investment grade foreign debt securities. May use forward foreign currency contracts and futures for hedging purposes. Up to 15% of assets may be in illiquid securities.
Year organized: 1991 (Mileage: 1995, PlanAhead: 1994)
Ticker symbol: AAIPX (PlanAhead)
Discount broker availability: *Fidelity, *Schwab, *Siebert, *White
Dividends paid: Income - December; Capital gains - December

Portfolio turnover (3 yrs): 15%, 19%, 21%
Management fee: from 0.60% of the first $10M (highest)
Administration fee: 0.25%
Expense ratio: PlanAhead Class: 1.17% (year ending 10/31/96), Mileage Class: 1.47% (year ending 10/31/97) (1.68% without waiver)

AMERICAN AADVANTAGE
MONEY MARKET FUND
(See first American Aadvantage listing for data common to all funds)

Portfolio manager: Michael W. Fields (1991)
Investment objective and policies: Current income consistent with stability of principal and liquidity. Invests in domestic and foreign corporate and government money market instruments.
Year organized: 1988 (Mileage: 1995, PlanAhead: 1994)
Deadline for same day wire purchase: 3 P.M.
Check redemptions: $100 minimum
Dividends paid: Income - declared daily, paid monthly
Management fee: 0.15%
Administration fee: 0.05%
Expense ratio: PlanAhead Class: 0.58% (year ending 10/31/96), Mileage Class: 0.67% (year ending 10/31/97) (0.74% without waiver)

AMERICAN AADVANTAGE MUNICIPAL
MONEY MARKET FUND
(See first American Aadvantage listing for data common to all funds)

Portfolio manager: Michael W. Fields (1993)
Investment objective and policies: Current income exempt from federal income tax, consistent with stability of principal and liquidity. Invests at least 80% of assets in tax-free municipal money market instruments.
Year organized: 1993 (Mileage: 1995, PlanAhead: 1994)
Deadline for same day wire purchase: 12 NN
Check redemptions: $100 minimum
Dividends paid: Income - declared daily, paid monthly
Management fee: 0.15%
Administration fee: 0.05%
Expense ratio: PlanAhead Class: 0.62% (year ending 10/31/96) (0.67% without waiver), Mileage Class: 0.65% (year ending 10/31/97) (0.78% without waiver)

AMERICAN AADVANTAGE
SHORT-TERM BOND FUND
(See first American Aadvantage listing for data common to all funds)

Portfolio managers: Michael W. Fields (1987), Benjamin L. Mayer (1995)
Investment objective and policies: Income and capital appreciation. Invests primarily in investment grade fixed-income government and corporate securities. Portfolio will generally maintain a dollar-weighted average maturity of less than three years. May invest in asset- and mortgage-backed securities and YankeeDollar and EuroDollar CDs, bonds and notes. Up to 15% of assets may be in illiquid securities.
Year organized: 1987 (Mileage: 1995, PlanAhead: 1994) (Name changed from Ltd-Term Inc 3/1/98)
Ticker symbol: AALPX (PlanAhead)
Discount broker availability: *Fidelity, *Schwab, *Siebert, *White
Dividends paid: Income - declared daily, paid monthly; Capital gains - December
Portfolio turnover (3 yrs): 282%, 304%, 183%
Management fee: 0.25%
Administration fee: 0.25%
Expense ratio: PlanAhead Class: 0.85% (year ending 10/31/96) (0.94% without waiver), Mileage Class: 0.85% (year ending 10/31/97) (3.01% without waiver)

AMERICAN AADVANTAGE U.S. TREASURY MONEY MARKET FUND

(See first American Aadvantage listing for data common to all funds)

Portfolio manager: Michael W. Fields (1992)
Investment objective and policies: Current income consistent with stability of principal and liquidity. Invests exclusively in short-term U.S. Treasury money market instruments and others insured by the U.S. Government.
Year organized: 1992 (Mileage: 1995, PlanAhead: 1994)
Deadline for same day wire purchase: 3 P.M.
Check redemptions: $100 minimum
Dividends paid: Income - declared daily, paid monthly
Management fee: 0.15%
Administration fee: 0.05%
Expense ratio: PlanAhead Class: 0.67% (year ending 10/31/96), Mileage Class: 0.62% (year ending 10/31/96) (0.78% without waiver)

AMERICAN CENTURY FUNDS ◆

(Data common to all American Century funds are shown below. See subsequent listings for data specific to individual funds.)

4500 Main Street
P.O. Box 419200
Kansas City, MO 64141-6200
800-345-2021, 816-531-5575
prices 800-345-8765
TDD 800-634-4113, in-state 816-443-3485
fax 816-340-7962
Internet: http://www.americancentury.com

Shareholder service hours: Full service: M-F 7 A.M.-7 P.M. CST; After hours service: prices, yields, balances, orders, last transaction, DJIA/index close, prospectuses, total returns
Adviser: American Century Investment Management Corp.
Transfer agent: American Century Services Corp.
Sales restrictions: On 9/3/96, the fund instituted multiple share classes. Advisor Class shares are sold with 12b-1 fees through distribution intermediaries (discount availability noted). Only the Investor class shares marketed directly by the fund are represented here.
Minimum purchase: Initial: $2,500, Subsequent: $50; IRA/Keogh: Initial: $1,000; Automatic investment plan: Initial: $50 (exceptions noted)
Wire orders accepted: Yes
Deadline for same day wire purchase: 4 P.M.
Qualified for sale in: All states (exceptions noted)
Telephone redemptions: Yes
Wire redemptions: Yes, $10 fee
Letter redemptions: Signature guarantee required over $25,000
Telephone switching: With other American Century funds except Giftrust, $100 minimum
Number of switches permitted: 6 per year per account (unlimited for money market funds)
Deadline for same day switch: 3 P.M. EST for Target Maturities Trust, 4 P.M. EST for others

Shareholder services: IRA, SEP-IRA, SIMPLE IRA, Keogh, 401(k), 403(b), corporate retirement plans, electronic funds transfer (except Giftrust), systematic withdrawal plan min. bal. req. $10,000
Management fees: Each fund is charged a "Complex Fee" and an "Investment Category Fee," of which there are three. The Complex Fee is determined by a fee schedule applied to all the assets managed by the Advisor, which ranges from 0.31% for the first $2.5B, to 0.29% over $1,250B. This fee now stands at 0.30%. The Investment Category Fees are determined by fee schedules based on the fund type, equity, bond or money market, and the amount of money the Advisor manages in each type. See each fund for its specific schedule.
IRA fees: Annual $10 (maximum of $30, regardless of number of accounts); waived if total IRA assets exceed $10,000
Keogh fees: Annual $10

AMERICAN CENTURY BALANCED FUND ◆

(See first American Century listing for data common to all funds)

Portfolio managers: Equity - James E. Stowers III (1996), Bruce A. Wimberly (1996), John R. Sykora (1997); Fixed-income - Norman E. Hoops (1989), Jeffrey L. Houston (1996)
Investment objective and policies: Capital growth and current income. Invests fully with approximately 60% of assets in common stocks having appreciation potential; the remaining 40% is in fixed-income securities (minimum 25% in fixed-income senior securities) with a weighted average maturity of three to ten years. At least 80% of debt obligations will be A rated or better with the remainder Baa or equivalent. May invest in securities of foreign issuers without limit, and use forward currency exchange contracts for hedging purposes.
Year organized: 1988 (name changed from Twentieth Century Balanced Investors Fund 1/1/97)
Ticker symbol: TWBIX
Group fund code: 031
Discount broker availability: Fidelity, *Schwab, Siebert, *White
Dividends paid: Income - March, June, September, December; Capital gains - December
Portfolio turnover (3 yrs): 110%, 130%, 85%
Management fee: 1.00%
Expense ratio: 1.00% (year ending 10/31/97)

AMERICAN CENTURY CAPITAL MANAGER FUND ◆

(Merged into American Century Strategic Allocation: Conservative 8/30/97)

AMERICAN CENTURY EQUITY GROWTH FUND ◆

(See first American Century listing for data common to all funds)

Portfolio managers: Jeffrey R. Tyler (1997), William Martin (1997)
Investment objective and policies: Long-term capital appreciation. Invests in large and small cap common stocks to deliver total return in excess of that of the S&P 500. May invest in securities of foreign issuers and use options and futures to hedge up to 20% of assets.
Year organized: 1991 (name changed from Benham Equity Growth Fund 1/1/97)
Ticker symbol: BEQGX
Group fund code: 982
Discount broker availability: Fidelity, *Schwab, Siebert, *White
Dividends paid: Income - March, June, September, December; Capital gains - December
Portfolio turnover (3 yrs): 161%, 131%, 126%
Management fee: 0.50% first $100M to 0.19% over $6.5B
Expense ratio: 0.67% (year ending 12/31/97)

AMERICAN CENTURY EQUITY INCOME FUND ◆

(See first American Century listing for data common to all funds)

Portfolio managers: Peter A. Zuger (1994), Phillip N. Davidson (1994)
Investment objective and policies: Current income; capital growth secondary. Invests primarily in dividend-paying common stocks of companies with favorable dividend-paying history. May have up to 25% of assets in securities of foreign issuers, including foreign debt securities. May use forward currency exchange contracts for hedging purposes, and may sell short.
Year organized: 1994 (name changed from Twentieth Century Equity Income Fund 1/1/97)
Ticker symbol: TWEIX
Group fund code: 038
Discount broker availability: Fidelity, *Schwab, Siebert, *White
Dividends paid: Income - March, June, September, December; Capital gains - December
Portfolio turnover (3 yrs): 159%, 170%, 45%
Management fee: 1.00%
Expense ratio: 1.00% (year ending 3/31/97)

AMERICAN CENTURY GLOBAL GOLD FUND ◆

(See first American Century listing for data common to all funds)

Sub-adviser: State Street Bank & Trust Co.
Portfolio manager: William Martin (1992)
Investment objective and policies: Total return: capital appreciation and current income. Invests in securities of companies principally engaged in mining, fabricating, processing, or otherwise dealing in gold throughout the world. Portfolio is constructed to match the risk characteristics of the market for gold and gold-related equity securities and, in turn, attempt to produce performance indicative of performance in the worldwide gold equities market. Will utilize such market indices as the FT-SE Gold Mines Index. At least 25% of assets and, during normal circumstances, 65% will be in gold companies.
Year organized: 1988 (name changed from Gold Equities Index Fund 2/96; policy changed from domestic to global strategy. Past results may be misleading. Name changed from Benham Global Gold Fund 1/1/97)
Ticker symbol: BGEIX
Group fund code: 980
Discount broker availability: Fidelity, *Schwab, Siebert, *White
Dividends paid: Income - June, December; Capital gains - December
Portfolio turnover (3 yrs): 28%, 45%, 28%
Management fee: 0.50% first $100M to 0.19% over $6.5B
Expense ratio: 0.67% (year ending 12/31/97)

AMERICAN CENTURY GLOBAL NATURAL RESOURCES FUND ◆

(See first American Century listing for data common to all funds)

Portfolio managers: William Martin (1994), Joseph Sterling (1997)
Investment objective and policies: Total return: capital growth and dividends. Invests primarily in the securities of companies engaged in the energy or basic materials industries that are part of the Dow Jones World Stock Index. Under normal market conditions, assets will be invested in the securities of at least three different countries. May hedge and invest in illiquid securities, ADRs and EDRs.
Year organized: 1994 (name changed from Benham Global Natural Resources Index Fund 1/1/97)
Ticker symbol: BGRIX
Group fund code: 984
Discount broker availability: Fidelity, *Schwab, Siebert, *White
Dividends paid: Income - June, December; Capital gains - December
Portfolio turnover (3 yrs): 41%, 53%, 39%
Management fee: 0.50% first $100M to 0.19% over $6.5B
Expense ratio: 0.73% (year ending 12/31/97)

AMERICAN CENTURY INCOME & GROWTH FUND ◆

(See first American Century listing for data common to all funds)

Portfolio managers: John Schniedwind (1997), Kurt Borgwardt (1997)
Investment objective and policies: Dividend growth, current income and capital appreciation. Invests in dividend paying common stocks with total return approximating that of the S&P 500.
Year organized: 1990 (name changed from Benham Income & Growth Fund 1/1/97)
Ticker symbol: BIGRX
Group fund code: 981
Discount broker availability: Fidelity, *Schwab, Siebert, *White
Dividends paid: Income - monthly; Capital gains - December
Portfolio turnover (3 yrs): 102%, 92%, 70%
Management fee: 0.50% first $100M to 0.19% over $6.5B
Expense ratio: 0.65% (year ending 12/31/97)

AMERICAN CENTURY REAL ESTATE SECURITIES FUND ◆

(See first American Century listing for data common to all funds)

Sub-adviser: RREEF Real Estate Securities Advisers, L.P.
Portfolio managers: Kim G. Redding (1995), Karen J. Knudson (1995), Mark L. Mallon (1997)
Investment objective and policies: Long-term capital appreciation; income secondary. Invests primarily in equity securities issued by real estate investment trusts (REITs) or in individual issues of companies deriving at least 50% of revenues or 50% of market value from the real estate industry. May invest in fixed-income securities without limit, and may invest up to 15% of assets in illiquid securities. Fund is non-diversified.
Year organized: 1995 (name changed from RREEF Real Estate Securities Fund 6/1/97 when American Century bought the fund; some statistical data represent predecessor fund)
Ticker symbol: REACX
Group fund code: 037
Discount broker availability: Fidelity, Schwab (only through financial advisers), Siebert, *White
Dividends paid: Income - quarterly; Capital gains - December
Portfolio turnover (2 yrs): 69%, 86%
Management fee: 1.20%
Expense ratio: 1.17% (year ending 10/31/97) (6.83% without waiver)

AMERICAN CENTURY STRATEGIC ALLOCATION: AGGRESSIVE ◆

(See first American Century listing for data common to all funds)

Lead portfolio manager: Jeffrey R. Tyler (1996)
Investment objective and policies: A high level of total return consistent with an aggressive asset mix; primarily long-term capital growth, with nominal current income to help cushion the volatility of the equity portfolio. Fund invests with an emphasis on equity holdings. Operates within the following asset allocation ranges: Cash - 0% to 15%; Bonds - 10% to 30%; Stocks - 60% to 90%. Will generally have more of a growth and international stock orientation than the moderate fund, and will invest between 15% and 35% of assets in foreign securities. May invest up to 10% of assets in junk bonds.
Year organized: 1996 (name changed from Twentieth Century Strategic Allocation: Aggressive 1/1/97)
Ticker symbol: TWSAX
Group fund code: 046
Discount broker availability: Fidelity, *Schwab, Siebert, *White
Dividends paid: Income - December; Capital gains - December
Portfolio turnover (2 yrs): 135%, 64%
Management fee: 1.20% first $1B, 1.00% over $1B
Expense ratio: 1.20% (year ending 11/30/97)

AMERICAN CENTURY STRATEGIC ALLOCATION: CONSERVATIVE ◆

(See first American Century listing for data common to all funds)

Lead portfolio manager: Jeffrey R. Tyler (1996)
Investment objective and policies: A high level of total return consistent with a conservative asset mix; primarily current, regular income with a potential for moderate long-term capital growth as a result of its stake in equity securities. Fund invests with an emphasis on quality bonds and money market securities over equity holdings. Operates within the following asset allocation ranges: Cash - 10% to 25%; Bonds - 38% to 52%; Stocks - 34% to 46% Will generally have more of a value and domestic stock orientation than the other two strategic allocation funds, but will invest between 7% and 17% of assets in foreign securities.
Year organized: 1996 (name changed from Twentieth Century Strategic Allocation: Conservative 1/1/97; absorbed American Century Capital Manager 8/30/97)
Ticker symbol: TWSCX
Group fund code: 044

Discount broker availability: *Schwab, *White
Dividends paid: Income - quarterly; Capital gains - December
Portfolio turnover (2 yrs): 124%, 44%
Management fee: 1.00% first $1B, 0.90% over $1B
Expense ratio: 1.00% (year ending 11/30/97)

AMERICAN CENTURY STRATEGIC ALLOCATION: MODERATE ◆

(See first American Century listing for data common to all funds)

Lead portfolio manager: Jeffrey R. Tyler (1996)
Investment objective and policies: A high level of total return consistent with a moderate asset mix; primarily long-term capital growth with a moderate level of regular income. Fund invests with an emphasis on equity holdings, but maintains a considerable stake in bonds to decrease overall price volatility and to moderate losses in declining markets. Operates within the following asset allocation ranges: Cash - 5% to 20%; Bonds - 20% to 40%; Stocks - 50% to 70%. Will generally invest between 10% and 30% of assets in foreign securities. May invest up to 5% of assets in junk bonds.
Year organized: 1996 (name changed from Twentieth Century Strategic Allocation: Moderate 1/1/97)
Ticker symbol: TWSMX
Group fund code: 045
Discount broker availability: Fidelity, *Schwab, Siebert, *White
Dividends paid: Income - quarterly; Capital gains - December
Portfolio turnover (2 yrs): 119%, 78%
Management fee: 1.10% first $1B, 1.00% over $1B
Expense ratio: 1.10% (year ending 11/30/97)

AMERICAN CENTURY UTILITIES FUND ◆

(See first American Century listing for data common to all funds)

Portfolio manager: John Schniedwind (1997), Kurt Borgwardt (1997), Joseph Sterling (1997)
Investment objective and policies: Current income and long-term growth of capital and income. Normally invests at least 75% of assets in equity securities of companies engaged in the utilities industry - providing electricity, natural gas, telecommunications services, pay television, water or sanitary services. Up to 25% may be in fixed-income securities, with 10% to 20% in utility bonds.
Year organized: 1993 (name changed from Benham Utilities Income Fund 1/1/97)
Ticker symbol: BULIX
Group fund code: 983
Discount broker availability: Fidelity, *Schwab, Siebert, *White
Dividends paid: Income - declared daily, paid monthly; Capital gains - December
Portfolio turnover (3 yrs): 92%, 93%, 68%
Management fee: 0.50% first $100M to 0.19% over $6.5B
Expense ratio: 0.72% (year ending 12/31/97)

AMERICAN CENTURY VALUE FUND ◆

(See first American Century listing for data common to all funds)

Portfolio managers: Peter A. Zuger (1993), Phillip N. Davidson (1993)
Investment objective and policies: Long-term capital growth; income secondary. Invests at least 80% of assets in equity securities of well established companies with intermediate to large market capitalizations believed undervalued. Up to 25% of assets may be invested in securities of foreign issuers either directly or indirectly via ADRs, and 15% in securities convertible into common stock. May use forward currency exchange contracts for hedging purposes, and may sell short.
Year organized: 1993 (name changed from Twentieth Century Value Fund 1/1/97)
Ticker symbol: TWVLX
Group fund code: 039

Discount broker availability: Fidelity, *Schwab, Siebert, *White
Dividends paid: Income - March, June, September, December; Capital gains - December
Portfolio turnover (3 yrs): 111%, 145%, 94%
Management fee: 1.00%
Expense ratio: 1.00% (year ending 3/31/97)

AMERICAN CENTURY - BENHAM ADJUSTABLE RATE GOVERNMENT SECURITIES FUND ◆

(Merged into Benham Short Term Government fund 9/2/97)

AMERICAN CENTURY - BENHAM ARIZONA INTERMEDIATE-TERM MUNICIPAL FUND ◆

(See first American Century listing for data common to all funds)

Portfolio manager: Colleen M. Denzler (1996)
Investment objective and policies: High current income exempt from Arizona and federal income taxes, consistent with prudent management and capital preservation. Invests at least 65% of assets in intermediate-term Arizona municipal obligations with a weighted average maturity of five to ten years. May also invest in other municipal obligations. Up to 100% of assets may be in securities subject to AMT tax treatment. Fund is non-diversified.
Year organized: 1994 (name changed from AZ Municipal Intermediate-Term Muni Fund 1/1/97)
Ticker symbol: BEAMX
Group fund code: 948
Minimum purchase: Initial: $5,000
Discount broker availability: Fidelity, *Schwab, Siebert, *White
Qualified for sale in: AZ, CA, CO, NV, OR, TX, WA
Dividends paid: Income - declared daily, paid monthly; Capital gains - December
Portfolio turnover (3 yrs): 81%, 36%, 33%
Management fee: 0.30% complex fee plus a category fee of 0.28% first $1B to 0.1625% over $50B
Expense ratio: 0.66% (year ending 5/31/97) (0.79% without waiver)

AMERICAN CENTURY - BENHAM BOND FUND ◆

(See first American Century listing for data common to all funds)

Portfolio managers: Norman E. Hoops (1989), Jeffrey L. Houston (1996)
Investment objective and policies: High current income. Invests primarily in investment grade bonds and other debt obligations of domestic and foreign issuers. There is no restriction as to the weighted average maturity of the portfolio, however it is primarily intermediate- and long-term bonds. May use futures and options for hedging purposes.
Year organized: 1987 (split 10 for 1 on 11/13/93; name changed from Twentieth Century Long-Term Bond 1/1/97; ten year or longer maturity restriction removed 3/1/97)
Ticker symbol: TWLBX
Group fund code: 027
Discount broker availability: Fidelity, *Schwab, Siebert, *White
Dividends paid: Income - declared daily, paid monthly; Capital gains - December
Portfolio turnover (3 yrs): 52%, 100%, 105%
Management fee: 0.80%
Expense ratio: 0.80% (year ending 10/31/97)

AMERICAN CENTURY - BENHAM CALIFORNIA HIGH-YIELD MUNICIPAL FUND ◆

(See first American Century listing for data common to all funds)

Portfolio manager: Steven M. Permut (1997)
Investment objective and policies: High current income exempt from federal and California income taxes consistent with its investment policies, which permit investment in lower-rated and unrated municipal securities. Invests in high yielding, long- and intermediate-term medium to lower grade California

municipal securities with a weighted average maturity of more than ten years. May invest in securities subject to AMT tax treatment.
Year organized: 1986 (name changed from CA Muni High-Yield Fund 1/1/97)
Ticker symbol: BCHYX
Group fund code: 933
Minimum purchase: Initial: $5,000
Discount broker availability: Fidelity, Schwab, Siebert, *White
Qualified for sale in: AZ, CA, CO, HI, NV, NM, OR, TX, UT, WA
Dividends paid: Income - declared daily, paid monthly; Capital gains - December
Portfolio turnover (3 yrs): 46%, 36%, 40%
Management fee: 0.30% complex fee plus a category fee of 0.31% first $1B to 0.1925% over $50B
Expense ratio: 0.50% (year ending 8/31/97)

AMERICAN CENTURY - BENHAM CALIFORNIA INSURED TAX-FREE FUND ◆
(See first American Century listing for data common to all funds)

Portfolio manager: G. David MacEwen (1991)
Investment objective and policies: High interest income exempt from federal and California income taxes consistent with safety of principal. Invests in long-term California municipal securities covered by insurance guaranteeing the timely payment of principal and interest with a weighted average maturity of more than ten years.
Year organized: 1986 (name changed from CA Tax-Free Insured Fund 1/1/97)
Ticker symbol: BCINX
Group fund code: 934
Minimum purchase: Initial: $5,000
Discount broker availability: Fidelity, Schwab, Siebert, *White
Qualified for sale in: AZ, CA, CO, HI, NV, NM, OR, TX, UT, WA
Dividends paid: Income - declared daily, paid monthly; Capital gains - December
Portfolio turnover (3 yrs): 46%, 43%, 40%
Management fee: 0.30% complex fee plus a category fee of 0.28% first $1B to 0.1625% over $50B
Expense ratio: 0.48% (year ending 8/31/97)

AMERICAN CENTURY - BENHAM CALIFORNIA INTERMEDIATE-TERM TAX-FREE FUND ◆
(See first American Century listing for data common to all funds)

Portfolio managers: Colleen M. Denzler (1996), Joel Silva (1993)
Investment objective and policies: High interest income exempt from federal and California income taxes, consistent with prudent investment management and capital conservation. Invests in California municipal securities of the three highest grades with a weighted average maturity of five to ten years.
Year organized: 1983 (name changed from CA Tax-Free Intermediate-Term Fund 1/1/97)
Ticker symbol: BCITX
Group fund code: 931
Minimum purchase: Initial: $5,000
Discount broker availability: Fidelity, Schwab, Siebert, *White
Qualified for sale in: AZ, CA, CO, HI, NV, NM, OR, TX, UT, WA
Dividends paid: Income - declared daily, paid monthly; Capital gains - December
Portfolio turnover (3 yrs): 42%, 36%, 25%
Management fee: 0.30% complex fee plus a category fee of 0.28% first $1B to 0.1625% over $50B
Expense ratio: 0.48% (year ending 8/31/97)

AMERICAN CENTURY - BENHAM CALIFORNIA LIMITED-TERM TAX-FREE FUND ◆
(See first American Century listing for data common to all funds)

Portfolio manager: Joel Silva (1993)
Investment objective and policies: High interest income exempt from federal and California income taxes, consistent with prudent investment management

and capital conservation. Invests in California municipal securities of the three highest grades with a weighted average maturity of one to five years.
Year organized: 1992 (name changed from California Tax-Free Short-Term Fund 5/96; name changed from CA Tax-Free Limited-Term Fund 1/1/97)
Ticker symbol: BCSTX
Group fund code: 936
Minimum purchase: Initial: $5,000
Discount broker availability: Fidelity, Schwab, Siebert, *White
Qualified for sale in: AZ, CA, CO, HI, NV, NM, OR, TX, UT, WA
Dividends paid: Income - declared daily, paid monthly; Capital gains - December
Portfolio turnover (3 yrs): 47%, 44%, 50%
Management fee: 0.30% complex fee plus a category fee of 0.28% first $1B to 0.1625% over $50B
Expense ratio: 0.49% (year ending 8/31/97)

AMERICAN CENTURY - BENHAM CALIFORNIA LONG-TERM TAX-FREE FUND ◆
(See first American Century listing for data common to all funds)

Portfolio manager: G. David MacEwen (1991)
Investment objective and policies: High interest income exempt from federal and California income taxes, consistent with prudent investment management and capital conservation. Invests in California municipal securities of the three highest grades with a weighted average maturity of ten years or longer.
Year organized: 1983 (name changed from CA Tax-Free Long-Term Fund 1/1/97)
Ticker symbol: BCLTX
Group fund code: 932
Minimum purchase: Initial: $5,000
Discount broker availability: Fidelity, Schwab, Siebert, *White
Qualified for sale in: AZ, CA, CO, HI, NV, NM, OR, TX, UT, WA
Dividends paid: Income - declared daily, paid monthly; Capital gains - December
Portfolio turnover (3 yrs): 50%, 42%, 60%
Management fee: 0.30% complex fee plus a category fee of 0.28% first $1B to 0.1625% over $50B
Expense ratio: 0.48% (year ending 8/31/97)

AMERICAN CENTURY - BENHAM CALIFORNIA MUNICIPAL MONEY MARKET FUND ◆
(See first American Century listing for data common to all funds)

Portfolio manager: Todd Pardula (1994)
Investment objective and policies: High interest income exempt from federal and California income taxes, consistent with prudent investment management and conservation of capital. Invests in money market instruments with at least Aa ratings and with a weighted average maturity of less than 60 days. Fund will normally invest 60% to 80% in obligations subject to alternative minimum tax (AMT), but may invest up to 100% in these instruments. Fund designed for individuals not subject to AMT taxes.
Year organized: 1990
Ticker symbol: BNCXX
Group fund code: 935
Qualified for sale in: AZ, CA, CO, HI, NV, NM, OR, TX, UT, WA
Check redemptions: $100 minimum
Dividends paid: Income - declared daily, paid monthly
Management fee: 0.30% complex fee plus a category fee of 0.27% first $1B to 0.1570% over $50B
Expense ratio: 0.52% (year ending 8/31/97)

AMERICAN CENTURY - BENHAM CALIFORNIA TAX-FREE MONEY MARKET FUND ◆
(See first American Century listing for data common to all funds)

Portfolio manager: Todd Pardula (1994)
Investment objective and policies: High interest income exempt from federal and California income

taxes, consistent with capital conservation. Invests in California municipal money market instruments.
Year organized: 1983
Ticker symbol: BCTXX
Group fund code: 930
Check redemptions: $100 minimum
Qualified for sale in: AZ, CA, CO, HI, NV, NM, OR, TX, UT, WA
Dividends paid: Income - declared daily, paid monthly
Management fee: 0.30% complex fee plus a category fee of 0.27% first $1B to 0.1570% over $50B
Expense ratio: 0.49% (year ending 8/31/97)

AMERICAN CENTURY - BENHAM CAPITAL PRESERVATION FUND ◆
(See first American Century listing for data common to all funds)

Portfolio manager: Amy O'Donnell (1997)
Investment objective and policies: High current income consistent with safety and liquidity. Invests exclusively in U.S. Treasury money market instruments guaranteed by the full faith and credit of the U.S. Government. Portfolio maintains a dollar-weighted average maturity of 60 days or less.
Year organized: 1972 (absorbed Capital Preservation II 8/30/97)
Ticker symbol: CPFXX
Group fund code: 901
Check redemptions: $100 minimum
Dividends paid: Income - declared daily, paid monthly
Management fee: 0.30% complex fee plus a category fee of 0.25% first $1B to 0.1370% over $50B
Expense ratio: 0.49% (year ending 3/31/97)

AMERICAN CENTURY - BENHAM CASH RESERVE ◆
(See first American Century listing for data common to all funds)

Portfolio managers: Denise Tabacco (1995), John F. Walsh (1997)
Investment objective and policies: Maximum current income consistent with preservation of principal and liquidity. Invests in money market instruments.
Year organized: 1985 (split 100 for 1 on 11/13/93; name changed from Twentieth Century Cash Reserve 1/1/97)
Ticker symbol: TWCXX
Group fund code: 026
Dividends paid: Income - declared daily, paid monthly
Check redemptions: $100 minimum
Management fee: 0.30% complex fee plus a category fee of 0.25% first $1B to 0.1370% over $50B
Expense ratio: 0.68% (year ending 10/31/97)

AMERICAN CENTURY - BENHAM FLORIDA INTERMEDIATE-TERM MUNICIPAL FUND ◆
(See first American Century listing for data common to all funds)

Portfolio manager: G. David MacEwen (1994)
Investment objective and policies: High current income exempt from federal income tax and the Florida intangible personal property tax, consistent with prudent investment management and capital conservation. Invests primarily in intermediate-term Florida municipal obligations for which the interest is a tax preference item for purposes of the AMT. The weighted average portfolio maturity is five to ten years. Fund is non-diversified.
Year organized: 1994 (name changed from FL Muni Intermediate-Term Fund 1/1/97)
Ticker symbol: ACBFX
Group fund code: 946
Minimum purchase: Initial: $5,000
Discount broker availability: Fidelity, *Schwab, Siebert, *White
Qualified for sale in: CA, FL, GA, IL, MI, NJ, NY, PA
Dividends paid: Income - declared daily, paid monthly; Capital gains - December
Portfolio turnover (3 yrs): 82%, 66%, 37%

Management fee: 0.30% complex fee plus a category fee of 0.28% first $1B to 0.1625% over $50B
Expense ratio: 0.65% (year ending 5/31/97) (0.86% without waiver)

AMERICAN CENTURY - BENHAM FLORIDA MUNICIPAL MONEY MARKET FUND ◆
(See first American Century listing for data common to all funds)

Portfolio manager: Brian E. Karcher (1996)
Investment objective and policies: High current income exempt from regular federal income tax and the Florida intangible personal property tax. Invests primarily in high-quality municipal money market instruments for which the interest is a tax preference item for purposes of the AMT.
Year organized: 1994
Ticker symbol: BEFXX
Group fund code: 945
Check redemptions: $100 minimum
Qualified for sale in: CA, FL, GA, IL, MI, NJ, NY, PA
Dividends paid: Income - declared daily, paid monthly
Management fee: 0.30% complex fee plus a category fee of 0.27% first $1B to 0.1570% over $50B
Expense ratio: 0.12% (year ending 5/31/97) (0.66% without waiver)

AMERICAN CENTURY - BENHAM GNMA FUND ◆
(See first American Century listing for data common to all funds)

Portfolio managers: C. Casey Colton (1994), David W. Schroeder (1996)
Investment objective and policies: High current income consistent with safety of principal and maintenance of liquidity. Invests primarily in mortgage-backed GNMA certificates endorsed by the Government National Mortgage Association.
Year organized: 1985 (name changed from GNMA Income Fund 1/1/97)
Ticker symbol: BGNMX
Group fund code: 970
Discount broker availability: Fidelity, *Schwab, Siebert, *White
Check redemptions: $100 minimum
Dividends paid: Income - declared daily, paid monthly; Capital gains - December
Portfolio turnover (3 yrs): 105%, 64%, 120%
Management fee: 0.30% complex fee plus a category fee of 0.36% first $1B to 0.2425% over $50B
Expense ratio: 0.55% (year ending 3/31/97)

AMERICAN CENTURY - BENHAM GOVERNMENT AGENCY MONEY MARKET FUND ◆
(See first American Century listing for data common to all funds)

Portfolio manager: Amy O'Donnell (1997)
Investment objective and policies: High current income exempt from state income taxes, consistent with safety of principal and maintenance of liquidity. Normally invests at least 65% of assets in money market securities issued by U.S. Government agencies and instrumentalities, and maintains a dollar-weighted average maturity of 90 days or less.
Year organized: 1989
Ticker symbol: BGAXX
Group fund code: 971
Check redemptions: $100 minimum
Dividends paid: Income - declared daily, paid monthly
Management fee: 0.30% complex fee plus a category fee of 0.25% first $1B to 0.1370% over $50B
Expense ratio: 0.57% (year ending 3/31/97)

AMERICAN CENTURY - BENHAM HIGH YIELD FUND ◆
(See first American Century listing for data common to all funds)

Portfolio managers: Norman E. Hoops (1997), Theresa C. Fennell (1997)

Investment objective and policies: High current income. Invests in a diversified portfolio of high-yielding corporate bonds, debentures and notes. Fund invests primarily in lower rated debt securities denominated in U.S. dollars and foreign currencies. May invest up to 40% of assets in foreign issues, and up to 20% of assets in common stock or other equity related securities. May write covered call options and invest in a variety of derivatives.
Year organized: 1997
Group fund code: 101
Discount broker availability: *Fidelity, *Schwab, Siebert, *White
Dividends paid: Income - declared daily, paid monthly; Capital gains - December
Management fee: 0.90%

AMERICAN CENTURY - BENHAM INFLATION-ADJUSTED TREASURY FUND ◆
(See first American Century listing for data common to all funds)

Portfolio manager: David W. Schroeder (1997)
Investment objective and policies: Total return consistent with investment in U.S. Treasury inflation adjusted securities. Invests at least 65% of assets in Inflation-Adjusted Securities that are backed by the full faith and credit of the U.S. Government, and indexed or otherwise structured by the U.S. Treasury to provide protection against inflation. There are no maturity or duration restrictions for the securities in which the fund may invest.
Year organized: 1997
Group fund code: 975
Discount broker availability: *Fidelity, *Schwab, *White
Dividends paid: Income - declared daily, paid monthly; Capital gains - annually
Management fee: 0.30% complex fee plus a category fee of 0.36% first $1B to 0.2425% over $50B

AMERICAN CENTURY - BENHAM INTERMEDIATE-TERM BOND FUND ◆
(See first American Century listing for data common to all funds)

Portfolio managers: Norman E. Hoops (1994), Jeffrey L. Houston (1996)
Investment objective and policies: Competitive level of current income. Invests primarily in investment grade corporate securities and other debt obligations of domestic and foreign issuers with a weighted average maturity of three to ten years. May use futures and options for hedging purposes.
Year organized: 1994 (name changed from Twentieth Century Intermediate-Term Bond Fund 1/1/97)
Ticker symbol: TWITX
Group fund code: 034
Discount broker availability: Fidelity, *Schwab, Siebert, *White
Dividends paid: Income - declared daily, paid monthly; Capital gains - December
Portfolio turnover (3 yrs): 99%, 87%, 133%
Management fee: 0.75%
Expense ratio: 0.75% (year ending 10/31/97)

AMERICAN CENTURY - BENHAM INTERMEDIATE-TERM GOVERNMENT FUND ◆
(Merged into Benham Intermediate Term Treasury 8/30/97)

AMERICAN CENTURY - BENHAM INTERMEDIATE-TERM TAX-FREE FUND ◆
(See first American Century listing for data common to all funds)

Portfolio managers: Joel Silva (1994), Colleen M. Denzler (1996)
Investment objective and policies: Income exempt

from regular federal income tax, consistent with prudent investment management and conservation of capital. Invests primarily in short- and intermediate-term tax exempt bonds with a weighted average maturity of five to ten years. May have up to 15% of assets in illiquid securities, and use futures and options for hedging purposes.
Year organized: 1987 (split 10 for 1 on 11/13/93; name changed from Twentieth Century Tax-Exempt Intermediate-Term Fund 1/1/97; absorbed Benham Inter-Term TF 8/30/97 and changed name from Inter-Term TE)
Ticker symbol: TWTIX
Group fund code: 028
Minimum purchase: Initial: $5,000
Discount broker availability: Fidelity, Siebert, *White
Dividends paid: Income - declared daily, paid monthly; Capital gains - December
Portfolio turnover (3 yrs): 35%, 39%, 32%
Management fee: 0.30% complex fee plus a category fee of 0.28% first $1B to 0.1625% over $50B
Expense ratio: 0.58% (year ending 10/31/97)

AMERICAN CENTURY - BENHAM INTERMEDIATE-TERM TREASURY FUND ◆
(See first American Century listing for data common to all funds)

Portfolio managers: David W. Schroeder (1992), C. Casey Colton (1996)
Investment objective and policies: High current income consistent with conservation of assets and safety. Invests primarily in U.S. Treasury notes, U.S. Treasury bills and repurchase agreements secured by U.S. Treasury securities with a weighted average maturity of 13 months to ten years. Dividends are tax-free in many states.
Year organized: 1980 (formerly Capital Preservation Treasury Note Trust; name changed from Treasury Note Fund 1/1/97; fund absorbed Inter-Term Government Bond 8/30/97)
Ticker symbol: CPTNX
Group fund code: 950
Discount broker availability: Fidelity, *Schwab, Siebert, *White
Dividends paid: Income - declared daily, paid monthly; Capital gains - December
Portfolio turnover (3 yrs): 110%, 168%, 92%
Management fee: 0.30% complex fee plus a category fee of 0.28% first $1B to 0.1625% over $50B
Expense ratio: 0.51% (year ending 3/31/97)

AMERICAN CENTURY - BENHAM INTERNATIONAL BOND FUND ◆
(See first American Century listing for data common to all funds)

Sub-adviser: J.P. Morgan Investment Management
Portfolio managers: David W. Schroeder (1997), Randy Merk (1997), Dominic Pegler (1997)
Investment objective and policies: High long-term total return: interest income, capital appreciation and currency gains, consistent with investment in the highest quality European government debt securities, as well as those of Australia, Canada and Japan. Invests primarily in AAA-rated bonds denominated in foreign currencies and issued by foreign governments and government agencies and by supranational organizations. Under normal circumstances at least 25% of assets will be in German government debt securities.
Year organized: 1992 (name and policy changed from European Government Bond 10/1/97; may now invest outside of Europe)
Ticker symbol: BEGBX
Group fund code: 992
Discount broker availability: *Schwab, *White
Dividends paid: Income - March, June, September, December; Capital gains - December
Portfolio turnover (3 yrs): 163%, 242%, 167%
Management fee: 0.30% complex fee plus a category fee of 0.36% first $1B to 0.2425% over $50B
Expense ratio: 0.84% (year ending 12/31/97)

AMERICAN CENTURY - BENHAM LIMITED-TERM BOND FUND ◆

(See first American Century listing for data common to all funds)

Portfolio managers: Norman E. Hoops (1994), Jeffrey L. Houston (1996)
Investment objective and policies: High current income. Invests primarily in investment grade bonds and other debt obligations of domestic and foreign issuers with a weighted average maturity of five years or less. May use futures and options for hedging purposes.
Year organized: 1994 (name changed from Twentieth Century Limited-Term Bond Fund 1/1/97)
Group fund code: 033
Discount broker availability: Fidelity, *Schwab, Siebert, *White
Dividends paid: Income - declared daily, paid monthly; Capital gains - December
Portfolio turnover (3 yrs): 109%, 121%, 116%
Management fee: 0.70%
Expense ratio: 0.69% (year ending 10/31/97)

AMERICAN CENTURY - BENHAM LIMITED-TERM TAX-FREE FUND ◆

(See first American Century listing for data common to all funds)

Portfolio managers: Joel Silva (1995), Colleen M. Denzler (1996)
Investment objective and policies: High income exempt from regular federal income tax, consistent with prudent investment management and capital conservation. Invests in shorter-term municipal bonds and other tax-exempt debt instruments with a weighted average maturity of five years or less. May have up to 15% of assets in illiquid securities, and use futures and options for hedging purposes.
Year organized: 1993 (name changed from Twentieth Century Tax-Exempt Short-Term Fund 1/1/97; average maturity increased from three to five years 3/1/97; changed name from Limited-Term Tax Exempt 8/30/97)
Ticker symbol: TWTSX
Group fund code: 032
Minimum purchase: Initial: $5,000
Discount broker availability: Fidelity, Siebert, *White
Check redemptions: $100 minimum
Dividends paid: Income - declared daily, paid monthly; Capital gains - December
Portfolio turnover (3 yrs): 74%, 68%, 78%
Management fee: 0.30% complex fee plus a category fee of 0.28% first $1B to 0.1625% over $50B
Expense ratio: 0.59% (year ending 10/31/97)

AMERICAN CENTURY - BENHAM LONG-TERM TAX-FREE FUND ◆

(See first American Century listing for data common to all funds)

Portfolio managers: G. David MacEwen (1991), Colleen M. Denzler (1996)
Investment objective and policies: High level of income exempt from regular federal income tax, consistent with prudent investment management and capital conservation. Invests in longer-term tax-exempt bonds with a weighted average maturity of ten years or more. May have up to 15% of assets in illiquid securities, and use futures and options for hedging purposes.
Year organized: 1987 (split 10 for 1 on 11/13/93; name changed from Twentieth Century Tax-Exempt Long-Term Fund 1/1/97; absorbed Benham Long-Term TF 8/30/97 and changed name from Long-Term TE)
Ticker symbol: TWTLX
Group fund code: 029
Minimum purchase: Initial: $5,000
Discount broker availability: Fidelity, Siebert, *White
Dividends paid: Income - declared daily, paid monthly; Capital gains - December
Portfolio turnover (3 yrs): 65%, 60%, 61%
Management fee: 0.30% complex fee plus a category fee of 0.28% first $1B to 0.1625% over $50B
Expense ratio: 0.58% (year ending 10/31/97)

AMERICAN CENTURY - BENHAM LONG-TERM TREASURY FUND ◆

(See first American Century listing for data common to all funds)

Portfolio managers: David W. Schroeder (1992), C. Casey Colton (1996)
Investment objective and policies: Consistent and high current income exempt from state taxes. Invests exclusively in securities issued or guaranteed by the U.S. Treasury and agencies or instrumentalities of the U.S. Government with remaining maturities of 10 years or more. Portfolio maintains a dollar-weighted average maturity of 20 to 30 years.
Year organized: 1992 (name changed from Long-Term Treasury & Agency Fund 1/1/97)
Ticker symbol: BLAGX
Group fund code: 974
Discount broker availability: Fidelity, *Schwab, Siebert, *White
Dividends paid: Income - declared daily, paid monthly; Capital gains - December
Portfolio turnover (3 yrs): 40%, 112%, 147%
Management fee: 0.30% complex fee plus a category fee of 0.28% first $1B to 0.1625% over $50B
Expense ratio: 0.60% (year ending 3/31/97)

AMERICAN CENTURY - BENHAM PRIME MONEY MARKET FUND ◆

(See first American Century listing for data common to all funds)

Portfolio managers: Denise Tabacco (1997), John Walsh (1997)
Investment objective and policies: High current income consistent with capital preservation. Invests in high quality U.S. dollar-denominated money market instruments of domestic and foreign issuers.
Year organized: 1993
Ticker symbol: BPRXX
Group fund code: 921
Check redemptions: $100 minimum
Dividends paid: Income - declared daily, paid monthly
Management fee: 0.30% complex fee plus a category fee of 0.37% first $1B to 0.2570% over $50B
Expense ratio: 0.50% (year ending 2/28/97)

AMERICAN CENTURY - BENHAM SHORT-TERM GOVERNMENT FUND ◆

(See first American Century listing for data common to all funds)

Portfolio managers: Robert V. Gahagan (1991), Newlin Rankin (1996)
Investment objective and policies: High current income consistent with limited price volatility. Invest in debt securities of the U.S. Government and its agencies. Portfolio maintains a dollar-weighted average maturity of three years or less. May invest in mortgage-related securities and have up to 15% of assets in illiquid securities.
Year organized: 1982 (name changed from U.S. Govts on 3/1/94; name changed from Twentieth Century U.S. Govts ST on 1/1/97; absorbed Benham Adjustable Rate Government Securities 8/30/97.)
Ticker symbol: TWUSX
Group fund code: 023
Discount broker availability: Fidelity, *Schwab, Siebert, *White
Dividends paid: Income - declared daily, paid monthly; Capital gains - December
Portfolio turnover (3 yrs): 293%, 246%, 128%
Management fee: 0.30% complex fee plus a category fee of 0.36% first $1B to 0.2425% over $50B
Expense ratio: 0.68% (year ending 10/31/97)

AMERICAN CENTURY - BENHAM SHORT-TERM TREASURY FUND ◆

(See first American Century listing for data common to all funds)

Portfolio managers: Robert V. Gahagan (1996), Newlin Rankin (1996)
Investment objective and policies: Highest current income exempt from state income taxes consistent with capital preservation. Invests exclusively in securities issued or guaranteed by the U.S. Treasury and agencies or instrumentalities of the U.S. Government

with remaining maturities of three years or less. Portfolio maintains a dollar-weighted average maturity of 13 months to three years.
Year organized: 1992 (name changed from Benham Short-Term Treasury and Agency Fund 1/1/97)
Ticker symbol: BSTAX
Group fund code: 973
Discount broker availability: Fidelity, *Schwab, Siebert, *White
Dividends paid: Income - declared daily, paid monthly; Capital gains - December
Portfolio turnover (3 yrs): 234%, 224%, 141%
Management fee: 0.30% complex fee plus a category fee of 0.28% first $1B to 0.1625% over $50B
Expense ratio: 0.61% (year ending 3/31/97)

AMERICAN CENTURY - BENHAM TARGET MATURITIES TRUST ◆

(See first American Century listing for data common to all funds)

Portfolio managers: David W. Schroeder (1990), C. Casey Colton (1996), Jeremy Fletcher (1997)
Investment objective and policies: Highest attainable investment return consistent with the credit-worthiness of U.S. Treasury securities and the professional management of reinvestment and market risk. Invests in zero coupon U.S. Treasury securities and in Treasury bills, notes and bonds placed in separate portfolios, each maturing within one year of a specified target maturity year.
Portfolios/maturity: 2000, 2005, 2010, 2015, 2020, 2025
Year organized: 1985, Target 2020 Portfolio in 1990, Target 2025 Portfolio in 1996
Ticker symbol: BTMTX (2000), BTFIX (2005), BTTNX (2010), BTFTX (2015), BTTTX (2020), BTTRX (2025)
Group fund code: 2000 (963), 2005 (964), 2010 (965), 2015 (966), 2020 (967), 2025 (968)
Deadline for same day wire purchase: 3 P.M.
Discount broker availability: Fidelity, *Schwab, Siebert, *White
Dividends paid: Income - December; Capital gains - December (Fund declares a reverse split for the value of the distributions at the same time to reflect the non-cash taxable distribution.)
Portfolio turnover (3 yrs): T2000 - 10%, 29%, 53%; T2005 - 15%, 31%, 34%; T2010 - 26%, 24%, 26%; T2015 - 21%, 17%, 70%; T2020 - 14%, 47%, 78%; T2025 - 58%, 61%
Management fee: 0.30% complex fee plus a category fee of 0.36% first $1B to 0.2425% over $50B
Expense ratio: T2000- 0.56%; T2005 - 0.57%; T2010- 0.62%; T2015 - 0.61%; T2020 - 0.53%; T2025 - 0.62% (year ending 9/30/97)

AMERICAN CENTURY - BENHAM TAX-FREE MONEY MARKET FUND ◆

(See first American Century listing for data common to all funds)

Portfolio manager: Brian E. Karcher (1995)
Investment objective and policies: High interest income exempt from federal income tax, consistent with prudent investment management and capital conservation. Invests in municipal money market instruments.
Year organized: 1984 (name changed from National Tax-Free MM Fund 1/1/97)
Ticker symbol: BNTXX
Group fund code: 941
Check redemptions: $100 minimum
Dividends paid: Income - declared daily, paid monthly
Management fee: 0.30% complex fee plus a category fee of 0.27% first $1B to 0.1570% over $50B
Expense ratio: 0.67% (year ending 5/31/97)

AMERICAN CENTURY - TWENTIETH CENTURY EMERGING MARKETS FUND ◆

(See first American Century listing for data common to all funds)

Portfolio managers: Mark S. Kopinski (1997), Michael J. Donnelly (1997)
Investment objective and policies: Long-term capital growth. Invests at least 90% of assets in a diversified portfolio of equity securities of companies in

emerging market countries (as defined by the International Finance Corp., the U.N., or the World Bank) and regions that are considered to have prospects for appreciation. May also invest in companies which derive a significant portion of their revenues from these markets. May invest up to 35% of assets in junk bonds. May engage in forward foreign currency contracts and sell short against the box.
Year organized: 1997
Group fund code: 043
Minimum purchase: Initial: $10,000
Discount broker availability: Fidelity, *Schwab, Siebert, *White
Dividends paid: Income - December; Capital gains - December
Management fee: 2.00% first $500M to 1.25% over $1B

AMERICAN CENTURY - TWENTIETH CENTURY GIFTRUST FUND ◆
(See first American Century listing for data common to all funds)

Portfolio managers: John D. Seitzer (1996), Christopher K. Boyd (1997)
Investment objective and policies: Capital growth. Invests at least 90% of assets in securities of domestic and foreign issuers believed to have above-average appreciation potential. May invest in securities of foreign issuers without limit, and use forward currency exchange contracts for hedging purposes. Designed for persons wishing to make gifts to children, charities or others.
Year organized: 1983 (name changed from Giftrust Investors Fund 1/1/97)
Ticker symbol: TWGTX
Group fund code: 025
Special sales restriction: Available only to persons executing the Twentieth Century Giftrust in which a grantor makes a gift to any individual, child, organization or charity. Trust is irrevocable and shares cannot be distributed before the specified maturity date, which must be at least ten years.
Minimum purchase: Initial: $500, Subsequent: $250
Portfolio turnover (3 yrs): 118%, 121%, 105%
Dividends paid: Income - December; Capital gains - December
Management fee: 1.00%
Expense ratio: 1.00% (year ending 10/31/97)
Special fees: $10 annual fee for accounts requiring income-tax returns, and a $100 fee for administrative functions when the trust matures

AMERICAN CENTURY - TWENTIETH CENTURY GROWTH FUND ◆
(See first American Century listing for data common to all funds)

Portfolio manager: C. Kim Goodwin (1997)
Investment objective and policies: Capital growth. Invests in securities of domestic and foreign issuers believed to have above-average appreciation potential. Growth, Ultra, and Vista all have the same objective, differing only in size and trading volume of companies in portfolio. The largest companies are typically allocated to Growth, and the smallest to Vista. May use forward currency exchange contracts for hedging purposes.
Year organized: 1957 (current objectives and policies established in 1971; name changed from Growth Investors Fund 1/1/97)
Ticker symbol: TWCGX
Group fund code: 020
Discount broker availability: Fidelity, *Schwab, Siebert, *White
Dividends paid: Income - December; Capital gains - December
Portfolio turnover (3 yrs): 75%, 122%, 141%
Management fee: 1.00%
Expense ratio: 1.00% (year ending 10/31/97)

AMERICAN CENTURY - TWENTIETH CENTURY HERITAGE FUND ◆
(See first American Century listing for data common to all funds)

Portfolio managers: Linda K. Peterson (1998), Harold S. Bradley (1998)
Investment objective and policies: Capital growth; income secondary. Invests in common stocks of

domestic and foreign issuers believed to have above-average appreciation potential. Stocks must have a record of paying cash dividends, but growth is the primary consideration and the dividends may not be significant. Select and Heritage have the same objective, differing only in size and trading volume of companies in portfolio. The larger companies are typically allocated to Select, and the smaller to Heritage.
Year organized: 1987 (name changed from Heritage Investors Fund 1/1/97)
Ticker symbol: TWHIX
Group fund code: 030
Discount broker availability: Fidelity, *Schwab, Siebert, *White
Dividends paid: Income - December; Capital gains - December
Portfolio turnover (3 yrs): 69%, 122%, 121%
Management fee: 1.00%
Expense ratio: 1.00% (year ending 10/31/97)

AMERICAN CENTURY - TWENTIETH CENTURY INTERNATIONAL DISCOVERY FUND ◆
(See first American Century listing for data common to all funds)

Portfolio managers: Henrik Strabo (1994), Michael J. Donnelly (1997), Mark S. Kopinski (1997)
Investment objective and policies: Capital growth. Invests primarily in equity securities of foreign companies with market capitalizations under $1B, in developed markets believed to have above-average appreciation potential, and companies in emerging market countries without regard to market capitalization. Normally invests at least 65% of assets in common stocks of issuers from at least three foreign countries without regard to geographic region. May invest up to 50% of assets in emerging markets countries. May use forward currency exchange contracts for hedging purposes.
Year organized: 1994 (name changed from International Emerging Growth Fund 9/3/96)
Ticker symbol: TWEGX
Group fund code: 042
Minimum purchase: Initial: $10,000
Discount broker availability: Schwab (only through financial advisers)
Redemption fee: 2% for shares held less than 180 days, payable to the fund
Dividends paid: Income - December; Capital gains - December
Portfolio turnover (3 yrs): 146%, 130%, 168%
Management fee: 1.75% first $500M to 1.20% over $1B
Expense ratio: 1.70% (year ending 11/30/97) (1.87% without waiver)

AMERICAN CENTURY - TWENTIETH CENTURY INTERNATIONAL GROWTH FUND ◆
(See first American Century listing for data common to all funds)

Portfolio managers: Henrik Strabo (1994), Michael J. Donnelly (1997), Mark S. Kopinski (1997)
Investment objective and policies: Capital growth. Invests in securities of foreign companies believed to have above-average appreciation potential. Invests primarily in common stocks but may also hold convertible securities, preferred stocks, bonds, notes and other debt securities of companies or obligations of domestic or foreign governments and their agencies. Normally invests at least 65% of assets in common stocks of issuers from at least three developed foreign countries without regard to geographic region. May use forward currency exchange contracts for hedging purposes.
Year organized: 1991 (name changed from International Equity Fund 1/1/97)
Ticker symbol: TWIEX
Group fund code: 041
Discount broker availability: Fidelity, *Schwab, Siebert, *White
Dividends paid: Income - December; Capital gains - December
Portfolio turnover (3 yrs): 163%, 158%, 169%
Management fee: 1.50% first $1B to 1.10% over $2B
Expense ratio: 1.38% (year ending 11/30/97) (1.56% without waiver)

AMERICAN CENTURY - TWENTIETH CENTURY NEW OPPORTUNITIES FUND ◆
(See American Century listing for data common to all funds)

Portfolio managers: John D. Seitzer (1996), Christopher K. Boyd (1997)
Investment objective and policies: Capital growth. Invests in securities of small- to mid-sized companies believed to have above-average appreciation potential based on fundamental and technical standards demonstrating accelerating earnings and revenues. Invests primarily in common stocks but may also hold convertible securities, preferred stocks, bonds, notes and other debt securities of companies or obligations of domestic or foreign governments and their agencies. Will normally invest 80% to 90% of assets in equities, and will limit debt securities to investment grade only. May use forward currency exchange contracts and a variety of other derivative instruments in an effort to enhance revenue and for hedging purposes.
Year organized: 1996
Ticker symbol: TWNOX
Group fund code: 036
Special sales restrictions: Fund is only offered to members of the Priority Investors Program, those with at least $100,000 in total assets invested with the company. Manager intends to close the fund when assets reach $400M.
Minimum purchase: Initial: $10,000; Maximum: $500,000
Dividends paid: Income - December; Capital gains - December
Portfolio turnover (1 yrs): 118%
Management fee: 1.50% first $1B to 1.10% over $2B
Expense ratio: 1.49% (ten months ending 10/31/97)

AMERICAN CENTURY - TWENTIETH CENTURY SELECT FUND ◆
(See first American Century listing for data common to all funds)

Portfolio managers: James E. Stowers, III (1995), Jean C. Ledford (1997)
Investment objective and policies: Capital growth; income secondary. Invests in common stocks of domestic and foreign issuers believed to have above-average appreciation potential. At least 80% of stocks must have a record of paying cash dividends, but growth is the primary consideration and the dividends may not be significant. Select and Heritage have the same objective, differing only in size and trading volume of companies in portfolio. The larger companies are typically allocated to Select, and the smaller to Heritage.
Year organized: 1957 (current objectives and policies established in 1971; name changed from Select Investors Fund 1/1/97)
Ticker symbol: TWCIX
Group fund code: 021
Discount broker availability: Fidelity, *Schwab, Siebert, *White
Dividends paid: Income - December; Capital gains - December
Portfolio turnover (3 yrs): 94%, 105%, 106%
Management fee: 1.00%
Expense ratio: 1.00% (year ending 10/31/97)

AMERICAN CENTURY - TWENTIETH CENTURY ULTRA FUND ◆
(See first American Century listing for data common to all funds)

Portfolio managers: James E. Stowers III (1981), Bruce A. Wimberly (1996), John R. Sykora (1997)
Investment objective and policies: Capital growth. Invests in securities of domestic and foreign issuers believed to have above-average appreciation potential. Growth, Ultra, and Vista all have the same objective, differing only in size and trading volume of companies in portfolio. The largest companies are typically allocated to Growth, and the smallest to Vista. May use forward currency exchange contracts for hedging purposes.
Year organized: 1981 (name changed from Ultra Investors Fund 1/1/97)

Ticker symbol: TWCUX
Group fund code: 022
Discount broker availability: Fidelity, *Schwab, Siebert, *White
Dividends paid: Income - December; Capital gains - December
Portfolio turnover (3 yrs): 107%, 87%, 87%
Management fee: 1.00%
Expense ratio: 1.00% (year ending 10/31/97)

AMERICAN CENTURY - TWENTIETH CENTURY VISTA FUND ◆
(See first American Century listing for data common to all funds)

Portfolio managers: Glenn A. Fogle (1993), Arnold Douville (1997)
Investment objective and policies: Capital growth. Invests in securities of domestic and foreign issuers believed to have above-average appreciation potential. Growth, Ultra, and Vista all have the same objective, differing only in size and trading volume of companies in portfolio. The largest companies are typically allocated to Growth, and the smallest to Vista. May use forward currency exchange contracts for hedging purposes.
Year organized: 1983 (name changed from Vista Investors Fund 1/1/97)
Ticker symbol: TWCVX
Group fund code: 024
Discount broker availability: Fidelity, *Schwab, Siebert, *White
Dividends paid: Income - December; Capital gains - December
Portfolio turnover (3 yrs): 96%, 91%, 89%
Management fee: 1.00%
Expense ratio: 1.00% (year ending 10/31/97)

AMERICAN EXPRESS STRATEGIST FUNDS
(Data common to all American Express Strategist funds are shown below. See subsequent listings for data specific to individual funds.)

IDS Tower 10
Minneapolis, MN 55440-0010
800-297-7378, 800-297-8800
TTY 800-710-5260
Internet: http://www.americanexpress.com

Shareholder service hours: Full service: M-F 8 A.M.-12 midnight; Sat. 10 A.M.-5 p.m.; Sun. 9 A.M.-9 P.M., EST. After hours service: balances, yields
Adviser: American Express Financial Corp.
Transfer agent: American Express Financial Corp.
Sales restrictions: An investor must first open an Investment Management Account maintained by American Express Financial Corp. There is no fee. Money is first deposited into this account, and shares may be purchased from there.
Minimum purchase: Initial: $2,000, Subsequent: $100; IRA/Keogh: Initial: $1,000 (exception noted)
Wire orders accepted: No
Qualified for sale in: All states
Telephone redemptions: Yes
Wire redemptions: Yes, however redemptions also must first pass through the Investment Management Account. $15 fee. (exception noted)
Letter redemptions: Signature guarantee not required
Redemption fee: Fund reserves the right to institute a 1% redemption fee for any shares held less than one year, but will not exercise the option until at least after the first year of operation.
Telephone switching: With other American Express Strategist funds
Deadline for same day switch: 3 P.M. EST
Number of switches permitted: 4 per year
Shareholder services: IRA, SEP-IRA, corporate retirement plans, automatic investment plan, electronic funds transfer, systematic withdrawal plan
Maintenance fee: $40 per year for any account with a balance below $5,000, and for any account that registers no transaction activity during any calendar year.
12b-1 distribution fee: 0.25% (0.20% for MM)
IRA fees: Closing $50

AMERICAN EXPRESS -STRATEGIST BALANCED FUND
(See first American Express Strategist listing for data common to all funds)

Portfolio managers: Edward Labenski (1987), Kurt Winters (1997)
Investment objective and policies: Balance of growth of capital and current income. Invests all of its investable assets in an underlying portfolio with the same objective. Invests as much as 65% of assets in common stock and no less than 35% of assets in senior securities, convertible securities, derivative instruments and money markets. Selects common stocks believed to be undervalued based on their perceived ability to provide current income and growth. At least 25% of assets are invested in debt obligations and convertibles. May invest up to 25% of assets in foreign securities, and up to 10% in illiquid issues. May use derivatives in an effort to enhance performance.
Year organized: 1940 (name changed from IDS Mutual Fund 5/96)
Dividends paid: Income - March, June, September, December; Capital gains - December
Portfolio turnover (2 yrs): 49%, 14%
Management fee: 0.53% first $1B to 0.43% over $6B, +/- up to 0.08% based on performance relative to the Lipper Balanced Fund Index
Expense ratio: 0.62% (year ending 9/30/97) (6.35% without waiver)

AMERICAN EXPRESS - STRATEGIST EMERGING MARKETS FUND
(See first American Express Strategist listing for data common to all funds)

Portfolio manager: Ian King (1996)
Investment objective and policies: Long-term growth of capital. Invests all of its investable assets in an underlying portfolio with the same objective. Invests at least 65% of assets in a diversified portfolio of common stock of companies located in or doing the predominance of their business in at least three different emerging markets countries as defined by the World Bank or the U.N. Balance may be invested in any other type of security. May invest up to 20% of assets in foreign bonds, up to 10% in junk bonds including Brady Bonds, and up to 10% in illiquid securities. May use derivatives in an effort to enhance performance.
Year organized: 1996
Dividends paid: Income - December; Capital gains - December
Management fee: 1.10% first $250M to 1.00% over $2B

AMERICAN EXPRESS - STRATEGIST EQUITY FUND
(See first American Express Strategist listing for data common to all funds)

Portfolio manager: Dick Warden (1995)
Investment objective and policies: Current income and growth of capital. Invests all of its investable assets in an underlying portfolio with the same objective. Invests at least 65% of assets in common stock of U.S. and foreign companies. Balance may be invested in any other type of security. May invest up to 25% of assets in foreign securities, and up to 10% in illiquid issues. May use derivatives in an effort to enhance performance.
Year organized: 1940 (name changed from IDS Stock Fund 5/96)
Dividends paid: Income - March, June, September, December; Capital gains - December
Portfolio turnover (2 yrs): 82%, 21%
Management fee: 0.53% first $500M to 0.40% over $6B, +/- up to 0.08% based on performance relative to the Lipper Growth and Income Fund Index
Expense ratio: 0.58% (year ending 9/30/97) (1.13% without waiver)

AMERICAN EXPRESS - STRATEGIST EQUITY INCOME FUND
(See first American Express Strategist listing for data common to all funds)

Portfolio manager: Kurt Winters (1997)
Investment objective and policies: High level of current income; steady growth of capital secondary.

Invests all of its investable assets in an underlying portfolio with the same objective. Invests at least 65% of assets in dividend-paying common and preferred stocks, often selected from the utility, financial, consumer and energy sectors. Balance may be invested in any other type of security. May invest up to 25% of assets in foreign securities, and up to 10% in illiquid issues. May use derivatives in an effort to enhance performance.
Year organized: 1990 (name changed from IDS Diversified Equity Income Fund 5/96)
Dividends paid: Income - March, June, September, December; Capital gains - December
Portfolio turnover (2 yrs): 81%, 17%
Management fee: 0.53% first $500M to 0.40% over $6B
Expense ratio: 1.07% (year ending 9/30/97) (4.53% without waiver)

AMERICAN EXPRESS - STRATEGIST GOVERNMENT INCOME FUND
(See first American Express Strategist listing for data common to all funds)

Portfolio manager: James Snyder (1993)
Investment objective and policies: High level of current income consistent with safety of principal. Invests all of its investable assets in an underlying portfolio with the same objective. Invests at least 65% of assets a diversified portfolio of short- to medium-term fixed-income securities of the U.S. Government, its agencies and instrumentalities; primarily mortgage backed instruments. May use derivatives in an effort to enhance performance.
Year organized: 1985 (name changed from IDS Federal Income Fund 5/96)
Dividends paid: Income - monthly; Capital gains - December
Portfolio turnover (3 yrs): not available
Management fee: 0.52% first $1B to 0.395% over $9B
Expense ratio: 1.10% (year ending 5/31/97) (includes waiver)

AMERICAN EXPRESS - STRATEGIST GROWTH FUND
(See first American Express Strategist listing for data common to all funds)

Portfolio manager: Mitsi Malevich (1992)
Investment objective and policies: Long-term capital growth. Invests all of its investable assets in an underlying portfolio with the same objective. Invests in a broadly diversified portfolio of common and convertible stocks of U.S. and foreign companies that appear to offer growth opportunities. May invest up to 25% of assets in foreign securities. May also invest in preferred stocks, debt securities, money markets, and use derivative instruments in an effort to enhance performance.
Year organized: 1972 (name changed from IDS Growth Fund 5/96)
Ticker symbol: STGRX
Dividends paid: Income - December; Capital gains - December
Portfolio turnover (2 yrs): 24%, 5%
Management fee: 0.60% first $1B to 0.50% over $6B, +/- up to 0.12% based on performance relative to the Lipper Growth Fund Index
Expense ratio: 1.01% (year ending 7/31/97) (1.03% without waiver)

AMERICAN EXPRESS - STRATEGIST GROWTH TRENDS FUND
(See first American Express Strategist listing for data common to all funds)

Portfolio manager: Gordon Fines (1991)
Investment objective and policies: Long-term capital growth. Invests all of its investable assets in an underlying portfolio with the same objective. Invests in a diversified portfolio of common and convertible stocks of U.S. and foreign companies that appear to offer significant growth opportunities due to dynamic market conditions affecting their operations. May

invest up to 30% of assets in foreign securities. May also invest in preferred stocks, debt securities, money markets, and use derivatives in an effort to enhance performance.
Year organized: 1968 (name changed from IDS New Dimensions Fund 5/96)
Ticker symbol: STGTX
Dividends paid: Income - December; Capital gains - December
Portfolio turnover (2 yrs): 32%, 7%
Management fee: 0.60% first $1B to 0.49% over $12B, +/- up to 0.12% based on performance relative to the Lipper Growth Fund Index
Expense ratio: 1.30% (year ending 7/31/96) (1.10% without waiver)

AMERICAN EXPRESS - STRATEGIST HIGH YIELD FUND
(See first American Express Strategist listing for data common to all funds)

Portfolio manager: Jack Utter (1985)
Investment objective and policies: High current return; capital growth secondary. Invests all of its investable assets in an underlying portfolio with the same objective. Invests primarily in junk bonds, and may invest in instruments in default. May also invest up to 10% of assets in common stocks, preferred stocks that do not pay dividends, and warrants to purchase common. May also purchase investment grade debt securities and convertibles, and use derivatives in an effort to enhance performance. May invest up to 25% of assets in foreign issues.
Year organized: 1983 (name changed from IDS Extra Income Fund 5/96)
Dividends paid: Income - monthly; Capital gains - December
Portfolio turnover (3 yrs): not available
Management fee: 0.59% first $1B to 0.465% over $9B
Expense ratio: 1.20% (year ending 5/31/97) (includes waiver)

AMERICAN EXPRESS - STRATEGIST MONEY MARKET FUND
(See first American Express Strategist listing for data common to all funds)

Sub-adviser: Reserve Management Co., Inc.
Investment objective and policies: High level of current income consistent with preservation of capital and liquidity. Invests in high grade U.S. and foreign government, corporate and bank short-term money market instruments.
Year organized: 1986
Minimum purchase: Initial: $20,000, Subsequent: $1,000
Wire orders accepted: Yes
Deadline for same day wire purchase: 2 P.M.
Telephone redemptions: Yes, $1,000 minimum
Wire redemptions: Yes, $20 fee for redemptions less than $10,000
Letter redemptions: $2 fee for less than $100
Check redemptions: Yes, $2 fee for check less than $100
Dividends paid: Income - declared and paid daily
Management fee: 0.80%
Maintenance fee: $5/month if balance drops below $15,000

AMERICAN EXPRESS - STRATEGIST QUALITY INCOME FUND
(See first American Express Strategist listing for data common to all funds)

Portfolio manager: Raymond Goodner (1985)
Investment objective and policies: Attractive total return; income plus capital appreciation. Invests all of its investable assets in an underlying portfolio with the same objective. Invests at least 90% of assets in a diversified portfolio of the four highest investment grade marketable corporate debt obligations, as well as unrated debt securities believed to be comparable. The remaining 10% of assets may be invested in common or preferred stocks, or convertibles. May use derivatives in an effort to enhance performance.

Year organized: 1945 (name changed from IDS Selective Income Fund 5/96)
Dividends paid: Income - monthly; Capital gains - December
Portfolio turnover (3 yrs): not available
Management fee: 0.52% first $1B to 0.395% over $9B
Expense ratio: 1.10% (year ending 5/31/97) (includes waiver)

AMERICAN EXPRESS - STRATEGIST SPECIAL GROWTH FUND
(See first American Express Strategist listing for data common to all funds)

Portfolio manager: Gurudutt M. Baliga (1996)
Investment objective and policies: Long-term capital growth. Invests all of its investable assets in an underlying portfolio with the same objective. Invests at least 65% of assets in equity securities of companies found in the S&P 500 Index that are perceived to be undervalued. May invest more than 25% of assets in companies involved in either the utilities or energy industry. May invest up to 20% of assets in foreign issues, but only if they are listed in the Index. May also invest in junk bonds and use derivatives in an attempt to enhance performance.
Year organized: 1996
Dividends paid: Income - December; Capital gains - December
Portfolio turnover (1 yrs): 171%
Management fee: 0.65% first $250M to 0.50% over $6B
Expense ratio: 1.36% (year ending 7/31/97) (3.17% without waiver)

AMERICAN EXPRESS - STRATEGIST TAX-FREE HIGH YIELD FUND
(See first American Express Strategist listing for data common to all funds)

Portfolio manager: Kurt Larson (1979)
Investment objective and policies: High current income exempt from federal income taxes. Invests all of its investable assets in an underlying portfolio with the same objective. Invests in a diversified portfolio of medium- and lower-quality bonds and notes issued by or on behalf of state and local government units. May also invest in money markets and derivative instruments.
Year organized: 1979 (name changed from IDS High Yield Tax Exempt Fund 5/96)
Dividends paid: Income - monthly; Capital gains - December
Portfolio turnover (1 yrs): 4%
Management fee: 0.49% first $1B to 0.36% over $9B
Expense ratio: 0.95% (year ending 11/30/97) (includes waiver)

AMERICAN EXPRESS - STRATEGIST TOTAL RETURN FUND
(See first American Express Strategist listing for data common to all funds)

Lead portfolio manager: Steve Merrell (1997)
Investment objective and policies: Maximum total return: growth of capital and current income. Invests all of its investable assets in an underlying portfolio with the same objective. Allocates assets among four asset classes; U.S. equity securities, 25% to 75%; U.S. and foreign debt securities, 10% to 50%; foreign equity securities, 10% to 50%; and cash, 0% to 30%. 'Neutral' mix for 1998 is deemed 39%, 40%, 21%, and 0% respectively; may be reset every 12 to 18 months. May invest up to 15% of assets in junk bonds, and a maximum of 50% of assets in foreign issues. May use derivatives in an effort to enhance performance.
Year organized: 1985 (name changed from IDS Managed Retirement Fund 5/96)
Dividends paid: Income - March, June, September, December; Capital gains - December
Portfolio turnover (2 yrs): 99%, 35%
Management fee: 0.53% first $500M to 0.40% over

$6B, +/- up to 0.08% based on performance relative to the Lipper Flexible Portfolio Fund Index
Expense ratio: 1.26% (year ending 9/30/97) (2.79% without waiver)

AMERICAN EXPRESS - STRATEGIST WORLD GROWTH FUND
(See first American Express Strategist listing for data common to all funds)

Portfolio manager: John O'Brien (1997)
Investment objective and policies: Long-term growth of capital. Invests all of its investable assets in an underlying portfolio with the same objective. Invests primarily in equity securities, primarily common stocks, of companies of all market capitalizations over $200M throughout the world, including the U.S. Companies are selected based on perceived growth potential rather than on geographic location. May invest up to 20% of assets in bonds, and up to 10% in illiquid securities. Fund may use derivative instruments in an effort to enhance performance and for hedging purposes.
Year organized: 1990 (name changed from IDS Global Growth Fund 5/96)
Dividends paid: Income - December; Capital gains - December
Portfolio turnover (2 yrs): 91%, 58%
Management fee: 0.80% first $250M to 0.675% over $2B
Expense ratio: 1.75% (year ending 10/31/97) (includes waiver)

AMERICAN EXPRESS - STRATEGIST WORLD INCOME FUND
(See first American Express Strategist listing for data common to all funds)

Portfolio manager: Ray Goodner (1989)
Investment objective and policies: High rate of total return: income and capital growth. Invests all of its investable assets in an underlying portfolio with the same objective. Invests at least 80% of assets in a combination of mostly high quality bonds (those rated B or better) and convertible securities from at least three different countries including the U.S. Assets are shifted according to perceived market opportunities or international currency flows. May use a variety of derivatives in an effort to enhance performance. Fund is non-diversified.
Year organized: 1989 (name changed from IDS Global Bond Fund 5/96)
Dividends paid: Income - March, June, September, December; Capital gains - December
Portfolio turnover (2 yrs): 33%, 24%
Management fee: 0.77% first $250M to 0.67% over $1B
Expense ratio: 1.35% (year ending 10/31/97) (includes waiver)

THE AMERICAN HERITAGE FUND, INC. ◆
1370 Avenue of the Americas
New York, NY 10019
800-828-5050, 212-397-3900
fax 212-397-4036

Adviser: American Heritage Management Corp.
Portfolio manager: Heiko H. Thieme (1990)
Transfer agent: American Data Services, Inc.
Investment objective and policies: Maximum capital growth. Generally invests up to 80% of assets in common stocks and securities convertible into common stocks. Up to 35% of assets may be in securities of foreign issuers and up to 15% in illiquid securities. May sell short (up to 35% of assets), leverage and hedge. Fund is non-diversified.
Year organized: 1951 (Present management 1990; absorbed Industry Fund of America in June, 1988)
Ticker symbol: AHERX
Minimum purchase: Initial: $2,500, Subsequent: $250; IRA: Initial: $2,000, Subsequent: None; Keogh: Initial: $1,000; Automatic investment plan: Initial: $100
Wire orders accepted: No
Discount broker availability: *Fidelity, Schwab, *Siebert, *White
Qualified for sale in: All states except AR, NE, WI

Letter redemptions: Signature guarantee required
Dividends paid: Income - December; Capital gains - December
Portfolio turnover (3 yrs): 470%, 606%, 620%
Shareholder services: IRA, Keogh, systematic withdrawal plan min. bal. req. $50,000
Management fee: 1.25% first $100M, 1.00% over $100M
Expense ratio: 6.42% (year ending 5/31/97)
IRA/Keogh fees: Annual $13, Closing $15

AMERICAN HERITAGE GROWTH FUND, INC. ◆
1370 Avenue of the Americas
New York, NY 10019
800-828-5050, 212-397-3900
fax 212-397-4036

Adviser: American Heritage Management Corp.
Portfolio manager: Heiko H. Thieme (1994)
Transfer agent: American Data Services, Inc.
Investment objectives and policies: Capital growth. Invests at least 80% of assets in common stocks and securities convertible into common stocks. Up to 35% of assets may be in securities of foreign issuers. May write covered call options for hedging purposes.
Year organized: 1994
Ticker symbol: AHEGX
Minimum purchase: Initial: $1,000, Subsequent: $250; IRA: Subsequent: None; Automatic investment plan: Initial: $100
Wire orders accepted: No
Discount broker availability: *Fidelity, *Siebert, *White
Qualified for sale in: All states except MO, NE
Letter redemptions: Signature guarantee required
Dividends paid: Income - December; Capital gains - December
Portfolio turnover (3 yrs): 1,378%, 4,263%, 3,214%
Shareholder services: IRA, Keogh, systematic withdrawal plan min. bal. req. $50,000
Management fee: 1.25% first $100M, 1.00% over $100M
Expense ratio: 2.81% (year ending 1/31/97) (includes waiver)
IRA/Keogh fees: Annual $13, Closing $15

AMERICAN TRUST ALLEGIANCE FUND ◆
One Court Street
Lebanon, NH 03766-1358
800-788-8806, 800-385-7003
800-229-2105, 603-448-6415
fax 516-951-0573

Adviser: American Trust Co.
Administrator: Investment Company Administration Corp.
Portfolio managers: Jeffrey M. Harris (1997), Paul H. Collins (1997)
Transfer agent: American Data Services, Inc.
Investment objectives and policies: Capital appreciation. Normally invests up to 85% of assets in a diversified portfolio of common stocks of domestic companies of all sizes that are perceived to offer long-term growth prospects. Fund will not invest in companies which derive more than 5% of their total revenues from tobacco, pharmaceuticals, biotechnology, medical diagnostic services or products, or gambling or liquor. This screen allows the fund to address the investment needs of Christian Scientists. Fund may invest in foreign issues that are publicly traded in the U.S.
Year organized: 1997
Minimum purchase: Initial: $2,500, Subsequent: $250; IRA: Initial: $1,000, Subsequent: $100; Automatic investment plan: Initial: $1,000, Subsequent: $100
Wire orders accepted: Yes
Deadline for same day wire purchase: 4 P.M.
Qualified for sale in: All states
Telephone redemptions: Yes, $1,000 minimum, $12 fee
Wire redemptions: Yes, $1,000 minimum, $12 fee
Letter redemptions: Signature guarantee required over $5,000

Dividends paid: Income - December; Capital gains - December
Shareholder services: IRA, systematic withdrawal plan
Management fee: 0.95%
Administration fee: 0.20% (minimum of $30,000)
IRA fee: Annual $15

AMERICA'S UTILITY FUND ◆
901 East Byrd Street
Richmond, VA 23219
800-487-3863, 800-382-0016
804-649-1315, fax 804-698-2781

Adviser: Mentor Investment Advisors, LLC (an indirect, wholly-owned subsidiary of First Union Corp.)
Portfolio manager: Team managed
Transfer agent: State Street Bank and Trust Co.
Investment objective and policies: Current income and moderate capital growth. Invests at least 65% of assets in securities (common stock, preferred stock and debt securities) of electric utility companies, electric utility holding companies, electric and gas combination utility companies and local and long distance telephone companies. Allocation among security types is adjusted to reflect changes in market and economic conditions that affects their relative ability to contribute to the fund's objective. Fund may invest in foreign securities, and may buy and sell foreign currencies and use foreign currency forward and futures contracts for hedging purposes.
Year organized: 1992
Ticker symbol: AMUTX
Minimum purchase: Initial: $1,000, Subsequent: $100; Automatic investment plan: Initial: $40, Subsequent: $40
Wire orders accepted: No
Qualified for sale in: All states except AK, AR, DE, ID, IA, ME, MT, NE, NV, NH, NM, ND, RI, SD, UT, VT
Letter redemptions: Signature guarantee required over $25,000
Dividends paid: Income - March, June, September, December; Capital gains - December
Portfolio turnover (3 yrs): 24%, 28%, 29%
Shareholder services: IRA, SEP-IRA
Management fee: 0.65%
Expense ratio: 1.27% (year ending 12/31/96) (1.36% without waiver)
IRA fees: Annual $10

AMERISTOCK MUTUAL FUND ◆
1480 I Moraga Road, Suite 200
Moraga, CA 94556
800-394-5064, 510-376-3490
fax 510-376-3490
Internet http://www.ameristock.com
e-mail: ndg@ameristock.com

Adviser: Ameristock Corp.
Portfolio manager: Nicholas D. Gerber (1995)
Transfer agent: Ameristock Corp.
Investment objective and policies: Total return: capital appreciation and current income. Invests at least 80% of assets in equity securities of large capitalization companies identified by value; fund ranks the largest by value, growth, price/earnings ratio and dividend yields, and buys them all in proportion. May also invest up to 10% of assets in other mutual funds, and use futures and options in an effort to enhance performance and for hedging purposes.
Year organized: 1995
Ticker symbol: AMSTX
Minimum purchase: Initial: $1,000, Subsequent: $100
Wire orders accepted: Yes
Deadline for same day wire purchase: 4 P.M.
Discount broker availability: Fidelity, Siebert, *White
Qualified for sale in: All states
Telephone redemptions: Yes
Wire redemptions: Yes, $100 minimum, $15 fee
Letter redemptions: Signature guarantee required over $25,000
Dividends paid: Income - July, December; Capital gains - July, December
Portfolio turnover (2 yrs): 22%, 7%
Shareholder services: IRA, electronic funds transfer

Management fee: 1.00%
Expense ratio: 0.56% (year ending 6/30/97) (1.06% without waiver)
IRA fees: Annual $15

AMTRUST VALUE FUND ◆
109-A Teakwood
P.O. Box 3467
Victoria, TX 77901
800-532-1146, 512-578-7778
fax 512-575-5097

Adviser: AmTrust Capital Resources, Inc.
Portfolio manager: James E. Baker (1993)
Transfer agent: AmTrust Capital Resources, Inc.
Investment objective and policies: Long-term capital growth; current income incidental. Invests primarily in common stocks of small to mid-size domestic companies with market capitalization of less than $1 billion, that are listed on a national securities exchange or NASDAQ. May invest in U.S. Government securities and other short-term interest-bearing securities for defensive purposes. May invest up to 15% of assets in illiquid securities and use options for hedging purposes.
Year organized: 1993
Minimum purchase: Initial: $250, Subsequent: $50
Wire orders accepted: Yes
Qualified for sale in: TX
Telephone redemptions: Yes, $30,000 maximum
Letter redemptions: Signature guarantee required over $30,000
Dividends paid: Income - December; Capital gains - December
Shareholder services: IRA, SEP-IRA, Keogh, 403(b), automatic investment plan
Portfolio turnover (3 yrs): 87%, 79%, 49%
Management fee: 1.50% under $2M to 1.25% over $10M
Expense ratio: 1.60% (year ending 6/30/97) (includes waiver)
IRA/Keogh fees: Annual $12

ANALYSTS INVESTMENT TRUST - FIXED INCOME FUND ◆
9200 Montgomery Road
Building D, Suite 13A
Cincinnati, OH 45242
513-792-5400, 513-984-3377
fax 513-984-2411

Adviser: Equity Analysts, Inc.
Portfolio manager: David Lee Manzler, Jr. (1993)
Transfer agent: Analysts Investment Trust
Investment objective and policies: High long-term income consistent with capital preservation. Invests primarily in investment grade, fixed-income securities - U.S. Government obligations, securities of foreign governments, domestic and foreign corporate debt securities, convertible bonds and repurchase agreements. Up to 50% of assets may be in securities of foreign issuers. Fund may use futures and options for hedging purposes.
Year organized: 1993
Minimum purchase: Initial: $1,000, Subsequent: $25; IRA/Keogh: Initial: $25
Wire orders accepted: Yes
Deadline for same day wire purchase: 3 P.M.
Qualified for sale in: IN, KY, OH
Telephone redemptions: Yes
Wire redemptions: Yes, $1,000 minimum, $11 fee
Letter redemptions: Signature guarantee required over $25,000
Telephone switching: With Analysts Stock Fund and Kemper Cash Account Trust money market funds
Number of switches permitted: Unlimited
Dividends paid: Income - March, June, September, December; Capital gains - December
Portfolio turnover (3 yrs): 22%, 18%, 23%
Shareholder services: IRA, SEP-IRA, Keogh, 401(k), 403(b), corporate retirement plans, systematic withdrawal plan min. bal. req. $10,000
Management fee: 1.50% first $20M to 0.75% over $100M
Expense ratio: 1.50% (year ending 7/31/97)
IRA/Keogh fees: None

ANALYSTS INVESTMENT TRUST - STOCK INCOME FUND ◆

9200 Montgomery Road
Building D, Suite 13A
Cincinnati, OH 45242
513-792-5400, 513-984-3377
fax 513-984-2411

Adviser: Equity Analysts, Inc.
Portfolio manager: David Lee Manzler, Jr. (1993)
Transfer agent: Analysts Investment Trust
Investment objective and policies: Long-term capital appreciation. Invests primarily in common stocks of companies in six categories - three domestic stock capitalization groups (over $1B, $500M to $1B, and under $500M), foreign stocks, real estate stocks and gold and other natural resources stocks - with maximum of 50% of assets in any single category. Fund may use futures and options for hedging purposes.
Year organized: 1993
Minimum purchase: Initial: $1,000, Subsequent: $25; IRA/Keogh: Initial: $25
Wire orders accepted: Yes
Deadline for same day wire purchase: 3 P.M.
Qualified for sale in: IN, KY, OH
Telephone redemptions: Yes
Wire redemptions: Yes, $1,000 minimum, $11 fee
Letter redemptions: Signature guarantee required over $25,000
Telephone switching: With Analysts Fixed Income Fund and Kemper Cash Account Trust money market funds
Number of switches permitted: Unlimited
Dividends paid: Income - March, June, September, December; Capital gains - December
Portfolio turnover (3 yrs): 6%, 32%, 5%
Shareholder services: IRA, SEP-IRA, Keogh, 401(k), 403(b), corporate retirement plans, systematic withdrawal plan min. bal. req. $10,000
Management fee: 2.00% first $20M to 0.75% over $100M
Expense ratio: 2.00% (year ending 7/31/97)
IRA/Keogh fees: None

ANALYTIC FUNDS ◆

(Data common to all Analytic funds are shown below. See subsequent listings for data specific to individual funds.)

700 South Flower Street, Suite 2400
Los Angeles, CA 90017
800-374-2633, 800-618-1872
213-688-3015
fax 213-688-8856

Shareholder service hours: Full service: M-F 7:30 A.M.-4 P.M. PST
Adviser: Analytic-TSA Global Asset Management, Inc.
Administrator: UAM Fund Services, Inc.
Transfer agent: Chase Global Funds Services, Inc.
Minimum purchase: Initial: $5,000, Subsequent: None; IRA/Keogh: Initial: None
Wire orders accepted: Yes
Deadline for same day wire purchase: 4 P.M.
Qualified for sale in: All states
Wire redemptions: Yes
Telephone redemptions: Yes (proceeds will be wired only)
Letter redemptions: Signature guarantee required
Telephone switching: With other Analytic funds
Number of switches permitted: Unlimited
Shareholder services: IRA, SEP-IRA, 401(k), corporate retirement plans, systematic withdrawal plan
Adminstration fee: 0.25% first $200M to 0.11% over $3B
IRA fees: None

ANALYTIC DEFENSIVE EQUITY FUND ◆

(See first Analytic listing for data common to all funds)

Portfolio managers: Charles L. Dobson (1978), Dennis M. Bein (1995), Harindra de Silva (1995)
Investment objective and policies: Greater long-term total return and smaller fluctuations in quarterly total return from a hedged common stock portfolio

than would be realized from a non-hedged portfolio. Invests primarily in dividend-paying common stocks on which options are traded on national securities exchanges and in securities convertible into common stocks, by selling covered call options and secured put options and by entering into closing purchase transactions. Also known as The Defensive Equity Portfolio.
Year organized: 1978 (name changed from Optioned Equity Fund 6/97)
Ticker symbol: ANALX
Group fund code: 67
Discount broker availability: *Fidelity, *Schwab, *White
Dividends paid: Income - March, June, September, December; Capital gains - December
Portfolio turnover (3 yrs): 76%, 43%, 32%
Management fee: 0.75% first $100M to 0.55% over $200M
Expense ratio: 1.30% (year ending 12/31/97)

ANALYTIC SERIES FUND - ENHANCED EQUITY PORTFOLIO ◆

(See first Analytic listing for data common to all funds)

Portfolio managers: Charles L. Dobson (1995), Dennis M. Bein (1996), Harindra de Silva (1996)
Investment objective and policies: Above-average total return. Invests primarily in a diversified portfolio of domestic common stocks of companies with market capitalizations of $1B or more, and options and futures that relate to such stocks. May invest up to 20% of assets in non-U.S. dollar denominated securities of foreign issuers and 35% in other mutual funds.
Year organized: 1992
Ticker symbol: ANEEX
Group fund code: 137
Discount broker availability: *Fidelity, *Schwab, *White
Dividends paid: Income - March, June, September, December; Capital gains - December
Portfolio turnover (3 yrs): 189%, 179%, 10%
Management fee: 0.60%
Expense ratio: 1.00% (year ending 12/31/97) (2.24% without waiver)

ANALYTIC SERIES FUND - MASTER FIXED INCOME PORTFOLIO ◆

(See first Analytic listing for data common to all funds)

Portfolio managers: Scott T. Barker (1996), Gregory M. McMurran (1996), Robert Bannon (1996)
Investment objective and policies: Above-average total return. Normally invests in a diversified portfolio of high grade U.S. Government, corporate, and mortgage-related fixed-income securities. Portfolio maintains a dollar-weighted average maturity of three to ten years. May have up to 20% of assets in non-U.S. dollar denominated securities of foreign issuers and 35% in other mutual funds.
Year organized: 1992
Ticker symbol: ANMFX
Group fund code: 136
Discount broker availability: *Fidelity, *Schwab, *White
Dividends paid: Income - declared daily, paid monthly; Capital gains - December
Portfolio turnover (3 yrs): 40%, 22%, 32%
Management fee: 0.45%
Expense ratio: 0.91% (year ending 12/31/97) (1.22% without waiver)

ANALYTIC SERIES FUND - SHORT TERM GOVERNMENT PORTFOLIO ◆

(See first Analytic listing for data common to all funds)

Portfolio managers: Scott T. Barker (1996), Gregory M. McMurran (1996), Robert Bannon (1996)
Investment objective and policies: High current income consistent with stability of market value and low credit risk. Normally invests at least 80% of assets in high grade U.S. Government securities. Portfolio maintains a dollar-weighted average maturity of one to three years. May have up to 20% of assets in securities

of foreign issuers and 20% in other mutual funds.
Year organized: 1992
Ticker symbol: ANSGX
Group fund code: 135
Discount broker availability: *Fidelity, *Schwab, *White
Dividends paid: Income - declared daily, paid monthly; Capital gains - December
Portfolio turnover (3 yrs): 34%, 31%, 10%
Management fee: 0.30%
Expense ratio: 0.60% (year ending 12/31/97) (7.80% without waiver)

AON FUNDS ◆

(Data common to all Aon funds are shown below. See subsequent listings for data specific to individual funds.)

123 North Wacker Drive, 29th Floor
Chicago, IL 60606-4703
800-266-3637, 800-392-4326
312-701-3300

Shareholder services: Full service: M-F 8 A.M.-7 P.M. CST; After hours service: prices, balances, orders, last transaction, prospectuses
Adviser: Aon Advisors, Inc.
Transfer agent: Firstar Trust Co.
Minimum purchase: Initial: $1,000, Subsequent: $100
Wire orders accepted: Yes
Deadline for same day wire purchase: 4 P.M. (1:30 P.M. for MM)
Qualified for sale in: All states except AL, AK, AR, HI, ID, KS, KY, LA, ME, MS, MT, NE, NV, NH, NM, ND, OK, PR, RI, SD, UT, WV, WY
Wire redemptions: Yes, $10 fee
Telephone redemptions: Yes
Letter redemptions: Signature guarantee required over $10,000
Telephone switching: With the same share class of other Aon funds
Number of switches permitted: Unlimited, 15 day hold, $5 fee
Shareholder services: IRA, SEP-IRA, Keogh, automatic investment plan, systematic withdrawal plan min. bal. req. $7,500
IRA fees: Annual $12.50/acct., Closing $15

AON ASSET ALLOCATION FUND ◆

(See first Aon listing for data common to all funds)

Portfolio manager: John G. Lagedrost (1994)
Investment objective and policies: Maximum total return: capital appreciation, dividends and interest. Invests in an allocated mix of stocks, bonds and money market instruments, the proportions of which are determined by perceived market conditions. May invest in common and preferred domestic and foreign stocks, convertible securities and warrants; and domestic and foreign debt securities including bonds, debentures and notes. May write covered call options in an effort to enhance performance.
Year organized: 1994
Ticker symbol: AONAX
Dividends paid: Income - quarterly; Capital gains - December
Portfolio turnover (3 yrs): 64%, 120%, 95%
Management fee: 0.65% first $250M to 0.45% over $500M
Expense ratio: 0.56% (year ending 10/31/97) (0.78% without waiver)

AON GOVERNMENT SECURITIES FUND ◆

(See first Aon listing for data common to all funds)

Portfolio manager: Francis P. Wren (1997)
Investment objective and policies: High current income with limited risk. Invests at least 80% of assets in intermediate- and long-term debt instruments issued or guaranteed by the U.S. Government, its agencies or instrumentalities. May invest up to 50% of assets in GNMA securities. May purchase and write covered put and call options on debt securities, and purchase and sell exchange traded interest rate futures contracts with options thereon.
Year organized: 1996

Ticker symbol: AGSYX
Dividends paid: Income - monthly; Capital gains - December
Portfolio turnover (1 yr): 136%
Management fee: 0.45% first $250M to 0.25% over $400M
Expense ratio: 0.46% (year ending 10/31/97) (0.65% without waiver)

AON INTERNATIONAL EQUITY FUND ◆
(See first Aon listing for data common to all funds)

Sub-adviser: Brinson Partners, Inc.
Investment objective and policies: Long-term capital appreciation. Invests in equity and equity-related securities and non-dollar debt securities of companies either organized outside of the U.S. or those having their principal operations outside of the U.S. May invest in sponsored or unsponsored ADRs, EDRs, or GDRs. Generally will only purchase issues listed on the MSCI-EAFE Index. May employ certain currency management derivative strategies both in an effort to enhance performance and for hedging purposes.
Year organized: 1996
Ticker symbol: AIEYX
Dividends paid: Income - December; Capital gains - December
Portfolio turnover (1 yr): 27%
Management fee: 0.95% first $100M to 0.85% over $200M
Expense ratio: 1.40% (year ending 10/31/97) (1.61% without waiver)

AON MONEY MARKET FUND ◆
(See first Aon listing for data common to all funds)

Portfolio manager: Keith C. Lemmer (1992)
Investment objective and policies: Maximum current income consistent with the preservation of capital and liquidity. Invests in short-term commercial paper and U.S. Government securities with maturities of less than one year.
Year organized: 1992
Ticker symbol: AONXX
Check redemptions: $500 minimum
Dividends paid: Income - declared daily, paid monthly
Management fee: 0.30%
Expense ratio: 0.22% (year ending 10/31/97) (0.40% without waiver)

AON REIT INDEX FUND ◆
(See first Aon listing for data common to all funds)

Portfolio manager: Robert E. Dunn (1996)
Investment objective and policies: Capital appreciation and accumulation of income that approximates the investment return of the Morgan Stanley REIT Index. Invests primarily in the equity REITs that are components of the Index, although will not necessarily own all of the issues comprising the Index. Will not invest directly in real estate. Will attempt to acheive a correlation of 0.95 relative to the return of the index, without taking into account expenses.
Year organized: 1996
Ticker symbol: AREYX
Dividends paid: Income - December; Capital gains - December
Portfolio turnover (1 yr): 22%
Management fee: 0.60% first $100M to 0.50% over $200M
Expense ratio: 0.51% (year ending 10/31/97) (0.82% without waiver)

AON S&P 500 INDEX FUND ◆
(See first Aon listing for data common to all funds)

Portfolio manager: Melissa A. Aton (1997)
Investment objective and policies: Total return approximating that of the return demonstrated by the group of funds that comprise the S&P 500 Index. Invests in all 500 stocks found on the index in approximately the same weightings. Will attempt to acheive a correlation of 0.95 relative to the return of the index,

without taking into account expenses. May use call and put options to rapidly adjust correlation while waiting for the most efficient time to adjust the portfolio to reflect the Index.
Year organized: 1996
Ticker symbol: ASPYX
Dividends paid: Income - December; Capital gains - December
Portfolio turnover (1 yr): 13%
Management fee: 0.30%
Expense ratio: 0.37% (year ending 10/31/97) (0.49% without waiver)

API TRUST
(Data common to all API Trust funds are shown below. See subsequent listings for data specific to individual funds.)

P.O. Box 2529
2303 Yorktown Avenue
Lynchburg, VA 24501
800-628-4077, 800-544-6060
804-846-1361, fax 804-846-1837

Adviser: Yorktown Management & Research Co., Inc.
Transfer agent: Fund Services, Inc.
Wire orders accepted: No
Qualified for sale in: All states except IA, WI
Letter redemptions: Signature guarantee required over $10,000
Shareholder services: Automatic investment plan, systematic withdrawal plan min. bal. req. $10,000

API TRUST CAPITAL INCOME FUND
(See first API Trust listing for data common to all funds)

Portfolio manager: David D. Basten (1988)
Investment objective and policies: High current income; growth of capital and income secondary. Invests at least 65% of assets in shares of underlying funds that seek to achieve an objective of high current income by investing in equity securities, including dividend-paying common stocks and convertible securities, long- or short-term bonds and other fixed-income securities. Normally invests between 25% to 50% of assets in global funds. May invest up to 25% of assets in underlying funds that leverage.
Year organized: 1988 (Income Fund prior to 2/22/91, which invested in individual securities; formerly Investment Grade Securities Fund)
Ticker symbol: APIGX
Discount broker availability: Fidelity, Siebert, *White
Dividends paid: Income - December; Capital gains - December
Portfolio turnover (3 yrs): 67%, 40%, 65%
Management fee: 0.60%
12b-1 distribution fee: 0.50%
Expense ratio: 1.77% (year ending 5/31/97) (2.38% without waiver)

API TRUST MULTIPLE INDEX TRUST FUND ◆
(See first API Trust listing for data common to all funds)

Portfolio manager: David D. Basten (1997)
Investment objective and policies: Maximum total return: capital growth and income. Invests at least 65% of assets in other open-end investment companies, (i.e., a 'fund of funds'), whose portfolios mirror those of one index or another of market securities from around the world. Normally invests in approximately 10 to 15 different funds representing as many as 6,600 companies, and may invest up to 25% of assets in a single fund. Underlying funds may be load funds. Funds are overweighted in areas believed to be poised for outperformance.
Year organized: 1997
Minimum purchase: Initial: $5,000, Subsequent: $1,000
Discount broker availability: White
Dividends paid: Income - annually; Capital gains - annually

Management fee: 0.70%
12b-1 distribution fee: 0.50% (not currently imposed)

API TRUST - TREASURIES TRUST ◆
(See first API Trust listing for data common to all funds)

Portfolio manager: David D. Basten (1997)
Investment objective and policies: Current income consistent with limited credit risk. Invests in obligations of the U.S. Treasury that are guaranteed as to principal and interest by the full faith and credit of the U.S. Government.
Year organized: 1997
Minimum purchase: Initial: $5,000, Subsequent: $1,000
Discount broker availability: White
Dividends paid: Income - quarterly; Capital gains - annually
Management fee: 0.40%
12b-1 distribution fee: 0.30% (not currently imposed)

AQUINAS FUNDS ◆
(Data common to all Aquinas funds are shown below. See subsequent listings for data specific to individual funds.)

5310 Harvest Hill Road, Suite 248
Dallas, TX 75230
800-423-6369, 972-233-6655
fax 972-661-0140

Adviser: Aquinas Investment Advisers, Inc. (a wholly-owned subsidiary of The Catholic Foundation)
Administrator: Sunstone Financial Group, Inc.
Transfer agent: DST Systems, Inc.
Minimum purchase: Initial: $500, Subsequent: $250; Automatic investment plan: Initial: $50, Subsequent: $50
Wire orders accepted: Yes
Telephone redemptions: Yes, $1,000 minimum
Wire redemptions: Yes, $1,000 minimum, $9 fee
Letter redemptions: Signature guarantee required over $25,000
Telephone switching: With other Aquinas funds, $1,000 minimum
Number of switches permitted: Unlimited
Shareholder services: IRA, 401(k), 403(b), directed dividends, systematic withdrawal plan min. bal. req. $10,000
Administration fee: 0.23% first $50M to 0.075% over $250M (for combined assets of all funds; $185,000 minimum)
IRA fees: Annual $12

AQUINAS BALANCED FUND ◆
(See first Aquinas listing for data common to all funds)

Sub-advisers: Team composed of sub-advisers of other Aquinas funds, except Sirach
Portfolio managers: Team of portfolio managers from other Aquinas funds (1994)
Investment objective and policies: Long-term capital growth consistent with reasonable risk. Invests in a diversified portfolio of common stocks of established companies (40% to 70% of assets), investment grade fixed-income securities (25% to 40%), and cash equivalents. With a neutral position of 65% stocks, 35% bonds, allocation will vary depending on market and economic conditions. May invest up to 20% of assets in foreign securities and use options and futures for hedging purposes.
Year organized: 1994
Ticker symbol: AQBLX
Discount broker availability: White
Qualified for sale in: AK, CA, CO, CT, DC, FL, GA, IL, IN, KS, KY, LA, MI, MN, MO, NE, NH, NJ, NM, NY, OH, OK, OR, PA, TX, UT, VA, VT, WV, WY
Dividends paid: Income - March, June, September, December; Capital gains - December
Portfolio turnover (3 yrs): 94%, 111%, 118%
Management fee: 1.00%
Expense ratio: 1.45% (year ending 12/31/97) (1.52% without waiver)

AQUINAS EQUITY GROWTH FUND ◆
(See first Aquinas listing for data common to all funds)

Sub-advisers: John McStay Investment Counsel, Sirach Capital Management, Inc.
Portfolio managers: Team managed
Investment objective and policies: Capital appreciation. Invests in a diversified portfolio of equity securities, primarily common stocks, of companies believed to have above average potential for growth in revenues, profits, or cash flow. May also invest in preferred stocks, convertible securities and warrants. May invest up to 20% of assets in securities of foreign issuers and use futures and options for hedging purposes.
Year organized: 1994
Ticker symbol: AQEGX
Discount broker availability: White
Qualified for sale in: All states
Dividends paid: Income - March, June, September, December; Capital gains - December
Portfolio turnover (3 yrs): 104%, 112%, 102%
Management fee: 0.80% (JMIC); 0.60% first $10M to 0.25% over $50M (Sirach)
Expense ratio: 1.49% (year ending 12/31/97)

AQUINAS EQUITY INCOME FUND ◆
(See first Aquinas listing for data common to all funds)

Sub-advisers: Beutel, Goodman Capital Management; NFJ Investment Group
Portfolio managers: Team managed
Investment objective and policies: Growth of capital and high current income. Invests at least 85% of assets in dividend-paying common stocks of large, conservative companies with market capitalizations of $2B or more. May invest up to 20% of assets in securities of foreign issuers and use futures and options for hedging purposes.
Year organized: 1994
Ticker symbol: AQEIX
Discount broker availability: White
Qualified for sale in: All states
Dividends paid: Income - March, June, September, December; Capital gains - December
Portfolio turnover (3 yrs): 42%, 32%, 40%
Management fee: 0.45% first $25M, 0.315% over $25M
Expense ratio: 1.37% (year ending 12/31/97)

AQUINAS FIXED INCOME FUND ◆
(See first Aquinas listing for data common to all funds)

Sub-advisers: Atlantic Asset Management Partners, LLC; Income Research & Management, Inc.
Portfolio managers: Team managed
Investment objective and policies: High current income with reasonable opportunity for capital appreciation. Invests primarily in a diversified portfolio of investment grade debt securities of government and corporate issuers, and in mortgage-backed securities. May invest up to 25% of assets in junk bonds, 20% in securities of foreign issuers and use futures and options for hedging purposes.
Year organized: 1994
Ticker symbol: AQFIX
Discount broker availability: White
Qualified for sale in: All states
Dividends paid: Income - declared and paid monthly; Capital gains - December
Portfolio turnover (3 yrs): 102%, 169%, 126%
Management fee: 0.38% fir $15M to 0.10% over $100M (AAM); o.40% firs $10M to 0.15% over $100M (IRM)
Expense ratio: 0.99% (year ending 12/31/96) (1.05% without waiver)

ARBOR FUND - OVB PORTFOLIOS
(See OVB Funds)

ARIEL INVESTMENT TRUST MUTUAL FUNDS
(Data common to all Ariel Trust funds are shown below. See subsequent listings for data specific to individual funds.)

307 North Michigan Avenue, Suite 500
Chicago, IL 60601
800-292-7435, 312-726-0140
fax 312-726-7473

Adviser: Ariel Capital Management, Inc.
Transfer agent: Investors Fiduciary Trust Co.
Minimum purchase: Initial $1,000, Subsequent $50; IRA/Keogh: Initial: $250; Automatic investment plan: Initial: $50
Wire orders accepted: Yes
Deadline for same day wire purchase: 4 P.M.
Qualified for sale in: All states
Telephone redemptions: Yes, $1,000 minimum
Wire redemptions: Yes, $1,000 minimum, $10 fee
Letter redemptions: Signature guarantee required over $25,000
Telephone switching: With other Ariel funds and Cash Resource money market funds
Number of switches permitted: May be limited to 5 per year
Shareholder services: IRA, SEP-IRA, Keogh, 401(k), 403(b), corporate retirement plans, electronic funds transfer (purchase only), systematic withdrawal plan min. bal. req. $10,000
IRA/Keogh fees: Annual $25

ARIEL APPRECIATION FUND
(See first Ariel Trust listing for data common to all funds)

Portfolio manager: Eric T. McKissack (1989)
Investment objective and policies: Long-term capital appreciation. Invests primarily in equity securities of relatively unkown undervalued companies with market capitalizations of $200M to $5B and the potential to achieve above average returns. May invest up to 20% of assets in bonds and other debt obligations or fixed-income obligations. Investments are environmentally and socially screened; avoids companies with poor environmental records or engaged in weapons manufacturing, nuclear energy production or doing business in South Africa.
Year organized: 1989 (name changed from Calvert-Ariel Appreciation fund in 1994)
Ticker symbol: CAAPX
Discount broker availability: *Fidelity, *Schwab, *Siebert, *White
Dividends paid: Income - December; Capital gains - December
Portfolio turnover (3 yrs): 19%, 26%, 18%
Management fee: 0.75% first $500M to 0.65% over $1B
12b-1 distribution fee: 0.25%
Expense ratio: 1.33% (year ending 9/30/97)

ARIEL GROWTH FUND
(See first Ariel Trust listing for data common to all funds)

Portfolio manager: John W. Rogers (1986)
Investment objective and policies: Long-term capital appreciation. Invests primarily in equity securities of undervalued companies with market capitalizations under $1.5B with high growth potential and the ability to achieve a high annual return on equity. May invest up to 20% of assets in bonds and other debt or fixed-income obligations. Investments are environmentally and socially screened; avoids investing in companies with poor environmental records or engaged in weapons manufacturing, nuclear energy production or doing business in South Africa.
Year organized: 1986 (name changed from Calvert-Ariel Growth Fund in 1994)
Ticker symbol: ARGFX
Discount broker availability: *Fidelity, *Schwab, *Siebert, *White
Dividends paid: Income - December; Capital gains - December
Portfolio turnover (3 yrs): 20%, 17%, 16%
Management fee: 0.65% first $500M to 0.55% over $1B
12b-1 distribution fee: 0.25%
Expense ratio: 1.25% (year ending 9/30/97)

ARIEL PREMIER BOND FUND
(See first Ariel Trust listing for data common to all funds)

Sub-adviser: Lincoln Capital Management Co.
Portfolio manager: Team managed
Investment objective and policies: Maximum total return; capital appreciation and income. Invests primarily in high quality, highly liquid fixed-income securities. Normally at least 80% of assets will be invested in such securities rated A or better. Implements decisions with regard to the level and direction of interest rates and by attempting to take advantage of perceived yield spread opportunities. May purchase any other type of income producing security, and may utilize derivatives, but only if the value of the derivative is based on an instrument in which the fund could invest directly.
Year organized: 1995 (investor class opened 2/1/97)
Discount broker availability: *Schwab, *White
Dividends paid: Income - declared daily, paid quarterly; Capital gains - annually
Portfolio turnover (1 yr): 218%
Management fee: 0.45%
12b-1 distribution fee: 0.25% (investor class only)
Expense ratio: 0.85% (eight months ending 9/30/97) (investor class)

ARK FUNDS
(Ark Funds were previously carried here due to a longstanding waiver of the loads. Effective 11/1/97, the waiver was removed. Funds are now load funds.)

ARMSTRONG ASSOCIATES ◆
750 North St. Paul
Suite 1300, L.B. 13
Dallas, TX 75201-3250
214-720-9101, fax 214-871-8948

Adviser: Portfolios, Inc.
Portfolio manager: C.K. Lawson (1967)
Transfer agent: Portfolios, Inc.
Investment objective and policies: Capital growth. Invests primarily in common stocks perceived to offer prospects for earnings growth or capital growth over a one to three year period, but may also invest in convertible securities and, in volatile markets, short-term debt instruments. Up to 15% of assets may be in illiquid securities.
Year organized: 1967
Ticker symbol: ARMSX
Minimum purchase: Initial: $250, Subsequent: None
Wire orders accepted: No
Discount broker availability: White
Qualified for sale in: CA, TX
Letter redemptions: Signature guarantee required
Dividends paid: Income - December; Capital gains - December
Portfolio turnover (3 yrs): 7%, 19%, 12%
Shareholder services: IRA, Keogh, corporate retirement plans, automatic investment plan, systematic withdrawal plan
Management fee: 0.80%
Expense ratio: 1.40% (year ending 6/30/97)
IRA/Keogh fees: Annual $7.50

ARTISAN FUNDS ◆
(Data common to all Artisan Funds are shown below. See subsequent listings for data specific to individual portfolios.)

1000 North Water Street, Suite 1770
Milwaukee, WI 53202
800-344-1770, 414-390-6100
fax 414-390-6139

Adviser: Artisan Partners, L.P.
Transfer agent: State Street Bank & Trust Co.
Minimum purchase: Initial: $1,000, Subsequent: $50; Automatic investment plan: Initial: $50
Wire orders accepted: Yes
Deadline for same day wire purchase: 4 P.M.
Qualified for sale in: All states
Telephone redemptions: Yes, $500 minimum

Wire redemptions: Yes, $5.00 fee
Letter redemptions: Signature guarantee required over $25,000
Telephone switching: With other Artisan Funds, $1,000 minimum
Number of switches permitted: Unlimited
Shareholder services: IRA, SEP-IRA, electronic funds transfer, systematic withdrawal plan min. bal. req. $5,000
IRA fees: Annual $10, Initial $5, Closing $10

ARTISAN INTERNATIONAL FUND ◆
(See first Artisan listing for data common to all funds)

Portfolio manager: Mark L. Yockey (1995)
Investment objective and policies: Maximum long-term capital growth. Invests generally in the common stocks of foreign companies perceived to have dominant or increasing market share in strong industries, and that are not trading at unsustainable or unusually high valuations. Countries are selected which are showing improving or rapidly increasing economic growth but do not appear to have overvalued markets. Fund may invest in other types of equity and debt securities without limit. May use options and futures and currency exchange transactions for hedging purposes.
Year organized: 1995
Ticker symbol: ARTIX
Discount broker availability: *Fidelity, *Schwab, *Siebert, *White
Dividends paid: Income - December; Capital gains - December
Portfolio turnover (1 yr): 104%
Management fee: 1.00% first $500M to 0.925% over $1B
Expense ratio: 1.61% (year ending 6/30/97)

ARTISAN MIDCAP FUND ◆
(See first Artisan listing for data common to all funds)

Portfolio manager: Andrew C. Stephens (1997)
Investment objective and policies: Maximum long-term capital growth. Invests primarily in equity securities, mostly common stocks, of companies with market capitalizations within the range of the S&P MidCap 400 Index, currently between $200M and $12B. This range will change as the index changes. Selections are made based on management's perception of identifiable 'franchise characteristics,' and perceptions of short-term undervaluation. May invest up to 25% of assets in foreign issues, including ADRs, up to 10% of assets in other investment companies, and up to 10% of assets in illiquid securities. May invest in debt securities without limit for defensive purposes, however any debt securities exceeding 35% of assets must be investment grade. May use a variety of derivative instruments for hedging, risk management or portfolio management purposes, but not for speculation.
Year organized: 1997
Discount broker availability: *Fidelity, *Schwab, *Siebert, *White
Dividends paid: Income - December; Capital gains - December
Management fee: 1.00% first $500M to 0.925% over $1B

ARTISAN SMALL CAP FUND ◆
(See first Artisan listing for data common to all funds)

Portfolio managers: Carlene Murphy Ziegler (1995), Millie Adams Hurwitz (1996)
Investment objective and policies: Maximum long-term capital growth. Invests at least 65% of assets in common stocks of small companies with market capitalizations of $1B or less that are perceived to be undervalued, out of favor or under-researched. May invest up to 25% of assets directly or indirectly in foreign securities, and may invest up to 35% of assets in debt obligations. May use options, futures or currency exchange contracts for hedging purposes.
Year organized: 1995
Ticker symbol: ARTSX
Special sales restrictions: Fund closed to new investors 2/27/96

Discount broker availability: *Fidelity, *Schwab, *Siebert, *White
Dividends paid: Income - December; Capital gains - December
Portfolio turnover (2 yrs): 87%, 105%
Management fee: 1.00% first $500M to 0.925% over $1B
Expense ratio: 1.41% (year ending 6/30/97)

ARTISAN SMALL CAP VALUE FUND ◆
(See first Artisan listing for data common to all funds)

Portfolio manager: Scott C. Satterwhite (1997)
Investment objective and policies: Maximum long-term capital growth. Invests at least 65% of assets in common stocks of small companies with market capitalizations of $1B or less that are perceived to be undervalued and under-researched. May invest up to 25% of assets directly or indirectly in foreign securities. May use options, futures or currency exchange contracts for hedging purposes.
Year organized: 1997
Ticker symbol: ARTVX
Sales restrictions: Fund will close when assets reach $400M
Discount broker availability: *Fidelity, *Schwab, *Siebert, *White
Dividends paid: Income - December; Capital gains - December
Management fee: 1.00% first $500M to 0.925% over $1B

ASIA HOUSE ASEAN GROWTH FUND
(Fund liquidated 8/97)

ASIA HOUSE FAR EAST GROWTH FUND
(Fund liquidated 8/97)

ASM INDEX 30 FUND ◆
15438 N. Florida Avenue, Suite 107
Tampa, FL 33613
800-445-2763, 813-963-3150
fax 813-968-4074

Adviser: Vector Index Advisors, Inc.
Portfolio manager: Steven H. Adler (1991)
Transfer agent: Star Bank, N.A.
Investment objective and policies: Total return: capital appreciation and current income. Invests in common stocks of large well-established companies, principally the 30 companies that comprise the Dow Jones Industrial Average (DJIA). Although the fund may invest in other companies, it is effectively an index fund that mirrors the performance of the DJIA.
Year organized: 1991 (name changed from ASM Fund 9/8/97)
Ticker symbol: ASMUX
Minimum purchase: Initial: $1,000, Subsequent: $100; IRA: Initial: $500
Wire orders accepted: Yes
Deadline for same day wire purchase: 3 P.M.
Discount broker availability: *Fidelity, *White
Qualified for sale in: All states except ND, SD
Wire redemptions: Yes, $1,000 minimum
Letter redemptions: Signature guarantee not required
Redemption fee: 0.75% if shareholder redeems shares more than 6 times per year
Telephone switching: With Flex-Fund Money Market Fund
Number of switches permitted: 6 round trips per year, 3 per quarter
Deadline for same day switch: 3; p.m.
Dividends paid: Income - March, June, September, December; Capital gains - December
Portfolio turnover (3 yrs): 265%, 391%, 340%
Shareholder services: IRA, automatic investment plan
Management fee: 0.60%
Expense ratio: 0.42% (year ending 10/31/97) (1.05% without waiver)
IRA/Keogh fees: Annual $8, Closing $7

ASSET MANAGEMENT FUNDS
(Data common to all Asset Management Fund portfolios are shown below. See subsequent listings for data specific to individual portfolios.)

111 East Wacker Drive
Chicago, IL 60601
800-527-3713, 312-856-0715
fax 312-938-2548

Adviser: Shay Assets Management, Inc.
Lead portfolio manager: Edward E. Sammons, Jr.
Transfer agent and administrator: PFPC, Inc.
Special sales restrictions: Designed for institutional investors, with objectives designed to comply with the regulatory and accounting guidelines necessary for financial institutions, but available to individual investors in specific states.
Minimum purchase: Initial: $10,000, Subsequent: None
Wire orders accepted: Yes
Deadline for same day wire purchase: 12 NN EST (1 P.M. EST for shareholders in the Pacific Time Zone)
Telephone redemptions: Yes
Wire redemptions: Yes
Letter redemptions: Signature guarantee required
Telephone switching: With other Asset Management Fund portfolios
Deadline for same day switch: 12 NN (1 P.M. EST for shareholders in the Pacific Time Zone)
Number of switches permitted: Unlimited
Dividends paid: Income - declared daily, paid monthly; Capital gains - December

ASSET MANAGEMENT FUND - ADJUSTABLE RATE MORTGAGE PORTFOLIO
(See first Asset Management listing for data common to all portfolios)

Investment objective and policies: High current income consistent with preservation of capital and liquidity. Invests at least 65% of assets in adjustable rate mortgage securities, with the remainder in U.S. Government or agency securities, private fixed rate mortgage-related securities, certificates of deposit, bankers acceptances with remaining maturities of nine months or less, and repurchase agreements. Fund maintains a weighted average maturity of one year or less.
Year organized: 1991
Ticker symbol: ASARX
Qualified for sale in: CO, CT, DC, FL, GA, IL, IN, LA, MS, NJ, NY, PA, TN, VA, WI, WY
Portfolio turnover (3 yrs): 74%, 60%, 68%
Management fee: 0.45% first $3B to 0.25% over $5B
12b-1 distribution fee: 0.25%
Expense ratio: 0.49% (year ending 10/31/97) (0.79% without waiver)

ASSET MANAGEMENT FUND - INTERMEDIATE MORTGAGE SECURITIES PORTFOLIO
(See first Asset Management listing for data common to all portfolios)

Investment objective and policies: High current income consistent with preservation of capital and liquidity. Invests at least 65% of assets in mortgage-related securities paying fixed or adjustable rates of interest. Portfolio maintains a dollar weighted average maturity of two to seven years.
Year organized: 1986 (name changed from Corporate Bond Portfolio on 6/2/92. Prior to name change Portfolio was invested primarily in investment grade corporate bonds.)
Ticker symbol: ASCPX
Qualified for sale in: CO, DC, FL, GA, IL, IN, NJ, NY, PA, TN, VA, WY
Portfolio turnover (3 yrs): 120%, 133%, 133%
Management fee: 0.35% first $500M to 0.10% over $1.5B
12b-1 distribution fee: 0.15%
Expense ratio: 0.49% (year ending 10/31/97) (0.59% without waiver)

ASSET MANAGEMENT FUND - MONEY MARKET PORTFOLIO
(See first Asset Management listing for data common to all portfolios)

Investment objective and policies: High current income consistent with preservation of capital and liquidity. Invests only in high quality assets that qualify as 'short-term liquid assets' for savings associations under the regulations of the Office of Thrift Supervision of the Department of the Treasury.
Year organized: 1982 (name changed from Short-Term Liquidity Portfolio in 10/94)
Ticker symbol: ASLXX
Qualified for sale in: CO, DC, FL, GA, IL, IN, NJ, NY, PA, TN, VA, WY
Management fee: 0.15% first $500M to 0.075% over $2B
12b-1 distribution fee: 0.15%
Expense ratio: 0.26% (year ending 10/31/97) (0.41% without waiver)

ASSET MANAGEMENT FUND - SHORT U.S. GOVERNMENT SECURITIES PORTFOLIO
(See first Asset Management listing for data common to all portfolios)

Investment objective and policies: High current income consistent with preservation of capital and liquidity. Invests only in high quality obligations that qualify as 'liquid assets' for savings associations under the current OTS Regulations. The portfolio invests at least 65% of assets in obligations issued by or fully guaranteed as to principal and interest by U.S. Government agencies or instrumentalities, certificates of deposit and other time deposits, bankers' acceptances with remaining maturities of nine months or less and repurchase agreements. The fund only invests in securities with remaining maturities of less than five years. Portfolio maintains an average dollar-weighted maturity of three years or less.
Year organized: 1982 (name changed from Intermediate-Term Liquidity Portfolio on 10/3/94)
Ticker symbol: ASITX
Qualified for sale in: CO, CT, DC, FL, GA, HI, IL, IN, NJ, NY, PA, TN, VA, WY
Portfolio turnover (3 yrs): 75%, 69%, 112%
Management fee: 0.25% first $500M to 0.10% over $1.5B
12b-1 distribution fee: 0.15%
Expense ratio: 0.50% (year ending 10/31/97)

ASSET MANAGEMENT FUND - U.S. GOVERNMENT MORTGAGE SECURITIES PORTFOLIO
(See first Asset Management listing for data common to all portfolios)

Investment objective and policies: High current income consistent with preservation of capital and liquidity. Invests at least 65% of assets in mortgage-related securities guaranteed by U.S. Government agencies or instrumentalities, with the remainder in U.S. Government or agency securities, certificates of deposit or other time deposits, repurchase agreements and interest rate futures contracts and options.
Year organized: 1984 (name changed from Mortgage Securities Performance Portfolio on 10/3/94)
Ticker symbol: ASMTX
Qualified for sale in: CO, DC, FL, GA, IL, IN, NJ, NY, PA, TN, VA, WI, WY
Portfolio turnover (3 yrs): 135%, 165%, 177%
Management fee: 0.25% first $500M to 0.10% over $1.5B
12b-1 distribution fee: 0.15%
Expense ratio: 0.53% (year ending 10/31/97)

AUSTIN GLOBAL EQUITY FUND ◆
375 Park Avenue, Suite 2207
New York, NY 10152
212-888-9292, 207-879-0001
fax 207-879-6206

Adviser: Austin Investment Management, Inc.
Portfolio manager: Peter Vlachos (1993)
Transfer agent and administrator: Forum Financial Corp.
Investment objective and policies: Capital appreciation. Invests primarily in common stocks and securities

convertible into common stocks of issuers based in the U.S., Europe, Japan and the Pacific Basin, perceived to have above average growth potential or attractive valuations. May invest in foreign securities directly and through use of ADRs. Will have at least 65% of assets invested in at least three countries, but no more than 25% in any one country, and at least 65% in common stock. Intends to have up to 25% of assets in the telecommunications sector. Up to 35% of assets may be in convertible securities. May use futures and options to hedge up to 25% of assets.
Year organized: 1993
Ticker symbol: AGEQX
Minimum purchase: Initial: $10,000, Subsequent: $2,500; IRA: Initial: $2,000, Subsequent: $1,000
Wire orders accepted: Yes
Deadline for same day wire purchase: 4 P.M.
Qualified for sale in: CA, CT, DC, FL, GA, HI, IL, MN, NH, NJ, NC, OH, PA, TX, VT, VA, WY
Telephone redemptions: Yes
Wire redemptions: Yes, $10,000 minimum
Letter redemptions: Signature guarantee required
Dividends paid: Income - annually; Capital gains - annually
Portfolio turnover (3 yrs): 45%, 94%, 35%
Shareholder services: IRA, SEP-IRA
Management fee: 1.50%
Administration fee: 0.25%
12b-1 distribution fee: Maximum of 0.25% (not currently imposed)
Expense ratio: 2.50% (year ending 6/30/97) (3.38% without waiver)
IRA fees: Annual $25

AVONDALE TOTAL RETURN FUND ◆
1105 Holliday
Wichita Falls, TX 76301
800-385-7003, 817-761-3777

Adviser: Herbert R. Smith, Inc.
Administrator: Investment Company Administration Corp.
Portfolio manager: Herbert R. Smith (1988)
Transfer agent: American Data Services, Inc.
Investment objective and policies: Maximum total return: income and capital growth consistent with reasonable risk. Invests primarily in higher quality fixed-income obligations, but may invest up to 85% of assets in common, convertible and preferred equity securities. Weighted average maturity of the portfolio will not exceed ten years, and no debt security will have an effective maturity exceeding 15 years. Up to 15% of assets may be in securities of foreign issuers.
Year organized: 1988
Ticker symbol: ATRFX
Minimum purchase: Initial: $1,000, Subsequent: $250; IRA/Keogh: Initial: $500, Subsequent $100; Automatic investment plan: Subsequent: $500
Wire orders accepted: Yes
Deadline for same day wire purchase: 4 P.M.
Qualified for sale in: AL, AR, CA, CO, DC, FL, GA, HI, IL, IN, MN, NM, NC, NY, OK, PA, TX, VA, WV, WY
Telephone redemptions: Yes
Wire redemptions: Yes, $1,000 minimum
Letter redemptions: Signature guarantee required
Dividends paid: Income - March, June, September, December; Capital gains - December
Portfolio turnover (3 yrs): 41%, 52%, 52%
Shareholder services: IRA, electronic funds transfer, systematic withdrawal plan min. bal. req. $10,000
Management fee: 0.70% first $200M to 0.50% over $500M
Administration fee: 0.15%
Expense ratio: 1.83% (year ending 3/31/97)
IRA fees: None

BABSON FUNDS ◆
(Data common to all Babson funds are shown below. See subsequent listings for data specific to individual funds.)

BMA Tower
700 Karnes Boulevard
Kansas City, MO 64108-3306
800-422-2766, 816-751-5900
Internet: http://www.jbfunds.com

Shareholder service hours: Full service: M-F 8 A.M.-4:30 P.M. CST; After hours service: prices,

yields, balances, last transaction, messages, DJIA, prospectuses, portfolio distributions
Adviser: Jones & Babson, Inc. (a wholly-owned subsidiary of Business Men's Assurance Company of America, itself a wholly-owned subsidiary of Assicurazioni Generali S.p.A., an insurance organization founded in 1831 based in Trieste, Italy)
Transfer agent: Jones & Babson, Inc.
Wire orders accepted: Yes, $1,000 minimum
Deadline for same day wire purchase: 4 P.M. (1 P.M. for money market funds)
Qualified for sale in: All states
Telephone redemptions: Money markets only, $1,000 minimum
Wire redemptions: Yes, $1,000 minimum, $10 fee
Letter redemptions: Signature guarantee required over $50,000
Telephone switching: With other Babson funds or the Buffalo funds, $1,000 minimum
Number of switches permitted: 15 day hold
Shareholder services: IRA, SEP-IRA, Keogh, corporate retirement plans, electronic funds transfer (purchase only), systematic withdrawal plan min. bal. req. $10,000
IRA fees: Annual $10, Closing $10
Keogh fees: Annual $15, Closing $15

D.L. BABSON BOND TRUST - PORTFOLIO L ◆
(See first Babson listing for data common to all funds)

Portfolio manager: Edward L. Martin (1984)
Investment objective and policies: Maximum current income and reasonable stability of principal. Normally invests at least 80% of assets in corporate bonds and U.S. Government or government guaranteed obligations with a weighted average maturity of more than five years. Up to 20% of assets may be in U.S. dollar-denominated Canadian Government or corporate debt securities.
Year organized: 1945 (formerly Babson Income Trust)
Ticker symbol: BABIX
Minimum purchase: Initial: $500, Subsequent: $50; IRA: Initial: $250; Keogh: Initial: $100; Automatic investment plan: Subsequent: $100
Discount broker availability: *Fidelity, *Schwab, *Siebert, *White
Dividends paid: Income - declared daily, paid monthly; Capital gains - December
Portfolio turnover (3 yrs): 59%, 61%, 50%
Management fee: 0.95%
Expense ratio: 0.97% (year ending 11/30/97)

D.L. BABSON BOND TRUST - PORTFOLIOS ◆
(See first Babson listing for data common to all funds)

Portfolio manager: Edward L. Martin (1988)
Investment objective and policies: Maximum current income and reasonable stability of principal. Normally invests at least 80% of assets in corporate bonds and U.S. Government or government guaranteed obligations with a weighted average maturity of two to five years. Up to 20% of assets may be in U.S. dollar-denominated Canadian Government or corporate debt securities.
Year organized: 1988
Ticker symbol: BBDSX
Minimum purchase: Initial: $500, Subsequent: $50; IRA: Initial: $250; Keogh: Initial: $100; Automatic investment plan: Subsequent: $100
Discount broker availability: *Fidelity, *Schwab, *Siebert, *White
Dividends paid: Income - declared daily, paid monthly; Capital gains - December
Portfolio turnover (3 yrs): 65%, 48%, 57%
Management fee: 0.95%
Expense ratio: 0.67% (year ending 11/30/97)

BABSON BUFFALO FUNDS ◆
(See Buffalo Funds)

BABSON ENTERPRISE FUND ◆
(See first Babson listing for data common to all funds)

Portfolio manager: Peter C. Schliemann (1985)
Investment objective and policies: Long-term, aggressive capital growth. Invests primarily in common stocks

of smaller, faster growing companies which at time of purchase are considered to be realistically valued in the smaller company sector of the market. Normally invests at least 80% of assets in this manner. Capitalizations range from $15 million to $300 million.
Year organized: 1983
Ticker symbol: BABEX
Special sales restrictions: Fund closed to new shareholders on 2/1/92. New accounts may not be initiated; existing accounts may be added to.
Minimum purchase: Initial: $1,000, Subsequent: $100; IRA: Initial: $250, Subsequent: $50; Keogh: Initial: $100, Subsequent: $50; Automatic investment plan: Subsequent: $50
Discount broker availability: Fidelity, Schwab, *White
Dividends paid: Income - December; Capital gains - December
Portfolio turnover (3 yrs): 22%, 24%, 13%
Management fee: 1.50% first $30M, 1.00% over $30M
Expense ratio: 1.08% (year ending 11/30/97)

BABSON ENTERPRISE FUND II ◆
(See first Babson listing for data common to all funds)

Portfolio managers: Peter C. Schliemann (1991), Lance F. James (1991)
Investment objective and policies: Long-term capital growth. Invests at least 65% of assets in common stocks of companies with market capitalizations between $250M and $1B; smaller, faster growing firms perceived at time of purchase to be realistically valued in the smaller company market sector. May also invest in U.S. Government agency issues subject to repurchase agreements.
Year organized: 1991
Ticker symbol: BAETX
Minimum purchase: Initial: $1,000, Subsequent: $100; IRA: Initial: $250, Subsequent: $50; Keogh: Initial: $100, Subsequent: $50; Automatic investment plan: Subsequent: $50
Discount broker availability: *Fidelity, *Schwab, *Siebert, *White
Dividends paid: Income - December; Capital gains - December
Portfolio turnover (3 yrs): 21%, 30%, 15%
Management fee: 1.50% first $30M, 1.00% over $30M
Expense ratio: 1.28% (year ending 11/30/97)

DAVID L. BABSON GROWTH FUND ◆
(See first Babson listing for data common to all funds)

Portfolio manager: James B. Gribbell (1996)
Investment objective and policies: Above-average total return over longer periods of time through the growth of both capital and dividend income; current yield secondary. Invests primarily in common stocks of progressive, well managed companies in growing industries. Fund tends to remain fully invested. May, however, invest without limit in convertibles, preferreds or investment grade bonds if deemed advisable.
Year organized: 1959 (formerly D.L. Babson Investment Fund)
Ticker symbol: BABSX
Minimum purchase: Initial: $500, Subsequent: $50; IRA: Initial $250; Keogh: Initial: $100; Automatic investment plan: Initial: $100, Subsequent: $50
Discount broker availability: *Fidelity, *Schwab, *Siebert, *White
Dividends paid: Income - June, December; Capital gains - June, December
Portfolio turnover (3 yrs): 20%, 33%, 17%
Management fee: 0.85% first $250M, 0.70% over $250M
Expense ratio: 0.83% (year ending 6/30/97)

D.L. BABSON MONEY MARKET FUND - FEDERAL PORTFOLIO ◆
(See first Babson listing for data common to all funds)

Portfolio manager: Brian F. Reynolds (1986)
Investment objective and policies: High income, safety of principal and liquidity. Invests in short-term, high quality debt instruments, U.S. Government oblig-

ations issued by the U.S. Treasury, other government agencies and instrumentalities, and repurchase agreements thereon.
Year organized: 1982
Minimum purchase: Initial: $1,000, Subsequent: $100; IRA: Initial: $250, Subsequent: $50; Keogh: Initial: $100, Subsequent: $50; Automatic investment plan: Initial: $100, Subsequent: $50
Check redemptions: $500 minimum
Dividends paid: Income - declared daily, paid monthly
Management fee: 0.85%
Expense ratio: 0.91% (year ending 6/30/97)

D.L. BABSON MONEY MARKET FUND - PRIME PORTFOLIO ◆
(See first Babson listing for data common to all funds)

Portfolio manager: Brian F. Reynolds (1986)
Investment objective and policies: High income, safety of principal and liquidity. Invests in short-term, high quality money market instruments.
Year organized: 1980
Ticker symbol: BMMXX
Minimum purchase: Initial: $1,000, Subsequent: $100; IRA: Initial: $250, Subsequent: $50; Keogh: Initial: $100, Subsequent: $50; Automatic investment plan: Initial: $100, Subsequent: $50
Check redemptions: $500 minimum
Dividends paid: Income - declared daily, paid monthly
Management fee: 0.85%
Expense ratio: 0.92% (year ending 6/30/97)

BABSON SHADOW STOCK FUND ◆
(See first Babson listing for data common to all funds)

Sub-adviser: Analytic Systems, Inc.
Portfolio managers: Peter C. Schliemann (1987), Roland W. Whitridge (1987)
Investment objective and policies: Long-term capital growth. Invests in a diversified portfolio of small company stocks called "Shadow Stocks." These are stocks that combine the characteristics of small stocks (as ranked by market capitalization - currently under $193M but this amount fluctuates- and other factors) and neglected stocks (those least held by institutions and least covered by analysts). Portfolio can be exposed to above average risk in anticipation of greater rewards. Will not purchase stocks with share prices below $5.
Year organized: 1987
Ticker symbol: SHSTX
Minimum purchase: Initial: $2,500, Subsequent: $100; IRA: Initial: $250, Subsequent: $50; Keogh: Initial: $100, Subsequent: $50; Automatic investment plan: Subsequent: $50
Discount broker availability: *Fidelity, *Schwab, *Siebert, *White
Dividends paid: Income - June; Capital gains - June
Portfolio turnover (3 yrs): 0%, 25%, 19%
Management fee: 1.00%
Expense ratio: 1.13% (year ending 6/30/97)

BABSON-STEWART IVORY INTERNATIONAL FUND ◆
(See first Babson listing for data common to all funds)

Investment counsel: Babson-Stewart Ivory International
Portfolio manager: John G.L. Wright (1988)
Investment objective and policies: Total return from market appreciation and current income. Invests primarily in a diversified portfolio of equity securities of established companies whose primary business is carried on outside the U.S. May purchase ADRs, EDRs, IDRs, and foreign stocks directly on foreign securities markets. May use forward foreign currency exchange contracts to protect against exchange rate fluctuations. Up to 20% of assets may be in companies located in developing countries, and up to 35% of assets may be in a single country.
Year organized: 1987
Ticker symbol: BAINX
Minimum purchase: Initial: $2,500, Subsequent: $100; IRA: Initial: $250, Subsequent: $50; Keogh: Initial: $100, Subsequent: $50; Automatic investment plan: Initial: $100, Subsequent: $50

Discount broker availability: *Fidelity, *Schwab, *Siebert, *White
Dividends paid: Income - June; Capital gains - June
Portfolio turnover (3 yrs): 40%, 33%, 37%
Management fee: 0.95%
Expense ratio: 1.19% (year ending 6/30/97)

D.L. BABSON TAX-FREE INCOME FUND - PORTFOLIO L ◆
(See first Babson listing for data common to all funds)

Portfolio manager: Joel M. Vernick (1986)
Investment objective and policies: High income exempt from federal income tax, consistent with capital preservation. Invests primarily in investment grade municipal securities and maintains a weighted average maturity of 10 to 25 years. Up to 20% of assets may be in securities subject to AMT tax treatment.
Year organized: 1980
Ticker symbol: BALTX
Minimum purchase: Initial: $1,000, Subsequent: $100; Automatic investment plan: Initial: $100, Subsequent: $50
Discount broker availability: *Fidelity, *Schwab, *Siebert, *White
Dividends paid: Income - declared daily, paid monthly; Capital gains - June, December
Portfolio turnover (3 yrs): 21%, 39%, 34%
Management fee: 0.95%
Expense ratio: 1.01% (year ending 6/30/97)

D.L. BABSON TAX-FREE INCOME FUND - PORTFOLIO MM ◆
(See first Babson listing for data common to all funds)

Portfolio manager: Joanne E. Keers (1989)
Investment objective and policies: High income exempt from federal income tax, consistent with preservation of capital and liquidity. Invests in investment grade municipal money market instruments. Up to 20% of assets may be in securities subject to AMT tax treatment.
Year organized: 1980
Minimum purchase: Initial: $1,000, Subsequent: $100; Automatic investment plan: Initial: $100, Subsequent: $50
Check redemptions: $500 minimum
Dividends paid: Income - declared daily, paid monthly
Management fee: 0.50%
Expense ratio: 0.58% (year ending 6/30/97)

D.L. BABSON TAX-FREE INCOME FUND - PORTFOLIO S ◆
(See first Babson listing for data common to all funds)

Portfolio manager: Joel M. Vernick (1986)
Investment objective and policies: High income exempt from federal income tax, consistent with capital preservation and price stability. Invests in investment grade municipal securities and maintains a weighted average maturity of two to five years; no issues are purchased with maturities of more than ten years. Up to 20% of assets may be in securities subject to AMT tax treatment.
Year organized: 1980
Ticker symbol: BBDSX
Minimum purchase: Initial: $1,000, Subsequent: $100; Automatic investment plan: Initial: $100, Subsequent: $50
Discount broker availability: *Fidelity, *Schwab, *Siebert, *White
Dividends paid: Income - declared daily, paid monthly; Capital gains - June, December
Portfolio turnover (3 yrs): 23%, 41%, 34%
Management fee: 0.95%
Expense ratio: 1.01% (year ending 6/30/97)

BABSON VALUE FUND ◆
(See first Babson listing for data common to all funds)

Portfolio manager: Roland W. Whitridge (1984)
Investment objective and policies: Long-term growth of capital and dividend income. Invests in common stocks which are considered undervalued in relation to earnings, dividends and assets. Includes

stocks that are unpopular and out of favor with general investors.
Year organized: 1984
Ticker symbol: BVALX
Minimum purchase: Initial: $1,000, Subsequent: $100; IRA: Initial: $250; Subsequent: $50; Keogh: Initial: $100, Subsequent: $50; Automatic investment plan: Subsequent: $50
Discount broker availability: *Fidelity, *Schwab, *Siebert, *White
Dividends paid: Income - March, June, September, December; Capital gains - December
Portfolio turnover (3 yrs): 17%, 11%, 6%
Management fee: 0.95%
Expense ratio: 0.97% (year ending 11/30/97)

BAILARD, BIEHL & KAISER FUNDS ◆
(Data common to all Bailard, Biehl & Kaiser funds are shown below. See subsequent listings for data specific to individual funds.)

950 Tower Lane, Suite 1900
Foster City, CA 94404-2131
800-882-8383
650-571-5800
fax 650-573-7128

Adviser: Bailard, Biehl & Kaiser, Inc.
Transfer agent: Chase Global Funds Services Co.
Minimum purchase: Initial: $5,000, Subsequent: $100
Wire orders accepted: Yes
Deadline for same day wire purchase: 4 P.M.
Telephone redemptions: Yes, $1,000 minimum
Wire redemptions: Yes, $1,000 minimum, ($10 fee for Diversa fund only)
Letter redemptions: Signature guarantee required over $50,000
Telephone switching: With other Bailard, Biehl & Kaiser funds
Number of switches permitted: Unlimited
Shareholder services: IRA, systematic withdrawal plan min. bal. req. $10,000
IRA fees: Annual $10, Initial $10

BAILARD, BIEHL & KAISER DIVERSA FUND ◆
(See first Bailard, Biehl & Kaiser listing for data common to all funds)

Portfolio managers: Peter M. Hill (1995), Arthur A. Micheletti (1991)
Investment objective and policies: Above average total return with below average risk through multiple asset allocation. Invests in up to nine classes of foreign and domestic securities - stocks, bonds, cash equivalents, real estate securities, precious metal-related securities and precious metals. Allocation varies with changing market conditions. May use forward currency transaction, futures contracts and options for hedging purposes.
Year organized: 1986
Ticker symbol: DVERX
Discount broker availability: Schwab
Qualified for sale in: AZ, CA, CO, CT, HI, MA, NV, NY, VA, WI
Dividends paid: Income - March, June, September, December; Capital gains - December
Portfolio turnover (3 yrs): 66%, 68%, 166%
Management fee: 0.95% first $75M to 0.65% over $150M
Expense ratio: 1.84% (year ending 9/30/97)

BAILARD, BIEHL & KAISER INTERNATIONAL BOND FUND ◆
(See first Bailard, Biehl & Kaiser listing for data common to all funds)

Portfolio managers: Arthur A. Micheletti (1991), Michael J. Faust (1993)
Investment objective and policies: Total return: long-term growth of capital and income. Invests primarily in fixed-income securities of foreign issuers, including corporations, governments, supra-national entities and U.S. issuers whose assets are primarily located or whose operations are primarily conducted outside the U.S., or whose securities are denominated in foreign currencies. May use forward currency contracts, options, futures contracts, options on futures contracts and swaps relating to debt securities and foreign currencies for hedging purposes.
Year organized: 1990 (name changed from Bailard, Biehl & Kaiser International Fixed Income Fund 1/26/96)
Ticker symbol: BBIFX
Discount broker availability: Schwab
Qualified for sale in: AZ, CA, CO, CT, HI, IL, MA, MD, NV, NY, PA, UT
Dividends paid: Income - March, June, September, December; Capital gains - December
Portfolio turnover (3 yrs): 33%, 61%, 179%
Management fee: 0.75%
Expense ratio: 1.35 (year ending 9/30/97)

BAILARD, BIEHL & KAISER INTERNATIONAL EQUITY FUND ◆
(See first Bailard, Biehl & Kaiser listing for data common to all funds)

Portfolio manager: Rosemary Macedo (1995)
Investment objective and policies: Long-term capital appreciation. Invests primarily in equity securities of foreign issuers, including U.S. companies whose assets are primarily located or whose operations are primarily conducted outside the U.S. May use forward currency contracts, options, futures contracts and options on futures contracts for hedging purposes.
Year organized: 1979 (name changed from The International Fund on 7/31/90)
Ticker symbol: BBIEX
Discount broker availability: Schwab
Qualified for sale in: AZ, CA, CO, CT, HI, MA, MD, NV, NY, PA, UT
Dividends paid: Income - December; Capital gains - December
Portfolio turnover (3 yrs): 67%, 103%, 174%
Management fee: 0.95%
Expense ratio: 1.44% (year ending 9/30/97)

BARON FUNDS
767 Fifth Avenue, 24th Floor
New York, NY 10153
800-442-3814, 800-992-2766
212-583-2100
fax 212-583-2150

Adviser: BAMCO, Inc.
Transfer agent: DST Systems, Inc.
Minimum purchase: Initial: $2,000, Subsequent: None; Automatic investment plan: Initial: $500, Subsequent $50
Wire orders accepted: Yes
Deadline for same day wire purchase: 11 A.M.
Qualified for sale in: All states
Telephone redemptions: Yes, $1,000 minimum
Wire redemptions: Yes, $1,000 minimum, $10 fee
Letter redemptions: Signature guarantee required over $25,000
Shareholder services: IRA, electronic funds transfer
12b-1 distribution fee: 0.25%
IRA fees: Annual $10, Initial $10, Closing $10

BARON ASSET FUND
(See first Baron listing for data common to all funds)

Portfolio manager: Ronald S. Baron (1987)
Investment objective and policies: Capital appreciation. Invests primarily in common stocks and other equity securities of companies with market capitalizations between $100M and $2B that are perceived to have undervalued assets or favorable growth prospects. May also invest in convertible bonds and debentures, preferred stocks, warrants and convertible preferred stocks. Fund may use options for hedging purposes.
Year organized: 1987
Ticker symbol: BARAX
Discount broker availability: *Fidelity, *Schwab, *Siebert, *White
Dividends paid: Income - December; Capital gains - December
Portfolio turnover (3 yrs): 13%, 19%, 35%
Management fee: 1.00%
Expense ratio: 1.30% (year ending 9/30/97)

BARON GROWTH & INCOME FUND
(See first Baron listing for data common to all funds)

Portfolio manager: Ronald S. Baron (1995)
Investment objective and policies: Capital appreciation; income secondary. Invests in equity securities of small (market capitalization $100M-$1B) and medium-sized ($1B-$2B) companies with undervalued assets or favorable growth prospects, and in corporate and government debt obligations. Up to 35% of assets may be in junk bonds and 15% in illiquid securities. May use options to increase income and hedge and sell short against the box. Holdings will generally be in companies with higher capitalizations than those in Baron Asset Fund.
Year organized: 1995
Ticker symbol: BGINX
Discount broker availability: *Fidelity, *Schwab, *Siebert, *White
Dividends paid: Income - December; Capital gains - December
Portfolio turnover (3 yrs): 25%, 40%, 41%
Management fee: 1.00%
Expense ratio: 1.40% (year ending 9/30/97)

BARON SMALL CAP FUND
(See first Baron listing for data common to all funds)

Portfolio manager: Clifford Greenberg (1997)
Investment objective and policies: Capital appreciation. Invests in equity securities of small companies with market capitalizations up to $1B with undervalued assets or favorable growth prospects, and in corporate and government debt obligations. Up to 35% of assets may be in junk bonds and 15% in illiquid securities. May use options to increase income and hedge and sell short against the box.
Year organized: 1997
Ticker symbol: BSCFX
Discount broker availability: *Fidelity, *Schwab, *Siebert, *White
Dividends paid: Income - December; Capital gains - December
Management fee: 1.00%

BARR ROSENBERG SERIES TRUST
(Data common to all Barr Rosenberg funds are shown below. See subsequent listings for data specific to individual funds.)

4 Orinda Way, Suite 300E
Orinda, CA 94563
800-447-3332, 510-253-6464
510-253-0141
Internet: http://www.riem.com

Shareholder service hours: Full service: M-F 8 A.M.-9 P.M. EST
Adviser: Rosenberg Institutional Equity Management
Administrator: BISYS Fund Services, Inc.
Lead portfolio manager: Barr Rosenberg (1996)
Transfer agent: BISYS Fund Services, Inc.
Special sales restrictions: Barr Rosenberg offers three classes of shares in each series; Institutional, Adviser and Select. **Select** is the only "retail" class for individual investors, therefore all non-performance data is relevant to the Select class. Historical performance and turnover data, however, is based on the portfolio for the **Institutional** class, which has existed since 1989.
Minimum purchase: Initial: $10,000, Subsequent: $500; Automatic investment plan: Subsequent $50
Wire orders accepted: Yes
Deadline for same day wire purchase: 4 P.M. (1 A.M. for Japan shares)
Qualified for sale in: All states
Sales charge: Each series is subject to two fund reimbursement fees; one at purchase and one at redemption. Each is payable to the fund, not the manager, and is levied "to eliminate the diluting effect such costs (transaction fees, costs of 'investing' money) would otherwise have on the net asset value of shares held by pre-existing (or remaining) shareholders." The fees are NOT levied on reinvestments of dividends and capital gains, distributions paid by the funds, in-kind investments, additional investments made by 401(k) participants and, curiously, investments made through the automatic investment plan. See individual funds for specific costs.

Telephone redemptions: Yes
Wire redemptions: Yes
Letter redemptions: Signature guarantee required over $25,000
Telephone switching: With the same class of shares in other Barr Rosenberg funds (fund reimbursement fees apply)
Number of switches permitted: Unlimited, 10 day hold
Shareholder services: IRA, systematic withdrawal plan min. bal. req. $12,000
Administration fee: 0.15% + $30,000 per fund
IRA fees: Annual $12, Initial $5, Closing $10

BARR ROSENBERG INTERNATIONAL SMALL CAPITALIZATION SERIES
(See first Barr Rosenberg listing for data common to all funds)

Investment objective and policies: Total return (capital appreciation and current income) greater than the Cazenove Rosenberg Global Smaller Companies Index excluding the U.S. (CRIEXUS). Normally invests at least 65% of assets in equity securities of companies with market capitalizations between $15M and $1B located outside the U.S. May invest up to 15% of assets in illiquid securities, and use currency futures contracts and purchase stock index futures for hedging purposes.
Year organized: 1996 (all classes)
Sales charge: 0.50% fund reimbursement fee
Redemption fee: 0.50% fund reimbursement fee
Discount broker availability: Fidelity, *Schwab, *White
Dividends paid: Income - December; Capital gains - December
Portfolio turnover (1 yr): 7%
Management fee: 1.00%
12b-1 distribution fee: Maximum of 0.50%
Expense ratio: 1.50% (6 months ending 3/31/97) (7.46% without waiver)

BARR ROSENBERG JAPAN SERIES
(See first Barr Rosenberg listing for data common to all funds)

Investment objective and policies: Total return (capital appreciation and current income) greater than the Tokyo Stock Price Index. Normally invests at least 90% of assets in equity securities of companies that are organized under the laws of Japan and that either have 50% or more of their assets in Japan or derive 50% or more of their revenues from Japan. It is fundamental, however, that the fund invest at least 65% of assets in "Japanese Securities" as described above. May invest up to 15% of assets in illiquid securities, and use currency futures contracts and purchase stock index futures for hedging purposes.
Year organized: 1996 (Select Shares; series began in 1989)
Sales charge: 0.50% fund reimbursement fee
Redemption fee: 0.50% fund reimbursement fee
Discount broker availability: Fidelity, *White
Dividends paid: Income - December; Capital gains - December
Portfolio turnover (3 yrs): 52%, 61%, 57%
Management fee: 1.00%
12b-1 distribution fee: Maximum of 0.50%
Expense ratio: 1.50% (year ending 3/31/97) (13.33% without waiver)

BARR ROSENBERG U.S. SMALL CAPITALIZATION SERIES
(See first Barr Rosenberg listing for data common to all funds)

Investment objective and policies: Total return (capital appreciation and current income) greater than the Russell 2000 Index. Normally invests the majority of assets in equity securities of companies with market capitalizations under $750M at the time of purchase. However, may invest without limit in common stocks of foreign issuers which are listed on a U.S. securities exchange or traded in the OTC market in the U.S. It is fundamental that the fund invest at least 65% of assets in "small capitalization" issues as described above.

May invest up to 15% of assets in illiquid securities and purchase stock index futures for hedging purposes.
Year organized: 1996 (Select Shares; series began in 1989)
Ticker symbol: BRSCX
Sales restrictions: fund closed to new investors 2/20/98
Sales charge: 0.25% fund reimbursement fee
Discount broker availability: Fidelity, *Schwab, *White
Redemption fee: 0.25% fund reimbursement fee
Dividends paid: Income - annually; Capital gains - annually
Portfolio turnover (3 yrs): 127%, 72%, 57%
Management fee: 0.90%
12b-1 distribution fee: Maximum of 0.50%
Expense ratio: 1.15% (year ending 3/31/97) (1.54% without waiver)

BARTLETT BASIC VALUE FUND ◆
(Became a multi-class load fund 7/21/97)

BARTLETT VALUE INTERNATIONAL FUND ◆
(Became a multi-class load fund 7/21/97)

BASCOM HILL BALANCED FUND ◆
(Fund merged into Mosaic Balanced Fund 6/13/97)

BASCOM HILL INVESTORS ◆
(Fund merged into Mosaic Investors Fund 6/13/97)

BEA ADVISOR FUNDS
(Data common to all BEA Advisor funds are shown below. See subsequent listings for data specific to individual funds.)

One Citicorp Center
153 East 53rd Street
New York, NY 10022
800-401-2230
fax 212-421-0453
Internet: http://www.beafunds.com

Shareholder service hours: Full service: M-F 8 A.M.-6 P.M. EST; After hours service: prices, yields, account balances, orders, last transaction, prospectuses, total returns
Adviser: BEA Assocs. (a wholly-owned subsidiary of Credit Suisse)
Administrator: PFPC Inc.
Transfer agent: State Street Bank & Trust Co.
Sales restrictions: Information here represents only the Advisor class of shares; the Institutional class requires $3M minimum. The Investor class is inactive; when available it will be no-load with higher 12b-1 fees.
Minimum purchase: Initial: $2,500, Subsequent: $250; IRA: Initial: $1,000, Subsequent: $100; Automatic investment plan: Initial: $1,000, Subsequent: $100
Wire orders accepted: Yes
Deadline for same day wire purchase: 4 P.M.
Qualified for sale in: All states
Telephone redemptions: Yes
Wire redemptions: Yes
Letter redemptions: Signature guarantee not required
Telephone switching: With other BEA Advisor funds
Number of switches permitted: Unlimited
Shareholder services: IRA, SEP-IRA
Administration fee: 0.125%
12b-1 distribution fee: 0.25%
IRA fees: Annual $10 (waived for balances over $10,000), Closing $10

BEA ADVISOR EMERGING MARKETS EQUITY FUND
(See first BEA Advisor listing for data common to all funds)

Lead portfolio manager: Richard W. Watt (1996)
Investment objective and policies: Long-term capital appreciation. Invests at least 80% of assets in equity securities of companies located in at least three emerging market countries as defined by the World

Bank, the International Finance Corporation or the United Nations, at least at the time of the investment. Will not necessarily seek to diversify holdings based on geography or levels of economic development. May invest the remainder of assets in corporate or government debt securities in emerging markets, including junk bonds. May borrow up to 33% of total assets, invest in securities of other investment companies, and engage in foreign currency hedging transactions.
Year organized: 1996 (Institutional class: 1993)
Discount broker availability: *Fidelity, Schwab (only through financial advisers), *White
Dividends paid: Income - December; Capital gains - December
Portfolio turnover (1 yr): 147%
Management fee: 1.00%
Expense ratio: 1.75% (10 months ending 8/31/97) (1.92% without waiver)

BEA ADVISOR GLOBAL TELECOMMUNICATIONS FUND
(See first BEA Advisor listing for data common to all funds)

Lead portfolio manager: Richard W. Watt (1996)
Investment objective and policies: Long-term capital appreciation. Invests at least 65% of assets in equity securities, including convertibles, of telecommunications companies, both foreign and domestic. The balance of assets may be invested in either equity or non-equity securities of companies outside of the industry. May borrow up to 33% of total assets, invest in securities of other investment companies, and engage in foreign currency hedging transactions.
Year organized: 1996
Discount broker availability: *Fidelity, Schwab (only through financial advisers), *White
Dividends paid: Income - December; Capital gains - December
Portfolio turnover (1 yr): 43%
Management fee: 1.00%
Expense ratio: 1.65% (10 months ending 8/31/97) (8.38% without waiver)

BEA ADVISOR HIGH YIELD FUND
(See first BEA Advisor listing for data common to all funds)

Portfolio managers: Team managed
Investment objective and policies: Long-term capital appreciation. Invests at least 65%, and up to 100%, of assets in corporate or government, foreign or domestic speculative high yield debt securities; "junk bonds." Fund has no restrictions regarding maturity or average durations. May borrow up to 33% of total assets, invest in securities of other investment companies, and engage in foreign currency hedging transactions.
Year organized: 1996 (Institutional class: 1993)
Discount broker availability: *Fidelity, Schwab (only through financial advisers), *White
Dividends paid: Income - March, June, September, December; Capital gains - December
Portfolio turnover (1 yr): 84%
Management fee: 0.70%
Expense ratio: 0.96% (10 months ending 8/31/97) (1.47% without waiver)

BEA ADVISOR INTERNATIONAL EQUITY FUND
(See first BEA Advisor listing for data common to all funds)

Lead portfolio manager: William P. Sterling (1996)
Investment objective and policies: Long-term capital appreciation. Invest at least 80% of assets in equity securities, including convertibles, of non-U.S. issuers. May invest without limit in emerging markets, however, intends to use only up to 40% of assets in such a manner. May invest up to 20% of assets in U.S. or foreign corporate or government debt securities, including junk bonds. May borrow up to 33% of total assets, invest in securities of other investment companies, and engage in foreign currency hedging transactions.
Year organized: 1996 (Institutional class: 1992)

Discount broker availability: *Fidelity, Schwab (only through financial advisers), *White
Dividends paid: Income - December; Capital gains - December
Portfolio turnover (1 yr): 126%
Management fee: 0.80%
Expense ratio: 1.43% (10 months ending 8/31/97) (1.53% without waiver)

THE BENDER GROWTH FUND ◆
(Fund has instituted a 1.00% 12b-1 distribution fee and a 1.00%, one year CDSC redemption fee for the Class C shares intended for individual investors)

THE BERGER FUNDS
(Data common to all Berger funds are shown below. See subsequent listings for data specific to individual funds.)

210 University Blvd., Suite 900
Denver, CO 80206
800-333-1001, 303-329-0200
shareholder services 800-551-5849
fax 303-331-8141
Internet: http://www.bergerfunds.com

Shareholder service hours: Full service: M-F 7:30 A.M.-6 P.M. CST. After hours service: prices, yields, balances, orders, last transaction, news and views, prospectuses
Adviser: Berger Assocs., Inc.
Transfer agent: DST Systems, Inc.
Minimum purchase: Initial: $2,000, Subsequent: $50
Wire orders accepted: Yes
Deadline for same day wire purchase: 4 P.M.
Qualified for sale in: All states
Telephone redemptions: Yes
Wire redemptions: Yes, $1,000 minimum, $10 fee
Letter redemptions: Signature guarantee required over $100,000
Telephone switching: With other Berger funds and the Kemper Cash Account Trust money funds
Number of switches permitted: 4 out per fund per year (MMs are unlimited)
Shareholder services: IRA, SEP-IRA, Keogh, 403(b), corporate retirement plans, automatic investment plan, directed dividends, electronic funds transfer, systematic withdrawal plan min. bal. req. $5,000
12b-1 distribution fee: 0.25%
IRA/Keogh fees: Annual $12 per account

THE BERGER BALANCED FUND
(See first Berger listing for data common to all funds)

Portfolio managers: Patrick S. Adams (1997), John B. Jares (1997)
Investment objective and policies: Capital appreciation and current income. Invests in a diversified portfolio of equity and fixed-income securities. The proportion of assets invested in each type varies according to perceived market conditions. Equities range from 50% to 75% and debt ranges from 25% to 50%, with a minimum of 25% of either type at all times. Equity is represented primarily by dividend paying mid- to large-cap companies although small caps may be represented, and debt is primarily government and corporate issues and preferred stocks. Both foreign and domestic securities are used. May invest without limit in convertibles, however only 20% of assets may be in convertibles of less than investment grade. May use options and futures and forward foreign currency contracts for hedging purposes.
Year organized: 1997
Ticker symbol: BEBAX
Group fund code: 213
Discount broker availability: *Fidelity, *Schwab, *White
Dividends paid: Income - March, June, September, December; Capital gains - December
Management fee: 0.70%

THE BERGER/BIAM INTERNATIONAL FUND
(See first Berger listing for data common to all funds)

Sub-adviser: BBOI Worldwide LLC (a joint venture between Berger Assocs., and Bank of Ireland Asset Management (U.S.) Ltd.)

Lead portfolio manager: Chris Reilly (1996)
Investment objective and policies: Capital appreciation. Fund invests all its assets in an underlying portfolio, which invests at least 65% of assets in equity securities of well established companies in at least five different countries outside the U.S. Companies will generally have market capitalizations exceeding $1B, and will be weighted towards Europe and the Far East. Fund has the freedom, however, to invest in companies of any size or in any country. May also invest in investment grade debt securities, and up to 20% of assets in convertible securities that are below investment grade. May invest up to 15% of assets in illiquid securities, and use forward foreign currency contracts for hedging purposes.
Year organized: 1996
Ticker symbol: BBINX
Group fund code: 660
Discount broker availability: *Fidelity, *Schwab, *White
Dividends paid: Income - December; Capital gains - December
Portfolio turnover (1 yr): 17%
Management fee: 0.90%
Expense ratio: 1.80% (11 months ending 9/30/97) (1.99% without waiver)

THE BERGER GROWTH AND INCOME FUND
(See first Berger listing for data common to all funds)

Portfolio managers: Patrick S. Adams (1997), Sheila J. Ohlsson (1997)
Investment objective and policies: Capital appreciation; moderate level of current income secondary. Invests primarily in common stocks of companies with favorable growth prospects that also provide current income. Fund also invests in government securities, corporate bonds, convertible securities and preferred stocks. Fund may invest in securities of foreign issuers without limit and use options, futures and forward foreign currency contracts for hedging purposes. Up to 15% of net assets may be in illiquid securities.
Year organized: 1966 (formerly the 101 Fund, then to Berger 101 Fund 6/19/90; changed to current name January 1996) (2 for 1 split on 12/15/89)
Ticker symbol: BEOOX
Group fund code: 44
Discount broker availability: *Fidelity, *Schwab, *Siebert, *White
Dividends paid: Income - March, June, September, December; Capital gains - December
Portfolio turnover (3 yrs): 173%, 112%, 85%
Management fee: 0.75%
Expense ratio: 1.50% (year ending 9/30/97) (1.51% without waiver)

THE BERGER MID CAP GROWTH FUND
(See first Berger listing for data common to all funds)

Portfolio manager: Amy Selner (1997)
Investment objective and policies: Capital appreciation. Invests at least 65% of assets in equity securities of foreign and domestic companies with market capitalizations between $1B and $5B perceived to offer strong earnings growth. The balance of the fund may be invested in companies of any size, or in government securities or other short-term investments. May invest up to 20% of assets in convertible securities rated below investment grade, and up to 15% in illiquid securities. May use options, futures and forward foreign currency contracts for hedging purposes.
Year organized: 1997
Group fund code: 215
Discount broker availability: *Fidelity, *Schwab, *Siebert, *White
Dividends paid: Income - December; Capital gains - December
Management fee: 0.75%

THE BERGER NEW GENERATION FUND
(See first Berger listing for data common to all funds)

Portfolio manager: William R. Keithler (1996)
Investment objective and policies: Capital appreciation. Invests primarily in equity securities of companies believed to have significant growth prospects,

particularly those who develop, manufacture, sell or provide new or innovative products, services or methods of doing business. May invest up to 15% of assets in unseasoned companies. Fund may also invest in securities of other types of companies, government securities, corporate bonds, convertible securities and preferred stocks. Fund may invest in securities of foreign issuers without limit, and use options, futures and forward foreign currency contracts for hedging purposes. Up to 15% of net assets may be in illiquid securities.
Year organized: 1996
Ticker symbol: BENGX
Group fund code: 344
Discount broker availability: *Fidelity, *Schwab, *White
Dividends paid: Income - December; Capital gains - December
Portfolio turnover (2 yrs): 184%, 474%
Management fee: 0.90%
Expense ratio: 1.87% (year ending 9/30/97) (1.89% without waiver)

THE BERGER ONE HUNDRED FUND
(See first Berger listing for data common to all funds)

Portfolio manager: Patrick S. Adams (1997)
Investment objective and policies: Long-term capital appreciation. Invests primarily in common stocks with emphasis on established companies with favorable growth prospects, regardless of size. May invest in convertible securities, government securities, preferred stocks and other senior securities. Fund may invest in securities of foreign issuers without limit, and use options, futures and forward foreign currency contracts for hedging purposes. Up to 15% of net assets may be in illiquid securities.
Year organized: 1966 (formerly the 100 Fund) (3 for 1 split on 12/15/89)
Ticker symbol: BEONX
Group fund code: 43
Discount broker availability: *Fidelity, *Schwab, *Siebert, *White
Dividends paid: Income - December; Capital gains - December
Portfolio turnover (3 yrs): 200%, 122%, 114%
Management fee: 0.75%
Expense ratio: 1.38% (year ending 9/30/97) (1.41% without waiver)

THE BERGER SELECT FUND
(See first Berger listing for data common to all funds)

Portfolio manager: Patrick S. Adams (1997)
Investment objective and policies: Capital appreciation. Invests the majority of its assets in the common stock of a core portfolio of twenty to thirty companies perceived to offer superior potential for earnings growth. Companies may be experiencing evolving product cycles, special situations or changing economic conditions creating pricing inefficiencies. May invest without limit in foreign securities and in companies with limited operating histories. May use options, futures and forward foreign currency contracts for hedging purposes. Fund is non-diversified.
Year organized: 1997
Group fund code: 214
Discount broker availability: *Fidelity, *Schwab, *Siebert, *White
Dividends paid: Income - December; Capital gains - December
Management fee: 0.75%

THE BERGER SMALL CAP VALUE FUND
(See first Berger listing for data common to all funds)

Sub-adviser: Perkins, Wolf, McDonnell & Co.
Portfolio manager: Robert H. Perkins (1985)
Investment objective and policies: Capital appreciation. Invests at least 655 of assets in companies with market capitalizations under $1B that are believed to have growth potential or to be undervalued relative to their assets. The balance of assets may be invested in companies of any size, or in government securities or other short-term investments. May invest in small

unseasoned companies and special situations. Fund is non-diversified. May use derivatives on a limited basis for hedging purposes.
Year organized: 1984 (1997 for investor shares) (split 10 for 1 on 9/28/94; name changed from the Omni Investment Fund 2/14/97)
Ticker symbol: BSCVX
Group fund code: 120
Sales restrictions: At 2/14/97, Small Cap Value became a two class fund, Investor and Institutional. Shareholders with accounts preceding this date are now holding Institutional shares and are paying no 12b-1 fees; they may continue to add to those positions. New retail accounts with minimums of less than $100,000 are now placed in Investor shares.
Discount broker availability: *Fidelity, *Schwab, *Siebert, *White
Dividends paid: Income - December; Capital gains - December
Portfolio turnover (3 yrs): 81%, 69%, 90% (composite history)
Management fee: 0.90%
Expense ratio: 1.65% (8 months ending 9/30/97) (1.66% without waiver) (new Investor shares cost basis)

THE BERGER SMALL COMPANY GROWTH FUND
(See first Berger listing for data common to all funds)

Portfolio manager: William R. Keithler (1993)
Investment objective and policies: Capital appreciation. Invests at least 65% of assets in equity securities of companies with market capitalizations under $1B that are perceived to offer the potential for rapid earnings growth. The balance of assets may be invested in larger companies, government securities, or other short-term investments. May invest securities of both domestic and foreign issuers and use options, futures and forward foreign currency contracts for hedging purposes. Up to 15% of net assets may be in illiquid securities.
Year organized: 1993
Ticker symbol: BESCX
Group fund code: 345
Sales restrictions: Fund closed to new investors 11/17/97.
Discount broker availability: *Fidelity, *Schwab, *Siebert, *White
Dividends paid: Income - December; Capital gains - December
Portfolio turnover (3 yrs): 111%, 91%, 109%
Management fee: 0.90%
Expense ratio: 1.66% (year ending 9/30/97) (1.67% without waiver)

SANFORD C. BERNSTEIN FUND, INC. ◆
(Data common to all Bernstein portfolios are shown below. See subsequent listings for data specific to individual portfolios.)

767 Fifth Avenue
New York, NY 10153
212-756-4097, fax 212-756-4404

Shareholder service hours: Full service: M-F 9 A.M.-5 P.M. EST
Adviser: Sanford C. Bernstein & Co., Inc.
Portfolio manager: Team managed
Transfer agent: State Street Bank & Trust Co.
Minimum purchase: Initial: $25,000, Subsequent: $5,000
Wire orders accepted: Yes
Deadline for same day wire purchase: 4 P.M.
Wire redemptions: Yes
Letter redemptions: Signature guarantee required
Dividends paid: Income - declared daily, paid monthly (except International Value and Emerging Markets); Capital gains - December
Shareholders services: IRA, Keogh, systematic withdrawal plan min. bal. req. $25,000
Administration fee: 0.10% (exceptions noted)
IRA fees: Annual $40
Keogh fees: Annual $60

BERNSTEIN CALIFORNIA MUNICIPAL PORTFOLIO ◆
(See first Bernstein listing for data common to all portfolios)

Investment objective and policies: Maximum return after federal and California state income taxes. At least 80% of assets in municipals, at least 65% in California obligations. May use non-municipal securities if they increase after-tax return (maximum federal and California) and use securities subject to AMT tax treatment without limit. May invest up to 10% in foreign securities, buy options, write covered options, and use futures contracts and options thereon.
Year organized: 1990
Ticker symbol: SNCAX
Qualified for sale in: CA, CO, DC, FL, GA, IL, IN, KY, LA, NE, NH, NJ, NC, OK, OR, PA, UT, WY
Portfolio turnover (3 yrs): 41%, 24%, 64%
Management fee: 0.50% first $1B, 0.45% over $1B
Expense ratio: 0.67% (year ending 9/30/97)

BERNSTEIN DIVERSIFIED MUNICIPAL PORTFOLIO ◆
(See first Bernstein listing for data common to all portfolios)

Investment objective and policies: Maximum total return after federal tax. Invests primarily in municipal securities with average weighted portfolio duration of three to six years. Adviser uses a variety of internally developed, quantitatively based valuation techniques. Fund may invest up to 10% in foreign securities, buy options, write covered options, and use futures contracts and options thereon for hedging purposes.
Year organized: 1989
Ticker symbol: SNDPX
Qualified for sale in: All states except SD
Portfolio turnover (3 yrs): 25%, 25%, 43%
Management fee: 0.50% first $1B, 0.45% over $1B
Expense ratio: 0.65% (year ending 9/30/97)

BERNSTEIN EMERGING MARKETS VALUE PORTFOLIO ◆
(See first Bernstein listing for data common to all portfolios)

Investment objective and policies: Long-term capital growth on a total return basis; capital appreciation plus dividends and interest. Invests primarily in equity securities, both directly and through ADRs, of both large and small companies domiciled, or with primary operations, in emerging markets countries. Portfolio will consist of securities perceived to be undervalued. The universe of possible countries is determined by the International Finance Corporation of the World Bank, and at least 65% of assets will be invested in at least three different qualifying countries. May also invest in fixed-income securities and use various derivative instruments both in an effort to enhance portfolio performance and for hedging purposes.
Year organized: 1995
Ticker symbol: SNEMX
Qualified for sale in: All states except MS, MT, SD
Purchase charge: 2.00% payable to the fund
Redemption fee: 2.00% payable to the fund
Dividends paid: Income - December; Capital gains - December
Portfolio turnover (2 yrs): 33%, 10%
Management fee: 1.25%
Administration fee: 0.25%
Expense ratio: 1.75% (year ending 9/30/97)

BERNSTEIN GOVERNMENT SHORT DURATION PORTFOLIO ◆
(See first Bernstein listing for data common to all portfolios)

Investment objective and policies: Higher return than money market funds and inflation, and limit state and local taxes. Invests primarily in securities of the U.S. Government and its agencies rated A or better, with an effective portfolio duration of one to three years. Fund may invest up to 10% in foreign securities, buy options, write covered options, and use futures contracts and options thereon for hedging purposes.

Year organized: 1989
Ticker symbol: SNGSX
Qualified for sale in: All states except SD, WA
Portfolio turnover (3 yrs): 80%, 155%, 49%
Management fee: 0.50% first $1B, 0.45% over $1B
Expense ratio: 0.69% (year ending 9/30/97)

BERNSTEIN INTERMEDIATE DURATION PORTFOLIO ◆
(See first Bernstein listing for data common to all portfolios)

Investment objective and policies: Current income consistent with a prudent level of credit risk. Invests at least 65% of assets in securities rated AA or higher, with an effective portfolio duration of three to six years. Fund may invest up to 10% in foreign securities, buy options, write covered options, and use futures contracts and options thereon for hedging purposes.
Year organized: 1989
Ticker symbol: SNIDX
Discount broker availability: Schwab
Qualified for sale in: All states
Portfolio turnover (3 yrs): 238%, 141%, 212%
Management fee: 0.50% first $1B, 0.45% over $1B
Expense ratio: 0.62% (year ending 9/30/97)

BERNSTEIN INTERNATIONAL VALUE PORTFOLIO ◆
(See first Bernstein listing for data common to all portfolios)

Investment objective and policies: Long-term capital appreciation and total return. Invests in equity securities of the 19 nations of the Morgan Stanley Capital International EAFE Index and Canada. Invests in 12 countries at a time on average (with a minimum of three countries), weighting each in proportion to the size of its economy. Stocks selected based on value characteristics for expected return. Fund hedges its current exposure to offset changes in foreign exchange rates.
Year organized: 1992
Ticker symbol: SNIVX
Discount broker availability: Schwab
Qualified for sale in: All states
Dividends paid: Income - December; Capital gains - December
Portfolio turnover (3 yrs): 26%, 22%, 30%
Management fee: 1.00% first $2B, 0.90% over $2B
Administration fee: 0.25%
Expense ratio: 1.27% (year ending 9/30/97)

BERNSTEIN NEW YORK MUNICIPAL PORTFOLIO ◆
(See first Bernstein listing for data common to all portfolios)

Investment objective and policies: Maximum after-tax total return for taxable residents of New York State. Invests at least 65% of assets in securities issued by New York State and its political subdivisions, instrumentalities, and agencies. Fund may use securities subject to AMT tax treatment without limit, invest up to 10% in foreign securities, buy options, write covered options, and use futures contracts and options thereon for hedging purposes.
Year organized: 1989
Ticker symbol: SNNYX
Qualified for sale in: CA, CO, CT, DC, FL, IL, IN, KY, LA, MI, MN, NE, NH, NJ, NY, NC, OK, OR, PA, TX, UT, WY
Portfolio turnover (3 yrs): 26%, 26%, 45%
Management fee: 0.50% first $1B, 0.45% over $1B
Expense ratio: 0.65% (year ending 9/30/97)

BERNSTEIN SHORT DURATION CALIFORNIA MUNICIPAL PORTFOLIO ◆
(See first Bernstein listing for data common to all portfolios)

Investment objective and policies: Maximum after-tax total return for taxable residents of California. Invests at least 65% of assets in securities issued by California State and its political subdivisions, instru-

mentalities, and agencies with a weighted average maturity of six to thirty months. May invest in securities subject to AMT tax treatment without limit.
Year organized: 1994
Ticker symbol: SDCMX
Qualified for sale in: CA, CO, DC, FL, GA, IL, IN, KY, LA, MN, NE, NH, NJ, NC, OH, OK, OR, PA, UT, VA, WY
Portfolio turnover (3 yrs): 75%, 61%, 89%
Management fee: 0.50%
Expense ratio: 0.74% (year ending 9/30/97)

BERNSTEIN SHORT DURATION DIVERSIFIED MUNICIPAL PORTFOLIO ◆
(See first Bernstein listing for data common to all portfolios)

Investment objective and policies: Maximum after-tax total return consistent with prudent level of credit risk. Invests no more than 25% of total assets in any one state. Portfolio maintains a weighted average maturity of six to thirty months. May invest in securities subject to AMT tax treatment without limit.
Year organized: 1994
Ticker symbol: SDDMX
Qualified for sale in: All states except SD
Portfolio turnover (3 yrs): 68%, 63%, 74%
Management fee: 0.50%
Expense ratio: 0.72% (year ending 9/30/97)

BERNSTEIN SHORT DURATION NEW YORK MUNICIPAL PORTFOLIO ◆
(See first Bernstein listing for data common to all portfolios)

Investment objective and policies: Maximum after-tax total return for taxable residents of New York. Invests at least 65% of assets in securities issued by New York State and its political subdivisions, instrumentalities, and agencies with a weighted average maturity of six to thirty months. May invest without limit in securities subject to AMT tax treatment.
Year organized: 1994
Ticker symbol: SDNYX
Qualified for sale in: CA, CO, DC, FL, GA, IL, IN, KY, LA, MN, NE, NH, NJ, NY, NC, OH, OK, OR, PA, UT, VA, WY
Portfolio turnover (3 yrs): 98%, 56%, 112%
Management fee: 0.50%
Expense ratio: 0.76% (year ending 9/30/97)

BERNSTEIN SHORT DURATION PLUS PORTFOLIO ◆
(See first Bernstein listing for data common to all portfolios)

Investment objective and policies: Exceed the total return of both money market funds and inflation. Invests in a diverse group of high-quality fixed-income municipal securities with an effective portfolio duration of one to three years. Differs from Short Duration by investing in highest pre-tax return obligations without regard to tax considerations of shareholders. Fund may invest up to 10% in foreign securities, buy options, write covered options, and use futures contracts and options thereon for hedging purposes.
Year organized: 1988
Ticker symbol: SNSDX
Qualified for sale in: All states except SD
Dividends paid: Income - declared daily, paid monthly
Portfolio turnover (3 yrs): 119%, 170%, 61%
Management fee: 0.50% first $1B, 0.45% over $1B
Expense ratio: 0.65% (year ending 9/30/97)

THE BERWYN FUND ◆
1189 Lancaster Avenue
Berwyn, PA 19312
800-824-2249, 610-640-4330
shareholder services 800-992-6757,
302-324-4495
fax 302-324-4499

Adviser: The Killen Group, Inc.
Portfolio manager: Robert E. Killen (1984)
Transfer agent: Rodney Square Management Corp.
Investment objective and policies: Long-term capi-

tal appreciation; current income secondary. Normally invests at least 80% of assets in common stocks believed undervalued. Fund may invest up to 20% of assets in fixed-income securities with potential for long-term capital appreciation, 10% in illiquid securities, and in real estate investment trusts. Fund is non-diversified.
Year organized: 1984
Ticker symbol: BERWX
Sales restrictions: Fund closed to new investors 1/1/98.
Minimum purchase: Initial: $10,000 (investor's aggregate with Berwyn Income), Subsequent: $250; IRA: Initial: $1,000; Keogh: None; Automatic investment plan: Initial: $50, Subsequent: $50
Wire orders accepted: Yes
Deadline for same day wire purchase: 2 P.M.
Discount broker availability: Fidelity, Schwab, Siebert
Qualified for sale in: All states
Telephone redemptions: Yes, $5,000 maximum
Wire redemptions: Yes, $1,000 minimum, $7 fee
Letter redemptions: Signature guarantee not required
Redemption fee: 1.00% for shares held less than 1 year, payable to the fund
Telephone switching: With Berwyn Income Fund, Rodney Square Money Market Fund, Rodney Square Tax Exempt Money Market Fund
Number of switches permitted: 4 per any 12 month period
Dividends paid: Income - December; Capital gains - December
Portfolio turnover (3 yrs): 32%, 32%, 24%
Shareholder services: IRA, Keogh, corporate retirement plans, systematic withdrawal plan
Management fee: 1.00%
Expense ratio: 1.21% (year ending 12/31/96)
IRA/Keogh fees: None

THE BERWYN INCOME FUND ◆
1189 Lancaster Avenue
Berwyn, PA 19312
800-824-2249, 610-640-4330
shareholder services 800-992-6757,
302-324-4495
fax 302-324-4499

Adviser: The Killen Group, Inc.
Portfolio manager: Edward A. Killen (1994)
Transfer agent: Rodney Square Management Corp.
Investment objective and policies: Current income with capital preservation. Invests primarily in fixed-income corporate securities, preferred stocks, securities of the U.S. Government, its agencies and instrumentalities, and common stocks paying cash dividends. May invest up to 100% of assets in junk bonds. May also invest up to 30% of assets in common stocks, and up to 10% in REITs.
Year organized: 1987
Ticker symbol: BERIX
Special sales restrictions: Fund closed to new shareholders on 8/15/95, reopened on 1/21/97.
Minimum purchase: Initial: $10,000 (investor's aggregate with Berwyn Fund), Subsequent: $250; IRA: Initial: $1,000; Keogh: None; Automatic investment plan: Initial: $50, Subsequent: $50
Wire orders accepted: Yes
Deadline for same day wire purchase: 2 P.M.
Discount broker availability: Fidelity, Schwab, Siebert, White
Qualified for sale in: All states
Telephone redemptions: Yes, $5,000 maximum
Wire redemptions: Yes, $1,000 minimum, $7 fee
Letter redemptions: Signature guarantee not required
Telephone switching: With Berwyn Fund (only if account was opened prior to 1/1/98), Rodney Square Money Market Fund, Rodney Square Tax Exempt Money Market Fund
Number of switches permitted: 4 per year
Dividends paid: Income - April, July, October, December; Capital gains - December
Portfolio turnover (3 yrs): 38%, 39%, 30%
Shareholder services: IRA, Keogh, corporate retirement plans, systematic withdrawal plan
Management fee: 0.50%
Expense ratio: 0.68% (year ending 12/31/96)
IRA/Keogh fees: None

BJURMAN MICRO-CAP GROWTH FUND
10100 Santa Monica Blvd., Suite 1200
Los Angeles, CA 90067-4103
800-227-7264, 310-553-6577
fax 310-553-4150

Adviser: George D. Bjurman & Assocs.
Lead portfolio manager: George D. Bjurman (1997)
Transfer agent and administrator: First Data Investors Services Group
Investment objective and policies: Capital appreciation. Invests primarily in equity securities of companies with market capitalizations between $30M and $300M at time of investment that are perceived to offer strong growth prospects. May invest without limit in relatively new and unseasoned companies, including IPOs. May use futures in an effort to enhance performance and for hedging purposes.
Year organized: 1997
Sales restrictions: Fund intends to close when assets reach $250M
Minimum purchase: Initial: $5,000, Subsequent: $500
Wire orders accepted: Yes
Deadline for same day wire purchase: 4 P.M.
Discount broker availability: *Schwab, *White
Qualified for sale in: All states
Telephone redemptions: Yes
Wire redemptions: Yes, $9 fee
Letter redemptions: Signature guarantee required over $10,000
Dividends paid: Income - December; Capital gains - December
Shareholder services: IRA, SEP-IRA, Keogh, 401(k), 403(b), automatic investment plan
12b-1 distribution fee: 0.25%
Management fee: 1.00%
IRA fees: Annual $12

BLANCHARD FUNDS
(Funds merged into Evergreen funds, a load company, in February of 1998)

BNY HAMILTON FUNDS
(Data common to all BNY Hamilton funds are shown below. See subsequent listings for data specific to individual funds.)

125 West 55th Street
New York, NY 10019
800-426-9363, 800-952-6276
212-495-1784

Shareholder service hours: Full service: M-F 8 A.M.-9 P.M. EST. After hours service: prices, yields, account balances, place orders, last transaction, prospectuses, total returns
Adviser: The Bank of New York
Administrator: BNY Hamilton Distributors, Inc. (a wholly-owned subsidiary of The BISYS Group, Inc.)
Transfer agent: BISYS Fund Services, Inc.
Minimum purchase: Initial: $2,000, Subsequent: $100; IRA: Initial: $250, Subsequent: $25; Automatic investment plan: Initial: $500, Subsequent: $50
Wire orders accepted: Yes
Deadline for same day wire purchase: 4 P.M.
Qualified for sale in: All states
Telephone redemptions: Yes
Wire redemptions: Yes
Letter redemptions: Signature guarantee not required (except MM)
Telephone switching: With other BNY Hamilton funds, minimum $500
Number of switches permitted: Unlimited
Shareholder services: IRA, SEP-IRA, systematic withdrawal plan min. bal. req. $10,000
Shareholder services fee: 0.25% (except for Treasury MM)
12b-1 distribution fee: 0.25% (except for Treasury MM)
IRA fees: None

BNY HAMILTON EQUITY INCOME FUND
(See first BNY Hamilton listing for data common to all funds)

Portfolio manager: Robert G. Knott, Jr. (1992)
Investment objective and policies: Long-term capital appreciation and a current yield greater than that of

the S&P 500 Index; equal emphasis placed on income and appreciation. Invests at least 65% of assets in equity or equity-related securities issued by domestic and foreign companies that pay dividends or interest. May invest up to 10% of assets in other investment companies. May use foreign currency contracts, options and futures, and purchase put contracts for hedging purposes.

Year organized: 1992
Ticker symbol: BNEIX
Discount broker availability: Fidelity, Siebert
Dividends paid: Income - monthly; Capital gains - December
Portfolio turnover (3 yrs): 65%, 58%, 58%
Management fee: 0.60%
Administration fee: 0.20% first $400M, 0.15% over $400M
Expense ratio: 1.01% (year ending 12/31/97)

BNY HAMILTON INTERMEDIATE GOVERNMENT FUND
(See first BNY Hamilton listing for data common to all funds)

Portfolio managers: Mark A. Hemenetz (1993), William Baird (1997)
Investment objective and policies: High current income consistent with preservation of capital, moderate stability in net asset value, and minimal credit risk. Invests at least 65% of assets in debt obligations either issued or guaranteed by the U.S. Government. Portfolio will have a dollar-weighted average maturity of not less than three or more than ten years. May invest in mortgage-backed securities, including CMOs, and asset-backed securities. May invest up to 10% of assets in other investment companies. May use options and futures for hedging purposes.
Year organized: 1992
Ticker symbol: BNIGX
Discount broker availability: Fidelity, Siebert
Check redemptions: $500 minimum
Dividends paid: Income - declared daily, paid monthly; Capital gains - December
Portfolio turnover (3 yrs): 41%, 57%, 48%
Management fee: 0.50%
Administration fee: 0.20% first $400M, 0.15% over $400M
Expense ratio: 1.08% (year ending 12/31/97) (1.11% without waiver)

BNY HAMILTON INTERMEDIATE INVESTMENT GRADE DEBT FUND
(See first BNY Hamilton listing for data common to all funds)

Portfolio manager: Christopher M. Capone (1997)
Investment objective and policies: High current income consistent with preservation of capital, moderate stability of net asset value, and maintenance of liquidity. Invests at least 65% of assets in investment grade corporate and government debt obligations. Fund maintains an average maturity of three to ten years, with the maximum average maturity of any single security at the time of purchase at less than 15 years. May use options and futures for hedging purposes.
Year organized: 1997
Discount broker availability: Fidelity, Siebert
Check redemptions: $500 minimum
Dividends paid: Income - declared daily, paid monthly; Capital gains - December
Portfolio turnover (1 yr): 81%
Management fee: 0.50%
Administration fee: 0.20% first $400M, 0.15% over $400M
Expense ratio: 1.06% (eight months ending 12/31/97)

BNY HAMILTON INTERMEDIATE NEW YORK TAX-EXEMPT FUND
(See first BNY Hamilton listing for data common to all funds)

Portfolio manager: Colleen M. Frey (1992)
Investment objective and policies: Income exempt from federal, NY state and NY city income taxes, while maintaining relatively stable principal. Will

attempt to invest 100%, and must invest at least 80% of assets in investment grade municipal debt obligations issued by New York State and the Commonwealth of Puerto Rico and their agencies and instrumentalities, all of which are exempt from federal, state and local taxes in New York. May, however, at times, invest more than 20% of assets in taxable debt securities. May invest up to 10% of assets in other investment companies. May use options and futures, and purchase put contracts without limit for hedging purposes.
Year organized: 1992
Ticker symbol: BNNYX
Discount broker availability: Fidelity, Siebert
Check redemptions: $500 minimum
Dividends paid: Income - declared daily, paid monthly; Capital gains - December
Portfolio turnover (3 yrs): 21%, 22%, 4%
Management fee: 0.50%
Administration fee: 0.20% first $400M, 0.15% over $400M
Expense ratio: 1.02% (year ending 12/31/97) (1.32% without waiver)

BNY HAMILTON INTERMEDIATE TAX-EXEMPT FUND
(See first BNY Hamilton listing for data common to all funds)

Portfolio manager: Jeffrey B. Noss (1997)
Investment objective and policies: Income exempt from regular federal income tax, while maintaining relative stability of principal. Invests primarily in municipal obligations issued by states, territories and possessions of the U.S. and the District of Columbia, whose interest incomes are exempt from federal taxes. Fund maintains an average maturity ranging from three to eight years. If necessary, fund may invest up to 20% of assets in taxable bonds.
Year organized: 1997
Discount broker availability: Fidelity, Siebert
Check redemptions: 500 minimum
Dividends paid: Income - declared daily, paid monthly; Capital gains - December
Portfolio turnover (1 yr): 30%
Management fee: 0.50%
Administration fee: 0.20% first $400M, 0.15% over $400M
Expense ratio: 1.15% (eight months ending 12/31/97)

BNY HAMILTON INTERNATIONAL EQUITY FUND
(See first BNY Hamilton listing for data common to all funds)

Sub-adviser: Indosuez International Investment Services
Portfolio managers: Jill Currie (1997), Eric Taze-Bernard (1997)
Investment objective and policies: Long-term capital appreciation. Invests primarily in equity securities of large, well capitalized non-U.S. issuers throughout the world. May also choose to gain exposure through ADRs. May focus up to 50% of assets in a single country, but ordinarily has at least 65% of assets diversified across at least three countries. May use foreign currency contracts, options and futures, and purchase put contracts for hedging purposes.
Year organized: 1997
Discount broker availability: Fidelity, Siebert
Dividends paid: Income - December; Capital gains - December
Portfolio turnover (1 yr): 36%
Management fee: 0.85%
Administration fee: 0.20% first $400M, 0.15% over $400M
Expense ratio: 1.52% (eight months ending 12/31/97) (1.75% without waiver)

BNY HAMILTON LARGE CAP GROWTH FUND
(See first BNY Hamilton listing for data common to all funds)

Portfolio manager: Charles C. Goodfellow (1997)
Investment objective and policies: Long-term capital appreciation; current income secondary. Invests

primarily in common stocks and convertibles of domestic and foreign companies with market capitalizations exceeding $3B that are believed to offer above average growth potential. Also invests in securities that offer a relatively high yield to serve as a resistance to downward pressure. May use foreign currency contracts, options and futures, and purchase put contracts for hedging purposes.
Year organized: 1997
Discount broker availability: Fidelity, Siebert
Dividends paid: Income - monthly; Capital gains - December
Portfolio turnover (1 yr): 37%
Management fee: 0.60%
Administration fee: 0.20% first $400M, 0.15% over $400M
Expense ratio: 1.07% (eight months ending 12/31/97) (1.16% without waiver)

BNY HAMILTON MONEY FUND (CLASSIC SHARES)
(See first BNY Hamilton listing for data common to all funds)

Portfolio manager: Richard Klingman (1997)
Investment objective and policies: High level of current income consistent with capital preservation and maintenance of liquidity. Invests principally in high quality short-term government, bank and corporate money market instruments.
Year organized: 1995 (Institutional class began in 1992)
Check redemptions: $500 minimum
Letter redemptions: Signature guarantee required over $50M
Dividends paid: Income - declared daily, paid monthly
Management fee: 0.10%
Administration fee: 0.10%
Expense ratio: 0.88% (year ending 12/31/97)

BNY HAMILTON SMALL CAP GROWTH FUND
(See first BNY Hamilton listing for data common to all funds)

Portfolio manager: John C. Lui (1997)
Investment objective and policies: Long-term capital appreciation. Invests in equity securities of both foreign and domestic companies with market capitalizations of less than $1.5B that are perceived to offer the potential for rapid growth. May use foreign currency contracts, options and futures, and purchase put contracts for hedging purposes.
Year organized: 1997
Discount broker availability: Fidelity, Siebert
Dividends paid: Income - December; Capital gains - December
Portfolio turnover (1 yr): 68%
Management fee: 0.75%
Administration fee: 0.20% first $400M, 0.15% over $400M
Expense ratio: 1.22% (eight months ending 12/31/97) (1.40% without waiver)

BOSTON PARTNERS FUNDS
(Data common to all Boston Partners funds are shown below. See subsequent listings for data specific to individual funds.)

One Financial Center, 43rd Floor
Boston, MA 02111
888-261-4073, 800-311-9783
617-832-8200, fax 617-832-8222

Adviser: Boston Partners Asset Management, L.P.
Transfer agent: PFPC Inc.
Sales restrictions: Funds are available in two classes of shares, Institutional ($100,000 minimum and lower 12b-1 fees) and Investor. A third class, Advisor, is slated for eventual launch. The only class we review here is Investor.
Minimum purchase: Initial: $2,500, Subsequent: $100
Wire orders accepted: Yes, $2,500 minimum
Deadline for same day wire purchase: 4 P.M.
Telephone redemptions: Yes

Letter redemptions: Signature guarantee required over $10,000
Telephone switching: With other Boston Partners funds
Number of switches permitted: 3 per year, at least 30 days apart
Shareholder services: IRA, SEP-IRA, automatic investment plan, systematic withdrawal plan min. bal. req. $10,000
IRA fees: Annual $10 per account

BOSTON PARTNERS BOND FUND

(See first Boston Partners listing for data common to all funds)

Lead portfolio manager: William R. Leach (1998)
Investment objective and policies: Maximize total return, with a secondary focus on current income. Invests at least 75% of assets in investment grade debt securities, including corporate and government obligations and mortgage- and asset-backed securities. Up to 25% of assets may be rated at the fifth or sixth level by the national rating agencies; bonds rated below the top four grades are considered speculative in nature, otherwise known as junk bonds. Fund is managed so that the average effective duration is generally within 5% of that of the Lehman Brothers Aggregate Bond Index. May invest up to 15% of assets in each of the following; collateralized mortgage obligations, Yankee Bonds, non-dollar denominated bonds of foreign or domestic issuers, and illiquid securities.
Year organized: 1998
Discount broker availability: *Fidelity, *Schwab, *White
Qualified for sale in: All states
Dividends paid: Income - monthly; Capital gains - December
Management fee: 0.40%
Administration fee: 0.125% ($75,000 minimum)
12b-1 distribution fee: Maximum of 0.25%

BOSTON PARTNERS LARGE CAP VALUE FUND

(See first Boston Partners listing for data common to all funds)

Portfolio managers: Mark E. Donovan (1997), Wayne S. Sharp (1997)
Investment objective and policies: Long-term capital growth; current income secondary. Invests at least 65% of assets in a diversified portfolio of equity securities of companies with market capitalizations of $1B or more that are perceived to be undervalued. Fund may invest the balance of assets in the equity securities of smaller companies, other investment companies, or in debt securities issued by U.S. banks, corporations or government agencies. May invest up to 25% of assets in a single industry and up to 20% of assets in foreign companies. May use futures and options and various other derivative instruments.
Year organized: 1997
Ticker symbol: BPLAX (institutional shares only)
Discount broker availability: *Fidelity, *Schwab, *White
Qualified for sale in: All states
Dividends paid: Income - December; Capital gains - December
Portfolio turnover (1 yr): 67%
Management fee: 0.75%
Administration fee: 0.125% ($75,000 minimum)
12b-1 distribution fee: Maximum of 0.25%
Expense ratio: 1.11% (eight months ending 8/31/97) (3.05% without waiver)

BOSTON PARTNERS MID CAP VALUE FUND

(See first Boston Partners listing for data common to all funds)

Portfolio manager: Wayne J. Archambo (1997)
Investment objective and policies: Long-term capital growth; current income secondary. Invests at least 65% of assets in a diversified portfolio of equity securities of companies with market capitalizations of between $200M and $4B that are perceived to be undervalued. Fund may invest the balance of assets in the equity securities of smaller or larger companies,

other investment companies, or in debt securities issued by U.S. banks, corporations or government agencies. May invest up to 25% of assets in a single industry and up to 20% of assets in foreign companies. May use futures and options and various other derivative instruments.
Year organized: 1997
Discount broker availability: *Fidelity, *Schwab, *White
Qualified for sale in: All states
Dividends paid: Income - December; Capital gains - December
Management fee: 0.80%
Administration fee: 0.125% ($75,000 minimum)
12b-1 distribution fee: Maximum of 0.25%
Expense ratio: 1.10% (three months ending 8/31/97) (12.62% without waiver)

BOSTON 1784 FUNDS ◆

(Data common to all Boston 1784 funds are shown below. See subsequent listings for data specific to individual funds.)

P.O. Box 8524
Boston, MA 02266-8524
800-252-1784
Internet: http://www.boston1784funds.com

Shareholder service hours: Full service: M-F 8 A.M.-8 P.M., Sat. 9 A.M.-4 P.M., EST; After hours service: prices, balances, orders, prospectuses
Adviser: BankBoston (a wholly-owned subsidiary of BankBoston Corp.)
Administrator: SEI Fund Resources
Transfer agent: Boston Financial Data Services
Minimum purchase: Initial: $1,000, Subsequent: $250; IRA/Keogh: Initial: $250; Automatic investment plan: Subsequent: $50
Wire orders accepted: Yes
Deadline for same day wire purchase: 4 P.M. (12 NN for money market funds)
Qualified for sale in: All states (exceptions noted)
Telephone redemptions: Yes
Wire redemptions: Yes, $12 fee
Letter redemptions: Signature guarantee required over $100,000
Telephone switching: With other Boston 1784 funds
Number of switches permitted: Unlimited
Shareholder services: IRA, SEP-IRA, Keogh, 401(k), electronic funds transfer, systematic withdrawal plan min. bal. req. $10,000
Administration fee: 0.85% first $5B, 0.45% over $5B (of complex aggregate)
12b-1 distribution fee: Maximum of 0.25% (not currently imposed; does not apply to Money Markets)
IRA/Keogh fees: Annual $15

BOSTON 1784 ASSET ALLOCATION FUND ◆

(See first Boston 1784 listing for data common to all funds)

Portfolio managers: Emmett M. Wright (1997), Michael R. Pelosi (1997)
Investment objective and policies: Favorable total return: current income and capital appreciation, consistent with capital preservation. Normally invests 30% to 70% of assets in equity securities of companies larger than $250M, 30% to 60% in investment grade intermediate- and long-term fixed-income securities, and 0% to 40% in short-term debt securities or money market instruments. Allocation of assets is adjusted to reflect perceived changes in economic and market conditions. May invest up to 25% of assets in foreign securities and 15% in illiquid securities. May use futures and options in an effort to increase return and for hedging purposes.
Year organized: 1993
Ticker symbol: SEAXX
Discount broker availability: Fidelity, Siebert, *White
Dividends paid: Income - quarterly; Capital gains - annually
Portfolio turnover (3 yrs): 24%, 40%, 67%
Management fee: 0.74%
Expense ratio: 1.07% (year ending 5/31/97) (1.37% without waiver)

BOSTON 1784 CONNECTICUT TAX-EXEMPT INCOME FUND ◆

(See first Boston 1784 listing for data common to all funds)

Portfolio managers: David H. Thompson (1995), Carl W. Pappo (1996)
Investment objective and policies: Current income exempt from federal and Connecticut state income taxes; capital preservation secondary. Invests primarily in investment grade Connecticut municipal securities. Portfolio generally maintains a dollar-weighted average maturity of five to ten years. May invest up to 20% of assets in securities subject to AMT tax treatment, and 15% in illiquid securities.
Year organized: 1994
Ticker symbol: SCTEX
Discount broker availability: Fidelity, *Schwab, Siebert, *White
Qualified for sale in: CT
Dividends paid: Income - declared daily, paid monthly; Capital gains - annually
Portfolio turnover (3 yrs): 4%, 20%, 36%
Management fee: 0.74%
Expense ratio: 0.76% (year ending 5/31/97) (1.17% without waiver)

BOSTON 1784 FLORIDA TAX-EXEMPT INCOME FUND ◆

(See first Boston 1784 listing for data common to all funds)

Portfolio managers: David H. Thompson (1997), Susan A. Sanderson (1997)
Investment objective and policies: Current income exempt from federal income and Florida personal intangible property taxes; capital preservation secondary. Invests primarily in investment grade Florida municipal securities. Portfolio generally maintains a dollar-weighted average maturity of five to ten years. May invest up to 20% of assets in securities subject to AMT tax treatment, and 15% in illiquid securities.
Year organized: 1997
Ticker symbol: SFTEX
Discount broker availability: Fidelity, Siebert, *White
Qualified for sale in: FL
Dividends paid: Income - declared daily, paid monthly; Capital gains - annually
Management fee: 0.74%

BOSTON 1784 GROWTH FUND ◆

(See first Boston 1784 listing for data common to all funds)

Portfolio managers: Eugene D. Takach (1996), Theodore E. Ober (1996)
Investment objective and policies: Long-term capital appreciation; income incidental. Invests at least 65% of assets in common stocks of U.S. and foreign issuers with market capitalizations of more than $250M. Emphasizes sound companies with records of growth in both earnings and dividends. May invest up to 35% of assets in non-convertible debt, preferred stocks or money markets. May also invest up to 25% of assets in securities of foreign issuers and 15% in illiquid securities. Fund may use futures and options in an effort to increase income and for hedging purposes.
Year organized: 1996
Ticker symbol: SEGRX
Discount broker availability: Fidelity, Siebert, *White
Dividends paid: Income - annually; Capital gains - annually
Portfolio turnover (1 yr): 57%
Management fee: 0.74%
Expense ratio: 0.77% (year ending 5/31/97) (1.15% without waiver)

BOSTON 1784 GROWTH AND INCOME FUND ◆

(See first Boston 1784 listing for data common to all funds)

Portfolio managers: Eugene D. Takach (1993), Theodore E. Ober (1993)
Investment objective and policies: Long-term capital growth; income secondary. Invests at least 65% of

assets in common stocks of U.S. and foreign issuers with market capitalizations of more than $250M. Emphasizes sound companies with records of growth in both earnings and dividends. May invest up to 25% of assets in securities of foreign issuers and 15% in illiquid securities. Fund may use futures and options in an effort to increase income and for hedging purposes.
Year organized: 1993
Ticker symbol: SEGWX
Discount broker availability: Fidelity, Siebert, *White
Dividends paid: Income - quarterly; Capital gains - annually
Portfolio turnover (3 yrs): 15%, 39%, 39%
Management fee: 0.74%
Expense ratio: 0.92% (year ending 5/31/97) (1.19% without waiver)

BOSTON 1784 INCOME FUND ◆
(See first Boston 1784 listing for data common to all funds)

Portfolio managers: Emmett M. Wright (1995), Todd A. Finkelstein (1997)
Investment objective and policies: Maximum current income; capital preservation. Invests primarily in investment grade debt securities. Portfolio generally maintains a dollar-weighted average maturity of seven to 30 years. May invest up to 30% of assets in securities of foreign issuers and 15% in illiquid securities. May use futures and options in an effort to increase income and for hedging purposes.
Year organized: 1994
Ticker symbol: SEINX
Discount broker availability: Fidelity, Siebert, *White
Dividends paid: Income - declared daily, paid monthly; Capital gains - annually
Portfolio turnover (3 yrs): 79%, 101%, 81%
Management fee: 0.74%
Expense ratio: 0.80% (year ending 5/31/97) (1.15% without waiver)

BOSTON 1784 INTERNATIONAL EQUITY FUND ◆
(See first Boston 1784 listing for data common to all funds)

Co-adviser: Kleinwort Benson Investment Management Americas, Inc.
Portfolio managers: Kenton J. Ide (1995), Juliet Cohn (1995)
Investment objective and policies: Long-term capital growth; income incidental. Invests at least 65% of assets in equity securities of issuers from at least three countries other than the U.S. Emphasizes companies with strong growth prospects and market capitalizations of at least $100M. May invest in emerging market countries and have up to 15% of assets in illiquid securities. Fund may use futures and options in an effort to increase income and for hedging purposes.
Year organized: 1995
Ticker symbol: SEEQX
Discount broker availability: Fidelity, Siebert, *White
Dividends paid: Income - annually; Capital gains - annually
Portfolio turnover (2 yrs): 23%, 16%
Management fee: 1.00%
Expense ratio: 1.27% (year ending 5/31/97) (1.52% without waiver)

BOSTON 1784 MASSACHUSETTS TAX-EXEMPT INCOME FUND ◆
(See first Boston 1784 listing for data common to all funds)

Portfolio manager: Susan A. Sanderson (1993)
Investment objective and policies: Current income exempt from federal and Massachusetts state income taxes, consistent with preservation of capital. Invests primarily in investment grade Massachusetts municipal securities. Portfolio generally maintains a dollar-weighted average maturity of five to ten years. May invest up to 20% of assets in securities subject to AMT tax treatment, and 15% in illiquid securities.

Year organized: 1993
Ticker symbol: SEMAX
Discount broker availability: Fidelity, *Schwab, Siebert, *White
Qualified for sale in: MA
Dividends paid: Income - declared daily, paid monthly; Capital gains - annually
Portfolio turnover (3 yrs): 9%, 47%, 35%
Management fee: 0.74%
Expense ratio: 0.79% (year ending 5/31/97) (1.18% without waiver)

BOSTON 1784 PRIME MONEY MARKET FUND ◆
(See first Boston 1784 listing for data common to all funds)

Portfolio managers: Mary K. Werler (1996), Lisa Winslow LeBoeuf (1996)
Investment objective and policies: Current income consistent with preservation of principal and liquidity. Invests primarily in high quality short-term money market securities issued by the U.S. Government, corporations, and bank obligations.
Year organized: 1991 (prior to 12/9/96 fund was BayFunds MM Portfolio)
Check redemptions: $250 minimum
Dividends paid: Income - declared daily, paid monthly
Management fee: 0.40%
Expense ratio: 0.65% (year ending 5/31/97) (0.75% without waiver)

BOSTON 1784 RHODE ISLAND TAX-EXEMPT INCOME FUND ◆
(See first Boston 1784 listing for data common to all funds)

Portfolio managers: David H. Thompson (1995), Carl W. Pappo (1996)
Investment objective and policies: Current income exempt from federal and Rhode Island state income taxes; capital preservation secondary. Invests primarily in investment grade Rhode Island municipal securities. Portfolio generally maintains a dollar-weighted average maturity of five to ten years. May invest up to 20% of assets in securities subject to AMT tax treatment, and 15% in illiquid securities.
Year organized: 1994
Ticker symbol: SERIX
Discount broker availability: Fidelity, *Schwab, Siebert, *White
Qualified for sale in: RI
Dividends paid: Income - declared daily, paid monthly; Capital gains - annually
Portfolio turnover (3 yrs): 8%, 20%, 58%
Management fee: 0.74%
Expense ratio: 0.79% (year ending 5/31/97) (1.21% without waiver)

BOSTON 1784 SHORT-TERM INCOME FUND ◆
(See first Boston 1784 listing for data common to all funds)

Portfolio manager: Mary K. Werler (1994)
Investment objective and policies: Maximum current income; capital preservation secondary. Invests primarily in investment grade debt securities. Portfolio generally maintains a dollar-weighted average maturity of three years or less. May invest up to 30% of assets in securities of foreign issuers and 15% in illiquid securities. May use futures and options in an effort to increase income and for hedging purposes.
Year organized: 1994
Ticker symbol: SESTX
Discount broker availability: Fidelity, Siebert, *White
Check redemptions: $250 minimum
Dividends paid: Income - declared daily, paid monthly; Capital gains - annually
Portfolio turnover (3 yrs): 128%, 95%, 85%
Management fee: 0.50%
Expense ratio: 0.63% (year ending 5/31/97) (0.93% without waiver)

BOSTON 1784 TAX-EXEMPT MEDIUM-TERM INCOME FUND ◆
(See first Boston 1784 listing for data common to all funds)

Portfolio managers: David H. Thompson (1993), Carl W. Pappo (1996)
Investment objective and policies: Current income exempt from federal income taxes, consistent with capital preservation. Invests primarily in investment grade municipal securities. Portfolio generally maintains a dollar-weighted average maturity of five to ten years. May invest up to 20% of assets in securities subject to AMT tax treatment, 15% in illiquid securities, and use futures and options for hedging purposes.
Year organized: 1993
Ticker symbol: SETMX
Discount broker availability: Fidelity, *Schwab, Siebert, *White
Dividends paid: Income - declared daily, paid monthly; Capital gains - annually
Portfolio turnover (3 yrs): 33%, 37%, 75%
Management fee: 0.74%
Expense ratio: 0.80% (year ending 5/31/97) (1.17% without waiver)

BOSTON 1784 TAX-FREE MONEY MARKET FUND ◆
(See first Boston 1784 listing for data common to all funds)

Portfolio manager: James L. Bosland (1993)
Investment objective and policies: Current income exempt from federal income taxes, consistent with preservation of principal and liquidity. Invests at least 80% of assets in investment grade municipal money market securities. May invest up to 20% of assets in taxable securities.
Year organized: 1993
Ticker symbol: SETXX
Check redemptions: $250 minimum
Dividends paid: Income - declared daily, paid monthly
Management fee: 0.40%
Expense ratio: 0.54% (year ending 5/31/97) (0.56% without waiver)

BOSTON 1784 U.S. GOVERNMENT MEDIUM-TERM INCOME FUND ◆
(See first Boston 1784 listing for data common to all funds)

Portfolio manager: Emmett M. Wright (1995)
Investment objective and policies: Current income consistent with capital preservation. Invests at least 65% of assets in obligations issued or guaranteed as to payment of principal and interest by the U.S. Government or its agencies or instrumentalities. Portfolio generally maintains a dollar-weighted average maturity of three to ten years. May invest substantially in mortgage-backed securities and have up to 15% of assets in illiquid securities. May use futures and options for hedging purposes.
Year organized: 1993
Ticker symbol: SEGTX
Discount broker availability: Fidelity, Siebert, *White
Dividends paid: Income - declared daily, paid monthly; Capital gains - annually
Portfolio turnover (3 yrs): 98%, 159%, 142%
Management fee: 0.74%
Expense ratio: 0.79% (year ending 5/31/97) (1.16% without waiver)

BOSTON 1784 U.S. TREASURY MONEY MARKET FUND ◆
(See first Boston 1784 listing for data common to all funds)

Portfolio managers: Emmett M. Wright (1997), Lisa Winslow LeBoeuf (1997)
Investment objective and policies: Current income consistent with preservation of principal and liquidity. Invests at least 65% of assets in money market securities issued by the U.S. Treasury. Balance is ordinarily invested in guaranteed issues of other government entities.

Year organized: 1993
Ticker symbol: STRXX
Check redemptions: $250 minimum
Dividends paid: Income - declared daily, paid monthly
Management fee: 0.40%
Expense ratio: 0.64% (year ending 5/31/97) (0.72% without waiver)

BRAMWELL GROWTH FUND
745 Fifth Avenue
New York NY 10151
800-272-6227, 212-308-0505
fax 212-308-2551

Adviser: Bramwell Capital Management, Inc.
Administrator: Sunstone Financial Group, Inc.
Portfolio manager: Elizabeth R. Bramwell (1994)
Transfer agent: Firstar Trust Co.
Investment objective and policies: Long-term capital growth; current income secondary. Invests in a diversified portfolio of equity securities of companies thought to have above average growth prospects, primarily common stock and high-grade securities convertible into common stock. May also hold cash or cash equivalents and invest in U.S. Government obligations. May hold up to 15% in illiquid or restricted securities, and up to 25% in securities of foreign issuers purchased either directly or through ADRs. May use short sales, options, futures and forward foreign currency contracts for hedging purposes.
Year organized: 1994
Ticker symbol: BRGRX
Minimum purchase: Initial: $1,000, Subsequent: $100; IRA: Initial: $500; Automatic investment plan: Initial: $50, Subsequent: $50
Wire orders accepted: Yes, $1,000 minimum
Deadline for same day wire purchase: 4 P.M.
Discount broker availability: *Fidelity, *Schwab, *Siebert, *White
Qualified for sale in: All states
Wire redemptions: Yes, $12 fee
Letter redemptions: Signature guarantee required over $25,000
Telephone switching: With Firstar Money Market Funds, $1,000 minimum
Number of switches permitted: Unlimited, $5 fee
Dividends paid: Income - December; Capital gains - December
Portfolio turnover (3 yrs): 82%, 118%, 80%
Shareholder services: IRA, SEP-IRA, electronic funds transfer
Management fee: 1.00%
Administration fee: 0.15% first $50M to 0.05% over $200M ($60,000 minimum)
12b-1 distribution fee: 0.25%
Expense ratio: 1.75% (year ending 6/30/97) (1.77% without waiver)
IRA fees: Annual $12.50, Closing $15

BRANDYWINE FUND ◆
3908 Kennett Pike
P.O. Box 4166
Greenville, DE 19807
800-656-3017, 302-656-6200
fax 302-656-7644
TDD 800-684-3416
e-mail: bfunds@friess.com

Shareholder service hours: Full service M-F 8 A.M.-7 P.M. CST; After hours service: prices, yields, account balances, orders, last transaction, messages, prospectuses
Adviser: Friess Assocs., Inc.
Portfolio manager: Foster S. Friess (1985)
Transfer agent: Firstar Trust Co.
Investment objective and policies: Long-term capital appreciation; current income secondary. Invests at least 70% of assets primarily in common stocks of well-financed issuers with records of profitability and strong earnings momentum. May invest up to 15% of assets in securities or ADRs of foreign issuers.
Year organized: 1985
Ticker symbol: BRWIX
Minimum purchase: Initial: $25,000; Subsequent: $1,000
Wire orders accepted: Yes
Deadline for same day wire purchase: 4 P.M.

Discount broker availability: Fidelity, Schwab, Siebert, White
Qualified for sale in: All states
Telephone redemptions: Yes
Wire redemptions: Yes, $1,000 minimum, $10 fee
Letter redemptions: Signature guarantee not required
Dividends paid: Income - October, December; Capital gains - October, December
Portfolio turnover (3 yrs): 192%, 203%, 194%
Shareholder services: Systematic withdrawal plan min. bal. req. $25,000
Management fee: 1.00%
Expense ratio: 1.04% (year ending 9/30/97)

BRANDYWINE BLUE FUND ◆
3908 Kennett Pike
P.O. Box 4166
Greenville, DE 19807
800-656-3017, 302-656-6200
fax 302-656-7644
TDD 800-684-3416
e-mail: bfunds@friess.com

Shareholder service hours: Full service M-F 8 A.M.-7 P.M. CST; After hours service: prices, yields, account balances, orders, last transaction, messages, prospectuses
Adviser: Friess Assocs., Inc.
Portfolio manager: Foster S. Friess (1991)
Transfer agent: Firstar Trust Co.
Investment objective and policies: Long-term capital appreciation; current income secondary. Invests primarily in common stocks of companies with market capitalization of more than $500M perceived to offer growth in share value. Uses same selection process as Brandywine fund but investments are held in larger companies. May invest up to 15% of assets in foreign issues.
Year organized: 1991
Ticker symbol: BLUEX
Minimum purchase: Initial: $100,000; Subsequent: $1,000
Wire orders accepted: Yes
Deadline for same day wire purchase: 4 P.M.
Discount broker availability: Fidelity, Schwab, Siebert, White
Qualified for sale in: All states
Telephone redemptions: Yes
Wire redemptions: Yes, $1,000 minimum, $10 fee
Letter redemptions: Signature guarantee not required
Dividends paid: Income - October, December; Capital gains - October, December
Portfolio turnover (3 yrs): 202%, 197%, 174%
Shareholder services: Systematic withdrawal plan min. bal. req. $100,000
Management fee: 1.00%
Expense ratio: 1.08% (year ending 9/30/97)

BRAZOS/JMIC REAL ESTATE SECURITIES PORTFOLIO ◆
5949 Sherry Lane, Suite 1600
Dallas, TX 75225
800-426-9157, 214-365-5200

Adviser: John McStay Investment Counsel, L.P.
Portfolio manager: John D. McStay (1996)
Transfer agent and administrator: PFPC, Inc.
Investment objective and policies: A balance of income and appreciation consistent with reasonable risk to principal. Invests primarily in equity securities of companies principally engaged in the real estate industry, defined as an organization if at least 50% of its assets, gross income or profit are attributed to some recognizable real estate activity. May invest up to 20% of assets in companies less than three years old, up to 10% in other investment companies, and up to 15% in illiquid securities.
Year organized: 1996
Ticker symbol: BJRSX
Minimum purchase: Initial: $10,000; Subsequent: $1,000; IRA: Initial: $2,000, Subsequent: $100
Wire orders accepted: Yes
Deadline for same day wire purchase: 4 P.M.
Discount broker availability: Fidelity, Schwab, White

Qualified for sale in: All states
Telephone redemptions: Yes
Wire redemptions: Yes
Letter redemptions: Signature guarantee not required
Redemption fee: 1% for shares held less than 90 days, payable to the fund
Telephone switching: With other Brazos funds
Number of switches permitted: Unlimited
Dividends paid: Income - annually; Capital gains - annually
Portfolio turnover (1 yr): 185%
Shareholder services: IRA
Management fee: 0.90%
Administration fee: 0.15% first $50M to 0.07% over $200M (minimum $32,500)
Expense ratio: 1.25% (year ending 10/31/97) (1.83% without waiver)
IRA fees: Annual $10, Closing $10

BRAZOS/JMIC SMALL CAP GROWTH SECURITIES PORTFOLIO ◆
5949 Sherry Lane, Suite 1600
Dallas, TX 75225
800-426-9157, 214-365-5200

Adviser: John McStay Investment Counsel, L.P.
Portfolio manager: John D. McStay (1996)
Transfer agent and administrator: PFPC, Inc.
Investment objective and policies: Maximum capital appreciation consistent with reasonable risk to principal. Invests at least 65% of assets in a diverse portfolio of equity securities of companies with market capitalizations ranging from $40M to $1.2B perceived to offer strong growth potential. May invest up to 20% of assets in companies less than three years old, up to 15% of assets in foreign holdings, and up to 15% in illiquid securities.
Year organized: 1996
Ticker symbol: BJSCX
Minimum purchase: Initial: $10,000; Subsequent: $1,000; IRA: Initial: $2,000, Subsequent: $100
Wire orders accepted: Yes
Deadline for same day wire purchase: 4 P.M.
Discount broker availability: Fidelity, Schwab, White
Qualified for sale in: All states
Telephone redemptions: Yes
Wire redemptions: Yes
Letter redemptions: Signature guarantee not required
Telephone switching: With other Brazos funds
Number of switches permitted: Unlimited
Dividends paid: Income - annually; Capital gains - annually
Portfolio turnover (1 yr): 148%
Shareholder services: IRA
Management fee: 0.90%
Administration fee: 0.15% first $50M to 0.07% over $200M (minimum $32,500)
Expense ratio: 1.35% (year ending 10/31/97) (1.80% without waiver)
IRA fees: Annual $10, Closing $10

BRIDGES INVESTMENT FUND ◆
8401 West Dodge Road, Suite 256
Omaha, NE 68114
402-397-4700, fax 402-397-8617

Adviser: Bridges Investment Counsel, Inc.
Portfolio manager: Edson Low Bridges, III (1997)
Transfer agent: Bridges Investor Services, Inc.
Investment objective and policies: Long-term capital appreciation; modest amount of current income secondary. Invests at least 60% of assets in common stocks and securities convertible into common stocks. May invest up to 40% of assets in non-convertible, fixed-income government and corporate securities, and up to 10% in securities of foreign issuers. May write covered call options on up to 10% of portfolio value, although it has never been done.
Year organized: 1963
Minimum purchase: Initial: $800, Subsequent: $200
Wire orders accepted: No
Qualified for sale in: NE
Letter redemptions: Signature guarantee required
Dividends paid: Income - January, April, July, October; Capital gains - December
Portfolio turnover (3 yrs): 8%, 7%, 10%

Shareholder services: IRA, Keogh, 401(k), corporate retirement plans
Management fee: 0.50%
Expense ratio: 0.87% (year ending 12/31/96)
IRA/Keogh fees: Annual $8, Closing $9.75

BRIDGEWAY FUNDS ◆
(Data common to all Bridgeway funds are shown below. See subsequent listings for data specific to individual funds.)

5650 Kirby Drive, Suite 141
Houston, TX 77005-2443
800-661-3550, 713-661-3500
fax 713-661-3587

Adviser: Bridgeway Capital Management, Inc.
Transfer agent: Bridgeway Fund, Inc.
Minimum purchase: Initial: $2,000, Subsequent: $500; Automatic investment plan: Initial: $200, Subsequent: $200 ($166 for IRAs)
Wire orders accepted: Yes
Deadline for same day wire purchase: 3 P.M.
Telephone redemptions: Yes
Wire redemptions: Yes, $15 fee
Letter redemptions: Signature guarantee required
Telephone switching: With other Bridgeway funds
Number of switches permitted: 4 per year
Deadline for same day switch: 3 P.M.
Shareholder services: IRA, systematic withdrawal plan
IRA fees: Annual $20

BRIDGEWAY AGGRESSIVE GROWTH PORTFOLIO ◆
(See first Bridgeway listing for data common to all funds)

Portfolio manager: John N.R. Montgomery (1994)
Investment objective and policies: Total return: capital growth and income exceeding the broad stock market at a level of total risk roughly equal to that of the stock market over periods greater than three years. Capital growth will be the largest portion of the return. Normally invests in common stocks and uses leverage to increase potential return. Uses futures and options on indexes and stocks to increase return and hedge.
Year organized: 1994
Ticker symbol: BRAGX
Discount broker availability: *Fidelity, White
Qualified for sale in: CA, DC, GA, HI, MI, NY, PA, TX, VA
Dividends paid: Income - December; Capital gains - December
Portfolio turnover (3 yrs): 139%, 168%, 140%
Management fee: 0.90% (+/- up to 0.70% relative to performance compared with the S&P 500 Index over 60 months)
Expense ratio: 2.00% (year ending 6/30/97) (includes waiver)

BRIDGEWAY SOCIAL RESPONSIBILITY PORTFOLIO ◆
(See first Bridgeway listing for data common to all funds)

Portfolio manager: John N.R. Montgomery (1994)
Investment objective and policies: Total return: capital growth and income exceeding the broad stock market at a level of total risk roughly equal to that of the stock market over periods of three years or more. Invests in equities of companies with social criteria measured by the Council on Economic Priorities including environmental record, charitable giving, workplace issues, military contracts and animal testing. Shareholders are then presented a survey of these securities and are asked to rank them, with the resulting rankings used to determine portfolio weighting. May leverage and use index futures and options for hedging purposes.
Year organized: 1994
Ticker symbol: BRSRX
Discount broker availability: *Fidelity, White
Qualified for sale in: CA, DC, GA, HI, MI, PA, TX, VA
Dividends paid: Income - December; Capital gains - December

Portfolio turnover (3 yrs): 36%, 84%, 72%
Management fee: 0.90% (+/- up to 0.70% relative to performance compared with the S&P 500 Index over 60 months)
Expense ratio: 1.50% (year ending 6/30/97) (includes waiver)

BRIDGEWAY ULTRA-SMALL COMPANY PORTFOLIO ◆
(See first Bridgeway listing for data common to all funds)

Portfolio manager: John N.R. Montgomery (1994)
Investment objective and policies: Total return: capital appreciation plus income. Invests primarily in equities of very small companies, those companies with market capitalizations less than the upper limit of the smallest 10% of the New York Stock Exchange. This number will vary with market fluctuations, and currently is about $86M. Fund may only purchase securities of larger firms if at least 65% of assets are invested at this level. May invest up to 5% of assets in unseasoned companies, and up to 10% of assets in foreign securities or ADRs.
Year organized: 1994
Ticker symbol: BRUSX
Special sales restrictions: Closed to new shareholders whenever assets are above $27.5M
Discount broker availability: *Fidelity, White
Qualified for sale in: CA, DC, GA, HI, MI, NY, PA, TX, VA
Dividends paid: Income - December; Capital gains - December
Portfolio turnover (3 yrs): 56%, 156%, 104%
Management fee: 0.90% (percentage will be based on $55M if assets exceed closing cap, resulting in an effective rate of 1.49%)
Expense ratio: 1.67% (year ending 6/30/97) (incudes waiver)

BROWN CAPITAL MANAGEMENT FUNDS ◆
(Data common to all Brown Capital funds are shown below. See subsequent listings for data specific to individual funds.)

809 Cathedral Street
Baltimore, MD 21201
800-525-3863, 410-837-3234
fax 410-837-6525

Adviser: Brown Capital Management, Inc.
Administrator: The Nottingham Co.
Transfer agent: NC Shareholder Services, LLC
Minimum purchase: Initial: $10,000, Subsequent: $500; IRA: Initial: $2,000; Automatic investment plan: Initial: $100, Subsequent: $100
Wire orders accepted: Yes
Deadline for same day wire purchase: 4 P.M.
Telephone redemptions: Yes
Wire redemptions: Yes, $5,000 minimum, $7 fee
Letter redemptions: Signature guarantee required over $50,000
Telephone switching: With other Brown Capital funds
Number of switches permitted: Unlimited but monitored
Shareholder services: IRA, systematic withdrawal plan min. bal. req. $10,000
Administration fee: 0.25% first $10M to 0.15% over $100M ($36,000 minimum)

BROWN CAPITAL MANAGEMENT BALANCED FUND ◆
(See first Brown Capital listing for data common to all funds)

Portfolio manager: Eddie C. Brown (1993)
Investment objective and policies: Maximum total return; capital appreciation and income. Invests in an allocated portfolio of equity securities, fixed-income obligations and cash. Maintains no less than 25% and no more than 75% of assets in bonds and cash. Equity securities are selected primarily for their capital appreciation potential, bonds for their income. Foreign securities are only held in the form of ADRs.
Year organized: 1993

Ticker symbol: BCBIX
Discount broker availability: *White
Qualified for sale in: AL, CA, CO, CT, DC, FL, GA, IL, IN, KS, MN, NC, NJ, NY, PA, VA
Dividends paid: Income - quarterly; Capital gains - December
Portfolio turnover (3 yrs): 46%, 44%, 10%
Management fee: 0.65% first $25M, 0.50% over $25M
Expense ratio: 1.20% (year ending 3/31/97) (2.85% without waiver)

BROWN CAPITAL MANAGEMENT EQUITY FUND ◆
(See first Brown Capital listing for data common to all funds)

Portfolio manager: Eddie C. Brown (1993)
Investment objective and policies: Capital appreciation; current income secondary. Invests generally 90% and always at least 65% of assets in equity securities perceived to be undervalued relative to their growth potential due to being unknown or out of favor. Foreign securities are only held in the form of ADRs.
Year organized: 1993
Ticker symbol: BCEIX
Discount broker availability: *White
Qualified for sale in: AL, CA, CO, CT, DC, FL, GA, IL, IN, KS, MN, NC, NJ, NY, PA, VA
Dividends paid: Income - quarterly; Capital gains - December
Portfolio turnover (3 yrs): 34%, 48%, 7%
Management fee: 0.65% first $25M, 0.50% over $25M
Expense ratio: 1.20% (year ending 3/31/97) (3.37% without waiver)

BROWN CAPITAL MANAGEMENT SMALL COMPANY FUND ◆
(See first Brown Capital listing for data common to all funds)

Portfolio manager: Eddie C. Brown (1993)
Investment objective and policies: Capital appreciation; current income secondary. Invests generally 90% and always at least 65% of assets in equity securities of companies with operating revenues of less than $250M whose current price to earnings ratio is below the prospective growth rate. Foreign securities are only held in the form of ADRs.
Year organized: 1993
Ticker symbol: BCSIX
Discount broker availability: *White
Qualified for sale in: AL, AR, CA, CO, CT, DC, FL, GA, IL, IN, KS, MN, NC, NJ, NY, PA, VA
Dividends paid: Income - quarterly; Capital gains - December
Portfolio turnover (3 yrs): 13%, 23%, 33%
Management fee: 1.00%
Expense ratio: 1.50% (year ending 3/31/97) (2.70% without waiver)

BRUCE FUND ◆
20 N. Wacker Drive, Suite 2414
Chicago, IL 60606
800-872-7823, 312-236-9160
prices/yields 800-347-8607
fax 312-236-9161

Adviser: Bruce and Co., Inc.
Portfolio manager: Robert B. Bruce (1983)
Transfer agent: Unified Advisers, Inc.
Investment objective and policies: Long-term capital growth; income secondary. Invests primarily in common stocks and bonds, but may also invest in convertible securities, preferred stocks, and other debt instruments and warrants. May purchase securities of unseasoned companies and invest without restriction in zero coupon bonds.
Year organized: 1968 (formerly Herold Fund)
Ticker symbol: BRUFX
Minimum purchase: Initial: $1,000, Subsequent: $500
Wire orders accepted: No
Qualified for sale in: CA, CO, GA, IL, IN, MN, MS, MO, NV, NJ, NY, VA, WA, WI
Letter redemptions: Signature guarantee required

Dividends paid: Income - December; Capital gains - December
Portfolio turnover (3 yrs): 4%, 12%, 19%
Shareholder services: IRA
Management fee: 1.00% first $20M to 0.50% over $100M
Expense ratio: 1.69% (year ending 6/30/97)
IRA fees: None

BRUNDAGE, STORY AND ROSE EQUITY FUND

312 Walnut Street, 21st Floor
Cincinnati, OH 45202-4094
800-543-8721, 800-320-2212
513-629-2000, fax 513-629-2901
prices 800-852-4052

Adviser: Brundage, Story and Rose, LLC
Portfolio manager: Gregory E. Ratte (1994)
Transfer agent and administrator: Countrywide Fund Services, Inc.
Investment objective and policies: Protection and enhancement of capital, current income and growth of income. Invests primarily in a diversified portfolio of dividend-paying common stocks and securities convertible into common stock perceived to offer reasonable valuations. Management uses a top-down trend analysis to begin the investment process, first identifying economic then sector trends. May also invest without limit in securities of foreign issuers, both directly and via ADRs, as well as in investment grade fixed-income obligations.
Year organized: 1991 (name changed from Growth & Income fund 1996)
Ticker symbol: BREQX
Minimum purchase: Initial: $1,000, Subsequent: None; IRA/Keogh: Initial: $250; Automatic investment plan: Initial: $50, Subsequent: $50
Wire orders accepted: Yes
Deadline for same day wire purchase: 4 P.M.
Discount broker availability: Schwab, White
Qualified for sale in: All states except AL, HI, IA, MS, MO, MT, NE, NV, NC, ND, PR, RI, SD, UT, WV
Telephone redemptions: Yes
Wire redemptions: Yes, $1,000 minimum, $8 fee
Letter redemptions: Signature guarantee required over $25,000
Telephone switching: With BSR Short/Intermediate Term Fixed-Income Fund, Midwest Group Tax Free Trust - Tax-Free Money and Short- Term Government Funds
Number of switches permitted: Unlimited
Dividends paid: Income - March, June, September, December; Capital gains - December
Portfolio turnover (3 yrs): 49%, 44%, 42%
Shareholder services: IRA, Keogh, 401(k), 403(b), corporate retirement plans, electronic funds transfer (redemption only), systematic withdrawal plan min. bal. req. $5,000
Management fee: 0.65%
Administrative fee: 0.20% first $50M to 0.15% over $100M ($12,000 minimum)
12b-1 distribution fee: Maximum of 0.25%
Expense ratio: 1.19% (year ending 11/30/97)
IRA fees: Annual $10
Keogh fees: Annual $35

BRUNDAGE, STORY AND ROSE SHORT/INTERMEDIATE TERM FIXED-INCOME FUND

312 Walnut Street, 21st Floor
Cincinnati, OH 45202-4094
800-543-8721, 800-320-2212
513-629-2000, fax 513-629-2901
prices 800-852-4052

Adviser: Brundage, Story and Rose, LLC
Portfolio manager: H. Dean Benner (1991)
Transfer agent and administrator: Countrywide Fund Services, Inc.
Investment objective and policies: Higher and more stable level of current income than a money market with more stability of principal than an intermediate- or long-term bond fund. Invests at least 90% of assets in investment grade short- and intermediate-term foreign and domestic corporate and government fixed-income securities with remaining maturities of

between one and ten years. Portfolio generally maintains a dollar-weighted average maturity of between two and five years. May invest up to 35% of assets in U.S. Government obligations having less than a year to maturity. May use futures and options to hedge up to 25% of total assets.
Year organized: 1991
Ticker symbol: BRSFX
Minimum purchase: Initial: $1,000, Subsequent: None; IRA/Keogh: Initial: $250; Automatic investment plan: Initial: $50, Subsequent: $50
Wire orders accepted: Yes
Deadline for same day wire purchase: 4 P.M.
Discount broker availability: Schwab, White
Qualified for sale in: All states except AL, AK, HI, ID, IA, MS, MO, MT, NE, NV, ND, PR, RI, SD, TN, UT, WV
Telephone redemptions: Yes
Wire redemptions: Yes, $1,000 minimum, $8 fee
Letter redemptions: Signature guarantee required over $25,000
Check redemptions: No minimum, $0.50 fee
Telephone switching: With BSR Equity Fund, Midwest Group Tax Free Trust - Tax-Free Money and Short- Term Government Funds
Number of switches permitted: Unlimited
Dividends paid: Income - declared and paid monthly; Capital gains - December
Portfolio turnover (3 yrs): 46%, 40%, 39%
Shareholder services: IRA, Keogh, 401(k), 403(b), corporate retirement plans, electronic funds transfer (redemption only), systematic withdrawal plan min. bal. req. $5,000
Management fee: 0.50%
Administrative fee: 0.20% first $50M to 0.15% over $100M ($12,000 minimum)
12b-1 distribution fee: Maximum of 0.25%
Expense ratio: 0.65% (year ending 11/30/97) (1.07% without waiver)
IRA fees: Annual $10
Keogh fees: Annual $35

BT MUTUAL FUNDS ◆

(Data common to all BT Investment funds are shown below. See subsequent listings for data specific to individual funds.)

280 Park Avenue
New York, NY 10017
800-730-1313, 212-250-2500

Adviser: Bankers Trust Co.
Transfer agent: Bankers Trust Co.
Investment objectives and policies: All of the BT funds participate in master/feeder structures, in which the assets of the various funds are invested in underlying portfolios with the same objectives. All data shown are for the funds, except management fees and portfolio turnover, which are for the portfolios.
Minimum purchase: Initial: $2,500, Subsequent: $250; IRA/Keogh: Initial: $500, Subsequent: $100; Automatic investment plan: Initial: $1,000, Subsequent: $100
Wire orders accepted: Yes
Deadline for same day wire purchase: 4 P.M.
Qualified for sale in: All states (exception noted)
Telephone redemptions: Yes
Wire redemptions: Yes, $1,000 minimum
Letter redemptions: Signature guarantee not required
Telephone switching: With other BT Funds, $100 minimum
Number of switches permitted: 4 outbound per fund per year
Shareholder services: IRA, SEP-IRA, Keogh, 401(k), 403(b), corporate retirement plans, electronic funds transfer, systematic withdrawal plan min. bal. req. $10,000
IRA fees: Annual $15 per social security #

BT ADVISOR - EAFE EQUITY INDEX FUND ◆

(See first BT Investment listing for data common to all funds)

Portfolio manager: Richard J. Vella (1996)
Investment objective and policies: Seeks to replicate as closely as possible (before expenses) the total

return of the Morgan Stanley Capital International Europe, Australia, Far East (EAFE) Index. The fund will be invested primarily in equity securities of the 1,100 enterprises located outside the U.S. that comprise the Index.
Year organized: 1996
Ticker symbol: BTAEX
Group fund code: 510
Discount broker availability: Fidelity, Schwab, Siebert, *White
Redemption fee: 0.50% for redemptions and exchanges, payable to the fund
Dividends paid: Income - annually; Capital gains - annually
Portfolio turnover (1 yr): 4%
Management fee: 0.25%
Expense ratio: 0.65% (6 months ending 12/31/96) (2.35% without waiver)

BT ADVISOR - SMALL CAP INDEX FUND ◆

(See first BT Investment listing for data common to all funds)

Portfolio manager: Frank Salerno (1996)
Investment objective and policies: Seeks to replicate as closely as possible (before expenses) the total return of the Russell 2000 Small Stock Index. The fund will include the common stock of one or more companies included in the Russell 2000, selected on the basis of computer-generated statistical data that are deemed representative of the industry diversification of the entire Index.
Year organized: 1996
Ticker symbol: BTSIX
Group fund code: 509
Redemption fee: 0.50% for redemptions and exchanges, payable to the fund
Discount broker availability: Fidelity, Siebert, *White
Dividends paid: Income - annually; Capital gains - annually
Portfolio turnover (1 yr): 16%
Management fee: 0.15%
Expense ratio: 0.45% (6 months ending 12/31/96) (23.14% without waiver)

BT ADVISOR - U.S. BOND INDEX FUND ◆

(See first BT Investment listing for data common to all funds)

Portfolio manager: Louis R. D'Arienzo (1997)
Investment objective and policies: Seeks to replicate as closely as possible (before expenses) the investment performance of the Lehman Brothers Aggregate Bond Index. The fund will be invested primarily in fixed-income securities of the U.S. Government or agencies thereof, publicly issued fixed rate domestic debt of industrial, financial and utility corporations, and U.S. dollar-denominated fixed-income securities of foreign and supranational agencies issued publicly in the U.S. May also invest in GNMAs, FNMAs and Federal Home Loan Mortgage issues.
Year organized: 1997
Group fund code: 507
Discount broker availability: Fidelity, Siebert, White
Dividends paid: Income - declared daily, paid monthly; Capital gains - annually
Management fee: 0.15%

BT INVESTMENT - CAPITAL APPRECIATION FUND ◆

(See first BT Investment listing for data common to all funds)

Portfolio manager: Anthony Takazawa (1996)
Investment objective and policies: Long-term growth; current income secondary. Invests primarily in common stocks of growth-oriented, medium sized domestic corporations with market capitalizations between $500M and $5B. Investments, however, are not restricted, and fund may invest in any opportunity perceived to offer long-term growth potential. May invest up to 25% of assets in similar foreign issues.

May use a variety of derivative instruments in an effort to improve performance and for hedging purposes.
Year organized: 1993
Ticker symbol: BTCAX
Group fund code: 465
Discount broker availability: Fidelity, Siebert, *White
Dividends paid: Income - quarterly; Capital gains - annually
Portfolio turnover (3 yrs): 167%, 271%, 175%
Management fee: 0.65%
Expense ratio: 1.25% (year ending 9/30/97) (1.54% without waiver)

BT INVESTMENT - CASH MANAGEMENT FUND ◆
(See first BT Investment listing for data common to all funds)

Investment objective and policies: High level of current income consistent with liquidity and the preservation of capital. Invests in high quality money market instruments including bank obligations, commercial paper, corporate debt obligations and repurchase agreements.
Year organized: 1988
Group fund code: 471
Check redemptions: Yes
Dividends paid: Income - declared daily, paid monthly; Capital gains - December
Management fee: 0.15%
Expense ratio: 0.75% (year ending 12/31/96) (0.78% without waiver)

BT INVESTMENT - GLOBAL HIGH YIELD SECURITIES FUND ◆
(See first BT Investment listing for data common to all funds)

Portfolio manager: Greg Hopper (1997)
Investment objective and policies: High current income; capital appreciation secondary. Invests in a non-diversified portfolio of Brady bonds, sovereign debt and junk bonds from both developed and emerging markets around the world. May not, however, invest more than 25% of assets in bonds rated lower than CCC or Caa; may invest up to 10% of assets in defaulted debt securities. May use a variety of derivative instruments in an effort to improve performance and for hedging purposes.
Year organized: 1993
Ticker symbol: BTGHX
Group fund code: 478
Discount broker availability: Fidelity, *Schwab, Siebert, *White
Dividends paid: Income - quarterly; Capital gains - annually
Portfolio turnover (3 yrs): 139%, 207%, 169%
Management fee: 0.80%
Expense ratio: 1.50% (year ending 9/30/97) (2.18% without waiver)

BT INVESTMENT - INTERMEDIATE TAX FREE FUND ◆
(See first BT Investment listing for data common to all funds)

Portfolio manager: Gary Pollack (1992)
Investment objective and policies: High level of current income exempt from federal income tax, consistent with moderate risk of capital. Seeks to maintain a current yield that is greater than that generally obtainable from a portfolio of short-term tax-exempt obligations. Attempts to invest 100% of assets in tax free issues, but may invest up to 20% of assets in taxable securities. Portfolio generally maintains a dollar-weighted average maturity of three to ten years. May use puts, zero coupon municipals, Rule 144A securities, and options and futures contracts.
Year organized: 1992
Ticker symbol: BTTFX
Group fund code: 467
Discount broker availability: Fidelity, *Schwab, Siebert, *White

Dividends paid: Income - declared daily, paid monthly; Capital gains - annually
Portfolio turnover (3 yrs): 170%, 130%, 95%
Management fee: 0.40%
Expense ratio: 0.85% (year ending 9/30/97) (1.15% without waiver)

BT INVESTMENT - INTERNATIONAL EQUITY FUND ◆
(See first BT Investment listing for data common to all funds)

Portfolio managers: Michael Levy (1995), Robert Reiner (1994), Julie Wang (1994)
Investment objective and policies: Long-term capital appreciation; current income incidental. Invests primarily in equity securities from established companies in at least three different developed markets outside the U.S. May also invest in emerging markets. May use options or futures based on an established country index to gain exposure without purchasing equities in a market. May use a variety of derivative instruments in an effort to improve performance and for hedging purposes.
Year organized: 1992
Ticker symbol: BTEQX
Group fund code: 463
Discount broker availability: Fidelity, *Schwab, Siebert, *White
Dividends paid: Income - annually; Capital gains - annually
Portfolio turnover (3 yrs): 63%, 68%, 21%
Management fee: 0.65%
Expense ratio: 1.50% (year ending 9/30/97) (1.68% without waiver)

BT INVESTMENT - LATIN AMERICAN EQUITY FUND ◆
(See first BT Investment listing for data common to all funds)

Portfolio managers: Michael Levy (1993), Maria-Elena Carrion (1993), Julie Wang (1994)
Investment objective and policies: Long-term capital appreciation; current income incidental. Invests primarily in equity securities of companies domiciled in or conducting a majority of their business in Latin America. At this time investments are restricted to the following countries: Argentina, Brazil, Chile, Colombia, Mexico, Peru and Venezuela; at least three countries must be represented. May invest up to 35% of assets in Latin American debt obligations. May use a variety of derivative instruments in an effort to improve performance and for hedging purposes.
Year organized: 1993
Ticker symbol: BTLAX
Group fund code: 497
Discount broker availability: Fidelity, *Schwab, Siebert, *White
Dividends paid: Income - annually; Capital gains - annually
Portfolio turnover (3 yrs): 122%, 171%, 161%
Management fee: 1.00%
Expense ratio: 2.00% (year ending 9/30/97) (2.44% without waiver)

BT INVESTMENT - LIFECYCLE LONG RANGE FUND ◆
(See first BT Investment listing for data common to all funds)

Portfolio manager: Philip J. Green (1997)
Investment objective and policies: High total return with reduced risk over the long term. Allocates 40% to 70% of assets to stocks, 25% to 55% in bonds and 0% to 25% in money market instruments. Neutral balance is 55% stocks, 35% bonds and 10% money market instruments. May invest up to 25% of assets in foreign issues, use forward currency exchange contracts, and a variety of derivative instruments in an effort to enhance performance and for hedging purposes.
Year organized: 1993
Ticker symbol: BTILX
Group fund code: 476
Discount broker availability: Fidelity, *Schwab, *White

Dividends paid: Income - April, July, October, December; Capital gains - December
Portfolio turnover (3 yrs): 137%, 154%, 92%
Management fee: 0.65%
Expense ratio: 1.00% (year ending 3/31/97) (1.45% without waiver)

BT INVESTMENT - LIFECYCLE MID RANGE FUND ◆
(See first BT Investment listing for data common to all funds)

Portfolio manager: Philip J. Green (1997)
Investment objective and policies: Long-term capital growth, current income, and growth of income, consistent with reasonable risk. Allocates 20% to 50% of assets to stocks, 30% to 60% to bonds and 0% to 50% to money market instruments. Neutral balance is 35% stocks, 45% bonds and 20% money market instruments. May invest up to 25% of assets in foreign issues, use forward currency exchange contracts, and a variety of derivative instruments in an effort to enhance performance and for hedging purposes.
Year organized: 1993
Ticker symbol: BTLRX
Group fund code: 475
Discount broker availability: Fidelity, *Schwab, *White
Dividends paid: Income - April, July, October, December; Capital gains - December
Portfolio turnover (3 yrs): 209%, 208%, 105%
Management fee: 0.65%
Expense ratio: 1.00% (year ending 3/31/97) (1.49% without waiver)

BT INVESTMENT - LIFECYCLE SHORT RANGE FUND ◆
(See first BT Investment listing for data common to all funds)

Portfolio manager: Philip J. Green (1997)
Investment objective and policies: High income over the long term, consistent with conservation of capital. Allocates 0% to 30% of assets to stocks, 35% to 70% to bonds and 0% to 65% to money market instruments. Neutral balance is 15% stocks, 55% bonds and 30% money market instruments. May invest up to 25% of assets in foreign issues, use forward currency exchange contracts, and a variety of derivative instruments in an effort to enhance performance and for hedging purposes.
Year organized: 1993
Ticker symbol: BTSRX
Group fund code: 474
Discount broker availability: Fidelity, *Schwab, *White
Dividends paid: Income - April, July, October, December; Capital gains - December
Portfolio turnover (3 yrs): 307%, 221%, 111%
Management fee: 0.65%
Expense ratio: 1.00% (year ending 3/31/97) (1.59% without waiver)

BT INVESTMENT - NEW YORK TAX FREE FUND ◆
(See first BT Investment listing for data common to all funds)

Investment objective and policies: High level of current income consistent with liquidity and the preservation of capital. Invests in high quality money market instruments, primarily municipal obligations of New York state and its subdivisions; all issuers which are exempt from New York State and New York City taxes.
Year organized: 1988
Group fund code: 470
Qualified for sale in: CA, CO, CT, FL, GA, IL, IN, KY, LA, MN, NY, NC, OK, OR, PA, WY
Check redemptions: Yes
Dividends paid: Income - declared daily, paid monthly; Capital gains - December
Management fee: 0.15%
Expense ratio: 0.75% (year ending 12/31/96) (0.84% without waiver)

BT INVESTMENT - PACIFIC BASIN EQUITY FUND ◆
(See first BT Investment listing for data common to all funds)

Portfolio managers: Paul Durham (1993), Julie Wang (1994)
Investment objective and policies: Long-term capital appreciation; current income incidental. Invests primarily in equity securities perceived to be undervalued from companies domiciled in or conducting a majority of their business in Pacific Rim countries other than Japan. Must include representation from at least three different companies. May invest up to 20% of assets in China. May use options or futures based on an established country index to gain exposure without purchasing equities in a market. May use a variety of derivative instruments in an effort to improve performance and for hedging purposes.
Year organized: 1993
Ticker symbol: BTBEX
Group fund code: 496
Discount broker availability: Fidelity, *Schwab, Siebert, *White
Dividends paid: Income - annually; Capital gains - annually
Portfolio turnover (3 yrs): 172%, 118%, 104%
Management fee: 0.75%
Expense ratio: 1.75% (year ending 9/30/97) (2.04% without waiver)

BT INVESTMENT - SMALL CAP FUND ◆
(See first BT Investment listing for data common to all funds)

Portfolio managers: Mary P. Dugan (1994), Timothy Woods (1993)
Investment objective and policies: Long-term capital appreciation; current income secondary. Invests primarily in equity securities of small companies perceived to have strong growth potential. Market capitalizations will be below $750M at the time of purchase. May invest up to 25% of assets in similar foreign securities. May use a variety of derivative instruments in an effort to improve performance and for hedging purposes.
Year organized: 1993
Ticker symbol: BTSCX
Group fund code: 498
Discount broker availability: Fidelity, *Schwab, Siebert, *White
Dividends paid: Income - annually; Capital gains - annually
Portfolio turnover (3 yrs): 188%, 159%, 161%
Management fee: 0.65%
Expense ratio: 1.25% (year ending 9/30/97) (1.28% without waiver)

BT INVESTMENT - TAX FREE MONEY FUND ◆
(See first BT Investment listing for data common to all funds)

Investment objective and policies: High level of current income consistent with liquidity and the preservation of capital. Invests in high quality money market instruments, primarily obligations issued by states and their political subdivisions that are exempt from federal income taxes.
Year organized: 1987
Group fund code: 469
Check redemptions: Yes
Dividends paid: Income - declared daily, paid monthly; Capital gains - December
Management fee: 0.15%
Expense ratio: 0.75% (year ending 12/31/96) (0.82% without waiver)

BT INVESTMENT - TREASURY MONEY FUND ◆
(See first BT Investment listing for data common to all funds)

Investment objective and policies: High level of current income consistent with liquidity and the preservation of capital. Invests exclusively in high quality money market instruments issued by the U.S. Treasury, and repurchase agreements collateralized by such obligations.
Year organized: 1988
Group fund code: 472
Check redemptions: Yes
Dividends paid: Income - declared daily, paid monthly; Capital gains - December
Management fee: 0.15%
Expense ratio: 0.75% (year ending 12/31/96) (0.76% without waiver)

BT INVESTMENT - UTILITY FUND ◆
(Fund liquidated 11/21/97)

BT PYRAMID - EQUITY APPRECIATION FUND ◆
(See first BT Investment listing for data common to all funds)

Portfolio manager: Anthony Takazawa (1996)
Investment objective and policies: Long-term capital growth; current income secondary. Invests primarily in common stocks of domestic companies perceived to offer strong growth potential. May, however, invest up to 25% of assets in foreign issues perceived to have similar strength. The market capitalization of companies acquired will generally fall within the parameters of S&P Mid-Cap 400 organizations. May use a variety of derivative instruments in an effort to enhance performance and for hedging purposes.
Year organized: 1993
Ticker symbol: BTEAX
Group fund code: 477
Discount broker availability: *Schwab
Dividends paid: Income - April, July, October, December; Capital gains - December
Portfolio turnover (3 yrs): 188%, 271%, 125%
Management fee: 0.65%
Expense ratio: 1.00% (year ending 9/30/97) (1.20% without waiver)

BT PYRAMID - EQUITY 500 INDEX FUND ◆
(See first BT Investment listing for data common to all funds)

Portfolio manager: Frank Salerno (1992)
Investment objective and policies: Seeks to replicate as closely as possible (before expenses) the total return of the S&P 500 index, which emphasizes large capitalization stocks. The fund will include the common stock of those companies included in the S&P 500, excluding Bankers Trust New York Corporation, selected on the basis of computer-generated statistical data that are deemed representative of the industry diversification of the entire Index.
Year organized: 1992
Ticker symbol: BTIIX
Group fund code: 462
Discount broker availability: Fidelity, *Schwab, Siebert, *White
Dividends paid: Income - quarterly; Capital gains - December
Portfolio turnover (2 yrs): 15%, 6%
Management fee: 0.10%
Expense ratio: 0.25% (year ending 12/31/96) (0.47% without waiver)

BT PYRAMID - INSTITUTIONAL ASSET MANAGEMENT FUND ◆
(See first BT Investment listing for data common to all funds)

Portfolio managers: Karen Keller (1993), Philip Green (1997)
Investment objective and policies: High long-term total return: income and capital growth, with reduced risk. Allocates 40% to 70% of assets to stocks, 25% to 55% to bonds, and 0% to 25% to short-term instruments, according to perceived market conditions. Neutral position is 55% stocks, 35% bonds, and 10% short-term positions. Bonds include government and corporate obligations, stocks may be of companies of any size. All security classes may allocate as much as 25% to foreign issues, and the entire portfolio may comprise up to 50% foreign instruments. May use a variety of derivative instruments in an effort to improve performance and for hedging purposes.
Year organized: 1993
Ticker symbol: BTAMX
Group fund code: 482
Dividends paid: Income - quarterly; Capital gains - December
Portfolio turnover (2 yrs): 137%, 154%
Management fee: 0.65%
Expense ratio: 0.60% (year ending 3/31/97) (0.96% without waiver)

BT PYRAMID - LIMITED TERM U.S. GOVERNMENT SECURITIES FUND ◆
(See first BT Investment listing for data common to all funds)

Portfolio manager: Louis M. Hudson (1994)
Investment objective and policies: High current income consistent with capital preservation. Invests exclusively in U.S. Government securities or repurchase agreements secured by U.S. Government securities. Portfolio generally maintains a dollar-weighted average maturity of seven years or less.
Year organized: 1992
Ticker symbol: BTLGX
Group fund code: 461
Discount broker availability: *Schwab, *White
Dividends paid: Income - declared daily, paid monthly; Capital gains - annually
Portfolio turnover (3 yrs): 383%, 314%, 246%
Management fee: 0.25%
Expense ratio: 0.60% (year ending 9/30/97) (0.75% without waiver)

BT PYRAMID MONEY MARKET FUND ◆
(See first BT Investment listing for data common to all funds)

Investment objective and policies: High level of current income consistent with liquidity and the preservation of capital. Invests in high quality money market instruments including bank obligations, commercial paper, corporate debt obligations and repurchase agreements.
Year organized: 1992
Group fund code: 460
Check redemptions: Yes
Dividends paid: Income - declared daily, paid monthly; Capital gains - December
Management fee: 0.30%
Expense ratio: 0.35% (year ending 12/31/96) (0.51% without waiver)

BUFFALO FUNDS ◆
(Data common to all Buffalo funds are shown below. See subsequent listings for data specific to individual funds.)

BMA Tower
700 Karnes Blvd.
Kansas City, MO 64108-3306
800-492-8332, 816-751-5900
Internet: http://www.jbfunds.com

Shareholder service hours: Full service: M-F 8 A.M.-4:30 P.M. CST; After hours service: prices, yields, account balances, last transaction, messages, prospectuses, portfolio distributions
Adviser: Jones & Babson, Inc. (a wholly-owned subsidiary of Business Men's Assurance Company of America, itself a wholly-owned subsidiary of Assicurazioni Generali S.p.A., an insurance organization founded in 1831 based in Trieste, Italy)
Portfolio manager: Kornitzer Capital Management, Inc.
Transfer agent: Jones & Babson, Inc.
Minimum purchase: Initial: $2,500, Subsequent: $100; IRA: Initial: $250
Wire orders accepted: Yes, $1,000 minimum
Deadline for same day wire purchase: 4 P.M.
Discount broker availability: Fidelity, *White
Qualified for sale in: All states
Letter redemptions: Signature guarantee required over $10,000

Telephone switching: With other Buffalo or Babson funds, $1,000 minimum

Number of switches permitted: Unlimited, 15 day hold

Shareholder services: IRA, SEP-IRA, corporate retirement plans, automatic investment plan, electronic funds transfer (purchase only), systematic withdrawal plan min. bal. req. $10,000

IRA fees: Annual $10, Closing $10

Keogh fees: Annual $15, Closing $15

BUFFALO BALANCED FUND ◆
(See first Buffalo fund for data common to all funds)

Investment objective and policies: Long-term capital growth and high current income. Invests primarily in common stocks of companies listed on the NYSE with market capitalizations exceeding $1B, and secondarily in convertible bonds and convertible preferred stock. May invest up to 75% of assets in debt securities rated as junk bonds. May write covered put and call options and invest in issues of the U.S. Government subject to repurchase agreements.

Year organized: 1994

Ticker symbol: BUFBX

Dividends paid: Income - March, June, September, December; Capital gains - December

Portfolio turnover (3 yrs): 56%, 61%, 33%

Management fee: 1.00%

Expense ratio: 1.05% (year ending 3/31/97)

BUFFALO EQUITY FUND ◆
(See first Buffalo fund for data common to all funds)

Investment objective and policies: Long-term capital appreciation; dividend income secondary. Invests in the common stock of a broad array of companies and industries, most if not all of which will have market capitalizations exceeding $1B. May purchase foreign securities through dollar-denominated ADRs, and may utilize covered call options for hedging purposes.

Year organized: 1995

Ticker symbol: BUFEX

Discount broker availability: *White

Dividends paid: Income - June, December; Capital gains - June, December

Portfolio turnover (2 yrs): 123%, 63%

Management fee: 1.00%

Expense ratio: 1.16% (year ending 3/31/97)

BUFFALO HIGH YIELD FUND ◆
(See first Buffalo fund for data common to all funds)

Investment objective and policies: High level of current income; capital growth secondary. Invests primarily in a diversified portfolio of high-yielding, fixed-income securities of any rating at or above "B". May invest up to 20% of assets in securities rated below "B," and as low as "D." Proportional allocation will change over time based on perception of economic conditions and underlying security values. The average maturity of the portfolio will generally be ten years, and will not likely exceed 15 years. May use covered call options for hedging purposes.

Year organized: 1995

Ticker symbol: BUFHX

Discount broker availability: *White

Dividends paid: Income - March, June, September, December; Capital gains - June, December

Portfolio turnover (2 yrs): 39%, 25%

Management fee: 1.00%

Expense ratio: 1.13% (year ending 3/31/97)

BUFFALO USA GLOBAL FUND ◆
(See first Buffalo fund for data common to all funds)

Investment objective and policies: Capital growth; income secondary. Invests primarily in companies based in the U.S. who receive greater than 40% of their revenues or pre-tax income from international operations, measured as of the preceding four complete quarters or the companies' most recently completed fiscal years. At least 65% of assets must be invested in at least three different countries. May use covered call options for hedging purposes.

Year organized: 1995

Ticker symbol: BUFGX

Discount broker availability: *White

Dividends paid: Income - June, December; Capital gains - June, December

Portfolio turnover (2 yrs): 88%, 123%

Management fee: 1.00%

Expense ratio: 1.13% (year ending 3/31/97)

BULL & BEAR FUNDS
(Data common to all Bull & Bear funds are shown below. See subsequent listings for data specific to individual funds.)

11 Hanover Square
New York, NY 10005
888-503-3863, 212-363-1100
shareholder services 888-503-8642
fax 212-363-1103
Internet: http://www.mutualfunds.net
e-mail: BulBear@aol.com

Adviser: Bull & Bear Advisors, Inc.

Transfer agent: DST Systems, Inc.

Minimum purchase: Initial: $1,000, Subsequent: $100; IRA: Initial: $500; Keogh: Initial: $1,000; Automatic investment plan: Initial: $100

Wire orders accepted: Yes, $1,000 minimum

Deadline for same day wire purchase: 4 P.M.

Qualified for sale in: All states

Telephone redemptions: Yes, $250 minimum

Wire redemptions: Yes, $1,000 minimum

Letter redemptions: Signature guarantee not required

Redemption fee: 1.00% shares held less than 30 days (except Dollar Reserves)

Telephone switching: With other Bull & Bear no-load funds, plus Rockwood Growth and Midas funds, $500 minimum

Number of switches permitted: Unlimited

Shareholder services: IRA, SEP-IRA, Keogh, 403(b), corporate retirement plans, directed dividends, electronic funds transfer, systematic withdrawal plan min. bal. req. $20,000

IRA/Keogh fees: Annual $10, Closing $20 (waived for account balances over $10,000 or automatic investment plans)

BULL & BEAR DOLLAR RESERVES ◆
(See first Bull & Bear listing for data common to all funds)

Portfolio manager: Steven A. Landis (1995)

Investment objective and policies: Maximum current income (which is generally free from income tax) consistent with preservation of capital and liquidity. Invests only in money market instruments issued or guaranteed as to principal and interest by the U.S. Government or its agencies or instrumentalities.

Year organized: 1977 (as Bear Fund); name and objective changed in 1980

Ticker symbol: BBDXX

Discount broker availability: Fidelity

Check redemptions: $250 minimum

Dividends paid: Income - declared daily, paid monthly

Management fee: 0.50% first $250M to 0.40% over $500M

12b-1 distribution fee: maximum of 0.25% (not currently imposed)

Expense ratio: 0.71% (year ending 6/30/97) (1.21% without waiver)

BULL & BEAR GOLD INVESTORS LTD.
(See first Bull & Bear listing for data common to all funds)

Portfolio manager: Investment committee (1997)

Investment objective and policies: Long-term capital appreciation; income secondary. Invests at least 65% of assets in gold, platinum and silver bullion and a global portfolio of securities of companies involved directly or indirectly in mining, processing or dealing in gold or other precious metals. May also invest in companies who own or develop natural resources and other basic commodities, growth companies, and U.S. Government securities. May use futures and options for hedging purposes.

Year organized: 1974 (formerly Golconda Investors)

Ticker symbol: BBGIX

Discount broker availability: Fidelity, Schwab, Siebert, *White

Dividends paid: Income - December; Capital gains - December

Portfolio turnover (3 yrs): 37%, 61%, 158%

Management fee: 1.00% first $10M to 0.50% over $500M

12b-1 distribution fee: 1.00%

Expense ratio: 2.77% (year ending 6/30/97)

BULL & BEAR SPECIAL EQUITIES FUND
(See first Bull & Bear listing for data common to all funds)

Portfolio manager: Investment committee (1997)

Investment objective and policies: Capital appreciation. Engages in such speculative activities as special situations, purchasing or writing put and call options, warrants, short selling and short-term trading. Investments may be in established as well as new and unseasoned companies. At least 65% of the fund will consist of equity securities of U.S. and foreign issuers. Up to 35% may be in corporate bonds, debentures or preferred stocks, both convertible and non-convertible, and U.S. Government or municipal securities. Up to 15% of assets may be in illiquid securities. Fund leverages and sells short.

Year organized: 1986

Ticker symbol: BBSEX

Discount broker availability: Fidelity, Schwab, Siebert, *White

Dividends paid: Income - December; Capital gains - December

Portfolio turnover (3 yrs): 311%, 319%, 309%

Management fee: 1.00% first $10M to 0.50% over $500M

12b-1 distribution fee: 1.00%

Expense ratio: 2.45% (year ending 12/31/96) (2.92% without waiver)

BULL & BEAR U.S. AND OVERSEAS FUND
(See first Bull & Bear listing for data common to all funds)

Portfolio manager: Investment committee (1997)

Investment objective and policies: Total return: long-term growth of capital and income. Invests in equity and debt securities of U.S. and overseas issuers. There is no limit on the percent of assets which may be invested for growth or income and the emphasis can be changed at any point in time. May invest up to 35% of assets in junk bonds. May use forward currency contracts, futures and options, and other derivative instruments in an effort to enhance returns and for hedging purposes.

Year organized: 1987 (name changed from Bull & Bear Overseas Fund on 2/26/92; fund split 2 for 1 on 2/25/92)

Ticker symbol: BBOSX

Discount broker availability: Fidelity, Schwab, Siebert, *White

Dividends paid: Income - December, Capital gains - December

Portfolio turnover (3 yrs): 255%, 214%, 212%

Management fee: 1.00% first $10M to 0.50% over $500M

12b-1 distribution fee: 1.00%

Expense ratio: 3.20% (year ending 12/31/96)

BULL & BEAR U.S. GOVERNMENT SECURITIES FUND
(Fund converted to a closed end fund in 1996)

BULLFINCH - UNRESTRICTED SERIES FUND ◆
8 East Street, Suite 200
Honeoye Falls, NY 14472
888-285-5346, 716-234-2080
fax 716-582-1856

Adviser: Carosa, Stanton & DePaolo Asset Management, LLC

Portfolio manager: Christopher Carosa (1997)

Transfer agent: Bullfinch Fund, Inc.
Investment objective and policies: Conservative long-term growth of capital. Invests primarily in exchange listed and over the counter common stocks, as well as U.S. Government obligations maturing within five years. Allocation between stocks and bonds is adjusted according to perceived market conditions. Equities are selected based on fundamental share price valuation analysis. Fund is non-diversified, and may invest up to 25% of assets in a single industry.
Year organized: 1997
Minimum purchase: Initial: $2,500, Subsequent: $250; IRA: Initial: $500, Subsequent: $50
Wire orders accepted: No
Qualified for sale in: NY
Telephone redemptions: No
Wire redemptions: No
Letter redemptions: Signature guarantee required (unless submitted in person)
Telephone switching: With Bullfinch - Western New York Series
Number of switches permitted: 3 per 6 month period
Dividends paid: Income - annually; Capital gains - annually
Shareholder services: IRA, electronic funds transfer (purchase only)
Management fee: 1.25% first $1M, 1.00% over $1M
IRA fees: None

BULLFINCH - WESTERN NEW YORK SERIES FUND ◆
8 East Street, Suite 200
Honeoye Falls, NY 14472
888-285-5346, 716-234-2080
fax 716-582-1856

Adviser: Carosa, Stanton & DePaolo Asset Management, LLC
Portfolio manager: Christopher Carosa (1997)
Transfer agent: Bullfinch Fund, Inc.
Investment objective and policies: Capital appreciation. Invests at least 65% of assets in equity securities of exchange listed and over the counter companies with an important economic presence in the Greater Western New york Region of New York State. Fund also invests in U.S. Government obligations maturing within five years. Allocation between stocks and bonds is adjusted according to perceived market conditions. Equities are selected based on fundamental share price valuation analysis. Fund is non-diversified, and may invest up to 25% of assets in a single industry.
Year organized: 1997
Minimum purchase: Initial: $2,500, Subsequent: $250; IRA: Initial: $500, Subsequent: $50
Wire orders accepted: No
Qualified for sale in: NY
Telephone redemptions: No
Wire redemptions: No
Letter redemptions: Signature guarantee required (unless submitted in person)
Telephone switching: With Bullfinch - Western New York Series
Number of switches permitted: 3 per 6 month period
Dividends paid: Income - annually; Capital gains - annually
Shareholder services: IRA, electronic funds transfer (purchase only)
Management fee: 1.25% first $1M, 1.00% over $1M
IRA fees: None

C/FUNDS GROUP ◆
(Data common to all Caldwell funds are shown below. See subsequent listings for data specific to individual funds.)

250 Tampa Avenue
Venice, FL 34285
800-338-9477, 941-488-6772
fax 941-496-4661
e-mail: CFUNDS@CTRUST.COM

Shareholder service hours: Full service: M-F 8 A.M.-5 P.M. EST
Adviser: Omnivest Research Corp.
Transfer agent: C/Funds Group, Inc.

Minimum purchase: Initial: None, Subsequent: None
Wire orders accepted: No
Qualified for sale in: FL
Telephone redemptions: Yes
Letter redemptions: Signature guarantee not required
Telephone switching: With other C/Funds Group funds
Number of switches permitted: Unlimited
Shareholder services: IRA, SEP-IRA, automatic investment plan, electronic funds transfer (purchase only)
IRA fees: None

C/FUNDS - ADAMS EQUITY FUND ◆
(See first Caldwell listing for data common to all funds)

Portfolio manager: Roland G. Caldwell (1995)
Investment objective and policies: High total return; capital growth with some current income that outperforms similar mutual funds that also invest a minimum of 65% of total assets in equities. Invests primarily in common stocks selected using a proprietary valuation process to identify undervalued companies. May invest in companies of all capitalization levels.
Year organized: 1995
Discount broker availability: *White
Dividends paid: Income - June, December; Capital gains - December
Portfolio turnover (1 yr): 65%
Management fee: 1.00%
Expense ratio: 1.36% (year ending 12/31/96)

C/FUND ◆
(See first Caldwell listing for data common to all funds)

Portfolio manager: Roland G. Caldwell (1985)
Investment objective and policies: Current income with some capital growth. Invests in equity securities - common stocks, convertible preferred stocks and convertible bonds - and fixed-income securities with allocation varying depending on economic or market conditions. Securities will most commonly be traded on the NYSE or NASDAQ.
Year organized: 1985
Discount broker availability: *White
Dividends paid: Income - June, December; Capital gains - December
Portfolio turnover (3 yrs): 11%, 5%, 24%
Management fee: 1.00%
Expense ratio: 1.90% (year ending 12/31/96)

C/FUNDS - C/GOVERNMENT FUND ◆
(See first Caldwell listing for data common to all funds)

Portfolio manager: Roland G. Caldwell (1992)
Investment objective and policies: Higher interest rate returns than available from government-only money market mutual funds. Invests exclusively in U.S. Treasury issues or in obligations issued by agencies of the U.S. Government with remaining maturities of two to ten years.
Year organized: 1992
Dividends paid: Income - monthly; Capital gains - December
Portfolio turnover (3 yrs): 60%, 125%, 122%
Management fee: 0.50%
Expense ratio: 1.02% (year ending 12/31/96)

C/FUNDS - C/GROWTH STOCK FUND ◆
(See first Caldwell listing for data common to all funds)

Portfolio manager: Roland G. Caldwell (1992)
Investment objective and policies: Maximum capital appreciation. Invests primarily in common stocks or equivalents of rapidly growing companies believed to have above average growth prospects regardless of their capitalizations or annual sales volumes. Fund uses proprietary analytical methodology to select companies for its portfolio.
Year organized: 1992
Discount broker availability: *White
Dividends paid: Income - June, December; Capital gains - December

Portfolio turnover (3 yrs): 4%, 16%, 37%
Management fee: 1.00%
Expense ratio: 1.90% (year ending 12/31/96)

C/FUNDS - C/TAX-FREE FUND ◆
(See first Caldwell listing for data common to all funds)

Portfolio manager: Roland G. Caldwell (1992)
Investment objective and policies: High interest income exempt from federal income tax. Invests in securities issued by states, municipalities and other governmental jurisdictions, mainly in the state of Florida, exempt from federal income tax with remaining maturities of 12 years or less.
Year organized: 1992
Dividends paid: Income - monthly; Capital gains - December
Portfolio turnover (3 yrs): 0%, 23%, 3%
Management fee: 0.50%
Expense ratio: 1.01% (year ending 12/31/96)

THE CALDWELL & ORKIN MARKET OPPORTUNITY FUND ◆
2050 Tower Place
3340 Peachtree Road, Northeast
Atlanta, GA 30326
800-237-7073, 800-543-8721
404-239-0707
shareholder services 513-629-2070
fax 404-237-8603, 404-842-7868
e-mail: cofunds@aol.com

Adviser: C&O Funds Advisor, Inc.
Portfolio manager: Michael B. Orkin (1992)
Transfer agent: Countrywide Fund Services, Inc.
Investment objective and policies: Long-term capital growth and short-term capital preservation, through investment selection and asset allocation; current income incidental. Seeks to outperform the NASDAQ Composite Index and the S&P 500 over time. Invests at least 80% of assets in common stocks of companies of all sizes perceived to show potential for capital growth, and up to 20% in bonds and cash. Assets are allocated according to perceived market conditions. Up to 25% of assets may be in equity securities or ADRs of foreign issuers. May initiate short positions worth up to 40% of assets in an effort to enhance returns and for hedging purposes.
Year organized: 1991 (fund was a passive OTC index fund from '91 to '92; name changed from Caldwell & Orkin Aggressive Growth Fund 8/29/96)
Ticker symbol: COAGX
Minimum purchase: Initial: $10,000, Subsequent $100; IRA/Keogh: Initial $2,000
Wire orders accepted: Yes
Deadline for same day wire purchase: 4 P.M.
Discount broker availability: Fidelity, Schwab, Siebert, White
Qualified for sale: All states
Telephone redemptions: Yes
Wire redemptions: Yes, $6 fee (advance signature guarantee required)
Letter redemptions: Signature guarantee not required
Redemption fee: 2.00% for shares held less than 6 months, payable to fund
Dividends paid: Income - April, December; Capital gains - April, December
Portfolio turnover (3 yrs): 229%, 222%, 331%
Shareholder services: IRA, Keogh, automatic investment plan
Management fee: 0.90% first $100M to 0.50% over $500M
Expense ratio: 1.34% (year ending 4/30/97)
IRA/Keogh fees: None

CALIFORNIA DAILY TAX FREE INCOME FUND ◆
600 Fifth Avenue, 8th Floor
New York, NY 10020
800-221-3079, 212-830-5220
prices/yields 212-830-5225
fax 212-830-5476

Adviser: Reich & Tang Asset Management, L.P.
Portfolio manager: Molly Flewharty (1987)
Transfer agent: Reich & Tang Services, L.P.

Investment objective and policies: High current interest income exempt from federal income tax and, to the extent possible, from California income taxes, consistent with preservation of capital and liquidity. Invests primarily in California municipal money market instruments. Fund is non-diversified.
Year organized: 1987
Ticker symbol: CFDXX
Special sales restrictions: Only class "B" shares of the fund are sold direct and without 12b-1 fees. Statistics represent "B" shares only.
Minimum purchase: Initial: $5,000, Subsequent: $100
Wire orders accepted: Yes
Deadline for same day wire purchase: 12 NN
Qualified for sale in: AZ, CA, CT, NY
Telephone redemptions: Yes
Wire redemptions: Yes, $1,000 minimum
Letter redemptions: Signature guarantee required
Check redemptions: $250 minimum
Telephone switching: With other Reich & Tang Money Market funds and R&T Equity Fund
Number of switches permitted: Unlimited, $1,000 minimum
Deadline for same day switch: 12 NN
Dividends paid: Income - declared daily, paid monthly
Shareholder services: Automatic investment plan, electronic funds transfer, systematic withdrawal plan
Management fee: 0.30%
Administration fee: 0.21%
Shareholder services fee: 0.20%
Expense ratio: 0.56% (year ending 12/31/96) (0.62% without waiver)

CALIFORNIA INVESTMENT TRUST FUND GROUP ◆
(Data common to all California Investment Trust funds are shown below. See subsequent listings for data specific to individual funds.)

44 Montgomery Street, Suite 2100
San Francisco, CA 94104
800-225-8778, 415-398-2727
TDD 800-864-3416, fax 415-421-2019
Internet: http://www.caltrust.com

Adviser: CCM Partners, L.P.
Transfer agent: Firstar Trust Co.
Minimum purchase: Initial: $10,000 ($5,000 for Index funds), Subsequent: $250; IRA/Keogh: Initial: None, Subsequent: None
Wire orders accepted: Yes
Deadline for same day wire purchase: 4 P.M.
Qualified for sale in: CA, HI, NV, OR
Telephone redemptions: Yes
Wire redemptions: Yes, $10 fee
Letter redemptions: Signature guarantee required
Telephone switching: With other California Investment Trust funds
Number of switches permitted: Unlimited
Check redemptions: $500 minimum (not for stock funds)
Shareholders services: IRA, Keogh, 403(b), corporate retirement plans, automatic investment plan, electronic funds transfer (redemption only), systematic withdrawal plan min. bal. req. $10,000
IRA/Keogh fees: Annual $12.50 ($25 maximum per social security number)

CALIFORNIA INVESTMENT TRUST: CALIFORNIA INSURED INTERMEDIATE FUND ◆
(See first California Investment Trust listing for data common to all funds)

Portfolio manager: Phillip W. McClanahan (1992)
Investment objective and policies: High income exempt from federal and California personal income taxes, consistent with prudent investment risk and safety of capital. Invests primarily in intermediate- and long-term California municipal securities that are covered by insurance guaranteeing the timely payment of principal and interest. Invests only in the two highest rated categories available. May invest up to 20% of assets in uninsured obligations, and up to 20% in other municipal obligations not exempt from California tax.

Year organized: 1992 (name changed from California Insured Tax-Free Income Fund in 1995)
Ticker symbol: CATFX
Discount broker availability: Schwab, *White
Dividends paid: Income - monthly; Capital gains - December
Portfolio turnover (3 yrs): 32%, 36%, 44%
Management fee: 0.50% first $100M to 0.40% over $500M
Expense ratio: 0.55% (year ending 8/31/97) (0.70% without waiver)

CALIFORNIA INVESTMENT TRUST: CALIFORNIA TAX-FREE INCOME FUND ◆
(See first California Investment Trust listing for data common to all funds)

Portfolio manager: Phillip W. McClanahan (1985)
Investment objective and policies: High income exempt from federal and California personal income taxes. Invests primarily in intermediate- and long-term California municipal securities rated within the four highest categories by S&P, Moody's or Fitch's. Portfolio generally maintains a dollar-weighted average maturity of five years or more. Up to 20% of assets may be in securities rated as low as the fourth investment grade category, and up to 20% in securities subject to AMT tax treatment.
Year organized: 1985
Ticker symbol: CFNTX
Discount broker availability: Schwab, *White
Dividends paid: Income - monthly; Capital gains - December
Portfolio turnover (3 yrs): 35%, 10%, 32%
Management fee: 0.50% first $100M to 0.40% over $500M
Expense ratio: 0.59% (year ending 8/31/97)

CALIFORNIA INVESTMENT TRUST: CALIFORNIA TAX-FREE MONEY MARKET FUND ◆
(See first California Investment Trust listing for data common to all funds)

Portfolio manager: Phillip W. McClanahan (1985)
Investment objective and policies: Highest current income achievable exempt from federal and California personal income taxes, consistent with capital preservation and liquidity. Invests in all types of high quality California municipal obligations, primarily in money market instruments. Up to 35% of assets may be in municipal obligations of other states, and up to 20% in securities subject to AMT tax treatment.
Year organized: 1985
Ticker symbol: CAXXX
Dividends paid: Income - declared daily; paid monthly
Management fee: 0.50% first $100M to 0.40% over $500M
Expense ratio: 0.40% (year ending 8/31/97) (0.61% without waiver)

CALIFORNIA INVESTMENT TRUST: EQUITY INCOME FUND ◆
(See first California Investment Trust listing for data common to all funds)

Sub-adviser: Bank of America Capital Management, Inc.
Investment objective and policies: High current income with an average yield of at least twice that of the companies which comprise the S&P 500 Index; price appreciation secondary. Invests at least 65% and usually 80% of assets in a diversified portfolio of income producing common stocks and other equity securities. May invest without limit in ADRs and REITs, and use futures contracts based on the S&P BARRA Value Index, the S&P 500 Index, and the S&P MidCap Index representing up to 35% of assets.
Year organized: 1997
Ticker symbol: EQTIX
Discount broker availability: Fidelity, Siebert, *White
Dividends paid: Income - March, June, September, December; Capital gains - December
Portfolio turnover (1 yr): 3%

Management fee: 0.50% first $500M to 0.40% over $1B
Expense ratio: 0.76% (year ending 8/31/97) (1.55% without waiver)

CALIFORNIA INVESTMENT TRUST: S&P 500 INDEX FUND ◆
(See first California Investment Trust listing for data common to all funds)

Sub-adviser: Bank of America Capital Management, Inc.
Investment objective and policies: Investment results that correlate by at least 0.85 (0.95 if assets exceed $25M) to the total return of the common stocks comprising the S&P 500 Composite Stock Price Index. Invests in a sub-set of the stocks included in the index, weighted to match their representation in the Index. Fund may omit or remove an issue from the portfolio if extraordinary circumstances are deemed to substantially impair the merit of the investment.
Year organized: 1992
Ticker symbol: SPFIX
Discount broker availability: Fidelity, Schwab, Siebert, *White
Dividends paid: Income - March, June, September, December; Capital gains - December
Portfolio turnover (3 yrs): 2%, 2%, 4%
Maintenance fee: $10 per year, $2.50 per quarter
Management fee: 0.25%
Expense ratio: 0.20% (year ending 8/31/97) (0.46% without waiver)

CALIFORNIA INVESTMENT TRUST: S&P MIDCAP INDEX FUND ◆
(See first California Investment Trust listing for data common to all funds)

Sub-adviser: Bank of America Capital Management, Inc.
Investment objective and policies: Investment results that correlate by at least 0.85 (0.95 if assets exceed $25M) to the total return of the common stocks comprising the S&P MidCap 400 Index. Invests in a sub-set of the stocks included in the index, weighted to match their representation in the Index. Fund may omit or remove an issue from the portfolio if extraordinary circumstances are deemed to substantially impair the merit of the investment.
Year organized: 1992
Ticker symbol: SPMIX
Discount broker availability: Fidelity, Schwab, Siebert, *White
Dividends paid: Income - March, June, September, December; Capital gains - December
Portfolio turnover (3 yrs): 18%, 18%, 12%
Maintenance fee: $10 per year, $2.50 per quarter
Management fee: 0.40%
Expense ratio: 0.40% (year ending 8/31/97) (0.61% without waiver)

CALIFORNIA INVESTMENT TRUST: S&P SMALLCAP INDEX FUND ◆
(See first California Investment Trust listing for data common to all funds)

Sub-adviser: Bank of America Capital Management, Inc.
Investment objective and policies: Investment results that correlate by at least 0.85 (0.95 if assets exceed $25M) to the total return of the common stocks comprising the S&P SmallCap 600 Index. Invests in a sub-set of the stocks included in the index, weighted to match their representation in the Index. Fund may omit or remove an issue from the portfolio if extraordinary circumstances are deemed to substantially impair the merit of the investment.
Year organized: 1997
Ticker symbol: SMCIX
Discount broker availability: Fidelity, Siebert, *White
Dividends paid: Income - March, June, September, December; Capital gains - December
Portfolio turnover (1 yr): 20%
Management fee: 0.50% first $500M to 0.40% over $1B
Expense ratio: 0.65% (year ending 8/31/97) (2.32% without waiver)

CALIFORNIA INVESTMENT TRUST: U.S. GOVERNMENT SECURITIES FUND ◆

(See first California Investment Trust listing for data common to all funds)

Portfolio manager: Phillip W. McClanahan (1985)
Investment objective and policies: High income consistent with preservation of capital, safety and liquidity. Invests at least 80% of assets in full faith and credit obligations of the U.S. Government and its agencies or instrumentalities, primarily GNMA certificates.
Year organized: 1985
Ticker symbol: CAUSX
Discount broker availability: Fidelity, Schwab, Siebert, *White
Dividends paid: Income - monthly: Capital gains - December
Portfolio turnover (3 yrs): 171%, 89%, 170%
Management fee: 0.50% first $100M to 0.40% over $500M
Expense ratio: 0.65% (year ending 8/31/97) (0.69% without waiver)

CALIFORNIA INVESTMENT TRUST: THE UNITED STATES TREASURY TRUST ◆

(See first California Investment Trust listing for data common to all funds)

Portfolio manager: Phillip W. McClanahan (1989)
Investment objective and policies: High current income exempt from income taxes of California and most other states, consistent with preservation of capital, safety and liquidity. Invests exclusively in short-term U.S. Treasury money market securities.
Year organized: 1989
Ticker symbol: UTSXX
Dividends paid: Income - declared daily, paid monthly
Management fee: 0.50% first $100M to 0.40% over $500M
Expense ratio: 0.40% (year ending 8/31/97) (0.64% without waiver)

CAPITOL SQUARE FUNDS ◆

(Fund family liquidated 9/26/97)

CAPPIELLO-RUSHMORE FUNDS ◆

(Data common to all Cappiello-Rushmore funds are shown below. See subsequent listings for data specific to individual funds.)

4922 Fairmont Avenue, Third Floor
Bethesda, MD 20814
800-343-3355, 800-622-1386
301-657-1500
prices/yields 800-451-2234
fax 301-657-1520

Shareholder service hours: Full service: M-F 8:30 A.M.-4:30 P.M. EST; After hours service: prices, yields
Adviser: McCullough, Andrews & Cappiello, Inc.
Administrator: Money Management Assocs.
Transfer agent: Rushmore Trust and Savings, FSB
Minimum purchase: Initial: $2,500 (total among all funds, $500 minimum per fund), Subsequent: None; IRA/Keogh: Initial: $500
Wire orders accepted: Yes
Deadline for same day wire purchase: 4 P.M.
Qualified for sale in: All states
Telephone redemptions: Yes
Wire redemptions: Yes, $5,000 minimum
Letter redemptions: Signature guarantee required over $100,000
Telephone switching: With other Cappiello-Rushmore funds and Rushmore funds
Number of switches permitted: 5 per year
Shareholder services: IRA, Keogh, 401(k), 403(b), corporate retirement plans, automatic investment plan
Maintenance fee: $5/month for balances below $500
IRA/Keogh fees: Annual $10, Closing $10

CAPPIELLO-RUSHMORE EMERGING GROWTH FUND ◆

(See first Cappiello-Rushmore listing for data common to all funds)

Portfolio managers: Frank A. Cappiello (1992), Robert F. McCullough (1992), David H. Andrews (1992)
Investment objective and policies: Capital appreciation. Invests primarily in common stocks, securities convertible into common stocks and warrants to purchase common stocks of companies with market capitalization of $750M or less. May invest 35% of assets in debt securities, 25% in larger capitalization stocks and 20% in securities of foreign issuers. May sell short.
Year organized: 1992
Ticker symbol: CREGX
Group fund code: 43
Discount broker availability: *Fidelity, *Schwab, *Siebert, *White
Dividends paid: Income - December; Capital gains - December
Portfolio turnover (3 yrs): 66%, 121%, 96%
Management fee: 0.50%
Administration fee: 1.00%
Expense ratio: 1.50% (year ending 6/30/97)

CAPPIELLO-RUSHMORE GOLD FUND ◆

(See first Cappiello-Rushmore listing for data common to all funds)

Portfolio managers: Frank A. Cappiello (1994), Robert F. McCullough (1994), David H. Andrews (1994)
Investment objective and policies: Capital appreciation. Invests primarily in equity securities of companies engaged in the mining, exploration, fabrication, processing, marketing and distribution of gold and companies that finance, manage, control or operate companies engaged in these activities. Fund also invests directly in gold bullion and in companies engaged in the foregoing activities with respect to silver, platinum and other precious metals and in diamonds and other precious minerals. May use futures and options and sell short.
Year organized: 1994
Ticker symbol: CRGDX
Group fund code: 44
Discount broker availability: *Fidelity, *Schwab, *Siebert, *White
Dividends paid: Income - December; Capital gains - December
Portfolio turnover (3 yrs): 108%, 59%, 51%
Management fee: 0.70%
Administration fee: 1.00%
Expense ratio: 1.70% (year ending 6/30/97)

CAPPIELLO-RUSHMORE GROWTH FUND ◆

(See first Cappiello-Rushmore listing for data common to all funds)

Portfolio managers: Frank A. Cappiello (1992), Robert F. McCullough (1992), David H. Andrews (1992)
Investment objective and policies: Capital appreciation. Invests primarily in common stocks, securities convertible into common stocks and warrants to purchase common stock. May invest 20% of assets in securities of foreign issuers. Fund may use options for hedging purposes, and sell short against the box.
Year organized: 1992
Ticker symbol: CRGRX
Group fund code: 42
Discount broker availability: *Fidelity, *Schwab, *Siebert, *White
Dividends paid: Income - December; Capital gains - December
Portfolio turnover (3 yrs): 42%, 75%, 71%
Management fee: 0.50%
Administration fee: 1.00%
Expense ratio: 1.50% (year ending 6/30/97)

CAPPIELLO-RUSHMORE UTILITY INCOME FUND ◆

(See first Cappiello-Rushmore listing for data common to all funds)

Portfolio managers: Frank A. Cappiello (1992), Robert F. McCullough (1992), David H. Andrews (1992)
Investment objective and policies: Current income with an opportunity for capital appreciation. Invests at least 65% of assets in securities of public utility companies. May invest 20% of assets in securities of foreign issuers. Fund may use options for hedging purposes, and sell short against the box.
Year organized: 1992
Ticker symbol: CRUTX
Group fund code: 41
Discount broker availability: *Fidelity, *Schwab, *Siebert, *White
Dividends paid: Income - March, June, September, December; Capital gains - December
Portfolio turnover (3 yrs): 17%, 45%, 147%
Management fee: 0.35%
Administration fee: 0.70%
Expense ratio: 1.05% (year ending 6/30/97)

CAPSTONE FUNDS

(Data common to all Capstone funds are shown below. See subsequent listings for data specific to individual funds.)

5847 San Felipe, Suite 4100
Houston, TX 77057
800-262-6631, 800-845-2340
713-260-9000, fax 713-260-9025

Administrator: Capstone Asset Management Co.
Transfer agent: First Data Investor Services Group
Minimum purchase: Initial: $200, Subsequent: None; IRA: Initial: None; Automatic investment plan: Initial: $25
Wire orders accepted: Yes
Deadline for same day wire purchase: 4 P.M.
Telephone redemptions: Yes, $1,000 minimum
Wire redemptions: Yes, $1,000 minimum
Letter redemptions: Signature guarantee not required
Telephone switching: With other Capstone funds
Number of switches permitted: 1 per month, 15 day hold
Shareholder services: IRA, SEP-IRA, systematic withdrawal plan min. bal. req. $5,000
IRA/Keogh fees: Annual $12

CAPSTONE GOVERNMENT INCOME FUND

(See first Capstone listing for data common to all funds)

Adviser: Capstone Asset Management Co.
Sub-adviser: New Castle Advisers, Inc.
Portfolio manager: Howard S. Potter (1992)
Investment objective and policies: High total return consistent with safety of principal. Invests primarily in debt obligations issued or guaranteed by the U.S. Government, its agencies or instrumentalities, with remaining maturities of three years or less. Fund uses futures and options for hedging purposes.
Year organized: 1968 (formerly Investors Income Fund, Inc. Name and objective changed on 1/8/91.)
Ticker symbol: CGVIX
Discount broker availability: *Fidelity, Schwab, Siebert, *White
Qualified for sale in: All states
Dividends paid: Income - December; Capital gains - December
Portfolio turnover (3 yrs): 563%, 615%, 310%
Management fee: 0.40% first $250M, 0.36% over $250M
Administration fee: 0.10%
12b-1 distribution fee: 0.20%
Expense ratio: 0.87% (year ending 11/31/97)

CAPSTONE GROWTH FUND
(See first Capstone listing for data common to all funds)

Adviser: Capstone Asset Management Co.
Portfolio manager: Albert P. Santa Luca (1994)
Investment objective and policies: Long-term capital appreciation. Invests primarily in common stocks of rapidly growing companies. May also invest in preferred stocks and convertible preferred stocks. May invest without limit in securities of foreign issuers, and use futures and options for hedging purposes.
Year organized: 1952 (formerly U.S. Trend Fund. Name and objective changed on 9/6/94. Prior performance may be misleading)
Ticker symbol: TRDFX
Discount broker availability: *Fidelity, Schwab, Siebert, *White
Qualified for sale in: All states
Dividends paid: Income - May, November; Capital gains - May, November
Portfolio turnover (3 yrs): 229%, 173%, 119%
Management fee: 0.75% first $50M, 0.60% over $50M
12b-1 distribution fee: Maximum of 0.25%
Expense ratio: 1.25% (year ending 10/31/97)

CAPSTONE JAPAN FUND
(See first Capstone listing for data common to all funds)

Adviser: FCA Corp.
Portfolio manager: Robert W. Scharar (1997)
Investment objective and policies: Total return: capital appreciation and current income. Invests primarily in equity securities in Japanese companies traded on the Tokyo Stock Exchange, and in securities whose primary business activities are in Japan. May also invest in ADRs traded in the U.S., and in debt obligations rated BBB or better that are payable in yen or are otherwise linked to the performance of the Japanese market or economy. May use futures and options for hedging purposes.
Year organized: 1989
Ticker symbol: CNJFX
Discount broker availability: *Fidelity, Schwab, Siebert, *White
Qualified for sale in: All states except AL, AK, DE, ID, IN, IA, KY, ME, MA, MS, MT, NE, ND, OR, RI, SC, TN, UT, WA
Dividends paid: Income - December; Capital gains - December
Portfolio turnover (3 yrs): 73%, 47%, 27%
Management fee: 0.75%
Administration fee: 0.20%
12b-1 distribution fee: Maximum of 0.25% (0.35% prior to 8/21/95)
Expense ratio: 4.55% (year ending 10/31/97) (5.46% without waiver)

CAPSTONE NEW ZEALAND FUND
(See first Capstone listing for data common to all funds)

Adviser: FCA Corp.
Portfolio manager: Robert W. Scharar (1991)
Investment objective and policies: Long-term capital appreciation and current income. Invests primarily in equity and debt securities and securities convertible into common stock of New Zealand issuers, or those who derive at least 50% of their revenues from goods or services produced or sold in New Zealand.
Year organized: 1991
Ticker symbol: CNZLX
Qualified for sale in: All states except AR, IN
Discount broker availability: *Fidelity, Schwab, Siebert, *White
Dividends paid: Income - December; Capital gains - December
Portfolio turnover (3 yrs): 24%, 38%, 38%
Management fee: 0.75%
Administration fee: 0.25%
12b-1 distribution fee: Maximum of 0.25%
Expense ratio: 2.50% (year ending 10/31/97) (2.89% without waiver)

CARL DOMINO EQUITY INCOME FUND ◆
580 Village Blvd., Suite 225
West Palm Beach, FL 33409
800-506-9922, 561-697-2723

Adviser: Carl Domino Assocs., L.P.
Administrator: AmeriPrime Financial Services, Inc.
Portfolio manager: Carl J. Domino (1995)
Transfer agent: American Data Services, Inc.
Investment objective and policies: Total return: long-term capital growth and current income. Invests primarily in income producing equity securities perceived to demonstrate less downside risk and volatility than the S&P 500 Index. Issues are selected with a conservative value and yield strategy consistent with capital preservation, with a particular trend toward those undervalued due to perceived temporary special circumstances.
Year organized: 1995
Minimum purchase: Initial: $2,000, Subsequent: $100; IRA: Subsequent: $50
Wire orders accepted: Yes
Deadline for same day wire purchase: 4 P.M.
Discount broker availability: Fidelity, *White
Qualified for sale in: CA, CO, CT, DC, FL, GA, IN, MI, NJ, NC, PA, TX, VA, WA
Telephone redemptions: Yes
Wire redemptions: Yes
Letter redemptions: Signature guarantee required
Dividends paid: Income - December; Capital gains - December
Portfolio turnover (2 yrs): 52%, 63%
Shareholder services: IRA, SEP-IRA
Management fee: 1.50% (advisor pays all expenses)
Administration fee: 0.10% first $50M to 0.05% over $100M ($30,000 minimum)
Expense ratio: 1.50% (year ending 10/31/97) (1.55% without waiver)
IRA fees: Annual $10, Initial $12 (transfers only), Closing $15

CASH RESOURCE TRUST FUNDS
(Data common to all Cash Resource Trust funds are shown below. See subsequent listings for data specific to individual funds.)

901 East Byrd Street
Richmond, VA 23219
800-382-0016

Adviser: Mentor Investment Advisors, LLC (an indirect wholly owned subsidiary of Wheat First Butcher Singer, Inc.)
Transfer agent: Investors Fiduciary Trust Co.
Sales restrictions: Sold primarily through broker/dealers and other financial institutions, but are available direct from the distributor or by switching from Oberweis.
Minimum purchase: Initial: None, Subsequent: None
Wire orders accepted: Yes
Deadline for same day wire purchase: 4 P.M.
Qualified for sale in: All states
Letter redemptions: Signature guarantee required
Telephone switching: With other Cash Resource Trust funds and Oberweis mutual funds
Number of switches permitted: 2 round trips per year, $1,000 minimum

CASH RESOURCE TRUST MONEY MARKET
(See first Cash Resource Trust listing for data common to all funds)

Investment objective and policies: Highest rate of current income consistent with preservation of capital and maintenance of liquidity. Invests in high quality money market instruments.
Year organized: 1993
Dividends paid: Income - declared and paid monthly
Management fee: 0.22% first $500M to 0.15% over $3B
12b-1 distribution fee: Maximum of 0.40%
Expense ratio: 0.82% (year ending 7/31/97)

CASH RESOURCE TRUST TAX EXEMPT MONEY MARKET
(See first Cash Resource Trust listing for data common to all funds)

Investment objective and policies: Highest rate of current income exempt from federal income tax, consistent with preservation of capital and maintenance of liquidity. Invests in short-term general and special tax exempt obligations issued by U.S. states, territories and their political subdivisions.
Year organized: 1993
Dividends paid: Income - declared and paid monthly
Management fee: 0.22% first $500M to 0.15% over $3B
12b-1 distribution fee: Maximum of 0.33%
Expense ratio: 0.76% (year ending 7/31/97)

CASH RESOURCE TRUST U.S. GOVERNMENT MONEY MARKET
(See first Cash Resource Trust listing for data common to all funds)

Investment objective and policies: Highest rate of current income consistent with preservation of capital and maintenance of liquidity. Invests exclusively in U.S. Treasury bills, notes and bonds, and other obligations issued or guaranteed by the U.S. Government, its agencies or instrumentalities.
Year organized: 1993
Dividends paid: Income - declared and paid monthly
Management fee: 0.22% first $500M to 0.15% over $3B
12b-1 distribution fee: Maximum of 0.40%
Expense ratio: 0.93% (year ending 7/31/97)

CENTURY SHARES TRUST ◆
One Liberty Square
Boston, MA 02109
800-303-1928, 617-482-3060
fax 617-542-9398
e-mail: century28@aol.com

Adviser: Century Capital Management, Inc.
Portfolio managers: Allan W. Fulkerson (1976), William W. Dyer, Jr. (1976)
Transfer agent: Boston Financial Data Services, Inc.
Investment objective and policies: Long-term growth of principal and income. Invests in a diversified portfolio of common stocks, or securities convertible into common stocks, of insurance companies and banks, insurance brokers and other companies providing services to, or closely related to, insurance companies and banks. No relative amounts of either bank or insurance securities are specified, although the portfolio trends toward insurance.
Year organized: 1928
Ticker symbol: CENSX
Minimum purchase: Initial $500, Subsequent $25
Wire orders accepted: Yes
Deadline for same day wire purchase: 4 P.M.
Discount broker availability: *Fidelity, *Schwab, *White
Qualified for sale in: All states
Letter redemptions: Signature guarantee required over $10,000
Dividends paid: Income - June, December; Capital gains - December
Portfolio turnover (3 yrs): 6%, 3%, 5%
Shareholder services: IRA, automatic investment plan
Management fee: 0.70% first $250M, 0.60 over $250M
Expense ratio: 0.82% (year ending 12/31/97)
IRA fees: Annual $10, Closing $10

CGM FUNDS ◆
(Data common to all CGM funds are shown below. See subsequent listings for data specific to individual funds.)

c/o CGM Investor Services
222 Berkeley Street, Suite 1013
Boston, MA 02116
800-345-4048, 617-859-7714
prices/yields 800-343-5678
fax 617-774-3522, 617-859-7295
Internet: http://www.cgmfunds.com

Shareholder service hours: Full service: M-F 8:30 A.M.-8:00 P.M. EST; After hours service: prices, prospectuses, dividends/cap gains

Adviser: Capital Growth Management, L.P.
Transfer agent: State Street Bank & Trust Co.
Minimum purchase: Initial: $2,500, Subsequent: $50; IRA/Keogh: Initial: $1,000
Wire orders accepted: Yes, $50,000 minimum for initial, otherwise subsequent only
Deadline for same day wire purchase: 4 P.M.
Qualified for sale in: All states
Telephone redemptions: Yes, $25,000 maximum
Wire redemptions: Yes, $5 fee
Letter redemptions: Signature guarantee required over $25,000
Telephone switching: With other CGM funds and New England money market funds, $1,000 minimum
Number of switches permitted: 2 round trips per year, $1,000 minimum
Shareholder services: IRA, SEP-IRA, 403(b), Keogh, automatic investment plan, corporate retirement plans, directed dividends, systematic withdrawal plan min. bal. req. $10,000
IRA/Keogh fees: Annual $10, Initial $5, Closing $5

CGM AMERICAN TAX FREE FUND ◆
(See first CGM listing for data common to all funds)

Portfolio manager: Janice H. Saul (1993)
Investment objective and policies: High current income exempt from federal income tax; capital appreciation secondary. Invests primarily in investment grade tax-exempt general obligation bonds, revenue bonds and notes issued by states, territories and possessions of the U.S. and their political subdivisions, agencies and instrumentalities, or by multi-state agencies or authorities. Up to 25% of assets may be in securities rated below investment grade.
Year organized: 1993
Ticker symbol: CGMAX
Group fund code: 39
Dividends paid: Income - declared and paid monthly; Capital gains - February, December
Portfolio turnover (3 yrs): 107%, 125%, 169%
Management fee: 0.60% first $500M to 0.45% over $1B
Expense ratio: 0.00% (year ending 12/31/96) (2.14% without waiver)

CGM CAPITAL DEVELOPMENT FUND ◆
(See first CGM listing for data common to all funds)

Portfolio manager: G. Kenneth Heebner (1976)
Investment objective and policies: Long-term capital appreciation. Invests fully in common stocks and securities convertible into common stocks of both established and new, smaller companies.
Year organized: 1960 (formerly Loomis-Sayles Capital Development Fund)
Ticker symbol: LOMCX
Group fund code: 36
Special sales restrictions: Available only to shareholders of the Fund as of 9/24/93 who have remained continuous shareholders since that date.
Discount broker availability: White
Dividends paid: Income - December; Capital gains - December
Portfolio turnover (3 yrs): 178%, 271%, 146%
Management fee: 1.00% first $500M to 0.80% over $1B
Expense ratio: 0.82% (year ending 12/31/96)

CGM FIXED INCOME FUND ◆
(See first CGM listing for data common to all funds)

Portfolio managers: G. Kenneth Heebner (1992), Janice H. Saul (1993)
Investment objective and policies: Maximum total return: current income and capital appreciation. Invests in fixed-income or variable-rate securities and preferred stocks that provide current income, capital appreciation, or a combination of both, that are perceived to be undervalued. Will invest primarily in investment grade debt securities, but may invest up to 20% of assets in foreign securities, 10% in illiquid securities, and 35% in junk bonds.

Year organized: 1992
Ticker symbol: CFXIX
Group fund code: 38
Discount broker availability: White
Dividends paid: Income - declared and paid monthly; Capital gains - February, December
Portfolio turnover (3 yrs): 149%, 148%, 129%
Management fee: 0.65% first $200M to 0.40% over $500M
Expense ratio: 0.85% (year ending 12/31/96) (1.26% without waiver)

CGM FOCUS FUND ◆
(See first CGM listing for data common to all funds)

Portfolio manager: G. Kenneth Heebner (1997)
Investment objective and policies: Long-term capital growth. Invests in a core position of 20 to 30 equity securities. Then uses a variety of derivative instruments, including shorts, index futures contracts, puts and calls, to attempt to capitalize on the movement in prices of various securities. Fund is non-diversified.
Year organized: 1997
Ticker symbol: CGMFX
Group fund code: 815
Discount broker availability: White
Dividends paid: Income - December; Capital gains - December
Management fee: 1.00% first $500M to 0.90% over $1B

CGM MUTUAL FUND ◆
(See first CGM listing for data common to all funds)

Portfolio manager: G. Kenneth Heebner (1981)
Investment objective and policies: Long-term capital appreciation with a prudent approach to protection of capital from undue risks. Current income, while considered, is incidental. Invests in equity and debt securities with allocation of assets adjusted to perceived changes in market conditions. Fund may invest up to 25% of assets in one industry segment, including the real estate industry, and up to 35% of assets in junk bonds.
Year organized: 1929 (formerly Loomis-Sayles Mutual Fund)
Ticker symbol: LOMMX
Group fund code: 35
Discount broker availability: White
Dividends paid: Income - April, July, October, December; Capital gains - December
Portfolio turnover (3 yrs): 192%, 291%, 173%
Management fee: 0.90% first $500M to 0.75% over $1B
Expense ratio: 0.87% (year ending 12/31/96)

CGM REALTY FUND ◆
(See first CGM listing for data common to all funds)

Portfolio manager: G. Kenneth Heebner (1994)
Investment objective and policies: Above-average income and long-term capital growth. Invests at least 65% of assets in equity securities of companies in the real estate industry, including REITs, real estate developers and brokers, and companies with significant real estate holdings. Up to 25% of assets may be in junk bonds, and up to 35% invested in securities outside the real estate industry. May invest up to 10% of assets in illiquid securities.
Year organized: 1994
Ticker symbol: CGMRX
Group fund code: 137
Discount broker availability: Schwab, White
Dividends paid: Income - April, July, October, December; Capital gains - December
Portfolio turnover (3 yrs): 85%, 47%
Management fee: 0.85% first $500M, 0.75% over $500M
Expense ratio: 1.00% (year ending 12/31/96) (1.25% without waiver)

CHICAGO TRUST FUNDS
(At presstime, company announced a name change to Alleghany Funds. Data common to all Chicago Trust funds are shown below. See subsequent listings for data specific to individual funds.)

171 North Clark Street
Chicago, IL 60601-3294
800-992-8151, 800-621-1919
312-223-2300, fax 312-223-5609

Adviser: The Chicago Trust Co.
Transfer agent: First Data Investor Services Group, Inc.
Minimum purchase: Initial: $2,500, Subsequent: $50; IRA: Initial: $500; Automatic investment plan: Initial: $50
Wire orders accepted: Yes
Deadline for same day wire purchase: 4 P.M. (1 P.M. for Money Market Fund)
Qualified for sale: All states
Telephone redemptions: Yes
Wire redemptions: Yes, $20 fee
Letter redemptions: Signature guarantee required over $10,000
Telephone switching: With other Chicago Trust and Montag & Caldwell funds
Number of switches permitted: Unlimited
Shareholder services: IRA, systematic withdrawal plan min. bal. req. $50,000
12b-1 distribution fee: 0.25% (n/app to money market)
IRA fees: Annual $12

CHICAGO TRUST BALANCED FUND
(See first Chicago Trust listing for data common to all funds)

Portfolio managers: David J. Cox (1997), Thomas J. Marthaler (1997)
Investment objective and policies: Growth of capital and current income through asset allocation. Invests in a varying combination of common, preferred and convertible preferred stocks; fixed-income securities including bonds and bonds convertible into stocks; and short-term interest bearing obligations. Will generally hold between 30% and 70% of assets in equities. May invest up to 30% of assets in foreign securities in the form of ADRs, and up to 20% of assets in junk bonds.
Year organized: 1995 (Name changed from CT&T Asset Allocation 10/30/95; name changed from Chicago Asset Allocation 7/1/97.)
Ticker symbol: CHTAX
Discount broker availability: *Fidelity, *Schwab, *White
Dividends paid: Income - March, June, September, December; Capital gains - December
Portfolio turnover (2 yrs): 35%, 34%
Management fee: 0.70%
Expense ratio: 1.07% (year ending 10/31/97) (1.13% without waiver)

CHICAGO TRUST BOND FUND
(See first Chicago Trust listing for data common to all funds)

Portfolio manager: Thomas J. Marthaler (1993)
Investment objective and policies: High current income consistent with prudent risk of capital. Invests primarily in bonds and other fixed-income securities with a weighted average maturity of three to ten years. Up to 20% of assets may be in junk bonds. May use futures and options for hedging purposes.
Year organized: 1993 (Name changed from CT&T Intermediate Fixed Income Fund 10/30/95; objective remains the same)
Ticker symbol: CHTBX
Discount broker availability: *Fidelity, *Schwab, *White
Dividends paid: Income - declared and paid monthly; Capital gains - December
Portfolio turnover (3 yrs): 18%, 42%, 68%
Management fee: 0.55%
Expense ratio: 0.80% (year ending 10/31/97) (1.02% without waiver)

CHICAGO TRUST GROWTH & INCOME FUND
(See first Chicago Trust listing for data common to all funds)

Portfolio managers: Jerold L. Stodden (1993), Nancy Scinto (1997)
Investment objective and policies: Long-term total return: capital growth and current income. Invests primarily in common stocks, preferred stocks, securities convertible into common stocks and fixed-income securities. Up to 20% of assets may be in ADRs & EDRs of foreign issuers and 15% in illiquid securities. May use futures and options for hedging purposes.
Year organized: 1993 (name changed from CT&T Growth & Income 10/30/95)
Ticker symbol: CHTIX
Discount broker availability: *Fidelity, *Schwab, *White
Dividends paid: Income - March, June, September, December; Capital gains - December
Portfolio turnover (3 yrs): 31%, 25%, 9%
Management fee: 0.70%
Expense ratio: 1.07% (year ending 10/31/97) (1.12% without waiver)

CHICAGO TRUST MONEY MARKET FUND ◆
(See first Chicago Trust listing for data common to all funds)

Portfolio manager: Fred H. Senft, Jr. (1993)
Investment objective and policies: High current income consistent with liquidity and stability of principal. Invests in money market instruments.
Year organized: 1993 (Name changed from CT&T Money Market Fund 10/30/95)
Ticker symbol: CITXX
Check redemptions: $500 minimum
Dividends paid: Income - declared daily, paid monthly
Management fee: 0.40%
Expense ratio: 0.50% (year ending 10/31/97) (0.56% without waiver)

CHICAGO TRUST MUNICIPAL BOND FUND
(See first Chicago Trust listing for data common to all funds)

Portfolio manager: Lois A. Pasquale (1993)
Investment objective and policies: High current income exempt from federal income tax, consistent with capital preservation. Invests substantially all assets in domestic municipal debt obligations with a weighted average maturity of 3 to 10 years. Up to 20% of assets may be in securities subject to AMT tax treatment, and up to 20% in junk bonds.
Year organized: 1993 (Name changed from CT&T Intermediate Municipal Bond 10/30/95; objective remains the same)
Ticker symbol: CHTMX
Discount broker availability: *Fidelity, *Schwab, *White
Dividends paid: Income - declared and paid monthly; Capital gains - December
Portfolio turnover (3 yrs): 16%, 27%, 43%
Management fee: 0.60%
Expense ratio: 0.90% (year ending 10/31/97) (1.64% without waiver)

CHICAGO TRUST TALON FUND
(See first Chicago Trust listing for data common to all funds)

Sub-adviser: Talon Asset Management, Inc.
Portfolio manager: Terrance D. Diamond (1994)
Investment objective and policies: Long-term total return through capital appreciation. Invests primarily in stocks of companies of varied capitalization levels with good growth prospects. May also invest preferred stock and debt securities. Up to 30% of assets may be in ADRs & EDRs of foreign issuers, 20% in junk bonds and 15% in illiquid securities. May use covered call options for hedging purposes.
Year organized: 1994
Ticker symbol: CHTTX

Discount broker availability: *Fidelity, *Schwab, *White
Dividends paid: Income - March, June, September, December; Capital gains - December
Portfolio turnover (3 yrs): 113%, 127%, 229%
Management fee: 0.80%
Expense ratio: 1.30% (year ending 10/31/97) (1.67% without waiver)

CITISELECT PORTFOLIOS
(Data common to all CitiSelect portfolios are shown below. See subsequent listings for data specific to individual portfolios.)

153 East 53rd Street
New York, NY 10043
888-275-2484, 800-721-1899
212-820-2380, 617-423-1679

Adviser: Citibank, N.A.
Sub-advisers: Franklin Advisory Services, Inc.; Hotchkis and Wiley; Miller, Anderson & Sherrerd, LLP; Pacific Investment Management Co. (PIMCO)
Transfer agent: State Street Bank & Trust Co.
Sales restrictions: CitiSelect funds are, in fact, no-loads; however, the only 'direct' means to purchase them is by opening a brokerage account with Citicorp Investment Services. There is no transaction fee for purchasing CitiSelect funds through this account, but other purchases may incur such fees.
Minimum purchase: Initial: $1,000, Subsequent: $250
Wire orders accepted: No
Qualified for sale in: All states except AK, MO
Telephone redemptions: Yes
Wire redemptions: Yes, $15 fee
Letter redemptions: Signature guarantee not required
Telephone switching: With other CitiSelect portfolios
Number of switches permitted: Unlimited
Shareholder services: automatic investment plan, electronic funds transfer
12b-1 distribution fee: 0.50%

CITISELECT 200 PORTFOLIO
(See first CitiSelect listing for data common to all portfolios)

Lead portfolio manager: Lawrence P. Keblusek (1996)
Investment objective and policies: Income; capital appreciation secondary. Invests in an asset allocated portfolio, with allocations adjusted according to perceived market conditions. Types of assets and their ranges are as follows: stocks, 25% to 45%; bonds, 35% to 55%; cash, 10% to 30%. Bonds are diversified between domestic and foreign corporate and government issues, and stocks are diversified between domestic and foreign large cap growth, large cap value, small cap growth and small cap value. May use options and futures and currency exchange contracts for hedging purposes.
Year organized: 1996
Dividends paid: Income - monthly; Capital gains - annually
Portfolio turnover (1 yr): 127%
Management fee: 1.00%
Expense ratio: 1.50% (year ending 12/31/97)

CITISELECT 300 PORTFOLIO
(See first CitiSelect listing for data common to all portfolios)

Lead portfolio manager: Lawrence P. Keblusek (1996)
Investment objective and policies: Balanced total return; income and capital appreciation. Invests in an asset allocated portfolio, with allocations adjusted according to perceived market conditions. Types of assets and their ranges are as follows: stocks, 40% to 60%; bonds, 35% to 55%; cash, 1% to 10%. Bonds are diversified between domestic and foreign corporate and government issues, and stocks are diversified

between domestic and foreign large cap growth, large cap value, small cap growth and small cap value. May use options and futures and currency exchange contracts for hedging purposes.
Year organized: 1996
Dividends paid: Income - quarterly; Capital gains - annually
Portfolio turnover (1 yr): 1.09%
Management fee: 1.00%
Expense ratio: 1.50% (year ending 12/31/97)

CITISELECT 400 PORTFOLIO
(See first CitiSelect listing for data common to all portfolios)

Lead portfolio manager: Lawrence P. Keblusek (1996)
Investment objective and policies: Capital appreciation; income secondary. Invests in an asset allocated portfolio, with allocations adjusted according to perceived market conditions. Types of assets and their ranges are as follows: stocks, 55% to 85%; bonds, 15% to 35%; cash, 1% to 10%. Bonds are diversified between domestic and foreign corporate and government issues, and stocks are diversified between domestic and foreign large cap growth, large cap value, small cap growth and small cap value. May use options and futures and currency exchange contracts for hedging purposes.
Year organized: 1996
Dividends paid: Income - annually; Capital gains - annually
Portfolio turnover (1 yr): 1.09%
Management fee: 1.00%
Expense ratio: 1.75% (year ending 12/31/97)

CITISELECT 500 PORTFOLIO
(See first CitiSelect listing for data common to all portfolios)

Lead portfolio manager: Lawrence P. Keblusek (1996)
Investment objective and policies: Long-term total return, with primary emphasis on capital appreciation; income secondary. Invests in an asset allocated portfolio, with allocations adjusted according to perceived market conditions. Types of assets and their ranges are as follows: stocks, 70% to 95%; bonds, 5% to 20%; cash, 1% to 10%. Bonds are diversified between domestic and foreign corporate and government issues, and stocks are diversified between domestic and foreign large cap growth, large cap value, small cap growth and small cap value. May use options and futures and currency exchange contracts for hedging purposes.
Year organized: 1996
Dividends paid: Income - annually; Capital gains - annually
Portfolio turnover (1 yr): 70%
Management fee: 1.00%
Expense ratio: 1.75% (year ending 12/31/97)

CITIZENS TRUST PORTFOLIOS
(Data common to all Citizens Trust portfolios are shown below. See subsequent listings for data specific to individual portfolios.)

One Harbor Place, Suite 525
Portsmouth, NH 03801
800-223-7010, 603-436-5152
fax 603-433-4209
Internet: http://www.efund.com
e-mail: welcome@efund.com

Adviser: Citizens Advisers
Transfer agent: PFPC Inc.
Common policies: All portfolios favor investments that support housing, education, farming, small business, and energy conservation. Avoid companies that pollute the environment, manufacture weapons, drain capital from the U.S. or support repressive regimes.
Minimum purchase: Initial: $2,500, Subsequent: $50, Automatic investment plan: Initial: $250
Wire orders accepted: Yes
Deadline for same day wire purchase: 2:30 P.M.
Qualified for sale in: All states
Telephone redemptions: Yes

Wire redemptions: Yes, $10 fee
Letter redemptions: Signature guarantee required
Telephone switching: All Citizens Trust portfolios, and the Working Assets Money Market
Number of switches permitted: Unlimited
Shareholder services: IRA, SEP-IRA, 403(b), electronic funds transfer, systematic withdrawal plan min. bal. req. $10,000
Maintenance fee: $3/quarter for balances below $2,500
12b-1 distribution fee: Maximum of 0.25%
IRA fees: Annual $10, $5 per additional account ($15 maximum)

CITIZENS EMERGING GROWTH PORTFOLIO
(See first Citizens Trust listing for data common to all portfolios)

Sub-adviser: GMG/Seneca Capital Management, LLC
Portfolio manager: Richard D. Little (1994)
Investment objective and policies: Long-term capital growth. Invests at least 65% of assets in common stocks of companies with market capitalizations averaging $2B, believed to demonstrate above-average growth potential. May also invest in short-term fixed-income securities.
Year organized: 1994 (name changed from Working Assets Emerging Growth 9/1/95)
Ticker symbol: WAEGX
Discount broker availability: *Fidelity, *Schwab, Siebert, *White
Dividends paid: Income - annually; Capital gains - annually
Portfolio turnover (3 yrs): 229%, 337%, 231%
Management fee: 1.00%
Expense ratio: 1.99% (year ending 6/30/97) (2.01% without waiver)

CITIZENS GLOBAL EQUITY PORTFOLIO
(See first Citizens Trust listing for data common to all portfolios)

Sub-adviser: Clemente Capital, Inc.
Portfolio managers: Lilia Clemente (1994), Tom Prappas (1994), Sevgi Ipek (1994)
Investment objective and policies: Long-term capital appreciation. Invests in common stocks of domestic and foreign companies of all sizes with above-average growth potential on stock exchanges from around the world. Plans to invest over 50% of assets in a minimum of three countries outside of the U.S., of which no more than half will be invested in emerging markets. May use currency exchanges for purposes of hedging.
Year organized: 1993 (name changed from Working Assets Global Equity 9/1/95)
Ticker symbol: WAGEX
Discount broker availability: *Fidelity, *Schwab, Siebert, *White
Dividends paid: Income - annually; Capital gains - annually
Portfolio turnover (3 yrs): 69%, 86%, 22%
Management fee: 1.00%
Expense ratio: 2.10% (year ending 6/30/97) (2.33% without waiver)

CITIZENS INCOME PORTFOLIO
(See first Citizens Trust listing for data common to all portfolios)

Sub-adviser: GMG/Seneca Capital Management, LLC
Portfolio manager: Gail P. Seneca (1992)
Investment objective and policies: Current income with assured monthly dividends. Invests in fixed-income securities with a weighted average maturity of five to fifteen years. Up to 35% of assets may be in junk bonds.
Year organized: 1992 (name changed from Working Assets Income 9/1/95)
Ticker symbol: WAIMX
Discount broker availability: *Fidelity, *Schwab, Siebert, *White

Dividends paid: Income - monthly; Capital gains - annually
Portfolio turnover (3 yrs): 65%, 41%, 46%
Management fee: 0.65%
Expense ratio: 1.41% (year ending 6/30/97) (1.47% without waiver)

CITIZENS INDEX PORTFOLIO
(See first Citizens Trust listing for data common to all portfolios)

Sub-adviser: RhumbLine Advisers, Inc.
Portfolio manager: Edwin Ek (1996)
Investment objective and policies: Long-term capital appreciation. Invests in the common stock of a market weighted, highly diversified portfolio of 300 companies believed to be the best in their industries according to Citizens Trust social responsibility screening process.
Year organized: 1995 (Formed from merger of Working Assets Balanced fund and Working Assets Growth fund 5/30/95; name changed from Working Assets Index 9/1/95)
Ticker symbol: WAIDX
Discount broker availability: *Fidelity, *Schwab, Siebert, *White
Dividends paid: Income - annually; Capital gains - annually
Portfolio turnover (3 yrs): 19%, 6%, 65%
Management fee: 0.50%
Expense ratio: 1.59% (year ending 6/30/97)

CLIPPER FUND ◆
9601 Wilshire Blvd., Suite 800
Beverly Hills, CA 90210
800-432-2504, 800-776-5033
310-247-3940
shareholder services 800-432-2504
fax 310-273-0514
Internet: http://www.clipperfund.com

Adviser: Pacific Financial Research, Inc.
Portfolio managers: James H. Gipson (1984), Michael C. Sandler (1984), Bruce Veaco (1986)
Transfer agent: National Financial Data Services
Investment objective and policies: Long-term capital growth. Invests in common stocks, convertible long-term corporate debt, and convertible preferred stocks believed undervalued as determined by fundamental considerations. Fund may invest up to 25% of assets in junk bonds, 15% in securities of foreign issuers and/or 10% in special situations. Fund is non-diversified.
Year organized: 1984
Ticker symbol: CFIMX
Minimum purchase: Initial: $5,000, Subsequent: $1,000; IRA: Initial: $2,000, Subsequent: $200; Automatic investment plan: Subsequent: $150
Wire orders accepted: Yes
Deadline for same day wire purchase: 4 P.M.
Discount broker availability: *Fidelity, Schwab, White
Qualified for sale in: All states
Telephone redemptions: Yes
Wire redemptions: Yes
Letter redemptions: Signature guarantee required
Dividends paid: Income - December; Capital gains - December
Portfolio turnover (3 yrs): 31%, 24%, 31%
Shareholder services: IRA, 403(b)
Management fee: 1.00%
Expense ratio: 1.08% (year ending 12/31/97)
IRA fees: Annual $10

CLOVER CAPITAL FUNDS ◆
(See TIP Funds)

CMA MONEY FUND
P.O. Box 9011
Princeton, NJ 08543
800-637-7455, 800-637-3863
800-262-4636
609-282-2800, fax 609-282-3466

Adviser: Fund Asset Management, Inc. (a subsidiary of Merrill Lynch Asset Management, Inc.)
Portfolio manager: Kevin McKenna (1989)

Transfer agent: Financial Data Services, Inc.
Investment objective and policies: Current income, preservation of capital and liquidity. Invests in money market securities.
Year organized: 1977
Ticker symbol: CMEXX
Special sales restrictions: Available to Merrill Lynch customers only
Minimum purchase: Initial: $20,000 in cash or securities, Subsequent: $1,000
Qualified for sale in: All states
Check redemptions: No minimum
Dividends paid: Income - declared and paid daily
Shareholders services: Fund is part of a central assets account
Service fee: $100 per year
Management fee: 0.50% first $500M to 0.375% over $1B
12b-1 distribution fee: 0.13%
Expense ratio: 0.56% (year ending 3/31/97)

COHEN & STEERS REALTY SHARES ◆
757 Third Avenue
New York, NY 10017
800-437-9912, 212-832-3232
fax 212-832-3622

Adviser: Cohen & Steers Capital Management, Inc.
Portfolio managers: Martin Cohen (1991), Robert H. Steers (1991)
Transfer agent: Chase Global Funds Services Co.
Investment objective and policies: Total return: approximately equal emphasis on current income and capital appreciation. Invests substantially all its assets in equity securities of real estate companies, including common and preferred stocks and convertible debt securities. May invest in REITs without limit, and invest up to 15% of assets in illiquid securities. May invest up to 10% of assets in foreign real estate, and use derivatives. Fund is non-diversified, and may purchase more than 10% of the voting stock of any company in which it chooses to invest, and may invest up to 25% of assets in one company.
Year organized: 1991
Ticker symbol: CSRSX
Minimum purchase: Initial: $10,000, Subsequent: $500
Wire orders accepted: Yes
Deadline for same day wire purchase: 3 P.M.
Discount broker availability: *Fidelity, *Schwab, *Siebert, *White
Qualified for sale in: All states
Telephone redemptions: Yes
Wire redemptions: Yes
Letter redemptions: Signature guarantee not required
Telephone switching: With Cohen & Steers Special Equity Fund
Number of switches permitted: 4 per year
Dividends paid: Income - March, June, September, December; Capital gains - December
Portfolio turnover (3 yrs): 40%, 33%, 23%
Management fee: 0.85%
Administration fee: 0.20%
Expense ratio: 1.05% (year ending 12/31/97) (1.06% without waiver)

COHEN & STEERS SPECIAL EQUITY FUND ◆
757 Third Avenue
New York, NY 10017
800-437-9912, 212-832-3232
fax 212-832-3622

Adviser: Cohen & Steers Capital Management, Inc.
Portfolio managers: Martin Cohen (1997), Robert H. Steers (1997)
Transfer agent: Chase Global Funds Services Co.
Investment objective and policies: Maximum long-term capital appreciation; current income incidental. Invests at least 65% of assets in a limited number of companies engaged in real estate or related businesses. May also invest up to 35% of assets in debt or equity securities of any other type of business or in derivatives.
Year organized: 1997
Minimum purchase: Initial: $10,000, Subsequent: $500

Wire orders accepted: Yes
Deadline for same day wire purchase: 3 P.M.
Discount broker availability: Fidelity, Schwab, White
Qualified for sale in: All states
Telephone redemptions: Yes
Wire redemptions: Yes
Letter redemptions: Signature guarantee not required
Redemption fee: 2.00% for shares held less than 1 year, payable to the fund
Telephone switching: With Cohen & Steers Realty Fund
Number of switches permitted: 4 per year
Dividends paid: Income - semi-annually; Capital gains - annually
Portfolio turnover (1 yr): 97%
Management fee: 0.90%
Administration fee: 0.20%
Expense ratio: 1.35% (eight months ending 12/31/97)

COLUMBIA FUNDS ◆
(Data common to all Columbia funds are shown below. See subsequent listings for data specific to individual funds.)

1301 S.W. Fifth Avenue
Portland, OR 97201
800-547-1707, 800-547-1037
503-222-3600
prices/yields 800-547-2170
fax 503-243-3286
Internet: http://www.columbiafunds.com
e-mail: inser@columbiafunds.com

Shareholder service hours: Full service: M-F 7:30 A.M.-5 P.M. PST; After hours service: prices, yields, account balances, last transaction, news, indices, prospectuses, total returns
Adviser: Columbia Funds Management Co. (a wholly-owned affiliate of Fleet Financial Group, Inc.)
Transfer agent: Columbia Trust Co.
Minimum purchase: Initial: $1,000 ($2,000 for Small Cap and Special Funds), Subsequent: $100; Automatic investment plan: Initial: $0, Subsequent: $50
Wire orders accepted: Yes
Deadline for same day wire purchase: 4 P.M.
Telephone redemptions: Yes
Wire redemptions: Yes, $1,000 minimum, $5 fee
Letter redemptions: Signature guarantee required over $50,000
Telephone switching: With other Columbia Funds
Number of switches permitted: 4 exchanges out per year
Shareholder services: IRA, SEP-IRA, Keogh, directed dividends, electronic funds transfer, systematic withdrawal plan min. bal. req. $5,000
IRA fees: Annual $25, (waived for balances over $25,000)
Keogh fees: Annual $50, Initial $100

COLUMBIA BALANCED FUND ◆
(See first Columbia Funds listing for data common to all funds)

Portfolio manager: Team managed
Investment objective and policies: High total return: capital growth and income. Invests 35% to 65% of assets in common stocks, and 35% to 65% in fixed-income securities, with mix based on expected relative returns as investment environment changes. At least 25% of assets are always in non-convertible fixed-income securities, with cash equivalents normally less than 10%. May invest up to 33% of assets in securities of foreign issuers, and use futures and options to hedge up to 25% of assets.
Year organized: 1991
Ticker symbol: CBALX
Group fund code: 208
Discount broker availability: Fidelity, Schwab, Siebert, White
Qualified for sale in: All states
Dividends paid: Income - March, June, September, December; Capital gains - December
Portfolio turnover (3 yrs): 149%, 133%, 108%
Management fee: 0.50%
Expense ratio: 0.68% (year ending 12/31/97)

COLUMBIA COMMON STOCK FUND ◆
(See first Columbia Funds listing for data common to all funds)

Portfolio manager: Team managed
Investment objective and policies: Capital growth and dividend income. Invests primarily in common stocks which management believes will increase in value in current economic environment. May invest up to 33% of assets in securities of foreign issuers and use futures and options to hedge up to 25% of assets.
Year organized: 1991
Ticker symbol: CMSTX
Group fund code: 107
Discount broker availability: Fidelity, Schwab, Siebert, White
Qualified for sale in: All states
Dividends paid: Income - March, June, September, December; Capital gains - December
Portfolio turnover (3 yrs): 90%, 111%, 75%
Management fee: 0.60%
Expense ratio: 0.77% (year ending 12/31/97)

COLUMBIA DAILY INCOME COMPANY ◆
(See first Columbia Funds listing for data common to all funds)

Portfolio manager: Leonard A. Aplet (1988)
Investment objective and policies: High current income consistent with preservation of capital and liquidity. Invests in bank, corporate and government money market instruments.
Year organized: 1974
Ticker symbol: CDIXX
Group fund code: 301
Qualified for sale in: All states
Check redemptions: $500 minimum
Dividends paid: Income - declared and paid daily
Management fee: 0.50% first $500M to 0.40% over $1B
Expense ratio: 0.63% (year ending 12/31/97)

COLUMBIA FIXED INCOME SECURITIES FUND ◆
(See first Columbia Funds listing for data common to all funds)

Portfolio managers: Leonard A. Aplet (1989), Jeffrey L. Rippey (1989)
Investment objective and policies: High current income consistent with capital conservation. Invests at least 95% of assets in a diversified portfolio of investment grade fixed-income securities such as bonds, debentures, government securities, GNMAs and repurchase agreements. May invest a portion of assets in collateralized mortgage obligations. Fund has no maturity restrictions, and it varies according to perceived market conditions.
Year organized: 1983
Ticker symbol: CFISX
Group fund code: 402
Discount broker availability: Fidelity, Schwab, Siebert, White
Qualified for sale in: All states
Dividends paid: Income - declared daily, paid monthly; Capital gains - December
Portfolio turnover (3 yrs): 196%, 178%, 137%
Management fee: 0.50%
Expense ratio: 0.66% (year ending 12/31/97)

COLUMBIA GROWTH FUND ◆
(See first Columbia Funds listing for data common to all funds)

Portfolio manager: Alexander S. Macmillan (1992)
Investment objective and policies: Capital growth. Invests primarily in common stocks believed undervalued. Up to 10% of assets may be in securities of foreign issuers in developed economies. May use futures and options to hedge up to 25% of assets.
Year organized: 1967
Ticker symbol: CLMBX
Group fund code: 103

Discount broker availability: Fidelity, Schwab, Siebert, White
Qualified for sale in: All states
Dividends paid: Income - December; Capital gains - December
Portfolio turnover (3 yrs): 96%, 75%, 95%
Management fee: 0.75% first $200M to 0.50% over $500M
Expense ratio: 0.71% (year ending 12/31/97)

COLUMBIA HIGH YIELD FUND ◆
(See first Columbia Funds listing for data common to all funds)

Portfolio manager: Jeffrey L. Rippey (1993)
Investment objective and policies: High current income; capital appreciation secondary. Invests primarily in lower-rated fixed-income securities such as bonds, debentures, government securities, GNMAs and repurchase agreements. Normally invests at least 65% of assets in junk bonds, although no more than 10% of assets are rated below "Caa" or "CCC". Fund has no maturity restrictions, and it varies according to perceived market conditions. May invest 10% of assets in fixed-income securities of foreign issuers, and use options to hedge up to 25% of assets.
Year organized: 1993
Ticker symbol: CMHYX
Group fund code: 410
Discount broker availability: Fidelity, Schwab, Siebert, White
Qualified for sale in: All states
Dividends paid: Income - declared daily, paid monthly; Capital gains - December
Portfolio turnover (3 yrs): 124%, 62%, 52%
Management fee: 0.60%
Expense ratio: 1.00% (year ending 12/31/97)

COLUMBIA INTERNATIONAL STOCK FUND ◆
(See first Columbia Funds listing for data common to all funds)

Portfolio manager: James M. McAlear (1992)
Investment objective and policies: Long-term capital appreciation. Invests at least 65% of assets in equity securities of companies from at least three countries other than the U.S. At least 75% of assets are invested in companies with more than $500M in capitalizaition and more than three years of operating history. Up to 35% of assets may be in securities of U.S. issuers if deemed necessary. May use foreign currency exchange contracts and options and futures for hedging purposes.
Year organized: 1992
Ticker symbol: CMISX
Group fund code: 109
Discount broker availability: Fidelity, Schwab, Siebert, White
Qualified for sale in: All states
Dividends paid: Income - December; Capital gains - December
Portfolio turnover (3 yrs): 122%, 129%, 156%
Management fee: 1.00%
Expense ratio: 1.62% (year ending 12/31/97)

COLUMBIA MUNICIPAL BOND FUND ◆
(See first Columbia Funds listing for data common to all funds)

Portfolio manager: Greta R. Clapp (1992)
Investment objective and policies: High current income exempt from federal and State of Oregon income taxes, consistent with capital conservation. Invests in municipal securities of which at least 60% are expected to be exempt from Oregon income taxes, primarily those issued by the state of Oregon or other Oregon issuers. Fund normally has a weighted average maturity of ten years or more. May invest up to 20% of assets in securities subject to federal income tax.
Year organized: 1984
Ticker symbol: CMBFX
Group fund code: 404
Discount broker availability: Fidelity, Schwab, Siebert, White

Qualified for sale in: CA, CO, DC, HI, ID, KY, NE, NV, NJ, NM, OK, OR, PA, SD, UT, WA
Dividends paid: Income - declared daily, paid monthly; Capital gains - December
Portfolio turnover (3 yrs): 17%, 19%, 21%
Management fee: 0.50%
Expense ratio: 0.57% (year ending 12/31/97)

COLUMBIA REAL ESTATE EQUITY FUND ◆
(See first Columbia Funds listing for data common to all funds)

Portfolio manager: David W. Jellison (1994)
Investment objective and policies: Above-average current income and capital growth. Invests at least 65% of assets in equity securities of companies principally engaged in the real estate industry - that own, construct, manage or sell residential, commercial or industrial real estate. May invest in real estate investment trusts (REITs) without limit, and have up to 35% of assets in non-real estate companies or non-convertible debt securities. May invest up to 20% of assets in securities of foreign real estate issuers. May use futures and options for hedging purposes.
Year organized: 1994
Ticker symbol: CREEX
Group fund code: 111
Discount broker availability: Fidelity, Schwab, Siebert, White
Qualified for sale in: All states
Dividends paid: Income - March, June, September, December; Capital gains - December
Portfolio turnover (3 yrs): 34%, 46%, 54%
Management fee: 0.75%
Expense ratio: 1.02% (year ending 12/31/97)

COLUMBIA SMALL CAP FUND ◆
(See first Columbia Funds listing for data common to all funds)

Portfolio manager: Richard J. Johnson (1996)
Investment objective and policies: Capital appreciation. Invests primarily in common stocks of companies with market capitalizations under $1B, based on 'top down' management appraisal of financial condition, quality of management, dynamics of the relevant industry, earnings growth and profit margins, sales trends, potential for new product development, dividend history and potential, financial ratios, and investment in R&D. May invest up to 25% of assets in securities of foreign issuers or ADRs, and up to 35% of assets in larger capitalization companies. May also invest in debt securities or convertible preferred that may be exchanged for small cap common. May use futures and options to hedge up to 25% of assets.
Year organized: 1996
Ticker symbol: CMSCX
Group fund code: 112
Discount broker availability: Fidelity, Schwab, Siebert, White
Qualified for sale in: All states
Dividends paid: Income - December; Capital gains - December
Portfolio turnover (1 yr): 172%
Management fee: 1.00%
Expense ratio: 1.46% (year ending 12/31/97)

COLUMBIA SPECIAL FUND ◆
(See first Columbia Funds listing for data common to all funds)

Portfolio manager: Alan J. Folkman (1997)
Investment objective and policies: Capital appreciation. Invests primarily in common stocks of smaller companies believed to have growth potential higher than the overall market (as measured by the S&P 500) albeit with a higher degree of risk. May invest in special situations such as new issues, companies undergoing management or technology changes, tender offers, leveraged buyouts, or mergers. May invest up to 33% of assets in securities of foreign issuers and use futures and options to hedge up to 25% of assets.

Year organized: 1985 (3 for 1 split on 2/1/92)
Ticker symbol: CLSPX
Group fund code: 105
Discount broker availability: Fidelity, Schwab, Siebert, White
Qualified for sale in: All states
Dividends paid: Income - December; Capital gains - December
Portfolio turnover (3 yrs): 166%, 150%, 183%
Management fee: 1.00% first $500M, 0.75% over $500M
Expense ratio: 0.98% (year ending 12/31/97)

COLUMBIA U.S. GOVERNMENT SECURITIES FUND ◆
(See first Columbia Funds listing for data common to all funds)

Portfolio manager: Jeffrey L. Rippey (1987)
Investment objective and policies: Capital preservation and a high level of income. Invests substantially all of its assets in U.S. Government obligations with remaining individual maturities of three years or less.
Year organized: 1986 (formerly U.S. Government Guaranteed Securities Fund)
Ticker symbol: CUGGX
Group fund code: 406
Discount broker availability: Fidelity, Siebert, White
Qualified for sale in: All states except AL, AR, DE, IN, KS, LA, ME, MA, MS, NH, ND, RI, SC, TN, VT, WV, WI
Dividends paid: Income - declared daily, paid monthly; Capital gains - December
Portfolio turnover (3 yrs): 184%, 179%, 253%
Management fee: 0.50%
Expense ratio: 0.87% (year ending 12/31/97)

CONCORDE INCOME FUND ◆
1500 Three Lincoln Centre
5430 LBJ Freeway
Dallas, TX 75240
800-294-1699, 972-387-8258
shareholder services 800-338-1579
fax 972-701-0530
e-mail: concorde@airmail.net

Adviser: Concorde Financial Corp.
Portfolio managers: Gary B. Wood (1996), John A. Stetter (1997)
Transfer agent: Firstar Trust Co.
Investment objective and policies: Current income; capital growth secondary. Invests primarily in investment grade U.S. dollar-denominated debt securities. Will invest between 20% and 50% of portfolio in U.S. Government or agency instruments with maturities ranging from two to ten years. May also invest in dividend paying common stocks, preferred stocks and convertible securities. Up to 25% of assets may be in foreign securities, 20% in ADRs of foreign issuers, 20% in junk bonds and 15% in illiquid securities. May use options for hedging purposes.
Year organized: 1996
Ticker symbol: COINX
Minimum purchase: Initial: $500, Subsequent: $100
Wire orders accepted: Yes, $500 minimum
Deadline for same day wire purchase: 11 A.M.
Discount broker availability: Schwab
Qualified for sale in: CA, FL, GA, IL, NY, NC, TX, WI
Telephone redemptions: Yes, $1,000 minimum
Wire redemptions: Yes, $1,000 minimum, $10 fee
Letter redemptions: Signature guarantee not required
Telephone switching: With Concorde Value Fund, $1,000 minimum
Number of switches permitted: Unlimited
Dividends paid: Income - March, June, September, December; Capital gains - December
Portfolio turnover (2 yrs): 20%, 30%
Shareholder services: IRA, SEP-IRA, Keogh, 401(k), 403(b), corporate retirement plans
Management fee: 0.70%
Expense ratio: 1.99% (year ending 9/30/97)
IRA/Keogh fees: Annual $12.50 ($25 maximum per tax ID)

CONCORDE VALUE FUND ◆
1500 Three Lincoln Centre
5430 LBJ Freeway
Dallas, TX 75240
800-294-1699, 972-387-8258
shareholder services 800-338-1579
fax 972-701-0530
e-mail: concorde@airmail.net

Adviser: Concorde Financial Corp.
Portfolio managers: Gary B. Wood (1987), John A. Stetter (1997)
Transfer agent: Firstar Trust Co.
Investment objective and policies: Long-term capital growth without exposing capital to undue risk. Invests primarily in out of favor common stocks, focusing on "value" approach characterized by low relative price/earnings or price/book value, high dividend yield, less than $500M capitalization and/or low analyst coverage. Up to 20% of assets may be in foreign securities and 20% in ADRs of foreign issuers. May use options for hedging purposes.
Year organized: 1987
Ticker symbol: CONVX
Minimum purchase: Initial: $500, Subsequent: $100
Wire orders accepted: Yes, $500 minimum
Deadline for same day wire purchase: 11 A.M.
Discount broker availability: Schwab
Qualified for sale in: CA, FL, GA, IL, NY, NC, TX, WI
Telephone redemptions: Yes, $1,000 minimum
Wire redemptions: Yes, $1,000 minimum, $10 fee
Letter redemptions: Signature guarantee not required
Telephone switching: With Concorde Income Fund, $1,000 minimum
Number of switches permitted: Unlimited
Dividends paid: Income - December; Capital gains - December
Portfolio turnover (3 yrs): 31%, 26%, 22%
Shareholder services: IRA, SEP-IRA, Keogh, 401(k), 403(b), corporate retirement plans
Management fee: 0.90%
Expense ratio: 1.60% (year ending 9/30/97)
IRA/Keogh fees: Annual $12.50 ($25 maximum per tax ID)

CONNECTICUT DAILY TAX FREE INCOME FUND ◆
600 Fifth Avenue, 8th Floor
New York, NY 10020
800-221-3079, 212-830-5220
prices/yields 212-830-5225
fax 212-830-5478

Adviser: Reich & Tang Asset Management, L.P.
Portfolio manager: Molly Flewharty (1985)
Transfer agent: Investors Fiduciary Trust Co.
Investment objective and policies: High current interest income exempt from federal income tax, and, to the extent possible, from Connecticut income taxes, consistent with preservation of capital and liquidity. Invests primarily in Connecticut municipal money market instruments.
Year organized: 1985
Ticker symbol: CTIXX
Special sales restrictions: Only class "B" shares of the fund are sold direct and without 12b-1 fees. Statistics represent "B" shares only.
Minimum purchase: Initial: $5,000, Subsequent: $100
Wire orders accepted: Yes
Deadline for same day wire purchase: 12 NN
Qualified for sale in: CT, MA, NJ, NY
Telephone redemptions: Yes
Wire redemptions: Yes, $1,000 minimum
Letter redemptions: Signature guarantee required
Check redemptions: $250 minimum
Telephone switching: With other Reich & Tang Money Market funds and R&T Equity Fund
Number of switches permitted: Unlimited, $1,000 minimum
Deadline for same day switch: 12 NN
Dividends paid: Income - declared daily, paid monthly

Shareholder services: Automatic investment plan, electronic funds transfer, systematic withdrawal plan
Management fee: 0.30%
Administration fee: 0.21%
Shareholder services fee: 0.20%
Expense ratio: 0.70% (year ending 1/31/97) (0.72% without waiver)

COPLEY FUND ◆
P.O. Box 3287
Fall River, MA 02722-3287
508-674-8459, fax 508-672-9348

Adviser: Copley Financial Services Corp.
Portfolio manager: Irving Levine (1978)
Transfer agent: Steadman Security Corp.
Investment objective and policies: Tax-advantaged accumulation of dividend income utilizing the Fund's 70% deduction from federal income taxes for dividends received; long-term capital growth secondary. Invests in securities with high, and increasing, dividend income. May invest in bonds or money market instruments for defensive purposes. Fund engages to a limited degree in an operating business in order to qualify for its tax treatment; proceeds of the business are included in the NAV.
Year organized: 1978 (Formerly Copley Tax-Managed Fund) (1 for 3 reverse split in 1983)
Ticker symbol: COPLX
Minimum purchase: Initial: $1,000, Subsequent: $100; IRA/Keogh: Initial: $100
Wire orders accepted: No
Qualified for sale in: All states
Letter redemptions: Signature guarantee required
Dividends paid: No distributions by policy - retained in NAV, and the fund pays corporate taxes.
Portfolio turnover (3 yrs): 9%, 5%, 31%
Shareholder services: IRA, Keogh, systematic withdrawal plan min. bal. req. $10,000
Management fee: 1.00% first $25M to 0.50% over $40M
Expense ratio: 1.00% (year ending 2/28/97) (1.08% without waiver)
IRA/Keogh fees: Annual $25

CORBIN SMALL CAP VALUE FUND ◆
1320 South University Drive, Suite 406
Fort Worth, TX 76107
800-924-6848

Adviser: Corbin & Co.
Administrator: AmeriPrime Financial Services, Inc.
Portfolio manager: David A. Corbin (1997)
Transfer agent: American Data Services, Inc.
Investment objective and policies: Long-term capital appreciation. Invests primarily in equity securities of companies with market capitalizations of less than $2B that are perceived to be undervalued.
Year organized: 1997
Minimum purchase: Initial: $2,000, Subsequent: $50
Wire orders accepted: Yes
Deadline for same day wire purchase: 4 P.M.
Discount broker availability: *Fidelity, *Schwab, *White
Qualified for sale in: All states
Telephone redemptions: Yes
Wire redemptions: Yes
Letter redemptions: Signature guarantee required
Dividends paid: Income - December; Capital gains - December
Shareholder services: IRA, SEP-IRA, automatic investment plan
Management fee: 1.25%
Administration fee: 0.10% first $50M to 0.05% over $100M ($30,000 minimum)
IRA fees: Annual $15, Closing $15

CORNERCAP BALANCED FUND ◆
1355 Peachtree Street, N.E.
Suite 1700
Atlanta GA 30309
888-813-8637, 800-728-0670
404-892-9313, 404-870-0700
fax 404-892-9353, 404-870-0770

Adviser: Cornerstone Capital Corp.
Portfolio managers: Thomas E. Quinn (1997), D. Ray Peebles (1997)
Transfer agent: Fortune Fund Administration, Inc.
Investment objective and policies: Capital appreciation and income. Invests 50% to 70% of assets in equity securities, primarily common stocks, preferred stocks and securities convertible to common stocks, selected from among 1,500 issues ranked according to fundamental factors proprietary to the manager. The balance of assets, generally about 30%, is invested in investment grade fixed-income obligations of any maturity, and cash reserves. Up to 25% of assets may be in securities of foreign issuers, represented primarily by ADRs. May sell short and use futures and options in an effort to enhance returns and for hedging purposes.
Year organized: 1997
Minimum purchase: Initial: $2,000, Subsequent: $250; Automatic investment plan: Initial: $250
Wire orders accepted: Yes
Deadline for same day wire purchase: 4 P.M.
Discount broker availability: *Schwab
Qualified for sale in: All states except AK, CT, ID, ME, MA, MT, NE, NV, NM, ND, OK, RI, SD, UT, VT, WY
Letter redemptions: Signature guarantee not required
Dividends paid: Income - April, December; Capital gains - December
Shareholder services: IRA, systematic withdrawal plan min. bal. req. $10,000
Management fee: 1.00%
12b-1 distribution fee: Maximum of 0.25% (not currently imposed)
IRA fees: Annual $10

CORNERCAP GROWTH FUND ◆
1355 Peachtree Street, N.E.
Suite 1700
Atlanta GA 30309
888-813-8637, 800-728-0670
404-892-9313, 404-870-0700
fax 404-892-9353, 404-870-0770

Adviser: Cornerstone Capital Corp.
Portfolio manager: Thomas E. Quinn (1992)
Transfer agent: Fortune Fund Administration, Inc.
Investment objective and policies: Long-term capital appreciation; income secondary. Invests at least 65% of assets in equity securities of foreign and domestic companies selected from among 1,500 issues ranked according to fundamental factors proprietary to the manager. Up to 20% of assets may be in securities of foreign issuers. May sell short, use futures and options and, for defensive purposes, invest in short-term debt instruments.
Year organized: 1986 (as Wealth Monitors Fund - name/management change to Sunshine Growth Trust 8/13/90; name/management changed to Cornerstone Growth 12/10/92; name changed to current 6/30/95)
Ticker symbol: CGRFX
Minimum purchase: Initial: $2,000, Subsequent: $250; Automatic investment plan: Initial: $250
Wire orders accepted: Yes
Deadline for same day wire purchase: 4 P.M.
Discount broker availability: Schwab, *White
Qualified for sale in: All states except AK, CT, ID, ME, MA, MT, NE, NV, NM, ND, OK, RI, SD, UT, VT, WY
Letter redemptions: Signature guarantee not required
Dividends paid: Income - April, December; Capital gains - December
Portfolio turnover (3 yrs): 37%, 41%, 55%
Shareholder services: IRA, systematic withdrawal plan min. bal. req. $10,000
Management fee: 1.00%

12b-1 distribution fee: Maximum of 0.25% (not currently imposed)
Expense ratio: 1.71% (year ending 3/31/97) (2.15% without waiver)
IRA fees: Annual $10

THE CRABBE HUSON FUNDS
(Data common to all Crabbe Huson funds are shown below. See subsequent listings for data specific to individual funds.)

121 S.W. Morrison, Suite 1400
Portland, OR 97204
800-541-9732, 800-638-3148
503-295-0919
prices/yields 800-235-2442
fax 503-295-2939
Internet: http://www.contrarian.com
e-mail: shareholder@chgroup.com

Shareholder service hours: Full service: M-F 6:30 A.M.-5 P.M. PST; After hours service: prices, yields, account balances, orders, last transaction, news, messages, indices, order prospectuses, total returns, portfolio comments
Adviser: The Crabbe Huson Group, Inc.
Transfer agent: State Street Bank & Trust Co.
Minimum purchase: Initial: $2,000, Subsequent: $500; Automatic investment plan: Subsequent: $100
Wire orders accepted: Yes
Deadline for same day wire purchase: 4 P.M.
Qualified for sale in: All states (except Oregon Tax-Free fund)
Telephone redemptions: Yes
Wire redemptions: Yes
Letter redemptions: Signature guarantee required over $15,000
Telephone switching: With other Crabbe Huson funds
Number of switches permitted: 10 per year
Shareholder services: IRA, Keogh, 401(k), corporate retirement plans, electronic funds transfer, systematic withdrawal plan min. bal. req. $5,000
12b-1 distribution fee: Maximum of 0.25%
IRA fees: Annual $15 per account (waived if aggregate value of accounts exceeds $25,000)
Keogh fees: None

THE CRABBE HUSON ASSET ALLOCATION FUND
(See first Crabbe Huson listing for data common to all funds)

Portfolio managers: Richard S. Huson (1988), John E. Maack, Jr. (1988), Robert E. Anton (1995), Marian L. Kessler (1995), Garth R. Nisbet (1996)
Investment objective and policies: Capital appreciation and income consistent with capital preservation. Invests in a variable mix of stocks, fixed-income securities, cash, and cash equivalents. Stock portion of portfolio will range from 20% to 75% according to market conditions.
Year organized: 1988
Ticker symbol: CHAAX
Group fund code: 613
Discount broker availability: *Fidelity, *Schwab, *Siebert, *White
Dividends paid: Income - January, April, July, October, December; Capital gains - December
Portfolio turnover (3 yrs): 119%, 252%, 226%
Management fee: 1.00% first $100M to 0.60% over $500M
Expense ratio: 1.42% (year ending 10/31/97) (1.55% without waiver)

THE CRABBE HUSON EQUITY FUND
(See first Crabbe Huson listing for data common to all funds)

Portfolio managers: Richard S. Huson (1989), John E. Maack, Jr. (1989), Marian L. Kessler (1995), Robert E. Anton (1995)

Investment objective and policies: Long-term capital appreciation. Invests at least 65% of assets in common stocks. Fund employs a basic value, contrarian approach in selecting stocks and focuses on mid to large capitalization companies. May invest up to 35% of assets in foreign securities. Fund may hedge.
Year organized: 1989
Ticker symbol: CHEYX
Group fund code: 614
Discount broker availability: *Fidelity, *Schwab, *Siebert, *White
Dividends paid: Income - December; Capital gains - December
Portfolio turnover (3 yrs): 129%, 117%, 92%
Management fee: 1.00% first $100M to 0.60% over $500M
Expense ratio: 1.42% (year ending 10/31/97) (1.44% without waiver)

THE CRABBE HUSON INCOME FUND
(See first Crabbe Huson listing for data common to all funds)

Portfolio managers: Richard S. Huson (1995), Garth R. Nisbet (1995)
Investment objective and policies: Current income consistent with capital preservation. Invests in a diversified portfolio of high quality fixed-income securities and preferred or convertible preferred stock. Up to 35% of assets may be in foreign securities.
Year organized: 1988
Ticker symbol: CHINX
Group fund code: 615
Discount broker availability: *Fidelity, *Schwab, *Siebert, *White
Dividends paid: Income - monthly; Capital gains - December
Portfolio turnover (3 yrs): 56%, 469%, 543%
Management fee: 0.75% first $100M to 0.50% over $500M
Expense ratio: 0.80% (year ending 10/31/97) (2.78% without waiver)

THE CRABBE HUSON OREGON TAX-FREE FUND
(See first Crabbe Huson listing for data common to all funds)

Portfolio managers: Richard S. Huson (1995), Garth R. Nisbet (1995)
Investment objective and policies: High income exempt from federal and Oregon income taxes, consistent with capital preservation. Invests at least 80% of assets in tax-exempt municipal bonds issued by the state of Oregon and its political subdivisions.
Year organized: 1983 (name changed from Oregon Municipal Bond 9/30/96)
Ticker symbol: ORBFX
Group fund code: 615
Discount broker availability: *Fidelity, *Schwab, *Siebert, *White
Qualified for sale in: OR
Dividends paid: Income - declared daily, paid monthly; Capital gains - December
Portfolio turnover (3 yrs): 17%, 16%, 23%
Management fee: 0.50% first $500M to 0.40% over $1B
Expense ratio: 0.98% (year ending 10/31/97) (1.10% without waiver)

THE CRABBE HUSON REAL ESTATE INVESTMENT FUND
(See first Crabbe Huson listing for data common to all funds)

Sub-adviser: AEW Capital Management, L.P. (a wholly-owned subsidiary of the New England Investment Cos., Inc.)
Portfolio managers: Richard S. Huson (1994), Jay L. Willoughby (1996)
Investment objective and policies: Capital appreciation and current income. Invests primarily in equity securities of real estate investment trusts (REITs) and other companies involved in real estate. May invest up to 25% in debt securities of real estate companies, mortgage-backed securities and short-term investments, and use futures and options for hedging purposes.
Year organized: 1994
Ticker symbol: CHREX
Group fund code: 618
Discount broker availability: *Fidelity, *Schwab, *Siebert, *White
Dividends paid: Income - January, April, July, October, December; Capital gains - December
Portfolio turnover (3 yrs): 80%, 120%, 60%
Management fee: 1.00% first $100M to 0.60% over $500M
Expense ratio: 1.50% (year ended 10/31/97) (1.76% without waiver)

THE CRABBE HUSON SMALL CAP FUND
(See first Crabbe Huson listing for data common to all funds)

Portfolio managers: James E. Crabbe (1996), John W. Johnson (1996)
Investment objective and policies: Long-term capital appreciation; current income secondary. Invests at least 65% of assets in a diversified portfolio of selected domestic and foreign securities representing special situations, particularly those perceived to have intact long-term financial structures but current, short-term difficulties which offer the opportunity to buy at substantial discounts. Market capitalizations will be under $1B. May invest up to 35% of assets in securities issued by foreign entities, 20% of assets in junk bonds, and up to 25% of assets in a single industry.
Year organized: 1996
Ticker symbol: CHSCX
Group fund code: 864
Discount broker availability: *Fidelity, *Schwab, *Siebert, *White
Dividends paid: Income - December; Capital gains - December
Portfolio turnover (2 yrs): 65%, 39%
Management fee: 1.00% first $100M to 0.60% over $500M
Expense ratio: 1.50% (year ending 10/31/97) (1.73% without waiver)

THE CRABBE HUSON SPECIAL FUND
(See first Crabbe Huson listing for data common to all funds)

Portfolio managers: James E. Crabbe (1987), John W. Johnson (1995)
Investment objective and policies: Long-term capital appreciation; current income secondary. Normally invests at least 75% of assets in stocks of sound domestic and foreign companies with short-term difficulties that have temporarily depressed the price of their securities. May also invest in preferred stocks and bonds. Fund may leverage and sell short.
Year organized: 1987 (name changed from Crabbe Huson Growth in March 1993)
Ticker symbol: CHSPX
Group fund code: 612
Discount broker availability: *Fidelity, *Schwab, *Siebert, *White
Dividends paid: Income - December; Capital gains - December
Portfolio turnover (3 yrs): 33%, 33%, 123%
Management fee: 1.00% first $100M to 0.60% over $500M
Expense ratio: 1.50% (year ending 10/31/97)

THE CRABBE HUSON U.S. GOVERNMENT INCOME FUND
(See first Crabbe Huson listing for data common to all funds)

Portfolio managers: Richard S. Huson (1995), Garth R. Nisbet (1995)
Investment objective and policies: High current income consistent with safety of principal. Invests substantially all assets in direct or indirect debt obligations of the U.S. Government, its agencies and instrumentalities. Up to 10% of assets may be in repurchase agreements covering direct obligations of the U.S. Government.

Year organized: 1988
Ticker symbol: CHUSX
Group fund code: 616
Discount broker availability: *Fidelity, *Schwab, *Siebert, *White
Dividends paid: Income - monthly; Capital gains - December
Portfolio turnover (3 yrs): 45%, 226%, 230%
Management fee: 0.50% first $500M to 0.40% over $1B
Expense ratio: 0.75% (year ending 10/31/97) (1.78% without waiver)

THE CRABBE HUSON U.S. GOVERNMENT MONEY MARKET FUND
(See first Crabbe Huson listing for data common to all funds)

Portfolio managers: Richard S. Huson (1995), Garth R. Nisbet (1995)
Investment objective and policies: Current income consistent with preservation of capital and liquidity. Invests in U.S. Government money market instruments.
Year organized: 1988 (name and objective changed from Crabbe Huson Money Market Fund on 2/23/93)
Ticker symbol: CHGXX
Group fund code: 617
Check redemptions: $500 minimum
Dividends paid: Income - declared daily, paid monthly
Management fee: 0.50% first $500M to 0.40% over $1B
Expense ratio: 0.70% (year ending 10/31/97) (1.14% without waiver)

CRM SMALL CAP VALUE FUND ◆
707 Westchester Avenue
White Plains, NY 10604
800-276-2883, 914-681-4470
shareholders 800-844-8258
fax 914-682-3618
Internet: http://www.secapl.com/crm
e-mail: cbarnett@crmmail.secapl.com

Adviser: CRM Advisors, LLC
Administrator: Forum Financial Services, Inc.
Portfolio managers: Ronald H. McGlynn (1995), Jay B. Abramson (1995)
Transfer agent: Forum Financial Corp.
Investment objective and policies: Long-term capital appreciation. Invests at least 75% of assets in equity securities of companies with small market capitalizations, less than $1B prior to purchase, that are perceived to be undervalued and are experiencing a fundamental change such as a divesture, restructuring or acquisition. Firms whose market capitalizations increase after purchase will still be considered small for purposes of this policy. Fund maintains a broad 25% per sector limit. May invest in ADRs, and up to 10% of assets may be in illiquid securities.
Year organized: 1995
Ticker symbol: CRMSX
Minimum purchase: Initial: $10,000, Subsequent: $100; IRA: Initial: $2,000; Automatic investment plan: Initial: $2,000
Wire orders accepted: Yes
Deadline for same day wire purchase: 4 P.M.
Discount broker availability: Fidelity, Siebert, White
Qualified for sale in: All states
Telephone redemptions: Yes
Wire redemptions: Yes, $10,000 minimum
Letter redemptions: Signature guarantee required
Telephone switching: With Forum Daily Assets Treasury Fund, $2,500 minimum
Number of switches permitted: Unlimited
Dividends paid: Income - December; Capital gains - December
Portfolio turnover (2 yrs): 99%, 111%
Shareholder services: IRA, electronic funds transfer
Management fee: 0.75%
Administration: 0.15%
Expense ratio: 1.50% (year ending 9/30/97)
IRA fees: Annual $10, Initial $10

CROFT-LEOMINSTER INCOME FUND ◆
207 E. Redwood Street, Suite 802
Baltimore, MD 21202
800-551-0990, 410-576-0100
prices/yields 800-746-3322
fax 410-576-8232
e-mail: 73464,1652@compuserve.com

Adviser: Croft-Leominster, Inc.
Portfolio managers: L. Gordon Croft (1995), Kent G. Croft (1995)
Transfer agent and administrator: American Data Services, Inc.
Investment objective and policies: High current income with moderate risk of principal. Invests primarily in a diversified portfolio of investment grade, fixed-income securities. May invest up to 34% of assets in high yield junk bonds, and up to 35% of assets in warrants and in investment grade convertible securities, preferred stocks and common stocks.
Year organized: 1995
Ticker symbol: CLINX
Group fund code: 19-0111
Minimum purchase: Initial: $2,000, Subsequent: $200; IRA/Keogh: Initial: $500
Wire orders accepted: Yes
Deadline for same day wire purchase: 4 P.M.
Discount broker availability: *White
Qualified for sale in: CA, CO, DC, FL, KS, MD, MN, MO, NJ, NY, PA, TN, VA
Letter redemptions: Signature guarantee required
Dividends paid: Income - January, April, July, October; Capital gains - December
Portfolio turnover (2 yrs): 14%, 14%
Management fee: 0.79%
12b-1 distribution fee: 0.25% (not currently imposed)
Expense ratio: 1.10% (year ending 4/30/97) (1.90% without waiver)
IRA fees: Annual $15
Keogh fees: None

CROFT-LEOMINSTER VALUE FUND
207 E. Redwood Street, Suite 802
Baltimore, MD 21202
800-551-0990, 410-576-0100
prices/yields 800-746-3322
fax 410-576-8232
e-mail: 73464,1652@compuserve.com

Adviser: Croft-Leominster, Inc.
Portfolio managers: L. Gordon Croft (1995), Kent G. Croft (1995)
Transfer agent and administrator: American Data Services, Inc.
Investment objective and policies: Capital growth. Invests at least 65% of assets in common stocks perceived to be undervalued. Employs a value oriented and, at times, contrarian approach to company analysis. Invests in mid-cap ($500M-$2B) and large-cap (over $2B) established companies. May invest up to 35% of assets in warrants, investment grade convertible securities, preferred stocks and corporate debt securities. May invest up to 10% of assets in junk bonds.
Year organized: 1995
Ticker symbol: CLVFX
Group fund code: 19-0110
Minimum purchase: Initial: $2,000, Subsequent: $200; IRA/Keogh: Initial: $500
Wire orders accepted: Yes
Deadline for same day wire purchase: 4 P.M.
Discount broker availability: *White
Qualified for sale in: CA, CO, DC, FL, MD, MN, MO, NJ, NY, OH, PA, VA
Letter redemptions: Signature guarantee required
Dividends paid: Income - December; Capital gains - December
Portfolio turnover (2 yrs): 106%, 65%
Management fee: 0.94%
12b-1 distribution fee: Maximum of 0.25%
Expense ratio: 1.50% (year ending 4/30/97) (5.41% without waiver)
IRA fees: Annual $15
Keogh fees: None

THE CROWLEY PORTFOLIO GROUP ◆
(Data common to all Crowley portfolios are shown below. See subsequent listings for data specific to individual portfolios.)

3201 B Millcreek Road
Wilmington, DE 19808
302-994-4700, fax 302-994-9495

Adviser: Crowley & Crowley Corp.
Transfer agent: The Crowley Financial Group, Inc.
Minimum purchase: Initial: $5,000, Subsequent: $1,000 (minimums are in the aggregate, not per fund, and family totals may be included)
Wire orders accepted: No
Qualified for sale in: DE, MD, NJ, PA
Letter redemptions: Signature guarantee required over $5,000
Dividends paid: Income - December; Capital gains - December
Shareholder services: IRA, Keogh
IRA/Keogh fees: None

THE CROWLEY DIVERSIFIED MANAGEMENT PORTFOLIO ◆
(See first Crowley listing for data common to all portfolios)

Portfolio manager: Robert A. Crowley (1995)
Investment objective and policies: High total return consistent with reasonable risk. Invests primarily in shares of other mutual funds, both open and closed - including sector funds and funds that impose sales charges and/or invest in foreign securities. Management utilizes market trend analysis in an effort to allocate funds to various equity funds. May invest up to 35% of assets in a fund that invests up to 35% of its assets in junk bonds. May allocate up to 5% of assets in futures and options for hedging purposes.
Year organized: 1995
Portfolio turnover (3 yrs): 0%, 21%, 0%
Management fee: 1.00%
Expense ratio: 1.87% (year ending 11/30/97)

THE CROWLEY GROWTH AND INCOME PORTFOLIO ◆
(See first Crowley listing for data common to all portfolios)

Portfolio manager: Robert A. Crowley (1989)
Investment objective and policies: Long-term capital growth; current income secondary. Invests primarily in dividend-paying common stocks and other equity securities perceived to offer the potential for earnings growth. Management utilizes market trend analysis in an effort to allocate funds to equities. May allocate up to 5% of assets in futures and options for hedging purposes.
Year organized: 1989 (name changed from Growth Portfolio 3/29/96; objective remained the same)
Portfolio turnover (3 yrs): 70%, 182%, 118%
Management fee: 1.00%
Expense ratio: 1.95% (year ending 11/30/97)

THE CROWLEY INCOME PORTFOLIO ◆
(See first Crowley listing for data common to all portfolios)

Portfolio manager: Robert A. Crowley (1989)
Investment objective and policies: Maximum current income consistent with prudent risk. Invests primarily in a diversified portfolio of investment grade debt securities of domestic corporate and government issuers, dividend-paying common stocks, and dollar-denominated debt obligations of foreign issuers. No more than 5% of assets are allocated to obligations in the fourth ranking of credit quality; the balance must rank in the highest three grades. Debt obligations will generally have remaining maturities of seven years or less, with one third at zero to two years, one third at two to four years, and a third at four to seven years. May allocate up to 5% of assets to futures and options for hedging purposes.
Year organized: 1989

Portfolio turnover (3 yrs): 23%, 66%, 31%
Management fee: 0.60%
Expense ratio: 1.39% (year ending 11/30/97)

THE CRUELTY FREE VALUE FUND
8260 Greensboro Drive, Suite 250
McLean, VA 22102
800-892-9626, 800-662-9992
703-883-0865, fax 703-506-0950
Internet: http://www.crueltyfree.com
e-mail: beaconga@ix.netcom.com

Adviser: Beacon Global Advisors, Inc.
Sub-advisers: Dreman Value Advisors, Inc., and Zurich Investment Management, Inc.
Lead portfolio manager: William F. Coughlin (1997)
Transfer agent: First Data Investor Services Group
Investment objective and policies: Capital appreciation. Invests primarily in common stocks selected through two screening processes. First, companies must demonstrate that their policies and practices do not: employ animal testing in their product development; indiscriminately endanger and abuse animals; sponsor inhumane animal events; slaughter animals, or have subsidiaries involved in such activities. Second, companies are screened using a value orientation, with attention to price/earnings and price-to-book ratios, and to above-average dividend yields. Most companies will have market capitalizations between $100M and $1B. May invest in foreign holdings through ADRs, and use short sales and sales against the box for hedging purposes.
Year organized: 1997
Minimum purchase: Initial: $1,000, Subsequent: $100; Automatic investment plan: Subsequent: $50
Wire orders accepted: Yes
Deadline for same day wire purchase: 4 P.M.
Qualified for sale in: All states
Telephone redemptions: Yes
Wire redemptions: Yes, $9 fee
Letter redemptions: Signature guarantee required over $10,000
Dividends paid: Income - November; Capital gains - November
Portfolio turnover (1 yr): 15%
Shareholder services: IRA, SEP-IRA
Management fee: 1.25% first $100M to 0.75% over $500M
Admnistration fee: 0.15% ($55,000 minimum)
12b-1 distribution fee: Maximum of 0.25%
Expense ratio: 1.95% (seven months ending 11/30/97) (29.69% without waiver)
IRA fees: Annual $12

THE CUTLER APPROVED LIST EQUITY FUND ◆
503 Airport Road
Medford, OR 97504
888-288-5374, 800-228-8537
541-770-9000
fax 541-779-0006
Internet: http://www.cutler.com
e-mail: info@cutler.com

Adviser: Cutler & Co., LLC
Administrator: Forum Administrative Services, LLC
Portfolio manager: Kenneth R. Cutler (1992)
Transfer agent: Forum Financial Corp.
Investment objective and policies: Current income with long-term capital appreciation. Invests at least 90% of assets in the common stock of every company listed in the Cutler & Company Approved List. In order to be on this list, each company must meet the following four criteria: must have paid dividends continuously for the last twenty years, without any reduction in the rate; has commercial paper rated Prime-1 and senior debt rated at least A by Moody's; has annual sales, assets and market value of at least $1B; and, has wide ownership among institutional investors and a very liquid market. Fund invests at least 65% of assets in the income producing equity securities in the list.
Year organized: 1992
Ticker symbol: CALEX
Minimum purchase: Initial: $25,000, Subsequent: None; IRA: Initial: $2,000
Wire orders accepted: Yes
Deadline for same day wire purchase: 4 P.M.

Discount broker availability: Fidelity, Siebert, *White
Qualified for sale in: All states
Telephone redemptions: Yes
Wire redemptions: Yes, $10,000 minimum
Letter redemptions: Signature guarantee required
Telephone switching: With Cutler Equity Income fund and the Forum Daily Assets Treasury money market fund
Number of switches permitted: Unlimited
Dividends paid: Income - March, June, September, December; Capital gains - December
Portfolio turnover (3 yrs): 4%, 9%, 23%
Shareholder services: IRA
Management fee: 0.75%
Administration fee: 0.10%
Shareholder services fee: Maximum of 0.25%
Expense ratio: 1.25% (year ending 6/30/97)
IRA/Keogh fees: Annual $10, Initial $10 (per customer)

THE CUTLER EQUITY INCOME FUND ◆
503 Airport Road
Medford, OR 97504
888-288-5374, 800-228-8537
541-770-9000
fax 541-779-0006
Internet: http://www.cutler.com
e-mail: info@cutler.com

Adviser: Cutler & Co., LLC
Administrator: Forum Administrative Services, LLC
Portfolio manager: Kenneth R. Cutler (1992)
Transfer agent: Forum Financial Corp.
Investment objective and policies: Current income as is consistent with diversification, and long-term capital appreciation. Invests all assets in the common stocks of approximately 20 to 30 companies found in the Approved List, and at least 65% of assets in income producing equity securities of the same companies. Portfolio consists of equal positions in each company, rebalanced periodically to maintain the equality.
Year organized: 1992
Ticker symbol: CEIFX
Minimum purchase: Initial: $25,000, Subsequent: None; IRA: Initial: $2,000
Wire orders accepted: Yes
Deadline for same day wire purchase: 4 P.M.
Discount broker availability: Fidelity, Siebert, *White
Qualified for sale in: All states
Telephone redemptions: Yes
Wire redemptions: Yes, $10,000 minimum
Letter redemptions: Signature guarantee required
Telephone switching: With Cutler Approved List fund and the Forum Daily Assets Treasury money market fund
Number of switches permitted: Unlimited
Dividends paid: Income - March, June, September, December; Capital gains - December
Portfolio turnover (3 yrs): 23%, 57%, 43%
Shareholder services: IRA
Management fee: 0.75%
Administration fee: 0.10%
Shareholder services fee: Maximum of 0.25%
Expense ratio: 1.17% (year ending 6/30/97)
IRA/Keogh fees: Annual $10, Initial $10 (per customer)

DAILY TAX FREE INCOME FUND ◆
600 Fifth Avenue, 8th Floor
New York, NY 10020
800-221-3079, 800-676-6779
212-830-5220
prices/yields 800-830-5225
fax 212-830-5478

Adviser: Reich & Tang Asset Management, L.P.
Sub-adviser: Thornburg Management Co., Inc.
Portfolio manager: Molly Flewharty (1984)
Transfer agent: Reich & Tang Services, L.P.
Investment objective and policies: High current interest income exempt from federal income tax, consistent with preservation of capital and liquidity. Invests in money market instruments issued by state and municipal governments and other tax-exempt issuers.
Year organized: 1982
Ticker symbol: DTIXX

Special sales restrictions: Only class "B" shares of the fund are sold direct and without 12b-1 fees. Statistics represent "B" shares only.
Minimum purchase: Initial: $5,000, Subsequent: $100
Wire orders accepted: Yes
Deadline for same day wire purchase: 12 NN
Qualified for sale in: All states except AR, PR
Telephone redemptions: Yes
Wire redemptions: Yes, $1,000 minimum
Letter redemptions: Signature guarantee required
Check redemptions: $250 minimum
Telephone switching: With other Reich & Tang Money Market funds and R&T Equity Fund
Number of switches permitted: Unlimited, $1,000 minimum
Deadline for same day switch: 12 NN
Dividends paid: Income - declared daily, paid monthly
Shareholder services: IRA, automatic investment plan, electronic funds transfer, systematic withdrawal plan
Management fee: 0.325% first $750M to 0.30% over $750M
Administration fee: 0.21% first $1.25B to 0.19% over $1.5B
Expense ratio: 0.66% (year ending 10/31/96) (0.97% without waiver)

DARUMA MID-CAP VALUE FUND ◆
237 Park Avenue, Suite 801
New York, NY 10017
800-435-5076, 212-808-2424
shareholder services 888-532-7862
fax 212-808-2480
Internet: http://www.darumany@aol.com

Adviser: CastleRock Capital Management, Inc.
Portfolio manager: Mariko O. Gordon (1996)
Transfer agent: American Data Services, Inc.
Investment objective and policies: Long-term capital appreciation; current income incidental. Invests at least 65% of assets in the common stocks of approximately 35 companies with market capitalizations between $500M and $7B, perceived to demonstrate conditions which, while not yet recognized in the share price, will cause positive changes in earnings growth. May also invest in convertible and non-convertible preferred stocks, bonds and warrants. May invest up to 25% of assets in one industry, up to 15% of assets in foreign securities or ADRs, and up to 15% of assets in illiquid securities. May use short sales "against the box" for hedging purposes. Daruma was the founder of Zen Buddhism.
Year organized: 1996
Minimum purchase: Initial: $1,000, Subsequent: $100; IRA/Keogh: Initial: $500; Automatic investment plan: Initial: $500
Wire orders accepted: Yes
Deadline for same day wire purchase: 4 P.M.
Qualified for sale in: AK, CA, CO, CT, DC, HI, IL, NJ, NY, OR, PA
Telephone redemptions: Yes
Wire redemptions: No
Letter redemptions: Signature guarantee not required
Dividends paid: Income - December; Capital gains - December
Portfolio turnover (1 yr): 46%
Shareholder services: IRA, SEP-IRA, Keogh
Management fee: 1.00% first $100M to 0.50% over $200M
Expense ratio: 1.49% (11 months ending 6/30/97) (5.10% without waiver)
IRA fees: $15 Annual, $12 Initial, $15 Closing

DAVENPORT EQUITY FUND ◆
One James Center
901 East Cary Street
Richmond, VA 23219-4037
800-281-3217, 804-780-2000

Adviser: Davenport & Co., LLC
Portfolio manager: Joseph L. Antrim (1998)
Transfer agent and administrator: Countrywide Fund Services, Inc.
Investment objective and policies: Long-term growth of capital; current income incidental. Invests in a well diversified portfolio of common stocks selected for their perceived growth potential. May also invest

in investment grade convertible preferred issues, and in shares of small and unseasoned companies. May invest up to 10% of assets either directly in foreign securities or through ADRs, but only those issues listed on a recognized exchange.
Year organized: 1998
Minimum purchase: Initial: $10,000, Subsequent: $1,000; IRA/Keogh: Initial: $2,000; Automatic investment plan: Subsequent: $100
Wire orders accepted: Yes
Deadline for same day wire purchase: 4 P.M.
Qualified for sale in: All states except AK, AZ, AR, DE, HI, ID, MA, MN, MO, MT, NE, NH, NM, NY, ND, OK, OR, PR, RI, SD, WI
Telephone redemptions: No
Wire redemptions: No
Letter redemptions: Signature guarantee not required
Dividends paid: Income - quarterly; Capital gains - annually
Shareholder services: Systematic withdrawal plan min. bal. req. $25,000
Management fee: 0.75%
Administration fee: 0.20% first $25M to 0.15% over $50M ($24,000 minimum)

DEAN WITTER FUNDS
(Data common to all Dean Witter funds are shown below. See subsequent listings for data specific to individual funds.)

Two World Trade Center
New York, NY 10048
800-869-3863, 800-869-6397
800-526-3143, 212-392-2550
prices/yields 800-869-7283

Adviser: Dean Witter InterCapital, Inc., a wholly-owned subsidiary of Dean Witter, Discover & Co.
Transfer agent: Dean Witter Trust Co.
Wire orders accepted: Yes
Deadline for same day wire purchase: 4 P.M. (12 NN for money market funds)
Qualified for sale in: All states
Telephone redemptions: Yes
Wire redemptions: Yes, $1,000 minimum
Letter redemptions: Signature guarantee not required
Telephone switching: With other Dean Witter funds, some of which have loads, and TCW/DW funds
Number of switches permitted: Unlimited
Shareholder services: IRA, Keogh, 403(b), corporate retirement plans, directed dividends, systematic withdrawal plan min. bal. req. $10,000 for bond funds, $5,000 for money market funds
IRA/Keogh fees: Annual $30

DEAN WITTER LIQUID ASSET FUND
(See first Dean Witter listing for data common to all funds)

Investment objective and policies: Income, capital preservation and liquidity. Invests in money market instruments.
Year organized: 1975 (formerly InterCapital Liquid Asset Fund)
Ticker symbol: DWLXX
Minimum purchase: Initial $5,000, Subsequent $100; IRA/Keogh: Initial: $1,000; Automatic investment plan: Initial: $100
Check redemptions: $500 minimum
Dividends paid: Income - declared daily, paid monthly
Management fee: 0.50% first $500M to 0.248% over $17.5B
12b-1 distribution fee: Maximum of 0.15%
Expense ratio: 0.63% (year ending 8/31/97)

DEAN WITTER SHORT-TERM BOND FUND ◆
(See first Dean Witter listing for data common to all funds)

Portfolio manager: Rochelle G. Siegel (1994)
Investment objective and policies: High current income consistent with capital preservation. Invests in short-term fixed-income securities with a weighted average maturity of less than three years. May invest in investment grade corporate and government fixed-income securities, mortgage- and asset-backed securities

and in preferred stocks. Up to 25% of assets may be in securities of foreign issuers.
Year organized: 1994
Ticker symbol: DWSBX
Minimum purchase: Initial $1,000, Subsequent $100; Automatic investment plan: Initial: $100
Dividends paid: Income - declared daily, paid monthly; Capital gains - December
Portfolio turnover (2 yrs): 64%, 74%
Management fee: 0.70%
12b-1 distribution fee: Maximum of 0.25% (not currently imposed)
Expense ratio: 0.80% (year ending 4/30/97) (includes waiver)

DEAN WITTER SHORT-TERM U.S. TREASURY TRUST
(See first Dean Witter listing for data common to all funds)

Portfolio manager: Rajesh K. Gupta (1991)
Investment objective and policies: High current income consistent with preservation of capital and liquidity. Invests exclusively in short-term fixed-income U.S. Treasury securities. Portfolio maintains a dollar-weighted average maturity of less than three years.
Year organized: 1991
Ticker symbol: DWSHX
Minimum purchase: Initial $10,000, Subsequent $100; Automatic investment plan: Initial: $100
Check redemptions $500 minimum
Dividends paid: Income - declared daily, paid monthly; Capital gains - December
Portfolio turnover (3 yrs): 21%, 63%, 30%
Management fee: 0.35%
12b-1 distribution fee: 0.35%
Expense ratio: 0.79% (year ending 5/31/97)

DELAFIELD FUND, INC. ◆
600 Fifth Avenue, 8th Floor
New York, NY 10020
800-676-6779, 800-221-3079
212-830-5220
prices/yields 212-830-5225
fax 212-830-5478
Internet: http://www.delafieldfund.com

Adviser: Reich & Tang Asset Management, L.P., Delafield Asset Management Division
Portfolio managers: J. Dennis Delafield (1993), Vincent Sellecchia (1993)
Transfer agent: Reich & Tang Services, L.P.
Investment objective and policies: Long-term capital preservation with growth sufficient to outpace inflation. Invests at least 65% of assets in equity securities of domestic companies believed undervalued or undergoing change that might cause their market value to grow faster than the overall economy. May invest up to 35% of assets in debt securities and preferred stocks offering opportunity for price appreciation, 15% in foreign securities and 15% in restricted securities. May use warrants and sell short.
Year organized: 1993
Ticker symbol: DEFIX
Minimum purchase: Initial: $5,000, Subsequent: None, IRA: Initial: $250; Automatic investment plan: Subsequent: $50
Discount broker availability: Fidelity, Schwab, White
Wire orders accepted: Yes
Deadline for same day wire purchases: 4 P.M.
Qualified for sale in: All states
Wire redemptions: Yes, $1,000 minimum
Letter redemptions: Signature guarantee required over $25,000 and on all 401k's and IRAs
Telephone switching: Class B shares of Reich & Tang Daily Tax Free Income Fund and the Short-Term Income Fund Inc. (U.S. Govt. Portfolio), $1,000 minimum
Number of switches permitted: Unlimited
Dividends paid: Income - June, December; Capital gains - December
Portfolio turnover (3 yrs): 76%, 70%, 43%
Shareholder services: IRA, electronic funds transfer, systematic withdrawal plan min. bal. req. $10,000
Management fee: 0.80%
12b-1 distribution fee: 0.25% (not currently imposed)
Shareholder services fee: 0.25%

Expense ratio: 1.29% (year ending 12/31/96) (1.49% without waiver)
IRA fees: Annual $10, Initial $10, Closing $10

DODGE & COX FUNDS ◆
(Data common to all Dodge & Cox funds are shown below. See subsequent listing for data specific to individual funds.)

One Sansome Street, 35th Floor
San Francisco, CA 94104
800-621-3979
shareholders 800-338-1579
prices 415-981-1710

Shareholder service hours: Full service: M-F 8 A.M.-7 P.M. CST; After hours service: prices, account balances
Adviser: Dodge & Cox
Portfolio managers: Investment policy committee
Transfer agent: Firstar Trust Co.
Minimum purchase: Initial: $2,500, Subsequent: $100; IRA: Initial: $1,000
Wire orders accepted: Yes
Deadline for same day wire purchase: 4 P.M.
Qualified for sale in: All states
Telephone redemptions: Yes
Wire redemptions: Yes, $12 fee
Letter redemptions: Signature guarantee not required
Telephone switching: With other Dodge & Cox funds, $1,000 minimum
Number of switches permitted: Unlimited
Dividends paid: Income - March, June, September, December; Capital gains - March, December
Shareholder services: IRA, automatic investment plan, electronic funds transfer, systematic withdrawal plan min. bal. req. $10,000
IRA fees: Annual $12.50

DODGE & COX BALANCED FUND ◆
(See first Dodge & Cox listing for data common to all funds)

Investment objective and policies: Regular income, conservation of principal and long-term growth of income and principal. Remains fully invested in a portfolio of common and preferred stocks, and fixed-income securities. Fund will hold no more than 75% of total assets in stocks. Bond portfolio generally includes U.S. Treasuries as well as mortgage-related and corporate issues. Allocation of assets varies depending on perceived market and economic conditions.
Year organized: 1931
Ticker symbol: DODBX
Discount broker availability: Fidelity, Schwab, Siebert, White
Portfolio turnover (3 yrs): 17%, 20%, 20%
Management fee: 0.50%
Expense ratio: 0.56% (year ending 12/31/96)

DODGE & COX INCOME FUND ◆
(See first Dodge & Cox listing for data common to all funds)

Investment objective and policies: High and stable rate of current income consistent with long-term capital preservation; capital appreciation secondary. Invests at least 80% of assets in a diversified portfolio of high quality bonds and other fixed-income securities. Up to 25% of assets may be in dollar-denominated securities of foreign issuers and 20% in junk bonds.
Year organized: 1989
Ticker symbol: DODIX
Discount broker availability: Fidelity, Schwab, Siebert, White
Portfolio turnover (3 yrs): 37%, 53%, 55%
Management fee: 0.50% first $100M, 0.40% over $100M
Expense ratio: 0.50% (year ending 12/31/96)

DODGE & COX STOCK FUND ◆
(See first Dodge & Cox listing for data common to all funds)

Investment objective and policies: Long-term growth of principal and income; reasonable current income secondary. Invests primarily in common and convertible stocks of well established companies perceived to have

positive earnings prospects not reflected in the purchase price. Effort is made to maintain representation in major economic sectors and areas with strong long-term profit potential. Up to 25% of assets may be concentrated in one industry, up to 20% in dollar-denominated, U.S. traded securities of foreign issuers, and up to 15% invested in illiquid securities.
Year organized: 1965
Ticker symbol: DODGX
Discount broker availability: Fidelity, Schwab, Siebert, White
Portfolio turnover (3 yrs): 10%, 13%, 7%
Management fee: 0.50%
Expense ratio: 0.59% (year ending 12/31/96)

DOMINI SOCIAL EQUITY FUND
129 Mount Auburn Street
Cambridge, MA 02138
800-782-4165, 212-352-9200
Internet: http://www.domini.com

Adviser: Domini Social Investments, LLC
Sub-adviser: Mellon Equity Assocs.
Portfolio manager: John R. O'Toole (1994)
Transfer agent: Fundamental Shareholder Services, Inc.
Investment objective and policies: Long-term total return which corresponds to the total return performance of the Domini Social Index, a capitalization weighted index of 400 stocks drawn from the S&P 500 (about 50%) and other domestic and foreign (ADRs) companies selected to exclude those with involvement in military weapons, tobacco and alcohol, gambling and nuclear power production or construction. Investment is made by reassigning assets to the underlying Domini Social Index Portfolio. The Trust will have at least 80% of its assets in securities comprising the Index, either directly or through the Domini Portfolio, and attempts to be fully invested at all times.
Year organized: 1991 (name changed from Domini Social Index Trust in 1993)
Ticker symbol: DSEFX
Minimum purchase: Initial: $1,000, Subsequent: None; IRA: Initial: $250; Automatic investment plan: Initial: $500, Subsequent: $25
Wire orders accepted: Yes
Deadline for same day wire purchase: 4 P.M.
Discount broker availability: Fidelity, Schwab, Siebert, *White
Qualified for sale in: All states
Telephone redemptions: Yes
Wire redemptions: Yes
Letter redemptions: Signature guarantee required over $50,000
Dividends paid: Income - June, December; Capital gains - December
Portfolio turnover (3 yrs): 1%, 5%, 6% (underlying portfolio)
Shareholder services: IRA, systematic withdrawal plan min. bal. req. $10,000
Management fee: 0.20%
12b-1 distribution fee: Maximum of 0.25%
Expense ratio: 0.98% (year ending 7/31/97) (0.92% without waiver)
IRA fees: Annual $10, Initial $10

DRESDNER RCM EQUITY FUNDS ◆
(See RCM Equity Funds)

DREYFUS FUNDS
(Data common to all Dreyfus funds are show below. See subsequent listings for data specific to individual funds.)

EAB Plaza
144 Glenn Curtis Boulevard, Plaza Level
Uniondale, NY 11556-0144
800-645-6561, 800-782-6620
718-895-1206, 516-794-5200
TDD 800-227-1341
International: 516-794-5452
Internet: http://www.dreyfus.com/funds
e-mail: info@dreyfus.com

Shareholder service hours: Full service: 7 days, 24 hours
Adviser: The Dreyfus Corporation (a wholly-owned subsidiary of Mellon Bank, N.A.)
Transfer agent: Dreyfus Transfer, Inc.
Minimum purchase: Initial: $2,500, Subsequent: $100; IRA/Keogh: Initial: $750, Subsequent: None;

Automatic investment plan: Initial: $100 (exceptions noted)

Wire orders accepted: Yes (minimums according to fund)

Deadline for same day wire purchase: 4 P.M. (exceptions noted)

Qualified for sale in: All states (exceptions noted)

Telephone redemptions: Yes

Wire redemptions: Yes, $1,000 minimum

Letter redemptions: Signature guarantee required over $100,000

Telephone switching: With other Dreyfus funds (index funds do not switch), $500 minimum (exceptions noted)

Deadline for same day switch: 4 P.M. (unless noted)

Number of switches permitted: Unlimited (exceptions noted)

Shareholder services: IRA, SEP-IRA, Keogh, 403(b), 401(k), corporate retirement plans, directed dividends, electronic funds transfer, systematic withdrawal plan min. bal. req. $5,000

IRA/Keogh fees: Annual $10 per fund with balance below $5,000 (maximum $25 per individual); Closing $10

DREYFUS A BONDS PLUS ◆
(See first Dreyfus listing for data common to all funds)

Lead portfolio manager: Kevin M. McClintock (1997)

Investment objective and policies: High current income consistent with preservation of capital and liquidity. Invests primarily in debt obligations of corporations, the U.S. Government and its agencies and instrumentalities, and major domestic banking institutions. At least 80% of assets are in corporate obligations rated A or better, and government guaranteed issues. Up to 15% of assets may be in illiquid securities and 10% in securities of foreign issuers.

Year organized: 1976

Ticker symbol: DRBDX

Group fund code: 084

Discount broker availability: *Fidelity, *Schwab, *Siebert, *White

Check redemptions: $500 minimum

Dividends paid: Income - declared and paid monthly; Capital gains - December

Portfolio turnover (3 yrs): 416%, 166%, 173%

Management fee: 0.65%

Shareholder services fee: 0.25%

Expense ratio: 0.96% (year ending 3/31/97)

DREYFUS AGGRESSIVE GROWTH FUND ◆
(See first Dreyfus listing for data common to all funds)

Lead portfolio manager: Michael L. Schonberg (1995)

Investment objective and policies: Capital growth. Invests primarily in equity securities of domestic and foreign issuers expected to show above average earnings or sales growth within the next 12 to 18 months, retention of earnings, and higher P/E ratios, without regard to market capitalization. Up to 30% of assets may be in foreign securities and 15% in illiquid securities. Money borrowed for leverage may equal up to 33 1/3% of total assets. May use options, futures and foreign currency transactions for hedging purposes, and sell short up to 25% of total assets.

Year organized: 1995 (name changed from Growth and Value - Aggressive Growth in 1996; absorbed Dreyfus Special Fund 4/18/97)

Ticker symbol: DGVAX

Group fund code: 256

Discount broker availability: *Fidelity, *Schwab, *Siebert, *White

Redemption fee: 1.00% for shares held less than 15 days, payable to the fund

Dividends paid: Income - annually; Capital gains - annually

Portfolio turnover (2 yrs): 76%, 125%

Management fee: 0.75%

Shareholder services fee: 0.25%

Expense ratio: 1.34% (year ending 8/31/97) (1.43% without waiver)

DREYFUS AGGRESSIVE VALUE FUND ◆
(See first Dreyfus listing for data common to all funds)

Lead portfolio manager: Timothy M. Ghriskey (1995)

Investment objective and policies: Capital appreciation. Invests primarily in equity securities of domestic and foreign issuers perceived to have low price to book ratios, and lower P/E ratios and higher than average dividend rates, without regard to market capitalization. A "strategic overlay " of up to 20% of assets emphasizes short selling (usually hedged with futures contracts), heavy industry weightings, and investment in small caps, corporate junk bonds, and private placements. Up to 30% of assets may be in securities of foreign companies not traded in the U.S., or in debt obligations of foreign governments, and 15% in illiquid securities. May use futures and options and foreign currency transactions for hedging purposes, and sell short up to 25% of total assets.

Year organized: 1995 (name changed from Growth and Value - Aggressive Value in 1996)

Ticker symbol: DAGVX

Group fund code: 257

Discount broker availability: *Fidelity, *Schwab, *Siebert, *White

Redemption fee: 1.00% for shares held less than 15 days, payable to the fund

Dividends paid: Income - annually; Capital gains - annually

Portfolio turnover (2 yrs): 121%, 261%

Management fee: 0.75%

Shareholder services fee: 0.25%

Expense ratio: 1.24% (year ending 8/31/97) (1.38% without waiver)

DREYFUS APPRECIATION FUND ◆
(See first Dreyfus listing for data common to all funds)

Sub-adviser: Fayez Sarofim & Co.

Lead portfolio manager: Fayez Sarofim (1990)

Investment objective and policies: Long-term capital growth consistent with capital preservation; current income secondary. Invests primarily in common stocks of domestic and foreign companies believed to offer the potential for above average growth and that seem to be undervalued. Also invests in common stocks with warrants attached, and debt securities of foreign governments. Focuses on firms with market capitalizations over $500M. Fund looks for new or innovative products, services or processes, economic or political changes, and corporate restructurings. May invest up to 10% of assets in securities of foreign companies and governments not traded in the U.S., and 15% in illiquid securities. May use foreign currency exchange contracts and write covered calls options on up to 20% of assets.

Year organized: 1984 (name changed from General Aggressive Growth Fund on 12/30/91) (split 2 for 1 on 3/9/92)

Ticker symbol: DGAGX

Group fund code: 141

Discount broker availability: *Fidelity, *Schwab, *Siebert, *White

Number of switches permitted: 4 outbound per calendar year

Dividends paid: Income - annually; Capital gains - annually

Portfolio turnover (3 yrs): 5%, 5%, 7%

Management fee: 0.55% first $25M to 0.275% over $300M

Shareholder services fee: 0.25%

Expense ratio: 0.91% (year ending 12/31/96)

DREYFUS ASSET ALLOCATION FUND ◆
(See first Dreyfus listing for data common to all funds)

Lead portfolio manager: Kevin M. McClintock (1997)

Investment objective and policies: Maximum total return: capital growth and current income. Fund follows an asset allocation strategy that reapportions holdings, sometimes frequently. Allocations range from 40% to 80% in common stocks of the S&P 500 Index, 20% to 60% in U.S. Treasury Notes and Bonds, and 0% to 40% money market instruments. Neutral position is 55% stocks, 35% bonds and 10% money markets. Fund is not managed as a balanced fund. Fund may invest up to 25% of assets directly in foreign equity securities and 30% in foreign debt issues, may leverage, sell short, and write covered options on up to 20% of assets. Fund is non-diversified.

Year organized: 1993 (name changed from Dreyfus Asset Allocation Fund in 1994; back from Asset Allocation Fund- Total Return Portfolio 8/96)

Ticker symbol: DRAAX

Group fund code: 550

Discount broker availability: Fidelity, Schwab, Siebert, *White

Number of switches permitted: 4 outbound per calendar year

Dividends paid: Income - December; Capital gains - December

Portfolio turnover (3 yrs): 223%, 370%, 160%

Management fee: 0.75%

Shareholder services fee: 0.25%

Expense ratio: 1.31% (year ending 4/30/97)

DREYFUS BALANCED FUND ◆
(See first Dreyfus listing for data common to all funds)

Lead portfolio manager: Douglas D. Ramos (1997)

Investment objective and policies: Long-term capital growth and current income, consistent with reasonable investment risk. Normally invests about 50% of assets (within a range of 45% to 65%) in equity securities and about 40% in debt securities (within a range of 25% to 55%), with a range of 0% to 25% of assets in short-term cash and cash equivalents. Equity securities include common and preferred stocks, convertible securities and warrants of companies generally exceeding $1B in market capitalization. Debt securities must be of investment grade, and will have a dollar-weighted average maturity of two to ten years. May invest in securities of foreign issuers and have up to 15% of assets in illiquid securities, and may leverage. Fund is non-diversified.

Year organized: 1992

Ticker symbol: DRBAX

Group fund code: 222

Discount broker availability: *Fidelity, *Schwab, *Siebert, *White

Number of switches permitted: 4 outbound per calendar year

Dividends paid: Income - March, June, September, December; Capital gains - December

Portfolio turnover (3 yrs): 236%, 186%, 72%

Management fee: 0.60%

Shareholder services fee: 0.25%

Expense ratio: 0.96% (year ending 8/31/97)

DREYFUS BASIC CALIFORNIA MUNICIPAL MONEY MARKET FUND ◆
(See first Dreyfus/Laurel listing for data common to all funds)

Lead portfolio manager: Angela M. Deni (1994)

Investment objective and policies: Maximum current income exempt from federal and California state personal income taxes, consistent with preservation of capital and liquidity. Invests primarily in high quality California municipal money market obligations. Designed to deliver extra high yields for long-term buy and hold investors by maintaining a lower than average expense ratio.

Year organized: 1988 (Name changed from Boston Company California Tax-Free Money Fund on 4/1/94, from Laurel California Tax-Free Money Fund on 10/17/94 and from Dreyfus/Laurel California Tax-Free Money Fund in 1995)

Ticker symbol: DCLXX

Group fund code: 307

Minimum purchase: Initial: $25,000, Subsequent: $1,000; IRA: Initial: $5,000, Subsequent: None

Deadline for same day wire purchase: 12 NN and 4 P.M. (two pricings)

Qualified for sale in: AZ, CA, CO, CT, DC, FL, GA, HI, IL, IN, MA, MI, MN, NV, NJ, NM, NY, OH, OR, PA, RI, TX, UT, VA, WA, WV, WY

Wire redemptions: Yes, $5,000 minimum, $5 fee

Check redemptions $1,000 minimum, $2 fee
Account closeout fee: $5
Telephone switching: $1,000 minimum
Number of switches permitted: 4 outbound per year, $5 fee
Dividends paid: Income - declared daily, paid monthly
Management fee: 0.45%
Expense ratio: 0.42% (year ending 6/30/97) (0.45% without waiver)

DREYFUS BASIC GNMA FUND ◆

(See first Dreyfus listing for data common to all funds)

Lead portfolio manager: Michael Hoeh (1997)
Investment objective and policies: High current income consistent with capital preservation. Invests at least 65% of assets in GNMA certificates backed by the full faith and credit of the U.S. May purchase CMOs and other securities issued or guaranteed by the U.S. Government, its agencies or instrumentalities. Fund may use a variety of derivatives in an effort to enhance performance and for hedging purposes. Designed to deliver extra high yields for long-term buy and hold investors by maintaining a lower than average expense ratio.
Year organized: 1987 (formerly Dreyfus Foreign Investors GNMA Fund. Name and objectives changed 8/23/91. Name changed from Dreyfus Investors GNMA Fund 11/1/95.)
Ticker symbol: DIGFX
Group fund code: 080
Minimum purchase: Initial: $10,000, Subsequent: $1,000; IRA/Keogh: Initial: $5,000
Discount broker availability: Fidelity, Siebert, White
Wire redemptions: Yes, $5,000 minimum, $5 fee
Check redemptions $1,000 minimum, $2 fee
Account closeout fee: $5
Telephone switching: $1,000 minimum
Number of switches permitted: 4 outbound per year, $5 fee
Dividends paid: Income - declared daily, paid monthly; Capital gains - annually
Portfolio turnover (3 yrs): 333%, 254%, 290%
Management fee: 0.60%
Shareholder services fee: 0.25%
Expense ratio: 0.65% (year ending 12/31/96) (1.17% without waiver)

DREYFUS BASIC INTERMEDIATE MUNICIPAL BOND PORTFOLIO ◆

(See first Dreyfus listing for data common to all funds)

Lead portfolio manager: Douglas J. Gaylor (1996)
Investment objective and policies: High current income exempt from federal income tax, consistent with capital preservation. Invests primarily in high quality municipal obligations. Portfolio maintains a dollar-weighted average maturity of three to ten years. Up to 35% of assets may be in junk bonds and 15% in illiquid securities. May use futures and options on 20% of assets and sell short on 25% of assets. Designed to deliver extra high yields for long-term buy and hold investors by maintaining a lower than average expense ratio.
Year organized: 1994
Ticker symbol: DBIMX
Group fund code: 126
Minimum purchase: Initial: $10,000, Subsequent: $1,000
Discount broker availability: White
Wire redemptions: Yes, $5,000 minimum, $5 fee
Check redemptions $1,000 minimum, $2 fee
Account closeout fee: $5
Telephone switching: $1,000 minimum
Number of switches permitted: 4 outbound per year, $5 fee
Dividends paid: Income - declared daily, paid monthly; Capital gains - annually
Portfolio turnover (3 yrs): 65%, 55%, 34%
Management fee: 0.60%
Shareholder services fee: Maximum of 0.25%
Expense ratio: 0.24% (year ending 8/31/97) (0.80% without waiver)

DREYFUS BASIC MASSACHUSETTS MUNICIPAL MONEY MARKET FUND ◆

(See first Dreyfus listing for data common to all funds)

Lead portfolio manager: Angela M. Deni (1994)
Investment objective and policies: Current income exempt from federal and Massachusetts personal income taxes, consistent with preservation of capital and liquidity. Invests primarily in high quality, short-term Massachusetts municipal money market obligations. Designed to deliver extra high yields for long-term buy and hold investors by maintaining a lower than average expense ratio.
Year organized: 1983 (Name changed from Boston Company Massachusetts Tax-Free Money Fund on 4/1/94, from Laurel Massachusetts Tax-Free Money Fund on 10/17/94 and from Dreyfus/Laurel Massachusetts Tax-Free Money Fund in 1996)
Ticker symbol: DMRXX
Group fund code: 715
Minimum purchase: Initial: $25,000, Subsequent: $1,000
Qualified for sale in: All states except AK, AR, DE, ID, IA, KS, KY, LA, MI, MS, MT, NE, NM, ND, OK, PR, SC, SD, TN
Wire redemptions: Yes, $5,000 minimum, $5 fee
Check redemptions $1,000 minimum, $2 fee
Account closeout fee: $5
Telephone switching: $1,000 minimum
Number of switches permitted: 4 outbound per year, $5 fee
Dividends paid: Income - declared daily, paid monthly
Management fee: 0.45%
Expense ratio: 0.37% (year ending 6/30/97) (0.46% without waiver)

DREYFUS BASIC MONEY MARKET FUND ◆

(See first Dreyfus listing for data common to all funds)

Lead portfolio manager: Patricia A. Larkin (1994)
Investment objective and policies: High current income consistent with preservation of capital and liquidity. Invests in high quality money market obligations. Designed to deliver extra high yields for long-term buy and hold investors by maintaining a lower than average expense ratio.
Year organized: 1992
Ticker symbol: DBAXX
Group fund code: 123
Minimum purchase: Initial: $25,000, Subsequent: $1,000
Wire redemptions: Yes, $5,000 minimum, $5 fee
Check redemptions $1,000 minimum, $2 fee
Account closeout fee: $5
Telephone switching: $1,000 minimum
Number of switches permitted: 4 outbound per year, $5 fee
Dividends paid: Income - declared daily, paid monthly
Management fee: 0.50%
Shareholder services fee: 0.25%
Expense ratio: 0.45% (year ending 2/28/97) (0.68% without waiver)

DREYFUS BASIC MUNICIPAL BOND PORTFOLIO ◆

(See first Dreyfus listing for data common to all funds)

Lead portfolio manager: Douglas J. Gaylor (1996)
Investment objective and policies: High current income exempt from federal income tax, consistent with capital preservation. Invests primarily in high quality municipal obligations with no limit on maturity. Up to 35% of assets may be in junk bonds and 15% in illiquid securities. May use futures and options on 20% of assets and sell short on 25% of assets. Designed to deliver extra high yields for long-term buy and hold investors by maintaining a lower than average expense ratio.
Year organized: 1994
Ticker symbol: DRMBX
Group fund code: 125

Minimum purchase: Initial: $10,000, Subsequent: $1,000
Discount broker availability: White
Wire redemptions: Yes, $5,000 minimum, $5 fee
Check redemptions $1,000 minimum, $2 fee
Account closeout fee: $5
Telephone switching: $1,000 minimum
Number of switches permitted: 4 outbound per year, $5 fee
Dividends paid: Income - declared daily, paid monthly; Capital gains - annually
Portfolio turnover (3 yrs): 101%, 59%, 59%
Management fee: 0.60%
Shareholder services fee: Maximum of 0.25%
Expense ratio: 0.26% (year ending 8/31/97) (0.84% without waiver)

DREYFUS BASIC MUNICIPAL MONEY MARKET PORTFOLIO ◆

(See first Dreyfus listing for data common to all funds)

Lead portfolio manager: Karen M. Hand (1991)
Investment objective and policies: High current income exempt from federal income tax, consistent with preservation of capital and liquidity. Invests in high quality municipal money market obligations. Designed to deliver extra high yields for long-term buy and hold investors by maintaining a lower than average expense ratio.
Year organized: 1991 (name changed from Dreyfus Investors Municipal Money Market Fund on 4/23/92)
Ticker symbol: DBMXX
Group fund code: 122
Minimum purchase: Initial: $25,000, Subsequent: $1,000
Deadline for same day wire purchase: 12 NN
Wire redemptions: Yes, $5,000 minimum, $5 fee
Check redemptions $1,000 minimum, $2 fee
Account closeout fee: $5
Telephone switching: $1,000 minimum
Deadline for same day switch: 12 NN
Number of switches permitted: 4 outbound per year, $5 fee
Dividends paid: Income - declared daily, paid monthly
Management fee: 0.50%
Shareholder services fee: Maximum of 0.25%
Expense ratio: 0.45% (year ending 8/31/97) (0.60% without waiver)

DREYFUS BASIC NEW JERSEY MUNICIPAL MONEY MARKET PORTFOLIO ◆

(See first Dreyfus listing for data common to all funds)

Lead portfolio manager: Karen M. Hand (1995)
Investment objective and policies: Maximum current income exempt from federal and New Jersey state personal income taxes, consistent with preservation of capital and liquidity. Invests primarily in high quality New Jersey municipal money market obligations. May invest in securities eligible for AMT tax treatment without limit. Designed to deliver extra high yields for long-term buy and hold investors by maintaining a lower than average expense ratio.
Year organized: 1995
Ticker symbol: DBJXX
Group fund code: 127
Minimum purchase: Initial: $25,000, Subsequent: $1,000
Deadline for same day wire purchase: 12 NN
Qualified for sale in: CA, CO, CT, DE, FL, GA, HI, IL, IN, KY, LA, MD, MN, NJ, NY, NC, OH, OR, PA, RI, UT, VA, WY
Wire redemptions: Yes, $5,000 minimum, $5 fee
Check redemptions $1,000 minimum, $2 fee
Account closeout fee: $5
Telephone switching: $1,000 minimum
Deadline for same day switch: 12 NN
Number of switches permitted: 4 outbound per year, $5 fee
Dividends paid: Income - declared daily, paid monthly
Management fee: 0.50%
Shareholder services fee: 0.25%
Expense ratio: 0.36% (year ending 8/31/97) (0.63% without waiver)

DREYFUS BASIC NEW YORK MUNICIPAL MONEY MARKET FUND ◆

(See first Dreyfus listing for data common to all funds)

Lead portfolio manager: Angela M. Deni (1994)
Investment objective and policies: Maximum current income exempt from federal, NY state and NY city personal income taxes, consistent with preservation of capital and liquidity. Invests primarily in high quality New York municipal money market obligations. Designed to deliver extra high yields for long-term buy and hold investors by maintaining a lower than average expense ratio.
Year organized: 1988 (name changed from Boston Company New York Tax-Free Money Fund on 4/1/94, from Laurel New York Tax-Free Money Fund on 10/17/94 and from Dreyfus/Laurel New York Tax Free Money Fund in 1995)
Ticker symbol: DNIXX
Group fund code: 316
Minimum purchase: Initial: $25,000, Subsequent: $1,000
Qualified for sale in: AZ, CA, CO, CT, DC, FL, GA, HI, IL, IN, MA, MN, NJ, NY, NC, OH, OR, PA, RI, TX, UT, VA, WV, WY
Wire redemptions: Yes, $5,000 minimum, $5 fee
Check redemptions $1,000 minimum, $2 fee
Account closeout fee: $5
Telephone switching: $1,000 minimum
Number of switches permitted: 4 outbound per year, $5 fee
Dividends paid: Income - declared daily, paid monthly
Management fee: 0.45%
Expense ratio: 0.41% (year ending 6/30/97) (0.45% without waiver)

DREYFUS BASIC U.S. GOVERNMENT MONEY MARKET FUND ◆

(See first Dreyfus listing for data common to all funds)

Lead portfolio manager: Patricia A. Larkin (1994)
Investment objective and policies: High current income consistent with preservation of capital and liquidity. Invests in high quality short-term U.S. Government securities and repurchase agreements. Designed to deliver extra high yields for long-term buy and hold investors by maintaining a lower than average expense ratio.
Year organized: 1992
Ticker symbol: DBGXX
Group fund code: 124
Minimum purchase: Initial: $25,000, Subsequent: $1,000
Wire redemptions: Yes, $5,000 minimum, $5 fee
Check redemptions $1,000 minimum, $2 fee
Account closeout fee: $5
Telephone switching: $1,000 minimum
Number of switches permitted: 4 outbound per year, $5 fee
Dividends paid: Income - declared daily, paid monthly
Management fee: 0.50%
Shareholder services fee: 0.25%
Expense ratio: 0.45% (year ending 2/28/97) (0.65% without waiver)

DREYFUS BOND MARKET INDEX FUND

(See first Dreyfus listing for data common to all funds)

Lead portfolio manager: Laurie A. Carroll (1993)
Investment objective and policies: Replicate the total return of the Lehman Brothers Government/Corporate Bond Index. Invests in a representative sample of the securities contained in the Index, selecting one or two issues to represent an entire "class" or type of securities in the Index.
Year organized: 1993 (name changed from Laurel Bond Market Index Fund on 10/17/94) (Investor shares began in 1994, Basic shares began in 1993 as Trust shares; became Basic shares 6/15/97)
Ticker symbol: DBIRX (Basic shares): DBMIX (Investor shares)

Group fund code: 710 (Basic shares): 310 (Investor shares)
Deadline for same day wire purchase: 12 NN and 4 P.M. (two pricings for Basic Shares, 4 P.M. for Investor shares)
Minimum purchase: Initial: $2,500 ($10,000 Basic). Subsequent: $100 ($1,000 Basic); IRA/Keogh: Initial: $750 ($5,000 Basic). Subsequent: None ($1,000 Basic); Automatic investment plan: Initial: $100 (n/a for Basic)
Discount broker availability: Fidelity, Siebert, *White
Check redemptions: $500 minimum
Dividends paid: Income - declared daily, paid monthly; Capital gains - annually
Portfolio turnover (3 yrs): 49%, 43%, 40%
Management fee: 0.40%
12b-1 distribution fee: 0.25% (Investor shares)
Expense ratio: 0.35% (Basic) 0.60% (Investor) (year ending 10/31/97)

DREYFUS CALIFORNIA INTERMEDIATE MUNICIPAL BOND FUND ◆

(See first Dreyfus listing for data common to all funds)

Lead portfolio manager: Monica S. Weiboldt (1996)
Investment objective and policies: High current income exempt from federal and California state income taxes, consistent with capital preservation. Invests primarily in California municipal bonds with at least 80% rated BBB or better. Portfolio maintains a dollar-weighted average maturity of three to ten years. Up to 15% of assets may be in illiquid securities. May use futures and options and sell short on 25% of assets.
Year organized: 1992
Ticker symbol: DCIMX
Group fund code: 902
Discount broker availability: *Fidelity, *Schwab, *Siebert, *White
Qualified for sale in: AL, AZ, CA, CT, DC, FL, HI, IL, MA, MI, NV, NJ, NY, OR, PA, TX, WA, WI, WY
Check redemptions: $500 minimum
Redemption fee: 1.00% for shares held less than 15 days, payable to the fund
Number of switches permitted: 4 outbound per year, $5 fee
Dividends paid: Income - declared daily, paid monthly; Capital gains - annually
Portfolio turnover (3 yrs): 36%, 41%, 17%
Management fee: 0.60%
Shareholder services fee: Maximum of 0.25%
Expense ratio: 0.78% (year ending 3/31/97) (0.82% without waiver)

DREYFUS CALIFORNIA TAX EXEMPT BOND FUND ◆

(See first Dreyfus listing for data common to all funds)

Lead portfolio manager: Joseph P. Darcy (1996)
Investment objective and policies: High current income exempt from federal and California state income taxes, consistent with capital preservation. Invests at least 80% of assets in California municipal bonds rated BBB or better. Up to 20% of assets may be in securities eligible for AMT tax treatment, 20% in junk bonds and 15% in illiquid securities.
Year organized: 1983
Ticker symbol: DRCAX
Group fund code: 928
Discount broker availability: *Fidelity, *Schwab, *Siebert, *White
Check redemptions: $500 minimum
Redemption fee: 0.10% for shares held less than 15 days, payable to the fund
Number of switches permitted: 4 outbound per calendar year
Dividends paid: Income - declared daily, paid monthly; Capital gains - annually
Portfolio turnover (3 yrs): 61%, 56%, 40%
Management fee: 0.60%
Shareholder services fee: 0.25%
Expense ratio: 0.73% (year ending 5/31/97)

DREYFUS CALIFORNIA TAX EXEMPT MONEY MARKET FUND ◆

(See first Dreyfus listing for data common to all funds)

Lead portfolio manager: Jill C. Shaffro (1994)
Investment objective and policies: High current income exempt from federal and California state income taxes, consistent with preservation of capital and liquidity. Invests in California money market instruments.
Year organized: 1986
Ticker symbol: DCTXX
Group fund code: 357
Qualified for sale in: AK, AZ, CA, CO, CT, DC, FL, HI, ID, IL, LA, MD, MA, MI, MN, MS, NE, NV, NJ, NM, NY, OH, OR, PA, TX, VA, WA, WY
Check redemptions: $500 minimum
Dividends paid: Income - declared daily, paid monthly
Management fee: 0.50%
Expense ratio: 0.66% (year ending 3/31/97)

DREYFUS CONNECTICUT INTERMEDIATE MUNICIPAL BOND FUND ◆

(See first Dreyfus listing for data common to all funds)

Lead portfolio manager: Stephen C. Kris (1992)
Investment objective and policies: High current income exempt from federal and Connecticut income taxes, consistent with capital preservation. Invests at least 80% of assets in debt securities of the state of Connecticut, its political subdivisions, authorities and corporations rated BBB or better. Portfolio maintains a dollar-weighted average maturity of three to ten years. Up to 20% of assets may be in junk bonds and 15% in illiquid securities. May use futures and options and sell short up to 25% of assets.
Year organized: 1992
Ticker symbol: DCTIX
Group fund code: 914
Discount broker availability: *Fidelity, *Schwab, *Siebert, *White
Qualified for sale in: AZ, CA, CT, DC, FL, HI, IL, MA, NJ, NY, TX, WY
Check redemptions: $500 minimum
Redemption fee: 1.00% for shares held less than 15 days, payable to the fund
Number of switches permitted: 4 outbound per calendar year
Dividends paid: Income - declared daily, paid monthly; Capital gains - annually
Portfolio turnover (3 yrs): 30%, 20%, 32%
Management fee: 0.60%
Shareholder services fee: 0.25%
Expense ratio: 0.78% (year ending 3/31/97) (0.84% without waiver)

DREYFUS CONNECTICUT MUNICIPAL MONEY MARKET FUND ◆

(See first Dreyfus listing for data common to all funds)

Lead portfolio manager: Jill C. Shaffro (1994)
Investment objective and policies: High current income exempt from federal and State of Connecticut income taxes, consistent with preservation of capital and liquidity. Invests in Connecticut money market instruments.
Year organized: 1990
Ticker symbol: DRCXX
Group fund code: 101
Deadline for same day wire purchase: 12 NN
Qualified for sale in: AZ, CA, CT, DE, DC, FL, HI, IL, MA, MI, NJ, NY, PA, RI, TX, WY
Check redemptions: $500 minimum
Dividends paid: Income - declared daily, paid monthly
Management fee: 0.50%
Shareholder services fee: 0.25%
Expense ratio: 0.65% (year ending 9/30/97) (0.69% without waiver)

DREYFUS CORE VALUE FUND

(Effective January 1/15/98, fund became Dreyfus Premier Core Value Fund, a multi-class load fund. Shareholders of record prior to the changeover may still buy in at NAV.)

DREYFUS DISCIPLINED EQUITY INCOME FUND

(Effective January 1/15/98, fund became Dreyfus Premier Large Company Stock Fund, a multi-class load fund. Shareholders of record prior to the changeover may still buy in at NAV.)

DREYFUS DISCIPLINED INTERMEDIATE BOND FUND

(See first Dreyfus listing for data common to all funds)

Lead portfolio manager: Ridgeway H. Powell (1995)
Investment objective and policies: High current income, consistent with capital preservation. Invests primarily in investment grade debt securities of domestic and foreign issuers, with a dollar-weighted average maturity of three to ten years. May have up to 15% of assets in illiquid securities and use futures and options for hedging purposes.
Year organized: 1995
Group fund code: 302 (Investor shares)
Special sales restrictions: Fund is offered in two classes; Institutional (previously Investor) and Restricted (previously Class R, or Retail). The former Retail shares converted to Restricted and are sold only to previous accountholders, without 12b-1 fees. Investor shares (previously Institutional) are sold with 12b-1 fees direct as well as through banks and brokers.
Deadline for same day wire purchase: 12 NN
Discount broker availability: Fidelity, Siebert, *White
Qualified for sale in: All states except AK, AZ, AR, MO, OH, PR, VT
Check redemptions: $500 minimum
Deadline for same day switch: 12 NN
Dividends paid: Income - declared daily, paid monthly; Capital gains - annually
Portfolio turnover (2 yrs) 144%, 198%
Management fee: 0.55%
12b-1 distribution fee: 0.25% (Institutional shares)
Expense ratio: 0.55% (Retail) 0.80% (Institutional) (year ending 10/31/97)

DREYFUS DISCIPLINED MIDCAP STOCK FUND

(Effective January 1/15/98, fund became Dreyfus Premier Midcap Stock Fund, a multi-class load fund. Shareholders of record prior to the changeover may still buy in at NAV.)

DREYFUS DISCIPLINED STOCK FUND

(See first Dreyfus listing for data common to all funds)

Lead portfolio manager: Bert J. Mullins (1987)
Investment objective and policies: Total return exceeding that of the S&P 500 Index. Invests in a broadly diversified portfolio of equity securities chosen by the application of quantitative security selection and risk control techniques. Up to 20% of assets may be in money market instruments and 15% in illiquid securities.
Year organized: 1987 (name changed from Laurel Stock Fund on 10/17/94; Investor Shares commenced 4/6/94.**Prior to 12/15/97,** fund was offered in two classes, Retail (R) or Institutional (I). It is now a single class fund. It retains the ticker symbol and fund code of the retail class, as well as the historic expense and performance information, but inherits the I class 12b-1 fee. . .)
Ticker symbol: DDSTX
Group fund code: 728
Deadline for same day wire purchase: 12 NN and 4 P.M. (two pricings)
Discount broker availability: Fidelity, Siebert, *White
Dividends paid: Income - February, May, August, November; Capital gains - December

Portfolio turnover (3 yrs): 69%, 64%, 60%
Management fee: 0.90%
12b-1 distribution fee: 0.25%
Shareholder services fee: 0.10%
Expense ratio: 0.90% (year ending 10/31/97)

DREYFUS EMERGING LEADERS FUND ◆

(See first Dreyfus listing for data common to all funds)

Portfolio managers: Paul Kandel (1996), Hilary R. Woods (1996)
Investment objective and policies: Capital growth. Invests primarily in equity securities of domestic and foreign issuers with market capitalizations of less than $750M with dominant market positions within major product lines, sustained records of achievement and strong financial condition. Fund also seeks companies with new or innovative products, services or processes which should enhance prospects for growth and future earnings. Up to 25% of assets may be in securities of foreign issuers and 15% in illiquid securities. May use futures and options and foreign currency transactions for hedging purposes and sell short up to 25% of total assets.
Year organized: 1995 (name changed from Growth and Value - Emerging Leaders in 1996)
Ticker symbol: DRELX
Group fund code: 259
Discount broker availability: *Fidelity, *Schwab, *Siebert, *White
Redemption fee: 1.00% for shares held less than 15 days, payable to the fund
Dividends paid: Income - annually; Capital gains - annually
Portfolio turnover (2 yrs): 198%, 204%
Management fee: 0.90%
Shareholder services fee: 0.25%
Expense ratio: 1.39% (year ending 8/31/97) (1.45% without waiver)

DREYFUS EMERGING MARKETS FUND ◆

(See first Dreyfus listing for data common to all funds)

Lead portfolio manager: D. Kirk Henry (1996)
Investment objective and policies: Long-term capital appreciation. Invests primarily in equity securities of foreign issuers in countries with emerging markets, as defined by the Morgan Stanley Capital International Emerging Markets Index. Companies are selected using a "value" classification based on price to book, price to earnings, and price to cash flow ratios. Fund is non-diversified. May invest in securities of supranational entities such as the World Bank, invest up to 15% of assets in illiquid securities, invest in closed-end investment companies to the extent that it offers entrance to otherwise inaccessible securities, and use a variety of derivative instruments for hedging purposes.
Year organized: 1996
Ticker symbol: DRFMX
Group fund code: 327
Deadline for same day wire purchase: 12 NN and 4 P.M. (two pricings)
Discount broker availability: Fidelity, Siebert, *White
Redemption fee: 1.00% for shares held less than 6 months, payable to the fund
Number of switches permitted: 4 outbound per year
Dividends paid: Income - December; Capital gains - December
Portfolio turnover (1 yr): 53%
Management fee: 1.25%
Shareholder services fee: 0.25%
Expense ratio: 1.85% (11 months ending 5/31/97) (2.21% without waiver)

DREYFUS EQUITY DIVIDEND FUND ◆

(See first Dreyfus listing for data common to all funds)

Lead portfolio manager: Timothy M. Ghriskey (1995)
Investment objective and policies: Current income; capital appreciation secondary. Invests primarily in

dividend-paying common stocks, preferred stocks and securities convertible into common stocks of domestic and foreign issuers. May also invest up to 35% of assets in non-dividend paying equity securities and in debt obligations of foreign and domestic issuers. Up to 20% of assets may be in illiquid securities. May use foreign currency transactions as a hedging device or as a an attempt to realize gains. May use futures and options for hedging purposes and sell short up to 25% of total assets.
Year organized: 1995
Group fund code: 042
Discount broker availability: *Fidelity, *Siebert, *White
Number of switches permitted: 4 outbound per year
Dividends paid: Income - quarterly; Capital gains - annually
Portfolio turnover (2 yrs): 80%, 99%
Management fee: 0.75%
Shareholder services fee: Maximum of 0.25%
Expense ratio: 1.27% (year ending 10/31/97) (2.63% without waiver)

DREYFUS FLORIDA INTERMEDIATE MUNICIPAL BOND FUND ◆

(See first Dreyfus listing for data common to all funds)

Lead portfolio manager: Stephen C. Kris (1992)
Investment objective and policies: High current income exempt from federal income tax and Florida intangible personal property tax, consistent with capital preservation. Invests at least 80% of assets in municipal obligations (rated A or better), and at least 65% in high quality Florida municipals. Portfolio maintains a dollar-weighted average maturity of three to ten years. May have more than 25% of assets in securities subject to AMT tax treatment, up to 20% in municipal junk bonds and up to 15% in illiquid securities. May invest more than 25% of assets in industrial development bonds. May use futures and options and sell short on up to 25% of assets.
Year organized: 1992
Ticker symbol: DFLIX
Group fund code: 740
Discount broker availability: *Fidelity, *Schwab, *Siebert, *White
Qualified for sale in: AZ, CA, CT, DC, FL, HI, IL, MA, NJ, NY, PA, TX, WI, WY
Check redemptions: $500 minimum
Redemption fee: 1.00% for shares held less than 15 days, payable to the fund
Number of switches permitted: 4 outbound per year
Dividends paid: Income - declared daily, paid monthly; Capital gains - annually
Portfolio turnover (3 yrs): 19%, 25%, 19%
Management fee: 0.60%
Shareholder services fee: 0.25%
Expense ratio: 0.80% (year ending 12/31/96)

DREYFUS FLORIDA MUNICIPAL MONEY MARKET FUND ◆

(See first Dreyfus listing for data common to all funds)

Lead portfolio manager: Jill C. Shaffro (1993)
Investment objective and policies: High current income exempt from federal income tax and Florida intangible personal property tax, consistent with preservation of capital and liquidity. Invests in Florida municipal money market instruments.
Year organized: 1993
Ticker symbol: DFMXX
Group fund code: 741
Deadline for same day wire purchase: 12 NN
Qualified for sale in: AZ, CA, CT, DC, FL, HI, IL, MA, NJ, NY, PA, TX, WY
Check redemptions: $500 minimum
Deadline for same day switch: 12 NN
Dividends paid: Income - declared daily, paid monthly
Management fee: 0.50%
Shareholder services fee: Maximum of 0.25%
Expense ratio: 0.57% (year ending 6/30/97) (0.77% without waiver)

THE DREYFUS FUND ◆

(See first Dreyfus listing for data common to all funds)

Lead portfolio manager: Timothy M. Ghriskey (1997)
Investment objective and policies: Long-term capital growth consistent with the preservation of capital; current income is an important secondary consideration. Fund leans toward full investment in common stocks of seasoned companies, but may invest in fixed-income securities. Up to 20% of assets may be in foreign securities and 15% in illiquid securities. May use foreign currency exchange transactions.
Year organized: 1951
Ticker symbol: DREVX
Group fund code: 026
Discount broker availability: *Fidelity, *Schwab, *Siebert, *White
Dividends paid: Income - quarterly; Capital gains - annually
Portfolio turnover (3 yrs): 221%, 269%, 28%
Management fee: 0.65% first $1.5B to 0.55% over $2.5B
Expense ratio: 0.73% (year ending 12/31/96)

DREYFUS - GENERAL CALIFORNIA MUNICIPAL BOND FUND ◆

(See first Dreyfus listing for data common to all funds)

Lead portfolio manager: A. Paul Disdier (1989)
Investment objective and policies: Maximum current income exempt from federal and California state income taxes, consistent with capital preservation. Invests at least 80% of assets in municipal bonds, and at least 65% of assets in California municipal obligations rated Baa or better. May invest without limit in securities subject to AMT tax treatment, and have up to 35% of assets in municipal junk bonds and 15% in illiquid securities. May use futures and options for hedging purposes.
Year organized: 1989
Ticker symbol: GCABX (Class A shares)
Group fund code: 131
Discount broker availability: *Fidelity, *Schwab, *Siebert, *White
Qualified for sale in: All states except AL, AR, DE, IN, IA, KS, KY, ME, MO, MT, NH, NC, ND, OK, PR, RI, SC, SD, TN, UT, VT, WV, WI
Check redemptions: $500 minimum
Redemption fee: 0.10% for shares held less than 15 days, payable to the fund
Dividends paid: Income - declared daily, paid monthly; Capital gains - annually
Portfolio turnover (3 yrs): 90%, 165%, 83%
Management fee: 0.60%
12b-1 distribution fee: 0.25% (not currently imposed)
Shareholder services fee: 0.25%
Expense ratio: 0.76% (year ending 9/30/97)

DREYFUS - GENERAL CALIFORNIA MUNICIPAL MONEY MARKET FUND ◆

(See first Dreyfus listing for data common to all funds)

Lead portfolio manager: Jill C. Shaffro (1994)
Investment objective and policies: Maximum income exempt from federal and California state income taxes, consistent with preservation of capital and liquidity. Invests primarily in money market debt securities of the state of California and its political subdivisions, authorities and corporations.
Year organized: 1986 (Formerly General California Tax-Exempt Money Market Fund)
Ticker symbol: GCAXX (Class A shares)
Group fund code: 573
Qualified for sale in: AZ, CA, CT, DC, FL, GA, HI, ID, IL, MD, MA, NV, NJ, NM, NY, NC, OH, OR, PA, TX, UT, VA, WA, WI, WY
Deadline for same day wire purchase: 12 NN and 4 P.M. (two pricings)
Check redemptions: $500 minimum
Dividends paid: Income - declared daily, paid monthly
Management fee: 0.50%
Shareholder services fee: 0.25%
Expense ratio: 0.64% (year ending 7/31/97)

DREYFUS - GENERAL GOVERNMENT SECURITIES MONEY MARKET FUND

(See first Dreyfus listing for data common to all funds)

Portfolio managers: Patricia A. Larkin (1996), Bernard W. Kiernan, Jr. (1996)
Investment objective and policies: Current income consistent with preservation of capital and liquidity. Invests in money market securities issued or guaranteed by the U.S. Government and repurchase agreements on such securities.
Year organized: 1983
Ticker symbol: GGSXX (Class A shares)
Group fund code: 975
Deadline for same day wire purchase: 12 NN and 4 P.M. (two pricings)
Check redemptions: $500 minimum
Dividends paid: Income - declared daily, paid monthly
Management fee: 0.50%
12b-1 distribution fee: 0.20%
Shareholder services fee: 0.25%
Expense ratio: 0.82% (year ending 1/31/97)

DREYFUS - GENERAL MONEY MARKET FUND

(See first Dreyfus listing for data common to all funds)

Portfolio managers: Patricia A. Larkin (1995), Bernard W. Kiernan, Jr. (1996)
Investment objective and policies: High current income consistent with preservation of capital and liquidity. Invests in money market securities issued or guaranteed by the U.S. Government, bank obligations, repurchase agreements and commercial paper. May invest in securities of foreign issuers.
Year organized: 1982
Ticker symbol: GMMXX
Group fund code: 196
Deadline for same day wire purchase: 12 NN and 4 P.M. (two pricings)
Discount broker availability: *Fidelity
Check redemptions: $500 minimum
Dividends paid: Income - declared daily, paid monthly
Management fee: 0.50%
12b-1 distribution fee: 0.20%
Shareholder services fee: 0.25%
Expense ratio: 0.84% (year ending 1/31/97)

DREYFUS - GENERAL MUNICIPAL BOND FUND

(See first Dreyfus listing for data common to all funds)

Lead portfolio manager: A. Paul Disdier (1988)
Investment objective and policies: Maximum current income exempt from Federal income tax, consistent with capital preservation. Invests at least 80% of assets in municipal obligations, and at least 65% of assets in bonds, debentures and other debt instruments. May invest without limit in securities subject to AMT tax treatment, and have up to 35% of assets in junk bonds and up to 15% in illiquid securities. May invest more than 25% of assets in industrial development bonds. May use futures and options for hedging purposes.
Year organized: 1984 (Formerly General Tax-Exempt Bond Fund)
Ticker symbol: GMBDX
Group fund code: 106
Discount broker availability: *Fidelity, *Schwab, *Siebert, *White
Check redemptions: $500 minimum
Redemption fee: 0.10% for shares held less than 15 days, payable to the fund
Dividends paid: Income - declared daily, paid monthly; Capital gains - February
Portfolio turnover (3 yrs): 116%, 115%, 68%
Management fee: 0.55%
12b-1 distribution fee: 0.20%
Expense ratio: 0.88% (year ending 2/28/97)

DREYFUS - GENERAL MUNICIPAL MONEY MARKET FUND ◆

(See first Dreyfus listing for data common to all funds)

Lead portfolio manager: Karen M. Hand (1987)
Investment objective and policies: Maximum income exempt from federal income tax, consistent with preservation of capital and liquidity. Invests in municipal money market obligations.
Year organized: 1983 (formerly General Tax Exempt Money Market Fund)
Ticker symbol: GTMXX (Class A shares)
Group fund code: 918
Deadline for same day wire purchase: 12 NN
Check redemptions: $500 minimum
Deadline for same day switch: 12 NN
Dividends paid: Income - declared daily, paid monthly
Management fee: 0.50%
Shareholder services fee: 0.25%
Expense ratio: 0.66% (year ending 11/30/96)

DREYFUS - GENERAL NEW YORK MUNICIPAL BOND FUND

(See first Dreyfus listing for data common to all funds)

Lead portfolio manager: Monica S. Wieboldt (1988)
Investment objective and policies: High current income exempt from federal, NY state and NY city income taxes, consistent with capital preservation. Invests at least 65% of assets in investment grade New York municipal obligations. May invest without limit in securities subject to AMT tax treatment, and have up to 35% of assets in municipal junk bonds and up to 15% in illiquid securities. May invest up to 25% of assets in industrial development bonds. May use futures and options for hedging purposes.
Year organized: 1984 (formerly General New York Tax Exempt Intermediate Bond Fund)
Ticker symbol: GNYMX
Group fund code: 949
Discount broker availability: *Fidelity, *Schwab, *Siebert
Qualified for sale in: CA, CT, DC, FL, HI, NV, NJ, NY, WY
Check redemptions: $500 minimum
Redemption fee: 0.10% for shares held less than 15 days, payable to the fund
Dividends paid: Income - declared daily, paid monthly; Capital gains - annually
Portfolio turnover (3 yrs): 66%, 80%, 66%
Management fee: 0.60%
12b-1 distribution fee: 0.20%
Expense ratio: 0.91% (year ending 10/31/97)

DREYFUS - GENERAL NEW YORK MUNICIPAL MONEY MARKET FUND ◆

(See first Dreyfus listing for data common to all funds)

Lead portfolio manager: Karen M. Hand (1987)
Investment objective and policies: Maximum income exempt from federal, NY state and NY city income taxes, consistent with preservation of capital and liquidity. Invests primarily in money market securities issued by New York state and city municipalities.
Year organized: 1984 (formerly Park Avenue New York Tax Exempt Money Market Fund and General New York Tax Exempt Money Market Fund)
Ticker symbol: GNMXX (Class A shares)
Group fund code: 574
Deadline for same day wire purchase: 12 NN
Qualified for sale in: CA, CT, DC, FL, HI, MA, NV, NH, NJ, NY, OH, PA, RI, VT, WY
Check redemptions: $500 minimum
Deadline for same day switch: 12 NN
Dividends paid: Income - declared daily, paid monthly
Management fee: 0.50%
Shareholder services fee: 0.25%
Expense ratio: 0.68% (year ending 11/30/96)

DREYFUS GLOBAL BOND FUND ◆
(See first Dreyfus listing for data common to all funds)

Sub-adviser: Pareto Partners
Lead portfolio manager: Christine V. Downton (1996)
Investment objective and policies: Total return: capital growth and income. Invests primarily in bonds and debentures of corporate, government and supranational issuers located throughout the world. Up to 35% of assets may be in junk bonds, 35% in securities of issuers in emerging markets and 15% in illiquid securities. May sell short up to 25% of total assets, leverage up to 33% of net assets, and use futures and options transactions on indices, securities and interest rates.
Year organized: 1994
Ticker symbol: DGBDX
Group fund code: 098
Discount broker availability: Fidelity, Siebert, *White
Number of switches permitted: 4 outbound per year
Dividends paid: Income - monthly; Capital gains - annually
Portfolio turnover (3 yrs): 81%, 21%, 4%
Management fee: 0.70%
Shareholder services fee: 0.25%
Expense ratio: 1.34% (year ending 11/30/96) (2.00% without waiver)

DREYFUS GLOBAL GROWTH FUND ◆
(See first Dreyfus listing for data common to all funds)

Lead portfolio manager: Ronald Chapman (1996)
Investment objective and policies: Capital growth. Invests primarily in a broadly diversified, asset allocated portfolio of common stocks of foreign and domestic issuers representing between 15 and 25 global equity markets, including emerging markets; attempts also to identify industrial sectors with high relative growth. May invest in common stocks of foreign companies which are not publicly traded in the U.S. and the debt securities of foreign governments. Up to 35% of assets may be in junk bonds and 15% in illiquid securities. Fund may sell short up to 25% of total assets, leverage up to 33% of net assets, and use options, futures and forward foreign currency contracts for hedging purposes. Fund is non-diversified.
Year organized: 1987 (name changed from Dreyfus Strategic World Investing, L.P. on 1/1/94. 3% load dropped in 1/96)
Ticker symbol: DSWIX
Group fund code: 033
Discount broker availability: Fidelity, Siebert, *White
Number of switches permitted: 4 outbound per year
Dividends paid: Income - annually; Capital gains - annually
Portfolio turnover (3 yrs): 163%, 225%, 147%
Management fee: 0.75%
Shareholder services fee: 0.25%
Expense ratio: 1.39% (year ending 12/31/96) (1.90% without waiver)

DREYFUS GNMA FUND
(See first Dreyfus listing for data common to all funds)

Lead portfolio manager: Michael Hoeh (1997)
Investment objective and policies: High current income consistent with capital preservation. Invests at least 65% of assets in GNMAs. Also invests in other mortgage related securities such as FNMAs and FHLMC instruments. Fund may also invest in other mortgage-related securities guaranteed by the full faith and credit of the United States, its agencies or instrumentalities. May leverage up to 33 1/3% of assets and use a variety of derivative instruments in an effort to enhance performance and for hedging purposes.
Year organized: 1985
Ticker symbol: DRGMX
Group fund code: 265
Discount broker availability: *Fidelity, *Schwab, *Siebert, *White
Check redemptions: $500 minimum
Dividends paid: Income - monthly; Capital gains - annually

Portfolio turnover (3 yrs): 324%, 144%, 363%
Management fee: 0.60%
12b-1 distribution fee: 0.20%
Expense ratio: 0.96% (year ending 4/30/97)

DREYFUS GROWTH AND INCOME FUND ◆
(See first Dreyfus listing for data common to all funds)

Lead portfolio manager: Douglas D. Ramos (1997)
Investment objective and policies: Long-term capital growth, current income and growth of income, consistent with reasonable investment risk. Invests in equity securities including ADRs, EDRs and warrants; investment grade debt securities; and money markets of domestic and foreign issuers. May have up to 35% of assets in junk bonds and 15% in illiquid securities. Fund may leverage 33 1/3% of assets, sell short on as much as 25% of assets, use futures and options and use foreign currency transactions in an effort to enhance performance and for hedging purposes.
Year organized: 1991
Ticker symbol: DGRIX
Group fund code: 010
Discount broker availability: *Fidelity, *Schwab, *Siebert, *White
Number of switches permitted: 4 outbound per year
Dividends paid: Income - quarterly; Capital gains - annually
Portfolio turnover (3 yrs): 129%, 131%, 132%
Management fee: 0.75%
Shareholder services fee: 0.25%
Expense ratio: 1.01% (year ending 10/31/97)

DREYFUS GROWTH OPPORTUNITY FUND ◆
(See first Dreyfus listing for data common to all funds)

Lead portfolio manager: Timothy M. Ghriskey (1995)
Investment objective and policies: Long-term capital growth consistent with capital preservation; income secondary. Invests primarily in common stocks of small domestic and foreign companies considered undervalued. Up to 15% of assets may be in illiquid securities and 25% in securities of foreign governments and companies not publicly traded in the U.S. May use futures and options and foreign currency transactions to hedge up to 20% of total assets, and sell short up to 25% of total assets.
Year organized: 1972 (formerly Dreyfus Number Nine)
Ticker symbol: DREQX
Group fund code: 018
Discount broker availability: *Fidelity, *Schwab, *Siebert, *White
Number of switches permitted: 4 outbound per year
Dividends paid: Income - annually; Capital gains - annually
Portfolio turnover (3 yrs): 137%, 268%, 243%
Management fee: 0.75%
Shareholder services fee: 0.25%
Expense ratio: 1.06% (year ending 2/28/97)

DREYFUS HIGH YIELD SECURITIES FUND ◆
(See first Dreyfus listing for data common to all funds)

Lead portfolio manager: Roger King (1996)
Investment objective and policies: Maximum total return; capital appreciation and current income. Invests primarily in lower rated fixed-income securities, commonly known as "junk bonds." Fund may invest without limit in government or corporate foreign issues including developing countries, and will invest without regard to maturity. May invest in investment grade securities for defensive purposes, and use derivative instruments in an effort to enhance portfolio performance and for hedging purposes.
Year organized: 1996
Ticker symbol: DHIYX
Group fund code: 043
Discount broker availability: *Fidelity, *Schwab, *White

Redemption fee: 1.00% for shares held less than six months, payable to the fund
Number of switches permitted: 4 outbound per year
Dividends paid: Income - quarterly; Capital gains - annually
Portfolio turnover (2 yrs): 253%, 234%
Management fee: 0.65%
Shareholder services fee: 0.25%
Expense ratio: 0.71% (year ending 10/31/97) (1.14% without waiver)

DREYFUS INSURED MUNICIPAL BOND FUND
(See first Dreyfus listing for data common to all funds)

Lead portfolio manager: Joseph P. Darcy (1996)
Investment objective and policies: High current income exempt from federal income tax, consistent with capital preservation. Invests primarily in investment grade municipal obligations that are insured as to timely payment of principal and interest. May invest without limit in securities subject to AMT tax treatment, and have up to 15% of assets in illiquid securities. May invest more than 25% of assets in industrial development bonds.
Year organized: 1985 (formerly Dreyfus Insured Tax Exempt Bond Fund)
Ticker symbol: DTBDX
Group fund code: 306
Discount broker availability: *Fidelity, *Schwab, *Siebert, *White
Check redemptions: $500 minimum
Redemption fee: 0.10% for shares held less than 15 days, payable to the fund
Number of switches permitted: 4 outbound per year
Dividends paid: Income - declared daily, paid monthly; Capital gains - annually
Portfolio turnover (3 yrs): 93%, 83%, 41%
Management fee: 0.60%
12b-1 distribution fee: 0.20%
Expense ratio: 0.80% (year ending 4/30/97) (0.97% without waiver)

DREYFUS INTERMEDIATE MUNICIPAL BOND FUND ◆
(See first Dreyfus listing for data common to all funds)

Lead portfolio manager: Monica S. Wieboldt (1985)
Investment objective and policies: High current income exempt from federal income tax, consistent with capital preservation. Invests at least 80% of assets in high quality municipal obligations rated A or better. The dollar-weighted average maturity of the portfolio ranges from three to ten years. May invest without limit in securities subject to AMT tax treatment, and have up to 20% of assets in junk bonds and 15% in illiquid securities. May use options and futures for hedging purposes.
Year organized: 1983 (formerly Dreyfus Intermediate Tax Exempt Bond Fund)
Ticker symbol: DITEX
Group fund code: 947
Discount broker availability: *Fidelity, *Schwab, *Siebert, *White
Check redemptions: $500 minimum
Redemption fee: 0.10% for shares held less than 15 days, payable to the fund
Number of switches permitted: 4 outbound per year
Dividends paid: Income - declared daily, paid monthly; Capital gains - September
Portfolio turnover (3 yrs): 47%, 49%, 42%
Management fee: 0.60%
Shareholder services fee: 0.25%
Expense ratio: 0.73% (year ending 5/31/97)

DREYFUS INTERMEDIATE TERM INCOME FUND ◆
(See first Dreyfus listing for data common to all funds)

Lead portfolio manager: Kevin M. McClintock (1996)
Investment objective and policies: High current income consistent with capital preservation. Invests primarily in a broad range of investment grade debt

securities of both corporate and government domestic and foreign issues. Normally will invest in a portfolio of securities with an effective duration between three and eight years, and an effective average portfolio maturity between five and ten years. May invest up to 35% of assets in "junk bonds." May invest without limit in subordinated mortgage-related securities, although it is not expected this category of instruments will exceed 20% of assets.
Year organized: 1996
Ticker symbol: DRITX
Group fund code: 082
Discount broker availability: *White
Check redemptions: $500 minimum
Number of switches permitted - 4 outbound per year
Dividends paid: Income - declared daily, paid monthly; Capital gains - annually
Portfolio turnover (2 yrs): 322%, 139%
Management fee: 0.75%
Shareholder services fee: 0.25%
Expense ratio: 0.52% (year ending 7/31/97) (1.50% without waiver)

DREYFUS INTERNATIONAL EQUITY ALLOCATION FUND
(See first Dreyfus listing for data common to all funds)

Lead portfolio manager: Charles J. Jacklin (1996)
Investment objective and policies: Total return exceeding that of the MSCI-EAFE Index. Invests in common stocks chosen from among the countries and industry sectors represented in the Index and may invest up to 20% of assets in emerging markets countries. Fund may use futures and options and hedge up to 25% of total assets. Up to 15% of assets may be in illiquid securities.
Year organized: 1994 (name changed from Laurel International Equity Allocation Fund on 10/17/94)
Ticker symbol: DIEAX (Investor shares)
Group fund code: 323 (Investor shares)
Special sales restrictions: Shares formerly known as "Retail" are now "Restricted" shares, and are only available to accounts existing prior to 8/21/97 (without 12b-1 fees). Only "Investor" shares, formerly known as "Institutional," are available to new accounts.
Discount broker availability: Fidelity, Siebert, *White
Number of switches permitted - 4 outbound per year
Dividends paid: Income - December; Capital gains - December
Portfolio turnover (3 yrs): 7%, 34%, 65%
Management fee: 1.25%
12b-1 distribution fee: 0.25% (Investor shares)
Expense ratio: 1.50% (Investor) 1.25% (Restricted) (year ending 10/31/97)

DREYFUS INTERNATIONAL GROWTH FUND
(See first Dreyfus listing for data common to all funds)

Lead portfolio manager: Ronald Chapman (1996)
Investment objective and policies: Capital growth. Normally invests at least 65% of assets in equity securities of non-U.S. issuers throughout the world. May invest in debt securities of foreign issuers believed to offer opportunities for capital growth. Will invest up to 30% of assets in emerging markets when this strategy provides a perceived advantage. Up to 15% of assets may be in illiquid securities. May write options on up to 20% of assets, use foreign currency exchange contracts, and use stock index futures and interest rate futures contracts and options thereon.
Year organized: 1993 (name changed from Dreyfus International Equity 10/96)
Ticker symbol: DITFX
Group fund code: 095
Discount broker availability: *Fidelity, *Schwab, *Siebert, *White
Dividends paid: Income - annually; Capital gains - annually
Portfolio turnover (3 yrs): 158%, 96%, 40%
Management fee: 0.75%
12b-1 distribution fee: 0.50%
Shareholder services fee: 0.25%
Expense ratio: 1.98% (year ending 5/31/97)

DREYFUS INTERNATIONAL STOCK INDEX FUND ◆
(See first Dreyfus listing for data common to all funds)

Lead portfolio manager: Susan Ellison (1997)
Investment objective and policies: Seeks to match the investment results of the MSCI-EAFE Index to a correlation of at least 0.95 not including expenses. Fund will invest in a representative sample of the issues found in the index, not in all of them, in an effort to approximate the characteristics of the benchmark without duplicating it entirely. May use foreign currency exchange contracts, and use stock index futures and interest rate futures contracts and options thereon.
Year organized: 1997
Ticker symbol: DIISX
Group fund code: 079
Discount broker availability: Fidelity, Siebert, *White
Redemption fee: 1.00% for shares held less than six months, payable to the fund
Dividends paid: Income - annually; Capital gains - annually
Management fee: 0.35%
Shareholder services fee: 0.25%
Expense ratio: 0.20% (4 months ending 10/31/97) (includes waiver)

DREYFUS INTERNATIONAL VALUE FUND ◆
(See first Dreyfus listing for data common to all funds)

Sub-adviser: The Boston Company Asset Management, Inc.
Lead portfolio manager: Sandor Cseh (1995)
Investment objective and policies: Long-term capital growth. Invests primarily in equity securities of foreign issuers with low price to book ratios, lower P/E ratios and higher than average dividend rates without regard to market capitalization. Up to 15% of assets may be in illiquid securities. May use futures and options and foreign currency transactions for hedging purposes.
Year organized: 1995 (name changed from Growth and Value - International Value in 1996)
Ticker symbol: DIVLX
Group fund code: 254
Discount broker availability: *Fidelity, *Schwab, *Siebert, *White
Redemption fee: 1.00% for shares held less than 15 days, payable to the fund
Dividends paid: Income - annually; Capital gains - annually
Portfolio turnover (2 yrs): 25%, 19%
Management fee: 1.00%
Shareholder services fee: 0.25%
Expense ratio: 1.49% (year ending 8/31/97) (1.52% without waiver)

DREYFUS LARGE COMPANY GROWTH FUND ◆
(See first Dreyfus listing for data common to all funds)

Lead portfolio manager: Michael L. Schonberg (1995)
Investment objective and policies: Capital growth. Invests primarily in equity securities of domestic and foreign issuers with market capitalizations of $900M to $90B with above average earnings or sales growth, retention of earnings and higher P/E ratios. Up to 15% of assets may be in illiquid securities. May leverage up to 33 1/3% of total assets, use futures and options and foreign currency transactions for hedging purposes and sell short up to 25% of total assets.
Year organized: 1993 (name changed from Dreyfus Focus Fund - Large Company Growth Portfolio in 1995; from Growth and Value - Large Company Growth in 1996)
Ticker symbol: DLCGX
Group fund code: 250
Discount broker availability: *Fidelity, *Schwab, *Siebert, *White
Redemption fee: 1.00% for shares held less than 15 days, payable to the fund
Dividends paid: Income - annually; Capital gains - annually
Portfolio turnover (3 yrs): 195%, 154%, 87%
Management fee: 0.75%
Shareholder services fee: 0.25%
Expense ratio: 1.20% (year ending 10/31/97) (1.53% without waiver)

DREYFUS LARGE COMPANY VALUE FUND ◆
(See first Dreyfus listing for data common to all funds)

Lead portfolio manager: Timothy M. Ghriskey (1995)
Investment objective and policies: Capital growth. Invests primarily in equity securities of domestic and foreign issuers with market capitalizations of $900M to $90B with low price to book ratios, lower P/E ratios and higher than average dividend rates. Up to 15% of assets may be in illiquid securities. May leverage up to 33 1/3% of total assets, use futures and options and foreign currency transactions for hedging purposes and sell short up to 25% of total assets.
Year organized: 1993 (name changed from Dreyfus Focus Fund - Large Company Value Portfolio in 1995; changed from Growth and Value - Large Company Value in 1996)
Ticker symbol: DLCVX
Group fund code: 251
Discount broker availability: *Fidelity, *Schwab, *Siebert, *White
Redemption fee: 1.00% for shares held less than 15 days, payable to the fund
Dividends paid: Income - annually; Capital gains - annually
Portfolio turnover (3 yrs): 110%, 186%, 144%
Management fee: 0.75%
Shareholder services fee: 0.25%
Expense ratio: 1.22% (year ending 10/31/97) (1.28% without waiver)

DREYFUS LIFETIME PORTFOLIOS - GROWTH PORTFOLIO ◆
(See first Dreyfus listing for data common to all funds)

Sub-adviser: Mellon Equity Assocs.
Lead portfolio manager: Steven A. Falci (1995)
Investment objective and policies: Capital growth. Invests in equity (target 80%; range of 65% to 100% of assets) and fixed-income (20%; ranges from 0% to 35% securities of domestic and foreign issuers with allocations adjusted to changes in market and economic conditions. Equity portion is divided into 80% large cap and 20% small cap stocks. May have up to 25% of assets in foreign securities and 15% in illiquid securities. Fund may use futures and options to hedge up to 20% of assets and take advantage of international currency fluctuations.
Year organized: 1995 (absorbed Asset Allocation - Growth portfolio 8/96)
Ticker symbol: DLGIX (Investor); DLGRX (Restricted)
Group fund code: 556 (Investor); 756 (Restricted)
Special sales restrictions: Shares formerly known as "Retail" are now "Restricted" shares, and are only available to accounts existing prior to 8/21/97 or to institutional accounts without shareholder services fees. Only "Investor" shares, formerly known as "Institutional," are available to individuals as new accounts.
Discount broker availability: *White
Dividends paid: Income - annually; Capital gains - annually
Portfolio turnover (3 yrs): 118%, 78%, 53%
Management fee: 0.75%
Shareholder services fee: 0.25%
Expense ratio: 1.06% (year ending 9/30/97) (1.33% without waiver) (restated expenses for Investor shares after adjusting for 0.25% fee. Restricted shares are 0.23% lower)

DREYFUS LIFETIME PORTFOLIOS - GROWTH AND INCOME PORTFOLIO ◆
(See first Dreyfus listing for data common to all funds)

Sub-adviser: Mellon Equity Assocs.
Lead portfolio manager: Steven A. Falci (1995)
Investment objective and policies: Maximum total return: capital growth and current income. Invests in equity (target 50%; ranges from 35% to 65% of assets) and fixed-income (50%; ranges from 35% to 65% securities of domestic and foreign issuers with allocations adjusted to changes in market and economic conditions. Equity portion is divided into 80% large cap and 20% small cap stocks. May have up to 15% of assets in foreign securities and 15% in illiquid securities. Fund may use futures and options to hedge up to 20% of assets and take advantage of international currency fluctuations.
Year organized: 1995
Ticker symbol: DGIIX (Investor); DGIRX (Restricted)
Group fund code: 552 (Investor); 752 (Restricted)
Special sales restrictions: Shares formerly known as "Retail" are now "Restricted" shares, and are only available to accounts existing prior to 8/21/97 or to institutional accounts without shareholder services fees. Only "Investor" shares, formerly known as "Institutional," are available to individuals as new accounts.
Discount broker availability: *White
Dividends paid: Income - annually; Capital gains - annually
Portfolio turnover (3 yrs): 108%, 123%, 34%
Management fee: 0.75%
Shareholder services fee: 0.25%
Expense ratio: 1.00% (year ending 9/30/97) (1.05% without waiver) (restated expenses for Investor shares after adjusting for 0.25% fee. Restricted shares are 0.22% lower)

DREYFUS LIFETIME PORTFOLIOS - INCOME PORTFOLIO ◆
(See first Dreyfus listing for data common to all funds)

Sub-adviser: Mellon Equity Assocs.
Lead portfolio manager: Steven A. Falci (1995)
Investment objective and policies: Maximum current income. Invests in equity (target 25% of assets) and fixed-income (75%) securities of domestic issuers with allocations adjusted to changes in market and economic conditions. Equity portion is exclusively in stocks of companies with market capitalizations greater than $1.4B. May have up to 15% of assets in illiquid securities. Fund may use futures and options to hedge up to 20% of assets.
Year organized: 1995 (absorbed Asset Allocation - Income portfolio 8/96)
Ticker symbol: DLIIX (Investor)
Group fund code: 555 (Investor); 755 (Restricted)
Special sales restrictions: Shares formerly known as "Retail" are now "Restricted" shares, and are only available to accounts existing prior to 8/21/97 or to institutional accounts without shareholder services fees. Only "Investor" shares, formerly known as "Institutional," are available to individuals as new accounts.
Discount broker availability: *White
Dividends paid: Income - annually; Capital gains - annually
Portfolio turnover (3 yrs): 72%, 33%, 6%
Management fee: 0.60%
Shareholder services fee: 0.25%
Expense ratio: 0.97% (year ending 9/30/97) (1.12% without waiver) (restated expenses for Investor shares after adjusting for 0.25% fee. Restricted shares are 0.29% lower)

DREYFUS LIQUID ASSETS ◆
(See first Dreyfus listing for data common to all funds)

Lead portfolio manager: Patricia A. Larkin (1994)
Investment objective and policies: High current income consistent with capital preservation. Invests in money market obligations. At least 25% of assets will be in bank time deposits, CDs and bankers acceptances.

Year organized: 1974
Ticker symbol: DLAXX
Group fund code: 039
Check redemptions: $500 minimum
Dividends paid: Income - declared and paid daily; Capital gains - annually
Management fee: 0.50% first $1.5B to 0.45% over $2.5B
Shareholder services fee: 0.25%
Expense ratio: 0.75% (year ending 12/31/96)

DREYFUS MASSACHUSETTS INTERMEDIATE MUNICIPAL BOND FUND ◆
(See first Dreyfus listing for data common to all funds)

Lead portfolio manager: Monica S. Wieboldt (1996)
Investment objective and policies: High current income exempt from federal and Massachusetts income taxes, consistent with capital preservation. Invests in debt securities of the state of Massachusetts, its political subdivisions, authorities and corporations, with at least 80% rated BBB or better. The dollar-weighted average maturity of the portfolio ranges from three to ten years. May invest without limit in securities subject to AMT tax treatment, and have up to 20% of assets in junk bonds and 15% in illiquid securities. May use futures and options and sell short on up to 25% of assets.
Year organized: 1992
Ticker symbol: DMAIX
Group fund code: 268
Discount broker availability: *Fidelity, *Schwab, *Siebert, *White
Qualified for sale in: AZ, CA, CT, DC, FL, HI, IL, MA, NH, NJ, NY, PA, RI, TX, WY
Check redemptions: $500 minimum
Redemption fee: 1.00% for shares held less than 15 days, payable to the fund
Dividends paid: Income - declared daily, paid monthly; Capital gains - annually
Portfolio turnover (3 yrs): 23%, 32%, 9%
Management fee: 0.60%
Shareholder services fee: 0.25%
Expense ratio: 0.80% (year ending 3/31/97) (0.90% without waiver)

DREYFUS MASSACHUSETTS MUNICIPAL MONEY MARKET FUND ◆
(See first Dreyfus listing for data common to all funds)

Lead portfolio manager: Jill C. Shaffro (1994)
Investment objective and policies: High current income exempt from federal and Massachusetts income taxes, consistent with preservation of capital and liquidity. Invests primarily in Massachusetts municipal money market instruments.
Year organized: 1991
Ticker symbol: DMAXX
Group fund code: 639
Qualified for sale in: AZ, CA, CO, CT, DC, FL, HI, ID, IL, MA, ME, MD, MI, MN, MO, NH, NJ, NY, OH, PA, RI, TX, VA, WY
Check redemptions: $500 minimum
Dividends paid: Income - declared daily, paid monthly; Capital gains - annually
Management fee: 0.50%
Shareholder services fee: 0.25%
Expense ratio: 0.60% (year ending 1/31/97) (0.66% without waiver)

DREYFUS MASSACHUSETTS TAX EXEMPT BOND FUND ◆
(See first Dreyfus listing for data common to all funds)

Lead portfolio manager: Joseph P. Darcy (1996)
Investment objective and policies: High current income exempt from federal and Massachusetts income taxes, consistent with capital preservation. Invests primarily in the debt securities of the

Commonwealth of Massachusetts and its political subdivisions, rated Baa or better. May have up to 20% of assets in securities subject to AMT tax treatment, 20% in junk bonds and 15% in illiquid securities.
Year organized: 1985
Ticker symbol: DMEBX
Group fund code: 267
Discount broker availability: *Fidelity, *Schwab, *Siebert, *White
Qualified for sale in: All states except AK, CO, GA, ID, IL, IA, KS, LA, MI, MS, MO, MT, NE, NM, ND, OK, PR, SD, UT, WA, WV, WI
Check redemptions: $500 minimum
Redemption fee: 1.00% for shares held less than 15 days, payable to the fund
Dividends paid: Income - declared daily, paid monthly; Capital gains - annually
Portfolio turnover (3 yrs): 38%, 61%, 38%
Management fee: 0.60%
Shareholder services fee: 0.25%
Expense ratio: 0.79% (year ending 5/31/97)

DREYFUS MIDCAP INDEX FUND ◆
(See first Dreyfus listing for data common to all funds)

Sub-adviser: Mellon Equity Assocs.
Lead portfolio manager: Steven A. Falci (1996)
Investment objective and policies: Provide investment results that correspond to the price and yield performance of common stocks of medium-sized domestic companies that comprise the S&P MidCap 400 Index. Fund attempts to be fully invested at all times in the stocks that comprise the Index in approximately the same weightings, and stock index futures.
Year organized: 1991 (name changed from Peoples S&P MidCap Index Fund on 11/13/95)
Ticker symbol: PESPX
Group fund code: 113
Discount broker availability: Fidelity, *Schwab, Siebert, *White
Redemption fee: 1.00% for shares held less than 6 months, payable to the fund
Dividends paid: Income - annually; Capital gains - annually
Portfolio turnover (3 yrs): 20%, 15%, 20%
Management fee: 0.25%
Shareholder services fee: 0.25%
Expense ratio: 0.50% (year ending 10/31/97) (0.59% without waiver)

DREYFUS MIDCAP VALUE FUND ◆
(See first Dreyfus listing for data common to all funds)

Sub-adviser: The Boston Company Asset Management, Inc.
Lead portfolio manager: Peter I. Higgins (1995)
Investment objective and policies: Investment results that exceed the total return of the stocks in the Russell MidCap Index. Invests primarily in equity securities of domestic and foreign issuers with market capitalizations of $400M to $4B with low price to book ratios, lower P/E ratios and higher than average dividend rates. Up to 15% of assets may be in securities of foreign issuers and 15% in illiquid securities. May use futures and options and foreign currency transactions for hedging purposes and sell short up to 25% of total assets.
Year organized: 1995 (name changed from Growth and Value - MidCap Value in 1996)
Ticker symbol: DMCVX
Group fund code: 258
Discount broker availability: *Fidelity, *Schwab, *Siebert, *White
Redemption fee: 1.00% for shares held less than 15 days, payable to the fund
Dividends paid: Income - annually; Capital gains - annually
Portfolio turnover (2 yrs): 155%, 267%
Management fee: 0.75%
Shareholder services fee: 0.25%
Expense ratio: 1.25% (year ending 8/31/97) (1.51% without waiver)

DREYFUS MONEY MARKET INSTRUMENTS - GOVERNMENT SECURITIES SERIES ◆

(See first Dreyfus listing for data common to all funds)

Portfolio managers: Patricia A. Larkin (1990), Bernard W. Kiernan, Jr. (1995)
Investment objective and policies: High current income consistent with the preservation of capital and liquidity. Invests only in money market securities issued or guaranteed by the U.S. Government.
Year organized: 1979
Ticker symbol: DMMXX
Group fund code: 008
Deadline for same day wire purchase: 12 NN and 4 P.M. (two pricings)
Check redemptions: $500 minimum
Dividends paid: Income - declared daily, paid monthly
Management fee: 0.50%
Shareholder services fee: 0.25%
Expense ratio: 0.90% (year ending 12/31/96)

DREYFUS MONEY MARKET INSTRUMENTS - MONEY MARKET SERIES ◆

(See first Dreyfus listing for data common to all funds)

Portfolio managers: Patricia A. Larkin (1990), Bernard W. Kiernan, Jr. (1995)
Investment objective and policies: High current income consistent with the preservation of capital and liquidity. Invests in money market instruments.
Year organized: 1975
Ticker symbol: DMIXX
Group fund code: 060
Minimum purchase: Initial: $50,000
Deadline for same day wire purchase: 12 NN and 4 P.M. (two pricings)
Check redemptions: $500 minimum
Dividends paid: Income - declared daily, paid monthly
Management fee: 0.50%
Shareholder services fee: 0.25%
Expense ratio: 0.93% (year ending 12/31/96)

DREYFUS MUNICIPAL BOND FUND ◆

(See first Dreyfus listing for data common to all funds)

Lead portfolio manager: Richard J. Moynihan (1976)
Investment objective and policies: High current income exempt from federal income tax, consistent with capital preservation. Invests at least 75% of assets in investment grade municipal bonds rated A or better. May invest without limit in securities subject to AMT tax treatment, and have up to 25% of assets in municipal junk bonds and 15% in illiquid securities. May use options and futures for hedging purposes.
Year organized: 1976 (name changed from Dreyfus Tax-Exempt Bond Fund on 4/20/92)
Ticker symbol: DRTAX
Group fund code: 054
Discount broker availability: *Fidelity, *Schwab, *Siebert, *White
Check redemptions: $500 minimum
Redemption fee: 0.10% for shares held less than 15 days, payable to the fund
Dividends paid: Income - declared daily, paid monthly; Capital gains - annually
Portfolio turnover (3 yrs): 67%, 64%, 52%
Management fee: 0.60%
Shareholder services fee: 0.25%
Expense ratio: 0.71% (year ending 8/31/97)

DREYFUS MUNICIPAL MONEY MARKET FUND ◆

(See first Dreyfus listing for data common to all funds)

Lead portfolio manager: Karen M. Hand (1987)
Investment objective and policies: High current income exempt from federal tax, consistent with preservation of capital and liquidity. Invests in high quality municipal money market obligations.
Year organized: 1980 (name changed from Dreyfus Tax Exempt Money Market Fund, Inc. on 5/29/91)
Ticker symbol: DTEXX
Group fund code: 910
Deadline for same day wire purchase: 12 NN
Check redemptions: $500 minimum
Deadline for same day switch: 12 NN
Dividends paid: Income - declared daily, paid monthly
Management fee: 0.50%
Shareholder services fee: 0.25%
Expense ratio: 0.65% (year ending 5/31/97)

DREYFUS NEW JERSEY INTERMEDIATE MUNICIPAL BOND FUND ◆

(See first Dreyfus listing for data common to all funds)

Lead portfolio manager: Stephen C. Kris (1992)
Investment objective and policies: High current income exempt from federal and New Jersey income taxes, consistent with capital preservation. Invests primarily in investment grade debt securities of the state of New Jersey, and its political subdivisions, authorities and corporations. Portfolio maintains a dollar-weighted average maturity ranging from three to ten years. May invest without limit in securities subject to AMT tax treatment, and have up to 20% of assets in junk bonds and 15% in illiquid securities. May use futures and options for hedging purposes.
Year organized: 1992
Ticker symbol: DNJIX
Group fund code: 751
Discount broker availability: *Fidelity, *Schwab, *Siebert, *White
Qualified for sale in: DC, FL, HI, NJ, NY, PA, WY
Check redemptions: $500 minimum
Redemption fee: 1.00% for shares held less than 15 days, payable to the fund
Dividends paid: Income - declared daily, paid monthly; Capital gains - annually
Portfolio turnover (3 yrs): 15%, 14%, 35%
Management fee: 0.60%
Shareholder services fee: 0.25%
Expense ratio: 0.78% (year ending 3/31/97)

DREYFUS NEW JERSEY MUNICIPAL BOND FUND

(See first Dreyfus listing for data common to all funds)

Lead portfolio manager: W. Michael Petty (1997)
Investment objective and policies: High current income exempt from federal and New Jersey income taxes, consistent with capital preservation. Invests primarily in investment grade municipal bonds issued principally by the State of New Jersey and its subdivisions. Portfolio maintains an average dollar-weighted average maturity of more than ten years. May invest without limit in securities subject to AMT tax treatment, and have up to 20% of assets in junk bonds and 15% in illiquid securities. May use options for hedging purposes.
Year organized: 1987 (originally Dreyfus New Jersey Tax Exempt Bond Fund, then Dreyfus New Jersey Tax Exempt Bond Fund)
Ticker symbol: DRNJX
Group fund code: 750
Discount broker availability: *Fidelity, *Schwab, *Siebert, *White
Qualified for sale in: AZ, CA, CT, DE, DC, FL, HI, IL, MA, NH, NJ, NM, NY, PA, RI, TX, VA, VT
Check redemptions: $500 minimum
Redemption fee: 1.00% for shares held less than 15 days, payable to the fund
Number of switches permitted: 4 outbound per year
Dividends paid: Income - declared daily, paid monthly; Capital gains - December
Portfolio turnover (3 yrs): 31%, 24%, 10%
Management fee: 0.60%
12b-1 distribution fee: 0.25%
Expense ratio: 0.80% (year ending 12/31/96) (0.94% without waiver)

DREYFUS NEW JERSEY MUNICIPAL MONEY MARKET FUND ◆

(See first Dreyfus listing for data common to all funds)

Lead portfolio manager: Karen M. Hand (1988)
Investment objective and policies: High current income exempt from federal and New Jersey income taxes, consistent with preservation of capital and liquidity. Invests in municipal money market instruments, principally of New Jersey and its subdivisions.
Year organized: 1988 (formerly Dreyfus New Jersey Tax Exempt MM Fund)
Ticker symbol: DNJXX
Group fund code: 758
Deadline for same day wire purchase: 12 NN
Qualified for sale in: AZ, CA, CT, DE, DC, FL, HI, IL, MA, NH, NJ, NY, PA, RI, TX, VT, WY
Check redemptions: $500 minimum
Deadline for same day switch: 12 NN
Dividends paid: Income - declared daily, paid monthly; Capital gains - annually
Management fee: 0.50%
Shareholder services fee: 0.25%
Expense ratio: 0.65% (year ending 1/31/97)

DREYFUS NEW LEADERS FUND ◆

(See first Dreyfus listing for data common to all funds)

Portfolio managers: Paul Kandel (1996), Hilary R. Woods (1996)
Investment objective and policies: Maximum capital appreciation. Invests primarily in common stocks of domestic and foreign companies with market capitalizations under $750M that are perceived to offer significant growth potential. Companies will have new or innovative products, services or processes. Fund also looks for economic or political changes and corporate restructurings, mergers and acquisitions. Up to 25% of assets may be in foreign securities and 15% in illiquid securities. May use currency exchange contracts, futures and options to hedge up to 20% of assets and sell short up to 25% of assets.
Year organized: 1985
Ticker symbol: DNLDX
Group fund code: 085
Discount broker availability: Fidelity, *Schwab, Siebert, *White
Redemption fee: 1.00% for shares held less than 6 months, payable to the fund
Dividends paid: Income - annually; Capital gains - annually
Portfolio turnover (3 yrs): 102%, 109%, 94%
Management fee: 1.00%
Shareholder services fee: 0.25%
Expense ratio: 1.17% (year ending 12/31/96)

DREYFUS NEW YORK INSURED TAX EXEMPT BOND FUND

(See first Dreyfus listing for data common to all funds)

Lead portfolio manager: Richard J. Moynihan (1996)
Investment objective and policies: High current income exempt from federal, NY state and NY city income taxes, consistent with capital preservation. Invests primarily in New York municipal obligations rated Baa or higher that are insured as to the timely payment of principal and interest. Up to 20% of assets may be in securities subject to AMT tax treatment, and 15% in illiquid securities. May invest more than 25% of assets in industrial development bonds. May use options and futures for hedging purposes.
Year organized: 1986
Ticker symbol: DNYBX
Group fund code: 577
Deadline for same day wire purchase: 12 NN
Discount broker availability: *Fidelity, *Schwab, *Siebert, *White
Qualified for sale in: CT, DC, FL, HI, MA, MO, NV, NH, NJ, NY, PA, RI, VT, WY
Check redemptions: $500 minimum
Redemption fee: 1.00% for shares held less than 15 days, payable to the fund
Deadline for same day switch: 12 NN
Number of switches permitted: 4 outbound per year

Dividends paid: Income - declared daily, paid monthly; Capital gains - annually
Portfolio turnover (3 yrs): 84%, 31%, 13%
Management fee: 0.60%
12b-1 distribution fee: 0.25%
Expense ratio: 1.02% (year ending 12/31/96)

DREYFUS NEW YORK TAX EXEMPT BOND FUND ◆
(See first Dreyfus listing for data common to all funds)

Lead portfolio manager: Samuel J. Weinstock (1997)
Investment objective and policies: High current income exempt from federal, NY state and NY city income taxes, consistent with capital preservation. Invests at least 80% of assets in municipal bonds, principally of New York State and its subdivisions rated Baa or better, without regard to maturity. Up to 20% of assets may be in securities subject to AMT tax treatment, up to 20% in junk bonds and 15% in illiquid securities. May use futures and options for hedging purposes and sell short up to 25% of assets.
Year organized: 1983
Ticker symbol: DRNYX
Group fund code: 980
Discount broker availability: *Fidelity, *Schwab, *Siebert, *White
Check redemptions: $500 minimum
Redemption fee: 0.10% for shares held less than 15 days, payable to the fund
Dividends paid: Income - declared daily, paid monthly; Capital gains - annually
Portfolio turnover (3 yrs): 74%, 82%, 49%
Management fee: 0.60%
Shareholder services fee: 0.25%
Expense ratio: 0.74% (year ending 5/31/97)

DREYFUS NEW YORK TAX EXEMPT INTERMEDIATE BOND FUND
(See first Dreyfus listing for data common to all funds)

Lead portfolio manager: Monica S. Wieboldt (1987)
Investment objective and policies: High current income exempt from federal, NY state and NY city income taxes, consistent with capital preservation. Invests at least 80% of assets in municipal bonds, principally of New York State and its subdivisions, rated Baa or better. Portfolio maintains a dollar-weighted average maturity of three to ten years. Up to 20% of assets may be in securities subject to AMT tax treatment, 20% in junk bonds and 15% in illiquid securities. May use futures and options for hedging purposes and sell short up to 25% of assets.
Year organized: 1987
Ticker symbol: DRNIX
Group fund code: 705
Deadline for same day wire purchase: 12 NN
Discount broker availability: *Fidelity, *Schwab, *Siebert, *White
Qualified for sale in: CT, DC, FL, HI, MA, NV, NH, NJ, NY, OK, PA, RI, VT, WY
Check redemptions: $500 minimum
Redemption fee: 1.00% for shares held less than 15 days, payable to the fund
Deadline for same day switch: 12 NN
Dividends paid: Income - declared daily, paid monthly; Capital gains - annually
Portfolio turnover (3 yrs): 45%, 47%, 30%
Management fee: 0.60%
12b-1 distribution fee: 0.25%
Expense ratio: 0.80% (year ending 5/31/97)

DREYFUS NEW YORK TAX EXEMPT MONEY MARKET FUND ◆
(See first Dreyfus listing for data common to all funds)

Lead portfolio manager: Karen M. Hand (1987)
Investment objective and policies: Current income exempt from federal, NY state, and NY city income taxes, consistent with the preservation of capital and liquidity. Invests in money market securities issued by the State of New York and its subdivisions.
Year organized: 1987

Ticker symbol: DNYXX
Group fund code: 273
Qualified for sale in: CA, CT, DC, FL, HI, IL, MA, NH, NJ, NV, NY, OK, PA, RI, TX, VA, VT, WA, WY
Check redemptions: $500 minimum
Dividends paid: Income - declared daily, paid monthly
Management fee: 0.50%
Shareholder services fee: 0.25%
Expense ratio: 0.68% (year ending 5/31/97)

DREYFUS 100% U.S. TREASURY INTERMEDIATE TERM FUND ◆
(See first Dreyfus listing for data common to all funds)

Lead portfolio manager: Gerald E. Thunelius (1994)
Investment objective and policies: Highest level of current income exempt from state and local income taxes, consistent with capital preservation. Invests in securities issued and guaranteed by the U.S. Government and its agencies. Portfolio maintains a dollar-weighted average maturity ranging from three to seven years.
Year organized: 1987 (name and objective changed from Dreyfus U.S. Govt. Intermediate Securities 10/24/91)
Ticker symbol: DRGIX
Group fund code: 072
Discount broker availability: Fidelity, Siebert, *White
Check redemptions: $500 minimum
Number of switches permitted: 4 outbound per year
Dividends paid: Income - declared daily, paid monthly; Capital gains - annually
Portfolio turnover (3 yrs): 728%, 493%, 697%
Management fee: 0.60%
Shareholder services fee: 0.25%
Expense ratio: 0.80% (year ending 12/31/96) (0.93% without waiver)

DREYFUS 100% U.S. TREASURY LONG-TERM FUND ◆
(See first Dreyfus listing for data common to all funds)

Lead portfolio manager: Gerald E. Thunelius (1994)
Investment objective and policies: Highest level of current income exempt from state and local income taxes, consistent with capital preservation. Invests in obligations of the U.S. Government and its agencies and instrumentalities. Portfolio maintains a dollar-weighted average maturity of more than ten years.
Year organized: 1987 (named and objective changed from Dreyfus U.S. Government Bond 10/24/91)
Ticker symbol: DRGBX
Group fund code: 073
Discount broker availability: Fidelity, Siebert, *White
Check redemptions: $500 minimum
Number of switches permitted: 4 outbound per year
Dividends paid: Income - declared daily, paid monthly; Capital gains - annually
Portfolio turnover (3 yrs): 765%, 634%, 1,213%
Management fee: 0.60%
Shareholder services fee: 0.25%
Expense ratio: 0.80% (year ending 12/31/96) (0.99% without waiver)

DREYFUS 100% U.S. TREASURY MONEY MARKET FUND ◆
(See first Dreyfus listing for data common to all funds)

Portfolio managers: Patricia A. Larkin (1994), Bernard W. Kiernan, Jr. (1996)
Investment objective and policies: Highest level of current income exempt from state and local income taxes, consistent with preservation of capital and liquidity. Invests in U.S. Government money market obligations.
Year organized: 1987 (formerly U.S. Guaranteed Money Market Account, L.P.)
Ticker symbol: DUSXX
Group fund code: 071
Check redemptions: $500 minimum

Dividends paid: Income - declared daily, paid monthly
Management fee: 0.50%
Shareholder services fee: 0.25%
Expense ratio: 0.73% (year ending 12/31/96)

DREYFUS 100% U.S. TREASURY SHORT-TERM FUND ◆
(See first Dreyfus listing for data common to all funds)

Lead portfolio manager: Gerald E. Thunelius (1994)
Investment objective and policies: Highest level of current income exempt from state and local income taxes, consistent with capital preservation. Invests only in U.S. Treasury securities. Portfolio maintains a dollar-weighted average maturity ranging from two to three years.
Year organized: 1987 (name and objective changed from Dreyfus Foreign Investors U.S. Government Bond on 10/1/91)
Ticker symbol: DRTSX
Group fund code: 081
Discount broker availability: Fidelity, Siebert, *White
Check redemptions: $500 minimum
Number of switches permitted: 4 outbound per year
Dividends paid: Income - declared daily, paid monthly; Capital gains - annually
Portfolio turnover (3 yrs): 540%, 480%, 499%
Management fee: 0.60%
Shareholder services fee: 0.25%
Expense ratio: 0.70% (year ending 12/31/96) (0.97% without waiver)

DREYFUS PENNSYLVANIA INTERMEDIATE MUNICIPAL BOND FUND ◆
(See first Dreyfus listing for data common to all funds)

Lead portfolio manager: Douglas J. Gaylor (1996)
Investment objective and policies: High current income exempt from federal and Pennsylvania income taxes, consistent with capital preservation. Invests primarily in investment grade debt securities of the state of Pennsylvania, its political subdivisions, authorities and corporations. Portfolio maintains a dollar-weighted average maturity of three to ten years. May invest without limit in securities subject to AMT tax treatment, and have up to 20% of assets in junk bonds and 15% in illiquid securities. May use futures and options for hedging purposes.
Year organized: 1993
Ticker symbol: DPABX
Group fund code: 105
Discount broker availability: Fidelity, *Schwab, Siebert, *White
Qualified for sale in: AZ, CA, CT, DE, DC, FL, HI, IL, MA, NJ, NY, OH, PA, TX, VA, WV, WY
Check redemptions: $500 minimum
Redemption fee: 1.00% for shares held less than 15 days, payable to the fund
Dividends paid: Income - declared daily, paid monthly; Capital gains - annually
Portfolio turnover (3 yrs): 54%, 5%, 20%
Management fee: 0.60%
Shareholder services fee: 0.25%
Expense ratio: 0.80% (year ending 11/30/96) (0.97% without waiver)

DREYFUS PENNSYLVANIA MUNICIPAL MONEY MARKET FUND ◆
(See first Dreyfus listing for data common to all funds)

Lead portfolio manager: Jill C. Shaffro (1991)
Investment objective and policies: High current income exempt from federal and Pennsylvania income taxes, consistent with preservation of capital and liquidity. Invests in municipal money market instruments, principally of Pennsylvania and its subdivisions.
Year organized: 1990
Ticker symbol: DPAXX
Group fund code: 104
Deadline for same day wire purchase: 12 NN

Qualified for sale in: AZ, CA, CT, DE, DC, FL, HI, IL, MA, MD, MI, NJ, NY, OH, PA, TX, VA, WV, WY
Check redemptions: $500 minimum
Deadline for same day switch: 12 NN
Dividends paid: Income - declared daily, paid monthly
Management fee: 0.50%
Shareholder services fee: 0.25%
Expense ratio: 0.66% (year ending 9/30/97)

DREYFUS REAL ESTATE MORTGAGE FUND ◆
(See first Dreyfus listing for data common to all funds)

Lead portfolio manager: Michael Hoeh (1997)
Investment objective and policies: Total return; capital appreciation and current income. Invests at least 65% of assets in mortgage-related securities, which are derivatives collateralized by pools of loans on commercial or residential real estate. May invest in U.S. dollar-denominated foreign securities, and may invest without limit in junk bonds. Portfolio will typically have an average effective duration ranging between two and six years.
Year organized: 1997
Ticker symbol: DREMX
Group fund code: 045
Minimum purchase: Initial: $10,000, Subsequent: $1,000; IRA/Keogh: Initial: $5,000; Automatic investment plan: Initial: $100
Discount broker availability: *White
Redemption fee: 1.00% for shares held less than six months, payable to the fund
Dividends paid: Income - quarterly; Capital gains - annually
Management fee: 0.65%
Shareholder services fee: 0.25%

DREYFUS S&P 500 INDEX FUND ◆
(See first Dreyfus listing for data common to all funds)

Sub-adviser: Mellon Equity Assocs.
Lead portfolio manager: Steven A. Falci (1995)
Investment objective and policies: Investment results that correspond to the price and yield performance of the common stocks that comprise the S&P 500. Invests in a representative mix of S&P 500 stocks to achieve income and capital gains on a par with the S&P 500 composite average. Fund may use stock index futures for hedging purposes.
Year organized: 1990 (name changed from Peoples Index Fund in 1995)
Ticker symbol: PEOPX
Group fund code: 078
Discount broker availability: *Fidelity, *Schwab, *Siebert, *White
Redemption fee: 1.00% for shares held less than six months, payable to the fund
Dividends paid: Income - annually; Capital gains - annually
Portfolio turnover (3 yrs): 2%, 5%, 4%
Management fee: 0.25%
Shareholder services fee: 0.25%
Expense ratio: 0.50% (year ending 10/31/97)

DREYFUS SHORT-INTERMEDIATE GOVERNMENT FUND ◆
(See first Dreyfus listing for data common to all funds)

Lead portfolio manager: Gerald E. Thunelius (1994)
Investment objective and policies: High current income consistent with capital preservation. Invests in securities issued or guaranteed by the U.S. Government or its agencies or instrumentalities, or repurchase agreements in respect thereof. Invests in a portfolio of securities that has an effective duration of approximately three years. May also invest up to 35% of assets in government guaranteed mortgage related securities. May have up to 15% of assets in illiquid securities and sell short up to 25% of assets.
Year organized: 1987
Ticker symbol: DSIGX
Group fund code: 542

Deadline for same day wire purchase: 12 NN
Discount broker availability: *Fidelity, *Schwab, *Siebert, *White
Check redemptions: $500 minimum
Deadline for same day switch: 12 NN
Dividends paid: Income - declared daily, paid monthly; Capital gains - annually
Portfolio turnover (3 yrs): 594%, 388%, 696%
Management fee: 0.50%
Shareholder services fee: 0.25%
Expense ratio: 0.74% (year ending 11/30/96)

DREYFUS SHORT-INTERMEDIATE MUNICIPAL BOND FUND
(See first Dreyfus listing for data common to all funds)

Lead portfolio manager: Samuel J. Weinstock (1987)
Investment objective and policies: High current income exempt from federal income tax, consistent with the preservation of capital. Invests primarily in investment grade municipal obligations with remaining durations of five years or less. Portfolio maintains a dollar-weighted average maturity of two to three years. May invest without limit in securities subject to AMT tax treatment, and have up to 15% of assets in illiquid securities. Fund may buy options on up to 5% of assets, write options on up to 20% of portfolio assets and use municipal bond index futures and options thereon.
Year organized: 1987 (name changed from Short-Intermediate Tax Exempt Bond Fund in 1993)
Ticker symbol: DSIBX
Group fund code: 591
Discount broker availability: *Fidelity, *Schwab, *Siebert, *White
Check redemptions: $500 minimum
Redemption fee: 0.10% for shares held less than 15 days, payable to the fund
Dividends paid: Income - declared daily, paid monthly; Capital gains - annually
Portfolio turnover (3 yrs): 48%, 44%, 37%
Management fee: 0.50%
12b-1 distribution fee: 0.10%
Expense ratio: 0.80% (year ending 3/31/97) (0.82% without waiver)

DREYFUS SHORT-TERM HIGH YIELD FUND ◆
(See first Dreyfus listing for data common to all funds)

Lead portfolio manager: Roger King (1996)
Investment objective and policies: High current income. Normally invests at least 65% of assets in debt instruments rated below investment grade, better known as "junk bonds," with a portfolio average effective duration of three years or less. Fund may invest without limit in corporate or government foreign issues. May use derivative instruments in an effort to enhance portfolio performance and for hedging purposes.
Year organized: 1996
Ticker symbol: DSHYX
Group fund code: 044
Discount broker availability: *Fidelity, *Schwab, *Siebert, *White
Dividends paid: Income - declared daily, paid monthly; Capital gains - annually
Portfolio turnover (2 yrs): 103%, 78%
Management fee: 0.65%
Shareholder services fee: 0.25%
Expense ratio: 1.09% (year ending 10/31/97) (1.11% without waiver)

DREYFUS SHORT-TERM INCOME FUND ◆
(See first Dreyfus listing for data common to all funds)

Lead portfolio manager: Kevin M. McClintock (1996)
Investment objective and policies: High current income consistent with capital preservation. Invests primarily in investment grade debt securities of domestic and foreign issuers. Portfolio maintains a

dollar-weighted average maturity of three years or less. May invest in bonds, debentures, notes, subordinated mortgage-related securities, asset-backed securities and municipal obligations. Up to 35% of assets may be in junk bonds, 30% in securities of foreign issuers, 20% in subordinated securities, and 15% in illiquid securities. May use futures and options for hedging purposes and may leverage.
Year organized: 1992
Ticker symbol: DSTIX
Group fund code: 083
Discount broker availability: *Fidelity, *Schwab, *Siebert, *White
Check redemptions: $500 minimum
Number of switches permitted: 4 outbound per year
Dividends paid: Income - declared daily, paid monthly; Capital gains - annually
Portfolio turnover (3 yrs): 293%, 291%, 512%
Management fee: 0.50%
Shareholder services fee: 0.20%
Expense ratio: 0.80% (year ending 7/31/97) (0.91% without waiver)

DREYFUS SMALL CAP STOCK INDEX FUND ◆
(See first Dreyfus listing for data common to all funds)

Lead portfolio manager: Steven A. Falci (1997)
Investment objective and policies: Seeks to match the investment results of the S&P SmallCap 600 Index to a correlation of at least 0.95 not including expenses. Fund will invest in a representative sample of the issues found in the index, not in all of them, in an effort to approximate the characteristics of the benchmark without duplicating in entirely. May use stock index futures and interest rate futures contracts and options thereon.
Year organized: 1997
Ticker symbol: DISSX
Group fund code: 077
Discount broker availability: Fidelity, Siebert, *White
Redemption fee: 1.00% for shares held less than six months, payable to fund
Dividends paid: Income - annually; Capital gains - annually
Management fee: 0.25%
Shareholder services fee: 0.25%
Expense ratio: 0.17% (four months ending 10/31/97) (includes waiver)

DREYFUS SMALL COMPANY VALUE FUND ◆
(See first Dreyfus listing for data common to all funds)

Sub-adviser: The Boston Company Asset Management, Inc.
Lead portfolio manager: Peter I. Higgins (1997)
Investment objective and policies: Capital growth. Invests primarily in equity securities of domestic and foreign issuers with market capitalizations of $90M to $900M with low price to book ratios, lower P/E ratios and higher than average dividend rates. Up to 15% of assets may be in illiquid securities. May leverage up to 33 1/3% of total assets, use futures and options and foreign currency transactions for hedging purposes and sell short up to 25% of total assets.
Year organized: 1993 (formerly Focus Small Company Value Fund; name changed from Growth and Value - Small Company Value in 1996)
Ticker symbol: DSCVX
Group fund code: 253
Sales restrictions: Fund will close to new investors when assets reach $500M
Discount broker availability: *Fidelity, *Schwab, *Siebert, *White
Redemption fee: 1.00% for shares held less than 15 days, payable to the fund
Dividends paid: Income - annually; Capital gains - annually
Portfolio turnover (3 yrs): 76%, 184%, 161%
Management fee: 0.75%
Shareholder services fee: 0.25%
Expense ratio: 1.23% (year ending 10/31/97) (1.28% without waiver)

DREYFUS SPECIAL GROWTH FUND
(Fund merged into Dreyfus Aggressive Growth Fund 4/18/97)

DREYFUS STRATEGIC INCOME FUND ◆
(See first Dreyfus listing for data common to all funds)

Distributor: Premier Mutual Fund Services, Inc.
Lead portfolio manager: Kevin M. McClintock (1995)
Investment objective and policies: Maximum current income. Invests at least 65% of assets in both corporate and government debt securities of domestic and foreign issuers. May invest up to 35% of assets in junk bonds, up to 30% in debt securities of foreign companies and governments, and up to 15% in illiquid securities. Fund may use a variety of derivative instruments in an effort to enhance portfolio performance and for hedging purposes.
Year organized: 1986
Ticker symbol: DSINX
Group fund code: 031
Minimum purchase: Initial: $2,500, Subsequent: $500
Discount broker availability: Fidelity, Siebert, *White
Dividends paid: Income - declared daily, paid monthly; Capital gains - annually
Portfolio turnover (3 yrs): 348%, 215%, 177%
Management fee: 0.60%
Shareholder services fee: 0.25%
Expense ratio: 1.03% (year ending 10/31/97)

DREYFUS TECHNOLOGY GROWTH FUND ◆
(See first Dreyfus listing for data common to all funds)

Portfolio managers: Mark Herskovitz (1997), Richard D. Wallman (1997)
Investment objective and policies: Capital appreciation. Invests at least 65% of assets in foreign and domestic equity securities of companies which provide or are expected to benefit from technological advances and improvements. May invest up to 25% of assets in foreign issues. Fund may use a variety of derivatives in an attempt to enhance performance and for hedging purposes.
Year organized: 1997
Group fund code: 255
Discount broker availability: *White
Redemption fee: 1.00% for funds held less than 15 days, payable to the fund
Dividends paid: Income - annually; Capital gains - annually
Management fee: 0.75%
Shareholder services fee: 0.25%

DREYFUS THIRD CENTURY FUND ◆
(See first Dreyfus listing for data common to all funds)

Sub-adviser: NCM Capital Management, Inc.
Portfolio managers: Maceo K. Sloan (1994), Stephon Jackson (1994), Eric W. Steedman (1996)
Investment objective and policies: Capital growth; current income secondary. Invests in equity securities of companies which not only meet traditional investment standards but also contribute to the enhancement of the quality of life in America. Companies are considered for their protection and improvement of the environment and natural resources, occupational health and safety, consumer protection and product purity, and equal employment opportunity. Up to 15% of assets may be in illiquid securities. May use options in an effort to increase income and for hedging purposes on up to 20% of assets.
Year organized: 1972
Ticker symbol: DRTHX
Group fund code: 035
Discount broker availability: *Fidelity, *Schwab, *Siebert, *White
Dividends paid: Income - annually; Capital gains - annually
Portfolio turnover (3 yrs): 67%, 92%, 134%
Management fee: 0.75%

Shareholder services fee: 0.25%
Expense ratio: 1.03% (year ending 5/31/97)

∗

DREYFUS WORLDWIDE DOLLAR MONEY MARKET FUND ◆
(See first Dreyfus listing for data common to all funds)

Lead portfolio manager: Patricia A. Larkin (1994)
Investment objective and policies: High current income consistent with preservation of capital and liquidity. Invests in dollar-denominated money market obligations issued around the world.
Year organized: 1989
Ticker symbol: DWDXX
Group fund code: 762
Check redemptions: $500 minimum
Dividends paid: Income - declared daily, paid monthly
Management fee: 0.50%
Shareholder services fee: 0.25%
Expense ratio: 0.75% (year ending 10/31/97)

DUPREE MUTUAL FUNDS ◆
(Data common to all Dupree series are shown below. See subsequent listing for data specific to individual series.)

P.O. Box 1149
Lexington, KY 40589-1149
800-866-0614, 606-254-7741
fax 606-254-1399
Internet: http://www.dupree-funds.com
e-mail: DupreeCo@AOL.com

Adviser: Dupree & Company, Inc.
Transfer agent: Dupree & Company, Inc.
Minimum purchase: Initial: $100, Subsequent: $100
Wire orders accepted: Yes
Deadline for same day wire purchase: 3 P.M.
Telephone redemptions: Yes
Wire redemptions: Yes, $500 minimum, $10 fee
Letter redemptions: Signature guarantee required
Telephone switching: With other Dupree funds
Number of switches permitted: Unlimited
Shareholder services: IRA (Intermediate Government Bond Series only), automatic investment plan, systematic withdrawal plan min. bal. req. $10,000
Management fee: 0.50% first $100M to 0.40% over $150M (except Intermediate Government Bond Series)
IRA fees: None

DUPREE INTERMEDIATE GOVERNMENT BOND SERIES ◆
(See first Dupree listing for data common to all series)

Portfolio managers: William T. Griggs II (1992), Dorine Kelly (1992)
Investment objective and policies: High current income and capital preservation. Invests in securities issued by the U.S. Government and its agencies or instrumentalities, collateralized repurchase agreements and bank accounts. Portfolio has a dollar-weighted average maturity of three to ten years. Fund is non-diversified.
Year organized: 1992
Ticker symbol: DPIGX
Discount broker availability: Fidelity, Siebert
Qualified for sale in: FL, IN, KY, NC, TN, TX
Check redemptions: $500 minimum
Dividends paid: Income - declared daily, paid monthly; Capital gains - December
Portfolio turnover (3 yrs): 41%, 34%, 75%
Management fee: 0.20%
Expense ratio: 0.50% (year ending 6/30/97) (0.56% without waiver)

DUPREE KENTUCKY TAX-FREE INCOME SERIES ◆
(See first Dupree listing for data common to all series)

Portfolio managers: William T. Griggs II (1979), Michelle M. Dragoo (1987)
Investment objective and policies: High current income exempt from federal and Kentucky income

taxes, and Kentucky ad valorem tax. Invests primarily in a diversified portfolio of investment grade Kentucky municipal securities. Portfolio maintains a dollar-weighted average maturity of ten years or more. Up to 20% of assets may be in unrated securities believed of investment grade quality.
Year organized: 1979 (name changed from Kentucky Tax-Free Income Fund in 1987)
Ticker symbol: KYTFX
Discount broker availability: Fidelity, Siebert
Qualified for sale in: FL, IN, KY, NC, TX
Dividends paid: Income - March, June, September, December; Capital gains - December
Portfolio turnover (3 yrs): 7%, 4%, 18%
Expense ratio: 0.63% (year ending 6/30/97)

DUPREE KENTUCKY TAX-FREE SHORT-TO-MEDIUM SERIES ◆
(See first Dupree listing for data common to all series)

Portfolio managers: William T. Griggs II (1987), Vince Harrison (1987)
Investment objective and policies: High current income exempt from federal and Kentucky income taxes, and Kentucky ad valorem tax. Invests primarily in investment grade Kentucky municipal securities. Portfolio maintains a dollar-weighted average maturity of two to five years. Up to 20% of assets may be in unrated securities believed of investment grade quality. Portfolio is non-diversified.
Year organized: 1987
Ticker symbol: KYSMX
Discount broker availability: Fidelity, Siebert
Qualified for sale in: FL, IN, KY, NC, TX
Check redemptions: $500 minimum
Dividends paid: Income - declared daily, paid monthly; Capital gains - December
Portfolio turnover (3 yrs): 20%, 58%, 4%
Expense ratio: 0.72% (year ending 6/30/97)

DUPREE NORTH CAROLINA TAX-FREE INCOME SERIES ◆
(See first Dupree listing for data common to all series)

Portfolio managers: William T. Griggs II (1995), Michelle M. Dragoo (1995)
Investment objective and policies: High current income exempt from federal and North Carolina personal income taxes. Invests primarily in investment grade North Carolina municipal securities. Portfolio maintains a dollar-weighted average maturity of ten years or more. Up to 20% of assets may be in unrated securities believed of investment grade quality. Portfolio is non-diversified.
Year organized: 1995
Discount broker availability: Fidelity, Siebert
Qualified for sale in: FL, IN, KY, NC
Dividends paid: Income - March, June, September, December; Capital gains - December
Portfolio turnover (2 yrs): 24%, 23%
Expense ratio: 0.25% (year ending 6/30/97) (0.81% without waiver)

DUPREE NORTH CAROLINA TAX-FREE SHORT-TO-MEDIUM SERIES ◆
(See first Dupree listing for data common to all series)

Portfolio managers: William T. Griggs II (1995), Vince Harrison (1995)
Investment objective and policies: High current income exempt from federal and North Carolina personal income taxes. Invests primarily in investment grade North Carolina municipal securities. Portfolio maintains a dollar-weighted average maturity of two to five years. Up to 20% of assets may be in unrated securities believed of investment grade quality. Portfolio is non-diversified.
Year organized: 1995
Discount broker availability: Fidelity, Siebert
Qualified for sale in: FL, IN, KY, NC
Check redemptions: $500 minimum
Dividends paid: Income - declared daily, paid monthly; Capital gains - December
Portfolio turnover (2 yrs): 17%, 17%
Expense ratio: 0.23% (year ending 6/30/97) (0.82% without waiver)

DUPREE TENNESSEE TAX-FREE INCOME SERIES ◆

(See first Dupree listing for data common to all series)

Portfolio managers: William T. Griggs II (1993), Michelle M. Dragoo (1993)
Investment objective and policies: High current income exempt from federal income tax and the Tennessee Hall tax. Invests primarily in a diversified portfolio of investment grade Tennessee municipal securities. Portfolio generally maintains a dollar-weighted average maturity of ten years or more. Up to 20% of assets may be in unrated securities believed of investment grade quality.
Year organized: 1993
Discount broker availability: Fidelity, Siebert
Qualified for sale in: FL, IN, KY, NC, TN
Dividends paid: Income - March, June, September, December; Capital gains - December
Portfolio turnover (3 yrs): 5%, 9%, 7%
Expense ratio: 0.55% (year ending 6/30/97) (0.77% without waiver)

DUPREE TENNESSEE TAX-FREE SHORT-TO-MEDIUM SERIES ◆

(See first Dupree listing for data common to all series)

Portfolio managers: William T. Griggs II (1994), Vince Harrison (1994)
Investment objective and policies: High current income exempt from federal income tax and the Tennessee Hall tax. Invests primarily in investment grade Tennessee municipal securities. Portfolio maintains a dollar-weighted average maturity of two to five years. Up to 20% of assets may be in unrated securities believed of investment grade quality. Portfolio is non-diversified.
Year organized: 1994
Discount broker availability: Fidelity, Siebert
Qualified for sale in: FL, IN, KY, NC, TN
Check redemptions: $500 minimum
Dividends paid: Income - declared daily, paid monthly; Capital gains - December
Portfolio turnover (3 yrs): 24%, 23%, 1%
Expense ratio: 0.47% (year ending 6/30/97) (0.85% without waiver)

E-FUND MONEY MARKET ◆

(Fund was merged into the Working Assets Money Fund 12/8/97)

EASTCLIFF FUNDS ◆

(Data common to all Eastcliff funds are shown below. See subsequent listings for data specific to individual funds.)

900 Second Avenue South, Suite 300
300 International Centre
Minneapolis, MN 55402
800-595-5519, 612-336-1444
TDD 800-684-3416

Shareholder service hours: Full service M-F 8 A.M.-7 P.M. CST; After hours service: prices, account balances, place orders, last transaction, messages, prospectuses
Adviser: Resource Capital Advisers, Inc.
Administrator: Fiduciary Management, Inc.
Transfer agent: Firstar Trust Co.
Minimum purchase: Initial: $1,000, Subsequent: $100; Automatic investment plan: Initial: $50, Subsequent: $50
Wire orders accepted: Yes
Deadline for same day wire purchase: 4 P.M.
Telephone redemptions: Yes
Wire redemptions: Yes, $12 fee
Letter redemptions: Signature guarantee not required
Shareholder services: IRA, SEP-IRA, Keogh, 401(k), 403(b), corporate retirement plans, electronic funds transfer (redemptions only), systematic withdrawal plan min. bal. req. $10,000
Administration fee: 0.20% first $30M to 0.05% over $60M (subject to a minimum for each fund)
12b-1 distribution fee: Maximum of 1.00% (not currently imposed)
IRA/Keogh fees: Annual $12.50, Closing $15

EASTCLIFF GROWTH FUND ◆

(See first Eastcliff listing for data common to all funds)

Sub-adviser: Winslow Capital Management, Inc.
Portfolio managers: Clark J. Winslow (1995), Gail M. Knappenberger (1995), Richard E. Pyle (1995)
Investment objective and policies: Long-term capital growth. Invests in a wide variety of domestic equity securities of companies of all sizes, generally those traded on an exchange or in the over-the-counter market. May invest up to 20% of assets in securities of foreign issuers, and up to 10% of assets in companies with less than three years of continuous operating history. May use options and futures for hedging purposes.
Year organized: 1995
Ticker symbol: EASGX
Qualified for sale in: AZ, CA, CO, DC, FL, GA, IL, MN, NE, NY, NC, PA, SD, WI
Dividends paid: Income - July, December; Capital gains - July, December
Portfolio turnover (2 yrs): 54%, 40%
Management fee: 1.00%
Expense ratio: 1.30% (year ending 6/30/97)

EASTCLIFF REGIONAL SMALL CAPITALIZATION VALUE FUND ◆

(See first Eastcliff listing for data common to all funds)

Sub-adviser: Woodland Partners, LLC
Portfolio managers: Elizabeth M. Lilly (1996), Richard J. Rinkoff (1996)
Investment objective and policies: Capital appreciation. Invests primarily in companies with market capitalizations under $1B which are headquartered in Minnesota, North and South Dakota, Montana, Wisconsin, Michigan, Iowa, Nebraska, Colorado, Illinois, Indiana and Ohio. Selections are based on: company specifics that grow shareholder value; experienced, shareholder-oriented management; and perceived undervaluation. May also invest up to 35% of assets without regard to geographic consideration or the issuers' market capitalization, or in debt securities. May use put and call options for hedging purposes.
Year organized: 1996
Qualified for sale in: AZ, CA, CO, CT, DC, FL, GA, IL, IA, MN, NE, NY, NC, ND, PA, SD, WA, WI
Dividends paid: Income - July, December; Capital gains - July, December
Portfolio turnover (1 yr): 29%
Management fee: 1.00%
Expense ratio: 1.30% (10 months ending 6/30/97) (1.60% without waiver)

EASTCLIFF TOTAL RETURN FUND ◆

(See first Eastcliff listing for data common to all funds)

Sub-adviser: Palm Beach Investment Advisers, Inc.
Portfolio managers: Thomas M. Keresey (1995), Patrice J. Neverett (1995)
Investment objective and policies: Maximum total return: capital appreciation and income consistent with reasonable risk. Invests without limitation in common stocks, preferred stocks, convertible stocks, and corporate and governmental debt securities. Mix of equity and debt securities will be adjusted to reflect changes in market and economic conditions. May invest up to 25% of assets in securities of foreign issuers.
Year organized: 1986 (originally ValSearch Total Return Fund. Name changed from Fiduciary Total Return Fund on 12/31/94)
Qualified for sale in: AZ, CA, CO, DC, FL, GA, IL, KS, MI, MN, MO, NY, NC, PA, SD, TX, WI
Dividends paid: Income - July, December; Capital gains - July, December
Portfolio turnover (3 yrs): 58%, 95%, 89%
Management fee: 1.00% first $30M, 0.75% over $30M
Expense ratio: 1.30% (year ending 6/30/97) (1.50% without waiver)

ECLIPSE FUNDS ◆

(Data common to all Eclipse funds are shown below. See subsequent listings for data specific to individual funds.)

P.O. Box 2196
Peachtree City, GA 30269
800-872-2710, 770-631-0414
fax 404-487-0676
Internet: http://www.eclipsefund.com

Adviser: Towneley Capital Management, Inc.
Administrator: NYLIFE Distributors, Inc.
Transfer agent: Investors Fiduciary Trust Co.
Minimum purchase: Initial: $1,000, Subsequent: None; Automatic investment plan: Initial: $50, Subsequent: $50
Wire orders accepted: Yes
Deadline for same day wire purchase: 3 P.M.
Qualified for sale in: All states
Telephone redemptions: Yes
Letter redemptions: Signature guarantee required
Telephone switching: With other Eclipse funds and Vista money market funds, $500 minimum
Number of switches permitted: Unlimited
Shareholder services: IRA, 403(b), systematic withdrawal plan min. bal. req. $10,000
IRA fees: None

ECLIPSE BALANCED FUND ◆

(See first Eclipse listing for data common to all funds)

Portfolio manager: Wesley G. McCain (1989)
Investment objective and policies: High total return: dividend and interest income and capital gains. Invests in an allocated portfolio of equity and fixed-income securities; at least 25% of assets are always in fixed-income securities, including U.S. and foreign government debt, investment grade corporate obligations, and mortgage- and asset-backed securities. The average total common stock market capitalization of the fund's equity holdings will approximate that of the S&P 500 Stock Composite Index. May invest up to 20% of assets in securities of foreign governments and supranational entities.
Year organized: 1989
Ticker symbol: EBALX
Discount broker availability: *Fidelity, *Schwab, *White
Dividends paid: Income - March, June, September, December; Capital gains - December
Portfolio turnover (3 yrs): 72%, 75%, 94%
Management fee: 0.80%
Administration fee: 0.15% first $50M + 0.12% between $50M and $100M + 0.05% between $100M and $750M + 0.02 over $750M (of combined assets of Balanced and Equity funds)
Expense ratio: 0.80% (year ending 12/31/96) (1.00% without waiver)

ECLIPSE EQUITY FUND ◆

(See first Eclipse listing for data common to all funds)

Portfolio manager: Wesley G. McCain (1987)
Investment objective and policies: High total return: dividend income and realized and unrealized capital gains. Normally invests at least 65% of assets in equity securities of North American companies listed on major exchanges or traded over the counter. In general companies will have an average market capitalization below the average of the S&P 500. Up to 20% of assets may be in securities of foreign issuers or depository receipts.
Year organized: 1987
Ticker symbol: EEQFX
Discount broker availability: *Fidelity, *White
Dividends paid: Income - December; Capital gains - December
Portfolio turnover (3 yrs): 82%, 74%, 92%
Management fee: 1.00%
Administration fee: 0.15% first $50M + 0.12% between $50M and $100M + 0.05% between $100M and $750M + 0.02 over $750M (of combined assets of Balanced and Equity funds)
Expense ratio: 1.15% (year ending 12/31/96)

ECLIPSE GROWTH AND INCOME FUND ◆
(See first Eclipse listing for data common to all funds)

Portfolio manager: Wesley G. McCain (1995)
Investment objective and policies: High total return: dividend and interest income and capital gains. Invests primarily in dividend-paying equity securities of North American companies listed on major exchanges or sold over the counter. In general companies will have an average market capitalization equal to the average of the S&P 500. May have up to 20% of assets in securities of foreign issuers or in depository receipts.
Year organized: 1995
Ticker symbol: ECGIX
Discount broker availability: *Fidelity, *Schwab
Dividends paid: Income - December; Capital gains - December
Portfolio turnover (2 yrs): 102%, 63%
Management fee: 0.90%
Administration fee: 0.10% first $100M; if assets exceed this, balance will be combined with those of Balanced and Equity funds and fee schedule shown there will be in force.
Expense ratio: 0.90% (year ending 12/31/96) (1.60% without waiver)

ECLIPSE ULTRA SHORT-TERM INCOME FUND ◆
(See first Eclipse listing for data common to all funds)

Portfolio manager: Wesley G. McCain (1995)
Investment objective and policies: High current income consistent with capital preservation and a relatively stable share price. Invests primarily in a diversified portfolio of high quality, short-term domestic government and corporate fixed-income securities. The portfolio will maintain a duration not to exceed one year. May invest without limit in collateralized mortgage obligations and multi-class pass-through securities, stripped mortgage-backed securities and collateralized mortgage obligation residuals. May have up to 10% of assets in foreign debt securities rated at least AA by S&P and Aa2 or better by Moody's.
Year organized: 1995
Ticker symbol: ECUIX
Dividends paid: Income - March, June, September, December; Capital gains - December
Portfolio turnover (2 yrs): 47%, 39%
Management fee: 0.40%
Administration fee: 0.10% first $100M; if assets exceed this, balance will be combined with those of Balanced and Equity funds, and fee schedule shown there will be in force.
Expense ratio: 0.00% (year ending 12/31/96) (0.41% without waiver)

1838 FUNDS ◆
(Data common to all 1838 funds are shown below. See subsequent listings for data specific to individual funds.)

Five Radnor Corporate Center, Suite 320
100 Matsonford Road
Radnor, PA 19087
800-884-1838, 610-293-4300

Adviser: 1838 Investment Advisors, L.P.
Transfer agent and administrator: Rodney Square Management Corp.
Minimum purchase: Initial: $1,000, Subsequent: None; IRA: Initial: None; Automatic investment plan: Subsequent: $50
Wire orders accepted: Yes
Deadline for same day wire purchase: 4; p.m.
Telephone redemptions: Yes
Wire redemptions: Yes, $1,000 minimum
Letter redemptions: Signature guarantee required
Shareholder services: IRA, systematic withdrawal plan min. bal. req. $10,000
Administration fee: 0.15% first $50M to 0.05% over $200M
IRA fees: Annual $10

1838 FIXED INCOME FUND ◆
(See first 1838 listing for data common to all funds)

Portfolio manager: Marcia Zercoe (1997)
Investment objective and policies: Maximum current income; growth secondary. Invests at least 65% of assets in a diversified portfolio of investment grade fixed-income obligations. Although there is no restriction on the maturity of a single issue, the portfolio generally maintains a dollar-weighted average maturity of seven to twelve years. May invest in asset-backed securities and CMOs. May use a variety of derivative instruments in an effort to enhance return and for hedging purposes.
Year organized: 1997
Qualified for sale in: AR, CA, CT, DE, DC, FL, GA, HI, IL, MD, MA, MN, NJ, NY, NC, OH, PA, TN, TX, VA
Dividends paid: Income - quarterly; Capital gains - annually
Management fee: 0.50%

1838 INTERNATIONAL EQUITY FUND ◆
(See first 1838 listing for data common to all funds)

Portfolio manager: Hans Van Der Berg (1995)
Investment objective and policies: Capital appreciation; income secondary. Invests at least 65% of assets in equity securities of issuers located in at least three countries other than the U.S., with the majority of selections coming from the developed markets of Europe and the Far East. Fund may invest without limit, though, in developing countries whose macroeconomic and political profiles are perceived to favor strong growth in market economies. Fund may use a variety of derivative instruments in an effort to enhance returns and for hedging purposes.
Year organized: 1995
Qualified for sale in: AR, CA, CT, DE, DC, FL, GA, HI, IL, MD, MA, MN, NJ, NY, NC, OH, PA, TX, VA
Dividends paid: Income - annually; Capital gains - annually
Portfolio turnover (2 yrs): 92%, 59%
Management fee: 0.75%
Expense ratio: 1.25% (year ending 10/31/97) (1.44% without waiver)

1838 SMALL CAP EQUITY FUND ◆
(See first 1838 listing for data common to all funds)

Portfolio manager: Edwin B. Powell (1996)
Investment objective and policies: Long-term growth. Invests at least 65% of assets in equity securities of companies with market capitalizations of $1B or less, that are perceived to be undervalued but show good potential for capital appreciation. May invest up to 20% of assets in foreign issues, and up to 15% in illiquid securities. May invest without limit in bonds if deemed beneficial. May use a variety of derivative instruments and foreign currency transactions for hedging purposes.
Year organized: 1996
Qualified for sale in: AR, CA, CT, DE, DC, FL, GA, HI, IL, MD, MA, MN, NJ, NY, NC, OH, PA, TN, TX, VA
Dividends paid: Income - annually; Capital gains - annually
Portfolio turnover (1 yr): 68%
Management fee: 0.75%
Expense ratio: 1.25% (year ending 10/31/97) (1.84% without waiver)

EMERALD FUNDS
(Data common to all Emerald funds are shown below. See subsequent listings for data specific to individual funds.)

9000 Southside Blvd., Building 100
Jacksonville, FL 32256
800-637-3759, 904-464-2877

Adviser: Barnett Capital Advisors, Inc. (a wholly-owned subsidiary of NationsBank Corp.)**At press time The Board of Trustees was considering a reorganization to fold the Emerald Funds into existing Nations Funds with similar objectives. Decision will be rendered on or before May 9, 1998.**
Transfer agent and administrator: BISYS Fund Services Ohio, Inc.
Minimum purchase: Initial: $1,000, Subsequent: $100; IRA: Subsequent: None; Keogh: Initial: None, Subsequent: None; Automatic investment plan: Initial: $50, Subsequent: $50
Wire orders accepted: Yes
Deadline for same day wire purchase: 4 P.M.
Discount broker availability: Fidelity, Siebert
Qualified for sale in: All states
Telephone redemptions: Yes
Wire redemptions: Yes, $1,000 minimum
Letter redemptions: Signature guarantee required over $10,000
Telephone switching: With other Emerald funds, $500 minimum
Number of switches permitted: Unlimited
Shareholder services: IRA, SEP-IRA, 401(k), 403(b), electronic funds transfer, systematic withdrawal plan min. bal. req. $5,000
Administration fee: 0.0775% first $5B to 0.05% over $10B of the aggregate value of the Emerald Funds; fee increases to 0.08% if value drops below $8B.
12b-1 distribution fee: 0.25%
IRA fees: Initial $10, Annual $10, Closing $10

EMERALD BALANCED FUND
(See first Emerald listing for data common to all funds)

Portfolio manager: G. Russell Creighton (1994)
Investment objective and policies: Total return; capital growth and current income. Allocates assets across three major asset groups: equity securities, fixed-income securities and cash equivalents, based on the relative attractiveness of each. Will invest at least 25% of assets in debt securities and cash at all times, and no more than 75% of assets in equity securities. Allocations will vary according to perceptions of the market. May invest up to 25% of assets in foreign holdings through ADRs and EDRs, and up to 10% of assets in other investment companies.
Year organized: 1994
Ticker symbol: EMLRX
Dividends paid: Income - quarterly; Capital gains - annually
Portfolio turnover (3 yrs): 106%, 87%, 33%
Management fee: 0.60%
Expense ratio: 1.06% (year ending 11/30/96) (1.35% without waiver)

EMERALD EQUITY FUND
(See first Emerald listing for data common to all funds)

Portfolio manager: G. Russell Creighton (1993)
Investment objective and policies: Long-term capital appreciation; dividend income growth secondary. Invests primarily in high-quality common stocks and equity securities selected on the basis of fundamental investment value and growth prospects. May, however, invest up to 15% of assets in convertible securities rated below investment grade. May use ADRs and EDRs to invest up to 25% of assets in foreign issues.
Year organized: 1991
Ticker symbol: EMEQX
Dividends paid: Income - quarterly; Capital gains - annually
Portfolio turnover (3 yrs): 89%, 104%, 113%
Management fee: 0.60%
Expense ratio: 1.27% (year ending 11/30/96) (1.28% without waiver)

EMERALD EQUITY VALUE FUND
(See first Emerald listing for data common to all funds)

Portfolio managers: Martin E. LaPrade (1995), Don W. Bryant (1997)
Investment objective and policies: Long-term capital appreciation; income secondary. Invests at least 75% of assets in common and preferred stock and securities convertible into common stock, that have a price/book value ratio below that of the median stock in the S&P 500 Composite Stock Price Index. Equity investments consist primarily of common stocks of companies having capitalizations that exceed $100M. May invest up to 25% of assets in foreign issues, either directly or through ADRs and EDRs. May write covered call options.

Year organized: 1995
Dividends paid: Income - quarterly; Capital gains - annually
Portfolio turnover (1 yr): 19%
Management fee: 0.60%
Expense ratio: 0.00% (11 months ending 11/30/96) (277.68% without waiver)

EMERALD FLORIDA TAX-EXEMPT FUND

(See first Emerald listing for data common to all funds)

Portfolio managers: Margaret L. Moore (1996), Douglas Byrne (1997)
Investment objective and policies: High tax-free income and current liquidity; long-term capital appreciation secondary. Invest primarily in municipal obligations that are rated at or above investment grade at the time of purchase. Securities that cease to be rated at investment grade will be disposed of in a quick and orderly fashion. Fund has the ability to invest in instruments of any maturity, but will generally invest primarily in obligations with remaining maturities of more than ten years.
Year organized: 1991
Ticker symbol: EMFLX
Dividends paid: Income - declared daily, paid monthly; Capital gains - December
Portfolio turnover (3 yrs): 152%, 89%, 89%
Management fee: 0.40%
Expense ratio: 0.92% (year ending 11/30/96) (1.06% without waiver)

EMERALD INTERNATIONAL EQUITY FUND

(See first Emerald listing for data common to all funds)

Sub-adviser: Brandes Investment Partners, L.P.
Portfolio manager: Donald W. Bryant (1996)
Investment objective and policies: Long-term capital appreciation; income incidental. Invests at least 65% of assets in equity securities of companies in least three countries outside the U.S. May invest more than 25% of assets in issues from any single country. May invest up to 35% of assets in short-term debt instruments. May use covered call options and purchase and write put and call options on foreign stock indices for hedging purposes.
Year organized: 1995
Dividends paid: Income - annually; Capital gains - annually
Portfolio turnover (1 yr): 50%
Management fee: 1.00%
Expense ratio: 0.00% (year ending 11/30/96) (57.40% without waiver)

EMERALD MANAGED BOND FUND

(See first Emerald listing for data common to all funds)

Portfolio manager: Jack A. Ablin (1998)
Investment objective and policies: High level of current income; capital appreciation secondary. Invests substantially all its assets in debt obligations such as bonds, debentures and cash equivalents; either government or corporate, domestic or international. Fund will purchase only those securities considered investment grade or better by at least one rating agency, or, if unrated, those believed to be of comparable quality. Up to 35% of assets may be in dollar-denominated debt obligations of foreign issuers. There is no restriction on the average weighted maturity of the fund, and it may be more or less than ten years.
Year organized: 1994
Ticker symbol: EMBRX
Dividends paid: Income - declared daily, paid monthly; Capital gains - December
Portfolio turnover (3 yrs): 97%, 92%, 83%
Management fee: 0.40%
Expense ratio: 0.91% (year ending 11/30/96) (1.59% without waiver)

EMERALD PRIME FUND

(See first Emerald listing for data common to all funds)

Portfolio manager: Jacqueline R. Lunsford (1991)
Investment objective and policies: High current income, liquidity and capital preservation. Invests in a broad range of short-term, dollar-denominated government, bank and corporate money market obligations that mature in 13 months or less.
Year organized: 1991
Dividends paid: Income - declared daily, paid monthly
Management fee: 0.25%
Expense ratio: 0.38% (year ending 11/30/96) (0.42% without waiver)

EMERALD SHORT-TERM FIXED INCOME FUND

(See first Emerald listing for data common to all funds)

Portfolio managers: Jeffery A. Greenert (1996), David Furfine (1997)
Investment objective and policies: Consistently positive current income with relative stability principal. Invests primarily in investment grade debt securities and high-quality money market instruments. Invests substantially all its assets in debt obligations such as bonds, debentures and cash equivalents; either government or corporate, domestic or international. Fund will purchase only those securities considered investment grade or better by at least one rating agency, or, if unrated, those believed to be of comparable quality. Mat purchase cash equivalents and repurchase agreements without limit. Up to 35% of assets may be in dollar-denominated debt obligations of foreign issuers. The average dollar-weighted maturity of the fund will not exceed three years.
Year organized: 1994
Ticker symbol: EMSRX
Dividends paid: Income - declared daily, paid monthly; Capital gains - December
Portfolio turnover (3 yrs): 138%, 33%, 0%
Management fee: 0.40%
Expense ratio: 0.80% (year ending 11/30/96) (2.33% without waiver)

EMERALD SMALL CAPITALIZATION FUND

(See first Emerald listing for data common to all funds)

Portfolio manager: Martin E. LaPrade (1998)
Investment objective and policies: Long-term capital appreciation. Invests primarily in equity securities and convertibles of companies with market capitalizations ranging from $50M to $2B. May invest up to 25% of total assets in foreign issues by utilizing ADRs and EDRs. May acquire warrants and rights.
Year organized: 1994
Ticker symbol: EMCRX
Dividends paid: Income - annually; Capital gains - annually
Portfolio turnover (3 yrs): 356%, 229%, 118%
Management fee: 1.00%
Expense ratio: 1.59% (year ending 11/30/96) (1.70% without waiver)

EMERALD TAX-EXEMPT FUND

(See first Emerald listing for data common to all funds)

Sub-adviser: Rodney Square Management Corp.
Portfolio manager: Jacqueline R. Lunsford (1991)
Investment objective and policies: High current income free of federal income tax, consistent with liquidity, capital preservation and a stable net asset value. Invests in high-quality debt obligations of states, territories and possessions of the U.S. and the District of Columbia, and of their agencies, authorities and instrumentalities. Only invests in dollar-denominated securities that mature in 13 months or less.
Year organized: 1991

Dividends paid: Income - declared daily, paid monthly
Management fee: 0.25%
Expense ratio: 0.34% (year ending 11/30/96) (0.45% without waiver)

EMERALD TREASURY FUND

(See first Emerald listing for data common to all funds)

Portfolio manager: Jacqueline R. Lunsford (1991)
Investment objective and policies: High current income, liquidity and capital preservation. Invests in a broad range of obligations issued by the U.S. Treasury or those to which the U.S. Government has pledged its full faith and credit to guarantee the payment of principal and interest. Invests in dollar-denominated securities that mature in 13 months or less.
Year organized: 1991
Dividends paid: Income - declared daily, paid monthly
Management fee: 0.25%
Expense ratio: 0.47% (year ending 11/30/96) (0.49% without waiver)

EMERALD U.S. GOVERNMENT SECURITIES FUND

(See first Emerald listing for data common to all funds)

Portfolio manager: Jeffery A. Greenert (1998)
Investment objective and policies: Consistent positive income. Invests principally in U.S. Government securities and repurchase agreements collateralized by such securities. Fund will maintain a dollar-weighted average maturity between five and ten years.
Year organized: 1991
Ticker symbol: EMUSX
Dividends paid: Income - declared daily, paid monthly; Capital gains - December
Portfolio turnover (3 yrs): 53%, 89%, 133%
Management fee: 0.40%
Expense ratio: 1.09% (year ending 11/30/96) (1.14% without waiver)

EMPIRE BUILDERS TAX FREE BOND FUND ◆

237 Park Avenue, Suite 910
New York, NY 10017
800-847-5886, 212-808-3900

Adviser: Glickenhaus & Co.
Portfolio manager: James R. Vaccacio (1986)
Transfer agent and administrator: BISYS Fund Services, Inc.
Investment objective and policies: High current return exempt from federal, New York state and New York city personal income taxes, consistent with capital preservation. Invests primarily in a portfolio of tax exempt bonds issued by the State of New York or its political subdivisions. May use futures and options for hedging purposes.
Year organized: 1983 (fund went no-load 1/4/95)
Ticker symbol: EMBTX
Sales restrictions: Fund instituted a two class structure 4/15/96, 'Builder' Class and 'Premier' Class; Premier is the new entity. The Builder Class offers a higher level of services and features. Premier Class offers fewer services and features and requires a higher minimum investment, but has a lower level of expenses. Historic performance and turnover reflects Builder Class.
Minimum purchase: Initial: $1,000 (Builder); $20,000 (Premier), Subsequent: $100 (Builder); $1,000 (Premier)
Wire orders accepted: Yes
Deadline for same day wire purchase: 4 P.M.
Qualified for sale in: AL, AZ, CA, CT, DC, FL, HI, KY, ME, MD, MA, MI, NV, NH, NJ, NY, OR, PA, TN, VT, VA, WA, WY
Telephone redemptions: Yes
Letter redemptions: Signature guarantee required over $25,000
Check redemptions: $500 minimum (Builder); $5 initial fee, $5,000 minimum, $1/check fee (Premier)
Dividends paid: Income - declared daily, paid monthly; Capital gains - annually

Portfolio turnover (3 yrs): 181%, 150%, 143%
Shareholder services: Automatic investment plan, systematic withdrawal plan min. bal. req. $5,000 (not available for Premier)
Management fee: 0.40% first $100M, 0.3333% over $100M
Administration fee: 0.20% first $100M, 0.14% over $100M
Expense ratio: 1.07% (Builder) 0.97% (Premier) (year ending 2/28/97)

EXCELSIOR FUNDS ◆
(Data common to all Excelsior funds are shown below. See subsequent listings for data specific to individual funds.)

114 West 47th Street
New York, NY 10036
800-446-1012, 617-557-8280
price/yield 800-233-9180

Adviser: United States Trust Company of New York
Administrators: Chase Global Funds Services Co., and Federated Administrative Services
Transfer agent: U.S. Trust New York
Special sales restrictions: These funds were load funds prior to 2/14/97.
Minimum purchase: Initial: $500, Subsequent: $50; IRA: Initial: $250; Keogh: Initial: None, Subsequent: None; Automatic investment plan: Initial: $50
Wire orders accepted: Yes
Deadline for same day wire purchase: 4 P.M.
Qualified for sale in: All states
Telephone redemptions: Yes, $500 minimum
Wire redemptions: Yes, $500 minimum
Letter redemptions: Signature guarantee required over $50,000
Telephone switching: With other Excelsior funds, $500 minimum
Number of switches permitted: 6 per year
Shareholder services: IRA, SEP-IRA, 401(k), 403(b), directed dividends, electronic funds transfer, systematic withdrawal plan min. bal. req. $10,000

EXCELSIOR BLENDED EQUITY FUND ◆
(See first Excelsior listing for data common to all funds)

Portfolio managers: David A. Tillson (1994), Bruce Tavel (1997), Leigh H. Weiss (1997)
Investment objective and policies: Long-term capital appreciation. Invests at least 65% of assets in a diversified portfolio of equity securities of companies of all sizes perceived to be undervalued. May invest up to 35% of assets in securities of other types such as investment grade debt, warrants, options and futures. May invest without limit in foreign securities, both directly and through ADRs, and engage in foreign currency exchange transactions for hedging purposes.
Year organized: 1985 (previously known as the Equity Fund)
Ticker symbol: UMEQX
Group fund code: 800
Discount broker availability: *Fidelity, *Schwab, *White
Dividends paid: Income - quarterly; Capital gains - annually
Portfolio turnover (3 yrs): 39%, 27%, 23%
Management fee: 0.75%
Administration fee: 0.20% first $200M to 0.15% over $400M
Expense ratio: 1.01% (year ending 3/31/97) (1.06% without waiver)

EXCELSIOR CALIFORNIA TAX EXEMPT INCOME FUND ◆
(See first Excelsior listing for data common to all funds)

Sub-adviser: U.S. Trust Company of California
Portfolio manager: Lois G. Ingham (1996)
Investment objective and policies: High level of current income exempt from federal income tax and, to the extent possible, exempt from California state personal income tax, consistent with relative stability of principal. Invests at least 65% of assets in

California municipal obligations. Portfolio maintains a dollar-weighted average maturity of three to ten years. May invest up to 20% of assets in securities subject to AMT tax treatment. May use futures contracts for hedging purposes. Fund is non-diversified.
Year organized: 1996
Ticker symbol: UMCAX
Group fund code: 809
Discount broker availability: *Fidelity, *White
Dividends paid: Income - declared daily, paid monthly; Capital gains - annually
Portfolio turnover (1 yr): 7%
Management fee: 0.50%
Administration fee: 0.20% first $200M to 0.15% over $400M
Expense ratio: 0.66% (6 months ending 3/31/97) (1.53% without waiver)

EXCELSIOR ENERGY AND NATURAL RESOURCES FUND ◆
(See first Excelsior listing for data common to all funds)

Portfolio manager: Michael E. Hoover (1995)
Investment objective and policies: Long-term capital appreciation. Invests at least 65% of assets in equity securities of domestic and foreign companies engaged in the energy and other natural resources groups of industries, such as mining, pipeline construction, petroleum production and agriculture. May invest up to 35% of assets in precious metals, including coins and bullion, although coins are not purchased for numismatic value. May also purchase investment grade debt obligations and use options and futures for hedging purposes. Fund is non-diversified.
Year organized: 1992 (previously known as the Long-Term Supply of Energy Fund)
Ticker symbol: UMESX
Group fund code: 813
Discount broker availability: *Fidelity, *Schwab, *White
Dividends paid: Income - annually; Capital gains - annually
Portfolio turnover (3 yrs): 87%, 43%, 31%
Management fee: 0.60%
Administration fee: 0.20% first $200M to 0.15% over $400M
Expense ratio: 0.93% (year ending 3/31/97) (0.98% without waiver)

EXCELSIOR GOVERNMENT MONEY FUND ◆
(See first Excelsior listing for data common to all funds)

Investment objective and policies: A high level of current income, consistent with liquidity and stability of principal. Invests in short-term obligations issued or guaranteed by the U.S. Government, its agencies or instrumentalities, and repurchase agreements collateralized thereon.
Year organized: 1985
Ticker symbol: UTGXX
Group fund code: 804
Dividends paid: Income - declared daily, paid monthly; Capital gains - annually
Management fee: 0.25%
Administration fee: 0.20% first $200M to 0.15% over $400M
Expense ratio: 0.47% (year ending 3/31/97) (0.51% without waiver)

EXCELSIOR INCOME AND GROWTH FUND ◆
(See first Excelsior listing for data common to all funds)

Portfolio manager: Richard L. Bayles (1990)
Investment objective and policies: Moderate current income; capital appreciation secondary. Invests a substantial portion of assets in both foreign and domestic equity securities that are expected to offer dividends and a constant source of moderate income. Fund also invests in debt obligations chosen primarily for their income potential, and may invest up to 35% of assets in junk bonds.
Year organized: 1987

Ticker symbol: UMIGX
Group fund code: 801
Discount broker availability: *Fidelity, *Schwab, *White
Dividends paid: Income - quarterly; Capital gains - annually
Portfolio turnover (3 yrs): 25%, 22%, 36%
Management fee: 0.75%
Administration fee: 0.20% first $200M to 0.15% over $400M
Expense ratio: 1.03% (year ending 3/31/97) (1.11% without waiver)

EXCELSIOR INTERMEDIATE-TERM MANAGED INCOME FUND ◆
(See first Excelsior listing for data common to all funds)

Portfolio manager: Alexander R. Powers (1997)
Investment objective and policies: High current income consistent with relative stability of principal. Invests at least 75% of assets in investment or premium grade corporate an government debt obligations ranked in the three highest categories, and money markets. Portfolio maintains a dollar-weighted average maturity of three to ten years. May invest up to 25% of assets in preferred stocks, dollar-denominated debt obligations of foreign issuers, and dollar-denominated debt obligations of U.S. companies issued outside the U.S. May invest up to 10% of assets in junk bonds, and use foreign currency exchange transactions for hedging purposes.
Year organized: 1992
Ticker symbol: UIMIX
Group fund code: 824
Discount broker availability: *Fidelity, *White
Dividends paid: Income - declared daily, paid monthly; Capital gains - annually
Portfolio turnover (3 yrs): 129%, 129%, 682%
Management fee: 0.35%
Administration fee: 0.20% first $200M to 0.15% over $400M
Expense ratio: 0.63% (year ending 3/31/97) (0.68% without waiver)

EXCELSIOR INTERMEDIATE-TERM TAX EXEMPT FUND ◆
(See first Excelsior listing for data common to all funds)

Portfolio manager: Kenneth J. McAlley (1995)
Investment objective and policies: High current interest income exempt from regular federal income tax, consistent with relative stability of principal. Invests substantially all its assets in municipal obligations. Ordinarily maintains a dollar-weighted average maturity of three to ten years, although there is no restriction on the remaining maturity of any individual issue. May use futures contracts for hedging purposes.
Year organized: 1985
Ticker symbol: UMITX
Group fund code: 807
Discount broker availability: *Fidelity, *White
Dividends paid: Income - declared daily, paid monthly; Capital gains - annually
Portfolio turnover (3 yrs): 28%, 50%, 362%
Management fee: 0.35%
Administration fee: 0.20% first $200M to 0.15% over $400M
Expense ratio: 0.58% (year ending 3/31/97) (0.64% without waiver)

EXCELSIOR INTERNATIONAL FUND ◆
(See first Excelsior listing for data common to all funds)

Portfolio manager: Rosemary Sagar (1996)
Investment objective and policies: Total return; capital appreciation and income. Invests at least 65% of assets in a diversified portfolio of equity securities representing companies from around the world believed to be positioned to benefit from global economic trends, promising technology, or changing geopolitical, economic or currency relationships. Weightings towards either capital gains or income are not fixed and may be modified according to perceived market conditions. May

use options, futures and forward foreign currency transactions for hedging purposes.
Year organized: 1987
Ticker symbol: UMINX
Group fund code: 802
Discount broker availability: *Fidelity, *White
Dividends paid: Income - semi-annually; Capital gains - annually
Portfolio turnover (3 yrs): 116%, 39%, 66%
Management fee: 1.00%
Administration fee: 0.20%
Expense ratio: 1.43% (year ending 3/31/97) (1.51% without waiver)

EXCELSIOR LARGE CAP GROWTH FUND ◆
(See first Excelsior listing for data common to all funds)

Portfolio manager: Team managed
Investment objective and policies: Superior risk-adjusted total return. Invests at least 65% of asset in equity securities of companies with market capitalizations exceeding $5B whose growth opportunities appear to exceed the overall market. May invest without limit in foreign securities, both directly and through sponsored and unsponsored ADRs. May also invest up to 35% of assets in other types of securities, including investment grade debt and warrants, and use options and futures in an effort to enhance performance and for hedging purposes.
Year organized: 1997
Ticker symbol: UMLGX
Group fund code: 833
Discount broker availability: *White
Dividends paid: Income - annually; Capital gains - annually
Management fee: 0.75%
Administration fee: 0.20% first $200M to 0.15% over $400M

EXCELSIOR LATIN AMERICA FUND ◆
(See first Excelsior listing for data common to all funds)

Portfolio manager: Rosemary Sagar (1996)
Investment objective and policies: Long-term capital appreciation. Invests at least 75% of assets in undervalued equity securities of regional companies believed to be positioned to benefit from global economic trends, promising technology, or changing geopolitical, economic or currency relationships. May also invest in investment grade debt obligations of foreign governments, with up to 25% of assets allocated to any single government. May use options, futures and forward foreign currency transactions for hedging purposes.
Year organized: 1992 (previously known as the Emerging Americas Fund)
Ticker symbol: UMEAX
Group fund code: 822
Discount broker availability: *Fidelity, *Schwab, *White
Dividends paid: Income - semi-annually; Capital gains - annually
Portfolio turnover (3 yrs): 73%, 54%, 69%
Management fee: 1.00%
Administration fee: 0.20%
Expense ratio: 1.48% (year ending 3/31/97) (1.56% without waiver)

EXCELSIOR LONG-TERM TAX EXEMPT FUND ◆
(See first Excelsior listing for data common to all funds)

Portfolio manager: Kenneth J. McAlley (1986)
Investment objective and policies: Maximum current interest income exempt from regular federal income tax over time, with a view toward relative stability of principal and preservation of capital. Invests substantially all its assets in municipal obligations. Portfolio generally maintains a dollar-weighted average maturity of ten to thirty years. May use futures contracts for hedging purposes.
Year organized: 1986
Ticker symbol: UMLTX
Group fund code: 808

Discount broker availability: *Fidelity, *Schwab, *White
Dividends paid: Income - declared daily, paid monthly; Capital gains - annually
Portfolio turnover (3 yrs): 125%, 185%, 214%
Management fee: 0.50%
Administration fee: 0.20% first $200M to 0.15% over $400M
Expense ratio: 0.74% (year ending 3/31/97) (0.81% without waiver)

EXCELSIOR MANAGED INCOME FUND ◆
(See first Excelsior listing for data common to all funds)

Portfolio manager: Alexander R. Powers (1997)
Investment objective and policies: Higher current income consistent with prudent risk of capital. Invests at least 75% of assets in investment grade corporate and government debt obligations ranked in the three highest categories, and money markets. The dollar-weighted average maturity of the fund varies according to perceived market conditions. May invest up to 25% of assets in preferred stocks, dollar-denominated debt obligations of foreign issuers, and dollar-denominated debt obligations of U.S. companies issued outside the U.S. May invest up to 25% of assets in junk bonds, and use foreign currency exchange transactions for hedging purposes.
Year organized: 1986
Ticker symbol: UMMGX
Group fund code: 805
Discount broker availability: *Fidelity, *Schwab, *White
Dividends paid: Income - declared daily, paid monthly; Capital gains - annually
Portfolio turnover (3 yrs): 238%, 165%, 492%
Management fee: 0.75%
Administration fee: 0.20% first $200M to 0.15% over $400M
Expense ratio: 0.90% (year ending 3/31/97) (1.04% without waiver)

EXCELSIOR MONEY FUND ◆
(See first Excelsior listing for data common to all funds)

Investment objective and policies: High level of current income, consistent with liquidity and stability of principal. Invests in short-term corporate, bank and government money market obligations.
Year organized: 1985
Ticker symbol: UTMXX
Group fund code: 803
Dividends paid: Income - declared daily, paid monthly; Capital gains - annually
Management fee: 0.25%
Administration fee: 0.20% first $200M to 0.15% over $400M
Expense ratio: 0.47% (year ending 3/31/97) (0.53% without waiver)

EXCELSIOR NEW YORK INTERMEDIATE-TERM TAX EXEMPT FUND ◆
(See first Excelsior listing for data common to all funds)

Portfolio manager: Kenneth J. McAlley (1995)
Investment objective and policies: High current income exempt from regular federal income tax and, to the extent possible, from NY State and NY City personal income taxes, consistent with relative stability of principal. Fund normally invests substantially all its assets in New York municipal obligations. While there is no restriction as to the remaining maturity of an individual issue, the portfolio generally maintains a dollar-weighted average maturity of three to ten years. Fund is non-diversified.
Year organized: 1990
Ticker symbol: UMNYX
Group fund code: 810
Discount broker availability: *Fidelity, *White
Dividends paid: Income - declared daily, paid monthly; Capital gains - annually
Portfolio turnover (3 yrs): 89%, 154%, 563%

Management fee: 0.50%
Administration fee: 0.20% first $200M to 0.15% over $400M
Expense ratio: 0.72% (year ending 3/31/97) (0.75% without waiver)

EXCELSIOR PACIFIC/ASIA FUND ◆
(See first Excelsior listing for data common to all funds)

Portfolio manager: Wendy Agnew (1996)
Investment objective and policies: Long-term capital appreciation. Invests at least 65% of assets in undervalued equity securities of regional companies believed to be positioned to benefit from global economic trends, promising technology, or changing geopolitical, economic or currency relationships. May also invest in investment grade debt obligations of foreign governments, with up to 25% of assets allocated to any single government. May use options, futures and forward foreign currency transactions for hedging purposes.
Year organized: 1992
Ticker symbol: USPAX
Group fund code: 820
Discount broker availability: *Fidelity, *White
Dividends paid: Income - semi-annually; Capital gains - annually
Portfolio turnover (3 yrs): 126%, 29%, 69%
Management fee: 1.00%
Administration fee: 0.20%
Expense ratio: 1.45% (year ending 3/31/97) (1.52% without waiver)

EXCELSIOR PAN EUROPEAN FUND ◆
(See first Excelsior listing for data common to all funds)

Portfolio manager: Rosemary Sagar (1996)
Investment objective and policies: Long-term capital appreciation. Invests at least 65% of assets in undervalued equity securities of regional companies believed to be positioned to benefit from global economic trends, promising technology, or changing geopolitical, economic or currency relationships. May also invest in investment grade debt obligations of foreign governments, with up to 25% of assets allocated to any single government. May use options, futures and forward foreign currency transactions for hedging purposes.
Year organized: 1992
Ticker symbol: UMPNX
Group fund code: 821
Discount broker availability: *Fidelity, *Schwab, *White
Dividends paid: Income - semi-annually; Capital gains - annually
Portfolio turnover (3 yrs): 82%, 42%, 47%
Management fee: 1.00%
Administration fee: 0.20%
Expense ratio: 1.45% (year ending 3/31/97) (1.52% without waiver)

EXCELSIOR REAL ESTATE FUND ◆
(See first Excelsior listing for data common to all funds)

Portfolio managers: Joan Ellis (1997), Katherine Ellis (1997)
Investment objective and policies: Current income and long-term capital appreciation. Invests primarily in hybrid and equity REITs, and other companies principally engaged in the real estate business. Fund is non-diversified. May invest without limit in foreign securities, both directly and through sponsored and unsponsored ADRs. May also invest up to 35% of assets in other types of securities, including investment grade debt and warrants, and use options and futures in an effort to enhance performance and for hedging purposes.
Year organized: 1997
Ticker symbol: UMREX
Group fund code: 834
Discount broker availability: *White
Dividends paid: Income - annually; Capital gains - annually
Management fee: 0.75%
Administration fee: 0.20% first $200M to 0.15% over $400M

EXCELSIOR SHORT-TERM GOVERNMENT SECURITIES FUND ◆

(See first Excelsior listing for data common to all funds)

Portfolio manager: G. Michael O'Neill III (1996)
Investment objective and policies: High current income consistent with stability of principal. Invests primarily in debt obligations issued or guaranteed by the U.S. Government, its agencies or instrumentalities, and repurchase agreements collateralized thereon. Invests with a view toward providing interest income which generally should be exempt from state and local personal income taxes in most states. Portfolio maintains a dollar-weighted average maturity of one to three years.
Year organized: 1992
Ticker symbol: UMGVX
Group fund code: 823
Discount broker availability: *Fidelity, *White
Dividends paid: Income - declared daily, paid monthly; Capital gains - annually
Portfolio turnover (3 yrs): 82%, 77%, 198%
Management fee: 0.30%
Administration fee: 0.20% first $200M to 0.15% over $400M
Expense ratio: 0.61% (year ending 3/31/97) (0.70% without waiver)

EXCELSIOR SHORT-TERM TAX EXEMPT SECURITIES FUND ◆

(See first Excelsior listing for data common to all funds)

Portfolio manager: Kenneth J. McAlley (1995)
Investment objective and policies: High current interest income exempt from regular federal income tax, consistent with relative stability of principal. Invests substantially all its assets in municipal obligations. Portfolio generally maintains a dollar-weighted average maturity of one to three years, although there is no restriction on the remaining maturity of any individual issue. May use futures contracts for hedging purposes.
Year organized: 1992
Ticker symbol: USSSX
Group fund code: 825
Discount broker availability: *Fidelity, *White
Dividends paid: Income - declared daily, paid monthly; Capital gains - annually
Portfolio turnover (3 yrs): 87%, 124%, 565%
Management fee: 0.30%
Administration fee: 0.20% first $200M to 0.15% over $400M
Expense ratio: 0.58% (year ending 3/31/97) (0.65% without waiver)

EXCELSIOR SMALL CAP FUND ◆

(See first Excelsior listing for data common to all funds)

Portfolio managers: John J. Knox (1997), Kenneth R. Marcus (1997)
Investment objective and policies: Long-term capital appreciation. Invests at least 65% of assets in equity securities of companies with market capitalizations of under $1B that are perceived to be undervalued or overlooked. May also invest in larger companies involved in new or potentially higher growth operations. May invest up to 35% of assets in securities of other types such as investment grade debt, warrants, options and futures. May invest without limit in foreign securities, both directly and through ADRs, and engage in foreign currency exchange transactions for hedging purposes.
Year organized: 1992 (previously known as the Early Life Cycle Fund)
Ticker symbol: UMLCX
Group fund code: 812
Discount broker availability: Fidelity, *White
Dividends paid: Income - quarterly; Capital gains - annually
Portfolio turnover (3 yrs): 55%, 38%, 42%
Management fee: 0.60%
Administration fee: 0.20% first $200M to 0.15% over $400M
Expense ratio: 0.94% (year ending 3/31/97) (1.02% without waiver)

EXCELSIOR TAX EXEMPT MONEY FUND ◆

(See first Excelsior listing for data common to all funds)

Investment objective and policies: Moderate level of current income exempt from regular federal income tax, consistent with liquidity and stability of principal. Invests in high quality, short-term municipal securities.
Year organized: 1985
Ticker symbol: USSXX
Group fund code: 806
Dividends paid: Income - declared daily, paid monthly; Capital gains - annually
Management fee: 0.25%
Administration fee: 0.20% first $200M to 0.15% over $400M
Expense ratio: 0.47% (year ending 3/31/97) (0.52% without waiver)

EXCELSIOR TREASURY MONEY FUND ◆

(See first Excelsior listing for data common to all funds)

Investment objective and policies: Current income, consistent with liquidity and stability of principal. Invests at least 65% of assets directly in short-term U.S. Treasuries, with a view towards providing interest income that is generally exempt from state and local income taxes.
Year organized: 1991
Ticker symbol: UTTXX
Group fund code: 811
Dividends paid: Income - declared daily, paid monthly; Capital gains - annually
Management fee: 0.30%
Administration fee: 0.20% first $200M to 0.15% over $400M
Expense ratio: 0.52% (year ending 3/31/97) (0.54% without waiver)

EXCELSIOR VALUE AND RESTRUCTURING FUND ◆

(See first Excelsior listing for data common to all funds)

Portfolio manager: David J. Williams (1992)
Investment objective and policies: Long-term capital appreciation. Invests at least 65% of assets in equity securities of companies of all sizes that are perceived to be undervalued and are undergoing reorganization or redeployment, such as mergers, consolidations, liquidations, etc. May invest up to 35% of assets in securities of other types such as investment grade debt, warrants, options and futures. May invest without limit in foreign securities, both directly and through ADRs, and engage in foreign currency exchange transactions for hedging purposes.
Year organized: 1992 (previously known as the Business and Industrial Restructuring Fund)
Ticker symbol: UMBIX
Group fund code: 818
Discount broker availability: *Fidelity, *Schwab, *White
Dividends paid: Income - quarterly; Capital gains - annually
Portfolio turnover (3 yrs): 62%, 56%, 82%
Management fee: 0.60%
Administration fee: 0.20% first $200M to 0.15% over $400M
Expense ratio: 0.91% (year ending 3/31/97) (0.95% without waiver)

FAIRMONT FUND ◆

1346 S. Third Street
Louisville, KY 40208
800-262-9936, 502-636-5633
fax 502-634-6025
Internet: http://www.fairmontfund.com
e-mail: fund@sachs.win.net

Adviser: The Sachs Co.
Portfolio manager: Morton H. Sachs (1981)
Transfer agent: The Fairmont Fund Trust

Investment objective and policies: Capital appreciation. Invests in equity securities of established companies perceived to be undervalued. Seeks out securities selling at a discount from historical prices and/or at below average price/earnings ratios. Up to 25% of assets may be in ADRs of foreign issuers.
Year organized: 1981 (3 for 1 split on 2/15/90, 4 for 1 split 11/30/86)
Ticker symbol: FAIMX
Minimum purchase: Initial: $1,000, Subsequent: None
Wire orders accepted: Yes
Deadline for same day wire purchase: 4 P.M.
Discount broker availability: Fidelity, Siebert, *White
Qualified for sale in: All states except AK, AZ, AR, DE, ID, IA, KS, LA, ME, MT, NE, NH, ND, OK, RI, SC, UT, VT, WV
Letter redemptions: Signature guarantee not required
Dividends paid: Income - December; Capital gains - December
Portfolio turnover (3 yrs): 183%, 237%, 247%
Shareholder services: IRA
Management fee: 2.00% first $10M to 1.00% over $30M (Advisor pays all expenses)
Expense ratio: 1.63% (year ending 12/31/97)
IRA fees: Annual $12, Initial $12

FAIRPORT FUNDS

(Data common to all Fairport funds are shown below. See subsequent listings for data specific to individual funds. Fund family was previously the Roulston Funds.)

4000 Chester Avenue
Cleveland, OH 44103
800-332-6459, 216-431-1000
prices/yields 610-239-4717
fax 216-431-3681, 610-239-4927
Internet: http://www.fairport.com
e-mail: chuckkiraly@roulston.com

Shareholder service hours: Full service: M-F 9 A.M.-7 P.M. EST; After hours service: prices, yields, account balances, orders, last transaction, messages, prospectuses
Adviser: Roulston & Co., Inc.
Administrator and transfer agent: First Data Investor Services Group
Minimum purchase: Initial: $250, Subsequent: $50
Wire orders accepted: Yes
Deadline for same day wire purchase: 4 P.M.
Qualified for sale in: All states
Telephone redemptions: Yes
Wire redemptions: Yes, $9 fee
Letter redemptions: Signature guarantee required over $25,000
Telephone switching: With other Fairport funds or Kemper Cash Account Trust money market fund
Number of switches permitted: Unlimited
Shareholder services: IRA, 401(k), directed dividends, electronic funds transfer, systematic withdrawal plan min. bal. req. $10,000
Administration fee: 0.19% first $50M to 0.06% over $100M
12b-1 distribution fee: 0.25%
IRA fees: Annual $25

FAIRPORT GOVERNMENT SECURITIES FUND

(See first Fairport listing for data common to all funds)

Portfolio managers: Joseph A. Harrison (1993), D. Keith Lockyer (1993)
Investment objective and policies: Current income consistent with capital preservation. Invests at least 65% of assets in mid- to intermediate-term fixed-income securities issued by the U.S. Government, its agencies and instrumentalities. Remainder of assets may be in corporate debt securities, short-term bank obligations, and U.S. dollar denominated debt securities of foreign government issuers. Fund maintains a dollar-weighted average maturity of three to ten years. May use options for hedging purposes.
Year organized: 1993
Ticker symbol: FPGSX

Discount broker availability: *Schwab, *White
Dividends paid: Income - declared daily, paid monthly; Capital gains - December
Portfolio turnover (3 yrs): 21%, 21%, 1%
Management fee: 0.25% first $100M, 0.125% over $100M
Expense ratio: 0.90% (year ending 10/31/97) (2.70% without waiver)

FAIRPORT GROWTH AND INCOME FUND
(See first Fairport listing for data common to all funds)

Portfolio managers: Joseph A. Harrison (1993), Elmer L. Meszaros (1997)
Investment objective and policies: Capital appreciation and current income. Invests primarily in common stocks of U.S. issuers but may also invest in warrants, rights and debt securities and convertible preferred stocks and U.S. dollar-denominated securities of foreign issuers, including ADRs. May use options for hedging purposes.
Year organized: 1993
Ticker symbol: FPGIX
Discount broker availability: *Schwab, *White
Dividends paid: Income - June, December; Capital gains - December
Portfolio turnover (3 yrs): 42%, 34%, 13%
Management fee: 0.75% first $100M, 0.50% over $100M
Expense ratio: 1.50% (year ending 10/31/97) (1.76% without waiver)

FAIRPORT MIDWEST GROWTH FUND
(See first Fairport listing for data common to all funds)

Portfolio manager: Norman F. Klopp (1993)
Investment objective and policies: Long-term capital appreciation. Invests at least 65% of assets in common stocks of companies headquartered or maintaining a substantial operating presence in the states or areas bordering the Great Lakes. May also invest in warrants, rights and debt securities and convertible preferred stocks and use options for hedging purposes.
Year organized: 1993
Ticker symbol: FPMGX
Discount broker availability: *Schwab, *White
Dividends paid: Income - June, December; Capital gains - December
Portfolio turnover (3 yrs): 41%, 58%, 47%
Management fee: 0.75% first $100M, 0.50% over $100M
Expense ratio: 1.38% (year ending 10/31/97) (1.58% without waiver)

FAM EQUITY INCOME FUND ◆
P.O. Box 399
111 N. Grand Street
Cobleskill, NY 12043
800-932-3271, 518-234-7400
prices/yields 800-453-4392
fax 518-234-7793
Internet: http://www.famfunds.com
e-mail: famfunds@global2000.net

Adviser: Fenimore Asset Management, Inc.
Portfolio managers: Thomas O. Putnam (1996), Paul C. Hogan (1996)
Transfer agent: Fenimore Asset Management Trust
Investment objective and policies: Maximum total return: capital appreciation and dividend income. Invests primarily in income-producing common stocks, but may also acquire convertible bonds and convertible preferred stocks with a bias toward small cap issues. Selects stocks of companies believed undervalued, with a favorable price to value relationship, as well as a focus on dividend yield. Does not utilize options or futures.
Year organized: 1996
Minimum purchase: Initial: $10,000, Subsequent: $50; IRA: Initial: $2,000
Wire orders accepted: Yes
Deadline for same day wire purchase: 4 P.M.
Discount broker availability: *Fidelity, *Schwab, *Siebert, *White

Qualified for sale in: All states
Letter redemptions: Signature guarantee required over $10,000
Dividends paid: Income - December; Capital gains - December
Portfolio turnover (1 yr): 16%
Shareholder services: IRA, SEP-IRA, 403(b), automatic investment plan, systematic withdrawal plan
Management fee: 1.00%
Expense ratio: 1.50% (year ending 12/31/97)
IRA fees: Annual $15 (waived for accounts over $10,000)

FAM VALUE FUND ◆
P.O. Box 399
111 N. Grand Street
Cobleskill, NY 12043
800-932-3271, 518-234-7400
prices/yields 800-453-4392
fax 518-234-7793
Internet: http://www.famfunds.com
e-mail: famfunds@global2000.net

Adviser: Fenimore Asset Management, Inc.
Portfolio managers: Thomas O. Putnam (1987), Diane C. Van Buren (1987)
Transfer agent: Fenimore Asset Management Trust
Investment objective and policies: Maximum total return: capital appreciation and dividend income. Invests primarily in income-producing common stocks, but may also acquire convertible bonds and convertible preferred stocks with a bias toward small cap issues. Selects stocks of companies believed undervalued, with a favorable price to value relationship, as well as a focus on dividend yield. Does not utilize options or futures.
Year organized: 1987
Ticker symbol: FAMVX
Minimum purchase: Initial: $2,000, Subsequent: $50; IRA: Initial: $100; Automatic investment plan: Initial: $500
Wire orders accepted: Yes
Deadline for same day wire purchase: 4 P.M.
Discount broker availability: *Fidelity, *Schwab, *Siebert, *White
Qualified for sale in: All states
Letter redemptions: Signature guarantee required over $10,000
Dividends paid: Income - December; Capital gains - December
Portfolio turnover (3 yrs): 10%, 10%, 2%
Shareholder services: IRA, SEP-IRA, 403(b), systematic withdrawal plan
Management fee: 1.00%
Expense ratio: 1.24% (year ending 12/31/97)
IRA fees: Annual $15 (waived for accounts over $10,000)

FASCIANO FUND ◆
190 South LaSalle Street, Suite 2800
Chicago, IL 60603
800-982-3533, 800-848-6050
312-444-6050, fax 312-444-6011

Adviser: Fasciano Co., Inc.
Portfolio manager: Michael F. Fasciano (1988)
Transfer agent: Firstar Trust Co.
Investment objective and policies: Long-term capital growth; current income secondary. Invests primarily in common stocks and convertible securities of companies with market capitalizations under $1B, believed undervalued in relation to expected sales and earnings increases on the basis of a three to five year horizon. May, however, invest in larger companies thought to offer long-term capital growth potential. May invest directly in foreign securities or by way of ADRs. May enter into forward currency transactions and sell short against the box for hedging purposes.
Year organized: 1988
Ticker symbol: FASCX
Minimum purchase: Initial: $1,000, Subsequent: $100, Automatic investment plan: Initial: $50, Subsequent: $50
Wire orders accepted: Yes
Deadline for same day wire purchase: 4 P.M.
Discount broker availability: *Schwab, White
Qualified for sale in: All states
Letter redemptions: Signature guarantee required over $20,000

Dividends paid: Income - December; Capital gains - December
Portfolio turnover (3 yrs): 41%, 46%, 38%
Shareholder services: IRA, SEP-IRA, systematic withdrawal plan min. bal. req. $10,000
Management fee: 1.00%
Expense ratio: 1.40% (year ending 6/30/97)
IRA fees: Annual $12.50

FBP CONTRARIAN BALANCED FUND ◆
800 Main Street, Suite 202
Lynchburg, VA 24505
800-327-9375, 800-443-4249
804-845-4900, fax 804-846-3846

Adviser: Flippin, Bruce, & Porter, Inc.
Portfolio manager: John T. Bruce (1990)
Transfer agent and administrator: Countrywide Fund Services, Inc.
Investment objective and policies: Long-term capital appreciation and current income. Invests in a balanced portfolio of equity and fixed-income securities, with at least 65% of assets in securities of companies believed undervalued according to a contrarian investment approach. Under normal circumstances 40% to 70% of assets are in equities, 25% to 50% in fixed-income securities and 0% to 35% in money market instruments. Equity assets are normally apportioned 25% to freshly identified contrarian companies, 50% to recovering companies and 25% to recovered companies.
Year organized: 1989 (name changed from FBP Contrarian Fund in 1993)
Ticker symbol: FBPBX
Minimum purchase: Initial: $25,000, Subsequent: $1,000; IRA/Keogh: Initial: $1,000, Subsequent: $300; Automatic investment plan: Subsequent: $100
Wire orders accepted: Yes
Deadline for same day wire purchase: 4 P.M.
Discount broker availability: Schwab
Qualified for sale in: All states except DE, HI, ID, IA, KS, KY, MA, MN, MS, MT, NE, NV, NH, ND, OK, PR, RI, SD, UT, VT, WY
Telephone redemptions: No
Wire redemptions: No
Letter redemptions: Signature guarantee not required
Dividends paid: Income - March, June, September, December; Capital gains - December
Portfolio turnover (3 yrs): 24%, 17%, 14%
Shareholder services: IRA, systematic withdrawal plan min. bal. req. $25,000
Management fee: 0.75% first $250M to 0.50% over $500M
Administration fee: 0.20% first $25M to 0.15% over $50M ($24,000 minimum)
Expense ratio: 1.08% (year ending 3/31/97)
IRA/Keogh fees: None

FBP CONTRARIAN EQUITY FUND ◆
800 Main Street, Suite 202
Lynchburg, VA 24505
800-327-9375, 800-443-4249
804-845-4900, fax 804-846-3846

Adviser: Flippin, Bruce, & Porter, Inc.
Portfolio manager: John T. Bruce (1993)
Transfer agent and administrator: Countrywide Fund Services, Inc.
Investment objective and policies: Long-term growth of capital; current income secondary. Invests primarily in a diversified portfolio of equity securities, with at least 70% of assets in securities of companies believed undervalued according to a contrarian investment approach. Under normal circumstances 70% to 100% of assets are in equities and 0% to 30% in money market instruments. Equity assets are normally apportioned 25% to freshly identified contrarian companies, 50% to recovering companies and 25% to recovered companies.
Year organized: 1993
Minimum purchase: Initial: $25,000, Subsequent: $1,000; IRA/Keogh: Initial: $1,000, Subsequent: $300; Automatic investment plan: Subsequent: $100
Wire orders accepted: Yes
Deadline for same day wire purchase: 4 P.M.
Qualified for sale in: All states except AL, DE, HI, ID, IA, KY, NE, NH, ND, OK, PR, SD, UT, WI, WY

Telephone redemptions: No
Wire redemptions: No
Letter redemptions: Signature guarantee not required
Dividends paid: Income - March, June, September, December; Capital gains - December
Portfolio turnover (3 yrs): 9%, 12%, 9%
Shareholder services: IRA, systematic withdrawal plan min. bal. req. $25,000
Management fee: 0.75% first $250M to 0.50% over $500M
Administration fee: 0.20% first $25M to 0.15% over $50M ($24,000 minimum)
Expense ratio: 1.21% (year ending 3/31/97) (1.25% without waiver)
IRA/Keogh fees: None

FBR FUNDS

(Data common to all FBR funds are shown below. See subsequent listings for data specific to individual funds.)

Potomac Tower
1001 Nineteenth Street North
Arlington, VA 22209-1722
888-888-0025, 800-821-3460
703-469-1200
interactive services 888-200-4710
fax 703-312-9721
Internet: http//www.fbrfunds.com
e-mail: info@fbrfunds.com

Shareholder service hours: Full service: M-F 8:30 A.M.-5:30 P.M. EST; After hours service: prices, prospectuses, total returns
Adviser: FBR Fund Advisers, Inc., an affiliate of Freidman, Billings, Ramsey & Co., Inc. (except MM)
Administrator: Bear Stearns Funds Management, Inc. (except MM)
Transfer agent: PFPC Inc.
Special sales restrictions: Effective 3/23/98, funds became multi-class load funds; shareholders of record prior to this date may continue to buy this class of shares at NAV.
Minimum purchase: Initial: $2,000; Subsequent: $100; IRA: Initial: $1,000
Wire orders accepted: Yes ($2,500 minimum for MM)
Deadline for same day wire purchase: 4:15 P.M. (12 NN for MM)
Qualified for sale in: All states except AZ, ID
Telephone redemption: Yes
Wire redemptions: Yes, $10,000 minimum, $15 fee
Letter redemptions: Signature guarantee required over $10,000
Redemption fee: 1.00% for shares held less than 90 days, payable to the fund
Telephone switching: With other FBR funds, and the FBR Money Market portfolio (Bedford Class shares of the RBB Fund), $100 minimum
Deadline for same day switch: 4:15 P.M. EST
Number of switches permitted: Unlimited
Shareholder services: IRA, automatic investment plan, directed dividends, systematic withdrawal plan min. bal. req. $10,000
Administration fee: 0.075% first $250M, 0.050% over $250M ($75,000 minimum)
IRA fees: Annual $10

FBR FINANCIAL SERVICES FUND

(See first FBR listing for data common to all funds)

Portfolio manager: David Ellison (1997)
Investment objective and policies: Capital appreciation. Normally invests at least 65% of assets in equity securities of companies providing both commercial and consumer financial services, as well as in securities of information and technology companies that provide services to the financial services industry. Will generally attempt to invest in companies with market capitalizations of less than $500M at the time of purchase. May, however, invest in debt securities without limit. May invest in foreign issues, short sales, and may use options and futures and various other derivative instruments.
Year organized: 1997
Ticker symbol: FBRFX

Discount broker availability: *Fidelity, *Schwab, *White
Dividends paid: Income - December; Capital gains - December
Portfolio turnover (1 yr): 50%
Management fee: 0.90%
12b-1 distribution fee: 0.25%
Expense ratio: 1.65% (ten months ending 10/31/97) (3.07% without waiver)

FBR MONEY MARKET FUND

(See first FBR listing for data common to all funds)

Adviser: PNC Institutional Management Corp.
Sub-adviser: PNC Bank, N.A.
Administrator: PNC Institutional Management Corp.
Investment objective and policies: High current income consistent with maintenance of liquidity and stability of principal. Shares represented here are "Bedford Shares," a class of shares which is a subset of the RBB Money Market Portfolio. Invests in a diversified portfolio of U.S. dollar-denominated money market instruments.
Year organized: 1988 (The Bedford Shares began in 1997)
Ticker symbol: BDMXX
Check redemptions: $250 minimum
Dividends paid: Income - declared daily, paid monthly
Management fee: 0.45% first $250M to 0.35% over $500M
12b-1 distribution fee: Maximum of 0.65%
Expense ratio: 0.97% (year ending 8/31/96) (1.14% without waiver)

FBR SMALL CAP FINANCIAL FUND

(See first FBR listing for data common to all funds)

Portfolio manager: David Ellison (1997)
Investment objective and policies: Capital appreciation. Normally invests at least 65% of assets in equity securities of companies providing both commercial and consumer financial services, focusing primarily on those investing in real estate through mortgages or other consumer loans. Will generally invest in companies with market capitalizations below $750M, and will focus particularly on companies with market capitalizations below $200M. May, however, invest in debt securities without limit. May invest in foreign issues, short sales, and may use options and futures and various other derivative instruments.
Year organized: 1997
Ticker symbol: FBRSX
Discount broker availability: *Fidelity, *Schwab, *White
Dividends paid: Income - December; Capital gains - December
Portfolio turnover (1 yr): 35%
Management fee: 0.90%
12b-1 distribution fee: 0.25%
Expense ratio: 1.65% (ten months ending 10/31/97) (3.08% without waiver)

FBR SMALL CAP GROWTH/VALUE FUND

(See first FBR listing for data common to all funds)

Portfolio manager: Charles T. Akre, Jr. (1997)
Investment objective and policies: Capital appreciation. Invests primarily in equity securities of companies with market capitalizations below $1B that are perceived to be undervalued but have a demonstrated record of achievement. May, however, invest in debt securities without limit. May invest in foreign issues, short sales, and may use options and futures and various other derivative instruments. Fund is non-diversified.
Year organized: 1997
Discount broker availability: *Fidelity, *Schwab, *White
Dividends paid: Income - December; Capital gains - December
Portfolio turnover (1 yr): 43%
Management fee: 0.90%
12b-1 distribution fee: 0.25%
Expense ratio: 1.65% (ten months ending 10/31/97) (5.49% without waiver)

FEDERATED FUNDS

(Data common to all Federated funds are shown below. See subsequent listings for data specific to individual funds.)

Federated Investors Tower
Pittsburgh, PA 15222-3779
800-341-7400, 800-245-2423
412-288-1948
fax 412-288-1982
Internet: http://www.federatedinvestors.com

Shareholder service hours: Full service: M-F 9 A.M.-5 P.M. EST
Adviser: Federated Management
Transfer agent: Federated Services Co.
Classes of shares: Some Federated funds offer Institutional Shares (sold directly without 12b-1 distribution fees) and Institutional Service Shares (sold to banks and other financial institutions with varying 12b-1 distribution fees). Where such multiple classes exist, data shown in listings are for Institutional shares.
Special sales restrictions: Designed for corporate investors, banks in a fiduciary, advisory, agency or custodial capacity, but open to individuals.
Minimum purchase: Initial: $25,000 (Institutional Shares, 90 days to achieve minimum level), $5,000 (Institutional Service Shares); Subsequent: $100; IRA/Keogh: Initial: $50; Subsequent: $50
Wire orders accepted: Yes
Deadline for same day wire purchase: 3 P.M.
Qualified for sale in: All states
Telephone redemption: Yes
Wire redemptions: Yes, $1,000 minimum
Letter redemptions: Signature guarantee required over $50,000

FEDERATED ARMS FUND ◆

(See first Federated listing for data common to all funds)

Portfolio managers: Kathleen M. Foody-Malus (1992), Susan M. Nason (1993), Todd A. Abraham (1995)
Investment objective and policies: Current income consistent with minimal volatility of principal. Invests at least 65% of assets in adjustable and floating rate mortgage securities issued or guaranteed as to payment of principal and interest by the U.S. Government, its agencies or instrumentalities. May invest in other government obligations and mortgage-related securities issued by private entities such as banks and companies related to the construction industry.
Year organized: 1985 (objective changed on 1/31/92 and name changed from U.S. Government Fund on 4/23/92. Prior performance may be misleading.)
Ticker symbols: FEUGX (Institutional), FASSX (Institutional Service)
Discount broker availability: *Fidelity, *Schwab, *Siebert, *White
Dividends paid: Income - declared daily, paid monthly; Capital gains - December
Management fee: 0.60%
Administration fee: 0.15% first $250M to 0.075% over $750M
Shareholder services fee: 0.25% (Institutional Service shares only)
Expense ratio: 0.55% (year ending 8/31/97)

FEDERATED BOND INDEX FUND ◆

(See first Federated listing for data common to all funds)

Sub-adviser: U.S. Trust Co. of New York
Portfolio manager: Susan M. Nason (1995)
Investment objective and policies: To provide investment results that correspond to the investment performance of the Lehman Brothers Aggregate Bond Index, a broad market-weighted index which encompasses U.S. Treasury and agency securities, corporate investment grade bonds, and mortgage-backed securities. Fund invests its entire asset base in a master feeder portfolio with exactly the same objectives and policies, however, the portfolio will not hold every issue in the index, but will attempt to hold a representative sample of the issues whose performance will correlate by a factor of at least 0.95.

Year organized: 1995
Ticker symbol: BDXIX (Institutional), BDXSX (Institutional Service)
Discount broker availability: Schwab (only through financial advisers)
Dividends paid: Income - declared daily, paid monthly; Capital gains - December
Portfolio turnover (2 yrs): 49%, 43%
Management fee: 0.60%
Administration fee: 0.10% first $250M to 0.070% over $750M
Shareholder services fee: 0.25% (Institutional Service shares only)
Expense ratio: 0.29% (year ending 5/31/97) (2.02% without waiver)

FEDERATED GNMA TRUST ◆
(See first Federated listing for data common to all funds)

Portfolio managers: Kathleen M. Foody-Malus (1993), Edward J. Tiedge (1995)
Investment objective and policies: Current income. Invests in U.S. Government obligations, with at least 65% of assets in instruments issued or guaranteed by the Government National Mortgage Association.
Year organized: 1982 (formerly Federated Government Trust)
Ticker symbols: FGMAX (Institutional), FGSSX (Institutional Service)
Discount broker availability: *Fidelity, *Schwab, *Siebert, *White
Dividends paid: Income - declared daily, paid monthly: Capital gains - December
Portfolio turnover (3 yrs): 63%, 43%, 136%
Management fee: 0.40%
Administration fee: 0.15% first $250M to 0.075% over $750M
Shareholder services fee: Maximum of 0.25%
Expense ratio: 0.60% (year ending 1/31/97) (0.80% without waiver)

FEDERATED HIGH YIELD TRUST ◆
(See first Federated listing for data common to all funds)

Portfolio managers: Mark E. Durbiano (1984), William F. Stotz (1997)
Investment objective and policies: High current income. Invests primarily in a diversified portfolio of lower-rated (BBB or lower) fixed rate corporate debt obligations. Up to 15% of assets may be in illiquid securities and 10% in foreign securities not publicly traded in the U.S. May use options in an effort to enhance returns and for hedging purposes.
Year organized: 1984
Ticker symbol: FHYTX
Discount broker availability: *Fidelity, *Schwab, *Siebert, *White
Dividends paid: Income - declared daily, paid monthly; Capital gains - December
Portfolio turnover (3 yrs): 81%, 87%, 99%
Management fee: 0.75%
Administration fee: 0.15% first $250M to 0.075% over $750M
Shareholder services fee: Maximum of 0.25%
Expense ratio: 0.88% (year ending 2/28/97) (1.16% without waiver)

FEDERATED INCOME TRUST ◆
(See first Federated listing for data common to all funds)

Portfolio managers: Kathleen M. Foody-Malus (1990), Edward J. Tiedge (1995)
Investment objective and policies: Current income. Invests exclusively in U.S. Government and agency securities and certain collateralized mortgage obligations (CMOs).
Year organized: 1982
Ticker symbols: FICMX (Institutional), FITSX (Institutional Service)
Discount broker availability: *Fidelity, *Schwab, *Siebert, *White

Dividends paid: Income - Declared daily, paid monthly; Capital gains - December
Portfolio turnover (3 yrs): 212%, 184%, 217%
Management fee: 0.40%
Administration fee: 0.15% first $250M to 0.075% over $750M
Shareholder services fee: Maximum of 0.25% (Institutional Service shares only)
Expense ratio: 0.58% (year ending 1/31/97)

FEDERATED INTERMEDIATE INCOME FUND ◆
(See first Federated listing for data common to all funds)

Portfolio managers: Susan M. Nason (1993), Joseph M. Balestrino (1994), John T. Gentry (1997)
Investment objective and policies: Current income. Invests exclusively in debt securities rated in one of the highest three categories by the nationally recognized rating organizations at the time of purchase. Securities subsequently downgraded may continue to be held at advisors discretion. Portfolio will normally maintain a dollar-weighted average maturity of three to ten years.
Year organized: 1993
Ticker symbols: FIIFX (Institutional), INISX (Institutional Service)
Discount broker availability: Fidelity, *Schwab, *White
Dividends paid: Income - declared daily, paid monthly; Capital gains - December
Portfolio turnover (3 yrs): 55%, 66%, 88%
Management fee: 0.50%
Administration fee: 0.15% first $250M to 0.075% over $750M
Expense ratio: 0.55% (year ending 4/30/97) (1.12% without waiver)

FEDERATED INTERMEDIATE MUNICIPAL TRUST ◆
(See first Federated listing for data common to all funds)

Portfolio managers: J. Scott Albrecht (1995), Mary Jo Ochson (1997)
Investment objective and policies: Current income exempt from federal income tax. Invests at least 80% of assets in municipal securities. Fund maintains a dollar-weighted average maturity of three to ten years. Up to 15% of assets may be in illiquid securities.
Year organized: 1985
Ticker symbol: FIMTX
Discount broker availability: *Fidelity, *Schwab, *Siebert, White
Dividends paid: Income - declared daily, paid monthly; Capital gains - December
Portfolio turnover (3 yrs): 33%, 19%, 11%
Management fee: 0.40%
Administration fee: 0.15% first $250M to 0.075% over $750M
Expense ratio: 0.57% (year ending 5/31/97) (1.03% without waiver)

FEDERATED MANAGED AGGRESSIVE GROWTH FUND ◆
(See first Federated listing for data common to all funds)

Lead portfolio manager: Charles A. Ritter (1994)
Investment objective and policies: Capital growth. Allocates investments among asset categories within predetermined ranges to maximize return as market conditions change. Invests 70% to 90% of assets in stocks, using large companies (40% to 60%); small companies (10% to 20%); and foreign companies (10% to 20%). Invests 10% to 30% in bonds, using U.S. Treasury securities (0% to 20%); mortgage-backed securities (0% to 10%); investment grade corporate bonds (0% to 10%); high-yield corporate bonds (0% to 10%); and foreign bonds (0% to 10%). Remaining 0% to 20% of assets will be in cash equivalents.
Year organized: 1994
Ticker symbol: FMGGX (Institutional), FMASX (Select)

Special sales information: Select shares are available for this fund with lower ($1,500) investment minimums; however, they carry a 0.50% 12b-1 fee.
Discount broker availability: *Fidelity, *Schwab, *Siebert, *White
Dividends paid: Income - March, June, September, December; Capital gains - December
Portfolio turnover (3 yrs): 86%, 139%, 77%
Management fee: 0.75%
Administration fee: 0.15% first $250M to 0.075% over $750M
Shareholder services fee: Maximum of 0.25%
Expense ratio: 1.05% (year ending 11/30/97) (includes waiver)

FEDERATED MANAGED GROWTH FUND ◆
(See first Federated listing for data common to all funds)

Lead portfolio manager: Charles A. Ritter (1994)
Investment objective and policies: Capital growth; current income secondary. Allocates investments among asset categories within predetermined ranges to maximize return as market conditions change. Invests 50% to 70% of assets in stocks using large companies (30% to 50%), small companies (5% to 15%), and foreign companies (5% to 15%). Invests 30% to 50% in bonds using U.S. Treasury securities (0% to 40%), mortgage-backed securities (0% to 15%), investment grade corporate bonds (0% to 15%), high-yield corporate bonds (0% to 15%) and foreign bonds (0% to 15%). Mandates regarding cash equivalents and utility stocks have been removed.
Year organized: 1994
Ticker symbol: FMGFX (Institutional), MGFUX (Select)
Special sales information: Select shares are available for this fund with lower ($1,500) investment minimums; however, they carry a 0.50% 12b-1 fee.
Discount broker availability: *Fidelity, *Schwab, *Siebert, *White
Dividends paid: Income - March, June, September, December; Capital gains - December
Portfolio turnover (3 yrs): 95%, 106%, 71%
Management fee: 0.75%
Administration fee: 0.15% first $250M to 0.075% over $750M
Shareholder services fee: Maximum of 0.25%
Expense ratio: 1.05% (year ending 11/30/97) (includes waiver)

FEDERATED MANAGED GROWTH AND INCOME FUND ◆
(See first Federated listing for data common to all funds)

Lead portfolio manager: Charles A. Ritter (1994)
Investment objective and policies: Current income and capital growth. Allocates investments among asset categories within predetermined ranges to maximize return as market conditions change. Invests 30% to 50% of assets in stocks using large companies (22.5% to 37.5%), utilities (2.5% to 7.5%), small companies (0% to 5%), and foreign companies (0% to 5%). Invests 50% to 70% in bonds using U.S. Treasury securities (0% to 56%), mortgage-backed securities (0% to 35%), investment grade corporate bonds (0% to 35%), high-yield corporate bonds (0% to 10%) and foreign bonds (0% to 10%). Mandate regarding cash reserve has been removed.
Year organized: 1994
Ticker symbol: FMRIX (Institutional), MGIFX (Select)
Special sales information: Select shares are available for this fund with lower ($1,500) investment minimums; however, they carry a 0.50% 12b-1 fee.
Discount broker availability: *Fidelity, *Schwab, *Siebert, *White
Dividends paid: Income - March, June, September, December; Capital gains - December
Portfolio turnover (3 yrs): 154%, 157%, 132%
Management fee: 0.75%
Administration fee: 0.15% first $250M to 0.075% over $750M
Shareholder services fee: Maximum of 0.25%
Expense ratio: 1.05% (year ending 11/30/97) (includes waiver)

FEDERATED MANAGED INCOME FUND ◆

(See first Federated listing for data common to all funds)

Lead portfolio manager: Charles A. Ritter (1994)
Investment objective and policies: Current income. Allocates investments among asset categories within predetermined ranges to maximize return as market conditions change. Invests 10% to 30% of assets in stocks using large companies (7.5% to 22.5%) and utilities (2.5% to 7.5%) Invests 70% to 90% in bonds using U.S. Treasury securities (0% to 72%), mortgage-backed securities (0% to 45%), investment grade corporate bonds (0% to 45%), high-yield corporate bonds (0% to 10%) and foreign bonds (0% to 10%). Mandate regarding cash reserves has been removed.
Year organized: 1994
Ticker symbol: FMIFX (Institutional), MINFX (Select)
Special sales information: Select shares are available for this fund with lower ($1,500) investment minimums; however, they carry a 0.50% 12b-1 fee.
Discount broker availability: *Fidelity, *Schwab, *Siebert, *White
Dividends paid: Income - declared and paid monthly; Capital gains - December
Management fee: 0.75%
Administration fee: 0.15% first $250M to 0.075% over $750M
Shareholder services fee: Maximum of 0.25%
Expense ratio: 0.80% (year ending 11/30/97) (includes waiver)

FEDERATED MAX-CAP FUND ◆

(See first Federated listing for data common to all funds)

Sub-adviser: ANB Investment Management and Trust Co.
Portfolio manager: Thomas Franks (1995)
Investment objective and policies: Total return: income and capital appreciation that correspond to the price and dividend performance of the S&P 500 Composite Stock Price Index. Normally invests at least 80% of assets in the stocks that comprise the S&P 500 Index with goal of achieving a total return correlation of between 0.95 and 1.00 with the performance of the Index.
Year organized: 1990 (name changed from S&P 500 Fund on 8/23/91)
Ticker symbols: FISPX (Institutional), FMXSX (Institutional Service)
Special sales information: Fund also has a new "Class C" share with lower ($10,000) initial minimums; however, it has a 1.00% redemption fee for shares held less than 2 months, and a 0.75% 12b-1 fee.
Discount broker availability: *Fidelity, Schwab, Siebert, *White
Dividends paid: Income - March, June, September, December; Capital gains - December
Portfolio turnover (3 yrs): 3%, 57%, 2%
Management fee: 0.30%
Shareholder services fee: Maximum of 0.25%
Expense ratio: 0.31% (year ending 10/31/97) (includes waiver)

FEDERATED MID-CAP FUND ◆

(See first Federated listing for data common to all funds)

Sub-adviser: ANB Investment Management and Trust Co.
Portfolio manager: Thomas Franks (1995)
Investment objective and policies: Total return: income and capital appreciation that corresponds to the price and dividend performance of the S&P 400 Mid-Cap Index of companies with market capitalization of $200M-$5B. Normally invests at least 80% of assets in the stocks that comprise the S&P 400 Mid-Cap Index with goal of achieving a total return correlation of between 0.95 and 1.00 with the performance of the Index.
Year organized: 1992
Ticker symbol: FMDCX
Discount broker availability: Fidelity, *Schwab, Siebert, *White

Dividends paid: Income - March, June, September, December; Capital gains - December
Portfolio turnover (3 yrs): 17%, 26%, 30%
Management fee: 0.40%
Shareholder services fee: Maximum of 0.25%
Expense ratio: 0.60% (year ending 10/31/97) (includes waiver)

FEDERATED MINI-CAP FUND ◆

(See first Federated listing for data common to all funds)

Sub-adviser: ANB Investment Management and Trust Co.
Portfolio manager: Thomas Franks (1995)
Investment objective and policies: Total return: income and capital appreciation that corresponds to the price and dividend performance of the Russell 2000 Index of small capitalization stocks. Normally invests at least 80% of assets in the stocks that comprise the Russell 2000 Index with goal of achieving a total return correlation of between 0.95 and 1.00 with the performance of the Index.
Year organized: 1992
Ticker symbol: FMCPX
Special sales information: Fund also has a new "Class C" share with lower ($10,000) initial minimums; however, it has a 1.00% redemption fee for shares held less than 2 months, and a 0.75% 12b-1 fee.
Discount broker availability: *Fidelity, *Schwab, Siebert, *White
Dividends paid: Income - March, June, September, December; Capital gains - December
Portfolio turnover (3 yrs): 42%, 42%, 32%
Management fee: 0.50%
Shareholder services fee: Maximum of 0.25%
Expense ratio: 0.82% (year ending 10/31/97) (includes waiver)

FEDERATED OHIO INTERMEDIATE MUNICIPAL TRUST ◆

(Fund merged into Federated OH Municipal Income Fund, a multi-class load fund, 7/14/97)

FEDERATED PENNSYLVANIA INTERMEDIATE MUNICIPAL TRUST ◆

(See first Federated listing for data common to all funds)

Portfolio manager: J. Scott Albrecht (1993)
Investment objective and policies: Current income exempt from regular federal income tax and the personal income taxes imposed by the Commonwealth of Pennsylvania. Invests at least 80% of its assets in a non-diversified portfolio of Pennsylvania municipal securities. Trust has a dollar-weighted average maturity of three to ten years.
Year organized: 1993
Ticker symbol: PIMTX
Discount broker availability: Fidelity, *Schwab, Siebert, *White
Dividends paid: Income - declared daily, paid monthly; Capital gains - December
Management fee: 0.50%
Administration fee: 0.15% first $250M to 0.075% over $750M
Expense ratio: 0.45% (year ending 5/31/97) (includes waiver)

FEDERATED SHORT-TERM INCOME FUND ◆

(See first Federated listing for data common to all funds)

Portfolio managers: Randall S. Bauer (1995), Robert K. Kinsey (1997)
Investment objective and policies: Current income. Invests primarily in short and medium-term high grade debt securities, and maintains a dollar-weighted average maturity of three years or less. May invest in corporate debt obligations, asset-backed securities, commercial paper, bank instruments, U.S. dollar denominated foreign debt securities, obligations of the U.S. Government and its agencies and instrumentalities, and money market instruments. Up to 15% of assets may be in illiquid securities.

Year organized: 1986 (name changed from Federated Floating Rate Trust on 12/31/91)
Ticker symbol: FSTIX (Institutional), FSISX (Institutional Service)
Discount broker availability: *Fidelity, *Schwab, *Siebert, *White
Dividends paid: Income - declared daily, paid monthly; Capital gains - December
Portfolio turnover (3 yrs): 55%, 77%, 38%
Management fee: 0.40%
Administration fee: 0.15% first $250M to 0.075% over $750M
Shareholder services fee: Maximum of 0.25%
Expense ratio: 0.56% (year ending 4/30/97) (0.84% without waiver)

FEDERATED SHORT-TERM MUNICIPAL TRUST ◆

(See first Federated listing for data common to all funds)

Portfolio managers: Jeff A. Kozemchak (1996), Mary Jo Ochson (1997)
Investment objective and policies: Dividend income exempt from federal regular income tax. Invests in municipal securities, and maintains a dollar-weighted average maturity of less than three years. Up to 15% of assets may be in illiquid securities.
Year organized: 1981 (name changed from Federated Short-Intermediate Municipal Trust in 1993)
Ticker symbols: FSHIX (Institutional), FSHSX (Institutional Service)
Discount broker availability: *Fidelity, *Schwab, *Siebert, *White
Dividends paid: Income - declared daily, paid monthly; Capital gains - December
Portfolio turnover (3 yrs): 50%, 20%, 33%
Management fee: 0.40%
Administration fee: 0.15% first $250M to 0.075% over $750M
Shareholder services fee: Maximum of 0.25%
Expense ratio: 0.47% (year ending 6/30/97)

FEDERATED STOCK TRUST ◆

(See first Federated listing for data common to all funds)

Portfolio managers: Scott B. Schermerhorn (1996), Michael P. Donnelly (1997)
Investment objective and policies: Growth of income and capital. Invests at least 80% of assets in a diversified portfolio of common stocks of high quality companies which are generally perceived to be the leaders in their respective industries. May also invest in other corporate securities of these companies, as well as U.S. Government securities, repurchase agreements, and money market instruments. May invest without limit in ADRs, and invest up to 10% of assets in illiquid securities.
Year organized: 1982
Ticker symbol: FSTKX
Discount broker availability: *Fidelity, *Schwab, Siebert, *White
Dividends paid: Income - quarterly; Capital gains - November
Portfolio turnover (3 yrs): 71%, 55%, 42%
Management fee: 0.75% first 500M to 0.40% over $2B
Administration fee: 0.15% first $250M to 0.075% over $750M
Shareholder services fee: Maximum of 0.25%
Expense ratio: 0.99% (year ending 10/31/97) (1.12% without waiver)

FEDERATED U.S. GOVERNMENT BOND FUND ◆

(See first Federated listing for data common to all funds)

Portfolio managers: Susan M. Nason (1994), Donald T. Ellenberger (1997)
Investment objective and policies: Total return: current income with some capital growth. Invests at least 65% of assets in U.S. Government bonds. May invest up to 10% of assets in restricted securities and use options and hedge up to 25% of total assets.

Year organized: 1985 (formerly Federated Bond Fund. Name and objective changed on 8/30/93)
Ticker symbol: FEDBX
Discount broker availability: Fidelity, *Schwab, Siebert, *White
Dividends paid: Income - declared daily, paid monthly, Capital gains - December
Portfolio turnover (3 yrs): 90%, 53%, 37%
Management fee: 0.60%
Administration fee: 0.15% first $250M to 0.075% over $750M
Shareholder services fee: Maximum of 0.25%
Expense ratio: 0.85% (includes 8/31/97) (1.21% without waiver)

FEDERATED U.S. GOVERNMENT SECURITIES FUND: 1-3 YEARS ◆
(See first Federated listing for data common to all funds)

Portfolio managers: Susan M. Nason (1991), Robert J. Ostrowski (1997)
Investment objective and policies: Current income. Invests in securities issued or guaranteed by the U.S. Government, its agencies or instrumentalities with remaining maturities of 3 1/2 years or less. Up to 15% of assets may be in illiquid securities.
Year organized: 1984 (name changed from Short-Intermediate Government Trust 5/1/95)
Ticker symbol: FSGVX (Institutional), FSGIX (Institutional Service)
Discount broker availability: *Fidelity, *Schwab, *Siebert, *White
Dividends paid: Income - declared daily, paid monthly; Capital gains - December
Portfolio turnover (3 yrs): 145%, 142%, 265%
Management fee: 0.40%
Administration fee: 0.15% first $250M to 0.075% over $750M
Shareholder services fee: Maximum of 0.25%
Expense ratio: 0.54% (year ending 2/28/97) (0.81% without waiver)

FEDERATED U.S. GOVERNMENT SECURITIES FUND: 2-5 YEARS ◆
(See first Federated listing for data common to all funds)

Portfolio managers: Susan M. Nason (1991), Robert J. Ostrowski (1997)
Investment objective and policies: Current income. Invests in U.S. Government and agency securities with remaining maturities of five years or less. Fund generally maintains a dollar-weighted average maturity of two to five years.
Year organized: 1983 (name changed from Intermediate Government Trust 5/1/95)
Ticker symbol: FIGTX (Institutional), FIGIX (Institutional Service)
Discount broker availability: *Fidelity, *Schwab, *Siebert, *White
Dividends paid: Income - declared daily, paid monthly; Capital gains - December
Portfolio turnover (3 yrs): 99%, 117%, 163%
Management fee: 0.40%
Administration fee: 0.15% first $250M to 0.075% over $750M
Shareholder services fee: Maximum of 0.25%
Expense ratio: 0.54% (year ending 1/31/97) (0.80% without waiver)

FEDERATED U.S. GOVERNMENT SECURITIES FUND: 5-10 YEARS ◆
(See first Federated listing for data common to all funds)

Portfolio managers: Susan M. Nason (1995), Donald T. Ellenberger (1997)
Investment objective and policies: Total return consistent with current income. Invests in U.S. Government and agency securities, and generally maintains a dollar-weighted average maturity of five to ten years, although may purchase securities with longer maturities.
Year organized: 1995
Ticker symbols: FGVIX (Institutional), FGVUX (Institutional Service)

Discount broker availability: Fidelity, *Schwab, Siebert, *White
Dividends paid: Income - declared daily, paid monthly; Capital gains - December
Portfolio turnover (2 yrs): 57%, 29%
Management fee: 0.50%
Administration fee: 0.15% first $250M to 0.075% over $750M
Expense ratio: 0.13% (year ending 2/28/97) (4.08% without waiver)

FIDELITY FUNDS
(Data common to all Fidelity funds are shown below. See subsequent listing for data specific to individual funds.)

82 Devonshire Street
Boston, MA 02109
800-544-8888, 617-523-1919
shareholder services 800-544-6666
exchange/redemptions 800-544-7777
account balances 800-544-7544
fund quotes (shareholders only) 800-544-8544
TDD 800-544-0111
Internet: http://www.fid-inv.com

Shareholder service hours: Full service: 7 days, 24 hours
Adviser: Fidelity Management & Research Co.
Transfer agent: Fidelity Service Co. (exceptions noted)
Minimum purchase: Initial: $2,500, Subsequent: $250; IRA/Keogh: Initial: $500; Automatic investment plan: Subsequent: $100 (exceptions noted)
Wire orders accepted: Yes
Deadline for same day wire purchase: 4 P.M. (exceptions noted)
Qualified for sale in: All states (exceptions noted)
Breakpoint pricing: Fidelity load funds (except Select Money Market and Foreign Currency Portfolios) will have load reduced from 3% to 2% for purchases from $250,000-$499,999; from 2% to 1% for purchases from $500,000-$999,999; and eliminated for purchases over $1M.
Telephone redemptions: Yes, fee may apply
Wire redemptions: Yes, $5,000 minimum, fee may apply
Letter redemptions: Signature guarantee required over $100,000
Telephone switching: With all open Fidelity retail funds except Fidelity Destiny, Congress St., and Exchange Fund, unless otherwise noted; fee may apply.
Number of switches permitted: Reserves right to limit switches to 4 per year (exceptions noted); on 10/18/90, Fidelity instituted a policy of reserving the right to refuse, without prior notice, any exchange which a fund would not be able to invest effectively, applicable to a number of funds normally used by market timers (exceptions noted)
Shareholder services: IRA, SEP-IRA, Keogh, 401(k), 403(b), corporate retirement plans, directed dividends, electronic funds transfer, systematic withdrawal plan min. bal. req. $10,000
Maintenance fee: $12 for each fund under $2,500, maximum of $24 (waived for shareholders with total Fidelity holdings in excess of $30,000, or for those using Fidelity's automatic investment plan.)
IRA/Keogh fees: Annual $12 for each fund under $2,500 (waived for IRA accounts with balances of $2,500 or more, for shareholders with total Fidelity holdings in excess of $30,000, or for those using Fidelity's automatic investment plan), Closing $10

FIDELITY AGGRESSIVE MUNICIPAL FUND ◆
(See Spartan Aggressive Muni; fund changed names 7/31/97)

FIDELITY ASSET MANAGER ◆
(See first Fidelity listing for data common to all funds)

Portfolio managers: Richard C. Habermann (1996), Charles S. Morrison (1997), John J. Todd (1996), Thomas M. Sprague (1998)
Investment objective and policies: High total return with reduced risk over the long term. Allocates its

assets among equities (10%-60% of assets), bonds (20%-70%) and money market instruments (0%-70%). Fund's neutral asset allocation is 50% stocks, 40% bonds, and 10% short-term/money market instruments. May invest up to 20% of assets in foreign equities; use forward, futures and options on futures in currencies; use options, futures and options on futures on stock, stock indexes and interest rates; sell short against the box; and hold zero coupon bonds.
Year organized: 1988
Ticker symbol: FASMX
Group fund code: 314
Discount broker availability: *Fidelity, Schwab, *Siebert, White
Dividends paid: Income - March, June, September, December; Capital gains - December
Portfolio turnover (3 yrs): 79%, 131%, 137%
Management fee: 0.25% plus group fee of 0.25% to 0.52%
Expense ratio: 0.78% (year ending 9/30/97) (0.79% without waiver)

FIDELITY ASSET MANAGER: GROWTH ◆
(See first Fidelity listing for data common to all funds)

Portfolio managers: Richard C. Habermann (1996), Charles S. Morrison (1997), John J. Todd (1996), Bradford F. Lewis (1998)
Investment objective and policies: Maximum long-term total return. Allocates assets among stocks (50%-100%), bonds (0%-50%), and money market instruments (0%-50%). Unlike Fidelity Asset Manager, there is no upper limit on the percent of assets invested in equities. Neutral distribution is 70% stocks, 25% bonds, and 5% short-term/money markets. One to three year maturity debt instruments are included as bonds. Fund may use foreign equities, options, futures and options on futures on stock, stock indexes and interest rates; sell short against the box; and hold zero coupon bonds. Shifts among classes are made gradually over time, with a single reallocation decision generally involving less than 20% of total assets.
Year organized: 1991
Ticker symbol: FASGX
Group fund code: 321
Discount broker availability: *Fidelity, Schwab, *Siebert, White
Dividends paid: Income - December; Capital gains - December
Portfolio turnover (3 yrs): 70%, 138%, 119%
Management fee: 0.30% plus group fee of 0.25% to 0.52%
Expense ratio: 0.86% (year ending 9/30/97) (0.87% without waiver)

FIDELITY ASSET MANAGER: INCOME ◆
(See first Fidelity listing for data common to all funds)

Portfolio managers: Richard C. Habermann (1996), Charles S. Morrison (1997), John J. Todd (1996), Bradford F. Lewis (1998)
Investment objective and policies: High current income. Allocates assets among stocks (10%-30% of assets), bonds (40%-60%), and money market instruments (10%-50%). Fund's neutral asset allocation is 20% stocks, 50% bonds, and 30% short-term/money market instruments. May invest up to 35% of assets in foreign debt securities. May use forward currency contracts, use options and futures, sell short against the box and hold zero coupon bonds.
Year organized: 1992
Ticker symbol: FASIX
Group fund code: 328
Discount broker availability: *Fidelity, Schwab, *Siebert, White
Dividends paid: Income - monthly; Capital gains - December
Portfolio turnover (3 yrs): 112%, 148%, 157%
Management fee: 0.30% plus group fee of 0.11% to 0.37%
Expense ratio: 0.76% (year ending 9/30/97) (0.77% without waiver)

FIDELITY BALANCED FUND ◆
(See first Fidelity listing for data common to all funds)

Portfolio managers: Stephen DuFour (1997), Kevin E. Grant (fixed-income) (1997)
Investment objective and policies: High current income consistent with capital preservation; moderate long-term capital growth secondary. Invests primarily in high yielding securities, including common stocks, preferred stocks and bonds. A neutral portfolio is 60% equities, 40% debt obligations. Debt will be rated the equivalent of Baa or better and always be at least 25% of assets. Fund may use foreign securities without limit and use a variety of derivative instruments for hedging purposes.
Year organized: 1986
Ticker symbol: FBALX
Group fund code: 304
Discount broker availability: *Fidelity, Schwab, *Siebert, White
Dividends paid: Income - March, June, September, December; Capital gains - September, December
Portfolio turnover (3 yrs): 70%, 247%, 269%
Management fee: 0.15% plus group fee of 0.25% to 0.52%
Expense ratio: 0.74% (year ending 7/31/97) (0.75% without waiver)

FIDELITY BLUE CHIP GROWTH FUND
(See first Fidelity listing for data common to all funds)

Portfolio manager: John B. McDowell (1996)
Investment objective and policies: Long-term capital appreciation. Invests at least 65% of assets in a diversified portfolio of well known and established companies with market capitalization of at least $200M if included in the S&P 500 or DJIA, or with capitalization of $1B or more if not listed on the indices. Stocks are chosen that are perceived to offer greater than average long-term earnings growth. Fund may invest in foreign securities, use currency exchange contracts, stock index futures and options on stocks and indexes, and leverage.
Year organized: 1987
Ticker symbol: FBGRX
Group fund code: 312
Sales charge: 3% (may be waived for retirement accounts using Fidelity prototype plans)
Discount broker availability: Fidelity, Schwab, Siebert, White
Redemption fee: Shares purchased before 10/12/90 are subject to a 1% deferred sales charge.
Dividends paid: Income - September, December; Capital gains - September, December
Portfolio turnover (3 yrs): 51%, 206%, 182%
Management fee: 0.30% plus group fee of 0.25% to 0.52% +/- performance fee of up to 0.20% relative to the S&P 500 Index over 36 months
Expense ratio: 0.78% (year ending 7/31/97) (0.80% without waiver)

FIDELITY CALIFORNIA INSURED MUNICIPAL INCOME FUND ◆
(Merged with Fidelity Spartan CA Muni Inc. 8/28/97)

FIDELITY CALIFORNIA MUNICIPAL INCOME FUND ◆
(Became Spartan California Muni Income 8/28/97)

FIDELITY CALIFORNIA MUNICIPAL MONEY MARKET FUND ◆
(See first Fidelity listing for data common to all funds)

Portfolio manager: Diane McLaughlin (1997)
Investment objective and policies: A high level of current income exempt from federal and California state income taxes. Invests in high quality short-term California municipal money market obligations.
Year organized: 1984 (name and objective change 2/2/86. Formerly Short-Term portfolio; name changed from Tax-Free Money Market Portfolio 2/1/96)
Ticker symbol: FCFXX
Group fund code: 097
Minimum purchase: Initial: $5,000, Subsequent: $250
Deadline for same day wire purchase: 12 NN

Discount broker availability: *Fidelity
Qualified for sale in: CA
Check redemptions: $500 minimum
Number of switches permitted: Unlimited
Dividends paid: Income - declared daily, paid monthly
Management fee: 0.25% plus group fee of 0.11% to 0.37%
12b-1 distribution fee: Yes (not currently imposed)
Expense ratio: 0.61% (year ending 2/28/97) (0.62% without waiver)

FIDELITY CANADA FUND
(See first Fidelity listing for data common to all funds)

Portfolio manager: Thomas Sweeney (1996)
Investment objective and policies: Long-term capital growth. Invests at least 65% of assets in equity and debt securities of issuers that have their principal activities in Canada or are registered in Canadian markets. May also invest without limit in U.S. issues. Fund may use currency exchange contracts, futures contracts and options, and hedge up to 25% of total assets.
Year organized: 1987
Ticker symbol: FICDX
Group fund code: 309
Sales charge: 3% (may be waived for retirement accounts using Fidelity prototype plans)
Discount broker availability: Fidelity, Schwab, Siebert, White
Redemption fee: 1.00% on shares purchased prior to 2/1/96; 1.5% on shares purchased after 2/1/96 if held less than 90 days, payable to the fund
Dividends paid: Income - December; Capital gains - December
Portfolio turnover (3 yrs): 139%, 139%, 75%
Management fee: 0.45% plus group fee of 0.25% to 0.52% +/- performance fee of up to 0.20% relative to Toronto Stock Exchange 300 Composite Index over 36 months
Expense ratio: 0.92% (year ending 10/31/97) (0.93% without waiver)

FIDELITY CAPITAL & INCOME FUND ◆
(See first Fidelity listing for data common to all funds)

Portfolio manager: David L. Glancy (1996)
Investment objective and policies: Income and capital growth. Invests in debt securities, convertible securities, and common and preferred stocks. Although the manager has broad discretion, the majority of assets are usually in debt instruments or convertible securities. Fund focuses on lower quality debt in troubled or uncertain companies foreign or domestic, or those already in default. Will exploit opportunities in bankruptcies, mergers, consolidations, liquidations, reorganizations and restructurings. Up to 15% of assets may be in illiquid securities.
Year organized: 1977 (formerly Fidelity High Income Fund (name and objective change as of 1/1/91)
Ticker symbol: FAGIX
Group fund code: 038
Discount broker availability: *Fidelity, Schwab, *Siebert, White
Redemption fee: 1.50% on shares held less than 365 days, payable to the fund
Dividends paid: Income - declared daily, paid monthly; Capital gains - June, December
Portfolio turnover (3 yrs): 309%, 119%, 78%
Management fee: 0.45% plus group fee of 0.11% to 0.37%
12b-1 distribution fee: Yes (not currently imposed)
Expense ratio: 0.86% (year ending 4/30/97) (0.87% without waiver)

FIDELITY CAPITAL APPRECIATION FUND ◆
(See first Fidelity listing for data common to all funds)

Portfolio manager: Harry Lange (1996)
Investment objective and policies: Capital appreciation. Invests primarily in a diversified portfolio of common stocks of companies of any size. Fund may, however, invest without limit in preferred stocks or debt instruments. Seeks opportunities in prospective

acquisitions, reorganizations, spinoffs, consolidations, and liquidations in any domestic or foreign market. May invest up to 10% of assets in illiquid securities, and use various derivative instruments for either increasing returns or for hedging purposes.
Year organized: 1986
Ticker symbol: FDCAX
Group fund code: 307
Discount broker availability: *Fidelity, Schwab, Siebert, White
Dividends paid: Income - December; Capital gains - December
Portfolio turnover (3 yrs): 176%, 205%, 87%
Management fee: 0.30% plus group fee of 0.25% to 0.52% +/- performance fee of up to 0.20% relative to the S&P 500 Index over 36 months
Expense ratio: 0.66% (year ending 10/31/97) (0.69% without waiver)

FIDELITY CASH RESERVES ◆
(See first Fidelity listing for data common to all funds)

Portfolio manager: John Todd (1997)
Investment objective and policies: High current income consistent with preservation of capital and liquidity. Invests in high-grade domestic and international money market instruments, and reverse repurchase agreements thereon.
Year organized: 1979
Ticker symbol: FDRXX
Group fund code: 055
Deadline for same day wire purchase: 12 NN
Discount broker availability: *Fidelity
Number of switches permitted: Unlimited
Check redemptions: $500 minimum
Dividends paid: Income - declared daily, paid monthly
Management fee: 0.03% plus group fee of 0.11% to 0.37% plus 6.0% of gross income for portion of fund's gross income in excess of 5% yield; (this item cannot exceed 0.24%)
12b-1 distribution fee: Yes (paid by adviser)
Expense ratio: 0.49% (year ending 11/30/97)

FIDELITY CONNECTICUT MUNICIPAL MONEY MARKET FUND ◆
(See first Fidelity listing for data common to all funds)

Portfolio manager: Scott A. Orr (1997)
Investment objective and policies: High current income exempt from federal and Connecticut income taxes. Invests in short-term municipal money markets whose interest is tax free in the State of Connecticut.
Year organized: 1989
Ticker symbol: FCMXX
Group fund code: 418
Minimum purchase: Initial: $5,000, Subsequent: $250
Deadline for same day wire purchase: 12 NN
Discount broker availability: *Fidelity
Qualified for sale in: CT, NJ, NY
Number of switches permitted: Unlimited
Check redemptions: $500 minimum
Dividends paid: Income - declared daily, paid monthly
Management fee: 0.25% plus group fee of 0.11% to 0.37%
12b-1 distribution fee: Yes (not currently imposed)
Expense ratio: 0.57% (year ending 11/30/97) (0.58% without waiver)

FIDELITY CONTRAFUND
(See first Fidelity listing for data common to all funds)

Portfolio manager: William Danoff (1990)
Investment objective and policies: Long-term capital appreciation. Invests primarily in common stocks and securities convertible into common stock of companies either believed to be undervalued due to an overly pessimistic appraisal by the public, or to those thought to be overlooked and not fully recognized. Management does have the flexibility, however, to invest in any kind of securities believed to offer potential capital appreciation. Fund may invest in foreign securities without limit, and use currency exchange contracts, stock index futures and options and hedge up to 25% of total assets.

Year organized: 1967
Ticker symbol: FCNTX
Group fund code: 022
Sales restrictions: Fund closed to new investors 4/3/98
Sales charge: 3% (may be waived for retirement accounts using Fidelity prototype plans)
Discount broker availability: Fidelity, Schwab, Siebert, White
Dividends paid: Income - February, December; Capital gains - February, December
Portfolio turnover (3 yrs): 144%, 159%, 223%
Management fee: 0.30% plus group fee of 0.25% to 0.52% +/- performance fee of up to 0.20% relative to the S&P 500 Index over 36 months
Expense ratio: 0.67% (year ending 12/31/97) (0.70% without waiver)

FIDELITY CONVERTIBLE SECURITIES FUND ◆
(See first Fidelity listing for data common to all funds)

Portfolio manager: David Felman (1997)
Investment objective and policies: High total return: current income and capital appreciation. Invests at least 65% of assets in securities convertible into common stock. Fund may also invest in common stocks, non-convertible securities, junk bonds, zero coupon bonds, restricted securities and pay-in-kind bonds. Fund may use foreign securities without limit, and invest up to 10% of assets in illiquid securities. May use options, futures, swaps, short sales and foreign currency exchange contracts for hedging purposes.
Year organized: 1987
Ticker symbol: FCVSX
Group fund code: 308
Discount broker availability: *Fidelity, Schwab, *Siebert, White
Dividends paid: Income - March, June, September, December; Capital gains - January, December
Portfolio turnover (3 yrs): 212%, 175%, 203%
Management fee: 0.20% plus group fee of 0.25% to 0.52% +/- performance fee of up to 0.15% relative to the Merrill Lynch Convertible Securities Index over 36 months
12b-1 distribution fee: Yes (paid by adviser)
Expense ratio: 0.73% (year ending 11/30/97) (0.74% without waiver)

FIDELITY DAILY INCOME TRUST ◆
(See first Fidelity listing for data common to all funds)

Portfolio manager: John J. Todd (1997)
Investment objective and policies: High current income consistent with preservation of capital and liquidity. Invests in a broadly diversified portfolio of high quality, domestic U.S. dollar denominated money market instruments.
Year organized: 1974
Ticker symbol: FDTXX
Group fund code: 031
Minimum purchase: Initial: $5,000, Subsequent: $500; IRA/Keogh: Initial: $500, Subsequent: $250
Deadline for same day wire purchase: 12 NN
Discount broker availability: *Fidelity
Number of switches permitted: Unlimited
Check redemptions: Yes, $1 fee to fund on non-U.S. shareholder checks less than $500
Dividends paid: Income - declared daily, paid monthly
Management fee: 0.10% first $2B to 0.05% over $6B plus 4% of fund's monthly income (bounded by 0.20% and 0.40% of total assets)
Expense ratio: 0.49% (year ending 8/31/97) (0.50% without waiver)

FIDELITY DISCIPLINED EQUITY FUND ◆
(See first Fidelity listing for data common to all funds)

Portfolio manager: Bradford F. Lewis (1988)
Investment objective and policies: Long-term capital growth. Invests at least 65% of assets in common stocks of domestic issuers and ADRs believed undervalued relative to their industries, as determined by a proprietary computer model supported by conventional fundamental research. Generally maintains S&P

sector weightings but targets stocks with greatest growth potential. Up to 35% of assets may be in foreign stocks, and the balance of assets not committed to primary policy may be invested in all types of domestic or foreign securities. Fund uses foreign currency exchange contracts, and futures and options, and may hedge up to 25% of total assets.
Year organized: 1988
Ticker symbol: FDEQX
Group fund code: 315
Discount broker availability: *Fidelity, Schwab, *Siebert, White
Dividends paid: Income - December; Capital gains - December
Portfolio turnover (3 yrs): 127%, 297%, 221%
Management fee: 0.30% plus group fee of 0.25% to 0.52% +/- performance fee of up to 0.20% relative to the S&P 500 Index over 36 months
12b-1 distribution fee: Yes (paid by adviser)
Expense ratio: 0.64% (year ending 10/31/97) (0.69% without waiver)

FIDELITY DIVERSIFIED INTERNATIONAL FUND ◆
(See first Fidelity listing for data common to all funds)

Portfolio manager: Gregory Fraser (1991)
Investment objective and policies: Capital growth. Invests primarily in equity securities of companies with market capitalizations exceeding $100M that are perceived to be undervalued and are located anywhere outside the U.S. Fund may, however, invest in smaller companies, in U.S. issues and in debt obligations of any quality. Equity selection based on computer-aided quantitative analysis supported by fundamental research. Invests in the major markets of the Morgan Stanley Capital International Europe, Australia, Far East (EAFE) Index. May use options and futures and currency exchange contracts, hedge up to 25% of total assets, and invest up to 35% of assets in junk bonds.
Year organized: 1991
Ticker symbol: FDIVX
Group fund code: 325
Discount broker availability: *Fidelity, Schwab, *Siebert, White
Dividends paid: Income - December; Capital gains - December
Portfolio turnover (3 yrs): 81%, 94%, 101%
Management fee: 0.45% plus group fee of 0.25% to 0.52% +/- performance fee of up to 0.20% relative to the MSCI-EAFE Index over 36 months
12b-1 distribution fee: Yes (not currently imposed)
Expense ratio: 1.23% (year ending 10/31/97) (1.25% without waiver)

FIDELITY DIVIDEND GROWTH FUND ◆
(See first Fidelity listing for data common to all funds)

Portfolio manager: Charles Mangum (1997)
Investment objective and policies: Capital appreciation. Invests at least 65% of assets in equity securities of growth companies with the potential to increase the dividend or to begin paying one. This income trend is used as an indicator of future growth, not as a goal in and of itself. Fund may invest in all types of equity securities, including common and preferred stock and securities convertible into common and preferred stock. May invest up to 35% of assets in junk bonds, other debt securities of all types and warrants. Fund may use foreign stocks, foreign currency exchange contracts, and stock index futures and options on up to 25% of assets.
Year organized: 1993
Ticker symbol: FDGFX
Group fund code: 330
Discount broker availability: *Fidelity, Schwab, *Siebert, White
Dividends paid: Income - September, December; Capital gains - September, December
Portfolio turnover (3 yrs): 141%, 129%, 162%
Management fee: 0.30% plus group fee of 0.25% to 0.52% +/- performance fee of up to 0.20% relative to the S&P 500 Index over 36 months
Expense ratio: 0.92% (year ending 7/31/97) (0.95 without waiver)

FIDELITY EMERGING GROWTH FUND
(See first Fidelity listing for data common to all funds)

Portfolio manager: Erin Sullivan (1997)
Investment objective and policies: Capital appreciation. Invests at least 65% of assets in equity securities of emerging growth companies of small to medium size (less than $1B market capitalization) with potential for accelerated earnings and revenue growth due to new products or technologies, new channels of distribution, revitalized management and/or industry conditions. May use convertibles, warrants and rights, foreign securities and closed-end investment companies. May hold restricted securities, use currency exchange contracts, futures and options thereon (up to 15% of assets), and sell short against the box (up to 15% of assets).
Year organized: 1990
Ticker symbol: FDEGX
Group fund code: 324
Sales charge: 3% (waived for retirement accounts using Fidelity prototype plans)
Discount broker availability: Fidelity, Schwab, Siebert, White
Redemption fee: 0.75% on shares held less than 90 days, payable to the fund
Dividends paid: Income - January, December; Capital gains - January, December
Portfolio turnover (3 yrs): 212%, 105%, 102%
Management fee: 0.35% plus group fee of 0.25% to 0.52% +/- performance fee of up to 0.20% relative to the Russell 2000 Index over 36 months
Expense ratio: 1.05% (year ending 11/30/97) (1.09% without waiver)

FIDELITY EMERGING MARKETS FUND ◆
(See first Fidelity listing for data common to all funds)

Portfolio manager: David C. Stewart (1997)
Investment objective: Long-term capital growth. Invests aggressively in a diversified portfolio of common stocks and other equity securities of foreign issuers in emerging economies and developing markets as defined by the International Finance Corporation and the World Bank. May use forward currency contracts, currency swaps and options to hedge up to 25% of total assets.
Year organized: 1990 (name changed from Fidelity International Opportunities Fund in February 1993)
Ticker symbol: FEMKX
Group fund code: 322
Sales charge: 3% (may be waived for retirement accounts using Fidelity prototype plans)
Discount broker availability: Fidelity, Schwab, Siebert, White
Redemption fee: 1.50% on shares held less than 90 days, payable to the fund
Dividends paid: Income - December; Capital gains - December
Portfolio turnover (3 yrs): 69%, 77%, 78%
Management fee: 0.45% plus group fee of 0.25% to 0.52%
Expense ratio: 1.35% (year ending 10/31/97) (1.36% without waiver)

FIDELITY EQUITY-INCOME FUND ◆
(See first Fidelity listing for data common to all funds)

Portfolio manager: Stephen R. Peterson (1993)
Investment objective and policies: Income exceeding the yield on the securities comprising the S&P 500, and some capital appreciation. Invests at least 65% of assets in income-producing common or preferred stocks of companies perceived to be undervalued. Debt obligations will normally be convertible. May invest up to 20% of assets in junk bonds, and foreign securities without limit. May use foreign currency exchange contracts and stock index futures and options as well as other derivative instruments to hedge up to 25% of total assets.
Year organized: 1966
Ticker symbol: FEQIX
Group fund code: 023
Discount broker availability: *Fidelity, Schwab, *Siebert, White
Dividends paid: Income - March, June, September, December; Capital gains - March, December

Portfolio turnover (3 yrs): 30%, 39%, 50%
Management fee: 0.16% plus group fee of 0.25% to 0.52%
Expense ratio: 0.66% (year ending 1/31/97) (0.68% without waiver)

FIDELITY EQUITY-INCOME II FUND ◆
(See first Fidelity listing for data common to all funds)

Portfolio manager: Bettina Doulton (1996)
Investment objective and policies: Reasonable income with potential for capital growth. Invests at least 65% of assets in income producing equity securities with goal of exceeding total return of the S&P 500. May invest up to 35% of assets in junk bonds, and up to 15% of assets in foreign securities. May use foreign currency exchange contracts and stock index futures and options to hedge up to 25% of total assets.
Year organized: 1990
Ticker symbol: FEQTX
Group fund code: 319
Discount broker availability: *Fidelity, Schwab, *Siebert, White
Dividends paid: Income - March, June, September, December; Capital gains - January, December
Portfolio turnover (3 yrs): 77%, 46%, 45%
Management fee: 0.20% plus group fee of 0.25% to 0.52%
Expense ratio: 0.68% (year ending 11/30/97) (0.70% without waiver)

FIDELITY EUROPE FUND
(See first Fidelity listing for data common to all funds)

Portfolio manager: Sally Walden (1992)
Investment objective and policies: Long-term capital growth. Invests at least 65% of assets in securities of companies which have their principal business activities in Western Europe. Fund will be invested in at least three countries. May use currency exchange contracts, futures contracts and options and hedge up to 25% of total assets.
Year organized: 1986 (Absorbed old Fidelity UK Fund 4/28/89)
Ticker symbol: FIEUX
Group fund code: 301
Sales charge: 3% (may be waived for retirement accounts using Fidelity prototype plans)
Discount broker availability: Fidelity, Schwab, Siebert, White
Redemption fee: 1% on shares held less than 90 days, payable to the fund
Portfolio turnover (3 yrs): 57%, 45%, 38%
Dividends paid: Income - December; Capital gains - December
Management fee: 0.45% plus group fee of 0.25% to 0.52% +/- performance fee of up to 0.20% relative to the MSCI-Europe Index over 36 months
Expense ratio: 1.18% (year ending 10/31/97) (1.19% without waiver)

FIDELITY EUROPE CAPITAL APPRECIATION FUND
(See first Fidelity listing for data common to all funds)

Portfolio manager: Kevin McCarey (1993)
Investment objective and policies: Long-term capital appreciation. Invests at least 65% of assets in securities of companies which have their principal business activities in Eastern and Western Europe. Fund will be invested in at least three countries. May use currency exchange contracts, futures contracts and options and hedge up to 25% of total assets. Up to 15% of assets may be in illiquid securities. Fund will invest more aggressively than Fidelity Europe Fund.
Year organized: 1993
Ticker symbol: FECAX
Group fund code: 341
Sales charge: 3% (may be waived for retirement accounts using Fidelity prototype plans)
Discount broker availability: Fidelity, Schwab, Siebert, White
Redemption fee: 1% on shares held less than 90 days, payable to the fund
Dividends paid: Income - December; Capital gains - December
Portfolio turnover (3 yrs): 189%, 155%, 176%

Management fee: 0.45% plus group fee of 0.25% to 0.52% +/- performance fee of +/- 0.20% relative to the MSCI Europe Index over 36 months
Expense ratio: 1.07% (year ending 10/31/97) (1.10% without waiver)

FIDELITY EXPORT AND MULTINATIONAL FUND
(See first Fidelity listing for data common to all funds)

Portfolio manager: Jason Weiner (1997)
Investment objective: Long-term capital appreciation. Invests at least 65% of assets in equity securities of U.S. companies with 10% or more of annual revenues from sale of exported goods or services or engaged in export-related businesses. May also invest in multinational companies that derive income from products and services originated in and distributed to countries outside the U.S. May use futures and options and hedge up to 25% of total assets. Fund is non-diversified.
Year organized: 1994 (name and objective changed 5/1/97 from Fidelity Export; past performance may be misleading)
Ticker symbol: FEXPX
Group fund code: 332
Sales charge: 3% (may waived for retirement accounts using Fidelity prototype plans)
Discount broker availability: Fidelity, Schwab, Siebert, White
Redemption fee: 0.75% for shares held less than 90 days, payable to the fund
Dividends paid: Income - October, December; Capital gains - October, December
Portfolio turnover (3 yrs): 429%, 313%, 245%
Management fee: 0.30% plus group fee of 0.25% to 0.52%
Expense ratio: 0.91% (year ending 8/31/97) (0.98% without waiver)

FIDELITY FIFTY FUND ◆
(See first Fidelity listing for data common to all funds)

Portfolio manager: Scott Stewart (1993)
Investment objective: Capital appreciation. Invests in common stocks and other equity securities of domestic and foreign companies believed to have the greatest growth potential. Fund will normally be invested in 50 to 60 stocks and is non-diversified. May use forward currency contracts, currency swap agreements and options to hedge up to 25% of assets.
Year organized: 1993
Ticker symbol: FFTYX
Group fund code: 500
Sales charge: 3% (may be waived for retirement accounts using Fidelity prototype plans, and for all shareholders through 12/31/98)
Discount broker availability: *Fidelity, Schwab, *Siebert, White
Dividends paid: Income - August, December; Capital gains - August, December
Portfolio turnover (3 yrs): 131%, 152%, 180%
Management fee: 0.30% plus group fee of 0.25% to 0.52% +/- performance fee of up to 0.20% relative to the S&P 500 Index over 36 months
Expense ratio: 0.84% (year ending 6/30/97)

FIDELITY FOREIGN CURRENCY PORTFOLIOS
(Partnerships liquidated 12/15/97)

FIDELITY FRANCE FUND
(See first Fidelity listing for data common to all funds)

Portfolio manager: Renaud Saleur (1995)
Investment objective and policies: Long-term capital growth. Invests at least 65% of assets in equity and debt securities of French issuers. The remainder of assets may be invested in securities of other European issuers. May have up 35% of assets in junk bonds and 15% in illiquid securities. Fund may use currency exchange contracts, futures contracts and options, and hedge up to 25% of assets. Fund is non-diversified.
Year organized: 1995
Group fund code: 345

Discount broker availability: Fidelity, Schwab, Siebert, White
Sales charge: 3% (may be waived for retirement accounts using Fidelity prototype plans)
Redemption fee: 1.50% on shares held less than 90 days, payable to the fund
Dividends paid: Income - December; Capital gains - December
Portfolio turnover (2 yrs): 150%, 129%
Management fee: 0.45% plus group fee of 0.25% to 0.52%
Expense ratio: 2.00% (year ending 10/31/97) (3.81% without waiver)

FIDELITY FREEDOM FUNDS ◆
(See first Fidelity listing for data common to all funds)

Portfolio managers: Scott Stewart (1996), Ren Cheng (1996)
Investment objective and policies: Objectives vary according to durations of portfolios. The portfolios are "funds of funds," managed to specific target dates; 2000, 2010, 2020 and 2030. Investors pick a target date closest to their retirement. Then, fund managers adjust the asset allocations of the portfolios over time by using as many as 17 different Fidelity funds as components; the longer the portfolio has until its termination date, the larger the amount of equity allocation, ranging from a (current) 43% share of the shortest duration to an 85% share for the longest. As investors get closer to retirement, the portfolio is managed more conservatively, and the investors who are unwilling, uninterested or unable to don't have to make allocation decisions for themselves. The funds do not liquidate at their appointed year. They continue to be allocated more and more conservatively until they match the Freedom Income Fund, at which point they will be merged into it.
Year organized: 1996
Group fund code: 370 (2000), 371 (2010), 372 (2020), 373 (2030)
Discount broker availability: *Fidelity
Dividends paid: Income - annually; Capital gains - annually
Portfolio turnover (1 yr): 19% (2000), 3% (2010), 21% (2020), 19% (2030)
Management fee: 0.10% (plus fees of underlying funds)
Expense ratio: 0.08% (6 months ending 3/31/97) (includes waiver)

FIDELITY FREEDOM INCOME FUND ◆
(See first Fidelity listing for data common to all funds)

Portfolio managers: Scott Stewart (1996), Ron Cheng (1996)
Investment objective and policies: Income; capital growth secondary. Invests in a manner similar to the time sensitive Freedom Funds, but is asset allocated for the current retiree; about 20% of its assets in equity funds, and about 40% each in fixed-income and money market funds. Also draws on as many as 17 different Fidelity funds as components, however the allocation will not continues to evolve towards total income. The goal is to ensure that investors who are unwilling, uninterested or unable to don't have to make allocation decisions for themselves.
Year organized: 1996
Group fund code: 369
Discount broker availability: *Fidelity
Dividends paid: Income - monthly; Capital gains - May, December
Portfolio turnover (1 yr): 32%
Management fee: 0.10% (plus fees of underlying funds)
Expense ratio: 0.08% (6 months ending 3/31/97) (includes waiver)

FIDELITY FUND ◆
(See first Fidelity listing for data common to all funds)

Portfolio manager: Beth Terrana (1993)
Investment objective and policies: Long-term capital growth with reasonable current income. Invests primarily in a diversified portfolio of common stocks and convertible securities of established domestic and foreign companies. Fund may use currency exchange

contracts, stock index futures, options, and options on futures to hedge up to 25% of total assets.
Year organized: 1930
Ticker symbol: FFIDX
Group fund code: 003
Discount broker availability: *Fidelity, Schwab, *Siebert, White
Dividends paid: Income - March, June, September, December; Capital gains - August, December
Portfolio turnover (3 yrs): 107%, 150%, 157%
Management fee: 0.09% plus group fee of 0.25% to 0.52%
12b-1 distribution fee: Yes (not currently imposed)
Expense ratio: 0.59% (year ending 6/30/97) (0.62% without waiver)

FIDELITY GERMANY FUND
(See first Fidelity listing for data common to all funds)

Portfolio manager: Alexandra Edzard (1996)
Investment objective and policies: Long-term capital growth. Invests at least 65% of assets in equity and debt securities of German issuers. The remainder of assets may be invested in securities of other European issuers. May have up 35% of assets in junk bonds and 15% in illiquid securities. Fund may use currency exchange contracts, futures contracts and options, and hedge up to 25% of total assets. Fund is non-diversified.
Year organized: 1995
Group fund code: 346
Discount broker availability: Fidelity, Schwab, Siebert, White
Sales charge: 3% (may be waived for retirement accounts using Fidelity prototype plans)
Redemption fee: 1.50% on shares held less than 90 days, payable to the fund
Dividends paid: Income - December; Capital gains - December
Portfolio turnover (2 yrs): 120%, 133%
Management fee: 0.45% plus group fee of 0.25% to 0.52%
Expense ratio: 2.00% (year ending 10/31/97) (2.26% without waiver)

FIDELITY GINNIE MAE PORTFOLIO ◆
(See first Fidelity listing for data common to all funds)

Portfolio manager: Curtis Hollingsworth (1997)
Investment objective and policies: High current income consistent with prudent investment risk. Invests at least 65% of assets in Government National Mortgage Association pass-through certificates. Remainder will be in any type of U.S. or foreign debt or other income-producing investments, including other types of mortgage securities, government or government agency securities, asset-backed securities, and corporate debt instruments. Portfolio is managed generally to react to changes in interest rates similarly to government bonds with maturities between two and ten years. All non-government debt securities will be rated within the three highest grades by Moody's or S&P.
Year organized: 1985
Ticker symbol: FGMNX
Group fund code: 015
Discount broker availability: *Fidelity, Schwab, *Siebert, White
Check redemptions: $500 minimum
Dividends paid: Income - declared daily, paid monthly; Capital gains - September, December
Portfolio turnover (3 yrs): 98%, 107%, 210%
Management fee: 0.30% plus group fee of 0.11% to 0.37%
12b-1 distribution fee: Yes (not currently imposed)
Expense ratio: 0.75% (year ending 7/31/97) (0.76% without waiver)

FIDELITY GLOBAL BALANCED FUND ◆
(See first Fidelity listing for data common to all funds)

Portfolio manager: Richard R. Mace, Jr. (1996)
Investment objective and policies: High current income consistent with capital preservation; moderate capital growth secondary. Invests in a broadly diversified portfolio of common stocks, fixed-income securities and money markets issued from anywhere in the

world. Fund adjusts distribution of assets to perceived market and economic conditions, with at least 25% of assets always held in fixed-income senior securities. Fund may use foreign securities without limit, and use currency exchange contracts, stock index futures and options and hedge up to 25% of total assets.
Year organized: 1993
Ticker symbol: FGBLX
Group fund code: 334
Discount broker availability: *Fidelity, Schwab, *Siebert, White
Dividends paid: Income - September, December; Capital gains - September, December
Portfolio turnover (3 yrs): 57%, 189%, 242%
Management fee: 0.45% plus group fee of 0.25% to 0.52%
Expense ratio: 1.49% (year ending 7/31/97) (1.51% without waiver)

FIDELITY GOVERNMENT SECURITIES FUND ◆
(See first Fidelity listing for data common to all funds)

Portfolio manager: Curtis Hollingsworth (1997)
Investment objective and policies: High current income consistent with principal preservation and free from state and local taxes. Invests primarily in obligations issued by the U.S. Government, its agencies or instrumentalities whose income is exempt from state and local taxes. Fund generally maintains an average maturity of between five and twelve years. Fund may use futures and options to hedge up to 25% of total assets.
Year organized: 1979
Ticker symbol: FGOVX
Group fund code: 054
Discount broker availability: *Fidelity, Schwab, *Siebert, White
Check redemptions: $500 minimum
Dividends paid: Income - declared daily, paid monthly; Capital gains - December
Portfolio turnover (3 yrs): 199%, 124%, 391%
Management fee: 0.30% plus group fee of 0.11% to 0.37%
12b-1 distribution fee: Yes (paid by adviser)
Expense ratio: 0.72% (year ending 9/30/97) (0.73% without waiver)

FIDELITY GROWTH & INCOME PORTFOLIO ◆
(See first Fidelity listing for data common to all funds)

Portfolio managers: Steven Kaye (1993), Louis Salemy (1997)
Investment objective and policies: High total return: long-term growth of capital and income, as well as current income, consistent with reasonable investment risk. Invests primarily in equity securities of companies which offer growth of earnings potential while paying current dividends. May, however, invest in any combination of common, convertible, or preferred stock, and fixed-income securities. May invest in foreign securities without limit, invest up to 35% of assets in junk bonds and up to 10% of assets in illiquid securities. May use a variety of derivative instruments in an effort to enhance performance and for hedging purposes.
Year organized: 1985
Ticker symbol: FGRIX
Group fund code: 027
Sales restrictions: Fund closed to new investors 4/3/98
Discount broker availability: *Fidelity, Schwab, *Siebert, White
Dividends paid: Income - March, June, September, December; Capital gains - September, December
Portfolio turnover (3 yrs): 38%, 41%, 67%
Management fee: 0.20% plus group fee of 0.25% to 0.52%
Expense ratio: 0.71% (year ending 7/31/97) (0.73% without waiver)

FIDELITY GROWTH COMPANY FUND ◆
(See first Fidelity listing for data common to all funds)

Portfolio manager: Steven S. Wymer (1997)
Investment objective and policies: Long-term capital appreciation. Invests primarily in common stocks

and securities convertible into common stocks of companies with above average growth potential. May be in emerging or mature industries with emphasis on the former. May use foreign securities and currency exchange contracts and stock index options, futures and options thereon. May hedge up to 25% of total assets.
Year organized: 1983 (formerly Fidelity Mercury Fund)
Ticker symbol: FDGRX
Group fund code: 025
Discount broker availability: *Fidelity, Schwab, *Siebert, White
Dividends paid: Income - January, December; Capital gains - January, December
Portfolio turnover (3 yrs): 93%, 78%, 97%
Management fee: 0.30% plus group fee of 0.25% to 0.52% +/- performance fee of up to 0.20% relative to the S&P 500 Index over 36 months
Expense ratio: 0.68% (year ending 11/30/97) (0.71% without waiver)

FIDELITY HONG KONG AND CHINA FUND
(See first Fidelity listing for data common to all funds)

Portfolio manager: Joseph Tse (1995)
Investment objective and policies: Long-term capital growth. Invests at least 65% of assets in equity and debt securities of Hong Kong and Chinese issuers. The balance of the portfolio may be invested in securities of other Southeast Asian issuers. May have up 35% of assets in junk bonds and 15% in illiquid securities. Fund may use currency exchange contracts, futures contracts and options, and hedge up to 25% of total assets. Fund is non-diversified.
Year organized: 1995
Ticker symbol: FHKCX
Group fund code: 352
Discount broker availability: Fidelity, Schwab, Siebert, White
Sales charge: 3% (may be waived for retirement accounts using Fidelity prototype plans)
Redemption fee: 1.50% on shares held less than 90 days, payable to the fund
Dividends paid: Income - December; Capital gains - December
Portfolio turnover (2 yrs): 174%, 118%
Management fee: 0.45% plus group fee of 0.25% to 0.52%
Expense ratio: 1.31% (year ending 10/31/97)

FIDELITY INSURED MUNICIPAL INCOME FUND ◆
(See Spartan Insured Muni Income Fund)

FIDELITY INTERMEDIATE BOND FUND ◆
(See first Fidelity listing for data common to all funds)

Portfolio manager: Christine J. Thompson (1995)
Investment objective and policies: High current income. Invests primarily in foreign and domestic high- and upper-medium-grade fixed-income obligations (BBB or better), while maintaining a dollar-weighted average maturity of three to ten years. Fund may use options, futures and options thereon, and currency exchange contracts. May hedge up to 25% of total assets.
Year organized: 1975 (name changed from Fidelity Thrift Trust on 9/1/87)
Ticker symbol: FTHRX
Group fund code: 032
Discount broker availability: *Fidelity, Schwab, *Siebert, White
Check redemptions: $500 minimum
Dividends paid: Income - declared daily, paid monthly; Capital gains - June, December
Portfolio turnover (3 yrs): 116%, 169%, 75%
Management fee: 0.30% plus group fee of 0.11% to 0.37%
Expense ratio: 0.69% (year ending 4/30/97) (0.71% without waiver)

FIDELITY INTERNATIONAL BOND FUND ◆

(See first Fidelity listing on page 284 for data common to all funds)

Portfolio managers: Ian Spreadbury (1996), John H. Carlson (1998), Luis Martins (1998)
Investment objective and policies: High total return. Invests at least 65% of assets in debt securities issued anywhere in the world outside the U.S., primarily in Australia, Canada, Japan, the Netherlands, New Zealand, and Western Europe. The portfolio maintains a dollar-weighted average maturity of 15 years or less. Up to 35% of assets may be in junk bonds and up to 35% in securities of emerging markets. May use currency exchange and futures contracts and options, as well as securities indexed to foreign currencies. May use options and futures on indexes.
Year organized: 1986 (name and policy changed from Global Bond 2/27/98)
Ticker symbol: FGBDX
Group fund code: 451
Discount broker availability: *Fidelity, Schwab, *Siebert, White
Check redemptions: $500 minimum
Dividends paid: Income - declared daily, paid monthly; Capital gains - February, December
Portfolio turnover (3 yrs): 74%, 91%, 322%
Management fee: 0.55% plus group fee of 0.11% to 0.37%
12b-1 distribution fee: Yes (not currently imposed)
Expense ratio: 1.27% (year ending 12/31/97)

FIDELITY INTERNATIONAL GROWTH AND INCOME FUND ◆

(See first Fidelity listing on page 284 for data common to all funds)

Portfolio manager: John R. Hickling (1996)
Investment objective and policies: Capital growth and current income. Normally invests at least 65% of assets in equity securities and bonds from at least six different countries, primarily in developed markets in Europe, the Far East, and the Pacific Basin. Also invests at least 25% of assets in debt securities rated Baa or better, with up to 20% in securities of U.S. issuers. May use currency exchange contracts, futures contracts and options, and hedge up to 25% of total assets.
Year organized: 1986
Ticker symbol: FIGRX
Group fund code: 305
Discount broker availability: *Fidelity, Schwab, *Siebert, White
Dividends paid: Income - December; Capital gains - December
Portfolio turnover (3 yrs): 70%, 95%, 141%
Management fee: 0.45% plus group fee of 0.25% to 0.52%
12b-1 distribution fee: Yes (not currently imposed)
Expense ratio: 1.15% (year ending 10/31/97) (1.17% without waiver)

FIDELITY INTERNATIONAL VALUE FUND ◆

(See first Fidelity listing on page 284 for data common to all funds)

Portfolio manager: Richard R. Mace, Jr. (1994)
Investment objective and policies: Long-term capital growth. Invests primarily in equity securities of foreign companies that are perceived to be undervalued. Diversification includes issues from at least three different countries, primarily in developed markets in Europe, the Far East, and the Pacific Basin. Up to 35% of assets may be in junk bonds and 15% in illiquid securities. May use currency exchange contracts, futures contracts and options, and hedge up to 25% of total assets.
Year organized: 1994
Ticker symbol: FIVFX
Group fund code: 335
Discount broker availability: *Fidelity, *Siebert, White
Dividends paid: Income - December; Capital gains - December
Portfolio turnover (3 yrs): 86%, 71%, 109%
Management fee: 0.45% plus group fee of 0.25% to

0.52% +/- performance fee of up to 0.20% relative to the MSCI-EAFE Index over 36 months
12b-1 distribution fee: Yes (not currently imposed)
Expense ratio: 1.28% (year ending 10/31/97) (1.30% without waiver)

FIDELITY INVESTMENT GRADE BOND FUND ◆

(See first Fidelity listing on page 284 for data common to all funds)

Portfolio manager: Kevin E. Grant (1997)
Investment objective and policies: High current income consistent with reasonable risk. Invests primarily in investment grade debt securities. Portfolio is managed generally to react to interest rates similarly to bonds with maturities between four and ten years. May use bonds, notes, convertible bonds, mortgage-related securities, domestic and foreign government and government agency securities, zero coupon bonds and preferred stocks. May invest up to 35% of assets in junk bonds and 20% in warrants. May use options and futures and hedge up to 25% of total assets.
Year organized: 1971 (formerly Fidelity Flexible Bond Fund, name changed 4/15/92. Previously Fidelity Corporate Bond Fund.)
Ticker symbol: FBNDX
Group fund code: 026
Discount broker availability: *Fidelity, Schwab, *Siebert, White
Check redemptions: $500 minimum
Dividends paid: Income - declared daily, paid monthly; Capital gains - June, December
Portfolio turnover (3 yrs): 120%, 134%, 90%
Management fee: 0.30% plus group fee of 0.11% to 0.37%
Expense ratio: 0.75% (year ending 4/30/97) (0.76% without waiver)

FIDELITY JAPAN FUND

(See first Fidelity listing on page 284 for data common to all funds)

Portfolio manager: Shigeki Makino (1994)
Investment objective and policies: Long-term capital growth. Invests at least 65% of assets in securities of issuers that have their principal activities in Japan or are organized under Japanese law. May invest in common and preferred stocks, securities convertible into stocks, equity securities of closed-end investment companies, and depository receipts of equity securities. May also invest in securities from other Southeast Asian issuers, and invest in Japanese debt securities and U.S. and foreign money market instruments for defensive purposes. May use options and futures to hedge up to 25% of assets.
Year organized: 1992
Ticker symbol: FJAPX
Group fund code: 350
Discount broker availability: Fidelity, Schwab, Siebert, White
Sales charge: 3% (may be waived for retirement accounts using Fidelity prototype plans)
Redemption fee: 1.50% on shares held less than 90 days, payable to the fund
Dividends paid: Income - December; Capital gains - December
Portfolio turnover (3 yrs): 70%, 83%, 86%
Management fee: 0.45% plus group fee of 0.25% to 0.52% +/- performance fee of up to 0.20% relative to the TOPIX, an index of stocks in the first section of the Tokyo Stock Exchange, over 36 months
Expense ratio: 1.40% (year ending 10/31/97) (1.42% without waiver)

FIDELITY JAPAN SMALL COMPANIES FUND

(See first Fidelity listing on page 284 for data common to all funds)

Portfolio manager: Kenichi Mizushita (1996)
Investment objective and policies: Long-term capital growth. Invests at least 65% of assets in equity and debt securities of Japanese issuers with market capitalizations of $100B Yen or less. The remainder of the portfolio may be invested in securities of other Southeast Asian issuers or larger-cap Japanese issues. May have up 35% of assets in junk bonds and 15% in illiquid securities. Fund may use currency exchange

---

contracts, futures contracts and options, and hedge up to 25% of total assets. Fund is non-diversified.
Year organized: 1995
Ticker symbol: FJSCX
Group fund code: 360
Discount broker availability: Fidelity, Schwab, Siebert, White
Sales charge: 3% (may be waived for retirement accounts using Fidelity prototype plans)
Redemption fee: 1.50% on shares held less than 90 days, payable to the fund
Dividends paid: Income - December; Capital gains - December
Portfolio turnover (2 yrs): 101%, 66%
Management fee: 0.45% plus group fee of 0.25% to 0.52%
Expense ratio: 1.34% (year ending 10/31/97) (1.35% without waiver)

FIDELITY LARGE CAP STOCK FUND ◆

(See first Fidelity listing on page 284 for data common to all funds)

Portfolio manager: Karen Firestone (1998)
Investment objective and policies: Long-term capital appreciation. Invests primarily in equity securities of both domestic and foreign companies with market capitalizations in excess of $1B at the time of purchase. Fund may invest up to 35% of assets in junk bonds, use currency exchange contracts, and stock index futures and options thereon. May hedge up to 25% of total assets.
Year organized: 1995
Ticker symbol: FLCSX
Group fund code: 338
Discount broker availability: *Fidelity, Schwab, *Siebert, White
Dividends paid: Income - June, December; Capital gains - June, December
Portfolio turnover (2 yrs): 110%, 155%
Management fee: 0.30% plus group fee of 0.25% to 0.52% +/- performance fee of up to 0.20% relative to the S&P 500 Index over 36 months
12b-1 distribution fee: Yes (not currently imposed)
Expense ratio: 0.99% (year ending 4/30/97) (1.01% without waiver)

FIDELITY LATIN AMERICA FUND

(See first Fidelity listing on page 284 for data common to all funds)

Portfolio manager: Patricia A. Satterthwaite (1993)
Investment objective and policies: High total return. Invests at least 65% of assets in securities of Latin American issuers, including Mexico and all countries in Central and South America. May invest in common and preferred stocks, securities convertible into stocks, equity securities of closed-end investment companies, depository receipts of equity securities, debt securities and U.S. and foreign money market instruments for defensive purposes. May use options and futures to hedge up to 25% of assets. May invest up to 15% of assets in illiquid securities.
Year organized: 1993
Ticker symbol: FLATX
Group fund code: 349
Sales charge: 3% (may be waived for retirement accounts using Fidelity prototype plans)
Discount broker availability: Fidelity, Schwab, Siebert, White
Redemption fee: 1.50% on shares held less than 90 days, payable to the fund
Portfolio turnover (3 yrs): 64%, 70%, 57%
Dividends paid: Income - December; Capital gains - December
Management fee: 0.45% plus group fee of 0.25% to 0.52%
Expense ratio: 1.29% (year ending 10/31/97) (1.30% without waiver)

FIDELITY LIMITED TERM MUNICIPAL INCOME FUND ◆

(See first Fidelity listing on page 284 for data common to all funds)

Portfolio manager: Norman Lind (1998)
Investment objective and policies: High current income exempt from federal income tax, consistent with preservation of principal. Invests at least 80% of

assets in high quality municipal obligations (Baa or higher) having individual maturities of 15 years or less. Portfolio maintains a dollar-weighted average maturity of three to ten years. May purchase an unlimited amount of securities subject to AMT tax treatment. May use futures and options and hedge up to 25% of total assets.
Year organized: 1977 (name changed from Limited Term Municipals 12/14/95; maturity changed from 12 years or less 9/97)
Ticker symbol: FLTMX
Group fund code: 036
Discount broker availability: *Fidelity, Schwab, *Siebert, White
Check redemptions: $500 minimum
Dividends paid: Income - declared daily, paid monthly; Capital gains - February, December
Portfolio turnover (3 yrs): 22%, 27%, 31%
Management fee: 0.10% plus 5% of gross income
12b-1 distribution fee: Yes (not currently imposed)
Expense ratio: 0.55% (year ending 12/31/97)

FIDELITY LOW-PRICED STOCK FUND
(See first Fidelity listing on page 284 for data common to all funds)

Portfolio manager: Joel Tillinghast (1989)
Investment objective and policies: Capital appreciation. Invests at least 65% of assets in common and preferred stocks priced at or below $25 per share at time of purchase that may be undervalued, overlooked or out of favor. Remainder of assets may be in higher priced equity securities, convertible securities and debt instruments. Fund may use foreign securities and currency exchange contracts, junk bonds, stock index futures and options, and sell short against the box. May hedge up to 25% of total assets.
Year organized: 1989
Ticker symbol: FLPSX
Group fund code: 316
Sales restrictions: Fund closed to new investors 4/3/98
Discount broker availability: Fidelity, Schwab, Siebert, White
Sales charge: 3% (may be waived for retirement accounts using Fidelity prototype plans)
Redemption fee: 1.50% for shares held less than 90 days, payable to the fund
Dividends paid: Income - September, December; Capital gains - September, December
Portfolio turnover (3 yrs): 45%, 79%, 65%
Management fee: 0.35% plus group fee of 0.25% to 0.52% +/- performance fee of up to 0.20% relative to the Russell 2000 Index over 36 months
Expense ratio: 1.02% (year ending 7/31/97)

FIDELITY MAGELLAN FUND
(See first Fidelity listing on page 284 for data common to all funds)

Portfolio manager: Robert E. Stansky (1996)
Investment objective and policies: Long-term capital appreciation. Invests primarily in common stocks and securities convertible into common stocks of domestic, foreign and multinational companies. Fund may invest up to 20% of assets in debt securities, use currency exchange contracts, and stock index futures and options thereon. May invest up to 40% of assets in companies operating exclusively in one foreign country, and up to 10% of assets in illiquid securities. May hedge up to 25% of total assets.
Year organized: 1963 (opened for general public sale 6/24/81)
Ticker symbol: FMAGX
Group fund code: 021
Sales restrictions: Fund closed to new investors 9/30/97
Sales charge: 3%
Discount broker availability: Fidelity, Schwab, Siebert, White
Dividends paid: Income - May, December; Capital gains - May, December
Portfolio turnover (3 yrs): 67%, 155%, 120%
Management fee: 0.30% plus group fee of 0.25% to 0.52% +/- performance fee of up to 0.20% relative to the S&P 500 Index over 36 months
Expense ratio: 0.64% (year ending 3/31/97) (0.66% without waiver)

FIDELITY MARKET INDEX FUND ◆
(See Fidelity Spartan Market Index fund)

FIDELITY MASSACHUSETTS MUNICIPAL INCOME FUND ◆
(See Fidelity Spartan Massachusetts Municipal Income Fund)

FIDELITY MASSACHUSETTS MUNICIPAL MONEY MARKET FUND ◆
(See first Fidelity listing on page 284 for data common to all funds)

Portfolio manager: Scott A. Orr (1997)
Investment objective and policies: High level of current income exempt from federal and Massachusetts personal income taxes, consistent with preservation of capital and liquidity. Invests primarily in high quality, short-term municipal money market obligations whose interest is free from Massachusetts personal income tax.
Year organized: 1983 (name changed from Tax-Free Money Market Portfolio 2/1/96)
Ticker symbol: FDMXX
Group fund code: 074
Minimum purchase: Initial: $5,000, Subsequent: $250
Deadline for same day wire purchase: 12 NN
Discount broker availability: *Fidelity
Qualified for sale in: MA
Number of switches permitted: Unlimited
Check redemptions: $500 minimum
Dividends paid: Income - declared daily, paid monthly
Management fee: 0.25% plus group fee of 0.11% to 0.37%
12b-1 distribution fee: Yes (not currently imposed)
Expense ratio: 0.57% (year ending 1/31/98)

FIDELITY MICHIGAN MUNICIPAL INCOME FUND ◆
(See Fidelity Spartan Michigan Muni Income Fund)

FIDELITY MICHIGAN MUNICIPAL MONEY MARKET FUND ◆
(See first Fidelity listing on page 284 for data common to all funds)

Portfolio manager: Diane McLaughlin (1997)
Investment objective and policies: High current income exempt from federal and Michigan state income taxes, consistent with preservation of capital and liquidity. Invests in high quality, short-term money market instruments whose interest is tax free in the State of Michigan.
Year organized: 1990 (name changed from Michigan Tax-Free Money Market Portfolio on 8/10/90)
Ticker symbol: FMIXX
Group fund code: 420
Minimum purchase: Initial: $5,000, Subsequent: $250
Deadline for same day wire purchase: 12 NN
Discount broker availability: *Fidelity
Qualified for sale in: MI
Number of switches permitted: Unlimited
Check redemptions: $500 minimum
Dividends paid: Income - declared daily, paid monthly
Management fee: 0.25% plus group fee of 0.11% to 0.37%
12b-1 distribution fee: Yes (not currently imposed)
Expense ratio: 0.61% (year ending 12/31/97)

FIDELITY MID-CAP STOCK FUND ◆
(See first Fidelity listing on page 284 for data common to all funds)

Portfolio manager: Katherine Collins (1997)
Investment objective and policies: Long-term capital appreciation. Invests primarily in common stocks and securities convertible into common stocks of companies with medium-sized market capitalizations within the range of the S&P Mid-Cap 400 Index, currently

between $500M and $5B, at the time of purchase. May use foreign securities and currency exchange contracts and stock index options, futures and options thereon. May hedge up to 25% of total assets.
Year organized: 1994
Ticker symbol: FMCSX
Group fund code: 337
Discount broker availability: *Fidelity, Schwab, *Siebert, White
Dividends paid: Income - June, December; Capital gains - June, December
Portfolio turnover (3 yrs): 155%, 179%, 163%
Management fee: 0.30% plus group fee of 0.25% to 0.52% +/- performance fee of up to 0.20% relative to the S&P MidCap 400 Index over 36 months
Expense ratio: 0.96% (year ending 4/30/97) (1.00% without waiver)

FIDELITY MINNESOTA MUNICIPAL INCOME FUND ◆
(See Fidelity Spartan Minnesota Municipal Income Fund)

FIDELITY MORTGAGE SECURITIES FUND ◆
(See first Fidelity listing on page 284 for data common to all funds)

Portfolio manager: Thomas Silvia (1997)
Investment objective and policies: High current income consistent with prudent investment risk. Invests at least 65% of assets in investment grade mortgage related securities. Potential for capital gains may also be considered. Invests in GNMA, FNMA, FHLMC, CMOs and debt obligations secured by mortgages on real estate. Remainder of assets may be in any type of U.S. or foreign debt or other income producing investments, including government or government agency securities, asset backed securities, and corporate debt instruments. All non-governmental debt securities must be rated within the three highest grades by the national rating agencies.
Year organized: 1984
Ticker symbol: FMSFX
Group fund code: 040
Sales restrictions: Mortgage Securities fund is now a multiple class Advisor load fund; this profile reflects ONLY the no load class which preceded the Advisor shares; only those shareholders with positions prior to 2/28/97 may still buy this class.
Discount broker availability: *Fidelity, Schwab, *Siebert, White
Dividends paid: Income - declared daily, paid monthly; Capital gains - September, December
Portfolio turnover (3 yrs): 149%, 221%, 329%
Management fee: 0.30% plus group fee of 0.11% to 0.37%
Expense ratio: 0.73% (year ending 7/31/97)

FIDELITY MUNICIPAL INCOME FUND ◆
(Fund became Spartan Muni Income Fund 10/23/97)

FIDELITY MUNICIPAL MONEY MARKET FUND ◆
(See first Fidelity listing on page 284 for data common to all funds)

Portfolio manager: Diane McLaughlin (1996)
Investment objective and policies: Current income exempt from federal income tax. Invests in high quality municipal money market obligations. Fund may invest up to 100% of assets in securities subject to the federal alternative minimum tax.
Year organized: 1980 (Name changed from Tax-Exempt MM Trust, and policy changed 5/1/96.)
Ticker symbol: FTEXX
Group fund code: 010
Minimum purchase: Initial: $5,000, Subsequent: $500
Deadline for same day wire purchase: 12 NN
Discount broker availability: *Fidelity
Number switches permitted: Unlimited
Check redemptions: No minimum
Dividends paid: Income - declared daily, paid monthly

Management fee: 0.15% plus group fee of 0.11% to 0.37%
12b-1 distribution fee: Yes (not currently imposed)
Expense ratio: 0.49% (year ending 10/31/97)

FIDELITY NEW JERSEY MUNICIPAL MONEY MARKET FUND ◆
(See first Fidelity listing on page 284 for data common to all funds)

Portfolio manager: Scott A. Orr (1997)
Investment objective and policies: High current income exempt from federal and New Jersey gross income taxes. Invests primarily in money market instruments issued by the State of New Jersey and its subdivisions. May invest in any amount of municipal securities that may be considered taxable under the alternative minimum tax.
Year organized: 1988 (name changed from New Jersey Tax-Free Money Market Portfolio 1/19/96)
Ticker symbol: FNJXX
Group fund code: 417
Minimum purchase: Initial: $5,000, Subsequent: $250
Deadline for same day wire purchase: 12 NN
Discount broker availability: *Fidelity
Qualified for sale in: NJ, NY, PA
Number of switches permitted: Unlimited
Check redemptions: $500 minimum
Dividends paid: Income - declared daily, paid monthly
Management fee: 0.25% plus group fee of 0.11% to 0.37%
12b-1 distribution fee: Yes (not currently imposed)
Expense ratio: 0.61% (year ending 11/30/97)

FIDELITY NEW MARKETS INCOME FUND ◆
(See first Fidelity listing on page 284 for data common to all funds)

Portfolio manager: John H. Carlson (1995)
Investment objective and policies: High current income; capital appreciation secondary. Invests at least 65% of assets in debt securities of issuers whose principal activities are in emerging markets countries. May invest in corporate debt securities, sovereign debt instruments issued by governments or governmental entities, and all types of domestic and foreign money market instruments. At any one time substantially all assets may be in securities of poor quality or in default. May use currency forward contracts, futures and options, and hedge up to 25% of total assets.
Year organized: 1993
Ticker symbol: FNMIX
Group fund code: 331
Discount broker availability: *Fidelity, *Siebert, White
Redemption fee: 1.00% for shares held less than 180 days, payable to the fund
Dividends paid: Income - declared daily, paid monthly; Capital gains - February, December
Portfolio turnover (3 yrs): 656%, 405%, 306%
Management fee: 0.55% plus group fee of 0.11% to 0.37%
12b-1 distribution fee: Yes (not currently imposed)
Expense ratio: 1.08% (year ending 12/31/97)

FIDELITY NEW MILLENNIUM FUND
(See first Fidelity listing on page 284 for data common to all funds)

Portfolio manager: Neal Miller (1992)
Investment objective and policies: Capital growth. Invests in equity securities of companies likely to benefit from social and economic change - in social attitudes, legislative actions, economic plans, demographics, and new product innovation. Although there is no restriction on company size, emphasis will be placed on small to medium capitalization companies, often those perceived as undervalued or out of favor. Fund may use foreign stocks, foreign currency exchange contracts, and stock index futures and options.
Year organized: 1992

Ticker symbol: FMILX
Group fund code: 300
Special sales restrictions: Fund closed to new investors 5/15/96.
Sales charge: 3%
Discount broker availability: Fidelity, Schwab, Siebert, White
Dividends paid: Income - January, December; Capital gains - January, December
Portfolio turnover (3 yrs): 142%, 158%, 176%
Management fee: 0.35% plus group fee of 0.25% to 0.52% +/- performance fee of up to 0.20% relative to the S&P 500 Index over 36 months
Expense ratio: 0.94% (year ending 11/30/97) (0.99% without waiver)

FIDELITY NEW YORK INSURED MUNICIPAL INCOME FUND ◆
(Fund merged into Spartan NY Muni Income 1/98)

FIDELITY NEW YORK MUNICIPAL INCOME FUND ◆
(Fund absorbed Spartan NY Intermediate, NY Insured Muni, and OLD Spartan NY Muni Income 1/98, then became a Spartan fund in March.)

FIDELITY NEW YORK MUNICIPAL MONEY MARKET FUND ◆
(See first Fidelity listing on page 284 for data common to all funds)

Portfolio manager: Diane McLaughlin (1997)
Investment objective and policies: Income exempt from federal, NY state and NY city income taxes. Invests primarily in investment grade New York municipal money market obligations.
Year organized: 1984 (formerly New York Short-term Portfolio; name changed from Tax-Free Money Market Portfolio 2/1/96)
Ticker symbol: FNYXX
Group fund code: 092
Minimum purchase: Initial: $5,000, Subsequent: $250
Deadline for same day wire purchase: 12 NN
Discount broker availability: *Fidelity
Qualified for sale in: CT, NJ, NY
Number of switches permitted: Unlimited
Check redemptions: $500 minimum
Dividends paid: Income - declared daily, paid monthly
Management fee: 0.25% plus group fee of 0.11 to 0.37%
12b-1 distribution fee: Yes (not currently imposed)
Expense ratio: 0.61% (year ending 1/31/97)

FIDELITY NORDIC FUND
(See first Fidelity listing on page 284 for data common to all funds)

Portfolio manager: Colin Stone (1995)
Investment objective and policies: Long-term capital growth. Invests at least 65% of assets in equity and debt securities of Danish, Finnish, Norwegian and Swedish issuers. The remainder may be invested in securities of other European issuers. May have up 35% of assets in junk bonds and 15% in illiquid securities. Fund may use currency exchange contracts, futures contracts and options, and hedge up to 25% of total assets. Fund is non-diversified.
Year organized: 1995
Ticker symbol: FNORX
Group fund code: 342
Discount broker availability: Fidelity, Schwab, Siebert, White
Sales charge: 3% (may be waived for retirement accounts using Fidelity prototype plans)
Redemption fee: 1.50% on shares held less than 90 days, payable to the fund
Dividends paid: Income - December; Capital gains - December
Portfolio turnover (2 yrs): 74%, 35%
Management fee: 0.45% plus group fee of 0.25% to 0.52%
Expense ratio: 1.42% (year ending 10/31/97)

FIDELITY OHIO MUNICIPAL INCOME FUND ◆
(See Fidelity Spartan Ohio Municipal Income Fund)

FIDELITY OHIO MUNICIPAL MONEY MARKET FUND ◆
(See first Fidelity listing on page 284 for data common to all funds)

Portfolio manager: Scott A. Orr (1996)
Investment objective and policies: High current income exempt from federal and Ohio state income taxes, consistent with a stable share price and ongoing liquidity. Invests in money market instruments issued by the state of Ohio.
Year organized: 1989 (name changed from Ohio Tax-Free Money Market Portfolio on 8/10/90)
Ticker symbol: FOMXX
Group fund code: 419
Minimum purchase: Initial: $5,000, Subsequent: $250
Deadline for same day wire purchase: 12 NN
Discount broker availability: *Fidelity
Qualified for sale in: OH
Number of switches permitted: Unlimited
Check redemptions: $500 minimum
Dividends paid: Income - declared daily, paid monthly
Management fee: 0.25% plus group fee of 0.11% to 0.37%
12b-1 distribution fee: Yes (not currently imposed)
Expense ratio: 0.59% (year ending 12/31/97)

FIDELITY OTC PORTFOLIO
(See first Fidelity listing on page 284 for data common to all funds)

Portfolio manager: Robert C. Bertelson (1997)
Investment objective and policies: Long-term capital appreciation. Invests at least 65% of assets in equity securities traded on the over-the-counter securities market. May invest up to 30% of assets in foreign securities, and use currency exchange contracts, and stock index futures and options thereon to hedge up to 25% of total assets.
Year organized: 1984
Ticker symbol: FOCPX
Group fund code: 093
Discount broker availability: Fidelity, Schwab, Siebert, White
Sales charge: 3% (may be waived for retirement accounts using Fidelity prototype plans)
Dividends paid: Income - September, December; Capital gains - September, December
Portfolio turnover (3 yrs): 147%, 133%, 62%
Management fee: 0.35% plus group fee of 0.25% to 0.52% +/- performance fee of up to 0.20% relative to the NASDAQ Composite Index over 36 months
Expense ratio: 0.84% (year ending 7/31/97) (0.85% without waiver)

FIDELITY OVERSEAS FUND ◆
(See first Fidelity listing on page 284 for data common to all funds)

Portfolio manager: Richard R. Mace, Jr. (1996)
Investment objective and policies: Long-term capital growth. Invests primarily in foreign securities. Normally, at least 65% of assets will be in securities from at least three different countries located in the Americas, the Far East and Pacific Basin, and Western Europe. May also invest in the U.S. Fund may use currency exchange contracts, futures contracts and options and hedge up to 25% of total assets.
Year organized: 1984
Ticker symbol: FOSFX
Group fund code: 094
Discount broker availability: *Fidelity, Schwab, *Siebert, White
Dividends paid: Income - December; Capital gains - December
Portfolio turnover (3 yrs): 68%, 82%, 49%
Management fee: 0.45% plus group fee of 0.25% to 0.52% +/- performance fee of up to 0.20% relative to the MSCI-EAFE Index over 36 months
12b-1 distribution fee: Yes (not currently imposed)
Expense ratio: 1.20% (year ending 10/31/97) (1.23% without waiver)

FIDELITY PACIFIC BASIN FUND
(See first Fidelity listing on page 284 for data common to all funds)

Portfolio manager: Shigeki Makino (1996)
Investment objective and policies: Long-term capital growth. Invests at least 65% of assets in securities of companies that have their principal business activities in the Pacific Basin. Fund will generally be invested in at least three countries. Fund may use currency exchange contracts, futures contracts and options and hedge up to 25% of total assets.
Year organized: 1986
Ticker symbol: FPBFX
Group fund code: 302
Discount broker availability: Fidelity, Schwab, Siebert, White
Sales charge: 3% (may be waived for retirement accounts using Fidelity prototype plans)
Redemption fee: 1% on shares held less than 90 days, payable to the fund
Dividends paid: Income - December; Capital gains - December
Portfolio turnover (3 yrs): 42%, 85%, 65%
Management fee: 0.45% plus group fee of 0.25% to 0.52% +/- performance fee of up to 0.20% relative to the MSCI Pacific Index over 36 months
Expense ratio: 1.31% (year ending 10/31/97) (1.32% without waiver)

FIDELITY PURITAN FUND ◆
(See first Fidelity listing on page 284 for data common to all funds)

Portfolio managers: Bettina Doulton (1996), Kevin E. Grant (fixed-income) (1996)
Investment objective and policies: High income consistent with capital preservation. Invests primarily in a broadly diversified portfolio of high yielding securities, including common stocks, preferred stocks and bonds. Invests at least 25% of assets in fixed-income securities, and the neutral position holds about 60% equities. May invest up to 35% of assets in junk bonds, use foreign stocks, currency exchange contracts and stock index futures and options thereon. May hedge up to 25% of total assets.
Year organized: 1947
Ticker symbol: FPURX
Group fund code: 004
Discount broker availability: *Fidelity, Schwab, *Siebert, White
Dividends paid: Income - March, June, September, December; Capital gains - September, December
Portfolio turnover (3 yrs): 80%, 139%, 76%
Management fee: 0.15% plus group fee of 0.25% to 0.52%
Expense ratio: 0.66% (year ending 7/31/97) (0.67% without waiver)

FIDELITY REAL ESTATE
INVESTMENT PORTFOLIO ◆
(See first Fidelity listing on page 284 for data common to all funds)

Portfolio manager: Barry A. Greenfield (1986)
Investment objective and policies: Above average income and long-term capital growth consistent with reasonable risk. Invests at least 65% of assets in equity securities of companies principally engaged in the real estate industry. Remainder will generally be in companies with real estate-related themes or in debt securities, but may invest in all types of foreign and domestic securities, although no more than 25% of assets may be in any one industry except real estate. May hold up to 35% of assets in junk bonds, and up to 10% in illiquid securities. May use foreign currency exchange contracts and various other derivative instruments in an effort to enhance performance and for hedging purposes. May hedge up to 25% of total assets. Fund is non-diversified.
Year organized: 1986 (a portfolio of Fidelity Devonshire Trust)
Ticker symbol: FRESX
Group fund code: 303
Discount broker availability: *Fidelity, Schwab, *Siebert, White
Redemption fee: 0.75% on shares held less than 90 days, payable to the fund

Dividends paid: Income - March, June, September, December; Capital gains - March, December
Portfolio turnover (3 yrs): 55%, 85%, 75%
Management fee: 0.30% plus group fee of 0.25% to 0.52%
12b-1 distribution fee: Yes (paid by adviser)
Expense ratio: 0.90% (year ending 1/31/97) (0.94% without waiver)

FIDELITY RETIREMENT
GROWTH FUND ◆
(See first Fidelity listing on page 284 for data common to all funds)

Portfolio manager: J. Fergus Shiel (1996)
Investment objective and policies: Capital appreciation. Capital gains will be realized without regard to shareholder tax liability. Invests primarily in common stocks, both domestic and foreign that are believed to offer potential growth. May also invest in bonds, preferred stocks, warrants, real estate investment trusts and closed-end investment companies. May use currency exchange contracts, options and futures contracts. May hedge up to 25% of total assets.
Year organized: 1983 (name changed from Fidelity Freedom Fund on 1/29/91)
Ticker symbol: FDFFX
Group fund code: 073
Special sales restrictions: Designed for tax-qualified retirement plans and tax-exempt organizations; orders are not accepted for "regular" accounts.
Discount broker availability: *Fidelity, Schwab, *Siebert, White
Dividends paid: Income - January, December; Capital gains - January, December
Portfolio turnover (3 yrs): 205%, 230%, 108%
Management fee: 0.30% plus group fee of 0.25% to 0.52% +/- performance fee of up to 0.20% relative to the S&P 500 Index over 36 months
Expense ratio: 0.59% (year ending 11/30/97) (0.64% without waiver)

FIDELITY SELECT PORTFOLIOS
(Data common to all Select portfolios are shown below. See subsequent listings for data specific to individual portfolios.)

Adviser: Fidelity Management & Research Co.
Transfer agent: Fidelity Service Co.
Investment policies: May invest in foreign securities without limit, use currency forward contracts, buy and sell options and futures contracts, hedge up to 25% of total assets, sell short against the box and invest in up to 10% of assets in illiquid securities and 5% in junk bonds. (except Money Market Portfolio)
Sales charge: 3% (except for certain employee benefit plans)
Minimum purchase: Initial: $2,500, Subsequent: $250; IRA/Keogh: Initial: $500, Subsequent: $250 (exceptions noted); Automatic investment plan: Subsequent: $100
Wire orders accepted: Yes
Deadline for same day wire purchase: 4 P.M.
Discount broker availability: Fidelity, Schwab, Siebert, White (except Select Money Market)
Qualified for sale in: All states
Telephone redemptions: Yes, $10 minimum
Wire redemptions: Yes, $5,000 minimum
Letter redemptions: Signature guarantee required over $100,000
Redemption fee: 1.00% on shares purchased prior to 10/12/90. 0.75% of the amount redeemed (maximum of $7.50 for shares held 30 days or longer).
Fund pricing: Hourly from 10 a.m. to 4 P.M. when the New York Stock Exchange is open
Telephone switching: With All open Fidelity retail funds except Fidelity Destiny, Congress St., and Exchange Funds
Number of switches permitted: Unlimited trades among Select portfolios, $250 minimum; 4 round trips per year to other Fidelity funds.
Charge for switching: Among Select equity portfolios: $15 per switch ($7.50 to Fidelity and $7.50 to the portfolio) for shares held 30 days or longer, $7.50 + 0.75% of the amount redeemed ($7.50 to Fidelity and remainder to the portfolio) for shares held less than 30 days - no charge for switches out of Select Money Market Portfolio.

Dividends paid: Income - April, December; Capital gains - April, December (except Money Market)
Shareholder services: IRA, Keogh, 403(b), 401(k), qualified pension and profit-sharing plans, automatic investment plan, directed dividends, electronic funds transfer, systematic withdrawal plan
Management fee: 0.30% plus group fee of 0.25% to 0.52%
IRA/Keogh fees: Annual $10 (waived for IRA accounts with balances of $5,000 or more), Closing $10

FIDELITY SELECT - AIR
TRANSPORTATION PORTFOLIO
(See first Select listing for data common to all portfolios)

Portfolio manager: Peter Saperstone (1997)
Investment objective and policies: Capital appreciation. Invests in companies engaged in the regional, national, and international movement of passengers, mail and freight via aircraft. Companies include airlines, air cargo and express delivery operators, freight forwarders, aviation service firms and manufacturers of aeronautical equipment.
Year organized: 1985
Ticker symbol: FSAIX
Group fund code: 034
Portfolio turnover (3 yrs): 469%, 504%, 200%
Expense ratio: 1.80% (year ending 2/28/97) (1.89% without waiver)

FIDELITY SELECT - AMERICAN
GOLD PORTFOLIO
(See first Select listing for data common to all portfolios)

Portfolio manager: George Domolky (1997)
Investment objective and policies: Capital appreciation. Invests in companies engaged in exploration, mining, processing, or dealing in gold, or, to a lesser degree, in silver, platinum, diamonds, or other precious metals and minerals. Normally at least 80% of assets will be invested in gold bullion or coins (up to 50%) and in securities of North, Central and South American companies engaged in gold related activities.
Year organized: 1985
Ticker symbol: FSAGX
Group fund code: 041
Portfolio turnover (3 yrs): 63%, 56%, 34%
Expense ratio: 1.42% (year ending 2/28/97) (1.44% without waiver)

FIDELITY SELECT -
AUTOMOTIVE PORTFOLIO
(See first Select listing for data common to all portfolios)

Portfolio manager: Albert Grosman (1997)
Investment objective and policies: Capital appreciation. Invests in companies engaged in the manufacturing, marketing, and selling of automobiles, trucks, specialty vehicles, parts, tires, and related services.
Year organized: 1986
Ticker symbol: FSAVX
Group fund code: 502
Portfolio turnover (3 yrs): 175%, 61%, 63%
Expense ratio: 1.52% (year ending 2/28/97) (1.56% without waiver)

FIDELITY SELECT - BIOTECHNOLOGY
PORTFOLIO
(See first Select listing for data common to all portfolios)

Portfolio manager: James M. Harmon (1997)
Investment objective and policies: Capital appreciation. Invests in companies engaged in the research, development, scale up and manufacture of various biotechnological products, services, and processes, including such technologies as genetic engineering, hybridoma and recombinant DNA techniques and monoclonal antibodies.
Year organized: 1985
Ticker symbol: FBIOX
Group fund code: 042
Portfolio turnover (3 yrs): 41%, 67%, 77%
Expense ratio: 1.56% (year ending 2/28/97) (1.57% without waiver)

FIDELITY SELECT - BROKERAGE AND INVESTMENT MANAGEMENT PORTFOLIO
(See first Select listing for data common to all portfolios)

Portfolio manager: Peter Fruzzetti (1997)
Investment objective and policies: Capital appreciation. Invests in companies engaged in stock brokerage, commodity brokerage, investment banking, tax-advantaged investment and investment sales, investment management or related investment advisory services.
Year organized: 1985
Ticker symbol: FSLBX
Group fund code: 068
Portfolio turnover (3 yrs): 16%, 166%, 139%
Expense ratio: 1.93% (year ending 2/28/97) (1.94% without waiver)

FIDELITY SELECT - BUSINESS SERVICES AND OUTSOURCING PORTFOLIO
(See first Select listing for data common to all portfolios)

Portfolio manager: Michael D. Tarlowe (1998)
Investment objective and policies: Capital appreciation. Invests in companies that provide business-related and outsourcing services to companies and other organizations. Such services as data processing and financial back office functions are included, as well as consulting firms.
Year organized: 1998
Group fund code: 353

FIDELITY SELECT - CHEMICALS PORTFOLIO
(See first Select listing for data common to all portfolios)

Portfolio manager: Audra J. Barranco (1997)
Investment objective and policies: Capital appreciation. Invests in companies engaged in the research, development, manufacture, or marketing of products, processes, or services related to the chemical process industries.
Year organized: 1985
Ticker symbol: FSCHX
Group fund code: 069
Portfolio turnover (3 yrs): 207%, 87%, 106%
Expense ratio: 1.81% (year ending 2/28/97) (1.83% without waiver)

FIDELITY SELECT - COMPUTERS PORTFOLIO
(See first Select listing for data common to all portfolios)

Portfolio manager: Michael Tempero (1997)
Investment objective and policies: Capital appreciation. Invests in companies engaged in the research, design, development, manufacture, or distribution of products, processes, or services which relate to currently available or experimental hardware technology within the computer industry.
Year organized: 1985
Ticker symbol: FDCPX
Group fund code: 007
Portfolio turnover (3 yrs): 255%, 129%, 189%
Expense ratio: 1.44% (year ending 2/28/97) (1.48% without waiver)

FIDELITY SELECT - CONSTRUCTION AND HOUSING PORTFOLIO
(See first Select listing for data common to all portfolios)

Portfolio manager: Yolanda S. McGettigan (1997)
Investment objective and policies: Capital appreciation. Invests in companies engaged in the design and construction of residential, commercial, industrial and public works facilities, as well as companies engaged in the manufacture, supply, distribution or sale of products or services to these construction industries.
Year organized: 1986 (formerly Housing Portfolio)
Ticker symbol: FSHOX
Group fund code: 511
Portfolio turnover (3 yrs): 270%, 139%, 45%
Expense ratio: 1.35% (year ending 2/28/97) (1.41% without waiver)

FIDELITY SELECT - CONSUMER INDUSTRIES PORTFOLIO
(See first Select listing for data common to all portfolios)

Portfolio manager: Douglas B. Chase (1997)
Investment objective and policies: Capital appreciation. Invests in companies engaged in the manufacture and distribution of goods and services for consumers, both domestically and internationally.
Year organized: 1990 (name changed from Consumer Products 7/18/96)
Ticker symbol: FSCPX
Group fund code: 517
Portfolio turnover (3 yrs): 340%, 601%, 190%
Expense ratio: 2.44% (year ending 2/28/97) (2.49% without waiver)

FIDELITY SELECT - CYCLICAL INDUSTRIES PORTFOLIO
(See first Select listing for data common to all portfolios)

Portfolio manager: Albert Ruback (1997)
Investment objective and policies: Capital appreciation. Invests in equity securities of companies engaged in the research, development, manufacture, distribution, supply or sale of materials, equipment, products or services related to cyclical industries. Fund is relatively sensitive to changes in the economic cycle and will typically benefit most from a strong economy.
Year organized: 1997
Group fund code: 515

FIDELITY SELECT - DEFENSE AND AEROSPACE PORTFOLIO
(See first Select listing for data common to all portfolios)

Portfolio manager: Peter Saperstone (1997)
Investment objective and policies: Capital appreciation. Invests in companies involved in the defense and aerospace industries. May include air transport, computer related services, communications systems and general aviation companies.
Year organized: 1984
Ticker symbol: FSDAX
Group fund code: 067
Portfolio turnover (3 yrs): 219%, 267%, 146%
Expense ratio: 1.81% (year ending 2/28/97) (1.84% without waiver)

FIDELITY SELECT - DEVELOPING COMMUNICATIONS PORTFOLIO
(See first Select listing for data common to all portfolios)

Portfolio manager: Andrew Kaplan (1998)
Investment objective and policies: Capital appreciation. Invests in companies engaged in the development, manufacture or sale of emerging communications services or equipment, such as cellular, paging, personal communications networks, facsimile, fiber optic transmission, voice mail, video conferencing, microwave, satellite, and others.
Year organized: 1990
Ticker symbol: FSDCX
Group fund code: 518
Portfolio turnover (3 yrs): 202%, 249%, 266%
Expense ratio: 1.62% (year ending 2/28/97) (1.64% without waiver)

FIDELITY SELECT - ELECTRONICS PORTFOLIO
(See first Select listing for data common to all portfolios)

Portfolio manager: Andrew Kaplan (1996)
Investment objective and policies: Capital appreciation. Invests in companies engaged in the design, manufacture, or sale of electronic components (semiconductors, connectors, printed circuit boards and other components); equipment vendors to electronic component manufacturers; electronic component distributors; and electronic instruments and electronic systems vendors.
Year organized: 1985
Ticker symbol: FSELX
Group fund code: 008
Portfolio turnover (3 yrs): 341%, 366%, 205%
Expense ratio: 1.29% (year ending 2/28/97) (1.33% without waiver)

FIDELITY SELECT - ENERGY PORTFOLIO
(See first Select listing for data common to all portfolios)

Portfolio manager: Lawrence D. Rakers (1997)
Investment objective and policies: Capital appreciation. Invests in companies in the energy field, including the conventional areas of oil, gas, electricity and coal, and newer sources of energy such as nuclear, geothermal, oil shale and solar power.
Year organized: 1981
Ticker symbol: FSENX
Group fund code: 060
Portfolio turnover (3 yrs): 87%, 97%, 106%
Expense ratio: 1.55% (year ending 2/28/97) (1.57% without waiver)

FIDELITY SELECT - ENERGY SERVICE PORTFOLIO
(See first Select listing for data common to all portfolios)

Portfolio manager: James F. Catudal (1998)
Investment objective and policies: Capital appreciation. Invests in companies in the energy service field, including those that provide services and equipment to the conventional areas of oil, gas, electricity and coal, and newer sources of energy such as nuclear, geothermal, oil shale and solar power. May include companies involved in providing services and equipment in the drilling process, drill bits, drilling rig equipment, etc.
Year organized: 1985
Ticker symbol: FSESX
Group fund code: 043
Portfolio turnover (3 yrs): 167%, 223%, 209%
Expense ratio: 1.45% (year ending 2/28/97) (1.47% without waiver)

FIDELITY SELECT - ENVIRONMENTAL SERVICES PORTFOLIO
(See first Select listing for data common to all portfolios)

Portfolio manager: Steven J. Buller (1997)
Investment objective and policies: Capital appreciation. Invests primarily in companies engaged in the research, development, manufacture or distribution of products, processes or services related to waste management or pollution control.
Year organized: 1989
Ticker symbol: FSLEX
Group fund code: 516
Portfolio turnover (3 yrs): 252%, 138%, 82%
Expense ratio: 2.11% (year ending 2/28/97) (2.18% without waiver)

FIDELITY SELECT - FINANCIAL SERVICES PORTFOLIO
(See first Select listing for data common to all portfolios)

Portfolio manager: Robert D. Ewing (1998)
Investment objective and policies: Capital appreciation. Invests in companies providing financial services to consumers and industry. A company is considered principally engaged in the industry if it derives more than 15% of revenues or profits from brokerage or investment management activities. Companies in the field include commercial banks, S & L's, consumer and industrial finance companies, securities brokerage, real estate, leasing and insurance companies.
Year organized: 1981
Ticker symbol: FIDSX
Group fund code: 066
Portfolio turnover (3 yrs): 80%, 125%, 107%
Expense ratio: 1.43% (year ending 2/28/97) (1.45% without waiver)

FIDELITY SELECT - FOOD AND AGRICULTURE PORTFOLIO
(See first Select listing for data common to all portfolios)

Portfolio manager: Scott Offen (1996)
Investment objective and policies: Capital appreciation. Invests in companies engaged in the manufacture, sale or distribution of food and beverage products, agricultural products, and products related to the development of new food technologies.

Year organized: 1985
Ticker symbol: FDFAX
Group fund code: 009
Portfolio turnover (3 yrs): 91%, 126%, 96%
Expense ratio: 1.50% (year ending 2/28/97) (1.52% without waiver)

FIDELITY SELECT - HEALTH CARE PORTFOLIO
(See first Select listing for data common to all portfolios)

Portfolio manager: Beso Sikharulidze (1997)
Investment objective and policies: Capital appreciation. Invests in companies engaged in the design, manufacture or sale of products or services used for or in connection with health care or medicine. Includes securities of pharmaceutical companies, firms designing manufacturing or selling medical, dental and optical products, etc.
Year organized: 1981
Ticker symbol: FSPHX
Group fund code: 063
Portfolio turnover (3 yrs): 59%, 54%, 151%
Expense ratio: 1.32% (year ending 2/28/97) (1.33% without waiver)

FIDELITY SELECT - HOME FINANCE PORTFOLIO
(See first Select listing for data common to all portfolios)

Portfolio manager: William Rubin (1996)
Investment objective and policies: Capital appreciation. Invests in companies engaged in accepting public deposits and investing in real estate, usually through mortgages and other consumer, commercial, and construction loans.
Year organized: 1985 (name changed from Savings and Loan Portfolio on 2/17/93)
Ticker symbol: FSVLX
Group fund code: 098
Portfolio turnover (3 yrs): 78%, 81%, 124%
Expense ratio: 1.34% (year ending 2/28/97) (1.38% without waiver)

FIDELITY SELECT - INDUSTRIAL EQUIPMENT PORTFOLIO
(See first Select listing for data common to all portfolios)

Portfolio manager: Simon Wolf (1997)
Investment objective and policies: Capital appreciation. Invests in companies engaged in the manufacture, distribution or service of products and equipment for the industrial sector, including integrated producers of capital equipment (such as general industry machinery, farm equipment and computers), parts suppliers and subcontractors.
Year organized: 1986 (formerly Capital Goods, and Automation and Machinery Portfolios. Renamed Industrial Technology Portfolio 10/26/90. Renamed Industrial Equipment Portfolio 6/29/92.)
Ticker symbol: FSCGX
Group fund code: 510
Portfolio turnover (3 yrs): 261%, 115%, 131%
Expense ratio: 1.44% (year ending 2/28/97) (1.51% without waiver)

FIDELITY SELECT - INDUSTRIAL MATERIALS PORTFOLIO
(See first Select listing for data common to all portfolios)

Portfolio manager: James F. Catudal (1997)
Investment objective and policies: Capital appreciation. Invests in companies engaged in the manufacture, mining, processing, or distribution of raw materials and intermediate goods used in the industrial sector.
Year organized: 1986
Ticker symbol: FSDPX
Group fund code: 509
Portfolio turnover (3 yrs): 105%, 138%, 139%
Expense ratio: 1.51% (year ending 2/28/97) (1.54% without waiver)

FIDELITY SELECT - INSURANCE PORTFOLIO
(See first Select listing for data common to all portfolios)

Portfolio manager: Thomas Allen (1997)
Investment objective and policies: Capital appreciation. Invests in companies engaged in underwriting, reinsuring, selling, distributing or placing of property and casualty, life or health insurance. May invest in insurance brokers, reciprocals and claims processors, multi-line companies that provide health and life coverages.
Year organized: 1985 (formerly Life Insurance and Property & Casualty Insurance Portfolios)
Ticker symbol: FSPCX
Group fund code: 045
Portfolio turnover (3 yrs): 142%, 164%, 265%
Expense ratio: 1.77% (year ending 2/28/97) (1.82% without waiver)

FIDELITY SELECT - LEISURE PORTFOLIO
(See first Select listing for data common to all portfolios)

Portfolio manager: Jeffrey A. Dorsey (1998)
Investment objective and policies: Capital appreciation. Invests in companies engaged in the design, production or distribution of goods or services in the leisure industries. This includes television and radio broadcast or manufacture, motion pictures, photography, musical instruments, publishing, sporting goods and camping, and sports arenas, among others.
Year organized: 1984
Ticker symbol: FDLSX
Group fund code: 062
Portfolio turnover (3 yrs): 127%, 141%, 103%
Expense ratio: 1.54% (year ending 2/28/97) (1.56% without waiver)

FIDELITY SELECT - MEDICAL DELIVERY PORTFOLIO
(See first Select listing for data common to all portfolios)

Portfolio manager: John R. Porter III (1998)
Investment objective and policies: Capital appreciation. Invests in companies engaged in the ownership or management of hospitals, nursing homes, health maintenance organizations, and other companies specializing in the delivery of health care services.
Year organized: 1986 (formerly Health Care Delivery Portfolio)
Ticker symbol: FSHCX
Group fund code: 505
Portfolio turnover (3 yrs): 78%, 132%, 123%
Expense ratio: 1.53% (year ending 2/28/97) (1.57% without waiver)

FIDELITY SELECT - MONEY MARKET PORTFOLIO
(See first Select listing for data common to all portfolios)

Portfolio manager: John Todd (1991)
Investment objective and policies: High current income consistent with the preservation of capital and liquidity. Invests primarily in short-term money market obligations rated Aa or better.
Year organized: 1985
Group fund code: 085
Discount broker availability: Schwab (exchanges only), Waterhouse (exchanges only)
Dividends paid: Income - declared daily, paid monthly
Management fee: 0.03% plus group fee of 0.11% to 0.37% plus 6.0% of the portion of the fund's gross income that represents a gross yield of more than 5.0% per year (up to a maximum of 0.24% of average net assets)
Expense ratio: 0.56% (year ending 2/28/97)

FIDELITY SELECT - MULTIMEDIA PORTFOLIO
(See first Select listing for data common to all portfolios)

Portfolio manager: Jeffrey A. Dorsey (1997)
Investment objective and policies: Capital appreciation. Invests in companies engaged in the development, production, sale, and distribution of goods or services used in the broadcasting and media industries. Includes broadcasters, film studios, cable TV companies and equipment providers and companies involved in emerging technologies such as cellular communications.
Year organized: 1986 (name changed from Broadcast and Media Portfolio on 4/30/94)
Ticker symbol: FBMPX
Group fund code: 503
Portfolio turnover (3 yrs): 99%, 223%, 107%
Expense ratio: 1.56% (year ending 2/28/97) (1.60% without waiver)

FIDELITY SELECT - NATURAL GAS PORTFOLIO
(See first Select listing for data common to all portfolios)

Portfolio manager: Victor Y. Thay (1997)
Investment objective and policies: Capital appreciation. Invests in companies engaged in the production, transmission, and distribution of natural gas, and involved in the exploration of potential natural gas sources, as well as those companies that provide services and equipment to natural gas producers, refineries, cogeneration facilities, converters, and distributors. Companies participating in new activities working toward technological advances in the natural gas field may also be considered.
Year organized: 1993
Ticker symbol: FSNGX
Group fund code: 513
Portfolio turnover (3 yrs): 283%, 79%, 177%
Expense ratio: 1.66% (year ending 2/28/97) (1.70% without waiver)

FIDELITY SELECT - NATURAL RESOURCES PORTFOLIO
(See first Select listing for data common to all portfolios)

Portfolio manager: Lawrence D. Rakers (1997)
Investment objective and policies: Capital appreciation. Invests in equity securities of companies that own or develop natural resources or supply goods or services to such companies.
Year organized: 1997
Group fund code: 514

FIDELITY SELECT - PAPER AND FOREST PRODUCTS PORTFOLIO
(See first Select listing for data common to all portfolios)

Portfolio manager: Douglas J. Lober (1997)
Investment objective and policies: Capital appreciation. Invests in companies engaged in the manufacture, research, sale, or distribution of paper products, packaging products, building materials such as lumber and paneling products, and other products related to the paper and forest products industry.
Year organized: 1986
Ticker symbol: FSPFX
Group fund code: 506
Portfolio turnover (3 yrs): 180%, 78%, 209%
Expense ratio: 2.16% (year ending 2/28/97) (2.19% without waiver)

FIDELITY SELECT - PRECIOUS METALS AND MINERALS PORTFOLIO
(See first Select listing for data common to all portfolios)

Portfolio manager: George Domolky (1997)
Investment objective and policies: Capital growth via non-diversified common stock investments. Includes securities of companies engaged in exploration, mining, processing or dealing in gold, silver, platinum, diamonds, etc. May invest up to 10% in gold bullion or coins, and up to 50% of assets in precious metals and securities indexed to the price of gold and other precious metals.
Year organized: 1981
Ticker symbol: FDPMX
Group fund code: 061
Portfolio turnover (3 yrs): 54%, 53%, 43%
Expense ratio: 1.61% (year ending 2/28/97) (1.62% without waiver)

FIDELITY SELECT - REGIONAL BANKS PORTFOLIO
(See first Select listing for data common to all portfolios)

Portfolio manager: Christine Schaulat (1998)
Investment objective and policies: Capital appreciation. Invests in companies engaged in accepting deposits and making commercial and principally non-mortgage consumer loans.
Year organized: 1986
Ticker symbol: FSRBX
Group fund code: 507
Portfolio turnover (3 yrs): 43%, 103%, 106%
Expense ratio: 1.45% (year ending 2/28/97) (1.46% without waiver)

FIDELITY SELECT - RETAILING PORTFOLIO
(See first Select listing for data common to all portfolios)

Portfolio manager: Ramin Arani (1997)
Investment objective and policies: Capital appreciation. Invests in companies engaged in merchandising finished goods and services primarily to individual consumers. May include general merchandise retailers, department stores, food, drug stores, speciality retailers and mail order operations.
Year organized: 1985
Ticker symbol: FSRPX
Group fund code: 046
Portfolio turnover (3 yrs): 278%, 235%, 481%
Expense ratio: 1.39% (year ending 2/28/97) (1.45% without waiver)

FIDELITY SELECT - SOFTWARE AND COMPUTER SERVICES PORTFOLIO
(See first Select listing for data common to all portfolios)

Portfolio manager: John R. Porter, III (1997)
Investment objective and policies: Capital appreciation. Invests in companies engaged in research, design, production, or distribution of products or processes that relate to software or information based services.
Year organized: 1985
Ticker symbol: FSCSX
Group fund code: 028
Portfolio turnover (3 yrs): 279%, 183%, 164%
Expense ratio: 1.51% (year ending 2/28/97) (1.54% without waiver)

FIDELITY SELECT - TECHNOLOGY PORTFOLIO
(See first Select listing for data common to all portfolios)

Portfolio manager: Adam Hetnarski (1996)
Investment objective and policies: Capital appreciation. Portfolio is comprised of securities believed to have or be developing products, processes or services which will provide or benefit significantly from technological advances and improvements including computers, communications, etc.
Year organized: 1981
Ticker symbol: FSPTX
Group fund code: 064
Portfolio turnover (3 yrs): 549%, 112%, 102%
Expense ratio: 1.44% (year ending 2/28/97) (1.49% without waiver)

FIDELITY SELECT - TELECOMMUNICATIONS PORTFOLIO
(See first Select listing for data common to all portfolios)

Portfolio manager: Nicholas Thakore (1996)
Investment objective and policies: Capital appreciation. Invests in companies engaged in the development, manufacture or sale of communications services or communications equipment including telephone operating companies, long distance telephone services, telegraph, satellite, microwave, cellular radio, paging, electronic mail and cable TV services companies.
Year organized: 1985
Ticker symbol: FSTCX
Group fund code: 096
Portfolio turnover (3 yrs): 175%, 89%, 107%
Expense ratio: 1.47% (year ending 2/28/97) (1.51% without waiver)

FIDELITY SELECT - TRANSPORTATION PORTFOLIO
(See first Select listing for data common to all portfolios)

Portfolio manager: Jean-Marc Berteaux (1997)
Investment objective and policies: Capital appreciation. Invests in companies engaged in providing transportation services and/or companies engaged in the design, manufacture, distribution or sale of transportation equipment.
Year organized: 1986
Ticker symbol: FSRFX
Group fund code: 512
Portfolio turnover (3 yrs): 148%, 175%, 178%
Expense ratio: 2.48% (year ending 2/28/97) (2.50% without waiver)

FIDELITY SELECT - UTILITIES GROWTH PORTFOLIO
(See first Select listing for data common to all portfolios)

Portfolio manager: Nicholas Thakore (1997)
Investment objective and policies: Capital appreciation. Invests in public utilities and companies engaged in the manufacture, production, generation, transmission and sale of gas and electric energy; and communications companies with telephone, telegraph, satellite and microwave facilities.
Year organized: 1981 (name changed from Utilities Portfolio on 8/3/94)
Ticker symbol: FSUTX
Group fund code: 065
Portfolio turnover (3 yrs): 31%, 65%, 24%
Expense ratio: 1.46% (year ending 2/28/97) (1.47% without waiver)

FIDELITY SHORT-INTERMEDIATE GOVERNMENT FUND ◆
(See first Fidelity listing on page 284 for data common to all funds)

Portfolio manager: Curtis Hollingsworth (1991)
Investment objective and policies: High current income consistent with capital preservation. Invests primarily in securities issued or guaranteed by the U.S. Government and its agencies as to principal and interest - including mortgage securities and repurchase agreements secured by these obligations. May use futures and options related to government and other high-quality securities. Fund maintains a dollar-weighted average maturity of two to five years.
Year organized: 1991 (Name changed from Limited Maturity Govt 10/16/92; as of 7/1/96, fund no longer invests exclusively in securities fully guaranteed by the U.S.; may now be secured only by the agencies)
Ticker symbol: FLMGX
Group fund code: 464
Discount broker availability: *Fidelity, *Siebert, White
Check redemptions: $500 minimum
Dividends paid: Income - declared daily, paid monthly; Capital gains - December
Portfolio turnover (3 yrs): 126%, 188%, 266%
Management fee: 0.30% plus group fee of 0.11% to 0.37%
12b-1 distribution fee: Yes (not currently imposed)
Expense ratio: 0.81% (year ending 9/30/97)

FIDELITY SHORT-TERM BOND FUND ◆
(See first Fidelity listing on page 284 for data common to all funds)

Portfolio manager: Andrew Dudley (1997)
Investment objective and policies: High current income consistent with capital preservation. Invests in investment grade, fixed-income securities, while maintaining a dollar-weighted average maturity of three years or less. May use foreign securities, currency forward contracts, options and futures contracts. May hedge up to 25% of total assets.
Year organized: 1986 (absorbed Short-Term World Bond fund 10/31/96)
Ticker symbol: FSHBX
Group fund code: 450
Discount broker availability: *Fidelity, *Siebert, White
Check redemptions $500 minimum

Dividends paid: Income - declared daily, paid monthly; Capital gains - June, December
Portfolio turnover (3 yrs): 104%, 151%, 113%
Management fee: 0.30% plus group fee of 0.11% to 0.37%
12b-1 distribution fee: Yes (not currently imposed)
Expense ratio: 0.70% (year ending 4/30/97)

FIDELITY SMALL CAP SELECTOR FUND
(See first Fidelity listing on page 284 for data common to all funds)

Portfolio manager: Bradford F. Lewis (1993)
Investment objective and policies: Long-term capital appreciation. Normally invests at least 65% of assets in stock of companies with market capitalizations similar to those in the Russell 2000 Index that are perceived to be undervalued. May invest in preferred stocks or convertibles, and debt securities. May use securities of foreign issuers, currency exchange contracts, stock index futures and options on stocks and indexes, and hedge up to 25% of total assets.
Year organized: 1993 (name changed from Small Cap Stock 1/1/98; also expanded the capitalization range of fund investment options.)
Ticker symbol: FDSCX
Group fund code: 336
Sales charge: 3% (waived for retirement accounts using Fidelity prototype plans)
Discount broker availability: Fidelity, Schwab, Siebert, White
Redemption fee: 1.50% for shares held less than 90 days, payable to the fund
Dividends paid: Income - June, December; Capital gains - June, December
Portfolio turnover (3 yrs): 176%, 192%, 182%
Management fee: 0.35% plus group fee of 0.25% to 0.52% +/- performance fee of up to 0.20% relative to the Russell 2000 Index over 36 months
Expense ratio: 0.90% (year ending 4/30/97) (0.95% without waiver)

FIDELITY SOUTHEAST ASIA FUND
(See first Fidelity listing on page 284 for data common to all funds)

Portfolio manager: Allan Liu (1993)
Investment objective and policies: Long-term capital growth. Invests at least 65% of assets in securities of Southeast Asian issuers. Southeast Asia is defined as all countries is Southeast Asia with the exceptions of Japan, Australia and New Zealand. Fund invests in common and preferred stocks, securities convertible into stocks, equity securities of closed-end investment companies, depository receipts of equity securities, debt securities and U.S. and foreign money market instruments for defensive purposes. May use options and futures to hedge up to 25% of assets. May invest up to 15% of assets in illiquid securities and up to 35% in junk bonds.
Year organized: 1993
Ticker symbol: FSEAX
Group fund code: 351
Sales charge: 3% (may be waived for retirement accounts using Fidelity prototype plans)
Discount broker availability: Fidelity, Schwab, Siebert, White
Redemption fee: 1.50% on shares held less than 90 days, payable to the fund
Dividends paid: Income - December; Capital gains - December
Portfolio turnover (3 yrs): 141%, 102%, 94%
Management fee: 0.45% plus group fee of 0.25% to 0.52%
Expense ratio: 1.32% (year ending 10/31/97)

FIDELITY SPARTAN AGGRESSIVE MUNICIPAL FUND ◆
(See first Fidelity listing on page 284 for data common to all funds)

Portfolio manager: George A. Fischer (1998)
Investment objective and policies: High current income exempt from federal income tax. Invests primarily in medium and lower quality municipal bonds rated A or lower, with maturities of 20 years or more.

May, however, invest in funds of higher quality if perceived return potential of primary investments is not commensurate with the risk. Fund may invest an unlimited amount of assets in securities subject to the alternative minimum tax (AMT securities), and up to 10% in obligations in default. May use futures and options and hedge up to 25% of total assets.

Year organized: 1985 (name changed from Aggressive Tax-Free 12/14/95 and objective adjusted to allow unlimited AMT securities; objective adjusted to allow more investment grade securities 6/24/96; absorbed old Spartan Aggressive Muni Fund 7/31/97, and was then renamed Spartan Aggressive Muni)
Ticker symbol: FATFX
Group fund code: 012
Sales restrictions: Fund closed to new investors 1/30/98 pending possible merger with Spartan Insured Municipal Income Fund and Spartan Municipal Income Fund. If accepted 7/15/98, merger will be complete by 9/1/98.
Minimum purchase: Initial: $10,000, Subsequent: $1,000; Automatic investment plan: Subsequent: $500
Discount broker availability: *Fidelity, White
Redemption fee: 1.00% for shares held less than 180 days
Dividends paid: Income - declared daily, paid monthly; Capital gains - February, December
Portfolio turnover (3 yrs): 49%, 35%, 39%
Management fee: 0.30% plus group fee of 0.11% to 0.37%
12b-1 distribution fee: Yes (not currently imposed)
Expense ratio: 0.55% (year ending 12/31/97) (0.56% without waiver)

FIDELITY SPARTAN ARIZONA MUNICIPAL INCOME FUND ◆
(See first Fidelity listing on page 284 for data common to all funds)

Portfolio manager: Jonathan D. Short (1995)
Investment objective and policies: High current income exempt from federal and Arizona state personal income taxes. Invests primarily in investment grade Arizona municipal bonds. Portfolio is generally managed to react to interest rate changes similarly to municipal bonds with maturities of between eight and eighteen years. Up to 1/3 of assets may be in obligations rated below Baa, but not lower than Caa. Fund may use futures contracts and options thereon and zero coupon bonds. Designed to deliver extra high yields for long-term buy and hold investors by maintaining a lower than average expense ratio.
Year organized: 1994
Group fund code: 434
Minimum purchase: Initial: $10,000, Subsequent: $1,000; Automatic investment plan: Subsequent: $500
Discount broker availability: *Fidelity
Qualified for sale in: AZ, CA, CO, NV, NM, NY, UT
Redemption fee: 0.50% on shares held less than 180 days, payable to the fund
Dividends paid: Income - declared daily, paid monthly (not paid in cash); Capital gains - October, December
Portfolio turnover (3 yrs): 27%, 32%, 56%
Management fee: 0.55%
12b-1 distribution fee: Yes (not currently imposed)
Expense ratio: 0.53% (year ending 8/31/97) (0.55% without waiver)

FIDELITY SPARTAN ARIZONA MUNICIPAL MONEY MARKET FUND ◆
(See first Fidelity listing on page 284 for data common to all funds)

Portfolio manager: Scott A. Orr (1997)
Investment objective and policies: High current income exempt from federal and Arizona state personal income taxes, consistent with capital preservation. Invests in Arizona municipal money market securities of two highest grades. Designed to deliver extra high yields for long-term buy and hold investors by maintaining a lower than average expense ratio.
Year organized: 1994
Ticker symbol: FSAXX
Group fund code: 433
Minimum purchase: Initial: $25,000, Subsequent: $1,000; Automatic investment plan: Subsequent: $500
Wire orders accepted: Yes, $5 fee
Discount broker availability: Fidelity

Qualified for sale in: AZ, CA, CO, NV, NM, NY, UT
Telephone redemptions: Yes, $5 fee including exchanges
Wire redemptions: Yes, $5 fee
Check redemptions: $1,000 minimum, $2 fee per check
Account closeout fee: $5
Fee waivers: All wire purchase/redemption, redemption, check writing and account closeout fees waived for Spartan accounts with balance of $50,000 or more at time of transaction.
Dividends paid: Income - declared daily, paid monthly
Management fee: 0.50%
12b-1 distribution fee: Yes (not currently imposed)
Expense ratio: 0.35% (year ending 8/31/97) (0.44% without waiver)

FIDELITY SPARTAN CALIFORNIA INTERMEDIATE MUNICIPAL INCOME FUND ◆
(Fund merged with Spartan CA Muni Income fund 8/21/97)

FIDELITY SPARTAN CALIFORNIA MUNICIPAL INCOME FUND ◆
(Fund merged into Fidelity CA Muni Income 8/14/97, which was, in turn, renamed Spartan California Municipal Income Fund)

FIDELITY SPARTAN CALIFORNIA MUNICIPAL INCOME FUND ◆
(See first Fidelity listing on page 284 for data common to all funds)

Portfolio manager: Jonathan D. Short (1995)
Investment objective and policies: High current income exempt from federal and California state income taxes. Invests primarily in investment grade California municipal bonds of any maturity. Managed to react to interest rate changes similarly to municipal bonds with remaining portfolio maturities ranging from eight to 18 years. May only invest one third of assets in bonds rated as low as BB, but not lower than B or equivalent. Fund may use options and futures to hedge up to 25% of assets, and zero coupon bonds.
Year organized: 1984 (name and objective changed 2/2/86; name changed from Tax-Free High Yield 2/1/96. Name changed from CA Muni Income 8/28/97, when fund absorbed old Spartan CA Muni Income, Spartan CA Inter Muni Income, and CA Insured Muni Inc.)
Ticker symbol: FCTFX
Group fund code: 091
Minimum purchase: Initial: $10,000, Subsequent: $1,000; Automatic investment plan: Subsequent: $500
Discount broker availability: *Fidelity, White
Qualified for sale in: CA
Check redemptions: $500 minimum
Redemption fee: 0.50% on shares held less than 180 days, payable to the fund
Dividends paid: Income - declared daily, paid monthly; Capital gains - April, December
Portfolio turnover (3 yrs): 17%, 37%, 29%
Management fee: 0.25% plus group fee of 0.11% to 0.37%
12b-1 distribution fee: Yes (not currently imposed)
Expense ratio: 0.57% (year ending 2/28/97)

FIDELITY SPARTAN CALIFORNIA MUNICIPAL MONEY MARKET FUND ◆
(See first Fidelity listing on page 284 for data common to all funds)

Portfolio manager: Diane McGlaughlin (1997)
Investment objective and policies: High current income exempt from federal and California state income taxes, consistent with capital preservation and price stability. Invests in California municipal money market securities of two highest grades. Designed to deliver extra high yields for long-term buy and hold investors by maintaining a lower than average expense ratio.
Year organized: 1989
Ticker symbol: FSPXX

Group fund code: 457
Minimum purchase: Initial: $25,000, Subsequent: $1,000; Automatic investment plan: Subsequent: $500
Wire orders accepted: Yes, $5 fee
Discount broker availability: Fidelity
Qualified for sale in: CA
Telephone redemptions: Yes, $5 fee including exchanges
Wire redemptions: Yes, $5 fee
Check redemptions: $1,000 minimum, $2 fee per check
Account closeout fee: $5
Fee waivers: All wire purchase/redemption, redemption, check writing and account closeout fees waived for Spartan accounts with balance of $50,000 or more at time of transaction.
Dividends paid: Income - declared daily, paid monthly
Management fee: 0.50%
12b-1 distribution fee: Yes (not currently imposed)
Expense ratio: 0.34% (year ending 2/28/97) (0.35% without waiver)

FIDELITY SPARTAN CONNECTICUT MUNICIPAL INCOME FUND ◆
(See first Fidelity listing on page 284 for data common to all funds)

Portfolio manager: George A. Fischer (1996)
Investment objective and policies: High current income exempt from federal and Connecticut state income taxes. Invests primarily in investment grade Connecticut municipal bonds. Managed to react to interest rate changes similarly to municipal bonds with remaining portfolio maturities ranging from eight to 18 years. Up to 1/3 of assets may be in obligations rated below Baa, but not lower than Caa. Fund may use futures contracts and options thereon and zero coupon bonds. Designed to deliver extra high yields for long-term buy and hold investors by maintaining a lower than average expense ratio.
Year organized: 1987 (name changed from Fidelity CT Tax-Free High Yield on 3/1/91; name changed from CT Municipal High Yield 1/16/96)
Ticker symbol: FICNX
Group fund code: 407
Minimum purchase: Initial: $10,000, Subsequent: $1,000; Automatic investment plan: Subsequent: $500
Discount broker availability: *Fidelity
Qualified for sale in: CT, NJ, NY
Redemption fee: 0.50% on shares held less than 180 days, payable to the fund
Dividends paid: Income - declared daily, paid monthly; Capital gains - January, December
Portfolio turnover (3 yrs): 12%, 30%, 39%
Management fee: 0.55%
12b-1 distribution fee: Yes (not currently imposed)
Expense ratio: 0.55% (year ending 11/30/97)

FIDELITY SPARTAN CONNECTICUT MUNICIPAL MONEY MARKET FUND ◆
(See first Fidelity listing on page 284 for data common to all funds)

Portfolio manager: Scott A. Orr (1997)
Investment objective and policies: High current income exempt from federal and Connecticut state income taxes, consistent with capital preservation. Invests in Connecticut municipal money market securities of the two highest grades. Designed to deliver extra high yields for long-term buy and hold investors by maintaining a lower than average expense ratio.
Year organized: 1991
Ticker symbol: SPCXX
Group fund code: 425
Minimum purchase: Initial: $25,000, Subsequent: $1,000; Automatic investment plan: Subsequent: $500
Wire orders accepted: Yes, $5 fee
Discount broker availability: Fidelity
Qualified for sale in: CT, NJ, NY
Telephone redemptions: Yes, $5 fee including exchanges
Wire redemptions: Yes, $5 fee
Check redemptions: $1,000 minimum, $2 fee per check
Account closeout fee: $5
Fee waivers: All wire purchase/redemption, redemption, check writing and account closeout fees waived

for Spartan accounts with balance of $50,000 or more at time of transaction.
Dividends paid: Income - declared daily, paid monthly
Management fee: 0.50%
12b-1 distribution fee: Yes (not currently imposed)
Expense ratio: 0.50% (year ending 11/30/97)

FIDELITY SPARTAN EXTENDED MARKET INDEX FUND ◆
(See first Fidelity listing on page 284 for data common to all funds)

Sub-adviser: Bankers Trust Co.
Investment objective and policies: Total return corresponding to at least 98% of the return of the Wilshire 4500 Equity Index, an index of mid- to small-capitalization U.S. companies. Invests at least 80% of assets in common stocks of companies that comprise the Index, which includes 6,500 domestic companies; all the companies of the Wilshire 5000 except for those included in the S&P 500. Fund may engage in the use of certain derivatives for hedging purposes.
Year organized: 1997
Group fund code: 398
Minimum purchase: Initial: $15,000, Subsequent: $1,000; Automatic investment plan: Subsequent: $500
Discount broker availability: *Fidelity
Qualified for sale in: All states
Sales charge: 0.75%, paid to fund
Dividends paid: Income - April, December; Capital gains - April, December
Management fee: 0.25%
12b-1 distribution fee: Yes (paid by adviser)

FIDELITY SPARTAN FLORIDA MUNICIPAL INCOME FUND ◆
(See first Fidelity listing on page 284 for data common to all funds)

Portfolio manager: Jonathan D. Short (1996)
Investment objective and policies: High current income exempt from federal income tax and Florida intangible personal property tax. Invests primarily in investment grade Florida municipal bonds. Managed to react to interest rate changes similarly to municipal bonds with remaining portfolio maturities ranging from eight to 18 years. Fund may use futures contracts and options thereon and zero coupon bonds. Designed to deliver extra high yields for long-term buy and hold investors by maintaining a lower than average expense ratio.
Year organized: 1992
Ticker symbol: FFLIX
Group fund code: 427
Minimum purchase: Initial: $10,000, Subsequent: $1,000; Automatic investment plan: Subsequent: $500
Discount broker availability: *Fidelity
Qualified for sale in: CT, FL, MA, NJ, NY, PA
Check redemptions: $1,000 minimum
Redemption fee: 0.50% on shares held less than 180 days, payable to the fund
Dividends paid: Income - declared daily, paid monthly; Capital gains - January, December
Portfolio turnover (3 yrs): 25%, 28%, 65%
Management fee: 0.55%
12b-1 distribution fee: Yes (not currently imposed)
Expense ratio: 0.55% (year ending 11/30/97)

FIDELITY SPARTAN FLORIDA MUNICIPAL MONEY MARKET FUND ◆
(See first Fidelity listing on page 284 for data common to all funds)

Portfolio manager: Scott A. Orr (1997)
Investment objective and policies: High level of current income exempt from federal income tax and Florida intangible personal property tax, consistent with capital preservation. Invests in Florida municipal money market securities of two highest grades. Designed to deliver extra high yields for long-term buy and hold investors by maintaining a lower than average expense ratio.
Year organized: 1992
Ticker symbol: FSFXX
Group fund code: 428

Minimum purchase: Initial: $25,000, Subsequent: $1,000; Automatic investment plan: Subsequent: $500
Wire orders accepted: Yes, $5 fee
Discount broker availability: Fidelity
Qualified for sale in: CT, FL, MA, NJ, NY, PA
Telephone redemptions: Yes, $5 fee including exchanges
Wire redemptions: Yes, $5 fee
Check redemptions: $1,000 minimum, $2 fee per check
Account closeout fee: $5
Fee waivers: All wire purchase/redemption, redemption, check writing and account closeout fees waived for Spartan accounts with balance of $50,000 or more at time of transaction.
Dividends paid: Income - declared daily, paid monthly
Management fee: 0.50%
12b-1 distribution fee: Yes (not currently imposed)
Expense ratio: 0.49% (year ending 11/30/97) (0.50% without waiver)

FIDELITY SPARTAN GINNIE MAE FUND ◆
(See first Fidelity listing on page 284 for data common to all funds)

Portfolio manager: Curtis Hollingsworth (1997)
Investment objective and policies: High current income consistent with prudent investment risk. Invests at least 65% of assets in mortgage certificates issued by the Government National Mortgage Association (GNMA, or Ginnie Mae). Managed to react to interest rate changes similarly to municipal bonds with remaining portfolio maturities ranging from two to ten years. Remainder will be in obligations guaranteed as to principal and interest by the U.S. Government. Designed to deliver extra high yields for long-term buy and hold investors by maintaining a lower than average expense ratio.
Year organized: 1990
Ticker symbol: SGNMX
Group fund code: 461
Minimum purchase: Initial: $10,000, Subsequent: $1,000; Automatic investment plan: Subsequent: $500
Wire orders accepted: Yes, $5 fee
Discount broker availability: *Fidelity, White
Telephone redemptions: Yes, $5 fee including exchanges
Wire redemptions: Yes, $5 fee
Check redemptions: $1,000 minimum, $2 fee per check
Account closeout fee: $5
Fee waivers: All wire purchase/redemption, redemption, check writing and account closeout fees waived for Spartan accounts with balance of $50,000 or more at time of transaction.
Dividends paid: Income - declared daily, paid monthly; Capital gains - October, December
Portfolio turnover (3 yrs): 104%, 115%, 229%
Management fee: 0.65%
12b-1 distribution fee: Yes (not currently imposed)
Expense ratio: 0.51% (year ending 8/31/97)

FIDELITY SPARTAN GOVERNMENT INCOME FUND ◆
(See first Fidelity listing on page 284 for data common to all funds)

Portfolio manager: Curtis Hollingsworth (1997)
Investment objective and policies: High current income. Invests exclusively in U.S. Government securities and repurchase agreements thereon. Managed to react to interest rate changes similarly to municipal bonds with remaining portfolio maturities ranging from five to twelve years. Fund may use futures contracts and options thereon. Designed to deliver extra high yields for long-term buy and hold investors by maintaining a lower than average expense ratio.
Year organized: 1988 (name changed from Spartan Govt Fund on 12/17/90); absorbed Spartan Long-Term Govt Bond 5/31/96)
Ticker symbol: SPGVX
Group fund code: 453
Minimum purchase: Initial: $10,000, Subsequent: $1,000; Automatic investment plan: Subsequent: $500
Wire orders accepted: Yes, $5 fee
Discount broker availability: *Fidelity, White

Telephone redemptions: Yes, $5 fee including exchanges
Wire redemptions: Yes, $5 fee
Check redemptions: $1,000 minimum, $2 fee per check
Account closeout fee: $5
Fee waivers: All wire purchase/redemption, redemption, check writing and account closeout fees waived for Spartan accounts with balance of $50,000 or more at time of transaction.
Dividends paid: Income - declared daily, paid monthly; Capital gains - June, December
Portfolio turnover (3 yrs): 135%, 114%, 303%
Management fee: 0.65%
Expense ratio: 0.60% (year ending 4/30/97)

FIDELITY SPARTAN HIGH INCOME FUND ◆
(See first Fidelity listing on page 284 for data common to all funds)

Portfolio manager: Thomas T. Soviero (1996)
Investment objective and policies: High current income. Invests at least 65% of assets in all types of income-producing debt securities, preferred stocks, and convertible securities, with a strategic lean towards high-yielding speculative junk bonds. May use futures contracts and options thereon, invest up to 10% of assets in securities in default, up to 15% in illiquid or restricted securities, and up to 20% in equity securities. May hedge up to 25% of total assets and sell short against the box. Designed to deliver extra high yields for long-term buy and hold investors by maintaining a lower than average expense ratio.
Year organized: 1990
Ticker symbol: SPHIX
Group fund code: 455
Minimum purchase: Initial: $10,000, Subsequent: $1,000; Automatic investment plan: Subsequent: $500
Wire orders accepted: Yes, $5 fee
Discount broker availability: *Fidelity
Telephone redemptions: Yes, $5 fee including exchanges
Wire redemptions: Yes, $5 fee
Redemption fee: 1.00% on shares held less than 270 days, payable to the fund
Account closeout fee: $5
Fee waivers: All wire purchase/redemption, redemption, check writing and account closeout fees waived for Spartan accounts with balance of $50,000 or more at time of transaction.
Dividends paid: Income - declared daily, paid monthly; Capital gains - June, December
Portfolio turnover (3 yrs): 102%, 170%, 172%
Management fee: 0.80%
12b-1 distribution fee: Yes (not currently imposed)
Expense ratio: 0.80% (year ending 4/30/97)

FIDELITY SPARTAN INSURED MUNICIPAL INCOME FUND ◆
(See first Fidelity listing on page 284 for data common to all funds)

Portfolio manager: George A. Fischer (1995)
Investment objective and policies: High income exempt from federal income tax, consistent with capital preservation. Invests primarily in municipal bonds covered by insurance guaranteeing the timely payment of principal and interest with a dollar-weighted average maturity of 20 years or longer. Up to 35% of assets may be invested in uninsured obligations with not more than 5% below investment grade. May use futures and options and hedge up to 25% of total assets. Designed to deliver extra high yields for long-term buy and hold investors by maintaining a lower than average expense ratio.
Year organized: 1985 (name changed from Fidelity Insured Tax-Free 2/96; name changed from Insured Muni Income and became a Spartan fund 4/1/97)
Ticker symbol: FMUIX
Group fund code: 013
Sales restrictions: Fund closed to new investors 1/30/98 pending possible merger with Spartan Aggressive Municipal Income Fund and Spartan Municipal Income Fund. If accepted 7/15/98, merger will be complete by 9/1/98.
Minimum purchase: Initial: $10,000, Subsequent: $1,000; Automatic investment plan: Subsequent: $500

Discount broker availability: *Fidelity, White
Check redemptions: $1,000 minimum
Dividends paid: Income - declared daily, paid monthly; Capital gains - February, December
Portfolio turnover (3 yrs): 24%, 31%, 61%
Management fee: 0.25% plus group fee of 0.11% to 0.37%
12b-1 distribution fee: Yes (not currently imposed)
Expense ratio: 0.57% (year ending 12/31/97) (includes waiver)

FIDELITY SPARTAN INTERMEDIATE MUNICIPAL INCOME FUND ◆

(See first Fidelity listing on page 284 for data common to all funds)

Portfolio manager: Norman Lind (1995)
Investment objective and policies: High current income exempt from federal income tax. Invests at least 80% of assets in municipal securities whose interest is exempt from federal income tax, primarily securities rated A or better by Moody's or S&P with a dollar-weighted average maturity of three to ten years. Managed to react to interest rate changes similarly to municipal bonds with remaining portfolio maturities ranging from seven to ten years. May invest without limit in lower quality bonds. Fund may use futures and options thereon and hedge up to 25% of total assets. Designed to deliver extra high yields for long-term buy and hold investors by maintaining a lower than average expense ratio.
Year organized: 1993
Ticker symbol: FSIMX
Group fund code: 443
Sales restrictions: Fund closed to new investors 4/1/97 in anticipation of a merger with Fidelity Limited-Term Muni Income.
Minimum purchase: Initial: $10,000, Subsequent: $1,000; Automatic investment plan: Subsequent: $500
Discount broker availability: *Fidelity, White
Check redemptions: $1,000 minimum
Dividends paid: Income - declared daily, paid monthly; Capital gains - October, December
Portfolio turnover (3 yrs): 20%, 64%, 44%
Management fee: 0.55%
12b-1 distribution fee: Yes (not currently imposed)
Expense ratio: 0.55% (year ending 8/31/97)

FIDELITY SPARTAN INTERNATIONAL INDEX FUND ◆

(See first Fidelity listing on page 284 for data common to all funds)

Sub-adviser: Bankers Trust Co.
Investment objective and policies: Total return corresponding to at least 98% of the return of the EAFE Index, a capitalization weighted index of companies found in 14 European countries as well as Australia, New Zealand, Hong Kong, Japan, Malaysia and Singapore. This index does not represent emerging markets. Invests at least 80% of assets in common stocks of companies that comprise the Index. Fund may engage in the use of certain derivatives for hedging purposes.
Year organized: 1997
Group fund code: 399
Minimum purchase: Initial: $15,000, Subsequent: $1,000; Automatic investment plan: Subsequent: $500
Discount broker availability: *Fidelity
Qualified for sale in: All states
Sales charge: 1.00%, paid to fund
Dividends paid: Income - April, December; Capital gains - April, December
Management fee: 0.40%
12b-1 distribution fee: Yes (paid by adviser)

FIDELITY SPARTAN INVESTMENT GRADE BOND FUND ◆

(See first Fidelity listing on page 284 for data common to all funds)

Portfolio manager: Kevin E. Grant (1997)
Investment objective and policies: High current income. Invests primarily in investment grade corporate debt securities issued by U.S. or foreign corporations, banks, or other business organizations. Fund

generally focuses on longer-term bonds, with a dollar-weighted average maturity of four to ten years. Designed to deliver extra high yields for long-term buy and hold investors by maintaining a lower than average expense ratio.
Year organized: 1992
Ticker symbol: FSIBX
Group fund code: 448
Minimum purchase: Initial: $10,000, Subsequent: $1,000; Automatic investment plan: Subsequent: $500
Wire orders accepted: Yes, $5 fee
Discount broker availability: *Fidelity, White
Telephone redemptions: Yes, $5 fee including exchanges
Wire redemptions: Yes, $5 fee
Check redemptions: $1,000 minimum, $2 fee per check
Account closeout fee: $5
Fee waivers: All wire purchase/redemption, redemption, check writing and account closeout fees waived for Spartan accounts with balance of $50,000 or more at time of transaction.
Dividends paid: Income - declared daily, paid monthly; Capital gains - June, December
Portfolio turnover (3 yrs): 194%, 169%, 147%
Management fee: 0.65%
12b-1 distribution fee: Yes (not currently imposed)
Expense ratio: 0.48% (year ending 9/30/97) (0.60% without waiver)

FIDELITY SPARTAN LIMITED MATURITY GOVERNMENT FUND ◆

(See first Fidelity listing on page 284 for data common to all funds)

Portfolio manager: Curtis Hollingsworth (1988)
Investment objective and policies: High current income consistent with capital preservation. Invests at least 65% of assets in obligations of the U.S. Government and its agencies. May invest up to 40% of assets in mortgage-backed securities. Fund normally maintains a dollar-weighted average maturity of one to four years, but may reach a maximum of ten years. Fund may use securities of foreign issuers, zero coupon bonds and pay in kind obligations and futures contracts and options thereon. May hedge up to 50% of total assets. Designed to deliver extra high yields for long-term buy and hold investors by maintaining a lower than average expense ratio.
Year organized: 1988 (formerly Short-Term Government. Name and objective changed in 1990)
Ticker symbol: FSTGX
Group fund code: 452
Minimum purchase: Initial: $10,000, Subsequent: $1,000; Automatic investment plan: Subsequent: $500
Wire orders accepted: Yes, $5 fee
Discount broker availability: *Fidelity, White
Telephone redemptions: Yes, $5 fee including exchanges
Wire redemptions: Yes, $5 fee
Check redemptions: $1,000 minimum, $2 fee per check
Account closeout fee: $5
Fee waivers: All wire purchase/redemption, redemption, check writing and account closeout fees waived for Spartan accounts with balance of $50,000 or more at time of transaction.
Dividends paid: Income - declared daily, paid monthly; Capital gains - September, December
Portfolio turnover (3 yrs): 105%, 105%, 210%
Management fee: 0.65%
12b-1 distribution fee: Yes (not currently imposed)
Expense ratio: 0.54% (year ending 7/31/97)

FIDELITY SPARTAN MARKET INDEX FUND ◆

(See first Fidelity listing on page 284 for data common to all funds)

Sub-adviser: Bankers Trust Co.
Portfolio manager: Jennifer Farrelly (1994)
Investment objective and policies: Investment results that correspond to the total return of the S&P 500 Index. Long-term correlation target is 0.98. Invests in equity securities of companies which compose the S&P 500 Index, allocated in approximately the same weightings

as the Index. Fund may use index futures and options and other derivative instruments to maintain fully invested position and for hedging purposes.
Year organized: 1990 (name changed from Fidelity Spartan Market Index 11/1/91; name changed back from Fidelity Market Index 4/18/97)
Ticker symbol: FSMKX
Group fund code: 317
Minimum purchase: Initial: $10,000, Subsequent: $1,000; Automatic investment plan: Subsequent: $500
Discount broker availability: *Fidelity, White
Check redemptions: $1,000 minimum
Redemption fee: 0.50% for shares held less than 90 days, payable to the fund
Dividends paid: Income - March, June, September, December; Capital gains - June, December
Portfolio turnover (3 yrs): 6%, 5%, 2%
Management fee: 0.45%
12b-1 distribution fee: Yes (not currently imposed)
Expense ratio: 0.44% (year ending 4/30/97)

FIDELITY SPARTAN MARYLAND MUNICIPAL INCOME FUND ◆

(See first Fidelity listing on page 284 for data common to all funds)

Portfolio manager: George A. Fischer (1998)
Investment objective and policies: Current income exempt from federal and Maryland state and county income taxes. Invests primarily in investment grade municipal bonds issued by the State of Maryland, with the portfolio maintaining a dollar-weighted average maturity ranging from eight to 18 years. Up to 5% of assets may be in junk bonds. Fund may use futures and options thereon and hedge up to 25% of total assets. Designed to deliver extra high yields for long-term buy and hold investors by maintaining a lower than average expense ratio.
Year organized: 1993
Ticker symbol: SMDMX
Group fund code: 429
Minimum purchase: Initial: $10,000, Subsequent: $1,000; Automatic investment plan: Subsequent: $500
Discount broker availability: *Fidelity
Qualified for sale in: DE, DC, HI, MD, NJ, VA, WY
Redemption fee: 0.50% on shares held less than 180 days, payable to the fund
Dividends paid: Income - declared daily, paid monthly; Capital gains - October, December
Portfolio turnover (3 yrs): 41%, 74%, 72%
Management fee: 0.55%
12b-1 distribution fee: Yes (not currently imposed)
Expense ratio: 0.54% (year ending 8/31/97) (0.55% without waiver)

FIDELITY SPARTAN MASSACHUSETTS MUNICIPAL INCOME FUND ◆

(See first Fidelity listing on page 284 for data common to all funds)

Portfolio manager: Jonathan D. Short (1997)
Investment objective and policies: Current income exempt from federal and Massachusetts personal income taxes. Invests at least 80% of assets in municipal obligations exempt from these income taxes, rated Baa or better. Portfolio maintains a dollar-weighted average maturity of 15 years or more, with obligations ranging from eight to 18 years. Fund may use zero coupon obligations and futures contracts and options thereon. May hedge up to 25% of total assets.
Year organized: 1983 (name changed from Tax-Free High Yield 2/1/96; name changed from MA Muni Income and became a Spartan fund 4/1/97)
Ticker symbol: FDMMX
Group fund code: 070
Discount broker availability: *Fidelity, White
Qualified for sale in: MA
Check redemptions: $500 minimum
Dividends paid: Income - declared daily, paid monthly; Capital gains - March, December
Portfolio turnover (3 yrs): 21%, 44%, 33%
Management fee: 0.25% plus group fee of 0.11% to 0.37%
12b-1 distribution fee: Yes (not currently imposed)
Expense ratio: 0.53% (year ending 1/31/98)

FIDELITY SPARTAN MASSACHUSETTS MUNICIPAL MONEY MARKET FUND ◆
(See first Fidelity listing on page 284 for data common to all funds)

Portfolio manager: Scott A. Orr (1997)
Investment objective and policies: High current income exempt from federal and Massachusetts personal income taxes, consistent with capital preservation. Invests at least 65% of assets in Massachusetts municipal money market securities. Designed to deliver extra high yields for long-term buy and hold investors by maintaining a lower than average expense ratio.
Year organized: 1991
Ticker symbol: FMSXX
Group fund code: 426
Minimum purchase: Initial: $25,000, Subsequent: $1,000; Automatic investment plan: Subsequent: $500
Wire orders accepted: Yes, $5 fee
Discount broker availability: Fidelity
Qualified for sale in: MA
Telephone redemptions: Yes, $5 fee including exchanges
Wire redemptions: Yes, $5 fee
Check redemptions: $1,000 minimum, $2 fee
Account closeout fee: $5
Fee waivers: All wire purchase/redemption, redemption, check writing and account closeout fees waived for Spartan accounts with balance of $50,000 or more at time of transaction.
Dividends paid: Income - declared daily, paid monthly
Management fee: 0.50%
12b-1 distribution fee: Yes (not currently imposed)
Expense ratio: 0.50% (year ending 1/31/98)

FIDELITY SPARTAN MICHIGAN MUNICIPAL INCOME FUND ◆
(See first Fidelity listing on page 284 for data common to all funds)

Portfolio manager: Norman Lind (1998)
Investment objective and policies: High current income exempt from federal and Michigan state personal income taxes. Invests primarily in investment grade Michigan municipal bonds. Managed to react to interest rate changes similarly to municipal bonds with remaining portfolio maturities ranging from eight to 18 years. Fund may use zero coupon obligations and futures contracts and options thereon. May hedge up to 25% of total assets.
Year organized: 1985 (name changed from Michigan Tax-Free High Yield 2/20/96; name changed from Michigan Muni and became a Spartan fund 4/1/97)
Ticker symbol: FMHTX
Group fund code: 081
Minimum purchase: Initial: $25,000, Subsequent: $1,000; Automatic investment plan: Subsequent: $500
Discount broker availability: *Fidelity, White
Qualified for sale in: MI
Check redemptions: $1,000 minimum
Dividends paid: Income - declared daily, paid monthly; Capital gains - February, December
Portfolio turnover (3 yrs): 16%, 29%, 29%
Management fee: 0.25% plus group fee of 0.11% to 0.37%
12b-1 distribution fee: Yes (not currently imposed)
Expense ratio: 0.56% (year ending 12/31/97)

FIDELITY SPARTAN MINNESOTA MUNICIPAL INCOME FUND ◆
(See first Fidelity listing on page 284 for data common to all funds)

Portfolio manager: Jonathan D. Short (1995)
Investment objective and policies: High current income exempt from federal and Minnesota state personal income taxes. Invests primarily in municipal obligations of the state of Minnesota or its political subdivisions, whose interest is exempt from federal and Minnesota taxes. Portfolio is managed to react to changes in interest rates similarly to municipal bonds with maturities ranging from eight to 18 years. Fund may use zero coupon obligations and futures contracts and options thereon. May hedge up to 25% of total assets.
Year organized: 1985 (name changed from MN Tax-Free 12/14/95; name changed from MN Muni Income and became a Spartan fund 4/1/97)
Ticker symbol: FIMIX
Group fund code: 082
Minimum purchase: Initial: $25,000, Subsequent: $1,000; Automatic investment plan: Subsequent: $500
Discount broker availability: *Fidelity, White
Qualified for sale in: MN
Check redemptions: $500 minimum
Dividends paid: Income - declared daily, paid monthly; Capital gains - February, December
Portfolio turnover (3 yrs): 18%, 17%, 49%
Management fee: 0.25% plus group fee of 0.11% to 0.37%
12b-1 distribution fee: Yes (not currently imposed)
Expense ratio: 0.56% (year ending 12/31/97)

FIDELITY SPARTAN MONEY MARKET FUND ◆
(See first Fidelity listing on page 284 for data common to all funds)

Portfolio manager: John Todd (1989)
Investment objective and policies: High current income. Invests in high quality, U.S. dollar-denominated money market instruments of domestic and foreign issuers. Designed to deliver extra high yields for long-term buy and hold investors by maintaining a lower than average expense ratio.
Year organized: 1989
Ticker symbol: SPRXX
Group fund code: 454
Minimum purchase: Initial: $20,000, Subsequent: $1,000; IRA/Keogh: Initial: $10,000; Automatic investment plan: Subsequent: $500
Wire orders accepted: Yes, $5 fee
Discount broker availability: *Fidelity
Telephone redemptions: Yes, $5 fee including exchanges
Wire redemptions: Yes, $5 fee
Check redemptions: $1,000 minimum, $2 fee per check
Account closeout fee: $5
Fee waivers: All wire purchase/redemption, redemption, check writing and account closeout fees waived for Spartan accounts with balance of $50,000 or more at time of transaction.
Dividends paid: Income - declared daily, paid monthly
Management fee: 0.45%
12b-1 distribution fee: Yes (paid by adviser)
Expense ratio: 0.45% (year ending 4/30/97)

FIDELITY SPARTAN MUNICIPAL INCOME FUND ◆
(See first Fidelity listing on page 284 for data common to all funds)

Portfolio manager: George A. Fischer (1998)
Investment objective and policies: High current income exempt from federal income tax. Invests primarily in investment grade municipal bonds. Portfolio is managed to react to changes in interest rates similarly to municipal bonds with maturities ranging from eight to 18 years. Up to 25% can be in bonds below BBB or unrated equivalent but no more than 5% may be in B or lower obligations. Up to 100% of assets may be in securities subject to the federal alternative minimum tax. May use futures and options to hedge up to 25% of total assets.
Year organized: 1977 (formerly Fidelity High Yield Munis, absorbed Fidelity Texas Tax-Free 6/29/90; name and investment policies changed from High Yield Tax-Free 6/24/96. Absorbed previous Spartan Muni Income and changed name from Fidelity Muni Income 10/23/97)
Ticker symbol: FHIGX
Group fund code: 037
Minimum purchase: Initial: $10,000, Subsequent: $1,000; Automatic investment plan: Subsequent: $500
Discount broker availability: *Fidelity, White
Redemption fee: 0.50% on shares held less than 180 days, payable to the fund
Dividends paid: Income - declared daily, paid monthly; Capital gains - January, December

FIDELITY SPARTAN MUNICIPAL INCOME FUND ◆
(Previous Spartan Muni Income fund merged into Muni Income, which was, in turn, renamed as the new Spartan Muni Income Fund)

FIDELITY SPARTAN MUNICIPAL MONEY FUND ◆
(See first Fidelity listing on page 284 for data common to all funds)

Portfolio manager: Diane McLaughlin (1997)
Investment objective and policies: High current income exempt from federal income tax, consistent with preservation of capital and liquidity. Invests in high-quality, short-term municipal money market obligations of all types. Designed to deliver extra high yields for long-term buy and hold investors by maintaining a lower than average expense ratio.
Year organized: 1991
Ticker symbol: FIMXX
Group fund code: 460
Minimum purchase: Initial: $25,000, Subsequent: $1,000; Automatic investment plan: Subsequent: $500
Wire orders accepted: Yes, $5 fee
Discount broker availability: Fidelity
Telephone redemptions: Yes, $5 fee including exchanges
Wire redemptions: Yes, $5 fee
Check redemptions: $1,000 minimum, $2 fee per check
Account closeout fee: $5
Fee waivers: All wire purchase/redemption, redemption, check writing and account closeout fees waived for Spartan accounts with balance of $50,000 or more at time of transaction.
Dividends paid: Income - declared daily, paid monthly
Management fee: 0.50%
12b-1 distribution fee: Yes (not currently imposed)
Expense ratio: 0.40% (year ending 8/31/97)

FIDELITY SPARTAN NEW JERSEY MUNICIPAL INCOME FUND ◆
(See first Fidelity listing on page 284 for data common to all funds)

Portfolio manager: Norman Lind (1997)
Investment objective and policies: High current income exempt from federal and New Jersey state income taxes. Invests primarily in investment grade municipal securities, and manages the fund so that it generally reacts to changes in interest rates similarly to municipal bonds with maturities between eight and eighteen years. Fund normally invests so that at least 80% of income is exempt from the stated taxes. Fund may use futures and options thereon and may hedge up to 25% of total assets. Designed to deliver extra high yields for long-term buy and hold investors by maintaining a lower than average expense ratio.
Year organized: 1988 (name changed from Fidelity NJ Tax-Free High Yield 3/1/91; name changed from Fidelity Spartan NJ Muni High Yield 1/19/96)
Ticker symbol: FNJHX
Group fund code: 416
Minimum purchase: Initial: $10,000, Subsequent: $1,000; Automatic investment plan: Subsequent: $500
Discount broker availability: *Fidelity
Qualified for sale in: NJ, NY, PA
Redemption fee: 0.50% on shares held less than 180 days, payable to the fund
Dividends paid: Income - declared daily, paid monthly; Capital gains - January, December
Portfolio turnover (3 yrs): 16%, 57%, 36%
Management fee: 0.55%
12b-1 distribution fee: Yes (not currently imposed)
Expense ratio: 0.55% (year ending 11/30/97)

Portfolio turnover (3 yrs): 31%, 53%, 50%
Management fee: 0.25% plus group fee of 0.11% to 0.37%
12b-1 distribution fee: Yes (not currently imposed)
Expense ratio: 0.53% (year ending 11/30/97)

FIDELITY SPARTAN NEW JERSEY MUNICIPAL MONEY MARKET FUND ◆
(See first Fidelity listing on page 284 for data common to all funds)

Portfolio manager: Scott A. Orr (1997)
Investment objective and policies: High current income exempt from federal and New Jersey state income taxes, consistent with capital preservation. Invests at least 65% of assets in New Jersey municipal money market securities, and normally invests so that at least 80% of fund income is free of federal tax. Designed to deliver extra high yields for long-term buy and hold investors by maintaining a lower than average expense ratio.
Year organized: 1990 (formerly Fidelity Tax-Exempt Money Market Trust)
Ticker symbol: FSJXX
Group fund code: 423
Minimum purchase: Initial: $25,000, Subsequent: $1,000; Automatic investment plan: Subsequent: $500
Wire orders accepted: Yes, $5 fee
Discount broker availability: Fidelity
Qualified for sale in: NJ, NY, PA
Telephone redemptions: Yes, $5 fee including exchanges
Wire redemptions: Yes, $5 fee
Check redemptions: $1,000 minimum, $2 fee per check
Account closeout fee: $5
Fee waivers: All wire purchase/redemption, redemption, check writing and account closeout fees waived for Spartan accounts with balance of $50,000 or more at time of transaction.
Dividends paid: Income - declared daily, paid monthly; Capital gains - December
Management fee: 0.50%
12b-1 distribution fee: Yes (not currently imposed)
Expense ratio: 0.50% (year ending 11/30/97)

FIDELITY SPARTAN NEW YORK INTERMEDIATE MUNICIPAL INCOME FUND ◆
(Merged into Fidelity NY Muni Income fund 1/15/98)

FIDELITY SPARTAN NEW YORK MUNICIPAL INCOME FUND ◆
(See first Fidelity listing on page 284 for data common to all funds)

Portfolio manager: Norman Lind (1993)
Investment objective and policies: Current income exempt from federal, NY state and NY city income taxes. Invests primarily in investment grade New York municipal bonds with a dollar-weighted average maturity of 15 years or more. Fund may use zero coupon bonds and futures and options thereon to hedge up to 25% of total assets.
Year organized: 1984 (name changed from NY Municipal Bond October 1985; name changed from Tax-Free High Yield 2/1/96; name changed from Fidelity NY Muni Income 1/98)
Ticker symbol: FTFMX
Group fund code: 071
Minimum purchase: Initial: $10,000, Subsequent: $1,000; Automatic investment plan: Subsequent: $500
Discount broker availability: *Fidelity, White
Qualified for sale in: CT, NJ, NY
Check redemptions: $500 minimum
Portfolio turnover (3 yrs): 44%, 83%, 34%
Dividends paid: Income - declared daily, paid monthly; Capital gains - March, December
Management fee: 0.25% plus group fee of 0.11% to 0.37%
12b-1 distribution fee: Yes (not currently imposed)
Expense ratio: 0.59% (year ending 1/31/97)

FIDELITY SPARTAN NEW YORK MUNICIPAL INCOME FUND ◆
(The OLD Spartan NY Muni fund merged into Fidelity NY Muni 1/98)

FIDELITY SPARTAN NEW YORK MUNICIPAL MONEY MARKET FUND ◆
(See first Fidelity listing on page 284 for data common to all funds)

Portfolio manager: Diane McLaughlin (1997)
Investment objective and policies: High current income exempt from federal, NY state and NY city personal income taxes consistent with capital preservation. Invests in the two highest grades of New York municipal money market securities. Designed to deliver extra high yields for long-term buy and hold investors, by maintaining a lower than average expense ratio.
Year organized: 1990
Ticker symbol: FSNXX
Group fund code: 422
Minimum purchase: Initial: $25,000, Subsequent: $1,000; Automatic investment plan: Subsequent: $500
Wire orders accepted: Yes, $5 fee
Discount broker availability: Fidelity
Qualified for sale in: CT, NJ, NY
Telephone redemptions: Yes, $5 fee including exchanges
Wire redemptions: Yes, $5 fee
Check redemptions: $1,000 minimum, $2 fee per check
Account closeout fee: $5
Dividends paid: Income - declared daily, paid monthly (not paid in cash)
Fee waivers: All wire purchase/redemption, redemption, check writing and account closeout fees waived for Spartan accounts with balance of $50,000 or more at time of transaction.
Management fee: 0.50%
12b-1 distribution fee: Yes (paid by adviser)
Expense ratio: 0.49% (year ending 1/30/97) (0.50% without waiver)

FIDELITY SPARTAN OHIO MUNICIPAL INCOME FUND ◆
(See first Fidelity listing on page 284 for data common to all funds)

Portfolio manager: George A. Fischer (1997)
Investment objective and policies: High current income exempt from federal and Ohio state income taxes. Invests primarily in longer-term, investment grade municipal bonds whose interest is tax exempt in Ohio, and manages the fund so that it generally reacts to changes in interest rates similarly to municipal bonds with maturities between eight and eighteen years. At least 80% of its income distributions will be exempt from federal and Ohio income taxes.
Year organized: 1985 (name changed from OH Tax-Free High Yield 2/96; name changed from OH Muni Income and became a Spartan fund 4/1/97)
Ticker symbol: FOHTX
Group fund code: 088
Minimum purchase: Initial: $10,000, Subsequent: $1,000; Automatic investment plan: Subsequent: $500
Discount broker availability: *Fidelity, White
Qualified for sale in: OH
Check redemptions: $500 minimum
Dividends paid: Income - declared daily, paid monthly; Capital gains - February, December
Portfolio turnover (3 yrs): 15%, 43%, 48%
Management fee: 0.25% plus group fee of 0.11% to 0.37%
12b-1 distribution plan: Yes (not currently imposed)
Expense ratio: 0.56% (year ending 12/31/97)

FIDELITY SPARTAN PENNSYLVANIA MUNICIPAL INCOME FUND ◆
(See first Fidelity listing on page 284 for data common to all funds)

Portfolio manager: Jonathan D. Short (1997)
Investment objective and policies: High current income exempt from federal and Pennsylvania income taxes. Invests primarily in longer-term, investment grade municipal securities whose interest is free from taxes in the Commonwealth of Pennsylvania, and manages the fund so that it generally reacts to changes in interest rates similarly to municipal bonds with maturities between eight and eighteen years. Fund may use zero coupon securities and futures contracts and options thereon. Designed to deliver extra high

yields for long-term buy and hold investors by maintaining a lower than average expense ratio.
Year organized: 1986 (converted to Spartan 1990; formerly Fidelity PA Tax-Free High Yield; name changed from PA Municipal High Yield 12/14/95)
Ticker symbol: FPXTX
Group fund code: 402
Minimum purchase: Initial: $10,000, Subsequent: $1,000; Automatic investment plan: Subsequent: $500
Wire orders accepted: Yes
Discount broker availability: *Fidelity
Qualified for sale in: PA
Telephone redemptions: Yes
Wire redemptions: Yes
Redemption fee: 0.50% on shares held less than 180 days, payable to the fund
Dividends paid: Income - declared daily, paid monthly; Capital gains - February, December
Portfolio turnover (3 yrs): 26%, 53%, 49%
Management fee: 0.55%
12b-1 distribution fee: Yes (not currently imposed)
Expense ratio: 0.55% (year ending 12/31/97)

FIDELITY SPARTAN PENNSYLVANIA MUNICIPAL MONEY MARKET FUND ◆
(See first Fidelity listing on page 284 for data common to all funds)

Portfolio manager: Diane McLaughlin (1997)
Investment objective and policies: High current income exempt from federal and Pennsylvania income taxes, consistent with capital preservation. Invests primarily in Pennsylvania municipal money market instruments. Designed to deliver extra high yields for long-term buy and hold investors by maintaining a lower than average expense ratio.
Year organized: 1986 (formerly Fidelity PA Tax-Free Money Market)
Ticker symbol: FPTXX
Group fund code: 401
Minimum purchase: Initial: $25,000, Subsequent: $1,000; Automatic investment plan: Subsequent: $500
Wire orders accepted: Yes, $5 fee
Discount broker availability: Fidelity
Qualified for sale in: PA
Telephone redemptions: Yes, $5 fee including exchanges
Wire redemptions: Yes, $5 fee
Check redemptions: $1,000 minimum, $2 fee per check
Account closeout fee: $5
Dividends paid: Income - declared daily, paid monthly
Fee waivers: All wire purchase/redemption, redemption, check writing and account closeout fees waived for Spartan accounts with balance of $50,000 or more at time of transaction.
Management fee: 0.50%
12b-1 distribution fee: Yes (not currently imposed)
Expense ratio: 0.50% (year ending 12/31/97)

FIDELITY SPARTAN SHORT-INTERMEDIATE GOVERNMENT FUND ◆
(See first Fidelity listing on page 284 for data common to all funds)

Portfolio manager: Curtis Hollingsworth (1992)
Investment objective and policies: High current income consistent with capital preservation. Invests exclusively in securities backed by the full faith and credit of the U.S. Government. Portfolio maintains a dollar-weighted average maturity of two to five years. Fund may use zero coupon securities and futures and options thereon and hedge up to 25% of total assets. Designed to deliver extra high yields for long-term buy and hold investors by maintaining a lower than average expense ratio.
Year organized: 1992
Ticker symbol: SPSIX
Group fund code: 474
Minimum purchase: Initial: $10,000, Subsequent: $1.000; Automatic investment plan: Subsequent: $500
Wire orders accepted: Yes, $5 fee
Discount broker availability: *Fidelity, White
Telephone redemptions: Yes, $5 fee including exchanges
Wire redemptions: Yes, $5 fee

Check redemptions: $1,000 minimum, $2 fee per check
Account closeout fee: $5
Fee waivers: All wire purchase/redemption, redemption, check writing and account closeout fees waived for Spartan accounts with balance of $50,000 or more at time of transaction.
Dividends paid: Income - declared daily, paid monthly; Capital gains - June, December
Portfolio turnover (3 yrs): 104%, 161%, 282%
Management fee: 0.65%
12b-1 distribution fee: Yes (not currently imposed)
Expense ratio: 0.65% (year ending 4/30/97)

FIDELITY SPARTAN SHORT-INTERMEDIATE MUNICIPAL INCOME FUND ◆
(See first Fidelity listing on page 284 for data common to all funds)

Portfolio manager: Norman Lind (1995)
Investment objective and policies: High current income exempt from federal income tax. Invests in municipal securities rated "BBB" or better, with a dollar-weighted average maturity of two to five years. May, however, invest up to 5% of assets in junk bonds. Fund may use zero coupon securities and futures and options thereon and hedge up to 25% of total assets. Designed to deliver extra high yields for long-term buy and hold investors by maintaining a lower than average expense ratio.
Year organized: 1986 (name changed from Short-Term Tax-Free 12/1/90; name changed from Short-Intermediate Municipal 2/20/96)
Ticker symbol: FSTFX
Group fund code: 404
Minimum purchase: Initial: $10,000, Subsequent: $1,000; Automatic investment plan: Subsequent: $500
Discount broker availability: *Fidelity, White
Check redemptions: $1,000 minimum
Dividends paid: Income - declared daily, paid monthly; Capital gains - October, December
Portfolio turnover (3 yrs): 32%, 78%, 51%
Management fee: 0.55%
12b-1 distribution fee: Yes (not currently imposed)
Expense ratio: 0.55% (year ending 8/31/97)

FIDELITY SPARTAN SHORT-TERM BOND FUND ◆
(See first Fidelity listing on page 284 for data common to all funds)

Portfolio manager: Andrew Dudley (1997)
Investment objective and policies: High current income consistent with capital preservation. Invests primarily in shorter-term investment grade debt securities including bonds, notes, and money market instruments, with a dollar-weighted average maturity of three years or less. Securities may be issued by any type of U.S. or foreign issuer, and may be denominated in U.S. dollars or foreign currencies. Designed to deliver extra high yields for long-term buy and hold investors, by maintaining a lower than average expense ratio.
Year organized: 1992 (name changed from Spartan Short-Term Bond 11/19/93; name changed back from Short-Term Income 2/1/96)
Ticker symbol: FTBDX
Group fund code: 449
Minimum purchase: Initial: $10,000, Subsequent: $1,000; Automatic investment plan: Subsequent: $500
Wire orders accepted: Yes, $5 fee
Discount broker availability: *Fidelity, White
Telephone redemptions: Yes, $5 fee including exchanges
Wire redemptions: Yes, $5 fee
Check redemptions: $1,000 minimum, $2 fee per check
Account closeout fee: $5
Fee waivers: All wire purchase/redemption, redemption, check writing and account closeout fees waived for Spartan accounts with balance of $50,000 or more at time of transaction.
Dividends paid: Income - declared daily, paid monthly; Capital gains - June, December
Portfolio turnover (3 yrs): 105%, 134%, 159%
Management fee: 0.65%
12b-1 distribution fee: Yes (not currently imposed)
Expense ratio: 0.50% (year ending 9/30/97) (0.66% without waiver)

FIDELITY SPARTAN TOTAL MARKET INDEX FUND ◆
(See first Fidelity listing on page 284 for data common to all funds)

Sub-adviser: Bankers Trust Co.
Investment objective and policies: Total return corresponding to at least 98% of the return of the Wilshire 5000 Equity Index, a capitalization weighted index of approximately 7,000 common stocks of U.S. companies. Invests at least 80% of assets in common stocks of companies that comprise the Index, which includes all the companies included in the S&P 500 except for the foreign components (Only about 4% of the S&P). The S&P 500 companies comprise about 70% of the weighting of the Wilshire 5000. Fund may engage in the use of certain derivatives for hedging purposes.
Year organized: 1997
Group fund code: 397
Minimum purchase: Initial: $15,000, Subsequent: $1,000; Automatic investment plan: Subsequent: $500
Discount broker availability: *Fidelity
Qualified for sale in: All states
Sales charge: 0.50%, paid to fund
Dividends paid: Income - April, December; Capital gains - April, December
Management fee: 0.25%
12b-1 distribution fee: Yes (paid by adviser)

FIDELITY SPARTAN U.S. GOVERNMENT MONEY MARKET FUND ◆
(See first Fidelity listing on page 284 for data common to all funds)

Portfolio manager: Robert A. Litterst (1997)
Investment objective and policies: High current income consistent with preservation of capital and liquidity. Invests exclusively in money market instruments issued by the U.S. Government and agencies, and repurchase agreements thereon. Designed to deliver extra high yields for long-term buy and hold investors by maintaining a lower than average expense ratio.
Year organized: 1990
Ticker symbol: SPAXX
Group fund code: 458
Minimum purchase: Initial: $20,000, Subsequent: $1,000; IRA/Keogh: Initial: $10,000; Automatic investment plan: Subsequent: $500
Wire orders accepted: Yes, $5 fee
Discount broker availability: *Fidelity
Telephone redemptions: Yes, $5 fee including exchanges
Wire redemptions: Yes, $5 fee
Check redemptions: $1,000 minimum, $2 fee per check
Account closeout fee: $5
Dividends paid: Income - declared daily, paid monthly
Fee waivers: All wire purchase/redemption, redemption, check writing and account closeout fees waived for Spartan accounts with balance of $50,000 or more at time of transaction.
Management fee: 0.45%
12b-1 distribution fee: Yes (paid by adviser)
Expense ratio: 0.45% (year ending 4/30/97)

FIDELITY SPARTAN U.S. TREASURY MONEY MARKET FUND ◆
(See first Fidelity listing on page 284 for data common to all funds)

Portfolio manager: Robert A. Litterst (1997)
Investment objective and policies: High current income consistent with security of principal and liquidity. Invests exclusively in U.S. Treasury and agency money market obligations backed by the full faith and credit of the U.S. Government. Designed to deliver extra high yields for long-term buy and hold investors by maintaining a lower than average expense ratio.
Year organized: 1988 (formerly Fidelity U.S. Treasury Money Market)
Ticker symbol: FDLXX

Group fund code: 415
Minimum purchase: Initial: $20,000, Subsequent: $1,000; IRA/Keogh: Initial: $10,000; Automatic investment plan: Subsequent: $500
Wire orders accepted: Yes, $5 fee
Discount broker availability: Fidelity
Telephone redemptions: Yes, $5 fee including exchanges
Wire redemptions: Yes, $5 fee
Check redemptions: $1,000 minimum, $2 fee per check
Account closeout fee: $5
Dividends paid: Income - declared daily, paid monthly
Fee waivers: All wire purchase/redemption, redemption, check writing and account closeout fees waived for Spartan accounts with balance of $50,000 or more at time of transaction.
Management fee: 0.45%
12b-1 distribution fee: Yes (paid by adviser)
Expense ratio: 0.45% (year ending 4/30/97)

FIDELITY STOCK SELECTOR FUND ◆
(See first Fidelity listing on page 284 for data common to all funds)

Portfolio manager: Bradford F. Lewis (1990)
Investment objective and policies: Capital growth. Invests at least 65% of assets in equity securities of domestic and foreign companies with market capitalizations of $100M or more believed undervalued relative to their industry norms. Companies are selected by computer-aided, quantitative analysis supported by fundamental research. Fund may use a variety of derivatives for hedging purposes, including currency exchange contracts and futures and options thereon.
Year organized: 1990
Ticker symbol: FDSSX
Group fund code: 320
Discount broker availability: *Fidelity, Schwab, *Siebert, White
Dividends paid: Income - December; Capital gains - December
Portfolio turnover (3 yrs): 117%, 247%, 220%
Management fee: 0.30% plus group fee of 0.25% to 0.52% +/- performance fee of up to 0.20% relative to the S&P 500 Index over 36 months
12b-1 distribution fee: Yes (paid by adviser)
Expense ratio: 0.69% (year ending 10/31/97) (0.74% without waiver)

FIDELITY TARGET TIMELINE FUND ◆
(See first Fidelity listing on page 284 for data common to all funds)

Portfolio manager: Christine J. Thompson (1996)
Investment objective and policies: A predictable rate of return within a specific period of time. The portfolios, maturing in 1999, 2001, and 2003, invest in U.S. dollar-denominated, fixed-income securities rated BBB and higher by Standard & Poor's, and are managed with the intent of providing a total return over their lifetimes that, on average, are within +/- 0.50% per year of the yield quoted as of the date of purchase. Securities will be selected whose average duration - or sensitivity to interest rates - approximates the amount of time remaining to the fund's target date. Rate of return assumes the investor holds the shares for the life of the fund and reinvests all distributions. Funds are non-diversified.
Year organized: 1996
Group fund code: Timeline 1999 (379), Timeline 2001 (381), Timeline 2003 (383)
Special sales information: These funds will each liquidate shortly after their target date.
Discount broker availability: *Fidelity
Redemption fee: 0.50% for shares held less than 90 days, payable to fund
Dividends paid: Income - declared daily, paid monthly; Capital gains - September, December
Portfolio turnover (2 yrs): 80%, 118% (1999), 97%, 93% (2001), 83%, 180% (2003)
Management fee: 0.30% plus group fee of 0.11% to 0.37%
Expense ratio: 0.34% (year ending 7/31/97) (0.35% without waiver)

FIDELITY TECHNOQUANT GROWTH FUND

(See first Fidelity listing on page 284 for data common to all funds)

Portfolio manager: Timothy A. Krochuk (1996)
Investment objective and policies: Long-term capital appreciation. Invests in equity securities, primarily common stocks, selected by computer-assisted artificial intelligence, using a combination of technical analysis of each issue and quantitative criteria of market activity in an attempt to predict future price movements. Fund may use a variety of derivatives for hedging purposes.
Year organized: 1996
Ticker symbol: FTQGX
Group fund code: 333
Sales charge: 3% (may be waived for retirement accounts using Fidelity prototype plans)
Discount broker availability: *Fidelity, White
Redemption fee: 0.75% for shares held 90 days or less, payable to the fund
Dividends paid: Income - December; Capital gains - December
Portfolio turnover (1 yr): 296%
Management fee: 0.30% plus group fee of 0.25% to 0.52% +/- performance fee of up to 0.20% relative to the S&P 500 Index over 36 months
Expense ratio: 1.24% (year ending 10/31/97) (0.74% without waiver)

FIDELITY TREND FUND ◆

(See first Fidelity listing on page 284 for data common to all funds)

Portfolio manager: Arieh Coll (1997)
Investment objective and policies: Long-term capital growth. Invests in securities of both established and smaller companies that will benefit from industry and/or market trends. May invest in any type of securities without restriction, including common stock, investment grade fixed-income securities or cash, in any proportion, depending on market and economic conditions. May invest in foreign securities without limit, and have up to 35% of assets in junk bonds and 10% in illiquid securities. May use futures and options and hedge up to 25% of total assets.
Year organized: 1958
Ticker symbol: FTRNX
Group fund code: 005
Discount broker availability: *Fidelity, Schwab, *Siebert, White
Dividends paid: Income - February, December; Capital gains - February, December
Portfolio turnover (3 yrs): 334%, 142%, 186%
Management fee: 0.30% plus group fee of 0.25% to 0.52% +/- performance fee of up to 0.20% relative to the S&P 500 Index over 36 months
12b-1 distribution fee: Yes (paid by adviser)
Expense ratio: 0.59% (year ending 12/31/97) (0.65% without waiver)

FIDELITY UNITED KINGDOM FUND

(See first Fidelity listing on page 284 for data common to all funds)

Portfolio manager: Simon Roberts (1997)
Investment objective and policies: Long-term capital growth. Invests at least 65% of assets in equity and debt securities of British issuers. The remainder may be invested in securities of other European issuers. May have up 35% of assets in junk bonds and 15% in illiquid securities. Fund may use currency exchange contracts, futures contracts and options, and hedge up to 25% of total assets. Fund is non-diversified.
Year organized: 1995
Group fund code: 344
Discount broker availability: Fidelity, Schwab, Siebert, White
Sales charge: 3% (may be waived for retirement accounts using Fidelity prototype plans)
Redemption fee: 1.50% on shares held less than 90 days, payable to the fund
Dividends paid: Income - December; Capital gains - December
Portfolio turnover (2 yrs): 96%, 50%
Management fee: 0.45% plus group fee of 0.25% to 0.52%
Expense ratio: 1.99% (year ending 10/31/97) (2.00% without waiver)

FIDELITY U.S. GOVERNMENT RESERVES ◆

(See first Fidelity listing on page 284 for data common to all funds)

Portfolio manager: Robert A. Litterst (1997)
Investment objective and policies: A high level of current income while maintaining a stable $1 share price. Invests exclusively in money market instruments issued or guaranteed by the U.S. Government, its agencies or instrumentalities, or reverse repurchase agreements thereon.
Year organized: 1981
Ticker symbol: FGRXX
Group fund code: 050
Deadline for same day wire purchase: 12 NN
Discount broker availability: *Fidelity
Number switches permitted: Unlimited
Check redemptions: $500 minimum
Dividends paid: Income - declared daily, paid monthly
Management fee: 0.03% plus group fee of 0.11% to 0.37% plus 6.0% of gross income for portion of fund's gross income in excess of 5% yield; (this item cannot exceed 0.24%)
12b-1 distribution fee: Yes (paid by adviser)
Expense ratio: 0.48% (year ending 11/30/97)

FIDELITY UTILITIES FUND ◆

(See first Fidelity listing on page 284 for data common to all funds)

Portfolio manager: Nicholas Thakore (1997)
Investment objective and policies: High total return through a combination of current income and capital appreciation. Invests at least 65% of assets in equity securities of public utilities. Debt will be rated A or better. Fund may use foreign securities and stock index futures and options thereon, and hedge up to 25% of total assets.
Year organized: 1987 (name changed from Utilities Income Fund on 8/3/94)
Ticker symbol: FIUIX
Group fund code: 311
Discount broker availability: *Fidelity, Schwab, *Siebert, White
Dividends paid: Income - March, June, September, December; Capital gains - March, December
Portfolio turnover (3 yrs): 57%, 56%, 98%
Management fee: 0.20% plus group fee of 0.25% to 0.52% +/- performance fee of up to 0.15% relative to the S&P Utilities Index over 36 months
Expense ratio: 0.85% (year ending 1/31/98) (0.87% without waiver)

FIDELITY VALUE FUND ◆

(See first Fidelity listing on page 284 for data common to all funds)

Portfolio manager: Richard B. Fentin (1996)
Investment objective and policies: Capital appreciation. Invests primarily in stocks and convertible securities of companies that possess valuable fixed assets or are believed to be undervalued. May invest in foreign securities without limit, and have up to 35% of assets in junk bonds and 10% in illiquid securities. May use futures and options and hedge up to 25% of total assets.
Year organized: 1978 (formerly Fidelity Discoverer Fund)
Ticker symbol: FDVLX
Group fund code: 039
Discount broker availability: *Fidelity, Schwab, *Siebert, White
Dividends paid: Income - December; Capital gains - December
Portfolio turnover (3 yrs): 56%, 112%, 125%
Management fee: 0.30% plus group fee of 0.25% to 0.52% +/- performance fee of 0.20% relative to S&P 500 Index over 36 months
12b-1 distribution fee: Yes (not currently imposed)
Expense ratio: 0.66% (year ending 10/31/97) (0.68% without waiver)

FIDELITY WORLDWIDE FUND ◆

(See first Fidelity listing on page 284 for data common to all funds)

Portfolio manager: Penelope Dobkin (1990)
Investment objective and policies: Capital growth. Invests primarily in equity securities worldwide. Fund will focus on developed countries in North America, Europe and the Pacific Basin. Assets are spread among at least three countries, one of which will be the U.S. May invest in both established and smaller companies. May also invest without limit in debt obligations, and up to 35% of assets may be in junk bonds. Fund may use currency exchange contracts, futures and options and hedge up to 25% of total assets.
Year organized: 1990
Ticker symbol: FWWFX
Group fund code: 318
Discount broker availability: *Fidelity, Schwab, *Siebert, White
Dividends paid: Income - December; Capital gains - December
Portfolio turnover (3 yrs): 85%, 49%, 70%
Management fee: 0.45% plus group fee of 0.25% to 0.52%
12b-1 distribution fee: Yes (not currently imposed)
Expense ratio: 1.16% (year ending 10/31/97) (1.18% without waiver)

FIDUCIARY CAPITAL GROWTH FUND ◆

225 East Mason Street
Milwaukee, WI 53202
800-338-1579, 800-811-5311
414-226-4555
TDD 800-684-3416
fax 414-226-4530

Adviser: Fiduciary Management, Inc.
Portfolio managers: Ted D. Kellner (1981), Donald S. Wilson (1981). Patrick J. English (1997)
Transfer agent: Firstar Trust Co.
Investment objective and policies: Long-term capital appreciation; current income secondary. Invests primarily in common stocks that are perceived to offer growth potential and are significantly underpriced relative to estimated market value of a corporation's assets less its liabilities. Up to 10% of assets may be in securities of foreign issuers.
Year organized: 1981
Ticker symbol: FCGFX
Minimum purchase: Initial: $1,000, Subsequent: $100; Automatic investment plan: Initial: $50, Subsequent: $50
Wire orders accepted: Yes
Deadline for same day wire purchase: 4 P.M.
Letter redemptions: Signature guarantee not required
Qualified for sale in: All states except AK, AR, ID, ME, MD, MA, MS, MT, NH, NC, ND, SD, WV
Dividends paid: Income - October, December; Capital gains - October, December
Portfolio turnover (3 yrs): 61%, 44%, 29%
Shareholder services: IRA, Keogh, 401(k), corporate retirement plans, systematic withdrawal plan min. bal. req. $10,000
Management fee: 1.00% first $30M, 0.75% over $30M
Expense ratio: 1.20% (year ending 9/30/97)
IRA/Keogh fees: Annual $12.50, Closing $15

59 WALL STREET FUNDS ◆

(See discount broker listed funds)

FIRST EAGLE FUND OF AMERICA ◆

1345 Avenue of the Americas
New York, NY 10105-4300
800-451-3623, 800-824-3863
212-698-3000
fax 212-299-4310

Adviser: Arnhold and S. Bleichroeder Advisers, Inc.
Portfolio managers: Harold J. Levy (1987), David L. Cohen (1989)
Transfer agent: BISYS Fund Services, Inc.
Investment objective and policies: Capital appreciation. Invests, in varying proportions, in domestic and

to a lesser extent foreign equity and debt securities deemed undervalued on an "intrinsic value" basis. Fund is non-diversified and will normally limit foreign holdings to 10% of total assets. May buy and sell options on stocks and indices and sell short.
Year organized: 1986
Ticker symbol: FEAFX
Special sales restrictions: Effective 3/2/98, the fund launched broker-sold Class C Shares which carry a 0.75% 12b-1 fee and a one year, 1.25% CDSC fee. Previous shares (profiled here) are now known as Y Shares, and are available at NAV directly from the fund.
Minimum purchase: Initial: $2,500 (waived for additional accounts for existing shareholders), Subsequent: $100 ; IRA: Initial: $500, Subsequent: None; Automatic investment plan: Subsequent $100
Wire orders accepted: Yes
Deadline for same day wire purchase: 4 P.M.
Discount broker availability: *Fidelity, *Schwab, *White
Qualified for sale in: AL, CA, CO, CT, DE, DC, FL, GA, HI, IL, IA, MA, MD, MI, MN, MO, MT, NE, NH, NJ, NY, NC, OH, OR, PA, RI, SC, TX, VT, WA
Telephone redemptions: Yes
Wire redemptions: Yes
Letter redemptions: Signature guarantee required
Dividends paid: Income - annually; Capital gains - annually
Portfolio turnover (3 yrs): 98%, 93%, 81%
Shareholder services: IRA, electronic funds transfer
Management fee: 1.00%
Shareholder services fee: Maximum of 0.25%
Expense ratio: 1.70% (year ending 10/31/97)
IRA fees: Annual $10, Initial $10, Closing $10

FIRST EAGLE INTERNATIONAL FUND ◆
1345 Avenue of the Americas
New York, NY 10105-4300
800-451-3623, 800-824-3863
212-698-3000
fax 212-299-4310

Adviser: Arnhold and S. Bleichroeder Advisers, Inc.
Portfolio manager: Arthur F. Lerner (1994)
Transfer agent: BISYS Fund Services, Inc.
Investment objective and policies: Capital appreciation. Normally invests at least 65% of assets in foreign equity and debt securities deemed undervalued on an "intrinsic value" basis. May also invest in domestic equity and debt securities, use futures and options on stocks and indices, hedge and leverage. Up to 15% of assets may be in illiquid securities. Fund is non-diversified.
Year organized: 1994
Special sales restrictions: Effective 3/2/98, the fund launched broker-sold Class C Shares which carry a 0.75% 12b-1 fee and a one year, 1.25% CDSC fee. Previous shares (profiled here) are now known as Y Shares, and are available at NAV directly from the fund.
Minimum purchase: Initial: $2,500 (waived for additional accounts for existing shareholders), Subsequent: $100 ; IRA: Initial: $500, Subsequent: None; Automatic investment plan: Subsequent $100
Wire orders accepted: Yes
Deadline for same day wire purchase: 4 P.M.
Discount broker availability: *Fidelity, *Schwab, *White
Qualified for sale in: AL, CA, CO, CT, DC, DE, FL, GA, HI, IL, MA, MD, MN, MO, MT, NE, NH, NJ, NY, NC, OH, OR, PA, RI, SC, TX, VT, WA
Telephone redemptions: Yes
Wire redemptions: Yes
Letter redemptions: Signature guarantee required over $5,000
Dividends paid: Income - annually; Capital gains - annually
Portfolio turnover (3 yrs): 54%, 101%, 166%
Shareholder services: IRA, electronic funds transfer
Management fee: 1.00%
Shareholder services fee: Maximum of 0.25%
Expense ratio: 2.25% (10 months ending 10/31/97)
IRA fees: Annual $10, Initial $10, Closing $10

FIRST HAWAII INTERMEDIATE MUNICIPAL FUND
2756 Woodlawn Drive, Suite 6-201
Honolulu, HI 96822
800-354-9654, 808-988-8088
fax 808-988-5770

Adviser: First Pacific Management Corp.
Portfolio managers: Terrence K.H. Lee (1994), Louis E. D'Avanzo (1994)
Transfer agent: First Pacific Bookkeeping, Inc.
Investment objective and policies: High current income exempt from regular federal and Hawaii state income taxes, consistent with capital preservation. Invests primarily in a diversified portfolio of investment grade municipal securities issued by the State of Hawaii or its political subdivisions, and certain other interstate and federal agencies whose interest payments are considered tax exempt. Portfolio generally maintains a dollar-weighted average maturity of between three and ten years. May invest up to 20% of assets in taxable securities.
Year organized: 1994 (absorbed Leahi Tax Free Income Trust 9/97)
Minimum purchase: Initial: $1,000, Subsequent: $100
Wire orders accepted: No
Qualified for sale in: CA, HI
Telephone redemptions: Yes
Wire redemptions: Yes
Letter redemptions: Signature guarantee required over $50,000
Dividends paid: Income - declared daily, paid monthly; Capital gains - December
Portfolio turnover (3 yrs): 17%, 18%, 10%
Management fee: 0.50%
12b-1 distribution fee: Maximum of 0.25%
Expense ratio: 0.86% (year ending 9/30/97) (1.43% without waiver)

FIRST HAWAII MUNICIPAL BOND FUND
2756 Woodlawn Drive, Suite 6-201
Honolulu, HI 96822
800-354-9654, 808-988-8088
fax 808-988-5770

Adviser: First Pacific Management Corp.
Portfolio managers: Terrence K.H. Lee (1988), Louis E. D'Avanzo (1991)
Transfer agent: First Pacific Bookkeeping, Inc.
Investment objective and policies: High current income exempt from regular federal and Hawaii state income taxes, consistent with capital preservation. Invests primarily in a diversified portfolio of investment grade municipal securities issued by the State of Hawaii or its political subdivisions, and certain other interstate and federal agencies whose interest payments are considered tax exempt. Portfolio generally maintains a dollar-weighted average maturity of between ten and 25 years. May invest up to 20% of assets in taxable securities.
Year organized: 1988
Minimum purchase: Initial: $1,000, Subsequent: $100
Wire orders accepted: No
Qualified for sale in: CA, HI
Telephone redemptions: Yes
Wire redemptions: Yes
Letter redemptions: Signature guarantee required over $50,000
Dividends paid: Income - declared daily, paid monthly; Capital gains - December
Portfolio turnover (3 yrs): 3%, 15%, 17%
Management fee: 0.50%
12b-1 distribution fee: Maximum of 0.25%
Expense ratio: 0.98% (year ending 9/30/97)

FIRST MUTUAL FUND
(See Trainer, Wortham First Mutual Funds)

FIRST OMAHA FUNDS
(Data common to all First Omaha funds are shown below. See subsequent listings for data specific to individual funds.)

One First National Center
Omaha, NE 68102-1576
800-662-4203, 402-341-0500
fax 402-633-3434

Adviser: First National Bank of Omaha
Administrator: Sunstone Financial Group, Inc.
Transfer agent: First National Bank of Omaha
Minimum purchase: Initial: $500, Subsequent: $50; Automatic investment plan: Initial: $100
Wire orders accepted: Yes, subsequent only
Deadline for same day wire purchase: 4 P.M.
Qualified for sale in: All states
Telephone redemptions: Yes
Wire redemptions: Yes
Letter redemptions: Signature guarantee not required
Telephone switching: With other First Omaha funds
Number of switches permitted: Unlimited
Shareholder services: IRA, electronic funds transfer, systematic withdrawal plan
Administration fee: 0.20%
Shareholder services fee: Maximum of 0.25%
12b-1 distribution plan: Maximum of 0.25%
IRA fees: None

FIRST OMAHA BALANCED FUND
(See first First Omaha listing for data common to all funds)

Lead portfolio manager: Vicki Hohenstein (1996)
Investment objective and policies: Capital appreciation and current income. Invests among the three major asset groups: common stocks, debt securities and cash equivalents. Allocation among these classes will vary depending on perceived market conditions. Normally the allocation is expected to approach 65% equities and 35% debt; however, the equity portion may range from 35% to 65%, and debt securities will rarely be less than 25%. May have up to 10% of assets in securities of foreign issuers and 10% in shares of other mutual funds.
Year organized: 1996 (Ownership of group changed in April 1995)
Ticker symbol: FOBAX
Dividends paid: Income - monthly; Capital gains - December
Portfolio turnover (1 yr): 6%
Management fee: 0.70%
Expense ratio: 1.16% (8 months ending 3/31/97) (3.04% without waiver)

FIRST OMAHA EQUITY FUND
(See first First Omaha listing for data common to all funds)

Lead portfolio manager: Vicki Hohenstein (1992)
Investment objective and policies: Long-term capital growth. Invests primarily in common stocks and securities convertible into common stocks of large capitalization companies with good earnings and dividend growth. May have up to 35% of assets in other equity securities and investment grade debt securities, 10% in securities of foreign issuers and 10% in shares of other mutual funds.
Year organized: 1975 (Ownership of group changed in April 1995)
Ticker symbol: FOEQX
Dividends paid: Income - monthly; Capital gains - December
Portfolio turnover (3 yrs): 26%, 27%, 16%
Management fee: 0.75%
Expense ratio: 1.04% (year ending 3/31/97) (1.10% without waiver)

FIRST OMAHA FIXED INCOME FUND
(See first First Omaha listing for data common to all funds)

Lead portfolio manager: Dick Chapman (1992)
Investment objective and policies: Current income consistent with capital preservation. Invests at least 65% of assets in investment grade bonds, debentures, notes, mortgage-related securities, state, municipal or industrial revenue bonds, U.S. Government and government agency obligations, and convertible securities. Up to 35% of assets may be in preferred stocks, 10% in securities of foreign issuers and 10% in shares of other mutual funds.
Year organized: 1975 (Ownership of group changed in April 1995)
Ticker symbol: FOFIX
Dividends paid: Income - monthly; Capital gains - December
Portfolio turnover (3 yrs): 13%, 37%, 13%
Management fee: 0.60%
Expense ratio: 0.89% (year ending 3/31/97) (1.00% without waiver)

FIRST OMAHA SHORT/INTERMEDIATE FIXED INCOME FUND
(See first First Omaha listing for data common to all funds)

Lead portfolio manager: Dick Chapman (1992)
Investment objective and policies: Current income consistent with capital preservation. Invests at least 65% of assets in investment grade bonds, debentures, notes, mortgage-related securities, state, municipal or industrial revenue bonds, U.S. Government and government agency obligations, and convertible securities. Portfolio maintains a dollar-weighted average maturity of two to five years. Up to 35% of assets may be in preferred stocks, 10% in securities of foreign issuers and 10% in shares of other mutual funds.
Year organized: 1991 (Ownership of group changed in April 1995)
Ticker symbol: FOSIX
Dividends paid: Income - monthly; Capital gains - December
Portfolio turnover (3 yrs): 5%, 41%, 21%
Management fee: 0.50%
Expense ratio: 0.97% (year ending 3/31/97) (1.08% without waiver)

FIRST OMAHA SMALL CAP VALUE FUND
(See first First Omaha listing for data common to all funds)

Lead portfolio manager: Marci Koory (1996)
Investment objective and policies: Long-term capital appreciation. Invests at least 65% of assets in common stock and convertible securities of companies having market capitalizations smaller than the largest 25% of companies traded on the New York Stock Exchange (approximately $1.5B) with perceived potential for capital appreciation based on records of earnings and dividend growth. May invest up to 35% of assets in equity securities of other types and other capitalizations, and debt securities within the four highest rating categories. May invest up to 10% of assets in foreign issues, either direct or through sponsored and unsponsored ADRs.
Year organized: 1996 (Ownership of group changed in April 1995)
Ticker symbol: FOSCX
Dividends paid: Income - monthly; Capital gains - December
Portfolio turnover (1 yr): 7%
Management fee: 0.85%
Expense ratio: 1.34% (10 months ending 3/31/97) (3.76% without waiver)

FIRST OMAHA U.S. GOVERNMENT OBLIGATIONS FUND
(See first First Omaha listing for data common to all funds)

Investment objective and policies: Maximum current income consistent with preservation of capital and liquidity. Invests primarily in high quality money mar-ket instruments issued by the U.S. Government, its agencies and its instrumentalities.
Year organized: 1991 (Ownership of group changed in April 1995)
Ticker symbol: FOGXX
Dividends paid: Income - declared daily, paid monthly
Management fee: 0.25%
Expense ratio: 0.58% (year ending 3/31/97) (0.59% without waiver)

FIRSTAR FUNDS
(Data common to all Firstar funds are shown below. See subsequent listings fro data specific to individual funds.)

615 East Michigan Street
P.O. Box 3011
Milwaukee, WI 53201-3011
800-982-8909, 800-228-1024
414-287-3808, fax 414-276-0604
Internet: http://www.firstarfunds.com

Adviser: FIRMCO (a wholly owned subsidiary of Firstar Corp.)
Co-administrators: Firstar Trust Co., and B.C. Ziegler & Co.
Transfer agent: Firstar Trust Co.
Special information: Fund family changed names from the Portico Funds 2/1/98.
Minimum purchase: Initial: $1,000, Subsequent: $50; IRA: Initial: $100
Wire orders accepted: Yes
Deadline for same day wire purchase: 3:00 P.M. CST
Qualified for sale in: All states
Telephone redemptions: Yes, $500 minimum
Wire redemptions: Yes, $12 fee
Letter redemptions: Signature guarantee required over $50,000
Check redemptions: $250 minimum
Telephone switching: With other Firstar funds, $1,000 minimum (all Firstar stock and bond funds have loads), the Bramwell Growth Fund, the Heartland funds, the Hennessy Balanced Fund, the Kenwood Growth and Income Fund, the Merriman funds, the O'Shaughnessy funds, the Primary funds, the Skyline Equity funds, the Thompson Plumb funds, and the Wasatch funds
Number of switches permitted: 4 per year
Dividends paid: Income - declared daily, paid monthly
Shareholder services: IRA, SEP-IRA, Keogh, 401(k), automatic investment plan, directed dividends, electronic funds transfer, systematic withdrawal plan min. bal. req. $5,000
Management fee: 0.50% first $2B, 0.40% over $2B
Administrative fee: 0.125% first $2B plus 0.10% over $2B (for aggregate total of all Firstar funds)
IRA/Keogh fees: Annual $12.50, Closing $15

FIRSTAR MONEY MARKET FUND
(See first Firstar listing for data common to all funds)

Investment objective and policies: Current income consistent with capital preservation, liquidity and price stability. Invests in a broad range of government, bank and commercial money market instruments.
Year organized: 1988 (formerly Elan Money Market Fund)
Ticker symbol: POMXX
12b-1 distribution fee: Maximum of 0.25%
Expense ratio: 0.60% (year ending 10/31/97)

FIRSTAR TAX-EXEMPT MONEY MARKET FUND ◆
(See first Firstar listing for data common to all funds)

Investment objective and policies: Current income exempt from federal income tax, consistent with capital preservation, liquidity and price stability. Invests in municipal money market instruments.
Year organized: 1988 (formerly Elan Tax-Exempt Money Market Fund)
Ticker symbol: POTXX
12b-1 distribution fee: Maximum of 0.25% (not currently imposed)

Expense ratio: 0.60% (year ending 10/31/97)

FIRSTAR U.S. GOVERNMENT MONEY MARKET FUND ◆
(See first Firstar listing for data common to all funds)

Investment objective and policies: Current income consistent with capital preservation, liquidity and price stability. Invests in money market obligations issued or guaranteed by the U.S. Government, its agencies or instrumentalities, and in repurchase agreements relating to such obligations, irrespective of state income tax considerations.
Year organized: 1988 (formerly Elan U.S. Government Money Market Fund)
Ticker symbol: POGXX
12b-1 distribution fee: Maximum of 0.25% (not currently imposed)
Expense ratio: 0.60% (year ending 10/31/97)

FIRSTAR U.S. TREASURY MONEY MARKET FUND ◆
(See first Firstar listing for data common to all funds)

Investment objective and policies: Current income exempt from state income taxes, consistent with capital preservation, liquidity and price stability. Invests in money market obligations issued or guaranteed by the U.S. Government, its agencies or instrumentalities, the interest income from which is generally exempt from state income taxation.
Year organized: 1991 (name changed from U.S. Federal Money Market Fund in 1994)
Ticker symbol: PUJXX
12b-1 distribution fee: Maximum of 0.25% (not currently imposed)
Expense ratio: 0.60% (year ending 10/31/97)

FIRSTHAND FUNDS ◆
(Data common to all Firsthand funds are shown below. See subsequent listings for data specific to individual funds. Funds were previously listed as Interactive Investments, or Technology Value)

101 Park Center Plaza, Suite 1300
San Jose, CA 95113
888-883-3863, 408-294-2200
shareholder services 888-884-2675
fax 408-490-0291
Internet: http://www.techfunds.com

Adviser: Interactive Research Advisers, Inc.
Transfer agent: Countrywide Fund Services, Inc.
Minimum purchase: Initial: $10,000, Subsequent: $50; IRA: Initial: $2,000
Wire orders accepted: Yes
Deadline for same day wire purchase: 4 P.M.
Qualified for sale in: All states
Letter redemptions: Signature guarantee required over $25,000
Telephone switching: With other Firsthand funds
Number of switches permitted: Unlimited
Shareholder services: IRA, automatic investment plan
Administration fee: 0.45% first $200M to 0.30% over $1B (paid to adviser)
IRA fees: Annual $25

FIRSTHAND - MEDICAL SPECIALISTS FUND ◆
(See first Firsthand listing for data common to all funds)

Portfolio manager: Kendrick W. Kam (1998)
Investment objective and policies: Long-term capital growth. A non-diversified fund which invests at least 65% of assets in equity securities of companies of any size in the health, biotech and medical technology fields, which are believed to have a strong a strong earnings growth outlook and the potential for capital appreciation. This includes such products and services as cardiovascular medical devices, minimally invasive surgical tools, pharmaceuticals including generic drugs, and managed care providers. May also

invest up to 10% of assets in 'special situations,' including: liquidations; reorganizations; recapitalizations or mergers; material litigation; technological breakthroughs; or new management or management policies. May invest up to 35% of assets in debt securities, 25% of assets in unseasoned companies, 15% in illiquid securities, and up to 15% of assets in foreign issues. May invest up to 25% in one company, and up to 50% in two companies. May use options in an effort to enhance return and for hedging purposes.
Year organized: 1998
Discount broker availability: *Fidelity, *Schwab, *White
Dividends paid: Income - December; Capital gains - December
Management fee: 1.50%

FIRSTHAND - TECHNOLOGY LEADERS FUND ◆
(See first Firsthand listing for data common to all funds)

Portfolio manager: Kevin M. Landis (1998)
Investment objective and policies: Long-term capital growth. A non-diversified fund which invests at least 65% of assets in equity securities of companies of any size in the high tech arena, which are believed to have the strongest competitive position in their sector. This includes companies in the semiconductor, computer, computer peripheral, software, telecommunications, and mass storage device segments of the high tech industry. May also invest up to 10% of assets in 'special situations,' including: liquidations; reorganizations; recapitalizations or mergers; material litigation; technological breakthroughs; or new management or management policies. May invest up to 35% of assets in debt securities, 25% of assets in unseasoned companies, 15% in illiquid securities, and up to 15% of assets in foreign issues. May invest up to 25% in one company, and up to 50% in two companies. May use options in an effort to enhance return and for hedging purposes.
Year organized: 1998
Discount broker availability: *Fidelity, *Schwab, *White
Dividends paid: Income - December; Capital gains - December
Management fee: 1.50%

FIRSTHAND - TECHNOLOGY VALUE FUND ◆
(See first Firsthand listing for data common to all funds)

Portfolio managers: Kendrick W. Kam (1994), Kevin M. Landis (1994)
Investment objective and policies: Long-term capital growth. A non-diversified fund which invests at least 65% of assets in equity securities of companies of any size in the electronic and medical technology fields, which are believed to be undervalued and have potential for capital appreciation based on balance sheet strength, the ability to generate earnings and a strong competitive position. May also invest up to 10% of assets in 'special situations,' including: liquidations; reorganizations; recapitalizations or mergers; material litigation; technological breakthroughs; or new management or management policies. May invest up to 35% of assets in debt securities, 25% of assets in unseasoned companies, 15% in illiquid securities, and up to 15% of assets in foreign issues. May invest up to 25% in one company, and up to 50% in two companies.
Year organized: 1994
Ticker symbol: TVFQX
Discount broker availability: *Fidelity, *Schwab, *White
Dividends paid: Income - December; Capital gains - December
Portfolio turnover (3 yrs): 101%, 43%, 45%
Management fee: 1.50%
Expense ratio: 1.93% (year ending 12/31/97)

THE FLEX-FUNDS
(Data common to all Flex-Funds are shown below. See subsequent listings for data specific to individual funds.)

6000 Memorial Drive
P.O. Box 7177
Dublin, OH 43017
800-325-3539, 614-766-2159
fax 614-766-6669
Internet: http://www.flexfunds.com
e-mail: info@flexfunds.com

Shareholder service hours: Full service: M-F 8 A.M.-5 P.M. EST; After hours service: prices, yields, messages, prospectuses
Adviser: R. Meeder & Assocs., Inc.
Transfer agent: Mutual Funds Service Co.
Minimum purchase: Initial: $2,500, Subsequent: $100; IRA: Initial: $500; Automatic investment plan: Initial: $100
Wire orders accepted: Yes
Deadline for same day wire purchase: 4 P.M. (3 P.M. for Money Market)
Telephone redemptions: Yes
Wire redemptions: Yes, $1,000 minimum
Letter redemptions: Signature guarantee required
Telephone switching: With other Flex-Fund funds
Number of switches permitted: Unlimited
Deadline for same day switch: 3 P.M. for MM
Shareholder services: IRA, SEP-IRA, 401(k), corporate retirement plans, electronic funds transfer (purchase only), systematic withdrawal plan min. bal. req. $10,000
IRA fees: Annual $5, Closing $7

THE FLEX-FUNDS - HIGHLANDS GROWTH FUND
(See first Flex-Fund listing for data common to all funds)

Sub-adviser: Sector Capital Management, LLC
Portfolio manager: William L. Gurner (1997)
Investment objective and policies: Long-term capital growth. Fund invests all of its assets in an underlying portfolio with identical objectives; it invests at least 70% of assets in common stocks selected from representatives of the S&P 500 Index perceived to show greater than average growth characteristics. Index companies are subdivided into ten industry sectors as determined by the sub-adviser, and each sector is then assigned to yet another sub-adviser for specialized analysis and management. Up to 30% of assets may be invested in securities of companies not listed in the index. Fund may hedge.
Year organized: 1985 (formerly Capital Gains portfolio; name changed from Growth Fund 1/6/97; simultaneous objective change; prior performance may be irrelevant. Name changed BACK to Growth from Highlander 6/97.)
Ticker symbol: FLCGX
Discount broker availability: Fidelity, *Schwab, Siebert, *White
Qualified for sale in: All states
Dividends paid: Income - March, June, September, December; Capital gains - December
Portfolio turnover (3 yrs): 82%, 338%, 103%
Management fee: 1.00% first $50M to 0.60% over $100M
12b-1 distribution fee: Maximum of 0.20%
Expense ratio: 1.65% (year ending 12/31/96)

THE FLEX-FUNDS - MONEY MARKET FUND
(See first Flex-Fund listing for data common to all funds)

Portfolio manager: Philip A. Voelker (1985)
Investment objective and policies: Income and stable asset values. Invests in an underlying portfolio with identical objectives, which, in turn, invests in a portfolio of high quality short-term money market instruments.
Year organized: 1985
Ticker symbol: FFMXX
Qualified for sale in: All states except: AK, ID, ME, MT, NV, NH, NM, ND, RI, SD, UT, VT, WV
Check redemptions: $100 minimum

Dividends paid: Income - declared daily, paid monthly
Management fee: 0.40% first $100M, 0.25% over $100M
12b-1 distribution fee: Maximum of 0.20%
Expense ratio: 0.40% (year ending 12/31/96) (0.58% without waiver)

THE FLEX-FUNDS - MUIRFIELD FUND
(See first Flex-Fund listing for data common to all funds)

Portfolio manager: Robert S. Meeder, Jr. (1988)
Investment objective and policies: Long-term capital growth; current income secondary. Fund invests all of its assets in an underlying portfolio with identical objectives; it invests in shares of other equity mutual funds which seek long-term growth, primarily no-loads. Fund may use index funds, sector funds and low load (maximum of 2%) funds. Fund will not use other Flex funds.
Year organized: 1988
Ticker symbol: FLMFX
Discount broker availability: Fidelity, *Schwab, Siebert, *White
Qualified for sale in: All states
Dividends paid: Income - March, June, September, December; Capital gains - December
Portfolio turnover (3 yrs): 186%, 168%, 280%
Management fee: 1.00% first $50M to 0.60% over $100M
12b-1 distribution fee: Maximum of 0.20%
Expense ratio: 1.19% (year ending 12/31/96)

THE FLEX-FUNDS - TOTAL RETURN UTILITIES FUND
(See first Flex-Fund listing for data common to all funds)

Sub-adviser: Miller/Howard Investments, Inc.
Portfolio manager: Lowell G. Miller (1995)
Investment objective and policies: High current income and growth of income; also capital appreciation when consistent with primary objective. Fund invests all of its assets in an underlying portfolio with identical objectives; it invests primarily in common stocks, preferred stocks, warrants and rights, and securities convertible into common or preferred stock of domestic and foreign utility companies with a commitment to dividend growth. Only invests in companies within the top decile of their industry that have no nuclear exposure. Up to 40% of assets may be in the telephone industry and 25% in securities of foreign issuers. Fund may hedge.
Year organized: 1995
Ticker symbol: FLRUX
Discount broker availability: *Schwab, *White
Qualified for sale in: All states except: AK, AR, HI, ID, IA, LA, ME, MS, MT, NE, NV, NH, NM, ND, PR, OK, SD, UT, VT, WV
Dividends paid: Income - monthly; Capital gains - December
Portfolio turnover (1 yr): 51%
Management fee: 1.00% first $50M to 0.60% over $100M
12b-1 distribution fee: Maximum of 0.25%
Expense ratio: 1.25% (year ending 12/31/96) (2.95% without waiver)

THE FLEX-FUNDS - U.S. GOVERNMENT BOND FUND
(See first Flex-Fund listing for data common to all funds)

Portfolio manager: Joseph Zarr (1996)
Investment objective and policies: Maximum current income. Fund invests all of its assets in an underlying portfolio with identical objectives; it invests only in high quality fixed-income government securities issued by the U.S. Government or its agencies or instrumentalities. Under stable market conditions, portfolio maintains a dollar-weighted average maturity of approximately ten years. Fund may hedge.
Year organized: 1985 (name and objective changed June 1996. Past data regarding Flex-Fund Bond Fund may be misleading.)
Ticker symbol: FLXBX

Discount broker availability: Fidelity, *Schwab, Siebert, *White
Qualified for sale in: All states except: AK, AR, CT, HI, ID, IA, LA, ME, MA, MS, MT, NE, NV, NH, NJ, ND, PR, OK, OR, RI, SC, SD, TN, UT, VT, WV
Dividends paid: Income - declared daily, paid monthly; Capital gains - December
Portfolio turnover (3 yrs): 779%, 232%, 708%
Management fee: 0.4% first $100M, 0.2% over $100M
12b-1 distribution fee: 0.20%
Expense ratio: 1.00% (year ending 12/31/96) (1.06% without waiver)

FLEX-PARTNERS - INTERNATIONAL EQUITY FUND
(See first Flex-Fund listing for data common to all funds)

Sub-adviser: Commercial Union Investment Management, Ltd.
Portfolio manager: David Keen (1997)
Investment objective and policies: Long-term capital growth. Fund invests primarily in equity securities of companies in both developed and developing foreign markets. Invests at least 70% of assets in common stocks selected from representatives of "developed" countries, and a maximum of 30% of assets in "developing markets. Fund may hedge currencies.
Year organized: 1997
Sales restrictions: Fund is being sold retail to new accounts with a 4% load. Only existing customers of the Flex-Fund family as of 12/31/97 (NOT other Flex-Partners funds though) may purchase this fund at NAV.
Discount broker availability: Fidelity
Qualified for sale in: AL, AZ, AR, CA, CO, FL, GA, IL, IN, KY, LA, MA, MI, MN, MS, MO, NJ, NY, NC, OH, PA, SC, TN, TX, VA, WA, WI
Dividends paid: Income - March, June, September, December; Capital gains - December
Management fee: 1.00%
12b-1 distribution fee: Maximum of 0.25%

FLORIDA DAILY MUNICIPAL INCOME FUND ◆
600 Fifth Avenue, 8th Floor
New York, NY 10020
800-676-6779, 212-830-5200
prices/yields 212-830-5225
fax 212-830-5476

Adviser: Reich & Tang Asset Management, L.P.
Portfolio manager: Molly Flewharty (1994)
Transfer agent: Reich & Tang Services, L.P.
Investment objective and policies: High current interest income exempt from federal income tax and, to the extent possible, from Florida intangible personal property tax, consistent with preservation of capital and liquidity. Invests primarily in Florida municipal money market instruments.
Year organized: 1994
Ticker symbol: FIAXX
Special sales restrictions: Only class "B" shares of the fund are sold direct and without 12b-1 fees. Statistics represent "B" shares only.
Minimum purchase: Initial: $5,000, Subsequent: $100
Wire orders accepted: Yes
Deadline for same day wire purchase: 12 NN
Qualified for sale in: FL, NY
Telephone redemptions: Yes
Wire redemptions: Yes, $1,000 minimum
Letter redemptions: Signature guarantee required
Check redemptions: $250 minimum
Telephone switching: With other Reich & Tang Money market funds and R&T Equity Fund
Number of switches permitted: Unlimited, $1,000 minimum
Dividends paid: Income - declared daily, paid monthly
Shareholder services: Automatic investment plan, systematic withdrawal plan
Management fee: 0.40%
Administration fee: 0.21%
Shareholder services fee: 0.25%
Expense ratio: 0.30% (year ending 8/31/97) (0.81% without waiver)

FLORIDA STREET BOND FUND ◆
247 Florida Street
Baton Rouge, LA 70801
800-890-5344, 504-343-9342

Adviser: CommonWealth Advisors, Inc.
Administrator: AmeriPrime Financial Services, Inc.
Portfolio manager: Walter A. Morales (1997)
Transfer agent: American Data Services, Inc.
Investment objective and policies: Long-term total return: high current income and long-term capital appreciation. Invests primarily in a non-diversified portfolio of high yield junk bonds, Brady bonds and sovereign debt from around the world. May, however, invest in preferred stock, convertible bonds and equity securities without regard to yield characteristics. May invest up to 25% of assets in bonds rated lower than CCC or Caa.
Year organized: 1997
Minimum purchase: Initial: $1,000, Subsequent: $100
Wire orders accepted: Yes
Deadline for same day wire purchase: 4 P.M.
Discount broker availability: Fidelity, Schwab, Siebert, *White
Qualified for sale in: All states
Telephone redemptions: Yes
Wire redemptions: Yes
Letter redemptions: Signature guarantee required
Dividends paid: Income - December; Capital gains - December
Shareholder services: IRA, SEP-IRA, automatic investment plan, systematic withdrawal plan min. bal. req. $10,000
Management fee: 1.10%
Administration fee: 0.05%
IRA fees: Annual $15

FLORIDA STREET GROWTH FUND ◆
247 Florida Street
Baton Rouge, LA 70801
800-890-5344, 504-343-9342

Adviser: CommonWealth Advisors, Inc.
Administrator: AmeriPrime Financial Services, Inc.
Portfolio manager: Richard L. Chauvin (1997)
Transfer agent: American Data Services, Inc.
Investment objective and policies: Long-term total return: Invests primarily in equity securities perceived to be undervalued, but may also invest in bonds and other debt securities perceived to be consistent with the fund objective.
Year organized: 1997
Minimum purchase: Initial: $1,000, Subsequent: $100
Wire orders accepted: Yes
Deadline for same day wire purchase: 4 P.M.
Discount broker availability: Fidelity, Schwab, Siebert, *White
Qualified for sale in: All states
Telephone redemptions: Yes
Wire redemptions: Yes
Letter redemptions: Signature guarantee required
Dividends paid: Income - December; Capital gains - December
Shareholder services: IRA, SEP-IRA, automatic investment plan, systematic withdrawal plan min. bal. req. $10,000
Management fee: 1.35%
Administration fee: 0.10% first $50M to 0.05% over $100M (minimum $25,000)
IRA fees: Annual $15

FLORIDA TAX FREE MONEY MARKET FUND ◆
100 Second Avenue South, Suite 800
St. Petersburg, FL 33701
800-557-7555, 813-825-7731
fax 813-895-8805

Adviser: William R. Hough & Co.
Portfolio manager: Investment committee
Transfer agent: William R. Hough & Co.
Investment objective and policies: High current income exempt from federal income tax and Florida intangible personal property tax, consistent with preservation of capital and liquidity. Invests in high

quality, short-term Florida municipal obligations. Fund is non-diversified.
Year organized: 1993
Ticker symbol: HFMXX
Minimum purchase: Initial: $1,000, Subsequent: $50; Automatic investment plan: Subsequent: $250
Wire orders accepted: Yes, $500 minimum
Deadline for same day wire purchase: 12 P.M.
Qualified for sale in: All states except AK, AR, ID, LA, MA, MO, NE, ND, PR, SD, WV
Telephone redemptions: Yes
Wire redemptions: Yes, $1,000 minimum, $10 fee
Letter redemptions: Signature guarantee required over $10,000
Check redemptions: No minimum, $0.80 per check after 3 each month
Telephone switching: With Hough Florida TaxFree ShortTerm fund, $500 minimum
Number of switches permitted: 4 outbound per year, 15 day hold
Dividends paid: Income - declared and paid monthly
Shareholder services: Electronic funds transfer, systematic withdrawal plan min. bal. req. $10,000
Management fee: 0.50%
12b-1 distribution fee: Maximum of 0.25% (not currently imposed)
Expense ratio: 0.20% (year ending 4/30/97) (0.78% without waiver)

FLORIDA TAX FREE SHORT-TERM FUND ◆
100 Second Avenue South, Suite 800
St. Petersburg, FL 33701
800-557-7555, 813-825-7731
fax 813-895-8805

Adviser: William R. Hough & Co.
Portfolio manager: Investment committee
Transfer agent: William R. Hough & Co.
Investment objective and policies: High current income exempt from federal income tax and Florida intangible personal property tax, consistent with preservation of capital and liquidity. Invests primarily in Florida municipal bonds with remaining maturities of less than six years at the time of purchase. Portfolio maintains a dollar-weighted average maturity of three years or less. May hedge up to 25% of assets and invest in reverse repurchase agreements, and buy and sell options and futures. Up to 20% of assets may be securities subject to AMT tax treatment. Fund is non-diversified.
Year organized: 1993
Minimum purchase: Initial: $1,000, Subsequent: $50; Automatic investment plan: Subsequent: $250
Wire orders accepted: Yes, $500 minimum
Deadline for same day wire purchase: 1 P.M.
Qualified for sale in: All states except AK, AR, ID, LA, MA, MO, NE, ND, PR, SD, WV
Telephone redemptions: Yes
Wire redemptions: Yes, $1,000 minimum, $10 fee
Letter redemptions: Signature guarantee required over $10,000
Check redemptions: No minimum, $0.80 per check after 3 each month
Telephone switching: With Hough Florida TaxFree Money Market fund, $500 minimum
Number of switches permitted: 4 outbound per year, 15 day hold
Dividends paid: Income - monthly; Capital gains - December
Portfolio turnover (3 yrs): 41%, 83%, 36%
Shareholder services: Electronic funds transfer, systematic withdrawal plan min. bal. req. $10,000
Management fee: 0.60%
12b-1 distribution fee: Maximum of 0.25% (not currently imposed)
Expense ratio: 0.20% (year ending 4/30/97) (1.18% without waiver)

FMC SELECT FUND ◆
437 Madison Avenue
New York, NY 10022
800-932-7781, 212-756-3100

Adviser: First Manhattan Co.
Administrator: SEI Fund Resources
Portfolio managers: Bernard C. Groveman (1995), A. Byron Nimocks (1995), William K. McElroy (1995)

Transfer agent: DST Systems, Inc.
Investment objective and policies: A favorable rate of return principally through capital appreciation, and, to a limited degree, through current income. Generally invests 75% to 85% of assets in equity securities, and the balance in fixed-income securities and money market instruments. Allocation is varied according to perceived market conditions. May sell short against the box, and use options and futures.
Year organized: 1995
Minimum purchase: Initial: $10,000, Subsequent: $1,000; Automatic investment plan: Subsequent: $100
Wire orders accepted: Yes
Deadline for same day wire purchase: 4 P.M.
Qualified for sale in: AZ, CA, CO, CT, DE, FL, GA, HI, IA, IL, IN, KS, KY, MD, MS, MN, NC, NH, NY, OH, PA, TX, VA, WA
Telephone redemptions: Yes
Wire redemptions: Yes, $10 fee
Letter redemptions: Signature guarantee not required
Dividends paid: Income - October, December; Capital gains - October, December
Portfolio turnover (2 yrs): 22%, 24%
Shareholder services: IRA, SEP-IRA, 401(k), electronic funds transfer (redemption only), systematic withdrawal plan min. bal. req. $25,000
Management fee: 1.00%
Expense ratio: 1.10% (year ending 10/31/97) (1.17% without waiver)
IRA fees: None

FMI FOCUS FUND ◆
225 East Maston Street
Milwaukee, WI 53202
800-811-5311, 414-226-4555
fax 414-226-4530

Adviser: Fiduciary Management, Inc.
Portfolio managers: Ted D. Kellner (1996), Richard E. Lane (1997)
Transfer agent: Firstar Trust Co.
Investment objective and policies: Capital appreciation. Invests primarily in common stocks and warrants, engages in short sales, invests in foreign securities which are traded in the U.S., and effects transactions in stock index futures contracts, options on stock index futures, and options on securities and stock indexes. Focuses on 40 securities or less perceived to offer greatest growth potential in one to two years; fund is non-diversified. Fund may leverage its investments.
Year organized: 1996
Minimum purchase: Initial: $1,000, Subsequent: $100; Automatic investment plan: Subsequent: $50
Wire orders accepted: Yes
Deadline for same day wire purchase: 4 P.M.
Qualified for sale in: AZ, CA, CO, DE, DC, IL, IN, KS, KY, MA, MI, MN, NJ, NY, OH, PA, TN, WA, WI
Letter redemptions: Signature guarantee not required
Dividends paid: Income - October, December; Capital gains - October, December
Portfolio turnover (1 yr): 298%
Shareholder services: IRA, SEP-IRA, 401(k), 403(b), systematic withdrawal plan min. bal. req. $10,000
Management fee: 1.00%
12b-1 distribution fee: 0.25% (not currently imposed)
Expense ratio: 2.75% (10 months ending 9/30/97) (6.38% without waiver)
IRA fees: Annual $12.50, Closing $15

FOCUS TRUST, INC. ◆
P.O. Box 407
Wayne, PA 19087
800-665-2550, 610-688-6558
Internet: http://www.focustrust.com

Adviser: Focus Capital Advisory, L.P.
Portfolio manager: Robert G. Hagstrom, Jr. (1995)
Transfer agent and administrator: First Data Investor Services Group
Investment objective and policies: Maximum long-term capital appreciation consistent with minimum

long-term risk to principal; income incidental. Invests primarily in a small group of common and preferred stocks and convertible securities. Stock will be selected based on perceptions of underlying value and held for the long term. May invest up to 10% of assets in illiquid securities and 15% in foreign issues, including ADRs and EDRs. Fund is non-diversified.
Year organized: 1995
Ticker symbol: FOCTX
Minimum purchase: Initial: $1,000, Subsequent: $100; Automatic investment plan: Subsequent: $50
Wire orders accepted: Yes
Deadline for same day wire purchase: 4 P.M.
Discount broker availability: Fidelity, Schwab, Siebert, White
Qualified for sale in: All states
Telephone redemptions: Yes
Wire redemptions: Yes, $9 fee
Letter redemptions: Signature guarantee required over $10,000
Redemption fee: 1.00% if held less than two years, payable to the fund
Dividends paid: Income - December; Capital gains - December
Portfolio turnover (2 yrs): 8%, 0%
Shareholder services: IRA, SEP-IRA, 401(k), 403(b), electronic funds transfer
Management fee: 0.70%
Administration fee: 0.15% first $50M to 0.05% over $100M
Expense ratio: 2.00% (year ending 12/31/96) (4.96% without waiver)

FONTAINE FUNDS ◆
(Data common to all Fontaine funds are shown below. See subsequent listings for data specific to individual funds.)

210 West Pennsylvania Avenue, Suite 240
Towson, MD 21204-5354
800-247-1550, 410-825-7890
fax 410-825-7945

Shareholder service hours: Full service: M-F 8:30 A.M.-5 P.M. EST; After hours service: prices, messages, account balances, last transaction, prospectuses
Adviser: Richard Fontaine Assocs., Inc.
Transfer agent: Richard Fontaine & Co., Inc.
Minimum purchase: Initial: $1,000, Subsequent: $100
Wire orders accepted: Yes
Deadline for same day wire purchase: 4 P.M.
Letter redemptions: Signature guarantee required over $10,000
Shareholder services: IRA, SEP-IRA, directed dividends, electronic funds transfer (purchase only)
IRA fees: None

FONTAINE CAPITAL APPRECIATION FUND ◆
(See first Fontaine listing for data common to all funds)

Portfolio manager: Richard H. Fontaine (1989)
Investment objective and policies: Long-term capital appreciation; current income secondary. Normally invests 80% of assets in common stocks of primarily domestic companies believed undervalued or out of favor with investors, focusing on price/book value relative to 10-15 year range. Up to 20% of assets may be in securities of foreign issuers from developed countries. Portfolio will switch to cash and fixed-income positions according to perceived market conditions.
Year organized: 1989
Ticker symbol: FAPPX
Discount broker availability: White
Qualified for sale in: CA, DE, DC, FL, IL, MD, MA, NH, NJ, NY, OH, OR, PA, TN, TX, WI
Dividends paid: Income - December; Capital gains - December
Portfolio turnover (3 yrs): 373%, 96%, 136%
Management fee: 0.95%
Expense ratio: 1.68% (year ending 12/31/97)

FONTAINE GLOBAL GROWTH FUND ◆
(See first Fontaine listing for data common to all funds)

Portfolio manager: Richard H. Fontaine (1992)
Investment objective and policies: Long-term capital growth. Invests primarily in equity and equity-related securities of established medium and large capitalization domestic and foreign issuers. Will normally have at least 65% of assets invested in at least three different developed countries in North America, Europe and the Pacific Basin, one of which may be the U.S.
Year organized: 1992
Ticker symbol: FONGX
Discount broker availability: White
Qualified for sale in: CA, DC, FL, IL, MD, NH, NJ, NY, OH, OR, PA, TX
Dividends paid: Income - December; Capital gains - December
Portfolio turnover (3 yrs): 253%, 101%, 114%
Management fee: 0.85%
Expense ratio: 2.00% (year ending 12/31/97)

FONTAINE GLOBAL INCOME FUND ◆
(See first Fontaine listing for data common to all funds)

Portfolio manager: Richard H. Fontaine (1992)
Investment objective and policies: High current income; capital appreciation secondary. Invests primarily in fixed-income securities of domestic and foreign issuers; high and medium quality bonds, debentures, and notes. Investments outside the U.S. will be principally in government and quasi-governmental issuers to maintain liquidity and reduce credit risk. May also use currency exchange transactions to reduce risk. To the extent not invested in fixed-income instruments, fund may invest in equity positions similar to those taken in the Global Growth portfolio.
Year organized: 1992
Ticker symbol: FOGIX
Discount broker availability: White
Qualified for sale in: CA, DC, FL, IL, MD, NH, NJ, NY, OH, OR, PA, TX
Dividends paid: Income - March, June, September, December; Capital gains - December
Portfolio turnover (3 yrs): 222%, 96%, 130%
Management fee: 0.75%
Expense ratio: 1.69% (year ending 12/31/97)

THE 44 WALL STREET EQUITY FUND ◆
(See Matterhorn Growth Fund)

FORUM DAILY ASSETS CASH FUND ◆
Two Portland Square
Portland, ME 04101
888-557-3200, 207-879-0001
shareholder services 800-943-6786

Adviser: Linden Asset Management, Inc.
Portfolio manager: Anthony R. Fischer, Jr. (1996)
Transfer agent and administrator: Forum Financial Corp.
Investment objective and policies: High current income consistent with the preservation of capital and liquidity. Invests in a broad spectrum of high quality short-term instruments issued by financial institutions, corporations or the U.S. Government, its instrumentalities or agencies. Only invests in issues with maturities of thirteen months or less.
Year organized: 1996
Ticker symbol: FACXX
Minimum purchase: Initial: $10,000, Subsequent: $500; IRA: Initial: $2,000; Automatic investment plan: Subsequent: $250
Wire orders accepted: $5,000 minimum
Deadline for same day wire purchase: 12 NN
Qualified for sale in: All states
Telephone redemptions: Yes
Wire redemptions: Yes, $5,000 minimum
Letter redemptions: Signature guarantee required
Telephone switching: With the Highland Growth fund, Payson funds, Sound Shore Fund, and other Forum (load) funds

Number of switches permitted: Unlimited, $2,500 minimum
Deadline for same day switch: 2 P.M.
Dividends paid: Income - declared daily, paid monthly
Shareholder services: IRA, systematic withdrawal plan
Management fee: 0.10%
Administration fee: 0.25% + $12,000
Expense ratio: 0.52% (year ending 8/31/97) (1.22% without waiver)
IRA fee: Annual $10, Initial $10

FORUM DAILY ASSETS TREASURY FUND ◆
Two Portland Square
Portland, ME 04101
888-557-3200, 207-879-0001
shareholder services 800-943-6786

Adviser: Forum Advisors, Inc.
Portfolio manager: Anthony R. Fischer, Jr. (1992)
Transfer agent and administrator: Forum Financial Corp.
Investment objective and policies: High current income consistent with preservation of capital and liquidity. Invests primarily in money market obligations issued or guaranteed by the U.S. Treasury or its agencies and instrumentalities.
Year organized: 1992
Ticker symbol: FODXX
Minimum purchase: Initial: $10,000, Subsequent: $500; IRA: Initial: $2,000; Automatic investment plan: Subsequent: $250
Wire orders accepted: Yes
Deadline for same day wire purchase: 12 NN
Qualified for sale in: AK, CA, CO, CT, DC, FL, GA, ID, IL, IN, KY, LA, ME, MA, MD, MI, MN, MO, NH, NJ, NY, NC, OH, OK, OR, PA, RI, TX, UT, VA, WA, WI, WY
Telephone redemptions: Yes
Wire redemptions: Yes, $5,000 minimum
Letter redemptions: Signature guarantee required
Telephone switching: With the Highland Growth fund, Payson funds, Sound Shore Fund, and other Forum (load) funds
Number of switches permitted: Unlimited, $2,500 minimum
Deadline for same day switch: 12 NN
Dividends paid: Income - declared daily, paid monthly
Shareholder services: IRA, systematic withdrawal plan
Management fee: 0.10%
Administration fee: 0.25% + $12,000
Expense ratio: 0.50% (year ending 8/31/97) (0.95% without waiver)
IRA fees: Annual $10, Initial $10

FOUNDERS FUNDS
(Data common to all Founders funds are shown below. See subsequent listings for data specific to individual funds.)

Founders Financial Center
2930 East Third Avenue
Denver, CO 80206-5002
800-525-2440, 800-947-3278
303-394-4404
prices/yields 800-232-8088
fax 303-394-4021
Internet: http://www.founders.com
e-mail: @founders.com

Shareholder service hours: Full service: M-F 7 A.M.-6:30 P.M., Sat 9 A.M.-2 P.M. MST; After hours service: prices, balances, place orders, last transactions, news, messages, prospectuses, indices, total returns
Adviser: Founders Asset Management, Inc.
Transfer agent: Investors Fiduciary Trust Co.
Minimum purchase: Initial: $1,000, Subsequent: $100; IRA/Keogh: Initial: $500; Automatic investment plan: Initial: $50, Subsequent: $50
Wire orders accepted: Yes
Deadline for same day wire purchase: 4 P.M.
Qualified for sale in: All states
Telephone redemptions: Yes, $100 minimum

Wire redemptions: Yes, $1,000 minimum, $6 fee
Letter redemptions: Signature guarantee required over $50,000
Telephone switching: With other Founders Funds, $100 minimum
Number of switches permitted: 4 round trips per year
Shareholder services: IRA, SEP-IRA, Keogh, 403(b), 401(k), corporate retirement plans, directed dividends, electronic funds transfer, systematic withdrawal plan min. bal. req. $5,000
Maintenance fee: $10/year for accounts with balances under $1,000
12b-1 distribution fees: Maximum of 0.25% (except MM)
IRA fees: Annual $10 per social security number (waived for accounts with at least $5,000 in assets)
Keogh fees: Annual $10

FOUNDERS BALANCED FUND
(See first Founders listing for data common to all funds)

Lead portfolio manager: Brian F. Kelly (1996)
Investment objective and policies: Current income and capital appreciation. Generally invests in dividend-paying common stocks, U.S. and foreign government obligations and corporate fixed-income securities. Using a minimum investment of 25% of assets in investment grade bonds and a maximum of 75% in equities, fund will vary allocation according to perceived market conditions. May elect to invest in non-dividend paying companies if there is a belief the companies offer a better prospect for capital appreciation. May have up to 30% of assets in foreign securities, 15% in illiquid securities and use futures and options for hedging purposes.
Year organized: 1963
Ticker symbol: FRINX
Group fund code: 376
Discount broker availability: *Fidelity, *Schwab, *Siebert, White
Dividends paid: Income - March, June, September, December; Capital gains - December
Portfolio turnover (3 yrs): 146%, 286%, 258%
Management fee: 0.65% first $250M to 0.50% over $750M
Expense ratio: 1.12% (year ending 12/31/96)

FOUNDERS BLUE CHIP FUND
(See first Founders listing for data common to all funds)

Lead portfolio manager: Brian F. Kelly (1996)
Investment objective and policies: Long-term growth of capital and income. Invests in common stocks of large companies with proven earnings and dividends records in sound financial condition. At least 65% of assets will be in "Blue Chips" in the DJIA, S&P 500, or NYSE with capitalizations over $1B. May have up to 30% of assets in foreign securities, 15% in illiquid securities and use futures and options for hedging purposes.
Year organized: 1938 (Name change 12/1/87, formerly Founders Mutual. Changed from a quasi-index fund in November 1983)
Ticker symbol: FRMUX
Group fund code: 375
Discount broker availability: *Fidelity, *Schwab, *Siebert, White
Dividends paid: Income - December; Capital gains - December
Portfolio turnover (3 yrs): 195%, 235%, 239%
Management fee: 0.65% first 250M to 0.50% over $750M
Expense ratio: 1.16% (year ending 12/31/96)

FOUNDERS DISCOVERY FUND
(See first Founders listing for data common to all funds)

Lead portfolio manager: Robert T. Ammann (1997)
Investment objective and policies: Capital appreciation. Invests primarily in common stocks of small, rapidly growing U.S. companies with market capitalizations or revenues between $10M and $500M. May

have up to 30% of assets in foreign securities, 15% in illiquid securities and use futures and options for hedging purposes.
Year organized: 1989
Ticker symbol: FDISX
Group fund code: 370
Discount broker availability: *Fidelity, *Schwab, *Siebert, White
Dividends paid: Income - December; Capital gains - December
Portfolio turnover (3 yrs): 106%, 118%, 72%
Management fee: 1.00% first $250M to 0.70% over $500M
Expense ratio: 1.59% (year ending 12/31/96)

FOUNDERS FRONTIER FUND
(See first Founders listing for data common to all funds)

Lead portfolio manager: Michael K. Haines (1990)
Investment objective and policies: Capital appreciation. Invests in domestic and foreign equities with at least 50% of assets in U.S. companies and no more than 25% in any one foreign country, but fund may be 100% invested in U.S. or foreign securities depending on opportunities. Buys common stocks of small and medium size companies with revenues or market capitalizations from $200M to $1.5B, but will not be restricted from owning large companies if they represent better prospects for capital appreciation. May have up to 30% of assets in foreign securities, 15% in illiquid securities and use futures and options for hedging purposes.
Year organized: 1987
Ticker symbol: FOUNX
Group fund code: 371
Discount broker availability: *Fidelity, *Schwab, *Siebert, White
Dividends paid: Income - December; Capital gains - December
Portfolio turnover (3 yrs): 85%, 92%, 72%
Management fee: 1.00% first $250M to 0.70% over $500M
Expense ratio: 1.53% (year ending 12/31/96)

FOUNDERS GOVERNMENT SECURITIES FUND
(See first Founders listing for data common to all funds)

Lead portfolio manager: Margaret Danuser (1996)
Investment objective and policies: Current income. Invests at least 65% of assets in obligations of the U.S. Government - Treasury bills, notes and bonds and Government National Mortgage Association pass-through securities. May also invest in obligations of other agencies or instrumentalities of the U.S. Government. May also invest in securities of foreign governments and/or their agencies, with a maximum of 25% of assets in securities of any one foreign country. May have up to 15% of assets in illiquid securities and use futures and options for hedging purposes.
Year organized: 1988
Ticker symbol: FGVSX
Group fund code: 377
Discount broker availability: *Fidelity, *Schwab, *Siebert, White
Check redemptions: $500 minimum
Dividends paid: Income - declared daily, paid monthly; Capital gains - December
Portfolio turnover (3 yrs): 166%, 141%, 379%
Management fee: 0.65% first $250M, 0.50% over $250M
Expense ratio: 1.29% (year ending 12/31/96)

FOUNDERS GROWTH FUND
(See first Founders listing for data common to all funds)

Lead portfolio manager: Edward F. Keely (1994)
Investment objective and policies: Long-term capital growth. Invests primarily in common stocks of well established, high-quality growth companies with strong performance records, solid market positions and reasonable financial strength, with continuous operating histories of three years or more. May have

up to 30% of assets in foreign securities, 15% in illiquid securities and use futures and options for hedging purposes.
Year organized: 1962
Ticker symbol: FRGRX
Group fund code: 374
Discount broker availability: *Fidelity, *Schwab, *Siebert, White
Dividends paid: Income - December; Capital gains - December
Portfolio turnover (3 yrs): 134%, 130%, 172%
Management fee: 1.00% first $30M to 0.65% over $500M
Expense ratio: 1.20% (year ending 12/31/96)

FOUNDERS INTERNATIONAL EQUITY FUND
(See first Founders listing for data common to all funds)

Portfolio manager: Douglas A. Loeffler (1997)
Investment objective and policies: Long-term capital growth. Invests primarily in foreign equity securities representing a minimum of three countries outside the U.S. Will represent countries throughout the world, and will not invest more than 50% of assets in any one country. May also invest in investment grade debt securities in ratios determined by the portfolio manager according to market conditions. May invest up to 15% of assets in illiquid securities, and use futures contracts, foreign currency futures contracts, and covered call options for hedging purposes.
Year organized: 1995
Ticker symbol: FOIEX
Group fund code: 381
Discount broker availability: *Fidelity, *Schwab, *Siebert, White
Dividends paid: Income - December; Capital gains - December
Portfolio turnover (1 yr): 71%
Management fee: 1.00% first $30M to 0.70% over $500M
Expense ratio: 2.00% (year ending 12/31/96) (2.52% without waiver)

FOUNDERS MONEY MARKET FUND ◆
(See first Founders listing for data common to all funds)

Lead portfolio manager: Margaret Danuser (1996)
Investment objective and policies: Maximum current income consistent with preservation of capital and liquidity. Invests in high-quality money market instruments. May also invest in dollar denominated foreign securities.
Year organized: 1981
Ticker symbol: FMMXX
Group fund code: 378
Discount broker availability: *Fidelity
Check redemptions: $500 minimum
Dividends paid: Income - declared daily, paid monthly
Management fee: 0.50% first $250M to 0.35% over $750M
Expense ratio: 0.88% (year ending 12/31/96)

FOUNDERS PASSPORT FUND
(See first Founders listing for data common to all funds)

Lead portfolio manager: Michael W. Gerding (1993)
Investment objective and policies: Capital appreciation. Invests primarily in securities issued by foreign companies with market capitalizations under $1B. Normally invests at least 65% of assets in securities from at least three countries. May invest in established and emerging economies around the world, including the U.S. May have up to 15% of assets in illiquid securities and use futures and options for hedging purposes.
Year organized: 1993
Ticker symbol: FPSSX
Group fund code: 379
Discount broker availability: *Fidelity, *Schwab, *Siebert, White

Dividends paid: Income - December; Capital gains - December
Portfolio turnover (3 yrs): 58%, 37%, 78%
Management fee: 1.00% first $250M to 0.70% over $500M
Expense ratio: 1.59% (year ending 12/31/96)

FOUNDERS SPECIAL FUND
(See first Founders listing for data common to all funds)

Portfolio managers: Michael K. Haines (1997), Douglas A. Loeffler (1997)
Investment objective and policies: Capital appreciation. Invests in common stocks of three categories of companies: small- to medium-sized companies, large companies, and foreign companies. Asset allocations between categories may be adjusted according to perceived market conditions. May have up to 30% of assets in foreign securities, 15% in illiquid securities and use futures and options for hedging purposes.
Year organized: 1961 (5 for 1 split 8/31/87)
Ticker symbol: FRSPX
Group fund code: 372
Discount broker availability: *Fidelity, *Schwab, *Siebert, White
Portfolio turnover (3 yrs): 186%, 263%, 272%
Dividends paid: Income - December; Capital gains - December
Management fee: 1.00% first $30M to $0.65% over $500M
Expense ratio: 1.36% (year ending 12/31/96)

FOUNDERS WORLDWIDE GROWTH FUND
(See first Founders listing for data common to all funds)

Lead portfolio manager: Michael W. Gerding (1990)
Investment objective and policies: Long-term capital growth. Primarily invests in equity securities of established growth companies around the world, including the U.S. Emphasizes common stocks of both emerging and established growth companies. At least 65% of assets will be invested in three or more countries, with no more than 50% in any country other than the U.S. May have up to 15% of assets in illiquid securities and use futures and options for hedging purposes.
Year organized: 1989
Ticker symbol: FWWGX
Group fund code: 373
Discount broker availability: *Fidelity, *Schwab, *Siebert, White
Portfolio turnover (3 yrs): 72%, 54%, 87%
Dividends paid: Income - December; Capital gains - December
Management fee: 1.00% first $250M to $0.70% over $500M
Expense ratio: 1.55% (year ending 12/31/96)

FOUNTAINHEAD SPECIAL VALUE FUND ◆
1980 Post Oak Blvd., Suite 2400
Houston, TX 77056-3898
800-868-9535, 713-961-0462

Adviser: Jenswold, King Assocs., Inc.
Administrator: AmeriPrime Financial Services, Inc.
Portfolio manager: Roger E. King (1996)
Transfer agent: American Data Services, Inc.
Investment objective and policies: Long-term capital growth. Invests primarily in a diversified portfolio of equity securities of domestic companies with market capitalizations between $500M and $5B that are perceived to be undervalued. May, however, invest in ADRs or debt obligations without limit at the discretion of management.
Year organized: 1996
Minimum purchase: Initial: $5,000, Subsequent: $1,000; IRA: Initial: $2,000
Wire orders accepted: Yes
Discount broker availability: Fidelity, *White
Deadline for same day wire purchase: 4 P.M.
Qualified for sale in: AZ, CA, CO, DC, FL, GA, IN, LA, MI, NV, NJ, NM, NY, NC, OR, PA, TX, VA, WY

Telephone redemptions: Yes
Wire redemptions: Yes
Letter redemptions: Signature guarantee required
Dividends paid: Income - December; Capital gains - December
Portfolio turnover (1 yr): 131%
Shareholder services: IRA, SEP-IRA, automatic investment plan
Management fee: 1.43%
Administration fee: 0.10% first $50M to 0.05% over $100M ($30,000 minimum)
Expense ratio: 0.97% (10 months ending 10/31/97) (8.25% without waiver)
IRA fees: Annual $15, Closing $12

FRANKLIN MONEY FUND ◆
777 Mariners Island Blvd.
P.O. Box 7777
San Mateo, CA 94403-7777
800-342-5236
shareholder services 800-632-2301
TDD 800-851-0637

Shareholder service hours: Full service M-F 5:30 A.M.- 8 P.M., Sat 6:30 ;a.m- 2:30 P.M., PST; After hours service: prices, yields, balances, orders, last transaction
Adviser: Franklin Advisers, Inc.
Transfer agent: Franklin/Templeton Investor Services, Inc.
Investment objective and policies: High current income consistent with preservation of capital and liquidity. Invests in an underlying portfolio with identical objectives which holds money market obligations issued or guaranteed by the U.S. Treasury or its agencies and instrumentalities, short-term bank obligations, municipal securities, corporate obligations or commercial paper.
Year organized: 1975
Group fund code: 111
Minimum purchase: Initial: $1,000, Subsequent: $25; IRA: Initial: None, Subsequent: None; Automatic investment plan: Initial: $250
Wire orders accepted: Yes
Deadline for same day wire purchase: 12 NN
Qualified for sale in: All states
Telephone redemptions: Yes
Wire redemptions: Yes, $1,000 minimum
Letter redemptions: Signature guarantee required over $50,000
Check redemptions: $100 minimum
Telephone switching: With other Franklin and Templeton (load) funds, and Mutual Series funds, which are available no-load to shareholders of record prior to the merger of the two companies.
Number of switches permitted: 2 per quarter, at least two weeks apart; $5 fee to anyone trading at these limits if trade is accepted.
Deadline for same day switch: 12 NN
Dividends paid: Income - declared daily, paid monthly
Shareholder services: IRA, SEP-IRA, 401(k), 403(b), directed dividends, electronic funds transfer, systematic withdrawal plan min. bal. req. $5,000
Management fee: 0.15%
Administration fee: 0.30%
Expense ratio: 0.75% (year ending 6/30/97)
IRA fees: Annual $10

FRANKLIN MUTUAL SERIES Z SHARES ◆
(See Mutual Series Funds)

FREMONT MUTUAL FUNDS
(Data common to all Fremont funds are shown below. See subsequent listings for data specific to individual funds.)

333 Market Street, Suite 2600
San Francisco, CA 94119
800-548-4539, 888-502-3253
415-284-8900
fax 415-284-8955

Shareholder service hours: Full service: M-F 5 A.M.-5 P.M. PST; After hours service: prices, yields, account balances, orders, last transaction, prospectuses, total returns, fund objectives

Adviser: Fremont Investment Advisors, Inc.
Transfer agent: National Financial Data Services
Minimum purchase: Initial: $2,000, Subsequent: $200; IRA/Keogh: Initial: $1,000, Subsequent: None; Automatic investment plan: Initial: None, Subsequent: $50
Wire orders accepted: Yes
Deadline for same day wire purchase: 4 P.M.
Qualified for sale in: All states (except CA Intermediate Tax-Free Fund)
Telephone redemptions: Yes
Wire redemptions: Yes, $10 fee
Letter redemptions: Signature guarantee required over $25,000
Telephone switching: With other Fremont funds
Number of switches permitted: Unlimited
Shareholder services: IRA, SEP-IRA, Keogh, 401(k), 403(b), corporate retirement plans, directed dividends, electronic funds transfer, systematic withdrawal plan min. bal. req. $1,500
IRA/Keogh fees: None

FREMONT BOND FUND ◆
(See first Fremont listing for data common to all funds)

Sub-adviser: Pacific Investment Management Co. (PIMCO)
Portfolio manager: William H. Gross (1994)
Investment objective and policies: Maximum total return consistent with capital preservation and prudent investment management. Invests primarily in high-quality, intermediate-term bonds issued by U.S. and foreign governments, supranational organizations such as the World Bank, corporations and mortgage-related and other asset-backed securities. At least 60% of total assets are in securities of U.S. issuers, and no more than 25% of assets may be from any other country. The average maturity of these securities varies between five and fifteen years. May use a wide variety of derivative instruments for hedging purposes.
Year organized: 1993 (name changed from Income Fund in 1994)
Ticker symbol: FBDFX
Discount broker availability: Fidelity, Schwab, White
Check redemption: $250 minimum
Dividends paid: Income - declared daily, paid monthly; Capital gains - December
Portfolio turnover (3 yrs): 191%, 154%, 21%
Management fee: 0.55%
Expense ratio: 0.61% (year ending 10/31/97) (0.76% without waiver)

FREMONT CALIFORNIA INTERMEDIATE TAX-FREE FUND ◆
(See first Fremont listing for data common to all funds)

Portfolio manager: William M. Feeney (1990)
Investment objective and policies: High current income exempt from federal and California state income taxes, consistent with prudent investment management. Invests in investment grade tax-exempt securities of the State of California and its municipalities. The portfolio maintains a dollar-weighted average maturity of three to ten years. Fund may also invest up to 5% of assets in mutual funds which invest in securities whose income is exempt from such taxes, and may, for defensive purposes, invest in U.S. Treasury securities without limit. Such securities are taxable by the State of California. May hedge up to 25% of total assets. Fund is non-diversified.
Year organized: 1990
Ticker symbol: FCATX
Discount broker availability: Schwab, White
Qualified for sale in: AZ, CA, CO, NV, NM, OR, TX, UT, WA
Check redemption: $250 minimum
Dividends paid: Income - declared daily, paid monthly; Capital gains - December
Portfolio turnover (3 yrs): 6%, 6%, 18%
Management fee: 0.55% first $25M to 0.35% over $150M
Expense ratio: 0.49% (year ending 10/31/97) (0.69% without waiver)

FREMONT EMERGING MARKETS FUND ◆
(See first Fremont listing for data common to all funds)

Sub-adviser: Nicholas/Applegate Capital Management (Hong Kong) LLC
Lead portfolio manager: Henry Thornton (1996)
Investment objective and policies: Long-term capital appreciation. A non-diversified fund which invests in equity securities of issuers located in or deriving their principal revenues from developing or emerging markets. Will normally invest at least 65% of assets in at least three different countries, but will not necessarily seek to diversify holdings based on variations in economic development or geography. A high concentration of the asset allocation will be in Asian markets. Fund may also invest without limit in debt securities of both governmental and corporate issuers in emerging markets which are rated Baa or higher by Moody's, or BBB or higher by S&P. Fund may use derivative instruments in search of appreciation or for hedging purposes.
Year organized: 1996
Discount broker availability: *Fidelity, *Schwab, *White
Dividends paid: Income - October; Capital gains - December
Portfolio turnover (1 yr): 208%
Management fee: 1.00
12b-1 distribution fee: 0.25% (not currently imposed)
Expense ratio: 0.26% (year ending 10/31/97) (2.63% without waiver)

FREMONT GLOBAL FUND ◆
(See first Fremont listing for data common to all funds)

Portfolio managers: Team managed
Investment objective and policies: Maximum total return: income and capital gains, with reduced risk. Fund allocates assets among seven classes - U.S. stocks, U.S. dollar denominated debt securities, foreign stocks, foreign bonds, real estate securities, precious metals, and cash equivalents - and adjusts allocation to changing market conditions. May use forward currency contracts, currency futures contracts, put and call options on currencies, and sell futures and options contracts on commodities. Fund may hedge.
Year organized: 1988 (name changed From Fremont Multi Asset Fund in 1993)
Ticker symbol: FMAFX
Discount broker availability: *Fidelity, *Schwab, *White
Dividends paid: Income - March, June, September, December; Capital gains December
Portfolio turnover (3 yrs): 48%, 71%, 83%
Management fee: 0.75%
Expense ratio: 0.85% (year ending 10/31/97)

FREMONT GROWTH FUND ◆
(See first Fremont listing for data common to all funds)

Portfolio managers: W. Kent Copa (1995), Peter F. Landini (1992), John B. Kosecoff (1996)
Investment objective and policies: Long-term capital growth; income incidental. Invests at least 65% of assets in U.S. common stocks. May also invest in securities convertible into common and preferred stocks. May invest up to 35% of assets in direct equity securities, ADRs and EDRs of foreign issuers. May use futures contracts, options on index futures and stock indices to hedge up to 25% of total assets, and may engage in foreign currency hedging.
Year organized: 1992 (name changed from Fremont Equity Fund in 1993)
Ticker symbol: FEQFX
Discount broker availability: *Fidelity, *Schwab, *White
Dividends paid: Income - October; Capital gains - December
Portfolio turnover (3 yrs): 48%, 129%, 108%
Management fee: 0.65%
Expense ratio: 0.85% (year ending 10/31/97)

FREMONT INTERNATIONAL GROWTH FUND ◆
(See first Fremont listing for data common to all funds)

Portfolio managers: Andrew L. Pang (1995), Robert J. Haddick (1995), Peter F. Landini (1995)
Investment objective and policies: Long-term capital growth. Invests primarily in equity securities of foreign companies believed undervalued. Will be invested in a minimum of three countries excluding the U.S. Up to 50% of total assets may be invested in the securities of small- to medium-sized companies ($25M-$2B) in developed and emerging markets. May invest more than 25% in securities issued by companies in Japan, the United Kingdom and/or Germany, and use ADRs and EDRs. May have up to 15% of assets in illiquid securities, and use forward currency futures and options for hedging purposes.
Year organized: 1994
Ticker symbol: FIGFX
Discount broker availability: *Fidelity, *Schwab, *White
Dividends paid: Income - September; Capital gains - December
Portfolio turnover (3 yrs): 95%, 74%, 32%
Management fee: 1.50%
Expense ratio: 1.50% (year ending 10/31/97)

FREMONT INTERNATIONAL SMALL CAP FUND ◆
(See first Fremont listing for data common to all funds)

Sub-adviser: Acadian Asset Management, Inc.
Portfolio manager: Dr. Gary L. Bergstrom (1994)
Investment objective and policies: Long-term capital appreciation. Invests primarily in equities of foreign companies in both developed and emerging markets, with market capitalizations under $1B. May invest more than 25% of assets in securities of companies in Japan, the United Kingdom and/or Germany, and up to 35% in firms from emerging markets. May use ADRs and EDRs, and have up to 15% of assets in illiquid securities. May use forward currency futures and options for hedging purposes.
Year organized: 1994
Ticker symbol: FRISX
Discount broker availability: *Fidelity, *Schwab, *White
Dividends paid: Income - October; Capital gains - December
Portfolio turnover (3 yrs): 56%, 74%, 96%
Management fee: 2.50% first $30M to 1.50% over $70M
Expense ratio: 1.50% (year ending 10/31/97)

FREMONT MONEY MARKET FUND ◆
(See first Fremont listing for data common to all funds)

Portfolio manager: Norman Gee (1988)
Investment objective and policies: Maximum current income consistent with preservation of capital and liquidity. Invests in money market instruments including Eurodollar certificates of deposit, and U.S. dollar denominated money market instruments of foreign financial institutions, corporations and governments.
Year organized: 1988
Ticker symbol: FRMXX
Check redemption: $250 minimum
Dividends paid: Income - declared daily, paid monthly
Management fee: 0.30% first $50M, 0.20% over $50M
Expense ratio: 0.30% (year ending 10/31/97) (0.45% without waiver)

FREMONT REAL ESTATE SECURITIES FUND
(See first Fremont listing for data common to all funds)

Sub-adviser: Kensington Investment Group, Inc.
Portfolio managers: John P. Kramer (1997), Paul Gray (1997)
Investment objective and policies: Total return: a combination of income and long-term capital appreci-

ation. Invests at least 65% of assets in equity securities of companies principally engaged in the real estate industry. A substantial portion of assets are invested in REITs, including equity, mortgage and hybrid types. May use options and futures for hedging purposes. Fund is non-diversified.
Year organized: 1997
Special sales restrictions: Fund will close to new investors whenever the asset value reaches 0.3% of the total market capitalization of the NAREIT All REITS Index, recalculated quarterly.
Discount broker availability: *White
Dividends paid: Income - October; Capital gains - December
Management fee: 1.00%
12b-1 distribution fee: 0.25%

FREMONT SELECT FUND
(See first Fremont listing for data common to all funds)

Portfolio managers: John B. Kosecoff (1997), Debra L. McNeill (1997), Peter F. Landini (1997)
Investment objective and policies: Long-term capital appreciation. Invests primarily in equity securities of established U.S.-based companies with mid-cap market capitalizations ranging from $1B to $9B that are perceived to offer strong growth characteristics at a relatively low price. Generally at least 80% of assets are concentrated in the common stocks of not more than 30 companies. May invest up to 25% of assets in a single industry sector, up to 15% in a single issuer, and up to 10% in foreign securities. May use options and futures. Fund is non-diversified.
Year organized: 1997
Discount broker availability: *White
Dividends paid: Income - October; Capital gains - December
Management fee: 1.00%
12b-1 distribution fee: 0.25%

FREMONT U.S. MICRO-CAP FUND ◆
(See first Fremont listing for data common to all funds)

Sub-adviser: Kern Capital Management, LLC
Lead portfolio manager: Robert E. Kern (1994)
Investment objective and policies: Long-term capital appreciation. Invests primarily in securities of emerging growth companies in the bottom 10% of the Wilshire 5000 Index, which currently have market capitalizations under $425M. Up to 25% of assets may be in securities, ADRs and EDRs of small foreign companies. May use futures and options to hedge up to 25% of total assets.
Year organized: 1994
Ticker symbol: FUSMX
Discount broker availability: *Fidelity, *Schwab, *White
Dividends paid: Income - September; Capital gains - December
Portfolio turnover (3 yrs): 125%, 81%, 144%
Management fee: 2.50% first $30M to 1.50% over $100M
Expense ratio: 1.88% (year ending 10/31/97) (1.90% without waiver)

FREMONT U.S. SMALL CAP FUND ◆
(See first Fremont listing for data common to all funds)

Sub-adviser: Kern Capital Management, LLC
Lead portfolio manager: David G. Kern (1997)
Investment objective and policies: Long-term capital appreciation. Invests primarily in common stocks of small, rapidly growing companies whose market capitalizations are in the lowest 20% of all U.S. companies. Currently this group has capitalizations of less than $2.6B. Up to 25% of assets may be in securities, ADRs and EDRs of small foreign companies, and up to 15% may be in illiquid securities. May use futures and options for hedging purposes.
Year organized: 1997
Discount broker availability: *Schwab, *White
Dividends paid: Income - October; Capital gains - December
Management fee: 1.00%

FTI FUNDS ◆
(Data common to all FTI funds are shown below. See subsequent listings for data specific to individual funds.)

Two World Trade Center
New York, NY 10048-0772
212-524-7300, 212-466-4100
Texas 800-356-2805

Adviser: Fiduciary International, Inc.
Transfer agent and administrator: Federated Services Co.
Minimum purchase: Initial: $10,000, Subsequent: None
Wire orders accepted: Yes
Deadline for same day wire purchase: 3 P.M.
Qualified for sale in: All states
Telephone redemptions: Yes
Wire redemptions: Yes, fee for redemptions of less than $5,000, or for redemptions exceeding one per month
Letter redemptions: Signature guarantee not required
Telephone switching: With other FTI funds
Number of switches permitted: Unlimited
Shareholder services fee: Maximum of 0.25% (not currently imposed)
Administration fee: 0.15% first $250M to 0.075% over $750M
12b-1 distribution fee: Maximum of 0.75% (not currently imposed)

FTI GLOBAL BOND FUND ◆
(See first FTI listing for data common to all funds)

Portfolio managers: Stuart Hochberger (1995), Anthony Gould (1995)
Investment objective and policies: Total return; capital appreciation and income. Invests primarily in a diversified portfolio of high quality government and corporate fixed-income instruments from at least three countries including the U.S. The average portfolio duration is three to ten years. May invest up to 10% of assets in instruments issued in emerging market countries, up to 35% of assets in asset- and mortgage-backed securities, up to 10% of assets in other investment companies, and up to 15% in illiquid securities. May use options, futures and foreign currency exchange contracts for hedging purposes.
Year organized: 1995
Discount broker availability: White
Dividends paid: Income - semi-annually; Capital gains - annually
Portfolio turnover (1 yr): 287%
Management fee: 0.70%
Expense ratio: 0.95% (11 months ending 11/30/96) (27.89% without waiver)

FTI INTERNATIONAL BOND FUND ◆
(See first FTI listing for data common to all funds)

Portfolio managers: Stuart Hochberger (1995), Anthony Gould (1995)
Investment objective and policies: Total return; capital appreciation and income. Invests primarily in a diversified portfolio of high quality government and corporate fixed-income instruments from at least three countries outside the U.S., primarily those of OECD members, although up to 10% of assets may be in issues of emerging countries. May invest up to 35% of assets in asset- and mortgage-backed securities, up to 10% of assets in other investment companies, and up to 15% in illiquid securities. May use options, futures and foreign currency exchange contracts for hedging purposes.
Year organized: 1995
Discount broker availability: White
Dividends paid: Income - semi-annually; Capital gains - annually
Portfolio turnover (1 yr): 190%
Management fee: 0.70%
Expense ratio: 1.20% (11 months ending 11/30/96) (5.83% without waiver)

FTI INTERNATIONAL EQUITY FUND ◆
(See first FTI listing for data common to all funds)

Portfolio managers: Sheila Coco (1995), William Yun (1995), Steven Miller (1995)
Investment objective and policies: Principal growth. Invests at least 65% of assets in a broadly diversified portfolio of equity and debt issues from at least three countries outside of the U.S. At least 65% of assets are in equity securities, and up to 35% are in debt issues. Invests primarily in industrialized countries represented in the MSCI EAFE Index, but may invest up to 20% of assets in common stocks of companies located in emerging market countries. May use forward currency exchange contracts and options and futures for hedging purposes.
Year organized: 1995
Ticker symbol: FTIEX
Discount broker availability: White
Dividends paid: Income - semi-annually; Capital gains - annually
Portfolio turnover (1 yr): 29%
Management fee: 1.00%
Expense ratio: 1.68% (11 months ending 11/30/96) (4.73% without waiver)

FTI SMALL CAPITALIZATION EQUITY FUND ◆
(See first FTI listing for data common to all funds)

Portfolio managers: Yvette Bockstein (1995), Helen Degener (1995), Grant Babyak (1995)
Investment objective and policies: Principal growth. Invests primarily in the common stock of companies with market capitalizations below $1.5B that are perceived to be undervalued or to have a growth rate faster than the U.S. economy in general. May also invest in convertible securities, preferred stocks and corporate bonds without limit. May invest up to 20% of assets in ADRs, up to 10% in foreign securities, and up to 15% in illiquid securities. Fund may use a variety of derivative instruments to implement its investment strategy and for hedging purposes.
Year organized: 1995
Ticker symbol: FTSCX
Discount broker availability: White
Dividends paid: Income - semi-annually; Capital gains - annually
Portfolio turnover (1 yr): 94%
Management fee: 1.00%
Expense ratio: 1.50% (year ending 11/30/97) (includes waiver)

FUNDAMENTAL FUNDS
(Data common to all Fundamental funds are shown below. See subsequent listings for data specific to individual funds.)

90 Washington Street, 19th Floor
New York, NY 10006
800-225-6864, 800-322-6864
212-635-3000
fax 212-635-5009

Adviser: Fundamental Portfolio Advisors, Inc.
Portfolio manager: Team managed
Transfer agent: Fundamental Shareholder Services, Inc.
Minimum purchase: Initial: $1,000, Subsequent: $100 (except U.S. Government Strategic Income); Automatic investment plan: Initial: $100, Subsequent: $50
Wire orders accepted: Yes
Deadline for same day wire purchase: 4 P.M.
Telephone redemptions: Yes
Wire redemptions: Yes, $5,000 minimum
Letter redemptions: Yes, Signature guarantee required over $50,000
Check redemptions: $100 minimum
Telephone switching: With other Fundamental funds, $1,000 minimum
Number of switches permitted: Unlimited
12b-1 distribution fee: 0.50%

FUNDAMENTAL CALIFORNIA MUNI FUND
(See first Fundamental listing for data common to all funds)

Investment objective and policies: High current income exempt from federal and California state income taxes, consistent with capital preservation. Invests at least 80% of assets in California municipal bonds of the four highest grades or notes in the three highest categories. Fund may leverage up to 20% of assets.
Year organized: 1984
Ticker symbol: CAMFX
Discount broker availability: *White
Qualified for sale in: CA, DC, HI, NJ, WY
Dividends paid: Income - declared daily, paid monthly; Capital gains - December
Management fee: 0.50% first $100M to 0.40% over $500M
Expense ratio: 3.20% (year ending 12/31/96)

FUNDAMENTAL FIXED-INCOME FUND: HIGH-YIELD MUNICIPAL BOND SERIES
(See first Fundamental listing for data common to all funds)

Investment objective and policies: High current income exempt from federal income tax. Invests at least 80% of assets in debt securities issued by or on behalf of states, territories, and possessions of the U.S. and D.C. and their political subdivisions. At least 65% of assets are invested in lower quality, high-yielding municipal bonds rated BB or lower by S&P or Ba or lower by Moody's or unrated instruments. Fund buys only issues with maturities of 20 years or more. Fund may not purchase obligations rated lower than C, or those not currently paying income. May use futures and options and leverage up to 1/3 of assets. Fund is non-diversified.
Year organized: 1987
Discount broker availability: *White
Qualified for sale in: CA, CO, CT, DC, FL, GA, HI, IL, IN, NJ, NY, NC, PA, VA, WY
Dividends paid: Income - declared daily, paid monthly; Capital gains - annually
Portfolio turnover (3 yrs): 139%, 44%, 75%
Management fee: 0.80% first $100M, to 0.70% over $500M
Expense ratio: 2.49% (year ending 12/31/96) (4.59% without waiver)

FUNDAMENTAL FIXED-INCOME FUND: TAX-FREE MONEY MARKET SERIES
(See first Fundamental listing for data common to all funds)

Investment objective and policies: High current income exempt from federal income tax, consistent with preservation of capital and liquidity. Invests at least 80% of assets in municipal money market securities rated Aa or better.
Year organized: 1987
Ticker symbol: FUNXX
Qualified for sale in: CA, CO, CT, DC, FL, GA, HI, IL, IN, NJ, NY, NC, PA, VA, WY
Dividends paid: income - declared daily, paid monthly
Management fee: 0.50% of first $100M to 0.40% over $500M

FUNDAMENTAL FIXED-INCOME FUND: U.S. GOVERNMENT STRATEGIC INCOME SERIES
(See first Fundamental listing for data common to all funds)

Investment objective and policies: High current income with minimum risk of principal and stability of NAV. Invests primarily in obligations issued or guaranteed by the U.S. Government, its agencies or instrumentalities. Portfolio generally maintains a dollar-weighted average maturity of three years or less. Fund may use futures and options and leverage up to 1/3 of assets.

Year organized: 1992
Ticker symbol: FUSIX
Minimum purchase: Initial: $2,500, Subsequent: $100; IRA: Initial: $2,000
Discount broker availability: *White
Qualified for sale in: All states except AL, AK, AR, ID, KS, KY, LA, MN, MO, MT, NE, NH, ND, OK, PR, RI, SC, SD, TN, TX, UT, WV
Dividends paid: Income - declared daily, paid monthly; Capital gains - December
Management fee: 0.75% first $500M, to 0.70% over $1B

FUNDAMENTAL NEW YORK MUNI FUND
(See first Fundamental listing for data common to all funds)

Investment objective and policies: High current income exempt from federal, NY state and NY city income taxes, consistent with capital preservation. Invests primarily in New York municipal bonds of the 4 highest grades or notes in the three highest categories. May invest up to 35% in obligations rated lower than Baa and as low as Caa, including zero coupon and pay-in-kind securities. May leverage, use financial futures and options thereon and use options on debt securities.
Year organized: 1981 (formerly New York Muni)
Ticker symbol: NYMFX
Discount broker availability: *White
Qualified for sale in: CA, CT, DC, FL, HI, NJ, NY, PA, WY
Dividends paid: Income - declared daily, paid monthly; Capital gains - December
Management fee: 0.50% first $100M to 0.40% over $500M

FUNDMANAGER FUNDS
(Effective 2/17/98, funds became 4.5% load funds. Shareholders prior to this data may continue to buy at NAV.)

GABELLI FUNDS
(Data common to all Gabelli funds are shown below. See subsequent listing for data specific to individual funds.)

One Corporate Center
Rye, NY 10580-1434
800-422-3554, 914-921-5100
fax 914-921-5118
Internet: http://www.gabelli.com
e-mail: info@gabelli.com

Shareholder service hours: Full service: M-F 9 A.M.-8 P.M. EST; After hours service: prices, yields, news and views, messages, index close, prospectuses, total returns
Adviser: Gabelli Funds, Inc.
Transfer agent: State Street Bank & Trust Co.
Minimum purchase: Initial: $1,000, Subsequent: None; Automatic investment plan: Initial: None, Subsequent: $100 (exceptions noted)
Wire orders accepted: Yes
Deadline for same day wire purchase: 3 P.M.
Qualified for sale in: All states (except ABC fund)
Telephone redemptions: Yes ($5 fee for MM redemptions under $5,000)
Wire redemptions: Yes, $1,000 minimum ($5 fee for MM redemptions under $5,000)
Letter redemptions: Signature guarantee required
Telephone switching: With other Gabelli funds, some of which have loads, and Westwood funds
Number of switches permitted: Unlimited
Dividends paid: Income - December; Capital gains - December (exception noted)
Shareholder services: IRA, electronic funds transfer (purchase only), systematic withdrawal plan min. bal. req. $10,000
Management fee: 1.00% (except U.S. Treasury Money Market Fund)
IRA fees: Annual $10 per social security number (waived for balances over $25,00)

THE GABELLI ABC FUND
(See first Gabelli listing for data common to all funds)

Portfolio manager: Mario J. Gabelli (1993)
Investment objective and policies: Total returns attractive to investors in various market conditions without excessive risk of capital loss. Invests in a mix of equity and debt securities of domestic and foreign issuers chosen for their attractive opportunities for appreciation or investment income. May invest without limit in companies for which a tender offer or exchange offer has been made or announced, and in securities of companies for which a merger, consolidation, liquidation or similar proposal has been announced. May invest up to 25% of assets in junk bonds and 15% in illiquid securities. Fund is non-diversified.
Year organized: 1993
Ticker symbol: GABCX
Special sales restrictions: Fund closed to new shareholders on 1/3/94, Reopened 11/21/94 to 1/3/95, closed again, reopened for one day, 1/2/96 with a new guarantee, then closed. Reopened with no guarantee and no sales load 1/2/97.
Discount broker availability: *Fidelity, *White
Qualified for sale in: All states
Portfolio turnover (3 yrs): 343%, 508%, 490%
12b-1 distribution fee: 0.25%
Expense ratio: 2.09% (year ending 12/31/96)

THE GABELLI ASSET FUND
(See first Gabelli listing for data common to all funds)

Portfolio manager: Mario J. Gabelli (1986)
Investment objective and policies: Long-term capital growth; current income secondary. Invests in equity securities believed to have good growth potential or to be undervalued. May invest up to 35% of assets in companies undergoing corporate reorganizations, 10% in closed-end mutual funds, and 25% in securities of foreign issuers. May invest up to 10% of assets in small companies with less than a three year history, including predecessors.
Year organized: 1986
Ticker symbol: GABAX
Discount broker availability: *Fidelity, *Schwab, Siebert, *White
Portfolio turnover (3 yrs): 22%, 15%, 26%
12b-1 distribution fee: Maximum of 0.25%
Expense ratio: 1.38% (year ending 12/31/97)

GABELLI EQUITY INCOME FUND
(See first Gabelli listing for data common to all funds)

Portfolio manager: Mario J. Gabelli (1992)
Investment objective and policies: High total return: capital appreciation and current income; emphasis on current income. Invests primarily in income producing securities which have; a better yield than the average of the S&P 500 Stock Index, as well as perceived capital gains potential. Normally invest at least 65% of assets in equity securities of this type, but may invest in any type of debt security without limit except junk bonds, which are limited to 35% of assets. May invest up to 35% of assets in foreign securities, and up to 65% of assets in announced corporate reorganizations. May invest up to 15% of assets in illiquid securities, and may use a variety of derivative instruments in an effort to enhance return and for hedging purposes.
Year organized: 1992
Ticker symbol: GABEX
Discount broker availability: *Fidelity, *Schwab, *Siebert, *White
Dividends paid: Income - quarterly; Capital gains - December
Portfolio turnover (3 yrs): 43%, 20%, 30%
12b-1 distribution fee: 0.25%
Expense ratio: 1.78% (year ending 9/30/97)

THE GABELLI GLOBAL CONVERTIBLE SECURITIES FUND
(See first Gabelli listing for data common to all funds)

Portfolio manager: A. Hartswell Woodson III (1994)
Investment objective and policies: Maximum total return: capital growth and current income. Invests at least 65% of assets in securities convertible into com-

mon stock or other equity securities of domestic and foreign companies. May invest without limit in junk bonds, 15% in illiquid securities and use futures and options and sell short.
Year organized: 1994
Ticker symbol: GAGCX
Discount broker availability: *Fidelity, *Schwab, *Siebert, *White
Portfolio turnover (3 yrs): 126%, 152%, 329%
12b-1 distribution fee: Maximum of 0.25%
Expense ratio: 2.35% (year ending 12/31/96)

THE GABELLI GLOBAL INTERACTIVE COUCH POTATO FUND
(See first Gabelli listing for data common to all funds)

Portfolio manager: Marc J. Gabelli (1996)
Investment objective and policies: Long-term capital appreciation; current income secondary. Invests at least 65% of assets in securities of companies involved with communications, creativity and copyright throughout the world. Such companies, which are participating in emerging technological advances in interactive services and products accessible through telephones, TVs, radios and personal computers, are typically in the communications, entertainment, media and publishing industries. May invest up to 25% of assets in junk bonds and 15% in illiquid securities, use futures and options, and sell short.
Year organized: 1994
Ticker symbol: GICPX
Discount broker availability: *Fidelity, *Schwab, *Siebert, *White
Portfolio turnover (3 yrs): 47%, 33%, 14%
12b-1 distribution fee: Maximum of 0.25%
Expense ratio: 2.06% (year ending 12/31/96)

THE GABELLI GLOBAL TELECOMMUNICATIONS FUND
(See first Gabelli listing for data common to all funds)

Portfolio managers: Mario J. Gabelli (1993), Marc J. Gabelli (1993), Ivan Arteaga (1993)
Investment objective and policies: Long-term capital appreciation; current income secondary. Invests at least 65% of assets in securities of companies involved with telecommunications throughout the world. May invest up to 25% of assets in junk bonds, 15% in illiquid securities and use futures and options and sell short.
Year organized: 1993
Ticker symbol: GABTX
Discount broker availability: *Fidelity, *Schwab, *Siebert, *White
Portfolio turnover (3 yrs): 7%, 24%, 14%
12b-1 distribution fee: Maximum of 0.25%
Expense ratio: 1.72% (year ending 12/31/96)

THE GABELLI GOLD FUND
(See first Gabelli listing for data common to all funds)

Portfolio manager: Caesar M.P. Bryan (1994)
Investment objective and policies: Long-term capital appreciation; current income incidental. Invests at least 65% of assets in equity securities of foreign and domestic issuers principally engaged in the exploration, mining, fabrication, processing, distribution or trading of gold or other precious metals. May have up to 15% of assets in illiquid securities. May use futures and options, forward foreign currency exchange transactions, currency swaps and sell short for hedging purposes.
Year organized: 1994
Ticker symbol: GOLDX
Special sales restrictions: Will increase its initial purchase minimum to $10,000 when it has either 10,000 shareholders or has over $100M in assets.
Discount broker availability: *Fidelity, *Schwab, *Siebert, *White
Portfolio turnover (2 yrs): 54%, 38%
12b-1 distribution fee: Maximum of 0.25%
Expense ratio: 2.17% (year ending 12/31/96)

THE GABELLI GROWTH FUND
(See first Gabelli listing for data common to all funds)

Portfolio manager: Howard F. Ward (1995)
Investment objective and policies: Long-term capital appreciation; current income secondary. Invests in a diversified portfolio of common stocks and securities convertible into common stocks with favorable earnings growth prospects that are perceived to be undervalued at prevailing market multiples. May also invest up to 35% of assets in securities for which a tender or exchange offer has been made or announced, and in securities of companies for which some type of major reorganization has been announced. Up to 25% of assets may be in securities of foreign issuers.
Year organized: 1987
Ticker symbol: GABGX
Discount broker availability: *Fidelity, *Schwab, *Siebert, *White
Portfolio turnover (3 yrs): 88%, 140%, 40%
12b-1 distribution fee: Maximum of 0.25%
Expense ratio: 1.43% (year ending 12/31/96)

THE GABELLI INTERNATIONAL GROWTH FUND
(See first Gabelli listing for data common to all funds)

Portfolio manager: Caesar M.P. Bryan (1995)
Investment objective and policies: Long-term capital appreciation: current income incidental. Invests primarily in equity securities of non-U.S. issuers. Will ordinarily invest in companies located in at least three countries outside of the U.S. Country allocation may be based on political stability, economic outlook or attempts to reduce volatility. May use foreign currency exchange transactions, currency swaps, futures contracts, options on futures, repurchase agreements, and covered put and call options for purposes of hedging.
Year organized: 1995
Ticker symbol: GIGRX
Special sales restrictions: Will increase its initial purchase minimum to $10,000 when it has either 10,000 shareholders or has over $100M in assets.
Discount broker availability: *Fidelity, *Schwab, *Siebert, *White
Portfolio turnover (1 yr): 30%
12b-1 distribution fee: Maximum of 0.25%
Expense ratio: 2.72% (year ending 12/31/96) (includes waiver)

THE GABELLI SMALL CAP GROWTH FUND
(See first Gabelli listing for data common to all funds)

Portfolio manager: Mario J. Gabelli (1992)
Investment objective and policies: Capital appreciation. Invests primarily in equity securities of smaller companies, with market capitalizations under $500M at the time of investment, believed to have prospects for rapid growth in earnings and/or revenues and above average capital appreciation. May, however, invest in any type of fixed-income debt security without limit. May invest up to 35% of assets in securities of non-U.S. issuers, and up to 65% of assets in announced corporate reorganizations. May invest up to 10% of assets in unseasoned issues, up to 10% in illiquid securities, and may use a variety of derivative instruments in an effort to enhance return and for hedging purposes.
Year organized: 1992
Ticker symbol: GABSX
Discount broker availability: *Fidelity, *Schwab, *Siebert, *White
Portfolio turnover (3 yrs): 14%, 11%, 17%
12b-1 distribution fee: 0.25%
Expense ratio: 1.62% (year ending 9/30/97)

THE GABELLI U.S. TREASURY MONEY MARKET FUND ◆
(See first Gabelli listing for data common to all funds)

Portfolio manager: Judith A. Raneri (1997)
Investment objective and policies: High current income consistent with preservation of principal and liquidity. Substantially all dividends are exempt from state and local, but not federal, taxes. Invests at least 65% (and often exclusively) in U.S. Treasury money market obligations and repurchase agreements collateralized by U.S. Treasury obligations.
Year organized: 1992
Ticker symbol: GABXX
Minimum purchase: Initial: $10,000 ($3,000 for shareholders of other Gabelli funds), Subsequent: None; IRA: Initial: $1,000; No automatic investment accepted.
Check redemptions: $500 minimum
Dividends paid: Income - declared daily, paid monthly
Management fee: 0.30%
Account closeout fee: $5
Expense ratio: 0.30% (year ending 9/30/97) (0.46% without waiver)

THE GABELLI WESTWOOD FUNDS
(See listing under Westwood)

GALAXY II FUNDS ◆
(Data common to all Galaxy II funds are listed below. See subsequent listings for data specific to individual funds.)

4400 Computer Drive
P.O. Box 5108
Westboro, MA 01581-5108
800-628-0414, 800-628-0413
Internet: http://www.galaxyfunds.com

Shareholder service hours: Full service: M-F 9 A.M.-5 P.M. EST; After hours service: orders, prospectuses, total returns
Adviser: Fleet Investment Advisors, Inc.
Transfer agent: First Data Investor Services Group, Inc.
Sales restrictions: Effective 12/2/95 all Galaxy bond and equity funds imposed a 3.75% load except index funds and money markets, which remain no-load.
Minimum purchase: Initial: $2,500, Subsequent $100; IRA/Keogh: Initial: $500; Automatic investment plan: Initial: $50, Subsequent: $50
Wire orders accepted: Yes
Deadline for same day wire purchase: 4 P.M. (11 A.M. for money market)
Qualified for sale in: All states
Telephone redemptions: Yes
Wire redemptions: Yes, $1,000 minimum, $5 fee
Letter redemptions: Signature guarantee required over $10,000 ($50,000 for MM)
Telephone switching: With other Galaxy II funds, $100 minimum
Number of switches permitted: 3 per year
Shareholder services: IRA, SEP-IRA, Keogh, 401(k), 403(b), electronic funds transfer, systematic withdrawal plan min. bal. req. $10,000
Administration fee: 0.30% (0.35% for Municipal Bond Fund)
IRA/Keogh fees: Annual $15, Closing $10

GALAXY II: LARGE COMPANY INDEX FUND ◆
(See first Galaxy II listing for data common to all funds)

Portfolio manager: Murphy van der Velde (1996)
Investment objective and policies: Investment results that match the price and yield performance of the stocks contained in the S&P 500 Composite Stock Price Index. Invests at least 80% of assets in a proportional representative mix of the S&P 500 stocks to achieve a total return approximately equal to the performance of the total Index.
Year organized: 1990 (name changed from IBM Large Company Index Fund in 1994)
Ticker symbol: ILCIX
Discount broker availability: Fidelity, Siebert, White
Dividends paid: Income - annually; Capital gains - annually
Portfolio turnover (3 yrs): 11%, 5%, 7%
Management fee: 0.10%
Expense ratio: 0.40% (year ending 3/31/97)

GALAXY: MONEY MARKET FUND ◆

(See first Galaxy II listing for data common to all funds)

Portfolio managers: Karen Arneil (1996), Thomas DeMarco (1996)
Investment objective and policies: High current income consistent with liquidity and stability of principal. Invests in high quality money market instruments.
Year organized: 1986
Special sales restrictions: The Galaxy Money Market offers two classes of shares, Retail and Trust. Only retail are offered direct to individuals; information here reflects costs and services for retail shares only.
Check redemptions: $250 minimum
Dividends paid: Income - declared daily, paid monthly
Management fee: 0.40%
12b-1 distribution fee: Maximum of 0.25% (not currently imposed)
Expense ratio: 0.69% (year ending 10/31/97) (0.73% without waiver)

GALAXY II: SMALL COMPANY INDEX FUND ◆

(See first Galaxy II listing for data common to all funds)

Portfolio manager: Murphy van der Velde (1996)
Investment objective and policies: Investment results that match the price and yield performance of the stocks with smaller capitalizations as represented by the Russell Special Small Company Index. Invests at least 80% of assets in a proportional representative mix of the Russell Special Small Company Index stocks to achieve a total return approximately equal to the performance of the total Index.
Year organized: 1990 (name changed from IBM Small Company Index Fund in 1994)
Ticker symbol: ISCIX
Discount broker availability: Fidelity, Siebert, White
Dividends paid: Income - annually; Capital gains - annually
Portfolio turnover (3 yrs): 8%, 14%, 10%
Management fee: 0.10%
Expense ratio: 0.40% (year ending 3/31/97)

GALAXY II: U.S. TREASURY INDEX FUND ◆

(See first Galaxy II listing for data common to all funds)

Portfolio manager: David Lindsay (1994)
Investment objective and policies: Investment results that match the price and yield performance of U.S. Treasury notes and bonds as represented by the U.S. Treasury component (U.S. Treasury Index) of the Salomon Brothers Broad Investment-Grade Bond Index. Invests at least 80% of assets in a proportional representative mix of U.S. Treasury obligations to achieve a total return approximately equal to the performance of the U.S. Treasury Index.
Year organized: 1991 (name changed from IBM U.S. Treasury Index Fund in 1994)
Ticker symbol: IMTIX
Discount broker availability: Fidelity, Siebert, White
Dividends paid: Income - declared daily, paid monthly; Capital gains - annually
Portfolio turnover (3 yrs): 39%, 35%, 50%
Management fee: 0.10%
Expense ratio: 0.40% (year ending 3/31/97)

GALAXY II: UTILITY INDEX FUND ◆

(See first Galaxy II listing for data common to all funds)

Portfolio manager: Murphy van der Velde (1996)
Investment objective and policies: Investment results that match the price and yield performance of the stocks included in the Russell 1000 Utility Index. Invests at least 80% of assets in a proportional representative mix of the Russell 1000 Utility Index stocks

to achieve a total return approximately equal to the performance of the total Index.
Year organized: 1993 (name changed from IBM Utility Index Fund in 1994)
Ticker symbol: IUTLX
Discount broker availability: Fidelity, Siebert, White
Dividends paid: Income - quarterly; Capital gains - annually
Portfolio turnover (3 yrs): 170%, 12%, 5%
Management fee: 0.10%
Expense ratio: 0.40% (year ending 3/31/97)

GATEWAY FUNDS ◆

(Data common to all Gateway funds are listed below. See subsequent listings for data specific to individual funds.)

400 TechneCenter Drive, Suite 220
Milford, OH 45150
800-354-6339, 800-354-5525
513-248-2700
fax 513-248-2699
Internet: http://www.gia.com

Shareholder service hours: Full service: M-F 9 A.M.-5 P.M. EST; After hours service: prices, prospectuses
Adviser: Gateway Investment Advisers, L.P.
Transfer agent: The Gateway Trust
Minimum purchase: Initial: $1,000, Subsequent: $100; IRA: Initial: $500
Wire orders accepted: Yes
Deadline for same day wire purchase: 4 P.M.
Qualified for sale in: All states (except Cincinnati Fund)
Telephone redemptions: Yes
Wire redemptions: Yes, $10 fee
Letter redemptions: Signature guarantee not required
Telephone switching: With other Gateway Funds and Kemper Cash Equivalent Money Market Funds
Number of switches permitted: 12 per year
Shareholder services: IRA, SEP-IRA, automatic investment plan, systematic withdrawal plan min. bal. req. $5,000
IRA fees: None

GATEWAY CINCINNATI FUND ◆

(See first Gateway listing for data common to all funds)

Portfolio manager: J. Patrick Rogers (1994)
Investment objective and policies: Long-term capital growth. Invests at least 65% of assets in the common stocks of companies with an important presence in the Greater Cincinnati Area - either headquartered in or ranking among the 25 largest employers in the Cincinnati area. Company must employ at least 50 people in the greater Cincinnati area, be traded on a national stock exchange, and have a market capitalization exceeding $5M. Fund uses a proprietary model to select stocks and allocate assets among chosen stocks.
Year organized: 1994
Ticker symbol: CINFX
Discount broker availability: *Fidelity, *Schwab, *White
Qualified for sale in: DC, FL, IN, KY, MD, NJ, OH, PA, TN
Dividends paid: Income - December; Capital gains - December
Portfolio turnover (2 yrs): 10%, 9%
Management fee: 0.50%
Expense ratio: 2.00% (year ending 12/31/96)

GATEWAY INDEX PLUS FUND ◆

(See first Gateway listing for data common to all funds)

Portfolio manager: J. Patrick Rogers (1994)
Investment objective and policies: High current return at a reduced level of risk. Invests in stocks included in the S&P 100 Index (OEX), and writes call options on this portfolio (currently the index versus individual issues). Also buys put options designed as insurance against a downward market correction. Prior to March 22, 1985, fund's objective was to invest in a

diversified portfolio of common stocks and sell covered call options on these stocks.
Year organized: 1977 (name changed from Gateway Option Income Fund 2/88; from Gateway Option Index Fund 3/90)
Ticker symbol: GATEX
Discount broker availability: *Fidelity, *Schwab, *White
Dividends paid: Income - March, June, September, December; Capital gains - December
Portfolio turnover (3 yrs): 17%, 5%, 4%
Management fee: 0.90% first $50M to 0.60% over $100M
Expense ratio: 1.14% (year ending 12/31/96)

GATEWAY MID CAP INDEX FUND ◆

(See first Gateway listing for data common to all funds)

Portfolio manager: J. Patrick Rogers (1994)
Investment objective and policies: Long-term capital growth; principal conservation secondary. Invests in the 400 stocks in the S&P 400 Midcap Index (in the proportions that they are represented in that index) and occasionally writes options on this portfolio to maximize return in up or down markets.
Year organized: 1992 (Name and objective changed from Gateway Capital Fund 12/93)
Ticker symbol: GMCIX
Discount broker availability: *Fidelity, *Schwab
Dividends paid: Income - December; Capital gains - December
Portfolio turnover (3 yrs): 14%, 18%, 8%
Management fee: 0.90% first $50M to 0.60% over $100M
Expense ratio: 2.00% (year ending 12/31/96)

GATEWAY SMALL CAP INDEX FUND ◆

(See first Gateway listing for data common to all funds)

Portfolio manager: J. Patrick Rogers (1994)
Investment objective and policies: Long-term capital growth. Invests in the 250 stocks in the Wilshire Small Cap Index in the same proportions that they are represented in that index. Fund may buy index put options to reduce the risk of principal loss and index call options to increase the potential for gain.
Year organized: 1993
Ticker symbol: GSCIX
Discount broker availability: *Fidelity, *Schwab, *White
Dividends paid: Income - December; Capital gains - December
Portfolio turnover (3 yrs): 20%, 20%, 39%
Management fee: 0.90% first $50M to 0.60% over $100M
Expense ratio: 1.50% (year ending 12/31/96)

GE FUNDS

(This series of GE funds are offered as multi-class load funds.)

GE - ELFUN FUNDS ◆

(Fund family will not provide data. Data common to all GE - Elfun funds are shown below. See subsequent listings for data specific to individual funds.)

3003 Summer Street
P.O. Box 120074
Stamford, CT 06912-0074
800-242-0134, 203-326-4040
prices/yields 800-843-3359

Adviser: General Electric Investment Corp.
Transfer agent: State Street Bank & Trust Co.
Special sales restrictions: Available to members of the Elfun Society and immediate families, General Electric board members, and GE and its subsidiaries. (Members are selected from active employees of the General Electric Co.)
Wire orders accepted: Yes
Deadline for same day wire purchase: 4 P.M.
Qualified for sale in: All states

Telephone redemptions: Yes, $1,000 minimum, $15 fee
Wire redemptions: Yes, $1,000 minimum, $15 fee
Letter redemptions: Signature guarantee required over $10,000
Telephone switching: With other GE - Elfun Funds
Number of switches permitted: Unlimited
Shareholder services: IRA, automatic investment plan, directed dividends, systematic withdrawal plan min. bal. req. $10,000, payroll deduction ($25 per month minimum)
IRA fees: None

GE - ELFUN DIVERSIFIED FUND ◆
(See first GE - Elfun listing for data common to all funds)

Investment objective and policies: High total return consistent with prudent investment management and capital preservation. Invests in common stocks, convertible securities, preferred stocks, investment grade taxable and non-taxable bonds, other registered investment companies, and restricted non-public securities with allocation adjusted to reflect changes in market and economic conditions. Up to 20% of assets may be in foreign securities not listed on U.S. exchanges. Fund may use forward contracts, futures and options for hedging purposes.
Year organized: 1987
Ticker symbol: ELDFX
Minimum purchase: Initial: $100, Subsequent: $25
Dividends paid: Income - December; Capital gains - December
Management fee: 0.08%

GE - ELFUN GLOBAL FUND ◆
(See first GE - Elfun listing for data common to all funds)

Investment objective and policies: Long-term capital growth and future income. Invests primarily in foreign securities with at least 65% of assets in securities listed on domestic and foreign exchanges - primarily stocks, convertible securities, and foreign denominated bonds - of at least three countries, including the U.S. Fund may use forward contracts, futures and options for hedging purposes.
Year organized: 1987
Ticker symbol: EGLBX
Minimum purchase: Initial: $100, Subsequent: $25
Dividends paid: Income - December Capital gains - December
Management fee: 0.13%

GE - ELFUN INCOME FUND ◆
(See first GE - Elfun listing for data common to all funds)

Investment objective and policies: High current income consistent with prudent investment management and capital preservation. Invests in both domestic and foreign issued bonds and debentures, government obligations and preferred and common stock. Up to 25% of assets may be in junk bonds. May use forward contracts, futures and options for hedging purposes.
Year organized: 1982
Ticker symbol: EINFX
Minimum purchase: Initial: None, Subsequent: None
Dividends paid: Income - declared daily, paid monthly; Capital gains - January
Management fee: 0.10%

GE - ELFUN MONEY MARKET FUND ◆
(See first GE - Elfun listing for data common to all funds)

Investment objective and policies: High current income consistent with prudent investment management and capital preservation. Invests in short-term money market instruments.
Year organized: 1990
Ticker symbol: EINXX
Minimum purchase: Initial: $100, Subsequent: $25

Check redemptions: $500 minimum, $20 fee to establish
Dividends paid: Income - declared daily, paid monthly
Management fee: 0.08%

GE - ELFUN TAX-EXEMPT INCOME FUND ◆
(See first GE - Elfun listing for data common to all funds)

Investment objective and policies: Current income exempt from federal income tax. Invests in high-grade municipal bonds. Up to 25% of assets may be in junk bonds and 20% in securities subject to AMT tax treatment. Fund may use futures and options for hedging purposes.
Year organized: 1977
Ticker symbol: ELFTX
Minimum purchase: Initial: None, Subsequent: None
Dividends paid: Income - declared daily, paid monthly; Capital gains - December
Management fee: 0.05%

GE - ELFUN TRUSTS ◆
(See first GE - Elfun listing for data common to all funds)

Investment objective and policies: Long-term capital growth, and future rather than current income. Fund may invest in any types of securities and in any proportions it deems proper or suitable. Normally will invest in equities and convertibles. May use futures and options for hedging purposes.
Year organized: 1935
Ticker symbol: ELFNX
Minimum purchase: Initial: None, Subsequent: None
Dividends paid: Income - December, Capital gains - December
Management fee: 0.06%

GENERAL ELECTRIC S&S LONG-TERM INTEREST FUND ◆
3003 Summer Street
P.O. Box 7900
Stamford, CT 06904
800-242-0134, 203-326-2300
prices/yields 800-843-3359

Adviser: General Electric Investment Corp.
Transfer agent: Elfun Mutual Funds
Investment objective and policies: High interest rate of return. Invests in debt securities consisting of corporate bonds and debentures, real estate sale, U.S. Government obligations, etc.
Special sales restrictions: Available to employees of General Electric Co. who are participants in the GE Savings & Security Program
Year organized: 1980
Ticker symbol: GESLX
Group fund code: 98
Minimum purchase: Initial: None, Subsequent: None
Qualified for sale in: All states
Letter redemptions: Signature guarantee not required
Dividends paid: Income - monthly
Shareholder services: IRA, Keogh

GENERAL ELECTRIC S&S PROGRAM MUTUAL FUND ◆
3003 Summer Street
P.O. Box 7900
Stamford, CT 06904
800-242-0134, 203-356-2300
prices/yields 800-843-3359

Adviser: General Electric Investment Corp.
Transfer agent: Elfun Mutual Funds
Investment objective and policies: Long-term growth of capital and income. Invests principally in common stocks and securities convertible into common stock of U.S. corporations. May invest in securi-

ties of foreign issuers, directly and through use of ADRs
Special sales restrictions: Available to employees of General Electric Co. who are participants in the GE Savings & Security Program
Year organized: 1967
Ticker symbol: GESSX
Group fund code: 97
Minimum purchase: Initial: None, Subsequent: None
Qualified for sale in: All states
Letter redemptions: Signature guarantee not required
Dividends paid: Income - January; Capital gains - January
Shareholder services: IRA, Keogh

GENERAL SECURITIES, INC. ◆
5100 Eden Avenue, Suite 204
Edina, MN 55436
800-577-9217, 800-939-9990
617-927-6799
fax 617-927-6897

Adviser: Robinson Capital Management, Inc.
Lead portfolio manager: John P. Robinson (1951)
Transfer agent: Investors Fiduciary Trust Co.
Investment objective and policies: Long-term capital appreciation and preservation of capital. Invests primarily in a diversified portfolio of common stocks of blue chip companies that have implemented Total Quality Management or Continuous Quality Management principles, but may also invest in preferred stocks and fixed-income securities. May use exchange traded options to hedge up to 25% of assets.
Year organized: 1951
Ticker symbol: GSECX
Minimum purchase: Initial: $1,500, Subsequent: $100; Automatic investment plan: Initial: $100
Wire orders accepted: Yes
Deadline for same day wire purchase: 12 NN
Discount broker availability: *White
Qualified for sale in: All states
Telephone redemptions: Yes
Wire redemptions: Yes, $2,500 minimum, $20 fee
Letter redemptions: Signature guarantee required over $50,000
Dividends paid: Income - February, May, August, November; Capital gains - November
Portfolio turnover (3 yrs): 20%, 18%, 24%
Shareholder services: IRA, SEP-IRA, Keogh, systematic withdrawal plan min. bal. req. $10,000
Management fee: 0.60% first $100M to 0.10% over $250M
Expense ratio: 1.44% (year ending 11/30/97)
IRA fees: Annual $12

GINTEL FUND ◆
6 Greenwich Office Park
Greenwich, CT 06831
800-243-5808, 800-344-3092
203-622-6400, prices 800-759-4171

Adviser: Gintel Asset Management, Inc.
Portfolio managers: Robert M. Gintel (1981), Cecil A. Godman III (1992)
Transfer agent: Chase Manhattan Bank, N.A.
Investment objective and policies: Capital appreciation. Invests in common stocks or securities convertible into common stock. Fund invests in major companies traded on the New York or American stock exchanges, or in the OTC market. Up to 20% of assets may be in securities of foreign issuers and 15% in illiquid securities. Fund leverages, sells short against the box and is non-diversified.
Year organized: 1981 (absorbed Gintel ERISA Fund 9/27/96)
Ticker symbol: GINLX
Minimum purchase: Initial: $5,000, Subsequent: None; IRA/Keogh: Initial: $2,000; Automatic investment plan: Subsequent: $100
Wire orders accepted: Yes
Deadline for same day wire purchase: 4 P.M.
Discount broker availability: *Fidelity, Schwab, Siebert, *White
Qualified for sale in: All states except AR, NE, OH, PR
Telephone redemptions: Yes

Wire redemptions: Yes, $1,000 minimum, $8 fee
Letter redemptions: Signature guarantee required
Telephone switching: With certain Chase money market and income funds
Number of switches permitted: Unlimited
Dividends paid: Income - December; Capital gains - December
Portfolio turnover (3 yrs): 61%, 55%, 70%
Shareholder services: IRA, SEP-IRA, Keogh, 401(k), 403(b), corporate retirement plans, systematic withdrawal plan min. bal. req. $10,000
Management fee: 1.00%
Expense ratio: 1.80% (year ending 12/31/96)
IRA/Keogh fees: Annual $10, Initial $5

GIT TRUSTS ◆
(See Mosaic Funds; name changed 5/12/97)

GLOBALT GROWTH FUND ◆
3060 Peachtree Road, N.W.
One Buckhead Plaza, Suite 225
Atlanta, GA 30305
800-831-9922, 404-364-2188

Adviser: GLOBALT Inc.
Administrator: AmeriPrime Financial Services, Inc.
Portfolio managers: Angela Z. Allen (1995), Samuel Allen (1995), Greg Paulette (1995)
Transfer agent: American Data Services, Inc.
Investment objective and policies: Long-term growth of capital; current income incidental but expected. Invests in a broad range of domestic equity securities perceived to offer superior growth potential. All companies selected, however, will be globally oriented, competing in both foreign and domestic economies, with at least 20% of revenues derived from operations or sales outside the U.S. Fund will not purchase foreign securities.
Year organized: 1995
Minimum purchase: Initial: $25,000; Subsequent: $5,000; IRA: Subsequent: $2,000
Wire orders accepted: Yes
Deadline for same day wire purchase: 4 P.M.
Discount broker availability: *Fidelity, *Schwab, *White
Qualified for sale in: AL, CA, CO, DC, FL, GA, IN, NC, PA, TN, VA, WY
Telephone redemptions: Yes
Wire redemptions: Yes
Letter redemptions: Signature guarantee required
Dividends paid: Income - December; Capital gains - December
Portfolio turnover (2 yrs): 110%, 66%
Shareholder services: IRA, SEP-IRA, automatic investment plan
Management fee: 1.17% (adviser pays all expenses)
Administration fee: 0.10% first $50M to 0.05% over $100M ($30,000 minimum)
Expense ratio: 1.17% (year ending 10/31/97) (1.19% without waiver)
IRA fees: Transfer fees, $12; Closing $15

GMO PELICAN FUND ◆
40 Rowes Wharf
Boston, MA 02110
800-447-3167, 617-346-7600

Adviser: Grantham, Mayo, Van Otterloo & Co.
Portfolio manager: Richard A. Mayo (1989)
Transfer agent: Boston Financial Data Services, Inc.
Investment objective and policies: Long-term capital growth; current income secondary. Invests primarily in equity securities of domestic companies with market capitalizations of more than $100M perceived to represent outstanding values relative to their market prices. Seeks to maintain a lower than average risk level relative to potential return through a portfolio with an average volatility below 1.0. Invests primarily in domestic equities, but may invest up to 25% of assets in foreign securities. May use derivative instruments for hedging purposes.
Year organized: 1989 (previously named the Pelican Fund)
Ticker symbol: PELFX

Minimum purchase: Initial: $5,000, Subsequent: None; IRA/Keogh: Initial: $1,000
Wire orders accepted: Yes
Deadline for same day wire purchase: 4 P.M.
Discount broker availability: Fidelity, Siebert
Qualified for sale in: All states except AL, AK, AZ, AR, HI, ID, IA, MN, MS, MO, MT, NE, NV, NJ, NM, NC, ND, OK, OR, SD, TN, TX, VT, WV, WY
Telephone redemptions: Yes, $5,000 minimum
Wire redemptions: Yes, $5,000 minimum
Letter redemptions: Signature guarantee required
Redemption fee: 0.50% for redemptions of at least $1 million within 30 days, if any of the redeemed shares were purchased within the 12 month period immediately preceding the 30 days.
Dividends paid: Income - quarterly; Capital gains - annually
Portfolio turnover (3 yrs): 40%, 49%, 39%
Shareholder services: IRA, SEP-IRA, Keogh, 401(k), systematic withdrawal plan min. bal. req. $5,000
Management fee: 0.90%
Expense ratio: 0.95% (year ending 2/29/97)
IRA/Keogh fees: None

GOVERNMENT CASH SERIES
Federated Investors Tower
Pittsburgh, PA 15222-3779
800-245-2423, 412-288-1948

Adviser: Federated Advisers
Portfolio manager: Susan M. Nason (1990)
Transfer agent: Federated Services Co.
Investment objective and policies: Income consistent with stability of principal and liquidity. Invests in short-term U.S. Government money market instruments.
Year organized: 1989
Ticker symbol: CTGXX
Minimum purchase: Initial: $10,000, Subsequent: $500; IRA: Initial: $1,000
Wire orders accepted: Yes
Deadline for same day wire purchase: 12 NN
Qualified for sale in: All states
Telephone redemptions: Yes
Wire redemptions: Yes, $1,000 minimum
Letter redemptions: Signature guarantee required over $50,000
Check redemptions: No minimum
Dividends paid: Income - declared daily, paid monthly
Shareholder services: IRA, systematic withdrawal plan, debit card
Management fee: 0.50%
12b-1 distribution fee: Maximum of 0.35%
Expense ratio: 0.99% (year ending 5/31/97) (includes waiver)

THE GOVERNMENT STREET FUNDS ◆
(Data common to all Government Street funds are shown below. See subsequent listings for data specific to individual funds.)

150 Government Street
P.O. Box 1307
Mobile, AL 36633
800-443-4249, 334-433-3709
prices/yields 800-852-4052

Adviser: T. Leavell & Assocs., Inc.
Administrator and transfer agent: Countrywide Fund Services, Inc.
Minimum purchase: Initial: $5,000, Subsequent: $500; IRA/Keogh: Initial: $1,000; Automatic investment plan: Subsequent: $100
Wire orders accepted: Yes
Deadline for same day wire purchase: 4 P.M.
Wire redemptions: Yes, $5,000 minimum
Letter redemptions: Signature guarantee not required
Shareholder services: IRA, Keogh, electronic funds transfer, systematic withdrawal plan min. bal. req. $10,000
IRA/Keogh fees: None

GOVERNMENT STREET ALABAMA TAX FREE BOND FUND ◆
(See first Government Street listing for data common to all funds)

Portfolio manager: Timothy S. Healey (1993)
Investment objective and policies: Current income exempt from federal and Alabama personal income taxes, consistent with capital preservation; capital appreciation is secondary. Normally invests at least 80% of assets in municipal bonds and notes and other debt instruments the interest on which is exempt from the taxes mentioned, and which are rated within the three highest grades. These are usually issued by the State of Alabama or its subdivisions, but may also come from Puerto Rico, the U.S. Virgin Islands, and Guam. The portfolio generally maintains a dollar-weighted average maturity of three to ten years. May also invest, however, in securities subject to AMT tax treatment, and up to 15% in illiquid securities.
Year organized: 1993
Qualified for sale in: AL, CA, FL, IL, TN
Dividends paid: Income - declared daily, paid monthly; Capital gains - December
Portfolio turnover (3 yrs): 6%, 4%, 36%
Management fee: 0.35% first $100M, 0.25% over $100M
Administration fee: 0.15% first $200M, 0.10% over $200M ($24,000 minimum)
Expense ratio: 0.66% (year ending 3/31/97) (0.78% without waiver)

GOVERNMENT STREET BOND FUND ◆
(See first Government Street listing for data common to all funds)

Portfolio manager: Mary Shannon Hope (1997)
Investment objective and policies: Current income and preservation of capital while protecting the portfolio against the effects of inflation; capital appreciation secondary. Invests in fixed-income securities of the four highest grades with at least 40% of assets in U.S. Government obligations. Fund maintains a weighted averaged maturity of three to seven years, with individual maturities ranging from one to 15 years. May invest without limit in ADRs of foreign issuers.
Year organized: 1991
Ticker symbol: GVSBX
Discount broker availability: Schwab
Qualified for sale in: AL, CA, CO, FL, GA, ID, IL, KY, MA, ME, MS, NY, NC, PA, SC, TN, VA, WV
Dividends paid: Income - monthly; Capital gains - December
Portfolio turnover (3 yrs): 20%, 10%, 11%
Management fee: 0.50% first $100M, 0.40% over $100M
Administration fee: 0.075% first $200M, 0.05% over $200M ($24,000 minimum)
Expense ratio: 0.75% (year ending 3/31/97)

GOVERNMENT STREET EQUITY FUND ◆
(See first Government Street listing for data common to all funds)

Portfolio manager: Thomas W. Leavell (1991)
Investment objective and policies: Capital appreciation through the compounding of dividends and capital gains; current income secondary. Invests primarily in a broadly diversified portfolio of common stocks of medium to large capitalization companies, with equal weightings given for growth and value companies. May invest without limit in sponsored ADRs of foreign issuers.
Year organized: 1991
Ticker symbol: GVEQX
Discount broker availability: Schwab
Qualified for sale in: AL, CA, CO, FL, GA, IL, KY, MS, MT, NY, NC, PA, SC, TN, TX, VA, WA, WV
Dividends paid: Income - March, June, September, December; Capital gains - December
Portfolio turnover (3 yrs): 20%, 31%, 55%
Management fee: 0.60% first $100M, 0.50% over $100M
Administration fee: 0.20% first $25M to 0.15% over $50M ($24,000 minimum)
Expense ratio: 0.89% (year ending 3/31/97)

GRADISON MUTUAL FUNDS

(Data common to all Gradison funds are shown below. See subsequent listings for data specific to individual funds.)

580 Walnut Street
Cincinnati, OH 45202
800-869-5999, 513-579-5000
fax 513-579-5847

Adviser: The Gradison Division of McDonald & Co. Securities, Inc.
Transfer agent: Gradison Mutual Funds
Minimum purchase: Initial: $1,000, Subsequent: $50
Wire orders accepted: Yes
Deadline for same day wire purchase: 4 P.M. (12 NN for U.S. Government Reserves)
Telephone redemptions: Yes
Wire redemptions: Yes, $1,000 minimum
Letter redemptions: Signature guarantee not required
Telephone switching: With other Gradison funds, and certain Federated tax-free state and federal money market funds
Number of switches permitted: Unlimited
Shareholder services: IRA, automatic investment plan, systematic withdrawal plan min. bal. req. $10,000
IRA fees: Annual $10, Initial $10, Closing $50, (Annual $30 and Initial $20 for a self-directed brokerage account)

GRADISON GOVERNMENT INCOME FUND

(See first Gradison listing for data common to all funds)

Portfolio managers: Michael J. Link (1987), C. Stephen Wesselkamper (1993)
Investment objective and policies: High current income. Invests in a portfolio of intermediate- and long-term obligations issued or guaranteed by the U.S. Government, its agencies or instrumentalities. Average maturity is adjusted according to perceived market conditions.
Year organized: 1987 (fund carried a 2% load until 7/7/97)
Ticker symbol: GGIFX
Qualified for sale in: All states except HI
Dividends paid: Income: declared daily, paid monthly; Capital gains - annually
Portfolio turnover (3 yrs): 13%, 16%, 21%
Management fee: 0.50%
12b-1 distribution fee: 0.25%
Expense ratio: 0.90% (year ending 12/31/96)

GRADISON GROWTH TRUST ESTABLISHED VALUE FUND

(See first Gradison listing for data common to all funds)

Portfolio managers: William J. Leugers, Jr. (1983), Daniel R. Shick (1996)
Investment objective and policies: Long-term capital growth. Invests in the common stocks of established companies with market capitalizations of at least $500M, selected from the S&P 500 and other markets, considered undervalued, selected on the basis of a disciplined portfolio construction and comprehensive computer modeling.
Year organized: 1983 (name changed from Gradison Established Growth Fund on 8/1/92)
Ticker symbol: GETGX
Discount broker availability: Schwab, White
Qualified for sale in: All states except HI
Dividends paid: Income: quarterly; Capital gains - annually
Portfolio turnover (3 yrs): 31%, 18%, 24%
Management fee: 0.65% first $100M to 0.45% over $200M
12b-1 distribution fee: 0.50%
Expense ratio: 1.12% (year ending 3/31/97)

GRADISON GROWTH TRUST GROWTH & INCOME FUND

(See first Gradison listing for data common to all funds)

Portfolio manager: Julian C. Ball (1995)
Investment objective and policies: Long-term capital growth, current income and growth of income consistent with reasonable risk. Invests primarily in the common stocks of dividend-paying companies perceived to be undervalued, with market capitalizations of $500M or more. May also invest in convertible securities and investment grade fixed-income instruments. May invest up to 25% of assets in a single industry sector.
Year organized: 1995
Ticker symbol: GRINX
Qualified for sale in: All states except HI
Dividends paid: Income - quarterly; Capital gains - annually
Portfolio turnover (2 yrs): 16%, 3%
Management fee: 0.65% first $100M to 0.45% over $200M
12b-1 distribution fee: 0.50%
Expense ratio: 1.50% (year ending 3/31/97) (1.84% without waiver)

GRADISON GROWTH TRUST INTERNATIONAL FUND ◆

(See first Gradison listing for data common to all funds)

Sub-adviser: Blairlogie Capital Management
Portfolio manager: Bradley E. Turner (1996)
Investment objective and policies: Capital growth. Invests primarily in a diversified portfolio of common stocks of non-U.S. companies. Will invest in both emerging markets and more developed countries. Approximately 30% of assets will be dedicated to issuers of at least three different emerging market countries, and allocation will be adjusted monthly to attempt to retain this percentage. May utilize ADRs, EDRs, and Global Depository Receipts, in addition to direct foreign issues. May use foreign currency contracts to hedge exchange rate risk, and certain derivative instruments for hedging purposes.
Year organized: 1995
Ticker symbol: INTFX
Qualified for sale in: All states except HI
Dividends paid: Income - annually; Capital gains - annually
Portfolio turnover (2 yrs): 92%, 72%
Management fee: 1.00% first $100M to 0.75% over $200M
12b-1 distribution fee: 0.50% (not currently imposed)
Expense ratio: 2.00% (year ending 3/31/97) (2.78% without waiver)

GRADISON GROWTH TRUST OPPORTUNITY VALUE FUND

(See first Gradison listing for data common to all funds)

Portfolio managers: William J. Leugers, Jr. (1983), Daniel R. Shick (1996)
Investment objective and policies: Long-term capital growth. Invests in the common stocks of smaller companies, generally with market capitalizations under $500M with potential for high earnings growth not currently reflected, selected on the basis of a disciplined portfolio construction and comprehensive computer modeling.
Year organized: 1983 (Formerly Gradison Emerging Growth Fund. Name changed from Gradison Opportunity Growth Fund on 8/1/92.)
Ticker symbol: GOGFX
Discount broker availability: Schwab, White
Qualified for sale in: All states except HI
Dividends paid: Income - semi-annually; Capital gains - annually
Portfolio turnover (3 yrs): 35%, 24%, 32%
Management fee: 0.65% first $100M to 0.45% over $200M
12b-1 distribution fee: 0.50%
Expense ratio: 1.36% (year ending 3/31/97)

GRADISON OHIO TAX-FREE INCOME FUND

(See first Gradison listing for data common to all funds)

Portfolio manager: Stephen C. Dilbone (1992)
Investment objective and policies: High level of after tax income consistent with preservation of capital and liquidity. Invests in obligations the interest from which is exempt from federal and Ohio state personal income tax. Fund tends to invest in longer term debt securities. May invest up to 20% of assets in securities subject to AMT tax treatment. Fund may hedge.
Year organized: 1992 (fund carried a 2% load until 7/7/97)
Ticker symbol: GMOTX
Qualified for sale in: OH
Dividends paid: Income: declared daily, paid monthly; Capital gains - annually
Portfolio turnover (3 yrs): 134%, 100%, 80%
Management fee: 0.50%
12b-1 distribution fee: 0.25%
Expense ratio: 0.96% (year ending 6/30/97)

GRADISON U.S. GOVERNMENT RESERVES

(See first Gradison listing for data common to all funds)

Portfolio managers: C. Stephen Wesselkamper (1993), Paul J. Weston (1993)
Investment objective and policies: Maximum current income consistent with preservation of capital and liquidity. Invests in money market securities issued or guaranteed as to principal and interest by the U.S. Government or its agencies or instrumentalities, and repurchase agreements in respect to these securities. Fund attempts to maximize the portion of its dividends not subject to state and local taxation.
Year organized: 1993
Ticker symbol: GMUXX
Qualified for sale in: All states
Check redemptions: No minimum ($0.30 fee under $100)
Dividends paid: Income: declared daily, paid monthly
Management fee: 0.50% first $400M to 0.35% over $2B
12b-1 distribution fee: Maximum of 0.20%
Expense ratio: 0.72% (year ending 9/30/97) (0.73% without waiver)

GRAND PRIX FUND

Wilton Executive Campus
15 River Road, Suite 220
Wilton, CT 06897
800-432-4741

Adviser: Target Holdings Corp., d.b.a. Target Investors
Administrator: Sunstone Financial Group, Inc.
Portfolio manager: Robert Zuccaro (1997)
Transfer agent: Sunstone Investor Services, LLC
Investment objective and policies: Capital appreciation. Invests primarily in an actively traded portfolio of common stocks and other equity securities of companies perceived to offer growth potential, without regard to market capitalization. Does focus mainly on small to mid cap companies as much as possible. May invest up to 35% of assets in cash or money markets, up to 20% in ADRs, and up to 10% in companies with less than three years operating history. May invest more than 25% of assets in a single sector, and may invest in fewer than 25 companies. Fund is non-diversified.
Year organized: 1997
Minimum purchase: Initial: $5,000; Subsequent: $1,000
Wire orders accepted: Yes
Deadline for same day wire purchase: 4 P.M.
Qualified for sale in: AK, CA, CO, GA, IL, IN, KY, LA, MN, NC, OH, OK, OR, PA, RI, UT, VA, WY
Telephone redemptions: Yes
Wire redemptions: Yes, $10 fee
Letter redemptions: Signature guarantee required over $10,000

Telephone switching: With the Fountain Square U.S. Treasury Obligations MM
Number of switches permitted: 5 per year
Dividends paid: Income - June, December; Capital gains - December
Shareholder services: IRA, SEP-IRA, automatic investment plan, electronic funds transfer
Management fee: 1.00%
12b-1 distribution fee: 0.25%
IRA fees: Annual $10, Closing $15

GREEN CENTURY BALANCED FUND
29 Temple Place, Suite 200
Boston, MA 02111
800-93-GREEN, 617-482-0800
prices/yields 800-882-8316
fax 617-422-0881

Adviser: Green Century Capital Management, Inc.
Sub-adviser: Winslow Management Co., a Division of Eaton Vance Management
Administrator: Sunstone Financial Group, Inc.
Portfolio manager: Jackson W. Robinson (1995)
Transfer agent: Investors Bank & Trust Co.
Investment objective and policies: Capital growth and income. Invests primarily in equities and fixed-income securities compatible with the fund's commitment to environmental responsibility. At least 25% of assets are in fixed-income senior securities, with a maximum of 75% of assets invested in equities. Seeks protection of capital by adjusting allocation of assets to changing economic and market conditions. Up to 25% of assets may be in securities of foreign issuers and up to 35% in junk bonds. May use futures and options to increase return and for hedging purposes.
Year organized: 1992
Ticker symbol: GCBLX
Minimum purchase: Initial: $2,000; Subsequent: $100; IRA: Initial: $500; Automatic investment plan: Initial: $50, Subsequent: $50
Wire orders accepted: Yes
Deadline for same day wire purchase: 4 P.M.
Discount broker availability: *Fidelity, *Siebert, White
Qualified for sale in: All states except AL, AR, ID, KS, NV, ND, OK, SC, SD
Telephone redemptions: Yes
Wire redemptions: Yes, $10 fee
Letter redemptions: Signature guarantee required
Telephone switching: With Green Century Equity Fund, $100 minimum
Number of switches permitted: Unlimited
Dividends paid: Income - June, December; Capital gains - December
Portfolio turnover (3 yrs): 109%, 136%, 16%
Shareholder services: IRA, SEP-IRA
Management fee: 0.40% +/- performance fee of up to 0.20% relative to the total return from Lipper Directors' Analytical Data Balanced Fund Average
12b-1 distribution fee: 0.25%
Expense ratio: 2.50% (year ending 6/30/97)
IRA fees: Annual $10

GREEN CENTURY EQUITY FUND ◆
29 Temple Place, Suite 200
Boston, MA 02111
800-93-GREEN, 617-482-0800
prices/yields 800-882-8316
fax 617-422-0881

Adviser: Domini Social Investments, LLC
Administrator: Sunstone Financial Group, Inc.
Sub-adviser: Mellon Equity Assocs. (1995)
Transfer agent: Investors Bank & Trust Co.
Investment objective and policies: Long-term total return. Invests all its assets in the Domini Social Index Portfolio, a diversified index portfolio with the same investment objective, which, in turn, invests in the common stock of companies that meet the social and environmental criteria of the Domini Social Index. As an index fund, the underlying portfolio is likely to change frequently.
Year organized: 1995
Minimum purchase: Initial: $2,000; Subsequent: $100; IRA: Initial: $500; Automatic investment plan: Initial: $50, Subsequent: $50
Wire orders accepted: Yes
Deadline for same day wire purchase: 4 P.M.

Discount broker availability: *Fidelity, *Siebert, White
Qualified for sale in: All states except AL, AR, ID, KS, NV, ND, OK, SC, SD
Telephone redemptions: Yes
Wire redemptions: Yes, $10 fee
Letter redemptions: Signature guarantee required
Telephone switching: With Green Century Balanced Fund, $100 minimum
Number of switches permitted: Unlimited
Dividends paid: Income - June, December; Capital gains - December
Turnover (2 yrs): 1%, 5% (for underlying portfolio)
Shareholder services: IRA, SEP-IRA
Management fee: 0.20%
Expense ratio: 1.50% (year ending 7/31/97)
IRA fees: Annual $10

GREENSPRING FUND ◆
2330 West Joppa Road, Suite 110
Lutherville, MD 21093-4641
800-366-3863, 410-823-5353
shareholder services 800-576-7498
fax 410-823-0903
e-mail: greenspring@corbyn.com

Shareholder service hours: Full service: M-F 9 A.M.-5 P.M. EST; After hours services: prices, account balances, last transaction, messages, prospectuses, div/cap gains distributions
Adviser: Key Equity Management Corp.
Portfolio manager: Charles vK. Carlson (1987)
Transfer agent: Rodney Square Management Corp.
Investment objective and policies: Long-term capital growth; current income secondary. Invests primarily in common stocks perceived to be undervalued, but may also invest in preferred stocks, illiquid securities, debt securities and money markets in an effort to enhance total return. May invest in foreign securities and junk bonds without limit. May use options and various derivative instruments to hedge up to 25% of net assets.
Year organized: 1982
Ticker symbol: GRSPX
Minimum purchase: Initial: $2,000, Subsequent: $100; IRA: Initial: $1,000; Automatic investment plan: Initial: $1,000
Wire orders accepted: Yes
Deadline for same day wire purchase: 4 P.M.
Discount broker availability: Fidelity, Schwab, Siebert, White
Qualified for sale in: All states except PR
Telephone redemptions: Yes
Wire redemptions: Yes
Letter redemptions: Signature guarantee required over $10,000
Dividends paid: Income - July, December; Capital gains - July, December
Portfolio turnover (3 yrs): 46%, 61%, 65%
Shareholder services: IRA, SEP-IRA, electronic funds transfer, systematic withdrawal plan min. bal. req. $10,000
Management fee: 0.75%
Expense ratio: 1.00% (year ending 12/31/97)
IRA fees: Annual $10

GUINNESS FLIGHT FUNDS ◆
(Data common to all Guinness Flight funds are shown below. See subsequent listings for data specific to individual funds.)

225 South Lake Avenue, Suite 777
Pasadena, CA 91101
800-915-6566, 800-434-5623, 626-795-0039
prices/yields 800-915-6564
fax 626-795-0593
Internet: http://www.gffunds.com
e-mail: mail@gffunds.com

Shareholder service hours: Full service: M-F 8 A.M.-6 P.M. EST; After hours service: prices, yields, account balances, orders, last transaction, news and views, messages, indices, prospectuses, total returns
Adviser: Guinness Flight Investment Management Ltd. (A division of Guinness Flight Hambro Asset Management of London)
Administrator: Investment Company Administration Corp.

Transfer agent: State Street Bank & Trust Co.
Minimum purchase: Initial: $2,500 ($1,000 for existing Guinness shareholders), Subsequent: $250; IRA: Initial: $1,000; Automatic investment plan: Initial: $100, Subsequent: $100
Wire orders accepted: Yes
Deadline for same day wire purchase: 4 P.M.
Qualified for sale in: All states
Telephone redemptions: Yes
Wire redemptions: Yes, $500 minimum, $10 fee
Letter redemptions: Signature guarantee required over $50,000
Redemption fee: 1.00% for shares held less than 30 days, payable to the fund (exception noted)
Telephone switching: With other Guinness Flight funds and SSgA Money Market Fund
Number of switches permitted: 4 per year
Shareholder services: IRA, electronic funds transfer (purchase only), systematic withdrawal plan min. bal. req. $1,000
Administration fee: 0.25% of aggregate assets ($80,000 minimum)
12b-1 distribution fee: Yes (not currently imposed)
IRA fees: Annual $10, Initial $5, Closing $10

GUINNESS FLIGHT ASIA BLUE CHIP FUND ◆
(See first Guinness Flight listing for data common to all funds)

Portfolio manager: Richard Farrell (1996)
Investment objective and policies: Long-term capital appreciation. Invests in equity securities of well established and sizable companies located in the Asian continent. Will invest between 65% and 100% of assets in Asian "blue chip" organizations. Invests in at least four different countries.
Year organized: 1996
Ticker symbol: GFABX
Group fund code: 990
Discount broker availability: *Fidelity, *Schwab, *Siebert, *White
Dividends paid: Income - June, December; Capital gains - June, December
Portfolio turnover (2 yrs): 35%, 11%
Management fee: 1.00%
Expense ratio: 1.98% (year ending 12/31/97) (4.41% without waiver)

GUINNESS FLIGHT ASIA SMALL CAP FUND ◆
(See first Guinness Flight listing for data common to all funds)

Portfolio managers: Robert Conlon (1998), Agnes Chow (1998)
Investment objective and policies: Long-term capital appreciation. Invests 65% to 100% of assets in smaller capitalization issuers located in the Asian continent, generally those with market caps of less than $1B. Invests in at least four different countries.
Year organized: 1996
Ticker symbol: GFASX
Group fund code: 991
Discount broker availability: *Fidelity, *Schwab, *Siebert, *White
Dividends paid: Income - June, December; Capital gains - June, December
Portfolio turnover (2 yrs): 52%, 22%
Management fee: 1.00%
Expense ratio: 1.76% (year ending 12/31/97) (1.80% without waiver)

GUINNESS FLIGHT CHINA & HONG KONG FUND ◆
(See first Guinness Flight listing for data common to all funds)

Portfolio managers: Lynda Johnstone (1994), Richard Farrell (1997), Edmund Harriss (1997)
Investment objective and policies: Long-term capital growth. Invests at least 85% of assets in equity securities primarily traded in China and Hong Kong. May invest in other mutual funds and restricted securities, and use foreign currency contracts, futures and options for hedging purposes. Up to 15% of assets may be in illiquid securities.

Year organized: 1994
Ticker symbol: GFCHX
Group fund code: 139
Discount broker availability: *Fidelity, *Schwab, *Siebert, *White
Dividends paid: Income - June, December; Capital gains - December
Portfolio turnover (3 yrs): 54%, 30%, 11%
Management fee: 1.00%
Expense ratio: 1.70% (year ending 12/31/97)

GUINNESS FLIGHT GLOBAL GOVERNMENT BOND FUND ◆

(See first Guinness Flight listing for data common to all funds)

Portfolio managers: John Stopford (1994), Michael Daley (1994)
Investment objective and policies: Current income with some capital growth. Invests primarily in government bonds issued by at least three countries, including the U.S. and supranational entities throughout the world. Up to 15% of assets may be in fixed-income securities of issuers in emerging markets and 15% in illiquid securities. May use foreign currency contracts and futures and options for hedging purposes.
Year organized: 1994
Group fund code: 140
Discount broker availability: *Fidelity, *Schwab, *Siebert, *White
Dividends paid: Income - declared and paid monthly; Capital gains - December
Portfolio turnover (3 yrs): 186%, 297%, 203%
Management fee: 0.75%
Expense ratio: 0.75% (year ending 12/31/97) (3.15% without waiver)

GUINNESS FLIGHT MAINLAND CHINA FUND ◆

(See first Guinness Flight listing for data common to all funds)

Portfolio manager: Lisa M. Chow (1998)
Investment objective and policies: Long-term capital growth. Invests between 65% and 100% of assets in equity securities primarily traded in China. Fund invests in "B" shares listed on the Shanghai or Shenzen stock exchanges, "H" shares listed on the Hong Kong Stock Exchange, Red Chips - companies listed in Hong Kong that are controlled by Chinese corporations, and "N" shares listed on the New York Stock Exchange. May invest in other mutual funds and restricted securities, and use forward foreign currency contracts, futures and options for hedging purposes. Up to 15% of assets may be in illiquid securities.
Year organized: 1997
Ticker symbol: GFMCX
Sales restrictions: Fund will close to new investors at $50M.
Discount broker availability: *Fidelity, *Schwab, *White
Redemption fee: 2.00% for shares held less than 60 days, payable to the fund
Dividends paid: Income - June, December; Capital gains - December
Management fee: 1.00%

GW&K EQUITY FUND

222 Berkeley Street
Boston, MA 02116
800-443-4249, 800-225-4236, 617-236-8900
shareholder services 888-495-3863
fax 617-236-1815

Adviser: Gannett Welsh & Kotler, Inc.
Portfolio manager: Edward B. White (1996)
Transfer agent: Countrywide Fund Services, Inc.
Investment objective and policies: Long-term total return: capital growth and growth of income. Invests primarily in a diversified portfolio of equity securities from companies of all sizes perceived to be undervalued and to offer long-term growth potential. Fund will purchase primarily stocks which pay dividends, although it may choose those perceived to offer long-term growth or the possibility of future income. May invest without limit in foreign securities that are publicly traded in the U.S., or in ADRs. May invest in preferred stocks and bonds without regard to quality ratings, but will not invest more than 5% of assets in junk bonds.
Year organized: 1996
Minimum purchase: Initial: $2,000, Subsequent: None; IRA: Initial: $1,000; Automatic investment plan: Initial: $100, Subsequent: $100
Wire orders accepted: Yes
Deadline for same day wire purchase: 4 P.M.
Discount broker availability: Fidelity
Qualified for sale in: AZ, CA, CO, CT, FL, GA, IL, IN, MA, MD, ME, NH, NJ, NY, OR, PA, RI, TX, VA, VT, WY (will register in any state if requested)
Letter redemptions: Signature guarantee required over $25,000
Telephone switching: With GW&K Government Securities fund and Countrywide Trust Short Term Government Income fund
Number of switches permitted: Unlimited
Dividends paid: Income - annually; Capital gains - annually
Portfolio turnover (1 yr): 13%
Shareholder services: IRA, SEP-IRA, Keogh, 401(k), 403(b), systematic withdrawal plan min. bal. req. $5,000
Management fee: 1.00%
12b-1 distribution fee: 0.25%
Expense ratio: 1.25% (nine months ending 9/30/97)
IRA fees: Annual $10, Closing $10

GW&K GOVERNMENT SECURITIES FUND

222 Berkeley Street
Boston, MA 02116
800-443-4249, 800-225-4236, 617-236-8900
shareholder services 888-495-3863
fax 617-236-1815

Adviser: Gannett Welsh & Kotler, Inc.
Portfolio manager: Jeanne M. Skettino (1996)
Transfer agent: Countrywide Fund Services, Inc.
Investment objective and policies: Total return: capital appreciation and income. Invests at least 65% of assets in debt obligations issued or guaranteed by the U.S. Government, its agencies or instrumentalities. May also invest up to 35% of assets in preferred stocks and debt securities not issued by the U.S., including corporate and bank debt, and U.S. dollar denominated foreign issues, without regard to national quality ratings. May invest up to 35% of assets in junk bonds, and up to 15% in foreign issues.
Year organized: 1996
Minimum purchase: Initial: $2,000, Subsequent: None; IRA: Initial: $1,000; Automatic investment plan: Initial: $100, Subsequent: $100
Wire orders accepted: Yes
Deadline for same day wire purchase: 4 P.M.
Discount broker availability: Fidelity
Qualified for sale in: AZ, CA, CO, CT, FL, GA, IL, IN, MA, MD, ME, NH, NJ, NY, OR, PA, RI, TX, VA, VT, WY (will register in any state if requested)
Letter redemptions: Signature guarantee required over $25,000
Telephone switching: With GW&K Equity fund and Countrywide Trust Short Term Government Income fund
Number of switches permitted: Unlimited
Dividends paid: Income - declared daily, paid monthly; Capital gains - annually
Portfolio turnover (1 yr): 44%
Shareholder services: IRA, SEP-IRA, Keogh, 401(k), 403(b), systematic withdrawal plan min. bal. req. $5,000
Management fee: 0.75%
12b-1 distribution fee: 0.25%
Expense ratio: 0.97% (nine months ending 9/30/97)
IRA fees: Annual $10, Closing $10

HARBOR FUNDS ◆

(Data common to all Harbor funds are shown below. See subsequent listings for data specific to individual funds.)

One SeaGate, 15th Floor
Toledo, OH 43666
800-422-1050, 419-247-2477
prices/yields 800-422-1065
fax 419-247-3093

Shareholder service hours: Full service: M-F 9 A.M.-5 P.M. EST; After hours service: prices, yields, prospectuses
Adviser: Harbor Capital Advisors, Inc. (a wholly-owned subsidiary of Owens-Illinois)
Transfer agent: Harbor Transfer, Inc.
Minimum purchase: Initial: $2,000, Subsequent: $500; IRA/Keogh: Initial: $500, Subsequent $100; Automatic investment plan: Initial: $500, Subsequent: $100
Wire orders accepted: Yes, $25,000 initial minimum
Deadline for same day wire purchase: 4 P.M.
Qualified for sale in: All states
Telephone redemptions: Yes
Wire redemptions: Yes
Letter redemptions: Signature guarantee required over $50,000
Telephone switching: With other open Harbor funds
Number of switches permitted: Unlimited, 15 day hold
Shareholder services: IRA, SEP-IRA, directed dividends, systematic withdrawal plan min. bal. req. $10,000
IRA fees: None

HARBOR BOND FUND ◆

(See first Harbor listing for data common to all funds)

Sub-adviser: Pacific Investment Management Co.
Portfolio managers: William H. Gross (1987), Dean Meiling (1994)
Investment objective and policies: Maximum total return consistent with capital preservation and prudent investment management. Invests primarily in investment grade fixed-income securities, and maintains a dollar-weighted average maturity of eight to fifteen years. May invest up to 40% of assets in debt securities of foreign issuers with maximum 20% of assets in debt securities denominated in currencies other than the U.S. dollar. May have up to 15% of assets in illiquid securities and use futures and options for hedging purposes.
Year organized: 1987
Ticker symbol: HABDX
Discount broker availability: Fidelity, Schwab, Siebert, White
Dividends paid: Income - March, June, September, December; Capital gains - December
Portfolio turnover (3 yrs): 203%, 193%, 89%
Management fee: 0.70%
Expense ratio: 0.70% (year ending 10/31/97) (includes waiver)

HARBOR CAPITAL APPRECIATION FUND ◆

(See first Harbor listing for data common to all funds)

Sub-adviser: Jennison Associates Capital Corp. (a wholly owned subsidiary of Prudential Insurance Co. of America)
Portfolio manager: Spiros Segalas (1990)
Investment objective and policies: Long-term capital growth. Invests in equities, including convertibles, of establish companies with above average growth prospects and market capitalizations over $1B. Companies selected will have superior absolute and relative earnings growth, high returns on equity and assets, and strong balance sheets. May invest up to 20% of assets in securities of foreign issuers, have up to 15% of assets in illiquid securities and use futures and options for hedging purposes.

Year organized: 1987 (name changed from Harbor U.S. Equities Fund on April 26, 1990)
Ticker symbol: HACAX
Discount broker availability: Fidelity, Schwab, Siebert, White
Dividends paid: Income - December; Capital gains - December
Portfolio turnover (3 yrs): 48%, 74%, 51%
Management fee: 0.60%
Expense ratio: 0.72% (year ending 10/31/97)

HARBOR GROWTH FUND ◆
(See first Harbor listing for data common to all funds)

Sub-adviser: Emerging Growth Advisors, Inc.
Portfolio manager: Peter Welles (1997)
Investment objective and policies: Long-term capital growth. Invests at least 65% of assets in a diversified portfolio of equity and equity-related securities of approximately 40 companies with market capitalizations or revenues not exceeding $500M at the time of purchase. Companies are selected based on their perceived long-term growth potential. May invest in securities of foreign issuers, have up to 15% of assets in illiquid securities and engage up to 25% of assets in short sales. May use a variety of derivative instruments in an effort to enhance performance and for hedging purposes.
Year organized: 1986 (investment policy changed 5/97; past performance may not be relevant)
Ticker symbol: HAGWX
Discount broker availability: Fidelity, Schwab, Siebert, White
Dividends paid: Income - December; Capital gains - December
Portfolio turnover (3 yrs): 216%, 88%, 88%
Management fee: 0.75%
Expense ratio: 0.98% (year ending 10/31/97)

HARBOR INTERNATIONAL FUND ◆
(See first Harbor listing for data common to all funds)

Sub-adviser: Northern Cross Investments Ltd.
Portfolio manager: Hakan Castegren (1987)
Investment objective and policies: Long-term total return based primarily on capital growth. Invests at least 65% of assets in equity securities of non-U.S. issuers, principally domiciled in Europe, the Pacific Basin and other more highly developed emerging industrialized countries. Fund must diversify across at least three different countries. May invest directly and use ADRs, EDRs, GDRs and IDRs. May have up to 15% of assets in illiquid securities and use futures and options for hedging purposes.
Year organized: 1987
Ticker symbol: HAINX
Special sales restrictions: Fund closed to new shareholders on 9/10/93
Discount broker availability: Fidelity, Schwab, Siebert, White
Dividends paid: Income - December; Capital gains - December
Portfolio turnover (3 yrs): 17%, 10%, 14%
Management fee: 0.85%
Expense ratio: 0.98% (year ending 10/31/97) (includes waiver)

HARBOR INTERNATIONAL GROWTH FUND ◆
(See first Harbor listing for data common to all funds)

Sub-adviser: Jennison Associates Capital Corp. (a wholly owned subsidiary of Prudential Insurance Co. of America)
Portfolio managers: Howard B. Moss (1993), Blair Boyer (1993)
Investment objective and policies: Long-term capital growth. Invests primarily in equity securities of a focused selection of non-U.S. issuers that demonstrate a tendency toward long-term secular growth. Normally invests at least 65% of assets in 30-40 selected stocks of issuers from at least three countries other than the U.S. May invest up to 40% of assets in companies in one of three designated industries - pharmaceuticals, banking, and telephone - with more than 25% of assets in either of the other two designated industries. Fund may invest directly and use ADRs,

EDRs, GDRs and IDRs. May have up to 15% of assets in illiquid securities and use futures and options for hedging purposes.
Year organized: 1993
Ticker symbol: HAIGX
Discount broker availability: Fidelity, Schwab, Siebert, White
Dividends paid: Income - December; Capital gains - December
Portfolio turnover (3 yrs): 55%, 75%, 42%
Management fee: 0.75%
Expense ratio: 1.10% (year ending 10/31/96)

HARBOR INTERNATIONAL FUND II ◆
(See first Harbor listing for data common to all funds)

Sub-adviser: Summit International Investments, Inc.
Portfolio manager: James J. LaTorre, Jr. (1996)
Investment objective and policies: Long-term total return based primarily on capital growth. Invests at least 65% of assets in equity securities of non-U.S. issuers, principally domiciled in Europe, the Pacific Basin and other more highly developed emerging industrialized countries. Fund must diversify across at least three different countries. May invest directly and use ADRs, EDRs, GDRs and IDRs. May have up to 15% of assets in illiquid securities, up to 10% in corporate, government and supranational fixed-income securities, and use a variety of derivative instruments for hedging purposes.
Year organized: 1996
Ticker symbol: HAIIX
Discount broker availability: Fidelity, Schwab, Siebert, White
Dividends paid: Income - December; Capital gains - December
Portfolio turnover (2 yrs): 3%, 3%
Management fee: 0.75%
Expense ratio: 1.17% (year ending 10/31/97) (includes waiver)

HARBOR MONEY MARKET FUND ◆
(See first Harbor listing for data common to all funds)

Sub-adviser: Fischer Francis Trees & Watts, Inc.
Portfolio manager: David Marmon (1994)
Investment objective and policies: High level of current income consistent with preservation of capital and liquidity. Invests in short-term foreign and domestic money market debt securities.
Year organized: 1987
Ticker symbol: HARXX
Dividends paid: Income - declared daily, paid monthly
Check redemptions: $500 minimum
Management fee: 0.30%
Expense ratio: 0.64% (year ending 10/31/96) (includes waiver)

HARBOR SHORT DURATION FUND ◆
(See first Harbor listing for data common to all funds)

Sub-adviser: Fischer Francis Trees & Watts, Inc.
Portfolio manager: Stewart Russell (1994)
Investment objective and policies: Maximum total return consistent with preservation of capital. Invests primarily in high-grade domestic and foreign corporate and government debt securities. Portfolio may invest in securities of any duration so long as it maintains a dollar-weighted average maturity of less than three years. May invest up to 40% of assets in debt securities of foreign issuers, with a maximum of 20% of assets in debt securities denominated in currencies other than the U.S. dollar. May have up to 15% of assets in illiquid securities and use futures and options for hedging purposes.
Year organized: 1992
Ticker symbol: HASDX
Discount broker availability: Fidelity, Schwab, Siebert, White
Dividends paid: Income - declared and paid monthly; Capital gains - December
Portfolio turnover (3 yrs): 1,484%, 1,278%, 3,108%
Management fee: 0.40%
Expense ratio: 0.99% (year ending 10/31/97) (includes waiver)

HARBOR VALUE FUND ◆
(See first Harbor listing for data common to all funds)

Sub-advisers: DePrince, Race & Zollo, Inc. (75% of assets), Richards & Tierney, Inc. (25% of assets)
Portfolio managers: Gregory M. DePrince (1994), David E. Tierney (1993)
Investment objective and policies: Maximum long-term total return with an emphasis on current income. DePrince invests primarily in dividend-paying common stocks of companies perceived to be undervalued that are traded on national exchanges. R&T selects stocks using quantitative analysis techniques that are intended to complement securities selected by DePrince' active management techniques. May have up to 15% of assets in non-dividend paying stocks, 15% in illiquid securities, invest without limit in foreign securities by means of ADRs, EDRs, GDRs and IDRs, and use a variety of derivative instruments for hedging purposes.
Year organized: 1986
Ticker symbol: HAVLX
Discount broker availability: Fidelity, Schwab, Siebert, White
Dividends paid: Income - March, June, September, December; Capital gains - December
Portfolio turnover (3 yrs): 44%, 132%, 136%
Management fee: 0.60%
Expense ratio: 0.83% (year ending 10/31/97)

THE HAVEN FUND
655 Third Avenue, 19th Floor
New York, NY 10017
800-844-4836, 800-428-3664
shareholder services 800-850-7163
212-953-2322, fax 212-818-9044

Adviser: Haven Capital Management, Inc.
Portfolio manager: Colin C. Ferenbach (1994)
Transfer agent and administrator: PFPC, Inc.
Investment objective and policies: Long-term capital growth. Invests at least 65% of assets in equity securities of domestic and foreign companies of any market capitalization that are perceived to be undervalued. May also invest in investment grade, fixed-income securities of domestic and foreign issuers. Up to 35% of assets may be in foreign securities (including ADRs), 15% in illiquid securities and 10% in closed end mutual funds. May use forward foreign currency contracts for hedging purposes.
Year organized: 1994
Ticker symbol: HAVEX
Minimum purchase: Initial: $2,500, Subsequent: $100; IRA: Initial: $2,000; Automatic investment plan: Initial: $1,000
Wire orders accepted: Yes
Deadline for same day wire purchase: 4 P.M.
Discount broker availability: Fidelity, *Schwab, Siebert, *White
Qualified for sale in: All states
Telephone redemptions: Yes, $500 minimum
Wire redemptions: Yes, $10,000 minimum
Letter redemptions: Signature guarantee required over $25,000
Dividends paid: Income - June, December; Capital gains - December
Portfolio turnover (3 yrs): 57%, 67%, 77%
Shareholder services: IRA
Management fee: 0.60%
Administration fee: 0.10%
12b-1 distribution fee: Maximum of 0.25%
Expense ratio: 1.33% (year ending 10/31/97)
IRA fees: Annual $10

HEARTLAND FUNDS
(Data common to all Heartland funds are shown below. See subsequent listings for data specific to individual funds.)

790 North Milwaukee Street
Milwaukee, WI 53202
800-432-7856, 800-478-3863
414-289-7000, 414-347-7777
prices/yields 800-248-1162
fax 414-347-0661

Adviser: Heartland Advisors, Inc.
Transfer agent: Firstar Trust Co.
Minimum purchase: Initial: $1,000, Subsequent:

$100; IRA/Keogh: Initial: $500, Subsequent: $50:
Automatic investment plan: Initial: $50, Subsequent:
$50
Wire orders accepted: Yes
Deadline for same day wire purchase: 4 P.M.
Qualified for sale in: All states (except tax-free bond
fund)
Telephone redemptions: Yes
Wire redemptions: Yes, $500 minimum, $10.00 fee
Letter redemptions: Signature guarantee required
over $25,000
Telephone switching: With other Heartland funds
and Firstar Money Market Funds, $1,000 minimum
Number of switches permitted: 4 per year
Shareholder services: IRA, directed dividends, sys-
tematic withdrawal plan min. bal. req. $25,000
IRA fees: Annual $12.50 ($25 maximum per social
security #, waived for balances over $10,000), Closing
$15

HEARTLAND HIGH-YIELD
MUNICIPAL BOND FUND

(See first Heartland listing for data common to all
funds)

Portfolio managers: Thomas J. Conlin (1997), Greg
D. Winston (1997)
Investment objective and policies: Maximum after-
tax total return by investing for a high level of current
income exempt from federal income tax. Invests pri-
marily in medium and lower quality municipal debt
obligations. Duration is unrestricted, but will generally
average over five years. May invest up to 10% of
assets in issues which are in default, and may invest
without limitation in obligations of higher quality.
Year organized: 1997
Ticker symbol: HRHYX
Discount broker availability: *Fidelity, *Schwab,
*White
Dividends paid: Income - declared and paid monthly;
Capital gains - annually
Portfolio turnover (1 yr): 439%
Management fee: 0.60%
12b-1 distribution fee: 0.10%
Expense ratio: 0.00% (year ending 12/31/97) (1.25%
without waiver)

HEARTLAND LARGE CAP
VALUE FUND

(See first Heartland listing for data common to all
funds)

Portfolio manager: James P. Holmes (1996)
Investment objective and policies: Long-term capital appreciation. Invests primarily in equity securities
of attractively priced, growing companies worldwide,
with market capitalizations over $1B. May also invest
up to 35% of assets in debt securities, including up to
15% in junk bonds. May invest in ADRs of foreign
issuers without limit, and have up to 25% of assets
directly in foreign securities. May use futures and
options to hedge up to 25% of total assets, and sell
short in an effort to enhance performance and for
hedging purposes.
Year organized: 1996
Ticker symbol: HRLCX
Discount broker availability: *Fidelity, *Schwab,
*White
Dividends paid: Income - December; Capital gains -
December
Portfolio turnover (1 yr): 30%
Management fee: 0.75%
12b-1 distribution fee: 0.25%
Expense ratio: 1.36% (year ending 12/31/97) (2.00%
without waiver)

HEARTLAND MID CAP VALUE FUND

(See first Heartland listing for data common to all
funds)

Portfolio manager: Michael A. Berry (1996)
Investment objective and policies: Long-term capital
appreciation. Invests primarily in equity securities of
attractively priced, growing companies worldwide, with
market capitalizations of between $500M and $1B. May
also invest up to 35% of assets in debt securities, including up to 15% in junk bonds. May invest in ADRs of

foreign issuers without limit, and have up to 25% of
assets directly in foreign securities. May use futures and
options to hedge up to 25% of total assets, may leverage
up to 25% of assets, and sell short in an effort to enhance
performance and for hedging purposes.
Year organized: 1996
Ticker symbol: HRMCX
Discount broker availability: *Fidelity, *Schwab,
*White
Dividends paid: Income - December; Capital gains -
December
Portfolio turnover (1 yr): 48%
Management fee: 0.75%
12b-1 distribution fee: 0.25%
Expense ratio: 1.29% (year ending 12/31/97) (1.32%
without waiver)

HEARTLAND SHORT DURATION
HIGH-YIELD MUNICIPAL FUND

(See first Heartland listing for data common to all
funds)

Portfolio managers: Thomas J. Conlin (1997), Greg
D. Winston (1907)
Investment objective and policies: High current
income exempt from federal income taxes, with a low
degree of share price fluctuation. Invests primarily in
short and intermediate term municipal obligations of
medium and lower quality. Maintains an average portfo-
lio duration of three years or less. May invest up to 10%
of assets in issues which are in default, and may invest
without limitation in obligations of higher quality.
Year organized: 1997
Ticker symbol: HRSDX
Discount broker availability: *Fidelity, *Schwab,
*White
Dividends paid: Income - declared and paid monthly;
Capital gains - annually
Portfolio turnover (1 yr): 175%
Management fee: 0.60%
12b-1 distribution fee: 0.10%
Expense ratio: 0.00% (year ending 12/31/97) (0.84%
without waiver)

HEARTLAND SMALL CAP
CONTRARIAN FUND

(See first Heartland listing for data common to all
funds)

Portfolio manager: William J. Nasgovitz (1995)
Investment objective and policies: Maximum long-
term capital growth. Invests primarily in equity securities of attractively priced, growing small companies
worldwide, with market capitalizations of less than
$500M. May invest up to 35% of assets in debt securi-
ties including junk bonds. May invest in ADRs of foreign issuers, and have up to 15% of assets directly in
foreign securities. May use futures and options to
hedge up to 25% of total assets, may leverage up to
25% of assets, and sell short in an effort to enhance
performance and for hedging purposes.
Year organized: 1995
Ticker symbol: HRSMX
Sales restrictions: Fund closed to new investors
10/31/97.
Discount broker availability: *Fidelity, *Schwab,
*Siebert, *White
Dividends paid: Income - December; Capital gains -
December
Portfolio turnover (3 yrs): 103%, 57%, 45%
Management fee: 0.75%
12b-1 distribution fee: 0.25%
Expense ratio: 1.30% (year ending 12/31/97)

HEARTLAND U.S. GOVERNMENT
SECURITIES FUND

(See first Heartland listing for data common to all
funds)

Portfolio managers: Patrick J. Retzer (1988),
Douglas S. Rogers (1996)
Investment objective and policies: High current
income consistent with liquidity and safety of principal. Invests essentially all assets in obligations issued
or guaranteed by the U.S. Government or by its agencies or instrumentalities. Average portfolio maturity is
between three and six years. May use futures and
options to hedge up to 25% of total assets.

Year organized: 1987 (name changed from U.S.
Government Fund in 1994; policy change removing
corporate exposure 3/31/97)
Ticker symbol: HRUSX
Discount broker availability: *Fidelity, *Schwab,
*Siebert, *White
Dividends paid: Income - declared daily, paid
monthly; Capital gains - December
Portfolio turnover (3 yrs): 143%, 30%, 97%
Management fee: 0.65% first $100M to 0.40% over
$500M
12b-1 distribution fee: 0.25%
Expense ratio: 0.87% (year ending 12/31/97) (1.20%
without waiver)

HEARTLAND VALUE FUND

(See first Heartland listing for data common to all
funds)

Portfolio managers: William J. Nasgovitz (1984),
Eric J. Miller (1997)
Investment objective and policies: Long-term capital appreciation. Invests primarily in equity securities
of small companies with market capitalizations of less
than $300M selected on a value basis. May invest in
ADRs of foreign issuers and have up to 15% of assets
directly in foreign securities. May use futures and
options to hedge up to 25% of total assets and sell
short.
Year organized: 1984
Ticker symbol: HRTVX
Special sales restrictions: Fund closed to new share-
holders on 7/1/95
Discount broker availability: *Fidelity, *Schwab,
*Siebert, *White
Dividends paid: Income - December; Capital gains -
December
Portfolio turnover (3 yrs): 55%, 31%, 31%
Management fee: 0.75%
12b-1 distribution fee: 0.25%
Expense ratio: 1.12% (year ending 12/31/97)

HEARTLAND VALUE PLUS FUND

(See first Heartland listing for data common to all
funds)

Portfolio managers: William J. Nasgovitz (1993),
Patrick J. Retzer (1997)
Investment objective and policies: Capital growth
and current income. Invests in equity and debt securities, with allocations adjusted from time to time based
on perceptions of economic conditions and investment
opportunities. Equity securities are primarily of companies with market capitalizations of under $750M
selected on a value basis. Up to 25% of assets may be
in junk bonds and 10% in REITs. May invest in ADRs
of foreign issuers, and have up to 15% of assets directly in foreign securities. May use futures and options to
hedge up to 25% of total assets and sell short.
Year organized: 1993 (name changed from Value &
Income 10/96; nominal policy revisions regarding
market capitalizations affected at the same time.)
Ticker symbol: HRVIX
Discount broker availability: *Fidelity, *Schwab,
*Siebert, *White
Dividends paid: Income - March, June, September,
December; Capital gains - December
Portfolio turnover (3 yrs): 74%, 73%, 150%
Management fee: 0.70%
12b-1 distribution fee: 0.25%
Expense ratio: 1.12% (year ending 12/31/97)

HEARTLAND WISCONSIN
TAX FREE FUND ◆

(See first Heartland listing for data common to all
funds)

Portfolio manager: Patrick J. Retzer (1992)
Investment objective and policies: High current
income exempt from federal and Wisconsin personal
income taxes. Invests primarily in Wisconsin municipal securities and general obligation bonds issued by
Puerto Rico, the Virgin Islands and Guam. Up to 25%
of assets may be in junk bonds and 20% in securities
subject to AMT tax treatment. May use futures and
options to hedge up to 40% of total assets.
Year organized: 1992

Ticker symbol: HRWIX
Discount broker availability: Fidelity, *Schwab, Siebert, *White
Qualified for sale in: WI
Dividends paid: Income - declared daily, paid monthly; Capital gains - December
Portfolio turnover (3 yrs): 8%, 14%, 22%
Management fee: 0.65%
Expense ratio: 0.80% (year ending 12/31/97)

THE HENLOPEN FUND ◆
Longwood Corporate Center, Suite 213
415 McFarlan Road
Kennett Square, PA 19348
800-922-0224, 610-925-0400

Adviser: Landis Assocs., Inc.
Administrator: Fiduciary Management, Inc.
Portfolio manager: Michael L. Hershey (1992)
Transfer agent: Firstar Trust Co.
Investment objective and policies: Long-term capital appreciation; current income secondary. Invests primarily in common stocks expected to appreciate significantly over a one to two year period. May invest in companies with market capitalizations ranging from less than $100M to over $5B. Up to 30% of assets may be in investment grade debt securities and 10% in securities of foreign issuers.
Year organized: 1992
Ticker symbol: HENLX
Minimum purchase: Initial: $10,000, Subsequent: $1,000; IRA: Initial: $2,000, Subsequent: $500; Automatic investment plan: Initial: $500, Subsequent: $100
Wire orders accepted: Yes
Deadline for same day wire purchase: 4 P.M.
Discount broker availability: *Schwab, *White
Qualified for sale in: All states
Telephone redemptions: Yes
Wire redemptions: Yes, $12 fee
Letter redemptions: Signature guarantee not required
Dividends paid: Income - July, December; Capital gains - July, December
Portfolio turnover (3 yrs): 141%, 178%, 148%
Shareholder services: IRA, SEP-IRA, Keogh, 401(k), 403(b), corporate retirement plans, electronic funds transfer (redemption only), systematic withdrawal plan min. bal. req. $50,000
Management fee: 1.00%
Administration fee: 0.20% first $30M to 0.05% over $60M
Expense ratio: 1.60% (year ending 6/30/97)
IRA/Keogh fees: Annual $12.50, Closing $15

HENNESSY BALANCED FUND
The Courtyard Square
750 Grant Avenue, Suite 100
Novato, CA 94945
800-966-4354, 415-899-1555
shareholder services 800-261-6950
fax 415-899-1559
e-mail: ejhmo@aol.com

Adviser: The Hennessy Management Co., L.P.
Portfolio manager: Neal J. Hennessy (1996)
Transfer agent: Firstar Trust Co.
Investment objective and policies: Capital appreciation and current income. Invests one half of portfolio in U.S. Treasury securities having a remaining maturity of approximately one year, and the other half in the ten highest yielding common stocks in the Dow Jones Industrial Average ("The Dogs of the Dow"), with the intent of obtaining substantially the same return as the DJIA but with less risk and volatility. Portfolio will be adjusted twice each month to rebalance stocks held for one year in light of their standing in the dividend return category; those stocks no longer representing the highest dividend yields will be sold.
Year organized: 1996
Ticker symbol: HBFBX
Minimum purchase: Initial: $1,000, Subsequent: $100
Wire orders accepted: Yes
Deadline for same day wire purchase: 4 P.M.
Discount broker availability: *Fidelity, *Schwab, *White
Qualified for sale in: All states

Telephone redemptions: Yes, $1,000 minimum
Wire redemptions: Yes, $1,000 minimum, $12 fee
Letter redemptions: Signature guarantee not required
Telephone switching: With Firstar Money Market Funds
Number of switches permitted: Unlimited but monitored, 2 day hold, $5 fee
Dividends paid: Income - March, June, September, December; Capital gains - December
Shareholder services: IRA, SEP-IRA, automatic investment plan, electronic funds transfer (purchase only), systematic withdrawal plan
Management fee: 0.85%
12b-1 fees: Maximum of 0.75%
Expense ratio: 1.90% (year ending 6/30/97) (2.48% without waiver)
IRA fees: Annual $12.50

HGK FIXED INCOME FUND ◆
P.O. Box 419009
Kansas City, MO 64141-6009
800-808-4921
shareholder services 800-932-7781

Adviser: HGK Asset Management, Inc.
Administrator: SEI Fund Resources
Portfolio managers: Gregory W. Lobo (1994), Anthony Santoliquido (1994), Patricia Bernabeo (1994)
Transfer agent: DST Systems, Inc.
Investment objective and policies: Total return; current income and capital appreciation consistent with the preservation of capital. Invests at least 65% of assets in investment grade, U.S. dollar-denominated fixed-income securities issued or guaranteed by the U.S. or foreign governments, or corporations. May invest up to 35% of assets in mortgage- and asset-backed securities, and up to 15% in restricted securities. Portfolio maintains an average duration of approximately five years.
Year organized: 1994
Minimum purchase: Initial: $2,000, Subsequent: $1,000; Automatic investment plan: Subsequent: $25
Wire orders accepted: Yes
Deadline for same day wire purchase: 4 P.M.
Qualified for sale in: AL, CA, CT, FL, GA, MD, MA, NJ, NY, NC, OH, PA, TN, VA, WA
Telephone redemptions: Yes
Wire redemptions: Yes, $10 fee
Letter redemptions: Signature guarantee not required
Dividends paid: Income - monthly; Capital gains - annually
Portfolio turnover (2 yrs): 264%, 300%
Shareholder services: Electronic funds transfer (redemptions only), systematic withdrawal plan min. bal. req. $50,000
Management fee: 0.50%
Administration fee: 0.20% ($75,000 minimum)
Expense ratio: 1.00% (year ending 10/31/97) (includes waiver)

HIGHLAND GROWTH FUND ◆
1248 Post Road
Fairfield, CT 06430
888-557-3200, 888-244-4452
203-319-3310
fax 203-319-3322
e-mail: highlandct@worldnet.att.net

Adviser: Highland Investment Group, L.P. (a wholly-owned subsidiary of BancBoston Ventures, Inc.)
Portfolio manager: Catherine C. Lawson (1997)
Transfer agent and administrator: Forum Financial Corp.
Investment objective and policies: Long-term capital appreciation. Invests primarily in equity securities of companies of all sizes perceived to demonstrate long-term growth prospects. May invest in start up firms. May invest in foreign securities and ADRs without limit, and invest up to 15% of assets in illiquid securities. May use reverse repurchase agreements, forward foreign currency exchange contracts, short sales against the box, and options and futures for hedging purposes.
Year organized: 1997
Minimum purchase: Initial: $1,000, Subsequent:

$50; IRA: Initial: $500; Automatic investment plan: Initial: $500
Wire orders accepted: Yes
Deadline for same day wire purchase: 4 P.M.
Discount broker availability: *Schwab, *White
Qualified for sale in: All states except NH
Telephone redemptions: Yes, $50 minimum
Wire redemptions: Yes, $10 fee
Letter redemptions: Signature guarantee required over $25,000
Telephone switching: With Forum Daily Assets Treasury Fund (and with the Highland Aggressive Growth fund when it opens)
Number of switches permitted: 5 per year
Dividends paid: Income - December; Capital gains - December
Shareholder services: IRA
Management fee: 1.15%
Administration fee: 0.10% first $100M, 0.05% over $100M ($40,000 minimum)
12b-1 distribution fee: Maximum of 0.25% (not currently imposed)
IRA fee: Annual $10, Initial $10

HOLLAND BALANCED FUND ◆
375 Park Avenue
New York, NY 10152
800-304-6552, 800-249-0763
212-486-2002
fax 212-486-0744

Adviser: Holland & Co., LLC
Administrator: AMT Capital Services, Inc.
Portfolio manager: Michael F. Holland (1995)
Transfer agent: Unified Advisers, Inc.
Investment objective and policies: High total return: capital appreciation and current income. Invests in a combined portfolio of equity and investment grade fixed-income securities. Under normal conditions, portfolio will maintain at least 50% of assets in equities and at least 25% of assets in debt securities, however manager has discretion to establish and adjust asset allocation according to perceived market conditions. May keep as much as 25% of assets in money market instruments, invest as much as 33% of assets in foreign issues, and invest without limit in fixed-income securities of any maturity. May invest up to 25% of assets in a single market sector, and up to 15% of assets in illiquid securities.
Year organized: 1995
Ticker symbol: HOLBX
Minimum purchase: Initial: $1,000, Subsequent: $500; Automatic investment plan: Subsequent: $100
Wire orders accepted: Yes
Deadline for same day wire purchase: 4 P.M.
Discount broker availability: White
Qualified for sale in: All states
Telephone redemptions: Yes
Wire redemptions: Yes
Letter redemptions: Signature guarantee required
Dividends paid: Income - April, July, October, December; Capital gains - December
Portfolio turnover (2 yrs): 5%, 5%
Shareholder services: IRA, electronic funds transfer (purchase only)
Management fee: 0.75%
Administration fee: 0.15% ($50,000 minimum)
Expense ratio: 1.50% (year ending 9/30/97) (2.55% without waiver)
IRA fees: Annual $10, Closing $10

HOMESTEAD FUNDS ◆
(Data common to all Homestead funds are shown below. See subsequent listings for data specific to individual funds.)

4301 Wilson Boulevard
Arlington, VA 22203
800-258-3030, 703-907-6039
fax 703-907-5526

Shareholder service hours: Full service: M-F 8:30 A.M.-5 P.M. EST; After hours service: prices
Adviser: RE Advisers Corp. (a wholly-owned subsidiary of National Rural Electric Cooperative Association)
Transfer agent: Rodney Square Management Corp.
Minimum purchase: Initial: $1,000, Subsequent:

$100; IRA: Initial: $200; Automatic investment plan: Initial: $50, Subsequent: None
Wire orders accepted: Yes
Deadline for same day wire purchase: 4 P.M.
Qualified for sale in: All states
Telephone redemptions: Yes
Letter redemptions: Signature guarantee required over $24,999
Telephone switching: With other Homestead funds, $1,000 minimum
Number of switches permitted: 1 per quarter
Shareholder services: IRA, SEP-IRA, electronic funds transfer, systematic withdrawal plan
IRA fees: Annual $10, Closing $10

HOMESTEAD DAILY INCOME FUND ◆
(See first Homestead listing for data common to all funds)

Portfolio manager: John J. Szczur (1993)
Investment objective and policies: Maximum current income consistent with preservation of capital and liquidity. Invests in high quality money market securities.
Year organized: 1990
Ticker symbol: HDIXX
Check redemptions: $100 minimum
Dividends paid: Income - declared daily, paid monthly
Management fee: 0.50%
Expense ratio: 0.75% (year ending 12/31/96) (includes waiver)

HOMESTEAD SHORT-TERM BOND FUND ◆
(See first Homestead listing for data common to all funds)

Portfolio manager: Douglas G. Kern (1991)
Investment objective and policies: High current income consistent with stability of principal and liquidity. Invests primarily in short-term debt securities rated within the three highest categories assigned by Moody's or S&P. Portfolio generally maintains a dollar-weighted average maturity of three years or less. May use options to hedge up to 25% of total assets.
Year organized: 1991
Ticker symbol: HOSBX
Discount broker availability: White
Dividends paid: Income - declared daily, paid monthly; Capital gains - December
Portfolio turnover (3 yrs): 35%, 13%, 14%
Management fee: 0.60%
Expense ratio: 0.75% (year ending 12/31/96) (includes waiver)

HOMESTEAD SHORT-TERM GOVERNMENT SECURITIES FUND ◆
(See first Homestead listing for data common to all funds)

Portfolio manager: Douglas G. Kern (1995)
Investment objective and policies: High current income consistent with stability of principal and liquidity. Invests primarily in short-term debt securities backed by the full faith and credit of the U.S. Government, including T-Bills, notes and bonds, and securities issued by agencies and instrumentalities guaranteed by the U.S. Government. Portfolio average maturity will not exceed three years.
Year organized: 1995
Discount broker availability: White
Dividends paid: Income - declared daily, paid monthly; Capital gains - December
Portfolio turnover (1 yr): 7%
Management fee: 0.45%
Expense ratio: 0.75% (year ending 12/31/96) (includes waiver)

HOMESTEAD VALUE FUND ◆
(See first Homestead listing for data common to all funds)

Portfolio manager: Stuart E. Teach (1990)
Investment objective and policies: Long-term capital growth and income for the conservative investor; current income secondary. Invests at least 80% of

assets in a carefully selected portfolio of common stocks of established companies believed undervalued. Up to 10% of assets may be invested in ADRs of foreign issuers. May use options to hedge up to 25% of total assets.
Year organized: 1990
Ticker symbol: HOVLX
Discount broker availability: *White
Dividends paid: Income - June, December; Capital gains - December
Portfolio turnover (3 yrs): 10%, 4%, 2%
Management fee: 0.65% first $200M to 0.40% over $400M
Expense ratio: 0.73% (year ending 12/31/96)

HOTCHKIS AND WILEY FUNDS ◆
(Data common to all Hotchkis and Wiley funds are shown below. See subsequent listing for data specific to individual funds.)

800 West Sixth Street, Fifth Floor
Los Angeles, CA 90017
800-236-4479, 213-362-8888
fax 213-623-7880
Internet: http://www.hotchkisandwiley.com

Shareholder service hours: Full service: M-F 8 A.M.-7 P.M. CST; After hours service: prices, balances, orders, last transaction, prospectuses
Adviser: Hotchkis and Wiley, A division of Merrill Lynch Capital Management Group
Transfer agent: Firstar Trust Co.
Year organized: Group changed name from Olympic Trust to Hotchkis and Wiley in 10/94
Minimum purchase: Initial: $10,000, Subsequent: None; IRA: Initial: $1,000; Automatic investment plan: Subsequent: $50
Qualified for sale in: All states
Wire orders accepted: Yes
Deadline for same day wire purchase: 4 P.M.
Telephone redemptions: Yes, $1,000 minimum
Wire redemptions: Yes, $1,000 minimum
Letter redemptions: Signature guarantee required over $50,000
Telephone switching: With other Hotchkis and Wiley funds, $1,000 minimum
Number of switches permitted: Unlimited
Shareholder services: IRA
IRA fees: Annual $12.50

HOTCHKIS AND WILEY BALANCED INCOME FUND ◆
(See first Hotchkis and Wiley listing for data common to all funds)

Portfolio managers: Roger DeBard (1985), Michael Sanchez (1996)
Investment objective and policies: High total return consistent with capital preservation in an attempt to earn at least 4% more than the Consumer Price Index. Allocates at least 20% of assets to equity securities for capital growth, and at least 25% to investment grade fixed-income securities for current income and share price stability. Also invests in money market obligations. Allocation of assets varies depending on market conditions. May invest up to 20% of assets in foreign securities.
Year organized: 1985 (formerly Olympic Total Return Series)
Ticker symbol: HWBAX
Discount broker availability: *Fidelity, *Schwab, *Siebert, *White
Dividends paid: Income - March, June, September, December; Capital gains - December
Portfolio turnover (3 yrs): 117%, 92%, 51%
Management fee: 0.75%
Expense ratio: 0.98% (year ending 6/30/97)

HOTCHKIS AND WILEY EQUITY INCOME FUND ◆
(See first Hotchkis and Wiley listing for data common to all funds)

Portfolio managers: Gail Bardin (1994), Sheldon Lieberman (1997)
Investment objective and policies: Current income, long-term income growth, and capital growth. Invests at least 80% of assets in income-producing equity

securities issued by companies with a record of earnings and dividends. Fund seeks an earnings yield 3% greater than the yield on long-term bonds, and a dividend yield which exceeds that of the composite yield for the S&P 500. May invest in foreign securities and use options and futures for hedging purposes.
Year organized: 1987
Ticker symbol: HWEQX
Discount broker availability: *Fidelity, *Schwab, *Siebert, *White
Dividends paid: Income - March, June, September, December; Capital gains - December
Portfolio turnover (3 yrs): 44%, 24%, 50%
Management fee: 0.75%
Expense ratio: 0.88% (year ending 6/30/97)

HOTCHKIS AND WILEY GLOBAL EQUITY FUND ◆
(See first Hotchkis and Wiley listing for data common to all funds)

Portfolio managers: Sarah H. Ketterer (1997), Patricia McKenna (1997)
Investment objective and policies: Current income, long-term income growth, and capital growth. Invests fully in equity securities of at least three countries, possibly including the U.S. No country other than the U.S. may represent more than 30% of assets. Companies are chosen from a universe of about twenty-one foreign markets on criteria relating to value, stability, and price/earnings ratio. At least 80% of assets will be invested in companies with a record of producing earnings and dividends. Earnings yield must exceed the long-term bond yield of the country be at least 300 basis points, and dividend yield must exceed market average for the parent country. May use currency options and forward foreign currency exchange contracts for hedging purposes.
Year organized: 1997
Discount broker availability: *Fidelity, *Schwab, *White
Dividends paid: Income - June, December; Capital gains - December
Portfolio turnover (1 yr): 18%
Management fee: 0.75%
Expense ratio: 1.00% (6 months ending 6/30/97) (4.43% without waiver)

HOTCHKIS AND WILEY INTERNATIONAL FUND ◆
(See first Hotchkis and Wiley listing for data common to all funds)

Portfolio managers: Sarah H. Ketterer (1990), Harry Hartford (1994), David Chambers (1996)
Investment objective and policies: Current income, long-term income growth, and capital growth. Invests at least 65% of assets in equity securities of companies from at least three non-U.S. countries. At least 80% of equity assets are income producing, with a record of dividend yield and earnings. Companies are chosen from a universe of about twenty-two developed foreign markets on criteria relating to value, stability, and price/earnings ratio. Earnings yield must exceed the long-term bond yield of the country by at least 300 basis points, and dividend yield must exceed market average for the parent country. May use currency options and forward foreign currency exchange contracts for hedging purposes.
Year organized: 1990
Ticker symbol: HWINX
Discount broker availability: *Fidelity, *Schwab, *Siebert, *White
Dividends paid: Income - June, December; Capital gains - December
Portfolio turnover (3 yrs): 18%, 12%, 24%
Management fee: 0.75%
Expense ratio: 1.00% (year ending 6/30/97) (1.07% without waiver)

HOTCHKIS AND WILEY LOW DURATION FUND ◆
(See first Hotchkis and Wiley listing for data common to all funds)

Portfolio managers: Roger DeBard (1996), Michael Sanchez (1996), John Queen (1997)
Investment objective and policies: High total return

consistent with capital preservation, with an emphasis on current yield. Invests at least 75% of assets in investment grade fixed-income securities, and maintains a dollar-weighted average maturity of one to five years and a portfolio duration of one to three years. Invests in government securities, corporate debt securities, commercial paper, mortgage and other asset-backed securities, variable and floating rate debt securities, bank CDs and repurchase agreements. May invest up to 15% of assets in non-U.S. dollar denominated securities of foreign issuers, 25% in securities of foreign issuers denominated in U.S. dollars and 25% in Eurodollar securities.

Year organized: 1993
Ticker symbol: HWLDX
Discount broker availability: *Fidelity, *Schwab, *Siebert, *White
Dividends paid: Income - declared daily, paid monthly; Capital gains - December
Portfolio turnover (3 yrs): 202%, 50%, 71%
Management fee: 0.46%
Expense ratio: 0.58% (year ending 6/30/97) (0.66% without waiver)

HOTCHKIS AND WILEY MID-CAP FUND ◆
(See first Hotchkis and Wiley listing for data common to all funds)

Portfolio managers: Michael Baxter (1997), James Miles (1997)
Investment objective and policies: Current income, long-term growth of income, and capital growth. Invests primarily in undervalued common stocks with capitalizations between $750M and $5B, earnings yield at least 3% greater than the yield on long-term bonds, dividend yield higher than the composite yield on the securities comprising the Russell Mid-Cap Index, and undervalued as determined by a low P/E relative to their expected growth rate. Fund will invest at least 50% of assets in income producing equity securities, and may invest up to 20% of assets in foreign securities.
Year organized: 1997
Discount broker availability: *Fidelity, *Schwab, *White
Dividends paid: Income - June, December; Capital gains - December
Portfolio turnover (1 yr): 23%
Management fee: 0.75%
Expense ratio: 1.00% (6 months ending 6/30/97) (8.26% without waiver)

HOTCHKIS AND WILEY SHORT-TERM INVESTMENT FUND ◆
(See first Hotchkis and Wiley listing for data common to all funds)

Portfolio managers: Roger DeBard (1996), Michael Sanchez (1996), John Queen (1997)
Investment objective and policies: High total return consistent with capital preservation. Invests at least 75% of assets in investment grade fixed-income securities, and maintains a dollar-weighted average maturity of three years or less and a portfolio duration which will generally not exceed one year. Invests in government securities, corporate debt securities, commercial paper, mortgage and other asset-backed securities, variable and floating rate debt securities, bank CDs and repurchase agreements. May invest up to 15% of assets in non-U.S. dollar denominated securities of foreign issuers, 25% in securities of foreign issuers denominated in U.S. dollars and 25% in Eurodollar securities.
Year organized: 1993
Ticker symbol: HWSTX
Discount broker availability: *Fidelity, Schwab, *Siebert, *White
Dividends paid: Income - declared daily, paid monthly; Capital gains - December
Portfolio turnover (3 yrs): 154%, 60%, 81%
Management fee: 0.40% first $100M to 0.25% over $500M
Expense ratio: 0.48% (year ending 6/30/97) (0.96% without waiver)

HOTCHKIS AND WILEY SMALL CAP FUND ◆
(See first Hotchkis and Wiley listing for data common to all funds)

Portfolio managers: James Miles (1995), David Green (1997)
Investment objective and policies: Capital appreciation. Invests primarily in undervalued common stocks with capitalizations of less than $1B, a projected high rate of growth in earnings per share over a five year horizon, a dividend yield higher than the Russell 2000 Index, and a return of equity higher than that of the S&P 500. Fund may invest up to 20% of assets in foreign securities.
Year organized: 1985 (formerly Olympic Series B)
Ticker symbol: HWSCX
Discount broker availability: *Fidelity, *Schwab, *Siebert, *White
Dividends paid: Income - December; Capital gains - December
Portfolio turnover (3 yrs): 88%, 119%, 81%
Management fee: 0.75%
Expense ratio: 1.00% (year ending 6/30/97) (1.30% without waiver)

HOTCHKIS AND WILEY TOTAL RETURN BOND FUND ◆
(See first Hotchkis and Wiley listing for data common to all funds)

Portfolio managers: Roger DeBard (1996), Michael Sanchez (1996), John Queen (1997)
Investment objective and policies: Maximum long-term total return. Invests at least 70% of assets in investment grade fixed-income securities believed to be undervalued. Portfolio maintains a dollar-weighted average maturity of two to fifteen years and an effective duration of two to eight years. Invests in government securities, corporate debt securities, commercial paper, mortgage and other asset-backed securities, variable and floating rate debt securities, bank CDs and repurchase agreements. May invest up to 30% of assets in junk bonds and 15% in emerging markets foreign securities.
Year organized: 1994 (Name changed from Total Return Fund 5/95)
Ticker symbol: HWTRX
Discount broker availability: *Fidelity, *Schwab, *Siebert, *White
Dividends paid: Income - declared daily, paid monthly; Capital gains - December
Portfolio turnover (3 yrs): 173%, 51%, 68%
Management fee: 0.55%
Expense ratio: 0.65% (year ending 6/30/97) (0.95% without waiver)

IAA TRUST COMPANY MUTUAL FUNDS
(Data common to all IAA Trust funds are shown below. See subsequent listings for data specific to individual funds.)

808 IAA Drive
Bloomington, IL 61702
800-245-2100, 800-245-4712
309-557-3222

Shareholder service hours: Full service: M-F 9 A.M.-7 P.M. EST; After hours service: prices, account balances, orders, last transaction
Adviser: IAA Trust Co. (a wholly-owned subsidiary of the Illinois Agricultural Association)
Transfer agent and administrator: First Data Investor Services Group
Sales information: IAA funds carried a 3% load prior to 10/28/96, when all loads except 12b-1 fees were dropped.
Minimum purchase: Initial: $1,000, Subsequent: $100; IRA: Initial: $100, Subsequent: None; Automatic investment plan: Subsequent: $25
Wire orders accepted: Yes, $1,000 minimum
Deadline for same day wire purchase: 12 NN
Qualified for sale in: FL, IL, MO
Telephone redemptions: Yes
Wire redemptions: Yes, $1,000 minimum
Letter redemptions: Signature guarantee required over $25,000

Telephone switching: With other IAA Trust funds
Number of switches permitted: Unlimited
Shareholder services: IRA, Keogh, 401(k), directed dividends, systematic withdrawal plan min. bal. req. $5,000
Administration fee: 0.15% first $50M to 0.05% over $100M
12b-1 distribution fee: 0.25% (MM not included)
IRA fees: Annual $15

IAA TRUST ASSET ALLOCATION FUND
(See first IAA Trust listing for data common to all funds)

Portfolio managers: John Jacobs (1978), Michael E. Marks (1993)
Investment objective and policies: Growth of capital and current income. Invests in a wide range of equity, debt and money market securities, with allocations adjusted according to perceived market conditions. Fixed-income investments will only be purchased if they are rated as one of the four highest grades, although downgraded issues may not necessarily be sold.
Year organized: 1978
Dividends paid: Income - June, December; Capital gains - June, December
Portfolio turnover (3 yrs): 19%, 34%, 21%
Management fee: 0.75%
Expense ratio: 1.46% (year ending 6/30/97)

IAA TRUST GROWTH FUND
(See first IAA Trust listing for data common to all funds)

Portfolio manager: Michael E. Marks (1997)
Investment objective and policies: Capital growth; current income secondary. Invests primarily in equity positions and convertible instruments with equity-like characteristics, but may invest in debt obligations and preferred stocks according to perceived market conditions. Issues are selected which are believed to be undervalued.
Year organized: 1966
Dividends paid: Income - June, December; Capital gains - June, December
Portfolio turnover (3 yrs): 31%, 33%, 32%
Management fee: 0.75%
Expense ratio: 1.16% (year ending 6/30/97)

IAA TRUST LONG-TERM BOND SERIES
(See first IAA Trust listing for data common to all funds)

Portfolio manager: John Jacobs (1997)
Investment objective and policies: Maximum current income and capital appreciation consistent with preservation of capital and the maintenance of liquidity. Invests at least 80% of assets in investment grade corporate and government debt obligations, with at least 65% invested in bonds. May invest up to 20% of assets in issues rated lower than A- by S&P and A3 by Moody's, and up to 10% of assets in foreign securities. Portfolio maintains a dollar-weighted average maturity exceeding ten years.
Year organized: 1997
Dividends paid: Income - June, December; Capital gains - June, December
Portfolio turnover (1 yr): 42%
Management fee: 0.75%
Expense ratio: 0.78% (6 months ending 6/30/97) (3.82% without waiver)

IAA TRUST MONEY MARKET SERIES ◆
(See first IAA Trust listing for data common to all funds)

Portfolio manager: Robert L. Sammer (1991)
Investment objective and policies: High current income consistent with maintaining liquidity and stability of principal. Invests only in high quality rated money market instruments maturing in one year or less.
Year organized: 1981

Check redemptions: $100 minimum
Dividends paid: Income - June, December; Capital gains - June, December
Management fee: 0.50%
Expense ratio: 0.94% (year ending 6/30/97)

IAA TRUST SHORT-TERM GOVERNMENT BOND SERIES
(See first IAA Trust listing for data common to all funds)

Portfolio manager: John Jacobs (1997)
Investment objective and policies: Maximum total return consistent with preservation of capital and prudent investment management. Invests at least 65% of assets in short-term domestic government bonds. Portfolio seeks to maintain a dollar-weighted average maturity of less than three years. May invest in long-term fixed rate bonds that allow the Series to tender (or "put") bonds to the issuer at specified intervals and receive face value for them.
Year organized: 1997
Dividends paid: Income - June, December; Capital gains - June, December
Portfolio turnover (1 yr): 0%
Management fee: 0.50%
Expense ratio: 0.76% (6 months ending 6/30/97) (3.88% without waiver)

IAA TRUST TAX EXEMPT BOND FUND
(See first IAA Trust listing for data common to all funds)

Portfolio manager: Mary S. Guinane (1981)
Investment objective and policies: High current income exempt from federal income tax, consistent with conservation of capital. Invests substantially all its assets in a diversified portfolio of debt obligations issued by the various domestic political entities and their subdivisions, or multi-state agencies or authorities.
Year organized: 1978
Dividends paid: Income - June, December; Capital gains - June, December
Portfolio turnover (3 yrs): 11%, 15%, 25%
Management fee: 0.50%
Expense ratio: 1.14% (year ending 6/30/97)

IAI FUNDS ◆
(Data common to all IAI funds are shown below. See subsequent listings for data specific to individual funds.)

3700 First Bank Place, 601 South Second Avenue
P.O. Box 357
Minneapolis, MN 55440-0357
800-945-3863, 612-376-2950
fax 612-376-2640
Internet: http://www.iaifunds.com

Shareholder service hours: Full service: M-F 7:30 A.M.-5:30 P.M. CST; After hours service: prices, yields, balances, last transaction, indices, prospectuses
Adviser: Investment Advisers, Inc. (a wholly-owned subsidiary of Lloyds TSB Group, plc)
Transfer agent: Investment Advisers, Inc.
Minimum purchase: Initial: $5,000 group total, $1,000 individual fund, Subsequent: $100; IRA: Initial: $2,000 group total, $1,000 individual fund
Wire orders accepted: Yes
Deadline for same day wire purchase: 4 P.M.
Qualified for sale in: All states
Telephone redemptions: Yes
Wire redemptions: Yes
Letter redemptions: Signature guarantee required over $50,000
Telephone switching: With other IAI funds
Number of switches permitted: 4 outbound per fund per year
Shareholder services: IRA, SEP-IRA, 401(k), 403(b), automatic investment plan, directed dividends, electronic funds transfer (redemption only), systematic withdrawal plan min. bal. req. $10,000
IRA fees: None

IAI BALANCED FUND ◆
(See first IAI listing for data common to all funds)

Portfolio managers: Larry R. Hill (1992), Donald J. Hoelting (1996)
Investment objective and policies: Maximum total return: capital appreciation and current income. Invests in common stocks (25% to 75% of assets), bonds (25% to 75%) and short-term instruments (0% to 50%), with a 60%/40% equity to debt ratio generally held as neutral. Allocation among asset categories varies depending on market conditions. fund also invests a portion of assets in private placement venture capital situations. May invest up to 15% of assets in illiquid securities and use foreign securities, options, futures contracts and currency exchange contracts. Fund may sell short.
Year organized: 1992
Ticker symbol: IABLX
Discount broker availability: *Fidelity, *Schwab, *Siebert, *White
Dividends paid: Income - June, December; Capital gains - June, December
Portfolio turnover (3 yrs): 191%, 194%, 257%
Management fee: 1.25% first $200M to 1.10% over $500M
Expense ratio: 1.25% (year ending 3/31/97)

IAI BOND FUND ◆
(See first IAI listing for data common to all funds)

Portfolio managers: Larry R. Hill (1984), Stephen C. Coleman (1996), Scott A. Bettin (1987)
Investment objective and policies: High current income consistent with capital preservation. Invests primarily in a diversified portfolio of investment grade bonds and other high quality debt securities. Up to 25% of assets may be in non-dollar denominated securities of foreign issuers, and up to 10% in junk bonds (although none are rated lower than B). May also invest up to 10% of assets in preferred or convertible stock issues. May use options, futures contracts, currency exchange contracts and sell short.
Year organized: 1977
Ticker symbol: IAIBX
Discount broker availability: *Fidelity, *Schwab, *Siebert, *White
Dividends paid: Income - monthly; Capital gains - December
Portfolio turnover (3 yrs): 482%, 342%, 425%
Management fee: 1.10% (adviser pays all expenses)
Expense ratio: 1.10% (year ending 11/30/97)

IAI CAPITAL APPRECIATION FUND ◆
(See first IAI listing for data common to all funds)

Portfolio manager: Martin J. Calihan (1996)
Investment objective and policies: Long-term capital appreciation. Invests primarily in equity securities of a diversified portfolio of companies perceived to be undervalued based on a proprietary valuation model. Will generally invest in companies with market capitalizations less than $5B, but may invest in companies of any size that offer strong earnings growth potential. May invest up to 15% of assets in foreign issues. May participate in venture capital limited partnerships and leveraged buyouts, and may use derivative instruments for hedging purposes.
Year organized: 1996
Ticker symbol: IACAX
Discount broker availability: *Fidelity, *Schwab, *Siebert, *White
Dividends paid: Income - June, December; Capital gains - June, December
Portfolio turnover (1 yr): 133%
Management fee: 1.40% first $250M to 1.30% over $500M
Expense ratio: 1.25% (year ending 3/31/97) (1.40% without waiver)

IAI DEVELOPING COUNTRIES FUND ◆
(See first IAI listing for data common to all funds)

Portfolio managers: Roy C. Gillson (1995), Sookyong Kwak (1996)
Investment objective and policies: Long-term capital appreciation. Invests primarily in equity securities

of companies domiciled or having substantial operations in developing foreign countries. May invest directly in foreign securities as well as in ADRs, EDRs and GDRs. May use options, futures contracts, currency exchange contracts and sell short.
Year organized: 1995
Ticker symbol: IADCX
Discount broker availability: *Fidelity, *Schwab, *Siebert, *White
Dividends paid: Income - June, December; Capital gains - June, December
Portfolio turnover (2 yrs): 61%, 42%
Management fee: 1.25% first $200M to 1.10% over $400M
Expense ratio: 2.00% (year ending 1/31/97)

IAI EMERGING GROWTH FUND ◆
(See first IAI listing for data common to all funds)

Portfolio manager: David Himebrook (1997)
Investment objective and policies: Long-term capital appreciation. Invests primarily in common stocks of small and medium sized companies (capitalization under $1B) in the early stages of their life cycles with proven or potential for above average growth. May invest in convertible securities, non-convertible preferred stocks and non-convertible debt securities. May invest in securities of foreign issuers with up to 10% of assets denominated in foreign currencies and 15% in illiquid securities. May use options, futures contracts, currency exchange contracts and sell short.
Year organized: 1991
Ticker symbol: IAEGX
Special sales restrictions: Fund closed to new shareholders 2/1/96; reopened 7/2/97
Discount broker availability: *Fidelity, *Schwab, *Siebert, *White
Dividends paid: Income - June, December; Capital gains - June, December
Portfolio turnover (3 yrs): 50%, 63%, 58%
Management fee: 1.25% first $200M to 1.10% over $500M
Expense ratio: 1.19% (year ending 3/31/97)

IAI GOVERNMENT FUND ◆
(See first IAI listing for data common to all funds)

Portfolio managers: Scott A. Bettin (1991), Stephen C. Coleman (1996)
Investment objective and policies: High current income consistent with capital preservation. Invests primarily in debt securities issued, guaranteed or collateralized by the U.S. Government, its agencies or instrumentalities. Fund will generally maintain a dollar-weighted average maturity of approximately ten years, although at times it may be substantially less. Up to 15% of assets may be in junk bonds. May invest in debt securities of foreign issuers and use options, futures contracts and currency exchange contracts. Fund may sell short.
Year organized: 1991
Ticker symbol: IAGVX
Discount broker availability: *Fidelity, *Schwab, *Siebert, *White
Dividends paid: Income - monthly; Capital gains - December
Portfolio turnover (3 yrs): 350%, 152%, 284%
Management fee: 1.10% (adviser pays all expenses)
Expense ratio: 1.10% (year ending 11/30/97)

IAI GROWTH FUND ◆
(See first IAI listing for data common to all funds)

Portfolio managers: David A. McDonald (1994), Mark C. Hoonsbeen (1997)
Investment objective and policies: Long-term capital appreciation. Invests primarily in equity securities of established companies expected to increase earnings at an above average rate. May also invest in government securities, investment grade corporate bonds and debentures, commercial paper, preferred stocks, CDs or other securities. Fund may invest in ADRs of foreign issuers and have up to 15% of assets in securities denominated in foreign currencies and 15% in illiquid securities. May use futures, options and currency exchange contracts and sell short.
Year organized: 1993

Ticker symbol: IAGRX
Discount broker availability: *Fidelity, *Schwab, *Siebert, *White
Dividends paid: Income - June, December; Capital gains - June, December
Portfolio turnover (3 yrs): 134%, 93%, 69%
Management fee: 1.25% first $200M to 1.00% over $500M
Expense ratio: 1.25% (year ending 3/31/97)

IAI GROWTH AND INCOME FUND ◆
(See first IAI listing for data common to all funds)

Portfolio manager: Donald J. Hoelting (1996)
Investment objective and policies: Long-term capital appreciation; income secondary. Invests primarily in a broadly diversified portfolio of common stocks. May also invest in convertible securities, non-convertible preferred stocks and non-convertible debt securities. May invest up to 10% of assets in securities of foreign issuers and up to 15% in illiquid securities. May use futures, options and currency exchange contracts and sell short.
Year organized: 1971 (name changed from IAI Stock Fund in 1993)
Ticker symbol: IASKX
Discount broker availability: *Fidelity, *Schwab, *Siebert, *White
Dividends paid: Income - June, December; Capital gains - June, December
Portfolio turnover (3 yrs): 51%, 89%, 79%
Management fee: 1.25% first $200M to 1.00% over $500M
Expense ratio: 1.25% (year ending 3/31/97)

IAI INTERNATIONAL FUND ◆
(See first IAI listing for data common to all funds)

Sub-adviser: IAI International Ltd.
Portfolio manager: Roy C. Gillson (1990)
Investment objective and policies: Capital appreciation; current income secondary. Invests at least 95% of assets in equity and equity-related securities of non-U.S. issuers. Typically, the fund invests in stocks representative of the Morgan Stanley EAFE Index, but may also invest in other countries. Fund may have more than 50% of its assets in Japan, more than 25% in the UK and more than 25% in Germany, but at least four economies will be represented at any one time. May use forward currency exchange contracts, futures and options and sell short.
Year organized: 1987
Ticker symbol: IAINX
Discount broker availability: *Fidelity, *Schwab, *Siebert, *White
Dividends paid: Income - June, December; Capital gains - June, December
Portfolio turnover (3 yrs): 32%, 39%, 28%
Management fee: 1.25% first $100M to 1.10% over $300M
Expense ratio: 1.65% (year ending 1/31/97)

IAI LATIN AMERICA FUND ◆
(See first IAI listing for data common to all funds)

Lead portfolio manager: Roy C. Gillson (1997)
Investment objective and policies: Long-term capital appreciation. Invests at least 50% of assets in equity securities of Latin American companies, and at least 65% of assets in Latin securities of any type, including private debt obligations, ADRs, GDRs and sovereign debt such as Brady bonds. May invest in restricted securities, or purchase securities not listed in any organized market. There is no minimum requirement for creditworthiness required for any securities. May use futures, options and currency exchange contracts and sell short for hedging purposes.
Year organized: 1996
Redemption fee: 2.00% for shares held less than 1 year, payable to the fund
Dividends paid: Income - annually; Capital gains - annually
Management fee: 3.00% first $100M to 2.65% over $500M

IAI MIDCAP GROWTH FUND ◆
(See first IAI listing for data common to all funds)

Portfolio manager: Mark C. Hoonsbeem (1997)
Investment objective and policies: Long-term capital appreciation. Invests primarily in equity securities of companies with market capitalization of $1B to $3B, with superior performance records, solid market positions, strong balance sheets and a management team capable of sustaining growth. May invest in securities of foreign issuers with up to 10% of assets in securities denominated in foreign currencies and 15% in illiquid securities. May use futures, options and currency exchange contracts and sell short.
Year organized: 1992
Ticker symbol: IAMCX
Discount broker availability: *Fidelity, *Schwab, *Siebert, *White
Dividends paid: Income - June, December; Capital gains - June, December
Portfolio turnover (3 yrs): 72%, 30%, 51%
Management fee: 1.25% first $200M to 1.10% over $500M
Expense ratio: 1.25% (year ending 3/31/97)

IAI MONEY MARKET FUND ◆
(See first IAI listing for data common to all funds)

Portfolio manager: Timothy A. Palmer (1993)
Investment objective and policies: High current income consistent with preservation of capital and liquidity. Invests in a diversified portfolio of money market instruments from both domestic and foreign issuers.
Year organized: 1993
Ticker symbol: IAIXX
Check redemptions: $500 minimum
Dividends paid: Income - declared daily, paid monthly
Management fee: 0.60%
Expense ratio: 0.56% (year ending 1/31/97) (0.63% without waiver)

IAI REGIONAL FUND ◆
(See first IAI listing for data common to all funds)

Portfolio manager: Mark C. Hoonsbeen (1994)
Investment objective and policies: Capital appreciation. Invests at least 80% of assets in equity securities of companies headquartered in Minnesota, Wisconsin, Iowa, Illinois, Nebraska, Montana, North Dakota or South Dakota. May invest in securities of foreign issuers, with up to 10% of assets in securities denominated in foreign currencies and 15% in illiquid securities. May use futures, options and currency exchange contracts and sell short.
Year organized: 1980
Ticker symbol: IARGX
Discount broker availability: *Fidelity, *Schwab, *Siebert, *White
Dividends paid: Income - June, December; Capital gains - June, December
Portfolio turnover (3 yrs): 61%, 90%, 150%
Management fee: 1.25% first $200M to 1.10% over $500M
Expense ratio: 1.21% (year ending 3/31/97)

IAI RESERVE FUND ◆
(See first IAI listing for data common to all funds)

Portfolio manager: Timothy A. Palmer (1991)
Investment objective and policies: High level of capital stability and liquidity and a high level of current income. Invests primarily in investment grade bonds and other debt securities with maturities of 25 months or less. Up to 15% of assets may be in non-dollar denominated securities of foreign issuers. May use futures, options and currency exchange contracts and sell short.
Year organized: 1986
Ticker symbol: IARVX
Discount broker availability: *Fidelity, *Schwab, *Siebert, *White
Check redemptions: $500 minimum
Dividends paid: Income - monthly; Capital gains - June, December

Portfolio turnover (3 yrs): 231%, 261%, 170%
Management fee: 0.85%
Expense ratio: 0.85% (year ending 1/31/97)

IAI VALUE FUND ◆
(See first IAI listing for data common to all funds)

Portfolio manager: Donald J. Hoelting (1996)
Investment objective and policies: Long-term capital appreciation. Invests primarily in stocks of out of favor companies believed undervalued and having unusual opportunities for capital growth due to such factors as changes in management, product line and markets for their goods. May invest up to 10% of assets in securities of foreign issuers and 15% in illiquid securities. May use futures, options and currency exchange contracts and sell short.
Year organized: 1983 (name changed from IAI Apollo Fund in Aug. 1991)
Ticker symbol: IAAPX
Discount broker availability: *Fidelity, *Schwab, *Siebert, *White
Dividends paid: Income - June, December; Capital gains - June, December
Portfolio turnover (3 yrs): 61%, 73%, 102%
Management fee: 1.25% first $200M to 1.10% over $500M
Expense ratio: 1.25% (year ending 3/31/97)

ICAP DISCRETIONARY EQUITY PORTFOLIO ◆
225 West Wacker Drive, Suite 2400
Chicago, IL 60606-1229
888-221-4227, 312-424-9100

Adviser: Institutional Capital Corp.
Administrator: Sunstone Financial Group, Inc.
Lead portfolio manager: Robert H. Lyon (1995)
Transfer agent: Sunstone Investor Services, LLC
Investment objective and policies: Total return superior to that of the S&P 500 with equal or less risk. Invests primarily in U.S. dollar denominated equity securities of companies with market capitalizations of at least $500M. May also invest up to 35% of assets in cash and short-term fixed-income securities. May invest without limit in ADRs or other dollar denominated foreign securities. May use options and futures for hedging purposes.
Year organized: 1995
Minimum purchase: Initial: $10,000, Subsequent: $1,000
Wire orders accepted: Yes
Deadline for same day wire purchase: 4 P.M.
Qualified for sale in: All states
Wire redemptions: Yes, $10 fee
Letter redemptions: Signature guarantee not required
Dividends paid: Income - quarterly; Capital gains - December
Portfolio turnover (2 yrs): 138%, 102%
Shareholder services: IRA, SEP-IRA, Keogh, 401(k), 403(b), corporate retirement plans, systematic withdrawal plan min. bal. req. $100,000
Management fee: 0.80%
Administration fee: 0.175% first $50M to 0.05% over $100M
Expense ratio: 0.80% (year ending 12/31/96) (1.11% without waiver)
IRA fees: None

ICAP EQUITY PORTFOLIO ◆
225 West Wacker Drive, Suite 2400
Chicago, IL 60606-1229
888-221-4227, 312-424-9100

Adviser: Institutional Capital Corp.
Administrator: Sunstone Financial Group, Inc.
Lead portfolio manager: Robert H. Lyon (1995)
Transfer agent: Sunstone Investor Services, LLC
Investment objective and policies: Total return superior to that of the S&P 500 with equal or less risk. Invests primarily in U.S. dollar denominated equity securities of companies with market capitalizations of at least $500M. Is, for all intents, fully invested at all

times; may only hold a maximum of 5% of assets in cash or short-term securities for redemption purposes. May invest without limit in ADRs or other dollar denominated foreign securities. May use options and futures for hedging purposes.
Year organized: 1995
Minimum purchase: Initial: $10,000, Subsequent: $1,000
Wire orders accepted: Yes
Deadline for same day wire purchase: 4 P.M.
Qualified for sale in: All states
Wire redemptions: Yes, $10 fee
Letter redemptions: Signature guarantee not required
Dividends paid: Income - quarterly; Capital gains - December
Portfolio turnover (2 yrs): 125%, 105%
Shareholder services: IRA, SEP-IRA, Keogh, 401(k), 403(b), corporate retirement plans, systematic withdrawal plan min. bal. req. $100,000
Management fee: 0.80%
Administration fee: 0.175% first $50M to 0.05% over $100M
Expense ratio: 0.80% (year ending 12/31/96) (0.97% without waiver)
IRA fees: None

ICM/ISABELLE SMALL-CAP VALUE FUND
One International Place, Suite 2401
Boston, MA 02110
800-472-6114, 617-310-5120
fax 617-310-5124
Internet: http://www.icmfunds.com
e-mail: info@icmfunds.com

Adviser: Ironwood Capital Management, LLC
Portfolio manager: Warren J. Isabelle (1998)
Transfer agent and administrator: First Data Corp.
Investment objective and policies: Capital appreciation. Invests at least 80% of assets in common stocks of companies with market capitalizations of less than $1B that are believed to be undervalued because they are out of favor or unknown. Typically holds 40 to 70 issues. Up to 20% of assets may be invested in larger companies, up to 20% in nonconvertible or convertible debt obligations, and up to 25% in stocks of foreign companies. May make short sales against the box, and use a variety of derivative instruments for hedging purposes.
Year organized: 1998
Special sales restrictions: Fund intends to close when assets reach $500M. Fund offers retail, "Investment Class" shares (profiled here), and "Institutional Class" shares with $500,000 minimums and no 12b-1 fees.
Minimum purchase: Initial: $1,000, Subsequent: $100
Wire orders accepted: Yes
Deadline for same day wire purchase: 4 P.M.
Qualified for sale in: All states
Telephone redemptions: Yes
Wire redemptions: $1,000 minimum, $20 fee
Letter redemptions: Signature guarantee required over $50,000
Dividends paid: Income - annually; Capital gains - annually
Shareholder services: Automatic investment plan, electronic funds transfer (purchase only)
Management fee: 1.00%
Administration fee: 0.12% first $150M, 0.15% next $350M, 0.12% next $150M, to 0.025% over $5B ($55,000 minimum)
12b-1 distribution fee: 0.25%

IMG BOND FUND
(IMG Merged with the Amcore Vintage Funds 2/16/98 and this fund became The Vintage Bond Fund.)

IMG CORE STOCK FUND
(Merged with the Amcore Vintage Equity Fund 2/16/98.)

IMS CAPITAL VALUE FUND ◆
10159 Southeast Sunnyside Road, Suite 330
Portland, OR 97015
800-934-5550, 503-639-9669
Internet: http://www.imscapital.com

Adviser: IMS Capital Management, Inc.
Administrator: AmeriPrime Financial Services, Inc.
Portfolio manager: Carl W. Marker (1996)
Transfer agent: American Data Services, Inc.
Investment objective and policies: Long-term capital growth. Invests primarily in a diversified portfolio of equity securities of large, high quality, dividend-paying U.S. companies with historic market capitalizations exceeding $1B. Attempts to purchase securities at historically low prices, when they are temporarily out of favor and contrary to conventional wisdom. May also invest in corporate and government fixed-income instruments, and may invest in foreign issues by using ADRs. May write covered call options for income.
Year organized: 1996
Ticker symbol: IMSCX
Minimum purchase: Initial: $5,000, Subsequent: $100; IRA: Initial: $2,000
Wire orders accepted: Yes
Deadline for same day wire purchase: 4 P.M.
Discount broker availability: Fidelity, Siebert, *White
Qualified for sale in: All states except MA, NH
Telephone redemptions: Yes
Wire redemptions: Yes
Letter redemptions: Signature guarantee required
Dividends paid: Income - December; Capital gains - December
Portfolio turnover (1 yr): 35%
Shareholder services: IRA, SEP-IRA, automatic investment plan
Management fee: 1.59%
Administration fee: 0.10% first $50M to 0.05% over $100M ($30,000 minimum)
Expense ratio: 1.97% (year ending 10/31/97) (2.54% without waiver)
IRA fees: Annual $15, Closing $15

INDEPENDENCE ONE MUTUAL FUNDS ◆
(Data common to all Independence One funds are shown below. See subsequent listings for data specific to individual funds.)

2777 Inkster Road
Mail Code 10-52
Farmington Hills, MI 48333-9065
800-334-2292
Texas residents only 800-618-8573

Adviser: Michigan National Bank/Independence One Capital Management Corp. (an indirect, wholly owned subsidiary of National Australia Bank Ltd.)
Transfer agent and administrator: Federated Services Co.
Minimum purchase: Initial: $1,000, Subsequent: $100
Wire orders accepted: Yes
Deadline for same day wire purchase: 4 P.M.
Qualified for sale in: All states
Telephone redemptions: Yes
Wire redemptions: Yes, fee if less than $5,000
Letter redemptions: Signature guarantee not required
Telephone switching: With other Independence One funds
Number of switches permitted: unlimited
Shareholder services: automatic investment plan, systematic withdrawal plan min. bal. req. $10,000
Administration fee: 0.150% first $250M to 0.075% over $750M

INDEPENDENCE ONE EQUITY PLUS FUND ◆
(See first Independence One listing for data common to all funds)

Sub-adviser: Sosnoff Sheridan Corp.
Portfolio manager: Sharon Dischinger (1995)
Investment objective and policies: Total return. Invests primarily in the stocks of companies compris-

ing the S&P 100 Index, with at least 80% of assets approximating the weightings found in the index. The balance of assets are primarily invested in additional shares of the same companies, but in different weightings as seen fit by management. May use options and futures for hedging purposes.
Year organized: 1995
Dividends paid: Income - quarterly; Capital gains - annually
Portfolio turnover (2 yrs): 8%, 6%
Management fee: 0.40%
Expense ratio: 0.40% (year ending 4/30/97) (0.70% without waiver)

INDEPENDENCE ONE FIXED INCOME FUND ◆
(See first Independence One listing for data common to all funds)

Portfolio manager: Bruce Beaumont (1998)
Investment objective and policies: Total return; income and capital gains. Invests primarily in a diversified portfolio of high grade, domestic government and corporate fixed-income securities. Fund maintains an average dollar-weighted maturity of between three and eight years. May use options and futures for hedging purposes.
Year organized: 1995
Dividends paid: Income - declared daily, paid monthly; Capital gains - annually
Portfolio turnover (2 yrs): 23%, 4%
Management fee: 0.75%
Expense ratio: 0.55% (year ending 4/30/97) (1.05% without waiver)

INDEPENDENCE ONE MICHIGAN MUNICIPAL BOND FUND ◆
(See first Independence One listing for data common to all funds)

Portfolio manager: Bruce Beaumont (1995)
Investment objective and policies: Current income exempt from federal regular and Michigan personal income taxes. Invests at least 80% of assets in investment grade fixed-income securities issued by or guaranteed by the State of Michigan, or its political instrumentalities, or, fixed-income securities issued by any political entity nationwide that enjoys federal and Michigan tax exempt status. Fund intends to qualify as an investment substantially exempt from the Michigan intangibles tax. Fund is non-diversified and can invest in obligations from a single issuer without limit.
Year organized: 1995
Dividends paid: Income - declared daily, paid monthly; Capital gains - annually
Portfolio turnover (2 yrs): 48%, 39%
Management fee: 0.75%
Expense ratio: 0.70% (year ending 4/30/97) (1.64% without waiver)

INDEPENDENCE ONE MICHIGAN MUNICIPAL CASH FUND ◆
(See first Independence One listing for data common to all funds)

Investment objective and policies: Current, stable income exempt from federal regular income tax and Michigan state income tax, consistent with stability of principal. Additionally, fund provides income exempt from the Michigan intangibles tax and income taxes of Michigan municipalities. Invests at least 80% of assets in Michigan municipal securities with remaining maturities of 397 days or less.
Year organized: 1989
Dividends paid: Income - declared daily, paid monthly
Management fee: 0.40%
12b-1 distribution fee: Maximum of 0.25% (not currently imposed)
Expense ratio: 0.48% (year ending 4/30/97) (0.68% without waiver)

INDEPENDENCE ONE PRIME MONEY MARKET FUND ◆

(See first Independence One listing for data common to all funds)

Investment objective and policies: Current income consistent with stability of principal. Invests in high quality money market instruments maturing in 397 days or less.
Year organized: 1989
Sales restrictions: Prime MM has "A" and "B" shares; "B" shares have no shareholder services fee but require a $1M minimum investment.
Dividends paid: Income - declared daily, paid monthly
Management fee: 0.40%
Shareholder services fee: 0.25%
Expense ratio: 0.60% (year ending 4/30/97) (0.85% without waiver)

INDEPENDENCE ONE U.S. GOVERNMENT SECURITIES FUND ◆

(See first Independence One listing for data common to all funds)

Portfolio manager: Bruce Beaumont (1995)
Investment objective and policies: High current income with consideration of long-term capital gains. Invests in fixed-income securities either issued or guaranteed by the U.S. Government, its agencies or instrumentalities.
Year organized: 1993
Dividends paid: Income - declared daily, paid monthly; Capital gains - annually
Portfolio turnover (3 yrs): 73%, 104%, 75%
Management fee: 0.70%
Expense ratio: 0.57% (year ending 4/30/97) (1.02% without waiver)

INDEPENDENCE ONE U.S. TREASURY MONEY MARKET FUND ◆

(See first Independence One listing for data common to all funds)

Investment objective and policies: Current income consistent with stability of principal. Invests in a portfolio of short-term U.S. treasury obligations.
Year organized: 1989
Dividends paid: Income - declared daily, paid monthly
Management fee: 0.40%
12b-1 distribution fee: Maximum of 0.25% (not currently imposed)
Expense ratio: 0.59% (year ending 4/30/97)

INFORMATION TECH 100 FUND ◆

160 Sansome Street, 17th Floor
San Francisco, CA 94104
800-385-7003, 415-705-7777
800-229-2105
fax 415-705-7775
Internet: http://www.bayisle.com
e-mail: infotech@bayisle.com

Adviser: Bay Isle Financial Corp.
Administrator: Investment Company Administration Corp.
Portfolio manager: William F.K. Schaff (1997)
Transfer agent: American Data Services, Inc.
Investment objective and policies: Capital appreciation. Invests primarily in the common stocks of the scientific and technology companies that comprise the Information Week 100 Index, as published in Information Week magazine. This index was created by the portfolio manager, who is a weekly columnist for the magazine, and should not be considered an index fund in the strictest sense. Management contributes 10% of its fees to 501(c)(3) approved charities. May invest without limit in foreign issues. May use options.
Year organized: 1997
Minimum purchase: Initial: $5,000, Subsequent: $1,000; IRA: Initial: $2,000, Subsequent: $500; Automatic investment plan: Initial: $2,000
Wire orders accepted: Yes
Deadline for same day wire purchase: 4 P.M.
Discount broker availability: *Schwab, *White

Qualified for sale in: All states
Telephone redemptions: Yes, $1,000 minimum, $12 fee
Wire redemptions: Yes, $1,000 minimum, $12 fee
Letter redemptions: Signature guarantee required over $5,000
Redemption fee: 1.00% for shares held less than 6 months (waived for IRAs)
Dividends paid: Income - December; Capital gains - December
Shareholder services: IRA, SEP-IRA, systematic withdrawal plan min. bal. req. $10,000
Management fee: 0.95%
Administration fee: 0.20% ($30,000 minimum)
IRA/Keogh fees: Annual $15, Initial $12, Closing $15

INTERACTIVE INVESTMENTS TECHNOLOGY VALUE FUND ◆

(See Firsthand Funds)

INVESCO FUNDS

(Data common to all INVESCO funds are shown below. See subsequent listings for data specific to individual funds.)

7800 East Union Avenue, Suite 800
Denver, CO 80237
800-525-8085, 303-930-6300
prices/yields 800-424-8085
Internet: http://www.invesco.com

Shareholder service hours: Full service: M-F 6 A.M.-6P.M., Sat., 10 A.M.-3 P.M. MST; After hours service: prices, yields, account balances, orders, last transaction, indexes, total returns, statements, tax forms
Adviser: INVESCO Funds Group, Inc. (name changed from Financial Programs, Inc. on 1/1/91. Fund names changed from Financial to INVESCO on 7/1/93.)
Transfer agent: INVESCO Funds Group, Inc.
Minimum purchase: Initial: $1,000, Subsequent: $50; Ira/Keogh: Initial: $250 (exceptions noted): Automatic investment plan: Initial: $50
Wire orders accepted: Yes
Deadline for same day wire purchase: 4 P.M.
Qualified for sale in: All states
Telephone redemptions: Yes
Wire redemptions: Yes, $1,000 minimum
Letter redemptions: Signature guarantee not required
Telephone switching: With other INVESCO funds
Number of switches permitted: 4 per fund per year, $250 minimum
Shareholder services: IRA, SEP-IRA, Keogh, 401(k), 403(b), corporate retirement plans, directed dividends, electronic funds transfer, systematic withdrawal plan min. bal. req. $10,000
IRA fees: Annual $10, Initial $5
Keogh fees: Annual $10

INVESCO ASIAN GROWTH FUND

(See first INVESCO listing for data common to all funds)

Portfolio manager: William Barron (1996)
Investment objective and policies: Capital appreciation. Invests at least 65% of assets in equity securities of companies domiciled in Asia excluding Japan. Fund has not established any minimum investment standards; holdings may be of any capitalization, industry, or limited history and thus should be considered speculative. Management may choose, although it is not likely, to invest up to 50% of assets in a single country. Invests the balance of assets in debt securities issued by the U.S. Government, Asian issuers, or foreign governments, including as much as 30% of assets in junk bonds. May use derivative instruments for hedging purposes.
Year organized: 1996
Ticker symbol: IVAGX
Group fund code: 41
Discount broker availability: *Schwab
Redemption fee: 1.00% for shares held less than 90 days, payable to the fund

Dividends paid: Income - July; Capital gains - December
Portfolio turnover (2 yrs): 161%, 2%
Management fee: 0.75% first $500M to 0.55% over $1B
12b-1 distribution fee: 0.25%
Expense ratio: 2.05% (year ending 7/31/97) (2.10% without waiver)

INVESCO BALANCED FUND

(See first INVESCO listing for data common to all funds)

Portfolio managers: Charles P. Mayer (1996), Donovan J. Paul (1994)
Investment objective and policies: High total return: capital appreciation and current income. Invests in equity and bond securities. Normally invests 50% to 70% of assets in equity securities (primarily common stocks with some preferred stocks and convertible securities). Remainder of assets are in fixed-income securities including cash reserves, with at least 25% of total assets in fixed-income senior securities. Up to 25% of assets may be invested directly foreign securities and 15% in illiquid securities. Fund may use futures and options for hedging purposes.
Year organized: 1993
Ticker symbol: IMABX
Group fund code: 71
Discount broker availability: *Fidelity, *Schwab, *White
Dividends paid: Income - January, April, July, October; Capital gains - December
Portfolio turnover (3 yrs): 155%, 259%, 255%
Management fee: 0.60% first $350M to 0.50% over $700M
12b-1 distribution fee: 0.25%
Expense ratio: 1.29% (year ending 7/31/97) (1.34% without waiver)

INVESCO CASH RESERVES ◆

(See first INVESCO listing for data common to all funds)

Portfolio manager: Richard R. Hinderlie (1993)
Investment objective and policies: Current income consistent with liquidity and safety of capital. Invests in money market instruments.
Year organized: 1976 (name changed from Daily Income Shares on 7/1/93)
Ticker symbol: FDSXX
Group fund code: 25
Check redemptions: $500 minimum
Dividends paid: Income - declared daily, paid monthly
Management fee: 0.50% first $300M to 0.30% over $500M
Expense ratio: 0.86% (year ending 5/31/97) (0.92% without waiver)

INVESCO DYNAMICS FUND

(See first INVESCO listing for data common to all funds)

Portfolio managers: Timothy J. Miller (1993), Thomas Wald (1997)
Investment objective and policies: Capital appreciation through aggressive investment policies. Invests primarily in common stocks, but may also invest in bonds, convertible debentures, and preferred stocks when deemed appropriate. May hold securities for relatively short periods, resulting in high turnover. Up to 25% of assets may be in non-dollar denominated foreign securities, and fund may invest in ADRs without limit.
Year organized: 1967
Ticker symbol: FIDYX
Group fund code: 20
Discount broker availability: *Fidelity, *Schwab, Siebert, *White
Dividends paid: Income - April, December; Capital gains - December
Portfolio turnover (3 yrs): 204%, 196%, 176%
Management fee: 0.60% first $350M to 0.50% over $700M
12b-1 distribution fee: 0.25%
Expense ratio: 1.16% (year ending 4/30/97)

INVESCO EMERGING MARKETS FUND
(See first INVESCO listing for data common to all funds)

Portfolio manager: Team managed
Investment objective and policies: Capital appreciation. Invests at least 65% of assets in equity securities of companies located in emerging markets countries as identified by the World Bank. This would generally exclude: the U.S., Canada, Japan, Australia, New Zealand, and the nations in Western Europe other than Greece and Turkey. Management may choose, although it is not likely, to invest up to 50% of assets in a single country. There are no limitations on the market capitalizations of a company. May also invest without limit in debt obligations if deemed advisable, including up to 35% of assets in junk bonds. May use foreign forward currency contracts and options and futures for hedging purposes.
Year organized: 1998
Dividends paid: Income - December; Capital gains - December
Management fee: 1.00% first $500M to 0.75% over $1B
12b-1 distribution fee: 0.25%

INVESCO EUROPEAN FUND ◆
(See first INVESCO listing for data common to all funds)

Portfolio manager: Team managed
Investment objective and policies: Capital appreciation. Invests at least 80% of assets in equity securities of companies domiciled in specific Western European countries, including: Belgium, Denmark, England, Finland, France, Germany, Italy, the Netherlands, Norway, Spain, Sweden, and Switzerland. There are no limitations on size of company or percentage of assets invested in companies domiciled in any one country.
Year organized: 1986 (name changed from Strategic - European Portfolio on 7/1/93)
Ticker symbol: FEURX
Group fund code: 56
Discount broker availability: *Fidelity, *Schwab, Siebert, *White
Dividends paid: Income - October, December; Capital gains - December
Portfolio turnover (3 yrs): 96%, 70%, 44%
Management fee: 0.75% first $350M to 0.55% over $700M
Expense ratio: 1.25% (year ending 10/31/97)

INVESCO EUROPEAN SMALL COMPANY FUND
(See first INVESCO listing for data common to all funds)

Portfolio managers: Andy Crossley (1995), Claire Griffiths (1995)
Investment objective and policies: Capital appreciation. Invests in equity securities of European companies whose market caps place them in the same size range as U.S. companies in the lowest 25% of market capitalizations, typically under $1B. Invests in at least five different countries, and may not invest more than 50% of assets in any one country.
Year organized: 1995
Ticker symbol: IVECX
Group fund code: 37
Discount broker availability: *Fidelity, *Schwab, Siebert, *White
Dividends paid: Income - July; Capital gains - December
Portfolio turnover (2 yrs): 87%, 141%
Management fee: 0.75% first $500M to 0.55% over $1B
12b-1 distribution fee: 0.25%
Expense ratio: 1.62% (year ending 7/31/97)

INVESCO GROWTH FUND
(See first INVESCO listing for data common to all funds)

Portfolio managers: Timothy J. Miller (1996), Trent E. May (1996)
Objective and policies: Long-term capital growth; income secondary. Invests primarily in common

stocks of companies representing major fields of business and industrial activity. May also invest in bonds, convertible debentures, and preferred stocks when deemed appropriate. Up to 25% of assets may be in non-dollar denominated foreign securities with securities of Canadian issuers and ADRs of other foreign issuers not subject to this limitation.
Year organized: 1935 (name changed from Industrial Fund on 7/1/93)
Ticker symbol: FLRFX
Group fund code: 10
Discount broker availability: *Fidelity, *Schwab, Siebert, *White
Dividends paid: Income - February, May, August, November; Capital gains - December
Portfolio turnover (3 yrs): 286%, 207%, 111%
Management fee: 0.60% first $350M to 0.50% over $700M
12b-1 distribution fee: 0.25%
Expense ratio: 1.07% (year ending 8/31/97)

INVESCO HIGH YIELD FUND
(See first INVESCO listing for data common to all funds)

Portfolio manager: Donovan J. Paul (1994)
Investment objective and policies: High current income. Invests primarily in bonds and other debt securities, including municipals, rated in the medium and lower categories (BB or lower, but not below CCC); may also invest up to 10% of assets in unrated and restricted securities.
Year organized: 1984 (name changed from Bond Shares - High Yield Portfolio on 7/1/93)
Ticker symbol: FHYPX
Group fund code: 31
Discount broker availability: *Fidelity, *Schwab, Siebert, *White
Dividends paid: Income - declared daily, paid monthly; Capital gains - December
Portfolio turnover (3 yrs): 129%, 266%, 201%
Management fee: 0.50% first $300M to 0.30% over $500M
12b-1 distribution fee: 0.25%
Expense ratio: 1.00% (year ending 8/31/97)

INVESCO INDUSTRIAL INCOME FUND
(See first INVESCO listing for data common to all funds)

Portfolio managers: Donovan J. Paul (1994), Charles P. Mayer (1993)
Investment objective and policies: Best possible current income; capital growth secondary. Invests at least 65% of assets in dividend-paying common stocks providing relatively high yield and stable return, with potential for long-term capital appreciation during normal markets. May invest up to 10% of assets in common stock that is not paying a dividend. May invest the balance in convertible bonds, preferred stocks, and straight debt securities. Up to 25% of assets may be in foreign debt securities and 15% in junk bonds.
Year organized: 1960
Ticker symbol: FIIIX
Group fund code: 15
Discount broker availability: *Fidelity, *Schwab, Siebert, *White
Dividends paid: Income - March, June, September, December; Capital gains - June, December
Portfolio turnover (3 yrs): 47%, 63%, 54%
Management fee: 0.60% first $350M to 0.40% over $4B
12b-1 distribution fee: 0.25%
Expense ratio: 0.95% (year ending 6/30/97) (0.98% without waiver)

INVESCO INTERMEDIATE GOVERNMENT BOND FUND ◆
(See first INVESCO listing for data common to all funds)

Portfolio managers: James O. Baker (1993), Ralph H. Jenkins, Jr. (1997)
Investment objective and policies: High total return without regard to federal income tax considerations. Invests at least 65% of assets in obligations of the U.S. Government, its agencies and instrumentalities that

have maturities of three to five years. Up to 35% of assets may be invested in investment grade corporate debt obligations. Fund may use interest rate futures and options thereon and covered options on portfolio securities.
Year organized: 1986 (prior to 1/1/91 fund was Institutional Income Fund, the successor to Shearwater Income, Inc.; 80 to 1 split 1/2/91.)
Ticker symbol: FIGBX
Group fund code: 47
Discount broker availability: *Fidelity, *Schwab, Siebert, *White
Dividends paid: Income - declared daily, paid monthly; Capital gains - December
Portfolio turnover (3 yrs): 37%, 63%, 92%
Management fee: 0.60% of first $500M to 0.40% over $1B
Expense ratio: 1.02% (year ending 8/31/97) (1.37% without waiver)

INVESCO INTERNATIONAL GROWTH FUND ◆
(See first INVESCO listing for data common to all funds)

Portfolio managers: Team managed
Investment objective and policies: High total return without regard to federal income tax considerations. Invests at least 65% of assets in foreign equities, generally in developed countries, of at least three different countries outside of the U.S. Up to 10% of assets can be in developing countries. Fund may use forward currency exchange contracts to manage exchange rate risk.
Year organized: 1987 (prior to 1/1/91 fund was Institutional International Fund; 80 to 1 split 1/2/91)
Ticker symbol: FSIGX
Group fund code: 49
Discount broker availability: *Fidelity, *Schwab, Siebert, *White
Dividends paid: Income - July; Capital gains - December
Portfolio turnover (3 yrs): 62%, 87%, 46%
Management fee: 1.00% of first $500M to 0.65% over $1B
Expense ratio: 1.71% (year ending 10/31/97)

INVESCO LATIN AMERICAN GROWTH FUND
(See first INVESCO listing for data common to all funds)

Lead portfolio managers: Peter Jarvis (1996), Jane Lyon (1996)
Investment objective and policies: Long-term capital appreciation. Invests at least 65% of assets in common stocks, and to a lesser degree, depository receipts, preferred stocks, and convertibles of Latin American issuers of all sizes. Companies are selected based on perceptions of strong earnings growth reflecting the underlying economic activity within the country in which they operate. Countries include Mexico, Central and South America, and the Spanish speaking islands of the Caribbean.
Year organized: 1995
Ticker symbol: IVSLX
Group fund code: 34
Discount broker availability: *Schwab
Redemption fee: 1.00% on shares held less than 90 days
Dividends paid: Income - July; Capital gains - December
Portfolio turnover (3 yrs): 72%, 29%, 30%
Management fee: 0.75% first $500M to 0.55% over $1B
12b-1 distribution fee: 0.25%
Expense ratio: 1.76% (year ending 7/31/97)

INVESCO MULTI-ASSET ALLOCATION FUND
(See first INVESCO listing for data common to all funds)

Portfolio manager: Robert Slotpole (1994)
Investment objective and policies: High total return: capital growth and current income. Fund allocates assets among six classes. Numbers in parens indicate

default weightings and range. Large cap stocks (35%, 0-70%), fixed-income (25%, 0-50%), small cap stocks, real estate stocks, international stocks and cash (all 10%, 0-30% each). Allocations are adjusted to reflect changes in economic and market conditions.
Year organized: 1993
Ticker symbol: IMAAX
Group fund code: 70
Discount broker availability: *Fidelity, *Schwab, Siebert, *White
Dividends paid: Income - January, April, July, October; Capital gains - December
Portfolio turnover (3 yrs): 98%, 92%, 79%
Management fee: 0.75% first $500M to 0.50% over $1B
12b-1 distribution fee: 0.25%
Expense ratio: 1.55% (year ending 7/31/97) (1.97% without waiver)

INVESCO PACIFIC BASIN FUND ◆
(See first INVESCO listing for data common to all funds)

Lead portfolio manager: Ana Tong (1997)
Investment objective and policies: Long-term capital appreciation. Invests at least 80% of assets in equity securities of companies domiciled in the following Far Eastern or Western Pacific countries: Japan, Australia, Hong Kong, Malaysia, Singapore and the Philippines. There are no limitations on size of company or percentage of assets invested in companies domiciled in any one country.
Year organized: 1984 (name changed from Strategic - Pacific Basin Portfolio on 7/1/93)
Ticker symbol: FPBSX
Group fund code: 54
Discount broker availability: *Fidelity, *Schwab, Siebert, *White
Dividends paid: Income - October; Capital gains - December
Portfolio turnover (3 yrs): 56%, 70%, 30%
Management fee: 0.75% first $350M to 0.55% over $700M
Expense ratio: 1.72% (year ending 10/31/97)

INVESCO REALTY FUND
(See first INVESCO listing for data common to all funds)

Sub-adviser: INVESCO Realty Advisors, Inc.
Portfolio managers: Joe V. Rodriguez, Jr. (1997), Todd A. Johnson (1997), James W. Trowbridge (1997)
Investment objective and policies: Above average current income; long-term capital appreciation secondary. Invests at least 80% of assets in a broadly diversified range of real estate markets and property types, in addition to REITs. May invest in real estate brokers, home builders, real estate developers and companies with significant involvement in the industry, such as building supply companies or financial institutions which write mortgages.
Year organized: 1997
Ticker symbol: IVSRX
Group fund code: 42
Discount broker availability: *Fidelity, *Schwab, *White
Dividends paid: Income - quarterly; Capital gains - December
Portfolio turnover (1 yr): 70%
Management fee: 0.75%
12b-1 distribution fee: Maximum of 0.25%
Expense ratio: 1.20% (seven months ending 7/31/97) (1.83% without waiver)

INVESCO S&P 500 FUND
(See first INVESCO listing for data common to all funds)

Sub-adviser: World Asset Management
Investment objective and policies: To provide both price performance and income comparable to the S&P 500 Composite Stock Index. Fund invests in the equity securities that comprise the Index in approximately the same weightings, and in other derivative instruments based upon the Index.
Year organized: 1997

Group fund code: 23 (Class II) 22 (Class I)
Special sales restrictions: Only class II shares are available at retail minimums. Class I shares are available with a minimum investment of $250,000.
Minimum purchase: Initial: $5,000
Redemption fee: 1.00% for shares held less than three months, payable to the fund
Dividends paid: Income - January, April, July, October; Capital gains - December
Management fee: 0.25%
12b-1 distribution fee: Maximum of 0.25% (Class II shares only)

INVESCO SELECT INCOME FUND
(See first INVESCO listing for data common to all funds)

Portfolio manager: Donovan J. Paul (1994)
Investment objective and policies: High current income. Invests at least 90% in marketable debt securities of established companies and government and municipal issues. At least 50% of assets will be in securities rated investment grade. Up to 50% may be invested in lower grade (Ba or less by Moody's, BB or less by S&P) or unrated securities.
Year organized: 1976 (formerly Bond Shares - Bond Shares Portfolio. Name changed from Bond Shares - Select Income Portfolio on 7/1/93)
Ticker symbol: FBDSX
Group fund code: 30
Discount broker availability: *Fidelity, *Schwab, Siebert, *White
Dividends paid: Income - declared daily, paid monthly; Capital gains - December
Portfolio turnover (3 yrs): 263%, 210%, 181%
Management fee: 0.55% first $300M to 0.35% over $500M
12b-1 distribution fee: 0.25%
Expense ratio: 1.03% (year ending 8/31/97) (1.21% without waiver)

INVESCO SHORT-TERM BOND FUND
(See first INVESCO listing for data common to all funds)

Portfolio managers: Richard R. Hinderlie (1993), Donovan J. Paul (1994)
Investment objective and policies: High current income consistent with minimum fluctuation in principal value and liquidity. Invests at least 65% of assets in all types of investment grade debt securities; fixed rate and variable corporate, government and government agency issues which may or may not be guaranteed. Up to 25% of assets may be invested in foreign debt securities; securities of Canadian issuers and ADRs of other foreign issuers are not subject to this limitation. May invest up to 15% of assets in junk bonds. Fund maintains a dollar-weighted average maturity of three years or less.
Year organized: 1993
Ticker symbol: INIBX
Group fund code: 33
Discount broker availability: *Fidelity, *Schwab, *White
Dividends paid: Income - declared daily, paid monthly; Capital gains - December
Portfolio turnover (3 yrs): 331%, 103%, 68%
Management fee: 0.50% first $300M to 0.30% over $500M
12b-1 distribution fee: 0.25%
Expense ratio: 0.83% (year ending 8/31/97) (1.84% without waiver)

INVESCO SMALL COMPANY GROWTH FUND
(See first INVESCO listing for data common to all funds)

Portfolio managers: Stacie L. Cowell (1997), Timothy J. Miller (1997), Trent E. May (1997)
Investment objective and policies: Long-term capital growth. Invests primarily in equity securities of emerging growth companies with market capitalization of less than $1B at time of purchase. Up to 25% of assets may be in non-dollar denominated foreign securities, although securities of Canadian issuers and ADRs of other foreign issuers not subject to this limi-

tation. Stocks selected are believed undervalued and/or to have earnings that may be expected to grow faster than the U.S. economy in general.
Year organized: 1991 (name changed from Emerging Growth 2/1/97)
Ticker symbol: FIEGX
Group fund code: 60
Discount broker availability: *Fidelity, *Schwab, Siebert, *White
Dividends paid: Income - May, December; Capital gains - December
Portfolio turnover (3 yrs): 216%, 221%, 228%
Management fee: 0.75% first $350M to 0.55% over $700M
12b-1 distribution fee: 0.25%
Expense ratio: 1.52% (year ending 5/31/97)

INVESCO SMALL COMPANY VALUE FUND ◆
(See first INVESCO listing for data common to all funds)

Portfolio manager: Robert Slotpole (1994)
Investment objective and policies: Long-term capital growth. Invests primarily in equity securities of U.S. companies smaller than the 1,000 U.S. companies having the largest capitalizations - generally in the $10M to $600M range, focusing on companies perceived to be undervalued by the market. Up to 25% of assets may be in foreign securities and 15% in illiquid securities. May use futures and options and hedge up to 25% of total assets.
Year organized: 1993 (name changed from Small Company Fund 2/1/97)
Ticker symbol: IDSCX
Group fund code: 74
Discount broker availability: *Fidelity, *Schwab, *White
Dividends paid: Income - January, April, July, October; Capital gains - December
Portfolio turnover (3 yrs): 147%, 156%, 73%
Management fee: 0.75%
Expense ratio: 1.25% (year ending 7/31/97)

INVESCO STRATEGIC - ENERGY PORTFOLIO
(See first INVESCO listing for data common to all funds)

Portfolio manager: John Segner (1997)
Investment objective and policies: Capital appreciation. Invests at least 80% of assets in common stocks and securities convertible into common stock of companies in oil, natural gas, coal, uranium, etc., transportation, distribution or processing services, production services, and research and development of energy, including energy conversion, conservation and pollution control. Up to 25% of assets may be in non-dollar denominated foreign securities, although securities of Canadian issuers and ADRs of other foreign issuers are not subject to this limitation. May invest up to 10% of assets in a single issuer, and use options and futures for hedging purposes.
Year organized: 1984
Ticker symbol: FSTEX
Group fund code: 50
Discount broker availability: *Fidelity, *Schwab, Siebert, *White
Dividends paid: Income - October; Capital gains - December
Portfolio turnover (3 yrs): 249%, 392%, 300%
Management fee: 0.75% first $350M to 0.55% over $700M
12b-1 distribution fee: Maximum of 0.25%
Expense ratio: 1.21% (year ending 10/31/97)

INVESCO STRATEGIC - ENVIRONMENTAL SERVICES PORTFOLIO
(See first INVESCO listing for data common to all funds)

Portfolio manager: Gerard F. Hallaren, Jr. (1996)
Investment objective and policies: Capital appreciation. Invests at least 80% of assets in common stocks and securities convertible into common stock of companies engaged in products and services concerning waste

management, pollution control and other companies offering products and services related to environmental concerns in the United States and foreign countries. May invest in securities of foreign issuers without limit. May invest up to 10% of assets in a single issuer, and use options and futures for hedging purposes.
Year organized: 1991
Ticker symbol: FSEVX
Group fund code: 59
Discount broker availability: *Fidelity, *Schwab, Siebert, *White
Dividends paid: Income - October; Capital gains - December
Portfolio turnover (3 yrs): 187%, 142%, 195%
Management fee: 0.75% first $350M to 0.55% over $700M
12b-1 distribution fee: Maximum of 0.25%
Expense ratio: 1.72% (year ending 10/31/97) (2.16% without waiver)

INVESCO STRATEGIC - FINANCIAL SERVICES PORTFOLIO
(See first INVESCO listing for data common to all funds)

Portfolio managers: Daniel B. Leonard (1996), Jeffrey G. Morris (1997)
Investment objective and policies: Capital appreciation. Invests at least 80% of assets in common stocks and securities convertible into common stock of companies primarily engaged in businesses involving financial services, including banks, savings and loans, finance companies, leasing, securities brokerage and insurance. Up to 25% of assets may be in non-dollar denominated foreign securities, although securities of Canadian issuers and ADRs of other foreign issuers are not subject to this limitation. May invest up to 10% of assets in a single issuer, and use options and futures for hedging purposes.
Year organized: 1986
Ticker symbol: FSFSX
Group fund code: 57
Discount broker availability: *Fidelity, *Schwab, Siebert, *White
Dividends paid: Income - October; Capital gains - December
Portfolio turnover (3 yrs): 96%, 141%, 171%
Management fee: 0.75% first $350M to 0.55% over $700M
12b-1 distribution fee: Maximum of 0.25%
Expense ratio: 0.99% (year ending 10/31/97)

INVESCO STRATEGIC - GOLD PORTFOLIO
(See first INVESCO listing for data common to all funds)

Portfolio manager: Daniel B. Leonard (1989)
Investment objective and policies: Long-term capital appreciation. Invests at least 80% of assets in common stocks and securities convertible into common stock of companies in mining, exploration, processing, dealing or investing in gold. Up to 10% of assets may be in gold bullion. May invest in securities of foreign issuers without limit. May invest up to 10% of assets in a single issuer, and use options and futures for hedging purposes.
Year organized: 1984
Ticker symbol: FGLDX
Group fund code: 51
Discount broker availability: *Fidelity, *Schwab, Siebert, *White
Dividends paid: Income - October; Capital gains - December
Portfolio turnover (3 yrs): 148%, 155%, 72%
Management fee: 0.75% first $350M to 0.55% over $700M
12b-1 distribution fee: Maximum of 0.25%
Expense ratio: 1.47% (year ending 10/31/97)

INVESCO STRATEGIC - HEALTH SCIENCES PORTFOLIO
(See first INVESCO listing for data common to all funds)

Portfolio manager: John R. Schroer (1994)
Investment objective and policies: Long-term capital appreciation. Invests at least 80% of assets in com-
mon stocks and securities convertible into common stock of companies in medical equipment, pharmaceuticals, health care facilities fields, and research and development in these fields. Up to 25% of assets may be in non-dollar denominated foreign securities, although securities of Canadian issuers and ADRs of other foreign issuers are not subject to this limitation. May invest up to 10% of assets in a single issuer, and use options and futures for hedging purposes.
Year organized: 1984
Ticker symbol: FHLSX
Group fund code: 52
Discount broker availability: *Fidelity, *Schwab, Siebert, *White
Dividends paid: Income - October; Capital gains - December
Portfolio turnover (3 yrs): 143%, 90%, 107%
Management fee: 0.75% first $350M to 0.55% over $700M
12b-1 distribution fee: Maximum of 0.25%
Expense ratio: 1.08% (year ending 10/31/97)

INVESCO STRATEGIC - LEISURE PORTFOLIO
(See first INVESCO listing for data common to all funds)

Portfolio manager: Mark Greenberg (1996)
Investment objective and policies: Capital appreciation. Invests at least 80% of assets in common stocks and securities convertible into common stock of companies in sporting goods, recreational equipment, photography, music, broadcasting, movie, hotel, casinos and amusement parks. Up to 25% of assets may be in non-dollar denominated foreign securities, although securities of Canadian issuers and ADRs of other foreign issuers are not subject to this limitation. May invest up to 10% of assets in a single issuer, and use options and futures for hedging purposes.
Year organized: 1984
Ticker symbol: FLISX
Group fund code: 53
Discount broker availability: *Fidelity, *Schwab, Siebert, *White
Dividends paid: Income - October; Capital gains - December
Portfolio turnover (3 yrs): 25%, 56%, 119%
Management fee: 0.75% first $350M to 0.55% over $700M
12b-1 distribution fee: Maximum of 0.25%
Expense ratio: 1.41% (year ending 10/31/97)

INVESCO STRATEGIC - TECHNOLOGY PORTFOLIO
(See first INVESCO listing for data common to all funds)

Portfolio managers: Daniel B. Leonard (1984), Gerard F. Hallaren, Jr. (1996)
Investment objective and policies: Capital appreciation. Invests at least 80% of assets in common stocks and securities convertible into common stock of companies principally engaged in the field of technology. Included are companies engaged in such fields as computers, communications, video, electronics, oceanography, office and factory automation, and robotics. Up to 25% of assets may be in non-dollar denominated foreign securities, although securities of Canadian issuers and ADRs of other foreign issuers are not subject to this limitation. May invest up to 10% of assets in a single issuer, and use options and futures for hedging purposes.
Year organized: 1984
Ticker symbol: FTCHX
Group fund code: 55
Discount broker availability: *Fidelity, *Schwab, Siebert, *White
Dividends paid: Income - October; Capital gains - December
Portfolio turnover (3 yrs): 237%, 168%, 191%
Management fee: 0.75% first $350M to 0.55% over $700M
12b-1 distribution fee: Maximum of 0.25%
Expense ratio: 1.05% (year ending 10/31/97)

INVESCO STRATEGIC - UTILITIES PORTFOLIO
(See first INVESCO listing for data common to all funds)

Portfolio manager: Brian B. Hayward (1997)
Investment objective and policies: Capital appreciation. Invests at least 80% of assets in common stocks and securities convertible into common stock of companies principally engaged in the public utilities industry. These may include companies which manufacture, produce, generate, transmit, or sell gas or electric energy; and companies engaged in various aspects of communications, such as telephone, telegraph, satellite, microwave, and the provision of other communication facilities, excluding broadcasting, for public use and benefit. Up to 25% of assets may be in non-dollar denominated foreign securities, although securities of Canadian issuers and ADRs of other foreign issuers are not subject to this limitation. May invest up to 10% of assets in a single issuer, and use options and futures for hedging purposes.
Year organized: 1986
Ticker symbol: FSTUX
Group fund code: 58
Discount broker availability: *Fidelity, *Schwab, Siebert, *White
Dividends paid: Income - October; Capital gains - December
Portfolio turnover (3 yrs): 55%, 141%, 185%
Management fee: 0.75% first $350M to 0.55% over $700M
12b-1 distribution fee: Maximum of 0.25%
Expense ratio: 1.22% (year ending 10/31/97) (1.27% without waiver)

INVESCO TAX-FREE INTERMEDIATE BOND FUND
(See first INVESCO listing for data common to all funds)

Portfolio manager: James S. Grabovac (1995)
Investment objective and policies: High current income exempt from federal income tax, consistent with capital preservation. Invests at least 80% of assets in municipal bonds within the four highest grades. Portfolio generally maintains a dollar-weighted average maturity of five to ten years. Up to 20% of assets may be in securities subject to AMT tax treatment. May use futures and options for hedging purposes.
Year organized: 1993
Ticker symbol: IVTIX
Group fund code: 36
Discount broker availability: *Fidelity, *Schwab, *White
Dividends paid: Income - declared daily, paid monthly; Capital gains - December
Portfolio turnover (3 yrs): 41%, 49%, 23%
Management fee: 0.50% first $300M to 0.30% over $500M
12b-1 distribution fee: 0.25%
Expense ratio: 0.84% (year ending 6/30/97) (2.43% without waiver)

INVESCO TAX-FREE LONG-TERM BOND FUND
(See first INVESCO listing for data common to all funds)

Portfolio manager: James S. Grabovac (1995)
Investment objective and policies: High current income exempt from federal income tax, consistent with capital preservation. Normally invests at least 80% of assets in municipal bonds within the four highest grades. Portfolio generally maintains a dollar-weighted average maturity of 20 years or more. May use futures for hedging purposes.
Year organized: 1981 (name changed from Tax-Free Income Shares on 7/1/93)
Ticker symbol: IVTIX
Group fund code: 35
Discount broker availability: *Fidelity, *Schwab, Siebert, *White
Dividends paid: Income - declared daily, paid monthly; Capital gains - December
Portfolio turnover (3 yrs): 123%, 146%, 99%
Management fee: 0.55% first $300M to 0.35% over $500M

12b-1 distribution fee: 0.25%
Expense ratio: 0.90% (year ending 6/30/97) (1.05% without waiver)

INVESCO TAX-FREE MONEY FUND ◆
(See first INVESCO listing for data common to all funds)

Portfolio manager: Ingeborg S. Cosby (1987)
Investment objective and policies: Current income exempt from federal income tax, consistent with preservation of capital and liquidity. Invests in municipal money market obligations issued by states and other municipalities.
Year organized: 1983
Ticker symbol: FFRXX
Group fund code: 40
Check redemptions: $500 minimum
Dividends paid: Income - declared daily, paid monthly
Management fee: 0.50% first $300M to 0.30% over $500M
Expense ratio: 0.76% (year ending 5/31/97) (1.01% without waiver)

INVESCO TOTAL RETURN FUND ◆
(See first INVESCO listing for data common to all funds)

Portfolio managers: Edward C. Mitchell (1987), David S. Griffin (1997)
Investment objective and policies: High total return without regard to federal income tax considerations. Maintains minimum of 30% in equities and 30% in fixed and variable debt obligations. The remaining 40% will vary in asset allocation according to business, economic and market conditions, determined systematically using current versus expected levels. Up to 25% of assets may be in securities of foreign issuers. May use futures and options for hedging purposes.
Year organized: 1987 (prior to 1/1/91 fund was Institutional Flex Fund; 80 to 1 split 1/2/91. Name changed from Flex Fund on 7/1/93)
Ticker symbol: FSFLX
Group fund code: 48
Discount broker availability: *Fidelity, *Schwab, Siebert, *White
Dividends paid: Income - February, May, August, November; Capital gains - December
Portfolio turnover (3 yrs): 4%, 10%, 30%
Management fee: 0.75% of first $500M to 0.50% over $1B
Expense ratio: 0.86% (year ending 8/31/97)

INVESCO U.S. GOVERNMENT MONEY FUND ◆
(See first INVESCO listing for data common to all funds)

Portfolio manager: Richard R. Hinderlie (1993)
Investment objective and policies: High current income consistent with liquidity and safety of capital. Invests only in money market obligations issued or guaranteed by the U.S. Government or its agencies or instrumentalities.
Year organized: 1991
Ticker symbol: FUGXX
Group fund code: 44
Check redemptions: $500 minimum
Dividends paid: Income - declared daily, paid monthly
Management fee: 0.50% of first $300M to 0.30% over $500M
Expense ratio: 0.86% (year ending 5/31/97) (1.06% without waiver)

INVESCO U.S. GOVERNMENT SECURITIES FUND
(See first INVESCO listing for data common to all funds)

Portfolio manager: Richard R. Hinderlie (1994)
Investment objective and policies: High current income. Invests at least 65% of assets in bonds and other debt securities issued or guaranteed by the U.S.

Government or its agencies or instrumentalities. May invest a substantial portion of its assets in GNMA certificates and use interest rate futures contracts for hedging purposes.
Year organized: 1986 (name changed from Bond Shares - U.S. Government Securities Portfolio on 7/1/93)
Ticker symbol: FBDGX
Group fund code: 32
Discount broker availability: *Fidelity, *Schwab, Siebert, *White
Dividends paid: Income - declared daily, paid monthly; Capital gains - December
Portfolio turnover (3 yrs): 139%, 212%, 99%
Management fee: 0.55% first $300M to 0.35% over $500M
12b-1 distribution fee: 0.25%
Expense ratio: 1.01% (year ending 8/31/97) (1.32% without waiver)

INVESCO VALUE EQUITY FUND ◆
(See first INVESCO listing for data common to all funds)

Portfolio manager: Michael C. Harhai (1993)
Investment objective and policies: High total return without regard to federal income tax considerations. Invests primarily in common stocks and, to a lesser extent, in convertible securities. Most of the common stocks pay regular dividends. Up to 35% of assets may be in investment grade debt securities and 25% in securities of foreign issuers.
Year organized: 1986 (name changed from Equity Fund on 7/1/93. Prior to 1/1/91 fund was Institutional Equity Fund, the successor to Shearwater Equity, Inc.; 80 to 1 split 1/2/91)
Ticker symbol: FSEQX
Group fund code: 46
Discount broker availability: *Fidelity, *Schwab, Siebert, *White
Dividends paid: Income - February, May, August, November; Capital gains - December
Portfolio turnover (3 yrs): 37%, 27%, 34%
Management fee: 0.75% of first $500M to 0.50% over $1B
Expense ratio: 1.04% (year ending 8/31/97)

INVESCO WORLDWIDE CAPITAL GOODS FUND
(See first INVESCO listing for data common to all funds)

Portfolio manager: John Segner (1998)
Investment objective and policies: Capital appreciation. Invests at least 65% of assets in equity securities of companies engaged in design, development, manufacture, distribution, sale or service of capital goods, or in the mining, processing, manufacture or distribution of raw materials and intermediate goods used by industry and agriculture. Invests in at least three countries, one of which may be the U.S. There are no limitations on percentage of assets invested in companies domiciled in any one country. Up to 15% of assets may be in illiquid securities. May use futures and options for hedging purposes.
Year organized: 1994
Ticker symbol: ISWGX
Group fund code: 38
Discount broker availability: *Fidelity, *Schwab, *White
Dividends paid: Income - July; Capital gains - December
Portfolio turnover (3 yrs): 192%, 247%, 193%
Management fee: 0.65% first $500M to 0.45% over $1B
12b-1 distribution fee: 0.25%
Expense ratio: 1.98% (year ending 7/31/97) (2.58% without waiver)

INVESCO WORLDWIDE COMMUNICATIONS FUND
(See first INVESCO listing for data common to all funds)

Lead portfolio manager: Brian B. Hayward (1997)
Investment objective and policies: Capital appreciation. Invests at least 65% of assets in equity securities

of companies engaged in design, development, manufacture, distribution or sale of communications services and equipment. May invest in companies involved in telephone service, wireless communications, local and wide area networks, fiber optic transmission, satellite communication, microwave transmission, television and movie programming, broadcasting and cable television. Invests in at least three countries, one of which may be the U.S. There are no limitations on percentage of assets invested in companies domiciled in any one country. Up to 15% of assets may be in illiquid securities. May use futures and options for hedging purposes.
Year organized: 1994
Ticker symbol: ISWCX
Group fund code: 39
Discount broker availability: *Fidelity, *Schwab, *White
Dividends paid: Income - July; Capital gains - December
Portfolio turnover (3 yrs): 96%, 157%, 215%
Management fee: 0.65% first $500M to 0.45% over $1B
12b-1 distribution fee: 0.25%
Expense ratio: 1.69% (year ending 7/31/97)

INVESTEK FIXED INCOME TRUST ◆
317 East Capitol Street
P.O. Box 2840
Jackson, MS 39207
800-525-3863, 601-949-3105
fax 919-972-1908

Adviser: Investek Capital Management, Inc.
Portfolio managers: Michael T. McRee (1991), Timothy L. Ellis (1991)
Transfer agent and administrator: The Nottingham Co.
Investment objective and policies: Maximum total return: capital appreciation and income, with capital preservation. Invests in a diversified portfolio of investment grade fixed-income securities perceived to be undervalued, including U.S. Government securities, mortgage pass-through certificates, collateralized mortgage obligations, asset backed securities, zero-coupon bonds, corporate bonds and floating rate securities. Fund generally maintains a portfolio duration between two and seven years, which is approximately equivalent to an effective maturity of three to twelve years. At least 90% of bonds in portfolio will be rated A or better by Moody's or S&P. May purchase ADRs without limit.
Year organized: 1991
Ticker symbol: IVFTX
Special sales restrictions: Designed primarily for institutional investors and high net worth individuals, but is open to anyone.
Minimum purchase: Initial: $50,000, Subsequent: $1,000; Automatic investment plan: Subsequent: $100
Wire orders accepted: Yes
Deadline for same day wire purchase: 4 P.M.
Qualified for sale in: AR, CA, CO, FL, GA, IL, IN, KY, LA, MN, MS, NC, NJ, NY, PA, TX, VA
Telephone redemptions: Yes (only with fax confirmation)
Wire redemptions: Yes, $5,000 minimum, $7 fee
Letter redemptions: Signature guarantee required over $50,000
Dividends paid: Income - monthly; Capital gains - December
Portfolio turnover (3 yrs): 33%, 17%, 20%
Shareholder services: Systematic withdrawal plan min. bal. req. $30,000
Management fee: 0.45%
Administration fee: 0.15% plus $21,000
Expense ratio: 0.90% (year ending 3/31/97) (1.20% without waiver)
IRA/Keogh fees: Annual $15

IPO PLUS AFTERMARKET FUND
325 Greenwich Avenue
Greenwich, CT 06830
888-476-3863, 203-622-2978
Internet: http://www.ipo-fund.com

Adviser: Renaissance Capital Corp.
Portfolio managers: Linda R. Killian (1997), Kathleen Shelton Smith (1997), William K. Smith (1997)

Transfer agent and administrator: Chase Global Services Co.

Investment objective and policies: Capital appreciation. Invests at least 65% of assets in a diversified portfolio of common stocks of initial public offerings both at the time of the initial offering and in the subsequent aftermarket trading. Aftermarket investments are limited only to issues exhibiting such characteristics as limited research, limited float, unseasoned trading, limited public ownership, limited operating history, or relative anonymity. May invest up to 35% of assets in common stocks of issues that are not IPOs. May invest up to 25% of assets in foreign issues, although foreign issues registered with the SEC and traded on a U.S. stock exchange may be purchased without limit. May use options, futures and short sales in an effort to enhance performance or for hedging purposes.

Year organized: 1997
Minimum purchase: Initial: $2,500, Subsequent: $100; IRA: Initial: $500
Wire orders accepted: Yes
Deadline for same day wire purchase: 4 P.M.
Qualified for sale in: All states except AR, FL, KY, MS, NM, OK, PR
Telephone redemptions: Yes
Wire redemptions: Yes, $10 fee
Letter redemptions: Signature guarantee required over $25,000
Redemption fee: 2.00% for shares held less than 90 days, payable to the fund
Dividends paid: Income - December; Capital gains - December
Shareholder services: IRA, SEP-IRA, SIMPLE IRA, automatic investment plan, electronic funds transfer
Management fee: 1.50%
Administration fee: 0.17%
12b-1 distribution fee: 0.50%
IRA fees: None

IPS MILLENNIUM FUND ◆
Two Centre Square
625 South Gay Street, Suite 630
Knoxville, TN 37902
800-232-9142, 423-524-1676
prices/yields 800-544-1842
fax 423-544-0630
Internet: http://www.ipsmillennium.com
e-mail: ipsalw@icx.net

Adviser: IPS Advisory, Inc.
Portfolio managers: Robert Loest (1995), Gregory A. D'Amico (1995)
Transfer agent: IPS Advisory, Inc.
Investment objective and policies: Long-term growth of capital and growth of income. Invests primarily in a diversified portfolio of U.S. common stocks believed to have higher than average long-term growth prospects and that appear to be undervalued, as well as companies with the potential to increase dividends and the ability to protect their dividend.
Year organized: 1995
Ticker symbol: IPSMX
Minimum purchase: Initial: $1,000, Subsequent: $100; Automatic investment plan: Initial: $100
Wire orders accepted: Yes
Deadline for same day wire purchase: 4:30 P.M.
Discount broker availability: *Fidelity, *Schwab, *Siebert, *White
Qualified for sale in: AL, DC, FL, GA, IL, IN, KS, KY, MO, NY, NC, OH, PR, SC, TN, TX, VA, WV
Letter redemptions: Signature guarantee required over $50,000
Dividends paid: Income - April, July, October, December; Capital gains - December
Portfolio turnover (3 yrs): 33%, 55%, 27%
Shareholder services: IRA, SEP-IRA, Keogh, 403(b), 401(k), corporate retirement plans, automatic investment plan, systematic withdrawal plan min. bal. req. $10,000
Management fee: 1.40% first $100M to 0.90% over $250M
Expense ratio: 1.40% (year ending 11/30/97) (Advisor pays all fund expenses)
IRA/Keogh fees: Annual $10, Initial $15, Closing $5

J.P. MORGAN FUNDS ◆
(Data common to all J.P. Morgan funds are shown below. See subsequent listings for data specific to individual funds.)

522 Fifth Avenue
New York, NY 10036
800-521-5411

Adviser: Morgan Guaranty Trust Co. (a wholly owned subsidiary of J.P. Morgan & Co., Inc.)
Administrator: Funds Distributor, Inc.
Transfer agent: State Street Bank and Trust Co.
Special information: In all cases where a fund is participating in a master/feeder arrangement, the advisor, reported management fees and portfolio turnover represent the underlying portfolio. **Prior to January 1, 1998, these funds were known as the JPM Pierpont Funds.**
Minimum purchase: Initial: $2,500, Subsequent: $500
Wire orders accepted: Yes
Deadline for same day wire purchase: 4 P.M. (exceptions noted)
Qualified for sale in: All states (exception noted)
Telephone redemptions: Yes
Wire redemptions: Yes
Letter redemptions: Signature guarantee not required
Telephone switching: With other J.P. Morgan funds
Deadline for same day switch: 4 P.M. (12 NN for TE MM, 1 P.M. for Federal MM)
Number of switches permitted: Unlimited
Shareholder services: IRA, Keogh, electronic funds transfer
IRA fees: Annual $10

J.P. MORGAN ASIA GROWTH FUND ◆
(Fund liquidated 12/12/97)

J.P. MORGAN BOND FUND ◆
(See first J.P. Morgan listing for data common to all funds)

Portfolio managers: William G. Tennille (1994), Connie J. Plaehn (1994)
Investment objective and policies: High total return consistent with moderate risk of capital and maintenance of liquidity. Fund uses a master/feeder structure and invests all of its investable assets in an underlying portfolio with identical objectives. Portfolio invests in a broadly diversified selection of U.S. Government and agency securities, corporate securities, private placements, asset-backed and mortgage-related securities. Portfolio is actively managed for duration, and will range between one year shorter and one year longer than the overall U.S. investment grade fixed-income universe. Fund may hedge.
Year organized: 1988
Ticker symbol: PPBDX
Discount broker availability: Fidelity, *Schwab, *White
Dividends paid: Income - monthly; Capital gains - December
Portfolio turnover (3 yrs): 93%, 186%, 293%
Management fee: 0.30%
Shareholder services fee: 0.20%
Expense ratio: 0.68% (year ending 10/31/97)

J.P. MORGAN DIVERSIFIED FUND ◆
(See first J.P. Morgan listing for data common to all funds)

Portfolio managers: Gerald H. Osterberg (1993), John M. Devlin (1993)
Investment objective and policies: High long-term total return; income plus realized and unrealized capital gains. Fund uses a master/feeder structure and invests all of its investable assets in an underlying portfolio with identical objectives. Portfolio normally invests approximately 65% of assets in equities and 35% in fixed-income securities, with allocations adjusted according to perceived market conditions. Equities will be primarily mid- to large-cap companies with an average market capitalization of $1.5B, with

about 3% of equities represented by small companies. Up to 30% of assets may be foreign issues. May use options and futures for hedging and risk management.
Year organized: 1993
Ticker symbol: PPDVX
Discount broker availability: Fidelity, *Schwab, *White
Dividends paid: Income - quarterly; Capital gains - September, December
Portfolio turnover (3 yrs): 100%, 144%, 136%
Management fee: 0.55%
Shareholder services fee: 0.25%
Expense ratio: 0.98% (year ending 6/30/97) (1.25% without waiver)

J.P. MORGAN EMERGING MARKETS DEBT FUND ◆
(See first J.P. Morgan listing for data common to all funds)

Portfolio manager: Eduardo L. Cortes (1997)
Investment objective and policies: High total return: realized and unrealized capital gains and income. Fund uses a master/feeder structure and invests all of its investable assets in an underlying portfolio with identical objectives. Portfolio invests at least 65% of assets in a selection of debt obligations issued by governments, government related agencies and corporate issuers located in emerging markets around the world. May invest without limit in junk bonds, and may buy securities denominated in any currency. May use forward foreign currency exchange contracts and a variety of derivatives for hedging purposes.
Year organized: 1997
Discount broker availability: Fidelity, *Schwab, *White
Dividends paid: Income - monthly; Capital gains - December
Management fee: 0.70%
Shareholder services fee: 0.25%

J.P. MORGAN EMERGING MARKETS EQUITY FUND ◆
(See first J.P. Morgan listing for data common to all funds)

Portfolio managers: Douglas J. Dooley (1993), Satyen Mehta (1993), Alejandro J. Baez-Sacasa (1995)
Investment objective and policies: High total return: realized and unrealized capital gains plus income. Fund uses a master/feeder structure and invests all of its investable assets in an underlying portfolio with identical objectives. Portfolio invests at least 65% of assets in equity securities of companies located in or doing at least 50% of their business in emerging markets countries, as defined by the IMF or the World Bank. Holdings are diversified across at least three countries. Portfolio only hedges foreign currencies occasionally. May invest up to 10% of assets in other investment companies. May use options and futures for hedging purposes.
Year organized: 1993
Ticker symbol: PPEEX
Discount broker availability: Fidelity, *Schwab, *White
Dividends paid: Income - December; Capital gains - December
Portfolio turnover (3 yrs): 55%, 31%, 41%
Management fee: 1.00%
Shareholder services fee: 0.25%
Expense ratio: 1.65% (year ending 10/31/97)

J.P. MORGAN EUROPEAN EQUITY FUND ◆
(See first J.P. Morgan listing for data common to all funds)

Portfolio managers: Paul A. Quinsee (1996), Rudolph Leuthold (1996)
Investment objective and policies: High total return: realized and unrealized capital gains plus income. Fund uses a master/feeder structure and invests all of its investable assets in an underlying portfolio with identical objectives. Portfolio invests at least 65% of assets in equity securities of companies from at least three 'developed' European countries, primarily com-

mon stock. May invest up to 5% of assets in emerging Eastern European economies or in Turkey. May use a variety of derivative instruments for hedging purposes.
Year organized: 1996 (underlying portfolio began in 1995)
Discount broker availability: Fidelity, *Schwab, *White
Dividends paid: Income - December; Capital gains - December
Portfolio turnover (2 yrs): 57%, 36%
Management fee: 0.65%
Shareholder services fee: 0.25%
Expense ratio: 1.42% (7 months ending 12/31/96) (2.50% without waiver)

J.P. MORGAN FEDERAL MONEY MARKET FUND ◆
(See first J.P. Morgan listing for data common to all funds)

Portfolio managers: Robert R. "Skip" Johnson (1993), Daniel B. Mulvey (1996)
Investment objective and policies: Current income consistent with preservation of capital and the maintenance of liquidity. Invests in short-term U.S. Treasury money market instruments, and those of certain other U.S. Government agencies.
Year organized: 1993
Deadline for same day wire purchase: 1 P.M.
Dividends paid: Income - declared daily, paid monthly; Capital gains - December
Management fee: 0.20% first $1B, 0.10% over $1B
Shareholder services fee: 0.15% first $2B, 0.10% over $2B
Expense ratio: 0.40% (year ending 10/31/97) (0.52% without waiver)

J.P. MORGAN INTERNATIONAL EQUITY FUND ◆
(See first J.P. Morgan listing for data common to all funds)

Portfolio managers: Paul A. Quinsee (1993), Nigel F. Emmett (1997), Anne H. Richards (1997)
Investment objective and policies: Long-term high total return: realized and unrealized capital gains plus income. Fund uses a master/feeder structure and invests all of its investable assets in an underlying portfolio with identical objectives. Portfolio invests at least 65% of assets in equity securities, principally common stocks, of companies located throughout the world excluding the U.S. Management intends to outperform the EAFE Index, with reduced volatility. Securities are selected on a quantitative basis. May use derivatives for hedging purposes, and will use forward foreign currency exchange contracts to hedge currencies.
Year organized: 1990
Ticker symbol: PPIEX
Discount broker availability: Fidelity, *Schwab, *White
Dividends paid: Income - December; Capital gains - December
Portfolio turnover (3 yrs): 67%, 57%, 59%
Management fee: 0.60%
Shareholder services fee: 0.25%
Expense ratio: 1.12% (year ending 10/31/97)

J.P. MORGAN INTERNATIONAL OPPORTUNITIES FUND ◆
(See first J.P. Morgan listing for data common to all funds)

Portfolio managers: Paul A. Quinsee (1997), Rudolph Leuthold (1997)
Investment objective and policies: Long-term high total return: realized and unrealized capital gains plus income. Fund uses a master/feeder structure and invests all of its investable assets in an underlying portfolio with identical objectives. Portfolio invests at least 65% of assets in equity securities of foreign issuers, excluding the U.S. Approximately 80% of equity holdings are in 'developed' countries, and 20% in 'emerging' markets, although this allocation may vary according to perceived market conditions. Portfolio will hedge currency exposure, and use a variety of derivative instruments to manage risk.

Year organized: 1997
Ticker symbol: PPIOX
Discount broker availability: Fidelity, *Schwab, *White
Dividends paid: Income - December; Capital gains - December
Portfolio turnover (1 yr): 72%
Management fee: 0.60%
Shareholder services fee: 0.25%
Expense ratio: 1.20% (nine months ending 11/30/97) (1.51% without waiver)

J.P. MORGAN JAPAN EQUITY FUND ◆
(See first J.P. Morgan listing for data common to all funds)

Portfolio managers: Masata Degawa (1996), Yukiko Sugimoto (1996)
Investment objective and policies: Long-term high total return: realized and unrealized capital gains plus income. Fund uses a master/feeder structure and invests all of its investable assets in an underlying portfolio with identical objectives. Portfolio invests at least 65% of assets in equity securities of Japanese companies represented in the First Section of the Tokyo stock exchange. Management intends to outperform the Tokyo Stock Price Index (TOPIX) Index with less volatility. Portfolio only hedges foreign currencies occasionally, but may use a variety of derivative instruments to manage risk. Portfolio is non-diversified.
Year organized: 1996
Discount broker availability: Fidelity, *Schwab, *White
Dividends paid: Income - December; Capital gains - December
Portfolio turnover (1 yr): 86%
Management fee: 0.65%
Shareholder services fee: 0.25%
Expense ratio: 1.43% (7 months ending 12/31/96) (2.51% without waiver)

J.P. MORGAN NEW YORK TOTAL RETURN BOND FUND ◆
(See first J.P. Morgan listing for data common to all funds)

Portfolio managers: Elaine B. Young (1997), Robert W. Meiselas (1997)
Investment objective and policies: High after tax total return for New York residents, consisting of current income and capital gains. Invests primarily in investment grade municipal securities of the state of New York and its subdivisions, but may invest in municipals from other states and the federal government as well. Generally the fund will maintain an average duration of three to seven years. Fund is non-diversified.
Year organized: 1994
Ticker symbol: PPNYX
Discount broker availability: Fidelity, *Schwab, *White
Qualified for sale in: CT, DC, NJ, NY
Dividends paid: Income - monthly; Capital gains - December
Portfolio turnover (3 yrs): 35%, 41%, 63%
Management fee: 0.30%
Shareholder services fee: 0.20%
Expense ratio: 0.75% (year ending 3/31/97) (0.81% without waiver)

J.P. MORGAN PRIME MONEY MARKET FUND ◆
(See first J.P. Morgan listing for data common to all funds)

Portfolio managers: Robert R. "Skip" Johnson (1988), Daniel B. Mulvey (1995)
Investment objective and policies: Maximum current income consistent with capital preservation and the maintenance of liquidity. Invests in a portfolio of high quality short-term money market instruments.
Year organized: 1982 (name changed from JPM Pierpont MM 5/12/97)
Dividends paid: Income - declared daily, paid monthly; Capital gains - December

Management fee: 0.20% first $1B, 0.10% over $1B
Shareholder services fee: 0.15% first $2B, 0.10% over $2B
Expense ratio: 0.38% (year ending 11/30/97)

J.P. MORGAN SHARES: CALIFORNIA BOND FUND ◆
(See first J.P. Morgan listing for data common to all funds)

Portfolio managers: Elaine B. Young (1997), Robert W. Meiselas (1997)
Investment objective and policies: High after tax total return for California residents, consistent with moderate risk of capital. Invests at least 65% of assets in California municipal bonds. Portfolio will generally have an average duration of three to ten years. May invest up to 35% of assets in non-municipal securities, and up to 10% of assets in junk bonds rated at least "B", and may hold them even if they are downgraded. Fund is non-diversified.
Year organized: 1997
Discount broker availability: *White
Dividends paid: Income - monthly; Capital gains - December
Management fee: 0.30%
Shareholder services fee: 0.25%

J.P. MORGAN SHARES: TAX AWARE DISCIPLINED EQUITY FUND ◆
(See first J.P. Morgan listing for data common to all funds)

Portfolio managers: Robin B. Chance (1997), Frederic A. Nelson (1997)
Investment objective and policies: Long-term high total return, consistent with sensitivity to the impact of capital gains taxes. Fund is normally fully invested, and must maintain at least 65% of assets in equity securities of medium- and large-sized domestic companies that are perceived to be undervalued. Fund generally invests in companies found in the top two quintiles of their industrial sectors, and may overweight or underweight sectors relative to the S&P 500. May invest up to 15% of assets in illiquid securities, up to 5% in foreign issues, and may use a variety of derivative instruments.
Year organized: 1997
Redemption fees: 2% for shares held less than one year, 1% for shares held less than five years, payable to fund
Dividends paid: Income - December; Capital gains - December
Portfolio turnover (1 yr): 35%
Management fee: 0.35%
Shareholder services fee: 0.25%
Expense ratio: 0.55% (nine months ending 10/31/97) (4.59% without waiver)

J.P. MORGAN SHARES: TAX AWARE U.S. EQUITY FUND ◆
(See first J.P. Morgan listing for data common to all funds)

Portfolio managers: Terry E. Banet (1996), Gordon B. Fowler (1996)
Investment objective and policies: Long-term high total return, consistent with sensitivity to the impact of capital gains taxes. Fund is normally fully invested, and must maintain at least 65% of assets in equity securities of medium- and large-sized domestic companies that are perceived to be undervalued. Fund generally invests in companies found in the top three quintiles of their industrial sectors, and generally will not overweight or underweight sectors relative to the S&P 500. May invest up to 15% of assets in illiquid securities, up to 5% in foreign issues, and may use a variety of derivative instruments.
Year organized: 1996
Discount broker availability: *Schwab, *White
Redemption fees: 2.00% for shares held less than one year, 1.00% for shares held less than five years, payable to fund
Dividends paid: Income - December; Capital gains - December
Management fee: 0.45%
Shareholder services fee: 0.25%

J.P. MORGAN SHORT TERM BOND FUND ◆

(See first J.P. Morgan listing for data common to all funds)

Portfolio managers: Connie J. Plaehn (1993), William G. Tennille (1994)
Investment objective and policies: High total return while attempting to limit the likelihood of negative quarterly returns, consistent with modest risk of capital and maintenance of liquidity. Fund is actively allocated across the broad spectrum of fixed-income markets using quantitative models to identify securities perceived to be undervalued. The average duration of the portfolio will generally range from one to three years. May invest up to 10% of assets in junk bonds rated at least B. May use forward foreign currency contracts and options and futures for hedging purposes.
Year organized: 1993
Discount broker availability: Fidelity, *Schwab, *White
Dividends paid: Income - monthly; Capital gains - December
Portfolio turnover (3 yrs): 219%, 191%, 177%
Management fee: 0.25%
Shareholder services fee: 0.20%
Expense ratio: 0.50% (year ending 10/31/97) (1.38% without waiver)

J.P. MORGAN TAX EXEMPT BOND FUND ◆

(See first J.P. Morgan listing for data common to all funds)

Portfolio managers: Elaine B. Young (1997), Robert W. Meiselas (1997)
Investment objective and policies: High level of current income exempt from federal income tax, consistent with moderate risk to capital and the maintenance of liquidity. Fund uses a master/feeder structure and invests all of its investable assets in an underlying portfolio with identical objectives. Portfolio invests at least 80% of assets in municipal securities which earn interest believed to be exempt from federal income tax. Portfolio will generally maintain an average duration of four to seven years. At times, portfolio may invest up to 20% of assets in taxable securities. May invest up to 10% of assets in junk bonds rated "B" or better at time of purchase, and may continue to hold these issues even if they are downgraded.
Year organized: 1984
Ticker symbol: PPTBX
Discount broker availability: Fidelity, *Schwab, *White
Dividends paid: Income - monthly; Capital gains - December
Portfolio turnover (3 yrs): 25%, 25%, 47%
Management fee: 0.30%
Shareholder services fee: 0.20%
Expense ratio: 0.64% (year ending 8/31/97)

J.P. MORGAN TAX EXEMPT MONEY MARKET FUND ◆

(See first J.P. Morgan listing for data common to all funds)

Portfolio managers: Daniel B. Mulvey (1995), Richard W. Oswald (1996)
Investment objective and policies: High level of current income exempt from federal income tax, consistent with a stable asset value and a high level of liquidity. Fund uses a master/feeder structure and invests all of its investable assets in an underlying portfolio with identical objectives. Portfolio invests in short-term municipal money market instruments which may, however, be subject to state and local income taxes.
Year organized: 1983
Deadline for same day wire purchase: 12 NN
Dividends paid: Income - declared daily, paid monthly; Capital gains - December
Management fee: 0.20% first $1B, 0.10% over $1B
Shareholder services fee: 0.15% first $2B, 0.10% over $2B
Expense ratio: 0.46% (year ending 8/31/97)

J.P. MORGAN U.S. EQUITY FUND ◆

(See first J.P. Morgan listing for data common to all funds)

Portfolio managers: William M. Riegel, Jr. (1993), Henry Cavanna (1997)
Investment objective and policies: High long-term total return: realized and unrealized capital gains and income. Fund uses a master/feeder structure and invests all of its investable assets in an underlying portfolio with identical objectives. Portfolio is generally fully invested in the common stock of medium- and large-sized U.S. companies perceived to be undervalued. Portfolio may maintain modestly overweighted or underweighted sector holdings relative to the S&P 500. May use options and futures for hedging purposes.
Year organized: 1985 (name changed from JPM Pierpont Equity 5/21/97)
Ticker symbol: PPEQX
Discount broker availability: Fidelity, *Schwab, *White
Dividends paid: Income - quarterly; Capital gains - August
Portfolio turnover (3 yrs): 99%, 85%, 71%
Management fee: 0.40%
Shareholder services fee: 0.25%
Expense ratio: 0.80% (year ending 5/31/97)

J.P. MORGAN U.S. SMALL COMPANY FUND ◆

(See first J.P. Morgan listing for data common to all funds)

Portfolio managers: James B. Otness (1993), Michael J. Kelly (1996), Candice Eggerss (1996)
Investment objective and policies: High long-term total return: realized and unrealized capital gains and income. Fund uses a master/feeder structure and invests all of its investable assets in an underlying portfolio with identical objectives. Portfolio invests primarily in the common stock of companies with market capitalizations in the range of those included in the Russell 2500 Index. May use options and futures for hedging purposes.
Year organized: 1985 (name changed from JPM Pierpont Capital Appreciation 5/21/97)
Ticker symbol: PPCAX
Discount broker availability: Fidelity, *Schwab, *White
Dividends paid: Income - biannually; Capital gains - August
Portfolio turnover (1 yr): 98%, 93%, 75%
Management fee: 0.60%
Shareholder services fee: 0.25%
Expense ratio: 0.90% (year ending 5/31/97) (1.03% without waiver)

J.P. MORGAN U.S. SMALL COMPANY OPPORTUNITIES FUND ◆

(See first J.P. Morgan listing for data common to all funds)

Portfolio manager: Marian U. Pardo (1997)
Investment objective and policies: Long-term capital appreciation. Fund uses a master/feeder structure and invests all of its investable assets in an underlying portfolio with identical objectives. Portfolio invests at least 65% of asset in equity securities of companies with market capitalizations of less than $2B at time of purchase, although the focus is on companies below $1.25B perceived to be undervalued. May invest in foreign securities without limit, up to 15% of assets in illiquid securities, up to 10% in other investment companies, and up to 10% in equity securities of medium- and large-sized companies. May use derivatives in an effort to enhance performance and for hedging purposes.
Year organized: 1997
Discount broker availability: Fidelity, *Schwab, *White
Dividends paid: Income - December; Capital gains - December
Management fee: 0.60%
Shareholder services fee: 0.25%

JAMESTOWN INTERNATIONAL EQUITY FUND ◆

6620 West Broad Street, Suite 300
Richmond, VA 23230
800-443-4249, 804-288-0404

Adviser: Lowe, Brockenbrough & Tattersall, Inc.
Sub-adviser: Oechsle International Advisors, L.P.
Portfolio managers: Kathleen Harris (1996), Walter Oechsle (1996)
Administrator and transfer agent: Countrywide Fund Services, Inc.
Investment objective and policies: Superior total return: capital growth and current income. Invests in a broadly diversified portfolio of equity securities from companies located outside the U.S. Fund uses a top down analysis to select countries, followed by a bottom up company analysis of any company with a market capitalization exceeding $50M. Primarily selects mid- to large-cap stocks. Generally diversifies across at least 12 countries, and is never out of any major EAFE market. Uses currency hedges for defense only. May use stock and currency options, futures, and forward foreign currency exchange contracts for hedging purposes.
Year organized: 1996
Minimum purchase: Initial: $5,000, Subsequent: $1,000; Automatic investment plan: Subsequent: $100
Wire orders accepted: Yes
Deadline for same day wire purchase: 4 P.M.
Qualified for sale in: All states
Letter redemptions: Signature guarantee not required
Dividends paid: Income - March, June, September, December; Capital gains - December
Portfolio turnover (1 yr): 70%
Shareholder services: Systematic withdrawal plan min. bal. req. $25,000
Management fee: 1.00%
Administration fee: 0.25%
Expense ratio: 1.60% (year ending 3/31/97) (1.71% without waiver)

JAMESTOWN TAX EXEMPT VIRGINIA FUND ◆

6620 West Broad Street, Suite 300
Richmond, VA 23230
800-443-4249, 804-288-0404

Adviser: Lowe, Brockenbrough & Tattersall, Inc.
Portfolio manager: Beth Ann Walk (1993)
Administrator and transfer agent: Countrywide Fund Services, Inc.
Investment objective and policies: Current income exempt from federal and Virginian personal income taxes, to preserve capital, to limit credit risk and to take advantage of opportunities to increase income and enhance value. Invests at least 75% of assets in bonds rated at least A or better. Portfolio duration ranges from two to fifteen years, with an average maturity that is longer than the average duration. May purchase bonds with a lower rating if it is thought they will be upgraded.
Year organized: 1993
Minimum purchase: Initial: $25,000, Subsequent: $500; Automatic investment plan: Subsequent: $100
Wire orders accepted: Yes
Deadline for same day wire purchase: 4 P.M.
Qualified for sale in: VA
Letter redemptions: Signature guarantee not required
Dividends paid: Income - declared daily, paid monthly; Capital gains - December
Portfolio turnover (3 yrs): 24%, 14%, 97%
Shareholder services: Systematic withdrawal plan min. bal. req. $25,000
Management fee: 0.40% first $250M to 0.30% over $500M
Administration fee: 0.15% first $200M, 0.10% over $200M ($2,000/mo. minimum)
Expense ratio: 0.75% (year ending 3/31/97) (0.88% without waiver)

JANUS FUNDS ◆

(Data common to all Janus funds are shown below. See subsequent listings for data specific to individual funds.)

100 Fillmore Street, Suite 300
Denver, CO 80206-4923
800-525-3713, 303-333-3863
prices/yields 888-979-7737
account information 800-525-6125
Quoteline 800-525-0024
Literature line 800-525-8983
fax 303-782-3055, TDD 800-525-0056
Internet: http://www.janus.com

Shareholder service hours: Full service: M-F 8 A.M.-10 P.M., Sat 10 A.M.-7 P.M. EST; After hours service: prices, yields, balances, orders, last transaction, indices, prospectuses, total returns
Adviser: Janus Capital Corp.
Transfer agent: Janus Service Corp.
Minimum purchase: Initial: $2,500, Subsequent: $100; IRA/Keogh: Initial: $500, Subsequent: $50; Automatic investment plan: Initial: $500
Wire orders accepted: Yes
Deadline for same day wire purchase: 4 P.M. (exceptions noted)
Telephone orders accepted: Yes
Qualified for sale in: All states
Telephone redemptions: Yes
Wire redemptions: Yes, $8 fee
Letter redemptions: Signature guarantee required over $100,000
Telephone switching: With other open retail Janus funds
Number of switches permitted: 4 per year out of each fund, $100 minimum; unlimited money market; $5 fee for each exchange over 4
Shareholder services: IRA, SEP-IRA, Keogh, 403(b), corporate retirement plans, directed dividends, electronic funds transfer, systematic withdrawal plan min. bal. req. $10,000
Maintenance fee: $10 per year for accounts with balances below $2,500 ($1,000 for accounts opened before 2/18/96)
IRA/Keogh fees: Annual $12 per fund, $24 maximum (or $100 lifetime for all IRA/Keogh account fund holdings)

JANUS BALANCED FUND ◆

(See first Janus listing for data common to all funds)

Portfolio manager: Blaine P. Rollins (1996)
Investment objective and policies: Long-term capital growth consistent with capital preservation and balanced by current income. Invests 40% to 60% of assets in equity securities selected for growth and 40% to 60% in fixed-income securities, generally short-term instruments. At least 25% of assets in fixed-income senior securities, including debt securities and preferred stocks. Up to 25% of assets may be in securities of foreign issuers but fund will not invest in foreign corporate debt securities. May use futures and options for hedging purposes.
Year organized: 1992
Ticker symbol: JABAX
Group fund code: 51
Discount broker availability: *Fidelity, *Schwab, *Siebert, *White
Dividends paid: Income - March, June, September, December; Capital gains - December
Portfolio turnover (3 yrs): 139%, 151%, 185%
Management fee: 0.75% first $270M to 0.65% over $500M
Expense ratio: 1.10% (year ending 10/31/97) (1.12% without waiver)

JANUS ENTERPRISE FUND ◆

(See first Janus listing for data common to all funds)

Portfolio manager: James P. Goff (1992)
Investment objective and policies: Long-term growth of capital consistent with capital preservation. Invests primarily in a non-diversified portfolio of medium-sized companies with market capitalizations of $1B to $7.5B, but may also invest in smaller and/or larger companies. May invest up to 25% of assets in securities of foreign issuers, and use futures and options for hedging purposes.
Year organized: 1992
Ticker symbol: JAENX
Group fund code: 50
Discount broker availability: *Fidelity, *Schwab, *Siebert, *White
Dividends paid: Income - December; Capital gains - December
Portfolio turnover (3 yrs): 111%, 93%, 194%
Management fee: 0.75% first $270M to 0.65% over $500M
Expense ratio: 1.04% (year ending 10/31/97) (1.07% without waiver)

JANUS EQUITY INCOME FUND ◆

(See first Janus listing for data common to all funds)

Portfolio manager: Blaine P. Rollins (1996)
Investment objective and policies: Long-term growth of capital and current income. Invests at least 65% of assets in income-producing equity securities of mature companies, with as much as 80% to 90% of assets in stocks. Will also hold a portion of assets in non-income-producing equities due to their growth potential. May invest up to 35% of net assets in junk bonds, 25% in mortgage- and asset-backed bonds, and 10% in zero-coupon bonds. May invest without limit in either equity or debt securities of foreign issuers, and use a variety of derivative instruments in an effort to enhance returns or for hedging purposes.
Year organized: 1996
Ticker symbol: JAEIX
Group fund code: 50
Discount broker availability: *Fidelity, *Schwab, *Siebert, *White
Dividends paid: Income - March, June, September, December; Capital gains - December
Portfolio turnover (2 yrs): 180%, 325%
Management fee: 0.75% first $270M to 0.65% over $500M
Expense ratio: 1.45% (year ending 10/31/97) (1.48% without waiver)

JANUS FEDERAL TAX EXEMPT FUND ◆

(See first Janus listing for data common to all funds)

Portfolio manager: Darrell W. Watters (1996)
Investment objective and policies: High current income exempt from federal income tax, consistent with capital preservation. Invests at least 80% of assets in municipal obligations whose interest is exempt from federal income tax. Up to 35% of assets may be in junk bonds, 20% in securities subject to AMT tax treatment, and 15% in illiquid securities.
Year organized: 1993
Ticker symbol: JATEX
Group fund code: 53
Discount broker availability: *Fidelity, *Schwab, *Siebert, *White
Dividends paid: Income - declared daily, paid monthly; Capital gains - December
Portfolio turnover (3 yrs): 304%, 225%, 164%
Management fee: 0.60% first $300M, 0.55% over $300M
Expense ratio: 0.66% (year ending 10/31/97) (1.11% without waiver)

JANUS FLEXIBLE INCOME FUND ◆

(See first Janus listing for data common to all funds)

Portfolio managers: Ronald V. Speaker (1991), Sandy R. Rufenacht (1996)
Investment objective and policies: Maximum total return consistent with capital preservation. Invests primarily in income-producing securities - debt securities, mortgage- or asset-backed securities, preferred stocks, income-producing common stocks and/or securities convertible into common stocks. Income will be the dominant component of total return. May invest in securities of foreign issuers and junk bonds without limit, and use futures and options for hedging purposes. Up to 15% of assets may be in illiquid securities.
Year organized: 1987

Ticker symbol: JAFIX
Group fund code: 49
Discount broker availability: *Fidelity, *Schwab, *Siebert, *White
Dividends paid: Income - declared daily, paid monthly; Capital gains - December
Portfolio turnover (3 yrs): 207%, 214%, 250%
Management fee: 0.65% first $300M, 0.55% over $300M
Expense ratio: 0.87% (year ending 10/31/97)

JANUS FUND ◆

(See first Janus listing for data common to all funds)

Portfolio managers: James P. Craig III (1986), David C. Decker (1997), Blaine P. Rollins (1997)
Investment objective and policies: Capital growth consistent with capital preservation. Invests primarily in common stocks of companies with favorable demand for their products and services operating in favorable competitive environments and regulatory climates, regardless of their size, although it trends toward large caps. May invest in foreign securities without limit. Up to 15% of assets may be in illiquid securities. Fund may use futures and options for hedging purposes.
Year organized: 1970
Ticker symbol: JANSX
Group fund code: 42
Discount broker availability: *Fidelity, *Schwab, *Siebert, *White
Dividends paid: Income - December; Capital gains - December
Portfolio turnover (3 yrs): 132%, 104%, 118%
Management fee: 0.75% first $270M to 0.65% over $500M
Expense ratio: 0.86% (year ending 10/31/97) (0.87% without waiver)

JANUS GOVERNMENT MONEY MARKET FUND ◆

(See first Janus listing for data common to all funds)

Portfolio manager: Sharon S. Pichler (1995)
Investment objective and policies: Maximum current income consistent with capital stability. Invests exclusively in obligations issued and/or guaranteed as to principal and interest by the U.S. Government, its agencies and instrumentalities, and repurchase agreements secured by such obligations.
Year organized: 1995
Group fund code: 38
Deadline for same day wire purchase: 3 P.M.
Check redemptions $250 minimum
Dividends paid: Income - declared daily, paid monthly
Management fee: 0.20%
Expense ratio: 0.60% (year ending 10/31/97) (0.70% without waiver)

JANUS GROWTH AND INCOME FUND ◆

(See first Janus listing for data common to all funds)

Portfolio manager: David J. Corkins (1997)
Investment objective and policies: Long-term capital growth and current income. Invests in a broadly diversified portfolio of equity securities, convertible securities and fixed-income securities of domestic and foreign issuers. Normally invests up to 75% (at least 25%) of assets based on capital growth potential and at least 25% based on income producing properties. Up to 35% of assets may be in junk bonds and 15% in illiquid securities. Fund may use futures and options for hedging purposes.
Year organized: 1991
Ticker symbol: JAGIX
Group fund code: 40
Discount broker availability: *Fidelity, *Schwab, *Siebert, *White
Dividends paid: Income - March, June, September, December; Capital gains - December
Portfolio turnover (3 yrs): 127%, 153%, 195%
Management fee: 0.75% first $270M to 0.65% over $500M
Expense ratio: 0.96% (year ending 10/31/97) (0.98% without waiver)

JANUS HIGH-YIELD FUND ◆
(See first Janus listing for data common to all funds)

Portfolio managers: Ronald V. Speaker (1995), Sandy R. Rufenacht (1996)
Investment objective and policies: High current income; capital appreciation secondary. Invests primarily in high-yield, high risk fixed-income securities, also known as 'junk bonds.' May also invest in government issues as well as common stock. May invest without limit in foreign securities. May invest up to 15% of assets in illiquid securities and use a variety of derivative instruments both in an effort to enhance performance and for hedging purposes.
Year organized: 1995
Ticker symbol: JAHYX
Group fund code: 57
Discount broker availability: *Fidelity, *Schwab, *Siebert, *White
Dividends paid: Income - declared daily, paid monthly; Capital gains - December
Portfolio turnover (2 yrs): 404%, 324%
Management fee: 0.75% first $300M, 0.65% over $300M
Expense ratio: 1.03% (year ending 10/31/97) (1.04% without waiver)

JANUS MERCURY FUND ◆
(See first Janus listing for data common to all funds)

Portfolio manager: Warren B. Lammert (1993)
Investment objective and policies: Long-term capital growth. Invests primarily in equity securities of companies believed to have strong earnings growth potential, with emphasis on those whose perceived potential has not been recognized by the market. May invest in securities of companies of any size, and those of foreign issuers without limit. Up to 15% of assets may be in illiquid securities. May use futures and options for hedging purposes.
Year organized: 1993
Ticker symbol: JAMRX
Group fund code: 48
Discount broker availability: *Fidelity, *Schwab, *Siebert, *White
Dividends paid: Income - December; Capital gains - December
Portfolio turnover (3 yrs): 157%, 177%, 201%
Management fee: 0.75% first $270M to 0.65% over $500M
Expense ratio: 0.96% (year ending 10/31/97) (0.98 without waiver)

JANUS MONEY MARKET FUND ◆
(See first Janus listing for data common to all funds)

Portfolio manager: Sharon S. Pichler (1995)
Investment objective and policies: Maximum current income consistent with capital stability. Invests in high quality commercial paper and obligations of financial institutions.
Year organized: 1995
Ticker symbol: JAMXX
Group fund code: 37
Deadline for same day wire purchase: 3 P.M.
Discount broker availability: *Fidelity
Check redemptions $250 minimum
Dividends paid: Income - declared daily, paid monthly
Management fee: 0.20%
Expense ratio: 0.60% (year ending 10/31/97) (0.70% without waiver)

JANUS OLYMPUS FUND ◆
(See first Janus listing for data common to all funds)

Portfolio manager: Claire W. Young (1997)
Investment objective and policies: Long-term capital growth. Invests in a non-diversified portfolio of common stocks of companies of any size, including established issuers and smaller, emerging growth companies. Preliminary selections are based on analysis of long-term economic and demographic trends. May also invest up to 35% of net assets in junk bonds, 25% in mortgage- and asset-backed bonds, and 10% in zero-coupon bonds. May invest without limit in equity

or debt securities of foreign issuers, and use a variety of derivative instruments in an effort to enhance returns or for hedging purposes.
Year organized: 1995
Ticker symbol: JAOLX
Group fund code: 56
Discount broker availability: *Fidelity, *Schwab, *Siebert, *White
Dividends paid: Income - December; Capital gains - December
Portfolio turnover (2 yrs): 244%, 303%
Management fee: 0.75% first $270M to 0.65% over $500M
Expense ratio: 1.03% (year ending 10/31/97) (1.06% without waiver)

JANUS OVERSEAS FUND ◆
(See first Janus listing for data common to all funds)

Portfolio managers: Helen Young Hayes (1994), Laurence J. Chang (1997)
Investment objective and policies: Long-term capital growth. Invests primarily in common stocks of foreign issuers, regardless of size, country of origin or place of principal business activity. May invest in fixed-income securities of foreign corporations, governments, government agencies and other government entities. Normally invests in securities of issuers from at least five different countries, excluding the U.S. Up to 15% of assets may be in illiquid securities. May use futures and options for hedging purposes.
Year organized: 1994
Ticker symbol: JAOSX
Group fund code: 54
Discount broker availability: *Fidelity, *Schwab, *Siebert, *White
Dividends paid: Income - December; Capital gains - December
Portfolio turnover (3 yrs): 72%, 71%, 188%
Management fee: 0.75% first $270M to 0.65% over $500M
Expense ratio: 1.01% (year ending 10/31/97) (1.03% without waiver)

JANUS SHORT-TERM BOND FUND ◆
(See first Janus listing for data common to all funds)

Portfolio manager: Sandy R. Rufenacht (1996)
Investment objective and policies: High current income consistent with capital preservation. Invests primarily in short- and intermediate-term investment grade fixed-income securities. Portfolio generally maintains a dollar-weighted average maturity of less than five years. May invest in foreign debt securities without limit. Up to 35% of assets may be in junk bonds and 15% in illiquid securities.
Year organized: 1992
Ticker symbol: JASBX
Group fund code: 52
Discount broker availability: *Fidelity, *Schwab, *Siebert, *White
Dividends paid: Income - declared daily, paid monthly; Capital gains - December
Portfolio turnover (3 yrs): 133%, 486%, 337%
Management fee: 0.65% first $300M, 0.55% over $300M
Expense ratio: 0.67% (year ending 10/31/97) (1.20% without waiver)

JANUS SPECIAL SITUATIONS FUND ◆
(See first Janus listing for data common to all funds)

Portfolio manager: David C. Decker (1996)
Investment objective and policies: Long-term growth. Invests primarily in common stocks of domestic and foreign companies of all types and sizes. Selection will be based on companies perceived to be overlooked or those that demonstrate that they have, or will have, excellent management and the capability of generating strong cash flow. Fund is non-diversified and may invest up to 25% of assets in a single industry or in a single issuer. May use a variety of derivative instruments in an effort to enhance performance and for hedging purposes.
Year organized: 1996
Ticker symbol: JASSX

Group fund code: 58
Discount broker availability: *Fidelity, *Schwab, *White
Dividends paid: Income - December; Capital gains - December
Portfolio turnover (1 yr): 146%
Management fee: 0.75% first $270M to 0.65% over $500M
Expense ratio: 1.18% (10 months ending 10/31/97) (1.20% without waiver)

JANUS TAX-EXEMPT MONEY MARKET FUND ◆
(See first Janus listing for data common to all funds)

Portfolio manager: Sharon S. Pichler (1995)
Investment objective and policies: Maximum current income exempt from federal income tax, consistent with capital stability. Invests primarily in municipal securities whose interest is exempt from federal income taxes including the alternative minimum tax. Fund reserves the right to invest up to 20% of assets in taxable securities.
Year organized: 1995
Ticker symbol: JATXX
Group fund code: 39
Deadline for same day wire purchase: 12 NN
Check redemptions $250 minimum
Dividends paid: Income - declared daily, paid monthly
Management fee: 0.20%
Expense ratio: 0.60% (year ending 10/31/97) (0.70% without waiver)

JANUS TWENTY FUND ◆
(See first Janus listing for data common to all funds)

Portfolio manager: Scott W. Schoelzel (1997)
Investment objective and policies: Capital growth consistent with capital preservation. Invests fully in a limited number of common stocks (generally 20 to 30) of companies with rapid growth potential, trending toward large, multinationals with internationally known brand recognition. May invest in ADRs of foreign companies and in non-dollar denominated foreign securities. Up to 35% of assets may be in junk bonds and 15% in illiquid securities. May use futures and options for hedging purposes. Fund is non-diversified.
Year organized: 1985 (name changed from Janus Value on 5/19/89)
Ticker symbol: JAVLX
Group fund code: 43
Special sales restrictions: Fund closed to new investors in 1992; reopened 11/95.
Discount broker availability: *Fidelity, *Schwab, *Siebert, *White
Dividends paid: Income - December; Capital gains - December
Portfolio turnover (3 yrs): 123%, 137%, 147%
Management fee: 0.75% first $270M to 0.65% over $500M
Expense ratio: 0.91% (year ending 10/31/97) (0.93% without waiver)

JANUS VENTURE FUND ◆
(See first Janus listing for data common to all funds)

Portfolio managers: James P. Craig III (1997), William H. Bales (1997), Jonathan D. Coleman (1997)
Investment objective and policies: Capital appreciation consistent with capital preservation. Invests in common stocks of companies with potentially strong growth in revenues, earnings and assets, primarily with market capitalization less than $1B or annual revenues of less than $500M at the time of purchase. Some will have limited operating histories (less than five years) and may depend on new products, services or processes. May invest in securities of foreign issuers without limit. Up to 35% of assets may be in junk bonds and 15% in illiquid securities. May use futures and options for hedging purposes. Fund is non-diversified.
Year organized: 1984
Ticker symbol: JAVTX
Group fund code: 45
Special sales restrictions: Fund closed to new shareholders 9/30/91.

Discount broker availability: *Fidelity, *Schwab, *Siebert, *White
Dividends paid: Income - December; Capital gains - December
Portfolio turnover (3 yrs): 146%, 136%, 113%
Management fee: 0.75% first $270M to 0.65% over $500M
Expense ratio: 0.92% (year ending 10/31/97) (0.94% without waiver)

JANUS WORLDWIDE FUND ◆
(See first Janus listing for data common to all funds)

Portfolio manager: Helen Young Hayes (1992)
Investment objective and policies: Long-term capital growth consistent with capital preservation. Invests primarily in a widely diversified portfolio of common stocks of foreign and domestic issuers, regardless of size, country of origin or place of principal business activity. May invest in fixed-income securities of corporations, domestic and foreign issuers, government agencies and other government entities. Normally invests in securities of issuers from at least five different countries, including the U.S., but usually holds very few domestic issues. Up to 35% of assets may be in junk bonds and 15% in illiquid securities. May use futures and options for hedging purposes.
Year organized: 1991
Ticker symbol: JAWWX
Group fund code: 41
Discount broker availability: *Fidelity, *Schwab, *Siebert, *White
Dividends paid: Income - December; Capital gains - December
Portfolio turnover (3 yrs): 79%, 80%, 142%
Management fee: 0.75% first $270M to 0.65% over $500M
Expense ratio: 0.95% (year ending 10/31/97) (0.97% without waiver)

THE JAPAN ALPHA FUND ◆
(Fund liquidated 12/31/97)

JAPAN FUND ◆
Shareholder Service Center
Two International Place
Boston, MA 02110-4103
800-225-2470, 800-535-2726
617-295-1000, prices 800-343-2890
TDD 800-543-7916, fax 617-261-4420

Adviser and manager: Scudder, Kemper Investments, Inc.
Investment research adviser: Nikko International Capital Mgmt. Co., Ltd.
Portfolio managers: Seung Kwak (1989), Elizabeth J. Allan (1991)
Transfer agent: Scudder Service Corp.
Investment objective and policies: Long-term capital growth. Invests primarily in equity securities, including ADRs, of Japanese companies - common stock, preferred stock, warrants, and convertible debentures. May, although, invest in government and corporate debt securities at will. May invest in affiliates of Japanese companies listed on non-Japanese exchanges, and issuers not organized under the laws of Japan but deriving 50% or more of their revenues from Japan. May use currency transactions, and futures and options for hedging purposes.
Year organized: 1962 (formerly a closed-end fund, open-ended 8/14/87)
Ticker symbol: SJPNX
Minimum purchase: Initial: $2,500, Subsequent: $100; IRA/Keogh: $500, Subsequent: $50; Automatic investment plan: Subsequent: $50
Wire orders accepted: Yes
Deadline for same day wire purchase: 4 P.M.
Discount broker availability: Fidelity, *Schwab, Siebert, *White
Qualified for sale in: All states
Telephone redemptions: Yes
Wire redemptions: Yes, $5 fee
Letter redemptions: Signature guarantee required over $100,000
Telephone switching: With all Scudder funds
Number of switches permitted: 4 round trips per year

Dividends paid: Income - December; Capital gains - March, December
Portfolio turnover (3 yrs): 73%, 70%, 74%
Shareholder services: IRA, SEP-IRA, Keogh, 401(k), 403(b), corporate retirement plans, electronic funds transfer, systematic withdrawal plan min. bal. req. $10,000
Maintenance fee: $10 per year for balances of less than $2,500 (waived for shareholders with aggregate Scudder accounts over $25,000)
Management fee: 0.85% first $100M to 0.65% over $600M
Expense ratio: 1.71% (year ending 12/31/96)
IRA fees: None
Keogh fees: Annual $10

THE JENSEN PORTFOLIO ◆
430 Pioneer Tower
888 S.W. Fifth Avenue
Portland, OR 97204-2018
800-221-4384, 503-274-2044
prices/yields 800-338-1579
fax 503-274-2031

Adviser: Jensen Investment Management, Inc.
Portfolio managers: Val E. Jensen (1992), Gary Hibler (1992), Robert Zagunis (1992)
Transfer agent: Firstar Trust Co.
Investment objective and policies: Long-term capital appreciation; increasing dividend income over time secondary. Invests primarily in common stocks of 20 to 30 companies selected by the adviser based on criteria that evaluate a company's current financial strength and potential for increasing long-term returns. May invest in securities of foreign issuers. Fund is non-diversified.
Year organized: 1992
Minimum purchase: Initial: $1,000, Subsequent: None; Automatic investment plan: Subsequent: $100
Wire orders accepted: Yes
Deadline for same day wire purchase: 4 P.M.
Discount broker availability: Schwab, White
Qualified for sale in: AZ, CA, ID, NV, OR, WA (will register in states with interest)
Letter redemptions: Signature guarantee required over $10,000
Dividends paid: Income - March, June, September, December; Capital gains - December
Portfolio turnover (3 yrs): 24%, 48%, 11%
Shareholder services: IRA, 403(b)
Management fee: 0.50%
Expense ratio: 1.00% (year ending 5/31/97)
IRA fees: Annual $12.50

JHAVERI VALUE FUND ◆
P.O. Box 16188
Cleveland, OH 44116
216-356-1565
fax 216-331-7040
e-mail: saumi19@mail.idt.net

Adviser: Investments Technology, Inc.
Portfolio manager: Ramesh C. Jhaveri (1995), Saumil R. Jhaveri (1995)
Transfer agent: Maxus Information Systems, Inc.
Investment objective and policies: Long-term capital appreciation; current income incidental. Invests in a broad range of common stocks selected using a proprietary investment model. Portfolio will be diversified across a broad range of companies and industries in an effort to limit risk. May invest in foreign companies through ADRs.
Year organized: 1995
Minimum purchase: Initial: $10,000, Subsequent: $1,000; IRA: Initial: $2,000
Wire orders accepted: Yes
Deadline for same day wire purchase: 12 NN
Qualified for sale in: AZ, DC, IN, NC, OH
Letter redemptions: Signature guarantee required
Dividends paid: Income - December; Capital gains - March, December
Portfolio turnover (2 yrs): 54%, 45%
Shareholder services: IRA, SEP-IRA
Management fee: 2.50% (Advisor pays all fund expenses)
Expense ratio: 2.50% (year ending 3/31/97) (includes waiver)
IRA fees: Annual $10

JURIKA & VOYLES BALANCED FUND ◆
Lake Merrit Plaza
1900 Harrison, Suite 700
Oakland, CA 94612-3517
800-852-1991, 800-458-7452
510-446-1991, fax 510-446-1983

Adviser: Jurika & Voyles, L.P.
Administrator: Investment Company Administration Corp.
Portfolio managers: William K. Jurika (1992), Peter Goetz (1996)
Transfer agent: State Street Bank & Trust Co.
Investment objective and policies: A balance of long-term capital appreciation and current income. Invests primarily in a diversified portfolio of stocks, bonds and cash equivalents, with allocations adjusted according to perceived market conditions. Equities comprise at least 40% to 70% of the portfolio, fixed-income instruments at least 25%, and cash 0% to 35%. Generally at least 80% of equity holdings will be of companies with market capitalizations exceeding $500M. May invest up to 25% of assets in foreign securities, and up to 25% in junk bonds.
Year organized: 1992
Ticker symbol: JVBAX
Minimum purchase: Initial: $10,000, Subsequent: $1,000; Automatic investment plan: Initial: $1,000
Wire orders accepted: Yes
Deadline for same day wire purchase: 4 P.M.
Discount broker availability: *Fidelity, *Schwab, *White
Qualified for sale in: All states
Telephone redemptions: Yes, $1,000 minimum
Wire redemptions: Yes, $10 fee
Letter redemptions: Signature guarantee required over $50,000
Telephone switching: With Jurika & Voyles Mini-Cap fund and Value Plus Growth fund (subject to its $250,000 minimum), and the SSgA Money Market
Number of switches permitted: Unlimited
Dividends paid: Income - quarterly; Capital gains - annually
Portfolio turnover (3 yrs): 92%, 69%, 54%
Shareholder services: Electronic funds transfer, systematic withdrawal plan
Shareholder services fees: 0.15%
Management fee: 0.70%
Expense ratio: 1.26% (year ending 6/30/97) (1.31% without waiver)

JURIKA & VOYLES MINI-CAP FUND ◆
Lake Merrit Plaza
1900 Harrison, Suite 700
Oakland, CA 94612-3517
800-852-1991, 800-458-7452
510-446-1991, fax 510-446-1983

Adviser: Jurika & Voyles, L.P.
Administrator: Investment Company Administration Corp.
Portfolio managers: Paul Meeks (1997), Guy Elliffe (1997)
Transfer agent: State Street Bank & Trust Co.
Investment objective and policies: Maximum long-term capital appreciation. Invests at least 65% of assets in common stock of companies with market capitalizations no larger than that of the largest issues included in the Russell 2000. Median and weighted average market capitalization of the portfolio remains primarily below $1B. May invest up to 25% of assets in foreign securities, and up to 35% of assets in debt securities, including as much as 25% in junk bonds.
Year organized: 1992
Ticker symbol: JVMCX
Minimum purchase: Initial: $10,000, Subsequent: $1,000; Automatic investment plan: Initial: $1,000
Wire orders accepted: Yes
Deadline for same day wire purchase: 4 P.M.
Discount broker availability: *Fidelity, *Schwab, *White
Qualified for sale in: All states
Telephone redemptions: Yes, $1,000 minimum
Wire redemptions: Yes, $10 fee
Letter redemptions: Signature guarantee required over $50,000
Telephone switching: With Jurika & Voyles Balanced fund and Value Plus Growth fund (subject to its $250,000 minimum), and the SSgA Money Market

Number of switches permitted: Unlimited
Dividends paid: Income - annually; Capital gains - annually
Portfolio turnover (3 yrs): 305%, 215%, 103%
Shareholder services: Electronic funds transfer, systematic withdrawal plan
Shareholder services fees: 0.25%
Management fee: 1.00%
Expense ratio: 1.50% (year ending 6/30/97)

KALMAR GROWTH WITH VALUE SMALL CAP FUND ◆

Barley Mill House
3701 Kennett Pike
Greenville, DE 19807
800-282-2319, 302-658-7575
fax 302-658-7513

Adviser: Kalmar Investment Advisers
Lead portfolio manager: Ford B. Draper, Jr. (1997)
Transfer agent and administrator: Rodney Square Management Corp.
Investment objective and policies: Long-term capital appreciation. Invests primarily in a diversified portfolio of common stocks of companies whose market capitalizations range from $50M to $1B at the time of purchase. Companies selected are perceived to afford future capital appreciation while currently selling at a reasonable or undervalued price. May invest up to 15% of assets in foreign issues, including ADRs, up to 15% in illiquid securities, and up to 5% of assets in junk bonds. May use options in an effort to enhance performance and for hedging purposes, and sell short against the box.
Year organized: 1997
Ticker symbol: KGSCX
Minimum purchase: Initial: $10,000, Subsequent: $1,000; IRA: Initial: $1,000, Subsequent: None; Automatic investment plan: Subsequent: $100
Wire orders accepted: Yes
Deadline for same day wire purchase: 4 P.M.
Discount broker availability: *Fidelity, Schwab (only through financial advisers)
Qualified for sale in: All states
Telephone redemptions: Yes
Wire redemptions: $1,000 minimum
Letter redemptions: Signature guarantee required over $25,000
Telephone switching: With the Kalmar Micro Cap fund when it opens
Number of switches permitted: Unlimited
Dividends paid: Income - annually; Capital gains - annually
Shareholder services: IRA, electronic funds transfer (redemption only), systematic withdrawal plan min. bal. req. $10,000
Management fee: 1.00%
Administration fee: 0.15% first $50M, 0.10% over $50M
IRA fees: Annual $10

KAMINSKI POLAND FUND

210 North Second Street, Suite 050
Minneapolis, MN 55401
888-765-3863, 888-229-2105
612-305-9026
fax 612-321-0928
Internet: http://www.polfund.com
e-mail: maciek@visi.com

Adviser: Kaminski Asset Management, Inc.
Administrator: Investment Company Administration Corp.
Portfolio manager: M.G. Kaminski (1997)
Transfer agent: American Data Services, Inc.
Investment objective and policies: Long-term capital appreciation. Invests at least 80% of assets in a portfolio of publicly traded equity securities of companies domiciled in Poland whose market capitalizations exceed $20M and whose record of annual earnings growth exceeds 10%. May also invest in shares of investment companies being formed as part of the privatization of state-owned companies. May invest without limit in short-term debt securities and money markets for defensive purposes. May buy or write options on equities and on stock indices, and may engage in foreign exchange transactions.
Year organized: 1997

Minimum purchase: Initial: $1,000, Subsequent: $250; Automatic investment plan: Subsequent: $50
Wire orders accepted: Yes
Deadline for same day wire purchase: 4 P.M.
Discount broker availability: *White
Qualified for sale in: All states
Telephone redemptions: Yes, $1,000 minimum, $12 fee
Wire redemptions: $1,000 minimum, $12 fee
Letter redemptions: Signature guarantee required over $5,000
Dividends paid: Income - December; Capital gains - December
Shareholder services: IRA, systematic withdrawal plan min. bal. req. $10,000
Management fee: 1.45% first $20M, 1.25% over $20M
Administration fee: 0.20% ($30,000 minimum)
12b-1 distribution fee: 0.25%
IRA fees: Annual $15, Initial $15, Closing $15

KAUFMANN FUND

140 East 45th Street, 43rd Floor
New York, NY 10017
800-261-0555, 212-922-0123
prices 212-661-4699
Internet: http://www.kaufmann.com

Adviser: Edgemont Asset Management Corp.
Portfolio managers: Hans P. Utsch (1986), Lawrence Auriana (1986)
Transfer agent: Boston Financial Data Services, Inc.
Investment objective and policies: Long-term capital appreciation. Invests primarily in common stocks of smaller companies with annual sales under $500M and, to a lesser extent, convertible preferred stocks and convertible bonds. Fund may sell short up to 25% of total assets, leverage up to 1/3 of assets, have up to 10% in restricted securities, 25% in foreign securities, 10% in other mutual funds, and write, purchase and/or sell puts and covered calls with aggregate premiums up to 10% of assets.
Year organized: 1967
Ticker symbol: KAUFX
Minimum purchase: Initial: $1,500, Subsequent: $100; IRA/Automatic investment plan: Initial: $500, Subsequent: $50
Wire orders accepted: Yes, $1,000 subsequent minimum, $9 fee
Deadline for same day wire purchase: 4 P.M.
Discount broker availability: *Fidelity, *Schwab, *Siebert, *White
Qualified for sale in: All states
Telephone redemptions: Yes
Letter redemptions: Signature guarantee required
Redemption fee: 0.20% on shares purchased after 2/1/85
Telephone switching: With The Reserve Money Market Fund, $1,000 minimum
Number of switches permitted: Unlimited (2/year for pension plans)
Dividends paid: Income - November; Capital gains - November
Portfolio turnover (3 yrs): 72%, 60%, 47%
Shareholder services: IRA, 401(k), 403(b), electronic funds transfer, systematic withdrawal plan min. bal. req. $5,000
Management fee: 1.50%
Shareholder services fee: Maximum of 0.25%
12b-1 distribution fee: Maximum of 0.75%
Expense ratio: 1.92% (year ending 12/31/96) (1.93% without waiver)
IRA fees: Annual $12 (waived for balances over $20,000)

KAYNE, ANDERSON FUNDS ◆

(Data common to all Kayne Anderson funds are shown below. See subsequent listings for data specific to individual funds.)

1800 Avenue of the Stars, Second Floor
Los Angeles, CA 90067
800-395-3807, 800-231-7414
310-556-2721

Adviser: Kayne, Anderson Investment Management
Administrator: Investment Company Administration Corp.
Transfer agent: Investors Bank and Trust Co.

Minimum purchase: Initial: $2,000, Subsequent: $250; IRA: Initial: $1,000, Subsequent: $200; Automatic investment plan: Subsequent: $100
Wire orders accepted: Yes
Deadline for same day wire purchase: 4 P.M.
Qualified for sale in: All states
Telephone redemptions: Yes, $1,000 minimum
Wire redemptions: Yes, $1,000 minimum, $7 fee
Letter redemptions: Signature guarantee required over $50,000
Telephone switching: With other Kayne Anderson funds
Number of switches permitted: Unlimited
Shareholder services: IRA, SEP-IRA, electronic funds transfer (redemption only), systematic withdrawal plan min. bal. req. $10,000
Administration fee: 0.075% first $40M to 0.01% over $120M ($30,000 minimum per fund)
IRA fee: $10 Annual

KAYNE, ANDERSON INTERMEDIATE TAX-FREE BOND FUND ◆

(See first Kayne Anderson listing for data common to all funds)

Portfolio manager: Mark E. Miller (1996)
Investment objective and policies: Current income exempt from federal income taxes, consistent with preservation of capital. Invests at least 80% of assets in investment grade municipal securities upon which the interest is tax exempt. Normally will maintain a dollar-weighted average maturity between three and ten years.
Year organized: 1996
Discount broker availability: Schwab (only through financial advisers)
Dividends paid: Income - declared daily, paid monthly; Capital gains - December
Management fee: 0.50%
Expense ratio: 0.95% (three months ending 12/31/96) (2.08% without waiver)

KAYNE, ANDERSON INTERMEDIATE TOTAL RETURN BOND FUND ◆

(See first Kayne Anderson listing for data common to all funds)

Portfolio manager: Mark E. Miller (1996)
Investment objective and policies: Total return: primarily through current income, with capital appreciation contributing secondarily. Invests primarily in domestic and foreign investment grade fixed-income securities and seeks to maintain an average maturity of three to ten years.
Year organized: 1996
Discount broker availability: Schwab (only through financial advisers)
Dividends paid: Income - monthly; Capital gains - December
Management fee: 0.50%
Expense ratio: 0.95% (three months ending 12/31/96) (2.10% without waiver)

KAYNE, ANDERSON INTERNATIONAL RISING DIVIDENDS FUND ◆

(See first Kayne Anderson listing for data common to all funds)

Portfolio manager: Jean-Baptiste Nadal (1996)
Investment objective and policies: Long-term capital appreciation; income secondary. Invests at least 65% of assets in equity securities, primarily common stocks, of companies outside of the U.S. with market capitalizations exceeding $1B, and demonstrating an increase in dividends in at least three of the last five years, with a maximum of 65% payout of current earnings. Furthermore, the companies should have increased dividends at a rate that would double them in ten years, and not cut them during this period.
Year organized: 1996
Discount broker availability: Schwab (only through financial advisers)
Dividends paid: Income - December; Capital gains - December
Management fee: 0.95%
Expense ratio: 1.40% (three months ending 12/31/96) (15.74% without waiver)

KAYNE, ANDERSON
RISING DIVIDENDS FUND ♦

(See first Kayne Anderson listing for data common to all funds)

Portfolio manager: Allan M. Rudnick (1996)
Investment objective and policies: Long-term capital appreciation; income secondary. Invests at least 65% of assets in equity securities, primarily common stocks, of companies demonstrating an increase in dividends in at least seven of the last ten years, with a maximum of 65% payout of current earnings. Furthermore, the companies should have increased dividends by at least 100% in the past ten years, and not cut them during this period.
Year organized: 1995
Ticker symbol: KARDX
Discount broker availability: Schwab (only through financial advisers), White
Dividends paid: Income - December; Capital gains - December
Portfolio turnover (2 yrs): 23%, 28%
Management fee: 0.75%
Expense ratio: 1.37% (year ending 12/31/96)

KAYNE, ANDERSON SMALL-MID CAP
RISING DIVIDENDS FUND ♦

(See first Kayne Anderson listing for data common to all funds)

Portfolio managers: Robert Schwarzkopf (1996), Sandi Gleason (1997)
Investment objective and policies: Long-term capital appreciation; income secondary. Invests at least 65% of assets in equity securities, primarily common stocks, of companies with market capitalizations ranging from $50M to $1B, demonstrating an increase in dividends in at least three of the last five years, with a maximum of 65% payout of current earnings. Furthermore, the companies should have increased dividends at a rate that would double them in ten years, and not cut them during this period.
Year organized: 1996
Discount broker availability: Schwab (only through financial advisers), White
Dividends paid: Income - December; Capital gains - December
Management fee: 0.85%
Expense ratio: 1.30% (three months ending 12/31/96) (18.91% without waiver)

KEMPER MONEY MARKET FUNDS

(Data common to all Kemper money market funds are shown below. See subsequent listings for data specific to individual funds.)

222 South Riverside Plaza
Chicago, IL 60606-5808
312-537-7000
800-621-1048, yields 800-972-3060
fax 312-537-6001
Internet: www.kemper.com

Adviser: Zurich Kemper Investments, Inc.
Transfer agent: The Kemper Service Co.
Special sales restrictions: These six funds represent two private label series managed by Kemper which are used primarily as omnibus accounts for mutual fund companies which do not have their own money market funds. See each fund listing for a partial list of companies involved. See Zurich Money funds for Kemper's direct offerings under their new names.
Wire orders accepted: Yes
Deadline for same day wire purchase: 11 A.M. CST
Qualified for sale in: All states
Telephone redemptions: Yes
Wire redemptions: Yes, $1,000 minimum
Letter redemptions: Signature guarantee required over $25,000
Telephone switching: With other Kemper Funds (which have loads), and other mutual fund families under special arrangement (see fund), $100 minimum
Number of switches: Unlimited
Dividends paid: Income - declared daily, paid monthly
Shareholder services: IRA, SEP-IRA, Keogh, 401(k), 403(b), corporate retirement plans, automatic investment plan, electronic funds transfer, systematic withdrawal plan min. bal. req. $5,000
IRA/Keogh fees: Annual $12 per account, $24 maximum per SSN#

KEMPER CASH ACCOUNT TRUST -
GOVERNMENT SECURITIES
PORTFOLIO

(See first Kemper listing for data common to all funds)
800-231-8568

Portfolio managers: Frank J. Rachwalski, Jr. (1990), John W. Stuebe (1990)
Investment objective and policies: Maximum current income consistent with stability of capital. Invests exclusively in money market obligations issued or guaranteed by the U.S. Government, its agencies or its instrumentalities.
Year organized: 1990
Ticker symbol: CAGXX
Minimum purchase: Initial: $1,000, Subsequent: $100; IRA/Keogh: Initial: $250, Subsequent: $50
Check redemptions: $500 minimum
Telephone switching: With Analysts Investment Trust, Berger, Fairport and Vontobel funds
Management fee: 0.22% first $500M to 0.15% over $3B (for all portfolios combined)
12b-1 distribution fee: 0.60%
Expense ratio: 0.92% (year ending 4/30/97) (0.99% without waiver)

KEMPER CASH ACCOUNT TRUST -
MONEY MARKET PORTFOLIO

(See first Kemper listing for data common to all funds)
800-231-8568

Portfolio managers: Frank J. Rachwalski, Jr. (1990), John W. Stuebe (1990)
Investment objective and policies: Maximum current income consistent with stability of capital. Invests in high quality money market instruments.
Year organized: 1990
Ticker symbol: CSAXX
Minimum purchase: Initial: $1,000, Subsequent: $100; IRA/Keogh: Initial: $250, Subsequent: $50
Check redemptions: $500 minimum
Telephone switching: With Analysts Investment Trust, Berger, Fairport and Vontobel funds
Management fee: 0.22% first $500M to 0.15% over $3B (for all portfolios combined)
12b-1 distribution fee: 0.60%
Expense ratio: 1.00% (year ending 4/30/97) (1.03% without waiver)

KEMPER CASH ACCOUNT TRUST -
TAX-EXEMPT PORTFOLIO

(See first Kemper listing for data common to all funds)
800-231-8568

Portfolio managers: Frank J. Rachwalski, Jr. (1990), John W. Stuebe (1990)
Investment objective and policies: Maximum current income exempt from federal income tax, consistent with stability of capital. Invests in a diversified portfolio of municipal money market instruments.
Year organized: 1990
Minimum purchase: Initial: $1,000, Subsequent: $100
Check redemptions: $500 minimum
Telephone switching: With Analysts Investment Trust, Berger, Fairport and Vontobel funds
Management fee: 0.22% first $500M to 0.15% over $3B (for all portfolios combined)
12b-1 distribution fee: 0.50%
Expense ratio: 0.81% (year ending 4/30/97) (0.96% without waiver)

KEMPER CASH EQUIVALENT FUND -
GOVERNMENT SECURITIES
PORTFOLIO

(See first Kemper listing for data common to all funds)
800-231-8568

Portfolio managers: Frank J. Rachwalski, Jr. (1979), John W. Stuebe (1982)
Investment objective and policies: Maximum current income consistent with stability of capital. Invests

exclusively in short-term obligations issued or guaranteed by the U.S. Treasury, or the U.S. Government and its agencies or instrumentalities. May also invest in repurchase agreements of such obligations.
Year organized: 1979
Ticker symbol: CQGXX
Minimum purchase: Initial: $1,000, Subsequent: $100; IRA/Keogh: Initial: $250
Check redemptions: $250 minimum
Telephone switching: With Gateway funds
Management fee: 0.22% first $500M to 0.15% over $3B (for all portfolios combined)
12b-1 distribution fee: Maximum of 0.40%
Expense ratio: 0.83% (year ending 7/31/97)

KEMPER CASH EQUIVALENT FUND -
MONEY MARKET PORTFOLIO

(See first Kemper listing for data common to all funds)
800-231-8568

Portfolio managers: Frank J. Rachwalski, Jr. (1979), John W. Stuebe (1979)
Investment objective and policies: Maximum current income consistent with stability of capital. Invests exclusively in short-term prime U.S. and Canadian commercial and bank money market instruments, and obligations guaranteed by the U.S. and Canadian Governments. Also invests in repurchase agreements on such obligations.
Year organized: 1979
Ticker symbol: CQMXX
Minimum purchase: Initial: $1,000, Subsequent: $100; IRA/Keogh: Initial: $250
Check redemptions: $250 minimum
Telephone switching: With Gateway funds
Management fee: 0.22% first $500M to 0.15% over $3B (for all portfolios combined)
12b-1 distribution fee: Maximum of 0.40%
Expense ratio: 0.93% (year ending 7/31/97)

KEMPER CASH EQUIVALENT FUND -
TAX-EXEMPT PORTFOLIO

(See first Kemper listing for data common to all funds)
800-231-8568

Portfolio managers: Frank J. Rachwalski, Jr. (1979), John W. Stuebe (1979)
Investment objective and policies: Maximum current income that is exempt from federal income taxes, consistent with stability of capital. Invests at least 80% of assets in short-term, investment grade municipal money market instruments ranked in the two highest grades. May invest up to 20% of assets in securities subject to AMT tax treatment.
Year organized: 1979
Ticker symbol: TEMXX
Minimum purchase: Initial: $1,000, Subsequent: $100
Check redemptions: $250 minimum
Telephone switching: With Gateway funds
Management fee: 0.22% first $500M to 0.15% over $3B (for all portfolios combined)
12b-1 distribution fee: Maximum of 0.33%
Expense ratio: 0.71% (year ending 7/31/97)

KEMPER MONEY FUNDS ♦

(See Zurich Money Funds)

KENT MUTUAL FUNDS

(Data common to all Kent funds are shown below. See subsequent listings for data specific to individual funds.)

One Vandenberg Center
Grand Rapids, MI 49503
800-633-5368, 616-771-5817

Adviser: Old Kent Bank (an indirect, wholly owned subsidiary of Old Kent Financial Corp.)
Administrator and transfer agent: BISYS Fund Services, Inc.
Sales restrictions: Fund is available in two share classes, Investment and Institutional. Only Investment shares are profiled here.

Minimum purchase: Initial: $1,000, Subsequent: None; IRA: Initial: $100; Automatic investment plan: Subsequent: $50
Wire orders accepted: Yes
Deadline for same day wire purchase: 4 P.M.
Telephone redemption: Yes
Wire redemptions: Yes, $2,500 minimum
Letter redemptions: Signature guarantee required over $50,000
Telephone switching: With the same share class of other Kent funds
Number of switches permitted: 5 per year, 3 per quarter
Shareholder services: IRA, SEP-IRA, electronic funds transfer, systematic withdrawal plan min. bal. req. $10,000
Administration fee: 0.185% of aggregate assets of $5B or less, to 0.135% over $7.5B ($45,000 minimum per fund)
IRA fees: None

KENT GOVERNMENT MONEY MARKET FUND ◆
(See first Kent listing for data common to all funds)

Investment objective and policies: Current income while preserving capital and maintaining liquidity. Invests in short-term securities issued by the U.S. Government, its agencies or instrumentalities, or repurchase agreements with respect to such securities.
Year organized: 1997
Qualified for sale in: AZ, CA, CO, DC, FL, GA, IL, IN, MI, MN, MS, MO, NJ, NY, NC, OH, PA, SD, TN, TX, WA, WI
Dividends paid: Income - declared daily, paid monthly
Management fee: 0.40%
12b-1 distribution fee: Maximum of 0.25% (not currently imposed)

KENT GROWTH AND INCOME FUND
(See first Kent listing for data common to all funds)

Portfolio managers: Michael A. Petersen (1992), David C. Eder (1992), Joseph T. Keating (1992)
Investment objective and policies: Long-term growth of capital; current income secondary. Invests primarily in the common stock of companies listed on the New York or American Stock Exchanges which have a net capitalization of at least $100M. May also invest in preferred stock or convertible bonds, and maintain up to 10% of assets in foreign securities or ADRs. May use options and futures for hedging purposes.
Year organized: 1992
Ticker symbol: KNVIX
Qualified for sale in: AL, AR, AZ, CA, CO, DC, FL, GA, IL, IN, MD, MI, MN, MS, MO, NJ, NM, NY, NC, OH, PA, SD, TN, TX, WA, WI
Dividends paid: Income - monthly; Capital gains - annually
Portfolio turnover (3 yrs): 39%, 58%, 28%
Management fee: 0.70%
12b-1 distribution fee: Maximum of 0.25%
Expense ratio: (1.09% year ending 12/31/96)

KENT INCOME FUND
(See first Kent listing for data common to all funds)

Portfolio managers: Mitchell L. Stapley (1995), Joseph T. Keating (1995)
Investment objective and policies: High current income consistent with the preservation of capital. Invests in a broad range of investment quality corporate and domestic fixed-income securities, maintaining a dollar-weighted average portfolio maturity between seven and twenty years.
Year organized: 1995
Qualified for sale in: AZ, CA, CO, DC, FL, GA, IL, IN, MD, MI, MN, MS, MO, NJ, NY, NC, OH, PA, SD, TN, TX, WA, WI
Dividends paid: Income - monthly; Capital gains - annually
Portfolio turnover (2 yrs): 102%, 50%
Management fee: 0.60%
12b-1 distribution fee: Maximum of 0.25%
Expense ratio: (1.08% year ending 12/31/96)

KENT INDEX EQUITY FUND
(See first Kent listing for data common to all funds)

Portfolio managers: Michael A. Petersen (1992), David C. Eder (1992), Joseph T. Keating (1992)
Investment objective and policies: Investment results which mirror the capital performance and dividend income of the S&P 500 Composite Stock Price Index. Invests in the common stock of companies comprising the benchmark index in approximately the same weightings. Will attempt to achieve a performance correlation of at least 0.95, not accounting for expenses. May use options and futures for hedging purposes.
Year organized: 1992
Ticker symbol: KNIDX
Qualified for sale in: AL, AZ, CA, CO, DC, FL, GA, IL, IN, MD, MI, MN, MS, MO, NJ, NM, NY, NC, OH, PA, SD, TN, TX, WA, WI
Dividends paid: Income - monthly; Capital gains - annually
Portfolio turnover (3 yrs): 2%, 3%, 50%
Management fee: 0.30%
12b-1 distribution fee: Maximum of 0.25%
Expense ratio: (0.49% year ending 12/31/96) (0.59% without waiver)

KENT INTERMEDIATE BOND FUND
(See first Kent listing for data common to all funds)

Portfolio managers: Mitchell L. Stapley (1992), Joseph T. Keating (1992)
Investment objective and policies: Current income consistent with the preservation of capital. Invests in a broad range of investment grade corporate and U.S. Government fixed-income instruments, maintaining a dollar-weighted average portfolio maturity between three and ten years.
Year organized: 1992
Ticker symbol: KNFVX
Qualified for sale in: AL, AZ, CA, CO, DC, FL, GA, IL, IN, MD, MI, MN, MS, MO, NJ, NY, NC, OH, PA, SD, TN, TX, WA, WI
Dividends paid: Income - monthly; Capital gains - annually
Portfolio turnover (3 yrs): 135%, 166%, 124%
Management fee: 0.55%
12b-1 distribution fee: Maximum of 0.25%
Expense ratio: (1.02% year ending 12/31/96) (1.03% without waiver)

KENT INTERMEDIATE TAX-FREE FUND
(See first Kent listing for data common to all funds)

Portfolio managers: Allan J. Meyers (1992), Joseph T. Keating (1992)
Investment objective and policies: Current income exempt from federal income tax, consistent with preservation of capital. Invests in a broadly diversified portfolio of municipal debt securities of any maturity. Fund will maintain a dollar-weighted average portfolio maturity between three and ten years.
Year organized: 1992
Ticker symbol: KNMBX
Qualified for sale in: AL, AZ, CA, CO, DC, FL, GA, IL, IN, LA, MI, MN, NJ, NM, NC, OH, PA, SD, WI
Dividends paid: Income - monthly; Capital gains - annually
Portfolio turnover (3 yrs): 35%, 6%, 36%
Management fee: 0.50%
12b-1 distribution fee: Maximum of 0.25%
Expense ratio: (0.98% year ending 12/31/96)

KENT INTERNATIONAL GROWTH FUND
(See first Kent listing for data common to all funds)

Portfolio managers: Michael A. Petersen (1992), David C. Eder (1992), Joseph T. Keating (1992)
Investment objective and policies: Long-term capital appreciation. Invests primarily in equity securities, mostly common and preferred stock, of companies diversified across at least three countries other than the U.S. Invests almost exclusively in companies in the developed world. Fund uses a top down country analysis to weight its allocations, shifting to countries per-

ceived to be undervalued. May purchase ADRs and use options and futures and forward foreign currency contracts for hedging purposes.
Year organized: 1992
Ticker symbol: KNIVX
Qualified for sale in: AL, AZ, CA, CO, DC, FL, GA, IL, IN, MD, MI, MN, MS, MO, NJ, NM, NY, NC, OH, PA, SD, TN, TX, WA, WI
Dividends paid: Income - annually; Capital gains - annually
Portfolio turnover (3 yrs): 13%, 6%, 20%
Management fee: 0.75%
12b-1 distribution fee: Maximum of 0.25%
Expense ratio: (1.34% year ending 12/31/96)

KENT LIMITED TERM TAX-FREE FUND
(See first Kent listing for data common to all funds)

Portfolio managers: Allan J. Meyers (1994), Michael J. Martin (1994), Joseph T. Keating (1994)
Investment objective and policies: Current income exempt from federal income tax, consistent with preservation of capital. Invests in a broadly diversified portfolio of municipal debt securities of any maturity less than ten years. Fund will maintain a dollar-weighted average portfolio maturity between one and three years.
Year organized: 1994
Ticker symbol: KLTIX
Qualified for sale in: AZ, CA, CO, DC, FL, GA, IL, IN, LA, MI, MN, NJ, NM, NC, OH, PA, SD, WI
Dividends paid: Income - monthly; Capital gains - annually
Portfolio turnover (2 yrs): 32%, 51%
Management fee: 0.45%
12b-1 distribution fee: Maximum of 0.25%
Expense ratio: (0.87% year ending 12/31/96) (0.97% without waiver)

KENT MICHIGAN MUNICIPAL BOND FUND
(See first Kent listing for data common to all funds)

Portfolio managers: Allan J. Meyers (1993), Michael J. Martin (1993), Joseph T. Keating (1993)
Investment objective and policies: Current income exempt from federal and Michigan personal income taxes, consistent with preservation of capital. Invests at least 65% of assets in municipal obligations issued by the state of Michigan or its political subdivisions. No obligation will have a remaining maturity of more than ten years, and the portfolio will maintain a dollar-weighted average between three and five years.
Year organized: 1993
Ticker symbol: KNMVX
Qualified for sale in: AZ, CA, CO, DC, FL, GA, IL, IN, MI, MN, NJ, NC, OH, PA, SD, WI
Dividends paid: Income - monthly; Capital gains - annually
Portfolio turnover (3 yrs): 24%, 42%, 27%
Management fee: 0.45%
12b-1 distribution fee: Maximum of 0.25%
Expense ratio: (0.85% year ending 12/31/96) (0.95% without waiver)

KENT MICHIGAN MUNICIPAL MONEY MARKET FUND ◆
(See first Kent listing for data common to all funds)

Investment objective and policies: Current income exempt from federal and Michigan personal income taxes, while preserving capital and maintaining liquidity. Invests at least 80% of assets in federally tax exempt municipal obligations, and at least 65% of assets in Michigan municipal obligations.
Year organized: 1992
Qualified for sale in: AZ, CA, CO, DC, FL, GA, IL, IN, MI, MN, NJ, NC, OH, PA, SD, TX, WI
Dividends paid: Income - declared daily, paid monthly
Management fee: 0.40%
12b-1 distribution fee: Maximum of 0.25% (not currently imposed)
Expense ratio: (0.54% year ending 12/31/96) (0.64% without waiver)

KENT MONEY MARKET FUND ◆
(See first Kent listing for data common to all funds)

Investment objective and policies: Current income while preserving capital and maintaining liquidity. Invests in a broad range of short-term government, bank and commercial money market obligations.
Year organized: 1992
Qualified for sale in: AZ, CA, CO, DC, FL, GA, IL, IN, MD, MI, MN, MS, MO, NJ, NY, NC, OH, PA, SD, TN, TX, WA, WI
Dividends paid: Income - declared daily, paid monthly
Management fee: 0.40%
12b-1 distribution fee: Maximum of 0.25% (not currently imposed)
Expense ratio: (0.52% year ending 12/31/96) (0.62% without waiver)

KENT SHORT TERM BOND FUND
(See first Kent listing for data common to all funds)

Portfolio managers: Mitchell L. Stapley (1992), Joseph T. Keating (1992)
Investment objective and policies: Current income consistent with the preservation of capital. Invests in a limited range of investment grade corporate and U.S. Government fixed-income instruments with remaining maturities of five years or less, and a dollar-weighted average portfolio maturity between one and three years.
Year organized: 1992
Ticker symbol: KNLIX
Qualified for sale in: AZ, CA, CO, DC, FL, GA, IL, IN, MD, MI, MN, MS, MO, NJ, NY, NC, OH, PA, SD, TN, TX, WA, WI
Dividends paid: Income - monthly; Capital gains - annually
Portfolio turnover (3 yrs): 32%, 75%, 56%
Management fee: 0.50%
12b-1 distribution fee: Maximum of 0.25%
Expense ratio: (0.85% year ending 12/31/96) (0.96% without waiver)

KENT SMALL COMPANY GROWTH FUND
(See first Kent listing for data common to all funds)

Portfolio managers: Michael A. Petersen (1992), David C. Eder (1992), Joseph T. Keating (1992)
Investment objective and policies: Long-term capital appreciation. Invests primarily in equity securities of companies traded in the U.S. securities markets whose market capitalizations are less than $1B. May use options and futures for hedging purposes.
Year organized: 1992
Ticker symbol: KNEMX
Qualified for sale in: AZ, CA, CO, DC, FL, GA, IL, IN, MD, MI, MN, MS, MO, NJ, NM, NY, NC, OH, PA, SD, TN, TX, WA, WI
Dividends paid: Income - monthly; Capital gains - annually
Portfolio turnover (3 yrs): 16%, 30%, 20%
Management fee: 0.70%
12b-1 distribution fee: Maximum of 0.25%
Expense ratio: (1.21% year ending 12/31/96)

KENT TAX-FREE INCOME FUND
(See first Kent listing for data common to all funds)

Portfolio managers: Allan J. Meyers (1995), Joseph T. Keating (1995)
Investment objective and policies: As high a level of current income exempt from federal income tax as is consistent with prudent investment risk and preservation of capital. Invests in a broadly diversified portfolio of municipal debt securities of any maturity. Fund will maintain a dollar-weighted average portfolio maturity between ten and twenty-five years.
Year organized: 1995
Qualified for sale in: AZ, CA, CO, FL, GA, IL, IN, MI, MN, NJ, NC, OH, PA, SD, WI
Dividends paid: Income - monthly; Capital gains - annually
Portfolio turnover (2 yrs): 40%, 10%
Management fee: 0.55%
12b-1 distribution fee: Maximum of 0.25%
Expense ratio: (1.07% year ending 12/31/96)

KENWOOD GROWTH AND INCOME FUND
10 South LaSalle Street, Suite 3610
Chicago, IL 60603
888-536-3863, 312-368-1666
fax 312-368-1769

Adviser: The Kenwood Group, Inc.
Portfolio manager: Barbara L. Bowles (1996)
Transfer agent and administrator: Firstar Trust Co.
Investment objective and policies: High overall total return: capital appreciation and current income. Invests at least 85% of assets in domestic equity securities issued by companies with mid-cap market capitalizations between $200M and $6.5B. Issues are purchased if perceived to be temporarily undervalued but have potential for growth and a good dividend stream. May invest up to 15% of assets in other securities, including investment grade debt securities, and up to 15% in illiquid issues.
Year organized: 1996
Minimum purchase: Initial: $2,000, Subsequent: $100; IRA: Initial: $250
Wire orders accepted: Yes
Deadline for same day wire purchase: 4 P.M.
Discount broker availability: *Schwab
Qualified for sale in: All states
Telephone redemptions: Yes
Wire redemptions: Yes, $10 fee
Letter redemptions: Signature guarantee required over $25,000
Telephone switching: With Firstar Money Market funds
Number of switches permitted: 5 per year, one day hold, $5 fee
Dividends paid: Income - annually; Capital gains - annually
Portfolio turnover (1 yr): 31%
Shareholder services: IRA, automatic investment plan
Management fee: 0.75% first $500M to 0.65% over $1B
Administration fee: 0.05% first $100M to 0.03% over $500M ($20,000 minimum)
12b-1 distribution fee: 0.25%
Expense ratio: 0.92% (year ending 4/30/97) (7.84% without waiver)
IRA fees: Closing $10

KEY MUTUAL FUNDS
(Funds merged into the Victory Fund family 3/98)

KIEWIT MUTUAL FUNDS ◆
(Data common to all Kiewit funds are shown below. See subsequent listings for data specific to individual funds.)

1000 Kiewit Plaza
Omaha, NE 68131
800-254-3948, 402-536-3665

Adviser: Kiewit Investment Management Corp.
Transfer agent: Rodney Square Management Corp.
Minimum purchase: Initial: $10,000, Subsequent: None
Wire orders accepted: Yes
Deadline for same day wire purchase: 4 P.M. (2 P.M. for MM)
Qualified for sale in: All states
Telephone redemption: Yes
Wire redemptions: Yes
Letter redemptions: Signature guarantee required
Telephone switching: With other Kiewit funds
Number of switches permitted: Unlimited
Shareholder services: IRA, SEP-IRA
IRA fees: Annual $10

KIEWIT EQUITY PORTFOLIO ◆
(See first Kiewit listing for data common to all funds)

Portfolio managers: Livingston Douglas (1997), Brian J. Mosher (1995)
Investment objective and policies: Long-term capital appreciation. Invests all its investable assets in a corresponding series of an underlying trust which invests at least 65% of assets in a diversified portfolio of equity securities perceived to be undervalued. May

participate in cyclical sector rotation based on perception of the economic cycle. May also invest in investment grade debt issues and ADRs without limit. May use put and call options for hedging purposes.
Year organized: 1995
Dividends paid: Income - annually; Capital gains - annually
Portfolio turnover (3 yrs): 26%, 17%, 0%
Management fee: 0.70%
Expense ratio: 0.80% (year ending 6/30/97) (0.94% without waiver)

KIEWIT INTERMEDIATE-TERM BOND PORTFOLIO ◆
(See first Kiewit listing for data common to all funds)

Portfolio managers: Brian J. Mosher (1994), Livingston Douglas (1997)
Investment objective and policies: High current income consistent with reasonable risk. Invests all its investable assets in a corresponding series of an underlying trust which invests virtually all its assets in U.S. Treasury, U.S. Government agency, mortgage-backed, asset-backed, and corporate debt securities. Portfolio will maintain an average effective maturity of between three and ten years. May use put and call options for hedging purposes.
Year organized: 1994
Dividends paid: Income - declared daily, paid monthly; Capital gains - annually
Portfolio turnover (3 yrs): 52%, 86%, 121%
Management fee: 0.40%
Expense ratio: 0.50% (year ending 6/30/97) (0.58% without waiver)

KIEWIT MONEY MARKET PORTFOLIO ◆
(See first Kiewit listing for data common to all funds)

Portfolio managers: Brian J. Mosher (1994), Livingston Douglas (1997)
Investment objective and policies: High current income consistent with maintenance of a stable share price. Invests all its investable assets in a corresponding series of an underlying trust which invests in U.S. dollar denominated money market instruments maturing in 13 months or less.
Year organized: 1994
Dividends paid: Income - declared daily, paid monthly
Management fee: 0.20%
Expense ratio: 0.20% (year ending 6/30/97) (0.27% without waiver)

KIEWIT SHORT-TERM GOVERNMENT PORTFOLIO ◆
(See first Kiewit listing for data common to all funds)

Portfolio managers: Brian J. Mosher (1994), Livingston Douglas (1997)
Investment objective and policies: High current income consistent with the maintenance of principal and liquidity. Invests all its investable assets in a corresponding series of an underlying trust which invests at least 65% of assets in U.S. Treasury and Government agency debt securities. Portfolio maintains a dollar-weighted average maturity between one and three years. May use put and call options for hedging purposes.
Year organized: 1994
Dividends paid: Income - declared daily, paid monthly; Capital gains - annually
Portfolio turnover (3 yrs): 44%, 58%, 70%
Management fee: 0.30%
Expense ratio: 0.30% (year ending 6/30/97) (0.44% without waiver)

KIEWIT TAX-EXEMPT PORTFOLIO ◆
(See first Kiewit listing for data common to all funds)

Portfolio managers: Brian J. Mosher (1994), Livingston Douglas (1997)
Investment objective and policies: High current income exempt from federal income tax, consistent with reasonable risk. Invests all its investable assets in a corresponding series of an underlying trust which

invests at least 80% of assets in investment grade, tax-exempt municipal securities.
Year organized: 1994
Dividends paid: Income - declared daily, paid monthly; Capital gains - annually
Portfolio turnover (3 yrs): 63%, 101%, 93%
Management fee: 0.40%
Expense ratio: 0.50% (year ending 6/30/97) (0.55% without waiver)

KOBREN INSIGHT FUNDS ◆
(Data common to all Kobren Insight funds are shown below. See subsequent listings for data specific to individual funds.)

20 William Street, Suite 310
P.O. Box 9150
Wellesley Hills, MA 02181
800-566-4274, 800-895-9936

Adviser: Insight Management, Inc.
Administrator: First Data Investor Services Group, Inc.
Portfolio manager: Eric M. Kobren (1996)
Transfer agent: First Data Investor Services Group, Inc.
Minimum purchase: Initial: $25,000, Subsequent: $1,000
Wire orders accepted: Yes
Deadline for same day wire purchase: 4 P.M.
Qualified for sale in: All states except HI
Telephone redemption: Yes
Wire redemptions: Yes, $10 fee
Letter redemptions: Signature guarantee required over $50,000
Telephone switching: With other Kobren Insight funds
Number of switches permitted: 4 per year
Shareholder services: IRA, SEP-IRA, 401(k), 403(b), automatic investment plan, electronic funds transfer (redemption only), systematic withdrawal plan min. bal. req. $25,000
Management fee: 0.75%
Administration fee: 0.25%
IRA fees: Annual $20, Closing $20

KOBREN INSIGHT CONSERVATIVE ALLOCATION FUND ◆
(See first Kobren Insight listing for data common to all funds)

Investment objective and policies: Enough long-term growth of capital to protect purchasing power in the face of inflation, while maintaining a level of volatility 30% lower than the S&P 500 over an entire market cycle. A "fund of funds," the portfolio uses an allocation strategy to invest primarily in other mutual funds, with allocations adjusted according to perceived market conditions. Invests at least 40% of assets in growth and growth and income funds, both foreign and domestic. Invests at least 20% of assets in income producing funds or securities. May invest up to 40% of assets directly in stocks, bonds, money market instruments, options or futures. May invest up to 35% of assets in junk bonds, and up to 15% in illiquid securities and use a variety of derivatives for hedging purposes.
Year organized: 1996
Discount broker availability: *Fidelity, Schwab, White
Dividends paid: Income - annually; Capital gains - annually
Portfolio turnover (1 yr): 13%
Expense ratio: 1.00% (year ending 12/31/97) (2.82% without waiver)

KOBREN INSIGHT GROWTH FUND ◆
(See first Kobren Insight listing for data common to all funds)

Investment objective and policies: Long-term growth of capital while maintaining a level of volatility about the same as the S&P 500. A "fund of funds," the portfolio uses an allocation strategy to invest primarily in other mutual funds, with allocations adjusted according to perceived market conditions. Invests at least 65% of assets in growth and growth and income

funds, both foreign and domestic. Invests up to 35% of assets in income producing funds or directly in stocks, bonds, money market instruments, options or futures. May invest up to 35% of assets in junk bonds, and up to 15% in illiquid securities and use a variety of derivatives for hedging purposes.
Year organized: 1996
Ticker symbol: KOGRX
Discount broker availability: *Fidelity, Schwab, White
Dividends paid: Income - annually; Capital gains - annually
Portfolio turnover (1 yr): 43%
Expense ratio: 0.89% (year ending 12/31/97) (1.28% without waiver)

KOBREN INSIGHT MODERATE GROWTH FUND ◆
(See first Kobren Insight listing for data common to all funds)

Investment objective and policies: Long-term growth of capital while maintaining a level of volatility 20% below that of the S&P 500 over a full market cycle. A "fund of funds," the portfolio uses an allocation strategy to invest primarily in other mutual funds, with allocations adjusted according to perceived market conditions. Invests at least 65% of assets in growth and growth and income funds, both foreign and domestic. Invests up to 35% of assets in income producing funds or directly in stocks, bonds, money market instruments, options or futures. May invest up to 35% of assets in junk bonds, and up to 15% in illiquid securities and use a variety of derivatives for hedging purposes.
Year organized: 1996
Discount broker availability: *Fidelity, Schwab, White
Dividends paid: Income - annually; Capital gains - annually
Portfolio turnover (1 yr): 14%
Expense ratio: 0.92% (year ending 12/31/97) (1.58% without waiver)

KPM EQUITY PORTFOLIO
10250 Regency Circle, Suite 500
Omaha, NE 68114
800-776-5782, 800-776-5777
402-392-7931, 402-397-5777
fax 402-392-8370

Adviser: KPM Investment Management, Inc. (an indirect, wholly owned subsidiary of Mutual of Omaha Insurance Co.)
Portfolio managers: Rodney D. Cerny (1994), Bruce H. Van Kooten (1997)
Transfer agent and administrator: Lancaster Administrative Services, Inc.
Investment objective and policies: Capital appreciation. Invests primarily in common stocks and securities convertible into common stock. Concentrates on large companies with capitalizations above $1B which are currently out of favor, and smaller companies with capitalizations between $100M and $1B that are not well received or followed by the financial research community. Up to 20% of assets may be in securities of foreign issuers. May use options for hedging purposes.
Year organized: 1994
Ticker symbol: KPMEX
Minimum purchase: Initial: $25,000 (in aggregate), Subsequent: None; IRA: Initial: $1,000
Wire orders accepted: Yes
Deadline for same day wire purchase: 2 P.M.
Qualified for sale in: CA, CO, CT, ID, IA, IL, MO, NE, TX, WI
Letter redemptions: Signature guarantee required
Telephone switching: With KPM Fixed Income Portfolio
Number of switches permitted: Unlimited
Dividends paid: Income - March, June, September, December; Capital gains - December
Portfolio turnover (3 yrs): 42%, 34%, 28%
Shareholder services: Systematic withdrawal plan min. bal. req. $50,000
Management fee: 0.80%
Administration fee: 0.25%
12b-1 distribution fee: 0.25%
Expense ratio: 1.45% (year ending 6/30/97)

KPM FIXED INCOME PORTFOLIO
10250 Regency Circle, Suite 500
Omaha, NE 68114
800-776-5782, 800-776-5777
402-392-7931, 402-397-5777
fax 402-392-8370

Adviser: KPM Investment Management, Inc. (an indirect, wholly owned subsidiary of Mutual of Omaha Insurance Co.)
Portfolio manager: Patrick M. Miner (1994)
Administrator and transfer agent: Lancaster Administrative Services, Inc.
Investment objective and policies: Current income; capital appreciation secondary. Invests only in investment grade, fixed-income securities. No maturity is mandated, but the dollar-weighted average maturity of the portfolio generally ranges from seven to ten years. Up to 20% of assets may be in securities of foreign issuers.
Year organized: 1994
Ticker symbol: KPMFX
Minimum purchase: Initial: $25,000 (in aggregate), Subsequent: None; IRA: Initial: $1,000
Wire orders accepted: Yes
Deadline for same day wire purchase: 2 P.M.
Qualified for sale in: CA, CO, ID, IA, IL, MO, NE, WI
Letter redemptions: Signature guarantee required
Telephone switching: With KPM Equity Portfolio
Number of switches permitted: Unlimited
Dividends paid: Income - March, June, September, December; Capital gains - December
Portfolio turnover (3 yrs): 26%, 20%, 40%
Shareholder services: Systematic withdrawal plan min. bal. req. $50,000
Management fee: 0.60%
Administration fee: 0.25%
12b-1 distribution fee: 0.25%
Expense ratio: 1.25% (year ending 6/30/97) (1.51% without waiver)

LAKE FOREST CORE EQUITY FUND ◆
One Westminster Place
Lake Forest, IL 60045-1821
888-295-5707, 847-295-5700
shareholder services 800-592-7722
fax 847-295-4243, 516-951-0573
Internet: http://www.lakeforestfunds.com
e-mail: lff@compuserve.com

Adviser: Boberski & Co.
Portfolio manager: Irving V. Boberski (1995)
Transfer agent: American Data Services, Inc.
Investment objective and policies: Long-term capital appreciation and current income. Invests primarily in equity securities of a broad range of companies with market capitalizations exceeding $1B, believed to have above average prospects for appreciation. Will also invest in dividend paying stocks to achieve current income goal. May also invest in foreign markets by using ADRs, and in fixed-income securities including government and/or corporate debt.
Year organized: 1995
Ticker symbol: LFCEX
Minimum purchase: Initial: $2,500, Subsequent: $500; IRA: Initial: $1,000; Automatic investment plan: Subsequent: $100
Wire orders accepted: Yes
Deadline for same day wire purchase: 11 A.M.
Discount broker availability: *White
Qualified for sale in: AZ, CA, CO, DC, FL, IL, IN, IA, MD, MI, MN, NY, OH, VA, WI
Telephone redemptions: Yes
Wire redemptions: Yes, $1,000 minimum, $15 fee
Letter redemptions: Signature guarantee required
Redemption fee: 0.10% for shares held less than 30 days
Telephone switching: With Lake Forest Money Market, $1,000 minimum
Number of switches permitted: Unlimited, $5 fee
Dividends paid: Income - quarterly; Capital gains - December
Portfolio turnover (2 yrs): 0%, 130%
Shareholder services: IRA, SEP-IRA, electronic funds transfer, systematic withdrawal plan min. bal. req. $10,000
Maintenance fee: $5 per month if balance falls below $2,500 due to redemptions (IRAs exempt)

Management fee: 1.25% (Adviser pays all expenses)
Expense ratio: 1.00% (year ending 2/29/97)
IRA fees: Annual, $12, Closing $15

LAKE FOREST
MONEY MARKET FUND ◆
One Westminster Place
Lake Forest, IL 60045-1821
888-295-5707, 847-295-5700
shareholder services 800-592-7722
fax 847-295-4243, 516-951-0573
Internet: http://www.lakeforestfunds.com
e-mail: lff@compuserve.com

Adviser: Boberski & Co.
Portfolio manager: Irving V. Boberski (1995)
Transfer agent: American Data Services, Inc.
Investment objective and policies: High level of current income consistent with liquidity and security of principal. Invests in the short-term obligations of the U.S. Government, its agencies or instrumentalities, as well as repurchase agreements involving these securities.
Year organized: 1995
Ticker symbol: LFMXX
Minimum purchase: Initial: $2,500, Subsequent: $500; IRA: Initial: $1,000; Automatic investment plan: Subsequent: $100
Wire orders accepted: Yes
Deadline for same day wire purchase: 11 A.M.
Qualified for sale in: AZ, CA, CO, FL, IL, IN, IA, MD, MI, MN, NY, OH, VA, WI
Telephone redemptions: Yes
Wire redemptions: Yes, $1,000 minimum, $15 fee
Letter redemptions: Signature guarantee required
Redemption fee: 0.10% for shares held less than 30 days
Telephone switching: With Lake Forest Core Equity, $1,000 minimum
Number of switches permitted: Unlimited, $5 fee
Dividends paid: Income - declared daily, paid monthly
Shareholder services: IRA, SEP-IRA, electronic funds transfer, systematic withdrawal plan min. bal. req. $10,000
Maintenance fee: $5 per month if balance falls below $2,500 due to redemptions (IRAs exempt)
Management fee: 0.50% (Adviser pays all expenses)
Expense ratio: 0.125% (year ending 2/28/97) (includes waiver)
IRA fees: Annual, $12, Closing $15

LANCASTER FUNDS
(Data common to all Lancaster funds are shown below. See subsequent listings for data specific to individual funds.)

1225 L Street
200 Centre Terrace
Lincoln, NE 68508
800-279-7437, 402-476-3000
fax 402-476-6909

Shareholder service hours: Full service: M-F 8 A.M.-5 P.M. CST
Adviser: Conley Smith, Inc.
Distributor: Smith Hayes Financial Services
Transfer agent and administrator: Lancaster Administrative Services, Inc.
Sales restrictions: Information here represents "Investor" shares. There are also "Select" shares which charge sliding front end loads instead of 12b-1 fees. Commissioned as follows: $1M-$25M, 3.9%; $25M-$50M, 2.5%; $50M-$100M, 1.3%; over $100M, no-load. Curiously, however, Select shares may be purchased at no-load if the investor uses the redemption proceeds of any U.S. mutual fund not distributed by Smith Hayes that had imposed front end or deferred sales charges.
Minimum purchase: Initial: $1,000, Subsequent: None
Wire orders accepted: Yes
Deadline for same day wire purchase: 4; p.m. EST (11 A.M. money market)
Letter redemptions: Signature guarantee required
Telephone switching: With other Lancaster funds,

including the Nebraska Tax-Free fund, which has a load
Number of switches permitted: Unlimited
Shareholder services: Systematic withdrawal plan min. bal. req. $5,000

LANCASTER CAPITAL
BUILDER FUND
(See first Lancaster listing for data common to all funds)

Portfolio manager: John H. Conley (1995)
Investment objective and policies: Long-term capital appreciation; current income secondary. Invests in a diversified portfolio of equity and fixed-income securities and cash or money market instruments, with at least 65% of assets in common and preferred stocks and securities convertible into common stocks. Selects investments based on a value and growth philosophy. May use are options for hedging purposes.
Year organized: 1995 (Initial funding came from combining assets of the Asset Allocation, Balanced and Value portfolios; name changed from Smith Hayes Capital Builder in 1996)
Qualified for sale in: AZ, CO, MN, NE, NY
Dividends paid: Income: June, December; Capital gains: December
Portfolio turnover (1 yr): 31%
Management fee: 0.75%
Administration fee: 0.25%
12b-1 distribution fee: 0.50%
Expense ratio: 1.84% (year ending 6/30/97)

LANCASTER CONVERTIBLE FUND
(See first Lancaster listing for data common to all funds)

Sub-adviser: Calamos Asset Management, Inc.
Portfolio manager: John P. Calamos (1988)
Investment objective and policies: Preservation of capital while maximizing total return: capital gains, interest and dividends. Invests at least 65% of assets in convertible corporate debt securities and/or convertible preferred stock. Up to 20% of assets may be in non-convertible income producing securities and up to 15% in warrants. Fund may hedge with put and call options on underlying stocks, index options, and limited offsetting short sales.
Year organized: 1988 (name changed from Smith Hayes Convertible in 1996)
Qualified for sale in: CO, MN, NE
Dividends paid: Income: June, December; Capital gains: December
Portfolio turnover (3 yrs): 79%, 51%, 66%
Management fee: 0.75%
Administration fee: 0.25%
12b-1 distribution fee: 0.50%
Expense ratio: 1.93% (year ending 6/30/97)

LANCASTER CRESTONE
SMALL CAP FUND
(See first Lancaster listing for data common to all funds)

Sub-adviser: Crestone Capital Management, Inc.
Portfolio manager: Kirk McCown (1992)
Investment objective and policies: Long-term capital appreciation. Invests primarily in stocks of companies with market capitalizations between $50M and $2B (majority of companies in the $350M-$600M range) showing above average growth, trading at low price/earnings ratios compared to the S&P 500, and exhibiting financial strength. May invest up to 25% of assets in one industry sector.
Year organized: 1992 (name changed from Smith Hayes Small Cap in 1996)
Qualified for sale in: CA, CO, MI, MN, NE, NY
Dividends paid: Income: June, December; Capital gains: December
Portfolio turnover (3 yrs): 150%, 87%, 75%
Management fee: 0.75%
Administration fee: 0.25%
12b-1 distribution fee: 0.50%
Expense ratio: 1.87% (year ending 6/30/97)

LANCASTER GOVERNMENT/QUALITY
BOND FUND
(See first Lancaster listing for data common to all funds)

Portfolio manager: John H. Conley (1995)
Investment objective and policies: Income and capital appreciation, consistent with capital preservation. Invests solely in U.S. Government securities, repurchases agreements on U.S. Government securities, and corporate bonds rated A or better by Moody's or S&P. Normally at least 65% of assets will be invested in Government securities. Weighted average maturity will not exceed ten years.
Year organized: 1988 (name changed from Smith Hayes Govt/Quality Bond in 1996)
Qualified for sale in: CO, MN, NE
Dividends paid: Income: June, December; Capital gains: December
Portfolio turnover (3 yrs): 36%, 9%, 218%
Management fee: 0.60%
Administration fee: 0.25%
12b-1 distribution fee: 0.25%
Expense ratio: 1.42% (year ending 6/30/97)

LANCASTER INSTITUTIONAL
MONEY MARKET PORTFOLIO
(See first Lancaster listing for data common to all funds)

Portfolio manager: John H. Conley (1992)
Investment objective and policies: Maximum current income consistent with preservation of capital and liquidity. Invests in high quality money market instruments.
Year organized: 1992 (minimum initial investment reduced from $500K to $1K on 6/22/95 and assets from Money Market Portfolio were merged into Institutional Money Market Fund; name changed from Smith Hayes Inst MM in 1996)
Qualified for sale in: CO, MN, NE
Dividends paid: Income: declared daily, paid monthly
Management fee: 0.10%
Administration fee: 0.12%
12b-1 distribution fee: 0.20%
Expense ratio: 0.57% (year ending 6/30/97)

THE LAZARD PORTFOLIOS
(Data common to all Lazard portfolios are shown below. See subsequent listings for data specific to individual portfolios.)

Thirty Rockefeller Plaza, 58th Floor
New York, NY 10020
800-823-6300, 212-632-6400
shareholder services 800-986-3455
fax 212-332-5785, 617-774-2792
Internet: http://www.lazardfunds.com
e-mail: lazardfunds@lazard.com

Shareholder service hours: Full service: 9 A.M.-6 P.M. EST; After hours service: prices, yields, news, messages, prospectuses, total returns
Adviser: Lazard Freres Asset Management
Transfer agent: Boston Financial Data Services, Inc.
Special sales restrictions: Historical data (including date of organization) provided here represents performance of institutional class shares only; purchase information represents a retail class of shares ("Open Shares") recently made available, which have lower minimums and 12b-1 fees. In many instances both classes are available through discount brokers.
Minimum purchase: Initial: $10,000, Subsequent: $1,000; Automatic investment plan: Subsequent: $250
Wire orders accepted: Yes
Deadline for same day wire purchase: 4 P.M.
Qualified for sale in: All states
Letter redemptions: Signature guarantee required over $50,000
Telephone switching: With other Lazard Funds, $1,000 minimum ($10,000 for new account funds)
Number of switches permitted: Unlimited, 7 day hold
Shareholder services: IRA (rollover only)
12b-1 distribution fees: 0.25%
IRA fees: Annual $12, Initial $5, Closing $10

LAZARD BANTAM VALUE PORTFOLIO
(See first Lazard listing for data common to all portfolios)

Lead portfolio managers: Herbert W. Gullquist (1996), Eileen Alexanderson (1996)
Investment objective and policies: Capital appreciation. Invests primarily in equity securities of companies with market capitalizations under $500M that are perceived to be undervalued. Foreign exposure, up to 10% of assets, is gained through investment in ADRs and GDRs. Those assets not invested in small cap issues will generally be invested in securities of larger companies or in investment grade debt securities or cash equivalents. May use a variety of derivative instruments in an effort to enhance performance and for hedging purposes. Portfolio is non-diversified.
Year organized: 1996
Group fund code: 654
Discount broker availability: *Schwab (only through financial advisers), *White
Dividends paid: Income - May, December; Capital gains - May, December
Portfolio turnover (1 yr): 262%
Management fee: 0.75%
Expense ratio: 1.05% (10 months ending 12/31/96) (1.91% without waiver)

LAZARD BOND PORTFOLIO
(See first Lazard listing for data common to all portfolios)

Lead portfolio managers: Thomas F. Dunn (1995), Ira O. Handler (1997)
Investment objective and policies: Capital growth and preservation. Invests in a range of bonds and fixed-income securities including U.S. Government, mortgage-backed, asset-backed, municipal, and corporate fixed-income securities. Portfolio distribution is not fixed, but will normally be held in debt instruments with maturities greater than one year. The effective duration ranges from two to seven years, but may be extended if deemed necessary. May invest up to 10% of assets in non-rated or junk bonds. May use options and futures in an effort to enhance performance and for hedging purposes. Portfolio is non-diversified.
Year organized: 1991
Ticker symbol: LZBDX
Group fund code: 648
Discount broker availability: Schwab (only through financial advisers)
Dividends paid: Income - declared daily, paid monthly; Capital gains - May, December
Portfolio turnover (3 yrs): 460%, 244%, 121%
Management fee: 0.50%
Expense ratio: 0.80% (year ending 12/31/96) (0.88% without waiver)

LAZARD EMERGING MARKETS PORTFOLIO
(See first Lazard listing for data common to all portfolios)

Lead portfolio managers: Herbert W. Gullquist (1994), John R. Reinsberg (1994)
Investment objective and policies: Long-term capital appreciation. Invests primarily in equity issues of companies located or doing significant business in emerging market economies as defined by the International Finance Corporation and the World Bank. Investments are held in at least three different countries not including the U.S., focusing on but not limited to Latin America, the Pacific Basin and Europe. May also own ADRs and GDRs relevant to emerging markets holdings. Portfolio is non-diversified.
Year organized: 1994
Group fund code: 652
Discount broker availability: *Schwab (only through financial advisers), *White
Dividends paid: Income - May, December; Capital gains - May, December
Portfolio turnover (3 yrs): 51%, 102%, 31%
Management fee: 1.00%
Expense ratio: 1.38% (year ending 12/31/96) (1.48% without waiver)

LAZARD EQUITY PORTFOLIO
(See first Lazard listing for data common to all portfolios)

Lead portfolio managers: Herbert W. Gullquist (1987), Michael S. Rome (1991)
Investment objective and policies: Capital appreciation. Invests primarily in equity securities of companies with relatively large capitalizations that appear to be undervalued. May hold up to 20% of assets in investment grade debt securities of the U.S. Government or of domestic corporations, and up to 10% of assets in foreign equity or debt securities either represented by ADRs or GDRs or traded in domestic markets. May use a variety of derivative instruments in an effort to enhance performance and for hedging purposes.
Year organized: 1987
Group fund code: 645
Discount broker availability: *Schwab (only through financial advisers), *White
Dividends paid: Income - February, May, August, November; Capital gains - May, December
Portfolio turnover (3 yrs): 66%, 81%, 67%
Management fee: 0.75%
Expense ratio: 0.89% (year ending 12/31/96)

LAZARD GLOBAL EQUITY PORTFOLIO
(See first Lazard listing for data common to all portfolios)

Lead portfolio managers: Herbert W. Gullquist (1996), John R. Reinsberg (1996), Michael S. Rome (1996)
Investment objective and policies: Capital appreciation. Invests in equity securities of worldwide companies with relatively large capitalization that are perceived to be undervalued. Will generally be diversified in at least four countries including the U.S., and will usually have at least 25% of assets in U.S. holdings. May invest up to 20% of assets in investment grade fixed-income securities and short-term money market instruments. May use a variety of derivative instruments in an effort to enhance performance and for hedging purposes. Portfolio is non-diversified.
Year organized: 1996
Group fund code: 653
Discount broker availability: *White
Dividends paid: Income - May, December; Capital gains - May, December
Portfolio turnover (1 yr): 74%
Management fee: 0.75%
Expense ratio: 1.05% (year ending 12/31/96) (5.06% without waiver)

LAZARD INTERNATIONAL EQUITY PORTFOLIO
(See first Lazard listing for data common to all portfolios)

Lead portfolio managers: Herbert W. Gullquist (1991), John R. Reinsberg (1992)
Investment objective and policies: Capital appreciation. Invests in equity securities of companies perceived to be undervalued. Holdings come from at least three non-U.S. countries, although there may be substantial investments in ADRs. May invest up to 20% of assets in fixed-income securities and short-term money market instruments. May use foreign currency forward exchange contracts to hedge against currency fluctuations, and a variety of derivative instruments in an effort to enhance performance and for hedging purposes. Portfolio is non-diversified.
Year organized: 1991
Group fund code: 646
Discount broker availability: *Schwab (only through financial advisers), *White
Dividends paid: Income - May, December; Capital gains - May, December
Portfolio turnover (3 yrs): 39%, 63%, 106%
Management fee: 0.75%
Expense ratio: 0.91% (year ending 12/31/96)

LAZARD INTERNATIONAL FIXED-INCOME PORTFOLIO
(See first Lazard listing for data common to all portfolios)

Lead portfolio managers: Thomas F. Dunn (1995), Ira O. Handler (1992)
Investment objective and policies: High total return: current income and capital appreciation consistent with prudent investment risk. Invests in fixed-income securities of varying maturities from companies within or governments of at least three different countries not including the U.S. Typically the portfolio's effective duration ranges between two and eight years. Since the focus is return and not stability of net asset value, average maturity of the portfolio will vary according to market conditions. May invest up to 15% of assets in junk bonds. May use a variety of derivative instruments in an effort to enhance income and for hedging purposes.
Year organized: 1991
Ticker symbol: LZIFX
Group fund code: 647
Discount broker availability: *White
Dividends paid: Income - declared daily, paid monthly; Capital gains - May, December
Portfolio turnover (3 yrs): 242%, 190%, 66%
Management fee: 0.75%
Expense ratio: 1.05% (year ending 12/31/96)

LAZARD INTERNATIONAL SMALL CAP PORTFOLIO
(See first Lazard listing for data common to all portfolios)

Lead portfolio managers: Herbert W. Gullquist (1993), John R. Reinsberg (1993)
Investment objective and policies: Capital appreciation. Invests primarily in equity securities of non-U.S. companies with market capitalizations under $1B that are perceived to be undervalued. Remaining assets are generally invested in larger companies or in investment grade debt obligations. May also invest in ADRs, GDRs and convertible securities. May use a variety of derivatives in an effort to enhance performance and for hedging purposes. Portfolio is non-diversified.
Year organized: 1993
Group fund code: 651
Discount broker availability: *White
Dividends paid: Income - May, December; Capital gains - May, December
Portfolio turnover (3 yrs): 101%, 118%, 113%
Management fee: 0.75%
Expense ratio: 1.12% (year ending 12/31/96)

LAZARD MID CAP PORTFOLIO
(See first Lazard listing for data common to all portfolios)

Lead portfolio managers: Herbert W. Gullquist (1997), Eileen Alexanderson (1997)
Investment objective and policies: Capital appreciation. Invests primarily in equity securities of U.S.-based companies with market capitalizations in the range of the Russell Midcap Index, generally $1B to $5B, perceived to be undervalued. Assets not so invested are generally invested in larger cap companies or investment grade debt issues. May invest up to 15% of assets in foreign issues, and use various derivative instruments for hedging purposes. Portfolio is non-diversified.
Year organized: 1997
Group fund code: 972
Discount broker availability: Fidelity
Dividends paid: Income - May, December; Capital gains - May, December
Management fee: 0.75%

LAZARD SMALL CAP PORTFOLIO
(See first Lazard listing for data common to all portfolios)

Lead portfolio managers: Herbert W. Gullquist (1991), Eileen Alexanderson (1991)
Investment objective and policies: Capital appreciation. Invests primarily in equity securities of U.S.-based companies with market capitalizations falling in

the range of the Russell 2000 Index, currently between $200M and $1B, which are perceived to be undervalued. May invest up to 10% of assets in unseasoned companies, and use various derivative instruments in an effort to enhance income and for hedging purposes. Portfolio is non-diversified.
Year organized: 1991 (absorbed Lazard Special Equity Portfolio 6/28/96)
Group fund code: 650
Discount broker availability: Fidelity, *Schwab (only through financial advisers), *White
Dividends paid: Income - May, December; Capital gains - May, December
Portfolio turnover (3 yrs): 51%, 70%, 70%
Management fee: 0.75%
Expense ratio: 0.84% (year ending 12/31/96)

LAZARD STRATEGIC YIELD PORTFOLIO
(See first Lazard listing for data common to all portfolios)

Lead portfolio managers: Thomas F. Dunn (1995), Ira O. Handler (1993)
Investment objective and policies: Total return: current income and capital appreciation. Invests primarily in an in an international portfolio of high yielding junk bonds, including emerging markets issues. Up to 50% of assets may be in non-U.S. debt securities, although fund may invest without limit in foreign issues denominated in U.S. dollars. Up to 5% of obligations held may be in default. May use put and call options, foreign exchange transactions and foreign currency forward exchange contracts for hedging purposes. Portfolio is non-diversified.
Year organized: 1991
Group fund code: 649
Discount broker availability: *Schwab (only through financial advisers), *White
Dividends paid: Income - declared daily, paid monthly; Capital gains - May, December
Portfolio turnover (3 yrs): 189%, 205%, 195%
Management fee: 0.75%
Expense ratio: 1.08% (year ending 12/31/96)

LEAHI TAX-FREE INCOME TRUST
(Fund was absorbed by First Hawaii Intermediate Municipal fund 9/97)

LEGG MASON FUNDS
(Data common to all Legg Mason funds are shown below. See subsequent listings for data specific to individual funds.)

111 South Calvert Street
P.O. Box 1476
Baltimore, MD 21203-1476
800-822-5544, 800-577-8589
410-539-0000
fax 410-539-3445
Internet: http://www.leggmason.com

Shareholder service hours: Full service: M-F 8:30 A.M.-6:30 P.M. EST; After hours service: prices, yields, messages, DJIA, prospectuses
Transfer agent: Boston Financial Data Services
Minimum purchase: Initial: $1,000, Subsequent: $100 (exceptions noted); Automatic investment plan: Initial: $50, Subsequent: $50
Sales restrictions: Data presented here represents "Primary" shares; "Navigator" shares are institutional only.
Telephone redemptions: Yes
Wire redemptions: Money market funds only, $18 fee
Letter redemptions: Signature guarantee required (exceptions noted)
Telephone switching: With same share class of other Legg Mason funds, $100 minimum
Number of switches permitted: 4 per year
Shareholders services: IRA, SEP-IRA, 401(k), corporate retirement plans, directed dividends, electronic funds transfer (purchase only), systematic withdrawal plan min. bal. req. $5,000
IRA fees: Annual $10, Closing $25

LEGG MASON AMERICAN LEADING COMPANIES TRUST
(See first Legg Mason listing for data common to all funds)

Adviser: Legg Mason Capital Management, Inc.
Portfolio manager: William H. Miller III (1997)
Investment objective and policies: Long-term capital appreciation and income consistent with prudent investment risk. Invests at least 75% of assets in dividend-paying common stocks of leading companies with market capitalizations of at least $2B. Up to 25% of assets may be foreign securities and 25% in debt securities. Fund may sell covered call options to generate additional income.
Year organized: 1993
Ticker symbol: LMALX
Wire orders accepted: No
Discount broker availability: *White
Qualified for sale in: All states except AK, ID, SD, PR
Dividends paid: Income - March, June, September, December; Capital gains - December
Portfolio turnover (3 yrs): 56%, 43%, 31%
Management fee: 0.75%
12b-1 distribution fee: Maximum of 1.00%
Expense ratio: 1.95% (year ending 3/31/97) (2.06% without waiver)

LEGG MASON BALANCED TRUST
(See first Legg Mason listing for data common to all funds)

Adviser: Bartlett & Co.
Portfolio managers: Dale H. Rabiner (1996), Woodrow H. Uible (1996)
Investment objective and policies: Total return: long-term capital appreciation and current income consistent with reasonable risk. Invests up to 75% of assets in equity securities, including closed end investment companies and ADRs and GDRs, and at least 25% of assets in fixed-income securities. May invest up to 15% of assets in illiquid securities and use various derivative instruments for hedging purposes.
Year organized: 1996
Wire orders accepted: No
Discount broker availability: *White
Qualified for sale in: All states except AK, ID, SD, PR
Dividends paid: Income - March, June, September, December; Capital gains - December
Portfolio turnover (1 yr): 5%
Management fee: 0.75%
12b-1 distribution fee: Maximum of 0.75%
Expense ratio: 1.85% (6 months ending 3/31/97) (3.03% without waiver)

LEGG MASON CASH RESERVE TRUST
(See first Legg Mason listing for data common to all funds)

Adviser: Western Asset Management Co.
Portfolio manager: Carl L. Eichstaedt (1994)
Investment objective and policies: Principal stability and current income. Invests in high quality money market instruments.
Year organized: 1979
Ticker symbol: LMCXX
Minimum purchase: Initial: $1,000, Subsequent: $500
Wire orders accepted: Yes, subsequent only
Qualified for sale in: All states
Letter redemptions: Signature guarantee required over $10,000
Check redemptions: $500 minimum
Dividends paid: Income: declared daily, paid monthly
Management fee: 0.50% first $500M to 0.40% over $2B
12b-1 distribution fee: Maximum of 0.15%
Expense ratio: 0.70% (year ending 8/31/96)

LEGG MASON EMERGING MARKETS TRUST
(See first Legg Mason listing for data common to all funds)

Adviser: Batterymarch Financial Management, Inc.
Portfolio manager: Investment Committee
Investment objective and policies: Long-term capital appreciation. Invests at least 65% of assets in equity securities of companies domiciled in or deriving a substantial percentage of their revenues from emerging markets countries as defined by the IMF or the World Bank. The balance of assets may be invested in any combination of equity or debt securities from any government or company anywhere in the world, including the U.S. May invest up to 10% of assets in other investment companies, and use ADRs to gain exposure to certain markets. May invest over 25% of assets in any one currency denomination, and up to 25% of assets in junk bonds. May use options and futures and forward foreign currency contracts for hedging purposes.
Year organized: 1996
Wire orders accepted: No
Qualified for sale in: All states except AK, PR, SD
Redemption fee: 2.00% for shares held less than one year
Dividends paid: Income - annually; Capital gains - annually
Portfolio turnover (1 yr): 46%
Management fee: 1.00%
12b-1 distribution fee: Maximum of 1.00%
Expense ratio: 2.50% (7 months ending 12/31/96) (includes waiver)

LEGG MASON GLOBAL GOVERNMENT TRUST
(See first Legg Mason listing for data common to all funds)

Adviser: Western Asset Management Co.
Portfolio manager: Keith J. Gardner (1993)
Investment objective and policies: Total return: capital appreciation and current income, consistent with prudent investment risk. Invests at least 75% of assets in debt obligations issued or guaranteed by foreign governments, the U.S. Government, their agencies, instrumentalities and political subdivisions. Up to 25% of assets may be in junk bonds and 15% in illiquid securities. May use options, futures and forward contracts to increase income and for hedging purposes.
Year organized: 1993
Ticker symbol: LMGGX
Wire orders accepted: No
Discount broker availability: *White
Qualified for sale in: All states except AK, PR, SD
Dividends paid: Income - declared daily, paid monthly; Capital gains - December
Portfolio turnover (3 yrs): 172%, 169%, 127%
Management fee: 0.75%
12b-1 distribution fee: 0.75%
Expense ratio: 1.86% (year ending 12/31/96)

LEGG MASON HIGH YIELD PORTFOLIO
(See first Legg Mason listing for data common to all funds)

Adviser: Western Asset Management Co.
Lead portfolio manager: Trudie D. Whitehead (1994)
Investment objective and policies: High current income; capital growth secondary. Invests primarily in high yield lower-rated corporate debt securities, preferred stock, convertible securities and mortgage- and asset-backed securities. Up to 25% of assets may be in securities of foreign issuers and 15% in illiquid securities. May use futures and options to increase income and for hedging purposes.
Year organized: 1994
Ticker symbol: LMHYX
Wire orders accepted: Yes, subsequent only
Discount broker availability: *White
Qualified for sale in: All states except AK, PR
Dividends paid: Income - declared and paid monthly; Capital gains - December
Portfolio turnover (3 yrs): 77%, 47%, 67%

Management fee: 0.65%
12b-1 distribution fee: 0.50%
Expense ratio: 1.35% (year ending 12/31/96)

LEGG MASON INTERNATIONAL EQUITY TRUST
(See first Legg Mason listing for data common to all funds)

Adviser: Batterymarch Financial Management, Inc.
Portfolio manager: Investment Committee
Investment objective and policies: Maximum long-term total return: capital appreciation and income. Invests primarily in common stocks of companies located outside of the U.S., including up to 35% of assets in emerging market securities. Under normal circumstances fund will remain broadly diversified and fully invested. May use options and futures for hedging purposes.
Year organized: 1995 (name and objective changed from Global Equity Trust 3/96)
Ticker symbol: LMGEX
Wire orders accepted: No
Discount broker availability: *White
Qualified for sale in: All states except AK, PR, SD
Dividends paid: Income - December; Capital gains - December
Portfolio turnover (2 yrs): 83%, 58%
Management fee: 0.75%
12b-1 distribution fee: 1.00%
Expense ratio: 2.25% (year ending 12/31/96)

LEGG MASON INVESTMENT GRADE INCOME PORTFOLIO
(See first Legg Mason listing for data common to all funds)

Adviser: Western Asset Management Co.
Lead portfolio manager: Kent S. Engel (1987)
Investment objective and policies: High current income. Invests primarily in investment grade debt securities of domestic and foreign corporate and government issuers. Up to 50% of assets may be in mortgage-related securities and 25% in junk bonds. May use futures and options to increase income and for hedging purposes.
Year organized: 1987
Ticker symbol: LMIGX
Wire orders accepted: Yes, subsequent only
Qualified for sale in: All states except AK, PR
Dividends paid: Income - declared daily, paid monthly; Capital gains - December
Portfolio turnover (3 yrs): 383%, 221%, 200%
Management fee: 0.60%
12b-1 distribution fee: 0.50%
Expense ratio: 0.97% (year ending 12/31/96) (includes waiver)

LEGG MASON SPECIAL INVESTMENT TRUST
(See first Legg Mason listing for data common to all funds)

Adviser: Legg Mason Fund Adviser, Inc.
Portfolio manager: William H. Miller III (1985)
Investment objective and policies: Capital appreciation. Invests primarily in equity securities of companies with market capitalizations under $1B which are generally out of favor or undervalued on an earnings or asset basis; undergoing significant change; and in which actual/anticipated reorganizations or restructuring are taking place (limited to 20% of assets). May have up to 35% of assets in junk bonds and 25% in foreign securities. May use futures and options in an effort to enhance income and for hedging purposes.
Year organized: 1985
Ticker symbol: LMASX
Wire orders accepted: No
Discount broker availability: *White
Qualified for sale in: All states except AK, PR
Dividends paid: Income - May, December; Capital gains - May, December
Portfolio turnover (3 yrs): 29%, 36%, 28%
Management fee: 1.00% first $100M to 0.65% over $1B
12b-1 distribution fee: Maximum of 1.00%
Expense ratio: 1.92% (year ending 3/31/97)

LEGG MASON TAX EXEMPT TRUST
(See first Legg Mason listing for data common to all funds)

Adviser: Legg Mason Fund Adviser, Inc.
Portfolio manager: Victoria Schwatka (1983)
Investment objective and policies: High current income exempt from federal income tax, consistent with preservation of capital and liquidity. Invests in short-term, high-quality municipal money market instruments exempt from federal income tax.
Year organized: 1982
Ticker symbol: LGMXX
Minimum purchase: Initial: $1,000, Subsequent: $500
Wire orders accepted: Yes, subsequent only
Qualified for sale in: All states except AK, PR
Letter redemptions: Signature guarantee required over $10,000
Check redemptions: $500 minimum
Dividends paid: Income: declared daily, paid monthly
Management fee: 0.50%
12b-1 distribution fee: Maximum of 0.20%
Expense ratio: 0.64% (year ending 12/31/96)

LEGG MASON TOTAL RETURN TRUST
(See first Legg Mason listing for data common to all funds)

Adviser: Legg Mason Fund Adviser, Inc.
Portfolio manager: Nancy T. Dennin (1992)
Investment objective and policies: Capital appreciation and current income consistent with reasonable risk. Invests primarily in dividend-paying common stocks and securities convertible into common stock of companies with potential for long-term growth. Up to 50% of assets may be in intermediate- and long-term debt securities and 25% in foreign securities. May use futures and options in an effort to enhance income and for hedging purposes.
Year organized: 1985
Ticker symbol: LMTRX
Wire orders accepted: No
Discount broker availability: *White
Qualified for sale in: All states except AK, PR
Dividends paid: Income - March, June, September, December; Capital gains - December
Portfolio turnover (3 yrs): 38%, 35%, 62%
Management fee: 0.75%
12b-1 distribution fee: Maximum of 1.00%
Expense ratio: 1.93% (year ending 3/31/97)

LEGG MASON U.S. GOVERNMENT INTERMEDIATE-TERM PORTFOLIO
(See first Legg Mason listing for data common to all funds)

Adviser: Western Asset Management Co.
Lead portfolio manager: Carl L. Eichstaedt (1994)
Investment objective and policies: High current income consistent with prudent investment risk and liquidity. Invests at least 75% of assets in debt obligations issued or guaranteed by the U.S. Government, its agencies or instrumentalities. Portfolio maintains a dollar-weighted average maturity of three to ten years. Up to 50% of assets may be in mortgage-backed securities and 25% in investment grade corporate debt securities. May invest in dollar-denominated securities of foreign issuers, and use futures and options in an effort to enhance income and for hedging purposes.
Year organized: 1987 (absorbed Bartlett Fixed Income and Short Term Bond funds 12/20/96)
Ticker symbol: LGINX
Wire orders accepted: Yes, subsequent only
Discount broker availability: *White
Qualified for sale in: All states except AK, PR
Dividends paid: Income - declared daily, paid monthly; Capital gains - December
Portfolio turnover (3 yrs): 354%, 290%, 315%
Management fee: 0.55%
12b-1 distribution fee: 0.50%
Expense ratio: 0.98% (year ending 12/31/96)

LEGG MASON U.S. GOVERNMENT MONEY MARKET PORTFOLIO
(See first Legg Mason listing for data common to all funds)

Adviser: Western Asset Management Co.
Lead portfolio manager: Carl L. Eichstaedt (1994)
Investment objective and policies: High current income consistent with conservation of principal and liquidity. Invests in money market debt obligations issued or guaranteed by the U.S. Government, its agencies or instrumentalities and in repurchase agreements secured by such instruments.
Year organized: 1989
Ticker symbol: LMGXX
Wire orders accepted: Yes, subsequent only
Qualified for sale in: All states except AK, PR
Letter redemptions: Signature guarantee required over $10,000
Check redemptions: $500 minimum
Dividends paid: Income: declared daily, paid monthly
Management fee: 0.50%
12b-1 distribution fee: Maximum of 0.20%
Expense ratio: 0.66% (year ending 12/31/96)

LEGG MASON VALUE TRUST
(See first Legg Mason listing for data common to all funds)

Adviser: Legg Mason Adviser, Inc.
Portfolio manager: William H. Miller, III (1982)
Investment objective and policies: Long-term capital growth. Invests primarily in common stocks perceived to be undervalued in relation to earnings power and/or asset value, with emphasis on companies with a record of earnings and dividends, reasonable return on equity and sound finances. Up to 25% of assets may be in foreign securities, 25% in long-term debt securities and 10% in junk bonds. May use futures and options in an effort to enhance income and for hedging purposes.
Year organized: 1982 (split 2 for 1 on 8/6/91)
Ticker symbol: LMVTX
Wire orders accepted: No
Discount broker availability: *White
Qualified for sale in: All states except AK, PR
Dividends paid: Income - May, July, October, December; Capital gains - May, December
Portfolio turnover (3 yrs): 11%, 20%, 20%
Management fee: 1.00% first $100M to 0.65% over $1B
12b-1 distribution fee: Maximum of 0.95%
Expense ratio: 1.77% (year ending 3/31/97)

LEONETTI BALANCED FUND ◆
1130 Lake Cook Road, Suite 105
Buffalo Grove, IL 60089-1974
800-454-0999, 800-385-7003
847-520-0999
fax 847-520-5475

Adviser: Leonetti & Assocs., Inc.
Administrator: Investment Company Administration Corp.
Portfolio managers: Michael E. Leonetti (1995), Craig T. Johnson (1995)
Transfer agent: American Data Services
Investment objective and policies: Total return: income and capital growth, consistent with capital preservation. Invests in equity securities and higher quality fixed-income obligations, the allocation of each being determined by interpretation of the market. Favors investments in out-of-favor blue chips, growth stocks that pay dividends with rising trends in earnings and revenues, and small companies with rapidly rising revenues and earnings. Fixed income obligations must be of investment grade.
Year organized: 1995
Ticker symbol: LEONX
Minimum purchase: Initial: $100, Subsequent: $100
Wire orders accepted: Yes
Deadline for same day wire purchases: 4 P.M.
Discount broker availability: Schwab, White
Qualified for sale in: All states except: AR, CT, MA, MD, NE, NM, NV, NY, SD, UT, VT
Telephone redemptions: Yes
Wire redemptions: Yes, $1,000 minimum

Letter redemptions: Signature guarantee required over $5,000
Dividends paid: Income - June; Capital gains - December
Portfolio turnover (2 yrs): 120%, 42%
Shareholder services: IRA, automatic investment plan, systematic withdrawal plan min. bal. req. $10,000
Management fee: 1.00%
Administration fee: 0.20% first $50M to 0.05% over $150M ($30,000 minimum)
Expense ratio: 2.29% (year ending 6/30/97)
IRA fee: None

LEPERCQ-ISTEL TRUST - LEPERCQ-ISTEL FUND
1675 Broadway
New York, NY 10019
800-497-1411, 800-655-7766
212-698-0749
fax 212-262-0155

Adviser: Lepercq, de Neuflize & Co. Inc.
Portfolio managers: Tsering Ngudu (1993), Andrew Merz Hanson (1993)
Transfer agent: Firstar Trust Co.
Investment objective and policies: Long-term capital growth; dividend income secondary. Invests primarily in equity securities of companies believed to be undergoing an unrecognized transformation, or those that are perceived to be undervalued. Market capitalization of target companies may be as low as $50M. May have up to 25% of assets in junk bonds and 20% in securities of foreign issuers, and use covered calls to hedge up to 25% of total assets. May write covered call options.
Year organized: 1953 (formerly Istel Fund, name changed 4/86. Now a series fund)
Ticker symbol: ISTLX
Minimum purchase: Initial: $1,000, Subsequent: $100 (waived for shareholders of record prior to 5/1/97); IRA: Initial: $500; Automatic investment plan: Initial: $50, Subsequent: $50
Wire orders accepted: Yes
Discount broker availability: Fidelity, *White
Qualified for sale in: All states
Letter redemptions: Signature guarantee required over $50,000
Dividends paid: Income - July, December; Capital gains - December
Portfolio turnover (3 yrs): 54%, 60%, 71%
Shareholder services: IRA, systematic withdrawal plan min. bal. req. 10,000
Management fee: 0.75%
Shareholder services fee: Maximum of 0.25%
12b-1 distribution fee: Maximum of 0.75%
Expense ratio: 1.65% (year ending 12/31/96) (1.71% without waiver)
IRA fees: None

LEUTHOLD CORE INVESTMENT FUND ◆
100 North 6th Street, Suite 700 A
Minneapolis, MN 55403
800-273-6886, 612-332-9141
TDD 800-684-3416
fax 612-332-0797

Adviser: Leuthold & Anderson, Inc.
Portfolio manager: Steven C. Leuthold (1995)
Transfer agent: Firstar Trust Co.
Investment objective and policies: High total return: capital growth and income consistent with reasonable long-term risk. Invests in common stocks and other equity securities, bonds and other fixed-income securities, and money markets. Allocation of these assets is determined in proportion to their risk and market conditions as evaluated by the adviser. General investment guidelines allow up to 70% of assets to be directed to either stocks or to bonds. May hold up to 25% of assets in securities of foreign issuers, up to 25% of assets in securities of other registered investment companies, and may hold junk bonds. May use options and futures in an effort to enhance performance and for hedging purposes.
Year organized: 1995 (name changed from Leuthold Asset Allocation 1/31/98)
Ticker symbol: LCORX

Minimum purchase: Initial: $10,000, Subsequent: $100; IRA: Initial: $1,000; Automatic investment plan: Subsequent: $50
Wire orders accepted: Yes
Deadline for same day wire purchase: 4; p.m.
Discount broker availability: Schwab (only through financial advisors), *White
Qualified for sale in: All states except AZ, AK, ID, KS, KY, LA, ME, MS, MO, OK, RI, SC, SD, TN, UT, WV
Telephone redemptions: Yes
Wire redemptions: Yes, $12 fee
Letter redemptions: Signature guarantee not required
Dividends paid: Income - March, June, September, December; Capital gains - December
Portfolio turnover (2 yrs): 36%, 103%
Shareholder services: IRA, electronic funds transfer, systematic withdrawal plan
Management fee: 0.90%
IRA fees: None
Expense ratio: 1.25% (year ending 9/30/97) (1.47% without waiver)

LEXINGTON FUNDS
(Data common to all Lexington funds are shown below. See subsequent listings for data specific to individual funds.)

Park 80 West, Plaza Two
Saddle Brook, NJ 07663
800-526-0056, 201-845-7300
prices/yields 800-526-0052
fax 201-845-3534
Internet:http://www.invest@lexfunds.com

Shareholder service hours: Full service: M-F 9 A.M.-5 P.M. EST; After hours service: prices, yields, balances, total returns, last transaction, prospectuses, statements, checkbooks, tax forms, exchanges
Adviser: Lexington Management Corp.
Transfer agent: State Street Bank and Trust Co.
Minimum purchase: Initial: $1,000 (exception noted), Subsequent: $50; IRA/Keogh: Initial: $250; Automatic investment plan: Initial $500
Wire orders accepted: Yes
Deadline for same day wire purchase: 4 P.M.
Qualified for sale in: All states (exception noted)
Telephone redemptions: Yes
Wire redemptions: Yes $1,000 minimum, $5 fee
Letter redemptions: Signature guarantee required over $25,000
Telephone switching: With other Lexington funds, $500 minimum
Number of switches permitted: Unlimited, 7 day hold
Shareholder services: IRA, SEP-IRA, Keogh, 401(k), 403(b), corporate retirement plans, systematic withdrawal plan min. bal. $10,000
IRA fees: Annual $12 (for all funds under the same social security number)
Keogh fees: None

LEXINGTON CONVERTIBLE SECURITIES FUND
(See first Lexington listing for data common to all funds)

Sub-adviser: Ariston Capital Management Corp.
Portfolio manager: Richard B. Russell (1988)
Investment objective and policies: High total return: capital appreciation, current income and capital preservation. Invests primarily in convertible securities including those rated as low as B, and may invest without limit in junk bonds. May also invest up to 35% of assets in common stocks and corporate and government debt securities, and up to 10% of assets in restricted securities. May use options to increase income and for hedging purposes, and may sell short.
Year organized: 1988 (As Concord Income Trust, a load fund. Current management since 5/15/92)
Ticker symbol: CNCVX
Group fund code: 283
Discount broker availability: *Fidelity, *Schwab, *Siebert, *White

Dividends paid: Income - March, June, September, December; Capital gains - December
Portfolio turnover (3 yrs): 30%, 18%, 11%
Management fee: 1.00%
12b-1 distribution fee: 0.25%
Expense ratio: 2.38% (year ending 12/31/97)

LEXINGTON CORPORATE LEADERS TRUST FUND ◆
(See first Lexington listing for data common to all funds)

Investment objective and policies: Long-term growth of capital and income. Invests in equal share amounts from a fixed list of blue chip corporations, currently 25, and therefore is not a managed portfolio.
Year organized: 1935 (as Corporate Leaders Trust Fund; name changed 10/31/88)
Ticker symbol: LEXCX
Group fund code: 268
Discount broker availability: *Fidelity, *Schwab, *Siebert, *White
Dividends paid: Income - June, December; Capital gains - June, December
Administration fee: 0.35%
Expense ratio: 0.62% (year ending 12/31/97)

LEXINGTON CROSBY SMALL CAP ASIA GROWTH FUND ◆
(See first Lexington listing for data common to all funds)

Sub-adviser: Crosby Asset Management (US), Inc.
Portfolio managers: Simon C.N. Thompson (1997), Christina Lam (1995)
Investment objective and policies: Long-term capital appreciation. Invests in common stocks and equivalents of companies with market capitalizations of less than $1B, domiciled in at least three countries in Asia. May also invest in Australia and New Zealand. May temporarily invest up to 100% of assets in debt obligations issued anywhere in the world. May use foreign currency exchange contracts, currency futures, options and futures for purposes of hedging up to 30% of assets and have up to 15% of assets in illiquid securities.
Year organized: 1995
Ticker symbol: LXCAX
Group fund code: 286
Discount broker availability: *Fidelity, *Schwab, *Siebert, *White
Dividends paid: Income - December; Capital gains - December
Portfolio turnover (3 yrs): 187%, 176%, 40%
Management fee: 1.25%
Shareholder services fee: Maximum of 0.25%
Expense ratio: 2.30% (year ending 12/31/97)

LEXINGTON GLOBAL FUND ◆
(See first Lexington listing for data common to all funds)

Portfolio managers: Alan H. Wapnick (1994), Richard T. Saler (1994)
Investment objective and policies: Long-term capital growth. Invests at least 65% of assets in common stocks of companies in at least three countries from around the world - primarily Western Europe and the Pacific Basin - and the U.S. May invest in companies located in developing nations without limit, and may invest in preferred stocks, bonds, and other debt obligations as management according to perceived market conditions. Fund may write covered calls and use spot currency purchases and forward currency contracts for hedging purposes.
Year organized: 1987
Ticker symbol: LXGLX
Group fund code: 270
Discount broker availability: *Fidelity, *Schwab, *Siebert, *White
Dividends paid: Income - December; Capital gains - December
Portfolio turnover (3 yrs): 117%, 128%, 166%
Management fee: 1.00%
Expense ratio: 1.75% (year ending 12/31/97)

LEXINGTON GNMA INCOME FUND ◆
(See first Lexington listing for data common to all funds)

Portfolio manager: Denis P. Jamison (1981)
Investment objective and policies: High current income consistent with liquidity and safety of principal. Invests at least 80% of assets in mortgage-backed, government guaranteed GNMA certificates.
Year organized: 1973 as Lexington Income Fund; present name and objective adopted 12/29/80
Ticker symbol: LEXNX
Group fund code: 274
Discount broker availability: *Fidelity, *Schwab, *Siebert, *White
Dividends paid: Income - declared and paid monthly; Capital gains - December
Portfolio turnover (3 yrs): 134%, 129%, 31%
Management fee: 0.60% first $150M to 0.40% over $800M
Shareholder services fee: Maximum of 0.25%
Expense ratio: 1.01% (year ending 12/31/97)

LEXINGTON GOLDFUND
(See first Lexington listing for data common to all funds)

Portfolio manager: Robert W. Radsch (1994)
Investment objective and policies: Capital appreciation and hedge against loss of buying power. Invests in gold and equity securities of companies engaged in mining or processing gold throughout the world. Securities of foreign issuers make up a substantial portion of the fund's assets. Up to 15% of assets may be in warrants.
Year organized: 1979 (formerly Goldfund)
Ticker symbol: LEXMX
Group fund code: 271
Discount broker availability: *Fidelity, *Schwab, *Siebert, *White
Dividends paid: Income - semi-annually; Capital gains - semi-annually
Portfolio turnover (3 yrs): 38%, 31%, 40%
Management fee: 1.00% first $50M, 0.75% over $50M
12b-1 distribution fee: 0.25%
Expense ratio: 1.65% (year ending 12/31/97)

LEXINGTON GROWTH & INCOME FUND
(See first Lexington listing for data common to all funds)

Portfolio manager: Alan H. Wapnick (1994)
Investment objective and policies: Long-term capital appreciation; income secondary. Invests in publicly traded common stocks and senior securities convertible into common stocks. Up to 20% of assets may be in securities of foreign issuers. May invest for defensive purposes in varying amounts of senior securities such as bonds, debentures and preferred stocks as dictated by market conditions.
Year organized: 1939 (name changed from Lexington Research Fund in May 1991)
Ticker symbol: LEXRX
Group fund code: 280
Discount broker availability: *Fidelity, *Schwab, *Siebert, *White
Dividends paid: Income - February, May, August, December; Capital gains - December
Portfolio turnover (3 yrs): 88%, 101%, 160%
Management fee: 0.75% first $100M to 0.40% over $250M
12b-1 distribution fee: 0.25%
Expense ratio: 1.17% (year ending 12/31/97)

LEXINGTON INTERNATIONAL FUND
(See first Lexington listing for data common to all funds)

Portfolio manager: Richard T. Saler (1994)
Investment objective and policies: Long-term capital growth. Invests assets in a diversified portfolio of common stocks and equivalents of companies domiciled in foreign countries, primarily Western Europe and the Pacific Basin. At least 65% of assets will be invested in at least three countries outside the U.S.

May also invest in preferred stocks, bonds, and other debt obligations, and is not required to maintain any particular proportion of equity or debt securities. May use forward currency contracts for hedging purposes, and write covered calls.
Year organized: 1994
Ticker symbol: LEXIX
Group fund code: 284
Discount broker availability: *Fidelity, *Schwab, *Siebert, *White
Dividends paid: Income - December; Capital gains - December
Portfolio turnover (3 yrs): 123%, 114%, 138%
Management fee: 1.00%
12b-1 distribution fee: 0.25%
Expense ratio: 2.15% (year ending 12/31/97)

LEXINGTON MONEY MARKET TRUST ◆
(See first Lexington listing for data common to all funds)

Portfolio manager: Denis P. Jamison (1981)
Investment objective and policies: High level of current income consistent with preservation of capital and liquidity. Invests in short-term money market instruments.
Year organized: 1976 (Name changed from Banner Redi-Resources Trust in 1979)
Ticker symbol: LMMXX
Group fund code: 277
Check redemptions: $100 minimum
Dividends paid: Income - declared daily, paid monthly
Management fee: 0.50% first $500M, 0.45% over $500M
Expense ratio: 1.00% (year ending 12/31/97) (1.04% without waiver)

LEXINGTON RAMIREZ GLOBAL INCOME FUND
(See first Lexington listing for data common to all funds)

Sub-adviser: MFR Advisors, Inc. (1995)
Portfolio managers: Denis P. Jamison (1986), Maria Fiorini Ramirez (1995)
Investment objective and policies: High current income; capital appreciation secondary. Invests primarily in lower-rated and unrated debt securities, whose credit quality is generally considered "junk bonds," issued by governments and companies in at least three countries including the U.S. May invest in mature and emerging markets all over the world. May invest in "Brady Bonds," which are debt restructurings created in emerging market economies. May use forward foreign currency contracts and futures and options to increase return and for hedging purposes. Fund is non-diversified.
Year organized: 1986 (Formerly Lexington Tax-Exempt Bond Trust. Name and objectives changed on 1/3/95. Prior performance should be ignored.)
Ticker symbol: LEBDX
Group fund code: 275
Discount broker availability: *Fidelity, *Schwab, *Siebert, *White
Dividends paid: Income - March, June, September, December; Capital gains - December
Portfolio turnover (3 yrs): 118%, 72%, 165%
Management fee: 1.00%
12b-1 distribution fee: 0.25%
Expense ratio: 1.50% (year ending 12/31/97) (2.17% without waiver)

LEXINGTON SMALLCAP VALUE FUND
(See first Lexington listing for data common to all funds)

Sub-adviser: Capital Technology, Inc.
Portfolio managers: Robb W. Rowe (1996), Dennis J. Hamilton (1996)
Investment objective and policies: Long-term capital appreciation. Invests in common stocks and equivalents of companies domiciled in the U.S. with market capitalizations below $1B, that are perceived to offer exceptional relative value and attractive prices. May also invest in Canadian or other foreign issues whose

shares trade in U.S. dollar-denominated markets. Up to 10% of assets may be invested in companies with market caps below $20M; above $1B; outside the U.S.; in ADRs; REITs; or cash.
Year organized: 1996
Ticker symbol: LESVX
Group fund code: 287
Discount broker availability: *Fidelity, *Schwab, *Siebert, *White
Dividends paid: Income - December; Capital gains - December
Portfolio turnover (2 yrs): 39%, 61%
Management fee: 1.00%
12b-1 distribution fee: 0.25%
Expense ratio: 2.57% (year ending 12/31/97)

LEXINGTON TAX FREE MONEY FUND ◆
(Fund liquidated 8/29/97)

LEXINGTON TROIKA DIALOG RUSSIA FUND
(See first Lexington listing for data common to all funds)

Sub-adviser: Troika Dialog Asset Management
Portfolio managers: Gavin Rankin (1996), Ruben Vardanian (1996), Richard M. Hisey (1997)
Investment objective and policies: Long-term capital appreciation. Invests primarily in equity securities of companies organized under the laws of; principally domiciled in; for which the principal equity securities market is in; at least 50% of revenues, profits, or investments come from; or at least 50% of assets are situated in Russia. Invests at least 65% of assets in such equity securities, and holds at least 20% of assets in highly liquid assets for liquidity, stability and to provide flexibility as the Russian market matures. May invest up to 35% of assets in Russian corporate or government debt securities, as well as corporate or governmental debt or equity securities outside of Russia. May utilize sponsored or unsponsored ADRs and GDRs. May use various derivatives to mitigate currency fluctuations and for hedging purposes.
Year organized: 1996
Ticker symbol: LETRX
Group fund code: 288
Minimum purchase: Initial: $5,000
Discount broker availability: *Fidelity, *Schwab, *Siebert, *White
Qualified for sale in: All states except SD
Redemption fee: 2.00% for shares held less than 365 days, payable to fund
Dividends paid: Income - December; Capital gains - December
Portfolio turnover (2 yrs): 67%, 116%
Management fee: 1.25%
12b-1 distribution fee: 0.25%
Expense ratio: 1.85% (year ending 12/31/97) (2.89% without waiver)

LEXINGTON WORLDWIDE EMERGING MARKETS FUND ◆
(See first Lexington listing for data common to all funds)

Portfolio manager: Richard T. Saler (1994)
Investment objective and policies: Long-term capital growth. Normally invests at least 65% of assets in equity securities of companies domiciled in, or doing business in, emerging countries and emerging markets. May also invest in preferred stocks, bonds and money market instruments of the U.S. Government and its agencies, and foreign and domestic companies. May use futures and options, and use "spot" currency purchases and forward currency exchanged contracts for hedging purposes.
Year organized: 1969 (formerly Lexington Growth Fund, name and objectives changed in July 1991. Prior performance data should be ignored.)
Ticker symbol: LEXGX
Group fund code: 273
Discount broker availability: *Fidelity, *Schwab, *Siebert, *White
Dividends paid: Income - December; Capital gains - December

Portfolio turnover (3 yrs): 112%, 86%, 93%
Management fee: 1.00%
Shareholder services fee: Maximum of 0.25%
Expense ratio: 1.82% (year ending 12/31/97)

LIGHTHOUSE CONTRARIAN FUND
10000 Memorial Drive, Suite 660
Houston, TX 77024
800-282-2340, 800-841-8238
713-688-6881
Internet: http://www.lightkeepers.com

Adviser: Lighthouse Capital Management, Inc.
Administrator: Investment Company Administration Corp.
Portfolio manager: Kevin P. Duffy (1995)
Transfer agent: American Data Services, Inc.
Investment objective and policies: Capital growth. Invests primarily in common stocks, convertible preferred stocks, convertible debt securities, and warrants of companies perceived to be undervalued or out of favor. May hold up to 25% of assets in fixed-income securities, including junk bonds. May invest in foreign securities without limit, and use options and short sales for hedging purposes.
Year organized: 1995 (name changed from Lighthouse Growth 11/15/97)
Ticker symbol: LGFTX
Minimum purchase: Initial: $2,000, Subsequent: $100
Wire orders accepted: Yes
Deadline for same day wire purchase: 4 P.M.
Discount broker availability: *Schwab
Qualified for sale in: All states
Telephone redemptions: Yes
Wire redemptions: Yes, $1,000 minimum, $7 fee
Letter redemptions: Signature guarantee required
Dividends paid: Income - August, December; Capital gains - August, December
Portfolio turnover (2 yrs): 22%, 21%
Shareholder services: IRA, automatic investment plan, systematic withdrawal plan min. bal. req. $10,000
Management fee: 1.25%
Administration fee: 0.20% under $50M to 0.05% over $150M ($30,000 minimum)
12b-1 distribution fee: 0.25%
Expense ratio: 2.00% (year ending 8/31/97) (2.24% without waiver)
IRA fees: Annual $15

LINDNER FUNDS ◆
(Data common to all Lindner funds are shown below. See subsequent listings for data specific to individual funds.)

7711 Carondelet Avenue, Suite 700
P.O. Box 11208
St. Louis, MO 63105
800-995-7777, 800-733-3769
314-727-5305
fax 314-727-1528
Internet: http://www.lindnerfunds.com
e-mail: customerservice@ryback.com

Shareholder service hours: Full service: M-F 8 A.M.-5 P.M. CST; After hours service: prices, yields
Adviser: Ryback Management Corp.
Transfer agent: Ryback Management Corp.
Special sales information: Lindner offers two classes of shares, "Investor" and "Institutional." The latter are available at minimums as low as $250, but are only distributed through institutional intermediaries, and they include 12b-1 distribution fees. The information here represents "Investor" shares, which are sold directly by the fund.
Minimum purchase: See individual fund; however, if you meet the required minimum for any one fund, you may open an account in another for as little as $500.
Wire orders accepted: Yes, subsequent only; any amount less than $1,000 is subject to a wire fee.
Deadline for same day wire purchase: 4 P.M.
Qualified for sale in: All states
Telephone redemptions: Yes
Wire redemptions: Yes, $10 fee

Letter redemptions: Signature guarantee not required
Telephone switching: With other Lindner funds
Number of switches: Unlimited
Shareholder services: IRA, electronic funds transfer, systematic withdrawal plan min. bal. req. $15,000
IRA fees: Annual $10

LINDNER BULWARK FUND ◆
(See first Lindner listing for data common to all funds)

Portfolio manager: Team managed (1997)
Investment objective and policies: Capital appreciation. Invests primarily in common stocks of domestic and foreign companies believed undervalued and selected with emphasis on capital preservation through periods of economic stress, including those engaged in the production of precious metals and other natural resources. Fund may purchase precious metals, use futures and options, and sell short. Up to 35% of assets may be in securities of foreign issuers, 35% in junk bonds and 15% in illiquid securities.
Year organized: 1994
Ticker symbol: LDNBX
Minimum purchase: Initial: $3,000, Subsequent: $100; IRA: Initial $250; Automatic investment plan: Subsequent: $50
Discount broker availability: *Fidelity, Schwab, Siebert, *White
Dividends paid: Income - December; Capital gains - December
Portfolio turnover (3 yrs): 458%, 140%, 123%
Management fee: 1.00%
Expense ratio: 1.20% (year ending 6/30/97)

LINDNER DIVIDEND FUND ◆
(See first Lindner listing for data common to all funds)

Portfolio manager: Eric E. Ryback (1984)
Investment objective and policies: Current income; capital appreciation secondary. Invests primarily in common stocks yielding substantial dividend income, preferred stocks and, to a lesser extent, corporate bonds and government debt securities. May invest up to 40% of assets in utility securities, 35% in junk bonds and 25% in real estate investment trusts (REITs).
Year organized: 1976 (Formerly Lindner Fund for Income)
Ticker symbol: LDDVX
Minimum purchase: Initial: $2,000, Subsequent: $100; IRA: Initial $250; Automatic investment plan: Subsequent: $50
Discount broker availability: *Fidelity, Schwab, Siebert, *White
Dividends paid: Income - January, April, July, October; Capital gains - December
Portfolio turnover (3 yrs): 40%, 30%, 11%
Management fee: 0.70% first $50M to 0.50% over $200M
Expense ratio: 0.60% (year ending 6/30/97)

LINDNER GOVERNMENT MONEY MARKET FUND ◆
(See first Lindner listing for data common to all funds)

Sub-adviser: Star Bank, N.A.
Investment objective and policies: High current income consistent with capital preservation and liquidity. Invests in a portfolio of high-quality, short-term securities issued or guaranteed by the U.S. Government, its agencies or instrumentalities, and in repurchase agreements relating to such types of securities.
Year organized: 1996
Minimum purchase: Initial: $2,000, Subsequent: $100; IRA: Initial $250; Automatic investment plan: Subsequent: $50
Check redemption: $500 minimum ($5,000 min. bal. req.)
Dividends paid: Income - declared daily, paid monthly
Management fee: 0.15%
Administration fee: 0.20%
Expense ratio: 0.43% (year ending 6/30/97)

LINDNER GROWTH FUND ◆
(See first Lindner listing for data common to all funds)

Portfolio managers: Robert A. Lange (1977), Eric E. Ryback (1984)
Investment objective and policies: Long-term capital appreciation; income secondary. Invests in common stocks and convertible securities. May invest in debt securities for defensive purposes. May invest up to 25% of assets in securities of foreign issuers, 25% in REITs, 15% in illiquid securities and 10% in junk bonds. Fund may leverage.
Year organized: 1973 (name changed from The Lindner Fund 6/30/95)
Ticker symbol: LDNRX
Minimum purchase: Initial: $2,000, Subsequent: $100; IRA: Initial $250; Automatic investment plan: Subsequent: $50
Discount broker availability: *Fidelity, Schwab, Siebert, *White
Dividends paid: Income - December; Capital gains - December
Portfolio turnover (3 yrs): 36%, 39%, 25%
Management fee: 0.70% first $50M to 0.50% over $400M, subject to incentive adjustment of +/- 0.20% depending on the fund's performance relative to the S&P 500 Index
Expense ratio: 0.44% (year ending 6/30/97)

LINDNER INTERNATIONAL FUND ◆
(See first Lindner listing for data common to all funds)

Portfolio managers: Eric E. Ryback (1995), Robert A. Lange (1995)
Investment objective and policies: Capital appreciation; current income secondary. Invests primarily in common stocks and securities convertible into common stock of financially strong foreign companies in at least three countries. Fund may purchase precious metals, use futures and options, and sell short. Up to 25% of assets may be in restricted securities, 15% in REITs and 15% in illiquid securities.
Year organized: 1995
Ticker symbol: LDINX
Minimum purchase: Initial: $3,000, Subsequent: $100; IRA: Initial $250; Automatic investment plan: Subsequent: $50
Discount broker availability: *Fidelity, Schwab, Siebert, *White
Dividends paid: Income - December; Capital gains - December
Portfolio turnover (2 yrs): 38%, 48%
Management fee: 1.00%
Expense ratio: 1.96% (year ending 6/30/97)

LINDNER/RYBACK SMALL-CAP FUND ◆
(See first Lindner listing for data common to all funds)

Portfolio managers: Eric E. Ryback (1994), Donald B. Wang (1996)
Investment objective and policies: Capital appreciation; current income secondary. Invests primarily in common stocks or securities convertible into common stock of companies with market capitalizations under $750M. Fund may purchase precious metals, use futures and options, and sell short. Up to 25% of assets may be in securities of foreign issuers, 20% in junk bonds and 15% in REITs.
Year organized: 1994
Ticker symbol: LDRSX
Minimum purchase: Initial: $3,000, Subsequent: $100; IRA: Initial $250; Automatic investment plan: Subsequent: $50
Discount broker availability: *Fidelity, Schwab, *White
Dividends paid: Income - December; Capital gains - December
Portfolio turnover (3 yrs): 49%, 103%, 159%
Management fee: 0.70% first $50M to 0.50% over $200M
Expense ratio: 0.96% (year ending 6/30/97)

LINDNER UTILITY FUND ◆
(See first Lindner listing for data common to all funds)

Portfolio managers: Eric E. Ryback (1993), Richard H. Eckenrodt, Jr. (1996)
Investment objective and policies: Current income;

capital appreciation secondary. Invests primarily in common stocks of domestic and foreign public utilities (gas, electric, telecommunications, cable TV, water, energy, etc.), securities convertible into common stock issued by utilities and other preferred stocks or bonds issued by utilities. May invest up to 35% of assets in securities of foreign issuers and 35% in junk bonds.
Year organized: 1993
Ticker symbol: LDUTX
Minimum purchase: Initial: $3,000, Subsequent: $100; IRA: Initial $250; Automatic investment plan: Subsequent: $50
Discount broker availability: *Fidelity, Schwab, Siebert, *White
Dividends paid: Income - January, April, July, October; Capital gains - December
Portfolio turnover (3 yrs): 86%, 99%, 191%
Management fee: 0.70% first $50M to 0.50% over $200M
Expense ratio: 0.89% (year ending 6/30/97)

THE LIPPER FUNDS
(Data common to all Lipper funds are shown below. See subsequent listings for data specific to individual funds.)

101 Park Avenue, 6th Floor
New York, NY 10178
800-547-7379, 212-883-6333

Adviser: Lipper & Co., LLC
Transfer agent and administrator: Chase Global Funds Services, Inc.
Minimum purchase: Initial: $10,000, Subsequent: $2,500; IRA: Initial: $2,000, Subsequent: $250; Automatic investment plan: Subsequent: $100
Sales restrictions: Funds are offered in three no-load classes; Premier (institutional), Retail, and Group Retirement. Only retail are covered here.
Wire orders accepted: Yes
Deadline for same day wire purchase: 4 P.M.
Qualified for sale in: All states
Telephone redemptions: Yes
Wire redemptions: Yes, $8 fee
Letter redemptions: Signature guarantee not required
Telephone switching: With other Lipper funds, and Chase Vista U.S. Government Money Market, $100 minimum
Number of switches: Unlimited
Shareholder services: IRA, 401(k), corporate retirement plans, systematic withdrawal plan
Administration fee: 0.20% first $200M to 0.05% over $400M
12b-1 distribution fee: 0.25%
IRA fees: None

LIPPER EUROPE EQUITY FUND
(See first Lipper listing for data common to all funds)

Sub-adviser: Prime Lipper Asset Management
Portfolio manager: Guido Guzzetti (1996)
Investment objective and policies: Capital appreciation. Invests primarily in a diversified portfolio of common stocks of approximately 100 large cap European companies perceived to have strong growth potential. May invest in ADRs, GDRs and EDRs, and use various derivative instruments for hedging purposes.
Year organized: 1996
Ticker symbol: PLEEX
Discount broker availability: *White
Dividends paid: Income - annually; Capital gains - annually
Portfolio turnover (1 yr): 34%
Management fee: 1.10%
Expense ratio: 1.85% (9 months ending 12/31/96) (2.07% without waiver)

LIPPER HIGH INCOME BOND FUND
(See first Lipper listing for data common to all funds)

Portfolio manager: Wayne Plewniak (1996)
Investment objective and policies: High current yield equal to approximately 3% to 5% more than U.S. Treasuries of the same maturity. Invests primarily in a diversified portfolio of high yield securities rated Baa to B or BBB to B, with maturities of less than ten

years. Securities whose ratings fall lower will be disposed of. May invest up to 20% of assets in common stocks or other equity securities. May invest in ADRs, GDRs and EDRs, and use various derivative instruments for hedging purposes.
Year organized: 1996
Ticker symbol: LHIBX
Discount broker availability: *White
Dividends paid: Income - monthly; Capital gains - annually
Portfolio turnover (1 yr): 74%
Management fee: 0.75%
Expense ratio: 1.25% (9 months ending 12/31/96) (1.59% without waiver)

LIPPER U.S. EQUITY FUND
(See first Lipper listing for data common to all funds)

Portfolio managers: Kenneth Lipper (1996), Nancy Friedman (1996), Michael Visovsky (1996)
Investment objective and policies: Capital appreciation. Invests primarily in a diversified portfolio of common stocks of domestic companies with market capitalizations exceeding $500M that are perceived to be undervalued. May invest up to 15% of assets in foreign securities by means of ADRs, GDRs and EDRs, and use various derivative instruments for hedging purposes.
Year organized: 1996
Discount broker availability: *White
Dividends paid: Income - annually; Capital gains - annually
Portfolio turnover (1 yr): 117%
Management fee: 0.85%
Expense ratio: 1.35% (year ending 12/31/96) (2.75% without waiver)

LKCM EQUITY PORTFOLIO ◆
301 Commerce Street, Suite 1600
Fort Worth, TX 76102
800-688-5526, 817-332-3235
fax 817-332-4630

Adviser: Luther King Capital Management Corp.
Portfolio manager: J. Luther King, Jr. (1996)
Transfer agent: Firstar Co.
Investment objective and policies: Maximum long-term capital appreciation. Invests primarily in equity securities of companies believed to have above average growth in revenues and/or earnings with high returns on shareholders' equity, as well as those perceived to be undervalued. May also invest in investment grade U.S. Government and corporate debt securities. May invest up to 10% of assets in other investment companies, and up to 7% of assets in illiquid securities.
Year organized: 1996
Ticker symbol: LKEQX
Minimum purchase: Initial: $10,000, Subsequent: $1,000; Automatic investment plan: Subsequent: $100
Wire orders accepted: Yes
Deadline for same day wire purchase: 4 P.M.
Qualified for sale in: All states
Telephone redemptions: Yes
Wire redemptions: Yes
Letter redemptions: Signature guarantee not required
Dividends paid: Income - December; Capital gains - December
Portfolio turnover (1 yr): 79%
Shareholder services: IRA, SEP-IRA
Management fee: 0.70%
Administration fee: 0.185% first $75M to 0.095% over $150M ($100,000 + .015% minimum)
Expense ratio: 0.80% (year ending 12/31/96)
IRA fees: Annual $10

LKCM SMALL CAP EQUITY PORTFOLIO ◆
301 Commerce Street, Suite 1600
Fort Worth, TX 76102
800-688-5526, 817-332-3235
fax 817-332-4630

Adviser: Luther King Capital Management Corp.
Portfolio managers: J. Luther King, Jr. (1995), David D. May (1995)
Transfer agent: Firstar Co.

Investment objective and policies: Maximum capital appreciation. Invests primarily in equity securities of smaller companies with market capitalizations under $1B. May invest in foreign securities, have up to 15% of assets in illiquid securities and 10% in other investment companies. May use foreign currency transactions, futures and options for hedging purposes.
Year organized: 1995
Ticker symbol: LKSCX
Minimum purchase: Initial: $10,000, Subsequent: $1,000; Automatic investment plan: Subsequent: $100
Wire orders accepted: Yes
Deadline for same day wire purchase: 4 P.M.
Qualified for sale in: All states
Telephone redemptions: Yes
Wire redemptions: Yes
Letter redemptions: Signature guarantee not required
Dividends paid: Income - December; Capital gains - December
Portfolio turnover (2 yrs): 66%, 57%
Shareholder services: IRA, SEP-IRA
Management fee: 0.75%
Administration fee: 0.215% first $75M to 0.095% over $150M ($145,000 + .015% minimum)
Expense ratio: 1.00% (year ending 12/31/96)
IRA fees: Annual $10

LMH FUND ◆
(See Matrix/LMH Value Fund)

LONGLEAF PARTNERS FUNDS ◆
(Data common to all Longleaf Partners funds are shown below. See subsequent listings for data specific to individual funds.)

6075 Poplar Avenue, Suite 900
Memphis, TN 38119
800-445-9469, 901-818-5100, 901-761-2474
shareholders 800-488-4191
prices/yields 800-378-3788
fax 901-818-5210, 901-763-2142

Shareholder service hours: Full service: M-F 8 A.M.-5 P.M. CST; After hours service: prices, yields, account balances, last transaction, prospectuses, total returns
Adviser: Southeastern Asset Management, Inc.
Transfer agent: National Financial Data Services
Minimum purchase: Initial: $10,000, Subsequent: None; Automatic investment plan: Subsequent: $100
Wire orders accepted: Yes
Deadline for same day wire purchase: 4 P.M.
Qualified for sale in: All states
Telephone redemptions: Yes
Wire redemptions: Yes
Letter redemptions: Signature guarantee required over $25,000
Shareholder services: IRA, SEP-IRA
IRA fees: Annual $10, Initial $15

LONGLEAF PARTNERS FUND ◆
(See first Longleaf Partners listing for data common to all funds)

Portfolio managers: O. Mason Hawkins (1987), G. Staley Cates (1994)
Investment objective and policies: Long-term capital growth; current income incidental. Invests primarily in common stocks of a limited number of companies perceived to be undervalued, with market capitalizations greater than $500M. Up to 20% of assets may be in securities of foreign issuers that are traded in U.S. markets, and up to 15% in illiquid and restricted securities. May write covered put and call options.
Year organized: 1987 (name changed from Southeastern Asset Management Value Trust in 1994)
Ticker symbol: LLPFX
Group fund code: 133
Special sales restrictions: Fund closed to new shareholders on 9/15/95
Discount broker availability: Fidelity, Schwab, White
Dividends paid: Income - December; Capital gains - December
Portfolio turnover (3 yrs): 38%, 33%, 13%
Management fee: 1.00% first $400M, 0.75% over $400M
Expense ratio: 0.94% (year ending 12/31/97)

LONGLEAF PARTNERS REALTY FUND ◆

(See first Longleaf Partners listing for data common to all funds)

Portfolio managers: O. Mason Hawkins (1996), G. Staley Cates (1996), C.T. Fitzpatrick III (1996)
Investment objective and policies: Maximum long-term total return; capital growth and current income. Invests primarily in equity securities of a limited number of companies which are engaged in business in the real estate industries, or in companies which own significant real estate assets. May also invest up to 35% of assets in equity or debt securities of companies in any other kind of business, or in money markets, options, futures, and currency contracts.
Year organized: 1996
Ticker symbol: LLREX
Group fund code: 135
Discount broker availability: Fidelity, Schwab, Siebert, White
Dividends paid: Income - December; Capital gains - December
Portfolio turnover (2 yrs): 29%, 4%
Management fee: 1.00%
Expense ratio: 1.20% (year ending 12/31/97)

LONGLEAF PARTNERS SMALL-CAP FUND ◆

(See first Longleaf Partners listing for data common to all funds)

Portfolio managers: O. Mason Hawkins (1991), G. Staley Cates (1991)
Investment objective and policies: Long-term capital growth; current income incidental. Invests primarily in common stocks of a limited number of companies with market capitalizations of $1B or less that are believed to be undervalued. Up to 20% of assets may be in securities of foreign issuers that are traded in U.S. markets, and up to 15% in illiquid and restricted securities. May write covered put and call options.
Year organized: 1988 (name changed from Southeastern Asset Management Small-Cap fund in 1994)
Ticker symbol: LLSCX
Group fund code: 134
Sales restrictions: Fund closed to new investors 8/1/97
Discount broker availability: Fidelity, Schwab, Siebert, White
Dividends paid: Income - December; Capital gains - December
Portfolio turnover (3 yrs): 17%, 28%, 33%
Management fee: 1.00% first $400M, 0.75% over $400M
Expense ratio: 1.09% (year ending 12/31/97)

LOOMIS SAYLES FUNDS

(See Discount Broker listings in the next section)

MAIRS & POWER BALANCED FUND ◆

W-2062 First National Bank Building
332 Minnesota Street
St. Paul, MN 55101-1363
800-304-7404, 612-222-8478
fax 612-222-8470

Adviser: Mairs and Power, Inc.
Portfolio manager: William B. Frels (1992)
Transfer agent: Mairs and Power, Inc.
Investment objective and policies: Regular current income with the possibility of modest long-term capital appreciation and moderate volatility. Invests in a diversified portfolio of bonds, preferred stocks, securities convertible into common stocks and common stocks. Allocations may vary according to perceived market conditions. Up to 20% of assets may be in junk bonds.
Year organized: 1961 (name changed from Mairs & Powers Income Fund in April 1997)
Ticker symbol: MAPOX
Minimum purchase: Initial: $2,500, Subsequent: $100; IRA: Initial: $1,000
Wire orders accepted: No
Qualified for sale in: CA, CO, DC, FL, MN, NJ, NY, ND, WI

Letter redemptions: Signature guarantee required over $10,000
Dividends paid: Income - March, June, September, December; Capital gains - December
Portfolio turnover (3 yrs): 8%, 4%, 17%
Shareholder services: IRA, SEP-IRA, Keogh, systematic withdrawal plan min. bal. req. $10,000
Management fee: 0.60%
Expense ratio: 1.08% (year ending 12/31/96)
IRA/Keogh fees: Annual $12, Initial $6, Closing $12

MAIRS & POWER GROWTH FUND ◆

W-2062 First National Bank Building
332 Minnesota Street
St. Paul, MN 55101-1363
800-304-7404, 612-222-8478
fax 612-222-8470

Adviser: Mairs and Power, Inc.
Portfolio manager: George A. Mairs, III (1980)
Transfer agent: Firstar Trust Co.
Investment objective and policies: Long-term capital appreciation. Invests primarily in a diversified portfolio of equity securities, principally common stocks, perceived to offer long-term growth potential. Issues are usually held for a period of at least one year. Remains reasonably fully invested at all times.
Year organized: 1958
Ticker symbol: MPGFX
Minimum purchase: Initial: $2,500, Subsequent: $100; IRA: Initial: $1,000
Wire orders accepted: No
Qualified for sale in: CA, CO, FL, IL, MN, NY, PA, TX, WI
Letter redemptions: Signature guarantee required over $10,000
Dividends paid: Income - June, December; Capital gains - December
Portfolio turnover (3 yrs): 3%, 4%, 5%
Shareholder services: IRA, SEP-IRA, Keogh, systematic withdrawal plan min. bal. req. $10,000
Management fee: 0.60%
Expense ratio: 0.89% (year ending 12/31/96)
IRA/Keogh fees: Annual $12, Initial $6, Closing $12

THE MANAGERS FUNDS ◆

(Data common to all Managers funds are shown below. See subsequent listings for data specific to individual funds.)

One Norwalk West
40 Richards Avenue
Norwalk, CT 06854-2325
800-835-3879, 203-857-5321
fax 203-857-5316
Internet: http://www.managers-funds.com

Shareholder service hours: Full service: M-F 8 A.M.-6 P.M. EST; After hours service: prices, yields, messages, prospectuses
Adviser: The Managers Funds, L.P.
Transfer agent: Boston Financial Data Services, Inc.
Minimum purchase: Initial: $2,000, Subsequent: None; IRA: Initial: $500; Automatic investment plan: Initial: $500, Subsequent: $100
Wire orders accepted: Yes
Deadline for same day wire purchase: 4 P.M. (3 P.M. for MM)
Qualified for sale in: All states
Telephone redemptions: Yes
Wire redemptions: Yes
Letter redemptions: Signature guarantee required over $25,000
Telephone switching: With other Managers funds
Number of switches permitted: unlimited
Shareholder services: IRA, electronic funds transfer, systematic withdrawal plan min. bal. req. $25,000
IRA fees: None

THE MANAGERS BOND FUND ◆

(See first Managers listing for data common to all funds)

Asset manager: Loomis, Sayles & Co., Inc.
Portfolio manager: Daniel J. Fuss (1984)
Investment objective and policies: Income. Invests in obligations of the U.S. Government and its agencies

and instrumentalities and corporate bonds, debentures, non-convertible preferred stocks, mortgage-related securities, asset-backed securities, Eurodollar certificates of deposit and Eurodollar bonds. Up to 20% of assets may be in variable rate interest securities and 10% in non-U.S. dollar denominated instruments. May have up to 15% of assets in illiquid securities, and use futures and options for hedging purposes.
Year organized: 1984 (name changed from Fixed Income Securities Fund in 1993)
Ticker symbol: MGFIX
Group fund code: 156
Discount broker availability: *Fidelity, *Schwab, *Siebert, *White
Dividends paid: Income - monthly; Capital gains - December
Portfolio turnover (3 yrs): 72%, 46%, 84%
Management fee: 0.625%
Expense ratio: 1.36% (year ending 12/31/96)

THE MANAGERS CAPITAL APPRECIATION FUND ◆

(See first Managers listing for data common to all funds)

Asset managers: Husic Capital Management; Essex Investment Management
Portfolio managers: Frank J. Husic (1996), Joseph McNay (1997)
Investment objective and policies: Long-term capital appreciation; income secondary. Invests primarily in common stock, securities convertible into common stocks, and securities having common stock characteristics such as rights and warrants. May have up to 15% of assets in illiquid securities, and use futures and options for hedging purposes.
Year organized: 1984
Ticker symbol: MGCAX
Group fund code: 152
Discount broker availability: *Fidelity, *Schwab, *Siebert, *White
Dividends paid: Income - December; Capital gains - December
Portfolio turnover (3 yrs): 172%, 134%, 122%
Management fee: 0.80%
Expense ratio: 1.33% (year ending 12/31/96)

THE MANAGERS GLOBAL BOND FUND ◆

(See first Managers listing for data common to all funds)

Asset manager: Rogge Global Partners
Portfolio manager: Olaf Rogge (1994)
Investment objective and policies: High total return: income and capital appreciation. Invests in investment grade domestic and foreign fixed-income securities issued by governments, corporations and supra-national organizations. Fund normally maintains a dollar-weighted average maturity of ten years or less. May have up to 15% of assets in illiquid securities, and use currency exchange contracts, options and futures for hedging purposes.
Year organized: 1994
Ticker symbol: MGGBX
Group fund code: 163
Discount broker availability: *Fidelity, *Schwab, *White
Dividends paid: Income - quarterly; Capital gains - December
Portfolio turnover (3 yrs): 202%, 214%, 266%
Management fee: 0.70%
Expense ratio: 1.57% (year ending 12/31/96)

THE MANAGERS INCOME EQUITY FUND ◆

(See first Managers listing for data common to all funds)

Asset managers: Scudder, Kemper Investments, Inc.; Chartwell Investment Partners
Portfolio managers: Robert T. Hoffman (1991), Harold Ofstie (1997)
Investment objective and policies: High current income. Invests at least 65% of assets in income producing equity securities - common stocks and securities convertible into common stocks such as bonds and

preferred stocks. May invest in fixed-income debt securities with maximum remaining maturities of 15 years or less. May have up to 15% of assets in illiquid securities, and use futures and options for hedging purposes.
Year organized: 1984
Ticker symbol: MGIEX
Group fund code: 154
Discount broker availability: *Fidelity, *Schwab, *Siebert, *White
Dividends paid: Income - monthly; Capital gains - December
Portfolio turnover (3 yrs): 33%, 36%, 46%
Management fee: 0.75%
Expense ratio: 1.44% (year ending 12/31/96)

THE MANAGERS INTERMEDIATE MORTGAGE FUND ◆
(See first Managers listing for data common to all funds)

Asset manager: Jennison Assocs. Capital Corp.
Portfolio managers: Michael Porreca (1994), John Feingold (1994)
Investment objective and policies: High current income. Invests at least 65% of assets in mortgage-related securities issued by governments, government-related and private organizations and at least 25% in the mortgage and mortgage finance industry. Fund maintains a dollar-weighted average maturity of three to ten years. May have up to 15% of assets in illiquid securities, and use futures and options for hedging purposes.
Year organized: 1986
Ticker symbol: MGIGX
Group fund code: 159
Discount broker availability: *Fidelity, *Schwab, *Siebert, *White
Dividends paid: Income - monthly; Capital gains - December
Portfolio turnover (3 yrs): 232%, 506%, 240%
Management fee: 0.45%
Expense ratio: 1.19% (year ending 12/31/96)

THE MANAGERS INTERNATIONAL EQUITY FUND ◆
(See first Managers listing for data common to all funds)

Asset managers: Scudder, Stevens & Clark, Inc.; Lazard, Freres & Co.
Portfolio managers: William E. Holzer (1989), John R. Reinsberg (1995)
Investment objective and policies: Long-term capital appreciation; income secondary. Invests primarily in equity securities of companies domiciled outside the U.S. May invest up to 35% of assets in equity and fixed-income debt securities of domestic companies when domestic returns are expected to be greater than those of non-U.S. equity securities. May have up to 15% of assets in illiquid securities, and use futures and options for hedging purposes.
Year organized: 1986
Ticker symbol: MGITX
Group fund code: 155
Discount broker availability: *Fidelity, *Schwab, *Siebert, *White
Dividends paid: Income - December; Capital gains - December
Portfolio turnover (3 yrs): 30%, 73%, 22%
Management fee: 0.90%
Expense ratio: 1.53% (year ending 12/31/96)

THE MANAGERS MONEY MARKET FUND ◆
(See first Managers listing for data common to all funds)

Asset manager (of the underlying portfolio): Morgan Guaranty Trust Co.
Portfolio manager: Robert R. "Skip" Johnson (1988)
Investment objective and policies: High current income consistent with preservation of capital and liquidity. Invests in money market instruments through a two-tiered, master feeder structure, into a portfolio with identical objectives and policies.
Year organized: 1984

Ticker symbol: MGMXX
Group fund code: 162
Dividends paid: Income - declared daily, paid monthly
Check redemptions: $500 minimum
Management fee: 0.20% first $1B, 0.10% over $1B
Expense ratio: 1.13% (year ending 12/31/96)

THE MANAGERS SHORT AND INTERMEDIATE BOND FUND ◆
(See first Managers listing for data common to all funds)

Asset manager: Standish, Ayer & Wood, Inc.
Portfolio manager: Howard B. Rubin (1984)
Investment objective and policies: High current income. Invests in obligations of the U.S. Government and its agencies and instrumentalities as well as corporate bonds, debentures, non-convertible fixed-income preferred stocks, mortgage-related securities, Eurodollar certificates of deposit and Eurodollar bonds. Portfolio maintains a dollar-weighted average maturity of one to five years. Up to 20% of assets may be in variable rate interest securities, 15% in illiquid securities and 10% in non-U.S. dollar denominated instruments. May use futures and options for hedging purposes.
Year organized: 1984 (name changed from Short and Intermediate Fixed Income Securities Fund in 1993)
Ticker symbol: MGSIX
Group fund code: 157
Discount broker availability: *Fidelity, *Schwab, *Siebert, *White
Dividends paid: Income - monthly; Capital gains - December
Portfolio turnover (3 yrs): 96%, 131%, 57%
Management fee: 0.50%
Expense ratio: 1.45% (year ending 12/31/96)

THE MANAGERS SHORT GOVERNMENT FUND ◆
(See first Managers listing for data common to all funds)

Asset manager: Jennison Assocs. Capital Corp.
Portfolio manager: Thomas P. Doyle (1994)
Investment objective and policies: High current income consistent with capital preservation. Invests at least 65% of assets in obligations of the U.S. Government and its agencies and instrumentalities with remainder in domestic and Eurodollar corporate bonds, commercial paper, bankers' acceptances, certificates of deposit, time deposits and repurchase agreements. Portfolio generally maintains a dollar-weighted average maturity of less than three years. May have up to 15% of assets in illiquid securities, and use futures and options for hedging purposes.
Year organized: 1987
Ticker symbol: MGSGX
Group fund code: 158
Discount broker availability: *Fidelity, *Schwab, *Siebert, *White
Dividends paid: Income - declared daily, paid monthly; Capital gains - December
Portfolio turnover (3 yrs): 169%, 238%, 140%
Management fee: 0.45%
Expense ratio: 1.17% (year ending 12/31/96)

THE MANAGERS SPECIAL EQUITY FUND ◆
(See first Managers listing for data common to all funds)

Asset managers: Pilgrim Baxter & Assocs.; Westport Asset Management, Inc.; Liberty Investment Management (formerly Eagle Investment Management), Kern Capital Management, LLC
Portfolio managers: Gary L. Pilgrim (1994), Andrew J. Knuth (1985), Tim Ebright (1985), Robert E. Kern (1997)
Investment objective and policies: Capital appreciation. Invests primarily in equity securities of companies expected to have superior earnings growth potential, generally with small- to medium- sized market capitalizations of under $1B. May invest up to 35% of assets in equities of larger companies believed to have

prospects for accelerated earnings growth, and have up to 15% of assets in illiquid securities. May use futures and options for hedging purposes.
Year organized: 1984
Ticker symbol: MGSEX
Group fund code: 153
Discount broker availability: *Fidelity, *Schwab, *Siebert, *White
Dividends paid: Income - December; Capital gains - December
Portfolio turnover (3 yrs): 56%, 65%, 66%
Management fee: 0.90%
Expense ratio: 1.43% (year ending 12/31/96)

MANOR INVESTMENT FUND ◆
15 Chester Commons
Malvern, PA 19355
800-787-3334, 610-722-3334

Adviser: Morris Capital Advisors, Inc.
Portfolio manager: Daniel A. Morris (1995)
Transfer agent: Morris Capital Advisors, Inc.
Investment objective and policies: Capital appreciation; moderate level of current income secondary. Invests in a diversified portfolio of common stocks and securities convertible into common stocks. Fund is non-diversified.
Year organized: 1995
Minimum purchase: Initial: $1,000, Subsequent: $100
Wire orders accepted: No
Qualified for sale in: DE, PA
Letter redemptions: Signature guarantee required
Dividends paid: Income - annually; Capital gains - annually
Portfolio turnover (1 yr): 14%
Shareholder services: IRA
Management fee: 1.00%
Expense ratio: 1.50% (year ending 12/31/96)
IRA fees: None

MARKMAN MULTIFUND TRUST ◆
(Data common to all Markman Multifund Trust funds are shown below. See subsequent listings for data specific to individual funds.)

6600 France Avenue South, Suite 565
Minneapolis, MN 55435
800-707-2771, 800-395-4848
800-232-4792, 513-629-2070
prices 800-536-8679
fax 513-629-2041
Internet: http://www.markman.com
e-mail: noloadmgr@aol.com

Adviser: Markman Capital Management, Inc.
Transfer agent and administrator: Countrywide Fund Services, Inc.
Portfolio manager: Robert J. Markman (1995)
Minimum purchase: Initial: $25,000, Subsequent: $500
Wire orders accepted: Yes
Deadline for same day wire purchase: 4 P.M.
Qualified for sale in: All states except PR
Telephone redemptions: Yes
Wire redemptions: Yes, $8 fee
Letter redemptions: Signature guarantee required over $25,000
Telephone switching: With other Markman funds
Number of switches permitted: Unlimited
Dividends paid: Income - December; Capital gains - December
Shareholder services: IRA, SEP-IRA, Keogh, 401(k), 403(b), automatic investment plan, corporate retirement plans, electronic funds transfer, systematic withdrawal plan min. bal. req. $25,000
Management fee: 0.95%
IRA/Keogh fees: None

MARKMAN MULTIFUND TRUST - AGGRESSIVE ALLOCATION PORTFO- LIO ◆
(See first Markman listing for data common to all funds)

Investment objective and policy: Capital appreciation without regard to current income. Invests at least 65% of assets in mutual funds with the same objective

that invest primarily in equity and debt securities. May also invest in mutual funds that invest primarily in short-term bonds and other fixed-income securities that offer a potential for capital appreciation. May invest up to 25% of assets in one fund.
Year organized: 1995
Ticker symbol: MMAGX
Discount broker availability: *Fidelity, *Schwab, Siebert, *White
Portfolio turnover (3 yrs): 141%, 340%, 204%
Expense ratio: 0.95% (year ending 12/31/97)

MARKMAN MULTIFUND TRUST - CONSERVATIVE ALLOCATION PORTFOLIO ◆
(See first Markman listing for data common to all funds)

Investment objective and policy: Current income; moderate capital growth secondary. Invests in mutual funds with the same objective that invest in equity and debt securities. May also invest in mutual funds that invest primarily in short-term bonds and other fixed-income securities that offer a potential for capital appreciation. May also invest in mutual funds that invest primarily in short-term bonds and other fixed-income securities that offer a potential for capital appreciation. May invest up to 25% of assets in one fund.
Year organized: 1995
Ticker symbol: MMCGX
Discount broker availability: *Fidelity, *Schwab, Siebert, *White
Portfolio turnover (3 yrs): 48%, 104%, 176%
Expense ratio: 0.95% (year ending 12/31/97)

MARKMAN MULTIFUND TRUST - MODERATE ALLOCATION PORTFOLIO ◆
(See first Markman listing for data common to all funds)

Investment objective and policy: Reasonable level of current income and capital growth. Invests in mutual funds with the same objective that invest in equity and debt securities. May also invest in mutual funds that invest primarily in short-term bonds and other fixed-income securities that offer a potential for capital appreciation. May invest up to 25% of assets in one fund.
Year organized: 1995
Ticker symbol: MMMGX
Discount broker availability: *Fidelity, *Schwab, Siebert, *White
Portfolio turnover (3 yrs): 82%, 280%, 141%
Expense ratio: 0.95% (year ending 12/31/97)

MARSHALL FUNDS
(Data common to all Marshall funds are shown below. See subsequent listings for data specific to individual funds.)

1000 North Water Street
P.O. Box 1348
Milwaukee, WI 53201-1348
800-618-8573, 800-236-3863
414-287-8555
fax 414-287-8511, TDD 800-209-3520
Internet: http://marshallfunds.com

Shareholder service hours: Full service: M-F 8 ;a.m-5 P.M. CST; After hours service: prices, yields, balances, orders, last transaction, news, messages, indices, prospectuses, total returns
Adviser: M&I Investment Management Corp.
Transfer agent and administrator: Federated Services Co.
Minimum purchase: Initial: $1,000, Subsequent: $50; Automatic investment plan: Initial: $100
Wire orders accepted: Yes
Deadline for same day wire purchase: 4 P.M. (1 P.M. for Money Market Fund)
Qualified for sale in: All states
Telephone redemptions: Yes
Wire redemptions: Yes, $1,000 minimum, $10 fee
Letter redemptions: Signature guarantee required over $50,000

Telephone switching: With other Marshall funds
Number of switches permitted: Unlimited
Shareholder services: IRA, SEP-IRA, Keogh, 401(k), 403(b), corporate retirement plans, electronic funds transfer, systematic withdrawal plan min. bal. req. $10,000
Administration fee: 0.150% first $250M to 0.075% over $750M
Shareholder services fee: 0.25% (except MM)
IRA/Keogh fees: Annual $10 per fund, $30 maximum

MARSHALL EQUITY INCOME FUND ◆
(See first Marshall listing for data common to all funds)

Portfolio manager: Bruce P. Hutson (1993)
Investment objective and policies: Above average dividend income with capital growth. Normally invests at least 65% of assets in dividend-paying common and preferred stocks Fund seeks to maintain a dividend level at least 1% higher than the composite of the stocks comprising the S&P 500. May also invest in convertible securities and government and corporate debt securities. Up to 20% of assets may be in ADRs of foreign issuers and 15% in illiquid securities.
Year organized: 1993
Ticker symbol: MREIX
Group fund code: 260
Discount broker availability: *Fidelity, *Schwab, *Siebert, *White
Dividends paid: Income - March, June, September, December; Capital gains - December
Portfolio turnover (3 yrs): 61%, 60%, 43%
Management fee: 0.75%
Expense ratio: 1.22% (year ending 8/31/97)

MARSHALL GOVERNMENT INCOME FUND ◆
(See first Marshall listing for data common to all funds)

Portfolio manager: Lawrence J. Pavelec (1993)
Investment objective and policies: Current income. Invests at least 65% of assets in U.S. Government securities guaranteed at to payment of principal and interest by the U.S. Government, its agencies or its instrumentalities. May also invest in mortgage-backed securities and use financial futures contracts, and options on financial futures contracts for hedging purposes. Up to 15% of assets may be in illiquid securities.
Year organized: 1992 (includes asset exchange from Newton Income Fund at date of inception)
Ticker symbol: MRGIX
Group fund code: 207
Discount broker availability: *Fidelity, *Siebert, *White
Dividends paid: Income - declared daily, paid monthly; Capital gains - December
Portfolio turnover (3 yrs): 299%, 268%, 360%
Management fee: 0.75%
Expense ratio: 0.86% (year ending 8/31/97) (1.24% without waiver)

MARSHALL INTERMEDIATE BOND FUND ◆
(See first Marshall listing for data common to all funds)

Portfolio manager: Mark D. Pittman (1994)
Investment objective and policies: Maximum total return consistent with current income. Invests in high-grade bonds and notes, and generally maintains a dollar-weighted average maturity of three to ten years with at least 65% of assets in bonds. May invest in debt securities of domestic issuers, obligations of the U.S., its agencies and its instrumentalities, commercial paper, certificates of deposit and other financial debt instruments. Up to 15% of assets may be in illiquid securities.
Year organized: 1992
Ticker symbol: MAIBX
Group fund code: 204
Discount broker availability: *Fidelity, *Siebert, *White

Dividends paid: Income - declared daily, paid monthly; Capital gains - December
Portfolio turnover (3 yrs): 144%, 201%, 232%
Management fee: 0.60%
Expense ratio: 0.72% (year ending 8/31/97) (1.03% without waiver)

MARSHALL INTERMEDIATE TAX-FREE FUND ◆
(See first Marshall listing for data common to all funds)

Portfolio manager: John D. Boritzke (1994)
Investment objective and policies: Maximum total return exempt from federal income tax, consistent with capital preservation. Invests in high-grade municipal securities, and generally maintains a dollar-weighted average maturity of three to ten years. May use options and futures to increase income and for hedging purposes. Up to 20% of assets may be in securities subject to AMT tax treatment, and 15% in illiquid securities.
Year organized: 1994
Ticker symbol: MITFX
Group fund code: 207
Discount broker availability: *Fidelity, *Siebert, *White
Dividends paid: Income - declared daily, paid monthly; Capital gains - December
Portfolio turnover (3 yrs): 53%, 41%, 105%
Management fee: 0.60%
Expense ratio: 0.61% (year ending 8/31/97) (1.15% without waiver)

MARSHALL INTERNATIONAL STOCK FUND ◆
(See first Marshall listing for data common to all funds)

Sub-adviser: Templeton Investment Counsel, Inc.
Portfolio manager: Gary R. Clemons (1995)
Investment objective and policies: Capital growth. Invests at least 65% of assets in common and preferred stocks of companies domiciled in at least three countries outside the U.S. May invest directly and use ADRs, GDRs and EDRs. Up to 35% of assets may be in foreign debt and convertible securities and 15% in illiquid securities. May use foreign currency exchange contracts and options on foreign currencies for hedging purposes.
Year organized: 1994
Ticker symbol: MRISX
Group fund code: 394
Discount broker availability: *Fidelity, *Schwab, *Siebert, *White
Dividends paid: Income - March, June, December; Capital gains - December
Portfolio turnover (3 yrs): 26%, 26%, 61%
Management fee: 1.00%
12b-1 distribution fee: Maximum of 0.25% (not currently imposed)
Expense ratio: 1.59% (year ending 8/31/97)

MARSHALL LARGE-CAP GROWTH AND INCOME FUND ◆
(See first Marshall listing for data common to all funds)

Portfolio manager: William J. O'Connor (1996)
Investment objective and policies: Capital growth and income. Invests at least 65% of assets in common and preferred stocks of companies with established markets, primarily companies whose equity securities generate income. Up to 20% of assets may be in ADRs of foreign issuers and 15% in illiquid securities.
Year organized: 1992 (includes asset exchange from Newton Growth Fund at date of inception; name changed from Stock Fund 6/1/97)
Ticker symbol: MASTX
Group fund code: 206
Discount broker availability: *Fidelity, *Schwab, *Siebert, *White
Dividends paid: Income - March, June, September, December; Capital gains - December
Portfolio turnover (3 yrs): 43%, 147%, 79%
Management fee: 0.75%
Expense ratio: 1.23% (year ending 8/31/97)

MARSHALL MID-CAP GROWTH FUND ◆

(See first Marshall listing for data common to all funds)

Portfolio manager: Steven D. Hayward (1993)
Investment objective and policies: Capital growth. Invests at least 65% of assets in common and preferred stocks of companies with market capitalizations between $200M and $7.5B. Fund invests primarily in companies with above-average earnings growth prospects or likely to benefit from significant changes in their internal structure, products, or market environment. Up to 20% of assets may be in ADRs of foreign issuers and 15% in illiquid securities.
Year organized: 1993 (name changed from Mid-Cap Stock Fund 6/1/97)
Ticker symbol: MRMSX
Group fund code: 261
Discount broker availability: *Fidelity, *Schwab, *Siebert, *White
Dividends paid: Income - March, June, September, December; Capital gains - December
Portfolio turnover (3 yrs): 211%, 189%, 157%
Management fee: 0.75%
Expense ratio: 1.24% (year ending 8/31/97)

MARSHALL MID-CAP VALUE FUND ◆

(See first Marshall listing for data common to all funds)

Portfolio managers: John C. Potter (1997), Matthew B. Fahey (1997)
Investment objective and policies: Long-term growth of capital and income. Invests at least 65% of assets in common stocks, securities convertible into common stocks and preferred stocks of medium to large capitalization companies. Fund seeks companies with price/earnings ratios less than the S&P 500, above average dividend yields, below average price to book value and unrecognized or undervalued assets. Up to 20% of assets may be in ADRs of foreign issuers and 15% in illiquid securities.
Year organized: 1993 (name changed from Value Equity Fund 6/1/97)
Ticker symbol: MRVEX
Group fund code: 262
Discount broker availability: *Fidelity, *Siebert, *White
Dividends paid: Income - March, June, September, December; Capital gains - December
Portfolio turnover (3 yrs): 55%, 67%, 78%
Management fee: 0.75%
Expense ratio: 1.23% (year ending 8/31/97)

MARSHALL MONEY MARKET FUND - CLASS A SHARES ◆

(See first Marshall listing for data common to all funds)

Portfolio manager: Richard M. Rokus (1992)
Investment objective and policies: Current income consistent with principal stability. Invests in high quality money market instruments. May invest in dollar-denominated Eurodollar commercial paper and other short-term debt instruments of foreign banks and other deposit institutions.
Year organized: 1992 (includes asset exchange from Newton Money Market Fund at date of inception)
Ticker symbol: MARXX
Group fund code: 200
Special sales restrictions: Sold to customers of M&I Corp. and its affiliates, or retail customers of institutions that have not entered into a marketing arrangement or do not provide sales and/or administrative services for the sale of Money Market Fund shares
Check redemptions: $250 minimum
Dividends paid: Income - declared daily, paid monthly
Management fee: 0.50%
Expense ratio: 0.41% (year ending 8/31/97) (0.67% without waiver)

MARSHALL MONEY MARKET FUND - CLASS B SHARES

(See first Marshall listing for data common to all Marshall funds. All information for Class B Shares is identical to that for Investment shares except as listed below.)

Year organized: 1992
Special sales restrictions: Sold through institutions and other entities that have entered into marketing arrangements to make Money Market Fund shares available to their clients, customers or other specified groups of investors, or that have agreed to provide sales and/or administrative services as agents for holders of Class B shares.
Ticker symbol: MABXX
12b-1 distribution fee: 0.30%
Expense ratio: 0.71% (year ending 8/31/97) (0.97% without waiver)

MARSHALL SHORT-TERM INCOME FUND ◆

(See first Marshall listing for data common to all funds)

Portfolio manager: Mark D. Pittman (1994)
Investment objective and policies: Maximum total return consistent with current income. Invests in high-grade bonds and notes, and generally maintains a dollar-weighted average maturity of six months to three years. May invest in debt securities of domestic issuers, obligations of the U.S. Government, its agencies and its instrumentalities, commercial paper, certificates of deposit and other financial debt instruments. Up to 15% of assets may be in illiquid securities.
Year organized: 1992
Ticker symbol: MSINX
Group fund code: 203
Discount broker availability: *Fidelity, *Siebert, *White
Dividends paid: Income - declared daily, paid monthly; Capital gains - December
Portfolio turnover (3 yrs): 101%, 144%, 194%
Management fee: 0.60%
Expense ratio: 0.49% (year ending 8/31/97) (1.08% without waiver)

MARSHALL SMALL-CAP GROWTH FUND ◆

(See first Marshall listing for data common to all funds)

Portfolio managers: David J. Lettenberger (1996), Steve D. Hayward (1996)
Investment objective and policies: Long-term capital appreciation. Invests primarily in common and preferred stocks of companies with market capitalizations below $1B. Invests in companies with perceived above average earnings growth or in companies where significant, fundamental changes are taking place. Compares performance to the Russell 2000 Index. May also invest in investment grade convertible securities, mortgage-backed securities, adjustable rate mortgage securities. May hold up to 20% of assets in ADRs and up to 15% of assets in illiquid securities. May use a variety of derivative instruments in an effort to enhance performance and for hedging purposes.
Year organized: 1996 (name changed from Small-Cap Stock Fund 6/1/97)
Ticker symbol: MRSCX
Group fund code: 612
Discount broker availability: *Fidelity, *Schwab, *Siebert, *White
Dividends paid: Income - March, June, September, December; Capital gains - December
Portfolio turnover (1 yr): 183%
Management fee: 1.00%
12b-1 distribution fee: Maximum of 0.25% (currently not imposed)
Expense ratio: 1.80% (year ending 8/31/97)

MARSICO FOCUS FUND ◆
1200 Seventeenth Street, Suite 1300
Denver, CO 80202
888-860-8686, 303-436-1300

Adviser: Marsico Capital Management, LLC
Administrator: Sunstone Financial Group, Inc.
Portfolio manager: Thomas F. Marsico (1997)
Transfer agent: Sunstone Investor Services, LLC
Investment objective and policies: Long-term growth of capital. Invests primarily in the common stocks of a select group of twenty to thirty stocks selected for their perceived growth potential. May also invest to a lesser degree in preferred stock, warrants convertible securities and debt obligations. May invest up to 25% of assets in mortgage- and asset-backed securities, up to 10% in zero coupon, pay-in-kind and step coupon securities, up to 15% in illiquid securities, up to 35% of assets in junk bonds, without limit in foreign securities (including those denominated in foreign currencies), and without limit in indexed/structured securities. May invest up to 25% of assets in a single issuer. May use a variety of derivative instruments for hedging purposes. Fund is non-diversified.
Year organized: 1997
Minimum purchase: Initial: $2,500, Subsequent: $100; IRA: Initial: $1,000; Automatic investment plan: Initial: $1,000, Subsequent: $50
Wire orders accepted: Yes
Deadline for same day wire purchase: 4 P.M.
Discount broker availability: *Fidelity, *Schwab, *White
Qualified for sale in: All states
Telephone redemptions: Yes, $500 minimum
Wire redemptions: Yes, $500 minimum, $10 fee
Letter redemptions: Signature guarantee required over $50,000
Telephone switching: With Marsico Growth & Income Fund and the Northern Money Market fund
Number of switches permitted: Six per year
Dividends paid: Income - annually; Capital gains - annually
Shareholder services: IRA, SEP-IRA, electronic funds transfer, systematic withdrawal plan min. bal. req. $10,000
Management fee: 0.85%
Administration fee: 0.14% ($62,500 minimum)
IRA fees: Annual $15, Closing $15

MARSICO GROWTH AND INCOME FUND ◆
1200 Seventeenth Street, Suite 1300
Denver, CO 80202
888-860-8686, 303-436-1300

Adviser: Marsico Capital Management, LLC
Administrator: Sunstone Financial Group, Inc.
Portfolio manager: Thomas F. Marsico (1997)
Transfer agent: Sunstone Investor Services, LLC
Investment objective and policies: Long-term growth of capital and a limited emphasis on current income. Invests up to 75% of assets (but may be as low as 25%) in a diversified portfolio of equity securities selected for their perceived growth potential, and at least 25% of assets in securities with perceived income potential. Allocation between elements may be allocated according to perceived market conditions. May invest up to 25% of assets in mortgage- and asset-backed securities, up to 10% in zero coupon, pay-in-kind and step coupon securities, up to 15% in illiquid securities, up to 35% of assets in junk bonds, without limit in foreign securities (including those denominated in foreign currencies), and without limit in indexed/structured securities. May use a variety of derivative instruments for hedging purposes. Fund is non-diversified.
Year organized: 1997
Minimum purchase: Initial: $2,500, Subsequent: $100; IRA: Initial: $1,000; Automatic investment plan: Initial: $1,000, Subsequent: $50
Wire orders accepted: Yes
Deadline for same day wire purchase: 4 P.M.
Discount broker availability: *Fidelity, *Schwab, *White
Qualified for sale in: All states
Telephone redemptions: Yes, $500 minimum
Wire redemptions: Yes, $500 minimum, $10 fee
Letter redemptions: Signature guarantee required over $50,000

Telephone switching: With Marsico Focus Fund and the Northern Money Market fund
Number of switches permitted: Six per year
Dividends paid: Income - annually; Capital gains - annually
Shareholder services: IRA, SEP-IRA, electronic funds transfer, systematic withdrawal plan min. bal. req. $10,000
Management fee: 0.85%
Administration fee: 0.14% ($62,500 minimum)
IRA fees: Annual $15, Closing $15

MASTERS' SELECT EQUITY FUND ◆
4 Orinda Way
Orinda, CA 94563
800-960-0188, 510-254-8999

Adviser: Litman/Gregory Fund Advisors, LLC
Sub-advisers: Davis Select Advisers, LP (20%); Societe Generale Asset Management Corp. (20%); Friess Assocs. (10%); Southeastern Asset Management (20%); Jennison Associates Capital Corp. (20%); Strong Capital Management, Inc. (10%)
Administrator: Investment Company Administration Corp.
Portfolio managers: Kenneth E. Gregory (1997), Shelby Davis (1997), Jean-Marie Eveillard (1997), Foster Friess (1997), Mason Hawkins (1997), Spiros Segalas (1997), Richard Weiss (1997)
Transfer agent: National Financial Data Services
Investment objective and policies: Long-term capital growth. Invests primarily in a diversified portfolio of U.S. equity securities of all market capitalizations. Fund is sub-advised by six different investment managers, each with a different stock picking discipline. Each runs a fixed percentage of the fund's portfolio, and invests in a maximum of 15 stocks. The portfolio is thus diversified across 75 to 90 stocks; undue duplication or over-concentration in sectors or industries will be resolved by the lead portfolio manager. Allocations will be maintained more or less within the percentage parameters shown above. Invests 20% to 30% of assets in small cap companies, up to 25% of assets in foreign issues, up to 10% of assets in junk bonds and 15% in illiquid securities. May use options for hedging purposes.
Year organized: 1997
Ticker symbol: MSEFX
Sales restrictions: Fund will close to new investors between $500M and $750M in assets
Minimum purchase: Initial: $5,000, Subsequent: $250; IRA: Initial: $1,000; Automatic investment plan: Initial: $2,500, Subsequent: $100
Wire orders accepted: Yes, $5,000 minimum
Deadline for same day wire purchase: 4 P.M.
Discount broker availability: Fidelity, Schwab, White
Qualified for sale in: All states
Telephone redemptions: Yes
Wire redemptions: Yes
Letter redemptions: Signature guarantee required over $25,000
Telephone switching: With Masters' Select Int'l Fund
Number of switches permitted: Monitored
Dividends paid: Income - December; Capital gains - December
Shareholder services: IRA, SEP-IRA, systematic withdrawal plan
Management fee: 1.10%: Adviser pays sub-advisers at the following rate on their allocated portion: Davis Select Advisers, LP (0.60%); Societe Generale Asset Management Corp. (0.75%); Friess Assocs. (1.00%); Southeaster Asset Management (0.75%); Jennison Associates Capital Corp. (0.75% first $10M to 0.35% over $40M); Strong Capital Management, Inc. (0.75%)
Administration fee: 0.10% first $100M to 0.0125% over $500M ($40,000 minimum)
IRA fees: Initial $5, Annual $15

MASTERS' SELECT INTERNATIONAL FUND ◆
4 Orinda Way
Orinda, CA 94563
800-960-0188, 510-254-8999

Adviser: Litman/Gregory Fund Advisors, LLC
Sub-advisers: Bee & Assocs., Inc. (10%); Janus Capital Corp. (22.5%); Harris Assocs., L.P. (22.5%); BPI Global Asset Management, LLP (22.5%); Artisan Partners, L.P. (22.5%)
Administrator: Investment Company Administration Corp.
Portfolio managers: Kenneth E. Gregory (1997), Bruce Bee (1997), Helen Young Hayes (1997), David G. Herro (1997), Daniel R. Jaworski (1997), Mark L. Yockey (1997)
Transfer agent: National Financial Data Services
Investment objective and policies: Long-term capital growth. Invests primarily in a diversified portfolio of foreign securities of all market capitalizations from at least five countries, with 60% to 90% in mid- and large-cap issues; it will include emerging markets. Fund is sub-advised by five different investment managers, each with a different stock picking discipline. Each runs a fixed percentage of the fund's portfolio, and invests in at least eight and as many as fifteen stocks. The portfolio is thus diversified across 50 to 75 stocks; undue duplication or overconcentration in sectors or industries will be resolved by the lead portfolio manager. Allocations will be maintained more or less within the percentage parameters shown above. Invests up to 35% of assets in short-term debt obligations, 10% of assets in junk bonds and 15% in illiquid securities. May use a variety of derivative instruments for hedging purposes.
Year organized: 1997
Sales restrictions: Fund will close to new investors between $600M and $1B in assets
Minimum purchase: Initial: $5,000, Subsequent: $250; IRA: Initial: $1,000; Automatic investment plan: Initial: $2,500, Subsequent: $100
Wire orders accepted: Yes, $5,000 minimum
Deadline for same day wire purchase: 4 P.M.
Discount broker availability: Fidelity, Schwab, White
Qualified for sale in: All states
Telephone redemptions: Yes
Wire redemptions: Yes
Letter redemptions: Signature guarantee required over $25,000
Telephone switching: With Masters' Select Equity Fund
Number of switches permitted: Monitored
Dividends paid: Income - December; Capital gains - December
Shareholder services: IRA, SEP-IRA, systematic withdrawal plan
Management fee: 1.10%: Adviser pays sub-advisers at an annual aggregate rate of 0.6175%
Administration fee: 0.10% first $100M to 0.0125% over $500M ($40,000 minimum)
IRA fees: Initial $5, Annual $15

MATHERS FUND ◆
100 Corporate North, Suite 201
Bannockburn, IL 60015-1253
800-962-3863, 847-295-7400
price/yields 800-235-7458
fax 847-295-7573

Adviser: Mathers and Co., Inc.
Portfolio managers: Henry G. Van der Eb, Jr. (1975), Anne E. Morrissy (1996), Robert J. Reynolds (1996)
Transfer agent: DST Systems, Inc.
Investment objective and policies: Long-term capital appreciation; current income secondary. Invests primarily in common stocks believed to have favorable growth prospects. May invest in securities of foreign issuers traded on U.S. securities markets without limit and have up to 10% of assets in securities not publicly traded in the U.S. Fund may hedge.
Year organized: 1965
Ticker symbol: MATRX
Minimum purchase: Initial: $1,000, Subsequent: $200; IRA/Keogh: Initial: $200, Subsequent: None; Automatic investment plan: Subsequent: $50
Wire orders accepted: Subsequent only
Deadline for same day wire purchase: 4 P.M.
Discount broker availability: Schwab, White
Qualified for sale in: All states
Letter redemptions: Signature guarantee required over $25,000
Dividends paid: Income - December; Capital gains - December
Portfolio turnover (3 yrs): 50%, 38%, 58%
Shareholder services: IRA, SEP-IRA, Keogh, systematic withdrawal plan

Management fee: 0.75% first $200M to 0.50% over $500M
Expense ratio: 1.07% (year ending 12/31/97)
IRA/Keogh fees: Annual $12

MATRIX EMERGING GROWTH FUND
300 Main Street
Cincinnati, OH 45202
800-385-7003, 800-877-3344
513-621-2875
fax 513-241-9448

Adviser: Sena Weller Rohs Williams, Inc.
Administrator: Investment Company Administration Corp.
Portfolio managers: Fred W. Weller (1995), Michael A. Coombe (1995)
Transfer agent: American Data Services, Inc.
Investment objective and policies: Long-term capital appreciation. Invests primarily in common stocks of companies perceived to show long-term growth potential, particularly smaller companies in their emerging or developing growth phase. Fund emphasizes companies in the fields of science and technology, but is not limited to them. May have up to 15% of assets in illiquid securities.
Year organized: 1995
Ticker symbol: MEGFX
Minimum purchase: Initial: $1,000, Subsequent: $100; IRA/Keogh: Initial: $500
Wire orders accepted: Yes
Deadline for same day wire purchase: 4 P.M.
Discount broker availability: *White
Qualified for sale in: CA, CO, DC, FL, GA, IL, IN, KY, NC, NJ, NY, OH, PA, TN, TX, UT, VA, WY
Telephone redemptions: Yes
Wire redemptions: Yes, $1,000 minimum
Telephone switching: With Matrix Growth Fund and Star Treasury Fund
Number of switches permitted: 12 per year
Dividends paid: Income - December; Capital gains - December
Portfolio turnover (2 yrs): 41%, 10%
Shareholder services: IRA, Keogh, 403(b), corporate retirement plans, automatic investment plan, electronic funds transfer, systematic withdrawal plan min. bal. req. $10,000
Management fee: 0.90% first $50M to 0.60% over $100M
Administration fee: $30,000 first $15M to 0.05% over $150M
12b-1 distribution fee: 0.25%
IRA/Keogh fees: None
Expense ratio: 2.00% (year ending 12/31/97) (includes waiver)

MATRIX GROWTH FUND
300 Main Street
Cincinnati, OH 45202
800-385-7003, 800-877-3344
513-621-2875
fax 513-241-9448

Adviser: Sena Weller Rohs Williams, Inc.
Administrator: Investment Company Administration Corp.
Portfolio managers: Peter H. Williams (1988), David P. Osborn (1994)
Transfer agent: American Data Services, Inc.
Investment objective and policies: Long-term capital appreciation; principal conservation secondary. Invests primarily in common stocks of companies with potential for rising earnings and stable or rising share prices. May purchase put options on up to 5% of assets for hedging purposes, or to attempt to retain unrealized gains. May have up to 15% of assets in illiquid securities.
Year organized: 1986 (originally Gateway Growth Plus Fund. Name changed to SWRW Growth Plus in 1992, and to current 1/1/94)
Ticker symbol: GATGX
Minimum purchase: Initial: $1,000, Subsequent: $100; IRA/Keogh: Initial: $500
Wire orders accepted: Yes
Deadline for same day wire purchase: 4 P.M.
Discount broker availability: Schwab, *White
Qualified for sale in: CA, CO, DC, FL, GA, IL, IN, KY, MI, MO, NC, NJ, NY, OH, PA, TN, TX, UT, VA, WA, WI, WY

Telephone redemptions: Yes
Wire redemptions: Yes, $1,000 minimum
Telephone switching: With Matrix Emerging Growth Fund and Star Treasury Fund
Number of switches permitted: 12 per year
Dividends paid: Income - December; Capital gains - December
Portfolio turnover (3 yrs): 0%, 27%, 25%
Shareholder services: IRA, Keogh, 403(b), corporate retirement plans, automatic investment plan, electronic funds transfer, systematic withdrawal plan min. bal. req. $10,000
Management fee: 0.90% first $50M to 0.60% over $100M
Administration fee: $30,000 first $15M to 0.05% over $150M
12b-1 distribution fee: 0.25%
Expense ratio: 1.75% (year ending 12/31/97) (includes waiver)
IRA/Keogh fees: None

MATRIX/LMH VALUE FUND ◆
444 Madison Avenue, Suite 302
New York, NY 10022
800-366-6223, 212-486-2004

Adviser: Matrix Asset Advisors, Inc.
Administrator: Investment Company Administration Corp.
Portfolio manager: David A. Katz (1996)
Transfer agent: Star Bank, N.A.
Investment objective and policies: Total return: capital appreciation and current income. Invests primarily in common stocks selected through Benjamin Graham valuation analysis or high yields relative to the S&P 400—typically stocks deemed undervalued. May also invest in preferred stocks and convertible securities and have up to 10% of assets in foreign securities. May use options for hedging purposes.
Year organized: 1983 (name changed from LMH Value Fund in Spring 1997)
Ticker symbol: LMHFX
Minimum purchase: Initial: $1,000, Subsequent: $100; IRA/Keogh: Initial: $500; Automatic investment plan: Initial $500
Wire orders accepted: Yes
Deadline for same day wire purchase: 4 P.M.
Discount broker availability: *Schwab, *White
Qualified for sale in: All states except SD, TX
Letter redemptions: Signature guarantee required over $5,000
Dividends paid: Income - December; Capital gains - December
Portfolio turnover (3 yrs): 129%, 57%, 34%
Shareholder services: IRA
Management fee: 1.00%
Expense ratio: 1.42% (year ending 6/30/97) (1.92% without waiver)
IRA fees: Annual $10

THE MATTERHORN GROWTH FUND
301 Oxford Valley Road, Suite 802B
Yardley, PA 19067
800-637-3901, 800-543-2875

Adviser: Matterhorn Asset Management Corp.
Administrator: Investment Company Administration Corp.
Portfolio manager: Gregory Alan Church (1996)
Transfer agent: American Data Services, Inc.
Investment objective and policies: Long-term capital appreciation. Invests in securities of companies of any market capitalization expected to grow faster than the average rate of companies in the S&P 500 Stock Price Index. Fund is non-diversified and employs leverage. May invest 10% of assets in securities of foreign issuers and use options in an effort to enhance return and for hedging purposes.
Year organized: 1980, present management 1988 (name changed from 44 Wall Street Equity Fund in 1996)
Ticker symbol: FWLEX
Minimum purchase: Initial: $1,000, Subsequent: $100
Wire orders accepted: Yes
Deadline for same day wire purchase: 4 P.M.
Discount broker availability: White

Qualified for sale in: CT, DC, FL, HI, IL, MD, MA, NJ, NY, PA, TX, VA, WA
Telephone redemptions: Yes
Wire redemption: Yes, $1,000 minimum
Letter redemptions: Signature guarantee required
Dividends paid: Income - annually, Capital gains - annually
Portfolio turnover (3 yrs): 131%, 88%, 72%
Shareholder services: IRA, 403(b), automatic investment plan, systematic withdrawal plan min. bal. req. $10,000
Management fee: 1.00%
12b-1 distribution fee: 0.25%
Administration fee: 0.10% (minimum $10,000)
Expense ratio: 4.00% (year ending 6/30/97)
IRA fees: Annual $10, Initial $10, Closing $10

MATTHEW 25 FUND ◆
605 Cloverly Avenue
Jenkintown, PA 19046
800-884-4458

Adviser: Matthew 25 Fund, Inc.
Portfolio manager: Mark Mullholland (1996)
Transfer agent: American Data Services, Inc.
Investment objective and policies: Long-term capital appreciation; current income secondary. Invests in common stock or securities convertible to common stock. Fund is non-diversified, and may invest up to 25% of assets in a single sector.
Year organized: 1996
Minimum purchase: Initial: $1,000, Subsequent: $100
Wire orders accepted: No
Qualified for sale in: NJ, PA
Letter redemptions: Signature guarantee required
Dividends paid: Income - annually, Capital gains - annually
Portfolio turnover (1 yr): 3%
Shareholder services: IRA
Management fee: 1.00%
Expense ratio: 1.34% (year ending 12/31/96)
IRA fees: Annual $40 (waived for balances over $5,000)

MATTHEWS INTERNATIONAL FUNDS ◆
(Data common to all Matthews funds are shown below. See subsequent listings for data specific to individual funds.)

655 Montgomery Street, Suite 1438
San Francisco, CA 94111
800-789-2742, 415-788-6036
shareholders 800-892-0382, 800-955-2742
fax 415-788-4804
Internet: http://www.micfunds.com

Adviser: Matthews International Capital Management, LLC
Transfer agent and administrator: First Data Investor Services Group
Sales restrictions: All Matthews funds except Convertibles have two classes of shares, "I" shares are sold direct and through discount brokers with no loads and no 12b-1 fees. "A" shares are sold through brokers with a 4.95% load. Only "I" shares are represented here.
Minimum purchase: Initial: $1,000, Subsequent: $250; IRA: Initial: $250, Subsequent: $50; Automatic investment plan: Subsequent: $100
Wire orders accepted: Yes
Deadline for same day wire purchase: 4 P.M.
Qualified for sale in: All states
Telephone redemptions: Yes
Wire redemptions: Yes, $9 fee
Letter redemptions: Signature guarantee required over $100,000
Redemption fee: 1.00% for shares held less than 90 days, payable to the funds
Telephone switching: With other Matthews International Funds, $1,000 minimum
Number of switches permitted: Unlimited
Shareholder services: IRA, SEP-IRA, 401(k), 403(b)
Management fee: 1.00%
Administration fee: 0.10% first $250M to 0.03% over $750M ($100,000 minimum per fund)
IRA fees: Annual $12

MATTHEWS ASIAN CONVERTIBLE SECURITIES FUND !
(See first Matthews listing for data common to all funds)

Portfolio manager: G. Paul Matthews (1994)
Investment objective and policies: Capital appreciation and current income. Invests at least 65% of its total assets in convertible securities of issuers from at least three countries in the Asian markets of Hong Kong, Japan, Singapore, South Korea, Taiwan, Indonesia, Malaysia, the Philippines, Thailand, China and India. Instruments will primarily be Euroconvertible securities denominated in U.S. dollars, Swiss francs or other currencies. Balance of assets may be invested in virtually any instrument anywhere in the world without limit, including the U.S. May invest in junk bonds without limit. May use options, futures and forward currency contracts for hedging purposes. Will not knowingly invest more than 15% of assets in illiquid securities.
Year organized: 1994
Ticker symbol: MACSX
Discount broker availability: *Fidelity, *Schwab, *White
Dividends paid: Income - June, December; Capital gains - December
Portfolio turnover (3 yrs): 50%, 88%, 122%
Expense ratio: 1.90% (year ending 8/31/97) (4.45% without waiver)

MATTHEWS DRAGON CENTURY CHINA FUND ◆
(See first Matthews listing for data common to all funds)

Portfolio manager: G. Paul Matthews (1998)
Investment objective and policies: Long-term capital appreciation. Invests at least 65% of its total assets in equity securities of Chinese companies of all sizes, including B shares, "H" shares and Red Chips in both China and Hong Kong. May invest up to 35% of assets in any other type of instrument anywhere in the world. May invest up to 10% of assets in securities rated below investment grade, including junk bonds. May use options, futures and forward currency contracts for hedging purposes. Will not knowingly invest more than 15% of assets in illiquid securities.
Year organized: 1998
Discount broker availability: *Schwab, *White
Dividends paid: Income - June, December; Capital gains - December

MATTHEWS KOREA FUND ◆
(See first Matthews listing for data common to all funds)

Sub-adviser: Daewoo Capital Management Co., Ltd.
Portfolio manager: G. Paul Matthews (1995)
Investment objective and policies: Long term capital appreciation. Invests primarily in equity securities of South Korean companies or those who derive at least 50% of their revenues or profits from, or have at least 50% of their assets located in, South Korea. The remaining assets may be invested in any security of any issuer without limit anywhere in the world, including up to 35% of assets in convertibles and up to 35% in junk bonds. May use options and futures for hedging purposes. Will not knowingly invest more than 10% of assets in illiquid securities.
Year organized: 1995
Ticker symbol: MAKOX
Discount broker availability: *Fidelity, *Schwab, *White
Dividends paid: Income - December; Capital gains - December
Portfolio turnover (3 yrs): 113%, 140%, 42%
Expense ratio: 2.50% (year ending 8/31/97) (2.90% without waiver)

MATTHEWS PACIFIC TIGER FUND ◆
(See first Matthews listing for data common to all funds)

Portfolio managers: G. Paul Matthews (1994), Mark W. Headley (1996)
Investment objective and policies: Maximum capi-

tal appreciation. Invests primarily in equity securities of issuers from at least three different countries in the Pacific Tiger markets (except Japan) of Hong Kong, Singapore, South Korea, Taiwan, Indonesia, Malaysia, the Philippines, Thailand, and China. Up to 35% of assets may be in securities of issuers outside the Pacific Tiger region, including the U.S., and 25% in convertible securities of Pacific Tiger issuers. May invest in ADRs, GDRs and EDRs, and use options, futures and forward currency contracts for hedging purposes. Will not knowingly invest more than 15% of assets in illiquid securities.
Year organized: 1994
Ticker symbol: MAPTX
Discount broker availability: *Fidelity, *Schwab, *White
Dividends paid: Income - December; Capital gains - December
Portfolio turnover (3 yrs): 71%, 125%, 93%
Expense ratio: 1.90% (year ending 8/31/97) (1.97% without waiver)

MAXIM CONTRARIAN FUND
(See NewCap Contrarian Fund)

MAXUS FUNDS
(Data common to all Maxus funds are shown below. See subsequent listings for data specific to individual funds.)

28601 Chagrin Blvd., Suite 500
Cleveland, OH 44122
888-896-2987, 216-687-1000

Adviser: Maxus Asset Management, Inc.
Transfer agent: Maxus Information Systems, Inc.
Minimum purchase: Initial: $1,000, Subsequent: $100
Wire orders accepted: Yes
Deadline for same day wire purchase: 4 P.M.
Telephone orders accepted: Yes
Telephone redemptions: Yes, $1,000 minimum
Wire redemptions: Yes, $1,000 minimum, $8 fee
Letter redemptions: Signature guarantee required
Telephone switching: With other Maxus funds
Number of switches permitted: Unlimited
Shareholder services: IRA, systematic withdrawal plan min. bal. req. $15,000
Management fee: 1.00% first $150M, 0.75% over $150M
12b-1 distribution fee: Maximum of 0.50%
IRA fees: Annual $8

MAXUS EQUITY FUND
(See first Maxus listing for data common to all funds)

Portfolio manager: Richard A. Barone (1989)
Investment objective and policies: Total return: income and capital appreciation. Invests in equity and debt securities. Normally at least 65% of assets will be in equity securities. Up to 35% of assets will be in investment grade debt securities. May invest in closed-end mutual funds and use options to increase return.
Year organized: 1989
Ticker symbol: MXSEX
Discount broker availability: Fidelity, Siebert, *White
Qualified for sale in: All states
Dividends paid: Income - December; Capital gains - December
Portfolio turnover (3 yrs): 89%, 111%, 173%
Expense ratio: 1.87% (year ending 12/31/97)

MAXUS INCOME FUND
(See first Maxus listing for data common to all funds)

Portfolio manager: Richard A. Barone (1985)
Investment objective and policies: High total return: income and capital appreciation, consistent with reasonable risk. Invests in debt securities and preferred and common stock. May invest in options and closed-end mutual funds. Fund will adjust mix of debt and equity securities to reflect changes in economic and market conditions.
Year organized: 1985 (formerly Maxus Fund)
Ticker symbol: MXSFX

Discount broker availability: Fidelity, Siebert, *White
Qualified for sale in: All states
Dividends paid: Income - monthly; Capital gains - December
Portfolio turnover (3 yrs): 70%, 78%, 121%
Expense ratio: 1.91% (year ending 12/31/97)

MAXUS LAUREATE FUND
(See first Maxus listing for data common to all funds)

Portfolio managers: Richard A. Barone (1994), Alan G. Miller (1994)
Investment objective and policies: High total return: income and capital appreciation, consistent with reasonable risk. Invests exclusively in shares of other open-end mutual funds and allocates assets among equity and bond funds adjusting mix to reflect changes in economic and market conditions.
Year organized: 1993 (name changed from Maxus Prism Fund in 1994)
Ticker symbol: MXSPX
Discount broker availability: Fidelity, Siebert, *White
Qualified for sale in: All states except TX
Dividends paid: Income - December; Capital gains - December
Portfolio turnover (3 yrs): 1,511%, 1,267%, 1,377%
Expense ratio: 2.49% (year ending 12/31/97)

MCM FUNDS ◆
(Data common to all McM funds are shown below. See subsequent listings for data specific to individual funds.)

One Bush Street, Suite 800
San Francisco, CA 94104
800-788-9485, 415-788-9300
shareholder services 800-831-1146
fax 415-616-9386
Internet: http://www.mcmfunds.com
e-mail: mcmfunds@mcmfunds.com

Adviser: McMorgan & Co.
Transfer agent: First Data Investor Services Group
Minimum purchase: Initial: $5,000, Subsequent: $250; Automatic investment plan: Subsequent: $100
Wire orders accepted: Yes
Deadline for same day wire purchase: 4 P.M. (1 P.M. for MM)
Qualified for sale in: AZ, AR, CA, CO, CT, DE, DC, FL, HI, IL, IN, IA, MA, ME, MD, NV, NY, OH, OR, PA, WA
Telephone redemptions: Yes
Wire redemptions: Yes, $9 fee for redemptions under $10,000
Letters redemptions: Signature guarantee required over $10,000
Telephone switching: With other McM funds
Number of switches permitted: Unlimited
Shareholder services: IRA, automatic investment plan, directed dividends, electronic funds transfer (redemptions only), systematic withdrawal plan min. bal. req. $10,000
IRA fees: Annual $12

MCM BALANCED FUND ◆
(See first McM listing for data common to all funds)

Portfolio manager: Team managed
Investment objective and policies: Capital appreciation, income and preservation of capital over a market cycle of three to five years. Invests in a diversified portfolio of common stocks and fixed-income securities. Normally invests 50% to 75% of assets in equity securities, with allocation adjusted according to perceived changes in market and economic conditions. Fund maintains at least 25% of assets in fixed-income securities. May invest in ADRs and EDRs of foreign issuers, and use futures and options in an effort to increase income and for hedging purposes.
Year organized: 1994
Ticker symbol: MCMBX
Dividends paid: Income - March, June, September, December; Capital gains - December

Portfolio turnover (3 yrs): 32%, 26%, 81%
Management fee: 0.45%
Expense ratio: 0.60% (year ending 6/30/97) (1.01% without waiver)

MCM EQUITY INVESTMENT FUND ◆
(See first McM listing for data common to all funds)

Portfolio manager: Team managed
Investment objective and policies: Above average total return over a market cycle of three to five years, consistent with reasonable risk. Invests primarily in common stocks of high quality blue chip domestic companies with earnings growth, dividend growth and capital appreciation potential. May have up to 15% of assets in ADRs and EDRs of foreign issuers, and use futures and options to increase income and for hedging purposes.
Year organized: 1994
Ticker symbol: MCMEX
Dividends paid: Income - March, June, September, December; Capital gains - December
Portfolio turnover (3 yrs): 1%, 1%, 2%
Management fee: 0.50%
Expense ratio: 0.75% (year ending 6/30/97) (0.88% without waiver)

MCM FIXED INCOME FUND ◆
(See first McM listing for data common to all funds)

Portfolio manager: Team managed
Investment objective and policies: Above average total return consistent with low risk to principal over a market cycle of three to five years. Invests primarily in intermediate and long-term investment grade corporate and government debt securities. Portfolio maintains a dollar-weighted average maturity of three to fifteen years. May invest in ADRs and EDRs of foreign issuers, and use futures and options in an effort to increase income and for hedging purposes.
Year organized: 1994
Ticker symbol: MCMFX
Dividends paid: Income - declared daily, paid monthly; Capital gains - December
Portfolio turnover (3 yrs): 32%, 38%, 151%
Management fee: 0.35%
Expense ratio: 0.50% (year ending 6/30/97) (1.57% without waiver)

MCM INTERMEDIATE FIXED INCOME FUND ◆
(See first McM listing for data common to all funds)

Portfolio manager: Team managed
Investment objective and policies: Above average total return consistent with low risk to principal and liquidity over a market cycle of three to five years. Invests primarily in short- and intermediate-term, investment grade government and corporate debt securities. Portfolio maintains a dollar-weighted average maturity of three to ten years. May invest in ADRs and EDRs of foreign issuers, and use futures and options to increase income and for hedging purposes.
Year organized: 1994
Ticker symbol: MCMNX
Dividends paid: Income - declared daily, paid monthly; Capital gains - December
Portfolio turnover (3 yrs): 36%, 75%, 227%
Management fee: 0.35%
Expense ratio: 0.50% (year ending 6/30/97) (0.59% without waiver)

MCM PRINCIPAL PRESERVATION FUND ◆
(See first McM listing for data common to all funds)

Portfolio manager: Team managed
Investment objective and policies: Maximum income consistent with stability of principal and liquidity. Invests high quality U.S. Treasury and other government money market instruments.
Year organized: 1994
Check redemptions: No minimum
Dividends paid: Income - declared daily, paid monthly

Management fee: 0.25%
Expense ratio: 0.30% (year ending 6/30/97) (0.77% without waiver)

THE MERGER FUND

100 Summit Lake Drive
Valhalla, NY 10595
800-343-8959, 914-741-5600
fax 914-741-5737

Adviser: Westchester Capital Management, Inc.
Portfolio managers: Frederick W. Green (1989), Bonnie L. Smith (1989)
Transfer agent: Firstar Trust Co.
Investment objective and policies: Maximum capital growth through risk arbitrage. Invests at least 65% of assets in companies which are acquisition or reorganization targets. Positions hedged through short sales and the use of put (limited to 25% of assets) and covered call options (limited to 50% of assets). Fund may leverage its assets up to 50%.
Year organized: 1982 (formerly Ayco Risk Fund)
Ticker symbol: MERFX
Special sales restrictions: Fund closed to new investors 6/1/96
Minimum purchase: Initial: $2,000, Subsequent: None; Keogh: Initial & Subsequent: None; Automatic investment plan: Subsequent: $100
Wire orders accepted: Yes
Deadline for same day wire purchase: 4 P.M.
Discount broker availability: *Fidelity, *Schwab, *Siebert, *White
Qualified for sale in: All states
Letters redemptions: Signature guarantee required over $25,000
Dividends paid: Income - December; Capital gains - December
Portfolio turnover (3 yrs): 271%, 406%, 419%
Shareholder services: IRA, Keogh, corporate retirement plans, systematic withdrawal plan min. bal. req. $10,000 ($15 annual fee)
Management fee: 1.00%
12b-1 distribution fee: Maximum of 0.25%
Expense ratio: 1.36% (10 months ending 9/30/97) (4.29% without waiver)
IRA/Keogh fees: Annual $12.50

MERIDIAN FUND ◆

60 East Sir Francis Drake Blvd.
Wood Island, Suite 306
Larkspur, CA 94939
800-446-6662, 415-461-6237

Adviser: Aster Capital Management, Inc.
Portfolio manager: Richard F. Aster, Jr. (1984)
Transfer agent: First Data Investor Services Group
Investment objective and policies: Long-term capital growth income incidental. Invests at least 65% of assets in equity and equity-related securities, primarily common stocks, of small- and medium-sized companies experiencing above average growth in revenues and earnings. May invest up to 10% of assets in ADRs of foreign companies.
Year organized: 1984
Ticker symbol: MERDX
Minimum purchase: Initial: $1,000, Subsequent: $50
Wire orders accepted: Yes
Deadline for same day wire purchase: 4 P.M.
Discount broker availability: Schwab, White
Qualified for sale in: All states
Telephone redemptions: Yes
Wire redemptions: Yes, $5,000 minimum
Letter redemptions: Signature guarantee required over $25,000
Telephone switching: With Meridian Value Fund
Number of switches permitted: Unlimited
Dividends paid: Income - September; Capital gains - September
Portfolio turnover (3 yrs): 37%, 34%, 29%
Shareholder services: IRA, automatic investment plan
Management fee: 1.00% first $50M, 0.75% over $50M
Expense ratio: 0.96% (year ending 6/30/97)
IRA fees: Annual $12

MERIDIAN VALUE FUND ◆

60 East Sir Francis Drake Blvd.
Wood Island, Suite 306
Larkspur, CA 94939
800-446-6662, 415-461-6237

Adviser: Aster Capital Management, Inc.
Portfolio managers: Richard F. Aster, Jr. (1994), Kevin C. O'Boyle (1997)
Transfer agent: First Data Investor Services Group
Investment objective and policies: Long-term capital growth. Invests in equity and equity-related securities, primarily common stocks, of companies believed undervalued in relation to their earning power or asset value. Up to 35% of assets may be in junk bonds, and 10% in ADRs of foreign companies.
Year organized: 1994
Ticker symbol: MVALX
Minimum purchase: Initial: $1,000, Subsequent: $50
Wire orders accepted: Yes
Deadline for same day wire purchase: 4 P.M.
Discount broker availability: Schwab, White
Qualified for sale in: All states
Telephone redemptions: Yes
Wire redemptions: Yes, $5,000 minimum
Letter redemptions: Signature guarantee required over $25,000
Telephone switching: With Meridian Fund
Number of switches permitted: Unlimited
Dividends paid: Income - September; Capital gains - September
Portfolio turnover (3 yrs): 144%, 125%, 77%
Shareholder services: IRA, automatic investment plan
Management fee: 1.00%
Expense ratio: 2.51% (year ending 6/30/97) (2.80% without waiver)
IRA fees: Annual $12

MERRILL LYNCH READY ASSETS TRUST

P.O. Box 9011
Princeton, NJ 08543-9011
800-221-7210, 609-282-2800
fax 609-282-3466
Internet: http://www.ML.com

Adviser: Merrill Lynch Asset Management, Inc.
Portfolio manager: John Ng (1988)
Transfer agent: Merrill Lynch Financial Data Services, Inc.
Investment objective and policies: Preservation of capital, liquidity, and income. Invests in high quality money market securities.
Year organized: 1975
Ticker symbol: MRAXX
Minimum purchase: Initial: $5,000, Subsequent: $1,000; IRA/Keogh: $250, Subsequent: None
Wire orders accepted: Yes
Deadline for same day wire purchase: 4 P.M.
Qualified for sale in: All states
Telephone redemptions: Yes
Wire redemptions: Yes, $5,000 minimum
Letter redemptions: Signature guarantee required
Telephone switching: With other Merrill Lynch funds, most of which have loads, $250 minimum
Number of switches permitted: Unlimited
Check redemptions: $500 minimum
Dividends paid: Income - declared and paid daily
Shareholder services: IRA, Keogh, corporate retirement plans, systematic withdrawal plan min. bal. req. $5,000
Management fee: 0.50% first $500M to 0.25% over $20B
12b-1 distribution fee: 0.125%
IRA/Keogh fees: See Merrill Lynch broker

MERRILL LYNCH RETIREMENT RESERVES MONEY FUND ◆

P.O. Box 9011
Princeton, NJ 08543-9011
800-221-7210, 609-282-2800
fax 609-282-3466

Adviser: Merrill Lynch Asset Management, Inc.
Portfolio manager: Christopher Ayoub (1988)
Transfer agent: Merrill Lynch Financial Data Services, Inc.
Investment objective and policies: Preservation of capital, liquidity, and income. Invests primarily in U.S. Government and agency securities, bank CDs, commercial paper, repurchase agreements and purchase and sale contracts with a weighted average maturity of 90 days or less.
Year organized: 1982
Special sales restrictions: Available to participants in self-directed retirement plans for which Merrill Lynch serves as passive custodian and certain independent pension, profit-sharing, annuity and other qualified plans.
Minimum purchase: None
Wire orders accepted: Yes
Deadline for same day wire purchase: 4 P.M.
Qualified for sale in: All states
Telephone redemptions: Yes
Wire redemptions: Yes, $5,000 minimum
Letter redemptions: Signature guarantee required
Telephone switching: With other Merrill Lynch funds, most of which have loads, $250 minimum
Number of switches permitted: Unlimited
Check redemptions: $500 minimum
Dividends paid: Income - declared and paid daily
Shareholder services: IRA, Keogh, corporate retirement plans, systematic withdrawal plan min. bal. req. $5,000
Management fee: 0.50% first $1B to 0.40% over $2B
Expense ratio: 0.60% (year ending 10/31/97)
IRA/Keogh fees: See Merrill Lynch broker

MERRIMAN FUNDS ◆

(Data common to all Merriman funds are shown below. See subsequent listings for data specific to individual funds.)

1200 Westlake Avenue North, Suite 700
Seattle, WA 98109
800-423-4893, 206-285-8877
prices/yields 800-224-4743
fax 206-286-2079

Shareholder service hours: Full service: M-F 7 A.M.-4 P.M. PST; After hours service: messages, prospectuses
Adviser: Merriman Investment Management Co.
Transfer agent: Firstar Trust Co.
Minimum purchase: Initial: $5,000, Subsequent: $100; IRA: Initial: $2,000; Automatic investment plan: Initial: None
Wire orders accepted: Yes
Deadline for same day wire purchase: 4 P.M.
Telephone redemptions: Yes
Wire redemptions: Yes, $12 fee
Letter redemptions: Signature guarantee required
Telephone switching: With other Merriman funds and Firstar money market funds, $1,000 minimum
Number of switches permitted: Unlimited, $5 fee
Shareholder services: IRA, SEP-IRA, Keogh, corporate retirement plans, electronic funds transfer, systematic withdrawal plan min. bal. req. $10,000
IRA/Keogh fees: Annual $12.50 ($25 maximum), Closing $15

MERRIMAN ASSET ALLOCATION FUND ◆

(See first Merriman listing for data common to all funds)

Portfolio managers: Paul A. Merriman (1989), William L. Notaro (1989)
Investment objective and policies: High total return consistent with reasonable risk. At least 25% and up to 100% of assets are invested in a diversified portfolio of other mutual funds, but can buy individual issues. Assets are allocated among domestic and foreign equities, domestic and foreign fixed-income securities, and precious metals. May use futures and options in an effort to enhance income and for hedging purposes. Extensively utilizes an independent market timing model for each sector.
Year organized: 1989
Ticker symbol: MTASX
Discount broker availability: Fidelity, *Schwab, Siebert, *White
Qualified for sale in: All states except AR, DE, ME, MS, NH, ND, RI, SD, UT, VT

Dividends paid: Income - December; Capital gains - December
Portfolio turnover (3 yrs): 162%, 205%, 288%
Management fee: 1.25% first $250M to 1.00% over $500M
Expense ratio: 1.78% (year ending 9/30/97)

MERRIMAN CAPITAL APPRECIATION FUND ◆
(See first Merriman listing for data common to all funds)

Portfolio managers: Paul A. Merriman (1989), William L. Notaro (1989)
Investment objective and policies: Capital appreciation. Invests at least 25% and up to 100% of assets in a diversified portfolio of other mutual funds, primarily aggressive growth and growth funds, but may use individual equities. Up to 35% may be in high quality money market instruments. May hedge substantially. Utilizes equity market timing model extensively.
Year organized: 1989
Ticker symbol: MNCAX
Discount broker availability: Fidelity, *Schwab, Siebert, *White
Qualified for sale in: All states except AR, DE, ME, MS, MT, NH, ND, RI, SD, UT, VT
Dividends paid: Income - December; Capital gains - December
Portfolio turnover (3 yrs): 114%, 255%, 146%
Management fee: 1.25% first $250M to 1.00% over $500M
Expense ratio: 1.78% (year ending 9/30/97)

MERRIMAN FLEXIBLE BOND FUND ◆
(See first Merriman listing for data common to all funds)

Portfolio managers: Paul A. Merriman (1988), William L. Notaro (1988)
Investment objective and policies: Income and capital preservation; capital growth secondary. Invests at least 25% and up to 100% of assets in a diversified portfolio of other mutual funds believed to enhance the fund's objectives. Those mutual funds will hold all types of debt securities. Fund may make direct investments in all types of debt securities other than convertible securities and preferred stocks. May use futures and options in an effort to enhance income and for hedging purposes.
Year organized: 1988 (formerly Government Fund. Name and objective changed in December 1992. Prior performance may be misleading)
Ticker symbol: MTGVX
Discount broker availability: Fidelity, *Schwab, Siebert, *White
Qualified for sale in: All states except AL, DE, ID, ME, MD, MA, MS, MT, NE, NV, NH, ND, RI, SC, SD, UT, VT
Dividends paid: Income - March, June, September, December; Capital gains - December
Portfolio turnover (3 yrs): 173%, 140%, 291%
Management fee: 1.00% first $250M to 0.75% over $500M
Expense ratio: 1.46% (year ending 9/30/97)

MERRIMAN GROWTH & INCOME FUND ◆
(See first Merriman listing for data common to all funds)

Portfolio managers: Paul A. Merriman (1988), William L. Notaro (1988)
Investment objective and policies: Long-term growth of capital and income; preservation of capital secondary. Invests at least 25% and up to 100% of assets in a diversified portfolio of other mutual funds believed to enhance the fund's objectives. Those mutual funds will hold primarily common stocks, bonds and securities convertible into common stocks, both domestic and foreign. Up to 35% of assets may be invested directly in U.S. Government securities and high quality money market instruments. May use futures and options in an effort to enhance income and for hedging purposes.

Year organized: 1988 (formerly Merriman Blue Chip Fund. Name and objective changed on 1/12/94. Prior performance may be misleading.)
Ticker symbol: MTBCX
Discount broker availability: Fidelity, *Schwab, Siebert, *White
Qualified for sale in: All states except AL, AR, CT, DE, ID, ME, MD, MA, MT, NE, NV, NH, ND, RI, SC, SD, UT, VT
Dividends paid: Income - December; Capital gains - December
Portfolio turnover (3 yrs): 105%, 133%, 79%
Management fee: 1.25% first $250M to 1.00% over $500M
Expense ratio: 1.71% (year ending 9/30/97)

MERRIMAN LEVERAGED GROWTH FUND ◆
(See first Merriman listing for data common to all funds)

Portfolio managers: Paul A. Merriman (1992), William L. Notaro (1992)
Investment objective and policies: Capital appreciation. Invests at least 25% and up to 100% of assets in other mutual funds, primarily aggressive growth and growth funds, but may use individual equities including securities convertible into common stocks. Up to 35% may be in high quality money market instruments. May hedge substantially. Utilizes proprietary market timing model extensively. With the exception of its use of leverage (borrowing), the policies of the Leveraged Growth Fund are the same as those of the Capital Appreciation Fund.
Year organized: 1992
Ticker symbol: MELGX
Discount broker availability: Fidelity, *Schwab, Siebert, *White
Qualified for sale in: All states except AL, AR, DE, ID, IA, ME, MS, MT, NH, NM, ND, RI, SD, UT, VT
Dividends paid: Income - December; Capital gains - December
Portfolio turnover (3 yrs): 130%, 247%, 88%
Management fee: 1.25% first $250M to 1.00% over $500M
Expense ratio: 4.13% (year ending 9/30/97)

METROPOLITAN WEST LOW DURATION BOND FUND ◆
10880 Wilshire Blvd., Suite 2020
Los Angeles, CA 90024
800-241-4671, 310-446-7727
fax 310-466-7733
Internet: http://www.mws.com/msw_funds.htm
e-mail: sdubchansky@mws.com

Adviser: Metropolitan West Asset Management
Portfolio managers: Laird R. Landmann (1997), Tad Rivelle (1997), Stephen Kane (1997)
Transfer agent: First Data Investor Services Group
Investment objective and policies: Maximum current income consistent with preservation of capital; capital appreciation secondary. Invests in a diversified portfolio of government and corporate fixed-income securities with a portfolio duration of from one to three years and a dollar-weighted average maturity ranging from one to five years. May invest up to 25% of assets in foreign issues denominated in U.S. dollars, and up to 15% of assets in foreign securities denominated in other currencies, including up to 10% in emerging market securities. May use a variety of derivative instruments in an effort to enhance performance and for hedging purposes.
Year organized: 1997
Ticker symbol: MWLDX
Minimum purchase: Initial: $5,000, Subsequent: $100; IRA: Initial: $1,000
Wire orders accepted: Yes
Deadline for same day wire purchase: 4 P.M.
Discount broker availability: *Schwab, *White
Qualified for sale in: All states
Telephone redemptions: Yes
Wire redemptions: Yes, $10 fee
Letter redemptions: Signature guarantee required over $50,000
Telephone switching: With Metropolitan West Total Return Bond fund

Number of switches permitted: Unlimited
Dividends paid: Income - declared daily, paid monthly; Capital gains - annually
Shareholder services: IRA
Management fee: 0.48%
12b-1 distribution fee: Maximum of 0.25% (not currently imposed)
IRA fees: Annual $12

METROPOLITAN WEST TOTAL RETURN BOND FUND ◆
10880 Wilshire Blvd., Suite 2020
Los Angeles, CA 90024
800-241-4671, 310-446-7727
fax 310-466-7733
Internet: http://www.mws.com/msw_funds.htm
e-mail: sdubchansky@mws.com

Adviser: Metropolitan West Asset Management
Portfolio managers: Laird R. Landmann (1997), Tad Rivelle (1997), Stephen Kane (1997)
Transfer agent: First Data Investor Services Group
Investment objective and policies: Maximum long-term total return. Invests in a diversified portfolio of corporate and government fixed-income securities with a portfolio duration of from two to eight years and a dollar-weighted average maturity ranging from two to fifteen years. Securities are selected which management perceives to be undervalued. May invest up to 25% of assets in foreign issues denominated in U.S. dollars, and up to 15% of assets in foreign securities denominated in other currencies, including up to 10% in emerging market securities. May use a variety of derivative instruments in an effort to enhance performance and for hedging purposes.
Year organized: 1997
Minimum purchase: Initial: $5,000, Subsequent: $100; IRA: Initial: $1,000
Wire orders accepted: Yes
Deadline for same day wire purchase: 4 P.M.
Discount broker availability: *Schwab, *White
Qualified for sale in: All states
Telephone redemptions: Yes, $10 fee
Wire redemptions: Yes, $10 fee
Letter redemptions: Signature guarantee required over $50,000
Telephone switching: With Metropolitan West Low Duration Bond fund
Number of switches permitted: Unlimited
Dividends paid: Income - declared daily, paid monthly; Capital gains - annually
Shareholder services: IRA
Management fee: 0.55%
12b-1 distribution fee: Maximum of 0.25% (not currently imposed)
IRA fees: Annual $12

MEYERS PRIDE VALUE FUND
8901 Wilshire Blvd.
Beverly Hills, CA 90211
800-410-3337, 310-657-9393

Adviser: Meyers Capital Management Co.
Portfolio manager: Shelly J. Meyers (1996)
Transfer agent and administrator: BISYS Fund Services, Inc.
Investment objective and policies: Long term capital appreciation. Invests in companies perceived to be undervalued, who also utilize progressive policies toward gay and lesbian employees, suppliers, vendors and customers in terms of innovative employee relationships and corporate citizenship. At minimum, they must have in place specific policies against sexual discrimination. This social objective currently limits the number of companies available for investment to approximately 350. Value-based approach focuses on long-term investment cycle which usually spans three to five years. May invest up to 15% of assets in illiquid securities and may use certain derivative instruments for hedging purposes.
Year organized: 1996
Minimum purchase: Initial: $1,000, Subsequent: $100; IRA: Initial: $250, Subsequent: $50; Automatic investment plan: Initial: $250; Subsequent: $50
Wire orders accepted: Yes, $1,000 minimum
Deadline for same day wire purchase: 4 P.M.
Discount broker availability: *White

Qualified for sale in: All states
Telephone redemptions: Yes
Wire redemptions: Yes
Letter redemptions: Signature guarantee not required
Dividends paid: Income - December; Capital gains - December
Portfolio turnover (1 yr): 42%
Shareholder services: IRA, systematic withdrawal plan min. bal. req. $12,000
Management fee: 1.00%
Administration fee: 0.15% first $100M to 0.06% over $1B ($60,000 minimum)
12b-1 distribution fee: 0.25%
Expense ratio: 2.09% (year ending 5/31/97) (41.61% without waiver)
IRA fees: Annual $12, Closing $10

MICHIGAN DAILY TAX FREE INCOME FUND ◆
600 Fifth Avenue, 8th Floor
New York, NY 10020
800-221-3079, 212-830-5220
prices/yields 212-830-5225
fax 212-830-5478

Adviser: Reich & Tang Asset Management, L.P.
Portfolio manager: Molly Flewharty (1987)
Transfer agent: Reich & Tang Services, L.P.
Investment objective and policies: High current interest income exempt from federal income tax, and, to the extent possible, from Michigan dividends and interest income taxes, consistent with preservation of capital and liquidity. Invests primarily in debt obligations issued by or on behalf of the State of Michigan and other municipal authorities. Up to 20% of assets may be in securities subject to AMT tax treatment.
Year organized: 1987
Ticker symbol: MIDXX
Special sales restrictions: Only class "B" shares of the fund are sold direct and without 12b-1 fees. Statistics represent "B" shares only.
Minimum purchase: Initial: $5,000, Subsequent: $100
Wire orders accepted: Yes
Deadline for same day wire purchase: 12 NN
Qualified for sale in: FL, IL, MI, MS, NY
Telephone redemptions: Yes
Wire redemptions: Yes, $1,000 minimum
Letter redemptions: Signature guarantee required
Check redemptions: $250 minimum
Telephone switching: With other Reich & Tang money market funds and the R&T Equity Fund
Deadline for same day switch: 12 NN
Number of switches permitted: Unlimited, $1,000 minimum
Dividends paid: Income - declared daily, paid monthly
Shareholder services: Automatic investment plan, electronic funds transfer, systematic withdrawal plan
Management fee: 0.30%
Administration fee: 0.21%
12b-1 distribution fee: Yes (not currently imposed)
Expense ratio: 0.60% (year ending 2/29/97) (0.68% without waiver)

MIDAS FUND
11 Hanover Square
New York, NY 10005-3452
800-400-6432, 800-345-0051
212-480-6432
shareholder services 888-503-8642
fax 212-363-1103
Internet: http://www.mutualfunds.net
e-mail: info@mutualfunds.net

Shareholder service hours: Full service: M-F 9 A.M.-5 P.M. EST; After hours service: prices, yields, account balances, orders, last transaction, messages, indexes, prospectuses
Adviser: Midas Management Corp.
Sub-adviser: Lion Resource Management Ltd.
Portfolio manager: Kjeld Thygesen (1992)
Transfer agent: DST Systems, Inc.
Investment objective and policies: Capital apprecia-

tion and protection against inflation; current income secondary. Invests primarily in securities of U.S. and Canadian firms directly or indirectly involved in the mining and production processes of precious metals or other natural resources, and in gold, silver or platinum bullion. May invest up to 20% of assets in mining securities of countries other than the U.S. or Canada. May only invest up to 10% of assets directly in bullion. Fund is non-diversified.
Year organized: 1986 (name changed from Excel Midas Gold Shares on 8/28/95)
Ticker symbol: EMGSX
Group fund code: 620
Minimum purchase: Initial: $1,000, Subsequent: $50; IRA: Initial: $500
Automatic investment plan: Initial: $50
Wire orders accepted: Yes
Deadline for same day wire purchase: 4 P.M.
Discount broker availability: *Fidelity, *Schwab, *Siebert, *White
Qualified for sale in: All states
Telephone redemptions: Yes, $250 minimum ($1,000 minimum if redemption is mailed)
Wire redemptions: Yes, $1,000 minimum
Letter redemptions: Signature guarantee not required
Redemption fee: 1.00% for shares held less than 30 days
Telephone switching: With Bull & Bear Dollar Reserves, Gold Investors, Special Equities, and Bull & Bear U.S. and Overseas; and Rockwood, $500 minimum, 30 day hold
Number of switches permitted: Unlimited
Dividends paid: Income - December; Capital gains - December
Portfolio turnover (3 yrs): 23%, 48%, 53%
Shareholder services: IRA, SEP-IRA, Keogh, 403(b), corporate retirement plans, electronic funds transfer, systematic withdrawal plan min. bal. req. $20,000
Management fee: 1.00% first $200M to 0.75% over $1B
12b-1 distribution fee: 0.25%
Expense ratio: 1.63% (year ending 12/31/96) (1.83% without waiver)
IRA fees: Annual $10, Closing $20 (waived for accounts with assets over $10,000, and for automatic investment plan accounts)

MONETTA FUNDS
(Data common to all Monetta funds are shown below. See subsequent listings for data specific to individual funds.)

1776-A South Naperville Road
Suite 207
Wheaton, IL 60187-8133
800-666-3882, 708-462-9800
shareholder services 800-241-9772
TDD 800-684-3416
fax 708-462-9433
Internet: http://www.monetta.com
e-mail: info@monetta.com

Shareholder service hours: Full service: M-F 8 A.M.-6 P.M. CST; After hours service: prices, yields, account balances, orders, last transaction, news, messages, indices, prospectuses, total returns
Adviser: Monetta Financial Services, Inc.
Transfer agent: Firstar Trust Co.
Minimum purchase: Initial: $1,000 aggregate, $250/fund; Subsequent: $50; IRA, Automatic investment plan: Initial: $50
Wire orders accepted: Yes, subsequent only
Deadline for same day wire purchase: 4 P.M.
Qualified for sale in: All states
Telephone redemptions: Yes
Wire redemptions: Yes, $12 fee
Letter redemptions: Signature guarantee required over $50,000
Telephone switching: With other Monetta funds, $250 minimum
Number of switches permitted: Unlimited, $5 fee
Shareholder services: IRA, SIMPLE-IRA, 401(k), 403(b), corporate retirement plans, systematic withdrawal plan min. bal. req. $10,000
IRA fees: Annual $12.50, Closing $15

MONETTA BALANCED FUND
(See first Monetta listing for data common to all funds)

Portfolio managers: Robert S. Bacarella (1996), Kevin D. Moore (1996)
Investment objective and policies: Total return: capital appreciation and current income, consistent with preservation of capital. Invests at least 80% of assets in a diversified portfolio of equity and fixed-income securities. At least 25% will be in fixed-income securities rated A or better, or guaranteed by the U.S. Government or its agencies and instrumentalities. May invest up to 10% of assets in junk bonds. May use covered call and put options and futures contracts in an effort to enhance revenues or for hedging purposes.
Year organized: 1995
Ticker symbol: MBALX
Discount broker availability: *Fidelity, *White
Dividends paid: Income - March, June, September, December; Capital gains - October
Portfolio turnover (1 yr): 118%
Management fee: 0.40%
Shareholder services fee: 0.25%
12b-1 distribution fee: 0.25%
Expense ratio: 1.40% (year ending 12/31/96)

MONETTA FUND ◆
(See first Monetta listing for data common to all funds)

Portfolio manager: Robert S. Bacarella (1986)
Investment objective and policies: Capital appreciation; income secondary. Invests at least 70% of assets in equity securities of small to medium size companies with market capitalization of $50M-$1B with growth potential and undervalued with respect to price/earnings ratio relative to estimated earnings growth rate. Remainder of assets are in dividend-paying equity securities and/or long-term debt securities.
Year organized: 1986
Ticker symbol: MONTX
Discount broker availability: *Fidelity, *White
Dividends paid: Income - December; Capital gains - October
Portfolio turnover (3 yrs): 205%, 272%, 191%
Management fee: 1.00%
Expense ratio: 1.38% (year ending 12/31/96)

MONETTA GOVERNMENT MONEY MARKET FUND ◆
(See first Monetta listing for data common to all funds)

Portfolio managers: Robert S. Bacarella (1996), Kevin D. Moore (1996)
Investment objective and policies: Maximum current income, consistent with safety of capital and liquidity. Invests in U.S. Government and agency money market instruments maturing in thirteen months or less.
Year organized: 1993
Ticker symbol: MONXX
Check redemptions: $500 minimum
Dividends paid: Income - declared daily, paid monthly
Management fee: 0.25%
Shareholder services fee: 0.10%
12b-1 distribution fee: Maximum of 0.10% (not currently imposed)
Expense ratio: 0.31% (year ending 12/31/96) (0.67% without waiver)

MONETTA INTERMEDIATE BOND FUND
(See first Monetta listing for data common to all funds)

Portfolio managers: Robert S. Bacarella (1996), Kevin D. Moore (1996)
Investment objective and policies: High current income consistent with capital preservation. Invests at least 70% of assets in investment grade debt securities of U.S. issuers and foreign issuers payable in U.S. dollars, securities issued or guaranteed by the U.S. Government or its agencies or instrumentalities, com-

mercial paper, variable rate demand notes and bank obligations. Fund maintains a dollar-weighted average maturity of three to ten years. May invest up to 20% of assets in junk bonds.
Year organized: 1993
Ticker symbol: MIBFX
Discount broker availability: *Fidelity, *White
Dividends paid: Income - declared and paid monthly; Capital gains - October
Portfolio turnover (3 yrs): 29%, 75%, 94%
Management fee: 0.35%
Shareholder services fee: 0.25%
12b-1 distribution fee: 0.25%
Expense ratio: 0.55% (year ending 12/31/96) (0.85% without waiver)

MONETTA LARGE-CAP EQUITY FUND
(See first Monetta listing for data common to all funds)

Portfolio managers: Robert S. Bacarella (1996), Kevin D. Moore (1996)
Investment objective and policies: Long-term capital growth. Invests primarily in common stocks of companies with market capitalizations over $5B using a "bottom-up" stock selection process. Normally invests at least 90% of assets in equities and 65% of assets in common stocks of large-cap companies.
Year organized: 1995
Ticker symbol: MLCEX
Discount broker availability: *Fidelity, *White
Dividends paid: Income - December; Capital gains - October
Portfolio turnover (1 yr): 153%
Management fee: 0.75%
Shareholder services fee: 0.25%
12b-1 distribution fee: 0.25%
Expense ratio: 1.51% (year ending 12/31/96)

MONETTA MID-CAP EQUITY FUND
(See first Monetta listing for data common to all funds)

Portfolio managers: Robert S. Bacarella (1996), Kevin D. Moore (1996)
Investment objective and policies: Long-term capital growth. Invests primarily in common stocks of medium sized companies with market capitalizations of $1B-$5B using a "bottom-up" stock selection process. Normally invests at least 90% of assets in equities and 65% of assets in common stocks of mid-cap companies.
Year organized: 1993
Ticker symbol: MMCEX
Discount broker availability: *Fidelity, *White
Dividends paid: Income - December; Capital gains - October
Portfolio turnover (3 yrs): 93%, 254%, 210%
Management fee: 0.75%
Shareholder services fee: 0.25%
12b-1 distribution fee: 0.25%
Expense ratio: 1.23% (year ending 12/31/96)

MONETTA SMALL-CAP EQUITY FUND
(See first Monetta listing for data common to all funds)

Portfolio managers: Robert S. Bacarella (1997), Kevin D. Moore (1997)
Investment objective and policies: Long-term capital growth. Invests primarily in common stocks of companies with market capitalizations ranging from $50M to $1B using a "bottom-up" stock selection process. Normally invests at least 90% of assets in equities and 65% of assets in common stocks of small-cap companies.
Year organized: 1997
Ticker symbol: MSCEX
Discount broker availability: *Fidelity, *White
Dividends paid: Income - December; Capital gains - October
Management fee: 0.75%
Shareholder services fee: 0.25%
12b-1 distribution fee: 0.25%

MONTAG & CALDWELL BALANCED FUND
171 North Clark Street
Chicago, IL 60601-3294
800-992-8151, 800-621-1919
312-223-2300, fax 312-223-5609

Adviser: Montag & Caldwell, Inc. (a wholly-owned subsidiary of the Alleghany Corp.)
Administrator: The Chicago Trust Co.
Portfolio manager: Ronald E. Canakaris (1994)
Transfer agent: First Data Investors Services Group, Inc.
Investment objective and policies: Long-term total return: capital appreciation and current income. Invests in a mix of common and preferred stocks, convertible and non-convertible debt securities, and short-term securities. Strategic allocation target is 50% to 70% equities, however allocation will vary according to perceived changes in market conditions. Up to 30% of assets may be in ADRs or EDRs, at least 25% will be in fixed-income securities with weighted average maturities normally ranging from three to ten years, and up to 15% may be in illiquid securities. May use futures and options for hedging purposes.
Year organized: 1994
Ticker symbol: MOBAX
Minimum purchase: Initial: $2,500, Subsequent: $50; IRA: Initial: $500; Automatic investment plan: Initial: $50
Wire orders accepted: Yes
Deadline for same day wire purchase: 4 P.M.
Discount broker availability: *Fidelity, *Schwab, *White
Qualified for sale: All states
Telephone redemptions: Yes
Wire redemptions: Yes, $20 fee
Letter redemptions: Signature guarantee required over $10,000
Telephone switching: With Chicago Trust funds and Montag & Caldwell Growth Fund
Number of switches permitted: Unlimited
Dividends paid: Income - March, June, September, December; Capital gains - December
Portfolio turnover (3 yrs): 28%, 44%, 27%
Shareholder services: IRA, systematic withdrawal plan min. bal. req. $50,000
Management fee: 0.75%
Administration fee: 0.06% first $2B to 0.04% over $3.5B
12b-1 distribution fee: 0.25%
Expense ratio: 1.25% (year ending 10/31/97) (1.33% without waiver)
IRA fees: Annual $12

MONTAG & CALDWELL GROWTH FUND
171 North Clark Street
Chicago, IL 60601-3294
800-992-8151, 800-621-1919
312-223-2300, fax 312-223-5609

Adviser: Montag & Caldwell, Inc. (a wholly-owned subsidiary of the Alleghany Corp.)
Administrator: The Chicago Trust Co.
Portfolio manager: Ronald E. Canakaris (1994)
Transfer agent: First Data Investors Services Group, Inc.
Investment objective and policies: Long-term capital appreciation; income secondary. Invests primarily in a combination of convertible and non-convertible debt securities, and convertible and non-convertible equity securities of companies of varied capitalization levels with strong earnings growth potential. Up to 30% of assets may be in ADRs and EDRs, and up to 15% in illiquid securities. May use futures and options for hedging purposes.
Year organized: 1994
Ticker symbol: MCGFX
Special sales restrictions: Information provided here is only for class "N" shares; Fund has class "I" shares, with $40 million minimum.
Minimum purchase: Initial: $2,500, Subsequent: $50; IRA: Initial: $500; Automatic investment plan: Initial: $50
Wire orders accepted: Yes
Deadline for same day wire purchase: 4 P.M.

Discount broker availability: *Fidelity, *Schwab, *White
Qualified for sale: All states
Telephone redemptions: Yes
Wire redemptions: Yes, $20 fee
Letter redemptions: Signature guarantee required over $10,000
Telephone switching: With Chicago Trust funds and Montag & Caldwell Balanced Fund
Number of switches permitted: Unlimited
Dividends paid: Income - March, June, September, December; Capital gains - December
Portfolio turnover (3 yrs): 19%, 26%, 34%
Shareholder services: IRA, systematic withdrawal plan min. bal. req. $50,000
Management fee: 0.80% first $800M, 0.60% over $800M
Administration fee: 0.06% first $2B to 0.04% over $3.5B
12b-1 distribution fee: 0.25%
Expense ratio: 1.23% (year ending 10/31/97) (1.25% without waiver)
IRA fees: Annual $12

MONTGOMERY FUNDS ◆
(Data common to all Montgomery funds are shown below. See subsequent listings for data specific to individual funds.)

101 California Street
San Francisco, CA 94111
800-572-3863, 415-248-6000
fax 415-248-6100
Internet: http://www.montgomeryfunds.com

Shareholder service hours: Full service: M-F 5 A.M.-6 P.M. PST; After hours service: prices, yields, account balances, orders, last transaction, news, messages, prospectuses, total returns
Adviser: Montgomery Asset Management, L.P. (a wholly-owned subsidiary of Commerzbank A.G.)
Transfer agent: Investors Fiduciary Trust Co./DST Systems, Inc.
Sales restrictions: All data quoted represent Class "R" Shares. Class "P" Shares commenced operations 3/12/96, but are only available through limited brokerage accounts.**Do not confuse these funds with the Montgomery Partners Series,** a multi-class load series by the same company sold by brokers.
Minimum purchase: Initial: $1,000, Subsequent: $100 (exception noted)
Wire orders accepted: Yes
Deadline for same day wire purchase: 4 P.M. (12 NN for MMs)
Qualified for sale in: All states (except California funds)
Telephone redemptions: Yes
Wire redemptions: Yes, $500 minimum, $10 fee
Letter redemptions: Signature guarantee required over $50,000
Telephone switching: With other open Montgomery funds
Number of switches permitted: 4 outbound per fund per year (does not apply to U.S. fixed-income or money market funds)
Shareholder services: IRA, automatic investment plan, directed dividends, electronic funds transfer, systematic withdrawal plan min. bal. req. $1,000
IRA fees: Annual $10 (waived for account balances over $10,000)

MONTGOMERY CALIFORNIA TAX-FREE INTERMEDIATE BOND FUND ◆
(See first Montgomery listing for data common to all funds)

Portfolio managers: William C. Stevens (1993), Peter D. Wilson (1996)
Investment objective and policies: Maximum current income exempt from federal and California personal income taxes, consistent with capital preservation and prudent investment management. Invests at least 80% of assets in California municipal securities that, at the time of purchase, are rated within the four

highest grades by Moody's or S&P. Portfolio maintains a dollar-weighted average maturity of five to ten years. Up to 20% of assets may be in securities subject to AMT tax treatment and 10% in illiquid securities.
Year organized: 1993 (name and objective changed from Tax-Free Short/Inter Fund in 1995)
Ticker symbol: MNCTX
Group fund code: 281
Discount broker availability: *Fidelity, *Schwab, *Siebert, *White
Qualified for sale in: CA
Check redemptions: $250 minimum
Dividends paid: Income - declared and paid daily; Capital gains - December
Portfolio turnover (3 yrs): 26%, 58%, 38%
Management fee: 0.50% first $500M, 0.40% over $500M
Expense ratio: 0.68% year ending 6/30/97) (1.18% without waiver)

MONTGOMERY CALIFORNIA TAX-FREE MONEY FUND ◆
(See first Montgomery listing for data common to all funds)

Portfolio managers: William C. Stevens (1996), Peter D. Wilson (1996)
Investment objective and policies: Maximum current income exempt from federal and California personal income taxes, consistent with preservation of capital and liquidity. Invests primarily in California municipal money market instruments. May invest up to 35% of assets in securities subject to AMT tax treatment.
Year organized: 1994
Ticker symbol: MCFXX
Group fund code: 292
Qualified for sale in: CA
Check redemptions: $250 minimum
Dividends paid: Income - declared and paid daily
Management fee: 0.40% first $500M, 0.30% over $500M
Expense ratio: 0.58% (year ending 6/30/97) (0.73% without waiver)

MONTGOMERY EMERGING ASIA FUND ◆
(See first Montgomery listing for data common to all funds)

Portfolio managers: Frank Chiang (1996), Josephine S. Jimenez (1996), Bryan L. Sudweeks (1996), Angeline Ee (1996)
Investment objective and policies: Capital appreciation. Invests at least 65% of assets in equity securities of companies with their principal activities in emerging market countries located in Asia, currently including Bangladesh, China, Hong Kong, India, Indonesia, Korea, Malaysia, Pakistan, the Philippines, Singapore, Sri Lanka, Taiwan, and Thailand. Normally invests in at least three of these countries with a maximum of 33% of assets in any one country. As part of the remaining 35% of its total assets, the fund may invest in more developed Asian countries such as Japan. May also invest up to 35% of assets in debt securities, including 5% in junk bonds. May use sponsored and unsponsored ADRs, EDRs and GDRs. May invest up to 10% of assets in other investment companies, up to 15% in illiquid securities, and use forward currency contracts and options and futures for hedging purposes.
Year organized: 1996
Ticker symbol: MNEAX
Group fund code: 648
Discount broker availability: *Fidelity, *Schwab, *Siebert, *White
Dividends paid: Income - December; Capital gains - December
Portfolio turnover (1 yr): 72%
Management fee: 1.25% first $500M to 1.00% over $1B
Expense ratio: 2.20% (9 months ending 6/30/97) (2.69% without waiver)

MONTGOMERY EMERGING MARKETS FUND ◆
(See first Montgomery listing for data common to all funds)

Portfolio managers: Josephine S. Jimenez (1992), Bryan L. Sudweeks (1992), Frank Chiang (1996), Angeline Ee (1996)
Investment objective and policies: Capital appreciation. Invests at least 65% of assets in equity securities of companies in countries having emerging markets. Fund uses a proprietary quantitative asset allocation model in conjunction with fundamental industry analysis and stock selection methods in making investments. Normally invests in at least six emerging market countries, with a maximum of 35% of assets in any one country. May invest no more than 20% of assets in equity securities of companies comprising the EAFE Index, and 15% in illiquid securities. May invest up to 35% of assets in debt securities, including up to 5% in junk bonds. May use options and futures for hedging purposes.
Year organized: 1992
Ticker symbol: MNEMX
Group fund code: 277
Discount broker availability: *Fidelity, *Schwab, *Siebert, *White
Dividends paid: Income - December; Capital gains - December
Portfolio turnover (3 yrs): 83%, 110%, 92%
Management fee: 1.25% first $250M, 1.00% over $250M
Expense ratio: 1.67% (year ending 6/30/97)

MONTGOMERY EQUITY INCOME FUND ◆
(See first Montgomery listing for data common to all funds)

Portfolio manager: John H. Brown (1994)
Investment objective and policies: Current income and capital appreciation. Invests primarily in equity securities of domestic companies, primarily those with market capitalization of $1B or more. Fund emphasizes investments in common stocks, but may also invest in other types of equity and equity derivative securities. Up to 20% of assets may be in equity or debt securities of foreign issuers and 15% in illiquid securities. May use options and futures for hedging purposes.
Year organized: 1994
Ticker symbol: MNEIX
Group fund code: 293
Discount broker availability: *Fidelity, *Schwab, *Siebert, *White
Dividends paid: Income - March, June, September, December; Capital gains - December
Portfolio turnover (3 yrs): 62%, 90%, 29%
Management fee: 0.60% first $500M, 0.50% over $500M
Expense ratio: 0.86% (year ending 6/30/97) (1.46% without waiver)

MONTGOMERY FEDERAL TAX-FREE MONEY FUND ◆
(See first Montgomery listing for data common to all funds)

Portfolio managers: William C. Stevens (1996), Peter D. Wilson (1996)
Investment objective and policies: Current income exempt from regular federal income tax, consistent with preservation of capital and liquidity. Invests at least 80% of assets in U.S. Treasury money market obligations issued or guaranteed by the U.S. Government, its agencies, or instrumentalities.
Year organized: 1996
Ticker symbol: MFFXX
Group fund code: 647
Check redemptions: $250 minimum
Dividends paid: Income - declared daily, paid monthly
Management fee: 0.40% first $500M to 0.30% over $500M
Expense ratio: 0.33% (11 months ending 6/30/97) (0.69% without waiver)

MONTGOMERY GLOBAL ASSET ALLOCATION FUND ◆
(See first Montgomery listing for data common to all funds)

Portfolio manager: Kevin T. Hamilton (1997)
Investment objective and policies: High total return; capital appreciation and income, while reducing risk. Invests in an active allocation portfolio of five different asset classes: domestic stocks, international developed market stocks, emerging market stocks, domestic dollar-denominated debt instruments, and cash or cash equivalents. A 'fund of funds,' portfolio invests in a diversified group of five other Montgomery funds.
Year organized: 1997
Group fund code: 649
Discount broker availability: *Fidelity, *Schwab
Dividends paid: Income - December; Capital gains - December
Portfolio turnover (1 yr): 89%
Management fee: 0.20%
Expense ratio: 0.47% (6 months ending 6/30/97) (4.84% without waiver)

MONTGOMERY GLOBAL COMMUNICATIONS FUND ◆
(See first Montgomery listing for data common to all funds)

Portfolio manager: Oscar A. Castro (1993)
Investment objective and policies: Capital appreciation. Invests at least 65% of assets in equity securities of communications companies, which may be of any size, throughout the world. A communications company is engaged in the development, manufacture or sale of communications equipment or services that derived at least 50% of either its revenues or earnings from these activities. Fund normally invests in at least three different countries with no country, other than the US, representing more than 40% of assets. May have up to 15% of assets in illiquid securities, and use options and futures for hedging purposes.
Year organized: 1993
Ticker symbol: MNGCX
Group fund code: 280
Discount broker availability: *Fidelity, *Schwab, *Siebert, *White
Dividends paid: Income - December; Capital gains - December
Portfolio turnover (3 yrs): 76%, 104%, 50%
Management fee: 1.25% first $250M, 1.00% over $250M
Expense ratio: 1.91% (year ending 6/30/97) (2.00% without waiver)

MONTGOMERY GLOBAL OPPORTUNITIES FUND ◆
(See first Montgomery listing for data common to all funds)

Portfolio managers: Oscar A. Castro (1993), John D. Boich (1993)
Investment objective and policies: Capital appreciation. Invests at least 65% of assets in equity securities of companies of any size throughout the world. Fund emphasizes common stocks of companies with total market capitalization of more than $1B, but may also invest in other types of equity and equity derivative securities. Fund normally invests in at least three different countries, with no country other than the U.S. representing more than 40% of assets. May have up to 15% of assets in illiquid securities. May leverage, and use options and futures for hedging purposes.
Year organized: 1993
Ticker symbol: MNGOX
Group fund code: 285
Discount broker availability: *Fidelity, *Schwab, *Siebert, *White
Dividends paid: Income - December; Capital gains - December
Portfolio turnover (3 yrs): 117%, 164%, 119%
Management fee: 1.25% first $500M to 1.00% over $1B
Expense ratio: 1.90% (year ending 6/30/97) (2.62% without waiver)

MONTGOMERY GOVERNMENT RESERVE FUND ◆

(See first Montgomery listing for data common to all funds)

Portfolio managers: Wi!liam C. Stevens (1992), Peter D. Wilson (1996)
Investment objective and policies: Current income consistent with preservation of capital and liquidity. Invests at least 65% of assets in U.S. Treasury money market obligations issued or guaranteed by the U.S. Government, its agencies, or instrumentalities.
Year organized: 1992
Ticker symbol: MNGXX
Group fund code: 278
Discount broker availability: *Fidelity
Check redemptions: $250 minimum
Dividends paid: Income - declared daily, paid monthly
Management fee: 0.40% first $250M to 0.20% over $500M
Expense ratio: 0.60% (year ending 6/30/97) (0.62% without waiver)

MONTGOMERY GROWTH FUND ◆

(See first Montgomery listing for data common to all funds)

Portfolio managers: Roger W. Honour (1993), Andrew G. Pratt (1994), Kathryn M. Peters (1996)
Investment objective and policies: Capital appreciation. Invests at least 65% of assets in equity securities of domestic companies, primarily those with market capitalization of $1B or more. Fund emphasizes investments in common stocks, but may also invest in other types of equity and equity derivative securities. Up to 35% of assets may be in investment grade debt securities and 15% in illiquid securities. May invest in ADRs and EDRs of foreign issuers, leverage and use options and futures for hedging purposes.
Year organized: 1993
Ticker symbol: MNGFX
Group fund code: 284
Discount broker availability: *Fidelity, *Schwab, *Siebert, *White
Dividends paid: Income - December; Capital gains - December
Portfolio turnover (3 yrs): 61%, 118%, 128%
Management fee: 1.00% first $500M to 0.80% over $1B
Expense ratio: 1.27% (year ending 6/30/97)

MONTGOMERY INTERNATIONAL GROWTH FUND ◆

(See first Montgomery listing for data common to all funds)

Portfolio managers: Oscar A. Castro (1995), John D. Boich (1995)
Investment objective and policies: Capital appreciation. Invests at least 65% of assets in equity securities, primarily common stocks, of non-U.S. companies with market capitalizations over $1B, with the remainder invested similarly in smaller capitalization non-U.S. and U.S. companies. Fund normally invests in at least three different countries, with no single country representing more than 40% of assets. May have up to 15% of assets in illiquid securities. May leverage and use options and futures for hedging purposes.
Year organized: 1995
Ticker symbol: MNIGX
Group fund code: 296
Discount broker availability: *Fidelity, *Schwab, *Siebert, *White
Dividends paid: Income - December; Capital gains - December
Portfolio turnover (2 yrs): 95%, 239%
Management fee: 1.10% first $500M to 0.90% over $1B
Expense ratio: 1.66% (year ending 6/30/97) (2.37% without waiver)

MONTGOMERY INTERNATIONAL SMALL CAP FUND ◆

(See first Montgomery listing for data common to all funds)

Portfolio manager: John D. Boich (1993)
Investment objective and policies: Capital appreciation. Invests at least 65% of assets in equity securities, primarily common stocks, of non-U.S. companies with market capitalizations under $1B, with remainder invested similarly in larger capitalization non-U.S. companies. Fund normally invests in at least three different countries, with no single country representing more than 40% of assets. May have up to 15% of assets in illiquid securities. May leverage and use options and futures for hedging purposes.
Year organized: 1993
Ticker symbol: MNISX
Group fund code: 283
Discount broker availability: *Fidelity, *Schwab, *Siebert, *White
Dividends paid: Income - December; Capital gains - December
Portfolio turnover (3 yrs): 85%, 177%, 156%
Management fee: 1.25% first $250M, 1.00% over $250M
Expense ratio: 1.90% (year ending 6/30/97) (2.60% without waiver)

MONTGOMERY JAPAN SMALL CAP FUND ◆

(See first Montgomery listing for data common to all funds)

Portfolio managers: John D. Boich (1997), Oscar A. Castro (1997)
Investment objective and policies: Long-term capital appreciation in excess of the returns of the Tokyo Stock Exchange Second Section Index and the JAS-DAQ OTC Index. Invests at least 65% of assets in equity securities of small companies that have their principal activities in Japan. Securities are selected from those ranked in the bottom quartile of the various Japanese markets, rendering a current market cap of approximately $2B. May invest up to 10% of assets in other investment companies, up to 15% in illiquid securities, and use various derivative instruments for hedging purposes.
Year organized: 1997
Group fund code: 653
Sales restrictions: Fund opened 7/1/97 to Montgomery employees only; never opened to public, then closed to new investors, period.
Dividends paid: Income - December; Capital gains - December
Management fee: 1.25% first $500M to 1.00% over $1B

MONTGOMERY LATIN AMERICA FUND ◆

(See first Montgomery listing for data common to all funds)

Portfolio manager: Jesus Isidoro Duarte (1997)
Investment objective and policies: Long-term capital appreciation. Invests at least 65% of assets in equity securities of companies that have their principal activities in Latin America, including Mexico, Central America, South America and the islands of the Caribbean. Maintains investments in at least three countries, and may have no more than 50% of assets in any one country except Brazil and Mexico, where the fund may invest up to 75% and 67%, respectively. Will only invest up to 15% of assets in Chile due to repatriation regulations. May also invest up to 35% of assets in high yield debt securities, including up to 15% in junk bonds. May invest up to 10% of assets in other investment companies, up to 15% in illiquid securities, and use various derivative instruments for hedging purposes.
Year organized: 1997
Group fund code: 652
Discount broker availability: *Fidelity, *Schwab, *Siebert, *White
Dividends paid: Income - December; Capital gains - December
Management fee: 1.25% first $500M to 1.00% over $1B

MONTGOMERY MICRO CAP FUND ◆

(See first Montgomery listing for data common to all funds)

Portfolio managers: Roger W. Honour (1994), Andrew G. Pratt (1994), Kathryn M. Peters (1996)
Investment objective and policies: Capital appreciation. Invests at least 65% of assets in equity securities of domestic companies with market capitalizations that would place them within the smallest 10% of the Wilshire 5000 Index; currently under $600M; with the perceived potential for rapid growth. May invest in ADRs and EDRs of foreign issuers, and have up to 15% of assets in illiquid securities. May leverage and use options and futures for hedging purposes.
Year organized: 1994
Ticker symbol: MNMCX
Group fund code: 294
Special sales restrictions: Fund closed to new investors 8/15/95.
Minimum purchase: Initial: $5,000, Subsequent: $500
Discount broker availability: *Fidelity, *Schwab, *White
Dividends paid: Income - December; Capital gains - December
Portfolio turnover (3 yrs): 79%, 89%, 37%
Management fee: 1.40% first $200M, 1.25% over $200M
Expense ratio: 1.71% (year ending 6/30/97)

MONTGOMERY SELECT 50 FUND ◆

(See first Montgomery listing for data common to all funds)

Portfolio managers: Kevin T. Hamilton (1995), Nancy Kukacka (1997)
Investment objective and policies: Capital appreciation. Invests at least 65% of assets in at least 50 different equity securities of companies of all sizes throughout the world. Portfolio is divided into five areas - U.S. Growth Equity, U.S. Small Cap, U.S. Equity Income, International and Emerging Markets. Normally invests in at least three countries, with no country other than the U.S. having more than 40% of assets. May invest in ADRs and EDRs of foreign issuers and have up to 15% of assets in illiquid securities. May leverage and use options and futures for hedging purposes.
Year organized: 1995
Ticker symbol: MNSFX
Group fund code: 295
Discount broker availability: *Fidelity, *Schwab, *Siebert, *White
Dividends paid: Income - December; Capital gains - December
Portfolio turnover (2 yrs): 158%, 106%
Management fee: 1.25% first $250M to 0.90% over $500M
Expense ratio: 1.82% (year ending 6/30/97) (1.92% without waiver)

MONTGOMERY SHORT DURATION GOVERNMENT BOND FUND ◆

(See first Montgomery listing for data common to all funds)

Portfolio managers: William C. Stevens (1992), Peter D. Wilson (1996)
Investment objective and policies: Maximum total return consistent with capital preservation and prudent investment risk. Invests at least 65% of assets in obligations issued or guaranteed by the U.S. Government, its agencies, or instrumentalities. Fund maintains a dollar-weighted average maturity of less than three years. May invest up to 35% of assets in cash, commercial paper and investment grade debt securities and have up to 15% of assets in illiquid securities. May leverage and use options and futures for hedging purposes.
Year organized: 1992 (name changed from Short Government Bond 2/14/97)
Ticker symbol: MNSGX
Group fund code: 279
Discount broker availability: *Fidelity, *Schwab, *Siebert, *White
Check redemptions: $250 minimum

Dividends paid: Income - declared daily, paid monthly; Capital gains - December
Portfolio turnover (3 yrs): 451%, 350%, 284%
Management fee: 0.50% first $500M, 0.40% over $500M
Expense ratio: 1.55% (year ending 6/30/97) (2.05% without waiver)

MONTGOMERY SMALL CAP FUND ◆
(See first Montgomery listing for data common to all funds)

Portfolio managers: Stuart O. Roberts (1990), Jerome C. Philpott (1996), Bradford D. Kidwell (1996)
Investment objective and policies: Capital appreciation. Invests at least 65% of assets in common stocks of U.S. companies with market capitalization under $1B perceived to have above average growth prospects. May invest in ADRs and EDRs of foreign issuers and have up to only 5% of assets in illiquid securities. May leverage and use options and futures for hedging purposes.
Year organized: 1990
Ticker symbol: MNSCX
Group fund code: 276
Special sales restriction: Fund closed to new investors 3/6/92.
Discount broker availability: *Fidelity, *Schwab, *White
Dividends paid: Income - December; Capital gains - December
Portfolio turnover (3 yrs): 59%, 80%, 85%
Management fee: 1.00% first $250M, 0.80% over $250M
Expense ratio: 1.20% (year ending 6/30/97)

MONTGOMERY SMALL CAP OPPORTUNITIES FUND ◆
(See first Montgomery listing for data common to all funds)

Portfolio managers: Roger W. Honour (1995), Andrew G. Pratt (1995), Kathryn M. Peters (1996)
Investment objective and policies: Capital appreciation. Invests at least 65% of assets in equity securities of U.S. companies with market capitalizations under $1B perceived to have above average growth prospects. May invest in ADRs and EDRs of foreign issuers and have up to 15% of assets in illiquid securities. May leverage and use options and futures for hedging purposes.
Year organized: 1995 (name changed from Small Cap II 3/29/96)
Ticker symbol: MNSOX
Group fund code: 645
Discount broker availability: *Fidelity, *Schwab, *Siebert, *White
Dividends paid: Income - December; Capital gains - December
Portfolio turnover (2 yrs): 155%, 81%
Management fee: 1.20% first $200M to 1.00% over $500M
Expense ratio: 1.50% (year ending 6/30/97) (1.75% without waiver)

MONTGOMERY TOTAL RETURN BOND FUND ◆
(See first Montgomery listing for data common to all funds)

Portfolio managers: William C. Stevens (1997), Peter D. Wilson (1997)
Investment objective and policies: Maximum total return: income and capital appreciation, consistent with preservation of capital and prudent investment management. Invests at least 65% of assets in a broad range of investment grade government and corporate bonds, mortgage-related securities, other asset-backed securities and money markets and cash instruments. May invest up to 20% of assets in foreign denominated securities, and beyond this limit in foreign issues denominated in U.S. currency. The dollar-weighted average maturity may be longer than three years, with

an effective duration between four and five and one half years.
Year organized: 1997
Ticker symbol: MNTRX
Group fund code: 650
Discount broker availability: *Fidelity, *Schwab, *Siebert, *White
Check redemptions: $250 minimum
Dividends paid: Income - declared daily, paid monthly; Capital gains - December
Management fee: 0.50% first $500M, 0.40% over $500M

MONTGOMERY U.S. ASSET ALLOCATION FUND ◆
(See first Montgomery listing for data common to all funds)

Lead portfolio manager: Kevin T. Hamilton (1997)
Investment objective and policies: High total return: current income and capital growth, with reduced risk. A "fund of funds," invests 20-80% of assets in the Montgomery Growth fund of domestic stocks, 20-80% in investment grade debt instruments by way of Montgomery Total Return Bond or other bond funds, and 0-50% in cash equivalents through the Montgomery Government Reserve fund, with allocation adjusted to reflect changes in market and economic conditions.
Year organized: 1994 (name changed from Strategic Allocation in 1994; fund assumed its "fund of funds" identity 6/97; prior performance and information may be misleading; name changed from Asset Allocation Fund 9/97)
Ticker symbol: MNAAX
Group fund code: 291
Discount broker availability: *Fidelity, *Schwab, *Siebert, *White
Dividends paid: Income - December; Capital gains - December
Portfolio turnover (3 yrs): 169%, 226%, 96%
Management fee: 0.00% (pro rata share of underlying funds)
Expense ratio: 1.43% (year ending 6/30/97) (1.49% without waiver)

MOSAIC FUNDS ◆
(Fund family changed name from GIT Investment Trusts 5/12/97. Data common to all Mosaic funds are shown below. See subsequent listings for data specific to individual portfolios.)

1655 Fort Myer Drive, Suite 1000
Arlington, VA 22209
888-670-3600, 800-767-0300
703-528-6500
automated price/yield 800-336-3063
fax 703-528-9143
Internet: http://www.mosaicfunds.com

Shareholder service hours: Full service: M-F 9 A.M.-6 P.M. EST; After hours service: prices, yields, balances, last transaction, total returns
Adviser: Bankers Finance Advisors, LLC (a wholly-owned subsidiary of Madison Investment Advisors, Inc.)
Transfer agent: GIT Investment Services, Inc.
Minimum purchase: Initial: $1,000 ($5,000 for Worldwide Growth Portfolio), Subsequent: $50; IRA/Keogh: Initial: $500; Automatic investment plan: Subsequent: $100
Wire orders accepted: Yes, $6 fee under $1,000
Deadline for same day wire purchase: 1 P.M.
Telephone redemptions: Yes
Wire redemptions: Yes, $10 fee under $10,000
Letter redemptions: Signature guarantee required over $50,000
Telephone switching: With other Mosaic funds
Number of switches permitted: Unlimited
Shareholder services: IRA, SIMPLE-IRA, Keogh, 401(k), 403(b), corporate retirement plans, systematic withdrawal plan no min. bal. req.
IRA fees: Annual $12 per shareholder
Keogh fees: Annual $15 per shareholder

MOSAIC BALANCED FUND ◆
(See first Mosaic listing for data common to all portfolios)

Portfolio managers: Jay R. Sekelsky (1990), Frank E. Burgess (1996)
Investment objective and policies: Current income and long-term growth of capital and income. Invests in an allocated mix of equity securities and investment grade U.S. Government and corporate debt issues perceived to offer long-term growth and income. Invests no more than 70% of assets in equities and no less than 25% in debt (not including convertible issues). Allocations vary according to management conception of market conditions. May purchase foreign securities and use covered call options.
Year organized: 1983 (Name changed from GIT Equity Income Portfolio 5/12/97; changed again from Equity Income 6/13/97 after merger with Bascom Hill Balanced; performance history from Balanced (the economic survivor), may be misleading.)
Ticker symbol: BHBFX
Group fund code: 86
Discount broker availability: *Schwab, White
Qualified for sale in: All states except NH, ND, PR, SD, VT
Dividends paid: Income - April, July, October, December; Capital gains - December
Portfolio turnover (3 yrs): 86%, 66%, 76%
Shareholder services fee: 0.30% first $10M to 0.17% over $50M
Management fee: 0.75%
Expense ratio: 1.42% (year ending 12/31/96)

MOSAIC BOND FUND ◆
(See first Mosaic listing for data common to all portfolios)

Portfolio managers: Christopher C. Berberet (1996), Jay R. Sekelsky (1996)
Investment objective and policies: Production of current income consistent with its quality standards, and capital preservation. Invests at least 65% of assets in investment grade corporate and government bonds, with the portfolio maintaining an average dollar-weighted maturity of ten years or less. Invests the balance of assets in money markets, with the allocation adjusted according to perceived market conditions.
Year organized: 1990 (Name changed from Madison Bond Fund 6/13/97; history is Madison, Mosaic is a reorganization; may be misleading.)
Ticker symbol: MBNDX
Group fund code: 38
Qualified for sale in: AZ, CA, CO, DC, FL, GA, IL, IN, KY, MI, MN, NH, NJ, NC, OH, PA, PR, SC, VA, VT, WI, WY
Check redemptions: Yes, $5 fee for checks under $500
Dividends paid: Income - declared daily, paid monthly; Capital gains - December
Portfolio turnover (3 yrs): 94%, 58%, 5%
Shareholder services fee: 0.30% first $10M to 0.17% over $50M
Management fee: 0.50%
Expense ratio: 1.51% (year ending 12/31/96)

MOSAIC FORESIGHT FUND ◆
(See first Mosaic listing for data common to all portfolios)

Portfolio manager: Frank E. Burgess (1996)
Investment objective and policies: Capital appreciation; capital preservation and reduced exposure to market risk secondary. Invests in a diversified asset allocated portfolio of stocks, bonds and cash. Stocks represented are of about 25 well established, high quality domestic companies with a demonstrated pattern of consistent growth. Management will shift into and out of equities, bonds and cash in 25% increments, not small units. Bonds are investment grade corporate and government issues with maturities of less than ten years.
Year organized: 1993 (Name changed from GIT Worldwide Growth Portfolio 5/12/97. On 1/1/98, the name and objective changed from Mosaic WW Growth to a domestic equity allocation fund. Past performance is not relevant.)
Ticker symbol: GEWWX

Group fund code: 88
Discount broker availability: *Schwab, White
Qualified for sale in: All states except NH, ND, SD, VT
Dividends paid: Income - March, December; Capital gains - March, December
Portfolio turnover (3 yrs): 47%, 78%, 65%
Management fee: 1.00%
Expense ratio: 2.50% (year ending 3/31/97) (3.00% without waiver)

MOSAIC GOVERNMENT FUND ◆
(See first Mosaic listing for data common to all portfolios)

Portfolio managers: Christopher C. Berberet (1996), Jay R. Sekelsky (1996)
Investment objective and policies: Current income. Invests exclusively in U.S. Government securities, including those issued or guaranteed by the U.S. Treasury, federal government agencies and instrumentalities with the portfolio maintaining an average dollar-weighted maturity of 20 years or longer. May invest 10% of assets in illiquid securities.
Year organized: 1983 (Formerly A-Rated Income; name changed from GIT Income Trust - Government Portfolio 5/12/97)
Ticker symbol: GIGVX
Group fund code: 58
Discount broker availability: *Schwab, White
Qualified for sale in: All states except NH, ND, PR, SD, VT
Check redemptions: Yes
Dividends paid: Income - declared daily, paid monthly; Capital gains - November
Portfolio turnover (3 yrs): 17%, 190%, 318%
Shareholder services fee: 0.30% first $10M to 0.17% over $50M
Management fee: 0.625%
Expense ratio: 1.43% (year ending 3/31/97)

MOSAIC GOVERNMENT MONEY MARKET TRUST ◆
(See first Mosaic listing for data common to all portfolios)

Portfolio manager: Christopher C. Berberet (1996)
Investment objective and policies: High current income consistent with stability of principal and liquidity. Invests solely in money market instruments issued or guaranteed by the U.S. Government, its agencies or its instrumentalities.
Year organized: 1979 (Name changed from GIT Government Investors Trust MM 5/12/97)
Ticker symbol: GITXX
Group fund code: 81
Qualified for sale in: All states except AK, AR, ID, MT, NE, NV, ND, OK, PR, SD, UT, VT
Check redemptions: Yes
Dividends paid: Income - declared daily, paid monthly
Management fee: 0.50%
Expense ratio: 0.90% (6 months ending 3/31/97) (changed fiscal yr from March)

MOSAIC HIGH YIELD FUND ◆
(See first Mosaic listing for data common to all portfolios)

Portfolio managers: Christopher C. Berberet (1996), Jay R. Sekelsky (1996)
Investment objective and policies: Current income. Invests in corporate bonds, notes and debentures (including convertibles), as well as U.S. Government securities, and generally maintains a dollar-weighted average maturity of 20 years or more. To obtain higher yields fund invests primarily in lower-rated securities ("junk bonds"), including those rated as low as "Caa" or "CCC." May invest up to 10% of assets in illiquid securities.
Year organized: 1983 (Name changed from GIT Maximum Income Portfolio 5/12/97)
Ticker symbol: GITMX
Group fund code: 48
Discount broker availability: *Schwab, White
Qualified for sale in: All states except NH, ND, PR, SD, VT

Check redemptions: Yes
Dividends paid: Income - declared daily, paid monthly; Capital gains - November
Portfolio turnover (3 yrs): 95%, 237%, 243%
Shareholder services fee: 0.30% first $10M to 0.17% over $50M
Management fee: 0.625%
Expense ratio: 1.44% (year ending 3/31/97)

MOSAIC INVESTORS FUND ◆
(See first Mosaic listing for data common to all portfolios)

Portfolio managers: Jay R. Sekelsky (1990), Frank E. Burgess (1996)
Investment objective and policies: Capital appreciation; current income secondary. Invests primarily in equity securities of established companies that may be undervalued or may have good management and significant growth potential. Fund may write covered calls and invest in foreign securities.
Year organized: 1983 (Name changed from GIT Select Growth Portfolio 5/12/97; merged with Bascom Hill Investors 6/13/97; performance history from Bascom Investors (the economic survivor), may be misleading.)
Ticker symbol: MINVX
Group fund code: 76
Discount broker availability: *Schwab, White
Qualified for sale in: All states except NH, ND, PR, SD, VT
Dividends paid: Income - December; Capital gains - December
Portfolio turnover (3 yrs): 81%, 58%, 54%
Shareholder services fee: 0.25% first $10M to 0.12% over $50M
Management fee: 0.75%
Expense ratio: 1.17% (year ending 12/31/96)

MOSAIC MID-CAP GROWTH FUND ◆
(See first Mosaic listing for data common to all portfolios)

Portfolio managers: Frank E. Burgess (1996), Jay R. Sekelsky (1996)
Investment objective and policies: Maximum capital appreciation. Invests primarily in equity securities of smaller, medium-sized companies that may offer rapid growth potential. Fund may write covered calls and invest in foreign securities.
Year organized: 1983 (Name changed from GIT Special Growth Portfolio 5/12/97)
Ticker symbol: GTSGX
Group fund code: 66
Discount broker availability: *Schwab, White
Qualified for sale in: All states except NH, ND, PR, SD, VT
Dividends paid: Income - December; Capital gains - December
Portfolio turnover (3 yrs): 127%, 21%, 4%
Shareholder services fee: 0.25% first $10M to 0.12% over $50M
Management fee: 0.75%
Expense ratio: 1.62% (year ending 3/31/97)

MOSAIC TAX-FREE ARIZONA FUND ◆
(See first Mosaic listing for data common to all portfolios)

Portfolio managers: Christopher C. Berberet (1996), Michael J. Peters (1996)
Investment objective and policies: Current income exempt from federal and Arizona state income taxes. Invests primarily in municipal securities issued by the state of Arizona. Up to 20% of assets may be invested in taxable securities, including those subject to AMT tax treatment.
Year organized: 1989 (Name changed from GIT Tax-Free AZ Portfolio 5/12/97)
Ticker symbol: GTAZX
Group fund code: 92
Discount broker availability: *Schwab, White
Qualified for sale in: AZ, CA, DC, FL, GA, IN, NJ, NC, OH, OR, PA, WV
Check redemptions: $5 fee for checks under $500

Dividends paid: Income - declared daily, paid monthly; Capital gains - November
Portfolio turnover (3 yrs): 32%, 9%, 24%
Management fee: 0.625%
Expense ratio: 1.11% (year ending 9/30/97)

MOSAIC TAX-FREE MARYLAND FUND ◆
(See first Mosaic listing for data common to all portfolios)

Portfolio managers: Christopher C. Berberet (1996), Michael J. Peters (1996)
Investment objective and policies: Current income exempt from federal and Maryland state income taxes. Invests primarily in municipal securities issued by the state of Maryland. Up to 20% of assets may be invested in taxable securities including those subject to AMT tax treatment.
Year organized: 1993 (Name changed from GIT Tax-Free MD Portfolio 5/12/97)
Ticker symbol: MTFMX
Group fund code: 74
Discount broker availability: White
Qualified for sale in: CA, DC, FL, GA, IN, MD, NJ, NC, OH, OR, PA, VA, WV
Check redemptions: $5 fee for checks under $500
Dividends paid: Income - declared daily, paid monthly; Capital gains - November
Portfolio turnover (3 yrs): 15%, 21%, 9%
Management fee: 0.625%
Expense ratio: 1.12% (year ending 9/30/97)

MOSAIC TAX-FREE MISSOURI FUND ◆
(See first Mosaic listing for data common to all portfolios)

Portfolio managers: Christopher C. Berberet (1996), Michael J. Peters (1996)
Investment objective and policies: Current income exempt from federal and Missouri state income taxes. Invests primarily in municipal securities issued by the state of Missouri. Up to 20% of assets may be invested in taxable securities including those subject to AMT tax treatment.
Year organized: 1989 (Name changed from GIT Tax-Free MO Portfolio 5/12/97)
Ticker symbol: GTMOX
Group fund code: 93
Discount broker availability: *Schwab, White
Qualified for sale in: CA, DC, FL, GA, IN, MO, NJ, NC, OH, OR, PA, VA, WV
Check redemptions: $5 fee for checks under $500
Dividends paid: Income - declared daily, paid monthly; Capital gains - November
Portfolio turnover (3 yrs): 41%, 21%, 16%
Management fee: 0.625%
Expense ratio: 1.02% (year ending 9/30/97)

MOSAIC TAX-FREE MONEY MARKET ◆
(See first Mosaic listing for data common to all portfolios)

Portfolio managers: Christopher C. Berberet (1996), Michael J. Peters (1996)
Investment objective and policies: Current income exempt from federal income tax, safety of principal and liquidity. Invests in short-term municipal money market securities. Up to 20% of assets may be invested in taxable securities including those subject to AMT tax treatment.
Year organized: 1982 (Name changed from GIT Tax-Free MM Portfolio 5/12/97)
Group fund code: 51
Qualified for sale in: All except AL, AR, DE, ID, IA, KS, KY, LA, ME, MI, MN, MS, MT, NE, NH, ND, OK, PR, RI, SD, UT, VT, WA
Check redemptions: $0.15 fee for checks under $500
Dividends paid: Income - declared daily, paid monthly
Management fee: 0.50%
Expense ratio: 0.83% (year ending 9/30/96) (0.95% without waiver)

MOSAIC TAX-FREE NATIONAL FUND ◆

(See first Mosaic listing for data common to all portfolios)

Portfolio managers: Christopher C. Berberet (1996), Michael J. Peters (1996)
Investment objective and policies: Current income exempt from federal income tax. Invests primarily in medium-grade municipal securities, and generally maintains a dollar-weighted average maturity of 15 years or more. Up to 20% of assets may be invested in taxable securities including those subject to AMT tax treatment.
Year organized: 1982 (name changed from GIT Tax-Free High Yield Portfolio on 2/1/94; changed from GIT Tax-Free National Portfolio 5/12/97)
Ticker symbol: GTFHX
Group fund code: 72
Discount broker availability: White
Qualified for sale in: All states
Check redemptions: $5 fee for checks under $500
Dividends paid: Income - declared daily, paid monthly; Capital gains - November
Portfolio turnover (3 yrs): 44%, 39%, 56%
Management fee: 0.625%
Expense ratio: 1.05% (year ending 9/30/97)

MOSAIC TAX-FREE VIRGINIA FUND ◆

(See first Mosaic listing for data common to all portfolios)

Portfolio managers: Christopher C. Berberet (1996), Michael J. Peters (1996)
Investment objective and policies: Current income exempt from federal and Virginia state income taxes. Invests primarily in municipal securities issued by the Commonwealth of Virginia. Up to 20% of assets may be invested in taxable securities including those subject to AMT tax treatment.
Year organized: 1987 (Name changed from GIT Tax-Free VA Portfolio 5/12/97)
Ticker symbol: GTVAX
Group fund code: 52
Discount broker availability: White
Qualified for sale in: CA, DC, FL, GA, IN, NJ, NC, OH, OR, PA, WV
Check redemptions: $5 fee for checks under $500
Dividends paid: Income - declared daily, paid monthly; Capital gains - November
Portfolio turnover (3 yrs): 28%, 28%, 55%
Management fee: 0.625%
Expense ratio: 1.05% (year ending 9/30/97)

M.S.B. FUND ◆

c/o Shay Financial Services Co.
111 East Wacker Drive, Suite 2600
Chicago, IL 60601
800-661-3938, 312-856-0711
212-573-9354
fax 212-573-9440

Adviser: Shay Assets Management Co.
Portfolio managers: Mark F. Trautman (1993), John J. McCabe (1991)
Transfer agent and administrator: PFPC Inc.
Investment objective and policies: Capital appreciation; income secondary. Invests in equity securities of companies with promising growth, earnings and dividend prospects. Normally invests at least 85% of assets in companies with market capitalization in excess of $500M.
Year organized: 1964
Ticker symbol: MSBFX
Minimum purchase: Initial: $50, Subsequent: $25
Wire orders accepted: Yes
Discount broker availability: *White
Qualified for sale in: All states
Telephone redemptions: Yes, $500 minimum
Wire redemptions: Yes, $15 fee
Letter redemptions: Signature guarantee required
Dividends paid: Income - March, June, September, December; Capital gains - December
Portfolio turnover (3 yrs): 45%, 68%, 62%
Shareholder services: IRA, SEP-IRA, automatic investment plan, systematic withdrawal plan

Management fee: 0.75% first $100M, 0.50% over $100M
Administration fee: 0.10% first $200M to 0.075% over $200M
Expense ratio: 1.41% (year ending 12/31/96) (1.61% without waiver)
IRA fees: Annual $10

THE MUHLENKAMP FUND ◆

12300 Perry Highway
P.O. Box 598
Wexford, PA 15090
800-860-3863, 724-935-5520
fax 724-935-4720
Internet: http://www.muhlenkamp.com
e-mail: fund@muhlenkamp.com

Adviser: Muhlenkamp & Co., Inc.
Portfolio manager: Ronald H. Muhlenkamp (1988)
Transfer agent: American Data Services, Inc.
Investment objective and policies: Maximum total return: current income and capital gains, consistent with reasonable risk. Invests primarily in a diversified portfolio of common stocks but may hold fixed-income securities when deemed appropriate. Employs "value" approach, using low price/earnings ratio, high return on equity and relative price to book criteria.
Year organized: 1988
Ticker symbol: MUHLX
Minimum purchase: Initial: $200, Subsequent: $100; IRA: Initial: None, Subsequent: None; Automatic investment plan: Subsequent: $50
Wire orders accepted: Yes
Discount broker availability: *Fidelity, *Schwab, *White
Qualified for sale in: All states
Letter redemptions: Signature guarantee not required
Dividends paid: Income - December; Capital gains - December
Shareholder services: IRA, systematic withdrawal plan min. bal. req. $5,000
Portfolio turnover (3 yrs): 17%, 23%, 26%
Management fee: 1.00%
Expense ratio: 1.56% (year ending 12/31/96)
IRA fees: Annual $10, Closing $15

MUIR CALIFORNIA TAX-FREE BOND FUND

(Fund merged into Citizens Trust Income fund 9/97)

MUNDER NETNET FUND

480 Pierce Street
Birmingham, MI 48009
800-438-5789, 800-468-6337
Internet: http://www.netnet.munder.com

Adviser: Munder Capital Management
Administrator: First Data Investor Services Group, Inc.
Portfolio manager: Team managed
Transfer agent: First Data Investor Services Group, Inc.
Investment objective and policies: Long-term capital appreciation. Invests primarily in equity securities of companies of any size engaged in the research, design, development, manufacturing, or engaged to a significant extent in the business of distributing products, processes or services for use with Internet and Intranet related businesses. May also invest up to 35% of assets in short-term money market instruments. May invest without limit in small, unseasoned, newly public companies, and in foreign securities. May use forward foreign currency exchange contracts and options and futures for hedging purposes.
Year organized: 1996
Minimum purchase: Initial: $1,000, Subsequent: $50; Automatic investment plan: Initial: $50
Wire orders accepted: Yes
Deadline for same day wire transfer: 4 P.M.
Qualified for sale in: All states
Telephone redemptions: Yes
Wire redemptions: Yes, $7.50 fee for redemptions under $5,000
Letter redemptions: Signature guarantee required over $50,000

Dividends paid: Income - annually; Capital gains - annually
Portfolio turnover (1 yr): 195%
Shareholder services: IRA, SEP-IRA, systematic withdrawal plan min. bal. req. $2,500
Management fee: 1.00%
Administration fee: 0.14% first $2.8B to 0.11% over $5B (aggregate of all funds to First Data)
12b-1 distribution fee: 0.25%
Expense ratio: 1.48% (10 months ending 6/30/97) (4.57% without waiver)
IRA fees: Annual $10

MUNICIPAL CASH SERIES

Federated Investors Tower
Pittsburgh, PA 15222-3779
800-245-2423, 412-288-1948

Adviser: Federated Advisers
Portfolio manager: Mary Jo Ochson (1989)
Transfer agent: State Street Bank & Trust Co.
Investment objective and policies: Current income exempt from federal income tax, consistent with principal stability. Invests in short-term municipal money market instruments.
Year organized: 1989
Ticker symbol: CMSXX
Minimum purchase: Initial: $10,000, Subsequent: $500; IRA: Initial: $1,000
Wire orders accepted: Yes
Deadline for same day wire purchase: 12 NN
Qualified for sale in: All states
Telephone redemptions: Yes
Wire redemptions: Yes, $1,000 minimum
Letter redemptions: Signature guarantee required over $50,000
Check redemptions: No minimum
Dividends paid: Income - declared daily, paid monthly
Shareholder services: IRA, systematic withdrawal plan
Management fee: 0.50%
12b-1 distribution fee: Maximum of 0.35%
Expense ratio: 0.99% (year ending 5/31/97) (includes waiver)

MUTUAL SERIES FUNDS ◆

(Data common to all Mutual Series funds are shown below. See subsequent listing for data specific to individual funds.)

51 John F. Kennedy Parkway
Short Hills, NJ 07078
800-448-3863, 800-342-5236
201-912-2001
fax 201-912-1048

Shareholder service hours: Full service: M-F 8 A.M.-7 P.M. EST; After hours service: prices, account balances, place orders, last transaction, news and views, messages, indices, prospectuses, total returns
Adviser: Franklin Mutual Advisers, Inc.
Portfolio managers: Michael F. Price (1975), Jeffrey A. Altman (1988), Robert L. Friedman (1988), Raymond Garea (1991), Peter A. Langerman (1986), Lawrence N. Sondike (1984)
Transfer agent: PFPC, Inc.
Investment objective and policies (except Discovery): Capital appreciation, which may occasionally be short-term; income secondary. Mutual Beacon, Shares, and Qualified all have growth-income objectives and similar portfolios, and tend to invest in securities of issuers with market capitalizations in excess of $500M, although they may invest in companies of any size. They differ in that Mutual Qualified is largely held by IRAs and pension plans. Thus, Qualified is the same as Shares, except it doesn't hold anything for tax reasons. Funds may invest up to 50% of assets in securities of companies involved in prospective mergers, consolidations, liquidations and reorganizations. All portfolios are invested in three categories. First, 60% of the portfolio is made up of stocks trading at large discounts from asset values. Another portion is deal oriented, i.e. merges, liquidations, tender offers, spinoffs, sales of assets, and exchange offers. A third category is bankruptcy situations.

Special sales restrictions: Funds have become part of the Franklin mutual fund complex. As such, they are now multi-class load funds also carrying 12b-1 fees as high as 0.75%. Only the "Z" class shares are discussed here; only the "Z" class shares are available at no-load, and then, only to shareholders with positions prior to the acquisition. The only exception is that you may buy "Z" shares for a new account if you invest $5M. Those shareholders may, however, continue to buy at the minimums listed here, and may exchange shares at NAV for other Franklin/Templeton funds, avoiding their loads.
Minimum purchase: Initial: $1,000, Subsequent: $25; IRA/Keogh: Initial: None
Wire orders accepted: Subsequent only, $1,000 minimum
Deadline for same day wire purchase: 4 P.M.
Qualified for sale in: All states
Telephone redemptions: Yes
Wire redemptions: Yes
Letter redemptions: Signature guarantee required over $50,000
Telephone switching: With other Mutual Series funds, "Z" shares only; qualified shareholders may transfer at NAV to any Franklin/Templeton fund
Number of switches permitted: Monitored; timers will be halted
Dividends paid: Income - June, December; Capital gains - June, December
Shareholder services: IRA, SEP-IRA, Keogh, 401(k), 403(b), corporate retirement plans, automatic investment plan, directed dividends, electronic funds transfer, systematic withdrawal plan min. bal. req. $5,000
IRA/Keogh fees: Annual $9 (currently waived)

MUTUAL BEACON FUND ◆
(See first Mutual Series listing for data common to all funds)

Year organized: 1962 (Formerly Beacon Growth Fund; performance record before 1985 should be disregarded. 3 for 1 split 2/3/97)
Ticker symbol: BEGRX
Group fund code: 76
Discount broker availability: Fidelity, Schwab, Siebert, White
Portfolio turnover (3 yrs): 55%, 67%, 73%
Management fee: 0.60%
Expense ratio: 0.74% (year ending 12/31/97) (0.77% without waiver)

MUTUAL DISCOVERY FUND ◆
(See first Mutual Series listing for data common to all funds)

Investment objective and policies: Long-term capital appreciation. Invests primarily in equity securities of small capitalization companies. Up to 50% of assets may be in securities of foreign issuers and 15% in illiquid debt securities. May invest in distressed first mortgage obligations and other debt secured by real property and sell short securities it does not own up to 5% of assets. May sell short against the box and hedge.
Year organized: 1992
Ticker symbol: MDISX
Group fund code: 77
Discount broker availability: Fidelity, Schwab, Siebert, White
Portfolio turnover (3 yrs): 58%, 80%, 73%
Management fee: 0.80%
Expense ratio: 0.98% (year ending 12/31/97) (1.00% without waiver)

MUTUAL EUROPEAN FUND ◆
(See first Mutual Series listing for data common to all funds)

Investment objective and policies: In addition to the fundamental policies noted above, it is important to note that the fund will invest at least 65% of assets in securities of issuers organized under the laws of, or whose principal business operations derive at least 50% of revenues from, European countries. Will ordinarily invest in at least five countries, but may invest in only one. Europe is given the broadest definition,

including all those portions of the former Soviet Union now considered Europe, as well as Scandinavia and the U.K. May also invest up to 35% of assets anywhere else in the world.
Year organized: 1996
Ticker symbol: MEURX
Group fund code: 78
Discount broker availability: Fidelity, Schwab, Siebert, White
Management fee: 0.80%
Expense ratio: 1.09% (6 months ending 12/31/96) (1.15% without waiver)

MUTUAL FINANCIAL SERVICES FUND ◆
(See first Mutual Series listing for data common to all funds)

Investment objective and policies: In addition to the fundamental policies noted above, it is important to note that the fund will invest at least 65% of assets in securities of issuers involved in the financial services industry, including banks, savings and loans, brokerage firms, investment advisors and credit card, finance and insurance companies.
Year organized: 1997
Ticker symbol: TEFAX
Group fund code: 79
Discount broker availability: Fidelity, Schwab, Siebert, White
Management fee: 0.80%

MUTUAL QUALIFIED FUND ◆
(See first Mutual Series listing for data common to all funds)

Year organized: 1980 (Formerly Mutual Qualified Income Fund; 2 for 1 split 2/3/97)
Ticker symbol: MQIFX
Group fund code: 75
Discount broker availability: Fidelity, Schwab, Siebert, White
Portfolio turnover (3 yrs): 65%, 76%, 68%
Management fee: 0.60%
Expense ratio: 0.75% (year ending 12/31/96) (0.78% without waiver)

MUTUAL SHARES FUND ◆
(See first Mutual Series listing for data common to all funds)

Year organized: 1949 (Formerly Mutual Shares Corporation; 5 for 1 split 2/3/97)
Ticker symbol: MUTHX
Group fund code: 74
Discount broker availability: Fidelity, Schwab, Siebert, White
Portfolio turnover (3 yrs): 58%, 79%, 67%
Management fee: 0.60%
Expense ratio: 0.70% (year ending 12/31/96) (0.72% without waiver)

NATIONS FUNDS
(Data common to all Nations funds are shown below. See subsequent listings for data specific to individual funds.)

c/o Stephens Inc.
One NationsBank Plaza, 33rd Floor
Charlotte, NC 28255
800-321-7854, 800-982-2271
Internet: http://www.nationsbank.com/nationsfunds

Adviser: NationsBanc Advisors, Inc.
Sub-adviser: Trade Street Assocs., Inc. (a wholly owned subsidiary of NationsBank), except for the international funds, sub-advised by Gartmore Global Partners (a joint venture with National Westminster Bank, plc).
Administrator: Stephens Inc.
Transfer agent: First Data Investor Services Group
Sales restrictions: This information is pertinent to INVESTOR A shares only; other classes of no-load shares are available, but only through institutions, banks or intermediaries. Nations has formed its own captive discount brokerage; to buy retail you must

open an account with them. Only existing account holders at the other discount brokerages may continue to add to those positions.
Minimum purchase: Initial: $1,000, Subsequent: $100; IRA: Initial: $500; Automatic investment plan: Subsequent: $25
Wire orders accepted: Yes
Deadline for same day wire purchase: 4 P.M.
Qualified for sale in: All states (except single state funds)
Telephone redemptions: Yes
Wire redemptions: Yes
Letter redemptions: Signature guarantee not required
Telephone switching: With the same share class of other Nations funds.
Number of switches permitted: Unlimited, $1,000 minimum
Shareholder services: IRA, SEP-IRA, 401(k), systematic withdrawal plan min. bal. req. $10,000
Administration fee: 0.10%
12b-1 distribution fee: 0.25%
IRA fees: Annual $35 (waived for balances over $10,000), Closing $10

NATIONS BALANCED ASSETS FUND
(See first Nations listing for data common to all funds)

Portfolio manager: Julie Hale (1995)
Investment objective and policies: Total return: growth of capital and current income, consistent with preservation of capital. Fund uses asset allocation strategies to invest in varying amounts in both foreign and domestic common stocks, fixed-income securities, and cash equivalents. Normally at least 25% of the portfolio will be in debt securities.
Year organized: 1992
Ticker symbol: NBAIX
Discount broker availability: Fidelity, Siebert, *White
Dividends paid: Income - quarterly; Capital gains - annually
Portfolio turnover (3 yrs): 264%, 83%, 174%
Management fee: 0.75%
Expense ratio: 1.25% (year ending 3/31/97)

NATIONS CAPITAL GROWTH FUND
(See first Nations listing for data common to all funds)

Portfolio manager: Philip J. Sanders (1995)
Investment objective and policies: Long-term capital appreciation; income secondary. Invests primarily in common stocks and equity securities of companies perceived to have above average appreciation potential. May invest up to 10% of assets in foreign issues.
Year organized: 1992
Ticker symbol: NCGIX
Discount broker availability: Fidelity, Siebert, *White
Dividends paid: Income - quarterly; Capital gains - annually
Portfolio turnover (3 yrs): 75%, 25%, 80%
Management fee: 0.75%
Expense ratio: 1.21% (year ending 3/31/97)

NATIONS DISCIPLINED EQUITY FUND
(See first Nations listing for data common to all funds)

Portfolio manager: Jeffery C. Moser (1995)
Investment objective and policies: Long-term capital appreciation. Invests at least 65% of assets in common stock of domestic companies considered to have the potential for significant increases in earnings per share. May invest the balance of assets in a broad range of foreign or domestic debt or equity issues, both government and corporate. Most companies will have market capitalizations exceeding $500M.
Year organized: 1995
Ticker symbol: NDEAX
Discount broker availability: Fidelity, Siebert, *White
Dividends paid: Income - quarterly; Capital gains - annually
Portfolio turnover (3 yrs): 120%, 47%, 124%
Management fee: 0.75%
Expense ratio: 1.29% (year ending 3/31/97)

NATIONS DIVERSIFIED INCOME FUND
(See first Nations listing for data common to all funds)

Portfolio manager: Mark S. Ahnrud (1992)
Investment objective and policies: High current income consistent with prudent investment risk. Invests in a diversified portfolio of investment grade government and corporate fixed-income securities. The average dollar-weighted maturity exceeds five years. May invest up to 25% of assets in foreign securities. May invest up to 35% of assets in debt securities rated "B."
Year organized: 1992
Ticker symbol: NDIAX
Discount broker availability: Fidelity, Siebert, *White
Dividends paid: Income - monthly; Capital gains - annually
Portfolio turnover (3 yrs): 278%, 69%, 96%
Management fee: 0.60%
Expense ratio: 1.00% (year ending 3/31/97) (1.10% without waiver

NATIONS EMERGING GROWTH FUND
(See first Nations listing for data common to all funds)

Portfolio manager: Scott A. Billeadeau (1997)
Investment objective and policies: Capital appreciation. Invests in equity securities of both domestic and foreign emerging growth companies perceived to have superior earnings growth rates. Market capitalizations will range from $50M to $1.5B. Portfolio will diversify across at least 75 to 100 issues.
Year organized: 1992
Ticker symbol: NEGAX
Discount broker availability: Fidelity, Siebert, *White
Dividends paid: Income - quarterly; Capital gains - annually
Portfolio turnover (3 yrs): 93%, 39%, 139%
Management fee: 0.75%
Expense ratio: 1.23% (year ending 3/31/97)

NATIONS EMERGING MARKETS FUND
(See first Nations listing for data common to all funds)

Portfolio manager: Philip Ehrmann (1995)
Investment objective and policies: Long-term capital growth. Invests primarily in equity securities of companies located in countries considered to have relatively low gross national product per capita compared to industrialized economies, as defined by the International Finance Corporation or the World Bank. May invest in investment grade debt securities as well. Will generally diversify into at least three countries, but may concentrate in one if conditions warrant. May use derivatives in an effort to enhance performance and for hedging purposes.
Year organized: 1995
Discount broker availability: Fidelity, Siebert, *White
Dividends paid: Income - quarterly; Capital gains - annually
Portfolio turnover (2 yrs): 31%, 17%
Management fee: 1.10%
Expense ratio: 1.99% (year ending 3/31/97)

NATIONS EQUITY INCOME FUND
(See first Nations listing for data common to all funds)

Portfolio manager: Eric S. Williams (1991)
Investment objective and policies: High current income; increasing dividend income or capital appreciation secondary. Invests primarily in equity securities, including convertibles, with a relatively high current yield. Companies must demonstrate at least five years of stable or increasing dividends, in addition to exhibiting other favorable financial characteristics. May also invest without limit in investment grade debt obligations, and have up to 10% of assets in foreign issued securities.
Year organized: 1991
Ticker symbol: NEQIX
Discount broker availability: Fidelity, Siebert, *White

Dividends paid: Income - quarterly; Capital gains - annually
Portfolio turnover (3 yrs): 102%, 59%, 158%
Management fee: 0.75% first $100M to 0.60% over $250M
Expense ratio: 1.16% (year ending 3/31/97)

NATIONS EQUITY INDEX FUND
(See first Nations listing for data common to all funds)

Portfolio manager: Greg W. Golden (1995)
Investment objective and policies: Total return: capital appreciation and current income, comparable (before expenses) to the total return of the S&P 500 Composite Price Index. Invests at least 80% of assets in equity securities which compose the S&P 500 Index, with an expected correlation of 0.95 on an annual basis. May also use debt securities indexed to the S&P 500, and swaps, options and futures to more closely match performance. May use a variety of derivative instruments for hedging purposes.
Year organized: 1995 (commencement of "A" shares)
Discount broker availability: Fidelity, Siebert
Dividends paid: Income - quarterly; Capital gains - annually
Portfolio turnover (3 yrs): 5%, 2%, 18%
Management fee: 0.50%
Expense ratio: 0.60% (year ending 3/31/97)

NATIONS FLORIDA INTERMEDIATE MUNICIPAL BOND FUND
(See first Nations listing for data common to all funds)

Portfolio manager: Michele M. Poirier (1992)
Investment objective and policies: High current income exempt from Federal and state taxes, consistent with moderate fluctuation of principal. Invests in investment grade, intermediate-term municipal securities. The average dollar-weighted maturity is between three and ten years; duration between five and six years. May use some derivatives for hedging purposes. Fund is non-diversified.
Year organized: 1992
Ticker symbol: NFIMX
Discount broker availability: Fidelity, Siebert, *White
Dividends paid: Income - declared daily, paid monthly; Capital gains - annually
Portfolio turnover (3 yrs): 16%, 18%, 27%
Management fee: 0.50%
Expense ratio: 0.70% (year ending 3/31/97) (1.01% without waiver)

NATIONS FLORIDA MUNICIPAL BOND FUND
(See first Nations listing for data common to all funds)

Portfolio manager: Michele M. Poirier (1993)
Investment objective and policies: High current income exempt from Federal and state taxes, with the potential for principal fluctuation. Invests in investment grade, long-term municipal securities. The average dollar-weighted maturity is greater than ten years and duration is greater than ten years. May use some derivatives for hedging purposes. Fund is non-diversified.
Year organized: 1993
Ticker symbol: NFDAX
Discount broker availability: Florida, Siebert, *White
Dividends paid: Income - declared daily, paid monthly; Capital gains - annually
Portfolio turnover (3 yrs): 23%, 7%, 13%
Management fee: 0.60%
Expense ratio: 0.80% (year ending 3/31/97) (1.13% without waiver)

NATIONS GEORGIA INTERMEDIATE MUNICIPAL BOND FUND
(See first Nations listing for data common to all funds)

Portfolio manager: Michele M. Poirier (1992)
Investment objective and policies: High current income exempt from Federal and state taxes, consistent with moderate fluctuation of principal. Invests in

investment grade, intermediate-term municipal securities. The average dollar-weighted maturity is between three and ten years; duration between five and six years. May use some derivatives for hedging purposes. Fund is non-diversified.
Year organized: 1992
Ticker symbol: NGIMX
Discount broker availability: Fidelity, Siebert, *White
Dividends paid: Income - declared daily, paid monthly; Capital gains - annually
Portfolio turnover (3 yrs): 9%, 3%, 17%
Management fee: 0.50%
Expense ratio: 0.70% (year ending 3/31/97) (1.00% without waivers)

NATIONS GEORGIA MUNICIPAL BOND FUND
(See first Nations listing for data common to all funds)

Portfolio manager: Michele M. Poirier (1993)
Investment objective and policies: High current income exempt from Federal and state taxes, with the potential for principal fluctuation. Invests in investment grade, long-term municipal securities. The average dollar-weighted maturity is greater than ten years and duration is greater than ten years. May use some derivatives for hedging purposes. Fund is non-diversified.
Year organized: 1993
Ticker symbol: NGAAX
Discount broker availability: *White
Dividends paid: Income - declared daily, paid monthly; Capital gains - annually
Portfolio turnover (3 yrs): 19%, 7%, 26%
Management fee: 0.60%
Expense ratio: 0.80% (year ending 3/31/97) (1.25% without waivers)

NATIONS GLOBAL GOVERNMENT INCOME FUND
(See first Nations listing for data common to all funds)

Portfolio manager: Mark Rimmer (1995)
Investment objective and policies: Current income. Invests primarily in insured debt securities of governments, banks, and supranational entities located in the major industrialized countries throughout the world. Will normally diversify among at least three countries, including the U.S., but must maintain at least 25% of assets in overseas markets.
Year organized: 1995
Ticker symbol: NGLBX
Discount broker availability: Fidelity, Siebert, *White
Dividends paid: Income - quarterly; Capital gains - annually
Portfolio turnover (2 yrs): 100%, 213%
Management fee: 0.70%
Expense ratio: 1.51% (year ending 3/31/97)

NATIONS GOVERNMENT MONEY MARKET FUND
(See first Nations listing for data common to all funds)

Portfolio manager: Sandra L. Duck (1993)
Investment objective and policies: High current income consistent with liquidity and stability of principal. Invests in short-term U.S. Government obligations. May also invest in securities of other investment companies.
Year organized: 1991
Ticker symbol: NGAXX
Dividends paid: Income - declared daily, paid monthly
Management fee: 0.40%
Expense ratio: 0.65% (year ending 3/31/97) (0.92% without waiver)

NATIONS GOVERNMENT SECURITIES FUND
(See first Nations listing for data common to all funds)

Portfolio manager: Christopher Gunster (1997)
Investment objective and policies: Current income and preservation of capital. Invests primarily in obligations issued or backed by the U.S. Government. The

average dollar-weighted maturity of the portfolio is between three and ten years; the duration between 3.5 and six years. May also invest in corporate convertible and non-convertible debt securities.
Year organized: 1991
Ticker symbol: NGVAX
Discount broker availability: Fidelity, Siebert, *White
Dividends paid: Income - declared daily, paid monthly; Capital gains - annually
Portfolio turnover (3 yrs): 468%, 199%, 413%
Management fee: 0.65% first $100M to 0.50% over $250M
Expense ratio: 1.05% (year ending 3/31/97) (1.19% without waiver)

NATIONS INTERMEDIATE MUNICIPAL BOND FUND
(See first Nations listing for data common to all funds)

Portfolio manager: Matthew M. Kiselak (1994)
Investment objective and policies: High current income exempt from Federal income tax, and consistent with moderate fluctuation of principal. Invests in investment grade intermediate-term municipal securities issued by or on behalf of states, territories, and possessions of the U.S., the District of Columbia, and their political subdivisions, agencies, instrumentalities and authorities. The average dollar-weighted maturity will be between three and ten years; the average duration between five and six years. May use some derivatives for hedging purposes. Fund is non-diversified.
Year organized: 1993
Ticker symbol: NITMX
Discount broker availability: Fidelity, Siebert, *White
Dividends paid: Income - declared daily, paid monthly; Capital gains - annually
Portfolio turnover (3 yrs): 21%, 4%, 31%
Management fee: 0.50%
Expense ratio: 0.70% (year ending 3/31/97) (1.01% without waiver)

NATIONS INTERNATIONAL EQUITY FUND
(See first Nations listing for data common to all funds)

Portfolio manager: Stephen Watson (1995)
Investment objective and policies: Long-term capital growth. Invests primarily in equity securities of large, established non-U.S. companies believed to have growth potential. May use ADRs, GDRs and EDRs to gain access to foreign issues. May invest up to 35% of assets in any other type of securities, including Eurodollar securities.
Year organized: 1992
Ticker symbol: NIIAX
Discount broker availability: Fidelity, Siebert, *White
Dividends paid: Income - quarterly; Capital gains - annually
Portfolio turnover (3 yrs): 36%, 26%, 92%
Management fee: 0.90%
Expense ratio: 1.41% (year ending 3/31/97)

NATIONS INTERNATIONAL GROWTH FUND
(See first Nations listing for data common to all funds)

Portfolio manager: Brian O'Neill (1997)
Investment objective and policies: Long-term capital growth. Invests at least 65% of assets in foreign equity securities listed on major exchanges, primarily in Europe and the Pacific Rim. May also invest up to 35% of assets in developing countries, and invest in debt securities listed in the top two categories by any nationally recognized rating agencies. May also use sponsored and unsponsored ADRs, EDRs, GDRs and ADSs.
Year organized: 1984(?) (fund began life as the Kleinwort Benson International Equity Fund; became the Pilot Kleinwort Benson Int'l Equity fund in 1993; became the Pilot International Equity fund "A" shares 8/31/95, and became the Nations Int'l Growth Fund 5/23/97.)
Dividends paid: Income - annually; Capital gains - annually

Portfolio turnover (3 yrs): 34%, 22%, 36%
Management fee: 0.90%
Expense ratio: 1.42% (year ending 5/16/97)

NATIONS LIFEGOAL BALANCED FUND
(See first Nations listing for data common to all funds)

Portfolio managers: E. Keith Wirtz (1996), C. Thomas Clapp (1996)
Investment objective and policies: Total return: capital appreciation and current income. A "fund of funds," this fund invests in an underlying selection of balanced equity and fixed-income funds also from Nations. Ranges of allocation are: large-cap domestic equity funds, 15% to 35%; small/mid-cap domestic equity funds, 10% to 20%; 'core' (developed nations) international equity funds, 5% to 15%; and 'core' bond funds, 40% to 60%.
Year organized: 1996
Discount broker availability: Fidelity, Siebert, *White
Dividends paid: Income - quarterly; Capital gains - annually
Portfolio turnover (1 yr): 1%
Management fee: 0.25%
Expense ratio: 0.50% (six months ending 3/31/97)

NATIONS LIFEGOAL GROWTH FUND
(See first Nations listing for data common to all funds)

Portfolio managers: E. Keith Wirtz (1996), C. Thomas Clapp (1996)
Investment objective and policies: Capital appreciation. A "fund of funds," this fund invests in an underlying selection of diversified equity funds also from Nations. Ranges of allocation are: large-cap domestic equity funds, 35% to 75%; small/mid-cap domestic equity funds, 20% to 35%; 'core' (developed nations) international equity funds, 10% to 20%; and non 'core' (emerging markets) international equity funds, 0% to 10%.
Year organized: 1996
Discount broker availability: Fidelity, Siebert, *White
Dividends paid: Income - quarterly; Capital gains - annually
Portfolio turnover (1 yr): 25%
Management fee: 0.25%
Expense ratio: 0.50% (six months ending 3/31/97)

NATIONS LIFEGOAL INCOME AND GROWTH FUND
(See first Nations listing for data common to all funds)

Portfolio managers: E. Keith Wirtz (1996), C. Thomas Clapp (1996)
Investment objective and policies: Current income and modest growth to protect against inflation and to preserve purchasing power. A "fund of funds," this fund invests in an underlying selection of funds weighted primarily towards fixed-income holdings, also from Nations. Ranges of allocation are: large-cap domestic equity funds, 10% to 30%; 'core' (developed nations) international equity funds, 0% to 10%; short duration bond funds, 50% to 90%; and money market funds, 0% to 20%.
Year organized: 1996
Discount broker availability: Fidelity, Siebert, *White
Dividends paid: Income - quarterly; Capital gains - annually
Portfolio turnover (1 yr): 2%
Management fee: 0.25%
Expense ratio: 0.50% (six months ending 3/31/97)

NATIONS MANAGED INDEX FUND
(See first Nations listing for data common to all funds)

Portfolio manager: Greg W. Golden (1996)
Investment objective and policies: Total return which exceeds the total return of the S&P 500 Composite Stock Price Index. Invests in common stocks of the companies that comprise the index, overweighting the top two deciles of the index universe, and underweighting or eliminating the lowest two deciles. Fund also employs tax efficiency strategies to

manage capital gains distributions. May also use derivatives in an effort to enhance return and for hedging purposes.
Year organized: 1996
Discount broker availability: Fidelity, *Schwab, Siebert, *White
Dividends paid: Income - quarterly; Capital gains - annually
Portfolio turnover (1 yr): 17%
Management fee: 0.10%
Expense ratio: 0.75% (eight months ending 3/31/97) (1.30% without waiver)

NATIONS MANAGED SMALL CAP INDEX FUND
(See first Nations listing for data common to all funds)

Portfolio manager: Greg W. Golden (1996)
Investment objective and policies: Long-term total return exceeding the total return of the S&P SmallCap 600 Index. Invests in common stocks of the companies that comprise the index, overweighting the top two deciles of the index universe, and underweighting or eliminating the lowest two deciles. Fund also employs tax efficiency strategies to manage capital gains distributions. May also use derivatives in an effort to enhance return and for hedging purposes.
Year organized: 1996
Discount broker availability: Fidelity, *Schwab, Siebert, *White
Dividends paid: Income - quarterly; Capital gains - annually
Portfolio turnover (1 yr): 18%
Management fee: 0.10%
Expense ratio: 0.75% (six months ending 3/31/97) (1.46% without waiver)

NATIONS MANAGED SMALL CAP VALUE INDEX FUND
(See first Nations listing for data common to all funds)

Portfolio managers: Greg W. Golden (1997), Jeffery C. Moser (1997)
Investment objective and policies: Long-term total return exceeding the total return of the S&P Barra SmallCap Value Index. Invests in common stocks of the companies that comprise the index, overweighting the top two deciles of the index universe, and underweighting or eliminating the lowest two deciles. Fund also employs tax efficiency strategies to manage capital gains distributions. May also use derivatives in an effort to enhance return and for hedging purposes.
Year organized: 1997
Dividends paid: Income - quarterly; Capital gains - annually
Management fee: 0.10%

NATIONS MANAGED VALUE INDEX FUND
(See first Nations listing for data common to all funds)

Portfolio managers: Greg W. Golden (1997), Jeffery C. Moser (1997)
Investment objective and policies: Long-term total return exceeding the total return of the S&P Barra Value Index. Invests in common stocks of the companies that comprise the index, overweighting the top two deciles of the index universe, and underweighting or eliminating the lowest two deciles. Fund also employs tax efficiency strategies to manage capital gains distributions. May also use derivatives in an effort to enhance return and for hedging purposes.
Year organized: 1997
Dividends paid: Income - quarterly; Capital gains - annually
Management fee: 0.10%

NATIONS MARSICO FOCUSED EQUITIES FUND
(See first Nations listing for data common to all funds)

Sub-adviser: Marsico Capital Management, LLC
Portfolio manager: Thomas F. Marsico (1997)
Investment objective and policies: Long-term growth of capital. Invests primarily in the common stocks of a select group of twenty to thirty stocks

selected for their perceived growth potential. May also invest to a lesser degree in preferred stock, warrants convertible securities and debt obligations. May invest up to 25% of assets in mortgage- and asset-backed securities, up to 10% in zero coupon, pay-in-kind and step coupon securities, up to 15% in illiquid securities, up to 35% of assets in junk bonds, without limit in foreign securities (including those denominated in foreign currencies), and without limit in indexed/structured securities. May invest up to 25% of assets in a single issuer. May use a variety of derivative instruments for hedging purposes. Fund is non-diversified.
Year organized: 1997
Dividends paid: Income - quarterly; Capital gains - annually
Management fee: 0.80%

NATIONS MARSICO GROWTH AND INCOME FUND
(See first Nations listing for data common to all funds)

Sub-adviser: Marsico Capital Management, LLC
Portfolio manager: Thomas F. Marsico (1997)
Investment objective and policies: Long-term growth of capital and a limited emphasis on current income. Invests up to 75% of assets (but may be as low as 25%) in a diversified portfolio of equity securities selected for their perceived growth potential, and at least 25% of assets in securities with perceived income potential. Allocation between elements may be allocated according to perceived market conditions. May invest up to 25% of assets in mortgage- and asset-backed securities, up to 10% in zero coupon, pay-in-kind and step coupon securities, up to 15% in illiquid securities, up to 35% of assets in junk bonds, without limit in foreign securities (including those denominated in foreign currencies), and without limit in indexed/structured securities. May use a variety of derivative instruments for hedging purposes. Fund is non-diversified.
Year organized: 1997
Dividends paid: Income - quarterly; Capital gains - annually
Management fee: 0.80%

NATIONS MARYLAND INTERMEDIATE MUNICIPAL BOND FUND
(See first Nations listing for data common to all funds)

Portfolio manager: Dawn Daggy-Mangerson (1997)
Investment objective and policies: High current income exempt from Federal and state taxes, consistent with moderate fluctuation of principal. Invests in investment grade, intermediate-term municipal securities. The average dollar-weighted maturity is between three and ten years; duration between five and six years. May use some derivatives for hedging purposes. Fund is non-diversified.
Year organized: 1990
Ticker symbol: NMDMX
Discount broker availability: Fidelity, Siebert, *White
Dividends paid: Income - declared daily, paid monthly; Capital gains - annually
Portfolio turnover (3 yrs): 10%, 4%, 11%
Management fee: 0.50%
Expense ratio: 0.70% (year ending 3/31/97) (0.98% without waiver)

NATIONS MARYLAND MUNICIPAL BOND FUND
(See first Nations listing for data common to all funds)

Portfolio manager: Dawn Daggy-Mangerson (1997)
Investment objective and policies: High current income exempt from Federal and state taxes, with the potential for principal fluctuation. Invests in investment grade, long-term municipal securities. The average dollar-weighted maturity is greater than ten years and duration is greater than ten years. May use some derivatives for hedging purposes. Fund is non-diversified.
Year organized: 1993
Ticker symbol: NMDIX
Discount broker availability: *White
Dividends paid: Income - declared daily, paid monthly; Capital gains - annually

Portfolio turnover (3 yrs): 18%, 7%, 11%
Management fee: 0.60%
Expense ratio: 0.80% (year ending 3/31/97) (1.32% without waiver)

NATIONS MUNICIPAL INCOME FUND
(See first Nations listing for data common to all funds)

Portfolio manager: Michele M. Poirier (1992)
Investment objective and policies: High current income exempt from Federal income tax, with the potential for principal fluctuation. Invests in investment grade, long-term municipal securities issued by or on behalf of states, territories, and possessions of the U.S., the District of Columbia, and their political subdivisions, agencies, instrumentalities and authorities. The average dollar-weighted maturity is be greater than ten years; the average duration between 7.5 and 9.5 years. May use some derivatives for hedging purposes. Fund is non-diversified.
Year organized: 1991
Ticker symbol: NMUIX
Discount broker availability: Fidelity, Siebert, *White
Dividends paid: Income - declared daily, paid monthly; Capital gains - annually
Portfolio turnover (3 yrs): 25%, 4%, 49%
Management fee: 0.60%
Expense ratio: 0.80% (year ending 3/31/97) (1.11% without waiver)

NATIONS NORTH CAROLINA INTERMEDIATE MUNICIPAL BOND FUND
(See first Nations listing for data common to all funds)

Portfolio manager: Matthew M. Kiselak (1995)
Investment objective and policies: High current income exempt from Federal and state taxes, consistent with moderate fluctuation of principal. Invests in investment grade, intermediate-term municipal securities. The average dollar-weighted maturity is between three and ten years; duration between five and six years. May use some derivatives for hedging purposes. Fund is non-diversified.
Year organized: 1992
Ticker symbol: NNCIX
Discount broker availability: Fidelity, Siebert, *White
Dividends paid: Income - declared daily, paid monthly; Capital gains - annually
Portfolio turnover (3 yrs): 26%, 3%, 57%
Management fee: 0.50%
Expense ratio: 0.70% (year ending 3/31/97) (1.02% without waiver)

NATIONS NORTH CAROLINA MUNICIPAL BOND FUND
(See first Nations listing for data common to all funds)

Portfolio manager: Matthew M. Kiselak (1995)
Investment objective and policies: High current income exempt from Federal and state taxes, with the potential for principal fluctuation. Invests in investment grade, long-term municipal securities. The average dollar-weighted maturity is greater than ten years and duration is greater than ten years. May use some derivatives for hedging purposes. Fund is non-diversified.
Year organized: 1993
Ticker symbol: NNCAX
Discount broker availability: Fidelity, Siebert, *White
Dividends paid: Income - declared daily, paid monthly; Capital gains - annually
Portfolio turnover (3 yrs): 28%, 22%, 40%
Management fee: 0.60%
Expense ratio: 0.80% (year ending 3/31/97) (1.14% without waiver)

NATIONS PACIFIC GROWTH FUND
(See first Nations listing for data common to all funds)

Portfolio manager: Seok Teoh (1995)
Investment objective and policies: Long-term capital growth. Invests primarily in securities of issuers located in or doing at least 50% of their business in the Far East

and the Pacific Basin, except for Japan. May invest in ADRs, GDRs and EDRs, and use puts and calls and forward foreign currency contracts in an effort to enhance performance and for hedging purposes.
Year organized: 1995
Discount broker availability: Fidelity, Siebert, *White
Dividends paid: Income - quarterly; Capital gains - annually
Portfolio turnover (2 yrs): 78%, 23%
Management fee: 0.90%
Expense ratio: 1.67% (year ending 3/31/97)

NATIONS PRIME MONEY MARKET FUND
(See first Nations listing for data common to all funds)

Portfolio manager: Martha L. Sherman (1990)
Investment objective and policies: Maximum current income consistent with the preservation of capital and the maintenance of liquidity. Invests in short-term government- and bank-issued money market instruments. May also invest in other investment companies.
Year organized: 1990
Ticker symbol: NPRXX
Dividends paid: Income - declared daily, paid monthly
Management fee: 0.25% first $250M, 0.20% over $250M
Expense ratio: 0.65% (year ending 3/31/97) (0.70% without waiver)

NATIONS SHORT-INTERMEDIATE GOVERNMENT FUND
(See first Nations listing for data common to all funds)

Portfolio manager: John Swaim (1992)
Investment objective and policies: High current income consistent with prudent investment risk. Invests virtually all assets in obligations issued or guaranteed by the U.S. Government. The average dollar-weighted maturity of the fund is three to five years, and the average duration will not exceed five years. May also invest in corporate convertible and non-convertible debt.
Year organized: 1991 (absorbed the Pilot Intermediate U.S. Govt. Securities fund 5/16/97)
Ticker symbol: NSIGX
Discount broker availability: Fidelity, Siebert, *White
Dividends paid: Income - declared daily, paid monthly; Capital gains - annually
Portfolio turnover (3 yrs): 529%, 189%, 328%
Management fee: 0.60%
Expense ratio: 0.83% (year ending 3/31/97) (1.03% without waiver)

NATIONS SHORT-TERM INCOME FUND
(See first Nations listing for data common to all funds)

Portfolio manager: Patrick Frith (1997)
Investment objective and policies: High current income consistent with prudent investment risk. Invests primarily in investment grade corporate bonds and mortgage backed bonds. The average dollar-weighted maturity and duration will generally not exceed three years. May invest up to 25% of assets in foreign issues.
Year organized: 1992
Ticker symbol: NSTRX
Discount broker availability: Fidelity, Siebert, *White
Dividends paid: Income - declared daily, paid monthly; Capital gains - annually
Portfolio turnover (3 yrs): 172%, 73%, 224%
Management fee: 0.60%
Expense ratio: 0.75% (year ending 3/31/97) (1.05% without waiver)

NATIONS SHORT-TERM MUNICIPAL INCOME FUND
(See first Nations listing for data common to all funds)

Portfolio manager: Dawn Daggy-Mangerson (1997)
Investment objective and policies: High current income exempt from Federal income tax, consistent

with minimal fluctuation of principal. Invests in investment grade, short-term municipal securities issued by or on behalf of states, territories and possessions of the U.S., the District of Columbia, and their political subdivisions, agencies, instrumentalities and authorities. The average dollar-weighted maturity is be less than three years; the average duration between 1.25 and 2.75 years. May use some derivatives for hedging purposes. Fund is non-diversified.
Year organized: 1993
Ticker symbol: NSMMX
Discount broker availability: Fidelity, Siebert, *White
Dividends paid: Income - declared daily, paid monthly; Capital gains - annually
Portfolio turnover (3 yrs): 80%, 16%, 82%
Management fee: 0.50%
Expense ratio: 0.60% (year ending 3/31/97) (1.04% without waiver)

NATIONS SMALL COMPANY GROWTH FUND
(See first Nations listing for data common to all funds)

Portfolio manager: Scott A. Billeadeau (1997)
Investment objective and policies: Long-term capital growth. Invests at least 65% of assets in equity securities of companies with market capitalizations of less than $1B that are thought to offer growth potential. Weighted median capitalization of fund holdings should not exceed 125% of that of the Russel 2000 Small Stock Index. May invest up to 35% of assets in larger concerns, and up to 10% of assets in investment grade debt obligations.
Year organized: 1995 (Nations acquired the Pilot Small Cap Equity fund 5/23/97 and merged it into this fund, which began then.)
Dividends paid: Income - monthly; Capital gains - annually
Portfolio turnover (2 yrs): 48%, 31%
Management fee: 1.00%
Expense ratio: 1.23% (year ending 5/16/97) (1.66% without waiver)

NATIONS SOUTH CAROLINA INTERMEDIATE MUNICIPAL BOND FUND
(See first Nations listing for data common to all funds)

Portfolio manager: Michele M. Poirier (1992)
Investment objective and policies: High current income exempt from Federal and state taxes, consistent with moderate fluctuation of principal. Invests in investment grade, intermediate-term municipal securities. The average dollar-weighted maturity is between three and ten years; duration between five and six years. May use some derivatives for hedging purposes. Fund is non-diversified.
Year organized: 1992
Ticker symbol: NSCIX
Discount broker availability: Fidelity, Siebert, *White
Dividends paid: Income - declared daily, paid monthly; Capital gains - annually
Portfolio turnover (3 yrs): 13%, 6%, 11%
Management fee: 0.50%
Expense ratio: 0.70% (year ending 3/31/97) (0.99% without waiver)

NATIONS SOUTH CAROLINA MUNICIPAL BOND FUND
(See first Nations listing for data common to all funds)

Portfolio manager: Michele M. Poirier (1993)
Investment objective and policies: High current income exempt from Federal and state taxes, with the potential for principal fluctuation. Invests in investment grade, long-term municipal securities. The average dollar-weighted maturity is greater than ten years and duration is greater than ten years. May use some derivatives for hedging purposes. Fund is non-diversified.
Year organized: 1993
Ticker symbol: NSCAX
Discount broker availability: Fidelity, Siebert, *White

Dividends paid: Income - declared daily, paid monthly; Capital gains - annually
Portfolio turnover (3 yrs): 30%, 20%, 13%
Management fee: 0.60%
Expense ratio: 0.80% (year ending 3/31/97) (0.99% without waiver)

NATIONS STRATEGIC FIXED INCOME FUND
(See first Nations listing for data common to all funds)

Portfolio manager: Mark S. Ahnrud (1993)
Investment objective and policies: Maximum total return. Actively manages investment grade fixed-income securities. May invest in corporate convertible and non-convertible debt, as well as U.S. Government issues and dollar-denominated debt securities from foreign entities. The average dollar-weighted maturity of the fund is generally ten years or less, and will never exceed 15 years.
Year organized: 1992 (absorbed the Pilot Diversified Bond Fund 5/16/97)
Ticker symbol: NSFAX
Discount broker availability: Fidelity, Siebert, *White
Dividends paid: Income - declared daily, paid monthly; Capital gains - annually
Portfolio turnover (3 yrs): 368%, 133%, 228%
Management fee: 0.60%
Expense ratio: 0.91% (year ending 3/31/97) (1.01% without waiver)

NATIONS TAX-EXEMPT MONEY MARKET FUND
(See first Nations listing for data common to all funds)

Portfolio manager: Melinda Allen Crosby (1992)
Investment objective and policies: High current income exempt from federal income taxes, consistent with liquidity and stability of principal. Invests in a diversified portfolio of obligations issued by or on the behalf of states, territories and possessions of the U.S. or the District of Columbia, or their agencies or instrumentalities.
Year organized: 1991
Ticker symbol: NTEXX
Dividends paid: Income - declared daily, paid monthly
Management fee: 0.40%
Expense ratio: 0.55% (year ending 3/31/97) (0.80% without waiver)

NATIONS TENNESSEE INTERMEDIATE MUNICIPAL BOND FUND
(See first Nations listing for data common to all funds)

Portfolio manager: Matthew M. Kiselak (1994)
Investment objective and policies: High current income exempt from Federal and state taxes, consistent with moderate fluctuation of principal. Invests in investment grade, intermediate-term municipal securities. The average dollar-weighted maturity is between three and ten years; duration between five and six years. May use some derivatives for hedging purposes. Fund is non-diversified.
Year organized: 1993
Discount broker availability: *White
Dividends paid: Income - declared daily, paid monthly; Capital gains - annually
Portfolio turnover (3 yrs): 28%, 3%, 34%
Management fee: 0.50%
Expense ratio: 0.70% (year ending 3/31/97) (1.13% without waiver)

NATIONS TENNESSEE MUNICIPAL BOND FUND
(See first Nations listing for data common to all funds)

Portfolio manager: Matthew M. Kiselak (1994)
Investment objective and policies: High current income exempt from Federal and state taxes, with the potential for principal fluctuation. Invests in investment grade, long-term municipal securities. The average dollar-weighted maturity is greater than ten years and duration is greater than ten years. May use some derivatives for hedging purposes. Fund is non-diversified.

Year organized: 1993
Discount broker availability: *White
Dividends paid: Income - declared daily, paid monthly; Capital gains - annually
Portfolio turnover (3 yrs): 31%, 2%, 45%
Management fee: 0.60%
Expense ratio: 0.80% (year ending 3/31/97) (1.44% without waiver)

NATIONS TEXAS INTERMEDIATE MUNICIPAL BOND FUND
(See first Nations listing for data common to all funds)

Portfolio manager: Matthew M. Kiselak (1994)
Investment objective and policies: High current income exempt from Federal and state taxes, consistent with moderate fluctuation of principal. Invests in investment grade, intermediate-term municipal securities. The average dollar-weighted maturity is between three and ten years; duration between five and six years. May use some derivatives for hedging purposes. Fund is non-diversified.
Year organized: 1993
Discount broker availability: *White
Dividends paid: Income - declared daily, paid monthly; Capital gains - annually
Portfolio turnover (3 yrs): 34%, 11%, 64%
Management fee: 0.50%
Expense ratio: 0.70% (year ending 3/31/97) (1.04% without waiver)

NATIONS TEXAS MUNICIPAL BOND FUND
(See first Nations listing for data common to all funds)

Portfolio manager: Matthew M. Kiselak (1994)
Investment objective and policies: High current income exempt from Federal and state taxes, with the potential for principal fluctuation. Invests in investment grade, long-term municipal securities. The average dollar-weighted maturity is greater than ten years and duration is greater than ten years. May use some derivatives for hedging purposes. Fund is non-diversified.
Year organized: 1993
Discount broker availability: *White
Dividends paid: Income - declared daily, paid monthly; Capital gains - annually
Portfolio turnover (3 yrs): 52%, 6%, 50%
Management fee: 0.60%
Expense ratio: 0.80% (year ending 3/31/97) (1.23% without waiver)

NATIONS TREASURY MONEY MARKET FUND
(See first Nations listing for data common to all funds)

Portfolio manager: Sandra L. Duck (1993)
Investment objective and policies: Maximum current income consistent with the preservation of capital and the maintenance of liquidity. Invest in short-term money market instruments issued or insured by the U.S. Treasury.
Year organized: 1990
Ticker symbol: NTSXX
Dividends paid: Income - declared daily, paid monthly
Management fee: 0.25% first $250M, 0.20% over $250M
Expense ratio: 0.65% (year ending 3/31/97) (0.70% without waiver)

NATIONS U.S. GOVERNMENT BOND FUND
(See first Nations listing for data common to all funds)

Sub-adviser: Boatmen's Capital Management, Inc.
Investment objective and policies: Current income consistent with reasonable risk. Invests primarily in debt obligations issued or guaranteed by the U.S. Government, its agencies or instrumentalities, or repurchase agreements thereon.
Year organized: 1995 (began as the Pilot U.S. Government Securities fund. Acquired by Nations and renamed 5/23/97.)
Dividends paid: Income - declared daily, paid monthly; Capital gains - annually

Portfolio turnover (3 yrs): 58%, 87%, 132%
Management fee: 0.60%
Expense ratio: 0.87% (year ending 5/16/97) (1.07% without waiver)

NATIONS VALUE FUND
(See first Nations listing for data common to all funds)

Portfolio manager: Sharon M. Herrmann (1989)
Investment objective and policies: Long-term capital growth; income secondary. Invests at least 65% of assets in common stocks of domestic companies with market capitalizations exceeding $300M that are perceived to be undervalued. Fund may also invest in foreign issues, and invest up to 20% of assets in investment grade, domestic corporate and government fixed-income securities.
Year organized: 1989
Ticker symbol: NVLEX
Discount broker availability: Fidelity, Siebert, *White
Dividends paid: Income - quarterly; Capital gains - annually
Portfolio turnover (3 yrs): 47%, 12%, 63%
Management fee: 0.75%
Expense ratio: 1.22% (year ending 3/31/97)

NATIONS VIRGINIA INTERMEDIATE MUNICIPAL BOND FUND
(See first Nations listing for data common to all funds)

Portfolio manager: Dawn Daggy-Mangerson (1997)
Investment objective and policies: High current income exempt from Federal and state taxes, consistent with moderate fluctuation of principal. Invests in investment grade, intermediate-term municipal securities. The average dollar-weighted maturity is between three and ten years; duration between five and six years. May use some derivatives for hedging purposes. Fund is non-diversified.
Year organized: 1989
Ticker symbol: NVAFX
Discount broker availability: Fidelity, Siebert, *White
Dividends paid: Income - declared daily, paid monthly; Capital gains - annually
Portfolio turnover (3 yrs): 20%, 2%, 22%
Management fee: 0.50%
Expense ratio: 0.70% (year ending 3/31/97) (0.94% without waiver)

NATIONS VIRGINIA MUNICIPAL BOND FUND
(See first Nations listing for data common to all funds)

Portfolio manager: Dawn Daggy-Mangerson (1997)
Investment objective and policies: High current income exempt from Federal and state taxes, with the potential for principal fluctuation. Invests in investment grade, long-term municipal securities. The average dollar-weighted maturity is greater than ten years and duration is greater than ten years. May use some derivatives for hedging purposes. Fund is non-diversified.
Year organized: 1993
Discount broker availability: Fidelity, Siebert, *White
Dividends paid: Income - declared daily, paid monthly; Capital gains - annually
Portfolio turnover (3 yrs): 37%, 8%, 16%
Management fee: 0.60%
Expense ratio: 0.80% (year ending 3/31/97) (1.18% without waiver)

NAVELLIER FUNDS
(Data common to all Navellier funds are shown below. See subsequent listings for data specific to individual funds.)

One East Liberty, Third Floor
Reno, NV 89501-2110
800-887-8671, 702-785-2300
shareholder services 800-622-1386
fax 702-785-2321
Internet: http://www.navellier.com

Adviser: Navellier Management, Inc.
Transfer agent: Rushmore Trust and Savings, FSB
Minimum purchase: Initial: $2,000, Subsequent: $100; IRA: Initial: $500

Wire orders accepted: Yes
Deadline for same day wire purchase: 4 P.M.
Qualified for sale in: All states (NE is broker only)
Telephone redemptions: Yes
Wire redemptions: Yes
Letter redemptions: Signature guarantee required over $1,000
Telephone switching: Performance funds may switch amongst one another (for open funds), but Series Aggressive Small Cap Equity cannot switch
Number of switches permitted: 1 per 30 days, 10 per year, $5 fee after 5 per year
Shareholder services: IRA, automatic investment plan, systematic withdrawal plan min. bal. req. $25,000
IRA fees: Annual $10, Closing $10 (or $100 one-time fee)

NAVELLIER PERFORMANCE: AGGRESSIVE GROWTH PORTFOLIO
(See first Navellier listing for data common to all funds)

Portfolio managers: Louis G. Navellier (1995), Alan Alpers (1995)
Investment objective and policies: Long-term capital appreciation. Invests primarily in equity securities of companies believed to be undervalued. Fund is non-diversified, and may invest up to 10% of assets in a single company and up to 25% of assets in one industry sector. May invest in companies of any market capitalization. May also invest up to 35% of assets in corporate and government debt securities of the four highest grades as rated by the national rating services. Any debt securities falling below this rating while held will be promptly disposed of. May make short sales against the box.
Year organized: 1995
Ticker symbol: NPFGX
Discount broker availability: *Fidelity, *Schwab, *Siebert, *White
Dividends paid: Income - December; Capital gains - December
Portfolio turnover (2 yrs): 247%, 169%
Management fee: 1.25%
12b-1 distribution fee: 0.25%
Expense ratio: 2.00% (year ending 12/31/97)

NAVELLIER PERFORMANCE: AGGRESSIVE SMALL CAP PORTFOLIO ◆
(See first Navellier listing for data common to all funds)

Portfolio managers: Louis G. Navellier (1997), Alan Alpers (1997)
Investment objective and policies: Long-term capital growth. Invests in equity securities of foreign and domestic issuers with market capitalizations below $1B, perceived to demonstrate strong appreciation potential. May invest up to 25% of assets in a single industry sector. May also invest up to 35% of assets in corporate and government debt securities of the four highest grades as rated by the national rating services. Any debt securities falling below this rating while held will be promptly disposed of. May make short sales against the box.
Year organized: 1997
Ticker symbol: NPMCX
Discount broker availability: *Fidelity, *Schwab, White
Dividends paid: Income - December; Capital gains - December
Management fee: 1.15%

NAVELLIER PERFORMANCE: AGGRESSIVE SMALL CAP EQUITY PORTFOLIO ◆
(See first Navellier listing for data common to all funds)

Portfolio managers: Louis G. Navellier (1997), Alan Alpers (1997)
Investment objective and policies: Long-term growth of capital. Invests in equity securities of for-

eign and domestic issuers that trade in the U.S. markets with market capitalizations above $1B and are perceived to demonstrate strong appreciation potential. May invest up to 25% of assets in a single industry sector. May also invest up to 35% of assets in corporate and government debt securities of the four highest grades as rated by the national rating services. Any debt securities falling below this rating while held will be promptly disposed of. May make short sales against the box.
Year organized: 1997
Discount broker availability: *Fidelity, *Schwab, White
Dividends paid: Income - December; Capital gains - December
Management fee: 1.15%

NAVELLIER PERFORMANCE: INTERNATIONAL EQUITY PORTFOLIO
(See first Navellier listing for data common to all funds)

Sub-adviser: Global Value Investors, Inc.
Portfolio manager: Ram Kolluri (1997)
Investment objective and policies: Long-term growth of capital. Invests at least 65% of assets in equity securities of companies which are perceived to offer growth opportunities at a reasonable price at the time of purchase. Holdings are diversified across at least three different foreign countries. May invest up to 35% of assets in non-equity securities. May use certain derivative instruments for hedging purposes.
Year organized: 1997
Discount broker availability: *Fidelity, *Schwab, *White
Dividends paid: Income - December; Capital gains - December
Management fee: 1.00%
12b-1 distribution fee: 0.25%

NAVELLIER PERFORMANCE: LARGE CAP GROWTH PORTFOLIO
(See first Navellier listing for data common to all funds)

Portfolio managers: Louis G. Navellier (1997), Alan Alpers (1997)
Investment objective and policies: Long-term capital growth. Invests at least 65% of assets in companies with market capitalizations exceeding $5B that are perceived to offer appreciation potential. As a non-diversified portfolio, fund may invest up to 10% of assets in one company and up to 25% in a single industry segment. May invest up to 10% of assets in illiquid securities and use "short sales against the box."
Year organized: 1997
Discount broker availability: *Fidelity, *Schwab
Dividends paid: Income - December; Capital gains - December
Management fee: 1.15%
12b-1 distribution fee: 0.25%

NAVELLIER PERFORMANCE: LARGE CAP VALUE PORTFOLIO
(See first Navellier listing for data common to all funds)

Portfolio managers: Louis G. Navellier (1997), Alan Alpers (1997)
Investment objective and policies: Long-term capital growth. Invests at least 65% of assets in equity securities traded in all U.S. markets, including dollar denominated foreign securities. Securities are primarily of companies with market capitalizations exceeding $5B that are perceived to be undervalued. May invest up to 10% of assets in illiquid securities and use "short sales against the box."
Year organized: 1997
Discount broker availability: *Fidelity, *Schwab
Dividends paid: Income - December; Capital gains - December
Management fee: 0.75%
12b-1 distribution fee: 0.25%

NAVELLIER PERFORMANCE: MID CAP GROWTH PORTFOLIO

(See first Navellier listing for data common to all funds)

Portfolio managers: Louis G. Navellier (1996), Alan Alpers (1996)
Investment objective and policies: Long-term capital growth. Invests in equity securities of companies traded in U.S. markets, including dollar-denominated foreign issues, with market capitalizations between $1B and $5B perceived to be undervalued. May invest up to 25% of assets in a single industry sector. May also invest up to 35% of assets in corporate and government debt securities of the four highest grades as rated by the national rating services without limit. Any debt securities falling below this rating while held will be promptly disposed of. May make short sales against the box.
Year organized: 1996
Discount broker availability: *Fidelity, *Schwab, Siebert, *White
Dividends paid: Income - December; Capital gains - December
Portfolio turnover (1 yr): 163%
Management fee: 1.25%
12b-1 distribution fee: 0.25%
Expense ratio: 2.00% (year ending 12/31/97)

NAVELLIER PERFORMANCE: SMALL CAP VALUE PORTFOLIO

(See first Navellier listing for data common to all funds)

Portfolio managers: Louis G. Navellier (1997), Alan Alpers (1997)
Investment objective and policies: Long-term capital growth. Invests at least 65% of assets in companies with market capitalizations of less than $1B that are perceived to be undervalued at the time of purchase. Invests in equity securities of companies traded on all U.S. markets, including dollar denominated foreign issues. May invest up to 10% of assets in illiquid securities and use "short sales against the box."
Year organized: 1997
Discount broker availability: *Fidelity, *Schwab
Dividends paid: Income - December; Capital gains - December
Management fee: 1.00%
12b-1 distribution fee: 0.25%

NAVELLIER SERIES: AGGRESSIVE SMALL CAP EQUITY PORTFOLIO

(See first Navellier listing for data common to all funds)

Portfolio manager: Louis G. Navellier (1997)
Investment objective and policies: Long-term growth of capital. Invests primarily in the common stock of domestic companies with market capitalizations of less than $1B that are perceived to offer capital appreciation. May invest up to 35% of assets in equity securities of larger companies as well, or up to 35% of assets in non-equity securities.
Year organized: 1994
Ticker symbol: NASCX
Special sales information: Prior to the end of 1997 this fund carried a 3% load; fund is now a no-load.
Discount broker availability: *Fidelity, *Schwab
Dividends paid: Income - December; Capital gains - December
Portfolio turnover (3 yrs): 184%, 137%, 170%
Management fee: 1.15%
12b-1 distribution fee: 0.25%
Expense ratio: 1.75% (year ending 12/31/97)

NEEDHAM GROWTH FUND

445 Park Avenue
New York, NY 10022
800-625-7071, 212-371-8300

Adviser: Needham Investment Management, LLC
Portfolio manager: Howard S. Schachter (1995)
Transfer agent: PFPC Inc.
Investment objective and policies: Long-term capital appreciation. Invests primarily in equity securities of companies perceived to present superior growth rates.

Fund will normally retain 65% of assets in this category, with the ability to invest the balance in other securities or cash. May invest up to 25% of assets in securities of foreign issuers, 15% in illiquid securities, 35% of assets in debt securities, and up to 10% of assets in junk bonds. May use a variety of derivative instruments for hedging purposes. Fund is non-diversified.
Year organized: 1995
Ticker symbol: NEEGX
Minimum purchase: Initial: $1,500, Subsequent: $100; IRA: Initial: $2,000; Automatic investment plan: Subsequent: $50
Wire orders accepted: Yes
Deadline for same day wire purchase: 4 P.M.
Discount broker availability: *Fidelity, *Schwab, *White
Qualified for sale in: All states except AL, IN, IA, ME, MN, NE, NM, NY, VT
Telephone redemptions: Yes (1 every 30 days), $1,000 minimum, $10,000 maximum
Wire redemptions: Yes, $5,000 minimum, $7.50 fee
Letter redemptions: Signature guarantee required over $50,000
Redemption fee: 0.50% for shares held less than 6 months
Dividends paid: Income - December; Capital gains - December
Portfolio turnover (1 yr): 569%
Shareholder services: IRA, SEP-IRA
Management fee: 1.25%
12b-1 distribution fee: 0.25%
Expense ratio: 2.50% (year ending 12/31/96)
IRA fees: Annual $10

NEUBERGER & BERMAN FUNDS ◆

(Data common to all Neuberger & Berman funds are shown below. See subsequent listings for data specific to individual funds.)

605 Third Avenue, 2nd Floor
New York, NY 10158-0180
800-877-9700, 212-476-8800
automated services 800-335-9366
fax 212-476-8848
Internet: http://www.nbfunds.com
e-mail: questions@nbfunds.com

Shareholder service hours: Full service: M-F 8 A.M.-8 P.M., Sat 8 A.M.-6 P.M. EST; After hours service: prices, yields, balances, orders, last transaction, news, messages, indices, prospectuses, total returns
Adviser: Neuberger & Berman Management, Inc.
Transfer agent: State Street Bank & Trust Co.
Objectives and policies: All funds invest their assets in underlying portfolios of the same objective. Expense ratios and administrative fees given here represent the 'fund;' portfolio turnover and management fees represent the underlying 'portfolio.'
Wire orders accepted: Yes, $1,000 subsequent minimum
Deadline for same day wire purchase: 4 P.M. (12 NN for money markets)
Qualified for sale in: All states (except New York Insured Intermediate)
Telephone redemptions: Yes, $500 minimum
Wire redemptions: Yes, $1,000 minimum, $8 fee
Letter redemptions: Signature guarantee required over $50,000
Telephone switching: With other Neuberger & Berman funds. $1,000 minimum ($2,000 if first investment in bond fund)
Number of switches permitted: Monitored
Shareholder services: IRA, SEP-IRA, Keogh, 401(k), 403(b), corporate retirement plans, electronic funds transfer, systematic withdrawal plan min. bal. req. $5,000
IRA/Keogh fees: Annual $12 for all accounts

NEUBERGER & BERMAN CASH RESERVES ◆

(See first Neuberger & Berman listing for data common to all funds)

Portfolio managers: Theodore P. Giuliano (1996), Josephine P. Mahaney (1993)
Investment objective and policies: Highest current income consistent with safety and liquidity. Invests in high-quality U.S. denominated money market instruments of both foreign and domestic issuers.

Year organized: 1988
Ticker symbol: NBCXX
Group fund code: 420
Minimum purchase: Initial: $2,000, Subsequent: $100; IRA/Keogh: Initial: $250; Automatic investment plan: Initial: $100
Check redemptions: $250 minimum
Dividends paid: Income - declared daily, paid monthly
Management fee: 0.52% first $500M to 0.42% over $2B
Expense ratio: 0.63% (year ending 10/31/97)

NEUBERGER & BERMAN FOCUS FUND ◆

(See first Neuberger & Berman listing for data common to all funds)

Portfolio managers: Kent C. Simons (1988), Kevin L. Risen (1996)
Investment objective and policies: Long-term capital appreciation. Invests in common stocks from 13 diversified economic sectors using a value oriented approach. Normally at least 90% of assets are in up to six sectors believed undervalued. May invest up to 10% of assets in foreign securities, up to 15% in illiquid securities, and use covered call options for hedging purposes.
Year organized: 1955 (formerly Energy Fund, name changed to Selected Sectors Plus Energy and objective changed in 1988. Name and objective changed to Selected Sectors 10/91, and to current name 1/1/95.)
Ticker symbol: NBSSX (NBFCX for Trust Shares)
Group fund code: 494
Minimum purchase: Initial: $1,000, Subsequent: $100; IRA/Keogh: Initial: $250; Automatic investment plan: Initial: $100
Discount broker availability: *Fidelity, *Schwab, *Siebert, *White
Dividends paid: Income - December; Capital gains - December
Portfolio turnover (3 yrs): 63%, 39%, 36%
Management fee: 0.55% first $250M to 0.425% over $1.5B
Administration fee: 0.26%
Expense ratio: 0.86% (year ending 8/31/97)

NEUBERGER & BERMAN GENESIS FUND ◆

(See first Neuberger & Berman listing for data common to all funds)

Portfolio managers: Judith M. Vale (1994), Robert W. D'Alelio (1997)
Investment objective and policies: Long-term capital growth. Invests primarily in a widely diversified portfolio of common stocks of small to mid-sized companies with market capitalizations of $1.5B or less, considered undervalued on a current earnings basis. May invest up to 10% of assets in foreign securities, up to 15% in illiquid securities, and use covered call options for hedging purposes.
Year organized: 1988
Ticker symbol: NBGNX (NBGEX for Trust Shares)
Group fund code: 493
Sales restrictions: Fund closed to new investors 3/6/98
Minimum purchase: Initial: $1,000, Subsequent: $100; IRA/Keogh: Initial: $250; Automatic investment plan: Initial: $100
Discount broker availability: *Fidelity, *Schwab, *Siebert, *White
Dividends paid: Income - December; Capital gains - December
Portfolio turnover (3 yrs): 18%, 21%, 37%
Management fee: 0.85% first $250M to 0.65% over $1B
Administration fee: 0.26%
Expense ratio: 1.16% (year ending 8/31/97) (1.26% without waiver)

NEUBERGER & BERMAN GOVERNMENT MONEY FUND ◆

(See first Neuberger & Berman listing for data common to all funds)

Portfolio managers: Theodore P. Giuliano (1996), Josephine P. Mahaney (1993)
Investment objective and policies: Highest available

current income consistent with maximum safety and liquidity. Invests in U.S. Treasury obligations and other money market instruments backed by the "full faith and credit" of the U.S. Government.
Year organized: 1983
Ticker symbol: NBGXX
Group fund code: 419
Minimum purchase: Initial: $2,000, Subsequent: $100; IRA/Keogh: Initial: $250; Automatic investment plan: Initial: $100
Check redemptions: $250 minimum
Dividends paid: Income - declared daily, paid monthly
Management fee: 0.52% first $500M to 0.42% over $2B
Expense ratio: 0.63% (year ending 10/31/97) (0.64% without waiver)

NEUBERGER & BERMAN GUARDIAN FUND ◆
(See first Neuberger & Berman listing for data common to all funds)

Portfolio managers: Kent C. Simons (1983), Kevin L. Risen (1995)
Investment objective and policies: Capital appreciation; current income secondary. Invests in dividend-paying common stocks of long-established, well-managed companies selected on a value basis. May invest up to 10% of assets in foreign securities, up to 15% in illiquid securities, and use covered call options for hedging purposes.
Year organized: 1950 (split 3 for 1 on 1/20/93)
Ticker symbol: NGUAX (NBGTX for Trust Shares)
Group fund code: 484
Minimum purchase: Initial: $1,000, Subsequent: $100; IRA/Keogh: Initial: $250; Automatic investment plan: Initial: $100
Discount broker availability: *Fidelity, *Schwab, *Siebert, *White
Dividends paid: Income - March, June, September, December; Capital gains - December
Portfolio turnover (3 yrs): 50%, 37%, 26%
Management fee: 0.55% first $250M to 0.425% over $1.5B
Administration fee: 0.26%
Expense ratio: 0.80% (year ending 8/31/97)

NEUBERGER & BERMAN HIGH YIELD BOND FUND ◆
(See first Neuberger & Berman listing for data common to all funds)

Portfolio manager: Team managed
Investment objective and policies: High current income; capital growth secondary. Invests at least 65% of assets in a diversified portfolio of lower-rated junk bonds. Portfolio has no limits on the minimum quality or duration of its holdings. May invest up to 25% of assets in foreign securities, up to 15% in illiquid securities, and use covered put and call options and interest rate futures contracts for hedging purposes.
Year organized: 1998
Minimum purchase: Initial: $2,000, Subsequent: $100; Automatic investment plan: Initial: $100
Dividends paid: Income - declared daily, paid monthly; Capital gains - December
Management fee: 0.38% first $500M to 0.28% over $1.5B
Administration fee: 0.26%

NEUBERGER & BERMAN INTERNATIONAL FUND ◆
(See first Neuberger & Berman listing for data common to all funds)

Portfolio manager: Valerie Chang (1997)
Investment objective and policies: Long-term capital appreciation. Invests primarily in equity securities of medium to large capitalization companies traded on foreign exchanges. Will normally invest in at least three countries with up to 50% of assets in Japan. May use ADRs, EDRs, GDRs and IDRs, use options and futures for hedging purposes, and sell short. Up to 15% of assets may be in illiquid securities and 10% in other mutual funds.
Year organized: 1994
Ticker symbol: NBISX
Group fund code: 341

Minimum purchase: Initial: $1,000, Subsequent: $100; IRA/Keogh: Initial: $250; Automatic investment plan: Initial: $100
Discount broker availability: *Fidelity, *Schwab, *Siebert, *White
Dividends paid: Income - December; Capital gains - December
Portfolio turnover (3 yrs): 37%, 45%, 41%
Management fee: 0.85% first $250M to 0.725% over $1.5B
Administration fee: 0.26%
Expense ratio: 1.70% (year ended 8/31/97)

NEUBERGER & BERMAN LIMITED MATURITY BOND FUND ◆
(See first Neuberger & Berman listing for data common to all funds)

Portfolio managers: Theodore P. Giuliano (1996), Thomas G. Wolfe (1995)
Investment objective and policies: High current income consistent with low risk to principal and liquidity; total return secondary. Invests primarily in short- to intermediate-term investment grade debt securities with a dollar-weighted average maturity of five years or less. May invest up to 10% of assets in securities rated below Baa or BBB, but none lower than B. May use options and futures in an effort to increase returns and for hedging purposes.
Year organized: 1986 (absorbed Ultra Short Bond fund 2/27/98)
Ticker symbol: NLMBX
Group fund code: 483
Minimum purchase: Initial: $2,000, Subsequent: $100; IRA/Keogh: Initial: $250; Automatic investment plan: Initial: $100
Discount broker availability: *Fidelity, *Schwab, *Siebert, *White
Dividends paid: Income - declared daily, paid monthly; Capital gains - December
Portfolio turnover (3 yrs): 89%, 169%, 88%
Management fee: 0.52% first $500M to 0.42% over $2B
Expense ratio: 0.70% (year ending 10/31/97)

NEUBERGER & BERMAN MANHATTAN FUND ◆
(See first Neuberger & Berman listing for data common to all funds)

Portfolio managers: Jennifer K. Silver (1997), Brooke A. Cobb (1997)
Investment objective and policies: Long-term capital appreciation. Invests primarily in common stocks and securities convertible into common stocks of companies of any size believed to have maximum potential for growth. May also invest in preferred stocks and debt securities with potential for capital growth. May invest up to 10% of assets in foreign securities, up to 15% in illiquid securities, and use covered call options for hedging purposes.
Year organized: 1966 (Neuberger-Berman management since 3/1/79)
Ticker symbol: NMANX (NBMTX for Trust Shares)
Group fund code: 491
Minimum purchase: Initial: $1,000, Subsequent: $100; IRA/Keogh: Initial: $250; Automatic investment plan: Initial: $100
Discount broker availability: *Fidelity, *Schwab, *Siebert, *White
Dividends paid: Income - December, Capital gains - December
Portfolio turnover (3 yrs): 89%, 53%, 44%
Management fee: 0.55% first $250M to 0.425% over $1.5B
Administration fee: 0.26%
Expense ratio: 0.98% (year ending 8/31/96) (0.99% without waiver)

NEUBERGER & BERMAN MUNICIPAL MONEY FUND ◆
(See first Neuberger & Berman listing for data common to all funds)

Portfolio managers: Theodore P. Giuliano (1996), Clara Del Pillar (1993)
Investment objective and policies: Maximum current income exempt from federal income tax, consis-

tent with safety and liquidity. Invests in short-term, tax-exempt municipal money market securities.
Year organized: 1984 (formerly Neuberger & Berman Tax-Free Money Fund)
Ticker symbol: NBTXX
Group fund code: 421
Minimum purchase: Initial: $2,000, Subsequent: $100; Automatic investment plan: Initial: $100
Check redemptions: $250 minimum
Dividends paid: Income - declared daily, paid monthly
Management fee: 0.52% first $500M to 0.42% over $2B
Expense ratio: 0.72% (year ending 10/31/97) (0.73% without waiver)

NEUBERGER & BERMAN MUNICIPAL SECURITIES TRUST ◆
(See first Neuberger & Berman listing for data common to all funds)

Portfolio managers: Theodore P. Giuliano (1996), Clara Del Pillar (1991)
Investment objective and policies: High current tax-exempt income with low risk to principal, limited price fluctuation and liquidity; total return secondary. Invests in municipal securities rated A or better, and maintains a dollar-weighted average maturity of 12 years or less.
Year organized: 1987
Ticker symbol: NBMUX
Group fund code: 423
Minimum purchase: Initial: $2,000, Subsequent: $100; Automatic investment plan: Initial: $100
Discount broker availability: *Schwab, *White
Dividends paid: Income - declared daily, paid monthly; Capital gains - December
Portfolio turnover (3 yrs): 22%, 3%, 66%
Management fee: 0.52% first $500M to 0.42% over $2B
Expense ratio: 0.65% (year ending 10/31/97) (0.66% without waiver)

NEUBERGER & BERMAN NEW YORK INSURED INTERMEDIATE FUND ◆
(Fund liquidated 10/24/97)

NEUBERGER & BERMAN PARTNERS FUND ◆
(See first Neuberger & Berman listing for data common to all funds)

Portfolio managers: Michael M. Kassen (1990), Robert I. Gendelman (1994)
Investment objective and policies: Capital growth with reasonable risk. Invests primarily in common stocks and other equity securities of established companies. Seeks securities believed undervalued based on fundamentals. May invest up to 10% of assets in foreign securities, up to 15% in illiquid securities, and use covered call options for hedging purposes.
Year organized: 1968 (Neuberger & Berman assumed management 1/20/75)
Ticker symbol: NPRTX (NBPTX for Trust Shares)
Group fund code: 492
Minimum purchase: Initial: $1,000, Subsequent: $100; IRA/Keogh: Initial: $250; Automatic investment plan: Initial: $100
Discount broker availability: *Fidelity, *Schwab, *Siebert, *White
Dividends paid: Income - December; Capital gains - December
Portfolio turnover (3 yrs): 77%, 96%, 98%
Management fee: 0.55% first $250M to 0.425% over $1.5B
Administration fee: 0.26%
Expense ratio: 0.81% (year ending 8/31/97)

NEUBERGER & BERMAN SOCIALLY RESPONSIVE FUND ◆
(See first Neuberger & Berman listing for data common to all funds)

Portfolio manager: Janet Prindle (1994)
Investment objective and policies: Long-term appreciation. Invests primarily in securities of companies whose

policies, practices, products and services meet social criteria believed to be characteristic of a better society. portfolio invests primarily in common stocks but may also invest in convertible securities, preferred stock and foreign securities and ADRs of foreign companies that meet the Social Policy. May use futures and options in an effort to enhance income and for hedging purposes, and sell short against the box.

Year organized: 1994
Ticker symbol: NBSRX
Group fund code: 342
Minimum purchase: Initial: $1,000, Subsequent: $100; IRA/Keogh: Initial: $250; Automatic investment plan: Initial: $100
Discount broker availability: *Fidelity, *Schwab, *White
Dividends paid: Income - December; Capital gains - December
Portfolio turnover (3 yrs): 51%, 53%, 58%
Management fee: 0.55% first $250M to 0.425% over $1.5B
Administration fee: 0.26%
Expense ratio: 1.48% (year ending 8/31/97) (1.69% without waiver)

NEUBERGER & BERMAN ULTRA SHORT BOND FUND ◆
(Merged into Limited Maturity fund 2/27/98)

NEWCAP CONTRARIAN FUND
23775 Commerce Park Road
Cleveland, OH 44122
888-816-2946, 216-514-5151

Adviser: Newport Investment Advisors, Inc.
Administrator: AmeriPrime Financial Services, Inc.
Portfolio manager: Kenneth M. Holeski (1996)
Transfer agent: American Data Services, Inc.
Investment objective and policies: Maximum long-term growth. Invests primarily in equity securities of domestic, multinational and foreign companies perceived to be undervalued. May invest in companies of any market capitalization. May invest up to 35% of assets in debt securities of any type or quality. May use a variety of derivative instruments in an effort to enhance performance or for hedging purposes. Fund is non-diversified.
Year organized: 1996 (name changed from Maxim Contrarian fund in 1997)
Minimum purchase: Initial: $2,500, Subsequent: $500; IRA: Initial: $1,000, Subsequent: $100
Wire orders accepted: Yes
Deadline for same day wire purchase: 4 P.M.
Discount broker availability: Fidelity, Siebert, *White
Qualified for sale in: CA, CO, DC, FL, GA, HI, IL, IN, KS, LA, MI, MN, MO, NY, NC, OH, PA, TX, VA, WY
Telephone redemptions: Yes
Wire redemptions: Yes
Letters redemptions: Signature guarantee required
Dividends paid: Income - December; Capital gains - December
Portfolio turnover (2 yrs): 146%, 92%
Shareholder services: IRA, SEP-IRA, automatic investment plan
Management fee: 2.50% (adviser pays all expenses except 12b-1 fee)
Administration fee: 0.10% first $50M to 0.05% over $100M ($30,000 minimum)
12b-1 distribution fee: 0.25%
Expense ratio: 2.83% (year ending 10/31/97)
IRA/Keogh fees: Transfer fee, $12, Closing $15

NEW ENGLAND MONEY MARKET FUNDS ◆
Data common to all New England money market funds are shown below. See subsequent listing for data specific to individual funds.)

399 Boylston Street
Boston, MA 02116
800-225-5478, 617-578-1400
yields 800-346-5984
fax 617-578-1191

Adviser: New England Funds Management, L.P. (a wholly owned subsidiary of the Nvest Cos., L.P.)
Sub-adviser: Back Bay Advisors, L.P.
Transfer agent: State Street Bank & Trust Co.

Minimum purchase: Initial: $1,000, Subsequent: $50; IRA/Keogh: Initial: $250; Automatic investment plan: Initial: $50
Wire orders accepted: Yes
Deadline for same day wire purchase: 4 P.M.
Qualified for sale in: All states
Telephone redemptions: Yes
Wire redemptions: Yes, $5 fee
Letter redemptions: Signature guarantee required over $100,000
Check redemptions: $250 minimum
Redemption fee: Certain shares acquired by exchange from Stock or Bond Series will have a CDSC fee based on class of shares and duration of holdings.
Telephone switching: With other New England funds (which have loads), Loomis Sayles funds, and CGM funds, $500 minimum
Number of switches permitted: Unlimited
Dividends paid: Income - declared daily, paid monthly
Shareholder services: IRA, Keogh, 401(k), 403(b), directed dividends, electronic funds transfer, systematic withdrawal plan min. bal. req. $5,000, VISA redemptions
IRA/Keogh fees: Annual $10 (per social security number)

NEW ENGLAND CASH MANAGEMENT TRUST - MONEY MARKET SERIES ◆
(See first New England listing for data common to all funds)

Portfolio manager: J. Scott Nicholson (1978)
Investment objective and policies: Current income consistent with preservation of capital and liquidity. Invests in high quality money market instruments.
Year organized: 1978
Ticker symbol: NELXX
Management fee: 0.425% first $500M to 0.25% over $2B
Expense ratio: 0.90% (year ending 6/30/97)

NEW ENGLAND CASH MANAGEMENT TRUST - U.S. GOVERNMENT SERIES ◆
(See first New England listing for data common to all funds)

Portfolio manager: J. Scott Nicholson (1982)
Investment objective and policies: Current income consistent with preservation of capital and liquidity. Invests only in obligations backed by the full faith and credit of the U.S. Government and in related repurchase agreements.
Year organized: 1982
Ticker symbol: NUSXX
Management fee: 0.425% first $500M to 0.25% over $2B
Expense ratio: 0.93% (year ending 6/30/97)

NEW ENGLAND TAX EXEMPT MONEY MARKET TRUST ◆
(See first New England listing for data common to all funds)

Portfolio manager: John E. Maloney (1992)
Investment objective and policies: Current income exempt from federal tax, consistent with preservation of capital and liquidity. Invests in high quality short-term fixed, variable and floating rate municipal obligations.
Year organized: 1983
Ticker symbol: NTMXX
Management fee: 0.40% first $100M, 0.30% over $100M
Expense ratio: 0.56% (year ending 6/30/97)

NEW JERSEY DAILY MUNICIPAL INCOME FUND ◆
600 Fifth Avenue, 8th Floor
New York, NY 10020
800-221-3079, 212-830-5200
fax 212-830-5478

Adviser: Reich & Tang Asset Management, L.P.
Portfolio manager: Molly Flewharty (1990)
Transfer agent: Reich & Tang Services, L.P.
Investment objective and policies: Interest income exempt from federal and New Jersey income taxes,

capital preservation, liquidity and stability of principal. Invests in a non-diversified portfolio of high quality, short-term New Jersey municipal obligations.
Year organized: 1990
Ticker symbol: NJDXX
Special sales restrictions: Only class "B" shares of the fund are sold direct and without 12b-1 fees. Statistics represent "B" shares only.
Minimum purchase: Initial: $5,000, Subsequent: $100
Wire orders accepted: Yes
Deadline for same day wire purchase: 12 NN
Qualified for sale in: DE, FL, NJ, NY, PA
Telephone redemptions: Yes
Wire redemptions: Yes, $1,000 minimum
Letter redemptions: Signature guarantee required
Check redemptions: $250 minimum
Telephone switching: With other Reich & Tang money market funds and the R&T Equity Fund
Number of switches permitted: Unlimited, $1,000 minimum
Deadline for same day switch: 12 NN
Check redemptions: $250 minimum
Dividends paid: Income - declared daily, paid monthly; Capital gains - December
Shareholder services: Automatic investment plan, electronic funds transfer, systematic withdrawal plan
Management fee: 0.30%
Administration fee: 0.21%
Shareholder services fee: 0.20%
Expense ratio: 0.61% (year ending 10/31/96)

NEW PROVIDENCE CAPITAL GROWTH FUND ◆
2859 Paces Ferry Road, Suite 2125
Atlanta, GA 30339
800-639-7768, 800-525-3863, 800-510-3128
770-333-0356, fax 770-333-9050
Internet: http://www.npcm.com

Adviser: New Providence Capital Management, LLC
Administrator: The Nottingham Co.
Portfolio managers: John K. Donaldson (1997), Kyle A. Tomlin (1997), Shannon D. Koogle (1997)
Transfer agent: NC Shareholder Services, LLC
Investment objective and policies: Long-term capital growth; current income secondary. Invests approximately 90% of assets in a portfolio of equity securities traded on domestic U.S. exchanges or on over-the-counter markets selected with a primary focus on quality earnings growth at a reasonable price. Minimum eligible market capitalizations are generally over $500M. May invest up to 10% of assets in foreign issues represented by ADRs but likely won't, and up to 10% in illiquid securities.
Year organized: 1997
Ticker symbol: NPCGX
Minimum purchase: Initial: $2,500, Subsequent: $250; IRA: Initial: $1,000; Automatic investment plan: Subsequent: $100
Wire orders accepted: Yes
Deadline for same day wire purchase: 4 P.M.
Qualified for sale in: All states except: AK, AR, DE, HI, IA, ID, KS, MO, MT, ND, NE, NV, NM, OK, OR, PR, RI, SD, UT, VT, WV (will register on request)
Telephone redemptions: Yes (with written confirmation by fax)
Wire redemptions: Yes, $5,000 minimum, $7 fee
Letters redemptions: Signature guarantee required over $50,000
Dividends paid: Income - quarterly; Capital gains - annually
Shareholder services: IRA, SEP-IRA, Keogh, systematic withdrawal plan min. bal. req. $2,500
Management fee: 0.75%
Administration fee: 0.125% first $50M to 0.075% over $100M ($50,000 minimum)
12b-1 distribution fee: 0.25% (currently not imposed)
IRA fees: Annual $15

NEW YORK DAILY TAX-FREE INCOME FUND ◆
600 Fifth Avenue, 8th Floor
New York, NY 10020
800-221-3079, 212-830-5220
fax 212-830-5478

Adviser: Reich & Tang Asset Management, L.P.
Portfolio manager: Molly Flewharty (1985)
Transfer agent: Reich & Tang Services, L.P.

Investment objective and policies: Interest income exempt from federal, NY state and NY city income taxes, capital preservation, liquidity and stability of principal. Invests in a non-diversified portfolio of high quality, short-term New York municipal obligations.
Year organized: 1984 (formerly Empire Tax Free Money Market)
Ticker symbol: NYDXX
Special sales restrictions: Only class "B" shares of the fund are sold direct and without 12b-1 fees. Statistics represent "B" shares only.
Minimum purchase: Initial: $5,000, Subsequent: $100
Wire orders accepted: Yes
Deadline for same day wire purchase: 12 NN
Qualified for sale in: CA, CT, FL, NJ, NY, VA
Telephone redemptions: Yes
Wire redemptions: Yes, $1,000 minimum
Letter redemptions: Signature guarantee required
Telephone switching: With other Reich & Tang money market funds and the R&T Equity Fund
Deadline for same day switch: 12 NN
Number of switches permitted: Unlimited, $1,000 minimum
Check redemptions: $250 minimum
Dividends paid: Income - declared daily, paid monthly; Capital gains - December
Shareholder services: Automatic investment plan, electronic funds transfer, systematic withdrawal plan
Management fee: 0.30%
Administration fee: 0.21%
Expense ratio: 0.62% (year ending 4/30/97)

n/i NUMERIC INVESTORS FAMILY OF MUTUAL FUNDS ◆
(Data common to all n/i numeric funds are shown below. See subsequent listings for data specific to individual funds.)

One Memorial Drive, Fourth Floor
Cambridge, MA 02142
800-686-3742, 617-577-1166
shareholder services 800-348-5031
fax 617-577-0475
Internet: http://www.numeric.com
e-mail: info@numeric.com

Adviser: Numeric Investors, L.P.
Co-administrators: Bear Stearns Funds Management, Inc., and PFPC Inc.
Transfer agent: PFPC Inc.
Minimum purchase required: Initial: $3,000, Subsequent: $100; IRA: Initial: $1,000; Automatic investment plan: Initial: $1,000
Wire orders accepted: Yes
Deadline for same day wire purchase: 4 P.M.
Qualified for sale in: All states
Telephone redemptions: Yes
Wire redemptions: Yes, $1,000 minimum
Letter redemptions: Signature guarantee required over $10,000
Telephone switching: With other n/i numeric funds if account holder is eligible (each closed fund has its own restrictions)
Number of switches permitted: 3 per year, 30 day hold
Shareholder services: IRA, electronic funds transfer (redemptions only), systematic withdrawal plan min. bal. req. $10,000
Administration fee: 0.325% first $150M, 0.295% over $150M
IRA/Keogh fees: Annual $10

n/i NUMERIC GROWTH FUND ◆
(See first n/i numeric listing for data common to all funds)

Portfolio managers: John C. Bogle, Jr. (1996), Shannon Vanderhoof (1996)
Investment objective and policies: Long-term capital appreciation. Invests primarily in common stock of firms with market capitalizations of $1B or less, or companies with substantial equity capital and higher than average earnings growth rates. Management utilizes a quantitative approach to investing, relying on proprietary computer data modeling techniques for stock selections. May engage in short sales and use var-

ious derivative instruments for hedging purposes. Fund will measure its performance against the Russell 2500 Growth Index (a growth-oriented subset of the Russell 2500, an index of stocks 501 through 3,000 in the Russell 3000, as ranked by total market capitalization.)
Year organized: 1996
Ticker symbol: NISGX
Special sales restrictions: Fund closed to new investors 8/8/97
Discount broker availability: Fidelity, Schwab, Siebert, White
Dividends paid: Income - December; Capital gains - December
Portfolio turnover (1 yr): 266%
Management fee: 0.75%
Expense ratio: 1.00 (year ending 8/31/97) (1.40% without waiver)

n/i NUMERIC GROWTH AND VALUE FUND ◆
(See first n/i numeric listing for data common to all funds)

Portfolio managers: John C. Bogle, Jr. (1996), Arup Datta (1996)
Investment objective and policies: Long-term capital appreciation. Invests primarily in common stock of companies where earnings per share are improving more rapidly than the earnings per share of the average company, as well as companies whose securities have market valuations which are lower than the average market valuations of securities, as measured by such characteristics as price to earnings ratios and price to book ratios. Management utilizes a quantitative approach to investing, relying on proprietary computer data modeling techniques for stock selections. May engage in short sales and use various derivative instruments for hedging purposes. Fund will measure its performance against the S&P MidCap 400 Index.
Year organized: 1996
Ticker symbol: NIGVX
Special sales restrictions: Fund will close when assets reach $200M
Discount broker availability: Fidelity, Schwab, Siebert, White
Dividends paid: Income - December; Capital gains - December
Portfolio turnover (1 yr): 264%
Management fee: 0.75%
Expense ratio: 1.00 (year ending 8/31/97) (1.81% without waiver)

n/i NUMERIC LARGER CAP VALUE FUND ◆
(See first n/i numeric listing for data common to all funds)

Portfolio managers: John C. Bogle, Jr. (1997), Arup Datta (1997)
Investment objective and policies: Long-term capital appreciation. Invests at least 65% of assets in common stock of companies with capitalizations exceeding $1B that are perceived to be undervalued. Management utilizes a quantitative approach to investing, relying on proprietary computer data modeling techniques for stock selections. May engage in short sales and use various derivative instruments for hedging purposes. The fund will measure its performance against the Russell 1000 Value Index.
Year organized: 1997
Discount broker availability: Fidelity, Schwab, Siebert, White
Dividends paid: Income - December; Capital gains - December
Management fee: 0.75%

n/i NUMERIC MICRO CAP FUND ◆
(See first n/i numeric listing for data common to all funds)

Portfolio managers: John C. Bogle, Jr. (1996), Shannon Vanderhoof (1996)
Investment objective and policies: Long-term capital appreciation. Invests primarily in common stock of companies with market capitalizations of $500M or

less, although the fund may invest in companies with higher market capitalization. Management utilizes a quantitative approach to investing, relying on proprietary computer data modeling techniques for stock selections. May engage in short sales and use various derivative instruments for hedging purposes. Fund will measure its performance against the Wilshire Small Company Growth Index, (a growth-oriented subset of the Small Company Universe, an index of stocks 751 through 2,500 in the Wilshire 2500, as ranked by total market capitalization.)
Year organized: 1996
Ticker symbol: NIMCX
Special sales restrictions: Fund closed to new investors 8/8/97; shareholders who held shares of this fund directly as of 9/12/97 may add up to $25,000 per fiscal year to existing accounts.
Discount broker availability: Fidelity, Schwab, Siebert, White
Dividends paid: Income - December; Capital gains - December
Portfolio turnover (1 yr): 233%
Management fee: 0.75%
Expense ratio: 1.00 (year ending 8/31/97) (1.40% without waiver)

NICHOLAS FUNDS ◆
(Data common to all Nicholas funds are shown below. See subsequent listings for data specific to individual funds.)

700 N. Water Street, Suite 1010
Milwaukee, WI 53202
800-544-6547, 800-227-5987, 414-272-6133
shareholder services 800-227-5987

Shareholder service hours: Full service: M-F 8:15 A.M.-4:30 P.M. CST; After hours service: prices, balances, last transactions, messages, prospectuses
Adviser: Nicholas Co., Inc.
Transfer agent: Firstar Trust Co.
Wire orders accepted: Yes
Deadline for same day wire purchase: 4 P.M.
Qualified for sale in: All states
Telephone redemptions: Yes, $500 minimum ($1,000 for Equity Income and Nicholas Funds)
Wire redemptions: Yes, $12 fee
Letter redemptions: Signature guarantee required over $100,000
Telephone switching: With other Nicholas funds, $1,000 minimum, $100,000 per account per day maximum
Number of switches permitted: 4 per year, $5 fee
Shareholder services: IRA, Keogh, systematic withdrawal plan min. bal. req. $10,000 (except Nicholas II and Money Market)
IRA/Keogh fees: Annual $12.50 per fund, $25 cap; Closing $15

NICHOLAS EQUITY INCOME FUND ◆
(See first Nicholas listing for data common to all funds)

Portfolio manager: Albert O. Nicholas (1993)
Investment objective and policies: Income greater than the composite dividend yield of the securities in the S&P 500; moderate long-term capital growth secondary. Invests at least 65% of assets in income producing equity securities - common stocks, preferred stocks and convertible securities. The balance of the portfolio is normally invested in corporate or government debt issues. Up to 20% of assets may be in repurchase agreements for defensive purposes.
Year organized: 1993
Ticker symbol: NSEIX
Group fund code: 022
Minimum purchase: Initial: $2,000, Subsequent: $100; Automatic investment plan: Subsequent: $50
Discount broker availability: Schwab
Dividends paid: Income - April, July, October, December; Capital gains - December
Portfolio turnover (3 yrs): 23%, 69%, 11%
Management fee: 0.70% first $50M, 0.60% over $50M
Expense ratio: 0.90% (year ending 3/31/97) (1.18% without waiver)

NICHOLAS FUND ◆

(See first Nicholas listing for data common to all funds)

Portfolio managers: Albert O. Nicholas (1969), David O. Nicholas (1996)
Investment objective and policies: Capital appreciation; income secondary. Invests primarily in common stocks of companies perceived to show favorable long-term growth potential, although debt securities and preferred stock may be acquired as deemed advisable. There are no minimum or maximum parameters required for any type of instrument selected for investment.
Year organized: 1969
Ticker symbol: NICSX
Group fund code: 023
Minimum purchase: Initial: $500, Subsequent: $100; Automatic investment plan: Subsequent: $100
Discount broker availability: Fidelity, Schwab, Siebert, White
Dividends paid: Income - May, December; Capital gains - May, December
Portfolio turnover (3 yrs): 15%, 26%, 30%
Management fee: 0.75% first $50M, 0.65% over $50M
Expense ratio: 0.72% (year ending 3/31/97)

NICHOLAS INCOME FUND ◆

(See first Nicholas listing for data common to all funds)

Portfolio manager: Albert O. Nicholas (1977)
Investment objective and policies: High current income. Invests primarily in junk bonds but still attempts to preserve capital and provide some long-term growth of capital and income. Invests in bonds, debentures, preferred stocks, securities convertible into common stocks, and common stocks. Will have 10% to 50% of assets in securities of electric companies and systems and may have up to 25% in real estate-related securities.
Year organized: 1929 (originally Wisconsin Investment Co.; changed to Wisconsin Fund, Inc. in 1955, to Wisconsin Income Fund in 1976; to current in 1983)
Ticker symbol: NCINX
Group fund code: 021
Minimum purchase: Initial: $500, Subsequent: $100; Automatic investment plan: Subsequent: $50
Discount broker availability: Fidelity, Schwab, Siebert, White
Dividend paid: Income - April, July, October, December; Capital gains - December
Portfolio turnover (3 yrs): 32%, 33%, 29%
Management fee: 0.50% first $50M to 0.30% over $100M
Expense ratio: 0.50% (year ending 12/31/97)

NICHOLAS LIMITED EDITION FUND ◆

(See first Nicholas listing for data common to all funds)

Portfolio manager: David O. Nicholas (1993)
Investment objective and policies: Long-term growth. Invests primarily in common stocks, and may invest in companies which carry greater risk because such stocks are not actively traded or the companies are smaller, out of favor, or have limited operating history upon which to base an evaluation of future performance. Fund name is derived from the fact that the fund is restricted in size to a maximum of 14 million shares, of which 10 million are available for purchase and 4 million reserved for reinvestment of capital gains and dividends.
Year organized: 1987
Ticker symbol: NCLEX
Group fund code: 027
Minimum purchase: Initial: $2,000; Subsequent: $100; Automatic investment plan: Subsequent: $50
Discount broker availability: Fidelity, Schwab, Siebert, White
Dividends paid: Income - December; Capital gains - December
Portfolio turnover (3 yrs): 37%, 32%, 36%
Management fee: 0.75%
Expense ratio: 0.86% (year ending 12/31/97)

NICHOLAS MONEY MARKET FUND ◆

(See first Nicholas listing for data common to all funds)

Portfolio manager: Jeffrey T. May (1988)
Investment objective and policies: Current income consistent with preservation of capital and liquidity. Invests in money market instruments.
Year organized: 1988
Ticker symbol: NICXX
Group fund code: 029
Minimum purchase: Initial: $2,000, Subsequent: $100; Automatic investment plan: Subsequent: $50
Dividends paid: Income - declared daily, paid monthly
Management fee: 0.30%
Expense ratio: 0.51% (year ending 12/31/97)

NICHOLAS II FUND ◆

(See first Nicholas listing for data common to all funds)

Portfolio manager: David O. Nicholas (1993)
Investment objective and policies: Long-term growth; income secondary. Invests primarily in common stocks perceived to have long-term growth prospects. Emphasizes stocks of small and medium sized companies with market capitalizations under $5B. May invest up to 25% of assets in one industry sector, up to 10% of assets in REITs, and up to 10% of assets in other investment companies.
Year organized: 1983
Ticker symbol: NCTWX
Group fund code: 025
Minimum purchase: Initial: $500, Subsequent: $100; Automatic investment plan: Subsequent: $50
Discount broker availability: Fidelity, Schwab, Siebert, White
Dividends paid: Income - December; Capital gains - December
Portfolio turnover (3 yrs): 30%, 24%, 20%
Management fee: 0.75% first $50M to 0.50% over $100M
Expense ratio: 0.61% (year ending 9/30/97)

NOMURA PACIFIC BASIN FUND ◆

180 Maiden Lane
New York, NY 10038
800-833-0018, 800-680-1836
212-509-8181
fax 212-509-8860

Advisers: Nomura Investment Management Co., Ltd., Nomura Capital Management (Singapore) Ltd.
Portfolio manager: Haruo Sawada (1997)
Transfer agent: State Street Bank & Trust Co.
Investment objective and policies: Long-term capital appreciation. Invests primarily in equity securities of companies domiciled in Japan and other Far Eastern and Western Pacific countries. Current income is not a consideration. Normally at least 70% of assets will consist of equity securities of Pacific Basin issuers - common stock and, to a lesser extent, securities convertible into common stock and rights to subscribe for common stock. May use up to 15% of assets for hedging purposes.
Year organized: 1985
Ticker symbol: NPBFX
Minimum purchase: Initial: $1,000, Subsequent: None
Wire orders accepted: Yes
Deadline for same day wire purchase: 4 P.M.
Discount broker availability: Schwab, White
Qualified for sale in: All states except AR, IA, ME, MT, NH, ND, OK, RI, SD, VT
Telephone redemptions: Yes
Letter redemptions: Signature guarantee required
Dividends paid: Income - May, December; Capital gains - May, December
Portfolio turnover (3 yrs): 45%, 49%, 76%
Shareholder services: IRA
Management fee: 0.75%
12b-1 distribution fee: Yes (not currently imposed)
Expense ratio: 2.21% (year ending 3/30/97)
IRA fees: Annual $40, Initial $25, Closing $100-$300

NORTH CAROLINA DAILY MUNICIPAL INCOME FUND

600 Fifth Avenue, 8th Floor
New York, NY 10020
800-221-3079, 800-676-6779
212-830-5200
fax 212-830-5478

Adviser: Reich & Tang Asset Management, L.P.
Portfolio manager: Molly Flewharty (1991)
Transfer agent: Reich & Tang Services, L.P.
Investment objective and policies: Interest income exempt from federal and North Carolina income taxes, consistent with capital preservation, liquidity and stability of principal. Invests primarily in a non-diversified portfolio of high quality, North Carolina municipal money market obligations.
Year organized: 1991
Ticker symbol: NCDXX
Special sales restrictions: Only class "B" shares of the fund are sold direct and without 12b-1 fees. At 8/31/97, however, there were no shares outstanding for this class. Only class "A" shares, available through financial intermediaries, is currently active. Statistics represent "A" shares only.
Minimum purchase: Initial: $5,000, Subsequent: $100
Wire orders accepted: Yes
Deadline for same day wire purchase: 12 NN
Qualified for sale in: AL, CA, CT, GA, NY, NC, OH, SC, VA, WV
Telephone redemptions: Yes
Wire redemptions: Yes
Letter redemptions: Signature guarantee required
Check redemptions: $250 minimum
Telephone switching: With other Reich & Tang money market funds and the R&T Equity Fund
Deadline for same day switch: 12 NN
Number of switches permitted: Unlimited, $1,000 minimum
Dividends paid: Income - declared daily, paid monthly
Shareholder services: Automatic investment plan, systematic withdrawal plan
Management fee: 0.40%
Administration fee: 0.21%
12b-1 distribution fee: 0.25%
Shareholder services fee: 0.25%
Expense ratio: 0.80% (year ending 8/31/97) (0.98% without waiver)

THE NORTH CAROLINA TAX FREE BOND FUND ◆

Post Office Drawer 5255
1272 Hendersonville Road
Asheville, NC 28813-5255
800-525-3863, 800-286-8038
fax 919-972-1908

Adviser: Boys, Arnold & Co., Inc.
Portfolio managers: Thomas C. Arnold (1993), John B. Kuhns (1993), Jon Vannice (1993)
Transfer agent and administrator: The Nottingham Co.
Investment objective and policies: Current income exempt from federal and North Carolina personal income taxes, consistent with capital preservation and protection from inflation; capital appreciation secondary. Invests at least 80% of assets in intermediate term North Carolina municipal bonds and notes and other debt instruments. At least 66% of assets are invested in debt obligations rated "A" or better. Fund is non-diversified.
Year organized: 1993
Ticker symbol: NCTFX
Minimum purchase: Initial: $1,000, Subsequent: $500; Automatic investment plan: Subsequent: $100
Wire orders accepted: Yes
Deadline for same day wire purchase: 4 P.M.
Discount broker availability: Schwab
Qualified for sale in: FL, NC, PA
Telephone redemptions: Yes (if confirmed by fax)
Wire redemptions: Yes, $5,000 minimum, $10 fee
Letter redemptions: Signature guarantee required over $50,000
Dividends paid: Income - monthly; Capital gains - December
Portfolio turnover (3 yrs): 20%, 10%, 83%

Shareholder services: Systematic withdrawal plan
min. bal. req. $10,000
Management fee: 0.35%
Administration fee: 0.15% plus $21,000
12b-1 distribution fee: 0.25% (not currently
imposed)
Expense ratio: 0.85% (year ending 8/31/97) (1.68%
without waiver)

NORTHEAST INVESTORS
GROWTH FUND ◆
50 Congress Street, Suite 1000
Boston, MA 02109
800-225-6704, 617-523-3588
fax 617-523-5412

Adviser: Northeast Management & Research Co., Inc.
Portfolio manager: William A. Oates, Jr. (1980)
Transfer agent: Northeast Investors Growth Fund
Investment objective and policies: Long-term
growth of both capital and future income. Fund main-
tains a flexible policy investing in common stocks,
convertibles, bonds and money market instruments,
varying the allocations according to perceived current
and future market conditions. Fund may leverage.
Year organized: 1980
Ticker symbol: NTHFX
Minimum purchase: Initial: $1,000, Subsequent:
None; IRA/Keogh: Initial: $500; Automatic invest-
ment plan: Subsequent: $50
Wire orders accepted: Yes
Deadline for same day wire purchase: 4 P.M.
Discount broker availability: Fidelity, Schwab,
Siebert, White
Qualified for sale in: All states
Letter redemptions: Signature guarantee required
over $5,000
Telephone switching: With Northeast Investors Trust
Number of switches permitted: Unlimited
Dividends paid: Income - December; Capital gains -
December
Portfolio turnover (3 yrs): 25%, 27%, 26%
Shareholder services: IRA, Keogh, 403(b), 401(k),
corporate retirement plans, electronic funds transfer,
systematic withdrawal plan
Management fee: 1.00% first $10M to 0.50% over
$30M
Expense ratio: 1.21% (year ending 12/31/96)
IRA/Keogh fees: Annual $10

NORTHEAST INVESTORS TRUST ◆
50 Congress Street, Suite 1000
Boston, MA 02109
800-225-6704, 617-523-3588
fax 617-523-5412

Adviser: Northeast Investors Trust
Portfolio managers: Ernest E. Monrad (1950), Bruce
H. Monrad (1989)
Transfer agent: Northeast Investors Trust
Investment objective and policies: Income; capital
appreciation secondary to the extent it is compatible
with the income objective. Invests primarily in bonds
but may also hold preferred stocks, dividend paying
common stocks, convertible securities and securities
with warrants attached. Fund may invest without limit
in junk bonds, and leverage.
Year organized: 1950
Ticker symbol: NTHEX
Minimum purchase: Initial: $1,000, Subsequent:
None; IRA/Keogh: Initial: $500; Automatic invest-
ment plan: Subsequent: $50
Wire orders accepted: Yes
Deadline for same day wire purchase: 4 P.M.
Discount broker availability: Fidelity, Schwab,
Siebert, White
Qualified for sale in: All states
Letter redemptions: Signature guarantee required
over $5,000
Telephone switching: With Northeast Investors
Growth Fund
Number of switches permitted: Unlimited
Dividends paid: Income - February, May, August,
November; Capital gains - December
Portfolio turnover (3 yrs): 32%, 41%, 73%

Shareholder services: IRA, Keogh, 403(b), 401(k),
corporate retirement plans, electronic funds transfer,
systematic withdrawal plan
Management fee: 0.50%
Expense ratio: 0.66% (year ending 9/30/96)
IRA/Keogh fees: Annual $10

NORTHERN FUNDS ◆
(Data common to all Northern funds are shown below.
See subsequent listings for data specific to individual
funds.)

50 South LaSalle Street
Chicago, IL 60675
800-595-9111, 312-630-6000
fax 312-630-0629
e-mail: northernfunds@execpc.com

Adviser: The Northern Trust Co.
Administrator: Sunstone Financial Group, Inc.
Transfer agent: The Northern Trust Co.
Minimum purchase: Initial: $2,500, Subsequent:
$50; IRA/Keogh: Initial: $500; Automatic investment
plan: Initial: $250
Wire orders accepted: Yes
Deadline for same day wire purchase: 4 P.M. (2 P.M.
for money market funds)
Qualified for sale in: All states (exceptions noted)
Telephone redemptions: Yes
Wire redemptions: Yes, $250 minimum, $15 fee
Letter redemptions: Signature guarantee required
over $50,000
Telephone switching: With other Northern funds,
$1,000 minimum
Number of switches permitted: 8 per year, 2 per
quarter
Shareholder services: IRA, Keogh, 401(k), corpo-
rate retirement plans, directed dividends, electronic
funds transfer (purchase only), systematic withdrawal
plan min. bal. req. $10,000
Administration fee: 0.15%
12b-1 distribution fee: Maximum of 0.25% (not currently imposed)
IRA/Keogh fees: None

NORTHERN CALIFORNIA MUNICIPAL
MONEY MARKET FUND ◆
(See first Northern listing for data common to all
funds)

Portfolio manager: Bradley C. Snyder (1997)
Investment objective and policies: High current
income exempt from federal and California state
income taxes, consistent with capital preservation.
Invests primarily in high-quality California municipal
money market instruments.
Year organized: 1994
Ticker symbol: NOCXX
Qualified for sale in: AZ, CA, CO, FL, GA, HI, ID,
IL, IN, KY, LA, MA, MN, MT, NV, NY, NC, OH,
OK, OR, PA, UT, VA, WA, WV, WY
Check redemptions: $250 minimum
Dividends paid: Income - declared daily, paid
monthly
Management fee: 0.60%
Expense ratio: 0.45% (year ending 3/31/97) (0.94%
without waiver)

NORTHERN CALIFORNIA
TAX-EXEMPT FUND ◆
(See first Northern listing for data common to all
funds)

Portfolio manager: Eric M. Bergson (1997)
Investment objective and policies: High level of
current income exempt from regular federal and state
income tax. Invests at least 65% of assets in municipal
instruments issued by the state of California and its
municipalities, as well as other securities exempt from
California tax. Portfolio maintains a dollar-weighted
average maturity ranging between ten and thirty years.
Up to 20% of assets may be in obligations which may
be taxable. May use options, futures and forward cur-

rency contracts in an effort to increase income and for
hedging purposes.
Year organized: 1997
Qualified for sale in: AZ, CA, CO, FL, GA, HI, ID,
IL, IN, KY, LA, MA, MN, MT, NV, NC, NY, OH,
OK, OR, PA, UT, VA, WA, WI, WV, WY
Dividends paid: Income - declared daily, paid
monthly; Capital gains - December
Management fee: 0.75%

NORTHERN FIXED INCOME FUND ◆
(See first Northern listing for data common to all
funds)

Portfolio manager: Michael J. Lannan (1994)
Investment objective and policies: High current
income. Invests primarily in investment grade fixed-
income securities, and maintains a dollar-weighted
average maturity of seven to twelve years. Up to 20%
of assets may be in obligations of issuers within a single foreign country. May use options, futures and forward currency contracts in an effort to increase
income and for hedging purposes.
Year organized: 1994
Ticker symbol: NOFIX
Discount broker availability: *White
Dividends paid: Income - declared daily, paid
monthly; Capital gains - December
Portfolio turnover (3 yrs): 88%, 116%, 55%
Management fee: 0.75%
Expense ratio: 0.90% (year ending 3/31/97) (1.12%
without waiver)

NORTHERN FLORIDA INTERMEDIATE
TAX-EXEMPT FUND ◆
(See first Northern listing for data common to all
funds)

Portfolio manager: Eric M. Bergson (1996)
Investment objective and policies: High level of
current income exempt from regular federal income
tax. Invests at least 65% of assets in municipal instruments issued by the state of Florida and its municipalities, as well as other securities exempt from the
Florida intangibles tax. Portfolio generally maintains a
dollar-weighted average maturity between three and
ten years. Up to 20% of assets may be in obligations
which may be taxable. May use options, futures and
forward currency contracts in an effort to increase
income and for hedging purposes.
Year organized: 1996
Ticker symbol: NOFTX
Discount broker availability: *White
Dividends paid: Income - declared daily, paid
monthly; Capital gains - December
Portfolio turnover (1 yr): 51%
Management fee: 0.75%
Expense ratio: 0.85% (8 months ending 3/31/97)
(2.31% without waiver)

NORTHERN GROWTH
EQUITY FUND ◆
(See first Northern listing for data common to all
funds)

Portfolio manager: Theodore Breckel (1995)
Investment objective and policies: Long-term capital growth. Invests primarily in common and preferred
stocks and convertible securities of companies with
above average growth prospects. May invest in securi-
ties of foreign issuers, including ADRs and EDRs, and
have up to 15% of assets in illiquid securities. May
use options and futures in an effort to increase income
and for hedging purposes.
Year organized: 1994
Ticker symbol: NOGEX
Discount broker availability: *White
Dividends paid: Income - March, June, September,
December; Capital gains - December
Portfolio turnover (3 yrs): 67%, 73%, 83%
Management fee: 1.00%
Expense ratio: 1.00% (year ending 3/31/97) (1.33%
without waiver)

NORTHERN INCOME EQUITY FUND ◆
(See first Northern listing for data common to all funds)

Portfolio manager: Theodore T. Southworth (1995)
Investment objective and policies: High current income; long-term capital growth secondary. Invests primarily in income-producing convertible and other equity securities. Up to 35% of assets may be in investment grade bonds and 35% in junk bonds and 15% in illiquid securities. May invest in securities of foreign issuers, including ADRs and EDRs. May use options and futures in an effort to increase income and for hedging purposes.
Year organized: 1994
Ticker symbol: NOIEX
Discount broker availability: *White
Dividends paid: Income - monthly; Capital gains - December
Portfolio turnover (3 yrs): 72%, 67%, 46%
Management fee: 1.00%
Expense ratio: 1.00% (year ending 3/31/97) (1.42% without waiver)

NORTHERN INTERMEDIATE TAX-EXEMPT FUND ◆
(See first Northern listing for data common to all funds)

Portfolio manager: Eric V. Boeckmann (1994)
Investment objective and policies: High current income exempt from federal income taxes, consistent with capital preservation. Invests primarily in high-quality municipal debt obligations, and maintains a dollar-weighted average maturity of three to ten years. Up to 20% of assets may be in securities subject to AMT tax treatment, and 15% in illiquid securities. May use options, futures and forward currency contracts in an effort to increase income and for hedging purposes.
Year organized: 1994
Ticker symbol: NOITX
Discount broker availability: *White
Dividends paid: Income - declared daily, paid monthly; Capital gains - December
Portfolio turnover (3 yrs): 61%, 138%, 79%
Management fee: 0.75%
Expense ratio: 0.85% (year ending 3/31/97) (1.07% without waiver)

NORTHERN INTERNATIONAL FIXED INCOME FUND ◆
(See first Northern listing for data common to all funds)

Portfolio manager: Michael J. Lannan (1994)
Investment objective and policies: High total return consistent with reasonable current income. Invests primarily in investment grade fixed-income securities of foreign issuers, and maintains a dollar-weighted average maturity of three to eleven years. May invest in ADRs and EDRs, and use options, futures and forward currency contracts in an effort to increase income and for hedging purposes. Up to 15% of assets may be in illiquid securities.
Year organized: 1994
Ticker symbol: NOIFX
Discount broker availability: *White
Dividends paid: Income - quarterly; Capital gains - December
Portfolio turnover (3 yrs): 38%, 52%, 43%
Management fee: 0.90%
Expense ratio: 1.15% (year ending 3/31/97) (1.96% without waiver)

NORTHERN INTERNATIONAL GROWTH EQUITY FUND ◆
(See first Northern listing for data common to all funds)

Portfolio manager: Robert A. LaFleur (1994)
Investment objective and policies: Long-term capital growth. Invests primarily in common and preferred stocks and convertible securities of foreign issuers with above average growth prospects. May invest in ADRs and EDRs, and use options, futures and forward currency contracts in an effort to increase income and

for hedging purposes. Up to 15% of assets may be in illiquid securities.
Year organized: 1994
Ticker symbol: NOIGX
Discount broker availability: *White
Dividends paid: Income - December; Capital gains - December
Portfolio turnover (3 yrs): 191%, 217%, 158%
Management fee: 1.20%
Expense ratio: 1.25% (year ending 3/31/97) (1.63% without waiver)

NORTHERN INTERNATIONAL SELECT EQUITY FUND ◆
(See first Northern listing for data common to all funds)

Portfolio managers: Robert A. LaFleur (1997), Svein Backer (1997)
Investment objective and policies: Long-term capital growth. Invests primarily in equity securities of foreign issuers with market capitalizations under $1B, believed to be growing faster than their markets and transacting a majority of their business in countries growing faster than the world average. May invest in ADRs and EDRs, and use options, futures and forward currency contracts in an effort to increase income and for hedging purposes. Up to 15% of assets may be in illiquid securities.
Year organized: 1994
Ticker symbol: NINEX
Discount broker availability: *White
Dividends paid: Income - December; Capital gains - December
Portfolio turnover (3 yrs): 98%, 177%, 98%
Management fee: 1.20%
Expense ratio: 1.25% (year ending 3/31/97) (1.66% without waiver)

NORTHERN MONEY MARKET FUND ◆
(See first Northern listing for data common to all funds)

Portfolio manager: Mary Ann Flynn (1994)
Investment objective and policies: Maximum current income consistent with preservation of capital and liquidity. Invests primarily in high-quality money market instruments.
Year organized: 1994
Ticker symbol: NORXX
Check redemptions: $250 minimum
Dividends paid: Income - declared daily, paid monthly
Management fee: 0.60%
Expense ratio: 0.55% (year ending 3/31/97) (0.90% without waiver)

NORTHERN MUNICIPAL MONEY MARKET FUND ◆
(See first Northern listing for data common to all funds)

Portfolio manager: Bradley C. Snyder (1994)
Investment objective and policies: Maximum current income exempt from federal income tax, consistent with preservation of capital and liquidity. Invests primarily in high-quality municipal money market instruments.
Year organized: 1994
Ticker symbol: NOMXX
Check redemptions: $250 minimum
Dividends paid: Income - declared daily, paid monthly
Management fee: 0.60%
Expense ratio: 0.55% (year ending 3/31/97) (0.90% without waiver)

NORTHERN SELECT EQUITY FUND ◆
(See first Northern listing for data common to all funds)

Portfolio manager: Robert N. Streed (1994)
Investment objective and policies: Long-term capital growth. Invests primarily in equity securities of companies with superior quality and growth characteristics and market capitalizations of more than $500M.

May invest in securities of foreign issuers, including ADRs and EDRs and have up to 15% of assets in illiquid securities. May use options and futures in an effort to increase income and for hedging purposes.
Year organized: 1994
Ticker symbol: NOEQX
Discount broker availability: *White
Dividends paid: Income - December; Capital gains - December
Portfolio turnover (3 yrs): 73%, 138%, 49%
Management fee: 1.20%
Expense ratio: 1.00% (year ending 3/31/97) (1.67% without waiver)

NORTHERN SMALL CAP FUND ◆
(See first Northern listing for data common to all funds)

Portfolio manager: Susan J. French (1994)
Investment objective and policies: Long-term capital growth. Invests primarily in equity securities of companies with market capitalizations lower than the median capitalization of stocks listed on the NYSE. May invest in securities of foreign issuers, including ADRs and EDRs and have up to 15% of assets in illiquid securities. May use options and futures in an effort to increase income and for hedging purposes.
Year organized: 1994 (name changed from Small Cap Growth in 1996)
Ticker symbol: NOSGX
Discount broker availability: *White
Dividends paid: Income - December; Capital gains - December
Portfolio turnover (3 yrs): 19%, 47%, 82%
Management fee: 1.20%
Expense ratio: 1.00% (year ending 3/31/97) (1.54% without waiver)

NORTHERN STOCK INDEX FUND ◆
(See first Northern listing for data common to all funds)

Portfolio manager: Mary Kay Wright (1996)
Investment objective and policies: Investment results approximating the aggregate price and performance of the securities included in the S&P 500 Index. Normally invests at least 65% of assets in the issues included in the index. Invests are selected passively using statistical selection processes in an attempt to achieve a correlation of 0.95 with the Index. May use options and futures in an attempt to more closely match performance.
Year organized: 1996
Ticker symbol: NOSIX
Discount broker availability: *White
Dividends paid: Income - December; Capital gains - December
Portfolio turnover (1 yr): 65%
Management fee: 0.60%
Expense ratio: 0.55% (6 months ending 3/31/97) (2.23% without waiver)

NORTHERN TAX-EXEMPT FUND ◆
(See first Northern listing for data common to all funds)

Portfolio manager: Peter J. Flood (1994)
Investment objective and policies: High current income exempt from federal income taxes, consistent with capital preservation. Invests primarily in high-quality municipal debt obligations, and maintains a dollar-weighted average maturity ranging from ten to 30 years. Up to 20% of assets may be in securities subject to AMT tax treatment, and 15% in illiquid securities. May use options, futures and forward currency contracts in an effort to increase income and for hedging purposes.
Year organized: 1994
Ticker symbol: NOTEX
Discount broker availability: *White
Dividends paid: Income - declared daily, paid monthly; Capital gains - December
Portfolio turnover (3 yrs): 8%, 60%, 55%
Management fee: 0.75%
Expense ratio: 0.85% (year ending 3/31/97) (1.10% without waiver)

NORTHERN TECHNOLOGY FUND ◆

(See first Northern listing for data common to all funds)

Portfolio managers: John B. Leo (1996), George J. Gilbert (1997), Jim Burkart (1997)
Investment objective and policies: Long-term capital appreciation. Invests at least 65% of assets in equity securities of companies that develop, produce or distribute products and services related to advances in technology, as determined by the Hambrecht and Quist Technology Index, the SoundView Technology Index, the technology grouping of the S&P 500 Index, or other similar indicators. Fund emphasizes issues of any market capitalization perceived to have the ability to outperform the market over a one to two year period. May invest up to 10% of assets directly in foreign issues, and up to 25% including ADRs.
Year organized: 1996
Ticker symbol: NTCHX
Discount broker availability: *White
Dividends paid: Income - December; Capital gains - December
Portfolio turnover (1 yr): 68%
Management fee: 1.20%
Expense ratio: 1.25% (year ending 3/31/97) (2.02% without waiver)

NORTHERN U.S. GOVERNMENT FUND ◆

(See first Northern listing for data common to all funds)

Portfolio manager: Monty M. Memler (1994)
Investment objective and policies: High current income. Invests primarily in securities issued or guaranteed by the U.S. Government or its agencies or instrumentalities, and maintains a dollar-weighted average maturity ranging from one to ten years. May use options, futures and forward currency contracts in an effort to increase income and for hedging purposes.
Year organized: 1994
Ticker symbol: NOUGX
Discount broker availability: *White
Dividends paid: Income - declared daily, paid monthly; Capital gains - December
Portfolio turnover (3 yrs): 83%, 112%, 42%
Management fee: 0.75%
Expense ratio: 0.90% (year ending 3/31/97) (1.09% without waiver)

NORTHERN U.S. GOVERNMENT MONEY MARKET FUND ◆

(See first Northern listing for data common to all funds)

Portfolio manager: Valerie J. Lokhorst (1997)
Investment objective and policies: Maximum current income consistent with preservation of capital and liquidity. Invests in money market instruments guaranteed as to payment of principal and interest by the U.S. Government, its agencies or instrumentalities, repurchase agreements relating to the above instruments and custodial receipts for such money market securities.
Year organized: 1994
Ticker symbol: NOGXX
Dividends paid: Income - declared daily, paid monthly
Check redemptions: $250 minimum
Management fee: 0.60%
Expense ratio: 0.55% (year ending 3/31/97) (0.96% without waiver)

NORTHERN U.S. GOVERNMENT SELECT MONEY MARKET FUND ◆

(See first Northern listing for data common to all funds)

Portfolio manager: Valerie J. Lokhorst (1997)
Investment objective and policies: Maximum current income consistent with preservation of capital and liquidity. Invests exclusively in money market instruments guaranteed as to payment of principal and interest by the U.S. Government, its agencies or instrumentalities.
Year organized: 1994

Ticker symbol: NOSXX
Check redemptions: $250 minimum
Dividends paid: Income - declared daily, paid monthly
Management fee: 0.60%
Expense ratio: 0.40% (year ending 3/31/97) (0.97% without waiver)

OAK HALL EQUITY FUND

122 East 42nd Street, 24th Floor
New York, NY 10168
800-625-4255, 212-455-9600
207-879-0001, fax 207-879-6206

Adviser: Oak Hall Capital Advisors, L.P.
Portfolio manager: Edward Cimilluca (1997)
Transfer agent and administrator: Forum Financial Corp.
Investment objective and policies: Capital appreciation. Invests primarily in common stocks and securities convertible into common stocks perceived to have above average growth potential or attractive valuations. May invest up to 25% of assets in junk bonds and 30% of assets in foreign securities. May hedge up to 25% of assets.
Year organized: 1992
Ticker symbol: OEHFX
Minimum purchase: Initial: $10,000, Subsequent: $5,000; IRA: Initial: $2,000, Subsequent: $250
Wire orders accepted: Yes
Deadline for same day wire purchase: 4 P.M.
Discount broker availability: Fidelity, Schwab, Siebert, White
Qualified for sale in: All states
Telephone redemptions: Yes
Ticker symbol: NOSIX
Wire redemptions: Yes, $10,000 minimum
Letter redemptions: Signature guarantee required
Dividends paid: Income - December; Capital gains - December
Portfolio turnover (3 yrs): 95%, 157%, 115%
Shareholder services: IRA
Management fee: 0.75%
Administration fee: 0.25%
12b-1 distribution fee: maximum of 0.20%
Expense ratio: 2.00% (year ending 3/31/97) (2.93% without waiver)
IRA fees: Annual $25

OAK VALUE FUND ◆

3100 Tower Boulevard, Suite 800
Durham, NC 27707
800-622-2474, 513-629-2000
800-680-4199, 919-419-1900
fax 919-419-1941, 513-629-2901

Adviser: Oak Value Capital Management, Inc.
Portfolio managers: David R. Carr, Jr. (1993), George W. Brumley, III (1993)
Transfer agent and administrator: Countrywide Fund Services, Inc.
Investment objective and policies: Capital appreciation; income secondary. Invests primarily in common and preferred stocks and convertibles of companies of any capitalization perceived to be undervalued relative to price for growth. May invest in securities of foreign issuers without limit, either directly or by means of ADRs, although it is likely this will not exceed 10%. May use covered call options for hedging purposes.
Year organized: 1993
Ticker symbol: OAKVX
Minimum purchase: Initial: $2,500, Subsequent: $100; IRA/Keogh: Initial: $1,000
Wire orders accepted: Yes
Deadline for same day wire purchase: 4 P.M.
Discount broker availability: *Fidelity, *Schwab, Siebert, *White
Qualified for sale in: All states except PR
Telephone redemptions: Yes (with fax confirmation)
Wire redemptions: Yes, $5,000 minimum
Letter redemptions: Signature guarantee required over $25,000
Dividends paid: Income - semi-annually; Capital gains - semi-annually
Portfolio turnover (3 yrs): 22%, 58%, 103%

Shareholder services: IRA, Keogh, automatic investment plan, systematic withdrawal plan min. bal. req. $10,000
Management fee: 0.90%
Administration fee: 0.125% first $100M, 0.10% over $100M
Expense ratio: 1.59% (year ending 6/31/97)
IRA/Keogh fees: Annual $10

THE OAKMARK FUNDS ◆

(Data common to all Oakmark funds are shown below. See subsequent listings for data specific to individual funds. **Note exceptions for Oakmark Units money funds.**)

Two North LaSalle Street, Suite 500
Chicago, IL 60602-3790
800-625-6275, 312-621-0600
prices 800-476-9625
telephone exchange 800-626-9392
fax 312-621-0582
Internet: http://www.oakmark.com

Shareholder service hours: Full service: M-F 8 A.M.- 6 P.M. EST; After hours service: prices, yields, account balances, last transaction, total returns, distributions
Adviser: Harris Assocs., L.P. (except money markets)
Transfer agent: State Street Bank & Trust Co.
Minimum purchase: Initial: $1,000 (except MM), Subsequent: $100
Wire orders accepted: Yes
Deadline for same day wire purchase: 2 P.M. (except MMs)
Qualified for sale in: All states
Telephone redemptions: Yes
Wire redemptions: Yes, $250 minimum, $5 fee
Letter redemptions: Signature guarantee required over $50,000
Telephone switching: With other Oakmark Funds and Oakmark Units of Goldman Sachs Money Market Trust; Government Portfolio, Tax-Exempt Diversified Portfolio and GS Short Duration Tax-Free Fund
Number of switches permitted: 4 per year, $5 fee to money market
Shareholder services: IRA, SEP-IRA, automatic investment plan, electronic funds transfer, directed dividends, systematic withdrawal plan min. bal. req. $25,000
IRA fees: Annual $10 per account ($20 maximum), Initial $5, Closing $10

OAKMARK EQUITY AND INCOME FUND ◆

(See first Oakmark listing for data common to all funds)

Portfolio manager: Clyde S. McGregor (1995)
Investment objective and policies: High current income and preservation and growth of capital. Invests in a diversified portfolio of equity and fixed-income securities, generally 50% to 65% equities, and 25% to 50% investment grade debt. May invest up to 10% of assets in foreign issues and up to 20% of assets in unrated, junk bonds. May sell short and engage in forward currency transactions for hedging purposes.
Year organized: 1995 (name changed from Oakmark Balanced fund 7/14/97)
Ticker symbol: OAKBX
Discount broker availability: *Fidelity, *Schwab, *White
Dividends paid: Income - December; Capital gains - December
Portfolio turnover (2 yrs): 53%, 66%
Management fee: 0.75%
Expense ratio: 1.50% (year ending 9/30/97)

OAKMARK FUND ◆

(See first Oakmark listing for data common to all funds)

Portfolio manager: Robert J. Sanborn (1991)
Investment objective and policies: Long-term capital appreciation. Invests primarily in common stocks and securities convertible into common stocks. May invest up to 25% of assets in junk bonds, 25% in for-

eign securities and 10% in other mutual funds. May use forward currency transactions and sell short.
Year organized: 1991
Ticker symbol: OAKMX
Discount broker availability: *Fidelity, *Schwab, *White
Dividends paid: Income - December; Capital gains - December
Portfolio turnover (3 yrs): 17%, 24%, 18%
Management fee: 1.00% first $2.5B to 0.90% over $5B
Expense ratio: 1.08% (year ending 9/30/97)

OAKMARK INTERNATIONAL FUND ◆
(See first Oakmark listing for data common to all funds)

Portfolio managers: David G. Herro (1992), Michael J. Welsh (1992)
Investment objective and policies: Long-term capital appreciation. Invests primarily in a diversified portfolio of equity securities of non-U.S. issuers. Fund may invest in securities of companies based in mature markets, less developed markets and in selected emerging markets. May invest 10% of assets in junk bonds and 10% in other investment companies holding foreign securities. May use forward currency transactions and sell short.
Year organized: 1992
Ticker symbol: OAKIX
Discount broker availability: *Fidelity, *Schwab, *White
Dividends paid: Income - December; Capital gains - December
Portfolio turnover (3 yrs): 61%, 42%, 26%
Management fee: 1.00% first $2.5B to 0.90% over $5B
Expense ratio: 1.26% (year ending 9/30/97)

OAKMARK INTERNATIONAL SMALL CAP FUND ◆
(See first Oakmark listing for data common to all funds)

Portfolio managers: David G. Herro (1995), Michael J. Welsh (1997)
Investment objective and policies: Long-term capital appreciation. Invests primarily in equity securities of non-U.S. issuers that have small market capitalizations or that are located in emerging markets. In those markets considered developed, the fund invests in companies with market capitalization of under $1B; in emerging markets, the fund will invest in companies of any capitalization. Attempts to invest in at least five countries outside of the U.S. May invest 10% of assets in junk bonds and 10% in other investment companies holding foreign securities. May use forward currency transactions and sell short.
Year organized: 1995 (name changed from International Emerging Value 3/1/97)
Ticker symbol: OAKEX
Discount broker availability: *Fidelity, *Schwab, *White
Dividends paid: Income - December; Capital gains - December
Portfolio turnover (2 yrs): 63%, 27%
Management fee: 1.25%
Expense ratio: 1.93% (year ending 9/30/97)

OAKMARK SELECT FUND ◆
(See first Oakmark listing for data common to all funds)

Portfolio manager: William C. Nygren (1996)
Investment objective and policies: Long-term capital appreciation. Invests primarily in a non-diversified portfolio of equity securities of U.S. companies. Rather than concentrate on one industry, fund intends to focus on seven to ten value-based "themes," concentrating holdings to between 15 and 25 companies, primarily mid- to large-cap firms, with as much as 50% of assets in the top five. May invest up to 25% of assets in foreign securities of any type. May invest 10% of assets in junk bonds and 10% in other investment companies holding foreign securities. May use forward currency transactions and sell short.
Year organized: 1996

Ticker symbol: OAKSX
Discount broker availability: *Fidelity, *Schwab, *White
Dividends paid: Income - December; Capital gains - December
Portfolio turnover (1 yr): 37%
Management fee: 1.00%
Expense ratio: 1.12% (year ending 9/30/97)

OAKMARK SMALL CAP FUND ◆
(See first Oakmark listing for data common to all funds)

Portfolio manager: Steven J. Reid (1995)
Investment objective and policies: Long-term capital appreciation. Invests primarily in equity securities of companies with market capitalizations of under $1B. May invest up to 25% of assets in foreign securities of any type. May invest 10% of assets in junk bonds and 10% in other investment companies holding foreign securities. May use forward currency transactions and sell short.
Year organized: 1995
Ticker symbol: OAKSX
Sales restrictions: Fund closed to new investors 6/20/97
Discount broker availability: *Fidelity, *Schwab, *White
Dividends paid: Income - December; Capital gains - December
Portfolio turnover (2 yrs): 27%, 23%
Management fee: 1.25%
Expense ratio: 1.37% (year ending 9/30/97)

OAKMARK UNITS - GOVERNMENT PORTFOLIO ◆
(ILA Service Units of Goldman Sachs Money Market Trust)
(See first Oakmark listing for data common to all funds)

Adviser: GSAM (a division of Goldman Sachs)
Transfer agent: Goldman Sachs
Investment objective and policies: High current income consistent with preservation of capital and maintenance of liquidity. Invests exclusively in high quality U.S. Government issued or guaranteed money market instruments.
Year organized: 1990 (ILA Service Units): 1981 (Goldman Sachs master fund; name changed from Goldman Sachs Institutional Liquid Assets Government Portfolio on 10/14/94)
Minimum purchase: Initial: $2,500
Deadline for same day wire purchase: 3 P.M.
Check redemptions: $500 minimum
Dividends paid: Income - declared daily, paid monthly
Management fee: 0.35%
Shareholder services fee: 0.40%
Expense ratio: 0.81% (year ending 12/31/96)

OAKMARK UNITS - TAX-EXEMPT DIVERSIFIED PORTFOLIO ◆
(ILA Service Units of Goldman Sachs Money Market Trust)
(See first Oakmark listing for data common to all funds)

Adviser: GSAM (a division of Goldman Sachs)
Transfer agent: Goldman Sachs
Investment objective and policies: Current income exempt from federal income tax, consistent with preservation of capital and liquidity. Invests in short-term municipal money market instruments issued by federal, state, local or District of Columbia governments, agencies or instrumentalities.
Year organized: 1990 (ILA Service Units): 1984 (Goldman Sachs master fund: name changed from Goldman Sachs Institutional Liquid Assets Tax-Exempt Diversified Portfolio on 10/14/94)
Minimum purchase: Initial: $2,500
Deadline for same day wire purchase: 1 P.M.
Check redemptions: $500 minimum
Dividends paid: Income - declared daily, paid monthly
Management fee: 0.35%
Shareholder services fee: 0.40%
Expense ratio: 0.71% (year ending 12/31/96)

OBERWEIS FUNDS
(Data common to all Oberweis funds are shown below. See subsequent listings for data specific to individual funds.)

951 Ice Cream Drive, Suite 200
North Aurora, IL 60542
800-323-6166, 630-801-6000
prices/shareholder services 800-245-7311
fax 708-896-5282

Shareholder service hours: Full service: M-F 7:30 A.M.-6 P.M. CST; After hours service: prices, yields, account balances, last transaction, total returns
Adviser: Oberweis Asset Management, Inc.
Transfer agent: Investors Fiduciary Trust Co.
Minimum purchase: Initial: $1,000, Subsequent: $100; Automatic investment plan: Initial: $100
Wire orders accepted: Yes
Deadline for same day wire purchase: 4 P.M.
Qualified for sale in: All states
Telephone redemptions: Yes
Wire redemptions: Yes, $6 fee
Letter redemptions: Signature guarantee required over $50,000
Telephone switching: With other Oberweis funds and the Cash Resource Trust money market funds, $1,000 minimum
Number of switches permitted: Unlimited
Shareholder services: IRA, electronic funds transfer (redemption only), systematic withdrawal plan min. bal. req. $10,000
12b-1 distribution fee: 0.25%
IRA fees: Annual $12

OBERWEIS EMERGING GROWTH PORTFOLIO
(See first Oberweis listing for data common to all funds)

Portfolio manager: James D. Oberweis (1987)
Investment objective and policies: Maximum capital appreciation. Invests at least 80% of assets in equity securities of companies whose capitalizations equals that of the lowest 30% of those listed on the NYSE (typically less than $1B), believed to have potential for above average long-term growth based on management's proprietary eight-point tracking analysis. The average market cap for the portfolio is about $600M. May buy common and preferred stocks, convertible securities and foreign securities. May use up to 10% of assets in restricted securities and hedge up to 25% of assets.
Year organized: 1987
Ticker symbol: OBEGX
Discount broker availability: *Fidelity, Schwab, *Siebert, *White
Dividends paid: Income - November; Capital gains - November
Portfolio turnover (3 yrs): 75%, 64%, 79%
Management fee: 0.85% first $50M, 0.80% over $50M (includes administrative fees)
Expense ratio: 1.44% (year ending 12/31/97)

OBERWEIS MICRO-CAP PORTFOLIO
(See first Oberweis listing for data common to all funds)

Portfolio manager: James D. Oberweis (1996)
Investment objective and policies: Maximum capital appreciation. Invests at least 80% of assets in companies with a market capitalization under $250M, and at least 50% in companies with market capitalizations under $100M at acquisition. Those selected are believed to have potential for above average long-term growth based on management's proprietary eight-point tracking analysis. The average market cap for the portfolio is about $100M. May buy common and preferred stocks, convertible securities and foreign securities. May use up to 10% of assets in restricted securities and hedge up to 25% of assets.
Year organized: 1996
Ticker symbol: OBMCX
Special sales restrictions: Fund closed to all investors 5/96; reopened 11/1/96; will close again if assets reach $60M.
Discount broker availability: Fidelity, Schwab, *White

Redemption fee: 0.25%, payable to the portfolio
Dividends paid: Income - November; Capital gains - November
Portfolio turnover (2 yrs): 89%, 70%
Management fee: 1.00% (includes administrative fees)
Expense ratio: 1.81% (year ending 12/31/97)

OBERWEIS MID-CAP PORTFOLIO
(See first Oberweis listing for data common to all funds)

Portfolio manager: James D. Oberweis (1996)
Investment objective and policies: Maximum capital appreciation. Invests in companies with market capitalization between $500M and $5B at acquisition, believed to have potential for above average long-term growth based on management's proprietary eight-point tracking analysis. May buy common and preferred stocks, convertible securities and foreign securities. May use up to 10% of assets in restricted securities and hedge up to 25% of assets.
Year organized: 1996
Ticker symbol: OBMDX
Discount broker availability: *Fidelity, Schwab, Siebert, *White
Redemption fee: 0.25%, payable to the portfolio
Dividends paid: Income - November; Capital gains - November
Portfolio turnover (1 yr): 106%
Management fee: 0.80% (includes administrative fees)
Expense ratio: 2.00% (year ending 12/31/97) (2.46% without waiver)

O'SHAUGHNESSY FUNDS ◆
(Data common to all O'Shaughnessy funds are shown below. See subsequent listings for data specific to individual funds.)

35 Mason Street
Greenwich, CT 06830
800-797-0773, 203-869-7148
fax 203-869-3674
Internet: http://www.osfunds.com

Adviser: O'Shaughnessy Capital Management, Inc.
Distributor: First Fund Distributors, Inc.
Administrator: Investment Company Administration Corp.
Transfer agent: Firstar Trust Co.
Minimum purchase: Initial: $5,000, Subsequent: $100; IRA: Initial: $500, Subsequent: $50
Wire orders accepted: Yes
Deadline for same day wire purchase: 4 P.M.
Qualified for sale in: All states
Telephone redemptions: Yes
Wire redemptions: Yes, $1,000 minimum $7.50 fee
Letter redemptions: Signature guarantee required over $10,000
Telephone switching: With other O'Shaughnessy funds, and the Firstar Money Market Funds ($5,000 minimum)
Number of switches permitted: Unlimited
Shareholder services: IRA, SEP-IRA, corporate retirement plans, automatic investment plan, systematic withdrawal plan min. bal. req. $10,000
Administration fee: 0.10% first $100M to 0.03% over $200M ($40M minimum)
IRA/Keogh fees: Annual $12.50, Closing $15

O'SHAUGHNESSY AGGRESSIVE GROWTH FUND ◆
(See first O'Shaughnessy listing for data common to all funds)

Portfolio manager: James P. O'Shaughnessy (1996)
Investment objective and policies: Capital appreciation. Invests primarily in common stocks of approximately 45 different companies with market capitalizations of any amount exceeding $150M, selected by a proprietary modeling system based on price/performance, earnings, and perceived future earnings. May invest as much as 25% of assets in foreign issues only through ADRs available on domestic exchanges. May

invest up to 25% of assets in one sector, and up to 15% of assets in illiquid securities. May use options and futures for hedging purposes.
Year organized: 1996
Ticker symbol: OSAGX
Discount broker availability: *Fidelity, *Schwab, *White
Dividends paid: Income - December; Capital gains - December
Portfolio turnover (1 yr): 105%
Management fee: 1.00%
Expense ratio: 1.36% (11 months ending 9/30/97) (6.41% without waiver)

O'SHAUGHNESSY CORNERSTONE GROWTH FUND ◆
(See first O'Shaughnessy listing for data common to all funds)

Portfolio manager: James P. O'Shaughnessy (1996)
Investment objective and policies: Long-term capital appreciation. Invests in the common stock of the 50 issues with the highest one-year price appreciation as of the date of purchase, as long as they have a price-to-sales ratio below 1.5 and annual earnings have increased in each of the past five years. Companies must be represented in the S&P Compustat database and have market capitalizations exceeding $150M. Manager must deviate from strategy to prevent industry sector concentration exceeding 25% of assets.
Year organized: 1996
Ticker symbol: OSCGX
Discount broker availability: *Fidelity, *Schwab, *White
Dividends paid: Income - December; Capital gains - December
Portfolio turnover (1 yr): 16%
Management fee: 0.74%
Expense ratio: 1.56% (11 months ending 9/30/97) (1.63% without waiver)

O'SHAUGHNESSY CORNERSTONE VALUE FUND ◆
(See first O'Shaughnessy listing for data common to all funds)

Portfolio manager: James P. O'Shaughnessy (1996)
Investment objective and policies: Total return: capital appreciation and current income. Invests in the 50 highest dividend yielding common stocks from a universe derived from the S&P Compustat database. Companies must not be utility companies, and must have: market capitalizations exceeding the average of those represented in the database; twelve months sales 50% greater than the average for the database; a number of shares outstanding which exceeds the average for the database; and cash flow exceeding the average for the database. Manager must deviate from strategy to prevent industry sector concentration exceeding 25% of assets.
Year organized: 1996
Ticker symbol: OSCVX
Discount broker availability: *Fidelity, *Schwab, *White
Dividends paid: Income - December; Capital gains - December
Portfolio turnover (1 yr): 2%
Management fee: 0.74%
Expense ratio: 1.85% (11 months ending 9/30/97) (2.66% without waiver)

O'SHAUGHNESSY DOGS OF THE MARKET FUND ◆
(See first O'Shaughnessy listing for data common to all funds)

Portfolio manager: James P. O'Shaughnessy (1996)
Investment objective and policies: Capital appreciation. Invests at least 30% of assets in the common stock of the ten highest-yielding companies contained in the Dow Jones Industrial Average. Remaining assets will be invested primarily in 30 to 40 additional stocks perceived to have substantially the same characteristics as the top ten, although they must have:

market capitalizations above $1B; sales, common shares outstanding, and cash flow higher than the average of all stocks in the market; and have dividend yields higher than the average of all the stocks in the market. May invest up to 25% of assets in ADRs, and up to 15% in illiquid securities. May invest up to 25% of total assets in any one industry. May use options and futures in an effort to enhance performance and for hedging purposes.
Year organized: 1996
Ticker symbol: OSDGX
Discount broker availability: *Fidelity, *Schwab, *White
Dividends paid: Income - December; Capital gains - December
Portfolio turnover (1 yr): 118%
Management fee: 0.90%
Expense ratio: 1.99% (11 months ending 9/30/97) (4.28% without waiver)

OVB FUNDS
(Data common to all OVB Funds are shown below. See subsequent listings for data specific to individual portfolios.)

One Valley Square
P.O. Box 1793
Charleston, WV 25326
800-545-6331, 800-354-8618

Adviser: One Valley Bank, N.A.
Administrator: SEI Fund Resources
Transfer agent: DST Systems, Inc.
Special sales restrictions: OVB funds are offered in two classes, "A" and "B" shares; "A" shares, offered to institutions, require a $100M minimum investment, and are offered without 12b-1 fees. Only "B" shares are represented here.
Minimum purchase: Initial $1,000, Subsequent $50; IRA/Keogh: Initial: $500; Automatic investment plan: Subsequent: $100
Wire orders accepted: Yes
Deadline for same day wire purchase: 4 P.M.
Qualified for sale in: CA, CT, DC, FL, GA, IL, IN, KY, LA, MD, MI, MS, NJ, NY, NC, OH, PA, SC, TX, VA, WV, WY
Telephone redemptions: Yes (Prime Obligations only)
Wire redemptions: Yes, $500 minimum, $10 fee
Letter redemptions: Signature guarantee required over $5,000
Telephone switching: With the same share class of other OVB funds
Number of switches permitted: Unlimited
Deadline for same day switch: 4 P.M. (12 NN for MM)
Shareholder services: IRA, Keogh, 401(k), corporate retirement plans, electronic funds transfer, systematic withdrawal plan min. bal. req. $10,000
Administration fee: 0.20% ($100,000 minimum per portfolio)
12b-1 distribution fee: 0.25%
IRA fee: $20 Annual

OVB CAPITAL APPRECIATION PORTFOLIO
(See first OVB listing for data common to all portfolios)

Portfolio manager: David P. Nolan (1993)
Investment objective and policies: Long-term capital growth. Invests primarily in equity securities of undervalued companies with established records of growth and market capitalizations of more than $1B, that are thought to have the potential to achieve above average returns. May invest in securities of foreign issuers traded in the U.S. or Canada without limit, and have up to 15% of assets in illiquid securities.
Year organized: 1993
Discount broker availability: White
Dividends paid: Income - March, June, September, December; Capital gains - December
Portfolio turnover (3 yrs): 90%, 119%, 107%
Management fee: 0.95%
Expense ratio: 1.27% (year ending 1/31/97) (1.52% without waiver)

OVB EMERGING GROWTH PORTFOLIO

(See first OVB listing for data common to all portfolios)

Portfolio manager: David P. Nolan (1993)
Investment objective and policies: Long-term capital growth. Invests primarily in equity securities of undervalued companies with market capitalizations of less than $1B that are thought to have the potential to achieve above average returns. May invest in securities of foreign issuers traded in the U.S. or Canada without limit, and have up to 15% of assets in illiquid securities.
Year organized: 1993
Discount broker availability: White
Dividends paid: Income - March, June, September, December; Capital gains - December
Portfolio turnover (3 yrs): 119%, 117%, 126%
Management fee: 0.95%
Expense ratio: 1.40% (year ending 1/31/97) (1.58% without waiver)

OVB EQUITY INCOME PORTFOLIO

(See first OVB listing for data common to all portfolios)

Portfolio manager: Buel S. Sears (1997)
Investment objective and policies: Current income; moderate capital appreciation secondary. Invests at least 65% of assets in both foreign and domestic dividend paying common stocks, preferred stocks, and preferred stocks and debt securities convertible into common stock. Will generally restrict selections to companies with market capitalizations exceeding $1B, and to securities actively traded in the U.S. either on major exchanges or over-the-counter. May invest up to 25% of assets in one industry sector, and up to 10% of assets in other investment companies. May use options and futures for hedging purposes.
Year organized: 1996
Discount broker availability: White
Dividends paid: Income - March, June, September, December; Capital gains - December
Portfolio turnover (1 yr): 10%
Management fee: 0.74%
Expense ratio: 1.45% (five months ending 7/31/97) (1.50% without waiver)

OVB GOVERNMENT SECURITIES PORTFOLIO

(See first OVB listing for data common to all portfolios)

Portfolio manager: James R. Thomas III (1993)
Investment objective and policies: Current income consistent with capital preservation. Invests primarily in debt obligations guaranteed as to principal and interest by the U.S. Government or its agencies and instrumentalities. Portfolio maintains a dollar-weighted average maturity of three to ten years. May also invest in investment grade corporate debt securities and mortgage- and asset-backed securities. Up to 20% of assets may be in common and preferred stocks of utility companies. May use futures and options for hedging purposes.
Year organized: 1993
Discount broker availability: White
Dividends paid: Income - declared daily, paid monthly; Capital gains - December
Portfolio turnover (3 yrs): 46%, 28%, 13%
Management fee: 0.75%
Expense ratio: 1.08% (year ending 1/31/97) (1.41% without waiver)

OVB PRIME OBLIGATIONS PORTFOLIO

(See first OVB listing for data common to all portfolios)

Sub-adviser: Wellington Management Corp.
Portfolio manager: Tim Smith (1993)
Investment objective and policies: Current income consistent with preservation of capital and a high degree of liquidity. Invests in high quality money market instruments.
Year organized: 1993
Check redemptions: $500 minimum

Dividends paid: Income - declared daily, paid monthly
Management fee: 0.25%
Expense ratio: 0.74% (year ending 1/31/97) (0.91% without waiver)

OVB WEST VIRGINIA TAX-EXEMPT INCOME PORTFOLIO

(See first OVB listing for data common to all portfolios)

Portfolio manager: James R. Thomas III (1993)
Investment objective and policies: Current income exempt from federal and West Virginia personal income taxes, consistent with capital preservation. Invests primarily in high quality municipal securities exempt from federal and West Virginia personal income taxes. Up to 20% of assets may be securities subject to AMT tax treatment. May use futures and options for hedging purposes.
Year organized: 1993
Discount broker availability: White
Dividends paid: Income - declared daily, paid monthly; Capital gains - December
Portfolio turnover (3 yrs): 26%, 43%, 28%
Management fee: 0.45%
Expense ratio: 1.00% (year ending 1/31/97) (1.10% without waiver)

PACIFIC HORIZON CALIFORNIA TAX-EXEMPT MONEY MARKET FUND ◆

555 California Street
San Francisco, CA 94104
800-346-2087
TTY/TDD 800-232-6299

Adviser: Bank of America National Trust and Savings Assn.
Administrator: The BISYS Group, Inc.
Transfer agent: DST Systems, Inc.
Investment objective and policies: High current income consistent with principal stability whose earnings are exempt from federal and California income taxes. Invests in high-grade money market instruments.
Year organized: 1987
Minimum purchase: Initial: $500, Subsequent: $50
Wire orders accepted: Yes
Deadline for same day wire purchase: 12 NN
Telephone orders accepted: Yes, $500 minimum
Qualified for sale in: All states
Telephone redemptions: Yes
Wire redemptions: Yes, $1,000 minimum
Letter redemptions: Signature guarantee required over $50,000
Check redemptions: $500 minimum
Telephone switching: With other Horizon funds (which have loads) and with Sefton Funds
Number of switches permitted: Unlimited
Dividends paid: Income - declared daily, paid monthly
Shareholder services: IRA, SEP-IRA, automatic investment plan, electronic funds transfer, systematic withdrawal plan min. bal. req. $5,000
Management fee: 0.10% first $3B to 0.08% over $5B
Administration fee: 0.10% first $7B to 0.08% over $10B
Expense ratio: 0.25% (year ending 2/28/97) (includes waiver)
IRA fees: Annual $25, Initial $25, Closing $50

PACIFIC HORIZON PRIME MONEY MARKET FUND ◆

555 California Street
San Francisco, CA 94104
800-346-2087
TTY/TDD 800-232-6299

Adviser: Bank of America National Trust and Savings Assn.
Administrator: The BISYS Group, Inc.
Transfer agent: DST Systems, Inc.
Investment objective and policies: High current income consistent with principal stability. Invests in

high-grade bank, corporate and government money market instruments.
Year organized: 1984
Group fund code: 062
Minimum purchase: Initial: $500, Subsequent: $50
Wire orders accepted: Yes
Deadline for same day wire purchase: 12 NN
Telephone orders accepted: Yes, $500 minimum
Qualified for sale in: All states
Telephone redemptions: Yes
Wire redemptions: Yes, $1,000 minimum
Letter redemptions: Signature guarantee required over $50,000
Check redemptions: $500 minimum
Telephone switching: With other Horizon funds (which have loads) and with Sefton Funds
Number of switches permitted: Unlimited
Dividends paid: Income - declared daily, paid monthly
Shareholder services: IRA, SEP-IRA, automatic investment plan, electronic funds transfer, systematic withdrawal plan min. bal. req. $5,000
Management fee: 0.10% first $3B to 0.08% over $5B
Administration fee: 0.10% first $7B to 0.08% over $10B
Expense ratio: 0.23% (year ending 2/28/97) (includes waiver)
IRA fees: Annual $25, Initial $25, Closing $50

PAINEWEBBER CASHFUND ◆

1285 Avenue of the Americas
New York, NY 10019
800-647-1568, 212-713-2000
or call local PaineWebber branch office
Internet: http://www.painewebber.com

Adviser: PaineWebber Inc.
Sub-adviser: Mitchell Hutchins Asset Management, Inc.
Portfolio manager: Susan P. Messina (1994)
Transfer agent: Provident Financial Processing Corp.
Investment objective and policies: Current income, stability of principal and high liquidity. Invests in high-grade money market instruments.
Year organized: 1978
Ticker symbol: PWCXX
Minimum purchase: Initial: $5,000, Subsequent: $500; IRA: Initial: $1,000
Wire orders accepted: Yes
Deadline for same day wire purchase: 2 P.M.
Qualified for sale in: All states
Telephone redemptions: Yes
Wire redemptions: Yes, $5,000 minimum
Letter redemptions: Signature guarantee required
Check redemptions: $500 minimum
Dividends paid: Income - declared daily, paid monthly
Shareholder services: IRA, Keogh
Management fee: 0.50% first $500M to 0.28% over $5.5B
Expense ratio: 0.60% (year ending 3/31/97)
IRA/Keogh fees: Annual $25, Initial $25, Closing $50

PAPP FUNDS ◆

(Data common to all Papp Funds are shown below. See subsequent listings for data specific to individual portfolios.)

4400 North 32nd Street, Suite 280
Phoenix, AZ 85018
800-421-4004, 602-956-1115
fax 602-956-1985
Internet: http://www.roypapp.com
e-mail: invest@roypapp.com

Shareholder service hours: Full service: M-F 8 A.M.-5 P.M. MST
Adviser: L. Roy Papp & Assocs.
Transfer agent: L. Roy Papp & Assocs.
Minimum purchase: Initial: $5,000, Subsequent: $1,000; IRA/Keogh: Initial $1,000
Letter redemptions: Signature guarantee required
Management fee: 1.00%

PAPP AMERICA-ABROAD FUND ◆
(See first Papp listing for data common to all portfolios)

Portfolio managers: L. Roy Papp (1991), Rosellen C. Papp (1997)
Investment objective and policies: Long-term capital growth. Invests in common stocks of U.S. companies that have substantial international activities, and up to 30% of its common stock assets in either common stocks or ADRs of foreign companies traded publicly in U.S. securities markets.
Year organized: 1991
Ticker symbol: PAAFX
Discount broker availability: *Fidelity, *Schwab, Siebert, *White
Qualified for sale in: All states except GU, PR
Dividends paid: Income - June, December; Capital gains - December
Portfolio turnover (3 yrs): 5%, 12%, 27%
Expense ratio: 1.11% (year ending 12/31/97)

PAPP AMERICA-PACIFIC RIM FUND ◆
(See first Papp listing for data common to all portfolios)

Portfolio managers: L. Roy Papp (1997), Rosellen C. Papp (1997)
Investment objective and policies: Long-term capital growth. Invests in common stocks of U.S. companies that have substantial business activities in the Pacific Rim countries, and up to 30% of its common stock assets may be in either common stocks or ADRs of foreign companies traded publicly in U.S. securities markets.
Year organized: 1997
Ticker symbol: PAPRX
Discount broker availability: *Fidelity, *Schwab, Siebert, *White
Qualified for sale in: All states except GU, PR
Dividends paid: Income - June, December; Capital gains - December

L. ROY PAPP STOCK FUND ◆
(See first Papp listing for data common to all portfolios)

Portfolio managers: L. Roy Papp (1989), Rosellen C. Papp (1997)
Investment objective and policies: Long-term capital growth. Invests in common stocks believed undervalued, including those considered speculative. May invest up to 5% of assets in convertible securities. Fund is normally fully invested.
Year organized: 1989
Ticker symbol: LRPSX
Discount broker availability: *Fidelity, *Schwab, Siebert, *White
Qualified for sale in: All states except GU, PR
Dividends paid: Income - June, December; Capital gains - December
Portfolio turnover (3 yrs): 14%, 22%, 20%
Expense ratio: 1.16% (year ending 12/31/96)

PARNASSUS INCOME FUND PORTFOLIOS ◆
(Data common to all Parnassus Income Fund portfolios are shown below. See subsequent listings for data specific to individual portfolios.)

One Market - Steuart Tower, Suite 1600
San Francisco, CA 94105
800-999-3505, 415-778-0200
Internet: http://www.parnassus.com/

Shareholder services: Full service: M-F 8:30 A.M.-5 P.M. PST; After hours service: prices, messages, prospectuses
Adviser: Parnassus Investments
Transfer agent: Parnassus Investments
Social policy: Adviser attempts to invest in companies which treat employees fairly, have sound environmental protection policies, support equal employment opportunity, provide quality products and services, are sensitive to the local communities in which they operate and engage in ethical business practices. Fund does not invest in companies that manufacture alcohol or

tobacco products, are involved with gambling, are weapons contractors, or generate electricity from nuclear power.
Minimum purchase: Initial: $2,000, Subsequent: $50; IRA: Initial: $500; Automatic investment plan: Initial: $500
Wire orders accepted: No
Letter redemptions: Signature guarantee not required
Telephone switching: With other Parnassus Income Fund portfolios, and the Parnassus Fund (which has a 3.5% load), $50 minimum
Number of switches permitted: Unlimited
Shareholder services: IRA, SEP-IRA
IRA/Keogh fees: Annual $15

PARNASSUS INCOME FUND - BALANCED PORTFOLIO ◆
(See first Parnassus listing for data common to all portfolios)

Portfolio manager: Jerome L. Dodson (1992)
Investment objective and policies: Current income and capital preservation; capital appreciation secondary. Invests in a diversified portfolio of fixed-income and equity securities with the allocation adjusted according to perceived market conditions. At least 25% of assets are in fixed-income securities. Up to 10% of assets may be in community development loan funds.
Year organized: 1992
Ticker symbol: PRBLX
Qualified for sale in: All states
Discount broker availability: Fidelity, Siebert, Schwab, *White
Dividends paid: Income - March, June, September, December; Capital gains - December
Portfolio turnover (3 yrs): 48%, 15%, 7%
Management fee: 0.75% first $30M to 0.65% over $100M
Expense ratio: 0.80% (year ending 12/31/96) (1.40% without waiver)

PARNASSUS INCOME FUND - CALIFORNIA TAX-EXEMPT PORTFOLIO ◆
(See first Parnassus listing for data common to all portfolios)

Portfolio managers: David Pogran (1992), Jerome L. Dodson (1992)
Investment objective and policies: High current income exempt from federal and California personal income taxes, while choosing a portfolio that will have a positive social and environmental impact. Invests in a diversified portfolio of tax-exempt investment grade securities issued by California state and local governments and by other public authorities. Up to 20% of assets may be in AMT securities.
Year organized: 1992
Ticker symbol: PRCLX
Qualified for sale in: CA
Discount broker availability: Fidelity, Siebert, *White
Dividends paid: Income - declared daily, paid monthly; Capital gains - December
Portfolio turnover (3 yrs): 0%, 13%, 12%
Management fee: 0.50% first $200M to 0.40% over $400M
Expense ratio: 0.54% (year ending 12/31/96) (1.00% without waiver)

PARNASSUS INCOME FUND - FIXED INCOME PORTFOLIO ◆
(See first Parnassus listing for data common to all portfolios)

Portfolio manager: Jerome L. Dodson (1992)
Investment objective and policies: High current income consistent with safety and capital preservation. Invests in a diversified portfolio of investment grade bonds and other fixed-income instruments. Portfolio maintains a weighted average maturity of 5 to 20 years depending on market conditions. Fund expects a substantial portion of its funds will be in FHLMC ("Freddie Mac"), FNMA ("Fannie Mae") and GNMA

securities. Up to 10% of assets may be in community development loan funds.
Year organized: 1992
Ticker symbol: PRFIX
Qualified for sale in: All states
Discount broker availability: Fidelity, Siebert, *White
Dividends paid: Income - declared daily, paid monthly; Capital gains - December
Portfolio turnover (3 yrs): 3%, 12%, 5%
Management fee: 0.50% first $200M to 0.40% over $400M
Expense ratio: 0.83% (year ending 12/31/96) (1.33% without waiver)

PATHFINDER FUND ◆
P.O. Box 75231
Los Angeles, CA 90075-0231
800-444-4778, 213-386-4049, 213-252-9000
shareholder services 800-207-0760
fax 213-386-4050

Adviser: Pathfinder Advisors
Portfolio manager: Edwin R. Bernstein (1989)
Transfer agent: Unified Advisers, Inc.
Investment objective and policies: Long-term capital growth. Invests substantially all of its assets in common stocks believed significantly undervalued, primarily of companies with market capitalizations under $500M. May write covered call options and utilize stock index options for hedging purposes. Up to 20% of assets may be in ADRs of foreign issuers.
Year organized: 1987 (formerly Prudent Speculator Leveraged Fund. Name and objective changed in July 1993. Name changed from Prudent Speculator Fund 4/3/96.)
Ticker symbol: PSLFX
Minimum purchase: Initial: $1; Subsequent: $25
Wire orders accepted: Yes
Deadline for same day wire purchase: 4 P.M.
Discount broker availability: *White
Qualified for sale in: All states except AR, DE, GU, KY, ME, MT, NE, NH, NM, ND, OK, PR, RI, SC, SD, TN, UT, VT, VI, WV, WY
Telephone redemptions: Yes
Letter redemptions: Signature guarantee required
Dividends paid: Income - December; Capital gains - December
Portfolio turnover (3 yrs): 131%, 119%, 60%
Shareholder services: IRA, SEP-IRA, automatic investment plan, systematic withdrawal plan min. bal. req $10,000
Management fee: 0.875%
12b-1 distribution fee: Maximum of 0.25% (not currently imposed)
Expense ratio: 1.37% (year ending 10/31/97) (4.14% without waiver)
IRA/Keogh fees: None

PAX WORLD FUND ◆
222 State Street
Portsmouth, NH 03801-3853
800-767-1729, 603-431-8022
shareholder services 800-372-7827
Internet: http://www.paxfund.com/
e-mail: paxworld@nh.ultranet.com

Adviser: Pax World Management Corp.
Portfolio manager: Anthony S. Brown (1971)
Transfer agent: PFPC, Inc.
Investment objective and policies: Income and capital preservation; long-term capital growth secondary. Normally invests about 60% of assets in common and preferred stock and 40% in bonds, but may adjust allocation according to perceived changes in market or economic conditions. Invests in companies that do *not* engage in manufacturing defense or weapons-related products, or are *not* in tobacco, liquor, or gambling industries. Invests in companies producing life-supportive goods and services.
Year organized: 1970
Ticker symbol: PAXWX
Minimum purchase: Initial: $250, Subsequent: $50
Wire orders accepted: Yes, subsequent only
Deadline for same day wire purchase: 4 P.M.
Discount broker availability: Fidelity, *Schwab, Siebert, *White
Qualified for sale in: All states

Telephone redemptions: Yes, $1,000 minimum
Letter redemptions: Signature guarantee required
Telephone switching: With Pax World Growth Fund, a load fund $100 minimum
Number of switches permitted: Unlimited
Dividends paid: Income - July, December; Capital gains - December
Portfolio turnover (3 yrs): 14%, 35%, 28%
Shareholder services: IRA, SEP-IRA, 403(b), automatic investment plan, electronic funds transfer (purchase only), systematic withdrawal plan min. bal. req. $10,000
Management fee: 0.75% first $25M, 0.50% over $25M
12b-1 distribution fee: Maximum of 0.25%
Expense ratio: 0.91% (year ending 12/31/97)
IRA fees: Annual $10

PAYDEN & RYGEL FUNDS ◆

(Data common to all Payden & Rygel funds are shown below. See subsequent listings for data specific to individual funds.)

333 South Grand Avenue, 32nd Floor
Los Angeles, CA 90071
800-572-9336, 213-625-1900
Internet: http://www.payden.com

Adviser: Payden & Rygel
Administrator: Treasury Plus, Inc.
Transfer agent: Investors Fiduciary Trust Co.
Special sales restrictions: Information here reflects only "R" shares; "S" shares, which have 12b-1 fees, are as yet unavailable.
Minimum purchase: Initial: $5,000, Subsequent: $1,000; IRA: Initial: $2,000; Automatic investment plan: Initial: $2,500, Subsequent: $250 (exceptions noted)
Wire orders accepted: Yes
Deadline for same day wire purchase: 4 P.M.
Qualified for sale in: All states
Telephone redemptions: Yes
Wire redemptions: Yes
Letter redemptions: Signature guarantee not required
Telephone switching: With other Payden & Rygel funds, $1,000 minimum
Number of switches permitted: Unlimited
Shareholder services: IRA, SEP-IRA, 403(b), corporate retirement plans
Administration fee: 0.06% (aggregate of all funds)
IRA fees: None

PAYDEN & RYGEL BUNKER HILL MONEY MARKET FUND ◆

(See first Payden & Rygel listing for data common to all funds)

Portfolio manager: Team managed
Investment objective and policies: High level of current income consistent with a stable share price, and the preservation of principal and liquidity. Invests in high quality corporate, bank and government short-term money market instruments and repurchase agreements thereon.
Year organized: 1997
Dividends paid: Income - declared daily, paid monthly
Management fee: 0.15%

PAYDEN & RYGEL EUROPEAN GROWTH AND INCOME FUND ◆

(See first Payden & Rygel listing for data common to all funds)

Sub-adviser: Scottish Widows Investment Management Ltd.
Portfolio manager: Team managed
Investment objective and policies: Growth of capital and some current income. Normally invests in the common stocks of approximately ten issuers located in each of France, Germany, the Netherlands and the U.K. The selections are those companies with the highest dividend yield chosen from the thirty companies in each country with the highest market capitalization. Fund is also known as "the Euro Dogs" fund.

Portfolio is rebalanced monthly after review of those issues selected one year previous.
Year organized: 1997
Discount broker availability: Schwab, *White
Dividends paid: Income - quarterly; Capital gains - annually
Portfolio turnover (1 yr): 9%
Management fee: 0.50% first $2B, 0.40% over $2B
Expense ratio: 0.69% (seven months ending 10/31/97) (2.48% without waiver)

PAYDEN & RYGEL GLOBAL BALANCED FUND ◆

(See first Payden & Rygel listing for data common to all funds)

Sub-adviser: Scottish Widows Investment Management Ltd.
Portfolio manager: Team managed
Investment objective and policies: High level of total return consistent with preservation of capital. Allocates assets among a common stock portfolio, a bond portfolio, and money market instruments, in proportions which reflect the adviser's judgement of anticipated returns and risks of each asset class. There are no limitations on the amount of assets which may be allocated to any class. Money market and debt securities may be in U.S. or non-U.S. denominated issues, and equity securities may be from anywhere in the world. At least 65% of the equity portfolio will be distributed throughout at least three countries. May use futures or options contracts on stock indexes, foreign currencies and bonds.
Year organized: 1996
Ticker symbol: PYGBX
Discount broker availability: Fidelity, *White
Dividends paid: Income - quarterly; Capital gains - annually
Portfolio turnover (1 yr): 211%
Management fee: 0.50% first $1B, 0.40% over $1B
Expense ratio: 0.70% (eleven months ending 10/31/97) (1.64% without waiver)

PAYDEN & RYGEL GLOBAL FIXED INCOME FUND ◆

(See first Payden & Rygel listing for data common to all funds)

Portfolio manager: Team managed
Investment objective and policies: High level of total return consistent with preservation of capital. Invests in high quality U.S. and foreign government notes, bonds, and corporate debt securities. Will maintain a dollar-weighted average maturity of ten years or less. May invest in a variety of derivative instruments in an effort to enhance performance and for hedging purposes.
Year organized: 1992
Ticker symbol: PYGFX
Discount broker availability: Fidelity, Schwab, *White
Dividends paid: Income - monthly; Capital gains - annually
Portfolio turnover (3 yrs): 289%, 176%, 227%
Management fee: 0.30% first $2B to 0.25% over $2B
Expense ratio: 0.49% (year ending 10/31/97)

PAYDEN & RYGEL GLOBAL SHORT BOND FUND ◆

(See first Payden & Rygel listing for data common to all funds)

Portfolio manager: Team managed
Investment objective and policies: High level of total return consistent with preservation of capital. Invests in both domestic and foreign government and corporate debt securities. Will also make substantial investments in foreign currency contracts in order to hedge foreign currency exposure. At least 65% of assets will be distributed in issues from at least three different countries. Securities will be, at the time of investment, considered high quality by at least one rating agency; if the rating of bonds of any country is lowered so that two or more agencies categorize the investments below AA, the fund will discontinue making investments in that country and liquidate any current holdings as soon as possible.

Year organized: 1996
Ticker symbol: PYGSX
Minimum purchase: Initial: $100,000 (accounts previous to this change may only add to them if the new investment will increase the value to this minimum)
Discount broker availability: *White
Dividends paid: Income - monthly; Capital gains - annually
Portfolio turnover (1 yr): 214%
Management fee: 0.30% first $2B to 0.25% over $2B
Expense ratio: 0.45% (year ending 10/31/97) (0.53% without waiver)

PAYDEN & RYGEL GROWTH & INCOME FUND ◆

(See first Payden & Rygel listing for data common to all funds)

Portfolio manager: Team managed
Investment objective and policies: Growth of capital and some current income. Invests at least 45% of its total assets in equity securities and the balance in equity-based derivative instruments such as SPDRs, stock index futures contracts, options on stocks and stock indexes, and equity swap contracts. Allocation to various categories will vary with perceived market conditions. Approximately 50% of total assets will be invested in the ten common stocks included in the Dow Jones Industrial Average which had the highest dividend rates during the previous calendar year.
Year organized: 1996
Ticker symbol: PDOGX
Discount broker availability: Fidelity, Schwab, *White
Dividends paid: Income - quarterly; Capital gains - annually
Portfolio turnover (1 yr): 2%
Management fee: 0.50% first $2B, 0.30% over $2B
Expense ratio: 0.54% (year ending 10/31/97) (0.89% without waiver)

PAYDEN & RYGEL GROWTH STOCK FUND ◆

(See first Payden & Rygel listing for data common to all funds)

Portfolio manager: Team managed
Investment objective and policies: Long-term capital appreciation. Invests primarily in common stocks of domestic companies with market capitalizations between $250M and $4B that are perceived to offer growth potential. May also invest up to 15% of assets in ADRs of foreign issuers traded in the U.S., and up to 25% of assets in S&P Depositary Receipts, known as SPDRs, or "Spiders." May use a variety of derivative instruments in an effort to enhance return and for hedging purposes.
Year organized: 1998
Dividends paid: Income - semi-annually; Capital gains - annually
Management fee: 0.60% first $1B, 0.50% over $2B

PAYDEN & RYGEL HIGH INCOME FUND ◆

(See first Payden & Rygel listing for data common to all funds)

Portfolio manager: Team managed
Investment objective and policies: High current income with the potential for capital appreciation. Invests at least 65% of assets in a diversified portfolio of junk bonds. Fund focuses on those issues believed to be at the low-risk end of the high yield spectrum, issued by companies thought to have stable to improving business prospects. May also invest up to 20% of assets in convertible bonds, preferred stocks, Brady bonds or bonds of issuers headquartered in emerging markets. The average maturity of the portfolio is generally less than eight years.
Year organized: 1998
Dividends paid: Income - monthly; Capital gains - annually
Management fee: 0.35%

PAYDEN & RYGEL INTERMEDIATE BOND FUND ◆

(See first Payden & Rygel listing for data common to all funds)

Portfolio manager: Team managed
Investment objective and policies: High total return consistent with preservation of capital. Invests in high quality debt obligations of the U.S. Treasury, U.S. Government agencies, foreign and domestic public corporations and mortgage-backed securities. Portfolio generally maintains a dollar-weighted average maturity of three to six years. May invest in a variety of derivative instruments in an effort to enhance performance and for hedging purposes.
Year organized: 1994
Ticker symbol: PYIMX
Minimum purchase: Initial: $100,000 (accounts previous to this change may only add to them if the new investment will increase the value to this minimum)
Discount broker availability: Fidelity, *White
Dividends paid: Income - monthly; Capital gains - annually
Portfolio turnover (3 yrs): 192%, 196%, 189%
Management fee: 0.28% first $1B, 0.25% over $1B
Expense ratio: 0.45% (year ending 10/31/97) (0.55% without waiver)

PAYDEN & RYGEL INTERNATIONAL BOND FUND ◆

(Fund liquidated 1/18/98)

PAYDEN & RYGEL INTERNATIONAL EQUITY FUND ◆

(See first Payden & Rygel listing for data common to all funds)

Sub-adviser: Scottish Widows Investment Management Ltd.
Portfolio manager: Team managed
Investment objective and policies: High level of total return consistent with preservation of capital. Invests in common and preferred equity securities in at least five countries outside of the U.S. Universe of available companies is determined primarily by determining if the long-term government debt of the firm's country is rated as investment grade, although as much as 20% of assets may be invested in countries that do not meet this criteria.
Year organized: 1996
Ticker symbol: PYIEX
Discount broker availability: Fidelity, *White
Dividends paid: Income - quarterly; Capital gains - annually
Portfolio turnover (1 yr): 66%
Management fee: 0.60% first $1B, 0.45% over $1B
Expense ratio: 0.90% (eleven months ending 10/31/97) (1.57% without waiver)

PAYDEN & RYGEL INVESTMENT QUALITY BOND FUND ◆

(See first Payden & Rygel listing for data common to all funds)

Portfolio manager: Team managed
Investment objective and policies: High total return consistent with preservation of capital. Invests in high quality debt obligations of the U.S. Treasury, U.S. Government agencies, foreign and domestic public corporations and mortgage-backed securities, with no limitations on maturity. May invest in a variety of derivative instruments in an effort to enhance performance and for hedging purposes.
Year organized: 1994 (name changed from Opportunity Fund 1996)
Ticker symbol: PYOPX
Discount broker availability: Fidelity, Schwab, *White
Dividends paid: Income - monthly; Capital gains - annually
Portfolio turnover (3 yrs): 317%, 197%, 252%
Management fee: 0.28% first $1B, 0.25% over $1B
Expense ratio: 0.45% (year ending 10/31/97) (0.53% without waiver)

PAYDEN & RYGEL LIMITED MATURITY FUND ◆

(See first Payden & Rygel listing for data common to all funds)

Portfolio manager: Team managed
Investment objective and policies: High total return consistent with preservation of capital that, over time, exceeds the return available from money market funds. Invests in high quality debt obligations of the U.S. Treasury, U.S. Government agencies, foreign and domestic public corporations and mortgage backed securities. Portfolio generally maintains a dollar-weighted average maturity of four to nine months, with a maximum average of one year. May invest in a variety of derivative instruments in an effort to enhance performance and for hedging purposes.
Year organized: 1994
Ticker symbol: PYLMX
Minimum purchase: Initial: $100,000 (accounts previous to this change may only add to them if the new investment will increase the value to this minimum)
Discount broker availability: *White
Check redemptions: Yes, $2 fee for balances below $25,000
Dividends paid: Income - monthly; Capital gains - annually
Portfolio turnover (3 yrs): 135%, 217%, 166%
Management fee: 0.28% first $1B, 0.25% over $1B
Expense ratio: 0.30% (year ending 10/31/97) (0.52% without waiver)

PAYDEN & RYGEL MARKET RETURN FUND ◆

(See first Payden & Rygel listing for data common to all funds)

Portfolio manager: Team managed
Investment objective and policies: Total return in excess of the S&P 500 Stock Index. Invests primarily in equity-based investments such as stock index futures contracts and equity swap contracts, as well as in fixed-income securities. Portfolio will generally consist of 80% investment grade, dollar-denominated foreign and domestic fixed-income instruments, both private and government. The average duration of the portfolio will be no more than five years.
Year organized: 1995 (name changed from Equity Market Tracking 2/7/96)
Ticker symbol: PYMRX
Discount broker availability: Fidelity, Schwab, *White
Dividends paid: Income - monthly; Capital gains - annually
Portfolio turnover (2 yrs): 140%, 146%
Management fee: 0.28% first $1B, 0.25% over $1B
Expense ratio: 0.45% (year ending 10/31/97) (0.96% without waiver)

PAYDEN & RYGEL SHORT BOND FUND ◆

(See first Payden & Rygel listing for data common to all funds)

Portfolio manager: Team managed
Investment objective and policies: High total return consistent with preservation of capital. Invests in high quality debt obligations of the U.S. Treasury, U.S. Government agencies, foreign and domestic public corporations and mortgage backed securities. Portfolio maintains a dollar-weighted average maturity of three years or less. May invest in a variety of derivative instruments in an effort to enhance performance and for hedging purposes.
Year organized: 1994
Ticker symbol: PYSBX
Minimum purchase: Initial: $100,000 (accounts previous to this change may only add to them if the new investment will increase the value to this minimum)
Discount broker availability: Schwab, *White
Dividends paid: Income - monthly; Capital gains - annually
Portfolio turnover (3 yrs): 208%, 212%, 170%
Management fee: 0.28% first $1B, 0.25% over $1B
Expense ratio: 0.40% (year ending 10/31/97) (0.49% without waiver)

PAYDEN & RYGEL SHORT DURATION TAX EXEMPT FUND ◆

(See first Payden & Rygel listing for data common to all funds)

Portfolio manager: Team managed
Investment objective and policies: Income exempt from federal income tax consistent with preservation of capital. Invests in debt obligations issued by state and local governments and other issuers that provide interest income exempt from federal income taxes. Portfolio maintains an average maturity of one to four years. May invest in a variety of derivative instruments in an effort to enhance performance and for hedging purposes.
Year organized: 1994
Ticker symbol: PYSDX
Discount broker availability: Fidelity, *White
Dividends paid: Income - monthly; Capital gains - annually
Portfolio turnover (3 yrs): 57%, 35%, 80%
Management fee: 0.32% first $500M to 0.25% over $1B
Expense ratio: 0.45% (year ending 10/31/97) (0.62% without waiver)

PAYDEN & RYGEL TAX EXEMPT BOND FUND ◆

(See first Payden & Rygel listing for data common to all funds)

Portfolio manager: Team managed
Investment objective and policies: Income exempt from federal income tax consistent with preservation of capital. Invests in debt obligations issued by state and local governments and other issuers that provide interest income exempt from federal income taxes. Portfolio is not constrained as to its average maturity, and the average dollar-weighted maturity may be adjusted according to perceived market conditions. May invest in a variety of derivative instruments in an effort to enhance performance and for hedging purposes.
Year organized: 1993
Ticker symbol: PYTEX
Discount broker availability: Fidelity, Schwab, *White
Dividends paid: Income - monthly; Capital gains - annually
Portfolio turnover (3 yrs): 42%, 23%, 42%
Management fee: 0.32% first $500M to 0.25% over $1B
Expense ratio: 0.45% (year ending 10/31/97) (0.59% without waiver)

PAYDEN & RYGEL TOTAL RETURN FUND ◆

(See first Payden & Rygel listing for data common to all funds)

Portfolio manager: Team managed
Investment objective and policies: High level of total return consistent with preservation of capital. Invest primarily in a diverse portfolio of fixed-income securities perceived to afford attractive yields and potential capital gains. Maturity and duration are actively managed according to perceived market conditions and long-term trends in interest rates and inflation. May invest in foreign debt issues, and use currency hedging.
Year organized: 1996
Ticker symbol: PYTRX
Minimum purchase: Initial: $100,000 (accounts previous to this change may only add to them if the new investment will increase the value to this minimum)
Discount broker availability: Fidelity, *White
Dividends paid: Income - monthly; Capital gains - annually
Portfolio turnover (1 yr): 206%
Management fee: 0.28% first $1B, 0.25% over $1B
Expense ratio: 0.45% (eleven months ending 10/31/97) (0.69% without waiver)

PAYDEN & RYGEL
U.S. GOVERNMENT FUND ◆
(See first Payden & Rygel listing for data common to all funds)

Portfolio manager: Team managed
Investment objective and policies: High total return consistent with preservation of capital. Invests in U.S. Treasury debt securities guaranteed by the full faith and credit of the U.S. Government, with maturities ranging from one day to ten years; average maturity is adjusted according to perceived changes in market conditions.
Year organized: 1995 (name changed from U.S. Treasury Fund 1/98)
Ticker symbol: PYTSX
Discount broker availability: Fidelity, *White
Dividends paid: Income - monthly; Capital gains - annually
Portfolio turnover (3 yrs): 160%, 152%, 87%
Management fee: 0.28% first $1B, 0.25% over $1B
Expense ratio: 0.45% (year ending 10/31/97) (0.63% without waiver)

PAYDEN & RYGEL VALUE
STOCK FUND ◆
(See first Payden & Rygel listing for data common to all funds)

Portfolio manager: Team managed
Investment objective and policies: Long-term capital appreciation. Invests primarily in common stocks of domestic companies with market capitalizations between $250M and $4B that are perceived to be undervalued. May also invest up to 15% of assets in ADRs of foreign issuers traded in the U.S., and up to 25% of assets in S&P Depositary Receipts, known as SPDRs, or "Spiders." May use a variety of derivative instruments in an effort to enhance return and for hedging purposes.
Year organized: 1998
Dividends paid: Income - semi-annually; Capital gains - annually
Management fee: 0.60% first $1B, 0.50% over $2B

PBHG FUNDS ◆
(Data common to all PBHG funds are shown below. See subsequent listings for data specific to individual funds.)

825 Duportail Road
Wayne, PA 19087
800-433-0051, 800-809-8008
610-341-9000, fax 610-687-1890
Internet: http://www.pbhgfunds.com

Adviser: Pilgrim Baxter & Assocs., Ltd.
Administrator: PBHG Fund Services
Distributor: SEI Financial Management Corp.
Transfer agent: DST Systems, Inc.
Special sales information: Certain PBHG funds are offering "Adviser" Class shares, with different fees structures. The funds we refer to here are "PBHG" Class shares.
Minimum purchase: Initial: $2,500, Subsequent: None; IRA/Keogh: Initial: $2,000; Automatic investment plan: Initial: $500, Subsequent: $25 (exceptions noted)
Wire orders accepted: Yes
Deadline for same day wire purchase: 4 P.M. (2 P.M. for Cash Reserves Fund)
Qualified for sale in: All states
Telephone redemptions: Yes
Wire redemptions: Yes, $10 fee
Letter redemptions: Signature guarantee required over $50,000
Telephone switching: With other PBHG funds
Number of switches permitted: Unlimited (only 4 outbound to Cash Reserve per portfolio per year)
Shareholder services: IRA, SEP-IRA, Keogh, 401(k), 403(b), corporate retirement plans, electronic funds transfer, systematic withdrawal plan min. bal. req. $5,000
Maintenance fee: $12 per account for balances below initial minimums
Administration fee: 0.15%
IRA/Keogh fees: Annual $10

PBHG CASH RESERVES ◆
(See first PBHG listing for data common to all funds)

Sub-adviser: Wellington Management Co., LLP
Investment objective and policies: Current income consistent with preservation of principal and liquidity. Invests in U.S. dollar-denominated money market securities of domestic and foreign issuers.
Year organized: 1995
Check redemptions: $250 minimum
Dividends paid: Income - declared daily, paid monthly
Management fee: 0.30%
Expense ratio: 0.68% (year ending 3/31/97)

PBHG CORE GROWTH FUND ◆
(See first PBHG listing for data common to all funds)

Portfolio managers: James D. McCall (1995), Ellen A. McGee (1997)
Investment objective and policies: Long-term capital growth. Invests primarily in equity securities of companies, without regard to market capitalization, believed to have superior long-term growth prospects and potential for long-term capital appreciation. Fund focuses on mid-cap companies poised for rapid growth. May have up to 15% of assets in securities of foreign issuers and 15% in illiquid securities.
Year organized: 1995
Ticker symbol: PBCRX
Discount broker availability: *Fidelity, *Schwab, *White
Dividends paid: Income - December; Capital gains - December
Portfolio turnover (2 yrs): 47%, 17%
Management fee: 0.85%
Expense ratio: 1.36% (year ending 3/31/97)

PBHG EMERGING GROWTH FUND ◆
(See first PBHG listing for data common to all funds)

Portfolio manager: Christine M. Baxter (1993)
Investment objective and policies: Long-term capital growth. Invests primarily in common stocks of domestic companies and ADRs of foreign concerns with market capitalizations ranging from $10M to $250M with demonstrable records of exceptional growth and prospects for continued strong growth. May invest up to 15% of assets in illiquid securities.
Year organized: 1993
Ticker symbol: PBEGX
Special sales restrictions: Fund closed to new shareholders on 3/31/95, reopened 5/1/96.
Discount broker availability: *Fidelity, *Schwab, *Siebert, *White
Dividends paid: Income - December; Capital gains - December
Portfolio turnover (3 yrs): 48%, 97%, 28%
Management fee: 0.85%
Expense ratio: 1.28% (year ending 3/31/97)

PBHG GROWTH FUND ◆
(See first PBHG listing for data common to all funds)

Portfolio manager: Gary L. Pilgrim (1985)
Investment objective and policies: Capital growth. Invests primarily in common stocks of companies with prospects for strong earnings growth and significant capital appreciation. Fund will normally have at least 65% of assets in companies with market capitalizations under $2B. May have up to 15% of assets in securities of foreign issuers and 15% in illiquid securities.
Year organized: 1985
Ticker symbol: PBHGX
Discount broker availability: *Fidelity, *Schwab, *Siebert, *White
Dividends paid: Income - December; Capital gains - December
Portfolio turnover (3 yrs): 65%, 45%, 119%
Management fee: 0.85%
Expense ratio: 1.25% (year ending 3/31/97)

PBHG INTERNATIONAL FUND ◆
(See first PBHG listing for data common to all funds)

Sub-adviser: Murray Johnstone International, Ltd.
Portfolio manager: Rodger F. Scullion (1995)
Investment objective and policies: Capital growth.

Invests at least 65% of assets in equity securities of non-U.S. issuers from at least three different countries. May have more than 25% of assets in securities of companies in emerging markets, more than 25% in securities of Japanese issuers and up to 15% in illiquid securities. May invest directly and use ADRs and GDRs. May use forward foreign currency contracts and options for hedging purposes.
Year organized: 1994
Ticker symbol: PBHIX
Discount broker availability: *Fidelity, *Schwab, *Siebert, *White
Dividends paid: Income - December; Capital gains - December
Portfolio turnover (3 yrs): 75%, 140%, 82%
Management fee: 1.00%
Expense ratio: 2.22% (year ending 3/31/97)

PBHG LARGE CAP GROWTH FUND ◆
(See first PBHG listing for data common to all funds)

Portfolio managers: James D. McCall (1995), Ellen A. McGee (1997)
Investment objective and policies: Long-term capital growth. Invests primarily in common stocks of companies with prospects for strong earnings growth and significant capital appreciation. Fund will normally have at least 65% of assets in companies with market capitalizations in excess of $1B (with a median capitalization of approximately $2.75B). May invest in ADRs and have up to 10% of assets in securities of foreign issuers not traded in the U.S. or Canada. May have up to 15% of assets in illiquid securities and use options for hedging purposes.
Year organized: 1995
Ticker symbol: PBHLX
Discount broker availability: *Fidelity, *Schwab, *Siebert, *White
Dividends paid: Income - December; Capital gains - December
Portfolio turnover (2 yrs): 52%, 117%
Management fee: 0.75%
Expense ratio: 1.23% (year ending 3/31/97)

PBHG LARGE CAP 20 FUND ◆
(See first PBHG listing for data common to all funds)

Portfolio managers: James D. McCall (1996), Ellen A. McGee (1997)
Investment objective and policies: Long-term capital growth. Invests primarily in common stocks of a limited number of no more than twenty companies with prospects for strong earnings growth and significant capital appreciation. Fund will normally have at least 65% of assets in companies with market capitalizations in excess of $1B. May invest in ADRs and have up to 40% of assets in securities of foreign issuers not traded in the U.S. or Canada. May have up to 15% of assets in illiquid securities and use options for hedging purposes.
Year organized: 1996
Ticker symbol: PLCPX
Discount broker availability: *Fidelity, *Schwab, *Siebert, *White
Dividends paid: Income - December; Capital gains - December
Portfolio turnover (1 yr): 44%
Management fee: 0.85%
Expense ratio: 1.50% (4 months ending 3/31/97)

PBHG LARGE CAP VALUE FUND ◆
(See first PBHG listing for data common to all funds)

Sub-adviser: Newbold's Asset Management, Inc.
Portfolio manager: James H. Farrell (1996)
Investment objective and policies: Long-term growth of capital and income; current income secondary. Invests at least 65% of assets in a diversified portfolio of equity securities of companies with market capitalization exceeding $1B perceived to be overlooked or undervalued. Generally will invest in issues from the U.S. or Canada, but may invest up to 15% of assets in foreign companies, including ADRs. May have up to 15% of assets in illiquid securities and use options for hedging purposes.
Year organized: 1996
Ticker symbol: PLCVX

Discount broker availability: *Fidelity, *Schwab, *Siebert, *White
Dividends paid: Income - December; Capital gains - December
Management fee: 0.65%
Expense ratio: 1.50% (3 months ending 3/31/97) (1.74% without waiver)

PBHG LIMITED FUND ◆
(See first PBHG listing for data common to all funds)

Portfolio manager: Christine M. Baxter (1996)
Investment objective and policies: Long-term capital appreciation. Invests primarily in a diversified portfolio of equity securities of companies with market capitalizations or annual revenues up to $250M, believed to have prospects for strong earnings growth and significant capital appreciation. Fund will normally purchase only securities traded in the U.S. or Canada, but may invest up to 15% of total assets in securities of foreign issuers including ADRs and foreign currency exchange contracts. May have up to 15% of assets in illiquid securities.
Year organized: 1996
Ticker symbol: PBLDX
Minimum purchase: Initial: $5,000
Special sales restrictions: Fund closed to new investors the day it opened, July 1, 1996.
Discount broker availability: *Schwab
Dividends paid: Income - December; Capital gains - December
Portfolio turnover (1 yr): 75%
Management fee: 1.00%
Expense ratio: 1.42% (9 months ending 3/31/97)

PBHG MID-CAP VALUE FUND ◆
(See first PBHG listing for data common to all funds)

Sub-adviser: Newbold's Asset Management, Inc.
Portfolio manager: Gary D. Haubold (1997)
Investment objective and policies: Above average total return over a three to five year market cycle, consistent with reasonable risk. Invests primarily in equity securities of companies with market capitalizations in the range of companies represented in the S&P Mid-Cap 400 Index, currently between $200M and $5B. Companies are selected that are perceived to be undervalued. Fund will normally purchase only securities traded in the U.S. or Canada, but may invest up to 15% of total assets in securities of foreign issuers including ADRs and foreign currency exchange contracts. May have up to 15% of assets in illiquid securities. May use futures contracts for hedging purposes.
Year organized: 1997
Ticker symbol: PBMCX
Discount broker availability: *Fidelity, *Schwab, *Siebert, *White
Dividends paid: Income - December; Capital gains - December
Management fee: 0.65%

PBHG SELECT EQUITY FUND ◆
(See first PBHG listing for data common to all funds)

Portfolio managers: James D. McCall (1995), Ellen A. McGee (1997)
Investment objective and policies: Long-term capital growth. Invests primarily in common stocks of companies with prospects for strong earnings growth and significant capital appreciation. Fund will normally have at least 65% of assets in a limited number (less than 30) of stocks of small, medium and large capitalization companies with strong earnings growth outlooks and potential for capital appreciation. May invest in ADRs and have up to 10% of assets in securities of foreign issuers not traded in the U.S. or Canada. May have up to 15% of assets in illiquid securities and use options for hedging purposes.
Year organized: 1995
Ticker symbol: PBHEX
Special sales restrictions: Closed to new investors 10/1/96; reopened 7/1/97
Discount broker availability: *Fidelity, *Schwab, *Siebert, *White
Dividends paid: Income - December; Capital gains - December

Portfolio turnover (2 yrs): 72%, 206%
Management fee: 0.85%
Expense ratio: 1.26% (year ending 3/31/97)

PBHG SMALL CAP VALUE FUND ◆
(See first PBHG listing for data common to all funds)

Sub-adviser: Newbold's Asset Management, Inc.
Portfolio manager: Gary D. Haubold (1997)
Investment objective and policies: Above average total return over a three to five year market cycle, consistent with reasonable risk. Invests primarily in equity securities of companies with market capitalizations within the range of companies represented in the Russell 2000 Index, currently between $57M and $610. Companies are selected that are perceived to be undervalued. Fund will normally purchase only securities traded in the U.S. or Canada, but may invest up to 15% of total assets in securities of foreign issuers including ADRs and foreign currency exchange contracts. May have up to 15% of assets in illiquid securities. May use futures contracts for hedging purposes.
Year organized: 1997
Ticker symbol: PBSVX
Discount broker availability: *Fidelity, *Schwab, *Siebert, *White
Dividends paid: Income - December; Capital gains - December
Management fee: 1.00%

PBHG STATEGIC SMALL COMPANY FUND ◆
(See first PBHG listing for data common to all funds)

Sub-adviser: Newbold's Asset Management, Inc.
Portfolio managers: James M. Smith (1996), Gary D. Haubold (1996)
Investment objective and policies: Long-term capital growth. Invests at least 65% of assets in a diversified portfolio of companies with market capitalizations under $750M at time of purchase. Selections will be made based on either a growth or value basis according to perceived market conditions. Generally will invest in securities of the U.S. and Canada, but may invest up to 15% of assets in foreign issues, including ADRs. May have up to 15% of assets in illiquid securities and use options for hedging purposes.
Year organized: 1996
Ticker symbol: PSSCX
Sales restrictions: Fund will close when assets reach $250M
Discount broker availability: *Fidelity, *Schwab, *Siebert, *White
Dividends paid: Income - December; Capital gains - December
Management fee: 1.00%
Expense ratio: 1.50% (3 months ending 3/31/97)

PBHG TECHNOLOGY AND COMMUNICATIONS FUND ◆
(See first PBHG listing for data common to all funds)

Portfolio managers: John F. Force (1995), James M. Smith (1995)
Investment objective and policies: Long-term capital growth; current income incidental. Invests primarily in common stocks of companies which rely extensively on technology or communications in their product development or operations, or which are expected to benefit from technological advances and improvements, and that may be experiencing exceptional growth in sales and earnings driven by technology- or communication-related products and services. May invest, in the aggregate, up to 10% of net assets in restricted securities and securities of foreign issuers traded outside the U.S. and Canada. May invest up to 15% of assets in illiquid securities. May purchase and sell options on stocks or stock indices for hedging purposes only.
Year organized: 1995
Ticker symbol: PBTCX
Discount broker availability: *Fidelity, *Schwab, *Siebert, *White
Dividends paid: Income - December; Capital gains - December
Portfolio turnover (2 yrs): 290%, 126%
Management fee: 0.85%
Expense ratio: 1.33% (year ending 3/31/97)

PC&J PERFORMANCE FUND ◆
300 Old Post Office
120 West Third Street, Suite 300
Dayton, OH 45402
937-223-0600, fax 937-461-6691

Adviser: Parker, Carlson & Johnson, Inc.
Portfolio managers: James M. Johnson (1983), Kathleen A. Carlson (1983)
Transfer agent: PC&J Service Corp.
Investment objective and policies: Long-term capital growth; current income secondary. Invests in common stocks. Seeks to identify undervalued stocks based on comparison of current P/E ratios to three to five year earnings growth rate. Up to 15% of assets may be in illiquid securities.
Year organized: 1983 (name changed from PDC&J Performance Fund in 1994)
Minimum purchase: Initial: $1,000, Subsequent: None; IRA/Keogh: Initial: $2,000
Wire orders accepted: Yes (written instructions required first)
Deadline for same day wire purchase: 4 P.M.
Qualified for sale in: OH
Wire redemptions: Yes
Letter redemptions: Signature guarantee not required
Telephone switching: With PC&J Preservation Fund
Number of switches permitted: Unlimited
Dividends paid: Income - December; Capital gains - December
Portfolio turnover (3 yrs): 22%, 64%, 77%
Shareholder services: IRA, Keogh
Management fee: 1.00%
12b-1 distribution fee: Yes (not currently imposed)
Expense ratio: 1.50% (year ending 12/31/97)
IRA/Keogh fees: Annual $20

PC&J PRESERVATION FUND ◆
300 Old Post Office
120 West Third Street, Suite 300
Dayton, OH 45402
937-223-0600, fax 937-461-6691

Adviser: Parker, Carlson & Johnson, Inc.
Portfolio managers: Kathleen A. Carlson (1985), James M. Johnson (1985)
Transfer agent: PC&J Service Corp.
Investment objective and policies: Preservation of capital by investing in fixed-income securities. Invests primarily in high grade corporate obligations, U.S. Government obligations, CDs, prime commercial paper and other securities believed of comparable quality. Portfolio generally maintains a dollar-weighted average maturity of less than ten years.
Year organized: 1985 (name changed from PDC&J Preservation Fund in 1994)
Minimum purchase: Initial: $1,000, Subsequent: None; IRA/Keogh: Initial: $2,000
Wire orders accepted: Yes (written instructions required first)
Deadline for same day wire purchase: 4 P.M.
Qualified for sale in: OH
Wire redemptions: Yes
Letter redemptions: Signature guarantee not required
Telephone switching: With PC&J Performance Fund
Number of switches permitted: Unlimited
Dividends paid: Income - December; Capital gains - December
Portfolio turnover (3 yrs): 31%, 29%, 26%
Shareholder services: IRA, Keogh
Management fee: 0.50%
12b-1 distribution fee: Yes (not currently imposed)
Expense ratio: 1.00% (year ending 12/31/97)
IRA/Keogh fees: Annual $20

PELICAN FUND ◆
(See GMO Pelican Fund)

PENNSYLVANIA DAILY MUNICIPAL INCOME FUND ◆
600 Fifth Avenue, 8th Floor
New York, NY 10020
800-221-3079, 800-676-6779
212-830-5200
fax 212-830-5478

Adviser: Reich & Tang Asset Management, L.P.
Portfolio manager: Molly Flewharty (1992)
Transfer agent: Reich & Tang Services, L.P.

Investment objective and policies: Interest income exempt from federal and Pennsylvania income taxes, consistent with capital preservation, liquidity and stability of principal. Invests primarily in a non-diversified portfolio of high quality, Pennsylvania municipal money market obligations.
Year organized: 1992
Ticker symbol: PDIXX
Special sales restrictions: Only class "B" shares of the fund are sold direct and without 12b-1 fees. Statistics represent "B" shares only.
Minimum purchase: Initial: $5,000, Subsequent: $100
Wire orders accepted: Yes
Deadline for same day wire purchase: 12 NN
Qualified for sale in: NY, PA
Telephone redemptions: Yes
Wire redemptions: Yes
Letter redemptions: Signature guarantee required
Check redemptions: $250 minimum
Telephone switching: With other Reich & Tang money market funds and the R&T Equity Fund
Deadline for same day switch: 12 NN
Number of switches permitted: Unlimited, $1,000 minimum
Dividends paid: Income - declared daily, paid monthly
Shareholder services: Automatic investment plan, systematic withdrawal plan
Management fee: 0.40%
Administration fee: 0.21% first $1.25B to 0.19% over $1.5B
Expense ratio: 0.42% (year ending 11/30/96) (0.69% without waiver)

PEREGRINE ASIA PACIFIC GROWTH FUND ◆
(Fund liquidated 2/23/98)

PERMANENT PORTFOLIO FUNDS ◆
(Data common to all Permanent Portfolios are shown below. See subsequent listings for data specific to individual portfolios.)

625 Second Street, Suite 102
Petaluma, CA 94952
800-341-8900, 800-531-5142
707-778-1000
fax 707-778-8804

Shareholder service hours: Full service: M-F 9 A.M.-5 P.M. EST
Adviser: World Money Managers
Transfer agent: Chase Global Funds Service Co.
Special accounting procedure: Funds apply special accounting with respect to redemptions and distributions to minimize taxable distributions and maximize capital gains versus ordinary income treatment under the tax laws.
Minimum purchase: Initial: $1,000, Subsequent: $100
Wire orders accepted: Yes, subsequent only
Deadline for same day wire purchase: 4 P.M.
Qualified for sale in: All states
Opening fee: $35 one-time start up fee
Telephone redemptions: Yes
Wire redemptions: Yes, $8 fee
Letter redemptions: Signature guarantee not required
Telephone switching: With other Permanent Portfolio funds
Number of switches permitted: Unlimited, $5 fee
Shareholder services: IRA, automatic investment plan, systematic withdrawal plan min. bal. req. $5,000
Maintenance fee: $1.50/month
Management fee: 0.25% on first $200M of each portfolio, PLUS, 0.875% on first $200M to 0.688% over $600M for total assets of all portfolios
IRA fees: Annual $8, Initial $5, Closing $10

PERMANENT PORTFOLIO FUND - AGGRESSIVE GROWTH PORTFOLIO ◆
(See first Permanent Portfolio listing for data common to all portfolios)

Portfolio manager: Terry Coxon (1990)
Investment objective and policies: Long-term capital appreciation in excess of the market as a whole. Invests fully at all times in stocks and warrants. At least 60% of

its portfolio will be listed on the New York Stock Exchange. Selection will be based on appreciation potential versus current income, involving high technology, new products, price volatility, and/or above-average growth in income, profits or sales.
Year organized: 1990
Ticker symbol: PAGRX
Discount broker availability: Schwab, *White
Dividends paid: Income - December; Capital gains - December
Portfolio turnover (3 yrs): 21%, 19%, 26%
Expense ratio: 1.33% (year ending 1/31/97)

PERMANENT PORTFOLIO FUND - PERMANENT PORTFOLIO ◆
(See first Permanent Portfolio listing for data common to all portfolios)

Portfolio manager: Terry Coxon (1982)
Investment objective and policies: To preserve and increase purchasing power value over the long term. Invests a fixed percentage, balanced continually, of its net assets in the following categories: gold (20%), silver (5%), Swiss francs (10%), stocks of U.S. and foreign real estate and natural resource companies (15%), aggressive growth stocks (15%), and dollar assets (35%).
Year organized: 1982
Ticker symbol: PRPFX
Discount broker availability: Schwab, *White
Dividends paid: Income - December; Capital gains - December
Portfolio turnover (3 yrs): 12%, 10%, 31%
Expense ratio: 1.49% (year ending 1/31/97)

PERMANENT PORTFOLIO FUND - TREASURY BILL PORTFOLIO ◆
(See first Permanent Portfolio listing for data common to all portfolios)

Portfolio manager: Terry Coxon (1987)
Investment objective and policies: High current income consistent with safety of principal. Invests in U.S. Treasury bills, U.S. Treasury bonds and notes having remaining maturities of 13 months or less. Unlike most money market funds, portfolio does not declare dividends daily. They are reinvested, which allows the NAV to rise.
Year organized: 1987
Ticker symbol: PRTBX
Discount broker availability: Schwab, *White
Check redemptions: No minimum, $1 per check
Dividends paid: Income - December; Capital gains - December
Expense ratio: 0.90% (year ending 1/31/97) (1.40% without waiver)

PERMANENT PORTFOLIO FUND - VERSATILE BOND PORTFOLIO ◆
(See first Permanent Portfolio listing for data common to all portfolios)

Portfolio manager: Terry Coxon (1991)
Investment objective and policies: High current income consistent with safety of principal. Invests in corporate bonds rated "A" or higher by S&P and having a remaining maturity of 24 months or less.
Year organized: 1991
Ticker symbol: PRVBX
Discount broker availability: Schwab, *White
Check redemptions: No minimum, $1 per check
Dividends paid: Income - December; Capital gains - December
Portfolio turnover (3 yrs): 102%, 52%, 75%
Expense ratio: 0.97% (year ending 1/31/97) (1.35% without waiver)

PERRITT MICRO CAP OPPORTUNITIES FUND ◆
120 South Riverside Plaza, Suite 1745
Chicago, IL 60606-3911
800-331-8936, 312-669-1650
shareholder services 800-332-3133
fax 312-669-1235
Internet: http://www.perrittcap.com
e-mail: perrittcap@perrittcap.com

Shareholder service hours: Full service: M-F 9 A.M.-5 P.M. CST
Adviser: Perritt Capital Management, Inc.

Portfolio managers: Gerald W. Perritt (1988), Michael J. Corbett (1996)
Transfer agent: Firstar Trust Co.
Investment objective and policies: Long-term capital growth. Invests primarily in equity securities of small companies with market capitalizations ranging from $10M to $300M, perceived to have rapid growth potential. More than 20% of assets may be in money market instruments for defensive purposes. May use options to hedge up to 25% of total assets.
Year organized: 1988 (name changed from Perritt Capital Growth 11/26/97)
Ticker symbol: PRCGX
Minimum purchase: Initial: $1,000, Subsequent: $50; IRA: Initial: $250; Automatic investment plan: Initial: $50
Wire orders accepted: Yes, $12 fee
Deadline for same day wire purchase: 1 P.M.
Discount broker availability: *Schwab, *White
Qualified for sale in: All states except AR, MT, NH, ND, SD, VT
Letter redemptions: Signature guarantee required over $10,000
Dividends paid: Income - December; Capital gains - December
Portfolio turnover (3 yrs): 83%, 58%, 67%
Shareholder services: IRA, SEP-IRA, Keogh, 401(k), 403(b), systematic withdrawal plan min. bal. req. $10,000
Management fee: 0.70%
Expense ratio: 1.52% (year ending 10/31/97)
IRA/Keogh fees: Annual $12.50, Closing $15

PHILADELPHIA FUND
1200 North Federal Highway, Suite 424
Boca Raton, FL 33432
800-749-9933, 800-525-6201
561-395-2155
fax 407-338-7590
Internet: http://www.netrunner.net/~philfund
e-mail: philfund@netrunner.net

Adviser: Baxter Financial Corp.
Portfolio manager: Donald H. Baxter (1987)
Transfer agent: American Data Services, Inc.
Investment objective and policies: Long-term growth of capital and income. Invests primarily in a diversified portfolio of common stocks traded on major U.S. security exchanges, but may acquire unlisted securities as well. May invest up to 20% of assets in foreign securities, and may hold investment grade fixed-income securities for defensive purposes. May use options and futures contracts in an effort to increase income and for hedging purposes.
Year organized: 1923
Ticker symbol: PHILX
Minimum purchase: Initial: $1,000, Subsequent: None; Automatic investment plan: Initial: $50, Subsequent: $50
Wire orders accepted: No
Qualified for sale in: All states except AZ, AR, DE, ID, KS, LA, MN, MT, NE, NH, NM, ND, OK, OR, SD, UT, WA, WI
Letter redemptions: Signature guarantee required
Check redemptions: Yes
Dividends paid: Income - March, June, September, December; Capital gains - December
Portfolio turnover (3 yrs): 17%, 14%, 59%
Shareholder services: IRA, Keogh, corporate retirement plans
Shareholder services fee: 0.25%
Management fee: 0.75% first $200M to 0.50% over $400M
12b-1 distribution fee: Maximum of 0.50%
Expense ratio: 1.53% (year ending 11/30/97)
IRA/Keogh fees: Annual $15, Closing $15

PIC FUNDS
300 North Lake Avenue
Pasadena, CA 91101-4106
800-618-7643, 626-449-8500
fax 626-577-2402

Adviser: Provident Investment Counsel, Inc. (an indirect, wholly owned subsidiary of United Asset Management Corp., UAM)
Administrator: Investment Company Administration Corp.

Transfer agent: Rodney Square Management Corp.
Sales restrictions: PIC funds are all subject to "hub and spoke" investment structuring. Each of the five funds listed below are invested in underlying portfolios with the identical policies and objectives. Portfolio information is for underlying unit; expenses are for funds. Funds with 12b-1 distribution fees are primarily used for retirement accounts.
Minimum purchase: Initial: $2,000, Subsequent: $250; IRA/Keogh: Initial: $500; Automatic investment plan: Initial: $250, Subsequent: $100
Wire orders accepted: Yes
Deadline for same day wire purchases: 4 P.M.
Qualified for sale in: All states
Telephone redemptions: Yes
Wire redemptions: Yes, $5,000 minimum
Letter redemptions: Signature guarantee required over $100,000
Telephone switching: With other PIC funds
Number of switches permitted: 4 per year
Shareholder services: IRA, SEP-IRA, 401(k), 403(b), corporate retirement plans, systematic withdrawal plan
Maintenance fee: $12 per year for balances below $2,500
Administration fee: 0.10%
IRA/Keogh fees: Annual $10

PIC GROWTH FUND ◆
(See first PIC Fund listing for data common to all portfolios)

Portfolio manager: Team managed
Investment objective and policies: Long-term growth of capital. Portfolio invests primarily in equity securities of companies currently experiencing an above average rate of earnings growth, that being a demonstrable five year average performance record of sales, earnings, pre-tax margins, return on equity and reinvestment rate all of which in the aggregate are 1.5 times the performance of the S&P 500 common stocks for the same period. May invest up to 20% of assets in foreign securities or ADRs, but only those listed on a national exchange or in NASDAQ. May use options and futures for hedging purposes.
Year organized: 1992 (name changed from PIC Institutional Growth 3/97)
Ticker symbol: PIPGX
Discount broker availability: Fidelity, *Schwab, *White
Dividends paid: Income - December; Capital gains - December
Portfolio turnover (3 yrs): 64%, 55%, 68%
Management fee: 0.80%
Expense ratio: 1.25% (year ending 10/31/97)

PIC MID CAP GROWTH FUND ◆
(See first PIC Fund listing for data common to all portfolios)

Lead portfolio manager: Evelyn Lapham (1998)
Investment objective and policies: Long-term growth of capital. Portfolio invests primarily in equity securities of companies with market capitalizations between $500M and $5B that are currently experiencing an above average rate of earnings growth. May invest up to 20% of assets in foreign securities or ADRs, but only those listed on a national exchange or in NASDAQ. May use options and futures for hedging purposes.
Year organized: 1998
Dividends paid: Income - December; Capital gains - December
Management fee: 0.70%

PIC PINNACLE BALANCED FUND
(See first PIC Fund listing for data common to all portfolios)

Portfolio manager: Team managed
Investment objective and policies: Total return: current income and growth of capital, while preserving capital. Portfolio invests primarily in equity securities of companies currently experiencing an above average rate of earnings growth, that being a demonstrable five year average performance record of sales, earnings, pretax margins, return on equity and reinvestment rate

all of which in the aggregate are 1.5 times the performance of the S&P 500 common stocks for the same period. Also invests at least 25% and as much as 70% of assets in fixed-income senior securities. May use options and futures for hedging purposes.
Year organized: 1992 (name changed from PIC Institutional Balanced 4/97)
Ticker symbol: PIPBX
Discount broker availability: Fidelity, *Schwab, *White
Dividends paid: Income - quarterly; Capital gains - December
Portfolio turnover (3 yrs): 104%, 54%, 106%
Management fee: 0.60%
12b-1 distribution fee: 0.25%
Expense ratio: 1.05% (year ending 10/31/97) (1.43% without waiver)

PIC PINNACLE GROWTH FUND
(See first PIC Fund listing for data common to all portfolios)

Portfolio manager: Team managed
Investment objective and policies: Long-term growth of capital. Portfolio invests primarily in equity securities of companies currently experiencing an above average rate of earnings growth, that being a demonstrable five year average performance record of sales, earnings, pretax margins, return on equity and reinvestment rate all of which in the aggregate are 1.5 times the performance of the S&P 500 common stocks for the same period. May invest up to 20% of assets in foreign securities or ADRs, but only those listed on a national exchange or in NASDAQ. May use options and futures for hedging purposes.
Year organized: 1997 (portfolio began in 1992)
Dividends paid: Income - December; Capital gains - December
Portfolio turnover (3 yrs): 68%, 64%, 55%
Management fee: 0.80%
12b-1 distribution fee: 0.25%
Expense ratio: 1.35% (nine months ending 10/31/97) (9.97% without waiver)

PIC PINNACLE SMALL COMPANY GROWTH FUND
(See first PIC Fund listing for data common to all portfolios)

Portfolio manager: Team managed
Investment objective and policies: Long-term growth of capital. Portfolio invests primarily in equity securities of companies with market capitalizations of less than $250M at acquisition. May invest up to 35% of assets in other types of securities and companies with higher capitalizations. May invest up to 20% of assets in foreign securities or ADRs, but only those listed on a national exchange or in NASDAQ. May use options and futures for hedging purposes.
Year organized: 1997 (portfolio began in 1992)
Dividends paid: Income - December; Capital gains - December
Portfolio turnover (3 yrs): 53%, 45%, 64%
Management fee: 0.80%
12b-1 distribution fee: 0.25%
Expense ratio: 1.55% (nine months ending 10/31/97) (11.55% without waiver)

PIC SMALL COMPANY GROWTH FUND ◆
(See first PIC Fund listing for data common to all portfolios)

Portfolio manager: Team managed
Investment objective and policies: Long-term growth of capital. Portfolio invests primarily in equity securities of companies with market capitalizations of less than $250M at acquisition. May invest up to 35% of assets in other types of securities and companies with higher capitalizations. May invest up to 20% of assets in foreign securities or ADRs, but only those listed on a national exchange or in NASDAQ. May use options and futures for hedging purposes.
Year organized: 1996 (portfolio began in 1992: name changed from PIC Institutional Small Cap 3/97)
Ticker symbol: PISMX
Discount broker availability: *Schwab, *White

Dividends paid: Income - December; Capital gains - December
Portfolio turnover (3 yrs): 53%, 45%, 64%
Management fee: 0.80%
Expense ratio: 1.45% (year ending 10/31/96) (1.86% without waiver)

PIN OAK AGGRESSIVE STOCK FUND ◆
c/o Oak Associates Funds
P.O. Box 419009
Kansas City, MO 64141-6009
888-462-5386
fax 330-668-2901
Internet: http://www.oakassociates.com

Adviser: Oak Associates, Ltd.
Administrator: SEI Fund Resources
Portfolio manager: James D. Oelschlager (1992)
Transfer agent: DST Systems, Inc.
Investment objective and policies: Long-term capital growth. Invests as fully as practicable in a diversified portfolio of common stocks of companies with market capitalizations between $100M and $1B. May also invest in warrants and rights, debt securities, convertible preferred stocks and ADRs. Up to 15% of assets may be in illiquid securities.
Year organized: 1992 (name changed from Advisors' Inner Circle - Pin Oak Aggressive Stock Fund in 1996)
Ticker symbol: POGSX
Minimum purchase: Initial: $2,000, Subsequent: $50; Automatic investment plan: Subsequent: $25
Wire orders accepted: Yes
Deadline for same day wire purchase: 4 P.M.
Discount broker availability: *Fidelity, *Schwab, *White
Qualified for sale in: All states
Telephone redemptions: Yes
Wire redemptions: Yes, $10 fee
Letter redemptions: Signature guarantee not required
Telephone switching: With White Oak Growth Stock Fund
Number of switches permitted: Unlimited
Dividends paid: Income - March, June, September, December; Capital gains - December
Portfolio turnover (3 yrs): 17%, 32%, 49%
Shareholder services: IRA, systematic withdrawal plan min. bal. req. $25,000
Management fee: 0.74%
Administration fee: 0.15% first $250M to 0.08% over $650M
Expense ratio: 0.99% (year ending 10/31/97) (1.23% without waiver)
IRA fees: Annual $25

PINNACLE FUND ◆
36 South Pennsylvania Street, Suite 610
Indianapolis, IN 46204
317-633-4080, 414-765-4124

Adviser: Heartland Capital Management, Inc.
Portfolio manager: Tom Maurath (1985)
Transfer agent: Firstar Trust Co.
Investment objective and policies: Long-term capital appreciation. Invests primarily in common stocks but may invest in fixed-income securities and money market instruments for defensive purposes.
Year organized: 1985 (split 2 for 1 on 10/9/89)
Ticker symbol: PINNX
Minimum purchase: Initial: $1,000, Subsequent: $100; Automatic investment plan: Subsequent: $50
Wire orders accepted: No
Qualified for sale in: All states except: AK, AZ, CT, DE, HI, KS, LA, MN, MS, MO, NH, NJ, OR, SD, VT, WI
Letter redemptions: Signature guarantee required over $5,000
Dividends paid: Income - December; Capital gains - December
Portfolio turnover (3 yrs): 50%, 91%, 85%
Shareholder services: IRA, electronic funds transfer (purchase only)
Management fee: 0.80%
Expense ratio: 1.45% (year ending 12/31/97)
IRA fees: Annual $10

PORTICO FUNDS
(See Firstar Funds; name changed 2/1/98)

PRAGMA PROVIDENCE FUND ◆
(Fund liquidated 2/27/98)

THE PREFERRED GROUP OF FUNDS ◆
(Data common to all Preferred funds are shown below. See subsequent listings for data specific to individual funds.)

1200 First Financial Plaza
411 Hamilton Boulevard
Peoria, IL 61602-1104
800-662-4769

Adviser: Caterpillar Investment Management Ltd.
Transfer agent: Boston Financial Data Services, Inc.
Minimum purchase: Initial: $1,000, Subsequent: $50; IRA: Initial $250; Automatic investment plan: Initial: $50
Wire orders accepted: Yes, $1,000 minimum
Deadline for same day wire purchase: 4 P.M.
Qualified for sale in: All states
Telephone redemptions: Yes
Wire redemptions: Yes, $100 minimum, $10 fee
Letter redemptions: Signature guarantee required over $50,000
Telephone switching: With other Preferred funds, 10 day hold
Number of switches permitted: Unlimited (fund reserves right to limit to 1 round trip every 120 days)
Shareholder services: IRA, SEP-IRA, electronic funds transfer, systematic withdrawal plan
IRA fees: Annual $10 per fund ($30 maximum, waived for accounts with assets of $5,000 or more)

PREFERRED ASSET ALLOCATION FUND ◆
(See first Preferred listing for data common to all funds)

Sub-advisers: Mellon Capital Management Corp. & PanAgora Asset Management, Inc.
Portfolio managers: Thomas B. Hazuka (1992), Edgar E. Peters (1992)
Investment objective and policies: Capital appreciation and current income. Invests in stocks, bonds and high quality money market instruments. Proportion allocated to any class is unlimited, and proportion allocated to each asset class will vary depending on changes in interest rates and other economic factors. Stocks are chosen primarily from issues that comprise the S&P 500 Index, and bonds are exclusively long-term U.S. Treasuries and other highly liquid obligations issued by the U.S. Government. May invest without limit in securities of foreign issuers traded in domestic securities markets, and invest up to 10% of assets in foreign securities. Up to 15% of assets may be in illiquid securities. May use a variety of derivative instruments and foreign currency contracts for hedging purposes.
Year organized: 1992
Ticker symbol: PFAAX
Discount broker availability: Fidelity, Siebert, White
Dividends paid: Income - quarterly; Capital gains - December
Portfolio turnover (3 yrs): 28%, 38%, 18%
Management fee: 0.70%
Expense ratio: 0.99% (year ending 6/30/97)

PREFERRED BALANCED FUND ◆
(Fund liquidated 10/97)

PREFERRED FIXED INCOME FUND ◆
(See first Preferred listing for data common to all funds)

Sub-adviser: J.P. Morgan Investment Management, Inc.
Portfolio manager: Paul L. Zemsky (1994)
Investment objective and policies: High level of current income. Invests primarily in a diversified portfolio of publicly traded domestic investment grade

debt securities - U.S. Treasury and agency obligations, mortgage-backed securities and corporate debt securities. Portfolio generally maintains a weighted average maturity of three to seven years, although variation is allowed. May invest without limit in securities of foreign issuers traded in domestic securities markets, and invest up to 10% of assets directly in foreign securities. Up to 15% of assets may be in illiquid securities. May sell short and use futures and options in an effort to increase current return and for hedging purposes.
Year organized: 1992
Ticker symbol: PFXIX
Discount broker availability: Fidelity, Siebert, White
Dividends paid: Income - declared daily, paid monthly; Capital gains - December
Portfolio turnover (3 yrs): 106%, 314%, 331%
Management fee: 0.50%
Expense ratio: 0.74% (year ending 6/30/97)

PREFERRED GROWTH FUND ◆
(See first Preferred listing for data common to all funds)

Sub-adviser: Jennison Associates Capital Corp.
Portfolio manager: Robert B. Corman (1998)
Investment objective and policies: Long-term capital appreciation. Invests at least 65% of assets in equity securities believed to offer potential for capital appreciation, including stocks of companies experiencing above average earnings growth. May invest without limit in securities of foreign issuers traded in domestic securities markets, and invest up to 10% of assets directly in foreign securities. Up to 15% of assets may be in illiquid securities. May use a variety of derivative instruments and foreign currency contracts for hedging purposes.
Year organized: 1992
Ticker symbol: PFGRX
Discount broker availability: Fidelity, Siebert, White
Dividends paid: Income - December; Capital gains - December
Portfolio turnover (3 yrs): 58%, 75%, 55%
Management fee: 0.75%
Expense ratio: 0.84% (year ending 6/30/97)

PREFERRED INTERNATIONAL FUND ◆
(See first Preferred listing for data common to all funds)

Sub-adviser: Mercator Asset Management, L.P.
Portfolio manager: Peter F. Spano (1992)
Investment objective and policies: Long-term capital appreciation. Invests primarily in equity securities traded principally on markets outside the U.S., including emerging markets, believed undervalued. Normally at least 65% of assets will be invested in at least three different countries not including the U.S. Up to 15% of assets may be in illiquid securities. May use a variety of derivative instruments and foreign currency contracts for hedging purposes.
Year organized: 1992
Ticker symbol: PFIFX
Discount broker availability: Fidelity, Siebert, White
Dividends paid: Income - December; Capital gains - December
Portfolio turnover (3 yrs): 13%, 20%, 29%
Management fee: 0.95%
Expense ratio: 1.25% (year ending 6/30/97)

PREFERRED MONEY MARKET FUND ◆
(See first Preferred listing for data common to all funds)

Sub-adviser: J.P. Morgan Investment Management, Inc.
Portfolio manager: Robert R. "Skip" Johnson (1992)
Investment objective and policies: Maximum current income consistent with preservation of capital and liquidity. Invests in a broad range of U.S. denominated government, bank and commercial money market instruments, although may invest in obligations of U.S. branches or subsidiaries of foreign banks, or foreign branches or subsidiaries of U.S. banks.
Year organized: 1992

Check redemptions: $250 minimum
Dividends paid: Income - declared daily, paid monthly
Management fee: 0.30%
Expense ratio: 0.48% (year ending 6/30/97)

PREFERRED SHORT-TERM GOVERNMENT SECURITIES FUND ◆
(See first Preferred listing for data common to all funds)

Sub-adviser: J.P. Morgan Investment Management, Inc.
Portfolio manager: Richard W. Oswald (1997)
Investment objective and policies: High level of current income consistent with capital preservation. Invests primarily in securities issued or guaranteed as to principal and interest by the U.S. Government, its agencies, authorities or instrumentalities. Under normal conditions not less than 65% of holdings will have a weighted average maturity of not more than three years, and fund typically purchases issues with remaining maturities of five years or less. Up to 15% of assets may be in illiquid securities. May sell short and use futures and options in an effort to increase current return and for hedging purposes.
Year organized: 1992
Ticker symbol: PFSGX
Discount broker availability: Fidelity, Siebert, White
Check redemptions: $250 minimum
Dividends paid: Income - declared daily, paid monthly; Capital gains - December
Portfolio turnover (3 yrs): 184%, 79%, 256%
Management fee: 0.35%
Expense ratio: 0.63% (year ending 6/30/97)

PREFERRED SMALL CAP FUND ◆
(See first Preferred listing for data common to all funds)

Portfolio manager: Todd M. Sheridan (1995)
Investment objective and policies: Long-term capital appreciation. Invests at least 65% of assets in common stock and other equity securities of companies with market capitalizations under $1B. May also invest in large capitalization companies, and purchase other types of securities such as government and corporate debt, or short-term money instruments. May invest without limit in securities of foreign issuers traded in domestic securities markets, and invest up to 10% of assets directly in foreign securities. Up to 15% of assets may be in illiquid securities. May use a variety of derivative instruments and foreign currency contracts for hedging purposes.
Year organized: 1995
Ticker symbol: PSMCX
Discount broker availability: Fidelity, Siebert
Dividends paid: Income - annually; Capital gains - annually
Portfolio turnover (2 yrs): 104%, 66%
Management fee: 0.75%
Expense ratio: 0.88% (year ending 6/30/97) (0.98% without waivers)

PREFERRED VALUE FUND ◆
(See first Preferred listing for data common to all funds)

Sub-adviser: Oppenheimer Capital
Portfolio manager: John G. Lindenthal (1992)
Investment objective and policies: Capital appreciation and current income. Invests at least 65% of assets in equity securities - common stocks, preferred stocks and convertible securities - believed undervalued that offer above-average potential for capital appreciation. May invest without limit in securities of foreign issuers traded in domestic securities markets, and invest up to 10% of assets directly in foreign securities. Up to 15% of assets may be in illiquid securities. May use a variety of derivative instruments and foreign currency contracts for hedging purposes.
Year organized: 1992
Ticker symbol: PFVLX
Discount broker availability: Fidelity, Siebert, White
Dividends paid: Income - December; Capital gains - December

Portfolio turnover (3 yrs): 7%, 17%, 29%
Management fee: 0.75%
Expense ratio: 0.85% (year ending 6/30/97)

T. ROWE PRICE FUNDS ◆

(Data common to all T. Rowe Price funds are shown below. See subsequent listings for data specific to individual funds.)

100 East Pratt Street
Baltimore, MD 21202
800-638-5660, 410-547-2308
shareholder services 800-225-5132,
410-625-6500
prices/yields 800-638-2587
TDD 800-367-0763, fax 410-345-1572
Internet http://www.troweprice.com

Shareholder service hours: Full service: M-F 8 A.M.-10 P.M., Sat-Sun 8:30 A.M.-5 P.M. EST; After hours service: prices, yields, balances, orders, last transaction, indices, prospectuses, total returns
Adviser: T. Rowe Price Assocs., Inc. (except International Equity Funds)
Transfer agent: State Street Bank & Trust Co.
Minimum purchase: Initial: $2,500, Subsequent: $100; IRA/Keogh: Initial: $1,000, Subsequent: $50; Automatic investment plan: Initial: $50, Subsequent: $50 (Except Summit funds)
Wire orders accepted: Yes
Deadline for same day wire purchase: 4 P.M.
Qualified for sale in: All states (exceptions noted)
Telephone redemptions: Yes
Wire redemptions: Yes, $5 fee under $5,000
Letter redemptions: Signature guarantee required over $100,000
Telephone switching: With other T. Rowe Price Funds
Number of switches permitted: 1 purchase and 1 sale per fund per 120 days, $100 minimum (except money funds)
Shareholder services: IRA, SEP-IRA, Keogh, 401(k), 403(b), corporate retirement plans, directed dividends, electronic funds transfer, systematic withdrawal plan min. bal. req. $10,000
Maintenance fee: $10 per year for balances below $2,000 ($500 for UGMA/UTMA); waived for accounts with aggregate balances exceeding $25,000
Management fee: Each fund pays a minimum amount plus a pro rata share, based on assets, of a group fee levied on total assets of all funds under management, ranging from 0.48% of the first $1B down to 0.31% over $34B.
IRA fees: Annual $10 (waived for accounts with assets of $50,000 or more), Closing $10
Keogh fees: Annual $10, Closing $10

T. ROWE PRICE BALANCED FUND ◆

(See first T. Rowe Price listing for data common to all funds)

Lead portfolio manager: Richard T. Whitney (1994)
Investment objective and policies: Long-term total return: capital growth and income, consistent with conservation of principal. Invests approximately 60% of assets in common stocks and about 40% in various fixed-income securities. Allocation may be adjusted according to perceived market conditions, however at least 25% of assets will always be invested in senior fixed-income obligations. May invest up to 20% of assets in mortgage-backed securities, 10% in junk bonds, 10% in stripped mortgage securities, 10% in hybrid instruments, and 25% in foreign securities. May use various derivatives in an effort to enhance performance and for hedging purposes.
Year organized: 1991 (absorbed Axe-Houghton Fund 'B' 8/31/92)
Ticker symbol: RPBAX
Discount broker availability: Fidelity, Schwab, Siebert, White
Dividends paid: Income - March, June, September, December; Capital gains - December
Portfolio turnover (3 yrs): 22%, 13%, 33%
Management fee: 0.15% + pro rata group fee
Expense ratio: 0.87% (year ending 12/31/96)

T. ROWE PRICE BLUE CHIP GROWTH FUND ◆

(See first T. Rowe Price listing for data common to all funds)

Lead portfolio manager: Larry J. Puglia (1993)
Investment objective and policies: Long-term total growth; current income secondary. Invests primarily in common stocks of well established, large-cap companies with potential for above-average growth in earnings. May invest in convertible securities, preferred stocks and fixed-income securities. Up to 20% of assets may be in foreign securities and 15% in illiquid securities. May use futures and options on up to 25% of assets.
Year organized: 1993
Ticker symbol: TRBCX
Discount broker availability: Fidelity, Schwab, Siebert, White
Dividends paid: Income - December; Capital gains - December
Portfolio turnover (3 yrs): 26%, 38%, 75%
Management fee: 0.30% + pro rata group fee
Expense ratio: 1.12% (year ending 12/31/96)

T. ROWE PRICE CALIFORNIA TAX-FREE BOND FUND ◆

(See first T. Rowe Price listing for data common to all funds)

Portfolio manager: Mary J. Miller (1990)
Investment objective and policies: Highest level of current income exempt from federal and California state income taxes, consistent with prudent portfolio management. Invests primarily in long-term municipal securities exempt from such taxes. Portfolio generally maintains a dollar-weighted average maturity greater than fifteen years. Fund may use a variety of derivative instruments, and invest up to 10% of assets in private placements. Up to 20% of assets may be in securities subject to AMT tax treatment.
Year organized: 1986
Ticker symbol: PRXCX
Discount broker availability: Fidelity, White
Qualified for sale in: AZ, CA, DC, HI, MD, NJ, NV, WY
Check redemptions: $500 minimum
Dividends paid: Income - declared daily, paid monthly; Capital gains - March, December
Portfolio turnover (3 yrs): 47%, 62%, 78%
Management fee: 0.10% + pro rata group fee
Expense ratio: 0.62% (year ending 2/28/97)

T. ROWE PRICE CALIFORNIA TAX-FREE MONEY FUND ◆

(See first T. Rowe Price listing for data common to all funds)

Portfolio manager: Patrice L. Berchtenbreiter Ely (1990)
Investment objective and policies: Capital preservation, liquidity and high current income exempt from federal and California state income taxes. Invests primarily in California municipal money market securities.
Year organized: 1986
Ticker symbol: PRXMX
Qualified for sale in: AZ, CA, DC, HI, MD, NJ, NV, WY
Check redemptions: $500 minimum
Dividends paid: Income - declared daily, paid monthly
Management fee: 0.10% + pro rata group fee
Expense ratio: 0.55% (year ending 2/28/97) (0.72% without waiver)

T. ROWE PRICE CAPITAL APPRECIATION FUND ◆

(See first T. Rowe Price listing for data common to all funds)

Lead portfolio manager: Richard P. Howard (1989)
Investment objective and policies: Maximum long-term capital appreciation. Invests primarily in common stocks of established companies perceived to be undervalued and out of favor. The core of the portfolio consists of long-term holdings bought at a discount;

opportunistic minority portions consist of positions expected to increase in price in the short term, but which may not be attractive as long-term holdings. May have up to 25% of assets in foreign securities, 15% in illiquid issues, and 15% in junk bonds. May use a variety of derivatives in an effort to enhance performance and for hedging purposes.
Year organized: 1986
Ticker symbol: PRWCX
Discount broker availability: Fidelity, Schwab, Siebert, White
Dividends paid: Income - December; Capital gains - December
Portfolio turnover (3 yrs): 48%, 44%, 47%
Management fee: 0.30% + pro rata group fee
Expense ratio: 0.64% (year ending 12/31/97)

T. ROWE PRICE CAPITAL OPPORTUNITY FUND ◆

(See first T. Rowe Price listing for data common to all funds)

Lead portfolio manager: John F. Wakeman (1994)
Investment objective and policies: Long-term capital appreciation. Invests primarily in common stocks of U.S. companies believed to be undervalued, with no limits on capitalization. May buy both growth and value stocks. Fund may have more than 5% of assets in stocks of a single company, and will usually invest in fewer than 50 different companies. May, however, invest in debt obligations without limit and without regard to quality, although the fund will hold no more than 10% of assets in junk bonds. May have up to 20% of assets in foreign securities, 15% in illiquid securities, 10% in hybrid instruments, and use options and futures in an effort to enhance performance and for hedging purposes.
Year organized: 1994
Ticker symbol: PRCOX
Discount broker availability: Fidelity, Schwab, Siebert, White
Dividends paid: Income - December; Capital gains - December
Portfolio turnover (2 yrs): 107%, 137%
Management fee: 0.45% + pro rata group fee
Expense ratio: 1.35% (year ending 12/31/96) (includes waiver)

T. ROWE PRICE CORPORATE INCOME FUND ◆

(See first T. Rowe Price listing for data common to all funds)

Lead portfolio manager: J. Peter Van Dyke (1995)
Investment objective and policies: High income; capital appreciation secondary. Invests at least 65% of assets in investment grade corporate debt securities, but may invest up to 35% of assets in the two highest categories of speculative-grade, high yield junk bonds. Portfolio generally maintains a dollar-weighted average maturity exceeding ten years. May also invest up to 25% of assets in foreign debt, and up to 25% of assets combined in convertible securities and preferred stocks in an effort to enhance income and capital appreciation.
Year organized: 1995
Ticker symbol: PRPIX
Check redemptions: $500 minimum
Discount broker availability: Fidelity, Siebert, White
Dividends paid: Income - declared daily, paid monthly; Capital gains - December
Portfolio turnover (2 yrs): 120%, 71%
Management fee: 0.15% + pro rata group fee
Expense ratio: 0.80% (year ending 5/31/97) (includes waiver)

T. ROWE PRICE DIVERSIFIED SMALL-CAP GROWTH FUND ◆

(See first T. Rowe Price listing for data common to all funds)

Lead portfolio manager: Richard T. Whitney (1997)
Investment objective and policies: Long-term capital appreciation. Invests in a broadly diversified portfolio of small-cap equity securities selected by utilizing proprietary computer models programmed to iden-

tify growth situations. Companies are smaller than 90% of those comprising the S&P 500 Index; currently limiting market capitalizations to those companies below $1.5B. May invest up to 10% of assets in foreign securities, up to 10% in hybrid instruments, and up to 15% in illiquid securities. May use options and futures for hedging purposes.
Year organized: 1997
Ticker symbol: PRDSX
Discount broker availability: Fidelity, Schwab, Siebert, White
Redemption fee: 1.00% for shares held less than 6 months, payable to the fund
Dividends paid: Income - December; Capital gains - December
Management fee: 0.35% + pro rata group fee

T. ROWE PRICE DIVIDEND GROWTH FUND ◆
(See first T. Rowe Price listing for data common to all funds)

Lead portfolio manager: William J. Stromberg (1992)
Investment objective and policies: Increasing dividend income, long-term capital growth and reasonable current income. Invests primarily in common stocks of dividend-paying companies with potential for increasing dividends and capital growth. May invest in convertible securities, preferred stocks and fixed-income securities. Up to 25% of assets in foreign securities, 15% in illiquid securities and 10% in derivatives. May use futures and options on up to 25% of assets.
Year organized: 1992
Ticker symbol: PRDGX
Discount broker availability: Fidelity, Schwab, Siebert, White
Dividends paid: Income - March, June, September, December; Capital gains - December
Portfolio turnover (3 yrs): 43%, 56%, 71%
Management fee: 0.20% + pro rata group fee
Expense ratio: 1.10% (year ending 12/31/96)

T. ROWE PRICE EMERGING MARKETS BOND FUND ◆
(See first T. Rowe Price listing for data common to all funds)

Adviser: Rowe Price-Fleming International, Inc.
Portfolio managers: Peter B. Askew (1994), Michael Conelius (1995), Christopher Rothery (1994)
Investment objective and policies: High current income and capital growth. Invests at least 65% of assets in high yield, high risk corporate and government fixed-income securities of issuers in emerging foreign markets. Since these issues are primarily in less developed countries and their bonds carry a greater degree of risk of default, they are often rated as junk bonds. There are no maturity restrictions, but the normal weighted average maturity is five to ten years. This may vary substantially, however, due to market conditions. Most assets are expected to be denominated in U.S. dollars, and the fund will not usually hedge currency holdings back to dollars. May invest up to 10% of assets in hybrid instruments, 15% in illiquid securities, and use a variety of foreign currency transactions.
Year organized: 1994
Ticker symbol: PREMX
Discount broker availability: Fidelity, Siebert, White
Check redemptions: $500 minimum
Dividends paid: Income - declared daily, paid monthly; Capital gains - December
Portfolio turnover (3 yrs): 88%, 169%, 274%
Management fee: 0.45% + pro rata group fee
Expense ratio: 1.25% (year ending 12/31/97) (includes waiver)

T. ROWE PRICE EMERGING MARKETS STOCK FUND ◆
(See first T. Rowe Price listing for data common to all funds)

Adviser: Rowe Price-Fleming International, Inc.
Lead portfolio manager: Martin G. Wade (1995)
Investment objective and policies: Long-term capi-

tal growth. Invests primarily in common stocks and other equity securities of large and small companies domiciled in or with primary operations in emerging market countries, as defined by the World Bank, International Finance Corporation, or the United Nations. Issues are selected primarily based upon perceived growth potential. May invest up to 10% of assets in hybrid instruments, and 15% in illiquid securities. May engage in foreign currency transactions in spot/forward markets, and use interest rate and currency futures and options for hedging purposes. Fund is non-diversified.
Year organized: 1995
Ticker symbol: PRMSX
Discount broker availability: Schwab
Redemption fee: 2.00% for shares held less than one year, payable to the fund
Dividends paid: Income - December; Capital gains - December
Portfolio turnover (3 yrs): 84%, 42%, 29%
Management fee: 0.75% + pro rata group fee
Expense ratio: 1.75% (year ending 10/31/97)

T. ROWE PRICE EQUITY INCOME FUND ◆
(See first T. Rowe Price listing for data common to all funds)

Lead portfolio manager: Brian C. Rogers (1985)
Investment objective and policies: Substantial dividend income and long-term capital appreciation. Invests at least 65% of assets in dividend-paying common stocks of established companies perceived to be undervalued and that show favorable prospects for increasing dividend income. Considering income as a major component of total return, it is expected the portfolio will provide a total yield higher than that of the S&P 500 Index over time. Up to 25% of assets may be in foreign securities, 10% in junk bonds, and 10% in hybrid instruments. May use options and futures and forward foreign currency transactions for hedging purposes.
Year organized: 1985
Ticker symbol: PRFDX
Discount broker availability: Fidelity, Schwab, Siebert, White
Dividends paid: Income - March, June, September, December; Capital gains - December
Portfolio turnover (3 yrs): 24%, 25%, 21%
Management fee: 0.25% + pro rata group fee
Expense ratio: 0.79% (year ending 12/31/97)

T. ROWE PRICE EQUITY INDEX 500 FUND ◆
(See first T. Rowe Price listing for data common to all funds)

Portfolio managers: Richard T. Whitney (1990), Kristen F. Culp (1998)
Investment objective and policies: Replicate the total return performance of the U.S. equities market as represented by the S&P 500 Composite Price Index. Fund invests in all 500 stocks in their approximate index weightings, producing a performance correlation to that of the Index of at least 0.95. May use stock index futures and options to maintain liquidity and a fully invested position.
Year organized: 1990 (name changed from Equity Index Fund 1/98)
Ticker symbol: PREIX
Discount broker availability: Schwab
Redemption fee: 0.50% for shares held less than 6 months, payable to the fund
Dividends paid: Income - March, June, September, December; Capital gains - December
Portfolio turnover (3 yrs): 1%, 1%, 1%
Management fee: 0.20%
Expense ratio: 0.40% (year ending 12/31/96) (0.44% without waiver)
Maintenance fee: $2.50 per quarter for balances of less than $10,000, even if the low balance is due to market fluctuations.

T. ROWE PRICE EUROPEAN STOCK FUND ◆
(See first T. Rowe Price listing for data common to all funds)

Adviser: Rowe Price-Fleming International, Inc.
Lead portfolio manager: Martin G. Wade (1990)
Investment objective and policies: Long-term capital growth; income secondary. Invests in equity securities issued by companies of all sizes domiciled in at least five countries in Europe. May also hold ADRs, EDRs, and ADSs. Up to 35% of assets may be in high-grade, non-dollar denominated debt securities or other types of equity securities. May invest up to 15% of assets in illiquid securities and 10% in hybrid instruments. Fund may use options and currency exchange contracts for hedging purposes.
Year organized: 1990
Ticker symbol: PRESX
Discount broker availability: Fidelity, Schwab, Siebert, White
Dividends paid: Income - December; Capital gains - December
Portfolio turnover (3 yrs): 18%, 14%, 17%
Management fee: 0.50% + pro rata group fee
Expense ratio: 1.06% (year ending 10/31/97)

T. ROWE PRICE EXTENDED EQUITY MARKET INDEX FUND ◆
(See first T. Rowe Price listing for data common to all funds)

Portfolio managers: Richard T. Whitney (1998), Kristen F. Culp (1998)
Investment objective and policies: Replicate the total return performance of the small and midsize U.S. equities market as represented by the Wilshire 4500 Equity Index. Fund invests in a representative sample of the 6700 stocks (entire market minus the S&P 500) in their approximate index weightings, producing a performance correlation to that of the Index of at least 0.95. May use stock index futures and options to maintain liquidity and a fully invested position.
Year organized: 1998
Redemption fee: 0.50% for shares held less than 6 months, payable to the fund
Dividends paid: Income - December; Capital gains - December
Management fee: 0.20%
Maintenance fee: $2.50 per quarter for balances of less than $10,000, even if the low balance is due to market fluctuations.

T. ROWE PRICE FINANCIAL SERVICES FUND ◆
(See first T. Rowe Price listing for data common to all funds)

Lead portfolio manager: Larry J. Puglia (1997)
Investment objective and policies: Long-term capital appreciation; income secondary. Invests primarily in equity securities issued by companies involved in the various, diversified segments of the financial services industry, including such companies as those ancillary to the industry but deriving at least 50% of their revenues from servicing it, such as software companies. Selections are based on perceived earnings growth, significant market share, seasoned management and undervalued shares. May invest up to 30% of assets in foreign issues. May invest up to 10% of assets in hybrid instruments, 15% of assets in illiquid securities, and use futures and options and foreign currency transactions for hedging purposes. Fund is non-diversified.
Year organized: 1996
Ticker symbol: PRISX
Discount broker availability: Fidelity, Siebert, White
Dividends paid: Income - December; Capital gains - December
Management fee: 0.35% + pro rata group fee
Expense ratio: 1.25% (3 months ending 12/31/96) (1.98% without waiver)

T. ROWE PRICE FLORIDA INSURED INTERMEDIATE TAX-FREE FUND ◆
(See first T. Rowe Price listing for data common to all funds)

Lead portfolio manager: Charles B. Hill (1994)
Investment objective and policies: High current income exempt from federal income tax and Florida intangible personal property tax. Invests primarily in investment grade Florida municipal bonds. Portfolio maintains a weighted average maturity of five to ten years. Bonds are insured as to timely payment of principal and interest.
Year organized: 1993
Ticker symbol: FLTFX
Discount broker availability: Fidelity, Siebert, White
Qualified for sale in: AL, CT, DC, FL, GA, IL, MD, MI, NJ, NY, PA, WY
Check redemptions: $500 minimum
Dividends paid: Income - declared daily, paid monthly; Capital gains - March, December
Portfolio turnover (3 yrs): 76%, 99%, 141%
Management fee: 0.05% + pro rata group fee
Expense ratio: 0.60% (year ending 2/28/97) (0.68% without waiver)

T. ROWE PRICE GEORGIA TAX-FREE BOND FUND ◆
(See first T. Rowe Price listing for data common to all funds)

Lead portfolio manager: Hugh D. McGuirk (1994)
Investment objective and policies: Highest level of current income exempt from federal and Georgia state income taxes, consistent with prudent portfolio management. Invests primarily in long-term investment grade Georgia municipal bonds. Portfolio maintains a dollar-weighted average maturity of more than fifteen years. May invest up to 15% of assets in illiquid securities, 10% in embedded interest rate swaps and caps, and 10% in residual interest bonds. May use options and futures in an effort to enhance performance and for hedging purposes. Fund is non-diversified.
Year organized: 1993
Ticker symbol: GTFBX
Discount broker availability: Fidelity, Schwab, Siebert, White
Qualified for sale in: AL, DC, FL, GA, HI, IL, MD, NJ, NC, SC, TN, VA, WY
Check redemptions: $500 minimum
Dividends paid: Income - declared daily, paid monthly; Capital gains - March, December
Portfolio turnover (3 yrs): 71%, 72%, 170%
Management fee: 0.10% + pro rata group fee
Expense ratio: 0.65% (year ending 2/28/97) (0.96% without waiver)

T. ROWE PRICE GLOBAL GOVERNMENT BOND FUND ◆
(See first T. Rowe Price listing for data common to all funds)

Adviser: Rowe Price-Fleming International, Inc.
Portfolio managers: Peter B. Askew (1994), Michael Conelius (1995), Christopher Rothery (1994)
Investment objective and policies: High current income; capital growth and principal protection secondary. Invests at least 65% of assets in U.S. and foreign high-quality (AA or better) government bonds, normally investing in assets diversified throughout at least three countries. The normal weighted average maturity of the portfolio is approximately seven years. May also hold U.S. and foreign corporate debt, including convertibles. May write and/or buy options on debt securities, indexes and currencies (up to 25% of assets); use index, interest rate and currency futures transactions and use private placements (up to 10% of assets). Fund will normally hedge 50% of foreign holdings using currency transactions.
Year organized: 1990 (absorbed Short-term Global Income fund 11/1/96)
Ticker symbol: RPGGX
Discount broker availability: Fidelity, Schwab, Siebert, White
Dividends paid: Income - declared daily, paid monthly Capital gains - December

Check redemptions: $500 minimum
Portfolio turnover (3 yrs): 153%, 263%, 291%
Management fee: 0.35% + pro rata group fee
Expense ratio: 1.20% (year ending 12/31/97) (includes waiver)

T. ROWE PRICE GLOBAL STOCK FUND ◆
(See first T. Rowe Price listing for data common to all funds)

Adviser: Rowe Price-Fleming International, Inc.
Lead portfolio manager: Martin G. Wade (1995)
Investment objective and policies: Long-term capital growth. Invests primarily in common stocks of established companies throughout the world, including the U.S. Fund will diversify broadly by investing in a variety of industries in developed, newly industrialized and emerging markets. Will normally invest in at least five countries including the U.S. May purchase stock without regard to market capitalization, but will focus first on large companies and second, on mid-cap issues. May invest up to 10% of assets in hybrid instruments, 15% in illiquid securities, and use a variety of derivative instruments for hedging purposes.
Year organized: 1995
Ticker symbol: PRGSX
Discount broker availability: Schwab, White
Dividends paid: Income - December; Capital gains - December
Portfolio turnover (2 yrs): 42%, 50%
Management fee: 0.35% + pro rata group fee
Expense ratio: 1.30% (year ending 10/31/97) (1.96% without waiver)

T. ROWE PRICE GNMA FUND ◆
(See first T. Rowe Price listing for data common to all funds)

Lead portfolio manager: J. Peter Van Dyke (1987)
Investment objective and policies: Highest level of current income consistent with maximum credit protection and moderate price fluctuation. Invests exclusively in securities backed by the full faith and credit of the U.S. Government, with at least 65% of assets in GNMA mortgage backed securities. Fund may also use interest rate futures and options in an effort to enhance yield and for hedging purposes.
Year organized: 1985
Ticker symbol: PRGMX
Check redemptions: $500 minimum
Discount broker availability: Fidelity, Schwab, Siebert, White
Dividends paid: Income - declared daily, paid monthly; Capital gains - December
Portfolio turnover (3 yrs): 116%, 114%, 121%
Management fee: 0.15% + pro rata group fee
Expense ratio: 0.74% (year ending 5/31/97)

T. ROWE PRICE GROWTH & INCOME FUND ◆
(See first T. Rowe Price listing for data common to all funds)

Lead portfolio manager: Stephen W. Boesel (1987)
Investment objective and policies: Long-term capital growth, reasonable current income, and the prospect of increasing future income. Invests primarily in dividend paying common stocks selected using both growth and value oriented approaches. May also invest in convertible and corporate debt securities and preferred stocks if deemed consistent with fund objective. Up to 25% of assets may be in securities of foreign issuers, 10% in junk bonds, 15% in illiquid securities and 10% in hybrid instruments. May use options and futures in an effort to enhance income and for hedging purposes.
Year organized: 1982
Ticker symbol: PRGIX
Discount broker availability: Fidelity, Schwab, Siebert, White
Dividends paid: Income - March, June, September, December; Capital gains - December
Portfolio turnover (3 yrs): 14%, 26%, 26%
Management fee: 0.25% + pro rata group fee
Expense ratio: 0.82% (year ending 12/31/96)

T. ROWE PRICE GROWTH STOCK FUND ◆
(See first T. Rowe Price listing for data common to all funds)

Lead portfolio manager: Robert W. Smith (1997)
Investment objective and policies: Long-term capital growth; increasing dividend income secondary. Invests primarily in a diversified portfolio of common stocks of well established domestic growth companies, generally those paying dividends. May, however, invest up to 30% of assets in securities of foreign issuers, 15% in illiquid securities and 10% in hybrid instruments. May use futures and options and foreign currency transactions in an effort to enhance performance and for hedging purposes.
Year organized: 1950
Ticker symbol: PRGFX
Discount broker availability: Fidelity, Schwab, Siebert, White
Dividends paid: Income - December; Capital gains - December
Portfolio turnover (3 yrs): 49%, 43%, 54%
Management fee: 0.25% + pro rata group fee
Expense ratio: 0.77% (year ending 12/31/96)

T. ROWE PRICE HEALTH SCIENCES FUND ◆
(See first T. Rowe Price listing for data common to all funds)

Lead portfolio manager: Joseph Klein III (1995)
Investment objective and policies: Long-term capital appreciation. Invests at least 65% of assets in the common stocks of companies engaged in the research, development, production, or distribution of products or services related to health care, medicine, or the life sciences. Looks for issues expected to grow faster than inflation and the economy in general. May invest up to 35% of assets in foreign securities, 15% in illiquid securities and 10% in hybrid instruments. May use foreign currency contracts, options and futures, and other derivative instruments in an effort to enhance performance and for hedging purposes.
Year organized: 1995
Ticker symbol: PRHSX
Discount broker availability: Fidelity, Schwab, Siebert, White
Dividends paid: Income - December; Capital gains - December
Portfolio turnover (1 yr): 133%
Management fee: 0.25% + pro rata group fee
Expense ratio: 1.35% (year ending 12/31/96) (1.43% without waiver)

T. ROWE PRICE HIGH YIELD FUND ◆
(See first T. Rowe Price listing for data common to all funds)

Lead portfolio manager: Mark J. Vaselkiv (1996)
Investment objective and policies: High current income; capital growth secondary. Invests at least 80% of assets in junk bonds and preferred stocks, and generally maintains a dollar-weighted average maturity of eight to twelve years. May invest up to 20% of assets in non-dollar denominated securities of foreign issuers and 10% in derivatives May use futures and options, sell short and hedge up to 25% of total assets.
Year organized: 1984 (name changed from High Yield Bond Fund in 1993)
Ticker symbol: PRHYX
Discount broker availability: Schwab, White
Check redemptions: $500 minimum
Redemption fee: 1.00% on shares held less than 1 year, payable to the fund
Dividends paid: Income - declared daily, paid monthly; Capital gains - March, December
Portfolio turnover (3 yrs): 111%, 100%, 74%
Management fee: 0.30% + pro rata group fee
Expense ratio: 0.84% (year ending 5/31/97)

T. ROWE PRICE INTERNATIONAL BOND FUND ◆
(See first T. Rowe Price listing for data common to all funds)

Adviser: Rowe Price-Fleming International, Inc.
Portfolio managers: Peter B. Askew (1994), Michael Conelius (1995), Christopher Rothery (1994)

Investment objective and policies: High current income with capital growth and protection of its principal value by actively managing its maturity structure and currency exposure. Invests at least 65% of assets in high quality, non-dollar-denominated fixed-income securities rated the equivalent of A or better. Up to 10% of assets may be in derivatives. Fund may hedge up to 50% of total assets in currencies in spot/forward markets, and use interest rate and currency futures and options on up to 25% of assets.
Year organized: 1986
Ticker symbol: RPIBX
Discount broker availability: Fidelity, Schwab, Siebert, White
Check redemptions: $500 minimum
Dividends paid: Income - declared daily, paid monthly; Capital gains - December
Portfolio turnover (3 yrs): 156%, 234%, 237%
Management fee: 0.35% + pro rata group fee
Expense ratio: 0.86% (year ending 12/31/97)

T. ROWE PRICE INTERNATIONAL DISCOVERY FUND ◆
(See first T. Rowe Price listing for data common to all funds)

Adviser: Rowe Price-Fleming International, Inc.
Lead portfolio manager: Martin G. Wade (1989)
Investment objective and policies: Long-term growth of capital. Invests primarily in common stocks of rapidly growing, small- and medium-sized foreign companies in developed and emerging markets. At least 65% of assets are in at least three countries, and fund generally holds at least 100 issues in at least ten countries. Up to 15% of assets may be in illiquid securities and 10% in hybrid instruments. May use spot/forward currency transactions, options on foreign currencies, and index and currency futures.
Year organized: 1988
Ticker symbol: PRIDX
Redemption fee: 2.00% for shares held less than one year, payable to the fund
Discount broker availability: Schwab
Dividends paid: Income - December; Capital gains - December
Portfolio turnover (3 yrs): 73%, 52%, 44%
Management fee: 0.75% + pro rata group fee
Expense ratio: 1.41% (year ending 10/31/97)

T. ROWE PRICE INTERNATIONAL STOCK FUND ◆
(See first T. Rowe Price listing for data common to all funds)

Adviser: Rowe Price-Fleming International, Inc.
Lead portfolio manager: Martin G. Wade (1989)
Investment objective and policies: Long-term growth of capital. Invests primarily in common stocks of established non-U.S. issuers in developed, newly industrialized and emerging markets. May, however, invest up to 35% of assets in other types of securities, including debt obligations, convertibles and preferred stock. Up to 15% of assets may be in illiquid securities and 10% in hybrid instruments. Fund may use spot/forward currency transactions and options and futures on foreign currencies.
Year organized: 1979 (2 for 1 stock split 8/31/87)
Ticker symbol: PRITX
Discount broker availability: Fidelity, Schwab, Siebert, White
Dividends paid: Income - December; Capital gains - December
Portfolio turnover (3 yrs): 16%, 12%, 18%
Management fee: 0.35% + pro rata group fee
Expense ratio: 0.85% (year ending 10/31/97)

T. ROWE PRICE JAPAN FUND ◆
(See first T. Rowe Price listing for data common to all funds)

Adviser: Rowe Price-Fleming International, Inc.
Lead portfolio manager: Martin G. Wade (1991)
Investment objective and policies: Long-term capital appreciation. Invests in a diversified portfolio of equity securities of established Japanese companies of all sizes that are perceived to have growth potential. Includes securities of companies domiciled in Japan or

with at least half their assets in Japan or deriving at least half their revenues from Japan. Up to 15% of assets may be in illiquid securities and 10% in hybrid instruments. Fund may use spot/forward currency transactions, and options and futures on foreign currencies. Up to 25% of assets may be in Japanese debt securities for defensive purposes.
Year organized: 1991
Ticker symbol: PRJPX
Discount broker availability: Fidelity, Schwab, Siebert, White
Dividends paid: Income - December; Capital gains - December
Portfolio turnover (3 yrs): 32%, 30%, 62%
Management fee: 0.50% + pro rata group fee
Expense ratio: 1.24% (year ending 10/31/97)

T. ROWE PRICE LATIN AMERICA FUND ◆
(See first T. Rowe Price listing for data common to all funds)

Adviser: Rowe Price-Fleming International, Inc.
Lead portfolio manager: Martin G. Wade (1993)
Investment objective and policies: Long-term capital growth. Invests in equity securities of both large and small companies in Latin America - primarily in Mexico, Brazil, Chile, Argentina, Venezuela and Columbia. Up to 15% of assets may be in illiquid securities and 10% in hybrid instruments. Fund may invest more than 25% of assets in the various Latin American telephone companies. Fund may use spot/forward currency transactions, and futures and options on foreign currencies. Fund is non-diversified.
Year organized: 1993
Ticker symbol: PRLAX
Discount broker availability: Schwab
Redemption fee: 2.00% for shares held less than one year, payable to the fund
Dividends paid: Income - December; Capital gains - December
Portfolio turnover (3 yrs) 33%, 22%, 19%
Management fee: 0.75% + pro rata group fee
Expense ratio: 1.47% (year ending 10/31/97)

T. ROWE PRICE MARYLAND SHORT-TERM TAX-FREE BOND FUND ◆
(See first T. Rowe Price listing for data common to all funds)

Lead portfolio manager: Charles B. Hill (1994)
Investment objective and policies: High level of current income exempt from federal and Maryland state and local income taxes, consistent with modest fluctuation in principal value. Invests at least 65% of assets in investment grade Maryland municipal securities. While there is no restriction on the maturity of any particular security, the portfolio maintains a dollar-weighted average maturity of less than three years. Up to 20% of assets may be in securities subject to AMT tax treatment, and up to 10% each in derivatives such as residual interest bonds or embedded interest rate swaps and caps. Fund is non-diversified.
Year organized: 1993
Ticker symbol: PRMDX
Discount broker availability: Fidelity, Schwab, Siebert, White
Qualified for sale in: DC, DE, FL, HI, MD, NJ, PA, VA, VT, WV, WY
Check redemptions: $500 minimum
Dividends paid: Income - declared daily, paid monthly; Capital gains - March, December
Portfolio turnover (3 yrs): 21%, 39%, 105%
Management fee: 0.10% + pro rata group fee
Expense ratio: 0.65% (year ending 2/28/97) (0.67% without waiver)

T. ROWE PRICE MARYLAND TAX-FREE BOND FUND ◆
(See first T. Rowe Price listing for data common to all funds)

Lead portfolio manager: Mary J. Miller (1990)
Investment objective and policies: The highest level current income exempt from federal and Maryland state and local income taxes, consistent with prudent portfolio management. Invests at least 65% of assets

in long-term investment grade Maryland municipal bonds. Portfolio maintains a dollar-weighted average maturity of more than 15 years. Up to 20% of assets may be in securities subject to AMT tax treatment, and up to 10% each in derivatives such as residual interest bonds or embedded interest rate swaps and caps. Fund is non-diversified.
Year organized: 1986
Ticker symbol: MDXBX
Discount broker availability: Fidelity, Schwab, Siebert, White
Qualified for sale in: DC, DE, FL, HI, MD, NJ, PA, VA, VT, WV, WY
Check redemptions: $500 minimum
Dividends paid: Income - declared daily, paid monthly; Capital gains - March, December
Portfolio turnover (3 yrs): 26%, 24%, 29%
Management fee: 0.10% + pro rata group fee
Expense ratio: 0.54% (year ending 2/28/97)

T. ROWE PRICE MEDIA AND TELECOMMUNICATIONS FUND ◆
(See first T. Rowe Price listing for data common to all funds)

Lead portfolio manager: Brian D. Stansky (1997)
Investment objective and policies: Long-term capital appreciation. Invests at least 65% of assets in a diversified portfolio of mid- and large-cap media and technology companies involved in the production and distribution of multimedia information, and up to 20% of assets may be in debt obligations of such firms. Issues are selected from companies with market capitalizations exceeding $500M that are perceived to have the greatest growth potential. May invest up to 35% of assets in foreign securities, up to 15% in illiquid securities, and up to 10% in hybrid instruments. May use options and futures and foreign currency contracts in an effort to enhance return and for hedging purposes.
Year organized: 1993 (originally New Age Media Fund, a closed-end fund; reorganized as open-ended fund with the new name 7/28/97; statistics through 12/96 represent closed-end fund.)
Ticker symbol: PRMTX
Discount broker availability: Schwab, White
Dividends paid: Income - December; Capital gains - December
Portfolio turnover (3 yrs): 103%, 119%, 134%
Management fee: 0.35% + pro rata group fee
Expense ratio: 1.22% (year ending 12/31/96)

T. ROWE PRICE MID-CAP GROWTH FUND ◆
(See first T. Rowe Price listing for data common to all funds)

Lead portfolio manager: Brian W.H. Berghuis (1992)
Investment objective and policies: Long-term capital growth. Invests at least 65% of assets in common stocks of companies whose market capitalization falls within the range of $300M and $5B that are perceived to offer above average growth potential. May invest up to 25% of assets in foreign securities, 15% in illiquid securities and 10% in hybrid instruments, and use stock index futures and options and foreign currency contracts in an effort to enhance performance and for hedging purposes.
Year organized: 1992
Ticker symbol: RPMGX
Discount broker availability: Fidelity, Schwab, Siebert, White
Dividends paid: Income - December; Capital gains - December
Portfolio turnover (3 yrs): 43%, 38%, 57%
Management fee: 0.35% + pro rata group fee
Expense ratio: 0.95% (year ending 12/31/97)

T. ROWE PRICE MID-CAP VALUE FUND ◆
(See first T. Rowe Price listing for data common to all funds)

Lead portfolio manager: Gregory A. McCrickard (1996)
Investment objective and policies: Long-term capital appreciation. Invests primarily in mid-sized companies with market capitalizations between $300M and $5B,

perceived to be undervalued relative to some combination of earnings, assets and cash flows. Will also seek value in companies undergoing restructurings and turnarounds. May invest in any type of security or instrument whose investment characteristics are consistent with the fund's investment program. May invest up to 20% of assets in foreign securities, 10% in hybrid instruments, and 15% in illiquid securities. May use futures and options for any reason, and foreign currency exchange contracts for hedging purposes.

Year organized: 1996
Ticker symbol: TRMCX
Discount broker availability: Fidelity, Siebert, White
Dividends paid: Income - December; Capital gains - December
Portfolio turnover (1 yr): 4%
Management fee: 0.35% + pro rata group fee
Expense ratio: 1.25% (6 months ending 12/31/96) (1.78% without waiver)

T. ROWE PRICE NEW AMERICA GROWTH FUND ◆
(See first T. Rowe Price listing for data common to all funds)

Lead portfolio manager: John H. Laporte (1985)
Investment objective and policies: Long-term capital growth. Invests most of its assets in common stocks of U.S. companies which operate in the service sector of the economy, without regard to capitalization size, including companies closely allied to service sector. May also invest up to 25% of assets in growth companies outside the service sector. May invest up to 15% of assets in foreign securities, 15% in illiquid securities and 10% in hybrid instruments, and use options and futures and foreign currency transactions in an effort to enhance performance and for hedging purposes.
Year organized: 1985
Ticker symbol: PRWAX
Discount broker availability: Fidelity, Schwab, Siebert, White
Dividends paid: Income - December; Capital gains - December
Portfolio turnover (3 yrs): 43%, 37%, 56%
Management fee: 0.35% + pro rata group fee
Expense ratio: 0.96% (year ending 12/31/97)

T. ROWE PRICE NEW ASIA FUND ◆
(See first T. Rowe Price listing for data common to all funds)

Adviser: Rowe Price-Fleming International, Inc.
Lead portfolio manager: Martin G. Wade (1990)
Investment objective and policies: Long-term capital growth. Invests primarily in large and small capitalization companies domiciled or operating primarily in Asia (excluding Japan) and the Pacific Basin, including Australia and New Zealand. Fund will hold securities in at least five different countries. May have up to 15% of assets in illiquid securities and 10% in hybrid instruments. May use spot/forward currency transactions, options and futures on foreign currencies, and index futures.
Year organized: 1990
Ticker symbol: PRASX
Discount broker availability: Fidelity, Schwab, Siebert, White
Discount broker availability: Schwab, White
Dividends paid: Income - December; Capital gains - December
Portfolio turnover (3 yrs): 42%, 42%, 66%
Management fee: 0.50% + pro rata group fee
Expense ratio: 1.10% (year ending 10/31/97)

T. ROWE PRICE NEW ERA FUND ◆
(See first T. Rowe Price listing for data common to all funds)

Lead portfolio manager: Charles M. Ober (1997)
Investment objective and policies: Long-term capital growth. Invests approximately two thirds of assets in common stocks of both domestic and foreign companies which own or develop natural resources and other basic commodities, and other selected non-resource growth companies. Fund focuses on companies whose

earnings and tangible assets could benefit from accelerating inflation. May invest up to 50% of assets in foreign securities, 10% in junk bonds, 15% in illiquid securities and 10% in hybrid instruments. May use options and futures and foreign currency contracts in an effort to enhance return and for hedging purposes.
Year organized: 1968
Ticker symbol: PRNEX
Discount broker availability: Fidelity, Schwab, Siebert, White
Dividends paid: Income - December; Capital gains - December
Portfolio turnover (3 yrs): 29%, 23%, 25%
Management fee: 0.25% + pro rata group fee
Expense ratio: 0.76% (year ending 12/31/96)

T. ROWE PRICE NEW HORIZONS FUND ◆
(See first T. Rowe Price listing for data common to all funds)

Lead portfolio manager: John H. Laporte (1988)
Investment objective and policies: Long-term capital growth. Invests primarily in a diversified portfolio of common stocks of small, rapidly growing domestic companies. Fund attempts to identify small firms before they are recognized by the market. May invest 10% of assets in foreign securities, 15% in illiquid securities and 10% in hybrid instruments. May use options and futures and foreign currency contracts in an effort to enhance performance and for hedging purposes.
Year organized: 1960
Ticker symbol: PRNHX
Special sales restrictions: Fund closed to new investors 6/18/96
Discount broker availability: Fidelity, Schwab, Siebert, White
Dividends paid: Income - December; Capital gains - December
Portfolio turnover (3 yrs): 41%, 56%, 44%
Management fee: 0.35% + pro rata group fee
Expense ratio: 0.90% (year ending 12/31/96)

T. ROWE PRICE NEW INCOME FUND ◆
(See first T. Rowe Price listing for data common to all funds)

Lead portfolio manager: Charles P. Smith (1986)
Investment objective and policies: High long-term income consistent with capital preservation. Invests at least 80% of assets in investment grade debt securities. Although there are no restrictions as to the maturity of individual issues, portfolio maintains a dollar-weighted average maturity of four to 15 years. Fund may invest without limit in mortgage-backed securities, and have up to 25% of assets in preferred and common stocks or equivalents, 20% in non-dollar denominated foreign fixed-income securities, 15% in illiquid securities, 10% in stripped mortgage securities, and 10% in hybrid instruments. May use foreign currency transactions and futures and options in an effort to enhance return or for hedging purposes. Fund will, under certain conditions, invest up to 50% of assets in any one of the following industries: gas utility, gas transmission utility, electric utility, telephone utility, and petroleum.
Year organized: 1973
Ticker symbol: PRCIX
Discount broker availability: Fidelity, Schwab, Siebert, White
Check redemptions: $500 minimum
Dividends paid: Income - declared daily, paid monthly; Capital gains - May, December
Portfolio turnover (3 yrs): 87%, 36%, 54%
Management fee: 0.15% + pro rata group fee
Expense ratio: 0.74% (year ending 5/31/97)

T. ROWE PRICE NEW JERSEY TAX-FREE BOND FUND ◆
(See first T. Rowe Price listing for data common to all funds)

Lead portfolio manager: William F. Snider (1997)
Investment objective and policies: High current income exempt from federal and New Jersey state and local income taxes, consistent with prudent portfolio management. Invests at least 65% of assets in long-term investment grade New Jersey municipal securi-

ties, and the income of at least 80% of assets must qualify as tax-free in New Jersey. Portfolio generally maintains a dollar-weighted average maturity exceeding 15 years. Up to 20% of assets may be subject to AMT treatment. May invest up to 10% of assets in residual interest bonds, 10% in embedded interest rate swaps and caps, and 15% in illiquid securities. Fund is non-diversified and may invest up to 25% of assets in the same industry sector.
Year organized: 1991
Ticker symbol: NJTFX
Discount broker availability: Fidelity, Schwab, Siebert, White
Qualified for sale in: DC, FL, HI, MA, NJ, WY
Check redemptions: $500 minimum
Dividends paid: Income - declared daily, paid monthly; Capital gains - March, December
Portfolio turnover (3 yrs): 79%, 98%, 139%
Management fee: 0.10% + pro rata group fee
Expense ratio: 0.65% (year ending 2/28/97) (0.75% without waiver)

T. ROWE PRICE NEW YORK TAX-FREE BOND FUND ◆
(See first T. Rowe Price listing for data common to all funds)

Lead portfolio manager: William F. Snider (1995)
Investment objective and policies: High current income exempt from federal, NY state and NY city income taxes, consistent with prudent portfolio management. Invests primarily in long-term, investment grade municipal securities exempt from such taxes, primarily from New York but also from Puerto Rico, Guam and the Virgin Islands. Portfolio generally maintains a dollar-weighted average maturity exceeding 15 years. Up to 20% of assets may be subject to AMT tax treatment. May invest up to 15% in illiquid securities, 10% in residual interest bonds and 10% in embedded interest rate swaps and caps. Fund is non-diversified and may invest up to 25% of assets in development bonds from the same industry sector.
Year organized: 1986
Ticker symbol: PRNYX
Qualified for sale in: CT, DE, DC, FL, HI, MD, MA, NJ, NY, PA, RI, VA, VT, WV, WY
Discount broker availability: Fidelity, Siebert, White
Check redemptions: $500 minimum
Dividends paid: Income - declared daily, paid monthly; Capital gains - March, December
Portfolio turnover (3 yrs): 97%, 116%, 134%
Management fee: 0.10% + pro rata group fee
Expense ratio: 0.65% (year ending 2/28/97) (includes waiver)

T. ROWE PRICE NEW YORK TAX-FREE MONEY FUND ◆
(See first T. Rowe Price listing for data common to all funds)

Portfolio manager: Patrice L. Berchtenbreiter Ely (1991)
Investment objective and policies: High current income exempt from federal, NY state and NY city income taxes consistent with preservation of capital and liquidity. Invests primarily in New York municipal money market securities ranked within the two highest categories of bond quality guidelines.
Year organized: 1986
Ticker symbol: NYTXX
Qualified for sale in: CT, DE, DC, FL, HI, MD, MA, NJ, NY, PA, RI, VA, VT, WV, WY
Check redemptions: $500 minimum
Dividends paid: Income - declared daily, paid monthly
Management fee: 0.10% + pro rata group fee
Expense ratio: 0.55% (year ending 2/28/97) (0.71% without waiver)

T. ROWE PRICE PERSONAL STRATEGY FUND - BALANCED ◆
(See first T. Rowe Price listing for data common to all funds)

Lead portfolio manager: J. Peter Van Dyke (1994)
Investment objective and policies: Highest total return: capital appreciation and income. Invests in a

diversified portfolio of 50% to 70% stocks, 20% to 40% bonds and 0% to 20% money market instruments. Neutral portfolio position is 60% stocks, 30% bonds and 10% money markets; adjustments are made according to perceived market conditions. Always invests at least 25% of assets in senior debt securities. Up to 35% of assets may be in securities of foreign issuers, 20% in junk bonds, 15% in illiquid securities, 10% in other mutual funds and 10% in hybrid instruments. May use futures and options, interest rate transactions, and foreign currency contracts in an effort to enhance performance and for hedging purposes.
Year organized: 1994
Ticker symbol: TRPBX
Discount broker availability: White
Dividends paid: Income - quarterly; Capital gains - December
Portfolio turnover (3 yrs): 54%, 48%, 26%
Management fee: 0.25% + pro rata group fee
Expense ratio: 1.05% (year ending 5/31/97) (1.10% without waiver)

T. ROWE PRICE PERSONAL STRATEGY FUND - GROWTH ◆
(See first T. Rowe Price listing for data common to all funds)

Lead portfolio manager: J. Peter Van Dyke (1994)
Investment objective and policies: Highest total return: primary emphasis on capital growth; income secondary. Invests in a diversified portfolio of 70% to 90% stocks, 10% to 30% bonds and money market instruments. Neutral portfolio position is 80% stocks and 20% bonds; adjustments are made according to perceived market conditions. Always invests at least 65% of assets in common stocks. Up to 35% of assets may be in securities of foreign issuers, 15% in junk bonds, 15% in illiquid securities, 10% in other mutual funds and 10% in hybrid instruments. May use futures and options, interest rate transactions, and foreign currency contracts in an effort to enhance performance and for hedging purposes.
Year organized: 1994
Ticker symbol: TRSGX
Discount broker availability: White
Dividends paid: Income - December; Capital gains - December
Portfolio turnover (3 yrs): 40%, 40%, 26%
Management fee: 0.30% + pro rata group fee
Expense ratio: 1.10% (year ending 5/31/97) (1.51% without waiver)

T. ROWE PRICE PERSONAL STRATEGY FUND - INCOME ◆
(See first T. Rowe Price listing for data common to all funds)

Lead portfolio manager: J. Peter Van Dyke (1994)
Investment objective and policies: Highest total return: primary emphasis on income, with some capital appreciation secondary. Invests in a diversified portfolio of 30% to 50% stocks, 30% to 50% bonds and 10% to 30% money market instruments. Neutral portfolio position is 40% stocks, 40% bonds and 20% money markets; adjustments are made according to perceived market conditions. Always invests at least 65% of assets in income producing bonds and dividend paying stocks. Up to 35% of assets may be in securities of foreign issuers, 25% in junk bonds, 25% in illiquid securities, 10% in other mutual funds and 10% in hybrid instruments. May use futures and options, interest rate transactions, and foreign currency contracts in an effort to enhance performance and for hedging purposes.
Year organized: 1994
Ticker symbol: PRSIX
Discount broker availability: White
Dividends paid: Income - quarterly; Capital gains - December
Portfolio turnover (3 yrs): 45%, 34%, 51%
Management fee: 0.15% + pro rata group fee
Expense ratio: 0.95% (year ending 5/31/97) (1.36% without waiver)

T. ROWE PRICE PRIME RESERVE FUND ◆
(See first T. Rowe Price listing for data common to all funds)

Lead portfolio manager: Edward A. Wiese (1990)
Investment objective and policies: Highest possible current income consistent with preservation of capital and liquidity. Invests in domestic and U.S. dollar-denominated foreign money market securities ranked in the two highest rating categories.
Year organized: 1975
Ticker symbol: PRRXX
Check redemptions: $500 minimum
Dividends paid: Income - declared daily, paid monthly
Management fee: 0.05% + pro rata group fee
Expense ratio: 0.64% (year ending 5/31/97)

T. ROWE PRICE REAL ESTATE FUND ◆
(See first T. Rowe Price listing for data common to all funds)

Lead portfolio manager: David M. Lee (1997)
Investment objective and policies: Long-term capital appreciation and current income. Invests at least 80% of assets in common stocks of companies with at least 50% of revenues or profits derived from, or assets committed to the real estate business, such as REITs, and real estate operating, development, management and finance companies. May also invest up to 20% of assets in firms which service the real estate industry, or in unrelated industries. May invest up to 25% of assets in foreign securities, 15% in illiquid securities and use futures and options on up to 25% of total assets.
Year organized: 1997
Redemption fee: 1.00% for shares held less than six months, payable to the fund.
Dividends paid: Income - December; Capital gains - December
Management fee: 0.35% + pro rata group fee

T. ROWE PRICE SCIENCE AND TECHNOLOGY FUND ◆
(See first T. Rowe Price listing for data common to all funds)

Lead portfolio manager: Charles A. Morris (1991)
Investment objective and policies: Long-term growth of capital. Invests primarily in common stocks of companies expected to benefit from the development, advancement, and use of science and technology. May invest up to 30% of assets in foreign securities, 15% in illiquid securities and 10% in derivatives and use futures and options on up to 25% of total assets.
Year organized: 1987
Ticker symbol: PRSCX
Discount broker availability: Fidelity, Schwab, Siebert, White
Dividends paid: Income - December; Capital gains - December
Portfolio turnover (3 yrs): 134%, 126%, 130%
Management fee: 0.35% + pro rata group fee
Expense ratio: 0.94% (year ending 12/31/97)

T. ROWE PRICE SHORT-TERM BOND FUND ◆
(See first T. Rowe Price listing for data common to all funds)

Lead portfolio manager: Edward A. Weise (1995)
Investment objective and policies: High income consistent with minimum fluctuation in principal and liquidity. Invests in short- and intermediate-term securities in the three highest rating categories. No security will have an effective duration exceeding seven years, and the portfolio maintains a weighted average maturity of less than three years. May concentrate up to 50% of assets in any one of the following industries: gas, electric or telephone utility; gas transmission; and petroleum. Fund may invest without limit in asset-backed securities, 15% in illiquid securities, up to 10% of assets in stripped mortgage securities, 10% in non-dollar denominated foreign fixed-income securities and 10% in hybrid instruments. May use foreign cur-

rency transactions and U.S. interest rate futures for hedging purposes, and use options on up to 25% of total assets.
Year organized: 1983
Ticker symbol: PRWBX
Check redemptions: $500 minimum
Discount broker availability: Fidelity, Schwab, Siebert, White
Dividends paid: Income - declared daily, paid monthly; Capital gains - December
Portfolio turnover (3 yrs): 104%, 119%, 137%
Management fee: 0.10% + pro rata group fee
Expense ratio: 0.74% (year ending 5/31/97)

T. ROWE PRICE SHORT-TERM U.S. GOVERNMENT FUND ◆
(See first T. Rowe Price listing for data common to all funds)

Lead portfolio manager: J. Peter Van Dyke (1992)
Investment objective and policies: High current income consistent with minimum fluctuation in share price. Invests at least 65% of assets in adjustable rate mortgage securities (ARMs) and collateralized mortgage obligations (CMOs). May also invest in high-quality fixed and adjustable rate mortgage and debt securities rated within the two highest credit categories. Up to 10% of assets may be in derivatives.
Year organized: 1991 (Name and objective changed from Adjustable Rate U.S. Government Fund in March 1995)
Ticker symbol: PRARX
Discount broker availability: Fidelity, Schwab, Siebert, White
Check redemptions: $500 minimum
Dividends paid: Income - declared daily, paid monthly; Capital gains - December
Portfolio turnover (3 yrs): 83%, 153%, 100%
Management fee: 0.10% + pro rata group fee
Expense ratio: 0.70% (year ending 5/31/97) (0.86% without waiver)

T. ROWE PRICE SMALL-CAP STOCK FUND ◆
(See first T. Rowe Price listing for data common to all funds)

Lead portfolio manager: Gregory A. McCrickard (1992)
Investment objective and policies: Long-term capital growth. Invests at least 65% of assets in stocks and equity-related securities traded in the U.S. with market capitalizations under $1B. Focuses on small rapidly growing companies which seem to offer growth potential and are perceived to be undervalued. May invest up to 15% of assets in illiquid securities, 10% in junk bonds, 10% in foreign securities, and 10% in hybrid instruments. May use options and futures and foreign currency transactions in an effort to enhance performance and for hedging purposes.
Year organized: 1956 (As the Over The Counter Securities Fund. Name changed in 1988 to the USF&G OTC Fund. Management and name changed to T. Rowe Price OTC Fund 8/31/92; name changed from OTC Fund 5/1/97)
Ticker symbol: OTCFX
Discount broker availability: Fidelity, Schwab, Siebert, White
Dividends paid: Income - December; Capital gains - December
Portfolio turnover (3 yrs): 23%, 31%, 58%
Management fee: 0.45% + pro rata group fee
Expense ratio: 1.02% (year ending 12/31/97)

T. ROWE PRICE SMALL-CAP VALUE FUND ◆
(See first T. Rowe Price listing for data common to all funds)

Lead portfolio manager: Preston G. Athey (1988)
Investment objective and policies: Long-term capital growth. Invests primarily in common stocks of companies with market capitalizations under $500M believed to be undervalued and to have good prospects for capital appreciation. Fund may invest up to 20% of assets in foreign securities, 15% in illiquid securities and 10% in hybrid instruments. May use options and futures and

foreign currency exchange transactions in an effort to enhance performance and for hedging purposes.
Year organized: 1988 (previously PEMCO, a New York limited partnership)
Ticker symbol: PRSVX
Special sales restrictions: Fund closed to new investors 3/1/96
Redemption fee: 1.00% for shares held less than one year, payable to the fund
Dividends paid: Income - December; Capital gains - December
Portfolio turnover (3 yrs): 15%, 15%, 18%
Management fee: 0.35% + pro rata group fee
Expense ratio: 0.87% (year ending 12/31/97)

T. ROWE PRICE SPECTRUM GROWTH FUND ◆
(See first T. Rowe Price listing for data common to all funds)

Lead portfolio manager: J. Peter Van Dyke (1990)
Investment objective and policies: Long-term growth of capital and income; current growth secondary. Invests primarily in a diversified group of seven T. Rowe Price mutual funds which invest principally in equity securities. Currently the funds it uses and the allocations are: Prime Reserve, 0% to 25%; Equity Income, 5% to 20%; Growth & Income, 5% to 20%; International Stock, 5% to 20%; New Era, 10% to 25%; New Horizons, 10% to 25%; and Growth Stock, 15% to 30%.
Year organized: 1990
Ticker symbol: PRSGX
Discount broker availability: Fidelity, Schwab, Siebert, White
Dividends paid: Income - December; Capital gains - December
Portfolio turnover (3 yrs): 3%, 7%, 21%
Management fee: No management fees except indirect fees allocated to shares of funds held.
Expense ratio: None (See expense ratios of underlying portfolio funds)

T. ROWE PRICE SPECTRUM INCOME FUND ◆
(See first T. Rowe Price listing for data common to all funds)

Lead portfolio manager: J. Peter Van Dyke (1990)
Investment objective and policies: High current income and capital preservation. Invests primarily in a diversified group of seven T. Rowe Price mutual funds which invest principally in fixed-income securities. Currently the funds it uses and the allocations are: Short-Term Bond, 0% to 15%; GNMA, 5% to 20%; International Bond, 5% to 20%; Equity Income, 10% to 25%; High Yield, 10% to 25%; Prime Reserve, 5% to 30%; and New Income, 15% to 30%.
Year organized: 1990
Ticker symbol: RPSIX
Discount broker availability: Fidelity, Schwab, Siebert, White
Dividends paid: Income - monthly; Capital gains - December
Check redemptions: $500 minimum
Portfolio turnover (3 yrs): 18%, 20%, 23%
Management fee: No management fees except indirect fees allocated to shares of funds held.
Expense ratio: None (See expense ratios of underlying portfolio funds)

T. ROWE PRICE SPECTRUM INTERNATIONAL FUND ◆
(See first T. Rowe Price listing for data common to all funds)

Sub-adviser: Rowe-Price Fleming International, Inc.
Lead portfolio manager: John R. Ford (1997)
Investment objective and policies: Long-term capital appreciation. Invests primarily in a group of T. Rowe Price international stock funds, and to a lesser degree in international bond funds. Allocation ranges include: International Stock Fund, 35% to 65%; International Discovery, 0% to 20%; Emerging Markets Stock, 0% to 20%; Japan, 0% to 30%; New Asia, 0% to 20%; European Stock, 0% to 30%; Latin

America, 0% to 15%; International Bond, 0% to 20%; Emerging Markets Bond, 0% to 15%; and Prime Reserve Fund, 0% to 25%.
Year organized: 1997
Ticker symbol: PSILX
Discount broker availability: Fidelity, Siebert, White
Dividends paid: Income - December; Capital gains - December
Management fee: No management fees except indirect fees allocated to shares of funds held.
Expense ratio: None (See expense ratios of underlying portfolio funds)

T. ROWE PRICE SUMMIT CASH RESERVE FUND ◆
(See first T. Rowe Price listing for data common to all funds)

Lead portfolio manager: Edward A. Wiese (1993)
Investment objective and policies: Highest level of current income consistent with preservation of capital and liquidity. Invests in domestic and U.S. dollar-denominated foreign money market securities ranked in the two highest rating categories. Designed to provide higher returns with low costs for long-term investors with substantial assets.
Year organized: 1993
Ticker symbol: TSCXX
Minimum purchase: Initial: $25,000, Subsequent: $1,000; IRA: Subsequent: $100
Check redemptions: $500 minimum
Dividends paid: Income - declared daily, paid monthly
Management fee: 0.45% (year ending 10/31/97) (covers all expenses)

T. ROWE PRICE SUMMIT GNMA FUND ◆
(See first T. Rowe Price listing for data common to all funds)

Lead portfolio manager: J. Peter Van Dyke (1993)
Investment objective and policies: High level of income and maximum credit protection. Invests at least 65% of assets in GNMA certificates guaranteed by the U.S. Government; the remainder of assets are invested in other government and corporate debt securities rated within the two highest rating categories. Portfolio maintains an effective average maturity of three to ten years. May have up to 15% of assets in illiquid securities, and up to 10% in stripped mortgage securities. May use options, futures and interest rate swaps. Designed to provide higher returns with low costs for long-term investors with substantial assets.
Year organized: 1993
Ticker symbol: PRSUX
Discount broker availability: White
Minimum purchase: Initial: $25,000, Subsequent: $1,000; IRA: Subsequent: $100
Check redemptions: $500 minimum
Dividends paid: Income - declared daily, paid monthly; Capital gains - October, December
Portfolio turnover (3 yrs): 112%, 136%, 174%
Management fee: 0.60% (year ending 10/31/97) (covers all expenses)

T. ROWE PRICE SUMMIT LIMITED TERM BOND FUND ◆
(See first T. Rowe Price listing for data common to all funds)

Lead portfolio manager: Edward A. Wiese (1993)
Investment objective and policies: High current income exempt from federal income tax. Invests at least 65% of assets in short- and intermediate-term investment grade bonds. Although there are no maturity restrictions on individual securities, the fund's dollar-weighted average maturity will not exceed five years. May have up to 10% of assets in junk bonds, up to 10% in stripped mortgage securities, 15% in illiquid securities, and use options, futures and interest rate swaps. Designed to provide higher returns with low costs for long-term investors with substantial assets.
Year organized: 1993
Ticker symbol: PRSBX
Discount broker availability: White

Minimum purchase: Initial: $25,000, Subsequent: $1,000; IRA: Subsequent: $100
Check redemptions: $500 minimum
Dividends paid: Income - declared daily, paid monthly; Capital gains - November
Portfolio turnover (3 yrs): 76%, 116%, 84%
Management fee: 0.55% (year ending 10/31/97) (covers all expenses)

T. ROWE PRICE SUMMIT MUNICIPAL INCOME FUND ◆
(See first T. Rowe Price listing for data common to all funds)

Lead portfolio manager: William T. Reynolds (1993)
Investment objective and policies: High income exempt from federal income tax. Invests primarily in long-term investment grade municipal securities. Average maturity is generally 15 years or longer. May have up to 20% of assets in junk bonds, and use securities that require AMT tax treatment without limit. Designed to provide higher returns with low costs for long-term investors with substantial assets.
Year organized: 1993
Ticker symbol: PRINX
Minimum purchase: Initial: $25,000, Subsequent: $1,000
Discount broker availability: White
Check redemptions: $500 minimum
Dividends paid: Income - declared daily, paid monthly; Capital gains - March, December
Portfolio turnover (3 yrs): 36%, 57%, 74%
Management fee: 0.50% (year ending 10/31/97) (covers all expenses)

T. ROWE PRICE SUMMIT MUNICIPAL INTERMEDIATE FUND ◆
(See first T. Rowe Price listing for data common to all funds)

Lead portfolio manager: Charles B. Hill (1993)
Investment objective and policies: High income exempt from federal income tax, consistent with moderate price fluctuation. Invests primarily in investment grade municipal securities. There is no restriction on the maturity of an individual security, but the portfolio maintains a dollar-weighted average maturity of between five and ten years. May have up to 10% of assets in junk bonds, and use securities that require AMT tax treatment without limit. Designed to provide higher returns with low costs for long-term investors with substantial assets.
Year organized: 1993
Ticker symbol: PRSMX
Minimum purchase: Initial: $25,000, Subsequent: $1,000
Discount broker availability: Fidelity, Siebert, White
Check redemptions: $500 minimum
Dividends paid: Income - declared daily, paid monthly; Capital gains - March, December
Portfolio turnover (3 yrs): 54%, 73%, 86%
Management fee: 0.65% (year ending 10/31/97) (covers all expenses)

T. ROWE PRICE SUMMIT MUNICIPAL MONEY MARKET FUND ◆
(See first T. Rowe Price listing for data common to all funds)

Lead portfolio manager: Patrice L. Berchtenbreiter Ely (1993)
Investment objective and policies: High current income exempt from federal income tax, consistent with preservation of capital and liquidity. Invests in municipal money market securities in the two highest rating categories. Designed to provide higher returns with low costs for long-term investors with substantial assets.
Year organized: 1993
Ticker symbol: TRSXX
Minimum purchase: Initial: $25,000, Subsequent: $1,000
Check redemptions: $500 minimum
Dividends paid: Income - declared daily, paid monthly
Management fee: 0.45% (year ending 10/31/97) (covers all expenses)

T. ROWE PRICE TAX-EFFICIENT BALANCED FUND ◆

(See first T. Rowe Price listing for data common to all funds)

Portfolio managers: Mary J. Miller (1997), Donald J. Peters (1997)
Investment objective and policies: Attractive long-term after tax returns comprised of capital appreciation and tax exempt current income, while maintaining minimal taxable distributions. Invests in a balanced portfolio of mid- to large-cap stocks selected using both growth and value characteristics from the 1,000 largest U.S. companies, and at least 50% tax exempt investment grade municipal bonds with maturities generally exceeding ten years. May invest up to 10% of assets in junk bonds, up to 25% in foreign issues, up to 15% in illiquid securities. May use certain derivative instruments for hedging purposes.
Year organized: 1997
Redemption fee: 1.00% for shares held less than one year, payable to the fund
Dividends paid: Income - (tax exempt): declared daily, paid quarterly; (taxable): annually; Capital gains - December
Management fee: 0.20% + pro rata group fee

T. ROWE PRICE TAX-EXEMPT MONEY FUND ◆

(See first T. Rowe Price listing for data common to all funds)

Lead portfolio manager: Patrice L. Berchtenbreiter Ely (1991)
Investment objective and policies: High current income exempt from federal income tax, consistent with preservation of capital and liquidity. Invests in short-term municipal money market securities with remaining maturities of one year or less.
Year organized: 1980
Ticker symbol: PTEXX
Check redemptions: $500 minimum
Dividends paid: Income - declared daily, paid monthly
Management fee: 0.10% + pro rata group fee
Expense ratio: 0.55% (year ending 2/28/97)

T. ROWE PRICE TAX-FREE HIGH YIELD FUND ◆

(See first T. Rowe Price listing for data common to all funds)

Lead portfolio manager: C. Stephen Wolfe II (1993)
Investment objective and policies: Maximum current income exempt from federal income tax. Invests primarily in long-term, high yielding, medium and lower quality municipal bonds, including as much as 10% of assets invested in bonds that are in default. The fund's dollar-weighted average maturity generally exceeds 15 years. Up to 25% of assets may be in issues representing the same industry sector, up to 15% in illiquid securities, and 10% in embedded interest rate swaps and caps.
Year organized: 1985
Ticker symbol: PRFHX
Discount broker availability: Fidelity, Schwab, Siebert, White
Check redemptions: $500 minimum
Dividends paid: Income - declared daily, paid monthly; Capital gains - December
Portfolio turnover (3 yrs): 37%, 39%, 60%
Management fee: 0.30% + pro rata group fee
Expense ratio: 0.74% (year ending 2/28/97)

T. ROWE PRICE TAX-FREE INCOME FUND ◆

(See first T. Rowe Price listing for data common to all funds)

Lead portfolio manager: Mary J. Miller (1997)
Investment objective and policies: High income exempt from federal income tax. Invests primarily in municipal securities in the four highest grades. Securities can be long, short, or intermediate term according to perceived market conditions. Portfolio generally maintains a dollar-weighted average maturity of more than 15 years. Up to 20% of securities may

be non-rated, but not below investment grade. Up to 25% of assets may be in issues representing the same industry sector, up to 15% in illiquid securities, and 10% in embedded interest rate swaps and caps.
Year organized: 1976
Ticker symbol: PRTAX
Discount broker availability: Fidelity, Schwab, Siebert, White
Check redemptions: $500 minimum
Dividends paid: Income - declared daily, paid monthly; Capital gains - December
Portfolio turnover (3 yrs): 41%, 49%, 49%
Management fee: 0.15% + pro rata group fee
Expense ratio: 0.57% (year ending 2/28/97)

T. ROWE PRICE TAX-FREE INSURED INTERMEDIATE BOND FUND ◆

(See first T. Rowe Price listing for data common to all funds)

Lead portfolio manager: Charles B. Hill (1994)
Investment objective and policies: High income exempt from federal income tax with minimal credit risk and greater principal stability than a long-term bond fund. Invests primarily in investment grade municipal bonds, insured as to timely payment of principal and interest. The dollar-weighted average maturity of the portfolio is five to ten years. Up to 25% of assets may be in issues representing the same industry sector, up to 15% in illiquid securities, and 10% in embedded interest rate swaps and caps.
Year organized: 1992
Ticker symbol: PTIBX
Discount broker availability: Fidelity, Schwab, Siebert, White
Check redemptions: $500 minimum
Dividends paid: Income - declared daily, paid monthly; Capital gains - December
Portfolio turnover (3 yrs): 77%, 64%, 171%
Management fee: 0.05% + pro rata group fee
Expense ratio: 0.65% (year ending 2/28/97) (0.70% without waiver)

T. ROWE PRICE TAX-FREE SHORT-INTERMEDIATE FUND ◆

(See first T. Rowe Price listing for data common to all funds)

Lead portfolio manager: Charles B. Hill (1995)
Investment objective and policies: High income exempt from federal income tax. Invests primarily in short and intermediate term municipal bonds. Portfolio maintains a dollar-weighted average maturity of between two and five years. None of the individual securities will have maturities greater than seven years. Up to 25% of assets may be in issues representing the same industry sector, up to 15% in illiquid securities, and 10% in embedded interest rate swaps and caps.
Year organized: 1983
Ticker symbol: PRFSX
Discount broker availability: Fidelity, Schwab, Siebert, White
Check redemptions: $500 minimum
Dividends paid: Income - declared daily, paid monthly; Capital gains - December
Portfolio turnover (3 yrs): 84%, 70%, 93%
Management fee: 0.10% + pro rata group fee
Expense ratio: 0.56% (year ending 2/28/97)

T. ROWE PRICE TOTAL EQUITY MARKET INDEX FUND ◆

(See first T. Rowe Price listing for data common to all funds)

Portfolio managers: Richard T. Whitney (1998), Kristen F. Culp (1998)
Investment objective and policies: Replicate the total return performance of the entire U.S. equities market as represented by the Wilshire 5000 Equity Index. Fund invests in a representative sample of the 7200 stocks in their approximate index weightings, producing a performance correlation to that of the Index of at least 0.95. May use stock index futures and options to maintain liquidity and a fully invested position.
Year organized: 1998

Redemption fee: 0.50% for shares held less than 6 months, payable to the fund
Dividends paid: Income - March, June, September, December; Capital gains - December
Management fee: 0.20%
Maintenance fee: $2.50 per quarter for balances of less than $10,000, even if the low balance is due to market fluctuations.

T. ROWE PRICE U.S. TREASURY INTERMEDIATE FUND ◆

(See first T. Rowe Price listing for data common to all funds)

Lead portfolio manager: Charles P. Smith (1989)
Investment objective and policies: High current income. Invests at least 85% of assets in U.S. Treasury securities and repurchase agreements thereon. Portfolio maintains a dollar-weighted average maturity of three to seven years. No individual security will have a remaining maturity in excess of ten years at time of purchase.
Year organized: 1989
Ticker symbol: PRTIX
Discount broker availability: Fidelity, Schwab, Siebert, White
Check redemptions: $500 minimum
Dividends paid: Income - declared daily, paid monthly; Capital gains - December
Portfolio turnover (3 yrs): 58%, 41%, 81%
Management fee: 0.05% + pro rata group fee
Expense ratio: 0.64% (year ending 5/31/97)

T. ROWE PRICE U.S. TREASURY LONG-TERM FUND ◆

(See first T. Rowe Price listing for data common to all funds)

Lead portfolio manager: J. Peter Van Dyke (1989)
Investment objective and policies: High current income. Invests at least 85% of assets in U.S. Treasury securities and repurchase agreements thereon. The fund's average maturity typically varies between 15 and 20 years, but may range from ten to 30 years.
Year organized: 1989
Ticker symbol: PRULX
Discount broker availability: Fidelity, Siebert, White
Check redemptions: $500 minimum
Dividends paid: Income - declared daily, paid monthly; Capital gains - December
Portfolio turnover (3 yrs): 68%, 60%, 99%
Management fee: 0.05% + pro rata group fee
Expense ratio: 0.80% (year ending 5/31/97)

T. ROWE PRICE U.S. TREASURY MONEY FUND ◆

(See first T. Rowe Price listing for data common to all funds)

Lead portfolio manager: Edward A. Wiese (1990)
Investment objective and policies: Highest current income consistent with safety of capital and liquidity. Invests in short-term U.S. Treasury securities, other money market securities carrying "full faith and credit" guarantee, and in repurchase agreements involving these securities.
Year organized: 1982
Ticker symbol: PRTXX
Check redemptions: $500 minimum
Dividends paid: Income - declared daily, paid monthly
Management fee: 0.05% + pro rata group fee
Expense ratio: 0.56% (year ending 5/31/97)

T. ROWE PRICE VALUE FUND ◆

(See first T. Rowe Price listing for data common to all funds)

Lead portfolio manager: Brian C. Rogers (1994)
Investment objective and policies: Long-term capital growth; income secondary. Invests primarily in common stocks believed undervalued. May also invest in convertible and corporate debt securities and preferred stocks. Up to 25% of assets may be in securities of foreign issuers, 15% in illiquid securities, 10% in

junk bonds and 10% in hybrid instruments. May use options, futures and foreign currency transactions in an effort to enhance return and for hedging purposes.
Year organized: 1994
Ticker symbol: TRVLX
Discount broker availability: Fidelity, Schwab, Siebert, White
Dividends paid: Income - March, June, September, December; Capital gains - December
Portfolio turnover (2 yrs): 68%, 90%
Management fee: 0.35% + pro rata group fee
Expense ratio: 1.13% (year ending 12/31/96)

T. ROWE PRICE VIRGINIA SHORT-TERM TAX-FREE BOND FUND ◆
(See first T. Rowe Price listing for data common to all funds)

Lead portfolio manager: Charles B. Hill (1994)
Investment objective and policies: High level of current income exempt from federal and Virginia state income taxes, consistent with modest fluctuation of the principal value. Invests primarily in investment grade Virginia municipal securities. Although there is no restriction on the remaining duration of any individual security, the fund's average maturity will not exceed three years. Up to 20% of assets may be in securities subject to AMT taxation, 15% in illiquid securities, 10% in residual interest bonds, and 10% in interest rate swaps and caps. Fund is non-diversified.
Year organized: 1995
Ticker symbol: PRVSX
Discount broker availability: Fidelity, Schwab, Siebert, White
Qualified for sale in: DC, HI, MD, NJ, VA, WY
Check redemptions: $500 minimum
Dividends paid: Income - declared daily, paid monthly; Capital gains - March, December
Portfolio turnover (2 yrs): 33%, 36%
Management fee: 0.10% + pro rata group fee
Expense ratio: 0.65% (year ending 2/28/97) (1.36% without waiver)

T. ROWE PRICE VIRGINIA TAX-FREE BOND FUND ◆
(See first T. Rowe Price listing for data common to all funds)

Lead portfolio manager: Hugh D. McGuirk (1997)
Investment objective and policies: High current income exempt from federal and Virginia state and local income taxes, consistent with prudent portfolio management. Invests primarily in long-term investment grade Virginia municipal bonds. The fund's average maturity generally exceed 15 years. Up to 20% of assets may be in securities subject to AMT taxation, 15% in illiquid securities, 10% in residual interest bonds, and 10% in interest rate swaps and caps. Fund is non-diversified.
Year organized: 1991
Ticker symbol: PRVAX
Discount broker availability: Fidelity, Schwab, Siebert, White
Qualified for sale in: DC, HI, MD, NJ, VA, WY
Check redemptions: $500 minimum
Dividends paid: Income - declared daily, paid monthly; Capital gains - March, December
Portfolio turnover (3 yrs): 66%, 94%, 89%
Management fee: 0.10% + pro rata group fee
Expense ratio: 0.65% (year ending 2/28/97)

PRIMARY TREND FUNDS ◆
(Data common to all Primary Trend funds are shown below. See subsequent listings for data specific to individual funds.)

First Financial Centre
700 North Water Street, Suite 420
Milwaukee, WI 53202
800-443-6544, 800-968-2122
414-271-7870, fax 414-271-2809

Shareholder service hours: Full service: M-F 8:30 A.M.-4:30 P.M. CST; After hours service: prices, account balances, orders, last transaction, prospectuses
Adviser: Arnold Investment Counsel, Inc.

Administrator: Sunstone Financial Group, Inc.
Transfer agent: Firstar Trust Co.
Minimum purchase: Initial: $500, Subsequent: $100; Automatic investment plan: Subsequent: $50
Wire orders accepted: Yes, $500 minimum
Deadline for same day wire purchase: 4 P.M.
Wire redemptions: No
Letter redemptions: Signature guarantee required over $10,000
Telephone switching: With other Primary Trend funds and Firstar Money Market Funds, $1,000 minimum
Number of switches permitted: 2 per 12 month period, $5 fee
Shareholder services: IRA, SEP-IRA, SIMPLE-IRA, Keogh, 401(k), 403(b), corporate retirement plans, directed dividends, systematic withdrawal plan min. bal. req. $25,000
IRA/Keogh fees: Annual $12.50, Closing $15

PRIMARY INCOME FUND ◆
(See first Primary Trend listing for data common to all funds)

Portfolio manager: Team managed
Investment objective and policies: High current income; capital appreciation secondary. Invests in a diversified portfolio of fixed-income securities of any maturity, and/or dividend-paying common and preferred stocks of well established companies with market capitalizations of $500M or more. Fund focuses on the utility industry, and may invest 100% of assets in it.
Year organized: 1989
Ticker symbol: PINFX
Qualified for sale in: CA, DC, FL, HI, IL, IN, KY, LA, MI, MN, NJ, NY, OH, OR, PA, TX, UT, WA, WI
Dividends paid: Income - declared daily, paid monthly; Capital gains - August, December
Portfolio turnover (3 yrs): 48%, 42%, 41%
Management fee: 0.74%
Expense ratio: 0.84% (year ending 6/30/97) (1.70% without waiver)

PRIMARY TREND FUND ◆
(See first Primary Trend listing for data common to all funds)

Portfolio manager: Team managed
Investment objective and policies: Maximum total return, a combination of capital growth and current income, without exposing capital to undue risk, as determined by the adviser. Fund invests in a flexibly allocated portfolio of cash, equities, or bonds in order to achieve this objective, with no minimum or maximum percentages of any asset type required. Fund endeavors to provide returns in excess of the inflation rate, the 90-day U.S. Treasury Bill rate, and the returns produced by popular stock market indices. Equity investments generally focus on undervalued companies with market capitalizations of $1B or more.
Year organized: 1986
Ticker symbol: PTFDX
Discount broker availability: Schwab
Qualified for sale in: AZ, CA, CO, DC, FL, HI, IL, IN, IA, KY, LA, MA, MI, MN, NJ, NY, OH, OR, PA, TX, UT, WA, WI
Dividends paid: Income - August, December; Capital gains - August, December
Portfolio turnover (3 yrs): 64%, 47%, 37%
Management fee: 0.74%
Expense ratio: 1.18% (year ending 6/30/97)

PRIMARY U.S. GOVERNMENT FUND ◆
(See first Primary Trend listing for data common to all funds)

Portfolio manager: Team managed
Investment objective and policies: High current income. Invests at least 80% of assets in a diversified portfolio of securities issued or guaranteed as to principal and interest by the U.S. Government and its agencies or instrumentalities. Portfolio will have a varying average maturity ranging from two to thirty years, depending on adviser's expectations regarding interest rates. May invest up to 20% of assets in investment grade corporate debt or commercial paper.

Year organized: 1989
Ticker symbol: PGUSX
Qualified for sale in: CA, DC, FL, IL, IN, KY, LA, MN, NJ, OH, OR, PA, TX, UT, WA, WI
Dividends paid: Income - declared daily, paid monthly; Capital gains - August, December
Portfolio turnover (3 yrs): 29%, 47%, 63%
Management fee: 0.65%
Expense ratio: 0.75% (year ending 6/30/97) (4.59% without waiver)

PRIME CASH SERIES
Federated Investors Tower
Pittsburgh, PA 15222-3779
800-245-0242, 412-288-1900
fax 412-288-1982

Adviser: Federated Advisers
Portfolio manager: Deborah Cunningham (1991)
Transfer agent: Federated Services Co.
Investment objective and policies: Income consistent with stability of principal and liquidity. Invests in high quality money market instruments.
Year organized: 1989
Ticker symbol: CTPXX
Minimum purchase: Initial: $10,000, Subsequent: $500; IRA: Initial: $1,000
Wire orders accepted: Yes
Deadline for same day wire purchase: 12 NN
Qualified for sale in: All states
Telephone redemptions: Yes
Wire redemptions: Yes, $10,000 minimum
Letter redemptions: Signature guarantee required over $50,000
Check redemptions: No minimum
Management fee: 0.50%
12b-1 distribution fee: Maximum of 0.35%
Expense ratio: 0.99% (year ending 5/31/96) (includes waiver)

PROFIT VALUE FUND
8720 Georgia Avenue, Suite 808
Silver Spring, MD 20910
888-335-6629, 301-951-9173
prices/yields 888-744-2337
fax 301-650-0608
Internet: http://www.profitfunds.com
e-mail: profitfunds@aol.com

Adviser: Investor Resources Group, Inc.
Administrator: SEI Fund Resources
Portfolio manager: Eugene A. Profit (1997)
Transfer agent: State Street Bank & Trust Co.
Investment objective and policies: High long-term total return: capital appreciation and increasing income; current income incidental. Invests primarily in common stocks of established companies with market capitalizations exceeding $1B. Selects investments based on low price/earnings ratios, strong balance sheet ratios, high and/or stable dividend yields, and low price/book ratios. Will gain foreign exposure through ADRs or other securities traded in U.S. markets. May also invest in convertible instruments of the four highest ratings.
Year organized: 1996
Minimum purchase: Initial: $2,500, Subsequent: $50; IRA: Initial: $1,000; Automatic investment plan: Initial: $500
Wire orders accepted: Yes
Deadline for same day wire purchase: 4 P.M.
Discount broker availability: *Fidelity, *White
Qualified for sale in: All states except AK, AR, CO, HI, ID, IA, KS, KY, MN, MT, NE, NV, NM, ND, OK, OR, RI, SD, UT, WA, WV, WI, WY
Letter redemptions: Signature guarantee required over $25,000
Dividends paid: Income - December; Capital gains - December
Portfolio turnover (1 yr): 10%
Shareholder services: IRA, SEP-IRA, systematic withdrawal plan min. bal. req. $5,000
Management fee: 1.25%
Administration fee: 0.15% first $50M to 0.10% over $100M ($65,000 minimum)
12b-1 distribution fee: Maximum of 0.25%
Expense ratio: 1.95% (eleven months ending 9/30/97) (18.57% without waiver)
IRA fees: None

PROFUNDS ◆

(Data common to all ProFunds are shown below. See subsequent listings for data specific to individual funds.)

7900 Wisconsin Avenue, Suite 300
Bethesda, MD 20814
888-776-3637

Adviser: ProFund Advisors, LLC (except MM)
Portfolio manager: William E. Seale (1997)
Transfer agent and administrator: BISYS Fund Services
Special sales restrictions: ProFunds are offered in two classes of shares, "Investor" and "Service." Service class shares are sold through various advisers and are available with initial minimums of $5,000. You must, however, pay the 1.00% shareholder services fee mentioned below for these shares. Information shown in this profile is for the direct marketed, self-directed "Investor" shares.
Minimum purchase: Initial: $15,000, Subsequent: None; Automatic investment plan: Subsequent: $1,000
Wire orders accepted: Yes
Deadline for same day wire purchase: 3:30 P.M.
Qualified for sale in: All states
Telephone redemptions: Yes, $1,000 minimum (from 8 A.M. to 3:50 P.M., and 4:30 P.M. to 9 P.M.)
Wire redemptions: $15 fee
Letter redemptions: Signature guarantee not required
Telephone switching: With the same share class of other ProFunds, $1,000 minimum
Deadline for same day switch: 3:50 P.M.
Number of switches permitted: Unlimited
Shareholder services: IRA, SEP-IRA, SIMPLE-IRA, ystematic withdrawal plan
Administration fee: 0.15% first $300M to 0.05% over $1B
IRA fees: Annual $15

BEAR PROFUND ◆

(See first ProFund listing for data common to all funds)

Investment objective and policies: Seeks to provide the opposite of the daily return of the S&P 500 benchmark index. A substantial portion of fund assets is devoted to engaging in short sales as well as options and futures trading using derivative instruments relative to the index. Fund is non-diversified.
Year organized: 1997
Discount broker availability: *White
Dividends paid: Income - annually; Capital gains - annually
Management fee: 0.75%
Shareholder services fee: Maximum of 1.00% (service class shares only)

BULL PROFUND ◆

(See first ProFund listing for data common to all funds)

Investment objective and policies: Seeks to match the daily return of the S&P 500 benchmark index. A substantial portion of fund assets is devoted to engaging in short sales as well as options and futures trading using derivative instruments relative to the index. Fund is non-diversified.
Year organized: 1997
Discount broker availability: *White
Dividends paid: Income - annually; Capital gains - annually
Management fee: 0.75%
Shareholder services fee: Maximum of 1.00% (service class shares only)

MONEY MARKET PROFUND ◆

(See first ProFund listing for data common to all funds)

Adviser: Bankers Trust Co.
Investment objective and policies: A high level of current income consistent with preservation of capital. Invests all its investable assets in an underlying money market portfolio with identical objectives at Bankers Trust.

Year organized: 1997
Check redemptions: $500 minimum
Dividends paid: Income - declared daily, paid monthly
Management fee: 0.35%
Shareholder services fee: Maximum of 1.00% (service class shares only)

ULTRABEAR PROFUND ◆

(See first ProFund listing for data common to all funds)

Investment objective and policies: Seeks to provide twice the inverse of the daily return of the S&P 500 benchmark index. A substantial portion of fund assets is devoted to engaging in short sales as well as options and futures trading using derivative instruments relative to the index. Fund is non-diversified.
Year organized: 1997
Discount broker availability: *White
Dividends paid: Income - annually; Capital gains - annually
Management fee: 0.75%
Shareholder services fee: Maximum of 1.00% (service class shares only)

ULTRABULL PROFUND ◆

(See first ProFund listing for data common to all funds)

Investment objective and policies: Seeks to double the daily return of the S&P 500 benchmark index. A substantial portion of fund assets is devoted to engaging in short sales as well as options and futures trading using derivative instruments relative to the index. Fund is non-diversified.
Year organized: 1997
Discount broker availability: *White
Dividends paid: Income - annually; Capital gains - annually
Management fee: 0.75%
Shareholder services fee: Maximum of 1.00% (service class shares only)

ULTRAOTC PROFUND ◆

(See first ProFund listing for data common to all funds)

Investment objective and policies: Seeks to double the daily return of the NASDAQ 100 benchmark index. A substantial portion of fund assets is devoted to engaging in short sales as well as options and futures trading using derivative instruments relative to the index. Fund is non-diversified.
Year organized: 1997
Discount broker availability: *White
Dividends paid: Income - annually; Capital gains - annually
Management fee: 0.75%
Shareholder services fee: Maximum of 1.00% (service class shares only)

PRUDENT BEAR FUND

8140 Walnut Hill Lane, Suite 405
Dallas, TX 75231-4336
888-778-2327, 214-696-5474
shareholder services 800-711-1848
Internet: http://www.pru-bear.com
e-mail: tice@tice.com

Adviser: David W. Tice & Assocs., Inc.
Administrator: Firstar Trust Co.
Portfolio manager: David W. Tice (1995)
Transfer agent: Firstar Trust Co.
Investment objective and policies: Capital appreciation. Attempts to achieve this objective in declining equity markets as well as in rising equity markets. Will invest primarily in common stocks and warrants, engage in short sales, and effect transactions in stock futures contracts, options on stock index futures contracts, and option on securities and stock indexes. Will utilize long or short equity positions to achieve capital appreciation determined relative to the direction of dividend yield of the stocks comprising the Standard & Poor's 500 index, overall market conditions, and the adviser's discretion. May invest up to 20% of assets in

foreign securities in the form of sponsored ADRs.
Year organized: 1995
Ticker symbol: BEARX
Minimum purchase: Initial: $5,000, Subsequent: $100; IRA: Initial: $1,000
Wire orders accepted: Yes
Deadline for same day wire purchase: 1 P.M.
Discount broker availability: *Fidelity, *Schwab, *White
Qualified for sale in: All states
Telephone redemptions: Yes, $1,000 minimum
Letter redemptions: Signature guarantee required
Dividends paid: Income - December; Capital gains - December
Portfolio turnover (2 yrs): 413%, 91%
Shareholder services: IRA, SEP-IRA, automatic investment plan, systematic withdrawal plan
Management fee: 1.25%
Administration fee: 0.05% first $100M to 0.03% over $500M
12b-1 distribution fee: Maximum of 0.25%
Expense ratio: 2.59% (year ending 9/30/97) (2.93% without waiver)
IRA fees: None

PRUDENT SPECULATOR FUND

(See the Pathfinder Fund)

PRUDENTIAL FUNDS

(Data common to all Prudential funds are shown below. See subsequent listings for data specific to individual funds.)

One Seaport Plaza
New York, NY 10292
800-225-1852, 908-417-7555
Internet: http://www.prudential.com

Adviser: Prudential Mutual Fund Management, Inc.
Transfer agent: Prudential Mutual Fund Services, Inc.
Minimum purchase: Initial: $2,500 ($1,000 for MoneyMart), Subsequent: $100; IRA/Keogh: None
Wire orders accepted: Yes, $1,000 minimum
Deadline for same day wire purchase: 12 NN (4 P.M. for Government Securities Trust - Short-Intermediate Term Series)
Qualified for sale in: All states
Wire redemptions: Yes
Letter redemptions: Signature guarantee required over $50,000
Telephone switching: With all Prudential funds (most of which have loads)
Number of switches permitted: Unlimited
Dividends paid: Income - declared daily, paid monthly; Capital gains - December (Government Securities Trust - Short-Intermediate Term Series only)
Shareholder services: IRA, Keogh, 401(k), 403(b), corporate retirement plans, automatic investment plan, systematic withdrawal plan min. bal. req. $10,000
IRA/Keogh fees: Annual $12, Initial $5, Closing $10

PRUDENTIAL GOVERNMENT SECURITIES TRUST - SHORT INTERMEDIATE TERM SERIES

(See first Prudential listing for data common to all funds)

Portfolio manager: Barbara L. Kenworthy (1996)
Investment objective and policies: High income consistent with reasonable safety. Invests at least 65% of assets in securities issued or guaranteed by the U.S. Government, its agencies or its instrumentalities. May invest up to 35% of assets in mortgage-backed issues or corporate debt. Portfolio maintains a dollar-weighted average maturity of two to five years.
Year organized: 1982 (name changed from Prudential-Bache Government Securities Trust in 1991)
Ticker symbol: PBGVX
Portfolio turnover (3 yrs): 132%, 217%, 431%
Management fee: 0.40%
12b-1 distribution fee: 0.25%
Expense ratio: 1.01% (year ending 11/30/96)

PRUDENTIAL GOVERNMENT SECURITIES TRUST - U.S. TREASURY MONEY MARKET SERIES
(See first Prudential listing for data common to all funds)

Portfolio manager: Bernard D. Whitesett II (1996)
Investment objective and policies: High current income consistent with preservation of capital and liquidity. Invests in money market instruments issued or guaranteed by the U.S. Government or its agencies or instrumentalities.
Year organized: 1982 (name changed from Prudential-Bache Government Securities Trust in 1991)
Ticker symbol: PBGXX
Management fee: 0.40%
12b-1 distribution fee: 0.125%
Expense ratio: 0.63% (year ending 11/30/96)

PRUDENTIAL MONEYMART ASSETS
(See first Prudential listing for data common to all funds)

Portfolio manager: Joseph M. Tully (1996)
Investment objective and policies: Maximum current income consistent with stability of capital and liquidity. Invests in money market instruments.
Year organized: 1976 (name changed from Prudential-Bache MoneyMart Assets in 1991)
Ticker symbol: PBMXX
Dividends paid: Income - declared daily, paid monthly
Management fee: 0.50% first $50M, 0.30% over $50M
12b-1 distribution fee: 0.125%
Expense ratio: 0.71% (year ending 12/31/96)

PRUDENTIAL TAX-FREE MONEY FUND
(See first Prudential listing for data common to all funds)

Portfolio manager: Rick Lynes (1987)
Investment objective and policies: High current income exempt from federal income taxes, consistent with capital preservation and liquidity. Invests in municipal money market obligations issued by states, territories and possessions of the U.S. and their subdivisions.
Year organized: 1979 (name changed from Prudential-Bache Tax-Free Money Fund in 1991)
Ticker symbol: PBFXX
Management fee: 0.50%
12b-1 distribution fee: 0.125%
Expense ratio: 0.80% (year ending 12/31/96)

PURISIMA TOTAL RETURN FUND
13100 Skyline Blvd.
Woodside, CA 94062-4547
800-841-2858, 415-851-3334
Internet: http://www.purisima.com

Adviser: Fisher Investments, Inc.
Portfolio manager: Kenneth L. Fisher (1996)
Transfer agent and administrator: Investment Company Administration Corp.
Investment objective and policies: High total return: capital appreciation and current income. Invests in an allocated portfolio of equity securities, corporate and government debt obligations, and short-term money market instruments. Allocation will be adjusted according to perceived market conditions. May use various options strategies for hedging purposes.
Year organized: 1996
Minimum purchase: Initial: $25,000, Subsequent: $5,000; IRA: Initial: $2,000, Subsequent: $100; Automatic investment plan: Subsequent: $100
Wire orders accepted: Yes
Deadline for same day wire purchase: 4 P.M.
Qualified for sale in: All states
Telephone redemptions: Yes, $500 minimum
Wire redemptions: Yes, $500 minimum, $10 fee
Letter redemptions: Signature guarantee required over $50,000
Dividends paid: Income - annually; Capital gains - annually
Portfolio turnover (1 yr): 1%

Shareholder services: IRA, SEP-IRA, electronic funds transfer, systematic withdrawal plan min. bal. req. $100,000
Management fee: 1.00%
12b-1 distribution fee: Maximum of 0.25%
Expense ratio: 1.50% (ten months ending 8/31/97) (20.97% without waiver)
IRA fees: Annual $10

QUAKER FAMILY OF FUNDS ◆
(Data common to all Quaker funds are shown below. See subsequent listings for data specific to individual funds.)

1288 Valley Forge Road, Suite 76
P.O. Box 987
Valley Forge, PA 19482
800-220-8888, 919-972-9922
610-917-9196
fax 919-972-1908, 610-935-8892
Internet: http://www.quakerfunds.com
e-mail: info@fundsrvs.com

Sponsor and distributor: Quaker Funds, Inc.
Transfer agent and administrator: The Nottingham Co.
Minimum purchase: Initial: $10,000 (aggregate), Subsequent: $250; IRA: Initial: $2,000; Automatic investment plan: Subsequent: $100
Wire orders accepted: Yes
Deadline for same day wire purchase: 4 P.M.
Telephone redemptions: Yes
Wire redemptions: Yes, $5,000 minimum, $7 fee
Letter redemptions: Signature guarantee required over $50,000
Telephone switching: With other Quaker funds and the Evergreen Money Market, requires fax confirmation
Number of switches permitted: Unlimited
Shareholder services: IRA, automatic investment plan, systematic withdrawal plan min. bal. req. $10,000
Administration fee: 0.175% first $50M to 0.125% over $100M (per fund)
12b-1 distribution fee: Maximum of 0.25% (not currently imposed) (paid by advisors)
IRA fees: Annual $15

QUAKER AGGRESSIVE GROWTH FUND ◆
(See first Quaker listing for data common to all funds)

Adviser: DG Capital Management, Inc.
Portfolio manager: Manu Daftary (1996)
Investment objective and policies: Long-term capital growth; current income incidental. Invests primarily in equity securities of a limited number of U.S. companies perceived to have superior prospects for growth. May use short sales valued to as much as 25% of assets. May use options for hedging purposes and make short sales against the box.
Year organized: 1996
Discount broker availability: *Fidelity, *White
Qualified for sale in: CA, CO, CT, DC, FL, MA, NJ, NY, NC, OH, PA, VA
Dividends paid: Income - December; Capital gains - December
Portfolio turnover (1 yr): 778%
Management fee: 0.75%
Expense ratio: 1.34% (7 months ending 6/30/97) (13.44% without waiver)

QUAKER CORE EQUITY FUND ◆
(See first Quaker listing for data common to all funds)

Adviser: West Chester Capital Advisors, Inc.
Portfolio managers: Bruce L. Marra (1996), Thomas F. McKeon (1996)
Investment objective and policies: Long-term capital growth; current income secondary. Invests primarily in equity securities of well established, large capitalization U.S. companies perceived to have strong financials and reasonable expectations for continued profit growth. The majority of holdings will have capitalizations exceeding $5B, aggregate trailing growth rates exceeding the S&P 500 average, dividend yields

in line with the S&P average, and price/earnings ratios approximating that of the S&P 500 average. Up to 25% of assets may not meet these conditions. May make short sales against the box.
Year organized: 1996
Dividends paid: Income - December; Capital gains - December
Discount broker availability: *Fidelity, *White
Qualified for sale in: CA, CO, FL, MD, NJ, NY, NC, OH, PA, VA
Portfolio turnover (1 yr): 11%
Management fee: 0.75%
Expense ratio: 1.35% (7 months ending 6/30/97) (21.30% without waiver)

QUAKER ENHANCED STOCK MARKET FUND ◆
(See first Quaker listing for data common to all funds)

Adviser: Fiduciary Asset Management Co.
Portfolio manager: John L. Dorian (1996)
Investment objective and policies: Long-term capital growth; current income incidental. Invests primarily in equity securities of U.S. companies in a portfolio whose diversification, capitalization and volatility levels approximate those of the S&P 500. May contain up to 300 issues and may not include all market sectors included in the S&P 500. May make short sales against the box.
Year organized: 1996
Qualified for sale in: CA, CO, FL, NJ, NY, NC, OH, PA, VA
Discount broker availability: *Fidelity, *White
Dividends paid: Income - December; Capital gains - December
Portfolio turnover (1 yr): 34%
Management fee: 0.50%
Expense ratio: 1.00% (7 months ending 6/30/97) (16.44% without waiver)

QUAKER FIXED INCOME FUND ◆
(See first Quaker listing for data common to all funds)

Adviser: Fiduciary Asset Management Co.
Portfolio managers: Wiley D. Angell (1996), Charles D. Walbrandt (1996)
Investment objective and policies: Current income, capital preservation and maximization of total returns. Invests primarily in a portfolio of investment grade, fixed-income securities selected on quantitative and qualitative terms relative to valuations against historic spreads and value relative to the yield curve. Duration may be lengthened or shortened according to variations in yield.
Year organized: 1996
Discount broker availability: *Fidelity, *White
Qualified for sale in: CA, CO, FL, MD, NJ, NY, NC, OH, PA, VA
Dividends paid: Income - monthly; Capital gains - December
Portfolio turnover (1 yr): 0%
Management fee: 0.45%
Expense ratio: 0.90% (7 months ending 6/30/97) (16.56% without waiver)

QUAKER MID-CAP VALUE FUND ◆
(See first Quaker listing for data common to all funds)

Adviser: Compu-Val Investments, Inc.
Portfolio managers: Christopher O'Keefe (1997), James Kalil (1997)
Investment objective and policies: Long-term capital growth; income incidental. Invests primarily in the equity securities of domestic companies exhibiting market capitalizations similar to those represented in the Russell Mid-Cap Index, under $6B. Companies are chosen according to perceived growth, value and momentum trends.
Year organized: 1997
Discount broker availability: *White
Qualified for sale in: AZ, CA, CO, DE, DC, FL, GA, IL, IN, LA, MD, MA, MO, NJ, NY, NC, OH, PA, SC, TX, VA
Dividends paid: Income - December; Capital gains - December
Management fee: 0.75%

QUAKER SECTOR ALLOCATION FUND ◆
(Fund liquidated Spring 1998)

QUAKER SMALL-CAP VALUE FUND ◆
(See first Quaker listing for data common to all funds)

Adviser: Aronson & Partners
Portfolio manager: Theodore R. Aronson (1996)
Investment objective and policies: Long-term capital growth; current income incidental. Invests in a broadly diversified number of U.S. equity securities of those companies perceived to show a high probability of superior total returns. Will generally hold between 140 to 160 companies with market capitalizations below $1B. May make short sales against the box.
Year organized: 1996
Discount broker availability: *Fidelity, *White
Qualified for sale in: AZ, CA, CO, CT, FL, MD, NJ, NY, NC, OH, PA, SC, VA
Dividends paid: Income - December; Capital gains - December
Portfolio turnover (1 yr): 91%
Management fee: 0.75%
Expense ratio: 1.31% (7 months ending 6/30/97) (10.50% without waiver)

QUANTITATIVE FUNDS
(Data common to all Quantitative funds are shown below. See subsequent listings for data specific to individual funds.)

55 Old Bedford Road
Lincoln, MA 01773
800-331-1244, 617-259-1144
fax 617-259-1166

Shareholder service hours: Full service: M-F 8:30 A.M.-6 P.M. EST; After hours service: prices, prospectuses
Manager: Quantitative Advisors, Inc. (formerly U.S. Boston Investment Management Corp.)
Transfer agent: Quantitative Institutional Services, Inc.
Sales restrictions: Funds have two share classes - Ordinary and Institutional. Institutional shares have minimum initial investments of $0.5M to $1.0M but do not impose either 12b-1 distribution fees or redemption fees. These may be purchased through discount brokers at lower minimums. All data listed here are for Ordinary shares.
Minimum purchase: Initial: $5,000, Subsequent: None; IRA: Initial: $1,000; Automatic investment plan: Initial: $1,000, Subsequent: $100
Wire orders accepted: Yes
Deadline for same day wire purchase: 4 P.M.
Telephone redemptions: Yes
Wire redemptions: Yes, $1,000 minimum
Letter redemptions: Signature guarantee required over $10,000
Redemption fee: 1.00% deferred sales charge (does not apply to Ordinary Shares of the Numeric II fund purchased after 8/1/96)
Telephone switching: With other Quantitative funds
Number of switches permitted: Unlimited
Shareholder services: IRA, SEP-IRA, 401(k), 403(b), systematic withdrawal plan min. bal. req. $10,000
IRA fees: Annual $15

QUANTITATIVE DISCIPLINED GROWTH FUND
(Fund liquidated 4/30/97)

QUANTITATIVE FOREIGN FRONTIER FUND
(See first Quantitative listing for data common to all funds)

Adviser: Independence International Assocs., Inc.
Portfolio managers: Lyle H. Davis (1994), David A. Umstead (1994)
Investment objective and policies: Long-term capital growth. Invests at least 65% of assets in common stock and securities convertible into common stock of issuers located in emerging markets. Will normally be invested in at least eight emerging markets. May use foreign currency futures to hedge against changes in exchange rates.

Year organized: 1994
Ticker symbol: QFFOX
Discount broker availability: Fidelity, Siebert, *White (only through financial advisers)
Qualified for sale in: All states except AL, AK, AR, DE, ID, IA, KS, ME, MS, MT, NE, NV, NH, NM, ND, OK, PR, SC, SD, WV, WI, WY
Dividends paid: Income - December; Capital gains - December
Portfolio turnover (3 yrs): 8%, 9%, 11%
Management fee: 0.80%
12b-1 distribution fee: 0.50%
Expense ratio: 2.68% (year ending 3/31/97)

QUANTITATIVE GROWTH AND INCOME FUND
(See first Quantitative listing for data common to all funds)

Adviser: State Street Global Advisors (a unit of State Street Bank & Trust Co.)
Portfolio managers: Steven M. Esielonis (1992), Douglas T. Holmes (1994), Charles Babin (1997)
Investment objective and policies: Long-term growth of capital and income. Invests primarily in dividend-paying common stocks of large companies with substantial equity capital. May invest in ADRs of foreign issuers, and use covered call options in an effort to increase return and hedge up to 25% of total assets.
Year organized: 1985
Ticker symbol: USBOX
Discount broker availability: *Fidelity, *White
Dividends paid: Income - December; Capital gains - December
Qualified for sale in: All states except AL, AK, AR, DE, ID, KS, ME, MS, MT, NE, NV, NH, ND, OK, PR, SC, SD, WV, WI, WY
Portfolio turnover (3 yrs): 98%, 152%, 121%
Management fee: 0.75%
12b-1 distribution fee: 0.50%
Expense ratio: 1.73% (year ending 3/31/97)

QUANTITATIVE INTERNATIONAL EQUITY FUND
(See first Quantitative listing for data common to all funds)

Adviser: Independence International Assocs., Inc.
Portfolio managers: Lyle H. Davis (1987), David A. Umsted (1987)
Investment objective and policies: Long-term growth of capital and income. Invests at least 65% of assets in equity securities and debt obligations of foreign companies and debt obligations of foreign governments. May use forward foreign currency contracts to hedge up to 25% of total assets.
Year organized: 1985 (name changed from Quantitative Boston Foreign Growth and Income Series in 1994)
Ticker symbol: USBFX
Discount broker availability: Fidelity, Siebert, *White
Qualified for sale in: All states except AL, AK, AR, DE, ID, IA, KS, ME, MS, MT, NE, NV, NH, NM, ND, OK, PR, SD, VT, WV, WI, WY
Dividends paid: Income - December; Capital gains - December
Portfolio turnover (3 yrs): 135%, 43%, 46%
Management fee: 1.00%
12b-1 distribution fee: 0.50%
Expense ratio: 2.20% (year ending 3/31/97)

QUANTITATIVE NUMERIC FUND
(See first Quantitative listing for data common to all funds)

Adviser: Columbia Partners, LLC, Investment Management
Portfolio manager: Robert A. von Pentz (1996)
Investment objective and policies: Long-term capital growth; income secondary. Invests primarily in common stocks with capitalizations under $800M that are perceived to have above average growth potential. May also purchase convertible securities and other investment grade fixed-income securities. May use futures and options in an effort to increase return and hedge up to 25% of total assets.
Year organized: 1992

Ticker symbol: USBNX
Discount broker availability: *Fidelity, *White
Qualified for sale in: All states except AK, AR, IA, KS, ME, MS, MT, NE, NV, NH, ND, OK, PR, SD, WV, WY
Dividends paid: Income - December; Capital gains - December
Portfolio turnover (3 yrs): 393%, 324%, 320%
Management fee: 1.00%
12b-1 distribution fee: 0.50%
Expense ratio: 1.97% (year ending 3/31/97)

QUANTITATIVE NUMERIC II FUND
(See first Quantitative listing for data common to all funds)

Adviser: Columbia Partners, LLC, Investment Management
Portfolio manager: Robert A. von Pentz (1996)
Investment objective and policies: Long-term capital growth. Invests primarily in common stocks of companies with medium capitalizations between $800M and $5B that are perceived to offer above average growth potential. May also purchase convertible securities and other investment grade fixed-income securities. May sell short on up to 25% of total assets, and use futures and options in an effort to increase return and hedge up to 25% of total assets.
Year organized: 1994
Ticker symbol: QNIIX
Discount broker availability: *Fidelity, *White
Qualified for sale in: All states except AK, AR, ID, IA, KS, ME, MS, MT, NE, NV, NH, NM, OK, PR, SD, VT, WV, WI, WY
Dividends paid: Income - December; Capital gains - December
Portfolio turnover (2 yrs): 162%, 181%
Management fee: 1.00%
12b-1 distribution fee: 0.25%
Expense ratio: 1.19% (year ending 3/31/97)

THE RAINBOW FUND ◆

33 Whitehall Street, 30th Floor
New York, NY 10004
212-349-6100

Adviser: Furman, Anderson & Co.
Portfolio manager: Robert M. Furman (1974)
Transfer agent: Investor Data Services
Investment objective and policies: Capital growth. Invests primarily in common stocks perceived to have growth potential. Up to 25% of assets may be in foreign securities. Fund may purchase ADRs of foreign issuers without limit, use options on securities and stock indexes in an effort to increase return and hedge up to 25% of total assets, use warrants and sell short. Fund is non-diversified.
Year organized: 1967 (10 for 1 split on 6/30/89)
Ticker symbol: RBOWX
Minimum purchase: Initial: $300, Subsequent: $50
Wire orders accepted: No
Qualified for sale in: NJ, NY
Letter redemptions: Signature guarantee required
Dividends paid: Income - December; Capital gains - December
Portfolio turnover (3 yrs): 90%, 46%, 102%
Shareholder services: IRA
Management fee: 0.625% first $2M to 0.375% over $5M
Expense ratio: 3.67% (year ending 10/31/97)
IRA fees: None

RAINIER PORTFOLIOS
(Data common to all Rainier portfolios are shown below. See subsequent listings for data specific to individual portfolios.)

601 Union Street, Suite 2801
Seattle, WA 98101
800-280-6111, 206-464-0400
prices/yields 800-248-6314
TDD 800-684-3416, fax 206-464-0616

Shareholder service hours: Full service: M-F 7:30 A.M.-4:30 P.M. PST; After hours service: prices, yields, account balances, orders, last transaction, messages, prospectuses, total returns

Adviser: Rainier Investment Management, Inc.
Administrator: Investment Company Administration Corp.
Transfer agent: Firstar Trust Co.
Minimum purchase: Initial: $25,000, Subsequent: $1,000
Wire orders accepted: Yes
Deadline for same day wire purchase: 4; p.m.
Telephone redemptions: Yes, $1,000 minimum
Wire redemptions: Yes, $1,000 minimum
Letter redemptions: Signature guarantee required over $50,000
Telephone switching: With other Rainier funds, and the Portico MM and U.S. Government MM funds
Number of switches permitted: Unlimited
Administration fee: 0.10% first $100M to 0.03% over $200M ($40,000 minimum)
Shareholder services: IRA, systematic withdrawal plan min. bal. req. $10,000
IRA/Keogh fees: Annual $12.50/account, $25 maximum

RAINIER BALANCED PORTFOLIO
(See first Rainier listing for data common to all portfolios)

Portfolio manager: Team managed
Investment objective and policies: Total return; long-term capital growth and current income. Invests in a mix of U.S. equity securities (35% to 65% of assets), intermediate-term fixed-income securities (35% to 55%) and cash equivalents (0% to 35%), with allocation adjusted to reflect changing market and economic conditions. May invest up to 20% of assets in U.S. dollar-denominated securities of foreign issuers and securities of foreign issuers listed and traded on domestic national securities exchanges. May invest up to 15% of assets in illiquid securities.
Year organized: 1994
Ticker symbol: RIMBX
Discount broker availability: *Fidelity, *Schwab, *Siebert, *White
Qualified for sale in: All states
Dividends paid: Income - March, June, September, December; Capital gains - June, December
Portfolio turnover (3 yrs): 134%, 115%, 92%
Management fee: 0.70%
12b-1 distribution fee: 0.25%
Expense ratio: (1.19% year ending 3/31/97) (1.31% without waiver)

RAINIER CORE EQUITY PORTFOLIO
(See first Rainier listing for data common to all portfolios)

Portfolio managers: James R. Margard (1994), David A. Veterane (1994), Peter M. Musser (1994)
Investment objective and policies: Maximum long-term capital appreciation. Invests primarily in a diversified portfolio of common stocks of U.S. companies within the S&P 500 Index perceived to have above average earnings and growth potential while selling at attractive valuations. May invest up to 20% of assets in U.S. dollar-denominated securities of foreign issuers and securities of foreign issuers listed and traded on domestic national securities exchanges. May invest up to 15% of assets in illiquid securities and 20% in short-term instruments.
Year organized: 1994
Ticker symbol: RIMEX
Discount broker availability: *Fidelity, *Schwab, *Siebert, *White
Qualified for sale in: All states
Dividends paid: Income - June, December; Capital gains - June, December
Portfolio turnover (3 yrs): 146%, 138%, 133%
Management fee: 0.75%
12b-1 distribution fee: 0.25%
Expense ratio: (1.18% year ending 3/31/97) (1.22% without waiver)

RAINIER INTERMEDIATE FIXED-INCOME PORTFOLIO
(See first Rainier listing for data common to all portfolios)

Portfolio managers: Patricia L. Frost (1994), Michael E. Raney (1994)
Investment objective and policies: Current income.

Invests primarily in investment grade government and corporate debt securities of U.S. issuers and foreign issuers denominated in U.S. dollars, with a weighted average maturity of three to ten years. May invest up to 20% of assets in U.S. dollar-denominated securities of foreign issuers and securities of foreign issuers listed and traded on domestic national securities exchanges. May invest up to 15% of assets in illiquid securities.
Year organized: 1994
Ticker symbol: RIMFX
Discount broker availability: Fidelity, Schwab, Siebert, *White
Qualified for sale in: All states
Dividends paid: Income - monthly; Capital gains - June, December
Portfolio turnover (3 yrs): 8%, 15%, 5%
Management fee: 0.50%
12b-1 distribution fee: 0.25%
Expense ratio: (0.95% year ending 3/31/97) (1.53% without waiver)

RAINIER SMALL/MID CAP EQUITY PORTFOLIO
(See first Rainier listing for data common to all portfolios)

Portfolio managers: James R. Margard (1994), David A. Veterane (1994), Peter M. Musser (1994)
Investment objective and policies: Maximum long-term capital appreciation. Invests primarily in common stocks of small and medium capitalization companies perceived to have above average earnings and growth potential while selling at attractive valuations. The capitalization ranges are determined by using the parameters of the Russell 2000 and Mid-Cap Indices. Generally the portfolio will hold between 15% and 40% of assets in small-cap and 60% to 80% of assets in mid-cap securities. A security that remains attractive may be held even if its capitalization exceeds these targets. May invest up to 20% of assets in U.S. dollar-denominated securities of foreign issuers and securities of foreign issuers listed and traded on domestic national securities exchanges. May invest up to 15% of assets in illiquid securities and 20% in short-term instruments.
Year organized: 1994
Ticker symbol: RIMSX
Discount broker availability: *Fidelity, *Schwab, *Siebert, *White
Qualified for sale in: All states
Dividends paid: Income - June, December; Capital gains - June, December
Portfolio turnover (3 yrs): 131%, 151%, 152%
Management fee: 0.85%
12b-1 distribution fee: 0.25%
Expense ratio: (1.33% year ending 3/31/97) (1.40% without waiver)

RCM EQUITY FUNDS ◆
(**At press time,** the funds had changed their name to Dresdner RCM Equity Funds. Data common to all Dresdner RCM Equity funds are shown below. See subsequent listings for data specific to individual portfolios.)

Four Embarcadero Center, Suite 3000
San Francisco, CA 94111-4189
800-726-7240, 415-954-5400
fax 415-954-8200

Adviser: Dresdner RCM Global Investors, LLC (a wholly-owned subsidiary of Dresdner Bank AG, of Frankfurt, Germany)
Transfer agent: State Street Bank and Trust Co.
Minimum purchase: Initial: $5,000, Subsequent: $250
Wire orders accepted: Yes
Deadline for same day wire purchase: 4; p.m.
Qualified for sale in: All states
Telephone redemptions: No
Wire redemptions: No
Letter redemptions: Signature guarantee not required
Shareholder services: electronic funds transfer (purchase only)

RCM BIOTECHNOLOGY FUND ◆
(See first Dresdner RCM Equity listing for data common to all portfolios)

Portfolio managers: Jeffrey J. Wiggins (1997), Selena A. Chaisson (1997)
Investment objective and policies: Long-term capital appreciation. Invests at least 65% of assets in equity and equity related securities of companies involved in biotechnology industries, including those involved in the research, development and manufacture of such products and services, that are believed to offer a high rate of growth. May invest without limit in foreign securities, although no more than 25% of assets may be invested in any one foreign country, no more than 15% of assets may be invested in emerging markets companies, and no more than 10% in any one emerging economy. May use foreign currency transactions, short sales against the box, and options for hedging purposes. Fund is non-diversified.
Year organized: 1997
Discount broker availability: *Fidelity, White
Dividends paid: Income - annually; Capital gains - annually
Management fee: 1.00% of first $500M to 0.90% over $1B
12b-1 distribution fee: 0.25% (not currently imposed)

RCM EMERGING MARKETS FUND ◆
(See first Dresdner RCM Equity listing for data common to all portfolios)

Portfolio managers: Ana Wiechers-Marshall (1997), William S. Stack (1997)
Investment objective and policies: Capital appreciation. Invests at least 80% of assets in equity and equity related securities of companies with market capitalizations exceeding $100M that are organized or headquartered in emerging markets countries as defined by the World Bank, The International Finance Corporation, or the United Nations. Management utilizes a top-down selection strategy in an effort to take advantage of market inefficiencies and the lack of correlation among emerging markets. May use a variety of foreign currency transactions for hedging purposes.
Year organized: 1997
Discount broker availability: *Fidelity, White
Dividends paid: Income - annually; Capital gains - annually
Management fee: 1.00%
12b-1 distribution fee: 0.25% (not currently imposed)

RCM GLOBAL HEALTH CARE FUND ◆
(See first Dresdner RCM Equity listing for data common to all portfolios)

Portfolio managers: Jeffrey J. Wiggins (1996), Selena A. Chaisson (1996)
Investment objective and policies: Capital appreciation. Invests primarily in equity and equity related securities of domestic and foreign companies in the health care sector and related industries that are perceived to have above average growth potential. May invest without limit in foreign markets, although may only invest up to 25% of assets in any one country, only 15% of assets in developing countries, and only 10% of assets in a single emerging market. May invest up to 10% of assets in debt obligations, and up to 15% in illiquid securities. May use options and futures, forward foreign currency exchanges and short sales against the box for hedging purposes.
Year organized: 1996
Discount broker availability: *Fidelity, White
Dividends paid: Income - annually; Capital gains - annually
Portfolio turnover (1 yr): 158%
Management fee: 1.00%
12b-1 distribution fee: 0.25% (not currently imposed)
Expense ratio: 1.50% (year ending 12/31/97) (2.93% without waiver)

RCM GLOBAL SMALL CAP FUND ◆
(See first Dresdner RCM Equity listing for data common to all portfolios)

Portfolio managers: David S. Plants (1996), Michael F. Malouf (1996)
Investment objective and policies: Capital appreciation. Invests primarily in equity and equity related securities of both foreign and domestic companies with market capitalizations of less than $1B at time of purchase that are perceived to have above average growth potential. Also invests in emerging growth companies and cyclical and semi-cyclical companies in developing economies. Invests without limit in foreign securities, and must be distributed throughout at least three countries, including the U.S. May invest up to 30% of assets in emerging markets, and up to 10% in any one emerging market country. May invest up to 10% of assets in debt obligations, and up to 15% in illiquid securities. May use options and futures, forward foreign currency exchanges and short sales against the box for hedging purposes.
Year organized: 1996
Discount broker availability: *Fidelity, White
Dividends paid: Income - annually; Capital gains - annually
Portfolio turnover (1 yr): 153%
Management fee: 1.00%
12b-1 distribution fee: 0.25% (not currently imposed)
Expense ratio: 1.75% (year ending 12/31/97) (3.09% without waiver)

RCM GLOBAL TECHNOLOGY FUND ◆
(See first Dresdner RCM Equity listing for data common to all portfolios)

Portfolio manager: Walter C. Price, Jr. (1995), Huachen Chen (1995)
Investment objective and policies: Long-term capital appreciation. Invests primarily in equity and equity related securities of technology companies of any size from around the world that are perceived to have above average growth potential. May invest up to 15% of assets in companies with market capitalizations of less than $100M. Must distribute investments through at least three countries in the world, none of which may be the U.S., although will not invest more than 25% of assets in any one country except Japan. May invest up to 20% of assets in emerging markets, but only 10% in any one emerging market country. May invest up to 10% of assets in debt obligations, and up to 15% in illiquid securities. May use options and futures, forward foreign currency exchanges and short sales against the box for hedging purposes.
Year organized: 1995
Discount broker availability: *Fidelity, White
Dividends paid: Income - annually; Capital gains - annually
Portfolio turnover (2 yrs): 189%, 156%
Management fee: 1.00%
12b-1 distribution fee: 0.25% (not currently imposed)
Expense ratio: 1.75% (year ending 12/31/97) (2.45% without waiver)

RCM LARGE CAP GROWTH FUND ◆
(See first Dresdner RCM Equity listing for data common to all portfolios)

Portfolio manager: John D. Leland (1996), Carson V. Levit (1996)
Investment objective and policies: Capital appreciation. Invests primarily in equity and equity related securities of companies with market capitalizations exceeding $1B at time of purchase that are perceived to have above average growth potential. May invest up to 20% of assets in foreign issues, including up to 10% in emerging markets. May invest up to 10% of assets in debt obligations, and up to 15% in illiquid securities. May use options and futures, forward foreign currency exchanges and short sales against the box for hedging purposes.
Year organized: 1996
Discount broker availability: *Fidelity, White
Dividends paid: Income - annually; Capital gains - annually

Management fee: 0.70%
12b-1 distribution fee: 0.15% (not currently imposed)

REICH & TANG EQUITY FUND
600 Fifth Avenue, 8th Floor
New York, NY 10020
800-221-3079, 212-830-5220
prices/yields 212-830-5225
fax 212-830-5350

Adviser: Reich & Tang Asset Management, L.P.
Portfolio managers: Robert F. Hoerle (1985), Steven M. Wilson (1993)
Transfer agent: Reich & Tang Services, L.P.
Investment objective and policies: Capital appreciation; current income secondary. Invests at least 65% of assets in equity securities believed undervalued. May invest up to 35% of assets in debt securities and preferred stocks offering opportunity for price appreciation. Up to 15% of assets may be in foreign securities and 10% in restricted securities.
Year organized: 1985
Ticker symbol: RCHTX
Minimum purchase: Initial: $5,000, Subsequent: None; IRA: Initial: $250; Automatic investment plan: Subsequent: $100
Wire orders accepted: Yes
Deadline for same day wire purchases: 4 P.M.
Discount broker availability: Schwab, *White
Qualified for sale in: All states except AK, DC, ID, IA, MS, MT, NM, ND, PR, SC, SD, TN, WV, WY
Telephone redemptions: Yes, $25,000 maximum
Wire redemptions: Yes
Letter redemptions: Signature guarantee required
Telephone switching: With other Reich & Tang funds, $1,000 minimum
Number of switches permitted: Unlimited
Dividends paid: Income - March, June, September, December; Capital gains - December
Portfolio turnover (3 yrs): 28%, 26%, 27%
Shareholder services: IRA, electronic funds transfer, systematic withdrawal plan min. bal. req. $10,000
Management fee: 0.80%
Administration fee: 0.20%
12b-1 distribution fee: Maximum of 0.05%
Expense ratio: 1.22% (year ending 12/31/96) (1.23% without waiver)
IRA fees: None

REMBRANDT FUNDS
(Data common to all Rembrandt funds are shown below. See subsequent listings for data specific to individual funds.)

208 South LaSalle Street, Fourth Floor
Chicago, IL 60604-1003
800-443-4725, 312-855-3350
Internet: http://www.rembrandtfunds.com

Shareholder service hours: Full service: M-F 8:30 A.M.-8 P.M. EST; After hours service: prices, yields, news, total returns
Adviser: ABN AMRO Asset Management (USA) Inc. (an indirect, wholly-owned subsidiary of ABN AMRO Holding N.V. of the Netherlands)
Transfer agent and administrator: First Data Corp.
Special sales restrictions: The Rembrandt funds are available in two share classes, "Common" and "Investor." Common shares were previously called "Trust" shares, and were only available to institutions. Investor shares were previously retail load funds carrying a 4.5% commission, sold through banks. Common shares are now sold direct and at discount brokers with no loads and lower minimums; Investor shares are still sold through the bank, with a 0.25% 12b-1 fee. Historic performance information and turnover reflects the old institutional class shares.
Minimum purchase: Initial: $2,000, Subsequent: $100; IRA: Initial: $1,000; Automatic investment plan: Subsequent: $50
Wire orders accepted: Yes
Deadline for same day wire purchases: 4 P.M. (1 P.M. for MMs)
Qualified for sale in: All states
Telephone redemptions: Yes
Wire redemptions: Yes, $1,000 minimum, $10 fee
Letter redemptions: Signature guarantee required over $5,000

Telephone switching: With the same class of other Rembrandt funds
Number of switches permitted: Unlimited
Shareholder services: IRA, electronic funds transfer, systematic withdrawal plan min. bal. req. $5,000
Maintenance fees: $10 per year low balance fee if under $15,000
IRA fees: None (except possible low balance fees)

REMBRANDT ASIAN TIGERS FUND ◆
(See first Rembrandt listing for data common to all funds)

Sub-adviser: ABN AMRO-NSM International Funds Management B.V.
Portfolio manager: Alex Ng (1995)
Investment objective and policies: Capital appreciation. Invests at least 65% of assets in equity securities traded on recognized stock exchanges of the countries of Asian other than Japan, and in equity securities of companies organized under the laws of those countries, including developing markets such as India, Pakistan, and Sri Lanka. Country allocations are not set; they are determined only by the relative attractiveness of stocks issued by companies within their borders. Remaining assets are invested in closed end companies that invest primarily in common stocks or money market instruments of Asian or European issuers. Fund may invest or hold a portion of assets in U.S. dollars or foreign currencies, and will usually hold some U.S. dollars. May use options and futures for hedging purposes.
Year organized: 1994
Ticker symbol: RATIX
Group fund code: 16
Discount broker availability: Fidelity, *White
Dividends paid: Income - annually; Capital gains - August
Portfolio turnover (3 yrs): 42%, 24%, 28%
Management fee: 1.00%
Expense ratio: 1.60% (year ending 12/31/97)

REMBRANDT BALANCED FUND ◆
(See first Rembrandt listing for data common to all funds)

Lead portfolio manager: Jac A. Cerney (1993)
Investment objective and policies: Favorable total return - current income and capital appreciation, consistent with preservation of capital. Invests at least 80% of assets in fixed-income and equity securities, with a minimum of 25% and maximum of 50% of assets in investment-grade, fixed-income securities. The allocation of assets are adjusted for changes in perceived market and economic conditions. Up to 15% of assets may be in foreign fixed-income obligations. There are no restrictions regarding maturity. Equity funds are either listed on national exchanges or actively traded in over the counter markets. May use options and futures for hedging purposes.
Year organized: 1993
Ticker symbol: RBTCX
Group fund code: 10
Discount broker availability: Fidelity, *White
Dividends paid: Income - monthly; Capital gains - August, December
Portfolio turnover (3 yrs): 111%, 104%, 85%
Management fee: 0.70%
Expense ratio: 0.93% (year ending 12/31/97)

REMBRANDT FIXED INCOME FUND ◆
(See first Rembrandt listing for data common to all funds)

Portfolio manager: Charles H. Self, III (1995)
Investment objective and policies: High total return relative to other funds with similar objectives from income and, to a lesser degree, capital growth. Invests as fully as feasible, and always at least 65%, of assets in quality intermediate- and long-term corporate and government fixed-income securities. Portfolio has no restrictions governing the maturity of any single instrument or of the entire portfolio, although the estimated average maturity of the portfolio is eight years. May invest in options and futures for hedging purposes.
Year organized: 1993
Ticker symbol: RTFTX

Group fund code: 5
Discount broker availability: Fidelity, *White
Dividends paid: Income - monthly; Capital gains - December
Portfolio turnover (3 yrs): 233%, 194%, 59%
Management fee: 0.60%
Expense ratio: 0.71% (year ending 12/31/97) (0.81% without waiver)

REMBRANDT GOVERNMENT MONEY MARKET FUND ◆
(See first Rembrandt listing for data common to all funds)

Portfolio manager: Karen Van Cleave (1994)
Investment objective and policies: Highest possible current income consistent with the preservation of capital and liquidity. Invests in high quality obligations of the U.S. Government or its agencies and instrumentalities. May also invest in repurchase agreements thereon.
Year organized: 1993
Ticker symbol: RGTXX
Group fund code: 2
Check redemptions: $100 minimum
Dividends paid: Income - declared daily, paid monthly
Management fee: 0.20%
Expense ratio: 0.32% (year ending 12/31/97) (0.40% without waiver)

REMBRANDT GROWTH FUND ◆
(See first Rembrandt listing for data common to all funds)

Portfolio manager: Keith Dibble (1993)
Investment objective and policies: High total return, primarily through capital appreciation. Invests at least 65% of assets in common stocks of domestic companies of any size that are thought to offer strong prospects for appreciation through growth in earnings. Securities are selected that are traded on national exchanges or actively in the over the counter market, and have an average daily trading volume in excess of $1M. May invest the balance of assets in convertibles or in dollar denominated equity securities of foreign firms, but only if they meet the same trading criteria as domestic issues. May use options and future for hedging purposes.
Year organized: 1993
Ticker symbol: RGTCX
Group fund code: 12
Discount broker availability: Fidelity, Siebert, *White
Dividends paid: Income - monthly; Capital gains - August, December
Portfolio turnover (3 yrs): 62%, 58%, 71%
Management fee: 0.80%
Expense ratio: 1.02% (year ending 12/31/97)

REMBRANDT INTERMEDIATE GOVERNMENT FIXED INCOME FUND ◆
(See first Rembrandt listing for data common to all funds)

Portfolio manager: Mark W. Karstrom (1996)
Investment objective and policies: High total return relative to other funds with similar objectives, from income and, to a lesser degree, capital growth, consistent with preservation of capital. Invests 100% of assets in short- to intermediate-term securities issued or guaranteed by the U.S. Government. Portfolio generally maintains a weighted average maturity of three to ten years; it may at times, though, fall under three years. May invest in options and futures for hedging purposes only.
Year organized: 1993 (name changed from Short/Intermediate Government Fixed Income Fund in 1995)
Ticker symbol: RIGTX
Group fund code: 6
Discount broker availability: Fidelity, Siebert, *White
Dividends paid: Income - monthly; Capital gains - December
Portfolio turnover (3 yrs): 283%, 179%, 115%

Management fee: 0.60%
Expense ratio: 0.71% (year ending 12/31/97) (0.81% without waiver)

REMBRANDT INTERNATIONAL EQUITY FUND ◆
(See first Rembrandt listing for data common to all funds)

Sub-adviser: ABN AMRO-NSM International Funds Management B.V.
Portfolio manager: Wypke Postma (1997)
Investment objective and policies: High total return: capital appreciation and current income. Invests at least 65% of assets in equity securities of issuers located in at least three countries other than the U.S. Fund intends to diversify investments among as many countries as possible in order to mitigate currency risk. May invest in both developed and emerging markets, when issues are available on either national exchanges or active over the counter markets. Balance of assets are invested in common stocks of closed end companies that invest primarily in international and U.S. common stocks, and money markets. Fund may invest or hold a portion of assets in U.S. dollars or foreign currencies, and will usually hold some U.S. dollars. May use options and futures for hedging purposes.
Year organized: 1993
Ticker symbol: RIEQX
Group fund code: 14
Discount broker availability: Fidelity, Siebert, *White
Dividends paid: Income - annually; Capital gains - December
Portfolio turnover (3 yrs): 17%, 9%, 11%
Management fee: 1.00%
Expense ratio: 1.35% (year ending 12/31/97)

REMBRANDT INTERNATIONAL FIXED INCOME FUND ◆
(See first Rembrandt listing for data common to all funds)

Sub-adviser: ABN AMRO-NSM International Funds Management B.V.
Portfolio manager: Wouter Weijand (1997)
Investment objective and policies: High total return from capital appreciation and income, relative to other funds with similar objectives. Invests as fully as is feasible in investment quality fixed-income securities denominated in foreign currencies (including the ECU) of at least three of the following countries: Austria, Australia, Belgium, Canada, Denmark, Finland, France, Germany, Ireland, Italy, Japan, Luxembourg, The Netherlands, New Zealand, Norway, Spain, Sweden, Switzerland and the United Kingdom. There are no restrictions regarding the maturity of a single instrument or of the entire portfolio. Fund may invest or hold a portion of assets in U.S. dollars or foreign currencies, and will usually hold some U.S. dollars. May use options and futures for hedging purposes.
Year organized: 1993 (name changed from Global Fixed Income 2/24/97)
Ticker symbol: RGFIX
Group fund code: 8
Discount broker availability: Fidelity, *White
Dividends paid: Income - annually; Capital gains - annually
Portfolio turnover (3 yrs): 52%, 85%, 105%
Management fee: 0.80%
Expense ratio: 1.22% (year ending 12/31/97)

REMBRANDT LATIN AMERICAN EQUITY FUND ◆
(See first Rembrandt listing for data common to all funds)

Sub-adviser: ABN AMRO-NSM International Funds Management B.V.
Portfolio manager: Luis M. Ribeiro, Jr. (1997)
Investment objective and policies: Long-term capital appreciation. Invests primarily in equity securities of companies organized in, or for which the principal securities trading market is in Latin America. The companies must have derived at least 50% of their activities in one of the last two fiscal years from within the Latin

American market. At this time, eligible countries include: Argentina, Bolivia, Brazil, Chile, Colombia, Costa Rica, the Dominican Republic, Ecuador, El Salvador, Guatemala, Honduras, Mexico, Nicaragua, Panama, Paraguay, Peru, Uruguay, Venezuela, and the Spanish-speaking islands of the Caribbean (not including Cuba and Haiti). May also invest in investment grade debt obligations of government agencies within the region, or of supranationals. Fund may invest or hold a portion of assets in U.S. dollars or foreign currencies, and will usually hold some U.S. dollars. May use a variety of derivative instruments for hedging purposes. Fund is non-diversified.
Year organized: 1996
Ticker symbol: RLAEX
Group fund code: 17
Discount broker availability: Fidelity
Dividends paid: Income - annually; Capital gains - December
Portfolio turnover (2 yrs): 45%, 10%
Management fee: 1.00%
Expense ratio: 1.50% (year ending 12/31/97)

REMBRANDT MONEY MARKET FUND ◆
(See first Rembrandt listing for data common to all funds)

Portfolio manager: Karen Van Cleave (1994)
Investment objective and policies: Highest current income possible consistent with the preservation of capital and liquidity. Invests exclusively in high quality corporate, bank and government money market instruments.
Year organized: 1993
Ticker symbol: RTTXX
Group fund code: 3
Check redemptions: $100 minimum
Dividends paid: Income - declared daily, paid monthly
Management fee: 0.35%
Expense ratio: 0.32% (year ending 12/31/97) (0.56% without waiver)

REMBRANDT REAL ESTATE FUND ◆
(See first Rembrandt listing for data common to all funds)

Portfolio manager: Nancy Droppelman (1997)
Investment objective and policies: High total return: capital growth and income. Invests at least 65% of assets in equity securities of domestic and foreign companies that are principally engaged in the real estate business, including REITs, real estate operating companies, real estate brokerages or developers, mortgage providers, and companies such as lumber and paper concerns, or hotels, who own large amounts of real estate. Fund does not invest directly in real estate. Balance of funds may be invested in any manner. Fund may invest without limit in foreign securities, and may engage in short sales. May use options and futures for hedging purposes.
Year organized: 1997
Group fund code: 18
Dividends paid: Income - monthly; Capital gains - annually
Management fee: 1.00%

REMBRANDT SMALL CAP FUND ◆
(See first Rembrandt listing for data common to all funds)

Portfolio manager: Marc G. Borghans (1997)
Investment objective and policies: High total return, primarily through capital appreciation. Invests at least 65% of assets in a diversified portfolio of common stocks of companies with market capitalizations under $1B that are believed to offer strong growth prospects and strong sales and earnings growth rates. Fund may invest without limit in foreign securities that fit the criteria necessary for inclusion. May use options and futures for hedging purposes.
Year organized: 1993
Ticker symbol: RSMCX
Group fund code: 13
Discount broker availability: Fidelity, Siebert, *White

Dividends paid: Income - monthly; Capital gains - August, December
Portfolio turnover (3 yrs): 170%, 158%, 142%
Management fee: 0.80%
Expense ratio: 1.04% (year ending 12/31/97)

REMBRANDT TAX-EXEMPT FIXED INCOME FUND ◆
(See first Rembrandt listing for data common to all funds)

Portfolio manager: Phillip P. Mierzwa (1997)
Investment objective and policies: High total return exempt from federal income tax, relative to other funds with similar objectives, consistent with preservation of capital. Invests as fully as possible in investment grade fixed-income municipal securities not subject to AMT tax treatment. May use options and futures for hedging purposes.
Year organized: 1993
Ticker symbol: RTETX
Group fund code: 7
Discount broker availability: Fidelity, Siebert, *White
Dividends paid: Income - monthly; Capital gains - annually
Portfolio turnover (3 yrs): 54%, 98%, 129%
Management fee: 0.60%
Expense ratio: 0.73% (year ending 12/31/97) (0.84% without waiver)

REMBRANDT TAX-EXEMPT MONEY MARKET FUND ◆
(See first Rembrandt listing for data common to all funds)

Portfolio manager: Phillip P. Mierzwa (1997)
Investment objective and policies: High current income exempt from federal regular and AMT income tax, consistent with the maintenance of principal value and a high degree of liquidity. Invests in all levels of eligible municipal money market instruments.
Year organized: 1993
Ticker symbol: RXTXX
Group fund code: 4
Check redemptions: $100 minimum
Dividends paid: Income - declared daily, paid monthly
Management fee: 0.35%
Expense ratio: 0.33% (year ending 12/31/97) (0.57% without waiver)

REMBRANDT TREASURY MONEY MARKET FUND ◆
(See first Rembrandt listing for data common to all funds)

Portfolio manager: Karen Van Cleave (1994)
Investment objective and policies: Current income consistent the preservation of capital and a high degree of liquidity. Invests exclusively in money market instruments issued by the U.S. Treasury, and the separately traded components that are transferable through the Federal Book Entry System (i.e., STRIPS).
Year organized: 1993
Ticker symbol: RTMXX
Group fund code: 1
Check redemptions: $100 minimum
Dividends paid: Income - declared daily, paid monthly
Management fee: 0.35%
Expense ratio: 0.33% (year ending 12/31/97) (0.57% without waiver)

REMBRANDT VALUE FUND ◆
(See first Rembrandt listing for data common to all funds)

Portfolio manager: Jac A. Cerney (1993)
Investment objective and policies: High level of total return through capital appreciation and current income. Invests at least 65% of assets in dividend-paying common stocks of companies believed to be undervalued, including U.S. dollar-denominated securities of foreign issuers, or sponsored ADRs if they are actively

traded on national exchanges or over the counter. May use options and futures for hedging purposes.
Year organized: 1993
Ticker symbol: RVALX
Group fund code: 11
Discount broker availability: Fidelity, Siebert, *White
Dividends paid: Income - monthly; Capital gains - August, December
Portfolio turnover (3 yrs): 79%, 58%, 37%
Management fee: 0.80%
Expense ratio: 1.01% (year ending 12/31/97)

RESERVE FUNDS
(Data common to all Reserve funds are shown below. See subsequent listing for data specific to individual funds.)

810 Seventh Avenue
New York, NY 10019
800-637-1700, 212-977-9982
fax 212-977-9897
Internet: http://www.reservefunds.com

Shareholder service hours: Full service: M-F 8:30 A.M.- 6 P.M. EST; After hours service: prices, yields, balances, orders, last transaction, news, messages, prospectuses, total returns, investment objectives
Adviser: Reserve Management Co., Inc.
Transfer agent: Resrv Partners, Inc.
Minimum purchase: Initial: $1,000, Subsequent: $100; IRA: Initial: $250; Automatic investment plan: Initial: $25, Subsequent: $25
Wire orders accepted: Yes, $1,000 minimum
Telephone redemptions: Yes, $2 fee for redemptions under $100
Wire redemptions: Yes, $10 fee under $10,000
Letter redemptions: Signature guarantee required over $5,000
Telephone switching: With other Reserve Group funds
Number of switches permitted: Unlimited, 15 day hold
Shareholder services: IRA, systematic withdrawal plan min. bal. req. $5,000
Maintenance fee: $5 per month for balances under $2,500 (shareholders have 12 months from the date of initial purchase to achieve this)
IRA fees: Annual $10 (waived for accounts over $10,000), Initial $10, Closing $10

THE RESERVE BLUE CHIP GROWTH FUND
(See first Reserve listing for data common to all funds)

Sub-adviser: Trainer, Wortham & Co., Inc.
Portfolio manager: Charles V. Moore (1996)
Investment objective and policies: Capital appreciation; income secondary. Invests at least 65% of assets in 'blue chip' U.S. common stocks believed to offer growth prospects. Fund may also invest without limit in both adjustable and fixed rate securities issued, guaranteed or collateralized by the U.S. Government or its subdivisions, and without limit in covered call options. Fund is non-diversified.
Year organized: 1996
Ticker symbol: RBCAX
Deadline for same day wire purchase: 4 P.M.
Discount broker availability: *Schwab, *White
Qualified for sale in: All states
Deadline for same day switch: 4 P.M.
Dividends paid: Income - quarterly; Capital gains - annually
Portfolio turnover (3 yrs): 109%, 72%, 68%
Management fee: 1.50%
12b-1 distribution fee: 0.25%
Expense ratio: 1.75% (year ending 5/31/97)

THE RESERVE CALIFORNIA TAX-EXEMPT FUND
(See first Reserve listing for data common to all funds)

Portfolio manager: Michael Sheridan (1995)
Investment objective and policies: High level of short-term interest income exempt from federal, state and local

income and or property taxes, consistent with preservation of capital and liquidity. Invests primarily in tax-exempt issues issued by the state and its' counties, municipalities, authorities or other political subdivisions.
Year organized: 1994
Ticker symbol: RTCXX
Deadline for same day wire purchase: 11 A.M.
Qualified for sale in: CA
Check redemptions: No minimum, $2 fee for less than $100
Deadline for same day switch: 11 A.M.
Dividends paid: Income - declared daily, paid monthly
Management fee: 0.50% first $500M to 0.40% over $400M
12b-1 distribution fee: 0.20%
Expense ratio: 1.03% (year ending 5/31/97)

THE RESERVE CONNECTICUT TAX-EXEMPT FUND
(See first Reserve listing for data common to all funds)

Portfolio manager: Michael Sheridan (1995)
Investment objective and policies: High level of short-term interest income exempt from federal, state and local income and or property taxes, consistent with preservation of capital and liquidity. Invests primarily in tax-exempt issues issued by the state and its' counties, municipalities, authorities or other political subdivisions.
Year organized: 1987
Ticker symbol: RCOXX
Deadline for same day wire purchase: 11 A.M.
Qualified for sale in: CT
Check redemptions: No minimum, $2 fee for less than $100
Deadline for same day switch: 11 A.M.
Dividends paid: Income - declared daily, paid monthly
Management fee: 0.50% first $500M to 0.40% over $400M
12b-1 distribution fee: 0.20%
Expense ratio: 0.97% (year ending 5/31/97)

THE RESERVE CONVERTIBLE SECURITIES FUND
(See first Reserve listing for data common to all funds)

Sub-adviser: New Vernon Advisers, Inc.
Portfolio manager: J. Peter Simon (1996)
Investment objective and policies: Capital appreciation and current income. Invests primarily in securities which are convertible into, or which derive their returns from, price changes in the common stock of an underlying corporate issuer. These include corporate debentures, convertible preferred stocks and derivative convertibles. Fund focuses on convertibles with underlying securities that are thought to be undervalued, and trades in both rated and unrated securities, as well as in busted convertibles. Fund may also invest without limit in both adjustable and fixed rate securities issued, guaranteed or collateralized by the U.S. Government or its subdivisions, and without limit in covered call options. Fund is non-diversified.
Year organized: 1996
Ticker symbol: RCSAX
Deadline for same day wire purchase: 4 P.M.
Discount broker availability: *Schwab, *White
Qualified for sale in: All states
Deadline for same day switch: 4 P.M.
Dividends paid: Income - quarterly; Capital gains - annually
Portfolio turnover (1 yr): 113%
Management fee: 1.50%
12b-1 distribution fee: 0.25%
Expense ratio: 0.52% (year ending 5/31/97) (2.36% without waiver)

THE RESERVE FLORIDA TAX-EXEMPT FUND
(See first Reserve listing for data common to all funds)

Portfolio manager: Michael Sheridan (1995)
Investment objective and policies: High level of short-term interest income exempt from federal, state and local

income and or property taxes, consistent with preservation of capital and liquidity. Invests primarily in tax-exempt issues issued by the state and its' counties, municipalities, authorities or other political subdivisions.
Year organized: 1996
Deadline for same day wire purchase: 11 A.M.
Qualified for sale in: FL
Check redemptions: No minimum, $2 fee for less than $100
Deadline for same day switch: 11 A.M.
Dividends paid: Income - declared daily, paid monthly
Management fee: 0.50% first $500M to 0.40% over $400M
12b-1 distribution fee: 0.20%
Expense ratio: 1.04% (eleven months ending 5/31/97)

THE RESERVE INFORMED INVESTORS GROWTH FUND
(See first Reserve listing for data common to all funds)

Sub-adviser: T.H. Fitzgerald & Co.
Portfolio manager: Thomas H. Fitzgerald, Jr. (1994)
Investment objective and policies: Capital growth; income secondary. Invests at least 65% of assets in a portfolio of seasoned, well managed, financially sound U.S. companies with demonstrated superior growth and earnings. Priority is given to companies with large volumes of stock are owned by management or outside investors, or where repurchasing on the open market is occurring (the "informed" investors.) Fund may also invest without limit in both adjustable and fixed rate securities issued, guaranteed or collateralized by the U.S. Government or its subdivisions, and without limit in covered call options. Fund is non-diversified.
Year organized: 1994
Ticker symbol: RIGAX
Deadline for same day wire purchase: 4 P.M.
Discount broker availability: *Schwab, *White
Qualified for sale in: All states
Deadline for same day switch: 4 P.M.
Dividends paid: Income - quarterly; Capital gains - annually
Portfolio turnover (3 yrs): 255%, 132%, 59%
Management fee: 1.50%
12b-1 distribution fee: 0.25%
Expense ratio: 1.75% (year ending 5/31/97)

THE RESERVE INTERNATIONAL EQUITY FUND
(See first Reserve listing for data common to all funds)

Sub-adviser: Pinnacle Associates, Ltd.
Portfolio manager: Nicholas Reitenbach (1995)
Investment objective and policies: Capital appreciation; income secondary. Invests at least 65% of assets in a diversified portfolio of 80 to 110 companies representing 15 to 23 countries outside the U.S. Focuses on high visibility firms that are often sector leaders or dominant in their niche. Fund may also invest without limit in both adjustable and fixed rate securities issued, guaranteed or collateralized by the U.S. Government or its subdivisions, and without limit in covered call options. Fund is non-diversified.
Year organized: 1995
Ticker symbol: RIEAX
Deadline for same day wire purchase: 4 P.M.
Discount broker availability: *Schwab, *White
Qualified for sale in: All states
Deadline for same day switch: 4 P.M.
Dividends paid: Income - quarterly; Capital gains - annually
Portfolio turnover (2 yrs): 52%, 70%
Management fee: 1.75%
12b-1 distribution fee: 0.25%
Expense ratio: 2.00% (year ending 5/31/97)

RESERVE - INTERSTATE TAX-EXEMPT FUND
(See first Reserve listing for data common to all funds)

Portfolio manager: Michael Sheridan (1995)
Investment objective and policies: Current income consistent with preservation of capital and liquidity.

Invests in short-term money market instruments issued by states, territories and possessions of the U.S. that are exempt from federal income taxes.
Year organized: 1983
Ticker symbol: RISXX
Deadline for same day wire purchase: 11 A.M.
Qualified for sale in: All states
Check redemptions: No minimum, $2 fee for less than $100
Deadline for same day switch: 11 A.M.
Management fee: 0.50% first $500M to 0.40% over $2B
12b-1 distribution fee: 0.20%
Expense ratio: 1.04% (year ending 5/31/97)

THE RESERVE LARGE-CAP VALUE FUND
(See first Reserve listing for data common to all funds)

Sub-adviser: Siphron Capital Management
Portfolio managers: David C. Siphron (1996), Peter D. Siphron (1996)
Investment objective and policies: Long-term capital appreciation. Invests in a diversified portfolio of large, high-quality U.S. companies with market capitalizations exceeding $5B that are believed to be undervalued. Fund may also invest without limit in both adjustable and fixed rate securities issued, guaranteed or collateralized by the U.S. Government or its subdivisions, and without limit in covered call options. Fund is non-diversified.
Year organized: 1996
Ticker symbol: RLVAX
Deadline for same day wire purchase: 4 P.M.
Discount broker availability: *Schwab, *White
Qualified for sale in: All states
Deadline for same day switch: 4 P.M.
Dividends paid: Income - quarterly; Capital gains - annually
Portfolio turnover (1 yr): 18%
Management fee: 1.50%
12b-1 distribution fee: 0.25%
Expense ratio: 1.75% (year ending 5/31/97)

THE RESERVE MASSACHUSETTS TAX-EXEMPT FUND
(See first Reserve listing for data common to all funds)

Portfolio manager: Michael Sheridan (1995)
Investment objective and policies: High level of short-term interest income exempt from federal, state and local income and or property taxes, consistent with preservation of capital and liquidity. Invests primarily in tax-exempt issues issued by the state and its' counties, municipalities, authorities or other political subdivisions.
Year organized: 1990
Deadline for same day wire purchase: 11 A.M.
Qualified for sale in: MA
Check redemptions: No minimum, $2 fee for less than $100
Deadline for same day switch: 11 A.M.
Dividends paid: Income - declared daily, paid monthly
Management fee: 0.50% first $500M to 0.40% over $400M
12b-1 distribution fee: 0.20%
Expense ratio: 0.79% (year ending 5/31/97)

THE RESERVE MID-CAP GROWTH FUND
(See first Reserve listing for data common to all funds)

Sub-adviser: Southern Capital Advisors
Portfolio manager: Richard A. McStay (1996)
Investment objective and policies: Capital appreciation. Invests in a portfolio of companies with a median market capitalization of about $1B; bounded by $150M to $5B outside parameters, that are thought to offer a strong potential for capital appreciation. May invest in special situations. Fund may also invest without limit in both adjustable and fixed rate securities issued, guaranteed or collateralized by the U.S.

Government or its subdivisions, and without limit in covered call options. Fund is non-diversified.
Year organized: 1996
Ticker symbol: RMCAX
Deadline for same day wire purchase: 4 P.M.
Discount broker availability: *Schwab, *White
Qualified for sale in: All states
Deadline for same day switch: 4 P.M.
Dividends paid: Income - quarterly; Capital gains - annually
Portfolio turnover (1 yr): 102%
Management fee: 1.50%
12b-1 distribution fee: 0.25%
Expense ratio: 1.75% (year ending 5/31/97)

THE RESERVE NEW JERSEY TAX-EXEMPT FUND
(See first Reserve listing for data common to all funds)

Portfolio manager: Michael Sheridan (1995)
Investment objective and policies: High level of short-term interest income exempt from federal, state and local income and or property taxes, consistent with preservation of capital and liquidity. Invests primarily in tax-exempt issues issued by the state and its' counties, municipalities, authorities or other political subdivisions.
Year organized: 1994
Ticker symbol: RNJXX
Deadline for same day wire purchase: 11 A.M.
Qualified for sale in: NJ
Check redemptions: No minimum, $2 fee for less than $100
Deadline for same day switch: 11 A.M.
Dividends paid: Income - declared daily, paid monthly
Management fee: 0.50% first $500M to 0.40% over $400M
12b-1 distribution fee: 0.20%
Expense ratio: 1.06% (year ending 5/31/97)

THE RESERVE NEW YORK TAX-EXEMPT FUND
(See first Reserve listing for data common to all funds)

Portfolio manager: Michael Sheridan (1995)
Investment objective and policies: High level of short-term interest income exempt from federal, state and local income and or property taxes, consistent with preservation of capital and liquidity. Invests primarily in tax-exempt issues issued by the state and its' counties, municipalities, authorities or other political subdivisions.
Year organized: 1987
Ticker symbol: RTEXX
Deadline for same day wire purchase: 11 A.M.
Qualified for sale in: NY
Check redemptions: No minimum, $2 fee for less than $100
Deadline for same day switch: 11 A.M.
Dividends paid: Income - declared daily, paid monthly
Management fee: 0.50% first $500M to 0.40% over $400M
12b-1 distribution fee: 0.20%
Expense ratio: 1.04% (year ending 5/31/97)

THE RESERVE PENNSYLVANIA TAX-EXEMPT FUND
(See first Reserve listing for data common to all funds)

Portfolio manager: Michael Sheridan (1995)
Investment objective and policies: High level of short-term interest income exempt from federal, state and local income and or property taxes, consistent with preservation of capital and liquidity. Invests primarily in tax-exempt issues issued by the state and its' counties, municipalities, authorities or other political subdivisions.
Year organized: 1997
Deadline for same day wire purchase: 11 A.M.
Qualified for sale in: PA
Check redemptions: No minimum, $2 fee for less than $100
Deadline for same day switch: 11 A.M.

Dividends paid: Income - declared daily, paid monthly
12b-1 distribution fee: 0.20%
Management fee: 0.50% first $500M to 0.40% over $400M

THE RESERVE PRIMARY FUND
(See first Reserve listing for data common to all funds)

Portfolio manager: Karen Quigley (1985)
Investment objective and policies: Current income consistent with preservation of capital and liquidity. Invests in short-term money market instruments.
Year organized: 1971
Ticker symbol: RFIXX
Deadline for same day wire purchase: 2 P.M.
Qualified for sale in: All states
Check redemptions: No minimum, $2 fee for less than $100
Deadline for same day switch: 2 P.M.
Dividends paid: Income - declared daily, paid monthly
Management fee: 0.50% first $500M to 0.40% over $2B
12b-1 distribution fee: 0.20%
Expense ratio: 0.98% (year ending 5/31/97)

THE RESERVE SMALL-CAP GROWTH FUND
(See first Reserve listing for data common to all funds)

Sub-adviser: Roanoke Asset Management
Portfolio manager: Edwin G. Vroom (1996), Brian J. O'Connor (1996), Adele S. Weisman (1996)
Investment objective and policies: Capital appreciation. Invests at least 65% of assets in a diversified portfolio of common stocks of companies with market capitalizations of less than $1B that are thought to be overlooked or misunderstood. Fund may also invest without limit in both adjustable and fixed rate securities issued, guaranteed or collateralized by the U.S. Government or its subdivisions, and without limit in covered call options. Fund is non-diversified.
Year organized: 1996
Ticker symbol: REGAX
Deadline for same day wire purchase: 4 P.M.
Discount broker availability: *White
Qualified for sale in: All states
Deadline for same day switch: 4 P.M.
Dividends paid: Income - quarterly; Capital gains - annually
Portfolio turnover (3 yrs): 28%, 38%, 43%
Management fee: 1.50%
12b-1 distribution fee: 0.25%
Expense ratio: 1.75% (year ending 5/31/97)

THE RESERVE U.S. GOVERNMENT FUND
(See first Reserve listing for data common to all funds)

Portfolio manager: Karen Quigley (1985)
Investment objective and policies: Current income consistent with preservation of capital and liquidity. Invests exclusively in marketable money market obligations issued or guaranteed by the U.S. Government or its agencies.
Year organized: 1981
Ticker symbol: RFGXX
Deadline for same day wire purchase: 2 P.M.
Qualified for sale in: All states
Check redemptions: No minimum, $2 fee for less than $100
Deadline for same day switch: 2 P.M.
Dividends paid: Income - declared daily, paid monthly
Management fee: 0.50% first $500M to 0.40% over $2B
12b-1 distribution fee: 0.20%
Expense ratio: 0.99% (year ending 5/31/97)

THE RESERVE U.S. TREASURY FUND
(See first Reserve listing for data common to all funds)

Portfolio manager: Karen Quigley (1985)
Investment objective and policies: Current income consistent with preservation of capital and liquidity. Invests exclusively in marketable money market obligations issued or guaranteed by the U.S. Government that provide income exempt from state and local income taxes.
Year organized: 1992
Ticker symbol: RUTXX
Deadline for same day wire purchase: 11 A.M.
Qualified for sale in: All states
Check redemptions: No minimum, $2 fee for less than $100
Deadline for same day switch: 11 A.M.
Dividends paid: Income - declared daily, paid monthly
Management fee: 0.80% (comprehensive fee covering advisory and all ordinary operating expenses)
12b-1 distribution fee: 0.20%
Expense ratio: 0.77% (year ending 5/31/97) (0.97% without waiver)

RETIREMENT SYSTEM FUNDS
(Effective 7/16/97, the Retirement System funds were reorganized as "Y" shares of the Enterprise Group of Funds, Inc., a multi-class load fund family.)

REYNOLDS FUNDS ◆
(Data common to all Reynolds funds are shown below. See subsequent listings for data specific to individual funds.)

Wood Island, Third Floor
80 East Sir Francis Drake Blvd.
Larkspur, CA 94939
800-773-9665, 800-338-1579
415-461-7860
TDD 800-684-3416

Shareholder service hours: Full service: M-F 8 A.M.- 7 P.M. CST; After hours service: prices, balances, orders, last transactions, prospectuses
Adviser: Reynolds Capital Management
Administrator: Fiduciary Management, Inc.
Transfer agent: Firstar Trust Co.
Minimum purchase: Initial: $1,000, Subsequent: $100; Automatic investment plan: Initial: $50, Subsequent: $50
Wire orders accepted: Yes
Deadline for same day wire purchase: 4 P.M.
Letter redemptions: Signature guarantee required over $25,000
Telephone switching: With other Reynolds funds, $1,000 minimum
Number of switches permitted: Unlimited
Shareholder services: IRA, SEP-IRA, SIMPLE-IRA, Keogh, 401(k), 403(b), corporate retirement plans, systematic withdrawal plan min. bal. req. $10,000
IRA/Keogh fees: Annual $12.50, Closing $15

REYNOLDS BLUE CHIP GROWTH FUND ◆
(See first Reynolds listing for data common to all funds)

Portfolio manager: Frederick L. Reynolds (1988)
Investment objective and policies: Long-term capital growth; current income secondary. Invests at least 65% of assets in common stocks of well established blue chip growth companies with at least $300M in market capitalization and listed in either the Dow Jones or S&P 500 Indexes. Up to 15% of assets may be in ADRs of foreign issuers, and up to 35% of assets may be invested in companies which are not blue chip firms. Fund may use index put and call options for hedging purposes.
Year organized: 1988
Ticker symbol: RBCGX
Discount broker availability: Fidelity, Schwab, Siebert, White
Qualified for sale in: All states except AR, MT, NE, NH, ND, WV

Dividends paid: Income - October, December; Capital gains - October, December
Portfolio turnover (3 yrs): 25%, 22%, 49%
Management fee: 1.00%
Administration fee: 0.20% first $30M, 0.10% over $30M
Expense ratio: 1.40% (year ending 9/30/97)

REYNOLDS MONEY MARKET FUND ◆
(See first Reynolds listing for data common to all funds)

Portfolio manager: Frederick L. Reynolds (1991)
Investment objective and policies: High current income consistent with preservation of capital and liquidity. Invests in money market instruments.
Year organized: 1991
Ticker symbol: REYXX
Qualified for sale in: All states except AL, AK, AZ, AR, DE, IA, KS, ME, MD, MA, MS, MD, MT, NE, NH, ND, OK, RI, SC, SD, TN, VT, WV, WA
Telephone redemptions: Yes, $1,000 minimum
Wire redemptions: Yes, $1,000 minimum, $10 fee
Check redemptions: $500 minimum
Dividends paid: Income - declared daily, paid monthly
Management fee: 0.50%
Administration fee: 0.10%
Expense ratio: 0.65% (year ending 9/30/97) (2.02% without waiver)

REYNOLDS OPPORTUNITY FUND ◆
(See first Reynolds listing for data common to all funds)

Portfolio manager: Frederick L. Reynolds (1992)
Investment objective and policies: Long-term capital growth. Invests primarily in securities of growth companies believed undervalued, without regard to size. May invest up to 25% of assets in ADRs of foreign companies traded in the U.S. and engages in options trading for hedging purposes.
Year organized: 1992
Ticker symbol: ROPPX
Discount broker availability: Fidelity, Siebert, White
Qualified for sale in: All states except AL, AK, AZ, AR, DE, ID, IA, KS, ME, MD, MA, MS, MO, MT, NE, NH, NM, ND, OK, RI, SC, SD, TN, VT, WV, WA
Dividends paid: Income - October, December; Capital gains - October, December
Portfolio turnover (3 yrs): 60%, 12%, 38%
Management fee: 1.00%
Administration fee: 0.20% first $30M, 0.10% over $30M
Expense ratio: 1.50% (year ending 9/30/97)

REYNOLDS U.S. GOVERNMENT BOND FUND ◆
(See first Reynolds listing for data common to all funds)

Portfolio manager: Frederick L. Reynolds (1992)
Investment objective and policies: High current income. Invests at least 65% of assets in securities issued or guaranteed by the U.S. Government or its agencies or instrumentalities, with a weighted average maturity of one to ten years. May invest in high quality corporate obligations.
Year organized: 1992
Ticker symbol: RUSGX
Discount broker availability: Fidelity, Siebert, White
Qualified for sale in: CA, CO, CT, DC, FL, GA, HI, IL, IN, KY, LA, MI, MN, NJ, NY, NC, OH, OR, PA, TX, UT, VA, WA, WY
Dividends paid: Income - declared daily, paid monthly; Capital gains - October, December
Portfolio turnover (3 yrs): 25%, 29%, 0%
Management fee: 0.75%
Administration fee: 0.10%
Expense ratio: 0.90% (year ending 9/30/97) (2.30% without waiver)

RIDGEWAY HELMS MILLENNIUM FUND ◆
303 Twin Dolphin Drive, Suite 530
Redwood Shores, CA 94065
800-801-5992, 888-229-2105
800-229-2105

Adviser: Ridgeway Helms Investment Management, LLC
Administrator: Investment Company Administration Corp.
Portfolio managers: Robert A. Dowlett (1997), N. Joseph Nahas (1997)
Transfer agent: American Data Services, Inc.
Investment objective and policies: Growth of capital. Invests in equity securities of companies of all sizes perceived to offer earnings growth in excess of the average of those companies comprising the S&P 500. Approximately 20% of fund holdings are of companies with market capitalizations below $500M. May engage in short selling and write or buy options on equities and stock indices.
Year organized: 1997
Minimum purchase: Initial: $2,500, Subsequent: $100; IRA: Initial: $1,000
Wire orders accepted: Yes, $10 fee
Deadline for same day wire purchase: 4 P.M.
Discount broker availability: White
Qualified for sale in: CA, VT
Telephone redemptions: Yes
Wire redemptions: Yes, $10 fee
Letter redemptions: Signature guarantee required over $5,000
Telephone switching: With RNC Money Market fund, $1,000 minimum
Deadline for same day switch: 2 P.M.
Number of switches permitted: Unlimited
Dividends paid: Income - December; Capital gains - December
Shareholder services: IRA, automatic investment plan, systematic withdrawal plan min. bal. req. $10,000
Management fee: 0.95%
Administration fee: 0.20% ($30,000 minimum)
IRA/Keogh fees: Annual $15

THE RIGHTIME FUND
The Forst Pavilion, Suite 1000
218 Glenside Avenue
Wyncote, PA 19095-1594
800-866-9393, 800-242-1421
610-887-8111

Adviser: Rightime Econometrics, Inc.
Portfolio managers: David J. Rights (1985), Anthony W. Soslow (1985), Denis N. Houser (1988)
Transfer agent: Lincoln Investment Planning, Inc.
Investment objective and policies: High total return consistent with reasonable risk. Invests in other mutual funds. May invest in funds with sales loads and use futures for hedging purposes. Fund will adopt an aggressive portfolio strategy in rising markets and a conservative strategy in declining markets.
Year organized: 1985
Ticker symbol: RTFDX
Minimum purchase: Initial (and Keogh): $1,000, Subsequent: $25; IRA: Initial: None
Wire orders accepted: Yes
Deadline for same day wire purchase: 5 P.M.
Qualified for sale in: All states except NH
Telephone redemptions: Yes
Wire redemptions: Yes
Letter redemptions: Signature guarantee required over $5,000
Telephone switching: With other Rightime funds, all of which have loads
Deadline for same day switch: 5 P.M.
Number of switches permitted: Unlimited
Dividends paid: Income - December; Capital gains - December
Portfolio turnover (3 yrs): 62%, 15%, 9%
Shareholder services: IRA, Keogh, 403(b), systematic withdrawal plan min. bal. req. $10,000
Management fee: 0.50%
Administration fee: 0.95%
12b-1 distribution fee: 0.75%
Expense ratio: 2.45% (year ending 10/31/97)
IRA/Keogh fees: Annual $10

RNC EQUITY FUND
11601 Wilshire Boulevard, 25th Floor
Los Angeles, CA 90025
800-385-7003, 310-553-8871

Adviser: RNC Capital Management Co. (an indirect subsidiary of Bank Austria Aktiengesellschaft)
Administrator: Investment Company Administration Corp.
Portfolio manager: John G. Marshall (1996)
Transfer agent: American Data Services, Inc.
Investment objective and policies: Above average total return consistent with reasonable risk. Normally stays fully invested in common stocks. May, however, purchase convertible preferred stocks, warrants, convertible debt obligations, or other debt obligations perceived to offer capital appreciation. Securities are selected based on growth in earnings. May invest up to 15% of assets in foreign securities through ADRs or EDRs. May use options in an effort to enhance performance and for hedging purposes.
Year organized: 1996
Minimum purchase: Initial: $1,000, Subsequent: $100; Automatic investment plan: Subsequent: $50
Wire orders accepted: Yes
Deadline for same day wire purchase: 4 P.M.
Qualified for sale in: All states
Telephone redemptions: Yes
Wire redemptions: Yes, $1,000 minimum
Letter redemptions: Signature guarantee required
Telephone switching: With RNC Money Market
Deadline for same day switch: 2 P.M.
Number of switches permitted: Unlimited
Dividends paid: Income - December; Capital gains - December
Shareholder services: IRA, systematic withdrawal plan min. bal. req. $10,000
Management fee: 1.00%
Administration fee: 0.10% first $100M to 0.03% over $200M ($40,000 minimum)
12b-1 distribution fee: 0.25%
IRA fees: Annual $12, Transfer $12, Closing $12

RNC MONEY MARKET FUND ◆
11601 Wilshire Boulevard, 25th Floor
Los Angeles, CA 90025
800-385-7003, 310-553-8871

Adviser: RNC Capital Management Co. (an indirect subsidiary of Bank Austria Aktiengesellschaft)
Administrator: Investment Company Administration Corp.
Portfolio manager: A. Robert Blais (1988)
Transfer agent: American Data Services, Inc.
Investment objective and policies: High current income consistent with preservation of capital and liquidity. Invests in a diversified portfolio of high-quality, short-term money market instruments.
Year organized: 1986 (previously known as RNC Liquid Assets Fund)
Minimum purchase: Initial: $1,000, Subsequent: $100; Automatic investment plan: Subsequent: $50
Wire orders accepted: Yes
Deadline for same day wire purchase: 4 P.M.
Qualified for sale in: All states
Telephone redemptions: Yes
Wire redemptions: Yes, $1,000 minimum
Letter redemptions: Signature guarantee required
Check redemptions: $500 minimum
Telephone switching: With RNC Equity Fund, and Ridgeway Helms Millennium fund
Deadline for same day switch: 2 P.M.
Number of switches permitted: Unlimited
Dividends paid: Income - declared daily, paid monthly
Shareholder services: IRA, systematic withdrawal plan min. bal. req. $10,000
Management fee: 0.41%
Administration fee: 0.10% first $100M to 0.03% over $200M ($40,000 minimum)
12b-1 distribution fee: 0.25% (not currently imposed)
Expense ratio: 0.90% (year ending 9/30/96)
IRA fees: Annual $12, Transfer $12, Closing $12

ROBERTSON STEPHENS FUNDS
(Data common to all Robertson Stephens funds are show below. See subsequent listings for data specific to individual funds.)

555 California Street, Suite 2600
San Francisco, CA 94104
800-766-3863, 415-781-9700
prices 800-624-8025
fax 415-433-7326
Internet: http://www.rsim.com
e-mail: funds@rsco.com

Shareholder service hours: Full service: M-F 6 A.M.-6 P.M.; Sat. 8 A.M.-3 P.M. PST; After hours service: prices, balances, news and views, prospectuses
Adviser: Robertson Stephens & Co. Investment Management, L.P.
Transfer agent: State Street Bank & Trust Co.
Special sales information: Effective May, 1997, these funds initiated Class "A" shares, the original no-load shares, and Class "C" shares which feature a 1% CDSC that lasts for a year. Only A shares are no-load, and only those are represented here.
Minimum purchase: Initial: $5,000, Subsequent: $100; IRA: Initial: $1,000, Subsequent: $1
Wire orders accepted: Yes
Deadline for same day wire purchase: 4 P.M.
Qualified for sale in: All states
Telephone redemption: Yes
Wire redemption: Yes, $9 fee
Letter redemptions: Signature guarantee not required
Telephone switching: With other Robertson Stephens funds
Number of switches permitted: 4 round trips per year
Shareholder services: IRA, automatic investment plan, electronic funds transfer
IRA fees: Annual $10

ROBERTSON STEPHENS CONTRARIAN FUND
(See first Robertson Stephens listing for data common to all funds)

Portfolio manager: Paul H. Stephens (1993)
Investment objective and policies: Long-term capital growth. Invests worldwide in equity securities of companies perceived to be attractively priced and growing. Fund seeks out overlooked companies, companies that have improved growth potential due to changed circumstances, companies that have declined in value and lost favor with investors, or firms that are temporarily out of favor due to short-term factors. Fund is non-diversified. Up to 35% of assets may be in debt obligations, including junk bonds, and 15% in illiquid securities. May use options, futures, and options thereon and hedge up to 25% of assets. Fund may borrow money to leverage positions and will short sell stocks when deemed appropriate.
Year organized: 1993
Ticker symbol: RSCOX
Discount broker availability: *Fidelity, *Schwab, *Siebert, *White
Dividends paid: Income - December; Capital gains - December
Portfolio turnover (3 yrs): 36%, 44%, 29%
Management fee: 1.50%
12b-1 distribution fee: 0.75%
Expense ratio: 2.48% (year ending 12/31/97)

ROBERTSON STEPHENS DEVELOPING COUNTRIES FUND
(See first Robertson Stephens listing for data common to all funds)

Portfolio manager: Michael C. Hoffman (1994)
Investment objective and policies: Long-term capital appreciation. Invests primarily in publicly traded equity securities, ADRs and GDRs of companies in emerging markets. Will also target companies perceived to be overvalued, and will sell short attempting to profit from devaluation. Fund is non-diversified. Up to 15% of assets may be in illiquid securities. May sell short up to 25% of assets and use options and futures

to hedge up to 25%. May borrow money to leverage positions.
Year organized: 1994 (name changed from Robertson Stephens Emerging Markets 6/95)
Ticker symbol: RSDCX
Discount broker availability: *Fidelity, *Schwab, *Siebert, *White
Dividends paid: Income - December; Capital gains - December
Portfolio turnover (3 yrs): 148%, 165%, 103%
Management fee: 1.25%
12b-1 distribution fee: Maximum of 0.50%
Expense ratio: 2.10% (year ending 12/31/97) (2.53% without waiver)

ROBERTSON STEPHENS DIVERSIFIED GROWTH FUND
(See first Robertson Stephens listing for data common to all funds)

Portfolio managers: John L. Wallace (1996), John H. Seabern (1996)
Investment objective and policies: Long-term capital growth. Invests in a broadly diversified portfolio of common and preferred stocks and warrants representing a wide variety of industry sectors, focused primarily on small- and mid-cap companies with capitalizations under $3B. Maintains, however, the flexibility to invest in companies of any size, and may invest in debt securities including junk bonds without limit. May also invest in foreign securities without limit, engage in short sales worth up to 25% of assets, and use futures and options both in an effort to enhance returns and for hedging purposes.
Year organized: 1996
Ticker symbol: RSDGX
Discount broker availability: *Fidelity, *Schwab, *Siebert, *White
Dividends paid: Income - December; Capital gains - December
Portfolio turnover (2 yrs): 370%, 69%
Management fee: 1.25%
12b-1 distribution fee: 0.25%
Expense ratio: 1.94% (year ending 12/31/97) (2.14% without waiver)

ROBERTSON STEPHENS EMERGING GROWTH FUND
(See first Robertson Stephens listing for data common to all funds)

Portfolio manager: James L. Callinan (1996)
Investment objective and policies: Long-term capital appreciation. Invests primarily in equity securities of emerging growth companies with above average growth prospects. Seeks to invest in companies that are growing at least 20% annually. Up to 35% of assets may be in securities of foreign issuers, and 35% in debt obligations of the U.S. Government, its agencies or instrumentalities.
Year organized: 1987 (formerly RCS Emerging Growth Fund)
Ticker symbol: RSEGX
Discount broker availability: *Fidelity, *Schwab, *Siebert, *White
Dividends paid: Income - December; Capital gains - December
Portfolio turnover (3 yrs): 462%, 270%, 147%
Management fee: 1.00%
12b-1 distribution fee: 0.25%
Expense ratio: 1.50% (year ending 12/31/97)

ROBERTSON STEPHENS GLOBAL LOW-PRICED STOCK FUND
(See first Robertson Stephens listing for data common to all funds)

Portfolio manager: Andrew P. Pilara (1998)
Investment objective and policies: Long-term capital growth. Invests in low priced stocks, generally below $10/share, of unrecognized or under-appreciated companies from around the world. May utilize short sales, and use futures and options for hedging purposes.
Year organized: 1995
Ticker symbol: RSLPX
Special sales information: AT PRESS TIME, fund

was soliciting proxies to merge Global Low-Priced Stock into another of the Global funds.
Discount broker availability: *Fidelity, *Schwab, *Siebert, *White
Dividends paid: Income - December; Capital gains - December
Portfolio turnover (2 yrs): 65%, 66%
Management fee: 1.25%
12b-1 distribution fee: 0.25%
Expense ratio: 1.95% (year ending 12/31/97)

ROBERTSON STEPHENS GLOBAL NATURAL RESOURCES FUND
(See first Robertson Stephens listing for data common to all funds)

Portfolio manager: Andrew P. Pilara, Jr. (1995)
Investment objective and policies: Long-term capital appreciation. Invests primarily in securities of issuers involved in the discovery, development, production or distribution of natural resources all over the world. Will normally invest at least 65% of assets in at least three countries, which may include the U.S. Otherwise, may invest in any other industry as deemed desirable to achieve fund objective. May use short sales, invest in debt securities, and use futures and options for hedging purposes.
Year organized: 1995
Ticker symbol: RSNRX
Discount broker availability: *Fidelity, *Schwab, *Siebert, *White
Dividends paid: Income - December; Capital gains - December
Portfolio turnover (2 yrs): 97%, 82%
Management fee: 1.25%
12b-1 distribution fee: 0.25%
Expense ratio: 1.81% (year ending 12/31/97) (1.82% without waiver)

ROBERTSON STEPHENS GLOBAL VALUE FUND
(See first Robertson Stephens listing for data common to all funds)

Portfolio manager: Andrew P. Pilara, Jr. (1997)
Investment objective and policies: Long-term growth. appreciation. Invests primarily in equity securities of issuers with market capitalizations of $1B or more from all over the world. Will normally invest at least 65% of assets in equities, selected using Graham & Dodd balance sheet analysis to identify stocks perceived to be undervalued. Fund is non-diversified. May invest without limit in fixed-income securities, and use futures and options for hedging purposes.
Year organized: 1997
Ticker symbol: RSGAX
Discount broker availability: *Fidelity, *Schwab, *Siebert, *White
Dividends paid: Income - December; Capital gains - December
Portfolio turnover (1 yr): 234%
Management fee: 1.00%
12b-1 distribution fee: 0.25%
Expense ratio: 1.95% (nine months ending 12/31/97) (3.21% without waiver)

ROBERTSON STEPHENS GROWTH & INCOME FUND
(See first Robertson Stephens listing for data common to all funds)

Portfolio manager: John L. Wallace (1995)
Investment objective and policies: Long-term total return: capital appreciation and income. Invests in the full range of equity and debt securities of small- and mid-cap companies with less than $3B capitalization and above average prospects for growth and current income. Utilizes the 'barbell' strategy; stocks, 5% to 25% bonds, and 0% to 15% cash. May sell short in an effort to enhance profits, and invest in lower-quality, high-yielding junk bonds. May use options and futures for hedging purposes.
Year organized: 1995
Ticker symbol: RSGIX
Discount broker availability: *Fidelity, *Schwab, *Siebert, *White
Dividends paid: Income - March, June, September, December; Capital gains - December
Portfolio turnover (3 yrs): 236%, 212%, 97%

Management fee: 1.25%
12b-1 distribution fee: 0.25%
Expense ratio: 1.30% (year ending 12/31/97) (1.72% without waiver)

ROBERTSON STEPHENS INFORMATION AGE FUND
(See first Robertson Stephens listing for data common to all funds)

Portfolio manager: Ronald E. Elijah (1995)
Investment objective and policies: Long-term capital appreciation. Invests aggressively in the information technology sector, primarily targeting small- to mid-cap companies involved in the development, production or distribution of products or services related to the processing, storage, transmission or presentation of information or data. May use short sales in an effort to enhance profits, and use futures and options for hedging purposes.
Year organized: 1995
Ticker symbol: RSIFX
Discount broker availability: *Fidelity, *Schwab, *Siebert, *White
Dividends paid: Income - December; Capital gains - December
Portfolio turnover (2 yrs): 369%, 452%
Management fee: 1.25%
12b-1 distribution fee: 0.25%
Expense ratio: 1.82% (year ending 12/31/97)

ROBERTSON STEPHENS MICROCAP GROWTH FUND
(See first Robertson Stephens listing for data common to all funds)

Portfolio managers: David J. Evans (1996), Rainerio Reyes (1997)
Investment objective and policies: Long-term capital appreciation. Invests primarily in companies with market capitalizations of $250M or less at the time of purchase. Focuses on selecting firms perceived to be mis-priced relative to their growth rate. May invest the balance of assets in companies of any size, or in investment grade debt securities. May engage in short sales and use options and futures in an effort to enhance returns or for hedging purposes.
Year organized: 1996
Ticker symbol: RSMGX
Special sales restrictions: Fund will close when assets reach $250M
Discount broker availability: *Fidelity, *Schwab, *Siebert, *White
Dividends paid: Income - December; Capital gains - December
Portfolio turnover (2 yrs): 170%, 22%
Management fee: 1.50%
12b-1 distribution fee: 0.25%
Expense ratio: 1.95% (year ending 12/31/97) (2.60% without waiver)

ROBERTSON STEPHENS PARTNERS FUND
(See first Robertson Stephens listing for data common to all funds)

Portfolio manager: Andrew P. Pilara, Jr. (1995)
Investment objective and policies: Long-term growth. Invests primarily in U.S. equity securities of small-cap companies with market capitalizations of less than $750M, using a value methodology combining Graham & Dodd balance sheet analysis with cash flow analysis. Fund is non-diversified. May invest in assets of foreign issuers, utilize any form of equity or debt security, or hold cash without limit. May use options and futures for hedging purposes.
Year organized: 1995
Ticker symbol: RSPFX
Sales restrictions: Fund will close when assets reach $250M.
Discount broker availability: *Fidelity, *Schwab, *Siebert, *White
Dividends paid: Income - December; Capital gains - December
Portfolio turnover (3 yrs): 78%, 101%, 71%
Management fee: 1.25%
12b-1 distribution fee: 0.25%
Expense ratio: 1.78% (year ending 12/31/97)

ROBERTSON STEPHENS VALUE + GROWTH FUND

(See first Robertson Stephens listing for data common to all funds)

Portfolio manager: Ronald E. Elijah (1992)
Investment objective and policies: Long-term capital appreciation. Invests primarily in equity securities of small- and medium-sized companies with capitalizations ranging from $750M to $2B and favorable growth prospects and modest valuations based on earnings and assets. May invest in securities of any domestic, multinational or foreign companies without limit. Up to 35% of assets may be in debt obligations of the U.S. Government, its agencies and its instrumentalities. May sell short up to 25% of assets and use options and futures to hedge up to 25%.
Year organized: 1992 (name changed from Value Plus Fund in 1994)
Ticker symbol: RSVPX
Discount broker availability: *Fidelity, *Schwab, *Siebert, *White
Dividends paid: Income - December; Capital gains - December
Portfolio turnover (3 yrs): 228%, 221%, 104%
Management fee: 1.00%
12b-1 distribution fee: 0.25%
Expense ratio: 1.44% (year ending 12/31/97)

THE ROCKHAVEN FUND
100 First Avenue, Suite 1050
Pittsburgh, PA 15222
888-229-2105, 800-522-3508

Adviser: Rockhaven Asset Management, LLC
Administrator: Investment Company Administration Corp.
Portfolio manager: Christopher H. Wiles (1997)
Transfer agent: American Data Services, Inc.
Investment objective and policies: Above average current income and capital appreciation. Invests at least 65% of assets in income producing equity securities, including common and preferred stocks and convertibles. Issues are selected on the perception of good value, attractive yield and the potential for dividend growth. May invest up to 35% of assets in fixed-income obligations and short-term issues. May invest without limit in debt securities rated C or higher, and may invest up to 50% of assets in convertibles rated as low as C. May invest up to 50% of assets in foreign securities if they are listed on a national exchange. May invest up to 15% of assets in illiquid securities, and write covered call options without limit.
Year organized: 1997
Minimum purchase: Initial: $1,000, Subsequent: $100
Wire orders accepted: Yes
Deadline for same day wire purchase: 4 P.M.
Discount broker availability: *White
Qualified for sale in: All states
Telephone redemptions: Yes
Wire redemptions: Yes, $1,000 minimum, $12 fee
Letter redemptions: Signature guarantee required over $5,000
Telephone switching: With the Rockhaven Premier Dividend fund, $1,000 minimum
Number of switches permitted: Unlimited
Dividends paid: Income - quarterly; Capital gains - December
Shareholder services: IRA, automatic investment plan
Management fee: 0.75%
Administration fee: 0.20% ($30,000 minimum)
12b-1 distribution fee: 0.25%
IRA fees: Annual $15

THE ROCKHAVEN PREMIER DIVIDEND FUND
100 First Avenue, Suite 1050
Pittsburgh, PA 15222
888-229-2105, 800-522-3508

Adviser: Rockhaven Asset Management, LLC
Administrator: Investment Company Administration Corp.
Portfolio manager: Christopher H. Wiles (1997)
Transfer agent: American Data Services, Inc.
Investment objective and policies: High current income; capital appreciation secondary. Invests at least 65% of assets in income producing equity securities, including common and preferred stocks and convertibles. Issues are selected on the perception of good value, attractive yield and the potential for dividend growth. Fund will likely maintain a higher percentage of convertibles than its sibling fund. May invest up to 35% of assets in fixed-income obligations and short-term issues. May invest without limit in debt securities rated C or higher, and may invest up to 50% of assets in convertibles rated as low as C. May invest up to 50% of assets in foreign securities if they are listed on a national exchange. May invest up to 15% of assets in illiquid securities, and write covered call options without limit.
Year organized: 1997
Minimum purchase: Initial: $1,000, Subsequent: $100
Wire orders accepted: Yes
Deadline for same day wire purchase: 4 P.M.
Discount broker availability: *White
Qualified for sale in: All states
Telephone redemptions: Yes
Wire redemptions: Yes, $1,000 minimum, $12 fee
Letter redemptions: Signature guarantee required over $5,000
Telephone switching: With the Rockhaven Fund, $1,000 minimum
Number of switches permitted: Unlimited
Dividends paid: Income - quarterly; Capital gains - December
Shareholder services: IRA, automatic investment plan
Management fee: 0.75%
Administration fee: 0.20% ($30,000 minimum)
12b-1 distribution fee: 0.25%
IRA fees: Annual $15

THE ROCKWOOD FUND ◆
545 Shoup Avenue, No. 303
Idaho Falls, ID 83405
888-762-5966, 208-522-5593

Adviser: Aspen Securities and Advisory, Inc.
Portfolio manager: Ross H. Farmer (1986)
Transfer agent: Aspen Securities and Advisory, Inc.
Investment objective and policies: Long-term capital appreciation. Current income incidental. Invests primarily in common, convertible, and preferred stock of companies perceived to be priced below intrinsic value. May invest up to 5% of assets in closed end investment companies, and up to 5% in unseasoned or illiquid issues.
Year organized: 1986 (name changed from Rockwood Growth in Spring 1997)
Ticker symbol: ROCKX
Minimum purchase: Initial: $100, Subsequent: None
Wire orders accepted: No
Discount broker availability: Fidelity, *Schwab, *White
Qualified for sale in: All states
Letter redemptions: Signature guarantee required
Dividends paid: Income - annually; Capital gains - annually
Portfolio turnover (3 yrs): 43%, 30%, 18%
Shareholder services: IRA
Management fee: 0.70%
Expense ratio: 2.73% (year ending 10/31/97) (includes waiver)
IRA/Keogh fees: Annual $10 (waived for balances over $10,000), Initial $100, Closing $20

ROYCE FUNDS ◆
(Data common to all Royce funds are shown below. See subsequent listings for data specific to individual funds.)

1414 Avenue of the Americas
New York, NY 10019
800-221-4268, 212-486-1445
800-841-1180 (for shareholders only)
fax 212-752-8875
Internet: http://www.roycefunds.com
e-mail: funds@roycenet.com

Shareholder service hours: Full service: M-F 8:30 A.M.-5:30 P.M. EST; After hours service: prices, balances, transactions, messages, prospectuses, total returns

Adviser: Royce & Assocs., Inc. (exception noted)
Transfer agent: State Street Bank & Trust Co. c/o NFDS
Minimum purchase: Initial: $2,000 (exceptions noted), Subsequent: $50; IRA: Initial: $500; Keogh: Initial: None; Automatic investment plan: Initial $500
Wire orders accepted: Yes
Deadline for same day wire purchase: 4 P.M.
Telephone redemptions: Yes
Wire redemptions: Yes, $1,000 minimum
Letter redemptions: Signature guarantee required over $50,000
Redemption fee: 1.00% on purchases held less than one year, payable to the fund (does not apply to GiftShares)
Telephone switching: With other Royce funds (except GiftShares)
Number of switches permitted: Unlimited
Shareholder services: IRA, 403(b), electronic funds transfer, systematic withdrawal plan min. bal. req. $25,000
IRA fees: Annual $15, Initial $5

ROYCE EQUITY INCOME FUND ◆
(Fund merged into Total Return Fund 6/17/97)

ROYCE FINANCIAL SERVICES FUND ◆
(See first Royce listing for data common to all funds)

Portfolio managers: Charles M. Royce (1994), Jack E. Fockler, Jr. (1994), W. Whitney George (1994)
Investment objective and policies: Long-term capital growth. Invests at least 65% of assets in common stocks and securities convertible into common stocks of domestic and foreign companies principally engaged in the financial services industries, selected on a value basis. Securities not so invested may be committed to equity or debt positions in any type of industry anywhere in the world. May invest in foreign securities without limit, may invest up to 20% of assets in other mutual funds that invest primarily in financial services companies, and 15% in illiquid securities. Fund is non-diversified.
Year organized: 1994 (name and objective changed 11/25/97 from Global Services; past results may not be relevant.)
Ticker symbol: RYGSX
Discount broker availability: *Fidelity, *Schwab, *Siebert, *White
Qualified for sale in: CA, CO, CT, DC, FL, GA, HI, IL, IN, ME, MD, MA, MI, MN, NJ, NY, NC, PA, TX, VA, WA, WV, WI, WY
Dividends paid: Income - December; Capital gains - December
Portfolio turnover (2 yrs): 81%, 106%
Management fee: 1.50%
12b-1 distribution fee: Maximum of 0.25% (not currently imposed)
Expense ratio: 1.56% (year ending 12/31/96) (3.31% without waiver)

ROYCE GIFTSHARES FUND
(Investment Class) ◆
(See first Royce listing for data common to all funds)

Portfolio managers: Charles M. Royce (1995), Jack E. Fockler, Jr. (1993), W. Whitney George (1993)
Investment objective and policies: Long-term capital appreciation. Invests at least 80% of assets in a limited portfolio of common and convertible securities of small- (under $1B) and micro- (under $300M) cap companies. Remainder of portfolio invested in securities of larger companies, and in non-convertible preferred stocks and debt securities. May invest up to 10% of assets in debt and/or equity securities of foreign issuers.
Year organized: 1995
Special sales restrictions: You may not open a GiftShares account for yourself or your spouse.
Minimum purchase: Initial: $5,000
Qualified for sale in: All states
Dividends paid: Income - December; Capital gains - December
Portfolio turnover (2 yrs): 64%, 93%
Management fee: 1.00%
Expense ratio: 1.49% (year ending 12/31/97) (3.82% without waiver)

ROYCE LOW-PRICED STOCK FUND ◆
(See first Royce listing for data common to all funds)

Portfolio managers: Charles M. Royce (1993), Jack E. Fockler, Jr. (1993), W. Whitney George (1993)
Investment objective and policies: Long-term capital growth. Invests primarily in common stocks and convertibles securities of small and medium-sized companies with shares trading at prices below $15 per share at the time of investment. At least 65% of these companies will have market capitalizations under $1B at the time of purchase. Balance of assets may be in issues of any size, or in debt securities. May invest up to 10% of assets in foreign issues.
Year organized: 1993
Ticker symbol: RYLPX
Discount broker availability: *Fidelity, *Schwab, *Siebert, *White
Qualified for sale in: All states
Dividends paid: Income - December; Capital gains - December
Portfolio turnover (3 yrs): 137%, 114%, 95%
Management fee: 1.50%
12b-1 distribution fee: Maximum of 0.25% (not currently imposed)
Expense ratio: 1.88% (year ending 12/31/96) (2.59% without waiver)

ROYCE MICRO-CAP FUND ◆
(See first Royce listing for data common to all funds)

Portfolio managers: Charles M. Royce (1991), Jack E. Fockler, Jr. (1993), W. Whitney George (1993)
Investment objective and policies: Long-term capital appreciation; income incidental. Invests at least 65% of assets in common stocks and convertible securities of companies with market capitalizations under $300M at the time of investment. The balance may be invested in securities of larger companies, in non-convertible preferred stocks, and in debt securities.
Year organized: 1991 (name changed from Royce OTC Fund on 12/27/94)
Ticker symbol: RYOTX
Sales restrictions: Fund limits cash inflow to $50M in any calendar six month period. Once the limit is reached, fund closes to new shareholders for the balance of the period.
Discount broker availability: *Fidelity, *Schwab, *Siebert, *White
Qualified for sale in: All states
Dividends paid: Income - December; Capital gains - December
Portfolio turnover (3 yrs): 38%, 70%, 25%
Management fee: 1.50%
Expense ratio: 1.49% (year ending 12/31/97) (1.80% without waiver)

ROYCE PENNSYLVANIA MUTUAL FUND (Investment Class) ◆
(See first Royce listing for data common to all funds)

Portfolio managers: Charles M. Royce (1973), Jack E. Fockler, Jr. (1993), W. Whitney George (1993)
Investment objective and policies: Long-term capital growth. Invests primarily in common stocks and convertible securities of companies with market capitalizations under $750M that are selected on a value basis. May use fixed-income securities and have up to 35% of assets in lowest investment grade category bonds.
Year organized: 1962 (DataQuest assumed management of fund in 1973; absorbed Value Fund 6/17/97)
Ticker symbol: PENNX
Sales restrictions: Fund now trades two classes of shares: former Value Fund shares are now "Consultant" class shares of the fund, with different fees and expenses, including a substantial 12b-1 fee and higher overall expenses.
Discount broker availability: *Fidelity, *Schwab, *Siebert, *White
Qualified for sale in: All states
Dividends paid: Income - December; Capital gains - December
Portfolio turnover (3 yrs): 18%, 29%, 10%
Management fee: 1.00% first $50M to 0.75% over $100M
Expense ratio: 1.05% (year ending 12/31/97)

ROYCE PMF II FUND (Investment Class) ◆
(See first Royce listing for data common to all funds)

Portfolio managers: Charles M. Royce (1996), Jack E. Fockler, Jr. (1996), W. Whitney George (1996)
Investment objective and policies: Long-term capital growth. Invests primarily in common stocks and convertible securities of small- and micro-cap companies (capitalizations under $1B) selected on a value basis. Capitalizations below $300M are considered micro-cap. May use fixed-income securities, and have up to 35% of assets in the lowest investment grade category of bonds or securities of domestic or foreign issues with higher capitalizations.
Year organized: 1996
Ticker symbol: RYPNX
Discount broker availability: Fidelity, *Schwab, Siebert, *White
Dividends paid: Income - December; Capital gains - December
Portfolio turnover (1 yr): 77%
Management fee: 1.00%
Expense ratio: 0.99% (year ending 12/31/97) (1.56% without waiver)

ROYCE PREMIER FUND ◆
(See first Royce listing for data common to all funds)

Portfolio managers: Charles M. Royce (1991), Jack E. Fockler, Jr. (1993), W. Whitney George (1993)
Investment objective and policies: Long-term capital growth; current income secondary. Invests primarily in a limited portfolio of common stocks and securities convertible into common stocks of small and medium-sized companies (market capitalizations under $1B). Companies are picked for superior financial characteristics and/or unusually attractive business prospects.
Year organized: 1991
Ticker symbol: RYPRX
Discount broker availability: *Fidelity, *Schwab, *Siebert, *White
Qualified for sale in: All states
Dividends paid: Income - December; Capital gains - December
Portfolio turnover (3 yrs): 18%, 34%, 39%
Management fee: 1.00%
Expense ratio: 1.24% (year ending 12/31/97)

ROYCE REVEST GROWTH AND INCOME FUND ◆
(See first Royce listing for data common to all funds)

50 Portland Pier
Portland, ME 04101
800-277-5573, 207-774-7455
fax 207-772-7370

Adviser: Royce, Ebright & Assocs., Inc.
Portfolio managers: Thomas R. Ebright (1994), Jennifer E. Goff (1994)
Investment objective and policies: Long-term growth; current income secondary. Invests at least 90% of assets in a broadly diversified portfolio of common stocks and securities convertible into common stocks. At least 80% of these will be income-producing, and 80% of these will be of small and medium-sized companies, with market capitalizations from $200M to $2B, selected on a value basis. The remainder of assets may be invested in companies of higher or lower market capitalizations, non-dividend paying common stocks, or in non-convertible fixed-income obligations.
Year organized: 1994
Ticker symbol: REGIX
Minimum purchase: Initial: $10,000
Special sales restriction: Fund will close to new shareholders on March 1st of any year following a December 31st with total assets exceeding $350M; new shareholders will only be able to resume purchases if fund assets drop to $250M or less at the end of any subsequent calendar quarter.
Discount broker availability: Fidelity, Schwab (only through financial advisers), Siebert
Qualified for sale in: All states
Dividends paid: Income - March, June, September, December; Capital gains - December

Portfolio turnover (3 yrs): 64%, 53%, 5%
Management fee: 1.00% first $50M, 0.75% over $50M
Shareholder services fee: 0.25%
Expense ratio: 1.29% (year ending 12/31/96)

ROYCE TOTAL RETURN FUND ◆
(See first Royce listing for data common to all funds)

Portfolio managers: Charles M. Royce (1993), Jack E. Fockler, Jr. (1993), W. Whitney George (1993)
Investment objective and policies: Long-term capital growth and current income. Invests primarily in dividend-paying common stocks and securities convertible into common stocks of small and medium-sized companies (capitalization under $1B), selected on a value basis.
Year organized: 1993 (absorbed Equity Income Fund 6/17/97)
Ticker symbol: RYTRX
Discount broker availability: *Fidelity, *Schwab, *Siebert, *White
Dividends paid: Income - December; Capital gains - December
Qualified for sale in: All states
Portfolio turnover (3 yrs): 111%, 68%, 88%
Management fee: 1.00%
12b-1 distribution fee: Maximum of 0.25% (not currently imposed)
Expense ratio: 1.25% (year ending 12/31/96) (2.23% without waiver)

ROYCE VALUE FUND
(Fund merged into Pennsylvania Mutual Fund 6/17/97)

RSI RETIREMENT TRUST FUNDS ◆
(Data common to all RSI Retirement Trust funds are shown below. See subsequent listings for data specific to individual funds.)

317 Madison Avenue
New York, NY 10017-5397
800-772-3615, 212-503-0100
fax 212-503-0198

Shareholder service hours: Full service: M-F 9 A.M.- 5 P.M. EST
Adviser: Retirement System Investors, Inc.
Transfer agent: Retirement System Consultants, Inc.
Special sales restrictions: Designed for corporate trusts exempt from taxation under Section 501(a) of the Internal Revenue Code of 1986 (tax-qualified retirement plans) and individual retirement trusts or custodial accounts exempt from taxation under Section 408(e) of the code (IRA Rollovers).
Minimum purchase: Initial: $2,000 (per Trust; $500 per fund), Subsequent: $500
Wire orders accepted: No
Qualified for sale in: CT, DE, DC, FL, IL, ME, MD, NH, NJ, NY, PA, RI
Letter redemptions: Signature guarantee required over $25,000
Dividends paid: None
IRA fees: None

RSI RETIREMENT TRUST - ACTIVELY MANAGED BOND FUND ◆
(See first RSI listing for data common to all funds)

Portfolio managers: Herbert Kuhl, Jr. (1990), Deborah A. Modzelewski (1995)
Investment objective and policies: Total return: income and capital appreciation in excess of the Lipper U.S. Government Bond Funds Average measured over a period of three to five years. Invests primarily in U.S. Government and agency securities, corporate debt securities rated A or better. Up to 20% of assets may be in securities of foreign issuers. May use futures and options for hedging purposes.
Year organized: 1983
Ticker symbol: RSIAX
Portfolio turnover (3 yrs): 17%, 18%, 9%
Management fee: 0.40% first $50M to 0.20% over $150M
Expense ratio: 0.80% (year ending 9/30/97)

RSI RETIREMENT TRUST - CORE EQUITY FUND ◆
(See first RSI listing for data common to all funds)

Portfolio manager: James P. Coughlin (1984)
Investment objective and policies: Total return: income and capital appreciation in excess of the Lipper Growth and Income Mutual Funds Average, measured over a period of three to five years. Invests at least 65% of assets in common stocks of companies with market capitalization in excess of $750M. Up to 20% of assets may be in securities of foreign issuers. May use futures and options for hedging purposes.
Year organized: 1983
Ticker symbol: RSICX
Portfolio turnover (3 yrs): 10%, 8%, 6%
Management fee: 0.60% first $50M to 0.40% over $200M
Expense ratio: 0.90% (year ending 9/30/97)

RSI RETIREMENT TRUST - EMERGING GROWTH EQUITY FUND ◆
(See first RSI listing for data common to all funds)

Sub-advisers: Friess Assocs., Inc., Putnam Advisory Co., Inc.
Portfolio manager: Richard M. Frucci (1994)
Investment objective and policies: Total return in excess of the Lipper Small Company Growth Mutual Fund Average, measured over a three to five year period. Invests at least 65% of assets in common stocks of rapidly growing companies, generally with market capitalizations from $50M to $750M. Up to 20% of assets may be in securities of foreign issuers. May use futures and options for hedging purposes.
Year organized: 1983
Ticker symbol: RSIGX
Portfolio turnover (3 yrs): 150%, 171%, 114%
Management fee: 1.20% (for assets managed by Friess), 1.20% first $25M and 0.95% over $25M (for assets managed by Putnam Advisory Co., Inc.)
Expense ratio: 1.98% (year ending 9/30/97)

RSI RETIREMENT TRUST - INTERMEDIATE-TERM BOND FUND ◆
(See first RSI listing for data common to all funds)

Portfolio managers: Herbert Kuhl, Jr. (1983), Deborah A. Modzelewski (1995)
Investment objective and policies: Total return: income and capital appreciation in excess of the Lipper Intermediate (five to ten year) U.S. Government Mutual Funds Average measured over a period of three to five years. Invests in a diversified portfolio of debt securities with a weighted average maturity of less than ten years. Up to 10% of assets may be in securities of foreign issuers. May use futures and options for hedging purposes.
Year organized: 1983
Ticker symbol: RSIBX
Portfolio turnover (3 yrs): 13%, 16%, 18%
Management fee: 0.40% first $50M to 0.20% over $150M
Expense ratio: 0.98% (year ending 9/30/97)

RSI RETIREMENT TRUST - INTERNATIONAL EQUITY FUND ◆
(See first RSI listing for data common to all funds)

Sub-adviser: Morgan Grenfell Investment Services Ltd.
Portfolio manager: William G.M. Thomas (1984)
Investment objective and policies: Total return: income and capital appreciation in excess of the Lipper International Mutual Funds Average measured over a period of three to five years. Invests primarily in equity securities of mid- and large-capitalization companies domiciled outside the U.S. May invest in securities of foreign governments and agencies and in U.S. companies which derive substantial income from operations outside the U.S. May use foreign currency transactions, options and futures for hedging purposes.
Year organized: 1984
Ticker symbol: RSTEX
Portfolio turnover (3 yrs): 51%, 51%, 44%

Management fee: 0.80% first $50M, 0.70% over $50M
Expense ratio: 1.96% (year ending 9/30/97)

RSI RETIREMENT TRUST - SHORT-TERM INVESTMENT FUND ◆
(See first RSI listing for data common to all funds)

Portfolio managers: John F. Meuser (1987), Deborah A. Modzelewski (1994)
Investment objective and policies: Current income and stability of principal. Invests in high quality short-term fixed-income securities with a weighted average maturity of one year or less. Up to 25% of assets may be in dollar-denominated securities of foreign issuers. May use futures and options for hedging purposes.
Year organized: 1983
Ticker symbol: RSISX
Management fee: 0.25% first $50M, 0.20% over $50M
Expense ratio: 0.80% (year ending 9/30/97) (includes waiver)

RSI RETIREMENT TRUST - VALUE EQUITY FUND ◆
(See first RSI listing for data common to all funds)

Portfolio manager: Chris R. Kaufman (1995)
Investment objective and policies: Total return: income and capital appreciation in excess of the Lipper Growth and Income Mutual Funds Average measured over a period of three to five years. Invests at least 65% of assets in common stocks of companies believed undervalued, generally with market capitalizations in excess of $750M. Up to 20% of assets may be in securities of foreign issuers. May use futures and options for hedging purposes.
Year organized: 1983
Ticker symbol: RSIVX
Portfolio turnover (3 yrs): 62%, 67%, 40%
Management fee: 0.60% first $10M to 0.10% over $150M
Expense ratio: 1.20% (year ending 9/30/97)

RUSHMORE FUNDS ◆
(Data common to all Rushmore Fund portfolios are shown below. See subsequent listings for data specific to individual portfolios.)

4922 Fairmont Avenue, Third Floor
Bethesda, MD 20814
800-343-3355, 800-622-1386
301-657-1500
prices/yields 800-451-2234
fax 301-657-1520

Shareholder service hours: Full service: M-F 8:30 A.M.-4:30 P.M. EST; After hours service: prices, yields
Adviser: Money Management Assocs.
Transfer agent: Rushmore Trust & Savings, FSB
Minimum purchase: Initial: $2,500 (total among all funds, $500 minimum per fund), Subsequent: None; IRA/Keogh: Initial: $500
Wire orders accepted: Yes
Telephone redemptions: Yes
Wire redemptions: Yes, $5,000 minimum
Letter redemptions: Signature guarantee required over $100,000
Telephone switching: With other Rushmore funds and Cappiello Rushmore funds
Number of switches permitted: 5 per year
Shareholder services: IRA, Keogh, 401(k), 403(b), corporate retirement plans, automatic investment plan
Maintenance fee: $5/month for balances below $500
IRA/Keogh fees: Annual $10, Closing $10

RUSHMORE AMERICAN GAS INDEX FUND ◆
(See first Rushmore listing for data common to all funds)

Administrator: American Gas Association
Portfolio managers: Daniel O'Connor (1989), Richard J. Garvey (1989)
Investment objective and policies: Total return that correlates to that of an index comprising the common

stocks of approximately 102 natural gas distribution and transmission company members who belong to the American Gas Association. A common stock index fund, issues are chosen solely on the basis of their statistical weighting in the Index.
Year organized: 1989
Ticker symbol: GASFX
Deadline for same day wire purchase: 4 P.M.
Discount broker availability: *Fidelity, *Schwab, *Siebert, *White
Qualified for sale in: All states except PR
Dividends paid: Income - March, June, September, December; Capital gains - June, December
Portfolio turnover (3 yrs): 8%, 10%, 8%
Management fee: 0.40%
Administration fees: 0.45%
Expense ratio: 0.85% (year ending 3/31/97)

RUSHMORE FUND FOR GOVERNMENT INVESTORS ◆
(See first Rushmore listing for data common to all funds)

Portfolio manager: Investment committee
Investment objective and policies: Current income with safety of principal. Invests exclusively in short-term debt securities issued by the U.S. Government, its agencies or instrumentalities, and repurchase agreements thereon.
Year organized: 1975 (absorbed Rushmore Money Market Portfolio 5/31/96)
Ticker symbol: FUSXX
Deadline for same day wire purchase: 12 NN
Check redemptions: Available on request
Qualified for sale in: All states except PR
Deadline for same day switch: 12 NN
Dividends paid: Income - declared daily, paid monthly
Management fee: 0.50% first $500M to 0.35% over $1B
Expense ratio: 0.74% (year ending 12/31/96)

RUSHMORE FUND FOR TAX FREE INVESTORS - MARYLAND TAX-FREE PORTFOLIO ◆
(See first Rushmore listing for data common to all funds)

Lead portfolio manager: Daniel O'Connor (1983)
Investment objective and policies: Current income exempt from federal and Maryland personal income taxes. Invests at least 80% of assets in high-quality, long-term Maryland municipal securities with a weighted average maturity of more than ten years.
Year organized: 1983 (objective and name change in 1991; formerly Fund for Tax-Free Investors - Long-Term Portfolio. Previous performance record may not be applicable.)
Ticker symbol: RSXLX
Deadline for same day wire purchase: 4 P.M.
Discount broker availability: *Fidelity, *Schwab, *Siebert, *White
Qualified for sale in: DC, GA, IL, MD, VA
Portfolio turnover (3 yrs): 31%, 37%, 38%
Dividends paid: Income - declared daily, paid monthly; Capital gains - December
Management fee: 0.625%
Expense ratio: 0.93% (year ending 12/31/96)

RUSHMORE FUND FOR TAX FREE INVESTORS - MONEY MARKET PORTFOLIO ◆
(See first Rushmore listing for data common to all funds)

Portfolio manager: Investment committee
Investment objective and policies: Current income exempt from federal income tax. Invests primarily in high-quality municipal money market securities.
Year organized: 1983
Ticker symbol: FFTXX
Deadline for same day wire purchase: 12 NN
Check redemptions: Available on request
Qualified for sale in: DC, GA, IL, MD, NY, PA, TX, VA
Deadline for same day switch: 12 NN

Dividends paid: Income - declared daily, paid monthly
Management fee: 0.50%
Expense ratio: 0.75% (year ending 12/31/96)

RUSHMORE FUND FOR TAX FREE INVESTORS - VIRGINIA TAX-FREE PORTFOLIO ◆
(See first Rushmore listing for data common to all funds)

Lead portfolio manager: Daniel O'Connor (1983)
Investment objective and policies: Current income exempt from federal and Virginia personal income taxes. Invests at least 80% of assets in high-quality long-term Virginia municipal securities with a weighted average maturity of more than ten years.
Year organized: 1983 (objective and name change in 1991; formerly Fund for Tax-Free Investors - Intermediate Term Portfolio)
Ticker symbol: RSXIX
Deadline for same day wire purchase: 4 P.M.
Discount broker availability: *Fidelity, *Schwab, *Siebert, *White
Qualified for sale in: DC, GA, IL, VA
Portfolio turnover (3 yrs): 46%, 55%, 33%
Dividends paid: Income - declared daily, paid monthly; Capital gains - December
Management fee: 0.625%
Expense ratio: 0.93% (year ending 12/31/96)

RUSHMORE - U.S. GOVERNMENT BOND PORTFOLIO ◆
(See first Rushmore listing for data common to all funds)

Lead portfolio manager: Daniel O'Connor (1985)
Investment objective and policies: Maximum current income consistent with safety of principal. Invests primarily in the current thirty-year U.S. Treasury bond, as well as other government agency securities and coupon securities (subject to a 10% limitation) and repurchase agreements thereon, with maturities of ten years of more.
Year organized: 1985 (name changed from U.S. Government Securities Long-Term Portfolio 1/96 after merging with Intermediate Term Portfolio; long-term objective remains the same)
Ticker symbol: RSGVX
Deadline for same day wire purchase: 4 P.M.
Discount broker availability: *Fidelity, *Schwab, *Siebert, *White
Qualified for sale in: All states except PR
Dividends paid: Income - declared daily, paid monthly; Capital gains: Short-term - quarterly, Long-term - December
Portfolio turnover (3 yrs): 19%, 85%, 63%
Management fee: 0.50%
Administration fee: 0.30%
Expense ratio: 0.80% (year ending 8/31/97)

RYDEX SERIES TRUST FUNDS ◆
(Data common to all Rydex funds are shown below. See subsequent listings for data specific to individual funds.)

6116 Executive Blvd., Suite 400
Bethesda, MD 20852
800-820-0888, 800-678-2873
301-468-8520
prices/yields 800-717-7776
fax 301-468-8585
Internet: http://www.rydexfunds.com
e-mail: acollins@rydexfunds.com

Shareholder service hours: Full service: M-F 8:30 A.M.-5:30 P.M. EST; After hours service: prices, yields
Adviser: PADCO Advisors, Inc.
Transfer agent: PADCO Service Co., Inc.
Special sales restrictions: Designed for professional money managers and investors who intend to follow an asset allocation or market-timing investment strategy, but is open to individuals with self directed accounts; investors using a registered investment advisor as an intermediary may open an account with a $15,000 minimum balance.
Minimum purchase: Initial: $25,000 (total among all

Rydex funds), Subsequent: None; Automatic investment plan: Subsequent: $50
Wire orders accepted: Yes
Deadline for same day wire purchase: (See fund)
Qualified for sale in: All states
Telephone redemptions: Yes
Wire redemptions: Yes, $15 fee for less than $5,000
Letter redemptions: Signature guarantee not required
Telephone switching: With other Rydex funds, $1,000 minimum
Number of switches permitted: Unlimited
Shareholder services: IRA, Keogh, 403(b), corporate retirement plans, electronic funds transfer
12b-1 distribution fee: Paid by advisor
IRA/Keogh fees: Annual $15, Closing $15

RYDEX HIGH YIELD FUND ◆
(See first Rydex listing for data common to all funds)

Sub-adviser: Loomis, Sayles & Co., L.P.
Portfolio managers: Stephanie S. Lord (1997), Steven J. Doherty (1997)
Investment objective and policies: Investment returns that correspond to the performance of the Merrill Lynch High Yield Master Index, a benchmark for high yield fixed-income securities. Fund invests in securities found in the index, as well as others expected to perform in a manner that will assist the fund's performance to track closely to the index.
Year organized: 1997
Ticker symbol: RYHYX
Deadline for same day wire purchase:: 2:15 P.M.
Discount broker availability: White
Deadline for same day switch: 2:15 P.M.
Dividends paid: Income - declared daily, paid monthly; Capital gains - annually
Management fee: 0.75%

RYDEX JUNO FUND ◆
(See first Rydex listing for data common to all funds)

Portfolio manager: Thomas Michael (1996)
Investment objective and policies: Total return before expenses that inversely correlates to the price movements of a benchmark U.S. Treasury debt instrument or futures contract on a specified debt instrument - currently the 30-year U.S. Treasury Bond. Fund is designed for investors speculating on anticipated decreases in the price of the long bond. Does not invest in traditional fixed-income securities but engages in short sales and options and futures transactions designed to benefit from declines in bond prices. Up to 15% of assets may be in illiquid securities. Fund is non-diversified.
Year organized: 1995
Ticker symbol: RYJUX
Deadline for same day wire purchase:: 3 P.M.
Discount broker availability: Fidelity, Schwab, Siebert, White
Deadline for same day switch: 2:45 P.M.
Dividends paid: Income - December; Capital gains - December
Portfolio turnover (2 yrs): 0%, 0% (short-term securities do not count as turnover)
Management fee: 0.90%
Expense ratio: 1.58% (year ending 3/31/97) (1.60% without waiver)

RYDEX NOVA FUND ◆
(See first Rydex listing for data common to all funds)

Portfolio manager: Thomas Michael (1994)
Investment objective and policies: Total return that corresponds to 150% of the performance of the S&P 500 Index. A substantial portion of assets will be devoted to investment techniques including index futures contracts, options on stock index futures contracts, and options on securities and stock indexes. Fund should outperform an S&P 500 Index fund when the underlying stocks are rising and increase losses to investors when such prices are declining. Fund is non-diversified.
Year organized: 1993 (formerly Rushmore Nova Portfolio. Current ownership acquired all assets of Rushmore Nova Portfolio on 5/20/93)
Ticker symbol: RYNVX

Deadline for same day wire purchase:: 3:45 P.M.
Discount broker availability: Fidelity, Schwab, Siebert, White
Deadline for same day switch: 3:45 P.M.
Dividends paid: Income - December; Capital gains - December
Portfolio turnover (3 yrs): 0%, 0%, 0% (short-term securities do not count as turnover)
Management fee: 0.75%
Expense ratio: 1.16% (year ending 3/31/97) (1.19% without waiver)

RYDEX OTC FUND ◆
(See first Rydex listing for data common to all funds)

Portfolio manager: Michael P. Byrum (1997)
Investment objective and policies: Total return that approximates the performance of the NASDAQ 100 Index. Invests in a representative mix of securities included in the NASDAQ 100 Index but is not an index fund. Up to 15% of assets may be in illiquid securities. Fund may use index options, stock index futures contracts and options in an effort to enhance total return and for hedging purposes. Fund is non-diversified.
Year organized: 1994
Ticker symbol: RYOCX
Deadline for same day wire purchase:: 3:45 P.M.
Discount broker availability: Fidelity, Schwab, Siebert, White
Deadline for same day switch: 3:45 P.M.
Dividends paid: Income - December; Capital gains - December
Portfolio turnover (3 yrs): 1,140%, 2,579% 2,241%
Management fee: 0.75%
Expense ratio: 1.27% (year ending 3/31/97)

RYDEX PRECIOUS METALS FUND ◆
(See first Rydex listing for data common to all funds)

Portfolio manager: T. Daniel Gillespie (1997)
Investment objective and policies: Total return that approximates the performance of the Philadelphia Stock Exchange Gold/Silver Index (the "XAU Index"). Invests in securities included in the Index and in other securities expected to perform in a manner that enables the fund to track closely the XAU Index. May purchase ADRs of issuers located outside the U.S. and Canada. Fund is non-diversified.
Year organized: 1993 (objective changed in 1995)
Ticker symbol: RYPMX
Deadline for same day wire purchase:: 3:30 P.M.
Discount broker availability: White
Deadline for same day switch: 3:30 P.M.
Dividends paid: Income - December; Capital gains - December
Portfolio turnover (3 yrs): 743%, 1,036%, 1,765%
Management fee: 0.75%
Expense ratio: 1.45% (year ending 3/31/97) (1.49% without waiver)

RYDEX URSA FUND ◆
(See first Rydex listing for data common to all funds)

Portfolio manager: Michael P. Byrum (1997)
Investment objective and policies: Investment results that inversely correlate to the performance to the total return of the S&P 500 Index. Fund is designed for investors speculating on anticipated decreases in the S&P 500 Index. Does not invest in traditional equity securities but engages in short sales and options and futures transactions designed to benefit from bear (hence the name Ursa) market declines in stock prices. Up to 15% of assets may be in illiquid securities. Fund is non-diversified.
Year organized: 1994
Ticker symbol: RYURX
Deadline for same day wire purchase:: 3:30 P.M.
Discount broker availability: Fidelity, Schwab, Siebert, White
Deadline for same day switch: 3:45 P.M.
Dividends paid: Income - December; Capital gains - December
Portfolio turnover (3 yrs): 0%, 0%, 0% (short-term securities do not count as turnover)
Management fee: 0.90%
Expense ratio: 1.34% (year ending 3/31/97) (1.36% without waiver)

RYDEX U.S. GOVERNMENT BOND FUND ◆
(See first Rydex listing for data common to all funds)

Portfolio manager: Anne Ruff (1997)
Investment objective and policies: To provide investment results that correspond to 120% of the price movement of the 30 year U.S. Treasury Bond, without consideration of interest paid. Invests primarily in debt obligations issued or guaranteed as to principal and interest by the U.S. Government, its agencies or instrumentalities. May use futures contracts and options thereon.
Year organized: 1994
Ticker symbol: RYGBX
Deadline for same day wire purchase:: 2:45 P.M.
Discount broker availability: Fidelity, Schwab, Siebert, White
Deadline for same day switch: 2:45 P.M.
Dividends paid: Income - declared daily, paid monthly; Capital gains - December
Portfolio turnover (3 yrs): 962%, 780%, 3,453%
Management fee: 0.50%
Expense ratio: 1.49% (year ending 3/31/97) (1.51% without waiver)

RYDEX U.S. GOVERNMENT MONEY MARKET FUND ◆
(See first Rydex listing for data common to all funds)

Portfolio manager: Anne Ruff (1997)
Investment objective and policies: High current income consistent with security of principal and liquidity. Invests primarily in money market instruments issued or guaranteed as to principal and interest by the U.S. Government, its agencies or instrumentalities.
Year organized: 1993
Ticker symbol RYMXX
Deadline for same day wire purchase:: 1 P.M.
Deadline for same day switch: 1 P.M.
Discount broker availability: Schwab (only through financial advisers)
Check redemptions: $500 minimum
Dividends paid: Income - declared daily, paid monthly
Management fee: 0.50%
Expense ratio: 0.86% (year ending 3/31/97)

SAFECO FUNDS ◆
(Data common to all SAFECO funds are shown below. See subsequent listings for data specific to individual funds.)

4333 Brooklyn Avenue N.E.
Seattle, WA 98105
800-426-6730, 206-545-5530
prices/yields 800-835-4391, 206-545-5113
TTY/TDD 800-438-8718
fax 206-545-7150
Internet: http://www.safecofunds.com
e-mail: mfunds@safeco.com

Shareholder service hours: Full service: M-F 5:30 A.M.-7 P.M. PST; After hours service: prices, yields, total returns, prospectuses, DJIA
Adviser: SAFECO Asset Management Co.
Transfer agent: SAFECO Services Corp.
Sales restrictions: SAFECO now offers multiple classes of many of their shares, referred to as No-Load, Advisor A, and Advisor "B" classes. A and "B" shares are sold through advisors, banks, etc. NO-LOAD shares are sold through fee-based advisors, discount brokers, or directly from the distributor. Information presented here is for NO-LOAD shares only.
Minimum purchase: Initial: $1,000, Subsequent: $100; IRA: Initial: $250; Keogh: Initial: $25, Subsequent: $25; Automatic investment plan: Initial: None, Subsequent: $100
Wire orders accepted: Yes
Deadline for same day wire purchase: 4 P.M.
Qualified for sale in: All states (exceptions noted)
Telephone redemptions: Yes
Wire redemptions: Yes, $1,000 minimum, $10 fee
Letter redemptions: Signature guarantee not required

Telephone switching: With other SAFECO funds, $1,000 minimum
Number of switches permitted: Unlimited
Shareholder services: IRA, SEP-IRA, Keogh, 401(k), 403(b), corporate retirement plans, electronic funds transfer, systematic withdrawal plan min. bal. req. $5,000
IRA fees: Annual $5
Keogh fees: None

SAFECO BALANCED FUND ◆
(See first SAFECO listing for data common to all funds)

Portfolio managers: Rex L. Bentley (1996), Lynette D. Savgold (1997), Michael Hughes (1997)
Investment objective and policies: Growth and income consistent with preservation of capital. Invests in an allocated mix of equity (50% to 70%) and fixed-income (at least 25%) securities, which will be altered occasionally in response to economic conditions in order to pursue the objective. Will not make changes to "time the market." May invest up to 35% of assets in convertible securities downgraded to below investment grade after purchase. May purchase ADRs and invest up to 10% of assets in foreign securities. May invest up to 10% of assets in REITs, and up to 10% of assets in restricted securities.
Year organized: 1996
Ticker symbol: SAFBX
Discount broker availability: *Fidelity, *Schwab, *Siebert, *White
Dividends paid: Income - March, June, September, December; Capital gains - March, June, September, December
Portfolio turnover (2 yrs): 101%, 144%
Management fee: 0.75% first $250M to 0.55% over $500M
Expense ratio: 1.23% (year ending 12/31/97)

SAFECO CALIFORNIA TAX-FREE INCOME FUND ◆
(See first SAFECO listing for data common to all funds)

Portfolio manager: Stephen C. Bauer (1983)
Investment objective and policies: High level of current income exempt from federal and California income taxes, consistent with relative stability of capital. Invests at least 80% of assets in investment grade securities exempt from federal and California taxes.
Year organized: 1983
Ticker symbol: SFCAX
Discount broker availability: *Fidelity, *Schwab, *Siebert, *White
Qualified for sale in: AZ, CA, NV
Dividends paid: Income - declared daily, paid monthly; Capital gains - March, December
Portfolio turnover (3 yrs): 10%, 11%, 16%
Management fee: 0.55% first $100M to 0.25% over $500M
Expense ratio: 0.68% (year ending 12/31/97)

SAFECO EQUITY FUND ◆
(See first SAFECO listing for data common to all funds)

Portfolio manager: Richard D. Meagley (1995)
Investment objective and policies: Long-term capital growth and reasonable current income. Invests primarily in common stocks, and securities convertible to common stock, taking a long-range investment viewpoint. May invest in ADRs of foreign issuers. Up to 35% of assets may be in convertible securities, all of which may be below investment grade.
Year organized: 1932
Ticker symbol: SAFQX
Discount broker availability: *Fidelity, *Schwab, *Siebert, *White
Dividends paid: Income - March, June, September, December; Capital gains - September, December
Portfolio turnover (3 yrs): 34%, 74%, 56%
Management fee: 0.75% first $100M to 0.45% over $500M
Expense ratio: 0.73% (year ending 12/31/97)

SAFECO GNMA FUND ◆
(See first SAFECO listing for data common to all funds)

Portfolio manager: Paul A. Stevenson (1988)
Investment objective and policies: High level of current income consistent with capital preservation. Invests at least 65% of assets in U.S. Government securities, primarily GNMAs, guaranteed at to timely payment of principal and interest by the full faith and credit of the U.S. Government. Up to 35% of assets may be in other investment grade government and corporate debt securities.
Year organized: 1986 (name changed from SAFECO U.S. Govt. Securities 2/1/94)
Ticker symbol: SFUSX
Discount broker availability: *Fidelity, *Schwab, *Siebert, *White
Dividends paid: Income - declared daily, paid monthly; Capital gains - September, December
Portfolio turnover (3 yrs): 83%, 48%, 131%
Management fee: 0.65% first $250M to 0.35% over $750M
Expense ratio: 0.93% (year ending 12/31/97)

SAFECO GROWTH FUND ◆
(See first SAFECO listing for data common to all funds)

Portfolio manager: Thomas M. Maguire (1989)
Investment objective and policies: Capital growth; income secondary. Invests primarily in common stocks selected for appreciation potential. May invest in ADRs of foreign issuers, securities convertible into common stock and investment grade debt securities.
Year organized: 1967
Ticker symbol: SAFGX
Discount broker availability: *Fidelity, *Schwab, *Siebert, *White
Dividends paid: Income - annually; Capital gains - September, December
Portfolio turnover (3 yrs): 83%, 125%, 110%
Management fee: 0.75% first $100M to 0.45% over $500M
Expense ratio: 0.85% (year ending 12/31/97)

SAFECO HIGH-YIELD BOND FUND ◆
(See first SAFECO listing for data common to all funds)

Portfolio manager: Robert Kern (1997)
Investment objective and policies: High current income. Invests in high-yield, fixed-income securities with maturities of one to 30 years with majority in the five to 15 year range. In and effort to increase yield, fund may invest up to 25% of assets in junk bonds and in unrated securities or those in default.
Year organized: 1988
Ticker symbol: SAFHX
Discount broker availability: *Fidelity, *Schwab, *Siebert, *White
Dividends paid: Income - declared daily, paid monthly; Capital gains - September, December
Portfolio turnover (3 yrs): 85%, 93%, 38%
Management fee: 0.65% first $250M to 0.35% over $750M
Expense ratio: 0.91% (year ending 12/31/97)

SAFECO INCOME FUND ◆
(See first SAFECO listing for data common to all funds)

Portfolio manager: Thomas E. Rath (1996)
Investment objective and policies: Current income; long-term capital growth secondary. Invests in common stocks, convertible and non-convertible preferred stock, bonds and debentures with emphasis on common stock. Fund may invest up to 35% of assets in junk bonds and 10% in Eurodollar bonds of U.S. issuers.
Year organized: 1969
Ticker symbol: SAFIX
Discount broker availability: *Fidelity, *Schwab, *Siebert, *White

Dividends paid: Income - March, June, September, December; Capital gains - September, December
Portfolio turnover (3 yrs): 52%, 50%, 31%
Management fee: 0.75% first $100M to 0.45% over $500M
Expense ratio: 0.85% (year ending 12/31/97)

SAFECO INSURED MUNICIPAL BOND FUND ◆
(See first SAFECO listing for data common to all funds)

Portfolio manager: Stephen C. Bauer (1993)
Investment objective and policies: Current income exempt from federal income tax, consistent with relative stability of capital. Invests at least 95% of assets in municipal bonds whose interest is exempt from federal income tax and are covered by insurance guaranteeing the timely payment of both principal and interest.
Year organized: 1993
Ticker symbol: SFIMX
Discount broker availability: *Fidelity, *Schwab, *Siebert, *White
Dividends paid: Income - declared daily, paid monthly; Capital gains - April, October
Portfolio turnover (3 yrs): 13%, 15%, 4%
Management fee: 0.65% first $250M to 0.35% over $750M
Expense ratio: 0.92% (year ending 12/31/97)

SAFECO INTERMEDIATE-TERM MUNICIPAL BOND FUND ◆
(See first SAFECO listing for data common to all funds)

Portfolio manager: Mary V. Metastasio (1996)
Investment objective and policies: Current income exempt from federal income tax, consistent with relative stability of capital. Invests at least 80% of assets in securities exempt from federal income tax, and at least 65% in municipal bonds of the four highest grades. Portfolio generally maintains an average dollar-weighted maturity of three to ten years.
Year organized: 1993
Ticker symbol: SFIBX
Discount broker availability: *Fidelity, *Schwab, *Siebert, *White
Dividends paid: Income - declared daily, paid monthly; Capital gains - April, October
Portfolio turnover (3 yrs): 11%, 13%, 9%
Management fee: 0.55% first $250M to 0.25% over $750M
Expense ratio: 0.83% (year ending 12/31/97)

SAFECO INTERMEDIATE-TERM U.S. TREASURY FUND ◆
(See first SAFECO listing for data common to all funds)

Portfolio manager: Ronald Spaulding (1997)
Investment objective and policies: High current income consistent with capital preservation. Invests at least 65% of assets in U.S. Treasury securities, with the remainder in other investment grade, fixed-income securities. Fund maintains a dollar-weighted average maturity of three to ten years.
Year organized: 1988 (name changed from Intermediate-Term Bond Fund on 1/31/93.)
Ticker symbol: SFIUX
Discount broker availability: *Fidelity, *Schwab, *Siebert, *White
Dividends paid: Income - declared daily, paid monthly; Capital gains - September, December
Portfolio turnover (3 yrs): 82%, 294%, 125%
Management fee: 0.55% first $250M to 0.25% over $750M
Expense ratio: 0.92% (year ending 12/31/97)

SAFECO INTERNATIONAL STOCK FUND ◆
(See first SAFECO listing for data common to all funds)

Sub-adviser: Bank of Ireland Asset Management (U.S.) Ltd.
Portfolio managers: Team managed

Investment objective and policies: Maximum long-term total return: capital appreciation and income. Invests at least 65% of assets in common stock of well established non-U.S. companies domiciled in at least five different countries. May invest in preferred stocks and convertible securities without limit, and may invest in debt securities issued by foreign governments or their agencies. May use derivatives for hedging purposes.
Year organized: 1996
Ticker symbol: SFISX
Discount broker availability: *Fidelity, *Schwab, *Siebert, *White
Dividends paid: Income - annually; Capital gains - annually
Portfolio turnover (2 yrs): 22%, 16%
Management fee: 1.10% first $250M to 0.90% over $500M
Expense ratio: 1.63% (year ending 12/31/97) (1.89% without waiver)

SAFECO MANAGED BOND FUND ◆
(See first SAFECO listing for data common to all funds)

Portfolio manager: Michael Hughes (1997)
Investment objective and policies: High total return consistent with relative stability of capital. Invests at least 65% of assets in investment grade fixed-income securities with remaining maturities of ten years or less, with at least 50% of assets committed to U.S. Government issued or guaranteed instruments. May invest up to 50% of assets in corporate debt securities or Eurodollar bonds, and may invest in asset-backed securities.
Year organized: 1994
Ticker symbol: SAMBX
Discount broker availability: *Fidelity, *White
Dividends paid: Income - declared daily, paid monthly; Capital gains - March, December
Portfolio turnover (3 yrs): 177%, 136%, 79%
Management fee: 0.50% first $250M to 0.35% over $250M
Expense ratio: 1.15% (year ending 12/31/97)

SAFECO MONEY MARKET FUND ◆
(See first SAFECO listing for data common to all funds)

Portfolio manager: Naomi Urata (1994)
Investment objective and policies: Current income consistent with preservation of capital and liquidity. Invests in high quality money market instruments maturing in thirteen months or less.
Year organized: 1981
Ticker symbol: SAFXX
Dividends paid: Income - declared daily, paid monthly
Check redemptions: $500 minimum
Management fee: 0.50% first $250M to 0.25% over $750M
Expense ratio: 0.78% (year ending 12/31/97)

SAFECO MUNICIPAL BOND FUND ◆
(See first SAFECO listing for data common to all funds)

Portfolio manager: Stephen C. Bauer (1981)
Investment objective and policies: Current income exempt from federal income tax, consistent with relative stability of capital. Invests at least 80% of assets in tax-exempt securities and at least 65% in municipal bonds of the four highest grades.
Year organized: 1981
Ticker symbol: SFCOX
Discount broker availability: Fidelity, Schwab, Siebert, White
Dividends paid: Income - declared daily, paid monthly; Capital gains - March, December
Portfolio turnover (3 yrs): 14%, 6%, 13%
Management fee: 0.55% first $100M to 0.25% over $500M
Expense ratio: 0.51% (year ending 12/31/97)

SAFECO NORTHWEST FUND ◆
(See first SAFECO listing for data common to all funds)

Portfolio manager: William B. Whitlow (1997)
Investment objective and policies: Long-term capital growth. Invests at least 65% of assets in securities issued by companies with principal executive offices in the Northwest (Washington, Alaska, Idaho, Oregon and Montana). Fund may use common stocks and securities convertible into common stock (rated Baa or better). Up to 35% of assets may be in junk bonds.
Year organized: 1991
Ticker symbol: SFNWX
Discount broker availability: *Fidelity, *Schwab, *Siebert, *White
Dividends paid: Income - annually; Capital gains - September, December
Portfolio turnover (3 yrs): 55%, 36%, 20%
Management fee: 0.75% first $250M to 0.45% over $750M
Expense ratio: 1.09% (year ending 12/31/97)

SAFECO SMALL COMPANY STOCK FUND ◆
(See first SAFECO listing for data common to all funds)

Portfolio manager: Greg Eisen (1996)
Investment objective and policies: Long-term capital growth. Invests at least 65% of assets in companies with total market capitalizations of less than $1B. May continue to hold securities as part of 65% portfolio share if market capitalizations exceeds this level after purchase. May purchase ADRs and invest up to 10% of assets in foreign securities. May invest up to 10% of assets in REITs, and up to 10% of assets in restricted securities.
Year organized: 1996
Ticker symbol: SFSCX
Discount broker availability: *Fidelity, *Schwab, *Siebert, *White
Dividends paid: Income - annually; Capital gains - annually
Portfolio turnover (2 yrs): 61%, 91%
Management fee: 0.85% first $250M to 0.65% over $500M
Expense ratio: 1.33% (year ending 12/31/97)

SAFECO TAX-FREE MONEY MARKET FUND ◆
(See first SAFECO listing for data common to all funds)

Portfolio manager: Mary V. Metastasio (1987)
Investment objective and policies: Current income exempt from federal income tax, consistent with a portfolio of high-quality, municipal money market obligations selected on the basis of liquidity and capital preservation.
Year organized: 1984
Ticker symbol: SFTXX
Dividends paid: Income - declared daily, paid monthly
Check redemptions: $500 minimum
Management fee: 0.50% first $100M to 0.20% over $500
Expense ratio: 0.72% (year ending 12/31/97)

SAFECO U.S. VALUE FUND ◆
(See first SAFECO listing for data common to all funds)

Portfolio managers: Rex L. Bentley (1997), Lynette D. Sagvold (1997)
Investment objective and policies: Long-term growth of capital and income. Invests primarily in common stock selected for potential appreciation and income using fundamental value analysis. Invests at least 65% of assets in common and preferred stock of U.S. companies. May also invest up to 35% of assets in convertible junk bonds. May invest up to 10% of assets in REITs, 10% in foreign securities, and up to 10% of assets in restricted securities.
Year organized: 1997

Discount broker availability: *Fidelity, *Schwab, *Siebert, *White
Dividends paid: Income - March, June, September, December; Capital gains - annually
Portfolio turnover (1 yr): 36%
Management fee: 0.85% first $250M to 0.55% over $500M
Expense ratio: 1.19% (eight months ending 12/31/97)

SAFECO WASHINGTON STATE MUNICIPAL BOND FUND ◆
(See first SAFECO listing for data common to all funds)

Portfolio manager: Beverly R. Denny (1996)
Investment objective and policies: Current income exempt from federal income tax, consistent with relative stability of capital. Invests at least 80% of assets in securities exempt from federal income tax and at least 65% in municipal bonds of the four highest grades. Fund will normally invest at least 65% of assets in municipal bonds issued by the state of Washington or one of its political subdivisions, municipalities, agencies, instrumentalities or public authorities. Management intends to buy and hold low-coupon, long-term bonds with maturities of twenty years or more.
Year organized: 1993
Ticker symbol: SAWBX
Qualified for sale in: AZ, CA, WA
Discount broker availability: *Fidelity, *Schwab, *Siebert, *White
Dividends paid: Income - declared daily, paid monthly; Capital gains - March, December
Portfolio turnover (3 yrs): 12%, 16%, 21%
Management fee: 0.65% first $250M to 0.35% over $750M
Expense ratio: 1.02% (year ending 12/31/97)

SALOMON BROTHERS ASSET OPPORTUNITY FUND ◆
7 World Trade Center, 38th Floor
New York, NY 10048
800-725-6666, 212-783-1301
fax 212-783-4334

Adviser: Salomon Brothers Asset Management, Inc.
Portfolio manager: Irving Brilliant (1979)
Transfer agent: First Data Investor Services Group, Inc.
Investment objective and policies: Long-term capital appreciation; current income secondary. Invests primarily in common stocks and convertible securities. Fund seeks companies believed undervalued, undergoing management and/or structural changes or likely to benefit from new technological, marketing or production methods or new or unique products or services. May buy restricted securities and leverage up to 1/3 of total assets. Fund is non-diversified.
Year organized: 1978 (formerly Lehman Opportunity)
Ticker symbol: SAOPX
Minimum purchase: Initial: $1,000, Subsequent: $100; IRA/Keogh: Initial: $250; Automatic investment plan: Initial: $50, Subsequent: $25
Wire orders accepted: Yes
Deadline for same day wire purchase: 4 P.M.
Discount broker availability: Fidelity, Schwab, Siebert, White
Qualified for sale in: All states
Telephone redemptions: Yes
Wire redemptions: Yes, $500 minimum
Letter redemptions: Signature guarantee required over $50,000
Telephone switching: Effective 3/1/97 the Opportunity fund switches with nothing.
Dividends paid: Income - December; Capital gains - December
Portfolio turnover (3 yrs): 4%, 5%, 8%
Shareholder services: IRA, SEP-IRA, Keogh, systematic withdrawal plan min. bal. req. $7,500
Management fee: 1.00%
Expense ratio: 1.16% (year ending 8/31/97)
IRA/Keogh fees: Annual $10, Initial $5, Closing $10

SAND HILL PORTFOLIO MANAGER FUND ◆
1500 Forest Avenue, Suite 223
Richmond, VA 23229
800-527-9500, 800-628-4077
804-285-8211
fax 804-285-8252

Adviser: Sand Hill Advisors, Inc.
Administrator: Commonwealth Shareholder Services, Inc.
Portfolio managers: Jane H. Williams (1995), David W. Cost, Jr. (1996)
Transfer agent: Fund Services, Inc.
Investment objective and policies: Maximum total return: realized and unrealized appreciation and income. Invests in a diversified portfolio of domestic and foreign equities, debt securities, and short-term investment vehicles. Asset allocations are selected based on perceived market conditions, with equities comprising the primary vehicle; bonds will be held to provide a degree of stability and to provide current income for future stock purchases. May invest up to 10% of assets in other investment companies and use various derivatives for hedging purposes or in an attempt to enhance potential gain.
Year organized: 1995
Ticker symbol: SHPMX
Minimum purchase: Initial: $25,000, Subsequent: $50
Wire orders accepted: Yes
Deadline for same day wire purchase: 2 P.M.
Discount broker availability: *Fidelity, *Siebert, *White
Qualified for sale in: CA, CO, ID, ME, MI, MN, OR, PA, VA
Telephone redemptions: Yes, $10 fee
Wire redemptions: Yes, $10 fee
Letter redemptions: Signature guarantee not required
Telephone switching: With Vontobel funds
Dividends paid: Income - December; Capital gains - December
Portfolio turnover (2 yrs): 33%, 41%
Shareholder services: IRA, automatic investment plan
Management fee: 1.00% first $100M, 0.75% over $100M
Administration fee: 0.20% ($15,000 minimum)
Expense ratio: 2.00% (year ending 12/31/96) (2.64% without waiver)
IRA fees: Annual $20

SCHOONER FUND ◆
(Fund liquidated 4/30/97)

SCHRODER CAPITAL FUNDS ◆
(Data common to all Schroder Capital Funds are shown below. See subsequent listings for data specific to individual funds.)

787 Seventh Avenue, 29th Floor
New York, NY 10019-6016
800-290-9826, 800-344-8332
212-641-3830, 207-879-6200
fax 207-879-6050

Adviser: Schroder Capital Management International, Inc.
Transfer agent: Forum Financial Corp.
Wire orders accepted: Yes
Deadline for same day wire purchase: 4 P.M.
Telephone redemptions: Yes
Wire redemptions: Yes
Letter redemptions: Signature guarantee required
Shareholder services: IRA, systematic withdrawal plan min. bal. req. $10,000
IRA fees: Annual: $10, Initial: $10

SCHRODER CAPITAL - INTERNATIONAL FUND ◆
(See first Schroder Capital listing for data common to all funds)

Portfolio managers: Mark J. Smith (1989), Michael M. Perelstein (1997)
Investment objective and policies: Long-term capital appreciation. Invests all its assets in a corresponding portfolio of Schroder Capital Funds with identical objectives, rather than investing directly in securities. Master portfolio invests primarily in equity securities of companies domiciled outside the U.S. May also invest in the securities of closed-end investment companies investing primarily in foreign securities, and in debt obligations of foreign governments, international organizations and foreign corporations. May use forward currency contracts.
Year organized: 1985 (formerly a portfolio of Fund Source; name changed from International Equity Fund 5/1/96)
Ticker symbol: SCIEX
Sales restrictions: Fund offers two classes of shares effective 5/16/96, Investor and Advisor. Advisor Shares are offered through intermediaries and have higher expenses. Information here represents Investor Shares. All shares existing prior to that date were converted to Investor Shares.
Minimum purchase: Initial: $10,000, Subsequent: $2,500; IRA: Initial: $2,000, Subsequent: $250
Discount broker availability: *White
Qualified for sale in: All states except AZ, HI, VT
Dividends paid: Income - annually; Capital gains - annually
Portfolio turnover (3 yrs): 56%, 61%, 25%
Management fee: 0.50% first $100M to 0.35% over $250M
12b-1 distribution fee: Maximum of 0.50% (not currently imposed)
Expense ratio: 0.99% (year ending 10/31/96) (1.04% without waiver)

SCHRODER CAPITAL - MICRO CAP FUND ◆
(See first Schroder Capital listing for data common to all funds)

Lead portfolio manager: Ira Unschuld (1997)
Investment objective and policies: Long-term capital appreciation. Invests all its assets in a corresponding portfolio of Schroder Capital Funds with identical objectives. Master portfolio invests primarily in equity securities of domestic companies with market capitalizations of less than $300M, usually those found in the bottom third of the Russell 2000 Growth Index. May use forward currency contracts, short sales, and options and futures for hedging purposes.
Year organized: 1997
Minimum purchase: Initial: $10,000, Subsequent: $2,500; IRA: Initial: $2,000, Subsequent: $250
Discount broker availability: *White
Qualified for sale in: All states except AZ, HI, VT
Dividends paid: Income - annually; Capital gains - annually
Management fee: 1.25%

SCHRODER CAPITAL - U.S. EQUITY FUND ◆
(See first Schroder Capital listing for data common to all funds)

Portfolio managers: Jane P. Lucas (1995), Paul Morris (1997)
Investment objective and policies: Capital growth; income secondary. Invests primarily in common stock and securities convertible into common stock, including securities with common stock purchase warrants attached, in such warrants themselves or in other rights to purchase common stock. Debt securities and non-convertible preferred stocks are normally limited to 15% of assets.
Year organized: 1970 (formerly Cheapside Dollar Fund)
Ticker symbol: SUSEX
Minimum purchase: Initial: $10,000, Subsequent: $2,500; IRA Initial: $2,000, Subsequent: $250
Discount broker availability: White
Qualified for sale in: CA, CO, DC, FL, GA, IL, IN, KS, KY, MN, MO, NJ, NY, NC, OH, OK, OR, PA, VA, WY
Dividends paid: Income - annually; Capital gains - annually
Portfolio turnover (3 yrs): 57%, 57%, 27%
Management fee: 0.75% first $100M, 0.50% over $100M
Expense ratio: 1.48% (year ending 10/31/97) (includes waiver)

SCHRODER CAPITAL - U.S. SMALLER COMPANIES FUND ◆

(See first Schroder Capital listing for data common to all funds)

Portfolio manager: Fariba Talebi (1993)
Investment objective and policies: Capital growth. Invests at least 65% of assets in equity securities of companies with market capitalizations under $1B perceived to have prospects for above average earnings growth. May invest up to 20% of assets in securities of unseasoned companies and 15% in illiquid securities. May hedge and sell short against the box.
Year organized: 1993
Ticker symbol: SCUIX
Sales restrictions: Fund offers two classes of shares effective 5/16/96, Investor and Advisor. Advisor Shares are offered through intermediaries and have higher expenses. Information here represents Investor Shares. All shares existing prior to that date were converted to Investor Shares.
Minimum purchase: Initial: $10,000, Subsequent: $2,500; IRA: Initial: $2,000
Discount broker availability: *White
Qualified for sale in: All states except AZ, HI, KY, MD, MA, MI, MN, NH, NM, TN, TX, VT
Dividends paid: Income - annually; Capital gains - annually
Management fee: 0.50% first $100M to 0.35% over $250M
Portfolio turnover (3 yrs): 34%, 59%, 93%
Administration fee: 0.25% of first $100M to 0.175% in excess of $250M
Expense ratio: 1.49% (year ending 5/31/97) (1.87% without waiver)

SCHRODER SERIES TRUST FUNDS ◆

(Series changed name from The Wertheim Funds 3/1/97).Data common to all Schroder Series funds are shown below. See subsequent listings for data specific to individual funds.)

787 Seventh Avenue
New York, NY 10019
800-464-3108, 212-641-3900

Adviser: Schroder Capital Management, Inc.
Transfer agent: Boston Financial Data Services, Inc.
Minimum purchase: Initial: $25,000 (total among all funds), Subsequent: $1,000
Wire orders accepted: Yes
Deadline for same day wire purchase: 4 P.M.
Qualified for sale in: All states except AR, AZ, IN, MN, MO, OH, SD, TX ,WI
Wire redemptions: Yes, $1,000 minimum
Letter redemptions: Signature guarantee required
Shareholder services: IRA, automatic investment plan
IRA fees: Annual: $12 per social security number

SCHRODER SERIES - HIGH YIELD INCOME FUND ◆

(Fund liquidated 7/8/97)

SCHRODER SERIES - INVESTMENT GRADE INCOME FUND ◆

(See first Schroder Series listing for data common to all funds)

Portfolio manager: Gary S. Zeltzer (1994)
Investment objective and policies: Current income consistent with capital preservation; capital growth secondary. Invests primarily in investment grade U.S. Government and corporate debt securities. The dollar-weighted average maturity of the fund varies from relatively short (under five years) to relatively long (more than ten years) depending on the interest rate outlook. May invest in securities of foreign issuers without limit, and use futures and options in an effort to enhance return and for hedging purposes.
Year organized: 1994 (name changed from Wertheim Investment Grade Income 3/1/97)
Ticker symbol: WSIGX
Discount broker availability: White
Dividends paid: Income - monthly; Capital gains - December
Portfolio turnover (3 yrs): 69%, 114%, 156%
Management fee: 0.50%
Expense ratio: 1.32% (year ending 10/31/97)

SCHRODER SERIES - LARGE CAP EQUITY FUND ◆

(See first Schroder Series listing for data common to all funds)

Portfolio manager: Paul Morris (1997)
Investment objective and policies: Long-term capital growth. Invests primarily in common and preferred stocks of undervalued companies with above average long-term growth potential. May invest in securities of foreign issuers without limit, and use futures and options in an effort to enhance return and for hedging purposes.
Year organized: 1994 (name changed from Equity Value 3/1/97)
Ticker symbol: WEQVX
Discount broker availability: White
Dividends paid: Income - December; Capital gains - December
Portfolio turnover (3 yrs): 56%, 83%, 103%
Management fee: 0.75%
Expense ratio: 1.21% (year ending 10/31/97)

SCHRODER SERIES - SHORT-TERM INVESTMENT FUND ◆

(See first Schroder Series listing for data common to all funds)

Portfolio manager: Gary S. Zeltzer (1994)
Investment objective and policies: High current income consistent with preservation of capital and liquidity. Invests primarily in investment grade U.S. Government and corporate debt securities with remaining maturities of three years or less, and maintains a dollar-weighted average maturity of one year or less. May invest in securities of foreign issuers without limit, and use futures and options in an effort to enhance return and for hedging purposes.
Year organized: 1994 (name changed from Wertheim Short-Term Investment 3/1/97)
Ticker symbol: WSTFX
Discount broker availability: White
Dividends paid: Income - declared daily, paid monthly; Capital gains - December
Portfolio turnover (3 yrs): 155%, 28%, 71%
Management fee: 0.40%
Expense ratio: 1.05% (year ending 10/31/97)

SCHRODER SERIES - SMALL CAPITALIZATION VALUE FUND ◆

(See first Schroder Series listing for data common to all funds)

Portfolio manager: Nancy B. Tooke (1994)
Investment objective and policies: Long-term capital growth. Invests primarily in common and preferred stocks of companies with market capitalizations under $1B believed to have above average long-term growth potential. May invest in securities of foreign issuers without limit, and use futures and options in an effort to enhance return and for hedging purposes.
Year organized: 1994 (name changed from Wertheim Small Cap Value 3/1/97)
Ticker symbol: WSCVX
Discount broker availability: White
Dividends paid: Income - December; Capital gains - December
Portfolio turnover (3 yrs): 82%, 46%, 19%
Management fee: 0.95%
Expense ratio: 1.32% (year ending 10/31/97)

SCHWAB FUNDS ◆

(Data common to all Schwab funds are shown below. See subsequent listings for data specific to individual funds.)

101 Montgomery Street
San Francisco, CA 94104
800-266-5623, 800-435-4000
415-627-7000, TDD 800-345-2550
Internet: http://www.schwab.com/funds

Shareholder service hours: Full service: 7 days, 24 hours
Adviser: Charles Schwab Investment Management, Inc.
Transfer agent: Charles Schwab & Co., Inc.

Special sales restrictions: Schwab has introduced multiple 'no-load' share classes for several of their funds; previously existing shares are now called "Investor" shares, and can still be purchased at old minimums. New "Select" shares are offered with minimum investments of $50,000, minimum balances of $40,000, and additional investment minimums of $1,000. The higher minimum shares come with lower expenses: .15% lower shareholder services fees, and some other waivers resulting in lower annual costs of 0.11% to about 0.26%. Those funds with Select shares available are noted. Costs shown are for Investor shares.
Minimum purchase: Initial: $1,000, Subsequent: $100; IRA/Keogh: Initial: $500 (exceptions noted)
Wire orders accepted: Yes
Deadline for same day wire purchase: 4 P.M.
Discount broker availability: *Schwab
Qualified for sale in: All states (except California and New York funds)
Telephone redemptions: Yes
Wire redemptions: Yes, $25 fee ($15 for MM funds) (exception noted)
Letter redemptions: Signature guarantee not required
Telephone switching: With the same share class of other Schwab funds and any mutual fund offered in the Schwab Mutual Fund Marketplace. No charge to other Schwab funds, regular Schwab transaction fees to non-Schwab funds.
Number of switches permitted: Unlimited
Maintenance fees: $7.50 per quarter for Schwab brokerage accounts. Waived if there has been at least one commissionable trade within the last six months, or the shareholder's combined balances exceed $10,000. $5 per month for Schwab One accounts. Waived if there has been at least two commissionable trades within the last twelve months, or the account balance exceeds $5,000. (Additional fees or variations noted)
Shareholder services: IRA, SEP-IRA, Keogh, 401(k), 403(b), corporate retirement plans, automatic investment plan, electronic funds transfer (purchase only)
IRA fees: Annual $29 (one fee regardless of number of funds held, waived for IRA accounts with assets of $10,000 or more)
Keogh fees: Annual $45 (one fee regardless of number of funds held, waived for accounts with assets of $10,000 or more)

SCHWAB ANALYTICS FUND ◆

(See first Schwab listing for data common to all funds)

Sub-adviser: Symphony Asset Management, Inc. (a wholly-owned subsidiary of BARRA, Inc.)
Portfolio managers: Geri Hom (1996), Praveen K. Gottipalli (1996)
Investment objective and policies: Maximum long-term capital growth producing an aggregate total return exceeding that of the S&P 500 Index over time. Invests in stocks of medium- and large-capitalization U.S. companies; those with capitalization above $500M. Utilizing quantitative techniques, proprietary software models and real time databases to structure and manage the portfolio, fund will apply three major sets of criteria to rank companies: stock price momentum and price/earnings ratio, reports of securities analysts whose recommendations historically have correlated most closely with a stock's actual performance, and unusual selling patterns by major company executives and shareholders. Portfolio will then be balanced to seek industry diversification similar to that of the S&P 500.
Year organized: 1996
Ticker symbol: SWANX
Dividends paid: Income - annually; Capital gains - annually
Portfolio turnover (1 yr): 120%
Shareholder services fee: 0.20%
Management fee: 0.74% first $1B to 0.64% over $2B
Expense ratio: 0.74% (year ending 10/31/97) (1.15% without waiver)

SCHWAB ASSET DIRECTOR - BALANCED GROWTH FUND ◆

(See first Schwab listing for data common to all funds)

Portfolio managers: Geri Hom (1995), Stephen B. Ward (1995), Kimon Daifotis (1997)
Investment objective and policies: Maximum total return: capital growth and income Invests in a diversified

mix of stocks (50% to 70% of assets), bonds (25% to 45%) and cash equivalents (0% to 25%) with the allocation adjusted to reflect perceived changes in market and economic conditions. The target mix is 60% stocks (30% large company, 15% small company and 15% international), 35% bonds and 5% cash equivalents. May use stock and index futures and options thereon, and engage in foreign currency exchange transactions for hedging purposes.
Year organized: 1995
Ticker symbol: SWBGX
Dividends paid: Income - December; Capital gains - December
Portfolio turnover (2 yrs): 104%, 44%
Shareholder services fee: 0.20%
Management fee: 0.74% first $1B to 0.64% over $2B
Expense ratio: 0.78% (year ending 10/31/97) (1.30% without waiver)

SCHWAB ASSET DIRECTOR - CONSERVATIVE GROWTH FUND ◆
(See first Schwab listing for data common to all funds)

Portfolio managers: Geri Hom (1995), Stephen B. Ward (1995), Kimon Daifotis (1997)
Investment objective and policies: Maximum total return: capital growth and income Invests in a diversified mix of stocks (30% to 50% of assets), bonds (45% to 65%) and cash equivalents (0% to 25%) with the allocation adjusted to reflect perceived changes in market and economic conditions. The target mix is 40% stocks (20% large company, 10% small company and 10% international), 55% bonds and 5% cash equivalents. May use stock and index futures and options thereon, and engage in foreign currency exchange transactions for hedging purposes.
Year organized: 1995
Ticker symbol: SWCGX
Dividends paid: Income - March, June, September, December; Capital gains - December
Portfolio turnover (2 yrs): 104%, 64%
Shareholder services fee: 0.20%
Management fee: 0.74% first $1B to 0.64% over $2B
Expense ratio: 0.81% (year ending 10/31/97) (1.65% without waiver)

SCHWAB ASSET DIRECTOR - HIGH GROWTH FUND ◆
(See first Schwab listing for data common to all funds)

Portfolio managers: Geri Hom (1995), Stephen B. Ward (1995), Kimon Daifotis (1997)
Investment objective and policies: Maximum total return: capital growth and income Invests in a diversified mix of stocks (65% to 95% of assets), bonds (0% to 30%) and cash equivalents (0% to 35%) with the allocation adjusted to reflect perceived changes in market and economic conditions. The target mix is 80% stocks (40% large company, 20% small company and 20% international), 15% bonds and 5% cash equivalents. May use stock and index futures and options thereon, and engage in foreign currency exchange transactions for hedging purposes.
Year organized: 1995
Ticker symbol: SWHGX
Dividends paid: Income - December; Capital gains - December
Portfolio turnover (2 yrs): 113%, 46%
Shareholder services fee: 0.20%
Management fee: 0.74% first $1B to 0.64% over $2B
Expense ratio: 0.75% (year ending 10/31/97) (1.24% without waiver)

SCHWAB CALIFORNIA LONG-TERM TAX-FREE BOND FUND ◆
(See first Schwab listing for data common to all funds)

Portfolio managers: Joanne Larkin (1992), Stephen B. Ward (1993)
Investment objective and policies: Current income exempt from federal and California personal income taxes, consistent with capital preservation. Invests at least 80% of assets in investment grade debt securities issued by or on behalf of the State of California, its

political subdivisions, agencies or authorities. Portfolio maintains a dollar-weighted average maturity of ten years or longer. Up to 20% of assets may be in securities subject to AMT tax treatment.
Year organized: 1992 (name changed from Schwab California Tax-Free Bond Fund on 4/21/93)
Ticker symbol: SWCAX
Qualified for sale in: CA, IL
Dividends paid: Income - declared daily, paid monthly; Capital gains - December
Portfolio turnover (3 yrs): 35%, 36%, 46%
Shareholder services fee: 0.20%
Management fee: 0.41%
Expense ratio: 0.49% (year ending 8/31/97) (0.82% without waiver)

SCHWAB CALIFORNIA MUNICIPAL MONEY FUND - SWEEP SHARES ◆
(See first Schwab listing for data common to all funds)

Portfolio manager: Charles Soulis (1997)
Investment objective and policies: Maximum current income exempt from federal and California personal income taxes, consistent with stability of capital and liquidity. Invests in a diversified portfolio of California municipal money market securities.
Year organized: 1990 (name changed from Schwab California Tax-Free Money Fund on 4/21/93; changed from CA Tax-Exempt Money Fund 1/2/97)
Ticker symbol: SWCXX
Qualified for sale in: CA, IL
Dividends paid: Income - declared daily, paid monthly
Shareholder services fee: 0.45%
Management fee: 0.46% first $1B to 0.40% over $2B
Expense ratio: 0.65% (year ending 12/31/97) (0.91% without waiver)

SCHWAB CALIFORNIA MUNICIPAL MONEY FUND - VALUE ADVANTAGE SHARES ◆
(See first Schwab listing for data common to all funds)

Portfolio manager: Charles Soulis (1997)
Investment objective and policies: Maximum current income exempt from federal and California personal income taxes, consistent with stability of capital and liquidity. Invests in a diversified portfolio of California municipal money market securities. Designed to deliver extra high yields for long-term buy and hold investors by maintaining a lower than average expense ratio.
Year organized: 1995 (name changed from CA Tax-Exempt Money Fund 1/2/97)
Ticker symbol: SWKXX
Minimum purchase: Initial: $25,000, Subsequent: $5,000
Qualified for sale in: CA, IL
Administrative fee: $5 for redemptions or exchanges of less than $5,000
Dividends paid: Income - declared daily, paid monthly
Shareholder services fee: 0.25%
Low balance fee: $5 per month if account balance is less than $20,000
Management fee: 0.46% first $1B to 0.40% over $2B
Expense ratio: 0.45% (year ending 12/31/97) (0.72% without waiver)

SCHWAB CALIFORNIA SHORT/INTERMEDIATE TAX-FREE BOND FUND ◆
(See first Schwab listing for data common to all funds)

Portfolio managers: Joanne Larkin (1993), Stephen B. Ward (1993)
Investment objective and policies: Current income exempt from federal and California personal income taxes, consistent with capital preservation. Invests at least 80% of assets in investment grade debt securities issued by or on behalf of the state of California, its political subdivisions, agencies and instrumentalities. Portfolio maintains a dollar-weighted average maturity of two to five years. Up to 20% of assets may be in securities subject to AMT tax treatment.

Year organized: 1993
Ticker symbol: SWCSX
Qualified for sale in: CA, IL
Dividends paid: Income - declared daily, paid monthly; Capital gains - December
Portfolio turnover (3 yrs): 23%, 20%, 62%
Shareholder services fee: 0.20%
Management fee: 0.41%
Expense ratio: 0.49% (year ending 8/31/97) (0.89% without waiver)

SCHWAB FLORIDA MUNICIPAL MONEY FUND - SWEEP SHARES ◆
(See first Schwab listing for data common to all funds)

Investment objective and policies: Maximum current income exempt from federal personal income tax, and, to the extent possible, from the Florida intangibles tax, consistent with stability of capital and liquidity. Invests in a diversified portfolio of Florida municipal money market securities.
Year organized: 1998
Qualified for sale in: FL
Dividends paid: Income - declared daily, paid monthly
Shareholder services fee: 0.45%
Management fee: 0.46% first $1B to 0.40% over $2B

SCHWAB GOVERNMENT MONEY FUND ◆
(See first Schwab listing for data common to all funds)

Portfolio manager: Amy Treanor (1997)
Investment objective and policies: Maximum current income consistent with stability of capital. Invests exclusively in U.S. Government money market obligations.
Year organized: 1990 (name changed from Schwab Government Securities Fund in 1993)
Ticker symbol: SWGXX
Dividends paid: Income - declared daily, paid monthly
Shareholder services fee: 0.45%
Management fee: 0.46% first $1B to 0.40% over $2B
Expense ratio: 0.75% (year ending 12/31/97) (0.92% without waiver)

SCHWAB INSTITUTIONAL ADVANTAGE MONEY FUND ◆
(See first Schwab listing for data common to all funds)

Investment objective and policies: Maximum current income consistent with stability of capital and liquidity. Invests in U.S. dollar-denominated money market instruments.
Special sales restrictions: Designed for retirement plans, plan participants and other institutional investors for investment of their own funds or funds for which they act in a fiduciary, agency or custodial capacity, but open to all investors.
Year organized: 1994
Ticker symbol: SWIXX
Minimum purchase: Initial: $25,000, Subsequent: $1
Dividends paid: Income - declared daily, paid monthly
Shareholder services fee: 0.25%
Management fee: 0.46% first $2B to 0.34% over $20B
Expense ratio: 0.50% (year ending 12/31/96) (0.88% without waiver)

SCHWAB INTERNATIONAL INDEX FUND ◆
(See first Schwab listing for data common to all funds)

Portfolio managers: Geri Hom (1995), Stephen B. Ward (1995)
Investment objective and policies: To match the total return of the Schwab International Index, an index created by Schwab to represent the performance of equity securities issued by large, publicly traded companies from countries around the world with major developed securities markets, excluding the U.S. Fund invests sub-

stantially all its assets in the roughly 350 stocks comprising the Index in approximately the same proportion as they are represented in the Index. Fund will not be automatically re-balanced to reflect changes in the index. May use stock and index futures and options thereon, and engage in foreign currency exchange transactions for hedging purposes.
Year organized: 1993
Ticker symbol: SWINX
Special sales information: Select shares available as noted above.
Redemption fee: 0.75% for shares held less than six months, payable to the fund
Dividends paid: Income - December; Capital gains - December
Portfolio turnover (3 yrs): 13%, 6%, 0%
Shareholder services fee: 0.20% (0.05% for Select Shares)
Management fee: 0.70% first $300M, 0.60% over $300M
Expense ratio: 0.61% (year ending 10/31/97) (1.13% without waiver)

SCHWAB LONG-TERM TAX-FREE BOND FUND ◆
(See first Schwab listing for data common to all funds)

Portfolio managers: Joanne Larkin (1992), Stephen B. Ward (1992)
Investment objective and policies: High level of current income exempt from federal income tax, consistent with capital preservation. Invests at least 80% of assets in investment grade debt securities issued by or on behalf of states, territories and possessions of the U.S. and their political subdivisions, agencies and instrumentalities. Portfolio maintains a dollar-weighted average maturity of more than ten years. Fund is non-diversified and may invest up to 25% of assets in obligations of a single issuer.
Year organized: 1992 (name changed from Schwab National Tax-Free Bond Fund on 4/21/93)
Ticker symbol: SWNTX
Dividends paid: Income - declared daily, paid monthly; Capital gains - December
Portfolio turnover (3 yrs): 61%, 50%, 70%
Shareholder services fee: 0.25%
Management fee: 0.41%
Expense ratio: 0.49% (year ending 8/31/97) (1.02% without waiver)

SCHWAB MONEY MARKET FUND ◆
(See first Schwab listing for data common to all funds)

Portfolio manager: Linda Klingman (1990)
Investment objective and policies: Maximum current income consistent with stability of capital and liquidity. Invests in U.S. dollar-denominated money market instruments.
Year organized: 1990
Ticker symbol: SWMXX
Dividends paid: Income - declared daily, paid monthly
Shareholder services fee: 0.45%
Management fee: 0.46% first $1B to 0.34% over $20B
Expense ratio: 0.75% (year ending 12/31/97) (0.87% without waiver)

SCHWAB MUNICIPAL MONEY FUND - SWEEP SHARES ◆
(See first Schwab listing for data common to all funds)

Portfolio manager: Walter Beveridge (1992)
Investment objective and policies: Maximum current income exempt from federal income tax, consistent with stability of capital and liquidity. Invests in municipal money market securities.
Year organized: 1990 (name changed from Tax-Exempt Money Fund 1/2/97)
Ticker symbol: SWXXX
Dividends paid: Income - declared daily, paid monthly
Shareholder services fee: 0.45%
Management fee: 0.46% first $1B to 0.40% over $2B
Expense ratio: 0.66% (year ending 12/31/97) (0.90% without waiver)

SCHWAB MUNICIPAL MONEY FUND - VALUE ADVANTAGE SHARES ◆
(See first Schwab listing for data common to all funds)

Portfolio manager: Walter Beveridge (1995)
Investment objective and policies: Maximum current income exempt from federal income taxes, consistent with stability of capital and liquidity. Invests in municipal money market securities. Designed to deliver extra high yields for long-term buy and hold investors by maintaining a lower than average expense ratio.
Year organized: 1995 (name changed from Tax-Exempt Money Fund 1/2/97)
Ticker symbol: SWTXX
Minimum purchase: Initial: $25,000, Subsequent: $5,000
Administrative fee: $5 for redemptions or exchanges of less than $5,000
Dividends paid: Income - declared daily, paid monthly
Low balance fee: $5 per month if account balance is less than $20,000
Shareholder services fee: 0.25%
Management fee: 0.46% first $1B to 0.40% over $2B
Expense ratio: 0.45% (year ending 12/31/97) (0.72% without waiver)

SCHWAB NEW JERSEY MUNICIPAL MONEY FUND - SWEEP SHARES ◆
(See first Schwab listing for data common to all funds)

Investment objective and policies: Maximum current income exempt from federal and New Jersey state personal income taxes, consistent with stability of capital and liquidity. Invests in a diversified portfolio of New Jersey municipal money market securities.
Year organized: 1998
Dividends paid: Income - declared daily, paid monthly
Shareholder services fee: 0.45%
Management fee: 0.46% first $1B to 0.40% over $2B

SCHWAB NEW YORK MUNICIPAL MONEY FUND - SWEEP SHARES ◆
(See first Schwab listing for data common to all funds)

Portfolio manager: Charles Soulis (1997)
Investment objective and policies: Maximum current income exempt from federal, NY State and NY City personal income taxes, consistent with stability of capital and liquidity. Invests in a diversified portfolio of New York municipal money market securities.
Year organized: 1995 (name changed from NY Tax-Exempt Money Fund 1/2/97)
Ticker symbol: SWNXX
Dividends paid: Income - declared daily, paid monthly
Shareholder services fee: 0.45%
Management fee: 0.46% first $1B to 0.40% over $2B
Expense ratio: 0.69% (year ending 12/31/97) (1.02% without waiver)

SCHWAB NEW YORK MUNICIPAL MONEY FUND - VALUE ADVANTAGE SHARES ◆
(See first Schwab listing for data common to all funds)

Portfolio manager: Charles Soulis (1997)
Investment objective and policies: Maximum current income exempt from federal, NY State and NY City personal income taxes, consistent with stability of capital and liquidity. Invests in a diversified portfolio of New York municipal money market securities. Designed to deliver extra high yields for long-term buy and hold investors by maintaining a lower than average expense ratio.
Year organized: 1995 (name changed from NY Tax-Exempt Money Fund 1/2/97)
Ticker symbol: SWYXX
Minimum purchase: Initial: $25,000, Subsequent: $5,000
Qualified for sale in: NY
Administrative fee: $5 for redemptions or exchanges of less than $5,000

Dividends paid: Income - declared daily, paid monthly
Shareholder services fee: 0.25%
Low balance fee: $5 per month if account balance is less than $20,000
Management fee: 0.46% first $1B to 0.40% over $2B
Expense ratio: 0.45% (year ending 12/31/97) (0.85% without waiver)

SCHWAB 1000 FUND ◆
(See first Schwab listing for data common to all funds)

Portfolio managers: Geri Hom (1995), Stephen B. Ward (1995)
Investment objective and policies: To match the total return of the Schwab 1000 index, an index created by Schwab which represents the top 1,000 U.S. companies, about 90% of U.S. stocks. Fund will not be automatically re-balanced to reflect changes in the index. Portfolio is managed for maximum tax efficiency, and has thus far never paid out a capital gain. Fund may purchase shares of other mutual funds and use stock and index futures and options thereon for hedging purposes.
Year organized: 1991
Ticker symbol: SNXFX
Special sales information: Select shares available as noted above.
Redemption fee: 0.50% for shares held less than six months, payable to the fund
Dividends paid: Income - December; Capital gains - December
Portfolio turnover (3 yrs): 2%, 2%, 2%
Shareholder services fee: 0.20% (0.05% for Select Shares)
Management fee: 0.30% of first $500M, 0.22% over $500M
Expense ratio: 0.46% (year ending 10/31/97) (0.50% without waiver)

SCHWAB ONESOURCE PORTFOLIO - BALANCED ALLOCATION FUND ◆
(See first Schwab listing for data common to all funds)

Portfolio managers: Cynthia Liu (1996), Stephen B. Ward (1996)
Investment objective and policies: Total return: capital growth and current income, with less volatility than the Growth Fund. Invests in a diversified, asset-allocated portfolio of other domestic and international mutual funds; neutral allocation mix is 60% stock, 35% bond and 5% money market funds, with defined ranges of 50% to 70% stock, 25% to 45% bond and 0% to 25% money market funds. Selection of the underlying funds is based on quantifiable variables such as historic total returns, volatility, expenses and size; fund focuses almost exclusively on funds available through the Schwab OneSource discount brokerage accounts.
Year organized: 1996
Ticker symbol: SWOBX
Dividends paid: Income - December; Capital gains - December
Shareholder services fee: 0.25% (not currently imposed)
Management fee: 0.74% of first $1B to 0.64% over $2B

SCHWAB ONESOURCE PORTFOLIO - GROWTH ALLOCATION FUND ◆
(See first Schwab listing for data common to all funds)

Portfolio managers: Cynthia Liu (1996), Stephen B. Ward (1996)
Investment objective and policies: Total return: capital growth and current income, with less volatility than with a portfolio comprised entirely of stock funds. Invests in a diversified, asset-allocated portfolio of other domestic and international mutual funds; neutral allocation mix is 80% stock, 15% bond and 5% money market funds, with defined ranges of 65% to 95% stock, 0% to 30% bond and 0% to 35% money market funds. Selection of the underlying funds is based on quantifiable variables such as historic total returns, volatility, expenses and size; fund focuses almost exclusively on funds available through the

Schwab OneSource discount brokerage accounts.
Year organized: 1996
Ticker symbol: SWOGX
Dividends paid: Income - December; Capital gains - December
Shareholder services fee: 0.25% (not currently imposed)
Management fee: 0.74% of first $1B to 0.64% over $2B

SCHWAB ONESOURCE PORTFOLIO - INTERNATIONAL FUND ◆
(See first Schwab listing for data common to all funds)

Portfolio managers: Cynthia Liu (1996), Stephen B. Ward (1996)
Investment objective and policies: Long-term capital appreciation. Invests in a diversified portfolio of international equity mutual funds. Selection of the underlying funds is based on quantifiable variables such as historic total returns, volatility, expenses and size; fund focuses almost exclusively on funds available through the Schwab OneSource discount brokerage accounts.
Year organized: 1996
Ticker symbol: SWOIX
Dividends paid: Income - December; Capital gains - December
Shareholder services fee: 0.25% (not currently imposed)
Management fee: 0.74% of first $1B to 0.64% over $2B

SCHWAB ONESOURCE PORTFOLIO - SMALL COMPANY FUND ◆
(See first Schwab listing for data common to all funds)

Portfolio managers: Cynthia Liu (1997), Stephen B. Ward (1997)
Investment objective and policies: Long-term capital appreciation. Invests in a diversified portfolio of small company equity funds. Selection of the underlying funds is based on quantifiable variables such as historic total returns, volatility, expenses and size; fund focuses almost exclusively on funds available through the Schwab OneSource discount brokerage accounts.
Year organized: 1997
Dividends paid: Income - December; Capital gains - December
Shareholder services fee: 0.25% (not currently imposed)
Management fee: 0.74% of first $1B to 0.64% over $2B

SCHWAB PENNSYLVANIA MUNICIPAL MONEY FUND - SWEEP SHARES ◆
(See first Schwab listing for data common to all funds)

Investment objective and policies: Maximum current income exempt from federal and Pennsylvania state personal income taxes, consistent with stability of capital and liquidity. Invests in a diversified portfolio of Pennsylvania municipal money market securities.
Year organized: 1998
Dividends paid: Income - declared daily, paid monthly
Shareholder services fee: 0.45%
Management fee: 0.46% first $1B to 0.40% over $2B

SCHWAB RETIREMENT MONEY FUND ◆
(See first Schwab listing for data common to all funds)

Portfolio managers: Linda Klingman (1994), Stephen B. Ward (1994)
Investment objective and policies: Maximum current income consistent with stability of capital and liquidity. Invests in money market instruments.
Special sales restrictions: Designed for retirement plans, plan participants and other institutional investors for investment of their own funds or funds for which they act in a fiduciary, agency or custodial capacity, but open to all investors.

Year organized: 1994
Ticker symbol: SWRXX
Minimum purchase: Initial: $1, Subsequent: $1
Dividends paid: Income - declared daily, paid monthly
Shareholder services fee: 0.25%
Management fee: 0.46% first $1B to 0.34% over $20B
Expense ratio: 0.73% (year ending 12/31/96) (0.88% without waiver)

SCHWAB S&P 500 FUND - E SHARES ◆
(See first Schwab listing for data common to all funds)

Portfolio managers: Geri Hom (1996), Stephen B. Ward (1996)
Investment objective and policies: Seeks to track the price and dividend performance of common stocks of U.S. companies as represented by the Standard & Poor's Composite Index of 500 Stocks. Invests primarily in equity securities of companies composing the Index. Fund is not actively managed; invests to track the index, however it does not re-balance the portfolio automatically; fund sells the highest tax cost securities first to minimize current realized capital gains, and trades only in round lots or large blocks of stocks to minimize expenses. May use options and futures to adjust its correlation to the Index.
Year organized: 1996
Ticker symbol: SWPEX
Special sales restrictions: Only available to clients of Schwab Institutional and the Trust Company, and to certain tax-advantaged retirement plans that can communicate with Schwab through SchwabLink. Transactions are not available by telephone, by wire, by mail or in person.
Dividends paid: Income - December; Capital gains - December
Portfolio turnover (1 yr): 3%
Shareholder services fee: 0.05%
Management fee: 0.36% first $1B to 0.31% over $3B
Expense ratio: 0.28% (year ending 10/31/97) (0.68% without waiver)

SCHWAB S&P 500 FUND - INVESTOR SHARES ◆
(See first Schwab listing for data common to all funds)

Portfolio managers: Geri Hom (1996), Stephen B. Ward (1996)
Investment objective and policies: Seeks to track the price and dividend performance of common stocks of U.S. companies as represented by the Standard & Poor's Composite Index of 500 Stocks. Invests primarily in equity securities of companies composing the Index. Fund is not actively managed; invests to track the index, however it does not re-balance the portfolio automatically; fund sells the highest tax cost securities first to minimize current realized capital gains, and trades only in round lots or large blocks of stocks to minimize expenses. May use options and futures to adjust its correlation to the Index.
Year organized: 1996
Ticker symbol: SWPEX
Special sales information: Select shares available as noted above.
Dividends paid: Income - December; Capital gains - December
Portfolio turnover (1 yr): 3%
Shareholder services fee: 0.20% (0.05% for Select Shares)
Management fee: 0.36% first $1B to 0.31% over $3B
Expense ratio: 0.38% (year ending 10/31/97) (0.70% without waiver)

SCHWAB SHORT/INTERMEDIATE TAX-FREE BOND FUND ◆
(See first Schwab listing for data common to all funds)

Portfolio managers: Joanne Larkin (1993), Stephen B. Ward (1993)
Investment objective and policies: High level of current income exempt from federal income tax, consistent with capital preservation. Invests at least 80% of assets in debt securities issued by or on behalf of

states, territories and possessions of the U.S. and their political subdivisions, agencies and instrumentalities. Portfolio maintains an average dollar-weighted maturity of two to five years. Fund is non-diversified and may invest up to 25% of assets in obligations of a single issuer.
Year organized: 1993
Ticker symbol: SWITX
Dividends paid: Income - declared daily, paid monthly; Capital gains - December
Portfolio turnover (3 yrs): 20%, 44%, 35%
Shareholder services fee: 0.20%
Management fee: 0.41%
Expense ratio: 0.49% (year ending 8/31/97) (0.96% without waiver)

SCHWAB SHORT-TERM BOND MARKET INDEX FUND ◆
(See first Schwab listing for data common to all funds)

Portfolio managers: Stephen B. Ward (1993), Kimon Daifotis (1997)
Investment objective and policies: High level of current income tracking the performance of the Lehman Brothers Mutual Fund Short (1-5) Government Corporate Index, consistent with capital preservation. Invests at least 80% of assets in the securities that make up the Index, a market-weighted index of investment grade debt securities with maturities ranging from one to five years, in an effort to achieve a correlation of 0.90 or better. May use options and futures and swap agreements for hedging purposes.
Year organized: 1991 (name changed from U.S. Government Bond Fund (Short/Intermediate Term) in 1993; name and objective changed from Short/Inter Govt. Bond Fund 11/1/97. Past performance may be irrelevant.)
Ticker symbol: SWBDX
Dividends paid: Income - declared daily, paid monthly; Capital gains - December
Portfolio turnover (3 yrs): 71%, 80%, 203%
Shareholder services fee: 0.20%
Management fee: 0.41%
Expense ratio: 0.49% (year ending 8/31/97) (0.82% without waiver)

SCHWAB SMALL-CAP INDEX FUND ◆
(See first Schwab listing for data common to all funds)

Portfolio managers: Geri Hom (1996), Stephen B. Ward (1993)
Investment objective and policies: To match the total return of the Schwab Small-Cap Index, an index created by Schwab to represent the performance of equity securities of small capitalization companies, as represented by the second 1,000 publicly traded companies listed in the U.S. Fund invests substantially all its assets in the stocks comprising the Index, in about the same weightings. May use stock and index futures and options thereon, and engage in foreign currency exchange transactions for hedging purposes.
Year organized: 1993
Ticker symbol: SWSMX
Special sales information: Select shares available as noted above.
Redemption fee: 0.50% for shares held less than six months, payable to the fund
Dividends paid: Income - December; Capital gains - December
Portfolio turnover (3 yrs): 23%, 23%, 24%
Shareholder services fee: 0.20% (0.05% for Select Shares)
Management fee: 0.50% first $300M, 0.45% over $300M
Expense ratio: 0.52% (year ending 10/31/97) (0.89% without waiver)

SCHWAB TOTAL BOND MARKET INDEX FUND ◆
(See first Schwab listing for data common to all funds)

Portfolio managers: Stephen B. Ward (1993), Kimon Daifotis (1997)
Investment objective and policies: High level of current income tracking the performance of the Lehman Brothers Aggregate Bond Index, consistent with capital preservation. Invests at least 80% of assets in the securi-

ties that make up the Index, a comprehensive market-weighted index of all investment grade debt securities with maturities greater than one year, in an effort to achieve a correlation of 0.9 or better. Securities must have a par amount outstanding of at least $100M, and be publicly traded. May use options and futures and swap agreements for hedging purposes.
Year organized: 1993 (name and objective changed from Long-Term Govt. Bond Fund 11/1/97. Past performance may be irrelevant.)
Ticker symbol: SWLBX
Dividends paid: Income - declared daily, paid monthly; Capital gains - December
Portfolio turnover (3 yrs): 51%, 66%, 240%
Shareholder services fee: 0.20%
Management fee: 0.41%
Expense ratio: 0.20% (year ending 8/31/97) (1.18% without waiver)

SCHWAB U.S. TREASURY MONEY FUND ◆
(See first Schwab listing for data common to all funds)

Portfolio manager: Amy Treanor (1997)
Investment objective and policies: High current income consistent with stability of capital and liquidity. Invests exclusively in U.S. Treasury notes, bills, and other direct obligations of the U.S. Treasury which mature in 13 months or less.
Year organized: 1991
Ticker symbol: SWUXX
Dividends paid: Income - declared daily, paid monthly
Shareholder services fee: 0.45%
Management fee: 0.46% first $1B to 0.40% over $2B
Expense ratio: 0.65% (year ending 12/31/97) (0.93% without waiver)

SCHWAB VALUE ADVANTAGE MONEY FUND ◆
(See first Schwab listing for data common to all funds)

Portfolio managers: Linda Klingman (1992), Stephen B. Ward (1992)
Investment objective and policies: Maximum current income consistent with stability of capital and liquidity. Invests in money market instruments. Designed to deliver extra high yields for long-term buy and hold investors by maintaining a lower than average expense ratio.
Year organized: 1992
Ticker symbol: SWVXX
Minimum purchase: Initial: $25,000, Subsequent: $5,000; IRA/Keogh: Initial: $15,000, Subsequent $2,000
Administration fee: $5 for redemptions or exchanges of less than $5,000
Dividends paid: Income - declared daily, paid monthly
Low balance fee: $5 per month if account balance is less than $20,000 ($15,000 for retirement accounts)
Shareholder services fee: 0.25%
Management fee: 0.46% first $1B to 0.34% over $20B
Expense ratio: 0.40% (year ending 12/31/96) (0.70% without waiver)

SCHWARTZ VALUE FUND ◆
3707 W. Maple Road
Bloomfield Hills, MI 48301
800-543-0407
248-644-8500, fax 248-644-4250

Adviser: Schwartz Investment Counsel, Inc.
Portfolio manager: George P. Schwartz (1993)
Transfer agent and administrator: Countrywide Fund Services, Inc.
Investment objective and policies: Long-term capital appreciation; income incidental. Invests primarily in common stocks perceived to be undervalued and chosen through fundamental analysis. May have substantial holdings in small capitalization companies, and may invest up to 10% of assets in unseasoned companies. May invest up to 15% of assets in foreign issues through ADRs, and up to 10% of asset in other investment companies.

Year organized: 1993 (name changed from The RCM Fund on 9/2/94)
Ticker symbol: RCMFX
Minimum purchase: Initial: $25,000, Subsequent: None
Wire orders accepted: Yes
Deadline for same day wire purchase: 4 P.M.
Discount broker availability: Schwab
Qualified for sale in: DC, FL, IL, MI, NY, OH
Wire redemptions: Yes
Letter redemptions: Signature guarantee required over $5,000
Dividends paid: Income - December; Capital gains - December
Portfolio turnover (3 yrs): 47%, 50%, 70%
Management fee: 1.50% first $75M to 1.00% over $100M
Administration fee: 0.22% first $25M to 0.15% over $100M
Expense ratio: 1.91% (year ending 12/31/97)

SCM PORTFOLIO FUND ◆
119 Maple Street
P.O. Box 947
Carrollton, GA 30117
770-834-5839

Adviser: SCM Associates, Inc.
Portfolio manager: Stephen C. McCutcheon (1988)
Transfer agent: SCM Associates, Inc.
Investment objective and policies: Total return: combination of capital appreciation and income consistent with preservation of principal. Invests in common stocks, bonds, money market funds, U.S. Government securities, CDs, and shares of other mutual funds. Fund allocates assets to generate real growth during favorable investment periods and emphasizes income and capital preservation during uncertain investment periods.
Year organized: 1988
Minimum purchase: Initial: $2,500, Subsequent: $250; IRA: Initial: $1,000, Subsequent: $100
Wire orders accepted: Yes, $2,500 minimum
Deadline for same day wire purchase: 2 P.M.
Qualified for sale in: AL, FL, GA
Wire redemptions: Yes, $15 fee (written request only)
Letter redemptions: Signature guarantee required
Redemption fee: 1.00% for shares held less than 6 months, payable to the fund
Dividends paid: Income - July, December; Capital gains - December
Portfolio turnover (3 yrs): 11%, 15%, 27%
Management fee: 0.74%
Expense ratio: 1.68% (year ending 12/31/96)
IRA fees: Annual $10, Closing $25

SCOUT FUNDS ◆
(Data common to all Scout funds are shown below. See subsequent listings for date specific to individual funds.)

BMA Tower
700 Karnes Blvd.
Kansas City, MO 64108-3306
800-996-2862, 816-751-5900
Internet: http://www.jbfunds.com

Shareholder service hours: Full service: M-F 8 A.M.-4:30 P.M. CST; After hours service: prices, yields, account balances, last transaction, messages, prospectuses, portfolio distributions
Adviser: UMB Bank, n.a.
Sub-adviser: Jones & Babson, Inc.
Transfer agent: Jones & Babson, Inc.
Special sales restrictions: Designed for customers of affiliated banks of UMB Financial Corporation, but open to all investors.
Minimum purchase: Initial: $1,000, Subsequent: $100; IRA/Keogh: Initial: $250, Subsequent: $50; Automatic investment plan: Initial: $100, Subsequent: $100
Wire orders accepted: Yes, ($500 minimum for subsequent)
Deadline for same day wire purchase: 4 P.M. (1 P.M. for money market funds)
Qualified for sale in: AR, AZ, CA, CO, DC, FL, HI, IL, IN, IA, KS, KY, MA, MN, MO, MT, NE, NJ, NY, OH, OK, PA, SD, TN, TX, WY

Letter redemptions: Signature guarantee required over $50,000
Telephone switching: With other Scout funds, $1,000 minimum
Number of switches permitted: Unlimited, 15 day hold
Shareholder services: IRA, Keogh, corporate retirement plans, electronic funds transfer, systematic withdrawal plan min. bal. req. $10,000
IRA fees: Annual $10, Closing $10
Keogh fees: Annual $15, Closing $15

SCOUT BALANCED FUND ◆
(See first Scout listing for data common to all funds)

Portfolio manager: Christopher P. Bloomstran (1995)
Investment objective and policies: Total return; long-term capital growth and high current income. Invests in a variable mix of equity securities (for growth) and fixed-income securities (for income) adjusted according to perceived market conditions. Normally the fund will invest at least 25% of total assets in equity securities and a minimum of 25% of assets in fixed-income senior obligations with an average maturity between five and seven years. May invest in foreign markets either directly or through ADRs, and may use repurchase agreements for hedging purposes.
Year organized: 1995
Discount broker availability: Fidelity, Siebert, White
Dividends paid: Income - June, December; Capital gains - June, December
Portfolio turnover (2 yrs): 14%, 5%
Management fee: 0.85%
Expense ratio: 0.85% (year ending 6/30/97)

SCOUT BOND FUND ◆
(See first Scout listing for data common to all funds)

Portfolio manager: George W. Root (1982)
Investment objective and policies: Maximum current income consistent with quality and maturity standards. Normally invests at least 80% of assets in a diversified portfolio of investment grade government and corporate bonds with remaining individual maturities of 20 years or less.
Year organized: 1982 (Name changed from UMB Bond Fund 4/30/95)
Ticker symbol: UMBBX
Discount broker availability: Fidelity, Siebert, White
Dividends paid: Income - declared daily, paid monthly; Capital gains - June, December
Portfolio turnover (3 yrs): 19%, 12%, 2%
Management fee: 0.85%
Expense ratio: 0.87% (year ending 6/30/97)

SCOUT MONEY MARKET FUND - FEDERAL PORTFOLIO ◆
(See first Scout listing for data common to all funds)

Portfolio manager: William A. Faust (1995)
Investment objective and policies: Maximum income consistent with safety of principal and liquidity. Invests in high quality short-term obligations of the U.S. Government, its agencies or instrumentalities.
Year organized: 1982 (Name changed from UMB Money Market 4/30/95)
Ticker symbol: UMFXX
Telephone redemptions: Yes, $500 minimum
Check redemptions: $500 minimum
Dividends paid: Income - declared daily, paid monthly
Management fee: 0.50%
Expense ratio: 0.52% (year ending 6/30/97)

SCOUT MONEY MARKET FUND - PRIME PORTFOLIO ◆
(See first Scout listing for data common to all funds)

Portfolio manager: William A. Faust (1995)
Investment objective and policies: Maximum income consistent with safety of principal and liquidity. Invests in any of the government obligations available to the Federal portfolio, as well as highly rated

short-term corporate debt obligations with less than one year remaining to maturity, and domestic short-term obligations of commercial banks.
Year organized: 1982 (Name changed from UMB Money Market 4/30/95)
Ticker symbol: UMPXX
Telephone redemptions: Yes, $500 minimum
Check redemptions: $500 minimum
Dividends paid: Income - declared daily, paid monthly
Management fee: 0.50%
Expense ratio: 0.51% (year ending 6/30/97)

SCOUT REGIONAL FUND ◆
(See first Scout listing for data common to all funds)

Portfolio manager: David B. Anderson (1991)
Investment objective and policies: Long-term growth of both capital and dividend income; current yield secondary. Invests at least 80% of assets in common stocks of smaller regional companies (with capitalizations under $1B) doing a substantial portion of their business in MO, KS, IA, NE, AR, OK, IL and CO, selected for their long-term growth potential.
Year organized: 1986 (formerly UMB Qualified Dividend Fund. Name and objectives changed 7/30/91. Name changed from UMB Heartland Fund on 4/30/95)
Ticker symbol: UMBHX
Discount broker availability: Fidelity, Siebert, White
Dividends paid: Income - June, December; Capital gains - June, December
Portfolio turnover (3 yrs): 20%, 29%, 37%
Management fee: 0.85%
Expense ratio: 0.87% (year ending 6/30/97)

SCOUT STOCK FUND ◆
(See first Scout listing for data common to all funds)

Portfolio manager: David B. Anderson (1982)
Investment objective and policies: Long-term growth of both capital and dividend income; current yield secondary. Invests at least 80% of assets in common stocks selected for earning power, dividend-paying ability and assets within industries that have demonstrated both a consistent and an above-average ability to increase their earnings and dividends and which have favorable prospects of sustaining such growth.
Year organized: 1982 (Name changed from UMB Stock Fund 4/30/95)
Ticker symbol: UMBSX
Discount broker availability: Fidelity, Siebert, White
Dividends paid: Income - June, December; Capital gains - June, December
Portfolio turnover (3 yrs): 16%, 28%, 52%
Management fee: 0.85%
Expense ratio: 0.86% (year ending 6/30/97)

SCOUT TAX-FREE MONEY MARKET FUND ◆
(See first Scout listing for data common to all funds)

Portfolio manager: Eric Kelley (1996)
Investment objective and policies: Highest level of income exempt from federal income tax, consistent with safety of principal and liquidity. Invests in high quality short-term municipal obligations.
Year organized: 1982 (Name changed from UMB Tax-Free Money Market 4/30/95)
Ticker symbol: UMTXX
Telephone redemptions: Yes, $500 minimum
Check redemptions: $500 minimum
Dividends paid: Income - declared daily, paid monthly
Management fee: 0.50%
Expense ratio: 0.55% (year ending 6/30/97)

SCOUT WORLDWIDE FUND ◆
(See first Scout listing for data common to all funds)

Portfolio manager: James L. Moffett (1993)
Investment objective and policies: Long-term growth of capital and income. Invests in equity securi-

ties of established foreign and domestic companies. Normally invests at least 65% of assets in equity securities of foreign issuers, primarily through ADRs. May also invest in EDRs, IDRs and directly in foreign securities. Up to 20% of assets may be in companies located in developing countries. May purchase foreign currencies and/or engage in forward foreign currency transactions for hedging purposes.
Year organized: 1993 (Name changed from UMB WorldWide Fund 4/30/95)
Ticker symbol: UMBWX
Discount broker availability: Fidelity, *Schwab, Siebert, White
Dividends paid: Income - June, December; Capital gains - June, December
Portfolio turnover (3 yrs): 18%, 5%, 27%
Management fee: 0.85%
Expense ratio: 0.86% (year ending 6/30/97)

SCUDDER FUNDS ◆
(Data common to all Scudder funds, except Scudder Fund, Inc. funds, are shown below. See subsequent listings for data specific to individual funds.)

P.O. Box 2291
Boston, MA 02107-2291
800-225-2470, 617-295-1000
shareholder services 800-225-5163
prices/yields 800-343-2890
TDD 800-543-7916, fax 617-261-4420
Internet: http://funds.scudder.com

Shareholder service hours: Full service: M-F 8 A.M.-8 P.M. EST; After hours service: prices, yields, balances, exchanges, redemptions, investment updates, prospectuses, last transaction, total returns
Adviser: Scudder, Kemper Investments, Inc.
Transfer agent: Scudder Service Corp.
Minimum purchase: Initial: $2,500, Subsequent: $100; IRA/Keogh: Initial: $1,000, Subsequent: $50; Automatic investment plan: Initial: $1,000, Subsequent: $100 (exceptions noted)
Wire orders accepted: Yes
Deadline for same day wire purchase: 4 P.M.
Qualified for sale in: All states (single state tax free exceptions noted)
Telephone redemptions: Yes
Wire redemptions: Yes, $5 fee
Letter redemptions: Signature guarantee required over $50,000
Check redemptions: Money funds only, $100 minimum
Telephone switching: With all Scudder funds
Number of switches permitted: 4 round trips per year
Shareholder services: IRA, SEP-IRA, Keogh, 401(k), 403(b), corporate retirement plans, electronic funds transfer, systematic withdrawal plan min. bal. req. $10,000
Maintenance fee: $10 per fund for balances below $2,500 (waived for shareholders with a combined household balance over $25,000, and for IRAs)
IRA fees: None
Keogh fees: Annual $10

SCUDDER BALANCED FUND ◆
(See first Scudder listing for data common to all funds)

Portfolio managers: Valerie F. Malter (1995), George Fraise (1997), Stephen A. Wohler (1997)
Investment objective and policies: Balance of growth and income and long-term capital preservation. Invests 50% to 75% of assets in common stocks and other equity securities, with the remaining 25% to 50% of assets in investment grade bonds and other fixed-income securities, including cash. Invests primarily in domestic companies with annual revenues or market capitalization of at least $600M believed to offer above average potential for price appreciation. At least 25% of assets are always invested in senior fixed-income securities. Allocation of assets adjusted to changing market conditions. Fund may use foreign securities, write covered calls, and use futures contracts and options thereon.

Year organized: 1993
Ticker symbol: SCBAX
Group fund code: 062
Discount broker availability: Fidelity, *Schwab, Siebert, *White
Dividends paid: Income - March, June, September, December; Capital gains - December
Portfolio turnover (3 yrs): 43%, 70%, 103%
Management fee: 0.70%
Expense ratio: 1.02% (year ending 12/31/97) (1.37% without waiver)

SCUDDER CALIFORNIA TAX FREE FUND ◆
(See first Scudder listing for data common to all funds)

Portfolio managers: Jeremy L. Ragus (1990), Christopher J. Mier (1997)
Investment objective and policies: Income exempt from both federal and California state income taxes. Invests at least 80% of assets in investment grade California state, municipal and local government obligations, but primarily AA and A. Up to 25% of assets may be in junk bonds and 20% in securities subject to AMT tax treatment. May use options, futures and options thereon.
Year organized: 1983
Ticker symbol: SCTFX
Group fund code: 043
Discount broker availability: Fidelity, *Schwab, Siebert, *White
Qualified for sale in: AZ, CA, CO, DC, FL, GA, HI, IL, IN, KS, MD, MA, MI, MO, NV, NJ, NY, NC, OH, OR, SC ,TX, VA, WA, WV, WI, WY
Dividends paid: Income - declared daily, paid monthly; Capital gains - June, November, December
Portfolio turnover (3 yrs): 71%, 49%, 87%
Management fee: 0.625% first $200M, 0.60% over $200M
Expense ratio: 0.78% (year ending 3/31/97)

SCUDDER CALIFORNIA TAX FREE MONEY FUND ◆
(See first Scudder listing for data common to all funds)

Portfolio managers: Frank J. Rachwalski, Jr. (1998), Jerri I. Cohen (1998)
Investment objective and policies: High current income exempt from both federal and California state income taxes. Invests at least 80% of assets in California state, municipal and local government money market instruments.
Year organized: 1987
Ticker symbol: SCAXX
Group fund code: 087
Qualified for sale in: AZ, CA, CO, DC, FL, GA, HI, ID, IL, IN, KS, MD, MA, MI, MO, NV, NJ, NY, NC, OH, OR, SC ,TX, VA, WA, WV, WI, WY
Dividends paid: Income - declared daily, paid monthly
Management fee: 0.50%
Expense ratio: 0.60% (year ending 3/31/97) (0.79% without waiver)

SCUDDER CASH INVESTMENT TRUST ◆
(See first Scudder listing for data common to all funds)

Portfolio managers: Frank J. Rachwalski, Jr. (1998), John W. Stuebe (1998)
Investment objective and policies: Stability of capital, liquidity and income. Invests in U.S. dollar-denominated short-term money market instruments.
Year organized: 1975
Ticker symbol: SCTXX
Group fund code: 065
Dividends paid: Income - declared daily, paid monthly
Management fee: 0.50% first $250M to 0.35% over $1B
Expense ratio: 0.86% (year ending 6/30/97)

SCUDDER CLASSIC GROWTH FUND ◆
(See first Scudder listing for data common to all funds)

Portfolio managers: William F. Gadsden (1996), Bruce F. Beaty (1996)
Investment objective and policies: Long-term capital appreciation and share value stability. Invests primarily in a diversified portfolio of medium- to large-capitalization stocks of established, high-quality U.S. companies with a record of strong, consistent earnings growth and above average prospects for appreciation, and like prospects going forward. May invest up to 20% of assets in investment grade debt securities, and up to 25% of assets in listed and unlisted foreign securities. May use a variety of derivative instruments in an effort to enhance performance or for hedging purposes.
Year organized: 1996
Ticker symbol: SCCGX
Group fund code: 058
Sales restrictions: Effective 4/15/98 this fund becomes a Kemper load fund. Only those shareholders with an existing account will be grandfathered into the no-load class. All new Scudder clients must buy load shares.
Discount broker availability: Fidelity, *Schwab, *White
Dividends paid: Income - December; Capital gains - December
Portfolio turnover (1 yr): 27%
Management fee: 0.75%
Expense ratio: 1.25% (year ending 8/31/97) (2.25% without waiver)

SCUDDER DEVELOPMENT FUND ◆
(See first Scudder listing for data common to all funds)

Portfolio managers: Roy C. McKay (1988), Peter Chin (1993)
Investment objective and policies: Above-average long-term capital growth. Invests in a diversified portfolio of equity securities of relatively small or little-known emerging growth companies perceived to show above-average growth potential. Up to 20% of assets may be in securities of foreign issuers. Fund may use a variety of derivatives in an effort to enhance performance and for hedging purposes.
Year organized: 1971
Ticker symbol: SCDVX
Group fund code: 067
Discount broker availability: Fidelity, Siebert, *White
Dividends paid: Income - December; Capital gains - December
Portfolio turnover (3 yrs): 52%, 59%, 42%
Management fee: 1.00% first $500M to 0.90% over $1B
Expense ratio: 1.36% (year ending 6/30/97)

SCUDDER EMERGING MARKETS GROWTH FUND ◆
(See first Scudder listing for data common to all funds)

Portfolio managers: Joyce E. Cornell (1996), Elizabeth J. Allan (1996), Tara C. Kenney (1996), Andre J. DeSimone (1997)
Investment objective and policies: Long-term capital growth. Invests primarily in equity securities of emerging markets around the globe, using top down fundamental research of the political and economic status of each country and region. Looks for companies believed to have exceptional business prospects and focuses on high growth potential, unrecognized value, market dominance, or unique franchises. Diversifies between at least three countries, but has no limitation on the amount the fund can invest in a specific country or region. Invests up to 35% of assets in debt securities issued anywhere in the world, and up to 35% of assets in equity issues of the U.S. and other developed markets. May use various derivative instruments for hedging purposes or in an effort to enhance potential gain.
Year organized: 1996
Ticker symbol: SEMGX
Group fund code: 079

Redemption fee: 2.00% for shares held less than one year, payable to the fund
Discount broker availability: *Schwab, *White
Dividends paid: Income - December; Capital gains - December
Portfolio turnover (2 yrs): 62%, 20%
Management fee: 1.25%
Expense ratio: 2.00% (year ending 10/31/97) (2.33% without waiver)

SCUDDER EMERGING MARKETS INCOME FUND ◆
(See first Scudder listing for data common to all funds)

Portfolio managers: Susan E. Dahl (1996), M. Isabel Saltzman (1993)
Investment objective and policies: High current income; long-term capital appreciation secondary. Invests primarily in high-yielding debt securities issued by governments and corporations in emerging markets. Many investments are weighted toward countries in Latin America - Argentina, Brazil, Mexico, and Venezuela - but fund may also invest in Asia, Africa, The Middle East and Eastern Europe. Normally invests in securities from at least three countries, but may invest up to 40% of assets in issuers of a single country. Fund may use futures and options in an effort to increase returns and for hedging purposes. Fund is non-diversified.
Year organized: 1993
Ticker symbol: SCEMX
Group fund code: 076
Discount broker availability: Fidelity, *Schwab, Siebert, *White
Dividends paid: Income - March, June, September, December; Capital gains - December
Portfolio turnover (3 yrs): 410%, 430%, 302%
Management fee: 1.00%
Expense ratio: 1.49% (year ending 10/31/97)

SCUDDER FINANCIAL SERVICES FUND ◆
(See first Scudder listing for data common to all funds)

Portfolio managers: Thaddeus W. Paluszek (1997), Peter A. Taylor (1997), William F. Truscott (1997)
Investment objective and policies: Long-term growth of capital. Invests at least 80% of assets in common stocks and other equity securities of companies who derive at least 50% of their assets, revenues, or net income from the financial services industries, including banks, insurance companies and investment firms. May invest up to 20% of assets in obligations of the U.S. Treasury, or other federal agency issues. May invest in both listed and unlisted foreign securities without limit, and may use a variety of derivative instruments in an effort to enhance performance and for hedging purposes. Fund is non-diversified.
Year organized: 1997
Redemption fee: 1.00% for shares held less than one year, payable to the fund
Dividends paid: Income - December; Capital gains - December
Management fee: 0.75%

SCUDDER GLOBAL BOND FUND ◆
(See first Scudder listing for data common to all funds)

Portfolio managers: Gary P. Johnson (1997), Adam M. Greshin (1995)
Investment objective and policies: Total return; emphasis on current income, capital appreciation secondary. Invests in at least 65% of assets in high grade money market instruments and short-term bonds from issuers found in at least three countries around the world, denominated in foreign currencies as well as the U.S. dollar. These obligations must be rated in the three highest grades by the national rating agencies. May invest up to 15% of assets in the fourth highest grade as well. Portfolio maintains a dollar-weighted average maturity of three years or less. May use a variety of derivatives in an effort to enhance performance and for hedging purposes.
Year organized: 1991 (Name and objective changed from Global Short-Term Income Fund 12/29/95. Past performance may be misleading.)

Ticker symbol: SSTGX
Group fund code: 061
Discount broker availability: Fidelity, *Schwab, Siebert, *White
Dividends paid: Income - declared daily, paid monthly; Capital gains - December
Portfolio turnover (3 yrs): 257%, 336%, 183%
Management fee: 0.75% first $1B, 0.70% over $1B
Expense ratio: 1.00% (year ending 10/31/97) (1.39% without waiver)

SCUDDER GLOBAL DISCOVERY FUND ◆
(See first Scudder listing for data common to all funds)

Lead portfolio manager: Gerald J. Moran (1991)
Investment objective and policies: Above average long-term capital appreciation. Invests at least 65% of assets in a widely diversified portfolio of equity securities of small companies throughout the world whose market capitalizations range from $50M to $2B; median capitalization will be $750M or less. Fund attempts to identify companies thought to offer long-term growth potential and who are undervalued due to market oversight or mispricing. These issues will generally represent the smallest 20% of companies in the world. May invest up to 35% of assets in larger companies, or in investment grade debt obligations from around the world. Fund may use a variety of derivative instruments in an effort to enhance performance and for hedging purposes.
Year organized: 1991 (Name changed from Global Small Company Fund 3/6/96)
Ticker symbol: SGSCX
Group fund code: 010
Sales restrictions: Effective 4/15/98 this fund becomes a Kemper load fund. Only those shareholders with an existing account will be grandfathered into the no-load class. All new Scudder clients must buy load shares.
Discount broker availability: Fidelity, *Schwab, Siebert, *White
Dividends paid: Income - December; Capital gains - December
Portfolio turnover (3 yrs): 61%, 63%, 44%
Management fee: 1.10%
Expense ratio: 1.63% (year ending 10/31/97)

SCUDDER GLOBAL FUND ◆
(See first Scudder listing for data common to all funds)

Portfolio managers: William E. Holzer (1986), Nicholas Bratt (1993), Diego Espinosa (1997)
Investment objective and policies: Long-term capital growth; income incidental. Invests in a diversified portfolio of equity securities of companies from at least three countries around the world, including the U.S. Seeks companies which will benefit from global economic trends, technologies, and currency changes. May also invest in investment grade debt securities of U.S. and foreign issuers. Fund may invest in closed-end investment companies holding foreign securities. May use a variety of derivative instruments in an effort to enhance performance and for hedging purposes.
Year organized: 1986
Ticker symbol: SCOBX
Group fund code: 007
Discount broker availability: Fidelity, *Schwab, Siebert, *White
Dividends paid: Income - September, December; Capital gains - September, December
Portfolio turnover (3 yrs): 41%, 29%, 44%
Management fee: 1.00% first $500M, 0.90% over $1B
Expense ratio: 1.37% (year ending 6/30/97)

SCUDDER GNMA FUND ◆
(See first Scudder listing for data common to all funds)

Portfolio managers: Richard L. Vandenberg (1998), Mark S. Boyadjian (1995), Scott S. Anthony (1997)
Investment objective and policies: High current income. Invests at least 65% of assets in a diversified portfolio of U.S. Government mortgage-backed securities (GNMAs) of varying maturities. Up to 35% of

assets may be invested in other U.S. Government securities and cash equivalents. Fund may use a variety of derivative instruments in an effort to enhance performance and for hedging purposes.
Year organized: 1985
Ticker symbol: SGMSX
Group fund code: 006
Discount broker availability: Fidelity, *Schwab, Siebert, *White
Dividends paid: Income - declared daily, paid monthly, Capital gains - June, December
Portfolio turnover (3 yrs): 188%, 158%, 221%
Management fee: 0.65% first $200M to 0.55% over $500M
Expense ratio: 0.96% (year ending 3/31/97)

SCUDDER GOLD FUND ◆
(See first Scudder listing for data common to all funds)

Portfolio managers: Clay L. Hoes (1997), William J. Wallace (1991)
Investment objective and policies: Maximum total return; capital appreciation and income. Invests at least 65% of assets in equity securities of companies engaged in the exploration, mining, fabrication, processing or distribution of gold, as well as in gold bullion and coins. Assets are invested primarily in Australia, Canada, South Africa and the U.S., as well as in the Cayman Islands. The remaining 35% of assets may be in other precious metals and related equities, and in debt securities. Up to 10% of assets may be committed directly to gold, silver, platinum and palladium bullion and in gold and silver coins. Fund may use a variety of derivative instruments in an effort to enhance performance and for hedging purposes. Fund is non-diversified.
Year organized: 1988
Ticker symbol: SCGDX
Group fund code: 019
Discount broker availability: Fidelity, *Schwab, Siebert, *White
Dividends paid: Income - December; Capital gains - December
Portfolio turnover (3 yrs): 39%, 30%, 42%
Management fee: 1.00%
Expense ratio: 1.60% (year ending 6/30/97)

SCUDDER GREATER EUROPE GROWTH FUND ◆
(See first Scudder listing for data common to all funds)

Portfolio managers: Carol L. Franklin (1994), Nicholas Bratt (1994), Joan R. Gregory (1994)
Investment objective and policies: Long-term capital growth; current income incidental. Invests at least 80% of assets in equity securities of issuers from at least three European countries, primarily from Western and Southern Europe. Fund may invest in less developed European markets in an effort to enhance returns, however. May invest up to 20% of assets in European junk bonds, and may use a variety of derivative instruments in an effort to enhance performance and for hedging purposes. Fund is non-diversified.
Year organized: 1994
Ticker symbol: SCGEX
Group fund code: 077
Discount broker availability: Fidelity, *Schwab, Siebert, *White
Dividends paid: Income - December; Capital gains - December
Portfolio turnover (3 yrs): 89%, 39%, 28%
Management fee: 1.00%
Expense ratio: 1.66% (year ending 10/31/97) (1.72% without waiver)

SCUDDER GROWTH AND INCOME FUND ◆
(See first Scudder listing for data common to all funds)

Lead portfolio manager: Robert T. Hoffman (1991)
Investment objective and policies: Long-term capital growth, current income, and growth of income. Invests primarily in dividend-paying common stocks, preferred stocks and convertible securities which are

thought to offer the prospect of growth of earnings. May invest in REITs and foreign securities without limit. May use a variety of derivative instruments in an effort to enhance returns and for hedging purposes.
Year organized: 1929 (formerly Scudder Common Stock Fund; name and objectives changed 11/13/84)
Ticker symbol: SCDGX
Group fund code: 064
Discount broker availability: Fidelity, *Schwab, Siebert, *White
Dividends paid: Income - March, June, September, December; Capital gains - December
Portfolio turnover (3 yrs): 22%, 27%, 27%
Management fee: 0.60% first $500M to 0.405% over $4.5B
Expense ratio: 0.76% (year ending 12/31/97)

SCUDDER HEALTH CARE FUND ◆
(See first Scudder listing for data common to all funds)

Portfolio managers: Kimberly Purvis (1998), James Fenger (1998)
Investment objective and policies: Long-term growth of capital. Invests at least 80% of assets in common stocks and other equity securities of companies who derive at least 50% of their assets, revenues, or net income from the health care industries, including hospitals, medical supply companies, equipment and support services, and medical, diagnostic, biochemical, and biotechnological research and development firms. May invest up to 20% of assets in obligations of the U.S. Treasury, or other federal agency issues. May invest in both listed and unlisted foreign securities without limit, and may use a variety of derivative instruments in an effort to enhance performance and for hedging purposes. Fund is non-diversified.
Year organized: 1998
Redemption fee: 1.00% for shares held less than one year, payable to the fund
Dividends paid: Income - December; Capital gains - December
Management fee: 0.85%

SCUDDER HIGH YIELD BOND FUND ◆
(See first Scudder listing for data common to all funds)

Portfolio managers: Kelly D. Babson (1996), Stephen A. Wohler (1996)
Investment objective and policies: High current income; capital appreciation secondary. Invests primarily in high-yield domestic junk bonds, and will focus on medium-term corporate bonds. Focuses on stable and improving credits with high relative yields that are candidates for upgrades. May invest with no limitation as to the maturity of any individual security, and without regard to the weighted average maturity of the portfolio. May also invest in a variety of other types of securities with consistent objectives. May invest up to 25% of assets in foreign securities, and use derivative instruments in an effort to enhance performance or for hedging purposes.
Year organized: 1996
Ticker symbol: SHBDX
Group fund code: 047
Discount broker availability: *Schwab
Redemption fee: 1.00% on shares held less than 1 year, payable to the fund
Dividends paid: Income - declared daily, paid monthly; Capital gains - November
Portfolio turnover (1 yr): 40%
Management fee: 0.70%
Expense ratio: 0.00% (eight months ending 2/28/97) (1.75% without waiver)

SCUDDER HIGH YIELD TAX FREE FUND ◆
(See first Scudder listing for data common to all funds)

Portfolio managers: Philip G. Condon (1987), Rebecca L. Wilson (1998)
Investment objective and policies: High current income exempt from regular federal income tax. Invests at least 50% of assets in a diversified portfolio

of municipal bonds ranked within the four highest ratings categories. May, however, invest as much as 50% of assets ranked lower than this, although none may fall below B. May invest up to 20% of assets in securities subject to AMT tax treatment. May use a variety of derivative instruments for hedging purposes.
Year organized: 1987
Ticker symbol: SHYTX
Group fund code: 008
Discount broker availability: Fidelity, *Schwab, Siebert, *White
Dividends paid: Income - declared daily, paid monthly; Capital gains - March, November
Portfolio turnover (3 yrs): 33%, 22%, 27%
Management fee: 0.65% first $300M, 0.60% over $300M
Expense ratio: 0.90% (year ending 12/31/97)

SCUDDER INCOME FUND ◆
(See first Scudder listing for data common to all funds)

Portfolio managers: Stephen A. Wohler (1994), Kelly D. Babson (1998), Robert S. Cessine (1998)
Investment objective and policies: Current income. Invests at least 65% of assets in a broadly diversified portfolio of investment grade fixed-income securities of all types, as well as in dividend-paying common stocks. Bonds will normally be ranked in the top three grades, but up to 20% of assets can be rated Baa or BBB or lower, but no lower than B. Fund may invest in foreign securities or zero coupon securities without limit. May use a variety of derivative instruments in an effort to enhance performance and for hedging purposes.
Year organized: 1928
Ticker symbol: SCSBX
Group fund code: 063
Discount broker availability: Fidelity, *Schwab, Siebert, *White
Dividends paid: Income - March, June, September, December; Capital gains - December
Portfolio turnover (3 yrs): 62%, 67%, 128%
Management fee: 0.65% first $200M to 0.55% over $500M
Expense ratio: 1.18% (year ending 12/31/96)

SCUDDER INTERNATIONAL BOND FUND ◆
(See first Scudder listing for data common to all funds)

Portfolio managers: Gary P. Johnson (1997), Adam M. Greshin (1988)
Investment objective and policies: Current income; protection and possible enhancement of principal value secondary. Invests at least 65% of assets in high-grade debt securities rated A or better that are denominated in foreign currencies, and actively manages currency, bond market and maturity exposure. Up to 35% of assets may be in U.S. debt securities. Generally invests in at least three different countries, but may choose to concentrate all holdings in just one. May use a variety of derivative instruments in an effort to increase performance and for hedging purposes. Fund is non-diversified.
Year organized: 1988
Ticker symbol: SCIBX
Group fund code: 018
Discount broker availability: Fidelity, *Schwab, Siebert, *White
Dividends paid: Income - declared daily, paid monthly; Capital gains - December
Portfolio turnover (3 yrs): 298%, 276%, 319%
Management fee: 0.85% first $1B to 0.80% over $1B
Expense ratio: 1.36% (year ending 6/30/97)

SCUDDER INTERNATIONAL FUND ◆
(See first Scudder listing for data common to all funds)

Lead portfolio manager: Irene T. Cheng (1997)
Investment objective and policies: Long-term capital growth. Invests primarily in a broadly diversified portfolio of equity securities of established foreign companies and economies perceived to show favorable growth prospects. Is always diversified across at

least three countries. May invest up to 20% of assets in fixed-income securities of foreign governments and companies, generally of investment grade quality, although 5% can be rated B or lower. May use a variety of derivative instruments in an effort to enhance performance and for hedging purposes.

Year organized: 1954
Ticker symbol: SCINX
Group fund code: 068
Discount broker availability: Fidelity, *Schwab, Siebert, *White
Dividends paid: Income - December; Capital gains - December
Portfolio turnover (3 yrs): 36%, 45%, 46%
Management fee: 0.90% first $500M to 0.70% over $3B
Expense ratio: 1.15% (year ending 3/31/97)

SCUDDER INTERNATIONAL GROWTH AND INCOME FUND ◆
(See first Scudder listing for data common to all funds)

Lead portfolio manager: Sheridan Reilly (1997)
Investment objective and policies: Long-term capital growth and current income. Invests primarily in equity securities of established foreign companies and economies with growth prospects that also pay high current dividends. Can invest throughout the world, but will emphasize investments in developed countries other than the U.S., investing at least 80% of assets in foreign equities. May invest up to 20% of assets in fixed-income securities of foreign governments and companies, generally of investment grade quality, although 5% can be rated B or lower. May use a variety of derivative instruments in an effort to enhance performance and for hedging purposes.
Year organized: 1997
Ticker symbol: SIGIX
Group fund code: 300
Discount broker availability: Fidelity, *Schwab, Siebert, *White
Dividends paid: Income - June, December; Capital gains - December
Management fee: 1.00%

SCUDDER LARGE COMPANY GROWTH FUND ◆
(See first Scudder listing for data common to all funds)

Portfolio managers: Valerie F. Malter (1995), George P. Fraise (1997)
Investment objective and policies: Long-term capital growth; current income incidental. Invests at least 65% of assets in a diversified portfolio of equity securities including common stocks, preferred stocks and convertible securities, of seasoned, financially strong U.S. growth companies with market capitalizations of at least $1B. Fund may, however, invest without limit in both listed and unlisted foreign securities when deemed beneficial. May also use a variety of derivative instruments in an effort to enhance performance and for hedging purposes.
Year organized: 1991 (name changed from Quality Growth 2/97)
Ticker symbol: SCQGX
Group fund code: 060
Discount broker availability: Fidelity, *Schwab, Siebert, *White
Dividends paid: Income - December; Capital gains - December
Portfolio turnover (3 yrs): 68%, 69%, 92%
Management fee: 0.70%
Expense ratio: 1.21% (year ending 10/31/97)

SCUDDER LARGE COMPANY VALUE FUND ◆
(See first Scudder listing for data common to all funds)

Portfolio managers: Kathleen T. Millard (1995), Lois R. Friedman Roman (1995)
Investment objective and policies: Maximum long-term capital appreciation. Invests in a broad range of marketable securities, principally common stocks, but also may use preferred stocks and investment grade

debt securities in keeping with its objective. Normally invests at least 65% of assets in equity securities of U.S. companies with market capitalizations of $1B or more that are perceived to be undervalued. May, however, invest in both listed and unlisted securities of foreign issuers without limit when deemed advisable. May use a variety of derivative instruments in an effort to enhance return and for hedging purposes.
Year organized: 1956 (as Scudder Special Fund; in 1982 Scudder Duo-Vest open-ended, changed name to Capital Growth, and merged with Special. Name changed from Capital Growth 2/1/97.)
Ticker symbol: SCDUX
Group fund code: 049
Discount broker availability: Fidelity, *Schwab, Siebert, *White
Dividends paid: Income - December; Capital gains - December
Portfolio turnover (3 yrs): 43%, 151%, 154%
Management fee: 0.75% first $500M to 0.55% over $1.5B
Expense ratio: 0.93% (year ending 9/30/97)

SCUDDER LATIN AMERICA FUND ◆
(See first Scudder listing for data common to all funds)

Portfolio managers: Edmund B. Games, Jr. (1992), Tara C. Kenney (1996), Paul Rogers (1996)
Investment objective and policies: Long-term capital appreciation. Fund seeks to benefit from economic and political trends throughout Latin America by investing at least 65% of assets in securities of Latin American issuers, with at least 50% in equity securities. May invest up to 35% of assets in equity securities of U.S. and other non-Latin American issuers. Fund may invest up to 10% of assets in closed-end mutual funds. May use a variety of derivative instruments in an effort to enhance return and for hedging purposes. Fund is non-diversified.
Year organized: 1992
Ticker symbol: SLAFX
Group fund code: 074
Discount broker availability: Fidelity, *Schwab, *White
Dividends paid: Income - December; Capital gains - December
Portfolio turnover (3 yrs): 42%, 22%, 40%
Management fee: 1.25% first $1B, 1.15% over $1B
Expense ratio: 1.89% (year ending 10/31/97)

SCUDDER LIMITED TERM TAX FREE FUND ◆
(See first Scudder listing for data common to all funds)

Portfolio managers: M. Ashton Patton (1994), K. Sue Cote (1998)
Investment objective and policies: High income exempt from regular federal income tax, consistent with stability of principal. Invests in a diversified portfolio of shorter-term municipal bonds ranked in the highest three grades. Portfolio generally maintains a dollar-weighted average maturity of one to five years, and only invests in securities with effective maturities of less than ten years at the time of purchase. May, if necessary, invest in securities subject to AMT tax treatment, but doesn't intend to. May use futures and options thereon and options on portfolio securities.
Year organized: 1994
Ticker symbol: SCLTX
Group fund code: 044
Discount broker availability: Fidelity, *Schwab, Siebert, *White
Dividends paid: Income - declared daily, paid monthly; Capital gains - March, December
Portfolio turnover (3 yrs): 18%, 38%, 38%
Management fee: 0.60%
Expense ratio: 0.75% (year ending 10/31/97) (0.83% without waiver)

SCUDDER MANAGED MUNICIPAL BONDS ◆
(See first Scudder listing for data common to all funds)

Portfolio managers: Philip G. Condon (1987), M. Ashton Patton (1998)
Investment objective and policies: Income exempt

from regular federal income tax. Invests at least 65% of assets in investment grade municipal bonds. Fund has the flexibility to vary its maturity according to perceived market conditions, and may invest up to 10% of assets in securities rated as low as B. May invest up to 20% of assets in taxable securities. Fund may use a variety of derivative instruments for hedging purposes.
Year organized: 1976
Ticker symbol: SCMBX
Group fund code: 066
Discount broker availability: Fidelity, *Schwab, Siebert, *White
Dividends paid: Income - declared daily, paid monthly; Capital gains - March, December
Portfolio turnover (3 yrs): 10%, 12%, 18%
Management fee: 0.55% first $200M to 0.475% over $700M
Expense ratio: 0.64% (year ending 12/31/97)

SCUDDER MASSACHUSETTS LIMITED TERM TAX FREE FUND ◆
(See first Scudder listing for data common to all funds)

Portfolio managers: Philip G. Condon (1994), Kathleen A. Meany (1994)
Investment objective and policies: High income exempt from federal and Massachusetts state income taxes, consistent with stability of principal. Invests in high grade (at least 80% rated A or better, none less than Baa) shorter-term Massachusetts municipal bonds, and maintains a dollar-weighted average maturity of one to five years. Up to 20% of assets may be in securities subject to AMT tax treatment. May use futures and options thereon, and options on portfolio securities.
Year organized: 1994
Ticker symbol: SMLFX
Group fund code: 041
Discount broker availability: Fidelity, *Schwab, Siebert, *White
Qualified for sale in: AZ, CA, CO, CT, DC, FL, GA, HI, IL, IN, ME, MD, MA, MN, NH, NJ, NY, NC, OH, PA, RI, TX, VT, VA, WV
Dividends paid: Income - declared daily, paid monthly; Capital gains - December
Portfolio turnover (3 yrs): 10%, 27%, 26%
Management fee: 0.60%
Expense ratio: 0.75% (year ending 10/31/97) (0.93% without waiver)

SCUDDER MASSACHUSETTS TAX FREE FUND ◆
(See first Scudder listing for data common to all funds)

Portfolio managers: Philip G. Condon (1989), Kathleen A. Meany (1988)
Investment objective and policies: Income exempt from regular federal and Massachusetts state income taxes. Invests at least 80% of assets in long-term (more than 10 years) investment grade Massachusetts state, municipal and local government obligations. May invest up to 25% of assets in junk bonds and 20% in securities subject to AMT tax treatment. Fund may use options, futures, and options thereon.
Year organized: 1987
Ticker symbol: SCMAX
Group fund code: 012
Discount broker availability: Fidelity, *Schwab, Siebert, *White
Qualified for sale in: AZ, CA, CO, CT, DC, FL, GA, HI, IL, IN, ME, MD, MA, MN, NH, NJ, NY, NC, OH, PA, RI, TX, VT, VA, WV
Portfolio turnover (3 yrs): 12%, 21%, 10%
Dividends paid: Income - declared daily, paid monthly; Capital gains - December
Management fee: 0.60%
Expense ratio: 0.76% (year ending 3/31/97)

SCUDDER MEDIUM TERM TAX FREE FUND ◆
(See first Scudder listing for data common to all funds)

Portfolio managers: M. Ashton Patton (1986), Philip G. Condon (1997)
Investment objective and policies: High income exempt from regular federal income tax while limiting

principal fluctuation. Invests primarily in high grade (at least 65% in the three highest grades, none less than the fourth grade) intermediate-term municipal bonds. Portfolio generally maintains a dollar-weighted average maturity of five to ten years, and only purchases securities with remaining maturities of less than 15 years. May use a variety of derivative instruments for hedging purposes.

Year organized: 1990 (formerly Tax Free Target Fund - 1990 Portfolio; performance data before 1990 may not be relevant. Absorbed Tax Free Target Fund 1993 and 1996 Portfolios 5/15/92.)
Ticker symbol: SCMTX
Group fund code: 045
Discount broker availability: Fidelity, *Schwab, Siebert, *White
Dividends paid: Income - declared daily, paid monthly; Capital gains - March, December
Portfolio turnover (3 yrs): 13%, 14%, 36%
Management fee: 0.60% first $500M, 0.50% over $500M
Expense ratio: 0.74% (year ending 12/31/97)

SCUDDER MICRO CAP FUND ◆
(See first Scudder listing for data common to all funds)

Portfolio managers: James M. Eysenbach (1996), Philip S. Fortuna (1996), Calvin S. Young (1997)
Investment objective and policies: Long-term capital growth. Invests primarily in a diversified portfolio of U.S. micro-cap stocks, with the median market capitalization of the portfolio maintained below $125M. Fund focuses on companies that, at the time of purchase, have a market cap smaller than the 3,000 largest U.S. companies. Selections are made with a bias toward companies demonstrating value pricing while maintaining reasonable growth prospects. May, however, purchase investment grade debt securities deemed consistent with fund objectives. May use a variety of derivative instruments in an effort to enhance performance and for hedging purposes.
Year organized: 1996
Ticker symbol: SCMCX
Group fund code: 048
Special sales restrictions: Fund closed to new investors 9/22/97
Discount broker availability: *Schwab
Redemption fee: 1.00% for shares held less than 1 year, payable to the fund (waived for non-IRA pension accounts)
Dividends paid: Income - December; Capital gains - December
Portfolio turnover (1 yr): 17%
Management fee: 075%
Expense ratio: 1.75% (year ending 8/31/97) (2.19% without waiver)

SCUDDER NEW YORK TAX FREE FUND ◆
(See first Scudder listing for data common to all funds)

Portfolio managers: Jeremy L. Ragus (1990), Christopher J. Mier (1997)
Investment objective and policies: Income exempt from federal, NY and NY city income taxes. Invests at least 80% of assets in New York state, municipal and local government obligations. May invest up to 25% of assets in junk bonds and 20% in securities subject to AMT tax treatment. Fund may use futures and options thereon for hedging purposes.
Year organized: 1983
Ticker symbol: SCYTX
Group fund code: 042
Discount broker availability: Fidelity, *Schwab, Siebert, *White
Qualified for sale in: AZ, CA, CO, CT, DE, DC, FL, GA, HI, IL, IN, MD, MA, MD, MN, MO, NH, NJ, NY, NC, OH, PA, RI, SC, TX, VT, VA, WV
Dividends paid: Income - declared daily, paid monthly; Capital gains - December
Portfolio turnover (3 yrs): 71%, 81%, 84%
Management fee: 0.625% first $200M, 0.60% over $200M
Expense ratio: 0.83% (year ending 3/31/97)

SCUDDER NEW YORK TAX FREE MONEY FUND ◆
(See first Scudder listing for data common to all funds)

Portfolio managers: Frank J. Rachwalski, Jr. (1998), Jerri I. Cohen (1998)
Investment objective and policies: High current income exempt from federal, NY state and NY city income taxes. Invests at least 80% of assets in New York state, municipal and local government money market obligations rated Aaa or Aa.
Year organized: 1987
Ticker symbol: SCNXX
Group fund code: 088
Qualified for sale in: AZ, CA, CO, CT, DE, DC, FL, GA, HI, IL, IN, MD, MA, MN, MO, NH, NJ, NY, NC, OH, PA, RI, SC, TX, VT, VA, WV
Dividends paid: Income - declared daily, paid monthly
Management fee: 0.50%
Expense ratio: 0.60% (year ending 3/31/97) (0.85% without waiver)

SCUDDER OHIO TAX FREE FUND ◆
(See first Scudder listing for data common to all funds)

Portfolio managers: Christopher J. Mier (1998), Rebecca L. Wilson (1997)
Investment objective and policies: Income exempt from federal and Ohio state income taxes. Invests at least 80% of assets in long-term Ohio state, municipal and local government obligations. May invest up to 25% of assets in junk bonds and 20% in securities subject to AMT tax treatment. Fund may use futures and options thereon for hedging purposes.
Year organized: 1987
Ticker symbol: SCOHX
Group fund code: 013
Discount broker availability: Fidelity, *Schwab, Siebert, *White
Qualified for sale in: AZ, CA, CO, DC, FL, GA, HI, IL, IN, KY, MD, MA, MN, MI, MN, NJ, NY, NC, OH, PA, TX, VA, WV
Dividends paid: Income - declared daily, paid monthly; Capital gains - December
Portfolio turnover (3 yrs): 10%, 20%, 20%
Management fee: 0.60%
Expense ratio: 0.50% (year ending 3/31/97) (0.88% without waiver)

SCUDDER PACIFIC OPPORTUNITIES FUND ◆
(See first Scudder listing for data common to all funds)

Portfolio managers: Elizabeth J. Allan (1994), Nicholas Bratt (1992), Theresa Gusman (1997)
Investment objective and policies: Long-term capital growth. Invests at least 65% of assets in equity securities of companies either domiciled in or conducting at least 50% of their business in Pacific Basin countries, excluding Japan. Fund intends to diversify holdings across at least three countries. May invest up to 35% of assets in foreign and domestic investment grade debt securities and 35% in U.S. and non-Pacific Basin equity securities. Fund may use a variety of derivative instruments in an effort to enhance returns and for hedging purposes. Fund is non-diversified.
Year organized: 1992
Ticker symbol: SCOPX
Group fund code: 073
Discount broker availability: Fidelity, *Schwab, Siebert, *White
Dividends paid: Income - December; Capital gains - December
Portfolio turnover (3 yrs): 97%, 95%, 64%
Management fee: 1.10%
Expense ratio: 1.94% (year ending 10/31/97)

SCUDDER PATHWAY SERIES: BALANCED PORTFOLIO ◆
(See first Scudder listing for data common to all funds)

Lead portfolio manager: Benjamin W. Thorndike (1996)
Investment objective and policies: A balance of growth and income. Invests in an underlying mix of money market, bond, and equity funds from the rest of the Scudder family. Normal balanced allocation is composed of 40% to 70% of assets in equity funds, 25% to 60% of assets in bond funds, and 0% to 10% of assets in money market funds, cash, or cash equivalents. Allocations will vary according to perceived market conditions.
Year organized: 1996
Ticker symbol: SPBAX
Group fund code: 081
Discount broker availability: Fidelity, *Schwab, Siebert, *White
Dividends paid: Income - March, June, September, December; Capital gains - December
Portfolio turnover (1 yr): 24%
Management fee: None (pro rata share of underlying funds)

SCUDDER PATHWAY SERIES: CONSERVATIVE PORTFOLIO ◆
(See first Scudder listing for data common to all funds)

Lead portfolio manager: Benjamin W. Thorndike (1996)
Investment objective and policies: Current income; long-term capital growth secondary. Invests in an underlying mix of money market, bond, and equity funds from the rest of the Scudder family. Normal conservative allocation is composed of 40% to 80% of assets in bond funds, 20% to 50% of assets in equity funds, and 0% to 15% of assets in money market funds, cash, or cash equivalent. Allocations will vary according to perceived market conditions.
Year organized: 1996
Group fund code: 080
Discount broker availability: Fidelity, *Schwab, Siebert, *White
Dividends paid: Income - March, June, September, December; Capital gains - December
Portfolio turnover (1 yr): 42%
Management fee: None (pro rata share of underlying funds)

SCUDDER PATHWAY SERIES: GROWTH PORTFOLIO ◆
(See first Scudder listing for data common to all funds)

Lead portfolio manager: Benjamin W. Thorndike (1996)
Investment objective and policies: Long-term capital growth. Invests in an underlying mix of money market, bond, and equity funds from the rest of the Scudder family. Normal growth allocation is composed of 60% to 90% of assets in equity funds, 10% to 40% of assets in bond funds, and 0% to 5% of assets in money market funds, cash, or cash equivalent. Allocations will vary according to perceived market conditions.
Year organized: 1996
Ticker symbol: SPGRX
Group fund code: 082
Discount broker availability: Fidelity, *Schwab, Siebert, *White
Dividends paid: Income - December; Capital gains - December
Portfolio turnover (1 yr): 15%
Management fee: None (pro rata share of underlying funds)

SCUDDER PATHWAY SERIES: INTERNATIONAL PORTFOLIO ◆
(See first Scudder listing for data common to all funds)

Lead portfolio manager: Benjamin W. Thorndike (1996)
Investment objective and policies: Maximum total return: current income and capital growth. Invests in a select mix of established global and international Scudder funds. At least 65% of assets are invested in funds with primarily non-domestic holdings, and at least 60% of total assets are invested in equity holdings. Balance of assets are invested in bond or money market funds, or cash.

Year organized: 1996
Ticker symbol: SPIPX
Group fund code: 083
Discount broker availability: Fidelity, *Schwab, Siebert, *White
Dividends paid: Income - December; Capital gains - December
Portfolio turnover (1 yr): 35%
Management fee: None (pro rata share of underlying funds)

SCUDDER PENNSYLVANIA TAX FREE FUND ◆
(See first Scudder listing for data common to all funds)

Portfolio managers: Philip G. Condon (1987), Rebecca L. Wilson (1997)
Investment objective and policies: Income exempt from federal and Pennsylvania state income taxes and property taxes. Invests at least 80% of assets in long-term Pennsylvania state, municipal and local government obligations. May invest up to 25% of assets in junk bonds and 20% in securities subject to AMT tax treatment. Fund may use futures and options thereon for hedging purposes.
Year organized: 1987
Ticker symbol: SCPAX
Group fund code: 015
Discount broker availability: Fidelity, *Schwab, Siebert, *White
Qualified for sale in: AZ, CA, CO, DE, DC, FL, GA, HI, IL, IN, KY, MD, MA, MN, NJ, NY, NC, OH, PA, TX, VA, WV
Dividends paid: Income - declared daily, paid monthly; Capital gains - December
Portfolio turnover (3 yrs): 12%, 11%, 26%
Management fee: 0.60%
Expense ratio: 0.50% (year ending 3/31/97) (0.92% without waiver)

SCUDDER PREMIUM MONEY MARKET SHARES ◆
(See first Scudder listing for data common to all funds)

Lead portfolio manager: Frank J. Rachwalski, Jr. (1998)
Investment objective and policies: Current income consistent with stability of principal and maintenance of liquidity. Invests in a high-grade portfolio of short-term money market securities.
Year organized: 1997
Minimum purchase: Initial: $25,000
Dividends paid: Income - declared daily, paid monthly
Management fee: 0.50% first $500M, 0.48% over $500M

SCUDDER S&P 500 INDEX FUND ◆
(See first Scudder listing for data common to all funds)

Sub-adviser: Bankers Trust Co.
Portfolio manager: Frank Salerno (1997)
Investment objective and policies: Investment results that, before expenses, correspond (at least 0.98) to the total return of common stocks publicly traded in the U.S. as represented by the S&P 500 Index. Using a master/feeder structure, the fund invests substantially all its assets in the Equity 500 Index portfolio, which has the same objective and policies. Weightings of the portfolio may not match the Index precisely, but will be structured to mirror the performance and avoid small transactions. May hold up to 20% of assets in short-term debt securities and money markets hedged with stock index futures and options.
Year organized: 1997 (1993 for underlying portfolio)
Group fund code: 301
Discount broker availability: *Schwab, *White
Dividends paid: Income - March, June, September, December; Capital gains - December
Portfolio turnover (3 yrs): 19%, 15%, 6%
Management fee: 0.10%
Expense ratio: 0.40% (four months ending 12/31/97) (4.42% without waiver)

SCUDDER SHORT-TERM BOND FUND ◆
(See first Scudder listing for data common to all funds)

Portfolio managers: Stephen A. Wohler (1998), Robert S. Cessine (1998)
Investment objective and policies: Current income consistent with stability of principal. Invests in high quality debt instruments, including mortgage-backed securities, and generally maintains a dollar-weighted average maturity of three years or less. At least 65% of assets will be in Aaa or Aa rated securities with no securities below Baa. May use foreign securities and currency exchange contracts. Fund may use options on portfolio securities and futures contracts and options thereon for hedging purposes.
Year organized: 1982 (formerly the three portfolios of the Scudder Target Fund; name and objectives changed on 7/3/89.)
Ticker symbol: SCSTX
Group fund code: 022
Discount broker availability: Fidelity, *Schwab, Siebert, *White
Dividends paid: Income - declared daily, paid monthly; Capital gains - December
Portfolio turnover (3 yrs): 39%, 62%, 101%
Management fee: 0.60% first $500M to 0.35% over $3B
Expense ratio: 0.86% (year ending 12/31/97)

SCUDDER SMALL COMPANY VALUE FUND ◆
(See first Scudder listing for data common to all funds)

Portfolio managers: Philip S. Fortuna (1995), James M. Eysenbach (1995), Calvin S. Young (1997)
Investment objective and policies: Long-term capital growth. Invests at least 90% of assets in a diversified portfolio of equity securities, principally common stocks, of small U.S. companies believed to be out of favor or undervalued relative to a long-term horizon. Companies selected are similar in size to those comprising the Russell 2000 Index. May use derivatives to enhance liquidity, increase market participation, and to manage transaction costs.
Year organized: 1995
Ticker symbol: SCSUX
Group fund code: 078
Discount broker availability: *Schwab
Redemption fee: 1.00% for shares held less than one year, payable to fund
Dividends paid: Income - December; Capital gains - December
Portfolio turnover (2 yrs): 44%, 34%
Management fee: 0.75%
Expense ratio: 1.50% (year ending 8/31/97) (1.63% without waiver)

SCUDDER TAX FREE MONEY FUND ◆
(See first Scudder listing for data common to all funds)

Portfolio managers: Frank J. Rachwalski, Jr. (1998), Jerri I. Cohen (1998)
Investment objective and policies: Income exempt from regular federal income tax, consistent with relative stability of principal. Invests at least 80% of assets in a diversified portfolio of short-term municipal money market securities ranked within the two highest rating categories. May invest up to 20% of assets in securities subject to AMT tax treatment.
Year organized: 1980
Ticker symbol: STFXX
Group fund code: 071
Dividends paid: Income - declared daily, paid monthly
Management fee: 0.50% first $500M, 0.48% over $500M
Expense ratio: 0.65% (year ending 12/31/97) (0.76% without waiver)

SCUDDER TECHNOLOGY FUND ◆
(See first Scudder listing for data common to all funds)

Lead portfolio manager: Brooks Dougherty (1998)
Investment objective and policies: Long-term growth of capital. Invests at least 80% of assets in common stocks and other equity securities of companies who derive at least 50% of their assets, revenues, or net income engaged in the development, production, or distribution of technology-related products or services, including computer hardware and software, technology-based service industry companies, semiconductors, office equipment and automation, data networking and telecommunications equipment, and internet-related products and services. May invest up to 20% of assets in obligations of the U.S. Treasury, or other federal agency issues. May invest in both listed and unlisted foreign securities without limit, and may use a variety of derivative instruments in an effort to enhance performance and for hedging purposes. Fund is non-diversified.
Year organized: 1998
Redemption fee: 1.00% for shares held less than one year, payable to the fund
Dividends paid: Income - December; Capital gains - December
Management fee: 0.85%

SCUDDER 21st CENTURY GROWTH FUND ◆
(See first Scudder listing for data common to all funds)

Portfolio managers: Peter Chin (1996), Roy C. McKay (1996)
Investment objective and policies: Long-term capital appreciation. Invests primarily in equity securities of small, emerging growth companies with market capitalizations of $750M or less. May, however, invest in preferred stocks when management anticipates that the capital appreciation will outperform common stocks over a selected time. May also invest in illiquid and foreign securities without limit, and use a variety of derivative instruments in an effort to enhance performance and for hedging purposes.
Year organized: 1996
Ticker symbol: SCTGX
Group fund code: 050
Discount broker availability: *Schwab
Redemption fee: 1.00% on shares held less than 1 year, payable to the fund (waived for non-IRA pension accounts)
Dividends paid: Income - December; Capital gains - December
Portfolio turnover (1 yr): 92%
Management fee: 1.00%
Expense ratio: 1.75% (year ending 8/31/97) (3.52% without waiver)

SCUDDER U.S. TREASURY MONEY FUND ◆
(See first Scudder listing for data common to all funds)

Portfolio managers: Frank J. Rachwalski, Jr. (1998), John W. Stuebe (1998)
Investment objective and policies: Safety, liquidity and stability of capital, consistent with current income. Invests exclusively in ultra short-term, unconditionally guaranteed high quality U.S. Government and government agency money market obligations. Fund is allowed a maximum average maturity of 90 days.
Year organized: 1981 (name changed from Government Money Fund 3/91)
Ticker symbol: SCGXX
Group fund code: 059
Dividends paid: Income - declared daily, paid monthly
Management fee: 0.50%
Expense ratio: 0.65% (year ending 6/30/97) (0.94% without waiver)

SCUDDER VALUE FUND ◆
(See first Scudder listing for data common to all funds)

Portfolio managers: Donald E. Hall (1992), William J. Wallace (1992)
Investment objective and policies: Long-term capital growth. Invests at least 80% of assets in equity securities of undervalued medium-to-large sized companies with annual revenues or market capitalizations of at least $600M that are thought to have above-average potential

for price appreciation. May also invest up to 20% of assets in debt obligations including junk bonds. Fund may invest without limit in both listed and unlisted foreign securities when deemed beneficial, and use a variety of derivative instruments in an effort to enhance returns and for hedging purposes.
Year organized: 1992
Ticker symbol: SCVAX
Group fund code: 075
Sales restrictions: Effective 4/15/98 this fund becomes a Kemper load fund. Only those shareholders with an existing account will be grandfathered into the no-load class. All new Scudder clients must buy load shares.
Discount broker availability: Fidelity, *Schwab, Siebert, *White
Dividends paid: Income - December; Capital gains - December
Portfolio turnover (3 yrs): 47%, 91%, 98%
Management fee: 0.70%
Expense ratio: 1.24% (year ending 9/30/97) (1.28% without waiver)

SCUDDER ZERO COUPON 2000 FUND ◆
(See first Scudder listing for data common to all funds)

Portfolio managers: Stephen A. Wohler (1994), Timothy G. Raney (1997)
Investment objective and policies: As high an investment return over a selected period as is consistent with investment in U.S. Government securities and the minimization of reinvestment risk. Seeks to return a reasonably assured targeted dollar amount, predictable at the time of investment, on a specific target date in the future. Invests in U. S. Government zero coupon securities and matures on the third Friday of December of the year 2000. At that time the fund will be converted to cash and distributed to shareholders.
Year organized: 1986
Ticker symbol: SGZTX
Group fund code: 089
Discount broker availability: Fidelity, *Schwab, Siebert
Dividends paid: Income - December; Capital gains - December
Portfolio turnover (3 yrs): 6%, 85%, 87%
Management fee: 0.60%
Expense ratio: 1.00% (year ending 12/31/97) (1.76% without waiver)

SEAFIRST RETIREMENT PORTFOLIO FUNDS ◆
(Merged into Pacific Horizon Funds; SRF shares are open only to previous shareholders)

SEFTON FUNDS ◆
(Data common to all Sefton funds are shown below. See subsequent listings for data specific to individual funds.)

2550 Fifth Avenue, Suite 808
San Diego, CA 92103
800-524-2276, 619-239-5600

Adviser: Sefton Capital Management
Administrator: The BISYS Group, Inc.
Transfer agent: BISYS Fund Services
Minimum purchase: Initial: $2,000 ($5,000 for MM), Subsequent: $50
Wire orders accepted: Yes
Deadline for same day wire purchase: 4 P.M.
Telephone redemptions: Yes
Letter redemptions: Signature guarantee required over $50,000
Wire redemptions: Yes
Telephone switching: With other Sefton funds, and Pacific Horizon Prime and California Tax Exempt MM Funds
Number of switches permitted: Unlimited
Shareholder services: IRA, automatic investment plan, electronic funds transfer, systematic withdrawal plan min. bal. req. $100,000
IRA fees: Annual $12, Initial $5, Closing $10

SEFTON CALIFORNIA TAX FREE FUND ◆
(See first Sefton listing for data common to all funds)

Portfolio managers: Ted Piorkowski (1995), Harley K. Sefton (1995)
Investment objective and policies: A high level of current income exempt from federal and California income taxes, consistent with capital preservation. Invests primarily in investment grade California municipal obligations such that the weighted average maturity of the portfolio is ten years or more. May invest up to 20% of assets in taxable securities. Fund is non-diversified.
Year organized: 1995
Ticker symbol: SCALX
Discount broker availability: *White
Qualified for sale in: CA, CO, DC, NJ, OH, VI
Dividends paid: Income - declared daily, paid monthly; Capital gains - annually
Portfolio turnover (2 yrs): 15%, 94%
Management fee: 0.60%
Administration fee: 0.15%
Expense ratio: 0.88% (year ending 3/31/97) (1.17% without waiver)

SEFTON EQUITY VALUE FUND ◆
(See first Sefton listing for data common to all funds)

Portfolio managers: Leif O. Sanchez (1995), Thomas C. Bowden (1995), Harley K. Sefton (1995)
Investment objective and policies: Long-term capital appreciation. Invests primarily in common and convertible stocks of both domestic and foreign companies perceived to be undervalued. May invest in any size company with market capitalization exceeding $50M. May invest up to 15% of assets directly in foreign securities and may invest in ADRs and EDRs. May use forward foreign currency contracts and use options and futures for hedging purposes.
Year organized: 1995
Ticker symbol: SEQVX
Discount broker availability: *White
Qualified for sale in: CA, CO, DC, KS, NJ, NY, OH, SC, VI, WA
Dividends paid: Income - quarterly; Capital gains - annually
Portfolio turnover (2 yrs): 78%, 63%
Management fee: 1.00%
Administration fee: 0.15%
Expense ratio: 1.52% (year ending 3/31/97) (1.56% without waiver)

SEFTON SMALL COMPANY VALUE FUND ◆
(See first Sefton listing for data common to all funds)

Portfolio managers: Leif O. Sanchez (1997), Thomas C. Bowden (1997), Harley K. Sefton (1997)
Investment objective and policies: Long-term capital appreciation. Invests primarily in common and convertible stocks of both domestic and foreign companies perceived to be undervalued. May invest in any size company with market capitalization exceeding $50M. May invest up to 15% of assets directly in foreign securities and may invest in ADRs and EDRs. May use forward foreign currency contracts and use options and futures for hedging purposes.
Year organized: 1997
Ticker symbol: SSLVX
Discount broker availability: *White
Qualified for sale in: AL, CA, CO, DC, KS, NJ, NY, OH, SC, VI, WA
Dividends paid: Income - quarterly; Capital gains - annually
Management fee: 1.25%
Administration fee: 0.15%

SEFTON U.S. GOVERNMENT FUND ◆
(See first Sefton listing for data common to all funds)

Portfolio managers: Harley K. Sefton (1995), Ted Piorkowski (1995)
Investment objective and policies: As high a level of current income as is consistent with preservation of capital. Invests at least 65% of assets in securities issued or guaranteed by the U.S. Government, its agencies or instrumentalities. May also invest in CDs, bankers acceptances, commercial paper, and corporate

debt if rated in one of the two highest categories by a nationally recognized statistical rating organization. Portfolio maintains an average dollar-weighted maturity ranging from five to ten years.
Year organized: 1995
Ticker symbol: SGVTX
Discount broker availability: *White
Qualified for sale in: CA, CO, DC, NJ, OH, VI, WA
Dividends paid: Income - declared daily, paid monthly; Capital gains - annually
Portfolio turnover (2 yrs): 12%, 45%
Management fee: 0.60%
Administration fee: 0.15%
Expense ratio: 1.09% (year ending 3/31/97) (1.39% without waiver)

THE SELECTED FUNDS
(Data common to all Selected funds are shown below. See subsequent listings for data specific to individual funds.)

124 East Marcy Street
Santa Fe, NM 87501
800-243-1575, 800-279-0279
505-820-3000
fax 505-820-3001
Internet: http://www.selected.com

Shareholder service hours: Full service: M-F 7 A.M.-4 P.M. MST; After hours service: prices, yields, balances, orders, last transaction, messages, prospectuses, total returns
Adviser: Davis Selected Advisers, L.P.
Transfer agent: Investors Fiduciary Trust Co.
Minimum purchase: Initial: $1,000, Subsequent: $100; IRA: Initial: $250; Keogh: Initial: $500
Wire orders accepted: Yes
Deadline for same day wire purchase: 4 P.M.
Qualified for sale in: All states
Telephone redemptions: Yes
Wire redemptions: Yes, $10,000 minimum ($1,000 for Daily Government Fund), $5 fee
Letter redemptions: Signature guarantee required over $25,000
Telephone switching: With other Selected funds
Number of switches permitted: 4 per year
Shareholder services: IRA, SEP-IRA, Keogh, 401(k), 403(b), 457, corporate retirement plans, automatic investment plan, electronic funds transfer, systematic withdrawal plan min. bal. req. $5,000
12b-1 distribution fee: 0.25%
IRA/Keogh fees: Annual $12

SELECTED AMERICAN SHARES
(See first Selected listing for data common to all funds)

Portfolio manager: Christopher C. Davis (1995)
Investment objective and policies: Capital growth and income. Invests primarily in common stocks and other equity securities of U.S. companies, generally with market capitalizations of more than $1B. May invest in fixed-income securities with up to 30% of assets in junk bonds. Up to 35% of assets may be in securities of foreign issuers and 15% in illiquid securities. Fund follows a conservative approach in selecting common stocks and fixed-income securities, some of which may be convertible into common stocks.
Year organized: 1933
Ticker symbol: SLASX
Group fund code: 305
Discount broker availability: *Fidelity, *Schwab, *Siebert, *White
Dividends paid: Income - March, June, September, December; Capital gains - September
Portfolio turnover (3 yrs): 29%, 27%, 23%
Management fee: 0.65% first $500M to 0.55% over $1B
Expense ratio: 1.03% (year ending 12/31/96)

SELECTED DAILY GOVERNMENT FUND
(See first Selected listing for data common to all funds)

Portfolio manager: Carolyn H. Spolidoro (1993)
Investment objective and policies: Current income consistent with capital preservation and liquidity.

Invests exclusively in short-term U.S. Government money market obligations.
Year organized: 1988
Ticker symbol: SDGXX
Group fund code: 301
Check redemptions: $250 minimum
Dividends paid: Income - declared daily, paid monthly
Management fee: 0.30%
Expense ratio: 0.75% (year ending 12/31/96)

SELECTED SPECIAL SHARES
(See first Selected listing for data common to all funds)

Sub-adviser: Bramwell Capital Management
Portfolio manager: Elizabeth R. Bramwell (1994)
Investment objective and policies: Capital growth. Invests primarily in common stocks and securities convertible into common stocks emphasizing companies with market capitalizations under $1B. Fund seeks companies with growth potential because of rapid growth of demand within their existing markets, expansion into new markets, new products, reduced competition, cost reduction programs and other favorable indicators. Up to 25% of assets may be in securities of foreign issuers and 15% in illiquid securities.
Year organized: 1968 (split 2 for 1 on 1/6/94)
Ticker symbol: SLSSX
Group fund code: 304
Discount broker availability: *Fidelity, *Schwab, *Siebert, *White
Dividends paid: Income - December; Capital gains - December
Portfolio turnover (3 yrs): 98%, 127%, 99%
Management fee: 0.70% first $50M to 0.60% over $250M
Expense ratio: 1.33% (year ending 12/31/96)

SELECTED U.S. GOVERNMENT INCOME FUND
(See first Selected listing for data common to all funds)

Portfolio manager: Carolyn H. Spolidoro (1995)
Investment objective and policies: Current income and short-term capital gains, consistent with capital preservation. Invests primarily in debt obligations of varying maturities issued or guaranteed by the U.S. Government, its agencies and instrumentalities.
Year organized: 1987 (formerly Government Total Return)
Ticker symbol: SSGTX
Group fund code: 303
Discount broker availability: *Fidelity, *Schwab, *Siebert, *White
Dividends paid: Income - monthly; Capital gains - annually
Portfolio turnover (3 yrs): 76%, 65%, 29%
Management fee: 0.50%
Expense ratio: 1.44% (year ending 12/31/96)

SENECA FUNDS
(Data common to all Seneca funds are shown below. See subsequent listings for data specific to individual funds.)

909 Montgomery Street, Suite 600
San Francisco, CA 94133
800-990-9331, 800-828-1212
415-677-5950, fax 415-956-4345
Internet: http://www.senecafunds.com
e-mail: emunson@gmgseneca

Shareholder service hours: Full service: M-F 8 A.M.-4 P.M. CST; After hours service: prices, messages
Adviser: GMG/Seneca Capital Management
Transfer agent: Investors Fiduciary Trust Co.
Minimum purchase: Initial: $1,000, Subsequent: $500; IRA/Keogh: Initial: $5000; Subsequent: $250; Automatic investment plan: Subsequent: $100
Wire orders accepted: Yes
Deadline for same day wire purchase: 4 P.M.
Qualified for sale in: All states
Telephone redemptions: Yes
Wire redemptions: Yes
Letter redemptions: signature guarantee required over $99,999

Redemption fee: 1.00% for shares held less than 90 days, payable to fund
Telephone switching: Other Seneca funds
Number of switches permitted: Unlimited
Shareholder services: IRA, SEP-IRA, Keogh, 401(k), 403(b), directed dividends, electronic funds transfer
12b-1 distribution fee: 0.25%
IRA/Keogh fees: Annual $12

SENECA BOND FUND
(See first Seneca listing for data common to all funds)

Portfolio managers: Gail P. Seneca (1996), Charles B. Dicke (1996)
Investment objective and policies: Total return: capital appreciation and current income. Fund seeks to outperform the Lehman Brothers Government/Corporate Index by investing in a diversified portfolio of corporate and U.S. Government bonds and other debt securities. Will normally maintain a dollar-weighted average maturity of between two and ten years, and a dollar-weighted average duration of between two and eight years. May invest up to 35% of assets in junk bonds and up to 20% of assets in foreign debt.
Year organized: 1996
Ticker symbol: SAVYX
Discount broker availability: *Fidelity, *Schwab
Dividends paid: Income - monthly; Capital gains - December
Portfolio turnover (2 yrs): 63%, 53%
Management fee: 0.50%
Expense ratio: 2.00% (year ending 9/30/97) (includes waiver)

SENECA GROWTH FUND
(See first Seneca listing for data common to all funds)

Portfolio managers: Gail P. Seneca (1996), Richard D. Little (1996)
Investment objective and policies: Capital appreciation; current income incidental. Fund seeks appreciation greater than that of the S&P 500 Index by investing primarily in common stocks of growth companies with demonstrated greater long-term earnings growth than the average company in the index, with the belief that earnings growth will correlate to growth in stock price. While their is no limit to market capitalization, fund will focus on large firms, many with capitalizations above $5B. May also invest in preferred, convertible and debt instruments, and warrants as deemed necessary by market conditions. May invest up to 20% of assets in securities of foreign issuers, and use derivative instruments for hedging purposes.
Year organized: 1996
Ticker symbol: SGCRX
Discount broker availability: *Fidelity, *Schwab, *Siebert, *White
Dividends paid: Income - annually; Capital gains - December
Portfolio turnover (2 yrs): 72%, 88%
Management fee: 0.70%
Expense ratio: 2.55% (year ending 9/30/97) (includes waiver)

SENECA MID-CAP EDGE FUND
(See first Seneca listing for data common to all funds)

Portfolio managers: Gail P. Seneca (1996), Richard D. Little (1996)
Investment objective and policies: Capital appreciation; current income incidental. Fund seeks appreciation greater than that of the S&P Mid-Cap Index by investing primarily in common stocks of growth companies with demonstrated greater long-term earnings growth than the average company in the index, with the belief that earnings growth will correlate to growth in stock price. While their is no limit to market capitalization, fund will focus on firms with capitalizations between $500M & $5B. May also invest in preferred, convertible and debt instruments, and warrants as deemed necessary by market conditions. May invest up to 20% of assets in securities of foreign issuers, and use derivative instruments for hedging purposes.
Year organized: 1996
Ticker symbol: EDGEX

Discount broker availability: *Fidelity, *Schwab, *Siebert, *White
Dividends paid: Income - annually; Capital gains - December
Portfolio turnover (2 yrs): 112%, 72%
Management fee: 0.80%
Expense ratio: 2.70% (year ending 9/30/97) (includes waiver)

SENECA REAL ESTATE SECURITIES FUND
(See first Seneca listing for data common to all funds)

Portfolio managers: Gail P. Seneca (1996), David A. Shapiro (1996)
Investment objective and policies: High total return: current income and long-term capital appreciation. Generally invests at least 65% of assets in equity or debt securities of issuers that are principally engaged in the U.S. real estate industry or in related businesses. Directly engaged firms are those deriving at least 50% of assets or income from ownership, construction, management or sale of real estate. Examples of related firms include REITs, mortgage REITs, manufacturers and distributors of building supplies, or financial institutions originating or servicing mortgage loans. Fund is non-diversified. The fund will not make direct investments in real estate, and may invest up to 35% of assets outside of its stated fundamental focus. May invest up to 35% of assets in junk bonds.
Year organized: 1996
Ticker symbol: REALX
Discount broker availability: *Fidelity, *Schwab, *Siebert, *White
Dividends paid: Income - quarterly; Capital gains - December
Portfolio turnover (2 yrs): 64%, 31%
Management fee: 0.85%
Expense ratio: 3.05% (year ending 9/30/97) (includes waiver)

SENTRY FUND ◆
1800 North Point Drive
Stevens Point, WI 54481
800-533-7827, 715-346-7048
fax 715-346-7283

Shareholder service hours: Full service: 8 A.M.-4:15 P.M. CST; After hours service: prices, indices, prospectuses
Adviser: Sentry Investment Management, Inc. (a wholly owned subsidiary of Sentry Insurance)
Portfolio manager: Keith E. Ringberg (1983)
Transfer agent: Sentry Equity Services, Inc.
Investment objective and policies: Long-term capital growth; income secondary. Invests in a diversified portfolio of common stocks and securities convertible into common stocks believed to offer favorable long-term growth prospects. May invest at times in bonds and preferred stocks if perceived to benefit fund objective. May invest up to 10% of assets in foreign issues.
Year organized: 1970 (fund had an 8.0% load prior to 3/1/91)
Ticker symbol: SNTRX
Minimum purchase: Initial: $500, Subsequent: $50; Automatic investment plan: Initial: $200, Subsequent: $20
Wire orders accepted: No
Qualified for sale in: All states except HI
Letter redemptions: Signature guarantee required over $5,000
Dividends paid: Income - June, December; Capital gains - December
Portfolio turnover (3 yrs): 28%, 27%, 16%
Shareholder services: IRA, systematic withdrawal plan min. bal. req. $5,000
Management fee: 0.75% first $150M to 09.45% over $500M
Expense ratio: 0.84% (year ending 10/31/96)
IRA fees: Annual $5, Initial $5, Closing $5

SEQUOIA FUND ◆
767 Fifth Avenue, Suite 4701
New York, NY 10153-4798
800-686-6884, 212-832-5280
fax 212-832-5280

Adviser: Ruane, Cunniff & Co., Inc.
Lead portfolio manager: William J. Ruane (1970)
Transfer agent: DST Systems, Inc.

Investment objective and policies: Capital growth. Invests in common stocks and securities convertible into common stocks believed undervalued using classic Graham and Dodd analysis which emphasizes balance sheet strength and earnings power. May invest up to 15% of assets in foreign securities, and 10% in restricted securities and special situations. Fund gives no weight to technical stock market studies. Fund is non-diversified.
Special sales restrictions: Fund has been closed to new shareholders since 12/23/82
Year organized: 1970
Ticker symbol: SEQUX
Minimum purchase: Subsequent: $50
Wire orders accepted: No
Qualified for sale in: All states
Telephone redemptions: Yes
Letter redemptions: Signature guarantee required
Dividends paid: Income - February, June, December; Capital gains - February, December
Portfolio turnover (3 yrs): 8%, 23%, 15%
Shareholder services: IRA, systematic withdrawal plan min. bal. req. $10,000
Management fee: 1.00%
Expense ratio: 1.00% (year ending 12/31/97)
IRA fees: Annual $12

1784 FUNDS ◆
(See Boston 1784 funds.)

SEXTANT FUNDS ◆
(Data common to all Sextant funds are shown below. See subsequent listings for data specific to individual funds.)

1300 North State Street
Bellingham, WA 98225-4730
800-728-8762, 360-734-9900
prices/yields 888-732-6262
fax 360-734-0755
Internet: http://www.saturna.com
e-mail: saturna@saturna.com

Shareholder service hours: Full service: M-F 6:30 A.M.-5 P.M. PST; After hours service: prices, messages, prospectuses
Adviser: Saturna Capital Corp.
Transfer agent: Saturna Capital Corp.
Minimum purchase: Initial: $1,000, Subsequent: $100; IRA/Keogh: Initial: $25, Subsequent: $25; Automatic investment plan: Subsequent $100
Wire orders accepted: Yes, $500 subsequent minimum
Deadline for same day wire transfer: 4 P.M.
Telephone redemptions: Yes
Wire redemptions: Yes, $5,000 minimum, $25 fee
Letter redemptions: Signature guarantee not required
Check redemptions: $500 minimum
Telephone switching: With Amana funds and other Sextant funds, $25 minimum
Number of switches permitted: Unlimited
Shareholder services: IRA, Keogh, corporate retirement plans, electronic funds transfer, systematic withdrawal plan
IRA/Keogh fees: None

SEXTANT BOND INCOME FUND ◆
(See first Sextant listing for data common to all funds)

Portfolio manager: Phelps S. McIlvaine (1994)
Investment objective and policies: High current income. Invests at least 65% of assets in corporate debt securities rated within the three highest grades, U.S. Government Securities, high quality commercial paper and bank obligations. Fund generally maintains a dollar-weighted average maturity of ten years or longer.
Year organized: 1993 (name and objectives changed from Washington Tax-Exempt Fund in 1995. Prior performance may be misleading)
Ticker symbol: SBIFX
Group fund code: 22
Qualified for sale in: CA, DC, ID, IL, OR, WA
Dividends paid: Income - declared daily, paid monthly; Capital gains - November
Portfolio turnover (3 yrs): 77%, 75%, 77%

Management fee: 0.60% plus performance adjustment of up to +/- 0.20%
Expense ratio: 0.21% (year ending 11/30/97) (includes waiver)

SEXTANT GROWTH FUND ◆
(See first Sextant listing for data common to all funds)

Portfolio manager: Nicholas F. Kaiser (1990)
Investment objective and policies: Capital growth. Invests primarily in U.S. common stocks, securities convertible into common stocks and preferred stocks. May invest in smaller or newer companies as well as well-seasoned companies of any size and, to a limited extent, in foreign companies.
Year organized: 1987 (Name and objective changed from Northwest Growth Fund in 1995. Prior performance may be misleading.)
Ticker symbol: SSGFX
Group fund code: 21
Qualified for sale in: AK, CA, DC, ID, IL, OR, WA
Dividends paid: Income - November; Capital gains - November
Portfolio turnover (3 yrs): 32%, 40%, 12%
Management fee: 0.60% plus performance adjustment of up to +/- 0.30%
Expense ratio: 0.53% (year ending 11/30/97) (includes waiver)

SEXTANT IDAHO
TAX-EXEMPT FUND ◆
(See first Sextant listing for data common to all funds)

Portfolio manager: Phelps S. McIlvaine (1995)
Investment objective and policies: Income exempt from federal and Idaho income taxes; capital preservation secondary. Invests at least 65% of assets in Idaho tax-exempt securities rate A or better, and maintains a widely ranging dollar-weighted average maturity of from six to fifteen years.
Year organized: 1987 (formerly Idaho Extended Maturity Tax-Exempt Fund)
Ticker symbol: NITEX
Group fund code: 20
Qualified for sale in: DC, ID, OR, WA
Dividends paid: Income - declared daily, paid monthly; Capital gains - November
Portfolio turnover (3 yrs): 3%, 28%, 36%
Management fee: 0.50%
Expense ratio: 0.40% (year ending 11/30/97)

SEXTANT INTERNATIONAL FUND ◆
(See first Sextant listing for data common to all funds)

Portfolio manager: Nicholas F. Kaiser (1995)
Investment objective and policies: Long-term capital growth. Invests primarily in common stocks, securities convertible into common stocks and preferred stocks of foreign issuers from at least three countries other than the U.S. Fund only invests in securities traded on U.S. markets and in ADRs. May invest in mature and emerging markets.
Year organized: 1995
Ticker symbol: SINTX
Qualified for sale in: CA, ID, IL, OR, WA
Dividends paid: Income - May, November; Capital gains - November
Portfolio turnover (1 yr): 11%
Management fee: 0.60% plus performance adjustment of up to +/- 0.30%
Expense ratio: 1.74% (year ending 11/30/97) (includes waiver)

SEXTANT SHORT-TERM BOND FUND ◆
(See first Sextant listing for data common to all funds)

Portfolio manager: Phelps S. McIlvaine (1995)
Investment objective and policies: High current income consistent with preservation of capital. Invests at least 65% of assets in corporate debt securities rated within the three highest grades, U.S. Government securities, high quality commercial paper and bank obligations. Fund generally maintains a dollar-weighted average maturity of three years or less.
Year organized: 1995
Group fund code: 24

Qualified for sale in: CA, DC, ID, IL, OR, WA
Dividends paid: Income - declared daily, paid monthly; Capital gains - November
Portfolio turnover (1 yr): 100%
Management fee: 0.60% plus performance adjustment of up to +/- 0.20%
Expense ratio: 0.85% (year ending 11/30/97) (includes waiver)

SHORT-TERM INCOME FUND -
MONEY MARKET PORTFOLIO ◆
600 Fifth Avenue, 8th Floor
New York, NY 10020
800-221-3079, 212-830-5220
prices/yields 212-830-5225
fax 212-830-5478

Adviser: Reich & Tang Asset Management, L.P.
Portfolio manager: Molly Flewharty (1981)
Transfer agent: Reich & Tang Services, L.P.
Investment objective and policies: High current income consistent with preservation of capital and liquidity. Invests in money market obligations with maturities of one year or less.
Year organized: 1981
Ticker symbol: STIXX
Special sales restrictions: Only class "B" shares of the fund are sold direct and without 12b-1 fees. Statistics represent "B" shares only.
Minimum purchase: Initial: $5,000, Subsequent: $100; IRA: Initial $250, Subsequent: None
Wire orders accepted: Yes
Deadline for same day wire purchase: 12 NN
Qualified for sale in: All states except MT, PR
Telephone redemptions: Yes
Wire redemptions: Yes, $1,000 minimum
Letter redemptions: Signature guarantee required
Check redemptions: $250 minimum
Telephone switching: With other Reich & Tang funds, $1,000 minimum
Number of switches permitted: Unlimited
Deadline for same day switch: 12 NN
Dividends paid: Income - declared daily, paid monthly
Shareholder services: IRA, automatic investment plan, electronic funds transfer, systematic withdrawal plan
Management fee: 0.30% first $750M to 0.27% over $1.5B
Administration fee: 0.21% first $1.25B to 0.19% over $1.5B
Expense ratio: 0.66% (year ending 8/31/97)
IRA fees: None

SHORT-TERM INCOME FUND -
U.S. GOVERNMENT PORTFOLIO ◆
600 Fifth Avenue, 8th Floor
New York, NY 10020
800-221-3079, 212-830-5220
prices/yields 212-830-5225
fax 212-830-5478

Adviser: Reich & Tang Asset Management, L.P.
Portfolio manager: Molly Flewharty (1982)
Transfer agent: Reich & Tang Services, L.P.
Investment objective and policies: High current income consistent with capital preservation and liquidity. Invests in obligations issued or guaranteed by the U.S. Government with maturities of one year or less or subject to repurchase within one year.
Year organized: 1982
Ticker symbol: SGVXX
Special sales restrictions: Only class "B" shares of the fund are sold direct and without 12b-1 fees. Statistics represent "B" shares only.
Minimum purchase: Initial: $5,000, Subsequent: $100; IRA: Initial $250, Subsequent: None
Wire orders accepted: Yes
Deadline for same day wire purchase: 12 NN
Qualified for sale in: All states except AL, DE, PR
Telephone redemptions: Yes
Wire redemptions: Yes, $1,000 minimum
Letter redemptions: Signature guarantee required
Telephone switching: With other Reich & Tang funds, $1,000 minimum
Number of switches permitted: Unlimited
Deadline for same day switch: 12 NN

Check redemptions: $250 minimum
Dividends paid: Income - declared daily, paid monthly
Shareholder services: IRA, automatic investment plan, electronic funds transfer, systematic withdrawal plan
Management fee: 0.275% first $250M, 0.25% over $250M
Administration fee: 0.21% first $1.25B to 0.19% over $1.5B
Expense ratio: 0.55% (year ending 8/31/97)
IRA fees: None

SIT FUNDS ◆

(Data common to all Sit funds are shown below. See subsequent listings for data specific to individual funds.)

4600 Norwest Center
90 South Seventh Street, Suite 4000
Minneapolis, MN 55402-4130
800-332-5580, 612-334-5888
fax 612-342-2111
Internet: http://www.sitfunds.com

Shareholder service hours: Full service: M-F 8 A.M.-5 P.M. CST; After hours service: prices, prospectuses
Adviser: Sit Investment Assocs., Inc.
Transfer agent: First Data Investor Services
Minimum purchase: Initial: $2,000, Subsequent: $100; IRA/Keogh: None; Automatic investment plan: Initial: $500
Wire orders accepted: Yes
Deadline for same day wire purchase: 4 P.M.
Qualified for sale in: All states (except Minnesota Tax-Free Income Fund)
Telephone redemptions: Yes
Wire redemptions: Yes, $8 fee
Letter redemptions: Signature guarantee not required
Telephone switching: With other Sit funds
Number of switches permitted: 4 exchanges out per year (unlimited for money market fund)
Shareholder services: IRA, SEP-IRA, Keogh, 401(k), corporate retirement plans, directed dividends, electronic funds transfer, systematic withdrawal plan
IRA fees: Annual $15, Initial $5
Keogh fees: None

SIT BALANCED FUND ◆

(See first Sit listing for data common to all funds)

Portfolio managers: Peter L. Mitchelson (1993), Bryce A. Doty (1997)
Investment objective and policies: Long-term growth of capital consistent with preservation of principal, and regular income. Invests 40% to 60% of assets in equity securities, 40% to 60% in fixed-income securities, and 0% to 20% in money market instruments. At least 25% of assets will be in fixed-income senior securities. Up to 25% of assets may be in junk bonds, 20% in ADRs of foreign issuers and 20% in foreign debt securities. May use futures and options in an effort to increase return and for hedging purposes.
Year organized: 1993
Ticker symbol: SIBAX
Discount broker availability: *Fidelity, *Schwab, *Siebert, *White
Dividends paid: Income - March, June, September, December; Capital gains - December
Portfolio turnover (3 yrs): 38%, 101%, 51%
Management fee: 1.00%
Expense ratio: 1.00% (year ending 6/30/97)

SIT BOND FUND ◆

(See first Sit listing for data common to all funds)

Portfolio managers: Michael C. Brilley (1993), Bryce A. Doty (1997)
Investment objective and policies: Maximum total return: income and capital growth, consistent with capital preservation. Invests in a diverse mix of government and corporate debt securities, mortgage and other asset-backed securities and other debt instruments. Portfolio generally maintains a dollar-weighted aver-

age maturity of 2 to 30 years. Up to 25% of assets may be in junk bonds, 20% in non-dollar denominated securities of foreign issuers and 15% in illiquid securities. May use options and futures for hedging purposes.
Year organized: 1993
Ticker symbol: SIBOX
Discount broker availability: *Fidelity, *Schwab, *Siebert, *White
Check redemptions: $250 minimum
Dividends paid: Income - declared daily, paid monthly; Capital gains - December
Portfolio turnover (3 yrs): 128%, 159%, 41%
Management fee: 0.80%
Expense ratio: 0.80% (year ending 3/31/97)

SIT DEVELOPING MARKETS GROWTH FUND ◆

(See first Sit listing for data common to all funds)

Sub-adviser: Sit/Kim International Investment Associates, Inc.
Portfolio managers: Eugene C. Sit (1994), Andrew B. Kim (1994)
Investment objective and policies: Long-term capital appreciation. Invests at least 65% of assets in equity securities - common and preferred stock, warrants and convertible securities - of companies located in developing market countries, generally as defined by the International Finance Corporation or the World Bank. May invest directly and in ADRs, EDRs and GDRs and use options on foreign securities and indices for hedging purposes. Up to 15% of assets may be in illiquid securities. May use currency contracts for hedging purposes.
Year organized: 1994
Ticker symbol: SDMGX
Discount broker availability: *Fidelity, *Schwab, *Siebert, *White
Dividends paid: Income - December; Capital gains - December
Portfolio turnover (3 yrs): 66%, 46%, 56%
Management fee: 2.00%
Expense ratio: 2.00% (year ending 6/31/97)

SIT INTERNATIONAL GROWTH FUND ◆

(See first Sit listing for data common to all funds)

Sub-adviser: Sit/Kim International Investment Assocs., Inc.
Portfolio managers: Eugene C. Sit (1991), Andrew B. Kim (1991)
Investment objective and policies: Long-term growth. Invests at least 90% of assets in equity securities of issuers domiciled outside the U.S. May invest up to 50% of assets in smaller- to medium-sized growth companies with market capitalizations between $25M and $2B. May have more than 25% of assets concentrated in Japan, the United Kingdom and/or Germany. May invest directly if foreign securities or use ADRs and EDRs. Up to 15% of assets may be in illiquid securities. May use currency contracts for hedging purposes.
Year organized: 1991
Ticker symbol: SNGRX
Discount broker availability: Fidelity, *Schwab, Siebert, *White
Dividends paid: Income - December; Capital gains - December
Portfolio turnover (3 yrs): 42%, 39%, 40%
Management fee: 1.85%
Expense ratio: 1.50% (year ending 6/30/97) (1.85% without waiver)

SIT LARGE CAP GROWTH FUND ◆

(See first Sit listing for data common to all funds)

Portfolio managers: Peter L. Mitchelson (1981), Ronald D. Sit (1995)
Investment objective and policies: Maximum long-term capital appreciation. Invests at least 65% of assets in equity securities, primarily common stocks of companies with market capitalizations exceeding $5B at the time of purchase perceived to show growth potential. May also invest in convertible securities, corporate bonds, debentures and government securities. Up to

20% of assets may be in equity and debt securities of foreign issuers and 15% in illiquid securities.
Year organized: 1981 (formerly "New Beginning" Income and Growth Fund. Name changed 11/1/93; name changed again from Sit Growth & Income Fund 11/1/96)
Ticker symbol: SNIGX
Discount broker availability: Fidelity, *Schwab, Siebert, *White
Dividends paid: Income - December; Capital gains - December
Portfolio turnover (3 yrs): 32%, 50%, 67%
Management fee: 1.00% first $30M to 0.50% over $100M
Expense ratio: 1.00% (year ending 6/30/97) (1.08% without waiver)

SIT MID CAP GROWTH FUND ◆

(See first Sit listing for data common to all funds)

Portfolio managers: Eugene C. Sit (1981), Erik S. Anderson (1985)
Investment objective and policies: Maximum long-term capital appreciation. Invests at least 65% of assets in a diversified portfolio of common stocks of companies with market capitalizations ranging from $500M to $5B at the time of purchase. May also invest in larger companies offering improved growth possibilities. Up to 20% of assets may be in ADRs of foreign issuers and 15% in illiquid securities.
Year organized: 1981 (name changed from Sit Growth Fund 11/1/96)
Ticker symbol: NBNGX
Discount broker availability: Fidelity, *Schwab, Siebert, *White
Dividends paid: Income - December; Capital gains - December
Portfolio turnover (3 yrs): 39%, 50%, 75%
Management fee: 1.25%
Expense ratio: 0.92% (year ending 6/30/97) (1.09% without waiver)

SIT MINNESOTA TAX-FREE INCOME FUND ◆

(See first Sit listing for data common to all funds)

Portfolio managers: Michael C. Brilley (1993), Debra A. Sit (1993)
Investment objective and policies: High level of current income exempt from federal and Minnesota personal income taxes, consistent with capital preservation. Invests primarily in investment grade Minnesota municipal bonds. Generally maintains a dollar-weighted average maturity of 4 to 28 years. Up to 30% of assets may be in junk bonds and 20% in securities subject to AMT tax treatment.
Year organized: 1993
Ticker symbol: SMTFX
Discount broker availability: *Fidelity, *Schwab, Siebert, *White
Qualified for sale in: MN
Check redemption: $250 minimum
Dividends paid: Income - declared daily, paid monthly; Capital gains - December
Portfolio turnover (3 yrs): 6%, 16%, 34%
Management fee: 0.80%
Expense ratio: 0.80% (year ending 3/31/97)

SIT MONEY MARKET FUND ◆

(See first Sit listing for data common to all funds)

Portfolio managers: Michael C. Brilley (1985), Paul J. Jungquist (1995)
Investment objective and policies: Maximum current income consistent with preservation of capital and liquidity. Invests in money market instruments.
Year organized: 1985 (formerly "New Beginning" Investment Reserve, a short-term bond fund. Name and objective changed 11/1/93)
Ticker symbol: SNIXX
Check redemption: $250 minimum
Dividends paid: Income - declared daily, paid monthly
Management fee: 0.80%
Expense ratio: 0.50% (year ending 3/31/97) (0.80% without waiver)

SIT REGIONAL GROWTH FUND ◆
(See first Sit listing for data common to all funds)

Portfolio manager: Eugene C. Sit (1997)
Investment objective and policies: Maximum long-term capital appreciation. Invests at least 80% of assets in common stocks of companies of all sizes that are perceived to offer long-term growth and have corporate headquarters in the twelve Upper Midwestern states, including: Minnesota, Iowa, Missouri, North Dakota, South Dakota, Nebraska, Kansas, Wisconsin, Illinois, Michigan, Indiana and Ohio. May invest up to 15% of assets in illiquid securities and use put and call options for hedging purposes.
Year organized: 1997
Dividends paid: Income - December; Capital gains - December
Management fee: 1.25%

SIT SCIENCE AND TECHNOLOGY GROWTH FUND ◆
(See first Sit listing for data common to all funds)

Portfolio manager: Eugene C. Sit (1997)
Investment objective and policies: Maximum long-term capital appreciation. Invests at least 80% of assets in a diversified portfolio of common stocks of companies of all sizes expected to benefit from the development, improvement, advancement and use of science and technology, and are perceived to have a high potential for long-term growth. May invest up to 20% of assets in foreign securities that are available as ADRs. May invest up to 15% of assets in illiquid securities and use put and call options for hedging purposes.
Year organized: 1997
Dividends paid: Income - December; Capital gains - December
Management fee: 1.50%

SIT SMALL CAP GROWTH FUND ◆
(See first Sit listing for data common to all funds)

Portfolio manager: Eugene C. Sit (1994)
Investment objective and policies: Maximum long-term capital appreciation. Invests primarily in common stocks of small companies with market capitalizations under $500M at the time of purchase. May also invest in preferred stocks, convertible securities and warrants. Up to 20% of assets may be in ADRs of foreign issuers and 15% in illiquid securities.
Year organized: 1994
Ticker symbol: SSMGX
Discount broker availability: *Fidelity, *Schwab, *Siebert, *White
Dividends paid: Income - December; Capital gains - December
Portfolio turnover (3 yrs): 58%, 70%, 49%
Management fee: 1.50%
Expense ratio: 1.50% (year ending 6/30/97)

SIT TAX-FREE INCOME FUND ◆
(See first Sit listing for data common to all funds)

Portfolio managers: Michael C. Brilley (1985), Debra A. Sit (1988)
Investment objective and policies: High current income exempt from federal income tax, consistent with capital preservation. Invests primarily in investment grade municipal bonds, and maintains a dollar-weighted average maturity of 5 to 22 years. Fund may trade up to 5% of assets in options on debt securities for hedging purposes and may use futures and options thereon to hedge against interest rate fluctuations (up to 5% of assets in margin). Up to 20% of assets may be in securities subject to AMT tax treatment.
Year organized: 1985 (formerly Sit New Beginning Yield Fund. Name and objective changed 9/15/88)
Ticker symbol: SNTIX
Discount broker availability: *Fidelity, *Schwab, Siebert, *White
Check redemption: $250 minimum
Dividends paid: Income - declared daily, paid monthly; Capital gains - December
Portfolio turnover (3 yrs): 10%, 26%, 13%
Management fee: 0.80%
Expense ratio: 0.77% (year ending 3/31/97) (0.80% without waiver)

SIT U.S. GOVERNMENT SECURITIES FUND ◆
(See first Sit listing for data common to all funds)

Portfolio managers: Michael C. Brilley (1987), Bryce A. Doty (1997)
Investment objective and policies: High current income and safety of principal. Invests solely in debt obligations issued, guaranteed or insured by the U.S. Government, its agencies or instrumentalities. Portfolio maintains a dollar-weighted average maturity ranging from 2 to 20 years.
Year organized: 1987
Ticker symbol: SNGVX
Discount broker availability: *Fidelity, *Schwab, Siebert, *White
Check redemptions: $250 minimum
Dividends paid: Income - declared daily, paid monthly; Capital gains - December
Portfolio turnover (3 yrs): 85%, 51%, 39%
Management fee: 1.00%
Expense ratio: 0.80% (year ending 3/31/97) (0.97% without waiver)

SKYLINE FUNDS ◆
(Data common to all Skyline funds are shown below. See subsequent listings for data specific to individual funds.)

311 South Wacker Drive, Suite 4500
Chicago, IL 60606
800-458-5222, 888-759-3863
312-913-0900
prices/yields 800-828-2759
fax 312-913-1980

Adviser: Skyline Asset Management, L.P.
Transfer agent: Firstar Trust Co.
Minimum purchase: Initial: $1,000, Subsequent: $100; Automatic investment plan: Subsequent: $50
Wire orders accepted: Yes
Deadline for same day wire purchase: 4 P.M.
Qualified for sale in: All states
Telephone redemptions: Yes
Wire redemptions: Yes, $250 minimum, $12 fee
Letter redemptions: Signature guarantee required over $10,000
Telephone switching: With other Skyline funds, Firstar Money Market Fund and Firstar U.S. Government Money Market Fund
Number of switches permitted: 4 per year, 15 day hold
Shareholder services: IRA, directed dividends, systematic withdrawal plan min. bal. req. $5,000
IRA fees: Annual $12.50

SKYLINE FUND - SMALL CAP CONTRARIAN PORTFOLIO ◆
(See first Skyline listing for data common to all funds)

Portfolio manager: Daren C. Heitman (1997)
Investment objective and policies: Long-term capital appreciation. Invests primarily in common stocks of companies with market capitalizations between $50M and $2B that are perceived to be undervalued relative to book value, sales or potential earnings. Generally will not overweight portfolio in any sector more than twice the weighting of the Russell 2000. While normally fully invested, fund may invest without limit in investment grade fixed-income instruments or cash.
Year organized: 1997
Discount broker availability: *Fidelity, *Schwab, *White
Dividends paid: Income - December; Capital gains - December
Management fee: 1.50% first $200M to 1.35% over $600M (covers all normal operating expenses)

SKYLINE FUND - SPECIAL EQUITIES PORTFOLIO ◆
(See first Skyline listing for data common to all funds)

Portfolio manager: William M. Dutton (1987)
Investment objective and policies: Maximum capital appreciation. Invests in common stocks with emphasis on small companies with market capitaliza-

tions under between $100M and $700M perceived to be undervalued relative to low price/earnings multiples, but showing strong current trends and earnings growth. While normally fully invested, fund may invest without limit in investment grade fixed-income instruments or cash.
Year organized: 1987
Ticker symbol: SKSEX
Special sales restrictions: Fund closed to new shareholders 12/11/92 and to additional investments by existing shareholders 3/22/93, except for IRAs; reopened to existing shareholders 1/2/96, and to all investors 4/24/96. Closed again to new investors 1/30/97.
Discount broker availability: *Fidelity, *Schwab, *Siebert, *White
Dividends paid: Income - December; Capital gains - December
Portfolio turnover (3 yrs): 62%, 130%, 71%
Management fee: 1.50% first $200M to 1.35% over $600M (covers all normal operating expenses)
Expense ratio: 1.48% (year ending 12/31/97)

SKYLINE FUND - SPECIAL EQUITIES II ◆
(See first Skyline listing for data common to all funds)

Portfolio manager: Kenneth S. Kailin (1993)
Investment objective and policies: Maximum capital appreciation. Invests in common stocks with emphasis on small and medium-sized companies with market capitalizations between $400M and $2B perceived to be undervalued relative to low price/earnings multiples, but showing strong current trends and earnings growth. While normally fully invested, fund may invest without limit in investment grade fixed-income instruments or cash.
Year organized: 1993
Ticker symbol: SPEQX
Discount broker availability: *Fidelity, *Schwab, *Siebert, *White
Dividends paid: Income - December; Capital gains - December
Portfolio turnover (3 yrs): 104%, 145%, 102%
Management fee: 1.50% first $200M to 1.35% over $600M (covers all normal operating expenses)
Expense ratio: 1.51% (year ending 12/31/97)

SMITH BARNEY MONEY FUNDS - CASH PORTFOLIO
388 Greenwich Street
New York, NY 10013
800-327-6748, 212-723-9218

Adviser: Mutual Management Corp., a subsidiary of Smith Barney, Harris, Upham & Co.
Portfolio manager: Tom Rivoir (1991)
Transfer agent: First Data Investor Services Group, Inc.
Investment objective and policies: Maximum current income and capital preservation. Invests in a portfolio of various high quality, short-term money market instruments.
Year organized: 1974 (name changed from National Liquid Reserves - Cash Portfolio on 6/6/91)
Ticker symbol: SBCXX
Minimum purchase: Initial: $1,000, Subsequent: $50; IRA/Keogh: Initial: $250, Subsequent: $100
Wire orders accepted: Yes
Deadline for same day wire purchase: 12 NN
Qualified for sale in: All states
Telephone redemptions: Yes
Wire redemptions: Yes
Letter redemptions: Signature guarantee required
Check redemptions: $500 minimum
Dividends paid: Income: declared daily, paid monthly
Shareholder services: Keogh, IRA, SEP-IRA, corporate retirement plans, 403(b), systematic withdrawal plan min. bal. req. $5,000
Management fee: 0.45% first $6B to 0.35% over $18B
12b-1 distribution fee: 0.10%
Expense ratio: 0.64% (year ending 12/31/96)
IRA fees: Annual $2.50, Initial $5, Closing $5 (before 59 1/2)

SMITH BREEDEN FUNDS ◆

(Data common to all Smith Breeden funds are shown below. See subsequent listings for data specific to individual funds.)

100 Europa Drive, Suite 200
Chapel Hill, NC 27514-2310
800-221-3137, 919-967-7221
prices/yields 800-221-3138
fax 919-933-3157
Internet: http://www.smithbreeden.com
e-mail: mtfd@smithbreeden.com

Shareholder service hours: Full service: M-F 9 A.M.-7 ;p.m EST; After hours service: prices, account balances, orders, last transaction, prospectuses
Adviser: Smith Breeden Assocs., Inc.
Transfer agent: First Data Investor Services Group
Minimum purchase: Initial: $1,000, Subsequent: $50; IRA: Initial: $350; Automatic investment plan: Initial: None
Wire orders accepted: Yes
Deadline for same day wire purchase: 4 P.M.
Qualified for sale in: All states
Telephone redemptions: Yes
Wire redemptions: Yes, $1,000 minimum, $9 fee
Letter redemptions: Signature guarantee required over $25,000
Telephone switching: With other Smith Breeden funds
Number of switches permitted: 5 per year
Shareholder services: IRA, Keogh, electronic funds transfer (redemption only), systematic withdrawal plan min. bal. req. $10,000
12b-1 distribution fee: Maximum of 0.25% (paid by advisor)
IRA fees: Annual $12 (waived for balances over $10,000)

SMITH BREEDEN EQUITY PLUS FUND ◆

(See first Smith Breeden listing for data common to all funds)

Portfolio manager: John B. Sprow (1992)
Investment objective and policies: Total return approximating the performance of the S&P 500. Invests primarily in equity swap contracts with major commercial banks and S&P futures contracts. May also invest in fixed-income securities issued or guaranteed by the U.S. Government, its agencies or instrumentalities, and mortgage-backed securities. Fund hedges.
Year organized: 1992 (name changed from Market Tracking Fund 8/1/96)
Ticker symbol: SBEPX
Discount broker availability: *Fidelity, *Schwab, *Siebert, *White
Dividends paid: Income - March, June, September, December; Capital gains - March, June, September, December
Portfolio turnover (3 yrs): 182%, 107%, 120%
Management fee: 0.70%
Expense ratio: 0.88% (year ending 3/31/97) (2.60% without waiver)

SMITH BREEDEN FINANCIAL SERVICES FUND ◆

(See first Smith Breeden listing for data common to all funds)

Portfolio managers: Douglas T. Breeden (1997), Michael J. Giarla (1997), Robert B. Perry (1997)
Investment objective and policies: Capital appreciation. Invests at least 65% of assets in a diversified portfolio of foreign and domestic equity securities of banks; thrift, finance and leasing companies; brokerage, investment banking and advisory firms; real estate-related firms; and insurance companies. Foreign investment is made primarily through ADRs. May buy or sell interest or stock index futures and options for hedging purposes.
Year organized: 1997
Discount broker availability: *Fidelity, *Schwab, *Siebert, *White
Dividends paid: Income - annually; Capital gains - annually
Management fee: 1.50%

SMITH BREEDEN INTERMEDIATE DURATION U.S. GOVERNMENT SERIES ◆

(See first Smith Breeden listing for data common to all funds)

Portfolio manager: Daniel C. Dektar (1992)
Investment objective and policies: Total return in excess of the major market indices for mortgage-backed securities. Invests at least 70% of assets in fixed-income securities issued or guaranteed by the U.S. Government or its agencies and instrumentalities. Fund hedges.
Year organized: 1992
Ticker symbol: SBIDX
Discount broker availability: *Fidelity, *Schwab, *Siebert, *White
Dividends paid: Income - declared daily, paid monthly; Capital gains - annually
Portfolio turnover (3 yrs): 409%, 193%, 557%
Management fee: 0.70%
Expense ratio: 0.88% (year ending 3/31/97) (1.16% without waiver)

SMITH BREEDEN SHORT DURATION U.S. GOVERNMENT SERIES ◆

(See first Smith Breeden listing for data common to all funds)

Portfolio manager: Daniel C. Dektar (1992)
Investment objective and policies: High level of current income consistent with a volatility of net asset value similar to that of a portfolio which invests exclusively in six month U.S. Treasury securities on a constant maturity basis. It is expected that the dollar-weighted average life of its portfolio securities will be longer than six months, sometimes significantly; the adviser may use the acquisition of debt obligations at a premium or discount, mortgage and interest-rate swaps, interest-rate caps and floors, and interest-rate futures and options to lengthen or shorten the option-adjusted duration of the portfolio assets.
Year organized: 1992
Ticker symbol: SBSHX
Discount broker availability: *Fidelity, *Schwab, *Siebert, *White
Check redemptions: $100 minimum
Dividends paid: Income - monthly; Capital gains - annually
Portfolio turnover (3 yrs): 556%, 225%, 47%
Management fee: 0.70%
Expense ratio: 0.78% (year ending 3/31/97) (0.93% without waiver)

SOUND SHORE FUND ◆

Eight Sound Shore Drive
P.O. Box 1810
Greenwich, CT 06836
800-551-1980, 800-754-8758
207-879-0001
prices 800-754-8757
fax 207-879-6206
Internet: http://www.soundshorefund.com

Adviser: Sound Shore Management, Inc.
Portfolio managers: Henry Burn III (1985), T. Gibbs Kane, Jr. (1985)
Transfer agent and administrator: Forum Financial Corp.
Investment objective and policies: Capital growth; current income secondary. Invests primarily in a diversified portfolio of common stocks of undervalued companies believed to display good growth potential. Fund generally only considers companies with market capitalizations exceeding $1B. May, however, invest in government and corporate debt issues or money markets without limit if deemed necessary or consistent with the fund objective in light of market conditions. Up to 10% of assets may be in securities of other investment companies.
Year organized: 1985
Ticker symbol: SSHFX
Minimum purchase: Initial: $10,000, Subsequent: None; IRA: Initial: $250; Automatic investment plan: Subsequent: $50
Wire orders accepted: Yes
Deadline for same day wire purchase: 4 P.M.

Discount broker availability: *Fidelity, *Schwab, *Siebert, *White
Qualified for sale in: All states
Telephone redemptions: Yes
Wire redemptions: Yes, $5,000 minimum
Letter redemptions: Signature guarantee required over $50,000
Telephone switching: With Forum Daily Assets Treasury Fund; and, Forum Investors Bond and TaxSaver Bond funds, both of which have loads, although the fees are not levied on inbound exchanges, $2,500 minimum
Number of switches permitted: Unlimited
Dividends paid: Income: June, December; Capital gains: December
Portfolio turnover (3 yrs): 53%, 69%, 53%
Shareholder services: IRA, electronic funds transfer, systematic withdrawal plan min. bal. req. $20,000
Management fee: 0.75%
Administration fee: 0.10%
Expense ratio: 1.08% (year ending 12/31/97)
IRA fees: Annual $10

SPECTRA FUND ◆

75 Maiden Lane
New York, NY 10038
800-711-6141, 212-806-8800
201-547-3600
fax 201-247-3628

Adviser: Fred Alger Management, Inc.
Portfolio managers: David D. Alger (1971), Seilai Khoo (1989), Ronald Tartaro (1990)
Transfer agent: Alger Shareholder Services, Inc.
Investment objective and policies: Capital appreciation. Invests primarily in common stocks of companies traded on domestic stock exchanges or in the over-the-counter market. May invest in companies that are still in the developmental stage, or older companies that appear to be entering a new stage of growth due to a variety of factors. Fund may invest up to 20% of assets in foreign issues, may hold as much as 15% of assets in money markets, and invest up to 15% of assets in illiquid securities. May use futures and options for hedging purposes. Fund is non-diversified.
Year organized: 1968 (Fund was closed-end from 1968 to 1975, open-end from 1975 to 1978, closed-end from 1978 to Feb. 12, 1996.)
Ticker symbol: SPECX
Minimum purchase: Initial: $1,000, Subsequent: $100; IRA: Initial: $250; Automatic investment plan: Initial: $100
Wire orders accepted: Yes
Deadline for same day wire purchase: 4 P.M.
Discount broker availability: *Fidelity, *White
Qualified for sale in: All states
Telephone redemptions: Yes
Wire redemptions: Yes, $2,500 minimum
Letter redemptions: Signature guarantee required over $5,000
Dividends paid: Income: December; Capital gains: December
Portfolio turnover (3 yrs): 197%, 197%, 207%
Shareholder services: IRA, SEP-IRA, Keogh, 401(k), 403(b), automatic investment plan, systematic withdrawal plan min. bal. req. $10,000
Shareholder services fee: 0.25%
Management fee: 1.50%
Expense ratio: 2.15% (year ending 10/31/97)
IRA fees: Annual $10

SSgA FUNDS

(Data common to all SSgA funds are shown below. See subsequent listings for data specific to individual funds.)

Two International Place, 35th Floor
Boston, MA 02110
800-647-7327, 800-997-7327
617-654-6089
fax 617-654-6011

Shareholder service hours: Full service: M-F 8 A.M.-4 P.M. EST; After hours service: prices, yields, account balances, orders, last transaction, prospectuses, total returns
Adviser: State Street Bank & Trust Co.
Administrator: Frank Russell Investment Management Co.

Transfer agent: State Street Bank & Trust Co.
Minimum purchase: Initial: $1,000, Subsequent: $100; IRA: Initial: $250
Wire orders accepted: Yes
Deadline for same day wire purchase: 4 P.M. (12 NN for money market funds)
Qualified for sale in: All states
Telephone redemptions: Yes
Wire redemptions: Yes, $1,000 minimum
Letter redemptions: Signature guarantee required over $50,000
Telephone switching: With other SSgA funds, $100 minimum
Number of switches permitted: Unlimited, 15 day hold
Shareholder services: IRA, automatic investment plan, directed dividends, electronic funds transfer (redemption only)
12b-1 distribution fee: Maximum of 0.25%
IRA fees: Annual $10 (waived for '97, though), Initial $10, Closing $10

SSgA ACTIVE INTERNATIONAL FUND
(See first SSgA listing for data common to all funds)

Lead portfolio manager: Robert Rubano (1995)
Investment objective and policies: Long-term capital growth. Invests primarily in equity securities of companies domiciled or doing substantial portions of their businesses in various foreign countries. Fund diversifies across at least ten different countries in order to reduce the volatility associated with specific markets. May use ADRs and EDRs, and futures and options for hedging purposes on up to 25% of total assets.
Year organized: 1995
Ticker symbol: SSAIX
Discount broker availability: Fidelity, Schwab (only through financial advisers), Siebert, *White
Dividends paid: Income - October; Capital gains - October
Portfolio turnover (3 yrs): 48%, 22%, 7%
Management fee: 0.75%
Expense ratio: 1.00% (year ending 8/31/97) (1.40% without waiver)

SSgA BOND MARKET FUND
(See first SSgA listing for data common to all funds)

Lead portfolio manager: John P. Kirby (1996)
Investment objective and policies: Maximum total return. Invests primarily in investment grade fixed-income securities of all types and all durations, either foreign or domestic, government or private. May use a variety of derivative instruments in an effort to enhance performance and for hedging purposes.
Year organized: 1996
Ticker symbol: SSBMX
Discount broker availability: Fidelity, Schwab (only through financial advisers), Siebert, *White
Dividends paid: Income - quarterly; Capital gains - October
Portfolio turnover (2 yrs): 453%, 314%
Management fee: 0.30%
Expense ratio: 0.50% (year ending 8/31/97) (0.74% without waiver)

SSgA EMERGING MARKETS FUND
(See first SSgA listing for data common to all funds)

Lead portfolio manager: Joshua Feuerman (1997)
Investment objective and policies: Maximum total return, primarily capital growth. Invests primarily in equity securities of companies domiciled, or doing a substantial portion of their business in emerging markets countries as defined by the IMF or the World Bank. Fund diversifies across companies in at least ten developing or emerging markets with gross domestic product per capita under $8,000. Up to 15% of assets may be in illiquid securities. May use ADRs and EDRs, and futures and options for hedging purposes on up to 10% of total assets.
Year organized: 1994
Ticker symbol: SSEMX

Discount broker availability: Fidelity, Schwab (only through financial advisers), Siebert, *White
Dividends paid: Income - October; Capital gains - October
Portfolio turnover (3 yrs): 15%, 4%, 20%
Management fee: 0.75%
Expense ratio: 1.25% (year ending 8/31/97) (1.51% without waiver)

SSgA GROWTH AND INCOME FUND
(See first SSgA listing for data common to all funds)

Lead portfolio manager: Brenton H. Dickson (1993)
Investment objective and policies: Long-term capital growth, current income and growth of income. Invests at least 65% of assets in common and preferred stock and convertibles of well established, publicly traded companies. May also invest in ADRs, fixed-income securities of domestic issuers and U.S. dollar-denominated debt securities of foreign issuers. Any debt securities purchased other than convertibles have a dollar-weighted average maturity of ten years or less. May have up to 15% of assets in illiquid securities and use futures and options to hedge up to 25% of total assets.
Year organized: 1993
Ticker symbol: SSGWX
Discount broker availability: Fidelity, Schwab (only through financial advisers), Siebert, *White
Dividends paid: Income - quarterly; Capital gains - October
Portfolio turnover (3 yrs): 30%, 38%, 39%
Management fee: 0.85%
Expense ratio: 0.95% (year ending 8/31/97) (1.21% without waiver)

SSgA INTERMEDIATE FUND
(See first SSgA listing for data common to all funds)

Lead portfolio manager: John P. Kirby (1996)
Investment objective and policies: High current income consistent with capital preservation. Invests primarily in investment grade debt securities, and maintains a dollar-weighted average maturity between three and ten years. May invest in U.S. Government securities, corporate debt securities of domestic and foreign issuers, mortgage- and asset-backed securities and instruments of U.S. and foreign banks. May use futures and options and hedge up to 25% of total assets.
Year organized: 1993
Ticker symbol: SSINX
Discount broker availability: Fidelity, Schwab (only through financial advisers), Siebert, *White
Dividends paid: Income - March, June September, December; Capital gains - October
Portfolio turnover (3 yrs): 243%, 222%, 26%
Management fee: 0.80%
Expense ratio: 0.60% (year ending 8/31/97) (1.30% without waiver)

SSgA LIFE SOLUTIONS BALANCED FUND
(See first SSgA listing for data common to all funds)

Lead portfolio manager: Agustin "Gus" J. Fleites (1997)
Investment objective and policies: A balance of growth of capital and income. Designed primarily for tax-advantaged retirement accounts and other long-term investment strategies. Fund is comprised of portions of at least six of the investment family's underlying funds. Allocation ranges are as follows; equities 40% to 80%; bonds 20% to 60%; short-term assets 0% to 20%, with adjustments made according to perceived market conditions relative to fund objective. If necessary, portfolio is rebalanced at least quarterly. May invest up to 20% in international equities.
Year organized: 1997
Ticker symbol: SSLGX
Discount broker availability: Fidelity, Siebert, White
Dividends paid: Income - October; Capital gains - October
Management fee: pro rata share of underlying funds

SSgA LIFE SOLUTIONS GROWTH FUND
(See first SSgA listing for data common to all funds)

Lead portfolio manager: Agustin "Gus" J. Fleites (1997)
Investment objective and policies: Long-term growth of capital. Designed primarily for tax-advantaged retirement accounts and other long-term investment strategies. Fund is comprised of portions of at least six of the investment family's underlying funds. Allocation ranges are as follows; equities 60% to 100%; bonds 0% to 40%; short-term assets 0% to 20%, with adjustments made according to perceived market conditions relative to fund objective. If necessary, portfolio is rebalanced at least quarterly. May invest up to 25% in international equities.
Year organized: 1997
Ticker symbol: SSLIX
Discount broker availability: Fidelity, Siebert, White
Dividends paid: Income - October; Capital gains - October
Management fee: pro rata share of underlying funds

SSgA LIFE SOLUTIONS INCOME AND GROWTH FUND
(See first SSgA listing for data common to all funds)

Lead portfolio manager: Agustin "Gus" J. Fleites (1997)
Investment objective and policies: Income; long-term growth of capital secondary. Designed primarily for tax-advantaged retirement accounts and other long-term investment strategies. Fund is comprised of portions of at least six of the investment family's underlying funds. Allocation ranges are as follows; equities 20% to 60%; bonds 40% to 80%; short-term assets 0% to 20%, with adjustments made according to perceived market conditions relative to fund objective. If necessary, portfolio is rebalanced at least quarterly. May invest up to 15% in international equities.
Year organized: 1997
Ticker symbol: SSMTX
Discount broker availability: Fidelity, Siebert, White
Dividends paid: Income - October; Capital gains - October
Management fee: pro rata share of underlying funds

SSgA MATRIX EQUITY FUND
(See first SSgA listing for data common to all funds)

Lead portfolio manager: Douglas Holmes (1992)
Investment objective and policies: Total return that exceeds the return of the S&P 500 Index over time. Invests primarily in common stocks selected on the basis of a proprietary analytical model. The model measures value and Wall Street sentiment to rank stocks on overall attractiveness. May have up to 15% of assets in illiquid securities and use futures and options and hedge up to 25% of total assets.
Year organized: 1992
Ticker symbol: SSMTX
Discount broker availability: Fidelity, Schwab (only through financial advisers), Siebert, *White
Dividends paid: Income - quarterly; Capital gains - October
Portfolio turnover (3 yrs): 117%, 151%, 130%
Management fee: 0.75%
Expense ratio: 0.58% (year ending 8/31/97) (0.94% without waiver)

SSgA MONEY MARKET FUND
(See first SSgA listing for data common to all funds)

Lead portfolio manager: Rena Williams (1994)
Investment objective and policies: Maximum current income consistent with preservation of capital and liquidity. Invests in high-quality money market instruments.
Year organized: 1988
Ticker symbol: SSMXX
Check redemptions: $500 minimum
Dividends paid: Income - declared daily, paid monthly
Management fee: 0.25%
Expense ratio: 0.39% (year ending 8/31/97)

SSgA S&P 500 INDEX FUND
(See first SSgA listing for data common to all funds)

Lead portfolio manager: James B. May (1995)
Investment objective and policies: Total return that replicates the return of the S&P 500 Index. Invests in the stocks comprising the S&P 500 Index in proportion to their weighting in the Index (will purchase a representative sampling of the S&P 500 Index stocks if assets are too low to purchase all 500 stocks).
Year organized: 1992
Ticker symbol: SVSPX
Discount broker availability: Fidelity, Schwab (only through financial advisers), Siebert, *White
Dividends paid: Income - quarterly; Capital gains - October
Portfolio turnover (3 yrs): 8%, 29%, 39%
Management fee: 0.10%
Expense ratio: 0.16% (year ending 8/31/97) (0.26% without waiver)

SSgA SMALL CAP FUND
(See first SSgA listing for data common to all funds)

Lead portfolio manager: Jeffrey Adams (1994)
Investment objective and policies: Maximum total return. Invests primarily in the stocks of domestic companies with market capitalizations of $50M to $3B selected using a proprietary analytical model based on the momentum of Wall Street sentiment. Sector and industry weightings tend to approximate those of the Russell 2000. May have up to 15% of assets in illiquid securities and use ADRs of foreign issuers. May use futures and options and hedge up to 25% of total assets.
Year organized: 1992 (Formerly S&P Midcap Index Fund. Name and objective changed on 11/22/94. Prior performance may be misleading.)
Ticker symbol: SVSCX
Discount broker availability: Fidelity, Schwab (only through financial advisers), Siebert, *White
Dividends paid: Income - October; Capital gains - October
Portfolio turnover (3 yrs): 144%, 77%, 193%
Management fee: 0.75%
Expense ratio: 1.00% (year ending 8/31/97) (1.09% without waiver)

SSgA TAX FREE MONEY MARKET FUND
(See first SSgA listing for data common to all funds)

Lead portfolio manager: James Donahue (1994)
Investment objective and policies: Maximum current income exempt from federal income taxes, consistent with preservation of capital and liquidity. Invests primarily in high-quality municipal money market instruments.
Year organized: 1994
Ticker symbol: STAXX
Check redemptions: $500 minimum
Dividends paid: Income - declared daily, paid monthly
Management fee: 0.25%
Expense ratio: 0.58% (year ending 8/31/97)

SSgA U.S. GOVERNMENT MONEY MARKET FUND
(See first SSgA listing for data common to all funds)

Lead portfolio manager: Lisa Hatfield (1994)
Investment objective and policies: Maximum current income consistent with preservation of capital and liquidity. Invests exclusively in high-quality money market instruments issued by the U.S. Government, its agencies and instrumentalities.
Year organized: 1991
Ticker symbol: SSGXX
Check redemptions: $500 minimum
Dividends paid: Income - declared daily, paid monthly
Management fee: 0.25%
Expense ratio: 0.44% (year ending 8/31/97)

SSgA YIELD PLUS FUND
(See first SSgA listing for data common to all funds)

Lead portfolio manager: Rena Williams (1996)
Investment objective and policies: Maximum current income consistent with preservation of liquidity. Invests in high-quality debt securities with a portfolio duration of less than one year. May invest in U.S. Government securities, instruments of U.S. and foreign banks, debt instruments issued by U.S. and foreign corporations, securities of foreign governments and supranational organizations, asset- and mortgage-backed securities and interest rate swaps. May have up to 15% of assets in illiquid securities and use futures and options and hedge up to 25% of total assets.
Year organized: 1992
Ticker symbol: SSYPX
Discount broker availability: Fidelity, Siebert, *White
Dividends paid: Income - declared daily, paid monthly; Capital gains - October
Portfolio turnover (3 yrs): 92%, 97%, 200%
Management fee: 0.25%
Expense ratio: 0.38% (year ending 8/31/97)

STAGECOACH FUNDS
(Funds were absorbed into Wells Fargo complex along with another family and became entirely load funds.)

STAR SELECT REIT PLUS FUND ◆
425 Walnut Street
Cincinnati, OH 45201
800-677-3863, 513-632-2005

Adviser: Star Bank, N.A.
Administrator: Unified Advisers, Inc.
Portfolio managers: Carolyn A. Baril (1997), Peter Sorrentino (1997)
Transfer agent: Unified Advisers, Inc.
Investment objective and policies: Above average income and long-term growth of capital. Invests at least 65% of assets in real estate investment trusts (REITs) 'plus' real estate related equity securities. Always maintains at least 50% of assets in equity, mortgage and/or hybrid REITs, but focuses on equity type REITs. When selecting debt issues with equity characteristics, fund only invests in convertible debentures rated A or better. May use options.
Year organized: 1997
Minimum purchase: Initial: $1,000, Subsequent: $25
Wire orders accepted: Yes
Deadline for same day wire purchase: 3:30 P.M.
Qualified for sale in: All states
Telephone redemptions: Yes
Wire redemptions: Yes
Letter redemptions: Signature guarantee not required
Dividends paid: Income: quarterly; Capital gains: annually
Shareholder services: IRA, SEP-IRA, SIMPLE-IRA, automatic investment plan, systematic withdrawal plan
Shareholder services fee: Maximum of 0.25%
Management fee: 0.75%
12b-1 distribution fee: Maximum of 0.25% (not currently imposed)
IRA fees: None

STATE FARM MUTUAL FUNDS ◆
(Data common to all State Farm funds are shown below. See subsequent listings for data specific to individual funds.)

One State Farm Plaza
Bloomington, IL 61710
800-447-0740, 309-766-2029
fax 309-766-2579

Shareholder service hours: Full service: M-F 7:30 A.M.-4:15 P.M. CST; After hours service: prices, prospectuses
Adviser: State Farm Investment Management Corp.
Transfer agent: State Farm Investment Management Corp.

Special sales restrictions: Offered only to agents and employees of State Farm Insurance Companies and their families.
Minimum purchase: Initial: $50, Subsequent: $50; Automatic investment plan: Initial: $20, Subsequent: $20 (except Municipal Bond)
Wire orders accepted: No
Qualified for sale in: All states
Telephone redemptions: Yes
Wire redemptions: Yes, $2,500 minimum, $7.50 fee
Letter redemptions: Signature guarantee required over $50,000
Telephone switching: With other State Farm funds
Number of switches permitted: Unlimited
Shareholder services: IRA, Keogh, systematic withdrawal plan min. bal. req. $5,000
IRA fees: Annual $1
Keogh fees: None

STATE FARM BALANCED FUND ◆
(See first State Farm listing for data common to all funds)

Lead portfolio manager: Kurt G. Moser (1991)
Investment objective and policies: Long-term capital growth and income. Invests in common stocks (up to 75% of assets), preferred stocks and bonds with proportions varying according to market conditions. May invest up to 25% of assets in securities of foreign issuers.
Year organized: 1967
Ticker symbol: STFBX
Dividends paid: Income - June, December; Capital gains - December
Portfolio turnover (3 yrs): 9%, 6%, 4%
Management fee: 0.20% first $100M to 0.10% over $200M
Expense ratio: 0.15% (year ending 11/30/96)

STATE FARM GROWTH FUND ◆
(See first State Farm listing for data common to all funds)

Lead portfolio manager: Kurt G. Moser (1991)
Investment objective and policies: Long-term growth of capital and income. Invests primarily in income producing equity-type securities. Remainder of assets may be in fixed-income securities such as U.S. Government obligations, investment grade bonds and debentures, preferred stocks and in foreign securities not traded in the U.S.
Year organized: 1967
Ticker symbol: STFGX
Dividends paid: Income - June, December; Capital gains - December
Portfolio turnover (3 yrs): 16%, 3%, 3%
Management fee: 0.20% first $100M to 0.10% over $200M
Expense ratio: 0.13% (year ending 11/30/96)

STATE FARM INTERIM FUND ◆
(See first State Farm listing for data common to all funds)

Lead portfolio manager: Kurt G. Moser (1988)
Investment objective and policies: High yield with relative price stability. Invests in high quality government and corporate debt securities, with short (less than five years) and intermediate term (five to fifteen years) maturities.
Year organized: 1977
Ticker symbol: SFITX
Dividends paid: Income - declared daily, paid March, June, September, December; Capital gains - December
Portfolio turnover (3 yrs): 17%, 17%, 15%
Management fee: 0.20% first $50M to 0.10% over $100M
Expense ratio: 0.23% (year ending 11/30/96)

STATE FARM MUNICIPAL BOND FUND ◆
(See first State Farm listing for data common to all funds)

Lead portfolio manager: Kurt G. Moser (1988)
Investment objective and policies: Income exempt from federal income tax consistent with prudent

investment management. Invests primarily in long-term municipal bonds, including revenue bonds, with individual maturities of longer than five years. Up to 30% of assets may be in lower-rated or non-rated municipal securities.
Year organized: 1977
Ticker symbol: SFBDX
Minimum purchase: Initial: $1,000, Subsequent: $500; Automatic investment plan: Subsequent: $100
Dividends paid: Income - declared daily, paid March, June, September, December; Capital gains - December
Portfolio turnover (3 yrs): 6%, 7%, 8%
Management fee: 0.20% first $50M to 0.10% over $100M
Expense ratio: 0.16% (year ending 11/30/96)

STEADMAN FUNDS

At press time a plan was being discussed to consolidate the Steadman funds into one fund and make it a closed end fund. (Data common to all Steadman funds are shown below. See subsequent listing for data specific to individual funds.)

1730 K Street, NW, Suite 904
Washington, DC 20006
800-424-8570, 202-223-1000

Adviser: Steadman Security Corp.
Transfer agent: Steadman Security Corp.
Special sales restrictions: All Steadman funds are closed to new shareholders.
Minimum purchase: Initial: $500, Subsequent: $25
Wire orders accepted: No
Deadline for same day wire purchase: 4 P.M.
Telephone redemptions: Yes
Wire redemption: Yes, $10,000 minimum
Letter redemptions: Signature guarantee required over $10,000
Telephone switching: With other Steadman funds
Number of switches permitted: Unlimited
Shareholder services: IRA, Keogh, 401(k), systematic withdrawal plan min. bal. req. $10,000
Management fee: 1.00% first $35M to 0.75% over $70M
12b-1 distribution fee: Maximum of 0.25%
IRA/Keogh fees: Annual $5, Initial $5, Closing $3.50

STEADMAN AMERICAN INDUSTRY FUND
(See first Steadman listing for data common to all funds)

Investment objective and policies: Long-term capital growth; income secondary. Invests in common stocks. Fund buys call options and leverages.
Year organized: 1959
Ticker symbol: SAMRX
Dividends paid: Income - April; Capital gains - annually
Expense ratio: 31.07% (year ending 6/30/97)

STEADMAN ASSOCIATED FUND
(See first Steadman listing for data common to all funds)

Investment objective and policies: Income commensurate with reasonable risk; long-term capital growth secondary. Fund leverages. Invests in bonds and stocks.
Year organized: 1939
Ticker symbol: SASSX
Dividends paid: Income - March, June, September, December; Capital gains - annually
Expense ratio: 12.42% (year ending 6/30/97)

STEADMAN INVESTMENT FUND
(See first Steadman listing for data common to all funds)

Investment objective and policies: Long-term capital appreciation; income secondary. Invests primarily in common stocks, leverages.
Year organized: 1956
Ticker symbol: SINVX

Dividends paid: Income - March; Capital gains - annually
Expense ratio: 16.47% (year ending 6/30/97)

STEADMAN TECHNOLOGY & GROWTH FUND
(See first Steadman listing for data common to all funds)

Investment objective and policies: Capital appreciation. Invests at least 80% of assets in common stocks of companies which are primarily engaged in matters related to the ocean environment and companies expected to benefit from technological advances in scientifically related fields. Fund leverages.
Year organized: 1968 (name changed from Steadman Oceanographic, Technology & Growth Fund in 1993)
Ticker symbol: SOCNX
Dividends paid: Income - March; Capital gains - annually
Expense ratio: 41.46% (year ending 6/30/97)

STEIN ROE FUNDS ◆
(Data common to all Stein Roe funds are shown below. See subsequent listings for data specific to individual funds.)

One South Wacker Drive, Suite 3200
Chicago, IL 60606
800-338-2550, 312-368-7800
fax 312-368-5631
Internet: http://www.steinroe.com

Shareholder service hours: Full service: M-F 7 A.M.-8 P.M. Sat-Sun 8 A.M.-5 ;p.m CST; After hours service: prices, yields, balances, orders, last transaction, news, DJIA, total returns, exchanges, redemptions, purchases
Adviser: Stein Roe & Farnham, Inc. (a wholly-owned subsidiary of Liberty Mutual Insurance Co.)
Transfer agent: Stein Roe Services, Inc.
Minimum purchase: Initial: $2,500, Subsequent: $100; IRA/Keogh: Initial: $500, Subsequent: $50; Automatic investment plan: Initial: $1,000, Subsequent: $50 (exception noted)
Wire orders accepted: Yes
Deadline for same day wire purchase: 4 P.M.
Qualified for sale in: All states
Telephone redemptions: Yes, $1,000 minimum
Wire redemptions: Yes, $1,000 minimum, $7 fee
Letter redemptions: Signature guarantee required
Telephone switching: With other Stein Roe funds, $50 minimum
Number of switches permitted: 4 round trips per year
Shareholder services: IRA, SEP-IRA, Keogh, corporate retirement plans, directed dividends, electronic funds transfer, systematic withdrawal plan min. bal. req. $10,000
IRA fees: None
Keogh fees: Annual $10, Initial $50, Closing $5

STEIN ROE BALANCED FUND ◆
(See first Stein Roe listing for data common to all funds)

Portfolio manager: Harvey B. Hirschhorn (1996)
Investment objective and policies: Long-term growth of capital and current income, consistent with reasonable risk. Invests in an allocated combination of equity and fixed-income securities, and cash. Ordinarily will maintain no more than 75% of assets in common stocks. Equity positions will only be held in companies with market caps exceeding $1B, and all debt securities are investment grade. May invest in ADRs without limit and have up to 25% of assets in foreign securities. May use futures and options in an effort to increase revenue and for hedging purposes.
Year organized: 1949 (formerly Stein Roe & Farnham Balanced Fund, name changed to Total Return Fund, then back to Stein Roe Balanced Fund 4/96. Objective changed 4/96 as well.)
Ticker symbol: SRFBX
Discount broker availability: *Fidelity, *Schwab, *Siebert, *White

Dividends paid: Income - March, June, September, December; Capital gains - December
Portfolio turnover (3 yrs): 15%, 87%, 45%
Management fee: 0.55% first $500M to 0.45% over $1B
Administration fee: 0.15% first $500M to 0.10% over $1B
Expense ratio: 1.05% (year ending 9/30/97)

STEIN ROE CAPITAL OPPORTUNITIES FUND ◆
(See first Stein Roe listing for data common to all funds)

Portfolio managers: Gloria J. Santella (1989), Eric S. Maddix (1996)
Investment objective and policies: Long-term capital appreciation. Invests in stocks of both seasoned and smaller companies with above-average earnings growth rates that may benefit from new products or services, technological developments or changes in management. May invest in ADRs without limit and have up to 25% of assets in foreign securities and 35% in debt securities, including junk bonds. May use futures and options in an effort to increase revenue and for hedging purposes.
Year organized: 1963 (split 2 for 1 on 8/25/95)
Ticker symbol: SRFCX
Special sales restrictions: Closed to new investors 9/30/96, reopened 3/31/97.
Discount broker availability: *Fidelity, *Schwab, *Siebert, *White
Dividends paid: Income - December; Capital gains - December
Portfolio turnover (3 yrs): 35%, 22%, 60%
Management fee: 0.75% first $500M to 0.60% over $1.5B
Administration fee: 0.15% first $500M to 0.075% over $1.5B
Expense ratio: 1.17% (year ending 9/30/97)

STEIN ROE CASH RESERVES FUND ◆
(See first Stein Roe listing for data common to all funds)

Portfolio manager: Jane M. Naeseth (1980)
Investment objective and policies: Maximum current income consistent with preservation of capital and liquidity. Invests in high quality dollar denominated corporate and government money market instruments.
Year organized: 1976
Ticker symbol: STCXX
Check redemptions: $50 minimum
Dividends paid: Income - declared daily, paid monthly
Management fee: 0.50% first $500M to 0.40% over $1B
Expense ratio: 0.77% (year ending 6/30/97)

STEIN ROE EMERGING MARKETS FUND ◆
(See first Stein Roe listing for data common to all funds)

Portfolio managers: Bruno Bertocci (1997), David P. Harris (1997)
Investment objective and policies: Long-term capital appreciation. Invests in securities of companies located in emerging markets countries that are perceived to be undervalued. Country selections are based on the BARRA Emerging Markets Model, and cannot be included in the MSCI-EAFE or the Financial Times Indexes. There is no limitation regarding the amount of assets which may be invested in any one country or any one region of the world. May invest up to 35% of assets in debt securities of any rated quality, and up to 5% of assets in Russian securities. May use a variety of derivative instruments in an effort to enhance performance and for hedging purposes.
Year organized: 1997
Ticker symbol: SRMAX
Discount broker availability: *Fidelity, *Schwab, *Siebert, *White
Redemption fee: 1.00% for shares held less than 90 days, payable to the fund
Dividends paid: Income - December; Capital gains - December
Management fee: 1.25%

STEIN ROE GOVERNMENT
INCOME FUND ◆
(Fund liquidated 10/17/97)

STEIN ROE GOVERNMENT
RESERVES FUND ◆
(Fund liquidated 10/17/97)

STEIN ROE GROWTH AND
INCOME FUND ◆
(See first Stein Roe listing for data common to all funds)

Portfolio manager: Daniel K. Cantor (1995)
Investment objective and policies: Capital growth. Invests primarily in common stocks, convertible securities and other equity-type investments of companies with market capitalizations of $1B or more. May invest in ADRs without limit and have up to 25% of assets in foreign securities and 35% in investment grade debt securities. May use futures and options in an effort to increase revenue and for hedging purposes.
Year organized: 1987 (Name changed from Prime Equities 2/1/96; objectives remain the same)
Ticker symbol: SRPEX
Discount broker availability: *Fidelity, *Schwab, *Siebert, *White
Dividends paid: Income - February, May, August, November, December; Capital gains - December
Portfolio turnover (3 yrs): 9%, 13%, 70%
Management fee: 0.60% first $500M to 0.50% over $1B
Administration fee: 0.15% first $500M to 0.10% over $1B
Expense ratio: 1.13% (year ending 9/30/97)

STEIN ROE GROWTH
OPPORTUNITIES FUND ◆
(See first Stein Roe listing for data common to all funds)

Portfolio managers: Gloria J. Santella (1997), Eric S. Maddix (1997), Arthur J. McQueen (1997)
Investment objective and policies: Long-term capital appreciation. Invests primarily in common stocks of companies of any size and from any industry, perceived to offer sustained earnings growth at an above average rate. May invest in ADRs without limit and have up to 25% of assets in foreign securities, and up to 35% in investment grade corporate and government debt securities. May use a broad array of derivative instruments in an effort to enhance performance and for hedging purposes.
Year organized: 1997
Ticker symbol: SRGOX
Discount broker availability: *Fidelity, *Schwab, *Siebert, *White
Dividends paid: Income - December; Capital gains - December
Management fee: 0.75% first $500M to 0.60% over $1B
Administration fee: 0.15% first $500M to 0.075% over $1.5B

STEIN ROE GROWTH STOCK FUND ◆
(See first Stein Roe listing for data common to all funds)

Sub-adviser: Adviser's Capital Management Group
Portfolio manager: Eric P. Gustafson (1994)
Investment objective and policies: Long-term capital appreciation. Invests at least 65% of assets in common stocks and other equity type securities perceived to offer long-term growth. May invest in ADRs without limit and have up to 25% of assets in foreign securities and 35% in investment grade debt securities. May use futures and options in an effort to increase revenue and for hedging purposes.
Year organized: 1958 (Formerly Stein Roe Stock. Name changed 2/1/95.)
Ticker symbol: SRFSX
Sales restrictions: Fund closed to new investors 10/15/97; Only those shareholders of record on this date may continue to invest; three other classes of the fund now exist, including load classes.

Discount broker availability: *Fidelity, *Schwab, *Siebert, *White
Dividends paid: Income - December; Capital gains - December
Portfolio turnover (3 yrs): 27%, 39%, 36%
Management fee: 0.60% first $500M to 0.50% over $1B
Administration fee: 0.15% first $500M to 0.10% over $1B
Expense ratio: 1.07% (year ending 9/30/97)

STEIN ROE HIGH-YIELD FUND ◆
(See first Stein Roe listing for data common to all funds)

Portfolio manager: Stephen F. Lockman (1997)
Investment objective and policies: Total return: high current income and capital growth. Invests primarily in high-yield, high-risk medium and lower quality debt securities bearing a high rate of interest income. Selection of issues is made using a proprietary credit rating system based upon comparative credit analyses of issuers within the same industry. May use a variety of derivatives in an effort to increase revenue and for hedging purposes.
Year organized: 1996
Discount broker availability: *Fidelity, *Schwab, *Siebert, *White
Dividends paid: Income - declared daily, paid monthly; Capital gains - December
Management fee: 0.15% first $500M to 0.125% over $500M
Expense ratio: 1.00% (eight months ending 6/30/97) (2.29% without waiver)

STEIN ROE HIGH-YIELD
MUNICIPALS FUND ◆
(See first Stein Roe listing for data common to all funds)

Portfolio manager: M. Jane McCart (1995)
Investment objective and policies: High current income exempt from regular federal personal income tax. Invests primarily in long-term medium- or lower-quality municipal securities bearing a high rate of interest income. May invest 100% of assets in securities subject to AMT tax treatment. May use futures and options in an effort to increase revenue and for hedging purposes.
Year organized: 1984
Ticker symbol: SRMFX
Discount broker availability: *Fidelity, *Schwab, *Siebert, *White
Dividends paid: Income - declared daily, paid monthly; Capital gains - December
Portfolio turnover (3 yrs): 11%, 34%, 23%
Management fee: 0.60% first $100M to 0.50% over $200M
Expense ratio: 0.77% (year ending 6/30/97)

STEIN ROE INCOME FUND ◆
(See first Stein Roe listing for data common to all funds)

Portfolio manager: Stephen F. Lockman (1997)
Investment objective and policies: High current income. Invests primarily in medium-quality debt securities. May also invest in higher-quality securities and have up to 40% of assets in junk bonds. May invest in preferred and common stocks and foreign and municipal securities. May invest in ADRs without limit and have 25% of assets in foreign securities. May use futures and options in an effort to increase revenue and for hedging purposes.
Year organized: 1986 (formerly Stein Roe High-Yield Bond Fund)
Ticker symbol: SRHBX
Discount broker availability: *Fidelity, *Schwab, *Siebert, *White
Dividends paid: Income - declared daily, paid monthly; Capital gains - December
Portfolio turnover (3 yrs): 138%, 135%, 64%
Management fee: 0.65% first $100M, 0.60% over $100M
Expense ratio: 0.84% (year ending 6/30/97) (0.85% without waiver)

STEIN ROE INTERMEDIATE
BOND FUND ◆
(See first Stein Roe listing for data common to all funds)

Portfolio manager: Michael T. Kennedy (1988)
Investment objective and policies: High current income consistent with capital preservation. Invests at least 60% of assets in corporate debt securities with the three highest ratings of Moody's or S&P including securities issued or guaranteed by the U.S. Government or its agencies and instrumentalities, commercial paper and bank obligations. Fund maintains a dollar-weighted average maturity of three to ten years. May invest in ADRs without limit and have 25% of assets in foreign securities. Up to 35% of assets may be in junk bonds. May use futures and options in an effort to increase revenue and for hedging purposes.
Year organized: 1978 (formerly Stein Roe Managed Bonds)
Ticker symbol: SRBFX
Discount broker availability: *Fidelity, *Schwab, *Siebert, *White
Dividends paid: Income - declared daily, paid monthly; Capital gains - December
Portfolio turnover (3 yrs): 210%, 202%, 162%
Management fee: 0.50%
Expense ratio: 0.73% (year ending 6/30/97) (0.75% without waiver)

STEIN ROE INTERMEDIATE
MUNICIPALS BOND FUND ◆
(See first Stein Roe listing for data common to all funds)

Portfolio manager: Joanne T. Costopoulos (1991)
Investment objective and policies: High current income exempt from federal income tax, consistent with capital preservation. Invests primarily in intermediate-term municipal bonds. Portfolio maintains a dollar-weighted average maturity of three to ten years. At least 75% of assets will be in municipal securities within the three highest ratings. Up to 100% of assets may be in securities subject to AMT tax treatment. May use futures and options in an effort to increase revenue and for hedging purposes.
Year organized: 1985
Ticker symbol: SRIMX
Discount broker availability: *Fidelity, *Schwab, *Siebert, *White
Dividends paid: Income - declared daily, paid monthly; Capital gains - December
Portfolio turnover (3 yrs): 44%, 66%, 67%
Management fee: 0.60% first $100M to 0.50% over $200M
Expense ratio: 0.70% (year ending 6/30/97) (0.82% without waiver)

STEIN ROE INTERNATIONAL
FUND ◆
(See first Stein Roe listing for data common to all funds)

Portfolio managers: Bruno Bertocci (1994), David P. Harris (1994)
Investment objective and policies: Long-term capital growth. Invests primarily in stocks and other equity securities of both seasoned and smaller companies from at least three countries outside the U.S. Up to 35% of assets may be in investment grade debt securities. May use futures and options in an effort to increase revenue and for hedging purposes.
Year organized: 1994
Ticker symbol: SRITX
Discount broker availability: *Fidelity, *Schwab, *Siebert, *White
Dividends paid: Income - December; Capital gains - December
Portfolio turnover (2 yrs): 59%, 48%
Management fee: 1.00%
Expense ratio: 1.55% (year ending 9/30/97) (includes waiver)

STEIN ROE MANAGED MUNICIPALS FUND ◆

(See first Stein Roe listing for data common to all funds)

Portfolio manager: M. Jane McCart (1991)
Investment objective and policies: High income exempt from federal income tax, consistent with capital preservation. Invests primarily in long-term municipal securities with maturities generally longer than 10 years. At least 75% of assets will be in municipal securities within the three highest ratings. Up to 100% of assets may be in securities subject to AMT tax treatment. May use futures and options in an effort to increase revenue and for hedging purposes.
Year organized: 1976 (formerly Tax-Exempt Bond Fund)
Ticker symbol: SRMMX
Discount broker availability: *Fidelity, *Schwab, *Siebert, *White
Dividends paid: Income - declared daily, paid monthly; Capital gains - December
Portfolio turnover (3 yrs): 16%, 40%, 33%
Management fee: 0.60% first $100M to 0.45% over $1B
Expense ratio: 0.73% (year ending 6/30/97)

STEIN ROE MUNICIPAL MONEY MARKET FUND ◆

(See first Stein Roe listing for data common to all funds)

Portfolio manager: Veronica M. Wallace (1995)
Investment objective and policies: Maximum current income exempt from federal income tax, consistent with stability of principal and liquidity. Invests primarily in short-term municipal money market securities.
Year organized: 1983 (name changed from Tax-Exempt Money Fund in October 1992)
Ticker symbol: STEXX
Check redemptions: $50 minimum
Dividends paid: Income - declared daily, paid monthly
Management fee: 0.25%
Administration fee: 0.50% first $500M to 0.40% over $1B
Expense ratio: 0.70% (year ending 6/30/97) (0.86% without waiver)

STEIN ROE SPECIAL FUND ◆

(See first Stein Roe listing for data common to all funds)

Portfolio manager: M. Gerard Sandel (1997)
Investment objective and policies: Capital appreciation. Invests in a diversified portfolio of stocks of seasoned and new companies, securities with limited marketability and securities of companies which should benefit from management change, new product or service development, or change in demand. Seeks above-average growth stocks with limited downside risk due to being undervalued, under-followed or out of favor. May invest in ADRs without limit and have up to 25% of assets in foreign securities and up to 35% in debt securities including junk bonds. May use futures and options in an effort to increase revenue and for hedging purposes.
Year organized: 1968
Ticker symbol: SRSPX
Discount broker availability: *Fidelity, *Schwab, *Siebert, *White
Dividends paid: Income - December; Capital gains - December
Portfolio turnover (3 yrs): 15%, 32%, 41%
Management fee: 0.75% first $500M to 0.60% over $1B
Administration fee: 0.15% first $500M to 0.075% over $1.5B
Expense ratio: 1.14% (year ending 9/30/97)

STEIN ROE SPECIAL VENTURE FUND ◆

(See first Stein Roe listing for data common to all funds)

Portfolio managers: John S. McLandsborough (1997), Richard B. Peterson (1994)
Investment objective and policies: Long-term capi-

tal appreciation. Invests primarily in stocks of entrepeneurially managed companies that represent special opportunities and have market capitalizations under $3B. May invest in ADRs without limit and have up to 25% of assets in foreign securities. May use futures and options in an effort to increase revenue and for hedging purposes.
Year organized: 1994
Ticker symbol: SRSVX
Discount broker availability: *Fidelity, *Schwab, *Siebert, *White
Dividends paid: Income - December; Capital gains - December
Portfolio turnover (3 yrs): 102%, 72%, 84%
Management fee: 0.90%
Expense ratio: 1.29% (year ending 9/30/97)

STEIN ROE YOUNG INVESTOR FUND ◆

(See first Stein Roe listing for data common to all funds)

Portfolio managers: Erik P. Gustafson (1995), David P. Brady (1995)
Investment objective and policies: Long-term capital appreciation. Invests primarily in common stocks and other equity type securities of companies perceived to have long-term appreciation potential and to affect the lives of young people. May invest in ADRs without limit, and have up to 25% of assets in foreign securities and up to 35% in investment grade debt securities. May use futures and options in an effort to increase revenue and for hedging purposes. Fund also seeks to educate its shareholders by providing materials regarding personal finance and investing as well as materials on the fund and its portfolio holdings.
Year organized: 1994
Ticker symbol: SRYIX
Minimum purchase: Initial: $2,500, Subsequent: $50; IRA/Keogh: Initial: $500; UG/TMA: Initial: $1,000; Automatic investment plan: Initial: None
Discount broker availability: *Fidelity, *Schwab, *Siebert, *White
Dividends paid: Income - December; Capital gains - December
Portfolio turnover (3 yrs): 22%, 98%, 55%
Management fee: 0.60% first $500M to 0.50% over $1B
Administration fee: 0.20% first $500M to 0.125% over $1B
Expense ratio: 1.43% (year ending 9/30/97) (1.49% without waiver)

STONEBRIDGE GROWTH FUND ◆

1801 Century Blvd., Suite 1800
Los Angeles, CA 90067
800-639-3935

Adviser: Stonebridge Capital Management, Inc.
Portfolio manager: Richard C. Barrett (1984)
Transfer agent: National Financial Data Services, Inc.
Investment objective and policies: Long-term capital growth and increased future income; current income secondary. Invests primarily in common stocks with a potential growth rate greater than the overall economy. Up to 20% of assets may be invested in securities of foreign issuers, either directly or through ADRs or closed end investment companies. Fund may sell up to 25% of total assets short against the box; write covered options, use futures contracts and hedge.
Year organized: 1958 (name changed from National Industries Fund in 1996)
Ticker symbol: NAIDX
Minimum purchase: Initial: $250, Subsequent: $25
Wire orders accepted: No
Qualified for sale in: All states except AK, IA, MA, NH, SD, UT, VT
Letter redemptions: Signature guarantee not required
Dividends paid: Income - December; Capital gains - December
Portfolio turnover (3 yrs): 41%, 38%, 36%

Shareholder services: Systematic withdrawal plan min. bal. req. $10,000
Management fee: 0.75% first $10M to 0.5625% over $25M
Expense ratio: 1.50% (year ending 11/30/97) (includes waiver)

STRATTON FUNDS ◆

(Data common to all Stratton funds are shown below. See subsequent listings for data specific to individual funds.)

Plymouth Meeting Executive Campus
610 W. Germantown Pike, Suite 300
Plymouth Meeting, PA 19462-1050
800-441-6580, 800-634-5726
800-578-8261, 610-941-0255
recorded services 800-472-4266
fax 610-239-4920
e-mail: horizon@fpsserv.com

Shareholder service hours: Full service: M-F 9 A.M.-7 P.M. EST; After hours service: prices, account balances, last transaction, total returns
Adviser: Stratton Management Co.
Transfer agent: First Data Investor Services Group
Minimum purchase: Initial: $2,000, Subsequent: $100; IRA/Keogh: Initial: None, Subsequent: None
Wire orders accepted: Yes
Deadline for same day wire purchase: 4 P.M.
Qualified for sale in: All states
Letter redemptions: Signature guarantee required over $10,000
Telephone switching: With other Stratton funds
Number of switches permitted: Unlimited
Shareholder services: IRA, Keogh, 403(b), corporate retirement plans, automatic investment plan, electronic funds transfer, systematic withdrawal plan min. bal. req. $10,000
IRA/Keogh fees: Annual $12

STRATTON GROWTH FUND ◆

(See first Stratton listing for data common to all funds)

Portfolio managers: James W. Stratton (1972), Gerard E. Heffernan (1997)
Investment objective and policies: Capital growth; current income secondary. Invests primarily in quality, value-oriented, domestic common stocks and securities convertible into common stock, and other equity securities. May invest in REITs.
Year organized: 1972
Ticker symbol: STRGX
Discount broker availability: Fidelity, Schwab, Siebert, White
Dividends paid: Income - June, December; Capital gains - June, December
Portfolio turnover (3 yrs): 34%, 20%, 15%
Management fee: 0.75%
Expense ratio: 1.11% (year ending 12/31/97)

STRATTON MONTHLY DIVIDEND REIT SHARES ◆

(See first Stratton listing for data common to all funds)

Portfolio managers: James W. Stratton (1980), John A. Affleck (1997)
Investment objective and policies: High dividend and interest income. Invests primarily in common stock and securities convertible into common stock of REITs. Invests at least 25% of assets in public utility companies in electric, gas, energy, water and telephone fields.
Year organized: 1971 (formerly Energy & Utility Shares, a fund that was closed-end until 1981. Name changed from Stratton Monthly Dividend Shares 12/97, policy changed to investing only in REITs. Past performance may be misleading.)
Ticker symbol: STMDX
Discount broker availability: Fidelity, Schwab, Siebert, White
Dividends paid: Income - monthly; Capital gains - December
Portfolio turnover (3 yrs): 42%, 69%, 53%
Management fee: 0.625%
Expense ratio: 1.02% (year ending 12/31/97)

STRATTON SMALL-CAP YIELD FUND ◆
(See first Stratton listing for data common to all funds)

Portfolio managers: James W. Stratton (1993), Frank H. Reichel III (1993)
Investment objective and policies: Dividend income and capital appreciation. Invests primarily in common stock and securities convertible into common stock of companies with market capitalizations under $500M that pay quarterly dividends at an above-average rate. May invest in REITs.
Year organized: 1993
Ticker symbol: STSCX
Discount broker availability: Fidelity, Schwab, Siebert, White
Dividends paid: Income - March, June, September, December; Capital gains - June, December
Portfolio turnover (3 yrs): 26%, 36%, 33%
Management fee: 0.75% plus performance fee of +/- up to 0.50% relative to Russell 2000 Index over 24 months
Expense ratio: 1.62% (year ending 12/31/97)

STRATTON SPECIAL VALUE FUND ◆
(See first Stratton listing for data common to all funds)

Portfolio managers: James W. Stratton (1997), James Van Dyke Quereau (1997)
Investment objective and policies: Capital appreciation. Invests primarily in common stock and securities convertible into common stock of under-researched, misunderstood companies of all sizes perceived to be undervalued by the market. May also invest in other types of securities with equity characteristics. May use short sales and options and futures for hedging purposes.
Year organized: 1997
Discount broker availability: Schwab
Dividends paid: Income - December; Capital gains - December
Management fee: 0.75% plus performance fee of +/- up to 0.50% relative to Russell 2000 Index over 24 months

STRATUS FUND PORTFOLIOS
(Became load funds 10/1/96)

STRONG FUNDS ◆
(Data common to all Strong funds are shown below. See subsequent listings for data specific to individual funds.)

One Hundred Heritage Reserve
P.O. Box 2936
Milwaukee, WI 53201
800-368-3863, 800-368-4777, 414-359-1400
prices/yields 800-368-3550
TDD 800-999-2780, 414-359-3700
fax 414-359-0802
Internet: http://www.strong-funds.com

Shareholder service hours: Full service: 7 days, 24 hours
Adviser: Strong Capital Management, Inc. (exception noted)
Transfer agent: Strong Capital Management, Inc.
Minimum purchase: Initial: (See fund); Automatic investment plan: Initial: None, Subsequent: $50
Wire orders accepted: Yes
Deadline for same day wire purchase: 4 P.M.
Qualified for sale in: All states
Telephone redemptions: Yes
Wire redemptions: Yes, $500 minimum, $10 fee
Letter redemptions: Signature guarantee required over $25,000
Telephone switching: With other Strong funds
Number of switches permitted: 5 per year, 3 per quarter
Shareholder services: IRA, SEP-IRA, Keogh, 401(k), 403(b), directed dividends, electronic funds transfer, systematic withdrawal plan min. bal. req. $5,000
IRA/Keogh fees: Annual $10, $30 maximum per SSN (waived for retirement accounts with more than $25,000 in Strong funds); Closing $10

STRONG ADVANTAGE FUND ◆
(See first Strong listing for data common to all funds)

Portfolio managers: Jeffrey A. Koch (1989), Lyle J. Fitterer (1997)
Investment objective and policies: High current income consistent with minimum fluctuation of principal. Invests in high-quality money market instruments and longer-term fixed-income securities and must maintain a dollar-weighted averaged maturity of 90 days to one year. May invest up to 25% of assets in securities of foreign issuers, and use futures and options for hedging purposes.
Year organized: 1988
Ticker symbol: STADX
Group fund code: 031
Minimum purchase: Initial: $2,500, Subsequent: $50; IRA/Keogh: Initial: $1,000
Discount broker availability: *Fidelity, *Schwab, *Siebert, *White
Check redemptions: $500 minimum
Dividends paid: Income - declared daily, paid monthly; Capital gains - March
Portfolio turnover (3 yrs): 155%, 17%, 305%
Management fee: 0.60%
Expense ratio: 0.80% (year ending 2/29/97)

STRONG AMERICAN UTILITIES FUND ◆
(See first Strong listing for data common to all funds)

Sub-adviser: W. H. Reaves & Co.
Portfolio managers: William H. Reaves (1993), William A. Ferer (1993), Ronald J. Sorenson (1993), Mark D. Luftig (1995)
Investment objective and policies: Current income and capital appreciation. Invests primarily in equity securities of domestic "public utility companies" (companies that engage in the manufacture, production, generation, transmission, sale and/or distribution of water, gas and electric energy), and companies engaged in the communications field excluding public broadcasting companies. Up to 25% of assets may be in equity securities of energy companies and 35% in securities of foreign issuers. May use futures and options in an effort to increase return and for hedging purposes. Fund is non-diversified.
Year organized: 1993
Ticker symbol: SAMUX
Group fund code: 038
Minimum purchase: Initial: $1,000, Subsequent: $50; IRA/Keogh: Initial: $250
Discount broker availability: *Fidelity, *Schwab, *Siebert, *White
Dividends paid: Income - March, June, September, December; Capital gains - March
Portfolio turnover (3 yrs): 62%, 84%, 56%
Management fee: 0.75%
Expense ratio: 1.10% (year ending 10/31/97)

STRONG ASIA PACIFIC FUND ◆
(See first Strong listing for data common to all funds)

Portfolio manager: Anthony L.T. Cragg (1992)
Investment objective and policies: Capital appreciation. Invests primarily in equity securities of issuers located in Asia or the Pacific Basin. Fund must diversify its holdings across companies from at least three countries. Up to 35% of assets may be in equity or investment grade debt securities of issuers located elsewhere in the world, including the U.S. Up to 15% of assets may be in illiquid securities. May use derivatives in an effort to enhance returns and for hedging purposes.
Year organized: 1992
Ticker symbol: SASPX
Group fund code: 040
Minimum purchase: Initial: $1,000, Subsequent: $50; IRA/Keogh: Initial: $250
Discount broker availability: *Fidelity, *Schwab, *Siebert, *White
Dividends paid: Income - March, June, September, December; Capital gains - March
Portfolio turnover (3 yrs): 97%, 91%, 104%
Management fee: 1.00%
Expense ratio: 2.00% (year ending 10/31/97)

STRONG ASSET ALLOCATION FUND ◆
(See first Strong listing for data common to all funds)

Portfolio managers: Bradley C. Tank (1993), Rimas M. Milaitis (1995), Jeffrey A. Koch (1994)
Investment objective and policies: High total return - income and capital appreciation - with reasonable risk. Invests 30% to 70% of assets in equity securities, 20% to 70% in bonds and 0% to 50% in cash equivalents. Neutral balance is 60% equity securities, 35% bonds, and 5% cash equivalents. Allocation will vary depending on market and economic conditions. Up to 35% of assets may be in junk bonds and 25% in securities of foreign issuers. May use futures and options in an effort to increase return and for hedging purposes.
Year organized: 1981 (name changed from Strong Investment Fund in 1994)
Ticker symbol: STAAX
Group fund code: 020
Minimum purchase: Initial: $250; Subsequent: $50
Discount broker availability: *Fidelity, *Schwab, *Siebert, *White
Dividends paid: Income - March, June, September, December; Capital gains - March
Portfolio turnover (3 yrs): 276%, 447%, 327%
Management fee: 0.85% first $35M, 0.80% over $35M
Expense ratio: 1.10% (year ending 10/31/96)

STRONG BLUE CHIP 100 FUND ◆
(See first Strong listing for data common to all funds)

Portfolio manager: Karen E. McGrath (1997)
Investment objective and policies: Total return; capital appreciation and income. Invests 50% of assets in the S&P 100, the largest blue chip stocks traded in the U.S., weighted by capitalization. The balance of the portfolio is invested in some or all of these blue chips according to perceived market conditions. May use a variety of derivative instruments for hedging purposes.
Year organized: 1997
Ticker symbol: SBCHX
Group fund code: 063
Minimum purchase: Initial: $2,500, Subsequent: $50; IRA/Keogh: Initial: $250
Discount broker availability: *Fidelity, *Schwab, *Siebert, *White
Dividends paid: Income - quarterly; Capital gains - annually
Management fee: 0.75%
Expense ratio: 1.00% (4 months ending 10/31/97) (2.0% without waiver)

STRONG COMMON STOCK FUND ◆
(See first Strong listing for data common to all funds)

Portfolio managers: Richard T. Weiss (1991), Marina T. Carlson (1993)
Investment objective and policies: Capital growth. Designed for employee benefit plan investment needs, including a "fully invested" position at all times. Invests at least 80% of assets in the common stocks and other equity securities of small and medium-sized companies that are perceived to be undervalued. May invest up to 25% of assets in both direct and depositary securities of foreign issuers, and up to 20% in debt obligations.
Year organized: 1989
Ticker symbol: STCSX
Group fund code: 032
Special sales restrictions: Closed to new shareholders on 3/19/93
Minimum purchase: Initial: $1,000, Subsequent: $50; IRA/Keogh: Initial: $250
Discount broker availability: *Fidelity, *Schwab, *Siebert, *White
Dividends paid: Income - March, June, September, December; Capital gains - March
Portfolio turnover (3 yrs): 117%, 91%, 92%
Management fee: 1.00%
Expense ratio: 1.20% (year ending 12/31/97)

STRONG CORPORATE BOND FUND ◆
(See first Strong listing for data common to all funds)

Portfolio managers: Jeffrey A. Koch (1992), John T. Bender (1996)
Investment objective and policies: Total return: high current income with a moderate degree of share price fluctuation. Invests at least 65% of assets in investment grade, corporate fixed-income securities. While there are no restrictions, the portfolio generally maintains a dollar-weighted average maturity of seven to twelve years. Up to 35% of assets may be in any other type of fixed-income security, up to 25% in foreign debt, and up to 25% of assets may be in junk bonds. May use futures and options in an effort to increase return and for hedging purposes.
Year organized: 1985 (name and objective changed from Strong Income Fund in 1995; lost equity component)
Ticker symbol: STCBX
Group fund code: 022
Minimum purchase: Initial: $2,500; Subsequent: $50; IRA/Keogh: Initial: $1,000
Discount broker availability: *Fidelity, *Schwab, *Siebert, *White
Check redemptions: $500 minimum
Dividends paid: Income - declared daily, paid monthly; Capital gains - March
Portfolio turnover (3 yrs): 542%, 673%, 621%
Management fee: 0.625%
Expense ratio: 1.00% (year ending 10/31/97)

STRONG DISCOVERY FUND ◆
(See first Strong listing for data common to all funds)

Portfolio managers: Richard S. Strong (1987), Charles A. Paquelet (1996)
Investment objective and policies: Capital growth. Invests more or less equally in equity securities of small, mid and large capitalization growth companies. May invest up to 100% of assets in debt securities when they offer potential for capital appreciation. Fund will, to a substantial degree, engage in trading operations based upon short-term market considerations, pursuing those firms perceived to benefit most from emerging trends. May invest up to 25% of assets in securities of foreign issuers. May use futures and options in an effort to increase return and for hedging purposes, and sell short against the box.
Year organized: 1987
Ticker symbol: STDIX
Group fund code: 030
Minimum purchase: Initial: $1,000, Subsequent: $50; IRA/Keogh: Initial: $250
Discount broker availability: *Fidelity, *Schwab, *Siebert, *White
Dividends paid: Income - March, June, September, December; Capital gains - March
Portfolio turnover (3 yrs): 170%, 793%, 516%
Management fee: 1.00%
Expense ratio: 1.40% (year ending 12/31/97)

STRONG DOW 30 VALUE FUND ◆
(See first Strong listing for data common to all funds)

Sub-adviser: Horizon Investment Services, LLC
Portfolio managers: Charles B. Carlson (1997), Richard J. Moroney (1997)
Investment objective and policies: Capital growth. Invests in the thirty blue chip companies which make up the Dow Jones Industrial Average. One half of the assets maintain the price-weighted positions dictated for each company by the Index. The other half of the fund's assets are overweighted to various Index stocks based on various technical analysis, primarily those that are the ten highest yielding, in other words "The Dogs of the Dow." Additionally, if there is evidence that the DJIA and the Dow Transportation Index are trending in the same direction, up to 20% of assets may be invested in cash or debt obligations as a market hedge.
Year organized: 1997
Group fund code: 070
Minimum purchase: Initial: $2,500, Subsequent: $50; IRA/Keogh: Initial: $250

Discount broker availability: *Fidelity, *Schwab, *Siebert, *White
Dividends paid: Income - March, June, September, December; Capital gains - annually
Management fee: 0.80%

STRONG EQUITY INCOME FUND ◆
(See first Strong listing for data common to all funds)

Portfolio manager: Rimas M. Milaitis (1995)
Investment objective and policies: Total return: capital growth and income. Invests at least 65% of assets in dividend-paying equity securities. May invest up to 35% of assets in intermediate- to long-term corporate or U.S. Government debt securities. May invest up to 10% of assets in non-investment grade, "junk" bonds. May use derivative instruments for hedging purposes.
Year organized: 1995
Ticker symbol: SEQIX
Group fund code: 056
Minimum purchase: Initial: $2,500, Subsequent: $50; IRA/Keogh: Initial: $250
Discount broker availability: *Fidelity, *Schwab, *Siebert, *White
Dividends paid: Income - March, June, September, December; Capital gains - March
Portfolio turnover (2 yrs): 153%, 158%
Management fee: 0.80%
Expense ratio: 1.10% (year ending 10/31/97)

STRONG GLOBAL HIGH YIELD BOND FUND ◆
(See first Strong listing for data common to all funds)

Portfolio managers: Shirish T. Malekar (1998), John T. Bender (1998), Jeffrey A. Koch (1998)
Investment objective and policies: Total return: high current income and capital appreciation. Invests at least 80% of assets in a diversified portfolio of medium- and lower-quality (junk bond) debt obligations from at least three different countries, including the U.S. Portfolio has no maturity restrictions, but is generally held at an average dollar-weighted maturity between seven and twelve years. At least 35% of assets are always domestic. May invest up to 20% of assets in common stocks and convertibles, and up to 10% of assets in debt obligations which are in default. May use a variety of derivative instruments in an effort to enhance performance and for hedging purposes.
Year organized: 1998
Minimum purchase: Initial: $1,000, Subsequent: $50; IRA/Keogh: Initial: $250
Dividends paid: Income - declared daily, monthly; Capital gains - annually
Management fee: 0.70%

STRONG GOVERNMENT SECURITIES FUND ◆
(See first Strong listing for data common to all funds)

Portfolio managers: Bradley C. Tank (1990), John T. Bender (1997)
Investment objective and policies: Total return: high current income with a moderate share price fluctuation. Invests at least 80% of assets in U.S. Government securities; the remainder is in other investment grade, fixed-income securities, including dollar-denominated foreign debt securities known as "Yankee Bonds." Fund maintains an average dollar-weighted maturity of five to ten years. May use futures and options in an attempt to increase return and for hedging purposes.
Year organized: 1986
Ticker symbol: STVSX
Group fund code: 025
Minimum purchase: Initial: $2,500, Subsequent: $50; IRA/Keogh: Initial: $1,000
Discount broker availability: *Fidelity, *Schwab, *Siebert, *White
Check redemptions: $500 minimum
Dividends paid: Income - declared daily, paid monthly; Capital gains - March
Portfolio turnover (3 yrs): 475%, 458%, 409%
Management fee: 0.60%
Expense ratio: 0.80% (year ending 10/31/97)

STRONG GROWTH FUND ◆
(See first Strong listing for data common to all funds)

Portfolio manager: Ronald C. Ognar (1993)
Investment objective and policies: Capital growth. Invests at least 65% of assets in equity securities believed to have above average growth prospects. Up to 25% of assets may be in securities of foreign issuers and 35% in investment grade debt securities. May use forward currency contracts, sell short against the box, and use futures and options in an attempt to increase return and for hedging purposes.
Year organized: 1993
Ticker symbol: SGROX
Group fund code: 041
Minimum purchase: Initial: $1,000, Subsequent: $50; IRA/Keogh: Initial: $250
Discount broker availability: *Fidelity, *Schwab, *Siebert, *White
Dividends paid: Income - March, June, September, December; Capital gains - March
Portfolio turnover (3 yrs): 296%, 295%, 321%
Management fee: 1.00%
Expense ratio: 1.30% (year ending 12/31/97)

STRONG GROWTH AND INCOME FUND ◆
(See first Strong listing for data common to all funds)

Portfolio manager: Rimas M. Milaitis (1995)
Investment objective and policies: Maximum total return: capital growth and income. Invests at least 65% of assets in equity securities, with a focus on those that pay current dividends and offer potential growth of earnings. May also invest up to 35% of assets in intermediate- to long-term corporate or U.S. Government bonds. May invest up to 15% of assets directly in securities of foreign issuers, or without limit in domestic market depositary receipts of foreign concerns. May use derivative instruments for hedging purposes.
Year organized: 1995
Ticker symbol: SGRIX
Group fund code: 052
Minimum purchase: Initial: $2,500, Subsequent: $50; IRA/Keogh: Initial: $250
Discount broker availability: *Fidelity, *Schwab, *Siebert, *White
Dividends paid: Income - March, June, September, December; Capital gains - March
Portfolio turnover (2 yrs): 238%, 174%
Management fee: 0.80%
Expense ratio: 1.20% (year ending 10/31/97)

STRONG GROWTH 20 FUND ◆
(See first Strong listing for data common to all funds)

Portfolio manager: Ronald C. Ognar (1997)
Investment objective and policies: Capital growth. Invests at least 65% of assets in equity securities, with a focus on 20 to 30 companies perceived to offer above average growth prospects. May also invest up to 35% of assets in intermediate- to long-term corporate or U.S. Government bonds. May invest up to 25% of assets directly in securities of foreign issuers or in domestic market depositary receipts of foreign concerns. May use derivative instruments for hedging purposes.
Year organized: 1997
Ticker symbol: SGRTX
Group fund code: 062
Minimum purchase: Initial: $2,500, Subsequent: $50; IRA/Keogh: Initial: $250
Discount broker availability: *Fidelity, *Schwab, *Siebert, *White
Dividends paid: Income - quarterly; Capital gains - annually
Portfolio turnover (1 yr): 250%
Management fee: 1.00%
Expense ratio: 1.40% (5 months ending 12/31/97)

STRONG HERITAGE MONEY FUND ◆
(See first Strong listing for data common to all funds)

Portfolio manager: Jay N. Mueller (1995)
Investment objective and policies: Maximum current income consistent with capital preservation and liquidity. Invests in money market instruments. Up to

25% of assets may be in securities of foreign issuers. Designed to deliver extra high yields for long-term buy and hold investors by maintaining a lower than average expense ratio.

Year organized: 1995
Ticker symbol: SHMXX
Group fund code: 049
Minimum purchase: Initial: $25,000, Subsequent: $1,000
Check redemptions: $1,000 minimum
Transaction fees: $3 for each redemption exchange or check, payable to the fund (waived for accounts with balances of $100,000 or more)
Dividends paid: Income - declared daily, paid monthly
Management fee: 0.50%
Expense ratio: 0.10% (year ending 2/29/97) (0.60% without waiver)

STRONG HIGH-YIELD BOND FUND ◆
(See first Strong listing for data common to all funds)

Portfolio manager: Jeffrey A. Koch (1995)
Investment objective and policies: Total return: high current income and capital growth. Invests primarily in medium- and lower- ("junk bond") quality debt obligations of corporate issuers. Under normal conditions the fund will maintain an average portfolio maturity of five to ten years. May also invest up to 10% of assets in debt obligations that are in default, and up to 20% of net assets in common stocks and securities convertible to common. May invest up to 25% of assets in foreign issues, and use futures and options in an attempt to increase return and for hedging purposes.
Year organized: 1995
Ticker symbol: STHYX
Group fund code: 053
Minimum purchase: Initial: $2,500, Subsequent: $50; IRA/Keogh: Initial: $1,000
Discount broker availability: *Fidelity, *Schwab, *Siebert, *White
Check redemptions: $500 minimum
Dividends paid: Income - declared daily, paid monthly; Capital gains - March
Portfolio turnover (2 yrs): 409%, 391%
Management fee: 0.625%
Expense ratio: 0.60% (year ending 10/31/97) (0.80% without waiver)

STRONG HIGH-YIELD MUNICIPAL BOND FUND ◆
(See first Strong listing for data common to all funds)

Portfolio manager: Mary-Kay H. Bourbulas (1993)
Investment objective and policies: High current income exempt from federal income taxes. Invests primarily in medium and lower ("junk bond") quality long-term municipal securities, and maintains a dollar-weighted average maturity ranging from 15 to 25 years. May invest without limit in securities subject to AMT tax treatment, have up to 15% of assets in illiquid securities and use futures and options in an effort to increase return and for hedging purposes.
Year organized: 1993
Ticker symbol: SHYLX
Group fund code: 039
Minimum purchase: Initial: $2,500, Subsequent: $50
Discount broker availability: *Fidelity, *Schwab, *Siebert, *White
Check redemptions: $500 minimum
Dividends paid: Income - declared daily, paid monthly; Capital gains - March
Portfolio turnover (3 yrs): 92%, 107%, 114%
Management fee: 0.60%
Expense ratio: 0.70% (year ending 8/31/97)

STRONG INDEX 500 FUND ◆
(See first Strong listing for data common to all funds)

Sub-adviser: Barclays Global Fund Advisors
Investment objective and policies: To approximate (before fees and expenses) the capitalization weighted total rate of return of that portion of the U.S. market for publicly traded common stocks composed of the

larger capitalized companies. Fund invests all of its investable assets in a feeder portfolio managed by the sub-adviser, with identical objectives. Master portfolio will weight investments identically to the weightings found in the S&P 500 Index, and may use derivatives for hedging purposes.
Year organized: 1997
Ticker symbol: SINEX
Group fund code: 061
Minimum purchase: Initial: $2,500, Subsequent: $50; IRA/Keogh: Initial: $1,000
Discount broker availability: Fidelity, Schwab, Siebert, White
Redemption fee: 0.50% for shares held less than six months, payable to fund
Dividends paid: Income - quarterly; Capital gains - annually
Shareholder services fee: 0.25%
Management fee: 0.05%

STRONG INTERNATIONAL BOND FUND ◆
(See first Strong listing for data common to all funds)

Portfolio manager: Shirish T. Malekar (1994)
Investment objective and policies: High total return: capital appreciation and income. Invests primarily in investment grade corporate and government debt securities of foreign issuers from at least three countries other than the U.S. Portfolio generally maintains a dollar-weighted average maturity of four to nine years. Up to 35% of assets may be in securities of U.S. issuers, 35% in junk bonds and 15% in illiquid securities. May use derivatives in an effort to enhance returns and for hedging purposes.
Year organized: 1994
Ticker symbol: SIBUX
Group fund code: 043
Minimum purchase: Initial: $1,000, Subsequent: $50; IRA/Keogh: Initial: $250
Discount broker availability: *Fidelity, *Schwab, *Siebert, *White
Check redemptions: $500 minimum
Dividends paid: Income - declared daily, paid monthly; Capital gains - March
Portfolio turnover (2 yrs): 208%, 258%, 473%
Management fee: 0.70%
Expense ratio: 0.70% (year ending 10/31/97) (1.50% without waiver)

STRONG INTERNATIONAL STOCK FUND ◆
(See first Strong listing for data common to all funds)

Portfolio manager: Anthony L.T. Cragg (1992)
Investment objective and policies: Long-term capital appreciation. Invests at least 65% and preferably 90% of assets in equity securities of issuers located outside the U.S. May invest in ADRs and EDRs without limit, and invest up to 35% of assets in equity and other securities of U.S. issuers and in non-convertible bonds and other debt securities issued by foreign government entities. Up to 15% of assets may be in illiquid securities. Fund may use currency contracts, futures and options in an effort to increase return and for hedging purposes.
Year organized: 1992
Ticker symbol: STISX
Group fund code: 035
Minimum purchase: Initial: $1,000, Subsequent: $50; IRA/Keogh: Initial: $250
Discount broker availability: *Fidelity, *Schwab, *Siebert, *White
Dividends paid: Income - March, June, September, December; Capital gains - March
Portfolio turnover (3 yrs): 144%, 109%, 102%
Management fee: 1.00%
Expense ratio: 1.60% (year ending 10/31/97)

STRONG LIMITED RESOURCES FUND ◆
(See first Strong listing for data common to all funds)

Sub-adviser: Scarborough Investment Advisers, LLC
Portfolio manager: Mark A. Baskir (1997)
Investment objective and policies: Total return: income and capital growth. Invests at least 80% of

assets in equity securities of issuers principally engaged in the energy and natural resources industries or those that furnish related supplies or services, with a focus on mid- to large-cap stocks that pay current dividends. Up to 20% of assets may be invested in any type of securities, including debt securities and equity securities of companies in any industry of any size. Up to 25% of assets may be in foreign issues, and up to 15% of assets may be in illiquid securities. Fund may use forward currency contracts, futures and options in an effort to increase return and for hedging purposes.
Year organized: 1997
Group fund code: 065
Minimum purchase: Initial: $2,500, Subsequent: $50; IRA/Keogh: Initial: $250
Discount broker availability: *Fidelity, *Schwab, *Siebert, *White
Dividends paid: Income - March, June, September, December; Capital gains - annually
Management fee: 1.00%

STRONG MID CAP FUND ◆
(See first Strong listing for data common to all funds)

Portfolio managers: Mary Lisanti (1996), Jeffrey M.K. Bernstein (1996)
Investment objective and policies: Capital growth. Invests at least 80% of assets in equity securities - common stocks, preferred stocks, convertible securities, warrants and rights - and at least 65% must be of issuers with market capitalizations between $800M and $5B at the time of purchase. May invest up to 25% of assets in foreign issues, up to 20% of assets in debt securities (including as much as 5% in junk bonds,) and up to 15% of assets may be in illiquid securities. Fund may use currency contracts and futures and options in an effort to increase return and for hedging purposes.
Year organized: 1996
Ticker symbol: SMDCX
Group fund code: 059
Minimum purchase: Initial: $2,500, Subsequent: $50; IRA/Keogh: Initial: $250
Discount broker availability: *Fidelity, *Schwab, *Siebert, *White
Dividends paid: Income - March, June, September, December; Capital gains - March
Portfolio turnover (1 yr): 305%
Management fee: 1.00%
Expense ratio: 1.60% (year ending 12/31/97)

STRONG MONEY MARKET FUND ◆
(See first Strong listing for data common to all funds)

Portfolio manager: Jay N. Mueller (1991)
Investment objective and policies: Current income, a stable share price, and daily liquidity. Invests in bank, corporate and government money market instruments. Up to 25% of assets may be invested directly or indirectly in securities of foreign issuers.
Year organized: 1985 (absorbed U.S. Govt MM in 1996)
Ticker symbol: SMNXX
Group fund code: 023
Minimum purchase: Initial: $1,000, Subsequent: $50
Check redemptions: $500 minimum
Dividends paid: Income - declared daily, paid monthly
Management fee: 0.50%
Expense ratio: 0.50% (year ending 10/31/97) (0.90% without waiver)

STRONG MUNICIPAL ADVANTAGE FUND ◆
(See first Strong listing for data common to all funds)

Portfolio manager: Steven D. Harrop (1995)
Investment objective and policies: High income exempt from federal income tax, consistent with a very low degree of share-price fluctuation. Invests at least 90% of assets in investment grade municipal securities issued by or on behalf of states, territories, and possessions of the U.S. and their political subdivisions, agencies and instrumentalities. Portfolio maintains a dollar-weighted average maturity of one year or less. May invest 10% of assets in BB rated junk bonds,

invest without limit in securities subject to AMT tax treatment, have up to 15% of assets in illiquid securities and use futures and options in an effort to increase return and for hedging purposes.
Year organized: 1995
Ticker symbol: SMUAX
Group fund code: 051
Minimum purchase: Initial: $2,500, Subsequent: $50
Discount broker availability: *Fidelity, *Schwab, *Siebert, *White
Check redemption: $500 minimum
Dividends paid: Income - declared daily, paid monthly; Capital gains - March
Portfolio turnover (2 yrs): 41%, 17%
Management fee: 0.60%
Expense ratio: 0.00% (year ending 2/29/97) (0.70% without waiver)

STRONG MUNICIPAL BOND FUND ◆
(See first Strong listing for data common to all funds)

Portfolio manager: Steven D. Harrop (1996)
Investment objective and policies: High current income exempt from federal income taxes with moderate share-price fluctuation. Invests primarily in investment grade municipal securities, and maintains a dollar-weighted average maturity ranging from 15 to 25 years. May invest without limit in securities subject to AMT tax treatment, have up to 15% of assets in illiquid securities and use futures and options in an effort to increase return and for hedging purposes.
Year organized: 1986 (formerly Strong Tax-Free Income Fund; absorbed Insured Muni Fund September 30, 1996)
Ticker symbol: SXFIX
Group fund code: 027
Minimum purchase: Initial: $2,500, Subsequent: $50
Discount broker availability: *Fidelity, *Schwab, *Siebert, *White
Check redemptions: $500 minimum
Dividends paid: Income - declared daily, paid monthly; Capital gains - March
Portfolio turnover (3 yrs): 85%, 173%, 514%
Management fee: 0.60%
Expense ratio: 0.80% (year ending 8/31/97)

STRONG MUNICIPAL MONEY MARKET FUND ◆
(See first Strong listing for data common to all funds)

Portfolio manager: Steven D. Harrop (1991)
Investment objective and policies: Maximum current income exempt from federal income taxes, consistent with preservation of capital and liquidity. Invests in municipal money market instruments. May invest without limit in securities subject to AMT tax treatment.
Year organized: 1986 (formerly Strong Tax-Free Money Market Fund)
Ticker symbol: SXFXX
Group fund code: 026
Minimum purchase: Initial: $2,500, Subsequent: $50
Check redemptions: $500 minimum
Dividends paid: Income - declared daily, paid monthly; Capital gains - March
Management fee: 0.50%
Expense ratio: 0.60% (year ending 2/29/97)

STRONG OPPORTUNITY FUND ◆
(See first Strong listing for data common to all funds)

Portfolio managers: Richard T. Weiss (1991), Marina T. Carlson (1993)
Investment objective and policies: Capital growth. Invests at least 70% of assets in equity securities of companies believed under-researched and attractively valued, with emphasis on medium- to large-capitalization companies. Up to 25% of assets may be in securities of foreign issuers, and up to 30% in investment grade debt obligations. May use futures and options in an effort to increase return and for hedging purposes, and sell short against the box.
Year organized: 1985
Ticker symbol: SOPFX

Group fund code: 024
Minimum purchase: Initial: $1,000, Subsequent: $50; IRA/Keogh: Initial: $250
Discount broker availability: *Fidelity, *Schwab, *Siebert, *White
Dividends paid: Income - March, June, September, December; Capital gains - March
Portfolio turnover (3 yrs): 94%, 103%, 93%
Management fee: 1.00%
Expense ratio: 1.20% (year ending 12/31/97)

STRONG SCHAFER BALANCED FUND ◆
(See first Strong listing for data common to all funds)

Sub-adviser: Schafer Capital Management, Inc.
Portfolio manager: David K. Schafer (1997)
Investment objective and policies: Total return: income and capital growth. Invests between 50% and 75% of assets in equity securities, primarily of large-cap value stocks, and at least 25% of assets in investment grade bonds. Neutral portfolio holdings are 60% stocks, 40% bonds. May invest up to 25% of assets in foreign issues, including both direct investments and depositary receipts such as ADRs. May use derivative instruments in an effort to enhance performance and for hedging purposes.
Year organized: 1997
Group fund code: 068
Minimum purchase: Initial: $2,500, Subsequent: $50; IRA/Keogh: Initial: $250
Discount broker availability: *Schwab, *White
Dividends paid: Income - December; Capital gains - March
Management fee: 1.00%

STRONG SCHAFER VALUE FUND ◆
(See first Strong listing for data common to all funds)

Adviser: Strong Schafer Capital Management, LLC
Portfolio manager: David K. Schafer (1985)
Investment objective and policies: Long-term capital appreciation; current income secondary. Invests primarily in equity securities of strong, established companies that are perceived to have a low stock market valuation at the time of purchase. Portfolio weights each holding approximately equally in an effort to mitigate manager risk. May invest up to 20% of assets in securities of foreign issuers.
Year organized: 1985 (name changed from Schafer Value Fund January 1996)
Ticker symbol: SCHVX
Group fund code: 057
Minimum purchase: Initial: $2,500, Subsequent: $50; IRA/Keogh: Initial: $250
Discount broker availability: *Fidelity, *Schwab, *Siebert, *White
Dividends paid: Income - December; Capital gains - March
Portfolio turnover (3 yrs): 23%, 18%, 33%
Management fee: 1.00%
Expense ratio: 1.20% (year ending 9/30/97)

STRONG SHORT-TERM BOND FUND ◆
(See first Strong listing for data common to all funds)

Portfolio managers: Bradley C. Tank (1990), Lyle J. Fitterer (1996), Shirish T. Malekar (1997)
Investment objective and policies: High income consistent with minimum fluctuation of principal value and current liquidity. Invests primarily in short- and intermediate-term investment grade corporate and government debt securities. Portfolio generally maintains a dollar-weighted average maturity of one to three years. May have up to 25% of assets in securities of foreign issuers, and use a variety of derivatives in an attempt to increase returns and for hedging purposes.
Year organized: 1987
Ticker symbol: SSTBX
Group fund code: 028
Minimum purchase: Initial: $2,500, Subsequent: $50; IRA/Keogh: Initial: $1,000
Discount broker availability: *Fidelity, *Schwab, *Siebert, *White
Check redemption: $500 minimum
Dividends paid: Income - declared daily, paid monthly; Capital gains - March

Portfolio turnover (3 yrs): 194%, 192%, 317%
Management fee: 0.625%
Expense ratio: 0.90% (year ending 10/31/97)

STRONG SHORT-TERM GLOBAL BOND FUND ◆
(See first Strong listing for data common to all funds)

Portfolio manager: Shirish T. Malekar (1994)
Investment objective and policies: High income with a low degree of share price fluctuation. Invests primarily in investment grade corporate and government debt securities of issuers from at least three countries including the U.S. At least 35% of its total assets are from U.S. issuers. Portfolio generally maintains a dollar-weighted average maturity of three years or less. Up to 35% of assets may be in junk bonds and 15% in illiquid securities. May use foreign forward currency contracts, futures and options in an effort to increase return and for hedging purposes.
Year organized: 1994
Ticker symbol: STGBX
Group fund code: 042
Minimum purchase: Initial: $1,000, Subsequent: $50; IRA/Keogh: Initial: $250
Discount broker availability: *Fidelity, *Schwab, *Siebert, *White
Check redemptions: $500 minimum
Dividends paid: Income - declared daily, paid monthly; Capital gains - March
Portfolio turnover (3 yrs): 168%, 180%, 437%
Management fee: 0.625%
Expense ratio: 0.70% (year ending 10/31/97) (1.00% without waiver)

STRONG SHORT-TERM HIGH YIELD BOND FUND ◆
(See first Strong listing for data common to all funds)

Portfolio manager: Jeffrey A. Koch (1997)
Investment objective and policies: Total return; a high level of current income with a moderate degree of share price fluctuation. Invests primarily in short- and intermediate- non-investment grade corporate and government debt securities (junk bonds) of domestic issuers. Portfolio generally maintains a dollar-weighted average maturity of between one and three years. May invest without limit in junk bonds. Up to 25% of assets may be in foreign issues and 15% in illiquid securities. May use foreign forward currency contracts, futures and options in an effort to increase return and for hedging purposes.
Year organized: 1997
Ticker symbol: STHBX
Group fund code: 064
Minimum purchase: Initial: $2,500, Subsequent: $50; IRA/Keogh: Initial: $1,000
Discount broker availability: *Fidelity, *Schwab, *Siebert, *White
Check redemptions: $500 minimum
Dividends paid: Income - monthly; Capital gains - annually
Management fee: 0.625%

STRONG SHORT-TERM HIGH YIELD MUNI FUND ◆
(See first Strong listing for data common to all funds)

Portfolio manager: Mary-Kay H. Bourbulas (1997)
Investment objective and policies: Total return; a high level of current income with a moderate degree of share price fluctuation. Invests at least 80% of assets in short- and intermediate- term medium- to lower grade municipal obligations, and maintains a dollar-weighted average maturity of between one and three years. May invest without limit in lower-grade junk bonds, and invest up to 10% of assets in issues in default. Up to 25% of assets may be in foreign issues and 15% in illiquid securities. May use foreign forward currency contracts and futures and options in an effort to increase return and for hedging purposes.
Year organized: 1997
Group fund code: 067
Minimum purchase: Initial: $2,500, Subsequent: $50
Discount broker availability: *Schwab, *White
Check redemptions: $500 minimum

Dividends paid: Income - monthly; Capital gains - annually
Management fee: 0.60%

STRONG SHORT-TERM MUNICIPAL BOND FUND ◆
(See first Strong listing for data common to all funds)

Portfolio manager: Steven D. Harrop (1995)
Investment objective and policies: High income exempt from federal income tax, consistent with capital preservation. Invests primarily in investment grade municipal securities issued by or on behalf of states, territories, and possessions of the U.S. and their political subdivisions, agencies and instrumentalities. Portfolio maintains a dollar-weighted average maturity of three years or less. May invest without limit in securities subject to AMT tax treatment, have up to 15% of assets in illiquid securities and use futures and options in an effort to increase return and for hedging purposes.
Year organized: 1991
Ticker symbol: STSMX
Group fund code: 033
Minimum purchase: Initial: $2,500, Subsequent: $50
Discount broker availability: *Fidelity, *Schwab, *Siebert, *White
Check redemption: $500 minimum
Dividends paid: Income - declared daily, paid monthly; Capital gains - March
Portfolio turnover (3 yrs): 26%, 38%, 227%
Management fee: 0.50%
Expense ratio: 0.70% (year ending 8/31/97)

STRONG SMALL CAP FUND ◆
(See first Strong listing for data common to all funds)

Portfolio manager: Mary Lisanti (1996)
Investment objective and policies: Capital growth. Invests primarily in equity securities of companies with market capitalizations of under $2B. Will normally invest at least 65% of assets in equity securities of firms which meet this criteria at the time of the investment. May invest up to 20% of assets in debt securities, and up to 25% of assets in the securities of foreign issuers, either directly or through depositary instruments. May use derivative instruments for hedging purposes.
Year organized: 1995
Ticker symbol: SCAPX
Group fund code: 054
Minimum purchase: Initial: $2,500, Subsequent: $50; IRA/Keogh: Initial: $250
Discount broker availability: *Fidelity, *Schwab, *Siebert, *White
Dividends paid: Income - March, June, September, December; Capital gains - March
Portfolio turnover (2 yrs): 593%, 420%
Management fee: 1.00%
Expense ratio: 1.40% (year ending 12/31/97)

STRONG SMALL CAP VALUE FUND ◆
(See first Strong listing for data common to all funds)

Portfolio manager: I. Charles Rinaldi (1997)
Investment objective and policies: Capital growth. Invests at least 80% of assets in equity securities of companies with market capitalizations of under $2B that are perceived to be undervalued. Will normally invest at least 65% of assets in equity securities of firms which meet this criteria at the time of the investment. May invest up to 20% of assets in debt securities, and up to 25% of assets in the securities of foreign issuers, either directly or through depositary instruments. May use derivative instruments for hedging purposes.
Year organized: 1997
Group fund code: 069
Minimum purchase: Initial: $2,500, Subsequent: $50; IRA/Keogh: Initial: $250
Discount broker availability: *Fidelity, *Schwab, *Siebert, *White
Dividends paid: Income - March, June, September, December; Capital gains - annually
Management fee: 1.00%

STRONG STEP ONE MONEY FUND ◆
(See first Strong listing for data common to all funds)

Portfolio manager: Jay N. Mueller (1998)
Investment objective and policies: Current income, a stable share price and daily liquidity. Invests in first tier corporate, bank and government money market instruments that present minimal credit risk. These may fall only into the highest rating category available.
Year organized: 1998
Special sales restrictions: Maximum investment allowed in this fund is $20,000, and you may open one regular and one IRA account. Upon investing in this account you will receive a series of educational materials designed to teach you how to reinvest your holdings into a diversified portfolio.
Minimum purchase: Initial: $1,000, Subsequent: $50; IRA/Keogh: Initial: $250
Dividends paid: Income - declared daily, paid monthly
Management fee: 0.50%

STRONG TOTAL RETURN FUND ◆
(See first Strong listing for data common to all funds)

Portfolio managers: Ronald C. Ognar (1993), Ian J. Rogers (1994)
Investment objective and policies: High total return: income and capital appreciation with reasonable risk. Invests in equity and fixed-income securities and may have up to 100% of assets in either category depending on market and economic conditions. Normally emphasizes investment in mid-sized and large companies with steady or growing dividends. May invest up to 25% of assets in foreign issues. May assume short-term trading posture when management perceives economic uncertainty. May use futures and options in an effort to increase return and for hedging purposes, and sell short against the box.
Year organized: 1981
Ticker symbol: STRFX
Group fund code: 021
Minimum purchase: Initial: $250, Subsequent: $50
Discount broker availability: *Fidelity, *Schwab, *Siebert, *White
Dividends paid: Income - March, June, September, December; Capital gains - March
Portfolio turnover (3 yrs): 405%, 502%, 299%
Management fee: 0.85% first $35M, 0.80% over $35M
Expense ratio: 1.10% (year ending 10/31/97)

STRONG VALUE FUND ◆
(See first Strong listing for data common to all funds)

Sub-adviser: Sloate, Weisman, Murray & Co., Inc.
Portfolio managers: Laura J. Sloate (1995), Jeffrey B. Cohen (1995)
Investment objective and policies: Capital growth. Invests in equity securities believed to be undervalued. May invest in companies of any size, but currently emphasizes medium- to large-capitalization companies. Will normally be fully invested in equities, but may invest up to 30% of assets in debt securities. May invest up to 10% of assets in foreign issues through depositary instruments.
Year organized: 1995
Ticker symbol: STVAX
Group fund code: 055
Minimum purchase: Initial: $2,500, Subsequent: $50; IRA/Keogh: Initial: $250
Discount broker availability: *Fidelity, *Schwab, *Siebert, *White
Dividends paid: Income - March, June, September, December; Capital gains - March
Portfolio turnover (2 yrs): 103%, 90%
Management fee: 1.00%
Expense ratio: 1.30% (year ending 12/31/97)

SWISSKEY FUNDS
(Data common to all Swisskey funds are shown below. See subsequent listings for data specific to individual funds.)

209 South LaSalle Street
Chicago, IL 60604-1295
800-448-2430, 312-223-7975
fax 312-239-4927
Internet: http://www.networth.galt.com/swisskey

Shareholder service hours: Full service: M-F 9 A.M.-7 P.M. EST; after hours service: prices
Adviser: Brinson Partners, Inc.
Transfer agent: First Data Investor Services Group
Year organized: SwissKey Funds was organized in 1995 as a retail share class of the Brinson Fund portfolios. Historic data and portfolio turnover percentages reflect Brinson institutional share class data, with expense ratios adjusted for SwissKey retail fee structures.
Minimum purchase: Initial: $1,000; Subsequent: $50
Wire orders accepted: Yes
Deadline for same day wire purchase: 4 P.M.
Qualified for sale in: All states
Telephone redemptions: Yes
Wire redemptions: Yes, $9 fee
Letter redemptions: Signature guarantee required over $5,000
Telephone switching: With other SwissKey funds
Number of switches permitted: Unlimited
Shareholder services: IRA, automatic investment plan, electronic funds transfer (redemption only), systematic withdrawal plan min. bal. req. $10,000
Administration fee: 0.15% first $75M to 0.05% over $500M
Shareholder services fee: 0.25%
IRA fees: Annual $12

SWISSKEY GLOBAL FUND
(See first SwissKey listing for data common to all funds)

Portfolio manager: Team managed
Investment objective and policies: Total return; capital appreciation and current income. Invests at least 65% of assets in equity and debt securities of issuers from at least three different countries, one of which may be the U.S., using an active asset allocation strategy. May use interest rate swaps, foreign currency contracts, and options and futures for hedging purposes. May invest in junk bonds.
Year organized: 1995 (SwissKey class); 1992 (Brinson class)
Ticker symbol: SKGLX
Dividends paid: Income - June, December; Capital gains - December
Portfolio turnover (3 yrs): 142%, 238%, 231%
Management fee: 0.80%
12b-1 distribution fee: Maximum of 0.65%
Expense ratio: 1.64% (year ending 6/30/97)

SWISSKEY GLOBAL BOND FUND
(See first SwissKey listing for data common to all funds)

Portfolio manager: Team managed
Investment objective and policies: Total return; capital appreciation and current income. Invests at least 65% of assets in debt securities with an initial maturity of more than one year, issued from at least three different countries, one of which may be the U.S. May use interest rate swaps, foreign currency contracts, and options and futures for hedging purposes. May invest in junk bonds.
Year organized: 1995 (SwissKey class); 1993 (Brinson class)
Ticker symbol: SKGBX
Dividends paid: Income - June, December; Capital gains - December
Portfolio turnover (3 yrs): 184%, 199%, 189%
Management fee: 0.75%
12b-1 distribution fee: Maximum of 0.65%
Expense ratio: 1.65% (year ending 6/30/97)

SWISSKEY GLOBAL EQUITY FUND
(See first SwissKey listing for data common to all funds)

Portfolio manager: Team managed
Investment objective and policies: Total return; capital appreciation and current income. Invests at least 65% of assets in equity securities of issuers in at least three countries, one of which may be the U.S. May use interest rate swaps, foreign currency contracts, and options and futures for hedging purposes.
Year organized: 1995 (SwissKey class); 1994 (Brinson class)
Ticker symbol: SKGEX
Dividends paid: Income - June, December; Capital gains - December
Portfolio turnover (3 yrs): 74%, 36%, 21%
Management fee: 0.80%
12b-1 distribution fee: Maximum of 0.65%
Expense ratio: 1.75% (year ending 6/30/97) (includes waiver)

SWISSKEY NON-U.S. EQUITY FUND
(See first SwissKey listing for data common to all funds)

Portfolio manager: Team managed
Investment objective and policies: Total return; capital appreciation and current income. Invests at least 65% of assets in equity securities of issuers in at least three countries other than the U.S. May use interest rate swaps, foreign currency contracts, and options and futures for hedging purposes.
Year organized: 1995 (SwissKey class); 1993 (Brinson class)
Ticker symbol: SKNEX
Dividends paid: Income - June, December; Capital gains - December
Portfolio turnover (3 yrs): 20%, 14%, 12%
Management fee: 0.80%
12b-1 distribution fee: Maximum of 0.65%
Expense ratio: 1.81% (year ending 6/30/97) (includes waiver)

SWISSKEY U.S. BALANCED FUND
(See first SwissKey listing for data common to all funds)

Portfolio manager: Team managed
Investment objective and policies: Total return; capital appreciation and current income. Invests in a wide range of equity, debt and money market securities issued in the U.S. using an active asset allocation strategy. At least 25% of assets will be invested in fixed-income securities. May use interest rate swaps for hedging purposes. May invest in junk bonds.
Year organized: 1995 (SwissKey class); 1994 (Brinson class)
Ticker symbol: SKBLX
Dividends paid: Income - June, December; Capital gains - December
Portfolio turnover (2 yrs): 240%, 196%
Management fee: 0.70%
12b-1 distribution fee: Maximum of 0.65%
Expense ratio: 1.30% (year ending 6/30/97) (includes waiver)

SWISSKEY U.S. BOND FUND
(See first SwissKey listing for data common to all funds)

Portfolio manager: Team managed
Investment objective and policies: Total return; capital appreciation and current income, while controlling risk. Invests at least 65% of assets in U.S. debt securities with an initial maturity of more than one year. May use interest rate swaps for hedging purposes. Up to 30% of assets may be in junk bonds.
Year organized: 1995 (SwissKey class); 1995 (Brinson class)
Ticker symbol: SKBDX
Dividends paid: Income - June, December; Capital gains - December
Portfolio turnover (1 yr): 363%
Management fee: 0.50%
12b-1 distribution fee: Maximum of 0.65%
Expense ratio: 1.07% (year ending 6/30/96) (4.07% without waiver)

SWISSKEY U.S. EQUITY FUND
(See first SwissKey listing for data common to all funds)

Portfolio manager: Team managed
Investment objective and policies: Total return; capital appreciation and current income, while controlling risk. Invests at least 65% of assets in equity securities issued by U.S. companies. May use options and futures for hedging purposes.
Year organized: 1995 (SwissKey class); 1994 (Brinson class)
Ticker symbol: SKEQX
Dividends paid: Income - June, December; Capital gains - December
Portfolio turnover (2 yrs): 36%, 33%
Management fee: 0.70%
12b-1 distribution fee: Maximum of 0.65%
Expense ratio: 1.32% (year ending 6/30/97) (includes waiver)

TECHNOLOGY VALUE FUND ◆
(See Firsthand Funds)

THIRD AVENUE FUNDS ◆
(Data common to all Third Avenue funds are shown below. See subsequent listings for data specific to individual funds.)

767 Third Avenue
New York, NY 10017-2023
800-443-1021, 212-888-6685
shareholder services 610-239-4600
fax 212-888-6757
Internet: http://www.mjwhitman.com

Adviser: EQSF Advisers, Inc.
Transfer agent: First Data Investor Services Group
Minimum purchase: Initial: $1,000, Subsequent: $1,000; IRA: Initial: $500, Subsequent: $200; Automatic investment plan: Subsequent: $200
Wire orders accepted: Yes
Deadline for same day wire purchase: 4 P.M.
Telephone redemptions: Yes, $1,000 minimum
Discount broker availability: *Fidelity, *Schwab, *Siebert, *White
Qualified for sale in: All states
Wire redemptions: Yes, $9 fee
Letter redemptions: Signature guarantee required over $5,000
Telephone switching: With other Third Avenue funds and the Cash Account Trust MM fund, $1,000 minimum
Number of switches permitted: Unlimited
Shareholder services: IRA, systematic withdrawal plan min. bal. req. $10,000
IRA fees: Annual $12

THIRD AVENUE HIGH YIELD FUND ◆
(See first Third Avenue listing for data common to all funds)

Portfolio manager: Margaret D. Patel (1998)
Investment objective and policies: Total return: capital appreciation and current income. Invests at least 65% of assets in fixed-income and other debt instruments rated below investment grade, also known as junk bonds. Fund will gain equity exposure through the use of convertible securities thought to be undervalued. Fund also invests in mortgage- and derivative-backed securities and issues that are in default. Only invests in foreign securities that are either issued as dollar-denominated ADRs or those who comply substantially with SEC disclosure requirements. May invest up to 15% of assets in illiquid securities, and engage in foreign currency hedging transactions.
Year organized: 1998
Redemption fee: 1.00% for shares held less than 1 year, payable to the fund
Dividends paid: Income - quarterly; Capital gains - December
Management fee: 0.90%

THIRD AVENUE SMALL-CAP VALUE FUND ◆
(See first Third Avenue listing for data common to all funds)

Portfolio managers: Martin J. Whitman (1997), Curtis Jensen (1997)
Investment objective and policies: Long-term capital appreciation. Invests exclusively in equity securities, with at least 65% of assets in companies with market capitalizations of less than $1B, perceived to be substantially undervalued. May invest in unseasoned companies, with less than three years of operating history. May invest in foreign securities without limit, up to 15% of assets in illiquid securities and 10% in other mutual funds. May use various currency transactions as a hedge against fluctuations in foreign currency valuations.
Year organized: 1997
Ticker symbol: TASCX
Dividends paid: Income - December; Capital gains - December
Portfolio turnover (1 yr): 7%
Management fee: 0.90%
Expense ratio: 1.65% (seven months ending 10/31/97)

THIRD AVENUE VALUE FUND ◆
(See first Third Avenue listing for data common to all funds)

Portfolio manager: Martin J. Whitman (1990)
Investment objective and policies: Long-term capital appreciation. Invests primarily in common stocks of companies perceived to be substantially undervalued, and in senior securities, such as preferred stocks and debt instruments, that have strong covenant protections and above-average current yields, yields to events, or yields to maturity. May invest in unseasoned companies, with less than three years of operating history, and invest in foreign securities without limit. Up to 35% of assets may be in junk bonds, 15% in illiquid securities and 10% in other mutual funds. May use various currency transactions as a hedge against fluctuations in foreign currency valuations.
Year organized: 1990
Ticker symbol: TAVFX
Qualified for sale in: All states
Dividends paid: Income - December; Capital gains - December
Portfolio turnover (3 yrs): 10%, 14%, 15%
Management fee: 0.90%
Expense ratio: 1.13% (year ending 10/31/97)

THOMAS WHITE WORLD FUND ◆
One Financial Place
440 South LaSalle Street, Suite 3900
Chicago, IL 60605-1028
800-811-0535, 312-663-8300
fax 312-663-8323
Internet: http://www.thomaswhite.com

Adviser: Lord Asset Management, Inc.
Portfolio manager: Thomas S. White, Jr. (1994)
Transfer agent: Firstar Trust Co.
Investment objective and policies: Long-term capital appreciation; income incidental. Invests in all types of equity and debt securities of companies and governments of any nation. Selects companies perceived to benefit from global economic trends, or promising technologies or products; selects countries based on perceived changes in geopolitical, currency, or economic relationships. Up to 25% of assets may be in a single industry segment, and up to 5% of assets in securities issued by any single company or government. May invest up to 15% of assets in illiquid securities. May leverage the portfolio and use derivative instruments for investment purposes.
Year organized: 1994
Ticker symbol: TWWDX
Minimum purchase: Initial: $2,500, Subsequent: $100; IRA: Initial: $1,500; Automatic investment plan: Initial: $1,000
Wire orders accepted: Yes
Deadline for same day wire purchase: 3 P.M.
Discount broker availability: *Fidelity, *Schwab, *White

Qualified for sale in: All states
Telephone redemptions: Yes
Wire redemptions: Yes, $15 fee
Letter redemptions: Signature guarantee required over $25,000
Dividends paid: Income - December; Capital gains - December
Portfolio turnover (3 yrs): 48%, 51%, 55%
Shareholder services: IRA, automatic investment plan, electronic funds transfer
Management fee: 1.00%
Expense ratio: 1.47% (year ending 10/31/97)
IRA fees: Annual $15

THOMPSON & PLUMB FUNDS ◆

(Data common to all Thompson & Plumb funds are shown below. See subsequent listings for data specific to individual funds.)

8201 Excelsior Drive, Suite 200
Madison, WI 53717
800-999-0887, 608-831-1300
prices 800-338-1579, fax 608-831-3455
Internet: http://www.thompsonplumb.com

Adviser: Thompson, Plumb & Assocs., Inc.
Transfer agent: Firstar Trust Co.
Minimum purchase: Initial: $1,000, Subsequent: $100; IRA/Keogh: Initial: $250; Automatic investment plan: Subsequent: $50
Wire orders accepted: Yes
Deadline for same day wire purchase: 4 P.M.
Qualified for sale in: All states
Wire redemptions: Yes
Letter redemptions: Signature guarantee required over $25,000
Telephone switching: With other Thompson & Plumb funds and Firstar Money Market Funds, $1,000 minimum
Number of switches permitted: Unlimited, 15 day hold, $5 fee
Shareholder services: IRA, SEP-IRA, 403(b), corporate retirement plans, systematic withdrawal plan min. bal. req. $10,000
IRA fees: Annual $12.50

THOMPSON & PLUMB BALANCED FUND ◆

(See first Thompson & Plumb listing for data common to all funds)

Portfolio manager: Thomas G. Plumb (1987)
Investment objective and policies: Total return: income and capital appreciation with reasonable risk. Invests in a diversified portfolio consisting of a combination of common stocks, variable rate obligations, and investment grade fixed-income securities. Up to 75% of assets will be in common stocks that are perceived to be undervalued, and ordinarily at least 25% of assets will be in fixed-income senior securities.
Year organized: 1987 (name changed from Thompson, Unger & Plumb Fund in 1992; name changed from Thompson, Unger & Plumb Balanced in 1995)
Ticker symbol: THPBX
Discount broker availability: *Schwab
Dividends paid: Income - December; Capital gains - December
Portfolio turnover (3 yrs): 77%, 135%, 111%
Management fee: 0.85% first $50M, 0.80% over $50M
Expense ratio: 1.40% (year ending 11/30/97)

THOMPSON & PLUMB BOND FUND ◆

(See first Thompson & Plumb listing for data common to all funds)

Portfolio manager: John W. Thompson (1992)
Investment objective and policies: High current income consistent with capital preservation. Invests in debt securities of U.S. and foreign issuers (payable in U.S. dollars) rated within the four highest grades by S&P or Moody's; securities issued or guaranteed by the U.S. Government, its agencies or instrumentalities, mortgage-related securities, commercial paper rated within the highest two categories, FDIC bank and thrift obligations, and short-term corporate obliga-

tions. Normally 65% of assets will be in the first two categories. Dollar-weighted average maturity will usually not exceed ten years.
Year organized: 1992 (name changed from Thompson, Unger & Plumb Bond in 1995)
Ticker symbol: THOPX
Dividends paid: Income - March, June, September, December; Capital gains - December
Portfolio turnover (3 yrs): 53%, 104%, 112%
Management fee: 0.65% first $50M, 0.60% over $50M
Expense ratio: 1.14% (year ending 11/30/97)

THOMPSON & PLUMB GROWTH FUND ◆

(See first Thompson & Plumb listing for data common to all funds)

Portfolio manager: John W. Thompson (1992)
Investment objective and policies: Long-term capital appreciation; current income secondary. Invests primarily in common stocks and convertible securities of companies believed to have above average potential for earnings and dividend growth. May also invest in convertible preferred and convertible fixed-income securities which are rated in the top four categories by S&P or Moody's. Up to 33% of assets may be in companies with capitalizations under $200M.
Year organized: 1992 (name changed from Thompson, Unger & Plumb Growth in 1995)
Ticker symbol: THPGX
Discount broker availability: *Schwab
Dividends paid: Income - December; Capital gains - December
Portfolio turnover (3 yrs): 78%, 102%, 87%
Management fee: 1.00% first $50M, 0.90% over $50M
Expense ratio: 1.52% (year ending 11/30/97)

TIAA-CREF FUNDS ◆

(Data common to all TIAA-CREF funds are shown below. See subsequent listings for data specific to individual funds.)

730 Third Avenue
New York, NY 10017-3206
800-223-1200, 800-842-2776
shareholder services 800-842-2252
Internet: http://www.tiaa-cref.org

Adviser: Teachers Advisors, Inc., a wholly-owned subsidiary of the Teachers Insurance and Annuity Association, College Retirement Equities Fund
Transfer agent: State Street Bank & Trust Co.
Minimum purchase: Initial: $250, Subsequent: $25; Automatic investment plan: Initial: $25
Wire orders accepted: Yes
Deadline for same day wire purchase: 4 P.M.
Qualified for sale in: All states
Telephone redemptions: Yes, $250 minimum
Wire redemptions: Yes, $5,000 minimum
Letter redemptions: Signature guarantee not required
Telephone switching: With other TIAA-CREF funds
Number of switches permitted: 12 per 12 month period
Shareholder services: Electronic funds transfer, directed dividends, systematic withdrawal plan min. bal. req. $5,000

TIAA-CREF BOND PLUS FUND ◆

(See first TIAA-CREF listing for data common to all portfolios)

Portfolio manager: Elizabeth D. Black (1997)
Investment objective and policies: Long-term return, primarily through high current income consistent with capital preservation. Normally invests at least 80% of assets in two categories of bonds; a diversified portfolio of investment grade domestic and foreign debt obligations, and securities or other instruments that provide a spread over the yield curve, such as illiquid securities or junk bonds. The second element comprises no more than 25% of assets, and illiquid securities no more than 15%. May also use options and futures and preferred stock consistent with the objective.

Year organized: 1997
Ticker symbol: TIPBX
Dividends paid: Income - monthly; Capital gains - annually
Portfolio turnover (1 yr): 144%
Management fee: 0.80%
Expense ratio: 0.14% (five months ending 12/31/97) (0.37% without waiver)

TIAA-CREF GROWTH & INCOME FUND ◆

(See first TIAA-CREF listing for data common to all portfolios)

Portfolio manager: Carlton N. Martin (1997)
Investment objective and policies: Long-term total return; capital appreciation and income. Invests at least 80% of assets in a broadly diversified portfolio of equity securities selected for their perceived income-producing potential. May invest up to 40% of assets in foreign securities. May use foreign forward currency contracts and options and futures for hedging purposes.
Year organized: 1997
Ticker symbol: TIGIX
Dividends paid: Income - quarterly; Capital gains - annually
Portfolio turnover (1 yr): 1%
Management fee: 0.93%
Expense ratio: 0.20% (five months ending 12/31/97) (0.43% without waiver)

TIAA-CREF GROWTH EQUITY FUND ◆

(See first TIAA-CREF listing for data common to all portfolios)

Portfolio manager: Jeffrey Siegel (1997)
Investment objective and policies: Long-term capital appreciation. Invests at least 80% of assets in equity securities of companies of all sizes perceived to offer the potential for capital appreciation. May invest in new and unseasoned companies as well as special situations such as acquisitions and reorganizations. May purchase foreign securities and debt obligations without limit if deemed viable, including up to 40% of assets in foreign issues. May use foreign forward currency contracts and options and futures for hedging purposes.
Year organized: 1997
Ticker symbol: TIGEX
Dividends paid: Income - annually; Capital gains - annually
Portfolio turnover (1 yr): 29%
Management fee: 0.95%
Expense ratio: 0.21% (five months ending 12/31/97) (0.44% without waiver)

TIAA-CREF INTERNATIONAL EQUITY FUND ◆

(See first TIAA-CREF listing for data common to all portfolios)

Portfolio manager: Chris Semenuk (1997)
Investment objective and policies: Long-term capital appreciation. Invests at least 80% of assets in a broadly diversified portfolio of equity securities of companies representing at least three different countries outside of the U.S. May use foreign forward currency contracts and options and futures for hedging purposes.
Year organized: 1997
Dividends paid: Income - annually; Capital gains - annually
Portfolio turnover (1 yr): 5%
Management fee: 0.99%
Expense ratio: 0.23% (five months ending 12/31/97) (0.46% without waiver)

TIAA-CREF MANAGED ALLOCATION FUND ◆

(See first TIAA-CREF listing for data common to all portfolios)

Portfolio managers: James G. Fleischmann (1997), Michael T. O'Kane (1997)
Investment objective and policies: Total return; capital appreciation and income. Invests all its investable

assets in an asset allocated portfolio of other TIAA-CREF funds. Normally at least 60% of assets are in Growth & Income, Growth Equity and International; 40% in Bond Plus. These allocations fluctuate up and down by as much as 15% depending on perceptions of market conditions. Fund is non-diversified.
Year organized: 1997
Ticker symbol: TIMAX
Dividends paid: Income - quarterly; Capital gains - quarterly
Portfolio turnover (1 yr): 0%
Management fee: 0.00%
Expense ratio: 0.00% (pays pro rata portion of underlying funds)

TIAA-CREF MONEY MARKET FUND ◆
(See first TIAA-CREF listing for data common to all portfolios)

Portfolio manager: Steven Traum (1997)
Investment objective and policies: High current income consistent with maintenance of liquidity and capital preservation. Invests in high quality short-term money market obligations maturing in 397 days or less.
Year organized: 1997
Dividends paid: Income - declared daily, paid monthly
Management fee: 0.79%
Expense ratio: 0.13% (five months ending 12/31/97) (0.36% without waiver)

THE TIMOTHY PLAN
(Fund became a multi-class load fund in 1997)

TIP FUNDS ◆
(Data common to all TIP funds are shown below. See subsequent listings for data specific to individual funds.)

One Freedom Valley Blvd.
Oaks, PA 19456
800-224-6312
fax 816-843-5784
Internet: http://www.turner-invest.com
e-mail: bmf@turner-invest.com

Shareholder service hours: Full service: M-F 8 A.M.-8 P.M. EST
Administrator: SEI Fund Resources
Transfer agent: DST Systems, Inc.
Minimum purchase: Initial: $2,500, Subsequent: $500; IRA: Initial: $2,000
Wire orders accepted: Yes
Deadline for same day wire purchase: 4 P.M.
Qualified for sale in: All states
Telephone redemptions: Yes
Wire redemptions: Yes, $10 fee
Letter redemptions: Signature guarantee required over $50,000
Telephone switching: With other TIP funds
Number of switches permitted: Unlimited
Shareholder services: IRA, automatic investment plan, electronic funds transfer, systematic withdrawal plan min. bal. req. $2,500
Administration fee: 0.12% first $75M to 0.075% over $600M ($75,000 minimum per fund)
IRA fees: Annual $25

TIP: CLOVER EQUITY VALUE FUND ◆
(See first TIP listing for data common to all portfolios)

11 Tobey Village Office Park
Pittsford, NY 14534-9912
800-226-9558, 800-808-4921
shareholder services 800-932-7781
716-385-6090
fax 716-385-9068

Adviser: Clover Capital Management, Inc.
Portfolio managers: Paul W. Spindler (1991), Michael E. Jones (1991)
Investment objective and policies: Long-term total return. Invests at least 70% of assets in equity securi-

ties, including common stocks, debt securities, convertible preferred stocks. Holdings selected are perceived to be undervalued relative to the market. Up to 20% of assets may be in ADRs, 25% in nonconvertible fixed-income securities and 30% in money market instruments.
Year organized: 1991 (name changed from Clover Capital Equity Value 6/25/97)
Ticker symbol: CCEVX
Group fund code: 891
Discount broker availability: *Fidelity, *Schwab, Siebert, *White
Dividends paid: Income - March, June, September, December; Capital gains - December
Portfolio turnover (3 yrs): 52%, 51%, 85%
Management fee: 0.74%
Expense ratio: 1.10% (year ending 9/30/97) (1.15% without waiver)

TIP: CLOVER FIXED INCOME FUND ◆
(See first TIP listing for data common to all portfolios)

11 Tobey Village Office Park
Pittsford, NY 14534-9912
800-226-9558, 800-808-4921
shareholder services 800-932-7781
716-385-6090
fax 716-385-9068

Adviser: Clover Capital Management, Inc.
Portfolio managers: Paul W. Spindler (1991), Richard J. Huxley (1991)
Investment objective and policies: High income consistent with reasonable risk to capital and volatility low in relation to long-term bonds. Invests at least 70% of assets in fixed-income securities consisting of U.S. Government and government agency and instrumentality obligations, investment grade corporate bonds and debentures and high-rated mortgage backed securities. Portfolio generally maintains a weighted average maturity of seven to nine years. Up to 10% of assets may be in dollar denominated fixed-income securities of foreign issuers.
Year organized: 1991 (name changed from Clover Capital Fixed Income 6/25/97)
Ticker symbol: TCFIX
Group fund code: 893
Discount broker availability: Fidelity, *Schwab, Siebert, *White
Dividends paid: Income - declared daily, paid monthly; Capital gains - December
Portfolio turnover (3 yrs): 12%, 25%, 36%
Management fee: 0.45%
Expense ratio: 0.75% (year ending 9/30/97) (1.02% without waiver)

TIP: CLOVER MAX CAP VALUE FUND ◆
(See first TIP listing for data common to all portfolios)

11 Tobey Village Office Park
Pittsford, NY 14534-9912
800-226-9558, 800-808-4921
shareholder services 800-932-7781
716-385-6090
fax 716-385-9068

Adviser: Clover Capital Management, Inc.
Portfolio managers: Paul W. Spindler (1997), Lawrence Creatura (1997)
Investment objective and policies: Long-term total return. Invests primarily in equity securities of the 500 largest capitalization companies (currently $5B and above) perceived to be undervalued due to a low stock price relative to book value and cash flow. May, however, invest up to 25% of assets in companies with smaller capitalizations, up to 25% of assets in nonconvertible fixed-income securities of any grade including junk bonds. May invest up to 10% of assets in ADRs. May use options and futures.
Year organized: 1997
Group fund code: 894
Discount broker availability: *White
Dividends paid: Income - March, June, September, December; Capital gains - December
Management fee: 0.74%

TIP: CLOVER SMALL CAP VALUE FUND ◆
(See first TIP listing for data common to all portfolios)

11 Tobey Village Office Park
Pittsford, NY 14534-9912
800-226-9558, 800-808-4921
shareholder services 800-932-7781
716-385-6090
fax 716-385-9068

Adviser: Clover Capital Management, Inc.
Portfolio managers: Michael E. Jones (1996), Lawrence Creatura (1996)
Investment objective and policies: Long-term total return. Invests at least 75% and as much as 100% in equity securities of U.S. companies with market capitalizations of $750M or less at time of purchase. May also invest in convertible and debt securities that are below investment grade, including issues in default. Fund selects stocks trading in the bottom 20% of valuation parameters, but only those listed on registered securities exchanges or the over-the-counter market in the U.S. May invest up to 15% of assets in illiquid securities, and up to 10% of assets in ADRs.
Year organized: 1996 (name changed from Clover Capital Small Cap Value 6/25/97)
Ticker symbol: TCSVX
Group fund code: 892
Discount broker availability: *Fidelity, *Schwab, *Siebert, *White
Dividends paid: Income - March, June, September, December; Capital gains - December
Portfolio turnover (2 yrs): 59%, 14%
Management fee: 0.85%
Expense ratio: 1.40% (year ending 9/30/97) (2.43% without waiver)

TIP: PENN CAPITAL SELECT FINANCIAL SERVICES FUND ◆
(See first TIP listing for data common to all portfolios)

52 Haddonfield-Berlin Road, Suite 1000
Cherry Hill, NJ 08034
609-354-1519

Adviser: Penn Capital Management Co., Inc.
Portfolio managers: Richard A. Hocker (1997), Scott D. Schumacher (1997)
Investment objective and policies: Long-term capital appreciation. Invests primarily in equity securities of companies principally engaged in the banking industry or the financial services sector, with at least 25% of assets focused on banking. Any funds not committed to these two areas may be invested in equity or fixed-income securities of any type, including up to 15% of assets in junk bonds and up to 15% in illiquid securities. May invest up to 20% of assets in ADRs. May use leverage, and a variety of derivative instruments.
Year organized: 1997
Group fund code: 880
Discount broker availability: *Schwab, *White
Dividends paid: Income - December; Capital gains - December
Management fee: 1.00%

TIP: PENN CAPITAL STRATEGIC HIGH YIELD BOND FUND ◆
(See first TIP listing for data common to all portfolios)

52 Haddonfield-Berlin Road, Suite 1000
Cherry Hill, NJ 08034
609-354-1519

Adviser: Penn Capital Management Co., Inc.
Portfolio managers: Richard A. Hocker (1998), Kathleen A. News (1998)
Investment objective and policies: Maximum income through high current yield; above average capital appreciation secondary. Invests at least 65% of assets in a diversified portfolio of high yield junk bonds, including those in default. Additional assets may be invested in equity securities and/or investment grade debt issues. May use a variety of derivative instruments and leverage.
Year organized: 1998
Group fund code: 889

Dividends paid: Income - December; Capital gains - December
Management fee: 0.75%

TIP: PENN CAPITAL VALUE PLUS FUND ◆
(See first TIP listing for data common to all portfolios)

52 Haddonfield-Berlin Road, Suite 1000
Cherry Hill, NJ 08034
609-354-1519

Adviser: Penn Capital Management Co., Inc.
Portfolio managers: Richard A. Hocker (1998), Scott D. Schumacher (1998)
Investment objective and policies: Capital appreciation and above average income with less risk than the S&P 500 Index. Approximately one third of assets are invested in large cap value equity securities (over $1B), one third in small cap value equity securities (less than $1B), and one third in high yield junk bonds and cash. May use a variety of derivative instruments and leverage.
Year organized: 1998
Group fund code: 890
Dividends paid: Income - December; Capital gains - December
Management fee: 1.00%

TIP: TARGET SELECT EQUITY FUND ◆
(See first TIP listing for data common to all portfolios)

1235 Westlakes Drive, Suite 350
Berwyn, PA 19312
800-224-6312, 800-424-4865
610-251-0268
fax 610-251-0731

Investment adviser: Turner Investment Partners, Inc.
Sub-advisers: Clover Capital Management Co., Inc., Penn Capital Management Co., Inc., Chartwell Investment Partners
Lead portfolio manager: Robert E. Turner (1992)
Investment objective and policies: Long-term capital appreciation. Invests primarily in equity securities of U.S. companies. The adviser and each sub-adviser will invest one fourth of fund assets in at least ten and no more than twenty stocks, thus creating a focused, concentrated portfolio of no more than eighty stocks. Up to 25% of assets may be in non-convertible fixed-income instruments, and up to 25% in money markets. May purchase foreign securities without limit, and use options and futures.
Year organized: 1998
Discount broker availability: *White
Dividends paid: Income - December; Capital gains - December
Management fee: 1.05%

TIP: TURNER GROWTH EQUITY FUND ◆
(See first TIP listing for data common to all funds)

1235 Westlakes Drive, Suite 350
Berwyn, PA 19312
800-224-6312, 800-424-4865
610-251-0268, fax 610-251-0731

Investment adviser: Turner Investment Partners, Inc.
Portfolio manager: Robert E. Turner (1992)
Investment objective and policies: Capital appreciation. Invests in a diversified portfolio of common stocks of issuers with market capitalizations below $1B, believed to have strong earnings potential with reasonable valuations. Fund will attempt to maintain sector weightings that approximate the concentrations represented in the S&P 500 Composite Stock Price Index. May use options and futures.
Year organized: 1992
Ticker symbol: TREGX
Group fund code: 896
Discount broker availability: *Fidelity, *Schwab, *White
Dividends paid: Income - March, June, September, December; Capital gains - December

Portfolio turnover (3 yrs): 178%, 148%, 178%
Management fee: 0.75%
Expense ratio: 1.02% (year ending 9/30/97) (1.05% without waiver)

TIP: TURNER MIDCAP GROWTH FUND ◆
(See first TIP listing for data common to all funds)

1235 Westlakes Drive, Suite 350
Berwyn, PA 19312
800-224-6312, 800-424-4865
610-251-0268, fax 610-251-0731

Investment adviser: Turner Investment Partners, Inc.
Portfolio managers: William H. Chenoweth (1996), Christopher K. McHugh (1996)
Investment objective and policies: Capital appreciation. Invests in a broadly diversified portfolio of mid-cap equity securities believed to have earnings momentum selected by a proprietary model based on fundamental and technical analysis. Fund will remain fully invested and sector neutral. May use options and futures.
Year organized: 1996
Ticker symbol: TMGFX
Group fund code: 899
Discount broker availability: *Fidelity, *Schwab, *White
Dividends paid: Income - December; Capital gains - December
Portfolio turnover (1 yr): 348%
Management fee: 0.75%
Expense ratio: 1.25% (year ending 9/30/97) (7.96% without waiver)

TIP: TURNER SMALL CAP GROWTH FUND ◆
(See first TIP listing for data common to all funds)

1235 Westlakes Drive, Suite 350
Berwyn, PA 19312
800-224-6312, 800-424-4865
610-251-0268, fax 610-251-0731

Investment adviser: Turner Investment Partners, Inc.
Portfolio manager: William H. Chenoweth (1994)
Investment objective and policies: Capital appreciation. Invests in a diversified portfolio of equity securities believed to have strong earnings potential with reasonable valuations. Fund will attempt to maintain sector weightings that approximate the concentrations represented in the Russell 2500 Index. May use options and futures.
Year organized: 1994
Ticker symbol: TSCEX
Group fund code: 897
Sales restrictions: Fund closed to new investors 8/30/97.
Discount broker availability: *Fidelity, *Schwab, *White
Dividends paid: Income - December; Capital gains - December
Portfolio turnover (3 yrs): 131%, 149%, 183%
Management fee: 1.00%
Expense ratio: 1.24% (year ending 9/30/97) (1.33% without waiver)

TIP: TURNER ULTRA LARGE CAP GROWTH FUND ◆
(See first TIP listing for data common to all funds)

1235 Westlakes Drive, Suite 350
Berwyn, PA 19312
800-224-6312, 800-424-4865
610-251-0268, fax 610-251-0731

Investment adviser: Turner Investment Partners, Inc.
Portfolio managers: Robert E. Turner (1997), John F. Hammerschmidt (1997)
Investment objective and policies: Capital appreciation. Invests in a diversified portfolio of common stocks of companies that, at the time of purchase, have market capitalizations exceeding $10B, that is perceived to have strong earnings potential. Fund will attempt to maintain sector weightings that approximate the concentrations represented in the Russell 200

Growth Index. Remaining assets may be invested in smaller capitalization stocks, warrants and rights. May invest up to 10% of assets in ADRs. May use options and futures.
Year organized: 1997
Group fund code: 900
Discount broker availability: *Fidelity, *Schwab, *White

Dividends paid: Income - December; Capital gains - December
Portfolio turnover (1 yr): 346%
Management fee: 0.75%
Expense ratio: 1.00% (eight months ending 9/30/97) (26.45% without waiver)

THE TITAN FINANCIAL SERVICES FUND

9672 Pennsylvania Avenue
Upper Marlboro, MD 20772
800-385-7003, 800-448-4826
301-599-7528
fax 301-951-0573
Internet: http://www.firstfund.com

Adviser: Titan Investment Advisors, LLC
Administrator: Investment Company Administration Corp.
Portfolio manager: Gilbert R. Giordano (1996)
Transfer agent: American Data Services, Inc.
Investment objective and policies: Capital appreciation; moderate income secondary. Invests at least 65% of assets in equity securities of companies involved in the financial services industries, that are perceived to be undervalued. May be heavily weighted in banking institutions with assets of $5B or less. Fund will also open deposit accounts with mutual savings and loan associations with the intent of subscribing to stock in the event the institutions go public. May invest up to 35% of assets in equity securities of other types of issuers, including debt securities of all types of issuers, and money markets. May invest up to 20% of assets in ADRs, and up to 15% in illiquid securities. May use options for hedging purposes.
Year organized: 1996
Ticker symbol: TITNX
Minimum purchase: Initial: $5,000, Subsequent: $100; IRA: Initial: $2,000
Wire orders accepted: Yes
Deadline for same day wire purchase: 4 P.M.
Discount broker availability: *Schwab
Qualified for sale in: All states except AK, AR, HI, ID, LA, ME, MA, MS, MT, NV, NH, NJ, NM, ND, OK, PR, RI, SD, TN, VT, WA, WI
Telephone redemptions: Yes
Wire redemptions: Yes, $1000 minimum
Letter redemptions: Signature guarantee not required
Redemption fee: 1.00% first year, 0.50% second year, payable to the fund
Dividends paid: Income - December; Capital gains - December
Portfolio turnover (1 yr): 98%
Shareholder services: IRA, systematic withdrawal plan
Management fee: 1.00%
Administration fee: 0.20% first $50M to 0.05% over $150M ($30,000 minimum)
12b-1 distribution fee: 0.25%
Expense ratio: 2.49% (11 months ending 4/30/97) (3.14% without waiver)

THE TORRAY FUND ◆

6610 Rockledge Drive, Suite 450
Bethesda, MD 20817
800-443-3036, 301-493-4600
fax 301-530-0642

Adviser: The Torray Corporation
Portfolio manager: Robert E. Torray (1990)
Transfer agent: The Torray Corp.
Investment objective and policies: Long-term total return consistent with prudent investment management. Fund intends to earn 15% per year compounded, measured over long periods (ten years or more). Invests in common stocks, convertible securities, cor-

porate bonds, U.S. Government securities and other fixed-income instruments believed undervalued. Allocation of assets will vary depending on perceived market conditions.
Year organized: 1990
Ticker symbol: TORYX
Minimum purchase: Initial: $10,000, Subsequent: $2,500
Wire orders accepted: Yes
Discount broker availability: Fidelity, Schwab, Siebert, White
Qualified for sale in: All states except AR, IA, MN, NM, PR, RI
Telephone redemptions: Yes
Wire redemptions: Yes, $10 fee
Letter redemptions: Signature guarantee not required
Dividends paid: Income - March, June, September, December; Capital gains - December
Portfolio turnover (3 yrs): 12%, 21%, 23%
Management fee: 1.00%
Expense ratio: 1.13% (year ending 12/31/97)

TRAINER, WORTHAM FIRST MUTUAL FUNDS
(Data common to all Trainer, Wortham funds are shown below. See subsequent listings for data specific to individual funds.)

845 Third Avenue, 6th Floor
New York, NY 10022
800-257-4414, 800-554-1156
800-775-0604, 212-759-7755
fax 212-583-9348

Adviser: Trainer, Wortham & Co., Inc.
Transfer agent and administrator: First Data Investor Services Group
Minimum purchase: Initial: $250, Subsequent: $50
Wire orders accepted: Yes
Deadline for same day wire purchase: 4 P.M.
Qualified for sale in: All states
Telephone redemptions: Yes
Wire redemptions: Yes, $9 fee
Letter redemptions: Signature guarantee required over $25,000
Telephone switching: With other Trainer, Wortham funds
Number of switches permitted: Unlimited
Shareholder services: IRA, automatic investment plan, electronic funds transfer (redemption only), systematic withdrawal plan min. bal. req. $5,000
Administration fee: 0.15% first $50M to 0.05% over $100M ($72,000 minimum)
IRA fees: Annual $12

TRAINER, WORTHAM EMERGING GROWTH FUND
(Fund liquidated in February 1998)

TRAINER, WORTHAM FIRST MUTUAL FUND
(See first Trainer, Wortham listing for data common to all funds)

Portfolio manager: David P. Como (1982)
Investment objective and policies: Capital appreciation; income secondary. Invests primarily in common stock and securities convertible into common stock, such as convertible bonds and preferred stock. Selects issues perceived to offer prospects for capital growth and growth of earnings and dividends. May invest up to 15% of assets in ADRs, and invest without limit in domestic government debt obligations.
Year organized: 1959
Ticker symbol: FMFDX
Dividends paid: Income - December; Capital gains - December
Portfolio turnover (3 yrs): 109%, 107%, 198%
Management fee: 0.75% first $40M, 0.50% over $40M
12b-1 distribution fee: 0.25%
Expense ratio: 1.87% (year ending 6/31/97)

TRAINER, WORTHAM TOTAL RETURN BOND FUND ◆
(See first Trainer, Wortham listing for data common to all funds)

Portfolio manager: John D. Knox (1996)
Investment objective and policies: Maximum total return consistent with preservation of capital. Invests in a broadly diversified portfolio of government and corporate domestic and foreign fixed-income instruments. At least 75% of investments must be rated at least "A", and the remaining 25% may be rated no lower than Baa by Moody's or BBB by S&P.
Year organized: 1996
Dividends paid: Income - annually; Capital gains - annually
Portfolio turnover (1 yr): 112%
Management fee: 0.45%
Expense ratio: 0.88% (9 months ending 6/30/97) (2.01% without waiver)

TRANSAMERICA PREMIER PORTFOLIO OF FUNDS (Investor Class)
(Data common to all Transamerica funds are shown below. See subsequent listings for data specific to individual funds.)

1150 South Olive Street, Suite T-900
Los Angeles, CA 90015
800-892-7587
Internet: http://funds.transamerica.com
e-mail: PremierFunds@transamerica.com

Shareholder service hours: Full service: 7 days, 6 A.M.-12 ;midnight EST
Adviser: Transamerica Investment Services, Inc.
Administrator: Transamerica Occidental Life Insurance Co.
Transfer agent: State Street Bank and Trust Co.
Minimum purchase: Initial: $1,000, Subsequent: $100; IRA/Keogh: Initial: $250, Subsequent: None; Automatic investment plan: Initial: $50, Subsequent: $50 (waived for pension accounts)
Wire orders accepted: Yes
Deadline for same day wire purchase: 4 P.M.
Qualified for sale in: All states
Telephone redemptions: Yes
Wire redemptions: Yes, $10 fee for transfers of $2,500 or less
Letter redemptions: Signature guarantee required over $50,000
Telephone switching: With other Transamerica funds of the same class
Number of switches permitted: 4 per year per fund
Shareholder services: IRA, Keogh, 401(k), 403(b), corporate retirement plans, directed dividends, electronic funds transfer, systematic withdrawal plan
IRA fees: Annual $10 per fund (maximum of $36, regardless of number of accounts); waived if total IRA assets exceed $5,000. Optional one-time, nonrefundable $100 fee for all accounts with same TIN#. Closing $10

TRANSAMERICA PREMIER AGGRESSIVE GROWTH FUND
(See first Transamerica listing for data common to all funds)

Lead portfolio manager: Philip Treick (1997)
Investment objective and policies: Maximum long-term capital appreciation. Invests at least 90% of assets in a non-diversified portfolio of domestic common stocks perceived to demonstrate growth potential. Issues may be selected without regard to market capitalization. May also invest in foreign securities, debt obligations and junk bonds. Up to 35% of assets may be invested in non-investment grade securities. May use a variety of derivative instruments in an effort to enhance performance and for hedging purposes.
Year organized: 1997
Ticker symbol: TPAGX
Discount broker availability: *Fidelity, *Schwab, *White
Dividends paid: Income - December; Capital gains - December
Management fee: 0.85% first $1B to 0.80% over $2B
12b-1 distribution fee: 0.25%

TRANSAMERICA PREMIER BALANCED FUND
(See first Transamerica listing for data common to all funds)

Portfolio managers: Bonds - Sharon K. Kilmer (1995), Stocks - Jeffrey S. Van Harte (1995)
Investment objective and policies: Long-term capital growth and current income; capital preservation secondary. Invests in a diversified selection of equity, debt and money market securities. Asset allocation is determined by perceived market conditions. Holds generally between 30% and 40% and no less than 25% of assets in nonconvertible debt securities, and normally no less than 60% to 70% in equity securities perceived to be undervalued. May invest up to 20% of assets in junk bonds and 20% in foreign securities. May use short sales, options, futures and other derivatives for purposes of hedging.
Year organized: 1995
Ticker symbol: TBAIX
Discount broker availability: *Fidelity, *Schwab, *White
Dividends paid: Income - March, June, September, December; Capital gains - December
Portfolio turnover (2 yrs): 19%, 16%
Management fee: 0.75% first $1B to 0.70% over $2B
12b-1 distribution fee: 0.25%
Expense ratio: 1.45% (year ending 12/31/96) (1.94% without waiver)

TRANSAMERICA PREMIER BOND FUND
(See first Transamerica listing for data common to all funds)

Portfolio manager: Sharon K. Kilmer (1995)
Investment objective and policies: Total return: income and capital growth. Invests in a diversified selection of corporate and government bonds and mortgage-backed securities. Attempts to identify securities with the potential to outperform similar ones by virtue of underlying credit strength or market mispricing. Normally invests at least 65% of assets in investment grade bonds, but may invest up to 35% of assets in junk bonds. May invest as much as 20% of assets in foreign securities. May use short sales, options, futures and other derivatives for purposes of hedging.
Year organized: 1995
Ticker symbol: TPBIX
Discount broker availability: *Fidelity, *Schwab, *White
Dividends paid: Income - monthly; Capital gains - December
Portfolio turnover (2 yrs): 7%, 19%
Management fee: 0.60% first $1B to 0.55% over $2B
12b-1 distribution fee: 0.25%
Expense ratio: 1.30% (year ending 12/31/96) (1.81% without waiver)

TRANSAMERICA PREMIER CASH RESERVE FUND
(See first Transamerica listing for data common to all funds)

Portfolio manager: Kevin J. Hickam (1995)
Investment objective and policies: Maximum current income consistent with liquidity and preservation of principal. Invests primarily in U.S. dollar-denominated money market instruments issued by U.S. and foreign issuers. Also invests in short-term corporate obligations.
Year organized: 1995
Ticker symbol: TPCXX
Check redemption: $250 minimum
Dividends paid: Income - declared daily, paid monthly
Management fee: 0.35%
12b-1 distribution fee: 0.10% (not currently imposed)
Expense ratio: 0.25% (year ending 12/31/97) (includes waiver)

TRANSAMERICA PREMIER
EQUITY FUND
(See first Transamerica listing for data common to all funds)

Portfolio manager: Glen E. Bickerstaff (1995)
Investment objective and policies: Maximum long-term growth. Invests primarily in common stocks of growth companies perceived to be premier companies that are undervalued. Also uses trend analysis of the U.S. economy as a determining factor in selection of securities. May invest as much as 20% of assets in foreign securities through the use of ADRs. May use short sales, options, futures and other derivatives for purposes of hedging.
Year organized: 1995
Ticker symbol: TEQUX
Discount broker availability: *Fidelity, *Schwab, *White
Dividends paid: Income - March, June, September, December; Capital gains - December
Portfolio turnover (2 yrs): 60%, 0%
Management fee: 0.85% first $1B to 0.80% over $2B
12b-1 distribution fee: 0.25%
Expense ratio: 1.50% (year ending 12/31/96) (1.95% without waiver)

TRANSAMERICA PREMIER
INDEX FUND
(See first Transamerica listing for data common to all funds)

Portfolio manager: Christopher J. Bonavico (1995)
Investment objective and policies: Seeks to track the performance of the Standard & Poor's 500 Composite Stock Price Index. Buys common stock solely based on market proportions of securities included in the index, excluding Transamerica Corporation. Typically, companies included in the index are the largest and most dominant firms in their industries. Fund routinely re-balances the composition as required to track the index. May use short sales, options, futures and other derivatives for purposes of hedging and to maintain liquidity.
Year organized: 1995
Ticker symbol: TPIIX
Discount broker availability: *Fidelity, White
Dividends paid: Income - March, June, September, December; Capital gains - December
Portfolio turnover (2 yrs): 94%, 4%
Management fee: 0.30%
12b-1 distribution fee: 0.10%
Expense ratio: 0.25% (year ending 12/31/97) (includes waiver)

TRANSAMERICA PREMIER
SHORT-INTERMEDIATE
GOVERNMENT FUND
(Fund liquidated 4/2/97)

TRANSAMERICA PREMIER
SMALL COMPANY FUND
(See first Transamerica listing for data common to all funds)

Lead portfolio manager: Philip Treick (1997)
Investment objective and policies: Maximum long-term growth. Invests at least 65% of assets in a diversified portfolio of domestic common stock consisting of companies with market capitalizations between $300M and $1B, or annual revenues of no more than $1B. Assets may be invested without limit, however, in a variety of foreign and domestic debt and equity securities. May invest up to 35% of assets in junk bonds, and may use derivatives.
Year organized: 1997
Ticker symbol: TPSCX
Discount broker availability: *Fidelity, *Schwab, *White
Dividends paid: Income - December; Capital gains - December
Management fee: 0.85% first $1B to 0.80% over $2B
12b-1 distribution fee: 0.25%

TREASURY CASH SERIES
Federated Investors Tower
Pittsburgh, PA 15222-3779
800-245-0242, 412-288-1900
fax 412-288-1982

Adviser: Federated Advisers
Portfolio manager: Deborah Cunningham (1994)
Transfer agent: Federated Securities Corp.
Investment objective and policies: Income consistent with stability of principal and liquidity. Invests in short-term U.S. Treasury money market obligations.
Year organized: 1990
Minimum purchase: Initial: $10,000, Subsequent: $500; IRA: Initial: $1,000
Wire orders accepted: Yes
Deadline for same day wire purchase: 12 NN
Qualified for sale in: All states
Telephone redemptions: Yes
Wire redemptions: Yes, $10,000 minimum
Letter redemptions: Signature guarantee required over $50,000
Check redemptions: No minimum
Management fee: 0.50%
12b-1 distribution fee: Maximum of 0.35%
Expense ratio: 0.99% (year ending 5/31/97) (includes waiver)

TRENT EQUITY FUND ◆
3101 North Elm Street, Suite 150
Greensboro, NC 27408
910-282-9302
fax 910-282-8272

Adviser: Trent Capital Management, Inc.
Administrator: Investment Company Administration Corp.
Portfolio manager: Robert V. May (1992), David C. Millikan (1992)
Transfer agent: American Data Services, Inc.
Investment objective and policies: Capital appreciation; current income secondary. Invests primarily in a diversified portfolio of common stocks, preferred stocks and convertible securities. Fund will try to limit holdings to approximately 35 companies. May invest up to 10% of assets in foreign issues, including sponsored ADRs traded on U.S. exchanges.
Year organized: 1992
Ticker symbol: TREFX
Minimum purchase: Initial: $1,000, Subsequent: $500; Automatic investment plan: Subsequent: $250
Wire orders accepted: Yes
Deadline for same day wire purchase: 4 P.M.
Qualified for sale in: CA, CO, DC, FL, GA, HI, IL, IN, KY, LA, MD, NJ, NY, NC, PA, VA, WV, WY
Telephone redemptions: Yes, $1,000 minimum
Wire redemptions: Yes, $1,000 minimum
Letter redemptions: Signature guarantee required
Dividends paid: Income - August, December; Capital gains - August, December
Portfolio turnover (3 yrs): 28%, 59%, 47%
Shareholder services: IRA, systematic withdrawal plan min. bal. req. $10,000
Management fee: 1.15%
Administration fee: 0.25% ($15,000 minimum)
Expense ratio: 1.75% (year ending 8/31/97) (includes waiver)
IRA fees: None

TURNER FUNDS
(See TIP Funds)

TWEEDY BROWNE AMERICAN
VALUE FUND ◆
52 Vanderbilt Avenue
New York, NY 10017
800-432-4789, 212-916-0600
prices 800-873-8242
fax 212-916-0666, 508-871-4057

Shareholder service hours: Full service: M-F 9 A.M.-5 P.M. EST; After hours service: prices, account balances, last transaction, prospectuses
Adviser: Tweedy Browne Co., L.P.
Portfolio managers: Christopher H. Browne (1993), William H. Browne (1993), John D. Spears (1993)

Transfer agent and administrator: First Data Investor Services Group, Inc.
Investment objective and policies: Long-term capital growth. Invests primarily in a diversified portfolio of domestic equity securities including common stocks, preferred stocks and convertible securities of companies believed undervalued. Will invest in companies of any size. Up to 20% of assets may be in foreign securities. May invest up to 15% of assets in junk bonds. May use futures, options, and currency transactions for hedging purposes and, to a limited extent, in an effort to enhance performance.
Year organized: 1993 (name changed from Value Fund on 10/1/94)
Ticker symbol: TWEBX
Group fund code: 002
Minimum purchase: Initial: $2,500, Subsequent: $250; IRA: Initial: $500
Wire orders accepted: Yes
Deadline for same day wire purchase: 4 P.M.
Discount broker availability: Fidelity, Schwab, Siebert, White
Qualified for sale in: All states
Telephone redemptions: Yes
Wire redemptions: Yes
Letter redemptions: Signature guarantee required over $5,000
Telephone switching: With Tweedy Browne Global Value Fund, $250 minimum
Number of switches permitted: Unlimited
Dividends paid: Income - December; Capital gains - December
Portfolio turnover (3 yrs): 16%, 9%, 4%
Shareholder services: IRA, automatic investment plan, electronic funds transfer
Management fee: 1.25%
Administration fee: 0.16% first $100M to 0.10% over $500M
Expense ratio: 1.39% (year ending 3/31/97) (1.52% without waiver)
IRA fees: Annual $10

TWEEDY BROWNE
GLOBAL VALUE FUND ◆
52 Vanderbilt Avenue
New York, NY 10017
800-432-4789, 212-916-0600
prices 800-873-8242
fax 212-916-0666, 508-871-4057

Shareholder service hours: Full service: M-F 9 A.M.-5 P.M. EST; After hours service: prices, account balances, last transaction, prospectuses
Adviser: Tweedy Browne Co., L.P.
Portfolio managers: Christopher H. Browne (1993), William H. Browne (1993), John D. Spears (1993)
Transfer agent and administrator: First Data Investor Services Group, Inc.
Investment objective and policies: Long-term capital growth; income incidental. Invests primarily in a diversified portfolio of equity securities including common stocks, preferred stocks and convertible securities of established companies believed undervalued, wherever they may be in the world. Will normally be invested in at least three countries, one of which may be the U.S. May invest up to 15% of assets in junk bonds. May use futures, options, and currency transactions for hedging purposes and, to a limited extent, in an effort to enhance performance.
Year organized: 1993
Ticker symbol: TBGVX
Group fund code: 001
Minimum purchase: Initial: $2,500, Subsequent: $250; IRA: Initial: $500
Wire orders accepted: Yes
Deadline for same day wire purchase: 4 P.M.
Discount broker availability: Fidelity, Schwab, Siebert, White
Qualified for sale in: All states
Telephone redemptions: Yes
Wire redemptions: Yes
Letter redemptions: Signature guarantee required over $5,000
Telephone switching: With Tweedy Browne American Value Fund, $250 minimum
Number of switches permitted: Unlimited
Dividends paid: Income - December; Capital gains - December
Portfolio turnover (3 yrs): 20%, 17%, 16%

Shareholder services: IRA, automatic investment plan, electronic funds transfer
Management fee: 1.25%
Administration fee: 0.20% first $80M to 0.12% over $500M
Expense ratio: 1.58% (year ending 3/31/97)
IRA fees: Annual $10

UAM FUNDS PORTFOLIOS

(Data common to all UAM portfolios are shown below. See subsequent listings for data specific to individual portfolios.)

The UAM Service Center
211 Congress Street
Boston, MA 02110
800-638-7983, 617-542-5440

Administrator: UAM Fund Services, Inc.
Transfer agent: Chase Global Funds Service Co.
Sales restrictions: Some UAM Funds are available in two share classes; institutional class, and institutional service class, which carry 12b-1 distribution fees. Those classes with 12b-1 fees are intended for UAM defined contribution plans only; unless otherwise indicated, shares profiled here that are sold direct or through discount brokerage accounts have no 12b-1 distribution fees. Fees are noted only for those funds which have the second class.
Minimum purchase: Initial: $2,500, Subsequent: $100; IRA: Initial: $500 (exceptions noted)
Wire orders accepted: Yes
Deadline for same day wire purchase: 4 P.M.
Qualified for sale in: All states (exceptions noted)
Telephone redemptions: Yes
Wire redemptions: Yes
Letter redemptions: Signature guarantee not required
Telephone switching: With the same share class of other UAM portfolios
Number of switches permitted: Unlimited
Shareholder services: IRA

UAM - BHM&S TOTAL RETURN BOND PORTFOLIO ◆

(See first UAM listing for data common to all portfolios)

Adviser: Barrow, Hanley, Mewhinney & Strauss, Inc.
Portfolio managers: John S. Williams (1995), David R. Hardin (1995), Stephen M. Milano (1995)
Investment objective and policies: Maximum long-term total return consistent with reasonable risk to principal. Invests at least 90% of assets in a diversified portfolio of investment grade fixed-income securities of varying maturities that are perceived to be undervalued. Portfolio average weighted maturity will generally be ten years or less. May invest up to 25% of assets in one industry sector, up to 10% of assets in other investment companies, and up to 15% of assets in illiquid securities.
Year organized: 1995
Ticker symbol: BHMSX (BHYYX service class)
Group fund code: 952 (926 service class)
Discount broker availability: Fidelity, *White
Qualified for sale in: All states
Dividends paid: Income - quarterly; Capital gains - annually
Portfolio turnover (2 yrs): 151%, 55%
Management fee: 0.35%
Administration fee: 0.23% first $200M to 0.09% over $3B
12b-1 distribution fee: Maximum of 0.25% (service class only)
Expense ratio: 0.55% (year ending 4/30/97) (0.57% without waiver)

UAM - C&B BALANCED PORTFOLIO ◆

(See first UAM listing for data common to all portfolios)

Adviser: Cooke & Bieler, Inc.
Portfolio managers: John J. Medveckis (1989), R. James O'Neil (1989), Peter A. Thompson (1989)
Investment objective and policies: Maximum long-

term total return, with minimal risk to principal. Invests in a combined portfolio of common stocks which have a consistency and predictability in their earnings growth, and investment grade fixed-income securities. Asset allocation will vary according to perceived market conditions; a neutral portfolio mix is 60% common stocks, 40% bonds, but portfolio always maintains at least 25% of assets as fixed-income senior securities. May invest up to 25% of assets in a single industry sector, up to 10% of assets in other investment companies, up to 10% in ADRs, and up to 10% in illiquid securities.
Year organized: 1989
Ticker symbol: CBBAX
Group fund code: 275
Discount broker availability: *Fidelity, *Schwab, *White
Dividends paid: Income - quarterly; Capital gains - annually
Portfolio turnover (3 yrs): 35%, 21%, 22%
Management fee: 0.62%
Administration fee: 0.25% first $200M to 0.11% over $3B
Expense ratio: 1.00% (year ending 10/31/97)

UAM - C&B EQUITY PORTFOLIO ◆

(See first UAM listing for data common to all portfolios)

Adviser: Cooke & Bieler, Inc.
Portfolio managers: John J. Medveckis (1990), R. James O'Neil (1990), Peter A. Thompson (1990)
Investment objective and policies: Maximum long-term total return with minimal risk to principal. Invests in common stocks of companies with strong financial positions which are perceived to be undervalued, but have consistency and predictability in their earnings growth. May also invest in convertible bonds or convertible preferred stocks. May invest up to 25% of assets in a single industry sector, up to 10% of assets in other investment companies, up to 10% in ADRs, and up to 10% in illiquid securities.
Year organized: 1990
Ticker symbol: CBEQX
Group fund code: 279
Discount broker availability: *Fidelity, *Schwab, *White
Dividends paid: Income - quarterly; Capital gains - annually
Portfolio turnover (3 yrs): 55%, 29%, 42%
Management fee: 0.62%
Administration fee: 0.23% first $200M to 0.09% over $3B
Expense ratio: 0.83% (year ending 10/31/97)

UAM - C&B EQUITY PORTFOLIO FOR TAXABLE INVESTORS ◆

(See first UAM listing for data common to all portfolios)

Adviser: Cooke & Bieler, Inc.
Portfolio managers: John J. Medveckis (1997), R. James O'Neil (1997), Peter A. Thompson (1997)
Investment objective and policies: Maximum long-term, after-tax total return, consistent with minimizing risk to principal. Invests in common stocks of companies of any size which have consistency and predictability in their earnings growth. Management utilizes investment techniques designed to minimize tax impact, such as avoiding realized capital gains. May invest up to 25% of assets in a single industry sector, up to 10% of assets in other investment companies, up to 10% in ADRs, and up to 10% in illiquid securities.
Year organized: 1997
Group fund code: 276
Discount broker availability: *Schwab, *White
Dividends paid: Income - quarterly; Capital gains - annually
Portfolio turnover (1 yr): 3%
Management fee: 0.62%
Administration fee: 0.23% first $200M to 0.09% over $3B
Expense ratio: 1.00% (9 months ending 10/31/97)

UAM - C&B MID CAP EQUITY PORTFOLIO ◆

(At press time, fund was not yet open)

UAM - CHICAGO ASSET MANAGEMENT INTERMEDIATE BOND PORTFOLIO ◆

(See first UAM listing for data common to all portfolios)

Adviser: Chicago Asset Management Co.
Portfolio managers: Jon F. Holsteen (1995), William W. Zimmer (1995), Gary R. Dhein (1997)
Investment objective and policies: High current income with moderate interest rate exposure. Invests in investment grade domestic corporate and government bonds with an average weighted maturity of three to ten years. May invest up to 15% of assets in illiquid securities, 10% of assets in junk bonds, and may invest without limit in foreign issues denominated in U.S. or other currencies. May use options in an effort to enhance performance, and may use options, futures and forward currency contracts for hedging purposes.
Year organized: 1995
Ticker symbol: CAMBX
Group fund code: 236
Minimum purchase: Initial: $2,000
Discount broker availability: *Fidelity, *Schwab, *White
Dividends paid: Income - quarterly; Capital gains - annually
Portfolio turnover (2 yrs): 31%, 24%
Management fee: 0.48%
Administration fee: 0.23% first $200M to 0.09% over $3B
Expense ratio: 0.80% (year ending 4/30/97)

UAM - CHICAGO ASSET MANAGEMENT VALUE/CONTRARIAN PORTFOLIO ◆

(See first UAM listing for data common to all portfolios)

Adviser: Chicago Asset Management Co.
Portfolio managers: Jon F. Holsteen (1994), Kevin J. McGrath (1994)
Investment objective and policies: Capital appreciation. Invests in common stock of large companies thought to be undervalued due to poor recent performance that are perceived to offer the potential for better than average performance in the future. Companies are primarily those with market capitalizations exceeding $1B. May invest up to 25% of assets in sponsored or unsponsored ADRs, up to 15% of assets in illiquid securities, and may use a variety of derivative instruments for hedging purposes.
Year organized: 1994
Ticker symbol: CAMEX
Group fund code: 235
Minimum purchase: Initial: $2,000
Discount broker availability: *Fidelity, *Schwab, *White
Dividends paid: Income - quarterly; Capital gains - annually
Portfolio turnover (2 yrs): 21%, 33%
Management fee: 0.625%
Administration fee: 0.25% first $200M to 0.11% over $3B
Expense ratio: 0.95% (year ending 4/30/97)

UAM - DSI BALANCED PORTFOLIO ◆

(See first UAM listing for data common to all portfolios)

Adviser: Dewey Square Investors Corp.
Portfolio managers: Team managed
Investment objective and policies: Maximum long-term capital growth consistent with reasonable risk to principal. Invests in a diversified portfolio of equity, fixed-income and money market securities, with allocations varying according to perceived market conditions. Portfolio will always maintain at least 25% of assets in senior, investment grade fixed-income obligations. Neutral is considered 60% equities and 40% bonds, although equities range from 40% to 75%; bonds from 25% to 60%, and cash from 0% to 25%. The fixed-income portion maintains an average dollar-weighted maturity between three and ten years. May invest without limit in foreign securities, and up to 10% of assets in junk bonds. May use options, futures and forward foreign currency transactions for hedging purposes.
Year organized: 1997

Ticker symbol: DSIZX
Group fund code: 283
Dividends paid: Income - quarterly; Capital gains - annually
Management fee: 0.45% first year, 0.55% second year, 0.65% thereafter
Administration fee: 0.25% first $200M to 0.11% over $3B

UAM - DSI DISCIPLINED VALUE PORTFOLIO ◆
(See first UAM listing for data common to all portfolios)

Adviser: Dewey Square Investors Corp.
Portfolio managers: Ronald L. McCullough (1989), Robert S. Stephenson (1993)
Investment objective and policies: Maximum long-term total return consistent with reasonable risk to principal. Invests at least 80% of assets in a diversified portfolio of common stocks of sound mid- to large-cap companies represented in the S&P 500 perceived to be currently undervalued but with improving fundamentals. May invest up to 20% of assets in foreign issues, up to 10% in other investment companies, and use futures and options for hedging purposes.
Year organized: 1989
Ticker symbol: DSIDX (DSVIX service class)
Group fund code: 280 (980 service class)
Discount broker availability: *Fidelity, *Schwab, *White
Qualified for sale in: All states: (SERVICE CLASS IN ALL STATES EXCEPT: AL, AR, ID, IA, KS, KY, LA, ME, MD, MI, MS, MT, NE, NV, NM, NY, ND, OH, OK, OR, PR, RI, SD, TN, TX, UT, WA, WV, WI)
Dividends paid: Income - quarterly; Capital gains - annually
Portfolio turnover (3 yrs): 126%, 135%, 121%
Management fee: 0.75% first $500M, 0.65% over $500M
Administration fee: 0.25% first $200M to 0.11% over $3B
12b-1 distribution fee: 0.25% (service class only)
Expense ratio: 1.05% (year ending 10/31/97)

UAM - DSI LIMITED MATURITY BOND PORTFOLIO ◆
(See first UAM listing for data common to all portfolios)

Adviser: Dewey Square Investors Corp.
Portfolio managers: G.A. David Gray (1994), Frederick C. Meltzer (1997)
Investment objective and policies: Maximum total return consistent with reasonable risk to principal. Invests at least 80% of assets in investment grade government and corporate fixed-income securities. Portfolio maintains a dollar-weighted average maturity of less than six years. Will only invest in municipal securities when the expected return equals or exceeds a taxable investment. May use options and futures for hedging purposes.
Year organized: 1989
Ticker symbol: DSILX
Group fund code: 281
Discount broker availability: *Fidelity, *Schwab, *White
Dividends paid: Income - quarterly; Capital gains - annually
Portfolio turnover (3 yrs): 51%, 121%, 126%
Management fee: 0.45% first $500M to 0.35% over $1B
Administration fee: 0.23% first $200M to 0.09% over $3B
Expense ratio: 0.94% (year ending 10/31/97) (0.95% without waiver)

UAM - DSI MONEY MARKET PORTFOLIO ◆
(See first UAM listing for data common to all portfolios)

Adviser: Dewey Square Investors Corp.
Portfolio managers: G.A. David Gray (1994), David J. Thompson (1997)
Investment objective and policies: Maximum current income consistent with the preservation of capital

and liquidity. Invests in short-term corporate, government and institutional investment grade money market obligations.
Year organized: 1989
Ticker symbol: DSMXX
Group fund code: 282
Sales restrictions: This profile represents Institutional Class shares only; no other class is available.
Dividends paid: Income - declared daily, paid monthly
Management fee: 0.40% first $500M, 0.35% over $500M
Administration fee: 0.21% first $200M to 0.07% over $3B
Expense ratio: 0.37% (year ending 10/31/97)

UAM - FMA SMALL COMPANY PORTFOLIO ◆
(See first UAM listing for data common to all portfolios)

Adviser: Fiduciary Management Assocs., Inc.
Lead portfolio manager: Patricia A. Falkowski (1993)
Investment objective and policies: Maximum long-term total return consistent with reasonable risk. Capital appreciation is expected to be the principal component of return. Invests primarily in a diversified portfolio of common stocks of relatively small companies with market capitalizations in the $50M to $1B range. Selections are made using a top down, thematically oriented momentum review of market trends. May invest up to 10% of assets in foreign securities, and up to 25% of assets in a single sector.
Year organized: 1991
Ticker symbol: FMACX
Group fund code: 285 (985 service class)
Minimum purchase: Initial: $25,000, Subsequent: $1,000
Discount broker availability: *Fidelity, *Schwab, White
Dividends paid: Income - quarterly; Capital gains - annually
Portfolio turnover (3 yrs): 86%, 106%, 170%
Management fee: 0.75%
Administration fee: 0.23% first $200M to 0.09% over $3B
12b-1 distribution fee: 0.40% (service class only)
Expense ratio: 1.03% (year ending 10/31/97)

UAM - FPA CRESCENT FUND ◆
(See first UAM listing for data common to all portfolios)

Adviser: First Pacific Advisors, Inc.
Portfolio manager: Steven Romick (1996)
Investment objective and policies: Total return: income and capital appreciation, consistent with reasonable risk. Invests primarily in equity securities believed to offer superior investment value, and fixed-income obligations such as securities issued by the U.S. Government and investment grade corporate debt. Up to 15% of assets may be in illiquid securities and 20% in securities of foreign issuers. May use futures and options for hedging purposes.
Year organized: 1993
Ticker symbol: FPACX (FPCBX service class)
Group fund code: 921 (922 service class)
Discount broker availability: *Fidelity, *Schwab, *White
Dividends paid: Income - June, December; Capital gains - June, December
Portfolio turnover (3 yrs): 45%, 100%, 101%
Management fee: 1.00%
Administration fee: 0.25% first $200M to 0.11% over $3B
12b-1 distribution fee: 0.25% (service class only)
Expense ratio: 1.57% (year ending 3/31/97)

UAM - HANSON EQUITY PORTFOLIO ◆
(See first UAM listing for data common to all portfolios)

Adviser: Hanson Investment Management Co.
Portfolio managers: Charles H. Raven (1997), David E. Post (1997), Steven E. Cutliffe (1997)
Investment objective and policies: Maximum long-term total return consistent with reasonable risk to principal. Invests at least 80% of assets in common

stocks of U.S. companies with market capitalizations exceeding $1B that are perceived to demonstrate strong growth characteristics but can be purchased at a reasonable price. May invest without limit in sponsored and unsponsored ADRs, invest up to 15% of assets in illiquid securities and up to 10% in other investment companies.
Year organized: 1997
Ticker symbol: HANSX
Group fund code: 220
Dividends paid: Income - annually; Capital gains - annually
Management fee: 0.70%
Administration fee: 0.23% first $200M to 0.09% over $3B

UAM - ICM EQUITY PORTFOLIO ◆
(See first UAM listing for data common to all portfolios)

Adviser: Investment Counselors of Maryland, Inc.
Portfolio managers: Robert F. Boyd (1998), William V. Heaphy (1998)
Investment objective and policies: Maximum long-term total return with reasonable risk to principal. Invests at least 80% of assets in common stocks of relatively large companies, virtually all exceeding the median market capitalization of the stocks listed on the NYSE, that are perceived to be undervalued. Capital return is likely to be the predominant component of the total return. May purchase sponsored ADRs that are traded in the U.S. without limit, however, will usually not comprise more than 20% of assets. May invest up to 10% of assets in illiquid securities, up to 10% in other investment companies, and use options and futures for hedging purposes.
Year organized: 1993
Ticker symbol: ICMEX
Group fund code: 266
Discount broker availability: *Fidelity, *Schwab, White
Dividends paid: Income - June, December; Capital gains - June, December
Portfolio turnover (3 yrs): 31%, 57%, 37%
Management fee: 0.625%
Administration fee: 0.25% first $200M to 0.11% over $3B
Expense ratio: 0.90% (year ending 10/31/97)

UAM - IRC ENHANCED INDEX PORTFOLIO ◆
(See first UAM listing for data common to all portfolios)

Adviser: Investment Research Co.
Portfolio managers: Team managed
Investment objective and policies: Total return exceeding that of the return earned by the companies in the S&P 500 Composite Price Index, while carefully controlling for risk. Uses a proprietary analytic technology to select a diversified portfolio of common stocks from within the S&P 500 universe. Invests in eight to ten stocks each in the nineteen industrial sectors identified by the adviser within the Index universe.
Year organized: 1996
Group fund code: 950
Discount broker availability: *Fidelity, *Schwab, *White
Dividends paid: Income - quarterly; Capital gains - annually
Portfolio turnover (2 yrs): 117%, 31%
Management fee: 0.70%
Administration fee: 0.23% first $200M to 0.09% over $3B
Expense ratio: 2.50% (year ending 4/30/97) (2.56% without waiver)

UAM - JACOBS INTERNATIONAL OCTAGON PORTFOLIO ◆
(See first UAM listing for data common to all portfolios)

Adviser: Jacobs Asset Management, Inc.
Portfolio managers: Daniel L. Jacobs (1997), Wai W. Chin (1997), Robert J. Jurgens (1997)
Investment objective and policies: Long-term capital appreciation. Invests at least 85% of assets in equity securities of companies in any and all markets outside the U.S. May invest across the entire spectrum of market capitalizations, but emphasizes small compa-

nies perceived to be undervalued. Emerging markets companies will comprise anywhere from 15% to 40% of assets. Normally approximately 50% of assets will be invested in small cap concerns, those with no more than $1B market capitalization. Equity securities may include ADRs, EDRs and GDRs. May use forward foreign currency exchange contracts for hedging purposes.
Year organized: 1997
Ticker symbol: JIOPX
Group fund code: 916
Discount broker availability: *Fidelity, *Schwab, *White
Dividends paid: Income - quarterly; Capital gains - annually
Management fee: 1.00%
Administration fee: 0.23% first $200M to 0.09% over $3B
Expense ratio: 1.75% (4 months ending 4/30/97)

UAM - MCKEE DOMESTIC EQUITY PORTFOLIO ◆
(See first UAM listing for data common to all portfolios)

Adviser: C.S. McKee & Co., Inc.
Portfolio manager: Walter C. Bean (1995)
Investment objective and policies: Superior long-term total return over a market cycle. Invests at least 65% of assets in a broadly diversified portfolio of equity securities of nationally listed domestic companies with medium to large market capitalizations. Invests in companies perceived to be undervalued due to earnings momentum or earnings surprise. May invest up to 10% of assets in foreign issues by means of ADRs. May invest up to 10% of assets in other investment companies and up to 10% in illiquid securities, and may use options and futures for hedging purposes.
Year organized: 1995
Ticker symbol: MKDEX
Group fund code: 246
Discount broker availability: *Fidelity, *White
Dividends paid: Income - quarterly; Capital gains - annually
Portfolio turnover (3 yrs): 47%, 42%, 27%
Management fee: 0.65%
Administration fee: 0.23% first $200M to 0.09% over $3B
Expense ratio: 0.94% (year ending 10/31/97)

UAM - MCKEE INTERNATIONAL EQUITY PORTFOLIO ◆
(See first UAM listing for data common to all portfolios)

Adviser: C.S. McKee & Co., Inc.
Portfolio manager: Walter C. Bean (1994)
Investment objective and policies: Superior long-term total return over a market cycle. Invests at least 65% of assets in equity securities of companies located in at least three countries other than the U.S. Issues are generally those traded on national exchanges, and portfolio will normally hold at least 50 stocks selected from at least five countries. Will be deliberately managed to maintain international and sector diversification. May invest up to 10% of assets in other investment companies and up to 10% in illiquid securities, and may use options, futures and forward currency exchange contracts for hedging purposes.
Year organized: 1994
Ticker symbol: MKIEX
Group fund code: 247
Discount broker availability: *Fidelity, *Schwab, *White
Dividends paid: Income - quarterly; Capital gains - annually
Portfolio turnover (3 yrs): 29%, 9%, 7%
Management fee: 0.70%
Administration fee: 0.25% first $200M to 0.11% over $3B
Expense ratio: 0.98% (year ending 10/31/97)

UAM - MCKEE SMALL CAP EQUITY PORTFOLIO ◆
(See first UAM listing for data common to all portfolios)

Adviser: C.S. McKee & Co., Inc.
Portfolio manager: Walter C. Bean (1997)
Investment objective and policies: Superior long-

term total return. Invests at least 65% (and usually 75%) of assets in a broadly diversified portfolio of equity securities of companies with market capitalizations of less than $1B at the time of purchase. Sectors weightings are guided broadly by those of the Russell 2000 Index, although actual holdings may vary from the index by as much as 50%. Fund usually will not exceed (but may) placing 10% of assets in foreign holdings through the use of ADRs. May invest up to 10% of assets in other investment companies, up to 15% in illiquid securities, and may use options, futures and forward currency exchange contracts for hedging purposes.
Year organized: 1997
Ticker symbol: MKSSX
Group fund code: 248
Discount broker availability: *White
Qualified for sale in: All states except CT
Dividends paid: Income - quarterly; Capital gains - annually
Management fee: 1.00%
Administration fee: 0.23% first $200M to 0.09% over $3B

UAM - MCKEE U.S. GOVERNMENT PORTFOLIO ◆
(See first UAM listing for data common to all portfolios)

Adviser: C.S. McKee & Co., Inc.
Portfolio manager: Joseph F. Bonomo, Jr. (1995)
Investment objective and policies: High current income consistent with preservation of capital. Invests at least 65% of assets in U.S. Treasury and Government agency securities. Average weighted maturity of portfolio is expected to fluctuate between five and 15 years since portfolio will be managed based on perceptions of interest rate changes. May invest up to 10% of assets in other investment companies and up to 10% in illiquid securities, and may use options and futures for hedging purposes.
Year organized: 1995
Ticker symbol: MKGBX
Group fund code: 245
Discount broker availability: *White
Dividends paid: Income - quarterly; Capital gains - annually
Portfolio turnover (3 yrs): 124%, 83%, 104%
Management fee: 0.45%
Administration fee: 0.23% first $200M to 0.09% over $3B
Expense ratio: 0.94% (year ending 10/31/97)

UAM - MJI INTERNATIONAL EQUITY PORTFOLIO ◆
(See first UAM listing for data common to all portfolios)

Adviser: Murray Johnstone International Ltd.
Portfolio manager: Rodger F. Scullion (1994)
Investment objective and policies: Maximum total return: capital appreciation and current income. Invests at least 65% of assets in equity securities of non-U.S. companies from at least three different countries listed on national exchanges or traded over the counter. They are chosen from markets identified through use of a proprietary system analyzing economic factors, stock prices in each market, market performance and trends in monetary policy. Once top down country allocation is determined, companies are selected that appear to be undervalued. May invest up to 15% of assets in illiquid securities and up to 10% in other investment companies. May use options in an effort to enhance performance, and may use options, futures and foreign currency exchange contracts for hedging purposes.
Year organized: 1994
Ticker symbol: MJIEX
Group fund code: 230 (930 service class)
Discount broker availability: *Fidelity, *Schwab, White
Dividends paid: Income - annually; Capital gains - annually
Portfolio turnover (3 yrs): 47%, 59%, 81%
Management fee: 0.75%
Administration fee: 0.25% first $200M to 0.11% over $3B
12b-1 distribution fee: Maximum of 0.75% (service class only) (not currently imposed)
Expense ratio: 1.50% (year ending 4/30/97)

UAM - NWQ BALANCED PORTFOLIO ◆
(See first UAM listing for data common to all portfolios)

Adviser: NWQ Investment Management Co.
Portfolio managers: Investment committee
Investment objective and policies: Consistent, above-average returns with minimal risk to principal. Invests in investment grade fixed-income securities and common stocks of companies with above-average statistical value that are believed to be undervalued. Mix is adjusted to reflect perceived changes in market and economic conditions. Neutral mix is considered 60% stocks, 30% fixed-income and 10% cash, but allocations may range from 30% to 75% stocks, 25% to 50% fixed-income, and 0% to 45% cash and equivalents. At least 25% is always invested in fixed-income obligations. May invest up to 10% of assets in junk bonds. May invest up to 15% of assets in illiquid securities and 10% in other investment companies.
Year organized: 1994
Ticker symbol: NWQLX (NWQBX service class)
Group fund code: 240 (940 service class)
Discount broker availability: *Fidelity, *Schwab (only through financial advisers), White
Dividends paid: Income - quarterly; Capital gains - annually
Portfolio turnover (3 yrs): 20%, 31%, 31%
Management fee: 0.70%
Administration fee: 0.25% first $200M to 0.11% over $3B
12b-1 distribution fee: Maximum of 0.75% (service class only)
Expense ratio: 1.00% (year ending 10/31/97)

UAM - NWQ SMALL CAP VALUE PORTFOLIO ◆
(See first UAM listing for data common to all portfolios)

Adviser: NWQ Investment Management Co.
Portfolio managers: Investment committee
Investment objective and policies: Long-term capital appreciation. Invests at least 65% of assets in equity securities of companies with market capitalizations between $50M and $1B at the time of purchase. Selections are based on top down sector momentum analysis and bottom up fundamental analysis. May invest up to 20% of assets in foreign issues traded on U.S. exchanges or in ADRs. May invest up to 15% of assets in illiquid securities and 10% in other investment companies.
Year organized: 1997
Group fund code: 243 (943 service class)
Dividends paid: Income - quarterly; Capital gains - annually
Management fee: 1.00%
Administration fee: 0.23% first $200M to 0.09% over $3B
12b-1 distribution fee: Maximum of 0.75% (service class only)

UAM - NWQ SPECIAL EQUITY PORTFOLIO ◆
(See first UAM listing for data common to all portfolios)

Adviser: NWQ Investment Management Co.
Portfolio manager: Jon D. Bosse (1997)
Investment objective and policies: Long-term capital appreciation. Invests at least 65% of assets in equity securities of companies perceived to be undervalued that appear to present some type of special catalyst situation that will turn them around. May invest up to 35% of assets either directly in foreign equity or fixed-income holdings, or through sponsored and unsponsored ADRs, and up to 15% of assets in junk bonds. May invest up to 15% of assets in illiquid securities and 10% in other investment companies, and use options, futures and currency futures contracts for hedging purposes.
Year organized: 1997
Group fund code: 242 (942 service class)
Dividends paid: Income - quarterly; Capital gains - annually
Management fee: 0.85%
Administration fee: 0.23% first $200M to 0.09% over $3B
12b-1 distribution fee: Maximum of 0.75% (service class only)

UAM - NWQ VALUE
EQUITY PORTFOLIO ◆
(See first UAM listing for data common to all portfolios)

Adviser: NWQ Investment Management Co.
Portfolio managers: Investment committee
Investment objective and policies: Consistent, superior total return with minimal risk to principal. Invests at least 65% of assets in common stocks of companies perceived to offer above-average statistical value in fundamentally attractive industries that seem to be undervalued at the time of purchase. May invest up to 10% of assets in companies with market capitalizations of less than $500M. May invest up to 20% of assets in securities of foreign companies that are traded on U.S. exchanges or through sponsored or unsponsored ADRs. May invest up to 15% of assets in illiquid securities and 10% in other investment companies.
Year organized: 1994
Ticker symbol: NWQEX
Group fund code: 241 (941 service class)
Discount broker availability: *Fidelity, *Schwab (only through financial advisers), White
Dividends paid: Income - quarterly; Capital gains - annually
Portfolio turnover (3 yrs): 31%, 25%, 4%
Management fee: 0.70%
Administration fee: 0.23% first $200M to 0.09% over $3B
12b-1 distribution fee: Maximum of 0.75% (service class only)
Expense ratio: 1.00% (year ending 10/31/97)

UAM - RICE, HALL, JAMES
SMALL CAP PORTFOLIO ◆
(See first UAM listing for data common to all portfolios)

Adviser: Rice, Hall, James & Assocs.
Lead portfolio managers: Thomas W. McDowell, Jr. (1994), Samuel R. Trozzo (1994)
Investment objective and policies: Maximum capital appreciation consistent with reasonable risk. Invests at least 65% of assets in a broadly diversified portfolio of common stocks of smaller companies with market capitalizations in the $40M to $500M range, focusing on growth stocks. May invest up to 15% of assets in foreign securities, up to 25% of assets in a single industry sector, and up to 10% in illiquid securities. May use options and futures for hedging purposes.
Year organized: 1994
Ticker symbol: RHJSX
Group fund code: 255
Discount broker availability: *Fidelity, *Schwab, *White
Dividends paid: Income - quarterly; Capital gains - annually
Portfolio turnover (3 yrs): 158%, 181%, 180%
Management fee: 0.75%
Administration fee: 0.23% first $200M to 0.09% over $3B
Expense ratio: 1.21% (year ending 10/31/97)

UAM - RICE, HALL, JAMES
SMALL/MID CAP PORTFOLIO ◆
(See first UAM listing for data common to all portfolios)

Adviser: Rice, Hall, James & Assocs.
Lead portfolio managers: Thomas W. McDowell, Jr. (1996), Samuel R. Trozzo (1996)
Investment objective and policies: Maximum capital appreciation consistent with reasonable risk. Invests at least 65% of assets in a broadly diversified portfolio of common stocks of smaller companies with market capitalizations in the $300M to $2.5B range, focusing on growth stocks. May invest up to 15% of assets in foreign securities, up to 25% of assets in a single industry sector, and up to 10% in illiquid securities. May use options and futures for hedging purposes.
Year organized: 1996
Ticker symbol: RHJMX
Group fund code: 256
Discount broker availability: *Fidelity, *Schwab, *White
Dividends paid: Income - quarterly; Capital gains - annually
Portfolio turnover (1 yr): 56%

Management fee: 0.80%
Administration fee: 0.23% first $200M to 0.09% over $3B
Expense ratio: 1.25% (year ending 10/31/97)

UAM - SAMI PREFERRED STOCK
INCOME PORTFOLIO ◆
(See first UAM listing for data common to all portfolios)

Adviser: Spectrum Asset Management, Inc.
Portfolio managers: Investment committee
Investment objective and policies: High level of dividend income consistent with capital preservation. Invests at least 65% of assets in a diversified portfolio of investment grade preferred utility securities of varying maturities which are hedged with U.S. Government securities futures. Also invests a significant portion of assets in preferred bank securities. Portfolio will generally hold up to 35% of assets in short-term instruments such as U.S. Treasuries. Management intends to hedge a significant portion of the preferred and fixed-income securities through the use of derivatives in an effort to substantially reduce price volatility.
Year organized: 1992
Ticker symbol: SAPSX
Group fund code: 291
Discount broker availability: *Fidelity, *Schwab, *White
Dividends paid: Income - monthly; Capital gains - annually
Portfolio turnover (3 yrs): 59%, 77%, 44%
Management fee: 0.70%
Administration fee: 0.25% first $200M to 0.11% over $3B
Expense ratio: 0.99% (year ending 10/31/97)

UAM - SIRACH BOND PORTFOLIO ◆
(See first UAM listing for data common to all portfolios)

Adviser: Sirach Capital Management, Inc.
Portfolio managers: Team managed
Investment objective and policies: Above-average total return consistent with reasonable risk to principal. Invests at least 75% of assets in a diversified mix of dollar denominated, investment grade corporate and government fixed-income securities of varying maturities. Portfolio generally maintains a dollar-weighted average maturity between eight and twelve years. May hold up to 10% of assets in a single issue. May use bond futures, bond options and interest rate futures contracts for hedging purposes.
Year organized: 1997
Ticker symbol: SBNDX
Group fund code: 264 (964 service class)
Discount broker availability: *Fidelity, *Schwab, *White
Dividends paid: Income - quarterly; Capital gains - annually
Management fee: 0.35%
Administration fee: 0.23% first $200M to 0.09% over $3B
12b-1 distribution fee: Maximum of 0.75% (service class only)

UAM - SIRACH EQUITY PORTFOLIO ◆
(See first UAM listing for data common to all portfolios)

Adviser: Sirach Capital Management, Inc.
Portfolio managers: Team managed
Investment objective and policies: Long-term capital growth with reasonable risk. Invests at least 90% of assets in equity securities, primarily common stocks, of companies of all market capitalizations perceived to have long-term growth potential. Up to 20% of assets may be in foreign securities represented by ADRs.
Year organized: 1996
Ticker symbol: SIEQX
Group fund code: 273 (973 service class)
Discount broker availability: *Fidelity, *Schwab, *White
Dividends paid: Income - quarterly; Capital gains - annually
Portfolio turnover (2 yrs): 89%, 34%
Management fee: 0.65%
Administration fee: 0.23% first $200M to 0.09% over $3B

12b-1 distribution fee: Maximum of 0.75% (service class only)
Expense ratio: 0.90% (year ending 10/31/97)

UAM - SIRACH FIXED
INCOME PORTFOLIO ◆
(Fund liquidated 12/9/97)

UAM - SIRACH GROWTH
PORTFOLIO ◆
(See first UAM listing for data common to all portfolios)

Adviser: Sirach Capital Management, Inc.
Portfolio managers: Team managed
Investment objective and policies: Long-term capital growth with reasonable risk. Invests primarily in common stocks of companies of all market capitalizations perceived to have long-term growth potential. Up to 20% of assets may be in foreign securities represented by ADRs.
Year organized: 1993
Ticker symbol: SGRWX (SGWSX service class)
Group fund code: 262 (962 service class)
Discount broker availability: *Fidelity, *Schwab, *White
Dividends paid: Income - quarterly; Capital gains - annually
Portfolio turnover (3 yrs): 138%, 151%, 119%
Management fee: 0.65%
Administration fee: 0.23% first $200M to 0.09% over $3B
12b-1 distribution fee: Maximum of 0.75% (service class only)
Expense ratio: 0.90% (year ending 10/31/97)

UAM - SIRACH SHORT TERM
RESERVES PORTFOLIO ◆
(Fund liquidated in December of 1997)

UAM - SIRACH SPECIAL
EQUITY PORTFOLIO ◆
(See first UAM listing for data common to all portfolios)

Adviser: Sirach Capital Management, Inc.
Portfolio managers: Team managed
Investment objective and policies: Maximum long-term capital growth with reasonable risk to capital. Invests primarily in common stocks of companies with market capitalizations between $100M to $2B. Up to 20% of assets may be in foreign securities represented by ADRs.
Year organized: 1989
Ticker symbol: SSEPX
Group fund code: 274 (974 service class)
Discount broker availability: *Fidelity, *Schwab, *White
Dividends paid: Income - quarterly; Capital gains - annually
Portfolio turnover (3 yrs): 114%, 129%, 137%
Management fee: 0.70%
Administration fee: 0.23% first $200M to 0.09% over $3B
12b-1 distribution fee: Maximum of 0.75% (service class only)
Expense ratio: 0.89% (year ending 10/31/97)

UAM - SIRACH STRATEGIC
BALANCED PORTFOLIO ◆
(See first UAM listing for data common to all portfolios)

Adviser: Sirach Capital Management, Inc.
Portfolio managers: Team managed
Investment objective and policies: Long-term capital growth with reasonable risk. Invests in a diversified portfolio of 35% to 70% common stocks and 25% to 50% fixed-income securities, with mix adjusted to reflect perceived changes in economic and market conditions. Neutral position will be a 50/50 split, however at least 25% of assets will always be invested in fixed-income senior securities including investment grade debt and preferred stock. Up to 20% of assets may be obligations of foreign governments, agencies or corporations denominated in dollars or other currencies.
Year organized: 1993

Ticker symbol: SSBAX
Group fund code: 260 (960 service class)
Discount broker availability: *Fidelity, *Schwab, *White
Dividends paid: Income - quarterly; Capital gains - annually
Portfolio turnover (3 yrs): 128%, 172%, 158%
Management fee: 0.65%
Administration fee: 0.25% first $200M to 0.11% over $3B
12b-1 distribution fee: Maximum of 0.75% (service class only)
Expense ratio: 0.97% (year ending 10/31/97)

UAM - STERLING PARTNERS BALANCED PORTFOLIO ◆
(See first UAM listing for data common to all portfolios)

Adviser: Sterling Capital Management, Inc.
Investment objective and policies: Maximum long-term total return consistent with reasonable risk to principal. Invests in a balanced portfolio of common stocks and fixed-income securities, with mix adjusted to reflect perceived changes to economic and market conditions. A neutral position is 60% equities, 40% fixed-income securities and cash. Will always hold at least 25% of assets in fixed-income senior securities. Equity securities are primarily of companies with market capitalizations exceeding $500M that are thought to be undervalued. May use options and futures for hedging purposes.
Year organized: 1991
Ticker symbol: SPBPX
Group fund code: 271
Discount broker availability: *Schwab, White
Qualified for sale in: All states (SERVICE CLASS ONLY IN AL, AK, AR, CA, CO, CT, DE, DC, FL, GA, HI, IL, IN, KS, MN, MO, NJ, NY, NC, PA, SC, TN, VA, WY
Dividends paid: Income - quarterly; Capital gains - annually
Portfolio turnover (3 yrs): 133%, 84%, 130%
Management fee: 0.75%
Administration fee: 0.25% first $200M to 0.11% over $3B
12b-1 distribution fee: 0.25% (service class only)
Expense ratio: 1.07% (year ending 10/31/97)

UAM - STERLING PARTNERS EQUITY PORTFOLIO ◆
(See first UAM listing for data common to all portfolios)

Adviser: Sterling Capital Management, Inc.
Investment objective and policies: Maximum long-term total return consistent with reasonable risk to principal. Invests at least 65% of assets in common stocks and other equity securities believed to be undervalued. Foreign issues may be held without limit, although usually no more than 20% of assets will be non-U.S., including ADRs. May use options and futures for hedging purposes.
Year organized: 1991
Ticker symbol: STEQX
Group fund code: 272
Discount broker availability: *Fidelity, *Schwab, White
Qualified for sale in: All states (SERVICE CLASS ONLY IN AL, AK, AR, CA, CO, CT, DE, DC, FL, GA, HI, IL, IN, KS, MN, MO, NJ, NY, NC, PA, SC, TN, VA, WY
Dividends paid: Income - quarterly; Capital gains - annually
Portfolio turnover (3 yrs): 57%, 78%, 135%
Management fee: 0.75%
Administration fee: 0.25% first $200M to 0.11% over $3B
12b-1 distribution fee: 0.25% (service class only)
Expense ratio: 0.99% (year ending 10/31/97)

UAM - STERLING PARTNERS SHORT-TERM FIXED INCOME PORTFOLIO ◆
(Fund liquidated December, 1997)

UAM - STERLING PARTNERS SMALL CAP VALUE PORTFOLIO ◆
(See first UAM listing for data common to all portfolios)

Adviser: Sterling Capital Management, Inc.
Investment objective and policies: Maximum long-term total return consistent with reasonable risk to principal. Invests at least 65% of assets in both domestic and foreign equity securities of companies with market capitalizations of $1B or less. May also take positions in distressed bonds with a high likelihood of future equity conversion. Issues are selected that are believed to be undervalued. May use options and futures for hedging purposes.
Year organized: 1997
Ticker symbol: SPSCX
Group fund code: 288
Discount broker availability: *Fidelity, *Schwab, *White
Dividends paid: Income - quarterly; Capital gains - annually
Portfolio turnover (1 yr): 50%
Management fee: 1.00%
Administration fee: 0.23% first $200M to 0.09% over $3B
Expense ratio: 1.25% (10 months ending 10/31/97)

UAM - TJ CORE EQUITY PORTFOLIO
(See first UAM listing for data common to all portfolios)

Adviser: Tom Johnson Investment Management, Inc.
Lead portfolio manager: Thomas E. Johnson (1995)
Investment objective and policies: Maximum total return consistent with reasonable risk to principal. Invests at least 65% of assets in equity securities, primarily common stock of companies with market capitalizations greater than $200M which are perceived to be undervalued. At least 80% of equity securities will be in companies with market capitalizations exceeding $800M. Up to 35% of assets may be in investment grade fixed-income obligations, and up to 20% in foreign issues.
Year organized: 1995
Ticker symbol: TJCEX (service class)
Group fund code: 925 (service class)
Discount broker availability: *Fidelity, *Schwab, *White
Dividends paid: Income - quarterly; Capital gains - annually
Portfolio turnover (3 yrs): 15%, 27%, 17%
Management fee: 0.75%
Administration fee: 0.23% first $200M to 0.09% over $3B
12b-1 distribution fee: Maximum of 0.75%
Expense ratio: 1.25% (year ending 4/30/97)

UAM - TS&W BALANCED PORTFOLIO ◆
(At press time, fund was not yet available)

UAM - TS&W EQUITY PORTFOLIO ◆
(See first UAM listing for data common to all portfolios)

Adviser: Thompson, Siegel & Walmsley, Inc.
Portfolio manager: Team managed
Investment objective and policies: Maximum long-term total return with reasonable risk. Invests in common stocks and other equity securities of relatively large companies believed undervalued. Up to 20% of assets may be securities of foreign issuers.
Year organized: 1992
Ticker symbol: TSWEX
Group fund code: 296
Discount broker availability: *Fidelity, *Schwab, White
Dividends paid: Income - quarterly; Capital gains - annually
Portfolio turnover (3 yrs): 42%, 40%, 17%
Management fee: 0.75%
Administration fee: 0.25% first $200M to 0.11% over $3B
Expense ratio: 0.99% (year ending 10/31/97)

UAM - TS&W FIXED INCOME PORTFOLIO ◆
(See first UAM listing for data common to all portfolios)

Adviser: Thompson, Siegel & Walmsley, Inc.
Portfolio manager: Team managed
Investment objective and policies: Maximum long-term total return with reasonable risk. Invests primarily in investment grade fixed-income securities of various maturities. Up to 20% of assets may be in securities of foreign issuers.
Year organized: 1992
Ticker symbol: TSWFX
Group fund code: 297
Discount broker availability: *Fidelity, *Schwab, White
Dividends paid: Income - declared daily, paid monthly; Capital gains - annually
Portfolio turnover (3 yrs): 36%, 59%, 29%
Management fee: 0.45%
Administration fee: 0.23% first $200M to 0.09% over $3B
Expense ratio: 0.72% (year ending 10/31/97)

UAM - TS&W INTERNATIONAL EQUITY PORTFOLIO ◆
(See first UAM listing for data common to all portfolios)

Adviser: Thompson, Siegel & Walmsley, Inc.
Portfolio managers: G.D. Rothenberg (1992), Stuart R. Davies (1992)
Investment objective and policies: Maximum long-term total return with reasonable risk. Invests primarily in common stocks and other equity securities of established companies in non-U.S. markets.
Year organized: 1992
Ticker symbol: TSWIX
Group fund code: 293
Discount broker availability: *Fidelity, *Schwab, White
Dividends paid: Income - annually; Capital gains - annually
Portfolio turnover (3 yrs): 45%, 25%, 23%
Management fee: 1.00%
Administration fee: 0.25% first $200M to 0.11% over $3B
Expense ratio: 1.30% (year ending 10/31/97)

UBS PRIVATE INVESTOR FUNDS ◆
(Data common to all UBS funds are shown below. See subsequent listings for data specific to individual funds.)

1345 Avenue of the Americas
New York, NY 10105
800-914-8566, 212-821-3000

Adviser: Union Bank of Switzerland, New York Branch
Administrators: Investors Fund Services (Ireland) Ltd., and Investors Bank & Trust Co.
Transfer agent: Investors Bank & Trust Co.
Minimum purchase: Initial: $25,000 ($10,000 if you own another UBS fund); Subsequent: $5,000; IRA/Keogh: Initial: $2,000, Subsequent: $500 (Fund may choose to aggregate the value of related shareholders' accounts to achieve minimums.)
Wire orders accepted: Yes
Deadline for same day wire purchase: 4 P.M.
Qualified for sale in: All states
Telephone redemptions: Yes
Wire redemptions: Yes
Letter redemptions: Signature guarantee required
Telephone switching: With other UBS funds of the same class
Number of switches permitted: Unlimited
Shareholder services: IRA, SEP-IRA

UBS BOND FUND ◆
(See first UBS listing for data common to all funds)

Portfolio manager: Louis N. Cohen (1996)
Investment objective and policies: High total return consistent with moderate risk of capital and maintenance of liquidity. Utilizing a master/feeder structure,

the fund invests all its assets in a corresponding portfolio which holds identical objectives and policies. Invests in debt securities from domestic and foreign corporations and governments. Portfolio duration is actively managed according to perceived market conditions. May use a variety of derivative instruments in an effort to enhance performance and for hedging purposes.
Year organized: 1996
Ticker symbol: UBSBX
Dividends paid: Income - declared daily, paid monthly; Capital gains - annually
Management fee: 0.80%
Expense ratio: 0.80% (9 months ending 12/31/96) (4.13% without waiver)

UBS INTERNATIONAL EQUITY FUND ◆
(See first UBS listing for data common to all funds)

Sub-adviser: UBS International Investment London Ltd.
Portfolio manager: Robin Apps (1996)
Investment objective and policies: High total return; capital growth and income. Utilizing a master/feeder structure, the fund invests all its assets in a corresponding portfolio which holds identical objectives and policies. Invests in a diversified portfolio of equity securities from foreign companies that are perceived to be undervalued. May use several derivative instruments in an effort to enhance performance and for hedging purposes.
Year organized: 1996
Ticker symbol: UBIEX
Dividends paid: Income - annually; Capital gains - annually
Management fee: 0.85%
Expense ratio: 1.39% (9 months ending 12/31/96) (3.05% without waiver)

UBS U.S. EQUITY FUND ◆
(See first UBS listing for data common to all funds)

Portfolio manager: Nancy C. Tengler (1996)
Investment objective and policies: Long-term capital appreciation and the potential for a high level of current income, with lower investment risk and volatility than is normally available from a portfolio of common stocks. Utilizing a master/feeder structure, the fund invests all its assets in a corresponding portfolio which holds identical objectives and policies. Invests at least 80% of assets in income-producing equity securities of domestic issuers, particularly those that generate high dividend income and are perceived to offer the potential for capital appreciation. May invest up to 20% of assets in short-term fixed-income securities and cash. May use options and futures for hedging purposes.
Year organized: 1996
Ticker symbol: UBUSX
Dividends paid: Income - annually; Capital gains - annually
Management fee: 0.60%
Expense ratio: 0.90% (9 months ending 12/31/96) (3.55% without waiver)

U.S. GLOBAL INVESTORS FUNDS
(Data common to all U.S. Global funds are shown below. See subsequent listings for data specific to individual funds.)

P.O. Box 781234
San Antonio, TX 78278-1234
800-873-8637, 210-308-1234
TDD 800-677-1212, 210-558-7249
fax 210-308-1217
Internet: http://www.usfunds.com
e-mail: shsrc@usfunds.com

Shareholder service hours: Full service: M-F 7:30 A.M.-5 P.M. CST; After hours service: prices, yields, balances, orders, last transaction, news, messages, DJIA, prospectuses, total returns
Adviser: U.S. Global Investors, Inc.
Transfer agent: United Shareholder Services, Inc.
Minimum purchase: Initial: $5,000, Subsequent: $50; IRA/Keogh: None; Automatic investment plan: Initial: $100, Subsequent: $30 (exceptions noted)

Wire orders accepted: Yes
Deadline for same day wire purchase: 4 P.M. (3 P.M. for Gold Shares)
Qualified for sale in: All states
Wire redemptions: Yes, with written instructions - $10 fee
Letter redemptions: Signature guarantee required over $15,000
Account closing fee: $10
Telephone switching: With other U.S. Global Investors funds
Number of switches permitted: Unlimited, $5 fee (3/quarter free for IRAs)
Shareholder services: IRA, SEP-IRA, Keogh, 403(b), 401(k), corporate retirement plans, electronic funds transfer, systematic withdrawal plan min. bal. req. $5,000
IRA fees: Annual $10 ($15 for SEP-IRA), Closing $10
Keogh fees: Annual $15, Initial $25, Closing $10

U.S. GLOBAL INVESTORS - ACCOLADE - ADRIAN DAY GLOBAL OPPORTUNITY FUND
(See first U.S. Global listing for data common to all funds)

Sub-adviser: Global Strategic Management, Inc.
Portfolio manager: Adrian Day (1997)
Investment objective and policies: Long-term capital growth. Invests at least 80% of assets in a diversified portfolio of primarily common stocks from blue chip companies throughout the world perceived to be undervalued. Additionally the fund searches for a variety of unrecognized contrarian investment in companies of any size or age. Fund will primarily invest in foreign issues, but may and will invest in U.S. securities. Fund may also invest in high yield and junk bonds. May use foreign currency hedging instruments.
Year organized: 1997
Discount broker availability: *Schwab, *White
Minimum purchase: Automatic investment plan: Initial: $1,000, Subsequent: $100
Telephone redemptions: Yes, to a money market account. Then you may write a check against that. Direct telephone redemption available to VIP customers.
Dividends paid: Income - annually; Capital gains - annually
Management fee: 1.00%
12b-1 distribution fee: 0.25%

U.S. GLOBAL INVESTORS - ACCOLADE - BONNEL GROWTH FUND
(See first U.S. Global listing for data common to all funds)

Sub-adviser: Bonnel, Inc.
Portfolio manager: Arthur J. Bonnel (1994)
Investment objective and policies: Long-term capital growth; any income incidental. Invests primarily in common stocks chosen for their appreciation potential on both fundamental and technical bases. Focuses on mid-cap companies with market capitalizations around $1B, but has no restrictions and may invest in companies of any size. Fund intends to stay fully invested. Up to 25% of assets may be in equity securities of foreign issuers listed on domestic or foreign exchanges. May invest up to 25% of assets in one industry, and use options for hedging purposes.
Year organized: 1994
Ticker symbol: ACBGX
Minimum purchase: Automatic investment plan: Initial: $1,000, Subsequent: $100
Discount broker availability: *Fidelity, *Schwab, *Siebert, *White
Telephone redemptions: Yes, to a money market account. Then you may write a check against that. Direct telephone redemption available to VIP customers.
Redemption fee: 0.25% for shares held less than 30 days, payable to the fund
Dividends paid: Income - June, December; Capital gains - December
Portfolio turnover (3 yrs): 239%, 212%, 145%
Management fee: 1.00%
12b-1 distribution fee: 0.25%
Expense ratio: 1.77% (year ending 9/30/97)

U.S. GLOBAL INVESTORS - ACCOLADE - REGENT EASTERN EUROPEAN FUND
(See first U.S. Global listing for data common to all funds)

Sub-adviser: Regent Fund Management, Ltd.
Lead portfolio manager: Dominic Bokor-Ingram (1997)
Investment objective and policies: Long-term capital growth. Invests at least 65% of assets in equity securities of companies located in or doing the majority of their business with the developing markets of Eastern Europe. May use ADRs and GDRs to achieve these ends. Additional assets may be used for a variety of equity or debt investments in companies of any size or age anywhere in the world. Fund will primarily invest in foreign issues, but may invest in U.S. securities for defensive purposes. May use foreign currency hedging instruments.
Year organized: 1997
Ticker symbol: EUROX
Discount broker availability: *Schwab, *White
Minimum purchase: Automatic investment plan: Initial: $1,000, Subsequent: $100
Telephone redemptions: Yes, to a money market account. Then you may write a check against that. Direct telephone redemption available to VIP customers.
Dividends paid: Income - annually; Capital gains - annually
Maintenance fee: $1 per month, payable quarterly, for balances below $5,000
Management fee: 1.25%
12b-1 distribution fee: 0.25%

U.S. GLOBAL INVESTORS ALL AMERICAN EQUITY FUND ◆
(See first U.S. Global listing for data common to all funds)

Portfolio manager: Bin Shi (1995)
Investment objective and policies: Capital appreciation. Invests at least 75% of assets in domestic common stocks with goal of exceeding the total return of the S&P 500 Stock Price index. May use index options and futures contracts on up to 35% of assets, and hedge up to 25% of assets.
Year organized: 1981 (name changed from Good & Bad Times Fund on 11/1/90)
Ticker symbol: GBTFX
Discount broker availability: Fidelity, Schwab, Siebert, *White
Telephone redemptions: Yes, to a money market account. Then you may write a check against that.
Redemption fee: 0.10% for shares held less than 14 days, payable to the fund
Dividends paid: Income - March, June, September, December; Capital gains - December
Portfolio turnover (3 yrs): 7%, 16%, 97%
Maintenance fee: $3 per quarter
Management fee: 0.75% first $250M, 0.50% over $250M
Expense ratio: 0.67% (year ending 6/30/97) (1.81% without waiver)

U.S. GLOBAL INVESTORS CHINA REGION OPPORTUNITY FUND ◆
(See first U.S. Global listing for data common to all funds)

Portfolio manager: Bin Shi (1996)
Investment objective and policies: Capital growth. Pursues investment opportunities directly in or related to the People's Republic of China. Invests primarily in securities of Chinese enterprises through the Shenzhen, Shanghai and Hong Kong stock exchanges. May also use securities of companies that have business associations in China and are listed on other China Region stock exchanges. May use ADRs and GDRs. Up to 15% of assets may be in unlisted securities.
Year organized: 1994
Ticker symbol: USCOX
Discount broker availability: *Schwab, *White
Telephone redemptions: Yes, to a money market account. Then you may write a check against that.
Redemption fee: 1% for shares held less than 180 days ·

Dividends paid: Income - March, June, September, December, Capital gains - December
Portfolio turnover (3 yrs): 24%, 26%, 53%
Management fee: 1.25%
Expense ratio: 2.22% (year ending 6/30/97) (2.54% without waiver)

U.S. GLOBAL INVESTORS GOLD SHARES FUND ◆
(See first U.S. Global listing for data common to all funds)

Portfolio manager: Ralph P. Aldis (1997)
Investment objective and policies: Capital growth with protection against inflation and monetary instability; current income secondary. Invests primarily in common stocks of companies involved in the exploration for, mining and processing of, or dealing in gold. Fund will invest a substantial portion of assets in South Africa. Fund may hold bullion.
Year organized: 1970 (present objective since July 1974)
Ticker symbol: USERX
Discount broker availability: Fidelity, Schwab, Siebert, White
Telephone redemptions: Yes, to a money market account. Then you may write a check against that. Direct telephone redemption available, $50,000 min. bal. req.
Redemption fee: 0.25% for shares held less than 14 days, payable to the fund
Dividends paid: Income - June, December; Capital gains - December
Portfolio turnover (3 yrs): 44%, 24%, 33%
Management fee: 0.75% first $250M, 0.50% over $250M
Expense ratio: 1.80% (year ending 6/30/97) (1.84% without waiver)

U.S. GLOBAL INVESTORS INCOME FUND ◆
(See first U.S. Global listing for data common to all funds)

Portfolio manager: Timothy Reynolds (1996)
Investment objective and policies: Capital preservation and current income; long-term capital appreciation secondary. Invests at least 80% of assets in income-producing securities - dividend-paying common stocks, securities convertible into common stocks, REITs, corporate debt securities, U.S. Government obligations and securities of foreign issuers traded in the U.S. Fund may use options and hedge up to 25% of total assets.
Year organized: 1983
Ticker symbol: USINX
Discount broker availability: *Fidelity, *Schwab, *Siebert, *White
Dividends paid: Income - March, June, September, December; Capital gains - December
Telephone redemptions: Yes, to a money market account. Then you may write a check against that.
Redemption fee: 0.10% for shares held less than 14 days, payable to the fund
Portfolio turnover (3 yrs): 88%, 51%, 7%
Account fee: $1 per month if balance is less than $1,000
Management fee: 0.75% first $250M, 0.50% over $250M
Expense ratio: 2.19% (year ending 6/30/97) (2.20% without waiver)

U.S. GLOBAL INVESTORS INTERMEDIATE TREASURY FUND ◆
(Fund liquidated 5/12/97)

U.S. GLOBAL INVESTORS MEGATRENDS FUND ◆
(See first U.S. Global listing for data common to all funds)

Sub-adviser: Money Growth Institute, Inc.
Portfolio manager: Stephen Leeb (1991)
Investment objective and policies: Long-term capi-

tal appreciation; current income secondary. Invests primarily in common stocks of established, larger companies believed to be undervalued that are selected using a proprietary market timing strategy. In no case will more than 5% of assets be invested in companies with market capitalizations of less than $300M. May move entirely into debt securities and/or money market instruments depending on perceived market conditions.
Year organized: 1991 (name changed from Leeb Personal Finance Fund 11/18/96)
Ticker symbol: MEGAX
Minimum purchase: Automatic investment plan: Initial: $1,000, Subsequent: $100
Discount broker availability: *Schwab, *White
Telephone redemptions: Yes, to a money market account. Then you may write a check against that. Direct telephone redemptions available to Chairman's Circle members.
Redemption fee: 0.25% for shares held less than 30 days, payable to the fund
Dividends paid: Income - June, December; Capital gains - June, December
Portfolio turnover (3 yrs): 62%, 115%, 163%
Management fee: 1.00%
Expense ratio: 1.88% (year ending 6/30/97) (1.97% without waiver)

U.S. GLOBAL INVESTORS NEAR-TERM TAX FREE FUND ◆
(See first U.S. Global listing for data common to all funds)

Lead portfolio manager: Creston King (1995)
Investment objective and policies: High current income exempt from federal income tax, consistent with capital preservation. Invests primarily in investment grade municipal securities rated Baa or better by Moody's or BBB or better by S&P, and generally maintains a weighted average maturity of five years or less.
Year organized: 1990 (name and objective changed from United Services California Double Tax Free Fund in 1993; previous data may be misleading)
Discount broker availability: Fidelity, Siebert, White
Dividends paid: Income - monthly; Capital gains - December
Telephone redemptions: Yes, to a money market account. Then you may write a check against that.
Portfolio turnover (3 yrs): 103%, 83%, 53%
Management fee: 0.50%
Expense ratio: 0.40% (year ending 6/30/97) (1.92% without waiver)

U.S. GLOBAL INVESTORS REAL ESTATE FUND ◆
(See first U.S. Global listing for data common to all funds)

Portfolio manager: Timothy Reynolds (1996)
Investment objective and policies: Long-term capital appreciation; current income secondary. Invests primarily in common and preferred stock of companies having at least 50% of their assets in or deriving at least 50% of their revenues from the ownership, construction, management or sale of residential, commercial or industrial real estate. Up to 35% of assets may be in securities of foreign issuers. Fund may use options and hedge up to 25% of total assets.
Year organized: 1987
Ticker symbol: UNREX
Discount broker availability: *Fidelity, *Schwab, *Siebert, *White
Dividends paid: Income - June, December; Capital gains - December
Telephone redemptions: Yes, to a money market account. Then you may write a check against that.
Redemption fee: 0.10% for shares held less than 14 days, payable to the fund
Portfolio turnover (3 yrs): 118%, 108%, 48%
Management fee: 0.75% first $250M, 0.50% over $250M
Expense ratio: 1.80% (year ending 6/30/97) (1.82% without waiver)

U.S. GLOBAL INVESTORS U.S. GLOBAL RESOURCES FUND ◆
(See first U.S. Global listing for data common to all funds)

Portfolio manager: Ralph P. Aldis (1992)
Investment objective and policies: Long-term capital growth with protection against inflation and monetary instability. Invests in common stocks of companies all over the world engaged in exploration, mining, processing, fabrication and distribution of natural resources of any kind—metals, timber, minerals and hydrocarbons.
Year organized: 1983 (formerly U.S. Prospector Fund. Name and policies changed on 1/26/90. 10 for 1 reverse split 10/1/90)
Ticker symbol: PSPFX
Discount broker availability: *Fidelity, *Schwab, *Siebert, *White
Telephone redemptions: Yes, to a money market account. Then you may write a check against that. Direct telephone redemption available, $50,000 min. bal. req.
Redemption fee: 0.25% for shares held less than 14 days, payable to the fund
Dividends paid: Income - December; Capital gains - December
Portfolio turnover (3 yrs): 52%, 117%, 50%
Management fee: 1.00% first $250M, 0.50% over $250M
Expense ratio: 2.30% (year ending 6/30/97) (2.34% without waiver)

U.S. GLOBAL INVESTORS U.S. GOVERNMENT SECURITIES SAVINGS FUND ◆
(See first U.S. Global listing for data common to all funds)

Lead portfolio manager: Creston King (1995)
Investment objective and policies: Highest yield consistent with safety of principal and liquidity. Invests exclusively in short-term money market obligations of the U.S. Government and its agencies and instrumentalities.
Year organized: 1986 (formerly GNMA Fund; name and objective change as of 11/1/90)
Ticker symbol: UGSXX
Dividends paid: Income - declared daily, paid daily
Check redemptions: $500 minimum
Telephone redemptions: yes
Management fee: 0.50% of first $250M, 0.375% over $250M
Expense ratio: 0.29% (year ending 6/30/97) (0.70% without waiver)

U.S. GLOBAL INVESTORS U.S. TAX FREE FUND ◆
(See first U.S. Global listing for data common to all funds)

Lead portfolio manager: Creston King (1995)
Investment objective and policies: High level of current income exempt from federal income tax, consistent with capital preservation. Invests primarily in investment grade municipal securities rated Baa or better by Moody's or BBB or better by S&P. In periods of accelerating inflation, maturities will be four to ten years; in periods when inflation is subsiding, maturities will be twenty to thirty years.
Year organized: 1984
Ticker symbol: USUTX
Discount broker availability: Schwab, White
Telephone redemptions: Yes, to a money market account. Then you may write a check against that.
Dividends paid: Income - monthly; Capital gains - December
Portfolio turnover (3 yrs): 87%, 69%, 21%
Management fee: 0.75% first $250M, 0.50% over $250M
Expense ratio: 0.40% (year ending 6/30/97) (1.46% without waiver)

U.S. GLOBAL INVESTORS
U.S. TREASURY SECURITIES
CASH FUND ◆
(See first U.S. Global listing for data common to all funds)

Lead portfolio manager: Creston King (1995)
Investment objective and policies: High current income consistent with safety and liquidity. Invests in U.S. Treasury money market securities and in repurchase agreements.
Year organized: 1982 (name changed from U.S. Treasury Securities Fund on 10/1/90)
Ticker symbol: USTXX
Check redemptions: No minimum
Telephone redemptions: yes
Dividends paid: Income - declared daily, paid daily
Management fee: 0.50% first $250M, 0.375% over $250M
Expense ratio: 1.04% (year ending 6/30/97)

U.S. GLOBAL INVESTORS
WORLD GOLD FUND ◆
(See first U.S. Global listing for data common to all funds)

Portfolio manager: Ralph P. Aldis (1997)
Investment objective and policies: Long-term capital growth with protection against inflation and monetary instability. Invests at least 65% of assets in the securities of companies involved in the exploration for, mining and processing of, or dealing in gold. At least 25% will be invested in companies engaged in natural resource operations. Fund will not invest in South Africa. Fund may hold bullion.
Year organized: 1985 (formerly New Prospector Fund. Name and investment policy changes, 10 for 1 reverse split, effected 10/1/90)
Ticker symbol: UNWPX
Discount broker availability: *Fidelity, *Schwab, *Siebert, *White
Telephone redemptions: Yes, to a money market account. Then you may write a check against that. Direct telephone redemption available, $50,000 min. bal. req.
Redemption fee: 0.25% for shares held less than 14 days, payable to the fund
Dividends paid: Income - December; Capital gains - December
Portfolio turnover (3 yrs): 40%, 26%, 28%
Management fee: 1.00% first $250M, 0.50% over $250M
Expense ratio: 1.52% (year ending 6/30/97) (1.54% without waiver)

U.S. GLOBAL LEADERS
GROWTH FUND ◆
630 Fifth Avenue
New York, NY 10111
800-282-2340, 212-765-5350
fax 516-951-0573
Internet: http://www.firstfund.com/pages/usglx.phtml

Adviser: Yeager, Wood & Marshall, Inc.
Administrator: Investment Company Administration Corp.
Portfolio managers: George M. Yeager (1995), Gordon M. Marchand (1995)
Transfer agent: American Data Services, Inc.
Investment objectives and policies: Capital growth. Invests in common stocks of American companies with substantial international activities, market leading positions in developed markets, and substantial, profitable positions in emerging markets. May also invest up to 25% of assets in ADRs of foreign concerns who fit the "global leader" profile. Fund is non-diversified.
Year organized: 1995
Ticker symbol: USGLX
Minimum purchase: Initial: $2,000, Subsequent: $1,000; Automatic investment plan: Subsequent: $250
Wire orders accepted: Yes
Deadline for same day wire purchase: 4 P.M.
Discount broker availability: *Fidelity, *Schwab, *Siebert, *White
Qualified for sale in: All states
Telephone redemptions: Yes, $1,000 minimum
Wire redemptions: Yes, $1,000 minimum, $7 fee
Letter redemptions: Signature guarantee required

Dividends paid: Income - December; Capital gains - December
Shareholder services: IRA, electronic funds transfer
Management fee: 1.00%
Administration fee: 0.20% first $50M to 0.05% over $150M ($30,000 minimum)
Expense ratio: 1.48% (year ending 6/30/97) (1.87% without waiver)
IRA fees: Annual $12

THE UNIFIED FUNDS
(These are the funds previously known as "The Vintage Funds." Fund family changed names February 2, 1998. Data common to all Unified funds are shown below. See subsequent listings for data specific to individual funds.)

429 North Pennsylvania Street
Indianapolis, IN 46204
800-408-4682
Internet: http://www.umcfund.com

Adviser: Unified Advisers, Inc. Also administers the V.O.I.C.E. (Vision for On-Going Investment in Charity and Education) program to support and supplement education in America, which provides a means for individual and institutional customers of the Vintage funds to cause contributions to be made to various not-for-profit organizations at no cost to the shareholder or the funds.
Administrator: Unified Advisers, Inc.
Distributor: Unified Management Corp.
Transfer agent: Unified Advisers, Inc.
Minimum purchase: Initial: $1,000, Subsequent: $100; IRA: Initial: $500; Subsequent: $50
Wire orders accepted: Yes
Deadline for same day wire purchase: 4 P.M.
Qualified for sale in: All states
Telephone redemptions: Yes, $100 minimum
Wire redemptions: Yes, $1,000 minimum, $15 fee
Letter redemptions: Signature guarantee required over $5,000
Telephone switching: With other Unified funds
Number of switches permitted: Unlimited
Shareholder services: IRA, SEP-IRA, 401(k), 403(b), corporate retirement plans, automatic investment plan, electronic funds transfer, systematic withdrawal plan
12b-1 distribution fee: 0.10%
Shareholder services fees: 0.15%
IRA fees: Annual $10

UNIFIED - FIRST LEXINGTON
BALANCED FUND
(See first Unified listing for data common to all funds)

Sub-adviser: Health Financial, Inc.
Portfolio manager: Dr. Gregory W. Kasten (1996)
Investment objective and policies: Long-term growth of capital and current income. Invests primarily in a diversified portfolio of other no-load mutual funds that invest in one of six financial asset classes, including: S&P 500 common stocks; smaller cap stocks as represented by the Wilshire 4500 Index; international stocks selected from the MSCI EAFE Index; real estate investment trusts as represented by the Morgan Stanley REIT Index; cash equivalents, and; long-term investment rated corporate and government bonds. Allocation is adjusted according to perceived market conditions.
Year organized: 1996 (name and objective changed from Municipal Fixed Income Fund 9/30/96)
Group fund code: 26
Discount broker availability: *Schwab
Dividends paid: Income - quarterly; Capital gains - annually
Management fee: 0.50%
Administration fee: 0.185%

UNIFIED - LAIDLAW FUND
(See first Unified listing for data common to all funds)

Sub-adviser: Fiduciary Counsel, Inc.
Portfolio manager: Jack R. Orben (1992)
Investment objective and policies: Growth of capital, current income and growth of income. Invests primarily in a diversified portfolio of common stocks, preferred stocks, and preferred stocks or corporate debt securities

convertible into common stocks of companies which offer the prospect of growth of earnings while paying current dividends. May also purchase securities that do not pay current dividends but which offer prospects for growth of capital and future income. May invest up to 25% of assets in any individual sector fund, up to 25% of assets in international securities, and write covered call options and secured put options.
Year organized: 1992 (created from a merge/conversion with Fiduciary Value Fund (a planned fund which had never been invested) and the Laidlaw Covenant Fund, purchased 12/20/96)
Group fund code: 23
Discount broker availability: *Schwab
Dividends paid: Income - quarterly; Capital gains - annually
Portfolio turnover (3 yrs): 61%, 73%, 107%
Management fee: 0.75%
Administration fee: 0.435%
Expense ratio: 2.44% (9 months ending 9/30/96) (4.81% without waiver)

UNIFIED - STARWOOD
STRATEGIC FUND
(See first Unified listing for data common to all funds)

Sub-adviser: Starwood Corp.
Portfolio manager: Andrew E. Beer (1996)
Investment objective and policies: Growth of capital; current income incidental. Invests primarily in a diversified portfolio of equity securities of seasoned, financially strong growth companies demonstrating market capitalization of at least $300M above average growth rates over an extended period, important market positions and attractive share prices. May invest up to 35% of assets in any individual sector fund, up to 25% of assets in international securities, and write covered call options and secured put options.
Year organized: 1996
Group fund code: 20
Discount broker availability: *Schwab
Dividends paid: Income - quarterly; Capital gains - annually
Portfolio turnover (1 yr): 170%
Management fee: 0.75%
Administration fee: 0.435%
Expense ratio: 15.25% (6 months ending 9/30/96) (15.99% without waiver)

UNIFIED - TAXABLE MONEY
MARKET FUND
(See first Unified listing for data common to all funds)

Sub-adviser: Fiduciary Counsel, Inc.
Portfolio manager: Jack R. Orben (1997)
Investment objective and policies: High level of current income consistent with the preservation of capital and maintenance of liquidity. Invests primarily in a diversified portfolio of high quality, short-term money market instruments.
Year organized: 1995
Group fund code: 30
Check redemptions: $250 minimum
Dividends paid: Income - declared and paid daily
Management fee: 0.50%
Administration fee: 0.185%
Expense ratio: 1.16% (year ending 9/30/96) (1.25% without waiver)

USAA FUNDS ◆
(Data common to all USAA funds are shown below. See subsequent listings for data specific to individual funds.)

USAA Building
9800 Fredericksburg Road
San Antonio, TX 78288
800-531-8448, 800-531-8181
210-456-7211, TDD 800-531-4327
prices/yields 800-531-8066
TDD 800-531-4327
touchtone account line 800-531-8777
fax 210-498-2889

Shareholder service hours: Full service: M-F 7:30 A.M.-8 P.M., Sat 8 A.M.-5 P.M. CST; After hours service: prices, yields, balances, orders, last transaction, news, messages, DJIA, prospectuses, total returns

Adviser: USAA Investment Management Co.
Transfer agent: DST Systems, Inc.
Wire orders accepted: Yes
Deadline for same day wire purchase: 4 P.M.
Qualified for sale in: All states (except single state tax-exempt funds)
Telephone redemptions: Yes, $50 minimum
Wire redemptions: Yes, $50 minimum, $10 fee
Letter redemptions: Signature guarantee not required
Telephone switching: With other USAA funds, $50 minimum
Number of switches permitted: 6 per year out of any fund (unlimited for short-term bond and money market funds)
Maintenance fee: Beginning in September 1998, $12 per year for account balances below $2,000; waived for UGMA/UTMA, automatic investment plans, non-IRA money market accounts, aggregate balance holders with balances in excess of $50,000, and all IRA accounts for the first year.
Shareholder services: IRA, SEP-IRA, 403(b), directed dividends, electronic funds transfer, systematic withdrawal plan min. bal. req. $5,000
IRA fees: Closing $20

USAA AGGRESSIVE GROWTH FUND ◆
(See first USAA listing for data common to all funds)

Portfolio managers: John K. Cabell, Jr. (1995), Eric M. Efron (1995)
Investment objective and policies: Capital appreciation. Invests in common stocks and other securities convertible into common stocks of smaller, emerging growth companies with market capitalizations of less than $500M. Up to 30% of assets may be in securities of foreign issuers and 15% in illiquid securities.
Year organized: 1981 (Formerly USAA Sunbelt Era. Prior to name change 2/89, fund concentrated investments in the Sunbelt region.)
Ticker symbol: USAUX
Group fund code: 38
Minimum purchase: Initial: $3,000, Subsequent: $50; IRA: Initial: $250; Automatic investment plan: Initial: None
Dividends paid: Income - September; Capital gains - September
Portfolio turnover (3 yrs): 57%, 44%, 138%
Management fee: 0.50% first $200M to 0.33% over $300M
Expense ratio: 0.74% (year ending 7/31/97)

USAA BALANCED STRATEGY FUND ◆
(See first USAA listing for data common to all funds)

Portfolio managers: R. David Ullom (stocks) (1995), Paul H. Lundmark (bonds) (1995), Pamela K. Bledsoe (money markets) (1996)
Investment objective and policies: High total return: long-term capital growth and current income with reduced risk over time. Invests 50% to 70% of assets in stocks, 30% to 50% in bonds and 0% to 10% in cash equivalents using as asset allocation strategy. Allocations are adjusted quarterly to address imbalances and reflect perceived market conditions. May invest in securities of foreign issuers and have up to 15% of assets in illiquid securities. Fund may hedge in forward currency markets.
Year organized: 1995
Ticker symbol: USBSX
Group fund code: 47
Minimum purchase: Initial: $3,000, Subsequent: $50; IRA: Initial: $250; Automatic investment plan: Initial: None
Dividends paid: Income - March, June, September, December; Capital gains - July
Portfolio turnover (2 yrs): 28%, 27%
Management fee: 0.75%
Expense ratio: 1.25% (year ending 5/31/97) (1.39% without waiver)

USAA CALIFORNIA BOND FUND ◆
(See first USAA listing for data common to all funds)

Portfolio manager: Robert R. Pariseau (1995)
Investment objective and policies: High interest income exempt from federal and California state income taxes. Invests primarily in investment grade California municipal securities, and maintains a dollar-weighted average maturity of more than ten years. Up to 20% of assets may be in securities subject to AMT tax treatment, and up to 15% in illiquid securities.
Year organized: 1989
Ticker symbol: USCBX
Group fund code: 60
Minimum purchase: Initial: $3,000, Subsequent: $50; Automatic investment plan: Subsequent: $50
Qualified for sale in: CA
Dividends paid: Income - declared daily, paid monthly; Capital gains - May
Portfolio turnover (3 yrs): 24%, 23%, 29%
Management fee: 0.50% first $50M to 0.30% over $100M (for assets of California Bond and Money Market funds combined)
Expense ratio: 0.41% (year ending 3/31/97)

USAA CALIFORNIA MONEY MARKET FUND ◆
(See first USAA listing for data common to all funds)

Portfolio manager: John C. Bonnell (1996)
Investment objective and policies: High interest income exempt from federal and California state income taxes. Invests in California municipal money market securities.
Year organized: 1989
Ticker symbol: UCAXX
Group fund code: 61
Minimum purchase: Initial: $3,000, Subsequent: $50; Automatic investment plan: Subsequent: $50
Qualified for sale in: CA
Check redemptions: $250 minimum ($5 setup fee)
Dividends paid: Income - declared daily, paid monthly
Management fee: 0.50% first $50M to 0.30% over $100M (for assets of California Bond and Money Market funds combined)
Expense ratio: 0.45% (year ending 3/31/97)

USAA CORNERSTONE STRATEGY FUND ◆
(See first USAA listing for data common to all funds)

Lead portfolio manager: Harry W. Miller (asset allocation) (1987) (Individual market segments managed by specialists)
Investment objective and policies: Preserve purchasing power of capital against inflation and achieve a "real," positive inflation-adjusted rate of return. Invests 0% to 10% of assets in gold stocks, and 22% to 28% in each of; foreign stocks, real estate stocks, U.S. Government securities, and domestic stocks that are perceived to be undervalued. Up to 15% of assets may be in illiquid securities.
Year organized: 1984 (Name changed from Cornerstone Fund in 1995)
Ticker symbol: USCRX
Group fund code: 51
Minimum purchase: Initial: $3,000, Subsequent: $50; IRA: Initial: $250; Automatic investment plan: Initial: None
Dividends paid: Income - July; Capital gains - July, November
Portfolio turnover (3 yrs): 35%, 36%, 33%
Management fee: 0.75%
Expense ratio: 1.06% (year ending 5/31/97)

USAA EMERGING MARKETS FUND ◆
(See first USAA listing for data common to all funds)

Portfolio manager: W. Travis Selmier II (1994)
Investment objective and policies: Capital appreciation. Invests at least 65% of assets in common stocks and other securities convertible into common stocks of emerging market companies. May use ADRs and GDRs and invest directly on foreign stock exchanges. Up to 15% of assets may be in illiquid securities. May use forward foreign currency contracts for hedging purposes.
Year organized: 1994
Ticker symbol: USEMX

Group fund code: 56
Minimum purchase: Initial: $3,000, Subsequent: $50; IRA: Initial: $250; Automatic investment plan: Initial: None
Dividends paid: Income - July; Capital gains - July, November
Portfolio turnover (3 yrs): 61%, 88%, 35%
Management fee: 1.00%
Expense ratio: 1.81% (year ending 5/31/97)

USAA FIRST START GROWTH FUND ◆
(See first USAA listing for data common to all funds)

Portfolio manager: Curt Rohrman (1997)
Investment objective and policies: Long-term capital appreciation. Invests at least 65% of assets in a broadly diversified portfolio of equity securities of companies whose products or services are likely to be familiar and recognizable to young investors. Does not invest in companies whose primary products or services are alcohol, tobacco or gambling activities. May invest up to 25% of assets in one industry sector. May invest in foreign securities without limit, invest in convertible junk bonds, and use foreign currency contracts and options and futures for hedging purposes.
Year organized: 1997
Group fund code: 32
Minimum purchase: Initial: $3,000, Subsequent: $20; IRA: Initial: $250; Automatic investment plan: Initial: None
Dividends paid: Income - September; Capital gains - September
Management fee: 0.75%

USAA FLORIDA TAX-FREE INCOME FUND ◆
(See first USAA listing for data common to all funds)

Portfolio manager: Robert R. Pariseau (1995)
Investment objective and policies: High current interest income exempt from federal income and Florida intangible personal property taxes. Invests primarily in investment-grade Florida municipal securities, and maintains a dollar-weighted average maturity of more than ten years. Up to 20% of assets may be in securities subject to AMT tax treatment, and up to 15% in illiquid securities.
Year organized: 1993
Ticker symbol: UFLTX
Group fund code: 66
Minimum purchase: Initial: $3,000, Subsequent: $50; Automatic investment plan: Subsequent: $50
Qualified for sale in: FL
Dividends paid: Income - declared daily, paid monthly; Capital gains - May, November
Portfolio turnover (3 yrs): 45%, 58%, 72%
Management fee: 0.50% first $50M to 0.30% over $100M (for assets of Florida Tax-Free Income and Money Market funds combined)
Expense ratio: 0.50% (year ending 3/31/97) (0.57% without waiver)

USAA FLORIDA TAX-FREE MONEY MARKET FUND ◆
(See first USAA listing for data common to all funds)

Portfolio manager: John C. Bonnell (1996)
Investment objective and policies: High current interest income exempt from federal income and Florida intangible personal property taxes, while preserving capital and maintaining liquidity. Invests in Florida municipal money market securities.
Year organized: 1993
Ticker symbol: UFLXX
Group fund code: 67
Minimum purchase: Initial: $3,000, Subsequent: $50; Automatic investment plan: Subsequent: $50
Qualified for sale in: FL
Check redemptions: $250 minimum
Dividends paid: Income - declared daily, paid monthly
Management fee: 0.50% first $50M to 0.30% over $100M (for assets of Florida Tax-Free Income and Money Market funds combined)
Expense ratio: 0.50% (year ending 3/31/97) (0.57% without waiver)

USAA GNMA TRUST ◆
(See first USAA listing for data common to all funds)

Portfolio manager: Kenneth E. Willmann (1995)
Investment objective and policies: High current income consistent with principal preservation. Invests in securities backed by the full faith and credit of the U.S. Government with at least 65% of assets in GNMA pass-through certificates; remaining 35% or less in obligations back by the full faith and credit of the U.S. Government.
Year organized: 1991
Ticker symbol: USGNX
Group fund code: 58
Minimum purchase: Initial: $3,000, Subsequent: $50; IRA: Initial $250; Automatic investment plan: Initial: None
Dividends paid: Income - declared daily, paid monthly; Capital gains - July, November
Portfolio turnover (3 yrs): 78%, 128%, 94%
Management fee: 0.125%
Expense ratio: 0.30% (year ending 5/31/97)

USAA GOLD FUND ◆
(See first USAA listing for data common to all funds)

Portfolio manager: Mark W. Johnson (1994)
Investment objective and policies: Long-term capital appreciation while protecting purchasing power of capital against inflation; current income secondary. Invests at least 80% of assets in equity securities of companies engaged in gold exploration, mining, or processing; remainder of assets in companies similarly engaged in silver, platinum, diamonds, and other precious metals and minerals. May invest in securities of foreign issuers and have up to 15% of assets in illiquid securities.
Year organized: 1984
Ticker symbol: USAGX
Group fund code: 50
Minimum purchase: Initial: $3,000, Subsequent: $50; IRA: Initial $250; Automatic investment plan: Initial: None
Dividends paid: Income - July; Capital gains - July, November
Portfolio turnover (3 yrs): 26%, 16%, 35%
Management fee: 0.75%
Expense ratio: 1.31% (year ending 5/31/97)

USAA GROWTH FUND ◆
(See first USAA listing for data common to all funds)

Portfolio manager: David G. Parsons (1994)
Investment objective and policies: Long-term capital growth; income and principal conservation secondary. Invests primarily in common stocks and securities convertible into common stocks of established companies perceived to have growth potential that have been undervalued in the market. May invest up to 30% of assets in securities of foreign issuers and 15% in illiquid securities.
Year organized: 1971
Ticker symbol: USAAX
Group fund code: 41
Minimum purchase: Initial: $3,000, Subsequent: $50; IRA: Initial $250; Automatic investment plan: Initial: None
Dividends paid: Income - September; Capital gains - September
Portfolio turnover (3 yrs): 75%, 62%, 70%
Management fee: 0.75%
Expense ratio: 0.97% (year ending 7/31/97)

USAA GROWTH & INCOME FUND ◆
(See first USAA listing for data common to all funds)

Portfolio manager: R. David Ullom (1993)
Investment objective and policies: Capital growth and current income. Invests primarily in dividend-paying common stocks and securities convertible into common stocks. May also invest in non-convertible debt securities and non-convertible preferred stocks. Up to 30% of assets in may be in securities of foreign issuers traded in the U.S. and 15% in illiquid securities.
Year organized: 1993
Ticker symbol: USGRX

Group fund code: 37
Minimum purchase: Initial: $3,000, Subsequent: $50; IRA: Initial $250; Automatic investment plan: Initial: None
Dividends paid: Income - March, June, September, December; Capital gains - September
Portfolio turnover (3 yrs): 15%, 16%, 19%
Management fee: 0.60%
Expense ratio: 0.89% (year ending 7/31/97)

USAA GROWTH AND TAX STRATEGY FUND ◆
(See first USAA listing for data common to all funds)

Portfolio managers: John W. Saunders, Jr. (asset allocation) (1989), Kenneth E. Willmann (1989) (bonds and MMs), Harry W. Miller (1995) (stocks)
Investment objective and policies: Conservative balance between income (at least 50% exempt from federal income tax) and long-term capital growth. Invests in 0% to 10% of assets in short-term tax-exempt securities, 41% to 59% in long-term tax exempt securities and 41% to 49% in basic value, blue chip stocks. Allocations are adjusted to reflect perceived changes in economic and market conditions, and portfolio is re-balanced at least quarterly. Up to 15% of assets may be in illiquid securities.
Year organized: 1989 (Name changed from Balanced Portfolio Fund in 1995)
Ticker symbol: USBLX
Group fund code: 53
Sales restrictions: Fund is not available for IRAs because the majority of income is tax exempt.
Minimum purchase: Initial: $3,000, Subsequent: $50; Automatic investment plan: Initial: None
Dividends paid: Income - March, June, September, December; Capital gains - July, November
Portfolio turnover (3 yrs): 194%, 203%, 266%
Management fee: 0.50%
Expense ratio: 0.74% (year ending 5/31/97)

USAA GROWTH STRATEGY FUND ◆
(See first USAA listing for data common to all funds)

Lead portfolio manager: David G. Parsons (asset allocation) (1995) (Individual market segments managed by specialists)
Investment objective and policies: High total return with reduced risk over time: emphasis on long-term capital appreciation, with income secondary. Invests 25% to 35% of assets in large cap stocks, 25% to 35% in small cap stocks, 15% to 25% in international stocks, 15% to 25% in bonds and 0% to 10% in cash equivalents using as asset allocation strategy. Allocations are adjusted at least quarterly to reflect perceived changes in economic and market conditions. May have up to 15% of assets in illiquid securities. Fund may hedge in forward currency markets.
Year organized: 1995
Ticker symbol: USGSX
Group fund code: 49
Minimum purchase: Initial: $3,000, Subsequent: $50; IRA: Initial: $250; Automatic investment: Initial: None
Dividends paid: Income - July; Capital gains - July
Portfolio turnover (2 yrs): 63%, 40%
Management fee: 0.75%
Expense ratio: 1.31% (year ending 5/31/97)

USAA INCOME FUND ◆
(See first USAA listing for data common to all funds)

Portfolio manager: John W. Saunders, Jr. (1985)
Investment objective and policies: Maximum current income without undue risk to principal. Invests in U.S. dollar-denominated securities selected for their high yields relative to the risk involved and interest rates. May invest in bonds, preferred and common stock or up to 100% in short-term securities. May have up to 15% of assets in illiquid securities.
Year organized: 1973
Minimum purchase: Initial: $3,000, Subsequent: $50; IRA: Initial: $250; Automatic investment: Initial: None

Ticker symbol: USAIX
Group fund code: 40
Dividends paid: Income - monthly, Capital gains - September
Portfolio turnover (3 yrs): 58%, 81%, 31%
Management fee: 0.24%
Expense ratio: 0.39% (year ending 7/31/97)

USAA INCOME STOCK FUND ◆
(See first USAA listing for data common to all funds)

Portfolio manager: Harry W. Miller (1989)
Investment objective and policies: Current income with prospect of increasing dividend income and the potential for capital appreciation. Invests primarily in higher than average dividend-paying common stocks of well established, large companies. May also invest in convertible securities and hedge on 5% of assets. May have up to 15% of assets in illiquid securities.
Year organized: 1987
Ticker symbol: USISX
Group fund code: 35
Minimum purchase: Initial: $3,000, Subsequent: $50; IRA: Initial: $250; Automatic investment plan: Initial: None
Dividends paid: Income - March, June, September, December; Capital gains - September
Portfolio turnover (3 yrs): 35%, 32%, 35%
Management fee: 0.50%
Expense ratio: 0.68% (year ending 7/31/97)

USAA INCOME STRATEGY FUND ◆
(See first USAA listing for data common to all funds)

Portfolio managers: John W. Saunders, Jr. (asset allocation and bonds) (1995), R. David Ullum (1995) (stocks), Pamela K. Bledsoe (1996) (MMs)
Investment objective and policies: High current income with reduced risk. Invests 15% to 25% of assets in stocks, 75% to 85% in bonds and 0% to 10% in cash equivalents using as asset allocation strategy. Allocations are adjusted at least quarterly to reflect perceived changes in economic and market conditions. May invest in securities of foreign issuers and have up to 15% of assets in illiquid securities. Fund may hedge in forward currency markets.
Year organized: 1995
Ticker symbol: USICX
Group fund code: 48
Minimum purchase: Initial: $3,000, Subsequent: $50; IRA: Initial: $250; Automatic investment plan: Initial: None
Dividends paid: Income - March, June, September, December; Capital gains - July, November
Portfolio turnover (2 yrs): 65%, 79%
Management fee: 0.50%
Expense ratio: 1.00% (year ending 5/31/97) (1.51% without waiver)

USAA INTERNATIONAL FUND ◆
(See first USAA listing for data common to all funds)

Portfolio managers: David G. Peebles (1988), W. Travis Selmier, II (1996), Albert C. Sebastian (1996)
Investment objective and policies: Capital appreciation; current income secondary. Invests at least 80% of assets in equity and equity convertible securities of companies organized and operating principally outside the U.S. Fund will invest in at least four different countries. Up to 15% of assets may be in illiquid securities. May use forward currency contracts for hedging purposes.
Year organized: 1988
Ticker symbol: USIFX
Group fund code: 52
Minimum purchase: Initial: $3,000, Subsequent: $50; IRA: Initial: $250; Automatic investment plan: Initial: None
Dividends paid: Income - July; Capital gains - July, November
Portfolio turnover (3 yrs): 46%, 70%, 64%
Management fee: 0.75%
Expense ratio: 1.09% (year ending 5/31/97)

USAA MONEY MARKET FUND ◆
(See first USAA listing for data common to all funds)

Portfolio manager: Pamela K. Bledsoe (1996)
Investment objective and policies: High income consistent with preservation of capital and liquidity. Invests in high quality dollar-denominated money market instruments of domestic and foreign issuers.
Year organized: 1981
Ticker symbol: USAXX
Group fund code: 42
Minimum purchase: Initial: $3,000, Subsequent: $50; IRA: Initial: $250; Automatic investment plan: Initial: None
Check redemptions: $250 minimum
Dividends paid: Income - declared daily, paid monthly
Management fee: 0.24%
Expense ratio: 0.45% (year ending 7/31/97) (0.49% without waiver)

USAA NEW YORK BOND FUND ◆
(See first USAA listing for data common to all funds)

Portfolio manager: Kenneth E. Willmann (1990)
Investment objective and policies: High current interest income exempt from federal, NY state and NY city income taxes. Invests primarily in investment grade New York municipal securities, and maintains a dollar-weighted average maturity of more than ten years. Up to 20% of assets may be in securities subject to AMT tax treatment, and up to 15% in illiquid securities.
Year organized: 1990
Ticker symbol: USNYX
Group fund code: 62
Minimum purchase: Initial: $3,000, Subsequent: $50; Automatic investment plan: Subsequent: $50
Qualified for sale in: NY
Dividends paid: Income - declared daily, paid monthly; Capital gains - May
Portfolio turnover (3 yrs): 41%, 75%, 75%
Management fee: 0.50% of first $50M to 0.30% over $100M (combined assets of New York Bond and Money Market funds)
Expense ratio: 0.50% (year ending 3/31/97) (0.66% without waiver)

USAA NEW YORK MONEY MARKET FUND ◆
(See first USAA listing for data common to all funds)

Portfolio manager: John C. Bonnell (1996)
Investment objective and policies: High current interest income exempt from federal, NY state and NY city income taxes. Invests primarily in New York municipal money market securities.
Year organized: 1982
Ticker symbol: UNYXX
Group fund code: 63
Minimum purchase: Initial: $3,000, Subsequent: $50; Automatic investment plan: Subsequent: $50
Qualified for sale in: NY
Check redemptions: $250 minimum
Dividends paid: Income - declared daily, paid monthly
Management fee: 0.50% of first $50M to 0.30% over $100M (combined assets of New York Bond and Money Market funds)
Expense ratio: 0.50% (year ending 3/31/97) (0.69% without waiver)

USAA S&P 500 INDEX FUND ◆
(See first USAA listing for data common to all funds)

Sub-adviser: Bankers Trust Co.
Portfolio manager: Frank Salerno (1996)
Investment objective and policies: Investment results that, before expenses, correspond to the total return of common stocks publicly traded in the U.S. as represented by the Standard & Poor's 500 Composite Stock Price Index. Fund accomplishes this by investing all of its investable assets in the Equity 500 Index Portfolio, which is a separate mutual fund advised by Bankers Trust Company with an identical objective.
Year organized: 1996
Ticker symbol: USSPX

Group fund code: 34
Minimum purchase: Initial: $3,000, Subsequent: $50; IRA: Initial: $2,000; Automatic investment plan: Subsequent: $50
Dividends paid: Income - quarterly; Capital gains - September
Portfolio turnover (2 yrs): 19%, 15%
Maintenance fee: $2.50/quarter (waived for balances over $10,000)
Management fee: 0.10%
Expense ratio: 0.18% (year ending 12/31/97) (0.25% without waiver)

USAA SCIENCE AND TECHNOLOGY FUND ◆
(See first USAA listing for data common to all funds)

Portfolio manager: Curt Rohrman (1997)
Investment objective and policies: Long-term capital appreciation. Invests at least 80% of assets in equity securities of companies perceived to benefit from the development of scientific and technological advances and improvements. May invest without limit in foreign issues. May invest up to 25% of assets in a single industry, and up to 15% in illiquid securities. May use forward currency contracts for hedging purposes.
Year organized: 1997
Ticker symbol: USSCX
Group fund code: 31
Minimum purchase: Initial: $3,000, Subsequent: $50; IRA: Initial: $250; Automatic investment plan: Initial: $100
Dividends paid: Income - September; Capital gains - September
Management fee: 0.75%

USAA SHORT-TERM BOND FUND ◆
(See first USAA listing for data common to all funds)

Portfolio manager: Paul H. Lundmark (1993)
Investment objective and policies: High current income consistent with capital preservation. Invests primarily in U.S. dollar-denominated investment grade debt securities, and maintains a dollar-weighted average maturity of three years or less. May invest in U.S. Government and government agency and instrumentality obligations, mortgage-backed securities, U.S. and foreign corporate debt securities, U.S. & foreign bank obligations, obligations of state and local governments and their agencies and instrumentalities, and asset-backed securities. Up to 15% of assets may be in illiquid securities.
Year organized: 1993
Ticker symbol: USSBX
Group fund code: 36
Minimum purchase: Initial: $3,000, Subsequent: $50; IRA: Initial: $250; Automatic investment plan: Initial: None
Check redemptions: $250 minimum
Dividends paid: Income - declared daily, paid monthly; Capital gains - September
Portfolio turnover (3 yrs): 28%, 67%, 103%
Management fee: 0.24%
Expense ratio: 0.50% (year ending 7/31/97) (0.61% without waiver)

USAA TAX EXEMPT INTERMEDIATE-TERM FUND ◆
(See first USAA listing for data common to all funds)

Portfolio manager: Clifford A. Gladson (1993)
Investment objective and policies: High interest income exempt from federal income tax. Invests in investment grade tax exempt securities having maturities of no more than twelve years. Fund maintains an overall weighted average maturity of three to ten years. Up to 20% of assets may be in securities subject to AMT tax treatment, and up to 15% in illiquid securities.
Year organized: 1982
Ticker symbol: USATX
Group fund code: 44
Minimum purchase: Initial: $3,000, Subsequent: $50; Automatic investment plan: Subsequent: $50
Dividends paid: Income - declared daily, paid monthly; Capital gains - May

---

Portfolio turnover (3 yrs): 23%, 28%, 27%
Management fee: 0.28%
Expense ratio: 0.37% (year ending 3/31/97)

USAA TAX EXEMPT LONG-TERM FUND ◆
(See first USAA listing for data common to all funds)

Portfolio manager: Kenneth E. Willmann (1982)
Investment objective and policies: High interest income exempt from federal tax. Invests in investment grade tax exempt securities, and maintains an average dollar-weighted maturity of ten years or more. Up to 20% of assets may be in securities subject to AMT tax treatment, and up to 15% in illiquid securities.
Year organized: 1982 (Formerly Tax-Exempt High Yield Fund. Name and objective changed 8/7/92)
Ticker symbol: USTEX
Group fund code: 43
Minimum purchase: Initial: $3,000, Subsequent: $50; Automatic investment plan: Subsequent: $50
Dividends paid: Income - declared daily, paid monthly; Capital gains - May
Portfolio turnover (3 yrs): 41%, 53%, 65%
Management fee: 0.28%
Expense ratio: 0.37% (year ending 3/31/97)

USAA TAX EXEMPT MONEY MARKET FUND ◆
(See first USAA listing for data common to all funds)

Portfolio manager: Thomas G. Ramos (1994)
Investment objective and policies: High interest income exempt from federal income tax. Invests in investment grade municipal money market securities.
Year organized: 1984
Ticker symbol: USEXX
Group fund code: 46
Minimum purchase: Initial: $3,000, Subsequent: $50; Automatic investment plan: Subsequent: $50
Check redemptions: $250 minimum
Dividends paid: Income - declared daily, paid monthly
Management fee: 0.28%
Expense ratio: 0.39% (year ending 3/31/97)

USAA TAX EXEMPT SHORT-TERM FUND ◆
(See first USAA listing for data common to all funds)

Portfolio manager: Clifford A. Gladson (1994)
Investment objective and policies: High interest income exempt from federal income tax. Invests in investment grade tax exempt securities having maturities of no more than five years. Fund maintains an overall weighted average maturity of less than three years. Up to 20% of assets may be in securities subject to AMT tax treatment, and up to 15% in illiquid securities.
Year organized: 1982
Ticker symbol: USSTX
Group fund code: 45
Minimum purchase: Initial: $3,000, Subsequent: $50; Automatic investment plan: Subsequent: $50
Check redemptions: $250 minimum
Dividends paid: Income - declared daily, paid monthly; Capital gains - May
Portfolio turnover (3 yrs): 28%, 36%, 33%
Management fee: 0.28%
Expense ratio: 0.41% (year ending 3/31/97)

USAA TEXAS TAX-FREE INCOME FUND ◆
(See first USAA listing for data common to all funds)

Portfolio manager: Robert R. Pariseau (1995)
Investment objective and policies: High current interest income exempt from federal income tax. If Texas ever implements an income tax, they will try to stay exempt from that as well. Invests primarily in investment grade Texas municipal securities, and maintains a dollar-weighted average maturity of more than ten years. Up to 20% of assets may be in securities subject to AMT tax treatment, and up to 15% in illiquid securities.

Year organized: 1994
Group fund code: 70
Minimum purchase: Initial: $3,000, Subsequent: $50; Automatic investment plan: Subsequent: $50
Qualified for sale in: TX
Dividends paid: Income - declared daily, paid monthly; Capital gains - May
Portfolio turnover (3 yrs): 86%, 71%, 50%
Management fee: 0.50% of first $50M to 0.30% over $100M (combined assets of Texas Tax-Free Income and Money Market funds)
Expense ratio: 0.50% (year ending 3/31/97) (1.35% without waiver)

USAA TEXAS TAX-FREE MONEY MARKET FUND ◆
(See first USAA listing for data common to all funds)

Portfolio manager: John C. Bonnell (1996)
Investment objective and policies: High current interest income exempt from federal income tax while preserving capital and maintaining liquidity. If Texas ever implements an income tax, they will try to stay exempt from that as well. Invests primarily in Texas municipal money market securities.
Year organized: 1994
Group fund code: 71
Minimum purchase: Initial: $3,000, Subsequent: $50; Automatic investment plan: Subsequent: $50
Qualified for sale in: TX
Check redemptions: $250 minimum
Dividends paid: Income - declared daily, paid monthly
Management fee: 0.50% of first $50M to 0.30% over $100M (combined assets of Texas Tax-Free Income and Money Market funds)
Expense ratio: 0.50% (year ending 3/31/97) (1.77% without waiver)

USAA TREASURY MONEY MARKET TRUST ◆
(See first USAA listing for data common to all funds)

Portfolio manager: Pamela K. Bledsoe (1996)
Investment objective and policies: Maximum current income while maintaining the highest degree of safety and liquidity. Invests exclusively in money market securities backed by the full faith and credit of the U.S. Government. At least 65% of assets are in Treasury bills, notes and bonds, and repurchase agreements thereon.
Year organized: 1991
Ticker symbol: UATXX
Group fund code: 59
Minimum purchase: Initial: $3,000, Subsequent: $50; IRA: Initial: $250; Automatic investment plan: Initial: None
Check redemptions: $250 minimum
Dividends paid: Income - declared daily, paid monthly
Management fee: 0.125%
Expense ratio: 0.375% (year ending 5/31/97) (0.39% without waiver)

USAA VIRGINIA BOND FUND ◆
(See first USAA listing for data common to all funds)

Portfolio manager: Robert R. Pariseau (1995)
Investment objective and policies: High current interest income exempt from federal and Virginia income taxes. Invests primarily in investment grade Virginia municipal securities, and maintains a dollar-weighted average maturity of more than ten years. Up to 20% of assets may be in securities subject to AMT tax treatment, and up to 15% in illiquid securities.
Year organized: 1990
Ticker symbol: USVAX
Group fund code: 64
Minimum purchase: Initial: $3,000, Subsequent: $50; Automatic investment plan: Subsequent: $50
Qualified for sale in: VA
Dividends paid: Income - declared daily, paid monthly; Capital gains - May
Portfolio turnover (3 yrs): 27%, 27%, 28%

Management fee: 0.50% of first $50M to 0.30% over $100M (combined assets of Virginia Bond and Money Market funds)
Expense ratio: 0.46% (year ending 3/31/97)

USAA VIRGINIA MONEY MARKET FUND ◆
(See first USAA listing for data common to all funds)

Portfolio manager: John C. Bonnell (1996)
Investment objective and policies: High current interest income exempt from federal and Virginia income taxes. Invests primarily in Virginia municipal money market securities.
Year organized: 1990
Ticker symbol: UVAXX
Group fund code: 65
Minimum purchase: Initial: $3,000, Subsequent: $50; Automatic investment plan: Subsequent: $50
Qualified for sale in: VA
Check redemptions: $250 minimum
Dividends paid: Income - declared daily, paid monthly
Management fee: 0.50% of first $50M to 0.30% over $100M (combined assets of Virginia Bond and Money Market funds)
Expense ratio: 0.50% (year ending 3/31/97) (0.53% without waiver)

USAA WORLD GROWTH FUND ◆
(See first USAA listing for data common to all funds)

Portfolio managers: David G. Peebles (1992) (asset allocation), R. David Ullom (1995) (domestic equity), Albert C. Sebastian (1996) (foreign), W. Travis Selmier II (1996) (foreign)
Investment objective and policies: Capital appreciation. Invests in common stocks and other equity securities of both foreign and domestic issuers, including securities convertible into common stocks. Normally invests in at least three countries, one of which may be the U.S. Up to 15% of assets may be in illiquid securities. May use forward foreign currency contracts for hedging purposes.
Year organized: 1992
Ticker symbol: USAWX
Group fund code: 54
Minimum purchase: Initial: $3,000, Subsequent: $50; IRA: Initial: $250; Automatic investment plan: Initial: None
Dividends paid: Income - July; Capital gains - July, November
Portfolio turnover (3 yrs): 50%, 61%, 59%
Management fee: 0.75%
Expense ratio: 1.20% (year ending 5/31/97)

VALLEY FORGE FUND, INC. ◆
1375 Anthony Wayne Drive
Valley Forge, PA 19087
800-548-1942, 610-688-6839

Adviser: Valley Forge Management Corp.
Portfolio manager: Bernard B. Klawans (1971)
Transfer agent: Valley Forge Fund, Inc.
Investment objective and policies: Capital appreciation; current income secondary. Invests in common stocks and convertible securities, primarily those traded on the New York Stock Exchange, but will invest temporarily in short-term debt securities to defend capital in periods of falling stock prices. Fund is non-diversified.
Year organized: 1971
Ticker symbol: VAFGX
Minimum purchase: Initial: $1,000, Subsequent: $100; IRA: Initial: $250
Wire orders accepted: Yes
Deadline for same day wire purchases: 4 P.M.
Qualified for sale in: All states
Wire redemptions: Yes, $20,000 minimum
Letter redemptions: Signature guarantee required
Dividends paid: Income - December; Capital gains - December
Portfolio turnover (3 yrs): 42%, 16%, 54%
Shareholder services: IRA
Management fee: 1.00%
Expense ratio: 1.38% (year ending 12/31/97)
IRA fees: None

VALUE LINE FUNDS
(Data common to all Value Line funds are shown below. See subsequent listings for data specific to individual funds.)

220 East 42nd Street
New York, NY 10017
800-223-0818, 800-243-2729
212-907-1500
prices/yields 800-243-2739
fax 212-818-9672
Internet: http://www.valueline.com

Shareholder service hours: Full service: M-F 8 A.M.-6 P.M. CST; After hours service: prices, yields, balances, last transaction, prospectuses, total returns, exchanges
Adviser: Value Line, Inc.
Transfer agent: State Street Bank & Trust Co.
Wire orders accepted: Yes, $1,000 minimum
Deadline for same day wire purchase: 4 P.M.
Qualified for sale in: All states (except NY Tax Exempt Trust)
Wire redemptions: Yes, $1,000 minimum
Letter redemptions: Signature guarantee required over $5,000
Telephone switching: With other Value Line Funds, $1,000 minimum
Number of switches permitted: 8 per year (excluding outbound money market switches)
Shareholder services: IRA, SEP-IRA, Keogh, 403(b), electronic funds transfer, systematic withdrawal plan min. bal. req. $5,000
IRA/Keogh fees: Annual $10, Closing $5

VALUE LINE AGGRESSIVE INCOME TRUST ◆
(See first Value Line listing for data common to all funds)

Portfolio manager: Investment committee
Investment objective and policies: Maximum current income; capital appreciation secondary. Invests at least 80% of assets in high yielding, lower-rated fixed-income corporate securities, often referred to as 'junk bonds,' that are issued by companies rated B++ or lower for relative financial strength in The Value Line Investment Survey. May write covered call options, sell short, and invest in financial futures contracts.
Year organized: 1986
Ticker symbol: VAGIX
Group fund code: 31
Minimum purchase: Initial: $1,000, Subsequent: $250; Automatic investment plan: Subsequent: $25
Discount broker availability: *Fidelity, Schwab, Siebert, *White
Telephone redemptions: Yes, $1,000 minimum
Check redemptions: $500 minimum
Dividends paid: Income - declared daily, paid monthly; Capital gains - December
Portfolio turnover (3 yrs): 276%, 284%, 221%
Management fee: 0.75% first $100M, 0.50% over $100M
Expense ratio: 1.10% (year ending 1/31/97)

THE VALUE LINE ASSET ALLOCATION FUND
(See first Value Line listing for data common to all funds)

Portfolio manager: Investment committee
Investment objective and policies: High total return: current income and capital appreciation, consistent with reasonable risk. Invests primarily in common stocks, bonds and money market instruments. Fund uses a computer model to allocate assets among equity, debt and money market securities according to perceived changes in economic and market conditions. May use futures contracts and options for hedging purposes, and sell short. There are no limits established regarding the amount of various types of assets required in the portfolio, however, the neutral mix is considered 55% equity, 35% debt and 10% money market.
Year organized: 1993
Ticker symbol: VLAAX
Group fund code: 17
Minimum purchase: Initial: $1,000, Subsequent: $100; Automatic investment plan: Subsequent: $25

Discount broker availability: *Fidelity, Siebert, *White
Dividends paid: Income - December; Capital gains - December
Portfolio turnover (3 yrs): 192%, 244%, 211%
Management fee: 0.65%
12b-1 distribution fee: 0.25%
Expense ratio: 1.23% (year ending 3/31/97)

THE VALUE LINE CASH FUND ◆
(See first Value Line listing for data common to all funds)

Portfolio manager: Investment committee
Investment objective and policies: As high a level of current income as is consistent with preservation of capital and liquidity. Invests in short-term money market instruments maturing in 397 days or less.
Year organized: 1979
Ticker symbol: VLCXX
Group fund code: 02
Minimum purchase: Initial: $1,000, Subsequent: $100; Automatic investment plan: Subsequent: $25
Telephone redemptions: Yes, $1,000 minimum
Check redemptions: $500 minimum
Dividends paid: Income - declared daily, paid monthly
Management fee: 0.40%
Expense ratio: 0.55% (year ending 12/31/97)

THE VALUE LINE CONVERTIBLE FUND ◆
(See first Value Line listing for data common to all funds)

Portfolio manager: Investment committee
Investment objective and policies: High current income with capital appreciation. Invests at least 70% of assets in convertible securities, i.e. bonds, debentures, corporate notes which are convertible into common stock. Balance of assets may be invested in non-convertible debt or equity securities, warrants, U.S. Government securities, repurchase agreements or other money market instruments. May write covered call options on up to 25% of total assets, and make short sales worth up to 10% of assets.
Year organized: 1985
Ticker symbol: VALCX
Group fund code: 04
Minimum purchase: Initial: $1,000, Subsequent: $250; Automatic investment plan: Subsequent: $25
Discount broker availability: *Fidelity, Schwab, Siebert, *White
Telephone redemptions: Yes, $1,000 minimum
Check redemptions: $500 minimum
Dividends paid: Income - March, June, September, December; Capital gains - December
Portfolio turnover (3 yrs): 164%, 129%, 87%
Management fee: 0.75%
Expense ratio: 1.01% (year ending 4/30/97)

THE VALUE LINE FUND ◆
(See first Value Line listing for data common to all funds)

Portfolio manager: Investment committee
Investment objective and policies: Long-term capital growth; current income secondary. Invests primarily in common stocks or securities convertible into common stock selected, where feasible, on the basis of the Value Line rankings of normal value. May use stock index futures and options thereon, covered call options, and hedge up to 25% of total assets.
Year organized: 1949
Ticker symbol: VLIFX
Group fund code: 05
Minimum purchase: Initial: $1,000, Subsequent: $100; Automatic investment plan: Subsequent: $25
Discount broker availability: *Fidelity, Schwab, Siebert, *White
Dividends paid: Income - March, June, September, December; Capital gains - December
Portfolio turnover (3 yrs): 54%, 78%, 150%
Management fee: 0.70% first $100M, 0.65% over $100M
Expense ratio: 0.80% (year ending 12/31/96)

THE VALUE LINE INCOME FUND ◆
(See first Value Line listing for data common to all funds)

Portfolio manager: Investment committee
Investment objective and policies: High income consistent with reasonable risk; capital growth secondary. Invests substantially all its assets in common stocks or securities convertible into common stock selected, where feasible, on the basis of the Value Line rankings of normal value. Fund may use restricted securities, foreign currency-denominated debt securities of domestic issuers, stock index futures contracts and options thereon, covered call options, and hedge up to 25% of total assets.
Year organized: 1952
Ticker symbol: VALIX
Group fund code: 01
Minimum purchase: Initial: $1,000, Subsequent: $100; Automatic investment plan: Subsequent: $25
Discount broker availability: *Fidelity, Schwab, Siebert, *White
Dividends paid: Income - March, June, September, December; Capital gains - December
Portfolio turnover (3 yrs): 83%, 76%, 56%
Management fee: 0.70% first $100M, 0.65% over $100M
Expense ratio: 0.93% (year ending 12/31/96)

THE VALUE LINE INTERMEDIATE BOND FUND
(Fund liquidated 9/19/97)

VALUE LINE LEVERAGED GROWTH INVESTORS ◆
(See first Value Line listing for data common to all funds)

Portfolio manager: Investment committee
Investment objective and policies: Capital growth. Invests in common stocks or securities convertible into common stock selected, where feasible, on the basis of the Value Line rankings of normal value. Fund leverages up to one third of assets and may use stock index futures contracts and options thereon, covered call options, and hedge up to 25% of total assets.
Year organized: 1972
Ticker symbol: VALLX
Group fund code: 29
Minimum purchase: Initial: $1,000, Subsequent: $100; Automatic investment plan: Subsequent: $25
Discount broker availability: *Fidelity, Schwab, Siebert, *White
Dividends paid: Income - December; Capital gains - December
Portfolio turnover (3 yrs): 34%, 54%, 49%
Management fee: 0.75%
Expense ratio: 0.87% (year ending 12/31/96)

VALUE LINE NEW YORK TAX EXEMPT TRUST ◆
(See first Value Line listing for data common to all funds)

Portfolio manager: Investment committee
Investment objective and policies: Maximum income, with at least 80% of it exempt from federal, NY State and NY City income taxes, while avoiding undue risk to principal. Invests primarily in New York State municipal and public authority debt obligations with a maturity of more than one year and rated within the four highest grades. Up to 20% of assets may be in taxable securities, non-New York tax-exempt securities, and futures and options.
Year organized: 1987
Ticker symbol: VLNYX
Group fund code: 08
Minimum purchase: Initial: $1,000, Subsequent: $250; Automatic investment plan: Subsequent: $25
Discount broker availability: *Fidelity, Siebert, *White
Qualified for sale in: CT, FL, NJ, NY
Telephone redemptions: Yes, $1,000 minimum
Check redemptions: $500 minimum
Dividends paid: Income - declared daily, paid monthly; Capital gains - December

Portfolio turnover (3 yrs): 86%, 119%, 105%
Management fee: 0.60%
Expense ratio: 0.92% (year ending 2/28/97)

THE VALUE LINE SMALL-CAP GROWTH FUND
(See first Value Line listing for data common to all funds)

Portfolio manager: Investment committee
Investment objective and policies: Long-term capital growth. Invests at least 65% of assets in common stocks or securities convertible into common stock of companies with market capitalizations under $1B selected, where feasible, on the basis of the Value Line rankings of normal value. May invest up to 35% of assets in cash, U.S. Government securities, or investment grade corporate debt obligations. May use stock index futures contracts and options, and hedge up to 25% of total assets.
Year organized: 1993
Ticker symbol: ULSCX
Group fund code: 16
Minimum purchase: Initial: $1,000, Subsequent: $100; Automatic investment plan: Subsequent: $25
Discount broker availability: *Fidelity, Siebert, *White
Dividends paid: Income - December; Capital gains - December
Portfolio turnover (3 yrs): 100%, 57%, 30%
Management fee: 0.75%
12b-1 distribution fee: 0.25%
Expense ratio: 1.87% (year ending 3/31/97)

THE VALUE LINE SPECIAL SITUATIONS FUND ◆
(See first Value Line listing for data common to all funds)

Portfolio manager: Investment committee
Investment objective and policies: Long-term capital growth. Invests in common stocks or securities convertible into common stocks, with at least 80% of the portfolio invested in "special situations;" those in which the adviser feels that unusual and potentially non-recurring factors will have a positive impact on the value of securities. May write covered call options in an effort to enhance performance or to hedge up to 25% of total assets.
Year organized: 1956
Ticker symbol: VALSX
Group fund code: 03
Minimum purchase: Initial: $1,000, Subsequent: $100; Automatic investment plan: Subsequent: $25
Discount broker availability: *Fidelity, Schwab, Siebert, *White
Dividends paid: Income - December; Capital gains - December
Portfolio turnover (3 yrs): 146%, 10%, 37%
Management fee: 0.75%
Expense ratio: 1.08% (year ending 12/31/96)

THE VALUE LINE TAX EXEMPT FUND - HIGH-YIELD PORTFOLIO ◆
(See first Value Line listing for data common to all funds)

Portfolio manager: Investment committee
Investment objective and policies: Maximum income exempt from federal income tax, while avoiding undue risk to principal; capital appreciation secondary. Invests primarily in investment grade municipal bonds, and maintains a weighted average portfolio maturity ranging from 10 to 40 years.
Year organized: 1984
Ticker symbol: VLHYX
Group fund code: 44
Minimum purchase: Initial: $1,000, Subsequent: $250; Automatic investment plan: Subsequent: $25
Discount broker availability: *Fidelity, Schwab, Siebert, *White
Dividends paid: Income - declared daily, paid monthly; Capital gains - December
Portfolio turnover (3 yrs): 73%, 95%, 60%
Management fee: 0.50%
Expense ratio: 0.60% (year ending 2/28/97)

THE VALUE LINE TAX EXEMPT FUND - MONEY MARKET PORTFOLIO ◆
(See first Value Line listing for data common to all funds)

Portfolio manager: Investment committee
Investment objective and policies: Maximum income exempt from federal income tax, while avoiding undue risk to principal. Invests primarily in investment grade municipal money market securities.
Year organized: 1984
Ticker symbol: VLTXX
Group fund code: 13
Minimum purchase: Initial: $1,000, Subsequent: $250; Automatic investment plan: Subsequent: $25
Telephone redemptions: Yes, $1,000 minimum
Check redemptions: $500 minimum
Dividends paid: Income - declared daily, paid monthly
Management fee: 0.50%
Expense ratio: 1.00% (year ending 2/28/97)

THE VALUE LINE U.S. GOVERNMENT SECURITIES FUND ◆
(See first Value Line listing for data common to all funds)

Portfolio manager: Investment committee
Investment objective and policies: Maximum income without undue risk to principal; capital preservation and possible capital appreciation secondary. Invests at least 80% of assets in issues of the U.S. Government and its agencies and instrumentalities. May also invest in private collateralized mortgage obligations (CMOs) and real estate mortgage investment conduits (REMICs) that are fully guaranteed by the government.
Year organized: 1981 (name changed from Value Line Bond Fund 4/86)
Ticker symbol: VALBX
Group fund code: 10
Minimum purchase: Initial: $1,000, Subsequent: $250; Automatic investment plan: Subsequent: $25
Discount broker availability: *Fidelity, Schwab, Siebert, *White
Telephone redemptions: Yes, $1,000 minimum
Check redemptions: $500 minimum
Dividends paid: Income - March, June, September, December; Capital gains - December
Portfolio turnover (3 yrs): 255%, 158%, 193%
Management fee: 0.50%
Expense ratio: 0.65% (year ending 8/31/97)

THE VALUE LINE U.S. MULTINATIONAL COMPANY FUND
(See first Value Line listing for data common to all funds)

Portfolio manager: Investment committee
Investment objective and policies: Maximum total return; capital appreciation and dividend and interest income. Invests at least 65% of assets in common or convertible stocks of U.S. companies that derive at least 25% of their sales from outside the country. Up to 35% of assets may be in cash, U.S. Government securities, or prime money market instruments. May write covered call options on as much as 25% of assets, invest up to 15% of assets in illiquid securities, and make short sales equal to as much as 10% of assets.
Year organized: 1995
Ticker symbol: ULUMX
Group fund code: 18
Minimum purchase: Initial: $1,000, Subsequent: $100; Automatic investment plan: Subsequent: $25
Discount broker availability: *Fidelity, Siebert, *White
Dividends paid: Income - December; Capital gains - December
Portfolio turnover (2 yrs): 56%, 17%
Management fee: 0.75%
12b-1 distribution fee: Maximum of 0.25%
Expense ratio: 0.40% (year ending 3/31/97) (1.97% without waiver)

VAN WAGONER FUNDS
(Data common to all Van Wagoner funds are shown below. See subsequent listings for data specific to individual funds.)

345 California Street, Suit 2450
San Francisco, CA 94104
800-228-2121, 415-835-5000
fax 415-835-5050
Internet: http://www.vanwagoner.com

Adviser: Van Wagoner Capital Management, Inc.
Portfolio manager: Garrett R. Van Wagoner
Transfer agent and administrator: Sunstone Financial Group, Inc.
Minimum purchase: Initial: $1,000, Subsequent: $50; IRA: Initial: $500; Automatic investment plan: Initial: $500
Wire orders accepted: Yes
Qualified for sale in: All states except MN, MO, NJ
Telephone redemptions: Yes, $500 minimum
Wire redemptions: Yes, $10 fee
Letter redemptions: Signature guarantee required over $50,000
Telephone switching: With other Van Wagoner Funds and with Northern U.S. Government Money Market Fund, $500 minimum
Number of switches permitted: 5 per year, 10 day hold, $5 fee
Shareholder services: IRA, SEP-IRA, 403(b), electronic funds transfer, systematic withdrawal plan min. bal. req. $10,000
IRA/Keogh fees: Annual $15, Closing $10

VAN WAGONER EMERGING GROWTH FUND
(See first Van Wagoner listing for data common to all funds)

Investment objective and policies: Long-term capital appreciation. Invests in equity securities of companies perceived to have the potential for above-average long-term growth in market value. May invest in companies of any size. Focuses on companies with innovative new products and services, strong management and a strong financial condition that appear to have the potential to sustain growth over several years. May invest in unseasoned companies with less than three years of operation. May invest without limit in foreign securities represented by sponsored and unsponsored ADRs. Fund may hedge.
Year organized: 1995
Ticker symbol: VWEGX
Discount broker availability: *Fidelity, *Schwab, *White
Dividends paid: Income - annually; Capital gains - annually
Portfolio turnover (2 yrs): 333%, 159%
Management fee: 1.25%
Administration fee: 0.18% first $50M to 0.03% over $250M ($61,667 minimum)
12b-1 distribution fee: Maximum of 0.25%
Expense ratio: 1.88% (year ending 12/31/97)

VAN WAGONER MICRO-CAP FUND
(See first Van Wagoner listing for data common to all funds)

Investment objective and policies: Capital appreciation. Invests primarily in companies with market capitalizations of less than $350M. Focuses generally on companies with strong management perceived to have the ability to grow significantly over the next several years, but who may still be in the developmental stage and have limited product lines. May invest in unseasoned companies with less than three years of operation. May invest without limit in foreign securities represented by sponsored and unsponsored ADRs. Fund may hedge.
Year organized: 1995
Ticker symbol: VWMCX
Discount broker availability: *Fidelity, *Schwab, *White
Dividends paid: Income - annually; Capital gains - annually
Portfolio turnover (2 yrs): 232%, 153%
Management fee: 1.50%

Administration fee: 0.18% first $50M to 0.03% over $250M ($61,667 minimum)
12b-1 distribution fee: Maximum of 0.25%
Expense ratio: 1.95% (year ending 12/31/97) (2.32% without waiver)

VAN WAGONER MID-CAP FUND
(See first Van Wagoner listing for data common to all funds)

Investment objective and policies: Capital appreciation. Invests primarily in equity securities of companies with market capitalizations between $500M and $5B. Will focus on more established companies still undergoing growth due to new, upgraded or improved products, services, or business operations. May invest in unseasoned companies with less than three years of operation. May invest without limit in foreign securities represented by sponsored and unsponsored ADRs. Fund may hedge.
Year organized: 1995
Ticker symbol: VWMDX
Discount broker availability: *Fidelity, *Schwab, *White
Dividends paid: Income - annually; Capital gains - annually
Portfolio turnover (2 yrs): 304%, 173%
Management fee: 1.00%
Administration fee: 0.18% first $50M to 0.03% over $250M ($61,667 minimum)
12b-1 distribution fee: Maximum of 0.25%
Expense ratio: 1.80% (year ending 12/31/97)

VAN WAGONER POST-VENTURE FUND
(See first Van Wagoner listing for data common to all funds)

Investment objective and policies: Capital appreciation. Invests primarily in equity securities of companies that have already moved beyond the stage of using venture capital to underwrite their new existence or the earliest stages of the development of new products, services, or business operations, or for part of a reorganization, restructuring or recapitalization. May invest in unseasoned companies with less than three years of operation. May invest without limit in foreign securities represented by sponsored and unsponsored ADRs. Fund may hedge.
Year organized: 1996
Ticker symbol: VWPVX
Discount broker availability: *Fidelity, *Schwab, *White
Dividends paid: Income - annually; Capital gains - annually
Portfolio turnover (1 yr): 317%
Management fee: 1.50%
Administration fee: 0.18% first $50M to 0.03% over $250M ($61,667 minimum)
12b-1 distribution fee: Maximum of 0.25%
Expense ratio: 1.95% (year ending 12/31/97) (2.69% without waiver)

VAN WAGONER TECHNOLOGY FUND
(See first Van Wagoner listing for data common to all funds)

Investment objective and policies: Long-term capital appreciation. Invests at least 65% of assets in equity securities of companies that are involved in the technology sectors, including but not limited to computers, computer services and software, communications, consumer electronics, cable television, pharmaceuticals, biotechnology, medical devices, semi-conductors, technical services, and robotics. May invest a significant amount of assets in very small companies, although only invests up to 10% of assets in unseasoned companies with less than three years of operation. May invest without limit in foreign securities which are traded in the U.S., either directly or represented by sponsored and unsponsored ADRs. Fund may use options and futures for hedging purposes.
Year organized: 1997
Dividends paid: Income - annually; Capital gains - annually
Management fee: 1.25%
Administration fee: 0.18% first $50M to 0.03% over $250M ($61,667 minimum)
12b-1 distribution fee: Maximum of 0.25%

VANGUARD FUNDS ◆

(Data common to all Vanguard funds are shown below. See subsequent listing for data specific to individual funds.)

P.O. Box 2600
Valley Forge, PA 19482
800-662-2739, 800-662-7447
610-669-1000, TDD 800-662-2738
Internet: http://www.vanguard.com
e-mail: online@vanguard.com

Shareholder service hours: Full service: M-F 8 A.M.-9 P.M., Sat 9 A.M.-4 P.M. EST; After hours service: prices, yields, balances, orders, last transaction, prospectuses, total returns
Adviser: Vanguard Group, Inc. (exceptions noted)
Transfer agent: The Vanguard Group, Inc.
Minimum purchase: Initial: $3,000, Subsequent: $100; IRA/Keogh: Initial: $1,000 (exceptions noted)
Wire orders accepted: Yes, $1,000 minimum
Deadline for same day wire purchase: 4 P.M. (12 NN for money market funds)
Qualified for sale in: All states (exceptions noted)
Telephone redemptions: Yes (not retirement accounts)
Wire redemptions: Yes, $1,000 minimum, $5 fee under $5,000
Letter redemptions: Signature guarantee required over $25,000 (exceptions noted)
Telephone switching: With other open Vanguard funds (exceptions noted)
Number of switches permitted: 2 per year per portfolio, at least 30 days apart (exceptions noted; does not apply to money markets)
Shareholder services: IRA, SEP-IRA, Keogh, 401(k), 403(b), corporate retirement plans, automatic investment plan, directed dividends, electronic funds transfer, systematic withdrawal plan min. bal. req. $10,000
Low balance fee: $10 per year for any individual fund balance below $2,500 ($500 for UGMA accounts); waived for investors whose aggregate Vanguard Fund assets total $50,000 or more, and for IRA and retirement accounts. (exceptions noted)
IRA/Keogh fees: Annual $10 (waived for IRA planholders with $50,000 or more in total Vanguard IRA assets or for any fund holding worth $5,000 or more), Initial $10

VANGUARD ADMIRAL INTERMEDIATE-TERM U.S. TREASURY PORTFOLIO ◆

(See first Vanguard listing for data common to all funds)

Portfolio managers: Ian A. MacKinnon (1992), Robert F. Auwaerter (1992)
Investment objective and policies: Current income consistent with preservation of capital and liquidity. Invests at least 65% of assets in U.S. Treasury bills, notes and bonds and at least 85% in other "full faith and credit" obligations of the U.S. Government. Portfolio maintains a dollar-weighted average maturity of five to ten years. May invest in government guaranteed collateralized mortgage obligations, and invest up to 15% of assets in illiquid securities. May use futures contracts and options and hedge up to 20% of assets. Designed to deliver extra high yields by maintaining a lower than average expense ratio.
Year organized: 1992
Ticker symbol: VAITX
Group fund code: 019
Minimum purchase: Initial: $50,000, Subsequent: $100
Minimum account balance: $50,000
Discount broker availability: Fidelity, Schwab, White
Check redemptions: $250 minimum
Dividends paid: Income - declared daily, paid monthly; Capital gains - annually
Portfolio turnover (3 yrs): 52%, 64%, 134%
Management fee: At cost
Expense ratio: 0.15% (year ending 1/31/97)

VANGUARD ADMIRAL LONG-TERM U.S. TREASURY PORTFOLIO ◆

(See first Vanguard listing for data common to all funds)

Portfolio managers: Ian A. MacKinnon (1992), Robert F. Auwaerter (1992)
Investment objective and policies: Current income consistent with preservation of capital and liquidity. Invests at least 65% of assets in U.S. Treasury bills, notes and bonds and at least 85% in other "full faith and credit" obligations of the U.S. Government. Portfolio maintains a dollar-weighted average maturity ranging from 15 to 30 years. May invest in government guaranteed collateralized mortgage obligations, and invest up to 15% of assets in illiquid securities. May use futures contracts and options and hedge up to 20% of assets. Designed to deliver extra high yields by maintaining a lower than average expense ratio.
Year organized: 1992
Ticker symbol: VALGX
Group fund code: 020
Minimum purchase: Initial: $50,000, Subsequent: $100
Minimum account balance: $50,000
Discount broker availability: Schwab, White
Check redemptions: $250 minimum
Dividends paid: Income - declared daily, paid monthly; Capital gains - annually
Portfolio turnover (3 yrs): 42%, 125%, 44%
Management fee: At cost
Expense ratio: 0.15% (year ending 1/31/97)

VANGUARD ADMIRAL SHORT-TERM U.S. TREASURY PORTFOLIO ◆

(See first Vanguard listing for data common to all funds)

Portfolio managers: Ian A. MacKinnon (1992), Robert F. Auwaerter (1992)
Investment objective and policies: Current income consistent with preservation of capital and liquidity. Invests at least 65% of assets in U.S. Treasury bills, notes and bonds and at least 85% in other "full faith and credit" obligations of the U.S. Government. Portfolio maintains a dollar-weighted average maturity of one to three years. May invest in government guaranteed collateralized mortgage obligations, and invest up to 15% of assets in illiquid securities. May use futures contracts and options and hedge up to 20% of assets. Designed to deliver extra high yields by maintaining a lower than average expense ratio.
Year organized: 1992
Ticker symbol: VASTX
Group fund code: 012
Minimum purchase: Initial: $50,000, Subsequent: $100
Minimum account balance: $50,000
Discount broker availability: Fidelity, Schwab, White
Check redemptions: $250 minimum
Dividends paid: Income - declared daily, paid monthly; Capital gains - annually
Portfolio turnover (3 yrs): 80%, 95%, 129%
Management fee: At cost
Expense ratio: 0.15% (year ending 1/31/97)

VANGUARD ADMIRAL U.S. TREASURY MONEY MARKET PORTFOLIO ◆

(See first Vanguard listing for data common to all funds)

Portfolio manager: David Glocke (1998)
Investment objective and policies: Current income consistent with preservation of capital and liquidity. Invests at least 85% of assets in U.S. Treasury notes and other "full faith and credit" obligations of the U.S. Government. Portfolio maintains a weighted average maturity of 90 days or less. Designed to deliver extra high yields by maintaining a lower than average expense ratio.
Year organized: 1992
Ticker symbol: VUSXX
Group fund code: 011
Minimum purchase: Initial: $50,000, Subsequent: $100
Minimum account balance: $50,000

Check redemptions: $250 minimum
Number of switches permitted: Unlimited
Dividends paid: Income - declared daily, paid monthly
Management fee: At cost
Expense ratio: 0.15% (year ending 1/31/97)

VANGUARD ASSET ALLOCATION FUND ◆

(See first Vanguard listing for data common to all funds)

Adviser: Mellon Capital Management Corp.
Portfolio managers: Thomas Loeb (1988), William L. Fouse (1988)
Investment objective and policies: Maximum total return. Invests in common stocks, bonds, and money market instruments in proportions consistent with their perceived returns and risks. Stock selections are restricted to an index paralleling performance of the S&P 500, and bond selections are restricted to long-term U.S. Treasuries with maturities generally in excess of twenty years. Allocation of asset types will vary with changing economic and market conditions, and are bound by no minimum or maximum holdings requirements. Fund may use stock and bond futures (initial margin limited to 5% of assets) and options and hedge up to 50% of assets.
Year organized: 1988
Ticker symbol: VAAPX
Group fund code: 078
Discount broker availability: Fidelity, Schwab, White
Dividends paid: Income - June, December; Capital gains - December
Portfolio turnover (3 yrs): 10%, 47%, 34%
Management fee: 0.20% first $100M to 0.10% over $1.5B +/- performance fee of 0.05% relative to a combined index including the S&P 500 and the Lehman Long U.S. Treasury Index over 36 months
Expense ratio: 0.49% (year ending 9/30/97)

VANGUARD BALANCED INDEX FUND ◆

(See first Vanguard listing for data common to all funds)

Portfolio manager: Team managed
Investment objective and policies: To replicate, with respect to 60% of its assets, the investment performance of the Wilshire 5000 Index of common stocks and, with respect to 40% of its assets, the investment performance of the Lehman Brothers Aggregate Bond Index of fixed-income securities. Management is quantitatively organized and not active. May invest up to 30% of assets in stock/bond/interest rate futures contracts and options only to invest uncommitted cash balances and to maintain liquidity, not for defensive or hedging purposes.
Year organized: 1992
Ticker symbol: VBINX
Group fund code: 002
Discount broker availability: Fidelity, Schwab, White
Telephone switching: None (mail only)
Dividends paid: Income - March, June, September, December; Capital gains - December
Portfolio turnover (3 yrs): 18%, 37%, 16%
Maintenance fee: $10 per year for accounts with balances under $10,000; waived for investors whose aggregate Vanguard Fund assets total $50,000 or more, and for IRA and retirement accounts.
Management fee: At cost
Expense ratio: 0.20% (year ending 12/31/97)

VANGUARD BOND INDEX FUND - INTERMEDIATE-TERM BOND PORTFOLIO ◆

(See first Vanguard listing for data common to all funds)

Portfolio manager: Kenneth E. Volpert (1994)
Investment objective and policies: To duplicate the total return of the Lehman Brothers Mutual Fund Intermediate (5-10) Government/Corporate Index. The

Index is a market-weighted index of U.S. Treasury and agency securities and investment grade corporate bonds, and maintains a weighted average maturity of five to ten years. Management is quantitatively organized and not active. Fund invests at least 80% of assets in a representative sample of the securities included in the Index. Fund may use bond/interest rate futures and options and hedge up to 20% of assets.
Year organized: 1994
Ticker symbol: VBIIX
Group fund code: 314
Discount broker availability: Fidelity
Check redemptions: $250 minimum
Dividends paid: Income - declared daily, paid monthly; Capital gains - January
Portfolio turnover (3 yrs): 56%, 80%, 71%
Maintenance fee: $10 per year for accounts with balances under $10,000; waived for investors whose aggregate Vanguard Fund assets total $50,000 or more, and for IRA and retirement accounts.
Management fee: At cost
Expense ratio: 0.20% (year ending 12/31/97)

VANGUARD BOND INDEX FUND - LONG-TERM BOND PORTFOLIO ◆
(See first Vanguard listing for data common to all funds)

Portfolio manager: Kenneth E. Volpert (1994)
Investment objective and policies: To duplicate the total return of the Lehman Brothers Mutual Fund Long (10+) Government/Corporate Index. The Index is a market-weighted index of U.S. Treasury and agency securities and investment grade corporate bonds, and maintains a weighted average maturity of more than ten years. Management is quantitatively organized and not active. Fund invests at least 80% of assets in a representative sample of the securities included in the Index. Fund may use bond/interest rate futures and options and hedge up to 20% of assets.
Year organized: 1994
Ticker symbol: VBLTX
Group fund code: 522
Discount broker availability: Fidelity
Check redemptions: $250 minimum
Dividends paid: Income - declared daily, paid monthly; Capital gains - December
Portfolio turnover (3 yrs): 58%, 46%, 45%
Maintenance fee: $10 per year for accounts with balances under $10,000; waived for investors whose aggregate Vanguard Fund assets total $50,000 or more, and for IRA and retirement accounts.
Management fee: At cost
Expense ratio: 0.20% (year ending 12/31/97)

VANGUARD BOND INDEX FUND - SHORT-TERM BOND PORTFOLIO ◆
(See first Vanguard listing for data common to all funds)

Portfolio manager: Kenneth E. Volpert (1994)
Investment objective and policies: To duplicate the total return of the Lehman Brothers Mutual Fund Short (1-5) Government/Corporate Index. The Index is a market-weighted index of U.S. Treasury and agency securities and investment grade corporate bonds, and maintains a weighted average maturity of one to five years. Management is quantitatively organized and not active. Fund invests at least 80% of assets in a representative sample of the securities included in the Index. Fund may use bond/interest rate futures and options and hedge up to 20% of assets.
Year organized: 1994
Ticker symbol: VBISX
Group fund code: 132
Discount broker availability: Fidelity
Check redemptions: $250 minimum
Dividends paid: Income - declared daily, paid monthly; Capital gains - December
Portfolio turnover (3 yrs): 88%, 65%, 65%
Maintenance fee: $10 per year for accounts with balances under $10,000; waived for investors whose aggregate Vanguard Fund assets total $50,000 or more, and for IRA and retirement accounts.
Management fee: At cost
Expense ratio: 0.20% (year ending 12/31/97)

VANGUARD BOND INDEX FUND - TOTAL BOND MARKET PORTFOLIO ◆
(See first Vanguard listing for data common to all funds)

Portfolio manager: Kenneth E. Volpert (1992)
Investment objective and policies: To duplicate the total return of the Lehman Brothers Aggregate Bond Index. Management is quantitatively organized and not active. The index consists of over 6,000 issues that have not less than one year to maturity, over $25 million in outstanding market value, and a rating of BBB or better for corporate debt. Fund invests at least 80% of assets in a representative sample of the securities included in the Index. Unlike the other portfolios of the Bond Index Fund, the Total Bond Market Portfolio may invest in GNMAs and other mortgage-backed securities. Fund may use bond or interest rate futures and options and hedge up to 20% of assets.
Year organized: 1986 (name changed from Vanguard Bond Market Fund on 5/3/93)
Ticker symbol: VBMFX
Group fund code: 084
Discount broker availability: Fidelity, Schwab, White
Check redemptions: $250 minimum
Dividends paid: Income - declared daily, paid monthly; Capital gains - December
Portfolio turnover (3 yrs): 39%, 39%, 36%
Maintenance fee: $10 per year for accounts with balances under $10,000; waived for investors whose aggregate Vanguard Fund assets total $50,000 or more, and for IRA and retirement accounts.
Management fee: At cost
Expense ratio: 0.20% (year ending 12/31/97)

VANGUARD CALIFORNIA INSURED TAX-FREE INTERMEDIATE-TERM PORTFOLIO ◆
(See first Vanguard listing for data common to all funds)

Portfolio manager: Reid O. Smith (1994)
Investment objective and policies: High income exempt from federal and California personal income taxes. Invests at least 65% of assets in long-term California municipal bonds, insured as to interest and principal payments, rated AA or better. May invest the remaining 20% of assets in uninsured California municipals. Portfolio maintains a dollar-weighted average maturity of seven to twelve years. Fund may invest up to 20% of assets in bonds subject to AMT tax treatment, use bond futures and options, and purchase taxable securities in unusual circumstances. May hedge up to 20% of assets.
Year organized: 1994
Ticker symbol: VCAIX
Group fund code: 100
Discount broker availability: Fidelity, Schwab, White
Qualified for sale in: CA
Check redemptions: $250 minimum
Dividends paid: Income - declared daily, paid monthly; Capital gains - December
Portfolio turnover (3 yrs): 10%, 21%, 11%
Management fee: At cost
Expense ratio: 0.18% (year ending 11/30/97)

VANGUARD CALIFORNIA INSURED TAX-FREE LONG-TERM PORTFOLIO ◆
(See first Vanguard listing for data common to all funds)

Portfolio manager: Reid O. Smith (1992)
Investment objective and policies: High income exempt from federal and California personal income taxes. Invests at least 80% of assets in long-term California municipal bonds, insured as to interest and principal payments, rated AA or better. May invest the remaining 20% of assets in uninsured California municipals. Portfolio maintains a dollar-weighted average maturity ranging from 15 to 25 years. Fund may invest up to 20% of assets in bonds subject to AMT tax treatment, use bond futures and options, and purchase taxable securities in unusual circumstances. May hedge up to 20% of assets.
Year organized: 1986 (formerly Vanguard California Insured Tax-Free Fund)

Ticker symbol: VCITX
Group fund code: 075
Discount broker availability: Fidelity, Schwab, White
Qualified for sale in: CA
Check redemptions: $250 minimum
Dividends paid: Income - declared daily, paid monthly; Capital gains - December
Portfolio turnover (3 yrs): 21%, 23%, 23%
Management fee: At cost
Expense ratio: 0.16% (year ending 11/30/97)

VANGUARD CALIFORNIA TAX-FREE MONEY MARKET PORTFOLIO ◆
(See first Vanguard listing for data common to all funds)

Portfolio manager: Pamela E. Wisehaupt-Tynan (1987)
Investment objective and policies: Current income exempt from federal and California personal income taxes. Invests in high quality California municipal money market securities. Up to 20% of assets may be in securities subject to AMT tax treatment.
Year organized: 1987
Ticker symbol: VCTXX
Group fund code: 062
Qualified for sale in: CA
Number of switches permitted: Unlimited
Check redemptions: $250 minimum
Dividends paid: Income - declared daily, paid monthly
Management fee: At cost
Expense ratio: 0.18% (year ending 11/30/97)

VANGUARD CONVERTIBLE SECURITIES FUND ◆
(See first Vanguard listing for data common to all funds)

Adviser: Oaktree Capital Management, LLC
Portfolio manager: Larry W. Keele (1996)
Investment objective and policies: High current income and long-term capital growth. Invests at least 80% of assets in a broadly diversified portfolio of convertible securities - corporate bonds and preferred stocks convertible into common stock - as well as in debt instruments with warrants or common stock attached. The remaining 20% may be in non-convertible corporate or U.S. Government fixed-income securities, common stocks, and selected money market instruments. Up to 15% of assets may be in dollar-denominated foreign securities. Fund may write covered call options on equity securities held.
Year organized: 1986
Ticker symbol: VCVSX
Group fund code: 082
Discount broker availability: Fidelity, Schwab, White
Dividends paid: Income: March, June, September, December; Capital gains - December
Portfolio turnover (3 yrs): 182%, 97%, 46%
Management fee: 0.425% first $100M to 0.325% over $400M +/- up to 50% of basic fee based on performance relative to the 36 month cumulative performance of the First Boston Convertible Index
Expense ratio: 0.67% (year ending 11/30/97)

VANGUARD EQUITY INCOME FUND ◆
(See first Vanguard listing for data common to all funds)

Advisers: Newell Assocs.; Spare, Kaplan, Bischel & Assocs.; John A. Levin & Co., Inc.
Portfolio managers: Roger D. Newell (1988), Anthony E. Spare (1995), Melody P. Sarnell (1995), Jeffrey A. Kigner (1995)
Investment objective and policies: High current income. Invests at least 80% of assets in a diversified portfolio of dividend paying equity securities of established, high-quality U.S. companies. Securities are selected based on the expectation that their income yield will exceed that of the S&P 500 Index by at least 50%, but the overall portfolio will maintain a price volatility less than that of the Index average. Potential for capital appreciation will also be considered in security selection. May invest up to 20% of assets in

cash or short-term fixed-income securities, and up to 15% of assets may be in illiquid securities. Fund may use up to 25% of assets in a single industry. Fund may use equity futures and options, and hedge up to 20% of assets.
Year organized: 1988
Ticker symbol: VEIPX
Group fund code: 065
Discount broker availability: Fidelity, Schwab, White
Dividends paid: Income - March, June, September, December; Capital gains - December
Portfolio turnover (3 yrs): 22%, 21%, 31%
Management fee: 0.20% first $250M to 0.08% over $1B (Newell; 70% of assets); 0.175% first $500M to 0.10% over $1B +/- up to 20% of basic fee based on performance relative to the return of the S&P/BARRA Value Index (Spare, Kaplan, Bischel; 15% of assets); 0.40% first $100M to 0.30% over $300M +/- up to 40% of basic fee based on performance relative to the 36 month cumulative performance of the S&P 500 Index (John A. Levin & Co.; 15% of assets)
Expense ratio: 0.45% (year ending 9/30/97)

VANGUARD EXPLORER FUND◆
(See first Vanguard listing for data common to all funds)

Advisers: Wellington Management Co., Granahan Investment Management, Inc., Chartwell Investment Partners, Vanguard Core Management
Portfolio managers: Kenneth L. Abrams (1994), John J. Granahan (1990), Edward N. Antoian (1997), George U. Sauter (1997)
Investment objective and policies: Long-term capital growth; income incidental. Invests primarily in a broadly diversified portfolio of equity securities, mostly common stocks, of relatively small, emerging or embryonic companies with market capitalizations of less than $1B. Fund may use equity futures and options, and hedge up to 20% of total assets. May invest up to 10% of assets in foreign securities and 15% in illiquid securities.
Year organized: 1967
Ticker symbol: VEXPX
Group fund code: 024
Discount broker availability: Fidelity, Schwab, White
Dividends paid: Income - December; Capital gains - December
Portfolio turnover (3 yrs): 84%, 51%, 66%
Management fee: 0.25% first $500M to 0.10% over $1B +/- adjustment of up to 50% of basic fee based on performance relative to the Small Company Growth Stock Index (WMC; 30% of assets): 0.30% first $500M to 0.10% over $1B +/- adjustment of basic fee based on performance relative to the Small Company Growth Stock Index (Granahan; 48% of assets); 0.40% first $250M to 0.20% over $500M +/- adjustment of up to 20% of basic fee based on performance relative to the Small Company Growth Stock Index (Chartwell; 10% of assets); Vanguard Core Group at cost
Expense ratio: 0.62% (year ending 10/31/97)

VANGUARD FIXED INCOME - GNMA PORTFOLIO ◆
(See first Vanguard listing for data common to all funds)

Adviser: Wellington Management Co., LLP
Portfolio manager: Paul D. Kaplan (1994)
Investment objective and policies: High current income, consistent with safety of principal and liquidity. Invests at least 80% of assets in GNMA mortgage-backed securities of the modified pass-through type. Remainder may be in other U.S. Treasury or U.S. Government agency securities as well as repurchase agreements collateralized by such securities. Fund generally maintains an intermediate average maturity, although no specific restrictions apply. May have up to 15% of assets in restricted securities, use bond futures contracts and options, and hedge up to 20% of assets.
Year organized: 1980
Ticker symbol: VFIIX
Group fund code: 036
Discount broker availability: Fidelity, Schwab, White

Check redemptions: $250 minimum
Dividends paid: Income - declared daily, paid monthly; Capital gains - December
Portfolio turnover (3 yrs): 12%, 7%, 35%
Management fee: 0.020% first $3B to 0.008% over $6B based on an aggregate of total assets for GNMA, High Yield Corporate and Long-Term Corporate portfolios
Expense ratio: 0.27% (year ending 1/31/97)

VANGUARD FIXED INCOME - HIGH YIELD CORPORATE PORTFOLIO ◆
(See first Vanguard listing for data common to all funds)

Adviser: Wellington Management Co., LLP
Portfolio manager: Earl E. McEvoy (1984)
Investment objective and policies: High level of current income. Invests in high yielding medium and lower quality "junk" bonds with at least 80% of assets rated "B" or higher. May invest up to 20% of assets in restricted securities and in dollar-denominated foreign securities. May use bond futures and options, and hedge up to 20% of assets.
Year organized: 1978 (name changed from High Yield Bond Portfolio 10/91)
Ticker symbol: VWEHX
Group fund code: 029
Discount broker availability: Schwab, White
Redemption fee: 1.00% on shares held less than 1 year, payable to the fund
Dividends paid: Income - declared daily, paid monthly; Capital gains - December
Portfolio turnover (3 yrs): 23%, 38%, 33%
Management fee: 0.060% first $1B to 0.025% over $3B based on an aggregate of total assets for GNMA, High Yield Corporate and Long-Term Corporate portfolios)
Expense ratio: 0.29% (year ending 1/31/97)

VANGUARD FIXED INCOME - INTERMEDIATE-TERM CORPORATE PORTFOLIO ◆
(See first Vanguard listing for data common to all funds)

Portfolio manager: Robert F. Auwaerter (1993)
Investment objective and policies: High current income consistent with minimum fluctuation in principal value and current liquidity. Invests primarily in short-term investment grade bonds. Portfolio maintains a dollar-weighted average maturity of five to ten years. May invest up to 15% of assets in restricted securities and in dollar-denominated foreign securities, use bond futures contracts and options and hedge up to 20% of assets.
Year organized: 1993
Ticker symbol: VFICX
Group fund code: 071
Discount broker availability: Fidelity, Schwab, White
Check redemptions: $250 minimum
Dividends paid: Income - declared daily, paid monthly; Capital gains - December
Portfolio turnover (3 yrs): 85%, 78%, 97%
Management fee: At cost
Expense ratio: 0.25% (year ending 1/31/97)

VANGUARD FIXED INCOME - INTERMEDIATE-TERM U.S. TREASURY PORTFOLIO ◆
(See first Vanguard listing for data common to all funds)

Portfolio manager: Robert F. Auwaerter (1992)
Investment objective and policies: High current income consistent with safety of principal and liquidity. Invests at least 85% of assets in U.S. Treasury notes and bonds and other "full faith and credit" obligations of the U.S. Government. Portfolio maintains a dollar-weighted average maturity of five to ten years. Remainder may be in other U.S. Treasury or U.S. Government agency securities as well as repurchase agreements collateralized by such securities. May invest up to 15% of assets in restricted securities, use bond futures contracts and options and hedge up to 20% of assets.

Year organized: 1991
Ticker symbol: VFITX
Group fund code: 035
Discount broker availability: Fidelity, Schwab, White
Check redemptions: $250 minimum
Dividends paid: Income - declared daily, paid monthly; Capital gains - December
Portfolio turnover (3 yrs): 42%, 56%, 128%
Management fee: At cost
Expense ratio: 0.25% (year ending 1/31/97)

VANGUARD FIXED INCOME - LONG-TERM CORPORATE PORTFOLIO ◆
(See first Vanguard listing for data common to all funds)

Adviser: Wellington Management Co., LLP
Portfolio manager: Earl E. McEvoy (1994)
Investment objective and policies: High current income consistent with capital preservation. Invests at least 80% of assets in bonds and other fixed-income securities of the four highest grades. Portfolio maintains a dollar-weighted average maturity of 15 to 25 years. May invest up to 15% of assets in restricted securities and in dollar-denominated foreign securities. May use bond futures and options and hedge up to 20% of assets.
Year organized: 1973 (name changed from Investment Grade Corporate Portfolio on 11/1/93 and from Investment Grade Bond Portfolio, in October 1991)
Ticker symbol: VWESX
Group fund code: 028
Discount broker availability: Fidelity, Schwab, White
Check redemptions: $250 minimum
Dividends paid: Income - declared daily, paid monthly; Capital gains - December
Portfolio turnover (3 yrs): 30%, 49%, 43%
Management fee: 0.040% first $1B to 0.015% over $3B based on an aggregate of total assets for GNMA, High Yield Corporate and Long-Term Corporate portfolios)
Expense ratio: 0.28% (year ending 1/31/97)

VANGUARD FIXED INCOME - LONG-TERM U.S. TREASURY PORTFOLIO ◆
(See first Vanguard listing for data common to all funds)

Portfolio manager: Robert F. Auwaerter (1994)
Investment objective and policies: High current income consistent with safety of principal and liquidity. Invests at least 85% of assets in long-term U.S. Treasury bonds and other "full faith and credit" obligations of the U.S. Government. Portfolio maintains a dollar-weighted average maturity of 15 to 30 years. Fund may use zero coupon bonds. Remainder may be in other U.S. Treasury or U.S. Government agency securities as well as repurchase agreements collateralized by such securities. May invest up to 15% of assets in restricted securities, use bond futures contracts and options and hedge up to 20% of assets.
Year organized: 1986 (name changed from U.S. Treasury Bond in Oct. 1991)
Ticker symbol: VUSTX
Group fund code: 083
Discount broker availability: Fidelity, Schwab, White
Check redemptions: $250 minimum
Dividends paid: Income - declared daily, paid monthly; Capital gains - December
Portfolio turnover (3 yrs): 31%, 105%, 85%
Management fee: At cost
Expense ratio: 0.25% (year ending 1/31/97)

VANGUARD FIXED INCOME - SHORT-TERM CORPORATE PORTFOLIO ◆
(See first Vanguard listing for data common to all funds)

Portfolio manager: Robert F. Auwaerter (1983)
Investment objective and policies: High current income consistent with minimum fluctuation in principal value and current liquidity. Invests primarily in

short-term investment grade bonds. Portfolio maintains a dollar-weighted average maturity of one to three years. Fund may invest up to 15% of assets in restricted securities and in dollar-denominated foreign securities, use bond futures contracts and options and hedge up to 20% of assets.

Year organized: 1982 (name changed from Short-Term Bond Portfolio in Oct. 1991)
Ticker symbol: VFSTX
Group fund code: 039
Discount broker availability: Fidelity, Schwab, White
Check redemptions: $250 minimum
Dividends paid: Income - declared daily, paid monthly; Capital gains - December
Portfolio turnover (3 yrs): 45%, 62%, 69%
Management fee: At cost
Expense ratio: 0.25% (year ending 1/31/97)

VANGUARD FIXED INCOME - SHORT-TERM FEDERAL PORTFOLIO ◆

(See first Vanguard listing for data common to all funds)

Portfolio manager: John W. Hollyer (1996)
Investment objective and policies: High current income consistent with safety of principal and liquidity. Invests primarily in U.S. Treasury bonds and other "full faith and credit" obligations of the United States Government. Portfolio maintains a dollar-weighted average maturity of one to three years. May invest up to 15% of assets in restricted securities, use bond futures contracts and options and hedge up to 20% of assets.
Year organized: 1987 (name changed from Short-Term Government Bond in Oct. 1991)
Ticker symbol: VSGBX
Group fund code: 049
Discount broker availability: Fidelity, Schwab, White
Check redemptions: $250 minimum
Dividends paid: Income - declared daily, paid monthly; Capital gains - December
Portfolio turnover (3 yrs): 57%, 74%, 57%
Management fee: At cost
Expense ratio: 0.25% (year ending 1/31/97)

VANGUARD FIXED INCOME - SHORT-TERM U.S. TREASURY PORTFOLIO ◆

(See first Vanguard listing for data common to all funds)

Portfolio manager: Robert F. Auwaerter (1996)
Investment objective and policies: High current income consistent with safety of principal and liquidity. Invests at least 85% of assets in U.S. Treasury bills, notes and bonds and other "full faith and credit" obligations of the U.S. Government. Portfolio maintains a dollar-weighted average maturity of one to three years. Remainder may be in other U.S. Treasury or U.S. Government agency securities as well as repurchase agreements collateralized by such securities. Fund may invest up to 15% of assets in restricted securities, use bond futures contracts and options and hedge up to 20% of assets.
Year organized: 1991
Ticker symbol: VFISX
Group fund code: 032
Discount broker availability: Fidelity, Schwab, White
Check redemptions: $250 minimum
Dividends paid: Income - declared daily, paid monthly; Capital gains - December
Portfolio turnover (3 yrs): 86%, 93%, 126%
Management fee: At cost
Expense ratio: 0.25% (year ending 1/31/97)

VANGUARD FLORIDA INSURED TAX-FREE FUND ◆

(See first Vanguard listing for data common to all funds)

Portfolio manager: Reid O. Smith (1992)
Investment objective and policies: High income exempt from federal personal income taxes and the

Florida intangible personal property tax. Invests at least 80% of assets in insured long-term Florida municipal securities. Portfolio generally maintains a dollar-weighted average maturity of 15 to 25 years. Fund may invest up to 20% of assets in bonds subject to AMT tax treatment, use bond futures and options, and purchase taxable securities in unusual circumstances. May hedge up to 20% of assets. Fund is non-diversified.

Year organized: 1992
Ticker symbol: VFLTX
Group fund code: 018
Discount broker availability: Fidelity, Schwab, White
Qualified for sale in: FL
Check redemptions: $250 minimum
Dividends paid: Income - declared daily, paid monthly; Capital gains - December
Portfolio turnover (3 yrs): 13%, 19%, 20%
Management fee: At cost
Expense ratio: 0.19% (year ending 11/30/97)

VANGUARD GROWTH AND INCOME PORTFOLIO ◆

(See first Vanguard listing for data common to all funds)

Adviser: Franklin Portfolio Assocs., LLC
Portfolio manager: John J. Nagorniak (1986)
Investment objective and policies: Total return greater than that of the aggregate U.S. stock market, as measured by the S&P 500 Index. Fund selects common stocks using quantitative investment techniques such as measures of earnings changes, relative value based on p/e ratios, dividend discount calculations, and measures of sensitivity to economic changes. Fund then constructs a portfolio that resembles the S&P 500 Index with at least 65% of its assets, but which is weighted toward its most attractive stocks. Fund may use futures contracts and options and hedge up to 20% of assets.
Year organized: 1986 (name changed from Vanguard Quantitative 4/30/97)
Ticker symbol: VQNPX
Group fund code: 093
Discount broker availability: Fidelity, Schwab, White
Telephone switching: None (mail only)
Dividends paid: Income - June, December; Capital gains - December
Portfolio turnover (3 yrs): 66%, 75%, 59%
Management fee: 0.30% first $100M, 0.15% over $100M +/- adjustment based on performance relative to the S&P 500
Expense ratio: 0.36% (year ending 12/31/97)

VANGUARD HORIZON FUND - AGGRESSIVE GROWTH PORTFOLIO ◆

(See first Vanguard listing for data common to all funds)

Portfolio manager: George U. Sauter (1995)
Investment objective and policies: Maximum long-term total return. Invests at least 65% of assets in equity securities of small domestic companies with market capitalizations of less than $1B and medium-sized domestic companies with market capitalizations between $1B and $5B. Fund uses proprietary quantitative valuation methodology to identify stocks with best total return potential. May use futures contracts for hedging purposes. Designed for investors with long-range investment goals.
Year organized: 1995
Ticker symbol: VHAGX
Group fund code: 114
Discount broker availability: Schwab
Redemption fee: 1.00% for shares held less than 5 years, payable to the fund
Dividends paid: Income - December; Capital gains - December
Portfolio turnover (2 yrs): 85%, 106%
Management fee: At cost
Expense ratio: 0.40% (year ending 10/31/97)

VANGUARD HORIZON FUND - CAPITAL OPPORTUNITY PORTFOLIO ◆

(See first Vanguard listing for data common to all funds)

Adviser: Primecap Capital Management
Portfolio managers: Howard B. Schow (1998), Theofanis A. Kolokotrones (1998), Mitchell J. Milias (1998)
Investment objective and policies: Maximum long-term total return. Invests primarily in a concentrated portfolio of equity securities of 25 to 50 small- to medium-sized companies whose market capitalizations are less than $5B, with rapid earnings growth prospects. May have up to 15% of assets in securities of foreign issuers and use futures and options and sell short for hedging purposes. Designed for investors with long-range investment goals.
Year organized: 1995
Ticker symbol: VHCOX
Group fund code: 111
Discount broker availability: Schwab
Redemption fee: 1.00% for shares held less than 5 years, payable to the fund
Dividends paid: Income - December; Capital gains - December
Portfolio turnover (2 yrs): 195%, 128%
Management fee: 0.50% first $50M to 0.15% over $10B
Expense ratio: 0.49% (year ending 10/31/97)

VANGUARD HORIZON FUND - GLOBAL ASSET ALLOCATION PORTFOLIO ◆

(See first Vanguard listing for data common to all funds)

Adviser: Strategic Investment Management
Portfolio manager: Michael J. Duffy (1995)
Investment objective and policies: Maximum long-term total return. Invests in stocks, bonds and cash equivalents primarily in nine major markets - U.S., Japan, U.K., Germany, France, Spain, Canada, Australia and Hong Kong, with a general 60%, 30%, 10% distribution respectively. The country allocation is adjusted to reflect changes in relative rate of return, and although generally 65% of assets are distributed across at least three countries, up to 50% of assets may be concentrated in a single asset class from a single country. Bond maturities range from one to thirty years. May invest up to 50% of net assets in futures contracts instead of directly holding securities. May use futures and options and forward currency contracts for hedging purposes. Designed for investors with long-range investment goals.
Year organized: 1995
Ticker symbol: VHAAX
Group fund code: 115
Redemption fee: 1.00% for shares held less than 5 years, payable to the fund
Dividends paid: Income - December; Capital gains - December
Portfolio turnover (2 yrs): 162%, 191%
Management fee: 0.40% first $250M to 0.20% over $1B +/- adjustment of up to 75% of basic fee based on performance relative to the Global Balanced Index)
Expense ratio: 0.54% (year ending 10/31/97)

VANGUARD HORIZON FUND - GLOBAL EQUITY PORTFOLIO ◆

(See first Vanguard listing for data common to all funds)

Adviser: Marathon Asset Management Ltd.
Portfolio manager: Jeremy J. Hosking (1995)
Investment objective and policies: Maximum long-term total return. Invests primarily in equity securities of U.S. and foreign issuers traded in the major stock markets, as well as in emerging markets. Adviser selects securities based on industry and company analysis rather than "top down" country allocation decisions, searching for companies perceived to offer attractive total return prospects. Emerging markets generally comprise less than 20% of assets. May use futures contracts and forward foreign currency contracts for hedging purposes. Designed for investors with long-range investment goals.
Year organized: 1995
Ticker symbol: VHGEX

Group fund code: 129
Redemption fee: 1.00% for shares held less than 5 years, payable to the fund
Dividends paid: Income - December; Capital gains - December
Portfolio turnover (2 yrs): 24%, 29%
Management fee: 0.45% first $100M to 0.25% over $250M +/- adjustment of up to 50% of basic fee based on performance relative to the Morgan Stanley Capital International All Country World Index)
Expense ratio: 0.71% (year ending 10/31/97)

VANGUARD INDEX TRUST - EXTENDED MARKET PORTFOLIO ◆
(See first Vanguard listing for data common to all funds)

Portfolio manager: George U. Sauter (1987)
Investment objective and policies: Investment results that correspond as closely as possible to the price and yield performance of the Wilshire 4500 Index, an index of over 5,000 small- and medium-sized companies traded on the NYSE, AMEX, or NASDAQ exchanges that are not included in the S&P 500. Fund may use futures and options to maintain a fully invested strategy, and hedge up to 20% of assets.
Year organized: 1987
Ticker symbol: VEXMX
Group fund code: 098
Sales charge: 0.25% payable to fund
Discount broker availability: Schwab, White
Telephone switching: (Only for retirement accounts; others by mail)
Dividends paid: Income - December; Capital gains - December
Portfolio turnover (3 yrs): 15%, 22%, 15%
Maintenance fee: $10 per year for accounts with balances under $10,000; waived for investors whose aggregate Vanguard Fund assets total $50,000 or more, and for IRA and retirement accounts.
Management fee: At cost
Expense ratio: 0.23% (year ending 12/31/97)

VANGUARD INDEX TRUST - 500 PORTFOLIO ◆
(See first Vanguard listing for data common to all funds)

Portfolio manager: George U. Sauter (1987)
Investment objective and policies: Investment results that correspond as closely as possible to the price and yield performance of the S&P 500 Composite Stock Price Index. Fund owns all of the stocks in the Index. Fund may use futures and options to maintain a fully invested strategy, and hedge up to 20% of assets.
Year organized: 1976 (formerly Vanguard Index Trust)
Ticker symbol: VFINX
Group fund code: 040
Discount broker availability: Fidelity, Schwab, White
Telephone switching: (Only for retirement accounts; others by mail)
Dividends paid: Income - March, June, September, December; Capital gains - December
Portfolio turnover (3 yrs): 5%, 5%, 4%
Maintenance fee: $10 per year for accounts with balances under $10,000; waived for investors whose aggregate Vanguard Fund assets total $50,000 or more, and for IRA and retirement accounts.
Management fee: At cost
Expense ratio: 0.19% (year ending 12/31/97)

VANGUARD INDEX TRUST - GROWTH PORTFOLIO ◆
(See first Vanguard listing for data common to all funds)

Portfolio manager: George U. Sauter (1992)
Investment objective and policies: Investment results that correspond as closely as possible to the price and yield performance of the S&P/BARRA Growth Index, which includes those stocks selected from the S&P 500 Index with higher than average growth potential and lower than average dividend

yield. Fund may use futures and options to maintain a fully invested strategy, and hedge up to 20% of assets.
Year organized: 1992
Ticker symbol: VIGRX
Group fund code: 009
Discount broker availability: Fidelity, Schwab, White
Telephone switching: (Only for retirement accounts; others by mail)
Dividends paid: Income - March, June, September, December; Capital gains - December
Portfolio turnover (3 yrs): 26%, 29%, 24%
Maintenance fee: $10 per year for accounts with balances under $10,000; waived for investors whose aggregate Vanguard Fund assets total $50,000 or more, and for IRA and retirement accounts.
Management fee: At cost
Expense ratio: 0.20% (year ending 12/31/97)

VANGUARD INDEX TRUST - SMALL CAPITALIZATION STOCK PORTFOLIO ◆
(See first Vanguard listing for data common to all funds)

Portfolio manager: George U. Sauter (1989)
Investment objective and policies: Investment results that correspond as closely as possible to the price and yield performance of the Russell 2000 Small Stock Index, an unmanaged index of small, generally unseasoned companies. Fund may use futures and options to maintain a fully invested strategy, and hedge up to 20% of assets.
Year organized: 1960 (formerly Naess & Thomas Special Fund, Inc. Name and objective changed to Vanguard Small Capitalization Stock Fund 9/89. Prior performance record may not be relevant.) (3 for 1 split on 2/23/90. Became part of Index Trust in 1994)
Ticker symbol: NAESX
Group fund code: 048
Sales charge: 0.50% payable to fund
Discount broker availability: Schwab, White
Telephone switching: (Only for retirement accounts; others by mail)
Dividends paid: Income - December; Capital gains - December
Portfolio turnover (3 yrs): 29%, 28%, 28%
Maintenance fee: $10 per year for accounts with balances under $10,000; waived for investors whose aggregate Vanguard Fund assets total $50,000 or more, and for IRA and retirement accounts.
Management fee: At cost
Expense ratio: 0.23% (year ending 12/31/97)

VANGUARD INDEX TRUST - TOTAL STOCK MARKET PORTFOLIO ◆
(See first Vanguard listing for data common to all funds)

Portfolio manager: George U. Sauter (1992)
Investment objective and policies: Investment results that correspond as closely as possible to the price and yield performance of the unmanaged Wilshire 5000 Index, the broadest stock index in the U.S. consisting of all the stocks traded on the New York and American Stock Exchanges and the NAS-DAQ OTC market. This portfolio is essentially a composite of the S&P 500 Portfolio and the Extended Market Portfolio, with a dollar allocation of 75% in S&P 500 stocks and 25% in Extended Market stocks. Fund may use futures and options to maintain a fully invested strategy, and hedge up to 20% of assets.
Year organized: 1992
Ticker symbol: VTSMX
Group fund code: 085
Discount broker availability: Fidelity, Schwab, White
Telephone switching: (Only for retirement accounts; others by mail)
Dividends paid: Income - March, June, September, December; Capital gains - December
Portfolio turnover (3 yrs): 2%, 3%, 3%
Maintenance fee: $10 per year for accounts with balances under $10,000; waived for investors whose aggregate Vanguard Fund assets total $50,000 or more, and for IRA and retirement accounts.
Management fee: At cost
Expense ratio: 0.20% (year ending 12/31/97)

VANGUARD INDEX TRUST - VALUE PORTFOLIO ◆
(See first Vanguard listing for data common to all funds)

Portfolio manager: George U. Sauter (1992)
Investment objective and policies: Investment results that correspond as closely as possible to the price and yield performance of the S&P/BARRA Value Index, which consists of stocks selected from the S&P 500 Index that offer higher than average dividend yields and are generally out of favor with investors. Fund may use futures and options to maintain a fully invested strategy, and hedge up to 20% of assets.
Year organized: 1992
Ticker symbol: VIVAX
Group fund code: 006
Discount broker availability: Fidelity, Schwab, White
Telephone switching: (Only for retirement accounts; others by mail)
Dividends paid: Income - March, June, September, December; Capital gains - December
Portfolio turnover (3 yrs): 25%, 29%, 27%
Maintenance fee: $10 per year for accounts with balances under $10,000; waived for investors whose aggregate Vanguard Fund assets total $50,000 or more, and for IRA and retirement accounts.
Management fee: At cost
Expense ratio: 0.20% (year ending 12/31/97)

VANGUARD INTERNATIONAL EQUITY INDEX FUND - EMERGING MARKETS PORTFOLIO ◆
(See first Vanguard listing for data common to all funds)

Portfolio manager: George U. Sauter (1994)
Investment objective and policies: Investment results that correspond to the price and yield performance of the Morgan Stanley Capital International Select Emerging Markets (Free) Index of companies located in 14 countries in Asia, Africa, Latin America and Europe. Invests in a statistically selected sample of the more than 500 securities which comprise the Index. Fund may use futures, options, warrants and forward currency contracts. Up to 15% of assets may be in illiquid securities.
Year organized: 1994
Ticker symbol: VEIEX
Group fund code: 533
Sales charge: 1.00%, payable to fund
Discount broker availability: Schwab (only through financial advisers)
Redemption fee: 1.00%, payable to the fund
Telephone switching: None (mail only)
Dividends paid: Income - December; Capital gains - December
Portfolio turnover (3 yrs): 19%, 1%, 3%
Maintenance fee: $10 per year for accounts with balances under $10,000; waived for investors whose aggregate Vanguard Fund assets total $50,000 or more, and for IRA and retirement accounts.
Management fee: At cost
Expense ratio: 0.57% (year ending 12/31/97)

VANGUARD INTERNATIONAL EQUITY INDEX FUND - EUROPEAN PORTFOLIO ◆
(See first Vanguard listing for data common to all funds)

Portfolio manager: George U. Sauter (1990)
Investment objective and policies: Investment results that correspond to the price and yield performance of the Morgan Stanley Capital International Europe Index of companies located in 14 European countries. Invests in a statistically selected sample of the more than 600 securities which comprise the Index. Fund may use futures, options, warrants and forward currency contracts. Up to 15% of assets may be in illiquid securities.
Year organized: 1990
Ticker symbol: VEURX
Group fund code: 079
Sales charge: 0.50%, payable to the fund
Discount broker availability: Schwab, White

Telephone switching: None (mail only)
Dividends paid: Income - December; Capital gains - December
Portfolio turnover (3 yrs): 3%, 4%, 2%
Maintenance fee: $10 per year for accounts with balances under $10,000; waived for investors whose aggregate Vanguard Fund assets total $50,000 or more, and for IRA and retirement accounts.
Management fee: At cost
Expense ratio: 0.31% (year ending 12/31/97)

VANGUARD INTERNATIONAL EQUITY INDEX FUND - PACIFIC PORTFOLIO ◆
(See first Vanguard listing for data common to all funds)

Portfolio manager: George U. Sauter (1990)
Investment objective and policies: Investment results that correspond to the price and yield performance of the Morgan Stanley Capital International Pacific (Free) Index of companies located in Australia, Japan, Hong Kong, Malaysia, New Zealand and Singapore. Invests in a statistically selected sample of the more than 500 securities which comprise the Index. Japanese securities will usually represent a very large component of the Pacific portfolio. Fund may use futures, options, warrants and forward currency contracts. Up to 15% of assets may be in illiquid securities.
Year organized: 1990
Ticker symbol: VPACX
Group fund code: 072
Sales charge: 0.50%, payable to the fund
Discount broker availability: Schwab, White
Telephone switching: None (mail only)
Dividends paid: Income - December; Capital gains - December
Portfolio turnover (3 yrs): 8%, 9%, 1%
Maintenance fee: $10 per year for accounts with balances under $10,000; waived for investors whose aggregate Vanguard Fund assets total $50,000 or more, and for IRA and retirement accounts.
Management fee: At cost
Expense ratio: 0.35% (year ending 12/31/97)

VANGUARD INTERNATIONAL GROWTH PORTFOLIO ◆
(See first Vanguard listing for data common to all funds)

Adviser: Schroder Capital Management International
Portfolio manager: Richard R. Foulkes (1981)
Investment objective and policies: Long-term capital appreciation. Maintains a fully invested posture in equity securities of companies based outside the U.S., traded in as many as 30 foreign markets. Adviser focuses on companies with consistent above-average earnings prospects not yet recognized by the market. Fund may use stock index futures and options and forward currency contracts. May hedge up to 20% of assets.
Year organized: 1961 (as Ivest Fund, primarily U.S. securities; fund changed to international securities in 1981; renamed Vanguard World and subdivided into two portfolios at 9/30/85; World was dropped from name 5/3/93; long-term performance history may be misleading.)
Ticker symbol: VWIGX
Group fund code: 081
Discount broker availability: Fidelity, Schwab, White
Dividends paid: Income - December; Capital gains - December
Portfolio turnover (3 yrs): 22%, 22%, 31%
Management fee: 0.35% first $50M to 0.125% over $1B +/- adjustment of up to 0.075% based on funds's performance relative to the MSCI EAFE Index over 36 months.
Expense ratio: 0.57% (year ending 8/31/97)

VANGUARD INTERNATIONAL VALUE PORTFOLIO ◆
(See first Vanguard listing for data common to all funds)

Adviser: UBS International Investment London Ltd.
Portfolio managers: Wilson Phillips (1996), Robin Apps (1996)

Investment objective and policies: Maximum long-term total return; capital growth and income. Invests at least 65% of assets in non-U.S. equity securities of mostly large- and medium-sized companies selected on the basis of adviser's proprietary scoring system for identifying undervalued securities. Fund concentrates in the five largest of more than 25 foreign markets. Fund may use stock futures, options, and forward currency contracts in an effort to increase returns and hedge up to 20% of assets.
Year organized: 1983 (formerly Vanguard Trustee's Commingled-Int'l Portfolio; name changed 5/3/93. Name changed from Vanguard Trustees Equity - International 4/30/97)
Ticker symbol: VTRIX
Group fund code: 046
Discount broker availability: Fidelity, Schwab, White
Dividends paid: Income - December; Capital gains - December
Portfolio turnover (3 yrs): 37%, 82%, 47%
Management fee: 0.475% first $50M to 0.110% over $1B +/- adjustment of up to 50% of basic fee based on performance relative to the MSCI-EAFE Index
Expense ratio: 0.49% (year ending 12/31/97)

VANGUARD LIFESTRATEGY FUNDS - CONSERVATIVE GROWTH PORTFOLIO ◆
(See first Vanguard listing for data common to all funds)

Investment objective and policies: Current income and low to moderate capital growth. Allocates assets in other Vanguard common stock and fixed-income mutual funds, including index funds, within an established range as follows: Stocks - 25% to 50%; Bonds - 30% to 55%; Reserves - 20% to 45%. (Reserves are comprised of Vanguard Fixed Income Securities Fund holdings and cash instruments held in The Vanguard Asset Allocation Fund.) Fund may use short-term, fixed-income instruments on a temporary basis. Fund is especially suited to tax-advantaged retirement accounts.
Year organized: 1994
Ticker symbol: VSCGX
Group fund code: 724
Discount broker availability: Fidelity, Schwab, White
Dividends paid: Income - March, June, September, December; Capital gains - December
Portfolio turnover (3 yrs): 1%, 2%, 1%
Management fee: None. (See fees of underlying portfolio funds)
Expense ratio: None. (See expense ratios of underlying portfolio funds)

VANGUARD LIFESTRATEGY FUNDS - GROWTH PORTFOLIO ◆
(See first Vanguard listing for data common to all funds)

Investment objective and policies: Capital growth. Invests in other Vanguard common stock and fixed-income mutual funds, including index funds, within an established range as follows: Stocks - 65% to 90%; Bonds - 10% to 35%; Reserves - 0% to 25%. (Reserves are comprised of Vanguard Fixed Income Securities Fund holdings and cash instruments held in The Vanguard Asset Allocation Fund.) Fund may use short-term, fixed-income instruments on a temporary basis. Fund is especially suited to tax-advantaged retirement accounts.
Year organized: 1994
Ticker symbol: VASGX
Group fund code: 122
Discount broker availability: Fidelity, Schwab, White
Dividends paid: Income - June, December; Capital gains - December
Portfolio turnover (3 yrs): 1%, 0%, 1%
Management fee: None. (See fees of underlying portfolio funds)
Expense ratio: None. (See expense ratios of underlying portfolio funds)

VANGUARD LIFESTRATEGY FUNDS - INCOME PORTFOLIO ◆
(See first Vanguard listing for data common to all funds)

Investment objective and policies: Current income. Invests in other Vanguard common stock and fixed-income mutual funds, including index funds, within an established range as follows: Stocks - 5% to 30%; Bonds - 50% to 75%; Reserves - 20% to 45%. (Reserves are comprised of Vanguard Fixed Income Securities Fund holdings and cash instruments held in The Vanguard Asset Allocation Fund.) Fund may use short-term, fixed-income instruments on a temporary basis. Fund is especially suited to tax-advantaged retirement accounts.
Year organized: 1994
Ticker symbol: VASIX
Group fund code: 723
Discount broker availability: Fidelity, Schwab, White
Dividends paid: Income - March, June, September, December; Capital gains - December
Portfolio turnover (3 yrs): 6%, 22%, 4%
Management fee: None. (See fees of underlying portfolio funds)
Expense ratio: None. (See expense ratios of underlying portfolio funds)

VANGUARD LIFESTRATEGY FUNDS - MODERATE GROWTH PORTFOLIO ◆
(See first Vanguard listing for data common to all funds)

Investment objective and policies: Capital growth and a reasonable level of current income. Invests in other Vanguard common stock and fixed-income mutual funds, including index funds, within an established range as follows: Stocks - 45% to 70%; Bonds - 30% to 55%; Reserves - 0% to 25%. (Reserves are comprised of Vanguard Fixed Income Securities Fund holdings and cash instruments held in The Vanguard Asset Allocation Fund.) Fund may use short-term, fixed-income instruments on a temporary basis. Fund is especially suited to tax-advantaged retirement accounts.
Year organized: 1994
Ticker symbol: VSMGX
Group fund code: 914
Discount broker availability: Fidelity, Schwab, White
Dividends paid: Income - June, December; Capital gains - December
Portfolio turnover (3 yrs): 2%, 3%, 1%
Management fee: None. (See fees of underlying portfolio funds)
Expense ratio: None. (See expense ratios of underlying portfolio funds)

VANGUARD MONEY MARKET RESERVES - FEDERAL PORTFOLIO ◆
(See first Vanguard listing for data common to all funds)

Portfolio managers: David R. Glocke (1998), Robert F. Auwaerter (1989)
Investment objective and policies: Current income consistent with preservation of capital and liquidity. Invests in short-term money market securities issued by the U.S. Treasury and agencies of the U.S. Government, and repurchase agreements thereon.
Year organized: 1981
Ticker symbol: VMFXX
Group fund code: 033
Check redemptions: $250 minimum
Number of switches permitted: Unlimited
Dividends paid: Income - declared daily, paid monthly
Management fee: At cost
Expense ratio: 0.32% (year ending 11/30/97)

VANGUARD MONEY MARKET RESERVES - PRIME PORTFOLIO ◆
(See first Vanguard listing for data common to all funds)

Portfolio managers: John W. Hollyer (1991), Robert F. Auwaerter (1991)
Investment objective and policies: Current income consistent with preservation of capital and liquidity.

Invests in high quality money market instruments issued by financial institutions, nonfinancial corporations and federal, state and local municipal governments. May utilize Eurodollar and Yankee bank obligations.
Year organized: 1975
Ticker symbol: VMMXX
Group fund code: 030
Check redemptions: $250 minimum
Number of switches permitted: Unlimited
Dividends paid: Income - declared daily, paid monthly
Management fee: At cost
Expense ratio: 0.32% (year ending 11/30/97)

VANGUARD MONEY MARKET RESERVES - U.S. TREASURY PORTFOLIO ◆
(See Vanguard Treasury Money Market Portfolio)

VANGUARD/MORGAN GROWTH FUND ◆
(See first Vanguard listing for data common to all funds)

Advisers: Wellington Management Co., Franklin Portfolio Assocs., Vanguard Core Management Group
Portfolio managers: Robert D. Rands (1994), John J. Nagorniak (1990), George U. Sauter (1993)
Investment objective and policies: Long-term capital growth. Invests primarily in common stocks of established growth companies, emerging growth companies and cyclical growth companies. Wellington and Vanguard Core use traditional (fundamental and relative valuation) methods of stock selection; Franklin uses quantitative techniques for stock selection designed to produce results which outperform Morningstar's Growth Fund Stock Index. Fund may use index futures and options to a limited extent, and hedge up to 20% of assets.
Year organized: 1968 (formerly W.L. Morgan Growth Fund)
Ticker symbol: VMRGX
Group fund code: 026
Discount broker availability: Fidelity, Schwab, White
Dividends paid: Income - December; Capital gains - December
Portfolio turnover (3 yrs): 76%, 73%, 76%
Management fee: WMC: 0.175% first $500M to 0.075% over $1B +/- adjustment of up to 50% of basic fee based on performance relative to the Morningstar Growth Fund Stock Index (39% of assets): Franklin; 0.25% first $100M to 0.10% over $500M (33% of assets): Vanguard; at cost (10% of assets)
Expense ratio: 0.48% (year ending 12/31/97)

VANGUARD MUNICIPAL BOND FUND - HIGH YIELD PORTFOLIO ◆
(See first Vanguard listing for data common to all funds)

Portfolio manager: Reid O. Smith (1996)
Investment objective and policies: High income exempt from federal income tax. Invests in lower average credit quality than Long-Term Portfolio: at least 80% are rated Baa or better, and up to 20% in lower "junk" or unrated bonds. Portfolio maintains a dollar-weighted average maturity ranging from 15 to 25 years. Fund may invest up to 20% in bonds subject to AMT tax treatment, use bond futures and options (initial margin limited to 5% of assets) and hedge up to 20% of assets.
Year organized: 1978
Ticker symbol: VWAHX
Group fund code: 044
Discount broker availability: Fidelity, Schwab, White
Check redemptions: $250 minimum
Dividends paid: Income - declared daily, paid monthly; Capital gains - December
Portfolio turnover (3 yrs): 27%, 19%, 33%
Management fee: At cost
Expense ratio: 0.19% (year ending 8/31/97)

VANGUARD MUNICIPAL BOND FUND - INSURED LONG-TERM PORTFOLIO ◆
(See first Vanguard listing for data common to all funds)

Portfolio manager: Reid O. Smith (1996)
Investment objective and policies: Income exempt from federal income tax. Invests at least 80% of assets in investment grade municipal bonds covered by insurance guaranteeing payment of principal and interest. Portfolio maintains a dollar-weighted average maturity of 15 to 25 years. Up to 20% may be in uninsured municipals with ratings of A or better. Fund may invest up to 20% in bonds subject to AMT tax treatment. May use bond futures and options (initial margin limited to 5% of assets) and hedge up to 20% of assets.
Year organized: 1984
Ticker symbol: VILPX
Group fund code: 058
Discount broker availability: Fidelity, Schwab, White
Check redemptions: $250 minimum
Dividends paid: Income - declared daily, paid monthly; Capital gains - December
Portfolio turnover (3 yrs): 18%, 18%, 7%
Management fee: At cost
Expense ratio: 0.19% (year ending 8/31/97)

VANGUARD MUNICIPAL BOND FUND - INTERMEDIATE-TERM PORTFOLIO ◆
(See first Vanguard listing for data common to all funds)

Portfolio manager: Christopher M. Ryon (1991)
Investment objective and policies: Income exempt from federal income tax, consistent with capital preservation and moderate share price fluctuation. Invests in investment grade municipal securities, at least 75% of which must be rated A or better. Portfolio maintains a dollar-weighted average maturity of seven to twelve years. Fund may invest up to 20% in bonds subject to AMT tax treatment. May use bond futures and options (initial margin limited to 5% of assets) and hedge up to 20% of assets.
Year organized: 1977
Ticker symbol: VWITX
Group fund code: 042
Discount broker availability: Fidelity, Schwab, White
Check redemptions: $250 minimum
Dividends paid: Income - declared daily, paid monthly; Capital gains - December
Portfolio turnover (3 yrs): 15%, 14%, 12%
Management fee: At cost
Expense ratio: 0.19% (year ending 8/31/97)

VANGUARD MUNICIPAL BOND FUND - LIMITED-TERM PORTFOLIO ◆
(See first Vanguard listing for data common to all funds)

Portfolio manager: Pamela E. Wisehaupt-Tynan (1997)
Investment objective and policies: High interest income exempt from federal income tax, consistent with capital conservation and moderate share price fluctuation. Invests primarily in investment grade municipal bonds with maturities of ten years or less. Portfolio maintains a dollar-weighted average maturity of two to five years. At least 75% of must be rated A or better. Fund may invest up to 20% in bonds subject to AMT tax treatment. May use bond futures and options (initial margin limited to 5% of assets) and hedge up to 20% of assets.
Year organized: 1987
Ticker symbol: VMLTX
Group fund code: 031
Discount broker availability: Fidelity, Schwab, White
Check redemptions: $250 minimum
Dividends paid: Income - declared daily, paid monthly; Capital gains - December
Portfolio turnover (3 yrs): 28%, 27%, 35%
Management fee: At cost
Expense ratio: 0.19% (year ending 8/31/97)

VANGUARD MUNICIPAL BOND FUND - LONG-TERM PORTFOLIO ◆
(See first Vanguard listing for data common to all funds)

Portfolio manager: Christopher M. Ryon (1996)
Investment objective and policies: Income exempt from federal income tax. Invests in investment grade municipal securities, at least 75% of which must be rated A or better. Portfolio maintains a dollar-weighted average maturity ranging from 15 to 25 years. Fund may invest up to 20% in bonds subject to AMT tax treatment. May use bond futures and options (initial margin limited to 5% of assets) and hedge up to 20% of assets.
Year organized: 1977
Ticker symbol: VWLTX
Group fund code: 043
Discount broker availability: Fidelity, Schwab, White
Check redemptions: $250 minimum
Dividends paid: Income - declared daily, paid monthly; Capital gains - December
Portfolio turnover (3 yrs): 9%, 26%, 35%
Management fee: At cost
Expense ratio: 0.19% (year ending 8/31/97)

VANGUARD MUNICIPAL BOND FUND - MONEY MARKET PORTFOLIO ◆
(See first Vanguard listing for data common to all funds)

Portfolio manager: Pamela E. Wisehaupt-Tynan (1987)
Investment objective and policies: Income exempt from federal income tax, consistent with a stable share price, preservation of capital and liquidity. Invests in high-quality municipal money market securities, and maintains a dollar-weighted average maturity of ninety days or less.
Year organized: 1980
Ticker symbol: VMSXX
Group fund code: 045
Check redemptions: $250 minimum
Dividends paid: Income - declared daily, paid monthly
Management fee: At cost
Expense ratio: 0.19% (year ending 8/31/97)

VANGUARD MUNICIPAL BOND FUND - SHORT-TERM PORTFOLIO ◆
(See first Vanguard listing for data common to all funds)

Portfolio manager: Pamela E. Wisehaupt-Tynan (1997)
Investment objective and policies: Income exempt from federal income tax, consistent with capital preservation. Invests in investment grade municipal securities with maturities of less than five years, at least 75% rated A or better, and maintains a dollar-weighted average maturity of one to two years. Fund may invest up to 20% in bonds subject to AMT tax treatment. May use bond futures and options (initial margin limited to 5% of assets) and hedge up to 20% of assets.
Year organized: 1977
Ticker symbol: VWSTX
Group fund code: 041
Discount broker availability: Fidelity, Schwab, White
Check redemptions: $250 minimum
Dividends paid: Income - declared daily, paid monthly; Capital gains - December
Portfolio turnover (3 yrs): 34%, 33%, 32%
Management fee: At cost
Expense ratio: 0.19% (year ending 8/31/97)

VANGUARD NEW JERSEY INSURED TAX-FREE LONG-TERM PORTFOLIO ◆
(See first Vanguard listing for data common to all funds)

Portfolio managers: Danine A. Mueller (1996)
Investment objective and policies: High current income exempt from federal and New Jersey state income taxes. Invests at least 80% of assets in long-term municipal bonds issued by New Jersey state and

local governments and covered by insurance guaranteeing payment of principal and interest. Portfolio maintains a dollar-weighted average maturity of 15 to 25 years. Fund may invest up to 20% in bonds subject to AMT tax treatment, use bond futures and options, and purchase taxable securities in unusual circumstances. May hedge up to 20% of assets.
Year organized: 1988
Ticker symbol: VNJTX
Group fund code: 014
Discount broker availability: Fidelity, Schwab, White
Qualified for sale in: NJ
Check redemptions: $250 minimum
Dividends paid: Income - declared daily, paid monthly; Capital gains - December
Portfolio turnover (3 yrs): 13%, 11%, 7%
Management fee: At cost
Expense ratio: 0.18% (year ending 11/30/97)

VANGUARD NEW JERSEY TAX-FREE MONEY MARKET PORTFOLIO ◆
(See first Vanguard listing for data common to all funds)

Portfolio manager: John M. Carbone (1996)
Investment objective and policies: Current income exempt from federal and New Jersey state income taxes. Invests in high quality New Jersey municipal money market securities.
Year organized: 1988
Ticker symbol: VNJXX
Group fund code: 095
Qualified for sale in: NJ
Check redemptions: $250 minimum
Dividends paid: Income - declared daily, paid monthly
Management fee: At cost
Expense ratio: 0.20% (year ending 11/30/97)

VANGUARD NEW YORK TAX-FREE FUND - INSURED LONG-TERM PORTFOLIO ◆
(See first Vanguard listing for data common to all funds)

Portfolio manager: Christopher M. Ryon (1997)
Investment objective and policies: High current income exempt from federal, NY state and NY city personal income taxes. Invests primarily in long-term municipal bonds issued by New York state and local municipalities which are covered by insurance guaranteeing payment of principal and interest. Portfolio maintains a dollar-weighted average maturity of 15 to 25 years. Fund may invest up to 20% in bonds subject to AMT tax treatment, use bond futures and options, and taxable securities in unusual circumstances. May hedge up to 20% of assets.
Year organized: 1986 (name changed from NY Insured Tax Free Fund 9/2/97)
Ticker symbol: VNYTX
Group fund code: 076
Discount broker availability: Fidelity, Schwab, White
Qualified for sale in: NY
Check redemptions: $250 minimum
Dividends paid: Income - declared daily, paid monthly; Capital gains - December
Portfolio turnover (3 yrs): 6%, 5%, 10%
Management fee: At cost
Expense ratio: 0.20% (year ending 11/30/97)

VANGUARD NEW YORK TAX-FREE FUND - MONEY MARKET PORTFOLIO ◆
(See first Vanguard listing for data common to all funds)

Portfolio manager: John M. Carbone (1997)
Investment objective and policies: Current income exempt from federal, NY state and NY city income taxes. Invests in high quality New York municipal money market securities.
Year organized: 1997
Ticker symbol: VYFXX

Group fund code: 163
Qualified for sale in: NY
Check redemptions: $250 minimum
Dividends paid: Income - declared daily, paid monthly
Management fee: At cost

VANGUARD OHIO INSURED TAX-FREE LONG-TERM PORTFOLIO ◆
(See first Vanguard listing for data common to all funds)

Portfolio manager: Danine A. Mueller (1996)
Investment objective and policies: High current income exempt from federal and Ohio state income taxes. Invests at least 80% of assets in long-term municipal bonds issued by Ohio and its local municipalities covered by insurance guaranteeing payment of principal and interest. Portfolio generally maintains a dollar-weighted average maturity of 15 to 25 years. Fund may invest up to 20% of assets in bonds subject to AMT tax treatment, use bond futures and options, and taxable securities in unusual circumstances. May hedge up to 20% of assets.
Year organized: 1990
Ticker symbol: VOHIX
Group fund code: 097
Discount broker availability: Fidelity, Schwab, White
Qualified for sale in: OH
Check redemptions: $250 minimum
Dividends paid: Income - declared daily, paid monthly; Capital gains - December
Portfolio turnover (3 yrs): 14%, 17%, 7%
Management fee: At cost
Expense ratio: 0.17% (year ending 11/30/97)

VANGUARD OHIO TAX-FREE MONEY MARKET PORTFOLIO ◆
(See first Vanguard listing for data common to all funds)

Portfolio manager: John M. Carbone (1996)
Investment objective and policies: Highest level of interest income exempt from federal and Ohio state income taxes. Invests in high-quality Ohio municipal money market securities.
Year organized: 1990
Ticker symbol: VOHXX
Group fund code: 096
Qualified for sale in: OH
Check redemptions: $250 minimum
Dividends paid: Income - declared daily, paid monthly; Capital gains - December
Management fee: At cost
Expense ratio: 0.19% (year ending 11/30/97)

VANGUARD PENNSYLVANIA INSURED TAX-FREE LONG-TERM PORTFOLIO ◆
(See first Vanguard listing for data common to all funds)

Portfolio manager: Danine A. Mueller (1996)
Investment objective and policies: High current income exempt from federal and Pennsylvania state income taxes. Invests at least 80% of assets in long-term municipal bonds issued by Pennsylvania and its local municipalities covered by insurance guaranteeing payment of principal and interest. Portfolio maintains a dollar-weighted average maturity of 15 to 25 years. Fund may invest up to 20% in bonds subject to AMT tax treatment, use bond futures and options, and purchase taxable securities in unusual circumstances. May hedge up to 20% of assets.
Year organized: 1986
Ticker symbol: VPAIX
Group fund code: 077
Discount broker availability: Fidelity, Schwab, White
Qualified for sale in: PA
Check redemptions: $250 minimum
Dividends paid: Income - declared daily, paid monthly; Capital gains - December
Portfolio turnover (3 yrs): 9%, 13%, 12%
Management fee: At cost
Expense ratio: 0.18% (year ending 11/30/97)

VANGUARD PENNSYLVANIA TAX-FREE MONEY MARKET PORTFOLIO ◆
(See first Vanguard listing for data common to all funds)

Portfolio manager: Pamela E. Wisehaupt Tynan (1996)
Investment objective and policies: Current income exempt from federal and Pennsylvania state income taxes. Invests in high quality short-term Pennsylvania municipal securities.
Year organized: 1988
Ticker symbol: VPTXX
Group fund code: 063
Qualified for sale in: PA
Check redemptions: $250 minimum
Dividends paid: Income - declared daily, paid monthly
Management fee: At cost
Expense ratio: 0.20% (year ending 11/30/97)

VANGUARD PREFERRED STOCK FUND ◆
(See first Vanguard listing for data common to all funds)

Adviser: Wellington Management Co., LLP
Portfolio manager: Earl E. McEvoy (1982)
Investment objective and policies: Maximum dividend income qualifying for the 70% corporate dividends received deduction under federal tax law. Invests at least 75% of assets in cumulative preferred stocks of domestic corporations rated Baa or better by Moody's or BBB or better by S&P. Remainder may be in similarly rated fixed-income securities, money markets, or preferred stocks with lower ratings. Suitable for corporations, tax-exempt organizations and employee benefit plans.
Year organized: 1975 (formerly Qualified Dividend Portfolio II)
Ticker symbol: VQIIX
Group fund code: 038
Discount broker availability: Fidelity, Schwab, White
Dividends paid: Income - March, June, September, December; Capital gains - December
Portfolio turnover (3 yrs): 34%, 31%, 20%
Management fee: 0.15% first $200M to 0.075% over $400M
Expense ratio: 0.37% (year ending 10/31/97)

VANGUARD PRIMECAP FUND ◆
(See first Vanguard listing for data common to all funds)

Adviser: Primecap Management Co.
Portfolio managers: Howard B. Schow (1984), Theofanis A. Kolokotrones (1984)
Investment objective and policies: Long-term capital growth; dividend income incidental. Invests at least 80% of assets in common stocks selected on the basis of several fundamental factors, primarily those thought to demonstrate favorable growth prospects which are undervalued. May also invest in convertible securities, stock index futures and options to a limited extent, and in certain short-term fixed-income securities. May use futures and options to hedge up to 20% of assets.
Year organized: 1984 (4 for 1 split on 2/28/90)
Ticker symbol: VPMCX
Group fund code: 059
Special sales restrictions: Fund closed to new shareholders on 3/7/95; Reopened 10/31/96.
Discount broker availability: Fidelity, Schwab, White
Dividends paid: Income - December; Capital gains - December
Portfolio turnover (3 yrs): 13%, 10%, 7%
Management fee: 0.50% first $50M to 0.15% over $10B
Expense ratio: 0.51% (year ending 12/31/97)

VANGUARD SELECTED VALUE FUND ◆
(See first Vanguard listing for data common to all funds)

Adviser: Barrow, Hanley, Mewhinney & Strauss, Inc.
Portfolio manager: James S. McClure (1996), John P. Harloe (1996)

Investment objective and policies: Long-term capital growth and income. Invests primarily in equity securities of a concentrated group of 30 to 40 mid-cap companies with market capitalizations of $1B to $7.5B that are perceived to be undervalued or out of favor. May also include minority positions in large- and small-cap companies. May use futures and options contracts for hedging purposes and to maintain liquidity.
Year organized: 1996
Ticker symbol: VASVX
Group fund code: 934
Discount broker availability: Schwab, White
Dividends paid: Income - December; Capital gains - December
Portfolio turnover (2 yrs): 32%, 25%
Management fee: 0.40% first $100M to 0.15% over $1B, +/- up to 50% based on comparison to the 36 month performance of the Russell Midcap Index. This range will take full effect in April, 1999. Transition rules will be in effect in the interim.
Expense ratio: 0.74% (year ending 10/31/97)

VANGUARD SPECIALIZED PORTFOLIOS ◆

(Data common to all Specialized Portfolios are shown below. See subsequent listings for data specific to individual portfolios.)

Investment objective and policies: Long-term capital appreciation. Invests primarily in equity securities of domestic companies. Comprises a series of portfolios, each concentrated in a particular industry or related group of industries. Each portfolio normally invests at least 80% of assets in equity securities of its industry category (75% for Utilities Income and 98% for REIT Index); may use stock futures and options, and hedge up to 20% of assets. Portfolios generally may invest up to 30% in foreign securities.
Redemption fee: 1.00% for shares held less than one year (except Utilities Income), including exchanges among the Specialized Portfolios, paid to the portfolio
Dividends paid: Income - March; Capital gains - March (except Utilities Income and REIT Index)

VANGUARD SPECIALIZED PORTFOLIOS - ENERGY ◆

(See first Specialized Portfolios listing for data common to all portfolios)

Adviser: Wellington Management Co., LLP
Portfolio manager: Ernst H. Von Metzsch (1984)
Investment objective and policies: Invests in companies engaged in the production, transmission, marketing, and control of energy, both conventional and alternative, as well as component products, research, conservation and pollution control related to energy. Electric utilities are specifically excluded.
Year organized: 1984
Ticker symbol: VGENX
Group fund code: 051
Discount broker availability: Schwab, White
Portfolio turnover (3 yrs): 19%, 15%, 21%
Management fee: 0.15% first $500M to 0.05% over $3B (based on the aggregate assets of all Specialized portfolios under Wellington)
Expense ratio: 0.38% (year ending 1/31/98)

VANGUARD SPECIALIZED PORTFOLIOS - GOLD & PRECIOUS METALS ◆

(See first Specialized Portfolios listing for data common to all portfolios)

Adviser: M&G Investment Management Ltd.
Portfolio manager: Graham E. French (1996)
Investment objective and policies: Invests in companies engaged in the exploration, mining, fabricating, processing or dealing in precious metals and minerals. Fund may use up to 20% of assets to purchase bullion and coin directly from banks and commodity exchange dealers. Fund may invest up to 100% in foreign securities.
Year organized: 1984
Ticker symbol: VGPMX
Group fund code: 053

Discount broker availability: Schwab, White
Portfolio turnover (3 yrs): 26%, 19%, 5%
Management fee: 0.30% first $100M to 0.20% over $400M
Expense ratio: 0.62% (year ending 1/31/98)

VANGUARD SPECIALIZED PORTFOLIOS - HEALTH CARE ◆

(See first Specialized Portfolios listing for data common to all portfolios)

Adviser: Wellington Management Co., LLP
Portfolio manager: Edward P. Owens (1984)
Investment objective and policies: Invests in companies engaged in the development, production or distribution of products and services related to the treatment or prevention of diseases and other medical infirmities. This includes companies involved in products, supplies, equipment, facility management and research.
Year organized: 1984
Ticker symbol: VGHCX
Group fund code: 052
Discount broker availability: Schwab, White
Portfolio turnover (3 yrs): 10%, 7%, 13%
Management fee: 0.15% first $500M to 0.05% over $3B (based on the aggregate assets of all Specialized portfolios under Wellington)
Expense ratio: 0.40% (year ending 1/31/98)

VANGUARD SPECIALIZED PORTFOLIOS - REIT INDEX ◆

(See first Specialized Portfolios listing for data common to all portfolios)

Adviser: Vanguard Core Management Group
Portfolio manager: George U. Sauter (1996)
Investment objective and policies: Also seeks a high level of current income. Invests at least 98% of assets in stocks issued by real estate investment trusts that comprise the Morgan Stanley REIT Index, a benchmark of more than 90 U.S. property trusts that invest in some 7,000 properties. Portfolio is passively invested to mirror the index, and is readjusted quarterly and each time a trust is added or removed from the benchmark.
Year organized: 1996
Ticker symbol: VGSIX
Discount broker availability: Schwab (only through financial advisers)
Telephone switching: Not available
Dividends paid: Income - March, June, September, December; Capital gains - December
Portfolio turnover (2 yrs): 2%, 0%
Management fee: At cost
Expense ratio: 0.24% (year ending 1/31/98)

VANGUARD SPECIALIZED PORTFOLIOS - UTILITIES INCOME ◆

(See first Specialized Portfolios listing for data common to all portfolios)

Adviser: Wellington Management Co., LLP
Portfolio managers: Mark J. Beckwith (1996), Earl E. McEvoy (1997)
Investment objective and policies: Also seeks a high level of current income. Invests at least 75% of assets in equity securities of companies engaged in the generation, transmission, or distribution of electricity, telecommunications, gas, or water. Remainder of assets in utility bonds rated A or better.
Year organized: 1992
Ticker symbol: VGSUX
Group fund code: 057
Discount broker availability: Fidelity, Schwab, White
Redemption fee: None
Dividends paid: Income - March, June, September, December; Capital gains - March
Portfolio turnover (3 yrs): 41%, 38%, 35%
Management fee: 0.15% first $500M to 0.05% over $3B (based on the aggregate assets of all Specialized portfolios under Wellington)
Expense ratio: 0.44% (year ending 1/31/98)

VANGUARD STAR FUND - STAR PORTFOLIO ◆

(See first Vanguard listing for data common to all funds)

Investment objective and policies: Maximum total return: capital growth and income. Invests in other Vanguard common stock and fixed-income mutual funds as follows: common stock 60% to 70% (Windsor, Windsor II, Explorer, Morgan Growth, U.S. Growth, PRIMECAP and Index Trust - 500); fixed-income 20% to 30% (GNMA and Long-Term Corporate); and money market 10% to 20% (Money Market Prime). Since inception, fund has targeted 62.5% equities, 25% bonds, and 12.5% money market funds versus market timing. Fund may use short-term, fixed-income instruments on a temporary basis. Fund is especially suited to tax-advantaged retirement accounts.
Year organized: 1985
Ticker symbol: VGSTX
Group fund code: 056
Minimum purchase: Initial: $1,000, Subsequent: $100
Discount broker availability: Schwab, White
Dividends paid: Income - June, December; Capital gains - December
Portfolio turnover (3 yrs): 15%, 18%, 13%
Management fee: None. (See fees of underlying portfolio funds)
Expense ratio: None. (See expense ratios of underlying portfolio funds)

VANGUARD TAX-MANAGED FUND - BALANCED PORTFOLIO ◆

(See first Vanguard listing for data common to all funds)

Portfolio managers: Ian A. MacKinnon (1994), Christopher M. Ryon (1994)
Investment objective and policies: Capital growth and reasonable current income while minimizing capital gains and taxable dividend distributions. Invests 50% to 55% of assets in investment grade intermediate-term municipal securities, and maintains a weighted average maturity of seven to twelve years. Remaining 45% to 50% of assets are in a statistical sample of the stocks included in the Russell 1000 Index with emphasis on stocks with low dividend yields. May use futures, options, warrants and forward currency contracts. Up to 15% of assets may be in illiquid securities. Fund is designed for long-term investors seeking to minimize the impact of taxes on their returns.
Year organized: 1994
Ticker symbol: VTMFX
Group fund code: 103
Minimum purchase: Initial: $10,000, Subsequent: $100
Minimum account balance: $10,000
Redemption fee: 2.00% for shares held less than 1 year, 1.00% for shares held between 1 and 5 years, payable to fund
Dividends paid: Income - March, June, September, December; Capital gains - December
Portfolio turnover (3 yrs): 7%, 5%, 5%
Management fee: At cost
Expense ratio: 0.17% (year ending 12/31/97)

VANGUARD TAX-MANAGED FUND - CAPITAL APPRECIATION PORTFOLIO ◆

(See first Vanguard listing for data common to all funds)

Portfolio manager: Ian A. MacKinnon (1994)
Investment objective and policies: Capital growth and reasonable current income while minimizing capital gains and taxable dividend distributions. Invests in a statistical sample of the stocks included in the Russell 1000 Index with emphasis on stocks with low dividend yields. May use futures, options, warrants and forward currency contracts. Up to 15% of assets may be in illiquid securities. Fund is designed for long-term investors seeking to minimize the impact of taxes on their returns.

Year organized: 1994
Ticker symbol: VMCAX
Group fund code: 102
Minimum purchase: Initial: $10,000, Subsequent: $100
Minimum account balance: $10,000
Redemption fee: 2.00% for shares held less than 1 year, 1.00% for shares held between 1 and 5 years, payable to fund
Dividends paid: Income - December; Capital gains - December
Portfolio turnover (3 yrs): 4%, 12%, 7%
Management fee: At cost
Expense ratio: 0.17% (year ending 12/31/97)

VANGUARD TAX-MANAGED FUND - GROWTH AND INCOME PORTFOLIO ◆
(See first Vanguard listing for data common to all funds)

Portfolio manager: Ian A. MacKinnon (1994)
Investment objective and policies: Long-term capital growth and moderate taxable current income while minimizing capital gains distributions. Invests in substantially all 500 stocks in the S&P 500 Index. Management techniques used to minimize the realization of capital gains may affect the proportion of assets in each stock compared to the Index and cause the Portfolios return to differ from the Index. May use futures, options, warrants and forward currency contracts. Up to 15% of assets may be in illiquid securities. Fund is designed for long-term investors seeking to minimize the impact of taxes on their returns.
Year organized: 1994
Ticker symbol: VTGIX
Group fund code: 101
Minimum purchase: Initial: $10,000, Subsequent: $100
Minimum account balance: $10,000
Redemption fee: 2.00% for shares held less than 1 year, 1.00% for shares held between 1 and 5 years, payable to fund
Dividends paid: Income - March, June, September, December; Capital gains - December
Portfolio turnover (3 yrs): 2%, 7%, 6%
Management fee: At cost
Expense ratio: 0.17% (year ending 12/31/97)

VANGUARD TOTAL INTERNATIONAL PORTFOLIO ◆
(See first Vanguard listing for data common to all funds)

Investment objective and policies: Attempts to provide investment results that correspond to the aggregate price and yield performance of the Morgan Stanley Capital International - Europe, Australia, and Far East (MSCI-EAFE) plus Select Emerging Markets (Free) Index; (also known as the MSCI-EAFE+EMF Index). The portfolio is a 'fund of funds' that invests in a combination of the Vanguard International Equity Index Fund-European, Pacific and Emerging Markets Portfolios. Recent allocation reflected 45% each in the European and Pacific Markets, and 10% in Emerging Markets; Portfolio will re-balance on a daily basis with net cash inflow to reflect the weightings of the underlying investments.
Year organized: 1996 (name changed from Star Fund - Total Int'l Portfolio in 1997)
Ticker symbol: VGTSX
Group fund code: 113
Sales charge: 0.50%, payable to the fund
Discount broker availability: Schwab
Telephone switching: None (mail only)
Dividends paid: Income - December; Capital gains - December
Portfolio turnover (2 yrs): 0%, 0%
Maintenance fee: $10 per year for accounts with balances under $10,000; waived for investors whose aggregate Vanguard Fund assets total $50,000 or more, and for IRA and retirement accounts.
Management fee: At cost
Expense ratio: None (See expense ratios of underlying portfolio funds)

VANGUARD TREASURY MONEY MARKET PORTFOLIO ◆
(See first Vanguard listing for data common to all funds)

Portfolio managers: David R. Glocke (1998), Robert F. Auwaerter (1990)
Investment objective and policies: Maximum current income consistent with preservation of capital and liquidity. Invests primarily in direct U.S. Treasury money market obligations as well as repurchase agreements backed by Treasury securities, and other obligations backed by the full faith and credit of the U.S. Government.
Year organized: 1983 (formerly Insured Portfolio. Name and objective changed 3/89. Name changed from Money Market Reserves - U.S. Treasury Portfolio 1/96)
Ticker symbol: VMPXX
Group fund code: 050
Check redemptions: $250 minimum
Number of switches permitted: Unlimited
Dividends paid: Income - declared daily, paid monthly
Management fee: At cost
Expense ratio: 0.32% (year ending 11/30/97)

VANGUARD TRUSTEES' EQUITY FUND - U.S. PORTFOLIO ◆
(See first Vanguard listing for data common to all funds)

Adviser: Geewax, Terker & Co.
Portfolio manager: John J. Geewax (1992)
Investment objective and policies: Long-term capital growth with some income. Invests 50% to 70% of assets in domestic common stocks considered undervalued, with the balance invested in growth-oriented common stocks. Fund will invest in companies of all market capitalizations, and will therefore not mirror any index. Adviser uses proprietary valuation and ranking system to select companies with best relative total return potential. Fund may use stock futures and options in an effort to increase returns and hedge up to 20% of assets.
Year organized: 1980 (formerly Vanguard Trustee's Commingled-U.S. Portfolio; name change 5/3/93)
Ticker symbol: VTRSX
Group fund code: 025
Discount broker availability: Fidelity, White
Dividends paid: Income - June, December; Capital gains - December
Portfolio turnover (3 yrs): 139%, 114%, 77%
Management fee: 0.40% +/- adjustment depending on performance relative to the S&P 500 over 36 months
Expense ratio: 0.53% (year ending 12/31/97)

VANGUARD U.S. GROWTH PORTFOLIO ◆
(See first Vanguard listing for data common to all funds)

Adviser: Lincoln Capital Management Co.
Portfolio managers: J. Parker Hall III (1987), David M. Fowler (1987)
Investment objective and policies: Long-term capital appreciation. Invests primarily in equity securities, including common stocks and convertibles, of high-quality, seasoned U.S. companies with above average growth prospects. Fund is normally fully invested. May use stock index futures and options to a limited extent, and hedge up to 20% of assets.
Year organized: 1959 (as Ivest Fund, primarily U.S. securities; fund changed to international securities investing in 1981; renamed Vanguard World and subdivided into two portfolios at 9/30/85; World was dropped from name on 5/3/93)
Ticker symbol: VWUSX
Group fund code: 023
Discount broker availability: Fidelity, Schwab, White
Dividends paid: Income - December; Capital gains - December
Portfolio turnover (3 yrs): 35%, 44%, 32%
Management fee: 0.40% first $25M to 0.10% over $2.5B
Expense ratio: 0.42% (year ending 8/31/97)

VANGUARD WELLESLEY INCOME FUND ◆
(See first Vanguard listing for data common to all funds)

Adviser: Wellington Management Co.
Portfolio managers: Earl E. McEvoy (1982) (fixed-income), John R. Ryan (1986) (equity)
Investment objective and policies: Current income consistent with reasonable risk; moderate growth of capital secondary. Generally invests about 60% of assets in investment grade fixed-income securities, with the remainder primarily in dividend paying common stocks. Fixed-income securities may include U.S. Government and corporate bonds and mortgage-backed securities as well as securities convertible into common stock. May invest in securities of foreign issuers denominated in the U.S. dollar, use stock and bond futures contracts and options, and hedge up to 20% of assets.
Year organized: 1970
Ticker symbol: VWINX
Group fund code: 027
Discount broker availability: Fidelity, Schwab, White
Dividends paid: Income - March, June, September, December; Capital gains - December
Portfolio turnover (3 yrs): 36%, 26%, 32%
Management fee: 0.10% first $1B to 0.03% over $10B +/- adjustment of up to 20% of basic fee based on performance relative to a 'composite' index consisting of components from the Lehman Long-Term Corporate AA or Better Bond Index, the S&P BARRA Value Index and the S&P Utilities Index.
Expense ratio: 0.31% (year ending 12/31/97)

VANGUARD WELLINGTON FUND ◆
(See first Vanguard listing for data common to all funds)

Adviser: Wellington Management Corp.
Portfolio managers: Ernst H. von Metzsch (1995), Paul D. Kaplan (1994)
Investment objective and policies: Conservation of capital, moderate long-term capital growth and moderate income. Invests in a balanced portfolio of 60% to 70% common stocks of undervalued mid- and large-cap companies, with the remaining 30% to 40% of assets in long-term, investment grade government and corporate fixed-income securities. May invest up to 10% of assets in foreign securities, use stock and bond index futures and options, and hedge up to 20% of assets.
Year organized: 1929
Ticker symbol: VWELX
Group fund code: 021
Discount broker availability: Fidelity, Schwab, White
Dividends paid: Income - March, June, September, December; Capital gains - December
Portfolio turnover (3 yrs): 27%, 30%, 24%
Management fee: 0.10% first $1B to 0.03% over $10B, +/- performance adjustment of up to 30% relative to a combined index comprised of the S&P Composite Stock Index and the Lehman Long-Term Corporate AA or Better Bond Index
Expense ratio: 0.29% (year ending 11/30/97)

VANGUARD WINDSOR FUND ◆
(See first Vanguard listing for data common to all funds)

Adviser: Wellington Management Co.
Portfolio manager: Charles T. Freeman (1996)
Investment objective and policies: Long-term growth of capital and income; current dividend income secondary. Invests primarily in common stocks of mid- and large-cap companies based on their fundamental values, principally underlying earnings power and dividend payout ratio. Stocks selected will generally fall within the characterization of undervalued or overlooked. May invest up to 20% of assets in foreign issues and may engage in currency transactions with respect to such investments. Fund may use stock futures contracts and options, and hedge up to 20% of assets.
Year organized: 1958 (absorbed Vanguard High Yield Stock Fund 2/91)

Ticker symbol: VWNDX
Group fund code: 022
Special sales restrictions: Fund is currently closed to new shareholders. Current shareholders are limited to an additional $25,000 per year.
Minimum purchase: Subsequent: $100
Discount broker availability: Fidelity, Schwab, White
Dividends paid: Income - June, December; Capital gains - December
Portfolio turnover (3 yrs): 61%, 34%, 32%
Management fee: 0.125% first $17.5B to 0.100% over $17.5B +/- adjustment of up to 67% of the fee for the first $17.5B and 90% of the fee for assets above $17.5B, based on performance relative to the S&P 500 Index over 36 months
Expense ratio: 0.27% (year ending 10/31/97)

VANGUARD WINDSOR II ◆
(See first Vanguard listing for data common to all funds)

Advisers: Barrow, Hanley, Mewhinney & Strauss, Inc.; Equinox Capital Management, Inc.; Tukman Capital Management, Inc.; and Core Management Group
Portfolio managers: James P. Barrow (1985), Ronald J. Ulrich (1991), Melvin T. Tukman (1991), George U. Sauter (1991)
Investment objective and policies: Long-term growth of capital; current dividend income secondary. Invests primarily in income producing equity securities of mid- to large-cap companies believed undervalued, based on relative price to earnings and price to book ratios rather than earnings expectations. Fund stays substantially fully invested. May use stock futures contracts and options, and hedge up to 20% of assets.
Year organized: 1985
Ticker symbol: VWNFX
Group fund code: 073
Discount broker availability: Fidelity, Schwab, White
Dividends paid: Income - June, December; Capital gains - December
Portfolio turnover (3 yrs): 30%, 32%, 30%
Management fee: BHM&S: O.30% first $200M to 0.125% over $1B +/- adjustment of up to 25% based on performance relative to S&P/BARRA Value Index; Equinox: 0.20% first $400M to 0.10% over $2B +/- adjustment of up to 50% based on performance relative to S&P 500 Composite Stock Index; Tukman: 0.40% first $25M to 0.15% over $1B +/- adjustment of up to 50% based on performance relative to S&P 500 Composite Stock Index; Vanguard Core Management: At cost
Expense ratio: 0.37% (year ending 10/31/97)

THE VINTAGE FUNDS
(Old funds previously known as "The Vintage Funds" are now the "Unified Funds.")

VINTAGE - AGGRESSIVE GROWTH FUND
(Fund liquidated)
(Old funds previously known as "The Vintage Funds" are now the "Unified Funds.")

VINTAGE - ASSET ALLOCATION FUND
(Fund liquidated)
(Old funds previously known as "The Vintage Funds" are now the "Unified Funds.")

VINTAGE - TAX-FREE MONEY MARKET FUND
(Fund liquidated)
(Old funds previously known as "The Vintage Funds" are now the "Unified Funds.")

VINTAGE MUTUAL FUNDS ◆
(Fund family absorbed the IMG Funds and changed their name from Amcore Vintage Funds 2/16/98. Data common to all Vintage funds are shown below. See subsequent listings for data specific to individual funds.)

501 Seventh Street
Rockford, IL 61104
800-438-6375, 815-968-6006
Internet: http://www.amcore.com

Adviser: Investors Management Group
Transfer agent and administrator: BISYS Fund Services Inc.
Minimum purchase: Initial: $1,000, Subsequent: $50; IRA: Subsequent: None; Automatic investment plan: Initial: $250, Subsequent: $25
Wire orders accepted: Yes, $1,000 minimum
Deadline for same day wire purchase: 4 P.M.
Telephone redemptions: Yes
Wire redemptions: Yes, $7.50 fee
Letter redemptions: Signature guarantee not required
Telephone switching: With other Vintage funds
Number of switches permitted: Unlimited
Deadline for same day switch: 4 P.M. (12 NN for U.S. Government Obligations)
Shareholder services: IRA, directed dividends, electronic funds transfer, systematic withdrawal plan
Shareholder services fee: 0.25%
Administration fee: 0.20%
12b-1 distribution fee: Maximum of 0.25% (not currently imposed)
IRA fees: Annual $15

VINTAGE AGGRESSIVE GROWTH FUND ◆
(See first Vintage listing for data common to all funds)

Portfolio managers: Julie A. O'Rourke (1995), Darrell C. Thompson (1995)
Investment objective and policies: Long-term capital growth. Invests primarily in equity securities of companies of any size which management perceives to demonstrate above average price appreciation potential, relative to other equity securities. May invest in sponsored or unsponsored ADRs of foreign issuers, U.S. Government obligations and repurchase agreements and use call options to hedge up to 15% of total assets.
Year organized: 1995
Ticker symbol: AVAGX
Discount broker availability: Fidelity, Siebert, *White
Qualified for sale in: CA, CO, DC, FL, GA, HI, IL, IN, MD, NJ, NY, OH, WI
Dividends paid: Income - March, June, September, December; Capital gains - December
Portfolio turnover (2 yrs): 45%, 4%
Management fee: 0.95%
Expense ratio: 1.63% (year ending 3/31/97) (1.88% without waiver)

VINTAGE BALANCED FUND ◆
(See first Vintage listing for data common to all funds)

Portfolio managers: Julie A. O'Rourke (1995), Elizabeth S. Pierson (1995), Darrell C. Thompson (1997)
Investment objective and policies: Long-term growth of capital and income. Invests in a diversified portfolio of equity and debt issues, with a maximum of 75% of assets in equity securities and a minimum of 25% in high quality fixed-income securities. Allocations are adjusted to reflect perceived changes in market and economic conditions. fixed-income obligations generally have stated or remaining maturities of 15 years or less, and the portfolio maintains a dollar-weighted average maturity of three to seven years. May invest in sponsored or unsponsored ADRs of foreign issuers and in U.S. Government obligations and repurchase agreements without limit. May invest up to 10% of assets in other mutual funds, and use options and futures for hedging purposes.
Year organized: 1995 (absorbed IMG Capital Value Total Return 2/16/98)
Ticker symbol: AMBFX

Discount broker availability: Fidelity, Siebert, *White
Qualified for sale in: CA, CO, DC, FL, GA, HI, IL, IN, MD, NJ, NY, OH, WI
Dividends paid: Income - March, June, September, December; Capital gains - December
Portfolio turnover (2 yrs): 38%, 62%
Management fee: 0.75%
Expense ratio: 1.55% (year ending 3/31/97) (1.80% without waiver)

VINTAGE BOND FUND ◆
(IMG Merged with the Amcore Vintage Funds 2/16/98 and this fund became The Vintage Bond Fund.)

Portfolio managers: Jeffrey D. Lorenzen (1996), Kathryn D. Beyer (1996)
Investment objective and policies: Income; capital appreciation secondary. Invests at least 75% of assets in a portfolio of investment grade fixed-income obligations. Portfolio will be invested in all types of fixed-income securities, but will always hold at least 65% bonds. Average maturity will range from four to ten years. May invest up to 25% of assets in junk bonds. May use options and futures and various derivatives.
Year organized: 1995 (name changed from IMG Bond fund 2/98; fund converted from a private account 7/95)
Qualified for sale in: IA, IL, NE
Dividends paid: Income - quarterly; Capital gains - annually
Portfolio turnover (2 yrs): 42%, 60%
Management fee: 0.30%
Expense ratio: 0.83% (year ending 4/30/97)

VINTAGE EQUITY FUND ◆
(See first Vintage listing for data common to all funds)

Portfolio managers: Darrell C. Thompson (1992), Julie A. O'Rourke (1997)
Investment objective and policies: Long-term capital appreciation. Invests at least 75% of assets in equity securities of large capitalization companies believed to have strong earnings potential, striving for high overall return while minimizing risk through the selection of quality, dividend-paying securities. May invest in sponsored or unsponsored ADRs of foreign issuers. May invest up to 25% in U.S. Government obligations and repurchase agreements thereon. May invest up to 10% of assets in other mutual funds, and use options and futures for hedging purposes.
Year organized: 1992 (absorbed IMG Core Stock fund 2/16/98)
Ticker symbol: AVEQX
Discount broker availability: Fidelity, Siebert, *White
Qualified for sale in: All state except AL, AK, DE, HI, ID, LA, ME, MS, MT, NV, NH, ND, OK, PR, RI, SD, VT
Dividends paid: Income - March, June, September, December; Capital gains - December
Portfolio turnover (3 yrs): 37%, 33%, 21%
Management fee: 0.75%
Expense ratio: 1.33% (year ending 3/31/97) (1.58% without waiver)

VINTAGE GOVERNMENT ASSETS FUND ◆
(See first Vintage listing for data common to all funds)

Portfolio manager: Elizabeth S. Pierson (1996)
Investment objective and policies: Current income consistent with liquidity and stability of principal. Invests exclusively in U.S. Treasury bills, notes and other short-term obligations issued or guaranteed by the U.S. Government or its agencies or instrumentalities, and repurchase agreements thereon.
Year organized: 1992 (name changed from U.S. Govt. Obligations 2/98)
Ticker symbol: AVGXX
Qualified for sale in: CA, CO, DC, FL, GA, HI, IL, IN, MD, NJ, NY, OH, WI
Check redemptions: $250 minimum
Dividends paid: Income - declared daily, paid monthly

Management fee: 0.40%
Expense ratio: 0.76% (year ending 3/31/97) (1.01% without waiver)

VINTAGE INCOME FUND ◆
(See first Vintage listing for data common to all funds)

Portfolio manager: Elizabeth S. Pierson (1996)
Investment objective and policies: Total return: capital appreciation and interest income, consistent with the production of current income and capital preservation. Invests at least 75% of assets in fixed-income corporate and government securities, rated within the three highest rating categories, with a stated or remaining maturity of 15 years or less, or longer if there is an unconditional put to sell or redeem within 15 years of purchase. Portfolio will generally maintain a weighted average maturity of four to ten years. May invest in dollar-denominated fixed-income foreign securities if they are traded in the U.S. market.
Year organized: 1992 (name changed from Fixed Income 2/98)
Ticker symbol: AVINX
Discount broker availability: Fidelity, Siebert, *White
Qualified for sale in: CA, CO, DC, FL, GA, HI, IL, IN, MD, NJ, NY, OH, WI
Dividends paid: Income - declared and paid monthly; Capital gains - December
Portfolio turnover (3 yrs): 60%, 113%, 32%
Management fee: 0.60%
Expense ratio: 1.20% (year ending 3/31/97) (1.45% without waiver)

VINTAGE LIMITED-TERM BOND FUND ◆
(See first Vintage listing for data common to all funds)

Portfolio manager: Elizabeth S. Pierson (1996)
Investment objective and policies: Long-term total return: capital appreciation and interest income. Invests at least 75% of assets in a diversified portfolio of fixed-income corporate and government securities, rated within the four highest rating categories, with a stated or remaining maturity of 15 years or less. Portfolio maintains a dollar-weighted average maturity of one to four years. May invest in dollar-denominated, fixed-income foreign securities. Up to 15% of assets may be in securities rated in the fourth rating category and 10% in Treasury Zero Coupon securities.
Year organized: 1995 (name changed from Fixed Total Return fund 3/98)
Ticker symbol: AFTRX
Discount broker availability: Fidelity, Siebert, *White
Qualified for sale in: CA, CO, DC, FL, GA, HI, IL, IN, MD, NJ, NY, OH, WI
Dividends paid: Income - declared and paid monthly; Capital gains - December
Portfolio turnover (2 yrs): 71%, 69%
Management fee: 0.75%
Expense ratio: 1.40% (year ending 3/31/97) (1.65% without waiver)

VINTAGE MUNICIPAL BOND FUND ◆
(See first Vintage listing for data common to all funds)

Portfolio manager: Elizabeth S. Pierson (1996)
Investment objective and policies: Current income exempt from federal income tax, consistent with capital preservation. Invests at least 80% of assets in municipal securities with a stated or remaining maturity of 25 years or less, or longer if there is an unconditional put to sell or redeem within 25 years of purchase. Portfolio will generally maintain a weighted average maturity of five to nine years. Up to 20% of assets may be in securities subject to AMT tax treatment, and up to 15% in illiquid securities.
Year organized: 1993 (name changed from Intermediate Tax-Free 2/98)
Ticker symbol: AVTFX
Discount broker availability: Fidelity, Siebert, *White

Qualified for sale in: CA, CO, DC, FL, GA, HI, IL, IN, MD, NJ, NY, OH, WI
Dividends paid: Income - declared and paid monthly; Capital gains - December
Portfolio turnover (3 yrs): 21%, 14%, 6%
Management fee: 0.60%
Expense ratio: 1.28% (year ending 3/31/97) (1.53% without waiver)

VISTA FUNDS
(Data common to all Vista funds are shown below. See subsequent listings for data specific to individual funds.)
P.O. Box 419392
Kansas City, MO 64141-6392
800-348-4782
Internet: http://www.vista-funds.com

Adviser: Chase Manhattan Bank, N.A.
Transfer agent: DST Systems, Inc.
Minimum purchase: Initial: $2,500, Subsequent: $100; IRA/Keogh: Initial: $1,000; Automatic investment plan: Initial: $250, Subsequent: $200
Wire orders accepted: Yes
Deadline for same day wire purchase: 4 P.M.
Qualified for sale in: All states
Telephone redemptions: Yes
Wire redemptions: Yes, $10 fee
Letter redemptions: Signature guarantee not required
Check redemptions: $500 minimum (except American Value)
Telephone switching: With other Vista funds, most of which have loads, and the Lipper Funds
Number of switches permitted: over 10 per year, or 3 per quarter, $5 fee per transaction
Shareholder services: IRA, SEP-IRA, Keogh, 401(k), 403(b), corporate retirement plans, electronic funds transfer, systematic withdrawal plan min. bal. req. $5,000
Administration fee: 0.15
Shareholder services fee: Maximum of 0.35%
IRA fees: Annual $15
Keogh fees: Annual $25

VISTA AMERICAN VALUE FUND
(See first Vista listing for data common to all funds)

Sub-adviser: Van Deventer & Hoch
Portfolio manager: Richard Trautwein (1995)
Investment objective and policies: Maximum total return; capital appreciation and income. Invests primarily in equity securities of large, well established domestic companies perceived to be undervalued, although fund may invest in any size company without regard to market capitalization. May invest up to 25% of assets in money markets, repurchase agreements, and cash. May invest up to 20% of assets in foreign issues, including ADRs. Fund may use various derivatives in an effort to enhance performance and for hedging purposes.
Year organized: 1995
Group fund code: 369
Discount broker availability: Fidelity
Dividends paid: Income - annually; Capital gains - annually
Portfolio turnover (1 yr): 11%
Management fee: 0.35%
12b-1 distribution fee: Maximum of 0.25% (not currently imposed)
Expense ratio: 1.37% (year ending 11/31/96)

VISTA CASH MANAGEMENT MONEY MARKET FUND ◆
(See first Vista listing for data common to all funds)

Sub-adviser: Texas Commerce Bank, N.A.
Investment objective and policies: High current income consistent with preservation of capital and liquidity. Invests in high quality short-term U.S. dollar denominated money market instruments.
Year organized: 1989
Group fund code: 223
Dividends paid: Income - declared daily, paid monthly

Management fee: 0.10%
Expense ratio: 0.60% (year ending 8/31/97) (includes waiver)

VISTA 100% U.S. TREASURY SECURITIES MONEY MARKET FUND
(See first Vista listing for data common to all funds)

Sub-adviser: Chase Asset Management, Inc.
Investment objective and policies: High current income consistent with preservation of capital and liquidity. Invests in high quality short-term direct obligations of the U.S. Treasury. Does NOT purchase issues from agencies or instrumentalities.
Year organized: 1991
Group fund code: 677
Dividends paid: Income - declared daily, paid monthly
Management fee: 0.10%
12b-1 distribution fee: Maximum of 0.10%
Expense ratio: 0.60% (year ending 8/31/97) (includes waiver)

VISTA TAX FREE MONEY MARKET FUND
(See first Vista listing for data common to all funds)

Sub-adviser: Texas Commerce Bank, N.A.
Investment objective and policies: High current income which is excluded from gross income for federal income tax purposes, and is consistent with preservation of capital and liquidity. Invests in a non-diversified portfolio of high quality short-term municipal obligations.
Year organized: 1987
Group fund code: 002
Dividends paid: Income - declared daily, paid monthly
Management fee: 0.10%
12b-1 distribution fee: Maximum of 0.10%
Expense ratio: 0.69% (year ending 8/31/97) (includes waiver)

VISTA TREASURY PLUS MONEY MARKET FUND
(See first Vista listing for data common to all funds)

Sub-adviser: Chase Asset Management, Inc.
Investment objective and policies: High current income consistent with preservation of capital and liquidity. Invests in high quality short-term obligations issued directly by the U.S. Treasury and in repurchase agreements fully collateralized by obligations issued or guaranteed by the U.S. Treasury.
Year organized: 1996
Group fund code: 678
Dividends paid: Income - declared daily, paid monthly
Management fee: 0.10%
12b-1 distribution fee: Maximum of 0.10%
Expense ratio: 0.59% (year ending 8/31/97) (includes waiver)

VISTA U.S. GOVERNMENT MONEY MARKET FUND
(See first Vista listing for data common to all funds)

Sub-adviser: Chase Asset Management, Inc.
Investment objective and policies: High current income consistent with preservation of capital and liquidity. Invests in high quality short-term obligations issued or guaranteed by the U.S. Treasury and agencies of the U.S. Government or its instrumentalities.
Year organized: 1993
Ticker symbol: VGMXX
Group fund code: 220
Dividends paid: Income - declared daily, paid monthly
Management fee: 0.10%
12b-1 distribution fee: Maximum of 0.10%
Expense ratio: 0.65% (year ending 8/31/97) (includes waiver)

VOLUMETRIC FUND ◆
87 Violet Drive
Pearl River, NY 10965
800-541-3863, 914-623-7637
fax 914-623-7732
Internet: http://www.volumetric.com
e-mail: info@volumetric.com

Adviser: Volumetric Advisers, Inc.
Portfolio managers: Gabriel J. Gibs (1978), Irene J. Zawitkoswki (1978)
Transfer agent: Volumetric Advisers, Inc.
Investment objective and policies: Capital growth with downside protection. Invests in a broadly diversified portfolio of large- and mid-cap common stocks, principally those listed on the NYSE, although it may invest in issues of other exchanges as well. Additionally, a cash position of 3% to 15% is maintained in neutral markets, with increases according to perceived market conditions. Management uses a proprietary methodology of technical analysis developed by founder Gabriel Gibs to quantitatively analyze the demand and supply for individual stocks by volume. The thesis is that volume aberrations from normal trading precede price movements. Stocks singled out are then researched on a traditional fundamental basis for inclusion in the portfolio.
Year organized: 1978 (opened to the public in 1987)
Ticker symbol: VOLMX
Minimum purchase: Initial: $500, Subsequent: $200; Automatic investment plan: Subsequent: $100
Wire orders accepted: No
Discount broker availability: *White
Qualified for sale in: All states
Telephone redemptions: Yes
Letter redemptions: Signature guarantee not required
Dividends paid: Income - December; Capital gains - December
Portfolio turnover (3 yrs): 213%, 154%, 159%
Shareholder services: IRA, SEP-IRA, corporate retirement plans
Management fee: 2.00% first $10M to 1.50% over $100M
Expense ratio: 1.96% (year ending 12/31/97)
IRA/Keogh fees: Annual $20 (waived for accounts with assets over $2,000)

VONTOBEL FUNDS ◆
(Data common to all Vontobel funds are shown below. See subsequent listings for data specific to individual funds.)

1500 Forest Avenue, Suite 223
Richmond, VA 23229
800-527-9500, 800-445-8872
804-285-8211
shareholder services 800-628-4077
fax 804-285-8251
Internet: http://www.vontobelfunds.com
e-mail: info@vontobelfunds.com

Shareholder service hours: Full service: M-F 9 ;a.m-5 ;p.m EST; After hours service: prices, account balances, orders, last transaction, messages, prospectuses, total returns
Adviser: Vontobel USA, Inc. (A wholly-owned subsidiary of Vontobel Holding Ltd., of Zurich, Switzerland)
Administrator: Commonwealth Shareholder Services, Inc.
Transfer agent: Fund Services, Inc.
Minimum purchase: Initial: $1,000, Subsequent: $50
Wire orders accepted: Yes
Deadline for same day wire purchases: 4 P.M.
Qualified for sale in: All states
Telephone redemptions: Yes, $10 fee
Wire redemptions: Yes, $10 fee
Letter redemptions: Signature guarantee not required
Telephone switching: With other Vontobel funds and the Kemper Cash Account Trust Money Market Funds, $10 fee
Number of switches permitted: Unlimited, $1,000 minimum
Shareholder services: IRA, automatic investment plan, electronic funds transfer, systematic withdrawal plan min. bal. req. $10,000

Maintenance fees: $10 per year for account balances of less than $1,000
Administration fee: 0.20%
IRA fees: Annual $10

VONTOBEL EASTERN EUROPEAN DEBT FUND ◆
(See first Vontobel listing for data common to all funds)

Portfolio manager: Volker Wehrle (1997)
Investment objective and policies: Maximum total return; capital growth and income. Invests primarily in a carefully selected and continuously managed non-diversified portfolio of corporate and government debt securities of issuers of the former Warsaw pact countries and the European successor states of the former Soviet Union. Fund will initially focus on Hungary, the Czech Republic, Slovakia, Poland, Slovenia and the Baltic States. Normally will hold 65% of assets in securities from these countries. Fund expects to expand to other countries in the region as newly developing markets mature. May invest in other investment companies. May use options, forward foreign currency exchange contracts, interest rate futures contracts, financial futures, currency futures and options thereon, and invest up to 10% of assets in restricted securities.
Year organized: 1997
Ticker symbol: VEEDX
Group fund code: 39
Discount broker availability: *Fidelity, *Schwab, *Siebert, *White
Redemption fee: 2.00% for shares held less than 6 months, payable to fund: you may switch to the money market for up to 30 days and switch back and receive the 2% back.
Dividends paid: Income - December; Capital gains - December
Management fee: 1.25% first $500M, 1.00% over $500M
Expense ratio: 2.19% (four months ending 12/31/97) (2.38% without waivers)

VONTOBEL EASTERN EUROPEAN EQUITY FUND ◆
(See first Vontobel listing for data common to all funds)

Portfolio manager: Luca Parmeggiani (1997)
Investment objective and policies: Capital appreciation. Invests primarily in a diversified portfolio of equity securities of issuers of the former Warsaw pact countries and the European successor states of the former Soviet Union. Fund will initially focus on Hungary, the Czech Republic, Slovakia, and Poland. Normally will hold 65% of assets in securities from these countries. Fund expects to expand to other countries in the region as newly developing markets mature. May use ADRs, EDRs, GDRs in lieu of direct investment. May invest in other investment companies. May use options, forward foreign currency exchange contracts, financial futures, currency futures and options thereon, and invest up to 10% of assets in restricted securities.
Year organized: 1996
Ticker symbol: VEEEX
Group fund code: 37
Discount broker availability: *Fidelity, *Schwab, *Siebert, *White
Redemption fee: 2.00% for shares held less than 6 months, payable to fund: you may switch to the money market for up to 30 days and switch back and receive the 2% back.
Dividends paid: Income - December; Capital gains - December
Portfolio turnover (2 yrs): 106%, 39%
Management fee: 1.25% first $500M, 1.00% over $500M
Expense ratio: 1.66% (year ending 12/31/97) (1.94% without waiver)

VONTOBEL EMERGING MARKETS EQUITY FUND ◆
(See first Vontobel listing for data common to all funds)

Portfolio manager: Fabrizio Pierallini (1997)
Investment objective and policies: Capital appreciation. Invests primarily in a diversified portfolio of

equity securities of issuers from countries generally considered to be emerging markets according to the World Bank or the International Finance Corporation. May use ADRs, EDRs, GDRs in lieu of direct investment. May invest in other investment companies. May use options, forward foreign currency exchange contracts, financial futures, currency futures and options thereon, and invest up to 10% of assets in restricted securities.
Year organized: 1997
Group fund code: 38
Discount broker availability: *Fidelity, *Schwab, *Siebert, *White
Redemption fee: 2.00% for shares held less than 6 months, payable to fund: you may switch to the money market for up to 30 days and switch back and receive the 2% back.
Dividends paid: Income - December; Capital gains - December
Management fee: 1.25% first $500M, 1.00% over $500M
Expense ratio: 2.20% (four months ending 12/31/97) (2.41% without waiver)

VONTOBEL INTERNATIONAL BOND FUND ◆
(See first Vontobel listing for data common to all funds)

Portfolio manager: Sven Rump (1994)
Investment objective and policies: Maximum total return: capital growth and income. Invests primarily in investment grade bonds issued by foreign governments and companies that are denominated in non-U.S. currencies, including bonds denominated in the European Currency Unit (ECU). Fund is non-diversified.
Year organized: 1994
Ticker symbol: VIBDX
Group fund code: 35
Discount broker availability: *Fidelity, *Schwab, *Siebert, *White
Dividends paid: Income - December; Capital gains - December
Portfolio turnover (3 yrs): 0%, 20%, 19%
Management fee: 1.00%
Expense ratio: 1.40% (year ending 12/31/97) (1.60% without waiver)

VONTOBEL INTERNATIONAL EQUITY FUND ◆
(See first Vontobel listing for data common to all funds)

Portfolio manager: Fabrizio Pierallini (1994)
Investment objective and policies: Capital appreciation. Invests primarily in a broadly diversified portfolio of equity securities of issuers of developed countries in Europe and the Pacific Basin. May however, invest without limit in emerging markets as well. May also use ADRs, options, currency futures and options thereon, and invest up to 10% of assets in restricted securities.
Year organized: 1985 (as Nicholson Growth Fund. Name changed to Tyndall-Newport Global Growth Fund 1/1/87 and T.V. EuroPacific Fund 7/6/90. Name changed to Europacific fund 3/7/91, to current 3/10/97.)
Ticker symbol: VNEPX
Discount broker availability: *Fidelity, *Schwab, *Siebert, *White
Dividends paid: Income - December; Capital gains - December
Portfolio turnover (3 yrs): 38%, 55%, 68%
Management fee: 1.00% first $100M, 0.75% over $100M
Expense ratio: 1.50% (year ending 12/31/97) (1.56% without waiver)

VONTOBEL U.S. VALUE FUND ◆
(See first Vontobel listing for data common to all funds)

Portfolio manager: Edwin D. Walczak (1990)
Investment objective and policies: Long-term capital appreciation in excess of the broad market. Invests primarily in equity securities - including convertible

bonds, warrants, debentures and convertible preferred stock - traded on U.S. exchanges. Priority is given to securities offering an attractive yield. Fund is non-diversified.

Year organized: 1990
Ticker symbol: VUSVX
Discount broker availability: *Fidelity, *Schwab, *Siebert, *White
Dividends paid: Income - December; Capital gains - December
Portfolio turnover (3 yrs): 90%, 108%, 96%
Management fee: 1.00% first $100M, 0.75% over $100M
Expense ratio: 1.58% (year ending 12/31/97) (1.61% without waiver)

WADE FUND ◆
5100 Poplar Avenue, Suite 2224
Memphis, TN 38137
901-682-4613

Adviser: Maury Wade & Co.
Portfolio manager: Maury Wade, Jr. (1973)
Transfer agent: Wade Fund, Inc.
Investment objective and policies: Long-term capital gains; income secondary. Invests primarily in common stocks perceived to show appreciation potential. Will only invest in established companies doing business for at least three years.
Year organized: 1949
Minimum purchase: Initial: $500, Subsequent: 1 share
Wire orders accepted: No
Qualified for sale in: TN
Letter redemptions: Signature guarantee required
Dividends paid: Income - December; Capital gains - December
Portfolio turnover (3 yrs): 0%, 0%, 0%
Management fee: 0.75%
Expense ratio: 2.86% (year ending 12/31/96)

WARBURG, PINCUS FUNDS
(Data common to all Warburg, Pincus funds are shown below. See subsequent listings for data specific to individual funds.)

466 Lexington Avenue
New York, NY 10017-3147
800-927-2874, 800-888-6878
800-257-5615, 212-878-0600
fax 212-878-9351
Internet: http://www.warburg.com

Shareholder service hours: Full service: M-F 8 A.M.-8 P.M., Sat., 8 A.M.-4 P.M. EST; After hours service: prices, balances, last transaction, messages, indexes, distributions
Adviser: Warburg, Pincus Asset Management, Inc.
Transfer agent: Boston Financial Data Services, Inc.
Sales restrictions: Several Warburg, Pincus funds are available in two classes of shares, institutional (known as Advisor) and common. Advisor shares are only available through financial intermediaries and retirement plans, and are generally more expensive. The Handbook reports only the performance for investors buying common shares directly from Warburg, Pincus or through the various discount brokerage firms.
Wire orders accepted: Yes
Deadline for same day wire purchase: 4 P.M.
Telephone redemptions: Yes
Wire redemptions: Yes, $100 minimum
Letter redemptions: Signature guarantee not required
Telephone switching: With other Warburg, Pincus funds
Number of switches permitted: 3 per month, $100 minimum
Shareholder services: IRA, SEP-IRA, directed dividends, systematic withdrawal plan
IRA fees: Annual $10/account holder (waived for accounts over $10,000)

WARBURG, PINCUS BALANCED FUND
(See first Warburg, Pincus listing for data common to all funds)

Lead portfolio managers: Dale C. Christensen (1988), Anthony G. Orphanos (1994)
Investment objective and policies: Maximum total return: long-term capital growth and current income, consistent with preservation of capital. Invests in a diversified portfolio of common stocks, convertible and non-convertible preferred stocks and debt securities. At all times fund has at least 25% of assets in equity securities and at least 25% in fixed-income securities. Allocations are determined and adjusted by as many as five different sector teams covering all asset classes. May have up to 15% of assets in illiquid securities.
Year organized: 1988 (name changed from RBB Balanced Portfolio on 10/1/94)
Ticker symbol: WAPBX
Group fund code: 22
Minimum purchase: Initial: $1,000, Subsequent: $100; IRA: Initial: $500; Automatic investment plan: Subsequent: $50
Discount broker availability: *Fidelity, *Schwab, *Siebert, *White
Qualified for sale in: All states
Dividends paid: Income - March, June, September, December; Capital gains - December
Portfolio turnover (3 yrs): 120%, 108%, 107%
Management fee: 0.90%
Administration fee: 0.25% first $500M to 0.15% over $1.5B
12b-1 distribution fee: 0.25%
Expense ratio: 1.35% (year ending 10/31/97) (2.03% without waiver)

WARBURG, PINCUS CAPITAL APPRECIATION FUND ◆
(See first Warburg, Pincus listing for data common to all funds)

Portfolio managers: George U. Wyper (1994), Susan L. Black (1994)
Investment objective and policies: Long-term capital appreciation. Invests at least 80% of assets in equity securities of financially strong domestic companies with perceived opportunities for growth through increased earning power and improved utilization or recognition of assets. Up to 20% of assets may be in foreign securities, and 20% in investment grade fixed-income instruments. May use options on stocks and indices, and interest rate and index futures and options thereon.
Year organized: 1987 (name changed from Counsellors Capital Appreciation Fund on 3/9/92)
Ticker symbol: CUCAX
Group fund code: 3
Minimum purchase: Initial: $2,500, Subsequent: $100; IRA: Initial: $500; Automatic investment plan: Subsequent: $50
Discount broker availability: *Fidelity, *Schwab, *Siebert, *White
Qualified for sale in: All states
Dividends paid: Income - December; Capital gains - December
Portfolio turnover (3 yrs): 238%, 171%, 146%
Management fee: 0.70%
Administration fee: 0.20% first $500M to 0.15% over $1.5B
12b-1 distribution fee: 0.25% (not currently imposed)
Expense ratio: 1.01% (year ending 10/31/97)

WARBURG, PINCUS CASH RESERVE FUND ◆
(See first Warburg, Pincus listing for data common to all funds)

Sub-adviser: PNC Institutional Management Corp.
Portfolio manager: Dale C. Christensen (1992)
Investment objective and policies: High current income consistent with liquidity and stability of principal. Invests in money market instruments.
Year organized: 1985 (name changed from Counsellors Cash Reserve Fund on 3/9/92)
Ticker symbol: CRFXX
Group fund code: 12
Minimum purchase: Initial: $1,000, Subsequent: $100; IRA: Initial: $500; Automatic investment plan: Subsequent: $50
Qualified for sale in: All states
Check redemptions: $500 minimum

Dividends paid: Income - declared daily, paid monthly
Management fee: 0.25%
Administration fee: 0.35%
12b-1 distribution fee: Yes (not currently imposed)
Expense ratio: 0.55% (year ending 2/28/97) (0.69% without waiver) (fiscal year changed to December at the end of 1997)

WARBURG, PINCUS EMERGING GROWTH FUND ◆
(See first Warburg, Pincus listing for data common to all funds)

Portfolio managers: Elizabeth B. Dater (1988), Stephen J. Lurito (1990), Medha Vora (1997)
Investment objective and policies: Maximum capital appreciation. Invests at least 65% of assets in common stocks and equivalents of small- to medium-sized companies that have passed their start up phase and are perceived to offer emerging or renewed growth potential. Fund also focuses on special situations such as acquisitions or consolidations, reorganizations or recapitalizations, mergers, liquidations, tenders, litigation or changes in corporate control. May have up to 20% of assets in foreign securities, 20% in fixed-income instruments, and use options and futures in an effort to enhance performance and for hedging purposes. Fund is non-diversified.
Year organized: 1988 (name changed from Counsellors Emerging Growth Fund on 3/9/92)
Ticker symbol: CUEGX
Group fund code: 5
Minimum purchase: Initial: $2,500, Subsequent: $100; IRA: Initial: $500; Automatic investment plan: Subsequent: $50
Discount broker availability: *Fidelity, *Schwab, *Siebert, *White
Qualified for sale in: All states
Dividends paid: Income - December; Capital gains - December
Portfolio turnover (3 yrs): 87%, 66%, 85%
Management fee: 0.90%
Administration fee: 0.20% first $500M to 0.15% over $1.5B
12b-1 distribution fee: 0.25% (not currently imposed)
Expense ratio: 1.22% (year ending 10/31/97)

WARBURG, PINCUS EMERGING MARKETS FUND
(See first Warburg, Pincus listing for data common to all funds)

Portfolio managers: Richard H. King (1994), Vincent J. McBride (1997)
Investment objective and policies: Capital growth. Invests at least 65% of assets in equity securities of issuers in emerging markets around the world, as defined by the International Financial Corporation or the World Bank. Normally invests in at least three countries outside the U.S., although country diversification is not a fundamental requirement. May invest in companies of any size, whether traded on or off a national exchange, and may invest in closed end investment companies that invest in foreign securities. May have up to 35% of assets in junk bonds and use swaps, currency exchange contracts, futures and options and sell short. Fund is non-diversified.
Year organized: 1994
Ticker symbol: WPEMX
Group fund code: 17
Minimum purchase: Initial: $2,500, Subsequent: $100; IRA: Initial: $500; Automatic investment plan: Subsequent: $50
Discount broker availability: *Fidelity, *Schwab, *Siebert, *White
Qualified for sale in: All states
Dividends paid: Income - December; Capital gains - December
Portfolio turnover (3 yrs): 92%, 62%, 69%
Management fee: 1.25%
Administration fee: 0.22% first $250M to 0.15% over $750M
12b-1 distribution fee: 0.25%
Expense ratio: 1.65% (year ending 10/31/97) (2.11% without waiver)

WARBURG, PINCUS FIXED INCOME FUND ◆
(See first Warburg, Pincus listing for data common to all funds)

Portfolio managers: Dale C. Christensen (1991), M. Anthony E. van Daalen (1992)
Investment objective and policies: High current income consistent with reasonable risk; capital appreciation secondary. Invests in a diversified portfolio of corporate bonds, debentures and notes, convertible debt securities, preferred stocks, and government obligations and repurchase agreements. Portfolio maintains a weighted average maturity of less than ten years. Under normal market conditions at least 65% of assets are investment grade. May invest up to 35% of assets in junk bonds, 35% in securities of foreign issuers, 10% in zero coupon bonds and 10% in restricted securities.
Year organized: 1987 (name changed from Counsellors Fixed Income Fund on 3/9/92)
Ticker symbol: CUFIX
Group fund code: 4
Minimum purchase: Initial: $2,500, Subsequent: $100; IRA: Initial: $500; Automatic investment plan: Subsequent: $50
Discount broker availability: *Fidelity, *Schwab, *Siebert, *White
Qualified for sale in: All states
Dividends paid: Income - declared daily, paid monthly; Capital gains - December
Portfolio turnover (3 yrs): 129%, 194%, 183%
Management fee: 0.50%
Administration fee: 0.15%
Expense ratio: 0.75% (year ending 10/31/97) (0.83% without waiver)

WARBURG, PINCUS GLOBAL FIXED INCOME FUND ◆
(See first Warburg, Pincus listing for data common to all funds)

Portfolio managers: Dale C. Christensen (1990), Laxmi C. Bhandari (1993)
Investment objective and policies: Maximum total return consistent with prudent management: a combination of interest income, currency gains and capital appreciation. Invests primarily in investment grade fixed-income securities, convertible securities and preferred stocks of government and corporate issuers denominated in various currencies, including the U.S. dollar. Portfolio maintains a weighted average maturity of three to ten years. At least three countries are represented, and no country other than the U.S. may comprise more than 40% of assets. In addition, no obligations of a single foreign government may comprise more than 25% of the portfolio. May invest up to 35% of assets in junk bonds, 20% in zero coupon securities, and 10% in illiquid securities; may write covered options on up to 25% of assets and sell short against the box.
Year organized: 1990 (name changed from Counsellors Global Fixed Income Fund on 3/9/92)
Ticker symbol: CGFIX
Group fund code: 8
Minimum purchase: Initial: $2,500, Subsequent: $100; IRA: Initial: $500; Automatic investment plan: Subsequent: $50
Discount broker availability: *Fidelity, *Schwab, *Siebert, *White
Qualified for sale in: All states
Dividends paid: Income - March, June, September, December; Capital gains - December
Portfolio turnover (3 yrs): 203%, 124%, 129%
Management fee: 1.00%
Administration fee: 0.22% first $250M to 0.15% over $750M
Expense ratio: 0.95% (year ending 10/31/97) (1.34% without waiver)

WARBURG, PINCUS GLOBAL POST-VENTURE CAPITAL FUND
(See first Warburg, Pincus listing for data common to all funds)

Sub-adviser: Abbott Capital Management, LLC
Portfolio managers: Elizabeth B. Dater (1996), Harold E. Sharon (1998)
Investment objective and policies: Long-term capi-

tal growth. Invests primarily in equity securities of U.S. and foreign issuers in the post-venture capital stage of their development. This could be newer companies beyond the start-up phase, or ongoing concerns undergoing recapitalization or restructuring. The venture capital investments will have been made within the previous ten years. May invest up to 35% of assets in assets that do not meet the definition of post-venture investments, and up to 10% of assets in securities of issuers involved in 'special situations' such as recapitalizations or restructurings. May invest up to 20% of assets in investment grade debt securities.
Year organized: 1996
Group fund code: 43
Minimum purchase: Initial: $2,500, Subsequent: $100; IRA: Initial: $500; Automatic investment plan: Subsequent: $50
Qualified for sale in: All states
Dividends paid: Income - December; Capital gains - December
Portfolio turnover (1 yr): 207%
Management fee: 1.25%
Administration fee: 0.22% first $250M to 0.15% over $750M
12b-1 distribution fee: 0.25%
Expense ratio: 1.65% (year ending 10/31/97) (8.14% without waiver)

WARBURG, PINCUS GROWTH & INCOME FUND ◆
(See first Warburg, Pincus listing for data common to all funds)

Portfolio manager: Brian S. Posner (1997)
Investment objective and policies: Long-term growth of capital and income and a reasonable current return. Invests primarily in income-producing securities such as dividend-paying equity securities, fixed-income securities and money market instruments. May invest in ADRs without limit, have up to 10% of assets in direct foreign securities and 15% in illiquid securities. May use options on stocks and indices, and interest rate and index futures and options thereon.
Year organized: 1988 (name changed from RBB Equity Growth and Income Portfolio on 9/30/93)
Ticker symbol: RBEGX
Group fund code: 1
Minimum purchase: Initial: $1,000, Subsequent: $100; IRA: Initial: $500; Automatic investment plan: Subsequent: $50
Discount broker availability: *Fidelity, *Schwab, *Siebert, *White
Qualified for sale in: All states
Dividends paid: Income - March, June, September, December; Capital gains - December
Portfolio turnover (3 yrs): 148%, 94%, 109%
Management fee: 0.75%
Administration fee: 0.20% first $125M, 0.25% over $125M
12b-1 distribution fee: 0.25% (not currently imposed)
Expense ratio: 1.18% (year ending 10/31/97)

WARBURG, PINCUS HEALTH SCIENCES FUND
(See first Warburg, Pincus listing for data common to all funds)

Portfolio managers: Susan L. Black (1996), Patricia F. Widner (1996)
Investment objective and policies: Capital appreciation. Invests at least 65% of assets in equity and debt securities of health sciences companies, and preferably 80%, as divided into four different categories; buyers, providers, suppliers and innovators. May invest in companies of any size. May invest up to 35% of assets in foreign issues, up to 20% in debt securities (including junk bonds), and up to 15% in illiquid securities. May use derivatives for hedging purposes.
Year organized: 1996
Ticker symbol: WPHSX
Minimum purchase: Initial: $2,500, Subsequent: $100; IRA: Initial: $500; Automatic investment plan: Subsequent: $50
Discount broker availability: *Fidelity, *Schwab, *Siebert, *White
Qualified for sale in: All states
Dividends paid: Income - December; Capital gains - December

Portfolio turnover (1 yr): 160%
Management fee: 1.00%
Administration fee: 0.20% first $500M to 0.15% over $1.5B
12b-1 distribution fee: 0.25%
Expense ratio: 1.59% (10 months ending 10/31/97) (3.42% without waiver)

WARBURG, PINCUS INTERMEDIATE MATURITY GOVERNMENT FUND ◆
(See first Warburg, Pincus listing for data common to all funds)

Portfolio managers: Dale C. Christensen (1989), M. Anthony E. van Daalen (1992)
Investment objective and policies: High current income consistent with capital preservation. Invests at least 65% of assets in intermediate-term U.S. Treasury bonds and notes and other obligations issued, guaranteed by, or backed by the U.S. Government, its agencies or instrumentalities. The fund maintains a weighted average maturity of three to ten years. Fund may use zero coupon bonds but is not authorized to use financial futures and options.
Year organized: 1988 (name changed from Counsellors Intermediate Maturity Government Fund on 3/9/92)
Ticker symbol: CUIGX
Group fund code: 6
Minimum purchase: Initial: $2,500, Subsequent: $100; IRA: Initial: $500; Automatic investment plan: Subsequent: $50
Discount broker availability: *Fidelity, *Schwab, *Siebert, *White
Qualified for sale in: All states
Dividends paid: Income - declared daily, paid monthly; Capital gains - December
Portfolio turnover (3 yrs): 104%, 164%, 106%
Management fee: 0.50%
Administration fee: 0.15%
Expense ratio: 0.60% (year ending 10/31/97) (0.93% without waiver)

WARBURG, PINCUS INTERNATIONAL EQUITY FUND ◆
(See first Warburg, Pincus listing for data common to all funds)

Lead portfolio manager: Richard H. King (1989)
Investment objective and policies: Long-term capital appreciation. Invests at least 65% of assets in a broadly diversified portfolio of equity securities of companies that have their principal business activities and interests outside of the U.S. Fund may invest in companies of any size, whether traded on or off a national securities exchange, and will diversify across at least three countries. May, however, invest a significant portion of assets in a single country. May invest in closed end investment companies that purchase foreign securities. May use swaps, forward currency contracts, and futures and options for hedging purposes.
Year organized: 1989 (name changed from Counsellors International Equity Fund on 3/9/92)
Ticker symbol: CUIEX
Group fund code: 7
Minimum purchase: Initial: $2,500, Subsequent: $100; IRA: Initial: $500; Automatic investment plan: Subsequent: $50
Discount broker availability: *Fidelity, *Schwab, *Siebert, *White
Qualified for sale in: All states
Dividends paid: Income - December; Capital gains - December
Portfolio turnover (3 yrs): 62%, 32%, 39%
Management fee: 1.00%
Administration fee: 0.22% first $250M to 0.15% over $750M
12b-1 distribution fee: Yes (not currently imposed)
Expense ratio: 1.32% (year ending 10/31/97)

WARBURG, PINCUS JAPAN GROWTH FUND
(See first Warburg, Pincus listing for data common to all funds)

Portfolio manager: P. Nicholas Edwards (1995)
Investment objective and policies: Long-term capital growth. Invests preferably 80% but no less than

65% of assets in direct equity securities and ADRs of Japanese issuers that appear to present attractive opportunities for growth or seem to be undervalued. May invest in companies of any size, whether traded on an exchange or over-the-counter. The portion of the fund not invested in Japan is generally invested in other Asian securities. May also invest up to 35% of assets in investment grade debt securities. May use currency hedging techniques to mitigate changes in the value of the yen against the dollar. May use swaps, options and futures and forward currency contracts for hedging purposes. Fund is non-diversified.
Year organized: 1995
Ticker symbol: WPJGX
Group fund code: 32
Minimum purchase: Initial: $2,500, Subsequent: $100; IRA: Initial: $500; Automatic investment plan: Subsequent: $50
Discount broker availability: *Fidelity, *Schwab, *Siebert, *White
Qualified for sale in: All states
Dividends paid: Income - December; Capital gains - December
Portfolio turnover (2 yrs): 94%, 52%
Management fee: 1.25%
Administration fee: 0.22% first $250M to 0.15% over $750M
12b-1 distribution fee: 0.25%
Expense ratio: 1.75% (year ending 10/31/97) (2.56% without waiver)

WARBURG, PINCUS JAPAN OTC FUND
(See first Warburg, Pincus listing for data common to all funds)

Portfolio managers: Richard H. King (1994), P. Nicholas Edwards (1997)
Investment objective and policies: Long-term capital appreciation. Invests at least 65% of assets in securities traded on the primary Japanese over-the-counter market, JASDAQ, or the Frontier Market. Up to 35% of assets may be in securities of other Asian issuers or exchange-traded Japanese firms, although no more than 10% of assets may be in any one other country. Fund may use swaps, currency exchange transactions and futures and options to hedge up to 25% of total assets. Fund is non-diversified.
Year organized: 1994
Ticker symbol: WPJPX
Group fund code: 19
Minimum purchase: Initial: $2,500, Subsequent: $100; IRA: Initial: $500; Automatic investment plan: Subsequent: $50
Discount broker availability: *Fidelity, *Schwab, *Siebert, *White
Qualified for sale in: All states
Dividends paid: Income - December; Capital gains - December
Portfolio turnover (3 yrs): 101%, 95%, 83%
Management fee: 1.25%
Administration fee: 0.22% first $250M to 0.15% over $750M
12b-1 distribution fee: 0.25%
Expense ratio: 1.75% (year ending 10/31/97) (2.26% without waiver)

WARBURG, PINCUS MAJOR FOREIGN MARKETS FUND
(See first Warburg, Pincus listing for data common to all funds)

Portfolio managers: Richard H. King (1997), P. Nicholas Edwards (1997), Harold W. Ehrlich (1997)
Investment objective and policies: Long-term capital appreciation. Invests at least 65% of assets in a diversified portfolio of equity securities of companies of any size having their principal business interests in countries represented, at least from time to time, in the Morgan Stanley EAFE Index. Fund is not an index fund, and does not seek to match the performance or weightings of the Index. Fund may occasionally invest a significant portion of assets in a single country. May invest up to 35% of assets in investment grade fixed-income obligations. May use a variety of derivative instruments in an effort to enhance return and for hedging purposes.
Year organized: 1997 (name changed from Managed EAFE Countries Fund 2/9/98)

Minimum purchase: Initial: $2,500, Subsequent: $100; IRA: Initial: $500; Automatic investment plan: Subsequent: $50
Discount broker availability: *Schwab
Qualified for sale in: All states
Dividends paid: Income - December; Capital gains - December
Management fee: 1.00%
Administration fee: 0.22% first $250M to 0.15% over $750M
12b-1 distribution fee: 0.25%

WARBURG, PINCUS NEW YORK INTERMEDIATE MUNICIPAL FUND ◆
(See first Warburg, Pincus listing for data common to all funds)

Portfolio managers: Sharon B. Parente (1992), Dale C. Christensen (1992)
Investment objective and policies: Maximum current interest income exempt from federal, NY state and NY city personal income taxes, consistent with prudent investment management and preservation of capital. Invests primarily in investment grade New York municipal bonds with remaining maturities of five to fifteen years. Fund maintains a weighted average maturity between three and ten years. Up to 20% of assets may be securities subject to AMT tax treatment. Fund is non-diversified.
Year organized: 1987 (name changed from Counsellors New York Municipal Bond Fund on 3/9/92)
Ticker symbol: CNMBX
Group fund code: 2
Minimum purchase: Initial: $2,500, Subsequent: $100; Automatic investment plan: Subsequent: $50
Discount broker availability: *Fidelity, *Schwab, *Siebert, *White
Qualified for sale in: CO, CT, DC, FL, HI, IL, ME, MA, NJ, NY, OK, PA, PR, RI, TN, WI
Dividends paid: Income - declared daily, paid monthly; Capital gains - December
Portfolio turnover (3 yrs): 70%, 69%, 106%
Management fee: 0.40%
Administration fee: 0.15%
Expense ratio: 0.60% (year ending 10/31/97) (0.68% without waiver)

WARBURG, PINCUS NEW YORK TAX EXEMPT FUND ◆
(See first Warburg, Pincus listing for data common to all funds)

Sub-adviser: PNC Institutional Management Corp.
Portfolio manager: Dale C. Christensen (1992)
Investment objective and policies: High current income exempt from federal, NY state, and NY city personal income taxes, consistent with preservation of capital and liquidity. Invests in New York municipal money market instruments.
Year organized: 1985 (name changed from Counsellors New York Tax Exempt Fund on 3/9/92)
Ticker symbol: COEXX
Group fund code: 13
Minimum purchase: Initial: $1,000, Subsequent: $100; Automatic investment plan: Subsequent: $50
Qualified for sale in: CO, CT, DC, FL, HI, ME, MD, MA, MI, NJ, NY, NC, OK, PA, RI, TN, TX, VA, WA
Check redemptions: $500 minimum
Dividends paid: Income - declared daily, paid monthly
Management fee: 0.25%
Administration fee: 0.35%
12b-1 distribution fee: Yes (not currently imposed)
Expense ratio: 0.55% (year ending 2/28/97) (0.72% without waiver) (fiscal year changed to December at the end of 1997)

WARBURG, PINCUS POST-VENTURE CAPITAL FUND
(See first Warburg, Pincus listing for data common to all funds)

Sub-adviser: Abbott Capital Management, LLC
Lead portfolio managers: Elizabeth B. Dater (1995), Stephen J. Lurito (1995)
Investment objective and policies: Long-term capital

growth. Invests primarily in equity securities of issuers in the post-venture capital stage of their development. This could be newer companies beyond the start-up phase, or ongoing concerns undergoing recapitalization or restructuring. The venture capital investments will have been made within the previous ten years. May invest up to 35% of assets in assets that do not meet the definition of post-venture investments, and up to 10% of assets in securities of issuers involved in 'special situations' such as recapitalizations or restructurings. Fund may hold securities of companies of any size, and may invest in companies with market capitalizations of less than $1B. May invest up to 20% of assets in investment grade debt obligations, and up to 20% in foreign securities.
Year organized: 1995
Ticker symbol: WPVCX
Group fund code: 29
Minimum purchase: Initial: $2,500, Subsequent: $100; IRA: Initial: $500; Automatic investment plan: Subsequent: $50
Discount broker availability: *Fidelity, *Schwab, *Siebert, *White
Qualified for sale in: All states
Dividends paid: Income - December; Capital gains - December
Portfolio turnover (2 yrs): 198%, 168%
Management fee: 1.25%
Administration fee: 0.20% first $500M to 0.15% over $1.5B
12b-1 distribution fee: 0.25%
Expense ratio: 1.65% (year ending 10/31/97) (2.05% without waiver)

WARBURG, PINCUS SMALL COMPANY GROWTH FUND
(See first Warburg, Pincus listing for data common to all funds)

Portfolio manager: Stephen J. Lurito (1996)
Investment objective and policies: Long-term capital growth. Invests at least 80% of assets in equity securities of domestic companies with market capitalizations of less than $1B that are perceived to present attractive opportunities for capital growth. May invest up to 20% of assets in foreign securities, and up to 20% of assets in investment grade debt securities. May use derivative instruments for hedging purposes.
Year organized: 1996
Ticker symbol: WSCGX
Special sales restrictions: Fund closed to new investors 11/7/97.
Minimum purchase: Initial: $2,500, Subsequent: $100; IRA: Initial: $500; Automatic investment plan: Subsequent: $50
Discount broker availability: *Fidelity, *Schwab, *Siebert, *White
Qualified for sale in: All states
Dividends paid: Income - December; Capital gains - December
Portfolio turnover (1 yr): 123%
Management fee: 1.00%
Administration fee: 0.20% first $500M to 0.15% over $1.5B
12b-1 distribution fee: 0.25%
Expense ratio: 1.40% (10 months ending 10/31/97) (5.06% without waiver)

WARBURG, PINCUS SMALL COMPANY VALUE FUND
(See first Warburg, Pincus listing for data common to all funds)

Portfolio managers: George U. Wyper (1995), Kyle F. Frey (1995)
Investment objective and policies: Long-term capital appreciation. Invests primarily in equity securities of companies with market capitalizations under $1B at the time of purchase that are perceived to be undervalued. May invest up to 20% of assets in foreign securities, and up to 20% of assets in investment grade debt securities. May use derivative instruments for hedging purposes.
Year organized: 1995
Ticker symbol: WPSVX
Group fund code: 34

Minimum purchase: Initial: $2,500, Subsequent: $100; IRA: Initial: $500; Automatic investment plan: Subsequent: $50
Discount broker availability: *Fidelity, *Schwab, *Siebert, *White
Qualified for sale in: All states
Dividends paid: Income - December; Capital gains - December
Portfolio turnover (2 yrs): 106%, 43%
Management fee: 1.00%
Administration fee: 0.20% first $500M to 0.15% over $1.5B
12b-1 distribution fee: 0.25%
Expense ratio: 1.70% (year ending 10/31/97) (1.73% without waiver)

WARBURG, PINCUS STRATEGIC VALUE FUND
(See first Warburg, Pincus listing for data common to all funds)

Portfolio manager: Anthony G. Orphanos (1996)
Investment objective and policies: Capital appreciation. Invests primarily in equity securities of companies or market sectors perceived to be undervalued. May invest in companies of any size, and may invest without limit in unseasoned companies and ADRs. May invest up to 20% of assets in debt securities, including those rated as low as C and D, for the purpose of seeking capital appreciation. May use foreign currency transactions and various derivative instruments in an effort to enhance performance and for hedging purposes.
Year organized: 1996
Ticker symbol: WSLVX
Minimum purchase: Initial: $2,500, Subsequent: $100; IRA: Initial: $500; Automatic investment plan: Subsequent: $50
Discount broker availability: *Fidelity, *Schwab, *White
Qualified for sale in: All states
Dividends paid: Income - December; Capital gains - December
Portfolio turnover (1 yr): 278%
Management fee: 1.00%
Administration fee: 0.10% first $500M to 0.05% over $1.5B
12b-1 distribution fee: 0.25%
Expense ratio: 1.45% (10 months ending 10/31/97) (3.97% without waiver)

WARBURG, PINCUS TAX FREE FUND
(Fund liquidated 10/26/97)

WASATCH FUNDS ◆
(Data common to all Wasatch funds are shown below. See subsequent listing for data specific to individual funds.)

68 South Main Street
Salt Lake City, UT 84101
800-551-1700, 801-533-0778
prices/yields 800-382-3616
fax 801-533-9828

Adviser: Wasatch Advisors, Inc.
Administrator: Sunstone Financial Group, Inc.
Transfer agent: Firstar Trust Co.
Minimum purchase: Initial: $2,000; Subsequent: $100; IRA/Keogh: Initial: $1,000, Subsequent: None; Automatic investment plan: Initial: $1,000, Subsequent: $50
Wire orders accepted: Yes
Deadline for same day wire purchase: 4 P.M.
Qualified for sale in: All states
Telephone redemptions: Yes, $1,000 minimum
Wire redemptions: Yes, $1,000 minimum, $7.50 fee
Letter redemptions: Signature guarantee required over $25,000
Telephone switching: With other Wasatch Funds and Northern U.S. Government Money Market Fund, $500 minimum, $5 fee
Number of switches permitted: Unlimited (subject to review)
Shareholder services: IRA, 403(b), electronic funds transfer, systematic withdrawal plan min. bal. req. $10,000
IRA: Annual $12.50

WASATCH AGGRESSIVE EQUITY FUND ◆
(See first Wasatch listing for data common to all funds)

Portfolio managers: Jeff Cardon (1997), Samuel S. Stewart, Jr. (1986)
Investment objective and policies: Long-term capital growth; income secondary. Invests at least 65% of assets in common stocks of companies believed to possess superior growth potential. Up to 10% of assets may be in foreign securities and 5% in companies in reorganization or buyout. The fund holds relatively few securities and is non-diversified.
Year organized: 1986
Ticker symbol: WAAEX
Special sales restrictions: Fund closed to new shareholders on 7/15/95
Discount broker availability: *Fidelity, *Schwab, *Siebert, *White
Dividends paid: Income - December; Capital gains - December
Portfolio turnover (3 yrs): 48%, 73%, 29%
Management fee: 1.00%
Administration fee: 0.20% first $50M to 0.05% over $100M
Expense ratio: 1.50% (year ending 9/30/97) (1.54% without waiver)

WASATCH GROWTH FUND ◆
(See first Wasatch listing for data common to all funds)

Portfolio managers: Samuel S. Stewart, Jr. (1986), Jeff Cardon (1986)
Investment objective and policies: Long-term growth of capital. Invests at least 65% of assets in common stock of companies believed to possess superior growth potential. Up to 10% of assets may be in foreign securities and 5% in companies in reorganization or buyout. The fund holds more securities than the Wasatch Aggressive Growth Fund and is diversified.
Year organized: 1986
Ticker symbol: WGROX
Discount broker availability: *Fidelity, *Schwab, *Siebert, *White
Dividends paid: Income - December; Capital gains - December
Portfolio turnover (3 yrs): 81%, 62%, 88%
Management fee: 1.00%
Administration fee: 0.20% first $50M to 0.05% over $100M
Expense ratio: 1.50% (year ending 9/30/97)

WASATCH-HOISINGTON U.S. TREASURY FUND ◆
(See first Wasatch listing for data common to all funds)

Sub-adviser: Hoisington Investment Management
Portfolio manager: Van Robert Hoisington (1996)
Investment objective and policies: To provide a real rate of return (i.e., a rate of return that exceeds inflation) over a business cycle. Invests in U.S. Treasuries with an emphasis on both income and capital appreciation. At least 90% of assets will be invested in U.S. Treasury Securities and in repurchase agreements collateralized by such securities. The remainder of the fund can also be invested in money market instruments, cash equivalents and cash. May use the entire range of maturities offered, with the effective duration of the fund ranging from less than a year to a maximum of 15 years, and a maturity ranging from less than a year to a maximum of 30 years.
Year organized: 1986 (name and objective changed from Wasatch Income Fund 6/21/96; past performance information should be disregarded)
Ticker symbol: WHOSX
Discount broker availability: *Fidelity, *Schwab, *Siebert, *White
Dividends paid: Income - December; Capital gains - December
Portfolio turnover (3 yrs): 19%, 30%, 43%
Management fee: 0.50%
Administration fee: 0.20% first $50M to 0.05% over $100M
Expense ratio: 0.75% (year ending 9/30/97) (1.22% without waiver)

WASATCH MICRO-CAP FUND ◆
(See first Wasatch listing for data common to all funds)

Portfolio managers: Robert Gardiner (1995), Samuel S. Stewart (1995)
Investment objective and policies: Long-term capital growth; income secondary. Invests at least 65% of assets in common stocks of small companies with market capitalizations under $150M believed to possess superior growth potential. Up to 10% of assets may be in foreign securities and 5% in companies in reorganization or buyout. The fund is non-diversified.
Year organized: 1995
Ticker symbol: WMICX
Sales restrictions: Closed to new investors 9/24/97
Discount broker availability: *Fidelity, *Schwab, *Siebert, *White
Dividends paid: Income - December; Capital gains - December
Portfolio turnover (2 yrs): 99%, 84%
Management fee: 2.00%
Administration fee: 0.20% first $25M to 0.05% over $50M
Expense ratio: 2.50% (year ending 9/30/97) (2.58% without waiver)

WASATCH MICRO-CAP VALUE FUND ◆
(See first Wasatch listing for data common to all funds)

Portfolio managers: Robert Gardiner (1997), Jeff Cardon (1997)
Investment objective and policies: Long-term capital growth; income secondary only when consistent with primary objective. Invests at least 65% of assets in common stocks of small companies with market capitalizations under $300M believed to be temporarily undervalued but have significant potential for appreciation. May invest up to 25% of assets in a single issue. Up to 15% of assets may be in foreign securities, either directly or through ADRs, up to 15% in illiquid securities, and up to 10% in companies in reorganization or buyout. The fund is non-diversified.
Year organized: 1997
Sales restrictions: Will close to new investors when assets reach $200M.
Discount broker availability: *Fidelity, *Schwab, *Siebert, *White
Dividends paid: Income - December; Capital gains - December
Management fee: 1.50%
Administration fee: 0.20% first $25M to 0.05% over $50M

WASATCH MID-CAP FUND ◆
(See first Wasatch listing for data common to all funds)

Portfolio managers: Karolyn Barker (1992), Samuel S. Stewart (1992)
Investment objective and policies: Long-term capital growth; income secondary. Invests at least 65% of assets in common stock of mid-size companies with market capitalizations from $400M to $2B believed to possess superior growth potential. Up to 10% of assets may be in foreign securities and 5% in companies in reorganization or buyout. The fund is non-diversified.
Year organized: 1992
Ticker symbol: WAMCX
Discount broker availability: *Fidelity, *Schwab, *Siebert, *White
Dividends paid: Income - December; Capital gains - December
Portfolio turnover (3 yrs): 103%, 121%, 46%
Management fee: 1.25%
Administration fee: 0.20% first $50M to 0.05% over $100M
Expense ratio: 1.75% (year ending 9/30/97) (1.89% without waiver)

WAYNE HUMMER FUNDS ◆

(Data common to all Wayne Hummer funds are shown below. See subsequent listings for data specific to individual funds.)

300 South Wacker Drive
Chicago, IL 60606-6607
800-621-4477, 312-431-1700
fax 312-431-6741
Internet: http://whummer.com

Shareholder service hours: Full service: M-F 8 A.M.-5 P.M. CST.
Adviser: Wayne Hummer Management Co.
Transfer agent: State Street Bank & Trust Co.
Wire order accepted: Yes
Deadline for same day wire purchases: 3 P.M.
Telephone redemptions: Yes
Wire redemptions: Yes, $15 fee
Letter redemptions: Signature guarantee not required
Telephone switching: With other Wayne Hummer funds
Number of switches permitted: Unlimited
Shareholder services: IRA, SEP-IRA, Keogh, 401(k), corporate retirement plans, electronic funds transfer (purchase only)
IRA/Keogh fees: Annual $36, Closing $50

WAYNE HUMMER GROWTH FUND ◆

(See first Wayne Hummer listing for data common to all funds)

Portfolio manager: Thomas J. Rowland (1987)
Investment objective and policies: Long-term capital growth; current income secondary. Invests primarily in a diversified portfolio of common stocks of companies perceived to offer the potential for long-term capital growth. May also invest in preferred stocks, bonds, and convertible debentures. May use options and futures for hedging purposes.
Year organized: 1983
Ticker symbol: WHGRX
Minimum purchase: Initial: $1,000, Subsequent: $500; IRA/Keogh: Initial: $500, Subsequent: $200; Automatic investment plan: Initial: $500, Subsequent: $100
Discount broker availability: *White
Qualified for sale in: All states
Dividends paid: Income - April, July, October, December; Capital gains - April, December
Portfolio turnover (3 yrs): 9%, 6%, 3%
Management fee: 0.80% first $100M to 0.50% over $250M
Expense ratio: 0.99% (year ending 3/31/97)

WAYNE HUMMER INCOME FUND ◆

(See first Wayne Hummer listing for data common to all funds)

Portfolio manager: David P. Poitras (1992)
Investment objective and policies: High current income consistent with prudent investment management. Invests primarily in investment grade corporate and government debt securities, or convertible securities, including dollar denominated debt securities of foreign issuers. The dollar-weighted average life of the portfolio is between three and ten years. Up to 15% of assets may be in illiquid securities. May use options and futures for hedging purposes.
Year organized: 1992
Ticker symbol: WHICX
Minimum purchase: Initial: $2,500, Subsequent: $1,000; IRA/Keogh: Initial: $2,000, Subsequent: $500; Automatic investment plan: Subsequent: $100
Qualified for sale in: All states except MO, NH
Dividends paid: Income - declared daily, paid monthly; Capital gains - April, December
Portfolio turnover (3 yrs): 39%, 46%, 32%
Management fee: 0.50% first $100M to 0.30% over $250M
Expense ratio: 1.01% (year ending 3/31/97)

WAYNE HUMMER MONEY FUND TRUST ◆

(See first Wayne Hummer listing for data common to all funds)

Portfolio manager: David P. Poitras (1986)
Investment objective and policies: Maximum current income consistent with preservation of capital and liquidity. Invests in money market instruments.
Year organized: 1981
Minimum purchase: Initial: $500, Subsequent: $100; Automatic investment plan: Subsequent: $100
Qualified for sale in: All states
Check redemptions: $500 minimum
Dividends paid: Income - declared daily, paid monthly
Management fee: 0.50% first $500M to 0.275% over $2.5B
Expense ratio: 0.74% (year ending 3/31/97)

WEITZ FUNDS ◆

(Data common to all Weitz funds are shown below. See subsequent listing for data specific to individual funds.)

One Pacific Place, Suite 600
1125 South 103 Street
Omaha, NE 68124-6008
800-232-4161, 402-391-1980
fax 402-391-2125

Shareholder service hours: Full service: M-F 8 A.M.-4:30 P.M. CST; After hours: prices, messages, prospectuses
Adviser: Wallace R. Weitz & Co.
Transfer agent: Wallace R. Weitz & Co.
Minimum purchase: (Except Weitz Partners Fund) Initial: $25,000 (total among all portfolios), Subsequent: None; IRA: Initial: $2,000, Subsequent: None
Wire orders accepted: Yes
Deadline for same day wire purchase: 3 P.M.
Letter redemptions: Signature guarantee not required
Telephone switching: With other Weitz Series portfolios and Partners Value Fund
Number of switches permitted: Unlimited
Shareholder services: IRA, 403(b), automatic investment plan, systematic withdrawal plan
IRA fees: Annual $20

WEITZ PARTNERS, INC. - PARTNERS VALUE FUND ◆

(See first Weitz listing for data common to all funds)

Portfolio manager: Wallace R. Weitz (1994)
Investment objective and policies: Capital appreciation. Invests primarily in common stocks, convertible bonds, and preferred stocks trading at prices perceived to be significantly below their estimated intrinsic, or "going concern" value. May also invest in bonds and other debt obligations of both corporate and governmental issuers. Up to 25% of assets may be in securities of foreign issuers. Fund is non-diversified. May write covered call options.
Year organized: 1994
Ticker symbol: WPVLX
Group fund code: 22
Minimum purchase: Initial: $100,000, Subsequent: $2,000
Qualified for sale in: All states except AK, AR, DE, HI, ID, IN, KS, KY, ME, MI, MS, NV, NH, OH, RI, SC, UT, VT, WV, WI
Dividends paid: Income - April, December; Capital gains - April, December
Portfolio turnover (3 yrs): 30%, 37%, 51%
Management fee: 1.00%
Expense ratio: 1.24% (year ending 12/31/97)

WEITZ SERIES FUND - FIXED INCOME PORTFOLIO ◆

(See first Weitz listing for data common to all funds)

Portfolio managers: Wallace R. Weitz (1988), Thomas D. Carney (1996)
Investment objective and policies: High current income consistent with capital preservation. Invests at least 65% of assets in fixed-income debt securities, and maintains a dollar-weighted average maturity of seven years or less. Securities will be in the top four categories as rated by Moody's or S&P. Up to 15% of assets may be in junk bonds. May use interest rate futures, bond index futures and options for hedging purposes.
Year organized: 1988
Ticker symbol: WEFIX
Group fund code: 02
Qualified for sale in: All states except AL, AK, DE, HI, ID, ME, MA, MS, MT, NV, NH, ND, RI, SC, TN, VT, WI
Dividends paid: Income - April, July, October, December; Capital gains - April, December
Portfolio turnover (3 yrs): 24%, 28%, 49%
Management fee: 0.50%
Expense ratio: 0.75% (year ending 3/31/97) (0.93% without waiver)

WEITZ SERIES FUND - GOVERNMENT MONEY MARKET PORTFOLIO ◆

(See first Weitz listing for data common to all funds)

Portfolio managers: Wallace R. Weitz (1991), Thomas D. Carney (1996)
Investment objective and policies: Current income consistent with preservation of capital and liquidity. Invests at least 90% of assets in money market instruments issued or guaranteed by the U.S. Government, its agencies and instrumentalities, and repurchase agreements thereon.
Year organized: 1991
Group fund code: 03
Qualified for sale in: All states except AL, AK, DE, HI, ID, KS, ME, MD, MA, MS, MT, NH, ND, RI, SC, TN, VT, WI
Dividends paid: Income - declared and paid monthly
Management fee: 0.50%
Expense ratio: 0.50% (year ending 3/31/97) (1.15% without waiver)

WEITZ SERIES FUND - HICKORY PORTFOLIO ◆

(See first Weitz listing for data common to all funds)

Portfolio manager: Richard F. Lawson (1993)
Investment objective and policies: Capital appreciation; income secondary. Invests primarily in common stocks, convertible bonds, and preferred stocks trading at prices significantly below their estimated intrinsic, or "going concern" value. May also invest in bonds and other debt obligations of both corporate and governmental issuers. Up to 25% of assets may be in securities of foreign issuers. Fund may hedge. Unlike the Value Portfolio, which has the same basic policies, the Hickory Portfolio is non-diversified.
Year organized: 1993
Ticker symbol: WEHIX
Group fund code: 04
Discount broker availability: White
Qualified for sale in: All states except: AL, DE, HI, ID, ME, MD, MS, MT, NV, NH, SC, VT, WI
Dividends paid: Income - April, December; Capital gains - April, December
Portfolio turnover (3 yrs): 28%, 28%, 20%
Management fee: 1.00%
Expense ratio: 1.50% (year ending 3/31/97) (1.56% without waiver)

WEITZ SERIES FUND - VALUE PORTFOLIO ◆

(See first Weitz listing for data common to all funds)

Portfolio manager: Wallace R. Weitz (1986)
Investment objective and policies: Capital appreciation; income secondary. Invests primarily in common stocks, convertible bonds, and preferred stocks trading at prices perceived to be significantly below their estimated intrinsic, or "going concern" value. May also invest in bonds and other debt obligations of both corporate and governmental issuers. Up to 25% of assets may be in securities of foreign issuers. Fund may hedge.
Year organized: 1986 (formerly Weitz Value Fund)
Ticker symbol: WVALX
Group fund code: 01

Discount broker availability: White
Qualified for sale in: All states except: AL, DE, HI, NH
Dividends paid: Income - April, December; Capital gains - April, December
Portfolio turnover (3 yrs): 39%, 40%, 28%
Management fee: 1.00%
Expense ratio: 1.29% (year ending 3/31/97)

WERTHEIM FUNDS ◆
(See Schroder Series Trust Funds)

WEST UNIVERSITY FUND ◆
3030 University Blvd.
Houston, TX 77005
800-465-5657, 713-666-1652
fax 713-666-4175
e-mail: westfunds@compuserve.com

Adviser: Cancelmo Capital Management, Inc.
Portfolio manager: Richard P. Cancelmo, Jr.
Transfer agent: West University Fund
Investment objective and policies: Income. Invests in income producing common stocks on which options are traded on national securities exchanges. Then sells covered call options and enters into closing purchase transactions with respect to certain of such call options. Invests in companies of all market capitalizations.
Year organized: 1996
Minimum purchase: Initial: $1,000, Subsequent: None; IRA: Initial: None
Wire orders accepted: No
Qualified for sale in: CO, CT, PA, TX
Letter redemptions: Signature guarantee not required
Dividends paid: Income - December; Capital gains - December
Portfolio turnover (1 yr): 101%
Shareholder services: IRA
Management fee: 1.00%
IRA/Keogh fees: Annual $12.50, Closing $15
Expense ratio: 1.82% (11 months ending 12/31/96)

WESTCORE FUNDS ◆
(Data common to all Westcore funds are shown below. See subsequent listings for data specific to individual funds.)

370 Seventeenth Street, Suite 3100
Denver, CO 80202
800-734-9378, 800-392-2673
303-595-9156
fax 303-623-7850
Internet: http://www.westcore.com

Shareholder service hours: Full service: M-F 7 A.M.-6 P.M. MST; After hours service: prices, yields, account balances, prospectuses
Adviser: Denver Investment Advisors, LLC
Transfer agent: State Street Bank & Trust Co.
Minimum purchase: Initial: $1,000, Subsequent: $50; IRA: Initial: $250; Automatic investment plan: Initial: $50
Wire orders accepted: Yes
Deadline for same day wire purchase: 4 P.M.
Qualified for sale in: All states (exception noted)
Telephone redemptions: Yes
Wire redemptions: Yes, $1,000 minimum
Letter redemptions: Signature guarantee required over $25,000
Telephone switching: With other Westcore funds and BlackRock Money Market Portfolio
Number of switches permitted: Unlimited
Shareholder services: IRA, SEP-IRA, electronic funds transfer, systematic withdrawal plan min. bal. req. $10,000
IRA/Keogh fees: Annual $10 per fund, maximum of $30

WESTCORE BLUE CHIP FUND ◆
(See first Westcore listing for data common to all funds)

Portfolio manager: Varilyn K. Schock (1991)
Investment objective and policies: Long-term total return: capital growth and current income. Invests pri-

---

marily in approximately 50 common stocks from a universe of the 300 largest dividend-paying companies headquartered in the U.S. May invest in U.S. dollar-denominated debt obligations of foreign issuers, have up to 15% of assets in illiquid securities and use futures and options for hedging purposes.
Year organized: 1988 (formerly the Westcore Modern Value Fund)
Ticker symbol: WTMVX
Group fund code: 204
Discount broker availability: *Fidelity, *Schwab, *White
Dividends paid: Income - March, June, September, December; Capital gains - December
Portfolio turnover (3 yrs): 43%, 65%, 62%
Management fee: 0.65%
Expense ratio: 1.15% (year ending 5/31/97) (1.21% without waiver)

WESTCORE COLORADO TAX-EXEMPT FUND ◆
(See first Westcore listing for data common to all funds)

Portfolio manager: Robert O. Lindig (1991)
Investment objective and policies: Income exempt from federal and Colorado state income taxes, consistent with safety and stability of principal. Invests primarily in high quality municipal obligations issued by the state of Colorado and its political subdivisions, and maintains a dollar-weighted average maturity of seven to ten years. At least 75% of assets will be covered by insurance guaranteeing the timely payment of interest and principal. Up to 20% of assets may be in securities subject to AMT tax treatment, and 15% in illiquid securities.
Year organized: 1991
Ticker symbol: WTCOX
Group fund code: 219
Discount broker availability: *Fidelity, *Schwab, *White
Qualified for sale in: CA, CO, FL, GA, ID, IL, IN, KY, LA, MN, OK, OR, NC, PA, UT, VA, WY
Dividends paid: Income - declared and paid monthly; Capital gains - December
Portfolio turnover (3 yrs): 31%, 10%, 3%
Management fee: 0.50%
Expense ratio: 0.50% (year ending 5/31/97) (1.21% without waiver)

WESTCORE GROWTH AND INCOME FUND ◆
(See first Westcore listing for data common to all funds)

Portfolio manager: Milford H. Schulhof, II (1995)
Investment objective and policies: Long-term total return: capital growth and current income. Invests primarily in equity securities of domestic companies selected for their potential for capital appreciation and ability to produce above average earnings and dividend growth. Up to 25% of assets may be in securities of foreign issuers, 15% in convertible securities rated below investment grade and 15% in illiquid securities. May use futures and options for hedging purposes.
Year organized: 1988 (formerly the Westcore Equity Income Fund)
Ticker symbol: WTEIX
Group fund code: 195
Discount broker availability: *Fidelity, *Schwab, *White
Dividends paid: Income - March, June, September, December; Capital gains - December
Portfolio turnover (3 yrs): 40%, 88%, 81%
Management fee: 0.65%
Expense ratio: 1.15% (year ending 5/31/97) (1.56% without waiver)

WESTCORE INTERMEDIATE-TERM BOND FUND ◆
(See first Westcore listing for data common to all funds)

Portfolio manager: Jerome R. Powers (1997)
Investment objective and policies: Current income with relatively small volatility of principal. Invests primarily in investment grade bonds and high quality debt obligations, and maintains a weighted average

---

maturity of three to six years. May invest in U.S. dollar-denominated debt obligations of foreign issuers, have up to 15% of assets in illiquid securities and use futures and options for hedging purposes.
Year organized: 1988
Ticker symbol: WTIBX
Group fund code: 198
Discount broker availability: *Fidelity, *Schwab, *White
Dividends paid: Income - declared and paid monthly; Capital gains - December
Portfolio turnover (3 yrs): 27%, 72%, 61%
Management fee: 0.45%
Expense ratio: 0.85% (year ending 5/31/97) (0.97% without waiver)

WESTCORE LONG-TERM BOND FUND ◆
(See first Westcore listing for data common to all funds)

Portfolio manager: Jerome R. Powers (1997)
Investment objective and policies: High long-term total return: income and capital growth. Invests primarily in investment grade debt obligations, and maintains a weighted average maturity of ten years or longer. May invest in U.S. dollar-denominated debt obligations of foreign issuers, have up to 15% of assets in illiquid securities and use futures and options for hedging purposes.
Year organized: 1988
Ticker symbol: WTLTX
Group fund code: 213
Discount broker availability: *Fidelity, *Schwab, *White
Dividends paid: Income - declared and paid monthly; Capital gains - December
Portfolio turnover (3 yrs): 28%, 33%, 25%
Management fee: 0.45%
Expense ratio: 0.95% (year ending 5/31/97) (1.15% without waiver)

WESTCORE MIDCO GROWTH FUND ◆
(See first Westcore listing for data common to all funds)

Portfolio manager: Todger Anderson (1986)
Investment objective and policies: Maximum long-term capital growth. Invests primarily in common stocks of medium-sized companies with market capitalizations of $100M to $3B. Up to 25% of assets may be in securities of foreign issuers, 15% in convertible securities rated below investment grade and 15% in illiquid securities. May use futures and options for hedging purposes.
Year organized: 1986
Ticker symbol: WTMGX
Group fund code: 200
Discount broker availability: *Fidelity, *Schwab, *White
Dividends paid: Income - December; Capital gains - December
Portfolio turnover (3 yrs): 61%, 63%, 50%
Management fee: 0.65%
Expense ratio: 1.14% (year ending 5/31/97)

WESTCORE SMALL-CAP OPPORTUNITY FUND ◆
(See first Westcore listing for data common to all funds)

Portfolio manager: Varilyn K. Schock (1993)
Investment objective and policies: Maximum long-term capital growth. Invests primarily in equity securities of small companies with market capitalizations of $1B or less. May invest in securities of foreign issuers without limit and have up to 15% of assets in convertible securities rated below investment grade and 15% in illiquid securities. May use futures and options for hedging purposes.
Year organized: 1993
Ticker symbol: WTSCX
Group fund code: 208
Discount broker availability: *Fidelity, *Schwab, *White
Dividends paid: Income - March, June, September, December; Capital gains - December

Portfolio turnover (3 yrs): 78%, 48%, 59%
Management fee: 1.00%
Expense ratio: 1.30% (year ending 5/31/97) (1.69% without waiver)

WESTON PORTFOLIOS - NEW CENTURY CAPITAL PORTFOLIO
Wellesley Office Park
20 William Street, Suite 330
Wellesley, MA 02181-4102
617-239-0445, 617-235-7055
fax 617-239-0741

Adviser: Weston Financial Group, Inc.
Portfolio managers: Wayne M. Grzecki (1995), Douglas A. Biggar (1989), Ronald A. Sugameli (1989)
Transfer agent: FPS Services, Inc.
Investment objective and policies: Capital growth; income secondary, both while managing risk. Invests primarily in other mutual funds which emphasize investments in growth stocks. Fund maintains varying levels of cash and cash equivalents depending on perceived market conditions. While it is not currently intended, the fund retains the right to invest directly in securities and fixed-income instruments if deemed necessary.
Year organized: 1989
Ticker symbol: NCCPX
Minimum purchase: Initial: $5,000, Subsequent: $100; IRA/Keogh: Initial: $1,000
Wire orders accepted: Yes
Deadline for same day wire purchase: 4 P.M.
Qualified for sale in: CO, CT, DC, FL, GA, HI, KS, ME, MD, MA, MN, NH, NJ, NY, NC, PA, RI, VA, WA, WY
Telephone redemptions: Yes, $5,000 minimum
Wire redemptions: Yes, $5,000 minimum, $9 fee
Letter redemptions: Signature guarantee required over $5,000
Telephone switching: With Weston New Century I
Number of switches permitted: 10 per year
Dividends paid: Income - December; Capital gains - December
Portfolio turnover (3 yrs): 196%, 214%, 206%
Shareholder services: IRA, Keogh, 401(k), 403(b), corporate retirement plans, systematic withdrawal plan min. bal. req. $10,000
Management fee: 1.00% first $100M, 0.75% over $100M
12b-1 distribution fee: 0.25%
Expense ratio: 1.52% (year ending 10/31/97)
IRA/Keogh fees: Annual $10

WESTON PORTFOLIOS - NEW CENTURY I PORTFOLIO
Wellesley Office Park
20 William Street, Suite 330
Wellesley, MA 02181-4102
617-239-0445, 617-235-7055
fax 617-239-0741

Adviser: Weston Financial Group, Inc.
Portfolio managers: Wayne M. Grzecki (1995), Douglas A. Biggar (1989), Ronald A. Sugameli (1989)
Transfer agent: FPS Services, Inc.
Investment objective and policies: Income; capital growth secondary, both while managing risk. Invests primarily in other mutual funds which emphasize investments in fixed-income securities, preferred stocks, and high dividend paying stocks. Fund maintains varying levels of cash and cash equivalents depending on perceived market conditions. While it is not currently intended, the fund retains the right to invest directly in securities and fixed-income instruments if deemed necessary.
Year organized: 1989
Ticker symbol: NCIPX
Minimum purchase: Initial: $5,000, Subsequent: $100; IRA/Keogh: Initial: $1,000
Wire orders accepted: Yes
Deadline for same day wire purchase: 4 P.M.
Qualified for sale in: CO, CT, DC, FL, GA, HI, ME, MD, MA, MN, NH, NJ, NY, NC, PA, RI, VA, WY
Telephone redemptions: Yes, $5,000 minimum
Wire redemptions: Yes, $5,000 minimum, $9 fee
Letter redemptions: Signature guarantee required over $5,000

Telephone switching: With Weston New Century Capital
Number of switches permitted: 10 per year
Dividends paid: Income - March, June, September, December; Capital gains - December
Portfolio turnover (3 yrs): 191%, 172%, 191%
Shareholder services: IRA, Keogh, 401(k), 403(b), corporate retirement plans, systematic withdrawal plan min. bal. req. $10,000
Management fee: 1.00% first $100M, 0.75% over $100M
12b-1 distribution fee: 0.25%
Expense ratio: 1.72% (year ending 10/31/97)
IRA/Keogh fees: Annual: $10

WESTPORT FUND ◆
253 Riverside Avenue
Westport, CT 06880-4816
888-593-7878, 203-227-3645
fax 513-629-2901, 203-226-6306

Adviser: Westport Advisers, LLC
Portfolio managers: Edmund H. Nicklin, Jr. (1997), Andrew J. Knuth (1997)
Transfer agent and administrator: Countrywide Fund Services, Inc.
Investment objective and policies: Total return: primarily capital appreciation, income secondarily. Invests in a broadly diversified portfolio of equity securities believed to be undervalued relative to the company's assets or its long-term earnings potential; the stock universe encompasses a broad range of company sizes, but the median market cap generally ranges from $1B to $5B. May invest without limit in sponsored and unsponsored ADRs, may invest up to 10% of assets in junk bonds, 15% in illiquid securities, and use options and futures for hedging purposes.
Year organized: 1997
Minimum purchase: Initial: $5,000, Subsequent: None; IRA: Initial: $2,000; Automatic investment plan: Initial: $1,000, Subsequent: $100
Wire orders accepted: Yes
Deadline for same day wire purchase: 4 P.M.
Qualified for sale in: All states
Telephone redemptions: Yes
Wire redemptions: Yes, $5,000 minimum, $9 fee
Letter redemptions: Signature guarantee required over $25,000
Dividends paid: Income - annually; Capital gains - annually
Shareholder services: IRA, electronic funds transfer (redemption only), systematic withdrawal plan min. bal. req. $10,000
Management fee: 0.90%
Administration fee: 0.125% first $50M to 0.075% over $150M ($12,000 minimum)
Shareholder services fee: Maximum of 0.25% (not currently imposed)
IRA/Keogh fees: Annual: $10

WESTPORT SMALL CAP FUND ◆
253 Riverside Avenue
Westport, CT 06880-4816
888-593-7878, 203-227-3645
fax 513-629-2901, 203-226-6306

Adviser: Westport Advisers, LLC
Portfolio managers: Edmund H. Nicklin, Jr. (1997), Andrew J. Knuth (1997)
Transfer agent and administrator: Countrywide Fund Services, Inc.
Investment objective and policies: Long-term capital appreciation. Invests at least 65% of assets in equity securities of companies with market capitalizations of less than $1B that are believed to be overlooked and undervalued. May invest without limit in sponsored and unsponsored ADRs, may invest up to 10% of assets in junk bonds, 15% in illiquid securities, and use options and futures for hedging purposes.
Year organized: 1997
Minimum purchase: Initial: $5,000, Subsequent: None; IRA: Initial: $2,000; Automatic investment plan: Initial: $1,000, Subsequent: $100
Wire orders accepted: Yes
Deadline for same day wire purchase: 4 P.M.
Qualified for sale in: All states
Telephone redemptions: Yes
Wire redemptions: Yes, $5,000 minimum, $9 fee

Letter redemptions: Signature guarantee required over $25,000
Dividends paid: Income - annually; Capital gains - annually
Shareholder services: IRA, electronic funds transfer (redemption only), systematic withdrawal plan min. bal. req. $10,000
Management fee: 1.00%
Administration fee: 0.125% first $50M to 0.075% over $150M ($12,000 minimum)
Shareholder services fee: Maximum of 0.25% (not currently imposed)
IRA/Keogh fees: Annual: $10

WESTWOOD FUNDS Retail Class
(Data common to all Westwood funds are shown below. See subsequent listings for data specific to individual funds.)

One Corporate Center
Rye, NY 10580-1434
800-422-3554, 914-921-5000
fax 914-921-5118
Internet: http://www.gabelli.com
e-mail: info@gabelli.com, or westw1@aol.com

Shareholder service hours: Full service: M-F 9 A.M.-8 P.M. EST; After hours service: prices, yields, account balances, messages, news and views, prospectuses
Adviser: Gabelli Advisers, LLC
Sub-adviser: Westwood Management Corp.
Distributor: Gabelli & Co., Inc.
Transfer agent: Boston Financial Data Services, Inc.
Sales restrictions: Certain of the Westwood funds also have a "Service" class, a different series which are sold with a 4% load through dealers. These shares HAVE LOADS. We only discuss the no-load "Retail" class here.
Minimum purchase: Initial: $1,000, Subsequent: None; Automatic investment plan: Initial: None, Subsequent: $100
Wire orders accepted: Yes
Deadline for same day wire purchase: 4 P.M.
Qualified for sale in: All states
Telephone redemptions: Yes
Wire redemptions: Yes, $1,000 minimum
Letter redemptions: Signature guarantee required
Telephone switching: With other Westwood funds, and Gabelli funds (some of which have loads)
Number of switches permitted: Unlimited
Shareholder services: IRA, SEP-IRA, electronic funds transfer, systematic withdrawal plan min. bal. req. $10,000
12b-1 distribution fee: 0.25%
IRA fees: Annual: $10 per social security number (waived for balances over $25,000)

WESTWOOD BALANCED FUND
(See first Westwood listing for data common to all funds)

Portfolio managers: Susan M. Byrne (1991), Patricia R. Fraze (1991)
Investment objective and policies: High total return: capital growth and current income, consistent with prudent investment risk. Invests 30% to 70% of assets in a diversified portfolio of equity securities of companies of all sizes thought to have above average growth prospects, and 30% to 70% in debt securities. Allocations are adjusted to reflect changes in market conditions. At least 25% of assets are in fixed-income senior securities, up to 25% may be in securities of foreign issuers, and up to 10% may be in junk bonds. May use futures and options in an effort to enhance income and for hedging purposes.
Year organized: 1991
Ticker symbol: WEBAX
Discount broker availability: *Fidelity, *Schwab, *Siebert, *White
Dividends paid: Income - March, June, September, December; Capital gains - December
Portfolio turnover (3 yrs): 110%, 111%, 133%
Management fee: 0.75%
Expense ratio: 1.28% (year ending 9/31/97) (1.36% without waiver)

WESTWOOD EQUITY FUND
(See first Westwood listing for data common to all funds)

Portfolio manager: Susan M. Byrne (1987)
Investment objective and policies: Capital appreciation; current income secondary. Invests at least 65% of assets in common stocks and securities convertible into common stocks of companies of all sizes over $100M that are thought to have above average growth prospects. May have up to 25% of assets in securities of foreign issuers and up to 10% in junk bonds. May use futures and options in an effort to enhance income and for hedging purposes.
Year organized: 1987
Ticker symbol: WESWX
Discount broker availability: *Fidelity, *Schwab, *Siebert, *White
Dividends paid: Income - December; Capital gains - December
Portfolio turnover (3 yrs): 61%, 106%, 107%
Management fee: 1.00%
Expense ratio: 1.53% (year ending 9/31/97) (1.59% without waiver)

WESTWOOD INTERMEDIATE BOND FUND
(See first Westwood listing for data common to all funds)

Portfolio manager: Douglas Lehman (1996)
Investment objective and policies: High total return: capital growth and current income consistent with maintenance of principal and liquidity. Invests primarily in investment grade domestic and foreign government and corporate debt securities. While there is no restrictions regarding the duration or maturity of any security, the portfolio generally maintains a dollar-weighted average maturity of three to ten years. Up to 25% of assets may be in securities of foreign issuers. May use futures and options in an effort to enhance income and for hedging purposes.
Year organized: 1991
Ticker symbol: WEIBX
Discount broker availability: *Fidelity, *Schwab, *Siebert, *White
Dividends paid: Income - declared daily, paid monthly; Capital gains - December
Portfolio turnover (3 yrs): 628%, 309%, 165%
Management fee: 0.60%
Expense ratio: 1.11% (year ending 9/31/97) (1.70% without waiver)

WESTWOOD REALTY FUND
(See first Westwood listing for data common to all funds)

Lead portfolio manager: Susan M. Byrne (1997)
Investment objective and policies: Long-term capital appreciation and current income. Invests at least 65% of assets in a geographically diversified portfolio of REITs and real estate operating companies with market capitalizations of no less than $50M at the time of investment. May also invest in real estate oriented firms as well, such as construction companies. May purchase equity, mortgage or hybrid REITs, and other types of real estate securities including common and preferred stocks, limited partnerships, and convertible securities. Up to 25% of assets may be in foreign issues, and up to 35% in domestic and foreign debt obligations. May use a variety of derivatives in an effort to enhance performance and for hedging purposes.
Year organized: 1997
Ticker symbol: WESRX
Discount broker availability: *Fidelity, *Schwab, *Siebert, *White
Dividends paid: Income - annually; Capital gains - annually
Management fee: 1.00%

WESTWOOD SMALL CAP EQUITY FUND
(See first Westwood listing for data common to all funds)

Portfolio manager: Lynda J. Calkin (1997)
Investment objective and policies: Long-term capital appreciation. Invests primarily in equity securities of companies with market capitalizations below $1B at the time of investment, including those without three years of operating history. May also invest up to 35% of assets in equities without regard to market capitalizations. May invest up to 25% of assets in foreign issues, either directly or through depositary receipts such as ADRs, and up to 35% of assets in foreign or domestic government or corporate debt obligations. May invest up to 10% of assets in junk bonds, and up to 15% in illiquid securities. May use a variety of derivatives in an effort to enhance performance and for hedging purposes.
Year organized: 1997
Ticker symbol: WESCX
Discount broker availability: *Fidelity, *Schwab, *Siebert, *White
Dividends paid: Income - annually; Capital gains - annually
Portfolio turnover (1 yr): 146%
Management fee: 1.00%
Expense ratio: 1.89% (6 months ending 9/30/97) (2.45% without waiver)

WHITE OAK GROWTH STOCK FUND ◆
c/o Oak Associates Funds
P.O. Box 419009
Kansas City, MO 64141-6009
888-462-5386
fax 330-668-2901
Internet: http://www.oakassociates.com

Adviser: Oak Associates, Ltd.
Administrator: SEI Fund Resources
Portfolio manager: James D. Oelschlager (1992)
Transfer agent: DST Systems, Inc.
Investment objective and policies: Long-term capital growth. Invests as fully as practicable in a diversified portfolio of common stocks of companies with market capitalizations of more than $1B. May also invest in warrants and rights, debt securities, convertible preferred stocks and ADRs. Up to 15% of assets may be in illiquid securities.
Year organized: 1992 (name changed from Advisors' Inner Circle - White Oak Growth Stock in 1996)
Ticker symbol: WOGSX
Minimum purchase: Initial: $2,000, Subsequent: $50; Automatic investment plan: Subsequent: $25
Wire orders accepted: Yes
Deadline for same day wire purchase: 4 P.M.
Discount broker availability: *Fidelity, *Schwab, *White
Qualified for sale in: All states
Telephone redemptions: Yes
Wire redemptions: Yes, $10 fee
Letter redemptions: Signature guarantee not required
Telephone switching: With Pin Oak Aggressive Stock Fund
Number of switches permitted: Unlimited
Dividends paid: Income - March, June, September, December; Capital gains - December
Portfolio turnover (3 yrs): 8%, 8%, 22%
Shareholder services: IRA, systematic withdrawal plan min. bal. req. $25,000
Management fee: 0.74%
Administration fee: 0.20
Expense ratio: 0.98% (year ending 10/31/97) (1.14% without waiver)
IRA fees: Annual $25

WILLIAM BLAIR MUTUAL FUNDS ◆
(Data common to all William Blair funds are shown below. See subsequent listings for data specific to individual funds.)

222 West Adams Street
Chicago, IL 60606
800-742-7272, 800-635-2886
312-364-8000, fax 312-236-1497
Internet: http://www.wmblair.com
e-mail: dn1@wmblair.com

Shareholder service hours: Full service: M-F 8:30 A.M.-4:30 P.M. CST; After hours service: prices, yields, prospectuses
Adviser: William Blair & Co., LLC
Transfer agent: State Street Bank & Trust Co.

Minimum purchase: Initial: $5,000, Subsequent: $1,000 ($1 for MM); IRA: Initial: $2,000; Automatic investment plan: Subsequent: $250 (new minimums took effect 1/96. Prior shareholders exempt.)
Wire orders accepted: Yes
Deadline for same day wire purchase: 4 P.M. (2 P.M. for MM)
Qualified for sale in: All states
Wire redemptions: Yes
Letter redemptions: Signature guarantee required over $5,000
Telephone switching: With other William Blair funds
Number of switches permitted: 4 per year
Shareholder services: IRA, SEP-IRA, corporate retirement plans, systematic withdrawal plan min. bal. req. $5,000
IRA fees: Initial $5, Annual $15, Closing $10

WILLIAM BLAIR MUTUAL FUND - GROWTH FUND ◆
(See first William Blair listing for data common to all funds)

Portfolio managers: Rocky Barber (1993), Mark A. Fuller III (1993)
Investment objective and policies: Long-term capital appreciation. Invests primarily in equity securities of well managed companies in growing industries - small, rapid growth companies, medium-sized companies of emerging investment quality and large well managed companies in industries growing faster than the GNP. May, however, invest in convertibles as well. May invest without limit in foreign issues.
Year organized: 1946 (2-1 split, 4/24/84) (name changed from Growth Industry Shares in May 1991)
Ticker symbol: WBGSX
Group fund code: 268
Discount broker availability: *Fidelity, *Schwab, *Siebert, *White
Dividends paid: Income - July, December; Capital gains - December
Portfolio turnover (3 yrs): 43%, 32%, 46%
Management fee: 0.75%
Expense ratio: 0.79% (year ending 12/31/96)

WILLIAM BLAIR MUTUAL FUND - INCOME FUND ◆
(See first William Blair listing for data common to all funds)

Portfolio manager: Bentley M. Myer (1991)
Investment objective and policies: High current income consistent with capital preservation. Invests primarily in a diversified portfolio of high grade intermediate-term debt securities - U.S. dollar denominated debt rated A- or better, obligations of or guaranteed by the U.S. Government, its agencies or instrumentalities, collateralized obligations and commercial paper. Portfolio maintains a dollar-weighted average maturity of three to seven years, and a duration of two to five years.
Year organized: 1990
Ticker symbol: WBRRX
Group fund code: 213
Discount broker availability: *Fidelity, *Schwab, *Siebert, *White
Dividends paid: Income - declared daily, paid monthly; Capital gains - December
Portfolio turnover (3 yrs): 66%, 54%, 63%
Management fee: 0.25% first $250M, 0.20% over $250M + 5.0% of the gross income earned
Expense ratio: 0.70% (year ending 12/31/96)

WILLIAM BLAIR MUTUAL FUND - INTERNATIONAL GROWTH FUND ◆
(See first William Blair listing for data common to all funds)

Portfolio manager: William G. Greig (1996)
Investment objective and policies: Long-term capital appreciation. Invests primarily in common and convertible stocks of companies domiciled outside the U.S. May also invest in ADRs, EDRs and GDRs. May use forward currency exchange contracts to protect against changes in foreign exchange rates, and foreign currency futures for hedging purposes. Normally

invests in at least six countries, but may have as much as 50% of assets in companies from a single developed country. May invest up to 30% of assets in emerging markets.
Year organized: 1992
Ticker symbol: WBIGX
Group fund code: 317
Discount broker availability: *Fidelity, *Schwab, *Siebert, *White
Dividends paid: Income - July, December; Capital gains - December
Portfolio turnover (3 yrs): 89%, 77%, 40%
Management fee: 1.10% first $250M, 0.95% over $250M
Expense ratio: 1.44% (year ending 12/31/96)

WILLIAM BLAIR MUTUAL FUND - READY RESERVES FUND ◆
(See first William Blair listing for data common to all funds)

Portfolio manager: Bentley M. Myer (1991)
Investment objective and policies: Maximum current income consistent with capital preservation. Invests exclusively in high quality money market instruments.
Year organized: 1988
Ticker symbol: WBRXX
Group fund code: 209
Telephone redemptions: Yes
Check redemption: $500 minimum
Dividends paid: Income - declared daily, paid monthly
Management fee: 0.625% first $250M to 0.55% over $2.5B
Expense ratio: 0.71% (year ending 12/31/96)

WILLIAM BLAIR MUTUAL FUND - VALUE DISCOVERY FUND ◆
(See first William Blair listing for data common to all funds)

Portfolio managers: Glen A. Kleczka (1996), Capucine Price (1996), David Mitchell (1996)
Investment objective and policies: Long-term capital appreciation. Invests primarily in common stock of small companies perceived to be undervalued. May also invest in preferred and convertible securities if they meet the investment criteria of management. May invest up to 5% of assets in foreign issues and ADRs, up to 15% of assets in REITs and up to 15% of assets in illiquid securities.
Year organized: 1996
Ticker symbol: WBVDX
Group fund code: 161
Discount broker availability: Fidelity, *Schwab, White
Dividends paid: Income - July, December; Capital gains - December
Management fee: 1.15%

WILSHIRE TARGET FUNDS
(Data common to all Wilshire Target funds are shown below. See subsequent listings for data specific to individual funds.)

1299 Ocean Avenue, Suite 700
Santa Monica, CA 90401-1085
888-200-6796, 310-451-3051
fax 310-458-3920
Internet: http://www.wilfunds.com

Adviser: Wilshire Assocs., Inc.
Portfolio manager: Thomas D. Stevens (1992)
Transfer agent and administrator: First Data Investor Services Group, Inc.
Special sales restrictions: Information here reflects "Investor" shares class of funds only.
Minimum purchase: Initial: $2,500, Subsequent: $100; IRA: Initial: $750
Wire orders accepted: Yes
Deadline for same day wire purchase: 4 P.M.
Telephone redemptions: Yes, $1,000 minimum
Wire redemptions: Yes, $1,000 minimum
Letter redemptions: Signature guarantee required

Telephone switch privileges: With the same class shares of other Wilshire Target portfolios, $500 minimum
Number of switches permitted: Unlimited
Shareholder services: IRA, SEP-IRA, Keogh, 403(b), automatic investment plan, electronic funds transfer (purchase only)
Management fee: 0.25%
Administration fee: 0.15% first $1B to 0.08% over $5B ($25,000 minimum per portfolio)
12b-1 distribution fee: Maximum of 0.25%
IRA fees: Annual $10

WILSHIRE TARGET FUNDS - LARGE COMPANY GROWTH PORTFOLIO
(See first Wilshire listing for data common to all funds)

Investment objective and policies: Investment results comparable to the performance of the companies from the Wilshire 5000 Index classified by Wilshire as large capitalization, growth companies. Invests in a representative mix of Wilshire 5000 companies with capitalizations of $1.2B or more and above average earnings or sales growth and relatively high P/E ratios. May use stock index futures for hedging purposes.
Year organized: 1992
Ticker symbol: DTLGX
Discount broker availability: Fidelity, Schwab, *White
Dividends paid: Income - annually; Capital gains - annually
Portfolio turnover (3 yrs): 43%, 44%, 30%
Expense ratio: 0.81% (year ending 8/31/97) (1.09% without waiver)

WILSHIRE TARGET FUNDS - LARGE COMPANY VALUE PORTFOLIO
(See first Wilshire listing for data common to all funds)

Investment objective and policies: Investment results comparable to the performance of the companies from the Wilshire 5000 Index classified by Wilshire as large capitalization, value companies. Invests in a representative mix of Wilshire 5000 companies with capitalizations of $1.2B or more and above average dividends in relation to price and relatively low P/E ratios. May use stock index futures for hedging purposes.
Year organized: 1992
Ticker symbol: DTLVX
Discount broker availability: Fidelity, Schwab, *White
Dividends paid: Income - annually; Capital gains - annually
Portfolio turnover (3 yrs): 65%, 56%, 58%
Expense ratio: 0.91% (year ending 8/31/97) (1.18% without waiver)

WILSHIRE TARGET FUNDS - SMALL COMPANY GROWTH PORTFOLIO
(See first Wilshire listing for data common to all funds)

Investment objective and policies: Investment results comparable to the performance of the companies from the Wilshire 5000 Index classified by Wilshire as small capitalization, growth companies. Invests in a representative mix of Wilshire 5000 companies with capitalizations less than $1.2B, above average earnings or sales growth, and relatively high P/E ratios. May use stock index futures for hedging purposes.
Year organized: 1992
Ticker symbol: DTSGX
Discount broker availability: Fidelity, Schwab, *White
Dividends paid: Income - annually; Capital gains - annually
Portfolio turnover (3 yrs): 105%, 87%, 111%
Expense ratio: 1.22% (year ending 8/31/97) (1.45% without waiver)

WILSHIRE TARGET FUNDS - SMALL COMPANY VALUE PORTFOLIO
(See first Wilshire listing for data common to all funds)

Investment objective and policies: Investment results comparable to the performance of the companies from the Wilshire 5000 Index classified by Wilshire as small capitalization, value companies. Invests in a representative mix of Wilshire 5000 companies with capitalizations of less than $1.2B, above average dividends in relation to price, and relatively low P/E ratios. May use stock index futures for hedging purposes.
Year organized: 1992
Ticker symbol: DTSVX
Discount broker availability: Fidelity, Schwab, *White
Dividends paid: Income - annually; Capital gains - annually
Portfolio turnover (3 yrs): 105%, 81%, 86%
Expense ratio: 0.86% (year ending 8/31/97) (1.15% without waiver)

WOMEN'S EQUITY MUTUAL FUND

850 Montgomery Street, Suite 100
San Francisco, CA 94133
800-385-7003, 415-547-9135

Adviser: Pro-Conscience Funds, Inc.
Sub-adviser: U.S. Trust Co. of Boston
Administrator: Investment Company Administration Corp.
Portfolio managers: Linda C.Y. Pei (1993), Maria McCormack (1997)
Transfer agent: American Data Services, Inc.
Investment objective and policies: Long-term capital growth. Invests primarily in equity securities of companies that satisfy certain social responsibility criteria and are proactive towards women's social and economic equality. Considerations include high quality products or services, fair employee relations, environmental sensitivity, sensitivity to minority issues, and contributions to the community. Proactivity considerations include progress in promoting women into management positions, having an above average percentage of women in its work force, having a woman chief executive, having benefit programs that address work/family concerns, chooses women-owned businesses as vendors or service providers, provides career development and training programs for women employees and promotes positive images of women in its product advertising. May have up to 20% of assets in securities of foreign issuers, and use foreign currency transactions for hedging purposes. May sell short.
Year organized: 1993
Ticker symbol: FEMMX
Minimum purchase: Initial: $1,000, Subsequent: $100; IRA: Initial $500; Automatic investment plan: Subsequent: $50
Wire orders accepted: Yes
Deadline for same day wire purchase: 4 P.M.
Discount broker availability: *Fidelity, Schwab, *Siebert, *White
Qualified for sale in: All states except AL, AR, DE, HI, IL, KY, LA, MS, NV, NH, OK, VT
Telephone redemptions: Yes
Wire redemptions: Yes, $1,000 minimum
Letter redemptions: Signature guarantee required
Dividends paid: Income - March, December; Capital gains - December
Portfolio turnover (3 yrs): 51%, 121%, 706%
Shareholder services: IRA, electronic funds transfer, systematic withdrawal plan min. bal. req. $10,000
Maintenance fee: $15 per year for automatic distribution service on IRAs
Management fee: 1.00%
Administration fee: 0.20% first $50M to 0.05% over $150M ($30,000 minimum)
12b-1 distribution fee: 0.25%
Expense ratio: 1.50% (year ending 3/31/97) (4.09% without waiver)
IRA fees: Annual $12, Closing $15

WORKING ASSETS MONEY MARKET PORTFOLIO

One Harbor Place, Suite 525
Portsmouth, NH 03801
800-223-7010, 603-436-5152
fax 603-433-4209
Internet: http://www.efund.com
e-mail: welcome@efund.com

Adviser: Citizens Advisers
Sub-adviser: GMG/Seneca Capital Management, LLC
Portfolio manager: Laura Povost (1997)
Transfer agent: PFPC Inc.
Investment objective and policies: High income consistent with liquidity and safety of capital, and concern with the social impact of investments. Invests in U.S. dollar denominated money market instruments. Fund favors investments that support housing, education, farming, small business, and energy conservation. It avoids investments in firms that pollute the environment, manufacture weapons, practice discrimination or invest in nations controlled by repressive regimes. A non-traditional fund, Working Assets offers an electronic debit card for instant access, and refunds 1% of every debit card purchase to the fund's portfolio to boost the rate of return.
Year organized: 1983
Ticker symbol: WKAXX
Special sales restrictions: Must hold a Citizens Access Account and all shareholders must maintain some form of direct deposit, automatic investment plan. Individual investors may only hold a maximum balance of $15,000 unless their monthly salary is higher.
Minimum purchase: Initial: $1,000, Subsequent: $50; Automatic Investment Plan: direct payroll deposit, $500 for all others
Wire orders accepted: Yes
Deadline for same day wire purchase: 2:30 P.M.
Discount broker availability: Schwab
Qualified for sale in: All states
Telephone redemptions: Yes
Wire redemptions: Yes, $10 fee
Letter redemptions: Signature guarantee required
ATM redemptions: No minimum, $0.65/transaction
Check redemptions: No minimum, $0.50 per check fee
Telephone switch privileges: With Citizens Trust portfolios and the Muir California Tax-Free Income Fund
Number of switches permitted: Unlimited
Dividends paid: Income - declared daily, paid monthly
Shareholder services: IRA, SEP-IRA, 403(b), electronic funds transfer, systematic withdrawal plan min. bal. req. $10,000
Maintenance fee: $3/quarter for balances below $2,500
Management fee: 0.35%
12b-1 distribution fee: 0.25%
Expense ratio: 1.25% (year ending 6/30/97) (1.39% without waiver)
IRA fees: Annual $10, $5 additional account (maximum $15)

WPG FUNDS ◆
(Data common to all WPG funds are shown below. See subsequent listings for data specific to individual funds.)

One New York Plaza
New York, NY 10004
800-223-3332, 212-908-9582
fax 212-908-9867

Shareholder service hours: Full service: M-F 9 A.M.-5 P.M. EST; After hours service: prices, prospectuses
Adviser: Weiss, Peck & Greer, LLC
Transfer agent: First Data Investor Services Group, Inc.
Minimum purchase: Initial: $2,500, Subsequent: $100; IRA/Keogh: Initial: $250, Subsequent: None (exceptions noted): Automatic investment plan: Subsequent: $50 (not available for Growth or Quantitative funds)
Wire orders accepted: Yes
Deadline for same day wire purchase: 4 P.M. (12 NN for money market funds)

Qualified for sale in: All states
Letter redemptions: Signature guarantee not required
Telephone switching: With other WPG Funds
Number of switches permitted: 6 per year
Shareholder services: IRA, SEP-IRA, Keogh, 401(k), corporate retirement plans, systematic withdrawal plan min. bal. req. $10,000 (except Growth and Quantitative Funds)
12b-1 distribution fee: Maximum of 0.25% (not currently imposed)
IRA/Keogh fees: Annual $15, Initial $10, Closing $10

WEISS, PECK & GREER INTERNATIONAL FUND ◆
(See first WPG listing for data common to all funds)

Sub-adviser: Hill Samuel Investment Management, Ltd. (a wholly owned subsidiary of Lloyds Investment Management Ltd.)
Portfolio manager: David Kiddie (1996)
Investment objective and policies: Long-term capital growth; current income secondary. Invests primarily in a diversifed portfolio of common stocks and equity-related securities of established larger capitalization companies who are located outside of the U.S. and whose shares are traded primarily outside the U.S. as well. Fund generally invests in at least three countries, including emerging markets. May use ADRs, EDRs and IDRs in addition to direct investment. May also invest in fixed-income securities of foreign governments or companies. Fund uses a variety of derivative instruments in an effort to enhance returns and for hedging purposes.
Year organized: 1989
Ticker symbol: WPGIX
Discount broker availability: *Fidelity, Schwab, Siebert, *White
Dividends paid: Income - March, June, September, December; Capital gains - December
Portfolio turnover (3 yrs): 55%, 85%, 56%
Management fee: 0.50% first $15M to 1.00% over $20M
Expense ratio: 1.89% (year ending 12/31/97)

WPG CORE BOND FUND ◆
(See first WPG listing for data common to all funds)

Portfolio manager: Daniel S. Vandivort (1995)
Investment objective and policies: High current return, consistent with capital preservation. Invests at least 80% of assets in investment grade corporate and government debt securities. Portfolio maintains an average maturity of three to twelve years. Fund may use futures and options for hedging purposes.
Year organized: 1986 (name changed from Government Securities Fund 1/20/98; policy changed to extend maturity and include corporate bonds. Past performance may be misleading.)
Ticker symbol: WPGVX
Minimum purchase: Initial: $25,000, Subsequent: $5,000
Discount broker availability: *Fidelity, Schwab, Siebert, *White
Dividends paid: Income - declared daily, paid monthly; Capital gains - December
Portfolio turnover (3 yrs): 330%, 333%, 375%
Management fee: 0.60% first $300M to 0.50% over $500M
Expense ratio: 0.86% (year ending 12/31/97)

WPG GOVERNMENT MONEY MARKET FUND ◆
(See first WPG listing for data common to all funds)

Portfolio managers: Daniel S. Vandivort (1996), Thomas J. Girard (1996)
Investment objective and policies: High current income consistent with preservation of capital and liquidity. Invests in short-term money market securities issued or guaranteed by the U.S. Government, its agencies, or instrumentalities, and repurchase agreements collateralized by such securities, maturing in one year or less.
Year organized: 1988 (name changed from WPG Short-Term Income Fund on 1/2/92)

Ticker symbol: WPSXX
Check redemptions: $500 minimum
Dividends paid: Income - declared daily, paid monthly
Management fee: 0.50% first $500M to 0.35% over $1.5B
Expense ratio: 0.81% (year ending 12/31/97)

WPG GROWTH FUND ◆
(See first WPG listing for data common to all funds)

Portfolio manager: Adam Starr (1998)
Investment objective and policies: Maximum capital appreciation. Invests at least 65% of assets in an aggressively managed, diversified portfolio of common stocks or convertibles of emerging growth companies with market capitalizations under $1B, and special situations. May invest without limit in securities of foreign issuers, and use options and futures for hedging purposes.
Year organized: 1985
Ticker symbol: WPGRX
Special sales restrictions: Fund is designed especially for institutional investors but is available to all investors.
Minimum purchase: Initial: $250,000, Subsequent: $25,000
Discount broker availability: *Fidelity, Schwab, Siebert, *White
Dividends paid: Income - December; Capital gains - December
Portfolio turnover (3 yrs): 84%, 122%, 119%
Management fee: 0.75%
Expense ratio: 1.12% (year ending 12/31/97)

WPG GROWTH AND INCOME FUND ◆
(See first WPG listing for data common to all funds)

Portfolio manager: A. Roy Knutsen (1992)
Investment objective and policies: Long-term capital growth, reasonable current income, and an increase of future income. Invests primarily in a diversified portfolio of income producing common and preferred stocks, and convertible securities of companies believed to offer better than average prospects of growing faster than the U.S. economy in general. May also invest up to 35% of assets in junk bonds. May invest in securities of foreign issuers without limit, and use a variety of derivative instruments for hedging purposes.
Year organized: 1979 (WPG Fund prior to 1/1/91, prior to that ADV Fund, prior to that American Dualvest—dual purpose fund)
Ticker symbol: WPGFX
Discount broker availability: *Fidelity, Schwab, Siebert, *White
Dividends paid: Income - March, June, September, December; Capital gains - December
Portfolio turnover (3 yrs): 70%, 72%, 79%
Management fee: 0.75%
Expense ratio: 1.06% (year ending 12/31/97)

WPG INTERMEDIATE MUNICIPAL BOND FUND ◆
(See first WPG listing for data common to all funds)

Portfolio managers: Arthur L. Schwartz (1993), S. Blake Miller (1993)
Investment objective and policies: High current income exempt from regular federal income tax, consistent with relative stability of principal. Invests at least 80% of assets in a diversified portfolio of investment grade municipal securities. Portfolio maintains a dollar-weighted average maturity of four to ten years. May invest in securities subject to AMT tax treatment.
Year organized: 1993
Ticker symbol: WPGMX
Discount broker availability: *Fidelity, *Schwab (only through financial advisers), Siebert, *White
Dividends paid: Income - declared daily, paid monthly; Capital gains - December
Portfolio turnover (3 yrs): 40%, 44%, 51%
Management fee: 0.00% under $17M, 0.50% over $17M
Expense ratio: 0.85% (year ending 12/31/97)

WPG QUANTITATIVE EQUITY FUND ◆
(See first WPG listing for data common to all funds)

Portfolio manager: Daniel J. Cardell (1996)
Investment objective and policies: Results that exceed the performance of publicly traded stocks in the aggregate as represented by the capitalization weighted S&P 500 Index. Invests in an "efficient" portfolio of stocks believed to maximize expected return for any risk level or minimize risk level for any expected return. Uses a proprietary computer model to select stocks from a list of 1,000 including the S&P 500 companies and other large cap concerns. May invest up to 35% of assets in short-term debt obligations, and use options and futures for hedging purposes.
Year organized: 1993
Ticker symbol: WPGQX
Minimum purchase: Initial: $5,000, Subsequent: $500; IRA/Keogh: Initial: $250, Subsequent: None
Discount broker availability: *Fidelity, *Schwab (only through financial advisers), Siebert, *White
Dividends paid: Income - December; Capital gains - December
Portfolio turnover (3 yrs): 78%, 61%, 26%
Management fee: 0.75%
Expense ratio: 1.03% (year ending 12/31/97)

WPG TAX FREE MONEY MARKET FUND ◆
(See first WPG listing for data common to all funds)

Portfolio managers: Janet A. Fiorenza (1988), Arthur L. Schwartz (1988)
Investment objective and policies: High current income exempt from regular federal income tax, consistent with preservation of capital and liquidity. Invests in high quality, short-term tax exempt money market instruments.
Year organized: 1988
Ticker symbol: WPTXX
Check redemptions: $500 minimum
Dividends paid: Income - declared daily, paid monthly
Management fee: 0.50% first $500M to 0.35% over $1.5B
Expense ratio: 0.74% (year ending 12/31/97)

WPG TUDOR FUND ◆
(See first WPG listing for data common to all funds)

Portfolio manager: Adam Starr (1998)
Investment objective and policies: Capital appreciation. Invests in a diversified portfolio of common stocks or equity related securities of companies believed to offer exceptional capital appreciation, including unseasoned companies (i.e., those with less than three years operating history.) In addition, the fund may invest in "special situations," those in which unusual and possibly unique developments may create a special opportunity for significant returns. May use a variety of derivative instruments in an effort to enhance returns and for hedging purposes.
Year organized: 1969
Ticker symbol: TUDRX
Discount broker availability: *Fidelity, Schwab, Siebert, *White
Dividends paid: Income - September; Capital gains - December
Portfolio turnover (3 yrs): 106%, 105%, 123%
Management fee: 0.90% first $300M to 0.75% over $500M
Expense ratio: 1.24% (year ending 12/31/97)

THE WRIGHT MANAGED FUNDS
(Data common to all Wright Managed funds are shown below. See subsequent listings for data specific to individual funds.)

1000 Lafayette Boulevard
Bridgeport, CT 06604
800-225-6265, 800-232-0013
617-482-8260
recorded services 800-888-9471
Internet: http://www.wisi.com
e-mail: funds@wisi.com

Shareholder service hours: Full service M-F 8:30 A.M.-5:30 P.M. EST; After hours service: prices, messages, prospectuses

Adviser: Wright Investors' Service, Inc.
Administrator: Eaton Vance Management
Portfolio managers: Team managed
Transfer agent: First Data Investor Services Group
Minimum purchase: Initial: $1,000, Subsequent: None; Automatic investment plan: Initial: $50, Subsequent: $50
Wire orders accepted: Yes
Deadline for same day wire purchase: 4 P.M. (3 P.M. for MM)
Qualified for sale in: All states
Telephone redemptions: Yes
Wire redemptions: Yes
Letter redemptions: Signature guarantee required
Telephone switching: With other Wright Funds, $1,000 minimum
Number of switches permitted: 4 round trips per year
Shareholder services: IRA, Keogh, 401(k), corporate retirement plans, systematic withdrawal plan min. bal. req. $10,000
Administration fee: 0.10% first $100M (0.20% for equity funds. 0.07% for U.S. Treasury MF) to 0.02% over $500M (all funds)
12b-1 distribution fee: Maximum of 0.20% (0.25% for Equifunds, n/app to MM)
IRA/Keogh fees: Annual $10

WRIGHT CURRENT INCOME FUND
(See first Wright listing for data common to all funds)

Investment objective and policies: High current income. Invests primarily in debt obligations issued or guaranteed by the U.S. Government or its agencies or instrumentalities, mortgage-related securities of governmental or federally chartered corporate issuers, and corporate debt securities rated A or better.
Year organized: 1987
Ticker symbol: WCIFX
Group fund code: 10
Discount broker availability: *Fidelity, *Schwab, *Siebert, *White
Dividends paid: Income - declared daily, paid monthly; Capital gains - December
Portfolio turnover (3 yrs): 3%, 9%, 26%
Management fee: 0.40% first $100M to 0.33% over $1B
Expense ratio: 0.89% (year ending 12/31/97)

WRIGHT EQUIFUND - BELGIUM/LUXEMBOURG
(See first Wright listing for data common to all funds)

Investment objective and policies: Total return: price appreciation and income. Invests in a broad based portfolio of equity securities from the publicly traded companies in the National Equity Index for their nation. Only securities with adequate public information will be considered acceptable.
Year organized: 1994
Ticker symbol: WEBEX
Group fund code: 14
Discount broker availability: *Fidelity, *Schwab, *Siebert, *White
Redemption fee: 1.5% for shares held less than 30 days, payable to the fund
Dividends paid: Income - December; Capital gains - December
Portfolio turnover (3 yrs): 8%, 34%, 38%
Management fee: 0.75% first $500M to 0.68% over $1B
Expense ratio: 2.17% (year ending 12/31/97) (2.60% without waiver)

WRIGHT EQUIFUND - BRITAIN
(See first Wright listing for data common to all funds)

Investment objective and policies: Total return: price appreciation and income. Invests in a broad based portfolio of equity securities from the publicly traded companies in the National Equity Index for their nation. Only securities with adequate public information will be considered acceptable.
Year organized: 1995
Ticker symbol: WEGBX
Group fund code: 31
Discount broker availability: *Fidelity, *Schwab, *Siebert, *White

Redemption fee: 1.5% for shares held less than 30 days, payable to the fund
Dividends paid: Income - December; Capital gains - December
Portfolio turnover (3 yrs): 78%, 93%, 42%
Management fee: 0.75% first $500M to 0.68% over $1B
Expense ratio: 2.26% (year ending 12/31/97) (6.39% without waiver)

WRIGHT EQUIFUND - GERMANY
(See first Wright listing for data common to all funds)

Investment objective and policies: Total return: price appreciation and income. Invests in a broad based portfolio of equity securities from the publicly traded companies in the National Equity Index for their nation. Only securities with adequate public information will be considered acceptable.
Year organized: 1995
Ticker symbol: WEDEX
Group fund code: 17
Discount broker availability: *Fidelity, *Schwab, *Siebert, *White
Redemption fee: 1.5% for shares held less than 30 days, payable to the fund
Dividends paid: Income - December; Capital gains - December
Portfolio turnover (3 yrs): 8%, 77%, 18%
Management fee: 0.75% first $500M to 0.68% over $1B
Expense ratio: 2.28% (year ending 12/31/97) (2.39% without waiver)

WRIGHT EQUIFUND - HONG KONG/CHINA
(See first Wright listing for data common to all funds)

Investment objective and policies: Total return: price appreciation and income. Invests in a broad based portfolio of equity securities from the publicly traded companies in the National Equity Index for their nation. Only securities with adequate public information will be considered acceptable.
Year organized: 1990 (name changed from just Hong Kong 7/31/97)
Ticker symbol: WEHKX
Group fund code: 21
Discount broker availability: *Fidelity, *Schwab, *Siebert, *White
Redemption fee: 1.5% for shares held less than 30 days, payable to the fund
Dividends paid: Income - December; Capital gains - December
Portfolio turnover (3 yrs): 56%, 65%, 100%
Management fee: 0.75% first $500M to 0.68% over $1B
Expense ratio: 1.96% (year ending 12/31/97)

WRIGHT EQUIFUND - ITALIAN
(See first Wright listing for data common to all funds)

Investment objective and policies: Total return: price appreciation and income. Invests in a broad based portfolio of equity securities from the publicly traded companies in the National Equity Index for their nation. Only securities with adequate public information will be considered acceptable.
Year organized: 1996
Discount broker availability: *Fidelity, *Schwab, *Siebert, *White
Redemption fee: 1.5% for shares held less than 30 days, payable to the fund
Dividends paid: Income - December; Capital gains - December
Portfolio turnover (2 yrs): 10%, 24%
Management fee: 0.75% first $500M to 0.68% over $1B
Expense ratio: 2.34% (year ending 12/31/97) (2.89% without waiver)

WRIGHT EQUIFUND - JAPAN
(See first Wright listing for data common to all funds)

Investment objective and policies: Total return: price appreciation and income. Invests in a broad based portfolio of equity securities from the publicly

traded companies in the National Equity Index for their nation. Only securities with adequate public information will be considered acceptable.
Year organized: 1994
Ticker symbol: WEJPX
Group fund code: 20
Discount broker availability: *Fidelity, *Schwab, *Siebert, *White
Redemption fee: 1.5% for shares held less than 30 days, payable to the fund
Dividends paid: Income - December; Capital gains - December
Portfolio turnover (3 yrs): 112%, 56%, 112%
Management fee: 0.75% first $500M to 0.68% over $1B
Expense ratio: 2.15% (year ending 12/31/97)

WRIGHT EQUIFUND - MEXICO
(See first Wright listing for data common to all funds)

Investment objective and policies: Total return: price appreciation and income. Invests in a broad based portfolio of equity securities from the publicly traded companies in the National Equity Index for their nation. Only securities with adequate public information will be considered acceptable.
Year organized: 1994
Ticker symbol: WEMEX
Group fund code: 30
Discount broker availability: *Fidelity, *Schwab, *Siebert, *White
Redemption fee: 1.5% for shares held less than 30 days, payable to the fund
Dividends paid: Income - December; Capital gains - December
Portfolio turnover (3 yrs): 113%, 63%, 110%
Management fee: 0.75% first $500M to 0.68% over $1B
Expense ratio: 1.61% (year ending 12/31/97)

WRIGHT EQUIFUND - NETHERLANDS
(See first Wright listing for data common to all funds)

Investment objective and policies: Total return: price appreciation and income. Invests in a broad based portfolio of equity securities from the publicly traded companies in the National Equity Index for their nation. Only securities with adequate public information will be considered acceptable.
Year organized: 1990
Ticker symbol: WENLX
Group fund code: 18
Discount broker availability: *Fidelity, *Schwab, *Siebert, *White
Redemption fee: 1.5% for shares held less than 30 days, payable to the fund
Dividends paid: Income - December; Capital gains - December
Portfolio turnover (3 yrs): 29%, 124%, 87%
Management fee: 0.75% first $500M to 0.68% over $1B
Expense ratio: 1.86% (year ending 12/31/97)

WRIGHT EQUIFUND - NORDIC
(See first Wright listing for data common to all funds)

Investment objective and policies: Total return: price appreciation and income. Invests in a broad based portfolio of equity securities from the publicly traded companies in the National Equity Index for their nation. Only securities with adequate public information will be considered acceptable.
Year organized: 1994
Ticker symbol: WENOX
Group fund code: 22
Discount broker availability: *Fidelity, *Schwab, *Siebert, *White
Redemption fee: 1.5% for shares held less than 30 days, payable to the fund
Dividends paid: Income - December; Capital gains - December
Portfolio turnover (3 yrs): 48%, 78%, 94%
Management fee: 0.75% first $500M to 0.68% over $1B
Expense ratio: 2.15% (year ending 12/31/97) (3.15% without waiver)

WRIGHT EQUIFUND - SWITZERLAND
(See first Wright listing for data common to all funds)

Investment objective and policies: Total return: price appreciation and income. Invests in a broad based portfolio of equity securities from the publicly traded companies in the National Equity Index for their nation. Only securities with adequate public information will be considered acceptable.
Year organized: 1994
Ticker symbol: WECHX
Group fund code: 24
Discount broker availability: *Fidelity, *Schwab, *Siebert, *White
Redemption fee: 1.5% for shares held less than 30 days, payable to the fund
Dividends paid: Income - December; Capital gains - December
Portfolio turnover (3 yrs): 112%, 55%, 95%
Management fee: 0.75% first $500M to 0.68% over $1B
Expense ratio: 2.28% (year ending 12/31/97) (3.68% without waiver)

WRIGHT INTERNATIONAL BLUE CHIP EQUITIES FUND
(See first Wright listing for data common to all funds)

Investment objective and policies: Long-term capital growth and reasonable current income. Invests at least 80% of assets in equity securities of well-established non-U.S. companies meeting strict quality standards. Invests in companies based in at least three foreign countries, but may use ADRs. May use futures and options to hedge both currencies and individual equity holdings. All companies are selected from the Approved Wright Investment List.
Year organized: 1989
Ticker symbol: WIBCX
Group fund code: 11
Discount broker availability: *Fidelity, *Schwab, *Siebert, *White
Dividends paid: Income - March, June, September, December; Capital gains - December
Portfolio turnover (3 yrs): 4%, 29%, 12%
Management fee: 0.75% first $100M to 0.68% over $1B
Expense ratio: 1.31% (year ending 12/31/97)

WRIGHT JUNIOR BLUE CHIP EQUITIES FUND
(See first Wright listing for data common to all funds)

Investment objective and policies: Total return. Invests at least 80% of assets in equity securities of smaller companies still experiencing their rapid growth period. All companies are selected from the Approved Wright Investment List.
Year organized: 1985
Ticker symbol: WJBEX
Group fund code: 6
Discount broker availability: *Fidelity, *Schwab, *Siebert, *White
Dividends paid: Income - March, June, September, December; Capital gains - December
Portfolio turnover (3 yrs): 25%, 41%, 40%
Management fee: 0.55% first $100M to 0.58% over $1B
Expense ratio: 1.18% (year ending 12/31/97) (1.62% without waiver)

WRIGHT MAJOR BLUE CHIP EQUITIES FUND
(See first Wright listing for data common to all funds)

Investment objective and policies: Total return. Invests at least 80% of assets in equity securities of larger-capitalization well-established companies meeting strict quality standards. All companies are selected from the Approved Wright Investment List. Those included are likely to have capitalization characteristics similar to that of the companies comprising the S&P 500.
Year organized: 1985 (name changed from Quality Core Equities fund 6/97)
Ticker symbol: WQCEX
Group fund code: 9

Discount broker availability: *Fidelity, *Schwab, *Siebert, *White
Dividends paid: Income - March, June, September, December; Capital gains - December
Portfolio turnover (3 yrs): 89%, 45%, 83%
Management fee: 0.45% first $100M to 0.48% over $1B
Expense ratio: 1.08% (year ending 12/31/97) (1.43% without waiver)

WRIGHT SELECTED BLUE CHIP EQUITIES FUND
(See first Wright listing for data common to all funds)

Investment objective and policies: Total return. Invests in equity securities of well-established companies meeting strict quality standards. Companies are chosen for likelihood of providing superior total investment return over the intermediate term. All companies are selected from the Approved Wright Investment List.
Year organized: 1982
Ticker symbol: WSBEX
Group fund code: 2
Discount broker availability: *Fidelity, *Schwab, *Siebert, *White
Dividends paid: Income - March, June, September, December; Capital gains - December
Portfolio turnover (3 yrs): 10%, 43%, 44%
Management fee: 0.55% first $100M to 0.58% over $1B
Expense ratio: 1.08% (year ending 12/31/97)

WRIGHT TOTAL RETURN BOND FUND
(See first Wright listing for data common to all funds)

Investment objective and policies: High current income. Invests in corporate bonds, government obligations, or other debt securities rated A or better with a weighted average maturity that, in the advisor's judgement, produces the best total return. May invest in both government and corporate investment grade fixed-income securities.
Year organized: 1983
Ticker symbol: WTRBX
Group fund code: 5
Discount broker availability: *Fidelity, *Schwab, *Siebert, *White
Dividends paid: Income - declared daily, paid monthly; Capital gains - December
Portfolio turnover (3 yrs): 34%, 96%, 50%
Management fee: 0.40% first $100M to 0.33% over $1B
Expense ratio: 0.90% (year ending 12/31/97)

WRIGHT U.S. TREASURY FUND
(See first Wright listing for data common to all funds)

Investment objective and policies: High current income. Invests at least 65% of assets in T-Bills, notes and bonds, and other obligations of the U.S. Government or its agencies or instrumentalities, guaranteed as to principal and interest by the full faith and credit of the U.S. Government. Fund maintains a dollar-weighted average maturity ranging from 10 to 20 years. Fund does not invest in mortgage-related securities.
Year organized: 1983 (name changed from Government Obligations in 1995)
Ticker symbol: WGOBX
Group fund code: 3
Discount broker availability: *Fidelity, *Schwab, *Siebert, *White
Dividends paid: Income - declared daily, paid monthly; Capital gains - December
Portfolio turnover (3 yrs): 1%, 65%, 8%
Management fee: 0.40% first $100M to 0.33% over $1B
Expense ratio: 1.01% (year ending 12/31/97)

WRIGHT U.S. TREASURY MONEY MARKET FUND ◆
(See first Wright listing for data common to all funds)

Investment objective and policies: High current income consistent with preservation of capital and liquidity. Invests exclusively in money market instru-

ments issued by the U.S. Government and its agencies that are backed by the full faith and credit of the U.S. Government; and in repurchase agreements relating to such securities.
Year organized: 1991
Ticker symbol: WUSXX
Group fund code: 29
Check redemptions: $500 minimum
Dividends paid: Income - declared daily, paid monthly
Management fee: 0.35% first $100M to 0.30% over $1B
Expense ratio: 0.45% (year ending 12/31/97) (0.59% without waiver)

WRIGHT U.S. TREASURY NEAR TERM FUND
(See first Wright listing for data common to all funds)

Investment objective and policies: High current income. Invests primarily in debt obligations issued or guaranteed by the U.S. Government or its agencies or instrumentalities, and FDIC-insured CDs and bankers acceptances. Fund maintains a weighted average maturity of less than five years.
Year organized: 1983 (name changed from Near Term Bond Fund in 1995)
Ticker symbol: WNTBX
Group fund code: 4
Discount broker availability: *Fidelity, *Schwab, *Siebert, *White
Dividends paid: Income - declared daily, paid monthly; Capital gains - December
Portfolio turnover (3 yrs): 4%, 28%, 21%
Management fee: 0.40% first $100M to 0.33% over $1B
Expense ratio: 0.87% (year ending 12/31/97)

WST GROWTH AND INCOME FUND ◆
One Commercial Place, Suite 1450
Norfolk, VA 23510
800-525-3863

Adviser: Wilbanks, Smith & Thomas Asset Management, Inc.
Administrator: The Nottingham Co.
Portfolio managers: Wayne F. Wilbanks (1997), L. Norfleet Smith, Jr. (1997), Norwood A. Thomas, Jr. (1997)
Transfer agent: NC Shareholder Services, LLC
Investment objective and policies: Maximum total return; any combination of capital appreciation, both realized and unrealized, and income. Invests primarily in a flexible portfolio of equity securities, fixed-income securities and money markets. Allocation is adjusted according to perceived market conditions, although the portion allotted to cash and bonds generally is not less than 10% or more than 30%. Equity securities are chosen first with a top-down approach, then using growth at a reasonable price strategies in an effort to secure capital appreciation; fixed-income obligations are 50% allocated to a Treasury duration strategy, 50% to issues perceived to be undervalued with an aim towards total return. May invest up to 15% of assets in junk bonds, and use options in an effort to enhance returns and for hedging purposes.
Year organized: 1997
Special sales information: This is the "institutional" class. A retail "investor" class is planned for the future, with an 0.50% 12b-1 fee.
Minimum purchase: Initial: $25,000; Subsequent: $500; IRA: Initial: $2,000; Automatic investment plan: Subsequent: $100
Wire orders accepted: Yes
Deadline for same day wire purchase: 4 P.M.
Qualified for sale in: AL, AZ, CT, DC, FL, GA, IL, NC, NJ, PA, VA
Telephone redemptions: Yes
Wire redemptions: Yes, $5,000 minimum, $7 fee
Letter redemptions: Signature guarantee required over $50,000
Dividends paid: Income - quarterly; Capital gains - annually
Shareholder services: Systematic withdrawal plan min. bal. req. $25,000
Management fee: 0.75% first $250M, 0.65% over $250M
Administration fee: 0.175% first $50M to 0.10% over $150M ($36,000 minimum)

WWW INTERNET FUND
131 Prosperous Street, Suite 17
Lexington, KY 40509
888-999-8331, 888-263-2204
606-263-2204
fax 606-263-1312
Internet: http://www.inetfund.com, or
http://www.webfund.com
e-mail: advisor@inetfund.com

Adviser: WWW Advisors, Inc.
Portfolio managers: Lawrence S. York (1996), James D. Greene (1996)
Transfer agent: American Data Services, Inc.
Investment objective and policies: Long-term capital appreciation. Invests primarily in equity securities of companies that are designing, developing or manufacturing hardware and software products or services for the Internet and the World Wide Web. Will normally invest at least 70% of assets in securities of this nature, with a 50/25/25% distribution across mature, mid-life and adolescent companies from these industries. May hold up to 20% of assets in foreign securities or ADRs, up to 15% of assets in illiquid securities, and use short sales and options for performance enhancement or for hedging purposes.
Year organized: 1996
Minimum purchase: Initial: $1,000, Subsequent: $100; IRA: Initial: $250; Automatic investment plan: Initial: $500, Subsequent: $25
Wire orders accepted: Yes
Deadline for same day wire purchase: 2 P.M.
Discount broker availability: *White
Qualified for sale in: CA, CO, FL, GA, IL, KY, ME, MA, NJ, NY, OH, PA, TX, VA, WA
Telephone redemptions: Yes
Wire redemptions: Yes, $500 minimum, $15 fee
Letter redemptions: Signature guarantee not required
Redemption fee: 1.00% for shares held less than one year, payable to the fund
Dividends paid: Income - annually; Capital gains - annually
Portfolio turnover (1 yr): 110%
Shareholder services: IRA, SEP-IRA
Maintenance fee: $15/year
Management fee: 1.00% with a maximum +/-0.50% performance bonus or penalty if return underperforms or exceeds percentage change in the S&P 500 Index by 2% to 3% or more
12b-1 distribution fee: Maximum of 0.50%
Expense ratio: 2.50% (11 months ending 6/30/97) (7.23% without waiver)
IRA fees: Annual $15, Initial $12, Closing $15

THE YACKTMAN FUND
303 West Madison Street, Suite 1925
Chicago, IL 60606
800-525-8258, 800-457-6033
fax 312-201-1216

Adviser: Yacktman Asset Management Co.
Administrator: Sunstone Financial Group, Inc.
Portfolio manager: Donald A. Yacktman (1992)
Transfer agent: Firstar Trust Co.
Investment objective and policies: Long-term capital growth; current income secondary. Invests primarily in common stocks and other equity securities, usually of companies with market capitalizations in excess of $1B, for growth, and money market instruments for income. May, however, invest in the top two levels of investment grade, fixed-income securities when they are perceived to offer a greater potential for capital growth. May also invest without limit in ADRs of foreign issuers.
Year organized: 1992
Ticker symbol: YACKX
Minimum purchase: Initial: $2,500, Subsequent: $100; IRA/Keogh: Initial: $500; Automatic investment plan: Initial: $500
Wire orders accepted: Yes
Deadline for same day wire purchase: 4 P.M.
Discount broker availability: *Fidelity, *Schwab, *Siebert, *White
Qualified for sale in: All states
Telephone redemptions: Yes, $1,000 minimum

Wire redemptions: Yes, $1,000 minimum, $12 fee
Letter redemptions: Signature guarantee required over $25,000
Telephone switching: With Firstar money market funds, $1,000 minimum
Number of switches permitted: Unlimited, $5 fee
Dividends paid: Income - March, June, September, December; Capital gains - December
Portfolio turnover (3 yrs): 69%, 59%, 55%
Shareholder services: IRA, SEP-IRA, Keogh, 401(k), 403(b), corporate retirement plans, systematic withdrawal plan min. bal. req. $10,000
Management fee: 0.65% first $500M to 0.55% over $1B
Administration fee: 0.15% first $50M to 0.025% over $100M
12b-1 distribution fee: Maximum of 0.25% (payments may be made only for eligible shareholder accounts established prior to 12/31/92)
Expense ratio: 0.86% (year ending 12/31/97) (0.90% without waiver)
IRA/Keogh fees: Annual $12.50

THE YACKTMAN FOCUSED FUND ◆
303 West Madison Street, Suite 1925
Chicago, IL 60606
800-525-8258, 800-457-6033
fax 312-201-1216

Adviser: Yacktman Asset Management Co.
Administrator: Sunstone Financial Group, Inc.
Portfolio manager: Donald A. Yacktman (1997)
Transfer agent: Firstar Trust Co.
Investment objective and policies: Long-term capital growth; current income secondary. Invests primarily in common stocks and other equity securities of a limited number of companies (usually no more than 25) with market capitalizations in excess of $1B, for growth, and money market instruments for income. May, however, invest in the top two levels of investment grade, fixed-income securities when they are perceived to offer a greater potential for capital growth. May also invest without limit in ADRs of foreign issuers.
Year organized: 1997
Minimum purchase: Initial: $2,500, Subsequent: $100; IRA/Keogh: Initial: $500; Automatic investment plan: Initial: $500
Wire orders accepted: Yes
Deadline for same day wire purchase: 4 P.M.
Discount broker availability: *Fidelity, *Schwab, *Siebert, *White
Qualified for sale in: All states
Telephone redemptions: Yes, $1,000 minimum
Wire redemptions: Yes, $1,000 minimum, $12 fee
Letter redemptions: Signature guarantee required over $25,000
Telephone switching: With Firstar money market funds, $1,000 minimum
Number of switches permitted: Unlimited, $5 fee
Dividends paid: Income - March, June, September, December; Capital gains - December
Portfolio turnover (1 yr): 60%
Shareholder services: IRA, SEP-IRA, Keogh, 401(k), 403(b), corporate retirement plans, systematic withdrawal plan min. bal. req. $10,000
Management fee: 1.00
Administration fee: 0.05%
Expense ratio: 1.25% (year ending 12/31/97) (1.71% without waiver)
IRA/Keogh fees: Annual $12.50

THE ZSA ASSET ALLOCATION FUND
355 South Woodward Avenue, Suite 200
Birmingham, MI 48009
800-525-3863, 810-647-5990
fax 919-442-4226, 810-647-0537

Adviser: Zaske, Sarafa & Assocs., Inc.
Portfolio manager: Arthur E. Zaske (1992)
Transfer agent and administrator: The Nottingham Co.

Investment objective and policies: Total return: realized and unrealized capital appreciation, and current income, consistent with moderate risk to capital. Invests in a flexible portfolio of equity securities (25% to 65% of assets), investment grade corporate and government fixed-income securities (20% to 60%), real estate equity securities (5% to 20%) and money market instruments (0% to 40%). Allocation among categories is adjusted to perceived changes in market and economic conditions. Fund may invest in ADRs of foreign issuers and use puts and calls and options and futures to hedge its portfolio.
Year organized: 1992 (name changed from Growth and Income Fund in 1994; absorbed Zsa Equity Fund 1/31/97)
Ticker symbol: ZSAAX
Minimum purchase: Initial: $10,000, Subsequent: $500; IRA/Keogh: Initial: $2,000; Automatic investment plan: Subsequent: $100
Wire orders accepted: Yes
Deadline for same day wire purchase: 4 P.M.
Qualified for sale in: AZ, CA, CO, DC, FL, GA, IA, IL, IN, MD, MI, MN, NC, NV, NJ, NY, OH, PA, TX, VA, WA, WI
Telephone redemptions: Yes
Wire redemptions: Yes, $5,000 minimum, $7 fee
Letter redemptions: Signature guarantee required over $50,000
Dividends paid: Income - March, June, September, December; Capital gains - December
Portfolio turnover (3 yrs): 10%, 68%, 131%
Shareholder services: IRA, SEP-IRA, systematic withdrawal plan min. bal. req. $10,000
Management fee: 1.00%
Administration fee: 0.25% first $10M to 0.15% over $100M
12b-1 distribution fee: Maximum of 0.25%
Expense ratio: 1.95% (year ending 3/31/97) (2.37% without waiver)
IRA fees: Annual $15

ZURICH MONEY FUNDS ◆
(Name changed from Kemper when company merged with Zurich in 1997. Data common to all Zurich money market funds are shown below. See subsequent listings for data specific to individual funds.)

222 South Riverside Plaza
Chicago, IL 60606-5808
800-537-6001
TDD 800-972-3006

Adviser: Zurich Kemper Investments, Inc.
Transfer agent: Investors Fiduciary Trust Co.
Minimum purchase: Initial: $1,000, Subsequent: $100; IRA/Keogh: Initial: $250, Subsequent: $50
Wire orders accepted: Yes
Deadline for same day wire purchase: 11 A.M. CST
Qualified for sale in: All states
Telephone redemptions: Yes
Wire redemptions: Yes, $1,000 minimum
Letter redemptions: Signature guarantee required over $25,000
Check redemptions: $500 minimum
Telephone switching: With other Zurich Funds (which have loads), and other mutual fund families under special arrangement (see fund), $100 minimum
Number of switches: Unlimited
Shareholder services: IRA, SEP-IRA, Keogh, 401(k), 403(b), corporate retirement plans, automatic investment plan, electronic funds transfer, systematic withdrawal plan min. bal. req. $5,000
IRA/Keogh fees: Annual $12 per account, $24 maximum per SSN#

ZURICH MONEY FUNDS - GOVERNMENT MONEY FUND ◆
(See first Zurich listing for data common to all funds)
Portfolio manager: Frank J. Rachwalski (1974)
Investment objective and policies: Maximum current income consistent with principal stability. Invests primarily in a portfolio of short-term obligations issued by the U.S. Government, its agencies or instrumentalities.
Year organized: 1974
Ticker symbol: KEGXX

Dividends paid: Income - declared daily, paid monthly
Management fee: 0.50% first $215M to 0.25% over $800M
Expense ratio: 0.44% (year ending 7/31/97)

ZURICH MONEY FUNDS - MONEY MARKET FUND ◆
(See first Zurich listing for data common to all funds)
800-537-6001
TDD 800-972-3006

Portfolio manager: Frank J. Rachwalski (1974)
Investment objective and policies: Maximum current income consistent with principal stability. Invests primarily in short-term commercial and bank money market instruments.
Year organized: 1974
Ticker symbol: KMMXX
Minimum purchase: Initial: $1,000, Subsequent: $100; IRA/Keogh: Initial: $250, Subsequent: $50
Check redemptions: $500 minimum
Management fee: 0.50% first $215M to 0.25% over $800M
Expense ratio: 0.45% (year ending 7/31/97)

ZURICH MONEY FUNDS - TAX FREE MONEY FUND ◆
(See first Zurich listing for data common to all funds)
800-537-6001
TDD 800-972-3006

Portfolio manager: Frank J. Rachwalski (1974)
Investment objective and policies: Maximum current income exempt from federal income taxes, consistent with principal stability. Invests primarily in short-term municipal money market instruments.
Year organized: 1974
Ticker symbol: KXMXX
Minimum purchase: Initial: $1,000, Subsequent: $100
Check redemptions: $500 minimum
Management fee: 0.50% first $215M to 0.25% over $800M
Expense ratio: 0.37% (year ending 7/31/97)

Late directory information

Following are Directory additions and changes received after the alphabetical directory listings were completed.

ALPINE INTERNATIONAL REAL ESTATE EQUITY FUND ◆
2500 Westchester Avenue
Purchase, NY 10577
888-785-5578, 914-641-2324

Adviser: Alpine Management & Research, LLC
Portfolio managers: Samuel A. Lieber (1995), Marc R. Halle (1995)
Transfer agent: BISYS Fund Services, Inc.
Investment objective and policies: Long-term capital growth; current income secondary. Normally invests in least 65% of assets in equity securities of non-U.S. issuers located in at least three countries outside of the United States which are principally engaged in the real estate industry or which own significant real estate assets. These may include, among others; REITs, (both equity and mortgage), real estate brokers and developers, and companies such as paper and lumber producers and hotel and entertainment companies which hold large tracts of real estate. Fund may also purchase investment grade debt obligations and money market instruments without limit, as well as equity securities of companies unrelated to real estate. May use a variety of derivative instruments including leverage in an effort to increase returns and for hedging purposes.
Year organized: 1995 (organized as Evergreen Global Real Estate Equity Fund; ownership and name changed 3/19/98)
Special sales information: Fund is offered no-load only through the purchase of "Y" shares for the time being; "A", "B", and "C" shares are still available in conjunction with past commitments to Evergreen. Historic performance, turnover and expense ratios reflect activity of predecessor.
Minimum purchase: Initial: $1,000; Subsequent: None; Automatic investment plan: Subsequent: $25
Wire orders accepted: Yes
Deadline for same day wire purchase: 4 ;p.m.
Qualified for sale in: All states
Telephone redemptions: Yes, $1,000 minimum
Wire redemptions: No
Letter redemptions: Signature guarantee required over $50,000
Dividends paid: Income - annually; Capital gains - annually
Portfolio turnover (3 yrs): 44%, 25%, 28%
Shareholder services: IRA, SEP-IRA, corporate retirement plans, electronic funds transfer (purchase only), systematic withdrawal plan min. bal. req. $10,000
Management fee: 1.00% first $750M to 0.80% over $1B
Expense ratio: 1.82% (year ending 10/31/97) (1.90% without waiver)

ALPINE U.S. REAL ESTATE EQUITY FUND ◆
2500 Westchester Avenue
Purchase, NY 10577
888-785-5578, 914-641-2324

Adviser: Alpine Management & Research, LLC
Portfolio managers: Samuel A. Lieber (1993), Marc R. Halle (1994)
Transfer agent: BISYS Fund Services, Inc.
Investment objective and policies: Long-term capital growth; current income secondary. Normally invests at least 65% of assets in equity securities of U.S. issuers which are principally engaged in the real estate industry or which own significant real estate assets. These may include, among others; REITs, (both equity and mortgage), real estate brokers and developers, and companies such as paper and lumber producers and hotel and entertainment companies which hold large tracts of real estate. Fund may also purchase investment grade debt obligations and money market instruments without limit, as well as equity securities of companies unrelated to real estate. May use a variety of derivative

instruments including leverage in an effort to increase returns and for hedging purposes.
Year organized: 1993 (organized as Evergreen U.S. Real Estate Equity Fund; ownership and name changed 3/19/98)
Special sales information: Fund is offered no-load only through the purchase of "Y" shares for the time being; "A", "B", and "C" shares are still available in conjunction with past commitments to Evergreen. Historic performance, turnover and expense ratios reflect activity of predecessor.
Minimum purchase: Initial: $1,000; Subsequent: None; Automatic investment plan: Subsequent: $25
Wire orders accepted: Yes
Deadline for same day wire purchase: 4 ;p.m.
Qualified for sale in: All states
Telephone redemptions: Yes, $1,000 minimum
Wire redemptions: No
Letter redemptions: Signature guarantee required over $50,000
Dividends paid: Income - annually; Capital gains - annually
Portfolio turnover (3 yrs): 205%, 169%, 115%
Shareholder services: IRA, SEP-IRA, corporate retirement plans, electronic funds transfer (purchase only), systematic withdrawal plan min. bal. req. $10,000
Management fee: 1.00% first $750M to 0.80% over $1B
Expense ratio: 1.50% (year ending 9/30/97) (2.26% without waiver)

AMERICAN AADVANTAGE INTERMEDIATE BOND FUND
(See first American Aadvantage listing for data common to all funds)

Sub-adviser: Barrow, Hanley, Mewhiney & Strauss, Inc.
Portfolio managers: Michael W. Fields (1996), Benjamin L. Mayer (1996)
Investment objective and policies: Income and capital appreciation. Invests primarily in investment grade fixed-income government and corporate securities. Portfolio will generally maintain a dollar-weighted average maturity of three to seven years, although there are no restrictions. May invest in asset- and mortgage-backed securities and YankeeDollar and EuroDollar CDs, bonds and notes. Up to 15% of assets may be in illiquid securities.
Year organized: 1996 (Mileage: 1998, PlanAhead: 1998)
Discount broker availability: Fidelity
Dividends paid: Income - declared daily, paid monthly; Capital gains - December
Management fee: from 0.25%
Administration fee: 0.25%

AMERICAN AADVANTAGE S&P 500 INDEX FUND
(See first American Aadvantage listing for data common to all funds)

Sub-adviser: Bankers Trust Co.
Investment objective and policies: Investment returns, before expenses, that seek to correspond to the total return of the companies that comprise the S&P 500 Index, with a correlation of at least 0.98. Portfolio is constructed so as to match as closely as possible the weightings utilized in the index.
Year organized: 1996 (Mileage: 1998, PlanAhead: 1998)
Dividends paid: Income - April, July, October; Capital gains - December
Management fee: from 0.10%
Administration fee: 0.25%

BLUE RIDGE TOTAL RETURN FUND ◆
84 Villa Road, Suite B37
Greenville, SC 29615
800-525-3863

Adviser: Blue Ridge Advisors, Inc.
Administrator: The Nottingham Co.
Portfolio managers: Jeffrey M. Doyon (1997), Allen R. Gillespie (1997)
Transfer agent: NC Shareholder Services, LLC
Investment objective and policies: Total return: capital appreciation and current income. Invests in a varying portfolio of equity securities and debt obligations; no fixed allocation strategy is employed, and no set capitalization is required to qualify for purchase. Generally, when seeking capital appreciation fund purchases companies with market capitalizations exceeding $1B. Income may be derived from fixed-income obligations or dividend paying stocks. May use a variety of derivative instruments in an effort to enhance income and for hedging purposes.
Year organized: 1997
Minimum purchase: Initial: $5,000; Subsequent: $100; IRA: Initial: $2,000; Automatic investment plan: Initial: $1,000
Wire orders accepted: Yes
Deadline for same day wire purchase: 4 ;p.m.
Qualified for sale in: MD, SC, VA
Telephone redemptions: Yes
Wire redemptions: Yes, $1,000 minimum, $8 fee
Letter redemptions: Signature guarantee required over $50,000
Dividends paid: Income - annually; Capital gains - annually
Shareholder services: IRA, electronic funds transfer, systematic withdrawal plan min. bal. req. $10,000
Management fee: 1.65% first $20M, 1.20% over $20M
IRA fees: Annual $15

BRAZOS/JMIC MICRO CAP GROWTH PORTFOLIO ◆
5949 Sherry Lane, Suite 1600
Dallas, TX 75225
800-426-9157, 214-365-5200

Adviser: John McStay Investment Counsel, L.P.
Lead portfolio manager: John D. McStay (1998)
Transfer agent and administrator: PFPC Inc.
Investment objective and policies: Maximum capital appreciation consistent with reasonable risk to principal. Invests at least 65% of assets in a diversified portfolio of equity securities of companies with market capitalizations that would place them in the smallest 10% of capitalizations in the domestic market as measured by the Wilshire 5000 Index; currently, less than $600M. Up to 35% of assets may be invested in equity securities of larger companies. May invest up to 25% of assets in foreign companies, and up to 20% in assets of companies less than three years old. May invest up to 10% in other investment companies, and up to 15% in illiquid securities. May engage in short sales and use options and futures for hedging purposes.
Year organized: 1998
Minimum purchase: Initial: $10,000; Subsequent: $1,000; IRA: Initial: $2,000, Subsequent: $100
Wire orders accepted: Yes
Deadline for same day wire purchase: 4 ;p.m.
Discount broker availability: *Schwab
Qualified for sale in: All states
Telephone redemptions: Yes
Wire redemptions: Yes
Letter redemptions: Signature guarantee not required
Telephone switching: With other Brazos funds
Number of switches permitted: Unlimited
Dividends paid: Income - annually; Capital gains - annually

Shareholder services: IRA
Management fee: 1.20%
Administration fee: 0.15% first $50M to 0.07% over 200M (minimum $32,500)
IRA fees: Annual $10, Closing $10

CHESAPEAKE CORE GROWTH FUND ◆

285 Wilmington-West Chester Pike
Chadds Ford, PA 19317
800-430-3863

Adviser: Gardner Lewis Asset Management
Administrator: The Nottingham Co.
Portfolio managers: W. Whitfield Gardner (1997), John L. Lewis, IV (1997)
Transfer agent: NC Shareholder Services, LLC
Investment objective and policies: Capital appreciation; income incidental. Invests at least 80% of assets in a diversified portfolio of foreign and domestic equity securities with a range of market capitalizations approximately similar to that of the largest 1,000 companies domiciled in the U.S. The balance of assets is not limited to any size firm. Management focuses on issues perceived to offer strong growth prospects, and those undergoing 'positive change.' May invest without limit in foreign securities offered on U.S. exchanges or through the purchase of ADRs.
Year organized: 1997
Minimum purchase: Initial: $25,000; Subsequent: $500; Automatic investment plan: Subsequent: $100
Wire orders accepted: Yes
Deadline for same day wire purchase: 4 ;p.m.
Qualified for sale in: CA, CO, DC, FL, GA, IL, IN, MN, MS, NC, OR, PA, SC, TN, VA, WV
Telephone redemptions: Yes
Wire redemptions: Yes, $5,000 minimum, $7 fee
Letter redemptions: Signature guarantee required over $50,000
Dividends paid: Income - annually; Capital gains - annually
Shareholder services: IRA, electronic funds transfer, systematic withdrawal plan min. bal. req. $25,000
Management fee: 1.00%
IRA fees: Annual $15

FIDELITY SMALL CAP STOCK FUND ◆

(See first Fidelity listing for data common to all funds)

Portfolio manager: Paul L. Antico (1998)
Investment objective and policies: Capital appreciation. Invests primarily in a diversified portfolio of common stocks of small cap companies perceived to offer strong growth prospects. Investments are geared primarily to the U.S. market, however fund may invest in foreign issues without limit.
Year organized: 1998
Group fund code: 340
Discount broker availability: *Fidelity
Redemption fee: 3.00% for shares held less than 3 years, payable to the fund
Dividends paid: Income - December; Capital gains - December
Management fee: 0.45% plus group fee of 0.25% to 0.52% +/- performance fee of up to 0.20% relative to the Russell 2000 Index

CHAPTER 12

Additional stock and bond funds available no-load through discount brokers

This section lists funds available through discount brokerage firms that are normally not available to individual investors. They include the following:

■ Institutional funds that either have minimum initial investments of $100,000 or more, or are not available to individual investors, that can be purchased through discount brokerage firms at lower ($25,000 or less) initial minimums. Most are available to all brokerage customers, with some exceptions.

■ Load funds that are available through discount brokerage firms at NAV. Most are available to all customers, with some exceptions.

Note: All load funds purchased at NAV through financial advisers at Jack White (except no transaction fee funds) incur a $100 transaction fee. White charges no transaction fee for redemptions. Charles Schwab charges its standard fees on both purchases and redemptions.

BLACKROCK CORE BOND - INSTITUTIONAL PORTFOLIO

345 Park Avenue
New York, NY 10154
800-227-7236, 212-754-5555
fax 212-754-8775
Internet: http://www.compassfunds.com

Adviser: PNC Asset Management Group, Inc.
Sub-adviser: BlackRock Financial Management, Inc.
Portfolio manager: Team managed
Investment objective and policies: Total return exceeding the total return of the Lehman Brothers Aggregate Index. Invests in a broad range of investment grade fixed-income government and corporate securities, with a fluctuation of the weighted average maturity of plus or minus 20% around the current duration of the Lehman Brothers Aggregate Index.
Year organized: 1992 (name changed from BFM Institutional Trust - Core Fixed Income in 1996. Fund family name changed from Compass Capital 2/2/98.)
Ticker symbol: BFMCX
Special sales restrictions: Designed primarily for institutional investors and high net worth individuals. Fund is available at NAV with lower initial and subsequent minimums through discount brokerage firms which have established accounts with BFM.
Discount broker availability: Fidelity, Schwab, White (only through financial advisers)
Minimum purchase through discount broker: Fidelity: $2,500; Schwab: $2,500; White: $5,000

BLACKROCK LOW DURATION BOND - INSTITUTIONAL PORTFOLIO

345 Park Avenue
New York, NY 10154
800-227-7236, 212-754-5555
fax 212-754-8775
Internet: http://www.compassfunds.com

Adviser: PNC Asset Management Group, Inc.
Sub-adviser: BlackRock Financial Management, Inc.
Portfolio manager: Team managed
Investment objective and policies: Total return exceeding the total return of the Merrill Lynch 1-3 Year Treasury Index. Invests in a broad range of investment grade fixed-income government and, to a lesser extent, corporate securities. Portfolio maintains a weighted average maturity of three years or less.
Year organized: 1992 (name changed from BFM Institutional Trust - Short Duration Portfolio in 1996; name changed from Short Govt. Bond in 1997. Fund family name changed from Compass Capital 2/2/98).
Ticker symbol: BFMSX
Special sales restrictions: Designed primarily for institutional investors and high net worth individuals. Fund is available at NAV with lower initial and subsequent minimums through discount brokerage firms which have established accounts with BFM.

Discount broker availability: Fidelity, Schwab, White (only through financial advisers)
Minimum purchase through discount broker: Fidelity: $2,500; Schwab: $2,500; White: $5,000

BRIDGEWAY ULTRA-LARGE 35 INDEX PORTFOLIO ◆

5650 Kirby Drive, Suite 141
Houston, TX 77005-2443
800-661-3550, 713-661-3500
fax 713-661-3587

Adviser: Bridgeway Capital Management, Inc.
Transfer agent: Bridgeway Fund, Inc.
Portfolio manager: John N.R. Montgomery (1997)
Investment objective and policies: Total return: capital appreciation and current income. Seeks to meet the total return of a proprietary index comprised of the largest 35 U.S. equities as of June 27, 1997 after excluding tobacco companies and ensuring reasonable industry diversification. Fund is managed with an effort to minimize the distribution of capital gains and costs. Incoming cash is invested so that company weightings are approximately equal. A company will be removed from the index if a) it is no longer one of the 35 largest, AND b) it would not create a capital gain. Otherwise a company which only meets one criterion remains as a 'dormant' holding whose representation will decline over time. No new monies are invested in dormant companies.
Year organized: 1997
Special sales information: Fund may be purchased direct from Bridgeway without transaction fees for $1M initial minimum, $250,000 subsequent.
Discount broker availability: Fidelity, White
Minimum purchase through discount broker: Fidelity: $2,500; White: $0
Redemption fee: Fund may impose a 2% redemptions fee, payable to the fund, for any redemptions made if the S&P 500 Index (without dividends) has declined more than 5% over the previous five trading days.

BRIDGEWAY ULTRA-SMALL INDEX PORTFOLIO ◆

5650 Kirby Drive, Suite 141
Houston, TX 77005-2443
800-661-3550, 713-661-3500
fax 713-661-3587

Adviser: Bridgeway Capital Management, Inc.
Transfer agent: Bridgeway Fund, Inc.
Portfolio manager: John N.R. Montgomery (1997)
Investment objective and policies: Total return: capital appreciation and current income. Fund seeks to meet the total return (less expenses) of the University of Chicago's Center for Research in Securities (CRSP) Cap-Based Portfolio 10 Index by investing in a representative sample of companies represented in the

index. Index comprises all common stocks listed on the New York, American and NASDAQ markets which are the size of stocks in the smallest 10% of the New York Stock Exchange (excluding unit investment trusts, closed-end funds, REITs, americus trusts, foreign stocks and ADRs).
Year organized: 1997
Special sales information: Fund may be purchased direct from Bridgeway without transaction fees for $1M initial minimum, $250,000 subsequent.
Discount broker availability: Fidelity, White
Minimum purchase through discount broker: Fidelity: $2,500; White: $0
Redemption fee: Fund may impose a 2% redemptions fee, payable to the fund, for any redemptions made if the S&P 500 Index (without dividends) has declined more than 5% over the previous five trading days.

THE BRINSON FUNDS ◆

(Data common to all Brinson funds are shown below. See subsequent listings for data specific to individual funds.)

209 South LaSalle Street
Chicago, IL 60604-1295
800-448-2430, 312-223-7975
fax 312-239-4927
Internet: http://www.networth.galt.com/swisskey

Adviser: Brinson Partners, Inc.
Special sales restrictions: Designed primarily for institutional investors and high net worth individuals, minimum investments are $1,000,000, with subsequent investment minimums of $2,500. You may, however, invest directly in the Brinson funds at $2,000 minimum for an IRA account. Otherwise, fund is available at lower initial and subsequent minimums through discount brokerage firms which have established accounts. A sibling fund, SwissKey, is also available directly from Brinson at lower minimums with 12b-1 distribution fees.
Discount broker availability: *Fidelity, *Schwab, *White
Minimum purchase through discount broker: Fidelity $2,500; Schwab: $2,500; White: $1,000

BRINSON GLOBAL FUND ◆

(See first Brinson listing for data common to all funds)

Portfolio manager: Team managed
Investment objective and policies: Total return; capital appreciation and current income. Invests at least 65% of assets in equity and debt securities of issuers from at least three different countries, one of which may be the U.S., using an active asset allocation strategy. May use interest rate swaps, foreign currency contracts, and options and futures for hedging purposes. May invest in junk bonds.
Year organized: 1992 (Brinson class)
Ticker symbol: BPGLX

BRINSON GLOBAL BOND FUND ◆

(See first Brinson listing for data common to all funds)

Portfolio manager: Team managed
Investment objective and policies: Total return; capital appreciation and current income. Invests at least 65% of assets in debt securities with an initial maturity of more than one year, issued from at least three different countries, one of which may be the U.S. May use interest rate swaps, foreign currency contracts, and options and futures for hedging purposes. May invest in junk bonds.
Year organized: 1993 (Brinson class)
Ticker symbol: BPGBX

BRINSON GLOBAL EQUITY FUND ◆
(See first Brinson listing for data common to all funds)

Portfolio manager: Team managed
Investment objective and policies: Total return; capital appreciation and current income. Invests at least 65% of assets in equity securities of issuers in at least three countries, one of which may be the U.S. May use interest rate swaps, foreign currency contracts, and options and futures for hedging purposes.
Year organized: 1994 (Brinson class)
Ticker symbol: BPGEX

BRINSON NON-U.S. EQUITY FUND ◆
(See first Brinson listing for data common to all funds)

Portfolio manager: Team managed
Investment objective and policies: Total return; capital appreciation and current income. Invests at least 65% of assets in equity securities of issuers in at least three countries other than the U.S. May use interest rate swaps, foreign currency contracts, and options and futures for hedging purposes.
Year organized: 1993 (Brinson class)
Ticker symbol: BNUEX

BRINSON U.S. BALANCED FUND ◆
(See first Brinson listing for data common to all funds)

Portfolio manager: Team managed
Investment objective and policies: Total return; capital appreciation and current income. Invests in a wide range of equity, debt and money market securities issued in the U.S. using an active asset allocation strategy. At least 25% of assets will be invested in fixed-income securities. May use interest rate swaps for hedging purposes. May invest in junk bonds.
Year organized: 1995 1994 (Brinson class)
Ticker symbol: BPBLX

BRINSON U.S. BOND FUND ◆
(See first Brinson listing for data common to all funds)

Portfolio manager: Team managed
Investment objective and policies: Total return; capital appreciation and current income, while controlling risk. Invests at least 65% of assets in U.S. debt securities with an initial maturity of more than one year. May use interest rate swaps for hedging purposes. Up to 30% of assets may be in junk bonds.
Year organized: 1995 (Brinson class)
Ticker symbol: BPBDX

BRINSON U.S. EQUITY FUND ◆
(See first Brinson listing for data common to all funds)

Portfolio manager: Team managed
Investment objective and policies: Total return; capital appreciation and current income, while controlling risk. Invests at least 65% of assets in equity securities issued by U.S. companies. May use options and futures for hedging purposes.
Year organized: 1994 (Brinson class)
Ticker symbol: BPEQX

COMPASS CAPITAL FUNDS
(Renamed the BlackRock funds 2/2/98)

DFA INVESTMENT DIMENSIONS GROUP PORTFOLIOS ◆
(Data common to all DFA portfolios are shown below. See subsequent listings for data specific to individual portfolios.)

1299 Ocean Avenue, 11th Floor
Santa Monica, CA 90401
800-342-6684, 310-395-8005

Adviser: Dimensional Fund Advisers, Inc.
Special sales restrictions: Designed for institutional investors only, but individuals may invest **ONLY through financial advisers** at discount brokerage firms.

Minimum purchase through discount broker:
Fidelity: $2,500 (one fund); Schwab: $2,500; Jack White: $250

DFA CONTINENTAL SMALL COMPANY PORTFOLIO ◆
(See first DFA listing for data common to all portfolios)

Investment objective and policies: Capital appreciation. Invests in a broad and diverse portfolio of equity securities of companies with market capitalizations in the bottom 50% of each country's equity market. Capitalizations may be no larger than the largest of the bottom 20% of companies listed in the Financial Times Actuaries World Index. Selects companies from the developed countries of Continental Europe.
Year organized: 1988
Ticker symbol: DFCSX
Sales charge: 1.00% payable to the fund
Discount broker availability: Schwab, White

DFA EMERGING MARKETS PORTFOLIO ◆
(See first DFA listing for data common to all portfolios)

Investment objective and policies: Capital appreciation. Invests in equity securities of larger companies domiciled in, or primarily doing business in, the twelve countries currently classified as emerging markets as defined by the International Finance Corporation. New countries may be added in the future after careful review of laws, customs and procedures. Countries are weighted approximately equally in the portfolio to afford maximum diversification, although management discretion may be used to supercede these equitable weightings.
Year organized: 1994
Ticker symbol: DFEMX
Sales charge: 0.50% payable to the fund
Discount broker availability: Schwab, White

DFA ENHANCED U.S. LARGE COMPANY PORTFOLIO ◆
(See first DFA listing for data common to all portfolios)

Investment objective and policies: To outperform the total return performance of the S&P 500 Index. Invests in a portfolio of high quality, short-term fixed-income securities, S&P futures contracts, and various derivatives. If the rate of return on the fixed-income portfolio exceeds the interest rate implicit in the futures price, the strategy may outperform the S&P 500 on a pre-tax total return basis.
Year organized: 1996
Ticker symbol: DFELX
Discount broker availability: Schwab, White

DFA FIVE YEAR GOVERNMENT PORTFOLIO ◆
(See first DFA listing for data common to all portfolios)

Investment objective and policies: Maximum total return: income and capital gains. Invests in U.S. Government and U.S. Government agency debt obligations which mature within five years from the settlement date. Employs a 'variable maturity' strategy which shifts the weighted average maturity of the portfolio in response to changes in the shape of the yield curve.
Year organized: 1987
Ticker symbol: DFFGX
Discount broker availability: Schwab, White

DFA GLOBAL FIXED INCOME PORTFOLIO ◆
(See first DFA listing for data common to all portfolios)

Investment objective and policies: Market rate of return with low relative volatility. Invests in high quality fixed-income obligations issued or guaranteed by the U.S. and foreign governments and/or agencies in at least three developed countries. Portfolio will acquire assets which mature within five years of the date of settlement. Employs forward foreign currency contracts to hedge exchange rate risk.

Year organized: 1990 (name changed from Global Bond Portfolio on 3/17/92)
Ticker symbol: DFGBX
Discount broker availability: Schwab, White

DFA INTERMEDIATE GOVERNMENT FIXED INCOME PORTFOLIO ◆
(See first DFA listing for data common to all portfolios)

Investment objective and policies: Current income consistent with capital preservation. Invests in high quality, non-callable intermediate term U.S. and foreign government obligations and futures contracts on U.S. Treasuries. Portfolio generally maintains an average weighted maturity of seven to ten years.
Year organized: 1990 (name changed from Intermediate Government Bond Portfolio on 3/17/92)
Ticker symbol: DFIGX
Discount broker availability: Schwab, White

DFA INTERNATIONAL HIGH BOOK TO MARKET PORTFOLIO ◆
(See first DFA listing for data common to all portfolios)

Investment objective and policies: Long-term capital appreciation. Invests in stocks of large non-U.S. companies with high book values in relation to their market values. Portfolio is market capitalization weighted.
Year organized: 1993
Ticker symbol: DFHBX
Discount broker availability: Schwab

DFA INTERNATIONAL SMALL CAP VALUE PORTFOLIO ◆
(See first DFA listing for data common to all portfolios)

Investment objective and policies: Long-term capital appreciation. Invests in stocks of small non-U.S. companies with high book values in relation to their market values, and market capitalizations generally under $800M. Fund invests primarily in small caps of developed countries. Portfolio is market capitalization weighted.
Year organized: 1994
Ticker symbol: DISVX
Sales charge: 0.70% payable to the fund
Discount broker availability: Schwab, White

DFA INTERNATIONAL SMALL COMPANY PORTFOLIO ◆
(See first DFA listing for data common to all portfolios)

Investment objective and policies: Long-term capital appreciation. A "fund of funds," this portfolio invests in the four modular small company portfolios already in the DFA family, with weightings approximately as follows: Japan, 27.5% - 42.5%; Continental Europe, 27.5% - 42.5%; United Kingdom, 7.5% - 22.5%; and Pacific Rim, 7.5% - 22.5%. Portfolio is automatically re-balanced semi-annually.
Year organized: 1996
Ticker symbol: DFISX
Sales charge: 0.70% payable to the fund
Discount broker availability: Schwab, White

DFA INTERNATIONAL VALUE PORTFOLIO ◆
(See first DFA listing for data common to all portfolios)

Investment objective and policies: Long-term capital appreciation. Invests in large capitalization stocks in developed countries with high book-to-market characteristics, perceived to be undervalued at time of purchase. Country weightings are roughly equivalent to EAFE index weightings, adjusted for a maximum 40% exposure to any one country. Companies falling in the top 30% book-to-market ratings of that country's firms, with market capitalizations over $800M, are eligible for purchase.
Year organized: 1994
Ticker symbol: DFIVX
Discount broker availability: Schwab, White

DFA JAPANESE SMALL COMPANY PORTFOLIO ◆
(See first DFA listing for data common to all portfolios)

Investment objective and policies: Capital appreciation. Invests in a broadly diversified, highly liquid portfolio of stocks of small Japanese companies, with market capitalizations not greater than the bottom half of the First Section of the Tokyo Stock Exchange.
Year organized: 1986
Ticker symbol: DFJSX
Sales charge: 0.50% payable to the fund
Discount broker availability: Schwab, White

DFA LARGE CAP INTERNATIONAL PORTFOLIO ◆
(See first DFA listing for data common to all portfolios)

Investment objective and policies: Long-term capital appreciation. Invests in stocks of large companies in at least three different developed countries in Europe, Australia and the Far East. Portfolio is market capitalization weighted.
Year organized: 1991
Ticker symbol: DFALX
Discount broker availability: Schwab, White

DFA ONE-YEAR FIXED INCOME PORTFOLIO ◆
(See first DFA listing for data common to all portfolios)

Investment objective and policies: Return in excess of the rate of inflation with minimum risk. Invests in high quality U.S. Government and bank obligations and commercial paper with a maximum maturity of two years and an average maturity of one year. Fund employs a 'variable maturity' strategy which shifts the weighted average maturity of the portfolio in response to changes in the shape of the yield curve.
Year organized: 1983 (formerly Inflation Hedge Portfolio A)
Ticker symbol: DFIHX
Discount broker availability: Fidelity, Schwab, White

DFA PACIFIC RIM SMALL COMPANY PORTFOLIO ◆
(See first DFA listing for data common to all portfolios)

Investment objective and policies: Capital appreciation. Invests in stocks of small companies located in the Pacific Rim, including Australia, New Zealand, Singapore, Hong Kong, Korea and Malaysia. Japan is excluded.
Year organized: 1993 name changed from Asia/Australia Portfolio in 1994)
Ticker symbol: DFRSX
Sales charge: 1.00% payable to the fund
Discount broker availability: Schwab, White

DFA/AEW REAL ESTATE SECURITIES PORTFOLIO ◆
(See first DFA listing for data common to all portfolios)

Investment objective and policies: Long-term capital appreciation. Invests primarily in readily marketable securities of companies whose principal activities include development, ownership, construction, management, or sale of residential, commercial or industrial real estate. Generally purchase equity REITs, not mortgage REITs. Generally tracks the National Association of Real Estate Investment Trust's Index, with the exception of the health care REITs.
Year organized: 1992
Ticker symbol: DFREX
Discount broker availability: Schwab, White

DFA TWO YEAR GLOBAL FIXED INCOME PORTFOLIO ◆
(See first DFA listing for data common to all portfolios)

Investment objective and policies: Income. Invests in high quality fixed-income instruments with a maximum maturity of two years, from issuers in the U.S. and other major developed countries. Exposure is limited to 30% of any single non-U.S. issuer. May use forward foreign currency contracts to hedge exchange rate risk.
Year organized: 1996
Ticker symbol: DFGFX
Discount broker availability: Schwab, White

DFA UNITED KINGDOM SMALL COMPANY PORTFOLIO ◆
(See first DFA listing for data common to all portfolios)

Investment objective and policies: Capital appreciation. Invests in readily marketable small cap stocks of companies trading in the bottom 50% of the Financial Times-Actuaries All Share Index on the International Stock Exchange of the U.K. and Ireland.
Year organized: 1986
Ticker symbol: DFUKX
Discount broker availability: Schwab, White

DFA U.S. LARGE CAP VALUE PORTFOLIO ◆
(See first DFA listing for data common to all portfolios)

Investment objective and policies: Long-term capital appreciation. Invests in common stocks of large U.S. companies with shares that have high book values in relation to their market values. Companies in the top half of the NYSE are ranked by their book-to-market ratio. Those falling into the top 30% are eligible for purchase, excluding utilities, ADRs, EDRs, REITs, limited partnerships, and investment companies.
Year organized: 1992 (name changed from U.S. Large Cap High Book to Market in 1993)
Ticker symbol: DFLVX
Discount broker availability: Schwab, White

DFA U.S. LARGE COMPANY PORTFOLIO ◆
(See first DFA listing for data common to all portfolios)

Investment objective and policies: To approximate the investment performance of the S&P 500 Index. Invests in all the stocks in the S&P 500 Index in approximately the same proportions as they are represented in the index.
Year organized: 1990
Ticker symbol: DFLCX
Discount broker availability: Schwab, White

DFA U.S. 6-10 SMALL COMPANY PORTFOLIO ◆
(See first DFA listing for data common to all portfolios)

Investment objective and policies: Long-term capital appreciation. Invests in readily marketable common stocks, as a quasi-index, of small companies found in the smallest 50% of NYSE companies. Companies with similar capitalizations in the NASDAQ or American Stock Exchanges are eligible as well.
Year organized: 1992
Ticker symbol: DFSTX
Discount broker availability: Schwab, White

DFA U.S. 9-10 SMALL COMPANY PORTFOLIO ◆
(See first DFA listing for data common to all portfolios)

Investment objective and policies: Long-term capital appreciation. Invests in readily marketable common stocks, as a quasi-index, of small companies found in the smallest 20% of NYSE companies. Companies with similar capitalizations in the NASDAQ or American Stock Exchanges are eligible as well.
Year organized: 1981 (formerly the Small Company Portfolio)
Ticker symbol: DFSCX
Discount broker availability: Schwab, White

DFA U.S. SMALL CAP VALUE PORTFOLIO ◆
(See first DFA listing for data common to all portfolios)

Investment objective and policies: Long-term capital appreciation. Invests in common stocks of small U.S. companies falling into the top 30% as ranked by book-to-market ratios, excluding utilities, ADRs, EDRs, REITs, limited partnerships, and investment companies.
Year organized: 1992 (name changed from U.S. Small Cap High Book to Market Portfolio in 1993)
Ticker symbol: DFSVX
Discount broker availability: Schwab

59 WALL STREET FUNDS ◆
(Data common to all 59 Wall Street funds are shown below. See subsequent listings for data specific to individual funds.)

Six St. James Avenue
Boston, MA 02116
800-625-5759, 617-423-0800
212-493-8100

Adviser: Brown Brothers Harriman & Co.
Transfer agent: State Street Bank & Trust Co.
Special sales restrictions: Designed principally for the investments of high net worth individual investors and institutions, with $100M minimum investment policies, funds are available at lower initial minimums through discount brokerage firms which have established accounts with the funds.
Minimum purchase through discount broker: Fidelity: $2,500; Schwab: $2,500; White: $2,500

59 WALL STREET EUROPEAN EQUITY FUND ◆
(See first 59 Wall Street listing for data common to all funds)

Portfolio managers: Team managed (1990)
Investment objective and policies: Capital appreciation; income secondary. Invests primarily in common stocks of companies based in the European Economic Community. May also invest in convertible securities, trust or limited partnership interests, rights and warrants. May invest directly or in ADRs and EDRs, and use futures and options for hedging purposes.
Year organized: 1990
Ticker symbol: FNEEX
Discount broker availability: *Fidelity, *Schwab, *White

59 WALL STREET INFLATION INDEXED SECURITIES FUND ◆
(See first 59 Wall Street listing for data common to all funds)

Portfolio managers: Team managed (1997)
Investment objective and policies: High income consistent with preservation of capital and liquidity. Invests primarily in investment grade debt securities, and maintains a weighted average maturity of two to four years. May invest in municipal securities and foreign government securities. Fund may hedge.
Year organized: 1992 (reorganized from Short/Intermediate Fixed Income 2/97; past performance irrelevant)
Ticker symbol: FNISX
Discount broker availability: *Fidelity, *Schwab, *White

59 WALL STREET PACIFIC BASIN EQUITY FUND ◆
(See first 59 Wall Street listing for data common to all funds)

Portfolio managers: Team managed (1990)
Investment objective and policies: Capital appreciation; income secondary. Invests primarily in common stocks of companies based in Pacific Basin countries. May also invest in convertible securities, trust or limited partnership interests, rights and warrants. May

invest directly or in ADRs and EDRs, and use futures and options for hedging purposes.
Year organized: 1990
Ticker symbol: FNPEX
Discount broker availability: *Fidelity, *Schwab, *White

59 WALL STREET SMALL COMPANY FUND ◆
(See first 59 Wall Street listing for data common to all funds)

Portfolio managers: Team managed (1995)
Investment objective and policies: Capital appreciation; income secondary. Invests primarily in an underlying portfolio with identical objectives and policies; investing in common stocks of small domestic companies with market capitalizations of $90M to $750M, chosen through use of a proprietary selection model. May also invest in convertible securities, trust or limited partnership interests, rights and warrants.
Year organized: 1991
Ticker symbol: FNSMX
Discount broker availability: *Fidelity, *Schwab, *White

59 WALL STREET TAX FREE SHORT/INTERMEDIATE FIXED INCOME FUND ◆
(See first 59 Wall Street listing for data common to all funds)

Portfolio managers: Barbara A. Brinkley (1992), Jeffrey A. Schoenfeld (1995), Sabrina T. Huffman (1995)
Investment objective and policies: High income exempt from federal income tax, consistent with preservation of capital and liquidity. Invests primarily in investment grade municipal securities, and maintains a weighted average maturity of three years or less.
Year organized: 1992
Ticker symbol: FNSIX
Discount broker availability: *Fidelity, *Schwab, *White

59 WALL STREET U.S. EQUITY FUND ◆
(See first 59 Wall Street listing for data common to all funds)

Portfolio managers: Team managed (1990)
Investment objective and policies: Superior long-term capital growth with some current income. Invests primarily in common stocks of companies traded on major U.S. stock exchanges. May also purchase convertible securities, rights, warrants and ADRs of foreign issuers. May use futures and options for hedging purposes.
Year organized: 1990
Ticker symbol: FWUEX
Discount broker availability: *Fidelity, *Schwab, *White

HARDING, LOEVNER FUNDS ◆
(Data common to all Harding, Loevner funds are shown below. See subsequent listings for data specific to individual portfolios.)

50 Division Street, Suite 401
Somerville, NJ 08876
212-332-5210, 908-218-7900
fax 212-332-5190

Adviser: Harding, Loevner Management, L.P.
Administrator: AMT Capital Services, Inc.
Special sales restrictions: Designed principally for the investments of high net worth individual investors and institutions, with $100M minimum investment policies, funds are available at lower initial minimums through discount brokerage firms which have established accounts with the funds.
Minimum purchase through discount broker: Schwab: $25,000; White: $25,000

HARDING, LOEVNER GLOBAL EQUITY PORTFOLIO ◆
(See first Harding, Loevner listing for data common to all portfolios)

Lead portfolio manager: Daniel D. Harding (1996)
Investment objective and policies: Long-term capital appreciation. Invests at least 65% of assets in equity securities (including ADRs and EDRs), closed-end investment companies, and rights and warrants issued by companies based both inside and outside the U.S. Will select at least one country each from the three groupings used to select investments for the International Portfolio, as well as selecting U.S. investments. May invest up to 35% of assets in short-term and other debt securities, up to 15% of assets in securities of U.S. companies, and up to 20% of assets in junk bonds. May use a variety of derivative instruments in an effort to increase portfolio performance and for hedging purposes.
Year organized: 1996
Discount broker availability: Schwab, White

HARDING, LOEVNER INTERNATIONAL EQUITY PORTFOLIO ◆
(See first Harding, Loevner listing for data common to all portfolios)

Lead portfolio manager: Daniel D. Harding (1996)
Investment objective and policies: Long-term capital appreciation. Invests at least 65% of assets in equity securities (including ADRs and EDRs), closed-end investment companies, and rights and warrants issued by companies based outside the U.S. Will invest in at least one country of each of three groups loosely defined as Europe, the Pacific Rim, and "emerging markets." May invest up to 35% of assets in short-term and other debt securities, up to 15% of assets in securities of U.S. companies, and up to 20% of assets in junk bonds. May use a variety of derivative instruments in an effort to increase portfolio performance and for hedging purposes.
Year organized: 1994 (name changed from AMT Capital Fund - HLM International Equity Portfolio 11/1/96)
Ticker symbol: AMTHX
Discount broker availability: Schwab, White

HARDING, LOEVNER MULTI-ASSET GLOBAL PORTFOLIO ◆
(See first Harding, Loevner listing for data common to all portfolios)

Lead portfolio manager: Daniel D. Harding (1996)
Investment objective and policies: Long-term capital appreciation and increasing current income. Invests in equity securities (including ADRs and EDRs), closed-end investment companies, and rights and warrants issued by companies based within at least three countries including the U.S., as well as both corporate and government debt securities from all. May use a variety of derivative instruments in an effort to increase portfolio performance and for hedging purposes.
Year organized: 1996
Discount broker availability: Schwab, White

LEXINGTON STRATEGIC INVESTMENTS FUND
Park 80 West Plaza Two
P.O. Box 1515
Saddle Brook, NJ 07663
800-526-0056, 201-845-7300
prices/yields 800-526-0052
fax 201-845-3534

Adviser: Lexington Management Corp.
Portfolio manager: Robert W. Radsch (1994)
Investment objective and policies: Capital appreciation; current income secondary. Invests in common stocks of companies engaged in exploration, mining, processing, fabrication and distribution of natural resources - hydrocarbons, minerals, and metals of silver, gold, uranium, platinum and copper. Will be structured so that at least 80% of its gross income is derived from outside the U.S., and at least 50% of the

value of its assets will be in securities of foreign corporations. May also invest in precious metals bullion.
Year organized: 1974 (name changed from Strategic Investments Fund June 8, 1992)
Ticker symbol: STIVX
Discount broker availability: *Fidelity, *Schwab, *White
Sales charge: 5.75% (available at NAV through discount brokers)
Minimum purchase through discount broker: Fidelity: $2,500; Schwab: $2,500; White: $1,000

LEXINGTON STRATEGIC SILVER FUND
Park 80 West Plaza Two
P.O. Box 1515
Saddle Brook, NJ 07663
800-526-0056, 201-845-7300
prices/yields 800-526-0052
fax 201-845-3534

Adviser: Lexington Management Corp.
Portfolio manager: Robert W. Radsch (1994)
Investment objective and policies: Maximum total return: long-term growth of capital and income. Invests at least 80% of assets in equity securities of established companies throughout the world engaged in exploration, mining, processing, fabrication or distribution of silver. May also invest in silver bullion and debt securities according to market dictates.
Year organized: 1984
Ticker symbol: STSLX
Discount broker availability: *Fidelity, *Schwab, *White
Sales charge: 5.75% (available at NAV through discount brokers)
Minimum purchase through discount broker: Fidelity: $2,500; Schwab: $2,500; White: $1,000

LOOMIS SAYLES FUNDS
(Data common to all Loomis Sayles funds are shown below. See subsequent listings for data specific to individual funds.)

One Financial Center, 34th Floor
Boston, MA 02111
800-633-3330, 800-626-9390
617-482-2450, fax 617-338-0761

Adviser: Loomis, Sayles & Co., L.P.
Transfer agent: State Street Bank & Trust Co.
Special sales restrictions: Effective 1/97, Loomis created a two class share system; Retail shares are available with a $250,000 minimum, and Institutional shares with a $1 million dollar minimum direct from the company. Only shareholders with prior accounts may open new accounts with regular minimums. To purchase retail shares at lower minimums for a new account, contact a discount broker.
Minimum purchase (SHAREHOLDERS PRIOR TO 1/97 ONLY): Initial: $2,500, Subsequent: $50; IRA: Initial: $250; Automatic investment plan: Initial: $1,000
Discount broker availability: *Fidelity, *Schwab, *White (EXCEPTIONS NOTED)
Minimum purchase through discount broker: $2,500

LOOMIS SAYLES BOND FUND
(See first Loomis Sayles listing for data common to all funds)

Portfolio managers: Daniel J. Fuss (1991), Kathleen C. Gaffney (1997)
Investment objective and policies: High total return: current income and capital appreciation. Invests primarily in investment grade debt securities, including securities convertible into common stocks. May invest up to 35% of assets in junk bonds, 20% in preferred stocks and 20% in securities of foreign issuers other than Canada, in which unlimited assets may be invested.
Year organized: 1991
Ticker symbol: LSBDX

LOOMIS SAYLES CORE VALUE FUND
(See first Loomis Sayles listing for data common to all funds)

Portfolio managers: Jeffrey W. Wardlow (1991), James L. Carroll (1997), Isaac H. Green (1997)
Investment objective and policies: Long-term growth of capital and income. Invests primarily in common stocks believed undervalued in relation to their earnings, dividends, asset and growth prospects. May invest up to 20% of assets in securities of foreign issuers.
Year organized: 1991 (name changed from Growth & Income 1/97)

LOOMIS SAYLES GLOBAL BOND FUND
(See first Loomis Sayles listing for data common to all funds)

Portfolio manager: E. John deBeer (1991)
Investment objective and policies: High total return: current income and capital appreciation. Invests primarily in investment grade fixed-income obligations, including securities convertible into common stocks, denominated in various currencies including U.S. dollars or in multi-currency units. Normally invests at least 65% of assets in bonds of issuers of at least three countries with maximum of 40% in one country. 100% of assets may be denominated in U.S. dollars. May invest up to 20% of assets in junk bonds. Fund may hedge.
Year organized: 1991

LOOMIS SAYLES GROWTH FUND
(See first Loomis Sayles listing for data common to all funds)

Portfolio manager: Jerome A. Castellini (1991)
Investment objective and policies: Long-term capital growth. Invests primarily in common stocks chosen for their growth potential. May invest in companies with small market capitalizations as well as larger companies. May invest up to 20% of assets in securities of foreign issuers.
Year organized: 1991
Ticker symbol: LSGRX

LOOMIS SAYLES HIGH YIELD FUND
(See first Loomis Sayles listing for data common to all funds)

Portfolio managers: Daniel J. Fuss (1996), Kathleen C. Gaffney (1996)
Investment objective and policies: High total return; current income and capital appreciation. Invests primarily in junk bonds, but may also invest up to 20% of assets in convertible bonds and preferred stocks, and up to 10% of assets may be in common stocks. May invest without limit in Canadian securities, and up to 50% of assets in securities of other foreign issuers. Will focus on low-rated securities that are likely to receive an upgrade of their credit rating. May use foreign currency exchange transactions and put and call options for hedging purposes.
Year organized: 1996
Redemption fee: 2.00% for shares held less than 1 year, payable to the fund

LOOMIS SAYLES INTERMEDIATE MATURITY FUND
(See first Loomis Sayles listing for data common to all funds)

Portfolio manager: Anthony J. Wilkins (1996)
Investment objective and policies: High total return: current income and capital appreciation. Invests at least 90% of assets in investment grade fixed-income securities of all types, and to maintain the portfolio average weighted maturity between three and ten years. May invest up to 10% of assets in junk bonds. May invest in Canadian securities without limit, and invest up to 20% of assets in other foreign issues. May use a variety of derivative instruments for hedging purposes.
Year organized: 1996

LOOMIS SAYLES INTERNATIONAL EQUITY FUND
(See first Loomis Sayles listing for data common to all funds)

Portfolio manager: Paul H. Drexler (1996)
Investment objective and policies: High total return: capital appreciation and current income. Invests primarily in equity securities of companies organized or headquartered outside the U.S. Normally invests at least 65% of assets in at least three countries outside the U.S. with maximum of 40% in any one country. Fund may hedge.
Year organized: 1991

LOOMIS SAYLES INVESTMENT GRADE BOND FUND
(See first Loomis Sayles listing for data common to all funds)

Portfolio manager: Daniel J. Fuss (1996)
Investment objective and policies: High total return: current income and capital appreciation. Invests at least 65% of total assets in investment grade fixed-income securities, including corporate and government issues. Up to 20% of assets may be in preferred stocks, and up to 10% in junk bonds. May invest in Canadian securities without limit, and invest up to 20% of assets in other foreign issues. May use a variety of derivative instruments for hedging purposes.
Year organized: 1996

LOOMIS SAYLES MID CAP GROWTH FUND
(See first Loomis Sayles listing for data common to all funds)

Portfolio managers: Jerome A. Castellini (1996), Scott S. Pape (1996)
Investment objective and policies: Long-term capital growth. Invests at least 65% of assets in equity securities of domestic equity securities of companies with market capitalizations between $500M and $5B, with a median portfolio capitalization of between $1B and $5B. May invest in Canadian securities without limit, and invest up to 20% of assets in other foreign issues. May use a variety of derivative instruments for hedging purposes.
Year organized: 1996

LOOMIS SAYLES MID CAP VALUE FUND
(See first Loomis Sayles listing for data common to all funds)

Portfolio managers: Jeffrey C. Petherick (1996), Gregg D. Watkins (1996), Dean A. Gulis (1997)
Investment objective and policies: Long-term capital growth. Invests at least 65% of assets in equity securities of domestic equity securities of companies with market capitalizations between $500M and $5B that are perceived to be undervalued. Portfolio maintains a median capitalization of between $1B and $5B. May invest in Canadian securities without limit, and invest up to 20% of assets in other foreign issues. May use a variety of derivative instruments for hedging purposes.
Year organized: 1996

LOOMIS SAYLES MUNICIPAL BOND FUND
(See first Loomis Sayles listing for data common to all funds)

Portfolio manager: Martha F. Hodgman (1993)
Investment objective and policies: High current income exempt from federal income tax, consistent with capital preservation. Invests in investment grade municipal securities with at least 80% of assets in issues rated A or better and at least 65% of assets in bonds.
Year organized: 1991
Special sales restrictions: Effective 1/1/97, fund is only available to new shareholders in Institutional Class Shares with $1M minimums. Shareholders with prior accounts may open new accounts with regular minimums.

LOOMIS SAYLES SHORT-TERM BOND FUND
(See first Loomis Sayles listing for data common to all funds)

Portfolio manager: John Hyll (1992)
Investment objective and policies: High total return: current income and capital appreciation, with relatively low fluctuation in NAV. Invests primarily in investment grade debt securities, including securities convertible into common stocks, and maintains a weighted average maturity of one to three years. May invest up to 20% of assets in junk bonds, 20% in non-convertible preferred stocks and 20% in securities of foreign issuers.
Year organized: 1992

LOOMIS SAYLES SMALL CAP GROWTH FUND
(See first Loomis Sayles listing for data common to all funds)

Portfolio managers: Christopher R. Ely (1996), Philip C. Fine (1996), David L. Smith (1996)
Investment objective and policies: Long-term capital growth. Invests in equity securities of small, rapidly growing companies with good earnings growth potential perceived to be trading at below market valuation levels. Normally invests at least 65% of assets in companies with market capitalizations of less than $500M. May invest in Canadian securities without limit, and invest up to 20% of assets in other foreign issues. May use a variety of derivative instruments for hedging purposes.
Year organized: 1996

LOOMIS SAYLES SMALL CAP VALUE FUND
(See first Loomis Sayles listing for data common to all funds)

Portfolio managers: Jeffrey C. Petherick (value) (1993), Mary C. Champagne (growth) (1995)
Investment objective and policies: Long-term capital growth. Invests in equity securities of companies with good earnings growth potential at below market valuation levels. Normally invests at least 65% of assets in companies with market capitalizations of less than $500M. May invest up to 20% of assets in securities of foreign issuers, and use foreign currency hedging transactions.
Year organized: 1991 (name changed from Small Cap Fund 1/97)
Ticker symbol: LSCRX

LOOMIS SAYLES STRATEGIC VALUE FUND
(See first Loomis Sayles listing for data common to all funds)

Portfolio manager: Philip J. Schettewi (1996)
Investment objective and policies: Long-term capital growth. Invests substantially all its assets in common stocks of companies perceived to be undervalued. Portfolio will be concentrated in 35 to 40 issues perceived to be best positioned to perform in the current and future market environment. May invest in Canadian securities without limit, and invest up to 20% of assets in other foreign issues. May use a variety of derivative instruments for hedging purposes.
Year organized: 1996

LOOMIS SAYLES U.S. GOVERNMENT SECURITIES FUND
(See first Loomis Sayles listing for data common to all funds)

Portfolio manager: Kent P. Newmark (1991)
Investment objective and policies: High total return: current income and capital appreciation. Invests in securities issued or guaranteed by the U.S. Government or its authorities, agencies or instrumentalities and in certificates representing undivided interests in the interest or principal of U.S. Treasury Securities. Invests at least 65% of assets in U.S. Government Securities.
Year organized: 1991
Ticker symbol: LSGSX

Special sales restrictions: Effective 1/1/97, fund is only available to new shareholders in Institutional Class Shares with $1M minimums. Shareholders with prior accounts may open new accounts with regular minimums.

LOOMIS SAYLES WORLDWIDE FUND
(See first Loomis Sayles listing for data common to all funds)

Portfolio managers: Quentin P. Faulkner (domestic stocks) (1996), Daniel J. Fuss (domestic bonds) (1996), E. John deBeer (foreign bonds) (1996), Paul H. Drexler (foreign stocks) (1996)
Investment objective and policies: Maximum total return: high current income and capital appreciation. Invests primarily in an allocated distribution of U.S. and foreign equity and debt securities, usually including at least three different countries. Allocation across the four sectors will be determined by the Loomis Sayles' Global Asset Allocation Group. May invest up to 35% of assets in junk bonds, CMOs and Rule 144A securities (privately offered securities that can be resold only to certain qualified institutional buyers). May engage in options and forward contract transactions for hedging purposes.
Year organized: 1996

MAINSTAY EAFE INDEX FUND ◆
51 Madison Avenue
New York, NY 10010
800-695-2126

Adviser: Monitor Capital Advisors, Inc. (a subsidiary of New York Life)
Portfolio manager: James Mehling (1992)
Investment objective and policies: Total investment results comparable to the Morgan Stanley Capital International Europe, Australia and Far East (EAFE) Index. Invests in a representative sample of the stocks in the Index.
Year organized: 1991 (Group name changed from New York Life Institutional in 1995)
Ticker symbol: NIEAX
Special sales restrictions: Designed for institutional investors only, but individuals may invest through discount broker.
Discount broker availability: Schwab
Minimum purchase through discount broker: $2,500

MAINSTAY VALUE EQUITY FUND ◆
51 Madison Avenue
New York, NY 10010
800-695-2126

Adviser: MacKay-Shields Financial Corp. (a subsidiary of New York Life)
Portfolio managers: Team managed
Investment objective and policies: Maximum total return: capital growth and current income. Invests in a equity securities of domestic and foreign issuers selected according to fundamental value analysis.
Year organized: 1991 (Group name changed from New York Life Institutional in 1995)
Ticker symbol: NIVEX
Special sales restrictions: Designed for institutional investors only, but individuals may invest through discount brokers.
Discount broker availability: Schwab
Minimum purchase through discount broker: $2,500

MAS FUNDS PORTFOLIOS ◆
(Data common to all MAS portfolios are shown below. See subsequent listings for data specific to individual portfolios.)

One Tower Bridge
West Conshohocken, PA 19428-2899
800-354-8185, 610-940-5000
prices 800-522-1525
fax 610-940-5098

Adviser: Miller, Anderson & Sherrerd, LLP
Special sales restrictions: Designed principally for the investments of tax-exempt fiduciary investors who are entrusted with the responsibility of investing assets held for the benefit of others. Funds are available at lower initial and subsequent minimums through discount brokerage firms which have established accounts with the MAS funds.
Minimum purchase through discount broker: Fidelity: $2,500; Schwab: $2,500; IRA: $1,000; White: None

MAS BALANCED PORTFOLIO ◆
(See first MAS listing for data common to all portfolios)

Portfolio manager: Team managed
Investment objective and policies: Above-average total return consistent with reasonable risk. Invests in common stocks and fixed-income securities with mix adjusted to reflect changes in economic and market conditions.
Year organized: 1992
Ticker symbol: MPBAX
Discount broker availability: Fidelity, Schwab, White

MAS DOMESTIC FIXED INCOME PORTFOLIO ◆
(See first MAS listing for data common to all portfolios)

Portfolio manager: Team managed
Investment objective and policies: Maximum total return consistent with capital conservation. Invests in corporate bonds, mortgage-backed securities and U.S. Government securities, and maintains a weighted average maturity of more than five years. Up to 20% of assets may be in junk bonds.
Year organized: 1992
Ticker symbol: MPSFX
Discount broker availability: Fidelity, Schwab

MAS EQUITY PORTFOLIO ◆
(See first MAS listing for data common to all portfolios)

Portfolio manager: Team managed
Investment objective and policies: Above-average total return consistent with reasonable risk. Invests in common stocks of companies with earnings and dividend growth potential greater than the economy in general and inflation.
Year organized: 1984
Ticker symbol: MPEQX
Discount broker availability: Fidelity, Schwab, White

MAS FIXED INCOME PORTFOLIO ◆
(See first MAS listing for data common to all portfolios)

Portfolio manager: Team managed
Investment objective and policies: Maximum total return consistent with capital conservation. Invests in corporate bonds, mortgage-backed securities and U.S. Government securities, and maintains a weighted average maturity of more than five years. Up to 20% of assets may be in junk bonds.
Year organized: 1984
Ticker symbol: MPFIX
Discount broker availability: Fidelity, Schwab, White

MAS FIXED INCOME II PORTFOLIO ◆
(See first MAS listing for data common to all portfolios)

Portfolio manager: Team managed
Investment objective and policies: Maximum total return consistent with capital conservation. Invests in investment grade corporate bonds, mortgage-backed securities and U.S. Government securities, and maintains a weighted average maturity of more than five years.
Year organized: 1984
Ticker symbol: MPFDX
Discount broker availability: White

MAS GLOBAL FIXED INCOME PORTFOLIO ◆
(See first MAS listing for data common to all portfolios)

Portfolio manager: Team managed
Investment objective and policies: Above average total return consistent with capital conservation. Invests in domestic and foreign corporate and government debt securities, from at least three countries including the U.S., and maintains a weighted average maturity of more than five years.
Year organized: 1993
Ticker symbol: MAGFX
Discount broker availability: Schwab, White

MAS HIGH-YIELD SECURITIES PORTFOLIO ◆
(See first MAS listing for data common to all portfolios)

Portfolio manager: Team managed
Investment objective and policies: Above average total return consistent with reasonable risk. Invests primarily in high yield corporate fixed-income securities, including junk bonds, and maintains a weighted average maturity of more than five years.
Year organized: 1989
Ticker symbol: MPHYX
Discount broker availability: Fidelity, Schwab, White

MAS INTERMEDIATE DURATION PORTFOLIO ◆
(See first MAS listing for data common to all portfolios)

Portfolio manager: Team managed
Investment objective and policies: Above average total return over a three to five year market cycle, consistent with reasonable risk. Invests in a diversified portfolio of U.S. Governments, investment grade corporate bonds, mortgage-backed securities and U.S. Government securities. Portfolio maintains a weighted average maturity of two to five years.
Year organized: 1994
Discount broker availability: White

MAS INTERNATIONAL EQUITY PORTFOLIO ◆
(See first MAS listing for data common to all portfolios)

Portfolio manager: Team managed
Investment objective and policies: Above-average total return consistent with reasonable risk. Invests in common stocks of companies based outside the U.S. chosen from the Morgan Stanley Capital International World ex-U.S. Index of more than 1,100 securities.
Year organized: 1988
Ticker symbol: MPIEX
Discount broker availability: Schwab, White

MAS INTERNATIONAL FIXED INCOME PORTFOLIO ◆
(See first MAS listing for data common to all portfolios)

Portfolio manager: Team managed
Investment objective and policies: Above average total return consistent with capital conservation. Invests in high quality foreign corporate and government securities, from at least three countries other than the U.S.. Portfolio maintains a weighted average maturity of more than five years.
Year organized: 1994
Ticker symbol: MPIFX
Discount broker availability: Schwab, White

MAS LIMITED DURATION PORTFOLIO ◆
(See first MAS listing for data common to all portfolios)

Portfolio manager: Team managed
Investment objective and policies: Maximum total return consistent with capital conservation. Invests in investment grade corporate bonds, mortgage-backed securities and U.S. Government securities. Portfolio maintains a weighted average maturity of one to three years.

Year organized: 1992
Ticker symbol: MPLDX
Discount broker availability: Schwab, White

MAS MID CAP GROWTH PORTFOLIO ◆
(See first MAS listing for data common to all portfolios)

Portfolio manager: Team managed
Investment objective and policies: Long-term capital growth with no emphasis on current income. Invests primarily in common stocks of smaller and medium size companies with market capitalizations from $300M to $2B and above average growth potential.
Year organized: 1990 (name changed from Emerging Growth Portfolio on 6/12/95)
Ticker symbol: MPEGX
Discount broker availability: Fidelity, Schwab, White

MAS MID CAP VALUE PORTFOLIO ◆
(See first MAS listing for data common to all portfolios)

Portfolio manager: Team managed
Investment objective and policies: Above-average total return over a market cycle of three to five years, consistent with reasonable risk. Invests in common stocks of companies with market capitalizations in the range of the S&P MidCap 400 Index that are perceived to be undervalued.
Year organized: 1994
Ticker symbol: MPMVX
Discount broker availability: Fidelity, Schwab, White

MAS MORTGAGE-BACKED SECURITIES PORTFOLIO ◆
(See first MAS listing for data common to all portfolios)

Portfolio manager: Team managed
Investment objective and policies: Maximum total return consistent with reasonable risk. Invests in mortgage-backed securities, and maintains a weighted average maturity of more than seven years.
Year organized: 1992
Ticker symbol: MPMBX
Discount broker availability: White

MAS MULTI-ASSET-CLASS PORTFOLIO ◆
(See first MAS listing for data common to all portfolios)

Portfolio manager: Team managed
Investment objective and policies: Above average total return consistent with reasonable risk. Invests in a mix of equity and debt securities of U.S. and foreign issuers with allocation adjusted to reflect changes in economic and market conditions.
Year organized: 1994
Ticker symbol: MPGBX
Discount broker availability: Fidelity, Schwab, White

MAS MUNICIPAL FIXED INCOME PORTFOLIO ◆
(See first MAS listing for data common to all portfolios)

Portfolio manager: Team managed
Investment objective and policies: Above-average total return consistent with capital conservation and current income exempt from federal income tax. Invests in municipal debt securities, and maintains a weighted average maturity ranging from ten to thirty years. Up to 20% of assets may be in junk bonds.
Year organized: 1992
Ticker symbol: MPMFX
Discount broker availability: White

MAS PA MUNICIPAL FIXED INCOME PORTFOLIO ◆
(See first MAS listing for data common to all portfolios)

Portfolio manager: Team managed
Investment objective and policies: Above average total return consistent with capital conservation and current income exempt from Federal and Pennsylvania personal income tax. Invests primarily in investment grade Pennsylvania municipal securities, and maintains a weighted average maturity ranging from ten to thirty years.
Year organized: 1992
Ticker symbol: MPPIX
Discount broker availability: White

MAS SMALL CAPITALIZATION VALUE PORTFOLIO ◆
(See first MAS listing for data common to all portfolios)

Portfolio manager: Team managed
Investment objective and policies: Above-average total return consistent with reasonable risk. Invests in common stocks of companies with market capitalizations of $50M to $800M, in the range of the companies represented in the Russell 2000 Small Stock Index believed undervalued.
Year organized: 1986
Ticker symbol: MPSCX
Sales restrictions: Closed to new investors
Discount broker availability: Fidelity, Schwab, White

MAS SPECIAL PURPOSE FIXED INCOME PORTFOLIO ◆
(See first MAS listing for data common to all portfolios)

Portfolio manager: Team managed
Investment objective and policies: Above-average total return over a market cycle of three to five years, consistent with reasonable risk. Invests primarily in a diversified portfolio of U.S. Government, corporate, mortgage-backed, or foreign debt obligations, and other fixed-income securities and derivatives. Portfolio is structured to complement an investment in one or more of the equity portfolios. Average weighted maturity of the portfolio will ordinarily exceed five years.
Year organized: 1992
Ticker symbol: MPSPX
Discount broker availability: White

MAS VALUE PORTFOLIO ◆
(See first MAS listing for data common to all portfolios)

Portfolio manager: Team managed
Investment objective and policies: Above-average total return consistent with reasonable risk. Invests in common stocks of companies with market capitalizations greater than $300M believed undervalued. Will generate higher income than Equity Portfolio.
Year organized: 1986
Ticker symbol: MPVLX
Sales restrictions: Fund closed to new investors 3/7/97.
Discount broker availability: Fidelity, Schwab, White

MORGAN GRENFELL FUNDS ◆
(Data common to all Morgan Grenfell funds are shown below. See subsequent listings for data specific to individual funds.)

885 Third Avenue
New York, NY 10022
800-814-3401

Adviser: Morgan Grenfell Capital Management, Inc.
Special sales restrictions: Designed primarily for institutions and high net worth individuals. Funds are available at lower initial and subsequent minimums through discount brokerage firms which have established accounts with the Morgan Grenfell funds.
Minimum purchase through discount broker: Fidelity: $2,500; Schwab: $2,500, White: $2,500

MORGAN GRENFELL EMERGING MARKETS DEBT FUND ◆
(See first Morgan Grenfell listing for data common to all funds)

Portfolio manager: Team managed
Investment objective and policies: Maximum total return. Invests primarily in any quality of fixed-income securities of issuers located in countries with emerging securities markets. May invest more than 25% of assets in each of Mexico and Brazil. May invest up to 35% of assets in fixed-income obligations issued or guaranteed by the U.S. Government.
Year organized: 1994
Ticker symbol: MGEIX
Discount broker availability: Fidelity, Schwab, White

MORGAN GRENFELL EMERGING MARKETS EQUITY FUND ◆
(See first Morgan Grenfell listing for data common to all funds)

Portfolio manager: Team managed
Investment objective and policies: Maximum capital appreciation. Invests primarily in equity and equity-related securities of companies located in countries with emerging securities markets. Fund may invest more than 25% of its total assets each in Brazil, Malaysia, and Mexico. May invest up to 35% of assets in fixed-income securities, cash, or cash equivalents.
Year organized: 1994
Discount broker availability: Fidelity, White

MORGAN GRENFELL EUROPEAN SMALL CAP EQUITY FUND ◆
(See first Morgan Grenfell listing for data common to all funds)

Portfolio manager: Team managed
Investment objective and policies: Maximum capital appreciation. Invests primarily in equity and equity-related securities of small capitalization companies in Europe, identified as those found in the bottom 25% market capitalizations of issuers listed on any European stock exchange or over the counter market.
Year organized: 1994
Discount broker availability: Fidelity, White

MORGAN GRENFELL FIXED INCOME FUND ◆
(See first Morgan Grenfell listing for data common to all funds)

Portfolio manager: David W. Baldt (1992)
Investment objective and policies: High income consistent with preservation of capital. Invests in investment grade fixed-income government and corporate securities, and maintains a weighted average maturity ranging from five to ten years. May invest up to 25% of assets in dollar denominated securities of non-U.S. issuers.
Year organized: 1992
Ticker symbol: MFINX
Discount broker availability: Fidelity, Schwab, White

MORGAN GRENFELL GLOBAL FIXED INCOME FUND ◆
(See first Morgan Grenfell listing for data common to all funds)

Portfolio manager: Team managed
Investment objective and policies: Maximum total return. Invests in fixed-income securities of issuers located in at least three countries which may include the U.S. May invest more than 25% of assets in each of Japan, the U.S., Germany and the United Kingdom.
Year organized: 1994
Ticker symbol: MGGFX
Discount broker availability: Fidelity, White

MORGAN GRENFELL INTERNATIONAL EQUITY FUND ◆
(See first Morgan Grenfell listing for data common to all funds)

Portfolio manager: Team managed
Investment objective and policies: Maximum capital appreciation. Invests primarily in equity and equity-related securities of companies located in countries other than the U.S. Will diversify at least 65% of assets across companies from at least three different

countries. May invest more than 25% of assets in each of Japan and the U.K. Up to 35% of assets may be in fixed-income obligations, cash, or cash equivalents, and equity instruments of U.S. issuers.
Year organized: 1995
Discount broker availability: Fidelity

MORGAN GRENFELL INTERNATIONAL FIXED INCOME FUND ◆
(See first Morgan Grenfell listing for data common to all funds)

Portfolio manager: Team managed
Investment objective and policies: Maximum total return. Invests in fixed-income securities of issuers located in at least three countries outside the U.S. May invest more than 25% of assets in each of France, Germany, Italy, Japan, and the U.K.
Year organized: 1994
Ticker symbol: MGIIX
Discount broker availability: Fidelity, White

MORGAN GRENFELL INTERNATIONAL SMALL CAP EQUITY FUND ◆
(See first Morgan Grenfell listing for data common to all funds)

Portfolio manager: Team managed
Investment objective and policies: Maximum capital appreciation. Invests primarily in equity and equity-related securities of small cap companies located in countries other than the U.S. Companies fall into the bottom 25% market capitalization ranking on a stock exchange or secondary market. May invest more than 25% of total assets each in Japan and the U.K. May invest up to 35% of assets in domestic or foreign debt obligations, or in domestic equities.
Year organized: 1994
Discount broker availability: Fidelity, White

MORGAN GRENFELL MUNICIPAL BOND FUND ◆
(See first Morgan Grenfell listing for data common to all funds)

Portfolio manager: David W. Baldt (1991)
Investment objective and policies: High income exempt from federal income tax, consistent with preservation of capital. Invests in a portfolio of municipal securities, and maintains a weighted average maturity ranging from five to ten years. May invest without limit in securities subject to AMT tax treatment.
Year organized: 1991
Ticker symbol: MGMBX
Discount broker availability: Fidelity, Schwab, White

MORGAN GRENFELL SHORT-TERM FIXED INCOME FUND ◆
(See first Morgan Grenfell listing for data common to all funds)

Portfolio manager: David W. Baldt (1995)
Investment objective and policies: High income consistent with preservation of capital. Invests in investment grade fixed-income government and corporate securities, and maintains a weighted average maturity of three years or less. May invest up to 25% of assets in dollar denominated securities of non-U.S. issuers.
Year organized: 1995
Discount broker availability: Fidelity, White

MORGAN GRENFELL SHORT-TERM MUNICIPAL BOND FUND ◆
(See first Morgan Grenfell listing for data common to all funds)

Portfolio manager: David W. Baldt (1995)
Investment objective and policies: High income exempt from federal income tax, consistent with preservation of capital. Invests in a portfolio of municipal securities, and maintains a weighted average maturity of three years or less. May invest without limit in securities subject to AMT tax treatment.
Year organized: 1995
Discount broker availability: Fidelity, Schwab, White

MORGAN GRENFELL SMALLER COMPANIES FUND ◆
(See first Morgan Grenfell listing for data common to all funds)

Portfolio manager: Team managed
Investment objective and policies: Maximum capital appreciation. Invests primarily in equity and equity-related securities of domestic companies whose capitalization falls into the bottom 20% of the Wilshire 5000 Index. Looks for issues believed to show greater than average growth potential as well as low valuations. May invest up to 35% of assets in fixed-income securities.
Year organized: 1995
Discount broker availability: Fidelity, Schwab, White

PIMCO FUNDS
(data common to all PIMCo funds are shown below. See subsequent listings for data specific to individual funds.)

840 Newport Center Drive, Suite 360
Newport Beach, CA 92660
800-927-4648, 714-760-4880
fax 714-644-4651

Adviser: PIMCo Advisors, L.P.
Special sales restrictions: PIMCo Institutional and PIMCo Funds merged in 1996. Previously designed to provide pension and profit sharing plans, endowments, employee benefit trusts, foundations, etc., with access to the services of Pacific Investment Management and its affiliates, most funds are now available retail through a multiple class structure, some of which still maintain a no-load class available through discount brokers. A few are still institutional only, and available at discount brokerage firms which have established accounts with PIMCo.

PIMCO BALANCED FUND ◆
(See first PIMCo listing for data common to all funds)

Sub-advisers: PIMCo Advisors, L.P., Cadence Capital Management, NFJ Investment Group (a subsidiary of PIMCo)
Portfolio manager: Team managed
Investment objective and policies: Total return consistent with prudent investment management. Invests 40% to 65% of assets in common stocks, at least 25% of assets in fixed-income obligations, and money markets.
Year organized: 1992 (name changed from Strategic Allocation Portfolio in 1993 and from PFAMCo Balanced Portfolio on 11/15/94)
Ticker symbol: PBLIX
Discount broker availability: *White: $1,000

PIMCO CAPITAL APPRECIATION FUND ◆
(See first PIMCo listing for data common to all funds)

Sub-adviser: Cadence Capital Management (a subsidiary of PIMCo)
Portfolio manager: Team managed
Investment objective and policies: Capital growth. Invests in common stocks of companies with market capitalizations exceeding $100M that show demonstrably improving fundamentals and are thought to be reasonably valued relative to the markets.
Year organized: 1991 (name changed from Cadence Capital Appreciation fund in 1997, from PFAMCo Capital Appreciation Portfolio on 11/15/94)
Ticker symbol: PAPIX
Discount broker availability: *White: $1,000; Schwab: $2,500

PIMCO CORE EQUITY FUND ◆
(See first PIMCo listing for data common to all funds)

Sub-adviser: Columbus Circle Investors (a subsidiary of PIMCo)
Portfolio manager: Team managed
Investment objective and policies: Long-term capital growth; income secondary. Invests in common stocks of approximately 40 to 50 companies with market capitalizations of at least $3B currently outperforming market expectations.
Year organized: 1994 (name changed from Columbus Circle Core Equity in 1997)
Ticker symbol: PCEAX
Discount broker availability: Fidelity: $2,500; *White: $1,000

PIMCO EMERGING MARKETS FUND
(See first PIMCo listing for data common to all funds)

Sub-adviser: Blairlogie Capital Management Ltd. (an indirect subsidiary of PIMCo)
Portfolio manager: James Smith (1993)
Investment objective and policies: Long-term capital growth. Invests primarily in common stocks of companies located in or doing the majority of their business in emerging markets countries as defined by the Morgan Stanley Capital International Emerging Markets Free Index, or by the United Nations or the IMF.
Year organized: 1993 (name changed from Blairlogie Emerging Markets fund in 1997, from PFAMCo Emerging Markets Portfolio on 11/15/94)
Ticker symbol: PEMIX
Discount broker availability: Schwab: $2,500; *White: $1,000

PIMCO EMERGING MARKETS BOND FUND
(See first PIMCo listing for data common to all funds)

Portfolio manager: Michael Rosborough (1997)
Investment objective and policies: Total return: current income and capital appreciation. Invests primarily in debt obligations of companies located in or governments of emerging markets countries as defined by the Morgan Stanley Capital International Emerging Markets Free Index, or by the United Nations or the IMF.
Year organized: 1997
Discount broker availability: Schwab: $2,500; *White: $1,000

PIMCO EQUITY INCOME FUND
(See first PIMCo listing for data common to all funds)

Sub-adviser: NFJ Investment Group (a subsidiary of PIMCo)
Investment objective and policies: Current income; capital appreciation secondary. Invests primarily in equity securities of companies with below average price to earnings ratios and higher dividend yields relative to their industry groups.
Year organized: 1991 (name changed from NFJ Equity Income fund in 1997, and from PFAMCo Equity Income Portfolio 11/15/94)
Ticker symbol: PEIIX
Discount broker availability: Schwab: $2,500; *White: $1,000

PIMCO FOREIGN BOND FUND
(See first PIMCo listing for data common to all funds)

Portfolio managers: John L. Hague (1992). Lee R. Thomas, III (1995)
Investment objective and policies: Maximum total return. Invests in fixed-income obligations of non-U.S. issuers from at least three different countries or currencies. Fund generally maintains an average maturity of three to six years.
Year organized: 1992
Ticker symbol: PFORX
Discount broker availability: Schwab (only through financial advisers): $2,500; *White: $1,000

PIMCO GLOBAL BOND FUND
(See first PIMCo listing for data common to all funds)

Portfolio managers: John L. Hague (1992). Lee R. Thomas, III (1995)
Investment objective and policies: Maximum total return. Invests in fixed-income obligations of U.S. and foreign issuers. Fund generally maintains an average maturity of three to eight years. Foreign bonds may range from 25% to 75% of assets.
Year organized: 1992
Ticker symbol: PIGLX
Discount broker availability: Fidelity: $2,500; Schwab (only through financial advisers): $2,500; *White: $1,000

PIMCO HIGH YIELD FUND
(See first PIMCo listing for data common to all funds)

Portfolio manager: Benjamin Trosky (1992)
Investment objective and policies: Maximum total return. Invests in fixed-income obligations of U.S. and foreign issuers rated below investment grade, but rated at least "B". Fund generally maintains an average maturity of two to six years. Foreign bonds may range from 25% to 75% of assets.
Year organized: 1992
Ticker symbol: PHIYX
Discount broker availability: Schwab (only through financial advisers): $2,500; *White: $1,000

PIMCO INNOVATION FUND
(See first PIMCo listing for data common to all funds)

Portfolio manager: Team managed
Investment objective and policies: Capital appreciation. Invests primarily in equity securities of companies that use innovative technologies to gain strategic competitive advantages in their industries, and companies that provide and service these technologies.
Year organized: 1994
Discount broker availability: *White: $1,000

PIMCO INTERNATIONAL DEVELOPED FUND
(See first PIMCo listing for data common to all funds)

Sub-adviser: Blairlogie Capital Management Ltd. (an indirect subsidiary of PIMCo)
Portfolio managers: James Smith (1993), Gavin Dobson (1993)
Investment objective and policies: Long-term capital growth. Invests primarily in common stocks of companies located in or doing the majority of their business in countries included in the Morgan Stanley Capital International EAFE Index.
Year organized: 1993 (name changed from Blairlogie International Active in 1997, from PFAMCo International Active Portfolio on 11/15/94)
Ticker symbol: PIAIX
Discount broker availability: Schwab: $2,500; *White: $1,000

PIMCO LONG-TERM U.S. GOVERNMENT FUND
(See first PIMCo listing for data common to all funds)

Portfolio manager: Pasi Hamalainen (1997)
Investment objective and policies: Maximum total return. Invests primarily in U.S. Government debt obligations rated at least "A" or better. Portfolio maintains an average maturity of eight years or more.
Year organized: 1991 (name changed from Long Duration fund 12/18/92)
Ticker symbol: PGOVX
Discount broker availability: Fidelity: $2,500; Schwab (only through financial advisers): $2,500; *White: $1,000

PIMCO LOW DURATION FUND
(See first PIMCo listing for data common to all funds)

Portfolio manager: William H. Gross (1987)
Investment objective and policies: Maximum total return consistent with reasonable risk. Invests in a diversified portfolio of domestic, investment grade fixed-income securities, and generally maintains a weighted average maturity of one to three years. May invest up to 20% of assets in foreign currencies, up to 10% in junk bonds, and may invest without limit in derivatives.
Year organized: 1987
Ticker symbol: PTLDX
Discount broker availability: Schwab (only through financial advisors): $2,500; *White: $1,000

PIMCO LOW DURATION FUND II ◆
(See first PIMCo listing for data common to all funds)

Portfolio manager: William H. Gross (1991)
Investment objective and policies: Maximum total return. Invests in domestic investment grade fixed-income securities, and maintains a weighted average portfolio duration of one to three years. May invest up to 20% of assets in foreign currencies, up to 10% in junk bonds, and may invest without limit in derivatives.
Year organized: 1991
Ticker symbol: PLDTX
Discount broker availability: Fidelity: $2,500; Schwab (only through financial advisors): $2,500; *White: $1,000

PIMCO MICRO CAP GROWTH FUND
(See first PIMCo listing for data common to all funds)

Portfolio managers: David B. Breed (1993), William B. Bannick (1993)
Investment objective and policies: Capital growth. Invests in common stocks of 80 to 100 companies with market capitalizations of under $100M that demonstrate improving fundamentals and are thought to be reasonably valued relative to the market.
Year organized: 1991 (name changed from Cadence Micro Cap Growth in 1997, and from PFAMCo Micro Cap Growth 11/15/94)
Ticker symbol: PMCIX
Special sales information: Fund closed to new investors.
Discount broker availability: Fidelity: $2,500; Schwab (only through financial advisors): $2,500; *White: $1,000

PIMCO MID CAP EQUITY FUND ◆
(See first PIMCo listing for data common to all funds)

Sub-adviser: Columbus Circle Investors (a subsidiary of PIMCo)
Investment objective and policies: Long-term capital growth. Invests in common stocks of approximately 40 to 60 companies with market capitalizations of at least $800M to $3B currently outperforming market expectations.
Year organized: 1994 (name changed from Columbus Circle Mid Cap Equity in 1997)
Discount broker availability: *White: $1,000

PIMCO MID CAP GROWTH FUND
(See first PIMCo listing for data common to all funds)

Sub-adviser: Columbus Circle Investors (a subsidiary of PIMCo)
Portfolio manager: Team managed
Investment objective and policies: Long-term capital growth. Invests in common stocks of companies with market capitalizations of at least $500M with demonstrably improving fundamentals that are thought to offer reasonable value relative to the market.
Year organized: 1994 (name changed from Columbus Circle Mid Cap Equity in 1997)
Ticker symbol: PMGIX
Discount broker availability: Schwab: $2,500; *White: $1,000

PIMCO SHORT-TERM FUND
(See first PIMCo listing for data common to all funds)

Portfolio manager: David H. Edington (1987)
Investment objective and policies: Maximum current income consistent with preservation of capital and daily liquidity. Invests in money market and other short-term instruments, and maintains a weighted average maturity of less than one year. May invest up to 20% of assets in foreign currencies, up to 10% in junk bonds, and may invest without limit in derivatives.
Year organized: 1987
Ticker symbol: PTSHX
Discount broker availability: Schwab (only through financial advisers): $2,500; *White: $1,000

PIMCO SMALL CAP GROWTH FUND ◆
(See first PIMCo listing for data common to all funds)

Sub-adviser: Cadence Capital Management (a subsidiary of PIMCo)
Portfolio managers: William B. Bannick (1993), David B. Breed (1993)
Investment objective and policies: Capital growth. Invests in stocks of 80 to 100 companies with market capitalizations of $50M to $500M with improving fundamentals and stocks reasonably valued by the market.
Year organized: 1991 (name changed from Cadence Small Cap Growth in 1996, and from PFAMCo Small Cap Growth Portfolio on 11/15/94)
Discount broker availability: Fidelity: $2,500

PIMCO SMALL CAP VALUE FUND
(See first PIMCo listing for data common to all funds)

Sub-adviser: NFJ Investment Group (a subsidiary of PIMCo)
Portfolio manager: Team managed
Investment objective and policies: Long-term growth of capital and income. Invests in common stocks of companies with market capitalizations between $50M and $500M with below average price to earnings ratios relative to their industry groups.
Year organized: 1991 (name changed from NFJ Small Cap Value in 1996, and from PFAMCo Small Cap Value Portfolio on 11/15/94)
Ticker symbol: PSVIX
Discount broker availability: *White: $1,000

PIMCO STOCKSPLUS FUND
(See first PIMCo listing for data common to all funds)

Portfolio manager: David H. Edington (1993)
Investment objective and policies: Total return exceeding that of the stocks that comprise the S&P 500. Invests in selected stocks represented within the Index, and in index options, futures and options on index futures based on the S&P. May at times be fully invested in derivatives.
Year organized: 1993
Ticker symbol: PSTKX
Discount broker availability: Schwab (only through financial advisers): $2,500; *White: $1,000

PIMCO TOTAL RETURN FUND
(See first PIMCo listing for data common to all funds)

Portfolio manager: William H. Gross (1987)
Investment objective and policies: Maximum total return. Invests in fixed-income securities, including corporate bonds, U.S. Government securities and mortgage-related securities. Portfolio maintains a weighted average maturity ranging from three to six years. Up to 20% of assets may be denominated in foreign currencies.
Year organized: 1987
Ticker symbol: PTTRX
Discount broker availability: Schwab (only through financial advisers): $2,500; *White: $1,000

PIMCO TOTAL RETURN II FUND
(See first PIMCo listing for data common to all funds)

Portfolio manager: William H. Gross (1991)
Investment objective and policies: Maximum total return. Invests in fixed-income securities, including corporate bonds, U.S. Government securities and mortgage-related securities. Portfolio maintains a weighted average maturity ranging from three to six years. Up to 20% of assets may be denominated in foreign currencies.

Year organized: 1991
Ticker symbol: PMBIX
Discount broker availability: Fidelity: $2,500; Schwab (only through financial advisers): $2,500; *White: $1,000

PIMCO TOTAL RETURN FUND III
(See first PIMCo listing for data common to all funds)

Portfolio manager: William H. Gross (1991)
Investment objective and policies: Total return exceeding that of the stocks that comprise the S&P 500. Invests in selected stocks represented within the Index, and in index options, futures and options on index futures based on the S&P.
Year organized: 1991 (name changed from Total Return South Africa-Free 8/92)
Ticker symbol: PTSAX
Discount broker availability: Schwab (only through financial advisers): $2,500; *White: $1,000

PIMCO VALUE FUND
(See first PIMCo listing for data common to all funds)

Investment objective and policies: Long-term capital growth. Invests in common stocks of approximately fifty companies with market capitalizations of at least $200M that have below average price earnings ratios relative to their industry groups.
Year organized: 1991 (name changed from Advisers NFJ Diversified Low P/E in 1996)
Ticker symbol: PDLIX
Discount broker availability: Schwab: $2,500; *White: $1,000

REA-GRAHAM BALANCED FUND
10966 Chalon Road
Los Angeles, CA 90077
800-433-1998, 310-208-2282

Adviser: James Buchanan Rea, Inc.
Portfolio managers: Dr. James B. Rea (1976), James B. Rea, Jr. (1979)
Investment objective and policies: Medium-term capital growth, income and safety. Invests in common stocks, preferred stocks, U.S. Government securities and money market instruments with allocation adjusted to reflect market conditions.
Year organized: 1976
Ticker symbol: REAGX
Sales charge: 4.75% (available at NAV through discount brokers)
Discount broker availability: Schwab
Minimum purchase through discount broker: $2,500

SEI PORTFOLIOS
(Data common to all SEI portfolios are shown below. See subsequent listings for data specific to individual portfolios.)

One Freedom Valley Drive
Oaks, PA 19456
800-342-5734, 610-254-1000

Adviser: SEI Financial Management Corp.
Special sales restrictions: Class A - Designed primarily for institutional investors. Funds are available at lower initial and subsequent minimums through discount brokerage firms which have established accounts with SEI.
Minimum purchase through discount broker: Fidelity: $2,500; Schwab (only through financial advisers): $2,500; White: None

SEI BALANCED PORTFOLIO - CLASS A
(See first SEI listing for data common to all portfolios)

Portfolio manager: Anthony R. Gray (1992)
Investment objective and policies: Total return consistent with preservation of capital. Invests in undervalued common stocks of large companies and fixed-income securities with mix adjusted to reflect changes in market and economic conditions.
Year organized: 1990
Ticker symbol: SEBAX
Discount broker availability: Fidelity, White

SEI BOND INDEX PORTFOLIO - CLASS A
(See first SEI listing for data common to all portfolios)

Sub-adviser: Mellon Bond Assocs.
Portfolio manager: Team managed
Investment objective and policies: Investment results approximating the total return of the Salomon Brothers Broad investment grade Bond Index. Invests in a representative sample of the securities which comprise the Index.
Year organized: 1986
Ticker symbol: BIPFX
Discount broker availability: Fidelity, Schwab (only through financial advisers), White

SEI BOND PORTFOLIO - CLASS A
(See first SEI listing for data common to all portfolios)

Portfolio manager: Team managed
Investment objective and policies: Current income consistent with capital preservation. Invests in U.S. Government and agency securities and investment grade corporate debt, and maintains a weighted average maturity of more than ten years.
Year organized: 1987
Ticker symbol: SEBDX
Sales charge: 3.50% (available at NAV through discount brokers)
Discount broker availability: Fidelity

SEI CAPITAL APPRECIATION PORTFOLIO - CLASS A
(See first SEI listing for data common to all portfolios)

Portfolio manager: Anthony R. Gray (1988)
Investment objective and policies: Capital growth; income incidental. Invests in common stocks and securities convertible into common stocks selected on factors believed favorable for long-term growth, i.e. historical returns on equity & earnings growth rates, focusing on sectors and industry cycles.
Year organized: 1988
Ticker symbol: SECAX
Sales charge: 5.00% (available at NAV through discount brokers)
Discount broker availability: Fidelity, Schwab (only through financial advisers), White

SEI CORE FIXED INCOME PORTFOLIO - CLASS A
(See first SEI listing for data common to all portfolios)

Portfolio manager: Team managed
Investment objective and policies: Current income. Invests in U.S. Government and agency securities and high-quality corporate bonds, and maintains a weighted average maturity ranging from five to ten years.
Year organized: 1987 (formerly Limited Volatility Portfolio. Name changed to Intermediate Bond Portfolio on 1/1/94 and to current on 1/1/95)
Ticker symbol: TRLVX
Sales charge: 4.50% (available at NAV through discount brokers)
Discount broker availability: Fidelity, Schwab (only through financial advisers), White

SEI CORPORATE DAILY INCOME PORTFOLIO - CLASS A
(See first SEI listing for data common to all portfolios)

Sub-adviser: Wellington Management Co.
Portfolio manager: John C. Keogh (1993)
Investment objective and policies: Higher current income than money market funds consistent with preservation of liquidity. Invests in high-quality debt obligations of U.S. issuers, and maintains a weighted average maturity of six to eighteen months.
Year organized: 1993
Ticker symbol: SECPX
Discount broker availability: White

SEI EMERGING MARKETS EQUITY PORTFOLIO - CLASS A
(See first SEI listing for data common to all portfolios)

Sub-adviser: Montgomery Asset Management, L.P.
Portfolio managers: Josephine S. Jimenez (1995), Bryan L. Sudweeks (1995)
Investment objective and policies: Capital growth. Invests in equity securities of companies in at least six emerging market countries with maximum of 35% of assets in any one emerging market country.
Year organized: 1995
Ticker symbol: SIEMX
Discount broker availability: Schwab (only through financial advisers), White

SEI EQUITY INCOME PORTFOLIO - CLASS A
(See first SEI listing for data common to all portfolios)

Sub-adviser: Merus Capital Management (a division of the Bank of California)
Portfolio manager: Thomas M. Arrington (1994)
Investment objective and policies: Current income and moderate capital growth secondary. Invests primarily in common stocks with high current yield and a low level of volatility relative to the market.
Year organized: 1993
Ticker symbol: SEEIX
Sales charge: 5.00% (available at NAV through discount brokers)
Discount broker availability: Fidelity, Schwab (only through financial advisers), White

SEI GNMA PORTFOLIO - CLASS A
(See first SEI listing for data common to all portfolios)

Sub-adviser: Wellington Management Co.
Portfolio manager: Paul D. Kaplan (1993)
Investment objective and policies: Current income consistent with preservation of capital and liquidity. Invests in U.S. Government and agency securities, primarily in GNMA instruments.
Year organized: 1993
Ticker symbol: SEGMX
Discount broker availability: Fidelity, White

SEI INTERMEDIATE-DURATION GOVERNMENT PORTFOLIO - CLASS A
(See first SEI listing for data common to all portfolios)

Sub-adviser: Wellington Management Co.
Portfolio manager: Thomas L. Pappas (1995)
Investment objective and policies: Current income consistent with preservation of capital and liquidity. Invests in high-quality fixed-income U.S. Government securities, and maintains a weighted average maturity of three to five years.
Year organized: 1993
Ticker symbol: TCPGX
Discount broker availability: Fidelity, White

SEI INTERMEDIATE-TERM MUNICIPAL PORTFOLIO - CLASS A
(See first SEI listing for data common to all portfolios)

Sub-adviser: Weiss, Peck & Greer Advisers, Inc.
Portfolio manager: Raymond Kubiak (1995)
Investment objective and policies: High current income exempt from federal income tax, consistent with capital preservation. Invests in high-quality municipal securities, and maintains a weighted average maturity ranging from three to ten years.
Year organized: 1993
Ticker symbol: SEIMX
Sales charge: 3.50% (available at NAV through discount brokers)
Discount broker availability: Fidelity, Schwab (only through financial advisers), White

SEI INTERNATIONAL EQUITY PORTFOLIO - CLASS A
(See first SEI listing for data common to all portfolios)

Sub-advisers: Yamaichi Capital, Farrell-Wako, Seligman Henderson, Lazard Freres
Portfolio manager: Team managed
Investment objective and policies: Long-term capital appreciation. Invests primarily in equity securities of non-U.S. issuers, both on recognized foreign exchanges and in over-the-counter markets. May also invest up to 50% of assets in foreign debt obligations.
Year organized: 1993 (name changed from International Portfolio in 1995; absorbed SEI European Equity and Pacific Basin Equity Portfolios in March 1996)
Ticker symbol: SEITX
Sales charge: 5.00% (available at NAV through discount brokers)
Discount broker availability: Fidelity, Schwab (only through financial advisers), White

SEI INTERNATIONAL FIXED INCOME PORTFOLIO - CLASS A
(See first SEI listing for data common to all portfolios)

Sub-adviser: Strategic Fixed Income, L.P.
Portfolio manager: Kenneth A. Windheim (1993)
Investment objective and policies: Capital growth and current income. Invests high quality non-U.S. dollar denominated government securities and corporate fixed-income securities or debt obligations.
Year organized: 1993
Ticker symbol: SEFIX
Discount broker availability: Fidelity, Schwab (only through financial advisers), White

SEI LARGE CAP GROWTH PORTFOLIO - CLASS A
(See first SEI listing for data common to all portfolios)

Sub-advisers: Alliance Capital Management, L.P., IDS Advisory Group, Inc.
Portfolio manager: Team managed
Investment objective and policies: Capital growth. Invests in common stocks of large capitalization companies thought to offer significant growth potential.
Year organized: 1994
Ticker symbol: SELCX
Discount broker availability: Fidelity, Schwab (only through financial advisers), White

SEI LARGE CAP VALUE PORTFOLIO - CLASS A
(See first SEI listing for data common to all portfolios)

Sub-adviser: Duff & Phelps Investment Management Co.
Portfolio manager: Team managed
Investment objective and policies: Long-term capital growth and moderate income. Invests in common stocks of large capitalization companies with low price-to-earnings multiples and above-average dividend yields relative to the market.
Year organized: 1987 (name changed from Managed Trust Value in 1994)
Ticker symbol: TRMVX
Discount broker availability: Fidelity, Schwab (only through financial advisers), White

SEI MID-CAP GROWTH PORTFOLIO - CLASS A
(See first SEI listing for data common to all portfolios)

Sub-adviser: Martingale Asset Management, Inc.
Portfolio manager: John Freeman (1995)
Investment objective and policies: Long-term capital growth. Invests in common stocks and securities convertible into common stocks of companies with market capitalizations of $500M to $5B.
Year organized: 1993 (name changed from Mid-Cap Growth Portfolio in 1995)
Ticker symbol: SEMCX
Sales charge: 5.00% (available at NAV through discount brokers)
Discount broker availability: Fidelity, Schwab (only through financial advisers), White

SEI PENNSYLVANIA MUNICIPAL PORTFOLIO - CLASS A
(See first SEI listing for data common to all portfolios)

Sub-adviser: Morgan Grenfell Capital Management, Inc.
Portfolio manager: David W. Baldt (1995)
Investment objective and policies: Current income exempt from federal and Pennsylvania income taxes, consistent with capital preservation. Invests in high-quality Pennsylvania municipal securities, and maintains a weighted average maturity of five to seven years.
Year organized: 1987
Ticker symbol: SEIPX
Discount broker availability: Fidelity, Schwab (only through financial advisers), White

SEI S&P 500 INDEX PORTFOLIO - CLASS A
(See first SEI listing for data common to all portfolios)

Portfolio manager: Team managed
Investment objective and policies: Investment results approximating the total return of the S&P 500. Invests in the common stocks of the companies in the S&P 500 in the same proportion as their representation in the Index.
Year organized: 1985
Ticker symbol: TRQIX
Discount broker availability: Fidelity, Schwab (only through financial advisers), White

SEI SHORT-DURATION GOVERNMENT PORTFOLIO - CLASS A
(See first SEI listing for data common to all portfolios)

Sub-adviser: Wellington Management Co.
Portfolio manager: John C. Keogh (1995)
Investment objective and policies: Current income consistent with preservation of capital and liquidity. Invests in high-quality fixed-income U.S. Government securities, and maintains a weighted average maturity of three years or less.
Year organized: 1993
Ticker symbol: TCSGX
Discount broker availability: Fidelity, White

SEI SMALL CAP GROWTH PORTFOLIO - CLASS A
(See first SEI listing for data common to all portfolios)

Sub-advisers: Investment Advisers, Inc.; Nicholas-Applegate Capital Management, Wall Street Associates, Furman Selz Capital Management, Matthew Price
Portfolio manager: Team managed
Investment objective and policies: Long-term capital growth. Invests in equity securities of companies with market capitalizations under $1B thought to offer the potential for above average capital growth. May also invest in investment grade debt obligations.
Year organized: 1988
Ticker symbol: SSCGX
Sales charge: 5.00% (available at NAV through discount brokers)
Discount broker availability: Fidelity, Schwab (only through financial advisers), White

SEI SMALL CAP VALUE PORTFOLIO - CLASS A
(See first SEI listing for data common to all portfolios)

Sub-adviser: 1838 Investment Advisors, L.P.
Portfolio managers: Edwin B. Powell (1994), Holly L. Guthrie (1994), Joseph T. Doyle (1994)
Investment objective and policies: Capital growth. Invests in equity securities of companies with market capitalizations under $1B believed to be undervalued.
Year organized: 1994
Ticker symbol: SESVX
Discount broker availability: Fidelity, Schwab (only through financial advisers), White

TIP INSTITUTIONAL TRUST SHORT DURATION GOVT FUNDS - ONE YEAR PORTFOLIO ◆
1981 N. Broadway, Suite 325
Walnut Creek, CA 94596
800-223-7110, 510-988-7110

Adviser: Tip Turner Investment Partners, Inc.
Portfolio manager: James I. Midanek (1994)
Investment objective and policies: Maximum total return consistent with capital preservation. Invests in obligations issued or guaranteed by the U.S. Government, its agencies and instrumentalities, and maintains a weighted average maturity of one year or less.
Year organized: 1994 (name and management changed from Solon due to a buyout by TIP Turner 1/98.)
Special sales restrictions: Designed for institutional investors but available through discount brokerage firms at reduced minimum investments.
Discount broker availability: Schwab
Minimum purchase through discount broker: $2,500

TIP INSTITUTIONAL TRUST SHORT DURATION GOVT FUNDS - THREE YEAR PORTFOLIO ◆
1981 N. Broadway, Suite 325
Walnut Creek, CA 94596
800-223-7110, 510-988-7110

Adviser: Tip Turner Investment Partners, Inc.
Portfolio manager: James I. Midanek (1994)
Investment objective and policies: Maximum total return consistent with capital preservation. Invests in obligations issued or guaranteed by the U.S. Government, its agencies and instrumentalities, and maintains a weighted average maturity of three years or less.
Year organized: 1994 (name and management changed from Solon due to a buyout by TIP Turner 1/98.)
Special sales restrictions: Designed for institutional investors but available through discount brokerage firms at reduced minimum investments.
Discount broker availability: Schwab
Minimum purchase through discount broker: $2,500

TOUCHSTONE FUNDS
(Data common to all Touchstone funds are shown below. See subsequent listings for data specific to individual funds.)

318 Broadway
Cincinnati, OH 45202
800-669-2796

Adviser: Touchstone Advisors, Inc.
Discount broker availability: Fidelity, *White (Class A shares only)
Minimum purchase through discount broker: Fidelity: $2,500 (does not offer Standby Income); Jack White: $2,000

TOUCHSTONE BALANCED FUND
(See first Touchstone listing for data common to all funds)

Sub-adviser: OpCap Advisers
Investment objective and policies: Growth of capital and income. Invests in common stocks (normally 60% of assets) and fixed-income securities (normally 40%) with allocation adjusted to reflect perceived changes in market and economic conditions. Up to 33% of assets may be in securities of foreign issuers.
Year organized: 1994
Ticker symbol: TBFAX
Sales charge: 5.75% (available at NAV through discount broker)

TOUCHSTONE BOND FUND
(See first Touchstone listing for data common to all funds)

Sub-adviser: Fort Washington Investment Advisors, Inc.
Portfolio managers: Roger Lanham (1994), Rance Duke (1994)

Investment objective and policies: High current income. Invests in investment grade bonds, and maintains an average weighted maturity ranging from five to fifteen years. Up to 35% of assets may be in junk bonds.
Year organized: 1994
Ticker symbol: TOBAX
Sales charge: 4.75% (available at NAV through discount broker)

TOUCHSTONE EMERGING GROWTH FUND

(See first Touchstone listing for data common to all funds)

Sub-advisers: David L. Babson & Co., Inc., Westfield Capital Management, Inc.
Investment objective and policies: Capital growth; income secondary. Invests primarily in common stocks of smaller, rapidly growing companies with market capitalizations less than the average of the companies in the S&P 500 Index. Up to 20% of assets may be in securities of foreign issuers.
Year organized: 1994
Ticker symbol: TEGAX
Sales charge: 5.75% (available at NAV through discount broker)

TOUCHSTONE GROWTH & INCOME FUND

(See first Touchstone listing for data common to all funds)

Sub-adviser: Scudder, Kemper Investments, Inc.
Portfolio managers: Lori J. Ensinger (1997), Robert T. Hoffman (1997)
Investment objective and policies: Growth of capital and income. Invests in common stocks (normally 60% of assets) and fixed-income securities (normally 40%) with allocation adjusted to reflect changes in market and economic conditions. Up to 33% of assets may be in securities of foreign issuers.
Year organized: 1994
Ticker symbol: TGIAX
Sales charge: 5.75% (available at NAV through discount broker)

TOUCHSTONE INCOME OPPORTUNITY FUND

(See first Touchstone listing for data common to all funds)

Sub-adviser: Alliance Capital Management, L.P.
Portfolio managers: Wayne Lyski (1994), Vicki Fuller (1994)
Investment objective and policies: High current income. Invests in high-yield non-investment grade debt securities of both U.S. and non-U.S. issuers. Up to 30% of assets may be denominated in currencies other than the U.S. dollar.
Year organized: 1994
Ticker symbol: TIOAX
Sales charge: 4.75% (available at NAV through discount broker)

TOUCHSTONE INTERNATIONAL EQUITY FUND

(See first Touchstone listing for data common to all funds)

Sub-adviser: BEA Associates
Portfolio manager: Emilio Bassini (1994)
Investment objective and policies: Long-term capital growth. Invests primarily in equity securities of companies based outside the U.S. Up to 40% of assets may be in securities of issuers in emerging markets and 35% in junk bonds.
Year organized: 1994
Ticker symbol: TIEAX
Sales charge: 5.75% (available at NAV through discount broker)

TOUCHSTONE MUNICIPAL BOND FUND

(Fund liquidated 4/2/97)

TOUCHSTONE STANDBY INCOME FUND ◆

(See first Touchstone listing for data common to all funds)

Sub-adviser: Fort Washington Investment Advisors, Inc.
Portfolio manager: Christopher J. Mahoney (1994)
Investment objective and policies: High current income consistent with relative stability of principal. Invests in money market interests and other corporate debt with no single security having a weighted average maturity of greater than five years. Up to 20% of assets may be denominated in currencies other than the U.S. dollar.
Year organized: 1994
Ticker symbol: TSTIX
Sales charge: None

UAM FUNDS PORTFOLIOS

(Data common to all UAM portfolios are shown below. See subsequent listings for data specific to individual portfolios.)

The UAM Service Center
211 Congress Street
Boston, MA 02110
800-638-7983, 617-542-5440

Administrator: Mutual Funds Service Co.
Special sales restrictions: These classes of shares are designed primarily for institutional investors. Funds are available at lower initial and subsequent minimums through discount brokerage firms which have established accounts with UAM. Other UAM funds are available direct, and are profiled in the main directory.
Discount broker availability: *Fidelity, *Schwab, *White
Minimum purchase through discount broker: Fidelity, $2,500; Schwab, $2,500; White, $2,000

UAM - ACADIAN EMERGING MARKETS PORTFOLIO ◆

(See first UAM listing for data common to all portfolios)

Adviser: Acadian Asset Management, Inc.
Lead portfolio manager: Ronald D. Frashure (1993)
Investment objective and policies: Long-term capital appreciation. Invests at least 65% of assets in common stocks of issuers domiciled in emerging countries, as identified by the IMF and the World Bank. Invests in a representative portfolio of the securities available in each country rather than to attempt to predict the relative performance of one security over another within each country. May use options, futures and foreign currency transactions for hedging purposes. Fund is non-diversified.
Year organized: 1993
Ticker symbol: AEMGX

UAM - ACADIAN INTERNATIONAL EQUITY PORTFOLIO ◆

(See first UAM listing for data common to all portfolios)

Adviser: Acadian Asset Management, Inc.
Lead portfolio manager: Ronald D. Frashure (1993)
Investment objective and policies: Maximum long-term total return that exceeds the performance of the Morgan Stanley EAFE Index in the long term, consistent with reasonable risk to principal. Invests at least 65% of assets in a diversified portfolio of equity securities of companies located in at least three countries other than the U.S. through direct investment, ADRs and EDRs. Will invest in both countries and companies not included in the benchmark Index.
Year organized: 1993
Ticker symbol: AIEQX

UAM - ICM FIXED INCOME PORTFOLIO ◆

(See first UAM listing for data common to all portfolios)

Adviser: Investment Counselors of Maryland, Inc.
Portfolio managers: Linda W. McCleary (1992), Daniel O. Shackelford (1993)
Investment objective and policies: Maximum long-term total return consistent with reasonable risk to principal. Invests primarily in domestic investment grade

corporate and government bonds of varying maturities. Portfolio weighted average maturity is adjusted according to perceived market conditions. May, however, purchase foreign issues without limit. May use options, futures and forward foreign currency contracts for hedging purposes.
Year organized: 1992
Ticker symbol: ICFIX

WESTERN ASSET TRUST FUNDS ◆

(Data common to all Western Asset portfolios are shown below. See subsequent listings for data specific to individual portfolios.)

117 East Colorado Boulevard
Pasadena, CA 91105
818-844-9400

Adviser: Western Asset Management Co.
Administrator: Legg Mason Fund Adviser, Inc.
Special sales restrictions: Designed for institutional investors and high net worth individuals, but available at lower initial and subsequent minimums through discount brokerage firms which have established accounts with Western Asset Trust funds.
Minimum purchase through discount broker: Schwab: $2,500; Jack White: $1,000

WESTERN ASSET TRUST CORE PORTFOLIO ◆

(See first Western Asset listing for data common to all portfolios)

Portfolio manager: Kent S. Engel (1990)
Investment objective and policies: Maximum total return: capital appreciation and income. Invests primarily in investment grade fixed-income government and corporate debt securities, and maintains a weighted average maturity of four to six years. Up to 25% of assets may be in U.S. dollar-denominated securities of foreign issuers.
Year organized: 1990 (name changed from Western Asset Full Range Duration in 1996)
Discount broker availability: Schwab, White
Ticker symbol: WATFX

WESTERN ASSET TRUST INTERMEDIATE DURATION PORTFOLIO ◆

(See first Western Asset listing for data common to all portfolios)

Portfolio manager: Stephen A. Walsh (1994)
Investment objective and policies: Maximum total return: capital appreciation and income. Invests primarily in investment grade fixed-income government and corporate debt securities, and maintains a weighted average maturity of two to four years. Up to 25% of assets may be in U.S. dollar-denominated securities of foreign issuers.
Year organized: 1990
Discount broker availability: Schwab, White
Ticker symbol: WATIX

WESTERN ASSET TRUST LIMITED DURATION PORTFOLIO ◆

(See first Western Asset listing for data common to all portfolios)

Portfolio manager: Carl L. Eichstaedt (1996)
Investment objective and policies: Maximum total return: capital appreciation and income. Invests primarily in investment grade fixed-income government and corporate debt securities, and generally maintains a weighted average maturity of about three years, and a target range of two to four years. Up to 25% of assets may be in U.S. dollar-denominated securities of foreign issuers.
Year organized: 1996
Discount broker availability: Schwab
Ticker symbol: WALDX

CHAPTER 13

Directory of discount brokers trading mutual funds

CHARLES SCHWAB & CO.
Mutual Fund Marketplace

Phone: 800-435-4000
Internet address: http://www.schwab.com
Trading hours: 24 hours a day; 3 P.M. EST for today's price.
No. of branch offices: 270
Minimum investment: $2,500 (most funds)
Small account fee: $7.50/qtr. for balances below $1,000
Reinvests dividends: Yes
IRA account fee: $29/year under $10,000: waived for accounts with automatic monthly investments, and for account holders with $50,000 + in total assets at Schwab
Margin rules: Schwab proprietary funds must be in the account 30 days, non-Schwab funds can be margined immediately.
Shorts funds: No
No. of Handbook funds traded: 1362
No. of NTF (no transaction fee) funds traded: 858
NTF Assets: $63 billion
No. of load funds available NAV & institutional w/low min: 120
NTF short-term trading rules: Shares held for at least 90 days can be sold without penalty. Standard fees will be charged on the sale only if held less than 90 days. A maximum of 15 short-term redemptions (less than 90 days) per calendar year will be allowed. If this is exceeded, all future transactions (i.e. both on the buy and sell side) could become commissionable.
Fee schedule for commissionable funds

Overriding minimum: $39 per trade.

Transaction Size	Transaction fees
$0-14,999	0.7% of principal
$15,000-99,999	0.7% on first $15,000
	0.2% on amount over $15,000
$100,000+	0.7% on first $15,000
	0.2% on amount between $15,000 & $100,000
	0.06% on amount over $100,000

Any load fund with commissions exceeding 4% incurs no transactions charges except the commission.

When placing simultaneous orders to sell one fund and purchase a new fund with the proceeds you pay the standard fee on the larger transaction and $25 on the corresponding buy or sell. Funds sales or redemption fees also apply.
Discount for online trades: 20% off transaction fee for non-NTF funds

FIDELITY BROKERAGE
FundsNetwork

Phone: 800-544-9697
Internet address: http://www.fidelity.com
Trading hours: 24 hours a day; 4 P.M. EST for today's price for Fidelity funds; 3 P.M. for non-Fidelity funds (there are exceptions); 3 P.M. for exchanges in the same family.
No. of branch offices: 82
Minimum investment: $2,500 (or higher according to fund); $500 for retirement accounts, $1,000 for college savings accounts
Small account fee: $12 per year per account if valued under $2,500 in November, wavied for investors with $30,000 + in Fidelity assets, and for accounts using systemtic investments, maximum of $24 per investor per year.
Reinvests dividends: Yes
IRA account fee: $12 per year per account if valued under $2,500 in November, maximum of $24 per investor per year.
Margin rules: Funds must be in account 30 days
Shorts funds: Yes
No. of Handbook funds traded: 1440
No. of NTF funds traded: 811
NTF Assets: $17B
No. of load funds available NAV & institutional w/low min: 75
NTF short-term trading rules: If 5 short-term redemptions of shares held less than 6 months are made within a 12-month period, Fidelity may apply a $35 transaction fee to subsequent short-term buys or sells made during the 12-month period initiated by the first redemption.
Fee schedule for commissionable funds

Transaction Size	Transaction fees
$0 - $5,000	$35
$5,000 +	$35 on first $5,000
	+ 0.2% on principal amount above $5,000
	up to max of $150 per trade

Minimum fee on commissionable funds: $35

Any load fund incurs no transactions charges except the commission.

Discount for online trades: $28.95 flat fee for all web transactions

JACK WHITE & CO.
Mutual Fund Network

Phone: 800-323-3263
Internet address: http://www.jackwhiteco.com
Trading hours: 24 hours per day, 7 day a week. 9 A.M. or 12:00 NN PST for today's price depending on fund.
No. of branch offices: 0
Minimum investment: According to fund
Small account fee: None
Reinvests dividends: Most funds
IRA account fee: $35 per year, under $10,000.
Margin rules: Available for most funds (except extremely volatile ones; e.g., T. Rowe Price New Asia) with NAV's over $5. Funds must be in account 30 days
Shorts funds: Yes, subject to availability; $15,000 equity required.
No. of Handbook funds traded: 1643
No. of NTF funds traded: 1289
NTF Assets: $4.5 billion
No. of load funds available NAV & institutional w/low min: 130
NTF short-term trading rules: Positions liquidated within 90 days of purchase are charged $50 penalty for redemptions of less than $100,000, $100 penalty for redemptions of $100,000 +. If a customer makes 15 short-term redemptions in a calendar year, regular transaction fees apply to all purchases and redemptions for the balance of the year.
Fee schedule for commissionable funds

Transaction Size	Transaction fees
All trades	$27 flat fee

Discount for online trades: $24 flat fee

WATERHOUSE SECURITIES
Mutual FundConnection

Phone: 800-934-4443
Internet address: http://www.waterhouse.com
Trading hours: Monday-Friday, 8:30 A.M. - 12 A.M. EST; 2 P.M. for today's price.
No. of branch offices: 120
Minimum investment: According to fund
Small account fee: None
Reinvests dividends: Yes
IRA account fee: None; $25 termination fee
Margin rules: Available for funds with NAV's over $4 1/8
Shorts funds: No
No. of NTF funds traded: 930
NTF Assets: $2.5B
NTF short-term trading rules: Transaction fee of $25 is reinstated on accounts if five or more short-term redemptions of funds held for six months or less are executed within a 12-month period.
Fee schedule for commissionable funds

Transaction Size	Transaction fees
All transactions	$25

IRA Transaction Size	Transaction fees
All transactions	$25

When placing simultaneous orders to sell one fund and purchase a new fund with the proceeds, you pay the standard fee on the sale, and $15 for the corresponding buy order.

Discount for online trades: none

MURIEL SIEBERT
FundExchange

Phone: 800-872-0666
Internet address: http://www.msiebert.com
Trading hours: Monday-Friday, 9 A.M. - 5 P.M.; 3 P.M. or 4 P.M. for today's price.
No. of branch offices: 7
Minimum investment: According to fund
Small account fee: None
Reinvests dividends: Yes
IRA account fee: $30 per year, waived for accounts over $10,000
Margin rules: Funds must be in account 30 days
Shorts funds: No
No. of Handbook funds traded: 1036
No. of NTF funds traded: 472
NTF Assets: Proprietary info
No. of load funds available NAV & institutional w/low min: 41
NTF minimum investments: $5,000; $2,000 for IRAs
NTF short-term trading rules: Minimum holding period to qualify for NTF: $2,000-$9,999 = 9 months, $10,000-$19,999 = 6 months, $20,000-$49,999 = 3 months, $50,000+ = 1 month.

Fee schedule for commissionable funds

Transaction Size	Transaction fees
All transactions	$35 flat fee

Discount for online trades: 10% off transaction fee for non-NTF funds

General information: All services provide consolidated monthly statements and insurance protection. Multiple trades reduce fees and holding periods.

Other discount brokers offering no-load fund trading

The following brokers also offer fund services. Contact them for details:

Discount broker	800 telephone	NTF?
Accutrade for Mutual Funds	800-228-3011	yes
American Express Financial Direct	800-297-2001	yes
American Century Brokerage	888-345-2071	yes
AmeriTrade	800-669-3900	yes
Andrew Peck	800-221-5873	no
Arnold Securities	800-328-4076	no
Bidwell & Co.	800-547-6337	yes
Bruno, Stolze & Co.	800-899-6878	no
Bull & Bear Securities	800-262-5800	no
Bush Burns Securities	800-821-4800	no
Discover Brokerage Direct	800-688-6896	yes
DLJ Direct	800-825-5723	yes
First Montauk	800-366-1500	yes
Freeman Welwood & Co.	800-729-7585	yes
Kennedy, Cabot & Co.	800-252-0090	yes
Marsh Block & Co.	800-366-1500	yes
National Discount	800-888-3999	yes
NationsBank Fund Solutions	800-926-1111	yes
Peremel & Co.	800-666-1440	yes
Quick & Reilly	800-221-4257	yes
R.J. Forbes Group, Inc.	800-754-7687	no
Scudder FundFolio	800-700-0820	yes
Seaport Securities	800-732-7678	no
Securities Research	800-327-3156	no
Southern Financial	800-476-3738	no
State Discount	800-222-5520	no
Sterling Investment Services	800-782-1522	no
T. Rowe Price Discount Brokerage	800-638-5660	yes
Summit Discount	800-631-1635	no
Thomas F. White	800-669-4483	no
Tuttle Securities	800-962-5489	yes
Unified Management Corp.	800-862-7283	no
USAA Brokerage Services	800-531-8628	yes
Vanguard Brokerage Services	800-992-8327	yes
Wall Street Access	800-925-5781	yes
Wall St. Discount	800-221-7990	no
York Securities	800-221-3154	yes

CHAPTER 14

Directory of portfolio managers
Arranged alphabetically

Portfolio Manager	Fund	Portfolio Manager	Fund
Ablin, Jack A.	Emerald Managed Bond	Bacarella, Robert S.	Monetta Balanced, Fund, Govt MM, Inter
Abraham, Todd A.	Federated ARMs		Bond, Large-Cap, Mid-Cap, Small Cap
Abrams, Kenneth L.	Vanguard Explorer	Backer, Svein	Northern Int'l Select Equity
Abramson, Jay B.	CRM Small Cap Value	Baez-Sacasa, Alejandro J.	JP Morgan Emerg Mkts Equity
Adam, Joel	Academy Value	Baird, William	BNY Hamilton Inter Govt
Adams, Jeffrey	SSgA Small Cap	Baker, James E.	Amtrust Value
Adams, Patrick S.	Berger Balanced,Gr & Inc, One Hundred,	Baker, James O.	INVESCO Inter Govt Bond
	Select	Baldt, David W.	Morgan Grenfell FI, Muni Bond, ST FI,
Adler, Steven H.	ASM Index 30		ST Muni; SEI PA Muni
Affleck, John A.	Stratton Monthly Dividend REIT Shares	Bales, William H.	Janus Venture
Agnew, Wendy	Excelsior Pacific/Asia	Balestrino, Joseph M.	Federated Inter Inc
Ahnrud, Mark S.	Nations Diversified Inc	Baliga, Gurudutt M.	AMEX Strategist Special Growth
Akre, Charles T., Jr.	FBR Small Cap Gr/Value	Ball, Julian C.	Gradison Growth Tr Gr & Inc
Albrecht, J. Scott	Federated Inter Muni Tr, PA Inter Muni	Banet, Terry E.	JP Morgan Shares: Tax Aware U.S. Equity
Aldis, Ralph P.	U.S. Global Investors U.S. Glbl Resources,	Bannick, William B.	PIMCo Micro Cap Gr, Sm Cap Gr
	U.S. Gold Shares,	Bannon, Robert	Analytic Master FI, ST Govt
	U.S. World Gold	Barber, Rocky	William Blair Mutual Growth
Alexanderson, Eileen	Lazard Bantam Value, Mid Cap, Small Cap	Bardin, Gail	Hotchkis and Wiley Equity Income
Alger, David D.	Spectra Fund	Baril, Carolyn A.	Star Select REIT Plus
Allan, Elizabeth J.	Japan Fund; Scudder Emerg Mkts Gr,	Barker, Karolyn	Wasatch Mid-Cap
	Pacific Opps	Barker, Scott T.	Analytic Master FI, ST Govt
Allen, Angela Z.	Globalt Growth	Baron, Ronald S.	Baron Asset, Growth & Inc
Allen, Samuel	Globalt Growth	Barone, Richard A.	Maxus Equity, Inc, Laureate
Allen, Thomas	Fidelity Sel Insurance	Barr, Dean S.	AIT Vision: U.S. Equity
Alpers, Alan	Navellier Aggr Growth, Aggr Small Cap,	Barranco, Audra J.	Fidelity Select Chemicals
	Aggr Small Cap Equity, Lg Cap Gr, Lg	Barrett, Richard C.	Stonebridge Growth
	Cap Val, Mid Cap Gr, Sm Cap Val	Barron, William	INVESCO Asian Growth
Altman, Jeffrey A.	Franklin Mutual Series	Barrow, James P.	Vanguard Windsor II
Ammann, Robert T.	Founders Discovery	Baskir, Mark A.	Strong Limited Resources
Anderson, David B.	Scout Regional, Stock	Bassini, Emilio	Touchstone Int'l Equity
Anderson, Erik S.	Sit Sm Cap Growth	Basten, David D.	API Trust Capital Inc, Multiple Index Trust,
Anderson, Todger	Westcore MIDCO Growth		Treasuries Trust
Andrews, David H.	Cappiello Rushmore Emerg Gr, Gold, Gr,	Bauer, Randall S.	Federated ST Inc
	Util Inc	Bauer, Stephen C.	SAFECO CA TF Inc, Insured Muni Bond,
Angell, Wiley D.	Quaker Fixed Inc		Muni Bond
Anthony, Scott S.	Scudder GNMA	Baxter, Christine M.	PBHG Emerging Gr, Ltd
Antico, Paul L.	Fidelity Small Cap Stock	Baxter, Donald H.	Philadelphia Fund
Antoian, Edward N.	Vanguard Explorer	Baxter, Michael	Hotchkis & Wiley Mid-Cap
Anton, Robert E.	Crabbe Huson Asset Alloc, Equity	Bayles, Richard L.	Excelsior Inc & Gr
Antrim, Joseph L.	Davenport Equity	Bean, Walter C.	UAM - McKee Domestic Equity, McKee
Aplet, Leonard A.	Columbia Daily Inc, Fixed Inc Securities		Int'l Equity, McKee Small Cap Equity
Apps, Robin	UBS Int'l Equity; Vanguard Int'l Value	Beaty, Bruce F.	AARP Capital Gr; Scudder Classic Gr
Arani, Ramin	Fidelity Sel Retailing	Beaumont, Bruce	Independence One Fixed Inc, MI Muni Bond,
Archambo, Wayne J.	Boston Partners Mid Cap Value		U.S. Govt Secs
Arneil, Karen	Galaxy MM	Beckwith, Mark J.	Vanguard Specialized Utilities Inc
Arnold, Thomas C.	North Carolina TF Bond	Bee, Bruce	Masters' Select Int'l
Aronson, Theodore R.	Quaker Small-Cap Value	Beer, Andrew E.	Unified Starwood Strategic
Arrington, Thomas M.	SEI Equity Inc	Bein, Dennis M.	Analytic Defensive Equity, Enhanced Equity
Arteaga, Ivan	Gabelli Global Telecomm	Bender, John T.	Strong Corp Bond, Glbl High Yield Bond,
Askew, Peter B.	Price, Rowe Emerg Mkts Bond, Glbl Govt		Govt Securities
	Bond, Int'l Bond	Benner, H. Dean	Brundage Story & Rose Sht/Inter FI
Aster, Richard F. Jr.	Meridian, Meridian Value	Bentley, Rex L.	SAFECO Bal, U.S. Value
Athey, Preston G.	Price, Rowe Small Cap Value	Berberet, Christopher C.	Mosaic Bond, Govt MM, Govt, High Yield,
Aton, Melissa A.	Aon REIT Index, S&P 500 Index		TF AZ, TF MD, TF MO, TF MM, TF
Auriana, Lawrence	Kaufmann Fund		National, TF VA
Auwaerter, Robert F.	Vanguard Admiral Inter-Term U.S. Treas,	Berchtenbreiter, Patrice L.	Price, Rowe CA TF MF, NY TF MF, Summit
	Admiral Long-Term U.S. Treas, Admiral		Muni MM, TE MF
	ST U.S. Treas, FI Inter Corp, FI Inter U.S.	Berghuis, Brian W.H.	Price, Rowe Mid Cap Growth
	Treas, FI LT U.S. Treas, FI ST U.S. Treas,	Bergson, Eric M.	Northern CA TE, FL Inter TE
	MM Res Fed, MM Res Prime, ST Corp,	Bergstrom, Gary L.	Fremont Int'l Small Cap
	Treasury MM	Bernabeo, Patricia	HGK Fixed Income
Ayoub, Christopher	Merrill Lynch Retirement Reserves MF	Bernstein, Edwin R.	Pathfinder
Babin, Charles	Quantitative Gr & Inc	Bernstein, Jeffrey M.K.	Strong Mid Cap
Babson, Kelly D.	AARP Bond Fund for Inc; Scudder High	Berry, Michael A.	Heartland Mid Cap Value
	Yield Bond, Inc	Berteaux, Jean-Marc	Fidelity Sel Transportation
Babyak, Grant	FTI Small Cap Equity	Bertelson, Robert C.	Fidelity OTC

Portfolio Manager	Fund
Bertocci, Bruno	Stein Roe Emerg Mkts, Int'l
Bettin, Scott A.	IAI Bond, Govt
Beveridge, Walter	Schwab Muni MF
Beyer, Kathryn D.	Vintage Bond
Bhandari, Laxmi C.	Warburg, Pincus Glbl FI
Bickerstaff, Glen E.	Transamerica Premier Equity
Biggar, Douglas A.	Weston New Century Capital, New Century I
Billeadeau, Scott A.	Nations Emerg Gr, Sm Co Gr
Bjurman, George D.	Bjurman Micro-Cap Growth
Black, Elizabeth D.	TIAA-CREF Bond Plus
Black, Susan L.	Warburg, Pincus Cap Apprec, Health Scis
Blais, A. Robert	RNC MM
Bledsoe, Pamela K.	USAA Bal Strategy, Inc Strategy, MM, Treas MM
Bloomstran, Christopher P.	Scout Balanced
Boberski, Irving V.	Lake Forest Core Equity, MM
Bockstein, Yvette	FTI Small Cap Equity
Boeckmann, Eric V.	Northern Inter TE
Boesel, Stephen W.	Price, Rowe Growth & Inc
Bogle, John C., Jr.	ni numeric Growth, Growth & Val, Larger Cap Value, Micro-Cap
Boich, John D.	Montgomery Glbl Oppor, Int'l Gr, Int'l Small Cap, Japan Sm Cap
Bokor-Ingram, Dominic	U.S. Global Investors - Accolade - Regents Eastern Euro
Bonavico, Christopher J.	Transamerica Premier Index
Bonnel, Arthur J.	U.S. Global Investors - Accolade - Bonnel Growth
Bonnell, John C.	USAA CA MM, FL TF MM, NY MM, TX TF MM, VA MM
Bonomo, Joseph F., Jr.	UAM - McKee U.S. Govt
Borghans, Marc G.	Rembrandt Small Cap
Borgwardt, Kurt	American Century Inc & Gr, Utilities
Boritzke, John D.	Marshall Inter TF
Bosland, James L.	Boston 1784 TF MM
Bosse, Jon D.	UAM - NWQ Special Equity
Bourbulas, Mary-Kay H.	Strong HY Muni Bond, ST HY Muni
Bowden, Thomas C.	Sefton Equity Value, Sm Co Value
Bowles, Barbara L.	Kenwood Gr & Inc
Boyadjian, Mark S.	Scudder GNMA
Boyd, Christopher K.	Amer Century - 20th Century Giftrust, New Opportunities
Boyd, Robert F.	UAM - ICM Equity
Boyer, Blair	Harbor Int'l Growth
Bradley, Harold S.	Amer Century - 20th Century Heritage
Brady, David P.	Stein Roe Young Investor
Bramwell, Elizabeth R.	Bramwell Growth; Selected Special Shares
Bratt, Nicholas	AARP Glbl Growth; Scudder Glbl, Greater Europe Gr, Pacific Opps
Breckel, Theodore	Northern Growth Equity
Breed, David B.	PIMCo Micro Cap Gr, Small Cap Gr
Breeden, Douglas T.	Smith Breeden Financial Svcs
Bridges, Edson Low III	Bridges Investment
Brilley, Michael C.	Sit Bond, MM, MN TF, TF Inc, U.S. Govt Sec
Brilliant, Irving	Salomon Brothers Asset Opportunity
Brinkley, Barbara A.	59 Wall St TF Short-Interm Fixed Inc
Brown, Anthony S.	Pax World
Brown, Eddie C.	Brown Capital Mgmt Bal, Equity, Sm Co
Brown, John H.	Montgomery Equity Inc
Browne, Christopher H.	Tweedy, Browne Amer Value, Glbl Value
Browne, William H.	Tweedy, Browne Amer Value, Glbl Value
Bruce, John T.	FBP Contrarian Bal, Equity
Bruce, Robert B.	Bruce Fund
Brumley, George W., III	Oak Value
Bruno, Salvatore J.	AARP Diversified Gr, Diversified Inc w/Gr
Bryan, Caesar M.P.	Gabelli Gold, Int'l Growth
Bryant, Don W.	Emerald Equity Value
Buller, Steven J.	Fidelity Sel Environmental Services
Burgess, Frank E.	Mosaic Balanced, Foresight, Investors, Mid-Cap Gr
Burkart, Jim	Northern Technology
Burn, Harry, III	Sound Shore
Byrne, Douglas	Emerald FL TE
Byrne, Susan M.	Westwood Bal, Equity
Byrum, Michael P.	Rydex OTC, Ursa

Portfolio Manager	Fund
Cabell, John K., Jr.	USAA Aggressive Gr
Calamos, John P.	Lancaster Convertible
Caldwell, Roland G.	C/Fund Adams Equity, C/Fund, C/Govt, C/Gr Stock, C/TF
Calihan, Martin J.	IAI Capital Apprec
Calkin, Lynda J.	Westwood SmallCap Equity
Callinan, James L.	Robertson Stephens Emerging Growth
Canakaris, Ronald E.	Montag & Caldwell Bal, Growth
Cancelmo, Richard P., Jr.	West University
Cantor, Daniel K.	Stein Roe Growth & Inc
Capone, Christopher M.	BNY Hamilton Inter Investment Grade
Cappelli, Robert J.	Advance Capital I Bal, Bond, Retirement Inc
Cappiello, Frank A.	Cappiello-Rushmore Emerg Gr, Gold, Gr, Utility Inc
Carbone, John M.	Vanguard NJ TF MM, NY TF MM, OH TF MM
Cardell, Daniel J.	WPG Quantitative Equity
Cardon, Jeff	Wasatch Aggr Gr, Gr, Micro-Cap Value
Carlson, Charles B.	Strong Dow 30 Value
Carlson, Charles vK.	Greenspring
Carlson, John H.	Fidelity Int'l Bond, New Markets Inc
Carlson, Kathleen A.	PC&J Performance, Preservation
Carlson, Marina T.	Strong Common Stock, Opportunity
Carney, Thomas D.	Weitz Series Fixed Inc, Govt MM
Carr, David R. Jr.	Oak Value
Carrion, Maria-Elena	BT Investment Latin American Equity
Carroll, James L.	Loomis-Sayles Core Value
Carroll, Laurie A.	Dreyfus Bond Market Index
Case, Douglas W.	AIT Vision: U.S. Equity
Castegren, Hakan	Harbor Int'l
Castellini, Jerome A.	Loomis-Sayles Growth, Mid-Cap Gr
Castro, Oscar A.	Montgomery Glbl Commun, Glbl Oppor, Int'l Gr, Japan Sm Cap
Cates, G. Staley	Longleaf Partners, Small Cap, Realty
Catudal, James F.	Fidelity Sel Energy Svc, Sel Industrial Materials
Cavanna, Henry	J.P. Morgan U.S. Equity
Cerney, Jac A.	Rembrandt Balanced, Value
Cerny, Rodney D.	KPM Equity Portfolio
Cessine, Robert S.	AARP Bond Fund for Inc, High Quality ST Bond; Scudder Income, ST Bond
Chaisson, Selena A.	Dresdner RCM Biotech, Global Health Care
Chambers, David	Hotchkis & Wiley Int'l
Champagne, Mary C.	Loomis-Sayles Small Cap Value
Chance, Robin B.	JP Morgan Shares: Tax Aware Disciplined Equity
Chang, Laurence J.	Janus Overseas
Chang, Valerie	Neuberger & Berman Int'l
Chaplin, Deborah A.	AARP Int'l Gr & Inc
Chapman, Dick	First Omaha Fixed Inc, Short-Interm Fixed Inc
Chapman, Ronald	Dreyfus Global Gr, Int'l Gr
Chase, Douglas B.	Fidelity Sel Consumer Inds
Chauvin, Richard L.	Florida Street Growth
Chen, Huachen	Dresdner RCM Global Tech
Cheng, Irene T.	AARP Int'l Gr & Inc; Scudder Int'l
Cheng, Ren	Fidelity Freedom Funds
Chenoweth, William H.	TIP: Turner Midcap Gr, Small Cap
Chiang, Frank	Montgomery Emerg Asia, Emerg Mkts
Chin, Peter	Scudder Development, 21st Century Growth
Chin, Wai W.	UAM - Jacobs Int'l Octagon
Chow, Agnes	Guinness Flight Asia Sm Cap
Chow, Lisa M.	Guinness Flight Mainland China
Christensen, Dale C.	Warburg, Pincus Bal, Cash Res, FI, Glbl FI, Inter Mat Govt, NY Inter Muni, NY TE MM
Church, Gregory A.	Matterhorn Gr
Cimilluca, Ed	Oak Hall Equity
Clapp, Greta R.	Columbia Muni Bond
Clapp, C. Thomas	Nations LifeGoal Bal, LifeGoal Gr, LifeGoal Inc & Gr
Clemente, Lilia	Citizens Global Equity
Clemons, Gary R.	Marshall Int'l Stock

511

512

Portfolio Manager	Fund
Draper, Ford B. Jr.	Kalmar Growth with Value Sm Cap
Drexler, Paul H.	Loomis Sayles Int'l Equity, Worldwide
Droppelman, Nancy	Rembrandt Real Estate
Duarte, Jesus Isidoro	Montgomery Latin America
Duck, Sandra L.	Nations Govt MM, Treasury
Dudley, Andrew	Fidelity ST Bond, Spartan ST Bond
Duffy, Kevin P.	Lighthouse Contrarian
Duffy, Michael J.	Vanguard Horizon Global Asset Alloc
DuFour, Stephen	Fidelity Balanced
Dugan, Mary P.	BT Investment Small Cap
Duke, Rance	Touchstone Bond
Dunn, Thomas F.	Lazard Bond, Int'l FI, Strategic Yield
Durbiano, Mark E.	Federated High Yield Tr
Durham, Paul	BT Investment Pacific Basin Equity
Dutton, William M.	Skyline Special Equities
Dyer, William W., Jr.	Century Shares Trust
Ebright, Thomas R.	Royce REvest Gr & Inc
Ebright, Tim	Managers Special Equity
Eckenrodt, Richard H., Jr.	Lindner Utility
Eckl, Nancy A.	American Aadvantage Bal, Gr & Inc, Int'l Equity
Eder, David C.	Kent Gr & Inc, Index Equity, Int'l Gr, Small Co Gr
Edington, David H.	PIMCo Short Term, StocksPlus
Edwards, P. Nicholas	Warburg, Pincus Japan Growth, Japan OTC, Major Foreign Markets
Edzard, Alexandra	Fidelity Germany
Ee, Angeline	Montgomery Emerg Asia, Emerg Mkts
Efron, Eric M.	USAA Aggressive Gr
Eggerss, Candice	JP Morgan U.S. Small Co
Ehrlich, Harold W.	Warburg, Pincus Major Foreign Markets
Ehrmann, Philip	Nations Emerging Mkts
Eichstaedt, Carl L.	Legg Mason Cash Reserve Tr, U.S. Govt Inter, U.S. Govt MM; Western Asset Ltd Dur
Eisen, Greg	SAFECO Small Co Stock
Ek, Edwin	Citizens Index
Elijah, Ronald E.	Robertson Stephens Info Age, Value + Gr
Ellenberger, Donald T.	Federated U.S. Govt Bond, U.S. Govt Secs 5-10 yrs
Elliffe, Guy	Jurika & Voyles Mini-Cap
Ellis, Joan	Excelsior Real Estate
Ellis, Katherine	Excelsior Real Estate
Ellis, Timothy L.	Investek Fixed Inc Trust
Ellison, David	FBR Financial Svcs, Small Cap Financial
Ellison, Susan	Dreyfus Int'l Stock Index
Ely Berchtenbreiter, Patrice	Price, Rowe CA TF MF, NY TF MF, Summit Muni MM, TE MF
Ely, Christopher R.	Loomis Sayles Small Cap Gr
Emmett, Nigel F.	JP Morgan Int'l Equity
Engel, Kent S.	Legg Mason Invest Grade Inc; Western Asset Full Range Dur
English, Patrick J.	Fiduciary Capital Gr
Ensinger, Lori J.	AARP Bal Stk & Bond, Growth & Inc; Touchstone Gr & Inc
Esielonis, Steven M.	Quantitative Gr & Inc
Espinosa, Diego	AARP Glbl Gr; Scudder Global
Evans, David J.	Robertson Stephens MicroCap
Eveillard, Jean-Marie	Masters' Select Equity
Ewing, Robert D.	Fidelity Sel Financial Svcs
Eysenbach, James M.	AARP Small Co Stock, U.S. Stock Index; Scudder MicroCap, Small Co Value
Fahey, Matthew B.	Marshall Mid Cap Value
Falci, Steven A.	Dreyfus LifeTime Gr, LifeTime Gr & Inc, LifeTime Inc, Midcap Index, S&P 500 Index, Small Cap Stock Index
Falkowski, Patricia A.	UAM - FMA Small Co
Farmer, Ross H.	Rockwood Fund
Farrell, James H., Jr.	PBHG Large Cap Val
Farrell, Richard	Guiness Flight Asia Blue Chip, China & Hong
Farrelly, Jennifer	Fidelity Spartan Market Index
Fasciano, Michael F.	Fasciano
Faulkner, Quentin P.	Loomis Sayles Worldwide
Faust, Michael J.	Bailard, Biehl & Kaiser Int'l Bond
Faust, William A.	Scout MM Fed, MM Prime
Feeney, William M.	Fremont CA Inter TF
Feingold, John	Managers Intermediate Mtge
Felman, David	Fidelity Convertible Securities
Fennell, Theresa C.	Amer Century - Benham High Yield
Fentin, Richard B.	Fidelity Value
Ferenbach, Colin C.	Haven
Ferer, William A.	Strong American Utilities
Feuerman, Joshua	SSgA Emerg Mkts
Fields, Michael W.	American AAdvantage Inter Bond, MM, Muni MM, Short-Term Bond, U.S. Govt MM
Fine, Philip C.	Loomis Sayles Small Cap Gr
Fines, Gordon	AMEX Strategist Growth Trends
Finkelstein, Todd A.	Boston 1784 Income
Fiorenza, Janet A.	WPG TF MM
Firestone, Karen	Fidelity Lg Cap Stock
Fischer, Anthony R., Jr.	Forum Daily Assets Cash, Daily Assets Treasury
Fischer, George A.	Fidelity Muni Bond, Spartan Aggr Muni, Spartan CT Muni Inc, Spartan Insured Muni Inc, Spartan MD Muni Inc, Spartan Muni Inc, Spartan OH Muni Inc
Fisher, Kenneth L.	Purisima Total Return
Fitterer, Lyle J.	Strong Advantage, Short-Term Bond
Fitzgerald, Thomas H., Jr.	Reserve Informed Investors Gr
Fitzpatrick, C.T. III	Longleaf Partners Realty
Fleischmann, James G.	TIAA-CREF Managed Alloc
Fleites, Agustin J. "Gus"	SSgA Lifesolutions Bal, Gr, Inc & Gr
Fletcher, Jeremy	Amer Century - Benham Target Funds
Flewharty, Molly	CA Daily TF, CT Daily TF, Daily TF, FL Daily Muni, MI Daily TF, NJ Daily Muni, NY Daily TF, NC Daily Muni, PA Daily Muni, ST Inc MM, ST Inc U.S. Govt
Flood, Peter J.	Northern - Tax Exempt
Flynn, Mary Ann	Northern MM
Fockler, Jack E., Jr.	Royce Financial Svcs, GiftShares, Low Priced Stock, Micro Cap, PA Mutual, PMF II, Premier, Total Return
Fogle, Glenn A.	Amer Century - 20th Century Vista
Folkman, Alan J.	Columbia Special
Fontaine, Richard H.	Fontaine Cap Appr, Glbl Gr, Glbl Inc
Foody-Malus, Kathleen M.	Federated ARMs, GNMA Tr, Inc Tr
Force, John F.	PBHG Technology & Communications
Ford, John R.	Price Spectrum Int'l
Fortuna, Philip S.	AARP Divers Gr, Divers Inc w/Gr, Small Co Stock, U.S. Stock Index; Scudder Micro Cap, Small Co Value
Foulkes, Richard R.	Vanguard Int'l Gr
Fouse, William L.	Vanguard Asset Allocation
Fowler, David M.	Vanguard U.S. Growth
Fowler, Gordon B.	JP Morgan Shares: Tax Aware U.S. Equity
Fraise, George P.	Scudder Bal
Franklin, Carol L.	Scudder Greater Europe Gr
Franks, Thomas	Federated Max-Cap, Mid-Cap, Mini-Cap
Fraser, Gregory	Fidelity Diversified Int'l
Frashur, Ronald D.	UAM - Acadian Emerg Mkts, Int'l Equity
Fraze, Patricia R.	Westwood Balanced
Freeman, Charles T.	Vanguard Windsor
Freeman, John	SEI Mid-Cap
Frels, William B.	Mairs & Power Balanced
French, Graham E.	Vanguard Special Gold & Precious Metals
French, Susan J.	Northern Small Cap Gr
Frey, Colleen M.	BNY Hamilton Inter NY TE
Frey, Kyle F.	Warburg, Pincus Sm Co Value
Friedman, Nancy	Lipper U.S. Equity
Friedman, Robert L.	Franklin Mutual Series
Friess, Foster S.	Brandywine, Brandywine Blue; Masters' Select Equity
Frith, Patrick	Nations Short-Term Inc
Frost, Patricia L.	Rainier Inter FI
Frucci, Richard M.	RSI Ret Trust Emerg Gr Equity
Fruzzetti, Peter	Fidelity Sel Brokerage & Investment
Fulkerson, Allan W.	Century Shares Trust
Fuller, Mark A. III	William Blair Mutual Growth
Fuller, Vicki	Touchstone Income Opportunity
Furfine, David	Emerald ST FI

Portfolio Manager	Fund	Portfolio Manager	Fund
Furman, Robert M.	Rainbow Fund	Green, Isaac H.	Loomis-Sayles Core Value
Fuss, Daniel J.	Loomis-Sayles Bond, High Yield, Invest Grade Bond, Worldwide; Managers Bond	Green, Philip J.	BT Investment Life Cycle Long Range, Life Cycle Mid Range, Life Cycle Short Range, BT Pyramid Inst Asset Mgmt
Gabelli, Marc J.	Gabelli Global Inter Couch Potato, Glbl Telecomm	Greenberg, Clifford	Baron Small Cap
Gabelli, Mario J.	Gabelli ABC, Asset, Equity Inc, Glbl Interactive Couch Potato, Global Telecomm, Small Cap Gr	Greenberg, Mark	INVESCO Strategic Leisure
		Greene, James D.	WWW Internet
		Greenert, Jeffery A.	Emerald ST Fixed Inc, U.S. Govt Secs
		Greenfield, Barry A.	Fidelity Real Estate
Gadsden, William F.	AARP Capital Gr; Scudder Classic Gr	Gregory, Joan R.	Scudder Greater Europe Gr
Gaffney, Kathleen C.	Loomis Sayles Bond, High Yield	Gregory, Kenneth E.	Masters' Select Equity, Int'l
Gahagan, Robert V.	Amer Century - ST Govt, ST Treas	Greig, William G.	William Blair Int'l Gr
Games, Edmund B., Jr.	Scudder Latin America	Greshin, Adam M.	Scudder Global Bond, Int'l Bond
Gardiner, Robert	Wasatch Micro Cap, Micro-Cap Value	Gribbell, James B.	Babson Growth
Gardner, Keith J.	Legg Mason Global Govt	Griffin, David S.	INVESCO Total Return
Gardner, W. Whitfield	Chesapeake Core Gr	Griffiths, Claire	INVESCO European Small Co
Garea, Raymond	Franklin Mutual Series	Griggs, William T. II	Dupree Inter Govt Bond, KY TF Inc, KY TF Sht-Med, NC TF Inc, NC Sht-Med, TN TF Inc, TN Sht-Med
Garvey, Richard J.	Rushmore American Gas Index		
Gaylor, Douglas J.	Dreyfus BASIC Inter Muni, BASIC Muni, PA Inter Muni		
		Grishan, Adam M.	Scudder Global Bond
Gee, Norman	Fremont MM	Grosman, Albert	Fidelity Sel Automotive
Geewax, John J.	Accessor Growth; Vanguard Trustees Equity U.S.	Gross, William H.	Fremont Bond; Harbor Bond; PIMCo Low Duration, Low Dur II, Total Return, Total Return II, Tot Ret III
Gendelman, Robert I.	Neuberger & Berman Partners		
Gentry, John T.	Federated Inter Inc		
George, Whitney W.	Royce Financial Svcs, GiftShares, Low Priced Stock, Micro Cap, PA Mutual, PMF II, Premier, Total Return	Groveman, Bernard C.	FMC Select
		Grzecki, Wayne M.	Weston New Century Capital, New Century I
		Guinane, Mary S.	IAA Trust TE Bond
Gerber, Nicholas D.	Ameristock Mutual Fund	Gulis, Dean A.	Loomi-Sayles Mid-Cap Value
Gerding, Michael W.	Founders Passport, Worldwide Gr	Gullquist, Herbert W.	Lazard Bantam Value, Emerg Mkts, Equity, Glbl Eq, Int'l Eq, Int'l Sm Cap, Mid Cap, Small Cap
Ghriskey, Timothy M.	Dreyfus Eq Div, Fund, Gr & Opportunity, Aggr Gr, Large Co Val		
Giarla, Michael J.	Smith Breeden Financial Svcs	Gunster, Christopher	Nations Govt Secs
Gibs, Gabriel J.	Volumetric	Gupta, Rajesh K.	Dean Witter ST U.S. Treas
Gilbert, George J.	Northern Technology	Gurner, William L.	Flex-Funds Highlands Growth
Gillespie, Allen R.	Blue Ridge Total Return	Gusman, Theresa	Scudder Pacific Opps
Gillespie, T. Daniel	Rydex Precious Metals	Gustafson, Eric P.	Stein Roe Growth Stock, Young Investor
Gillson, Roy C.	IAI Developing Countries, Int'l, Latin America	Guthrie, Holly L.	SEI Small Cap Value
		Guzzetti, Guido	Lipper Europe Equity
Gintel, Robert M.	Gintel Fund	Habermann, Richard C.	Fidelity Asset Mgr, Asset Mgr Gr, Asset Mgr Inc
Giordano, Gilbert R.	Titan Financial Services		
Gipson, James H.	Clipper	Haddick, Robert J.	Fremont Int'l Growth
Girard, Thomas J.	WPG Govt MM	Hagstrom, Robert G., Jr.	Focus Trust
Giuliano, Theodore P.	Neuberger & Berman Cash Res, Govt MM, Ltd Mat Bond, Muni MM, Muni Securities Trust	Hague, John L.	PIMCo Foreign Bond, Glbl Bond
		Haines, Michael K.	Founders Frontier, Special
		Hale, Julie	Nations Balanced Assets
Gladson, Clifford A.	USAA TE Intermediate,TE ST	Hall, Donald E.	Scudder Value
Glancy, David L.	Fidelity Capital & Inc	Hall, J. Parker III	Vanguard U.S. Growth
Gleason, Sandi	Kayne, Anderson Small-Mid Cap Rising Divs	Hallaren, Gerard F., Jr.	INVESCO Strategic Environ Svcs, Strategic Technology
Glocke, David R.	Vanguard Admiral U.S. Treas MM, MM Reserves Federal, Treasury MM	Halle, Marc R.	Alpine Int'l Real Estate, U.S. Real Estate
		Hallett, Simon	Stalwart Int'l Equity
Godman, Cecil A. III	Gintel	Hamalainen, Pasi	PIMCo LT U.S. Govt Bond
Goetz, Peter	Jurika & Voyles Balanced	Hamilton, Dennis J.	Lexington Small Cap Val
Goff, James P.	Janus Enterprise	Hamilton, Kevin T.	Montgomery Global Asset Alloc, Select 50, U.S. Asset Alloc
Goff, Jennifer E.	Royce REvest Gr & Inc		
Golden, Greg W.	Nations Equity Index, Managed Index, Managed Sm Cap Index, Managed Sm Cap Value Idx, Managed Value Idx	Hammerschmidt, John F.	TIP: Turner Ultra Large Cap
		Hand, Karen M.	Dreyfus Basic Muni MM, Basic NJ Muni MM, Gen'l Muni MM, Gen'l NY Muni MM, Muni MM, NJ Muni MM, NY TE MM
Goodfellow, Charles C.	BNY Hamilton Lg Cap Gr		
Goodner, Raymond	AMEX Strategist Quality Inc, World Inc	Handler, Ira O.	Lazard Bond, Int'l FI, Strategic Yield
Goodwin, C. Kim	Amer Century: 20th Century Gr	Hanson, Andrew Merz	Lepercq-Istel Fund
Gordon, Mariko O.	Daruma Mid-Cap Value	Hardin, David R.	UAM - BHM&S Total Return Bond
Gottipalli, Praveen K.	Accessor Small to Mid Cap, Schwab Analytics	Harding, Daniel D.	Harding, Loevner Glbl Equity, Int'l Equity, Multi-Asset Glbl
Gould, Anthony	FTI Glbl Bond, Int'l Bond	Harhai, Michael C.	INVESCO Value Equity
Grabovac, James S.	INVESCO TF Inter Bond, TF LT Bond	Harloe, John P.	Vanguard Selected Value
Granahan, John J.	Vanguard Explorer	Harmon, James M.	Fidelity Sel Biotech
Grant, Karla D.	AARP Divsfd Gr, Divsfd Inc w/Gr	Harper, Robert H.	Stalwart Core Equity
Grant, Kevin E.	Fidelity Bal, Inv Grade Bond, Puritan, Spartan Inv Grade Inc	Harris, David P.	Stein Roe Emerg Mkts, Int'l
		Harris, Edmund	Guinness Flight China & Hong Kong
Gray, Anthony R.	SEI Bal, Cap Appreciation	Harris, Jeffrey M.	American Trust Allegiance
Gray, G.A. David	UAM - DSI Ltd Maturity, MM	Harris, Kathleen	Jamestown Int'l Equity
Gray, Paul	Fremont Real Estate Secs	Harrison, Joseph A.	Fairport Govt Sec, Gr & Inc
Green, David	Hotchkis & Wiley Sm Cap	Harrison, Vince	Dupree KY TF Short-Med, NC TF Short-Med, TN TF Short-Med
Green, Frederick W.	Merger Fund		

Portfolio Manager	Fund
Harrop, Steven D.	Strong Muni MM, Muni Advantage MM, Muni Bond, ST Muni Bond
Hartford, Harry	Hotchkis and Wiley Int'l
Hatfield, Lisa	SSgA U.S. Govt MM
Haubold, Gary D.	PBHG Mid-Cap Value, Small Cap Value, Strategic Small Cap
Hawkins, O. Mason	Longleaf Partners Fund, Small Cap, Realty; Masters Select Equity
Hayes, Helen Young	Janus Overseas, Worldwide; Masters's Select Int'l
Hayward, Brian B.	INVESCO Strategic Utilities, Worldwide Commun
Hayward, Steven D.	Marshall Mid-Cap Gr, Small-Cap Gr
Hazuka, Thomas B.	Preferred Asset Alloc
Headley, Mark W.	Matthews Pacific Tiger
Healey, Timothy S.	Government Street AL TF Bond
Heaphy, William V.	UAM - ICM Equity
Heebner, G. Kenneth	CGM Cap Devel, Fixed Inc, Focus, Mutual, Realty
Heffernan, Gerard E.	Stratton Growth
Heitman, Daren C.	Skyline Small Cap Contrarian
Hemenetz, Mark A.	BNY Hamilton Interm Govt
Hennessy, Neal J.	Henncssy Balanced
Henry, D. Kirk	Dreyfus Emerging Mkts
Herrman, Sharon M.	Nations Value
Herro, David G.	Oakmark Int'l, Int'l Small Cap; Masters' Select Int'l
Hershey, Michael L.	Henlopen Fund
Herskovitz, Mark	Dreyfus Technology Growth
Hetnarski, Adam	Fidelity Select Tech
Hibler, Gary	Jensen Portfolio
Hickam, Kevin J.	Transamerica Premier Cash Res
Hickling, John R.	Fidelity Int'l Growth & Inc
Higgins, Peter I.	Dreyfus MidCap Value, Small Co Value
Hill, Charles B.	Price, Rowe FL Insured TF, MD ST TF, Summit Muni Inter, TF Insured Inter, TF Short-Inter, VA ST TF
Hill, Larry R.	IAI Balanced, Bond
Hill, Peter M.	BBK Diversa
Himebrook, David	IAI Emerg Gr
Hinderlie, Richard R.	INVESCO Cash Res, ST Bond, U.S. Govt MM, U.S. Govt Sec
Hirschhorn, Harvey B.	Stein Roe Balanced
Hisey, Richard M.	Lexington Troika Dialog Russia
Hochberger, Stuart	FTI Glbl Bond, Int'l Bond
Hocker, Richard A.	TIP: Penn Capital Select Financial Svcs, Strategic High Yield Bond, Value Plus
Hodgman, Martha F.	Loomis-Sayles Muni Bond
Hoeh, Michael	Dreyfus Basic GNMA, GNMA, Real Estate Mortgage
Hoerle, Robert F.	Reich & Tang Equity
Hoelting, Donald	IAI Balanced, Gr & Inc, Value
Hoes, Clay L.	Scudder Gold
Hoffman, Michael C.	Robertson Stephens Developing Countries
Hoffman, Robert T.	AARP Bal Stock & Bond, Gr & Inc; Scudder Gr & Inc; Managers Inc Equity; Touchstone Gr & Inc
Hogan, Paul C.	FAM Equity Inc
Hogan, Terence M.	Acorn
Hohenstein, Vicki	First Omaha Balanced, Equity
Hoisington, Van Robert	Wasatch-Hoisington U.S. Treasury
Holeski, Kenneth M.	NewCap Contrarian
Holland, Michael F.	Holland Balanced
Hollingsworth, Curtis	Fidelity GNMA, Govt Secs, SI Govt, Spartan GNMA, Spartan Govt Inc, Spartan Ltd Mat Govt, Spartan SI Govt
Hollyer, John W.	Vanguard FI Short-Term Fed, MM Res Prime
Holmes, Douglas	SSgA Matrix Equity
Holmes, Douglas T.	Quantitative Gr & Inc
Holmes, James P.	Heartland Lg Cap Val
Holsteen, Jon F.	UAM - Chicago Asset Mgmt Value/Contrarian, Chicago Asset Mgmt Inter Bond

Portfolio Manager	Fund
Holzer, William E.	AARP Glbl Gr; Scudder Glbl; Managers Int'l Equity
Hom, Geri	Schwab Analytics, Asset Dir Bal, Asset Dir Cons Gr, Asset Dir High Gr, Int'l Index, 1000, S&P 500, Small Cap Index
Honour, Roger W.	Montgomery Gr, Micro Cap, Small Cap Opps
Hopper, Greg	BT Investments Glbl High Yield Secs
Hoonsbeen, Mark C.	IAI Growth, MidCap Gr, Regional
Hoops, Norman E.	Amer Century Bal; Amer Century - Benham Bond, High Yield, Inter Bond, Ltd Trm Bond
Hoover, Michael E.	Excelsior Energy and Natural Resources
Hope, Mary Shannon	Government Street Bond
Hosking, Jeremy J.	Vanguard Horizon Global Equity
Houser, Denis N.	Rightime Fund
Houston, Jeffrey L.	Amer Century Bal; Amer Century - Benham Bond, Inter-Term Bond, Ltd-Term Bond
Howard, Richard P.	Price, Rowe Capital Apprec
Hudson, Louis M.	Accessor Short-Inter FI; BT Pyramid Ltd Term U.S. Govt
Huffman, Sabrina T.	59 Wall St TF Short/Inter FI
Hughes, Michael	SAFECO Bal, Managed Bond
Hurwitz, Millie Adams	Artisan Small Cap
Husic, Frank J.	Managers Cap Apprec
Huson, Richard S.	Crabbe Huson Asset Alloc, Equity, Inc, OR Muni Bond, Real Estate, U.S. Govt Inc, U.S. Govt MM
Hutson, Bruce P.	Marshall Equity Inc
Huxley, Richard J.	TIP: Clover FI
Hyll, John	Loomis-Sayles ST Bond
Ide, Kenton J.	Boston 1784 Int'l Equity
Ingham, Lois G.	Excelsior CA TE Inc
Ipek, Sevgi	Citizens Global Equity
Isabelle, Warren J.	ICM/Isabelle Small-Cap Value
Jacklin, Charles J.	Dreyfus Int'l Equity Alloc
Jackson, Stephon	Dreyfus Third Century
Jacobs, Daniel L.	UAM - Jacobs Int'l Octagon
Jacobs, John	IAA Trust Asset Alloc, LT Bond, ST Govt Bond
Jacques, William E.	Accessor Value and Inc
James, Lance F.	Babson Enterprise II
Jamison, Denis P.	Lexington GNMA Inc, MM Tr, Ramirez Glbl Inc
Jares, John B.	Berger Balanced
Jarvis, Peter	INVESCO Latin Amer Gr
Jawarski, Daniel R.	Masters' Select Int'l
Jellison, David W.	Columbia Real Estate Equity
Jenkins, Ralph H.	INVESCO Inter Govt Bond
Jensen, Curtis	Third Ave Small-Cap Value
Jensen, Val E.	Jensen Portfolio
Jhaveri, Ramesh C.	Jhaveri Value
Jhaveri, Saumil R.	Jhaveri Value
Jimenez, Josephine S.	Montgomery Emerg Asia, Emerg Mkts, SEI Emerg Mkts Eq
Johnson, Gary P.	Scudder Global Bond, Int'l Bond
Johnson, Craig T.	Leonetti Balanced
Johnson, James M.	PC&J Performance, Preservation
Johnson, John W.	Crabbe Huson Small Cap, Special
Johnson, Mark W.	USAA Gold
Johnson, Richard J.	Columbia Small Cap
Johnson, Robert R. "Skip"	JP Morgan Federal MM, Prime MM; Managers MM; Preferred MM
Johnson, Thomas E.	UAM - TJ Core Equity
Johnson, Todd A.	INVESCO Realty
Johnstone, Lynda	Guinness Flight China & Hong Kong
Jones, Michael E.	TIP: Clover Equity Val, Sm Cap Value
Joseph, Marc	AARP Int'l Gr & Inc
Jungquist, Paul J.	Sit MM
Jurgens, Robert J.	UAM - Jacobs Int'l Octagon
Jurika, William K.	Jurika & Voyles Balanced
Kailin, Kenneth S.	Skyline Special Equities II
Kaiser, Nicholas F.	Amana Growth, Income; Sextant Gr, Int'l
Kalil, James	Quaker Mid-Cap Value
Kam, Kendrick W.	Firsthand - Medical Specialists, Technology Value
Kaminski, M.G.	Kaminski Poland Fund

Portfolio Manager	Fund
Lemmer, Keith C.	Aon MM
Leo, John B.	Northern Technology
Leonard, Daniel B.	INVESCO Strat Fin Svcs, Gold, Strat Technology
Leonetti, Michael E.	Leonetti Balanced
Lerner, Arthur F.	First Eagle Int'l
Lettenberger, David J.	Marshall Small-Cap Gr
Leugers, William J., Jr.	Gradison Growth Tr Estab Val, Oppor Val
Leuthold, Rudolph	JP Morgan Euro Equity, Int'l Opps
Leuthold, Steven C.	Leuthold Core Investment
Levine, Irving	Copley Fund
Levit, Carson V.	Dresdner RCM Large Cap
Levy, Harold J.	First Eagle Fund of America
Levy, Michael	BT Investment Int'l Equity, Latin Amer Equity
Lewis, Bradford F.	Fidelity Asset Mgr: Growth, Asset Mgr: Income, Disciplined Eq, Small Cap Selector, Stock Selector
Lewis, John L., IV	Chesapeake Core Gr
Lieber, Samuel A.	Alpine Int'l Real Estate, U.S. Real Estate
Lieberman, Sheldon	Hotchkis and Wiley Equity Inc
Lilly, Elizabeth M.	Eastcliff Regional Sm Cap Val
Lind, Norman	Fidelity Ltd Term Muni Inc, Spartan Inter Muni Inc, Spartan MI Muni Inc, Spartan NJ Muni Inc, Spartan NY Muni Inc, Spartan Short-Inter Muni Inc
Lindenthal, John G.	Preferred Value
Lindig, Robert O.	Westcore CO TE
Lindsay, David	Galaxy Fund II U.S. Treas Index
Link, Michael J.	Gradison Govt Inc
Lipper, Kenneth	Lipper U.S. Equity
Lisanti, Mary	Strong Mid Cap, Small Cap
Litterst, Robert A.	Fidelity Spartan U.S. Govt MM, Spartan U.S. Treas MM, U.S. Govt Res
Little, Richard D.	Citizens Emerg Gr; Seneca Gr, Mid-Cap EDGE
Liu, Allan	Fidelity Southeast Asia
Liu, Cynthia	Schwab OneSource Portfolios Bal Alloc, Growth Alloc, Int'l, Sm Co
Lober, Douglas J.	Fidelity Sel Paper & Forest Products
Lobo, Gregory W.	HGK Fixed Inc
Lockman, Stephen F.	Stein Roe High Yield, Inc
Lockyer, D. Keith	Fairport Govt Secs
Loeb, Thomas	Vanguard Asset Allocation
Loeffler, Douglas A.	Founders Special
Loest, Robert	IPS Millenium
Lokhorst, Valerie J.	Northern U.S. Govt MM, U.S. Govt Select MM
Lord, Stephanie S.	Rydex High Yield
Lorenzen, Jeffrey D.	Vintage Bond
Lucas, Jane P.	Schroder Capital - U.S. Equity
Luftig, Mark D.	Strong American Utilities
Lui, John C.	BNY Hamilton Sm Cap Gr
Lundmark, Paul H.	USAA Bal Strategy, ST Bond
Lundsford, Jacqueline R.	Emerald Prime, TE, Treasury
Lurito, Stephen J.	Warburg, Pincus Emerg Gr, Post-Venture Capital, Small Co Gr
Lynes, Rick	Prudential TF MF
Lyon, Jane	INVESCO Latin Amer Gr
Lyon, Robert H.	ICAP Discretionary Equity, Equity
Lyski, Wayne	Touchstone Income Opp
Maack, John E. Jr.	Crabbe Huson Asset Alloc, Equity
Mace, Richard R., Jr.	Fidelity Glbl Bal, Int'l Value, Overseas
Macedo, Rosemary	BBK Int'l Equity
MacEwen, G. David	Amer Century CA Ins TF, CA Ltd-Trm TF, FL Inter Muni, LT TF
MacKinnon, Ian A.	Vanguard Admiral IT U.S. Treas, Admiral LT U.S. Treas, Tax Managed Bal, Tax Managed Cap App, Tax Managed Gr & Inc
Macmillan, Alexander S.	Columbia Growth
Maddix, Eric S.	Stein Roe Capital Opps, Growth Opps
Maguire, Thomas M.	SAFECO Growth
Mahaney, Josephine P.	Neuberger & Berman Cash Res, Govt MM
Mahoney, Christopher J.	Touchstone Standby Income

Portfolio Manager	Fund
Mairs, George A. III	Mairs & Power Growth
Makino, Shigeki	Fidelity Japan, Pacific Basin
Malekar, Shirish T.	Strong Glbl High Yield Bond, Int'l Bond, ST Bond, ST Glbl Bond
Malevich, Mitzi	AMEX Strategist Growth
Mallon, Mark L.	Amer Century Real Estate
Maloney, John E.	New England TE MM
Malouf, Michael F.	Dresdner RCM Global Sm Cap
Malter, Valerie F.	Scudder Bal, Large Co Gr
Mangum, Charles	Fidelity Dividend Gr
Manzler, David Lee, Jr.	Analysts Investors FI, Stock
Marchand, Gordon M.	U.S. Global Leaders Growth
Marcus, Kenneth R.	Excelsior Small Cap
Margard, James R.	Rainier Core Eq, Small/Mid Cap Eq
Marker, Carl W.	IMS Capital Value
Markman, Robert J.	Markman MultiFund Tr Aggr Alloc, Conserv Alloc, Moderate Alloc
Marks, Michael E.	IAA Trust Asset Alloc, Gr
Marmon, David	Harbor MM
Marra, Bruce L.	Quaker Core Equity
Marshall, John G.	RNC Equity
Marsico, Thomas F.	Marsico Focused, Gr & Inc; Nations Marsico Focused Equities, Marsico Gr & Inc
Marthaler, Thomas J.	Chicago Trust Balanced, Bond
Martin, Carlton N.	TIAA-CREF Gr & Inc
Martin, Edward L.	Babson Bond Tr L, Bond Tr S
Martin, Michael J.	Kent Ltd Term TF, MI Muni Bond
Martin, William	American Century Equity Gr, Glbl Natural Resources Index, Glbl Gold
Martins, Luis	Fidelity Int'l Bond
Matthews, G. Paul	Matthews Asian Conv Sec, Korea, Pacific Tiger
Maurath, Tom	Pinnacle Fund
May, David D.	LKCM Small Cap Equity
May, James B.	SSgA S&P 500 Index
May, Jeffrey T.	Nicholas MM
May, Robert V.	Trent Equity
May, Trent E.	INVESCO Growth, Sm Co Gr
Mayer, Benjamin L.	American AAdvantage Inter Bond, Short-Term Bond
Mayer, Charles P.	INVESCO Balanced, Industrial Inc
Mayo, Richard A.	GMO Pelican Fund
McAlear, James M.	Columbia Int'l Stock
McAlley, Kenneth J.	Excelsior Inter-Term TE, LT TE, NY Inter-Term TE, ST TE
McBride, Vincent J.	Warburg, Pincus Emerg Mkts
McCabe, John J.	MSB Fund
McCain, Wesley G.	Eclipse Bal, Equity, Gr & Inc, Ultra ST Inc
McCall, James D.	PBHG Core Gr, Large Cap Gr, Large Cap 20, Select Eq
McCarey, Kevin	Fidelity Europe Capital Appreciation
McCart, M. Jane	Stein Roe HY Munis, Managed Munis
McClanahan, Phillip W.	California Inv Tr CA Ins Inter, CA TF Inc, CA TF MM, U.S. Govt Sec, U.S. Treas Tr
McCleary, Linda W.	UAM - ICM Fixed Inc
McClintock, Kevin M.	Dreyfus A Bonds Plus, Asset Alloc, Inter Term Inc, ST Income, Strategic Inc
McClure, James S.	Vanguard Selected Value
McCormack, Maria	Pro-Conscience Women's Equity
McCown, Kirk	Lancaster Crestone Small Cap
McCrickard, Gregory A.	Price, Rowe MidCap Value, Small Cap Stock
McCullough, Robert F.	Cappiello Rushmore Emerg Gr, Gold, Gr, Util Inc
McCullough, Ronald L.	UAM - DSI Disciplined Value
McCutcheon, Stephen C.	SCM Portfolio
McDonald, David A.	IAI Growth
McDowell, John B.	Fidelity Blue Chip Gr
McDowell, Thomas W., Jr.	UAM - Rice, Hall, James Small Cap, Sm/Mid Cap
McElroy, William K.	FMC Select
McEvoy, Earl E.	Vanguard FI HY Corp, FI LT Corp, Preferred Stock, Special Util Inc, Wellesley Inc
McGee, Ellen A.	PBHG Core Gr, Lg Cap Gr, Lg Cap 20, Select Equity
McGettigan, Yolanda S.	Fidelity Sel Construction and Housing
McGlynn Ronald H.	CRM Small Cap Value

Portfolio Manager	Fund
McGrath, Karen E.	Strong Blue Chip 100
McGrath, Kevin J.	UAM - Chicago Asset Mgmt Value Contrarian
McGregor, Clyde S.	Oakmark Equity and Income
McGuirk, Hugh D.	Price, Rowe GA TF Bond, VA TF
McHugh, Christopher K.	TIP: Turner Midcap
McIlvaine, Phelps S.	Sextant Bond Inc, ID TE, ST Bond
McKay, Roy C.	Scudder Development, 21st Century Growth
McKenna, Kevin	CMA Money
McKenna, Patricia	Hotchkis & Wiley Glbl Equity
McKeon, Thomas F.	Quaker Core Equity
McKissack, Eric T.	Ariel Appreciation
McLandsborough, John S.	Stein Roe Special Venture
McLaughlin, Diane	Fidelity CA Muni MM, MI Muni MM, Muni MM, NY Muni MM, Spartan CA Muni MM, Spartan Muni MF, Spartan NY Muni MM
McMurram, Gregory M.	Analytic Master FI, ST Govt
McNay, Joseph	Managers Cap App
McNeill, Debra L.	Fremont Select
McQuaid, Charles P.	Acorn
McQueen, Arthur J.	Stein Roe Growth Opps
McRee, Michael T.	Investek Fixed Inc Tr
McStay, John D.	Brazos/JMIC Micro Cap Gr, Real Estate, Small Cap Gr
McStay, Richard A.	Reserve Mid-Cap Gr
Meagley, Richard D.	SAFECO Equity
Meany, Kathleen A.	Scudder MA Ltd Term TF, MA TF
Medveckis, John J.	UAM - C&B Bal, C&B Equity, C&B Equity for Taxable Investors
Meeder, Robert S. Jr.	Flex-Fund Muirfield
Meeks, Paul	Jurika & Voyles Mini-Cap
Mehling, James A.	MainStay Inst EAFE Index
Mehta, Satyen	JP Morgan Emerg Mkts Equity
Meiling, Dean	Harbor Bond
Meiselas, Robert W.	JP Morgan NY Total Return Bond, TE Bond;JP Morgan Shares: CA Bond
Meltzer, Frederick C.	UAM - DSI Ltd Maturity Bond
Memler, Monty M.	Northern U.S. Govt
Merk, Randy	American Century - Benham Int'l Bond
Merrell, Steve	AMEX Strategist Total Return
Merriman, Paul A.	Merriman Asset Alloc, Cap Appr, Flexible Bond, Gr & Inc, Leveraged Gr
Messina, Susan P.	Paine Webber Cashfund
Meszaros, Elmer L.	Fairport Gr & Inc
Metastasio, Mary V.	SAFECO Inter-Term Muni Bond, TF MM
Meuser, John F.	RSI Ret Trust ST Invest
Meyers, Allan J.	Kent Inter TF, Ltd Term TF, MI Muni Bond, TF Inc
Meyers, Shelly J.	Meyers Pride Value
Michael, Thomas	Rydex Juno, Nova
Micheletti, Arthur A.	Bailard Biehl & Kaiser Diversa, Int'l Bond
Midanek, James I.	TIP Institutional Trust Short Dur Govt Funds 1 Yr, 3 Yr
Mier, Christopher J.	Scudder CA TF, NY TF, OH TF
Mierzwa, Phillip P.	Rembrandt TE FI, TE MM
Milaitis, Rimas M.	Strong Asset Alloc, Equity Inc, Gr & Inc
Milano, Stephen M.	UAM - BHM&S Total Return Bond
Miles, James	Hotchkis and Wiley Mid-Cap, Small Cap
Milias Mitchell J.	Vanguard Horizons Cap Opportunity
Millard, Kathleen T.	AARP Gr & Inc; Scudder Large Co Value
Miller, Alan G.	Maxus Laureate
Miller, Eric J.	Heartland Value
Miller, Harry W.	USAA Cornerstone Strategy, Gr & Tax Strategy, Inc Stock
Miller, Lowell G.	Flex-Fund Total Ret Utilities
Miller, Mark	Kayne Anderson Inter Total Return, Inter TF
Miller, Mary J.	Price, Rowe CA TF Bond, MD TF Bond, Tax-Efficient Bal, TF Inc
Miller, Neal	Fidelity New Millenium
Miller, S. Blake	WPG Inter Muni Bond
Miller, Steven	FTI Int'l Equity
Miller, Timothy J.	INVESCO Dynamics, Growth, Sm Co Gr
Miller, William H. III	Legg Mason America's Leading Cos., Special Inv Tr, Value Tr

Portfolio Manager	Fund
Millikan, David C.	Trent Equity
Miner, Patrick M.	KPM FI Portfolio
Mitchell, David	William Blair Value Discovery
Mitchell, Edward C.	INVESCO Total Return
Mitchelson, Peter L.	Sit Balanced, Lg Cap Gr
Mizushita, Kenichi	Fidelity Japan Small Cos
Modzelewski, Deborah A.	RSI Actively Managed Bond, Inter-Term Bond, Short-Term Invest
Moffett, James L.	Scout Worldwide
Mohn, Robert A.	Acorn USA
Monrad, Bruce H.	Northeast Investors Trust
Monrad, Ernest E.	Northeast Investors Trust
Montgomery, John N.R.	Bridgeway Aggr Gr, Social Responsibility, Ultra Lg 35 Index, Ultra Sm Co, Ultra Sm Index
Moore, Charles V.	Reserve Blue Chip Gr
Moore, Kevin D.	Monetta Bal, Lg-Cap, Govt MM, Inter Bond, Mid-Cap, Small-Cap
Moore, Margaret L.	Emerald Fl TE
Morales, Walter A.	Florida Street Bond
Moran, Gerald J.	Scudder Global Small Co
Moroney, Richard J.	Strong Dow 30 Value
Morris, Charles A.	Price, Rowe Science & Technology
Morris, Daniel A.	Manor Investment Fund
Morris, Jeffrey G.	INVESCO Strategic Financial Svcs
Morris, Paul	Schroder Capital - U.S. Equity; Schroder Series Lg Cap Equity
Morrison, Charles S.	Fidelity Asset Mgr, Asset Mgr Gr, Asset Mgr Inc
Morrissy, Anne E.	Mathers Fund
Moser, Jeffery C.	Nations Disciplined Equity
Moser, Kurt G.	State Farm Bal, Growth, Interim, Muni Bond
Mosher, Brian J.	Kiewit Equity, Inter-Term Bond, MM, ST Govt, Tax-Exempt
Moss, Howard B.	Harbor Int'l Growth
Moynihan, Richard J.	Dreyfus Muni Bond, NY Insured TE Bond
Mueller, Danine A.	Vanguard NJ Ins TF LT, OH Ins TF, PA Ins TF LT
Mueller, Jay N.	Strong Heritage MF, MM, Step One MF
Muhlenkamp, Ronald H.	Muhlenkamp Fund
Mullholland, Mark	Matthew 25 Fund
Mullins, Bert J.	Dreyfus Disciplined Stock
Mulvey, Daniel B.	JP Morgan Federal MM, Prime MM, TE MM
Musser, Peter M.	Rainier Core Equity, Small/Mid Cap Equity
Myer, Bentley M.	William Blair Mutual Inc, Ready Reserves
Nadal, Jean-Baptiste	Kayne Anderson Int'l Rising Dividends
Naeseth, Jane M.	Stein Roe Cash Reserves
Nagorniak, John J.	Vanguard Gr & Inc, Morgan Gr
Nahas, N. Joseph	Ridgeway Helms Millenium
Nasgovitz, William J.	Heartland Sm Cap Contrarian, Val, Val & Inc, WI TF
Nason, Susan M.	Federated ARMs, Bond Index, Inter Inc, U.S. Govt Bond, U.S. Govt Sec 1-3, U.S. Govt Sec 2-5, U.S. Govt Sec 5-10
Navellier, Louis G.	Navellier Perf: Aggr Gr, Aggr Small Cap, Aggr Small Cap Equity, Lg Cap Gr, Lg Cap Val, Mid Cap Gr, Sm Cap Val; Series: Aggr Sm Cap
Nelson, Frederic A.	JP Morgan Shares: Tax Aware Disciplined Equity
Neverett, Patrice J.	Eastcliff Total Return
Newell, Roger D.	Vanguard Equity Inc
Newmark, Kent P.	Loomis-Sayles U.S. Govt Securities
News, Kathleen A.	TIP: Penn Capital Strategic High Yield Bond
Ng, Alex	Rembrandt Asian Tigers
Ng, John	Merrill Lynch Ready Assets Tr
Ngudu, Tsering	Lepercq-Istel Fund
Nicholas, Albert O.	Nicholas Eq Inc, Fund, Inc
Nicholas, David O.	Nicholas Fund, Ltd Edition, II
Nicholson, J. Scott	New England Cash Mgmt Tr MM, U.S. Govt
Nicklin, Edmund H., Jr.	Westport Fund, Small Cap
Nimocks, A. Byron	FMC Select
Nisbet, Garth R.	Crabbe Huson Asset Alloc, Inc, OR Muni Bond, U.S. Govt Inc, U.S. Govt MM
Nolan, David P.	OVB Cap Appr, Emerg Gr

Portfolio Manager	Fund	Portfolio Manager	Fund
Noss, Jeffrey B.	BNY Hamilton Inter TE	Pavelec, Lawrence J.	Marshall Govt Inc
Notaro, William L.	Merriman Asset Alloc, Cap Appr, Flexible Bond, Gr & Inc, Leveraged Gr	Peebles, D. Ray	CornerCap Bal
		Peebles, David G.	USAA Int'l, World Gr
Nygren, William C.	Oakmark Select	Peebles, Douglas J.	Alliance World Income
Oates, William A. Jr.	Northeast Investors Gr	Pegler, Dominic	Amer Century - Benham Int'l Bond
Ober, Charles M.	Price, Rowe New Era	Pei, Linda C.Y.	Women's Equity
Ober, Theodore E.	Boston 1784 Gr, Gr & Inc	Pekin, Sheldon M.	Stalwart U.S. Govt Secs
Oberweis, James D.	Oberweis Emerg Gr, Micro-Cap, Mid-Cap	Pelosi, Michael R.	Boston 1784 Asset Alloc
Oberweis, James W.	Oberweis Mid-Cap	Perelstein, Michael M.	Schroder Capital - Int'l
O'Boyle, Kevin C.	Meridian Value	Perkins, Robert H.	Berger Small Cap Value
O'Brien, John	AMEX Strategist World Gr	Permut, Steven M.	Amer Century - Benham CA HY Muni
Ochson, Mary Jo	Federated Inter Muni Trust; Municipal Cash Series, ST Muni Trust	Perritt, Gerald W.	Perritt Capital Growth
		Perry, Robert B.	Smith Breeden Financial Svcs
O'Connor, Brian J.	Reserve Sm Cap Growth	Peters, Donald J.	Price Rowe Tax-Efficient Balanced
O'Connor, Daniel	Rushmore American Gas Index, TF MD, TF VA, U.S. Govt Bond	Peters, Edgar E.	Preferred Asset Allocation
		Peters, Kathryn M.	Montgomery Growth, Micro Cap, Small Cap
O'Connor, William J.	Marshall Lg Cap Gr & Inc	Peters, Michael J.	Mosaic TF AZ, TF MD, TF MO, TF MM, TF National, TF VA
O'Donnell, Amy	Amer Century - Benham Capital Pres, Govt Agency		
		Petersen, Michael A.	Kent Gr & Inc, Index Equity, Int'l Gr, Small Co Gr
Oechsle, Walter	Jamestown Int'l Equity		
Oelschlager, James D.	Pin Oak Aggr Stock; White Oak Gr Stock	Peterson, Linda K.	Amer Century - 20th Century Heritage
Offen, Scott	Fidelity Select Food & Agriculture	Peterson, Richard B.	Stein Roe Special Venture
Ofstie, Harold	Managers Income Equity	Peterson, Stephen R.	Fidelity Equity Inc
Ognar, Ronald C.	Strong Growth, Growth 20, Total Return	Petherick, Jeffrey C.	Loomis-Sayles Mid-Cap Val, Small Cap Value
Ohlsson, Sheila J.	Berger Gr & Inc		
O'Kane, Michael T.	TIAA-CREF Managed Alloc	Petty, W. Michael	Dreyfus NJ Muni Bond
O'Keefe, Christopher	Quaker Mid-Cap Value	Phillips, Wilson	Vanguard Int'l Value
O'Neil, R. James	UAM - C&B Bal, C&B Equity, C&B Equity for Taxable Investors	Philpott, Jerome C.	Montgomery Small Cap
		Pichler, Sharon S.	Janus Govt MM, MM, TE MM
O'Neill, Brian	Nations Int'l Gr	Pierallini, Fabrizio	Vontobel Emerg Mkts Equity, Int'l Equity
O'Neill, G. Michael III	Excelsior Govt Secs	Pierson, Elizabeth S.	Vintage Bal, FI, Govt Assets, Inter TF, Ltd-Term Bond
Orkin, Michael B.	Caldwell & Orkin Market Opportunity		
O'Rourke, Julie A.	Vintage Aggressive Gr, Bal, Equity	Pilara, Andrew P., Jr.	Robertson Stephens Glbl Low-Priced Stk, Glbl Natural Resources, Glbl Value, Partners
Orben, Jack R.	Unified Laidlaw, Taxable MM		
Orphanos, Anthony G.	Warburg Pincus Bal, Strategic Val		
Orr, Scott A.	Fidelity CT Muni MM, MA Muni MM, NJ Muni MM, OH Muni MM, Spartan AZ Muni MM, Spartan CT Muni MM, Spartan FL Muni MM, Spartan MA Muni MM, Spartan NJ Muni MM	Pilgrim, Gary L.	PBHG Growth; Managers Special Equity
		Piorkowski, Ted	Sefton CA TF, U.S. Govt
		Pittman, Mark D.	Marshall Inter Bond, ST Inc
		Plaehn, Connie J.	JP Morgan Bond, ST Bond
		Plants, David S.	Dresdner RCM Global Sm Cap
Osborn, David P.	Matrix Growth	Plewniak, Wayne	Lipper High Income
Osterberg, Gerald H.	JP Morgan Diversified	Plumb, Thomas G.	Thompson & Plumb Balanced
Ostrowski, Robert J.	Federated U.S. Govt Secs 1-3 yrs, U.S. Govt Secs 2-5 yrs	Pogran, David	Parnassus CA TE
		Poirier, Michele M.	Nations FL Inter Muni, FL Muni, GA Inter Muni, GA Muni, Muni Inc, SC Inter Muni, SC Muni
Oswald, Richard W.	JP Morgan TE MM; Preferred ST Govt		
Otness, James B.	JP Morgan U.S. Small Co		
O'Toole, John R.	Domini Social Equity	Poitras, David P.	Wayne Hummer Income, MF Tr
Ouimet, Christopher P.	Accessor Growth	Pollack, Gary	BT Investment Intermediate TF
Owens, Edward P.	Vanguard Special Health Care	Porreca, Michael	Managers Intermediate Mtge
Palmer, Timothy A.	IAI MM, Reserve	Porter, John R., III	Fidelity Sel Medical Delivery, Sel Software & Computer Svcs
Paluszek, Thaddeus W.	Scudder Financial Svcs		
Pang, Andrew L.	Fremont Int'l Growth	Posner, Brian S.	Warburg, Pincus Gr & Inc
Pape, Scott S.	Loomis Sayles Mid-Cap Gr	Post, David E.	UAM - Hanson Equity
Papp, L. Roy	Papp, L. Roy America-Abroad, America-Pacific Rim, Stock	Postma, Wypke	Rembrandt Int'l Equity
		Potter, Howard S.	Capstone Govt Income
Papp, Rosellen C.	Papp, L. Roy America Abroad, America-Pacific Rim, Stock	Potter, John C.	Marshall Mid Cap Value
		Povost, Laura	Working Assets MM
Pappas, Thomas L.	SEI Inter Dur Govt	Powell, Edwin B.	1838 Small Cap Equity; SEI Small Cap Value
Pappo, Carl W.	Boston 1784 CT TE, RI TE, TE Med-Term Inc	Powell, Ridgeway H.	Dreyfus Disciplined Inter Bond
		Powers, Alexander R.	Excelsior Inter-Term Managed Inc, Managed Inc
Paquelet, Charles A.	Strong Discovery		
Pardo, Marian U.	JP Morgan U.S. Small Co Opps	Powers, Jerome R.	Westcore Inter Bond, Long Bond
Pardula, Todd	Amer Century - Benham CA Muni MM, CA TF MM	Prappas, Tom	Citizens Global Equity
		Pratt, Andrew G.	Montgomery Growth, Micro Cap, Sm Cap Opps
Parente, Sharon B.	Warburg, Pincus NY Inter Muni		
Pariseau, Robert R.	USAA CA Bond, FL TF Inc, TX TF Inc, VA Bond	Price, Capucine	William Blair Value Discovery
		Price, Michael F.	Franklin Mutual Beacon, Discovery, Europe, Qualified, Shares
Parmeggiani, Luca	Vontobel Eastern Euro Equity		
Parsons, David G.	USAA Growth, Growth Strategy	Price, Walter C., Jr.	Dresdner RCM Global Tech
Pasquale, Lois	Chicago Trust Muni Bond	Prindle, Janet	Neuberger & Berman Socially Responsive
Patel, Margaret D.	Third Avenue High Yield	Profit, Eugene A.	Profit Value
Patton, M. Ashton	AARP Insured TF Gen'l Bond; Scudder Ltd Term TF, Managed Munis, Medium Term TF	Puglia, Larry J.	Price, Rowe Blue Chip Gr, Financial Svcs
		Putnam, Thomas O.	FAM Equity Inc, Value
		Pyle, Richard E.	Eastcliff Growth
Paul, Donovan J.	INVESCO Bal, HY, Industrial Inc, Select Inc, ST Bond	Queen, John	Hotchkis & Wiley Low Duration, Short Term Investment, Tot Return Bond
Paulette, Greg	Globalt Growth	Quereau, James Van Dyke	Stratton Special Value

Portfolio Manager	Fund
Quigley, Karen	Reserve Primary, U.S. Govt, U.S. Treas
Quinn, Thomas E.	CornerCap Bal, Growth
Quinn, William F.	American Aadvantage Bal, Gr & Inc, Int'l Equity
Quinsee, Paul A.	JP Morgan Euro Equity, Int'l Equity, Int'l Opps
Rabiner, Dale H.	Legg Mason Balanced
Rachwalski, Frank J.	AARP High Quality MF, High Quality TF MF; Kemper Cash Acct Tr Govt Secs, MM, TE MM; Kemper Cash Equivalent Govt MM, MM, TF MM; Scudder CA TF MF, Cash Investment Tr, NY TF MF, Prime MM, TF MF, U.S.Treasury MF
Radsch, Robert W.	Lexington Goldfund, Strategic Investments, Strategic Silver
Ragus, Jeremy L.	Scudder CA TF Bond, NY TF
Rakers, Lawrence D.	Fidelity Sel Energy, Sel Natural Resources
Ramirez, Maria Fiorini	Lexington Ramirez Global Inc
Ramos, Douglas D.	Dreyfus Balanced, Gr & Inc
Ramos, Thomas G.	USAA TE Fund MM
Rands, Robert D.	Vanguard Morgan Gr
Raneri, Judith A.	Gabelli U.S. Treasury MM
Raney, Michael E.	Rainier Inter Fixed Inc
Raney, Timothy G.	Scudder Zero Coupon 2000
Rankin, Gavin	Lexington Troika Dialog Russia
Rankin, Newlin	Amer Century - Benham ST Govt, ST Treas
Rath, Thomas E.	SAFECO Income
Ratte, Gregory E.	Brundage, Story & Rose Equity
Raven, Charles H.	UAM - Hanson Equity
Rea, Dr. James B.	Rea-Graham Balanced
Rea, James B., Jr.	Rea-Graham Balanced
Reaves, William H.	Strong American Utilities
Redding, Kim G.	American Century Real Estate
Reichel, Frank H. III	Stratton Small Cap Yield
Reid, Steven J.	Oakmark Small Cap
Reigel, Susan L.	AIT Vision: U.S. Equity
Reilly, Chris	Berger/BIAM Int'l
Reilly, Sheridan	AARP Int'l Gr & Inc; Scudder Int'l Gr & Inc
Reiner, Robert	BT Investment Int'l Equity
Reinsberg, John R.	Lazard Emerg Mkts, Glbl Eq, Int'l Eq, Int'l Sm Cap, Managers Int'l Equity
Reitenbach, Nicholas	Reserve Int'l Equity
Retzer, Patrick J.	Heartland U.S. Govt Sec, Value Plus, WI TF
Reyes, Rainerio	Robertson Stephens MicroCap Gr
Reynolds, Brian F.	Babson MM Fed, MM Prime
Reynolds, Frederick L.	Reynolds Blue Chip Gr, MM, Opportunity, U.S. Govt Bond
Reynolds, Robert J.	Mathers Fund
Reynolds, Timothy	U.S. Global Investors Income, Real Estate
Reynolds, William T.	Price, Rowe Summit Muni Inc
Ribeiro, Luis M., Jr.	Rembrandt Latin American Equity
Richards, Anne H.	JP Morgan Int'l Equity
Riegel, William M.	JP Morgan U.S. Equity
Rights, David N.	Rightime
Rimmer, Mark	Nations Glbl Govt
Rinaldi, I. Charles	Strong Small Cap Value
Ringberg, Keith E.	Sentry Fund
Rinkoff, Richard J.	Eastcliff Regional Sm Cap Value
Rippey, Jeffrey L.	Columbia High Yield, U.S. Govt Securities, Fixed Inc Securities
Risen, Kevin L.	Neuberger & Berman Focus, Guardian
Ritter, Charles A.	Federated Managed Aggr Gr, Managed Gr, Managed Gr & Inc, Managed Inc
Rivelle, Tad	Metropolitan West Low Duration Bond, Total Return Bond
Rivoir, Tom	Smith Barney Money Cash Port
Roberts, Simon	Fidelity United Kingdom
Roberts, Stuart O.	Montgomery Small Cap
Robinson, Jackson W.	Green Century Balanced
Robinson, John P.	General Securities
Rodriguez, Joe V., Jr.	INVESCO Realty
Rogers, Brian C.	Price, Rowe Equity Inc, Value
Rogers, Douglas S.	Heartland U.S. Govt Securities
Rogers, Ian J.	Strong Total Return
Rogers, J. Patrick	Gateway Cincinnati, Index Plus, Mid Cap Index, Sm Cap Index
Rogers, John W.	Ariel Growth

Portfolio Manager	Fund
Rogers, Paul	Scudder Latin America
Rogge, Olaf	Managers Global Bond
Rohrman, Curt	USAA First Growth, Sci & Tech
Rokus, Richard M.	Marshall MM
Rollins, Blaine P.	Janus Balanced, Equity Inc, Fund
Roman, Lois R. Friedman	Scudder Large Co Value
Rome, Michael S.	Lazard Equity, Glbl Equity
Romick, Steven	UAM - FPA Crescent
Root, George W.	Scout Bond
Rosborough, Michael	PIMCo Emerg Mkts Bond
Rosenberg, Barr	Barr Rosenberg Int'l Small Cap, Japan, U.S. Small Cap
Rothenberg, G.D.	UAM - TS&W Int'l Equity
Rothery, Christopher	Price, Rowe Emerg Mkts Bond, Glbl Govt Bond, Int'l Bond
Rowe, Robb W.	Lexington Small Cap Value
Rowland, Thomas J.	Wayne Hummer Growth
Royce, Charles M.	Royce Financial Svcs, GiftShares, Low Priced Stock, Micro-Cap, PA Mutual, PMF II, Premier, Tot Return
Ruane, William J.	Sequoia Fund
Ruback, Albert	Fidelity Sel Cyclical Industries
Rubano, Robert	SSgA Active Int'l
Rubin, Howard B.	Managers Short & Inter Bond
Rubin, William	Fidelity Sel Home Finance
Rudnick, Allan M.	Kayne, Anderson Rising Dividends
Rufenacht, Sandy R.	Janus Flex Inc, High Yield, ST Bond
Ruff, Anne	Rydex U.S. Govt Bond, U.S. Govt MM
Rump, Sven	Vontobel Int'l Bond
Russell, Richard B.	Lexington Convertible Securities
Russell, Stewart	Harbor Short Duration
Ryan, John R.	Vanguard Wellesley Inc
Ryback, Eric E.	Lindner Dividend, Growth, Int'l, Utility, Lindner/Ryback Sm Cap
Ryon, Christopher M.	Vanguard Muni Inter, Muni LT, NY Insured LT, Tax Managed Bal
Sachs, Morton H.	Fairmont
Sagar, Rosemary	Excelsior Int'l, Latin America, Pan European
Sagvold, Lynette D.	SAFECO Bal, U.S. Value
Salemy, Louis	Fidelity Gr & Inc
Saler, Richard T.	Lexington Glbl, Int'l, World Emerg Mkts
Salerno, Frank	BT Advisor Small Cap Index, BT Pyramid Equity 500 Index; Scudder S&P 500 Index; USAA S&P 500 Index
Saleur, Renaud	Fidelity France
Saltzman, M. Isabel	Scudder Emerging Mkts Inc
Sammer, Robert L.	IAA Trust MM
Sammons, Edward E., Jr.	Asset Mgmt Financial Adj Rate Mtge, Inter Mtge Sec, MM, ST U.S. Govt Sec, U.S. Govt Mtge Sec
Sanborn, Robert J.	Oakmark Fund
Sanchez, Leif O.	Sefton Equity Value, Sm Co Value
Sanchez, Michael	Hotchkis & Wiley Bal, Low Dur, ST Invstmnt, Total Return Bond
Sandel, M. Gerard	Stein Roe Special
Sanders, Philip J.	Nations Capital Gr
Sanderson, Susan A.	Boston 1784 FL TE Inc, MA TE Inc
Sandler, Michael C.	Clipper Fund
Santa Luca, Albert P.	Capstone Growth
Santella, Gloria J.	Stein Roe Capital Opps, Growth Opps
Santoliquido, Anthony	HGK Fixed Income
Saperstone, Peter	Fidelity Select Air Transport, Sel Def & Aerospace
Sarnell, Melody P.	Vanguard Equity Inc
Sarofim, Fayez	Dreyfus Appreciation
Satterthwaite, Patricia A.	Fidelity Latin America
Satterwhite, Scott C.	Artisan Sm Cap Value
Saul, Janice H.	CGM American TF, FI
Saunders, John W., Jr.	USAA Inc, Gr & Tax Strategy, Inc Strategy
Sauter, George U.	Vanguard Explorer, Horizon Aggr Gr, Index Tr 500, Index Tr Extended Mkt, Index Tr Gr, Index Tr Sm Cap, Index Tr Tot Stock Mkt, Index Tr Value, Int'l Eq Index Emerg Mkts, Int'l Eq Index Europe, Int'l Eq Index Pacific, Morgan Growth, Windsor II, Special REIT Idx
Sawada, Haruo	Nomura Pacific Basin

Portfolio Manager	Fund	Portfolio Manager	Fund
Schachter, Howard S.	Needham Growth	Short, Jonathan D.	Fidelity Spartan AZ Muni Inc, Spartan CA Muni Inc, Spartan FL Muni Inc, Spartan MA Muni Inc, Spartan MN Muni Inc, Spartan PA Muni Inc
Schafer, David K.	Strong Schafer Value, Schafer Balanced		
Schaff, William F.K.	Information Tech 100		
Scharar, Robert W.	Capstone Japan, New Zealand	Siegel, Jeffrey	TIAA-CREF Gr Equity
Schaulat, Christine	Fidelity Sel Regional Banks	Siegel, Rochelle G.	Dean Witter ST Bond
Schermerhorn, Scott B.	Federated Stock Trust	Sikharulidze, Beso	Fidelity Sel Health Care
Schettewi, Philip J.	Loomis Sayles Strategic Value	Silva, Joel	Amer Century - Benham CA Inter-Term TF,CA Ltd-Term TF, Inter-Term TF, Ltd-Term TF, LT TF, ST TE
Schliemann, Peter C.	Babson Enterprise, Enterprise II, Shadow Stock		
Schniedwind, John	American Century Inc & Gr, Utilities	Silver, Jennifer K.	Neuberger & Berman Manhattan
Schock, Varilyn K.	Westcore Blue Chip, Small-Cap Opp	Silvia, Thomas	Fidelity Mortgage Securities
Schoelzel, Scott W.	Janus Twenty	Sim, R. Dalton	INVESCO Strategic Financial Svcs
Schoenfeld, Jeffrey A.	59 Wall St Tax Free Sht/Inter FI	Simon, J. Peter	Reserve Convertible Secs
Schonberg, Michael L.	Dreyfus Aggr Gr, Large Co Gr	Simons, Kent C.	Neuberger & Berman Focus, Guardian
Schow, Howard B.	Vanguard Horizon Capital Opportunities, Primecap	Singer, Richard A.	Stalwart Income
		Siphron, David C.	Reserve Lg Cap Value
Schroeder, David W.	Amer Century - Benham Bond, Inflation-Adj Treas, Inter Govt, Inter Treas, Int'l Bond, LT Treas, GNMA, Target Maturities 2000-2025	Siphron, Peter D.	Reserve Lg Cap Value
		Sit, Debra A.	Sit MN TF, TF Inc
		Sit, Eugene C.	Sit Devel Mkts Gr, Int'l Gr, Regional Gr, Sci & Tech Gr, Sm Cap Gr
Schroer, John R.	INVESCO Strat Health Sciences	Sit, Ronald D.	Sit Lg Cap Growth
Schulhof, Milford H., II	Westcore Gr & Inc	Skettino, Jeanne M.	GW&K Govt Securities
Schumacher, Scott D.	TIP: Penn Capital Select Financial Svcs, Value Plus	Sloan, Maceo K.	Dreyfus Third Century
		Sloate, Laura J.	Strong Value
Schwartz, Arthur L.	WPG Inter Muni, TF MM	Slotpole, Robert	INVESCO Multi-Asset Allocation, Sm Co Value
Schwartz, George P.	Schwartz Value		
Schwarzkopf, Robert	Kayne Anderson Small-Mid Cap Rising Dividends	Smith, Bonnie L.	Merger Fund
		Smith, Charles P.	Price, Rowe New Inc, U.S. Treas Inter Bond
Schwatka, Victoria	Legg Mason TE Tr	Smith, David L.	Loomis Sayles Small Cap Gr
Scinto, Nancy	Chicago Trust Gr & Inc	Smith, Herbert R.	Avondale Total Return
Scullion, Rodger F.	PBHG Int'l; UAM - MJI Int'l Equity	Smith, James	PIMCo Emerg Mkts, Int'l Developed
Seabern, John H.	Robertson Stephens Dvsfd Gr	Smith, James M.	PBHG Small Co, Technology & Commun
Seale, William E.	ProFunds Bear, Bull, MM, UltraBear, Ultra Bull, Ultra OTC	Smith, Kathleen Shelton	IPO Plus Aftermarket
		Smith, L. Norfleet, Jr.	WST Growth & Inc
Sears, Buel S.	OVB Equity Inc	Smith, Mark J.	Schroder Capital - Int'l
Sebastian, Albert C.	USAA Int'l, World Growth	Smith, Reid O.	Vanguard CA TF Ins Inter, CA TF Ins LT, FL Ins TF, Muni High Yld, Muni Insured LT
Sefton, Harley K.	Sefton CA TF, Equity Value, Sm Co Value, U.S. Govt		
		Smith, Robert W.	Price, Rowe Growth Stock
Segalas, Spiros	Harbor Capital Apprec; Masters' Select Equity	Smith, Tim	Arbor OVB Prime Obligations
		Smith, William K.	IPO Plus Aftermarket
Segner, John	INVESCO Strategic Energy, Worldwide Capital Goods	Snider, William F.	Price, Rowe NJ TF Bond, NY TF Bond
		Snyder, Bradley C.	Northern CA Muni MM, Muni MM
Seitzer, John D.	Amer Century - 20th Century New Opps	Snyder, James	AMEX Strategist Govt Inc
Sekelsky, Jay R.	Mosaic Balanced, Bond, Govt, High Yield, Investors, Mid-Cap Gr	Sondike, Lawrence N.	Franklin Mutual Series
		Sorenson, Ronald J.	Strong American Utilities
Self, Charles H., III	Rembrandt FI	Sorrentino, Peter	Star Select REIT Plus
Sellecchia, Vincent	Delafield	Soslow, Anthony W.	Rightime Fund
Selmier, W. Travis, II	USAA Emerging Mkts, Int'l, World Gr	Soulis, Charles	Schwab CA Muni MF, NY Muni MF
Selner, Amy	Berger Mid Cap Gr	Southworth, Theodore T.	Northern Income Equity
Semenuk, Chris	TIAA-CREFF Int'l Equity	Soviero, Thomas T.	Fidelity Spartan High Inc
Senft, Fred H., Jr.	Chicago Trust MM	Spano, Peter F.	Preferred Int'l
Seneca, Gail P.	Citizens Inc; Seneca Bond, Growth, Mid-Cap EDGE, RE Secs	Spare, Anthony E.	Vanguard Equity Inc
		Spaulding, Ronald	SAFECO Inter-Term U.S. Treasury
Shackelford, Daniel O.	UAM - ICM Fixed Inc	Speaker, Ronald V.	Janus Flexible Inc, HY
Shaffro, Jill C.	Dreyfus CA TE MM, CT Muni MM, FL Muni MM, General CA Muni MM, MA Muni MM, PA Muni MM	Spears, John D.	Tweedy, Browne Amer Value, Glbl Value
		Spindler, Paul W.	TIP: Clover Equity Value, FI, Max Cap Value
		Spolidoro, Carolyn H.	Selected Daily Govt, U.S. Govt Inc
Shapiro, David A.	Seneca Real Estate Secs	Sprague, Thomas	Fidelity Asset Manager
Sharon, Harold E.	Warburg, Pincus Glbl Post-Venture Capital	Spreadbury, Ian	Fidelity Int'l Bond
		Sprow, John B.	Smith Breeden Market Tracking
Sharp, Wayne S.	Boston Partners Lg Cap Value	Stack, William S.	Dresdner RCM Emerg Mkts
Sheehan, Patrick	Accessor Inter FI	Stansky, Brian D.	Price, Rowe Media & Telecomm
Sheridan, Michael	Reserve CA TE MM, CT TE MM, FL TE MM, Interstate TE MM, MA TE MM, NJ TE MM, NY TE MM, PA TE MM	Stansky, Robert E.	Fidelity Magellan
		Stapley, Mitchell L.	Kent Inc, Inter Bond, ST Bond
		Stark, Douglas E.	Accessor Value and Income
		Starr, Adam	WPG Growth, Tudor
Sheridan, Todd M.	Preferred Sm Cap	Steedman, Eric W.	Dreyfus Third Century
Sherman, Martha L.	Nations Prime MM	Steers, Robert H.	Cohen & Steers Realty, Special Equity
Shi, Bin	U.S. Global Investors All American Eq, China Region Opp	Stephens, Andrew C.	Artisan Mid Cap
		Stephens, Paul H.	Robertson Stephens Contrarian
Shick, Daniel R.	Gradison Growth Tr Established Val, Opportunity Val	Stephenson, Robert S.	UAM - DSI Disciplined Value
		Sterling, Joseph	American Century Glbl Natural Resources, Utilities
Shiel, J. Fergus	Fidelity Retirement Gr		
Shoemaker, John C.	Advance Capital I Bal, Bond, Retirement Inc	Sterling, William P.	BEA Advisor Int'l Equity
		Stetter, John A.	Concorde Inc, Value

Portfolio Manager	Fund	Portfolio Manager	Fund
Stevens, Thomas D.	Wilshire Target Large Co Gr, Large Co Val, Sm Co Gr, Sm Co Val	Thompson, Peter A.	UAM - C&B Balanced, C&B Equity, C&B Equity for Taxable Investors
Stevens, William C.	Montgomery CA TF Inter, CA TF MM, Federal TF MF, Govt Res MM, Short Dur Govt Bond, Total Ret Bond	Thompson, Simon C.N.	Lexington Crosby Sm Cap Asia
		Thorndike, Benjamin W.	AARP Growth & Income; Scudder Pathway Series
Stevenson, Paul A.	SAFECO GNMA	Thornton, Henry	Fremont Emerging Mkts
Stewart, David C.	Fidelity Emerging Mkts	Thunelius, Gerald E.	Dreyfus 100% U.S. Treas Inter, 100% U.S. Treas Long, 100% U.S. Treas Short, Short-Inter Govt Fund
Stewart, Samuel S.	Stalwart Aggr Equity		
Stewart, Samuel S., Jr.	Wasatch Aggr Eq, Growth, Micro Cap, Mid-Cap		
Stewart, Scott	Fidelity Fifty, Freedom Funds	Thygesen, Kjeld R.	Midas Fund
Stodden, Jerold L.	Chicago Trust Gr & Inc	Tice, David W.	Prudent Bear
Stone, Colin	Fidelity Nordic	Tierney, David E.	Harbor Value
Stopford, John	Guiness Flight Glbl Govt Bond	Tillinghast, Joel	Fidelity Low-Priced Stock
Stotz, William F.	Federated High Yield	Tillson, David A.	Excelsior Blended Equity
Stowers, James E., III	Amer Century Bal; Amer Century - 20th Century Select, Ultra	Todd, John J.	Fidelity Asset Mgr, Asset Mgr Gr, Asset Mgr Inc, Cash Reserves, Daily Inc Tr, Sel MM, Spartan MM
Strabo, Henrik	Amer Century - 20th Century Int'l Discovery, Int'l Gr		
Stratton, James W.	Stratton Growth, Monthly Div REIT Sh, Sm Cap Yield, Special Value	Tomlin, Kyle A.	New Providence Capital Gr
		Tong, Ana	INVESCO Pacific Basin
Streed, Robert N.	Northern Select Equity	Tooke, Nancy B.	Schroder Series Small Cap Value
Stromberg, William J.	Price, Rowe Dividend Gr	Torray, Robert E.	Torray Fund
Strong, Richard S.	Strong Discovery	Traum, Steven	TIAA-CREF MM
Stuebe, John W.	Kemper Cash Account Tr Govt Secs, MM, Tax-Exempt, Cash Equiv Govt Secs, MM, Tax-Exempt; Scudder Cash Investment Trust, U.S. Treasury MF	Trautman, Mark F.	MSB Fund
		Trautwein, Richard	Vista American Value
		Treanor, Amy	Schwab Govt MM, U.S. Treas MF
		Treick, Philip	Transamerica Premier Aggr Gr, Sm Co
Sudweeks, Bryan L.	Montgomery Emerg Asia, Emerg Mkts; SEI Emerg Mkts Equity	Trosky, Benjamin	PIMCo High Yield
		Trowbridge, James W.	INVESCO Realty
Sugameli, Ronald A.	Weston New Century Capital, New Century I	Trozzo, Samuel R.	UAM - Rice, Hall, James Small Cap, Sm/Mid Cap
Sugimoto, Yukiko	JP Morgan Japan Equity	Truscott, William F.	Scudder Financial Svcs
Sullivan, Erin	Fidelity Emerging Gr	Tse, Joseph	Fidelity Hong Kong and China
Swaim, John	Nations Short/Inter Govt	Tukman, Melvin T.	Vanguard Windsor II
Sweeney, Thomas	Fidelity Canada	Tully, Joseph M.	Prudential MoneyMart Assets
Sykora, John R.	Amer Century Balanced, Amer Century: 20th Century Ultra	Turner, Bradley E.	Gradison Growth Tr Int'l
		Turner, Robert E.	TIP: Target Select Equity; TIP: Turner Growth Equity, Ultra Large Cap
Szczur, John J.	Homestead Daily Inc		
Tabacco, Denise	Amer Century - Benham Prime MM	Tyler, Jeffrey R.	American Century Equity Gr, Strategic Alloc Funds
Tajbakhsh, Shahram	AARP Diversified Gr, Diversified Inc w/Gr		
		Uible, Woodrow H.	Legg Mason Balanced
Takach, Eugene D.	Boston 1784 Gr, Gr & Inc	Ullom, R. David	USAA Bal Strategy, Gr & Inc, Inc Strategy, World Gr
Takazawa, Anthony	BT Investment Cap App, BT Pyramid Equity Apprec		
		Ulrich, Ronald J.	Vanguard Windsor II
Talebi, Fariba	Schroder Capital - U.S. Smaller Cos	Umstead, David A.	Quantitative Foreign Frontier, Int'l Eq
Tank, Bradley C.	Strong Asset Alloc, Govt Sec, ST Bond	Unschuld, Ira	Schroder Capital - MicroCap
Tarlowe, Michael D.	Fidelity Sel Business Svcs & Outsourcing	Urata, Naomi	SAFECO MM
Tartaro, Ronald	Spectra Fund	Utsch, Hans T.	Kaufmann
Tavel, Bruce	Excelsior Blended Equity	Utter, Jack	AMEX Strategist High Yield
Taylor, Peter A.	Scudder Financial Svcs	Vaccacio, James R.	Empire Builder TF Bond
Taze-Bernard, Eric	BNY Hamilton Int'l Equity	Vale, Judith M.	Neuberger & Berman Genesis
Teach, Stuart E.	Homestead Value	Van Buren, Diane C.	FAM Value
Teidge, Edward J.	Federated GNMA Tr, Inc Tr	Van Cleave, Karen	Rembrandt Govt MM, MM, Treas MM
Tempero, Michael	Fidelity Sel Computers	van Daalen, M. Anthony E.	Warburg, Pincus FI, Inter Mat Govt
Tengler, Nancy C.	UBS U.S. Equity	Van Der Berg, Hans	1838 Int'l Equity
Tennille, William G.	JP Morgan Bond, ST Bond	van der Velde, Murphy	Galaxy II Large Co Index, Small Co Index, Utility Index
Teoh, Seok	Nations Pacific Gr		
Terrana, Beth	Fidelity Fund	Van Dyke, J. Peter	Price, Rowe Corp Inc, GNMA, Personal Strat Bal, Personal Strat Gr, Personal Strat Inc, ST U.S. Govt, Spectrum Gr, Spectrum Inc, Summit GNMA, U.S. Treas LT
Thakore, Nicholas	Fidelity Sel Telecomm, Sel Utilities Gr, Utilities		
Thay, Victor Y.	Fidelity Sel Natural Gas		
Thieme, Heiko H.	American Heritage, Growth	Van Harte, Jeffrey S.	Transamerica Premier Balanced
Thomas, James R., III	OVB Govt Sec, WV TE Inc	Van Kooten, Bruce H.	KPM Equity
Thomas, Lee R., III	PIMCo Foreign Bond, Glbl Bond	Van Wagoner, Garrett R.	Van Wagoner Emerg Gr, Micro-Cap, Mid Cap, Post-Venture
Thomas, Norwood A., Jr.	WST Growth & Inc		
Thomas, William G.M.	RSI Ret Trust Int'l Equity	Vandenberg, Richard L.	AARP GNMA & Treasury, Scudder GNMA
Thompson, Christine J.	Fidelity Inter Bond, Target Timeline	Van der Eb, Harry G. Jr.	Mathers
Thompson, Darrell C.	Vintage Aggressive Gr, Bal, Equity	Vanderhooft, Shannon	ni numeric Growth, Micro Cap
Thompson, David H.	Boston 1784 CT TE Inc, FL TE Inc, RI TE Inc, TE Medium Term	Vandivort, Daniel S.	WPG Core Bond, Govt MM
		Vannice, Jon	North Carolina TF Bond
Thompson, David J.	UAM - DSI MM	Vardanian, Ruben	Lexington Troika Dialog
Thompson, John W.	Thompson & Plumb Bond, Gr	Vaselkiv, Mark J.	Price, Rowe High Yield
		Veaco, Bruce	Clipper
		Vella, Richard J.	BT Advisor EAFE Equity Index

Portfolio Manager	Fund
Vernick, Joel M.	Babson TF Inc L, TF Inc S
Veterane, David A.	Rainier Core Eq, Small/Mid Cap Eq
Visovsky, Michael	Lipper U.S. Equity
Vlachos, Peter	Austin Global Equity
Voelker, Philip A.	Flex-Fund MM
Volpert, Kenneth E.	Vanguard Bond Index Inter-Term, Bond Index LT, Bond Index ST, Bond Index Total Bond Mkt
Von Metzsch, Ernst H.	Vanguard Special Energy, Wellington
von Pentz, Robert A.	Quantitative Numeric, Numeric II
Vora, Medha	Warburg, Pincus Emerg Gr
Vroom, Edwin G.	Reserve Sm Cap Growth
Wade, Martin G.	Price, Rowe Emerg Mkts Stock, European Stock, Glbl Stock, Int'l Discovery, Int'l Stock, Japan, Latin America, New Asia
Wade, Maury Jr.	Wade Fund
Wakeman, John F.	Price, Rowe Capital Opp
Walbrandt, Charles D.	Quaker Fixed Inc
Walczak, Edwin D.	Vontobel U.S. Value
Wald, Thomas	INVESCO Dynamics
Walden, Sally	Fidelity Europe
Walk, Beth Ann	Jamestown TE Virginia
Wallace, John L.	Robertson Stephens Diversified Gr, Gr & Inc
Wallace, Veronica M.	Stein Roe Muni Money
Wallace, William J.	Scudder Gold, Value
Wallman, Richard D.	Dreyfus Technology Growth
Walsh, John	Amer Century - Benham Prime MM
Walsh, Stephen A.	Western Asset Inter Dur
Wanger, Ralph L. Jr.	Acorn, Acorn Int'l
Wapnick, Alan H.	Lexington Global, Gr & Inc
Ward, Howard F.	Gabelli Growth
Ward, Stephen B.	Schwab - Asset Director Bal, Asset Dir Cons Gr, Asset Dir High Gr, CA LT TF Bond, CA S/I TF Bond, Int'l Index, LT Govt Bond, LT TF Bond, OneSource Portfolios Bal, Growth, Int'l & Sm Co; Retirement MF, S/I Govt Bond, S/I TF Bond, Value Adv MF, 1000, S&P 500, Small Cap Index
Wardlow, Jeffrey W.	Loomis-Sayles Core Value
Warden, Dick	AMEX Strategist Equity
Watkins, Gregg D.	Loomis Sayles Mid-Cap Val
Watson, Stephen	Nations Int'l Equity
Watt, Richard W.	BEA Advisor Emerging Mkts, Glbl Telecom
Watters, Darrell W.	Janus Fed TE
Wehrle, Volker	Vontobel Eastern Euro Debt
Weichers-Marshall, Ana	Dresdner RCM Emerg Mkts
Weijand, Wouter	Rembrandt Int'l FI
Weiner, Jason	Fidelity Contrafund II, Export and Multinational
Weinstock, Samuel J.	Dreyfus NY TE, S-I Muni Bond
Weise, Edward A.	Price, Rowe ST Bond
Weisman, Adele S.	Reserve Sm Cap Growth
Weiss, Leigh H.	Excelsior Blended Equity
Weiss, Richard T.	Masters' Select Equity; Strong Common Stock, Opportunity
Weitz, Wallace R.	Weitz FI, Govt MM, Partners Value, Value
Weller, Fred W.	Matrix Emerg Gr
Welles, Peter	Harbor Growth
Welsh, Michael J.	Oakmark Int'l, Int'l Small Cap
Werler, Mary K.	Boston 1784 Prime MM, ST Inc
Wesselkamper, C. Stephen	Gradison Govt Inc,Growth Tr U.S. Govt Res
Weston, Paul J.	Gradison U.S. Govt Res
White, Edward M.	GW&K Equity
White, Thomas S., Jr.	Thomas White World Fund
Whitehead, Trudie D.	Legg Mason HY Bond
Whitesett, Bernard D., II	Prudential Govt Secs Tr, U.S. Treas MM
Whitlow, William B.	SAFECO Northwest
Whitman, Martin J.	Third Avenue Value
Whitney, Richard T.	Advance Capital I Bal, Eq Gr; Price, Rowe Bal, Dvsfd Sm-Cap Gr, Eq Index 500, Extended Equity Market Idx, Total Equity Mkt Idx
Whitridge, Roland W.	Babson Shadow Stock, Value

Portfolio Manager	Fund
Widner, Patricia F.	Warburg, Pincus Health Scis
Wieboldt, Monica S.	Dreyfus CA Inter Muni Bond, General NY Muni Bond, Inter Muni Bond, MA Inter Muni, NY TE Interm
Wiese, Edward A.	Price,Rowe Prime Res, Summit Cash Res, Summit Ltd Trm Bond, U.S. Treas MF
Wiggins, Jeffrey J.	Dresdner RCM Biotech, Global Health Care
Wilbanks, Wayne F.	WST Growth & Inc
Wiles, Christopher H.	Rockhaven Fund, Rockhaven Premier Dividend
Wilkins, Anthony J.	Loomis Sayles Intermediate Maturity
Williams, David J.	Excelsior Value & Restructuring
Williams, Eric S.	Nations Equity Inc
Williams, Jane H.	Sand Hill Portfolio Manager
Williams, John S.	UAM - BHM&S Total Return Bond
Williams, Peter H.	Matrix Growth
Williams, Rena	SSgA MM, TF MM, Yield Plus
Willmann, Kenneth E.	USAA GNMA Tr, Gr & Tax Strategy, NY Bond, TE Fund LT
Willoughby, Jay L.	Crabbe Huson Real Estate Investment
Wilson, Donald S.	Fiduciary Capital Gr
Wilson, Peter D.	Montgomery CA TF Inter Bond, CA TF MF, Federal TF MF, Govt Res, Short Dur Govt Bond, Total Ret Bond
Wilson, Rebecca L.	Scudder HY TF, OH TF, PA TF
Wilson, Steven M.	Reich & Tang Equity
Wimberly, Bruce A.	Amer Century Bal; Amer Century -20th Century Ultra
Windheim, Kenneth A.	SEI Int'l FI
Winslow, Clark J.	Eastcliff Growth
Winston, Greg D.	Heartland High Yield Muni, Short Dur High Yield
Winters, Kurt	AMEX Strategist Balanced, Equity Inc
Wirtz, E. Keith	Nations LifeGoal Bal, LifeGoal Gr, LifeGoal Inc & Gr
Wisehaupt-Tynan, Pamela E.	Vanguard CA TF MM, Muni Ltd-Term, Muni MM, Muni Short-Term, PA TF MM
Wohler, Stephen A.	AARP Bal Stock & Bond, Bond Fund for Inc, High Quality ST Bond; Scudder Bal, High Yield Bond, Income, ST Bond, Zero Coupon 2000
Wolf, Simon	Fidelity Sel Industrial Equipment
Wolfe, C. Stephen II	Price, Rowe TF High Yield
Wolfe, Thomas G.	Neuberger & Berman Ltd Mat Bond
Wood, Gary B.	Concorde Income,Value
Woods, Hilary R.	Dreyfus Emerg Leaders, New Leaders
Woods, Timothy	BT Investment Sm Cap
Woodson, A. Hartswell III	Gabelli Glbl Conv Sec
Wren, Francis P.	Aon Govt Securities
Wright, Emmett M.	Boston 1784 Asset Alloc, Income, U.S. Govt Med Term Inc, U.S. Treas MM
Wright, John G. L.	Babson Stewart Ivory Int'l
Wright, Mary Kay	Northern Stock Index
Wymer, Steven S.	Fidelity Growth Co
Wyper, George U.	Warburg, Pincus Cap Appr, Sm Co Value
Yacktman, Donald A.	Yacktman Fund
Yeager, George M.	U.S. Global Leaders Growth
Yockey, Mark, L.	Artisan Int'l; Masters' Select Int'l
York, Lawrence S.	WWW Internet
Young, Calvin S.	Scudder Micro Cap, Sm Co Value
Young, Claire W.	Janus Olympus
Young, Elaine B.	JP Morgan NY Total Return Bond, TE Bond; JP Morgan Shares: CA Bond
Yun, William	FTI Int'l Equity
Zagunis, Robert	Jensen Portfolio
Zarr, Joseph	Flex-Fund U.S. Govt Bond
Zaske, Arthur E.	ZSA Asset Alloc, Equity
Zawitkowski, Irene J.	Volumetric Fund
Zell, Leah Joy	Acorn International
Zeltzer, Gary S.	Schroder Series Inv Grade Inc, ST Investment
Zemsky, Paul L.	Preferred FI
Zercoe, Marcia	1838 Fixed Inc
Ziegler, Carlene Murphy	Artisan Small Cap
Zimmer, William W.	UAM - Chicago Asset Mgmt Inter Bond
Zuccaro, Robert	Grand Prix Fund
Zuger, Peter A.	American Century Eq Inc, Value

CHAPTER 15

Geographical guide to no-load funds

State/City	Funds
Alabama	
Mobile	Government Street group
Arizona	
Phoenix	L. Roy Papp group
California	
Beverly Hills	Clipper Fund
	Meyers Pride Value Fund
Foster City	Bailard, Biehl & Kaiser (BBK) group
Larkspur	Meridian group
	Reynolds group
Los Angeles	Analytic group
	Bjurman Micro Cap Growth Fund
	Crescent Fund
	Hotchkis & Wiley group
	Kayne, Anderson group
	Metropolitan West group
	Pathfinder Fund
	Payden & Rygel group
	Rea-Graham Balanced
	RNC group
	Stonebridge Growth Fund
	Transamerica Premier group
Moraga	Ameristock Mutual
Newport Beach	PIMCO group
Novato	Hennessy Balanced Fund
Oakland	Jurika & Voyles group
Orinda	Barr Rosenberg Series
	Masters' Select group
Pasadena	Guinness Flight group
	PIC group
	Western Asset Trust group
Petaluma	Permanent Portfolio group
Redwood Shores	Ridgeway Helms Millenium Fund
San Diego	Sefton group
San Francisco	California Investment Trust group
	Citizens Trust group
	Dodge & Cox group
	Dresdner RCM group
	Fremont group
	Information Tech 100 Fund
	Matthews group
	McM group
	Montgomery group
	Pacific Horizon
	Parnassus Income group
	Robertson Stephens group
	Schwab group
	Seneca group
	Van Wagoner group
	Women's Equity Fund
San Jose	Firsthand group
San Mateo	Franklin group
Santa Monica	DFA group
	Wilshire Target group
Walnut Creek	TIP (formerly Solon) Institutional
Woodside	Purisima Total Return
Colorado	
Denver	Berger group
	Founders group
	INVESCO group
	Janus group
	Marsico group
	Westcore group
Connecticut	
Bridgeport	Wright group
Fairfield	Highland Growth Fund
Greenwich	Gintel Fund

State/City	Funds
	IPO Plus Aftermarket Fund
	O'Shaughnessy group
	Sound Shore Fund
	Trainer, Wortham group
Norwalk	Managers group
Stamford	General Electric group
Westport	Westport group
Wilton	Grand Prix Fund
Delaware	
Greenville	Brandywine group
	Kalmar Gr w/Value Sm Cap
Wilmington	Crowley Portfolio group
District of Columbia	
Washington	Steadman group
Florida	
Boca Raton	Philadelphia Fund
Clearwater	AIT Vision U.S. Equity
Jacksonville	Emerald (Barnett) group
St. Petersburg	Florida Tax Free (Hough) group
Tampa	ASM Index 30 Fund
Venice	C/Funds (Caldwell) group
West Palm Beach	Carl Domino Equity Inc Fund
Georgia	
Atlanta	Caldwell & Orkin Agg Gr Fund
	Cornercap (Cornerstone) group
	Globalt Growth Fund
	New Providence Capital Gr
Carrollton	SCM Portfolio
Peachtree City	Eclipse group
Hawaii	
Honolulu	First Hawaii group
Idaho	
Idaho Falls	Rockwood Fund
Illinois	
Bannockburn	Mathers Fund
Bloomington	IAA Trust Co. group
	State Farm group
Buffalo Grove	Leonetti Balanced Fund
Chicago	Acorn group
	AON Advisors group
	Ariel Investment Trust group
	Asset Management (Shay) group
	Brinson group
	Bruce Fund
	Chicago Trust (Alleghany) group
	Fasciano Fund
	ICAP group
	Kemper group
	Kenwood Gr & Inc
	Montag & Caldwell group
	M.S.B. Fund
	Northern group
	Oakmark group
	Perritt Micro Cap Opps
	Rembrandt group
	Skyline group
	Stein Roe group
	SwissKey group
	Thomas White World Fund
	Wayne Hummer group
	William Blair group
	Yacktman group
	Zurich MM group
Lake Forest	Lake Forest group

State/City	Funds
North Aurora	Oberweis group
Peoria	Preferred group
Rockford	Vintage group
Wheaton	Monetta group
Indiana	
Indianapolis	Pinnacle Fund
	Unified group
Kentucky	
Lexington	Dupree group
	WWW Internet Fund
Louisville	Fairmont Fund
Louisiana	
Baton Rouge	Florida Street group
Maine	
Portland	Forum group
Maryland	
Baltimore	Brown Capital Management group
	Croft-Leominster group
	Legg Mason group
	T. Rowe Price group
Bethesda	Cappiello-Rushmore group
	ProFunds group
	Rydex group
	Torray Fund
Lutherville	Greenspring Fund
Silver Spring	Profit Value Fund
Towson	Fontaine group
Upper Marlboro	Titan Financial Svcs Fund
Massachusetts	
Boston	AARP group
	Boston Partners group
	Boston 1784 group
	Century Shares Trust
	CGM group
	Domini Social Equity Fund
	Fidelity group
	59 Wall St. group
	(GMO) Pelican Fund
	Green Century group
	GWK (Gannett, Welsh & Kotler) group
	ICM/Isabelle Sm Cap Value
	Loomis Sayles group
	New England group
	Northeast Investors group
	Scudder group
	SSgA group
	UAM group
Cambridge	ni Numeric group
Fall River	Copley Fund
Lincoln	Quantitative group
Wellesley	Weston Portfolios group
Wellesley Hills	Kobren Insight group
Westboro	Galaxy group
Michigan	
Birmingham	Munder NetNet Fund
	Zsa Asset Allocation Fund
Bloomfield Hills	Schwartz Value Fund
Farmington Hills	Independence One group
Grand Rapids	Kent group
Southfield	Advance Capital I group
Minnesota	
Edina	General Securities
Minneapolis	American Express Strategist group
	Eastcliff group
	IAI group
	Kaminski Poland Fund
	Leuthold Core Investment
	Markman Multifund Trust
	SIT group
St. Paul	Mairs & Power group

State/City	Funds
Mississippi	
Jackson	Investek Fixed Income
Missouri	
Kansas City	American Century group
	American Century (Benham) group
	American Century (20th Century) group
	Babson group
	Buffalo group
	HGK Fixed Income Fund
	Pin Oak Aggr Growth Fund
	Scout group
	Vista group
	White Oak Growth Fund
St. Louis	Lindner group
Nebraska	
Lincoln	Lancaster group
Omaha	Bridges Investment Fund
	First Omaha group
	Kiewit group
	KPM group
	Weitz group
Nevada	
Reno	Navellier group
New Hampshire	
Lebanon	American Trust Allegiance Fund
Portsmouth	Citizens Trust group
	Pax World Fund
	Working Assets MM
New Jersey	
Saddle Brook	Lexington group
Short Hills	(Franklin) Mutual Series group
Somerville	Harding, Loevner group
New Mexico	
Santa Fe	The Selected group
New York	
Cobleskill	FAM group
Honeoye Falls	Bullfinch funds
New York	Alliance World Income
	American Heritage group
	Austin Global Equity
	Baron group
	BEA Advisors group
	Bernstein group
	BlackRock Financial
	BNY Hamilton group
	Bramwell Growth Fund
	BT (Bankers Trust) group
	Bull & Bear group
	Citiselect Portfolios
	Cohen & Steers group
	Daruma Mid-Cap Value Fund
	Dean Witter group
	Delafield Fund
	Empire Builders TF Bond
	Excelsior group
	First Eagle group
	FMC Select Fund
	FTI group
	Fundamental group
	Haven Fund
	Holland Balanced Fund
	J.P. Morgan group
	Kaufmann Fund
	Lazard group
	Lepercq-Istel Fund
	Lipper group
	Mainstay group
	Matrix/LMH Value Fund
	Midas Fund
	Morgan Grenfell group
	Needham Growth Fund
	Neuberger & Berman group

State/City	Funds
	Nomura Pacific Basin
	Oak Hall Equity Fund
	PaineWebber group
	Prudential group
	Rainbow Fund
	Reich & Tang group
	Reserve group
	Royce group
	RSI Retirement group
	Salomon Brothers group
	Schroder Capital group
	Schroder Series group
	Sequoia Fund
	Smith Barney group
	Spectra Fund
	TCW/DW group
	Third Avenue group
	TIAA-CREF group
	Trainer, Wortham group
	Tweedy Browne group
	U.S. Global Leaders
	UBS Private Investors group
	Value Line group
	Warburg Pincus group
	Weiss, Peck & Greer (WPG) group
Pearl River	Volumetric Fund
Pittsford	TIP (Clover Capital) group
Purchase	Alpine group
Rye	Gabelli group
	(Gabelli) Westwood group
Uniondale	Dreyfus group
Valhalla	Merger Fund
White Plains	CRM Small Cap Value
North Carolina	
Asheville	North Carolina Tax-Free Bond
Chapel Hill	Smith Breeden group
Charlotte	Nations group
Durham	Oak Value Fund
Greensboro	Trent Equity Fund
Rocky Mount	Nottingham Investment Trust
Ohio	
Cincinnati	Analysts Investment Trust group
	Brundage Story & Rose group
	Gradison group
	Matrix group
	Star Select REIT Plus Fund
	Touchstone group
Cleveland	Fairport group
	Jhaveri Value Fund
	NewCap Contrarian
	Maxus group
Dayton	PC&J group
Dublin	Flex-Funds group
Milford	Gateway group
Toledo	Harbor group
Oregon	
Medford	Cutler group
Portland	Columbia group
	Crabbe Huson group
	IMS Capital Value
	Jensen Portfolio
Pennsylvania	
Berwyn	Berwyn group
Chadds Ford	Chesapeake Core Gr Fund
Jenkintown	Matthews 25 Fund
Kennett Square	Henlopen Fund
Malvern	Manor Investment
Oaks	SEI group
	TIP (Turner) group
Pittsburgh	Federated group
	Rockhaven group
Plymouth Meeting	Stratton group
Radnor	1838 Investment group
Valley Forge	Quaker group
	Valley Forge Fund

State/City	Funds
	Vanguard group
Wayne	Focus Trust
	PBHG group
West Conshohocken	MAS group
Wexford	Muhlenkamp Fund
Wyncote	Rightime Fund
Yardley	Matterhorn Growth Fund
South Carolina	
Greenville	Blue Ridge Total Return Fund
Tennessee	
Knoxville	IPS Millenium Fund
Memphis	Longleaf group
	Wade Fund
Texas	
Dallas	Aquinas group
	Armstrong Assocs.
	Brazos/JMIC group
	Concorde group
	Prudent Bear Fund
Ft. Worth	American AAdvantage group
	Corbin Sm Cap Value Fund
	LKCM group
Houston	Bridgeway group
	Capstone group
	Fountainhead Special Value
	Lighthouse Contrarian
	West University Fund
San Antonio	U.S. Global Investors group
	USAA group
Victoria	Amtrust Value Fund
Waco	Academy Value Fund
Wichita Falls	Avondale Total Return Fund
Utah	
Salt Lake City	Wasatch group
Virginia	
Alexandria	AFBA Five Star group
Arlington	FBR group
	Homestead group
	Mosaic group
Lynchburg	American Pension Investors group
	FBP Contrarian group
McLean	Cruelty Free Value
Norfolk	WST Growth & Inc Fund
Richmond	America's Utility Fund
	Cash Resource Trust
	Davenport Equity
	Jamestown group
	Sand Hill Portfolio Manager
	Vontobel group
	World Funds group
Washington	
Bellingham	Amana group
	Saturna Capital group
	Sextant group
Seattle	Accessor group
	Merriman group
	Rainier group
	SAFECO group
West Virginia	
Charleston	OVB (One Valley Bank) group
Wisconsin	
Madison	Thompson & Plumb group
Milwaukee	Artisan group
	Fiduciary Capital Growth
	Firstar group
	FMI Focus Fund
	Heartland group
	Marshall group
	Nicholas group
	Primary group
	Strong group
Stevens Point	Sentry Fund

Section IV

Appendixes

Index and passively managed funds

Fund	Index	Comments	1997 % return	Expense ratio %	Annual turnover %
S&P 500 funds					
AARP US Stk Idx	S&P 500	500 large and medium size cos.	—	0.50	15
Amer AAdv Mileage S&P 500 Idx	S&P 500	500 large and medium size cos.	33.1	0.55	—
AON S&P 500 Idx	S&P 500	500 large and medium size cos.	32.8	0.37	13
BT Pyramid:Eqty 500 Idx	S&P 500	500 large and medium size cos.	33.0	0.25	6
CA Inv Tr-S&P 500 Idx	S&P 500	500 large and medium size cos.	33.0	0.20	2
DFA US Lrg Co‡	S&P 500	500 large and medium size cos.	33.1	0.21	14
Dreyfus S&P 500 Idx	S&P 500	500 large and medium size cos.	32.6	0.50	2
Federated Max Cap	S&P 500	500 large and medium size cos.	32.7	0.31	3
Fidelity Spart Market Idx	S&P 500	500 large and medium size cos.	33.0	0.19	2
Galaxy II Lrg Co Idx	S&P 500	500 large and medium size cos.	32.8	0.40	5
Invesco S&P 500 Idx II	S&P 500	500 large and medium size cos.	—	0.55	—
Kent Idx Eqty	S&P 500	500 large and medium size cos.	32.2	0.74	2
Nations Eqty Idx	S&P 500	500 large and medium size cos.	33.2	0.60	5
Northern Stock Idx	S&P 500	500 large and medium size cos.	32.7	0.55	—
Price Eqty 500 Idx	S&P 500	500 large and medium size cos.	32.9	0.40	1
Schwab S&P 500(Inv)	S&P 500	500 large and medium size cos.	32.5	0.38	5
Scudder S&P 500 Idx	S&P 500	500 large and medium size cos.	—	0.40	—
SEI Idx S&P 500	S&P 500	500 large and medium size cos.	32.8	0.40	2
SSgA S&P 500	S&P 500	500 large and medium size cos.	33.1	0.16	8
Strong S&P 500 Idx	S&P 500	500 large and medium size cos.	—	0.45	—
Transamerica Prem Idx	S&P 500	500 large and medium size cos.	33.1	0.35	94
USAA S&P 500 Idx	S&P 500	500 large and medium size cos.	33.0	0.18	15
Vangd Idx 500	S&P 500	500 large and medium size cos.	33.2	0.20	5
Other large company indexes					
ASM Idx 30	DJIA	Unweighted Dow look alike	24.5	0.42	265
Bridgeway Ult Lrg 35 Idx	Ultra Large Cap 35	35 largest US stocks	—	0.15	0
DFA US Lrg Cap Val‡		US stocks with high book to market	28.1	0.36	20
Fidelity Spart Total Mkt Idx†	Wilshire 5000	Broadest Idx, covers all US stocks	—	0.25	—
Lexington Corp Ldrs		26 blue chip stocks	23.1	0.63	—
Price Total Mkt Eqty Idx	Wilshire 5000	Broadest Idx, covers all US stocks	—	0.40	—
Schwab 1000(Inv)		1000 largest US cos.	31.9	0.47	2
Vangd Idx Growth	S&P/BARRA Growth	S&P 500 cos. w/hi price/book ratios	36.3	0.20	29
Vangd Idx Total Stk Mkt†	Wilshire 5000	Broadest Idx, covers all US stocks	31.0	0.22	3
Vangd Idx Value	S&P/BARRA Value	Cos. in S&P 500 w/low price/book ratios	29.8	0.20	29
Wilshire Target Lg Growth	Wilshire 5000	Growth cos. w/$1.2 billion + market cap	32.2	0.81	43
Wilshire Target Lg Value	Wilshire 5000	Value cos. w/$1.2 billion + market cap	30.2	0.91	65
MidCap indexes					
CA Inv Tr-S&P MidCap	S&P MidCap 400	Stocks w\median market caps of $800M	31.9	0.40	18
Dreyfus MidCap Idx	S&P MidCap 400	Stocks w\market caps from $50M to $10B	31.6	0.50	20
Federated Mid Cap	S&P MidCap 400	Stocks w\median market caps of $800M	31.1	0.60	26
Fidelity Spart Extd Mkt Idx†	Wilshire 4500	Wishire 5000 minus S&P 500	—	0.25	—
Gateway MidCap Idx	S&P MidCap 400	Mid-size stocks, may use options	25.0	2.00	14
Price Extd Eqty Mkt Idx	Wilshire 4500	Wishire 5000 minus S&P 500	—	0.40	—
Vangd Idx Extend Mkt†	Wilshire 4500	Wishire 5000 minus S&P 500	26.7	0.25	22
Small cap indexes					
Bridgeway Ult Sm Idx	CRSP Portfolio 10	Smallest 10% of US cos.	—	0.75	66
BT Advs:Sm Cap Idx	Russell 2000	Sample of stocks in Russell 2000	25.1	0.45	16
CA Inv Tr-Sm Cap Idx	S&P SmallCap 600	Stocks w\market caps from $40M to $2.7B	24.1	0.65	—
DFA U.S. Small Cap Value‡		Value stocks w\high book to market	30.8	0.61	15
DFA U.S. Small Co (6-10)‡		Bottom 5 deciles US stocks	24.2	0.48	32
DFA U.S. Small Co (9-10)‡		Bottom 2 deciles US stocks	22.8	0.61	24
Dreyfus Sm Cap Stk Idx	S&P SmallCap 600	Stocks w\market caps from $40M to $2.7B	—	0.50	—

Fund	Index	Comments	1997 % return	Expense ratio %	Annual turnover %
Federated Mini-Cap Idx	Russell 2000	Cos. with avg market cap of $180M	20.4	0.74	42
Galaxy II Small Cap Idx	Russell Small Cap	3000 largest cos. excluding S&P 500	23.6	0.40	14
Gateway Small Cap Idx	Wilshire Small Cap	250 Small size cos.	20.6	1.50	20
Schwab Small Cap Idx		1000 cos. w/market caps from $150M-$600M	25.7	0.52	23
Vangd Idx Sm Cap†	Russell 2000	Small cos. with avg market cap of $200M	24.5	0.25	28
Wilshire Target Sm Co Gro	Wilshire 5000	Growth cos. w/less than $1.2B market cap	11.7	1.22	105
Wilshire Target Sm Co Val	Wilshire 5000	Value cos. w/less than $1.2B market cap	31.2	0.86	105
Specialized indexes					
AON REIT Idx	MS-REIT	US property trusts in MS-REIT Idx	18.8	0.51	22
Citizens Idx Portfolio		300 social and environmental stocks	35.0	1.59	19
DFA Real Estate Sec‡	NAREIT Idx	All REITs in NAREIT except health care	19.3	0.71	11
Domini Social Equity Fund		400 social stocks, half from S&P 500	36.0	0.98	5
Galaxy II Util Idx	Russell Utility	121 large utility stocks	28.5	0.40	12
Information Tech 100 Idx	Information Week 100	Info tech cos. in the IW 100 Idx	—	1.50	4
Rushmore Amer Gas Idx	AGA Idx	110 cos. in the American Gas Assn.	24.2	0.85	8
Vangd Spec-REIT Idx	MS REIT	US property trusts in MS-REIT Idx	18.6	0.36	0
International indexes					
BT Advs: EAFE Eqty Indx	MSCI-EAFE	Apprx. 1000 Europe, Aust. & Far East cos.	1.9	0.65	4
DFA Continental Sm Co‡		Small cos. on European continent	11.7	0.73	10
DFA Japan Small Co‡	1st Tier Tokyo Exchange	Bottom 1/2 of 1st tier Tokyo Exchange	-54.9	0.72	8
DFA Lg Cap Int'l‡		Large cos. in EAFE	5.5	0.58	7
DFA Pacific Rim Sm Co‡		Small cos. in Singapore, Hong Kong, Australia, Malaysia	-42.1	0.84	6
DFA U.K. Small Co‡	Financial Times Idx	Bottom half of United Kingdom Idx	3.5	0.72	8
Dreyfus Int'l Stk Idx	MSCI-EAFE	Apprx. 1000 Europe, Aust. & Far East cos.	—	0.60	—
Fidelity Spart Int'l Idx†	MSCI-EAFE	Apprx. 1000 Europe, Aust. & Far East cos.	—	0.35	—
Mainstay Inst EAFE Idx	MSCI-EAFE	Sample of 350 stocks in EAFE Idx	0.4	0.94	4
Schwab Int'l Idx (Inv)		350 large cos. excluding US & S. Africa	7.3	0.61	13
Vangd Int'l Idx-Emg Mkts†	MSCI Selected Emg Mkts Free	Cos. in 14 SE Asia, Latin Amer. & Eur. countries	-16.8	0.60	1
Vangd Int'l Idx-Europe†	MSCI-Europe	600 stocks in 14 European countries	24.2	0.35	4
Vangd Int'l Idx-Pacific†	MSCI-Pacific	Morgan Stanley large cap Pacific stocks	-25.7	0.35	9
Vangd:Tot Int'l Port†	MSCI-EAFE+ Select EMF	Morgan Stanley EAFE + selected emg mkts	-0.8	0.00	0
Bond and balanced indexes					
BT Advs:US Bond Idx	Lehman Aggregate Bond	US gov & agency, US corp, & foreign gov bds	—	0.35	—
Dreyfus Bond Mkt Idx	Lehman Govt/Corp Bond	Sample of US investment grade debt market	9.2	0.60	49
Federated Bond Idx	Lehman Aggregate	US gov & agency, US corp, & foreign gov bds	9.0	0.29	49
Galaxy II US Treas Idx	Salomon US Treasury	US Treas notes/bonds w/1+ yrs maturities	9.3	0.40	35
Schwab ST Bd Mkt Idx	Lehman Short Corp/ Govt Bond	Gov/corp bonds w/avg maturities 1-5 yrs	7.1	0.49	71
Schwab Tot Bd Mkt Idx	Lehman Long Corp/ Govt Bond	Gov/corp bonds w/avg maturities 10+ yrs	10.0	0.61	51
SEI Bond Idx	Lehman Aggregate Bond	US gov & agency, US corp, & foreign gov bds	9.4	0.30	46
Vangd Balanced Idx	Wilshire 5000/Lehman Aggregate Bd	60% Vangd Total Stk Mkt, 40% Total Bd Mkt	22.2	0.20	37
Vangd Bond Idx-Inter Bd	Lehman Inter Corp/ Govt Bond	5-10 year bonds	9.4	0.20	80
Vangd Bond Idx-Long Bd	Lehman Inter Corp/Govt Bond	10+ year bonds	14.3	0.20	46
Vangd Bond Idx-Short Bd	Lehman Short Corp/ Govt Bond	1-5 year bonds	7.0	0.20	65
Vangd Bond Idx-Tot Bd Mkt	Lehman Aggregate Bond Idx	US gov & agency, US corp, & foreign gov bds	9.4	0.20	39

Summary of no- and low-load sector and industry funds

Agriculture: Fidelity Food and Agriculture.

Communications: BEA Advisor Global Telecommunications, Fidelity Developing Communications, Fidelity Multimedia, Fidelity Telecommunications, Gabelli Global Interactive Couch Potato, Gabelli Global Telecommunications, Invesco World Communications, Montgomery Global Communications, T. Rowe Price Media & Telecommunications, Robertson Stephens Information Age.

Consumer: Fidelity Consumer Industries, Fidelity Retailing.

Defense and Aerospace: Fidelity Defense & Aerospace.

Energy: Excelsior Energy & Natural Resources, Fidelity Energy, Fidelity Energy Services, Fidelity Natural Gas, Invesco Energy, Rushmore American Gas Index, Vanguard Energy.

Environment: Fidelity Environmental Services, Invesco Environmental Services.

Financial Services: Century Shares Trust, FBR Financial Services, FBR Small Cap Financial Services, Fidelity Brokerage and Investment Management, Fidelity Financial Services, Fidelity Home Finance, Fidelity Insurance, Fidelity Regional Banks, Invesco Financial Services, Mutual Series: Financial Services, T.Rowe Price Financial Services, Royce Financial Services, Scudder Financial Services, Smith Breeden Financial Services, TIP: Penn Capital Select Financial Services, Titan Financial Services

Health/Biotechnology: Dresdner RCM Biotech, Dresdner RCM Global Health Care, Fidelity Biotechnology, Fidelity Health Care, Fidelity Medical Delivery, Firsthand Medical Specialists, Invesco Health, T. Rowe Price Health Sciences, Scudder Health Care, Vanguard Health Care, Warburg Pincus Health Sciences.

Housing: Fidelity Construction and Housing.

Industrial: Fidelity Automotive, Fidelity Chemicals, Fidelity Cyclical Industries, Fidelity Industrial Equipment, Fidelity Industrial Materials, Fidelity Paper & Forest Products, Invesco Worldwide Capital Goods.

Leisure: Fidelity Leisure, Invesco Leisure.

Natural Resources: American Century Global Natural Resources, Fidelity Natural Resources, T. Rowe Price New Era, Robertson Stephens Global Natural Resources, Strong Limited Resources, U.S. Global Investors: Global Resources.

Precious Metals: American Century Global Gold, Bull & Bear Gold Investors, Cappiello-Rushmore Gold, Fidelity American Gold, Fidelity Precious Metals and Minerals, Gabelli Gold, Invesco Gold, Lexington Goldfund, Midas Gold, Rydex Precious Metals, Scudder Gold, USAA Gold, U.S. Global Investors: Gold Shares, U.S. Global Investors World Gold, Vanguard Gold & Precious Metals.

Real Estate: Alpine International Real Estate, Alpine U.S. Real Estate, American Century Real Estate Securities, AON REIT Index, Brazos/JMIC Real Estate, CGM Realty, Cohen & Steers Realty, Cohen & Steers Special Equity, Columbia Real Estate Equity, Crabbe Huson Real Estate Investment, DFA/AEW Real Estate Securities, Dreyfus Real Estate Mortgage, Excelsior Real Estate, Fidelity Real Estate, Fremont Real Estate Securities, Invesco Realty, Longleaf Partners Realty, T. Rowe Price Real Estate, Rembrandt Real Estate, Seneca Real Estate, Stratton Monthly Dividend REIT Shares, U.S. Global Investors: Real Estate, Vanguard REIT Index, Westwood Realty.

Technology: Dresdner RCM Global Technology, Dreyfus Technology Growth, Fidelity Business Services & Outsourcing, Fidelity Computers, Fidelity Electronics, Fidelity Software and Computer Services, Fidelity Technology, Firsthand Technology Leaders, Firsthand Technology Value Fund, Information Technology 100 Index, Invesco Technology, Munder NetNet, Northern Technology, PBHG Technology & Communications, PIMCo Innovation, T. Rowe Price Science & Technology, Scudder Technology, USAA Science and Technology, Van Wagoner Technology, WWW Internet Fund.

Transportation: Fidelity Air Transportation, Fidelity Transportation.

Utilities: America's Utility Fund, American Century Utilities, Capiello-Rushmore Utility Income, Fidelity Utilities, Fidelity Utilities Growth, Flex-Fund Total Return Utilities, Galaxy II Utility Index, Invesco Utilities, Lindner Utility, Strong American Utilities, U.S. Global Investors: Income, Vanguard Utilities Income.

Top 50 no-load fund groups

Ranked by 1997 assets of funds listed in Chapter 7 of the Handbook

Rank	Fund Group	1997	1996	Rank	Fund Group	1997	1996
1	Fidelity Investments	$409,558	$332,921	26	Berger Funds	$5,714	$3,260
2	Vanguard Funds Group	309,865	230,699	27	Acorn Funds	5,500	4,678
3	T Rowe Price Funds	82,443	65,262	28	JP Morgan Funds	5,353	1,446
4	American Century Mutual Funds	59,783	50,649	29	Excelsior Funds	5,019	2,225
5	Schwab Funds	54,519	43,012	30	Montgomery Funds	4,975	2,953
6	Janus Funds	48,636	34,169	31	Founders Funds	4,595	3,339
7	Dreyfus Mutual Funds	48,034	44,842	32	Baron Funds	4,475	1,570
8	Scudder Funds	42,462	34,187	33	Longleaf Partners Funds	4,258	2,708
9	USAA Investment Management	22,048	18,571	34	Jones & Babson Funds	4,135	1,843
10	Strong Funds	21,686	17,702	35	Boston 1784 Funds	4,073	4,446
11	Invesco Funds Group	16,608	13,784	36	Marshall Funds	3,996	2,937
12	Neuberger & Berman Funds	14,142	11,223	37	Reserve Funds	3,961	3,944
13	Oakmark Funds	11,178	5,935	38	SAFECO Funds	3,660	2,288
14	Sanford Bernstein & Co	10,517	7,803	39	Nations Funds	3,540	2,263
15	Harbor Funds	10,177	7,424	40	Banker's Trust (BT) Mutual Funds	3,485	1,616
16	Dodge & Cox Funds	9,869	6,415	41	Gabelli Funds	3,416	2,469
17	SSgA Funds	9,354	6,731	42	Lindner/Ryback Management	3,274	3,946
18	Pilgrim, Baxter(PBHG) Mutual Funds	8,983	9,730	43	Heartland Funds	3,111	2,142
19	Legg Mason Funds	8,927	6,151	44	State Farm Funds	3,040	2,249
20	Federated Funds	7,534	14,366	45	Galaxy Funds	3,034	2,960
21	Stein Roe Funds	7,088	6,588	46	Capital Growth Management(CGM) Funds	2,558	2,064
22	Nicholas Funds	7,009	5,327	47	United Asset Management(UAM) Funds	2,480	1,677
23	Northern Funds	6,831	4,284	48	The Selected Funds	2,417	1,560
24	Warburg Pincus Funds	6,606	6,711	49	Gradison Mutual Funds	2,406	2,059
25	Columbia Funds	6,577	5,768	50	Robertson Stephens Funds	2,351	2,732

Top 30 fund groups — load and no-load*

Rank	Fund Group	Assets ($ mil)	Market share %	Rank	Fund Group	Assets ($ mil)	Market share %
1	Fidelity Investments	$555,261	12.37%	16	SEI Investments	83,103	1.85%
2	Vanguard Group	337,397	7.51%	17	AIM Group	81,133	1.81%
3	Capital Research	241,914	5.39%	18	Prudential Mutual Funds	78,400	1.75%
4	Merrill Lynch	193,473	4.31%	19	Alliance Capital	67,884	1.51%
5	Putnam Funds	174,930	3.90%	20	American Century Investments	60,959	1.36%
6	Franklin/Templeton	170,606	3.80%	21	SchwabFunds	55,460	1.24%
7	TIAA-CREF	120,408	2.68%	22	Massachusetts Financial Services	55,080	1.23%
8	Federated Investors	112,362	2.50%	23	Janus Funds	51,267	1.14%
9	Smith Barney	96,374	2.15%	24	BISYS Fund Services	49,290	1.10%
10	Dreyfus Corporation	90,124	2.01%	25	Evergreen Funds	40,008	0.89%
11	Dean Witter InterCapital	89,939	2.00%	26	Van Kampen American Capital	37,615	0.84%
12	Scudder Kemper Investments	89,885	2.00%	27	Goldman Sachs & Co.	34,753	0.77%
13	IDS Mutual Funds	89,620	2.00%	28	PNC Financial Services	34,194	0.76%
14	T Rowe Price Funds	86,706	1.93%	29	Vista Mutual Funds	32,660	0.73%
15	Oppenheimer/MassMutual	85,448	1.90%	30	PaineWebber	32,600	0.73%

Source: Investment Company Institute

*Includes load funds at mixed-groups.

Combined effective federal and state marginal tax rates on dividends

State	28%	Marginal federal rate 31%	36%	39.6%	Highest listed rate
Alabama*	30.59	33.38	38.05	41.42	5
Alaska	28.00	31.00	36.00	39.60	0
Arizona	31.72	34.57	39.31	42.72	5
Arkansas	33.04	35.83	40.48	43.83	7
California	34.70	37.42	41.95	45.22	9
Colorado	31.60	34.45	39.20	42.62	5
Connecticut	31.24	34.11	38.88	42.32	5
Delaware	32.97	35.76	40.42	43.77	7
District of Columbia	34.84	37.56	42.08	45.34	10
Florida	28.00	31.00	36.00	39.60	0
Georgia	32.32	35.14	39.84	43.22	6
Hawaii	35.20	37.90	42.40	45.64	10
Idaho	33.90	36.66	41.25	44.55	8
Illinois	30.16	33.07	37.92	41.41	3
Indiana	30.45	33.35	38.18	41.65	3
Iowa*	33.17	35.75	40.09	43.24	10
Kansas	32.64	35.45	40.13	43.50	6
Kentucky	32.32	35.14	39.84	43.22	6
Louisana*	31.11	33.86	38.46	41.79	6
Maine	34.12	36.87	41.44	44.73	9
Maryland	31.60	34.45	39.20	42.62	5
Massachusetts	36.64	39.28	43.68	46.85	12
Michigan	31.17	34.04	38.82	42.26	4
Minnesota	34.12	36.87	41.44	44.73	9
Mississippi	31.60	34.45	39.20	42.62	5
Missouri*	31.11	33.86	38.46	41.79	6
Montana*	33.70	36.24	40.51	43.61	11
Nebraska	33.03	35.82	40.47	43.82	7
Nevada	28.00	31.00	36.00	39.60	0
New Hampshire	31.60	34.45	39.20	42.62	5
New Jersey	32.59	35.40	40.08	43.45	6
New Mexico	34.12	36.87	41.44	44.73	9
New York	32.93	35.73	40.38	43.74	7
New York City	36.14	38.80	43.24	46.43	11
North Carolina	33.58	36.35	40.96	44.28	8
North Dakota*	34.22	36.71	40.92	43.96	12
Ohio	33.04	35.83	40.48	43.83	7
Oklahoma*	31.63	34.33	38.87	41.16	7
Oregon*	32.67	35.28	39.69	42.88	9
Pennsylvania	30.02	32.93	37.79	41.29	3
Rhode Island**	33.15	36.42	41.77	45.53	0
South Carolina	33.04	35.83	40.48	43.83	7
South Dakota	28.00	31.00	36.00	39.60	0
Tennessee	32.32	35.14	39.84	43.22	6
Texas	28.00	31.00	36.00	39.60	0
Utah*	31.63	34.33	38.87	41.16	7
Vermont***	32.71	35.96	41.28	45.04	0
Virginia	32.14	34.97	39.68	43.07	6
Washington	28.00	31.00	36.00	39.60	0
West Virginia	32.68	35.49	40.16	43.53	7
Wisconsin	32.99	35.78	40.44	43.79	7
Wyoming	28.00	31.00	36.00	39.60	0

* Takes into consideration the applicable deduction of federal taxes at the state level...................................

** State tax is 27.5% of federal liability

*** State tax is 25% of federal liability

Source: Deloitte & Touche

Industry assets (millions)

Year	All Funds	All Funds Excluding Sht Term Funds	All No-Load Funds	Money Market Funds	No-Load Funds Excluding Sht-term funds	No-Load Percentage (Excl Sht-term)
1997	$4,489,918	$3,430,898	$2,177,911	$1,059,020	$1,118,891	32.6%
1996	$3,539,200	$2,637,398	$1,729,866	$901,808	$828,060	31.4
1995	2,820,355	2,067,337	1,409,021	753,018	656,003	31.7
1994	2,168,681	1,550,490	1,098,302	567,720	482,690	31.1
1993	2,077,767	1,510,047	1,015,408	567,720	447,688	29.6*
1992	1,602,731	1,055,209	934,960	547,522	387,438	36.7*
1991	1,354,280	807,001	845,240	547,279	284,234	35.2
1990	1,018,298	525,397	684,937	492,901	187,335	35.6
1989	942,793	511,130	619,671	431,663	173,414	33.9
1988	807,134	481,370	474,172	325,764	148,408	30.8
1987	763,976	463,725	438,538	300,251	138,287	29.8
1986	701,788	424,088	420,937	277,700	143,237	33.8
1985	520,310	289,071	331,698	231,239	100,459	34.8
1984	346,955	149,211	251,772	197,744	54,028	36.2
1983	278,351	119,420	199,407	158,931	40,476	33.9
1982	282,758	80,432	227,801	202,326	25,475	31.7
1981	240,786	59,356	199,606	181,430	18,176	30.6
1980	136,135	61,449	93,383	74,686	18,697	30.4
1979	96,901	51,456	60,651	45,445	15,206	29.6
1978	57,493	46,827	22,051	10,666	11,385	24.3
1977	50,605	46,744	14,545	3,861	10,684	22.9
1976	52,732	49,078	11,222	3,655	7,567	15.4
1975	46,807	43,117	9,229	3,690	5,540	12.8
1974	37,376	34,913	6,867	2,462	4,405	12.6
1973	47,639	47,626	6,006	13	5,993	12.6
1972	61,326	61,326	7,419	—	7,419	12.1
1971	56,889	56,889	5,854	—	5,854	10.3
1970	48,971	48,971	4,112	—	4,112	8.4
1969	49,041	49,041	3,799	—	3,799	7.7
1968	52,912	52,912	3,464	—	3,464	6.5
1967	44,827	44,827	2,489	—	2,489	5.6
1966	35,076	35,076	1,975	—	1,975	5.6
1965	34,991	34,991	1,512	—	1,512	4.3
1964	28,963	28,963	1,257	—	1,257	4.3
1963	24,485	24,485	1,116	—	1,116	4.6

Includes low-loads before 1993

No-load mutual fund sales
As a percent of total mutual fund sales
(Excluding short-term funds)

Year	Total Fund Sales* ($ Mil.)	Total No-Load Sales (Mil.)	No-Load As A Percent	Year	Total Fund Sales* ($ Mil.)	Total No-Load Sales (Mil.)	No-Load As A Percent
1997	$885,334	$423,000	47.8%	1984	49,946	20,077	40.2
1996	690,816	311,614	45.1	1983	$50,112	$24,708	49.3%
1995	477,234	201,559	42.2	1982	17,849	7,498	42.0
1994	473,976	192,053	40.5	1981	11,926	5,483	46.0
1993	510,686	200,362	39.2	1980	11,208	5,301	47.3
1992	362,478	160,419	44.3	1979	8,039	4,247	52.8
1991	234,454	103,767	44.3	1978	7,818	3,917	50.1
1990	149,513	62,414	41.7	1977	6,962	3,360	48.3
1989	135,488	55,224	40.1	1976	4,724	1,401	29.7
1988	87,234	33,363	38.2	1975	3,506	816	23.3
1987	183,639	75,450	41.1	1974	3,269	734	22.5
1986	217,382	81,698	37.6	1973	4,642	1,091	23.5
1985	116,543	45,820	39.3	1972	5,080	1,021	20.1

Source: ICI, Donoghue's Money Fund Report, The No-Load Fund Association, The No-Load Fund Investor

The power of compound growth

■ The tables in this chapter illustrate the power of compound growth. Table 1 shows how an initial investment will multiply into thousands of dollars in your lifetime. The table is set up to show how much $10,000 will grow to in a given number of years at various rates of return with annual compounding. To use it, first estimate the rate of growth your investment will achieve and the number of years it will be invested. Figures in the body of the table will tell you how much wealth will accumulate. In addition, you can determine the rate of growth needed for $10,000 to grow to a target sum over a given period of time. For example, if you need $31,000 ten years from now for college expenses, then run your finger down the first column of the table to the line showing total value after ten years. Then look across till you find the number closest to $31,000—in this case, $31,058. Then note the percentage at the top of the column. In this example, it is 12%, the annual compounded rate you need to achieve your goal.

Similarly, table 1 can be used to determine how much money you will need at retirement. First assume an inflation rate and note the number of years you have before retirement. Then divide the applicable number in the table by 10,000. For example, if you assume a 5% inflation rate, and you will be retiring in 10 years, divide 16,289 (10th figure in the first column) by 10,000 to get 1.6289. If you will need $2,000 per month in today's dollars to live on, multiply $2,000 by 1.6289 to get $3,258. That's what you will need in the inflated dollars of a decade from now.

It is important to understand that past growth rates should be used for forecasting only after careful consideration of the basic reasons for the observed growth patterns as well as for any new factors that may change the growth rates.

Table 2 illustrates the far greater growth when $1,000 is deposited at the beginning of every year

and compounded annually at various growth rates. The base in this table is $1,000 (not $10,000 as in the first table) since this amount can be multiplied by two to easily obtain the size nest egg that can be accumulated with maximum IRA contributions. Multiply by other factors if you are contributing less. If the sum is deposited at the end of the year rather than at the beginning, then the resulting growth can be obtained by taking the year earlier figure and adding $1,000. For frequent periodic deposits via a payroll deduction plan, growth will fall in between the two methods described.

Tables 3 and 4 provide the flip side of tables 1 and 2. Where the first two tables show future value, the last two show present value. Table 3 calculates the present value of $1,000 at various rates of interest. Use table 3 when you want to determine the amount of one initial investment needed in order to accumulate $1,000 over various periods of times at various interest rates. For example, if you will need $1,000 in ten years and expect a 10% growth rate, you can realize this growth objective by investing $386 and letting it grow for ten years. Other growth targets can by obtained by multiplying the annual amounts by the ratio of your target sum over $1,000.

Table 4 calculates the present value of annual investments made over a period of one or more years. Use table 4 when you want to determine the size of annual investments needed in order to accumulate $1,000 at a target date at various interest rates. For example, if you will need $1,000 in ten years and expect a 10% growth rate, you can realize this growth objective by investing $57.04 at the beginning of each year for ten years. Other growth targets can by obtained by multiplying the annual amounts by the ratio of your target sum over $1,000. Table 4 is known as a table of sinking fund payments. Tables 3 and 4 are simply the reciprocals of tables 1 and 2.

Table 1

What $10,000 will be worth in a given number of years

% increase compounded annually

Year	5%	6%	7%	8%	9%	10%	11%	12%	13%	14%	15%	16%	17%	18%	19%	20%
1	10,500	10,600	10,700	10,800	10,900	11,000	11,100	11,200	11,300	11,400	11,500	11,600	11,700	11,800	11,900	12,000
2	11,025	11,236	11,449	11,664	11,881	12,100	12,321	12,544	12,769	12,996	13,225	13,456	13,689	13,924	14,161	14,400
3	11,576	11,910	12,250	12,597	12,950	13,310	13,676	14,049	14,429	14,815	15,209	15,609	16,016	16,430	16,852	17,280
4	12,155	12,625	13,108	13,605	14,116	14,641	15,181	15,735	16,305	16,890	17,490	18,106	18,739	19,388	20,053	20,736
5	12,763	13,382	14,026	14,693	15,386	16,105	16,851	17,623	18,424	19,254	20,114	21,003	21,924	22,878	23,864	24,883
6	13,401	14,185	15,007	15,869	16,771	17,716	18,704	19,738	20,820	21,950	23,131	24,364	25,652	26,996	28,398	29,860
7	14,071	15,036	16,058	17,138	18,280	19,487	20,762	22,107	23,526	25,023	26,600	28,262	30,012	31,855	33,793	35,832
8	14,775	15,938	17,182	18,509	19,926	21,436	23,045	24,760	26,584	28,526	30,590	32,784	35,115	37,589	40,214	42,998
9	15,513	16,895	18,385	19,990	21,719	23,579	25,580	27,731	30,040	32,519	35,179	38,030	41,084	44,355	47,854	51,598
10	16,289	17,908	19,672	21,589	23,674	25,937	28,394	31,058	33,946	37,072	40,456	44,114	48,068	52,338	56,947	61,917
11	17,103	18,983	21,049	23,316	25,804	28,531	31,518	34,785	38,359	42,262	46,524	51,173	56,240	61,759	67,767	74,301
12	17,959	20,122	22,522	25,182	28,127	31,384	34,985	38,960	43,345	48,179	53,503	59,360	65,801	72,876	80,642	89,161
13	18,856	21,329	24,098	27,196	30,658	34,523	38,833	43,635	48,980	54,924	61,528	68,858	76,987	85,994	95,964	106,993
14	19,799	22,609	25,785	29,372	33,417	37,975	43,104	48,871	55,348	62,613	70,757	79,875	90,075	101,472	114,198	128,392
15	20,789	23,966	27,590	31,722	36,425	41,772	47,846	54,736	62,543	71,379	81,371	92,655	105,387	119,737	135,895	154,070
16	21,829	25,404	29,522	34,259	39,703	45,950	53,109	61,304	70,673	81,372	93,576	107,480	123,303	141,290	161,715	184,884
17	22,920	26,928	31,588	37,000	43,276	50,545	58,951	68,660	79,861	92,765	107,613	124,677	144,265	166,722	192,441	221,861
18	24,066	28,543	33,799	39,960	47,171	55,599	65,436	76,900	90,243	105,752	123,755	144,625	168,790	196,733	229,005	266,233
19	25,270	30,256	36,165	43,157	51,417	61,159	72,633	86,128	101,974	120,557	142,318	167,765	197,484	232,144	272,516	319,480
20	26,533	32,071	38,697	46,610	56,044	67,275	80,623	96,463	115,231	137,435	163,665	194,608	231,056	273,930	324,294	383,376
21	27,860	33,996	41,406	50,338	61,088	74,002	89,492	108,038	130,211	156,676	188,215	225,745	270,336	323,238	385,910	460,051
22	29,253	36,035	44,304	54,365	66,586	81,403	99,336	121,003	147,138	178,610	216,447	261,864	316,293	381,421	459,233	552,061
23	30,715	38,197	47,405	58,715	72,579	89,543	110,263	135,523	166,266	203,616	248,915	303,762	370,062	450,076	546,487	662,474
24	32,251	40,489	50,724	63,412	79,111	98,497	122,392	151,786	187,881	232,122	286,252	352,364	432,973	531,090	650,320	794,968
25	33,864	42,919	54,274	68,485	86,231	108,347	135,855	170,001	212,305	264,619	329,190	408,742	506,578	626,686	773,881	953,962

Table 2

What $1,000 deposited annually will grow to in a given number of years

% increase compounded annually

Year	5%	6%	7%	8%	9%	10%	11%	12%	13%	14%	15%	16%	17%	18%	19%	20%
1	1,050	1,060	1,070	1,080	1,090	1,100	1,110	1,120	1,130	1,140	1,150	1,160	1,170	1,180	1,190	1,200
2	2,153	2,184	2,215	2,246	2,278	2,310	2,342	2,374	2,407	2,440	2,473	2,506	2,539	2,572	2,606	2,640
3	3,310	3,375	3,440	3,506	3,573	3,641	3,710	3,779	3,850	3,921	3,993	4,066	4,141	4,215	4,291	4,368
4	4,526	4,637	4,751	4,867	4,985	5,105	5,228	5,353	5,480	5,610	5,742	5,877	6,014	6,154	6,297	6,442
5	5,802	5,975	6,153	6,336	6,523	6,716	6,913	7,115	7,323	7,536	7,754	7,977	8,207	8,442	8,683	8,930
6	7,142	7,394	7,654	7,923	8,200	8,487	8,783	9,089	9,405	9,730	10,067	10,414	10,772	11,142	11,523	11,916
7	8,549	8,897	9,260	9,637	10,028	10,436	10,859	11,300	11,757	12,233	12,727	13,240	13,773	14,327	14,902	15,499
8	10,027	10,491	10,978	11,488	12,021	12,579	13,164	13,776	14,416	15,085	15,786	16,519	17,285	18,086	18,923	19,799
9	11,578	12,181	12,816	13,487	14,193	14,937	15,722	16,549	17,420	18,337	19,304	20,321	21,393	22,521	23,709	24,959
10	13,207	13,972	14,784	15,645	16,560	17,531	18,561	19,655	20,814	22,045	23,349	24,733	26,200	27,755	29,404	31,150
11	14,917	15,870	16,888	17,977	19,141	20,384	21,713	23,133	24,650	26,271	28,002	29,850	31,824	33,931	36,180	38,581
12	16,713	17,882	19,141	20,495	21,953	23,523	25,212	27,029	28,985	31,089	33,352	35,786	38,404	41,219	44,244	47,497
13	18,599	20,015	21,550	23,215	25,019	26,975	29,095	31,393	33,883	36,581	39,505	42,672	46,103	49,818	53,841	58,196
14	20,579	22,276	24,129	26,152	28,361	30,772	33,405	36,280	39,417	42,842	46,580	50,660	55,110	59,965	65,261	71,035
15	22,657	24,673	26,888	29,324	32,003	34,950	38,190	41,753	45,672	49,980	54,717	59,925	65,649	71,939	78,850	86,442
16	24,840	27,213	29,840	32,750	35,974	39,545	43,501	47,884	52,739	58,118	64,075	70,673	77,979	86,068	95,022	104,931
17	27,132	29,906	32,999	36,450	40,301	44,599	49,396	54,750	60,725	67,394	74,836	83,141	92,406	102,740	114,266	127,117
18	29,539	32,760	36,379	40,446	45,018	50,159	55,939	62,440	69,749	77,969	87,212	97,603	109,285	122,414	137,166	153,740
19	32,066	35,786	39,995	44,762	50,160	56,275	63,203	71,052	79,947	90,025	101,444	114,380	129,033	145,628	164,418	185,688
20	34,719	38,993	43,865	49,423	55,765	63,002	71,265	80,699	91,470	103,768	117,810	133,841	152,139	173,021	196,847	224,026
21	37,505	42,392	48,006	54,457	61,873	70,403	80,214	91,503	104,491	119,436	136,632	156,415	179,172	205,345	235,438	270,031
22	40,430	45,996	52,436	59,893	68,532	78,543	90,148	103,603	119,205	137,297	158,276	182,601	210,801	243,487	281,362	325,237
23	43,502	49,816	57,177	65,765	75,790	87,497	101,174	117,155	135,831	157,659	183,168	212,978	247,808	288,494	336,010	391,484
24	46,727	53,865	62,249	72,106	83,701	97,347	113,413	132,334	154,620	180,871	211,793	248,214	291,105	341,603	401,042	470,981
25	50,113	58,156	67,676	78,954	92,324	108,182	126,999	149,334	175,850	207,333	244,712	289,088	341,763	404,272	478,431	566,377

Table 3

What $1,000 in the future is worth today (present value)

Year	5%	6%	7%	8%	9%	10%	11%	12%	13%	14%	15%	16%	17%	18%	19%	20%
1	952	943	935	926	917	909	901	893	885	877	870	862	855	847	840	833
2	907	890	873	857	842	826	812	797	783	769	756	743	731	718	706	694
3	864	840	816	794	772	751	731	712	693	765	658	641	624	609	593	579
4	823	792	763	735	708	683	659	636	613	592	572	552	534	516	499	482
5	784	747	713	681	650	621	593	567	543	519	497	476	456	437	419	402
6	746	705	666	630	596	564	535	507	480	456	432	410	390	370	352	335
7	711	665	623	583	547	513	482	452	425	400	376	354	333	314	296	279
8	677	627	582	540	502	467	434	404	376	351	327	305	285	266	249	233
9	645	592	544	500	460	424	391	361	333	308	284	263	243	225	209	194
10	614	558	508	463	422	386	352	322	295	270	247	227	208	191	176	162
11	585	527	475	429	388	350	317	287	261	237	215	195	178	162	148	135
12	557	497	444	397	356	319	286	257	231	208	187	168	152	137	124	112
13	530	469	415	368	326	290	258	229	204	182	163	145	130	116	104	93
14	505	442	388	340	299	263	232	205	181	160	141	125	111	99	88	78
15	481	417	362	315	275	239	209	183	160	140	123	108	95	84	74	65
16	458	394	339	292	252	218	188	163	141	123	107	93	81	71	62	54
17	436	371	317	270	231	198	170	146	125	108	93	80	69	60	52	45
18	416	350	296	250	212	180	153	130	111	95	81	69	59	51	44	38
19	396	331	277	232	194	164	138	116	98	83	70	60	51	43	37	31
20	377	312	258	215	178	149	124	104	87	73	61	51	43	37	31	26
21	359	294	242	199	164	135	112	93	77	64	53	44	37	31	26	22
22	342	278	226	184	150	123	101	83	68	56	46	38	32	26	22	18
23	326	262	211	170	138	112	91	74	60	49	40	33	27	22	18	15
24	310	247	197	158	126	102	82	66	53	43	35	28	23	19	15	13
25	295	233	184	146	116	92	74	59	47	38	30	24	20	16	13	10

Table 4

Periodic investments that will grow to $1,000 at a future date

Year	5%	6%	7%	8%	9%	10%	11%	12%	13%	14%	15%	16%	17%	18%	19%	20%
1	952.38	943.40	934.58	925.93	917.43	909.09	900.90	892.86	884.96	877.19	869.57	862.07	854.70	847.46	840.34	833.33
2	464.58	457.96	451.49	445.16	438.96	432.90	426.97	421.16	415.47	409.90	404.45	399.11	393.87	388.74	383.72	378.79
3	302.10	296.33	290.70	285.22	279.87	274.65	269.56	264.60	259.75	255.03	250.41	245.91	241.52	237.22	233.03	228.94
4	220.96	215.65	210.49	205.48	200.61	195.88	191.29	186.82	182.47	178.25	174.14	170.15	166.27	162.49	158.82	155.24
5	172.36	167.36	162.51	157.83	153.30	148.91	144.66	140.54	136.56	132.70	128.97	125.35	121.85	118.46	115.17	111.98
6	140.02	135.25	130.65	126.22	121.94	117.82	113.85	110.02	106.33	102.77	99.34	96.03	92.83	89.75	86.79	83.92
7	116.97	112.39	107.99	103.77	99.72	95.82	92.09	88.50	85.05	81.75	78.57	75.53	72.60	69.80	67.10	64.52
8	99.74	95.32	91.09	87.05	83.19	79.49	75.96	72.59	69.37	66.29	63.35	60.54	57.85	55.29	52.84	50.51
9	86.37	82.10	78.02	74.15	70.46	66.95	63.61	60.43	57.41	54.53	51.80	49.21	46.74	44.40	42.18	40.07
10	75.72	71.57	67.64	63.92	60.39	57.04	53.88	50.88	48.04	45.36	42.83	40.43	38.17	36.03	34.01	32.10
11	67.04	63.01	59.21	55.63	52.24	49.06	46.05	43.23	40.57	38.07	35.71	33.50	31.42	29.47	27.64	25.92
12	59.83	55.92	52.24	48.79	45.55	42.51	39.66	37.00	34.50	32.17	29.98	27.94	26.04	24.26	22.60	21.05
13	53.77	49.96	46.40	43.08	39.97	37.07	34.37	31.85	29.51	27.34	25.31	23.43	21.69	20.07	18.57	17.18
14	48.59	44.89	41.44	38.24	35.26	32.50	29.94	27.56	25.37	23.34	21.47	19.74	18.15	16.68	15.32	14.08
15	44.14	40.53	37.19	34.10	31.25	28.61	26.18	23.95	21.90	20.01	18.28	16.69	15.23	13.90	12.68	11.57
16	40.26	36.75	33.51	30.53	27.80	25.29	22.99	20.88	18.96	17.21	15.61	14.15	12.82	11.62	10.52	9.53
17	36.86	33.44	30.30	27.43	24.81	22.42	20.24	18.26	16.47	14.84	13.36	12.03	10.82	9.73	8.75	7.87
18	33.85	30.53	27.49	24.72	22.21	19.94	17.88	16.02	14.34	12.83	11.47	10.25	9.15	8.17	7.29	6.50
19	31.19	27.94	25.00	22.34	19.94	17.77	15.82	14.07	12.51	11.11	9.86	8.74	7.75	6.87	6.08	5.39
20	28.80	25.65	22.80	20.23	17.93	15.87	14.03	12.39	10.93	9.64	8.49	7.47	6.57	5.78	5.08	4.46
21	26.66	23.59	20.83	18.36	16.16	14.20	12.47	10.93	9.57	8.37	7.32	6.39	5.58	4.87	4.25	3.70
22	24.73	21.74	19.07	16.70	14.59	12.73	11.09	9.65	8.39	7.28	6.32	5.48	4.74	4.11	3.55	3.07
23	22.99	20.07	17.49	15.21	13.19	11.43	9.88	8.54	7.36	6.34	5.46	4.70	4.04	3.47	2.98	2.55
24	21.40	18.57	16.06	13.87	11.95	10.27	8.82	7.56	6.47	5.53	4.72	4.03	3.44	2.93	2.49	2.12
25	19.95	17.20	14.78	12.67	10.83	9.24	7.87	6.70	5.69	4.82	4.09	3.46	2.93	2.47	2.09	1.77